"SECRETARIAT, HIS LAST PORTRAIT" BY TONY LEONARD

CHAMPIONS

THE LIVES, TIMES, AND PAST PERFORMANCES

OF THE

20TH CENTURY'S GREATEST

THOROUGHBREDS

BY THE EDITORS OF DAILY RACING FORM

Published by
Daily Racing Form Press
100 Broadway, 7th Floor
New York, NY 10005

ISBN: 0-9648493-9-9
Library of Congress Catalog Card Number: 00-043198

Cover photo by Tony Leonard
Back cover "Man o' War," oil on canvas, 1979, by Anthony M. Alonso
Cover design by Chris Donofry
Text design by Neuwirth and Associates
Printed in the United States of America

CONTENTS

Acknowledgments

A work such as "Champions" could not have been completed without considerable help from many varied resources. Information for British, European, South African, and some South American races was supplied by the International Racing Bureau. Detailed race lines on the Chilean starts by Iceberg II, Cougar II and Gran Kan were supplied by Racing Manager Beltran A. Montt of the Sociedad Hipodromo Chile S.A. Alan Shuback provided invaluable assistance in obtaining and sorting of foreign race records and past performances.

Data for starts that predate the publication of *Daily Racing Form* were obtained from Goodwin's Guide to the Turf, which ceased production in 1908. Some past performances created from *Daily Racing Form* charts also contain supplementary data from Goodwin's, primarily information regarding purses, which were often listed in incomplete fashion in very early *Daily Racing Form* charts.

Additional photographs were provided from collections maintained by the Keeneland library, the National Museum of Racing, the New York Racing Association and the California Thoroughbred Breeders' Association. Other photographs are by Michael J. Marten.

Oil reproductions of Man o' War and Forego are courtesy of Anthony M. Alonso.

The cover photograph of Secretariat winning the 1973 Kentucky Derby was taken by Tony Leonard.

Past performances were proofread by Steve Hill, Dan Illman, Chuck Kuehhas, Paul Malecki, Pat Mannion, Pam Ohanesian, Barbara Ransom, and Carmine Sicuranza.

Pauline Neuwirth and Serg Andreyev of Neuwirth and Associates were responsible for layout and design.

The text was edited by Robin Foster.

"Champions" would not have been possible without the dedication and perseverance of Paula Welch, who not only conceived the idea of collecting the past performances of the 20th century's greatest horses into one volume, but assembled many of them with her bare hands. The existence of this book owes greatly to her tireless efforts.

FOREWORD

Past performances are the lifeblood of Thoroughbred racing. The information carried in these unique profiles has been invaluable to bettors, breeders, horsemen, and the industry in general for most of the last 100 years. In North America, over $15 billion a year is wagered based on the dozens of data elements contained in the past-performance line.

As indispensable as past performances are to everyday life in the Thoroughbred industry, their enduring value lies in their role as the chronicle of the sport. A picture might be worth a thousand words, but a single past-performance line has an even more profound value in relating the rich lore of the racehorse. Most of us have seen and been thrilled by the video image of Secretariat's victory in the 1973 Belmont Stakes, but the magnitude of the performance is amplified in the printed running line:

ing eyewitnesses, who has seen Native Dancer's loss to Dark Star in the 1953 Kentucky Derby, or Count Fleet's spectacular sweep of the 1943 Triple Crown, or Seabiscuit's match-race victory over War Admiral in the 1938 Pimlico Special, or any of the 21 races in the career of the immortal Man o' War?

Here, for the first time anywhere, are the lifetime past performances of the greatest Thoroughbreds in the modern era. The careers of 487 horses, from Domino to Daylami, are represented. The list includes every elected champion since the first balloting began in 1936, as well as most of the significant horses of the late 19th and early 20th centuries and a handful of championship-caliber horses who were never elected for divisional honors.

Champions is, pure and simple, a time capsule of American racing. The past performances, from decade to decade, illuminate the changing land-

Secretariat	ch. c. 1970, by Bold Ruler (Nasrullah)–Somethingroyal, by Princequillo			Lifetime record: 21 16 3 1 $1,316,808
	Own.– Meadow Stable			
	Br.– Meadow Stud Inc (Va)			
	Tr.– L. Laurin			
9Jun73- 8Bel fst 1½ :461 1:094 1:59 2:24 Belmont-G1	1 1 1hd 120 128 131 Turcotte R	126 b *.10 113-05	Secretariat1263 1TwiceaPrince126¾MyGlInt12613	Ridden out 5

In addition, not all of the countless memorable moments of Thoroughbred racing have been captured in moving pictures. Other than a few remain-

scape of the sport–the slow but eventual improvement of the breed, and the dominance of great jockeys and horsemen.

The past-performance profile has undergone many alterations since Daily Racing Form began publishing in 1894, and it wasn't until the late 1960's that the format evolved into the one bettors are familiar with today. Significant modifications were instituted in 1992 and again in 1998, as the art and science of handicapping took on greater dimension and the demand grew for more and better information. Some of those changes have been woven into the reconstruction of past performances that predate the "modern era."

The supplementing of recent generations of data enhancements is part of what makes *Champions* an important work. For turf historians and true fans of the sport, it is an opportunity to view some very dated material through the lens of modern technology. This, however, is not the colorization of Casablanca or the restoration of The Last Supper. The retrieval and supplementing of data to the past performances was done with an archaeologist's pick and shovel rather than by any high-tech means. No piece of information was extrapolated, and only source material was used. Rummaging through musty, tattered bound volumes of *Daily Racing Form* as well as ancient chart books and copies of The American Racing Manual, Paula Welch assembled the great majority of past performances in this volume.

Champions also provides a narrative history of Thoroughbred racing. While the essence of racing performance is in the numbers, 100 years of this sport cannot truly be revealed without insight and anecdote as well. *Champions* employs today's finest turf writers to recount the glorious moments, and even some of the inglorious. Steven Crist, Joe Hirsch, Jay Hovdey, Jay Privman, and the other chapter authors have covered racing for an aggregate of well over 100 years, and have seen many of the great horses in this book come and go.

Out of the thousands of Thoroughbreds foaled in North America each year, only a few accomplish enough to earn the title of champion. Inclusion in this book may not make every honoree immortal, but it acknowledges that for at least one splendid season, each one stood apart and was called the best.

—**Irwin Cohen**

FOUNDATIONS

1890'S–1920'S

by Paula Welch

EVOLUTION IS A GRADUAL process. It is easy to compare something now and then to see how it has changed, but it is not so easy to pinpoint the precise moment that the change occurred.

During the 1800's, horse racing in the United States went from being a sport characterized by relatively tiny purses and hard campaigns at advanced ages to one of astronomical purses offered to the very young, with the spotlight shifting from grueling heat racing for older horses to so-called dashes for younger ones. While there are many milestones marking this transformation, it is not unreasonable to single out August 29, 1893, as one day in particular that racing in this country took shape in its modern form. In the 1:12⅖ that it took the undefeated Domino to negotiate about six furlongs in the Futurity Stakes at Sheepshead Bay, the past was erased and the present took its place.

In the course of securing the rich race, worth almost $49,000 to the winner, Domino became America's leading earning horse, unseating the still–racing Kingston in one quick blow. Then a 9-year-old, Kingston would retire a year later with 89 victories, which still stands as an American record.

That tally, and his final lifetime earnings of $138,917, required 138 starts during nine seasons. The 2-year-old Domino surpassed Kingston's total earnings in just seven starts over barely three months.

Kingston and Domino were tied together not just as former leading earner and successor, but by a man who was one of the dominant influences on American racing of his time. James R. Keene, who had twice earned a fortune in stocks and once lost it, bred Kingston. When he and his son, Foxhall, merged their racing stables, he became the co–owner of Domino, whom the younger Keene had bought as a yearling for $3,000. Keene had campaigned stars such as Spendthrift years before, and in the 1890's, with a lost fortune recovered, much glory lay ahead – and it all started with Domino.

The pedigree of Domino's sire, Himyar, reflected the culture clash that was occurring in the mid-19th century in American racing and breeding. Heat racing had begun falling out of favor in England decades earlier, and American breeders looked there for sources of speed. Eclipse, a stakes winner at 2 and 3, brought speed with him when imported to the United States, and among his offspring was Alarm, a record setter at a mile.

Himyar was by the sprinter-miler Alarm out of the Lexington mare Hira. The most dominant stallion the United States has ever seen, Lexington was the leading sire from 1861 through 1874, and twice again thereafter. During his racing career in the 1850's, he covered four miles in 7:19¾ against time and won 6 of 7 official races, all run in heats at distances ranging from one to four miles. Himyar, however, was more a speedster like his sire, and he transmitted that quality in abundance to his greatest son, Domino.

As brilliant as the "Black Whirlwind" was, he had an obvious weakness: stamina. Beaten just once in 19 starts at a mile or less, he won only one race at nine furlongs or more, and that was a dead heat in a match race.

Domino suffered the worst defeat of his career in the 1½-mile American Derby, fighting an effort by jockey Fred Taral to rate him and finishing last. The younger Keene claimed the colt had exited the race lame, and it was two months before he ran again. This debacle did not discourage the Keenes and trainer Billy Lakeland from trying Domino in routes again at 4, with little success. Kept to shorter distances, he remained a dominant force.

With his prodigious fleetness came a dose of unsoundness. After spectacular speed trials as a yearling, the colt suffered bowed tendons and always raced in bandages. A bad foot troubled him at 3 and 4 and, eventually, he refused to train on it and was retired to Keene's Castleton Stud near Lexington, Kentucky.

Domino was not only a star on the racetrack, but also became a significant influence in American pedigrees.

Domino – against tremendous odds – became a significant influence in American pedigrees. He died in 1897, the year his first crop was born, and despite siring only 20 foals – and only four surviving colts who were not gelded – Domino's name peppers the distant recesses of pedigrees of virtually every Thoroughbred alive today. From those two small crops, Domino produced eight stakes winners, and despite his own distance limitations, his offspring included Cap and Bells, who was the first American-bred to win the English Oaks, and Commando, winner of the Belmont.

Domino's first crop of five foals, which included three stakes winners, were 2-year-olds of 1899; Commando was a member of the second and last crop and he proved an immediate sensation, winning five straight races before losing his last outing of the season under a notably careless ride.

James Rowe Sr., a leading jockey of his day, had become an enormously successful trainer, developing stars such as Hindoo and Miss Woodford – even before joining forces with Keene. He had ridden two winners of the Belmont and eventually would train eight of them, more than anyone else in history. He sent Commando into the then-11-furlong classic for his 3-year-old debut, and the colt galloped to victory over the two rivals that dared to challenge him. An easy win in the Carlton followed, and then came the Lawrence Realization. According to accounts, Commando was lame before the race, and after a game but losing effort behind The Parader, whom he had beaten easily in the Belmont, the colt was virtually broken down. It was to be his last start.

Like Domino, Commando proved both an astonishingly successful stallion and a tragically unlucky one. He died of tetanus in 1905, siring just 27 foals in the end. This small total included 10 stakes winners, headlined by the fabulous Colin.

Barely a year and a month separate Colin's first and last racecourse appearances, but in that brief time, he established himself as one of the sport's superstars. Observers rated him the best American racehorse ever – better than stablemate Sysonby, and better, some would later maintain, than Man o' War.

Colin, the last major undefeated horse in America for 80 years, won the Belmont Stakes in a driving rainstorm over a sloppy track, despite suffering from severe soundness problems.

He went undefeated in 15 starts, his two close calls attributable to the sporadic leg troubles that eventually would end his career.

Only once was Colin challenged in 12 races at 2 – in the Eclipse, his third start. A week before, he had easily won his debut and in the intervening days had set a track record in the National Stallion Stakes. In the Eclipse, however, he never was able to get a clear lead and won by a head, emerging from the race with sore shins. That didn't prevent the Keene colt from returning after a short rest to sweep through nine more races before the season's end, setting an American record at seven furlongs in his 2-year-old finale.

Colin won the Withers in his return at 3, but after a swift 1¼-mile workout, it was announced that he had bowed tendons in his forelegs and would not run in the Belmont. In a last-minute surprise, however, he contested the race, held in a driving rainstorm over a sloppy track. The weather conditions prevented a time from being taken and also made it impossible to discern the horses until the final quarter-mile, in which Colin lost all but a head of a five-length lead, just edging Fair Play for the victory. The chart noted that rider error nearly cost Colin the win; jockey Joe Notter claimed that he was told to give the colt an easy race and that Colin had little left to offer against Fair Play's late run.

Antigambling legislation was passed on June 11, 1908, severely restricting betting in New York, but 20,000 were reported to be on hand at Sheepshead Bay for Colin's finale, a comfortable victory in the Tidal Handicap.

Like many American-owned racehorses of the day, Colin was sent to England, but he never raced there. After an impressive trial as a 4-year-old, he proved irretrievably broken down.

Unlike Commando and Domino, Colin lived to an advanced age, but he proved unable to produce a worthy successor on the track. Although other sons of Commando – Ultimus, Celt, and Peter Pan – were much more successful stallions, it is Colin who provides the sire-line link from Domino to the present, through Neddie, grandsire of Alsab and progenitor of the sire line that leads to Ack Ack.

Among the best of Keene's fillies was Maskette, whose somewhat disappointing 4-year-old campaign could not erase her accomplishments at 2 and 3. A daughter of the Domino stallion Disguise out of a Hamburg mare, Maskette suffered her only defeat at 2 behind the year's best 2-year-old colt, Sir Martin, who was subsequently sold for $70,000 and sent to England. Keene reportedly proclaimed her the fastest horse he yet had bred. Following her retirement, Maskette produced an Ultimus filly in the United States before being sold and sent to France.

One of the last stars campaigned by Keene was Sweep. By Ben Brush and out of the Domino mare Pink Domino, Sweep went 9 for 13 and was never unplaced in a career highlighted by victories in the Futurity, Belmont, and Lawrence Realization.

A two-time leading sire, Sweep produced good stallions in Eternal and The Porter, but his lasting prominence in pedigrees is mainly through his daughters. He is the broodmare sire of Triple Crown winners War Admiral and Whirlaway, of champion El Chico, and of Kentucky Derby winner Bubbling Over, among others.

Not all of the Keenes' superstars were homebred descendants of Domino, however. Sysonby was bred in England by American Marcus Daly, who had bought Optime and sent her to dual classicist Melton. Daly died before the foal was born, however, and when his England-based stock was auctioned, the elder Keene purchased the mare. Sysonby was foaled at Castleton Stud the following February.

It was fortuitous that Sysonby campaigned in America in Keene colors at all. James Keene wanted to sell the colt as a yearling, but Foxhall convinced him otherwise; later, Sysonby was slated to be shipped to England to race, but Rowe bundled up the little bay colt so it would be thought that he was in too poor a condition to make the trip. Actually, there was nothing wrong with him.

In fact, unlike Domino, Commando, and Colin, Sysonby was not troubled by unsoundness. He won the Lawrence Realization off three days' rest and won stakes races from 5½ furlongs to 2¼ miles. In most of his victories, he was not under urging at the end; the exception was a dead heat for

The versatile Sysonby won stakes races from 5 ½ furlongs to 2 ¼ miles, and lost only once in his career.

first in the Metropolitan Handicap, his 3-year-old debut, in which he gave 10 pounds to the older Race King. His lone defeat, to the good filly Artful in the 1904 Futurity, was later ascribed to foul play.

It was intended to race Sysonby at 4, but an irritating skin condition kept him sidelined through the spring. He suddenly developed a high fever and died shortly thereafter of blood poisoning. For Castleton, which had lost its two best stallions early, the ill fortune continued.

Racing in New York persisted until 1910, with betting on a man-to-man basis, until further legislation prohibited even that. Racing would not return to the state until 1913, and some storied tracks, such as Sheepshead Bay and Gravesend, shut down, never to reopen. Although he maintained a few horses in England, Keene sold his American interests, and he died before racing returned to Belmont in May 1913.

Henry of Navarre may have been the best of his time going long. As a 3-year-old, he won the Belmont and Travers, and also won the Suburban among other major stakes as a handicap star.

Henry of Navarre had not been good enough to beat Domino at a mile in the 1894 Withers, but after winning 11 of his next 12 starts, including the Belmont and the Travers, he was ready for a rematch. Gravesend featured a match race between the 3-year-old stars at nine furlongs, in which they hit the finish line together. Their connections opted against a runoff, and the race stood as a dead heat. It would be Domino's only victory beyond a mile, and the last time he got that close to Henry of Navarre at the finish of a race.

A week later, Henry of Navarre lost narrowly to the older Clifford, a horse Domino had beaten in a one-mile match race, thus setting up a contest among the three early the following month to determine the season's best. Longshot Henry of Navarre won, dueling Domino into defeat and holding off Clifford late; favored Domino finished last with an injured foot.

Midway through his 4-year-old season, Henry of Navarre was purchased by August Belmont II for $35,000. Although the colt won 6 of 8 starts for Belmont, including the 1896 Suburban Handicap

despite suffering a career-ending injury, he didn't come close to earning back his purchase price. After a disappointing career at stud, he was given away to the U.S. government for its cavalry program.

Belmont had more bad luck with Beldame, whom he bred but leased as a 2-year-old to Newton Bennington. She won 12 of 14 starts at 3 for Bennington, dominating fillies in the 1904 Gazelle and the Alabama and squashing older males in the Saratoga Cup and the First and Second Specials. Belmont reacquired her in time for her 4-year-old season, during which she took the Suburban but won only 2 of 10 starts. (Belmont's poor luck would hold; the very best horse he ever bred, and among the best horses anyone ever bred, would be sold as a yearling in 1918 for $5,000. That horse was Man o' War.)

Earlier on the very card in which Domino's career had come to a close with a whimper behind Henry of Navarre in the 1895 First Special, the sport's newest sensation exploded onto the scene. Ben Brush had been a star in the Midwest, winning his first five starts easily, but had come up short in New York, losing three of his first four starts there. In the Holly Handicap, he began an eight-race winning streak that would include the Champagne and the 1896 Kentucky Derby.

Roseben, "The Big Train," was a prodigious weight-carrier, once winning while spotting the runner-up 60 pounds. His seven-furlong record of 1:22 set in 1906 stood for 41 years.

Following the impressive Holly Handicap victory, the colt was bought by Mike Dwyer, who, with his brother, Phil, had campaigned a long stream of American champions such as Kingston, Hindoo, Miss Woodford, and Hanover, as well as Ben Brush's sire, Bramble. Mike had parted company with his brother and Ben Brush would be the last major horse he would own.

In his final start, Ben Brush, then 4, failed to give 36 pounds to a John E. Madden 2-year-old named Plaudit in an all-ages race, losing by a head to a colt who would go on to win the Kentucky Derby. After the race, Ben Brush was sold to James Keene to stand at Castleton Stud. He proved to be both an outstanding sire and a sire of sires; the leading stallion of 1909, he was represented by classic winners Delhi and Sweep. Sweep and Broomstick would lead the annual sire list themselves for five years between them.

Madden would figure prominently in the story of another 2-year-old of 1897: In 1895, the year that Domino retired, a near-relative was born who would later be hailed as the best of his crop. By Hanover out of a half-sister to Domino, Hamburg was purchased as a youngster by Madden, who was in the process of switching from Standardbred to Thoroughbred racing.

Although he lost 4 of his 16 starts at 2, Hamburg was considered far and away the standout of his generation. He won 10 stakes races, under 127 pounds or more in eight of them and once under 135 pounds, giving 15 to Futurity winner L'Alouette. He closed his campaign with six starts in a little more than two weeks, winning the last four. Late in the year, Marcus Daly purchased Hamburg for just over $40,000, an American record for a Thoroughbred in training. With the proceeds, Madden purchased Hamburg Place near Lexington.

Early the next season, it looked as if the wily Madden had come out best in the deal. The colt he kept, Plaudit, won the Kentucky Derby, while Hamburg was beaten in the Belmont in his season debut by Bowling Brook, whom he had handled easily at 2. But Hamburg, under the care of Domino's former trainer, Billy Lakeland, never lost again, capping his career with a victory over Plaudit in the Lawrence Realization and annihilating older horses in the 2¼-mile Brighton Cup by a margin officially estimated at 100 lengths.

Hamburg was America's leading sire in 1905, but his lasting contribution to the breed came with his daughters, such as the stellar racer Artful, who gave Sysonby his lone defeat, and Jersey Lightning, dam of Regret.

■ ■ ■

If Domino represented the modern era of American racing, with its new emphasis on youthful brilliance and shorter campaigns, there was still room for troupers such as Imp, Roseben, and Pan Zareta.

Imp, a handicap mare referred to as My Coal Black Lady after a popular song of the time, contested 96 races at 2, 3, and 4 before achieving national prominence as a 5-year-old in 1899.

Little more than a sprinter at first, the Ohio-bred proved a useful middle-distance stakes horse at the Chicago-area tracks at 4, but it was at 5, when she became the first filly or mare to win the Suburban, that she secured her place in history. Succeeding where legendary females such as Firenze had failed, Imp not only won the 1¼-mile handicap classic by daylight but also set a stakes record of 2:05⅗. Before her career ended, she set track records at 10, 12, and 14 furlongs in New York, and in addition to her Suburban score she won 16 other stakes, including the Advance, the Brighton Handicap, and the First and Second Specials.

The itinerant Pam Zareta was a brilliant weight-carrying mare who won a record 76 times while racing over 24 different tracks.

Roseben, "The Big Train," was renowned for his speed and weight-carrying ability: The huge gelding once won a six-furlong race in near-track-record time while giving the runner-up 60 pounds, and he won four times under 147 pounds and 38 times under 126 or more. He set records at six, seven, and 7½ furlongs, and at Belmont Park in 1906, he established an American record of 1:22 for seven furlongs around a turn, taking almost three seconds off the previous mark of 1:24⅘. The American record would last for 41 years, while the track record survived until 1957, when Bold Ruler finally laid it to rest.

Considering that he was a brilliant sprinter, Roseben reached prominence surprisingly late in life. Over 17 hands at maturity, the big horse raced just once at 2 and finished up the track. It was not until his 19th start that he finally won a stakes race, the Toboggan Handicap at the brand-new Belmont facility. Among the beaten was Race King, who had finished in a dead heat with Sysonby in the opening-day Metropolitan Handicap.

Between 1905 and 1907, Roseben was in the top three nearly 90 percent of the time despite weight assignments of up to 150 pounds. He was retired after bowing a tendon in 1909, ending his career with 52 victories from 111 starts.

From the fringes of racing in 1912 came one of the sport's enduring legends, the female equivalent to Roseben. Pan Zareta was a record-setting, weight-carrying sprinter who ran at 24 different tracks in Mexico, Canada, and eight states during her six-year career. Although she set a track record at a mile, she was most effective at six furlongs and under. She never won a race of significance, and aside from a victory over Old Rosebud early in his first comeback, she never defeated a top-level horse. What she did was run fast and win often.

Pan Zareta's dam, Caddie Griffith, was the offspring of the Thoroughbred stallion Rancocas out of a mare of somewhat more questionable breeding, and neither Caddie Griffith nor her famous daughter appears in the American Stud Book. That didn't keep Pan Zareta out of the winner's circle, which she visited 76 times – more than any other mare in U.S. racing history.

Ultimately, "Panzy," named after Panzy Zareta, the daughter of the former mayor of Juarez, set six track records at distances ranging from five furlongs to a mile, including a world record at five furlongs that would stand until 1951. She won under 146 pounds – giving 46 pounds to the runner-up – and carried 126 pounds or more 48 times, including 21 of her victories. Despite this, and a pronounced dislike of off tracks, Pan Zareta finished in the top three 128 times – 85 percent of her starts.

Pan Zareta died of pneumonia while in training at Fair Grounds, where she was buried.

Having outlived Mike Dwyer and James Keene, for whom he had trained a long stream of champions, and having waited out the dark days of no racing in New York, James Rowe was back on May 30, 1913, opening day at Belmont, with a new star for Harry Payne Whitney. Like many top American owners, Whitney had kept a stable in England, and among his better horses campaigning there was Whisk Broom. Classic-placed behind Neil Gow at 3, the Broomstick colt was a decent stakes-class performer in his adopted home.

The 6-year-old, racing in his native country under the name Whisk Broom II, came with a glowing reputation that earned him high weight in the opening-day Metropolitan Handicap, and he didn't disappoint. After his Met Mile victory, he took the Brooklyn and Suburban Handicaps before being sidelined by injury, sweeping the series that would later be recognized as the Handicap Triple Crown.

Whisk Broom II's U.S. finale was a performance that would earn him "greatest ever" accolades from contemporary observers, but the achievement had its share of controversy. Under 139 pounds, the horse officially traveled the 1¼ miles of the Suburban in 2:00, almost three seconds faster than the American record of the time set by his sire. But no independent clocker matched W. H. Barretto's official time. Among those on hand was James Fitzsimmons, who timed the race in 2:02⅗ – still an American record.

The following year, Whitney and Rowe had the country's best 2-year-old in the filly Regret, who proved her superiority in a rapid succession of three stakes victories against colts. Between August 8 and August 22, she won the Saratoga Special, Sanford, and Hopeful and was put away for the season.

Rowe, who had sent out Commando to win the Belmont in his 3-year-old debut, brought the filly back in the 1915 Kentucky Derby, where she was favored despite a nine-month layoff and the fact that she had never run farther than six furlongs. She won easily, leading throughout.

Whisk Broom II wins the Suburban Handicap under 139 pounds, going a mile and a quarter in 2:00, almost three seconds faster than the American record.

On one hand, Regret was campaigned in remarkably conservative fashion – in four years of racing, she had only 11 starts. But much was asked of her in most of those starts. At 4, she suffered the worst of two career losses when she took on an outstanding field in the 1¼-mile Saratoga Handicap in her first start in nearly a year, a race in which she led early and stopped abruptly, finishing 16 lengths behind Stromboli. Her other defeat came in the 1917 Brooklyn Handicap.

The Brooklyn featured a matchup of three Kentucky Derby winners – Regret, year-older Old Rosebud, and 3-year-old Omar Khayyam – and three of the best handicap horses of the time in Stromboli, Roamer, and Regret's stablemate, Borrow. Whitney had declared that he wanted to win with the mare, but in the stretch, with Regret on the lead and Old Rosebud looming dangerously, Willie Knapp aboard Borrow drove on to victory in track-record time over his own stablemate. Regret had been able to hold off Old Rosebud but fell a nose short against Borrow.

Roamer was not at his best for the 1917 Brooklyn, finishing fifth, but the tough gelding had done enough to prove his worth before the race. Even at 6, he still had important races yet to win. In fact, just a week before, he had beaten Borrow by daylight in the Excelsior Handicap.

Like Regret, he had scored his first stakes win in the Saratoga Special at 2 and went on to greatness at 3, winning 12 of 16 starts. The versatile runner had beaten older horses at seven furlongs in the Carter Handicap, won the Travers by 10, and so sufficiently scared away the opposition that he took the 1½-mile Autumn Weight-for-Age in a walkover. During the season, he set track records at seven, nine, and 10 furlongs. He was again dominant at 4 but afterward had to settle for being among a top-class set of handicap horses rather than being the leader.

With his best behind him, Roamer nevertheless had one particularly notable performance left in him even after the 1917 Brooklyn. At 7, after lowering his own 1¼-mile record at Saratoga, he ran a mile around two turns at Saratoga against time in 1:34⅖, becoming the first horse in history to run a

Despite being off for nine months and never having raced beyond six furlongs, Regret became the first filly to win the Kentucky Derby, in 1915.

sub-1:35 mile around at least one turn. Years before, Salvator had set the standard of 1:35½ on a straight course; the track record at Saratoga at the time was 1:36⅕.

In the winter after his 8-year-old season, the only year he failed to win a stakes event, Roamer died as a result of a paddock accident.

As good as Roamer was, he had an old rival who was, more often than not, better. He would try Old Rosebud 11 times over his career, with the latter finishing in front of him on six occasions.

Old Rosebud and Roamer met on the track for the first time as 2-year-olds in Kentucky, and though Roamer would go on to be a stakes-winning juvenile, he was no match for Old Rosebud, clearly the best 2-year-old of the year. It was not Roamer who would prove Old Rosebud's nemesis at 2, however, but Little Nephew, who was responsible for both of the gelding's losses that season. After losing the Bashford Manor, Old Rosebud romped through nine straight races before minor injury ended his campaign in August.

After a prep-race victory, Old Rosebud went to Churchill Downs for the Kentucky Derby, which was only then beginning to surge into prominence under Matt Winn, and there he won by eight

A bowed tendon sidelined 1914 Kentucky Derby winner Old Rosebud for more than 2 ½ years, but he came back as a star going shorter distances.

lengths while setting a track record. It was to be his last hurrah for quite some time, however, as he came out of his next start, the Withers, dead lame. A bowed tendon put the gelding on the sidelines for more than 2½ years.

In early 1917, Old Rosebud made it back to the track, and it wasn't long before he had established himself at the top again. The Derby record holder was no longer capable of handling 1¼ miles – he was unplaced both times he tried – but at shorter distances, he won 15 of 19 and was not worse than third. Then, injury intervened again and he sat out the 1918 season.

Returned to the races again the following year, Old Rosebud continued to win, but never again at the stakes level. In 1921, at age 10, he had only a couple of starts, both claiming events. When he pulled up lame winning the second, he was sidelined one last time, and after two races in his final comeback try, he broke down in a workout and was destroyed two days later.

Old Rosebud was in fact the first of five Kentucky Derby winners foaled at the farm named for Hamburg. Madden sold Old Rosebud as a yearling, but the second member of the quintet, the well-bred Sir Barton, raced for Madden at

2 until Commander J. K. L. Ross purchased the Star Shoot colt.

Madden had high expectations for Sir Barton; he was a half-brother to Sir Martin, who had handed Maskette her only loss at 2. Sir Barton debuted in a stakes event, and he showed little. Madden nevertheless sent him to Saratoga, where he ran even worse. He had not earned a penny when Ross, who already had bought a better 2-year-old in Billy Kelly, purchased him. In his final start of the season, though, he was a late-running second in the Futurity, at last showing a glimmer of his true racing ability.

Sir Barton made his 3-year-old debut in the Kentucky Derby, in which he did two things he had never before done: show speed from the gate and win. The Derby was contested in the mud and Sir Barton was getting weight from race favorites Eternal and Billy Kelly, but he returned four days later to beat Eternal at equal weights on a fast track in the Preakness. Victories in the Withers and the Belmont followed, though Sir Barton would not be recognized as America's first Triple Crown winner for years.

At the time, Sir Barton was best known for a race he lost – the famous match race against Man o' War at Kenilworth Park in October 1920. Before that, however, Sir Barton had put together a brilliant

In between Sir Barton's not-yet-recognized sweep of the Triple Crown and his match race loss to Man o' War was a brilliant four-race winning streak which included a track-record victory over Exterminator in the Saratoga Cup.

four-race winning streak that included a track-record victory in the 1¼-mile Saratoga Handicap against Exterminator and an American-record performance in the 1³⁄₁₆-mile Merchants' and Citizens', also at Saratoga. Man o' War had tied the former record in winning the Travers and had won the Miller Stakes in a second slower time than the latter, causing interest in a match race between the country's best 3- and 4-year-old. The showdown proved anticlimactic as Sir Barton never offered a challenge to his younger rival, who galloped to an easy victory. It was generally reported that Sir Barton, who suffered from the bad feet common to Star Shoot offspring, was not at his best on the hard track.

The Merchants' and Citizens' was to prove the last highlight for Sir Barton. He never won another race, losing his final three starts after the match race, and after a mediocre career at stud, he died in Wyoming in 1937 as a U.S. Army Remount stallion.

The Madden-bred Paul Jones won the Derby that Man o' War skipped, and the following year, Grey Lag almost gave Madden a chance at three in a row, but a stone bruise caused the colt to be scratched from the race.

Grey Lag was sold as a yearling to trainer Max Hirsch, who campaigned him until Sam Hildreth and Harry F. Sinclair purchased him for $50,000 after his victory in the Champagne. The colt raced

in trainer Hildreth's name for the remainder of his 2-year-old season, then in the name of Sinclair's Rancocas Stable thereafter. A good 2-year-old but a notch below the best of his crop, the son of Star Shoot returned to dominate the division for the next three years.

Starting with the Belmont, Grey Lag won eight straight stakes events, six of them in July alone, before losing his final three outings of the season. During the streak, he beat older horses, including Exterminator, in the Brooklyn Handicap, equaled an American record, and set a Canadian record. Like Sir Barton, he was troubled by bad feet and had two short campaigns at 4 and 5, losing only twice before being retired.

After proving a failure at stud, siring only a handful of foals before becoming sterile, he was back at the track at 9, when he won both starts, and at 10, when he only won 1 of 4. Retired once again to a supposed life of ease, the old horse changed ownership and eventually ended up racing three years later in claiming races in Canada, in which he was unable to win. When news of the matter reached Sinclair, the 13-year-old was bought back and sent, finally, to retirement at Rancocas.

Only two years after Grey Lag missed his Derby, another Madden-bred, Rancocas-owned horse earned the roses at Churchill Downs. This was Zev, who had lost the Preakness as the favorite the week before and was sent off at 19-1 in the Derby.

A good 2-year-old, Zev entered the Preakness having never gone beyond six furlongs, and his dismal showing in the nine-furlong event suggested that he could not handle the distance. A midweek sprint victory proved his fitness but did little to convince anyone that he could manage 10 furlongs. His front-running Derby victory did, however, and Zev kept on winning despite added distance. The Belmont at 1⅜ miles was no problem, nor was the 1⅝-mile Lawrence Realization.

Having established himself as the best 3-year-old in the country, Zev took on Epsom Derby winner Papyrus in a 1½-mile match race at Belmont in October. The International Race, worth a fabulous

Grey Lag's stellar career was interrupted several times by injury and once by a failed attempt at stud duty.

$100,000, was contested in deep slop, and Zev won it in a romp by five lengths.

Despite all that he had accomplished, the Latonia Championship nearly upended Zev's season. In the 1¾-mile race, In Memoriam replaced Zev as the division's leader in the eyes of many when he won by six lengths. A later match race between the two was inconclusive, won by a nose in rather unimpressive fashion by Zev over the Kentucky-based colt. Many went away feeling that In Memoriam was better, but Zev had won 12 of 14, including many of the season's most important contests, and his 3-year-old season earnings alone were enough to eclipse Man o' War as the country's leading money winner.

Zev returned to the races at 4 and won a pair of stakes, but he was no longer the kingpin. He took part in two of the three International Specials with French invader Epinard but failed to finish in the top three in either of them. On the day of the climactic International Special #3, he was in action, but in a sprint allowance, not the day's feature.

Instead, the star of the International Special #3 was the 3-year-old gelding Sarazen. By the remarkably inbred High Time, who was the product of a son of two Domino offspring bred to a Domino mare, Sarazen had been an undefeated sensation at 2 and was among the best of the crop at 3. In the International Special #3, he was trying 10 furlongs for the first time and proved spectacularly able, winning decisively in a brilliant 2:00⅗. Given the controversial nature of Whisk Broom II's 1913 Suburban record timing, it was probably the fastest 10 furlongs in the history of the sport.

Midway through his 5-year-old season, Sarazen began to sulk habitually in his races. After taking the Mount Vernon Handicap in July 1926, he never won another race. Eventually his connections, despairing of ever getting the horse to run again, retired him after he lost 16 straight over three seasons.

Also in action in the International Special #3 was another Madden-bred, the 3-year-old filly Princess Doreen. Already she had accounted for the Kentucky Oaks by disqualification, with Preakness winner Nellie Morse among the beaten, and an easy victory in the Coaching Club American Oaks. She came into the race with two straight stakes victories against older males and was well regarded in the Special, going off at 5-1. It was Sarazen's day to shine, however, and Princess Doreen finished a well-beaten fifth. But in years to come, when Sarazen's best days were behind him, the tough mare still had important races to win. Racing almost entirely in open company, Princess Doreen was a perennial star of the Midwest and competitive against the best in the East, winning races such as the Saratoga Handicap, Bowie Handicap, and the valuable Independence Handicap at Latonia twice.

In 1925, Princess Doreen passed Miss Woodford to become America's leading female earner, and the well-traveled mare ultimately retired in 1927 with $174,745 from 34 wins in 94 starts.

Just a week after Princess Doreen won the Coaching Club American

Princess Doreen, a winner 34 times in 94 starts, retired in 1927 as the richest female of all time, with $174,745 in earnings.

Oaks, a legendary career came quietly to a close in Canada. At 9, the great gelding Exterminator was long past his prime, but he was still good enough to win 3 of 7 outings, all three in different countries. A career that had seen him win 50 of 100 starts, recording victories in 33 stakes at distances ranging from six furlongs to 2¼ miles, ended with a third-place finish at Dorval Park.

Exterminator had won a pair of races at 2 without looking like a future star, but while in training at 3 he caught the eye of Henry McDaniel, who trained Kentucky Derby favorite Sun Briar for Willis Sharpe Kilmer. In the days before the 1918 Derby, Exterminator was purchased by Kilmer for $15,000 from J. C. Milam, who had obtained him as a yearling for $1,500. Although Exterminator was supposedly purchased as a workmate for Sun Briar, it was Exterminator who represented Kilmer in the Derby, and the gelding won as the longshot in an eight-horse field. He would not win again until the fall, eventually closing the season with a narrow victory in the 2¼-mile Latonia Cup.

Early in his 4-year-old campaign, Exterminator returned to the site of his Derby triumph to take the Kentucky Handicap over 10 furlongs but failed to win another stakes race at less than 1¾ miles through a long, hard campaign. His late season was highlighted by a victory in the Pimlico Cup over 2¼ miles, a race he would win the next two years.

Over the next three seasons, the marathon star, who previously had been outrun at middle distances against better company, suddenly proved dangerously proficient at all distances. At nine furlongs, he won the Brooklyn and Long Beach Handicaps, the latter twice in track-record time; at 9½, the Merchants' and Citizens' Handicap; and at 10, the Toronto Autumn Cup three straight years. Such was the respect for him that in 33 starts at ages 6 and 7, he never carried less than 126 pounds.

In a brief three-start campaign at 8, Exterminator earned his final stakes triumph in the Philadelphia Handicap, and he was no longer capable of winning against stakes company at 9. But with the last few thousand dollars he earned that season, he inched past Man o' War's former earnings record to retire with $252,996, good enough to place him second behind Zev among American runners.

Exterminator beat almost all of the good horses of his day, but although they competed at the same track on the same day on more than one occasion, Exterminator and the mighty Man o' War never met.

In fact, Man o' War raced only one horse not foaled in 1917 during his entire career, and that occurred in his final start, when he decisively

A moderate horse at 3, Exterminator won the Kentucky Derby as a longshot, but didn't really hit his stride until he turned 5.

MAN O' WAR
Anthony M. Alonso ©1979

Man o' War was so dominant that few horses would run against him. He won the Lawrence Realization by 100 lengths against just one other rival.

downed 1919 Triple Crown winner Sir Barton in the match race. But while his competition was limited, his performances were so brilliant that by the time he retired he was hailed almost universally as the best racehorse ever bred in the United States.

A son of Fair Play, who had almost beaten the great Colin in the 1908 Belmont, Man o' War was generally regarded as the best racehorse since that Keene runner by the end of his 2-year-old campaign. He had suffered one defeat in 10 starts when he was away poorly in the Sanford Memorial at Saratoga, losing by a half-length to Upset. He won under 130 pounds on five occasions while winning races at five to six furlongs, but the closest he came to a track record at 2 was in his lone loss.

The big red colt's performances at 3, virtually unvarying demonstrations of brilliance, effectively established him as a legend. After winning his season debut in the Preakness, he set five American records at distances ranging from a mile to 1⅝ miles while winning many of the most important races of the season. He won the Lawrence Realization by 100 lengths and took the Potomac Handicap under 138 pounds, believed to be the highest weight carried to victory by a 3-year-old in a flat race at a major track since at least the Civil War. So dominant was Man o' War that few would run their horses against him. Only once after the Preakness did he face as many as four rivals.

Man o' War's career ended with an anticlimactic gallop over Sir Barton in the $75,000 Kenilworth Park Gold Cup, at that time the richest horse race in history. It was enough to propel his earnings to nearly $250,000, well past Domino's standing record. Concerned about the weights that would be assigned to the colt in further campaigns, owner Samuel D. Riddle retired his champion shortly thereafter.

Man o' War made an immediate impression at stud. From his first crop, he sired American Flag, Maid at Arms, and Florence Nightingale, winners of the Belmont, Alabama, and Coaching Club American Oaks, respectively. From the second crop came Travers winner Mars, another CCA Oaks winner in Edith Cavell, and Crusader, the best of Man o' War's early foals.

Although he had previously won a stakes, it wasn't until the 1926 Suburban Handicap that Crusader began his ascent. Part of a favored entry with stablemate American Flag and under a feathery 104 pounds as a 3-year-old against his elders, he led American Flag home five lengths in front, then returned a week later to win the Belmont. The other highlight of a successful classic season was his victory in the Jockey Club Gold Cup, in which he produced a final quarter of just under 23 seconds to win the two-mile race going away.

He returned at 4 to win the Suburban by an even wider margin, but in his next outing he was kicked at the start and never returned to his best form. He already had done enough to earn a place in the record books, however. No other horse has won the Suburban Handicap, Belmont, and Jockey Club Gold Cup in the same season and it would be close to 60 years before Devil His Due won consecutive runnings of the Suburban, once America's premier contest for older horses.

Crusader went to stud amid great expectations but proved a dismal failure. Although Man o' War would eventually establish a surviving sire line, it would not be through Crusader or his other best racing son, War Admiral, but through War Relic, grandsire of sprint champion Intentionally.

As the 1920's drew to a close, racing lost one of its most noteworthy figures when James Rowe Sr. died in August 1929. Rowe had seen a heroic age of American racing from many angles: He had ridden classic winners during his stint as a racing official, he had set the field for Domino's Futurity on its way, and he had trained many of the legends of his time. Rowe had been a constant in a period of change, and his passing served well to mark the ending of an era.

CHAMPIONS

PAST PERFORMANCES
1890's–1920's

Beldame

ch. f. 1901, by Octagon (Rayon d'Or)–Bella–Donna, by Hermit — **Lifetime record: 31 17 6 4 $102,570**

Own.– A. Belmont
Br.– August Belmont (Ky)
Tr.– A.J. Joyner

19Aug05- 4Sar	fst	1¾	:51 2:08 2:341 3:004	3↑ Sar Cup 7.5k	1	1	12	1hd	21½	21½	O'Neill F	121 w	3.60	84-11	Caughnawaga1271½Beldame1213Cairngorm113	Gamely	3
8Aug05- 4Sar	fst	1	:244 :483 1:13 1:392	3↑ Delaware H 2.6k	1	1	1hd	31	46	52½	O'Neill F	122 w	3.20	89-13	MollyBrnt1132DollySpnkr108noCrngorm109hd	Fast pace,tired	7
31Jly05- 4Sar	sl	1¼	:474 1:132 1:41 2:07	3↑ Saratoga H 10k	8	6	65¼	51½	44	33½	O'Neill F	120 w	4.50e	86-15	Caughnawaga1193WaterLight108½Beldm1208	Wide,game at end	9
8Jly05- 4Bri	sly	1¼	:482 1:131 1:391 2:044	3↑ Brighton H 25k	4	4	42½	44	36	39	O'Neill F	125 w	3.20	81-12	Artful1031Ort Wells1258Beldame1253	Impeded first turn	7
5Jly05- 4Bri	fst	1	:243 :483 1:131 1:381	3↑ Brighton Mile 3.8k	1	1	11½	11½	1½	2¾	O'Neill F	121 w	*.80	98-08	OrtWells126¾Beldame1217Delhi1268	Sulked when challenged	4
	Previously trained by F. Burlew																
24Jun05- 4She	hy	1⅜	:494 1:151 1:411 2:204	3↑ Advance 15k	3	1	11½	11½	1hd	2no	O'Neill F	121 w	*.20	84-14	Agile111noBeldame12150Graziallo126	Just missed	3
15Jun05- 4She	fst	1¼	:484 1:133 1:393 2:052	3↑ Suburban H 20k	3	2	23	22	11½	11	O'Neill F	123 w	3.50	96-07	Beldame1231Proper1094First Mason118¾	Easily	11
8Jun05- 4Gra	hy	1¼	:49 1:144 1:413 2:073	3↑ Standard 5.8k	2	2	2nk	2hd	1hd	11	O'Neill F	121 w	*.70	89-15	Beldame1211Cairngorm11110MajorDaingerfld128	Dueled,best	3
5Jun05- 3Gra	fst	1 1/16	:24 :48 1:133 1:47	3↑ Handicap 1405	7	1	1½	11½	1nk	21½	O'Neill F	126 w	4.00	93-08	Garnish1071½Beldame1264Kehailan1024	Second best	12
4May05- 4Bel	fst	1	:253 :49 1:413	3↑ Metropolitan H 12k	4	3	33	33½	72	915	O'Neill F	122 w	4.00	--	[DH]Sysonby107[DH]Race King975Colonial Girl1114	Tired	12
	Previously owned by N. Bennington																
24Sep04- 4Gra	fst	1½	:50 1:153 2:073 2:352	3↑ Second Spl 5.7k	4	1	12	13	16	15	O'Neill F	112 w	*.55	88-10	Beldame1125Broomstick1101McChesney121hd	Easing up	4
19Sep04- 4Gra	fst	1¼	:484 1:14 1:402 2:06	3↑ First Spl 5.9k	2	1	14	13	12	11½	O'Neill F	114 w	*1.00	97-06	Beldame1141½Caughnawaga1263Stalwart11710	Easily	5
7Sep04- 4She	fst	1⅜	:49 1:142 1:402 2:193	September 4.8k	4	2	11½	12	13	12½	O'Neill F	123	*1.20	97-05	Beldame1232½Graziallo122¾Ort Wells1261	Easily	4
30Aug04- 4She	fst	1⅛	:49 1:141 1:402 1:53	Dolphin 3.6k	3	1	12	12	13	14	O'Neill F	126 w	*.14	96-09	Beldame1264Ormonde's Right1143Aurumaster1052		4
	Repelled stretch challenge																
20Aug04- 4Sar	sly	1¾	:50 2:082 2:36 3:034	3↑ Sar Cup 10k	5	1	16	15	14	14	O'Neill F	108 w	*1.80	71-21	Beldame1084Africandr126½ThPckt1262	Never fully extended	5
4Aug04- 4Sar	fst	1⅛	:49 1:14 1:402 1:533	Ⓕ Alabama 5k	1	1	15	16	18	16	O'Neill F	124 w	*.05	89-08	Beldame1246Dimple1164Ishlana116	Easing up late	3
6Jly04- 4Bri	fst	1	:241 :48 1:123 1:38	3↑ Test H 5k	1	3	21½	22	22	21	O'Neill F	115 w	1.40	99-07	Hermis1331Beldame1155Dainty1034	Off slowly,poor ride	5
30Jun04- 2She	gd	1	:242 :48 1:13 1:392	3↑ Ⓕ Alw 1140	2	1	16	16	14	12	O'Neill F	111 w	*.35	92-05	Beldame1112Lux Casta1105Hortensia1013	Bumped at start	6
22Jun04- 4She	fst	1⅛	:483 1:14 1:41 1:542	Ⓕ Mermaid 6.3k	6	1	13	15	16	17	O'Neill F	126 w	*.60	89-11	Beldame1267Little Em1112½Possession1113½	Easing up	6
9Jun04- 4Gra	sly	1 1/16	:24 :50 1:173 1:523	Ⓕ Gazelle 4.6k	4	1	12	13	15	110	O'Neill F	124 w	*.17	67-27	Beldame12410Graceful1211Little Em1135	Easily	5
1Jun04- 1Gra	sly	*6f	:234 :481 1:11	3↑ Ⓕ Alw 1220	3	3	32	21	11	11	O'Neill F	106 w	*.50	88-17	Beldame1061Mamie Worth1155Graceful1016	Easily	8
21May04- 4MP	fst	1	:243 :50 1:153 1:411	Ⓕ Ladies 5.6k	4	1	11½	1½	14	1¾	Hildebrand	121 w	*.60	87-10	Beldame121¾Audience1215Marjoram12110		4
	Bolted before start and returned to stable area,won easing up																
5May04- 4MP	fst	1	:242 :48 1:142 1:40	3↑ Metropolitan H 13k	9	7	73¼	77	45	34	Brennan A	98 w	20.00	89-09	Irish Lad1232Toboggan1032Beldame98½	Gamely	17
15Apr04- 4Aqu	fst	7f	:24 :494 1:141 1:27	3↑ Carter H 8.7k	5	1	11	11	11¼	12	O'Neill F	103 w	7.00	96-09	Beldame1032Peter Paul985Wotan1001½	Speed in reserve	17
5Nov03- 5Aqu	sly	6f	:251 1:154	Handicap 880	-	2	11½	11½	11	14	O'Neill F	121 w	1.70	90-11	Beldame1214Harangue1221Palette1056	Easily	5
	Previously owned by A. Belmont;previously trained by J. Hyland																
3Oct03- 3MP	fst	*6f	1:102	Nursery H 7.6k	-	2	51¾	62¼	61½	42½	Cochran H	116 w	15.00	89-11	Race King1141½Grenade115hdDivination108¾	Finished fast	12
28Sep03- 3MP	gd	*6f	1:101	Ⓕ Matron 7k	-	4	57½	44½	43½	32	Cochran H	123 w	6.00e	90-07	Armenia112hdFor Luck1092Beldame123½	Fast finish	8
2Sep03- 3She	gd	*6f	1:124	Ⓕ Great Filly 17k	-	2	32½	2½	2½	1hd	Bullman	116wb	15.00	76-20	Beldame116hdOcean Tide116noMineola1166	Dueled,just up	15
22Aug03- 5Sar	fst	5½f	:232 :47 1:002 1:07	Alw 740	-	11	75¾	55	77¾	68	Bullman	114 w	9.00	87-00	Hamburg Belle1141½Long Shot1171½Race King1172	Bad start	11
1Jly03- 4She	fst	5f	1:012	Ⓕ Vernal 4.9k	-	3	11	11	12	11	Bullman	107 w	*.90e	85-15	Beldame1071Monsoon107hdTepee107hd	Gamely	13
10Jun03- 3Gra	my	5f	:244 :50 1:03	Ⓕ Clover 2.6k	-	12	76¼	72½	32	21½	Minder	112 w	*2.50	81-20	Contentous1121½Bldm112½Mordll1124	Bad start,fast finish	12

Ben Brush

b. c. 1893, by Bramble (Bonnie Scotland)–Roseville, by Reform — **Lifetime record: 40 25 5 5 $65,217**

Own.– Michael F. Dwyer
Br.– Clay & Woodford (Ky)
Tr.– Hardy Campbell

29Sep97- 4Gra	fst	1 1/16	:25 :49½ 1:14½ 1:47½	2↑ Alw 1050	-	4	42½	32	33	2hd	Simms	126	*.29	--	Plaudit90hdBenBrush126hdDr.Ctltt1143	Driving throughout	5
25Sep97- 4Gra	gd	1¼	:53½ 1:18¾ 1:43½ 2:10	3↑ Second Spl 2.3k	-	1	1½	1¾	12	13	Simms	126	*.80	--	Ben Brush1263Ornament117	Best,good ride	2
23Sep97- 3Gra	hy	1		2↑ Alw 340	-	1	1	1	1	1	Simms	120	-	--	Ben Brush120	Walked over	1
	No times taken																
18Sep97- 4Gra	sl	1 1/16	:25 :50¼ 1:16 1:48¼	3↑ First Spl 2.5k	-	2	23	22½	1½	12	Simms	120	*1.00	--	Ben Brush1202Hastings1205Requital120	Easily	3
14Sep97- 4Gra	gd	1¼	:50 1:15½ 1:42¾ 2:08	3↑ Oriental H 3k	-	2	22	2½	1½	2no	Simms	127	4.00	--	Havoc113noBen Brush1272½Maurice99½	Used early	8
4Sep97- 4She	hy	1⅛	:511 1:17 1:421 1:55	3↑ Omnium H 2k	-	2	1hd	1hd	1½	1¾	Simms	126	3.00	--	Ben Brush126¾Hastings1231Clifford127½	Best,handily	7
30Aug97- 5She	gd	1⅛	:503 1:154 1:432 1:561	3↑ Handicap 1170	-	9	64¾	72¾	53	31	Hewitt	127	3.50	--	Sir Walter117hdFree Advice1081Ben Brush1274	Bad ride	10
21Aug97- 5Bri	gd	2¼	:52½ 2:38½ 2:51½ 3:56½	3↑ Brighton Cup 5k	-	3	35	35	35	310	Simms	130	*.60	--	TheFriar115hdSunnySlope11110BenBrush130	Challenged,quit	3
10Aug97- 4Sar	fst	1¼	:50¼ 1:15¾ 1:41¾ 2:07½	3↑ Citizens' 2.5k	-	2	21	21½	2½	11	Simms	126	2.00	--	Ben Brush1261Clifford1264Howard Mann126	Gamely	4
31Jly97- 3Sar	hy	1	:26 :51 1:16½ 1:44	2↑ Midsummer H 2k	-	3	31¼	31¾	45	31	Simms	126	*1.40	--	Sir Walter111hdHavoc1121Ben Brush1266	Pulled up lame	7
12Jly97- 4Bri	gd	1¼	:49¼ 1:14¼ 1:41¼ 2:09	3↑ Brighton H 2.5k	-	2	2½	2hd	11	12	Simms	126	1.00	--	Ben Brush1262The Friar1076Volley98	Easily	3
8Jly97- 4She	gd	1⅛	:504 1:16 1:411 1:542	3↑ Long Island H 2k	-	3	21½	31	33½	42½	Simms	126	2.50	--	Clifford127½Sir Walter1092Lehman114hd		5
	Eased up,passed late for 3rd																
5Jly97- 5She	gd	1	:242 :49 1:15 1:41	3↑ Sheepshead Bay H 1.5k	-	8	7	7	8	69¾	Simms	128	2.00	--	Havoc108nkLehman111½The Swain101.58	Eased up late	10
	Other margins unavailable																
22Jun97- 4She	gd	1¼	:511 1:161 1:464 2:071	3↑ Suburban H 7.5k	-	4	41½	3½	1½	11	Simms	123	*2.00	--	Ben Brush1231The Winner115½Havoc1028	Best,handily	9
17Jun97- 5Gra	gd	1	:25 :50¼ 1:15¾ 1:41¾	3↑ Alw 660	-	3	32½	2hd	12	13	Simms	118	*.60	--	Ben Brush1183Belmar1205The Swain108½	Much the best	5
12Jun97- 5Gra	hy	1 1/16	:25½ :51 1:17 1:48¼	3↑ Alw 680	-	4	51½	31	3½	2nk	Simms	118	3.00	--	Premier118nkBen Brush1181Caldron91hd	All out	10
18Aug96- 3She	gd	1	:262 :523 1:174 1:42	3↑ Handicap 890	-	4	31	32	1nk	1no	Simms	111	*.90	--	[D]Ben Brush111noSouffle1003Hanwell112½		4
	Disqualified																
15Aug96- 3She	gd	6f-FC	:251 :494 1:021 1:15	3↑ Fall H 1.5k	-	5	64½	64½	62¼	4nk	Simms	113	5.00	--	Gotham121hdHanwell110hdBuck Massie121hd	Closed gap	8
25Jun96- 4Lat	hy	1½	:53 1:20¼ 2:13¼ 2:40½	Lat Derby 13k	-	5	21	2hd	1½	11½	Simms	122	*.25e	--	Ben Brush1221½Ben Eder1225Loki1223	Entry much best	5
20Jun96- 4StL	fst	1½	:51½ 1:17 2:08 2:34	National Derby 20k	-	3	23	22	2hd	2hd	Simms	127	*1.00e	--	PrinceLief127hdBenBrush1275BenEder1228	All out effort	7
13Jun96- 4Oky	fst	1⅛	:50½ 1:15 1:40¾ 1:54	Buckeye 7k	-	3	2½	2hd	1hd	1hd	Simms	122	1.60	--	Ben Brush122hdPrince Lief1252Loki1191	Dueled,good ride	4
21May96- 4Oky	gd	1¼	:52 1:17 1:42 2:08¼	Oakley Derby 12k	-	4	31¼	31½	22	31½	Simms	122	*.50e	--	Prince Lief1171½Ben Eder122hdBen Brush1221½	Not enough	5
16May96- 4CD	my	1	:27 :53 1:19 1:44¼	Schulte 2k	-	1	1½	12	1nk	110	Thorpe	122	*.40	--	[DH]Ben Brush122[DH]Lady Inez11710Semper Ego11510	Driving	4
16May96- 0CD	my	1	:25½ :50¾ 1:16¼ 1:43	Run-Off	-	1	11	12	11	11	Thorpe	122	.90	--	Ben Brush1221Lady Inez117	Easily	2
	Run off of dead heat																
6May96- 3CD	fst	1¼	:49½ 1:15½ 1:42 2:07¾	Ky Derby 6k	-	4	21½	21½	11	1no	Simms	117	*.50	--	Ben Brush117noBen Eder1175Semper Ego1175	Driving,lasted	8
31Oct95- 4MP	gd	7f	:25¼ :49½ 1:02¼ 1:27	Champagne 3k	-	2	2hd	24	1nk	1½	Simms	120	*.33	--	Ben Brush120½Prince Lief1104Merry Prince1108	Handily	5
19Oct95- 3MP	fst	6f-EC	:24½ :49¼ 1:01½ 1:14	Albany 2k	-	2	11	1½	1nk	1¾	Simms	128	*.10	--	Ben Brush128¾Merry Prince1158Cassette1054	Very easily	4
15Oct95- 4MP	sly	6f-EC	:25½ :51¾ 1:04½ 1:11¾	Nursery H 3.2k	-	4	31½	2½	2hd	1½	Simms	127	*.80	--	Ben Brush127½Hazlet111½Woodvine1044	Handily	6
12Oct95- 1Gra	hy	6f	:25¾ 1:03 1:17½	2↑ Handicap 650	-	1	1hd	11	11	11½	Simms	108	*.30	--	Ben Brush1081½Salvable98nkCuckoo973	Cantering	5
5Oct95- 3Gra	fst	6f	:24¼ 1:01½ 1:15½	Prospect H 3k	-	2	2nk	1nk	11	12	Simms	124	*1.00	--	Ben Brush1242Crescendo1211½Handspring125nk	Handily	7

30Sep95- 5Gra	fst 5½f	:25¼ :50½ 1:04¼ 1:11	Alw 500	- 1 2hd 1½ 1½	1½	Simms	118	*.35	- -	Ben Brush118½Margrave1132Karma103	In a canter 3
	Previously owned and trained by Ed Brown & Eugene Leigh										
17Sep95- 3Gra	gd 5f	:23¾ :48¼ 1:01½	Holly H 2k	- 3 21 1nk 1½	11	Williams R	121	3.50	- -	Ben Brush1211Margrave1152Crescendo1221	Easily 7
14Sep95- 4She	gd *6f-FC	1:101	Great Eastern H 5k	- -	8	Williams R	126	4.50	- -	One I Love122hdMargrave110½Hazlet112hd	Never a threat 13
10Sep95- 4She	fst 7f	1:26	Flatbush 3k	- -	22	Williams R	110	3.00	- -	Requital1152Ben Brush1103Crescendo115	Led til late 4
5Sep95- 1She	fst 5f	1:002	Handicap 700	- -	11	Williams R	114	*.45	- -	BenBrush1141Mussulman95hdIntermission101.5hd	Led,easily 5
27Aug95- 1She	fst 6f	1:131 2↑	Alw 590	- -	35	Perkins	103	*.40	- -	RightRoyal824FlorettaIV103.51BenBrush103	Never a threat 6
23Jly95- 4Oky	fst 5½f	1:08	Diamond 3.5k	- -	11	Williams R	125	*.50	- -	Ben Brush1251Ben Eder1232Prince Lief111	Easily 5
9Jly95- 4Oky	fst 5f	1:02¼	©Emerald 2.5k	- -	12	Williams R	123	*.60	- -	Ben Brush1232Ramiro118hdBen Holladay118	Easily 5
6Jun95- 4Lat	gd 5f	:25 :49½ 1:02¾	©Harold 2.7k	- 3 22 21 2½	13	Williams R	121	*.60	- -	Ben Brush1213Nimrod111½The Dragon1111	Galloping 6
15May95- 4CD	hy 4½f	:25¼ :51¼ :58	©Cadet 2k	- 1 1nk 1½ 11	13	Williams R	118	*1.60	- -	Ben Brush1182Del Coronado115hdBen Eder118½	Easily 6
7May95- 2CD	fst 5f	1:02¼	©Alw 400	- -	15	Perkins	108	1.60	- -	Ben Brush1085Captive1134Concession113	5

Black Maria

blk. f. 1923, by Black Toney (Peter Pan)–Bird Loose, by Sardanapale

Lifetime record: 52 18 14 6 $110,350

Own.– W.R. Coe
Br.– E.R. Bradley (Ky)
Tr.– J. Lowe

21Nov28- 5Bow	gd 1 1/16	:25 :501 1:15 1:464 3↑	Handicap 1900	2 3 32 34¼ 35	37½	Bejshak J	117wb	4.30	81-14	Victorian120½Misstep1187Black Maria117	Outrun late 3
6Nov28- 5Pim	gd 1½	:493 1:153 2:072 2:342 3↑	Bowie H 13k	7 6 68½ 615 617	623¾	Fator L	116wb	9.65	57-21	Genie1171½Display1266Edith Cavell104nk	Never a factor 7
27Oct28- 5Lrl	fst 1¼	:463 1:12 1:373 2:033 3↑	Washington H 32k	9 10 1011 115 106¼	105¾	Fator L	122wb	*2.65e	86-11	Mike Hall124hdDisplay1262½Sir Harry113½	Tired 13
13Oct28- 5Lrl	fst 1	:234 :474 1:131 1:384 2↑	Laurel 14k	8 9 913 97 34½	2nk	Barnes E	113wb	8.20	94-12	Osmand123nkBlackMaria1131PrincessTina107½	Crowded start 9
8Oct28- 5Lrl	fst 6f	:23 :464 1:122 2↑	Handicap 1500	7 3 52¾ 75¼ 76¾	65	Barnes E	125wb	6.10	90-13	Knapsack104.5hdPrince of Wales1281½Wellet1051½	Outrun 8
25Aug28- 5Sar	my 1 3/16	:50 1:16 1:43 2:031 3↑	Merchants & Cits H 9k	3 2 12 1½ 1nk	2nk	Fator L	123wb	*1.10	62-34	ChanceShot123nkBlackMr1236Dngrous11015	Rushed up,gamely 4
11Aug28- 5Sar	fst 1¼	:471 1:124 1:39 2:06 3↑	Whitney 8.2k	1 2 21½ 21 1nk	1¾	Fator L	121wb	1.50	79-19	Black Maria121¾Chance Shot1264Whiskery12615	Driving 4
30Jly28- 5Sar	gd 1¼	:483 1:13 1:39 2:06 3↑	Saratoga H 9.7k	5 2 21 2hd 1hd	21½	Fator L	115wb	10.00	77-15	Chance Shot1221½Black Maria1152Edith Cavell1061½	Gamely 8
16Jun28- 4Aqu	fst 1⅛	:464 1:13 1:372 1:511 3↑	Brooklyn H 17k	9 6 64¼ 53¼ 55	64¼	Fator L	114wb	*2.20	83-21	Black Panther105½Victorian112½Diavolo1061½	Poor effort 9
12Jun28- 4Aqu	fst 1	:233 :47 1:123 1:383 3↑	Handicap 1200	2 2 13 15 13	12	Fator L	126wb	*.45	87-17	BlackMaria1262Dangerous11515Lasso'Gowrie109	Won eased 3
2Jun28- 4Bel	fst 1¼	:483 1:13 1:40 2:063 3↑	Suburban H 17k	2 3 43 86¾ 811	917½	Fator L	120wb	5.00	49-26	Dolan1054Chance Shot120½Scapa Flow120no	Quit 9
24May28- 4Bel	fst 6½f	:224 :47 1:12 1:184 3↑	ⒻHandicap 1275	3 5 43 21 23	22	Coltiletti F	126wb	*1.60	90-17	BlackCurl1202BlackMaria1262Snobbish988	Tired in stretch 5
	Previously trained by W.H. Karrick										
29Oct27- 5Lrl	fst 1¼	:47 1:114 1:372 2:022 3↑	Washington H 36k	5 2 2hd 2hd 2hd	2hd	Coltiletti F	117wb	4.20	98-10	Display112hdBlack Maria1171Mars1281	Just missed 9
15Oct27- 5Lrl	fst 1	:233 :47 1:133 1:381 2↑	Laurel 13k	5 8 62 62 21	2nk	Coltiletti F	117wb	3.85	97-14	Osmand115nkBlack Maria1171Macaw1161½	Getting to winner 8
8Oct27- 4Jam	sly 1 1/16	:233 :492 1:133 1:451 3↑	Continental H 6k	1 2 1hd 2hd 1hd	11½	Fator L	125wb	*.08	87-17	Black Maria1251½Rip Rap105	Won under restraint 2
1Oct27- 4Aqu	fst 1⅛	:47 1:12 1:36 1:494 3↑	Aqueduct H 7.4k	1 3 21 2½ 1½	12	Fator L	122wb	*.40	94-14	BlackMaria1222ⒹKentuckyII1062LightCarbin1082	Drew away 4
24Sep27- 4Aqu	fst 1⅛	:474 1:124 1:37 1:504 3↑	Edgemere H 7k	2 1 11½ 11½ 11½	12	Coltiletti F	116wb	*.55	89-12	BlackMaria1162LghtCrbn10810Pnuts122	Won under restraint 3
7Sep27- 4Bel	fst 1	:232 :462 1:111 1:372 2↑	Manhattan H 5.2k	8 2 2½ 2½ 2½	51	Coltiletti F	118wb	*2.00	89-14	Valorous114nkKiev109noOsmand117½	Forced pace,tired late 9
27Aug27- 5Sar	sly 1 3/16	:49 1:141 1:393 1:591 3↑	Merchants & Cits H 9.7k	4 1 11 1hd 2hd	21	McAuliffe D	116wb	*1.50e	81-19	Chance Play1241Black Maria1164Pompey1174	Tired 6
9Aug27- 4Sar	hy 1	:242 :474 1:134 1:403 3↑	Delaware H 5.3k	4 3 35 22 22	44¾	Coltiletti F	120wb	*.17e	73-26	LightCarbin106nkByrd1001½Pompy1193	Tired badly in drive 5
1Aug27- 5Sar	hy 1¼	:503 1:153 1:403 2:073 3↑	Saratoga H 9.5k	5 2 21 1nk 1hd	21½	Coltiletti F	119wb	3.20	69-21	Mars1221½Black Maria1193Light Carbine1073	Second best 5
4Jly27- 4Aqu	fst 7f	:23 :461 1:112 1:241 3↑	Carter H 10k	9 9 93½ 41½ 21½	2nk	Sande E	124wb	4.00e	94-10	HappyArgo119nkBlckMr1243Mcw124hd	Swerved final furlong 14
18Jun27- 4Aqu	fst 1⅛	:471 1:12 1:36 1:484 3↑	Brooklyn H 17k	3 5 44 35 47	76¼	Coltiletti F	123wb	7.00e	93-09	Peanuts112hdChance Play1214Display1121	Poor effort 10
4Jun27- 4Bel	fst 1¼	:464 1:11 1:371 2:022 3↑	Suburban H 15k	3 2 1hd 1hd 22	27	Coltiletti F	120wb	3.00	81-14	Crusadr1277BlckMaria1202Macw1202	Forced pace,no match 8
30May27- 4Bel	fst 1	:231 :47 1:112 1:372 3↑	Metropolitan H 9.7k	1 5 31¼ 21 21	11	Coltiletti F	116wb	4.00	90-16	BlackMaria1161Osmnd1122Vlorous108.55	Forced wide,gamely 8
21May27- 5Bel	gd 1	:231 :464 1:122 1:394 3↑	ⒻLadies H 4.4k	1 3 33½ 21½ 1nk	15	Coltiletti F	127wb	*.45	78-24	Black Maria1275Jumbo110½Corvette1111½	Cantering 5
14May27- 1Jam	fst 6f	:24 :471 1:121 3↑	ⒻHandicap 1255	2 4 2no 21 1hd	11½	Breuning B	126wb	*.60	94-07	BlackMaria1261½Accomplish1041Corvette115no	Won eased up 4
6Oct26- 4Jam	sly 1 1/16	:242 :473 1:122 1:452 3↑	October H 4.4k	3 1 14 13 14	12	McAuliffe D	115wb	*.65e	86-19	Black Maria1152Sanford1065Pompey1164	Won eased up 5
2Oct26- 5HdG	hy 1 1/16	:241 :484 1:134 1:47	Potomac H 16k	3 2 2½ 21 21	4¾	Johnson A	116 w	1.35e	88-21	ChancePlay123¾Gffsmn112hdPompy121no	Tired final furlong 6
25Sep26- 4Aqu	my 1⅛	:472 1:12 1:371 1:512 3↑	Aqueduct H 7.4k	1 1 12 15 14	15	Callahan J	112wb	*.13e	88-26	Black Maria1125Pompey1184Dazzler1008	Speed in reserve 5
18Sep26- 4Aqu	fst 1⅛	:454 1:102 1:36 1:483 3↑	Edgemere H 7.5k	4 2 11½ 11 11½	31¾	Fator L	113wb	*.35e	100-11	Peanuts114nkPompey1181½Black Maria113hd	Resolutely 7
14Sep26- 6Bel	fst 1¼	:484 1:121 1:37 2:024 3↑	Twin City H 5.9k	7 1 12 12 15	14	Fator L	110wb	4.50	86-17	BlackMaria1104Sanford108.5hdEdithCvll1051½	Won eased up 7
6Sep26- 6Bel	my 1¼	:473 1:123 1:391 2:074	ⒻChampion Filly 5.5k	1 1 12 14 16	15	Fator L	123wb	*.40	61-28	Black Maria1235Rapture123	Eased final 16th 2
24Aug26- 4Sar	my 1 3/16	:49 1:142 1:393 1:593	Huron H 5.1k	1 4 42½ 21½ 33	36½	Breuning B	112wb	6.00	73-20	Crusader1261½Espino1145Black Maria1124	Tired 7
19Aug26- 4Sar	fst 1	:242 :481 1:141 1:392	Sar Sales 3.8k	4 3 1hd 11½ 12	15	Breuning B	115wb	*.30	84-19	Black Maria1155Nomad1202Nurmi120hd	In a canter 4
10Aug26- 4Sar	fst 1¼	:473 1:131 1:392 2:06	ⒻAlabama 12k	3 1 13 11 1hd	22	Breuning B	126wb	2.50	77-15	Rapture1242Black Maria12610Ruthenia1174	Tired,gamely 6
31Jly26- 6Was	fst 1½	:48 1:131 2:043 2:301	American Derby 106k	4 4 35 42½ 33	34	Breuning B	116wb	2.80	- -	Boot to Boot1212Display1262Black Maria1166	Tired,gamely 5
24Jly26- 5Was	gd 1⅛	:49 1:134 1:394 1:54	ⒻIll Oaks 11k	3 1 13 16 16	16	Breuning B	121wb	*.10	- -	Black Maria1216In Bounds11610Spanish Star116	Cantering 3
3Jly26- 5Lat	fst 1¼	:464 1:121 1:38 2:03	ⒻLat Oaks 13k	4 3 21 2½ 21	21½	Mortensen A	126wb	3.70	87-11	EdithCavell1261½BlackMaria1262Helen'sBb121½	Outfinished 10
9Jun26- 4Bel	fst 1⅜	:50 1:154 1:412 2:203	ⒻC C A Oaks 13k	1 1 31 2½ 22	22	Fator L	121wb	*1.20	66-33	EdithCavell1172BlackMaria1214Rptur1177	Challenged,tired 6
31May26- 5CD	sly 1⅛	:491 1:143 1:414 1:552	ⒻKy Oaks 13k	6 2 2½	14	Mortensen A	121wb	4.00	72-20	BlckMria1214DarkPhantom116hdHelen'sBab1163	Going away 10
22May26- 4Bel	fst 1	:233 :473 1:132 1:384 3↑	ⒻLadies H 4k	5 1 11½ 13 11½	12	Fator L	120wb	7.00	83-20	Black Maria1202Extra Dry1197Rapture1222	Easily 7
5May26- 4Pim	fst 1 1/16	:234 :483 1:133 1:454	ⒻPim Oaks 6k	5 8 86 75¾ 611	312	Fator L	113wb	*1.15	81-17	Rapture11312Ingrid121hdBlack Maria1131½	8
	Outrun early,finished well										
1May26- 4Jam	fst 1 70	:234 :483 1:123 1:42	Wood 10k	7 4 42 44 44	46½	Mortensen A	105wb	*.29e	89-09	Pompey1201½Navigator1204Espino1101	Rated,outside 7
	Geldings not eligible;Previously campaigned in name of Shoshone Stable										
12Oct25- 3Jam	fst 5½f	:23 :47 1:054	ⒻHiawatha H 3.9k	5 5 56¾ 45¼ 33	42¼	Fator L	126wb	*1.00	93-12	Ethereal108hdPatricJ.121hdMdl1072	Hard ridden,slow gain 5
14Sep25- 4Bel	fst 5½f	:232 :473 1:053	ⒻTomboy H 4.6k	5 5 54½ 43 22	21½	Kummer C	125 w	5.00	92-16	Ruthenia1171½Black Maria1254Martha Washington1141	10
	Shuffled back,wide,finished fast										
5Sep25- 5Bel	fst 6f	:233 :471 1:12	Clm	2 2 21½ 24 23	11	Fator L	108wb	8.00	92-11	BlackMaria1081ColorSergeant1104RockStar1181	Going away 7
29Aug25- 3Sar	fst 6½f	:23 :461 1:113 1:174	Hopeful 51k	14 14 147¾ 1314 118½	915¼	Fator M	112wb	*3.20e	97-10	Pompey1275FlightofTime1254ChancePlay1223	Not a factor 15
25Aug25- 6Sar	fst 6½f	:23 :47 1:131 1:191	Alw 1000	6 3 21 11½ 13	14	Callahan J	99wb	3.60	105-11	Black Maria994Nurmi108noBlondin108½	Easily 7
15Aug25- 3Sar	hy 6f	:23 :48 1:152	ⒻSpinaway 8.9k	12 12 1220 1217 76¾	55¼	Fator L	109 w	4.50e	70-31	Cinema1121Asn1122Ruthn113nk	Left at start,closed ground 13
11Aug25- 6Sar	gd 5f	:233 :473 1:004	Alw 1000	8 10 98¼ 105¾ 62½	35	Fator L	108wb	6.00e	80-19	Rockslide118hdRemedy1135BlackMari1083	Began in a tangle 10
5Aug25- 6Sar	sl 5½f	:233 :474 1:072	Md Sp Wt	10 15 138 1313 1013	1016	Fairbrother C	115wb	40.00	70-17	Haste1182Vespasian1185Blondin1181	Not a factor 17

Colin

b. c. 1905, by Commando (Domino)–Pastorella, by Springfield — **Lifetime record: 15 15 0 0 $180,912**

Own.– J.R. Keene
Br.– James R. Keene (Ky)
Tr.– J. Rowe

20Jun08- 4She	fst 1¼	:47 1:113 1:38 2:04	Tidal 20k	3	1	12	11½	13	12	Notter	126	w	*.20	103-06	Colin1262Dorante1264Stamin1218	Bore out,tiring slightly	4
30May08- 3Bel	sly 1⅜		Belmont 25k	2	-			11½	1hd	Notter	126	w	*.50	- -	Colin126hdFair Play12615King James12610	Eased up	4
	Driving rainstorm,no time taken																
23May08- 4Bel	hy 1	:24 :48 1:14 1:41	Withers 14k	2	1	13	13	14	12	Notter	126	w	*.40	82-19	Colin1262Fair Play126¾King James1268	Eased up	6
16Oct07- 3Bel	fst 7f-Str	1:23	Champagne 7.2k	2	1	13	14	15	16	Miller W	122	w	*.14	103-06	Colin1226Stamina119	Drawing away	2
7Oct07- 2Bel	fst 6f-Str	1:12	©Matron 10k	3	1	24	15	14	13	Miller W	129	w	*.14	90-11	Colin1293Fair Play1224Royal Tourist119½	Easing up	4
30Sep07- 4Bri	my 6f	:242 :474 1:123	©Produce (2nd half) 12k	1	1	11½	14	14	15	Miller W	125	w	*.25	96-13	Colin1255Fair Play119hdRoyal Tourist11920	Eased up	4
7Sep07- 3She	fst 7f-FC	1:244	Flatbush 10k	6	1	11½	11½	13	13	Miller W	120	w	*.35e	100-00	Colin1203Celt1055Bar None1051½	Hard held	7
31Aug07- 4She	fst 6f-FC	1:111	Futurity 28k	5	1	21	22	1½	11½	Miller W	125	w	*.33	97-03	Coln1251½BrNon1171Chpultpc1171½	Blocked,as rider pleased	8
14Aug07- 3Sar	fst 6f	:241 :482 1:13	Grand Union Hotel 10k	3	4	2hd	2hd	1hd	12	Miller W	127	w	*.13e	95-05	Colin1272Jim Gaffney1123Ben Fleet1171	Hard held	6
10Aug07- 3Sar	fst 6f	:233 :47 :582 1:12	Sar Spl 9.5k	2	2	1hd	1hd	11	11	Miller W	122	w	*.40	100-04	Colin1221Uncle122	Decisively	2
27Jly07- 4Bri	fst 6f	:232 :471 1:121	Brighton Junior 15k	2	2	1½	11½	11½	11½	Miller W	127	w	*.65	99-06	Coln1271½Chpultpc1256BrNon112½	Repelled stretch challenge	8
29Jun07- 3She	sl 6f-FC	1:122	Great Trial 25k	7	2	21	11	12	12	Miller W	129	w	*2.60e	91-09	Colin1292Meelick1221½Monopolist1221½	Mild restraint	14
5Jun07- 3Bel	my 5½f-Str	1:063	Eclipse 9.2k	6	2	1nk	1hd	1hd	1hd	Mountain	125	w	*.60	94-07	Colin125hdBeaucoup11710WvCrst1175	Under pressure,gamely	6
1Jun07- 3Bel	fst 5f-Str	:58	National Stallion 10k	3	1	11½	11½	12	13	Miller W	122	w	*.75	102-00	Colin1223Bar None1174Ben Fleet122hd	Never threatened	6
29May07- 2Bel	gd 5f-Str	1:01	Md Sp Wt	10	1	12	13	12	12	Miller W	110	w	*1.20	87-17	Colin1102Bar None1108Harcourt1101½	Easily	23

Commando

b. c. 1898, by Domino (Himyar)–Emma C., by Darebin — **Lifetime record: 9 7 2 0 $58,196**

Own.– J.R. Keene
Br.– James R. Keene (Ky)
Tr.– James Rowe

4Jly01- 4She	my 1⅝	:492 1:433 2:10 2:494	Lawrence Realizatn 16k	-	2	24	21	1½	22	Spencer	121		*.20	91-13	TheParader1262Cmmndo12112Mortllo116hd	Tired badly,game	4
	Previously owned by J.R. & F.P. Keene																
1Jun01- 4Gra	fst 1	:242 :482 1:13 1:392	Carlton 5k	-	1	11	1¾	14	14	Spencer	126		*.20	106-08	Commando1264Blues111	Never extended	2
23May01- 4MP	fst 1⅜	:502 1:162 2:21	Belmont 13k	-	1	1hd	1¾	13	1½	Spencer	126		*.70	101-12	Commando126½The Parader12650All Green126	Tired at end	3
20Oct00- 3MP	fst *6f-EC	1:101	Matron 21k	-	3	11½	1½	12	2½	Spencer	125		*.40	91-09	Beau Gallant125½Commando125nkThe Parader1173	Poor ride	10
11Sep00- 3Gra	fst 6f	:231 :472 1:003 1:134	Jr Champion 15k	-	3	11	1½	11½	11	Spencer	127		*.33e	98-07	Commando1271Bellario117hdOlympian1072	Eased up at end	7
7Aug00- 5Bri	fst 6f	:233 :48 1:002 1:131	Brighton Junior 10k	-	1	2hd	1hd	1hd	1hd	Spencer	125		*.20e	100-02	Commando125hdOlympian1121½All Green1122	Best	5
6Jly00- 3Bri	fst 6f	:234 :474 1:141	Montauk 3k	-	1	13	13	15	18	Spencer	122		*.07	95-02	Commando1228Cresson1076Bedeck107	Outclassed rest	3
30Jun00- 3She	fst *6f-FC	1:114	Great Trial 20k	-	9	1½	14	14	13	Spencer	122		*1.80e	81-15	Commando1223The Parader1222Elkhorn1171½	Eased up	11
25Jun00- 3She	fst *6f-FC	1:092	Zephyr 1.1k	-	4	1hd	11	11½	11½	Spencer	112		*.70	93-05	Commando1121½Holstein112½King Pepper1126	Much the best	5

Crusader

ch. c. 1923, by Man o' War (Fair Play)–Star Fancy, by Star Shoot — **Lifetime record: 42 18 8 4 $203,261**

Own.– Glen Riddle Stable
Br.– Samuel D. Riddle (Ky)
Tr.– G. Conway

27Oct28- 5Lrl	fst 1¼	:463 1:12 1:373 2:033	3↑ Washington H 32k	1	6	77½	72¾	75¾	63½	Walls P	122	wb	5.65	88-11	Mike Hall124hdDisplay1262½Sir Harry113½	Outrun	13
24Oct28- 5Lrl	fst 1 1/16	:232 :47 1:124 1:452	3↑ Alw 2000	5	3	35¼	21	23	2½	Walls P	111	wb	1.75	89-20	Victorian114½Crusader1116Display1208	Gamely	5
11Oct28- 5Haw	fst 1¼	:473 1:12 1:371 2:03	3↑ Haw Gold Cup 26k	6	7	46½	51½	53½	32	Walls P	126	wb	2.91	103-06	Display126noMike Hall1262Crusader126hd	Hard urged	9
29Sep28- 5HdG	sly 1⅛	:48 1:131 1:411 1:534	3↑ H de Grace Cup H 24k	3	8	88	78	78½	33	Walls P	124	wb	4.05	78-19	Osmand121½Sun Beau1142½Crusader1241½	Outrun early	8
26Sep28- 6HdG	fst 1 1/16	:231 :474 1:122 1:442	3↑ Alw 2000	4	5	35½	33	22	23	Walls P	117	wb	3.25	98-14	Victorian1133Crusdr1173StrollngPlyr106.51	Game,no match	6
19Sep28- 4HdG	my 1 70	:22 :46 1:122 1:444	3↑ Alw 2500	6	3	36	24	23	24	Walls P	117	wb	3.00	82-19	Victorian1154Crusader117hdSun Beau1075	Game,tiring	6
30Jly28- 5Sar	gd 1¼	:483 1:13 1:39 2:06	3↑ Saratoga H 9.7k	2	6	55½	52	52¾	55	Workman R	127	wb	4.00	74-15	Chance Shot1221½Black Maria1152Edith Cavell1061½	Tired	8
29Oct27- 5Lrl	fst 1¼	:47 1:114 1:372 2:022	3↑ Washington H 36k	2	8	84½	62½	41½	42	Sande E	128	wb	*3.30	96-10	Display112hdBlack Maria1171Mars1281	Impeded,tired	9
24Oct27- 5Lrl	fst 1⅛	:473 1:12 1:392 1:514	3↑ Handicap 2000	1	5	51¼	43	42½	21	Sande E	130	wb	*1.00	88-16	[D]Mars1281Crusader1302½Gaffsman1161		6
	Placed first by disqualification																
18Oct27- 5Lrl	sly 1⅛	:492 1:151 1:403 1:532	3↑ Handicap 2000	2	1	1½	1½	1½	11	Sande E	126	wb	*.30	81-23	Crusader1261Sir Harry112hdDolan105	Handily	3
1Oct27- 5HdG	fst 1⅛	:47 1:123 1:383 1:52	3↑ H de Grace Cup H 24k	3	6	64¼	42¼	32½	43¾	Sande E	129	wb	*.75	86-14	ChancePly1241EdthCvll1031½Bostonn1131¼	Tired,eased late	7
28Sep27- 5HdG	fst 1 1/16	:242 :483 1:132 1:454	3↑ Delaware H 2k	1	3	32	21	1nk	13	Sande E	128	wb	*.45	95-16	Crusader1283Bostonian1171Navigtor1052½	As rider pleased	4
18Jun27- 4Aqu	fst 1⅛	:471 1:12 1:36 1:484	3↑ Brooklyn H 17k	4	8	88¼	45½	79¼	66¼	Sande E	132	wb	*1.10	93-09	Peanuts112hdChance Play1214Display1121	No threat	10
4Jun27- 4Bel	fst 1¼	:464 1:11 1:371 2:022	3↑ Suburban H 15k	5	5	43	3nk	12	17	Kummer C	127	wb	3.00	88-14	Crusader1277Black Maria1202Macaw1202	Won easily	8
14May27- 4Jam	fst 1 1/16	:24 :474 1:122 1:44	3↑ Excelsior H 7.7k	4	4	55	45½	44	43½	Fator L	127	wb	*.33	89-07	Amber Jack1022½Cherry Pie110hdNavigator1081	Poor effort	5
23Apr27- 5HdG	gd 1 1/16	:232 :473 1:132 1:452	3↑ Philadelphia H 12k	3	5	31	32	53¼	53	Fator L	128	wb	*.80	94-14	Single Foot114½Canter112hdMontferrat1031½		10
	Traffic on turn,dropped back																
13Nov26- 4Pim	fst 2¼	:50 2:34 3:01 3:521	3↑ Pim Cup H 12k	1	3	416	38¼	2½	22½	Sande E	126	wb	*.25	101-15	Edith Cavell932½Crusader12640Princess Doreen110hd		4
	Rated,tired late																
1Nov26- 4Pim	my 1½	:49 1:144 2:06 2:323	Riggs Mem H 30k	2	3	64	2½	11½	11¼	Sande E	130	wb	*.65	90-12	Crusader1301¼Mars1195Gaffsman1101½	Rated,easily	7
23Oct26- 5Lrl	sl 1¼	:472 1:123 1:392 2:052	Maryland H 12k	1	1	52	31¼	1nk	13	Ellis G	126	wb	*.45	83-17	Crusader1263Chance Play1195Gaffsman10812	Won easing up	5
16Oct26- 5Lrl	fst 1	:23 :472 1:123 1:38	2↑ Laurel 14k	8	7	82½	53	52¼	43	Coltiletti F	124	wb	*1.75	95-11	Croyden107.52Sarazen126hdMrs1171	Shuffled back 1st turn	11
25Sep26- 5HdG	fst 1⅛	:473 1:122 1:38 1:50	3↑ Havre de Grace H 17k	8	7	63½	31	11	15	Sande E	122	wb	*.85	100-06	Crusader1225Son of John108hdDisplay114nk	In a canter	12
11Sep26- 5Bel	fst 2	:502 2:36 3:024 3:26	3↑ J C Gold Cup 17k	2	2	23	22	21½	11½	Maiben J	114	wb	*1.40	79-17	Crusader1141½Espino1145Altawood125no	Going away	5
4Sep26- 5Bel	fst 1⅝	:481 1:392 2:044 2:423	Lawrence Realizatn 29k	5	2	12	12	11½	2hd	Maiben J	126	wb	*.80	91-16	Espino126hdCrusader1265Mars12615	Outfinished	5
24Aug26- 4Sar	my 1 3/16	:49 1:142 1:393 1:593	Huron H 5.1k	7	1	11	11½	13	11½	Sande E	126	wb	*.55	80-20	Crusader1261½Espino1145Black Maria1124	Speed to spare	7
14Aug26- 5Sar	fst 1¼	:463 1:123 1:383 2:043	Travers 18k	4	6	43½	22	31¼	44½	Sande E	129	wb	*.80	81-16	Mrs1231½Pompy1231½Dsply1231½	Left at start,rushed up,tired	8
24Jly26- 6CI	fst 1¼	:464 1:112 1:362 2:02	Cincinnati Derby 28k	3	3	21½	2hd	13	13	Sande E	126	wb	*.80	101-09	Crsdr1263Dsply126½BoottoBoot1262	Wide 1st turn,drew away	8
3Jly26- 4Aqu	fst 1½	:491 1:14 2:052 2:293	Dwyer 19k	2	5	57½	43	21	1no	Sande E	123	wb	1.60e	127-07	Crusader123noChance Play1203Espino1084	Just up	5
12Jun26- 5Bel	sly 1½	:50 1:14 2:063 2:321	Belmont 56k	2	2	51¾	34	2½	11	Johnson A	126	wb	*.70	83-22	Crusader1261Espino1264Haste1262	Handily	9
5Jun26- 4Bel	fst 1¼	:47 1:114 1:373 2:03	3↑ Suburban H 16k	2	3	21½	1nk	15	15	Callahan J	104	wb	*1.00e	85-17	Crusadr1045AmrcnFlg1241KngSolomon'sSl1071½	In a canter	9
26May26- 4Bel	fst 1	:232 :464 1:112 1:373	Withers 25k	4	13	106¼	98¼	56½	21	Johnson A	118	wb	7.00	88-24	Haste1181Crusader118hdEspino1181½	Impeded,finished fast	15
20May26- 3Jam	fst 6f	:233 :473 1:12	3↑ Handicap 1260	5	2	21½	21	22	21	Johnson A	126	wb	2.00	94-12	Claptrap1201Crusader1263Pheasant112hd	Gamely	5
	Previously trained by G.R. Tompkins																
6Nov25- 4Pim	fst 1	:232 :472 1:13 1:404	Pim Futurity 61k	2	13	1215	1212	78½	53	Johnson A	117	w	3.45e	81-19	Canter117noBubblingOver1221½Disply1191	Crowded 1st turn	14
	Geldings not eligible																
24Oct25- 4Lrl	hy 1	:241 :492 1:152 1:414	Manor H 14k	4	1	11½	13	16	110	Johnson A	116	wb	7.55e	79-28	Crusader11610Corvette107½Blondin1094	In a canter	10
10Oct25- 5Lrl	fst 6f	:234 :48 1:141	National 7.5k	4	2	66	47	34	31¼	Johnson A	115	b	*.45e	85-20	Gaffsman1181¼Corvtt112hdCrusdr1154	Finished with a rush	6
30Sep25- 4HdG	fst 5½f	:231 :47 1:06	Alw 1300	2	6	64¾	35	21½	13½	Callahan J	114	w	2.10	96-14	Crusader1143½UrsaMajor1176TheEngineer1081	Won eased up	6
26Sep25- 4HdG	fst 6f	:231 :472 1:122	Alw 1300	3	1	54½	31	26	37	Johnson A	112	wb	1.35	86-17	Macaw1127Welshot106noCrusader1126	Tiring	7

8Sep25- 5Bel	my 5½f	:243 :482	1:072	Alw 1000	6 6 43½ 31¼ 3¾	14	Johnson A	117wb	*1.60	85-22	Crusader1174Deviner1122Mars1124	Easily 9
3Jun25- 6Bel	fst 5f-Str		:582	Alw 1200	4 4 2½ 2hd	11	Maiben J	107wb	2.20	86-17	Crusader1071Mars1071Sandstorm107no	Finished fast 9
28May25- 3Bel	fst 4½f-Str		:52	Alw 1200	1 3 21 2½	2½	Johnson A	112 w	3.00	94-08	Punjab112½Crusader1124Euclid1152	Tired in drive 7
13May25- 1Pim	fst 4½f	:232 :473	:542	Md Sp Wt	8 6 54½ 45 21½	1hd	Johnson A	115 w	12.75	96-04	Crusader115hdGaffsman1152Zeppelin1153	Wide,just up 9
1May25- 2Pim	sl 4f	:233	:493	Md Alw 1500	6 6 64 56½	77¼	Scobie E	115 w	25.05	83-11	Welshot115hdShampoo1121½Foretell1155	Never a factor 12
16Apr25- 3HdG	fst 4f	:23	:471	©Md Sp Wt	2 10 1319 1017	817	Babin G	118 w	39.55	82-01	Canter118½Fiddlstcks1183HrvyStdmn1181½	Crowded at start 14

Domino

br. c. 1891, by Himyar (Alarm)–Mannie Gray, by Enquirer — **Lifetime record: 25 19 2 1 $193,550**

Own.– J.R. & F.P. Keene
Br.– Maj B.G. Thomas (Ky)
Tr.– William Lakeland

17Sep95- 4Gra	gd 1¼	:53 1:17½ 1:43½ 2:09	3↑ First Spl 2.5k	- 4 53 4¾ 51¼	56¼	Taral	122	5.00	- -	Henry of Navarre1221½Clifford117nkSir Walter1103	5
11Sep95- 5She	fst 1⅛	1:532	Swpst 3500	- -	2nk	Taral	122	1.60	- -	Henry of Navarre122nkDomino1223Rey el Santa Anita122	3
	Led,just missed										
24Aug95- 2She	fst *6f-FC	1:094	3↑ Fall H 1.5k	- -	2hd	Taral	133	*.70	- -	Butterflies109hdDomino1336ReyDelCarrrs112	Dueled,missed 8
29Jun95- 4She	gd 1	:26 :493 1:134 1:411	3↑ Sheepshead Bay H 1.5k	- 1 12 12	12	Taral	127	*1.40	- -	Domino1272Dorian118hdSir Walter1232	Handily 6
22Jun95- 4She	fst *6f-FC :233 :473 :59	1:10	3↑ Coney Island H 1.5k	- 2 11 11	12	Taral	120	*1.20	- -	Domino1202Wernberg116hdRedskin109nk	Very easily 6
18Jun95- 1She	fst 5½f	:24¾ :50 1:01¾ 1:08	3↑ Alw 720	- 2 21 2½ 2nk	13	Taral	122	*.50	- -	Domino1223Factotum112hdRey del Carreras1091	Easily 5
15Jun95- 4She	fst 1¼	:51½ 1:17 1:42 2:074	3↑ Suburban H 6.2k	- 3 3¾ 3½ 21½	43¼	Taral	123	*.40	- -	Lazzarone1151½Sir Walter1261½Song and Dance103nk	6
	Eased up after mile										
15May95- 1Gra	hy 6f	1:17	2↑ Swpst 690	- -	12	Taral	122	*.50	- -	Domino1222Wernberg112¾Patrician112	Led final ¼,easily 4
6Oct94- 5MP	fst 1⅛	1:52¼	3↑ Special 5k	- -	310¾	Taral	113	*1.20	- -	Henry of Navarre113¾Clifford12210Domino113	Led,faltered 3
15Sep94- 5Gra	gd 1⅛	1:55½	3rd Spl 5k	- -	1ʟ	Taral	122	*.55	- -	[DH]Domino122[DH]Henry of Navarre122	Led,dueled late 2
11Sep94- 4Gra	gd 6f	1:13¾	2↑ Culver 2.1k	- -	11½	Taral	116	*.25	- -	Domino1161½Stonenell12210Lissak91	Led final ¼ 3
6Sep94- 5She	fst 1	1:392	3↑ Match Race 5k	- -	1¾	Taral	112	1.05	- -	Domino112¾Clifford122	Led,drawing away 2
30Aug94- 4She	fst 1	1:401	3↑ Ocean H 2k	- -	1hd	Taral	116	*.65	- -	Domino116hdDucat1141½Saragossa106	Easily 4
27Aug94- 4She	fst *6f-FC	1:10	Flying 1.9k	- -	13	Taral	130	*.55	- -	Domino1303Peacemaker1195Harrington112	6
23Jun94- 3OWP	fst 1½	:52¼ 1:19¾ 2:10 2:36	American Derby 25k	- -	9	Taral	125	*1.40	- -	ReyelSantaAnita1226SntorGrdy1222Dspot122	Never a threat 9
12Jun94- 4MP	fst 1	1:40	Withers 7.9k	- -	1hd	Taral	122	1.80	- -	Domino122hdHenry of Navarre1223Dobbins122	Driving 5
29Sep93- 3MP	fst 6f	1:09	Matron 27k	- -	11	Taral	128	*.25	- -	Domino1281Peacemaker109.53Jack of Spades121	11
	Dueled,drew away rapidly										
31Aug93- 0She	fst *6f-FC	1:123	Match Race 22k	- -	1ʟ	Taral	118	-	- -	[DH]Domino118[DH]Dobbins118	Dueled throughout 2
	Match and mutuels called off - off at odds of *.50										
29Aug93- 4She	hy *6f-FC	1:124	Futurity 56k	- -	1hd	Taral	130	*1.20	- -	Domino130hdGallilee115hdDobbins130	Rapid finish 20
19Aug93- 4OMP	gd 6f-Str	1:14½	Produce 22k	- -	1¾	Taral	128	*.50	- -	Domino128¾Discount108nkDeclare118	Led throughout 11
13Jly93- 3OWP	fst 6f	1:14	Hyde Park 18k	- -	12	Taral	123	*.20e	- -	Domino1232Peter the Great118nkVassal123	Handily 9
27Jun93- 3She	hy *6f-FC	1:14	Great Trial 26k	- -	1nk	Garrison	125	*.60	- -	Domino125nkHyderAbad1182Dobbns125	Led throughout,easily 9
10Jun93- 4MP	fst 6f	1:12¾	Great Eclipse 20k	- -	12	Taral	118	*.33	- -	Domino1182Dobbins118¾Declare118	Led throughout 6
27May93- 3Gra	fst 5f	1:01¾	Great American	- -	14	Taral	118	*1.00	- -	Domino1184Dobbins1181Joe Ripley119	8
22May93- 2Gra	fst 5f	1:02	Swpst	- -	16	Taral	112	*.80	- -	Domino1126Fonso111¾Patrician111	Led throughout 13

Exterminator

ch. g. 1915, by McGee (White Knight)–Fair Empress, by Jim Gore — **Lifetime record: 100 50 17 17 $252,996**

Own.– W.S. Kilmer
Br.– F.D. Knight (Ky)
Tr.– H. McDaniel

21Jun24- 5Dor	gd 1116	:232 :474 1:132 1:47	3↑ Queen's Hotel H 3k	4 3 31¼ 3¾ 42½	35½	Wallace J	113 w	*1.30	84-13	SpotCash1282½ForestLor1033Extrmntor113nk	Pulled up lame 5
7Jun24- 6BB	gd 1	:232 :473 1:132 1:394	3↑ Alw 1000	1 4 21½ 21 22	11	Wallace J	111 w	1.85	90-14	Exterminator1111Golden Rule11340Opperman1116	Handily 5
1May24- 6Pim	fst 1	:242 :483 1:13 1:383	3↑ Handicap 2000	4 5 42½ 55¼ 46¼	310½	Johnson A	126 w	4.80	84-11	Martingale120½SpicndSpn10610Extrmntor1261	Always outrun 6
19Apr24- 5HdG	hy 1116	:232 :482 1:153 1:492	3↑ Philadelphia H 5.1k	6 5 65½ 63 56¾	58¼	Johnson A	125 w	*1.20e	69-25	SpotCash111hdFlintStone118nkNewHampshire1124	No mishap 6
17Apr24- 5HdG	fst 1 70	:244 :49 1:14 1:44	3↑ Alw 2000	2 2 21½ 1hd 1hd	1½	Walls P	107 w	*.50	92-11	Exterminator107½GoldenSpher103½SttngSun10615	Ridden out 5
30Mar24- 6Tij	fst 1¼	:474 1:124 1:39 2:052	3↑ Coffroth H 51k	11 7 65¾ 54½ 53	41½	Johnson A	130 w	*1.60e	97-14	Runstar123noOsprey123noCherryTree1171½	Challenged,tired 18
17Feb24- 4Tij	fst 1 70	:241 :483 1:133 1:443	4↑ Alw 700	4 2 2¾ 21 11	11	Johnson A	113 w	*.30	89-12	Extermintor1131Suprcrgo1161VnPtrck1011	Gentle hand ride 5
	Previously trained by W. Shields										
28Apr23- 5HdG	my 1 70	:242 :493 1:143 1:452	3↑ Handicap 2500	3 4 31½ 21 2½	2no	Johnson A	132 w	*1.10	85-21	Chickvl101noExtrmntor1321PulJons10810	Getting to winner 5
21Apr23- 5HdG	fst 1116	:24 :48 1:123 1:454	3↑ Philadelphia H 5.1k	2 4 53½ 42½ 2¾	1nk	McAtee L	129 w	*.80	95-10	Exterminator129nkPaul Jones1092Fair Phantom107nk	Gamely 6
16Apr23- 4HdG	my 6f	:24 :49 1:15	3↑ Harford H 5.1k	4 5 64 62¾ 42½	31¼	Sande E	132 w	3.70	80-32	Blazes106nkCareful116½Exterminator1326	Finished fast 8
	Previously trained by E. Wayland										
11Nov22- 4Pim	fst 2¼	:50 2:34 3:04 3:532	3↑ Pim Cup H 10k	5 2 2hd 46 418	331½	Marineli B	126 w	*.65	66-13	CaptanAlcock1061½PulJons9930Extrmntor126100	Forced pace 5
28Oct22- 5Lrl	fst 1¼	:47 1:122 1:382 2:044	3↑ Washington H 28k	8 5 54 44½ 45	43½	Johnson A	132 w	*.90	82-17	Oceanic104½Lucky Hour1202Paragon II1211	Finished fast 8
21Oct22- 5Lrl	fst 1	:244 :49 1:14 1:40	2↑ Laurel 13k	1 5 53 42 31½	12½	Johnson A	132 w	2.25	88-15	Extermintor1322½[D]PrgonII1251½Trystr123hd	Won easing up 8
14Oct22- 4Lrl	fst 6f	:23 :47 1:124	3↑ Handicap 2000	8 2 86¾ 64½ 65	41½	Johnson A	133 w	*2.25	92-16	CalamityJane113hdOnWatch1241TipptyWtcht112½	Steady gain 8
30Sep22- 5Haw	fst 1¼	:514 1:183 1:451 2:10	Special	- 1 1 1 1	1	Johnson A	126 w	-	73-19	Exterminator126	Good run 1
	Race against time										
20Sep22- 5OW	fst 1¼	:463 1:113 1:382 2:051	3↑ Toronto Aut Cup H 16k	5 5 53¼ 42½ 3½	11½	Johnson A	132 w	*.80	95-09	Exterminator1321½Guy102hdBitofWhit1001	Rated,going away 8
31Aug22- 4Sar	gd 1¾	:50 2:10 2:35 3:002	3↑ Sar Cup 8.3k	1 1 11 11 11	1nk	Johnson A	126 w	1.40	80-18	Exterminatr126nkMdHttr12612BonHomm126	Outstayed rivals 3
1Aug22- 4Sar	fst 1¼	:481 1:123 1:38 2:031	3↑ Saratoga H 9.2k	1 4 52 53½ 57	510¼	Johnson A	137 w	5.00	83-09	Grey Lag130½Bon Homme1091½Prudery1146	Hard ridden 5
4Jly22- 5Lat	gd 1½	:482 1:122 2:041 2:302	3↑ Independence H 18k	2 4 44½ 59½ 68	612	Johnson A	140 w	*.90	84-14	Firebrand1163Devastation1026Minto II1161	8
	Appeared in distress after mile										
16Jun22- 4Aqu	fst 1⅛	:473 1:123 1:37 1:50	3↑ Brooklyn H 9.8k	2 3 32 2½ 2hd	1hd	Johnson A	135 w	1.50	95-10	Exterminator135hdGreyLag1264PollyAnn103hd	Strong finish 5
13Jun22- 4Bel	fst 1116	:234 :48 1:131 1:44	3↑ Handicap 1635	5 4 21½ 22 11	11½	Johnson A	135 w	1.40	96-12	Exterminator1351½Mad Hatter1286Devastation102nk	Rated 6
5Jun22- 4Bel	gd 1⅛	:47 1:122 1:382 1:522	3↑ Handicap 1470	2 1 1no 1½ 1½	1½	Johnson A	133 w	*.07	83-11	Exterminator133½Be Frank107	Won hard held 2
27May22- 5CD	sl 1¼	:48 1:122 1:382 2:042	3↑ Kentucky H 12k	1 2 2hd 11 11½	11½	Johnson A	138 w	*.45	94-15	Exterminator1381½Firebrand1195Blarney Stone958	Easily 4
20May22- 5CD	fst 1⅛	:471 1:12 1:37 1:50	3↑ Clark H 13k	5 4 51½ 2nk 1½	11½	Johnson A	133 w	*.60	99-10	Exterminator1331½Lady Madcap1111Rouleau1074	Drew away 9
6May22- 6Pim	sl 1116	:243 :493 1:14 1:454	3↑ Pim Spring H 5.6k	3 2 21 1nk 1hd	1hd	Johnson A	133 w	*.75	97-18	Exterminator133hdBoniface12510Registrar1022	Hard drive 7
22Apr22- 5HdG	fst 1116	:244 :483 1:141 1:45	3↑ Philadelphia H 5.5k	2 2 31¼ 31½ 2hd	2no	Johnson A	133 w	*.65	99-09	Boniface122noExterminator1336BungaBuck110nk	Cut off ⅜ 6
15Apr22- 4HdG	hy 6f	:234 :481 1:141	3↑ Harford H 5.2k	7 4 64½ 43 42	11	Johnson A	132wb	4.95	85-24	Exterminator1321Billy Kelly1321Dexterous1021	Going away 12
	Previously trained by W. Knapp										
12Nov21- 5Pim	hy 2¼	:55 2:462 3:12 4:081	3↑ Pim Cup H 9.8k	1 1 1½ 1½ 1hd	1hd	Johnson A	126 w	*.70	- -	Exterminator126hdBoniface12120Lady Emmeline96	Held on 3
29Oct21- 5Lxt	fst 1½	:502 1:161 2:07 2:313	3↑ Lex Cup H 6.2k	5 3 33 23 32½	36½	Johnson A	135 w	*.80	84-10	Firbrnd1181½UntdVrd1055Extrmntor1352	Tired under impost 5
22Oct21- 4Lrl	fst 1¼	:471 1:12 1:382 2:042	3↑ Handicap 2038	6 3 37 34 2nk	11	Johnson A	132 w	*1.65	88-14	Exterminator1321My Dear1151½Bygone Days961½	Driving 6
8Oct21- 4Lrl	sly 1½	:483 1:141 2:06 2:35	3↑ Annapolis H 12k	6 4 1hd 21 33	38½	Kelsay W	135 w	*2.15	64-23	ThePorter1202½MyDer1146Extrmntr1351½	Eased when beaten 8
24Sep21- 5OW	fst 1¼	:48 1:132 1:383 2:051	3↑ Toronto Aut Cup H 7.9k	6 4 43½ 2½ 1½	1nk	Kelsay W	137 w	*1.40	95-12	Exterminator137nkMy Dear1172Golden Sphere1061	Gamely 9

16Sep21- 4Bel	fst	2	:493 2:352 3:02 3:291	3↑ Autumn Gold Cup H 5.7k	2	2	1hd	11	13	16	Kelsay W	130	w	*.33	63-19	Exterminator1306Bellsolar104	In a canter	2
31Aug21- 4Sar	sl	1¾	:554 2:132 2:393 3:043	3↑ Sar Cup 4.5k	-	1	1	1	1	1	Kelsay W	126	w	-	59-22	Exterminator126	Galloped	1
Walkover																		
27Aug21- 4Sar	fst	1 3/16	:472 1:114 1:373 1:572	3↑ Merchants & Cits H 8.7k	6	5	51¾	21	1½	11	Kelsay W	130	w	6.00	91-10	Exterminator1301MadHattr132¾Bllsolr104hd	Outside,gamely	7
Previously trained by F. Curtis																		
12Jly21- 4Wnr	fst	1⅛	:471 1:12 1:382 1:512	3↑ Frontier H 12k	7	4	51¾	32½	31½	32	Simpson R	132	w	4.20	97-07	BestPal1191½IrishKiss108½Extrmntor1328	Closed with rush	8
9Jly21- 5Lat	fst	1 3/16	:473 1:122 1:373 1:561	3↑ Daniel Boone H 14k	7	4	21	1½	21½	32	Haynes E	135	w	2.20	100-08	Best Pal1191La Rablee1061Exterminator1356		8
Cut off by winner final ⅛																		
4Jly21- 5Lat	fst	1½	:493 1:141 2:052 2:301	3↑ Independence H 19k	5	3	32	21	1½	11	Haynes E	130	w	*.55	97-07	Exterminator1301Woodtrap1111½La Rablee1086	Handily	7
Previously trained by W. McDaniel																		
17Jun21- 4Aqu	gd	1⅛	:462 1:11 1:362 1:494	3↑ Brooklyn H 9.8k	10	7	74	42½	42½	33	Ensor L	129	w	4.00	94-08	GreyLag1121½JohnP.Grier1241½Extrmntor1291	Inside,gamely	11
4Jun21- 4Bel	fst	1¼	:473 1:12 1:361 2:021	3↑ Suburban H 11k	8	5	58½	59½	59½	58¾	Johnson A	133	w	*1.20	80-09	Audacious120¾MadHattr1306SennngsPrk110no	Always outrun	8
21May21- 4Jam	fst	1⅛	:48 1:123 1:372 1:50	3↑ Long Beach H 5.8k	3	2	21½	1hd	1½	1¾	Johnson A	130	w	*1.00	106-03	Exterminator130¾Mad Hatter1305Cirrus1287	Drew clear	4
14May21- 4Jam	my	1 1/16	:233 :481 1:14 1:471	3↑ Excelsior H 10k	1	5	53	42½	31½	21	Johnson A	129	w	3.60	89-15	Blazes1181Exterminator1296Naturalist126¾	Slow late gain	7
7May21- 4Jam	fst	1 1/16	:233 :472 1:12 1:45	3↑ Kings County H 6.1k	3	3	44½	35	25	23	Haynes E	129	w	2.20	98-08	MadHatter1243Extrmintr1293YllowHnd1101½	Closed gamely	5
12Nov20- 4Pim	fst	2¼	:472 2:321 2:583 3:53	3↑ Pim Cup H 10k	2	3	21	11	1½	1no	Ensor L	126	w	*.75	20- -	Exterminator126noBonifc11410PulJons110.56	Rated,all out	7
8Nov20- 4Pim	fst	1½	:483 1:142 2:051 2:313	3↑ Bowie H 11k	3	7	73½	53½	63¾	53½	Fairbrother C	135	w	2.80	94-08	Mad Hatter120noBoniface1221½The Porter128no	In a pocket	9
20Oct20- 5OW	hy	2¼	:513 2:393 3:094 4:044	3↑ Ont Jockey Club Cup 7.7k	1	1	22	22	1nk	11¼	Fairbrother C	134	w	*.15	49-26	Exterminator1341¼Bondage1106St. Germain901½	Easily	4
25Sep20- 5OW	fst	1¼	:482 1:133 1:394 2:042	3↑ Toronto Aut Cup 7.8k	4	2	11	11	1½	1hd	Fairbrother C	132	w	*.25	99-10	Exterminator132hdMy Dear9212Bondage1081	Driving	5
Previously trained by J.S. Healey																		
15Sep20- 4Bel	fst	2	:482 2:293 3:214	3↑ Autumn Gold Cup 6.3k	2	3	32½	32	2½	1hd	Fairbrother C	128	w	*.70	- -	Exterminator128hdDamask982½Cleopatra105	Rated,driving	3
31Aug20- 4Sar	sl	1¾	:502 2:043 2:294 2:562	3↑ Sar Cup 5.6k	2	1	11	11½	13	16	Fairbrother C	126	w	*.55	108-12	Exterminator1266Cleopatra111	Easily	2
28Aug20- 4Wnr	fst	1 1/16	:23 :472 1:12 1:444	3↑ George Hendrie H 8.6k	4	3	31½	31¼	2½	11	Fairbrother C	131	w	*1.15	98-09	Exterminator1311Wildair1143My Dear95hd	Rated,going away	6
21Aug20- 4Wnr	sl	1⅛	:48 1:132 1:384 1:511	3↑ Wnr Jockey Club H 11k	1	3	21½	21½	2nk	11¼	Fairbrother C	125	w	2.50	100-17	Exterminator1251¼Wildair11010Boniface130nk	Drew away	7
14Aug20- 4Sar	gd	1⅛	:484 1:14 1:402 1:531	3↑ Champlain H 4.1k	1	4	21	31½	1½	21½	Schuttinger A	128	w	*2.20	82-19	Gnome1091½Extrminatr1281MadHatter1175	Inside,no match	7
2Aug20- 4Sar	fst	1¼	:474 1:11 1:36 2:014	3↑ Saratoga H 6.7k	3	5	54¼	21½	22½	22	Schuttinger A	126	w	7.00	100-06	SirBarton1292Exterminator1263Wildar1153	Gamely,no match	5
14Jly20- 4Wnr	hy	1⅛	:492 1:182 1:47 2:011	3↑ Frontier H 12k	5	3	44	22	32½	32½	Davies T	127	w	*1.25	47-48	Slippery Elm109½The Porter1292Exterminator1275	Tired	8
3Jly20- 4Aqu	my	1⅛	:481 1:124 1:373 1:501	3↑ Brookdale H 4.2k	2	3	3½	21	2½	11½	Schuttinger A	129	w	2.00	96-11	Exterminator1291½Cirrus1234Gladiator1126	Hard ridden	4
29Jun20- 4Aqu	fst	1 1/16	:233 :462 1:11 1:44	3↑ Handicap 1290	3	3	34	33	31	1¾	Schuttinger A	126	w	3.00	101-18	Exterminator126¾Naturalist120½Wildair11412	Drew away	5
24Jun20- 4Aqu	fst	1⅛	:47 1:11 1:363 1:50	3↑ Brooklyn H 7.3k	7	7	75	76	46	48¼	Schuttinger A	124	w	6.00	89-09	Cirrus108hdBoniface1228Mad Hatter115hd	Steadily	7
19Jun20- 4Jam	gd	1⅛	:474 1:13 1:382 1:511	3↑ Long Beach H 4k	2	3	1½	11	11	11	Schuttinger A	119	w	2.20	102-06	Exterminator1191Cirrus1098Naturalist1203	Handily	5
5Jun20- 4Bel	my	1¼	:52 1:163 1:432 2:093	3↑ Suburban H 7.8k	5	5	58½	46½	47	36	Rice T	123	w	*2.20	46-30	Paul Jones106hdBoniface1156Exterminator123½	Game try	5
29May20- 5Bel	fst	1 1/16	:242 :48 1:13 1:443	3↑ Handicap 1605	4	3	21½	31	1½	2nk	Davies T	128	w	*2.00	97-10	Alibi107nkExterminator1282Sea Mint98no	Led,tired	5
Previously trained by H. McDaniel																		
13Nov19- 4Pim	hy	2¼	:523 2:50 3:182 4:13	3↑ Pim Cup H 4.9k	1	1	22	14	12	14	Kummer C	121	w	*1.00	- -	Extrminatr1214RoycRools1058½Woodtrp1023	Won easing up	3
8Nov19- 4Pim	fst	1½	:493 1:15 2:072 2:334	3↑ Bowie H 10k	5	3	52¾	55½	511	513½	Kummer C	128	w	2.90	73-11	Royce Rools1071½Cudgel1314Mad Hatter1132	Quit badly	5
18Oct19- 5Lat	hy	2¼	:54 2:50 3:184 4:17	3↑ Lat Cup 8.7k	4	3	11	2hd	21½	22	Knapp W	134	w	*.45	- -	Be Frank1222Exterminator13420Legal10520	Tired	4
11Oct19- 4Lrl	fst	1½	:473 1:13 2:033 2:293	3↑ Annapolis H 8.3k	3	3	34½	21	21½	2hd	Knapp W	128	w	2.05	107-06	Thunderclp108hdExtrmntor1283Cudgl1321	Getting to winner	5
3Oct19- 3Lrl	fst	1 1/16	:242 :49 1:153 1:461	3↑ Alw 1200	2	1	11	1hd	1½	1nk	Knapp W	120	w	*.05	86-15	Exterminator120nkOrestes12010Douglass S.113	Hard ridden	3
27Sep19- 5HdG	fst	1⅛	:471 1:122 1:373 1:50	3↑ Havre de Grace H 10k	5	6	64¾	4¾	41¾	2½	Knapp W	126	w	10.50	105-05	Cudgel129½Extrmntr126noSrBrton1242	Impeded,game finish	8
22Sep19- 5HdG	fst	1 1/16	:24 :48 1:13 1:45	3↑ Purse 2527	1	2	22	21½	21	1¾	Schuttinger A	124	w	5.05	100-11	Exterminator124¾Cudgel1291Slippery Elm993	Gamely	5
11Sep19- 4HdG	my	1 70	:25 :49 1:143 1:45	3↑ Harford County H 5.4k	4	2	3½	23	24	24	Schuttinger A	125	w	*.35	83-25	The Porter1214Exterminator1258Slippery Elm1033	No match	5
30Aug19- 4Sar	sl	1¾	:48 2:07 2:32 2:58	3↑ Sar Cup 6.3k	3	1	11½	12	1½	11½	Schuttinger A	126	w	2.50	100-14	Extrmntr1261½Purchs11650ThTrump116	Challenged,drew away	3
23Aug19- 4Sar	fst	1 3/16	:484 1:133 1:372 1:572	3↑ Merchants & Cits H 3.4k	1	1	11	2½	32½	33	Loftus J	126	w	*1.10e	90-08	Cudgel1321Star Master1222Exterminator1261½	No menace	5
9Aug19- 4Sar	fst	1⅛	:48 1:123 1:371 1:50	3↑ Champlain H 3.4k	6	4	42¼	31	21	21	Loftus J	120	w	*.90e	106-09	SunBriar1281Extermintor120½Hollstr1151½	Not hard ridden	6
5Aug19- 4Sar	fst	1	:232 :462 1:112 1:361	3↑ Delaware H 3.4k	6	5	44½	34	33½	31	Loftus J	121	w	*1.20e	99-08	FairyWand107hdSunBriar1281Exterminator121½	Fast finish	8
14Jun19- 4Jam	fst	1 1/16	:244 :482 1:13 1:452	3↑ Excelsior H 4.8k	8	5	44½	45½	68	53¾	Loftus J	124	w	8.00	96-07	Naturalist1221Star Master1191Boniface108nk	No threat	8
7Jun19- 4Bel	fst	1¼	:463 1:113 1:38 2:021	3↑ Suburban H 6.7k	1	4	57½	75¼	76¾	55¼	Rice T	128	w	5.00	84-16	Corn Tassel108nkSweep On1081½Boniface1073	Outrun	8
24May19- 5CD	hy	1¼	:482 1:143 1:42 2:102	3↑ Kentucky H 14k	1	4	1½	1hd	1hd	31	Morys J	134	w	*2.15	64-31	Midway1221Beaverkill108noExterminator1342	Gamely	7
22May19- 6CD	my	1	:25 :50 1:153 1:423	3↑ Handicap 1660	4	1	11½	12	11½	15	Morys J	134	w	*.60	74-39	Exterminator1345Flyaway97nkDrastic11210	Ridden out	4
15May19- 4CD	fst	1	:25 :493 1:143 1:391	3↑ Alw 1800	4	1	1½	11	2hd	2no	Morys J	115	w	*.20	91-11	Under Fire103noExterminator1151½Bribed Voter1088		4
Tight restraint,tired																		
8May19- 4Lxt	my	1¼	:493 1:152 1:42 2:073	3↑ Camden H 2.5k	1	1	11	11	11	11	Morys J	132	w	*.35	81-28	Exterminator1321Midway118	Drawing away	2
1May19- 4Lxt	hy	1 1/16	:243 :491 1:16 1:502	3↑ Ben Ali H 2.9k	4	3	21½	21½	11½	13	Morys J	124	w	*.60	70-33	Exterminator1243AmericanAc996Mdwy120hd	As rider pleased	5
31Mar19- 4OP	fst	6f	:233 :48 1:124	3↑ Handicap 800	3	1	31½	32	1hd	11½	Haynes E	123	w	*1.00	96-09	Extrmntor1231½UltmThul1141¼A.N.Akn1072	As rider pleased	6
22Mar19- 4OP	fst	1 70	:242 :48 1:13 1:432	3↑ Handicap 800	2	2	2½	11½	11½	13	Schuttinger A	126	w	*.80	109-09	Exterminator1263Lucky B.1111½Drastic1113	Won eased up	4
28Nov18- 5Lat	my	1 1/16	:243 :493 1:153 1:503	2↑ Handicap 2090	2	4	3½	12	14	12½	Loftus J	126	w	*.85	64-37	Exterminator1262½Drastic1046WrMchn1095	As rider pleased	4
23Nov18- 5Lat	hy	2¼	:54 2:433 3:11 4:063	3↑ Lat Cup H 8.9k	6	6	11½	11	1hd	1no	Loftus J	121	w	*1.25	- -	Exterminator121noBeaverkill1105Moscowa1153	Gamely	6
12Nov18- 4Pim	fst	1½	:49 1:142 2:043 2:311	3↑ Bowie H 12k	4	5	1½	24	22	31¼	Loftus J	120	w	6.85	102-06	GeorgeSmith130¾OmarKhayyam115½Extrmntr1206	Resolutely	15
6Nov18- 4Pim	fst	1¼	:492 1:141 1:393 2:053	Pim Autumn H 5.4k	2	2	1hd	2hd	11	1½	Ensor L	118	w	3.20	99-09	Extrmntor118½Forground107nkThPortr1276	Outstayed rivals	5
31Oct18- 4Lrl	hy	1⅛	:50 1:16 1:414 1:542	3↑ National H 3k	1	1	1nk	1nk	1nk	2hd	Knapp W	117	w	1.75	76-25	Midway117hdExterminator11720Tombolo98	Wide	3
26Oct18- 6Lrl	fst	1⅛	:49 1:141 1:393 1:521	Ellicott City H 2.5k	5	1	1nk	13	11½	12½	Knapp W	113	w	*.30	87-08	Extermintor1132½Aurum104.51½RdSox105.5nk	Never extended	5
12Oct18- 5Lrl	gd	1⅛	:49 1:143 1:402 1:512	3↑ Washington H 2.5k	3	1	1¾	22	32	33½	Knapp W	114	w	3.15	87-13	Midway111.52Cudgel1301½Exterminator113.51½	Tired badly	4
8Oct18- 4Lrl	fst	1 1/16	:231 :464 1:124 1:441	Carrollton H 1.9k	4	1	1nk	1½	1½	1hd	Knapp W	118	w	12.70	96-11	Exterminator118hdThe Porter1265Sunny Slope1304	Gamely	4
4Oct18- 4Lrl	fst	1 1/16	:24 :481 1:15 1:461	3↑ Alw 1408	4	1	12	11½	11	11	Kummer C	103	w	*.65	86-11	Exterminator1031Franklin1122John I. Day100no	Ridden out	4
30Aug18- 4Sar	hy	1¼	:501 1:171 1:451 2:122	3↑ Handicap 1313	4	2	22	42½	47	39½	Knapp W	115	w	*2.20	48-34	Ticket1061½Bondage1068Extermntr1151½	Impeded by winner	5
17Aug18- 4Sar	fst	1¼	:49 1:133 1:382 2:031	Travers 10k	2	2	44½	47	48	412	Schuttinger A	123	w	*1.10e	92-05	Sun Briar120hdJohren1266War Cloud1266	Outrun	4
3Aug18- 4Sar	fst	1 3/16	:483 1:132 1:383 1:563	Kenner 4k	3	2	32½	33	31¾	22	Knapp W	129	w	5.00	105-02	Enfilade1142Exterminator129nkTippityWitch1235	Game try	5
22Jun18- 5Lat	fst	1½	:494 1:142 2:063 2:33	Lat Derby 12k	5	4	42½	35½	31½	22	Knapp W	124	w	8.75	85-11	Johren1272Exterminator124½Frecuttr1228	Hard ridden late	6
25May18- 4BPT	fst	1		3↑ Turf and Field H .7k	-	-				21	Knapp W	122		*.45	- -	Kilts II1261Exterminator1221Square Dealer1262	Driving	6
No time taken																		
11May18- 5CD	my	1¼	:491 1:161 1:433 2:104	Ky Derby 18k	5	5	42½	1hd	2hd	11	Knapp W	114	w	29.60	63-25	Exterminator1141Escoba1178Viva America1134	Saved ground	8
Previously owned and trained by J.C. Milam																		
26Jly17- 2Knw	fst	5½f	:233 :473 1:004 1:071	Alw 800	3	7	64¾	45	66¾	4½	Morys J	112	w	*1.55	102-00	MissBryn112noOwnRoeO'Neil104½Salvstr112no	Finished fast	11
17Jly17- 3Wnr	hy	5½f	:244 :51 1:052 1:13	Alw 800	2	6	43½	3nk	13	11	Kelsay W	105	w	7.85	63-41	Exterminator1051Fern Handley1031Lady Eileen1103	Handily	6
14Jly17- 2Wnr	gd	5f	:23 :473 1:011	Alw 800	11	3	48	79¾	49	410	Morys J	105	w	14.35	84-18	Jack Hare Jr.1111High Cost1153Viva America1156	Bumped	11
30Jun17- 1Lat	fst	6f	:233 :483 1:144	Md Sp Wt	2	2	12	12	11½	13	Morys J	109	w	5.20	81-12	Exterminator1093Mistress Polly1091Quito112½	Easily	12

Grey Lag

ch. c. 1918, by Star Shoot (Isinglass)–Miss Minnie, by Meddler — **Lifetime record: 47 25 9 6 $136,715**

Own.– Mrs J. Casson
Br.– Mr John E. Madden (Ky)
Tr.– W. Casson

1Jly31- 6Dor	fst	1⅛	:493 1:152 1:421 1:541	3↑ Clm	1 6 913 914 914 917¾	Fisher D	113wb	10.10	69-11	AlLivingston112hdJunMoon1044HghPlyr109nk	Never a factor	10
24Jun31- 3Dor	fst	6f	1:121	3↑ Clm	3 10 98¼ 98 96½ 710	Fisher D	115wb	22.10	82-15	Scotland110¾Zaidee1073Hogarty110¾	No factor	10
18Jun31- 6BB	fst	7f	:234 :49 1:142 1:273	3↑ Clm 2000	2 1 2hd 31½ 36 38	Simpson R	116wb	9.15	76-21	Scotland1125FairOrb1153GreyLg116hd	Hard ridden,game try	10
13Jun31- 2BB	fst	6f	:233 :482 1:141	3↑ Clm 2500	8 12 1212 1214 912 76¾	Drake V	115wb	18.90	79-18	Wacket1151½Vacillate1131½Zaidee107½	Closed fast	12
Previously owned by Rancocas Stable;previously trained by S.C. Hildreth												
12May28- 4Jam	fst	1 1/16	:24 :48 1:13 1:462	3↑ Excelsior H 7.7k	1 1 11 2hd 31¼ 33	Sande E	118wb	*.90e	78-15	Brown Flash114noHerodian1053Grey Lag118hd	Showed speed	6
4May28- 4Jam	fst	1 1/16	:23 :464 1:122 1:463	3↑ Handicap 1250	1 4 49 45¾ 11 13	Fator L	120wb	*1.10	80-13	GreyLg1203ChrryP1172Flmkr1105	Rated early,won easing up	5
30Apr28- 2Jam	hy	1 70	:243 :494 1:15 1:46	3↑ Alw 1000	3 4 43 42½ 42¼ 33½	Fator L	128wb	6.00	72-23	Gormond1181½Ironsides1152Grey Lag128½	Rated,gamely	7
25Apr28- 6Jam	sl	1 1/16	:24 :483 1:14 1:48	3↑ Handicap 1350	3 4 48 410 48½ 49	Pasc'ma A	126wb	*1.20	64-22	Retaliate1112Sanford1186Oh Say1101	Pulled up lame	4
22Jun27- 3Aqu	fst	1	:241 :473 1:121 1:374	3↑ Alw 1000	4 3 21½ 21 11 13	Fator L	122wb	*.17	91-11	Grey Lag1223Our General1191½John J. Williams1151		6
Easily,pulled up lame												
17Jun27- 2Aqu	fst	1	:233 :47 1:12 1:38	3↑ Alw 1000	5 2 2½ 21½ 12 12	Fator L	115wb	*.50	90-14	GreyLag1152LordBroom111hdRoyalPlay1158	Under restraint	5
2Jun23- 4Bel	fst	1¼	:483 1:132 1:373 2:03	3↑ Suburban H 10k	3 3 32 2hd 11½ 11½	Sande E	135wb	*.33e	85-14	Grey Lag1351½Snob II1152Exodus1092	Easily	6
24May23- 4Bel	fst	1	:232 :464 1:113 1:38	3↑ Metropolitan H 9.2k	7 5 32 1½ 13½ 13	Sande E	133wb	*1.40e	88-10	Grey Lag1333Dinna Care107hdExodus110½	Won eased up	7
19May23- 4Jam	fst	1 1/16	:233 :473 1:113 1:43	3↑ Long Beach H 6k	1 2 23 23 23 22	Fator M	133wb	*.65	104-06	SnobII116.52GreyLag1338KingAlbrt100.52	Steady late gain	5
12May23- 4Jam	fst	1 1/16	:24 :48 1:123 1:45	3↑ Excelsior H 7.3k	3 1 12 12 13 13	Fator L	130wb	*.50	96-06	Grey Lag1303Exodus1114Prince James112nk	Won eased up	6
5May23- 4Jam	fst	1 1/16	:24 :481 1:123 1:444	3↑ Kings County H 5.9k	3 2 22 21 1½ 11¾	Sande E	128wb	*.60	97-07	Grey Lag1281¾Snob II11110Prince James1204	Going away	4
1Aug22- 4Sar	fst	1¼	:481 1:123 1:38 2:031	3↑ Saratoga H 9.2k	5 5 41½ 2½ 11 1½	Fator L	130wb	*.70	93-09	Grey Lag130½Bon Homme1091¼Prudery1146	Hard ridden late	5
19Jly22- 4Emp	gd	1 70	:24 :483 1:14 1:452	3↑ Mount Kisco 4.1k	2 2 21 12 13 12¼	Fator L	125wb	*.08	87-14	Grey Lag1252¼Letterman102	Won under pull	2
8Jly22- 4Emp	sl	1⅛	:484 1:142 1:402 1:54	3↑ Empire City H 8k	3 4 42 42½ 1½ 11½	Fator L	132wb	*1.00	85-13	GreyLg1321½BonHomme111¾Devastton1021½	Rated,going away	5
24Jun22- 4Aqu	fst	1	:233 :464 1:102 1:38	3↑ Queens County H 7.9k	3 2 33 31 3½ 11½	Fator L	127wb	*.40	90-13	GreyLg1271½SenningsPark1203CaptanAlcock112¾	Going away	5
16Jun22- 4Aqu	fst	1⅛	:473 1:123 1:37 1:50	3↑ Brooklyn H 9.8k	1 2 21 1½ 1hd 2hd	Fator L	126wb	*.70	95-10	Exterminator135hdGrey Lag1264Polly Ann103hd	Gamely	5
9Jun22- 4Bel	fst	1	:231 :462 1:102 1:36	3↑ Handicap 1588	3 2 21 1hd 1no 12	Fator L	126wb	*.60	98-12	GreyLag1262Frigate1051Bersglr1095	Long drive,going away	5
17Sep21- 5Lat	my	1¾	:481 2:09 2:47 3:053	Lat Championship 29k	2 2 21 21 31½ 43¼	Fator L	126wb	*.60	53-29	SportngBlood1262BlckSrvnt1261Humphry126nk	Disliked going	5
10Sep21- 4Bel	fst	2	:48 2:292 2:552 3:222	3↑ J C Gold Cup 13k	4 3 33 23 24 22½	Fator L	114wb	*.60e	94-04	Mad Hatter1252½Grey Lag11415Touch Me Not1148	Rated	4
3Sep21- 4Bel	fst	1⅝	:474 1:39 2:043 2:431	Lawrence Realizatn 20k	2 4 2½ 21½ 22 21½	Fator L	126wb	*.70	83-09	TouchMNot1261½GryLg1265SprtngBlood12120	Rated,tired late	4
Geldings not eligible												
30Jly21- 5Dev	fst	1⅛	:472 1:112 1:38 1:50	Dev Int'l 21k	1 2 22 22 2½ 1no	Sande E	126wb	*.48	113-03	GreyLag126noBlackServnt1238BygonDys1172	In final stride	5
26Jly21- 4Emp	fst	1 70	:244 :474 1:122 1:434	3↑ Mount Kisco 4.3k	2 1 12½ 14 16 17	Sande E	121wb	*.03	95-08	Grey Lag1217Copper Demon111	Won easing up	2
23Jly21- 4Emp	fst	1 1/16	:232 :47 1:122 1:45	Knickerbocker H 5.1k	3 3 31¾ 11½ 12½ 12½	Sande E	135wb	*.29e	98-09	Grey Lg1352½Careful1083Copper Demon11012	Won easing up	4
16Jly21- 4Emp	sl	1¼	:493 1:133 1:403 2:071	Emp Derby 8k	3 4 21½ 11 12 1¾	Fator L	129wb	*.25e	84-16	GryLg129¾SportngBlood1115CopprDmon11015	Hard ridden late	4
11Jly21- 6Emp	gd	1	:25 :482 1:134 1:40	Alw 1200	2 3 2½ 11 11½ 13	Sande E	130wb	*.10	93-08	Grey Lag1303Quecreek11310Parader110	Cantering	3
7Jly21- 4Aqu	fst	1⅛	:461 1:101 1:352 1:49	Dwyer 8.6k	5 4 22 11 13 14	Sande E	123wb	*.40	101-06	GreyLag1234SportingBlood1124CopperDemon1081	Easing up	6
17Jun21- 4Aqu	gd	1⅛	:462 1:11 1:362 1:494	3↑ Brooklyn H 9.8k	1 5 63 31 1½ 11½	Fator L	112 w	*2.00	97-08	GreyLag1121½JohnP.Grier1241½Exterminator1291	Going away	11
11Jun21- 4Bel	fst	1⅜	:47 1:113 1:37 2:164	Belmont 10k	3 4 21½ 1½ 13 13	Sande E	126wb	2.00	87-12	GreyLag1263Sporting Blood126hdLeonardo II12610		4
Slight restraint late												
2Jun21- 4Bel	fst	1	:23 :46 1:102 1:372	Withers 6.4k	1 4 32½ 21 25 34½	Sande E	118 w	*1.00	87-09	Leonardo II1182Sporting Blood1182½Grey Lag1181½		7
Tired final furlong												
31May21- 2Bel	fst	6f	:232 :463 1:121	Handicap 1345	8 6 62¾ 31 1½ 11	Sande E	126 w	*1.10	92-12	GreyLag1261DryMoon1061Messins1071	Slow start,going away	9
Previously owned by S.C. Hildreth												
6Nov20- 5CD	fst	1	:233 :47 1:122 1:382	Ky Jockey Club 26k	2 6 32 31½ 22 21	Sande E	122 w	5.30	94-11	Tryster1221GreyLag1221BehaveYourself1225	Gamely,tiring	6
21Oct20- 4Emp	fst	5½f	:223 :463 1:00 1:06	Autumn Days 3.3k	3 3 44 45½ 32½ 1½	Ensor L	125 w	*.45	99-10	Grey Lag125½Mulciber1226Curfew118hd	Gamely	5
11Oct20- 4Jam	fst	6f	:24 :48 1:13	Oceanus H 4.2k	3 1 1hd 1hd 21½ 22	Fator L	128 w	*1.80	92-11	Mulciber1112Grey Lag1283Knobbie1256	Tired late	6
6Oct20- 4Jam	fst	6f	:24 :48 1:13	Remsen H 4.6k	4 2 21½ 2hd 31 1nk	Ensor L	123 w	*.70	94-11	Grey Lag123nkKnobbie1221½Care Free1091½	Forced wide	5
28Sep20- 4Aqu	sly	6f	:234 :48 1:134	Babylon H 5.1k	4 4 44½ 43½ 34 35	Ensor L	126 w	*.70	81-19	Knobbie1163½Mulciber1091½Grey Lag1263	Slow to begin	4
20Sep20- 4Aqu	fst	6f	:24 :473 1:13	Oakdale H 4.7k	1 1 1½ 21 22 21½	Fator L	126 w	*1.00	88-15	Knobbie1061½Grey Lag1262Dry Moon1126	Gamely	5
Previously owned and trained by M. Hirsch												
14Sep20- 4Bel	fst	7f-Str	1:242	Champagne 5.7k	3 4 42½ 21 11½ 16	Ensor L	111.5 w	*1.00	90-17	Grey Lag111.56Banksia105.51Our Flag115¾	Rated,easily	6
11Sep20- 3Bel	fst	6f-Str	1:121	Futurity 42k	5 15 107 104¼ 31½	Pierce J	119 w	15.00	80-21	Step Lightly1161Star Voter127½Grey Lag119hd	Closed gap	18
8Sep20- 1Bel	fst	5½f-Str	1:072	Handicap 1488	8 8 51¼ 32 1hd	Ensor L	114 w	4.50	82-23	Grey Lag114hdQuecreek109noStar Voter125½	Vigorous ride	8
4Sep20- 3Bel	fst	6f-Str	1:103	Nursery H 6.4k	10 7 64 67 44¾	Johnson A	112 w	4.00	85-13	Hildur1143Smoke Screen1151Oriole118¾	Finished fast	12
31Aug20- 3Sar	sl	6f	:223 :464 1:122	Hopeful 38k	11 12 1411 1315 1112 1012¼	McAtee L	115 w	30.00	78-12	Leonardo II115hdPrudery127½Oriole1155	No factor	15
26Aug20- 6Sar	fst	5½f	:222 :461 :591 1:051	Alw 1000	10 3 21 2hd 21½ 21	Kelsay W	108.5 w	*2.00	96-06	Broom Spun107.51Grey Lag108.52Normal1158	Chased winner	10
18Aug20- 6Sar	fst	6f	:233 :481 1:133	Md Sp Wt	3 6 44 54½ 52½ 2nk	Ponce C	115 w	50.00	84-13	Dartmoor115nkGrey Lag1151Bermont1151	Gaining	14

Hamburg

b. c. 1895, by Hanover (Hindoo)–Lady Reel, by Fellowcraft — **Lifetime record: 21 16 3 2 $61,455**

Own.– Marcus Daly
Br.– C.J. Enright (Ky)
Tr.– William Lakeland

30Jly98- 5Bri	hy	2¼	:55¼ 2:42¼ 3:08¼ 4:02¾	3↑ Brighton Cup 7.5k	- 1 150 150 150 1100	Sloan T	112	*.05e	69-15	Hamburg112100Ogden13010Howard Mann133	Easing up	3
4Jly98- 5She	gd	1⅝	:494 1:17 1:43 2:511	Lawrence Realizatn 16k	- 1 13 16 16 12	Sloan T	122	*.90	86-13	Hamburg1222Plaudit12210George Boyd1121	Easing up late	6
23Jun98- 4She	gd	7f	:232 :47 1:13 1:271	Swift 1.7k	- 1 13 110 110 18	Taral	126	*.20	91-11	Hamburg1268Lotrr1166Murllo116	Very easily,eased up late	3
8Jun98- 3Gra	gd	1 1/16	:25¼ :49¼ 1:14¼ 1:49	3↑ Spring Spl .8k	- 1 16 18 18 18	Sloan T	105	*.80	90-13	Hamburg1058SlyFox1084Hndbll105	Galloping,easing up late	3
26May98- 4MP	my	1⅜	:53 1:19½ 1:47¾ 2:32	Belmont 9.7k	- 2 2hd 21½ 35 316	Taral	122	*1.00	40-51	BowlngBrook1228Prvous1228Hmbrg12240	Eased last furlong	4
Previously owned and trained by John E. Madden												
16Sep97- 3Gra	sl	6f	:24 :48¼ 1:15	Excelsior 2.5k	- 2 11½ 12 13 12	Taral	115	*.17	--	Hamburg1152Handbll115½EstrGft115½	Easily,pulled up lame	4
14Sep97- 3Gra	gd	6f	:24 :49 1:15	Prospect 3k	- 3 12 11½ 12 12	Taral	127	*.60	--	Hamburg1272Handball122hdArchduke1154	Very easily	7
11Sep97- 3She	gd	*6f-FC	:24 :482 1:00 1:101	Great Eastern H 5k	- 1 12 12 12 11½	Taral	135	*1.60	--	Hamburg1351½Kitefoot111½Briar Sweet1092	Easily	14
6Sep97- 3She	gd	*6f-FC	1:11	Autumn 3k	- 1 1hd 1½ 13 12½	Taral	129	*1.40	--	Hamburg1292½Archduke1223The Huguenot1223	Easing up	6
4Sep97- 3She	hy	7f	:244 :491 1:144 1:281	Flatbush 3k	- 2 2hd 1½ 1hd 2hd	Taral	120	*.60	--	Previous115hdHamburg120½Firearm115½	Rated,hung	9
1Sep97- 3She	gd	7f	:232 :473 1:133 1:263	2↑ Flight 2.5k	- 1 11½ 11½ 2hd 22	Simms	105	2.00	--	Requital1252Hamburg10510Flying Dutchman1256	Gamely	4
21Aug97- 4Bri	gd	6f	:23½ :48½ 1:00½ 1:14¼	Electric H 2k	- 1 11½ 11½ 13 11½	Simms	132	*.17	--	Hmbrg1321½Hndbll12010FrstFrut8810	Never extended,easing up	5
17Aug97- 4Bri	fst	6f	:24 :48¼ 1:15	Rising Generation 2k	- 1 13 14 15 13	Simms	127	*.13	--	Hamburg1273CentralTrust12210JuliusCaesar1108	Easing up	6
7Aug97- 3Sar	sl	6f	:24¾ :50 1:15	Grand Union Hotel 2k	- 2 2½ 2½ 11 2hd	Wilhite	129	*.33	--	Archduke117hdHamburg12915Harvey117	Driving,poor ride	3
4Aug97- 3Sar	sl	5f	:24 :47 1:01½	Congress Hall 2k	- 4 22 2¾ 1hd 11	Wilhite	134	*1.00	--	Hamburg1341Archduke1198Harvey119½	Easily	7
28Jly97- 3Sar	hy	4f	:24¾ :50	Flash 2k	- 2 3½ 1hd 11½	Wilhite	129	*.50	--	Hamburg1291½Handball129hdLoiterer1225	Galloping	4
10Jly97- 3She	fst	*6f-FC	:233 :481 1:002 1:111	Double Event (2) 5k	- 2 21 1hd 12 12	Wilhite	129	*1.20	--	Hamburg1292Uriel1223Mont d'Or122½	Easily	10

5Jly97- 4She	gd	*6f-FC	:251 :511 1:121	Great Trial 20k	- 2 2½ 21 13	14	Wilhite	122	6.00	--	Hamburg1224Previous1292George Keene1222	Much best 12
22Jun97- 3She	gd	5½f-FC	:252 :504 1:03 1:091	Double Event (1) 5k	- 5 3nk 22 51½	33½	Wilhite	122	*.80	--	Bowling Brook122½Laudeman1173Hamburg122nk	Bumped 8
15Jun97- 5Gra	fst	5f	:25¼ :49¾ 1:02¼	Alw 700	- 1 12 12 13	12	Wilhite	122	*2.00	--	Hamburg1222Previous122nkColonial Dame1013	Fast start 7
9Jun97- 1Gra	hy	5f	:24 :49¾ 1:03¼	Alw 710	- 2 11 11 11	11	Wilhite	104	2.00	--	Hamburg1041Previous1151Swango104½	Handily 8

Henry of Navarre

ch. c. 1891, by Knight of Ellerslie (Eolus)–Moss Rose, by The Ill-Used — **Lifetime record: 42 29 8 3 $68,985**

Own.– August Belmont II
Br.– L.O. Appleby (NJ)
Tr.– John J. Hyland

23Jun96- 4She	fst	1¼	:51¾ 1:163 1:414 2:07 3↑	Suburban H 7.5k	- 6 2hd 2½ 2nk	11	Griffin	129	2.00	--	HenryofNavarre1291ThCommonr113½Clfford1261	Driving,best 7
21May96- 3MP	sl	1	:27 :53¾ 1:19¼ 1:44 3↑	Alw 500	- 2 22 2nk 1½	13	Griffin	126	-	--	Henry of Navarre1263Mingo II10120Ventanna98	Very easily 3
Odds not offered on Henry of Navarre												
24Oct95- 5MP	fst	1¾	:55¾ 2:37½ 3:02 3↑	Municipal H 3.5k	- 2 2nk 11 11	11	Griffin	130	*.60	--	HenryofNavarre1301ReyelSantaAnt1268Clfford12815	Handily 4
15Oct95- 5MP	sly	1¼	:55½ 1:20 1:42½ 2:07 3↑	Manhattan H 3.5k	- 4 42¼ 32 3½	11	Griffin	127	*1.20	--	HenryofNavarre1271CounterTenor1002SirWalter1076	Handily 4
21Sep95- 4Gra	fst	1¼	:55½ 1:19½ 1:43½ 2:07½ 3↑	Oriental H 3k	- 7 5 51¼ 41¼	32½	Griffin	128	*1.20	--	Clifford1211SirExcess1071½HenryofNavrr1284	Lacked speed 7
17Sep95- 4Gra	gd	1¼	:53 1:17½ 1:43½ 2:09 3↑	First Spl 2.5k	- 3 31½ 3nk 2hd	11½	Griffin	122	*1.80	--	HenryofNavarre1221½Clifford117nkSirWalter1103	Handily 5
11Sep95- 5She	fst	1⅛	1:532	Swpst 3500	- -	1nk	Perkins	122	*1.00	--	HenryofNavarre122nkDomino1223ReyelSantaAnit122	Cleverly 3
2Sep95- 4She	fst	1¼	2:07 3↑	Twin City H 2.2k	- -	22	Perkins	127	*.60	--	Rey el Santa Anita1202Henry of Navarre1278Sir Excess115	4
Second best;Previously owned and trained by B. McClelland												
13Jly95- 20ky	fst	1	:50 1:02¾ 1:15¼ 1:40¾ 3↑	Alw 500	- 1 1½ 1½ 11	11	Perkins	110	*.04	--	Henry of Navarre1101Orinda1053Lehman11010	Easily 5
29Jun95- 40ky	fst	1⅛	:51½ 1:17¼ 1:43 1:55½ 3↑	Country Club 2.5k	- 2 22 21½ 1½	12	Perkins	125	*.20	--	Henry of Navarre1252Lehman112hd[D]Selika1071	4
11Jun95- 4Lat	fst	1⅛	:50½ 1:16 1:42 1:55 3↑	Merchant 1.9k	- 3 32 22 2hd	1hd	Perkins	117	*.04	--	Henry of Navarre117hdBrendoo9710Ray S117	Under a pull 3
23May95- 1Lat	fst	1	1:41¾ 3↑	Alw 500	- -	1¾	Perkins	117	*.17	--	Henry of Navarre117¾Selika107¾Tariff Reform109	6
6Oct94- 5MP	fst	1⅛	1:52¼ 3↑	Special 5k	- -	1¾	Clayton A	113	4.00	--	HenryofNavarre113¾Clifford12210Domino113	Led final ½ 3
22Sep94- 4Gra	fst	1⅛	1:54¾ 3↑	2nd Spl 1.8k	- -	2no	Doggett	112	*.40	--	Clifford122noHenry of Navarre112	Led to ¼ 2
15Sep94- 5Gra	gd	1⅛	1:55½	3rd Spl 5k	- -	1↓	Doggett	122	1.80	--	[DH]Domino122[DH]Henry of Navarre122	Dueled last 3f 2
5Sep94- 5She	fst	1 3/16	2:023 2↑	Bay 3.2k	- -	1nk	Taral	112	*.60	--	Henry of Navarre112nkBanquet11912Yo Tambien119	4
25Aug94- 3She	fst	1⅛	1:534	Dolphin 1.9k	- -	1hd	Clayton A	122	*1.20	--	Henry of Navarre122hdDorian1106Sir Knight106.5	4
18Aug94- 3Sar	fst	1	1:43	Iroquois 2.5k	- -	11½	Clayton	122	*.20	--	Henry of Navarre1221½Peacemaker1191½Lakeshore110	4
14Aug94- 2Sar	gd	6½f	1:20¼	Alw 600	- -	11	Clayton	122	*.22	--	Henry of Navarre1221Potentate1154Lakeshore112	3
7Aug94- 4Sar	fst	1⅛	1:53¾	Foxhall 2.5k	- -	13	Clayton	122	*.90	--	HenryofNavarre1223JohnCooper1224ReyelSantaAnita122	3
23Jly94- 4Sar	gd	1¼	2:10¼	Travers 3k	- -	1½	Taral	125	*.33	--	HenryofNavarre125½JoeRipley1104ReyelSantaAnita125	5
7Jly94- 3She	gd	1⅛	1:55 3↑	Handicap 1145	- -	11	Doggett	112	*.33	--	Henry of Navarre1121Herald1081½Redskin99	6
5Jly94- 4She	fst	1⅛	1:561	Spindrift 2.5k	- -	11	Doggett	125	*.90	--	Henry of Navarre1251Dorian1128Our Jack112	4
3Jly94- 1She	fst	7f	1:262 3↑	Alw 1165	- -	13	Jones H	103	*.90	--	HnryofNvrr1033Glnmoyn1093MrryMonrch106	Led throughout 3
21Jun94- 5She	fst	1¼	2:061 3↑	Suburban H 16k	- -	5	Perkins J	108	6.00	--	Ramapo1201Banquet1192Sport114	Prominent early 12
19Jun94- 4MP	fst	1⅛	1:56½	Belmont 7.4k	- -	11½	Simms	117	*.10	--	HenryofNavarre1171½Prig11910Assign115	Led final furlong 3
15Jun94- 1MP	fst	6f	1:11 3↑	Swpst 1180	- -	11½	Perkins	107	*.40	--	HenryofNavarre1071½Melba108hdMerryMonarch113	Led late 5
12Jun94- 4MP	fst	1	1:40	Withers 7.9k	- -	2hd	Garrison	122	*1.30	--	Domino122hdHenry of Navarre1223Dobbins122	Driving 5
2Jun94- 4MP	gd	1⅛	1:52½ 3↑	Metropolitan H 7.6k	- -	33½	Doggett	106	5.00	--	Ramapo1171½Roche1052HnryofNavrr106	Late bid,not enough 12
29May94- 4Gra	gd	1⅛	1:55¼	Fort Hamilton H	- -	21½	Doggett	121	4.00	--	JohnCooper1101½HenryofNavarre1212Hornpipe122	Late bid 11
21May94- 4Gra	hy	1⅛	1:58 3↑	Standard 2.5k	- -	21½	Griffin	106	*.33	--	Don Alonzo1221½Henry of Navarre106	Led for mile 2
15May94- 4Gra	fst	1¼	2:07¼ 3↑	Brooklyn H 25k	- -	21	Clayton A	100	7.00	--	Dr. Rice1121Henry of Navarre1002Sir Walter120	14
Prominent throughout												
19Sep93- 3Gra	fst	6f	1:15	Algeria H	- -	12	Taral	116	*1.40	--	Henry of Navarre1162Dobbins1231½Ornus100	11
2Sep93- 2She	gd	5f	1:012	Dash 2.4k	- -	1hd	Bryant	115	*2.00	--	HenryofNavarr115hdPotntt1042Wrnbrg104	Led final furlong 13
1Sep93- 6She	gd	7f(T)	1:30	Golden Rod 1.3k	- -	1½	Bryant	110	*.40	--	Henry of Navarre110½Figaro1104Queenlike110	Led,easily 6
19Aug93- 20MP	gd	6f-Str	1:15	Alw 1060	- -	11	Bryant	119	*.33	--	HnryofNvrr1191Illuson104.56Ornus119	Pressed pace,galloping 5
12Aug93- 20MP	fst	5f-Str	:58¾	Alw 1120	- -	11½	Hamilton	119	*.40	--	HenryofNavarre1191½Senella1191½Dorian119	Led throughout 8
8Aug93- 30MP	fst	6f-Str	1:13¼	Jr Champion 23k	- -	31¼	Overton	118	8.00	--	Senator Grady1181Hornpipe118nkHenry of Navarre118	8
5Aug93- 30MP	sl	6f-Str	1:13¼	Select 5.7k	- -	2½	Hamilton	113	8.00	--	Senator Grady113½Henry of Navarre113¾Hornpipe118	9
Led early,pressed pace late												
25Jly93- 30MP	fst	5½f-Str	1:05	Sapling 8k	- -	21½↓	Hamilton	111	8.00	--	SenatorGrady1111½[DH]HyderAbad118[DH]HenryofNavarre111	6
8May93- 3Lxt	hy	5f	1:04½	Breeders	- -	1½	Bryant	118	5.50	--	Henry of Navarre118½La Joya1205Lazzarone118	6
1May93- 3Lxt	hy	5f	1:07¼	Melbourne	- -	6		118	4.00	--	La Joya115nkLazzarone118nkOh No115	7

Hermis

ch. c. 1899, by Hermence (Isonomy)–Katy of the West, by Spendthrift — **Lifetime record: 55 29 8 6 $84,135**

Own.– E.R. Thomas
Br.– H.A. Engman (Ky)
Tr.– J. Shields

27Jly05- 4Bri	fst	1	:24 :474 1:131 1:391 3↑	Test H 4.1k	5 2 2hd 21½ 57½	512	Redfern	132wb	*1.20	82-11	Wild Mint109hdHambrg Belle1232Buttling1044	Wide,bumped 5
15Jly05- 3Bri	fst	1⅛	:48 1:13 1:39 1:52 3↑	Islip H 3k	10 1 11 11 11½	1½	Redfern	132wb	*2.60	95-06	Hermis132½Buttling1022½Bad News114hd	Gamely 10
11Jly05- 2Bri	fst	6f	:24 :474 1:131 4↑	Alw 1080	5 1 14 14 13	11	Knapp W	125wb	*.33	94-08	Hermis1251Jocund1153½Incubator1153	Cantered 6
6Jly04- 4Bri	fst	1	:241 :48 1:123 1:38 3↑	Test H 5k	2 1 11½ 12 12	11	Redfern	133wb	*1.30	100-07	Hermis1331Beldame1155Dainty1034	Bore out,best 5
25Jun04- 4StL	hy	1¼	:50½ 1:16½ 1:43 2:09½ 3↑	World's Fair H 50k	2 1 16 15 21	23	Redfern	130wb	*1.60	75-32	Colonial Girl973Hermis1306Moharib1038	No match 12
16Jun04- 4She	fst	1¼	:482 1:13 1:382 2:05 3↑	Suburban H 20k	6 1 11 13 13	12½	Redfern	127wb	4.00	98-06	Hermis1272½The Picket124noIrish Lad12710	Very easily 6
14Jun04- 4Gra	fst	1⅛	:49 1:132 1:391 1:524 3↑	Brookdale H 4.2k	3 1 12 11½ 12	11	Redfern	125wb	*.60	96-08	Hermis1251½Dainty1005Africander1272½	Won easing up 5
7Jun04- 4Gra	my	1¼	:50 1:16 1:43 2:10 3↑	Standard 6.3k	2 1 2hd 35 32½	325¾	Phillips H	128wb	1.50	51-24	MajorDaingerfild128¾Afrcndr12625Hrms1283½	Brushed,eased 6
26May04- 4Gra	fst	1¼	:482 1:13 1:392 2:063 3↑	Brooklyn H 20k	6 2 2hd 21 2hd	43	Redfern	127wb	4.00	91-06	ThePckt119hdIrshLd1252Propr1101	Carried wide final turn 16
21May04- 6MP	fst	1	:24 :483 1:141 1:392 3↑	Handicap 1365	6 1 1hd 12 15	14	Redfern	128wb	7.00	96-10	Hermis1284Toboggan1134Hello97¾	In a canter 7
29Oct03- 4Aqu	fst	1⅛	:49 1:141 1:401 1:53 2↑	Edgemere 1.7k	- 1 13 12 12	14	Redfern	126wb	*.14	105-00	Hermis1264Stolen Moments11515Warranted126	In a canter 3
20Oct03- 4Bri	fst	2¼	:49 2:33 2:592 3:532 3↑	Brighton Cup 8.8k	- 1 1½ 11½ 1hd	18	Redfern	124wb	1.60	79-10	Hermis1248MajorDaingerfield1243Ignitr12420	Won eased up 4
13Oct03- 4Bri	gd	1½	:49 1:141 2:053 2:321 3↑	Cup Preliminary 2.4k	- 1 11½ 11½ 12	11	Fuller	126wb	*.65	106-05	Hermis1261Major Daingerfield12620Igniter126	Rated,best 3
3Oct03- 1MP	fst	7f	:25 :492 1:132 1:26 2↑	Alw 1120	- 2 22 21 2hd	2hd	Redfern	122wb	*.20	100-05	MamieWorth107hdHrmis1222HighChancellor1103	Just missed 4
1Oct03- 6MP	fst	1⅛	:484 1:142 1:40 1:522 3↑	Handicap 1255	- 1 11½ 13 1½	11½	Fuller	134wb	*1.10	95-07	Hermis1341½RiverPirate1101½Colonsay861	Speed in reserve 5
25Sep03- 4Gra	fst	1 1/16	:233 :474 1:141 1:461 2↑	Handicap 1285	- 1 13 12 13	13	Fuller	134wb	*.50	99-06	Hermis1343Colonsay86½Mabel Richardson95¾	Speed to spare 7
7Sep03- 4She	fst	1¼	:474 1:122 1:383 2:043 3↑	Twin City H 7.2k	- 1 16 14 2hd	21½	Odom	129wb	4.00e	100-00	McChesney1291½Hermis1291His Eminence1004	Second best 12
5Sep03- 4She	fst	1½	:491 1:143 2:05 2:313 3↑	Century 20k	- 1 1hd 24 35½	412½	Odom	126wb	*1.80	89-02	Water Bay1262½The Picket1154Heno1266	Tired badly 5
2Sep03- 4She	gd	1	:232 :471 1:122 1:394 3↑	Ocean H 2.6k	- 1 11½ 12 12	1½	Odom	127wb	*.60	90-10	Hermis127½Molly Brant1051½Douro1193	Driving,sulked 8
18Aug03- 4Sar	fst	1⅛	:49 1:131 1:383 1:513 3↑	Merchants & Citizens 7k	- 3 12 13 13	1½	Odom	124wb	1.60	99-02	Hermis1243Irish Lad1206Rigodon1035	Easily 4
15Aug03- 4Sar	fst	1¼	:482 1:132 1:384 2:05 3↑	Sar Champion 6.9k	- 2 21 2½ 21½	21½	Odom	126wb	4.00	101-09	Irish Lad1161½Hermis1261½Heno1263	No match 4

13Aug03- 1Sar	gd	7f	:233 :482 1:144 1:282	2↑ Handicap 960	- 3	22 2½ 2½	11	Odom	128wb	*.50	83-21	Hermis1281Molly Brant1036Rigodon1148	Away slowly	4
8Aug03- 1Sar	sl	7f	:24 :474 1:141 1:282	2↑ Handicap 810	- 1	14 15 110	112	Rice	126wb	3.20	83-24	Hermis12612Major Daingerfield1242½Stamping Ground1088		5
	Won eased up													
3Aug03- 4Sar	fst	1¼	:491 1:142 1:401 2:053	3↑ Saratoga H 12k	- 2	2hd 21 77¼	714¼	Rice	123ws	7.00	86-06	WaterBoy127¾HunterRaine1073Caughnawg1091½	Quit after 7f	11
24Jun03- 7She	yl	1 1/16Ⓣ	:252 :514 1:184 1:53	3↑ Alw 1040	- 4	21½ 2hd 34	33½	Rice	126 w	*.45	62-34	FlorhamQun961½FlyngJb1012Hrms126¾	Bad start,poor effort	5
18Jun03- 4She	sly	1¼	:492 1:152 1:43 2:102	3↑ Suburban H 19k	- 1	2hd 32 96¼	1224¼	Redfern	128wsb	10.00e	49-25	Africander110hdHrbrt1184HuntrRn986	Pulled up after mile	15
12Jun03- 2Gra	my	1 1/16	:233 :473 1:134 1:471	3↑ Alw 1080	- 2	22 22½ 23	2¾	Rice	106wb	*.29	93-17	RiverPirate91¾Hrms10620StmpngGround86	Rated,closed gap	3
3Jun03- 4Gra	fst	1 1/16	:232 :472 1:132 1:46	3↑ Handicap 1370	- 3	21 21½ 22	57	Burns T	126 w	*.60	93-07	Dublin1141½Water Boy1112½Herbert1101	Tired	7
	Previously owned by L.V. Bell;previously trained by J. McCorm'ck													
13Oct02- 3MP	cpy	1¼	:504 1:16 1:42 2:081	2↑ Mamaroneck H 2.5k	- 2	32½ 31½ 1hd	11½	Rice	126 w	*2.00	87-13	Hermis1261½Warranted87½Advance Guard1243		6
	Unruly start,wide turn,speed to spare													
7Oct02- 5MP	fst	1¼	:51 1:172 2:061	Jerome H 2.9k	- 3	32½ 33 2hd	13	Rice	126 w	*.50	97-08	Hermis1263Hunter Raine100hdOom Paul1101½	Won easing up	4
2Oct02- 4Gra	gd	1 1/16	:244 :50 1:154 1:48	Ocean View H 2.1k	- 2	41½ 31 1hd	13	Rice	126 w	2.50	90-14	Hermis1263Huntressa98hdIgniter1161	Easily	4
15Sep02- 4Gra	fst	1¼	:491 1:143 1:401 2:061	3↑ First Spl 3.6k	- 2	21½ 21 1hd	11½	Odom	117ws	3.00	96-07	Hermis1171½Articulate1261Gunfire114hd	Easily	6
28Aug02- 3Sar	fst	1⅛	:482 1:132 1:384 1:512	Saranac H 5k	- 2	21 2hd 1hd	1hd	Rice	122 w	10.00	104-02	Hermis122hdWhiskey King1043Cunard115no	Driving	10
9Aug02- 4Sar	cpy	1⅛	:493 1:15 1:413 1:544	Travers 10k	- 5	54¾ 52¾ 4½	1hd	Rice	111 w	*.90	87-13	Hermis111hdGold Cure116noCunard1111	Wide,going away	7
	Previously owned by H.M. Ziegler,trainer C. Hughes													
4Aug02- 1Sar	gd	7f	:243 :491 1:15 1:28	2↑ Alw 860	- 2	31 2hd 1hd	12	Odom	110 w	*1.40	90-06	Hermis1102Monograph119½Maud Gonne1142	Easily	14
21Jly02- 1Bri	my	1 1/16	:251 :51 1:174 1:51	3↑ Alw 885	- 1	11½ 11½ 13	14	Wonderly	114 w	*.03	71-23	Hermis1144Fair Knight106	Hard held	2
17Jly02- 3Bri	fst	1 1/16	:234 :48 1:131 1:46	Alw 960	- 1	1½ 1hd 11½	14	Wonderly	116 w	*.70	96-05	Hermis1164LadySterling111hdParExcellence1114	Much best	5
21Jun02- 30WP	sl	1½	:501 1:171 2:102 2:401	American Derby 25k	- 12	1247 1253 -	-	McCue	122 w	10.00	- -	Wyth1221½LucnApplby1223Alddn1223	Faltered,pulled up lame	12
5Jun02- 2Gra	fst	1½	:494 1:162 2:071 2:333	3↑ Handicap 1605	- 6	63 52¾ 62¾	31¼	Shea	98 w	7.00	96-07	Monarka106¾WaterCur104½Hrms98no	Poor ride,finished fast	8
2Jun02- 5Gra	fst	1 1/16	:234 :482 1:14 1:463	3↑ Handicap 1125	- 5	42¼ 62½ 32¾	32¼	Jackson L	114 w	6.00	95-08	Highlander110¾Colonel Bill891½Hermis1142½	Bad start	9
	Previously owned by H.A. Engman													
28May02- 4Gra	hy	1 1/16	:234 :483 1:15 1:481	3↑ Handicap 1085	- 2	21½ 31 21	11	Jackson L	108 w	*1.80	89-15	Hermis1081Himself1103Oom Paul116¾	Impeded,up with rush	5
26May02- 5Gra	fst	1 1/16	:24 :482 1:133 1:462	Alw 1060	- 3	3½ 41¼ 21½	21	Jackson L	109 w	3.00	97-06	Hyphen1091Hermis10915Bessie McCarthy10410	Good finish	4
12Nov01- 5Lat	my	6f	:25¼ :51 1:18½	Alw 300	- 6	51¼ 41¼ 1½	14	Lyne	110	*.60e	73-33	Hermis1104Kaloma1152Moderator103½	Easily	6
9Nov01- 2Lat	fst	5½f	:24 :49 1:01¾ 1:08	Alw 300	- 1	2hd 1½ 1½	12	Lyne	107	5.00	96-12	Hermis1072Inventor1072Setauket1072	Easily	7
31Oct01- 2Lat	fst	5½f	:24 :49½ 1:01½ 1:08	©Alw 300	- 4	21 21½ 21	3½	Lyne	109	2.60	95-08	BalmofGilead106.5noHarryNew109½Hrms109½	Bumped stretch	10
28Oct01- 5Lat	fst	5½f	:23¾ :49½ 1:01¾ 1:08	©Alw 250	- 1	22 22 41½	14	Lyne	106	7.00	96-11	Hermis1064Inventor106½Harry New1105	Easily	11
26Oct01- 3Lat	fst	5f	:24 :49 1:01½	Alw 300	- 9	52½ 53½ 32	23	Lyne	105	10.00	98-06	Jack Rattlin1133Hermis1051Inventor1051	Tiring,swerved	12
26Sep01- 6Haw	fst	6f	:24 :48½ 1:14	Alw 400	- 8	43 42¼ 43	69¾	Coburn	112	4.00	83-08	TommyFostr1122½Emathion109nkRosePlume1122	Not a factor	10
18Sep01- 7Haw	gd	6½f	:25 :49¾ 1:15½ 1:22¼	Alw 400	- 5	87¼ 810 -	-	Jackson L	110	13.00	- -	SouthTrimble105¾DarkSecret1101St.Tmmny1101	Cut off,fell	9
	Previously owned by W.A. Engman													
16Sep01- 2Haw	gd	5f	:24½ :49½ 1:02¾	Alw 500	- 5	55½ 33½ 34½	21½	Jackson L	102	12.00	82-19	Evening Star1041½Hermis1021Amirante1076	Finished well	8
30Aug01- 1Haw	fst	5½f	:24¾ :49 1:02 1:09	©Md Alw 400	- 4	21½ 21½ 12	13	Winkfield J	109	*2.00	90-13	Hermis1093Huzzah1132½Tommy Foster1061	As rider pleased	11
13Aug01- 1Hrm	fst	6f	:242 :492 1:153	©Md Alw 400	- 2	14 13 12	32	Knight T	110	4.50	81-09	Landseer1081Ravensbury1101Hermis1101	Tired	15
6Aug01- 1Hrm	fst	5f	:492 1:014	©Md Alw 400	- 12	78½ 72¾ 51½	55¼	Mitchell C	106	*2.60	83-12	Emathion1051Landseer1021Pompey1063	Nearly left	15
2Aug01- 1Haw	fst	5½f	:25¼ :50¼ 1:03¼ 1:10	©Md Alw 400	- 9	32½ 31½ 2nk	43	Nutt	107	12.00	82-13	Harry Wilson1122Fullen104hdHuzzah1071	Faltered late	12
22Jly01- 2Haw	fst	5f	:25 :49¾ 1:02½	Alw 400	- 12	1027 1020 1015	1017	Dominick	103	20.00	68-10	RedTip1104ISamuelson103hdBrdg115½	Slow start,closed gap	13

Imp

br. or blk. f. 1894, by Wagner (Prince Charlie)–Fondling, by Fonso

Lifetime record: 171 62 35 29 $70,119

Own.– Daniel R. Harness

Br.– D.R. Harness (Oh)

Tr.– P. Wimmer

9Nov01- 4Aqu	fst	1 1/16	:234 :482 1:142 1:474	2↑ Farmingdale H .8k	- 5	54¼ 53½ 44½	66¼	Odom	126	*1.50	92-10	Oom Paul1122Ben Mac Dhui1142Handicapper982	Poor effort	6
7Nov01- 1Aqu	fst	7f	:242 :483 1:14 1:274	2↑ Oakdale H .8k	- 6	72¾ 71½ 62	51¼	Odom	126	2.60	83-12	Paul Clifford113hdShoreham1001Unmasked120hd	Closed gap	9
5Nov01- 4Aqu	gd	1 1/16	:243 :50 1:491	2↑ Idlewild H .8k	- 2	1hd 2hd 2hd	2¾	Odom	126	*2.00	90-11	Potente110¾Imp1262St. Finnan115hd	Good try	5
26Oct01- 4MP	fst	2¼	:50 2:351 3:56	3↑ Morris Park 4.7k	- 3	32 46½ 612	517	Bullman	121	7.00	90-05	GoldHeels1112Hernando111noWtrColor1113	Lacked condition	8
25Oct01- 6MP	fst	1¼	:514 1:17 1:42 2:072	3↑ Handicap 1045	- 1	12 12 13	14	Odom	122	5.00	91-10	Imp1224Advance Guard1264Rafaello1053	Never extended	4
22Oct01- 5MP	fst	1	:252 :50 1:15 1:40	3↑ Handicap 660	- 1	1nk 1hd 1hd	1hd	Shaw	109	3.50	95-09	Imp109hdSt. Finnan1046Decanter1142	Driving	5
19Oct01- 3MP	fst	*6f-EC	1:10	2↑ Handicap 885	- 7	8 78¾ 73½	77	Bullman	116	15.00	86-09	Rockwater99½Roxane1091BelleofLxngton103½	Never a factor	10
6Sep01- 6She	fst	1½Ⓣ	:50 1:161 2:08 2:332	3↑ Handicap 1445	- 1	1nk 45 48½	422½	Fairgood	110	3.50	81-00	Trigger97½Baron Pepper1022Maid of Harlem9220	Speed,quit	4
2Sep01- 4She	gd	1¼	:491 1:143 1:404 2:07	3↑ Twin City H 6.3k	- 2	33 43 64¼	78½	Woods J	117	10.00	81-07	Herbert116hdTerminus108½Trigger951	Disliked going	10
24Aug01- 4Sar	my	1⅝	:51 1:45 2:522	3↑ Sar Cup 5k	- 2	23 315 325	338	Odom	122	2.60	- -	Blues1138Baron Pepper11330Imp122	Disliked going	3
20Aug01- 3Sar	fst	1 1/16	:243 :491 1:15 1:464	3↑ Alw 770	- 1	1hd 21 21½	26	Fairgood	111	*1.20	87-06	Roe Hampton1066Imp11112The Rhymer985	Poor ride	4
13Aug01- 4Sar	fst	1 70	:243 :494 1:161 1:452	3↑ Alw 790	- 2	21 21 21	1¾	Fairgood	113	*.90	- -	Imp113¾Smoke11312Admonition110	Poor ride,much best	3
5Aug01- 4Sar	fst	1⅛	:493 1:15 1:403 1:531	3↑ Saratoga H 10k	- 5	4¾ 42¼ 34	53½	Odom	123	20.00	91-09	Rockton1162Water Cure1071Water Color115nk	Good try	11
	Previously trained by C.E. Brossman,owned by Harness & Brossman													
23Nov00- 6Ben	fst	1 100	:252 :50 1:163 1:492	3↑ Handicap 445	- 1	1½ 1hd 2hd	2no	Rutter	123	*.90	93-07	First Whip112noImp1234Asquith99no	Tired	4
14Nov00- 1Aqu	fst	*7f	:232 :483 1:14 1:252	2↑ Handicap 585	- 6	53¼ 55¼ 41	31	Rutter	126	*3.00	95-08	Bastile95hdTrumpet1171Imp1262	Hung	12
8Nov00- 4Aqu	fst	1½	:501 1:17 2:092 2:373	2↑ Alw 525	- 1	1¾ 1½ 2hd	21½	Burns T	123	*.50	108-06	McMeekin1171½Imp12312Compensation126	Saved ground	3
3Nov00- 4Emp	hy	1⅛	:501 1:151 1:411 1:55	2↑ Wakefield H 1.4k	- 3	52¼ 52¾ 510	611¼	Burns T	126	4.00	- -	James1121KingBarleycorn1062PinkCoat107no	Disliked going	6
1Nov00- 6Emp	sl	1 1/16	:243 :483 1:15 1:474	2↑ Handicap 700	- 2	1hd 1hd 2½	21½	Burns T	128	2.00	- -	McMeekin1131½Imp1282Herbert1061	Disliked going	5
25Oct00- 4Emp	sl	1 1/16	:25 :481 1:141 1:47	3↑ ⒻMahopac H 1.1k	- 1	1½ 11 11½	11½	Burns T	126	*.70	- -	Imp1261½Kamara104hdOneck Queen951	Won easing up	4
22Oct00- 4Emp	fst	1¼	:484 1:13 1:39 2:04	2↑ Emp City H 3.2k	- 1	1hd 1hd 1½	2hd	O'Conner	124	*1.60	- -	Charentus106hdImp1241Pink Coat105no	Just missed	7
13Oct00- 5MP	fst	1¾	:49 2:084 2:333 2:583	3↑ Municipal H 3.9k	- 1	1½ 12 11½	2hd	Burns T	126	4.00	103-05	Ethelbert126hdImp1266Maid of Harlem1005	Gamely	5
22Sep00- 4Gra	fst	1⅛	:484 1:142 1:404 1:534	2↑ Occidental H 2.3k	- 2	1hd 4¾ 73¼	79¾	McJoynt	126	*3.00	86-07	PinkCoat1021½JckPont1163Chrntus103hd	Tired under impost	9
15Sep00- 4Gra	fst	1½	:502 1:17 2:083 2:341	3↑ Second Spl 3.2k	- 1	11 11 11	11	Burns T	118	7.00	99-06	Imp1181Kinley Mack126noEthelbert1211	Handily	4
11Sep00- 4Gra	fst	1¼	:512 1:171 1:431 2:081	3↑ First Spl 3.1k	- 1	11 11 1hd	34	Odom	123	*.90	86-07	Kinley Mack126hdMcMeekin1174Imp123	Speed,tired	3
3Sep00- 6She	fst	1 1/16Ⓣ	:242 :483 1:143 1:464	3↑ Handicap 1120	- 1	11½ 1½ 1hd	11½	Odom	128	3.50	101-00	Imp1281½Intrusive1171½Maximo Gomez1148	Gamely	6
4Aug00- 4Bri	fst	2¼	:501 2:323 2:574 3:491	3↑ Brighton Cup 8.3k	- 1	14 16 11½	2¾	Jenkins	121	8.00	135-00	Ethelbert124¾Imp12110Sidney Lucas10910	Good try	4
1Aug00- 6Bri	fst	1⅛	:483 1:141 1:40 1:53	3↑ Alw 880	- 1	2hd 2hd 22	23	Clawson	121	*.70	104-00	Belle of Troy1063Imp1212Gonfalon106no	Second best	5
25Jly00- 4Bri	fst	1	:24 :481 1:142 1:40	3↑ Islip 2.5k	- 1	2hd 2hd 35½	35½	Mitchell	121	2.20	92-05	Ethlbrt1264SkyScrpr1071½Imp121	Speed,tired,pulled up lame	3
23Jly00- 2Bri	fst	1⅛	:472 1:122 1:393 1:53	3↑ Alw 670	- 2	22 23 1hd	11½	Mitchell	115	*.45	107-00	Imp1151½Water Cure902Plucky95	Easily	3
7Jly00- 4Bri	fst	1¼	:473 1:13 1:382 2:043	3↑ Brighton H 11k	- 5	44 3nk 31	32	Odom	129	8.00	102-03	Jack Point1091½The Kentuckian109½Imp1293	Good effort	9
3Jly00- 4She	fst	1⅛	:50 1:144 1:404 1:54	3↑ Long Island H 2.5k	- 4	2hd 1hd 2hd	2no	Odom	130	*2.20	95-08	Charentus99noImp130noGreyfeld1006	Driving	6
30Jun00- 4She	fst	1¾	:491 2:05 2:32 2:591	3↑ Advance 5.3k	- 1	120 130 130	130	Odom	113	*.10	110-01	Imp11330MaidofHarlem1038PostHst95	Restrained throughout	3
23Jun00- 4She	fst	1	:24 :49 1:144 1:404	3↑ Sheepshead Bay H 2k	- 3	64¼ 54½ 23	34	Tabor	133	6.00	87-09	Greyfeld911Bendoran1213Imp133hd	Tired under impost	10
20Jun00- 3She	fst	1 3/16	:501 1:153 1:413 2:003	3↑ Handicap 1270	- 1	12 11½ 11½	11½	Tabor	131	*.80	98-09	Imp1311½Col. Roosevelt1016David Garrick1135	Easily	4
16Jun00- 4She	fst	1¼	:491 1:15 1:411 2:064	3↑ Suburban H 10k	- 2	21 2hd 42	410½	O'Conner	128	4.00	80-09	Kinley Mack1251½Ethelbert1304Gulden1005	Speed,tired	10
13Jun00- 2Gra	fst	1¼	:50 1:152 1:413 2:08	3↑ Handicap 1080	- 1	12 13 13	11½	Tabor	126	*1.40	91-08	Imp1261½Gulden99noLothario106no	Easily	7

5Jun00- 4Gra	fst	1⅛	:49 1:141 1:404 1:541	3↑ Brookdale H 2k	-	2	2½	2hd	1hd	2no	O'Connor	127	*.70	94-08	Jean Beraud127noImp1271½Charentus101hd	Gamely 4
30May00- 4Gra	fst	1 1/16	:25 :492 1:144 1:464	3↑ Parkway H 2.1k	-	1	1hd	12	1hd	12	O'Connor	124	*1.80	97-04	Imp1242Kinley Mack1274Survivor104hd	Easily 6
26May00- 4Gra	hy	1¼	:491 1:161 1:431 2:10	3↑ Brooklyn H 10k	-	4	32	41¼	61½	64¾	Clawson	128	8.00	76-15	Kinley Mack1221Rafaello113¾Herbert98hd	Disliked going 9
15May00- 1MP	fst	6½f	:234 :494 1:143 1:21	3↑ Alw 590	-	3	31	31	3½	31¾	Clay P	124	*.90	93-07	Vulcain1131Unmasked103¾Imp1241½	Urged,not enough 6
9May00- 4MP	sl	7f	:244 :511 1:164 1:30¼	3↑ Ⓕ Alw 690	-	2	32	3½	41¾	25	Vest	129	*.60	74-28	SparrowWing1135Imp129noStarChime106no	Poor ride,outrun 5
5May00- 4MP	fst	1	:234 :483 1:15 1:41¼	3↑ Metropolitan H 7.7k	-	7	51¾	32	22	33	Clawson	127	8.00	86-13	Ethelbert1263Box121noImp1271½	Driving 11
14Apr00- 5Ben	sl	7f	:242 :494 1:162 1:31	3↑ 2nd Ben Spring H 1.1k	-	2	31½	43	43½	35	Clay	132	*1.10	85-13	Charentus1125Boney Boy116hdImp132nk	Impeded 4
2Apr00- 4Ben	gd	6f	:241 :50 1:03 1:161	3↑ 1st Bennings Spring H .9k	-	1	3nk	3nk	41¼	31½	Clay P	132	*1.20	91-09	Boney Boy106½Charentus1101Imp132hd	Impeded½ 7
30Sep99- 4Gra	fst	1¼	:492 1:141 1:41 2:073	2↑ Oriental H 2.5k	-	1	12	12	14	14	Clay P	128	*.50	94-08	Imp1284Charentus106	Eased in stretch 2
23Sep99- 4Gra	fst	1½	:50 1:16 2:08 2:34	2↑ Second Spl 3.3k	-	1	12	13	15	11½	Clay P	124	3.50	107-04	Imp1241½BenHolldy12110ThBchlor118hd	Eased final furlong 4
16Sep99- 4Gra	fst	1⅛	:49 1:143 1:411 1:542	3↑ Occidental H 2.3k	-	2	1hd	2hd	31	53¼	Clay P	129	3.50	95-06	Previous122hdCharentus1091Prince McClurg115hd	Tired 7
12Sep99- 4Gra	gd	1¼	:494 1:15 1:42 2:094	3↑ First Spl 3.5k	-	2	2nk	1nk	11½	12	Clay P	119	*1.60	83-11	Imp1192May Hempstead1121½Maxine119¾	Restrained at end 6
4Sep99- 4She	gd	1¼	:491 1:16 1:44 2:10	3↑ Twin City H 6k	-	1	1hd	2hd	6	8	Clay P	130	4.00	--	Previous1144Bangle1201½Bannockburn1261	Disliked footing 9
1Sep99- 6She	fst	1¼Ⓣ	:49 1:141 1:401 2:071	3↑ Turf H 1.7k	-	1	13	14	12	12	Clay P	128	3.00	100-00	Imp1282Decanter1173Bon Ino973	Never threatened 6
30Aug99- 4She	fst	1	:242 :482 1:141 1:401	3↑ Ocean H 1.5k	-	1	1hd	1hd	1hd	1hd	Clay P	123	8.00	94-09	Imp123hdCharentus1092Batten112hd	Driving 9
26Aug99- 3She	fst	6f	:232 :473 1:132	3↑ Fall H 1.5k	-	1	2hd	2hd	21	33½	Clay	124	5.00	91-10	Previous111½Batten1143Imp1242	Outpaced 7
31Jly99- 5Bri	fst	1	:241 :482 1:141 1:403	3↑ Islip 2.3k	-	2	31	21	2hd	1hd	Clay	111	1.80	95-05	Imp111hdFirearm1132Peep o' Day1114	Just up 4
24Jly99- 3Bri	hy	1 1/16	:25 :502 1:162 1:50	3↑ Handicap 775	-	1	2nk	41	34½	46	Clay P	124	3.50	79-15	Kirkwood1041½Maxine1144Tamor98½	Poor ride 4
18Jly99- 3Bri	fst	1	:25 :501 1:16 1:412	3↑ Handicap 735	-	1	11	1½	1½	1½	Clay P	126	*1.00	91-08	Imp126½Charentus1065Cambrian1052	Driving 4
11Jly99- 4Bri	fst	6f	:232 :481 1:012 1:144	2↑ Flight H 1.8k	-	5	53	65¾	66¼	44	Clay P	126	6.00	88-08	Firearm1082Bendoran1262Swiftmas115hd	Finished fast 6
6Jly99- 4Bri	fst	1¼	:491 1:143 1:40 2:052	3↑ Brighton H 9.9k	-	1	11	11	11	11	O'Leary	115	8.00	110-02	Imp1151Ethelbert1071Bangle112nk	Mild drive 7
3Jly99- 3She	fst	1⅛	:50 1:144 1:401 1:53	3↑ Handicap 1080	-	1	11	11	1hd	32	Turner N	126	*3.50	98-04	Tragedian1062Survivor107hdImp1264	Driving 7
29Jun99- 4She	hy	1⅛	:49 1:15 1:411 1:541	3↑ Long Island H 2k	-	1	11	1hd	1hd	34½	O'Leary	119	2.60	89-06	Bangle1093Maxine1131½Imp1195	Dueled,tired 5
24Jun99- 4She	fst	1	:232 :471 1:123 1:394	3↑ Sheepshead Bay H 1.5k	-	2	25	35	33¼	78¼	Taral	125	3.50	88-06	Fly by Night108¾Azucena982Bendoran123hd	Weakened 9
20Jun99- 4She	fst	6f	:234 :472 1:00 1:132	3↑ Coney Island H 1.5k	-	4	47	45½	23	21½	Taral	128	*3.50	93-10	Bendoran1181½Imp1282St. Cloud122nk	Second best 12
17Jun99- 4She	fst	1¼	:492 1:141 1:393 2:054	3↑ Suburban H 10k	-	3	31	11	13	12	Turner N	114	6.00	96-06	Imp1142Bannockburn1123Warrenton114nk	Never threatened 13
14Jun99- 2Gra	fst	1⅛	:494 1:151 1:41 1:534	3↑ Handicap 1100	-	1	12	13	14	13	Clawson	126	3.20	101-06	Imp1263Pirate M.971Warrenton1251	Never extended 6
8Jun99- 2Gra	fst	1 1/16	:24 :49 1:152 1:49	3↑ Ⓕ Alw 700	-	4	21	11	1½	11½	Taral	123	3.50	90-08	Imp1231½Gaze983Azucena106½	Easily 7
5Jun99- 5Gra	fst	1 1/16	:251 :503 1:152 1:483	3↑ Handicap 875	-	2	21	31½	33	34½	Mitchell	122	4.00	87-07	Intrusive1123Charentus1101½Imp1222	Weak handling 9
27May99- 4Gra	fst	1¼	:491 1:142 1:392 2:061	3↑ Brooklyn H 10k	-	5	53½	62¼	15	15	Clayton	110	15.00	--	Banastar1103Lanky Bob1051Filigrane982	Outrun 16
23May99- 6MP	fst	1⅛	:502 1:15 1:41 1:533	3↑ Handicap 850	-	2	2hd	2hd	11	11	Taral	125	*2.00	89-05	Imp1251Glonoine108hdJefferson1083	Handily 8
18May99- 5MP	fst	6½f	:24 :49 1:14 1:202	3↑ Claremont Hwt H 1.5k	-	3	1nk	11	11	3½	Taral	119	*3.50	100-01	Kinnikinnick124½Dr. Eichberg106hdImp1191	Good effort 8
16May99- 4MP	fst	7f	:24 :492 1:141 1:263	3↑ New Rochelle H 1.6k	-	5	31¼	41	2nk	22	Taral	112	5.00	102-01	Previous1132Imp1122Kingdon112no	Good try 10
13May99- 5MP	fst	1 1/16	:26 :51 1:153 1:471	3↑ Handicap 900	-	9	4¾	2nk	2½	2¾	O'Connor	113	4.00	95-04	Don D'Oro128¾Imp1136Free Lance105½	Second best 10
11May99- 6MP	my	1	:251 :501 1:16 1:43	3↑ Handicap 880	-	1	22	22	25	42¾	Taral	117	*1.60	84-10	Don D'Oro1222Twinkler98½Charentus107nk	Tired 6
9May99- 4MP	fst	*6f-EC	:231 :47 :58 1:09	3↑ Toboggan H 2.1k	-	4	2½	63¼	63½	8	McGlone	120	8.00	--	Banastar116¾Sanders1213Octagon1303	Pulled up 10
6May99- 4MP	fst	1	:242 :49 1:14 1:394	3↑ Metropolitan H 8.2k	-	5	52¼	41¾	42	43	McGlone	112	6.00	100-00	Filigrane1022Ethelbert106hdSanders1101	Outrun 14
12Apr99- 5Ben	fst	1 1/16	:254 :501 1:161 1:503	3↑ Handicap 350	-	1	12	14	13	13	McGlone	126	1.60	--	Imp1263Alice Farley1161Double Dummy109hd	Cantering 5
8Apr99- 5Ben	sl	1 100	:25 :51 1:194 1:522	3↑ Handicap 335	-	2	1hd	21½	43	412	Scherrer	126	*.50	--	Beau Ideal1002Imperator1046Alice Farley1144	Weakened 5
15Nov98- 3Lak	hy	1 1/16	:25¼ :52 1:19 1:53½	3↑ Handicap 400	-	1	15	112	16	18	McNickle	116	1.40	68-27	Imp1168Macy1142Al Fresco97	Galloping 3
14Nov98- 3Lak	hy	6f	:26¼ :52½ 1:05 1:17½	3↑ Handicap 400	-	1	2nk	2nk	2½	23	McNickle	125	*.60	81-29	O'Connell1173Imp1255Timemakr1113	Carried wide by winner 6
8Nov98- 4Lak	gd	1⅛	:50 1:14½ 1:42 1:55¾	Handicap 400	-	1	1¾	13	11	15	McNickle	112	1.40	88-14	Imp1125Macy1163Storm King992	Easily 5
5Nov98- 4Lak	hy	1 1/16	:25¼ :50¾ 1:16½ 1:52¾	3↑ Handicap 400	-	1	2¾	23	24	35	Ellis	115	*.90	67-25	Macy1113Storm King972Imp1155	Dull effort 4
29Oct98- 4Lak	hy	1 100	:25¼ :50¼ 1:15¾ 1:46¼	Alw 400	-	1	12	12	1nk	21½	Sheppard	119	3.00	--	Macy1041½Imp1198Storm King96¾	Second best 5
12Oct98- 3Haw	sl	7f	:25½ :50 1:15¾ 1:29	3↑ Dash 1.3k	-	2	1½	11½	12½	11	Rutter	118	*.60	--	Imp1181May W.1024Lady Ellerslie976	Hand ride 5
1Oct98- 4Hrm	gd	6f	:23¼ :47¾ 1:01 1:13	2↑ Speed 1.5k	-	3	24	25	23	12½	Rutter	115	*.60	96-10	Imp1152½Frank Bell923Traverser1132½	In hand 5
28Sep98- 4Hrm	gd	1 70	:24¾ :49¾ 1:15¼ 1:44½	Alw 400	-	1	15	18	13	11	Rutter	119	*.70	94-15	Imp1191Dare II947Carnero945	Easily 4
19Sep98- 4Hrm	gd	7f	:25 :49¾ 1:15¼ 1:27¾	3↑ Austin 1.7k	-	1	1nk	1hd	11½	12½	Rutter	119	3.50	92-16	Imp1192½Hugh Penny1082Found95no	Easily 9
17Sep98- 3Haw	hy	1⅛	:53 1:19 1:47¼ 2:01½	3↑ Monadnock 1.1k	-	1	12	15	11½	12	McNickle	114	*.95	--	Imp1142Hugh Penny114	Easily 2
12Sep98- 3Haw	fst	1⅛	:49¾ 1:14¾ 1:40½ 1:53	3↑ Alw 500	-	1	12	16	15	12	McNickle	109	1.80	--	Imp1092Crocket9910John Bright1072	Eased up 5
8Sep98- 3Haw	gd	1	:26 :51 1:16½ 1:42	4↑ Alw 500	-	2	2½	1nk	21	25	Conley	111	4.50	--	Hugh Penny1115Imp1116David1042	Good try 5
3Sep98- 5Hrm	fst	1 70	:25 :50¼ 1:15¾ 1:44	Alw 400	-	2	2hd	21	33½	410½	Sheppard	112	9.00	85-07	Storm King981David Tenny1121½What Next1008	Stopped 4
1Sep98- 3Hrm	fst	6f	:24 :48¾ 1:01 1:13¾	3↑ Alw 400	-	3	32	34	34½	34¾	Sheppard	109	4.50	88-07	EugeniaWickes1044FloraLouis98¾Imp1092	Driving,lost whip 7
30Jly98- 5Hrm	hy	6f	:24¾ :50¼ 1:03¾ 1:17¼	3↑ Alw 400	-	2	25	23	24	25	Thorpe	112	*1.00	70-36	Mary Black1055Imp11250Storm King117100	Good try 4
23Jly98- 3OWP	fst	1¼	:48¼ 1:13¼ 1:39 2:04½	3↑ Wheeler H 5.4k	-	3	44	56	44¾	721¼	Reiff L	115	15.00	--	Algol1075Goodrich107½Pink Coat109¾	No threat 10
16Jly98- 5OWP	fst	1	:24½ :48¾ 1:13½ 1:39	3↑ Alw 400	-	3	1nk	1nk	2hd	22	Caywood	109	*.70	--	Azucena972Imp1098Miss Gussie97nk	Wide,careless ride 5
11Jly98- 5OWP	fst	6¼f	:24 :49 1:13¾ 1:17	3↑ Alw 500	-	3	22	22	31¾	42½	Turner N	112	*1.00	--	Satsuma109nkAlgol1171½Abuse119¾	Dull 5
9Jly98- 2OWP	fst	1⅛	:48¼ 1:14 1:39¼ 1:51¾	4↑ Alw 595	-	1	11½	12	11½	11½	Caywood	112	1.30	--	Imp1121½Macy117	Best 2
5Jly98- 3OWP	fst	1 1/16	:25 :50¼ 1:15¾ 1:46	3↑ Alw 600	-	1	11	12½	12	13	Caywood	110	*.55	--	Imp1103The Devil10010The Roman110	Easily 3
2Jly98- 3OWP	fst	1⅛	:49½ 1:14¼ 1:39¼ 1:51¾	3↑ Oakwood H 2.4k	-	1	1¾	11½	1nk	31½	Caywood	118	7.00	--	Fervor103noWhat Er Lou1081½Imp1186	Faltered late 6
22Jun98- 1She	gd	6½f	:232 :49 1:153 1:221	3↑ HiW H 845	-	4	33	43	54½	68	McCafferty	135	6.00	78-16	Swiftmas1201Hanlon106½Mainstay1123	Eased up late 10
18Jun98- 4She	gd	1¼	:51 1:16 1:412 2:081	3↑ Suburban H 10k	-	6	4nk	21	31	610½	Clawson	102	5.00	73-14	Tillo119½Semper Ego106hdOgden1093	Faltered 11
13Jun98- 2Gra	gd	1⅛	:51 1:16 1:41¾ 1:55½	3↑ Handicap 875	-	1	11½	11½	11½	11	Spencer	108	2.00	93-10	Imp1081Havoc1261½Knight of the Garter934	Tiring 5
3Jun98- 5Hrm	fst	6f	:24½ :48½ 1:01 1:14¼	3↑ Handicap 400	-	2	21	22½	21½	11½	Martin W	124	*.50	90-17	Imp1241½Dave Waldo108¾Cherry Leaf955	Driving 6
30May98- 5Hrm	sl	1 1/16	:25 :51¼ 1:18¼ 1:51½	3↑ Memorial Day H 1.9k	-	1	14	16	13	110	Caywood	118	*.80	70-31	Imp11810Dr. Sheppard10925Goodrich100	Won eased up 3
24May98- 5Hrm	gd	1	:26 :49¾ 1:16½ 1:44	3↑ Alw 500	-	1	11	11½	12½	1¾	Turner N	105	*.25	73-21	Imp105¾Frank Thompson946J.H.C.11012	Won eased up 4
21May98- 6Lak	hy	1⅛	:52 1:18¾ 1:45¾ 1:59¼	3↑ Handicap 400	-	1	13	15	18	16	Turner N	117	*.50	70-29	Imp1176Moncreith1055Banquo II10510	Won eased up 4
18May98- 5Lak	hy	1 1/16	:24¾ :50½ 1:16¾ 1:54½	4↑ Alw 400	-	1	115	125	120	16	Turner N	102	*.17	63-29	Imp1026Kirk108noArrezzo10210	Won pulled up 4
7May98- 5Lak	fst	5f	:23¼ :48½ 1:01	3↑ Alw 400	-	1	22½	33¼	32¼	22	Turner N	109	*.70	93-10	Abuse1102Imp1094Peter McCue951½	Outrun,driving 8
5May98- 4Lak	sly	1	:24¼ :49¾ 1:16¼ 1:44	3↑ Alw 400	-	1	18	115	112	112	Sheppard	102	*.25	81-23	Imp10212Dr. Sheppard107nkMyth1045	Won eased up 4
22Apr98- 4Nwp	fst	5½f	:22¼ :46¾ 1:00¾ 1:07	3↑ Alw 250	-	5	79	67½	44½	11	Sheppard	111	*.40	101-10	Imp1111Richard J.104noAunt Bird943	Driving 10
21Apr98- 3Nwp	fst	1	:25 :49¾ 1:14½ 1:40	3↑ Handicap 450	-	1	12	15	13	12	Sheppard	116	*1.60	100-08	Imp1162What Next110½Marito895	Easily 8
12Apr98- 3Nwp	fst	1 50	:24 :48¾ 1:13½ 1:43	3↑ Alw 250	-	1	12	12	1½	13	Sheppard	106	*1.00	107-03	Imp1063What Next1082Sister Stella1038	In a gallop 8
9Apr98- 1Nwp	fst	6f	:24½ :49 1:02¼ 1:15	4↑ Alw 250	-	2	1nk	11	12	16	Sheppard	109	*1.20	88-16	Imp1096Lufra112½Box1212	Galloping 5
	Previously owned by Daniel R. Brossman															
15Nov97- 5Lak	hy	1	:25 :50¼ 1:17¼ 1:45	3↑ Handicap 400	-	1	18	18	112	115	Waldo	80	*.60	--	Imp8015Harry Thoburn808Ben Waddell821	Easily 5
12Nov97- 4Lak	gd	7f	:24¼ :48¼ 1:14 1:26¾	3↑ Alw 400	-	1	1¾	12	12	14	Dupee	90	1.60	--	Imp904The Elector1043Laureate90	Speed to spare 3
9Nov97- 3Lak	my	7f	:25½ :51 1:18½ 1:32	3↑ Alw 400	-	2	1nk	2nk	2nk	21½	Dupee	104	1.30	--	Laureate1091½Imp1048LadyCallhn1003	Handicapped by going 8
6Nov97- 5Lak	fst	5f	:23½ :48½ 1:01	2↑ Alw 400	-	2	31¾	32½	3¾	21½	Dupee	105	4.00	--	Abuse1131½Imp1053Lady Callahan103nk	Good try 8
4Nov97- 5Lak	fst	7f	:24½ :48¾ 1:15 1:27¾	3↑ Alw 400	-	4	21	2nk	1½	1¾	Dupee	89	6.00	--	Imp89¾Gath1071Timemaker1001½	Hand ride 5
1Nov97- 3Lak	hy	7f	:24¼ :49 1:16½ 1:30¼	3↑ Alw 400	-	4	42½	42¼	44¼	46	Dupee	90	7.00	--	Macy922May W924Lady Callahan100no	Tired,disliked going 8
23Oct97- 4Hrm	fst	5½f	:23½ :49 1:01¼ 1:07½	2↑ Handicap 400	-	4	41¾	63	56¾	511¼	Burns T	103	4.00	--	Gath1181St. Alfonses D854Judge Wardell97nk	Poor effort 6

21Oct97- 5Hrm	fst	6f	:23½ :48 1:00½ 1:13¾	3↑ Alw 400	-	2	31¾	32¼	44	49	Clay	104	7.00	- -	Timemaker1052May W1023Abuse1124	Showed little	4
19Oct97- 6Hrm	fst	7f	:23¾ :48½ 1:14¼ 1:27	2↑ Alw 400	-	1	1nk	1nk	2nk	67	Everett	104	7.00	- -	May W102½Lieber Karl943Gath119no	Dueled,tired	7
16Oct97- 5Hrm	fst	6f	:24¼ :48½ 1:01¼ 1:13¼	2↑ Speed .6k	-	1	2nk	32¾	41	41½	Everett	105	30.00	- -	May W102noGath117no[D]Flora Louise871½	Impeded stretch	5

Placed third through disqualification

12Oct97- 3Hrm	hy	5½f	:25¾ :52 1:05¾ 1:12¾	3↑ Alw 400	-	4	32¾	313	312	316	Clay	99	3.00	- -	Gath1146B & W10210Imp9912	Disliked going	4
9Oct97- 5Hrm	fst	5½f	:23 :48½ 1:01 1:07¼	2↑ Alw 400	-	1	31	32¾	41¼	45	Clay	102	4.50	- -	Flora Louise881Charm1074Judge Wardell88hd	Good effort	5
18Sep97- 4Hrm	gd	6f	:24½ :49½ 1:01¼ 1:13½	2↑ Alw 400	-	3	44	44¼	21½	21	Connolly	105	4.00	- -	Harry Duke1071Imp1052½The Swain1076	Driving	8
15Sep97- 4Hrm	fst	6f	:24 :48½ 1:01¾ 1:14½	3↑ Handicap 400	-	2	41¼	43¼	31½	46½	Clay	115	*1.60	- -	Laureate110½Preston983Simmons983	Poor ride	5
11Sep97- 5Hrm	fst	6f	:24 :48½ 1:00½ 1:13¼	2↑ Alw 400	-	1	12½	1½	1nk	11½	Clay	108	4.50	- -	Imp1081½HrryDuk109½Prsbytrn885	Rated,drew away cleverly	5
9Sep97- 5Hrm	fst	7f	:24½ :49¾ 1:14½ 1:26¾	3↑ Alw 400	-	1	11	1¾	1nk	1no	Clay	104	6.00	- -	Imp104noThe Swain104½Macy1011½	Tired,well ridden	5
2Sep97- 4Hrm	fst	6f	:23½ :47½ 1:00¾ 1:13	3↑ Alw 400	-	1	11	11	1½	1½	Clay	97	*1.40	- -	Imp97½Harry Duke105.5¾Abuse11310	All out drive	4
30Aug97- 5Hrm	fst	7f	:22¾ :47 1:12½ 1:26¼	2↑ Alw 400	-	1	18	16	12	11	Clay	97	*1.10	- -	Imp971Fretful1046Irene Woods1094	Tiring	5
28Aug97- 5Hrm	fst	6f	:23¾ :48½ 1:00¼ 1:12¾	2↑ Alw 400	-	1	13	11½	1nk	2½	Clay	99	8.00	- -	Flora Louise85½Imp991½Timemaker110hd	Driving	5
24Aug97- 3Hrm	fst	6½f	:23½ :48¾ 1:13¼ 1:19¾	2↑ Alw 400	-	3	2½	2¾	3nk	34½	Clay	103	8.00	- -	Timemaker1081½Irene Woods1103Imp103hd	Used,tired	5
19Aug97- 4Hrm	fst	1	:24 :48 1:13½ 1:40	Alw 400	-	2	2½	2hd	21½	35½	Woods J	89	7.00	- -	Lady Callahan892½Serrano963Imp89hd	Appeared lame	4
16Aug97- 3Hrm	fst	1	:24 :49 1:13¾ 1:39¾	Alw 400	-	2	2hd	2hd	21½	37½	Caywood	102	1.60	- -	Lady Callahan981½Dunois986Imp10210	Dueled,tired	6
13Aug97- 4Hrm	fst	7f	:24¼ :49 1:14½ 1:27¾	3↑ Alw 400	-	1	1¾	12	11½	15	Burns T	97	5.00	- -	Imp975Greyhurst1042½Nimrod1072	Handily	7
11Aug97- 6Hrm	fst	6f	:24¼ :48¼ 1:01¼ 1:13¾	3↑ Alw 400	-	6	57¾	46	53	53	Hicks J	95	8.00	- -	IreneWoods1091½LadyCallahn95noThDuc105no	Never a threat	11
29Jly97- 4Oky	fst	7f	:23¾ :48¼ 1:14¼ 1:27	Ohio Selling 1k	-	1	1hd	2½	2hd	33½	Everett	97	8.00	- -	Taluca1031½Remember Me902Imp971	Gave way	6
27Jly97- 4Oky	hy	6f	:24½ :49 1:16½	Press 1.5k	-	1	2½	21	22	21	Piggott	103	2.50	- -	Abe Furst1081Imp1035Eugenia Wickes103	Driving,no match	3
17Jly97- 6Oky	hy	6½f	:25 :50¼ 1:16½ 1:23½	3↑ Alw 300	-	6	66½	614	611	717½	Reiff C	103	3.00	- -	Box984Arlington1064Geyser1063	Bad start	7
8Jly97- 5Oky	fst	1	:25¼ :50 1:15½ 1:43	ⒻAlw 350	-	1	1½	11	12	1hd	Reiff C	104	2.50	- -	Imp104hdPerformance1041½BelleBramble1078	Tiring,held on	5
1Jly97- 1Oky	fst	6f	:24½ :49¼ 1:14½	3↑ Inaugural Dash .5k	-	2	42	42½	31½	42½	Burns T	98	4.00	- -	Panmure101hdGeyser1061Boanerges1131½	No threat	7
29Jun97- 5Lat	fst	1	:24½ :48¾ 1:14¼ 1:41¾	Clm	-	3	2½	1nk	32	45	Everett	97	3.50	- -	LordZeni1041½Viscount932AbFurst1021½	Stopped in stretch	6
24Jun97- 5Lat	fst	1	:24½ :49 1:15 1:41¾	Handicap 500	-	2	2no	11	12	21	Burns T	97	5.00	- -	Donna Rita951Imp972Boanerges1142	Second best	4
14Jun97- 4Lat	fst	1	:24½ :48½ 1:13¾ 1:41¼	3↑ Alw 300	-	2	2½	2½	21	53½	Burns T	102	3.00	- -	Cavalero1071½FredBarr102.51JoClrk100no	Stopped in drive	8
10Jun97- 4Lat	fst	6f	:24¼ :49 1:14¼	3↑ Milldale 1.5k	-	6	52¼	33	44½	62½	Nutt	111	20.00	- -	Taluca101.51Byron McClelland112½Pete114hd	No threat	8
8Jun97- 5Lat	gd	6f	:24¼ :49 1:14½	3↑ Alw 300	-	1	11	11	1½	2hd	Nutt	106	*1.40	- -	Geyser97hdImp1062Orimar973	Speed,just missed	8
1Jun97- 4Lat	fst	6f	:24½ :48¾ 1:14	3↑ Handicap 480	-	1	11	12	11½	11½	Everett	104	10.00	- -	Imp1041½Byron McClelland1061Sangamon100hd	Cleverly	8
29May97- 5Lat	fst	6f	:24¼ :48½ 1:13¾	3↑ Alw 350	-	2	22	2½	21	2½	Burns T	100	15.00	- -	Pete109½Imp1001Sharon1103	No match	10
26May97- 6Lat	gd	6f	:24½ :49 1:14	3↑ Clm	-	3	41	55½	31½	512	Hill J	103	8.00	- -	J.A. Gray1091½Balk Line108.5hdW C T10910	Bid,tired	10
18May97- 4Nwp	fst	6f	:24 :48¾ 1:01¾ 1:14½	ⒻAlw 250	-	2	22	41½	31	4nk	Sheedy	115	5.00	- -	Suisun105noHer Excellency115noTrimuda105no	Driving	8
15May97- 4Nwp	fst	7f	:23¾ :48¾ 1:15¼ 1:28½	3↑ Clm 1500	-	1	11	12	1½	21	Sheedy	105	*2.00	- -	Irksome1051Imp105½Miss Ross105½	Stopped when challenged	9
13May97- 1Nwp	gd	6f	:25 :50 1:03 1:16¼	Alw 250	-	3	21	11	11	1½	Sheedy	109	2.00	- -	Imp109½Box1092Myth1062	Handily	6
7May97- 1Nwp	fst	5f	:24 :49 1:02	Alw 250	-	3	64½	44½	43	31	Knapp	112	3.00	- -	Lady Juliet1071Her Excellency107hdImp1123	Good try	9
4May97- 4Nwp	hy	7f	:25 :51½ 1:19½ 1:34¼	3↑ Clm 1400	-	1	12	12	12	12	Hill J	104	3.50	- -	Imp1042J H C1026Banquo II986	Handily	8
1May97- 2Nwp	sly	1	:27¼ :54 1:20¼ 1:46½	3↑ Alw 250	-	1	13	11	2½	26	Chenault	86	1.60	- -	Skate1046Imp863Jamboree1083	Used,tired	8
29Apr97- 6Nwp	fst	6f	:23½ :48½ 1:01½ 1:14½	3↑ Clm 1200	-	1	11	12	13	13	Reiff C	105	*2.50	- -	Imp1053J. Walter100nkGooding1111	Easily	8
19Apr97- 4Nwp	gd	6f	:23¾ :48 1:01½ 1:14¾	3↑ Alw 300	-	1	35	36	55	49	Hill J	100	10.00	- -	Flotow1053Winker1055Abe Furst1101	Outrun	6
16Apr97- 3Nwp	hy	1 50	:25¼ :51¼ 1:17¼ 1:50	3↑ Clm 1500	-	1	11	1½	2½	33½	Reiff C	101	2.50	- -	John Sullivan103½Parson1043Imp1018	Weakened	6
14Apr97- 1Nwp	hy	6f	:25 :50½ 1:05 1:19¾	ⒻAlw 250	-	2	1hd	13	12	15	Hill J	115	*.70	- -	Imp1155Adalid1158Carlotta C.1156	Much best	8
10Apr97- 3Nwp	sl	1	:25½ :52 1:20¾ 1:50¾	ⒻQueen City Oaks 1.3k	-	1	12	2hd	1½	49	Reiff C	112	12.00	- -	Faunette107hdNannieL'sSister1121PanchitaII1128	Stopped	5
8Apr97- 1Nwp	hy	6f	:25 :50½ 1:04 1:19	Alw 300	-	3	2½	24	36	54½	Scherrer	102	*.90	- -	Vengeance104½Suydam1072Cynthia II1021	Stopped	6
1Apr97- 4Nwp	fst	1	1:41¾	Alw 300	-	-	1	1	1	33½	Scherrer	107	3.50	- -	Winker109½Vengeance1043Imp107		9
25Jly96- 5Lat	sl	5½f	:25 :51½ 1:11¾	ⒻAlw 400	-	3	1hd	1½	1nk	36	Sherrin	115	*2.20	- -	Truelight1121Lady Keith1005Imp115no	Quit badly	6
24Jly96- 2Lat	hy	5f	:26 :53¼ 1:06¾	ⒻAlw 300	-	1	1½	12½	15	12½	Sherrin	112	*1.30	- -	Imp1122½Black Heart105.51Carlotta C112no	Never extended	13
14Jly96- 5Lat	sly	5f	:25¾ :51¼ 1:04	ⒻAlw 400	-	1	12	12	12	13	Sherrin	107	*2.00	- -	Imp1073Carlotta C1072Pouting1074	Easily	8
9Jly96- 5Lat	hy	5f	:26 :52¼ 1:05½	ⒻAlw 400	-	2	1½	1hd	12	21	Sherrin	107	7.00	- -	Mertie Reed1071Imp1071Adowa1103	Tiring badly	9
7Jly96- 4Lat	sl	5f	:25 :49¾ 1:01¾	ⒻClipsetta 2.5k	-	4	43	54½	34½	48½	Van Kuren	110	15.00	- -	Midlight105½EugeniaWcks1188BllBrmbl115hd	Never a threat	9
23Jun96- 3Oky	hy	5f	:25 :50 1:04	Alw 400	-	1	1½	2hd	21	22	Thorpe	112	*1.20	- -	Orion1152Imp1125Red115hd	Second best	6
15Jun96- 3Oky	gd	5f	:24¼ :49¼ 1:03	Alw 400	-	3	54¼	1no	2½	41	Snedeker	110	6.00	- -	Burlsqu1131ChrryLf108noOron113no	Taken up,altered course	8
12Jun96- 3Oky	gd	5f	:24 :48½ 1:02½	Alw 400	-	2	31	2½	21	22	Snedeker	108	3.00	- -	Eugenia Wickes1072Imp1083Cavalero110hd	Outrun	7
2Jun96- 1Oky	fst	5f	:24¼ :49 1:01¾	ⒻAlw 400	-	1	1hd	11½	11	2½	Thorpe	115	3.00	- -	White Frost105½Imp1156Charina1052	Used in pace	6
26May96- 4Oky	sl	4f	:24½ :50¾	ⒻSapphire 2.5k	-	2		32	32	33	Perkins	115	4.00	- -	Cleophus1202Amiable1151Imp1151	No threat to winner	5
22May96- 1Oky	sl	4f	:25 :50¾	ⒻMd Sp Wt	-	4		12	15	11	Snedeker	110	2.50	- -	Imp1101Dulcenea1055Scarf Pin1055	Urged at end	8

Man o' War

ch. c. 1917, by Fair Play (Hastings)–Mahubah, by Rock Sand

Lifetime record: 21 20 1 0 $249,465

Own.– S.D. Riddle

Br.– August Belmont (Ky)

Tr.– L. Feustel

12Oct20- 4Knw	fst	1¼	:46² 1:11⁴ 1:37² 2:03	3↑ Ken Park Gold Cup 75k	2	1	12	15	16	17	Kummer C	120	w	*.05	132-03	Man o' War1207Sir Barton126	Never extended	2
18Sep20- 5HdG	fst	1 1/16	:23 :47³ 1:11³ 1:44⁴	Potomac H 10k	4	1	11½	11	11½	11½	Kummer C	138	w	*.15	101-16	Man o' War1381½Wildair10815Blazes104.52	Easing late	4
11Sep20- 4Bel	fst	1½	:49³ 1:14¹ 2:03² 2:28⁴	3↑ Jockey Club 6.8k	2	1	15	18	112	115	Kummer C	118	w	*.01	117-02	Man o' War11815Damask118	Under a pull	2
4Sep20- 4Bel	fst	1⅝	:47⁴ 1:38² 2:03³ 2:40⁴	Lawrence Realizatn 16k	2	1	120	130	150	1100	Kummer C	126	w	*.01	134-00	Man o' War126100Hoodwink116	Restrained at end	2
21Aug20- 4Sar	fst	1¼	:46³ 1:10 1:35³ 2:01⁴	Travers 12k	1	1	12	14	14	12½	Schuttinger A	129	w	*.22	102-08	Mano'War1292½Upset1237JohnP.Grier115	Restrained in str	3
7Aug20- 4Sar	fst	1 3/16	:48¹ 1:12⁴ 1:37⁴ 1:56³	Miller 5.7k	2	1	11½	13	14	16	Sande E	131	w	*.03	97-09	Mano'War1316Donnacona1194KingAlbert114	Never extended	3
10Jly20- 4Aqu	fst	1⅛	:46 1:09³ 1:36 1:49¹	Dwyer 5.5k	1	1	1hd	1hd	1½	11½	Kummer C	126	w	*.20	101-08	Man o' War1261½John P. Grier108	Hard ridden,drew away	2
22Jun20- 4Jam	gd	1	:25³ :49 1:14¹ 1:41³	Stuyvesant H 4.5k	1	1	14	17	18	18	Kummer C	135	w	*.01	86-13	Man o' War1358Yellow Hand103	Eased final ⅛	2
12Jun20- 4Bel	fst	1⅜	2:14¹	Belmont 9.2k	1	1	12	17	112	120	Kummer C	126	w	*.04	116-10	Man o' War12620Donnacona126	Taken up final 1/16	2
29May20- 4Bel	fst	1	:24 :47¹ 1:11 1:35⁴	Withers 5.8k	2	1	11½	12	12	12	Kummer C	118	w	*.14	104-10	Man o' War1182Wildair11812David Harum118	Won under pull	3
18May20- 4Pim	fst	1⅛	:47³ 1:12² 1:38¹ 1:51³	Preakness 29k	7	1	11½	14	12	11½	Kummer C	126	w	*.80	97-10	Man o' War1261½Upset1225Wildair1145	Speed in reserve	9
13Sep19- 3Bel	fst	6f-Str	1:11³	Futurity 31k	8	2	31½	1½	12	12½	Loftus J	127	w	*.50	85-21	Mano'War1272½JohnP.Grier1174Dominiqu122nk	Won easing up	10
30Aug19- 3Sar	sl	6f	:23 :47 1:13	Hopeful 29k	3	4	22	21	15	14	Loftus J	130	w	*.45	87-14	Man o' War1304Cleopatra1124Constancy1242	Easily	8
23Aug19- 3Sar	fst	6f	:22³ :46² 1:12	Grand Union Hotel 9.8k	2	3	1hd	13	13	11	Loftus J	130	w	*.55	92-08	Man o' War1301Upset1254Blazes122½	Eased final 16th	10
13Aug19- 4Sar	fst	6f	:23¹ :46⁴ 1:11¹	Sanford Memorial 4.9k	6	5	41½	32	31½	2½	Loftus J	130	w	*.55	95-09	Upst115½Mno'Wr1303GoldnBroom1302	Slow start,gaining	7
2Aug19- 3Sar	fst	6f	:23 :47¹ 1:12²	U S Hotel 9.8k	8	1	13	13	14	12	Loftus J	130	w	*.90	90-13	Man o' War1302Upset1151Homely1121	Eased final 16th	10
5Jly19- 3Aqu	fst	6f	:23³ :47² 1:13	Tremont 5.8k	2	2	11	11	11½	11	Loftus J	130	w	*.10	90-12	Man o' War1301Ralco11520Ace of Aces112	Never extended	3
23Jun19- 3Aqu	fst	5f	1:01³	Hudson 3.4k	2	1	1½	11	11	11½	Loftus J	130	w	*.10e	83-12	Mano'War1301½VioletTip1094Shoal11512	Broke thru barrier	5
21Jun19- 3Jam	gd	5½f	:23¹ :47³ 1:00¹ 1:06³	Youthful 4.8k	4	3	11	12	14	12½	Loftus J	120	w	*.50	92-09	Mno'War1202½OnWtch1082LdyBrumml10510	Easing final 16th	4
9Jun19- 4Bel	sl	5½f-Str	1:05³	Keene Mem 5.2k	3	2	2½	3¾	31	13	Loftus J	115	w	*.70	91-17	Man o' War1153On Watch115½Anniversary1154	Drew away	6
6Jun19- 6Bel	fst	5f-Str	:59	Md Sp Wt	7	1	2nk	2½	13	16	Loftus J	115	w	*.60	83-18	Man o' War1156Retrieve112½Neddam1154	Easily	7

Maskette

br. f. 1906, by Disguise (Domino)–Biturica, by Hamburg — Lifetime record: 17 12 3 0 $77,090
Own.– J.R. Keene
Br.– James R. Keene (Ky)
Tr.– J. Rowe

6Aug10- 4Sar gd 1 :244 :48 1:124 1:40 3↑ Delaware H 6 2 21 31½ 45½ 513½ Notter 125 w *.50 74-14 SirJohnJohnson124hdStanlyFy1045Dnoscr105½ Quit after 5f 6
23Jun10- 4She fst 1 :232 :472 1:12 1:373 3↑ Sheepshead Bay H 2k 4 3 31½ 21½ 21½ 2½ Powers V 123 w 1.80 99-05 King James129½Maskette1238Czar110hd Gamely,impeded late 6
9Jun10- 5Gra fst 1 1/16 :241 :481 1:131 1:463 3↑ ⒻHandicap 1 1 11 11½ 12 11 Powers V 128 w *.14 94-07 Maskette1281Hill Top10310Imitator953 Won easing up 5
13May10- 4Bel fst 1 :233 :472 1:122 1:374 3↑ Metropolitan H 5 3 21½ 2hd 1½ 68 Butwell 123 w 2.50 90-03 Fashion Plate1051Prince Imperial971Jack Atkin129½ Tired 9
5May10- 4Aqu fst 6½f :224 :472 1:111 1:18 3↑ Handicap 2 2 1hd 1½ 1hd 1nk Butwell 122 w *.33 109-00 Maskett122nkDlmtn105½RockyO'Brn10715 Not fully extended 4
26Oct09- 4Aqu fst 1 1/16 :24 :49 1:132 1:482 2↑ Aqueduct H 2.5k 3 1 11 1½ 1hd 2no Butwell 126 w *.25 85-16 Firestone113noMaskette1261Olambala119hd Just missed 4
12Oct09- 4Jam gd 1⅛ :50 1:15 1:413 1:542 2↑ Pierrepont H 2.5k 5 4 1hd 11½ 11½ 12 Butwell 124 w *.50 92-12 Maskette1242Huck981½Firston118¾ Bad start,wide 1st turn 6
5Aug09- 4Sar sly 1⅛ :50 1:17 1:453 1:592 ⒻAlabama 5k 3 1 12 13 12 11½ Scoville 124 w *.30 60-27 Maskette1241½MissKearney1163Petticot1163 Disliked going 6
7Jly09- 4She fst 1⅛ :472 1:122 1:383 1:52 ⒻMermaid 1 1 11½ 11½ 12 13 Scoville 126 w *.13 97-03 Maskette1263Lady Bedford1116Petticoat111 Won easing up 3
17Jun09- 3Gra fst 1 1/16 :244 :482 1:14 1:48 ⒻGazelle 1 1 12 11½ 11 12 Scoville 121 w *.25 87-14 Maskette1212Petticoat1112Lady Bedford1116 Much best 4
20May09- 4Bel fst 1 :241 :482 1:133 1:39 ⒻLadies 4 1 11 16 13 15 Butwell 121 w *.25e 92-08 Maskette1215Lady Bedford1214Field Mouse1214 Much best 4
8Oct08- 3Bel fst 6f-Str 1:204 ⒻMatron 6.5k 2 2 2hd 1hd 11 11½ Notter 124 - - Masktt1241½Afflcton106 Stablemates cantered throughout 2
5Sep08- 3She fst 7f-FC 1:252 Flatbush 13k 5 2 2½ 1½ 2½ 24 Notter 117 w *.50e 93-10 Sir Martin1154Maskette1171½Fayette1152 Bumped,tired 5
2Sep08- 3She fst 6f-FC 1:123 ⒻGreat Filly 12k 2 2 1½ 12 12 11 Notter 127 w *.25e 90-10 Maskette1271Wedding Bells1194Lady Bedford116hd Easily 5
29Aug08- 4She fst 6f-FC 1:111 Futurity 29k 3 2 11 12 12 13 Notter 118 w *.70e 97-06 Maskette1183Sir Martin127hdHelmet1234 Never extended 9
5Aug08- 3Sar fst 5½f :222 :47 :584 1:054 ⒻSpinaway 10k 5 2 1½ 1½ 11 11½ Notter 112 w *.29e 101-18 Masktte1121½WeddngBlls112noMssHubbrd1122 Much the best 6
3Aug08- 6Sar fst 5½f :23 :472 :593 1:063 Alw 455 6 7 31 21 32 1½ Notter 101 w *.25 97-10 Maskette101½Miss Kearney1036Louise Bell99½ 8
Open to fillies and geldings

Old Rosebud

b. g. 1911, by Uncle (Star Shoot)–Ivory Bells, by Himyar — Lifetime record: 80 40 13 8 $74,729
Own.– F.D. Weir
Br.– J.E. Madden (Ky)
Tr.– F.D. Weir

17May22- 1Jam fst 6f :242 :493 1:15 3↑ Alw 1000 6 7 2hd 22 33 79¼ Sande E 110 w 5.00 74-10 Victor S.1071Ogarite96.53Ting-a-Ling1101 Quit badly 11
6May22- 6Jam gd 5½f :24 :483 1:011 1:073 3↑ Clm 3 5 42 2½ 12 2½ Sande E 114 w *1.60 86-10 Liberty Girl109½Old Rosebud1141½Dare1063 Rated,tired 8
6Sep21- 1Bel fst 6½f :233 :471 1:13 1:193 3↑ Clm 3 2 32 2½ 11½ 13 Fator L 110 w 6.00 88-09 Old Rosebud1103Old Sinner114hdGem972 Pulled up lame 9
20Apr21- 3HdG fst 6f :232 :473 1:133 3↑ Clm 3 3 21½ 2nk 21 63¾ McAtee L 111 w *1.25 84-16 Panaman108nkPickwick1171Uncle's Lassie1091½ Speed,tired 9
14Jun20- 5Jam fst 5½f :231 :464 :593 1:053 3↑ Handicap 1620 9 10 77 78 69 69½ McCabe J 119 w 10.00 87-06 PeterPiper1303IrishDream1051½Liond'Or1262 Never a factor 10
31May20- 4Bel fst 6f-Str 1:093 3↑ Toboggan H 4k 2 4 65 64 66½ 55½ McCabe J 113wb 8.00 87-11 Lion d'Or107.5hdMotor Cop128noNaturalist1264 Swerved 7
27May20- 4Bel fst 6f-Str 1:112 3↑ Handicap 1195 2 1 31½ 22 21 11½ McCabe J 123wb 5.00 84-13 Old Rosebud1231½Peter Piper134½Leading Star1104 Easily 8
22May20- 6Jam sl 6f :244 :49 1:15 3↑ Handicap 1155 1 7 52¾ 53 2½ 2hd McCabe J 124wb 6.00 84-15 Padriac116hdOldRosbud124½Tcklsh1241½ Hard ridden,gamely 8
15May20- 4Jam sl 6f :233 :464 1:122 3↑ Paumonok H 4.8k 2 2 32 21 24 44½ McCabe J 111wb 12.00 92-13 Dunboyne1152Billy Kelly126½Ticklish107.52 Speed,tired 9
27Apr20- 3HdG my 6f :24 :473 1:141 4↑ Alw 1200 3 4 13 11 1hd 21¼ McCabe J 116wb 3.40 84-26 WarPennant109.51¼OldRosebud1165Quietude1102 4
Speed,gave way
20Apr20- 4HdG fst 6f :232 :464 1:131 3↑ Alw 1674 7 4 43¾ 43½ 43½ 56 McCabe J 116 w 7.35 84-11 Dr. Clark104½Fruit Cake1112½War Pennant1083 Speed,tired 7
16Apr20- 5HdG gd 6f :234 :473 1:13 3↑ Harford H 5.6k 5 6 43 42½ 67¼ 611¾ McCabe J 122 w 15.95 79-15 BillyKelly127nkStarMaster1228MidnghtSun1051 Speed,tired 7
29Nov19- 4Bow fst 1 :243 :484 1:152 1:422 2↑ Handicap 1500 3 1 11 11 1½ 2nk Stirling D 117 w 5.30e 93-13 Slippery Elm112nkOld Rosebud1171Ballet Dancer II1034 7
Tired in drive
27Nov19- 5Bow fst 1 1/16 :25 :50 1:15 1:493 2↑ Thanksgiving H 2.6k 5 3 65½ 64½ 31¾ 31½ Stirling D 117 w 6.50 90-14 Ormonda118noSlippery Elm1111½Old Rosebud117½ Resolutely 7
25Nov19- 5Bow fst 1 70 :243 :50 1:143 1:46 3↑ Handicap 1500 2 2 22 24 22 35 Stirling D 120 w 16.45 91-10 Ophelia1144Salvestra1081Old Rosebud1201½ Tired late 5
22Nov19- 3Bow fst 6½f :232 :464 1:132 1:20 2↑ Handicap 1200 5 4 2hd 21½ 23 25 McCabe J 122 w 3.30 91-12 Flags1285Old Rosebud122hdQuietude1041 Held place 5
15Nov19- 3Bow fst 7f :231 :472 1:134 1:272 2↑ Alw 1000 1 2 1½ 11½ 12 12 McCabe J 112 w *.70 95-13 OldRosebud1122CharlieLeydecker1028ArrahGoOn1022 Easily 6
12Nov19- 5Pim hy 6f :234 :481 1:144 2↑ Handicap 1863 1 4 11 1nk 2½ 35½ McCabe J 113 w 2.70 79-26 TippityWtcht1041½Dr.Johnson934OldRosbud1136 Tired badly 4
21Oct19- 3Emp fst *6f :224 :464 1:10 2↑ Handicap 1199 8 1 21 2½ 13 12 McCabe J 126 w 4.50 89-12 Old Rosebud1262Flags1321Bill McCloy111nk Won easing up 9
15Oct19- 4Emp hy *6f :232 :484 1:112 3↑ Kingsbridge Hwt H 2.9k 2 7 63 52¼ 64 65¼ Fairbrother C 125 w 3.50e 77-24 FruitCake120hdPickwick120hdUltimaThul1182 Always beaten 7
13Oct19- 3Emp hy *6f :23 :472 1:103 2↑ Alw 1361 3 1 2hd 48 44½ 47 McCabe J 116 w 4.00 79-19 Ormonda103hdUltima Thule1075Flags1062 Tired 6
11Oct19- 6Jam fst 6f :231 :472 1:123 2↑ Handicap 920 3 8 43½ 44 33 33½ McCabe J 126 w 3.60 92-09 Flags1162Arnold1111½Old Rosebud1262 Away poorly 8
23Sep19- 3Aqu my 7f :24 :483 1:13 1:262 2↑ Handicap 1658 4 1 11 12 12 12 McCabe J 111 w *1.20 83-18 Old Rosebud1112Nutcracker1061Homely956 As rider pleased 5
17Sep19- 4Aqu fst 6f :231 :471 1:114 3↑ Arverne H 3.2k 5 5 34 42 41¾ 41¾ McCabe J 118 w 12.00 94-10 Lord Brighton114hdEnfilade1121½Hollister123nk No mishap 7
15Sep19- 1Aqu fst 6½f :23 :47 1:113 1:182 2↑ Handicap 1920 8 12 87½ 87½ 76½ 77½ McCabe J 120 w 20.00 90-10 FaryWnd1121CornTssl113noHollstr1251 Close quarters late 13
4Sep19- 3Bel gd 6f-Str 1:113 2↑ Autumn Hwt H 3.5k 4 - - - - - McCabe J 126 w 20.00 - - Naturalist140noBillyKelly1243Enfilade1161½ Left at post 7
1Sep19- 1Bel fst 6f :23 :464 1:103 3↑ Alw 1025 3 4 31 45½ 44 59½ McCabe J 123 w 7.00 94-03 Lucullite1305Peter Piper1134Fruit Cake108½ Tired late 7
29Aug19- 2Sar fst 6f :23 :464 1:113 3↑ Handicap 1145 7 2 1hd 11½ 11 33 McCabe J 125 w 10.00 92-10 Startling1121Lord Brighton1102[D]Old Rosebud125½ Tired 7
Impeded rival turn;Disqualified
26Jly19- 4Emp fst 1 1/16 :233 :474 1:132 1:453 3↑ Yonkers H 2.9k 1 1 1nk 43 56½ 518½ Loftus J 127 w 3.00 76-11 Bally1092Roamer1203Spur1131½ Eased when beaten 5
17Jly19- 4Emp gd 1 :241 :482 1:132 1:402 3↑ Mount Vernon H 2.9k 4 3 22 23 23 24 Lunsford H 126 w 4.00 87-18 Lucullite1274Old Rosebud1261Sun Briar1288 Chased winner 4
5Jly19- 4Lat fst 1 :24 :48 1:364 3↑ Handicap 2000 2 1 1nk 11 1½ 2nk Murray T 126 w 1.45 103-06 SenningsPark118nkOldRosebd12610Ginger1003 Saved ground 4
1Jly19- 5Lat fst 1 1/16 :233 :464 1:114 1:434 3↑ Handicap 2500 1 1 1½ 1½ 2½ 32½ Howard J 128 w 3.20 95-09 BarneyShannon1022VivaAmerica108½OldRosebud128hd Tired 7
25Jun19- 4Lat my 6f :233 :474 1:14 3↑ Handicap 2500 2 5 67 611 613 516 Van Dusen C 133 w *1.50 69-25 Beaverkill1081Top Coat1011Green Grass1058 Poor effort 6
12Jun19- 4Lat fst 6f :23 :462 1:111 3↑ Alw 2000 2 2 21 2nk 1hd 1hd Murray T 117 w *.50 99-10 OldRsbd117hdTopo'th'Mornng1128BroomPddlr110.51½ Gamely 6
5Jun19- 4Lat fst 1 :242 :481 1:13 1:382 3↑ Sp Wt 1868 7 1 11½ 11½ 13 11½ Murray T 118 w *.30 95-10 Old Rosebud1181½Buford1182Dodge1155 Won easing up 7
27May19- 3Bel fst 6f :233 :471 1:122 3↑ Alw 920 2 3 2½ 11 11 11½ Loftus J 128 w *.25 95-07 OldRosebud1281½CrystalFord107½Crimper1131½ Unruly start 10
22May19- 1Bel sly 5½f-Str 1:074 3↑ Alw 930 3 3 32 11 12 16 Dreyer J 124 w *.33 80-19 OldRosebud1246BullyBoy1152½BillMcCloy11815 In a canter 4
15May19- 4Jam fst 6f :231 :471 1:122 3↑ Paumonok H 5.8k 14 6 57 43 32 21½ Dreyer J 134 w 7.00 95-08 Flgs1261½OldRosbud1341½Lucullt119½ Interference at start 14
10May19- 5Pim hy 6f :233 :483 1:162 3↑ Handicap 1120 6 5 32¼ 32¼ 32 21 Dreyer J 132 w *1.15 76-25 Papp1111Old Rosebud132nkL'Errant105nk Poor ride 7
6May19- 6Pim fst 1 :243 :492 1:152 1:42 3↑ Alw 1000 2 1 14 14 1nk 2no Dreyer J 124 w *.30 85-15 Sweep On108noOld Rosebud1246Polka Dot9015 Tiring 6
1May19- 6Pim sly 6f 1:15 3↑ Alw 1078 1 - 11½ 12 Dreyer J 118 w *.45 84-18 Old Rosebud1182Flags1185Peter Piper1183 In a canter 7
Early calls unavailable due to fog
25Apr19- 3HdG gd 5½f :233 :472 1:002 1:063 3↑ Alw 1176 1 4 11½ 11½ 12 12 Dreyer J 123 w 1.45 94-16 OldRosebud1232Bonifc118½Mlkmd110hd Restrained final ⅛ 7
17Sep17- 4Aqu fst 1 1/16 :244 :48 1:121 1:443 3↑ Bayview H 1.6k 4 1 11 12 12 12 Peak C 133 w *1.30 100-06 OldRosebud1332Capra105nkStraghtForwrd1031 Easing at end 7
7Aug17- 4Sar fst 1 :233 :471 1:133 1:382 3↑ Delaware H 3.5k 2 3 32 21 2½ 1hd Molesworth G 133 w 2.60 95-10 Old Rosebud133hdCapra104½Roamer1274 Gamely 6
1Aug17- 4Sar my 1¼ :503 1:154 1:412 2:061 3↑ Saratoga H 5.8k 4 4 32½ 32 56 512½ Molesworth G 132 w *1.70 76-14 Roamer122½Spur1231Ticket1071 Rated,tired 7
24Jly17- 5Knw fst 1 70 :234 :474 1:131 1:432 3↑ Handicap 1200 1 2 2½ 2½ 1nk 12 Molesworth G 132 w *.15 108-00 Old Rosebud1322Kinney108hdFranklin107½ Easily 6
14Jly17- 4Wnr gd 1⅛ :493 1:15 1:403 1:541 3↑ Frontier H 13k 3 2 31 11 11 11½ Molesworth G 129 w 3.25 85-18 Old Rosebud1291½Boots1293Hodge1175 Hard ridden 8
9Jly17- 4Aqu sl 1 1/16 :241 :48 1:124 1:462 3↑ Handicap 1625 3 3 1nk 11 1½ 1nk Knapp W 130 w *.80 91-13 Old Rosebud130nkBromo1205Chiclet110 Gamely 3
4Jly17- 4Aqu fst 7f :24 :481 1:124 1:254 3↑ Carter H 3.4k 1 1 11 11½ 11 1½ Schuttinger A 130 w *2.20 93-11 OldRosebud130½Bromo122noTheFinn130½ Repelled challenges 9
30Jun17- 4Aqu fst 1 :241 :464 1:114 1:373 3↑ Queens County H 4.3k 1 2 1hd 11 11½ 11½ Robinson F 125 w *2.40 94-12 Old Rosebud1251½Roamer1291½Chiclet1102 Easily 7

Date	Cond	Dist	Fractions	Race	Calls	Jockey	Wt	Odds	Speed	Company / Comment	Field
25Jun17- 4Aqu	fst	1⅛	:47 1:122 1:363 1:492	3↑ Brooklyn H 5.8k	5 5 54½ 42½ 32 31	Connelly D	120 w	8.00	102-04	Borrow117noRgrt1221OldRosbud1201 Gamely,swerved last ¼	11
11Jun17- 5Lat	fst	1 1/16	:241 :484 1:14 1:45	3↑ Inaugural H 3k	4 3 31½ 2hd 11½ 12	Connelly D	124 w	*2.30	92-13	OldRosebd1242KingGorn1191½Mdwy1031 Rated,won easing up	6
2Jun17- 5DoP	gd	1¼	:474 1:121 1:384 2:041	3↑ Kentucky H 14k	2 1 2hd 21 75¾ 913	Connelly D	120 w	*1.80	80-13	King Gorin108nkCudgel103½Roamer1262 Speed,tired	11
30May17- 5DoP	fst	1⅛	:49 1:13 1:381 1:511	3↑ Handicap 1000	4 2 2hd 1½ 11 11½	Connelly D	126 w	*1.00	99-09	Old Rosebud1261½King Gorin1131Hodge1215 Easily	5
26May17- 5DoP	fst	1 1/16	:25 :492 1:13 1:45	3↑ Alw 1000	5 2 2hd 11½ 15 11½	Connelly D	115 w	*.65	94-09	Old Rosebud1151½Leo Skolny1114Pif Jr.116no Won eased up	5
19May17- 5CD	fst	1 1/16	:25 :493 1:13 1:451	3↑ Clark H 2.8k	2 1 1½ 11 1½ 11	Connelly D	117 w	3.85	96-14	OldRosbd1171Romr1288Embrodry1061½ Rated,ridden strongly	4
12May17- 3CD	fst	1 1/16	:234 :473 1:123 1:443	4↑ Alw 1000	1 1 1½ 1½ 21 36½	Connelly D	119 w	*.50	92-06	Roamer1191½Ed Crump1225Old Rosebud1196 Tired badly	4
6Apr17- 3OP	fst	7f	:24 :47 1:121 1:251	3↑ Alw 500	- 2 11½ 11½ 13 12	Molesworth G	105 w	*.90	105-06	Old Rosebud1052Robert Bradley106.52Pan Zareta103	3
			Won under restraint								
30Mar17- 4Esx	fst	1	:24 :473 1:13 1:384	3↑ Handicap 750	- 1 11½ 13 11½ 1hd	Peak C	130 w	*.55	106-01	Old Rosebud130hdLittle String101noGordon Russell10112	6
			Careless ride								
24Mar17- 3OP	fst	6f	:233 :471 1:123	3↑ Handicap 600	- 6 33½ 21½ 21½ 36	Peak C	137 w	1.30	95-05	PanZareta113hdColonelVenn1236OldRosbd137hd Away poorly	6
12Mar17- 4OP	sl	6f	:24 :474 1:15	3↑ Handicap 500	- 2 13 15 11 13	Peak C	130 w	*.55	89-22	Old Rosebud1303David Craig106nkBob Hensley1121	5
			Won under restraint								
8Mar17- 4OP	gd	6f	:234 :474 1:131	3↑ Handicap 500	- 2 11½ 11½ 11½ 12	Peak C	120 w	*.80	98-13	Old Rosebud1201Aldebaran1065Robert Bradley108nk Easily	6
18Feb17- 4Jua	fst	5½f	:232 :474 1:001 1:062	3↑ Handicap	- - 2	Molesworth G	122		- -	Zim108Old Rosebud122Belle Bird90	5
30May14- 4Bel	fst	1	:232 :474 1:133 1:394	Withers 3.4k	3 1 11 3½ 56¼ 516	McCabe J	115 w	*.20	72-14	Charlestonian115noGainer1188Roamr1155 Bore out far turn	5
9May14- 4CD	fst	1¼	:474 1:13 1:384 2:032	Ky Derby 12k	6 1 11½ 12 16 18	McCabe J	114 w	*.85	107-09	Old Rosebud1148Hodge1141½Bronzewing1174 Hard held	7
25Apr14- 4Lxt	sl	1	:242 :48 1:152 1:42	Alw 600	5 1 12 13 16 16	McCabe J	112 w	*.30	77-22	Old Rosebud1126Christophine985Ivan Gardner1126	7
			Under restraint throughout								
13Aug13- 3Sar	fst	6f	:232 :472 1:132	U S Hotel 2.8k	1 2 13 16 14 13	McCabe J	125 w	*.17	91-08	OldRsbd1253BlckBroom1071½PomttBlu1111½ Easing up at end	6
2Aug13- 3Sar	fst	5½f	:23 :472 1:00 1:07	Flash 1.1k	4 1 12 11½ 12 12	McCabe J	124 w	*.60	94-09	Old Rosebud1242Stromboli11210Black Broom1093 Easily	6
5Jly13- 4Lat	fst	6f	:232 :464 1:124	Cincinnati Trophy 5.7k	2 3 12 16 18 16	McCabe J	124 w	*.25	95-07	Old Rosebud1246Pebeco11140'Hagan114hd In a canter	4
18Jun13- 4Lat	my	5f	:234 :493 1:013	©Harold 3.5k	2 1 11 13 14 15	McCabe J	120 w	*.15	87-20	Old Rosebud1205Big Spirit10640'Hagan113 Easily	3
7Jun13- 4DoP	fst	5f	:23 :462 :582	Spring Trial 4.5k	5 1 11½ 11 11½ 12	McCabe J	115 w	*.55	113-04	Old Rosebud1152Little Nephew11810Imperator1213 Easily	5
4Jun13- 3DoP	fst	5f	:231 :463 :583	Alw 850	1 2 21 21½ 11½ 11	McCabe J	115 w	*.45	112-00	Old Rosebud1151Little Nephew1188Roamer1005 Easily	5
31May13- 3DoP	fst	5f	:224 :462 :584	Sp Wt 1030	2 2 2nk 2nk 11½ 14	McCabe J	112 w	2.20	111-00	OldRosebd1124LittleNephew1121½Imprtor112 Won easing up	3
26May13- 2DoP	fst	5f	:23 :47 1:002	Alw 750	3 2 11½ 12 14 16	McCabe J	111 w	*.25	103-00	OldRosbud1116Vndrgrft1143BlckToney1142 Eased up last 1/16	5
23May13- 6CD	hy	4½f	:23 :474 :542	Alw 600	2 1 110 110 110	McCabe J	115 w	*.45	92-08	Old Rosebud11510The Norman1113Harwood1051 Easily	7
19May13- 4CD	gd	4½f	:232 :463 :53	©Bashford Manor 1k	3 2 2hd 2hd 21	McCabe J	118 w	*.55	98-07	Little Nephew1181Old Rosebud11810Black Toney1188	5
			Impeded start,wide,tired								
17May13- 2CD	hy	4½f	:234 :48 :54	Alw 600	2 1 13 14 16	Peak C	115 w	*.40	94-06	OldRosebd1156Roamer1085BraveCunardr10512 Won easing up	5
1May13- 4Lxt	fst	4½f	:233 :472 :534	Idle Hour 1.6k	3 2 2hd 11½ 2hd	McCabe J	115 w	*.50	99-05	Little Nephew115hdOld Rosebud1156Francis1101½ Gamely	9
5Mar13- 1Jua	fst	4f	:232 :47	Alw 300	8 3 22 13 15	McCabe J	118 w	*.40	96-04	Old Rosebud1185Shadrach1152½Gladys Y.1073 Won easing up	8
9Feb13- 4Jua	hy	3½f	:243 :43	©Yucatan .9k	5 3 12½ 16	Peak C	110 w	3.00	82-18	Old Rosebud1106Blarney1181½Manganese1182½ In a canter	6

Pan Zareta

ch. f. 1910, by Abe Frank (Hanover)–Caddie Griffith, by Rancocas

Lifetime record: 151 76 31 21 $39,082

Own.– J. Marrone
Br.– J.F. Newman (Tx)
Tr.– J.C. Kirkpatrick

Date	Cond	Dist	Fractions	Race	Calls	Jockey	Wt	Odds	Speed	Company / Comment	Field
10Nov17- 4Lat	fst	6f	:23 :462 1:114	2↑ Handicap 1580	3 3 63 42 1½ 2nk	Willis O	123wb	4.60	96-08	Atalanta109nkPan Zareta1233Solly1291 Impeded	7
7Nov17- 5Lat	fst	6f	:224 :463 1:114	2↑ Ladies H 2.1k	3 7 53 43¼ 54½ 67½	Gentry L	125wb	2.75	88-09	Solly1221½Atalanta1053Ocean Sweep105hd Quit badly	8
29Oct17- 5Lat	my	6f	:24 :481 1:15	2↑ Handicap 1000	1 3 52¼ 55 41¾ 44¼	Garner M	127wb	6.00	76-28	Harry Kelly113hdJ.J. Murdock113nkFruit Cake1104 Outrun	7
26Oct17- 5Lat	sl	6f	:231 :464 1:123	3↑ Handicap 1000	2 1 1hd 1hd 12 1½	Garner M	122wb	3.00	92-19	Pan Zareta122½J.J. Murdock1104Phocion1075 Tiring	5
22Oct17- 5Lat	fst	6f	:23 :464 1:113	2↑ Handicap 1000	3 5 42½ 3¾ 62¾ 55	Garner M	126wb	*1.30	92-11	Atalanta1001½BelieveMeBoys106hdBradley'sChoice1132 Outrun	8
15Oct17- 4Lat	gd	6f	:23 :464 1:123	2↑ Handicap 1000	3 3 2hd 22 4nk 55¼	Garner M	128wb	3.25	87-13	Believe Me Boys100nkPrince of Como1191½Vogue1202	6
			Dropped out after ½								
4Oct17- 4CD	sl	6f	:232 :471 1:13	3↑ Falls City H 2.7k	5 1 11½ 11½ 11 31	Garner M	131wb	5.70	89-20	Vogue1131Bradley's Choice108hdPan Zareta1312 Tired	10
28Sep17- 5DoP	fst	6f	:23 :461 1:12	2↑ Handicap 1000	3 3 1½ 34½ 25 56¼	Howard J	133wb	*1.70	87-14	Prince of Como108.55Vogue110nkBelieve Me Boys99½ Tired	6
26Sep17- 4DoP	fst	6f	:223 :453 1:121	3↑ Alw 1000	1 3 21½ 21½ 11 11	Garner M	123wb	*1.35	92-09	Pan Zareta1231Marion Goosby112½Blind Baggage1263	5
			Rated,won restrained								
20Sep17- 4Lxt	fst	6f	:23 :462 1:12	3↑ Alw 650	2 1 11½ 11½ 11 1nk	Garner M	115wb	1.15	96-10	Pan Zareta115nkBlind Baggage11812Franklin1056 Lasted	6
15Sep17- 3Lxt	fst	6f	:232 :473 1:124	3↑ Handicap 700	4 1 11 11½ 12 11½	Howard J	125wb	*.80	92-14	Pan Zareta1251½Marion Goosby1145John Jr.1091 Easily	5
12Sep17- 1Lxt	fst	6f	:233 :474 1:14	3↑ Alw 700	4 3 1hd 2hd 2½ 41¼	Howard J	125wb	2.35	85-12	Blind Baggage128nkMarion Goosby115hdJohn Jr.1031 Tired	6
			Previously owned and trained by E.T. Colton								
6Aug17- 2Sar	fst	6f	:231 :474 1:132	3↑ Handicap 875	3 3 32 23 32½ 64¼	Mott A	142wb	4.50	84-14	Corn Tassel112hdHigh Noon120hdTom McTaggart1121½ Tired	14
31Jly17- 3Emp	fst	*6f	:222 :463 1:082	3↑ Handicap 600	4 2 11½ 11½ 12 11	Mott A	140wb	3.20	98-04	Pan Zareta1401High Noon122hdLeochares1263 Gamely	6
26Jly17- 3Emp	fst	*6f	:23 :47 1:092	3↑ Katonah H 1.1k	5 7 2hd 2hd 11 1¾	Mott A	137wb	4.50	93-08	Pan Zareta137¾Leochares127hdWhimsy1143 Dueled,gamely	7
20Jly17- 4Emp	fst	*6f	:23 :483 1:102	3↑ ⒻHandicap 660	1 2 11 1hd 13 12	Mott A	135wb	*1.60	88-11	Pan Zareta1352Capra1272½Diamond1001 Dueled	6
5Jly17- 5Aqu	fst	6½f	:23 :471 1:121 1:19	3↑ Handicap 710	5 3 11 11 2½ 21½	Mott A	135wb	3.00	93-11	Startling1241½PanZart135nkⒹWhmsy1184 Hard ridden,tired	6
29Jun17- 2Aqu	sly	6½f	:24 :474 1:144 1:22	3↑ ⒻHandicap 670	4 5 44½ 33 2½ 1½	Mott A	123 w	4.00	80-24	PanZarta123½RhineMaiden1082FairyWand1032 Saved ground	7
26Jun17- 1Aqu	fst	6½f	:23 :471 1:121 1:19	3↑ Alw 700	4 2 1hd 21½ 35 513	Troxler R	128wb	*2.00	82-14	Bromo1192Hank O'Day1238Madame Curie103no Quit badly	8
19Jun17- 5Jam	fst	5½f	:23 :473 :593 1:053	3↑ Handicap 815	3 1 11½ 11 12 12	Troxler R	128wb	10.00	102-07	PanZrta1282Topo'th'Morning1401HighNoon1371½ Drew away	10
21May17- 7OW	fst	6f	:231 :472 1:133	3↑ ⒻAlw 840	7 1 1½ 1hd 11 12	Mott A	125wb	7.15	90-11	Pan Zareta1252Arriet116nkGraphic103nk Easily	7
18May17- 4Dev	fst	6f	:234 :49 1:13	3↑ Handicap 1000	6 6 53½ 43½ 42½ 33½	Mott A	132wb	*1.50	91-15	Skiles Knob105½Tiajan983Pan Zareta1322 Slow start,tired	6
16May17- 4Dev	fst	5½f	:234 :481 1:01 1:074	3↑ Handicap 1000	3 7 43½ 44½ 33½ 33	Mott A	130wb	*.90	90-18	Etruscan1161ArthurMiddleton1002PanZareta1303 Slow start	8
14May17- 4Dev	fst	6f	:242 :49 1:152	3↑ Handicap 1000	4 7 42½ 36 21 1hd	Mott A	126wb	*1.15	83-25	Pan Zareta126hdEtruscan1085Pesky1101 Flat-footed start	8
9Apr17- 4OP	fst	6f	:24 :483 1:132	3↑ Handicap 550	- 6 41 41 3½ 2no	Dominick J	126wb	*.80	97-10	Opportunity104noPanZrt126noCaneRun110hd Away slowly,wide	6
6Apr17- 3OP	fst	7f	:24 :47 1:121 1:251	3↑ Alw 500	- 3 21½ 21½ 23 34	Lykes L	103wb	2.60	101-06	Old Rosebud1052Robert Bradley106.52Pan Zareta103	3
			Away slowly,tired								
3Apr17- 3OP	fst	6f	:233 :48 1:131	3↑ Handicap 700	- 1 32 31¾ 3¾ 31¾	Peak C	126wb	1.60	96-08	CaneRun1011½MarieMiller106nkPanZareta1265 Tired,gamely	4
			Previously owned by H.S. Newman, trained by E. Foucon								
28Mar17- 5OP	fst	6f	:233 :47 1:122	3↑ Handicap 600	- 3 2hd 1hd 11 11½	Kederis J	120wb	*.70	102-08	Pan Zareta1201½Hanovia116½Wise Man1022 Briefly urged	6
24Mar17- 3OP	fst	6f	:233 :471 1:123	3↑ Handicap 600	- 1 13 11½ 11½ 1hd	Kederis J	113wb	*1.00	101-05	PanZarta113hdColonelVennie1236OldRosbd137hd Hard ridden	6
20Mar17- 4OP	fst	6f	:232 :471 1:121	3↑ Handicap 600	- 3 31 32 21 2½	Kederis J	112wb	5.00	102-08	Brumley106.5½PanZareta112½JackO'Dowd105hd Finished fast	8
17Feb17- 3FG	fst	1	:234 1:132 1:40	3↑ Alw 600	- 2 2hd 2½ 64½ 816½	Lykes L	103 ws	*2.60	72-14	Half Rock109hdWise Man1046McAdoo1061 Tired badly	9
15Feb17- 5FG	sl	6f	:234 :473 1:14	3↑ Handicap 700	- 3 1hd 21 21 31½	Kederis J	116 ws	2.50	88-17	J.J.Murdock1111½RobertBradley108hdPanZareta1161 Tired	7
12Jan17- 4FG	fst	1	:24 :48 1:132 1:404	4↑ Alw 500	- 1 11½ 1½ 21 32	Kederis J	106wb	*.80	83-15	DavidCraig1041½Woodstone97½PanZaret1063 Tired after ¾	7
4Jan17- 4FG	sl	6f	:233 :48 1:151	3↑ Handicap 600	- 1 2nk 21½ 3½ 42	Kederis J	122wb	*.80	82-21	BarsandStars1001½PrinceofComo114hdArchPlotter95½ Tired	5
30Mar16- 4OP	fst	5½f	:233 :481 1:002 1:07	3↑ Handicap 500	1 1 1hd 2hd 1½ 11½	Murphy F	142wb	*.80	96-09	PanZareta1421½MarsCassidy110noKorfhage110no Hard ridden	5
17Mar16- 4OP	fst	6f	:231 :473 1:124	3↑ Handicap 300	3 1 1½ 1½ 1½ 11	Kederis J	135wb	*.80	100-06	PanZareta1351Korfhage1071½Dr.Larrick126nk Saved ground	5

11Mar16-4OP	fst	1	:25	:49	1:14^{3}	1:39	3↑ Handicap 300	2	1	$1^{\frac12}$	$1^{\frac12}$	1^{1}	1^{3}	Kederis J	118wb	*.60	103-05	PanZaret118^{3}Grumpy106^{nk}BobHnsly102^{nk}	Finished easing up	6
4Mar16-5FG	fst	6f	:22^{4}	:46^{3}		1:12^{1}	5↑ Sp Wt 600	1	1	2^{hd}	2^{1}	2^{1}	$2^{\frac34}$	Garner M	110wb	1.10	98-05	Bringhurst110$^{\frac34}$Pan Zareta110	Tired	2
26Feb16-4FG	fst	$1\frac{1}{16}$	:23^{4}	:47^{4}	1:13^{3}	1:45^{3}	3↑ New Orleans Hotel H 3.9k	11	1	$1^{1\frac12}$	1^{2}	$1^{\frac12}$	3^{2}	Kederis J	115wb	6.00	94-08	Marion Goosby110^{2}Skeerface103^{hd}Pan Zareta115^{hd}	Tired	14
23Feb16-4FG	fst	1	:23^{3}	:47^{1}	1:12^{3}	1:39^{1}	5↑ Sp Wt 600	1	2	$2^{\frac12}$	$1^{\frac12}$	1^{2}	1^{2}	Kederis J	108wb	*.65	97-07	Pan Zareta108^{2}J.J. Lillis108	Rated	2
19Feb16-4FG	fst	$1\frac{1}{16}$	:23^{3}	:47^{4}	1:12^{2}	1:45	3↑ Merchants H 3.3k	14	1	$1^{1\frac12}$	$1^{1\frac12}$	1^{2}	3^{1}	Kederis J	112wb	6.00	98-04	MarionGoosby103^{1}SkeerFace98^{hd}PnZareta112^{hd}	Not enough	15
5Feb16-3FG	fst	5½f	:22^{4}	:47	:59^{2}	1:06^{1}	3↑ Handicap 600	8	3	$5^{3\frac12}$	$4^{2\frac12}$	$4^{\frac34}$	$1^{\frac12}$	Kederis J	140wb	*1.40	98-06	Pan Zareta140$^{\frac12}$J.J. Lillis125^{no}Carbide108^{3}	Gamely	11
29Jan16-3FG	gd	6f	:23	:47^{3}		1:13^{2}	3↑ Handicap 600	1	2	3^{1}	3^{1}	$1^{1\frac12}$	$1^{1\frac12}$	Kederis J	124wb	*1.60	93-13	PnZareta124$^{1\frac12}$MronGoosby105$^{\frac12}$Dr.Lrrck110^{hd}	Won easing up	6
15Jan16-3FG	fst	6f	:23^{1}	:46^{3}		1:12	3↑ Handicap 500	4	4	3^{nk}	2^{hd}	$3^{1\frac12}$	3^{3}	Kederis J	126wb	*1.40	97-06	J.J. Lillis108$^{1\frac12}$Bringhurst113$^{1\frac12}$Pan Zareta126^{4}	Gamely	6
7Jan16-4FG	fst	6f	:23	:47^{2}		1:12^{3}	3↑ Handicap 400	6	5	2^{nk}	1^{hd}	$1^{\frac12}$	$1^{\frac12}$	Kederis J	124wb	*.80	97-08	Pan Zareta124$^{\frac12}$Ahara106.5$^{\frac12}$Carbide103^{no}	Hard ridden	6
5Oct15-3CD	hy	6f	:24^{1}	:48		1:14	3↑ ⒻAlw 700	4	1	1^{2}	1^{4}	1^{6}	1^{6}	Kederis J	110wb	*.50	85-18	Pan Zareta110^{6}Vogue100^{6}Lady J. Grey103^{6}		4
	Imped rivals at start,won easily																			
29Sep15-4CD	gd	6f	:23^{4}	:47^{4}		1:13^{1}	3↑ Falls City H 2.8k	7	5	$1^{1\frac12}$	1^{1}	2^{nk}	$3^{1\frac12}$	Rice T	125wb	3.50	87-14	PrinceHermis108^{no}Vogue107$^{1\frac12}$PanZareta125$^{\frac12}$	Tired near end	11
22Sep15-6OW	fst	6f	:22	:45^{4}		1:11^{4}	2↑ Handicap 745	3	2	2^{1}	3^{2}	3^{2}	$3^{1\frac12}$	Rice T	126wb	*1.00	97-09	Water Lady105^{hd}Kewessa110$^{1\frac12}$Pan Zareta126^{1}	Rated,tired	6
20Sep15-6OW	fst	7f	:24	:47^{3}	1:13^{1}	1:26^{3}	2↑ ⒻHandicap 640	4	1	1^{nk}	1^{2}	1^{3}	$1^{1\frac12}$	Rice T	124wb	*.70	99-11	Pan Zareta124$^{1\frac12}$Water Lady108^{no}Venetia107^{4}	Won easing up	5
16Sep15-4Dor	fst	6f	:22^{4}	:46^{3}		1:11	2↑ Handicap 600	1	1	2^{hd}	1^{nk}	1^{nk}	2no	Smyth J	123wb	*1.00	112-00	Back Bay113^{no}Pan Zareta123$^{\frac12}$Kewessa109$^{1\frac12}$	Just missed	5
8Sep15-5BB	sly	6f	:23^{1}	:47^{3}		1:13^{3}	2↑ Handicap 640	5	2	3^{3}	3^{6}	2^{2}	2^{nk}	Rice T	125wb	3.50	94-16	Water Lady102^{nk}Pan Zareta125^{1}Venetia106$^{\frac12}$	Good try	7
2Sep15-5BB	fst	7f	:23	:47	1:12	1:25	2↑ Handicap 700	7	2	2^{4}	2^{4}	$2^{\frac12}$	2^{2}	Cooper F	122wb	*1.50	95-11	Back Bay107^{2}Pan Zareta122$^{\frac12}$Ten Point124$^{\frac12}$	Led,tired	8
26Aug15-4Con	gd	6f	:23^{4}	:48^{1}		1:14^{2}	2↑ Handicap 500	2	2	1^{hd}	2^{hd}	$1^{\frac12}$	$2^{\frac12}$	Cooper F	129wb	*1.60	95-15	SirEdgar107$^{\frac12}$PanZareta129$^{1\frac12}$BackBy110^{3}	Saved ground,tired	5
10Aug15-4FE	gd	6f	:22^{4}	:47		1:14^{1}	3↑ Handicap 700	2	5	$4^{2\frac14}$	3^{2}	$4^{2\frac14}$	$3^{2\frac12}$	Cooper F	130 w	*.75	83-21	Kewessa102$^{1\frac12}$Sir Edgar103^{1}Pan Zareta130$^{\frac34}$	Outrun	7
28Jly15-5Ham	sly	6f	:23^{4}	:48^{4}		1:14^{2}	3↑ Handicap 670	5	1	2^{nk}	5^{9}	5^{15}	5^{11}	Cooper F	139wb	*1.40	72-20	Dr. Larrick100^{2}Ed Howard97^{no}Carbide106^{1}	Quit	5
24Jly15-3Ham	fst	6f	:23^{3}	:47^{2}		1:11^{4}	3↑ Handicap 680	4	3	2^{2}	$2^{\frac12}$	1^{nk}	2^{nk}	Cooper F	140wb	*.70	96-04	SirEdgar99^{nk}PanZareta140$^{\frac34}$Dr.Larrick101^{hd}	Resolute drive	8
20Jly15-3Wnr	fst	6f	:24^{1}	:47^{3}		1:12^{2}	3↑ Handicap 700	4	4	$1^{\frac12}$	$1^{1\frac12}$	1^{4}	$1^{1\frac12}$	Cooper F	136wb	*.60	98-11	PanZrta136$^{1\frac12}$Commonada105^{1}Ed Howard98^{hd}	Won easing up	5
14Jly15-3Wnr	fst	6f	:23^{2}	:46^{3}		1:11^{2}	3↑ Alw 700	3	3	$1^{1\frac12}$	1^{1}	$1^{1\frac12}$	1^{2}	Cooper F	118wb	*.80	103-07	Pan Zareta118^{2}Back Bay103^{2}Iron Mask108^{4}	Easily	6
28Jun15-3Ham	fst	5½f	:23^{1}	:47	:59^{4}	1:06^{1}	3↑ Handicap 690	2	3	1^{hd}	1^{1}	1^{3}	1^{5}	Cooper F	131wb	*1.60	98-12	Pan Zareta131^{5}Sir Edgar95.5^{2}Ed Howard99$^{\frac12}$	Drew away	9
25Jun15-3Ham	fst	6f	:22^{3}	:47^{1}		1:12^{2}	3↑ Handicap 680	3	5	2^{2}	3^{1}	$3^{2\frac14}$	$1^{\frac12}$	Cooper F	127wb	2.20	93-10	PnZreta127$^{\frac12}$Carbide96$^{2\frac12}$Kewessa107^{6}	Inside move,drew clear	7
	Previously owned by J.F. Newman & H.S. Newman																			
22Jun15-3Con	gd	6f	:24	:48^{2}		1:14^{4}	3↑ Handicap 500	4	1	2^{hd}	$1^{1\frac12}$	1^{3}	1^{hd}	Cooper F	129wb	*1.60	94-09	PanZarta129^{hd}SouthernMaid94^{5}BckBy116^{4}	Ridden out,lasted	5
17Jun15-5Con	sl	6f	:24	:48^{3}		1:14^{1}	3↑ Handicap 500	2	3	2^{2}	2^{1}	$2^{1\frac12}$	$3^{1\frac12}$	Burns G	134wb	*1.20	95-15	Recoil90^{hd}Back Bay116$^{1\frac12}$Pan Zareta134^{3}	Tired	4
9Jun15-3BB	fst	6f	:24	:47^{4}		1:13^{3}	3↑ Handicap 630	2	1	1^{1}	1^{hd}	$1^{\frac12}$	1^{1}	Burns G	134wb	*.80	94-14	Pan Zareta134^{1}Carbide105$^{2\frac12}$Deposit104^{nk}	Swerved ⅛	5
28May15-4OW	fst	6f	:22^{2}	:46^{3}		1:12^{2}	3↑ Handicap 770	1	1	2^{hd}	$1^{\frac12}$	1^{3}	1^{1}	Rice T	129wb	*1.05	96-10	Pan Zareta129^{1}Kewessa112^{3}Back Bay117$^{\frac12}$	Ridden out	6
24May15-7OW	fst	6f	:23	:47^{1}		1:13	3↑ ⒻAlw 630	4	1	1^{2}	1^{2}	1^{3}	1^{2}	Rice T	123wb	*.10	93-09	Pan Zareta123^{2}Recoil113$^{1\frac12}$Shyness103^{1}	Under restraint	6
	Previously trained by H.S. Newman																			
26Mar15-4Jua	fst	6f	:23^{2}	:47		1:11^{4}	3↑ Handicap 300	2	2	$1^{\frac12}$	1^{nk}	$1^{\frac34}$	1^{nk}	Loftus J	146wb	*.80	89-17	PanZrta146^{nk}Seneca100^{3}Kootny115$^{2\frac12}$	Ridden out vigorously	5
22Mar15-4Jua	fst	5½f	:22^{1}	:46	:59	1:05^{2}	3↑ Handicap 300	5	4	2^{2}	$2^{1\frac12}$	1^{1}	$1^{2\frac12}$	Loftus J	140wb	*.70	90-16	PanZarta140$^{2\frac12}$Kootenay112$^{1\frac12}$Manganese95$^{1\frac12}$	Won easing up	7
7Mar15-4Jua	fst	7f	:23^{2}	:46^{3}	1:12^{1}	1:24^{3}	3↑ Dos Republicas H 1.4k	6	2	2^{2}	$2^{2\frac12}$	1^{nk}	2^{hd}	Loftus J	135wb	*1.40	94-13	Kootenay107^{hd}Pan Zareta135$^{\frac12}$Rash112$^{1\frac12}$	Gamely	12
21Feb15-5Jua	gd	1	:24^{1}	:49	1:15^{4}	1:41^{3}	3↑ Alw 400	6	2	$1^{1\frac12}$	1^{3}	$1^{2\frac12}$	1^{1}	Rice T	108wb	*.70	76-24	PnZreta108^{1}Roadmstr103^{5}GnrlMrchmont104^{1}	Easing up late	7
10Feb15-3Jua	fst	5f	:21^{3}	:44^{4}		:57^{1}	3↑ Sp Wt 400	2	2	2^{3}	$2^{2\frac12}$	2^{hd}	1^{2}	Loftus J	120 w	*.50	105-07	Pan Zareta120^{2}Joe Blair110	Rated,easing late	2
18Jan15-4Jua	fst	5½f	:23	:47^{1}	:59^{4}	1:06^{2}	3↑ Handicap 400	1	1	1^{2}	1^{3}	1^{2}	1^{3}	Loftus J	136wb	*.13	85-19	Pan Zareta136^{3}Little Will92^{1}New Haven103^{4}	Won easing up	4
13Dec14-4Jua	fst	6f	:23^{2}	:47^{3}		1:11^{1}	2↑ Handicap 500	2	2	$1^{1\frac12}$	1^{2}	$1^{2\frac12}$	1^{hd}	Loftus J	132wb	*.70	92-14	PnZrt132^{hd}Hocnir116^{3}SirDyke96$^{1\frac12}$	Eased late,almost caught	4
	Previously trained by E. Foucon																			
10Oct14-3CD	my	6f	:23^{3}	:47^{2}		1:13	3↑ Alw 600	4	3	$1^{1\frac12}$	$1^{1\frac12}$	1^{2}	$1^{1\frac12}$	Loftus J	112wb	*.40	90-18	Pan Zareta112$^{1\frac12}$Bob Hensley106^{6}Korfhage103^{8}	Cantering	7
2Oct14-4DoP	fst	6f	:23	:46^{1}		1:11^{2}	3↑ Handicap 760	1	3	$1^{\frac12}$	1^{1}	1^{nk}	1^{hd}	Loftus J	116wb	3.35	97-10	PanZareta116^{hd}LeoSkolny106^{nk}Leochares113^{4}	Saved ground	6
26Sep14-2OW	fst	6f	:22^{1}	:45^{3}		1:11^{3}	2↑ Handicap 725	5	1	2^{1}	2^{2}	2^{nk}	2^{nk}	Burns G	122wb	*1.12	101-05	BackBay117^{nk}PanZareta122^{6}SouthernMaid100^{2}	Second best	5
19Sep14-1OW	fst	6f	:24^{4}	:46^{3}		1:12	2↑ Handicap 730	1	4	1^{nk}	$2^{\frac12}$	$2^{1\frac12}$	$2^{1\frac12}$	Burns G	124wb	*1.35	97-10	Back Bay115$^{1\frac12}$Pan Zareta124$^{1\frac12}$Rockville106^{2}	Tired	6
14Sep14-4Dor	fst	6f	:23^{3}	:48^{2}		1:14^{4}	3↑ Rapids H 1.7k	3	1	1^{2}	1^{1}	1^{nk}	2^{hd}	Burns G	126wb	*1.40	99-07	Water Lady91^{hd}Pan Zareta126^{4}Brave Cunarder94^{1}	Gamely	5
28Aug14-4Con	fst	6f	:24	:48^{4}		1:14	2↑ Handicap 600	1	4	1^{3}	1^{2}	1^{4}	$1^{\frac34}$	Callahan J	120wb	*1.80	98-09	Pan Zareta120$^{\frac34}$Back Bay115^{2}Southern Maid105^{5}	Tiring	8
5Aug14-6FE	fst	6f	:22^{4}	:46^{1}	:58^{4}	1:11^{2}	3↑ Alw 600	5	1	2^{hd}	2^{nk}	$3^{\frac12}$	$4^{2\frac12}$	Burns G	115wb	*1.50	99-04	Leochares102^{2}BackBy102$^{\frac12}$LttlNphw104^{hd}	Tired under impost	7
31Jly14-4Ham	fst	5½f	:24^{1}	:48^{2}	:59^{4}	1:05^{4}	3↑ Handicap 650	2	1	$1^{1\frac12}$	$1^{\frac12}$	1^{1}	1^{3}	Burns G	126wb	*2.00	100-10	PanZareta126^{3}Useeit100$^{\frac12}$KnightsDiffer103^{1}	Won easing up	5
29Jly14-1Ham	fst	6f	:23^{3}	:48^{1}		1:13	3↑ Handicap 740	1	2	$1^{1\frac12}$	1^{2}	1^{2}	1^{2}	Burns G	123wb	*.90	90-13	PanZrta123^{2}Nightstck117$^{\frac12}$MovngPctur97$^{1\frac12}$	Never extended	4
25Jly14-5Ham	fst	6f	:23^{3}	:46^{2}		1:12^{2}	3↑ Handicap 690	3	2	2^{nk}	$2^{\frac12}$	$2^{1\frac12}$	2^{2}	Burns G	124wb	*2.60	91-09	Back Bay112^{2}Pan Zareta124^{nk}Elwah100$^{\frac12}$	Game try	8
21Jly14-4Wnr	fst	6f	:23^{4}	:47^{2}		1:12	3↑ Handicap 700	1	1	1^{1}	$1^{1\frac12}$	1^{2}	1^{nk}	Burns G	120wb	2.50	100-04	Pan Zareta120^{nk}Back Bay111^{2}Miramichi103^{2}	Hard ridden	5
8Jly14-5FE	fst	6f	:22^{4}	:47		1:13	3↑ Handicap 600	4	1	$1^{\frac12}$	$1^{\frac12}$	1^{4}	1^{2}	Burns G	119wb	1.50	94-09	PanZarta119^{2}MeetingHous124^{nk}Shrwood114^{6}	Easing up late	4
4Jly14-5FE	fst	6f	:23^{2}	:47^{2}		1:12^{3}	3↑ Alw 700	5	3	$4^{1\frac12}$	$3^{1\frac12}$	$2^{\frac12}$	2^{1}	Burns G	112wb	*.80	95-08	SouthrnMaid102^{1}PanZarta112^{nk}MeetngHouse117^{8}	Wide,tired	5
27Jun14-1Ham	fst	6f	:24	:48^{3}		1:12^{1}	3↑ Alw 530	2	4	2^{2}	2^{2}	2^{1}	2^{3}	Callahan J	109wb	*.40	91-08	Back Bay112^{3}Pan Zareta109$^{1\frac12}$Dorothy Dean115^{3}	Lost whip	6
25Jun14-3Ham	fst	6f	:23^{1}	:46^{4}		1:12	3↑ Alw 640	7	2	$2^{\frac12}$	2^{1}	$1^{\frac12}$	1no	Callahan J	106wb	*1.00	95-08	Pan Zareta106^{no}Nightstick105^{3}Marjorie A.107^{6}	Lasted	7
20Jun14-5Con	sl	6f	:24^{1}	:49^{3}		1:16^{2}	3↑ Handicap 500	5	3	3^{2}	2^{nk}	1^{2}	1^{1}	Peak C	117 w	5.00	88-23	Pan Zareta117^{1}Sir Blaise104^{1}Fathom104^{4}	Ridden out	9
11Jun14-4Dor	fst	6f	:23^{4}	:48^{4}		1:14^{4}	3↑ Caughnawaga H 2.2k	8	2	1^{nk}	$1^{\frac12}$	1^{3}	$4^{3\frac14}$	Peak C	120wb	*3.00	104-00	Bwana Tumbo112^{hd}Sherwood112^{3}Marjorie A.112^{nk}	Tired	9
2Jun14-3BB	fst	6f	:23^{3}	:47^{4}		1:12^{4}	3↑ Handicap 755	5	3	$3^{2\frac12}$	2^{nk}	$1^{1\frac12}$	$2^{\frac12}$	Peak C	126wb	3.60	97-15	SirBlaise109$^{\frac12}$PanZareta126^{4}Recol102^{no}	Tired under impost	7
29May14-3OW	fst	6f	:23	:47^{4}		1:13	3↑ Handicap 820	4	2	2^{hd}	1^{hd}	$2^{1\frac12}$	3^{6}	Peak C	126wb	4.20	88-12	Cabaret115^{2}Marjorie A.112^{4}Pan Zareta126^{hd}	Dueled,tired	11
	Previously trained by H.S. Newman																			
22Mar14-4Jua	fst	5½f	:23	:47^{2}	:59^{1}	1:05^{2}	3↑ Handicap 500	4	4	$5^{3\frac34}$	3^{3}	3^{4}	$4^{2\frac12}$	Woods H	132wb	*.60	99-05	Lady Panchita98$^{\frac12}$Seneca108^{1}Furlong100^{1}	Tired	6
17Mar14-4Jua	fst	7f	:22^{3}	:46^{1}	1:11^{3}	1:24^{1}	3↑ Handicap 500	4	1	$1^{2\frac12}$	$1^{2\frac12}$	1^{2}	1^{2}	Cavanaugh H	122wb	*.60	101-09	PanZarta122^{2}NewHaven95^{nk}Swish87^{2}	Went to knees at start	5
11Mar14-4Jua	fst	1	:23^{2}	:45^{2}	1:11^{3}	1:36^{4}	3↑ Handicap 600	4	3	2^{hd}	2^{hd}	$3^{1\frac14}$	5^{6}	Cavanaugh H	126wb	4.00	97-06	Christophine102^{1}BertGetty105^{2}Curlicue102^{no}		7
	Forced pace,tired																			
8Mar14-4Jua	fst	7f	:23^{2}	:46	1:10^{2}	1:24	3↑ Dos Republicas H 1.4k	6	1	1^{hd}	2^{nk}	2^{nk}	$3^{1\frac34}$	Van Dusen C	130wb	*2.00	100-01	Orb105^{1}Dorothy Dean122$^{\frac34}$Pan Zareta130^{nk}	Tired	7
16Feb14-4Jua	fst	7f	:23^{1}	:46^{4}	1:11^{4}	1:24	3↑ Handicap 400	3	1	$1^{1\frac12}$	1^{2}	$1^{2\frac12}$	$2^{\frac34}$	Van Dusen C	135wb	2.20	101-05	Dorothy Dean112$^{\frac34}$Pan Zareta135$^{\frac12}$Barsac112^{4}	Resolute	6
13Feb14-4Jua	fst	6f	:22^{2}	:47^{1}		1:12	3↑ Handicap 400	4	3	1^{2}	$1^{2\frac12}$	1^{3}	1^{3}	Van Dusen C	132wb	*.80	96-06	Pan Zareta132^{3}Cosgrove102^{nk}Colquitt97$^{2\frac12}$	Never extended	4
27Jan14-4Jua	fst	6f	:22^{2}	:47		1:11^{3}	3↑ Handicap 400	2	3	$1^{\frac34}$	1^{1}	$1^{2\frac12}$	1^{1}	Loftus J	124wb	*.50	98-11	Pan Zareta124^{1}New Haven100^{no}Barsac103$^{1\frac12}$	Eased last 100y	5
4Jan14-3Jua	fst	6f	:21^{3}	:45	:56^{4}	1:09^{3}	3↑ Alw 500	1	1	$2^{\frac12}$	$2^{2\frac12}$	$2^{2\frac12}$	2^{5}	Kirschbaum C	110wb	1.50	103-02	Iron Mask115^{5}Pan Zareta110	No match	2
13Dec13-4Jua	fst	5½f	:22^{2}	:46^{1}	:58^{3}	1:04^{3}	2↑ Handicap 500	1	2	$1^{\frac34}$	1^{2}	$1^{2\frac12}$	$1^{1\frac12}$	Kirschbaum C	126 w	*.80	103-03	Pan Zareta126$^{1\frac12}$Useeit105^{2}Orb92^{9}	Won easing up	4
6Dec13-4Jua	fst	5½f	:22^{2}	:46^{1}	:58^{2}	1:04^{3}	2↑ Handicap 500	2	1	1^{1}	1^{2}	$1^{2\frac12}$	$1^{2\frac12}$	Kirschbaum C	124wb	*1.00	103-06	Pan Zareta124$^{2\frac12}$Florence Roberts112$^{1\frac12}$Gold of Ophir102^{2}		4
	Won easing up																			
2Dec13-4Jua	fst	6f	:22^{3}	:47^{1}		1:11^{4}	2↑ Handicap 500	5	1	2^{hd}	1^{hd}	1^{nk}	$2^{\frac34}$	Kirschbaum C	124wb	*1.00	96-06	VestedRights102$^{\frac34}$PnZrt124^{nk}HnryWlbnk101$^{\frac12}$	Led,just missed	8
27Nov13-4Jua	fst	6f	:22^{4}	:47		1:12	2↑ Juarez H 1.4k	4	1	$1^{1\frac12}$	$1^{1\frac12}$	1^{2}	1^{hd}	Kirschbaum C	118wb	*1.60	96-08	Pan Zareta118^{hd}Mimorioso105^{4}Useeit110^{nk}	Gamely	10
	Previously owned by J.F. Newman																			
23Oct13-2Dal	sl	6f	:28^{3}	:58^{3}		1:29	Handicap 300	-	-				$5^{13\frac34}$	Small R	122		- -	Furlong116^{nk}Husky Lad104^{3}Suffragist106^{10}		5
21Oct13-3Dal	sl	6f	:25^{3}	:52		1:19	3↑ Alw 200	-	-				1^{3}	Small R	119		- -	Pan Zareta119^{3}Furlong122^{3}Suffragist115^{4}		7
3Oct13-4DoP	fst	6f	:23	:46^{3}		1:10^{4}	3↑ Handicap 760	2	3	1^{nk}	$6^{6\frac34}$	$6^{9\frac14}$	$6^{14\frac14}$	Taylor WW	108wb	40.00	89-05	Leochares109^{5}Helios108^{nk}Iron Mask132^{1}	Dropped back	6
20Sep13-1OW	fst	6f	:23^{3}	:47^{3}		1:12^{4}	2↑ Handicap 745	5	2	2^{hd}	1^{1}	$1^{\frac12}$	$2^{1\frac12}$	Peak C	119wb	1.95	93-09	Rockville105$^{1\frac12}$Pan Zareta119$^{\frac12}$Plate Glass126^{1}	Tired	6
11Sep13-3BB	fst	6f	:24	:47^{3}		1:12^{4}	2↑ Handicap 625	2	2	$1^{1\frac12}$	$1^{1\frac12}$	1^{4}	1^{3}	Peak C	116wb	*.70	98-10	Pan Zareta116^{3}Sir Blaise105$^{\frac12}$Cowl104^{3}	Easily	5
1Sep13-2Con	fst	5½f	:23	:47^{3}	1:00^{2}	1:06^{4}	2↑ Handicap 655	1	4	$2^{1\frac12}$	$2^{1\frac12}$	2^{2}	$1^{1\frac12}$	Kederis J	115wb	*1.60	104-02	Pan Zareta115$^{1\frac12}$Three Links102^{1}Sir Blaise110^{1}	Handily	5
29Aug13-4Con	sl	6f	:24	:48		1:14	3↑ Handicap 600	5	2	2^{nk}	1^{2}	1^{2}	1^{1}	Kederis J	110wb	*1.80	101-05	Pan Zareta110^{1}Towton Field103$^{1\frac12}$Yorkville102^{4}	Easily	6

Race	Cond	Dist	Fractions	Time	Age / Race	PP	St	1st	2nd	Str	Fin	Jockey	Wt	Odds	Speed	Top three finishers	Comment	Fld
27Aug13- 3Con	hy	6f	:242 :50	1:152	2↑ Handicap 600	4	2	11	1½	11½	11½	Kederis J	105wb	*.80	94-12	Pan Zareta1051½Sherwood1146Sir Blaise112½	Gamely	5
22Aug13- 4Wnr	hy	6f	:243 :494	1:174	2↑ St. Clair H 1.4k	1	3	21½	31¼	33½	22	Kederis J	104wb	3.00	69-35	Flabbergast1082PanZareta1044HelenBarbee1141	Second best	4
19Aug13- 1Wnr	fst	6f	:24 :471	1:122	Alw 600	3	3	2hd	2½	2nk	2nk	Kederis J	100wb	2.00	98-04	[D]Great Britain107nkPan Zareta1003Grosvenor1021½		4
	Carried wide by winner;Placed first by disqualification																	
11Aug13- 3FE	hy	6f	:24 :49	1:171	3↑ Alw 600	4	2	11	1hd	11	11	Kederis J	98.5 w	*1.10	73-36	Pan Zareta98.51Joe Knight108.5hdDuquesne1081½	Gamely	6
6Aug13- 5FE	fst	6f	:223 :462	1:13	3↑ Alw 600	1	3	21	2½	31½	41¾	Callahan J	96.5 w	7.00	92-07	Calgary100hdUseeit105.5hdLeochares1111½	Tired	6
2Aug13- 3Ham	fst	6f	:231 :472	1:123	3↑ Alw 635	1	3	11½	1hd	1½	2hd	Callahan J	99 w	3.00	92-07	MarjorieA.102hdPanZareta994SirBlaise1123	Tiring,gamely	5
28Jly13- 6Ham	fst	6f	:233 :464	1:113	3↑ Handicap 755	1	5	1hd	2hd	11½	31½	Gross C	103.5 w	*2.20	95-06	Sir Blaise107½Sun Queen1051Pan Zareta103.5hd	Slow start	5
26Jly13- 4Ham	fst	6f	:241 :473	1:113	3↑ Alw 640	4	3	21	32½	34½	24	Kederis J	98 w	6.00	93-05	Leochares1044Pan Zareta98hdTen Point1123	Good try	8
23Jly13- 1Wnr	fst	6f	:232 :471	1:122	3↑ Alw 600	5	2	11½	11½	1nk	2hd	Kederis J	98 w	3.50	98-05	Plate Glass113hdPan Zareta985Sir Blaise1091½	Held well	8
18Jly13- 3Wnr	hy	6f	:25 :494	1:17	Alw 600	4	4	31	34	31¾	32	Gross C	106 w	10.00	73-32	MovingPicture102.5noLeochars1122PnZrt10610	Saved ground	4
1Jly13- 4Lat	fst	6f	:23 :464	1:122	3↑ Handicap 870	3	2	1hd	31	31	21	Kederis J	100 w	3.40	96-09	Casey Jones1141Pan Zareta100noBenanet1055	Came on again	6
28Jun13- 4Lat	fst	6f	:23 :462	1:112	3↑ Quickstep 3.4k	2	4	22	24	24	57	Kederis J	100 w	10.50f	95-07	Helios1083Presumption109hdGowell1103	Tired badly	11
24Jun13- 4Lat	hy	6f	:232 :482	1:141	Alw 700	1	1	11½	1½	2½	42¼	Estep	105 w	3.80	86-19	Helios108hdUSteppa1102Benanet108hd	In deep going,tiring	7
18Jun13- 5Lat	my	6f	:24 :484	1:134	Alw 700	2	4	42½	35½	33	35¼	Kederis J	107 w	7.40	85-20	Maria C.1025Flying Tom109nkPan Zareta107hd	Game finish	8
20May13- 3CD	fst	6f	:232 :47	1:124	Alw 700	1	1	77	712	77¾	715¼	Gross C	107 w	5.10	77-09	Silver Bill1042McCorkle1102Flying Tom106hd		8
	Knocked out of contention at start																	
17May13- 3CD	hy	6f	:233 :472	1:14	3↑ Handicap 700	2	2	21½	33½	49	413	Gross C	104 w	9.00	73-18	HelenBarbee1121SamulR.Myr105.54JimBasey1138	Quit after ¼	4
2Mar13- 4Jua	fst	6f	:232 :48	1:131	Chapultepec H 1.1k	1	2	11	1½	12	12	Loftus J	122 w	*2.00	90-12	Pan Zareta1222Colquitt95¾Truly1122	Won easing up	10
22Feb13- 4Jua	fst	5½f	:222 :461 :594	1:061	3↑ Handicap 400	2	1	22½	23	22½	21	Gross C	106 w	*1.20	94-15	Pride of Lismore1121Pan Zareta1062Kootenay1021	Gaining	5
5Feb13- 4Jua	fst	6f	:23 :471	1:122	Alw 300	1	2	3½	41½	3nk	11	Gross C	114 w	3.00	94-11	Pan Zareta1141Truly98hdEl Palomar1163	Rated,going away	7
2Feb13- 4Jua	fst	6f	:222 :471	1:131	Chihuahua 1.1k	6	4	21½	2nk	1¾	1½	Rightmire	112 w	*.80	90-10	PanZareta112½TheCindr112¾Gskt1002½	Stumbled badly start	6
25Jan13- 5Jua	fst	6f	:23 :481	1:131	Alw 300	1	2	1½	11	11	11	Gross C	110 w	*.60	90-11	PanZareta1101Truly1072½GordonRussell1081	Never extended	5
19Jan13- 4Jua	sl	6f	:231 :483	1:141	3↑ Rio Grande 1.1k	5	5	1¾	31¼	22	1no	Gross C	102 w	9.00	85-21	Pan Zareta102noFlorence Roberts1002Chapultepec108½		10
	Taken back,game finish																	
17Dec12- 1Jua	fst	5½f	:232 :481 1:004	1:071	Alw 300	1	1	2½	21	1hd	1½	Gross C	112 w	*.80	90-12	PanZareta112½Mrs.Gamp1095TheCinder1082	Impeded ½ post	5
14Dec12- 4Jua	fst	5½f	:24 :482 1:003	1:07	2↑ Handicap 400	1	2	11½	1nk	11½	1hd	Hill	95 w	*1.80	91-12	Pan Zareta95hdLady Panchita100¾Pawhuska1096	Gamely	5
11Dec12- 1Jua	gd	5f	:24 :483	1:013	Clm	2	1	12	11	13	13	Gross C	112 w	*1.00	82-19	Pan Zareta1123Real Star104¾Bula Welsh100¾	Easily	6
24Sep12- 3Hel	fst	5f		1:02	Wonderland H .4k	-	-				32½	Rooney	119		- -	Envy1152O'Konite107½Pan Zareta1193	Driving	6
4Sep12- 3Bue	sly	5f	:241 :492	1:02	Handicap 350	-	-				11	Rooney	116	*1.60	87-17	Pan Zareta1161Gasket1015Mollie Richards1075	Handily	6
22Aug12- 1Bue	fst	5f	:234 :483	1:003	Clm	7	1	2hd	1nk	12½	12½	Buxton	115 w	*.40	94-07	PnZrta1152½Coeurd'Alen1052½JohnHurie107½	Won easing up	7
17Aug12- 3Bue	sl	5f	:241 :483	1:01	Handicap 350	5	3	2nk	1hd	11½	2½	Buxton	115 w	*2.00e	91-11	Orlin Kripp115½Pan Zareta1152Envy115hd	No match	6
6Aug12- 3Bue	fst	4f	:24	:473	Alw 300	3	2		12	1½	11	Buxton	109 w	*.75e	94-11	Pan Zareta1091Envy1091Al Bloch110no	Swerved in str	5
23Jly12- 2Lag	fst	5f	:231 :472	1:002	Clm	5	4	12	13	14	14	Buxton	109 w	*.65	95-03	Pan Zareta1094Auto Run1051Bells1042	Never extended	8
9Jly12- 2Lag	fst	4½f	:23 :46	:524	Alw 300	4	4	22½	22	22½	24	Anderson E	109 w	1.80e	104-05	FloralPark1074PanZareta1093OrlinKripp1043	Chased winner	7
4Jly12- 2Lag	fst	4f	:233	:49	Alw 300	6	4		12	12½	12	Gross C	117 w	1.30	93-07	Pan Zareta1172John Hurie1124O'Konite1077	Easily	6
19Jun12- 3CDA	fst	5f	:234 :483	1:012	Alw 300	2	4	11	11½	1¾	1¾	Carter	103 w	*.40e	93-04	PanZareta103¾Camia99noVestedRights1036	Hard ridden late	7
14May12- 1CDA	fst	4f	:241	:49	Clm	7	6		13	13	14	Buxton	107 w	*.60	93-00	PanZareta1074VelieForty106¾JessiPortr1084	Won easing up	7
2Mar12- 1Jua	fst	4f	:232	:472	Alw 300	1	4		21½	23	33½	Murray A	110 w	3.50	90-06	Inquieta115½Negligee1083Pan Zareta1108	Tired	5
11Feb12- 1Jua	fst	4f	:23	:48	Alw 300	4	2		1hd	1hd	1¾•	Prior	117 w	*1.60	91-09	[DH]StoutHeart105[DH]PanZrta117¾Oldsmobl1023	Stretch duel	5
31Jan12- 1Jua	fst	3½f	:223	:401	Alw 300	8	2			1nk	12	Murray A	112 w	4.00	96-04	PanZareta1122Palatable115nkOldsmobile1053	Bore out turn	9
14Jan12- 4Jua	fst	3½f	:23	:402	Ⓕ Senoritas .7k	1	2		22	1nk	1¾	Borel	110 w	*1.40	95-05	Pan Zareta110¾Truly1103Velie Forty1156	Bore out,gamely	5
10Jan12- 1Jua	fst	3f	:233	:361	Ⓕ Alw 300	3	7			45	2¾	Murray A	110 w	10.00	- -	Velie Forty110¾Pan Zareta1101Tildy Wolffarth1103		11
	May have won if kept straight																	
7Jan12- 1Jua	fst	3f	:222	:342	Alw 300	7	8			76¾	78¾	Murray A	110 w	5.00e	- -	Hawthorne1153Palatable1132½Pat Gannon1101½	Greenly	10

Princess Doreen

b. f. 1921, by Spanish Prince II (Ugly)–Lady Doreen, by Ogden

Lifetime record: 94 34 15 17 $174,745

Own.– Audley Farm Stable

Br.– J.E. Madden (Ky)

Tr.– K. Spence

Race	Cond	Dist	Fractions	Time	Age / Race	PP	St	1st	2nd	Str	Fin	Jockey	Wt	Odds	Speed	Top three finishers	Comment	Fld
24Nov27- 5Bow	fst	1 3/16	:482 1:131 1:391	1:59	3↑ Thanksgiving H 12k	9	6	51¾	52	83½	86	Ambrose E	118 w	5.40	86-02	BlackPanther111noDisplay1264LightView103.5nk	Poor effort	10
26Oct27- 5Lrl	fst	1 1/16	:232 :47 1:124	1:444	3↑ Alw 2000	3	4	53¼	4¾	42½	41	Ellis G	117wb	2.60	92-12	Display123noBostonian1141Jock114no	Good try	7
24Oct27- 5Lrl	fst	1⅛	:473 1:12 1:392	1:514	3↑ Handicap 2000	2	2	3nk	32	32½	44½	Ellis G	116wb	4.65	84-16	[D]Mars1281Crusader1302½Gaffsman1161	Used,tired	6
	Placed third by disqualification																	
3Sep27- 4Haw	fst	1 1/16	:231 :47 1:12	1:44	3↑ Oak Park H 6.3k	2	1	11½	11½	11½	32½	Pool E	128wb	*1.35	97-10	Chicago116½Flat Iron1262Princess Doreen1282		5
	Set fast pace,tired late																	
27Aug27- 5Haw	fst	1 1/16	:232 :47 1:123	1:45	3↑ Greater Chicago H 5k	2	1	12	13	11	11½	Pool E	124wb	*.97	95-11	Princess Doreen1241½Mix-Up101nkChicago1171½	Hand ride	6
10Aug27- 5LF	fst	1 1/16	:233 :47 1:113	1:433	3↑ Handicap 1800	3	1	13	16	16	13	Pool E	118wb	2.07	98-11	Princess Doreen1183Handy Mandy1084Yeddo105hd	Cantering	8
6Aug27- 5LF	fst	1	:232 :453 1:11	1:363	3↑ Steger H 8.4k	12	8	96	94	73¼	77	Crump W	120 w	3.91	90-09	Chicago1102Nor'Easter1141½Cudgeller1081	Never a factor	13
23Jly27- 5LF	fst	1 1/16	:24 :472 1:13	1:442	3↑ Marquette H 8.1k	8	8	63	87	118½	1223½	Crump W	123 w	*1.99	70-09	Rothermel109½Chicago108hdNor'Easter1075	Impeded	14
9Jly27- 5LF	fst	1¼	:483 1:122 1:38	2:041	3↑ Lincoln H 30k	11	6	2hd	32	33	35½	Crump W	122 w	9.12	107-03	ChancePlay1221½FlatIron1214PrincessDoreen122hd	All out	13
4Jly27- 5Lat	fst	1 3/16	:471 1:123 1:374	1:562	3↑ Independence H 15k	6	3	61¾	62¼	2½	1no	Crump W	120 w	6.00	97-10	PrincessDoren120noRhnock1102Prcusson100hd	Tiring,gamely	13
25Jun27- 6FP	fst	1 1/16	:232 :474 1:13	1:453	3↑ Hotel Statler H 7.3k	6	1	2nk	23	21	2no	Legere E	122 w	*.90	97-10	Banton106noPrincssDreen122½Helen'sBabe1171½	Just missed	6
17Jun27- 5FP	fst	6f	:231 :463	1:121	3↑ Handicap 1235	4	3	21	21½	21	1hd	Legere E	126 w	*.55	98-11	PrincssDrn126hdReputation112hdLoungr1108	Gamely,up late	4
25Nov26- 4Bow	fst	1 3/16	:473 1:122 1:373	1:572	3↑ Thanksgiving H 12k	1	5	74½	1214	1211	1317	McTague J	118 w	11.00	106-00	Backbone114nkPeanuts1215Joy Smoke121hd	Tired badly	13
13Nov26- 4Pim	fst	2¼	:50 2:34 3:01	3:521	3↑ Pim Cup H 12k	2	2	212	28	331	342½	McTague J	110 w	6.90e	61-15	EdithCavell932½Crusader12640PrincessDoreen110hd	Outrun	4
12Nov26- 5Pim	fst	1⅛	:492 1:143 1:402	1:54	2↑ Serial WFA #3 5.2k	1	1	1nk	2hd	21½	21½	McTague J	123 w	2.30	83-16	Mars1201½Princess Doreen123	No match	2
6Nov26- 4Pim	fst	1½	:50 1:15 2:043	2:311	3↑ Bowie H 13k	5	2	63	31	2½	22	McTague J	112 w	10.60e	95-13	Peanuts1152PrincessDoren1121Dsply1172½	Challenged,tired	11
3Nov26- 5Pim	fst	1 3/16	:48 1:132 1:392	1:59	3↑ Handicap 1550	3	4	42	42	2hd	1nk	McTague J	115 w	3.85	97-14	PrincessDoreen115nkSeventhSon105hdJoySmoke1192	Lasted	8
30Oct26- 5Lrl	fst	1¼	:472 1:123 1:373	2:03	3↑ Washington H 29k	7	5	72	103¼	105¾	95½	Lang C	113 w	11.65	89-10	Mars118½Peanuts114½Display1141½	No factor	13
27Oct26- 5Lrl	fst	1 70	:232 :473 1:124	1:422	3↑ Purse 2000	2	2	21	2nk	2½	31½	Lang C	116 w	5.20	97-14	Gaffsman1121PrinceofWales116½PrncssDorn116hd	Raced well	5
16Oct26- 5Lrl	fst	1	:23 :472 1:123	1:38	2↑ Laurel 14k	5	4	51¾	43	74¼	85¾	McTague J	117 w	35.75	92-11	Croyden107.52Sarazen126hdMars1171	No factor	11
5Oct26- 5Lrl	fst	6f	:222 :461	1:113	3↑ Capitol H 7.7k	11	6	1113	107	84½	62¼	McTague J	117 w	7.15e	97-06	Prince of Wales1071Noah119hdCroyden114hd	Closed gap	13
25Sep26- 5HdG	fst	1⅛	:473 1:122 1:38	1:50	3↑ Havre de Grace H 17k	1	8	96¼	96¼	1012	812¼	Lang C	115 w	25.05	88-06	Crusader1225Son of John108hdDisplay114nk	Never a factor	12
15Sep26- 4OW	my	1¼	:492 1:142 1:413	2:07	3↑ Toronto Aut Cup H 10k	7	8	75	84¼	66	63¼	McTague J	120 w	3.55	83-16	Edisto122hdGaffsman1081Harry Baker105nk	Always beaten	13
28Aug26- 5Sar	sl	1¾	:50 2:09 2:34	3:002	3↑ Sar Cup 9.1k	3	1	11½	11	31	37	Sande E	121 w	7.00	73-20	Espino1162Display1165PrincessDoreen12110	Rated,no match	5
21Aug26- 5Sar	fst	1 3/16	:483 1:132 1:394	1:59	3↑ Merchants & Cits H 9.4k	2	1	12	2hd	23	44½	McTague J	123 w	*1.50	78-16	Flagstaff1082Peanuts1172Blondin109½	Tired	5
30Jly26- 4Sar	my	1¼	:49 1:141 1:402	2:082	3↑ Saratoga H 10k	7	1	15	15	15	14	McTge J	116 w	20.00	67-24	PrincessDoren1164Blondn1083KngSolomon'sSl1093	Cantering	8
5Jly26- 5Lat	gd	1 3/16	:463 1:113 1:374	1:571	3↑ Independence H 14k	2	8	67	53¼	1hd	2½	McTague J	124 w	3.80e	92-11	Rothermel103½Princess Doreen1241Rhinock1084	Second best	8
19Jun26- 5Lat	fst	1 1/16	:231 :463 1:12	1:433	3↑ Enquirer H 7.9k	5	4	54	54	55½	510	Scobie E	127 w	*1.30e	86-12	Barcolo107hdRhinock1063Heln'sBabe1002	Tired under impost	8
8Jun26- 5Lat	fst	6f	:223 :46	1:12	3↑ Ⓕ Alw 1615	2	4	55	34½	2½	11½	Scobie E	113 w	*.50	89-16	PrincessDoreen1131½Teak1054LittleVstor1151½	Wide,easily	6
3Jun26- 5Lat	fst	1 1/16	:241 :472 1:124	1:45	3↑ Inaugural H 7.8k	1	4	32¼	22	2½	11½	Legere E	122 w	*.60	89-12	PrincssDrn1221½Trymore1088Tangara1091½	Wide into stretch	8

22May26- 5CD	fst	1¼	:472 1:124 1:391 2:043	3↑ Grainger Mem H 14k	5	5	55	32¼	21½	21½	ZcchiniR	123	w	7.20	91-12	King Nadi1191½Princess Doreen1235Captain Hal1222		7
	Finished well,no match																	
19May26- 5CD	fst	6f	:224 :462 1:12	3↑ Handicap 1868	3	4	55	57	42½	44	Zucchini R	118	w	5.30	91-14	King Nadi1171Arcady1102Lee O. Cotner1171	Good effort	6
3May26- 5Pim	fst	1 3/16	:474 1:132 1:383 2:004	3↑ Dixie H 32k	1	4	55	64¼	86¼	98¾	Lang C	118	w	10.00	79-14	Sarazen128nkSunPal1051GeneralThtchr118nk	Never a factor	11
4Apr26- 8Tij	fst	1 70	:224 :464 1:114 1:414	3↑ Handicap 1200	1	2	21½	2½	11	1no	McTague J	120	w	*1.60	101-10	Princess Doreen120noSanford923Cherry Tree115no	Lasted	7
28Mar26- 7Tij	fst	1¼	:461 1:101 1:354 2:023	3↑ Coffroth H 80k	4	5	615	517	612	714¼	Sande E	123	w	2.20	97-10	Carlaris1008Roycrofter1001Cherry Tree1134	Outrun	9
24Mar26- 6Tij	fst	1⅛	:482 1:124 1:381 1:504	3↑ Handicap 1000	3	4	41¼	41¾	31½	1hd	McTague J	120	w	*.90	105-10	PrincessDorn120hdKntuckyCrdnl1121½Roycroftr1033	Just up	5
21Mar26- 7Tij	fst	1⅛	:463 1:103 1:363 1:492	3↑ Handicap 1500	1	2	22½	24	23	43	McTague J	123	w	5.00	109-10	Carlaris1061½Kentucky Cardinal112hdCherry Tree1151½		8
	Dropped back late																	
25Feb26- 7Tij	fst	6f	:224 :463 1:114	3↑ Handicap 1000	3	5	55¼	54½	43	35½	McTague J	123	w	*1.50e	89-17	Glister951½Serenader1184PrincessDoreen1232	Finished fast	6
26Nov25- 5Bow	fst	1 3/16	:492 1:14 1:412 2:021	3↑ Thanksgiving H 12k	6	3	43½	32½	31¼	22	Lang C	117	w	*3.05e	97-12	JoySmoke1142PrincessDorn117nkSenatorNorrs109hd	Gamely	13
21Nov25- 4Bow	fst	1	:24 :482 1:133 1:402	2↑ G D Bryan Mem H 18k	1	5	42½	43¼	3¾	32½	Stutts H	117	w	3.95	100-05	Sarazen1261Joy Smoke1151½Princess Doreen117nk		15
	In close start,gamely																	
14Nov25- 4Pim	gd	2¼	:503 2:38 3:023 3:58	3↑ Pim Cup H 11k	4	1	11	11	2hd	32	Lang C	116	w	*.90e	73-23	Rockminister102½Harrovin1121½PrncssDorn1166	Good effort	6
10Nov25- 5Pim	fst	1½	:493 1:15 2:063 2:342	3↑ Bowie H 12k	5	3	42¼	11	14	12	Lang C	118	w	2.75	81-17	PrincessDoreen1182AgaKhan1211MyOwn115nk	Won easing up	6
31Oct25- 5Lrl	sly	1¼	:482 1:14 1:423 2:094	3↑ Washington H 29k	5	6	52¾	43	46½	410	Stutts H	119	w	7.30	51-36	Joy Smoke1123Big Blaze1226Aga Khan1221	Tired	8
19Sep25- 5Lat	fst	6f	:224 :454 1:112	3↑ Autumn H 6.7k	9	1	105	83	21	1no	Stutts H	133	w	*3.60	92-12	PrincessDoreen133noArcady1111BrownSugr1131	Wide,just up	10
12Sep25- 5Lat	fst	1 1/16	:242 :48 1:13 1:451	3↑ Covington H 6.5k	5	7	31	1½	13	11½	Stutts H	130	w	2.00	88-13	PrincessDoreen1301½Starbeck1033NancyLanghorn107½		7
	Won easing up																	
7Sep25- 5CI	fst	1⅛	:472 1:112 1:371 1:492	3↑ Cincinnati Enquirer H 10k	6	7	74	2hd	11	1½	Stutts H	129	w	5.10	- -	PrincssDreen129½KentckyCardinal1101Boon Companion113hd		8
	Slow to start,wide																	
22Aug25- 4Haw	fst	1 3/16	:473 1:12 1:363 1:562	3↑ Chicago Spl 22k	3	2	21½	21½	3½	33	Stutts H	121	w	2.60	101-06	Mad Play1261Kentucky Cardinal1182Princess Doreen1218		5
	Forced wide,tired																	
15Aug25- 5CI	gd	1 3/16	:481 1:13 1:394 1:592	3↑ Western Hills H 7.9k	5	1	13	15	15	15	Stutts H	126	w	*.45	- -	Princess Doreen1265Tall Grass98nkOld Slip1022	Easily	5
8Aug25- 6Tdn	sl	1	:24 :482 1:141 1:40	3↑ Flint Stone Mem H 10k	9	8	53	42½	43½	32	Stutts H	129	w	*.60	- -	John T.D.104hdCherry Pie1142Princess Doreen1291½		9
	Slow to start,tired																	
1Aug25- 4CI	fst	1 1/16	:242 :48 1:12 1:433	3↑ Commercial Trib H 6.4k	4	2	2hd	13	12	11½	Stutts H	124	w	*.25	- -	PrincessDrn1241½GustofHonor1061NncyLnghrn103hd	Rated	4
18Jly25- 6CI	fst	1⅛	:463 1:102 1:354 1:491	3↑ Handicap 1800	4	1	12	12	11½	1½	Stutts H	122	w	*1.20	- -	PrincessDoreen122½SirPeter1174KingGorinII1026	Driving	4
11Jly25- 5CI	gd	1 1/16	:234 :471 1:114 1:44	3↑ Cin Times-Star H 6.5k	3	2	21	11½	12	11	Stutts H	118	w	*.50	- -	Princess Doreen1181King Gorin II1052Tangara99hd		5
	Won under restraint																	
4Jly25- 4Lat	gd	1 3/16	:47 1:114 1:374 1:573	3↑ Independence H 14k	9	1	110	110	15	13	Stutts H	115	w	4.55	91-16	Princess Doreen1153Progress1024King Gorin II1072	Easily	9
1Jly25- 5Lat	fst	1 70	:23 :464 1:104 1:421	3↑ Handicap 1700	1	2	22	21	21½	21½	Stutts H	114	w	*.65	96-12	SirPeter1071½PrcssDrn1146Graeme1056	Gamely,no match	5
27Jun25- 4Lat	fst	6f	:231 :464 1:121	3↑ Handicap 1765	3	1	2hd	11	12	11½	Stutts H	113	w	*1.15	88-15	PrincessDoreen1131½LordGranite108½Lathrop1005		4
	Won easing up																	
18Jun25- 4Lat	gd	6f	:232 :463 1:122	3↑ Alw 1720	6	1	1hd	12	12	12	Scobie E	109	w	*1.50	87-13	PrincessDoren1092Dudly109noDryMoon1094	As rider pleased	6
13Jun25- 5Lat	fst	1 1/16	:243 :481 1:132 1:443	3↑ Enquirer H 7.4k	1	3	31	42	3¾	33	Garner M	112	w	*1.30	88-13	Sir Peter1031½Guest of Honor1081½Princess Doreen112hd		6
	Finished gamely																	
2Jun25- 5Lat	fst	1 1/16	:24 :464 1:113 1:44	3↑ Inaugural H 7.5k	5	3	43½	32½	2½	32	Lang C	113	w	3.20	92-09	CaptainHal110noHopeless1072PrincssDorn1131	Tired at end	11
23May25- 5CD	fst	1¼	:473 1:12 1:38 2:041	3↑ Grainger Mem H 13k	7	4	46	34	1hd	31½	Connelly D	112	w	3.35	93-09	King Nadi102hdCaptain Hal1091½Princess Doreen1121		7
	Impeded by runner-up																	
15May25- 6CD	fst	1 1/16	:242 :482 1:131 1:441	3↑ Handicap 2500	6	1	1nk	32	2½	2½	Pool E	113	w	*2.10	98-12	BeauButlr108½PrncssDrn1136Stanwix1046	Getting to winner	6
1May25- 5Pim	sl	1 3/16	:482 1:133 1:403 2:02	3↑ Dixie H 33k	11	9	73¾	126½	1216	1320½	Lang C	115	w	8.45f	61-24	Sarazen1301¼Spot Cash115½Joy Smoke1043	Never a factor	14
25Apr25- 5HdG	fst	1 70	:231 :472 1:122 1:42	3↑ Handicap 2000	3	3	33	31½	43½	45¾	Lang C	112	w	*1.05	96-03	Transmute1123TenMinutes1061¼TheRollCll1011½	Hard ridden	8
15Apr25- 5HdG	gd	6f	:223 :46 1:122	3↑ Harford H 5.7k	7	4	57½	58	33½	33½	Lang C	110	w	12.85f	90-14	Noah1051½Leopardess1102PrincessDoren1101	Tired in drive	8
22Nov24- 5Bow	hy	1	:242 :49 1:142 1:421	2↑ G D Bryan Mem H 11k	11	9	108¼	44½	42½	22	Stutts H	109	w	7.10	92-14	Donaghee1102PrincessDrn1093MssWhsk96hd	Closed big gap	15
17Nov24- 4Bow	fst	1⅛	:493 1:142 1:412 1:552	Prince George H 7.9k	3	2	22	21½	22	25	Lang C	112	w	*.35	98-07	Donaghee1095PrincessDrn1122PrinceHamlet963	Tired badly	5
6Nov24- 7Pim	fst	1 1/16	:23 :463 1:12 1:452	Ⓕ Alw 1300	1	1	16	110	18	15	Lang C	123	w	*.85	95-12	PrincessDoreen1235PrscllRuly1235Sunyr108	Never extended	3
1Nov24- 5Lrl	fst	1¼	:462 1:114 1:381 2:041	3↑ Washington H 31k	6	4	43½	53¼	67¼	75½	Stutts H	110	w	20.55	83-14	Big Blaze1061¼Aga Khan106noRustic107hd	Good effort	10
25Oct24- 5CD	fst	1⅛	:473 1:133 1:384 1:513	3↑ Falls City H 6.6k	5	6	55½	12	12	13	Stutts H	113	w	4.80	91-14	PrincessDrn1133Hopeless1076JustDavid102½	Won easing up	7
18Oct24- 4Lat	fst	1	:233 :472 1:112 1:362	3↑ Handicap 1800	3	2	21½	2½	2nk	31¾	Stutts H	115	w	2.30	99-08	Zev129nkPostillion981½Princess Doreen115	Tired	3
11Oct24- 5Lat	fst	1¼	:451 1:102 1:354 2:004	3↑ Int'l Spl #3 65k	8	6	53¼	52	55½	59½	Stutts H	117	w	5.15	98-07	Sarazen1201½Epinard126noMad Play120no	Outrun	8
13Sep24- 5Lat	gd	1 1/16	:223 :471 1:114 1:441	3↑ Covington H 6.6k	5	3	1½	15	14	15	Stutts H	114	w	*.60e	94-15	Princess Doreen1145Graeme1091J.G. Denny1043	Easily	8
1Sep24- 4Haw	fst	1¼	:481 1:124 1:383 2:042	3↑ Labor Day H 6.3k	2	1	11	12	14	18	Stutts H	119	w	*.35	99-04	PrincessDrn1198Laveen1091PrinceTiiTii106nk	Much the best	7
23Aug24- 4Haw	fst	1 3/16	:47 1:12 1:373 1:571	3↑ Chicago Spl 15k	3	3	21½	2nk	2nk	2nk	Stutts H	113	w	1.30	114-07	Giblon118nkPrincess Doreen1135Hopeless12615	Wide,gamely	5
12Aug24- 4Sar	sly	1¼	:502 1:161 1:413 2:084	Ⓕ Alabama 12k	2	2	21½	21	21	21	Stutts H	126	w	*.40	64-23	Priscilla Ruley1171Princess Doreen1262½Sunayr117		3
	Rated,second best																	
6Aug24- 3Sar	my	1	:24 :47 1:134 1:401	3↑ Handicap 1305	1	4	34½		1½	12	Stutts H	122	w	*1.10	80-20	Princess Doreen1222Initiate1148Sunayr1112	Going away	7
	Second call unavailable due to rain storm																	
5Jly24- 5Lat	fst	1¼	:47 1:121 1:374 2:022	Ⓕ Lat Oaks 11k	4	1	12	12	1hd	2nk	Stutts H	130	w	*.60	101-06	Befuddle121nkPrincssDorn13012Lvn1218	Tired under impost	4
13Jun24- 4Bel	fst	1⅜	:472 1:124 1:384 2:191	Ⓕ C C A Oaks 14k	8	3	31	2½	11	12	Stutts H	121	w	4.00	75-12	Princess Doreen1212Relentless114½Priscilla Ruley111hd		9
	Won easing up																	
31May24- 5CD	fst	1⅛	:48 1:132 1:39 1:514	Ⓕ Ky Oaks 12k	3	5	53	52	2½	22	Stutts H	116	w	5.40	88-11	[D]Glide1162Princess Doreen116½Nellie Morse121hd		8
	Close quarters final turn;Placed first by disqualification																	
27May24- 5CD	my	7f	:233 :473 1:131 1:264	Ⓕ Alw 1558	1	2	11½	13	13	12	Stutts H	112	w	3.70	82-25	Princess Doreen1122Beautiful Agnes1011½Befuddle1076		6
	Speed in reserve																	
17May24- 3CD	fst	1	:221 :452 1:102 1:363	3↑ Handicap 2000	6	4	53¼	45½	45	57	Kennedy B	100	w	16.35	91-09	Actuary1104Moonraker1101½Ten-Lec109½	Needed race	8
13May24- 5CD	gd	1	:23 :46 1:112 1:374	Alw 2000	1	4	66	75½	69	616¼	Stutts H	114	w	34.15	76-11	BlackGold1198WildAster119nkKingGorinII1191	Brief speed	8
14Nov23- 5CD	fst	6f	:223 :46 1:12	Handicap 1500	7	5	32	1hd	13	13	Pool E	111	w	5.15e	95-13	Princess Drn1113Chilhowee112nkBattlCrk115no	easily	7
12Nov23- 6CD	fst	6f	:231 :472 1:13	Alw 1100	1	6	41¾	31	2hd	11½	Pool E	112	w	3.00e	90-13	Princess Doreen1121½Clarence1081Stage Coach105no		11
	Saved ground,drew away																	
9Nov23- 6CD	gd	6f	:232 :472 1:124	Ⓕ Alw 1200	4	3	1hd	12	1hd	1hd	Scobie E	115	w	*1.20	91-16	PrincessDoreen115hdBeautifulAgns103hdMhJong1061½	Lasted	9
23Oct23- 5Lat	fst	6f	:23 :464 1:124	Handicap 1700	7	4	63½	75	65½	65¼	Scobie E	109	w	3.50	81-16	ColonelGilmore111.5nkBeauButler1122Glide1051	Poor effort	7
16Oct23- 4Lat	fst	1	:233 :481 1:132 1:384	Alw 1700	7	1	11	2½	53½	511¾	Woods L	99	w	3.25e	78-13	Dare Say952Beau Butler1071½King Gorin II102nk	Tired	8
13Oct23- 4Lat	fst	6f	:23 :462 1:12	Fort Thomas H 7.9k	7	3	31	1½	2hd	2no	Scobie E	109	w	9.10	90-11	Chilhowee118noPrincessDoreen1091Sanola108nk	Just missed	13
3Oct23- 6Lat	fst	5½f	:23 :473 1:001 1:07	Ⓕ Alw 1500	2	4	21	2nk	1½	12	Scobie E	115	w	*1.45e	92-12	PrincssDoreen1152MahJong110nkButfulAgns1102	Going away	8
2Oct23- 2Lat	fst	5½f	:23 :471 :594 1:07	Md Clm	9	6	3½	11½	11½	12	Scobie E	115	w	*.70e	92-11	PrincessDoreen1152BreakfastBell115½PhyllsLous1153	Easily	12
10Sep23- 4Bel	fst	6f	:232 :461 1:113	Ⓕ Matron 5.2k	1	5	42	42¼	44	32	Scobie E	105.5	w	*3.60	92-06	Tree Top109hdNellie Morse1222Princess Doreen105.51		13
	Eased in final strides																	
5Sep23- 3Bel	fst	5½f	:461 :591 1:051	Ⓕ Tomboy H 4.8k	1	1	43	54½	69	43	Pool W	106	w	*2.00	93-08	Lady Diana1071½Tree Top1091Anna MarroneII123½	Crowded	9
30Aug23- 6Sar	gd	5½f	:232 :472 :594 1:06	Md Alw 1000	7	5	55	55¼	44½	2no	Pool W	112	w	8.00	93-10	Sun Pal115noPrincess Doreen1123Mr. Mutt115½	Just missed	8
25Aug23- 3Sar	fst	6f	:224 :462 1:123	Ⓕ Spinaway 9.1k	3	10	96¾	97	109¼	98	Pool W	109	w	6.00	81-07	AnnaMarroneII117nkNellMors1241TrTop112nk	Never a factor	11
21Aug23- 6Sar	fst	5f	:224 :454 :584	Alw 1000	5	8	96	96¾	68	44	Pool W	105	w	*1.60e	91-11	TreeTop106.51LadyDiana1102DearMaria1051	Finished fast	9

Regret

ch. f. 1912, by Broomstick (Ben Brush)–Jersey Lightning, by Hamburg — **Lifetime record: 11 9 1 0 $35,093**

Own.– H.P. Whitney
Br.– H.P. Whitney (NJ)
Tr.– J. Rowe

25Sep17- 1Aqu	fst	7f	:234 :472 1:112 1:241	2↑ Handicap 764	2	1	12	12	13	13	Robinson F	127	w	*.08	101-09	Regret1273Ima Frank109	Speed in reserve	2
10Jly17- 4Aqu	gd	1 1/16	:241 :48 1:152 1:452	3↑ (F)Gazelle H 3.1k	6	1	12	13	13	13	Loftus J	129	w	*.17	96-11	Regret1293Bayberry Candle123hdWistful1051	Won eased up	6
25Jun17- 4Aqu	fst	1⅛	:47 1:122 1:363 1:492	3↑ Brooklyn H 5.8k	3	1	12	11	11½	2no	Robinson F	122	w	3.60e	103-04	Borrow117noRegret1221Old Rosebud1201	Overconfident ride	11
31May17- 3Bel	fst	5½f-Str	1:042	3↑ (F)Alw 880	2	1	11	13	15	18	Robinson F	128	w	*.17	97-09	Regret1288YankeeWitch118½Admiration1061½	Won pulling up	5
18Aug16- 3Sar	fst	1	:25 :49 1:14 1:392	3↑ Alw 710	4	1	11½	13	12	11½	Keogh F	107.5	w	*.07	90-10	Regret107.51½Flittergold1154Polroma1041½	Under restraint throughout	5
31Jly16- 4Sar	fst	1¼	:50 1:144 1:40 2:051	3↑ Saratoga H 4.8k	6	1	11	2nk	21½	816	Notter J	123	w	*.90	78-10	Stromboli1211½EdCrump1231½FriarRock107hd	Set pace,tired	8
17Aug15- 4Sar	gd	1	:25 :49 1:151 1:42	Saranac H 1.4k	2	1	12	11	12	11½	Notter J	123	w	*.33	77-21	Rgrt1231½TrlbyJury1143LdyRotha1061	Under stout restraint	8
8May15- 5CD	fst	1¼	:483 1:133 1:392 2:052	Ky Derby 14k	2	1	1½	1½	11½	12	Notter J	112	w	*2.65	90-09	Regret1122Pebbles1172Sharpshooter1141	Won easing up	16
22Aug14- 3Sar	hy	6f	:241 :491 1:162	Hopeful 10k	2	2	56½	66¾	31½	1½	Notter J	127	w	*1.60	76-27	Regret127½AndrewM.1143Pebbles1304	In heavy going,gamely	11
15Aug14- 3Sar	sl	6f	:23 :471 1:132	Sanford Mem 3.4k	1	3	11	12	11½	11½	Notter J	127	w	*.80e	91-17	Rgrt1271½Solly1132DinahDo1075	Under restraint throughout	8
8Aug14- 3Sar	fst	6f	:23 :47 1:113	Sar Spl 4.1k	8	1	13	1½	12	11	Notter J	119	w	*1.60e	100-03	Regret1191Pebbles1223Paris122no	Speed in reserve	8

Roamer

b. g. 1911, by Knight Errant (Trenton)–Rose Tree II, by Bona Vista — **Lifetime record: 98 39 26 9 $98,828**

Own.– A. Miller
Br.– Clay Brothers (Ky)
Tr.– A.J. Goldsborough

26Jly19- 4Emp	fst	1 1/16	:233 :474 1:132 1:453	3↑ Yonkers H 2.9k	3	2	2nk	11	2hd	22	Schuttinger A	120	wb	2.60	93-11	Bally1092Roamer1203Spur1131½	Tired	5
11Jly19- 2Aqu	gd	6f	:233 :472 1:12	3↑ Handicap 1468	3	3	31½	3¾	32¼	1¾	Schuttinger A	114	wb	4.00	95-12	Roamer114¾Sun Briar1302L'Errant98.58	Driving	4
21Jun19- 4Jam	gd	1 1/16	:242 :48 1:133 1:46	3↑ Long Beach H 4.8k	5	4	43	66	611	711½	Schuttinger A	116	w	8.00	85-09	Naturalist128½Lanius1153Star Master1221	Speed,eased up	7
14Jun19- 4Jam	fst	1 1/16	:244 :482 1:13 1:452	3↑ Excelsior H 4.8k	6	2	22	23	34½	611¾	Schuttinger A	121	wb	7.00	88-07	Naturalist1221Star Master1191Boniface108nk	Tired badly	8
9Jun19- 5Bel	sl	1	:242 :48 1:133 1:374	3↑ Alw 879	3	3	33½	37	36	315	Schuttinger A	122	wb	3.00	79-20	Lucullite1145Natural Bridge10110Roamer122	Not a factor	3
4Jun19- 4Bel	fst	1	:241 :472 1:123 1:372	3↑ Alw 1340	2	1	13	14	11	21	Schuttinger A	127	wb	*.14	95-08	Natural Bridge971Roamer12715Henry G.100	Tired under confident ride	3
19Oct18- 4Emp	fst	1 1/16	:243 :484 1:123 1:462	3↑ Pelham Bay H 2k	1	4	21½	21	21½	21	Schuttinger A	126	wb	*1.80	90-08	Naturalist1231Roamer126hdCorn Tassel109no	Wide on turn	4
16Oct18- 4Emp	fst	1 70	:24 :474 1:133 1:43	2↑ Scarsdale H 2.1k	3	3	21½	22	22	32	Schuttinger A	128	wb	*.90	97-07	War Cloud1171½Corn Tassel109½Roamer1286	Bumped 1st turn	4
12Oct18- 4Jam	fst	1⅛	:483 1:131 1:382 1:513	3↑ Continental H 2.8k	3	1	12	11½	11	2½	Schuttinger A	127	wb	3.50	101-06	Star Master115½Roamer1271George Smith1285	Gamely	4
5Oct18- 4Jam	fst	1⅛	:49 1:14 1:393 1:523	3↑ Pierrepont H 3.3k	3	3	21½	2½	2½	1nk	Schuttinger A	127	wb	*.55	97-08	Roamer127nkManister Toi1031War Cloud121	Rated	3
28Sep18- 4Aqu	fst	1⅛	:474 1:13 1:381 1:501	3↑ Edgemere H 3.4k	2	2	21	11	1nk	34¼	Robinson F	130	wb	3.20	92-15	George Smith1234War Cloud124nkRoamer1305	Wide,tired	5
31Aug18- 4Sar	hy	1¾	:502 2:081 2:342 3:021	3↑ Sar Cup 5.9k	2	2	21½	21	24	25	Schuttinger A	127	wb	1.60	74-15	Johren1135Roamer127	Tired	2
21Aug18- 0Sar	fst	1	:233 :46 1:101 1:344	Special .5k	1	1	1	1	1	1	Schuttinger A	110	wb	-	113-00	Roamer110	Outran pacesetter from start; Race against time	1
1Aug18- 4Sar	fst	1¼	:481 1:12 1:371 2:021	3↑ Saratoga H 6.8k	6	4	22	21½	13	13	Robinson F	129	wb	3.60	109-02	Roamer1293Cudgel1332Bondage105nk	Won easing up	6
17Jly18- 4Emp	gd	1	:25 :484 1:144 1:401	3↑ Mount Vernon H 2.9k	1	3	31½	31	3¾	12	Lyke L	133	wb	*.40	92-11	Roamer1332Old Koenig1262Papp112	Rated,drew away	3
13Jly18- 4Emp	fst	1⅛	:48 1:123 1:383 1:51	3↑ Emp City H 4.8k	3	1	11½	15	15	18	Lyke L	128	wb	*.55e	100-07	Roamer1288Hollister1143Spur1166	In a canter	4
4Jly18- 4Aqu	fst	7f	:224 :464 1:102 1:234	3↑ Carter H 3.4k	3	4	53	32	32	2nk	Lyke L	130	wb	*1.30	102-03	OldKoenig122nkRoamr1301½Polymelian1282	Impeded at start	9
29Jun18- 4Aqu	fst	1	:23 :463 1:111 1:363	3↑ Queens County H 4.3k	2	1	13	12	12	12½	Lyke L	123	wb	*.60	99-08	Rmr1232½TomMcTaggart1094HandGrenad1051	Won easing up	6
24Jun18- 4Aqu	fst	1⅛	:473 1:13 1:373 1:501	3↑ Brooklyn H 5.8k	7	1	13	12	11½	21	Schuttinger A	120	wb	6.00e	95-05	Cudgel1291Roamer1202½George Smith1223	Held well	8
17Jun18- 4Jam	fst	1 1/16	:233 :473 1:122 1:452	3↑ Excelsior H 4.8k	2	3	31½	43	3¾	22	Loftus J	120	wb	*3.20	98-08	George Smith1172Roamer120noWesty Hogan1221½	Gamely	11
30May18- 4Bel	sly	6f-Str	1:10	3↑ Toboggan H 4.4k	3	6	75¼	87½	88½	97½	Schuttinger A	130	wb	8.00	85-11	Naturalist1071½MotorCop1131½OldKoeng1202	Never a factor	11
27May18- 4Bel	fst	1	:232 :472 1:131 1:382	3↑ Metropolitan H 4.8k	2	1	11	1nk	2½	56	Schuttinger A	126	wb	3.00	85-13	TrompeLaMort1021½OldKoenig1181PriscillaMullns104½	Tired	8
5Nov17- 4Pim	fst	1 3/16	:473 1:124 1:39 1:584	3↑ Monumental H 2.2k	1	1	11½	21½	45	48	Schuttinger A	129	wb	*.55	96-05	Spur118noWalnut Hall109noHendrie1168	Tired badly	5
1Nov17- 4Pim	sl	1 1/16	:233 :481 1:133 1:47	3↑ Arlington H 2.3k	5	2	21½	1hd	12	12	Schuttinger A	126	wb	*.95	95-16	Roamer1262Sunbonnet1151Ed Roche106¾	Speed in reserve	7
17Oct17- 5Lrl	fst	1 1/16	:232 :473 1:124 1:443	2↑ Handicap 1309	3	1	13	15	14	14	Schuttinger A	126	wb	*.30	94-10	Romr1264Wstful1113PrscllMullns1065	Restrained throughout	6
6Oct17- 4Aqu	sl	1 1/16	:25 :492 1:14 1:471	3↑ Edgemere H 2k	1	1	1hd	2½	22	22½	McTaggart J	130	wb	*.50	84-14	Chiclet1142½Roamer1306Capra108	Tired	3
29Sep17- 4Aqu	fst	1⅛	:462 1:112 1:364 1:501	3↑ Aqueduct H 2.8k	2	1	11	12	12	13	Schuttinger A	127	wb	*.33	96-12	Roamer1273Manister Toi108hdRunes101	Won easing up	3
21Sep17- 4Aqu	fst	1 1/16	:244 :492 1:141 1:443	2↑ Handicap 1018	2	1	15	12	11	13½	Schuttinger A	126	wb	*.50	100-07	Roamer1263½Runes1031½Daddy's Choice104hd	Drew away	4
7Aug17- 4Sar	fst	1	:233 :471 1:133 1:382	3↑ Delaware H 3.5k	3	4	53½	32	31½	3½	Butwell J	127	wb	*1.50	94-10	Old Rosebud133hdCapra104½Roamer1274	Tired	6
1Aug17- 4Sar	my	1¼	:503 1:154 1:412 2:061	3↑ Saratoga H 5.8k	3	1	1½	11	11	1½	Butwell J	122	wb	5.00	89-14	Roamer122½Spur1231Ticket1071	Hard ridden	7
18Jly17- 4Emp	sl	1	:25 :492 1:143 1:401	3↑ Mount Vernon H 2.9k	2	1	11	11	1hd	41½	Schuttinger A	125	wb	*.70	90-16	St. Isidore1111½Daddy's Choice107noWistful101no	Tired when challenged	6
13Jly17- 4Emp	hy	1⅛	:511 1:17 1:432 1:563	3↑ Emp City H 4.8k	4	1	1½	1hd	1hd	44	Schuttinger A	126	wb	*1.70	68-29	Spur1122Borrow124½Daddy's Choice1021½	Tired	4
7Jly17- 4Aqu	fst	1⅛	:471 1:114 1:362 1:492	3↑ Brookdale H 4.4k	8	1	12	1½	1½	2½	Buxton M	126	wb	3.00e	99-11	Boots127½Roamer1262Borrow124¾	Held gamely	8
30Jun17- 4Aqu	fst	1	:241 :464 1:114 1:373	3↑ Queens County H 4.3k	3	4	31	21	21½	21½	Schuttinger A	129	wb	3.50	92-12	Old Rosebud1251½Roamer1291½Chiclet1102	Gamely,no match	7
25Jun17- 4Aqu	fst	1⅛	:47 1:122 1:363 1:492	3↑ Brooklyn H 5.8k	6	4	32½	21	53½	53½	Schuttinger A	128	wb	4.00	99-04	Borrow117noRegret1221Old Rosebud1201	Tired badly	11
18Jun17- 4Jam	fst	1 1/16	:241 :48 1:123 1:452	3↑ Excelsior H 3.4k	4	1	2hd	2hd	2hd	11½	Schuttinger A	123	w	3.00	101-07	Roamer1231½Borrow117hdOld Koenig1124	Drew away	9
2Jun17- 5DoP	gd	1¼	:474 1:121 1:384 2:041	3↑ Kentucky H 14k	5	3	3½	11	3nk	3¾	Schuttinger A	126	wb	4.80	92-13	King Gorin108nkCudgel103½Roamer1262	No mishaps	11
19May17- 5CD	fst	1 1/16	:25 :493 1:13 1:451	3↑ Clark H 2.8k	3	2	2½	21	2½	21	Goose R	128	wb	*.45	95-14	Old Rosebd1171Roamer1288Embroidery1061½	Stumbled start	4
12May17- 3CD	fst	1 1/16	:234 :473 1:123 1:443	4↑ Alw 1000	4	2	2½	2½	11	11½	Schuttinger A	119	wb	4.20	99-06	Roamer1191½Ed Crump1225Old Rosebud1196	Won easing up	4
7Oct16- 4Lrl	fst	1 1/16	:233 :473 1:124 1:432	3↑ Baltimore H 2.8k	6	2	21	31	89¼	812	Byrne G	124	wb	3.15	89-04	Boots1161Spur1181½Stromboli1252	Tired	9
23Sep16- 4HdG	sl	1⅛	:483 1:141 1:392 1:521	3↑ Havre de Grace H 3.8k	5	3	73¾	55½	53½	54½	Davies T	126	wb	4.25	90-15	The Finn1291Spur117.5½Borrow1181	Crowded	8
16Sep16- 4HdG	gd	1 1/16	:241 :49 1:143 1:453	3↑ Chesterbrook H 3.9k	4	4	51¼	42	23	22	Loftus J	126	wb	1.90	97-15	The Finn1252Roamer1262Stromboli1261	Forced wide,gamely	8
4Sep16- 4Bel	fst	1½	2:391	3↑ Municipal H 2.5k	2	1	11	11	1½	2½	Butwell J	124	wb	*.60	64-25	Stromboli123½Roamer124	Gamely,tiring	2
26Aug16- 4Sar	gd	1¾	:55 2:363 3:03	3↑ Sar Cup 3.7k	1	1	32½	21	2hd	22	Butwell J	127	wb	4.50	73-20	Friar Rock1132Roamer1276The Finn126	Saved ground,tired	3
19Aug16- 4Sar	fst	1 3/16	:48 1:132 1:38 1:58	3↑ Merchants & Cits H 2.4k	2	1	11	1hd	22	35	Butwell J	127	wb	*1.20	95-06	The Finn1233Ed Crump1182Roamer127½	Saved ground	5
29Jly16- 4Emp	fst	1	:25 :491 1:133 1:39	3↑ Mount Vernon H 2.6k	5	2	31¼	32½	43½	44½	Butwell J	130	wb	*1.10	94-11	Boots104.52½He Will117½Spur1141½	Rated,no gain	5
22Jly16- 4Emp	sly	1⅛	:502 1:162 1:43 1:56	3↑ Yonkers H 2.3k	1	1	11	11	11	1¾	Butwell J	127	wb	4.00	75-23	Roamer127¾Spur1115Ed Crump1231	Easing up late	4
12Jly16- 4Emp	fst	1⅛	:482 1:13 1:391 1:511	3↑ Emp City H 4.2k	7	5	52½	31	1hd	21	Butwell J	129	wb	*1.40	98-10	ShortGrass1271Roamer129hdSpur1051	Tired when challenged	9
1Jly16- 4Aqu	fst	1	:23 :461 1:104 1:362	3↑ Queens County H 3.4k	5	1	11	11	11	23	Butwell J	129	wb	*1.40	99-09	Short Grass1143Roamer1291½Gainer1083	Gamely	9
24Jun16- 4Aqu	fst	1⅛	:47 1:11 1:372 1:50	3↑ Brooklyn H 4.8k	4	5	43½	42	31	56¾	Butwell J	131	wb	*2.20	96-09	Friar Rock1082Pennant1231½Slumber II111nk	Tired	8
3Jun16- 5DoP	fst	1¼	:481 1:131 1:39 2:043	3↑ Kentucky H 13k	10	5	2hd	11½	1½	2½	Butwell J	132	wb	*3.90	90-11	Ed Crump121½Roamer1321Water Witch1071	Tired	11
20May16- 4Jam	fst	1 1/16	:24 :472 1:123 1:453	3↑ Kings County H 3.4k	10	1	2hd	42	46¼	912	Butwell J	133	wb	*1.40	88-07	Capra98½The Finn1203Boots106½	Tired	10
30Oct15- 4Lrl	fst	1⅛	:472 1:114 1:381 1:50	3↑ National H 3k	3	1	11	12	13	13	Butwell J	132	wb	*1.00	98-09	Roamer1323Stromboli1231½Short Grass1236	Won easing up	4
18Sep15- 4HdG	fst	1⅛	:483 1:133 1:391 1:511	3↑ Havre de Grace H 1.8k	1	1	13	12	12	13	Butwell J	129	wb	*.65	104-09	Roamer1293Slumber II1131½Stromboli1201	Speed in reserve	4
28Aug15- 4Sar	fst	1¾	:491 2:083 2:352 3:014	3↑ Sar Cup 2.4k	2	1	1½	12	15	18	Butwell J	123	wb	*.13	81-14	Roamer1238Virile12410Star Gaze127	Under restraint	4
21Aug15- 4Sar	fst	1 3/16	:49 1:14 1:391 1:59	3↑ Merchants & Cits H 1.9k	3	1	11	11½	11½	1½	Butwell J	129	wb	*1.40	95-11	Roamer129½Borrow1233Stromboli1215	Gamely	8
14Aug15- 4Sar	sl	1⅛	:494 1:153 1:42 1:552	3↑ Champlain H 2.4k	2	3	34½	33½	45	49¾	Butwell J	132	wb	*.75	70-25	Star Jasmine110¾Gainer1145Stromboli1244	Never a threat	6

2Aug15- 4Sar	fst	1¼	:48 1:132 1:392 2:042	3↑ Saratoga H 2.9k	2 1 12 13 15 110	Butwell J	128wb	*3.00	98-11	Roamer12810Saratoga1031StarJsmn103½	Won under restraint	7
24Jly15- 4Bel	fst	1⅛	:473 1:13 1:382 1:513	3↑ Emp City H 3.5k	2 2 2½ 44 56½ 710¼	Butwell J	129wb	*.80	88-18	Gainer1092AddieM.995SamJackson105¾	Close quarters early	7
10Jly15- 4Aqu	fst	1⅛	:473 1:12 1:373 1:503	3↑ Brookdale H 2.5k	1 1 11½ 12 13 15	Butwell J	128wb	*.55	107-10	Roamer1285Stromboli12410Rock View114	In a canter	3
5Jly15- 4Aqu	sly	7f	:242 :482 1:144 1:30	3↑ Carter H 2.4k	2 8 89¾ 710 69½ 612	Butwell J	130wb	*2.50	62-30	Phosphor1161Pomette Bleu1041Leo Skolny1053		8
	Shuffled back at start,not persevered with											
29Jun15- 4Aqu	fst	1	:232 :462 1:132 1:392	3↑ Queens County H 2.8k	6 3 32 31½ 21 1no	Butwell J	127wb	*1.10	93-12	Roamer127noStromboli125½Harmonicon1214	Gamely	6
26Jun15- 4Aqu	fst	1⅛	:48 1:12 1:38 1:503	3↑ Brooklyn H 4.8k	3 1 13 12 2hd 21	Butwell J	125wb	*1.50	106-06	Tartar1031Roamer125hdBorrow1286	Tired in drive	6
29May15- 4DoP	hy	1¼	:493 1:151 1:432 2:102	3↑ Kentucky H 13k	3 1 11 1nk 43 814¼	Butwell J	127wb	*1.65	48-33	Borrow1261½Hodge109½Prince Hermis103no	Tired badly	9
8May15- 4CD	fst	1	:233 :472 1:123 1:39	3↑ Alw 700	4 2 11½ 11½ 11½ 1½	Butwell J	112wb	*.30	92-09	Romr112½ShortGrss108hdPrncHrms104hd	Won under restraint	8
10Oct14- 4Lrl	fst	1⅛	:463 1:113 1:363 1:493	3↑ Washington H 2.5k	3 1 12 12 12 11½	Butwell J	124wb	*1.40	105-02	Roamer1241½Tartar1022Buskin1101½	As rider pleased	6
1Oct14- 4Lrl	fst	1 1/16	:232 :47 1:121 1:433	3↑ Baltimore H 2.7k	7 1 12 11½ 1hd 21½	Butwell J	123wb	*.73	102-04	Stromboli1171½Roamer1235Tartar1041	Tired late	10
19Sep14- 4Bel	fst	1½	3:04	3↑ Autumn WFA .8k	1 1 1 1 1 1	Butwell J	112wb	-	- -	Roamer112	Walked over	1
12Sep14- 4Bel	fst	1¼	:483 1:14 1:393 2:04	3↑ Municipal H 2.7k	2 1 11 12 11½ 11	Butwell J	122wb	*.20	80-12	Roamer1221Addie M.981½Pandean1042	Tiring,ridden out	4
5Sep14- 3Syr	fst	1¼	:472 1:112 1:361 2:02	3↑ State Fair 10k	1 1 11½ 13 14 18	Butwell J	114wb	*.07	- -	Roamer1148Gainer117	In a canter	2
25Aug14- 4Sar	gd	1¼	:503 1:153 1:411 2:064	Huron H 3.2k	3 1 11½ 12 13 14	Butwell J	128wb	*.50	89-15	Roamer1284Punch Bowl1092Gainer1145	In a canter	4
8Aug14- 4Sar	fst	1¼	1:141 1:392 2:04	Travers 3.5k	3 1 11 13 15 110	Butwell J	123wb	*1.10	103-03	Roamer12310Surprising126¾Gainer121no	Cantering	7
22Jly14- 4Emp	fst	1½	:532 2:133 2:401	Midsummer 3.4k	1 1 12 13 14 13	Butwell J	123wb	*.02	69-13	Roamer1233Robert Oliver123	Hard held throughout	2
18Jly14- 4Emp	gd	1⅛	:49 1:14 1:41 1:54	3↑ Emp City H 3.9k	1 1 11 11½ 1½ 31	Butwell J	116wb	*.90	84-15	Buckhorn1201G.M.Mllr104hdRomr1166	Tired when challenged	5
9Jly14- 4Aqu	fst	1¼	:49 1:14 2:053	Brooklyn Derby 2.8k	2 1 11½ 12 14 18	Butwell J	117wb	*.70	119-04	Roamer1178Gainer1205Charlestonin123	Won under restraint	3
1Jly14- 3Aqu	fst	7f	:224 :463 1:12 1:25	3↑ Handicap 580	2 1 11½ 12 12 12½	Butwell J	115wb	*.65	105-07	Roamer1152½Hocnir1028HestrPrynn1003	Won under restraint	7
27Jun14- 4Aqu	fst	7f	:231 :47 1:121 1:244	3↑ Carter H 2.4k	8 1 15 13 12 12	Buxton M	109wb	6.00	106-06	Roamer1092Borrow1293Flying Fairy1173	Won easing up	12
20Jun14- 2Bel	fst	6f-Str	1:13	3↑ Handicap 625	9 1 11 12 13 13	Butwell J	107wb	4.50	78-19	Roamer1073Yankee Notions1021½Hester Prynne100nk	Easily	9
11Jun14- 4Bel	fst	6f-Str	1:121	3↑ Toboggan 3k	9 14 108¾ 1312 1314 1424½	Kederis J	106 w	20.00	57-23	Rock View126nkFiginny1001½Ten Point1283	Never a factor	15
30May14- 4Bel	fst	1	:232 :474 1:133 1:394	Withers 3.4k	4 4 42¾ 2½ 3¾ 38	Davies T	115 w	10.00	80-14	Charlestonian115noGainer1188Roamer1155	Ran well	5
27May14- 3Bel	sly	6f		3↑ Handicap 570	1 1 1½ 14	Turner C	104 w	*1.40	- -	Roamer1044Yankee Notions1142Leo Skolny1076	Easily	6
	No time taken,rainstorm prevented view of horses											
30Oct13- 3Lrl	gd	5½f	:24 :484 1:014 1:081	Handicap 620	5 1 2nk 3nk 32½ 43	Wolfe H	111 w	2.00	93-13	Gotelus124hdBraveCunarder1022WaterLdy96.51	Showed speed	7
17Oct13- 3Lrl	fst	5½f	:233 :472 1:002 1:064	Handicap 625	5 1 55½ 42¾ 42¼ 67½	Musgrave P	114 w	5.00	95-08	Surprising1171Gainer1253Addie M.109hd	Stumbled start	6
23Sep13- 4HdG	fst	5½f	:23 :48 1:003 1:07	Eastern Shore H 1.5k	8 1 54¾ 67½ 64¾ 810	Glass J	121 w	*2.50	82-12	Tranid1022Northerner1021½Uncle Mun1091	Impeded	9
16Sep13- 4HdG	fst	5½f	:223 :472 1:00 1:062	Lafayette H 1.5k	1 3 22 22 21½ 21½	Byrne G	123 w	*3.00	93-11	Gainer1201½Roamer1231Mr.Sniggs1081½	No match for winner	9
27Aug13- 4Sar	sl	6f	:233 :482 1:15	Adirondack H 2.4k	4 1 41½ 56 55½ 52½	Byrne G	118 w	4.00	80-17	Little Nephew125¾Black Broom116¾Spearhead106hd		9
	Shuffled back start											
20Aug13- 1Sar	fst	6f	:234 :473 1:123	2↑ Handicap 630	2 3 21 21 31¼ 21½	Byrne G	105 w	3.50	93-09	Isirose1061½Roamer105noSebago120hd	Gamely	7
15Aug13- 2Sar	fst	5½f	:224 :593 1:063	Handicap 635	9 3 41¼ 41½ 64½ 812	Byrne G	123 w	3.00	84-07	Gracilla1061Uncle Mun110½Flittergold120½	Tired	11
9Aug13- 3Sar	fst	6f	:232 :47 1:13	Sar Spl 6k	10 2 1hd 2hd 1hd 11½	Byrne G	119 w	7.00	93-08	Roamer1191½Gainer1222Black Toney1221	Going away	12
5Aug13- 1Sar	fst	5½f	:23 :471 1:002 1:064	Handicap 615	5 1 21½ 21½ 21½ 21	Byrne G	107 w	6.00	94-13	Little Nephew1201Roamer1071½Surprising1153	No match	8
	Previously owned by Clay Brothers;previously trained by F. Brooks											
15Jly13- 3Bel	fst	5½f-Str	1:07	Clm 2000	5 6 11 12 13 14	McTaggart T	109 w	2.50	85-13	Roamer1094Delft1093Gallop112¾	Much best	8
19Jun13- 3Lat	gd	5½f	:233 :474 1:003 1:07	Alw 670	4 3 55 55½ 56½ 512	Martin E	112 w	*1.70	80-09	Bringhurst1122BootsandSaddle115noMinda1065	Dropped back	6
11Jun13- 2Lat	fst	5f	:233 :482 1:004	Alw 710	1 1 13 14 16 16	Martin E	109 w	*.55	91-07	Roamer1096Candy Box1091½O'Reilly109no	Much best	8
4Jun13- 3DoP	fst	5f	:231 :463 :583	Alw 850	2 3 33 39½ 39½ 39	Callahan J	100 w	21.00	103-00	Old Rosebud1151Little Nephew1188Roamer1005	Best of rest	5
17May13- 2CD	hy	4½f	:234 :48 :54	Alw 600	5 2 23 24 26	Taplin	108 w	5.00	88-06	OldRosebud1156Roamer1085BraveCunarder10512	Second best	5
13May13- 2CD	fst	4½f	:24 :482 :54	©Alw 600	3 1 2nk 22 25	Ganz	109 w	*.35	89-05	The Norman1105Roamer1093Old Ben1085	Tired	5
6May13- 5Lxt	fst	4½f	:233 :48 :543	©Alw 390	4 1 1½ 1hd 2nk	Ganz	111 w	1.90	95-05	Imperatore109nkRoamer1115Bird Man112nk	Tired	4
1May13- 2Lxt	fst	4½f	:241 :49 :552	Md Sp Wt	7 5 11 12 15	Ganz	111.5wb	*.65	91-05	Roamer111.55Destino1121½Tiktok112nk	Easily	11

Roseben

b. g. 1901, by Ben Strome (Bend Or)–Rose Leaf, by Duke of Montrose

Lifetime record: 111 52 25 12 $74,910

Own.– D.C. Johnson
Br.– Mrs T.J. Carson (Ky)
Tr.– F.D. Weir

1Jly09- 2She	fst	7f	:24 :471 1:131 1:26	3↑ Clm	6 1 12 12½ 1½ 22½	Dugan E	105wb	5.00	91-06	Nimbus1112½Roseben1054Casque94½	Quit badly	7
2Jun09- 6Bel	sly	6f	:24 :474 1:13	3↑ Clm	7 6 52 45 33 23	McIntyre J	110wb	*1.80	90-07	Dreamer1083Roseben110hdSirJohnJohnson113½	Belated rally	10
29May09- 3Bel	gd	6½f	:224 :48 1:14 1:201	3↑ Clm 1000	4 3 32 31 11 13	McIntyre J	115wb	1.60	86-10	Roseben1153Black Mate1104McCarter113hd	Won easing up	4
20May09- 3Bel	fst	6f-Str	1:103	3↑ Norwood Selling	6 5 4¾ 42 63 54½	McIntyre J	111wb	*1.80	85-08	Chapultepec118½Dreamer1111½Horace E.111½	Poor effort	8
31Mar09- 4Oak	sl	*6f-FC	1:12	3↑ Clm 1500	6 2 22½ 1nk 1¾ 13	Walsh A	107wb	*.90	84-16	Roseben1073Westbury107noBellwether1111	Easily	9
22Feb09- 4SAP	fst	6f	:23 :46 :59 1:114	3↑ Speed H 6k	6 4 2hd 32 32 22	Walsh A	139 w	4.00	97-03	King James1422Roseben139hdMagazine126½	Resolute finish	10
30Jan09- 4SAP	fst	6f	:224 :463 :582 1:113	3↑ Alhambra H 2.5k	5 5 52½ 43 55 52¼	Goldstein	129wb	10.00	98-05	Jack Atkin138nkDominus Arvi1131Magazine1071	Gamely	11
23Jan09- 6Oak	sly	*6f-FC	1:123	3↑ Handicap 600	4 4 21 15 14 14	Mentry	130wb	*.50	81-19	Roseben1304Rose Queen917Sevenfull935	Flatfooted start	4
16Jan09- 4Oak	sly	6½f	:232 :49 1:151 1:22	3↑ Andrew Selling	4 4 31 2hd 2½ 2hd	Goldstein	119wb	4.60	82-27	BoogerRed100hdRosbn1195Bllwthr1021	Slow start,weak ride	8
9Jan09- 4Oak	hy	7f	:24 :484 1:162 1:29	3↑ Follansbee Hwt H	2 3 24 26 24 57	Lee J	145wb	4.00e	74-25	SmileyCorbett1303GracG.110noLghtWool1362	Failed to stay	9
19Dec08- 6Oak	gd	*6f-FC	1:091	2↑ Handicap 600	3 6 58 57¼ 58¼ 57½	Miller W	140wb	*1.20	90-06	Pajaroita108½Smiley Corbett1123Berry Maid1144	Outrun	8
14Dec08- 4Oak	hy	7f	:23 :481 1:15 1:274	2↑ Alw 700	1 2 2nk 12 2½ 22	McCarthy D	107wb	*.20	85-22	Firestone1062Roseben1074Hanbridge1066	Broke slowly	5
12Dec08- 6Oak	hy	*6f-FC	1:104	2↑ Handicap 600	1 2 12 13 13 13	Miller W	135wb	*.60	90-10	Rosebn1353CollctorJssup1005RoylTourst1153	Won easing up	7
5Dec08- 6Oak	my	*6f-FC	1:103	2↑ Handicap 600	3 5 43¼ 14 16 14	Holmes	128wb	*.55	91-09	Roseben1284Berry Maid1152Collector Jessup1027		5
	Unready for start,won easing up											
26Nov08- 3Oak	sl	*6f-FC	1:103	2↑ Alw 500	4 3 12½ 13 13 14	Holmes	112wb	*.80	91-09	Rosebn1124CollctorJssup11012J.C.Core1075	Won under pull	6
25Sep08- 5Gra	fst	*6f	:221 :472 1:00 1:10	3↑ Clm 3000	5 2 13 13 14 13	Notter	123wb	*.50	92-10	Roseben1233Stargowan100½Saracinesca1018	Never extended	8
15Sep08- 4Gra	fst	*6f	:224 :471 :594 1:093	3↑ Bayshore Selling	3 4 22 22 23 34½	Holmes	123wb	2.00	89-09	Besom1044Westbury108½Roseben1235	Pulled up sore	4
10Sep08- 4She	fst	7f	:24 :473 1:122 1:26	2↑ Flight 5k	5 5 31½ 31 43 59¼	Garner	122wb	*1.60	85-08	BabyWolf1074HalfSovereign1054Arcite110¾	Tired,pulled up	5
5Sep08- 1She	fst	6½f	:22 :47 1:122 1:192	2↑ HiW H 795	6 4 33½ 32½ 13 15	Garner	140wb	*2.50	95-01	Roseben1405Tom McGrath1173De Mund1231	Drew away	16
29Aug08- 3She	fst	6½f	:222 :464 1:11 1:181	3↑ Fall H 1.4k	4 3 813 814 811 916¼	Garner	129wb	*1.00	85-01	Half Sovereign984Dorante1095Westbury1091	Rough trip	10
20Aug08- 3Emp	fst	6f	:222 :46 1:122	3↑ Handicap 675	5 1 1hd 2hd 21 2¾	Garner	128wb	6.00	- -	Nimbus111¾Roseben1282Rialto1036	Not urged	5
6Jly08- 2She	fst	7f	:231 :464 1:12 1:254	3↑ Handicap 720	2 1 11½ 12 21 31¾	Garner	130wb	*3.00	93-05	Peter Quince1121Dreamer118¾Roseben1301½	Tired	9
3Jly08- 5She	fst	6½f(T)	:222 :474 1:121 1:183	3↑ Alw 590	5 4 1hd 2½ 2nk 2hd	Garner	127wb	*.60	106-00	Nimbus106hdRoseben1271Peter Quince1141	Wide,just missed	7
27Jun08- 1She	fst	6½f	:221 :47 1:12 1:19	3↑ HiW H 755	7 5 32 32 32½ 22	Notter	142wb	*1.20	95-05	Westbury1062Roseben142¾De Mund1192	Away slowly	11
25Jun08- 1She	fst	6½f	:231 :491 1:12 1:19	3↑ Alw 580	4 1 1½ 12 12 11½	Notter	137wb	*1.60	97-04	Roseben1371½Bouquet1025Jubilee1128	Never extended	4
22Jun08- 4She	fst	6f-FC	1:12	3↑ Coney Island H 4.5k	8 12 106¼ 105¼ 95¼ 912¼	Garner	140wb	6.00	81-10	Dreamer1121Jack Atkin1353De Mund115hd	Away poorly	13
18Jun08- 4Gra	fst	*6f	:222 :473 :593 1:091	2↑ Handicap 1090	4 8 824 714 711 612	Garner	142wb	*.80	84-08	Rialto1002Pantoufle1071Bat Masterson1041		8
	Caught in barrier,closed gap											
11Jun08- 6Gra	fst	*6f	:221 :472 :594 1:093	2↑ Handicap 1080	4 3 42 42 41 31	Notter	142wb	*.70	93-05	Dreamer110hdBat Masterson971Roseben1423	Held well	6
5Jun08- 1Gra	fst	*6f	:23 :472 :591 1:091	2↑ Handicap 1100	2 1 12 13 13 14	Notter	135wb	*.65	96-05	Roseben1354Pantoufle1094Gold Lady1131	Never extended	7
1Jun08- 1Gra	fst	*6f	:222 :473 1:00 1:10	2↑ Handicap 1120	1 4 22 21½ 2hd 1nk	Notter	130wb	*2.60	92-08	Roseben130nkBerry Maid1092King Cobalt1114	Going away	10

26May08-5Bel	fst	6f	:24^2 :48^1	1:13^2	3↑ Handicap 1070	8	4	$2^{\frac12}$	$2^{1\frac12}$	2^2	2^4	Shaw	132wb	*1.60	87-12	Royal Tourist112^{4}Roseben132$^{\frac12}$Pantoufle114$^{1\frac12}$		8
	Impeded by barrier,held 2nd																	
22May08-3Bel	sly	6½f	:23^3 :48^3 1:14^1	1:21^1	3↑ Claremont H 2.7k	4	2	2^{hd}	2^{hd}	3^2	$3^{5\frac12}$	Shaw	129wb	*2.00	75-24	Priscillian111$^{1\frac12}$King Cobalt102^{4}Roseben129^5	Tired badly	5
20May08-1Bel	sly	6f		1:15	3↑ HiW H 1050	2	1	$1^{1\frac12}$	1^2	1^3	1^6	Shaw	140wb	1.60	83-21	Roseben140^{6}Aletheuo127^{5}King Sol116^3	Cantering	4
16May08-4Bel	gd	6f-Str		1:11^3	3↑ Toboggan H 4.9k	4	9	$10^{4\frac34}$	10^6	$10^{6\frac14}$	$10^{7\frac34}$	Shaw	130wb	5.00	84-06	BerryMaid100^{nk}BabyWolf118^{nk}Restgouch105^2	Never a threat	13
30Apr08-4Jam	fst	6f	:24^2 :48^2	1:12^3	3↑ Paumonok H 2.1k	6	1	$3^{\frac12}$	$3^{1\frac12}$	$6^{5\frac12}$	6^{10}	Shaw	130wb	*1.50	88-10	RedRiver113^{2}Restigouche104$^{\frac12}$Rlto102^2	Quit,not ridden out	6
27Apr08-2Aqu	fst	5f-Str		:59^2	3↑ Alw 890	1	5	$6^{5\frac14}$	5^4	$4^{3\frac12}$	4^3	Shaw	130wb	*1.60	95-01	Berry Maid104^{no}King Cobalt99$^{1\frac12}$Red River118$^{1\frac12}$	Impeded	7
12Sep07-4She	hy	7f	:23^4 :47^2 1:12^4	1:25^3	2↑ Flight 5.8k	5	1	$1^{1\frac12}$	1^3	1^2	1^2	Knapp W	110wb	*1.00	96-15	Roseben110^{2}Far West112^{10}Keator109^8	Easily	5
10Sep07-1She	fst	6f	:24 :47^3	1:12^3	2↑ Alw 1300	1	2	2^3	$1^{\frac12}$	1^1	$1^{\frac34}$	Knapp W	137wb	*.20	97-07	Roseben137$^{\frac34}$Veil113^{6}First Premium123$^{\frac12}$	Lasted	8
3Sep07-1She	my	6f	:24^3 :49	1:14^3	2↑ Alw 1340	6	1	1^2	1^4	1^5	1^3	Knapp W	132wb	*.60	87-21	Roseben132^{3}Firestone110$^{2\frac12}$King Cole115^4	Never extended	8
25Jly07-3Bri	fst	6f	:23 :47	1:12^1	3↑ Handicap 1105	1	2	1^1	$2^{1\frac12}$	$2^{1\frac12}$	$2^{1\frac12}$	Martin J	150wb	*1.00	97-03	Ben Ban92$^{1\frac12}$Roseben150^{1}Red River108^{hd}	Tired,gamely	9
17Jly07-1Bri	fst	6f	:23^2 :47	1:12^1	2↑ Handicap 1330	2	3	$1^{1\frac12}$	1^3	1^3	1^2	Martin J	147wb	*2.20	99-07	Roseben147^{2}Smoker87$^{\frac34}$Dreamer116^{hd}	Never extended	9
10Jly07-1Bri	fst	6f	:23^3 :47^1	1:12	3↑ Handicap 1365	10	3	1^1	$1^{1\frac12}$	$1^{\frac12}$	1^1	Martin J	140wb	4.00	100-02	Roseben140^{1}Suffrage127^{5}Herodotus103^{hd}	Handily	12
6Jly07-1She	fst	6f	:24 :47^4	1:12^4	3↑ HiW H 1290	3	1	$1^{\frac12}$	$1^{\frac12}$	2^{nk}	2^3	Martin J	140wb	*.50	93-07	Dreamer113^{3}Roseben140^{4}Comedienne102^6	Quit	7
3Jly07-1She	fst	6f	:24^1 :48^1	1:13^4	3↑ Alw 1060	1	1	$2^{1\frac12}$	2^2	1^1	1^4	Martin J	130wb	*.20	91-12	Roseben130^{4}Haensel107^{3}Berwick107$^{\frac34}$	Easily	6
24Jun07-4She	fst	1			3↑ Equality 5.5k	6	1	$1^{\frac12}$	1^1	2^{hd}	3^2	Martin J	115wb	*2.00	- -	Frank Gill115$^{1\frac12}$Charles Edward107$^{\frac12}$Roseben115^2	Tired	10
	No time taken due to fog																	
22Jun07-1She	fst	6f	:24^2 :48	1:13	3↑ HiW H 1275	4	5	2^1	$2^{1\frac12}$	2^{nk}	2^2	Martin J	140wb	*.45	93-12	Prince Hamburg120^{2}Roseben140^{10}La Londe94$^{\frac12}$	Away slowly	5
20Jun07-2She	fst	6f	:23^3 :47^4	1:12^4	3↑ Alw 1090	1	1	$1^{1\frac12}$	1^3	1^3	1^1	Martin J	137wb	*1.20	96-07	Roseben137^{1}Prince Hamburg123^{5}Gold Lady105^{10}	Easing up	5
16May07-5Bel	fst	6f-Str		1:12^4	3↑ Crotona H 2.7k	3	6	$6^{3\frac12}$	6^4	$6^{3\frac34}$	$6^{4\frac14}$	Martin J	140wb	*1.20	82-11	Suffrage113^{2}Jack Atkin106$^{1\frac12}$Pantoufle103^{hd}	No gain	11
9May07-3Bel	hy	1	:24^1 :48^2 1:14	1:40^4	3↑ Metropolitan H 13k	1	4	$4^{2\frac12}$	4^1	1^{hd}	$3^{3\frac12}$	Martin J	124wsb	*1.60	79-26	Glorifier119$^{1\frac12}$Okenite99^{2}Roseben124^{hd}	Tired	15
15Apr07-4Aqu	sl	7f	:25 :48^4 1:15	1:28^1	3↑ Carter H 10k	5	15	1^2	1^1	$8^{3\frac14}$	$2^{1\frac12}$	Beckman	135wsb	8.00	87-10	Glorifir119$^{1\frac12}$Rosbn135^{no}DonDgo108$^{1\frac12}$	Bumped,finished fast	16
12Nov06-4Aqu	sly	7f	:25 :49 1:14^3	1:27^2	2↑ Bayview H 2.1k	3	1	$1^{1\frac12}$	1^1	$1^{\frac12}$	1^2	Shaw	146wb	2.20	93-14	Roseben146^{2}Oxford119^{6}Ormonde's Right104^2	Ridden out	5
5Nov06-1Aqu	fst	6f	:24 :48	1:12^4	2↑ Handicap 905	5	1	1^{hd}	$1^{\frac12}$	1^3	$1^{2\frac12}$	Shaw	147wb	*.55	100-05	Roseben147$^{2\frac12}$Zienap95^{6}Gambrinus100^{hd}	Easily	5
31Oct06-4Jam	my	6f	:24 :48^4	1:13^4	2↑ Richmond H 2k	2	2	$1^{\frac34}$	$1^{1\frac12}$	$2^{\frac12}$	$3^{1\frac12}$	Shaw	148wb	*.33	90-15	Oxford121^{no}[D]Jacobite114$^{1\frac12}$Rosebn148^8	Tiring,impeded str	4
	Placed second by disqualification																	
16Oct06-5Bel	fst	7f	:23^4 :46^4 1:10^2	1:22	2↑ Alw 1130	2	1	1^8	1^{10}	1^{20}	1^{20}	Shaw	126wb	*.01	116-00	Roseben126^{20}Beauclare85	Ridden out	2
12Oct06-3Bel	fst	6f-Str		1:12^1	2↑ Manhattan H 3.2k	2	1	1^2	1^3	1^4	1^6	Shaw	147wb	*1.00	93-12	Roseben147^{6}Suffrage111$^{\frac34}$Handzarra112^{10}	Won easing up	5
19Sep06-1Gra	fst	*6f	:22^2 :47^4 1:02	1:10	2↑ Handicap 1145	4	3	1^2	$1^{\frac12}$	1^{hd}	2^2	Lyne	150wb	*.45	91-10	Comedienne109^{2}Roseben150$^{1\frac12}$Wtrgrss107^2	Tired,good effort	5
15Sep06-1She	fst	6f	:24 :47^2	1:12^3	2↑ HiW H 1390	6	1	$1^{\frac12}$	1^1	1^{hd}	$1^{\frac34}$	Lyne	144wb	*.33	99-08	Roseben144$^{\frac34}$Suffrage100^{3}Far West115^1	Never extended	11
13Sep06-4She	gd	7f	:23^3 :46^2 1:13	1:26^1	2↑ Flight 5.9k	5	2	1^3	$1^{2\frac12}$	1^3	1^3	Lyne	122wb	*.33	96-09	Roseben122^{3}Sanfara105^{8}Deutschland110^4	Never extended	5
6Sep06-1She	fst	6f	:23^2 :47	1:12^1	2↑ Alw 1130	5	1	$1^{1\frac12}$	1^4	1^5	1^6	Shaw	137wb	*.33	101-05	Roseben137^{6}Rusk115^{1}Pretension130^{hd}	In a canter	8
1Sep06-3She	fst	6f	:24 :47^3	1:12^2	3↑ Fall H 3.5k	5	2	$1^{\frac12}$	1^2	1^2	1^2	Lyne	132 w	3.50	100-04	Roseben132^{2}Neva Lee107^{1}Ormondale116^{hd}	Never extended	11
5Jly06-5She	fst	6f	:24 :47^3	1:12^4	3↑ Alw 1060	3	2	$2^{\frac34}$	$2^{\frac34}$	1^{hd}	2^{hd}	Lyne	137 w	2.20	98-14	Kiamesha128^{hd}Roseben137$^{\frac12}$Hndzrr113^8	Bore out,just missed	4
28Jun06-1She	fst	6f	:24 :47^1	1:12^2	3↑ Alw 1050	3	5	3^2	3^3	3^4	$3^{4\frac12}$	Lyne	137wb	*.90	95-00	Kiamesha113^{4}Handzarra113$^{\frac12}$Roseben137^{hd}	Bad start	5
25Jun06-2She	fst	6½f	:22^2 :47 1:13	1:19	3↑ Alw 1070	4	3	1^1	$1^{\frac12}$	$1^{\frac12}$	2^4	O'Neill F	137wb	1.80	93-05	Timber112^{4}Roseben137^{2}Handzarra115^2	Disliked going	5
22Jun06-4She	fst	6f	:24 :47^4	1:12^2	3↑ Coney Island H 4k	5	5	4^3	3^4	3^4	3^3	Miller W	143wb	*1.40	97-04	King'sDaughter113^{1}PrinceHmburg124^{2}Rsbn143$^{1\frac12}$	Away badly	8
18Jun06-1Gra	my	*6f	:23^4 :48^4 1:01^4	1:11^3	2↑ Handicap 1355	3	5	$5^{2\frac12}$	$3^{1\frac14}$	3^2	$3^{2\frac12}$	Lyne	149wb	3.50	82-20	Shot Gun130$^{1\frac12}$Bohemia103^{1}Roseben149^2	Rated,belated rally	7
21May06-4Gra	fst	1¼	:48^4 1:13 1:39^2	2:05^3	3↑ Brooklyn H 20k	2	2	$1^{1\frac12}$	1^2	2^3	$7^{7\frac34}$	Lyne	119wb	20.00	90-09	Tokalon108^{no}Dandelion107^{2}ThePicket120^4	Tired after mile	14
19May06-1Bel	fst	7½f	:23^1 :47^1 1:12^4	1:32^1	3↑ Handicap 1080	3	1	1^2	1^2	$1^{1\frac12}$	$1^{\frac12}$	Lyne	133 w	*.60	113-00	Roseben133$^{\frac12}$Tommy Waddell106^{3}Cinna97$^{\frac12}$	Driving	5
17May06-1Bel	fst	6f	:24^3 :48^2	1:13	3↑ HiW H 1125	5	3	3^2	3^1	$4^{1\frac12}$	2^{nk}	Lyne	140wb	*.90	93-11	Guiding Star112^{nk}Roseben140^{2}Samson104^2	Troubled trip	8
10May06-3Bel	gd	1	:24^2 :47 1:13^4	1:39	3↑ Metropolitan H 13k	17	1	$1^{\frac12}$	$1^{\frac12}$	2^{hd}	$5^{4\frac14}$	Lyne	129wb	*3.50	88-12	Grapple106$^{\frac34}$Dandelion108^{hd}Oxford109^3	Gamely,tiring	22
28Apr06-4Jam	fst	1$\frac{1}{16}$	:24^1 :49^2 1:14^3	1:47^1	3↑ Excelsior H 10k	6	1	$1^{1\frac12}$	1^2	$2^{1\frac12}$	$5^{4\frac12}$	Lyne	120wb	*.70	87-07	MerryLark106$^{1\frac12}$Ormonde'sRight111^{1}EugeniaBurch110$^{1\frac12}$	Quit	10
25Apr06-4Aqu	fst	1	:23^1 :48 1:13^4	1:40^1	3↑ Sterling 2.4k	2	1	1^4	1^4	1^6	1^2	Lyne	127wb	*.80	89-09	Roseben127^{2}Ram's Horn126^{6}Phil Finch127^8	Never extended	4
16Apr06-4Aqu	fst	7f	:23^4 :47^4 1:13^2	1:26^2	3↑ Carter H 10k	12	1	1^1	1^3	1^2	1^{hd}	Lyne	129wb	*2.20	98-03	Roseben129^{hd}Southern Cross106^{1}Red Knight108^{no}	Held on	13
13Oct05-6Bel	fst	6f	:23^2 :47^4	1:12^1	2↑ Alw 1050	3	1	1^8	1^{12}	1^{15}	1^{20}	O'Neill F	130wb	*.04	- -	Roseben130^{20}Consideration115^{4}Torchello110	Won easily	3
10Oct05-5Bel	fst	7f	:24^4 :48^2	1:25^1	2↑ Alw 1150	3	1	1^8	1^{10}	1^{10}	1^{10}	O'Neill F	126wb	*.05	- -	Roseben126^{10}Chimney Sweep107^{hd}Monet109	Won easing up	3
6Oct05-3Bel	fst	6f	:24 :47	1:11^3	2↑ Manhattan H 2.5k	2	1	$1^{1\frac12}$	1^1	1^2	1^5	O'Neill F	147wb	*.60	- -	Roseben147^{5}Aeronaut105^{6}Race King104^4	Never extended	5
4Oct05-5Bel	fst	6f	:23^3 :47^3	1:12	2↑ Bronx Highweight H 2.2k	7	1	1^1	1^1	1^2	1^5	O'Neill F	140wb	*1.10	- -	Roseben140^{5}Ancestor90$^{\frac34}$RaceKing103$^{\frac12}$	Never fully extended	9
18Sep05-3Gra	my	*6f	:24^2 :48^3 1:01^4	1:11^1	2↑ Handicap 1210	2	3	2^{nk}	1^{hd}	$1^{1\frac12}$	$1^{1\frac12}$	Lyne	137wb	*1.80	87-17	Roseben137$^{1\frac12}$Schulamite104$^{\frac12}$NnnHodg115^{nk}	Bad start,easily	10
15Sep05-1Gra	fst	*6f	:22^2 :48 1:00	1:09^2	2↑ Handicap 1130	5	1	$1^{\frac12}$	1^2	1^2	1^5	O'Neill F	132wb	2.00	96-10	Roseben132^{5}Lady Amelia122$^{\frac34}$Rapid Water119$^{1\frac12}$	In a canter	6
31Aug05-2She	sl	6f	:25 :49	1:14^1	2↑ Alw 1040	2	1	1^{hd}	2^1	2^3	2^5	O'Neill F	137 w	*.29	86-10	Jocund120^{5}Roseben137^{6}Blucher116	Wide,poor effort	3
26Aug05-3She	sl	6f	:24^4 :49	1:14^1	3↑ Fall H 3.5k	5	1	4^2	3^2	$3^{1\frac12}$	2^1	O'Neill F	129 w	*.90	90-12	PrinceHamburg112^{1}Rosbn129^{hd}LadyAmel123^6	Troubled trip	11
22Aug05-1Sar	fst	6f	:23^4 :48	1:13	2↑ Handicap 935	7	2	1^1	1^1	$1^{\frac12}$	1^{hd}	O'Neill F	140 w	3.60	96-09	Roseben140^{hd}Marjoram104^{6}Right and True108^{hd}	Lasted	12
8Aug05-4Sar	fst	1	:24^4 :48^3 1:13	1:39^2	3↑ Delaware H 2.6k	3	2	2^{hd}	5^3	6^8	$6^{8\frac12}$	Buchanan W	120 w	3.50	83-13	MollyBrant113^{2}DollySpanker108^{no}Cairngorm109^{hd}	Pulled up	7
25Jly05-3Bri	fst	6f	:24^4 :49	1:14^4	3↑ Alw 1070	1	2	1^{hd}	1^{hd}	1^4	$1^{1\frac12}$	Lyne	137 w	*.13	86-10	Roseben137$^{1\frac12}$Israelite110^{1}Robador105^5	Won eased up	7
15Jly05-6Bri	fst	6f	:24^1 :48	1:13	3↑ Handicap 1170	2	1	$1^{\frac12}$	$1^{1\frac12}$	1^2	$1^{1\frac12}$	O'Neill F	140 w	*1.20	95-06	Roseben140$^{1\frac12}$Incantation105$^{1\frac12}$Lady Uncas100$^{\frac12}$	Easily	13
5Jly05-1Bri	fst	6f	:23^1 :47^2	1:12^2	3↑ Alw 1330	2	2	2^2	2^1	2^{hd}	$1^{3\frac12}$	O'Neill F	135 ws	*1.00	98-08	Roseben135$^{3\frac12}$Lady Amelia123^{no}Bad News115^8	Won easing up	8
1Jly05-2She	sl	6f	:24^2 :48^1	1:13	3↑ HiW H 1380	8	3	$2^{1\frac12}$	2^1	2^1	1^1	O'Neill F	140 ws	*1.60	97-08	Roseben140^{1}Druid105^{10}Prince Hamburg110^{hd}	Handily	15
24Jun05-2She	hy	6f	:24 :48^4	1:14^4	3↑ HiW H 1405	4	1	3^2	3^2	$1^{1\frac12}$	1^6	O'Neill F	137 ws	*1.50	88-14	Roseben137^{6}SparklingStar112^{hd}DmondFlush104^5	Wide,easily	8
	Previously trained by C. Oxx																	
16Jun05-4She	fst	6f	:23^4 :47^2	1:12^3	3↑ Coney Island H 3.8k	10	4	2^{hd}	2^1	$2^{1\frac12}$	2^2	O'Neill F	120 ws	4.00	97-05	HamburgBelle124^{2}Roseben120$^{1\frac12}$WildMnt113$^{1\frac12}$	Tired,bore out	13
14Jun05-1Gra	gd	*6f	:22^4 1:00^3	1:10	2↑ Handicap 1350	9	2	$3^{2\frac12}$	3^2	$3^{1\frac14}$	3^3	O'Neill F	123 w	5.00	90-10	Marjoram104^{3}Incantation95^{hd}Roseben123$^{1\frac12}$	Careless ride	9
22May05-1Bel	fst	7f-Str		1:28^2	3↑ HiW H 1130	3	3	$5^{1\frac12}$	3^{nk}	$1^{\frac12}$	1^2	O'Neill F	140 ws	*1.60	- -	Roseben140^{2}Neptunus117$^{\frac12}$Delcanta116^4	Won easing up	8
15May05-4Bel	gd	6½f	:24 :48 1:13^4	1:20^4	3↑ Claremont H 2.4k	3	2	3^1	3^1	3^1	$1^{1\frac12}$	Burns T	115 ws	*2.40e	- -	Roseben115$^{1\frac12}$Race King106^{2}Oxford108^{hd}	Going away	8
8May05-4Bel	gd	6f-Str		1:13	3↑ Crotona H 2.1k	6	2	$2^{\frac12}$	3^{nk}	$3^{\frac12}$	$6^{22\frac14}$	O'Neill F	115 w	5.00	- -	Wild Mint105^{hd}Spring108^{hd}Sparkling Star89^8		10
	Stumbled,bumped badly late str																	
6May05-4Bel	gd	6f-Str		1:13	3↑ Toboggan H 3.2k	1	2	$1^{\frac12}$	1^1	1^{hd}	1no	O'Neill F	112 w	8.00	- -	Roseben112^{no}Sparkling Star87$^{1\frac12}$Pasadena105$^{\frac12}$	Lasted	12
22Apr05-4Aqu	fst	1	:24^3 :48^3 1:14	1:39^1	3↑ Queens County H 2.1k	9	4	$4^{5\frac12}$	4^3	$4^{1\frac12}$	4^7	O'Neill F	122	6.00	87-04	St. Valentine112^{hd}Rapid Water125^{5}Sinister104^2	Tired	10
15Apr05-4Aqu	fst	7f	:24^2 :47^2 1:13	1:26^4	3↑ Carter H 8.1k	3	3	3^2	$6^{3\frac14}$	$2^{\frac12}$	$2^{\frac34}$	Fuller	113 w	10.00	95-08	Ormonde'sRight110$^{\frac34}$Rosbn113^{5}LttlEm105$^{\frac34}$	Getting to winner	18
4Apr05-4Ben	fst	6f	:24^4 :49^3	1:15	3↑ Alw 540	1	1	1^{hd}	2^{hd}	1^{hd}	1^{hd}	Fuller	122 w	1.40	93-12	Roseben122^{hd}Santa Catalina102^{8}Monacodor101	Went wide	3
1Apr05-3Ben	fst	6f	:24 :48^2	1:14	3↑ Alw 565	2	2	$1^{1\frac12}$	$2^{1\frac12}$	$2^{\frac12}$	2^2	Fuller	115 w	*.55	96-11	Santa Catalina92^{2}Roseben115	No mishap	2
27Mar05-1Ben	gd	5½f	:24^2 :49^4 1:04^1	1:10^4	3↑ Handicap 595	2	1	3^1	$2^{1\frac12}$	$1^{\frac12}$	1no	Fuller	128 w	*2.00	83-28	Roseben128^{no}Rockland93^{8}Right and True114^3	Gamely	6
17Feb05-3OP	hy	5½f	:25^2 :50^4	1:11^1	3↑ Alw 600	4	5	2^7	$2^{2\frac12}$	1^2	1^5	Smithson	98 w	*.33	- -	Roseben98^{5}Incense91$^{1\frac12}$Grenade98^{15}	In a canter	5
1Feb05-4Esx	hy	6f	:25 :50½	1:18	3↑ Handicap 600	2	3	$3^{1\frac12}$	$2^{\frac12}$	3^1	$3^{\frac12}$	Hildebrand	130 w	*.60	75-32	Mame Worth120^{hd}Toscan121$^{\frac12}$Roseben130^{25}	Weak ride	5
18Jan05-4Esx	my	6f	:25 :50½	1:18	3↑ Handicap 500	2	2	1^2	1^5	1^{10}	1^{12}	Smithson	117 w	*1.00	76-24	Roseben117^{12}Buttons120^{10}Neversuch98^6	Won eased up	5
24Nov04-4FG	fst	6f	:24^4 :47^2	1:13^3	2↑ Inaugural H 2.2k	4	2	1^{hd}	$1^{\frac12}$	2^{hd}	2^3	Gannon	116 w	12.00	91-08	Floral King118^{3}Roseben116^{hd}Ram's Horn101^1	Tired	13
12Nov04-1Aqu	hy	6f	:25 :50^4	1:16^2	2↑ Handicap 880	6	7	$4^{1\frac12}$	$4^{1\frac12}$	$4^{\frac34}$	4^1	Martin J	114 w	6.00	81-16	Atwood105$^{\frac12}$Ascension119^{hd}Monet112$^{\frac12}$	Good try	11
9Nov04-1Aqu	hy	7f	:25 :49^3 1:15	1:28	2↑ Handicap 785	3	2	2^3	$3^{3\frac12}$	4^2	$3^{\frac12}$	Martin J	122 w	2.20	90-12	Bank105^{hd}Monet118$^{\frac12}$Roseben122^2	Bumped	5
4Nov04-3Aqu	fst	6f	:25 :48^1	1:13^3	Handicap 775	3	1	$1^{\frac12}$	1^1	$1^{\frac12}$	$1^{\frac12}$	Martin J	123 w	1.20	96-03	Roseben123$^{\frac12}$Crown Prince120^{5}Rob Roy112	Gamely	3
31Oct04-1Jam	fst	6f	:23^4 :47^2	1:13	Handicap 855	3	3	2^{hd}	2^{hd}	1^{hd}	1no	O'Neill F	106 w	*1.00	98-04	Roseben106^{no}Crown Prince108^{6}Rapid Water126	Driving	3
24Oct04-3Jam	fst	6f	:24 :47^4	1:13^2	Handicap 885	6	1	1^1	1^1	1^{hd}	2^{nk}	O'Neill F	108 w	4.00	95-06	Crown Prince105^{nk}Roseben108$^{\frac12}$Israelite107^5	Gamely	6
	Previously owned by J.A. Drake;previously trained by E. Wishard																	

11Oct04- 1MP sl 6½f :242 :49 1:16 1:23 3↑ Md Alw 1050 14 4 14 14 14 13 O'Neill F 107 w *1.20e 82-18 Roseben1073Water Pansy108¾Tide1071½ Easily 14
21Sep04- 1Gra gd *6f :241 :483 1:013 1:113 2↑ Handicap 1185 10 12 88¼ 86¾ 88½ 89¼ Sperling 98 w 100.00 76-16 Invincible98½Divination982½Shot Gun125nk Away badly 14
7Jly04- 2Bri my 6f :24 :482 1:144 Alw 1090 4 5 42 48 410 416½ Sperling 98 w *2.20e 69-19 Mineola1061½Jocund1085EtTuBrute10810 Showed brief speed 5
28Apr03- 4Nvl fst 4½f :23¼ :48¾ :56 ©Alw 300 - 11 10 10 10 Meade T 107 8.00e -- Council1038EmperorofIndia1051Paris107hd Never a factor 11

Sarazen

ch. g. 1921, by High Time (Ultimus)–Rush Box, by Box **Lifetime record: 55 27 2 6 $225,000**
Own.– Fair Stable
Br.– M.E. Johnston (Ky)
Tr.– A.B. Gordon

9Jun28- 4Bel fst 1 :24 :474 1:13 1:394 3↑ Alw 1265 2 2 31¼ 42½ 33¼ 33 Pasc'ma A 126 w *1.60 75-23 Ingrid1122Knapsack1121Sarazen126hd Impeded,sulked 4
30May28- 3Bel fst 7f :23 :463 1:12 1:253 3↑ Handicap 2115 3 6 64¼ 53¾ 53¾ 31¾ Fields G 120 w 15.00 80-21 BlackCurl113nkBuddyBauer1111½Sarazen120nk Finished well 10
26May28- 4Bel sly 1 :23 :47 1:133 1:40 3↑ Metropolitan H 10k 4 7 722 713 613 616 Fields G 124 w 20.00 61-25 Nimba1141½ChanceShot1184ScapFlow1251½ Refused to extend 7
21May28- 4Bel hy 6f :231 :48 1:144 3↑ Handicap 1375 4 6 1115 106¼ 85¾ 45¾ Fator L 126 w 8.00 72-28 IndianLovCll107¾Byrd1144GnrlDskn1011 Dropped back start 13
Previously trained by M. Hirsch
17May28- 4Bel fst 6f-WC 1:112 3↑ Toboggan H 10k 8 3 52¼ 62½ 64½ 79¼ Pasc'ma A 126 w 15.00 85-07 Osmand124nkScapa Flow1241½Happy Argo125hd No factor 9
1Aug27- 4Sar hy 7f :233 :472 1:133 1:262 3↑ Handicap 1365 4 7 64¼ 53 54 413½ O'Donell S 127 w 4.00 72-21 Pompey1186Brown Bud1021½Byrd1006 Sulked late 7
4Jly27- 4Aqu fst 7f :23 :461 1:112 1:241 3↑ Carter H 10k 2 5 62¼ 74½ 118 97½ O'Donell S 129 w 7.00e 86-10 Happy Argo119nkBlack Maria1243Macaw124hd No factor 14
2May27- 4Pim fst 1 3/16 :473 1:132 1:39 1:592 3↑ Dixie H 34k 6 9 114 158 1516 1425¼ O'Donell S 127 w 12.35 70-17 Mars124½Display120½Edisto1132 Never a factor 15
27Apr27- 4Jam gd 6f :232 :472 1:13 3↑ Handicap 1320 8 6 41¼ 2hd 21½ 32¼ O'Donell S 130 w 2.20 88-16 Cntnkrous107nkCelidon1172Srzn130hd Fractious before start 8
20Nov26- 5Bow hy 1 :242 :492 1:152 1:43 2↑ G D Bryan Mem H 26k 5 8 85½ 89 86½ 86 O'Donell S 126 w *2.60 81-16 Glister104nkBackbone114½Willie K.94hd Impeded 15
2Nov26- 4Pim fst 6f :23 :464 1:122 2↑ Fall Serial WFA #1 3.9k 3 2 41 41¾ 45 47¾ O'Donell S 130 w 3.05 84-16 Croyden1271½Prince of Wales1271¼Nedana1275 Sulked 6
16Oct26- 5Lrl fst 1 :23 :472 1:123 1:38 2↑ Laurel 14k 10 5 2½ 21 21½ 22 O'Donell S 126 w 9.10 96-11 Croyden107.52Sarazen126hdMars1171 Second best 11
2Oct26- 4Jam fst 1 1/16 :24 :481 1:13 1:44 3↑ Continental H 6.4k 1 3 42 43 34¼ 37 O'Donell S 128 w *1.70 86-11 Catalan1154High Star1063Sarazen1281½ Ran well 7
25Sep26- 5HdG fst 1⅛ :473 1:122 1:38 1:50 3↑ Havre de Grace H 17k 3 2 21½ 21 21 45¼ O'Donell S 127 w 5.35 95-06 Crusader1225Son of John108hdDisplay114nk Tired late 12
4Aug26- 4Sar sl 1 :24 :473 1:13 1:40 3↑ Delaware H 5.6k 8 3 2½ 21½ 4¾ 97½ O'Donell S 130 w 4.00 73-21 Single Foot115noDress Parade1163Rock Man108hd 9
Impeded,quit,not persevered with
30Jly26- 4Sar my 1¼ :49 1:141 1:402 2:082 3↑ Saratoga H 10k 3 3 25 38 511 514 Weiner F 129 w 3.20 53-24 PrincssDoreen1164Blondin1083KingSolomon'sSeal1093 Tired 8
10Jly26- 4Emp fst 1 70 :241 :481 1:13 1:424 3↑ Mount Vernon H 6.4k 5 3 42½ 31½ 1nk 11½ Weiner F 128 w *2.20 99-06 Sarazen1281½Senalado112½Single Foot1121½ Going away 6
5Jly26- 4Aqu fst 7f :231 :464 1:112 1:243 3↑ Carter H 10k 2 7 69 67¼ 67½ 66¾ Weiner F 132 w 4.00 85-15 DHMacaw123DHNedana1191½Extra Dry99.54 Dwelt 7
14Jun26- 4Aqu fst 1⅛ :463 1:122 1:382 1:502 3↑ Brooklyn H 14k 1 1 11 11½ 1nk 66 Weiner F 130 w 5.00 87-10 Single Foot110noPeanuts1114Dangerous108hd Tired 10
31May26- 4Bel gd 1 :232 :463 1:124 1:38 3↑ Metropolitan H 10k 1 2 21½ 2nk 1nk 11 Weiner F 129 w 4.00 87-19 Sarazen1291Senalado115½Rock Star1052 Held on 10
3May26- 5Pim fst 1 3/16 :474 1:132 1:383 2:004 3↑ Dixie H 32k 3 1 11 11 12 1nk Weiner F 128 w *1.80e 88-14 Sarazen128nkSun Pal1051General Thatcher118nk Ridden out 11
28Apr26- 4HdG fst 6f :23 :463 1:122 3↑ Handicap 1500 2 6 57¾ 58¼ 55¼ 55 Weiner F 130 w *.80 88-12 Sun Pal982Postillion94noTamarind92no Worked extra ¼ 6
20Apr26- 5HdG fst 1 70 :242 :492 1:133 1:444 3↑ Handicap 2000 2 2 21 2½ 1nk 1hd Weiner F 128 w *.90 86-17 Sarazen128hdJoy Smoke1182½Edisto111.56 Ridden out 4
21Nov25- 4Bow fst 1 :24 :482 1:133 1:402 2↑ G D Bryan Mem H 18k 14 3 32½ 2nk 1½ 11 Weiner F 126 w *3.35 103-05 Sarazen1261JoySmoke1151½PrincessDoreen117nk Going away 15
10Nov25- 4Pim fst 6f :23 :472 1:13 3↑ Handicap 1500 4 5 89 84¾ 62¼ 41½ Weiner F 129 w *.85 87-17 Bigheart103nkWorthmore132nkLuckyPlay1221 9
Finished fastest of all
6Oct25- 5Lrl fst 6f :231 :47 1:12 3↑ Capital H 6.6k 1 4 67 68½ 58¼ 35 Sande E 132 w *1.05 92-12 WisCounsllor130hdSnglFoot1125Srzn1324 Fractious at post 7
28Sep25- 4Aqu fst 6f :24 :47 1:113 3↑ Arverne H 4.2k 2 2 11 12 13 11½ Sande E 130 w *2.00 96-11 Sarzn1301½ExtraDry98½AnnaMarroneII114no Never threatened 5
5Aug25- 4Sar sl 1 :241 :48 1:124 1:384 3↑ Delaware H 4.3k 4 2 2nk 2nk 43¾ 723½ Sande E 130wb *2.50 63-17 Blind Play106.52Mad Play1332Big Blaze1175 Tired,eased 8
30Jly25- 4Emp fst *6f :214 :463 :591 1:082 3↑ Fleetwing H 5.1k 1 1 2hd 13 13 1½ Sande E 130wb *1.40 97-18 Sarazen130½Lucky Play1154Worthmore126½ 6
Fractious,unseated rider before start,ridden out
2Jly25- 4Aqu fst 7f :223 :462 1:11 1:242 3↑ Carter H 9.6k 1 5 54¾ 53¼ 56 56 Sande E 132 w *.75 87-12 SilvrFox1141Worthmor1282CndyKd105.5no Refused to extend 5
22May25- 4Bel fst 1 :222 :453 1:102 1:37 3↑ Metropolitan H 10k 1 7 74¾ 64¼ 78¾ 713½ Sande E 128 w *1.00 78-10 Sting1142Shuffle Along1124Serenader106hd In close early 8
1May25- 5Pim sl 1 3/16 :482 1:133 1:403 2:02 3↑ Dixie H 33k 6 1 1½ 11 12 11¼ Sande E 130 w *1.25 82-24 Sarazen1301¼Spot Cash115½Joy Smoke1043 Easily 14
21Apr25- 5HdG fst 6f :223 :46 1:11 3↑ Handicap 2000 1 5 42 2hd 11 11½ Sande E 129 w *.65 101-09 Sarazn1291½BigBlaze115¾ThVintner1098 Under light restraint 6
1Nov24- 5Lrl fst 1¼ :462 1:114 1:381 2:041 3↑ Washington H 31k 9 3 32½ 31 3¾ 51½ Babin G 126 w *1.10 87-14 BigBlaze1061¼AgaKhan106noRustic107hd Pressed pace,tired 10
25Oct24- 5Lrl fst 1¼ :45 1:102 1:364 2:022 Maryland H 12k 4 2 23 21 21 1hd Babin G 126 w *.60 98-11 Sarazen126hdRustic1071½Aga Khan1083½ Tiring,held on 6
11Oct24- 5Lat fst 1¼ :451 1:102 1:354 2:004 3↑ Int'l Spl #3 65k 3 2 2nk 11 11 11½ Babin G 120 w 5.70 108-07 Sarazen1201½Epinard126noMad Play120no Easily 8
24Sep24- 4Aqu fst 6f :232 :464 1:112 3↑ Arverne H 4.5k 5 4 31¾ 21 2½ 11 Babin G 128 w *.60 97-11 Sarazen1281Zev130noMiss Star1144 Speed in reserve 5
12Sep24- 4Bel fst 6f :23 :46 1:113 2↑ Fall Highweight H 5.4k 12 9 96¾ 64¼ 43¼ 3½ Maiben J 135 w *1.20 93-12 Worthmore126½ShuffleAlong125hdSarazen1353 Slow to start 12
1Sep24- 5Bel fst 1 :23 :47 1:113 1:362 2↑ Manhattan H 4.4k 1 2 24 21½ 11½ 11 Maiben J 122 w *.45 94-11 Sarazen1221Cherry Pie1085Mad Play116 Won easing up 3
26Aug24- 4Sar my 1 3/16 :50 1:163 1:44 2:024 Huron H 4.9k 5 1 11 11 11 11½ Maiben J 126 w *2.20 64-32 Sarazen1261½Aga Khan1122Big Blaze1154 Easily 5
9Aug24- 4Sar gd 1 :234 :47 1:121 1:373 Saranac H 9.7k 6 4 31 21 3½ 1½ Maiben J 120 w *1.40 93-17 Sarazen120½Klondyke1141½Wise Counsellor1222 Away slowly 7
30Jly24- 4Emp fst *6f :221 :461 :591 1:082 3↑ Fleetwing H 5.4k 2 3 32 11½ 13 13 Maiben J 126 w *.45 97-07 Sarazen1263H.T. Waters110hdMiss Star11810 Won easing up 4
12Jly24- 4Emp fst 1 :24 :473 1:132 1:38 3↑ Mt. Vernon H 8.1k 4 4 11½ 1½ 2½ 68½ McAtee L 120 w *1.20 92-10 Ordinance112.5¾Sunsini1022Mad Play1152 Eased in stretch 7
4Jly24- 4Aqu fst 7f :23 :463 1:11 1:233 3↑ Carter H 8.4k 6 6 11½ 11½ 12 12½ Sande E 118 w *1.60 97-12 Sarazen1182½Brainstorm112½Ordinance1153 Won eased up 7
2May24- 4Jam fst 6f :233 :463 1:12 3↑ Handicap 1335 5 1 31½ 31½ 31½ 21¼ Kummer C 115 w *.33 95-06 Bracadale1071¼Sarazen115½Brainstorm1084 Slow gain 8
5Nov23- 5Pim gd 1 :24 :482 1:132 1:40 2↑ Fall Serial #2 3.5k 2 1 11½ 12 13 11½ Callahan J 100 w *.15 90-13 Sarazen1001½GeneralThatcher1206Blazes126 Never extended 3
26Oct23- 5Lrl gd 6f :233 :48 1:14 Lrl Spl 15k 2 1 14 15 16 12 Sande E 118 w *.30 88-22 Sarazen1182Happy Thoughts115 Won eased up 2
6Oct23- 5Lrl fst 6f :23 :474 1:122 National 7.3k 3 2 21½ 2½ 12 11½ Kummer C 122 w *.10 96-10 Sarazen1221½Moon Star112nkAga Khan1084 Easily 5
2Oct23- 6Lrl fst 1 :24 :481 1:133 1:383 2↑ Alw 2000 1 1 12 12 13 12 Callahan J 91 w *.35 95-10 Sarazen912Flagstaff1094Bigheart115hd As rider pleased 4
20Sep23- 4Aqu fst 6f :232 :463 1:12 Oakdale H 5.2k 3 1 11½ 12 12 12 Kummer C 127 w *.35 95-12 Sarazen1272Sun Pal1083½Elvina113¾ Easily 5
12Sep23- 4Bel fst 7f :23 :461 1:103 1:243 Champagne 6.8k 3 1 11 12 15 12 Sande E 112 w *.30 87-11 Sarazen1122Aga Khan107hdSunspero1191½ Under restraint 9
7Sep23- 3Bel fst 5½f :23 :454 :59 1:05 Alw 1000 3 1 12 13 15 14½ Sande E 118 w *.33 97-06 Sarazen1184½McAuliffe1081½Bonaparte118hd Under restraint 11
Previously owned by P.T. Chinn; previously trained by C.E. Patterson
28Aug23- 6Sar my 5½f :244 :472 1:054 Alw 1000 6 1 11½ 11½ 13 14 Garner M 115 w *.90 94-13 Sarazen1154H.T. Waters1154Bob Tail115hd Never extended 6
19Jly23- 1Haw fst 5f :23 :462 :591 Alw 700 2 1 11½ 14 15 18 Garner M 108 w *1.20e 101-04 Sarazen1088Sanola1131Time Exposure1032 As rider pleased 6
7Jly23- 1Haw hy 5f :25 :502 1:052 Md Sp Wt 6 5 3¾ 11½ 12 12½ Martinez P 115 w *1.40 70-31 Sarazen1152½Brandeis1151½No Lady1152 Under restraint 7

Sir Barton

ch. c. 1916, by Star Shoot (Isinglass)–Lady Sterling, by Hanover — **Lifetime record: 31 13 6 5 $116,857**

Own.– J.K.L. Ross
Br.– Madden & Gooch (Ky)
Tr.– H.G. Bedwell

Date	Cond	Dist	Fractions	Race	Calls	Jockey	Wt	Odds	Speed	Top finishers	Comment	Field
10Nov20- 4Pim	fst	1⅛	:473 1:122 1:382 1:513	2↑ Fall Serial #3 4.2k	3 1 47½ 35 31¼ 21½	Keogh F	126 w	1.65e	95-10	Billy Kelly126 1½Sir Barton126noMad Hatter1265	Led early,good finish	5
5Nov20- 4Pim	fst	1	:234 :473 1:12 1:38	2↑ Fall Serial #2 3.6k	1 1 2nk 24 33½ 31¼	Keogh F	126wb	*.45e	104-04	Mad Hatter1261Billy Kelly126nkSir Barton1265	Led early,fast finish	4
23Oct20- 3Lrl	fst	1	:233 :474 1:14 1:40	2↑ Laurel 11k	5 2 2½ 33 31½ 32	O'Brien WJ	125wb	*.85	86-18	Blazes1201ThePorter1251SirBarton125no	Forced early pace	6
12Oct20- 4Knw	fst	1¼	:462 1:114 1:372 2:03	3↑ Ken Park Gold Cup 75k	1 2 22 25 26 27	Keogh F	126wb	5.55	125-03	Man o' War1207Sir Barton126	Unable to gain	2
28Aug20- 4Sar	fst	1 3/16	:472 1:123 1:362 1:553	3↑ Merchants & Cits H 6.7k	2 1 1¾ 11 1hd 1no	Sande E	133wb	*.80	102-03	Sir Barton133noGnome1153Jack Stuart109	Saved ground	3
11Aug20- 5FE	sl	1¼	:473 1:122 1:383 2:06	3↑ Dominion H 11k	3 1 1hd 11 12 11½	Sande E	134wb	*.25	84-18	Sir Barton1341½Bondage1173The Porter1244	Mild hand ride	4
2Aug20- 4Sar	fst	1¼	:474 1:11 1:36 2:014	3↑ Saratoga H 6.7k	2 1 1hd 11½ 12½ 12	Sande E	129wb	2.60	102-06	SirBarton1292Extrmntor1263Wldr1153	Drew clear,easing up	5
4May20- 5Pim	fst	1	:243 :492 1:143 1:404	4↑ Rennert H 2.5k	2 2 2nk 2hd 1½ 11	Sande E	132wb	*.60	91-15	Sir Barton1321Foreground1135Bondage103.56	All out	5
30Apr20- 4HdG	fst	1 1/16	:234 :48 1:122 1:452	3↑ Philadelphia H 5.4k	9 3 42 42½ 43¼ 41½	Kummer C	132wb	*.55e	96-13	CrystlFord100nkStrMstr127nkBllyKlly1261	Finished gamely	10
27Apr20- 5HdG	my	1 1/16	:25 :501 1:153 1:49	3↑ Marathon H 2k	3 2 23 24 33 34	Sande E	135wb	*.30	76-26	Wildair110noBolster1064Sir Barton135	Wide,tired	3
24Apr20- 3HdG	fst	6f	:231 :474 1:131	3↑ Handicap 1845	2 4 11 12½ 11 11½	Kummer C	133wb	*.65e	90-11	SirBarton1331½Mlkmd1222Tcklsh1023	Slight restraint late	7
19Apr20- 5HdG	gd	6f	:234 :472 1:133	3↑ Belair H 2.7k	4 1 2½ 2nk 3nk 42½	Kummer C	133wb	*.25e	85-21	Billy Kelly1321¼War Mask107nkTicklish1031	Speed,tired	6
11Nov19- 4Pim	sly	1⅛	:493 1:143 1:42 1:563	2↑ Fall Serial #3 4k	3 2 1½ 12 13 13	Kummer C	120wb	*.30e	72-28	Sir Barton1203Billy Kelly1204Lucullite126	Easily	3
7Nov19- 4Pim	fst	1	:24 :482 1:142 1:40	2↑ Fall Serial #2 3.1k	2 1 1nk 2hd 1½ 12	Kummer C	120wb	2.60e	95-15	SirBarton1202ThePorter1265BillyKelly120nk	Won easing up	4
5Nov19- 4Pim	sl	1¼	:503 1:154 1:424 2:091	Autumn H 5.4k	5 4 43½ 31¼ 36 312	Loftus J	132wb	*.45e	69-26	Mad Hatter1114Bridesman1078Sir Barton13212	Tired,eased	5
4Oct19- 4Lrl	fst	1¼	:463 1:12 1:373 2:022	Maryland H 11k	6 4 51¾ 31 2½ 12	Loftus J	133wb	*1.25	98-08	SrBrtn1332MdHttr1061½Audcous118½	Forced wide,going away	6
27Sep19- 5HdG	fst	1⅛	:471 1:122 1:373 1:50	3↑ Havre de Grace H 10k	8 1 13 1½ 2½ 3½	Metcalf J	124wb	*.75e	105-05	Cudgel129½Exterminator126noSirBrton1242	Held resolutely	8
24Sep19- 4HdG	hy	1	:242 :49 1:151 1:422	3↑ Alw 2708	3 2 2hd 24 23 25	Sande E	110wb	*.60	- -	ThePorter1145SirBarton1103WarMask1008	Gamely,no match	5
13Sep19- 5HdG	gd	1 1/16	:242 :492 1:15 1:462	Potomac H 10k	5 1 11 13 11 11½	Nolan T	132wb	*.15e	93-10	SirBarton1321½BillyKelly125hdMlkmd117nk	Outran the rest	5
11Sep19- 3HdG	my	6f	:233 :482 1:14	3↑ Alw 1115	1 5 12 11 2nk 21	Troxler R	120wb	*.10e	87-25	Billy Kelly1201Sir Barton120hdMidnight Sun1052	Tired	7
10Jly19- 4Aqu	sly	1⅛	:481 1:132 1:39 1:523	Dwyer 5.8k	3 1 11½ 11 1½ 23	Loftus J	127wb	*.80	81-21	Purchase1183Sir Barton12715Crystal Ford109	Tired	3
11Jun19- 4Bel	fst	1⅜	2:172	Belmont 14k	1 2 23 21 13 15	Loftus J	126wb	*.35	102-05	Sir Barton1265Sweep On1268Natural Bridge126	Fast start, eased up late	3
24May19- 4Bel	gd	1	:24 :48 1:13 1:384	Withers 9k	2 1 21½ 22 11 12½	Loftus J	118wb	*.35	89-12	SirBrton1182½Etrnl1188PstorlSwn118½	Rated,eased up late	6
14May19- 4Pim	fst	1⅛	:471 1:13 1:391 1:53	Preakness 30k	8 1 11 12 16 14	Loftus J	126wb	*1.40e	90-11	Sir Barton1264Eternal1263Sweep On1262	eased up at finish	12
10May19- 5CD	hy	1¼	:482 1:14 1:414 2:094	Ky Derby 24k	1 1 1½ 12 1½ 15	Loftus J	112wb	2.60e	68-28	SirBarton112.55BillyKelly1191UnderFire1221	Rated,easily	12
14Sep18- 3Bel	fst	6f-Str	1:124	Futurity 29k	13 6 47½ 31 21½ 22½	Sande E	117wb	15.00	76-19	Dunboyne1272½Sir Barton117½Purchase1192	Held second	15
31Aug18- 3Sar	hy	6f	:232 :481 1:133	Hopeful 35k	6 13 15 17 17 16	Sande E	115 w	12.00	- -	Eternal1153Daydue1158War Marvel115hd	Never a factor. Beaten lengths unavailable;Previously owned by J.E. Madden;previously trained by W.S. Walker	20
14Aug18- 4Sar	sly	6f	:232 :484 1:143	Sanford Mem 4.9k	7 7 711 710 710 719	Collins A	112wb	25.00	63-25	BillyKelly1308Liond'Or1155ColonelLvngston1222	No factor	8
3Aug18- 3Sar	fst	6f	:23 :471 1:122	U S Hotel 11k	11 13 1111 98½ 108¾ 916	Collins A	112 w	25.00	77-02	Billy Kelly1271½Dunboyne1301½Terentia1241½	No factor	14
1Aug18- 3Sar	fst	5½f	:222 :464 :583 1:053	Flash 5.1k	9 11 1019 1116 118½ 915½	Collins A	107 w	8.00	84-02	BillyKelly1195LadyRosebud113½StarRealm1101½	Slow start	15
6Jly18- 3Aqu	fst	6f	:233 :473 1:124	Tremont 6.8k	7 8 74½ 76 77 56	Collins A	112 w	8.00	85-10	Lord Brighton1251Sweep On1153War Pennant1121	Greenly	9

Sweep

br. c. 1907, by Ben Brush (Bramble)–Pink Domino, by Domino — **Lifetime record: 13 9 2 2 $63,948**

Own.– J.R. Keene
Br.– James R. Keene (Ky)
Tr.– J. Rowe

Date	Cond	Dist	Fractions	Race	Calls	Jockey	Wt	Odds	Speed	Top finishers	Comment	Field
4Jly10- 4She	fst	1⅝	:501 1:47 2:27 2:53	Lawrence Realization	3 1 110 115 12 15	Notter	126 w	*.01e	60-18	Sweep1265Suffragist1165Hindoo Star116	eased up	3
14Jun10- 4Gra	gd	1¼	:461 1:14 1:402 2:07	Brooklyn Derby 3k	4 2 21½ 41½ 33½ 34	Powers V	126 w	*.70	78-12	Dalmatian1221PrinceImperial1223Swep126hd	Failed to stay	4
8Jun10- 4Gra	fst	1	:242 :483 1:134 1:391	Carlton 2.5k	6 1 12 11½ 12 1¾	Powers V	126 w	*.90	98-10	Sweep126¾ThTurk1265Dlmtn1224	Easily withstood challenge	6
30May10- 4Bel	fst	1⅜	:51 1:16 1:41 2:22	Belmont	1 1 14 15 15 16	Butwell	126 w	*.10	90-10	Sweep1266Duke of Ormonde126	Never extended	2
14May10- 2Bel	fst	7f	:241 :483 1:132 1:261	Alw	4 2 21 21½ 1½ 12	Butwell	121 w	*.17	79-23	Sweep1212KngOlympn1162Sndrian11510	Carried out in stretch	5
30Aug09- 4She	fst	6f-FC	1:114	Futurity	12 2 32½ 31 11½ 16	Butwell	126 w	*.90e	94-08	Sweep1266Candleberry117½Grasmere1221½	Impeded,drew off when clear	13
14Aug09- 3Sar	fst	6f	:233 :472 1:131	Hopeful	9 5 53¼ 42½ 31 21½	Butwell	130 w	*1.30e	91-08	RockyO'Brn1221½Sweep130¾Barleythpe115½	Slow start	9
12Aug09- 1Sar	fst	6f	:233 :472 1:124	Handicap	7 5 2½ 1½ 11 1hd	Butwell	120 w	*1.50	95-07	Sweep120hdLouiseS.1072Fauntleroy109¾	Away badly,impeded	12
7Aug09- 3Sar	gd	6f	:25 :49 1:154	Sar Spl	1 3 33½ 34 32 23	Scoville	122 w	*.90	77-21	Waldo1223Sweep122hdHerkmr122	Slow start,just up for 2nd	3
3Jly09- 3She	fst	6f-FC	1:132	Great Trial 2.5k	3 1 1hd 2½ 32 36	Scoville	130 w	*.45	80-14	Dalmatian122hdLovetie1226Sweep1302	Set pace,tired	6
31May09- 3Bel	fst	5½f-Str	1:081	Natl Stallion	5 2 12 13 15 18	Burns G	122 w	*.90	79-21	Sweep1228Newmarket122½Big Stick122½	Won easing up	5
29May09- 1Bel	gd	5f-Str	1:012	Alw	1 1 11 12 14 15	Scoville	119 w	*.33	83-20	Sweep1195Medallion1221Perry Johnson1142	Never extended	9
20May09- 1Bel	fst	5f-Str	:584	©Md Sp Wt	5 5 1½ 1hd 12 18	Butwell	110 w	*1.10	96-08	Sweep1108Beau Nash1104Firebox111hd	Easily	7

Sysonby

b. c. 1902, by Melton (Master Kildaire)–Optime, by Orme — **Lifetime record: 15 14 0 1 $184,438**

Own.– J.R. Keene
Br.– Marcus Daly (Ky)
Tr.– J. Rowe

Date	Cond	Dist	Fractions	Race	Calls	Jockey	Wt	Odds	Speed	Top finishers	Comment	Field
9Sep05- 4She	fst	2¼	:491 2:341 2:594 3:54	3↑ Annual Champion 25k	3 1 12 12 14 14	Nicol	115 w	*.17	98-08	Sysonby1154Oiseau10825Broomstick119	With ease	3
2Sep05- 4She	gd	1½	:51 1:183 2:092 2:35	3↑ Century 20k	1 1 12 13 13 12	Nicol	115 w	*.05	81-12	Sysnby1152Broomstick1261½EurgeniaBurch123no	Very easily	4
12Aug05- 4Sar	gd	1¼	:482 1:132 1:394 2:07	3↑ Great Republic 50k	5 2 1½ 13 15 13	Nicol	119 w	*.45	90-12	Sysonby1193Oiseau1161Broomstick12620	Away slowly	5
29Jly05- 4Bri	fst	1½	:493 1:154 2:063 2:331	Brighton Derby 15k	3 1 11½ 13 13 15	Nicol	126 w	*.25	95-06	Sysonby1265Agile12630Pasadena118	Easing up	3
20Jly05- 4Bri	fst	1¼	:491 1:15 1:411 2:062	Iroquois 7.5k	1 1 11½ 11½ 13 11½	Martin J	126 w	*.03	82-08	Sysonby1261½Migraine11615Pasadena119	Easily	3
4Jly05- 4She	fst	1⅝	:474 1:394 2:06 2:47	Lawrence Realizatn 20k	4 1 12 12½ 15 15	Nicol	126 w	*.40	91-06	Sysonby1265Tanya1213Migraine1166	Easing up	4
1Jly05- 4She	sl	1¼	:49 1:141 1:40 2:07	3↑ Commonwealth H 15k	1 1 12 12 13 14	Nicol	111 w	*1.00	88-08	Sysonby1114Proper1143Mabel Richardson958	Kicked at post	6
17Jun05- 4She	fst	1¼	:483 1:133 1:392 2:05	Tidal 20k	3 1 14 14 13 15	Nicol	126 w	*.90	98-08	Sysonby1265Agile1264Cairngorm12612	Easily	4
4May05- 4Bel	fst	1	:253 :49 1:413	3↑ Metropolitan H 12k	12 1 11½ 11½ 11½ 15ᵈ	Shaw	107 w	*2.00	- -	[DH]Sysonby107[DH]RaceKing975ColonialGirl1114	Hand ridden	12
19Sep04- 3Gra	fst	*6f	:231 :48 1:093	Jr Champion 10k	3 2 14 11 15 13	Redfern	127 w	*.33e	95-06	Sysonby1273Wild Mint1171Cairngorm110hd	Easing up	5
27Aug04- 4She	fst	6f-FC	1:114	Futurity 48k	16 8 12 1hd 21½ 35	Redfern	127 w	*.65e	76-17	Artful1145Tradition127hdSysonby1273	Broke sideways,slow into stride	16
6Aug04- 3Sar	fst	5½f	:223 :471 1:00 1:07	Sar Spl 10k	1 2 13 15 15 16	Redfern	122 w	*.05	95-06	Sysonby1226Hot Shot1224Britisher122	Easily	3
1Aug04- 3Sar	fst	5½f	:233 :474 1:001 1:064	Flash 6k	4 1 13 15 15 16	Redfern	125 w	*.40e	96-05	Sysonby1256Augur1192Glorifier1255	Easing up	4
16Jly04- 4Bri	fst	6f	:24 :481 1:13	Brighton Junior 15k	4 7 2hd 11½ 13 14	Martin J	112 w	*.80e	95-03	Sysnby1124Jonquil107½Britisher1123	Away last,under a pull	7
14Jly04- 6Bri	fst	5½f	:232 :48 1:004 1:074	Md Sp Wt	6 1 11½ 12 13 16	Martin J	107 w	*.60	94-12	Sysonby1076Linda Lee104noGotowin1041½	Under restraint	11

Whisk Broom II

ch. c. 1907, by Broomstick (Ben Brush)–Audience, by Sir Dixon — Lifetime record: 26 10 7 1 $38,545

Own.– H.P. Whitney
Br.– Clarence H. Mackay (Ky)
Tr.– James Rowe

Date/Track	Cond./Dist.	Fractions/Time	Race	Running line	Fin	Jockey	Wt	Odds	Figs	Top finishers	Comment	Starters
28Jun13- 4Bel	fst 1¼	:471 1:12 1:364 2:00	3↑ Suburban H 3.5k	4 2 23 1hd 1nk	1½	Notter	139 w	*.40	121-00	Whisk Broom II139½Lahore1125Meridian1193	Fully extended	6
21Jun13- 4Bel	fst 1¼	:482 1:131 1:39 2:032	3↑ Brooklyn H 3.6k	6 1 11½ 1½ 12	11½	Notter	130 w	*.50	104-06	Whisk Broom II1301½G.M. Miller1061½Sam Jackson108½		7
	Loafed in stretch											
30May13- 4Bel	fst 1	1:39	3↑ Metropolitan H 4k	1 11 10 45½ 12	11½	Notter	126	*1.60	92-08	Whisk Broom II1261½G.M. Miller1003Meridian120½		12
	Previously trained by Andrew Jackson Joyner											
30Oct12♦ Newmarket(GB)	gd 1⅛Ⓣ Str	1:554	3↑ Cambridgeshire H Hcp5800		7	Maher D	130	33.00		Adam Bede110½La Boheme II1071Drinmore100		20
16Oct12♦ Newmarket(GB)	gd 1Ⓣ Str	1:402	3↑ Select Stakes Stk1340		2no	Maher D	132	*.65		Long Set132noWhisk Broom II1326The Story132		4
3Oct12♦ Newmarket(GB)	gd 5fⓉ Str		2↑ Snailwell Stakes Alw800		1	Maher D	138	-		Whisk Broom II138	Walkover.Time not taken	1
19Jun12♦ Ascot(GB)	gd *7½fⓉ Str	1:413	3↑ Royal Hunt Cup H Hcp10700		6	Maher D	133	10.00		Eton Boy1083Long Set1301½Matelot97		28
28May12♦ Hurst Park(GB)	gd 7fⓉ Str		3↑ Victoria Cup H Hcp5200		11½	Maher D	128	*2.50		Whisk Broom II1281½Prince San1043Eton Boy111	Time not taken	14
11May12♦ Kempton(GB)	hd 1¼Ⓣ RH	2:054	3↑ Great Jubilee H Hcp12000		24	Maher D	125	7.50		Bachelor's Hope1004Whisk Broom II1256Mustapha121		12
8Sep11♦ Derby(GB)	gd 1Ⓣ Str		3↑ Peril of the Peak H Hcp4000		1nk	Martin JH	126	4.50		Whisk Broom II126nkSunspot1221½Mustapha122	Time not taken	12
14Jly11♦ Sandown(GB)	gd 1¼Ⓣ RH	2:09	3↑ Eclipse Stakes Stk40000		4	Martin JH	134	9.00		Swynford1404Lemberg1404Pietri125	Started slowly	7
28Jun11♦ Newmarket(GB)	gd 1Ⓣ Str	1:41	3↑ Duke of Cambridge H Hcp4000		2hd	Martin JH	126	7.00		Bannockburn103hdWhisk Broom II126½Sandal96		13
10Jun11♦ Manchester(GB)	gd 6fⓉ Str	1:111	3↑ Salford Borough H Hcp4000		11½	Martin JH	123	14.25		Whisk Broom II1231½Great Surprise994Spinner86		8
29Apr11♦ Hurst Park(GB)	gd 7fⓉ Str	1:302	3↑ Victoria Cup H Hcp5000		5	Martin JH	117	4.50		Spanish Prince1124Orphah1012Golden Rod119		9
26Oct10♦ Newmarket(GB)	gd 1⅛Ⓣ Str	1:562	3↑ Cambridgeshire H Hcp6300		4	Martin JH	110	*3.00		Christmas Daisy1141½Mustapha118¾Halcyon109		21
12Oct10♦ Newmarket(GB)	gd 1Ⓣ Str	1:41	3↑ Select Stakes Stk1300		14	Martin JH	124	*.25		Whisk Broom II1244Dean Swift131St Crispin109		3
21Jly10♦ Aintree(GB)	gd 1¼Ⓣ LH	2:073	Knowsley Dinner Stakes Stk4000		2hd	Martin JH	126	1.60		Willonyx122hdWhisk Broom II1261½Merry Task126		4
17Jun10♦ Ascot(GB)	gd 1½Ⓣ RH		3↑ Hardwicke Stakes Stk15200		6	Martin JH	117	*2.25		Swynford105¾Marajax1102Sanctuary112	Time not taken	7
14Jun10♦ Ascot(GB)	gd *7½fⓉ Str	1:42	3↑ Trial Stakes Alw2500		12	Martin JH	106	*.30		Whisk Broom II1062Dean Swift1263Yellow Slave111		8
27Apr10♦ Newmarket(GB)	gd 1Ⓣ Str	1:402	2000 Guineas Stakes Stk27200		32	Martin JH	126	14.25		Neil Gow126noLemberg1262Whisk Broom II126		13
14Apr10♦ Newmarket(GB)	gd 1Ⓣ Str	1:44	Craven Stakes Stk2180		23	Martin JH	129	6.00		Neil Gow1323Whisk Broom II129nkTressady132		6
28Oct09♦ Newmarket(GB)	hy 7fⓉ Str	1:314	Dewhurst Plate Stk6500		25	Martin JH	125	2.75		Lemberg1315Whisk Broom II125		2
15Oct09♦ Newmarket(GB)	gd 6fⓉ Str	1:144	Middle Park Plate Stk13300		2nk	Martin JH	126	3.50		Lemberg129nkWhisk Broom II126¾Admiral Hawke129		8
7Sep09♦ Doncaster(GB)	sf *5½fⓉ Str	1:094	Champagne Stakes Stk6920		4	Martin JH	126	7.00		Neil Gow1261½Admiral Hawke1261Lemberg126		4
24Aug09♦ York(GB)	sf 5fⓉ Str	1:024	Prince of Wales Plate Alw4000		12	Martin JH	119	3.00		Whisk Broom II1192Galatine1242Woolacombe119		10
2Aug09♦ Sandown(GB)	gd 5fⓉ Str	1:054	Holiday Stakes Alw1600		4	Martin JH	115	8.00		MountFelix116¾BlueBlazes1124Unnamed filly byCyllene123		7

Zev

br. c. 1920, by The Finn (Ogden)–Miss Kearney, by Planudes — Lifetime record: 43 23 8 5 $313,639

Own.– Rancocas Stable
Br.– J.E. Madden (Ky)
Tr.– S.C. Hildreth

Date/Track	Cond./Dist.	Fractions/Time	Race	Running line	Fin	Jockey	Wt	Odds	Figs	Top finishers	Comment	Starters
8Nov24- 4Pim	fst 1	:23 :472 1:123 1:392	2↑ Fall Serial #2 4.3k	4 3 36½ 33 33¼	34	Fator L	126wb	*1.10	87-14	Sun Flag1203Master Charlie1001Zev126nk	Rated,tired	4
7Nov24- 3Pim	fst 6f	:222 :453 1:111	2↑ Alw 2000	3 5 52½ 41¼ 1½	4nk	Fator L	125wb	*.65	98-10	Swinging90noMainmast115nkShuffle Along125no	Wide,tired	6
4Nov24- 4Pim	fst 6f	:223 :462 1:12	2↑ Fall Serial #1 3.8k	4 1 23 21½ 2½	1½	Fator L	130wb	*.35	94-12	Zev130½Goshawk1304½Lucky Play127½	Drew away	4
18Oct24- 4Lat	fst 1	:233 :472 1:112 1:362	3↑ Handicap 1800	1 3 33 34½ 31¾	1nk	Fator L	129wb	*.55	101-08	Zv129nkPostllon981½PrncssDorn115	Appeared beaten,just up	3
13Oct24- 5Lat	fst 6f	:231 :454 1:101	3↑ Alw 1800	1 3 21 1nk 11	12	Fator L	117wb	*35	98-10	Zev1172Baffling1176Best Pal117no	Easily	4
11Oct24- 3Lat	fst 6f	:231 :462 1:104	3↑ Alw 1615	6 2 11½ 11 12	12	Fator L	110wb	1.30	95-07	Zev1102Pegasus115½AliceB.Gown1091½	Won under restraint	6
10Oct24- 5Lat	fst 6f	:23 :461 1:111	3↑ Alw 1660	6 3 1hd 1½ 11	11	Fator L	108wb	*.70	93-13	Zev1081SnooksieBradly101hdRightonTime1108	Finished well	7
4Oct24- 4Jam	fst 1⅛	:473 1:123 1:373 1:493	3↑ Continental H 7.1k	5 1 1hd 1hd 33½	34¼	Kummer C	127wb	*.60e	98-07	MadPlay1154PriscillRuly106nkZv127nk	Tired,came on again	6
1Oct24- 4Jam	sl 1 1/16	:242 :472 1:123 1:444	3↑ Interborough H 5.3k	1 1 1½ 1nk 11	22	Fator L	130wb	*1.00e	89-15	Big Blaze1082Zev130¾Stanwix1023	Wide,tired under impost	5
27Sep24- 4Aqu	fst 1	:23 :454 1:103 1:362	3↑ Int'l Spl #2 35k	4 3 45¼ 44½ 45¼	43½	Fator L	126 w	5.00	94-09	Ladkin119noEpinard1261½Wise Counsellor1192	Outrun	6
24Sep24- 4Aqu	fst 6f	:232 :464 1:112	3↑ Arverne H 4.5k	1 1 43¼ 43½ 43	21	Fator L	130 w	8.00	96-11	Sarazen1281Zev130noMiss Star1144	Finished fast	5
8Sep24- 3Bel	fst 6f	:23 :461 1:122	2↑ Handicap 1420	8 9 911 97¼ 913	913¾	Fator L	130wb	*.80e	76-15	[D]Shuffle Along1141¼Rival1121½Dinna Care1172		9
	Unprepared for start,left,not persevered with											
1Sep24- 4Bel	fst 6f	:23 :46 1:114	3↑ Int'l Spl #1 36k	8 6 42¾ 2nk 2hd	56¼	Fator L	130wb	4.00	87-11	WiseCounsellor125¾Epnrd1303Ladkin1251	Tired final furlong	9
14Jun24- 4Aqu	fst 1⅛	:471 1:123 1:373 1:504	3↑ Brooklyn H 9.9k	5 2 2½ 2½ 2½	73¾	Sande E	130wb	*1.80e	87-07	Hephaistos106½Sunsini1021[D]Dunlin111hd	Impeded,tired	12
10May24- 4Jam	sl 1 1/16	:24 :474 1:13 1:46	3↑ Excelsior H 7.3k	1 3 21½ 32½ 3¾	31	Fator L	133wb	*.50e	84-17	Rialto115hdSunsini1021Zev1333	Wide,tired	6
3May24- 4Jam	fst 1 1/16	:234 :48 1:123 1:44	3↑ Kings County H 6.7k	3 1 11 11 12	12	Sande E	130wb	*.17e	95-08	Zev1302Mad Play107½Sunsini10210	Easily	5
29Apr24- 4Jam	fst 6f	:23 :47 1:113	3↑ Paumonok H 5.8k	1 1 21 22 22	23	Sande E	130wb	*.45e	95-07	St. James1123Zev1302½Dunlin1196	Close quarters early	8
17Nov23- 6CD	fst 1¼	:50 1:152 1:411 2:063	©Match Race 30k	2 2 21½ 21 11½	1no	Sande E	126wb	*.40	83-13	Zev126noIn Memoriam126	Lasted	2
8Nov23- 3Pim	gd 1⅛	:492 1:15 1:404 1:533	2↑ Fall Serial #3 3.9k	3 2 2nk 12 12	13	Sande E	120wb	*.15	87-15	Zev1203Homestretch12010Tryster126	Easily	3
3Nov23- 5Lat	fst 1¾	:491 2:081 2:344 3:004	Lat Championship 61k	2 1 11½ 12 21½	26	Sande E	126wb	*.40	68-18	In Memoriam1266Zev12610My Own126	Tired final ½	4
31Oct23- 4Emp	sl 1	:243 :473 1:132 1:403	2↑ Aut Championship 11k	3 2 31 11 12	14	Sande E	120wb	*.07e	88-11	Zev1204Bracadale101.515Tryster126	Speed in reserve	4

Date/Track	Cond/Dist	Fractions	Race (value)	Running line (PP St ¼ ½ Str Fin)	Jockey	Wt	Odds	SR	Top finishers	Comment
20Oct23- 4Bel	sly 1½	:50² 1:15 2:07³ 2:35²	International Race 105k	1 1 1^1 $1^{1\frac12}$ 1^3 1^5	Sande E	126wb	*.80	67-19	Zev126^5Papyrus126	Ridden out 2
8Sep23- 4Bel	fst 1⅝	:47 1:37² 2:03² 2:44³	Lawrence Realizatn 27k	3 2 2^2 2^2 1^2 $1^{2\frac12}$	Sande E	126wb	*.33	81-12	Zev$126^{2\frac12}$Untidy$123^{\frac12}$Rialto119^1	Won easing up 5
1Sep23- 1Bel	fst 6f	:22³ :46¹ 1:11¹	Alw 1238 3↑	1 1 1^{hd} $1^{\frac12}$ 1^2 $1^{2\frac12}$	Sande E	125wb	*.17	97-06	Zev$125^{2\frac12}$Bigheart112^1Runviso$110^{\frac12}$	In a canter 4
23Jun23- 4Aqu	fst 1	:22² :46 1:11 1:37 3↑	Queens County H 8.6k	7 1 1^1 1^1 1^2 $1^{3\frac12}$	Sande E	117 w	*.65e	95-13	Zev$117^{3\frac12}$Dunlin107^2Nedna$103^{\frac34}$	Going away 8
9Jun23- 4Bel	gd 1⅜	:47² 1:12⁴ 1:38¹ 2:19	Belmont 46k	2 1 1^2 1^5 1^4 $1^{1\frac12}$	Sande E	126wb	*.80	76-17	Zev$126^{1\frac12}$Chickvale$126^{3\frac12}$Rialto$126^{\frac12}$	Tiring late 8
26May23- 4Bel	fst 1	:23 :46⁴ 1:11 1:37²	Withers 20k	5 1 1^1 1^2 1^3 $1^{\frac12}$	Sande E	118wb	*.90	91-09	Zev$118^{\frac12}$Martingale$118^{4\frac12}$Barbary Bush$118^{2\frac12}$	7
			Eased up, almost caught							
19May23- 5CD	fst 1¼	:47² 1:12² 1:39 2:05²	Ky Derby 63k	10 1 1^2 $1^{\frac12}$ 1^2 $1^{1\frac12}$	Sande E	126wb	19.20	89-11	Zev126^1Martingale126^1Vigil126^1	Gamely 21
15May23- 4Jam	gd 6f	:23³ :46⁴ 1:12 3↑	Rainbow H 4.1k	7 3 1^2 1^2 1^2 $1^{\frac12}$	Sande E	114wb	2.40e	96-11	Zev$114^{\frac12}$Dominique125^{no}Rigel107^{no}	Best 8
12May23- 4Pim	fst 1⅛	:47⁴ 1:13 1:39⁴ 1:53³	Preakness 62k	6 3 $4^{2\frac12}$ 11^{18} 12^{29} $12^{26\frac14}$	Sande E	126wb	*4.35	61-12	Vigil$114^{1\frac12}$General Thatcher114^1Rialto114^{hd}	Quit 13
			Geldings not eligible							
2May23- 4Jam	fst 6f	:23¹ :46³ 1:12 3↑	Paumonok H 5.8k	1 2 $1^{\frac12}$ 1^2 $1^{2\frac12}$ 1^{nk}	Fator L	109wb	*2.50	96-07	Zev109^{nk}Dominique123^6Galantman106.5^{no}	10
			Tired, hard hand ride							
16Sep22- 3Bel	fst 6f-Str	1:11	Futurity 55k	15 3 $2^{1\frac12}$ 2^3	Sande E	124 w	*5.00	85-12	Sally's Alley116^3Zev$124^{\frac12}$Wilderness119^1	Tired 23
31Aug22- 3Sar	gd 6f	:23² :47² 1:12²	Hopeful 43k	12 2 2^{hd} 1^1 1^1 $3^{1\frac12}$	Sande E	130wb	5.00	89-18	Dunlin115^3Goshawk$130^{\frac12}$Zev130^1	Saved ground, tired 12
28Aug22- 4Sar	hy 6f	:23⁴ :48² 1:15³	Albany H 4.9k	2 5 $1^{1\frac12}$ 1^2 1^3 $1^{2\frac12}$	Sande E	126wb	*.60	74-31	Zev$126^{2\frac12}$Vigil106^5Boys Believe Me110^4	Never threatened 6
19Aug22- 3Sar	hy 6f	:23⁴ :47⁴ 1:15	Grand Union Hotel 12k	3 4 1^1 1^4 1^2 1^2	Fator L	115wb	*2.20e	77-31	Zev115^2Dunlin115^2Bud Lerner127^2	Ridden out 10
15Aug22- 3Sar	fst 5f	:23¹ :46¹ :59	Alw 1476	11 4 1^1 1^1 1^4 $1^{\frac12}$	Sande E	125wb	*2.50e	94-11	Zev$125^{\frac12}$Enchantment115^2Dunlin119^2	Ridden out 11
8Aug22- 6Sar	hy 5f	:24 :49 1:03	Alw 1000	5 2 1^2 1^3 1^5 1^4	Fator L	115wb	*.60	74-34	Zev115^4Wilderness110^3Nassau115^8	Easily 5
5Aug22- 6Sar	hy 5½f	:24 :48 1:02 1:08²	Md Sp Wt	4 3 1^3 1^5 1^8 1^5	Sande E	115wb	*1.40	81-29	Zev115^5Dougheregan115^6Beatitude$112^{\frac12}$	Won eased up 14
1Aug22- 6Sar	fst 5f	:23⁴ :46³ :59³	Md Sp Wt	17 7 $2^{2\frac12}$ $2^{1\frac12}$ 2^1 $2^{3\frac12}$	Sande E	115wb	*2.00	87-09	Comixa$112^{3\frac12}$Zev$115^{2\frac12}$Betty Beall112^2	Chased winner 20
21Jly22- 6Emp	fst 5½f	:22³ :46⁴ :59⁴ 1:06	Alw 1058	2 1 $1^{2\frac12}$ 1^1 1^1 $2^{\frac34}$	Fator L	104wb	1.80	98-09	Dunlin$103^{\frac34}$Zev104^4William Tell103^{12}	Tired late 5
19Jun22- 6Aqu	gd 5f	1:00	Md Sp Wt	3 10 $2^{1\frac12}$ 3^2	Sande E	115wb	*1.60e	87-12	Cyclops115^2General Thatcher115^{hd}Zev$115^{1\frac12}$	Tired 18
17Jun22- 3Aqu	fst 5f	:59²	Hudson H 6.5k	2 6 $3^{2\frac12}$ $2^{\frac12}$ $4^{2\frac34}$	Fator L	112 w	2.60	89-14	Sunference114^{nk}Cherry Pie130^2Bud Lerner$127^{\frac12}$	Tired 13
14Jun22- 6Bel	fst 5f-Str	:57⁴	Alw 1113	4 2 3^1 3^2 2no	Fator L	108wb	*.22e	89-16	Prince Regent108^{no}Zev108^1Whirlwind115^8	Just missed 6

LEGACIES
THE 1930'S

by Glenye Cain

EW DECADES HAVE had such a diverse and lasting impact on North American racing as the 1930's. The prevalence of racetracks around the country, the shapes of our prime circuits, and some of our most prestigious stakes races have their roots in the thirties, as do several of the conveniences that racegoers today take for

"The Fox of Belair," Gallant Fox, kicked off the 1930's by winning the Triple Crown. The tall, talented colt lured legendary jockey Earl Sande out of retirement to ride him as a 3-year-old.

granted. From starting gate to photo finish, the thirties left an impressive legacy for the Thoroughbred sport – in bloodstock, history, and mechanical invention.

After the Crash, the nation was slipping deeper into the economic devastation that drove hordes of people out of work and into breadlines. State governments were also hungry, but for tax revenue, and they saw a convenient opportunity in the daily attendance figures at places such as Pimlico, Belmont, and Churchill Downs. If citizens across the nation wanted diversion, their state governments, hunting for income, would give it to them in the form of more racetracks.

Thus began, paradoxically, a Depression boom as racing, demonized and shunned the generation before, was revived state by state to help fund government. Maryland, Kentucky, New York, and New England had been the predominant racing venues, but in the thirties racing appeared (or reappeared) in other areas, too. In New Hampshire, Thoroughbreds returned to Rockingham Park, while Massachusetts built Suffolk Downs. Rhode Island got Narragansett Park, and racing came to Delaware. In Kentucky, Keeneland debuted. Out west, still a relatively new frontier for racing,

California opened Santa Anita, Del Mar, Hollywood, and Bay Meadows that decade, and Texas got Arlington Downs. In south Florida, Tropical Park joined Hialeah in the Miami market in 1931, followed by Gulfstream Park in 1939.

The growth spurred unprecedented tinkering, too, as regulation-minded states looked for better ways to run the races for the benefit of the public; the electric timer and the photo-finish camera were among the developments in the 1930's, the amplified race call began and became an audio icon in the decade, and experimentation with starting gates ultimately resulted in the gate we know today.

Suddenly, racing was everywhere – and so were the opportunities for owners and trainers to make a little purse money, though the purse money was exactly that: little. In 1932, thanks to the general economic condition, the average purse slipped from $1,100 to $920, making it harder for racing stables to offset their expenses and for great racehorses to set new earnings records. At the top of the world's earnings list was Sun Beau, who had won much of his money by 1929, when he already was the nation's top older horse. When he retired in October 1931, Sun Beau had amassed a lifetime bankroll of $376,744. The horses that followed him in the 1930's were racing in a trench, so to speak, and it wasn't until 1940 that Seabiscuit finally climbed past Sun Beau's purse mark.

The history of the Thoroughbred is as cyclical as any other, and the decade of the thirties is especially rich in sporting and bloodstock regenerations. As new tracks sprang up, young members of old families took the helms of stables, while great racehorses went to stud and sired or produced another generation of champions. Some of the legacies of that time have faded in the 60 years since, but others are still etched in our collective memory and in the record books.

The Fox of Belair was his nickname. It is appropriate that the names of Gallant Fox and Belair Stud should be linked so closely, because together they dominated the 1930's and produced one of the era's most famous racing dynasties.

Gallant Fox was, in a sense, the bellwether for the era, a propitious sign. How better to begin a decade, after all, than with a Triple Crown winner? In 1930, thanks to Belair's blaze-faced bay colt, turf writers dusted off the record books and created a royal designation for sweeping the Kentucky Derby, Preakness, and Belmont Stakes. Sir Barton had been the first to do so 11 years before, when the feat was highly notable but not titled; Gallant Fox's repetition of it prompted someone to christen the events racing's Triple Crown.

In 1929, Gallant Fox had been a lanky, ungainly 2-year-old who, it was hoped, would help justify a risk taken in 1925 by Belair owner William Woodward Sr. Gallant Fox, out of Belair's Celt mare Marguerite, was a member of the first American crop sired by the English stallion Sir Gallahad III, whom Woodward and three other men, including Arthur B. Hancock Sr., had purchased in partnership for the fantastic sum of $125,000 and imported to stand at Hancock's Claiborne Farm.

Gallant Fox proved to be a talented, but not champion, 2-year-old, winning just two stakes. But his large size and awkward manner suggested that time and distance would bring him along. The hint was strong enough to induce three-time leading jockey Earl Sande to come out of retirement to ride the colt at 3, and he even forwent his usual monthly retainer on the agreement that he would instead get 10 percent of Gallant Fox's earnings.

The speculation paid off like a slot machine. Returning from winter quarters in April 1930, Gallant Fox was mature, coordinated, and practically invincible. After winning his season debut in the Wood Memorial by four lengths, he skated through the Preakness on May 9, the Derby just 10 days later, and the Belmont on June 7. And he went on from there, knitting together a skein of stakes wins that galvanized his reputation as an unbeatable foe.

He was not invulnerable, however, and the story of the one that got away has always stained Gallant

Fox's record like a brushstroke gone awry across a fine oil. It happened, as so many legendary defeats have, at Saratoga, when Gallant Fox, now the undisputed king of the 3-year-olds, met what should have been a docile field of three rivals in the 1930 Travers. Sent off the 1–2 favorite for the race over a heavy, muddy strip, Gallant Fox hooked into an early duel with Whichone, who had finished second to him in the Belmont. On the turn, the pair drifted wide, and into the breach stepped one of the turf's most unlikely spoilers: a 100-1 shot named Jim Dandy. Spurting through on the inside, Jim Dandy took the fastest route home and sailed in eight lengths ahead of the "invincible" 3-year-old, with Whichone another six lengths back. It was, without a doubt, Jim Dandy's finest hour – he made half of his career earnings in the Travers – and Gallant Fox's most humiliating one.

Still, when he retired at the end of the season, Gallant Fox had a bed of laurels on which to rest: He was the first horse ever to earn more than $300,000 in a single season, his career earnings totaled $328,165, and he was the first Triple Crown winner in 11 years. He had repaid everyone associated with him, from the casual bettor to Earl Sande, whose 10-percent deal netted him more than 3½ times the amount his monthly retainer would have brought.

Gallant Fox marked a turning point for his owner as well. Belair's white silks with red dots had been carried to new heights on the colt's back and he had resoundingly justified the investment in Sir Gallahad III. In fact, Sir Gallahad became a four-time leading sire in his adopted country, and his runners later included two stakes-winning full brothers to Gallant Fox: Foxbrough, who was a champion 2-year-old in England, and Fighting Fox. What Woodward suspected but didn't know at the time was that Gallant Fox also would add immense value to Belair's thirties legacy with his own progeny.

Four years later, Omaha, one of just 18 foals from Gallant Fox's first crop, arrived in trainer Sunny Jim Fitzsimmons's barn. Omaha, though chestnut, had his sire's flashy blaze and big frame. Like

Gallant Fox, he was awkward and long-striding, which augured better success at 3 than at 2. He matured into a long, elegant horse and set experts nodding in anticipation when he scored his first time out at 3, but enthusiasm dampened slightly when he failed to reproduce his sire's win in the Wood Memorial the following week; he finished third.

Between Gallant Fox's 1930 Derby and his son's in 1935, the race's purse had plummeted from $60,000 to $49,000. Nonetheless, after the winter-book favorite, Chance Sun, bowed out with an injury, the Derby appeared up for grabs, and 18 contested the race. Omaha was sent off at 4-1 and won, as the chart said, "easily," a word that also described his victories in the Preakness and the Belmont.

After Omaha's Triple Crown, newspaper columnist W. J. Macbeth noted that "Fitzsimmons is anxious to have Omaha duplicate all of Gallant Fox's stakes victories and to retrieve the sire's reputation in the Travers at Saratoga." That hope failed. Omaha, who could not win at Saratoga at 2, never ran there at all at 3, then was shipped to England, where he won two good races and narrowly lost

After an eventful early 3-year-old campaign, Granville won the Belmont and every succeeding race in which he ran in 1936 to become the first elected Horse of the Year.

the Ascot Gold Cup. But in winning the Triple Crown, Omaha offset Gallant Fox's black-mark Travers with an honor that was equally indelible: with Omaha, Gallant Fox became the only Triple Crown winner to date to sire a Triple Crown winner, and he did it in his first crop of runners.

While Omaha was winning the 1935 Triple Crown, a 2-year-old son of Gallant Fox was also in the hands of "Mr. Fitz" and training for his career debut at Saratoga. Named Granville, the colt showed some talent when he ran third in his first stakes, the Babylon Handicap, in September. Behind him in sixth place that day, incidentally, was another Fiztsimmons trainee, a hard-campaigned but obscure 2-year-old named Seabiscuit, who was making his 26th start.

Granville hit the board several times at 2, winning just once, in a $1,000 allowance race, and he was put away for the season having failed to raise any eyebrows. Typical of his sire and Omaha, however, Granville rocketed out of the barn at 3. He won his 1936 debut by five lengths under a hold and was nosed out in the Wood Memorial, suggesting that a third Triple Crown for the Gallant Fox males could be in the offing.

But in the Derby, now run before the Preakness, Granville bobbled at the start, and any Triple Crown hopes hit the track with jockey Jimmy Stout. Granville galloped off, stirrups flopping empty on their leathers, as front-runner Bold Venture won by a head from Brevity. Nor did Granville win the Preakness, though he came close: Having gained the lead in the stretch, he battled a fierce challenge by Bold Venture but could not hold the Derby winner off and lost by a nose. Two weeks later, he veered from the Triple Crown path to try older horses in the Suburban and was handed another nose defeat by the well-regarded Firethorn. But that 1¼-mile performance – and Bold Venture's retirement after he bowed a tendon in the Preakness – set Granville up well for the Belmont six days later, when he finally came out on the right side of a close decision. Pushed to his limit by longshot Mr. Bones, Granville dug in and kept his nose in front at the wire.

Granville never lost again, and that year he helped atone for his sire's Travers defeat. It was a messy victory that was threatened by the stewards: Granville won by a head, but only after hampering second-placed Sun Teddy. The officials, in a quirky decision, let the result stand after determining that Granville also had been bothered earlier by another horse and thus was already at a disadvantage when he bumped Sun Teddy.

In his next start, Granville defeated the great handicapper Discovery by eight lengths in the Saratoga Cup, a much-hyped match race. Discovery was the 4-5 choice in the 1¼-mile contest, which was run over a sloppy track at weight-for-age conditions. Carrying 116 pounds to Discovery's 126, Granville jumped out to an early lead and won by eight. There were extenuating circumstances, however, as Discovery was found to have thrown a shoe in Saratoga's deep going.

Granville won once more, easily taking the Lawrence Realization. Crowned Horse of the Year – the first so named – he retired, the most successful member of Gallant Fox's 19-horse second crop, which also included the good English stakes winner Flares.

From 1930 through 1936, Gallant Fox, in one way or another, was responsible for some of the finest racetrack performances of the decade. Having contributed, along with Fitzsimmons and his prodigious talents, to Belair's dominance of the era, Gallant Fox promptly lost cachet as a stallion, slipping off the top 20 sires list and finally getting 20 stakes winners from 320 foals.

Gallant Fox's own sire, ultimately, provided a more comprehensive breeding legacy. Sir Gallahad III appears early in the pedigrees of several other greats from the 1930's. His daughter La France, mated with the good handicapper Jamestown, produced Johnstown, who was purchased by Belair and won the Derby and Belmont. Laura Gal, another daughter of Sir Gallahad III owned by W. L. Brann's Branncastle Farm, produced Johnstown's chief rival, Challedon, a two-time Horse of the Year. And a son of Sir Gallahad III, Insco, sired two of the era's best fillies, Herbert Woolf's homebreds

Inscoelda and Unerring, whose long and distinguished records extended into the early 1940's.

Among the swells in Pimlico's clubhouse on November 5, 1930, was young Cornelius Vanderbilt Whitney, who was hoping not to be noticed. It was the day of the Pimlico Futurity, and the assembled throng that raw, damp afternoon was focused on the coming race, which pitted the country's top 2-year-olds against each other; the outcome would almost certainly settle the divisional crown. C. V. Whitney, who previously had not cared one way or the other about racing, found himself in the strange position of owning one of the leading contenders, a great crowd-pleaser later nicknamed the Chocolate Soldier – Equipoise.

It was, in fact, C. V. Whitney's first day at the races as an owner, and he was in that capacity to fulfill a family obligation. Whitney had arrived in the sport almost by accident 10 days earlier on the death of his father, the renowned owner-breeder Harry Payne Whitney, who had left a string of racehorses and his breeding stock. The younger Whitney, 31, encouraged by another great Thoroughbred sportsman, Joseph E. Widener, took his father's place at the helm.

Equipoise, the popular "Chocolate Soldier," was one of the first horses to run in the colors of C. V. Whitney.

The heir to Harry Payne Whitney's stable may have hoped for a relatively quiet entrance into his father's sport, but he got more fanfare, and probably more fun, than he bargained for. At the Pimlico Futurity, the stewards insisted that he and trainer Freddy Hopkins view the race from their stand, and when Whitney finally consented, the crowd, catching sight of him, broke into a spontaneous ovation.

As it happened, Equipoise's most contentious rival that day – all season, in fact – was also owned by a Whitney. Helen Hay Whitney, widow of C. V.'s uncle, Payne, campaigned the immensely popular Twenty Grand under the name of her Greentree Stable. Twenty Grand had beaten Equipoise twice, both times over a fast track at a mile. This time, the two were meeting at 1 1/16 miles over a muddy strip, and the betting crowd gave Equipoise the edge.

The Futurity was more than the expected coronation; it was one of the decade's epic clashes, and those who saw Equipoise's victory in it never forgot it. Not just beaten but distanced after sideswiping another horse at the break, C.V. Whitney's liver chestnut unexpectedly shot forward and started passing his rivals with a mere half-mile left in the race. Strenuously, yard by yard, he began picking up the 2-year-old championship for his new owner. He caught Twenty Grand in the stretch, matched strides with him, and those two joined the leader, Mate. As they swept past the wire, Equipoise was a half-length in front of Twenty Grand, with Mate a neck farther back.

In the running, Equipoise had gotten a bad start, been shuffled back into the deepest going, lost both front shoes, cut a front foot, popped open a recurring quarter crack, and still won. He retired for the season after the Futurity with top earnings for his division, $156,835. Even so, there were some who argued that Whitney's aunt owned the better horse, especially considering that, during his earlier defeat of Equipoise in the Kentucky Jockey Club Stakes, Twenty Grand had posted the fastest mile time, 1:36, that had ever been run by a 2-year-old in the United States.

Twenty Grand and Equipoise met only once the following year, when Mate beat them both to win the Preakness. Twenty Grand was second that day, but went on to win the Derby from Sweep All a week later, with Mate third. Equipoise, fourth in the Preakness, withdrew from the Derby and sat out the rest of the year with his troublesome quarter crack, which sometimes bled so badly that "you could track him all the way back to the barn," according to George Mohr, who worked as a teenager in trainer Al Weston's stable at Pimlico, across the horse path from Equipoise's barn.

Despite Equipoise's layoff, C.V. Whitney's stable was far from dormant in 1931. Just a month after Equipoise left the track, Whitney entered a 2-year-old Dis Donc filly in her first race, the five-furlong Clover Stakes at Aqueduct. Carrying 107 pounds, Top Flight cruised home by a length over Polonaise, who had 122 pounds. Top Flight proved the performance was a result of talent rather than a break in the weights when she traveled to

Arlington Park for the Lassie Stakes. Carrying 120 pounds, the same as Polonaise, Top Flight won again, this time by five while giving seven pounds to second-placed Modern Queen and three to third runner Princess Camellia. Polonaise finished fourth.

Top Flight provided plenty of entertainment for the Whitney stable the rest of the year, and plenty of dust for her competitors. She went on to be undefeated in 1931, skipping home by 1¼ lengths against colts in the Saratoga Special, by five again in the Spinaway, and by 1¼ in the Matron, seemingly oblivious to her 127-pound burden. In the fall, Top Flight stepped back into the boys division and handily whipped them again, coasting clear of well-regarded Mad Pursuit and Morfair, who both carried 122 to her 127, in Belmont's six-furlong Futurity. A month later, she beat males yet again – by the uncharacteristically slender margin of a neck – at 1 1/16 miles in the

Twenty Grand, winner of two legs of the Triple Crown in 1931, was a brilliant 3-year-old, defeating handicap star Sun Beau by 10 lengths in the Saratoga Cup.

Pimlico Futurity. Behind her that day was Burgoo King, who went on to win the Derby the following year.

While one Whitney runner sewed up the 2-year-old division, another Whitney horse pocketed the 3-year-old title with nearly equal ease. Greentree's trainer, Thomas W. Murphy, had resigned but offered a reported $125,000 to take Twenty Grand with him. Mrs. Whitney refused and was amply rewarded, as the St. Germans colt proceeded to win the Belmont (by 10), the Dwyer, and the Travers, with a third in the Arlington Classic for good measure. True proof of his hardiness came in the Saratoga Cup, when he faced the reigning handicap king, 6-year-old Sun Beau, who was enjoying a banner season that made him the world's leading earner in his last year at the races. Twenty Grand beat him by 10 in a gallop, then followed up by airing in the Lawrence Realization and the Jockey Club Gold Cup. In the latter, he hit his left front pastern, injuring the splint bone and tendon, and he hung up his bridle for the year.

Mrs. Whitney's Greentree Stable, which she started with her husband, Payne, in 1911, was a turf dynasty that had built its foundation with steeplechasers. Though her watermelon-pink silks with black-striped sleeves became increasingly prominent on the flat, Mrs. Whitney's stable in the 1930's also fielded one of the prominent jumpers of the era, Jungle King. The connection points to yet another breeding legacy of the time, that of the horse St. Germans. Payne Whitney had bought the English horse for $125,000 in 1925 – the same price and year of Sir Gallahad III's acquisition.

St. Germans sired both Jungle King and Twenty Grand, and the latter nearly single-handedly boosted the stallion to the top of America's sire list in 1931. Jungle King began as a flat runner but proved more successful over fences; despite a four-year career, though, he never quite equaled the dominance of another steeplechase champion of the time, Joe Widener's Bushranger, who won 11 of 21 career starts and carried 172 pounds to victory in the 1936 Grand National. Jungle King, carrying 140, lost his rider in that contest, precluding a true battle.

C. V. Whitney and his aunt Helen were to keep the Whitney name in the fore throughout the thirties, though their standard-bearers, Equipoise and Twenty Grand, did not meet again until their careers were near an end, in 1935.

Santa Anita Park near Los Angeles had opened on Christmas Day, 1934, to much fanfare, and the new hot spot, in an effort to attract horses from around the country and Mexico for high-class winter racing, was staging its inaugural $100,000-added Santa Anita Handicap in February. When the race had been announced, many greeted the plan with skepticism, but the horses pointing for it included a number of great runners from the East, among them old rivals Twenty Grand, Mate, and Equipoise, who was gunning for Sun Beau's all-time earnings title.

The story behind Twenty Grand's appearance was a sad one. Greentree trainer James Rowe Jr. had died soon after the 1931 Jockey Club Gold Cup, and his replacement, William Brennan, brought the now-4-year-old Twenty Grand back from his injury to start twice in 1932, but to little avail. He won his seasonal debut, but then pulled up lame in the slop at Laurel after running second. Deemed too valuable to risk any longer, he was retired to stud, where he was found to be infertile. Mrs. Whitney returned him to the racetrack in 1935. He was 7.

Equipoise also was struggling increasingly with his fragile feet and notorious quarter crack, which had required much of one hoof to be cut away and regrown. But heart and talent still got him to the wire. In a February 18 prep for the Santa Anita Handicap, Equipoise, carrying 125 and giving nine pounds to Twenty Grand, beat the Greentree runner by one length. But he also bothered him, resulting in Equipoise's third career disqualification. The crowd nonetheless saw that Twenty Grand was no longer the horse he had been, and five days later, they favored Equipoise – highweight at 130 pounds to Twenty Grand's 126 – among the 20 runners in the big event.

It was the last race for the three-time handicap champion. Breaking slowly from the gate, Equipoise was positioned to strike as the field headed home, but this time a tendon failed him, and he never improved from seventh. Twenty Grand finished a distant tenth. Fred Alger's Azucar, a former steeplechaser carrying 117, had lifted the prize. In doing so, Azucar made $108,400, the most a horse had ever earned in a single race; it would have been more than enough to catapult Equipoise past Sun Beau's famous earnings mark. Even the winner did not escape unscathed, though. It was reported some days later in the Detroit News that Azucar had been "slightly burned by electric wires when he became frightened and ran away after the finish of the Santa Anita Handicap."

And so the two great Whitney horses left the track, at least in America. Equipoise was retired with 29 wins from 51 starts, and total purses of $338,610, some $40,000 short of the world record. Twenty Grand was sent briefly to trainer Cecil Boyd-Rochfort in England, where he was easily put away by local runners in two races. In the fall of 1935, the old hero was taken home and turned out to pasture.

In 1935, the public and racing press hungered for a successor to Equipoise, and they found one in Discovery, who had never met Equipoise, though their careers had overlapped. This changing of the guard in the handicap division was reflected in the Thoroughbred industry's human leadership, as well.

On September 22, 1933, Alfred Gwynne Vanderbilt turned 21 and became, officially, a millionaire in his own right. Like his cousin C.V. Whitney, Vanderbilt also inherited a foothold in Thoroughbred racing, which he was to parlay into a role of immense influence. On his 21st birthday, he received a $2 million installment, the first of four, from the estate of his father, who had died on the Lusitania, as well as a birthday gift from his mother: her Sagamore Farm in Maryland and all of its Thoroughbreds.

Vanderbilt moved quickly to bolster Sagamore's homebreds with outside purchases. Discovery, a good 2-year-old of 1933, was among the early

draftees. Bred and owned early by Mr. and Mrs. Walter Salmon, Discovery had been the subject of some haggling before Vanderbilt, preparing to board the Aquitania at the start of a safari journey, made a final offer of $25,000. On November 2, 1933, Vanderbilt received an answer via his mother in a Cunard Line telegraph: "Discovery yours ok love Mother." Two days later, Discovery carried Alfred Vanderbilt's silks for the first time, getting within a neck of Chicstraw in Pimlico's Walden Handicap, his final start as a 2-year-old. Six lengths farther back that afternoon was Cavalcade, who would prove to be Discovery's nemesis the following year.

Prepping for the Derby, Discovery had a public work between races at Havre de Grace on April 21, 1934. Joined by a stablemate midway through it, Discovery went three-quarters in 1:12 ⅖, prompting the three clockers on duty, each sure he'd made an error, to quickly compare times. Discovery zipped past the wire under a tight hold in a final mile time of 1:37⅘, a second better than the track record. Vanderbilt and trainer J. H. Stotler "expressed satisfaction with the trial," *Daily Racing Form* noted.

Discovery was overshadowed by Cavalcade during his 3-year-old season, but went on to become a superior weight-carrier and handicap champion.

Cavalcade spoiled Discovery's Derby hopes, however. Discovery finished second, then came back to be third behind High Quest and Cavalcade in the Preakness. He was forced to skip the Belmont; the Salmons had never nominated him, and the deadline was past when Vanderbilt acquired him.

Stotler and Vanderbilt turned their attention to the late-season races, where Discovery was untouchable against almost all comers. Running at a dozen tracks in the Northeast and Midwest, he won half his 16 starts in 1934, six of them stakes. In his easiest race, the Whitney, he carried just 105 pounds and won off by 10; after that, he never carried less than 119. By the end of the season, his weight assignment reached 130 for the Maryland Handicap, and he won that, too, by a half-length over Good Goods.

There was one runner, however, he had been unable to beat all year long: Cavalcade. Mrs. Isabel Dodge Sloane's Brookmeade Stable campaigned the Lancegaye colt through a brilliant season that was further gilded by his routine drubbing of the obviously high-caliber Discovery. Even when he gave Discovery weight, as he did in the Detroit and American Derbies, Cavalcade beat Vanderbilt's colt. "Cavalcade strikes human fancy hardest by the destruction and havoc he causes among his rivals with one short but very explosive burst of speed," the *Form*'s Norris Royden wrote after Cavalcade, conceding five pounds, beat Discovery for the sixth and final time that season in the Arlington Classic.

With Cavalcade out the rest of 1934 with a hoof ailment, Discovery took advantage and won 5 of 7 races, setting a world record of 1:55 for 1 3/16 miles in the Rhode Island Handicap. On the heels of Equipoise's retirement, he was hailed as the Chocolate Soldier's successor.

Discovery met Cavalcade only once more, in the 1935 Suburban, when Cavalcade lost his rider at the start. Head Play won under 114 pounds, with Discovery, carrying 123, second. Though he returned in 1936 for two races at Narragansett and his stable kept hope alive that he was training to meet the best of the day, Cavalcade never won again and was retired.

The years 1935 and '36 belonged to Discovery, whose burdens had crept up to groaning levels. In 1935, he won five times carrying more than 130 pounds. In one of those races, Saratoga's 1 3/16-mile Merchants' and Citizens' Handicap, often thought to be his best performance, he lugged 139 pounds to a two-length score.

Northeastern handicappers, trainer Stotler felt, were especially harsh on Discovery. In 1936, after he had lost the Santa Anita Handicap thanks to getting bumped, he was given 135 pounds for his first race back at Aqueduct, which he won by four. Ten days later, on June 27, he aced his third consecutive Brooklyn Handicap, carrying 136. His assignments reached their peak in the 1936 Merchants' and Citizens', where he lugged 143 pounds over a sloppy track and finished fifth. The situation prompted a group of owners to call for a 138-pound ceiling on handicaps, citing the weight put on Discovery as "bad practice."

Vanderbilt generally remained quiet about the loads Discovery was asked to haul. "I wanted to see how good he was," he said 60 years later. In reference to the outcome of the Merchants' and Citizens', he added, "The thing I liked about that was that after he got beaten, they said he sulked, which said to me that they thought if he'd tried he could have done it."

When he retired at the end of the season, Discovery had won $195,287 and 27 races from 67 starts. He was third or better 47 times, he set a world mark, and he carried 130 pounds or more into the winner's circle nine times. In that respect, at least, he was able to beat Cavalcade, who never ran under more than 127.

As for Discovery's legacy, Vanderbilt noted in 1999, "In a way, the most important thing about Discovery is that for probably 20 years, give or take a little, the two major stallions in North America were Native Dancer and Bold Ruler. Both of them were out of Discovery mares."

Vanderbilt, too, made lasting contributions to the sport. As the head of Pimlico, and later

War Admiral, the great Man o' War's best son, was undefeated in eight starts as a 3-year-old.

Belmont, he brought innovation in track management. He helped usher in parimutuel wagering to New York, among other things, and sought to improve customer service for race fans. One of his first moves in power at Pimlico was to remove the infield hill that gave the track the moniker Old Hilltop and obstructed many fans' view of the backstretch; another was the installation of a public-address system. He also developed a stable full of talented runners, including the champion Now What, whom Stotler called the best filly he ever trained. She flew the Vanderbilt flag high late in the decade by winning the Astoria, Demoiselle, Arlington Lassie, and Spinaway Stakes in 1939.

On November 1, 1938, Vanderbilt, who was just 27 but had already acquired controlling interest in Pimlico, fulfilled something of a coup for the track by staging a match race between War Admiral and Seabiscuit, by far the best handicap horses of the day. Belmont Park previously had tried to put the match on for a $100,000 purse, but that event fell apart when owner Charles S. Howard withdrew Seabiscuit. Amid suggestions that he was ducking

War Admiral, Howard agreed to Vanderbilt's suggestion to run the two in the $15,000 Pimlico Special.

The match race marked a neat conjunction in the revival of a great name from the 1920's: Man o' War. War Admiral, who carried the black and gold silks of Man o' War's owner-breeder, Samuel D. Riddle, was a Triple Crown-winning son of the great horse; Seabiscuit, by hot-blooded Hard Tack, was a grandson of Man o' War campaigned by Howard, a California-based Buick dealer. The Pimlico Special was the first and only meeting of two of the decade's best horses.

War Admiral, for his part, was the best thing Man o' War had sired. At 2, he was overshadowed by the precocious champion Pompoon. But as a 3-year-old of 1937, he literally could not be caught. He was undefeated in eight starts – with Pompoon second to him twice. In the Belmont Stakes, War Admiral had clinched both the Triple Crown and a reputation for courage: Stumbling at the start, he had torn off a section of his right front hoof, which bled profusely. Driven on to the lead, he finished three lengths in front. Along the way, he had broken his sire's 17-year track record for 1½ miles, lowering the mark by one-fifth to 2:28⅗, which also was an American record for the distance.

At 4, War Admiral won eight races leading up to the Pimlico Special. He had little trouble with his competition, though the champion filly Esposa ran him to a neck in the sloppy Saratoga Handicap.

Setting records was old hat to Seabiscuit, who spent much of 1937 lowering track marks from Santa Anita to Suffolk Downs. Originally trained by Sunny Jim Fitzsimmons for the Wheatley Stable of Mrs. Henry Carnegie Phipps and her brother, Ogden Mills, he evidently failed to impress his connections at 2 and 3; he started 35 times at 2 and could have been claimed for $2,500 more than once. Shortly after a victory in the Mohawk Claiming Stakes at Saratoga in August 1936, in which he was entered for a $6,000 tag, the Wheatley principals happily sold the 3-year-old colt to Howard for $7,500.

Under the care of Silent Tom Smith, Seabiscuit gradually developed into something almost otherworldly. By the time the 5-year-old horse met War Admiral in the 1938 Pimlico Special, he owned track marks over a mile, 1 3/16, and 1 1/8 at Bay Meadows (1:36, 1:55 4/5, and 1:49); 1 1/8 miles at Santa Anita (1:48 4/5); 1 1/16 miles at Empire State (1:44 1/5); 1 1/8 miles at Suffolk (1:49); 1 3/16 miles at Pimlico (1:57 2/5); 1 1/4 miles at Hollywood (2:03 4/5); and 1 1/8 miles at Del Mar (1:49).

Since War Admiral had been known to kick up a fuss at the starting gate, Riddle insisted on a walk-up start for the Pimlico Special. He also demanded that the race be run without the participation of starter James Milton, whom he disliked. At Milton's own request, he was temporarily replaced by George Cassidy of New York

The start, everyone knew, was crucial. Tom Smith knew it, and he knew that Seabiscuit, who sometimes was a slow starter, was at a disadvantage in this regard. The week of the race, according to fellow trainer George Mohr, who also was stabled at Pimlico by this time, "They'd gallop Seabiscuit around, pull him up, then let him walk four or five strides and break him off sharp."

After two attempts at a true start, and in front of a record crowd of 40,000, War Admiral and Seabiscuit put on a memorable race. Seabiscuit was struck twice by jockey George Woolf, who was substituting for injured regular rider Red Pollard, and unexpectedly jumped to the lead, tracked by War Admiral 2 1/2 lengths behind. At the three-quarter mark in the 1 3/16-mile contest, jockey Charley Kurtsinger plied whip and heel to War Admiral, who hooked Seabiscuit at the half. It appeared to be over for Seabiscuit as War Admiral headed him for

Seabiscuit returns to the winner's circle following his victory over War Admiral in the 1938 Pimlico Special. The popular star trumped the 1937 Triple Crown winner by four lengths in track-record time.

about 100 yards. But Seabiscuit switched into high gear, and at the top of the stretch, he began drawing away powerfully, though War Admiral was under vigorous whipping. At the wire, it was Seabiscuit by four lengths in a track-record time of 1:56⅗. The defeat cost War Admiral the championship that season, though he won the Rhode Island Handicap 11 days later. He only raced once the following season, taking a Hialeah allowance, before retiring with a wrenched ankle.

Seabiscuit took the winter off after the Pimlico Special but returned in 1939 for a special task. It was his owner's fond hope to win the Santa Anita Handicap. The race had been an annual heartbreaker for him with Seabiscuit, who lost by a nose twice, to Rosemont in 1936 and to Stagehand in 1938. Unfortunately, Seabiscuit returned lame from a prep race, and he took the rest of the year off, at least from racing: While at his owner's northern California farm, he was bred to a handful of mares. Howard, as it happened, got lucky in the race anyway: His imported Kayak II drew away to win, and, in Seabiscuit's absence, proceeded to lock up the year's handicap championship. Seabiscuit would return briefly in 1940, finally surpassing Sun Beau's record and winning the Santa Anita Handicap on his third try.

Seabiscuit and War Admiral were not the only horses descended from Man o' War and his own sire, Fair Play, in the 1930's. Sun Beau was out of a Fair Play mare, as was Stagehand, who beat Pompoon and Bull Lea in addition to Seabiscuit. Discovery and Now What were by sons of Fair Play.

In their bloodlines and their ownership, many of the great runners of the 1930's harked back to an older world in racing that would one day fade almost entirely from view. The monarchies of the turf would eventually be replaced by increasingly diverse ownership interests, an upswing in strictly commercial breeding, and a more egalitarian clubhouse. But these champions of the 1930's, while representing the legacies that brought them into being, also created legacies of their own. They passed Fair Play's name into the future, but they also contributed their own to future pedigrees of import. Even if they proved infertile or unsuccessful at stud, like Twenty Grand, their place in the record books made them standards, marks for future runners to aim for.

And, perhaps as importantly, they lifted the sport and the people who watched them run. The colts were men's men, never-say-die warriors; the fillies were courageous and glamorous, too, exemplified by the brilliance and class of Top Flight, so merciless against all comers, and the Blue Larkspur blazer Myrtlewood, who won 15 of her 22 starts, including nine stakes and two matches, and set three track records.

In general, the greatest Depression-era runners were, in some respects, like the survivors who filled grandstands to watch them run: hard-bitten, tough, and burdened by misfortune or physical frailty, as in Equipoise's case, or, in Discovery's case, by crushing weight. And still they fought hard, playing out on racing's stage the allegories of the era: struggle and win, or at least go down fighting.

CHAMPIONS

PAST PERFORMANCES

THE 1930's

•1936•
•2-YEAR-OLD MALE *Pompoon* •3-YEAR-OLD MALE *Granville* •HANDICAP HORSE *Discovery*
•SPRINTER *Myrtlewood* •STEEPLECHASE *Bushranger*
•**HORSE OF THE YEAR** Granville

•1937•
•2-YEAR-OLD MALE *Menow* •3-YEAR-OLD MALE *War Admiral* •HANDICAP HORSE *Seabiscuit*
•STEEPLECHASE *Jungle King*
•**HORSE OF THE YEAR** War Admiral

•1938•
•2-YEAR-OLD MALE *El Chico* •2-YEAR-OLD FILLY *Inscoelda* •3-YEAR-OLD MALE *Stagehand*
•HANDICAP HORSE *Seabiscuit* •HANDICAP MARE *Marica*
•**HORSE OF THE YEAR** Seabiscuit

•1939•
•2-YEAR-OLD MALE *Bimelech* •2-YEAR-OLD FILLY *Now What* •3-YEAR-OLD MALE *Challedon*
•3-YEAR-OLD FILLY *Unerring* •HANDICAP HORSE *Kayak II* •HANDICAP MARE *Lady Maryland*
•**HORSE OF THE YEAR** Challedon

Bushranger

ch. g. 1930, by Stefan the Great (The Tetrarch)–War Path, by Man o' War — **Lifetime record: 21 11 3 1 $20,635**

Own.– J.E. Widener
Br.– Joseph E. Widener (Ky)
Tr.– J.H. Lewis

3Oct36- 2Bel	fst *3	S'Chase 5:47	4↑ Grand National H 7.5k	5	4	45½	21	1½	12	Little H	172 w	*1.00	- -	Bushranger1722Rioter15610Amagansett157nk	Speed to spare	5
26Sep36- 2Bel	fst *2½	S'Chase 4:461	4↑ Brook H 3.7k	6	1	11	1nk	13	15	Little H	165 w	*1.80	- -	Bushrangr1655Rioter1573GoldenMeadow1547	Speed to spare	6
17Sep36- 2Bel	fst *2	S'Chase 3:423	3↑ Broad Hollow H 1.9k	4	2	11½	12	11½	11½	Little H	159 w	*.60	- -	Bushranger1591½Prattler13910Spinach143	Much the best	4
30May36- 2Bel	fst *2	S'Chase 3:433	4↑ Corinthian H 1.9k	2	1	14	1hd	11	12	Little H	157 w	*.75	- -	Bushranger1572Birmingham1391½Jungle King143		3
	Bobbled several fences,won in hand															
16May36- 6Bel	fst 1 1/16	:234 :473 1:123 1:441	3↑ Handicap 1230	6	5	53½	57	55¾	58¼	Wright WD	123wb	4.00	82-14	Rust107nkEsposa1073Chance Ray1102	Quit	7
5Nov35- 3Bel	gd 1½	:481 1:133 2:062 2:323	3↑ Whitney Trophy H 1.5k	1	3	22	21½	1hd	13	Wright WD	118 w	*1.50	- -	Bushranger1183Fortification105noChance Ray10040		4
	Fractious post,speed to spare															
30Sep35- 2Bel	fst *2	S'Chase 3:45	3↑ Broad Hollow H 1.8k	2	1	16	13	1hd	11	Little H	153 w	*.50	- -	Bushranger1531Amagansett154	Speed in reserve	2
25May35- 2Bel	fst *2	S'Chase 3:421	4↑ C L Appleton Mem 3.7k	7	3	53¾	43½	11	11½	Little H	143 w	*1.80	- -	Bushranger1431½Rideaway1402Spinach1421½	Speed to spare	8
18May35- 2Bel	fst *2	S'Chase 3:41	4↑ International H 2.1k	2	1	25	21½	22	21½	Little H	142 w	2.20	- -	Amagansett1431½Bushrangr1426JunglKng14810	Finished well	5
	Previously trained by D. Byers															
12Nov34- 1Pim	fst 2	S'Chase 3:452	4↑ Alw 1000	6	1	11	1hd	1hd	11¼	Little H	140 w	*1.30	- -	Bushranger1401¼Amagansett14210Help Me1384	Drawing away	7
5Nov34- 1Pim	sl 2	S'Chase 3:54	4↑ Alw 1000	2	2	1nk	11	11½	12	Little H	135 w	2.40	- -	Bushranger1352Snap Back14312Nesconset13315	Won in hand	6
17Sep34- 5Aqu	sly 1	:234 :481 1:133 1:381	2↑ Md Sp Wt	5	2	32	33½	21½	1no	Wright WD	120 w	3.00	89-10	Bushranger120noParma1053Sir Thomas1174		6
	Up final strides,impeded rival															
3Sep34- 2Bel	fst *2	S'Chase 3:452	3↑ Broad Hollow H 2.2k	7	6	511	-	-	-	Bauman A	137 w	2.00	- -	RockLad1427ThistlePlay135noPoppyman1356	Lost rider 9th	7
9Jun34- 2Bel	fst *2	S'Chase 3:42	4↑ Alw 1000	3	1	13	11½	1nk	11½	Bauman A	133 w	*1.40	- -	Bushranger1331½Nesconset13720Dock Light13620		5
	Bad landing 8th,recovered															
30May34- 2Bel	fst *2	S'Chase 3:472	4↑ Alw 1000	4	1	21	11	2hd	21½	Bauman A	136 w	2.50	- -	Nsconst1361½Bshrngr13650HolHgh1354	Saved ground,gamely	7
16May34- 2Bel	gd *2	S'Chase 3:442	4↑ International H 2.4k	5	3	43¼	42¾	-	-	Slate F	130 w	*1.40e	- -	Amagansett1305RockyRun131.55Benedictn142hd	Fell at 11th	8
	Previously trained by H. McDaniel															
8Nov32- 2Pim	hy 1 70	:24 :491 1:152 1:471	2↑ Md Sp Wt	5	3	33½	36	39	314	Studley W	108wb	3.90	61-27	BandWagon10812FrenchKnight1082Bshrngr1085	No excuses	12
3Nov32- 1Pim	gd 1 70	:24 :492 1:143 1:464	©Md Sp Wt	12	2	1hd	1hd	1hd	2no	Garner M	116wb	3.20	77-17	PolarBrush116noBushrngr1161½JudgJudy1161½	Dueled,gamely	12
24Oct32- 1Lrl	fst 6f	:233 :482 1:144	©Md Sp Wt	3	8	73¼	83¾	64¼	52¼	Garner M	115 w	4.10	80-12	Sky Haven115noChatterfol1152Band Wagon115hd	Fast finish	12
10Aug32- 3Sar	fst 5½f	:231 :471 1:001 1:07	Alw 800	6	12	79½	64½	67¼	65	Garner M	110 w	3.60	83-16	WeddingRing1151Sarada1101JungleKing1202	Dwelt at start	12
4Aug32- 6Sar	my 5½f	:233 :482 1:02 1:09	Md Sp Wt	9	10	88¾	87½	66	56½	Garner M	117 w	7.00	71-26	RushHour1171½Pompoleon1174CarrytheNws1171	Slow to start	11

Cavalcade

br. c. 1931, by Lancegaye (Swynford)–Hastily, by Hurry On — **Lifetime record: 22 8 5 3 $127,165**

Own.– Brookmeade Stable
Br.– F. Wallis Armstrong Sr (NJ)
Tr.– R.A. Smith

12Sep36- 5Nar	fst 1 1/16	:24 :481 1:132 1:444	3↑ Handicap 1400	2	6	78¼	816	915	923	Woolf G	120wb	4.10	70-13	Sun Teddy119½Mountainy Man1081Pundit103.5hd	Outrun	9
9Sep36- 5Nar	fst 1 1/16	:233 :472 1:123 1:441	3↑ Alw 1100	4	6	69¼	59½	58	612¼	Woolf G	121 w	*.60	84-08	Chancing106nkPiccolo1103Boston Brook1061	No excuses	7
30May35- 5Bel	fst 1¼	:46 1:103 1:361 2:02	3↑ Suburban H 15k	4	-	-	-	-	-	Gilbert J	127 w	*1.40	- -	Head Play1141½Discovery1233Only One1103	Lost rider	7
22May35- 4Bel	fst 1	:234 :471 1:112 1:371	3↑ Handicap 1230	1	3	24	24	24	23	Gilbert J	127 w	*.50	86-09	Head Play1143Cavalcade12710Carry Over1045	Evenly	4
14Jly34- 6AP	fst 1¼	:473 1:12 1:363 2:024	Classic 40k	6	7	78	31	13	14	Garner M	126 w	*.37e	95-08	Cavalcade1264Discovery121½Hadagal1213	In hand	9
16Jun34- 6Det	fst 1 3/16	:473 1:124 1:393 1:581	Det Derby 29k	7	11	106¾	1110	63	11½	Garner M	126 w	*.50e	107-04	Cavalcade1261½Plight1232New Deal1193	Handily	12
2Jun34- 6Was	fst 1¼	:464 1:114 1:381 2:04	American Derby 28k	1	9	89¾	64	1hd	12	Garner M	126 w	*1.07e	90-09	Cavalcade1262Discovery1186Singing Wood1211	Drew out	9
12May34- 5Pim	fst 1 3/16	:473 1:122 1:373 1:581	Preakness 29k	5	7	64¾	53½	2hd	2no	Garner M	126 w	*.45e	99-11	High Quest126noCavalcade1261Discovery1261½	Gaining	7
	Geldings not eligible															
5May34- 6CD	fst 1¼	:471 1:121 1:372 2:04	Ky Derby 36k	8	11	77½	32	2nk	12½	Garner M	126 w	*1.50e	89-11	Cavalcade1262½Discovery1264Agrarian126no	Handily	13
28Apr34- 5HdG	fst 1 1/16	:232 :47 1:113 1:433	Chesapeake 9.3k	8	3	1½	11	12	11¼	Garner M	119 w	*1.10e	102-07	Cavalcade1191¼Agrarian114noDiscovery114½	Driving	9
25Apr34- 5HdG	fst 1 70	:233 :473 1:123 1:414	Alw 1000	6	4	32½	22	11½	12	Garner M	113 w	*1.55e	100-07	Cavalcade1132Agrarian1064Jabot1081½	Easily	7
4Nov33- 4Pim	fst 1 1/16	:233 :473 1:12 1:443	Walden H 6.5k	6	8	53¾	57¼	38	36¼	Jones R	121 w	*3.00	93-07	Chicstraw118nkDiscovery1136Cavalcade1213	Closed fast	10
28Oct33- 4Lrl	fst 1	:232 :473 1:123 1:384	S Lowe Jenkins H 3.8k	3	4	72¼	52¼	32½	21	Bellizzi D	118 w	4.80	91-11	Bazaar1161Cavalcade118noVicar1063	Belated rush	8
7Oct33- 5Lrl	fst 6f	:23 :462 1:114	Richard Johnson 3.8k	3	6	64¼	62¼	43½	44	Bellizzi D	112 w	2.70	93-11	Chicstraw1161½WiseDughtr1191Dscovry1131½	Closed stoutly	6
3Oct33- 4Lrl	fst 5½f	:233 :472 1:061	Alw 800	4	6	55½	53¾	3½	11	Meade D	122 w	*1.00	92-14	Cavalcade1221Cant Remember1071Polly Egret1072	Drew out	6
27Sep33- 5HdG	fst 6f	:224 :46 1:113	Eastern Shore H 13k	1	9	94¼	84¾	31	21	Bellizzi D	115 w	8.00e	96-12	HighQuest1171Cavalcade1151WiseDaughtr1221½	Belated rush	9
23Aug33- 4Sar	hy 6f	:233 :482 1:15	Sanford 3.5k	3	2	31¾	31¾	2nk	22	Fronk W	123 w	*3.50e	75-27	FirstMinstrel1132Cavalcade123noSoonOver1165	Game finish	10
8Aug33- 3Sar	fst 5½f	:231 :464 1:06	Sar Sales 2.4k	4	8	68¾	54¼	32	34	Bellizzi D	122 w	6.00e	89-11	WiseDaughter1193BlackBuddy1221Cavalcade1222	Closed fast	8
5Aug33- 3Sar	gd 6f	:233 :474 1:14	U S Hotel 8.1k	4	6	61½	62	42¼	46¾	Horn F	125 w	4.00e	75-19	Red Wagon1171¼Black Buddy1274Sainted1151½	Shuffled back	7
1Jly33- 6AP	my 5½f	:23 :483 1:013 1:084	Hyde Park 14k	14	13	107½	84¼	34½	1nk	Bellizzi D	112 w	90.57f	77-34	Cavalcade112nkSinging Wood1141Dartle1176	Hard drive	14
28Jun33- 1AP	fst 5½f	:223 :453 :573 1:043	©Md Sp Wt	6	9	88¼	613	511	37½	Bellizzi D	118 w	6.73	90-09	Singing Wood1186Sir Ten1181½Cavalcade1183	Closed fast	10
27May33- 3Bel	fst 4½f-WC	:523	Alw 600	2	5		41½	41¼	45	Bellizzi D	112 w	12.00	87-10	Billy M.118noFoghound112noSalaam1155	Tired	8

Challedon

b. c. 1936, by Challenger II (Swynford)–Laura Gal, by Sir Gallahad III — **Lifetime record: 44 20 7 6 $334,660**

Own.– W.L. Brann
Br.– Branncastle Farm (Md)
Tr.– E.A. Christmas

17Nov42- 6Bow	fst 1⅛	:494 1:153 1:414 1:554	3↑ Handicap 1035	1	4	33	31	31	55	Keiper P	122wb	*2.10	79-19	SirAlfred1071½KsrofAudly1162½AbbPrr111½	Tired at finish	5
4Nov42- 7Pim	gd 1 1/16	:232 :473 1:131 1:47	3↑ Handicap 2000	4	2	11½	1hd	2hd	32¼	Woolf G	122wb	2.90	81-23	Ksar of Audley107nkBushwhacker1152Challedon122½	Tired	7
17Oct42- 7Lrl	sl 1 1/16	:243 :493 1:151 1:474	3↑ Handicap 2500	2	3	44½	46½	44¾	58	Woolf G	120 w	2.65	70-28	Equifox108.51¼Rosetown1113He Rolls1143	Tired	5
26Sep42- 5HdG	fst 1⅛	:473 1:12 1:373 1:50	3↑ Havre de Grace H 18k	2	6	78¾	810	811	814½	Woolf G	122 w	*1.30e	84-12	TolaRose109½Aonbarr1141½Pctor1164	Outrun,pulled up sore	9
26May42- 6Bel	fst 1⅛	:47 1:12 1:362 1:484	3↑ Handicap 3035	4	3	32½	2hd	22	25	Woolf G	126 w	1.25	93-08	Shut Out1125Challedon1264Reading II1185	Second best	4
6May42- 6Pim	fst 1 3/16	:472 1:114 1:374 1:57	3↑ Dixie H 25k	6	7	713	710	3nk	41¼	Woolf G	124 w	5.90	97-12	Whirlaway128¾Attention124½Mioland126hd	Weakened	8
25Apr42- 5HdG	fst 1 1/16	:241 :482 1:13 1:452	3↑ Philadelphia H 11k	6	7	78¼	73¾	31½	1no	Woolf G	122 w	3.20	91-21	Challedon122noMioland1241½Cape Cod1123	Hard drive	7
18Apr42- 7HdG	fst 1 1/16	:24 :483 1:132 1:452	3↑ Handicap 3000	4	4	42½	33	32	2hd	Woolf G	124wb	*.80	91-18	Alaking112hdChalledon1243Warlock1081½	Just missed	6
7Mar42- 6Hia	fst 1¼	:47 1:122 1:374 2:051	3↑ Widener H 67k	12	14	1614	129¾	103¾	61½	Woolf G	126wb	13.85e	81-17	The Rhymer111hdBest Seller112hdOlympus107nk	Off slowly	17
28Feb42- 5Hia	fst 1⅛	:462 1:112 1:364 1:493	4↑ Sp Wt 2500	8	5	73¾	73½	66	56¼	Woolf G	122wb	3.55e	87-14	Market Wise1201½Attention120½War Relic120nk	No mishaps	9
24Feb42- 6Hia	sl 7f	:224 :463 1:114 1:243	4↑ Alw 1400	5	4	58¼	43½	32	13	Woolf G	117 w	*1.25	89-21	Challedon1173Signator110hdDoublrab1094	Going away	6
16Feb42- 6Hia	fst 1⅛	:483 1:123 1:373 1:504	4↑ Alw 1400	4	5	54½	44	41¾	25	Woolf G	126 w	*.65	82-23	Ponty1065Challedon126noChoppy Sea1063	Dwelt at start	6
7Feb42- 7Hia	fst 7f	:231 :463 1:113 1:24	4↑ Alw 1500	2	6	57	37	34	22	Woolf G	124 w	14.55	90-13	SheriffCulkin1052Challedon1241¼WarRelic1226	Closed fast	7
	Previously trained by L.T. Whitehill															
4Jly41- 7Hol	fst 1⅛	:462 1:104 1:364 1:492	3↑ American H 22k	8	8	97¾	106¾	99	88	Woolf G	126 w	*2.60	90-09	Mioland126noWoof Woof1141Big Pebble117½	Dull effort	10
1Mar41- 6SA	sly 1¼	:47 1:121 1:383 2:052	3↑ S Anita H 124k	7	7	107	1322	1322	1417¾	Woolf G	130 w	3.20	61-29	Bay View108nkMioland1244Bolingbroke1062	Outrun	16

22Feb41- 6SA	sl	1 1/16	:234 :473 1:121 1:452	3↑ San Antonio H 12k	11 9 910 1014 815 77	Woolf G	128 w	3.70	78-23	Mioland128noHysterical1111Bay View1051	Raced wide 11
Previously trained by G.D. Cameron											
1Nov40- 7Pim	sl	1 3/16	:52 1:18 1:444 2:031	3↑ Pim Spl 10k	2 1 13 12½ 12½ 12	Woolf G	126 w	*.20	67-24	Challedon1262Can't Wait126	Easily 2
28Sep40- 5HdG	fst	1⅛	:483 1:124 1:38 1:502	3↑ Havre de Grace H 16k	1 3 43¼ 31 1hd 13	Woolf G	130 w	*.25	97-13	Challdn1303HoneyCloud110½MaskedGeneral1125	Going away 4
21Sep40- 6Nar	fst	1 3/16	:472 1:13 1:381 1:57	3↑ Nar Spl 31k	1 3 48 31 12 2½	Woolf G	130 w	*.70	89-16	Hash122½Challedon130½Viscounty1165	Tired badly 9
Previously trained by L.J. Schaefer											
27Aug40- 5Sar	fst	1¼	:484 1:131 1:381 2:031	3↑ Whitney 3.7k	3 1 22 21 1hd 1no	Woolf G	126 w	*.20	93-14	Challdon126noIsoltr1267¾DuskyFox117	Driving,forced wide 3
27Jly40- 7Hol	fst	1¼	:461 1:11 1:36 2:02	3↑ Hol Gold Cup 53k	9 6 89½ 53 23 11¼	Woolf G	133 w	2.70	103-07	Challedon1331¼Specify1172½Can't Wait1151½	Going away 11
17Jly40- 7Suf	fst	1⅛	:471 1:104 1:353 1:49	3↑ Mass H 65k	8 8 87¾ 64¾ 64¾ 32½	Woolf G	130 w	*.90	97-12	Eight Thirty1261Hash1151½Challedon130½	Closed fast 11
9Jly40- 0Suf	fst	1 1/16	:243 :474 1:121 1:441	4↑ Alw 1500	2 1 11 11½ 13 12½	Woolf G	126 w	-	95-12	Challedon1262½Many Stings118	Easily 2
1Nov39- 5Pim	gd	1 3/16	:512 1:163 1:404 1:59	3↑ Pim Spl 10k	2 2 11 1½ 2hd 1½	Arcaro E	120 w	*.45	88-19	Challedon120½Kayak II12612Cravat126	Going away 3
21Oct39- 5Lrl	fst	1¼	:47 1:112 1:363 2:023	Maryland H 8.8k	4 1 45½ 1hd 12 14	Woolf G	128 w	*.15	97-14	Challedon1284General Mowlee1001Hostility1066	Going away 5
10Oct39- 5Kee	fst	1 3/16	:471 1:114 1:361 1:543	3↑ Tranter 5.4k	5 5 53¾ 2hd 12 14	Woolf G	120 w	*.40	144-02	Challedon1204Hash1168Chief Onaway1082	Ridden out 5
30Sep39- 5HdG	my	1⅛	:482 1:141 1:40 1:523	3↑ Havre de Grace H 18k	1 3 33 31½ 12 14	Woolf G	122 w	*.70	86-22	Challedon1224RobertL.107nkManieO'Hara105.51½	Going away 6
16Sep39- 6Haw	fst	1¼	:471 1:12 1:373 2:031	3↑ Haw Gold Cup H 16k	4 5 65 42 1½ 1¾	Richards H	120 w	*.30	92-12	Challedon120¾Gridiron106noChief Onaway108¾	Drew away 8
2Sep39- 5Nar	fst	1 3/16	:482 1:124 1:374 1:563	3↑ Nar Spl H 31k	6 6 64½ 52 1½ 13	Richards H	118 w	2.60	92-14	Challedon1183Kayak II1284Sorteado116½	Going away 6
26Aug39- 5Nar	hy	1⅛	:472 1:131 1:394 1:524	J C Thornton Mem H 6.1k	2 6 66¾ 32 21 21½	Richards H	128 w	*.55	81-23	Porter's Mite1161½Challedon1282½Montsin10410	No excuse 6
22Jly39- 6AP	fst	1¼	:47 1:112 1:36 2:02	Classic 47k	4 4 59½ 21½ 1½ 1nk	Richards H	126 w	13.60	96-11	Challedon126nkSun Lover1216Johnstown1262	Hard drive 5
12Jly39- 7Suf	sly	1⅛	:482 1:13 1:391 1:52	3↑ Mass H 68k	8 11 118¼ 97 66¾ 46	Richards H	113 w	*1.30	79-19	Fighting Fox113½Pompoon1203Burning Star1102½	Late foot 12
4Jly39- 6Suf	fst	1 3/16	:464 1:104 1:37 1:562	Yankee H 18k	2 4 68 45 11 11	Richards H	124 w	*.90	99-11	Challedon1241Hash1172Silent Witness106no	Easily 6
24Jun39- 5Del	fst	1 1/16	:24 :472 1:13 1:444	Kent H 12k	1 6 63¾ 52 32 32	Seabo G	126 w	*1.90	93-11	SunLover117noEightThirty1202Challedon1261½	Closed well 9
17Jun39- 5Aqu	fst	1⅛	:46 1:103 1:353 1:482	Dwyer 12k	1 2 22 24 23 37	Seabo G	126 w	8.00	92-05	Johnstown1261Sun Lover1166Challedon1266	Weakened 5
13May39- 6Pim	my	1 3/16	:473 1:133 1:394 1:594	Preakness 70k	2 2 44½ 34½ 11½ 11¼	Seabo G	126 w	6.20	84-19	Challedon1261¼Gilded Knight1263Volitant1263	Ridden out 6
6May39- 7CD	fst	1¼	:472 1:124 1:38 2:032	Ky Derby 56k	7 5 78 45 35 28	Seabo G	126 w	6.60	84-11	Johnstown1268Challedn1261Heather Broom126½	Good effort 8
22Apr39- 5HdG	fst	1 1/16	:232 :48 1:131 1:453	Chesapeake 17k	3 8 77¾ 53 44½ 32½	Seabo G	122 w	*2.60	87-14	Gilded Knight1141Impound1191½Challedon1221½	Closed fast 9
12Nov38- 6Pim	fst	1 1/16	:232 :473 1:124 1:454	Pim Futurity 33k	3 7 64¾ 33½ 2hd 11½	Seabo G	119 w	3.95	91-13	Challedon1191½ThirdDegree1191GildedKnght1222	Going away 8
Geldings not eligible											
29Oct38- 6Nar	hy	1 70	:231 :47 1:14 1:462	New England Fut 42k	6 6 64¼ 1hd 13 12	Seabo G	114 w	14.70	73-30	Challedon1142Impound114nkGilded Knight1144	Handily 7
Geldings not eligible											
15Oct38- 4Lrl	fst	6f	:234 :473 1:132	[S]Md Futurity 6.4k	7 5 71¾ 62¾ 31 1no	Seabo G	111 w	*2.30	87-12	Challedon111noWar Moon1091Mystery Miss1133	Just up 12
17Sep38- 5HdG	fst	6f	:232 :464 1:124	Eastern Shore H 15k	7 13 138¼ 138¼ 1215 126½	Laidley O	116 w	8.25	82-14	Time Alone1091Sweet Nancy110hdT.M. Dorsett112½	Outrun 15
7Sep38- 2Nar	fst	6f	:224 :462 1:121	Md Sp Wt	3 3 11½ 13 14 14	Laidley O	116 w	2.50	90-11	Challedon1164Greedan1162½Top Queen1132	Much best 8
6Jly38- 5Del	fst	5½f	:234 :49 1:004 1:072	Alw 1000	2 4 53¾ 54¼ 47 36	Laidley O	112 w	31.10	89-11	Birch Rod1182Buds Bell1154Challedon112hd	Closed fast 7

Discovery

ch. c. 1931, by Display (Fair Play)–Ariadne, by Light Brigade
Own.– A.G. Vanderbilt
Br.– Mereworth Stud (Ky)
Tr.– J.H. Stotler

Lifetime record: 63 27 10 10 $195,287

30Sep36- 5HdG	sly	1⅛	:48 1:131 1:373 1:51	3↑ Havre de Grace H 11k	1 4 44 45½ 46½ 54½	Bejshak J	128wsb	*.75	89-16	RomnSldier1182WhereAway1102DrkHop110½	Not enough late 8
16Sep36- 5Nar	fst	1 3/16	:48 1:123 1:373 1:562	3↑ Nar Spl 37k	5 8 88½ 87¾ 32 2hd	Bejshak J	130wb	*1.55	93-11	Rosemont121hdDiscovery1301½Time Supply1216	Just missed 8
29Aug36- 5Sar	sly	1¾	:502 2:083 2:341 3:004	3↑ Sar Cup 7.7k	1 2 21½ 21 25 28	Bejshak J	126 w	*.40	63-22	Granville1168Discovery126	Outrun 2
22Aug36- 5Sar	my	1¼	:483 1:131 1:392 2:064	3↑ Whitney 4.4k	1 1 410 13 15 110	Bejshak J	126wsb	*.20	75-27	Discovery12610Esposa1218Rust1061	Eased up 4
Geldings not eligible											
8Aug36- 5Sar	sl	1 3/16	:492 1:143 1:403 2:002	3↑ Merchants & Cits H 11k	4 4 44½ 32½ 55¼ 56½	Bejshak J	143wsb	*.70	69-22	Esposa1001Count Arthur107hdMantagna1081½	Tired 5
5Aug36- 4Sar	fst	1	:241 :481 1:132 1:384	3↑ Wilson 4.5k	1 1 12 15 14 18	Bejshak J	126wsb	*.04e	87-17	Discovery1268St. Bernard115.55Purple Knight114	Easily 3
Geldings not eligible											
1Aug36- 5Sar	fst	1¼	:48 1:121 1:382 2:05	3↑ Saratoga H 10k	1 3 12 13 14 16	Bejshak J	132wsb	*.60e	84-12	Discovery1326Mantagna1091½Isolater103nk	Easily 6
22Jly36- 5Suf	fst	1⅛	:472 1:12 1:373 1:494	3↑ Mass H 32k	2 7 102¾ 94½ 78¾ 89½	Fallon L	136wsb	*1.10e	88-07	Time Supply1213Gov. Sholtz1003Stand Pat1191	Impeded 11
4Jly36- 6AP	fst	1⅛	:474 1:12 1:371 1:493	3↑ Stars & Stripes H 13k	5 8 77¼ 88 810 98¾	Fallon L	138wsb	*1.00	90-09	Stand Pat1161½Corinto108noWhopper122no	Swerved 12
27Jun36- 5Aqu	fst	1⅛	:472 1:122 1:372 1:50	3↑ Brooklyn H 14k	3 4 23 22 21½ 14	Fallon L	136wb	*.29e	91-12	Discovery1364Good Gamble1104Roman Soldier126hd	Easily 5
17Jun36- 4Aqu	fst	1⅛	:47 1:113 1:371 1:50	3↑ Handicap 1165	2 2 12 14 14 14	Fallon L	135wb	*.45	91-13	Discovery1354Palma1063Observant110	Easily 3
22Feb36- 6SA	gd	1¼	:46 1:104 1:372 2:041	3↑ S Anita H 122k	12 12 109 114½ 108½ 75¾	Bejshak J	130wsb	*1.50	84-17	Top Row116½Time Supply114½Rosemont116½	Bumped 15
8Feb36- 6SA	fst	1⅛	:472 1:12 1:37 1:492	3↑ San Antonio H 8.6k	8 6 52¾ 51¼ 46 58	Bejshak J	138wsb	*.70e	93-10	TimeSupply1166PompeysPillar1051ArlCross106½	Dull effort 9
1Feb36- 6SA	sly	1 1/16	:232 :472 1:122 1:452	3↑ San Carlos H 5.7k	3 6 59 46½ 2½ 15	Bejshak J	130wsb	*.60	87-20	Discovery1305Ariel Cross1065Beefsteak1041½	Easily best 6
26Oct35- 5Lrl	fst	1¼	:461 1:113 1:371 2:023	3↑ Washington H 12k	7 9 99¾ 63½ 53½ 45	Bejshak J	138wsb	*.65	92-13	Firethorn1193CountArthur112noOnlyOne1142	Closed ground 9
22Oct35- 6Cl	my	1¼	:483 1:133 1:392 2:062	3↑ Cincinnati H 12k	6 5 35 16 110 112	Bejshak J	132wb	*.20	78-26	Discovry13212GoldenRockII10412OpenHearth1031	Much best 6
16Oct35- 6Suf	fst	1⅛	:473 1:12 1:364 1:492	3↑ Mass H 27k	7 3 31 2hd 3nk 3nk	Bejshak J	138wsb	*.70	112-02	Top Row116nkWhopper108noDiscovery1382	Good effort 8
5Oct35- 6Haw	fst	1¼	:472 1:112 1:372 2:042	3↑ Haw Gold Cup 16k	3 1 21 14 15 18	Bejshak J	126wsb	*.10	86-11	Discovery1263Top Dog1208Spanish Babe1174	Eased up 4
24Aug35- 5Sar	fst	1¼	:48 1:13 1:38 2:043	3↑ Whitney 4.3k	2 1 22 1hd 11 12	Bejshak J	126wsb	*.10e	86-14	Discovery1262Esposa1001½Good Goods1147	Easily 4
Geldings not eligible											
21Aug35- 5Nar	fst	1 3/16	:484 1:123 1:37 1:554	3↑ Nar Spl 30k	2 1 11½ 2hd 21 21½	Bejshak J	139wsb	*.25	94-08	Top Row1101½Discovery1391Howard1072	No mishap 5
10Aug35- 5Sar	fst	1 3/16	:482 1:132 1:38 1:572	3↑ Merchants & Cits H 10k	5 1 12 12 12 12	Bejshak J	139wsb	*.60e	91-14	Discovery1392Stand Pat1172Top Row1175	In hand 6
31Jly35- 4Sar	fst	1	:244 :48 1:121 1:371	3↑ Wilson 4.5k	2 2 2hd 13 13 16	Bejshak J	126wb	*.10e	95-11	Discovery1266Identify122nkPsychic Bid112	Eased up 3
Geldings not eligible											
27Jly35- 6AP	fst	1¼	:472 1:11 1:36 2:011	3↑ Arlington H 12k	6 5 32 1½ 13 15	Bejshak J	135wsb	*.30	103-06	Discovery1355Stand Pat1154Riskulus1162	Easily 7
20Jly35- 6Suf	gd	1⅛	:484 1:133 1:392 1:514	3↑ Bunker Hill H 10k	5 3 2hd 13 16 115	Bejshak J	131wsb	*.20	--	Discovery13115Gov.Sholtz1071AdvisingAnna103½	Galloping 5
13Jly35- 5Emp	sl	1⅛	:484 1:13 1:39 1:53	3↑ Butler H 15k	4 4 48 33½ 31¾ 11½	Bejshak J	132wsb	*.90	90-11	Discovery1321½Only One1132Top Row1163	Easily 6
4Jly35- 6AP	gd	1⅛	:482 1:13 1:382 1:504	3↑ Stars & Stripes H 12k	4 4 2½ 1hd 13 16	Bejshak J	126wsb	*.30	93-18	Discovery1266Chief Cherokee1061½Riskulus1182	Easily 8
29Jun35- 6Det	my	1 3/16	:464 1:12 1:381 1:581	3↑ Det Challenge Cup 13k	1 1 16 110 118 130	Bejshak J	126wb	*.20	100-25	Discovery12630Azucar127	Easily 2
22Jun35- 5Aqu	fst	1⅛	:461 1:112 1:353 1:481	3↑ Brooklyn H 13k	2 2 22 21½ 1nk 18	Bejshak J	123wb	5.00	102-13	Discovery1238King Saxon1274Omaha1146	Driven out 6
15Jun35- 5Rkm	my	1⅛	:47 1:122 1:39 1:522	3↑ Rock Park H 10k	1 4 22 33 32½ 33	Bejshak J	128wsb	*1.20e	84-18	Identify1138Dark Hope113hdDiscovery1282½	Closed well 11
10Jun35- 5Aqu	gd	1	:232 :463 1:113 1:371	3↑ Queens County H 4.7k	5 4 42½ 43¾ 43¾ 57	Bejshak J	123wsb	2.60	87-09	King Saxon1181Only One1103Singing Wood113hd	Faltered 6
30May35- 5Bel	fst	1¼	:46 1:103 1:361 2:02	3↑ Suburban H 15k	6 6 68 66½ 42¾ 21½	Bejshak J	123wsb	2.60e	88-12	Head Play1141½Discovery1233Only One1103	Closed well 7
18May35- 4Bel	fst	1	:233 :471 1:121 1:381	3↑ Metropolitan H 8.8k	4 5 52¼ 43¾ 43½ 41	Bejshak J	127wsb	5.00	83-16	King Saxon118nkSinging Wood114nkOnly One113½	Swerved 9
15May35- 4Bel	fst	6f-WC	1:113	3↑ Toboggan H 5.2k	12 7 53 44½ 52½	Bejshak J	130wb	*1.80e	86-11	Identify1081½Ajaccio1161Pompeys Pillar102no	Evenly 12
20Oct34- 5Lrl	fst	1¼	:461 1:102 1:364 2:03	Maryland H 6k	3 1 11½ 12 13 1½	Bejshak J	130wsb	*.30	95-09	Discovery130½Good Goods1095Maine Chance105nk	Hard drive 5
29Sep34- 5HdG	fst	1⅛	:473 1:114 1:38 1:504	3↑ Havre de Grace H 12k	5 9 62½ 32 33 31	Bejshak J	126wsb	*.55	94-10	Faireno122noAzucar1081Discovery1261½	Impeded 9
15Sep34- 5HdG	gd	1 1/16	:243 :49 1:134 1:451	Potomac H 11k	5 5 32½ 3½ 14 14	Bejshak J	128wsb	*.60	92-17	Discovery1284Chicstraw116noOnly One1061	Easily 6
3Sep34- 6Nar	fst	1 3/16	:472 1:132 1:373 1:55	3↑ Rhode Island H 16k	1 5 11½ 11½ 12 16	Bejshak J	119wsb	*1.00	--	Discovery1192Hadagal1192½Good Goods1041	Easily 6
1Sep34- 5Rkm	fst	1 1/16	:234 :474 1:131 1:431	3↑ Bennington H 10k	8 10 86 54 65¼ 56½	Bejshak J	124wb	*.40	98-07	Advising Anna1022Fleam1073Larranaga1131½	Impeded 10
25Aug34- 5Sar	hy	1¼	:503 1:162 1:413 2:074	3↑ Whitney 3.3k	3 1 23 13 15 110	Meade D	105wb	*.33	70-24	Discovery10510Fleam1074Time Clock1121	Eased up 4
14Aug34- 4Sar	fst	1 3/16	:481 1:122 1:373 1:571	Kenner 2.4k	2 1 15 16 13 12	Bejshak J	113wsb	*.10	92-10	Discovery1132Somebody1068Cleves106	Easily 3
14Jly34- 6AP	fst	1¼	:473 1:12 1:363 2:024	Classic 40k	4 1 43½ 2hd 23 24	Bejshak J	121wsb	4.91	91-08	Cavalcade1264Discovery121½Hadagal1213	Held well 9

4Jly34- 4Aqu	fst 1⅛	:481 1:13 1:373 1:494 3↑	Brooklyn H 4.3k	4 2 21 23 22 16	Bejshak J	113wb	*.60	94-14	Discovery1136Dark Secret1266Fleam1081	Easily	4
28Jun34- 4Aqu	fst 7f	:232 :464 1:112 1:233	Alw 1200	4 2 2hd 12 13 16	Bejshak J	112wsb	*1.80	97-10	Discovery1126Fleam1103Somebody1153	In hand	7
16Jun34- 6Det	fst 1 3/16	:473 1:124 1:393 1:581	Det Derby 29k	2 1 64 53¼ 108 1114½	Workman R	119wsb	3.50	92-04	Cavalcade1261½Plight1232New Deal1193	Outrun	12
2Jun34- 6Was	fst 1¼	:464 1:114 1:381 2:04	American Derby 28k	6 6 57½ 42 2hd 22	Bejshak J	118wb	2.74	88-09	Cavalcade1262Discovery1186Singing Wood1211	Troubled	9
25May34- 3Bel	sly 7f	:232 :471 1:12 1:25	Alw 1000	6 1 14 15 16 110	Bejshak J	112wsb	*.20	85-17	Discovery11210War Letter115½Rebel Yell1093	In hand	7
12May34- 5Pim	fst 1 3/16	:473 1:122 1:373 1:581	Preakness 29k	2 2 31 32 3nk 31	Bejshak J	126wsb	7.40	98-11	High Quest126noCavalcade1261Discovery1261½	Gamely	7
	Geldings not eligible										
5May34- 6CD	fst 1¼	:471 1:121 1:372 2:04	Ky Derby 36k	6 4 33 12 1nk 22½	Bejshak J	126wb	12.10	86-11	Cavalcade1262½Discovery1264Agrarian126no	Held well	13
28Apr34- 5HdG	fst 1 1/16	:232 :47 1:113 1:433	Chesapeake 9.3k	1 2 31 21 22 31¼	Bejshak J	114wb	3.60	101-07	Cavalcade1191¼Agrarian114noDiscovery114½	Faltered	9
4Nov33- 4Pim	fst 1 1/16	:233 :473 1:12 1:443	Walden H 6.5k	7 3 2hd 1hd 2hd 2nk	Humphries L	113wb	4.40	99-07	Chicstraw118nkDiscovery1136Cavalcade1213	Just missed	10
	Previously owned by A. Pons,previously trained by J.R. Pryce										
28Oct33- 6Lat	fst 1	:232 :464 1:124 1:394	Ky Jockey Club 19k	10 5 36 35½ 24 22½	Allen CE	122wb	3.60	80-18	Mata Hari1192½Discovery1222Collateral1222½	Closed well	11
21Oct33- 6Lat	fst 6f-FC	:222 :461 :592 1:093	Breeders' Futurity 21k	6 5 86½ 79½ 47½ 32¾	Allen CE	122wb	3.20	98-18	Mata Hari1242½Giggling119nkDiscovery122no	Belated rush	12
7Oct33- 5Lrl	fst 6f	:23 :462 1:114	Richard Johnson 3.8k	1 4 53¾ 31½ 31½ 32½	Steffen E	113wb	13.60	94-11	Chicstraw1161½WiseDughtr1191Dscovry1131½	Close quarters	6
27Sep33- 5HdG	fst 6f	:224 :46 1:113	Eastern Shore H 13k	8 5 62 63¾ 66½ 66	Steffen E	116wb	25.90	91-12	High Quest1171Cavalcade1151Wise Daughter1221½	Even race	9
21Sep33- 4HdG	fst 6f	:233 :472 1:122	Alw 800	3 1 2½ 21 1½ 12½	Gilbert J	113wb	*.80	93-11	Discovery1132½Prince Pompey1134Collateral115hd	Easily	6
2Sep33- 4Sar	fst 6½f	:232 :47 1:121 1:19	Hopeful 38k	3 14 106 98¼ 85 34	Gilbert J	117wb	15.00	86-14	Bazaar1194High Quest117noDiscovery117no	Belated rush	14
28Aug33- 5Sar	gd 6f	:232 :474 1:13	Alw 600	2 3 34 32 31¼ 33½	Robertson A	111wb	12.00	83-19	High Quest1112Soon Over1181½Discovery1113	Closed well	8
29Jly33- 5AP	fst 6f	:223 :46 1:111	Arl Futurity 42k	4 6 84¾ 811 711 710½	Corbett C	117wb	69.33	84-11	Far Star1161¼Hadagal1176Singing Wood1171½	Outrun	8
18Jly33- 4AP	fst 5½f	:23 :463 :592 1:053	Alw 800	3 5 31½ 21 21½ 23	Jones R	115wb	3.52	90-13	Hadagal1153Discovery115½Spy Hill1111	Closed well	7
6Jly33- 1AP	fst 5½f	:223 :463 :592 1:06	©Md Sp Wt	11 6 52½ 31½ 11 15	Jones R	118wb	6.98	91-12	Discovery1185GoldSignet118nkCottonClub1181	Easily best	12
28Jun33- 1AP	fst 5½f	:223 :453 :573 1:043	©Md Sp Wt	7 6 3½ 36½ 48½ 511½	Woolf G	118wb	*2.40	86-09	Singing Wood1186Sir Ten1181½Cavalcade1183	Tired	10
8Jun33- 5Bel	fst 5f-WC	1:00	Md Sp Wt	2 1 31 31 32½	Mills H	115wb	*1.50	77-14	Galabang1152½Willow King115noDiscovery115nk	Faltered	7
3Jun33- 6Bel	fst 5f-WC	:593	Md Sp Wt	1 7 55¼ 46 48¾	Robertson A	117 w	3.60	73-19	Watch Her1147Koterito1171½Galabang117nk	Closed well	8

El Chico

ch. c. 1936, by John P. Grier (Whisk Broom II)–La Chica, by Sweep **Lifetime record: 18 9 3 1 $88,050**

Own.– W. Ziegler Jr
Br.– Leslie Combs Jr trustee (Ky)
Tr.– M. Brady

7Oct39- 4Lrl	fst 6f	:233 :463 1:114 3↑	Handicap 1500	5 3 41¼ 52 62¼ 52¼	Wall N	117 w	3.10	93-14	Joe Schenck114hdAllegro1111½Bill Farnsworth119nk		7
	Hard urged,no excuse										
3Oct39- 5Lrl	my 6f	:243 :483 1:132 3↑	Capital H 9.3k	5 2 3nk 73½ 88½ 810	Wall N	119 w	3.85	77-22	Sun Egret1201½Clodion1121½Rough Time122½	Tired	8
23Sep39- 5HdG	fst 1 1/16	:24 :472 1:124 1:444	Potomac H 11k	1 1 11 11 2½ 33¼	Wall N	115 w	6.70	91-15	Third Degree1143Porter's Mite116nkEl Chico1151½	Tired	7
13Sep39- 5Aqu	fst 6½f	:222 :453 1:101 1:163 3↑	Bay Shore H 7.6k	9 7 54 41½ 2nk 68½	Workman R	126 w	*2.60e	91-08	ThirdDegree1161½BillFarnsworth1213WsBrrstr106hd	Impeded	12
14Aug39- 5Nar	fst 6f	:223 :46 1:11 3↑	Nar H 6.7k	3 5 61½ 1hd 1½ 2no	Wall N	115 w	*.35	96-12	Olney108noEl Chico1152½Prairie Dog103hd	No excuse	10
10Aug39- 5Sar	fst 6f	:224 :461 1:103	Alw 1000	4 1 11½ 13 14 13	Wall N	119 w	*.33	99-08	ElChico1193ThirdDegree1162NoCompetition1192	Easily best	4
1Aug39- 5Sar	fst 1	:232 :471 1:112 1:373 3↑	Alw 1200	3 1 14 15 16 15	Wall N	105 w	*.90	93-12	El Chico1055Pernie113noMy Porter1094	Much best	7
30May39- 3Bel	fst 6f	:224 :462 1:12	Alw 1200	3 3 21 1hd 2hd 22	Wall N	117 w	*.50	88-20	Golden Voyage1132El Chico1171½Black Bun1136	Hung	4
6May39- 7CD	fst 1¼	:472 1:124 1:38 2:032	Ky Derby 56k	1 1 22 613 617 623½	Wall N	126 w	8.20	68-11	Johnstown1268Challedon1261Heather Broom126½	Quit	8
29Apr39- 5Jam	fst 1 70	:23 :464 1:112 1:42	Wood Memorial 24k	4 5 59½ 58½ 613 615¼	Wall N	120 w	3.60	79-11	Johnstown1208Volitant1201Impound120¾	Impeded	8
15Apr39- 4Jam	fst 6f	:223 :46 1:112	Alw 1200	3 1 1½ 11 1hd 2no	Wall N	116 w	*.14e	95-14	Gilded Knight116noEl Chico1163Sea Captain1135	Not urged	5
10Sep38- 5Aqu	fst 6½f	:224 :46 1:114 1:18	Jr Champion 13k	2 2 1hd 1hd 2hd 11	Wall N	122 w	*.45	96-06	El Chico1221Volitant114noJohnstown1145	Driving	4
27Aug38- 4Sar	fst 6½f	:231 :463 1:121 1:182	Hopeful 48k	10 1 11 14 12 12	Wall N	126 w	*.33	93-08	El Chico1262Ariel Toy1161Johnstown116hd	In hand	11
6Aug38- 4Sar	fst 6f	:224 :46 1:102	Sar Spl 8k	8 1 11½ 11½ 11 13	Wall N	122 w	*.40	100-05	El Chico1223Eight Thirty1224Third Degree1225	Going away	8
30Jly38- 4Sar	sl 6f	:224 :47 1:131	U S Hotel 12k	6 3 1½ 12 13 18	Wall N	122 w	*2.00	86-16	El Chico1228Invader1162Eight Thirty122no	Much best	11
25Jun38- 4Aqu	fst 6f	:23 :47 1:131	Great American 4.7k	1 1 34½ 34½ 3¾ 14	Wall N	119 w	2.50e	88-12	El Chico1194Lovely Night1154Maeline1191	Going away	6
11Jun38- 5Del	fst 5f	:224 :46 :591	Dover 7.1k	10 4 31 21½ 1½ 11	Wall N	122 w	*2.40	100-03	El Chico1221Star Runner1164Cherry Jam1162	Drew out	10
16Apr38- 4Jam	fst 5f	:231 :474 1:00	Youthful 4.2k	3 3 11½ 1nk 11½ 14	Wall N	114 w	*2.20	93-13	El Chico1144Jack Horner119hdWise Shine1141	Going away	8

Equipoise

ch. c. 1928, by Pennant (Peter Pan)–Swinging, by Broomstick **Lifetime record: 51 29 10 4 $338,610**

Own.– C.V. Whitney
Br.– H.P. Whitney (Ky)
Tr.– T.J. Healey

23Feb35- 6SA	fst 1¼	:45 1:10 1:36 2:021 3↑	S Anita H 125k	19 12 1213 1213 74¼ 77½	Workman R	130wb	*1.70e	- -	Azucar1172Ladysman1171Time Supply1182		20
	Off slowly,close quarters										
18Feb35- 5SA	fst 1 1/16	:24 :473 1:12 1:432 3↑	Handicap 1200	4 3 31½ 31 1hd 11	Workman R	125wb	*.60	- -	[D]Equipos1251TwntyGrnd1163Srd1051½	Bumped rival,bore in	5
	Disqualified										
13Feb35- 5SA	fst 1	:23 :463 1:102 1:363 3↑	Handicap 1000	5 5 45 33 3½ 21	Workman R	128wb	*.30	- -	Sweping Light1091Equipoise128nkTed Clark1111½	Impeded	8
6Nov34- 3Bel	sly 1¼	:493 1:143 1:404 2:063 3↑	Whitney Trophy H 5.5k	5 1 51 21½ 2hd 11½	Workman R	128wb	*.55	67-23	Equipoise1281½Faireno1222Mr. Khayyam1204	Ridden out	6
31Oct34- 6Nar	fst 6f	:23 :453 1:104 3↑	Invitation 5.1k	5 2 45½ 44½ 43¾ 3½	Workman R	130wb	*.45	100-07	Okapi130½All Forlorn127noEquipoise130hd	Closed fast	5
30May34- 5Bel	fst 1¼	:471 1:12 1:371 2:023 3↑	Suburban H 7.4k	1 4 53¼ 31¼ 2½ 2no	Robertson A	134wb	*.50	87-16	Ladysman114noEquipoise13410War Glory1151½	Just missed	8
19May34- 4Bel	fst 1	:233 :47 1:112 1:37 3↑	Metropolitan H 4.3k	6 8 82¾ 4½ 1hd 12	Workman R	132wb	*.70	90-15	[D]Equipoise1322Mr.Khyym1191SunArchr1065	Swerved stretch	9
	Disqualified										
5May34- 5Pim	fst 1 3/16	:483 1:14 1:40 2:014 3↑	Dixie H 5.9k	4 1 2nk 2½ 14 11½	Workman R	130wb	*.10	81-19	Equipoise1301½Chatmoss1103Flaming Mamie1027	Easily	4
21Apr34- 5HdG	fst 1 1/16	:232 :472 1:122 1:442 3↑	Philadelphia H 8.4k	4 4 32½ 21 11½ 11	Workman R	130wb	*.50	98-08	Equipoise1301Springsteel1174Larranaga1136	In hand	5
30Sep33- 5HdG	fst 1⅛	:48 1:114 1:371 1:494 3↑	Havre de Grace H 11k	1 4 42 31½ 21 21	Workman R	132wb	*1.60	100-09	Osculator1041Equipoise1321½Mate1101½	Closed well	9
16Sep33- 5Bel	my 2	:50 2:341 3:251 3↑	J C Gold Cup 8.1k	1 2 21½ 21 31¼ 312	Workman R	125wb	*.45	71-16	Dark Secret1254Gusto1258Equipoise1257	No excuses	4
2Sep33- 5Sar	fst 1¾	:52 2:092 2:344 3:00 3↑	Sar Cup 6.9k	3 2 21½ 21 11 11½	Workman R	126 w	*.12	75-14	Equipoise1261½Gusto1268Keep Out118	Going away	3
24Aug33- 6Haw	fst 1¼	:483 1:132 1:383 2:024 3↑	Haw Gold Cup 27k	3 1 33 2½ 1hd 12	Workman R	126wb	*.18	94-14	Equipoise1262GallantSir1261½Mr.Khayyam1171½	Going away	5
3Aug33- 5Sar	fst 1	:242 :48 1:133 1:39 3↑	Wilson 3.3k	3 3 31¾ 3nk 1hd 13	Workman R	126wb	*.20	86-15	Equipoise1263Tambour1062Mate1113	Eased up	5
22Jly33- 6AP	fst 1¼	:471 1:114 1:37 2:023 3↑	Arlington H 12k	4 5 42 31½ 2nk 11½	Workman R	135wb	*.75	96-13	Equipoise1351½Watch Him1065Gallant Sir125no	Going away	7
7Jun33- 4Bel	fst 1¼	:47 1:111 1:36 2:02 3↑	Suburban H 8.9k	7 2 43½ 21½ 2hd 12	Workman R	132wb	*.40	90-18	Equipoise1322Osculator1076Apprentice112nk	Eased up	7
3Jun33- 5Bel	fst 1	:232 :464 1:114 1:372 3↑	Metropolitan H 5.8k	7 5 32 2½ 11 14	Workman R	128wb	*.90	88-15	Equipoise1284Okapi1021Scotch Gold1061	Eased up	10
22Apr33- 5HdG	fst 1 1/16	:232 :472 1:12 1:443 3↑	Philadelphia H 8.9k	1 5 43 41¼ 12 11½	Workman R	128wb	*.90	99-05	Equipoise1281½Tred Avon1122Osculator1051	Won easily	8
	Previously trained by F. Hopkins										
29Oct32- 5Lrl	gd 1¼	:48 1:134 1:393 2:053 3↑	Washington H 18k	6 4 86 21 2½ 2hd	Workman R	129wb	*1.10	82-25	Tred Avon112hdEquipoise129noMate1126	Finished fast	9
15Oct32- 5Lrl	fst 1	:233 :473 1:13 1:371 2↑	Laurel 7.1k	1 7 54 41½ 3½ 31½	Workman R	126wb	*.70	100-11	Jack High118noGallant Sir1081½Equipoise1263	No excuse	7
1Oct32- 5HdG	fst 1⅛	:461 1:11 1:364 1:501 3↑	H de Grace Cup H 26k	4 6 34½ 2½ 11½ 11	Workman R	128wb	*1.05	99-06	Equipoise1281Gallant Sir1073Tred Avon1103	Handily	13
24Sep32- 3HdG	gd 6f	:23 :464 1:12 3↑	Handicap 1500	3 5 54 53½ 58½ 59	Workman R	129wb	*.65	86-08	Pairbypair107½Jack High1231½Con Amore1125	Dull effort	5
13Aug32- 5Sar	fst 1¼	:50 1:142 1:40 2:053 3↑	Whitney 6.9k	2 1 11½ 14 14 13	Workman R	126wb	*.14	81-16	Equipoise1263Gusto1178Rocky News116	Easily	3
6Aug32- 5Sar	fst 1	:233 :462 1:113 1:381 3↑	Wilson 7.8k	2 3 32¼ 31 11 12	Workman R	126wb	*.13	90-11	Equipoise1262Blind Bowboy1216Pompeius113	Easily	3
23Jly32- 6AP	fst 1¼	:48 1:13 1:372 2:021 3↑	Arlington H 27k	3 4 32½ 2½ 2hd 2nk	Workman R	134wb	*.82	98-08	Plucky Play111nkEquipoise1346Pittsburgher1053	Hard try	6

9Jly32- 6AP	fst 1¼	:482 1:131 1:37 2:024 3↑	Arl Gold Cup 24k	3 1 21½ 12½ 15 14	Workman R	126wb	*.24	95-04	Equipoise1264Gusto1143½Mate126	Easily	3
4Jly32- 5AP	hy 1⅛	:492 1:15 1:412 1:544 3↑	Stars & Stripes H 27k	1 2 1hd 1hd 13 1¾	Workman R	129wb	*.34	73-31	Equipoise129¾Tred Avon1075Dr. Freeland1103	Easily	6
30Jun32- 5AP	fst 1	:231 :46 1:091 1:342 3↑	Handicap 1450	1 2 21½ 21½ 21 13	Workman R	128wb	*.90	106-02	Equipoise1283Jamestown1183½Spanish Play106	Easily	3
21May32- 4Bel	fst 1	:224 :462 1:102 1:37 3↑	Metropolitan H 9k	6 5 33¼ 21½ 2hd 12½	Workman R	127 w	*.60	90-15	Equipoise1272½Sun Meadow1181½Mate1284	Easily	7
12May32- 4Bel	fst 6f-WC	1:093 3↑	Toboggan H 8.2k	10 6 21 1hd 11	Workman R	129wb	*1.00	99-02	Equipoise1291Ironclad1081½Helianthus1104	Handily	10
16Apr32- 5HdG	fst 6f	:232 :472 1:122 3↑	Harford H 13k	9 5 72¼ 41½ 11½ 13	Workman R	128wb	*.55	93-16	Equipoise1283Happy Scot106.5hdEvening1051	Easily	12
13Apr32- 4Bow	fst 5f	:231 :46 :592 3↑	Handicap 1400	7 2 51¾ 31½ 2nk 1½	Workman R	126wb	*1.40	109-14	Equipoise126½Hygro112½Brandon Mint1046	Drew out	7
9May31- 5Pim	fst 1 3/16	:483 1:132 1:383 1:59	Preakness 58k	2 7 63½ 62¼ 41¾ 42¾	Workman R	126wb	1.95	94-10	Mate1261½Twenty Grand126nkLadder1261	Impeded early	7
	Geldings not eligible										
25Apr31- 5HdG	fst 1 1/16	:24 :483 1:143 1:464	Cheseapeake 13k	6 6 64½ 62¼ 611 613½	Robertson A	122wb	*.15	74-13	Anchors Aweigh114noSoll Gills1143Levante1121	Distressed	6
13Apr31- 4HdG	fst 6f	:231 :47 1:113	Alw 1400	4 1 21 2½ 11½ 12½	Robertson A	123wb	*.25	97-14	Equipoise1232½Panetian1084DarkHero1083	Outclassed field	5
5Nov30- 5Pim	my 1 1/16	:234 :482 1:142 1:483	Pim Futurity 58k	2 8 87½ 54¾ 22 1½	Workman R	119wb	*.95	79-26	Equipoise119½TwentyGrand119nkMat1194	Driving,great rush	8
	Geldings not eligible;Previously owned by H.P. Whitney										
16Oct30- 5CD	fst 1	:231 :464 1:111 1:36	Ky Jockey Club 31k	4 2 2½ 12 2hd 2no	Workman R	122wb	*.76	101-13	Twenty Grand122noEquipoise12210Knight's Call1225		7
	Going best at end										
4Oct30- 3Aqu	fst 1	:233 :473 1:13 1:38	Jr Champion 9.8k	4 5 53½ 31¾ 21 21	Workman R	122wb	*.20	89-15	Twenty Grand1111Equipoise1223Ormesby1168	Driving	7
27Sep30- 5HdG	fst 6f	:224 :463 1:122	Eastern Shore H 31k	2 8 52 2½ 11 15	Workman R	126wb	*.60e	93-12	Equipoise1265Don Leon1192½Magnifico110hd	Closed fast	15
13Sep30- 4Bel	fst *7f-WC	1:203	Futurity 114k	7 6 2nk 32 2hd	Workman R	130wb	3.60	92-11	Jamestown130hdEquipoise1303Mate1221	Driving,interfered	15
	Geldings not eligible										
6Sep30- 4Bel	fst *7f-WC	1:214	Champagne 7.6k	9 6 2½ 1hd 2hd	Workman R	132 w	*1.20	86-15	Mate119hdEquipoise1323Sunny Lassie1135	Driving,faltered	10
9Aug30- 4Sar	fst 6f	:23 :46 1:112	Sar Spl 14k	1 4 21½ 21½ 21½ 22½	Workman R	122wb	*.70	92-09	Jamestown1222½Eqpoise1228SunMedow1222	Not good enough	4
21Jun30- 3Aqu	fst 5f	1:001	Great American 16k	3 1 11 12 12	Workman R	130wb	*.45e	86-15	Equpos1302Polydorus1154Hlnthus1152½	Cleverly,mild drive	7
7Jun30- 3Bel	fst 5f-WC	:593	National Stallion 26k	7 4 21 13 16	Workman R	122wb	*.40e	82-20	Equipoise1226Polydorus1222Baba Kenny119hd	Easily	8
27May30- 4Bel	gd 5f-WC	:59	Juvenile 17k	1 4 34 31½ 1nk	Workman R	125wb	*.40e	85-24	Equipoise125nkHappy Scot122½Panasette1146	Driving	7
17May30- 3Bel	sl 4½f-WC	:523	Keene Mem 8.6k	2 2 3½ 2hd 12	Workman R	122wb	*.60	92-13	Equipoise1222Happy Scot1228Avaricious1172	Easily	5
10May30- 3Jam	fst 5f	:231 :47 :591	Youthful 11k	1 2 4¾ 1nk 11 14	Workman R	117wb	3.50	97-14	[D]Equipoise1174Vander Pool1254Chouette1254	Drew away	8
	Disqualified for impeding runner-up										
2May30- 5Pim	fst 4½f	:223 :47 :534	Pim Nursery 7.6k	2 2 - - - -	Workman R	122 w	*1.65	- -	Happy Scot1224Up1225St. Agnes1191		8
	Stumbled after start,lost rider										
23Apr30- 5HdG	fst 4½f	:23 :463 :53	Aberdeen 15k	7 9 55¼ 32¼ 34	Robertson A	122 w	4.25e	96-05	Vander Pool1221Up1173Equipoise1221½	Driving,closed well	10
15Apr30- 2HdG	fst 4½f	:233 :481 :542	Alw 1200	1 2 1½ 11½ 11½	Robertson A	118 w	*.90	93-07	Equipoise1181½Schooner1123Uncle Sam1121	Driving	15
7Apr30- 3Bow	hy 4f	:232 :481	Alw 1200	8 4 1hd 1nk 14	Robertson A	111 w	*2.15	92-08	Equipoise1114Glidelia1103Dry Dock112hd	Won easily	11

Gallant Fox

b. c. 1927, by Sir Gallahad III (Teddy)–Marguerite, by Celt **Lifetime record: 17 11 3 2 $328,165**

Own.– Belair Stud Stable
Br.– Belair Stud (Ky)
Tr.– J. Fitzsimmons

17Sep30- 4Bel	fst 2	:50 2:34 3:242 3↑	J C Gold Cup 13k	3 2 21 11 11½ 13	Sande E	118.5wb	*.04e	87-19	Gallant Fox118.53Yarn11412Frisius125	Speed in reserve	3
6Sep30- 3Bel	fst 1⅝	:483 1:374 2:024 2:411	Lawrence Realizatn 33k	2 2 22 22 1nk 1hd	Sande E	126wb	*.70	98-12	Gallant Fox126hdQuestionnaire1235Yarn1163	Outlasted	4
30Aug30- 5Sar	fst 1¾	:483 2:052 2:30 2:56 3↑	Sar Cup 10k	5 3 35½ 22 11 11½	Sande E	117.5wb	*.20e	95-06	Gallant Fox117.51½Frisius1261Gone Away1165	In hand late	6
16Aug30- 5Sar	hy 1¼	1:133 1:42 2:08	Travers 33k	4 4 2½ 21½ 23 28	Sande E	126wb	*.50	61-26	Jim Dandy1208Gallant Fox1266Whichone1263	Wide,no match	4
12Jly30- 5AP	fst 1¼	:474 1:122 1:372 2:034	Classic 78k	3 4 21½ 1hd 1½ 1nk	Sande E	126wb	*.32	99-00	GallntFox126nkGllntKnght1236NdO.12110	Hard stretch duel	6
28Jun30- 4Aqu	gd 1½	:49 1:142 2:063 2:322	Dwyer 15k	2 1 22 11½ 12 11½	Sande E	126wb	*.13e	86-18	Gallant Fox1261½Xenofol1107Limbus110nk	Loafed	5
7Jun30- 5Bel	gd 1½	:501 1:16 2:07 2:313	Belmont 77k	1 2 12 12 11 13	Sande E	126wb	1.60	86-18	GallantFox1263Whichon1263Qustonnr12620	Speed in reserve	4
17May30- 5CD	gd 1¼	:474 1:14 1:404 2:073	Ky Derby 60k	7 8 43 12 12 12	Sande E	126wb	*1.19	78-15	GallantFox1262GallantKnght1262NdO.1261	Speed in reserve	15
9May30- 5Pim	fst 1 3/16	:48 1:133 1:39 2:003	Preakness 61k	1 2 87 3nk 1hd 1¾	Sande E	126wb	*1.00	89-20	Gallant Fox126¾Crack Brigade1266Snowflake1211½		11
	Geldings not eligible										
26Apr30- 4Jam	fst 1 70	:243 :483 1:142 1:433	Wood Memorial 13k	1 3 32 3¾ 1nk 14	Sande E	120wb	*1.60	88-18	GallantFox1204CrackBrigad1201½DsrtLght1205	Drawing away	5
28Sep29- 3Aqu	fst 1	:24 :473 1:12 1:38	Jr Champion 9.5k	3 3 45 35 1½ 12	Maiben J	116wb	*.90	90-17	GallantFox1162DesrtLght1118SrJohrn1111	Speed in reserve	4
14Sep29- 4Bel	fst *7f-WC	1:193	Futurity 119k	12 11 23 33½ 33	McAuliffe D	122wb	20.00	94-09	Whichone1253Hi-Jack122noGallant Fox122no	Held well	17
10Sep29- 3Bel	gd 6f-WC	1:113	Alw 1200	6 3 4nk 21 2nk	McAuliffe D	120wb	*2.00	93-14	Polygamous117nkGallant Fox1201½Stanton115½		12
	Impeded,swerved,finished fast										
3Aug29- 3Sar	fst 6f	:232 :47 1:12	U S Hotel 16k	10 8 21½ 2hd 2hd 21½	Burke JH	122wb	2.00	90-16	Caruso1221½GallantFox1223Hi-Jck1146	No match for winner	10
29Jly29- 3Sar	fst 5½f	:23 :47 1:06	Flash 6.8k	3 8 64½ 66½ 33 11½	Burke JH	112wb	10.00	93-08	GllntFox1121½Cruso1254H-Jck112hd	Outrun early,drawing away	13
29Jun29- 3Aqu	gd 6f	:24 :472 1:144	Tremont 15k	6 12 1212 1111 119¾ 86¾	McAuliffe D	110wb	3.50	73-22	SarznII1251Moktm125hdPromthus1153	Dropped back at start	13
24Jun29- 5Aqu	fst 5f	1:004	Alw 1000	6 8 88½ 32 31	Burke JH	113wb	*2.40e	82-20	Desert Light113½Peto118½Gallant Fox1133	Greenly	10

Granville

b. c. 1933, by Gallant Fox (Sir Gallahad III)–Gravita, by Sarmatian **Lifetime record: 18 8 4 3 $111,820**

Own.– Belair Stud
Br.– Belair Stud (Ky)
Tr.– J. Fitzsimmons

26Sep36- 5Bel	fst 1⅝	:48 1:38 2:034 2:433	Lawrence Realizatn 23k	1 1 23 11 13 12	Stout J	126wb	*.13	86-16	Granville1262GiantKiller1161½MmoryBook126½	In hand late	5
	Geldings not eligible										
29Aug36- 5Sar	sly 1¾	:502 2:083 2:341 3:004 3↑	Sar Cup 7.7k	2 1 11½ 11 15 18	Stout J	116wb	1.80	71-22	Granville1168Discovery126	Easily	2
15Aug36- 5Sar	my 1¼	:49 1:133 1:394 2:054	Travers 19k	5 3 32¼ 31 2hd 1hd	Stout J	127wb	*1.00e	80-19	Granville127hdSun Teddy1224Count Morse1122	Hard drive	5
11Aug36- 5Sar	gd 1 3/16	:482 1:133 1:394 1:583	Kenner 5k	1 1 25 22 2hd 1nk	Stout J	126wb	*.60	85-17	Granville126nkMemory Book1231½Pullman108	Hard drive	3
25Jly36- 6AP	fst 1¼	:47 1:112 1:371 2:031	Classic 35k	1 3 41½ 3½ 1hd 12½	Stout J	126wb	*1.60e	90-12	Granville1262½Mr. Bones1211¼Hollyrood1234	Going away	10
6Jun36- 5Bel	fst 1½	:493 1:14 2:051 2:30	Belmont 41k	9 6 65¼ 41¼ 2hd 1no	Stout J	126wb	3.20e	94-09	Granville126noMr. Bones1268Hollyrood126½	Just up	10
30May36- 5Bel	fst 1¼	:474 1:13 1:382 2:043 3↑	Suburban H 15k	2 3 34 12 11½ 2no	Stout J	108wb	*2.50e	77-19	Firethorn116noGranville1082Whopper1191	Just missed	12
16May36- 5Pim	fst 1 3/16	:473 1:123 1:39 1:59	Preakness 31k	11 6 2hd 1½ 2hd 2no	Stout J	126wb	3.95e	95-17	BoldVenture126noGranville1268JeanBart126hd	Just missed	11
2May36- 6CD	fst 1¼	:474 1:123 1:374 2:033	Ky Derby 37k	4 - - - - -	Stout J	126wb	10.60e	- -	Bold Venture126hdBrevity1266Indian Broom1263	Lost rider	14
25Apr36- 5Jam	fst 1 70	:233 :471 1:12 1:431	Wood Memorial 14k	1 3 31½ 2hd 11 2no	Stout J	117wb	*1.00e	90-16	Teufel112noGranville1176Delphinium1171	Nosed out	7
21Apr36- 4Jam	fst 1 70	:234 :473 1:122 1:432	Alw 1200	2 1 11 11 13 15	Stout J	110wb	1.50e	89-14	Granville1105Ned Reigh1141Pullman110nk	Eased up	5
12Oct35- 4Bel	fst 6½f-WC	1:172	Futurity 84k	1 1 115 52½ 62¼	Rainey C	122wb	3.60e	94-04	Tintagel1221Hollyrood122noJean Bart122hd	Went well	18
3Oct35- 5Bel	fst 6½f-WC	1:172	Champagne 5.9k	12 11 41½ 35 35	Merritt R	113wb	*1.80e	91-09	Brevity113noSnark1135Granville113hd	Closed gamely	14
13Sep35- 6Aqu	fst 6f	:234 :481 1:124	Alw 1000	2 3 76¾ 55 42¾ 13	Litzenberger E	107wb	*1.30e	90-12	Granville1073Go Home112noDark Wizard112hd	Easily	11
7Sep35- 5Aqu	gd 6½f	:23 :463 1:121 1:183	Jr Champion 8.7k	3 4 89¾ 75 67½ 53¾	Litzenberger E	105 w	2.60e	90-11	Ned Reigh115½The Fighter1172Pullman110nk	Impeded	9
2Sep35- 3Aqu	fst 6f	:241 :49 1:12	Babylon H 4.2k	6 5 46½ 43 32¼ 3hd	Wright WD	114 w	1.50e	94-09	NedReigh116noSpeedtoSpare115noGranville1145	Game finish	6
22Aug35- 4Sar	fst 5½f	:231 :473 1:07	Alw 1000	10 7 85 73¼ 23 21	Malley T	110 w	3.60	87-16	BoldVenture114.51Granvill1102Trnsportr110hd	Game finish	12
16Aug35- 3Sar	fst 5½f	:232 :472 1:06	Alw 1000	10 2 2nk 42¾ 42¼ 33½	Malley T	108 w	15.00e	89-13	Brevity1082Aneroid1131½Granville108hd	Closed gamely	13

Inscoelda

br. f. 1936, by Insco (Sir Gallahad III)–Griselda, by Wrack — **Lifetime record: 42 12 4 8 $38,970**

Own.– King Ranch
Br.– Herbert M. Woolf (Kan)
Tr.– W.J. Hirsch

3Feb42- 6Hia	fst 7f	:232 :472 1:121 1:25	4↑ ⓕAlw 1500	2 5 44½ 55½ 54½	58	Garza I	109wb	12.75	79-16	Transient993Moon Maiden1051Silvestra1031½	Some str gain	8
Previously trained by M. Hirsch												
21Oct41- 5Emp	fst 1⅛	:49 1:14 1:394 1:524	3↑ Hannibal H 3.5k	1 2 21 21½ 2hd	11	Garza I	108wb	5.60	86-12	Inscoelda1081Hypocrite1212City Talk110hd	Drew out	5
Previously owned by Woolford Farm;previously trained by R.O. Higdon												
10Oct41- 5Jam	sly 6f	:23 :472 1:131	3↑ ⓕAlw 2000	6 7 79¾ 78½ 63	31½↓	Strickler W	103wb	5.05	84-21	YarrowMaid117¾FivtoOn117¾[DH]DrkImp111	Dwelt,fast finish	7
5Sep41- 6Aqu	fst 6f	:23 :462 1:113	3↑ ⓕAlw 2000	4 7 88 711 76½	57½	Strickler W	105wb	5.50	88-11	Pelisse1053½Thorn Apple1052Fleetborough112hd	Outrun	9
25Jly41- 4AP	fst 6f	:23 :462 1:122	3↑ Alw 1200	2 2 43 3½ 2½	1nk	Strickler W	106wb	4.30	85-18	Inscoelda106nkJack Twink105hdWoodsaw1112	Hard drive	7
12Nov40- 6Pim	sly 1 1/16	:241 :481 1:143 1:503	3↑ ⓕLady Baltimore H 3.4k	4 6 69½ 68½ 69½	512¾	Vedder RL	116wb	5.95	54-34	Rosetown1095Bright View104nkRaise Up1111½	Outrun	6
5Nov40- 6Pim	fst 1 3/16	:481 1:121 1:384 1:593	3↑ Riggs H 13k	4 2 77 88¼ 97¼	89½	Vedder RL	110wb	16.75	75-21	Rough Pass1053Burning Star113½War Beauty1011½	Outrun	10
22Oct40- 5Emp	fst 1 1/16	:234 :474 1:123 1:444	3↑ Handicap 3030	4 5 610 610 52¾	44¼	Vedder RL	109wb	3.45	91-08	Get Off1221½No Sir1122Foxbrough118¾	No excuse	6
5Oct40- 3Bel	fst 1 1/16	:223 :461 1:104 1:432	3↑ Handicap 1520	4 3 46 36 32½	2nk↓	Vedder RL	114wb	8.85	94-09	ThirdCovey116nk[DH]Volitant119[DH]Inscold1148	Finished well	4
21Sep40- 5Aqu	fst 1⅛	:472 1:12 1:372 1:504	3↑ ⓕBeldame H 19k	7 15 1414 139 1111	1011¾	Vedder RL	116wb	20.65	90-02	Fairy Chant1191¼Dotted Swiss1141Dolly Val1212½	Outrun	16
12Sep40- 4Aqu	fst 7f	:23 :47 1:122 1:244	3↑ Handicap 2030	4 3 31½ 1hd 1hd	11	Roberts P	107wb	13.25	92-09	Inscoelda1071Roman Flag119¾Dini1201	Drew out	4
17Aug40- 6Was	gd 1	:233 :471 1:122 1:383	3↑ ⓕBeverly H 5.9k	3 3 32½ 55½ 56½	57¼	Ashcroft J	113 w	5.40	78-31	BusyMorn1152Montsin1152½ShineO'Night1122	Close quarters	8
31Jly40- 7Was	fst 1	:232 :471 1:114 1:371	3↑ Handicap 1200	4 3 43 31½ 42	34	Craig A	108 w	*.90e	88-12	Detroit Bull110hdTown Boy1044Inscoelda108nk	Weakened	8
29Jun40- 6AP	fst 1	:224 :451 1:10 1:361	3↑ ⓕArl Matron H 9.1k	8 11 98½ 89 77¼	45	Richard J	108 w	*.90e	86-18	Shine O'Night1033Montsin1101Manie O'Hara1091	Late foot	14
25Jun40- 5AP	fst 1	:23 :46 1:102 1:371	3↑ Alw 1200	3 2 22 23 11½	12¾	Richard J	109 w	2.70	86-16	Inscoelda1092¾Bucking116½Loque1012	Going away	5
30May40- 6LF	sl 1 1/16	:252 :51 1:17 1:503	3↑ F S Peabody Mem H 5.8k	3 2 22 21 42	44	Vedder RL	110 w	4.00	59-34	Mucho Gusto1121½Shot Put110½Gray Jack1092	Tired	7
6May40- 6CD	gd 7f	:232 :472 1:132 1:271	3↑ Alw 1000	9 4 33½ 21½ 1hd	11½	Roberts P	110 w	*2.30	80-23	Inscoelda1101½TrueStar1102SouthlandBeau115nk	Going away	9
2Mar40- 6Hia	fst 1¼	:471 1:111 1:363 2:03	3↑ Widener H 66k	6 13 1113 1011 1422	1516¾	Roberts P	110 w	25.15e	77-09	Many Stings1091Big Pebble1065[DH]Day Off110	Outrun	16
21Feb40- 6Hia	fst 7f	:23 :471 1:113 1:241	3↑ Handicap 1500	3 7 73¼ 73¾ 64	52½	Smith FA	112 w	4.60e	89-13	Armor Bearer107¾Dunade1111½Dolly Val109hd	Off slowly	7
14Feb40- 5Hia	fst 6½f	:233 :472 1:111 1:172	3↑ Handicap 1500	2 4 32½ 42½ 45½	35¼	Smith FA	111 w	*1.60e	87-12	Many Stings118nkArmor Bearer1095Inscoelda1111½		5
No response late,worked mile in 1:37												
26Jan40- 6Hia	fst 7f	:232 :471 1:123 1:251	4↑ Alw 1200	1 6 53½ 32 23	2¾	Ryan P	112 w	*2.20	86-13	[D]MythicalKing110¾Inscold1121¼Bllotr102.55	Impeded turn	8
Placed first through disqualification												
11Jan40- 6Hia	fst 7f	:23 :462 1:111 1:242	4↑ Alw 1200	7 7 911 910 88¾	65	Ryan P	109 w	28.45	86-10	Napper Tandy1161Galsun1042One Jest1091½	Outrun	10
8Nov39- 6Pim	fst 1 1/16	:24 :483 1:14 1:472	3↑ ⓕLady Baltimore H 3.9k	2 6 73¾ 63 97¾	99¾	Robertson A	113 w	*1.55e	73-21	Manie O'Hara1084Bala Ormont109½Hostility110½	No excuse	12
26Oct39- 5Lrl	fst 6f	:231 :47 1:123	3↑ Handicap 1200	3 5 55½ 54¼ 45½	54¼	Ryan P	108 w	41.70	87-16	Allegro114hdBill Farnsworth1172½Cravat1241½	No mishaps	6
Previously trained by B.A. Jones												
4Feb39- 5Hia	fst 7f	:223 :454 1:104 1:234	Bahamas H 6.5k	4 10 106¾ 106¼ 75½	73¾	Smith FA	121 w	*2.00e	90-09	RoyalPam113nkTechnician1192ErlyMorn112hd	Close quarters	12
28Jan39- 6Hia	fst 7f	:23 :462 1:111 1:234	Alw 1200	2 5 52¼ 52¼ 42	41	Yarberry W	112 w	*1.85	93-11	Cherry Jam113nkHeather Time114½Search110nk	Good try	6
8Nov38- 5Pim	sl 1 1/16	:233 :482 1:143 1:49	Walden 10k	5 8 52¼ 31½ 22	1hd	Longden J	116 w	4.75	75-34	Inscoelda116hdVolitant1164Ciencia1101½	Just up	9
22Oct38- 4Lrl	sl 1	:241 :48 1:142 1:41	ⓕSelima 29k	14 16 104½ 51½ 2hd	2¾	Gilbert J	119 w	4.60	80-16	Big Hurry114¾Inscoelda1191½Dinner Date1221	Weakened	16
11Oct38- 4Jam	fst 6f	:23 :473 1:12	ⓕAlw 1000	5 6 66½ 46 45	34½	Rollins C	122 w	2.60e	87-13	SmartCrack1091½Matterhorn1143Inscoelda122hd	Closed fast	6
27Sep38- 4Bel	fst 6f-WC	1:103	Handicap 1265	2 1 64½ 44½	38	Rollins C	117 w	4.50	86-06	Johnstown1225Birch Rod1123Inscoelda117hd	Closed well	7
16Jly38- 6AP	fst 6f	:223 :454 1:113	ⓕArl Lassie 26k	5 7 65½ 45½ 1hd	11	Rollins C	117 w	*.90e	89-07	Inscoelda1171Dinner Date1172½Unerring1195	Drew out	9
12Jly38- 4AP	fst 5½f	:23 :46 :583 1:044	ⓕAlw 1000	8 2 22 21½ 11	14	Rollins C	112 w	3.80	97-12	Inscoelda1124Bold Fay1093Smart Trick115no	Going away	8
17Jun38- 5LF	fst 5f	:233 :472 1:00	Alw 1000	6 6 54½ 43 21½	11½	Rollins C	107 w	3.60e	99-15	Inscoelda1071½Maetown110nkBala Ormont105hd	Going away	9
30May38- 6CD	fst 5f	:232 :462 :59	Bashford Manor 7.1k	5 3 99 811 62½	66¾	Dotter R	119 w	3.10e	93-13	Royal Pam1192Unerring119hdCherry Jam1223	Outrun	11
3May38- 1CD	fst 4½f	:23 :464 :532	ⓕAlw 800	5 5 21 2½	1¾	Perkins C	107 w	*.90	95-08	Inscold107¾Espn113.56MssAlrt1102	Awkward start,drew out	6
30Apr38- 4CD	sl 4½f	:233 :473 :541	Alw 800	4 6 612 69½	56¼	Perkins C	106 w	4.50	85-12	American Byrd113¾Dolly Whisk1104Range Dust1151½	Outrun	7
26Feb38- 1Hia	fst 3f	:22 :34	Alw 800	6 7 63½	21	Haas L	112 w	3.10e	--	CherryJam1151Inscoelda112noSweetPatrice112nk	Great rush	9
17Feb38- 1Hia	fst 3f	:221 :343	ⓕAlw 800	8 5 45	3hd	Haas L	118 w	4.45e	--	OddesaBeulah118noSwetPtrc118hdInscold1182	Strong finish	12
11Feb38- 1Hia	fst 3f	:221 :344	Md Sp Wt	11 5 2hd	12½	Haas L	113 w	*1.00f	--	Inscoelda1132½Pradis116noHenryels Pick1162	Going away	13
28Jan38- 1Hia	fst 3f	:221 :334	ⓕAlw 800	2 7 45	32	Haas L	114 w	5.30	--	CharlotteGirl1181KentyMiss1181Inscoelda1145	Closed gap	7
20Jan38- 1Hia	fst 3f	:223 :344	Md Sp Wt	8 6 41	2½	Haas L	113	*1.25	--	HigherBracket116½Inscoelda1131½Matown1113	Strong finish	9
12Jan38- 1Hia	fst 3f	:223 :343	ⓕMd Sp Wt	14 8 46½	35½	Haas L	118	7.75f	--	CharlotteGirl1181½SweetPatrc1184Inscold1185	Closed well	14

Johnstown

b. c. 1936, by Jamestown (St. James)–La France, by Sir Gallahad III — **Lifetime record: 21 14 0 3 $169,315**

Own.– Belair Stud
Br.– A.B. Hancock Sr. (Ky)
Tr.– J. Fitzsimmons

22Jly39- 6AP	fst 1¼	:47 1:112 1:36 2:02	Classic 47k	1 2 13 11½ 31½	36¼	Stout J	126wb	*.20	90-11	Challedon126nkSun Lover1216Johnstown1262	Tired badly	5
17Jun39- 5Aqu	fst 1⅛	:46 1:103 1:353 1:482	Dwyer 12k	2 1 12 14 13	11	Stout J	126wb	*.20	99-05	Johnstown1261Sun Lover1166Challedon1266	Ridden out	5
3Jun39- 5Bel	fst 1½	:481 1:122 2:023 2:293	Belmont 45k	1 1 11½ 16 14	15	Stout J	126wb	*.13e	95-12	Johnstown1265Belay1261½Gilded Knight1261½	In hand	6
27May39- 5Bel	fst 1	:23 :461 1:10 1:354	Withers 19k	2 1 14 14 16	16	Stout J	118wb	*.13e	96-10	Johnstown1186Hash118hdPorter's Mite1186	Much best	5
Geldings not eligible												
13May39- 6Pim	my 1 3/16	:473 1:133 1:394 1:594	Preakness 70k	4 1 11½ 11½ 59	511¼	Stout J	126wb	*.45e	73-19	Challedon1261¼GildedKnight1263Volitnt1263	Stopped badly	6
6May39- 7CD	fst 1¼	:472 1:124 1:38 2:032	Ky Derby 56k	5 2 12 14 15	18	Stout J	126wb	*.60	92-11	Johnstown1268Challedon1261HthrBroom126½	Under restraint	8
29Apr39- 5Jam	fst 1 70	:23 :464 1:112 1:42	Wood Memorial 24k	6 2 21½ 11½ 15	18	Stout J	120wb	*.55	94-11	Johnstown1208Volitant1201Impound120¾	Much left	8
25Apr39- 4Jam	fst 1 70	:23 :463 1:111 1:404	Alw 1500	1 1 13 14 16	16	Stout J	120wb	*.33	102-06	Johnstwn1206LovlyNght1136EghtThrty11620	Under restraint	4
15Apr39- 5Jam	fst 6f	:221 :452 1:111	3↑ Paumonok H 9.5k	2 1 11½ 14 14	16	Stout J	112wb	*1.30	96-14	Johnstown1126Pagliacci1073EarlyDelivry1161½	Easily best	6
22Oct38- 5Kee	fst 6f	:223 :462 1:112	Breeders' Futurity 14k	5 3 3½ 31 2hd	1no	Stout J	119wb	*.60	97-09	Johnstown119noAllegro117hdLightspur1171¼	Hard drive	7
15Oct38- 5Jam	fst 6f	:223 :454 1:11	Remsen H 8.8k	1 1 1nk 13 16	17	Stout J	126wb	*.80e	97-11	Johnstown1267Lovely Night1224Beau James1203	Much best	6
8Oct38- 5Lrl	fst 6f	:23 :461 1:114	Richard Johnson 7.5k	2 4 2hd 1hd 13	1nk	Stout J	115wb	*1.25	95-11	Johnstown115nkImpound1123Time Alone1221½	Hard drive	7
1Oct38- 4Bel	fst 6½f-WC	1:164	Futurity 69k	3 1 32½ 43	43	Stout J	119wb	*2.00	85-12	Porter'sMite119½EightThirty1221½ThirdDgr1191	No mishaps	11
Geldings not eligible												
27Sep38- 4Bel	fst 6f-WC	1:103	Handicap 1265	6 4 1hd 13	15	Stout J	122wb	*.60	94-06	Johnstown1225Birch Rod1123Inscoelda117hd	Much best	7
10Sep38- 5Aqu	fst 6½f	:224 :46 1:114 1:18	Jr Champion 13k	3 3 2hd 2hd 1hd	31	Stout J	114wb	2.50	95-06	El Chico1221Volitant114noJohnstown1145	Good effort	4
5Sep38- 4Aqu	fst 6f	:224 :461 1:111	Babylon H 4k	5 4 1nk 11 13	14	Stout J	119wb	5.00	98-07	Johnstown1194Birch Rod1151T.M. Dorsett1121½	Much best	10
27Aug38- 4Sar	fst 6½f	:231 :463 1:121 1:182	Hopeful 48k	9 6 92¾ 34½ 42½	33	Stout J	116 w	15.00	90-08	El Chico1262Ariel Toy1161Johnstown116hd	Closed well	11
22Aug38- 4Sar	fst 6f	:23 :472 1:132	Alw 1000	6 7 53½ 51¼ 2hd	1hd	Stout J	116 w	*2.20e	85-15	Johnstown116hdPontius116no[D]RollandToss116½	Hard drive	14
25Jly38- 4Sar	fst 5½f	:223 :462 1:051	Flash 5.9k	3 5 42 42½ 42¾	47	Stout J	110 w	*2.60e	90-06	Eight Thirty117hdMaeline1193Ariel Toy1104	No mishap	15
27Apr38- 3Jam	fst 5f	:23 :461 :592	ⓒMd Sp Wt	4 2 1½ 11 12	11½	Stout J	117 w	*1.50	96-12	Johnstown1171½Hash1174King Cotton1173	Never headed	10
23Apr38- 4Jam	fst 5f	:23 :473 1:003	Alw 1000	4 4 2hd 31 43½	42¾	Stout J	111 w	*.70	87-11	Our Mat1142Rosemain112nkKate Smith114½	Raced greenly	5

Jungle King

b. g. 1930, by St. Germans (Swynford)–Leopardess, by Dominant
Own.– Greentree Stable
Br.– Greentree Stable (Ky)
Tr.– V. Powers

Lifetime record: 77 15 13 11 $32,605

13Aug38- 2Sar	gd *2	S'Chase	4:134 3↑ North American H 2.6k	3	3	35½	33	414	417	Collins W	148	w	3.60	--	Ossabaw1426Gay Charles1363Ship Executive1408	Faltered	4
18Jun38- 2Aqu	sly *2½	S'Chase	5:003 4↑ Old Glory H 2k	1	1	11	11	15	18	Little H	143	w	3.00	--	Jungle King1438Yemasee160	Easily	3
11Jun38- 2Aqu	fst *2	S'Chase	4:054 4↑ Lion Heart H 1.7k	2	4	23	33	49	418	Little H	147	w	1.20e	--	Yemasee1566Gay Charles1394Sumatra1418	Challenged,quit	4
4Jun38- 2Bel	fst *2½	S'Chase	4:451 4↑ Meadow Brook H 2.1k	2	5	31½	55	411	412	Collins W	150	w	*1.20e	--	Rioter1511SailorBeware1598LittleMarty1473	Rated,no gain	6
30May38- 2Bel	fst *2	S'Chase	3:462 4↑ Corinthian H 4.2k	2	3	55½	23	25	45	Collins W	149	w	*1.50e	--	Annibal1463NationalAnthem1401½RedRain152½	Faltered late	8
14May38- 2Bel	fst *2	S'Chase	3:44 4↑ International H 2k	5	5	55½	44½	43½	35	Little H	149	w	4.50	--	RedRain1401NationalAnthem1394JungleKing1491	No threat	6
8Nov37- 4Pim	fst 2½	S'Chase	4:531 4↑ Manley Mem H 6.5k	1	5	58½	46	2hd	2no	Little H	143	w	*2.40	--	[D]LittleMarty148noJungleKing14312CduII146½	Forced wide	7
	Placed first through disqualification																
2Nov37- 4Bel	fst *2½	S'Chase	4:474 4↑ Temple Gwathmey H 2.6k	3	2	32	2½	14	11½	Little H	147	w	*1.30e	--	Jungle King1471½Cadeau II1473Galsac1502	Speed to spare	5
20Oct37- 4Lrl	my *2	S'Chase	4:211 3↑ Chevy Chase H 3.3k	2	5	57	44	417	416½	Little H	146	w	*2.15e	--	Cadeau II1414Swimalong138½Rideaway14412	No factor	8
4Sep37- 2Aqu	fst *2½	S'Chase	4:472 4↑ Glendale H 5.8k	3	3	59½	49½	522	525	Baldwin E	146	w	*.60e	--	Yemasee1404Galsac1486National Anthem1408	Rated,no gain	6
28Aug37- 1Sar	hy *2½	S'Chase	5:102 4↑ Saratoga H 3.8k	2	4	37	35	33¼	34	Baldwin E	147	w	1.80e	--	Galsac145noLondon Town1464Jungle King147	Gamely	4
21Aug37- 1Sar	fst *2	S'Chase	4:153 3↑ Beverwyck H 2.4k	3	3	25	2hd	12	14	Baldwin E	142	w	*.08e	--	Jungle King1424Galsac142	Speed in reserve	3
14Aug37- 1Sar	fst *2	S'Chase	4:111 3↑ North American H 2.7k	6	2	314	315	38¼	37	Baldwin E	143	w	2.50e	--	Sailor Beware1453London Town1494Jungle King143	Outrun	6
26Jun37- 2Aqu	fst *2½	S'Chase	4:544 4↑ Old Glory H 2.8k	1	3	41¼	21	11	12½	Collins W	140	w	5.00	--	JungleKing1402½MaskedKnight144½St.Francis1548	Drew away	8
17Jun37- 2Aqu	fst *2	S'Chase	4:064 4↑ Handicap 1380	2	7	84	63½	76½	612½	Collins W	140	w	*4.00	--	Masked Knight1371½Prattler139noSaluda1436		10
	Bad landing 13th,faltered																
5Jun37- 2Bel	fst *2½	S'Chase	4:432 4↑ Meadow Brook H 2.2k	5	8	62¼	61½	69¼	617	Collins W	142	w	5.00	--	Birmingham1422ShipExecutiv1426St.Frncs1403	Bobbled 14th	10
29May37- 2Bel	fst *2	S'Chase	3:441 4↑ Corinthian H 2.1k	1	5	35	31	11½	13	Collins W	140	w	4.00	--	Jungle King1403Rioter1644Saluda14410	Easily	5
15May37- 2Bel	my *2	S'Chase	3:45 4↑ International H 2.1k	1	5	24	23	49	516	Collins W	143	w	7.00	--	Rioter1592Birminghm1408Rhdmnthus1484	Faltered final ¼	5
3Nov36- 4Bel	fst 2½	S'Chase	4:484 4↑ Temple Gwathmey H 2.1k	1	2	25	21	21	21½	McGinnis P	139	w	*1.00e	--	Sailor Beware1421½Jungle King1393Arc Light1546	No match	4
21Oct36- 4Lrl	fst *2	S'Chase	3:551 3↑ Chevy Chase H 2.9k	1	4	43	42½	49½	411	Collins W	141	w	8.35	--	Rioter1602Lord Johnson1351Birmingham1408	No threat	4
12Oct36- 2Lrl	fst *2	S'Chase	3:553 3↑ Handicap 1000	1	4	43	21	21½	21½	Collins W	140	w	5.45	--	Amagansett1601½JngleKing1401½Brmnghm1403	Finished well	6
3Oct36- 2Bel	fst *3	S'Chase	5:47 4↑ Grand National H 7.5k	4	5	59½	-	-	-	Collins W	140	w	20.00	--	Bushranger1722Rioter15610Amaganstt157nk	Lost rider 13th	5
26Sep36- 2Bel	fst *2½	S'Chase	4:461 4↑ Brook H 3.7k	5	5	55	55¼	412	415	Collins W	143	w	20.00	--	Bushranger1655Rioter1573Golden Meadow1547	No excuse	6
23Sep36- 2Bel	fst *2	S'Chase	3:494 3↑ Alw 1000	4	2	22	43¼	414	415	Baldwin E	151	w	4.00	--	Golden Meadow1474St. Francis1525Navarino1486	No excuse	4
29Aug36- 2Sar	sly *2½	S'Chase	5:242 4↑ Sar H 3.3k	4	4	47	-	-	-	Collins W	142	w	*1.40	--	Rioter1501½Birmingham14012Redshank142	Fell at 13th	4
22Aug36- 1Sar	my *2	S'Chase	4:224 3↑ North American H 2.2k	3	3	33	22	12	13	Collins W	140	w	*1.20	--	JungleKing1403NtonlAnthm139½Prttlr1384	Drew away easily	4
13Aug36- 2Sar	fst *2	S'Chase	4:104 4↑ Alw 900	2	2	22	21½	1nk	2no	Baldwin E	142	w	1.20	--	Prattler137noJungle King142	Saved ground,gamely	3
5Aug36- 2Sar	fst *2	S'Chase	4:064 4↑ Alw 1000	1	3	35½	34½	36	312	Collins W	148	w	2.20	--	Golden Meadow1438Escapade1524Jungle King14812	Hung	5
1Aug36- 2Sar	fst *2	S'Chase	4:12 3↑ Beverwyck H 2.1k	1	4	42¾	34¼	23	23	Collins W	142	w	4.00	--	Rioter1463Jungle King14212National Anthem1426	No match	4
6Jun36- 2Bel	fst *2½	S'Chase	4:48 4↑ Meadow Brook H 1.9k	3	3	35	36½	23	22	Collins W	143	w	1.80	--	NationalAnthem1352JungleKing1433SnapBack146	Slow start	3
30May36- 2Bel	fst *2	S'Chase	3:433 4↑ Corinthian H 1.9k	3	3	38	2hd	21	33½	Collins W	143	w	8.00	--	Bushranger1572Birmingham1391½JungleKing143	Bid,faltered	3
5Oct35- 2Bel	fst *2½	S'Chase	4:464 4↑ Brook H 3.2k	3	-	-	-	-	-	Williams F	143	w	1.60e	--	ArcLight1544BorderWarrant138	Pulled up lame after 1st	4
31Aug35- 2Sar	fst *2½	S'Chase	5:084 4↑ Sar H 3.8k	6	7	713	64¾	32	11½	Williams F	139	w	*2.20	--	Jungle King1391½Red Flash1443Amagansett1504	Driving	7
24Aug35- 2Sar	fst *2	S'Chase	4:14 3↑ Alw 1200	8	6	41¾	21	1nk	2nk	Collins W	150	w	*2.20	--	Driver130nkJungle King1505Benedictine1542	Gamely	8
17Aug35- 2Sar	fst *2	S'Chase	4:15 3↑ North American H 2.4k	4	4	32¼	42½	24	35½	Collins W	138	w	4.50	--	Rhadamanthus1452½Amaganstt1483JnglKng1388	Bid,faltered	5
14Aug35- 2Sar	gd *2	S'Chase	4:183 3↑ Alw 1000	4	3	2nk	2nk	140	140	Collins W	141	w	*1.40	--	Jungle King14140Staunch Pal136Galyarrow133	Easily	5
1Aug35- 2Sar	fst *2	S'Chase	4:183 3↑ Beverwyck H 2.4k	4	-	-	-	-	-	Collins W	136	w	*1.60e	--	Red Flash142½Amagansett1496Spinach1402	Lost rider 3rd	8
8Jun35- 2Bel	gd *2½	S'Chase	4:442 4↑ Meadow Brook H 2.2k	1	4	35	33	21½	34¼	Collins W	139	w	4.00	--	IrishBullet1564ArcLight155nkJungleKng1392	Faltered late	6
25May35- 2Bel	fst *2	S'Chase	3:421 4↑ C L Appleton Cup 3.7k	6	8	77¼	78	616	615	Collins W	150	w	12.00	--	Bushranger1431½Rideaway1402Spinach1421½		8
	Impeded by riderless horse																
18May35- 2Bel	fst *2	S'Chase	3:41 4↑ International H 2.1k	3	4	49	45¾	38	37½	Collins W	148	w	10.00	--	Amagansett1431½Bushrngr1426JunglKng14810	Outrun on flat	5
6Nov34- 4Bel	sly *2½	S'Chase	5:043 4↑ Temple Gwathmey H 2.4k	1	4	21	2hd	2nk	2hd	Collins W	142	w	4.00	--	Kummel136hdJungle King14210Bagatelle141½	Finished well	6
24Oct34- 3Lrl	fst *2	S'Chase	3:55 3↑ Chevy Chase H 2.9k	2	3	43	31½	1hd	1nk	Collins W	136	w	5.40	--	JungleKing136nkTanaringo1391Rideaway1431½	Game in drive	6
22Sep34- 2Aqu	sly 2	S'Chase	4:07 3↑ Handicap 1670	2	2	13	15	16	112	Collins W	132	w	5.00	--	Jungle King13212National Anthem135	In hand	3
20Sep34- 2Aqu	fst 2	S'Chase	3:564 3↑ Md Sp Wt	2	2	3½	12	23	27	Collins W	145	w	*.90e	--	Black Bean1337Jungle King14510Lei1456	Swerved	7
30Aug34- 2Sar	hy *2	S'Chase	4:133 3↑ Md Sp Wt	4	4	613	614	618	512	Collins W	142	w	3.50e	--	National Anthem1332Axon1354Surf Board1321	No mishap	10
	Previously trained by M.C. Lilly																
5Jun34- 5Det	fst 1	:243 :482 1:131 1:391	3↑ Alw 800	7	5	43½	45	55½	55	Jacobs J	106	w	7.20	94-08	Bamboula1032½Money Getter99hdDark Conquest1042		7
	Lost ground throughout																
21May34- 5Det	fst 1	:24 :473 1:122 1:371	3↑ Alw 1000	2	4	44	45	45½	48½	Jacobs J	104	w	5.30	100-02	Elf Lock89.5½Polydorus1065Projectile1063	No factor	5
7May34- 4Pim	fst 1 70	:233 :48 1:132 1:44	3↑ Alw 800	9	7	73¼	65¼	35½	34	Jacobs J	117	w	8.00e	87-13	Sea Fox1171Swiftsport106.53Jungle King1171	Good try	10
30Apr34- 6Pim	fst 6f	:232 :472 1:12	3↑ Alw 800	7	6	67	69½	611	69¾	Jacobs J	118	wb	26.25	84-14	CrowningGlory118¾BrightHaven1022HappyGo1042½	No threat	8
14Apr34- 5Bow	fst 1 70	:234 :482 1:133 1:46	3↑ Handicap 1500	6	6	52¼	53	511	58½	Coucci S	103	wb	4.80	76-21	Gay World120½Chatmoss1062½Chance Flight1084	No threat	7
10Mar34- 5Hia	fst 1⅛	:461 1:102 1:353 1:482	3↑ J McLennan Mem H 2.4k	5	3	46½	46	69	614	Stout J	102	wb	11.20	90-04	BlessedEvent1112Somebody1011½FlyingSailor1054	Quit late	6
3Mar34- 5Hia	fst 1¼	:474 1:122 1:37 2:024	3↑ Jockey Club H 3.5k	5	4	21½	22	44½	55½	Porter E	100	wb	15.40	98-01	BlessedEvent1081Springsteel1262BigBeu107.51½	Speed,quit	9
6Feb34- 5Hia	fst 1	:233 :464 1:114 1:38	4↑ Alw 1000	3	4	53¾	54¾	44	42½	Coucci S	113	w	3.90	87-10	Repaid115nkMountain Elk110¾Big Beau1121½	Saved ground	5
3Feb34- 6Hia	fst 1	:231 :463 1:114 1:371	3↑ Handicap 1000	6	5	65	63¼	65¼	67¼	Coucci S	105	w	*1.20e	87-08	SwpngLght116nkCurco110½MdFrmp1092½	Not persevered with	7
26Jan34- 5Hia	fst 1	:234 :464 1:111 1:364	4↑ Alw 1000	6	2	41½	43¼	34	36½	Coucci S	102	w	*1.20	89-05	Repaid103½Pastry1076Jungle King1022	Pinched back	6
28Jun33- 6AP	fst 1	:23 :463 1:111 1:37	Alw 1000	1	4	42½	44½	2½	21	Coucci S	108	w	*1.63	86-09	Esseff1041JungleKng1085Pompolon107½	Impeded after start	6
17Jun33- 5Aqu	fst 1	:24 :482 1:133 1:38	Alw 800	3	3	32½	31¾	32	23	Coucci S	112	w	2.20	87-14	Balios1123Jungle King1123Caesars Ghost1071		5
	Blocked,knocked off stride																
11Mar33- 5Hia	fst 1⅛	:47 1:113 1:37 1:493	Florida Derby 13k	2	5	32	41¾	22	23	Coucci S	118	w	*.80	102-01	Charley O.1183Jungle King1182½Inlander1164	No match	10
4Mar33- 6Hia	fst 1	:233 :47 1:11 1:364	Alw 1000	6	5	54	54	41½	1½	Coucci S	120	w	2.35	98-00	Jungle King120½Pot Au Brooms110nkCharacter1201	Driving	7
11Feb33- 4Hia	fst 7f	:23 :463 1:133 1:253	Bahamas 2.9k	5	5	64¼	63¼	42	2hd	Coucci S	122	w	3.15	89-10	Character121hdJungleKng1221½Algr113hd	Getting to winner	8
3Feb33- 4Hia	fst 1	:233 :47 1:12 1:381	Alw 1000	3	2	23	2½	11½	12½	Coucci S	111	w	2.90	91-14	Jungle King1112½Bubbler107nkPre War1061½	Easily	7
28Jan33- 4Hia	fst 6f	:23 :462 1:121	Hialeah 3k	6	7	87¼	67½	59	44½	Coucci S	114	w	14.30	86-09	Character1161½GoldBasis111hdThePelican1163	Hard ridden	9
23Jan33- 4Hia	fst 6f	:232 :47 1:124	Alw 1000	5	2	52½	42½	31	1hd	Coucci S	110	w	5.35	88-13	Jungle King110hdBubbler110noDaudet110hd	Up late	9
	Previously trained by W. Brennan																
18Nov32- 3Bow	my 6f	:232 :473 1:13	Alw 1000	2	6	128¾	1214	1116	811¼	Jones R	111	wb	32.95	77-22	Filter1081½Cruising1081Character1113	No factor	12
9Nov32- 3Pim	hy 1 70	:242 :50 1:172 1:501	Alw 1000	1	3	52¾	54¾	54	53¼	Kurtsinger C	111	wb	14.25	57-35	SilentShot114hdWhiteThorn1141½BurningFeet114nk	Good try	11
3Nov32- 4Pim	gd 6f	:232 :473 1:13	Pim Home-Bred 1.5k	2	5	62½	64¼	67	54½	Kurtsinger C	113	wb	69.75	84-17	Iseult1102Acautaw1152The Pelican113½	No mishap	10
14Oct32- 5Lrl	fst 1 70	:233 :482 1:132 1:442	Alw 1200	11	3	31	63¾	912	1012	Kurtsinger C	110	wb	13.20	77-15	Mr. Khayyam110hdPoppyman1152Keep Out1103	Quit	11
10Oct32- 3Lrl	gd 6f	:233 :483 1:142	Alw 1000	8	7	84¼	85¾	45½	43	Kurtsinger C	110	wb	15.65f	81-21	BoldLover110½Snaplock1142BrightShadow109.5½	Fast finish	12
21Sep32- 3HdG	fst 6f	:23 :461 1:114	Alw 1200	7	3	74¼	85¾	109¼	1010½	Kurtsinger C	108	wb	17.05	85-10	Poppyman110hdWhite Lies1055Okapi108hd	No factor	11
10Sep32- 3Bel	fst *7f-WC	1:204	Champagne 5k	3	2	1½	52¾	712	65	Robertson A	116	wb	5.00e	86-12	Dynastic1191Kerry Patch116noDe Valera1102	Quit,mate won	9

24Aug32- 3Sar	fst	5½f	:23 :463 :593 1:062	Alw 800	2 2 51¾ 53¼ 51¾	2no	Workman R	118wb	15.00	91-09	Bold Lover108noJungle King1181Llandaff111nk	Driving	9
18Aug32- 3Sar	sly	6f	:231 :471 1:124	Grab Bag H 3.4k	8 7 109¾ 1012 95½	98¾	Coucci S	120wb	15.00	79-13	Sun Archer1153Garden Message1121½Grand Time125no		10
Struggled in going													
10Aug32- 3Sar	fst	5½f	:231 :471 1:001 1:07	Alw 800	5 5 35 32½ 43	32	Kurtsinger C	120wb	5.00e	86-16	Wedding Ring1151Sarada1101Jungle King1202	Tired	12
6Aug32- 3Sar	fst	6f	:23 :47 1:123	U S Hotel 13k	10 1 63¾ 85 85½	79½	Kurtsinger C	118wb	30.00	79-11	Ladysman1253De Valera1142Happy Gal122½	Early speed	10
2Aug32- 6Sar	fst	5½f	:231 :464 1:00 1:064	©Md Sp Wt	9 5 47 45¼ 43¼	1no	Kurtsinger C	116wb	*2.00	89-12	JunglKng116noBlssdEvnt116½CrckFlyr1161	Away in a tangle	12
9Jun32- 3Bel	fst	5f-WC	1:001	Alw 1000	9 6 52¾ 51¼	43	Kurtsinger C	108wb	10.00	76-17	CrzyJn1131RomnHoldy116½LoughPort1161½	Blocked final ⅛	11
4Jun32- 6Bel	fst	4½f-WC	:52	Alw 1000	2 5 88¼ 915	813½	Kurtsinger C	112 w	8.00	81-08	Kerry Patch1121Bronze Saint112noPuchero1122	Outrun	9

Kayak II (Arg)

br. c. 1935, by Congreve (Copyright)–Mosquita, by Your Majesty
Lifetime record: 26 14 8 1 $213,205

Own.– C.S. Howard
Br.– J.V. Roca (Arg)
Tr.– T. Smith

16Jan41- 6SA	gd	6f	:223 :462 1:111	4↑ Alw 2500	1 5 56 31½ 3½	21½	Haas L	126wb	*.90	91-14	Augury1151½Kayak II1261Carmenita1052½		7
Wide,worked mile in 1:37 4/5													
2Sep40- 6Was	fst	1¼	:494 1:144 1:391 2:04	3↑ Wash Park H 31k	5 5 53½ 56 68	610¾	Adams J	130wb	*.80	79-14	War Plumage110¾Viscounty1183Burning Star1094	Gave way	6
3Aug40- 7Hol	fst	1½	:481 1:131 2:041 2:301	3↑ Sunset H 20k	7 4 55 32½ 2½	1hd	Adams J	131wb	*1.40e	94-06	Kayak II131hdSpecify1161½Big Flash1093	Hard drive	8
27Jly40- 7Hol	fst	1¼	:461 1:11 1:36 2:02	3↑ Hol Gold Cup 53k	11 8 67 73¾ 67¾	79¾	Rodriguez E	133wb	*1.10e	93-07	Challedon1331¼Specify1172½Can't Wait1151½	No excuse	11
2Mar40- 6SA	fst	1¼	:471 1:111 1:36 2:011	3↑ S Anita H 121k	2 13 1311 62½ 31½	21½	Haas L	129wb	*.70e	99-11	Seabiscuit1301½Kayak II1291Whichcee1141½	Good effort	13
24Feb40- 6SA	fst	1 1/16	:231 :464 1:111 1:422	3↑ S Antonio H 13k	5 10 95 54½ 42	22½	Shelhamer A	128wb	*1.70e	97-07	Seabiscuit1242½Kayak II128½Viscounty1104	Closed strong	13
17Feb40- 6SA	fst	7f	:223 :453 1:103 1:232	3↑ San Carlos H 12k	7 9 72¾ 63½ 710	87½	Adams J	130wb	*.80e	87-14	Specify1151¼Lassator105hdViscounty1093	Dull effort	11
1Jan40- 6SA	fst	1	:224 :463 1:112 1:372	3↑ New Year H 11k	7 5 33 33½ 23	24	Adams J	128wb	*.80	87-16	Whichcee1164Kayak II1284Heelfly1172	Second best	7
15Nov39- 6Pim	fst	1⅝	:494 1:402 2:05 2:442	3↑ Bowie H 12k	3 3 49½ 35 2hd	12	Woolf G	126wb	*.40	104-10	Kayak II1262Heelfly113noChallephen1131	Going away	8
1Nov39- 5Pim	gd	1 3/16	:512 1:163 1:404 1:59	3↑ Pim Spl 10k	3 1 21 2½ 1hd	2½	Woolf G	126wb	2.55	87-19	Challedon120½Kayak II12612Cravat126	Second best	3
21Oct39- 5Jam	fst	1 1/16	:231 :47 1:121 1:45	3↑ Continental H 12k	4 3 45½ 33 2½	11	Adams J	128wb	*.90	88-13	Kayak II1281Hash118noJourney On1124	Eased up	6
2Sep39- 5Nar	fst	1 3/16	:482 1:124 1:374 1:563	3↑ Nar Spl H 31k	3 2 31¾ 3nk 2½	23	Woolf G	128wb	*.50e	89-14	Challedon1183Kayak II1284Sorteado116½	Led,no excuse	6
22Jly39- 7Hol	fst	1¼	:472 1:121 1:371 2:023	3↑ Hol Gold Cup 52k	4 4 32 1hd 14	15	Woolf G	125wb	*.40	106-10	Kayak II1255Cravat126¾Specify118nk	Easily	7
4Jly39- 7Hol	fst	1⅛	:47 1:114 1:371 1:494	3↑ American H 15k	4 2 21 13 12½	15	Woolf G	120wb	*.60	101-10	Kayak II1205Gosum1073½Olimpo107no	Going away	8
4Mar39- 6SA	fst	1¼	:461 1:102 1:353 2:012	3↑ S Anita H 126k	16 10 73¾ 43½ 31½	11¼	Adams J	110wb	*3.00e	101-11	Kayak II1101¼Whichcee1121Main Man1171½	Going away	16
18Feb39- 6SA	fst	1 1/16	:231 :464 1:11 1:422	3↑ San Carlos H 13k	10 5 54½ 32 22½	1no	Adams J	110wb	4.20	102-11	Kayak II110noSpecify1194½Whichcee1124½	Just up	13
14Feb39- 5SA	fst	1 1/16	:231 :463 1:104 1:423	4↑ Alw 2000	2 2 2hd 1½ 12	34¼	Craigmyle J	120wb	*.30	97-06	Bottle Top1071¼Patty Cake1053Kayak II1205	Tired badly	6
25Jan39- 7SA	fst	1	:224 :462 1:11 1:36	4↑ Alw 1500	7 1 15 14 16	14½	Neves R	118wb	*.60	99-08	Kayak II1184½Quick Devil1181½Masker1152½	Easily best	8
14Jan39- 4SA	fst	6f	:221 :453 1:102	4↑ Handicap 1500	1 7 68½ 47 32	1hd	Neves R	116wb	*2.00	98-07	Kayak II116hdFirst Kiss1064½Lavengro1151	Just up	8
15Nov38- 4Pim	fst	6f	:23 :462 1:12	Alw 1200	6 3 2hd 21 1nk	1¾	Peters M	116wb	*1.00	94-15	Kayak II116¾Rissa104hdRoar113hd	Drew out	8
29Oct38- 2Lrl	hy	1 70	:234 :48 1:15 1:464	Alw 1100	5 2 1hd 13 11	21	Smith FA	118wb	*.70	74-30	SunAlexandria1151KayakII1184JohnOne1182	Tired in drive	5
17Oct38- 6Lrl	fst	1 70	:233 :463 1:121 1:423	Alw 1100	7 1 13 12 12	1nk	Smith FA	112wb	*1.25	96-13	Kayak II112nkPernie1121John One112½	Just lasted	7
13Oct38- 5Lrl	fst	6f	:231 :464 1:121	Alw 1200	1 5 11 11½ 12	11	Smith FA	110wb	2.95	93-13	Kayak II1101Court Dance107nkRissa1071	Driving	8
27Jun38- 6Suf	sly	1 70	:231 :47 1:114 1:433	Alw 1000	5 1 11½ 12 13	12½	Smith FA	113wb	*1.90	88-20	Kayak II1132½Mama's Boy1071Landlubber104no	In hand	6
23Jun38- 1Suf	fst	6f	:23 :453 1:11	3↑ Md Sp Wt	5 3 11½ 12 12½	15	Smith FA	110wb	*1.70	93-13	Kayak II1105Sport Heel1101½Running Scale1053	Going away	9
10Jun38- 6Aqu	fst	6½f	:233 :47 1:122 1:192	3↑ Md Sp Wt	7 6 2hd 11 1hd	22	Pollard J	118 w	3.00	88-13	Billy Van Nuys1182Kayak II1182Trojan Racket1262	Hung	7

Lady Maryland

gr. f. 1934, by Sir Greysteel (Roi Herode)–Palestra, by Prince Palatine
Lifetime record: 82 18 14 14 $31,067

Own.– G. Ring
Br.– Mrs Helena S. Raskob (Md)
Tr.– A.G. Robertson

12Oct40- 3Jam	fst	6f	:224 :462 1:121	3↑ ⒻAlw 2000	7 8 817 819 814	813	Seabo G	114 w	10.45	78-13	Dini1221½Flota105½Colosseum1141¼	Never a factor	8
Previously trained by L.G. Bedwell													
22Jun40- 6Del	fst	1 1/16	:233 :464 1:113 1:451	3↑ ⒻNewcastle H 13k	10 12 105¾ 117 1113	1010¾	Driscoll D	124 w	7.65	82-08	Tedbriar108.5½War Beauty1062Orcades107hd	Outrun	12
7Jun40- 6Bel	fst	1 1/16	:224 :453 1:103 1:433	3↑ ⒻTop Flight H 7.9k	4 8 67 64¼ 53	56½	Charlton C	126 w	4.45e	86-15	True Call1071Piquet106hdDolly Val120½	No mishap	9
27May40- 6Bel	fst	1 1/16	:231 :464 1:111 1:441	3↑ ⒻHandicap 2040	2 6 69½ 58½ 23	1hd	Charlton C	122 w	*1.50e	90-13	Lady Maryland122hdRosetown105½One Jest1174	Hard drive	8
16May40- 5Bel	fst	7f	:23 :461 1:121 1:25	3↑ ⒻHandicap 2035	1 3 32 33½ 23	2hd	Charlton C	122 w	*1.10	85-16	Torchlight116hdLadyMrylnd1226HstyWddng1062	Just missed	5
11May40- 5Pim	fst	6f	:223 :464 1:12	3↑ WFBR H 1.5k	4 4 54½ 41½ 1½	12	Charlton C	114 w	2.30	94-15	LadyMrylnd1142SlowMotion1223LegalLight1122	Going away	7
6May40- 6Pim	fst	6f	:222 :454 1:112	3↑ Jennings H 6k	1 6 42¾ 64¾ 53¼	43	Charlton C	111 w	8.45	94-15	BattleJack120½SpeedtoSpare1182SlowMotion117½	No mishap	9
29Apr40- 6Pim	fst	6f	:222 :46 1:111	3↑ Baltimore Spring H 3.2k	6 6 56 43 32	31¼	Charlton C	111 w	5.05	97-17	BattleJack1171SpeedtoSpar118nkLdyMrylnd1111	Closed fast	6
15Apr40- 5HdG	fst	6f	:234 :462 1:12	3↑ Harford H 6.7k	5 8 913 96½ 94½	45	Charlton C	111 w	7.25e	88-14	Sun Egret1222Battle Jack1152Jay Jay1141	Late foot	10
30Jan40- 5Hia	fst	7f	:23 :462 1:103 1:232	4↑ ⒻAlw 1200	4 7 54½ 55½ 42¾	51¼	Durando C	115 w	3.30	95-09	Flying Lill115nkDolly Val115hdUnerring118½	Swerved	8
27Jan40- 4Hia	fst	6f	:224 :463 1:102	4↑ Alw 1400	3 4 55½ 55½ 32½	33	Smith FA	111 w	7.10	94-12	EasyMon1142TheChief108.51LadyMaryland1115	Closed well	5
17Jan40- 6Hia	fst	6f	:23 :461 1:10	3↑ Handicap 1500	4 6 74¼ 74½ 55½	43½	Donoso R	113 w	7.15	95-07	Easy Mon1133Mar Le108½Speed to Spare118no	Late foot	7
10Jan40- 6Hia	gd	6f	:221 :453 1:114	3↑ Inaugural H 6.7k	4 13 1320 1325 1123	1119¾	Smith FA	115 w	6.10	70-18	Maetall114hdCardinalis1103Great Union120hd	Dull race	13
11Nov39- 6Pim	fst	6f	:221 :453 1:112	3↑ Ritchie H 7.5k	12 8 76 53½ 41½	1hd	Smith FA	108 w	9.10	97-12	Lady Maryland108hdJay Jay113noAirflame1102	Hard drive	12
7Nov39- 6Pim	gd	6f	:224 :464 1:13	2↑ ⓈHeiser H 3.1k	1 1 43¾ 52¼ 31½	2hd	Robertson A	111 w	10.80	89-25	SlowMotion116hdLadyMrylnd111noSpdtoSpr1181	Just missed	6
3Nov39- 5Pim	fst	1 1/16	:241 :484 1:14 1:464	3↑ Handicap 1500	5 4 43¼ 31½ 21½	21	Shelhamer A	115 w	*1.25	85-17	FlyingLee1111LadyMrylnd1152NoCompetiton1093	No excuse	5
21Oct39- 6Lrl	fst	1 1/16	:232 :464 1:122 1:45	3↑ Handicap 1500	4 4 42¾ 32 45½	45¼	Peters M	112 w	1.95	87-14	Challephen1111Nedayr116nkManie O'Hara1034	No excuse	6
14Oct39- 5Lrl	fst	1	:232 :463 1:12 1:374	2↑ Laurel 9.7k	7 7 74½ 63½ 34	34	Robertson A	111 w	5.90	92-13	Sun Egret1184Nedayr113hdLady Maryland1114	Closed well	8
Previously trained by P.D. Watts													
7Oct39- 6Lrl	fst	1 1/16	:232 :472 1:123 1:443	3↑ Handicap 2000	5 3 4¾ 2½ 2hd	2nk	Robertson A	111 w	4.40	94-14	WarMinstrel109nkLadyMaryland1112RobertL.1113	Game try	6
3Oct39- 5Lrl	my	6f	:243 :483 1:132	3↑ Capital H 9.3k	6 8 88¼ 86½ 78	79	Hardy L	110 w	20.40	78-22	Sun Egret1201½Clodion1121½Rough Time122½	Outrun	8
25Sep39- 4HdG	fst	6f	:232 :462 1:121	3↑ Handicap 1200	4 4 43¼ 43 21	2nk	Hardy L	116 w	3.35	92-17	BunnyBaby104nkLadyMaryland1161RobertL.1164	Just missed	5
18Sep39- 5HdG	fst	6f	:23 :463 1:114	3↑ Susquehanna H 2.5k	3 10 107 107¼ 105½	82¾	Stevenson C	116 w	11.95	91-12	Sun Egret120½Jay Jay115hdRedlin116½	Off slowly	11
9Sep39- 5Aqu	fst	1 1/16	:233 :462 1:103 1:43	3↑ ⒻBeldame H 13k	6 8 74¾ 42 41¾	63¾	Arcaro E	124 w	8.00	94-03	Nellie Bly102noUnerring1203Bala Ormont115hd	No mishap	18
5Sep39- 5Aqu	fst	7f	:231 :464 1:121 1:243	3↑ ⒻAlw 1200	3 5 65¾ 52¼ 3¾	12	Arcaro E	115 w	3.20	91-10	Lady Maryland1152Pixey Dell1154Chicluna105½	Going away	5
7Aug39- 5Sar	fst	1	:242 :481 1:124 1:381	3↑ ⒻHandicap 1230	1 5 57½ 57 52¼	67½	Peters M	122 w	6.00	82-11	Solar Flight1021½Hostility1121One Jest1122	No excuse	7
29Jly39- 5Emp	sly	1 1/16	:24 :473 1:123 1:453	3↑ Yonkers H 9.9k	6 6 68½ 67½ 57¼	58½	Peters M	112 w	12.00	84-16	Sickle T.108hdHe Did116½The Chief1165	Outrun	7
1Jly39- 5AP	fst	1	:23 :454 1:103 1:363	3↑ ⒻArl Matron H 6.1k	5 6 65½ 44 35	34¼	Smith G	120 w	7.00	85-17	FlyingLill107nkUnerring1084LadyMaryland1202	Closed well	9
10Jun39- 6Del	fst	1 1/16	:24 :48 1:124 1:46	3↑ ⒻNewcastle H 12k	2 9 82¾ 72¾ 2hd	3nk	Smith G	118 w	4.40	89-11	ShangayLily113noBunnyBaby108nkLadyMrylnd118no	Game try	12
3Jun39- 7Del	fst	1 70	:232 :472 1:123 1:431	4↑ ⒻAlw 1000	2 4 42½ 41¾ 1½	1¾	Smith G	117 w	2.45	100-07	LadyMaryland117¾PixeyDell1134ShortDistanc1031½	Drew out	7
30May39- 5Del	fst	6f	:23 :46 1:114	3↑ Wilmington H 5.4k	2 6 74½ 75¾ 54¾	32	Smith G	108 w	4.95	97-07	FightingFox1261Preeminent1131LdyMrylnd108hd	Closed fast	8
20May39- 5Bel	fst	1	:231 :463 1:12 1:371	3↑ Metropolitan H 10k	6 6 65½ 56 69¾	67½	Smith G	109 w	10.00	81-13	Knickerbocker1001½Heelfly116noJacola115hd	Outrun	8
11May39- 6Pim	fst	6f	:23 :463 1:121	3↑ ⒻCarroll H 3.3k	2 5 43½ 3½ 11½	14	Smith G	116 w	*2.05	93-16	Lady Maryland1164Rehearsal1151Bunny Baby1143	Easily	7
6May39- 4Pim	fst	6f	:23 :463 1:122	3↑ Handicap 1200	1 6 83¾ 64¾ 43	1nk	Smith G	110 w	6.15	92-15	LadyMaryland110nkSlowMotion111noRehersl1111½	Hard drive	9
15Apr39- 5HdG	fst	6f	:23 :463 1:114	3↑ Harford H 7k	6 13 135½ 135¼ 129¼	119½	Smith G	109 w	5.40f	84-15	Sun Egret1164Fighting Fox1221Old Rosebush1141½	Outrun	14

8Apr39- 4Bow gd 6f :232:473 1:14 3↑ Handicap 1065 8 2 97¾ 53¾ 41½ 31¾ Smith G 110 w 8.40 81-23 Pagliacci1121½Drudgery115nkLady Maryland110hd Late foot 10
30Mar39- 5Bow sly 6f :231:472 1:131 3↑ Rowe Mem H 6.3k 9 9 97½ 99 911 76¾ Mora H 108 w 16.90 80-25 Rough Time1161½Benjam1083Old Rosebush116hd Outrun 10
16Nov38- 5Bow fst 6f :231:472 1:12 2↑ W P Burch Mem H 2.6k 11 2 73½ 65 84 62¾ Seabo G 112 w 16.20 90-22 HoneyCloud1151½Clingendaal112noRyeBeach121no No mishap 13
11Nov38- 6Pim fst 6f :23 :462 1:121 3↑ Ritchie H 7.5k 7 13 94 51¾ 32 2¾ Yarberry W 109 w 19.70 92-16 HoneyCloud110¾LadyMaryland109¾HighLark107½ Closed fast 14
7Nov38- 6Pim hy 1 70 :233:483 1:142 1:46 3↑ [S]Heiser H 2.7k 3 3 3nk 11 1½ 1¾ Wall N 115 w 2.25 81-26 Lady Maryland115¾Unheralded1076Toddle On111 Drew out 3
2Nov38- 6Pim fst 6f :23 :463 1:114 2↑ Baltimore Autumn H 3.8k 3 9 82¾ 92 42 32¼ Yarberry W 107 w 32.05 93-13 SunEgrt1142Mowr116no[DH]TheFightr126 Close quarters early 11
17Oct38- 5Lrl fst 1 1/16 :232:471 1:122 1:444 3↑ Alw 1200 4 2 23 22 22 21½ Renick J 109 w 3.60 91-13 Conquer1201½LadyMrylnd1093SirJimJames1201 Good effort 5
12Oct38- 5Lrl fst 1 70 :232:47 1:123 1:431 3↑ Handicap 1200 4 6 66½ 43¼ 32 3½ Renick J 111 w 4.95 92-16 JohnOne111.5noJourneyOn111½LadyMrylnd1114 Strong finish 6
5Oct38- 4Lrl fst 6f :231:463 1:123 3↑ Handicap 1200 5 4 42½ 31¼ 31 3hd Scheih F 113 w 2.65 91-14 Benjam115noHappy Code108noLady Maryland1132 Game try 6
24Sep38- 4HdG fst 6f :234:47 1:12 3↑ Clm 4500 8 4 43 32 2nk 2¾ Dupps L 112 w 3.15 92-10 Infidox114¾Lady Maryland1123Carvola1041½ Weakened 9
16Sep38- 4HdG fst 6f :241:472 1:121 3↑ Susquehanna H 2.5k 4 9 95¾ 85¼ 75½ 54 Seabo G 108 w 13.40 88-16 Lavengro114noSunEgret1131MaskedGnrl1141½ Close quarters 10
20Aug38- 4Nar fst 6f :231:462 1:104 3↑ Clm 6000 5 4 33½ 33 2½ 1hd Krovitz H 95 w *2.20 97-09 Lady Maryland95hdHappy Knot1041Pordina101½ Hard drive 6
3Aug38- 5Nar fst 1 70 :233:472 1:114 1:422 3↑ [F]Mary Dyer H 6.7k 10 2 3nk 21½ 44 67½ Scheih F 107wb 23.55 85-14 Marica1292Patty Cake112noFair Stein1142 Tired 10
1Aug38- 5Nar fst 6f :23 :452 1:104 3↑ Nar H 6.6k 1 10 106½ 107½ 106 104¾ Smith E 112wb 33.80 92-14 Accolade1132Merry Lassie1101The Fighter114hd Outpaced 11
18Jly38- 4Emp fst 5¾f :231:464 1:09 3↑ Handicap 1030 2 4 44 33½ 31¼ 1nk Wall N 117wb *1.50 94-12 Lady Maryland117nkSunport120noLakeview1091½ Just up 5
7Jly38- 6Del fst 6f :241:461 1:12 3↑ Handicap 2000 3 7 51¾ 5½ 42 43¼ Vedder RL 113wb 7.10 95-11 James A.108¾Sun Egret1201½Bull Whip1111 No mishaps 10
18Jun38- 4Del fst 6f :224:46 1:12 3↑ Alw 1200 1 4 31¼ 31 2½ 21 Wall N 111wb 7.80 97-10 Sun Egret1131Lady Maryland111hdNedayr113no Good effort 5
15Jun38- 5Del fst 6f :24 :473 1:131 3↑ Handicap 1000 1 3 21 2nk 12 11 Vedder RL 108wb 8.60 92-11 Lady Maryland1081Sun Celerina1081Conquer1263 Driving 7
Previously owned by B.B. Archer
8Jun38- 5Del sl 6f :24 :473 1:142 4↑ Clm 4000 1 4 2hd 11½ 11½ 1no Wall N 115wb 2.00 86-16 LadyMaryland115noWinningChance1154Crvol1141½ Hard drive 5
Previously trained by B.B. Archer
11May38- 3Pim fst 6f :231:473 1:124 4↑ Clm 3250 5 4 21½ 2½ 14 11 Wall N 112wb 2.80 90-13 LadyMaryland1121ChiefCherokee1172Tddy'sStr107hd Driving 7
6May38- 2Pim fst 6f :232:472 1:122 4↑ Clm c-2500 6 8 73¾ 41¾ 21½ 2hd Adleman W 114wb *1.55 92-13 PostageDue121hdLadyMaryland1145Sachem1181½ Just missed 8
Claimed from Mrs R.H. Heighe, trainer J.A. Boniface
3May38- 3Pim fst 6f :232:473 1:122 4↑ [F]Clm 2250 5 8 52¼ 32 1½ 15 Adleman W 108wb *2.25 92-11 Lady Maryland1085Sheknows1111½Deflate1152 Going away 10
27Apr38- 2HdG fst 6f :232:473 1:13 4↑ Clm 2500 8 11 72 3nk 1hd 3nk Adleman W 108wb 5.20f 88-18 Golden Vein115nkEarly Times118noLady Maryland1081 Hung 12
22Mar38- 4TrP fst 6f :223:461 1:114 4↑ Clm 2500 4 5 85¼ 75¼ 62¼ 31½ Adleman W 106wb 6.30 89-11 [DH]Mixwell113[DH]Ladfield1161½LadyMaryland106nk Great rush 8
17Mar38- 7TrP fst 5½f :23 :462 1:061 4↑ Clm 2500 1 6 75¾ 65½ 43½ 32½ Adleman W 106wb 4.80 86-14 Rebekah1111½Mixwell1161Lady Maryland106hd Closed fast 8
14Mar38- 6TrP fst 6f :23 :462 1:12 4↑ Clm 3000 1 6 53½ 54½ 42½ 53¾ Adleman W 106wb 9.60 86-14 Noble Boy1141½My Kin109noGold Buckle1141½ Hung 7
12Feb38- 3Hia fst 6½f :23 :463 1:133 1:181 4↑ Clm 3500 5 3 53½ 42½ 56 88½ Kurtsinger C 110wb 7.15 79-14 Sunphantom110nkSachem111¾My Kin1102 No excuse 9
3Feb38- 4Hia fst 6f :23 :46 1:112 4↑ Clm 4000 6 7 710 78 78 611 Adleman W 106wb 4.30 81-18 Indomitable1133Time Signal1142Max B.1131 Outrun 8
24Jan38- 6Hia fst 1 :234:464 1:111 1:373 4↑ Alw 1200 4 4 32 31 68½ 1014½ Smith FA 96wb 16.05 73-19 Mucho Gusto1161½Maecloud921Pageboy1141½ Quit 11
19Jan38- 4Hia fst 6f :223:461 1:112 3↑ Handicap 1000 2 8 72¾ 74¼ 46½ 46 Adleman W 118wb 14.35 86-16 Joyride1101Black River124hdGene Wagers1165 No mishaps 11
27Jly37- 5Sar sl 6f :24 :473 1:14 Seneca Claiming 4k 7 2 54½ 52¼ 41¼ 43½ Wagner J 109wb 4.00 78-19 Golden Era108½Mahdi106noBitter Berry1053 No mishaps 7
3Jly37- 4Del fst 6f :233:463 1:131 [F]Alw 1000 5 2 32 32 2hd 1hd Adelman W 106wb *1.20 - - LadyMaryland106hdEarlyAutumn1034CareFor1035 Hard drive 6
26Jun37- 4Del fst 6f :23 :462 1:123 Clm 4000 2 1 41¼ 3½ 1hd 14 McDermott P 104wb *1.20 - - LadyMaryland1044CareFor101hdAlexandrine1051 Going away 5
15Jun37- 6Aqu fst 7f :233:48 1:121 1:244 Handicap 1055 4 3 34 35 33½ 24 Ray W 106wb 7.00 87-15 Drudgery1184LadyMaryland106½EarlySettlr1072 Closed well 5
4Jun37- 5Bel fst 1 :233:471 1:12 1:374 3↑ Handicap 1065 8 1 2hd 2hd 55¾ 610½ Peters M 111wb 4.00 75-14 Buginarug109½Danger Point1042Night Bud1105 Speed,quit 8
29May37- 4Bel fst 6f :223:454 1:12 [F]Alw 1000 1 3 45 55 32½ 34½ Hanford C 111wb 6.00 85-17 North Riding1151½Rosenna1113Lady Maryland111½ Wide 7
11May37- 5Bel fst 6f :23 :464 1:13 [F]Alw 1000 7 4 33 32½ 2½ 22½ Peters M 113wb 10.00 86-19 NorthRiding1172½LadyMaryland1134Flyanett109hd Wide,hung 7
30Apr37- 6Pim fst 6f :232:473 1:134 Alw 1000 3 3 3½ 2hd 42 54¾ Peters M 111wb 11.75 80-21 Carnarvon112.5½PrairiDog111nkGrndPly1114 Faltered drive 7
19Apr37- 3HdG fst 6f :233:48 1:144 [F]Alw 1000 2 3 1hd 1hd 1hd 1½ Peters M 110wb 8.95 79-24 Lady Maryland110.5½Care For112½My Elsie1124 7
Driving,slowly drew clear
18Sep36- 2HdG fst 6f :24 :482 1:144 Alw 1000 1 5 43½ 43½ 43½ 6¾ Renick J 111wb 18.45f 78-18 Alexandrine108noAngloSaxon111hdLiveGrant117no No factor 12
30Jly36- 3Sar fst 5½f :232:482 1:082 [F]Md Sp Wt 2 2 43¼ 3¾ 1nk 11 Fallon L 115wb 15.00 81-14 Lady Maryland1151Janeen115hdCare For1151½ Wide 14
20Jun36- 1Aqu fst 5f 1:002 [F]Md Sp Wt 5 2 63 62¾ 65¾ Richards H 115wb 4.00 79-09 Devil's Pace1102Sunfeathers115hdCeltic Legend1153 11
Slow into stride
4Jun36- 3Bel fst 4½f-WC :523 [F]Md Sp Wt 14 7 11½ 1hd 42 Peters M 112wb 50.00 90-15 Richmond Rose1121Premiere1121Scottish Mary112hd 14
Faltered under urging
1Jun36- 1Bel fst 5f-WC 1:001 Clm 3500 6 7 75½ 77¼ 713 Peters M 113wb 15.00 66-16 Pass 'Em By1141½Papenie1191½Thomas C.1115 Trailed 7
25Feb36- 2Hia fst 3f :344 Md Sp Wt 13 2 22 2hd Renick J 113wb 5.95f - - BravoCaruso116hdLadyMaryland1132MayRo1141 Just missed 13
13Feb36- 2Hia gd 3f :35 [F]Alw 800 6 3 55½ 47½ Renick S 115 w 19.40 - - Owaller1182Moss Gal1181½Little Empress1184 No mishaps 7
5Feb36- 2Hia fst 3f :35 Clm 2500 1 1 1½ 21½ Meade D 113 w 4.55 - - Oddesa Girl1151½Lady Maryland1131½Greedy113hd Bore out 14
27Jan36- 2Hia fst 3f :34 [F]Md Sp Wt 2 3 44 45½ Workman R 116 w 73.90 - - Owaller116½Peggy Porter116noClouds1165 Evenly 12

Marica

blk. f. 1933, by Epinard (Badajoz)–Canberra, by Craigangower **Lifetime record: 44 19 7 6 $48,825**
Own.– French Lick Springs Stable
Br.– Thomas D. Taggart (Ky)
Tr.– J.H Johnson

14Feb39- 6SA fst 1 :223:453 1:102 1:353 4↑ Alw 1900 3 2 31¾ 37 39 38¼ Dotter R 113wb 6.60 93-06 Today1042¼Seabiscuit1286Marica113 Tired 3
Trained in 1938 by H. Oots & H. Wells
28Sep38- 5HdG fst 1⅛ :472 1:122 1:372 1:50 3↑ Havre de Grace H 11k 5 4 43 56½ 711 712½ Dotter R 124wb 14.00 86-16 Seabiscuit1282½SavageBeauty1031Mnow1201½ Close quarters 8
3Sep38- 5Nar fst 1 3/16 :472 1:122 1:363 1:561 3↑ Nar Spl 33k 10 5 31¼ 32½ 1011 1019 Dotter R 128wb 3.30 75-09 Stagehand1191Bull Lea1133Cravat1084 Tired 10
22Aug38- 5Sar fst 1 :23 :463 1:12 1:38 3↑ [F]Handicap 1240 4 3 23 11 11½ 12 Gilbert J 128wb *.65 91-15 Marica1282Idle Miss1125Rust1095 Easily 4
3Aug38- 5Nar fst 1 70 :233:472 1:114 1:422 3↑ [F]Mary Dyer H 6.7k 2 6 1hd 11½ 12½ 12 Dotter R 129wb *.50 93-14 Marica1292Patty Cake112noFair Stein1142 In hand 10
9Jly38- 6Del fst 1¼ :48 1:121 1:362 2:033 3↑ Sussex H 11k 1 1 13 13 11½ 1½ Dotter R 125wb *1.00e 103-08 Marica125½Tatterdemalion1173Isolater116no Driving 6
18Jun38- 6Del fst 1 1/16 :25 :484 1:121 1:453 3↑ [F]Newcastle H 11k 3 1 11½ 11½ 13 11 Dotter R 125wb 1.90 91-10 Marica1251Savage Beauty109½Esposa1203 Eased up 6
Previously trained by H. Wells
14Oct37- 6Kee fst 1¼ :464 1:114 1:38 2:042 3↑ Breeders H 7.4k 2 1 15 14 13 1nk Dotter R 118wb 1.10 98-08 Marica118nkCount Arthur126 Hard drive 2
11Sep37- 6Haw gd 1¼ :472 1:121 1:374 2:042 3↑ Haw Gold Cup H 16k 10 6 42½ 54½ 69 67¼ Dotter R 120wb 2.70 79-16 Sahri II110hdInfantry116noDellor1142 Bore over badly 12
4Sep37- 5LF fst 6f :23 :461 1:104 3↑ Calumet H 3k 4 1 42 34½ 33½ 2nk Dotter R 127wb *.60 98-10 BienFait112nkMaric1272MssDolphn102.54 Getting to winner 7
14Aug37- 6LF fst 1 :232:46 1:094 1:352 3↑ F S Peabody Mem H 3.1k 3 5 2½ 1hd 11½ 11¼ Dotter R 122wb *1.40 97-08 Marica1221¼Deliberator118noDellor1103 Speed in reserve 8
7Aug37- 6LF fst 6f :221:444 1:102 3↑ Crete H 3.2k 7 10 64½ 45½ 23 13 Dotter R 117wb 2.20 100-05 Marica1173Bien Fait1142½Main Man1061 Ridden out 11
27Jly37- 5AP fst 1 :224:464 1:111 1:36 4↑ Alw 1500 2 3 32½ 2½ 1½ 12 Dotter R 105wb 3.30 92-14 Marica1052Infantry1126Sir Jim James110hd Easily 5
14Jly37- 6AP fst 1 :231:461 1:103 1:354 3↑ Handicap 1200 5 1 11½ 1½ 1hd 2½ Dotter R 112wb *1.00 92-12 Grand Manitou114½Marica1123Preeminent1181 Bore out 5
3Jly37- 6AP fst 1 :23 :453 1:101 1:364 3↑ [F]Arl Matron H 6.5k 8 5 42½ 4¾ 22 1hd Dotter R 122wb 3.10 88-13 Marica122hdShatterproof109¾Schoolmom1051 Willingly 13
17Apr37- 6Kee fst 6f :224:461 1:112 3↑ Phoenix H 4.1k 2 5 43 42 22 2¾ Dotter R 110wb *1.80 96-06 Preeminent110¾Marica1102Capt. Cal1173 Impeded 10
Previously owned by H. Oots; previously trained by C. Houbre
20Mar37- 4OP fst 5¾f 1:08 3↑ Handicap 1000 9 2 73¾ 52½ 21½ 11½ Dotter R 116wb *1.40 97-05 Marica1161½Cardarrone112hdMiss Ginbar99½ Strong finish 11
22Feb37- 5SA fst 6f :221:452 1:103 3↑ Handicap 1235 2 6 45 43½ 21 1no Dotter R 104wb *1.50 97-10 Marica104noSilk Mask107¾Delphinium1102 Just up 7

Date	Cond	Dist	Times	Race	Running line	Jockey	Wt	Odds	Speed	Top finishers	Comment
5Jan37- 6SA	fst	6f	:221 :454 1:104	3↑ ⒻHandicap 1545	1 6 53½ 51¾ 21 11¼	Dotter R	112wb	4.30	96-15	Marica1121¼Bay Bubble1102Uppermost112½	Going away 8
Previously trained by H. Wells											
23Oct36- 4Kee	gd	6f	:231 :463 1:114	3↑ Alw 1000	5 2 63¼ 66 46½ 33½	Dotter R	103wb	*1.40	--	Pelerine1082½Dusty Dawn1201Marica1033	Closed fast 6
20Oct36- 6Kee	sl	6f	:231 :482 1:134	Alw 1000	3 4 35 33 3½ 11½	Dotter R	105wb	*.90	--	Marica1051½Pelerine111¾Gleeman1136	Going away 6
15Oct36- 5Kee	fst	6f	:223 :461 1:104	3↑ Keene H 2.4k	5 3 44 45 33 2¾	Dotter R	101wb	3.00	--	Myrtlewood128¾Marica1012Gleeman112¾	Closed well 5
7Oct36- 6LF	fst	6f	:222 :454 1:104	3↑ Handicap 800	9 3 21½ 22 11 16	Dotter R	103wb	6.00	98-12	Marica1036PanicRelif1093ColonlEd1101½	Drew away rapidly 11
1Oct36- 6LF	hy	6f	:233 :474 1:152	Alw 1000	6 1 59 511 513 512	Dotter R	107wb	3.40	63-38	Billbo1103Panic Relief1082Kentucky Blues1095	Outrun 6
24Sep36- 5LF	fst	6f	:223 :46 1:11	3↑ ⒻAlw 800	4 7 67½ 66 65½ 42¾	Dotter R	103wb	6.00	94-09	Kentucky Blues104nkSilverette108½Slim Rosie1102	7
Stumbled badly start											
9Sep36- 5LF	fst	7f	:23 :461 1:111 1:233	3↑ Handicap 800	7 4 42½ 43½ 43¼ 31	Dotter R	105 w	*1.80	95-07	Colonel Ed108noTracker118.51Marica1051	Closed fast 12
4Sep36- 4Was	sl	6f	:233 :481 1:134	3↑ Handicap 1000	3 6 65½ 53½ 32 22	Dotter R	105 w	6.70	84-22	Mucho Gusto1152Marica105½Noble Count1011	Closed fast 7
5Aug36- 4Was	gd	7f	:231 :471 1:12 1:25	3↑ Handicap 1100	3 3 31½ 31½ 56¼ 77	Dotter R	105 w	8.30	86-09	Bartering Kate110noReaping1073½Salaam1121½	Quit 8
17Jly36- 5Emp	fst	1 1/16	:241 :48 1:13 1:461	3↑ ⒻHandicap 1220	4 2 2nk 41½ 43¼ 45½	Dotter R	105 w	15.00	86-14	Jesting1202Tabitha106½Paradisical1103	No excuse 4
10Jly36- 4Emp	fst	1 70	:233 :47 1:121 1:44	3↑ ⒻHandicap 1230	5 3 36 54¾ 510 59	Dotter R	104 w	3.20	81-10	Vicaress1211½Tabitha1071½Pretty Night1101	Quit 5
27Jun36- 6Lat	fst	1⅛	:47 1:124 1:381 1:501	ⒻLat Oaks 5.9k	7 3 21 21 1hd 21	Hanka W	116 w	14.00	92-14	Sparta1161Marica1164Gorgeous Lady116½	Gamely 8
20Jun36- 5Haw	fst	1 1/16	:24 :481 1:134 1:452	3↑ Alw 1000	3 1 11½ 12 1½ 1hd	Dotter R	92 w	3.70	91-14	Marica92hdSalaam1125Buck Langhorne1091	Just lasted 7
9Jun36- 6Haw	fst	6f	:23 :463 1:121	3↑ ⒻAlw 1000	7 7 52¾ 43½ 42¼ 32	Nolan J	103 w	8.40	90-14	Bird Flower1112Nellie Flag111noMarica1035	Closed well 7
5Jun36- 6Haw	fst	6½f	:23 :471 1:123 1:19	3↑ Alw 1000	2 3 21 21 2½ 21½	Nolan J	100 w	3.00	91-16	Where Away1171½Marica1004Money Getter112no	Closed well 7
28May36- 5Haw	fst	6f	:232 :473 1:124	3↑ ⒻAlw 1000	2 4 21½ 32½ 33¼ 33	Nolan J	101 w	6.20	86-13	Forever Yours1081Sandstone992Marica1016	Saved ground 6
16May36- 6CD	fst	1⅛	:473 1:124 1:384 1:523	ⒻKy Oaks 6.3k	9 1 11 1½ 32 107¾	Haas L	116 w	10.90f	78-08	Two Bob1164Threadneedle116½Seventh Heaven1161½	Quit 12
13May36- 6CD	my	1	:224 :473 1:14 1:414	ⒻAlw 1000	3 3 1hd 1hd 3nk 31½	Hanka W	107 w	4.10	68-29	Threadneedle109.5½Stepinanna1071Marica1073	Weakened 8
Previously trained by C. Houbre											
8May36- 6CD	fst	7f	:224 :462 1:114 1:252	ⒻAlw 1000	7 9 108 108½ 86¾ 77½	Hanka W	108 w	16.00	81-15	Mary Terry108noDora May110½Brendard1102	Closed gap 11
31Aug35- 6Dad	fst	6f	:233 :472 1:12	Handicap 1000	5 1 11½ 1½ 1½ 1½	Mayer J	112 w	4.40	96-07	Marica112½Boston Pal1153Emileo1132	Driving 7
24Aug35- 5Dad	fst	5½f	:23 :463 :59 1:052	Alw 700	6 3 1½ 1hd 11 1no	Mayer J	110 w	3.00	99-05	Marica110noBoston Pal113½Emileo110½	Hard drive 7
12Aug35- 5Dad	fst	5f	:232 :471 1:00	Alw 600	4 1 13 13 14 15	Mayer J	109 w	*.90	97-08	Marica1095Insulated106noStepinanna104nk	Eased up 8
9Aug35- 2Dad	fst	5f	:232 :473 1:002	ⒻMd Sp Wt	8 2 11 11½ 13 15	Mayer J	115 w	*2.10e	95-08	Marica1155Spectrum1151½Haeheart1153	Eased up 12
Previously trained by H. Wells											
14May35- 4CD	sly	4½f	:233 :473 :544	Clm 3000	3 10 818 819 817	Hanka W	106 w	110.60	72-11	Bushmaster1042½Glitter Glow1081½Barbara A1076	Outrun 10
9May35- 2CD	fst	4½f	:232 :473 :534	ⒻMd Sp Wt	9 12 1216 912 88	Hanka W	115 w	12.90e	86-06	Out Put1151½Monks Gold1151½Parsley115½	Off slow 12

Menow

dk. b. c. 1935, by Pharamond II (Phalaris)–Alcibiades, by Supremus

Lifetime record: 17 7 3 3 $140,100

Own.– H.P. Headley
Br.– Hal Price Headley (Ky)
Tr.– D.A. Headley

Date	Cond	Dist	Times	Race	Running line	Jockey	Wt	Odds	Speed	Top finishers	Comment
28Sep38- 5HdG	fst	1⅛	:472 1:122 1:372 1:50	3↑ Havre de Grace H 11k	8 1 11½ 1½ 32½ 33½	Haas L	120wb	5.25	95-16	Seabiscuit1282½Savage Beauty1031Menow1201½	Went lame 8
24Sep38- 5HdG	fst	1 1/16	:23 :463 1:122 1:44	Potomac H 11k	9 1 11½ 11½ 11½ 11	Workman R	122wb	3.05	98-10	Menow1221Bull Lea1182Sun Egret112hd	Under drive 9
17Sep38- 5Bel	fst	1	:223 :451 1:11 1:362	Jerome H 6.8k	1 2 24 25 44 46¼	Workman R	126wb	*1.20	87-12	Cravat115nkCan't Wait1164The Chief1192	Stopped 6
23Jly38- 6AP	sl	1¼	:48 1:124 1:382 2:061	Classic 34k	2 1 1½ 2½ 33 56	Wall N	123wb	2.10	69-26	Nedayr1211Bull Lea1211¼Cravat1233	Tired 8
29Jun38- 6Suf	hy	1⅛	:481 1:132 1:393 1:523	3↑ Mass H 59k	5 1 12 14 13 18	Wall N	107wb	10.40	82-28	Menow1078Busy K.107nkWar Minstrel106no	Easily 6
21May38- 5Bel	fst	1	:23 :462 1:113 1:372	Withers 18k	5 1 1½ 14 14 12	Kurtsinger C	118wb	*.60e	88-13	Menow1182Thanksgiving1184Redbreast1182	Eased up 9
14May38- 5Pim	sly	1 3/16	:48 1:132 1:40 1:594	Preakness 68k	3 2 1½ 12 23 37	Workman R	126wb	7.20	81-20	Dauber1267Cravat126hdMenow1263	Tired badly 9
7May38- 7CD	fst	1¼	:472 1:122 1:381 2:044	Ky Derby 57k	10 7 12 11½ 23 46	Workman R	126wb	8.50	79-16	Lawrin1261Dauber1265Can't Wait126no	Swerved,tired 10
28Apr38- 6Kee	fst	1⅛	:472 1:113 1:363 1:493	Blue Grass 8.3k	4 1 11½ 1½ 1½ 2nk	Robertson A	123wb	1.70e	113-08	Bull Lea121nkMenow1238Redbreast1235	No excuse 4
21Apr38- 5Kee	fst	1 1/16	:24 :48 1:122 1:44	ⒸAlw 1200	3 4 32 33 34 34½	Stevenson C	118wb	*.30	99-10	Bull Lea1123Birthday1081½Menow11830	Off poorly 4
15Apr38- 4Kee	fst	6f	:231 :462 1:112	Handicap 1500	3 3 11½ 12 11½ 11½	Kurtsinger C	122wb	*.10	97-13	Menow1221½King's Heir1126Sweep Royal1093	Eased up 4
20Oct37- 4Bel	fst	6½f-WC	1:151	Futurity 70k	8 7 11½ 12 14	Kurtsinger C	119wb	1.80e	106-00	Menow1194Tiger126hdFighting Fox122nk	Easily best 12
Geldings not eligible											
18Sep37- 4Bel	fst	6½f-WC	1:171	Champagne 5.2k	6 4 13 14 14	Kurtsinger C	113wb	12.00	96-08	Menow1134Bull Lea1161½Fighting Fox1221	Easily best 9
31Jly37- 5AP	fst	6f	:221 :453 1:114	Arl Futurity 40k	6 7 64½ 54½ 68 74	Corbett C	117wb	9.10e	84-16	DHTeddy's Comet117DHTiger1221C-Note117½	Outrun 8
26Jun37- 6Was	fst	6f	:222 :453 1:11	Was Futurity 34k	4 5 31½ 21½ 21½ 22	Westrope J	117wb	1.90e	95-10	Tiger1172Menow1172Bourbon King117½	Second best 8
18Jun37- 4Was	hy	5½f	:244 :50 1:033 1:11	ⒸMd Sp Wt	1 1 2hd 1½ 1½ 1no	Balaski L	118 w	*1.70	71-37	Menow118noPharacase1186Chatter Wrack1181	Hard drive 7
9Jun37- 3Was	sly	5½f	:232 :481 1:013 1:084	Alw 900	2 2 1½ 31½ 35½ 22	Haas L	111 w	5.40	80-21	Employer1082Menow1111Lillian Roth1132	No excuse 6

Myrtlewood

b. f. 1932, by Blue Larkspur (Black Servant)–Frizeur, by Sweeper

Lifetime record: 22 15 4 2 $40,620

Own.– B. Combs
Br.– Brownell Combs (Ky)
Tr.– R.A. Kindred

Date	Cond	Dist	Times	Race	Running line	Jockey	Wt	Odds	Speed	Top finishers	Comment
24Oct36- 6Kee	fst	6f	:222 :46 1:114	3↑ ⒻMatch Race	1 2 2hd 11 12 13	South G	118 w	*.30	--	Myrtlewood1183Miss Merriment118	Won in hand 2
No purse											
17Oct36- 5Kee	my	1 1/16	:24 :473 1:131 1:484	3↑ ⒻAshland 2.7k	3 1 16 18 18 112	South G	126 w	*.50	--	Myrtlewood12612Sparta111.54Wise Bessa110	Eased near end 3
15Oct36- 5Kee	fst	6f	:223 :461 1:104	3↑ Keen H 2.4k	2 4 1½ 12 12 1¾	South G	128 w	*.50	--	Myrtlewood128¾Marica1012Gleeman112¾	Eased final 1/16 5
5Sep36- 6Det	fst	6f	:223 :452 1:103	3↑ Cadillac H 3.6k	4 3 1hd 2hd 2hd 1hd	Burke JH	128 w	*.80	101-07	Myrtlwood128hdBoldLover110noExhbt111½	Won drawing away 10
22Aug36- 6Det	fst	1 1/16	:24 :47 1:113 1:432	3↑ Motor City H 5.7k	9 2 12 12 12 13	South G	122 w	*.90	103-08	Myrtlewood1223Professor Paul95nkCristate1061	Easily 11
8Aug36- 6Was	fst	1	:222 :452 1:094 1:353	3↑ Lakeside H 6.3k	4 1 11½ 14 14 13	South G	120 w	*2.10	100-04	Myrtlewood1203Where Away114nkThreadneedle1061	Easily 11
4Jly36- 6AP	fst	1⅛	:474 1:12 1:371 1:493	3↑ Stars & Stripes H 13k	6 1 1hd 31 31¼ 52	Fisher HW	110 w	13.40	97-09	Stand Pat1161½Corinto108noWhopper122no	Impeded 12
13Jun36- 6Haw	fst	6½f	:224 :463 1:113 1:181	3↑ Haw Sprint H 5.9k	1 4 11 11½ 14 11	Fisher HW	119 w	*1.10	97-13	Myrtlewood1191Billy Bee115nkBilly Jones114no	Handily 8
30May36- 6Lat	fst	6f	:222 :462 1:112	3↑ Quickstep H 6k	2 5 2hd 11½ 13 14	Fisher HW	116 w	*1.70	92-16	Myrtlewood1164Dusty Dawn117½Silk Mask1081½	Easily 9
23May36- 5Lat	fst	6f	:222 :462 1:111	3↑ Handicap 1000	6 2 2hd 2hd 21½ 23	Fisher HW	116 w	*.90	90-12	Likewise1083Myrtlewood1162Gilbert Elston103½	Impeded 7
12Oct35- 6CI	fst	6f	:22 :452 1:091	Match Race 3k	2 2 11½ 11 1nk 2no	McCoy J	110wb	*.30	105-09	Clang110noMyrtlewood110	Hard drive 2
25Sep35- 0Haw	fst	6f	:224 :46 1:104	Match Race 3k	2 2 2hd 1hd 1hd 1no	McCoy J	110 w	*.40	99-11	Myrtlewood110noClang110	Hard drive 2
7Sep35- 6Haw	fst	6f	:223 :46 1:103	3↑ Haw Sprint H 6.2k	5 3 53 43¾ 31½ 1nk	McCoy J	115 w	*1.20	100-08	Myrtlewood115nkWest Main114nkClang1121½	Driving 10
24Aug35- 6LF	fst	1 1/16	:23 :464 1:11 1:441	3↑ Lincoln H 6.1k	8 2 1hd 11½ 12 2nk	McCoy J	114 w	*1.40	95-11	SwepngLght114nkMrtlwood114hdPrncTorch114nk	Just missed 10
17Aug35- 6LF	fst	1	:23 :454 1:101 1:363	3↑ F S Peabody Mem H 6.4k	3 1 11 11½ 12 11½	McCoy J	111 w	*3.50	91-11	Myrtlewood1111½Clang1101½Tearout108no	In hand 13
10Aug35- 6LF	sl	6f	:233 :473 1:152	3↑ Crete H 6.4k	12 5 53 54½ 52¾ 3nk	South G	112 w	*1.90	75-29	SlimRosie108hdWestMain112hdMyrtlewood1121½	Closed fast 14
22Jly35- 4AP	fst	6f	:22 :45 1:092	ⒻAlw 1000	3 3 1½ 11½ 12 13	South G	113 w	3.40	104-07	Myrtlewood1133Toro Nancy1103Recovery1061½	Easily 6
16Jly35- 4AP	fst	7f	:222 :45 1:10 1:231	ⒻAlw 1000	1 1 14 14 13 1hd	South G	103 w	6.80	97-10	Myrtlewood103hdBanish Fear1056Toro Nancy1173	Driving 8
27Oct34- 6CD	fst	1	:224 :463 1:112 1:372	Ky Jockey Club 11k	7 2 2hd 31½ 33 36½	South G	119 w	8.90	85-13	Nellie Flag1191½Good Flavor1225Myrtlewood1193	Weakened 9
25Oct34- 5CD	gd	6f	:224 :461 1:13	Alw 500	6 2 1½ 22 22 11	South G	106 w	*4.10	90-18	Myrtlewood1061¼Grey Streak113¾Upside Down1122½	Driving 10
20Oct34- 5CD	fst	5½f	:23 :463 :593 1:06	Alw 600	1 4 12 11 11½ 2¾	Fowler G	105 w	5.20	92-08	Hastinola105¾Myrtlewood105½No Saint1101	Weakened 7
8Jun34- 2Lat	fst	5f	:232 :483 1:012	ⒻMd Sp Wt	8 6 11 11½ 11½ 11½	Meyer C	115 w	8.90	88-16	Myrtlewood1151½Ruths Hope1152Mary T.1153	Easily 11

Now What

ch. f. 1937, by Chance Play (Fair Play)–That's That, by High Time

Own.– A.G. Vanderbilt
Br.– Three D's Stock Farm (Ky)
Tr.– L. McCoy

Lifetime record: 19 5 4 0 $37,045

29Oct40- 5Lrl	gd 6f	:23 :472	1:133 3 ↑	ⒻAlw 1200	3 7	63½ 63½ 53	42½	Wall N	103wb	5.20	83-19	ThornAppl102¾OPly107¹Soldrtt109⁹ Closed ground,no threat 11
30Sep40- 6Bel	fst 6f	:224 :463	1:113 3 ↑	ⒻAlw 1500	4 4	42¾ 53	63¾ 88	Canning W	104wb	8.85	84-15	Colosseum115¾ⒹDinner Date110²¹Rosetown109¹½ Tired 8
23Sep40- 6Bel	fst 6f	:231 :471	1:12 3 ↑	ⒻAlw 1500	1 6	42½ 42½ 3½	4nk	Longden J	108wb	3.15	90-17	Colosseum111no War Regalia113nk Dinner Date110hd Good try 7
11Sep40- 5Aqu	fst 6f	:223 :462	1:114	Handicap 1530	4 4	33 36	43¾ 4	Bierman C	110wb	2.95	95-10	Witchlike114¹Rosetown110¹½Red Dock122³ Weakened 4
3Sep40- 5Aqu	fst 6f	:223 :47	1:12³ 3 ↑	ⒻAlw 1500	3 4	33½ 2¹ 3nk	24¾	Bierman C	110wb	7.35	89-12	Dotted Swiss105⁴¾Now What110²One Jest117¾ Weakened 7
19Aug40- 5Sar	sly 6f	:224 :47	1:12 3 ↑	ⒻAlw 1500	2 5	3¹ 41¾ 63¼	57	Finnegan J	100wb	*1.20	85-11	Glorious Time106²¾Colosseum112²Rosetown109³½ Faltered 9
8Aug40- 6Sar	fst 6f	:223 :463	1:11 3 ↑	ⒻHandicap 1530	5 3	32 32	32	James B	113wb	4.60	95-12	Wait for Baby109²Now What113½Redlin122⁴ Second best 6
2Aug40- 5Sar	fst 7f	:224 :461	1:114 1:242	ⒻTest 3.9k	6 2	23 32½ 53½	89	Longden J	120wb	21.90	85-13	Piquet123hdFairy Chant126²Inkling114²½ Stopped 10
29Jly40- 6Sar	fst 6f	:223 :461	1:11 3 ↑	ⒻAlw 1500	7 6	32½ 22 33½	711½	James B	112wb	7.75	85-08	Dini123³ⒹⒽRedlin116ⒹⒽLittle Risk115² Tired 11
4May40- 6Pim	sl 1¹⁄₁₆	:233 :483	1:152 1:494	ⒻPim Oaks 14k	11 4	1¹¹ 42½ 815	924	Workman R	121 w	4.60	47-31	Fairy Chant121¹¹True Call121⁴Discerning121¹ Tired 13
30Apr40- 6Pim	fst 6f	:223 :461	1:123	Rennert H 3.5k	6 2	1hd 1hd 1hd	61½	Workman R	121 w	*1.95	90-15	Domkin112no Ship Biscuit109½Merry Knight122nk Faltered 8
19Aug39- 6Sar	fst 6f	:23 :464	1:131	ⒻSpinaway 10k	6 2	1¹ 14 12	1½	Workman R	122wb	4.00	86-19	Now What122½Piquet113¹½Jeanne d'Arc113¹ Ridden out 9
12Aug39- 3Sar	fst 6f	:223 :461	1:104	Sar Spl 9k	8 1	2nk 21 21½	44½	Westrope J	119wb	7.00	93-06	Bimelech122³Briar Sharp122½Andy K.122¹ Tired 8
15Jly39- 6AP	fst 6f	:23 :47	1:13	ⒻArl Lassie 27k	1 4	1¹ 13 12	1nk	Workman R	122wb	*1.30	82-17	Now What122nk War Beauty117²Piquet117nk Just lasted 10
4Jly39- 4Emp	fst 5½f	:223 :461	1:09	ⒻDemoiselle 4.1k	4 1	14 14 15	16	Workman R	119wb	*1.80	94-06	Now What119⁶Piquet113⁵Ponemah113¹½ Much best 7
14Jun39- 4Aqu	fst 5f		:581	ⒻAstoria 4.4k	3 2	12 11½ 1½	1½	Workman R	116 w	*.80	96-11	Now What116.5½Us113⁴Fairy Chant119½ Driving 5
27May39- 4Bel	fst 5f-WC		:574	Juvenile 5.6k	5 3	1¹ 11½ 2nk		Fallon L	113 w	2.00	91-11	Cockerel119½Now What113³Gannet116⁴ Tired badly 11
20May39- 3Bel	fst 4½f-WC		:521	ⒻMd Sp Wt	8 4	1½ 1nk 11½		Fallon L	116 w	3.00e	94-10	Now What116¹½Rosetown116³Thorn Apple116hd Going away 15
12May39- 6Pim	fst 5f	:223 :473	1:01	Pim Nursery 6.5k	4 2	11½ 12 1½	2½	Fallon L	119 w	4.25	95-15	Cockerel122½NowWhat119¹½Imprudnt119½ Impeded,good try 6

Omaha

ch. c. 1932, by Gallant Fox (Sir Gallahad III)–Flambino, by Wrack

Own.– Belair Stud Stable
Br.– William Woodward Sr (Ky)
Tr.– Cecil Boyd–Rochfort

Lifetime record: 22 9 7 2 $154,755

2Jly36◆	Newmarket(GB) gd 1½⑯RH	2:343 3 ↑	Princess of Wales's Stakes 10000		2nk	Beasley P	134	*.70		Tak Ajbar120nkOmaha134⁵Esquemelling112 6
										Unruly pre-start,tracked in 3rd,led 3f out to 1f out,came again
18Jun36◆	Ascot(GB) sf 2½⑯RH	4:332 4 ↑	Ascot Gold Cup 17500		2no	Beasley P	126	*1.35		Quashed126noOmaha126⁵Bokbul126 9
										Rated in 4th,bid over 1f out,dueled,just failed
30May36◆	Kempton(GB) fm2⑯RH	3:441 4 ↑	Queen's Plate Hcp2000		1nk	Beasley P	130	*.90		Omaha130nkBobsleigh123⁶Silverlit113 5
										Tracked very slow pace,dueled 1f out,prevailed
9May36◆	Kempton(GB) gd 1½⑯RH	2:362 4 ↑	Victor Wild Stakes Alw4000		11½	Beasley P	129	*.80		Omaha129½Montrose126⁵Lobau119 6
	Previously trained by James Fitzsimmons									
20Jly35- 6AP	fst 1¼	:472 1:122 1:354 2:012	Classic 35k	7 7 88 2½ 11½	11½	Wright WD	126wb	*.40	102-03	Omaha126¹½St. Bernard121hdBloodroot113³ Wide 10
29Jun35- 5Aqu	fst 1⅛	:473 1:114 1:37 1:491	Dwyer 11k	2 2 22 2½ 2hd	11½	Wright WD	126wb	*.70	97-14	Omaha126¹½Good Gamble114⁶Cheshire116⁵ Easily 5
22Jun35- 5Aqu	fst 1⅛	:461 1:112 1:353 1:481 3 ↑	Brooklyn H 13k	3 4 411 38½ 35¼	312	Wright WD	114wb	*1.00	90-13	Discovery123⁸King Saxon127⁴Omaha114⁶ Evenly 6
8Jun35- 5Bel	sly 1½	:482 1:133 2:05 2:303	Belmont 43k	3 5 34½ 43½ 2nk	11½	Saunders W	126wb	*.70e	91-15	Omaha126¹½Firethorn126⁸Rosemont126¹ Easily 5
25May35- 4Bel	fst 1	:233 :464 1:11 1:363	Withers 29k	2 7 52½ 42½ 2nk	12	Saunders W	118wb	*.50	90-13	Omaha118½Today126⁸Firethorn126⁶ Easily 8
11May35- 6Pim	fst 1⅜	:473 1:122 1:38 1:582	Preakness 29k	6 6 69 45 16	16	Saunders W	126wb	*.95	98-16	Omaha126⁶Firethorn126⁶Psychic Bid126² Easily 8
4May35- 6CD	gd 1¼	:473 1:132 1:383 2:05	Ky Derby 49k	10 12 96½ 12 11½	11½	Saunders W	126wb	4.00	84-11	Omaha126¹½Roman Soldier126⁴Whiskolo126¹½ Easily 18
27Apr35- 4Jam	fst 1 70	:231 :464 1:112 1:424	Wood Memorial 14k	2 11 916 711 54½	32	Saunders W	112wb	3.20	90-11	Today112²Plat Eye122noOmaha112³ Closed fast 12
22Apr35- 4Jam	fst 1 70	:234 :482 1:124 1:43	Alw 10000	2 4 31½ 2hd 2½	2hd	Saunders W	110wb	*.55	98-10	Omaha110²Black Gift105hdThorson111.58 Easily easy 4
29Sep34- 4Aqu	fst 1	:231 :462 1:114 1:363	Jr Champion 5k	3 4 46½ 44½ 21½	2hd	Kurtsinger C	111wb	*1.00	97-08	Sailor Beware116hdOmaha111⁸Abner111¹ Game rush 5
15Sep34- 3Bel	my 6½f-WC		1:173	Futurity 92k	13 13 53½ 54½ 45		Kurtsinger C	122wb	5.00	94-05	Chance Sun122⁴Balladier122½Plat Eye125½ Closed fast 14
6Sep34- 4Bel	fst 6½f-WC		1:163	Champagne 4.4k	12 10 22 21½ 2no		Humphries L	117wb	*1.00e	104-07	Balladier124noOmaha117³Plat Eye126⁴ Gaining 12
1Sep34- 3Sar	fst 6½f	:232 :472 1:123 1:184	Hopeful 29k	9 10 73½ 83½ 74	42	Kurtsinger C	117wb	5.00e	84-15	Psychic Bid122³Rosemont117³Esposa114hd Closed gap 16
22Aug34- 3Sar	fst 6f	:224 :463	1:121	Sanford 3.4k	3 9 77½ 68¾ 46	22	Humphries L	113wb	4.00	89-12	Psychic Bid113²Omaha113¹½Boxthorn122¹ Game rush 9
11Aug34- 3Sar	fst 6f	:23 :47	1:121	Sar Spl 6.7k	1 6 77½ 79½ 55¼	42	Malley T	122wb	6.00	89-11	Boxthorn121²Plat Eye122hdToday122¹ Late speed 7
4Aug34- 3Sar	fst 6f	:23 :47	1:13	U S Hotel 6.9k	2 9 108³ 109½ 77¼	45¾	Malley T	117wb	8.00	81-17	Balladier117²½Today117nkPolar Flight115³ Late speed 10
23Jun34- 1Aqu	fst 5f		:583	Alw 1200	3 2 4¹½ 2hd	1hd	Stout J	110wb	*.90	94-12	Omaha110hdAllen Z.117¹Moisson117¹ Bore in 5
18Jun34- 1Aqu	fst 5f		1:01	Md Sp Wt	13 4 3 3nk 2no		Stout J	115wb	20.00	82-17	Sir Lamorak115noOmaha115½Nubs115² Closed fast 14

Pompoon

b. c. 1934, by Pompey (Sun Briar)–Oonagh, by Friar Rock

Own.– J.H. Louchheim
Br.– W.R. Coe (Ky)
Tr.– J. Loftus

Lifetime record: 26 10 8 1 $153,060

2Aug39- 5Sar	fst 1	:233 :471 1:114 1:37 3 ↑	Wilson 4.4k	3 4 47 44 43¼	24	Arcaro E	126wb	3.00	92-08	Eight Thirty118⁴Pompoon126nkMain Man126⁵ Outrun early 4
	Geldings not eligible											
12Jly39- 7Suf	sly 1⅛	:482 1:13 1:391 1:52 3 ↑	Mass H 68k	1 4 41¾ 2½ 2½	2½	Eccard R	120wb	10.20	85-19	FightingFox113½Pompoon120³BurningStar110²½ Good effort 12
24Jun39- 5Suf	hy 1½	:252 :50 1:154 1:493 3 ↑	Handicap 1500	4 4 22 24 26	26	Eccard R	126wb	*1.00	62-36	Pagliacci120½Pompoon126⁸Silent Witness107² 2nd best 4
30May39- 5Bel	fst 1¼	:474 1:121 1:371 2:024 3 ↑	Suburban H 24k	2 4 41½ 31 54¾	43½	Richards H	121wb	6.00	81-18	Cravat121²Thanksgiving120¹½Handcuff110hd Faltered 6
10May39- 6Pim	gd 1¾	:473 1:123 1:383 1:583 3 ↑	Dixie 28k	5 5 42½ 3½ 66¾	88¾	Richards H	125wb	5.65	81-18	Sir Damion113²¾Tatterdemalion111¹Jacola117¹ Tired 14
3May39- 6Pim	fst 1¹⁄₁₆	:233 :473 1:13 1:45 3 ↑	Gittings H 3.3k	2 3 35 41¾ 58¼	511½	Wright WD	126 w	*.85	83-17	Heelfly114⁶Aethelwold110³Kenty112¹ No mishaps 6
25Jun38- 5Aqu	fst 1¼	:46 1:104 1:35 1:482 3 ↑	Brooklyn H 25k	3 8 815 715 61½	612½	Woolf G	126 w	3.50	86-12	The Chief105⁶Stagehand117¹Guilotine106² Sore 10
28May38- 5Bel	fst 1¼	:472 1:113 1:361 2:012 3 ↑	Suburban H 24k	5 4 52¾ 44½ 32½	2no	Woolf G	126 w	*.70	93-15	Snark120noPompoon128²Aneroid120nk Just missed 6
11May38- 5Pim	fst 1⅝	:472 1:12 1:372 1:564 3 ↑	Dixie Handicap 26k	7 8 713 58½ 2hd	14	Woolf G	118 w	*3.05	103-13	Pompoon118⁴Busy K.110nkMasked General106.5½ Easily 12
5Mar38- 6SA	fst 1¼	:461 1:111 1:364 2:013 3 ↑	S Anita H 126k	11 10 75¼ 53 45½	36	Gilbert J	120 w	4.00	97-12	Stagehand100noSeabiscuit130⁶Pompoon120² Closed well 18
19Feb38- 6SA	sl 1¼	:474 1:12 1:45 1:494 3 ↑	San Carlos H 6.3k	2 5 43¼ 2hd 1hd	11	Gilbert J	124 w	*.70	89-26	Pompoon124¹Star Shadow107½He Did114³ Drew out 10
28Jan38- 6SA	fst 7f	:223 :452 1:101 1:23 4 ↑	Alw 1500	5 2 21 11 15	15	Gilbert J	120 w	*.40	97-14	Pompoon120⁵Ligaroti116²½Fairy Hill120⁶ In hand 8
	Previously trained by C.F. Clarke											
24Jly37- 6AP	sl 1¼	:481 1:133 1:381 2:054	Classic 34k	5 2 21½ 42¼ 56	55½	Wright WD	121 w	*1.20	71-26	Flying Scot123½Eagle Pass118¹½Burning Star118² Tired 7
5Jun37- 5Bel	fst 1⅜	:471 1:12¹ 2:012 2:283	Belmont 46k	3 3 511 411 618	618	Richards H	126 w	3.50	83-06	War Admiral126³Sceneshifter126¹⁰Vamoose126² No excuse 7
15May37- 6Pim	fst 1¾	:47 1:122 1:373 1:582	Preakness 55k	7 3 52¼ 21 2hd	2nk	Wright WD	126 w	4.80	98-16	War Admiral126⁸Pompoon126⁸Flying Scot126² Game try 8
8May37- 6CD	fst 1¼	:464 1:121 1:372 2:031	Ky Derby 62k	14 6 54½ 21½ 2½	21¾	Richards H	126 w	8.00	91-11	WarAdmirl126¹¾Pompoon126⁸ReapingRewrd126³ Second best 20
1May37- 5Jam	fst 1 70	:231 :47 1:124 1:424	Wood Memorial 26k	4 6 64½ 54½ 55¼	55¼	Richards H	120 w	*.60	86-10	Melodist120¹Sir Damion120²Jewell Dorsett115¹ No mishaps 10
15Apr37- 4Jam	fst 6f	:23 :462	1:11 3 ↑	Paumonok H 9.9k	4 4 52¼ 52¼ 1nk	1nk	Richards H	116 w	*2.00	97-11	Pompoon116nkTintagel120⁵Fraidy Cat115½ Hard drive 10
28Oct36- 6Nar	fst 1 70	:231 :47 1:12 1:413	New England Futurity 45k	6 4 2nk 11 2½	2nk	Workman R	122 w	*.30	97-13	ReapingReward117nkPompn122²⁰OceanRoll114⁴ Good effort 7

3Oct36- 4Bel	fst 6½f-WC	1:162	Futurity 72k	11 2 2hd 11½ 14	Richards H	127 w	*1.60	101-00	Pompoon1274Privlgd125nkFlyngCross122hd	Speed in reserve 17
12Sep36- 4Aqu	fst 6½f	:232 :471 1:114 1:181	Jr Champion 7.2k	5 5 31¼ 2nk 2½ 11	Richards H	119 w	*.29	96-11	Pompoon1191FlyingScot11010Tedious1101	Bore in,drew away 5
3Sep36- 4Aqu	fst 6f	:232 :472 1:121	Alw 1000	3 3 2½ 11 12 14	Richards H	122 w	*.29	93-13	Pompoon1224Dogaway113¾Talked About1055	Good effort 4
27Aug36- 5Sar	fst 5½f	:233 :47 1:054	®Handicap 1245	5 3 2nk 31 2nk 2½	Peters M	130 w	*.60	93-12	No Sir116½Pompoon1304Third Count1191	Good effort 5
	Property of lady owners									
6Jun36- 4Bel	fst 5f-WC	:59	National Stallion 16k	7 4 3½ 1hd 11½	Peters M	122 w	*2.50	85-14	Pompoon1221½Fencing1221War Admiral122hd	Drew away 10
29May36- 3Bel	fst 5f-WC	:591	Alw 900	10 4 11 13 14	Peters M	112 w	*1.30	84-20	Pompoon1124Your Honor1155All Agog109hd	Easily 10
29Apr36- 1Pim	fst 4½f	:231 :472 :54	Md Sp Wt	1 1 1½ 1hd 12	Peters M	116 w	2.40	97-05	Pompoon1162Sonny Joe1165Banjorine1132	Going away 12

Seabiscuit

b. c. 1933, by Hard Tack (Man o' War)–Swing On, by Whisk Broom II **Lifetime record: 89 33 15 13 $437,730**

Own.– C.S. Howard
Br.– Wheatley Stable (Ky)
Tr.– T. Smith

2Mar40- 6SA	fst 1¼	:471 1:111 1:36 2:011 3↑	S Anita H 121k	12 5 21 2hd 1hd 11½	Pollard J	130wb	*.70e	101-11	Seabiscuit1301½Kayak II1291Whichcee1141½	13
	Avoided trouble first turn									
24Feb40- 6SA	fst 1 1/16	:231 :464 1:111 1:422 3↑	S Antonio H 13k	10 5 2½ 2½ 1½ 12½	Pollard J	124wb	*1.70e	100-07	Seabiscuit1242½Kayak II128½Viscounty1104	Much best 13
17Feb40- 6SA	fst 7f	:223 :453 1:103 1:232 3↑	San Carlos H 12k	1 2 94 85¼ 69 66¾	Pollard J	127wb	*.80e	88-14	Specify1151¼Lassator105hdViscounty1093	Close quarters 11
9Feb40- 6SA	fst 7f	:224 :454 1:103 1:23 4↑	Handicap 2000	2 5 52¼ 63¾ 43¼ 33	Pollard J	128wb	*1.00	94-13	Heelfly1181Sun Egret1152Seabiscuit1283	Close quarters 8
14Feb39- 6SA	fst 1	:223 :453 1:102 1:353 4↑	Alw 1900	1 3 2nk 23 23 22¼	Woolf G	128wb	*.20	99-06	Today1042¼Seabiscuit1286Marica113	Went lame 3
1Nov38- 6Pim	fst 1 3/16	:473 1:114 1:364 1:563 3↑	Pim Spl 15k	2 1 11 1no 1½ 14	Woolf G	120wb	2.20	101-08	Seabiscuit1204War Admiral120	Driving,best 2
15Oct38- 5Lrl	fst 1	:231 :472 1:121 1:37 2↑	Laurel 10k	6 8 63½ 41¼ 21½ 22½	Woolf G	126wsb	*.60	98-12	Jacola1022½Seabiscuit1263The Chief1164	Second best 12
28Sep38- 5HdG	fst 1⅛	:472 1:122 1:372 1:50 3↑	Havre de Grace H 11k	6 5 32½ 2½ 11 12½	Woolf G	128wb	*.55	99-16	Seabiscuit1282½Savage Beauty1031Menow1201½	Going away 8
20Sep38- 5Bel	my 1½	:49 1:14 2:051 2:31 3↑	Manhattan H 6k	4 1 52¾ 53½ 34¼ 33	Woolf G	128wb	*1.20	85-12	Isolater108hdRegal Lily1083Seabiscuit12810	Forced wide 5
12Aug38- 5Dmr	fst 1⅛	:462 1:104 1:361 1:49 3↑	Match Race 25k	1 2 2hd 1hd 1hd 1no	Woolf G	130wb	-	124-02	Seabiscuit130noLigaroti115	Driving 2
16Jly38- 7Hol	fst 1¼	:471 1:112 1:373 2:034 3↑	Hol Gold Cup 55k	7 8 912 48 24 11½	Woolf G	133wb	*.70	- -	Seabiscuit1331½Specify109noWhichcee1145	Going away 10
4Jly38- 6AP	sl 1⅛	:484 1:143 1:41 1:541 3↑	Stars & Stripes H 12k	10 7 97¾ 67 42½ 23½	Woolf G	130wb	*.90	72-30	WarMinstrel1073½Seabiscut130½Arb'sArrow1114	Closed fast 10
16Apr38- 7BM	fst 1⅛	:474 1:114 1:37 1:49 3↑	Bay Meadows H 16k	7 2 21 2hd 11 13	Woolf G	133wb	*.20e	107-10	Seabiscuit1333Gosum1131¾Today112no	Going away 7
27Mar38- 8AC	fst 1⅛	:47 1:114 1:37 1:502 3↑	Agua Caliente H 13k	1 1 1½ 11½ 13 12	Rich'son N	130wb	*.30	97-13	Seabiscuit1302Gray Jack103hdLittle Nymph984½	Eased up 8
5Mar38- 6SA	fst 1¼	:461 1:111 1:364 2:013 3↑	S Anita H 126k	12 14 127½ 1hd 1hd 2no	Woolf G	130wb	*1.90	103-12	Stagehand100noSeabisct1306Pmpoon1202	Impeded,game try 18
26Feb38- 6SA	fst 1⅛	:47 1:113 1:371 1:50 3↑	San Antonio H 9.2k	5 5 46 42½ 3½ 2no	Workman R	130wb	*.40e	94-12	Aneroid118noSeabiscuit1301½IndianBroom108hd	Just missed 13
11Nov37- 6Pim	fst 1⅝	:501 1:41 2:062 2:451 3↑	Bowie H 12k	8 3 52¾ 41¼ 1hd 2no	Pollard J	130wb	*1.25	107-11	Esposa115noSeabiscuit1301¼Burning Star1141	Game try 8
5Nov37- 5Pim	fst 1 3/16	:47 1:113 1:37 1:572 3↑	Riggs H 12k	11 4 55½ 4¾ 1½ 1nk	Pollard J	130wb	*.40e	103-11	Seabiscuit130nkBurningStar114¾CaballroII116½	Hard drive 11
	Previously owned by Mrs C.S. Howard									
16Oct37- 5Lrl	fst 1	:24 :471 1:121 1:372 2↑	Laurel 9.6k	7 3 2hd 2nk 1hd 11½•	Pollard J	126wb	*.70	99-14	DHSeabiscuit126DHHeelfly1141½Deliberator1161	Gamely 7
12Oct37- 5Jam	fst 1 1/16	:24 :48 1:124 1:444 3↑	Continental H 12k	2 1 1hd 1nk 12 15	Pollard J	130wb	*.80	89-20	Seabiscuit1305Caballero II1172Moon Side1121	Easily 12
11Sep37- 5Nar	sly 1 3/16	:473 1:12 1:38 1:57 3↑	Nar Spl H 33k	5 4 46½ 21½ 33½ 32½	Pollard J	132wb	*.85	87-16	Calumet Dick1151Snark1171½Seabiscuit1324	Weakened 6
7Aug37- 5Suf	fst 1⅛	:47 1:11 1:36 1:49 3↑	Mass H 70k	3 3 22½ 21 1nk 11	Pollard J	130wb	*1.00	102-06	Seabiscuit1301CaballeroII1081FairKnghtss1082½	Drove out 13
24Jly37- 5Emp	fst 1 1/16	:233 :472 1:113 1:441 3↑	Yonkers H 10k	2 2 22 1hd 11½ 14	Pollard J	129wb	*1.00	102-12	Seabiscuit1294Jesting1083Corinto1093	Going away 6
10Jly37- 5Emp	fst 1 3/16	:48 1:12 1:382 1:583 3↑	Butler H 25k	1 2 1½ 1½ 11½ 11½	Pollard J	126wb	*.90	98-08	Seabiscuit1261½Thorson1073Corinto1091	Driving,best 6
26Jun37- 5Aqu	fst 1⅛	:47 1:112 1:37 1:501 3↑	Brooklyn H 25k	1 1 11 1½ 1hd 1no	Pollard J	122wb	3.20	90-14	Seabiscuit122noAneroid1225Memory Book1143	Hard drive 9
22May37- 7BM	fst 1 1/16	:24 :473 1:11 1:443 3↑	Bay Meadows H 11k	8 2 2nk 21 1½ 11¼	Pollard J	127wb	*.10e	87-15	Seabiscuit1271¼Exhibit105noWatersplash1031	Going away 8
17Apr37- 6Tan	fst 1⅛	:452 1:103 1:36 1:484 3↑	Marchbank H 11k	7 1 15 12 14 13	Pollard J	124wb	*.40	94-08	Seabiscuit1243Grand Manitou110hdSobriety1095	Easily 7
6Mar37- 6SA	fst 1⅛	:463 1:11 1:361 1:484 3↑	S Juan Capistrano H 12k	2 2 21½ 2hd 14 17	Pollard J	120wb	*1.50	103-08	Seabiscuit1207GrandManitou108¾SpecialAgent116nk	Easily 10
27Feb37- 6SA	gd 1¼	:454 1:104 1:364 2:024 3↑	S Anita H 125k	3 9 44½ 41½ 1hd 2no	Pollard J	114 w	6.40	97-13	Rosemont124noSeabiscuit1141Indian Broom1162½	Nosed out 18
20Feb37- 6SA	fst 1⅛	:464 1:11 1:372 1:501 3↑	San Antonio H 9.4k	11 14 128¾ 129¼ 98¾ 53¾	Pollard J	115wb	2.30	92-11	Rosemnt122¾StarShadow106½SpecialAgent1171	Forced wide 16
9Feb37- 6SA	fst 7f	:224 :452 1:104 1:231 4↑	Handicap 1545	5 1 1½ 11 1½ 14½	Pollard J	112wb	3.20	96-13	Seabiscuit1124½Sir Emerson104nkTime Supply1185	Easily 6
12Dec36- 7BM	fst 1 3/16	:47 1:112 1:364 1:554 2↑	World's Fair H 11k	4 3 15 13 13 15	Pollard J	113wb	*1.10	- -	Seabiscuit1135Wildland1012½GiantKiller1071½	Easily best 7
28Nov36- 7BM	fst 1	:232 :464 1:112 1:36 2↑	Bay Bridge H 2.7k	6 8 51¾ 22 1hd 15	Pollard J	116wb	*2.20	106-07	Seabiscuit1165Uppermost114½Velociter107nk	Eased up 8
31Oct36- 4Emp	fst 1⅛	:491 1:14 1:392 1:52 3↑	Yorktown H 6.5k	7 6 54 66½ 33½ 31¾	Pollard J	119wb	8.00	93-11	Thorson112nkPiccolo1071½Seabiscuit1193	Closed fast 8
24Oct36- 4Emp	fst 1 70	:233 :473 1:121 1:44 3↑	Scarsdale H 7.3k	2 7 84¾ 88¾ 63¾ 1no	Pollard J	116wb	12.00e	90-13	Seabiscuit116noJesting112hdPiccolo105.53	Just up 11
17Oct36- 6RD	my 1 1/16	:26 :51 1:18 1:562 3↑	East Hills H 2.7k	4 2 22 24 23 32½	Pollard J	116wb	3.20	29-59	MuchoGusto1111½SafeandSound1031Sebscut1162½	Closed well 6
3Oct36- 5RD	fst 1 1/16	:232 :464 1:113 1:44 3↑	Western Hills H 2.8k	7 4 52¼ 53½ 43½ 31½	Pollard J	116wb	4.90	92-16	Marynell100½Cristate1081Seabiscuit1161	Closed fast 8
26Sep36- 6Det	fst 1 1/16	:243 :483 1:13 1:442 3↑	Hendrie H 2.8k	2 2 2½ 11 12 14	Pollard J	115wb	2.10	98-12	Seabiscuit1154Cristate1142½Safe and Sound1083	Easily 6
19Sep36- 6Det	fst 1 1/16	:243 :483 1:133 1:46 3↑	De La Salle H 2.8k	7 1 11 31 63½ 63¾	Pollard J	115wb	*1.60	86-13	Cristate106hdProfessor Paul105hdParadisical1091½	Quit 8
7Sep36- 6Det	fst 1⅛	:47 1:12 1:38 1:504 3↑	Governor's H 5.6k	12 3 2hd 2hd 1½ 1nk	Pollard J	109wb	4.90	96-13	Seabiscuit109nkProfessor Paul991½Azucar1123	Driving 12
2Sep36- 6Det	sl 1 70	:243 :484 1:14 1:44 3↑	Handicap 1200	3 1 1hd 41¼ 31 3½	Pollard J	114wb	3.90	89-18	ProfessorPaul104noSafeandSound102½Seabsct1142½	Impeded 8
22Aug36- 6Det	fst 1 1/16	:24 :47 1:113 1:432 3↑	Motor City H 5.7k	3 1 33 78 65 44¼	Pollard J	110wb	13.20	99-08	Myrtlewood1223Professor Paul95nkCristate1061	Tired 11
	Previously owned by Wheatley Stable;previously trained by J. Fitzsimmons									
10Aug36- 6Sar	gd 1⅛	:482 1:132 1:401 1:54 3↑	Handicap 1070	1 1 12 12 13 14	Stout J	112wb	*.90	80-17	Seabiscuit1124Treford110	Easily 2
3Aug36- 5Sar	fst 1	:242 :481 1:124 1:382 3↑	Mohawk Claiming 6k	1 1 11½ 11 13 16	Stout J	109wb	4.00	89-15	Seabiscuit1096Ann O'Ruley1122Balkan Land1092	Easily 7
25Jly36- 5Suf	fst 1⅛	:473 1:122 1:381 1:511	Miles Standish H 3k	1 2 24 31¾ 33½ 44¼	Kopel F	115wb	5.90	87-08	Kearsarge99nkTatterdemalion113.54BrownTop109no	Faltered 7
29Jun36- 4Suf	fst 6f	:224 :453 1:114	Alw 1000	2 8 64¾ 62¾ 34 11½	Knott K	115wb	12.60	96-11	Seabiscuit1151½Deliberate115½Liberal1153	Handily 12
24Jun36- 5Suf	sl 6f	:234 :48 1:134	Commonwealth H 3.2k	6 13 128 1212 109¼ 1010¾	Kopel F	115wb	29.40	75-21	PartySpirit107nkIndomitable1054SpeedtoSpare114½	Outrun 13
1Jun36- 5Bel	fst 1 1/16	:24 :474 1:13 1:45 3↑	Handicap 1240	5 6 67¼ 65½ 65 66¼	Hanford I	112wb	*1.60e	80-16	Gallant Prince1161½Brown Twig114hdGillie114nk	Stumbled 6
27May36- 5Rkm	sly 1	:234 :473 1:132 1:411	New Hampshire H 4k	9 11 129 129½ 129 129½	Kopel F	116wb	8.40	71-16	Faust103noGallant Gay110.5noParty Spirit1112	Outrun 15
18May36- 5Nar	fst 1 1/16	:234 :472 1:123 1:441	Alw 1200	7 1 11 1hd 1½ 13	Kopel F	111wb	2.60	96-11	Seabiscuit1113Piccolo1063Swamp Angel1113½	Easily 7
13May36- 5Nar	fst 1 1/16	:234 :472 1:123 1:444	Providence H 3.8k	8 1 12½ 21 31¼ 42½	Kopel F	115wb	4.20	90-13	Tugboat Frank1102Piccolo108noGallant Gay109½	No excuse 8
8May36- 4Jam	fst 6f	:231 :47 1:12	Alw 1000	4 6 77 77¾ 53½ 42¾	Stout J	113wb	*2.40	89-14	Gleeman1101½Wha Hae1131Stubbs116nk	Finished fast 7
23Apr36- 4Jam	fst 6f	:233 :471 1:121	Handicap 1220	4 4 48 47½ 33½ 37	Hanford I	120wb	*.50	84-17	Goldeneye1053Chancer1054Seabiscuit1203	No excuse 4
18Apr36- 3Jam	fst 6f	:224 :462 1:12	Alw 1000	1 1 22 25 21½ 21½	Hanford I	105wb	5.00	90-13	Tintagel1181½Seabiscuit1054Hollyrood1188	Good effort 5
11Nov35- 6Pim	my 1 1/16	:24 :491 1:143 1:494	Walden H 11k	10 7 108¾ 1012 915 66	Kopel F	108wb	14.45	65-27	Ned Reigh116½Challephen107hdWise Duke112½	No excuse 10
26Oct35- 5Nar	fst 6f	:223 :451 1:111	Pawtucket H 6k	4 4 43½ 44 43¾ 2½	Stout J	117wb	*1.85	95-10	Clocks111½Seabiscuit1171½Crossbow II1211	Finished fast 5
23Oct35- 5Emp	fst 5¾f	:23 :47 1:084	Ardsley H 3.7k	4 3 2hd 2hd 11 13	Kopel F	112wb	4.00	95-13	Seabiscuit1123Neap1072Wha Hae115½	Easily 6
16Oct35- 5Agm	fst 6f	:234 :46 1:112	Springfield H 2.8k	8 1 12 11½ 11 11	Stout J	109wb	8.00	- -	Seabiscuit1091BrightPlumage117hdInfidox1171½	Ridden out 8
2Oct35- 4Suf	fst 6f	:231 :462 1:121	Constitution H 9.2k	10 10 95½ 107 108¼ 1010	Woolf G	115wb	21.90	84-08	Infidox110nkClocks110nkSparta109½	Outrun 10
21Sep35- 3Jam	fst 6f	:233 :464 1:12	Remsen H 4.7k	2 11 1115 1014 912 97¾	Horn F	112wb	7.00e	84-12	The Fighter122noTeufel1122Postage Due1241½	Off slowly 11
14Sep35- 4HdG	fst 6f	:232 :474 1:13	Eastern Shore H 14k	6 7 85¼ 92½ 64½ 41½	Rosengarten C	112wb	38.50e	86-11	Postage Due117½Wise Duke115noMaerial1201	Forced wide 14
9Sep35- 6Aqu	fst 6f	:233 :48 1:131	Alw 1000	4 4 11 11½ 12 13	Kopel F	115wb	12.00	88-13	Seabiscuit1153Count Morse1095Dark Wizard1122	Easily 8
4Sep35- 3Aqu	sly 6f	:232 :473 1:122	Alw 1000	5 3 46¾ 45½ 54½ 36	Kopel F	110wb	10.00	86-10	PhantomFox106noPullman1146Seabiscuit110nk	Finished well 7
2Sep35- 3Aqu	fst 6f	:241 :49 1:12	Babylon H 4.2k	5 6 511 67 67¾ 612	Horn F	112wb	1.50e	82-09	NedReigh116noSpeedtoSpare115noGranville1145	No excuse 6
26Aug35- 4Sar	fst 6f	:23 :47 1:12	Alw 1000	5 8 812 86¼ 66 68½	Horn F	112wb	25.00	83-10	BoldVenture1151½GrandSlam1223Valvctorn1152	Dropped back 9

Date/Race	Cond	Dist	Times	Race	Calls	Fin	Jockey	Wt	Odds	Speed	Top finishers	Comment	Field
14Aug35- 5Sar	gd	5½f	:231 :473 1:071	Alw 1000	11 13 1313 139¾ 106½	95¼	Gilbert J	112wb	6.00e	82-14	Maerial1181Lovely Girl1042Speed109no	Off slowly	13
27Jly35- 6Suf	fst	6f	:233 :463 1:122	Bay State 3.7k	4 6 31½ 52¼ 32½	43	Stout J	123wb	13.60	- -	BlackHighbrow1113NouveauRiche108noSt.Lous108no	Faltered	7
22Jly35- 3Suf	fst	6f	:231 :454 1:112	Alw 1000	5 5 21 2½ 22½	21½	Stout J	115wb	*1.70	- -	Black Highbrow1151½Seabiscuit1158Nedvive112½	Gamely	5
15Jly35- 5Suf	fst	6f	:232 :472 1:131	Mayflower 3k	4 8 52¼ 42¼ 62½	44	Horn F	123wb	15.00	- -	Maerial1232Jair111½Tugboat Frank1111½	No excuse	9
4Jly35- 5Nar	fst	5f	:223 :46 :593	Old Colony 6.7k	3 4 42 45 44¾	52½	Stout J	117wb	*1.40	101-07	BrightandEarly1141Swashbuckler114½Chllphn1121	No excuse	6
26Jun35- 5Nar	fst	5f	:223 :454 :593	Watch Hill Claiming 5k	6 5 2½ 11½ 11	12	Horn F	108wb	*1.70	104-08	Seabiscuit1082Infidox1081Zowie1022	Easily	8
22Jun35- 2Nar	fst	5f	:231 :464 1:003	Alw 1000	9 5 1½ 12 11½	12	Stout J	110wb	*2.55	99-12	Seabiscuit1102Ned Reigh1102½Tugboat Frank1151½	Easily	9
11Jun35- 1Rkm	hy	5f	:234 :49 1:02	Md Sp Wt	3 8 1½ 21½ 24	26	Stout J	116wb	*.60	78-18	Jubilee Jim1166Seabiscuit1162½Sky Pirate1162	Gamely	8
8Jun35- 4Rkm	fst	5f	:231 :462 :594	Juvenile H 5.7k	2 8 74¼ 65 31¾	31¼	Stout J	103wb	30.20	94-12	WinterSport1051PostageDue124nkSeabiscuit103½	Good effort	12
1Jun35- 1Rkm	fst	5f	:23 :461 1:011	Md Sp Wt	5 7 21 21½ 23	23	Stout J	116wb	7.75	85-14	Swashbuckler1163Seabiscuit1161½Sobriety1163	Good effort	12
28May35- 1Rkm	fst	5f	:232 :474 1:011	Md Sp Wt	2 11 98¼ 97¾ 34½	42½	Stout J	116wb	*2.05	85-11	SandyMack1161½Browbeatn1131TugboatFrnk116hd	Closed gap	11
21May35- 2Rkm	fst	5f	:231 :473 1:004	Alw 800	7 9 76¼ 87½ 31¼	3nk	Stout J	106wb	9.85	90-13	Microbe114nkBlackMistress111noSeabiscut1061	Closed fast	9
4May35- 1Jam	fst	5f	:233 :472 1:002	Md Sp Wt	2 2 57½ 55¼ 64½	68	Burke JH	115wb	2.00e	83-11	Pullman1151½Knowing115½Royal Fox1155	Shuffled	8
1May35- 4Jam	fst	5f	:231 :473 1:01	Alw 1000	4 6 69¼ 56½ 53¾	2½	Horn F	110wb	10.00	87-15	Galsac116½Seabiscuit110noTransitLady110no	Finished fast	6
Previously trained by G. Tappen													
25Apr35- 2HdG	fst	4½f	:232 :473 :542	Clm 4000	5 2 51¾ 44½	4½	Workman R	114wb	3.50	92-07	Cherry Stone115noHiatus110hdProsy113½	Finished fast	11
22Apr35- 2HdG	fst	4½f	:232 :473 :542	Clm 2500	6 7 89¼ 47½	33½	Peters M	116wb	11.95	89-07	Hiatus113½Deliberate1143Seabiscuit1161½	Close quarters	13
13Apr35- 3Bow	my	4f	:234 :492	Md Sp Wt	8 7 712 66¼	35½	Horn F	115wb	7.35	80-13	ParaguayTea1122½PatseyBegone1123Sebscut1151½	Off slowly	9
10Apr35- 4Bow	my	4f	:233 :492	Alw 800	9 10 911 97¾	87¼	Horn F	110wb	30.35	79-15	VictoriousAnn112hdWinterSport1151½Ste.Louise1121	Outrun	12
4Apr35- 1Bow	sl	4f	:24 :493	©Md Sp Wt	1 1 58½ 35½	21½	Horn F	115wb	3.80	83-15	Borsa1151½Seabiscuit1153Green Mist1151	Finished gamely	8
Previously trained by V. Mara													
8Mar35- 1Hia	fst	3f	:344	Alw 1000	12 10 63¼	43½	Horn F	113wb	4.50f	- -	VctorousAnn1102WllwWood113hdTwoEdgd1131½	Finished fast	14
5Mar35- 1Hia	fst	3f	:343	Alw 800	8 8 83¾	85	Horn F	109wb	49.50	- -	James City1191½Grand Slam108nkBright Light114hd	Impeded	13
27Feb35- 1Hia	fst	3f	:341	Clm 2500	2 1 73¾	63	Horn F	108 w	11.35	- -	Black Bess100noTransit110noEdri1051½	No excuse	11
22Jan35- 2Hia	fst	3f	:351	Clm 2500	10 6 53¾	22	Stout J	110	9.50	- -	ClappingJane1072Seabiscuit110hdSpart107nk	Finished fast	12
19Jan35- 1Hia	fst	3f	:343	Alw 1000	5 6 55¾	44½	Stout J	110	16.85e	- -	Wha Hae1131Wise Duke1103Blue Donna107½	Good effort	10

Stagehand

b. c. 1935, by Sickle (Phalaris)–Stagecraft, by Fair Play

Lifetime record: 25 9 3 6 $200,110

Own.– Maxwell Howard
Br.– J.E. Widener (Ky)
Tr.– Earl Sande

Date/Race	Cond	Dist	Times	Race	Calls	Fin	Jockey	Wt	Odds	Speed	Top finishers	Comment	Field
4Mar39- 6Hia	fst	1¼	:48 1:123 1:361 2:022	3↑ Widener H 60k	3 7 78 55¼ 36	32¾	Stout J	126wb	*.35	94-03	Bull Lea1192½Sir Damion114nkStagehand1265		7
Slow start,steady late gain													
18Feb39- 5Hia	fst	1⅛	:47 1:104 1:353 1:481	3↑ McLennan Mem H 8.6k	7 9 88 77¼ 34	1nk	Stout J	126wb	*2.05	100-05	Stagehand126nkBull Lea1224Mythical King112½	Just up	9
10Sep38- 5Nar	fst	1⅛	:472 1:112 1:37 1:492	3↑ Governor's H 12k	4 6 66 11½ 15	16	Westrope J	124wb	*.45e	101-07	Stagehand1246Two Bob1001½Thanksgiving1155	Much best	6
3Sep38- 5Nar	fst	1 3/16	:472 1:122 1:363 1:561	3↑ Nar Spl 33k	1 9 97¾ 85½ 2hd	11	Westrope J	119wb	*1.15e	94-09	Stagehand1191Bull Lea1133Cravat1084	Drew out	10
27Aug38- 5Nar	fst	1⅛	:473 1:112 1:362 1:501	J C Thornton Mem H 13k	12 7 75½ 55 44¼	3nk	Westrope J	126wb	*1.75	97-07	Bull Lea116nkPurple King104hdStagehand1261½	Closed fast	12
13Aug38- 5Sar	gd	1¼	:482 1:132 1:39 2:033	Travers 19k	5 8 713 65 63¾	45½	Westrope J	127 w	3.50	85-11	Thanksgiving1174Jolly Tar112½Fighting Fox1241	Late foot	9
23Jly38- 6AP	sl	1¼	:48 1:124 1:382 2:061	Classic 34k	5 8 815 512 59	45¼	Westrope J	126 w	*1.30e	70-26	Nedayr1211Bull Lea1211¼Cravat1233	Late foot	8
9Jly38- 5Emp	fst	1⅛	:474 1:123 1:382 1:51	Emp City H 12k	3 8 88 66½ 51	1nk	Westrope J	124 w	*1.60	100-06	Stagehand124nkFighting Fox120½Galapas106hd	Just up	8
25Jun38- 5Aqu	fst	1⅛	:46 1:104 1:35 1:482	3↑ Brooklyn H 25k	2 9 916 917 511	26	Westrope J	110 w	*1.00e	93-12	The Chief1056Stagehand1103Unfailing1062	Closed fast	10
18Jun38- 5Aqu	sly	1⅛	:46 1:11 1:353 1:482	Dwyer 12k	4 3 411 412 47	38	Westrope J	126 w	*.70e	91-08	The Chief1194Mythical King1194Stagehand1264	Went well	4
3May38- 5CD	fst	1	:23 :461 1:103 1:354	Derby Trial 3k	7 6 43 42½ 35	35	Westrope J	118 w	*.50e	95-13	The Chief117hdLawrin1185Stagehand1182	Hung	8
5Mar38- 6SA	fst	1¼	:461 1:111 1:364 2:013	3↑ S Anita H 126k	3 5 95½ 42½ 3nk	1no	Wall N	100 w	3.60e	103-12	Stagehand100noSeabiscuit1306Pompoon1202	Hard drive	18
22Feb38- 6SA	fst	1⅛	:47 1:113 1:374 1:502	SA Derby 59k	13 12 1112 79 41½	1½	Westrope J	118 w	5.60	92-12	Stagehand118½Dauber118½Sun Egret1185	Hard drive	15
15Feb38- 6SA	sl	1	:234 :48 1:132 1:393	Handicap 1500	1 6 610 67½ 3nk	1no	Westrope J	112 w	2.80	81-25	Stagehand112noCan't Wait1181½Dauber1165	Just up	6
8Jan38- 5SA	fst	1	:224 :464 1:122 1:382	Alw 1200	1 9 816 511 22	12½	Westrope J	116 w	*2.50	87-14	Stagehand1162½Solarium1132½Grim Reaper1131½	Going away	10
5Jan38- 3SA	fst	1	:233 :473 1:123 1:374	Alw 1200	5 5 52 32 1hd	12	Westrope J	111 w	*1.00	90-09	Stagehand1112Basque1125Godspeed1078	Going away	6
1Jan38- 2SA	fst	7f	:231 :463 1:12 1:242	Md Sp Wt	4 9 73¾ 61¾ 32½	2½	Westrope J	118 w	4.20	89-08	GipsyMinstrel118½Stagehand1184Galltor1181	Strong finish	11
20Oct37- 3Bel	fst	7f	:232 :471 1:132 1:26	Md Sp Wt	5 9 915 97¼ 72½	31½	Stout J	115wb	8.00	78-15	Alps115½[D]Bonnie Sea1151Stagehand115no	Fast finish	9
Placed second													
21Sep37- 4Bel	fst	6f-WC	1:114	Alw 1200	1 2 54½ 68½	512	Balaski L	108wb	25.00	76-18	Tiger1254Pumpkin1193Great Union1121	Outrun	6
18Sep37- 3Bel	fst	5½f-WC	1:051	©Md Sp Wt	3 8 1711 1710	1715	Balaski L	116wb	8.00	73-08	Dah He1161½Gentle Savage116hdJubal Junior1164	Outrun	19
23Aug37- 4Sar	fst	6f	:231 :471 1:131	©Md Sp Wt	1 1 96¾ 98¾ 76¾	43½	Balaski L	117 w	12.00	82-15	DanCupid117½GrassCutter1172[D]SturdyDuke1171	Held well	16
Placed third													
4Aug37- 6Sar	fst	5½f	:233 :473 1:082	©Md Sp Wt	16 14 109¼ 87½ 88¼	56	Westrope J	117 w	12.00	75-18	Gallery God1171Pit Bull1173Minimum1171	Late foot	17
31Jly37- 4Sar	my	6f	:233 :48 1:143	U S Hotel 9.4k	6 8 811 812 75¾	77¾	Westrope J	113 w	20.00	71-23	Chaps116nkMountain Ridge116hdRed Glare1131	Outrun	8
28Jly37- 7Sar	fst	5½f	:232 :473 1:074	Alw 1000	4 5 57 69½ 65½	32	Peters M	112 w	12.00	82-15	Chaps1172Jack Be Nimble112hdStagehand1121	Belated rush	7
6Jly37- 4Emp	fst	5f	:23 :473 1:012	©Md Sp Wt	4 10 1011 1011 96¾	94¾	Pollard J	116 w	15.00	86-12	Flying Ariel1161Stephen Jay116hdCal Rainey116hd	Outrun	12

Sun Beau

b. c. 1925, by Sun Briar (Sundridge)–Beautiful Lady, by Fair Play

Lifetime record: 74 33 12 10 $376,744

Own.– W.S. Kilmer
Br.– Mr W.S. Kilmer (Va)
Tr.– J. Whyte

Date/Race	Cond	Dist	Times	Race	Calls	Fin	Jockey	Wt	Odds	Speed	Top finishers	Comment	Field
8Oct31- 5Haw	fst	1¼	:483 1:122 1:39 2:05	3↑ Haw Gold Cup 27k	2 4 1hd 11 1½	11½	Maiben J	126wb	1.53	83-16	Sun Beau1261½Mate1206Plucky Play1264	Handily	4
3Oct31- 6Haw	fst	1 1/16	:25 :484 1:132 1:463	3↑ Mid-West H 5k	5 6 52¼ 42 42	62¼	Maiben J	126wb	*.48	83-18	UncommnGold108½JimDndy1021½Kincsen109no	Wide,weakened	7
5Sep31- 5Sar	sl	1¾	:523 2:083 2:333 3:011	3↑ Sar Cup 9.7k	2 3 24 28 28	210	Phillips C	126wb	2.00	59-21	TwentyGrand11810SunBeau126nkSirAshley118	Under urging	3
Geldings not eligible													
29Aug31- 5LF	gd	1¼	:47 1:12 1:38 2:05	3↑ Lincoln H 28k	4 8 55½ 31½ 11½	11½	Phillips C	129wb	*.94	93-15	Sun Beau1291½Plucky Play1141The Nut1096	Brisk hand ride	8
8Aug31- 6Haw	fst	1⅛	:48 1:124 1:371 1:492	3↑ Haw H 30k	7 5 2½ 11 1hd	21½	Phillips C	131wb	*.71	98-14	PluckyPlay1061½SunBeau1314PaulBunyan1074	Tired last ⅛	7
1Aug31- 5AP	fst	1¼	:47 1:114 1:362 2:031	3↑ Arlington H 34k	1 2 32 21½ 2½	13	Phillips C	128wb	*.63	102-06	Sun Beau1283Satin Spar1052½Plucky Play1091	Easily	7
25Jly31- 5AP	fst	1¼	:472 1:113 1:362 2:014	3↑ Arl Cup 26k	1 3 34½ 1hd 11	13½	Phillips C	126 w	*.94	109-02	Sun Beau1263½Mike Hall1262½Gallant Knight1266	Easily	4
18Jly31- 5AP	fst	1⅛	:47 1:112 1:363 1:492	3↑ Handicap 2000	2 2 11½ 11 11	14	Phillips C	125wb	*.97	100-05	SunBeau1254MikeHll1111½Mrts101no	Challenged turn,easily	5
Previously trained by A. Schuttinger													
7Jly31- 5AP	fst	1	:223 :454 1:093 1:361	3↑ Handicap 2000	4 3 33½ 34½ 33½	31¼	Watters E	124wb	*1.58	96-07	Morsel1051BestMan101nkSunBu1243	Finished fastest of all	5
18Apr31- 5HdG	fst	1 1/16	:232 :473 1:13 1:444	3↑ Philadelphia H 12k	1 3 2hd 13 13	11½	Kurtsinger C	129wb	*.30	98-11	Sun Beau1291½Paul Bunyan108½Fortunate Youth1032	Easily	6
15Apr31- 4HdG	fst	1 70	:232 :473 1:122 1:423	4↑ Alw 2000	1 1 13 14 18	16	Kurtsinger C	120wb	*.30	97-11	SunBeau1206WilliamT.1092½Folkng10615	Eased up final ⅛	4
Previously trained by W.A. Crawford													
22Mar31-12AC	fst	1¼	:464 1:111 1:363 2:03	3↑ Aqua Caliente H 117k	4 8 53 11½ 1½	56¼	Coltiletti F	129wb	*.60	95-08	MkHll116nkThChoctw922PluckyPly110hd	Blocked early,tired	10
1Mar31- 6AC	fst	1⅛	:47 1:12 1:372 1:502	3↑ Fashion 6.7k	9 4 34 31 2hd	13	Coltiletti F	130wb	*.30e	97-13	Sun Beau1303Pigeon Hole115nkAlexander Pantages1101	easily	11
19Feb31- 5AC	fst	6f	:223 :454 1:11	3↑ Alw 1000	10 7 95½ 31½ 11½	12½	Coltiletti F	120wb	*2.00e	98-11	Sun Beau1202½Crofton975Nellie Custis1054		11
Easily,worked additional ¼ mile													

22Nov30- 5Bow	fst	1 1/16	:232 :48 1:123 1:46	3↑ Southern Maryland H 41k	9	9	73	73½	42	11½	Coltiletti F	127wb	*1.90	91-14	Sun Beau1271½Valenciennes1081Lady Broadcast1102		9
	Took lead with rush																
11Nov30- 5Pim	fst	1½	:503 1:153 2:063 2:324	3↑ Bowie H 12k	8	7	21	21	21	31¼	Coltiletti F	130wb	*.90	88-12	Inception1081WilliamT.109nkSunBeu1304	Wide,lacked rally	8
1Nov30- 5Lrl	fst	1¼	:47 1:113 1:363 2:024	3↑ Washington H 31k	3	3	64½	21	2nk	11	Coltiletti F	126wb	*1.75	96-11	Sun Beau1261Vanity1072Hot Toddy1102½	Best in str drive	12
29Oct30- 6Lrl	sl	1 1/16	:233 :48 1:133 1:454	3↑ Handicap 2000	4	4	21	21½	23	21½	Coltiletti F	126wb	*.65	86-18	Vanity1101½Sun Beau1263½Jim Dandy1068	Driving	5
18Oct30- 5Lrl	fst	1	:23 :463 1:111 1:382	2↑ Laurel 14k	8	9	83	41½	43½	41½	Coltiletti F	122wb	2.35	94-12	Conclave1051½The Heathen122hdNed O.108no	Used early	10
11Oct30- 5Haw	fst	1¼	:472 1:124 1:38 2:043	3↑ Haw Gold Cup 30k	8	7	44½	2½	1½	11	Coltiletti F	126wb	*2.03	85-14	SunBeau1261PigeonHole1262½Alcibiades117no	Rated,driving	8
4Oct30- 5HdG	fst	1⅛	:473 1:114 1:38 1:51	3↑ H de Grace Cup H 25k	6	6	44	45	45	24	Coltiletti F	126wb	*1.40	91-14	Spinach1164Sun Beau126hdDr. Freeland1061	All out drive	11
20Sep30- 6OW	fst	1¼	:474 1:132 1:392 2:054	3↑ Toronto Aut Cup 8.1k	6	7	65¾	2½	2nk	11	Coltiletti F	132wb	*1.15	92-12	Sun Beau1321Sandy Ford1114Solace1181	Won in hand	9
13Sep30- 5Bel	fst	1 1/16	:231 :47 1:113 1:43	3↑ Handicap 1555	5	4	2hd	2hd	1hd	1¾	Coltiletti F	126wb	*.25	96-08	Sun Beau126¾William T.1102Folking1053	Speed in reserve	5
4Sep30- 2Bel	gd	1	:24 :48 1:12 1:374	3↑ Alw 1200	4	2	21	2½	11	13	Coltiletti F	120wb	*.90	86-12	Sun Beau1203Sun Edwin1206Titus1091½	Wide,easily	4
	Previously trained by W. Irvine																
26Jly30- 5AP	sly	1¼	:473 1:124 1:392 2:073	3↑ Arlington H 44k	3	6	911	1019	1027	1026	Schaefer L	125wb	*3.15	54-20	Pigeon Hole1051Curate1083The Nut1142½	Disliked going	11
23Jly30- 5AP	fst	1	:233 :47 1:12 1:361	3↑ Alw 2000	1	3	21	2½	2hd	12½	Schaefer L	117wb	*2.63	106-03	Sun Beau1172½Brown Wisdom1084Silverdale110½		6
	Easily,worked add'l furlong																
19Jly30- 5AP	fst	1¼	:48 1:122 1:37 2:034	3↑ Arl Cup 32k	3	4	52¾	43	46	46¼	Schaefer L	126wb	2.82	93-00	BlueLarkspur1263½Petee-Wrack126nkToro1262½	No late gain	5
12Jly30- 6AP	fst	1⅛	:48 1:13 1:374 1:504	3↑ Alw 2000	4	4	2hd	2hd	2hd	1½	Schaefer L	117wb	*.73	98-00	Sun Beau117½Paul Bunyan1101Petee-Wrack1124	Gamely	5
4Jly30- 5AP	fst	1⅛	:472 1:12 1:37 1:492	3↑ Stars & Stripes H 33k	2	3	32	31	31½	3½	Schaefer L	125wb	7.30	104-02	Blue Larkspur121½Misstep124noSun Beau1255	Held well	16
28Jun30- 5Was	fst	1¼	:484 1:133 1:382 2:043	3↑ F S Peabody Mem H 14k	1	1	11	2½	86½	1017	Coltiletti F	126wb	*1.82	81-08	PaulBunyan115noIronsides1061½LadyBrodcst1011	Quit badly	10
21Jun30- 4Aqu	fst	1⅛	:473 1:13 1:373 1:51	3↑ Brookdale H 8.2k	4	4	42	31½	2½	32	Coltiletti F	126wb	4.50	86-15	Jack High123hdSortie1202Sun Beau1264	Wide,tired	5
17Jun30- 4Aqu	fst	1⅛	:494 1:162 1:404 1:521	3↑ Handicap 1260	2	3	31	32½	21	11	Coltiletti F	126wb	*.25	82-16	Sun Beau1261Apple Cart105½Bannerette103	Troubled trip	4
9Jun30- 4Bel	my	1	:231 :47 1:112 1:383	3↑ Alw 1400	1	2	21	21½	24	21½	Coltiletti F	125wb	1.60	80-21	Caruso1101½Sun Beau125	Resolute finish	2
23Nov29- 4Bow	sl	1 1/16	:233 :473 1:124 1:462	2↑ Southern Maryland H 46k	2	2	2nk	2nk	56½	910¾	Coltiletti F	127wb	2.35	78-15	Bateau113noVictorian1221Balko1114	Quit	13
26Oct29- 5Lrl	fst	1¼	:463 1:112 1:37 2:024	3↑ Washington H 31k	7	5	94¼	2hd	1½	12	Coltiletti F	125wb	*2.65	96-12	Sun Beau1252Distraction120hdDisplay120hd	Saved ground	10
22Oct29- 5Lrl	sly	1 1/16	:243 :493 1:16 1:492	3↑ Alw 1800	2	2	1nk	1nk	1½	1hd	Coltiletti F	118wb	*.35	70-26	Sun Beau118hdLativich104	Hand ride	2
7Oct29- 5Haw	fst	1¼	:474 1:113 1:361 2:013	3↑ Haw Gold Cup 28k	2	5	46½	3nk	2hd	11½	Coltiletti F	126wb	7.67	107-11	Sun Beau1261½Misstep1264Diavolo1263	Easily	6
2Oct29- 5HdG	hy	1⅛	:492 1:143 1:413 1:553	3↑ H de Grace Cup H 24k	8	6	32¾	21	1nk	11	Coltiletti F	117wb	4.50	72-27	Sun Beau1171Glen Wild107hdBateau1164	Ridden out	9
28Sep29- 4Aqu	fst	1⅛	:48 1:124 1:372 1:50	3↑ Aqueduct H 7.1k	1	2	21½	22	1nk	11	Coltiletti F	116wb	8.00	93-17	Sun Beau1161Diavolo127¾Live Oak104	Driving	3
	Previously trained by C.W. Carroll																
21Sep29- 5OW	fst	1¼	:492 1:143 1:412 2:061	3↑ Toronto Aut Cup H 10k	9	7	42½	32	34	36½	Coltiletti F	122wb	*1.30	83-19	Gaffsman1122½Saxon1144SunBeu1222	Restrained,tired badly	9
13Sep29- 4Bel	fst	1⅛	:473 1:112 1:354 1:482	3↑ Handicap 1570	7	3	21	2½	21½	22	Coltiletti F	126wb	*1.50	101-03	Hot Toddy1102Sun Beau1264Fair Ball1055	Tired late	7
5Sep29- 5Bel	fst	1	:243 :48 1:12 1:37	3↑ Handicap 1255	4	2	21	2½	21½	1hd	Coltiletti F	126wb	2.20	92-09	Sun Beau126hdCoin Collector1124Soul of Honor1085		4
	Up in final strides;Previously trained by W. Irvine																
20Jly29- 5AP	fst	1⅛	:471 1:12 1:373 1:502	3↑ Arlington H 29k	4	10	108	119½	129¾	129½	Johnson A	118wb	*3.54	92-04	Misstep123hdDisplay1151BuddyBauer1141	Stumbled 1st turn	12
17Jly29- 5AP	fst	1	:244 :484 1:13 1:373	3↑ Handicap 2000	2	7	42½	32½	32	2nk	Legere E	116wb	6.47	109-00	Misstep122nkSunBeau1161½Republc115hd	Wide,finished fast	9
	Previously trained by J.O. Burttschell																
4Jly29- 5AP	fst	1⅛	:471 1:113 1:37 1:503	3↑ Stars & Stripes H 20k	4	5	44	33	33	33	Legere E	120wb	5.76	98-08	Dowagiac1082Misstep1251Sun Beau1202	Traffic,wide	13
	Previously trained by A.G. Blakely																
15Jun29- 4Aqu	fst	1⅛	:462 1:122 1:372 1:503	3↑ Brooklyn H 18k	2	3	53¾	41½	32½	34½	Legere E	124wb	7.00	85-16	Light Carbine971½Diavolo1203Sun Beau124hd	Good try	12
12Jun29- 4Aqu	fst	1 1/16	:232 :471 1:13 1:454	3↑ Handicap 1250	1	3	33½	34½	33	34½	Legere E	126wb	*3.00	81-19	Light Carbine1001½Sepoy1003Sun Beau1264	Tired	6
24Nov28- 4Bow	fst	1 1/16	:232 :473 1:122 1:441	2↑ G D Bryan Mem H 50k	14	11	128½	53½	65½	612¼	Craigmyle J	119wb	4.60	90-07	Misstep114hdVictorian1186Nassak1164	Off slowly,wide	16
16Nov28- 4Bow	fst	1 1/16	:233 :48 1:121 1:452	Prince Georges H 12k	4	3	34	34	34	21½	Craigmyle J	126wb	2.35	94-08	Nassak1161½Sun Beau126½Distraction1062½	Gamely	9
27Oct28- 5Lat	sl	1¾	:484 2:062 2:332 3:003	Lat Championship 33k	2	4	46	22	11½	12½	Craigmyle J	126wb	*.57	70-25	Sun Beau1262½Sortie12615Lawley12620	Easing up at end	4
	Previously trained by W. Short																
20Oct28- 5Lrl	fst	1¼	:463 1:123 1:38 2:051	Maryland H 19k	7	8	75¾	42½	3nk	15	Craigmyle J	116wb	6.15	84-19	Sun Beau1165Sortie110hdPetee-Wrack1161½	Easily	11
11Oct28- 5Haw	fst	1¼	:473 1:12 1:371 2:03	3↑ Haw Gold Cup 26k	9	5	21½	2½	11½	52¼	O'Donell S	120wb	7.89	103-06	Display126noMike Hall1262Crusader126hd	Tired late	9
29Sep28- 5HdG	sly	1⅛	:48 1:131 1:411 1:534	3↑ H de Grace Cup H 24k	4	7	65½	55	44	2½	Maiben J	114wb	8.25	80-19	Osmand121½Sun Beau1142½Crusader1241½	Wide,gaining	8
22Sep28- 4HdG	fst	1 1/16	:23 :472 1:12 1:46	Potomac H 23k	6	6	1hd	11½	11½	11	Craigmyle J	114wb	8.50	93-10	Sun Beau1141Victorian1252½Princess Tina1081		8
	Saved ground,ridden out																
19Sep28- 4HdG	my	1 70	:22 :46 1:122 1:444	3↑ Alw 2500	1	6	611	59	47½	34	Craigmyle J	107wb	13.40	82-19	Victorian1154Crusader117hdSunBeu1075	Just missed second	6
4Aug28- 4Sar	fst	1 3/16	:494 1:15 1:401 1:59	3↑ Miller 6.3k	4	3	21½	21½	42¾	58½	Craigmyle J	115wb	2.60	74-14	Reigh Count1272Gerard1155Penalo1151	Quit	5
30Jly28- 5Sar	gd	1¼	:483 1:13 1:39 2:06	3↑ Saratoga H 9.7k	8	4	43½	41¾	42¼	45	Craigmyle J	109wb	4.50	74-15	Chance Shot1221½Black Maria1152Edith Cavell1061½	Tiring	8
7Jly28- 5LF	fst	1¼	:484 1:13 1:392 2:053	3↑ Lincoln H 32k	12	7	95	51¼	2½	2½	Craigmyle J	111wb	14.10	92-10	Toro115½Sun Beau1114Flat Iron118½	No match	15
30Jun28- 4Aqu	gd	1½	:501 1:16 2:073 2:313	Dwyer 25k	2	1	21½	32¼	32½	26	Craigmyle J	110wb	2.60	84-14	Genie1106Sun Beau1101Ironsides1171	Driving	6
	Geldings not eligible																
27Jun28- 4Aqu	fst	1	:234 :473 1:132 1:382	3↑ Handicap 1285	8	6	41½	2nk	1hd	12	Craigmyle J	126wb	5.00	88-19	SunBeau1262Tantvy1081[D]Byrd1201	Outside move,going away	9
15Jun28- 2Aqu	gd	1	:24 :494 1:14 1:384	3↑ Alw 1000	5	3	3½	3nk	1½	12	Craigmyle J	114wb	5.00	86-16	Sun Beau1142St. Henell113noSocial Mug1213	Going away	7
9Jun28- 5Bel	fst	1½	:481 1:133 2:061 2:331	Belmont 74k	1	1	1hd	1hd	613	616	McAtee L	126wb	10.00	62-23	Vito1263Genie1263Diavolo126hd	Dueled,tired badly	6
1Jun28- 2Bel	fst	1⅛	:463 1:12 1:384 1:531	3↑ Alw 1200	7	1	12	13	11	11	McAtee L	111wb	*2.20	79-22	Sun Beau1111Sepoy118½Danthonia1091½	Saved ground	7
19May28- 5CD	hy	1¼	:493 1:154 1:432 2:102	Ky Derby 65k	18	16	1813	1411	1020	1119	Craigmyle J	126wb	38.42	45-26	Reigh Count1263Misstep1262Toro1264	Never a factor	22
11May28- 4Pim	fst	1 3/16	:472 1:13 1:384 2:001	Preakness 70k	6	10	104¾	43½	53¾	55½	Craigmyle J	126wb	17.85	85-14	Victorian126noToro1262½Solace1263	Wide	18
	Geldings not eligible																
8May28- 5Pim	fst	1 70	:232 :48 1:133 1:453	Alw 1500	6	6	52¼	52¾	63¼	1hd	Craigmyle J	112wb	20.75	83-32	Sun Beau112hdDon Q108hdSolace116½	Up in final strides	6
30Apr28- 5HdG	fst	1 1/16	:233 :473 1:122 1:451	Chesapeake 12k	7	5	52½	52¾	1013	1017¼	Craigmyle J	114 w	17.80f	80-13	Bobashela1104Typhoon1224Sortie1222	Crowded	11
27Apr28- 5HdG	gd	1 70	:24 :482 1:13 1:44	Alw 2000	7	7	73½	65½	610	613¼	Craigmyle J	111wb	7.70	77-19	Strolling Player111noToro1148Solace1145	Began slowly	7
24Apr28- 3HdG	hy	6f	:25 :503 1:172	Alw 1200	1	4	3¾	2hd	11½	13	Craigmyle J	106wb	*.50	68-39	Sun Beau1063Water Lad1081War Whoop1115	Easily	5
21Apr28- 3HdG	fst	6f	:232 :473 1:132	3↑ Handicap 1400	4	5	41¼	2hd	1nk	2hd	Craigmyle J	114wb	5.55	88-19	Contemplate113hdSunBeau1145Montferrt120½	Tired last ⅛	6
	Previously trained by G.E. Phillips																
4Nov27- 5Pim	my	1	:24 :483 1:142 1:414	Pim Futurity 61k	5	15	1312	1212	1112	75½	Craigmyle J	122wb	18.95e	73-24	Glade114hdPetee-Wrack119nk[D]Bateau1161½	No factor	15
	Geldings not eligible																
29Oct27- 4Lrl	fst	1	:231 :472 1:133 1:39	Manor H 15k	7	10	103¾	114½	1111	1011¼	GdwinP	107 w	*1.80e	82-10	Eugene S.1051Toro1153Sun Friar1113	Taken up start	11
27Oct27- 4Lrl	fst	1	:231 :47 1:13 1:384	2↑ Alw 1400	6	2	2nk	1hd	11½	1½	GdwinP	103wb	17.20	94-18	Sun Beau103½Fairy Maiden1091Eugene S.1034	Handily	9
	Previously trained by C.W. Carroll																
21Oct27- 2Lrl	sl	6f	:232 :48 1:144	Md Sp Wt	2	6	63¾	54½	43½	44¼	Craigmyle J	115wb	10.35	79-25	[D]ScotchandSoda115nkBobashela1153BarNon1151	Good effort	7
	Placed third by disqualification																

Top Flight

dk.br. f. 1929, by Dis Donc (Sardanapale)–Flyatit, by Peter Pan — Lifetime record: 16 12 0 0 $275,900

Own.– C.V. Whitney
Br.– H.P. Whitney (Ky)
Tr.– T.J. Healy

24Sep32- 5HdG	fst 1 1/16	:23 :47 1:123 1:45	Potomac H 25k	2 3 41¼ 41½ 42 42	Workman R	118wb	*1.90	95-08	DarkSecret110¹Osculator110noGallantSir111¹	Under urging 12
14Sep32- 4Bel	fst 1	:23 :464 1:114 1:374 2↑	ⒻLadies H 2.9k	5 2 2½ 2hd 11½ 11½	Workman R	126wb	*.80	86-17	Top Flight1261½Parry1145Risque1183	Speed to spare 7
30Aug32- 4Sar	fst 1	:231 :461 1:11 1:374 3↑	Delaware H 4.5k	3 1 11 2nk 32½ 45	Workman R	120wb	3.00	87-11	Flagstone104.51Morfr1233TrdAvon1161	Eased up when tired 4
17Aug32- 4Sar	fst 1¼	:234 :473 1:123 2:062	ⒻAlabama 15k	3 2 23 21 13 14	Workman R	126wb	*.40	77-14	Top Flight1264Parry1166Laughing Queen1214	Drawing away 4
16Jly32- 5AP	fst 1¼	:47 1:11 1:37 2:033	Classic 88k	8 3 11½ 1hd 2hd 57	Workman R	118wb	*1.82	84-08	Gusto1263Stepenfetcht1212Evrgold1212	Little left at end 12
2Jly32- 5AP	fst 1⅛	:473 1:12 1:372 1:504	ⒻArl Oaks 18k	5 1 11 11 12 12	Workman R	121wb	*.84	93-06	Top Flight1212Evening121½Parry118hd	Easily 8
9Jun32- 4Bel	fst 1⅜	:484 1:134 1:412 2:201	ⒻC C A Oaks 18k	9 3 21½ 21 2nk 1¾	Workman R	121wb	*.20	70-21	Top Flight121¾Argosie1141Unique1143	Loafing,just held 10
14May32- 5Bel	fst 1	:23 :47 1:12 1:39	ⒻAcorn 15k	1 1 11 12 14 16	Workman R	121wb	*.80	80-20	Top Flight1216Parry1142Unique1144	Drew away 7
30Apr32- 4Jam	fst 1 70	:231 :473 1:12 1:43	Wood Memorial 13k	3 3 32 35 46¼ 47½	Robertson A	115 w	*.50	83-11	Universe120½Economic1203Curacao1144	Tired badly 10
7Nov31- 4Pim	fst 1 1/16	:232 :471 1:122 1:444	Pim Futurity 64k	9 4 2hd 2hd 1½ 1nk	Workman R	119 w	*1.10	98-07	Top Flight119nkTick On1193Burgoo King119no	Lasted 12
	Geldings not eligible									
19Sep31- 4Bel	fst *7f-WC	1:21	Futurity 107k	10 4 2hd 1nk 12½	Workman R	127 w	*1.20e	90-10	TpFlght1272½MdPursut1221Mrfr1221	Drew off under pressure 12
9Sep31- 3Bel	fst 6f-WC	1:113	ⒻMatron 26k	2 1 1hd 1hd 11½	Workman R	127 w	*.17	89-16	Top Flight1271½Parry1191½Pintail1156	Speed to spare 7
22Aug31- 3Sar	fst 6f	:232 :47 1:123	ⒻSpinaway 10k	5 1 11½ 11½ 13 15	Workman R	127 w	*.55	89-10	TopFlight1275DinnerTime1111½Brocado115no	Speed to spare 8
15Aug31- 4Sar	fst 6f	:23 :462 1:12	Sar Spl 11k	2 7 1½ 11 12 11¼	Workman R	119 w	*.70	92-12	TopFlight1191¼IndianRunnr1222Curco1221	Speed in reserve 7
8Jly31- 4AP	fst 5½f	:221 :453 :583 1:051	ⒻLassie 22k	6 3 1½ 13 14 15	Robertson A	120 w	*1.90	99-09	TopFlight1205ModernQueen113½PrincessCml1171	Easily best 15
17Jun31- 4Aqu	my 5f	:58	ⒻClover 6.7k	6 5 1½ 1½ 11	Robertson A	107 w	*2.50e	97-20	Top Flight1071Polonaise1221Brocado112½	Held 12

Twenty Grand

b. c. 1928, by St. Germans (Swynford)–Bonus, by All Gold — Lifetime record: 25 14 4 3 $261,790

Own.– Greentree Stable
Br.– Greentree Stable (Ky)
Tr.– Cecil Boyd–Rochfort

29Oct35♦ Newmarket(GB)	gd 1½ⓉRH	2:35 3↑	Rutland Hcp Hcp1600	-	Childs J	133	20.00		Lobau108½Pharillon111½Linace115 — Never a factor;Exact finish position unavailable	11
18Jun35♦ Ascot(GB)	gd 1ⓉStr	1:44 3↑	Queen Anne Stakes Stk7200	7	Beasy M	124	16.50		Fair Trial1093Solerina992Monico109 — Chased leaders throughout;Beaten lengths unavailable,	22
	Previously trained by W. Brennan									
23Feb35- 6SA	fst 1¼	:45 1:10 1:36 2:021 3↑	S Anita H 125k	7 11 910 1415 1311 109¾	Coucci S	126wb	10.30	--	Azucar1172Ladysman1171Time Supply1182	Never a contender 20
18Feb35- 5SA	fst 1 1/16	:24 :473 1:12 1:432 3↑	Handicap 1200	3 1 11 11 2hd 21	Coucci S	116wb	4.00	--	ⒹEquipoise1251Twenty Grand1163Sarada1051½	5
	Placed first by disqualification									
25Jan35- 6SA	fst 7f	:224 :453 1:094 1:222 3↑	Handicap 1200	3 2 21½ 22½ 35 33½	Coucci S	122 w	*1.20	--	High Glee1132Mate1201½Twenty Grand1223½	Lame 4
5Oct32- 5Lrl	sl 1 1/16	:242 :492 1:142 1:483 3↑	Handicap 1200	3 4 2½ 1hd 2½ 21½	Kurtsinger C	126 w	*.65	72-25	Mad Frump1081½Twenty Grand126½War Hero112½	6
	Faltered,pulled up lame									
15Sep32- 4Bel	fst 1	:234 :464 1:113 1:364 3↑	Alw 900	4 3 33 23 21 1½	Kurtsinger C	125 w	*.80	91-10	Twenty Grand125½Masked Knight11820Pin Tail1014	Driving 4
	Previously trained by J. Rowe Jr									
19Sep31- 5Bel	fst 2	:501 2:37 2:562 3:232 3↑	J C Gold Cup 13k	2 2 22 13 15 13	Kurtsinger C	114 w	*.02	92-09	TwntyGrnd1143Blenheim1147Barometr114	Easily,much best 3
12Sep31- 5Bel	fst 1⅝	:48 1:38 2:022 2:411	Lawrence Realizatn 33k	3 4 36 2½ 13 16	Kurtsinger C	126 w	*.07	98-04	TwentyGrand1266SunMeadow1235SirAshley1231	Easily,best 4
5Sep31- 5Sar	sl 1¾	:523 2:083 2:333 3:011 3↑	Sar Cup 9.7k	3 1 14 18 18 110	McAtee L	118 w	*.40	69-21	TwentyGrand11810SunBeau126nkSirAshley118	Easily,best 3
	Geldings not eligible									
22Aug31- 5Sar	fst 1¼	:481 1:13 1:384 2:043	Travers 39k	5 5 56½ 2hd 11½ 11¾	McAtee L	126 w	*.14e	86-10	TwntyGrand1261¾St.Bridux1204SunMdow1205	Easily,in hand 5
	Geldings not eligible									
18Jly31- 4AP	fst 1¼	:471 1:12 1:371 2:022	Classic 85k	7 7 74¾ 44 36½ 34	Kurtsinger C	126 w	*.38e	102-05	Mate1264Spanish Play123noTwenty Grand1265	7
	Came wide,finished fast									
4Jly31- 4Aqu	fst 1½	:512 1:16 2:08 2:342	Dwyer 15k	3 1 22 22 1nk 12	Kurtsinger C	126 w	*.02	76-20	Twenty Grand1262Blenheim1124Barometer110	Easily best 3
13Jun31- 5Bel	fst 1½	:49 1:142 2:03 2:293	Belmont 69k	1 3 33 2hd 13 110	Kurtsinger C	126 w	*.80	96-12	TwentyGrand12610SunMeadow126noJamestown126	Cantered 3
16May31- 5CD	fst 1¼	:472 1:12 1:372 2:014	Ky Derby 58k	5 9 104½ 2½ 11 14	Kurtsinger C	126 w	*.88e	107-02	Twenty Grand1264Sweep All1263Mate1264	Easily 12
9May31- 5Pim	fst 1 3/16	:483 1:132 1:383 1:59	Preakness 58k	1 1 73¾ 51½ 31½ 21½	Kurtsinger C	126 w	*1.75e	95-10	Mate1261½Twenty Grand126nkLadder1261	Impeded 7
	Geldings not eligible									
2May31- 4Jam	fst 1 70	:233 :47 1:122 1:423	Wood Memorial 13k	2 4 58 48 24 1½	Kurtsinger C	120 w	*.60	93-09	Twenty Grand120½Clock Tower1106Camper1106	Driving 6
	Previously trained by T.W. Murphy									
14Nov30- 5Pim	my 1 1/16	:234 :483 1:134 1:474	Walden H 13k	1 5 53½ 42¼ 42 31¼	Walls P	125 w	*.95e	82-22	Mate125¾Sweep All105½Twenty Grand1252½	Finished fast 5
5Nov30- 5Pim	my 1 1/16	:234 :482 1:142 1:483	Pim Futurity 58k	8 6 63 64¾ 42¾ 2½	Kurtsinger C	119 w	3.40	78-26	Equipoise119½Twenty Grand119nkMate1194	Finished fast 8
	Geldings not eligible									
16Oct30- 5CD	fst 1	:231 :464 1:111 1:36	Ky Jockey Club 31k	1 7 43 22 1hd 1no	Kurtsinger C	122 w	2.77	101-13	TwentyGrand122noEquipoise12210Knight'sCall1225	Driving 7
4Oct30- 3Aqu	fst 1	:233 :473 1:13 1:38	Jr Champion 9.8k	7 7 65¼ 53¾ 32½ 11	Kurtsinger C	111 w	7.00	90-15	Twenty Grand1111Equipoise1223Ormesby1168	Driving 7
25Sep30- 4Aqu	fst 6f	:233 :472 1:124	Babylon H 6.8k	5 4 74½ 53¼ 52¾ 43½	Walls P	111 w	*3.20	86-14	Ormesby1162hdRollin In1102Gigantic1071½	No mishaps 13
18Sep30- 5Aqu	fst 5f	1:00	Alw 1000	3 5 42¼ 12 13	Garner M	113 w	5.00	87-17	Twenty Grand1133Laddie116nkCamper1222	Easily 10
11Jly30- 6Emp	fst 5f	:232 :474 1:004	Alw 1000	2 5 58 55 44 21	Robertson A	115 w	1.40e	93-13	Phantom Star1101Twenty Grand115½Jamison1103	Closed fast 9
30Apr30- 5Jam	fst 5f	:24 :482 1:014	Md Sp Wt	7 4 31 2½ 11½ 15	McAtee L	118 w	*.70	84-18	Twenty Grand1185Soarer1151½Black Shirt1182	Easily 11

Unerring

br. f. 1936, by Insco (Sir Gallahad III)–Margaret Lawrence, by Vulcain — Lifetime record: 57 16 13 7 $31,350

Own.– Woolford Farm
Br.– Herbert M. Woolf (Kan)
Tr.– R.O. Higdon

17Oct41- 5Emp	fst 1 1/16	:233 :471 1:123 1:453 3↑	Alw 2500	6 7 53¾ 53¾ 43 63½	Strickler W	112 w	3.05	87-12	Spanish Duke1141½Sun Eager1071Lovely Night111½	Faltered 7
13Oct41- 5Jam	fst 6f	:224 :461 1:12 2↑	ⒻCorrection H 8.9k	1 5 65 55½ 43 3½	Strickler W	112 w	12.95	91-16	WiseNiece109nkDevil'sGirl112½Unerrng112nk	Strong finish 9
7Oct41- 6Jam	fst 1 1/16	:242 :481 1:133 1:452 3↑	Handicap 3030	1 1 1hd 21 21 22	Strickler W	104 w	8.10	84-14	Dit1222Unerring104¾Birch Rod118¾	Weakened 5
3Oct41- 6Bel	sly 1 1/16	3↑	Alw 2500	6 1 21 2hd 1hd 1¾	Strickler W	103 w	16.55	--	Unerring103¾Hypocrite1205Tex Hygro1051	Drew out 7
	Time not taken									
29Sep41- 6Bel	fst 1	:234 :47 1:12 1:364 3↑	Alw 2500	3 1 1hd 1hd 42½ 410½	Strickler W	103 w	14.35	80-12	The Rhymer104½Llanero1044Vintage Port1066	Tired 8
22Sep41- 5Bel	fst 6f	:224 :463 1:113 3↑	ⒻAlw 2000	1 6 97¼ 87 87 74¼	Vedder RL	112 w	*1.05e	88-10	Five to One1031Dark Imp1102Fleetborough1051	Outrun 10
15Sep41- 6Aqu	fst 6f	:224 :464 1:12 3↑	ⒻAlw 2000	5 5 54¾ 55 42 2¾	Strickler W	108 w	10.40	93-16	Oasis116¾Unerring108nkPelisse111no	Closed fast 5
6Aug41- 7Was	fst 6f	:223 :463 1:112 3↑	Handicap 1200	2 4 55 53½ 53 42	Strickler W	113 w	3.70	92-11	Malisco1101Woodsaw112noBoysy1101	No mishaps 7
21May41- 6LF	fst 6f	:233 :473 1:134 3↑	ⒻAlw 1010	1 4 1hd 1hd 11½ 11¼	McCombs K	116 w	4.00	82-25	Unerring1161¼Montsin1111½Shine O'Night111½	Driving 7
12May41- 6CD	fst 7f	:232 :47 1:122 1:253 3↑	Alw 1000	3 1 1hd 1hd 1½ 43¼	McCombs K	111 w	7.00	85-15	Topic1102ValdinaGroom1101DancingLight116nk	Tired badly 7
1May41- 6CD	fst 1	:232 :463 1:113 1:363 3↑	Churchill Downs H 3k	3 6 42 77¾ 711 716½	McCombs K	108wb	8.30	79-14	My Bill1004Potranco1165Betty's Bobby109¾	Shuffled back 8
18Apr41- 4Kee	sl 6f	:23 :472 1:131 3↑	ⒻAlw 1200	2 5 63¾ 58 44¼ 34¾	McCombs K	121wb	3.90	81-21	Laatokka105¾Mattie J.1134Unerring121no	Wide 6

Date	Cond/Dist	Fractions	Race	PP	St	1st	2nd	Str	Fin	Jockey	Wt	Odds	Speed	Top Finishers	Comment	Fld
10Apr41- 5Kee	fst 6f	:23 :463 1:121	3↑ Phoenix H 3.6k	3	6	66	69	56	59½	Vedder RL	110wb	8.60	81-18	Cherry Jam111hdSmacked1016Parasang1221½	Outrun	7
28Feb41- 6Hia	fst 1⅛	:463 1:112 1:374 1:503	3↑ ⒻEvening H 6.5k	1	3	21	43	42½	54¼	Vedder RL	114wb	3.50e	84-18	Dorimar115nkJeanne d'Arc1023Silvestra102hd	Weakened	13
8Feb41- 6Hia	gd 7f	:224 :453 1:104 1:232	3↑ ⒻBlack Helen H 6.5k	1	3	35½	55	56½	69½	Vedder RL	121wb	4.60e	86-13	Sweet Willow1164Silvestra1052Up the Hill102½	Tired	13
28Jan41- 6Hia	fst 7f	:231 :47 1:112 1:24	4↑ ⒻAlw 1500	3	1	11½	12	12	1nk	Vedder RL	114wb	*.80	93-11	Unerring114nkPretty Pet1115Harp Weaver1081½	Just lasted	5
22Jan41- 5Hia	fst 6½f	:223 :453 1:10 1:163	3↑ Handicap 1600	2	2	31½	31¾	31½	2hd	Vedder RL	111wb	3.30	96-07	ClydeTolson115hdUnerring111nkSundodger110hd	Just missed	7
14Jan41- 6Hia	fst 6f	:223 :451 1:112	4↑ ⒻAlw 1500	6	4	41¾	36	33½	2¾	Vedder RL	114wb	6.45	91-15	Aerial Bomb108¾Unerring1141½Sassy Lady114½	Closed fast	10
17Sep40- 4Aqu	fst 6f	:223 :464 1:112	3↑ Handicap 2035	6	3	31½	32	32	2hd	Meade D	108wb	3.55e	100-07	Dr. Whinny122hdUnerring108nkVolitant1123	Just missed	7
10Sep40- 5Aqu	fst 6f	:223 :464 1:12	4↑ Handicap 1535	3	4	44	46	46	44½	Roberts P	110wb	1.70e	92-10	Rifted Clouds114noWatch Over122½Archworth1064	No mishap	6
8Aug40- 6Was	fst 6f	:223 :46 1:112	3↑ Handicap 1200	3	5	53½	55½	54½	54½	Eads W	112 w	1.90e	90-10	Float Away105hdTalked About1131½Morcarine1081	Outrun	6
16Jly40- 6AP	fst 7f	:233 :47 1:12 1:253	3↑ Alw 1200	1	1	1hd	2½	21½	2½	Eads W	110 w	*1.10	81-16	Talked About114½Unerring1105Co-Sport1082	Forced back	6
6Jly40- 7AP	fst 1	:234 :472 1:113 1:364	3↑ Alw 1200	4	1	11½	1½	1hd	2½	Richard J	113 w	*.80	87-12	Van109½Unerring11310Olympus1132¼	Weakened	5
29Jun40- 6AP	fst 1	:224 :451 1:10 1:361	3↑ ⒻArl Matron H 9.1k	12	8	73¼	42½	43¾	77¼	Bierman C	118 w	*.90e	84-18	Shine O'Night1033Montsin1101Manie O'Hara1091	Impeded	14
17Apr40- 5Kee	sly 6f	:23 :464 1:122	3↑ Handicap 1500	4	2	43	42¼	11½	13	Vedder RL	117 w	*2.10	90-22	Unerring1173Royal Blue109nkSmart Crack106hd	Going away	5
14Feb40- 5Hia	fst 6½f	:233 :472 1:111 1:172	3↑ Handicap 1500	3	2	1½	2½	35	56¾	Wright WD	116 w	*1.60e	85-12	Many Stings118nkArmor Bearer1095Inscoelda1111½		5
	Swerved final ¼,worked mile in 1:38															
30Jan40- 5Hia	fst 7f	:23 :462 1:103 1:232	4↑ ⒻAlw 1200	7	4	41½	32	31¼	3nk	Ryan P	118 w	*2.05	96-09	Flying Lill115nkDolly Val115hdUnerring118½	Swerved	8
16Jan40- 6Hia	fst 7f	:232 :47 1:112 1:24	4↑ ⒻAlw 1400	3	1	1hd	1½	1½	1nk	Ryan P	115 w	*1.80	93-09	Unerring115nkDolly Val1091One Jest108nk	Hard drive	8
8Nov39- 6Pim	fst 1 1/16	:24 :483 1:14 1:472	3↑ ⒻLady Baltimore H 3.9k	3	4	42	51½	43	76¼	Ryan P	118 w	*1.55e	77-21	Manie O'Hara1084Bala Ormont109½Hostility110½	Tired	12
18Oct39- 5Lrl	fst 1 70	:233 :472 1:133 1:424	3↑ Handicap 1500	3	3	11½	2hd	2hd	2hd	Ryan P	108 w	*1.25	95-14	War Minstrel112hdUnerring1085Pernie107½	Game try	6
23Sep39- 5HdG	fst 1 1/16	:24 :472 1:124 1:444	Potomac H 11k	7	4	42½	41½	43	44¾	Ryan P	114 w	4.25	89-15	ThirdDegree1143Porter'sMite116nkElChico1151½	No mishap	7
9Sep39- 5Aqu	fst 1 1/16	:233 :462 1:103 1:43	3↑ ⒻBeldame H 13k	3	1	1½	1½	11	2no	Ryan P	120 w	7.00	98-03	NellieBly102noUnerring1203BalOrmont115hd	Tired in drive	18
31Aug39- 0Was	fst 1	:23 :46 1:104 1:374	ⒻMatch Race 6.2k	2	2	2nk	1½	12	12	Ryan P	110 w	*.70	89-13	Unerring1102Flying Lill110	Handily	2
26Aug39- 7Was	fst 6f	:224 :464 1:114	3↑ Handicap 1000	5	2	2hd	2hd	11	3½	Ryan P	114 w	*.70e	92-12	Robert L.118nkGrass Cutter111nkUnerring1143	Tired badly	9
	Previously trained by B.A. Jones															
15Jly39- 3AP	fst 1	:233 :47 1:11 1:363	Alw 1500	2	1	11½	12	14	12½	Longden J	109 w	*.80e	89-17	Unerring1092½Technician123hdSun Lover1201½	In hand	7
1Jly39- 5AP	fst 1	:23 :454 1:103 1:363	3↑ ⒻArl Matron H 6.1k	8	3	32½	31	21	2nk	Yarberry W	108 w	*1.90	89-17	FlyingLill107nkUnerring1084LadyMaryland1202	Forced wide	9
26Jun39- 6AP	fst 1	:234 :471 1:113 1:37	Alw 1200	7	1	11½	13	16	19	Caffarella M	102 w	*1.00	87-14	Unerring1029Yale O' Nine1122Chief Onaway1184	Much best	7
19Jun39- 5LF	fst 6f	:23 :462 1:121	Alw 800	3	3	32	1hd	11	11¼	Caffarella M	102 w	*2.20	90-16	Unerring1021¼Olney1101½Carla1095	Handily	8
14Jun39- 5LF	gd 7f	:232 :464 1:123 1:254	Alw 800	2	2	21	31½	22	2nk	Hanke E	103 w	*1.50	85-26	Carla111nkUnerring1034Calexico1163	Just missed	7
17May39- 7CD	fst 6½f	:23 :462 1:113 1:182	Alw 800	5	3	32	2½	1½	12	Dupuy H	102 w	*1.80	89-13	Unerring1022American Byrd112hdOlney1123	Drew out	7
1May39- 5CD	fst 6f	:223 :46 1:12	ⒻAlw 800	8	3	21½	21	31	21½	Hanford I	110 w	*3.70e	91-17	FlyingLill1051½Unerrng110nkBurgooMss112.5hd	Good effort	8
17Oct38- 4Emp	fst 5½f	:223 :47 1:053	ⒻAlw 1000	6	6	65	56	56¼	67½	Baird R	114 w	8.00	90-09	Ciencia111noThrottle Wide1115Red Eye1112	Outrun	6
11Oct38- 4Jam	fst 6f	:23 :473 1:12	ⒻAlw 1000	3	1	33½	57½	58	58½	Baird R	109 w	2.60e	83-13	Smart Crack1091½Matterhorn1143Inscoelda122hd	Outrun	6
3Oct38- 4Jam	fst 6f	:231 :472 1:132	ⒻAlw 1200	1	1	21½	35	34½	36½	Rollins C	115 w	10.00	78-15	Smart Crack1145Red Eye1121½Unerring1158	Weakened	5
30Jly38- 6AP	gd 6f	:231 :463 1:12	Arl Futurity 41k	7	3	31	53½	78	77¾	Perkins C	116 w	4.60e	79-18	Thingumabob1175No Competition1171½Hants117½	Tired	10
16Jly38- 6AP	fst 6f	:223 :454 1:113	ⒻArl Lassie 26k	2	5	76	67½	45	33½	James B	119 w	*.90e	85-07	Inscoelda1171Dinner Date1172½Unerring1195	Closed fast	9
4Jly38- 5Hol	fst 5½f	:232 :471 :593 1:06	Starlet 2.8k	3	1	22½	3½	1hd	11½	Adams J	119 w	*.60	--	Unerring1191½Kenty Miss1132½Valley Lass1162½	Easily	5
30Jun38- 3Hol	fst 5f	:231 :473 1:002	Alw 900	2	3	2hd	1hd	1hd	11½	Adams J	118 w	*.20	--	Unerring1181½Pugknows113nkMorning Breeze1132½	Easily	7
21Jun38- 3Hol	fst 5½f	:232 :474 1:063	Alw 1000	3	3	2hd	2hd	1hd	1¾	Perkins C	117 w	*1.10	--	Unerring117¾Bang1146Kenty Miss1083	Handily	6
30May38- 6CD	fst 5f	:232 :462 :59	Bashford Manor 7.1k	2	1	2½	44	41½	22	Perkins C	119 w	3.10e	98-13	Royal Pam1192Unerring119hdCherry Jam1223	Closed well	11
13May38- 4CD	fst 4½f	:224 :462 :531	Alw 800	6	6		2½	2hd	11½	Perkins C	108 w	*1.60	96-07	Unrrng1081½RangeDust1161½AmericanByrd116hd	Going away	6
10May38- 4CD	fst 4½f	:23 :472 :542	Alw 800	1	2		36	35½	1nk	Perkins C	110 w	3.00	90-11	Unerring110nkSteady Don1181¼Tack Point1131½	Hard drive	6
2Mar38- 1Hia	fst 3f	:221 :342	Alw 800	2	4			43	32	Anderson I	114 w	7.40	--	Selmalad117noThird Degree1172Unerring1141½	Closed fast	7
26Feb38- 1Hia	fst 3f	:22 :34	Alw 800	3	4			52½	41¼	Anderson I	112 w	3.10e	--	CherryJam1151Inscoelda112noSweetPtrc112nk	Strong finish	9
12Feb38- 6Hia	fst 3f	:22 :341	ⒻNursery #2 3.4k	5	4			63¼	53¾	Haas L	116 w	4.10	--	Charlotte Girl119½Sweet Patrice1161¼Throttle Wide116hd		7
	Close quarters															
8Feb38- 1Hia	fst 3f	:221 :343	ⒻMd Sp Wt	11	3			4¾	12	Haas L	116 w	*2.05e	--	Unerring1162Sister Reigh116hdCatechism116no	Going away	12
5Feb38- 1Hia	fst 3f	:22 :334	Alw 800	4	6			67½	46	Haas L	113 w	9.00	--	Hireling1182Sweet Patrice115hdSelmalad1184	Late foot	7

War Admiral

br. c. 1934, by Man o' War (Fair Play)–Brushup, by Sweep

Own.– Glen Riddle Farm Stable

Br.– Samuel D. Riddle (Ky)

Tr.– G. Conway

Lifetime record: 26 21 3 1 $273,240

Date	Cond/Dist	Fractions	Race	PP	St	1st	2nd	Str	Fin	Jockey	Wt	Odds	Speed	Top Finishers	Comment	Fld
18Feb39- 6Hia	fst 7f	:233 :464 1:104 1:224	4↑ Alw 1500	2	1	11½	11½	1½	1½	Wright WD	126 w	*.20	99-05	WarAdmrl126½Psturzd11912SndyBoot110	Mild hand ride late	3
12Nov38- 5Nar	fst 1⅛	:472 1:113 1:372 1:512	3↑ Rhode Island H 11k	6	2	1nk	12½	16	12½	Kurtsinger C	127 w	*.20	91-17	War Admiral1272½Mucho Gusto1151Busy K.112no	Eased up	6
1Nov38- 6Pim	fst 1 3/16	:473 1:114 1:364 1:563	3↑ Pim Spl 15k	1	2	21	2no	2½	24	Kurtsinger C	120 w	*.25	97-08	Seabiscuit1204War Admiral120	No excuse	2
1Oct38- 5Bel	fst 2	:522 2:343 2:591 3:244	3↑ J C Gold Cup 7k	2	1	11½	12	12	13	Wright WD	124 w	*.08	85-12	War Admiral1243Magic Hour11710Jolly Tar1173	Galloping	3
	Geldings not eligible															
27Aug38- 5Sar	fst 1¾	:484 2:051 2:302 2:554	3↑ Sar Cup 8.3k	3	1	11½	11½	11½	14	Peters M	126 w	*.33	96-08	War Admiral1264Esposa12110Anaflame111	Easily	3
20Aug38- 5Sar	fst 1¼	:473 1:123 1:38 2:034	3↑ Whitney 3.7k	3	1	13	12	11	11	Wright WD	126 w	*.33	90-11	War Admiral1261Esposa12110Fighting Fox117	Handily	3
	Geldings not eligible															
30Jly38- 5Sar	sl 1¼	:491 1:14 1:39 2:06	3↑ Saratoga H 10k	5	1	12	11	12	1nk	Kurtsinger C	130 w	*.70	79-16	War Admiral130nkEsposa1165Isolater105.54	Under drive	5
27Jly38- 5Sar	my 1	:24 :481 1:13 1:392	3↑ Wilson 3.9k	3	2	1½	11½	13	18	Kurtsinger C	126 w	*.60	84-19	War Admiral1268Fighting Fox1161½Esposa121	Much best	3
	Geldings not eligible															
29Jun38- 6Suf	hy 1⅛	:481 1:132 1:393 1:523	3↑ Mass H 59k	6	4	32½	24	33	48¼	Kurtsinger C	130 w	*.40	74-28	Menow1078Busy K.107nkWar Minstrel106no	Weakened	6
6Jun38- 5Aqu	fst 1	:23 :461 1:112 1:364	3↑ Queens County H 6.1k	1	2	22	21	11½	11	Kurtsinger C	132 w	*.55	96-14	War Admiral1321Snark1267Danger Point1121½	Driving	4
5Mar38- 6Hia	fst 1¼	:471 1:113 1:37 2:034	3↑ Widener H 63k	13	3	11	13	15	11½	Kurtsinger C	130 w	*.35	90-12	War Admiral1301½Zevson104½War Minstrel1111	Eased up	13
19Feb38- 5Hia	fst 7f	:23 :452 1:101 1:234	4↑ Alw 1100	6	3	2nk	11½	14	11½	Kurtsinger C	122	*.30	94-13	WarAdmiral1221½SirOracle1166CaballeroII1102½	Eased up	6
3Nov37- 5Pim	fst 1 3/16	:462 1:112 1:38 1:584	Pim Spl H 8.2k	1	2	31	21½	12	11½	Kurtsinger C	128 w	*.05	96-13	WarAdmrl1281½MaskedGenrl1004WrMnstrl109no	Won driving	4
30Oct37- 5Lrl	gd 1¼	:48 1:13 1:384 2:044	3↑ Washington H 19k	7	3	11	13	11½	11½	Kurtsinger C	126 w	*.65	86-22	War Admiral1261½Heelfly1192Burning Star1183	Easily	7
26Oct37- 5Lrl	fst 1 1/16	:241 :48 1:131 1:46	3↑ Alw 1200	8	1	13	13	14	12½	Kurtsinger C	106 w	*.40	87-21	War Admiral1062½Aneroid1134Floradora107hd	Easily	8
5Jun37- 5Bel	fst 1½	:48 1:121 2:021 2:283	Belmont 46k	7	2	13	14	13	13	Kurtsinger C	126 w	*.90	101-06	War Admiral1263Sceneshifter12610Vamoose1262	Easily best	7
15May37- 6Pim	gd 1 3/16	:47 1:122 1:373 1:582	Preakness 55k	1	2	11	11	1hd	1hd	Kurtsinger C	126 w	*.35	98-16	War Admiral126hdPompoon1268Flying Scot1262	Hard drive	8
8May37- 6CD	fst 1¼	:464 1:122 1:372 2:031	Ky Derby 62k	1	2	11½	11½	13	11¾	Kurtsinger C	126 w	*1.60	93-11	War Admiral1261¾Pompoon1268Reaping Reward1263	In hand	20
24Apr37- 5HdG	fst 1 1/16	:232 :472 1:113 1:45	Chesapeake 11k	3	1	11	12	14	16	Kurtsinger C	119 w	*.65e	93-15	WarAdmiral1196CourtScandal119½OverthTop1142	Easily best	7
14Apr37- 4HdG	fst 6f	:23 :461 1:112	Alw 1000	2	1	1hd	12	13	12½	Kurtsinger C	120 w	*.75	96-16	War Admiral1202½Clingendaal1116Airflame1173	In hand	6
10Oct36- 5Lrl	my 6f	:232 :473 1:123	Richard Johnson H 5k	2	2	1hd	2½	22	21½	Kurtsinger C	124 w	*.80	89-23	BottleCap1191½WarAdmiral1248YellowTulp1141½	Closed well	10
19Sep36- 5HdG	fst 6f	:223 :454 1:11	Eastern Shore H 14k	15	1	11½	14	14	15	Kurtsinger C	118 w	7.85	98-12	War Admiral1185Orientalist116hdRex Flag115hd	Easily	15
1Jly36- 5Aqu	fst 6f	:232 :473 1:123	Great American 5.4k	6	3	1hd	1hd	1hd	21½	Kurtsinger C	115 w	2.00	89-15	Fairy Hill1131½War Admiral1152Maedic115½	Weakened	8
6Jun36- 4Bel	fst 5f-WC	:59	National Stallion 16k	6	2		53½	31½	32½	Westrope J	122 w	3.00	82-14	Pompoon1221½Fencing1221War Admiral122hd	Closed gamely	10
21May36- 3Bel	fst 5f-WC	:584	©Alw 900	6	3		1hd	11	12	Westrope J	113 w	10.00	86-18	War Admiral1132Scintillator1135Papenie1161	Going away	8
25Apr36- 1HdG	fst 4½f	:233 :483 :551	Md Sp Wt	9	4		2hd	2½	1no	Peters M	114 w	7.50	89-11	War Admiral114noSonny Joe1141Ground Oak1142½	Hard drive	10

WAR HORSES

THE 1940's

by David Grening

WO OF THE MAJOR themes for Thoroughbred racing in the 1940's were established on September 1, 1939. It was the day trainer Ben A. Jones and his son Jimmy went to work for Warren and Lucille Wright's Calumet Farm. On the same day, German armed forces invaded Poland, essentially kicking off World War II.

The merger of the Joneses and the Wrights helped turn Calumet into the dominant stable of the forties. In a decade that spawned four Triple Crown winners, two – Whirlaway in 1941 and Citation in 1948 – wore the devil's-red and blue silks of Calumet. All told, the farm produced nine champion Thoroughbreds in the forties, garnering 19 titles, including five Horse of the Year trophies. In 7 of the 10 seasons, Calumet was the leading money-winning owner, three times topping the $1 million plateau.

Meanwhile, as the war grew in stature – and America's role in it increased – Thoroughbred racing did its part to aid the effort. In addition to contributing millions of dollars to the cause, the country's racetracks were often used by U.S. armed forces during nonracing periods. Toward the end of the war, in 1945, the government shut down racing for four months. The sport had enjoyed a great

renaissance until then, and fans came back in droves when racing resumed that May.

Calumet's Whirlaway and John D. Hertz's Count Fleet, the 1943 Triple Crown winner, whetted fans' appetites in the first half of the decade. In the second half, racing enthusiasts were treated to a pair of Triple Crown winners that included Citation, arguably the top Thoroughbred of all time. The bay son of Bull Lea topped Calumet's

Whirlaway was the first of two Triple Crown winners to fly the Calumet Farm colors in the 1940's. The devil's-red and blue silks were atop nine champions during the decade.

amazing run with a 16-race winning streak that began on April 17, 1948, and lasted through January 11, 1950. Despite an injury that sidelined him a year, Citation became the first million-dollar earner in the sport and set a standard for greatness that few, if any, would ever match.

Warren Wright Sr., heir to the Calumet Baking Powder Company, began racing Thoroughbreds in 1932. Unable to achieve his lofty goals with trainers Bert Williams and Frank Kearns, Wright and his wife, Lucille, summoned Ben and Jimmy Jones, who had paired to win the 1938 Kentucky Derby with Lawrin, to the Drake Hotel in Chicago for a breakfast meeting in July 1939.

"'We want to win the Kentucky Derby,'" Jimmy Jones recalled Lucille Wright saying at the beginning of the discussion. "We said, 'We do, too.'"

The Joneses, who had had a falling-out with their primary owner, Herbert Woolf, accepted the Wrights' offer on the spot and went to work on September 1.

Success came swiftly for the new team. On January 10, 1940, opening day at Hialeah, Ben Jones sent out three winners for Calumet. A week later, he had four straight winners, three in major handicaps. Calumet won 75 races in 1940, second only to the 112 of Mrs. Emil Denemark. Calumet's earnings of $148,470 ranked third behind Charles S. Howard and the Greentree Stable of Mrs. Payne Whitney.

Almost half of that amount belonged to a 2-year-old son of Epsom Derby winner Blenheim II, a prolific yet problematic colt named Whirlaway. Overcoming a tendency to bear out in the stretch, Whirlaway won 7 of 16 starts that year, including the Saratoga Special, the Hopeful, and the Breeders' Futurity. He was denied a championship by Woodvale Farm's Our Boots, who only won 3 of 6 starts but finished ahead of Whirlaway 3 of the 4 times they met.

Despite the success of 1940, the Wright-Jones relationship almost did not make it past the next spring.

Whirlaway had finished first and third in two February allowance races to begin his 3-year-old season. Ben Jones, unhappy with the way Whirlaway had been training, decided to skip the Flamingo Stakes and wait for the Tropical Park meet. On March 28, six days after another third-place finish and five weeks before the Kentucky Derby, he entered the colt in a 5 ½-furlong dash. Wright, who was vacationing in the Florida Keys, was surprised to see Whirlaway's name in the entries for so short a race and rushed to Tropical Park to confront the trainer.

"We sat there and argued with the old man until it was too late to scratch him," Jimmy Jones said. "We won that argument. Then the horse, luckily, got up in the last few strides and won his race. Everybody congratulated [Wright]. He got into the spirit of things, shook hands, and said to us, 'I'm going to tell you fellas, I'm never going to bother you again.' But he did."

In Kentucky, Whirlaway's problems persisted. He bore out in the Blue Grass Stakes and was beaten six lengths by Our Boots. He did it again in the Derby Trial, five days before the Kentucky Derby. In a move that exemplified his greatness, Ben Jones saw fit to make an equipment change.

He decided to use a one-eyed blinker, with the cup on the outside, so that the vision in Whirlaway's right eye would be restricted. It would force the colt to rely more on his jockey, giving the rider added control. On the day before the Derby, Jones tested his experiment with Whirlaway's new rider, Eddie Arcaro. Arcaro, although under contract to Greentree, was available to ride Whirlaway because Greentree had no contender that year. Jones instructed Arcaro to blow Whirlaway out through the Churchill Downs stretch, then sat atop his pony and positioned himself 10 feet off the inside rail. He told Arcaro to bring Whirlaway through the opening.

"I had some doubts," Arcaro was quoted as saying. "But if that old man was game enough to sit there and risk me running him over, I was game enough to go through that narrow opening.

Whirlaway handled it perfectly and I felt we had a great shot in the Derby."

The next day, Whirlaway rallied from far back to win the Kentucky Derby by a record eight lengths in a track-record time of 2:01⅖ for 1¼ miles. A week later, he came from last to take the Preakness before whipping three opponents in the June 7 Belmont Stakes to become the sport's fifth Triple Crown winner. Whirlaway won 13 of 20 starts in 1941 and was voted 3-year-old champion and Horse of the Year. Calumet was the country's leading owner with $475,091, a single-season record the stable would shatter three years later.

In 1942, Whirlaway won 12 of 22 starts, including the Massachusetts Handicap on July 15; that victory pushed his earnings to $454,336 and enabled him to surpass Seabiscuit ($437,730) as the sport's all-time leading money winner. He was voted champion handicap horse and repeated as Horse of the Year despite losing 2 of 3 meetings to Albert Sabath's 3-year-old Alsab, who nosed out Whirlaway in a match race at Narragansett Park in Rhode Island. Alsab, who had compiled a 10-race winning streak in 1941 to be named the champion 2-year-old, was voted the top 3-year-old although Shut Out beat him in both the Kentucky Derby and the Belmont.

On June 28, 1943, two days after Whirlaway pulled up sore in the Equipoise Mile, Wright announced the horse's retirement. He finished his career with 32 wins from 60 starts and earnings of $561,161. Within a week, however, it was clear that Calumet's domination was not about to stop. On June 30, Mar-Kell won her eighth race of the season, the Cinderella Handicap, en route to being named that year's champion handicap mare. Still, there was an even more talented filly in the barn.

Twilight Tear, who won 4 of 6 starts as a 2-year-old in 1943, won 11 consecutive races from March 10 through July 22, 1944, and became the first filly to be awarded Horse of the Year honors. (Busher, owned by Col. Edward R. Bradley's Idle Hour Stock Farm, duplicated the feat the next year.) Her streak culminated with a victory in the Arlington

Classic, in which she beat four colts. Among them was her stablemate Pensive, who had given Calumet its second Kentucky Derby trophy earlier that year.

All in all, Twilight Tear won 14 of 17 starts in 1944, highlighted by a six-length victory against two colts in the Pimlico Special. She was beset by bleeding problems throughout her career, according to Jimmy Jones, and when she bled in an allowance race at Washington Park in August 1945, she was retired.

Twilight Tear was among the first crop of Bull Lea, who went on to sire seven Calumet champions of the decade. Bull Lea was purchased by Warren Wright for $14,000 at the Saratoga yearling sales of 1936. Many bidders stayed away from the colt because of his four white feet, which, in those days, were deemed to be a bad sign. Bull Lea went on to bank more than $90,000 and was the leading sire in 5 of the 7 years from 1947 through 1953.

In addition to Twilight Tear, Bull Lea's first crop included a dynamo named Armed. Bad ankles sidelined him as a 2-year-old, and his ornery behavior forced his castration before he ever raced. At one point, Calumet made him a lead pony. But

Twilight Tear won 11 straight races in 1944 en route to becoming the first filly to be voted Horse of the Year.

after a while, he shed his nasty disposition and developed into a champion.

Armed had an unspectacular 3-year-old season, winning 3 of 7 outings. In 1945, he came to hand, winning 10 of 15 starts, but only three stakes. Meanwhile, Mrs. Ethel D. Jacobs's Stymie won eight stakes and outpolled Armed for top handicap horse honors.

Stymie and Armed began a two-year rivalry in 1946, with the Calumet runner defeating Stymie twice. On May 30, a crowd of 60,631 – then a New York record – watched Armed, under 130 pounds and spotting Stymie seven, win the Suburban Handicap decisively. Armed won 11 of 18 starts that year and was voted top handicap horse. The Horse of the Year, however, was Assault, the 3-year-old who had swept the Triple Crown.

Armed returned in 1947 and not only captured his second handicap division title, but also was named Horse of the Year. He won 11 of 17 starts, set two track records, and finished worse than third only once – in the Santa Anita Handicap, when he was flown cross-country from Florida and may not have overcome the trip. The brown gelding, who carried a minimum of 130 pounds in 21 of 35 races over his two championship seasons, proved durable enough to race until the age of 9. His

The great handicap champion Armed blossomed as a 4-year-old, winning 10 of 15 races. He would go on to win consecutive handicap titles in 1946 and 1947.

career, which ended on a winning note in an allowance race at Gulfstream, concluded with a record of 41-20-10 from 81 starts and career earnings of $817,475.

"He was probably the best handicap horse of his time," Jimmy Jones said. "But, he wasn't a great horse. To be great, you got to be able to do everything great. Armed couldn't handle off tracks, for instance."

While Armed ruled the handicap ranks in 1947, Calumet had a dynamic pair of 2-year-olds to dominate their respective divisions. A filly named Bewitch and a colt named Citation would be awarded championships as Calumet won 100 races and earned $1,402,436, a mark that stood for 22 years.

Citation was 5 for 5 and Bewitch was 7 for 7 when the two met in the Washington Park Futurity on August 16. Free America, another Calumet colt, was 3 for 4, and the three-ply entry was 1-5 at the windows. Bewitch used her dazzling speed to win by a length, although many believe that had jockey Steve Brooks so desired, he could have gotten Citation home. Free America finished third.

"I told the riders we would split the jocks' fee three ways; whoever is in front, leave them alone," Jones related. "I didn't want them to be beating up these horses. Each of the losing riders said, 'If I could have hit my horse a time or two I would have won.'"

Citation defeated Bewitch in Belmont's Futurity and finished his season with a three-length romp in the Pimlico Futurity. He was a unanimous choice for champion 2-year-old colt. Citation, who was primarily trained by Jimmy Jones, began his 3-year-old career by defeating older horses in his first start. Among his victims in the six-furlong race was Armed, whom he would beat again in the Seminole Handicap nine days later.

Returning to his own division, Citation won two more races, the Everglades and the Flamingo, as he competed four times in 26 days during February. After his victory in the Flamingo, Wright was offered $250,000 for Citation. Upon hearing of the offer, Jimmy Jones was quoted as saying, "Whoever buys this horse has got to buy me too, because I'm going with him."

Citation lost his regular jockey in March when Albert Snider drowned while fishing in the Florida Keys. Jones said Snider "fit Citation better than anybody." Eddie Arcaro, who became Citation's rider, lost the first time he rode him when they were carried wide in the Chesapeake Trial at Havre de Grace and finished second to a colt called Saggy. Citation proved the result a fluke five days later when he beat Saggy by 15½ lengths in the Chesapeake Stakes. Thus began the bay colt's 16-race winning streak, which of course included the 1948 Triple Crown.

In the Derby, Citation followed stablemate Coaltown until the stretch, when Arcaro began a steady hand ride that propelled him past Coaltown and on to a 3½-length victory. Two weeks later, against only three rivals in the Preakness, Citation went wire to wire, winning by 5½ lengths. In need of activity before the Belmont, he set a track record winning the Jersey Stakes at Garden State in a track record of 2:03 for 10 furlongs.

Then came the Belmont. A slight stumble at the start provided the lone anxious moment as Citation again went gate to wire, winning by eight lengths in a gallop that was only three-fifths of a second off the track record. He missed some of the summer with a strained back, but went on to win nine more races that year, including the Jockey Club Gold Cup, which he won under double wraps.

"Truly the best one we ever had," Jimmy Jones said. "I never saw a better one."

His last race of 1948 was the 1¼-mile Tanforan Handicap at Tanforan Park in San Francisco. Jimmy Jones was not keen on running Citation there, but was doing a friend a favor. Eugene Mori had taken over the track and wanted to turn San Francisco into a racing center, and there was no better way to do that than have the sport's brightest star shine on your racetrack.

Citation romped in a six-furlong prep on December 3; eight days later, he treated 24,809 fans to a track record of 2:02⅖ in his five-length victory in the Tanforan Handicap, but the race proved to be his undoing. According to Jones, there was concrete on the bottom of the racing strip and Citation injured his ankle. He would never be the same. In the winter of 1949, over Jones's objection, Wright had a veterinarian pin-fire the ankle. It didn't help. Citation would not race that year, and when he came back, he was a mere shell of his former self. While he did win his first start back – his 16th victory in a row – he would only take one of his next 12. Of course, the lone triumph was spectacular, as he set a world record of 1:33⅗ in the Golden Gate Mile.

Determined to make Citation the first equine millionaire, Wright, whose health was failing, opted to keep him in training. The owner died on December 28, 1950, but the quest continued under the direction of his widow, and seven months later Citation topped the million-dollar mark by winning the Hollywood Gold Cup. He promptly was retired with earnings of $1,085,760.

"He would have been better off if he had never run in those races in California," Jones said. "He should never be judged on his races after that injury."

While Citation did not race in 1949, it hardly prevented Calumet from maintaining its status as the nation's leading money-winning owner; the stable had another talented Bull Lea colt in Coaltown, who might have been every bit as good as Citation if not for wind problems.

After living in Citation's shadow during his 3-year-old campaign, Coaltown established his own greatness in 1949 by winning 12 of 15 starts and setting a world record of 1:34 in the one-mile Whirlaway Stakes at Washington Park. While he was not good enough to handle the 3-year-old champion, Capot, he was still named the top handicap horse.

In fact, Calumet ended 1949 with four champions, as Bewitch was named top handicap mare and Two Lea and Wistful shared 3-year-old filly honors.

As the 1940's began, racing was flourishing, with new highs for attendance and handle being established on a regular basis. One of the most signifi-

Considered by some to be the greatest Thoroughbred of all time, Citation had a long list of accomplishments, including winning the Triple Crown in 1948, going a record 16 straight races without defeat, and becoming the first horse to earn $1 million.

cant developments of the decade came at the outset, when New York legalized parimutuel wagering and more than $100,000,000 was bet during that first year, far exceeding expectations. Record crowds were going to Jamaica and Belmont, and records were also being set at tracks in Maryland and Florida.

If World War II threatened to end that prosperity, racing did its best not to let that happen. In March 1942, four months after the bombing of Pearl Harbor resulted in the United States' complete participation in the war, the Thoroughbred Racing Associations was formed "for purpose of aiding government financially and in other ways." From that association, the Turf Committee of America was born, and under the leadership of New York Racing Commissioner Herbert Bayard Swope, a plan for racing to help the war-relief effort was devised.

A goal of $2 million was established, to be obtained in three ways. First, each track would donate a percentage of its profits for certain racing periods. Second, there would be days at each meet when all profits would go to the fund. Third, a self-imposed assessment on per capita attendance would be donated.

Racing contributed $3.19 million to the war effort in 1942 and surpassed that with more than $5 million in 1943. On October 2, 1943, Belmont Park hosted a "Back the Attack" day, with admission to the grandstand by purchase of a $25 war bond, or a $100 bond for clubhouse admission. An estimated $25,000,000 in bonds were sold. Such a response evoked a telegram of praise and appreciation from Henry Morgenthau, secretary of the treasury.

The U.S. armed forces took over several racetracks, including Hialeah, Fair Grounds, and Santa Anita, for varying war-related purposes. Santa Anita was used as an ordnance school, and later as a processing facility for local Japanese Americans, who were then sent to more permanent internment camps. Stalls served as actual living quarters. Tanforan Park, in San Francisco, was used by the Navy as a training base.

Race meetings were consolidated – and in some cases, canceled – as a way to conserve gas and rubber products. The 1943 Arlington meet was held at Washington Park. Belmont Park hosted the Saratoga meet for three years from 1943-45. Ak-Sar-Ben canceled its meeting in order not to interfere with the Army's operations at Ak-Sar-Ben Field.

In 1944, with racetracks still prospering, the sport contributed more than $8 million to the war-relief effort. However, in December, James F. Byrnes, director of War Mobilization and Reconversion, issued a request that racing cease by January 3, 1945. Tropical Park and Fair Grounds, the only tracks in operation at the time, put an end to their meetings. Racing was shut down for more than four months.

On May 12, action resumed at Narragansett Park in Rhode Island and Sportsman's Park in Illinois. Santa Anita, which had not raced since late 1941, opened on May 15 and offered free admission to those who purchased war bonds. On May 30, the track welcomed a record crowd of 76,649. New marks were also established at Jamaica (64,537) and Delaware Park (28,000) that day.

The Triple Crown was run in three successive weeks, with Fred Hooper's Hoop Jr. winning the Kentucky Derby on June 9, Mrs. P. A. B. Widener's Polynesian winning the Preakness on June 16, and Walter Jeffords's Pavot taking the Belmont on June 23.

That fall, with fans still purchasing millions of dollars of war bonds, racing showed it had recovered from the war when in September, Belmont Park established a world record in parimutuel wagering as $5,016,745 was bet on an eight-race card. A single-race record of $763,127 was wagered on the nightcap.

In 1942, the United States initiated a gasoline-rationing program that meant fans could only attend races by streetcar or horse-drawn vehicles. That didn't stop them from coming out to the track, especially on the occasions when Count Fleet raced.

Count Fleet's career only lasted 370 days – from June 1, 1942, through June 5, 1943 – but what a glorious 370 days they were. Never off the board in 21 career starts, the John Hertz-bred and -owned colt won 10 of 15 races as a 2-year-old en route to a divisional title.

Amazingly, Hertz, the rental-car and Yellow Cab magnate, almost sold the son of Reigh Count for

$4,500 because of his difficult temperament. Jockey Johnny Longden convinced the owner not to sell. "The colt is dangerous," Hertz said. "I'm afraid he'll do you serious injury." Longden replied, "I'm not afraid of him." Satisfied, Hertz decided to keep Count Fleet.

By the fall of that year, Hertz was glad he had. In late September, while preparing for the Futurity at Belmont, the colt worked six furlongs in 1:08 ⅗, a full second faster than the track record. He would finish third in the Futurity.

Count Fleet made amends a week later with a six-length victory in the Champagne Stakes. He covered a mile in 1:34 ⅘, a world record for a 2-year-old. His stakes record would last for 34 years. After closing out his season with three more dominant victories, Count Fleet was assigned top weight of 132 pounds on the Experimental Free Handicap, still the highest assignment since the handicap's debut in 1933.

With Tropical Park ending its 1943 race meeting on January 8 to aid the government's gasoline-conservation plan, Count Fleet was sent to Oaklawn Park instead, where he trained for six weeks, and then on to Belmont. Trainer Don Cameron did not bring Count Fleet to the races for his 3-year-old

Triple Crown winner Count Fleet was almost sold by owner John D. Hertz for $4,500. The Reigh Count colt would win 16 of 21 starts, including a then-record 25-length victory in the Belmont, the final race of his career.

debut until April 13, when he won an allowance race at Jamaica that served as a prep for the Wood Memorial. He then took the Wood four days later, slicing two seconds off the stakes record, but came out of the race with a gash in his left hind leg and was pulled up bleeding.

Cameron had two weeks to work on the injury, and by the first Saturday in May, Count Fleet was ready to go. Despite the transportation restrictions, a crowd of 61,700 fans showed up at Churchill Downs for what was dubbed the Streetcar Derby. They got what they came for as Count Fleet, at odds of 1-2, soared to a three-length victory. A week later, against only three rivals, he galloped to an eight-length score in the Preakness. With a month before the Belmont, Cameron opted to run Count Fleet in the Withers, and he whipped two opponents by five lengths.

As expected, the Belmont turned into a coronation for Count Fleet. Before a crowd of 19,290, he beat only two rivals by 25 lengths in stakes-record time of 2:28⅕ to become racing's sixth Triple Crown winner. Unfortunately, he came out of the race with an ankle injury. Eventually, Cameron would

announce that the tendon was affected as well, and Count Fleet would never race again.

"He was the best horse I ever rode," Longden said. "The best horse I ever saw."

On August 6, 1945, the day the United States dropped an atomic bomb on Hiroshima, Japan, a chestnut colt named Assault burst on the scene with a nose victory at 70-1 in the Flash Stakes, the opening-day feature at the Saratoga-at-Belmont meeting. It was one of only two victories that Assault, the King Ranch-bred and -owned son of 1936 Kentucky Derby and Preakness winner Bold Venture, tallied in his 2-year-old season.

Assault was a colt whose will to win helped him overcome myriad physical problems. As a weanling at Robert J. Kleberg Jr.'s King Ranch in Texas, he stepped on a sharp object that pierced his right front foot. As a result, he developed an unorthodox gait, which made him quite difficult to train. Max Hirsch, who had also handled Bold Venture, once said, "I didn't think he'd train at all. But, he's never shown any sign that it hurts him. When he walks or trots, you'd think he was going to fall down. I think that while the foot still hurt him, he got in the habit of protecting it with an awkward gait, and now he keeps it up. But he gallops true. There isn't a thing wrong with his action when he goes fast."

Assault, whose other injuries included several splints, an unreliable knee, and a wrenched ankle, did not make his 3-year-old debut until April 9, when he won the six-furlong Experimental Handicap at Jamaica. Eleven days later, against a strong headwind that caused some horses trouble, Assault scored by 2¼ lengths in the Wood Memorial. A muddy track may have compromised him when he finished a nonthreatening fourth in the Derby Trial at Churchill on April 30.

Four days later, Assault bounced back and roared to an eight-length victory in the Kentucky Derby. A premature move by jockey Warren Mehrtens nearly cost the colt the Preakness, a race he won by a neck over the traffic-troubled, late-

Assault overcame numerous physical problems to win the Triple Crown in 1946 and went on to have a solid season as a handicapper in 1947.

closing Lord Boswell. The Belmont, in which Lord Boswell was favored, was not nearly so close, as Assault bounded clear to a three-length victory over Natchez.

In the fall of his 3-year-old season, after being sidelined for six weeks, Assault met up with another of the walking wounded – Stymie, who at one time was owned by King Ranch. The two began a prolonged rivalry that lasted for the next two years. In 1946, Stymie beat Assault in 2 of 3 meetings. The next year, Assault defeated Stymie 4 of 5 times.

One of those races in 1947 was the Butler Handicap at Jamaica. Assault, who was 4 for 4 for the year and had a six-race winning streak dating back to November 9, 1946, was assigned 135 pounds by racing secretary John Campbell. He was conceding nine pounds to Stymie and 18 to Gallorette, the 1946 champion handicap mare. Assault, who by this time was being ridden by Eddie Arcaro, was moving into contention when Arcaro was forced to take up to avoid a tiring Risolator. Turning for home, Assault was last. In the stretch, Arcaro had him running again, but he was knocked off stride and back to last with a furlong to go. Somehow, he managed a third run, squeezed through horses, and defeated Stymie by a head.

Eleven years later, *Daily Racing Form* columnist Leon Rasmussen wrote, "When a lightly weighted horse gets thrown off stride, it's not too difficult for his rider to get him going again, but when it happens to a highweight, only a superior horse can answer the extra demand successfully. Therefore, when the talk turns to great races, Assault's Butler in 1947 receives my award for the best individual performance by a horse in my time."

With as many ailments as Assault had, it was remarkable that he lasted as long as he did, finally retiring after making three starts in late 1950 off a year layoff. He retired with 18 wins from 42 races and earnings of $675,470. "He was always crippled, and a horse with less determination would have quit," said King Ranch veterinarian Dr. James Northway.

Even in retirement, Assault had physical problems. He was sterile and was never able to produce any offspring. He died at the age of 28 on September 1, 1971.

"I never trained a better horse," said Max Hirsch.

While Stymie was almost as good, it certainly wasn't apparent from the beginning. Few horses were as durable as this one, who raced 131 times in a seven-year career that saw him go from frog to Prince Charming.

Hirsch had turned Stymie's dam, Stop Watch, over to King Ranch, but had not completed the necessary paperwork by the time the foal arrived in 1941, so he was officially credited with being the breeder of the colt. Stymie had a nasty disposition as a young horse and it obviously affected his ability. He had not shown much to his trainer, who put Stymie in claiming races in 2 of his first 3 starts.

On June 2, 1943, Hirsch Jacobs – the leading trainer in number of races won for 9 of the previous 10 years – put in a claim slip and took Stymie for $1,500 for his wife, Ethel. The son of Equestrian needed 10 more tries to finally find the winner's circle. Through his first two years of racing, Stymie had won just 7 of 50 starts, not one of them a stakes event. Thanks mainly to the government's ban on racing in early 1945, Stymie went nearly seven months between his 3-year-old finale and his 4-year-old debut. The rest appeared to do him a world of good.

A rejuvenated Stymie won his first stakes on June 2, 1945, taking the Grey Lag Handicap at Jamaica. He would go on to win seven more stakes that year en route to being named champion handicap horse. Stymie excelled as a 5-year-old as well, winning 8 of 20 starts and finishing out of the money only once. He equaled the track record for nine furlongs at Jamaica and set a track mark for 1⅜ miles there that same season.

In 1947, Stymie won seven stakes races and kept alternating with Assault as the all-time leading money-winning Thoroughbred. Although Assault had his number, defeating him in 4 of 5 meetings, Stymie would finish the year as the leading money earner after winning the Gallant Fox Handicap in October.

In July 1948, Stymie fractured a sesamoid at Monmouth Park with his bankroll at $911,335, the highest of any Thoroughbred. His connections tried to make him the first million-dollar earner,

The working-class hero Stymie was claimed for $1,500 by Hall of Fame trainer Hirsch Jacobs. At the time of his retirement he was the richest Thoroughbred ever.

but after five starts in the fall of 1949, it was evident it was not going to happen. He retired with $918,485 in earnings, a figure that would be eclipsed by Citation 15 months later.

In many respects, Stymie may have embodied the sport better than any horse of the decade. A warrior with the utmost courage, Stymie overcame a number of obstacles and not only succeeded, but also flourished. His career interrupted by the war-related ban on racing, Stymie was much better in the second half of the decade than he was in the first.

And despite fears to the contrary, so was racing. Having drawn fans in record numbers – buoyed by the exploits of wartime Triple Crown winners Whirlaway and Count Fleet – racing not only survived, but also prospered following the four-month government shutdown in 1945. Tracks throughout the country continued to boom during the last half of the decade. The success of Calumet Farm, as well as that of King Ranch, helped give full flight to the big-stable era and sent racing into the 1950's as the true Sport of Kings.

Champions

Past Performances

THE 1940'S

•1940•
•2-Year-Old Male *Our Boots* •2-Year-Old Filly *Level Best* •3-Year-Old Male *Bimelech*
•Handicap Horse *Challedon* •Handicap Mare *War Plumage*
•**HORSE OF THE YEAR** Challedon

•1941•
•2-Year-Old Male *Alsab* •2-Year-Old Filly *Petrify* •3-Year-Old Male *Whirlaway*
•3-Year-Old Filly *Painted Veil* •Handicap Horse *Mioland* •Handicap Mare *Fairy Chant*
•Steeplechase *Speculate*
•**HORSE OF THE YEAR** Whirlaway

•1942•
•2-Year-Old Male *Count Fleet* •2-Year-Old Filly *Ask Me Now* •3-Year-Old Male *Alsab*
•3-Year-Old Filly *Vagrancy* •Handicap Horse *Whirlaway* •Handicap Mare *Vagrancy* •Steeplechase *Elkridge*
•**HORSE OF THE YEAR** Whirlaway

•1943•
•2-Year-Old Male *Platter* •2-Year-Old Filly *Duranza* •3-Year-Old Male *Count Fleet*
•3-Year-Old Filly *Stefanita* •Handicap Horse *Market Wise, Devil Diver* •Handicap Mare *Mar-Kell*
•Steeplechase *Brother Jones*
•**HORSE OF THE YEAR** Count Fleet

•1944•
•2-Year-Old Male *Pavot* •2-Year-Old Filly *Busher* •3-Year-Old Male *By Jimminy*
•3-Year-Old Filly *Twilight Tear* •Handicap Horse *Devil Diver* •Handicap Mare *Twilight Tear*
•Steeplechase *Rouge Dragon*
•**HORSE OF THE YEAR** Twilight Tear

•1945•
•2-Year-Old Male *Star Pilot* •2-Year-Old Filly *Beaugay* •3-Year-Old Male *Fighting Step*
•3-Year-Old Filly *Busher* •Handicap Horse *Stymie* •Handicap Mare *Busher* •Steeplechase *Mercator*
•**HORSE OF THE YEAR** Busher

•1946•
•2-Year-Old Male *Double Jay* •2-Year-Old Filly *First Flight* •3-Year-Old Male *Assault*
•3-Year-Old Filly *Bridal Flower* •Handicap Horse *Armed* •Handicap Mare *Gallorette* •Steeplechase *Elkridge*
•**HORSE OF THE YEAR** Assault

•1947•
•2-Year-Old Male *Citation* •2-Year-Old Filly *Bewitch* •3-Year-Old Male *Phalanx*
•3-Year-Old Filly *But Why Not* •Handicap Horse *Armed* •Handicap Mare *But Why Not*
•Sprinter *Polynesian* •Steeplechase *War Battle*
•**HORSE OF THE YEAR** Armed

•1948•
•2-Year-Old Male *Blue Peter* •2-Year-Old Filly *Myrtle Charm* •3-Year-Old Male *Citation*
•3-Year-Old Filly *Miss Request* •Handicap Horse *Citation* •Handicap Mare *Conniver*
•Sprinter *Coaltown* •Steeplechase *American Way*
•**HORSE OF THE YEAR** Citation

•1949•
•2-Year-Old Male *Hill Prince* •2-Year-Old Filly *Bed o' Roses* •3-Year-Old Male *Capot*
•3-Year-Old Filly *Two Lea, Wistful* •Handicap Horse *Coaltown* •Handicap Mare *Bewitch*
•Sprinter *Delegate, Royal Governor* •Steeplechase *Trough Hill*
•**HORSE OF THE YEAR** Capot

Alsab

b. c. 1939, by Good Goods (Neddie)–Winds Chant, by Wildair

Lifetime record: 51 25 11 5 $350,015

Own.– Mrs A. Sabath
Br.– Thomas Piatt (Ky)
Tr.– A. Swenke

13May44- 5Bel	fst 6f	:222 :453 1:103 3↑	Handicap 4085	6 6 67¾ 78¼ 57 44½	Haas L	126wb	11.80	92-10	Bossut1164Adultr112noShtOut132½	Finished well,pulled up sore	7
13Nov43- 6Pim	fst 1 3/16	:484 1:141 1:402 2:00 3↑	Bryan & O'Hara H 19k	6 3 77¾ 77¾ 51½ 2nk	Woolf G	122wb	*1.10	82-31	Stefanita117nkAlsab1223Son of Peace1131	Fast finish	9
8Nov43- 8Pim	sly 1 1/16	:241 :494 1:161 1:494 3↑	Alw 2000	1 2 31 52½ 2nk 13	Woolf G	122wb	*2.30	69-28	Alsab1223Abrasion1172Rascal110nk	In hand late	7
30Oct43- 8Pim	sl 6f	:224 :463 1:13 3↑	Alw 3500	4 9 912 917 915 815¼	Woolf G	123 w	7.15	73-27	QuienEs1162½ReapngGlory107nkPompon113hd	Showed nothing	9
14Aug43- 6Nar	sl 1 1/16	:254 :49 1:14 1:464 3↑	King Philip H 6.5k	6 11 119¾ 77¾ 68¾ 47½	Woolf G	126wb	*.60	75-26	Some Chance1102Eire1042½Air Master1043	No threat	11
9Aug43- 6Nar	fst 6f	:23 :462 1:111 3↑	Pawtucket H 6k	8 7 87 85¼ 63¾ 32¾	Woolf G	124wb	*3.80	92-13	Cherrydale1092½ValdinaAlph115nkAlsb124½	Rapid late gain	8
11Nov42- 5Bel	fst 1¼	:474 1:121 1:372 2:021 3↑	Handicap 10350	2 6 77 52 3nk 1¾	Woolf G	126wb	*.75	89-16	Alsab126¾Boysy113½Bon Jour1022	Pulled up lame	7
31Oct42- 5Emp	fst 1 3/16	:484 1:122 1:374 1:562 3↑	Westchester H 28k	1 4 814 714 55¼ 3nk	Bierman C	124wb	*1.15	98-07	RvrInd114nkTolRos108noAlsb1241½	Inside,finished fastest	8
21Oct42- 5Jam	fst 1 5/8	:501 1:41 2:06 2:441 3↑	Gallant Fox H 16k	3 4 45 35 21½ 21	Bierman C	124wb	*1.05	93-13	DarkDiscovery1001Alsab1241½Mrrg1215	Wearing down winner	6
10Oct42- 6Bel	fst 2¼	:49 2:292 2:542 3:471 3↑	New York H 30k	10 5 711 31 2hd 1hd	Bierman C	121wb	4.25	99-07	Alsab121hdObash1061¼Whirlaway1305	Driving	12
3Oct42- 6Bel	fst 2	:523 2:32 2:562 3:213 3↑	J C Gold Cup 27k	1 2 2½ 1hd 11½ 2¾	Bierman C	117wb	2.80	95-05	Whirlaway124¾Alsab1178Bolingbroke12415	2nd best	4
	Geldings not eligible										
29Sep42- 7Bel	fst 1 5/8	:484 1:393 2:043 2:42	Lawrence Realizatn 11k	2 2 59 54½ 3¾ 13½	Woolf G	126wb	*.25	94-08	Alsab1263½Vagrancy1153Trrrch110nk	Blocked str,drew away	5
19Sep42- 7Nar	fst 1 3/16	:502 1:141 1:383 1:562 3↑	Match Race 25k	2 1 11½ 12 11 1no	Bierman C	119wb	1.60	93-11	Alsab119noWhirlaway126	Just enough	2
7Sep42- 7Was	fst 1¼	:47 1:11 1:36 2:022 3↑	Wash Park H 32k	6 3 815 63¾ 41½ 21	Robertson A	121wb	*.90	97-11	Mrrg1141Alsb121nkThumbsUp102nk	Wide,bearing in str,gamely	9
29Aug42- 7Was	sl 1¼	:481 1:132 1:393 2:063	American Derby 78k	4 2 513 53½ 11½ 13½	Woolf G	126wb	*.70	77-25	Alsab1263½With Regards1211½Anticlimax1212	Saved ground	7
20Aug42- 6Was	fst 1	:231 :464 1:113 1:361	Dick Welles H 5.3k	5 3 32½ 3nk 1hd 1½	Woolf G	128wb	*.60	97-12	Alsb128½King's Abby1125SomMn1002½	Lost ground,ridden out	6
15Aug42- 7Was	fst 7f	:223 :454 1:111 1:241 3↑	Handicap 3500	1 7 77¼ 65½ 2hd 1½	Richard J	120wb	3.40	95-12	Alsab120½Sales Talk1016Air Master111½	Carried out	7
8Aug42- 5Was	fst 6f	:224 :454 1:11 3↑	Handicap 2500	5 3 55 67 43½ 43½	James B	120wb	*1.90	92-15	Defense1081¼Sales Talk1061½Woof Woof117¾	Outrun	6
6Jun42- 6Bel	fst 1½	:481 1:123 2:031 2:291	Belmont 53k	1 1 55¼ 21 21½ 22	James B	126wb	*.40	94-09	Shut Out1262Alsab1264Lochinvar1266	No late gain	7
	Geldings not eligible										
23May42- 6Bel	fst 1	:231 :461 1:11 1:361	Withers 20k	4 7 75¾ 42¾ 1½ 12½	James B	126wb	*.75	94-08	Alsab1262½Lochinvar126noFairaris126½	Easily	9
	Geldings not eligible										
9May42- 6Pim	fst 1 3/16	:47 1:112 1:371 1:57	Preakness 75k	8 7 97¾ 94¼ 32½ 11	James B	126wb	*2.05	98-06	Alsab1261[DH]Requested126[DH]Sun Again126¾	Driving	10
2May42- 7CD	fst 1¼	:472 1:123 1:39 2:042	Ky Derby 76k	7 5 1011 42½ 42½ 22¼	James B	126wb	5.10	83-09	Shut Out1262¼Alsab126hdValdina Orphan1261½	Just up	15
28Apr42- 4CD	fst 1	:233 :47 1:123 1:364	Derby Trial 3.1k	7 8 65½ 45½ 33 33¾	James B	118wb	*1.60	91-16	Valdina Orphan111nkSun Again1183½Alsab1182½	No rally	8
	Worked out nine furlongs in 1:54										
18Apr42- 6HdG	fst 1 1/16	:234 :481 1:132 1:463	Chesapeake 18k	3 10 97½ 87¾ 32½ 21	James B	122wb	*.95	84-18	Colchis1161Alsab1221½Requested119hd	Gamely	11
13Apr42- 5HdG	fst 6f	:23 :464 1:122	Chesapeake Trial 3.7k	3 6 69 68¼ 64¼ 2½	Schmidl A	126wb	2.05	90-15	Colchis118½Alsab126½Seamanlike114hd	Away slowly	6
7Mar42- 6Hia	fst 1¼	:47 1:122 1:374 2:051 3↑	Widener H 67k	7 12 88½ 52½ 4¾ 51½	Thompson B	109wb	7.85	81-17	The Rhymer111hdBest Seller112hdOlympus107nk	Hung	17
28Feb42- 6Hia	fst 1⅛	:464 1:12 1:374 1:502	Flamingo 35k	3 10 98¾ 54½ 44 38	Vedder RL	126wb	3.40	81-14	Requested1224Redthorn1164Alsab1263	Outside	16
14Feb42- 4Hia	fst 1	:232 :463 1:104 1:363	Alw 1500	6 6 59 46½ 46½ 46¼	Arcaro E	126wb	*.75	--	BrightWillie1183SirWar1141¾Incoming1021½	Slow late gain	6
7Feb42- 6Hia	fst 7f	:232 :464 1:114 1:243	Bahamas H 6.2k	9 8 99 95¼ 74¾ 65¼	McCreary C	128wb	*.65	84-13	AmericanWolf1144FirstFiddle115noFggrtout114hd	Wide turn	10
12Nov41- 6Pim	fst 1 1/16	:23 :464 1:11 1:443	Walden 10k	5 2 2hd 2hd 11½ 1nk	Vedder RL	122wb	*.10	97-12	Alsab122nkBlessMe1131¼FairCall1161½	Tired,just held on	6
18Oct41- 5Lrl	fst 1 1/16	:234 :482 1:132 1:454	S Lowe Jenkins 7k	3 3 32 1nk 12 14¼	Vedder RL	124wb	*.10	88-16	Alsab1244¼Colchis1183Sweep Swinger1154	Easily	4
4Oct41- 5Bel	gd 1	:231 :46 1:104 1:352	Champagne 13k	6 4 31½ 2hd 13 17	Bierman C	122wb	*.60	98-11	Alsab1227Requested1162½Flaught110nk	Blocked ½ pole	7
23Sep41- 4Bel	fst 6½f	:231 :462 1:094 1:16	Match Race 10k	2 2 21 21 11½ 13½	Vedder RL	122wb	.85	106-07	Alsab1223½Requested122	Ridden out	2
13Sep41- 6HdG	fst 6f	:224 :462 1:123	Eastern Shore H 13k	7 8 83½ 65½ 32½ 13[illegible]	Vedder RL	126wb	*.60	90-18	[DH]Alsab126[DH]Colchis1173Flaught106½	Fast finish	10
6Sep41- 6Was	gd 6f	:223 :463 1:12	Prairie State 5.8k	6 4 42½ 3nk 12 13¼	Vedder RL	126wb	*.30	91-20	Alsab1263¼MissDogwood1143FirstofAll1171	Speed to spare	6
16Aug41- 6Was	fst 6f	:223 :463 1:11	Wash Park Futurity 42k	2 1 41½ 31½ 1hd 1¾	Vedder RL	119wb	*.50	96-10	Alsab119¾Contradiction1172Valdina Orphan1172½	Handily	9
9Aug41- 5Was	fst 5½f	:221 :453 :582 1:05	Wash Park Juvenile 3.2k	5 7 97¼ 72½ 1hd 1¾	Vedder RL	126wb	*.50	100-07	Alsab126¾Valdina Orphan1171Questvive1141	Driving	11
31Jly41- 6AP	gd 6f	:232 :472 1:124	Hyde Park 6.5k	3 3 41½ 1hd 15 15	Vedder RL	122wb	*.40	83-21	Alsab1225Sweep Swinger117hdValdina Orphan1174	Easily	9
19Jly41- 7Suf	fst 5½f	:23 :46 :582 1:051	Mayflower 21k	6 1 43¼ 31½ 11 12¼	Vedder RL	119wb	*.60	100-11	Alsab1192¼Syl's Jimmy110¾Eternal Bull119¾	handily	7
5Jly41- 7Suf	fst 5f	:22 :453 :583	©Miles Standish 10k	8 8 84¾ 65¼ 43½ 2½	Vedder RL	119wb	*1.00	100-09	Eternal Bull114½Alsab1192¾Bold Question117no		8
	Away slowly,getting to winner										
25Jun41- 6AP	fst 5½f	:223 :463 :583 1:044	Primer 3.5k	3 5 74¼ 43 1hd 17	Vedder RL	122wb	*1.20	97-12	Alsab1227Valdina Orphan1172Memphis114no		12
	Outrun early,speed in reserve										
31May41- 6LF	sl 5f	:231 :474 1:01	Joliet 6.5k	4 6 99 69 41½ 15	Pool E	122wb	3.90	90-24	Alsab1225Kirwin122hdValdina Orphan122hd	Blocked	13
21May41- 4LF	fst 5f	:23 :463 1:00	Alw 1010	6 4 56½ 57½ 43½ 2½	Craig A	115 w	*1.50	94-25	Valdina Alpha111½Alsab115nkOmathon1131½	Belated rally	6
10May41- 4CD	fst 5f	:231 :461 :592	Alw 1000	6 6 31½ 22 1½ 12½	Thompson B	110 w	*1.10	98-12	Alsab1102½Alohort1113Bayridge1113	Wide,drifted out	6
8May41- 5CD	sl 4½f	:232 :472 :541	Alw 1000	5 5 43½ 31½ 2no	Thompson B	113 w	2.70	91-12	Omathon112noAlszb1133½Famed1096		5
	Slow start,impeded by winner										
2May41- 6CD	fst 5f	:223 :463 :593	©Bashford Manor 3.5k	9 6 75¼ 710 46½ 42¾	Marinelli J	122 w	9.70	94-11	Black Raider1271½Omathon1221¼Bayridge117no		10
	Lost ground turn,good finish										
18Apr41- 5Kee	sl *4f	:47	[R]Sp Wt 1500	6 1 2½ 11½ 12	Marinelli J	115 w	5.50	95-06	Alsab1152Some Chance1153Topnard115½	Speed in reserve	8
8Apr41- 4TrP	gd 4f	:232 :471	Alw 1000	10 10 41½ 73 42	Howell R	116 w	4.35	92-06	MissShopper103½SonIslm1111½Drwby116hd	Wide,gradual gain	10
28Mar41- 1TrP	fst 4f	:233 :472	©Md Sp Wt	1 3 31½ 32½ 11	Howell R	116 w	4.60	93-07	Alsab1161Scotch Broth1161½Ask Me1161	Saved ground	12
21Mar41- 1TrP	sly 4f	:232 :481	©Md Sp Wt	6 9 98 77 31½	Howell R	116 w	74.45	87-11	Patriot116hdAlohort1161½Alsab116hd	Finished fastest	9
25Feb41- 1Hia	sly 3f	:222 :332	©Md Sp Wt	1 13 1419 1415¼	Bodiou A	118 w	72.85	--	Scotland Light1181Methodical118½Requested118½	Outrun	14

American Way

b. g. 1942, by Gino (Tetratema)–Sunchance, by Chance Shot

Lifetime record: 45 12 10 7 $100,982

Own.– Rokeby Stable
Br.– Paul Mellon
Tr.– J.T. Skinner

27Jun52- 6Del	fst *2½	S'Chase 4:44 4↑	Indian River H 12k	1 5 523 421 425½ 428	Field T	140ws	8.40	--	Jam15220Monkey Wrench1342The Mast1616	Trailed	5
11Jun52- 6Bel	fst *2¼	S'Chase 4:163 4↑	Temple Gwathmey H 16k	5 8 83½ 78½ 511 616	Field T	141ws	13.85	--	The Mast153¾Oedipus1631¼Navy Gun1497	No menace	9
3Jun52- 3Bel	fst *2	S'Chase 3:483 4↑	Alw 4500	6 6 57 510 57½ 43½	Field T	148ws	12.45	--	Hot1431½Flaming Comet1401½Gerrymander135½	No mishap	7
4Oct51- 5Bel	fst *2½	S'Chase 4:45 4↑	Brook H 16k	10 9 911 917 924 932	Field T	140ws	11.35	--	Oedipus1613Palaja1387Lone Fisherman148nk	Jumped poorly	12
25Sep51- 3Bel	sf *2	S'Chase 3:53 3↑	Alw 3500	6 7 63¾ 11 13 11	Field T	146ws	3.20e	--	American Way1461Eolus1422Syracuse Lad1421	Driving	8
11Oct50- 6Bel	fst *2¼	S'Chase 4:182 4↑	Temple Gwathmey H 11k	2 4 2½ 35½ 311 316	Field T	145ws	6.25	--	Tourist List13810Oedipus1536American Way1454	Tired	5
6Oct50- 5Bel	fst *3	S'Chase 5:422 4↑	Grand National H 23k	1 7 57½ 618 742 834	McDonald RS	145ws	1.85e	--	Trough Hill1502¼Oedipus1534Pontius Pilate1502½	Tired	9
28Sep50- 3Bel	fst *2	S'Chase 3:434 4↑	Handicap 4045	6 6 630 637 640 6136	McDonald RS	146ws	2.40e	--	SeaLegs1433Genancoke1433Sergt.Peace1394	Almost fell 4th	6
1Jun50- 5Bel	sl *2	S'Chase 4:03 4↑	Corinthian H 9.1k	5 2 43½ 48½ 48½ 48[illegible]	Field T	148ws	*1.95	--	Adaptable1411½Hot1403½Monkey Wrench1353	Dull try	7
25May50- 5Bel	fst *2	S'Chase 3:44 4↑	C L Appleton 9k	4 5 37 35 34 37	Field T	145 w	3.80	--	Darjeeling1302Hot1355American Way1455½	Even effort	7
17May50- 3Bel	fst *2	S'Chase 3:473 4↑	Handicap 4555	2 6 618 615 516 69	Field T	148 w	4.30	--	Phiblant1332Hot1392Irish Monkey1391½	Jumped poorly	7
10Nov49- 5Pim	fst *2½	S'Chase 4:482 4↑	Manly H 8.2k	2 4 412 411 314 314	Field T	152ws	*1.20e	--	His Boots1458Trough Hill1566American Way1526	Bobbled	5

20Oct49- 5Lrl	fst	*2½	S'Chase	4:452	4↑ Chevy Chase H 11k	1	4	44½	31	22	31½	Field T	152 ws	1.60e	--	LockandKey1401¼HisBoots145nkAmericnWay1521½	Went well 6
14Oct49- 3Lrl	fst	*2	S'Chase	3:522	4↑ Alw 5000	5	4	45½	44½	21	22	Field T	153 ws	2.30e	--	LarkyDay1532AmericanWay1532½TouristList1468	Closed well 6
7Oct49- 6Bel	fst	*3	S'Chase	5:483	4↑ Grand National H 22k	1	4	410	51¾	49	513	Field T	154 ws	*1.20e	--	His Boots1412½Trough Hill1588Tourist List1462	No mishap 7
29Sep49- 5Bel	sl	*2½	S'Chase	4:521	4↑ Brook H 15k	1	3	47½	22	21	210	Field T	151 ws	4.35e	--	TroughHill15310AmercnWy1511½HsBoots1429	Finished tiring 8
15Sep49- 5Aqu	fst	*2½	S'Chase	4:563	4↑ Glendale H 11k	2	3	315	319	419	421½	Field T	152 w	*1.00e	--	His Boots13520Rapier130½My Good Man1351	No mishap 7
1Sep49- 4Aqu	sl	*2	S'Chase	3:534	3↑ Harbor Hill H 11k	5	4	412	23	11½	12	Field T	148 w	2.30e	--	American Way1482Repose137¾His Boots13710	Ridden out 8
2Jun49- 4Bel	fst	*2	S'Chase	3:44	4↑ Corinthian H 9.4k	6	6	58½	66¾	23	36	Field T	146 w	4.35e	--	Trough Hill1476Elkridge149hdAmerican Way1463½	Weakened 10
10Nov48- 5Pim	gd	3	S'Chase	6:104	4↑ Manly H 18k	7	3	320	21½	210	215	Marzani D	152 w	*.80e	--	Adaptable14415American Way15215Point Bleu1468	Went well 9
28Oct48- 5Lrl	fst	*2½	S'Chase	4:474	4↑ Chevy Chase H 18k	4	3	317	36	11½	11	Marzani D	148 w	*1.50e	--	American Way1481Sun Bath1354Trough Hill1475	Cleverly 8
14Oct48- 5Lrl	fst	*2	S'Chase	3:531	3↑ Butler H 13k	8	9	68½	39½	37½	39½	Field T	149 w	*2.40e	--	Drift1346The Heir1493½American Way1493	Good effort 12
1Oct48- 5Bel	gd	*3	S'Chase	5:50	4↑ Grand Nat'l H 31k	3	5	79½	711	31½	11	Marzani D	144 w	*2.30e	--	American Way1441Tourist List1502Trough Hill1476	Driving 14
23Sep48- 5Bel	fst	*2½	S'Chase	4:471	4↑ Brook H 19k	10	4	53½	78½	44½	33½	Marzani D	143 w	3.45e	--	Trough Hill1422Elkridge1561½American Way1432	Good try 11
16Jly48- 5Aqu	fst	*2½	S'Chase	4:534	4↑ Hitchcock H 11k	3	5	48¼	33	21½	21	Field T	145 w	2.45	--	SunBath1371AmericanWay1454TouristList1432	Strong finish 6
24Jun48- 5Del	gd	*2	S'Chase	3:50	4↑ Georgetown H 12k	2	4	310	316	21	12½	Marzani D	144 w	3.95e	--	AmericnWay1442½Genancoke145nkFlotngIsl14010	Going away 8
17Jun48- 1Del	sl	*2	S'Chase	3:552	4↑ Alw 4000	1	4	513	413	26	28	Bland W Jr	151 w	*1.65e	--	War Battle1558American Way1516Lieut. Well155¾	Went well 5
12Jun48- 3Bel	fst	*2	S'Chase	3:492	4↑ Alw 4500	4	3	33	23	22	25	Bland W Jr	150 w	*2.20	--	Sun Bath1405American Way1502½Cash1362	Went well 6
12May48- 5Pim	fst	2	S'Chase	3:471	4↑ Jervis Spencer H 12k	5	6	628	-	-	-	Bland W	149 w	*1.10e	--	Lieut. Well1441½Canford13812Adaptable1501½	Fell 7
5May48- 3Pim	hy	2	S'Chase	4:132	4↑ Alw 4500	3	3	317	310	11	12	Bland W	150 w	*.70e	--	American Way1502Genancoke1512Floating Isle1531½	Handily 6
29May47- 5Del	fst	*2	S'Chase	4:03	4↑ Tom Roby 13k	8	6	54½	32	14	112	Bland W Jr	149 w	2.50e	--	AmericanWay14912TouristPride1351½TouristList1462	Easily 10
7May47- 5Pim	gd	*2	S'Chase	3:59	4↑ Jervis Spencer H 17k	3	5	612	514	513	517	Field T	140 w	4.50	--	Lieut.Well1448Fleettown141noFloatingIsle1411	No mishap 7
29Apr47- 3Pim	fst	*2	S'Chase	3:544	4↑ Alw 4000	6	2	212	311	1hd	1¾	Field T	147 w	*1.90	--	American Way147¾Adaptable1431½Allier1351	Driving 7
16Nov46- 5Mid	fst	*2½	S'Chase	4:341	4↑ Handicap 2415	5	4	518	1½	1½	11½	Bland W	150 w	-e	--	American Way1501½Caddie16015Lady Janice14030	Driving 5
8Nov46- 3Pim	fst	2	S'Chase	3:564	3↑ Alw 3500	4	6	55½	31	2½	2hd	Field T	149 w	1.85e	--	NeatPleat146hdAmericanWay14910FrCrystl14720	Just missed 6
4Nov46- 3Pim	fst	2	S'Chase	4:00	4↑ Alw 3500	6	2	22	22	13	11	Field T	142 w	4.30e	--	American Way1421Refugio1474Genancoke146.510	Driving 7
11Oct46- 3Bel	fst	*2	S'Chase	3:521	3↑ Alw 4000	5	5	513	511	25	26	Field T	147 w	*1.40	--	LittleSammie1436AmericnWay1478GalaReigh15215	No threat 5
18Sep46- 5Aqu	fst	*2½	S'Chase	4:512	4↑ Glendale H 11k	6	4	42½	65½	413	411½	Field T	136 w	9.00	--	Chesapeake1361½Nvgt150hdKnght'sQust14710	Speed,faltered 6
10Sep46- 3Aqu	fst	*2	S'Chase	3:46	3↑ Alw 3500	1	4	23	11½	13	13	Field T	138 w	2.05	--	AmericanWay1383FredericII1382½GreekFlag151½	Drew away 5
24Jun46- 2Del	fst	*2	S'Chase	3:502	4↑ Alw 3500	1	3	37	25	22	23½	Field T	135 w	8.65	--	SoldierSong1403½AmericnWy1352Rfugo142¾	Bad landing 13th 5
14Jun46- 2Del	fst	*2	S'Chase	3:591	4↑ Clm 3000	6	5	55¼	57	1hd	11½	Field T	139 w	7.75	--	American Way1391½Strawride1482Ducker1341½	Driving 9
27May46- 3Bel	my	*2	S'Chase	4:16	4↑ Md Sp Wt	2	3	34¼	28	5	5	Bland W	146 w	2.35	--	Tetrol13915Chancefield1427Chen13920	5
	Fell 11th,remounted and finished course																
9May46- 3Pim	fst	*2	S'Chase	3:574	4↑ Md Sp Wt	6	-	-	-	-	-	Bland W	146 w	1.85e	--	[D]Tetrol1462BigThr14620FuntlroyRun146100	Lost rider 1st 11
3May46- 3Pim	fst	*2	S'Chase	4:023	4↑ Md Sp Wt	1	6	87½	66½	28	2½	Bland W Jr	145 w	4.85	--	Military Man150½American Way14512George Corn14140	9
	Bobbled badly 11th																
13Apr46- 1Mid	fst	*1½	Hurdles	2:40	3↑ Alw 400	5	1	12	1hd	22½	412¾	Field T	134 ws	8.00	--	Binder1534Equirita1388Nobby138¾	Weakened 7

Armed

br. g. 1941, by Bull Lea (Bull Dog)–Armful, by Chance Shot **Lifetime record: 81 41 20 10 $817,475**

Own.– Calumet Farm
Br.– Calumet Farm (Ky)
Tr.– B.A. Jones

22Mar50- 6GP	fst	1 1/16	:23 :461 1:103 1:43	4↑ Alw 3000	4	5	46	31	1hd	11	Scurlock O	117 w	2.05	101-07	Armed1171Stud Poker114noHarbourton116hd	Won easily 6
11Mar50- 6GP	fst	1⅛	:473 1:123 1:374 1:492	3↑ Handicap 7500	2	3	33½	52½	4¾	2hd	Nelson E	111 w	*.40e	97-09	Wynford II112hdArmed111hdBewitch1232½	Held gamely 6
11Feb50- 6Hia	fst	1⅛	:463 1:111 1:37 1:501	3↑ McLennan H 33k	8	10	85	95	86¼	67	Scurlock O	112 w	*.55e	80-17	Three Rings1171Royal Governor1161Coaltown1321	Blocked 11
21Jan50- 6Hia	fst	1⅛	:471 1:113 1:364 1:492	3↑ Royal Palm H 11k	7	3	31½	2½	2½	2¾	Scurlock O	121 w	*1.20	90-18	Three Rings120¾Armed1211Renown II1153	Good effort 7
14Jan50- 7TrP	fst	1 1/16	:243 :482 1:123 1:433	4↑ Alw 2500	2	1	1½	1hd	11	12	Scurlock O	117 w	*.30	94-12	Armed1172Appease Not1176First Nighter117nk	Going away 6
3Jan50- 6TrP	fst	6f	:222 :452 1:101	4↑ Alw 2500	6	5	75½	44½	32	2½	Scurlock O	112 w	1.90e	95-14	Kay Gibson107½Armed1121Too Sunny1053	Gaining fast 9
	Previously trained by H.A. Jones															
5Sep49- 6Was	sl	1¼	:473 1:122 1:373 2:034	3↑ Wash Park H 52k	4	2	31½	2½	21	2¾	Scurlock O	110 w	*.10e	82-19	Coaltown130¾Armed1101Lithe102.524¼	Raced outside 4
23Jly49- 6AP	gd	1¼	:463 1:11 1:361 2:032	3↑ Arlington H 54k	3	3	48½	36	37	34	Scurlock O	113 w	*.40e	84-19	Coaltown1303Star Reward1161Armed1135	Closed well 6
4Jly49- 6AP	fst	1⅛	:472 1:103 1:352 1:482	3↑ Stars & Stripes H 54k	2	4	42	33	34	21¼	Scurlock O	110 w	*.40e	103-09	Coaltown1301¼Armed110½Star Reward121½	Good effort 6
30Jun49- 6AP	fst	7f	:23 :462 1:111 1:234	4↑ Alw 3500	2	7	51¾	41¼	1½	13	Brooks S	122 w	*1.80	91-09	Armed1223Trixie111noBest Prospect110½	Going away 7
20Jun49- 7AP	fst	6f	:223 :452 1:091	4↑ Alw 5000	6	7	96¾	99¼	810	710	Scurlock O	114 w	*1.00e	91-09	CarraraMarble1046Bewitch1151½StarReward118hd	Raced wide 10
	Previously trained by B.A. Jones															
21May49- 7CD	gd	7f	:233 :463 1:113 1:25	3↑ Churchill Downs H 11k	2	3	46	44½	33	21¼	Johnson WL	118 w	-e	90-18	Free America1201¼Armed1182¾Phar Mon1081½	Closed well 4
	No wagering															
5May49- 6CD	fst	1 1/16	:252 :502 1:143 1:451	3↑ Clark H 10k	4	1	12	33	32½	35	Glisson G	120 w	.90e	89-14	Shy Guy123hdFree America1155Armed12012	Weakened 4
2May49- 6CD	fst	6f	:232 :464 1:122	4↑ Alw 2500	6	1	54½	45½	22	13¼	Glisson G	113 w	*.20	91-16	Armed1133¼Best Prospect1161½Pomp's Gal1133	Going away 8
	Previously trained by H.A. Jones															
19Mar49- 6GP	fst	1¼	:45 1:09 1:341 1:594	3↑ Gulf Park H 20k	7	3	38	312	39	37½	Nelson E	116 w	*.10e	100-06	Coaltown1287Three Rings118½Armed1162½	Went well 9
8Mar49- 7GP	fst	7f	:24 :471 1:112 1:232	4↑ Alw 2500	1	3	2hd	1hd	11½	11¼	Nelson E	117 w	*.60	96-08	Armed1171¼Manna H.117½Control1171½	Easily 8
17Feb49- 4Hia	fst	7f	:232 :461 1:103 1:231	4↑ Alw 3500	5	4	54¼	56½	45¾	32½	Nelson E	119 w	*.70	93-12	Rare Jewel1102½Happy C.112hdArmed1191½	Closed well 7
9Feb49- 5Hia	fst	6f	:223 :454 1:11	4↑ Alw 3500	5	1	74¾	61¾	7¾	32¼	Civitello B	119 w	2.10	91-13	Column1151½Tight Squeeze113¾Armed119nk	Closed well 8
21Feb48- 6Hia	fst	1¼	:47 1:11 1:354 2:01	3↑ Widener H 62k	7	2	64	53	53¾	45½	Snider A	130 w	1.65	97-10	El Mono112hdStud Poker1032½Bug Juice1073	Mild rally 9
14Feb48- 6Hia	fst	1⅛	:463 1:104 1:36 1:482	3↑ McLennan H 31k	9	7	53½	64¾	54	31¾	Dodson D	128 w	*.35	97-10	El Mono112hdRiskolater1121¾Armed1281	Closed fast 9
11Feb48- 6Hia	fst	7f	:232 :46 1:101 1:23	3↑ Seminole H 12k	7	6	55¼	53½	43	31¼	Dodson D	128 w	*.40e	96-16	Citation1121Delegate123nkArmed1282	Closed fast 9
2Feb48- 6Hia	fst	6f	:223 :454 1:102	3↑ Alw 5000	3	3	77	78	76¼	66¼	Dodson D	130 w	*.20e	90-10	Citation1131Kitchen Police1101¾Say Blue1071½	Raced wide 7
15Jan48- 6GP	fst	1¼	:462 1:111 1:362 2:02	3↑ Gulf Park H 27k	3	2	34	21½	21	2no	Dodson D	130 w	*.15	97-17	Rampart108noArmed1302½Incline1102½	Just missed 6
2Jan48- 6GP	fst	6f	:231 :46 1:111	4↑ Alw 3500	2	4	47	38	34	1½	Dodson D	124 w	*.45	94-15	Armed124½Stageboy1072Mangohick1172½	Handily 5
31Oct47- 6Pim	sl	1 3/16	:472 1:122 1:384 1:582	3↑ Pim Spl 25k	2	1	31½	31½	3½	33¼	Dodson D	126 w	*.20e	87-24	Fervent120nkCosmic Bomb1203Armed1267	No excuse 4
9Oct47- 6Bel	fst	1	:232 :461 1:104 1:36	3↑ Sysonby Mile 27k	2	1	2hd	2hd	2nk	11¼	Snider A	126 w	*.35	94-15	Armed1261¼With Pleasure12615Ensueno126	Drew out 3
27Sep47- 6Bel	fst	1¼	:471 1:113 1:363 2:024	3↑ Special 100k	2	1	14	12	13	18	Dodson D	126 w	-	86-10	Armed1268Assault126	Much best 2
22Sep47- 5Bel	sly	6f	:231 :463 1:11	3↑ Alw 6500	4	1	32¼	32	31¾	22½	Dodson D	130 w	1.30	92-14	Polynesian1262½Armed1308Ensueno11430	Finished fast 4
1Sep47- 6Was	fst	1¼	:471 1:114 1:372 2:02	3↑ Wash Park H 55k	5	4	2hd	1hd	11	13½	Dodson D	130 w	*.70	95-12	Armed1303¼Honeymoon1111¼With Pleasure1233	Easily 7
20Aug47- 7Was	fst	1⅛	:483 1:123 1:361 1:483	3↑ Whirlaway 43k	4	2	1hd	12	1½	1½	Dodson D	130 w	*.30	104-08	Armed130½With Pleasure1264Service Pilot110hd	Driving 6
9Aug47- 6Was	fst	1	:23 :454 1:102 1:354	3↑ Sheridan H 33k	5	8	87	44½	34½	22	Dodson D	132 w	*.50	94-08	With Pleasure1242Armed132½Rippey112½	Good effort 10
19Jly47- 6AP	fst	1¼	:471 1:113 1:362 2:022	3↑ Arlington H 55k	7	4	11½	12½	13	11	Dodson D	130 w	*.40	93-12	Armed1301Bridal Flower1112¼Challenge Me1142	Driving 8
4Jly47- 6AP	fst	1⅛	:47 1:113 1:36 1:491	3↑ Stars & Stripes H 55k	1	2	32	21	1½	12	Dodson D	130 w	*.50	101-05	Armed1302With Pleasure1173Mighty Story114nk	In hand 7
28Jun47- 6AP	fst	1	:23 :453 1:093 1:35	3↑ Equipoise Mile H 33k	6	4	46½	33½	21	2nk	Dodson D	130 w	*.20	97-08	With Pleasure116nkArmed1303Mighty Story114¾	Just missed 9
21Jun47- 6AP	fst	6f	:223 :45 1:094	3↑ Domino H 29k	5	12	85½	66	34½	21	Dodson D	132 w	*1.20e	97-11	With Pleasure1141Armed132½Spy Song1207½	Closed fast 14
22Mar47- 6GP	fst	1¼	:451 1:094 1:344 2:012	3↑ Gulf Park H 30k	2	2	22	14	16	11	Dodson D	129 w	*.60e	122-00	Armed1291Pot o' Luck1172Concordian116¾	Eased up 10
1Mar47- 7SA	fst	1¼	:452 1:101 1:351 2:014	3↑ S Anita H 133k	14	4	52¼	2½	21½	52¼	Dodson D	129 w	*1.10	95-09	Olhaverry1161¼Stitch Again112½Pere Time108hd	Impeded 22
22Feb47- 6Hia	fst	1¼	:474 1:112 1:36 2:013	3↑ Widener H 61k	6	3	1hd	13	12½	12	Dodson D	129 w	*.25	101-11	Armed1292Talon1224½Let's Dance1154	Handily 6

84 CHAMPIONS

Date	Cond/Dist	Fractions	Race	PP/Positions	Jockey	Wt	Odds/Figures	Top finishers	Comment
15Feb47- 6Hia	gd 1⅛	:464 1:111 1:364 1:50	3↑ McLennan H 31k	8 3 2hd 2hd 11 14	Dodson D	130 w	*.25 91-16	Armed1304Eternal Reward1181½Westminster1208	Eased up 8
8Feb47- 3Hia	fst 6f	:224 :461 1:102	3↑ Handicap 5000	4 3 52½ 4¾ 3nk 11	Dodson D	130 w	*.80 96-15	Armed1301Lets Dance116½Pujante1245½	Drew out 5
1Feb47- 3Hia	fst 6f	:221 :451 1:101	4↑ Alw 5000	1 5 54¼ 54 32½ 1hd	Dodson D	128wb	*1.20 97-08	Armed128hdHornbeam1161½Shiny Penny1162½	Just up 5
14Sep46- 6Nar	fst 1 3/16	:46 1:102 1:36 1:543	3↑ Nar Spl 38k	2 3 23 22 22½ 33¾	Dodson D	130 w	*.50 98-16	Lucky Draw1233½Pavot123nkArmed1305	Weakened 4

Previously trained by B.A. Jones

Date	Cond/Dist	Fractions	Race	PP/Positions	Jockey	Wt	Odds/Figures	Top finishers	Comment
2Sep46- 6Was	fst 1¼	:462 1:11 1:353 2:01	3↑ Wash Park H 56k	1 1 32 11 11½ 13¾	Dodson D	130 w	*.80e 104-03	Armed1303¾Challenge Me1121Take Wing1102	Easily 10
21Aug46- 6Was	sl 1⅛	:48 1:122 1:374 1:511	3↑ Whirlaway 45k	5 3 31½ 31½ 2hd 11¼	Dodson D	130 w	*.50e 92-18	Armed1301¼Challenge Me1202Silvery Moon1113	Drew out 11
3Aug46- 6Was	fst 1	:224 :45 1:094 1:35	3↑ Sheridan H 34k	10 4 51¾ 42¼ 11 14	Pierson NL	130 w	*.60e 103-07	Armed1304Brookfield124¾Challenge Me112¾	Easily 10
31Jly46- 6Was	gd 6f	:223 :46 1:104	3↑ Quick Step 22k	3 5 55½ 46 35½ 22½	Pierson NL	130 w	1.70 93-11	FightingFrank108.52½Armed1306ThreeDots124hd	Closed fast 5
20Jly46- 6AP	fst 1¼	:464 1:11 1:353 2:01	3↑ Arlington H 56k	4 2 43½ 1½ 1½ 2nk	Dodson D	130 w	*.50 101-09	Historian112nkArmed1303Take Wing1112½	Game try 9

Previously trained by H.A. Jones

Date	Cond/Dist	Fractions	Race	PP/Positions	Jockey	Wt	Odds/Figures	Top finishers	Comment
26Jun46- 6AP	fst 1	:231 :46 1:112 1:371	3↑ Equipoise Mile H 34k	11 10 106 84 74¼ 3¾	Dodson D	132 w	*.70 85-14	Witch Sir110¾Old Kentuck106hdArmed132no	Close quarters 12
30May46- 6Bel	fst 1¼	:482 1:123 1:373 2:02	3↑ Suburban H 60k	7 6 55 41½ 2nk 12½	Dodson D	130 w	*1.05 90-16	Armed1302½Reply Paid110noStymie1231	Going away 11
10May46- 6Pim	fst 1 3/16	:494 1:141 1:384 1:582	3↑ Dixie H 34k	4 4 2¾ 1½ 13 13½	Dodson D	130 w	*.65 90-23	Armed1303½Stymie1242½Trymenow1172	Galloping 6
3May46- 6Pim	fst 6f	:222 :461 1:123	3↑ Jennings H 8.9k	6 6 66½ 65½ 63 4¾	Snellings A	132 w	*.95 89-23	New Moon115nkBrookfield122nkThe Doge117nk	Off slowly 6
20Apr46- 6HdG	fst 1 1/16	:233 :473 1:12 1:431	3↑ Philadelphia H 23k	6 4 32 21½ 2½ 11¼	Dodson D	129 w	*.35 102-11	Armed1291¼Ellis1153½Bobanet1193	Ridden out 6
15Apr46- 5HdG	fst 6f	:224 :461 1:111	3↑ Harford H 8.7k	4 5 67½ 65 52½ 21¼	Snellings A	129 w	*.60 96-15	Bobanet1161¼Armed1292Alexs1121½	Forced wide,closed fast 6

Previously trained by B.A. Jones

Date	Cond/Dist	Fractions	Race	PP/Positions	Jockey	Wt	Odds/Figures	Top finishers	Comment
30Mar46- 6TrP	fst 1⅛	:462 1:103 1:361 1:483	3↑ Double Event (2) 21k	4 5 42 41½ 2nk 1hd	Dodson D	126 w	*.30 102-10	Armed126hdHistorian1085Occupy1115	Driving 5
23Mar46- 6TrP	fst 1⅛	:462 1:102 1:354 1:483	3↑ Double Event (1) 22k	5 6 55¼ 22½ 2hd 11½	Dodson D	126 w	*.45 102-08	Armed1261½Occupy111¾Historian1088	Ridden out 7
2Mar46- 6Hia	gd 1¼	:464 1:111 1:36 2:022	3↑ Widener H 63k	3 2 34 14 15 14½	Dodson D	128 w	2.20 97-13	Armed1284½Concordian1094Reply Paid1141	Easily 8
16Feb46- 6Hia	fst 1⅛	:461 1:103 1:36 1:483	3↑ McLennan H 32k	6 6 43 45 33 25	Dodson D	128 w	*.55 93-14	Concordian1165Armed1283Bob Mann1102½	Went well 9
6Feb46- 7Hia	fst 7f	:233 :463 1:11 1:234	3↑ Handicap 5000	4 3 23½ 23 21½ 1nk	Dodson D	130 w	*.80e 93-17	Armed130nkBuzfuz1302½Pot o' Luck1204	Driving 6
26Jan46- 3Hia	fst 6f	:231 :462 1:102	4↑ Alw 4000	9 1 41¾ 31 1hd 1nk	Dodson D	126 w	*.45 97-08	Armed126nkNowadays1155Trouble Sands1122	Eased up 10
17Nov45- 6Pim	gd 1 3/16	:493 1:142 1:391 1:584	3↑ Pim Spl 25k	2 2 43½ 31½ 15 14	Dodson D	126 w	*.60e 88-20	Armed1264First Fiddle1262Stymie1261¼	Well in hand 7
10Nov45- 5Pim	fst 1⅛	:471 1:114 1:373 1:513	3↑ Handicap 5000	1 3 33 2hd 11 11¾	Dodson D	128 w	*.60e 97-14	Armed1281¾Rampart104hdGallorette1132	Eased up late 5
30Oct45- 6Pim	fst 6f	:223 :46 1:114	3↑ Alw 3500	5 6 33 22 1hd 1½	Dodson D	124 w	*.70 94-19	Armed124½Quarter Moon1215Jimmie1132	In hand late 7
20Oct45- 6Lrl	fst 1¼	:464 1:12 1:381 2:042	3↑ Washington H 29k	2 1 36½ 2hd 12½ 13½	Dodson D	124 w	*1.25 88-20	Armed1243½Dinner Party1061¼Good Morning105hd	Galloping 9
6Oct45- 6Lrl	sl 1⅛	:473 1:123 1:393 1:521	3↑ Havre de Grace H 17k	4 2 22 11 11 2¾	Dodson D	126 w	*1.90 86-23	Gay Bit113¾Armed1266Dinner Party1094	2nd best 9
17Sep45- 6Bel	fst 6f-WC	:221 :443 1:084	2↑ Fall Highweight H 10k	2 4 43½ 45 21	Dodson D	135 w	1.95 96-03	True North1401Armed1354Breezing Home1201½	Driving 4
3Sep45- 7Was	fst 1¼	:463 1:103 1:361 2:014	3↑ Wash Park H 57k	5 7 65¼ 44 23 21½	Dodson D	120 w	3.30e 99-12	Busher1151½Armed1201Take Wing1125	Driving 13
1Sep45- 7Was	sl 6f	:23 :47 1:113	3↑ Chicago H 22k	8 8 53½ 44½ 36 22½	Dodson D	123 w	*1.70 89-21	Three Dots1242½Armed1231Ariel Lad114hd	Away slowly 9
18Aug45- 5Was	fst 7f	:224 :462 1:103 1:233	3↑ Alw 4000	3 2 21½ 21½ 11 13	Dodson D	119 w	*.40 95-14	Armed1193ChallengeMe115noDailyTroubl1193	Speed to spare 4
8Aug45- 6Was	fst 7f	:222 :46 1:111 1:234	3↑ Sheridan H (Div 2) 16k	1 2 32 21 21 18	Dodson D	111 w	*1.40 94-14	Armd1118EspinoGold108hdThreeDots126hd	Drew away quickly 8
21Jly45- 6Was	fst 6f	:23 :46 1:113	3↑ Alw 4000	2 4 53½ 44¼ 43 11½	Dodson D	116 w	*2.10 92-12	Armed1161½Quick Reward1052Legislator108hd	In hand 6
14Jly45- 5Was	sly 7f	:234 :473 1:12 1:251	4↑ Alw 3000	3 2 22 21 14 12¼	Dodson D	118 w	*1.10 87-19	Armed1182¼Happy Pilot1133Miss Lark110.5½	In hand late 7
3Jly45- 4Was	fst 7f	:224 :462 1:12 1:251	4↑ Alw 2500	1 3 23 23 1hd 12	Dodson D	118 w	*.50 87-14	Armed1182Tawny Lady1083Five A.M.1112	Speed in reserve 10
27Jun45- 5Was	sl 7f	:24 :483 1:151 1:292	4↑ Alw 2500	1 3 31½ 2hd 15 14	Dodson D	117 w	*.70 66-34	Armed1174Oberver1153½Havaheart110¾	In hand 8
2Jun45- 6Jam	sly 6f	:231 :463 1:113	3↑ Handicap 3480	9 10 1010 108¾ 98¼ 56½	Jemas N	109 w	32.50 87-10	Unchallengd1122ComncheePeak1181½JeanMircl1221	No speed 11
4Nov44- 6Pim	fst 6f	:222 :46 1:114	2↑ Janney H 6.3k	3 6 69½ 76½ 75½ 65	Smith FA	110 w	15.45 89-15	Salto116hdChallamore1212Adroit1161	No factor 7
26Jun44- 6Was	fst 6f	:222 :454 1:103	3↑ Alw 2500	3 6 58 611 514 47½	McCreary C	104 w	4.80 90-09	Occupation1201½Tellmenow1053Bright Willie1173	Mild gain 6
19Jun44- 5Was	sl 6f	:232 :474 1:124	Alw 2500	1 4 1hd 1hd 11 11	McCreary C	111 w	4.20 87-24	Armed1111Sirde1204Sirius1111¼	Driving 8
3May44- 6Pim	fst 6f	:221 :453 1:113	Rennert H 7k	7 4 32 43 68 89¾	Smith FA	118 w	*.40e 85-17	Twilight Tear1181½Galactic1083Ideal Gift112.52	Quit 10
15Apr44- 7Pim	sly 6f	:23 :474 1:152	Alw 3500	1 3 11½ 1hd 21½ 22	McCreary C	110 w	2.00 74-32	Director J.E.1142Armed1104Gramps Image1144	Faltered str 6
4Mar44- 3Hia	fst 7f	:23 :461 1:122 1:262	Alw 1800	5 3 43½ 22 2½ 13	McCreary C	118 w	*.25e 80-21	Armed1183Herald115noRay G.1183	Easily 7
28Feb44- 2Hia	fst 6f	:233 :473 1:123	Md Sp Wt	11 5 31½ 31 11½ 18	Arcaro E	120 w	*1.95 86-26	Armed1208Saguaro1202½Change Here120hd	Speed to spare 11

Askmenow

br. f. 1940, by Menow (Pharamond II)–Conclave, by Friar Rock

Lifetime record: 27 8 7 4 $138,135

Own.– H.P. Headley

Br.– Hal Price Headley (Ky)

Tr.– K. Osborne

Date	Cond/Dist	Fractions	Race	PP/Positions	Jockey	Wt	Odds/Figures	Top finishers	Comment
18Sep43- 6Aqu	fst 1⅛	:474 1:132 1:383 1:513	3↑ ⒻBeldame H 28k	11 9 107 95¾ 75 65	Woolf G	119wb	5.65e 84-14	Mar-Kell1261Stefanita1162Vagrancy122½	Slow to begin 11
28Aug43- 6Was	sl 1¼	:491 1:141 1:41 2:07	American Derby 73k	1 1 21½ 22 1½ 1hd	Woolf G	115wb	3.80 75-27	Askmenw115hdBoldCptn11712FmousVctory117½	Tiring,lasted 7
21Aug43- 6Was	fst 1⅛	:474 1:112 1:374 1:51	3↑ ⒻBeverly H 11k	8 7 56½ 44½ 22 1nk	Woolf G	115wb	2.30e 93-11	Askmnw115nkMar-Kell1251¼Burgoo Maid1092½	Saved ground 8
4Aug43- 6Bel	fst 1¼	:471 1:121 1:381 2:042	ⒻAlabama 17k	1 2 21 21 21½ 21¾	Woolf G	124wb	1.10 76-15	Stefanita1171¾Askmenow12420Tack Room114	No match 3
24Jly43- 6Was	fst 1¼	:472 1:121 1:371 2:043	Classic 70k	4 4 33½ 46 46 410	Bierman C	115wb	5.40e 77-14	Slide Rule1201Bourmont1174Chop Chop1235	Faltered 8
19Jly43- 6Was	gd 1⅛	:482 1:14 1:403 1:533	Alw 5000	5 3 35½ 2½ 2½ 1½	Bierman C	113wb	3.30e 80-22	Askmenow113½Occupation118noBourmont112.510	Driving 7
10Jly43- 6Was	fst 1	:232 :464 1:123 1:381	3↑ ⒻArl Matron H 12k	10 5 52¼ 31 12 1nk	Bierman C	109wb	5.30 87-17	Askmenow109nkMar-Kell1262½Pomayya1181	Gamely 10
30Jun43- 6Was	fst 7f	:23 :464 1:113 1:242	3↑ ⒻCinderella H 6.3k	2 1 1½ 1hd 32 31¼	Bierman C	110wb	4.50 93-17	Mar-Kell122½Hometown106¾Askmenow1103	10

Drifted out into str,came on again when straightened

Date	Cond/Dist	Fractions	Race	PP/Positions	Jockey	Wt	Odds/Figures	Top finishers	Comment
23Jun43- 6Was	fst 6f	:231 :471 1:124	ⒻPrincess Doreen 6k	3 4 55 55½ 43 21¼	Bierman C	121wb	3.60 86-16	Valdina Marl1151¼Askmenow121noWiseasyou109¾	8

Lost ground,late rush

Date	Cond/Dist	Fractions	Race	PP/Positions	Jockey	Wt	Odds/Figures	Top finishers	Comment
26May43- 6Bel	sly 1½	:484 1:142 2:073 2:35	ⒻCCA Oaks 18k	3 1 22 2nk 1hd 23½	Bierman C	121wb	*1.55e 59-25	TooTimly1213½Askmnw1212½LaReigh1217	Drifted out final ⅛ 6
19May43- 6Bel	sly 1	:232 :472 1:121 1:383	ⒻAcorn 14k	7 5 65¼ 55 43½ 44½	Bierman C	121wb	*1.90e 76-20	Nellie L.1212La Reigh1211½Stefanita1211	No rally late 13
5May43- 6Pim	fst 1 1/16	:231 :471 1:12 1:454	ⒻPim Oaks 13k	10 4 32 21½ 1½ 11	Bierman C	121wb	*2.30e 89-14	Askmenow1211Too Timely1212Pomrose121nk	Easily 10
14Apr43- 6CD	sl 6f	:232 :474 1:141	ⒻAshland 3.4k	4 5 64½ 43 45½ 35¾	Bierman C	121 w	*.90e 76-27	ValdinaMarl118¾Nppy1155Askmnow1211	Close quarters early 6
24Oct42- 5Lrl	fst 1 1/16	:232 :481 1:142 1:464	ⒻSelima 25k	5 2 31½ 21 11 11½	Bierman C	111wb	3.55e 83-20	Askmenow1111½Good Morning119hdTooTimly1143	9

Forced wide,handily

Date	Cond/Dist	Fractions	Race	PP/Positions	Jockey	Wt	Odds/Figures	Top finishers	Comment
3Oct42- 4Bel	fst 6½f-W	:222 :443 1:083 1:151	Futurity 69k	8 7 33 23 24 25	Bierman C	116wb	27.80 91-04	Occupation1265Askmenow116hdCount Fleet1191½	Driving 10

Geldings not eligible

Date	Cond/Dist	Fractions	Race	PP/Positions	Jockey	Wt	Odds/Figures	Top finishers	Comment
26Sep42- 4Bel	fst 6f-WC	:222 :45 1:091	ⒻMatron 12k	8 8 62¼ 2hd 1hd 21	Haas L	114wb	9.25e 100-00	Good Morning1091Askmenow1141½Navigating1142	Gamely 20
21Sep42- 7Bel	fst 6f-WC	:224 :46 1:11	ⒻAlw 2000	3 5 74 3nk 3nk 53¼	Haas L	115wb	6.70 89-06	Samaritan111hdStefanita119nkCape May1111	Inside,blocked 13
15Aug42- 6Sar	fst 6f	:23 :464 1:123	ⒻSpinaway 10k	1 2 1nk 11 12 21	Wright WD	113wb	3.35 88-13	Our Page1131Askmenow1134Wuskenin113no	Driving 13
11Aug42- 6Sar	sl 5½f	:231 :472 1:001 1:072	ⒻAlw 1200	5 2 21 2nk 1nk 16	Arcaro E	115wb	4.85 86-19	Askmenow1156Navigating115noAdventurous114hd	Easily 8
11Jly42- 6AP	gd 6f	:23 :471 1:133	ⒻArl Lassie 34k	9 1 2hd 2½ 25 26	McCombs K	117wb	11.00e 73-30	Fad1176Askmenow1171Miss Barbara117½	Bore out turn 13
7Jly42- 5AP	fst 5½f	:223 :472 1:001 1:063	ⒻAlw 1500	2 2 11 1½ 31 56	Wright WD	116wb	12.40 82-13	MissBarbara1163½EvenStitch116¾BlenheimGirl116nk	Tired 7
27Jun42- 6Del	my 5f	:224 :471 1:01	ⒻPolly Drummond 8.4k	6 8 79 68 713 711¾	Roberts P	113wb	8.70e 78-19	Fair Weather1221½La Reigh122hdParachutist1132	Outrun 8
20Jun42- 7Suf	gd 5f	:23 :472 1:002	ⒻBetsy Ross 9.4k	3 2 21 1nk 1hd 32	Howell R	111wb	2.70e 89-14	La Reigh111hdTellmenow1112Askmenow111¾	Weakened 7
10Jun42- 5Aqu	fst 5f	:232 :47 1:00	ⒻAlw 2000	2 4 32½ 1½ 3½ 44½	Zufelt F	118wb	8.45 91-11	The Watch1183Witchwater1131½Mountain Pass113no	Tired 6
29Apr42- 4Jam	fst 5f	:23 :463 1:003	ⒻRosedale 7.7k	6 7 65 77½ 76¾ 712	Meade D	115wb	2.85 78-09	Hurriette111noOptimism1152Sonorous1121	Never close 8
22Apr42- 4Jam	fst 5f	:231 :463 1:00	ⒻAlw 2000	3 1 1½ 12 12 11¼	Meade D	109wb	3.40 93-11	Askmenow1091¼The Watch1162Hurriette1081¼	In hand 11
18Apr42- 3Jam	fst 5f	:23 :47 1:014	ⒻMd Sp Wt	5 5 41½ 22 23 35¾	Meade D	115wb	*2.25 78-19	Optimism1153½Good Morning1152¼Askmenow1151	Faltered 11

Assault

ch. c. 1943, by Bold Venture (St. Germans)–Igual, by Equipoise — **Lifetime record: 42 18 6 7 $675,470**

Own.– King Ranch
Br.– King Ranch (Tex)
Tr.– W.J. Hirsch

9Dec50- 7Hol	fst 1¼	:463 1:101 1:35 1:594 3↑	Hol Gold Cup 137k	5 2	53½	53¾	44½	710¼	Gilbert J	121wb	37.95	91-09	Noor1301Palestinian1223Hill Prince1301	8
	Carried wide,rallied,flattened out													
1Dec50- 7Hol	fst 1⅛	:48 1:114 1:361 1:48 3↑	Alw 5000	1 1	2hd	1½	23	38	Boland W	112wb	1.90	93-11	Noor1247Palestinian1201Assault1121	Weakened 5
22Nov50- 7Hol	fst 7f	:222 :451 1:093 1:224 3↑	Alw 4000	1 1	11½	12½	14	12	Arcaro E	120wb	2.90	95-16	Assault1202Repeluz1162Bernbrook1131	Easing up 7
	Previously trained by M. Hirsch													
15Oct49- 6Jam	fst 1 1/16	:242 :48 1:124 1:442 3↑	Grey Lag H 29k	10 8	87¼	85	84¼	86¼	Arcaro E	123wb	4.75e	85-16	Royal Governor1141Three Rings116hdCapot121nk	No rally 12
24Sep49- 6Bel	fst 1½	:49 1:13 2:022 2:28 3↑	Manhattan H 29k	7 4	66	611	79¼	714	Gorman D	126wb	*2.15	84-13	Donor118¾My Request1258Stunts114hd	Wide,outrun 7
10Sep49- 6Aqu	fst 1⅛	:473 1:12 1:37 1:504 3↑	Edgemere H 22k	3 9	916	914	48½	33¾	Gorman D	124wb	*2.50	89-16	My Request1193Stunts115¾Assault124½	Closed fast 9
13Aug49- 7Suf	hy 1¼	:482 1:133 1:393 2:043 3↑	Mass H 59k	5 2	21	3¾	3¾	43	Gorman D	125wb	*.40	87-27	FirstNighter104nkGoingAway103¾MichgnIII1172	Lost ground 5
2Jly49- 6Aqu	fst 1¼	:484 1:13 1:372 2:024 3↑	Brooklyn H 58k	7 5	42	2½	11½	1¾	Gorman D	122wb	*.95e	93-14	Assault122¾Vulcan's Forge129nkFlying Missel117¾	Driving 10
24Jun49- 5Aqu	fst 7f	:231 :46 1:12 1:262 4↑	Alw 4000	4 2	32	1½	1hd	2no	Boland W	119wb	*.35	80-27	Michigan III115noAssault1194Spats1082	Weak ride 5
21Feb48- 6Hia	fst 1¼	:47 1:11 1:354 2:01 3↑	Widener H 62k	1 5	85¾	31	42¼	57	Arcaro E	130wb	*1.15	96-10	El Mono112hdStud Poker1032½Bug Juice1073	Faltered 9
14Feb48- 5Hia	fst 7f	:233 :47 1:113 1:234 4↑	Alw 5000	1 4	33	21½	2½	1hd	Mehrtens W	126wb	*.40	93-10	Assault128hdRampart1097Star Pilot1169	Not urged 4
27Sep47- 6Bel	fst 1¼	:471 1:113 1:363 2:024 3↑	Special 100k	1 2	24	22	23	28	Arcaro E	126wb	-	78-10	Armed1268Assault126	Outrun 2
19Jly47- 6Bel	sly 1⅝	:483 1:39 2:042 2:423 3↑	Gold Cup 109k	2 2	418	45½	21½	34¼	Arcaro E	126wb	*.55	87-14	Stymie126nkNatchez1264Assault1261	Swerved,tired 7
	Geldings not eligible													
12Jly47- 5Jam	fst 1 3/16	:49 1:134 1:381 1:563 3↑	Butler H 54k	5 2	45	44½	51	1hd	Arcaro E	135wb	*.45	93-09	Assault135hdStymie1261¾Gallorette117nk	Hard drive 5
21Jun47- 6Aqu	fst 1¼	:472 1:121 1:38 2:033 3↑	Brooklyn H 55k	2 1	414	45½	2½	13	Arcaro E	133wb	*.45	89-14	Assault1333Stymie1244Larky Day1101	Easily 5
30May47- 6Bel	fst 1¼	:472 1:114 1:364 2:014 3↑	Suburban H 57k	2 4	46½	26	21½	12	Arcaro E	130wb	*1.10	91-09	Assault1302Natchez1207Talon1131	Going away 7
9May47- 6Pim	fst 1 3/16	:474 1:122 1:384 1:574 3↑	Dixie H 35k	7 1	56½	54¼	2hd	1½	Arcaro E	129wb	*.40e	93-20	Assault129½Rico Monte1203Talon1152	Hand ride 7
3May47- 5Jam	fst 1⅛	:47 1:112 1:363 1:494 3↑	Grey Lag H 46k	2 6	68½	41½	4nk	1nk	Mehrtens W	128wb	*1.25	99-13	Asslt128nkLetsDanc110nkConcdnc1202	Bumped,forced wide 8
	Daily Racing Form time,1:49 1/5													
9Nov46- 5Jam	gd 1 3/16	:472 1:112 1:373 1:562 3↑	Westchester H 56k	4 5	69½	510	11½	12	Arcaro E	122wb	1.65	94-17	Assault1222½Lucky Draw1284Lets Dance1041½	Cleverly 6
1Nov46- 6Pim	fst 1 3/16	:481 1:132 1:39 1:57 3↑	Pim Spl 25k	3 3	314	39½	11	16	Arcaro E	120wb	2.80	97-16	Assault1206Stymie1263Bridal Flower117½	Easily 4
26Oct46- 5Jam	fst 1⅝	:462 1:373 2:03 2:424 3↑	Gallant Fox H 85k	10 6	57½	11	35½	34½	Mehrtens W	114wb	4.90	96-11	Stymie1262½Rico Monte1162Assault1148	Weakened 11
19Oct46- 5Jam	fst 1 3/16	:473 1:123 1:39 1:572	Roamer H 31k	7 11	96¾	75¼	2nk	2½	Mehrtens W	126wb	*1.40	88-13	Bridal Flower118½Assault1261½Risolater109nk	Hung 12
25Sep46- 6Bel	fst 1½	:493 1:143 2:032 2:292 3↑	Manhattan H 28k	2 3	54¼	53¾	44¾	33¾	Mehrtens W	116wb	1.90	87-13	Stymie126¾Pavot1213[DH]Flareback1131	Came on again 8
14Sep46- 5GS	fst 1⅛	:472 1:121 1:363 1:491	Jersey H 31k	5 6	65½	31	2hd	2½	Mehrtens W	126wb	*.70	98-09	Mahout114½Assault1263Blue Yonder1131¼	No excuse 7
7Sep46- 6Aqu	fst 1⅛	:48 1:123 1:39 1:514	Discovery H 28k	4 8	812	67	57¼	33½	Mehrtens W	126wb	*.70e	84-14	Mighty Story1152½Mahout1121Assault126¾	Forced wide 9
27Jly46- 6AP	fst 1¼	:491 1:123 1:364 2:023	Classic 94k	2 2	33½	48½	610½	68¼	Mehrtens W	126wb	*.70	85-09	The Dude1191¼Sgt. Spence1192½Mighty Story1222	Sulked 6
15Jun46- 6Aqu	fst 1¼	:481 1:14 1:411 2:064	Dwyer 58k	6 4	59¼	33½	2nk	14½	Mehrtens W	126wb	*.40	73-23	Assault1264½Windfields116½Lord Boswell1211½	Easily 6
1Jun46- 6Bel	fst 1½	:493 1:141 2:04 2:304	Belmont 110k	1 7	45¼	33½	32	13	Mehrtens W	126wb	1.40	84-13	Assault1263Natchez1262Cable126hd	Going away 7
	Geldings not eligible													
11May46- 6Pim	fst 1 3/16	:48 1:13 1:40 2:012	Preakness 131k	5 6	65	3½	14	1nk	Mehrtens W	126wb	*1.40	75-20	Assault126nkLord Boswell1263½Hampden1264	Ridden out 10
4May46- 7CD	sl 1¼	:48 1:141 1:404 2:063	Ky Derby 113k	2 3	54	32	12½	18	Mehrtens W	126wb	8.20	74-22	Assault1268Spy Song126hdHampden1261	Drew away 17
30Apr46- 5CD	my 1	:223 :463 1:123 1:401	Derby Trial 13k	5 5	410	47½	47½	44½	Mehrtens W	118wb	4.50	73-32	Rippey110nkSpy Song1184With Pleasure118nk	Closed ground 10
20Apr46- 5Jam	fst 1 1/16	:233 :47 1:113 1:463	Wood Memorial 31k	11 3	35	34	2hd	12¼	Mehrtens W	126wb	8.85	80-18	Assault1262¼Hampden126½Marine Victory1261	Going away 14
	Daily Racing Form time,1:47 1/5													
9Apr46- 5Jam	fst 6f	:23 :47 1:12	Exp Free H 1 11k	6 6	31½	1½	13	14½	Mehrtens W	116wb	9.10	91-17	Assault1164½IslamPrince114½LarkmeadAndy110nk	Hand ride 11
8Oct45- 5Jam	fst 6f	:23 :463 1:12	Alw 5000	4 5	43¼	31	2hd	23	Mehrtens W	117wb	2.15	89-15	Lord Boswell1173Assault1174Landlord1112½	No match 5
12Sep45- 6Aqu	fst 6½f	:231 :464 1:122 1:18	Cowdin 31k	8 9	117	88	54½	44	Mehrtens W	120wsb	34.40	91-14	Knockdown1141½Revokd1261SouthernPrd1201½	Finished well 13
5Sep45- 6Aqu	fst 6f	:223 :463 1:121	Babylon H 14k	6 6	31¼	21	21	34	Mehrtens W	119wb	10.90	87-17	Southern Pride1201Tidy Bid1133Assault119nk	Hung 9
6Aug45- 4Bel	sly 5½f-W	:221 :452 1:044	Flash 15k	11 1		2nk	42¾	1no	Mehrtens W	113wb	70.60	90-10	Assault113noMist o' Gold122noMush Mush117hd	Driving 12
18Jly45- 5Jam	fst 6f	:23 :461 1:121	©East View 12k	1 5	53¾	45½	53½	58½	Mehrtens W	118 w	18.05	82-15	Misto'Gold1221½SouthrnPride1183Degage1222	Saved ground 14
12Jly45- 5Aqu	fst 5½f	:223 :463 1:072	©Alw 3000	2 2	1hd	21	2½	11¼	Mehrtens W	111wb	4.65	87-19	Assault1111¼Happy C.116¾Darby Darius1161¼	7
	Saved ground,ridden out													
23Jun45- 2Bel	fst 4½f-W	:231 :464 :53	©Md Sp Wt	16 3		11½	21	23	Mehrtens W	116wb	23.95	87-12	Mist o' Gold1163Assault1161Uncle Mac1161½	No mishap 23
12Jun45- 1Bel	fst 4½f-W	:251 :471 :533	©Md Sp Wt	12 4		4¾	62¾	51¾	Mehrtens W	116 w	79.25	85-12	Leeway109hdChallenge Play1161½The Heir116hd	Early speed 15
4Jun45- 4Bel	sly 4½f-W	:224 :462 :531	©Md Sp Wt	13 8		118	1114	1214½	Stout J	116 w	17.30	74-13	Grandpa Max1164The Heir1161½Skylighter1161	Evenly 21

Beaugay

b. f. 1943, by Stimulus (Ultimus)–Risk, by Sir Gallahad III — **Lifetime record: 18 9 3 0 $148,070**

Own.– Maine Chance Farm
Br.– Arthur B. Hancock Sr (Ky)
Tr.– J.W. Smith

29May48- 5Del	fst 6f	:223 :46 1:113 3↑	Wilmington H 13k	10 13	115	85½	95¾	85¾	Nash R	119 w	5.75	88-09	Itsabet1132½[DH]Phar Mon114[DH]Mity Me1121	14
	Slow into stride,no threat													
1May48- 5Jam	fst 6f	:232 :463 1:121 3↑	Interborough H 22k	5 1	2hd	4¾	3nk	93¾	Nash R	121 w	*2.25	86-20	Miss Disco1091Tavistock106nkKitchen Police114nk	Quit 9
17Apr48- 5GS	fst 6f	:23 :463 1:114 3↑	ⒻColonial H 20k	8 1	1hd	1hd	1hd	2no	Dodson D	122 w	*1.90	90-17	Itsabet110noBeaugay1224½Bogle1151½	Game try 13
11Nov47- 4Jam	fst 6f	:233 :462 1:113 3↑	Can't Wait H 10k	2 3	1hd	21½	3½	44	Dodson D	125 w	*.95	89-19	Miss Disco1071½Buzfuz126½Gestapo1082	Gave way 6
29Oct47- 5Jam	sly 6f	:231 :46 1:112 2↑	New Rochelle H 23k	5 2	11	11	11	11	Dodson D	117 w	6.90	94-17	Beaugay1171With Pleasure1322½Buzfuz1251	Driving 9
15Oct47- 5Jam	fst 6f	:232 :47 1:12 2↑	ⒻCorrection H 17k	10 3	2nk	1½	11	21	Adams J	123wb	4.40	90-17	Miss Kimo1261Beaugay1232Miss Disco110hd	Held on well 11
22Sep47- 6Bel	sly 6f-WC	:223 :454 1:104 2↑	Fall Highweight H 30k	10 5	1nk	42	31½	43¼	Dodson D	124 w	6.55	84-14	Rippey131noPipette1142½Ben Lewis103¾	No mishap 12
7Oct46- 5GS	fst 6f	:223 :461 1:103 3↑	ⒻColonial H (Div 1) 11k	2 4	2hd	3nk	11½	12	Guerin E	122 w	*.70	98-11	Beaugay1222Forgetmenow1111¼Athene113hd	Going away 8
18Sep46- 6Aqu	fst 6f	:222 :461 1:102	Alw 4500	5 1	21½	2½	1nk	11	Guerin E	115 w	2.85	100-16	Beaugay1151High Lea114½Pep Well1222½	Drew out 6
7Aug46- 6Was	fst 7f	:214 :443 1:10 1:23	ⒻArtful H 27k	5 2	1½	1½	2½	47¾	Adams J	121wb	*1.00e	90-09	Athenia1161¼Widow's Peak111½Trixie1056	Gave way 9
22Jun46- 6AP	gd 6f	:223 :454 1:121	ⒻPrincess Doreen 29k	7 3	1½	31	2½	21¼	Brooks S	121 w	*.90	85-22	SeaSnack1181¼Beaugay1213½RomanBelle110½	Close quarters 15
	Previously trained by T. Smith													
29Sep45- 4Bel	gd 6½f-W	:221 :451 1:103 1:171	Futurity 65k	11 4		1hd	21½	-	Dodson D	123 w	*.70e	- -	Star Pilot1261Athene1161Mighty Story1192	Bolted,fell 11
	Geldings not eligible													
22Sep45- 4Bel	fst 6f-WC	:221 :443 1:092	ⒻMatron 28k	4 1		2nk	31	1nk	Kirkland A	123 w	*.70	94-07	Beaugay123nkEnfilade119nkAthene1153	Driving 11
11Aug45- 6Was	sl 6f	:223 :46 1:13	ⒻPrincess Pat 42k	4 2	1½	13	15	16	Dodson D	119 w	*.40	85-18	Beaugay1196Enfilade1192½Breezy Louise1152	Easing up 6
18Jly45- 6Was	fst 6f	:222 :462 1:121	ⒻArl Lassie 44k	6 2	2hd	1hd	1½	11¼	Adams J	119 w	*.40	89-10	Beaugay1191¼Enfilade1193Aladear1193	Carried out 9
14Jun45- 6Del	fst 5f	:222 :453 :58	ⒻPolly Drummond 8.6k	2 1	11	1hd	1hd	12	Adams J	119 w	*.20	105-12	Beaugay1192Aladear1143Mamanie1138	Easily best 5
5Jun45- 6Bel	gd 4½f-W	:221 :452 :514	ⒻFashion 5.9k	3 1		1nk	11½	13½	Adams J	114 w	1.75	96-10	Beaugay1143½Enfilade11915Datura110	Swerved start,easily 3
22May45- 3Jam	fst 5f	:23 :47 :594	ⒻMd Sp Wt	8 2	1nk	11½	14	17	Adams J	115 w	3.95	91-14	Bugy1157Srongrl1151BonnBryl1154	Drew away final furlong 12

Bewitch

br. f. 1945, by Bull Lea (Bull Dog)–Potheen, by Wildair

Own.– Calumet Farm

Br.– Calumet Farm (Ky)

Tr.– H.A. Jones

Lifetime record: 55 20 10 11 $462,605

Date/Race	Cond	Dist	Fractions	Race	Calls	Jockey	Wt	Odds	Figs	Top finishers	Comment
3Sep51- 7Was	fst	1	:222 :443 1:09 1:343	3↑ Wash Park H 159k	16 19 1918 1925 1615 1615¼	Brooks S	113wb	7.30	82-07	Curandero115noOil Capitol1161½County Delight1231½	19
			Auxiliary gate opened over a second after main gate								
29Aug51- 7Was	fst	1	:222 :45 1:094 1:354	3↑ (F)Beverly H 28k	7 9 99½ 1011 77 55½	Dodson D	124wb	*1.70e	84-13	Wistful1261¼War Talk1141¼Lithe1241	No mishap 10
18Aug51- 6Was	fst	7f	:22 :442 1:09 1:212	3↑ Clang H 22k	3 10 911 1012 913 811	Brooks S	118wb	*1.50e	89-07	Lithe1152Seaward110hdWine List1161	Bore in 10
21Jly51- 7Hol	fst	1⅝	:483 1:383 2:032 2:42	3↑ Sunset H 57k	5 3 33½ 53¼ 711 710	Brooks S	110 w	*1.70	84-10	Alderman112noMocopo1066Stormy Cloud105no	Outrun 10
14Jly51- 7Hol	fst	1¼	:464 1:103 2:01	3↑ Hol Gold Cup 137k	4 7 79½ 54 44 24	Lasswell G	108 w	*.35e	90-10	Citation1204Bewitch108noBe Fleet1221	Good effort 10
7Jly51- 7Hol	fst	1 1/16	:231 :462 1:104 1:424	3↑ (F)Vanity H 28k	3 6 57¾ 35 2½ 1¾	Brooks S	125 w	*.35	94-08	Bewitch125¾Fleet Rings1064Great Dream1081½	Driving 7
4Jly51- 7Hol	fst	1⅛	:464 1:11 1:36 1:482	3↑ American H 56k	8 6 63½ 5¾ 1hd 2½	Lasswell G	106 w	*.75e	97-07	Citation123½Bewitch1062¾Sturdy One112¾	Good effort 8
23Jun51- 7Hol	fst	1 1/16	:224 :454 1:102 1:421	3↑ Inglewood H 29k	7 8 89 74¼ 51¾ 4nk	Smith FA	107 w	3.50e	97-08	Sturdy One109hdAll Blue111noBe Fleet123nk	Closed fast 8
30May51- 7Hol	fst	1 1/16	:222 :45 1:101 1:42	3↑ Argonaut H 30k	4 10 1015 87 46½ 43¾	Brooks S	109 w	*.45e	94-08	Be Fleet1183Citation121nkSturdy One111½	Late foot 10
26May51- 6Hol	fst	7f	:221 :444 1:094 1:222	3↑ Handicap 10000	3 9 99 85¾ 75¾ 11¾	Smith FA	110 w	*.70e	97-10	Bewitch1101¾Be Fleet119¾Special Touch123no	Going away 9
19Apr51- 8BM	fst	1	:234 :471 1:114 1:363	3↑ Handicap 5000	3 5 63¼ 54 53 31	Brooks S	110 w	3.65	96-11	Sturdy One109noAlderman1061Bewitch110no	Held well 6
31Mar51- 8BM	fst	1 1/16	:232 :464 1:11 1:431	3↑ San Fran Country H 30k	3 8 87¾ 88½ 74¼ 73	Brooks S	110wb	*1.55	91-11	BeFleet1191¼BullreighJr.113½VinoFno110nk	Close quarters 10
17Mar51- 8BM	fst	1 1/16	:232 :464 1:111 1:43	3↑ St. Patrick's Day H 29k	3 7 76¾ 64½ 42½ 2no	Brooks S	110wb	2.75	95-12	Manyunk113noBewitch110nkSturdy One109nk	Bold finish 8
3Mar51- 7SA	gd	1¼	:462 1:11 1:364 2:023	3↑ S Anita H 135k	7 3 1315 1111 912 611	Brooks S	111 w	*2.85e	76-24	Moonrush114nkNext Move1162¾Sudan111hd	Slow to settle 14
20Jan51- 7SA	fst	1⅛	:461 1:11 1:361 1:483	3↑ (F)S Margarita H 60k	5 6 56 33½ 22 21	Brooks S	122 w	3.20e	97-16	SpecialTouch1141Bewitch1221¼Bdo'Ross1251½	Strong finish 8
2Dec50- 7Hol	fst	1⅛	:47 1:111 1:362 1:492	3↑ (F)Vanity H 30k	7 7 76¾ 44½ 33 22¼	Brooks S	124 w	2.65e	92-11	Next Move1282¼Bewitch1241Wistful125½	Bore in 9
18Nov50- 6Hol	fst	1	:223 :454 1:102 1:36	3↑ Handicap 10000	2 5 54½ 53½ 32½ 31¼	Brooks S	115 w	*.75e	96-09	Curandero1151Valquest112nkBewitch1151	Finished strong 9
7Nov50- 7Hol	fst	7f	:221 :444 1:091 1:221	3↑ Premiere H 33k	7 14 94¾ 84¾ 64½ 3nk	Brooks S	114 w	9.30	98-12	Star Fiddle108noYour Host125nkBewitch114nk	Forced wide 14
14Oct50- 6GS	fst	1 1/16	:232 :471 1:112 1:434	3↑ (F)Vineland H 24k	13 11 106¾ 78½ 57½ 32½	Brooks S	122 w	*1.20	91-12	Almahmoud1082Lithe118½Bewitch1221½	Closed fast 14
28Sep50- 6Bel	fst	1 1/16	:232 :463 1:11 1:424	3↑ (F)Handicap 5060	4 6 53 32 2hd 11	Brooks S	122 w	2.20	97-11	Bewitch1221Night Game1102¼Jazz Baby113nk	Ridden out 8
23Sep50- 7Bel	fst	6f	:224 :463 1:111	3↑ (F)Handicap 5070	5 9 97 89 66½ 44¾	Brooks S	121 w	3.70	89-15	Sweet Dream118noMiss Highbrow1101¼Ouija1103½	No excuse 10
11Mar50- 6GP	fst	1⅛	:473 1:123 1:374 1:492	3↑ Handicap 7500	4 4 54½ 42 1hd 3nk	Scurlock O	123 w	*.40e	97-09	Wynford II112hdArmed111hdBewitch1232½	Lugged in 6
2Mar50- 6Hia	fst	1⅛	:454 1:103 1:353 1:48	3↑ (F)Black Helen H 19k	2 5 34½ 2hd 14 17	Scurlock O	126 w	*.70	98-10	Bewitch1267Roman Candle1092Yoncalla1041½	Impeded,best 10
15Feb50- 6Hia	fst	7f	:224 :451 1:102 1:23	3↑ (F)Columbiana H 9.6k	6 7 76½ 85¼ 43 2no	Scurlock O	126 w	*1.40	97-13	Fighting Fan118noBewitch126¾Nell K.124¾	Just missed 11
3Feb50- 6Hia	fst	6f	:222 :46 1:104	4↑ (F)Alw 4000	3 3 35½ 33 2hd 11	Culmone J	119 w	*.45	94-12	[D]Bewitch1191Fighting Fan110hdAllie's Pal1166	Bore in 5
			Disqualified and placed third								
11Jan50- 5TrP	fst	6f	:224 :46 1:103	4↑ (F)Alw 2000	5 5 44½ 42 32 31	Scurlock O	116 w	*.90	93-13	Fighting Fan114noNo Strings1111Bewitch1161½	Good effort 6
15Oct49- 6GS	fst	1 1/16	:224 :461 1:112 1:443	3↑ (F)Vineland H 24k	6 13 1211 58½ 44½ 1¾	Brooks S	126 w	*1.40	90-16	Bewitch126¾Imacomin111¾Lithe1073	Drew out 14
3Oct49- 6Bel	fst	1½	:482 1:131 2:033 2:294	3↑ (F)Ladies H 35k	8 12 129¾ 64¼ 63¼ 41¾	Brooks S	126 w	*1.95	87-14	Gaffery114noMiss Request119nkAdile1151½	Blocked 12
17Sep49- 6Aqu	fst	1⅛	:48 1:124 1:384 1:524	3↑ (F)Beldame H 72k	17 15 1316 1213 86½ 52¾	Scurlock O	126 w	*2.45	80-17	MissRequest1131[D]Harmonc1121¼Plundr108hd	Slow to settle 18
			Placed fourth by disqualification								
31Aug49- 6Was	fst	1	:223 :444 1:09 1:342	3↑ (F)Beverly H 27k	4 7 54½ 41½ 22 1nk	Brooks S	125 w	*1.20	98-13	Bewitch125nkStole1046Evanstep111½	Just up 9
6Aug49- 6Was	fst	7f	:213 :44 1:084 1:222	3↑ (F)Misty Isle H 28k	10 8 87¾ 34½ 21½ 1½	Brooks S	121 w	*1.40	98-08	Bewitch121½Dandilly1171½Stole107nk	Driving 12
27Jly49- 6AP	gd	1	:232 :462 1:102 1:361	3↑ (F)Arl Matron H 27k	7 2 21 22 22½ 23½	Brooks S	121 w	*1.00	87-20	Lithe1023½Bewitch1216Danada Gift112¾	Went well 8
19Jly49- 6AP	fst	7f	:23 :453 1:102 1:232	3↑ (F)Handicap 4500	3 4 44 33 2hd 2½	Brooks S	122 w	*.70	92-13	Roman Candle105½Bewitch1221½Brownian1104	Hung 6
2Jly49- 6AP	fst	6f	:222 :45 1:10	3↑ (F)Modesty 28k	2 7 93¾ 85 56 53½	Scurlock O	123 w	*1.40e	93-10	No Strings101½Two Lea1112Dandilly1081	No mishap 10
27Jun49- 6AP	fst	6f	:23 :46 1:104	4↑ (F)Alw 5000	7 5 54 64¾ 2½ 2½	Brooks S	120 w	*.90	92-17	Loriot108½Bewitch1202Blue Helen108nk	Blocked turn 8
20Jun49- 7AP	fst	6f	:223 :452 1:091	4↑ Alw 5000	5 3 52¼ 51¼ 24 26	Brooks S	115 w	*1.00e	95-09	CarraraMarble1046Bewitch1151½StarReward118hd	Went well 10
			Previously trained by B.A. Jones								
30Apr49- 6CD	fst	6f	:222 :452 1:102	3↑ Inaugural H 10k	5 2 44 23 1hd 14½	Glisson G	115 w	*.40e	101-14	Bewitch1154½Enforcer110noSouthern Pride104hd	Easily 7
19Apr49- 5Kee	fst	6½f	:23 :462 1:112 1:181	3↑ Handicap 3500	1 5 43½ 54½ 32 3nk	McCreary C	113 w	*1.10	--	Plumper108hdJohns Joy107hdBewitch1135	Strong finish 8
			Previously trained by H.A. Jones								
19Mar49- 5GP	fst	6f	:23 :46 1:102	4↑ Alw 3000	4 3 3½ 41¾ 3nk 3½	Nelson E	105 w	*.80	97-06	Carrara Marble120½High Shine112noBewitch1058	Weakened 9
11Aug48- 7Was	sl	7f	:222 :453 1:102 1:243	(F)Artful H 27k	3 7 54½ 44½ 11 12	Pierson NL	122 w	*.90e	87-16	Bewitch1222Blue Helen1091Miss Mommy1133	Driving 8
21Jly48- 7AP	fst	1	:233 :46 1:10 1:352	Dick Welles 28k	9 2 42½ 32 31 32¼	Pierson NL	118 w	*.80e	93-14	Papa Redbird117hdShy Guy1202½Bewitch1182¼	No excuse 10
14Jly48- 7AP	fst	1	:23 :46 1:11 1:364	(F)Cleopatra H 28k	5 5 65¼ 52¼ 1½ 14	Pierson NL	122 w	*.70e	88-19	Bewitch1224Alablue110¾Ann's Lee1101¼	Easily,bore in 12
3Jly48- 7AP	fst	6f	:214 :443 1:101	3↑ (F)Modesty 29k	16 15 96¾ 69 32 11¼	Woodhouse H	107 w	*1.40e	96-09	Bewitch1071¼Tre Vit1132Bogle1092¼	Drew out 18
23Jun48- 7AP	my	6f	:224 :453 1:114	(F)Princess Doreen 28k	6 3 63 66 65½ 52¾	Pierson NL	121 w	*.90	85-19	Miss Mommy121½Silly Gyp112¾Ann's Lee114nk	No excuse 13
			Previously trained by B.A. Jones								
10Apr48- 6Kee	fst	6f	:223 :462 1:12	(F)Ashland 12k	4 1 21 2½ 1hd 1no	Pierson NL	121 w	*.20	92-14	Bewitch121noSilly Gyp115¾Lea Lark1121½	Strong hand ride 4
			Previously trained by H.A. Jones								
4Oct47- 4Bel	fst	6½f-W	:221 :444 1:092 1:154	Futurity 106k	9 3 53 23 33¼	Westrope J	123 w	*.85e	90-10	Citation1223Whirling Fox114nkBewitch1231	Close quarters 14
			Geldings not eligible								
27Sep47- 4Bel	fst	6f-WC	:222 :451 1:101	(F)Matron 46k	9 3 3nk 3nk 1nk	Dodson D	123 w	*.35	90-10	[D]Bewitch123nkInheritance1152Vaudeville115hd	Bore in 10
			Disqualified and placed last								
16Aug47- 6Was	fst	6f	:223 :45 1:102	Was Futurity 78k	2 1 1hd 14 14 11	Dodson D	119 w	*.20e	98-07	Bewitch1191Citation118hdFree America1182	Ridden out 10
9Aug47- 7Was	fst	6f	:224 :453 1:11	(F)Princess Pat 57k	3 1 1hd 14 13 13	Dodson D	119 w	*.30	95-08	Bewitch1193Boswell Lady1154Shy Katie112½	Easily 6
23Jly47- 7AP	fst	6f	:221 :441 1:104	(F)Arl Lassie 58k	1 2 12 13 15 12¾	Dodson D	119 w	*.30e	93-07	Bewitch1192¾Boswell Lady1192¼Lea Lark1192¼	In hand 9
23Jun47- 6AP	fst	5½f	:22 :45 :572 1:04	(F)Pollyanna 20k	2 1 2½ 1hd 14 15	Dodson D	119 w	*.20e	101-10	Bewitch1195Kandy Comfort1163Whirl Some1162	Easily 13
16Jun47- 6AP	fst	5½f	:224 :463 :59 1:05	Hyde Park 23k	2 2 11 14 15 18	Dodson D	119 w	*.50e	96-16	Bewitch1198Loujac116½May Reward116hd	Easily 12
			Previously trained by B.A. Jones								
30Apr47- 6CD	gd	5f	:23 :47 1:003	(F)Debutante 13k	6 4 32 12 16 18	Dodson D	119 w	*.70	92-26	Bewitch1198Pelt1142Loriot1192	Easily 7
17Apr47- 5Kee	fst	*4f	:46	Sp Wt 3000	4 5 32 2hd 1nk	Dodson D	113 w	*.50	100-01	Bewitch113nkCircus Clown115¾Hilda1126	Hard drive 8
10Apr47- 1Kee	fst	*4f	:461	(F)Md Sp Wt	1 5 11 12½ 16	Dodson D	116 w	2.60	99-01	Bewitch1166Blue Helen1161½Bobalee1164½	Easily 11

Bimelech

b. c. 1937, by Black Toney (Peter Pan)–La Troienne, by Teddy — **Lifetime record: 15 11 2 1 $248,745**

Own.– E.R. Bradley
Br.– Idle Hour Stock Farm (Ky)
Tr.– W. Hurley

1Mar41- 6Hia	fst 1¼	:464 1:111 1:362 2:024	3↑	Widener H 65k	5	1	31½	2hd	1hd	42½	Meade D	126 w	*.75	92-12	BigPebble109hdGetOff1151½Hltl1081	Saved ground,led,hung	14
22Feb41- 5Hia	fst 1⅛	:492 1:132 1:38 1:494	4↑	Sp Wt 2500	1	1	11½	11½	11½	11	Meade D	116 w	*.35	92-08	Bimelech1161Hash1185Shot Put1182	Easily	4
20Jly40- 6AP	fst 1¼	:471 1:114 1:37 2:03		Classic 49k	1	1	21½	33½	39	310	Smith FA	126 w	*.60	81-13	Sirocco1217Gallahadion1263Bimelech1268	Weakened	6
8Jun40- 6Bel	fst 1½	:482 1:134 1:381 2:293		Belmont 42k	1	1	21½	1hd	1½	1¾	Smith FA	126 w	*1.35	94-12	Bimelech126¾Your Choice1261Andy K.1268	Drew out	6
18May40- 6Bel	fst 1	:23 :46 1:112 1:371		Withers 20k	6	4	41¾	21½	21½	21½	Smith FA	118 w	*.20	87-15	Corydon1181½Bimelech118noRoman1188	Hung	8
	Geldings not eligible																
11May40- 6Pim	fst 1 3/16	:47 1:12 1:384 1:583		Preakness 70k	5	1	11	11½	11½	13	Smith FA	126 w	*.90	90-15	Bimelech1263Mioland1261½Gallahadion1262	Going away	9
4May40- 7CD	fst 1¼	:48 1:124 1:383 2:05		Ky Derby 72k	2	1	21½	1hd	1½	21½	Smith FA	126 w	*.40	82-14	Gallahadion1261½Bimelech126noDit1261	Weakened	8
30Apr40- 4CD	gd 1	:224 :462 1:112 1:38		Derby Trial 3k	4	1	11	12	12	12¼	Smith FA	118 w	*.10	89-21	Bimelech1182¼Gallahadion1155Sirocco1126	Easily	8
25Apr40- 6Kee	fst 1⅛	:463 1:113 1:372 1:51		Blue Grass 8.5k	3	1	11½	12	13	12½	Smith FA	123 w	*.10e	92-15	Bimelech1232½Roman1233Bashful Duck121	In hand	3
4Nov39- 6Pim	fst 1 1/16	:231 :474 1:131 1:451		Pim Futurity 38k	5	2	21	2hd	11	14	Smith FA	122 w	*.40	94-12	Bimelech1224Rough Pass1225Straight Lead1227	Going away	7
	Geldings not eligible																
7Oct39- 4Bel	fst 6½f-WC	1:164		Futurity 67k	6	4	1hd	12	12	11½	Smith FA	126 w	*.50	88-12	Bimelech1261½Calory1194Call to Colors1192	In hand	7
	Geldings not eligible																
2Sep39- 5Sar	fst 6½f	:23 :461 1:121 1:184		Hopeful 39k	2	9	65¾	56	42¼	1nk	Smith FA	122 w	*.60e	91-09	Bimelech122nkAndyK.1263BoyAngler119nk	Impeded start,str	9
12Aug39- 3Sar	fst 6f	:223 :461 1:104		Sar Spl 9k	4	2	1nk	11	11½	13	Smith FA	122 w	*1.40	98-06	Bimelech1223Briar Sharp122½Andy K.1221	Going away	8
14Jly39- 4Emp	sl 5½f	:224 :462 1:062		Alw 1000	2	3	1½	11½	13	16	Smith FA	117 w	*.60	94-15	Bimelech1176Last Frontier1122Big Flash1126	Much best	5
28Jun39- 4Suf	fst 5f	:224 :46 :591		Md Sp Wt	5	2	2nk	1hd	11½	13	Smith FA	118 w	*1.80	98-16	Bimelech1183Smart Bet1183½Buenos Suerte1183	Easily	8

Blue Peter

b. c. 1946, by War Admiral (Man o' War)–Carillon, by Case Ace — **Lifetime record: 10 8 0 2 $189,185**

Own.– J.M. Roebling
Br.– Joseph M. Roebling (Ky)
Tr.– A. Schuttinger

25Sep48- 5Bel	fst 6½f-W	:22 :441 1:081 1:143		Futurity 113k	10	1		2hd	11½	1½	Guerin E	126wb	2.40e	99-03	BluPtr126½MrtlChrm1237SportPg118½	Driving	12
	Geldings not eligible																
28Aug48- 6Sar	fst 6½f	:232 :47 1:12 1:191		Hopeful 58k	5	2	11	11½	11½	13	Guerin E	126wb	*1.05e	89-12	Blue Peter1263Sport Page1141Curandero114hd	Easily	7
	Daily Racing Form time,1:19 4/5																
14Aug48- 5Sar	fst 6f	:224 :464 :59 1:13		Sar Spl 11k	1	1	11½	13	13	13½	Guerin E	122wb	*.40	83-17	Blue Peter1223½Sport Page1228Entrust1226	Ridden out	4
28Jly48- 5Mth	fst 6f	:221 :462 1:124		Sapling 14k	4	1	16	16	16	16	Guerin E	122wb	*.30e	84-21	Blue Peter1226Harbourton111½Razzmatazz1116	Galloping	7
31May48- 5GS	sly 5f	:222 :453 :584		Garden State 20k	5	1	2hd	1hd	11½	14½	Wright WD	122wb	*1.20	108-15	Blue Peter1224½Noble Impulse1171Irish Sun1227	Easily	5
22May48- 5GS	fst 5f	:222 :462 :583		©William Penn 14k	9	2	12	12½	1½	1¾	Wright WD	117wb	*1.10	109-17	Blue Peter117¾Noble Impulse11710Eatontown1101	Drew out	9
18May48- 4GS	fst 5f	:224 :464 :591		Alw 3500	6	3	12	11	12	13	Wright WD	117wb	*1.40e	106-19	Blue Peter1173Noble Impulse1151Mr. Jay1151½	Easily	10
1May48- 4Jam	fst 5f	:23 :464 1:002		Youthful 19k	3	6	41¾	3½	41¼	32½	Miller P	117wb	4.40	85-20	Eternal World117hdArise1172½Blue Peter1171	Went well	8
24Apr48- 4GS	fst 4½f	:224 :461 :521		Alw 3500	1	3		1hd	1½	13	Miller P	113wb	6.30	- -	Blue Peter1133Mr. Jay1161½Egretta1134	Ridden out	7
17Apr48- 2GS	fst 4½f	:232 :48 :542		©Md Sp Wt	4	9		2hd	32	35	Miller P	120wb	3.20e	- -	Rookwood1202Deep Fen1203Blue Peter120nk	Weakened	12

Bridal Flower

b. f. 1943, by Challenger II (Swynford)–Big Hurry, by Black Toney — **Lifetime record: 44 13 8 12 $222,055**

Own.– King Ranch
Br.– Idle Hour Stock Farm Co (Ky)
Tr.– W.J. Hirsch

5Mar48- 7SA	fst 1⅛	:464 1:113 1:37 1:493	4↑	Handicap 20000	8	5	75¾	75¾	46	45	Peterson M	110 w	*2.10e	90-11	HnkH.1151Brookfld1254ElLobo109no	Forced wide,closed gamely	10
28Feb48- 7SA	fst 1¼	:464 1:114 1:371 2:032	3↑	S Anita H 139k	12	9	43½	77½	913	99¾	Mehrtens W	111 w	18.20	79-22	Talon122noOn Trust1211¾Double Jay1181¼	Forced wide	14
20Feb48- 7SA	fst 1	:231 :462 1:111 1:372	4↑	Alw 7500	4	4	66½	66	55	31¾	Westrope J	113 w	6.05	89-15	Brabancon1151Hank H.120¾Bridal Flower1131	Closed fast	6
14Feb48- 7SA	fst 1⅛	:461 1:102 1:364 1:492	3↑	San Antonio H 69k	9	14	118	1411	1310	118¼	Lt'berg W	114 w	29.80	88-10	Talon122nkDouble Jay1182¼On Trust126½	No factor	18
	Previously trained by M. Hirsch																
8Nov47- 5Jam	sly 1 3/16	:474 1:121 1:384 1:591	3↑	Westchester H 57k	2	2	55	45½	32	11	Mehrtens W	108 w	5.25	80-22	Bridal Flower1081With Pleasure1301½Donor112hd	Drew out	8
6Nov47- 6Pim	hy 1 1/16	:234 :474 1:13 1:464	3↑	ⒻLady Baltimore H 12k	7	3	35½	31	12	19	Mehrtens W	112 w	3.10	84-31	Bridal Flower1129Irisen114hdEarshot117no	Much the best	7
18Oct47- 6Lrl	fst 1¼	:462 1:113 1:38 2:032	3↑	Washington H 29k	5	3	34	34	37	38½	Kirk C	113 w	5.70e	84-20	LoyalLegion1138BlueYonder113.5½BridlFlowr1134	Weakened	6
11Oct47- 6GS	fst 1⅛	:47 1:104 1:36 1:482	3↑	Trenton H 62k	3	5	56½	57	48½	413½	Mehrtens W	116wb	10.10	89-10	Cosmic Bomb1205Double Jay1188Earshot116½	Close quarters	7
4Oct47- 6GS	fst 1 1/16	:232 :472 1:113 1:423	3↑	ⒻVineland H 31k	1	5	54½	55½	59½	515¾	Mehrtens W	118wb	2.05	84-08	Miss Kimo11710Camargo1141½Letmenow111¾	No factor	7
1Oct47- 6Bel	fst 7f	:232 :464 1:111 1:232	2↑	Vosburgh H 28k	3	5	42¼	41¾	4¾	22½	Arcaro E	114wb	7.00	90-14	With Pleasure1322½Bridal Flower1141½Rabies1053	Swerved	8
26Sep47- 6Bel	fst 1	:231 :463 1:113 1:37	3↑	ⒻHandicap 10115	13	5	53	42¼	4¾	32¼	Arcaro E	122wb	*2.30	87-20	CosmicMissile116nkMissKimo1192BridlFlowr122no	No mishap	13
20Sep47- 7Aqu	fst 1⅛	:483 1:131 1:383 1:514	3↑	ⒻBeldame H (Div 2) 60k	2	1	11	11½	1hd	54	Westrope J	118wb	*1.15e	84-12	But Why Not120noMiss Grillo1262Elpis123hd	Tired	11
13Sep47- 6Aqu	fst 1⅛	:502 1:143 1:392 1:522	3↑	Edgemere H 27k	3	2	21½	3nk	1½	32½	Arcaro E	113wb	6.55	82-13	Elpis1141½Stymie1341Bridal Flower1131½	Tired	4
1Sep47- 6Aqu	fst 1 1/16	:242 :474 1:124 1:442	3↑	Aqueduct H 29k	7	2	24	1hd	1hd	44½	Arcaro E	114wb	6.50	87-13	Stymie132½Gallorette122hdElpis1144	Faltered stretch	11
4Aug47- 6Sar	fst 1	:23 :46 1:10 1:352	3↑	Wilson 23k	5	3	35	36½	42½	45	Mehrtens W	112wb	3.90	99-08	Gallorette1121¼Hornbeam1123King Dorsett112¾	Steadied	5
19Jly47- 6AP	fst 1¼	:471 1:113 1:362 2:022	3↑	Arlington H 55k	8	5	21½	22½	23	21	Mehrtens W	111wb	8.10	92-12	Armed1301Bridal Flower1112¼Challenge Me1142	Second best	8
9Jly47- 5Jam	fst 1 1/16	:233 :471 1:121 1:441	3↑	ⒻComely H 28k	4	9	88¾	76½	56¾	512¼	Mehrtens W	126wb	2.55	80-14	Elpis113hdRisolater1212War Date118nk	No menace	9
7Jun47- 5Del	gd 1 1/16	:23 :473 1:132 1:463	3↑	ⒻNew Castle H 30k	6	8	84¼	64¼	4¾	32¾	Mehrtens W	125wb	*2.00	77-21	Elpis1082Rampart111¾Bridal Flower125nk	Close quarters	11
28May47- 6Bel	fst 1 1/16	:224 :454 1:104 1:433	3↑	ⒻTop Flight H 25k	10	7	64¾	76½	1113	1113½	Mehrtens W	126wb	*1.55	79-18	Rytina1041Miss Grillo123nkBe Faithful1211	Flattened out	12
2May47- 5Jam	gd 1 1/16	:232 :473 1:12 1:451	3↑	ⒻHandicap 10050	2	4	47¼	42½	1hd	11½	Mehrtens W	122wb	*.30	87-17	Bridal Flower1221½Be Faithful1216Aladear1114	Easily	5
24Apr47- 5Jam	fst 6f	:232 :47 1:114	3↑	ⒻHandicap 6025	5	4	53¾	32	31	1no	Mehrtens W	122wb	*.90	92-14	Bridal Flower122noRytina1135Recce1206	Driving	5
	Previously owned by J.R. Bradley;previously trained by J.W. Smith																
1Nov46- 6Pim	fst 1 3/16	:481 1:132 1:39 1:57	3↑	Pim Spl 25k	4	1	12	11½	32½	39	DeLara A	117wb	4.25	88-16	Assault1206Stymie1263Bridal Flower117½	Tired	4
19Oct46- 5Jam	fst 1 3/16	:473 1:123 1:39 1:572		Roamer H 31k	2	2	11½	11	1nk	1½	DeLara A	118wb	3.45	89-13	Bridal Flower118½Assault1261½Risolater109nk	Driving	12
15Oct46- 7Bel	fst 1	:233 :461 1:103 1:363	2↑	Turf & Field H 10k	1	2	33½	35½	24	31	DeLara A	115 w	4.15	90-19	Polynesian126¾Coincidence123nkBridalFlower1158	Good try	4
21Sep46- 7Aqu	sly 1⅛	:471 1:122 1:383 1:521	3↑	ⒻBeldame H (Div 2) 56k	8	5	41¼	32	21	11¼	DeLara A	114wb	*2.45	86-13	BridalFlower1141¼Aladear1062½JupitrLght108no	Going away	10
21Aug46- 6Sar	fst 1¼	:473 1:122 1:38 2:041		ⒻAlabama 28k	5	6	58½	21½	21½	23	DeLara A	124wb	*1.25	85-10	Hypnotic1243Bridal Flower124hdAlma Mater1085	Hung	7
	Previously owned by E.R. Bradley																
9Aug46- 6Sar	fst 7f	:222 :444 1:103 1:232		ⒻTest 9.5k	1	7	77½	75¼	32	3¾	DeLara A	123wb	4.70	98-10	RedShoes123nkUpperLevel1111½BridlFlowr1232	Finished fast	11
24Jly46- 5Jam	my 6f	:23 :461 1:11		Handicap 7065	1	2	31½	3nk	2nk	3½	Wright WD	115wb	3.85	95-14	Inroc123noMaster Bid112½Bridal Flower115hd	Hung	9
6Jly46- 5Jam	fst 1 1/16	:24 :47 1:114 1:441	3↑	ⒻComely H 23k	5	2	21½	21	3nk	32¾	DeLara A	116wb	*1.35	89-10	Bonnie Beryl114¾Hypnotic1142Bridal Flower1161½	Weakened	9
29Jun46- 6Del	fst 1 1/16	:232 :47 1:114 1:434	3↑	ⒻNew Castle H 28k	4	2	12	12½	12½	14½	DeLara A	111wb	*1.05	94-13	Bridal Flower1114½Surosa1144Mahmoudess1141¼	Easily	6
20Jun46- 6Aqu	fst 1 1/16	:242 :48 1:13 1:462		ⒻGazelle 23k	2	2	21½	1½	12	16	DeLara A	111wb	12.20	82-23	BridalFlower1116Hypnotic1216BonnBryl1161½	Much the best	6
14Jun46- 6Aqu	fst 1 1/16	:24 :481 1:143 1:47		ⒻAlw 8000	1	3	36	25	23	26	DeLara A	112wb	*1.05	73-22	Hypnotic1186Bridal Flower1126Mush Mush1073	Went well	5
4Jun46- 6Bel	fst 6f	:23 :463 1:103		ⒻAlw 5500	3	3	2nk	2nk	1hd	1no	DeLara A	109wb	*1.30	97-11	Bridal Flower109noAladear1083½Mush Mush1072	Hard drive	5
25May46- 7Bel	fst 6f	:223 :462 1:113		Alw 4500	9	6	31½	21½	2hd	1nk	DeLara A	112wb	*1.25	92-14	BridlFlowr112nkSkylghtr1123½Drbyd'Amour117no	Hard drive	9

11May46- 5Bel fst 6f :223 :463 1:114 Alw 4500 2 6 63¼ 43½ 31½ 23½ Jessop JD 113wb 3.25 87-14 LarkmeadAndy1183½BridlFlower1131¼HieHeel1221¼ Went well 10
17Nov45- 5Pim gd 1 1/16 :233 :481 1:134 1:481 ⒻMarguerite 27k 3 3 33 1hd 31½ 21 Dodson D 116wb 8.70 76-20 Challadette1191Bridal Flower116¾Athene1166 Gamely 4
12Nov45- 3Pim fst 1 1/16 :233 :474 1:131 1:473 ⒻAlw 5000 2 1 14 12 1hd 22½ Dodson D 111.5wb *.45 77-26 Challadette1132½BridalFlower111.55Dtrb1056 Used in pace 6
25Oct45- 4Pim gd 6f :23 :463 1:124 ⒻAlw 2500 7 4 1½ 11 11½ 15 Young S 118 w 2.60 89-19 BridalFlower1185StellarRol115nkArlSong1184 In hand late 11
13Oct45- 6Lrl fst 1 1/16 :232 :473 1:143 1:472 ⒻSelima 40k 2 4 31½ 23 24 35 Dodson D 111wb 7.75 75-20 Athene1114½Edified111½Bridal Flower1115 No rally 9
28Sep45- 4Bel sly 6f-WC:231 :46 1:112 ⒻAlw 5000 4 4 3½ 32 46 Arcaro E 114 w 2.45 78-21 Pure Gold1141Datura1142Aladear1143 Even effort 5
18Sep45- 4Bel sly 6f-WC:214 :443 1:092 ⒻAlw 2500 2 77½ 44½ 35 McCreary C 119 w 5.00 89-08 Athene1194Pure Gold1191Bridal Flower1192 Slow start 8
Start obscured by rain
23Aug45- 6Bel fst 6f-WC:221 :444 1:091 ⒻSpinaway 20k 7 9 97 64¾ 2¾ Lindberg H 109 w 3.45 94-05 Sopranist110¾BridalFlower109nkRedShos1142 Finished well 14
15Aug45- 4Bel fst 6f-WC:224 :46 1:111 ⒻAlw 3500 2 4 52½ 42¾ 1¾ Lindberg H 115 w *.60 85-13 Bridal Flower115¾Harem1153Rytina1152½ Impeded start 9
8Aug45- 2Bel gd 5½f-W:224 :461 1:042 ⒻMd Sp Wt 2 3 52¼ 4¾ 1¾ Lindberg H 115 w 6.00 92-13 BridalFlower115¾Athenia1155DutchCut1151¼ Impeded early 14

Brother Jones

b. g. 1936, by Petee-Wrack (Wrack)-Maridel, by Durbar II — **Lifetime record: 40 10 10 5 $48,200**
Own.- H.E. Talbott
Br.- A.B. Hancock (Va)
Tr.- W.R. Miller

10Aug45- 3Bel fst *2 S'Chase 3:491 4↑ Shillelah 6.1k 9 7 86¾ 54½ 58 48 Mallison W 145ws 7.90 -- Raylywn1361RougeDragn1521Merctor1376 Saved ground late 10
6Aug45- 3Bel hy *2 S'Chase 4:084 4↑ Alw 3000 8 11 717 65¾ 34 1hd Mallison E 139ws 4.75 -- Brother Jones139hdMercator1373Boojum II149nk Driving 14
27Sep44- 5Bel fst *2½ S'Chase 4:552 4↑ Brook H 8.8k 2 4 73¼ 44 719 727½ Walker G 159ws 2.90 -- RougeDrgn1603BurmaRoad1365GrekFlg1341½ Pulled up lame 9
31May44- 5Bel fst *2½ S'Chase 4:52 4↑ Meadow Brook H 7k 4 4 43½ 32 22 23½ Walker G 161ws *1.95 -- Iron Shot1593½Brother Jones1616Knight's Quest1473 6
Bad landing 14th
23May44- 5Bel fst *2 S'Chase 3:502 4↑ Corinthian H 4.8k 3 7 52½ 41½ 33 1hd Walker G 158ws 5.30 -- Brother Jones158hdIron Shot158nkKnight's Quest1482½ 7
Between leaders,driving
6Oct43- 3Bel fst *3 S'Chase 5:533 4↑ Grand National H 18k 11 4 54¼ 42¼ 12 16 Walker G 150ws *2.85 -- Brother Jones1506Invader145½[DH]Caddie137 Easily 12
15Sep43- 3Aqu gd *2½ S'Chase 5:012 4↑ Glendale H 8.6k 5 4 44 32 1hd 11½ Walker G 146ws *2.05 -- Brother Jones1461½Invader145½Parma1358 Impeded 6
25Aug43- 3Bel fst *2½ S'Chase 4:471 4↑ Saratoga H 6.2k 1 5 57¼ 25 3¾ 2½ O'Neill S 146ws 10.65 -- Iron Shot148½Brother Jones1461½Corrigan1497 Fast finish 8
18Aug43- 3Bel fst *2 S'Chase 3:463 3↑ Beverwyck H 4.1k 8 8 98¼ 89¼ 57½ 38½ Walker G 147ws 3.75 -- RougeDragon145½IronShot1458BrothrJons1471½ Steady gain 10
11Aug43- 3Bel gd *2 S'Chase 3:52 3↑ North American H 3.8k 2 4 33½ 410 32½ 21¼ O'Neill S 146ws 2.60 -- Elkridge1511¼Brother Jones1462½Redlands1391 6
Lost stirrup 9th,recovered
23Jun43- 3Aqu fst *2½ S'Chase 4:53 4↑ Hitchcock H 6.1k 8 7 514 67 33 23 Walker G 143ws 4.85 -- Corrigan1423Brother Jones1432Invader1501½ Fast finish 8
9Jun43- 3Aqu my *2 S'Chase 3:511 4↑ Lion Heart H 3.8k 6 4 35½ 45 43½ 46 Walker G 145ws *1.35 -- Knght'sQust1452Invdr150noIronShot1474 Bothered 1st turn 9
1Jun43- 3Bel my *2½ S'Chase 5:181 4↑ Meadow Brook H 6.1k 1 2 21½ 2nk 112 112 Walker G 141ws *1.90 -- Brother Jones14112Frederic II1402Cottesmore1501½ Easily 7
25May43- 3Bel fst *2 S'Chase 3:521 4↑ Corinthian H 3.9k 4 7 54 52¾ 31½ 2nk Walker G 139ws 11.55 -- Invader145nkBrother Jones1394Boojum II1385 Inside,hung 8
11May43- 3Bel fst *2 S'Chase 3:461 4↑ International H 3.9k 7 5 725 820 48 48½ Walker G 140ws 13.10 -- Iron Shot1444Knight's Quest1483Invader1501½ No mishap 9
14Nov42- 6Bel fst *2½ S'Chase 5:03 4↑ Temple Gwathmey H 3.4k 3 5 42½ 32 31½ 2¾ Cruz H 142ws 3.00 -- Iron Shot144¾Brother Jones142½Cottesmore1561½ 10
Bothered by riderless horse
21Oct42- 3Lrl sl *2½ S'Chase 5:313 4↑ Chevy Chase H 6.4k 6 2 2½ 21½ 112 114 O'Neill S 134ws 12.55 -- BrotherJones13414StrollingOn1304Cadd1394 Speed to spare 8
28Aug42- 3Sar fst *2½ S'Chase 5:114 4↑ Saratoga H 4.3k 1 5 42¾ 44 2hd 31¼ Cruz H 138ws 5.25 -- Iron Shot136nkElkridge1491Brother Jones1385 Driving 5
22Aug42- 3Sar fst *2 S'Chase 4:202 3↑ Handicap 1200 2 4 35 33 3¾ 11½ Cruz H 145ws 7.30 -- Brother Jones1451½Good Chance1412½Boojum II144¾ 7
Jumped well,driving
15Aug42- 1Sar fst *2 S'Chase 4:192 3↑ Alw 1200 1 3 621 3nk 32½ 34 Cruz H 149ws 3.55 -- FayCottage1422½BoojumII1441½BrothrJons1492 Bid,faltered 6
4Jly42- 6PiR fst *2 S'Chase 4:162 4↑ Handicap 1650 6 5 1½ 11 11 15 Cruz H 146ws *1.50 -- Brother Jones1465Parma14425Chuckatuck14715 Driving 7
25Jun42- 3Del fst *2 S'Chase 3:474 4↑ Alw 4000 5 5 43½ 26 25 2½ Cruz H 155 w 4.60 -- Similar143½Brother Jones1558Caddie142hd Finished well 8
13Jun42- 1Aqu gd *2 S'Chase 3:484 4↑ Alw 1500 3 6 68 33½ - - Maier F 137 w 12.25 -- TheBeak1422½GoodChance1504PcoBlncoII1376 Lost rider 9th 8
15Nov41- 3MTP fst *2½ S'Chase 5:49 4↑ Handicap 1285 1 6 510 511 49 412½ Collins W 145 w 5.00e -- Corrigan156hdCastletown14710BigRebel1392½ Showed little 6
4Nov41- 5Bel fst *2½ S'Chase 4:571 4↑ Temple Gwathmey H 3.1k 3 5 512 49 310 23 Collins W 138 w 9.80 -- Parma1413BrotherJons138hdErndPrs139 Trailed,good finish 6
22Oct41- 2Lrl fst *2½ S'Chase 5:062 4↑ Chevy Chase H 6.3k 5 5 518 517 319 320 Jennings E 138 w 11.40 -- War Lance13315Fay Cottage1375Brother Jones138 Trailed 5
16Oct41- 2Lrl fst *2 S'Chase 3:54 3↑ Alw 1000 6 4 318 317 512 510½ Walker G 149 w *2.20 -- Rouge Dragon1356Bagpipe1451Frederic II1433 No rally 6
4Oct41- 1Bel my *2 S'Chase 3:573 3↑ Handicap 1500 4 2 21 42½ 51¼ 2hd Bauman A 144 w 4.15 -- National Anthem141hdBrother Jones1441Millrace143hd 9
Poor landing 10th,late gain
27Sep41- 2MBr *2 S'Chase 4↑ Purse 1440 7 7 76¼ - - - Miller R 145 w -e -- Fay Cottage1443The Beak1355Bagpipe138½ Lost rider 9
No time taken,no wagering
14Jun41- 6PiR fst *2 S'Chase 4:21 4↑ Handicap 1725 3 4 32½ 32½ 18 115 Gayer J 136 w 6.85 -- Brother Jones13615Kellsboro1405Little Cottage II1433 6
Rated,speed to spare
5Jun41- 1Bel my *2 S'Chase 4:042 4↑ Alw 1500 1 3 24 22 15 112 Gayer J 138 w 9.00 -- BrotherJons13812Smoon1457Kllsboro15010 Speed in reserve 8
26May41- 1Bel fst *2 S'Chase 3:481 4↑ Alw 1500 1 4 23 22 23 22 Gayer J 144 w 5.05 -- West Haddon1522Brother Jones1445Frederic II142100 7
Gained under urging
13May41- 1Bel fst 2 S'Chase 3:492 4↑ Clm 1500 6 6 515 513 311 310 Gayer J 139 w 33.00 -- Night Heron1398Coxswain1512Brother Jones13915 6
No early speed,gained under urging
21Jun40- 3Del fst *2 S'Chase 3:53 4↑ Sp Wt 1000 7 4 3¾ 21½ 45½ 415 Robey T 144wb 45.05 -- Deanslaw1511Red Gauntlet14412Scurry Along1522 Tired 8
15Jun40- 6UH fst *1¼ 2:01 3↑ Alw 500 7 8 108 94¼ 94 814 Wing W 145 w 184.00 -- Torch Song145½Navy1492Roustabout158½ No factor 11
23May40- 4Bel sly *2 S'Chase 3:572 4↑ Spring Maiden 4.9k 9 15 1216 1125 712 714¾ Gayer J 138ws 9.50f -- Massa1372Fay Cottage1552Star Bramble1445 Never a threat 16
6May39- 3Jam fst 1 70 :234 :48 1:13 1:432 3↑ Md Sp Wt 3 6 613 615 611 622¾ Balaski L 115wb 60.00 64-11 Gino Rex1153Generalis115¾Burnup1154 Outrun 6
26Apr39- 5Jam fst 1 70 :233 :474 1:13 1:43 3↑ Md Sp Wt 3 5 59 69½ 612 618 Faust F 113 w 60.00 73-14 Challenge1134Black Demon1134Burnup113hd Never a factor 6
18Nov38- 1Bow fst 5½f :233 :48 1:013 1:082 ©Md Sp Wt 5 12 1214 1214 65 63½ Yarberry W 111wb 54.35 80-23 One-Tenth111noSir Mowlee1161½Key Man1161 Broke slowly 12
10Oct38- 4Jam fst 5½f :223 :461 1:054 ©Md Sp Wt 12 12 1223 1224 1218 1224¼ Pikor A 117wb 40.00 67-15 Hy Camp1175Day Off1174Sky Flier112no No speed 12

Busher

ch. f. 1942, by War Admiral (Man o' War)-Baby League, by Bubbling Over — **Lifetime record: 21 15 3 1 $334,035**
Own.-L.B. Mayer
Br.- Idle Hour Stock Farm Co (Ky)
Tr.- G. Philpot

2Jan47- 7SA fst 6f :223 :454 1:10 4↑ ⒻAlw 7500 2 6 63 66 56½ 55 Westrope J 118 w *1.00 92-12 Miss Doreen1142Monsoon1141¼Going With Me1111 6
Dwelt,under urging at finish,worked seven furlongs;Previously trained by G.M. Odom
6Oct45- 7Hol fst 1 1/16 :23 :463 1:111 1:434 3↑ ⒻVanity H 27k 2 4 49 25 11½ 12 Longden J 126 w *.35e 93-09 Busher1262Canina1144Paula's Lulu113hd Speed in reserve 9
29Sep45- 7Hol fst 1⅛ :462 1:11 1:371 1:501 Hol Derby 57k 13 6 64¾ 4¾ 1½ 11½ Longden J 123 w *.65 94-09 Bushr1231½Mano'Glory1121QuickRewrd1212 Bumped 1st turn 14
15Sep45- 7Hol fst 1 :223 :46 1:112 1:373 Will Rogers H 30k 1 3 3½ 43 3½ 2hd Longden J 123 w *.35 93-11 Quick Reward112hdBusher123½War Allies1103 Driving 14
3Sep45- 7Was fst 1¼ :463 1:103 1:361 2:014 3↑ Wash Park H 57k 4 3 33 13 13 11½ Longden J 115 w *1.40 101-12 Busher1151½Armed1201Take Wing1125 Driving 13
29Aug45- 7Was gd 1 :23 :453 1:104 1:374 3↑ ⒻMatch Race 25k 1 2 1hd 2nk 1hd 1¾ Longden J 115 w *.50 89-21 Busher115¾Durazna115 Inside,vigorous ride 2
18Aug45- 7Was fst 1⅛ :463 1:12 1:373 1:512 3↑ ⒻBeverly H 32k 6 6 57½ 34½ 32½ 33¾ Longden J 128 w *.40e 87-14 Durazna1162½Letmenow1021½Busher1284 No threat 8
4Aug45- 7Was fst 1¼ :491 1:14 1:39 2:034 3↑ Arlington H 54k 2 1 12 11 13 14½ Longden J 113 w *1.10 91-12 Busher1134½Take Wing110noSirde114no Speed in reserve 8
25Jly45- 6Was fst 1 :233 :47 1:112 1:372 ⒻCleopatra H 26k 9 4 2hd 12 12 14½ Bailey W 126 w *.90 91-18 Busher1264½Twosy1162War Date1222½ Speed in reserve 9

4Jly45-6SA	fst 1 1/16	:224 :461 1:103 1:43	3↑ ⒻS Margarita H 53k	2	5	56	44	3nk	11½	Longden J	126 w	*.75e	97-09	Busher1261½Whirlabout123½Canina1172	Easily 10
23Jun45-6SA	fst 1⅛	:46 1:11 1:372 1:50	S Anita Derby 54k	8	4	32½	1hd	13	2½	Longden J	121 w	*.55	93-09	Bymeabond119½Busher1211Best Effort1265	Wide turn 8
9Jun45-6SA	fst 1	:223 :454 1:101 1:363	San Vicente 27k	4	4	43½	21½	1hd	11¼	Longden J	121 w	*.60e	95-10	Busher1211¼Sea Sovereign1217Bismarck Sea1212	8
Impeded by riderless horse															
2Jun45-6SA	fst 7f	:23 :454 1:104 1:233	ⒻS Susanna 27k	1	2	2½	11	16	17	Longden J	121 w	*.15	94-15	Busher1217Mist115½Glory Time1152	As rider pleased 7
26May45-5SA	fst 6f	:224 :463 1:12	ⒻAlw 4000	6	5	1hd	13	15	15	Longden J	121 w	*.20	89-19	Busher1215Glory Time1154Mist1153½	As rider pleased 8
Previously owned by E.R. Bradley;previously trained by J.W. Smith															
14Oct44-6Lrl	sl 1 1/16	:233 :474 1:141 1:493	ⒻSelima 29k	3	4	32	23	11½	13	Arcaro E	117 w	*.90	69-34	Busher1173Ace Card1192½Gallorette1144	Off slowly 10
23Sep44-4Bel	fst 6f-WC	:222 :451 1:092	ⒻMatron 27k	12	1		51¾	1hd	1nk	Arcaro E	119 w	*1.40	94-11	Busher119nkTwosy1151¼Price Level1234	Driving 12
19Sep44-5Bel	fst 6f-WC	:222 :443 1:083	ⒻAlw 3500	9	5		42½	3¼	2hd	Woolf G	119 w	*1.00e	98-05	Nomadic108hdBusher1192Thine1082½	Fast finish 12
30Aug44-6Bel	fst 6f-WC	:224 :46 1:113	ⒻAdirondack H 10k	11	4		31½	31¼	12	Arcaro E	123 w	*2.20	88-18	Busher1232War Date114½Leslie Grey116nk	Bobbled start 12
16Aug44-6Bel	fst 6f	:222 :462 1:121	ⒻSpinaway 18k	7	12	1111	96¼	74¼	43¾	Zufelt F	114 w	*1.20e	85-12	Price Level1152½Ace Card119nkSafeguard1111	Fast finish 12
2Aug44-3Bel	fst 5½f-W	:224 :454 1:042	ⒻAlw 3000	7	2		2½	11	14½	Young S	115 w	8.25	92-09	Bushr1154½ScotchPlns1151¼Conn'sGrl110¾	Speed in reserve 7
30May44-2Bel	fst 4½f-W	:23 :463 :524	ⒻMd Sp Wt	12	1		21½	1hd	1½	Atkinson T	115 w	*2.25e	91-09	Busher115½Pin Up Girl115hdFaint Heart115hd	Driving 13

But Why Not

b. f. 1944, by Blue Larkspur (Black Servant)–Be Like Mom, by Sickle

Lifetime record: 46 12 7 5 $295,155

Own.– King Ranch
Br.– Idle Hour Stock Farm Co (Ky)
Tr.– Max Hirsch

10Apr50-6Jam	fst 6f	:23 :461 1:111	3↑ ⒻCorrection H 18k	3	6	83½	85¾	82¾	106¼	Boland W	123wb	10.00	89-12	Sweet Dream123½Nell K.1263Fighting Fan121nk	No factor 14
Previously trained by W.J. Hirsch															
25Feb50-7SA	fst 1¼	:462 1:11 1:351 2:00	3↑ S Anita H 135k	8	5	54	43½	56	57	Boland W	111wb	52.00	99-11	Noor1101¼Citation1321Two Lea113nk	Wide,tired 11
22Feb50-7SA	fst 7f	:222 :452 1:11 1:231	4↑ Handicap 10000	2	2	21	21½	2hd	1¾	Boland W	110wb	9.65	93-17	But Why Not110¾Bolero1203Top's Boy1112½	Driving 7
13Feb50-7SA	fst 1	:232 :471 1:112 1:364	4↑ Handicap 8000	5	3	41¾	43½	52½	51¾	Boland W	110wb	4.35	91-13	Old Rockport118hdMoonrush118hdManyunk1201	No mishap 6
4Feb50-6SA	fst 1⅛	:471 1:114 1:372 1:501	4↑ Handicap 5000	3	1	1½	1hd	2hd	3½	Boland W	118wb	5.25	91-14	SafeArrival116½Top'sBoy117noButWhyNot1182½	Hard urged 9
25Jan50-7SA	fst 1	:223 :461 1:112 1:373	4↑ Handicap 5000	8	5	56½	55	65	44	Arcaro E	115wb	*2.20	85-17	Fervent1201¼Knockdown1201¼Autocrat1111½	Close quarters 8
14Jan50-7SA	my 1⅛	:472 1:121 1:393 1:524	3↑ ⒻS Margarita H 59k	4	2	21½	32½	31½	34½	Glisson G	116wb	8.85	74-21	Two Lea1262Gaffery1182½But Why Not1163½	Lost whip 8
29Dec49-7SA	fst 6f	:232 :47 1:111	3↑ ⒻAlw 5000	5	3	21½	21½	22	31½	Boland W	111wb	19.30	89-21	Two Lea119hdSweet Dream1161½But Why Not1114	Hung 7
Previously trained by M. Hirsch															
12Nov49-6Jam	fst 1 3/16	:471 1:113 1:37 1:564	3↑ Westchester H 29k	4	1	43½	43½	52½	66½	Boland W	112wb	21.15	85-17	ThreeRings116nkDelegate120hdRoyalGovernor1235	Weakened 11
29Oct49-6GS	sly 1⅛	:473 1:123 1:392 1:522	3↑ Trenton H 31k	6	5	79	1327	1330	1336	Gilbert J	116wb	11.60	44-26	Sky Miracle113hdChains1113Three Rings1157	Quit 13
22Oct49-6Jam	fst 1 1/16	:233 :471 1:121 1:451	3↑ ⒻComely H 29k	6	5	35	34	31½	21¼	Boland W	116wb	9.05	86-17	Lithe1071¼But Why Not1162Gaffery116no	Good effort 12
15Oct49-6GS	fst 1 1/16	:224 :461 1:112 1:443	3↑ ⒻVineland H 24k	5	11	99¼	911	910	67	Gilbert J	118 w	4.50	83-16	Bewitch126¾Imacomin111¾Lithe1073	No mishap 14
17Sep49-6Aqu	fst 1⅛	:48 1:124 1:384 1:524	3↑ ⒻBeldame H 72k	18	3	34	43½	56¼	108¼	Gorman D	125wb	8.65e	75-17	Miss Request1131[D]Harmonica1121¼Plunder108hd	Tired 18
10Sep49-5Aqu	fst 7f	:24 :472 1:12 1:25	3↑ Handicap 4040	4	3	42½	56	55	44½	Gorman D	122 w	3.15	83-16	Arise1143Paddleduck112½Young Peter118¾	No mishap 5
16Jly49-6Jam	fst 1 3/16	:472 1:122 1:372 1:571	3↑ Butler H 58k	10	8	33½	76¼	78¼	77¼	Guerin E	118 w	3.25e	83-14	Conniver112noPalestinian1143Stunts1051	Outrun 10
2Jly49-6Aqu	fst 1¼	:484 1:13 1:372 2:024	3↑ Brooklyn H 58k	3	1	72¾	73¾	75¼	53¼	Guerin E	120 w	*.95e	90-14	Assault122¾Vulcan'sForge129nkFlyingMissel117¾	No mishap 10
8Jun49-6Bel	fst 1 1/16	:24 :464 1:112 1:433	3↑ ⒻTop Flight H 16k	3	2	23½	21	11½	13½	Gorman D	126 w	*1.10	93-13	ButWhyNot1263½Paddleduck119¾Allie's Pal1141	Going away 5
30May49-6Bel	fst 1¼	:48 1:123 1:38 2:03	3↑ Suburban H 61k	10	2	11	2hd	22	22½	Gorman D	117 w	3.30e	82-17	Vulcan'sForge1242½BtWhyNot1174FlyingMssl108½	Went well 13
14May49-6Bel	fst 1	:23 :461 1:11 1:362	3↑ Metropolitan H 30k	9	2	63¼	75¼	43½	31¾	Mehrtens W	119 w	5.35	90-15	LoserWepr1051½Vulcn'sForg126nkBtWhyNot1191	Closed fast 10
5May49-6Jam	fst 1 1/16	:25 :484 1:13 1:444	3↑ ⒻFirenze H 28k	1	2	22	22	21	12	Gorman D	116 w	7.80e	89-18	But Why Not1162Allie's Pal111½Conniver1263	Drew out 9
30Apr49-6Jam	fst 1 3/16	:472 1:112 1:363 1:561	3↑ Gallant Fox H 56k	1	2	32	35	613	613	Mehrtens W	110wb	6.95e	82-13	Coaltown1307Vulcan's Forge1192Three Rings1131	Tired 6
Daily Racing Form time,1:55 4/5															
27Apr49-6Jam	fst 6f	:232 :464 1:114	3↑ ⒻCorrection H 17k	4	4	63¾	76¼	42½	53½	Arcaro E	119wb	3.65e	88-15	Ocean Brief117hdAlfoxie110¾Paddleduck1112½	No mishap 10
2Apr49-5Jam	fst 5½f	:23 :463 1:052	4↑ Alw 5000	4	6	66	67½	69	34½	Mehrtens W	108wb	6.00	86-16	Tavistock1183LocalBand1111½ButWhyNot108nk	Closed fast 7
15Nov48-4Jam	fst 1 1/16	:25 :482 1:142 1:472	3↑ Alw 5000	7	2	1hd	1½	3nk	21¼	Scurlock O	110wb	2.25	75-25	Mother1101¼But Why Not110hdRinaldo108hd	Held well 7
30Oct48-6Jam	fst 1 3/16	:48 1:123 1:38 1:574	3↑ Westchester H 57k	2	3	34½	76¾	812	817	Picou C	117wb	5.75e	70-22	Better Self1191War Trophy110nkPhalanx126no	Quit 8
27Oct48-6Jam	fst 1 1/16	:242 :48 1:13 1:45	3↑ ⒻComely H 29k	8	2	31¾	42¼	97	915	Gorman D	119wb	15.05	73-25	Conniver1231¼Miss Request1205Carolyn A.1182	Quit 10
22Sep48-6Bel	fst 7f	:224 :452 1:103 1:234	2↑ Vosburgh H 31k	9	6	64½	74¼	64¾	85	Mehrtens W	118wb	5.85e	86-17	Colosal1181Spy Song1292½First Flight124hd	No factor 14
15May48-5Jam	fst 1 3/16	:48 1:122 1:373 1:571	3↑ Gallant Fox H 87k	5	5	45½	63¾	74½	88¼	Jessop JD	115wb	8.90	82-15	Faultless118hdFervent125¼Gallorette1173½	Tired 10
30Apr48-5Jam	fst 1 1/16	:25 :49 1:133 1:462	4↑ ⒻHandicap 7540	6	4	35	44	43½	24	Mehrtens W	121wb	*.80	77-17	Harmonica1124But Why Not121noCarolyn A.1131½	Stumbled 6
25Oct47-5Jam	fst 1⅝	:50 1:41 2:053 2:442	3↑ Gallant Fox H 83k	3	2	12	23	44	67½	Mehrtens W	112wb	5.75	84-13	Stymie1251¾Talon1253½Miss Grillo117no	Tired 9
20Oct47-5Jam	fst 1 3/16	:473 1:121 1:383 1:581	Roamer H 30k	5	5	21½	31½	88¾	814½	Arcaro E	121wb	3.20	70-17	Cosmic Bomb128nkDouble Jay1201Flashco1041½	Impeded 10
7Oct47-6Bel	fst 1½	:473 1:123 2:042 2:293	3↑ ⒻLadies H 60k	7	7	2nk	1½	21	25	Arcaro E	121wb	2.85e	85-14	Snow Goose1135But Why Not1211Gallorette123hd	Weakened 12
20Sep47-7Aqu	fst 1⅛	:483 1:131 1:383 1:514	3↑ ⒻBeldame H (Div 2) 60k	11	8	105¼	72¾	4½	1no	Arcaro E	120wb	*1.15e	88-12	But Why Not120noMiss Grillo1262Elpis123hd	Hard drive 11
20Aug47-6Sar	fst 1¼	:472 1:13 1:384 2:05	ⒻAlabama 25k	8	7	48	22	1hd	1nk	Guerin E	126wb	*.70e	83-16	BtWhyNt126nkCosmicMissile1227BeeAnnMac1124	Hard drive 9
26Jly47-6AP	fst 1¼	:473 1:12 1:354 2:014	Arl Classic 93k	2	1	11	11½	11	1¾	Mehrtens W	117wb	5.10	96-06	But Why Not117¾Fervent1221Cosmic Bomb1197½	Held well 7
21Jly47-7AP	gd 1	:23 :46 1:11 1:373	3↑ ⒻArl Matron H 35k	2	2	32	21	11½	1½	Mehrtens W	114wb	*1.50	84-15	But Why Not114½Say Blue111nkCamargo1123	In hand 14
5Jly47-5Jam	fst 1 3/16	:483 1:13 1:39 1:574	Empire City 56k	4	5	41½	31¾	2nk	22¼	Mehrtens W	111 w	5.40	85-15	Phalanx1262¼But Why Not111½Harmonica116hd	Weakened 7
14Jun47-6Aqu	fst 1¼	:474 1:13 1:391 2:054	Dwyer 58k	5	6	56½	53¼	2hd	2nk	Mehrtens W	111 w	6.00	78-16	Phalanx126nkBut Why Not1117Brabancon1161½	Game try 9
20May47-6Bel	my 1⅜	:483 1:14 1:40 2:181	ⒻC C A Oaks 65k	12	1	64¾	33	35	43¼	Mehrtens W	121 w	*.70	77-24	Harmonica121nkCosmicMissile1213SnowGoose121hd	Weakened 14
13May47-6Bel	fst 1	:223 :454 1:12 1:38	ⒻAcorn 19k	6	4	43½	41¼	2nk	12	Mehrtens W	121 w	2.00	84-17	But Why Not1212Harmonica1214Alrenie121hd	Going away 13
9May47-7Pim	fst 1 1/16	:233 :48 1:133 1:462	ⒻPim Oaks 26k	5	1	11	1½	1hd	11¼	Mehrtens W	121 w	3.90	86-20	But Why Not1211¼Cosmic Missile1215Oberod121hd	Drew out 10
28Apr47-4Jam	fst 6f	:23 :462 1:113	ⒻAlw 4500	4	2	21½	21	2nk	12½	Mehrtens W	109 w	4.65	93-16	But Why Not1092½By Sea1131Cuisine1094	Driving 5
Previously owned by J.R. Bradley;previously trained by J.W. Smith															
26Oct46-2Lrl	sly 6f	:23 :48 1:14	Alw 2500	6	1	2½	11	1½	1nk	De Lara A	115 w	*.85	84-25	But Why Not115nkLittle Harp1138Gemsbok1131¼	Driving 6
19Oct46-4Jam	fst 6f	:23 :464 1:122	ⒻFrizette 20k	10	8	76¼	55½	54¼	52½	Robertson J	108 w	2.80e	86-13	Bimlette110nkCarolyn A.122½Pipette119nk	Even effort 11
14Oct46-3Bel	fst 5½f-W	:221 :45 1:032	ⒻMd Sp Wt	12	7		3½	1½	11	De Lara A	115 w	4.70	97-06	But Why Not1151Telk112nkMuti115½	Ridden out 20
4Oct46-6Bel	fst 6f-WC	:224 :46 1:102	ⒻAlw 4000	15	4		61¼	104¼	86¾	De Lara A	109 w	47.05	82-11	CosmicMissle1191¼GracieVe1191ShortRgn1191	Showed speed 15

By Jimminy

br. c. 1941, by Pharamond II (Phalaris)–Buginarug, by Blue Larkspur

Lifetime record: 21 9 4 3 $181,120

Own.– Alfred P. Parker
Br.– Idle Hour Stock Farm Co (Ky)
Tr.– J.W. Smith

26Sep44-6Bel	fst 1⅝	:492 1:391 2:043 2:431	Lawrence Realizatn 17k	2	1	11½	12	12	13½	Woolf G	126wb	*.30	88-12	By Jimminy1263½Bounding Home126	Saved ground 2
Geldings not eligible															
26Aug44-6Was	fst 1¼	:482 1:123 1:371 2:03	American Derby 79k	2	2	11½	14	14	16	Woolf G	122 w	*1.20	95-09	ByJmmny1226OldKentuck118nkNlsonDunstn118hd	Ridden out 5
12Aug44-6Bel	fst 1¼	:471 1:114 1:373 2:032	Travers 30k	1	3	2hd	12	11	11	Arcaro E	126wb	*.75	83-16	By Jimminy1261Free Lance112¾Bounding Home1262	Driving 5
Geldings not eligible															
8Jly44-5Jam	fst 1 3/16	:464 1:113 1:37 1:561	Empire City 56k	5	3	22	21½	33	33	Atkinson T	120wb	*.45	97-10	StirUp120½LuckyDraw1202½ByJimminy1202	Drifted out str 7
24Jun44-6Aqu	fst 1¼	:463 1:12 1:38 2:032	Dwyer 56k	9	4	1nk	11½	12	14	Atkinson T	114wb	*.95	90-15	By Jimminy1144Stir Up1205Lucky Draw1201	Ridden out 9
17Jun44-6Aqu	fst 1 1/16	:24 :474 1:132 1:452	Shevlin 12k	4	1	12	11½	11½	14	Atkinson T	116wb	2.15	87-15	By Jimminy1164Stir Up122hdStymie1085	Easily 12

Date/Race	Cond	Dist	Fractions	Race	PP	St	1st	2nd	Str	Fin	Jockey	Wt	Odds	Spd	Top finishers	Comment
12Jun44- 6Aqu	fst	7f	:23 :46 1:11 1:224	Handicap 4980	5	2	21	21	2½	13	Atkinson T	116wb	3.25	98-16	By Jimminy1163Lucky Draw1266Stymie1161½	Easily 5
Daily Racing Form time,1:23 1/5																
30May44- 5Bel	fst	6f	:223 :462 1:112	Handicap 4490	5	5	43½	43	41½	41¾	Young S	121wb	*1.40	91-16	Rodney Stone121noFreezout1151½Sky Tracer116nk	Wide,hung 5
20May44- 6Bel	fst	1	:231 :461 1:113 1:38	Withers 21k	3	4	31½	32	22	23	Young S	126wb	3.85	81-14	WhoGoesThere1263ByJmmny126noBoyKnight126nk	No match 13
Geldings not eligible																
16May44- 6Bel	fst	6f	:224 :462 1:111	Handicap 4090	6	6	73	64	43	12	Atkinson T	118wb	4.65	94-15	ByJimminy1182Ravnl1111½Jmm115hd	Between leaders,driving 7
15Apr44- 6CD	gd	6f	:224 :461 1:114	3↑ Phoenix H 6.1k	6	3	54½	68	55½	511¼	Adams J	111 w	4.90	83-19	RomanSox1081¼AmbrLight1142CoronaCorona1074	No threat 7
3Nov43- 6Pim	my	1 1/16	:232 :48 1:141 1:473	Pim Futurity 38k	6	2	22½	2½	1½	2½	Givens C	119wb	5.20	79-30	Platter119½By Jimminy1198Smolensko1222	Gamely 8
Geldings not eligible																
22Oct43- 5Pim	fst	6f	:223 :463 1:133	Alw 2000	5	5	32¼	31¾	3nk	13	Givens C	120wb	*1.60	85-24	By Jimminy1203Dustman1171¼Vim1172½	Easily 11
13Oct43- 6Pim	fst	6f	:224 :463 1:132	Richard Johnson 6.8k	8	4	41¼	32	43¾	32½	Young S	122wb	2.15	83-17	DirectorJ.E.1152RoyalPrince115½ByJmmny1221	Wide,driving 8
2Oct43- 4Bel	sly	6½f-W	:231 :461 1:111 1:174	Futurity 68k	4	7		2½	32	86½	Young S	122wb	40.90	76-17	Occupy1261¼Rodney Stone1221Platter1142	Early speed 11
Geldings not eligible																
25Sep43- 2Bel	fst	6f-WC	:224 :454 1:10	©Alw 2300	11	2		3½	41¾	25	Young S	119wb	7.75	91-04	Pensive1155By Jimminy1195Great Ripple115hd	No match 18
28Aug43- 4Bel	gd	6½f	:223 :463 1:113 1:182	Hopeful 42k	11	5	31½	21½	22	34	Givens C	122wb	*1.30e	84-12	Bee Mac1193Boy Knight1221By Jimminy122nk	Bid,faltered 12
Previously owned by E.R. Bradley																
21Aug43- 4Bel	fst	6f	:224 :464 1:124	Grand Union Hotel 13k	3	7	83½	61¼	3½	1nk	Givens C	112wb	7.05e	86-11	By Jimminy112nkSmolensko1161½Boy Knight1221½	Driving 13
17Aug43- 6Bel	fst	6f-WC	:231 :464 1:12	Albany H 7.2k	2	3		52	41	23	Young S	110wb	8.45	83-14	Rodney Stone1193ByJimminy110hdTropea1194	Impeded start 6
9Aug43- 6Bel	fst	6f	:23 :462 1:112	Alw 2500	3	2	77¾	711	77¾	57½	Young S	112 w	31.20	85-12	Ravenala1121½Stir Up1124Home Flight1122	No factor 8
29Jly43- 5Bel	gd	5½f-W	:231 :464 1:054	©Alw 1800	4	8		115	95¼	613	Young S	111 w	14.75e	72-16	Home Flight116½Stir Up1161½Hercules1165	No factor 12

Capot

br. c. 1946, by Menow (Pharamond II)–Piquet, by St. Germans — **Lifetime record: 28 12 4 7 $345,260**

Own.– Greentree Stable
Br.– Greentree Stud Inc (Ky)
Tr.– J.M. Gaver

Date/Race	Cond	Dist	Fractions	Race	PP	St	1st	2nd	Str	Fin	Jockey	Wt	Odds	Spd	Top finishers	Comment
5Aug50- 6Sar	sly	1¼	:482 1:141 1:403 2:063	3↑ Whitney 23k	3	1	11	2½	41½	46¼	Atkinson T	120wb	*1.15	69-19	Piet1161Sun Bahram1164Adile1151¼	Bore out,weakened 6
1Aug50- 6Sar	fst	1	:233 :464 1:114 1:382	3↑ Wilson 17k	5	1	1hd	1hd	1hd	11	Atkinson T	120wb	*.65	85-16	Capot1201Donor110noArise1101	Ridden out 7
5Jly50- 6Jam	fst	6f	:224 :453 1:092	3↑ Fleetwing H 22k	1	2	43½	75¼	56	36	Guerin E	128wb	2.35e	98-06	Sheilas Reward116hdGuillotine1156Capot1281	Closed well 9
28Oct49- 7Pim	fst	1 3/16	:461 1:104 1:363 1:564	3↑ Pim Spl 15k	1	1	11	12	16	112	Atkinson T	120wb	1.50	96-13	Capot12012Coaltown126	Easily 2
15Oct49- 6Jam	fst	1 1/16	:242 :48 1:124 1:442	3↑ Grey Lag H 29k	2	2	2hd	2hd	3½	31	Atkinson T	121wb	*1.50	90-16	Royal Governor1141Three Rings116hdCapot121nk	Hung 12
5Oct49- 6Bel	fst	1	:224 :453 1:103 1:353	3↑ Sysonby 23k	2	2	2½	2½	1hd	11½	Atkinson T	120wb	3.40	96-13	Capot1201½Coaltown1263Manyunk126	Drew clear 3
21Sep49- 6Bel	fst	1	:23 :461 1:111 1:364	Jerome H 24k	2	2	2hd	1½	2½	1no	Atkinson T	126wb	*1.70	90-14	Capot126noArise1162Double Brandy109¾	Hard drive 11
8Aug49- 6Sar	fst	7f	:224 :452 1:102 1:232	Handicap 4065	2	4	2hd	34	43¼	37	Atkinson T	126wb	*.85	92-11	Halt1101Daiquari1066Capot1263½	No rally 6
30Jly49- 6AP	gd	1¼	:461 1:104 1:364 2:031	Arl Classic 87k	2	2	38	56	510	515	Atkinson T	126wb	4.50	74-19	Ponder1263Admiral Lea1193Palestinian1266	Tired 6
9Jly49- 6Jam	fst	1 3/16	:474 1:123 1:373 1:571	Emp City H 56k	2	1	2½	21½	34	33¾	Atkinson T	130wb	*1.15e	86-16	Palestinian1252½Reveille1131¼Capot130nk	No excuse 7
2Jly49- 6Del	fst	1⅛	:463 1:104 1:36 1:482	Leonard Richards 31k	1	3	32½	32	32	1½	Atkinson T	126wb	*.10e	103-08	DCapt126½SunBahrm115½DWnLst1195	Saved ground,driving 4
Disqualified and placed third due to inference caused by entrymate																
11Jun49- 6Bel	fst	1½	:514 1:152 2:043 2:301	Belmont 91k	7	5	11½	11	11	1½	Atkinson T	126wb	5.60	87-13	Capot126½Ponder126½Palestinian12612	Driving 8
Geldings not eligible																
4Jun49- 6Bel	fst	1⅛	:453 1:093 1:362 1:492	Peter Pan H 18k	6	2	2½	3½	43	710	Atkinson T	128wb	*1.15	84-18	Ponder123¾Colonel Mike1136Old Rockport119¾	No excuse 9
14May49- 6Pim	fst	1 3/16	:462 1:103 1:363 1:56	Preakness 110k	1	2	22	22	2hd	1hd	Atkinson T	126wb	2.50	102-08	Capot126hdPalestinian1263Noble Impulse126no	Hard drive 9
7May49- 7CD	fst	1¼	:462 1:123 1:383 2:041	Ky Derby 119k	9	5	21½	21	13	23	Atkinson T	126wb	13.10e	83-15	Ponder1263Capot1264½Palestinian1262	Tired 14
3May49- 6CD	fst	1	:222 :452 1:101 1:372	Derby Trial 12k	6	3	44½	45	37	36¾	Atkinson T	118wb	3.90	85-11	Olympia1181¼Ponder1105½Capot1184	Tired 7
23Apr49- 6Jam	sly	1 1/16	:233 :47 1:12 1:45	Wood Memorial 46k	3	2	22½	32	35	36¼	Atkinson T	126wb	5.40	82-14	Olympia126nkPalestinian1266Capot126¾	Went well 8
16Apr49- 6HdG	fst	1 1/16	:231 :471 1:121 1:451	Chesapeake 35k	4	2	2½	1hd	11	1no	Atkinson T	122wb	*.70	87-20	Capot122noSlam Bang1161½Swap Out1142	Hard urged 6
7Apr49- 6Jam	fst	6f	:23 :46 1:114	3↑ Handicap 6530	2	3	32	25	24	25	Atkinson T	114wb	*.65	87-21	Buzfuz1225Capot114½Energetic1187	Ridden out 4
6Nov48- 7Pim	sl	1 1/16	:23 :464 1:12 1:454	Pim Futurity 57k	7	1	1½	11	12	13½	Atkinson T	119wb	*1.30	89-25	Capot1193½Slam Bang122nkSun Bahram1221½	Easily 9
30Oct48- 4Pim	fst	1 1/16	:224 :461 1:103 1:423	Alw 4000	5	2	21½	21½	1hd	1½	Atkinson T	122wb	*.40	105-00	DCapot122½SlamBang1164SunBahrm115.51½	Bumped rival str 5
Disqualified and placed second																
20Oct48- 6Jam	fst	6f	:23 :464 1:121	Wakefield 17k	5	4	43¼	43	2hd	11	Atkinson T	122wb	*.95	90-24	Capot1221Entrust11410Prince Quest1224	Drew out 7
2Oct48- 5Bel	fst	1	:23 :46 1:112 1:371	Champagne 33k	6	3	1hd	1hd	1½	1½	Atkinson T	110wb	3.15	88-09	Capot110½Stone Age111½Flying Disc1074	Driving 9
27Sep48- 7Bel	fst	1	:232 :462 1:114 1:372	Alw 5000	6	1	11½	12	13	17	Atkinson T	111wb	*2.60e	87-15	Capot1117Benvenuto1112Dry Fly114nk	Easily 11
20Sep48- 5Bel	fst	6f-WC	:223 :452 1:103	Futurity Trial 10k	1	6		2hd	115¼	99¼	Atkinson T	118 w	40.00	79-12	Ocean Drive118¾Olympia1183Roman Bout1131	Early foot 17
16Sep48- 4Bel	fst	6f-WC	:223 :452 1:101	Alw 4000	15	11		71¼	63¼	119¼	Atkinson T	118 w	5.30	81-15	Roman Bout1082Whirl Awhile118hdEntrust118hd	Tired 20
22May48- 4Bel	fst	5f-WC	:232 :47 :591	Alw 5000	5	2		1hd	2nk	11½	Atkinson T	111 w	2.95	84-14	Capot1111½Mirabeau1146Amarillo Kid1131½	Drew out 6
18May48- 2Bel	sl	4½f-W	:232 :48 :543	©Md Sp Wt	10	7		4¾	2hd	22	Atkinson T	116 w	19.65	80-16	Mirabeau1162Capot116½Illuminable116hd	Weakened 21

Citation

b. c. 1945, by Bull Lea (Bull Dog)–Hydroplane II, by Hyperion — **Lifetime record: 45 32 10 2 $1,085,760**

Own.– Calumet Farm
Br.– Calumet Farm (Ky)
Tr.– H.A. Jones

Date/Race	Cond	Dist	Fractions	Race	PP	St	1st	2nd	Str	Fin	Jockey	Wt	Odds	Spd	Top finishers	Comment
14Jly51- 7Hol	fst	1¼	:464 1:103 2:01	3↑ Hol Gold Cup 137k	10	6	33	12	13	14	Brooks S	120 w	*.35e	94-10	Citation1204Bewitch108noBe Fleet1221	Ridden out 10
4Jly51- 7Hol	fst	1⅛	:464 1:11 1:36 1:482	3↑ American H 56k	5	5	52½	4nk	2hd	1½	Brooks S	123 w	*.75e	98-07	Citation123½Bewitch1062¾Sturdy One112¾	Driving 8
14Jun51- 7Hol	fst	1	:232 :463 1:104 1:354	4↑ Handicap 15000	3	3	31	1hd	1½	1½	Brooks S	120 w	*.95	98-10	Citation120½Be Fleet123¾Sturdy One110½	Driving 5
30May51- 7Hol	fst	1 1/16	:222 :45 1:101 1:42	3↑ Argonaut H 30k	6	5	59½	44	24	23	Smith FA	121 w	*.45e	95-08	Be Fleet1183Citation121nkSturdy One111½	Closed well 10
11May51- 7Hol	fst	6f	:221 :452 :573 1:10	3↑ Premiere H 18k	3	8	86¼	96¼	84	52¾	Brooks S	120 w	*1.15	93-12	SpecilTouch122nkMnyunk1141½BullrghJr.1101	Closed ground 10
26Apr51- 8BM	fst	6f	:223 :453 1:094	3↑ Alw 3000	2	5	55	43½	33	32¼	Brooks S	120 w	*.60	97-10	Pancho Supreme1181¼A Lark1181Citation1203½	No excuse 5
18Apr51- 8BM	fst	6f	:223 :453 1:094	4↑ Alw 3250	4	3	46	43½	32	31	Brooks S	120 w	*.55	98-13	A Lark109noPancho Supreme1201Citation1202¼	Good effort 6
24Jun50- 8GG	fst	1¼	:451 1:091 1:34 1:581	3↑ Golden Gate H 57k	3	2	313	37	34	23	Brooks S	126 w	1.20	105-12	Noor1273Citation1261On Trust1032½	No excuse 5
17Jun50- 8GG	fst	1⅛	:463 1:093 1:344 1:464	3↑ Forty-Niners H 10k	3	2	21½	1hd	1hd	2nk	Brooks S	128 w	*.50	104-08	Noor123nkCitation1283Roman In1112	Outgamed 5
3Jun50- 8GG	fst	1	:221 :441 1:073 1:333	3↑ GG Mile H 23k	6	2	22	2½	1hd	1¾	Brooks S	128 w	*.60	104-08	Citation128¾Bolero1235On Trust116nk	Driving 6
17May50- 7GG	fst	6f	:22 :442 1:082	4↑ Alw 4000	4	5	55	52¾	21½	2¾	Glisson G	120 w	*.25	99-10	Roman In120¾Citation1201¼Blue Border1173	Forced wide 6
4Mar50- 7SA	fst	1¾	:474 2:023 2:271 2:524	3↑ S Juan Capistrano H 64k	8	4	2hd	1hd	1hd	2no	Brooks S	130 w	*.60	127-06	Noor117noCitation13012½Mocopo107hd	Just failed 8
25Feb50- 7SA	fst	1¼	:462 1:11 1:351 2:00	3↑ S Anita H 135k	5	7	64	32½	32	21¼	Arcaro E	132 w	*.35e	105-11	Noor1101¼Citation1321Two Lea113nk	Close quarters 11
11Feb50- 7SA	gd	1⅛	:471 1:113 1:372 1:501	3↑ San Antonio H 60k	7	4	35	22	2½	21	Arcaro E	130 w	*.45e	91-17	Ponder1281Citation130½Noor114¾	Forced wide 9
26Jan50- 7SA	fst	6f	:223 :46 1:104	4↑ Handicap 6000	4	1	42¼	31½	2hd	2nk	Brooks S	130 w	*.25	93-15	Miche114nkCitation1303½Huon Kid107½	Close quarters 6
11Jan50- 4SA	sly	6f	:223 :461 1:112	4↑ Alw 5000	3	4	33	31½	3nk	11½	Brooks S	124 w	*.15	90-19	Citation1241½Bold Gallant112nkRoman In1163½	Drew away 4
11Dec48- 7Tan	gd	1¼	:48 1:13 1:373 2:024	3↑ Tanforan H 54k	2	2	11½	11½	13½	15	Arcaro E	123 w	*.05	103-12	Citation1235Stepfather1102½See-tee-see1172	Easily best 7
3Dec48- 7Tan	my	6f	:231 :463 1:12	Alw 5000	4	5	21½	2hd	11½	11½	Arcaro E	126 w	*.10	95-23	Citation1261½Bold Gallant1122Barsard1095	In hand 5
29Oct48- 6Pim	fst	1 3/16	:504 1:152 1:421 1:594	3↑ Pim Spl 10k	1	1	1	1	1	1	Arcaro E	120 w		83-11	Citation120	Breezing 1
Walkover																

16Oct48- 7Bel	fst 1⅝	:48 1:382 2:034 2:424 3↑	Gold Cup 111k	8 3 33 12 14 12	Arcaro E	119 w	*.15	90-19	Citation1192Phalanx1265Carolyn A.123½	In hand	9
	Geldings not eligible										
2Oct48- 6Bel	fst 2	:48 2:294 2:562 3:213 3↑	J C Gold Cup 108k	7 1 15 18 18 17	Arcaro E	117 w	*.30	96-09	Citation1177Phalanx12412Beauchef124hd	Easily	7
	Geldings not eligible										
29Sep48- 6Bel	fst 1	:224 :452 1:101 1:36 3↑	Sysonby Mile 29k	6 4 46 12 12 13	Arcaro E	119 w	*.10e	94-14	Citation1193First Flight123nkCoaltown1194	Eased up	6
28Aug48- 7Was	fst 1¼	:462 1:10 1:353 2:013	American Derby 88k	1 1 21½ 11½ 1hd 11	Arcaro E	126 w	*.10e	95-10	Citation1261Free America1181Volcanic1182	Driving	5
21Aug48- 4Was	fst 6f	:223 :45 1:104	Alw 4000	4 3 22 21 11 12½	Pierson NL	120 w	*.20	93-09	Citation1202½King Rhymer1141¼Speculation1176½	Easily	4
5Jly48- 7AP	fst 1⅛	:464 1:104 1:354 1:491 3↑	Stars & Stripes H 56k	6 5 53½ 3½ 11½ 12	Arcaro E	119 w	*.30e	100-07	Citation1192Eternal Reward116nkPellicle106hd	Driving	9
12Jun48- 6Bel	fst 1½	:482 1:123 2:023 2:281	Belmont 117k	1 1 1hd 14 15 18	Arcaro E	126 w	*.20	97-10	Citation1268Better Self126½Escadru1265	Much the best	8
	Geldings not eligible										
29May48- 6GS	fst 1¼	:47 1:113 1:36 2:03	Jersey 61k	4 4 1hd 13 18 111	Arcaro E	126 w	*.10	108-11	Citation12611Macbeth114¾DBovard114¾	Eased up	5
15May48- 6Pim	hy 1 3/16	:502 1:16 1:43 2:022	Preakness 134k	4 1 11½ 12 12½ 15½	Arcaro E	126 w	*.10	70-43	Citation1265½Vulcan's Forge1263½Bovard126nk	Galloping	4
	Previously trained by B.A. Jones										
1May48- 7CD	sly 1¼	:463 1:112 1:38 2:052	Ky Derby 111k	1 2 26 2½ 12 13½	Arcaro E	126 w	*.40e	80-22	Citation1263½Coaltown1263My Request1261½	Drew away	6
27Apr48- 5CD	fst 1	:23 :46 1:103 1:372	Derby Trial 12k	2 2 2½ 12 11½ 11¼	Arcaro E	118 w	*.10	92-23	Citation1181¼Escadru118½Eagle Look11020	Easily	4
	Previously trained by H.A. Jones										
17Apr48- 6HdG	gd 1 1/16	:24 :483 1:132 1:454	Chesapeake 29k	4 3 31 11 13 14½	Arcaro E	122 w	*.20	84-16	Citation1224½Bovard1195Dr. Almac1196	Easily	4
12Apr48- 6HdG	my 6f	:233 :47 1:122	Chesapeake Trial 12k	6 1 41¾ 41½ 22 21	Arcaro E	126 w	*.30	88-27	Saggy1221Citation1264Dr. Almac1221½	Carried wide	6
28Feb48- 6Hia	fst 1⅛	:462 1:103 1:354 1:484	Flamingo 62k	4 4 1hd 1hd 13 16	Snider A	126 w	*.20	97-09	Citation1266Big Dial1184Saggy1221	Easily	7
18Feb48- 6Hia	fst 1⅛	:454 1:10 1:352 1:49	Everglades H 10k	1 2 23 1½ 11 11	Snider A	126 w	*.15	96-11	Citation1261Hypnos1094Silverling112	Easily	3
11Feb48- 6Hia	fst 7f	:232 :46 1:101 1:23 3↑	Seminole H 12k	8 2 2hd 2hd 1hd 11	Snider A	112 w	*.40e	97-16	Citation1121Delegate123nkArmed1282	Drew out	9
2Feb48- 6Hia	fst 6f	:223 :454 1:102 3↑	Alw 5000	2 7 2hd 2hd 1hd 11	Snider A	113 w	*.20e	96-10	Citation1131Kitchen Police1101¾Say Blue1071½	Handily	7
8Nov47- 5Pim	my 1 1/16	:234 :483 1:14 1:484	Pim Futurity 48k	4 2 31½ 2hd 1½ 11½	Dodson D	119 w	*.40	74-41	Citation1191½Better Self1198Ace Admiral1222	Ridden out	5
4Oct47- 4Bel	fst 6½f-W	:221 :444 1:092 1:154	Futurity 106k	14 4 31½ 13 13	Snider A	122 w	*.85e	93-10	Citation1223Whirling Fox114nkBewitch1231	Easily	14
	Geldings not eligible										
30Sep47- 4Bel	fst 6f-WC	:233 :453 1:11	Futurity Trial 10k	2 9 71 61¼ 11	Snider A	116 w	2.10	86-16	Citation1161Gasparilla116nkUp Beat116hd	Drew away	14
16Aug47- 6Was	fst 6f	:223 :45 1:102	Was Futurity 78k	5 3 44 47 36 21	Brooks S	118 w	*.20e	97-07	Bewitch1191Citation118hdFree America1182	Good effort	10
30Jly47- 7Was	fst 6f	:224 :453 1:103	Elementary 24k	10 5 21½ 1½ 11 12	Dodson D	122 w	*1.40	97-07	Citation1222Salmagundi110noBillings113nk	Going away	10
24Jly47- 5AP	fst 5f	:223 :453 :58	Alw 4000	2 4 42 43½ 32 1½	Dodson D	117 w	2.20	102-12	Citation117½Kandy Comfort1141½Queen Hairan1142	Driving	8
21May47- 5HdG	gd 5f	:23 :464 :591	Alw 3500	1 4 22 23 22 11¾	Snider A	119 w	*.40	99-18	Citation1191¾Little Tony1138Grand Entry1163	Going away	6
3May47- 4Pim	fst 5f	:231 :481 1:011	Alw 3500	1 1 11 1hd 1½ 13½	Snider A	119 w	*1.00	95-19	Citation1193½Newsweekly1191Still Champ119nk	Going away	6
22Apr47- 3HdG	sl 4½f	:23 :482 :542	©Md Sp Wt	2 2 35 33 1½	Snider A	120 w	*1.60	93-07	Citation120½Sunday Beau120nkBrass Band120no	Driving	11

Coaltown

b. c. 1945, by Bull Lea (Bull Dog)–Easy Lass, by Blenheim II — **Lifetime record: 39 23 6 3 $415,675**

Own.– Calumet Farm
Br.– Calumet Farm (Ky)
Tr.– H.A. Jones

30Jly51- 6Was	fst 6f	:221 :452 1:093 3↑	Drexel H 16k	4 3 42½ 54 79 79¼	Brooks S	124wb	*1.80	89-10	JohnsJoy124½WineList1121½Yllmntown1131½	Had little left	7
30May51- 7Hol	fst 1 1/16	:222 :45 1:101 1:42 3↑	Argonaut H 30k	1 1 14 11½ 79½ 915	Shoemaker W	125wb	*.45e	83-08	Be Fleet1183Citation121nkSturdy One111½	Stopped	10
26May51- 6Hol	fst 7f	:221 :444 1:094 1:222 3↑	Handicap 10000	1 4 11 11 1hd 64½	Brooks S	127wb	*.70e	92-10	Bewitch1101¾Be Fleet119¾Special Touch123no	Tired badly	9
5May51- 9BM	gd 6f	:222 :452 1:10 3↑	Children's Hospitl H 29k	6 6 41½ 2hd 1hd 12	Shoemaker W	123wb	*1.10	98-20	Coaltown1232SpecialTouch1242½BullrghJr.109no	Going away	8
7Apr51- 9BM	fst 6f	:221 :451 1:094 3↑	Art Sparks H 17k	3 5 1hd 2hd 1hd 1no	Brooks S	121wb	2.45	99-08	Coaltown121noSpecial Touch1242¼Manyunk1151¼	Hard drive	8
24Mar51- 8BM	fst 6f	:223 :451 1:10 3↑	Alameda H 18k	7 9 93¾ 85½ 107¼ 95¾	Brooks S	126wb	*1.35	92-08	SpecialTouch1211¼KitCrson118¾BullrghJr.118no	Raced wide	12
17Feb51- 7SA	fst 1⅛	:453 1:101 1:363 1:492 3↑	San Antonio H 68k	11 8 86¼ 84¾ 1416 1414¾	Brooks S	126wb	*1.55e	79-17	All Blue111¾Sudan109hdNext Move119½	Outrun	16
16Dec50- 6Hol	fst 6f	:221 :45 1:091 3↑	Alw 5000	6 1 1hd 1hd 11 12½	Brooks S	124 w	2.35e	100-12	Coaltown1242½Star Fiddle124nkBolero124nk	Ridden out	6
	Previously trained by B.A. Jones										
13Apr50- 6Kee	fst 6f	:221 :454 1:104 3↑	Phoenix H 12k	2 5 55 54 55 57	Scurlock O	130 w	*.50	91-12	Mount Marcy115noKing Bay107101' Skipper113no	Outrun	6
25Feb50- 6Hia	sl 1¼	:48 1:122 1:382 2:06 3↑	Widener H 61k	1 1 11½ 25 46½ 510	Scurlock O	132 w	*.70	65-27	Royal Governor118nkArise1096Going Away1104	Tired badly	6
11Feb50- 6Hia	fst 1⅛	:463 1:111 1:37 1:501 3↑	McLennan H 33k	9 3 31 2hd 2hd 32	Mehrtens W	132 w	*.55e	85-17	Three Rings1171Royal Governor1161Coaltown1321	Tired	11
	Previously trained by H.A. Jones										
28Oct49- 7Pim	fst 1 3/16	:461 1:104 1:363 1:564 3↑	Pim Spl 15k	2 2 21 22 26 212	Brooks S	126wb	*.30	84-13	Capot12012Coaltown126	Outrun	2
5Oct49- 6Bel	fst 1	:224 :453 1:103 1:353 3↑	Sysonby 23k	1 1 1½ 1½ 2hd 21½	Brooks S	126 w	*.10	94-13	Capot1201½Coaltown1263Manyunk126	Bore out,tired	3
5Sep49- 6Was	sl 1¼	:473 1:122 1:373 2:034 3↑	Wash Park H 52k	3 4 2hd 1½ 11 1¾	Brooks S	130 w	*.10e	83-19	Coaltown130¾Armed1101Lithe102.524¼	Handily	4
20Aug49- 6Was	fst 1	:222 :451 1:083 1:34 3↑	Whirlaway 32k	5 1 11 13 14 12¼	Brooks S	130 w	*.30e	105-03	Coaltown1302¼Ponder118½Star Reward1143	Easily	5
23Jly49- 6AP	gd 1¼	:463 1:11 1:361 2:032 3↑	Arlington H 54k	1 4 12 16 15 13	Brooks S	130 w	*.40e	88-19	Coaltown1303Star Reward1161Armed1135	Easily	6
4Jly49- 6AP	fst 1⅛	:472 1:103 1:352 1:482 3↑	Stars & Stripes H 54k	3 1 1hd 1hd 12 11¼	Brooks S	130 w	*.40e	104-09	Coaltown1301¼Armed110½Star Reward121½	Ridden out	6
25Jun49- 6AP	fst 1	:222 :442 1:083 1:35 3↑	Equipoise Mile H 27k	2 4 33 32 2hd 23	Brooks S	132 w	*.30e	94-12	StarReward1163Coaltown1322CarraraMarble112hd	Weakened	8
11Jun49- 6Nar	fst 1 3/16	:472 1:111 1:361 1:57 3↑	Roger Williams H 16k	3 3 12 18 115 112	Scurlock O	130 w	*.10	88-14	Coaltwn13012GrandEntry104noFncyFlyr1052½	Much the best	5
30Apr49- 6Jam	fst 1 3/16	:472 1:112 1:363 1:561 3↑	Gallant Fox H 56k	5 3 21 11 15 17	Brooks S	130 w	*.25	95-13	Coaltwn1307Vulcan'sForge1192ThreRngs1131	Much the best	6
	Daily Racing Form time, 1:55 4/5										
23Apr49- 6HdG	my 1 1/16	:272 :531 1:183 1:521 3↑	Edward Burke H 6.3k	1 1 1 1 1 1	Brooks S	130		--	Coaltown130	Walkover	1
19Mar49- 6GP	fst 1¼	:45 1:09 1:341 1:594 3↑	Gulf Park H 20k	6 1 15 110 18 17	Scurlock O	128 w	*.10e	108-06	Coaltown1287Three Rings118½Armed1162½	Much the best	9
26Feb49- 7Hia	fst 1¼	:472 1:112 1:363 2:02 3↑	Widener H 60k	5 3 15 13 13½ 12	Atkinson T	123 w	*.05e	95-10	Coaltown1232Shy Guy120½Faultless117¾	Easily	6
19Feb49- 6Hia	fst 1⅛	:461 1:093 1:344 1:482 3↑	McLennan H 31k	4 1 14 13 14 14	Atkinson T	124 w	*.10e	96-14	Coaltown1244Faultless115½Shy Guy120¾	Eased up	8
14Feb49- 5Hia	fst 1⅛	:454 1:084 1:341 1:473 4↑	Alw 4000	4 1 110 112 112 110	Nelson E	114 w	*.20e	103-14	Coaltown11410Three Rings1161½Free America1081¾	Eased up	6
5Feb49- 5Hia	fst 6f	:222 :452 1:101 4↑	Alw 3500	1 8 11 11 11¾ 12½	Pierson NL	120 w	*.20e	97-14	Coaltown1202½Free America106nkTavistock1083½	Easily	8
29Sep48- 6Bel	fst 1	:224 :452 1:101 1:36 3↑	Sysonby Mile 29k	3 3 34½ 44½ 34 33¼	Pierson NL	119 w	*.10e	91-14	Citation1193First Flight123nkCoaltown1194	Went well	6

Conniver

br. f. 1944, by Discovery (Display)–The Schemer, by Challenger II — **Lifetime record: 56 15 3 6 $227,825**

Own.– H. La Montagne
Br.– Alfred G. Vanderbilt (Md)
Tr.– W. Post

17Sep49- 6Aqu	fst 1⅛	:48 1:124 1:384 1:524 3↑	ⒻBeldame H 72k	5 16 1416 1519 97 63	Dodson D	125 w	4.95	80-17	MissRequest1131DHrmonc1121¼Plundr108hd	Closed gap late	18
3Sep49- 6Aqu	fst 1 1/16	:243 :482 1:123 1:46 3↑	Aqueduct H 23k	8 14 1412 1313 105 63½	Kirkland A	115 w	11.30	80-19	WineList114½DLoserWeeper114¾Riverln107½	Close quarters	14
20Aug49- 6Sar	fst 1¼	:471 1:114 1:364 2:04 3↑	Saratoga H 30k	10 10 818 1014 1115 1113	Adams J	118wb	6.40	75-13	Donor117nkStunts112½My Request1232	Dull effort	12
30Jly49- 6Jam	fst 1 3/16	:474 1:124 1:372 1:574 3↑	Merchants & Cits H 22k	2 7 59 51¼ 32½ 41¾	Kirkland A	118wb	2.65	85-18	Chains106nkMy Request126½High Trend1021	Weakened	7
16Jly49- 6Jam	fst 1 3/16	:472 1:122 1:372 1:571 3↑	Butler H 58k	1 6 88½ 86¼ 33 1no	Kirkland A	112wb	16.50	90-14	Conniver112noPalestinian1143Stunts1051	Hard drive	10
8Jly49- 6Jam	fst 1⅛	:491 1:133 1:383 1:512 3↑	Handicap 6030	3 3 1½ 12 11 1hd	Arcaro E	122wb	1.70	91-18	Conniver122hdLoser Weeper1171½Bug Juice1139	Just lasted	5
2Jly49- 6Aqu	fst 1¼	:484 1:13 1:372 2:024 3↑	Brooklyn H 58k	8 7 52½ 62¾ 54 74½	Glisson G	114wb	11.65	88-14	Assault122¾Vulcan's Forge129nkFlying Missel117¾	Outrun	10
13Jun49- 6Aqu	fst 1 1/16	:25 :49 1:134 1:472 3↑	Queens County H 22k	9 6 65½ 56½ 43 24	Arcaro E	114wb	3.00	73-29	Three Rings1104Conniver114nkBug Juice1073	Good effort	9
8Jun49- 6Bel	fst 1 1/16	:24 :464 1:112 1:433 3↑	ⒻTop Flight H 16k	1 4 44½ 43½ 44 45¼	Arcaro E	123 w	1.90	88-13	But Why Not1263½Paddleduck119¾Allie's Pal1141	No mishap	5
30May49- 6Bel	fst 1¼	:48 1:123 1:38 2:03 3↑	Suburban H 61k	12 6 84¾ 128 1215 1215	James B	120 w	6.80	70-17	Vulcan'sForge1242½ButWhyNot1174FlyingMissel108½	Outrun	13

Date	Cond	Dist	Times	Race	PP	St	1st	2nd	Str	Fin	Jockey	Wt	Eqp	Odds	Speed-Var	Top finishers	Comment	Field
5May49-6Jam	fst	1 1/16	:25 :484 1:13 1:444	3↑ ⒻFirenze H 28k	6	8	55	66¼	34	32½	Guerin E	126	w	*1.35	86-18	But Why Not1162Allie's Pal111½Conniver1263	Closed well	9
27Apr49-6Jam	fst	6f	:232 :464 1:114	3↑ ⒻCorrection H 17k	7	9	87¾	87¾	106¼	75½	Howell R	126	w	*2.40e	86-15	OceanBrief117hdAlfoxie110¾Paddlduck1112½	Dwelt at start	10
16Apr49-5Jam	fst	6f	:232 :463 1:13	3↑ ⒻHandicap 6065	3	7	78¾	47½	22½	1¾	Guerin E	122	w	1.80e	86-18	Conniver122¾Itsabet118½Allie's Pal118hd	Drew out	7
13Nov48-6Jam	fst	1 3/16	:484 1:13 1:38 1:58	3↑ Butler H 85k	9	8	814	813	812	817	Guerin E	125	w	3.35	69-20	Donor1171½Phalanx1261Better Self121½	Outrun	9
27Oct48-6Jam	fst	1 1/16	:242 :48 1:13 1:45	3↑ ⒻComely H 29k	10	8	813	85¼	2½	11¼	Guerin E	123	w	3.35	88-25	Conniver1231¼Miss Request1205Carolyn A.1182	Drew out	10
12Oct48-6Jam	fst	1 1/16	:24 :471 1:12 1:444	3↑ Questionnaire H 29k	5	10	1012	107	62¾	53	James B	123	w	6.30	86-18	Donor115noCarolyn A.111½Bug Juice1082	Sluggish	11
2Oct48-6Bel	fst	2	:48 2:294 2:562 3:213	3↑ J C Gold Cup 108k	1	4	411	28	311	521	Dodson D	121	w	13.15	75-09	Citation1177Phalanx12412Beauchef124hd	Stopped	7
	Geldings not eligible																	
28Sep48-6Bel	fst	1½	:473 1:122 2:04 2:30	3↑ ⒻLadies H 58k	3	9	912	72	611	512	Dodson D	126	w	*1.15	76-14	Miss Request1144Gallorette1211Honeymoon1231	No excuse	9
11Sep48-6Aqu	gd	1⅛	:482 1:131 1:39 1:522	3↑ ⒻBeldame H 68k	11	13	137½	95¼	51¼	13½	Dodson D	121	w	*2.35	85-20	Conniver1213½Harmonica114½Gallorette124nk	Easily	14
31Jly48-5Jam	fst	1 3/16	:483 1:14 1:392 1:59	3↑ Merchants & Cits H 22k	6	6	47	44½	1½	2¾	Atkinson T	126	w	*1.00	80-22	Beauchef117¾Conniver1261½Vertigo II1171¾	Weakened	7
17Jly48-6Aqu	fst	1¼	:502 1:16 1:404 2:054	3↑ Brooklyn H 57k	6	4	22	21	1hd	1hd	Atkinson T	114	w	2.00	78-21	Conniver114hdGallorette1193Stymie1302	Hard drive	6
10Jly48-6Aqu	fst	1 1/16	:243 :473 1:114 1:433	3↑ ⒻVagrancy H 29k	3	5	58	43	2nk	15	Atkinson T	121	w	*1.65	96-13	Conniver1215Harmonica1202Casa Camara1051	Easily	8
3Jly48-6Nar	fst	1 70	:23 :462 1:113 1:414	3↑ Governor's H 13k	6	11	99	95¾	75½	43¼	Zehr F	122	w	*.60	93-08	Reborn112½Willing Spirit1121Misleader1151¾	Late foot	11
26Jun48-6Aqu	fst	1 1/16	:251 :493 1:133 1:452	3↑ Aqueduct H 28k	2	6	54½	31¼	1nk	2hd	Zufelt F	117	w	2.70	87-18	Stymie130hdConniver1173½Double Jay1262½	Game try	7
3Jun48-6Bel	fst	1	:234 :464 1:114 1:371	3↑ ⒻHandicap 7535	3	3	32	11½	13	16	Zufelt F	119	w	*2.05	88-14	Conniver1196Red Stamp1093½Miss Kimo120hd	Easily	5
28May48-6Bel	fst	1⅛	:463 1:111 1:371 1:503	3↑ ⒻHandicap 7530	2	1	16	15	14	12	Zufelt F	116	w	1.30	88-15	Conniver1162Challe Anne1081¾Miss Grillo1265	In hand	5
21May48-6Bel	fst	1	:241 :472 1:121 1:374	4↑ ⒻHandicap 7350	3	1	11	13	13	11½	James B	110	w	1.85	85-20	Conniver1101½Honeymoon1173½Grillette1083½	Driving	4
6May48-5Jam	fst	1 1/16	:242 :49 1:133 1:452	4↑ Handicap 6530	1	3	2½	2hd	21	3¾	Jessop JD	111	w	1.55	85-14	Lord Grillo112¾Donor122hdConniver111	Faltered	3
28Apr48-6Jam	fst	1 1/16	:243 :49 1:14 1:464	4↑ Handicap 5565	2	8	66¾	52¾	1hd	1¾	Jessop JD	118	w	*.95	79-19	Conniver118¾Dangerous Age1112Master Mind1191	Drew out	10
22Apr48-5Jam	fst	1 1/16	:243 :49 1:14 1:464	3↑ Handicap 5530	4	2	22	2½	12	15	Jessop JD	114	w	*2.10	79-22	Conniver1145Misleader1202East Light1182	Easily	5
2Apr48-5Jam	my	5½f	:223 :464 1:07	4↑ ⒻAlw 5000	6	6	67¼	54	34¾	33¼	Jessop JD	108	w	4.85e	80-26	OceanBrief1172½DarkVenus108¾Conniver1082	Dwelt at start	6
6Nov47-6Jam	sly	1 1/16	:244 :49 1:141 1:473	Alw 4500	6	5	42¾	42¾	64	34½	Atkinson T	119	w	2.20	70-19	CleanSlate1151½ShortReign1163Conniver1191½	Closed fast	9
30Oct47-6Jam	sly	1 1/16	:242 :483 1:14 1:474	3↑ ⒻAlw 4500	1	5	43	4nk	1hd	11¼	Atkinson T	108	w	3.50	74-22	Conniver1081¼Short Reign1103Head Smart1122	Drew out	7
24Oct47-4Jam	fst	6f	:233 :47 1:122	Alw 4500	4	5	58¾	56½	45½	33¼	Arcaro E	114	w	3.20e	86-19	By Sea118nkDark Venus1143Conniver1141	Closed fast	5
13Oct47-4Bel	fst	1	:233 :47 1:122 1:383	3↑ Clm 8000	5	5	65¼	31½	42¾	42¾	Renick J	102	w	4.20	78-21	ScotchSecret108½BuffetSupper1112FrindorFo112nk	Faltered	8
7Oct47-7Bel	fst	1	:233 :463 1:12 1:381	Alw 5000	3	6	56½	75¾	66	54¼	Allgaier H	115	w	3.75e	79-14	Trilby115¾CaptainDorsett118hdRoyalLover1111½	No mishap	8
30Sep47-7Bel	fst	1	:231 :474 1:121 1:374	ⒻAlw 4000	9	9	83	84	1210	1212½	Allgaier H	117	w	11.80e	72-12	Legendra105hdTrilby1174Dancing Margot1051½	No factor	14
8Sep47-5GS	fst	6f	:224 :461 1:104	Alw 4000	7	8	78	69	59	512	Wilson HB	113	wb	19.40	85-13	Danada Capt.113hdWhipsaw1165Eternallea1192	No factor	8
29Aug47-6GS	fst	6f	:224 :471 1:131	ⒻAlw 4000	8	9	97	95¼	76	54¼	Lynch J	112.5	w	36.65	81-16	IDeclare1092GoingAiry116hdFrantie'sBid109¾	Off slowly	9
25Aug47-8GS	fst	1	:24 :472 1:122 1:381	Alw 4000	8	6	56½	67	610	611¾	Wilson HB	111	wb	49.35	84-06	High Trend114nkEnd of Strife1178Glen Heather1163	Outrun	8
16Aug47-6Sar	sly	6f	:23 :463 1:13	Alw 4000	6	8	811	718	615	613½	Allgaier H	112	w	32.45	69-20	Mangohick1214½Indicate1172½Supper Date1211	Outrun	8
9Aug47-8Sar	fst	1	:234 :474 1:12 1:382	Alw 4000	7	6	5¾	42½	78¾	712½	Allgaier H	114	w	31.00	76-09	Dinner Hour109nkTrapeze1133Daily Dip113hd	No factor	8
18Jly47-6Bel	fst	1	:23 :46 1:12 1:381	ⒻAlw 4500	6	9	87	96	1016	1015¾	Allgaier H	118	w	23.10	67-15	Quarantaine1141½BrightSong112½BimItt1126	Never a factor	11
25Jun47-4Jam	sly	6f	:233 :461 1:111	Alw 4500	3	5	65½	42½	42¼	57½	Allgaier H	118	w	17.55	87-13	OceanBrief1132Parhelion1234Rinldo1141½	Inside,no menace	7
17Jun47-5Aqu	fst	1 1/16	:244 :482 1:131 1:471	3↑ ⒻHandicap 5020	3	3	33	32¼	41¼	42¼	Sneller J	105	w	5.20	76-22	Mahmoudess1131Kay Gibson118nkClover Lea1171	No mishap	4
24May47-8Bel	fst	1	:233 :472 1:132 1:393	Alw 4500	3	3	31	1hd	1hd	54	Allgaier H	117	w	33.60	72-19	Khyber Pass1162Leander119noTrapeze116hd	Speed,quit	7
13May47-6Bel	fst	1	:223 :454 1:12 1:38	ⒻAcorn 19k	13	7	53¾	52¾	1113	1118¾	Allgaier H	121	w	143.55	65-17	But Why Not1212Harmonica1214Alrenie121hd	No factor	13
5May47-5Bel	my	1	:233 :473 1:133 1:404	Alw 5000	1	3	2½	41¼	47	411½	Allgaier H	114	wb	*1.80	58-25	Green Dragon1193Rappahannock1132½Marble Arch1136	Quit	5
23Apr47-6Jam	fst	1 1/16	:242 :482 1:133 1:471	Alw 4000	7	2	1hd	2hd	1hd	1½	Allgaier H	113	w	10.25	77-12	Conniver113½Atom Buster1211½Dorothy B. Jr.11410	Driving	7
16Apr47-2Jam	sly	6f	:24 :48 1:132	ⒻMd Sp Wt	6	4	3½	1hd	1hd	13	Allgaier H	115	w	6.35	84-16	[DH]Conniver115[DH]AppianVia1153PuffofSmoke110¾	Hung late	6
2Oct46-4Bel	fst	6f-WC	:231 :464 1:122	ⒻMd Sp Wt	3	10		103¾	104¾	135¾	Donoso R	115	w	28.10	73-25	Easy Living1151½C'est Tout115nkSnowfall1151	No factor	22
23Sep46-1Bel	fst	5½f-W	:221 :444 1:03	ⒻMd Sp Wt	17	4		41¼	64	55¼	Donoso R	115	w	19.40	94-02	Valse d'Or1151¼Bimlette1151Muti1153	Raced well	22
28Aug46-1Sar	fst	5½f	:222 :452 :581 1:044	ⒻMd Sp Wt	5	9	87¼	88½	611	511	Arcaro E	115	w	9.40	88-05	Blue Eyed Momo115hdMuti1155Mae Agnes1162	No threat	13
6Aug46-2Sar	fst	5½f	:231 :47 :592 1:052	ⒻMd Sp Wt	2	8	66	66½	76½	1010½	Guerin E	115	w	7.10	85-12	Tea Olive1156Farfalina115hd[DH]Hat Girl115	Even effort	15
1Jun46-1Bel	fst	5f-WC	:222 :45 :572	ⒻMd Sp Wt	17	3		1hd	31½	33¼	Permane R	115	w	*1.40f	90-05	DancingMargot1151¼Mother1102Conniver1151½	Faltered late	18
23May46-4Bel	fst	5f-WC	:222 :453 :581	ⒻMd Sp Wt	13	8		72¾	62¾	64½	Mehrtens W	115	w	4.15f	84-15	Pipette1151Dancing Margot115noWar Fan1151½	Good try	17

Count Fleet

br. c. 1940, by Reigh Count (Sunreigh)–Quickly, by Haste

Lifetime record: 21 16 4 1 $250,300

Own.– Mrs J. Hertz
Br.– Mrs John D. Hertz (Ky)
Tr.– G.D. Cameron

Date	Cond	Dist	Times	Race	PP	St	1st	2nd	Str	Fin	Jockey	Wt	Eqp	Odds	Speed-Var	Top finishers	Comment	Field
5Jun43-6Bel	fst	1½	:48 1:123 2:033 2:281	Belmont 42k	2	1	18	120	120	125	Longden J	126	wb	*.05	97-12	CountFleet12625FairyManhurst126¾Deseronto126	Galloping	3
	Geldings not eligible																	
22May43-6Bel	my	1	:23 :462 1:103 1:36	Withers 17k	2	1	11½	13	12	15	Longden J	126	wb	*.05	94-21	Count Fleet1265Slide Rule12612Tip-Toe126	Wide,easily	3
	Geldings not eligible																	
8May43-6Pim	gd	1 3/16	:472 1:114 1:381 1:572	Preakness 60k	2	1	14	14	15	18	Longden J	126	wb	*.15	95-15	Count Fleet1268Blue Swords1265Vincentive12620	Easily	4
1May43-7CD	fst	1¼	:463 1:123 1:373 2:04	Ky Derby 72k	5	1	1hd	12	12	13	Longden J	126	wb	*.40	87-12	Count Fleet1263Blue Swords1266Slide Rule1266	Handily	10
17Apr43-5Jam	fst	1 1/16	:232 :464 1:112 1:43	Wood Mem 28k	4	1	14	14	14	13½	Longden J	126	wb	*.25	98-06	Count Fleet1263½Blue Swords1267Twoses1212	Much the best	8
13Apr43-5Jam	sly	1 70	:234 :472 1:124 1:424	Alw 3000	8	4	31½	22	2hd	13½	Longden J	122	wb	*.15	90-19	CountFlt1223½Bossut1135Towsr113hd	Forced wide first turn	8
10Nov42-6Pim	gd	1 1/16	:231 :473 1:12 1:444	Walden 12k	3	1	18	115	125	130	Longden J	122	w	*.10	94-14	Count Fleet12230Uncle Billies11315Rough Doc1131	Easily	4
31Oct42-6Pim	fst	1 1/16	:231 :462 1:11 1:433	Pim Futurity 34k	3	2	2hd	1½	13	15	Longden J	119	wb	1.25	100-06	Count Fleet1195Occupation1224Vincentive122		3
	Geldings not eligible																	
20Oct42-5Jam	fst	1 70	:234 :473 1:13 1:44	Alw 5000	5	5	1hd	14	15	16	Longden J	122	wb	*.25	84-16	Count Fleet1226Towser1162½Jack S.L.1133	Easily	8
10Oct42-5Bel	fst	1	:231 :46 1:10 1:344	Champagne 12k	8	1	12	13	13	16	Longden J	116	wb	*1.05	101-07	Count Fleet1166Blue Swords1197Attendant1101	Easily	8
3Oct42-4Bel	fst	6½f-W	:222 :443 1:083 1:151	Futurity 69k	7	9	22	34	34	35	Longden J	119	wb	*1.55	91-04	Occupation1265Askmenow116hdCount Fleet1191½	Gamely	10
	Geldings not eligible																	
24Sep42-6Bel	fst	6f-WC	:23 :461 1:103	Alw 2000	9	12	51¾	53	21	12½	Longden J	122	wb	*1.40	94-06	CountFleet1222½BullsEye111nkJackS.L.111hd	Swerved start	13
15Sep42-5Aqu	fst	6f	:224 :462 1:12	Alw 2500	2	1	21½	33	31	1nk	Longden J	118	wb	*.70	92-12	CntFlt118nkVrySnooty1124NoondySun1121½	Bumped,driving	10
15Aug42-6Was	fst	6f	:222 :454 1:12	Wash Park Futurity 68k	11	9	75	54¼	22	2nk	Longden J	117	wb	4.80	91-12	Occupation122nkCntFleet1175BluSwords117hd	Wide,bumped	11
11Aug42-6Was	gd	6f	:23 :463 1:13	Alw 1800	6	5	3½	2½	1½	1nk	Longden J	119	wb	*.50	86-20	CountFleet119nkBlueSwords1084Hygrohour1223	Forced wide	9
22Jly42-5Emp	fst	5¾f	:232 :463 1:074	Wakefield 6.8k	4	1	31¼	11	12	14	Longden J	116	wb	*.65	98-10	CountFleet1164Rurales1132GoldShower1229	Speed to spare	4
15Jly42-5Emp	fst	5¾f	:23 :454 1:08	©East View 7.1k	6	5	52	21½	22	21	Longden J	116	wb	*.50	96-09	Gold Shower1161Count Fleet1167Rurales1122	Gamely	6
4Jly42-4Emp	fst	5½f	:23 :462 :592 1:054	Alw 2000	5	5	53¾	42½	11	15	Longden J	111	wb	*1.15	97-07	Count Fleet1115Samhar1143Bullpen114hd	Drew away easily	6
19Jun42-3Aqu	fst	5½f	:23 :471 1:06	©Md Sp Wt	8	6	3¾	2½	3½	14	Longden J	116	wb	*.75	97-08	CountFleet1164SewrdBound1161Crst116nk	Bore out str turn	10
15Jun42-5Aqu	fst	5½f	:23 :473 1:061	Md Sp Wt	9	8	63	44½	22	21½	Longden J	116	wb	*1.35	94-12	Supermont1161½Count Fleet1163Quiz116nk	Trouble early	14
1Jun42-5Bel	fst	5f-WC	:572	©Md Sp Wt	13	5	3½	3½	32½	21½	Longden J	116	wb	4.10	91-07	DoveShoot1161½CountFlet116noSuprmont116nk	Swerved start	16

Delegate

ch. g. 1944, by Maeda (Pennant)–Brides Veil, by Polymelian

Own.– Woolford Farm

Br.– Herbert M. Woolf (Kan)

Tr.– W. Stephens

Lifetime record: 134 31 21 26 $277,530

Date-Race	Track	Fractions	Time	Race	Running line	Jockey	Wt	Odds	Figs	Top three	Comment	Fld
6Apr54- 4Jam	fst 6f	:234 :473	1:123	4↑ Clm 10000	1 6 - - - -	Boland W	113wb	*1.50	- -	DeepRiver122hdRunner-up1154½YllowMst108½	Pulled up lame	6
13Feb54- 3Hia	fst 6f	:222 :453	1:101	4↑ Clm 13000	3 7 713 78 54 35½	Boland W	113wb	*1.10	91-09	Ruthred1092½Dean Cavy1163Delegate113no	Mild rally	7
6Feb54- 9Hia	fst 6f	:223 :454	1:111	4↑ Clm 15000	10 12 129¼ 118¼ 85¼ 3nk	Boland W	111wb	4.45	92-11	Chombro113nkSanfoin108noDelegate111½	Late speed	12
30Jan54- 6Hia	fst 6f	:222 :454	1:11	4↑ Clm 13000	1 10 911 89¼ 56½ 33½	Boland W	115wb	4.05	89-12	Easy Paddy114½Ignition1073Delegate115¾	Closed gamely	10
26Jan54- 7Hia	fst 6f	:223 :454	1:103	4↑ Alw 4500	5 11 109¼ 87¼ 63¾ 52	Boland W	112wb	16.95	93-13	Jet Master1151Judge J.B.112noRush Prince1151	Late rally	11
25Dec53- 7TrP	fst 1⅛	:462 1:11 1:371	1:501	3↑ Christmas H 9.1k	6 10 814 78 79 78½	Madden D	111wsb	33.95	81-11	MarkedGame109hdQuickFire1071GulfStream1102½	No threat	13
12Dec53- 7TrP	fst 1 1/16	:233 :471 1:114	1:443	3↑ Ponce de Leon H 8.8k	10 8 74¾ 52 78 87½	Madden D	113wsb	11.25	81-13	Andre1161Capeador109½Marked Game111½	Tired	12
27Oct53- 4Jam	gd 6f	:224 :461	1:114	4↑ Alw 5000	6 6 613 512 58½ 1no	Boland W	120wsb	*1.55	88-17	Delegate120noMohammedan120¾Rae's Reward113½	Just up	6
19Oct53- 6Jam	fst 6f	:23 :454	1:11	2↑ New Rochelle H 22k	10 10 1015 1015 812 78	McCreary C	106wsb	11.15	84-17	White Skies1282¾Hilarious110½Do Report1132½	No factor	10
12Oct53- 6Jam	fst 6f	:23 :462	1:113	3↑ Interborough H 23k	9 9 914 89¼ 710 62¾	McCreary C	108wsb	17.90	86-20	White Skies126hdDo Report112¾Hilarious1101½	Off slowly	9
25Sep53- 5Bel	fst 6f	:223 :462	1:113	4↑ Alw 5000	2 10 1111 1113 56½ 42¼	McCreary C	118wsb	6.75	88-15	Tea-Makr118noThsSd106hdColdCommnd1182¼	Not enough late	12
11Sep53- 6Aqu	fst 7f	:232 :461 1:111	1:234	3↑ Handicap 6060	4 8 99½ 87¾ 45½ 35½	McCreary C	122wsb	*2.20	85-14	Impasse1135½GameChance115noDelegate1222½	Close quarters	10
3Sep53- 7Aqu	fst 6f	:23 :462	1:12	3↑ Clm 12500	2 7 77 58 44½ 1no	Woodhouse H	117wsb	*1.20	92-17	Delegate117noThis Side1176Fancy Bonnet109nk	Just up	8
18Jly53- 3Jam	fst 5½f	:224 :461 :581	1:043	3↑ Clm 12500	7 8 813 79½ 67½ 31¼	Boland W	119wsb	*1.75	94-12	JessLinthicum117½Reprimand114¾Delegt119nk	Closed gamely	8
2Jly53- 6Aqu	fst 6f	:224 :454	1:111	3↑ Handicap 6040	1 6 611 611 47 33	Boland W	118wsb	4.85	93-15	Contribution1141½Hyphasis1221½Delegate1183¼	Late speed	6
27Jun53- 6Aqu	fst 7f	:22 :443 1:092	1:22	3↑ Carter H 59k	8 9 914 912 914 912	Boland W	110wb	25.75	88-09	Tom Fool1352Squared Away1222¼Eatontown1131¼	Trailed	9
13Jun53- 2Bel	fst 6f	:224 :463	1:114	4↑ OClm 12500	1 2 78 66 2½ 12	Boland W	122wsb	*1.40	90-11	Delegate1222Blinker Light118¾All Is Well126½	Drew out	7
27May53- 6Bel	fst 6f-WC	:214 :443	1:101	3↑ Roseben H 23k	1 9 911 916 97½	Boland W	112wb	17.05	82-09	SquaredAway1241¼DarkPeter1221½Sagittarius115hd	Trailed	9
6May53- 6Bel	gd 6f-WC	:221 :444	1:10	3↑ Toboggan H 30k	9 9 74½ 62¾ 52	Anderson P	113wb	7.15e	89-12	Tuscany122noHyphasis116½Dark Peter122nk	Lost bandage	9
21Apr53- 7Jam	fst 6f	:231 :463	1:114	3↑ Handicap 6055	1 8 816 714 612 44¾	Anderson P	122wb	2.55	83-19	Indian Land119noCount Flame1112½Sun Rene1112¼	Late rush	9
11Apr53- 6Jam	fst 6f	:223 :453	1:11	3↑ Jamaica H 23k	7 9 912 911 95¼ 32	Anderson P	115wsb	11.75	90-15	Sagittarius113hdTuscany1242Delegate115½	Closed fast	9
2Apr53- 3Jam	fst 6f	:233 :47	1:114	4↑ Clm 12500	1 3 58½ 45 4¾ 11	Anderson P	120wsb	*.60	88-16	Delegate1201Dictionary1134Harpes1172	Drew out	5
19Feb53- 7Hia	fst 1⅛	:464 1:11 1:37	1:502	4↑ Alw 5000	1 10 107 76½ 54 21½	McCreary C	122wsb	*1.90	82-13	GreatCaptain1081½Delegate122¾WnnngFlt1112	Closed gamely	10
7Feb53- 3Hia	my 6f	:223 :464	1:124	4↑ Clm 20000	5 5 57½ 55½ 3½ 16	McCreary C	118wsb	2.35	84-34	Delegate1186Roaming116nkWar Phar1181½	Easily	5
28Jan53- 7Hia	fst 7f	:224 :46 1:111	1:242	3↑ Palm Beach H 20k	4 13 1311 1111 1011 77¼	Boland W	111wsb	20.30	81-20	OilCapitol107nkBattlefield123½NimbleFox1141½	No mishap	14
16Jan53- 7Hia	fst 6f	:223 :461	1:11	3↑ Hia Inaugural H 19k	9 12 118½ 911 89¼ 79¼	Anderson P	119wb	7.90e	84-21	Nimble Fox1071¾Sagittarius1181½Starecase120½	No factor	12
3Jan53- 7TrP	gd 1 1/16	:224 :46 1:104	1:44	3↑ Robert E Lee H 30k	11 15 1517 1211 1216 98	Anderson P	117wsb	8.95	84-19	Elixir1103Recline1162Topside108no	No menace	15
27Dec52- 7TrP	fst 6f	:222 :451	1:102	3↑ E R Bradley H 17k	13 10 118½ 108¾ 87½ 42¼	Anderson P	122wsb	19.40	93-15	Sagittarius114nkEatontown1151Starecase1231	Closed fast	13
3Dec52- 7TrP	fst 6f	:223 :452	1:102	3↑ Alligator H 9k	5 14 149 1415 1212 117½	Anderson P	126wsb	7.10	87-18	Jet Fleet119hdCongo King1142Recover110no	Off slowly	14
11Nov52- 6Jam	fst 6f	:223 :454	1:11	2↑ Autumn Day H 22k	4 7 77½ 66¼ 53½ 2¾	Anderson P	119wsb	3.50	91-16	Squared Away119¾Delegate119½Tea-Maker1261½	Gaining	7
20Oct52- 6Jam	fst 6f	:224 :453	1:104	2↑ New Rochelle H 22k	2 9 97¾ 85¾ 63½ 11½	Anderson P	114wsb	3.55e	93-20	Delegate1141½Tea-Maker126¾War King1111½	Going away	9
6Oct52- 6Jam	fst 6f	:23 :46	1:11	2↑ Interborough H 23k	7 11 118¾ 117½ 95½ 41¾	Boland W	114wsb	4.50e	90-15	SquaredAway118½Tea-Maker124noTruePattrn1061¼	Late rally	11
1Oct52- 7Bel	fst 6f	:222 :462	1:113	3↑ Handicap 6070	7 8 89¼ 88½ 65¼ 2no	Boland W	122wsb	4.35	91-15	Jazerant117noDelegate122hdNullify1051¾	Just missed	8
24Sep52- 5Bel	fst 6f	:231 :471	1:114	3↑ Handicap 6045	4 5 53¾ 42¼ 43¼ 33½	Boland W	126wsb	*1.35	86-15	Roman Fair1141Acefull1122½Delegate1261	No rally	6
15Sep52- 6Bel	fst 6f-WC	:22 :441	1:082	2↑ Fall Highweight H 24k	5 15 147¼ 91¼ 62¾	Boland W	132wsb	32.85	96-03	Hitex130½Tea-Maker140½Papoose117nk	Off slowly	15
8Sep52- 6Aqu	fst 7f	:223 :451 1:102	1:24	3↑ Bay Shore H 17k	11 11 118¾ 1111 97 95¾	Boland W	114wsb	16.70	84-20	NextMove1151FirstGlance111nkSquaredAway1202	Slow start	12
29Jly52- 5Jam	fst 1 1/16	:25 :481 1:13	1:444	3↑ Handicap 6535	5 6 69 42 1hd 1hd	Boland W	121wsb	2.75	88-19	Delegate121hdBe Gracious1101Lone Eagle1162½	Driving	6
16Jly52- 6Jam	fst 6f	:23 :454	1:101	3↑ Fleetwing H 21k	6 6 66½ 67 66 55¾	Scurlock O	113wsb	13.75	90-16	Tea-Maker114¾Squared Away1202½Arise1221	Outrun	6
4Jly52- 6Aqu	fst 7f	:221 :443 1:09	1:22	3↑ Carter H 29k	4 10 108½ 108 914 79¾	Errico C	116wsb	13.70	92-09	NorthernStar1152CraftyAdmirl1202½ToMrkt123no	Slow start	10
21Jun52- 5Aqu	fst 6f	:222 :452	1:102	3↑ Handicap 7540	2 4 49½ 410 46½ 35	Boland W	120wsb	2.05	95-11	Squared Away1225Tea-Maker121noDelegate1201½	Late rally	4
13Jun52- 6Aqu	fst 6f	:23 :463	1:112	3↑ Handicap 7530	5 5 56 52¼ 41 1no	Boland W	118wsb	2.35	95-14	Delegate118noSheilasReward1261¼HeapBigChief1052	Just up	5
7Jun52- 5Bel	fst 6f	:223 :461	1:104	3↑ Handicap 7540	3 7 77¼ 76 53½ 2¾	Boland W	113wsb	11.20	94-14	First Glance112¾Delegate113½Tea-Maker121no	Late speed	7
29Apr52- 6Bel	gd 6f-WC	:221 :443	1:091	3↑ Toboggan H 23k	2 8 86¼ 66 67¾	Boland W	118wsb	7.10	87-05	DarkPeter108½CraftyAdmiral1182½Tea-Maker1202	Slow start	8
16Apr52- 6Jam	gd 6f	:23 :46	1:111	3↑ Jamaica H 17k	3 9 97¾ 95¼ 85¼ 32½	Boland W	114wsb	12.85	88-15	Tea-Maker1122½Northern Star115noDelegate1142	Late foot	9
11Apr52- 6Jam	fst 6f	:23 :46	1:113	3↑ Mettlesome H 7.9k	5 8 67½ 55¾ 45¼ 1hd	Boland W	111wsb	4.20	89-21	Delegate111hdBryan G.1261Tea-Maker1153	Just up	8
1Apr52- 6Jam	fst 6f	:222 :453	1:094	3↑ Paumonok H 29k	8 11 108¼ 87¾ 88¾ 65¾	Jemas N	110wsb	18.90	92-13	Woodchuck1193½Squared Away116½[D]Jumbo116¾	Late rally	11
4Mar52- 7GP	fst 6f	:22 :442	1:093	3↑ Inaugural H 8.8k	14 15 149¾ 108¼ 66 32¾	Jemas N	119wsb	8.80e	94-11	Tripoli113¾Eatontown1142Delegate119nk	Off slowly	15
28Feb52- 7Hia	fst 6f	:222 :452	1:103	4↑ Alw 4000	1 5 34 36 58½ 57¾	Jemas N	118wsb	2.35	87-12	Hi Billee1162½Prop118nkSuleiman1123½	Tired	7
16Feb52- 6Hia	fst 7f	:224 :452 1:10	1:232	4↑ Alw 5000	6 9 88 810 711 56¼	Jemas N	118wsb	9.65	89-16	Crafty Admiral119nkYildiz1222½Eatontown1161	Forced wide	10
23Jan52- 7Hia	fst 7f	:223 :444 1:091	1:22	3↑ Palm Beach H 13k	5 5 56 56½ 47 59	Woodhouse H	118wsb	6.30	93-12	CraftyAdmiral1072Woodchuck1163OilCapitol1122	No menace	10
17Jan52- 7Hia	fst 6f	:221 :452	1:10	3↑ Hia Inaugural H 13k	8 13 128¾ 118¼ 77¾ 75¼	Woodhouse H	122wsb	6.70	93-12	Spartan Valor121hdJumbo1182Woodchuck1192½	Raced wide	14
12Nov51- 6Jam	fst 6f	:231 :454	1:111	2↑ Autumn Day H 17k	6 9 98¼ 76¼ 76½ 31¼	McCreary C	120wsb	5.90	90-20	Tea-Maker115½Guillotine126¾Delegate120hd	Closed gamely	9
3Nov51- 7Jam	sly 6f	:222 :452	1:121	3↑ Handicap 5065	3 7 79½ 68½ 65¼ 2no	McCreary C	119wsb	*2.20	86-17	Assignment105noDelegate119½Atalanta104½	Just missed	7
19Oct51- 6Jam	fst 6f	:223 :452	1:101	2↑ New Rochelle H 17k	7 11 117¼ 85¼ 63¼ 21½	Woodhouse H	116wsb	9.80	94-15	Squared Away1151½Delegate116½Guillotine1261½	Late rush	12
10Oct51- 5Bel	fst 5½f-W	:22 :441	1:013	3↑ Handicap 4565	8 7 41 11 13	Woodhouse H	113wsb	5.45	106-00	Delegate1133Guillotine132¾Tea-Maker123nk	Driving	8
24Sep51- 6Bel	fst 6f-WC	:222 :443	1:09	2↑ Fall Highweight H 25k	15 15 167¼ 61 42	Woodhouse H	120wsb	15.50	94-07	Guillotine134noSquared Away1262Ferd128no	Off slowly	18
9Aug51- 7Atl	fst 6f	:222 :452	1:092	4↑ Alw 4500	3 7 53½ 43 36 46¾	Boulmetis S	124wsb	*1.90	91-11	Istan1144Chloe1192Vamanos121¾	Weakened	7
31Jly51- 6Jam	fst 6f	:232 :462	1:111	3↑ Handicap 5040	4 5 55 42½ 42 33¼	Mehrtens W	112wsb	7.85	88-16	Repetoire1232¼Mighty Quest1081Delegate1124	Hung	5
18Jly51- 6Jam	fst 6f	:231 :462	1:112	3↑ Fleetwing H 22k	3 9 85¾ 63¼ 62¼ 53¼	Boland W	112wsb	13.95	87-16	More Sun110hdTea-Maker1221½Arise1301½	No rally	9
4Jly51- 6Aqu	fst 7f	:223 :452 1:101	1:232	3↑ Carter H 23k	2 8 811 88¼ 85¼ 76	Boland W	114wsb	14.05	89-17	Arise1221More Sun1081¼Piet1231	Dull try	9
6Jun51- 6Bel	fst 6f-WC	:222 :444	1:084	3↑ Roseben H 12k	7 9 94½ 3½ 1nk	Boland W	111wsb	9.50	97-04	Delegate111nkMiche116noTea-Maker126¾	Just lasted	10
19May51- 6Bel	fst 1	:23 :453 1:10	1:352	3↑ Metropolitan H 36k	13 9 52¼ 42 65½ 64½	Boland W	110wsb	10.65f	92-06	Casemate115½Piet123½Lights Up1221	Forced wide	13
14May51- 6Bel	fst 6f-WC	:222 :444	1:092	3↑ Toboggan H 24k	13 13 132½ 3nk 42	Scurlock O	111wsb	13.95	92-06	Hyphasis110noTea-Maker1231Casemate1191	Weakened	14
7Apr51- 6Jam	fst 1 1/16	:231 :463 1:111	1:441	3↑ Excelsior H 29k	3 5 51¾ 51¼ 85¾ 64	Scurlock O	114wb	4.65	87-12	Lotowhite116hdFerd123¾Great Circle1191¼	Raced wide	11
2Apr51- 6Jam	fst 6f	:223 :46	1:111	3↑ Paumonok H 29k	8 5 52¾ 31 3¾ 31¼	Scurlock O	114wsb	5.20	90-15	Ferd116¾Casemate119½Delegate1141¼	Held well	11
5Mar51- 7GP	fst 6f	:222 :444	1:101	3↑ Inaugural H 7.5k	1 9 65¾ 66½ 55 2¾	Madden D	118wsb	12.70	93-11	Hyphasis118¾Delegate1181Lextown1201½	Finished fast	10
22Feb51- 7Hia	fst 7f	:224 :453 1:102	1:232	4↑ Alw 4500	3 - - - - -	Batcheller L	118wb	2.25	- -	Hyphasis1196Prop124½Black George1192	Refused to break	8
10Feb51- 7Hia	fst 1⅛	:453 1:103 1:361	1:492	3↑ McLennan H 36k	15 8 74¾ 53½ 34½ 66¼	Atkinson T	114wb	9.80	85-14	Gangway1091¼Mount Marcy114hdSunglow1172½	Faltered	15
24Jan51- 7Hia	fst 7f	:222 :451 1:104	1:234	3↑ Palm Beach H 10k	2 12 86¾ 55¼ 41½ 22	Atkinson T	120wb	*2.90	91-17	AmericanGlory1112Delegate120nkMountMrcy114hd	Off slowly	13
17Jan51- 7Hia	fst 6f	:221 :451	1:103	3↑ Inaugural H (Div 2) 9k	4 8 84¼ 66¾ 34 23	Scurlock O	122wb	4.80	92-12	Valpam1213Delegate122noNell K.119½	Closed fast	8
14Nov50- 6Jam	fst 1 1/16	:24 :47 1:113	1:442	3↑ Alw 5000	6 4 43¾ 21½ 11½ 21½	Scurlock O	120wb	*1.55	88-17	Ted M.1061½Delegate1203½Uncle Edgar1201¼	Weakened	7
2Nov50- 6Jam	fst 1 1/16	:234 :47 1:111	1:442	3↑ Handicap 5050	2 6 33 2hd 11 12½	Scurlock O	122wb	3.75	90-15	Delegate1222½Crystal Boot1131Wine List118½	Ridden out	7
25Oct50- 6Jam	gd 6f	:23 :46	1:111	2↑ New Rochelle H 17k	2 12 105 115½ 115¾ 86	Scurlock O	117wb	8.60	85-19	MagicWords1131SheilasReward124¾Tea-Makr1252	No factor	12
12Oct50- 6Jam	sly 6f	:23 :46	1:12	3↑ Interborough H 17k	9 9 97¼ 97¼ 86¼ 62	Atkinson T	119wb	3.80	85-18	SheilasRewrd120¾MgcWords112½WsconsnBoy109nk	Closed gap	10
25Sep50- 6Bel	fst 7f	:223 :453 1:102	1:23	2↑ Vosburgh H 18k	1 10 108½ 118¼ 87 66¼	Scurlock O	118wb	6.95	89-15	Tea-Maker1181¼More Sun106½Piet124nk	Close quarters	12
18Sep50- 6Bel	fst 6f-WC	:221 :443	1:084	2↑ Fall Highweight H 25k	3 9 8¾ 72 22	Scurlock O	128wb	17.90	95-06	Arise1332Delegate128nkRoyal Governor129½	Game effort	14
7Sep50- 6Aqu	fst 6f	:224 :454	1:11	3↑ Handicap 4055	5 8 84½ 73¾ 66 54	Scurlock O	122wb	3.45	93-09	Mangohick1173DarkFavorite1051FrindlyFrnk108no	No excuse	11

Previously trained by J.A. Nerud

Date/Race	Cond	Dist	Fractions	Race	Running line	Jockey	Wt	Odds	Speed	Top finishers	Comment
20May50- 6Bel	sly	1	:23 :452 1:102 1:363	3↑ Metropolitan H 31k	8 6 43½ 42½ 44 96¾	Scurlock O	117wb	11.25	84-13	Greek Ship106½Piet121¾Cochise121¼	Tired 11
13May50- 5Bel	fst	7f	:23 :454 1:101 1:23	3↑ Handicap 5050	5 5 64¼ 57 49 36	Scurlock O	122wb	3.30	89-11	Cochise1205Three Rings1221Delegate122hd	Sluggish start 7
29Apr50- 6Jam	gd	1 3/16	:473 1:12 1:372 1:57	3↑ Gallant Fox H 60k	4 8 83¾ 65 74¾ 77	Atkinson T	118wb	4.05	84-14	BetterSelf1161¼ChicleII120hdLoserWeeper109nk	No menace 13
8Apr50- 6Jam	fst	1 1/16	:241 :473 1:112 1:434	3↑ Excelsior H 24k	7 8 86 54¼ 54 33	Errico C	119wb	3.15	91-10	Arise1161½Olympia1261½Delegate1191	Finished well 10
1Apr50- 6Jam	fst	6f	:222 :461 1:104	3↑ Paumonok H 30k	13 8 54¾ 41½ 53¾ 31¾	Woodhouse H	122 w	3.90	95-14	Olympia1241¼Arise118½Delegate1223	Forced wide 15
20Mar50- 6GP	gd	6f	:223 :451 1:103	4↑ Alw 3000	1 6 53 42 2½ 1½	Stout J	112wb	*.50	97-18	Delegate112½Almenow1192½Appease Not111½	Driving 6
12Nov49- 6Jam	fst	1 3/16	:471 1:113 1:37 1:564	3↑ Westchester H 29k	3 8 88 57½ 31 2nk	Errico C	120wb	6.75	92-17	ThreeRings116nkDelegate120hdRoylGovrnor1235	Just missed 11
2Nov49- 6Jam	sly	6f	:232 :462 1:112	2↑ New Rochelle H 17k	2 7 61¾ 51¾ 13 16	Arcaro E	122wb	*1.25	94-19	Delegate1226Better Self124noLithe109no	Easily 8
12Oct49- 6Jam	fst	6f	:224 :461 1:111	3↑ Interborough H 17k	9 8 84¾ 42½ 31 21	Arcaro E	122wb	*2.25	94-15	Royal Governor1191Delegate122noPipette1121½	Good effort 10
6Sep49- 6Haw	fst	6f	:222 :453 1:101	3↑ Haw Inaugural H 12k	2 8 42 42 1hd 2¾	Brooks S	122wb	*1.70	101-06	Star Reward124¾Delegate122noBlue Helen109no	Good try 10
1Aug49- 6Was	fst	7f	:22 :443 1:09 1:221	3↑ Clang H 23k	11 9 94½ 64¼ 32 22¼	Brooks S	121wb	*2.50	97-10	Colosal1102¼Delegate1212¼Carrara Marble118hd	Good try 12
13Jly49- 6AP	fst	6f	:224 :452 1:104	3↑ Myrtlewood H 27k	2 3 42 32 42¼ 77½	Scurlock O	124wb	*1.90	85-17	Dandilly1083½WithPleasur1192¼RoylBlood112no	Forced back 9
4Jly49- 6AP	fst	1⅛	:472 1:103 1:352 1:482	3↑ Stars & Stripes H 54k	5 3 2hd 2hd 22 42¼	Garner W	110wb	6.30	102-09	Coaltown1301¼Armed110½Star Reward121½	Faltered 6
18Jun49- 6Det	hy	1 1/16	:243 :484 1:151 1:48	3↑ Governor's H 23k	5 2 21 2hd 1hd 2½	Nelson E	119wb	3.10	75-35	Vulcan's Forge128½Delegate1191¼Syndicate1086	Weakened 6
28May49- 6Was	fst	6½f	:223 :453 1:101 1:171	3↑ Steger H 11k	1 5 51¾ 31½ 1hd 12	Nelson E	125 w	*1.40	98-12	Delegate1252Blue Helen1081¼Enforcer1102½	Going away 10
16May49- 6Was	gd	6f	:224 :46 1:111	3↑ Crete H 10k	4 4 41¼ 12 11½ 12½	Nelson E	122wb	*.70	90-28	Delegate1222½Enforcer110nkWithPleasure120½	Wide,driving 6
9Feb49- 6Hia	fst	7f	:23 :452 1:093 1:223	3↑ Seminole H 11k	1 1 1hd 11 12 1hd	Brooks S	125wb	*1.20	99-13	Delegate125hdBlue Border1161Bug Juice1143	Hard drive 6
26Jan49- 6Hia	fst	7f	:231 :453 1:091 1:23	3↑ Palm Beach H 12k	2 8 74¾ 77 63½ 31	Nelson E	126wb	*1.50	96-12	BlueBorder1131BugJuice110hdDelegate126nk	Strong finish 10
17Jan49- 6Hia	fst	6f	:223 :452 1:104	3↑ Hia Inaugural H 12k	8 5 51¼ 52¼ 21½ 1nk	Nelson E	122wb	*1.45	94-14	Delegate122nkKitchenPolice1102¾CircusClown118½	Just up 9
3Jan49- 6TrP	fst	6f	:214 :442 1:094	4↑ Alw 2500	7 5 54½ 54½ 2hd 17	Nelson E	115wb	*1.55	98-16	Delegate1157Coyote122nkLoriot1121¼	Drew away 8
12Oct48- 7Haw	fst	6½f	:224 :461 1:113 1:182	3↑ Haw Sprint H 22k	9 6 53½ 21 2hd 1nk	Nelson E	116wb	*3.00	92-25	Delegate116nkCarrara Marble1098Blue Helen1081	Just up 10
2Oct48- 7Haw	fst	1¼	:473 1:123 1:391 2:06	3↑ Haw Gold Cup 57k	5 2 12 12 31½ 66¼	Parnell W	117wb	10.20e	72-20	Billings1221¼Sun Herod124hd[D]Happy Issue1101	Tired 12
18Sep48- 7Haw	fst	1 1/16	:241 :473 1:122 1:46	3↑ Haw Autumn H 22k	8 6 32 32 24 35	Skoronski A	118wb	2.90	83-15	Billings1165May Reward113noDelegate118nk	Faltered 11
11Sep48- 7Haw	fst	6f	:221 :453 1:114	3↑ Haw Speed H 24k	6 10 96½ 85 51¼ 41¾	Skoronski A	117wb	*3.20	92-20	Billings111nkCarrara Marble104½Bullish1111	Late drive 17
7Jly48- 7AP	fst	6f	:223 :45 1:103	3↑ Domino H 22k	6 3 34½ 33½ 32 42½	Brooks S	117wb	*1.00	91-15	Preoccupy1101¼Plumper111¾Fighting Frank119½	No excuse 6
26Jun48- 6AP	fst	1	:232 :454 1:094 1:351	3↑ Equipoise Mile H 33k	4 4 31½ 2hd 2hd 42	Keene H	119wb	4.50	94-06	Fervent124noMighty Story109¾Loujac1051¼	Faltered 11
21Jun48- 6AP	fst	6f	:224 :444 1:094	3↑ Handicap 5000	5 3 44 34 23 2hd	Keene H	120wb	*1.30	98-05	Mighty Story112hdDelegate120hdPhar Mon1161	Just missed 8
29May48- 6Was	fst	6½f	:223 :453 1:111 1:174	3↑ Steger H 11k	10 2 64 73¼ 2hd 1¾	Skoronski A	118wb	*1.70	95-17	Delegate118¾Eternal Reward1172½Tidy Sum113¾	In hand 10
17May48- 6Was	gd	6f	:23 :462 1:112	3↑ Crete H 11k	1 2 31½ 31½ 73½ 87¼	Skoronski A	121wb	*1.50	83-21	Eternal Reward1122Tre Vit111½Air Rate1092	Tired 13
Previously trained by R.O. Higdon											
27Mar48- 6TrP	fst	1⅛	:484 1:122 1:363 1:493	3↑ Double Event H (2) 16k	3 2 2hd 2hd 2hd 2nk	Richard J	119wb	*1.00	93-14	Colosal113nkDelegate1195½Childeric1075	No mishap 4
20Mar48- 6TrP	fst	1⅛	:472 1:112 1:362 1:492	3↑ Double Event H (1) 17k	8 2 11 13 1½ 31	Dodson D	119wb	2.10	93-13	Colosal113hdFervent1251Delegate119½	Swung wide 8
6Mar48- 6TrP	fst	1 1/16	:234 :474 1:113 1:431	3↑ Coral Gables H 11k	2 2 1hd 14 16 15	Dodson D	116wb	*1.00	96-12	Delegate1165Stud Poker115hdRespingo1143	Eased up 4
11Feb48- 6Hia	fst	7f	:232 :46 1:101 1:23	3↑ Seminole H 12k	6 3 1hd 1hd 2hd 21	Atkinson T	123wb	3.90	96-16	Citation1121Delegate123nkArmed1282	Weakened 9
24Jan48- 6Hia	my	7f	:231 :462 1:114 1:242	3↑ Palm Beach H 11k	5 3 43¾ 2hd 1½ 12	Atkinson T	118wb	1.90	90-28	Delegate1182Bug Juice1102½Lets Dance1101½	Going away 6
16Jan48- 5Hia	fst	6f	:224 :453 1:094	3↑ Hia Inaugural H 11k	4 2 31 31 3½ 1nk	Jessop JD	117wb	3.45	99-07	Delegate117nkBuzfuz1271¼El Mono1201	Hard drive 6
10Jan48- 6GP	fst	6f	:232 :462 1:111	3↑ Suwannee River H 11k	8 4 51¼ 3nk 2hd 21	Jessop JD	114wb	6.55	93-15	Buzfuz1221Delegate1143½Gestapo111nk	Raced well 9
1Dec47- 6GP	gd	6f	:231 :472 1:12	3↑ Inaugural H 9.2k	3 9 32 2hd 2hd 1nk	Scurlock D	109wb	6.95	90-24	Delegate109nkNance's Ace1141½Iodine1075	Driving 10
4Oct47- 6Haw	fst	6½f	:223 :451 1:104 1:174	3↑ Haw Sprint H 22k	2 8 52¾ 66 65¼ 65	Jemas N	105wb	10.60	90-17	Fighting Frank122noSpy Song1351Plumper1131½	No factor 9
27Sep47- 6Haw	fst	6f	:224 :462 1:111	3↑ Handicap 4500	4 3 2½ 2½ 2nk 2no	Jemas N	106wb	3.30	97-11	Proud Ruler103noDelegate1064½Education117hd	Game try 5
20Sep47- 5Haw	fst	6f	:224 :461 1:11	3↑ Handicap 4500	6 4 3½ 3nk 12 1no	Jemas N	106wb	*1.00	98-09	Delegate106noLove Sonnet1092Proud Ruler1006	Hard drive 7
13Sep47- 7Haw	gd	6f	:222 :461 1:122	3↑ Haw Speed H 22k	1 5 21 31 33½ 36½	Jemas N	103wb	17.40	84-19	SpySng1323½Educatn1133Dlgt103¾	Saved ground,weakened 8
3Sep47- 6Haw	fst	6f	:221 :452 1:11	3↑ Handicap 4500	2 7 22½ 23 33 35	Jemas N	105wb	*2.40	93-14	Bogle1094Jack S.L.1141Delegate1052	Weakened 9
18Aug47- 7Was	fst	6f	:223 :444 1:092	3↑ Great Western H 27k	3 6 55 66½ 711 713	Jemas N	105wb	16.30	90-07	Rippey1151Spy Song1291½Quick Reward1133½	Outrun 7
28Jly47- 7Was	fst	6f	:223 :452 1:094	3↑ Quick Step 22k	4 4 44 46½ 48½ 68½	Jessop JD	116wb	7.30	92-09	WithPleasure130½SpySong1302½Rippey1274½	Speed,faltered 8
3Jly47- 6AP	fst	6f	:223 :45 1:101	3↑ Alw 5000	3 5 1½ 13 12½ 31	Scurlock O	109wb	3.90	95-08	Quick Reward118½Air Patrol118½Delegate1092	Faltered 6
Previously trained by E. Anspach											
17Mar47- 6GP	fst	6f	:222 :451 1:104	Magic City H 5.6k	3 3 31½ 32 11 12½	Watson R	124wb	*.75	99-07	Delegate1242½Imperator1203Secnav1222	Easily 5
12Mar47- 4GP	fst	6f	:222 :453 1:103	Alw 3000	9 3 1hd 12 14 13½	Watson R	120wb	*.65	100-05	Dlgate1203½AtomicPowr1126PnnyRwrd109nk	Speed to spare 10
22Feb47- 5Hia	fst	1⅛	:464 1:113 1:371 1:494	Alw 5000	5 2 2½ 32½ 37 518½	Watson R	117wb	3.95	73-11	BulletProof1091½Faultlss11312Cpt.Ptrck1034¾	Flattened out 5
12Feb47- 5Hia	fst	7f	:224 :452 1:102 1:233	©Alw 4000	4 1 11½ 11½ 1½ 31¼	Watson R	122wb	5.75	93-12	Faultless122nkBullet Proof1131Delegate1227	Gamely 8
17Aug46- 6Was	my	6f	:224 :462 1:121	Wash Park Futurity 79k	11 6 41 2½ 22 35¾	Scurlock O	118wb	13.60	83-21	Education1183¼Jett-Jett1182½Delegate1181	Bid,failed 12
3Aug46- 7Was	fst	6f	:222 :452 1:111	Elementary 24k	10 9 64 64½ 42½ 46½	Anderson I	125 w	10.80	87-07	Education122hdColonelO'F1254John'sPrd1202½	Bid,faltered 11
24Jly46- 6AP	fst	6f	:224 :46 1:112	©Primer 23k	1 3 11½ 12 13 11¼	Scurlock O	119 w	11.40	90-14	Delegate1191¼Education122hdJohn's Pride119hd	Driving 11
13Jly46- 6AP	fst	6f	:22 :45 1:104	Arl Futurity 79k	7 14 98½ 911 96¾ 95	Scurlock O	122 w	14.40	88-09	CosmicBomb122¾JetPilot1223ColonelO'F122no	No response 15
6Jly46- 3AP	fst	5½f	:223 :461 :583 1:044	Alw 4000	1 4 42½ 43½ 34½ 34¾	Anderson I	117 w	4.60	92-09	Educton1232½Twt'sBoy1232¼Dlgt117hd	No rally,drifted out 5
26Jun46- 2AP	fst	5f	:23 :462 :591	Alw 3500	7 5 51¼ 53 42 1½	Scurlock O	118 w	4.30	96-14	Delegate118½Springtd1152½Bullsh1182	Bothered repeatedly 10
8Jun46- 3Haw	fst	5f	:23 :473 1:011	Md Sp Wt	5 4 11 13 16 18	Scurlock O	118 w	4.00	89-14	Delegate1188Miniver118hdGrand Fellow1183	Speed to spare 6
1Jun46- 1Haw	my	5f	:241 :491 1:022	Md Sp Wt	2 6 54 54½ 46 45½	Scurlock O	118 w	25.60	77-20	Galloway1184Masico Lad1181½Ranahead115no	Closed well 8

Devil Diver

b. c. 1939, by St. Germans (Swynford)–Dabchick, by Royal Minstrel **Lifetime record: 47 22 12 3 $261,064**

Own.– Greentree Stable
Br.– Greentree Farm (Ky)
Tr.– John M. Gaver

Date/Race	Cond	Dist	Fractions	Race	Running line	Jockey	Wt	Odds	Speed	Top finishers	Comment
4Jly45- 5Bel	fst	1¼	:464 1:104 1:363 2:021	3↑ Brooklyn H 56k	2 5 32 42¼ 2½ 21¼	Arcaro E	132wb	*1.25	88-12	Stymie1161¼Devil Diver1322½Olympic Zenith1102	Held well 9
16Jun45- 6Bel	fst	1¼	:502 1:142 1:39 2:04	3↑ Suburban H 52k	1 1 1½ 11½ 12 12	Arcaro E	132wb	*.50	80-15	DevlDvr1322Stym119nkOlympcZnth1061½	Under pressure late 4
9Jun45- 6Bel	fst	1	:234 :47 1:113 1:362	3↑ Metropolitan H 27k	5 4 31½ 32 11 14	Atkinson T	129wb	*.55	92-12	Devil Diver1294Alex Barth123½Boy Knight112¾	Easily 7
4Jun45- 6Bel	sly	6f-WC	:23 :462 1:11	3↑ Toboggan H 16k	6 1 62¼ 41¼ 23 22½	Arcaro E	135wb	*.85	83-13	Apache1292½Devil Diver1354Mrs. Ames1071	No match 9
24May45- 5Jam	fst	6f	:231 :462 1:104	3↑ Paumonok H 8.3k	3 7 55½ 41¾ 31½ 11¼	Arcaro E	132wb	*1.30	98-12	Devil Diver1321¼Apache1292½Alex Barth121hd	Fast finish 7
1Nov44- 7Pim	fst	1 3/16	:481 1:122 1:372 1:563	3↑ Pim Spl 25k	3 2 23 24 24 26	Arcaro E	126wb	1.55	93-12	Twilight Tear1176Devil Diver12610Megogo120	Mild bid 3
21Oct44- 5Jam	sly	1⅝	:483 1:391 2:051 2:46	3↑ Gallant Fox H 55k	2 1 35 33 55 510	Arcaro E	124wb	*3.00	75-15	Some Chance1161Pyracanth1053Stymie1121	Tired 10
30Sep44- 6Bel	fst	2	:513 2:351 3:01 3:271	3↑ J C Gold Cup 26k	2 2 2½ 2hd 21½ 33	Arcaro E	125wb	*1.45	65-17	Bolingbroke1253Strategic125hdDevil Diver125¾	Tired late 4
Geldings not eligible											
23Sep44- 6Bel	fst	1½	:553 1:221 2:132 2:363	3↑ Manhattan H 15k	3 2 3½ 1hd 11½ 11¼	Arcaro E	125wb	2.00	55-17	DevlDvr1251¼Crbou102hdBolngbrok126nk	Outsprinted rivals 4
16Sep44- 6Nar	fst	1 3/16	:463 1:111 1:364 1:56	3↑ Nar Spl 30k	13 5 74½ 64¼ 75 53½	Arcaro E	130wb	*1.30e	91-12	Paperboy1101Alex Barth117hdCastleman1131½	No response 13
26Aug44- 6Bel	fst	1	:232 :463 1:111 1:361	3↑ Wilson 17k	5 2 21½ 2½ 1hd 12½	Atkinson T	117wb	*.25	93-11	Devil Diver1172½Bull Reigh1121Wait a Bit1124	Drew away 5
19Aug44- 6Bel	fst	1¼	:48 1:114 1:37 2:021	3↑ Saratoga H 53k	4 5 51¾ 52¾ 73¼ 67	Arcaro E	135wb	*2.45	82-13	Paperboy103hdAlex Barth1161½Bolingbroke1181	Tired 7
15Aug44- 6Bel	fst	1¼	:481 1:114 1:364 2:02	3↑ Whitney 16k	4 1 1hd 12 11 1½	Arcaro E	117wb	*.25	90-17	DevilDiver117½Princequillo1173½Bolngbrok1172	Ridden out 4
31Jly44- 6Bel	fst	7f	:234 :463 1:104 1:233	3↑ American Legion H 7.8k	1 2 2nk 1nk 11 12½	Arcaro E	136wb	*.25	92-12	Devil Diver1362½Bull Reigh1054Bourmont108	Easily 3
13May44- 6Bel	fst	1	:23 :453 1:103 1:354	3↑ Metropolitan H 13k	5 5 54¾ 33 21 11½	Atkinson T	134wb	*.50e	95-10	Devil Diver1341½Alquest109¾Boysy1081¼	Driving 7
8May44- 6Bel	gd	6f-WC	:23 :464 1:123	3↑ Toboggan H 6.7k	2 3 53½ 52 3nk 11¼	Arcaro E	134wb	*.70e	83-16	Devil Diver1341¼Signator120hdBrownie1142	Drew away 7

Date	Trk	Dist	Fractions	Race	PP	St	1C	2C	Str	Fin	Jockey	Wt	Odds	Fig	Top Three	Comment	Fld
8Apr44- 5Jam	gd	6f	:223 :461 1:111	3↑ Paumonok H 9.2k	1	4	42¼	45	34½	11½	Atkinson T	130wb	3.15	96-16	Devil Diver1301½Apache1301Brownie112¾	Bore over,driving	10
5Jly43- 7Was	my	1⅛	:491 1:14 1:401 1:533	3↑ Stars & Stripes H 59k	10	5	43½	44½	44¾	55¾	Woolf G	124wb	*1.90	74-31	Rounders1161Thumbs Up113hdMarriage1164	No response	10
26Jun43- 6Aqu	fst	1¼	:481 1:132 1:383 2:032	3↑ Brooklyn H 33k	8	5	54	32	1½	11½	Brooks S	123wb	*.95e	90-12	Devil Diver1231½Market Wise128¾Don Bingo1133	Driving	9
12Jun43- 6Aqu	fst	7f	:23 :461 1:112 1:24	3↑ Carter H 9.7k	6	7	78½	712	82	1hd	Woolf G	126wb	*3.55	95-12	Devil Diver126hdMarriage1181Doublrab118nk	Driving	10
31May43- 6Bel	fst	1¼	:47 1:111 1:361 2:012	3↑ Suburban H 38k	11	1	52¼	64¾	63¼	55½	Gilbert J	121wb	*2.45e	87-12	Don Bingo1042[D]Market Wise1282½Attention121hd	Bothered	17
15May43- 6Bel	fst	1	:23 :463 1:103 1:363	3↑ Metropolitan H 14k	9	5	53½	33½	31½	11¼	Woolf G	117wb	*1.60e	91-16	DevlDivr1171¼Mrrg116¾ThumbsUp1172	Outside,drawing away	11
10May43- 6Bel	fst	6f-WC	1:10	3↑ Toboggan H 7.4k	6	7	107	72	3nk	11	Woolf G	116wb	2.55e	96-05	Devil Diver1161With Regards118noThumbs Up1161		12
	Between horses,drew away																
24Apr43- 5Jam	fst	1 1/16	:242 :481 1:131 1:442	3↑ Excelsior H 12k	7	8	85¾	87½	811	511	Gilbert J	115wb	5.00	80-15	Riverland1245Minee-Mo1082½Marrig121no	Outside,no threat	11
17Apr43- 4Jam	fst	6f	:23 :461 1:111	3↑ Handicap 2530	3	3	42	32½	34	2nk	Gilbert J	121wb	*1.75	96-06	Doublrab123nkDevilDivr1213Rqustd1211½	Getting to winner	6
10Apr43- 6Jam	fst	6f	:224 :454 1:121	3↑ Paumonok H (Div 2) 8.8k	6	8	914	813	78	54	McCreary C	123wb	*1.55	87-17	With Regards126hdPompion1143Boysy118hd	Outrun,late gain	9
17Oct42- 6Jam	fst	1 1/16	:233 :472 1:123 1:443	3↑ Continental H 11k	7	8	98¾	109	1011	109¾	Haas L	119wb	4.30e	80-14	[D]Riverland121noBoysy1141½Doublrab119½	Never a factor	12
1Oct42- 6Bel	fst	7f	:23 :461 1:103 1:23	2↑ Vosburgh H 8.9k	1	4	52¼	51½	22	21	Haas L	124wb	*1.50e	94-08	Parasang1121DvlDvr1246Rostown1121½	Close quarters early	7
25Sep42- 6Bel	fst	1	:234 :471 1:111 1:36	Alw 2500	3	2	2hd	1nk	2hd	1½	Haas L	116wb	*.45	95-08	DevilDiver116½PrtyBustr1111½ScotlndLght1135	Bumped turn	7
22Sep42- 6Bel	fst	1	:233 :464 1:111 1:362	Jerome H 8.9k	2	5	34	34½	32	3nk	Haas L	126wb	*1.15	93-11	King'sAbbey112nkBlessMe122noDevlDvr1262½	Inside,driving	7
7Sep42- 5Aqu	fst	5½f	:224 :461 :583 1:05	3↑ Handicap 3555	1	4	22	33½	42½	1½	Arcaro E	140wb	*2.10	102-04	Devil Diver140½Dogpatch126noVain Prince1161½	Drew away	5
19May42- 4Bel	fst	7f	:232 :463 1:111 1:231	Handicap 2530	4	2	21	21	2½	1hd	Arcaro E	126wb	*1.45	94-12	Devil Diver126hdDogpatch1156First Fiddle117¾	Hard drive	4
9May42- 6Pim	fst	1 3/16	:47 1:112 1:371 1:57	Preakness 75k	1	1	32	52¾	812	813	Arcaro E	126wb	2.40e	85-06	Alsb1261[DH]Requestd126[DH]SunAgn126¾	Close quarters,tired	10
2May42- 7CD	fst	1¼	:472 1:123 1:39 2:042	Ky Derby 76k	5	2	54¼	53	54½	67¼	Arcaro E	126wb	*1.90e	78-09	Shut Out1262¼Alsab126hdValdina Orphan1261½	Saved ground	15
9Apr42- 5Kee	my	6f	:234 :48 1:132	3↑ Phoenix H 3.4k	2	1	1hd	1hd	1hd	1hd	Arcaro E	113.5 w	1.30	85-26	Devil Diver113.5hdWhirlaway1281½Sun Again1122	Driving	5
1Nov41- 6Pim	sly	1 1/16	:232 :474 1:132 1:472	Pim Futurity 38k	8	2	2hd	1hd	23	26	Westrope J	119wb	*1.15e	77-26	Contradiction1226DevilDiver1191ChiqutM1191½	Second best	8
	Geldings not eligible																
18Oct41- 6Kee	my	6f	:231 :464 1:114	Breeders' Futurity 12k	3	3	32	32½	21	11	McCreary C	122wb	3.00	93-16	Devil Diver1221Miss Dogwood1143Dogpatch1175	Drew out	4
	Geldings not eligible																
11Oct41- 4Jam	gd	6f	:224 :461 1:124	Remsen H 12k	1	1	11	21	21	2½	Robertson A	124wb	*.75	87-25	Apache110½Devil Diver1242Contradiction119½	Good effort	9
27Sep41- 7Bel	fst	6½f-WC	1:164	Futurity 72k	2	5	11	11½	1½	2½	Skelly J	126wb	*1.45e	87-12	Some Chance122½Devil Diver1261Caduceus119hd	Good effort	14
	Geldings not eligible																
23Sep41- 5Bel	fst	6f-WC	1:10	Fut Trial (Div 1) 5k	8	1	11	12	1hd	21¼	Skelly J	122wb	*.70e	96-04	Dogpatch1111¼DevlDvr1221½Contrdcton1221½	Tired,bore out	8
30Aug41- 4Sar	fst	6½f	:224 :461 1:113 1:183	Hopeful 41k	1	1	12	12	1nk	12	Skelly J	119wb	*.40e	92-12	DevilDiver1192ShutOut1221½Amphitheatre1221¼	Going away	8
23Aug41- 5Sar	fst	6f	:23 :47 1:121	Grand Union Hotel 11k	2	2	11	2nk	31¾	34½	Meade D	119wb	*.65e	86-19	Shut Out1163½Requested1261Devil Diver1192½	Went well	7
13Aug41- 6Sar	fst	6f	:224 :464 1:124	Sanford 6.6k	2	3	11	2hd	1hd	1¾	Meade D	114wb	3.30	88-14	Devil Diver114¾Ramillies110hdColchis117hd	Drew out	10
8Aug41- 3Sar	fst	5½f	:23 :463 1:053	©Md Sp Wt	8	1	1hd	12	11½	12	Meade D	116wb	*1.50	95-12	Devil Diver1162Ramillies1164Fair Call1164	Easily	19
4Aug41- 3Sar	fst	5½f	:232 :472 1:064	©Md Sp Wt	9	6	1hd	1nk	1½	2hd	Meade D	116wb	*1.70	89-14	Nipsickle116hdDevil Diver1161Wishbone1162½	Hung	19
29Jly41- 3Sar	gd	5½f	:231 :471 1:07	©Md Sp Wt	8	5	55	62¾	31½	2¾	Meade D	116 w	*1.50	87-17	Sundial116¾Devil Diver116¾Anytime1161½	Closed fast	12
30May41- 3Bel	fst	5f	:224 :462 :584	©Alw 1500	7	4	1hd	1hd	1hd	21½	Arcaro E	111 w	*2.00	- -	SoldierSong1111½DevilDiver111hdEarlynSmart116½	Weakened	7

Double Jay

dk br. c. 1944, by Balladier (Black Toney)–Broomshot, by Whisk Broom II

Lifetime record: 48 17 9 9 $299,005

Own.– J.V. Tigani
Br.– John W. Stanley (Ky)
Tr.– W. Molter

Date	Trk	Dist	Fractions	Race	PP	St	1C	2C	Str	Fin	Jockey	Wt	Odds	Fig	Top Three	Comment	Fld
26Jan50- 7SA	fst	6f	:223 :46 1:104	4↑ Handicap 6000	2	6	610	613	69¼	612½	Gilbert J	116wb	25.95	80-15	Miche114nkCitation1303½Huon Kid107½		6
	Trailed,appeared sore afterward																
17Jan50- 7SA	gd	6f	:223 :461 1:113	4↑ Handicap 6000	3	5	56	58	56	44	Gilbert J	120wb	5.05	85-19	Johns Joy122nkOn Trust118¾Blue Border1163	No mishaps	5
	Previously trained by W.L. McCue																
16Jly49- 7SA	fst	1¼	:461 1:103 1:351 2:011	3↑ Hol Gold Cup H 136k	8	4	21½	31	36	75¼	Bierman C	116wb	3.85	95-12	Solidarity1151¼Ace Admiral1151½Pretal112¾	Tired	11
4Jly49- 7SA	fst	1⅛	:472 1:112 1:361 1:483	3↑ American H 56k	3	3	31½	21	2½	11	Bierman C	119wb	5.95	100-11	Double Jay1191Solidarity1172Dinner Gong122nk	Driving	8
25Jun49- 7SA	fst	1 1/16	:231 :461 1:103 1:424	3↑ Inglewood H 29k	8	7	54	51¾	5¾	4nk	Bierman C	122wb	3.60	94-10	Ace Admiral124hdPretal110noAmble In112hd	Close quarters	9
18Jun49- 6SA	fst	7f	:22 :444 1:094 1:222	3↑ Alw 10000	4	8	64	51¾	11	12	Bierman C	113wb	3.40	97-10	Double Jay1132On Trust1223May Reward1071½	In hand	8
30May49- 7SA	fst	1 1/16	:232 :463 1:103 1:422	3↑ Argonaut H 29k	7	3	32½	45	45½	46¾	Bierman C	120wb	2.25	89-13	AceAdmirl1191½Bymeabnd1101¼DnnrGong1244	Wide,weakened	7
25May49- 7SA	fst	7f	:221 :444 1:093 1:223	3↑ Handicap 7500	6	5	42	2½	2hd	12½	Bierman C	120wb	9.20	96-09	Double Jay1202½The Shaker1141Bymeabond115nk	Wide	7
21Aug48- 7Nar	fst	1 1/16	:242 :483 1:122 1:451	4↑ Alw 3500	4	5	22	21½	31½	32¾	Keiper P	120wb	*.50	88-12	WrTrophy110nkPrfctBhrm1132½DoublJy1201¾	Bid,drifted out	8
14Aug48- 6Suf	fst	1¼	:462 1:111 1:36 2:023	3↑ Mass H 67k	4	8	65¾	52½	62¼	32	Stout J	123wb	7.20	109-13	Beauchef1151¼Harmonica110¾DoubleJay123hd	Close quarters	12
	Previously trained by Claude Feltner																
10Jly48- 5Mth	fst	1⅛	:463 1:104 1:371 1:502	3↑ Omnibus H 18k	1	3	32½	43	45½	49¼	James B	124wb	*1.50	92-16	Flash Burn111nkLucky Draw1246½Faraway1102½	Tired	6
26Jun48- 6Aqu	fst	1 1/16	:251 :493 1:133 1:452	3↑ Aqueduct H 28k	4	3	21	1nk	2hd	33½	James B	126wb	6.25	83-18	Stymie130hdConniver1173½Double Jay1262½	Weakened	7
	Previously owned by Ridgewood Stable																
8May48- 6Pim	sl	1 3/16	:49 1:141 1:404 2:013	3↑ Dixie H 31k	5	7	76¾	85¼	65¾	76¼	Gilbert J	124wb	4.40	68-41	Fervent1211½Stymie1272½Incline107no	Quit	9
24Apr48- 5GS	fst	1⅛	:471 1:112 1:362 1:494	3↑ Trenton H 31k	2	4	33	33	31½	1½	Gilbert J	124wb	*1.10	93-08	Double Jay124½Tide Rips109nkElpis115¾	Driving	9
17Apr48- 5Jam	fst	1 1/16	:243 :482 1:132 1:46	3↑ Excelsior H 29k	8	2	21	21	21	2¾	Scurlock O	125wb	*1.60	82-20	Knockdown114¾Double Jay1252½Stymie1284	Close quarters	9
9Apr48- 5Jam	fst	1 1/16	:252 :49 1:132 1:472	3↑ Handicap 7535	5	2	21	11½	11½	13½	Arcaro E	126wb	*1.15	76-28	Double Jay1263½Elpis1191¼Lets Dance1151	Easily	5
28Feb48- 7SA	fst	1¼	:464 1:114 1:371 2:032	3↑ S Anita H 139k	6	11	75¼	33	33½	31¾	Gilbert J	118wb	7.75	87-22	Talon122noOn Trust1211¾Double Jay1181¼	Went well	14
14Feb48- 7SA	fst	1⅛	:461 1:102 1:364 1:492	3↑ San Antonio H 69k	1	5	74¼	31½	31½	2nk	Gilbert J	118wb	6.90	96-10	Talon122nkDouble Jay1182¼On Trust126½	Best of others	18
31Jan48- 7SA	fst	1¼	:471 1:113 1:364 2:031	Maturity 130k	11	11	63	53½	43	31½	Gilbert J	118wb	3.40	88-15	Flashco113nkOn Trust1251¼Double Jay1181¼	Finished well	13
23Jan48- 7SA	fst	6f	:22 :451 1:103	4↑ Handicap 10000	4	7	68½	67½	64¾	61¼	Gilbert J	122wb	*1.30	92-15	Ocean Brief114¾Bogle114noHubble Bubble110nk	No excuse	7
15Jan48- 7SA	fst	6f	:22 :451 1:11	4↑ Handicap 10000	6	7	713	615	48	44	Gilbert J	121wb	4.20	88-12	War Allies116nkBogle1091½Bymeabond1122¾	Late foot	7
	Previously trained by Charles Feltner																
29Nov47- 6Bow	fst	1 3/16	:493 1:133 1:392 1:593	3↑ Bryan & O'Hara H 22k	7	7	2hd	11½	2hd	3¾	Breen J	123wb	1.50e	88-18	Incline107¾Gallorette124hdDouble Jay123hd	Held on well	7
22Nov47- 6Bow	fst	1 1/16	:242 :483 1:132 1:46	2↑ Prince George Aut H 11k	3	1	1hd	1hd	1hd	1no	Breen J	120wb	*.30e	91-20	Double Jay120noMaster Bid1033Incline106nk	Hard drive	5
7Nov47- 6Pim	gd	1 3/16	:493 1:143 1:411 2:01	3↑ Riggs H 29k	4	3	21	21½	1½	12¼	Gilbert J	115wb	*1.20	77-29	DoubleJay1152¼FlashBurn1091LoyalLgon1181¼	Rated,driving	5
1Nov47- 5Jam	gd	1 1/16	:24 :472 1:121 1:443	3↑ Scarsdale H 30k	9	9	108	75¼	33½	32½	Gilbert J	118wb	3.95	87-17	WithPleasure1292Gallorette119½DoubleJay1182	Fast finish	12
20Oct47- 5Jam	fst	1 3/16	:473 1:121 1:383 1:581	Roamer H 30k	9	9	74¼	73¾	2½	2nk	Gilbert J	120wb	9.85	85-17	CosmcBomb128nkDblJy1201Flshco1041½	Steadied,led briefly	10
11Oct47- 6GS	fst	1⅛	:47 1:104 1:36 1:482	3↑ Trenton H 62k	2	3	22	21½	23	25	Gilbert J	118wb	*.90	98-10	Cosmic Bomb1205Double Jay1188Earshot116½	Impeded start	7
1Oct47- 6GS	fst	6f	:223 :453 1:103	Benjamin Franklin H 12k	5	3	42½	21	1½	14	Gilbert J	126wb	*.80	98-11	DoubleJay1264GlenHeathr1121MstrMnd1121½	Speed to spare	6
20Sep47- 5GS	fst	1⅛	:464 1:111 1:363 1:493	Jersey H 36k	5	2	22	2½	1hd	12½	Gilbert J	114wb	1.80	97-10	Double Jay1142½Fervent1252Lighthouse1097	Handily	5
13Sep47- 6GS	fst	1⅛	:463 1:104 1:373 1:511	Alw 5000	5	2	25	24	22	12½	Gilbert J	118wb	*.65	89-08	Double Jay1182½Lighthouse1123Camargo1182	Worked 1¼	5
6Sep47- 6Aqu	gd	1⅛	:483 1:123 1:38 1:511	Discovery H 28k	6	3	31¾	11½	1nk	2no	Gilbert J	115wb	34.35	91-13	Cosmic Bomb126noDouble Jay1151Phalanx1281	Held well	9
25Aug47- 6GS	fst	6f	:222 :452 1:094	3↑ Camden H 11k	2	6	42	52½	45	46½	Gilbert J	115wb	7.85e	95-06	Polynesian1295Air Patrol123nkThe Doge1191¼	Weakened	6
12Aug47- 7Sar	fst	6f	:23 :462 1:111	Alw 4000	2	4	3½	11½	11	11	Gilbert J	116wb	*.95	92-13	DoubleJay1161Mitym1181½Mr.John1096	Worked mile 1:38 1/5	9
2Aug47- 5Jam	fst	1 1/16	:242 :482 1:132 1:464	Handicap 15275	10	2	1½	1½	31½	62¾	Givens C	121wb	*2.65	76-20	ColonelO'F122hdPickMeUp1041OurTommy1111½	Tired badly	11
26Jly47- 4Jam	fst	6f	:224 :46 1:112	3↑ Handicap 10250	4	5	52¾	42¼	41¾	23	Givens C	114wb	7.35	91-14	Hornbm1243DoublJy114hdKngDorstt120nk	No threat to winner	7
	Previously trained by W.L. McCue																
3May47- 7CD	sl	1¼	:49 1:142 1:402 2:064	Ky Derby 109k	2	7	42	1223	1218	1224	Gilbert J	126wb	47.30	49-23	Jet Pilot126hdPhalanx126hdFaultless1261	Pulled up sore	13

29Apr47- 5CD	fst	1	:23 :462 1:114 1:373	Derby Trial 12k	6	1	11	1hd	42½	56½	Gilbert J	119wb	3.60	84-17	Faultless118hdStar Reward1103Cosmic Bomb1183	Gave way	6
26Apr47- 5CD	fst	6f	:224 :462 1:114	Alw 3000	1	6	32½	32	35	33¾	Gilbert J	126wb	*1.00	90-13	King Bay1141¼On Trust1262½Double Jay1261¾		6

Away slowly,worked mile in 1:41

2Nov46- 6CD	fst	1	:224 :462 1:112 1:37	Ky Jockey Club 31k	1	1	1½	1½	1hd	13	Gilbert J	122wb	2.70	94-11	Double Jay1223Education1227Patmiboy1162½	Going away	8
19Oct46- 6GS	fst	6f	:222 :454 1:11	Garden State 33k	4	8	31½	11	13	11½	Gilbert J	122 w	2.05	96-16	Double Jay1221½World Trade1104Mityme1192	Ridden out	11
28Sep46- 6Nar	fst	6f	:23 :46 1:113	J H Connors Mem 20k	7	2	2½	1nk	11½	11¼	Gilbert J	117wb	5.20	93-12	Double Jay1171¼Miss Kimo119¾Donor1223	Driving	14
18Sep46- 6Nar	fst	6f	:223 :452 1:11	ⒸNewport 9.7k	6	3	1nk	11½	1nk	1no	Gilbert J	113 w	*1.40	96-14	Double Jay113noBastogne1108First Sentry1141½	Hard drive	12
25May46- 5Nar	fst	5f	:23 :462 :591	Nar Nursery 10k	4	5	2hd	2hd	2½	2hd	Keiper P	114 w	4.20e	99-10	Fleet West110hdDouble Jay1141Mel Eppley1143	Just missed	12
11May46- 3Nar	fst	5f	:223 :453 :591	Alw 2500	6	8	21½	2½	1½	1no	Maschek F	115 w	*.60e	99-08	Double Jay115noSilee1151½Gay Pet113½	Hard drive	8
25Apr46- 3Nar	fst	4f	:24 :473	ⒸMd Sp Wt	9	7		31¾	1nk	12½	Maschek F	118 w	*1.30	99-01	Double Jay1182½Gemsbok1181½Noble Cyclops1181	Easily	9

Previously trained by L.J. Schaefer

4Mar46- 4Hia	fst	3f	:221 :332	Hia Juvenile (Div 1) 13k	5	4			21½	31	Dodson D	114 w	11.75	--	Tweet's Boy1141Transair117hdDouble Jay114½	Sharp effort	10
28Feb46- 1Hia	fst	3f	:222 :34	ⒸMd Sp Wt	13	4			54¼	21½	Wall N	120 w	2.90f	--	Eternal War1201½Double Jay120½Tweet's Boy1201	Good try	14
22Feb46- 1Hia	sl	3f	:223 :342	ⒸMd Sp Wt	7	4			43½	21½↓	Wall N	118 w	*2.70	--	Milkwagonjoe1181½[DH]DbleJay118[DH]Stmulus1181½	Held well	14

Durazna

b. f. 1941, by Bull Lea (Bull Dog)–Myrtlewood, by Blue Larkspur **Lifetime record: 19 9 2 4 $70,201**

Own.– Brownell Combs
Br.– Brownell Combs (Ky)
Tr.– J.M. Goode

3Sep45- 7Was	fst	1¼	:463 1:103 1:361 2:014	3↑ Wash Park H 57k	7	2	1hd	54½	1323	1328¼	Thompson B	117 w	17.80	73-12	Busher1151½Armed1201TakeWng1125	Faltered,not ridden out	13
29Aug45- 7Was	gd	1	:23 :453 1:104 1:374	3↑ ⒻMatch Race 25k	2	1	2hd	1nk	2hd	2¾	Woolf G	115 w	1.10	88-21	Busher115¾Durazna115	Tired late	2
18Aug45- 7Was	fst	1⅛	:463 1:12 1:373 1:512	3↑ ⒻBeverly H 32k	7	3	34	23	1½	12½	Woolf G	116 w	11.90	91-14	Durazna1162½Letmenow1021¼Busher1284	Ridden out	8
8Aug45- 5Was	fst	7f	:23 :461 1:111 1:24	3↑ Sheridan H (Div 1) 16k	9	2	11	12	14	17	Woolf G	113 w	4.10	93-14	Durazna1137Challenge Me111½Bolus1111½	Speed in reserve	9
1Aug45- 6Was	my	1	:231 :472 1:123 1:392	3↑ ⒻArl Matron H 27k	9	1	21	2½	2hd	36	Woolf G	117 w	5.30	75-33	War Date1134Whirlabout1202Durazna1172	Tired	9
26Jly45- 6Was	fst	6f	:222 :453 1:104	3↑ Myrtlewood H 17k	10	7	41½	32	34½	66¼	Adams J	119 w	8.20	90-11	Three Dots120½Burgoo Maid1091¼Fighting Don1081	Tired	13
14Jly45- 6Was	sly	1	:233 :473 1:114 1:384	3↑ ⒻModesty H 22k	4	1	11	11	13	32¾	South G	120 w	7.50	81-19	War Date110½Night Shadow1142¼Durazna1201¾	Tired	12
27Jun45- 6Was	sl	6f	:232 :482 1:141	3↑ Clang H 11k	5	2	11	1hd	1½	1no	South G	116 w	4.60	79-34	Durazna116noSigma Kappa1066Daily Trouble1113	Driving	10
15Jun45- 6CD	fst	6f	:224 :461 1:122	4↑ Alw 2000	1	1	1nk	1nk	2½	21½	South G	109.5 w	*.70	89-18	Zacapet1101½Durazna109.51¼Busyridge1124	Tired	4
28Jun44- 6Was	fst	6f	:222 :453 1:103	ⒻPrincess Doreen 11k	3	1	31½	34½	32½	47¾	Higley J	118 w	3.20	90-09	Twilight Tear1211½Bell Song1106Harriet Sue114nk	Tired	6
20Jun44- 4Was	fst	6f	:231 :47 1:114	ⒻAlw 3000	5	1	2hd	1hd	1½	11¼	Higley J	117 w	*.50	92-10	Durazna1171¼Harriet Sue1132½Bell Song109.5¾	Handily	5
23Oct43- 6CD	fst	6f	:23 :463 1:113	Breeders' Futurity 14k	2	1	1hd	1hd	1hd	12	Higley J	116 w	*2.00e	95-16	Durazna1162Occupy12217Mr. Rabbit117	In hand	3
25Sep43- 6Haw	gd	6f	:222 :47 1:131	Haw Juv H 6.2k	9	3	66¾	22	1hd	1no	Higley J	120 w	*2.20	87-15	Durazna120noCaptnEdd1121½Zcpt1161	Crowded rivals,lasted	11
13Sep43- 5Haw	sly	6f	:233 :48 1:142	ⒻAlw 1300	6	2	31	1hd	11½	14	Higley J	118 w	*.50	81-24	Durazna1184Harriet Sue1151½Miss Fluff1104	Wide,easily	7
26Aug43- 6Was	sly	6f	:232 :481 1:144	Prairie State 6k	1	1	1hd	1hd	12	15	Higley J	108 w	14.40	77-32	Durazna1085Occupy118½All Bright1111	Ridden out	9
18Aug43- 6Was	fst	6f	:224 :463 1:122	Wash Juveniles 6.2k	7	5	1½	2hd	11½	31	Higley J	105wb	11.60	88-15	Alorter114¾Doggone109nkDurazna105¾	Tired	9
10Aug43- 1Was	fst	5½f	:231 :471 :591 1:062	ⒻMd Sp Wt	9	6	1hd	2nk	1½	13½	Whiting L	115 w	3.30	93-13	Durazna1153½Brown Flame115¾Iron Maiden115½	Easily	12
25Jun43- 1Was	fst	5½f	:224 :473 1:003 1:073	ⒻMd Sp Wt	5	4	32	32	31½	31¾	Whiting L	115 w	5.60	85-17	Twilight Tear115¾Letmenow1151Durazna1153	Saved ground	12
19Jun43- 4Haw	fst	5f	:231 :472 1:001	Md Sp Wt	4	2	1hd	1hd	21½	45	Burns G	113 w	3.60	89-14	American Flyer1162½Zacapet1161½Valdina Clown1161		10

Saved ground,tired

Elkridge

b. g. 1938, by Mate (Prince Pal)–Best by Test, by Black Toney **Lifetime record: 123 31 18 15 $230,680**

Own.– K. Miller
Br.– Joseph F. Flanagan (Md)
Tr.– K. Miller

12Oct51- 5Bel	sf	*3	S'Chase 5:501	4↑ Grand National H 24k	8	6	913	733	749	769	Smithwick P	141 w	15.50	--	Oedips1651½NavyGun1402½BannerWvs14045	Bad landing 11th	10
4Oct51- 5Bel	fst	*2½	S'Chase 4:45	4↑ Brook H 16k	5	6	77½	515	510	410	Smithwick P	143 w	28.05	--	Oedipus1613Palaja1387Lone Fisherman148nk	No excuse	12
27Sep51- 5Bel	fst	*2	S'Chase 3:43	3↑ Broad Hollow H 12k	6	7	615	410	917	825	Harr C	140 w	45.60	--	Oedipus1587Palaja1342Genancoke1412½	Gave way	11
16Aug51- 5Sar	hy	*2	S'Chase 4:484	3↑ North American H 6.1k	6	2	411	564	5114	5130	Adams FD	142wb	4.95	--	Cherwell13415Lone Fisherman14710Extra Points14030	Quit	6
12Jly51- 5Aqu	hd	*2	S'Chase 3:441	4↑ Hitchcock 11k	2	6	716	725	743	756	Zimmerman J	144wb	10.10	--	Genncoke1352¼[D]LarkyDay147nkSemperEadm140½	Dull effort	7
3Jly51- 3Del	fst	*2½	S'Chase 4:471	4↑ Indian River H 11k	3	1	210	215	215	212	Adams FD	147 w	1.80	--	CrooningWind13712Elkridge1471½TouristList140	No mishap	4
27Jun51- 5Del	fst	*2	S'Chase 3:404	4↑ Georgetown H 12k	3	6	615	513	523	419	Smithwick P	148 w	3.15	--	Crooning Wind1304Oedipus15812Genancoke1373	Outrun	6
14Jun51- 5Bel	sl	*2½	S'Chase 4:56	4↑ Meadow Brook H 11k	4	3	32½	46	312	37½	Smithwick P	150 w	3.15	--	Titien II1401½Lone Fisherman1496Elkridge15012	No excuse	5
7Jun51- 5Bel	fst	*2	S'Chase 3:432	4↑ Corinthian H 8.7k	1	2	39	33½	37	312¾	Smithwick P	150 w	3.95	--	Oedipus156¾Lone Fisherman14812Elkridge1501	Tired	4
18May51- 5Bel	fst	*2	S'Chase 3:42	4↑ International H 9k	4	4	321	420	38	311	Smithwick P	149 w	7.45	--	Pontius Pilate1524Oedipus1547Elkridge1493½	Closed well	7
22Sep50- 5Bel	sf	*2	S'Chase 3:482	3↑ Broad Hollow H 11k	4	6	613	613	22	21¼	Adams FD	152 w	4.85	--	Oedipus1471¼Elkridge1521¼Trough Hill1505	Stout effort	10
25Aug50- 5Sar	fst	*2½	S'Chase 5:082	4↑ Saratoga H 11k	3	1	12	12	11	13	Adams FD	150 w	4.35	--	Elkridge1503Lone Fisherman1356Oedipus147nk	Handily	6
18Aug50- 5Sar	fst	*2	S'Chase 4:082	3↑ Beverwyck H 9.1k	2	3	37	411	333	328	Adams FD	146 w	7.60	--	Pontius Pilate13815Oedipus14313Elkridge14640	No threat	6
10Aug50- 5Sar	fst	*2	S'Chase 4:094	3↑ North American H 6.4k	6	2	32	512	636	636	Adams FD	149 w	*1.75	--	TheHeir143nkHamptonRoads14510Scuttleman1354	Done early	6
30Jun50- 5Del	gd	*2½	S'Chase 4:51	4↑ Indian River H 12k	1	1	23	25	11½	19	Adams FD	154 w	2.35	--	Elkridge1549Sun Bath1504Monkey Wrench137	Easily	6
22Jun50- 5Del	fst	*2	S'Chase 3:463	4↑ Georgetown H 12k	1	3	35	35	31	1½	Adams FD	148 w	3.75	--	Elkridge148½Darjeeling1502Genancoke1427	Driving	8
8Jun50- 5Bel	fst	*2½	S'Chase 4:473	4↑ Meadow Brook H 11k	6	2	24	22½	25	26	Adams FD	145 w	12.65	--	Darjeeling1436Elkridge1455Adaptable148hd	Went well	7
10Nov49- 5Pim	fst	*2½	S'Chase 4:482	4↑ Manly H 8.2k	4	1	1hd	1hd	422	420	Adams FD	145 w	9.80	--	His Boots1458Trough Hill1566American Way1526	Tired	5
3Nov49- 5Pim	gd	*2	S'Chase 3:554	3↑ Battleship H 8.4k	1	7	743	763	668	664	Ansteatt B	150wb	15.90	--	Trough Hill15410Fleettown14620Luan Casca13910	Distanced	7
11Oct49- 6Bel	fst	*2¼	S'Chase 4:191	4↑ Temple Gwathmey H 11k	4	3	49½	619	739	739	Ansteatt B	156wb	7.30	--	Hampton Roads152½Sun Bath1575Lock and Key1437	Tired	7
7Oct49- 6Bel	fst	*3	S'Chase 5:483	4↑ Grand National H 22k	2	5	513	2hd	515	620	Ansteatt B	152wb	10.15	--	His Boots1412½Trough Hill1588Tourist List1462	Tired	7
29Sep49- 5Bel	sl	*2½	S'Chase 4:521	4↑ Brook H 15k	6	2	24	42½	768	798	Ansteatt B	157wb	5.40	--	Trough Hill15310American Way151½His Boots1429	Quit	8
22Sep49- 4Bel	fst	*2	S'Chase 3:44	3↑ Broad Hollow H 11k	5	7	721	727	736	625	Smithwick P	157wb	*1.85	--	Sun Bath1496Hampton Roads141¾Trough Hill1522	Outrun	7
1Jly49- 5Del	fst	*2½	S'Chase 4:453	4↑ Indian River H 12k	3	5	422	48	12	13	Smithwick P	156wb	*1.00	--	Elkridge1563Sun Bath1361¼Tourist List14820	Ridden out	5
23Jun49- 5Del	fst	*2	S'Chase 3:461	4↑ Georgetown H 12k	5	4	37	28	2hd	16	Smithwick P	152wb	2.25	--	Elkridge1526Genancoke1455Sun Bath13725	Handily	5
9Jun49- 4Bel	fst	*2½	S'Chase 4:433	4↑ Meadow Brook H 11k	7	2	210	312	25	12	Smithwick P	147wb	7.45	--	Elkridge1472Trough Hill1518Rank1404	Going away	7
2Jun49- 4Bel	fst	*2	S'Chase 3:44	4↑ Corinthian H 9.4k	4	2	12	2hd	34½	26	Ansteatt B	149wb	21.85	--	Trough Hill1476Elkridge149hdAmerican Way1463½	Weakened	10
12May49- 5Bel	fst	*2	S'Chase 3:504	4↑ International H 9k	1	5	23	21½	417	428	Rich J	149wb	7.50	--	Homogenize1396Fleettown1498Lieut. Well14514	Quit	7
10Nov48- 5Pim	gd	3	S'Chase 6:104	4↑ Manly H 18k	6	9	940	827	533	542	Rich J	150wb	16.80	--	Adaptable14415American Way15215Point Bleu1468	Far back	9
3Nov48- 5Pim	fst	2	S'Chase 3:513	3↑ Battleship H 12k	9	4	99½	813	716	719	Rich J	152wb	7.70	--	Genancoke1403½The Heir147noTourist List1475	Outrun	9
14Oct48- 5Lrl	fst	*2	S'Chase 3:531	3↑ Butler H 13k	12	4	35	-	-	-	Bosley J III	153wb	9.60	--	Drift1346The Heir1493½American Way1493	Fell 10th	12
1Oct48- 5Bel	gd	*3	S'Chase 5:50	4↑ Grand Nat'l H 31k	12	9	810	611	621	728	Bosley J III	156wb	6.55	--	AmericanWay1441TouristList1502TroughHill1476	No factor	14
23Sep48- 5Bel	fst	*2½	S'Chase 4:471	4↑ Brook H 19k	7	3	31½	1nk	21½	22	Bosley J III	156 w	3.35	--	Trough Hill1422Elkridge1561½American Way1432	No excuse	11
16Sep48- 5Bel	fst	*2	S'Chase 3:441	3↑ Broad Hollow H 19k	9	12	1120	1122	56½	46	Rich J	155wb	3.15	--	The Heir1482Little Sammie1381Genancoke1453	Off slowly	12
27Aug48- 5Sar	fst	*2½	S'Chase 5:11	4↑ Saratoga H 11k	6	6	623	513	21	34¼	Rich J	156wb	*1.90	--	Tourist List1421¼The Heir1483Elkridge1568	Tired	6
12Aug48- 5Sar	fst	*2	S'Chase 4:141	3↑ North American H 8.9k	4	7	725	514	1nk	11½	Rich J	152wb	*2.55	--	Elkridge1521½Fleettown151hdThe Heir14620	Driving	7
5Aug48- 5Sar	fst	*2	S'Chase 4:141	4↑ Shillelah 8.7k	2	4	423	37	1	1	Rich J	154wb	*1.90	--	Elkridge154Sun Bath154Floating Isle150	Galloping	5

Other finishers remounted after falling or losing rider at final fence

9Jly48- 5Aqu	fst	*2	S'Chase	3:444	4↑ Lion Heart H 11k	6	2	21	1½	53¾	514	Bosley J III	153wb	*1.55	--	The Heir1421½Fleettown15110Genancoke147¾	Bobbled	6
2Jly48- 5Del	fst	*2½	S'Chase	4:522	4↑ Indian River H 12k	3	2	220	220	12	12	Bosley J III	151wb	3.55	--	Elkridge1512Tourist List1423Floating Isle14110	Driving	7
16Jun48- 6Bel	fst	*2½	S'Chase	4:512	4↑ Temple Gwathmey H 16k	4	2	26	23	2hd	21	Bosley J III	151wb	7.05	--	Adaptable1501Elkridge1514Floating Isle14012	Good try	7
10Jun48- 5Bel	fst	*2½	S'Chase	4:462	4↑ Meadow Brook H 17k	6	1	13	1½	3½	35	Bosley J III	152wb	3.60	--	Adaptable1463Canford1422Elkridge1521½	Tired	6
3Jun48- 5Bel	fst	*2	S'Chase	3:471	4↑ Corinthian H 11k	5	3	33½	41½	24	34	Bosley J III	153wb	9.45	--	Fleettown1473½The Heir142½Elkridge1534	Weakened	8
20May48- 5Bel	fst	*2	S'Chase	3:463	4↑ International H 11k	7	3	39	414	933	940	Bosley J III	154wb	11.25	--	Fleettown1413½Canford1422½The Heir1382½	Quit	10
4Nov47- 5Pim	hy	2	S'Chase	4:131	3↑ Battleship H 11k	3	5	56½	58	518	521¼	Roberts E	155wb	2.70	--	GrekFlg1365TourstLst141nkFlotngIsl14515	Bad landing 3rd	5
29Oct47- 5Lrl	gd	*2½	S'Chase	4:542	4↑ Chevy Chase H 18k	6	7	617	614	314	215	McGovern J	154wb	4.50	--	Sun Bath13915Elkridge154½Trough Hill1478	Closed well	7
17Oct47- 6Lrl	fst	*2	S'Chase	3:52	3↑ Butler H 11k	1	1	11	23	451	452½	Miller R	161wb	1.50	--	Trough Hill141hdSun Bath1372½Allier13750	Stopped	5
2Oct47- 5Bel	fst	*3	S'Chase	5:413	4↑ Grand National 29k	8	1	22	210	620	621¼	Brown N	162wb	*1.05e	--	Adaptable147hdWar Battle163nkTrough Hill1394	Quit	8
17Sep47- 5Aqu	fst	*2½	S'Chase	4:571	4↑ Glendale H 11k	6	1	21	11	11	12	Brown N	161wb	4.05	--	Elkridge1612Trough Hill1392Delhi Dan1385	Ridden out	7
5Sep47- 5Aqu	sl	*2	S'Chase	3:541	3↑ Harbor Hill H 11k	7	1	1½	21	411	49	Brown N	163wb	2.95	--	Floating Isle1451½Big Sun1321½Genancoke1386	Tired	7
26Jun47- 5Del	fst	*2	S'Chase	3:48	4↑ Georgetown H 13k	10	1	11	1hd	44½	57	Brown N	162wb	2.45	--	Genancoke135½TouristList1373½FloatingIsle137hd	Weakened	12
5Jun47- 5Aqu	fst	*2	S'Chase	3:441	4↑ Lion Heart H 10k	2	1	12	14	11	11	Brown N	158wb	2.85	--	Elkridge1581Fleettown1426Floating Isle14420	Jumped well	4
28May47- 5Bel	fst	*2½	S'Chase	4:464	4↑ Meadow Brook 17k	6	4	54¼	624	644	650	People C Jr	158wb	*1.15e	--	WarBattle15612Flttown14112FlotngIsl147no	Never a factor	6
5Nov46- 5Pim	fst	2	S'Chase	3:512	3↑ Battleship H 11k	3	2	2½	21	611	610¾	Roberts E	159wb	*.90e	--	Galley Boy1321½War Battle1481¼Tourist List1351	Quit	6
15Oct46- 6Bel	fst	*3	S'Chase	5:422	4↑ Temple Gwathmey H 21k	4	4	427	215	215	230	Roberts E	158wb	*1.35e	--	War Battle13830Elkridge1582½Chesapeake1403	Next best	5
3Oct46- 5Bel	fst	*3	S'Chase	5:484	4↑ Grand National H 30k	8	5	414	21	12	14	Roberts E	151wb	11.20	--	Elkridge1514Burma Road1622Refugio1343	Easily	10
26Sep46- 5Bel	fst	*2½	S'Chase	4:494	4↑ Brook H 19k	5	4	32½	53½	819	819	Russell EA	154 w	6.60	--	Burma Road1562½Caddie142noGreat Flare1385	Lost iron	11
16Aug46- 5Sar	fst	*2	S'Chase	4:154	3↑ North America H 5.4k	3	2	23	21	2hd	15	Adams FD	151ws	*.85	--	Elkridge1515Last1354Boojum II142	Easily	4
3Jly46- 3Del	fst	*2½	S'Chase	4:463	4↑ Indian River H 12k	6	4	22	25	37	38	Davis J	149wb	3.00	--	Rouge Dragon1573½Delhi Dan1374½Elkridge1492½	Went well	6
27Jun46- 3Del	fst	*2	S'Chase	3:483	4↑ Georgetown H 12k	5	3	26	24	23	23½	Davis J	149wb	4.55	--	Rouge Dragon1523½Elkridge1498Beneksar1366	Went well	6
22Jun46- 3Aqu	fst	*2	S'Chase	3:421	4↑ Handicap 4500	4	1	12	14	11½	1nk	Russell EA	155wb	*1.35e	--	Elkridge155nkWar Battle1461Lancastrian1402	Just lasted	5
10May46- 5Bel	fst	*2	S'Chase	3:45	4↑ International H 8.6k	6	6	624	622	637	635½	Jennings E	153wb	3.65	--	Fleettown1351Annotator1362½Mercator1557	Outrun	6
28Nov45- 5Pim	sly	2½	S'Chase	5:252	4↑ Manly H 12k	7	5	715	812	727	744	Adams FD	153wb	2.85e	--	PursuitPlane1325BurmaRoad13912GekFlg1384	Never a factor	10
21Nov45- 5Pim	sl	*2	S'Chase	3:544	3↑ Battleship H 12k	6	6	515	24	24	1no	Adams FD	146wb	9.65	--	Elkridge146noNavigate1368Caddie1465	Driving	7
12Oct45- 3Lrl	fst	*2	S'Chase	3:54	3↑ Butler H 6.4k	6	7	718	711	839	845	Adams FD	149wb	3.40	--	Great Flare1302Floating Isle15115Bill Coffman1334	Tired	9
26Sep45- 5Bel	fst	*2½	S'Chase	4:484	4↑ Brook H 9.3k	4	6	913	35	48½	38	Adams FD	148wb	5.30	--	Raylywn1376Rouge Dragon1552Elkridge148no	Fast finish	10
20Sep45- 5Bel	gd	*2	S'Chase	3:551	3↑ Broad Hollow H 6.1k	2	7	715	712	79½	715¾	Riles S	150wb	4.15	--	Boojum II1382Caddie138¾Raylywn137hd	Bad landing 4th	7
11Sep45- 5Aqu	my	*2½	S'Chase	4:511	4↑ Glendale H 8.6k	5	5	34½	45½	46	410½	Owen W	153wb	3.75	--	FloatingIsle150nkMerctor1437SoldrSong1403	Flattened out	5
4Sep45- 5Aqu	fst	*2	S'Chase	3:42	3↑ Harbor Hill H 6k	5	4	414	35½	2hd	2½	Owen W	153wb	4.05	--	Mercator140½Elkridge1533Floating Isle1512½	Driving	7
31Aug45- 5Bel	fst	*2½	S'Chase	4:51	4↑ Saratoga H 9.1k	5	2	32	21½	510	58¾	Owens W	156wb	*2.75	--	RougeDrgn152nkSoldierSong139noBurmaRod141hd	No mishap	9
24Aug45- 5Bel	sl	*2	S'Chase	3:494	3↑ Beverwyck H 5.9k	7	7	711	719	514	415	Owen W	158wb	*1.45e	--	War Battle1352Boojum II1373Floating Isle15210	Late gain	7
17Aug45- 4Bel	fst	*2	S'Chase	3:45	3↑ North American H 16k	6	3	45	56½	21	3¾	Owen W	158wb	3.85e	--	FloatingIsle149nkChesapeake136½Elkridg1581	Saved ground	10
10Aug45- 3Bel	fst	*2	S'Chase	3:491	4↑ Shillelah 6.1k	2	10	108½	813	713	611	Harrison JS	158wb	3.05	--	Raylywn1361Rouge Dragon1521Mercator1376	Outrun	10
3Jly45- 3Del	gd	*2½	S'Chase	5:033	4↑ Indian River H 12k	5	4	510	33½	11½	13½	Harrison JS	157wb	*3.85	--	Elkridge1573½Royal Archer1461Beneksar1302	Easily	8
27Jun45- 3Del	fst	*2	S'Chase	3:503	4↑ Georgetown H 12k	6	4	45½	56	48½	36½	Harrison JS	159wb	4.55	--	Iron Shot150½Rouge Dragon1596Elkridge159½	Mild rally	8
23Jun45- 3Bel	fst	*2½	S'Chase	4:56	4↑ Meadow Brook H 8.4k	1	3	48	57	23	22½	Harrison JS	160wb	1.80	--	Floating Isle1472½Elkridge160hdIron Shot1485	No match	6
	Daily Racing Form time, 4:53 4/5																		
12Jun45- 5Bel	fst	*2	S'Chase	3:49	4↑ CL Appleton 5.7k	3	5	53	41¾	14	1hd	Harrison JS	158wb	2.65	--	Elkridge158hdFloating Isle1496Mercator13910	Just held	8
6Nov44- 6Bel	fst	*3	S'Chase	5:57	4↑ Temple Gwathmey H 15k	5	3	21	45	-	-	Harrison JS	164wb	4.55	--	Burma Road1391¾Parma135hdAhmisk143nk	Lost rider 15th	7
18Oct44- 3Lrl	fst	*2	S'Chase	4:002	3↑ Butler H 6.5k	7	7	54¼	65¾	46	45	Harrison JS	166wb	*1.60	--	Raylywn132hdAhmisk1402Boojum II1403	Impeded by faller	10
4Oct44- 5Bel	fst	*3	S'Chase	5:541	4↑ Grand National H 16k	4	3	54½	54	33½	37	Harrison JS	167wb	*.80	--	Burma Road136hdRouge Dragon1647Elkridge1678	Faltered	6
20Sep44- 5Bel	fst	*2	S'Chase	3:533	3↑ Broad Hollow H 5.8k	4	3	39	37	2½	13	Harrison JS	161wb	*1.30	--	Elkridg1613BllCoffmn14012IronShot16010	Speed in reserve	6
1Sep44- 5Bel	fst	*2½	S'Chase	4:491	4↑ Saratoga H 8.5k	5	5	57¼	53¾	14	18	Harrison JS	155wb	*1.25	--	Elkridge1558Bridlespur1321Invader1404	Easily	5
11Aug44- 5Bel	fst	*2	S'Chase	3:48	4↑ Shillelah 5.7k	6	4	42½	32	11	11½	Harrison JS	146wb	*1.05	--	Elkridge1461½Mercator1417FloatngIsl13510	Bothered early	7
4Aug44- 3Bel	fst	*2	S'Chase	3:491	4↑ Handicap 3000	7	2	32½	38	2½	11¼	Harrison JS	154wb	4.60	--	Elkridge1541¼FrederclI1401½BurmRod1382	Speed in reserve	10
15Jun44- 7Aqu	fst	1¼	:492 1:143 1:42	2:083	3↑ Md Sp Wt	3	2	610	511	611	614¼	Meade D	121wb	4.90	50-18	General War113nkRanging1207Oceanus1131	No mishap	7
1Nov43- 5Pim	fst	2	S'Chase	3:571	3↑ Battleship H 6.9k	8	4	44¾	68	625	625½	Penrod J	147wb	6.25	--	Knight's Quest1411Invader144½Mercator1392	Outrun	10
26Oct43- 5Pim	sly	2½	S'Chase	5:181	4↑ Chevy Chase H 9.3k	6	4	616	732	-	-	Penrod J	150wb	*1.60	--	Uncle Seaweed137¾Caddie13820Invader1453		7
	Outrun,jumped poorly,left course																		
18Oct43- 5Pim	gd	2	S'Chase	3:56	3↑ Gov Ogle H 6.6k	4	5	33½	3½	-	-	Morlan L	150 w	6.65	--	Rouge Dragon1531Caddie1376Greek Flag1373	Lost rider	9
6Oct43- 3Bel	fst	*3	S'Chase	5:533	4↑ Grand National H 18k	9	3	22	32	44½	36½•	Riles S	150wb	12.05	--	Brother Jones1506Invader145½[DH]Caddie137hd	No mishap	12
29Sep43- 3Bel	fst	*2½	S'Chase	4:50	4↑ Brook H 6.6k	6	8	54	1016	1023	1022½	Hayhurst R	153wb	4.50	--	RougeDrgn1473Knght'sQust140noBnkNot1381	Never a factor	10
22Sep43- 3Bel	fst	*2	S'Chase	3:524	3↑ Broad Hollow H 4k	5	2	21½	21	43½	22	Harrison JS	154wb	3.95	--	Silver Birch1352Elkridge1543Caddie1391	Belated rally	7
15Sep43- 3Aqu	gd	*2½	S'Chase	5:012	4↑ Glendale H 8.6k	1	2	12	12	529	540	Scott A	156wb	5.30	--	Brother Jones1461½Invader145½Parma1358	Tired	6
1Sep43- 3Aqu	fst	*2	S'Chase	3:441	3↑ Harbor Hill H 4.9k	4	2	24	22	12	14	Harrison JS	151wb	5.95	--	Elkridge1514Knight'sQuest1451½BnkNot1396	Speed to spare	6
25Aug43- 3Bel	fst	*2½	S'Chase	4:471	4↑ Saratoga H 6.2k	7	4	34¼	35½	59¾	614	Cruz H	154wb	6.30	--	Iron Shot148½Brother Jones1461½Corrigan1497	Bobbled	8
18Aug43- 3Bel	fst	*2	S'Chase	3:463	3↑ Beverwyck H 4.1k	10	6	87¼	42½	35	410	Smiley J	155wb	5.15	--	RougDrgn145½IronShot1458BrothrJns1471½	Bad landing 11th	10
11Aug43- 3Bel	gd	*2	S'Chase	3:52	3↑ North American H 3.8k	3	3	43½	21	11	11¼	Cruz H	151wb	*2.30	--	Elkridge1511¼Brother Jones1462½Redlands1391	Drifted out	6
4Aug43- 3Bel	fst	*2	S'Chase	3:482	4↑ Shillelah 3.9k	1	8	622	44¾	24	22½	Marzani D	150wb	5.55	--	Delhi Dan1502½Elkridge1507Speculate1326	Checked	10
25May43- 3Bel	fst	*2	S'Chase	3:521	4↑ Corinthian H 3.9k	1	8	711	811	612	619¼	Owen W	157wb	7.85	--	Invader145nkBrotherJones1394BoojumII1385	Never a factor	8
18May43- 5Bel	fst	*2	S'Chase	3:494	4↑ CL Appleton 3.9k	1	6	58	36½	45½	48½	Leonard W	161wb	10.55	--	RougeDragon1443Knight'sQuest1492½Redlands1523	Faltered	8
11May43- 3Bel	fst	*2	S'Chase	3:461	4↑ International H 3.9k	9	6	423	719	718	718	Harrison JS	159wb	5.75	--	IronShot1444Knight'sQuest1483Invadr1501½	Never a factor	9
5May43- 6Jam	fst	1 1/16	:24 :48 1:123	1:45	3↑ Handicap 2540	1	5	56½	511	59½	612	Givens C	107 w	24.25	76-18	Tip-Toe1103Haile112noPlantagenet1105	No mishap	6
1May43- 4Jam	fst	1 70	:243 :481 1:15	1:461	3↑ Md Sp Wt	7	5	42½	32	33½	35	Lindberg H	122wb	4.50	68-19	Deseronto1134Minefinder1131Elkridge1224	Hard urged	10
19Apr43- 4Jam	gd	6f	:232 :481	1:141	3↑ Md Sp Wt	2	6	53	78½	711	78	Woolf G	126wb	5.05	73-22	Miracle Kin113½Stargoo113hdCamptown1131½	Evenly	14
9Nov42- 5Pim	gd	2½	S'Chase	5:061	4↑ Manly H 6.7k	3	5	58½	77¾	3nk	11½	Harrison JS	157wb	3.85	--	Elkridge1571½Nayr132½Iron Shot1406	Jumped well,driving	9
2Nov42- 5Pim	fst	2	S'Chase	4:14	3↑ Battleship H 3.5k	2	2	67½	76	11½	13	Harrison JS	151wb	4.80	--	Elkrdg1513IronShot139½RdInds1373	Outside,speed to spare	8
21Oct42- 3Lrl	sl	*2½	S'Chase	5:313	4↑ Chevy Chase H 6.4k	8	7	711	525	651	654	Harrison JS	153wb	2.15	--	Brother Jones13414Strolling On1304Caddie1394	Outrun	8
14Oct42- 3Lrl	sl	*2	S'Chase	4:183	3↑ Governor Ogle H 4.4k	4	4	49	12	18	18	Harrison JS	148wb	*1.55	--	Elkridge1488RedInds1398StrollngOn13312	Speed in reserve	5
7Oct42- 3Bel	fst	*3	S'Chase	6:051	4↑ Grand National H 17k	8	6	825	-	-	-	Harrison JS	147 w	5.15	--	Cottesmore1557Cupid13430Iron Shot1391	Fell 12th	9
23Sep42- 3Bel	fst	*2	S'Chase	3:483	3↑ Broad Hollow H 3.9k	3	4	42¾	45¾	1½	13½	Harrison JS	145wb	7.15	--	Elkridge1453½LovelyNight1525RougeDragon1372½	Ridden out	7
9Sep42- 3Aqu	sl	*2½	S'Chase	6:002	4↑ Glendale H 5.9k	3	3	313	210	517	518	Scott A	148wb	4.20	--	Mandingham1582Iron Shot1415Parma1346	Bobbled,tired	5
2Sep42- 3Aqu	fst	*2	S'Chase	3:494	3↑ Harbor Hill H 3.7k	3	3	32	35½	32	2nk	Penrod J	149 w	*1.40	--	Good Chance136nkElkridge149¾Cottesmore1627	Closed fast	4
28Aug42- 3Sar	fst	*2½	S'Chase	5:114	4↑ Saratoga H 4.3k	5	1	11½	2hd	1hd	2nk	Penrod J	149wb	*1.35	--	IronShot136nkElkridge1491BrotherJones1385	Wide into str	5
21Aug42- 3Sar	fst	*2	S'Chase	4:153	3↑ Beverwyck H 3.4k	3	4	37	22	1hd	2no	Penrod J	150wb	*1.05	--	Invader143noElkridge1507Iron Shot1374	Gamely	5
14Aug42- 1Sar	fst	*2	S'Chase	4:193	3↑ North American H 3.3k	5	2	25	3nk	15	17	Penrod J	146wb	2.85	--	Elkridge1467TheBeak1431IronShot143100	Drew away easily	5
7Aug42- 1Sar	fst	*2	S'Chase	4:14	4↑ Shillelah H 3k	2	1	12	21	-	-	Cruz H	150wb	1.95	--	LovelyNight13825IronShot15012RedInds147	Lost rider 15th	5
1Jly42- 3Del	fst	*2½	S'Chase	4:541	4↑ Indian River H 8k	1	1	13	11½	12	13	Cruz H	141wb	*.95	--	Elkridge1413Good Chance1415Caddie133		5
	Bothered by riderless horse																		
24Jun42- 3Del	fst	*2	S'Chase	3:47	4↑ Georgetown H 8.6k	2	3	47	25	25	26	Cruz H	142wb	5.90	--	Deanslaw1396Elkridge1426Ossabaw1474	Best of rest	5

11Jun42- 3Aqu fst *2 S'Chase 3:413 4↑ Hitchcock H 6.3k 7 7 713 719 34¼ 35 Clements HW 144wb 9.85 -- Bath155hdMandingham1565Elkridge1446 Finished well 7
2Jun42- 5Bel fst *2½ S'Chase 4:434 4↑ Meadow Brook H 6.6k 1 2 55¼ 52½ 2hd 2¾ Cruz H 139wb 8.75 -- Invdr139¾Elkrdg1396StrwBoss1424 Bothered by winner last ⅛ 7
23May42- 3Bel fst *2 S'Chase 3:444 4↑ Handicap 2000 7 6 514 44¼ - - Clements HW 145wb 4.75 -- Sussex1552Deanslaw1465Straw Boss1534 Lost rider 11th 7
16May42- 3Bel fst *2 S'Chase 3:433 4↑ Alw 1500 1 4 513 28 12 14 Clements HW 139wb 26.25 -- Elkridge1394Loughtrea1432Frozen North1435 Drew away 9
12May42- 5Bel fst *2 S'Chase 3:434 4↑ International H 4.3k 7 2 66½ 715 719 821½ McGovern J 133wb 60.30 -- Cottesmore1574Redlands140½Ossabaw152¾ Outrun 8
1May42- 5Pim fst 2 S'Chase 3:493 4↑ Jervis Spencer H 3.4k 3 2 48 621 840 750 Brown N 136 w 18.85 -- Bath14110Cottesmore1573Redlands14010 Outrun 8
Previously owned by Thomas Hitchcock;previously trained by P. Green
24Sep41- 1Bel fst *2 S'Chase 3:52 3↑ Md Sp Wt 3 3 2hd 11½ 16 17 Scott A 134 w *1.40 -- Elkridge134.57Pico Blanco II1495Glen-Na-Mona1492 9
Lost ground,in hand

Fairy Chant

ch. f. 1937, by Chance Shot (Fair Play)–Star Fairy, by The Satrap — Lifetime record: 42 10 8 8 $81,985
Own.– Foxcatcher Farm
Br.– William du Pont Jr (Ky)
Tr.– R.E. Handlen

13Sep41- 6Aqu fst 1⅛ :481 1:122 1:381 1:51 3↑ ⒻBeldame H 19k 13 7 109¼ 86½ 31½ 1no Anderson I 123wb 7.05 97-08 Fairy Chant123noImperatrice1161Rosetown1261 14
Traffic,up in closing strides
9Sep41- 6Aqu fst 1 1/16 :242 :482 1:124 1:44 3↑ ⒻAlw 3000 5 5 513 59 34 34 Anderson I 120wb 4.40 90-12 Rostown1163Oss1111FryChnt1203 Slow to start,saved ground 5
26Aug41- 6Sar my 1⅛ :504 1:153 1:404 1:532 3↑ ⒻDiana H 3.5k 2 3 37 22 33 35¾ James B 126wb 2.35 77-20 Rosetown118¾Dorimar1195Fairy Chant1266 Went well 5
2Aug41- 6Sar fst 1 3/16 :484 1:132 1:393 1:584 3↑ Merchants & Cits H 6.9k 1 4 47 31¾ 3½ 56¾ James B 112wb 4.35 77-19 Fenelon126hdAndy K.1172½Corydon108hd Stopped 7
29Jly41- 6Sar gd 1 :24 :48 1:124 1:384 3↑ Wilson 7.1k 2 4 32 32 31½ 31¼ Donoso R 112wb 6.25 86-17 Parasang1171Fenelon120nkFairy Chant11215 Good effort 4
12Jly41- 7Suf sly 1 1/16 :234 :473 1:13 1:46 3↑ ⒻHannah Dustin H 13k 3 8 65 41½ 12½ 12¾ James B 120wb 8.00 86-21 FairyChant1202¾UptheHill1062ShineO'Night116hd Easily 10
5Jly41- 6Del my 1 1/16 :233 :48 1:141 1:49 3↑ ⒻNew Castle H 13k 11 8 611 47½ 36 34½ James B 126wb 7.45 69-28 DottedSwiss1143BalaOrmont1161½FairyChnt1262 Closed fast 13
28Jun41- 6Del fst 1 1/16 :233 :473 1:12 1:44 3↑ Handicap 2000 2 6 57½ 42½ 44¼ 58½ Peters M 118wb 5.30 90-03 Sailor King1102Busy Morn111noRed Dock1191½ Tired 6
1Mar41- 6SA sly 1¼ :47 1:121 1:383 2:052 3↑ S Anita H 124k 15 14 1313 1012 1013 910¼ Richards H 112wb 24.60 69-29 Bay View108nkAugury1244Bolingbroke1062 Outrun 16
15Feb41- 6SA my 1 1/16 :241 :483 1:133 1:471 4↑ ⒻS Margarita 11k 1 7 79½ 66½ 54 43 James B 120wb *.60 73-29 Omelet116nkAugury1201¼Barrancosa1131½ Poor ride 7
7Feb41- 6SA my 1 1/16 :234 :482 1:124 1:46 4↑ Handicap 2500 2 5 31½ 13 14 12½ James B 118wb *.70 82-21 FairyChant1182½DuskyDuke1104JusticeM.1102 Easily best 5
25Jan41- 7SA sl 1 :234 :471 1:124 1:392 4↑ Alw 2500 4 6 35 33 32 33¾ James B 113wb 6.40 77-25 Vino Puro1203Gen'l Manager112¾Fairy Chant1136 Weakened 7
5Oct40- 7Bel fst 2¼ :484 2:313 2:571 3:484 3↑ New York H 59k 13 7 911 94 1122 1126½ Anderson I 111wb 16.95 84-09 Shot Put106nkEquitable94¾High Fidelity97nk Outrun 17
1Oct40- 6Bel fst 1½ :471 1:124 2:05 2:30 3↑ ⒻLadies H 17k 7 12 1121 96¼ 41½ 31½ Anderson I 123wb *2.85 90-12 Salaminia115½Pretty Pet1141Fairy Chant1232¾ Closed fast 12
21Sep40- 5Aqu fst 1⅛ :472 1:12 1:372 1:504 3↑ ⒻBeldame H 19k 5 9 88¾ 65½ 3½ 11¼ Anderson I 119wb *3.50 102-02 FairyChant1191¼DottedSwiss1141DollyVal1212½ Going away 16
13Sep40- 5Aqu fst 1 1/16 :25 :50 1:142 1:45 3↑ ⒻAlw 2000 4 4 45¼ 44½ 32 2no Anderson I 113wb 3.05 89-09 Little Risk108noFairy Chant1132¾Piquet1083¼ Just missed 5
28Aug40- 5Sar fst 1⅛ :481 1:131 1:383 1:52 3↑ ⒻDiana H 3.2k 3 6 65¾ 44½ 2hd 2hd Anderson I 118wb *1.30 90-13 Piquet116hdFairy Chant1183Rosetown1101 Game try 6
10Aug40- 6Sar fst 1¼ :49 1:14 1:392 2:044 ⒻAlabama 12k 2 6 611 42¼ 2hd 21½ Anderson I 124 w 3.70 83-10 Salaminia1111½Fairy Chant1241Piquet1223¼ Forced wide 6
2Aug40- 5Sar fst 7f :224 :461 1:114 1:242 ⒻTest 3.9k 9 4 46 21 12 2hd James B 126wb 9.45 94-13 Piquet123hdFairy Chant1262Inkling1142½ Tired badly 10
26Jun40- 5Aqu sly 1 1/16 1:46 ⒻGazelle 6.9k 9 8 15 James B 121wb 7.35 -- Fairy Chant1215Raise Up1093Rosetown112¾ Easily 11
Further information unavailable due to blinding rainstorm
22Jun40- 6Del fst 1 1/16 :233 :464 1:113 1:451 3↑ ⒻNewcastle H 13k 12 10 63½ 42 54 54 Peters M 112wb 7.20 89-08 Tedbriar108.5½War Beauty1062Orcades107hd No mishaps 12
13Jun40- 6Del fst 1⅛ :484 1:13 1:392 1:522 ⒻDel Oaks 6.1k 6 6 5¾ 41¼ 42½ 33 Peters M 119wb 3.85 95-10 Piquet1101Rosetown1132Fairy Chant1191 Closed fast 7
1Jun40- 6Bel my 1⅜ :481 1:124 1:384 2:19 ⒻC C A Oaks 15k 1 8 21 1nk 57½ 713½ Wright WD 121wb *1.80 62-21 Damaged Goods121hdRosetown1213Dipsy Doodle121hd Quit 9
22May40- 6Bel fst 1 :223 :46 1:111 1:37 ⒻAcorn 14k 10 10 1012 84 22 25 Wright WD 121wb *2.05 85-18 Damaged Goods1215Fairy Chant1214War Beauty1212 Bore in 11
4May40- 6Pim sl 1 1/16 :233 :483 1:152 1:494 ⒻPim Oaks 14k 10 11 84 21 2nk 11 Neves R 121wb *2.90 71-31 Fairy Chant1211True Call1214Discerning1211 Drew out 13
29Apr40- 5Pim fst 1 70 :231 :473 1:124 1:432 ⒻAlw 1500 4 8 42½ 2hd 11 2no Peters M 115wb 4.75 94-17 True Call112noFairy Chant1156Witchlike112½ Bore out 8
22Feb40- 6SA fst 1⅛ :463 1:112 1:374 1:513 S Anita Derby 61k 5 7 54¾ 65 716 1110¾ Peters M 115wb 8.60e 75-16 Sweepida1201¼Royal Crusader1201Weigh Anchor120hd Tired 17
3Feb40- 6SA my 1 1/16 :24 :474 1:124 1:464 3↑ ⒻS Margarita H 12k 4 1 13 13 15 13½ Dodson D 103 w 14.40 78-26 Fairy Chant1033½Omelet1101½Sweet Nancy1082 In hand 10
27Jan40- 5SA fst 1 :223 :461 1:112 1:38 Alw 1500 5 7 73 97¾ 916 919 McRoberts R 103wb 7.10 69-12 Mioland1142½Gallahadion1061The Gob108½ Outrun 10
20Jan40- 6SA fst 7f :222 :454 1:114 1:251 ⒻS Susana 12k 9 9 94¾ 55 46¼ 69¾ Peters M 115 w 2.80 76-14 Augury1214Less Time1123½Wanna Hygro1122 Tired 12
28Oct39- 4Lrl gd 1 :242 :48 1:144 1:414 ⒻSelima 29k 3 5 53 4¾ 41¾ 41¼ Peters M 114 w *2.30 75-24 WarBeauty114noTedbriar114nkMissFerdinand1221 No excuse 11
16Oct39- 5Lrl fst 1 70 :241 :483 1:132 1:44 ⒻAlw 1200 6 6 3nk 3nk 2hd 2½ Peters M 114 w *1.30 88-13 Dewy Dawn108½Fairy Chant1141½Baby Sister1081½ Weakened 7
6Oct39- 5Lrl fst 6f :234 :472 1:13 ⒻAlw 1100 9 1 64¼ 41¼ 1nk 1nk Peters M 119 w 12.55 89-18 Fairy Chant119nkYarnith1072Thorn Apple1071 Hard drive 10
23Sep39- 3Bel fst 6f-WC 1:12 ⒻMatron 17k 6 1 75 78 610 Peters M 115 w 5.00 77-13 Miss Ferdinand1154Piquet115½Thorn Apple1151½ Outrun 10
14Jun39- 4Aqu sly 5f :581 ⒻAstoria 4.4k 5 5 55½ 34½ 34½ Peters M 119 w 8.00 91-11 Now What116.5½Us1134Fairy Chant119½ Closed well 5
8Jun39- 3Del fst 5f :231 :472 1:004 Alw 1000 3 5 53½ 31¼ 1½ 12½ Peters M 117 w 3.20 92-13 Fairy Chant1172½Victory Morn1181Cutter1152 Going away 9
1Jun39- 4Del sl 5f :24 :49 1:032 ⒻAlw 1000 5 5 44¼ 44½ 42½ 21 Peters M 116 w 2.55 78-26 MadanCapet1161Fairy Chant1163Spanked111½ Closed fast 5
13May39- 4Bel fst 4½f-WC :52 ⒻFashion 4.9k 8 8 31 43 55½ Peters M 116 w 12.00 89-05 Perida1163Us1161½Rancho's Girl1161 Tired 10
22Apr39- 4Jam fst 5f :223 :471 1:002 ⒻRosedale 4k 6 6 69 611 612 614½ Peters M 119 w 2.20 76-14 Spanked1134Rancho's Girl116½Pilot Biscuit1164 Outrun 6
11Feb39- 4Hia fst 3f :222 :341 Everglades 3.7k 6 5 42 1no Peters M 114 w 11.90 -- Fairy Chant114noDrury Lane116noMaedrew114hd Just up 10
23Jan39- 1Hia fst 3f :221 :34 ⒻMd Sp Wt 13 7 53½ 41 Peters M 116 w 2.90f -- ValdinaBess116½Marandan116hdAnnieAlone116½ Good effort 13
16Jan39- 1Hia gd 3f :222 :334 ⒻMd Sp Wt 7 9 105¾ 106¾ Peters M 117 w *2.10 -- FlyngGlee1171HastyTriumph117noDmgdGoods1171½ Bad start 12

Fighting Step

ch. c. 1942, by Fighting Fox (Sir Gallahad III)–Stepinanna, by Misstep — Lifetime record: 35 13 8 5 $157,715
Own.– Murlogg Farn
Br.– Mrs R.J. Murphy & Miss Susan E. Kellogg (Ind)
Tr.– C. Norman

20Jly46- 6AP fst 1¼ :464 1:11 1:353 2:01 3↑ Arlington H 56k 3 1 2½ 44½ 69 710½ South G 119 w 12.50 90-09 Historian112nkArmed1303Take Wing1112½ Early speed 9
4Jly46- 6AP fst 1⅛ :462 1:113 1:37 1:492 3↑ Stars & Stripes H 57k 2 2 22 22 109½ 1012½ South G 122 w 3.10 87-11 WitchSir115noRichmondJac1094½OldKentuck108no Quit badly 11
26Jun46- 6AP fst 1 :231 :46 1:112 1:371 3↑ Equipoise Mile H 34k 6 8 84½ 42½ 53¾ 51 South G 126 w 6.80 85-14 WitchSr110¾OldKntuck106hdArmd132no Close quarters drive 12
19Jun46- 6AP hy 7f :234 :473 1:133 1:271 3↑ Clang H 23k 9 7 51¾ 31 11 1nk South G 121 w *2.70 74-31 FightngStep121nkWalkieTalkie1094SigmaKappa103no Gamely 12
30May46- 6Bel fst 1¼ :482 1:123 1:373 2:02 3↑ Suburban H 60k 9 2 11½ 11 1nk 54¾ South G 118 w 21.75 85-16 Armed1302½Reply Paid110noStymie1231 Faltered late 11
20May46- 6Bel fst 1 :234 :47 1:112 1:364 3↑ Sp Wt 10000 1 1 12 2hd 2hd 1² South G 121 w 1.50 90-20 DHFightingStep121DHSirde1222ReplyPaid121 Led,hung late 3
11May46- 6Bel fst 1 :224 :451 1:104 1:37 3↑ Metropolitan H 31k 7 10 1112 129½ 83¾ 51½ Adams J 123 w 3.65 87-14 Gallorette110noSirde124noFirst Fiddle126½ Impeded turn 14
4May46- 5Jam fst 1⅛ :462 1:12 1:37 1:493 3↑ Grey Lag H 35k 6 2 2½ 2hd 41¾ 35½ Adams J 126 w 5.25 94-10 Stymie1272Bounding Home1053½Fighting Step1261¾ Faltered 7
27Apr46- 5Jam sly 1 1/16 :24 :47 1:114 1:45 3↑ Excelsior H 18k 4 3 32½ 43 21 1½ Adams J 123 w *.85 88-16 Fighting Step123½King Dorsett1154Lets Dance1111 9
Impeded final turn
18Apr46- 5Jam fst 1 1/16 :242 :481 1:12 1:431 4↑ Alw 7500 4 1 12 2hd 21½ 22½ Arcaro E 119 w *.60 94-13 Stymie1142½FightingStep11912OlympicZenith1145¼ No match 4
Daily Racing Form time,1:43 3/5
6Apr46- 5Jam fst 6f :222 :46 1:104 3↑ Paumonok H 11k 7 7 53½ 32 2½ 1¾ South G 120 w 4.00 97-12 Fighting Step120¾Buzfuz1262Play Pretty1096 Going away 8
23Feb46- 5FG fst 5½f :223 :453 :582 1:051 3↑ WFA 2000 4 4 55½ 44½ 22½ 2¾ South G 126 w *.70 98-13 Scholrshp126¾FghtngStp1264MnyLnds1263 Getting to winner 7
20Oct45- 6CD fst 6f :23 :463 1:123 3↑ Autumn H 6.4k 8 4 31 31 31 1nk South G 123 w *.50e 90-22 Fighting Step123nkSirius1141Harriet Sue1071¼ Hard urged 12
15Sep45- 7Haw sl 1 1/16 :24 :48 1:14 1:462 3↑ Haw Autumn H 12k 1 4 53½ 3½ 12 14 South G 120 w *.80 86-22 FightingStep1204SigmaKappa1023½Devlu114½ Speed to spare 13
8Sep45- 8Haw fst 1 1/16 :241 :472 1:12 1:442 3↑ Handicap 3000 1 1 16 14 14 14 South G 118 w *.40 96-10 FightingStep1184K.Do-Do1035SunnyJck101nk Speed to spare 7
25Aug45- 7Was fst 1¼ :48 1:13 1:37 2:024 American Derby 86k 7 4 11½ 12 13 11½ South G 118 w 14.80 96-07 FightngStep1181½WarJp1182½Poto'Luck122hd Weakened late 9
20Aug45- 6Was fst 7f :224 :453 1:094 1:224 3↑ Alw 3500 5 1 1½ 1½ 1hd 1no South G 109 w *1.00 99-12 Fighting Step109noQuick Reward1073Icangetit1115 Driving 6

11Aug45- 7Was	gd 1	:223 :453 1:11 1:38	Dick Welles H 32k	7 6 43 32½ 22 33	Bailey W	116 w	2.50e	85-15	AirSailor118½WarJp125½FghtngStp116½	Vigorous handling	9
30Jly45- 6Was	sl 1	:224 :473 1:114 1:38	Constitution 20k	3 8 74 54 31½ 2½	South G	115 w	5.80	87-21	WarJeep121½FightingStp1154SSwllow1245	Getting to winner	9
23Jly45- 6Was	fst 1	:233 :462 1:111 1:362	Alw 3500	3 1 12 11½ 12 2no	South G	118 w	*.90	96-11	Icngtt118noFghtngStp11812ArtRo1181½	Saved ground,gamely	6
14Jly45- 7Was	sly 1¼	:48 1:133 1:39 2:054	Classic 84k	1 2 33½ 2½ 1hd 33¼	South G	119 w	4.00e	78-19	Poto'Luck1191¼AirSailr1192FightngStp1192	Wide,weakened	7
7Jly45- 7Was	fst 7f	:223 :46 1:12 1:25	Skokie H 22k	6 9 63½ 79 42½ 32¾	South G	116 w	6.30	85-18	WarJeep1181½Poto'Lck1191¼FightngStp116nk	Saved ground	11
25Jun45- 3Was	sly 6f	:233 :49 1:143	Alw 2500	2 1 21 11½ 15 16	South G	120 w	*.50	77-28	FightingStp1206InthBg112noJstngFox1174	Speed in reserve	5
15Jun45- 5CD	fst 6f	:23 :463 1:12	Alw 1800	4 5 1hd 11 11½ 13½	South G	113 w	*.40e	93-18	FightingStep1133½RoiRouge113½Bergolatr1131½	Wide,easily	5
9Jun45- 7CD	my 1¼	:48 1:14 1:41 2:07	Ky Derby 76k	13 11 142 46½ 816 818½	South G	126 w	19.80	53-28	HoopJr.1266Poto'Luck126¾DarbyDieppe126nk	Tired,swerved	16
2Jun45- 6CD	gd 1⅛	:49 1:14 1:40 1:532	Blue Grass 13k	3 4 42½ 62¾ 42½ 22¼	South G	123 w	17.10	80-17	Darby Dieppe1212¼Fighting Step123noAir Sailor123¾		10
		Close quarters str									
22May45- 6CD	fst 7f	:23 :462 1:114 1:252	Alw 2500	4 2 21 21 2nk 2no	South G	115 w	5.80	89-18	AirSailor119noFightingStep115nkJoe'sChoice1051½	Driving	6
2Sep44- 6Det	gd 6f	:231 :47 1:13	©Capt M Britt H 4k	7 5 54½ 54¼ 35½ 24½	Caffarella M	108 w	4.15	78-20	Unconditional1164½Fighting Step108noCrack Reward1124		7
		Strong finish									
26Aug44- 6Det	fst 6f	:224 :46 1:12	Moslem Temple H 10k	6 4 52½ 76 54½ 52¾	Mojena C	112 w	61.50	85-15	AirSailor1202DarbyDunedn112noUncondtonl116¾	Good finish	10
19Aug44- 5Det	fst 6f	:23 :461 1:122	Handicap 4000	2 6 31 63¾ 65 57¾	Burns G	114wb	20.80	78-16	Beaucaire1131½Unconditional1162½RegalMaid1113	No factor	7
29Jly44- 6Det	fst 6f	:224 :463 1:122	©Alw 5000	4 7 53 65¾ 65¼ 59½	Glidewell P	118 w	7.80	76-15	Tiger Man106noAir Sailor1186Good Ground1032½	No threat	7
17Jun44- 5Det	fst 5f	:23 :463 :592	Handicap 3000	7 3 2hd 2hd 1hd 33½	Adams J	115 w	*1.30	90-14	Misweet104½Quintero1153Fighting Step1154	No excuse	7
10Jun44- 4Det	my 4½f	:232 :48 :544	Handicap 3000	6 4 32½ 21½ 1¾	Adams J	112 w	*1.05	88-12	Fighting Step112¾Quintero116hdAgrarian-U116nk	Just up	8
29May44- 3Det	fst 4½f	:231 :471 :541	Md Sp Wt	10 4 42 2nk 15	Adams J	117 w	*2.00	91-09	Fighting Step1175Crack Reward117½Hi Gallant117nk	Easily	12
13May44- 1CD	fst 5f	:231 :473 1:012	Md Sp Wt	6 4 11½ 1hd 2hd 2¾	Adams J	116 w	15.90	87-17	Errard116¾FightingStep1163SeeD.1163	Greenly,drifted out	12

First Flight

b. f. 1944, by Mahmoud (Blenheim II)–Fly Swatter, by Dis Donc

Lifetime record: 24 11 3 3 $197,965

Own.– C.V. Whitney
Br.– C.V. Whitney (Ky)
Tr.– S.E. Veitch

15Nov48- 6Jam	fst 6f	:23 :463 1:123	2↑ New Rochelle H 28k	7 6 41½ 2hd 3nk 3nk	Clark S	125 w	*2.35	88-25	MissDisco112noBuzfuz121nkFirstFlght1251	Prominent,tired	7
27Oct48- 6Jam	fst 1$\frac{1}{16}$	:242 :48 1:13 1:45	3↑ ©Comely H 29k	5 6 67¼ 63¾ 42 812	Clark S	126 w	2.95	76-25	Conniver1231¼Miss Request1205Carolyn A.1182	Quit	10
15Oct48- 6Bel	fst 1	:233 :47 1:114 1:372	3↑ ©Handicap 10055	2 4 53¼ 42 21 1hd	Clark S	126 w	*.60	87-22	FirstFlight126hdSweetDream1147Paddleduck1094	Hard drive	5
4Oct48- 6Jam	fst 6f	:233 :471 1:121	3↑ Fleetwing H 29k	9 9 95¼ 64 82¼ 3½	Clark S	126 w	2.75	89-19	Buzfuz115hdRoyalGovrnor106½FrstFlght126no	Finished fast	10
29Sep48- 6Bel	fst 1	:224 :452 1:101 1:36	3↑ Sysonby Mile 29k	4 5 510 55 22 23	Clark S	123 w	7.30	91-14	Citation1193First Flight123nkCoaltown1194	Closed well	6
22Sep48- 6Bel	fst 7f	:224 :452 1:103 1:234	2↑ Vosburgh H 31k	13 13 1214 129¾ 106½ 33½	Donoso R	124 w	4.15	87-17	Colosal1181Spy Song1292½First Flight124hd	Poor start	14
13Sep48- 6Bel	fst 6f-WC	:22 :442 1:083	2↑ Fall Highweight H 31k	13 2 5¾ 61½ 11¼	Arcaro E	123 w	3.35e	98-05	First Flight1231¼Big Story1243Blue Border1241	Easily	17
2Aug48- 5Sar	fst 6f	:223 :463 1:122	3↑ ©Alw 4500	3 7 76 75¼ 73½ 41	Clark S	116wb	*1.70	85-18	GreyFlight114nkSnowGoose121nkWatermill114½	Closed fast	10
22Jly48- 5Jam	fst 5½f	:23 :454 :594 1:044	3↑ Handicap 5555	4 2 32 22 22 1½	Clark S	117wb	4.25	94-16	First Flight117½Grey Flight112nkMiss Disco1154	Driving	5
19Jun48- 5Del	my 1$\frac{1}{16}$	:242 :482 1:141 1:49	3↑ ©New Castle H 29k	3 4 32 52½ 69½ 617	Clark S	118wb	6.60	51-31	Miss Grillo1192½Elpis1191¾Rampart1176	Quit	7
9Jun48- 6Bel	fst 1$\frac{1}{16}$	:233 :463 1:112 1:43	3↑ ©Top Flight H 24k	6 7 65½ 55 43½ 57½	Clark S	120 w	*2.05	88-18	Honeymoon124noRed Shoes1085Gallorette126½	Faltered	10
2Jun48- 7Bel	fst 1	:23 :454 1:111 1:38	4↑ Alw 5000	5 3 33½ 22 22 12½	Clark S	114 w	2.65	84-22	First Flight1142½Mangohick1222Bullet Proof1143½	Easily	6
15Oct47- 5Jam	fst 6f	:232 :47 1:12	2↑ ©Correction H 17k	6 10 1114 1114 94 43	Guerin E	116wb	4.00e	88-17	Miss Kimo1261Beaugay1232Miss Disco110hd	Sluggish early	11
24Sep47- 6Bel	fst 1	:231 :46 1:11 1:372	Jerome H 30k	1 2 1nk 21 73¼ 78¼	Allgaier H	112wb	7.75	79-18	Donor115nkCosmic Bomb1261½Cornish Knight1132	Tired	12
15Sep47- 5Aqu	sly 7f	:241 :471 1:121 1:25	3↑ ©Alw 6000	2 2 2hd 2hd 1hd 2nk	Donoso R	114 w	*.50	87-16	Quarantaine103nkFirstFlight1141¼LittleAnn1087	Went well	4
8Aug47- 6Sar	fst 7f	:223 :452 1:11 1:242	©Test 10k	3 5 33½ 43¼ 105 88	Arcaro E	120 w	*.45e	86-11	MissDisco110¾Frantie'sBid112¾OcenBrf1101	Close quarters	15
23Jly47- 6Mth	gd 1$\frac{1}{16}$	:231 :471 1:124 1:46	©Mth Oaks 13k	1 4 33 11 12½ 12½	Arcaro E	117 w	*.55e	92-15	First Flight1172½Frantie's Bid1133½Whipsaw1131½	In hand	11
18Jly47- 4Bel	fst 6f	:222 :461 1:112	Alw 5000	6 2 1hd 11 11½ 1no	Arcaro E	121 w	*.45	93-15	First Flight121noColonel O'F1226Nassau1181		7
		Held on,worked seven furlongs									
5Oct46- 4Bel	fst 6½f-W	:224 :452 1:084 1:151	Futurity 93k	1 6 83¾ 2hd 11¾	Arcaro E	123 w	*.85e	96-07	First Flight1231¾I Will126hdJet Pilot1225	Going away	13
		Geldings not eligible									
28Sep46- 4Bel	fst 6f-WC	:223 :45 1:083	©Matron 44k	3 6 2nk 1hd 12¼	Arcaro E	123 w	*.75e	98-07	First Flight1232¼Pipette1231Quarantaine115½	Drew out	10
24Sep46- 4Bel	sly 5½f-W	:223 :451 1:032	©Alw 4000	5 4 2nk 1hd 1¾	Arcaro E	119 w	*1.55	97-07	FirstFlight119¾TeaOlive1141¼CosmicMissile1145	Drew out	10
8Jun46- 4Bel	fst 5½f-W	:223 :452 1:043	©Astoria 14k	8 1 4½ 2nk 11½ 13¼	Miller P	119 w	*1.15	91-12	FirstFlight1193¼MissKimo1221DarkVenus115hd	Going away	10
18May46- 4Bel	fst 5f-WC	:222 :45 :573	Juvenile 14k	2 8 71¾ 33 23	Kirkland A	119 w	*1.00e	89-06	EternalWr1223FrstFlght1191CornshKnght113no	Inside route	12
7May46- 6Bel	fst 4½f-W	:221 :45 :51	©Fashion 14k	10 3 1hd 1½ 11¼	Kirkland A	110 w	4.15	100-06	First Flight1101¼Miss Kimo1195Miss Disco1191	Drew out	11

Gallorette

ch. f. 1942, by Challenger II (Swynford)–Gallette, by Sir Gallahad III

Lifetime record: 72 21 20 13 $445,535

Own.– Mrs M.A. Moore
Br.– Preston M. Burch (Md)
Tr.– E.A. Christmas

12Oct48- 6Jam	fst 1$\frac{1}{16}$	:24 :471 1:12 1:444	3↑ Questionnaire H 29k	3 4 76¾ 96 98¼ 99	Kirkland A	121 w	5.90	80-18	Donor115noCarolyn A.111½Bug Juice1082	Couldn't keep up	11
28Sep48- 6Bel	fst 1½	:473 1:122 2:04 2:30	3↑ ©Ladies H 58k	2 2 56¾ 3nk 22 24	Jessop JD	121 w	4.05	84-14	Miss Request1144Gallorette1211Honeymoon1231	Went well	9
22Sep48- 6Bel	fst 7f	:224 :452 1:103 1:234	2↑ Vosburgh H 31k	1 8 107½ 106¼ 75 64¾	Jessop JD	120 w	6.45	86-17	Colosal1181Spy Song1292½First Flight124hd	Dull effort	14
11Sep48- 6Aqu	gd 1⅛	:482 1:131 1:39 1:522	3↑ ©Beldame H 68k	7 9 105¾ 74¾ 62¾ 34	Jessop JD	124wb	3.20	81-20	Conniver1213½Harmonica114½Gallorette124nk	Closed fast	14
		Previously owned by W.L. Brann									
21Aug48- 6Sar	fst 1¼	:474 1:12 1:372 2:031	3↑ Saratoga H 29k	1 2 47 45 63¾ 55¾	Jessop JD	122 w	3.60	86-13	Loyal Legion1181Bug Juice106nkSnow Goose120½	Tired	7
7Aug48- 6Sar	gd 1¼	:494 1:133 1:391 2:051	3↑ Whitney 22k	2 4 35 33 31¾ 1¾	Kirkland A	115 w	*.90	82-27	Gallorette115¾Loyal Legion1128Natchez1142	Drew out	4
3Aug48- 6Sar	fst 1	:231 :462 1:121 1:382	3↑ Wilson 17k	7 8 87¾ 76½ 3¾ 11¼	Jessop JD	115 w	2.90	85-17	Gallorette1151¼Mount Marcy1054Miss Disco1091½	Drew out	10
17Jly48- 6Aqu	fst 1¼	:502 1:16 1:404 2:054	3↑ Brooklyn H 57k	5 2 33 32 2hd 2hd	Jessop JD	119 w	5.50	78-21	Conniver114hdGallorette1193Stymie1302	Game try	6
3Jly48- 6Aqu	fst 7f	:23 :461 1:102 1:232	3↑ Carter H 29k	7 6 64½ 55¼ 53½ 1hd	Jessop JD	122 w	4.25	95-13	Gallorette122hdRippey1321¼Skylighter1101¼	Hard drive	8
9Jun48- 6Bel	fst 1$\frac{1}{16}$	:233 :463 1:112 1:43	3↑ ©Top Flight H 24k	2 3 3½ 31 31½ 35	Arcaro E	126 w	2.10	91-18	Honeymoon124noRed Shoes1085Gallorette126½	Forced back	10
22May48- 6Bel	fst 1	:233 :463 1:112 1:364	3↑ Metropolitan H 30k	8 7 75¼ 67¾ 45 43¾	Arcaro E	118 w	*2.30	86-14	Stymie126¾Colosal1171½Rippey1241½	No mishap	9
15May48- 5Jam	fst 1$\frac{3}{16}$	:48 1:122 1:373 1:571	3↑ Gallant Fox H 87k	1 2 11 11½ 2hd 3½	Atkinson T	117 w	10.15	89-15	Faultless118hdFervent125½Gallorette1173½	Close quarters	10
8May48- 5Jam	gd 1$\frac{1}{16}$	:243 :483 1:131 1:464	3↑ ©Firenze H 28k	2 2 31 2½ 31 22½	Jessop JD	126 w	*1.70	76-21	Carolyn A.1142½Gallorette126nkRed Shoes1073	Hung	6
30Apr48- 6Jam	fst 1$\frac{1}{16}$	:24 :482 1:13 1:464	4↑ Alw 5000	5 3 23 2hd 11 1¾	Jessop JD	115 w	*.30	79-17	Gallorette115¾Calvados1201½Lets Dance1205	Easily	5
24Apr48- 4Jam	fst 6f	:23 :462 1:114	3↑ Handicap 6570	6 8 53 56¼ 31¼ 2nk	Jessop JD	120 w	13.55	92-18	Rippey126nkGallorette120nkKitchenPolice1161	Good effort	8
29Nov47- 6Bow	fst 1$\frac{3}{16}$	:493 1:133 1:392 1:593	3↑ Bryan & O'Hara H 22k	2 4 41½ 43½ 1hd 2¾	Kirkland A	124 w	*1.20	88-18	Incline107¾Gallorette124hdDouble Jay123hd	Lacked room	7
8Nov47- 5Jam	sly 1$\frac{3}{16}$	:474 1:121 1:384 1:591	3↑ Westchester H 57k	3 4 21½ 22 2½ 52½	Atkinson T	118 w	5.15	77-22	Bridal Flower1081With Pleasure1301½Donor112hd	Tired	8
1Nov47- 5Jam	gd 1$\frac{1}{16}$	:24 :472 1:121 1:443	3↑ Scarsdale H 30k	6 10 97½ 43½ 23 22	Guerin E	119 w	10.50	88-17	WithPleasure1292Gallorette119½DoubleJay1182	Good effort	12
7Oct47- 6Bel	fst 1½	:473 1:123 2:042 2:293	3↑ ©Ladies H 60k	10 8 45¾ 3½ 52 36	Jessop JD	123 w	8.60e	84-14	Snow Goose1135But Why Not1211Gallorette123hd	Weakened	12
20Sep47- 6Aqu	fst 1⅛	:483 1:131 1:384 1:52	3↑ ©Beldame (Div 1) 59k	1 4 53½ 21 2nk 22½	Jessop JD	126 w	*1.85	84-12	SnowGoose1062½Gallorette1262½Crmrgo1122½	Determined bid	10
13Sep47- 6Aqu	fst 1⅛	:502 1:143 1:392 1:522	3↑ Edgemere H 27k	2 1 11½ 2nk 41¾ 44	Jessop JD	122 w	2.50	81-13	Elpis1141½Stymie1341Bridal Flower1131½	Tired badly	4
1Sep47- 6Aqu	fst 1$\frac{1}{16}$	:242 :474 1:124 1:442	3↑ Aqueduct H 29k	5 4 47 3nk 31½ 2½	Jessop JD	122wb	2.45	91-13	Stymie132½Gallorette122hdElpis1144	Held well	11
23Aug47- 6Sar	fst 1¼	:48 1:114 1:37 2:032	3↑ Saratoga H 33k	2 2 11 1nk 1hd 2nk	Guerin E	122 w	*.80	91-11	Rico Monte124nkGallorette12212Boss105	Hung late	3
9Aug47- 6Sar	fst 1¼	:491 1:133 1:393 2:023	3↑ Whitney 27k	3 1 12 1½ 1nk 2hd	Arcaro E	112 w	2.05	95-09	Rico Monte113hdGallorette1121½Stymie126	Held well	3
4Aug47- 6Sar	fst 1	:23 :46 1:10 1:352	3↑ Wilson 23k	3 4 47 48½ 31½ 11¼	Jessop JD	112 w	*1.45	104-08	Gallorette1121¼Hornbeam1123KngDorstt112¾	Steadied early	5

26Jly47- 5Mth	fst	1¼	:473 1:12 1:363 2:011	3↑ Mth Park H 29k	4	2	42½	32½	34½	38½	James B	119	w	*1.35	94-02	Round View1127Talon112½Gallorette119hd	Flattened out	6
12Jly47- 5Jam	fst	1 3/16	:49 1:134 1:381 1:563	3↑ Butler H 54k	2	4	31	33	4½	31¾	Guerin E	117	w	9.20	91-09	Assault135hdStymie1261¾Gallorette117nk	Swerved turn	5
3Jly47- 5Jam	fst	1 1/16	:241 :482 1:132 1:452	3↑ ⒻHandicap 7530	4	2	22	21	1½	11¼	Guerin E	128	w	*.80	86-16	Gallorette1281¼Kay Gibson1082½Elpis1142	Mild urging	4
7Jun47- 6Aqu	sly	7f	:23 :461 1:10 1:23	3↑ Carter H 28k	2	5	56½	54¾	52¼	33¼	James B	123	w	*2.25	94-09	Rippey112nkInroc1183Gallorette1232	Fast finish	8
2Jun47- 6Aqu	fst	1 1/16	:242 :482 1:124 1:452	3↑ Queens County H 21k	5	2	21	2hd	1hd	1nk	Jessop JD	119	w	1.70	87-19	Gallorette119nkStymie128noMangoneo1046	Driving	6
10May47- 6Bel	fst	1	:23 :464 1:112 1:372	3↑ Metropolitan H 30k	7	8	98¼	89¼	76¼	32	Givens C	116	w	8.95	85-15	Stymie1241BrownMogl1131Gllortt1161½	Bumped str,swerved	12
26Apr47- 5Jam	fst	1 1/16	:24 :473 1:114 1:44	3↑ Excelsior H 22k	2	5	64	51¾	53¾	58½	Wilson HB	118	w	6.55	84-10	Coincidence1155Polynesian126½Lets Dance1121	No menace	8
19Apr47- 4Jam	fst	6f	:23 :46 1:112	3↑ Handicap 6525	1	3	22	48	45¾	45	Jessop JD	121	w	6.45	89-10	Polynesin1301¾Buzfuz1201¼TdyBd1032	Worked mile 1:42 3/5	5
9Nov46- 5Jam	gd	1 3/16	:472 1:112 1:373 1:562	3↑ Westchester H 56k	3	4	38	48¼	66¾	69	Atkinson T	118	w	8.70	85-17	Assault1222½Lucky Draw1284Lets Dance1041½	No mishap	6
26Oct46- 6GS	sly	1⅛	:464 1:112 1:373 1:503	3↑ Trenton H 64k	12	6	66	55¼	86	88¾	Jessop JD	121	w	*2.35	83-19	Turbine115nkPolynesian123½Man o' Glory1162	No excuse	12
12Oct46- 4Bel	sly	1	:23 :453 1:102 1:353	3↑ Sysonby 25k	4	3	32½	23	26	212	Jessop JD	117	w	2.35	84-14	Lucky Draw12012Gallorette1171½War Date1172	Went well	4
21Sep46- 6Aqu	sly	1⅛	:474 1:124 1:382 1:512	3↑ ⒻBeldame H (Div 1) 56k	2	7	41¼	1hd	1½	1½	Jessop JD	126	w	*.80	90-13	Gallorette126½War Date1131¼Kay Gibson1056	Ridden out	10
14Sep46- 6Aqu	fst	1⅛	:474 1:13 1:38 1:502	3↑ Edgemere H 28k	1	3	32½	52¼	41¾	21½	Jessop JD	123	w	2.15	93-13	Stymie1211½Gallorette1231¼King Dorsett1156	Closed fast	8
9Sep46- 6Aqu	fst	7f	:223 :45 1:10 1:232	3↑ Bay Shore H 18k	2	4	73¼	77¼	53¼	1nk	Jessop JD	124	w	6.20	95-18	Gallorette124nkKing Dorsett1201½Polynesian1301	Just up	9
19Aug46- 6Sar	sly	1	:25 :493 1:14 1:39	3↑ Alw 6650	3	2	22	32	35¼	35¾	Jessop JD	121	w	*1.30	80-20	King Dorsett119¾Stymie1195Gallorette121	Tired	3
5Aug46- 6Sar	fst	1	:23 :461 1:111 1:363	3↑ Wilson 24k	4	7	79½	63¼	53½	2nk	Wilson HB	121	w	6.65	98-08	Pavot126nkGallorette121nkLarky Day112hd	Just missed	11
13Jly46- 5Jam	fst	1 3/16	:47 1:111 1:361 1:551	3↑ Butler H 57k	3	3	31½	32½	1½	2hd	Jessop JD	116	w	6.15	104-08	Lucky Draw105hdGallorette1161½Stymie126¾	Game try	9
4Jly46- 6Suf	fst	1⅛	:473 1:123 1:373 1:494	3↑ Mass H 66k	11	7	74¼	51½	21½	33¾	Jessop JD	119	w	*2.20	88-13	Pavot1202¼Dinner Party1131½Gallorette1192¾	Weakened	11
22Jun46- 6Aqu	fst	1¼	:48 1:131 1:393 2:05	3↑ Brooklyn H 58k	8	7	43½	2½	1½	1nk	Jessop JD	118	w	3.15	82-24	Gallorette118nkStymie1284½Burning Dream110½	Hard drive	8
15Jun46- 6Del	gd	1¼	:473 1:122 1:38 2:041	3↑ Sussex H 29k	5	3	31½	33½	22½	22	Jessop JD	113	w	3.55	92-16	Pavot1152Gallorette1131Stymie1262	Good effort	8
11Jun46- 6Del	fst	1 1/16	:241 :473 1:111 1:43	4↑ Alw 3500	4	1	11½	1½	12	11¼	Jessop JD	120	w	*.70	98-14	Gallorette1201¼War Trophy1146George Case120¾	Easily	4
29May46- 6Bel	fst	1 1/16	:224 :454 1:103 1:431	3↑ ⒻTop Flight H 24k	7	3	32½	42	31½	52¾	Jessop JD	128	w	*2.25	92-13	Sicily113nkSurosa1131¼Recce1181	Close quarters	11
24May46- 6Bel	fst	1	:231 :462 1:112 1:372	3↑ ⒻHandicap 8050	6	2	2½	2hd	11½	12	Jessop JD	122	w	*.90	87-14	Gallrette1222Mahmoudess109nkDarbyDunedn112hd	Drew away	6
11May46- 6Bel	fst	1	:224 :451 1:104 1:37	3↑ Metropolitan H 31k	6	8	1010	104½	4½	1no	Jessop JD	110	w	9.60	89-14	Gallorette110noSirde124noFirst Fiddle126½	Just up	14
4May46- 5Jam	fst	1⅛	:462 1:12 1:37 1:493	3↑ Grey Lag H 35k	7	1	1½	1hd	3nk	47¼	Donoso R	114	w	14.45	93-10	Stymie1272Bounding Home1053½Fighting Step1261¾	Bore in	7
27Apr46- 5Jam	sly	1 1/16	:24 :47 1:114 1:45	3↑ Excelsior H 18k	1	4	43½	32½	33	45½	Kirkland A	116	w	6.15	82-16	Fighting Step123½King Dorsett1154Lets Dance1111	Tired	9
17Nov45- 6Pim	gd	1 3/16	:493 1:142 1:391 1:584	3↑ Pim Spl 25k	7	3	33½	42½	55¾	47¼	Atkinson T	117	wb	16.15	81-20	Armed1264First Fiddle1262Stymie1261¼	No rally late	7
10Nov45- 5Pim	fst	1⅛	:471 1:114 1:373 1:513	3↑ Handicap 5000	4	2	22	1hd	21	31¾	Scawthorn K	113	w	2.50	95-14	Armed1281¾Rampart104hdGallorette1132	Outgamed for place	5
3Nov45- 5Jam	fst	1 3/16	:48 1:113 1:371 1:564	3↑ Westchester H 56k	6	2	45½	34	53½	44	Haskell L	116	w	22.20	92-10	Stymie125hdBuzfuz1162Olympic Zenith1172	Not enough late	10
27Oct45- 7Pim	fst	1 1/16	:241 :482 1:131 1:453	3↑ Handicap 3500	7	5	54½	53½	53¼	53	McCreary C	124	w	3.25	87-17	Salvo120½Polynesian1262He Rolls115hd	Failed to rally	7
8Sep45- 6Aqu	fst	1⅛	:471 1:113 1:373 1:512	Discovery H 28k	1	3	34	33	2½	77	Atkinson T	120	w	*2.00	83-13	[D]Bobanet115hdWar Jeep122½Chief Barker1162	Tired	11
25Aug45- 5GS	sl	1⅛	:473 1:122 1:381 1:514	Jersey H 32k	2	5	46	45¼	11	52¾	Permane R	121	w	*.95	83-18	Trymenow118nkBuzfuz1152½Turbine114no	Faltered	8
21Jly45- 5Jam	fst	1 3/16	:472 1:112 1:37 1:564	Empire City 57k	9	4	35½	32½	1nk	1¾	Atkinson T	116	w	3.00	96-08	Gallorette116¾Pavot1263Post Graduate1163	Drew away	11
14Jly45- 5Aqu	fst	1¼	:481 1:13 1:393 2:051	Dwyer 56k	1	3	33	21½	2hd	2no	Kirkland A	116	w	6.65	81-18	Wildlife116noGallorette116½Esteem11610	Bid,just missed	6
28Jun45- 6Del	fst	1⅛	:474 1:124 1:383 1:51	ⒻDel Oaks 13k	4	3	11½	11	11	13	Arcaro E	119	w	*.60	94-08	Gallorette1193Elpis119½Monsoon11312	Speed to spare	5
16Jun45- 7Pim	fst	1 1/16	:24 :48 1:114 1:442	ⒻPim Oaks 22k	6	3	22	21	2½	1¾	Woolf G	121	w	*.85	96-08	Gallorette121¾Recce121¾Be Faithful1216	Driving	6
7Jun45- 6Bel	fst	1	:23 :47 1:114 1:38	ⒻAcorn 11k	7	3	22	21½	11½	11½	Arcaro E	121	w	1.25	84-21	Gallorette1211½Monsoon1216Recce1212	Swerved,driving	7
30May45- 5Jam	fst	1 1/16	:24 :47 1:12 1:454	Wood Mem (Div 1) 27k	7	4	47	43¾	1hd	22	Atkinson T	121	w	10.85	82-16	Jeep1262Gallorette1212½Dockstader1261½	Driving	9
22May45- 5Jam	fst	6f	:232 :462 1:123	Alw 4000	11	5	2hd	11	11½	11¾	Arcaro E	113	w	12.85	89-14	Gallorette1131¾Hitem1171½War Trophy113hd	Driving	14
7Nov44- 5Pim	fst	1 70	:224 :47 1:123 1:442	Alw 2500	3	3	34	23	2hd	23½	Gilbert J	114	w	*.95e	85-17	Brookfield1133½Gallortt1145Mndru1105	Swerved repeatedly	6
3Nov44- 5Pim	fst	6f	:222 :46 1:12	ⒻAlw 3000	4	5	31½	2½	1hd	2½	Scawthorn K	116	wb	2.85	92-28	Monsoon116½Gallorette1163Connie's Girl1121	Driving	8
14Oct44- 6Lrl	sl	1 1/16	:233 :474 1:141 1:493	ⒻSelima 29k	1	2	22	44	33½	35½	Woolf G	114	w	3.65	63-34	Busher1173Ace Card1192½Gallorette1144	Held well	10
9Oct44- 4Lrl	sl	1 70	:241 :491 1:164 1:491	ⒻAlw 3000	4	2	21	11	14	15	Dodson D	114	w	3.50	63-37	Gallorette1145Whetstone112nkSweetChms1143	Eased up late	6
4Oct44- 6Lrl	hy	6f	:23 :481 1:151	[S]Maryland Futurity 6k	1	4	32	22	1hd	2no	Dodson D	110	w	*.60e	78-33	Petee Dee111noGallorette1104Sheltie1111	Just missed	8
28Sep44- 5Lrl	fst	6f	:224 :471 1:14	[S]Alw 2000	1	3	12	13	13	16	Dodson D	115	w	*.80	84-21	Gallorette1156Run Bud Run1182Abiel1181	Easily	8
20Sep44- 1Lrl	sl	5½f	:233 :484 1:02 1:09	ⒻMd Sp Wt	4	3	12	14	14	12	Dodson D	115	w	*1.30	78-28	Gallorette1152Chronoflit1156FourQuns1151½	Mild pressure	11
14Sep44- 1Lrl	hy	6f	:233 :492 1:173	Md Sp Wt	8	7	42½	21	1½	33¼	Dodson D	115	w	46.35	63-44	Director118nkWar Trophy1133Gallorette1151	Tired	12

Level Best

ch. f. 1938, by Equipoise (Pennant)–Speed Boat, by Man o' War

Lifetime record: 28 12 6 3 $64,230

Own.– C. Oglebay
Br.– Samuel D. Riddle (Ky)
Tr.– J.P. Jones

12Oct42- 6Lrl	fst	1⅛	:473 1:122 1:381 1:51	3↑ ⒻQueen Isabella H 6.1k	2	6	619	616	621	623½	Young S	114	wb	10.50	69-12	Vgrncy1263Lotopos1022Rostown1224	Fractious,broke in air	6
6Oct42- 6Bel	gd	1½	:481 1:133 2:054 2:311	3↑ ⒻLadies H 16k	10	6	12	11	21	810¾	Meade D	117	wb	20.50	75-13	Vagrancy1261¼Dark Discovery1081¼Loveday1175	Tired	10
19Sep42- 6Aqu	sly	1⅛	:472 1:121 1:373 1:50	3↑ ⒻBeldame H 17k	6	7	77½	69½	98¼	916½	Longden J	120	w	9.20	80-06	[DH]Vagrancy119[DH]Barrancosa1164Rosetown126hd	Outrun	10
12Sep42- 6GS	sl	1 1/16	:25 :494 1:142 1:472	3↑ ⒻVineland H 12k	4	2	2½	2hd	2½	2¾	Ensor L	115	wb	2.50	- -	Rosetown121¾Level Best1153½Dark Discovery1095	Weakened	6
5Sep42- 5GS	fst	6f	:224 :462 1:104	3↑ ⒻColonial H 5.9k	1	5	53½	31	2½	21¼	Meade D	121	w	*1.25	- -	Zaca Gray1131¼Level Best1215Taunt1121	Weakened	6
11Jly42- 7Suf	gd	1 1/16	:23 :46 1:112 1:444	3↑ ⒻHannah Dustin H 13k	4	4	44	913	915	1021	Gilbert J	118	wb	*2.30	71-15	Loveday112½Spiral Pass1021Red Moon1112¼	Weakened	10
4Jly42- 6Del	gd	1 1/16	:234 :482 1:124 1:453	3↑ ⒻNew Castle H 12k	3	1	11	11	2hd	611¾	Meade D	125	w	*1.80	79-09	Monida112nkRosetown1195War Hazard1232	Tired badly	8
23Jun42- 5Del	fst	6f	:223 :461 1:113	4↑ Alw 2080	2	2	32	22	2½	1hd	Meade D	119	w	*.80	95-07	Level Best119hdThe Finest1212½Madigama1176	Hard drive	5
13Jun42- 6Aqu	fst	7f	:223 :451 1:094 1:23	3↑ Carter H 9.8k	5	3	31½	56	76½	912½	Meade D	121	w	2.90	87-08	Doublrab120hdSwing and Sway112¾Whirlaway1301½	Impeded	9
4Jun42- 6Bel	fst	1 1/16	:231 :46 1:104 1:424	3↑ ⒻTop Flight H 7k	8	1	11	11	11½	11¾	Meade D	123	w	*2.90	97-09	Level Best1231¾Up the Hill1141Transient1121½	In hand	9
30May42- 7Bel	fst	7f	:232 :463 1:112 1:233	3↑ ⒻHandicap 2525	2	1	2hd	2hd	1hd	21½	Meade D	122	w	2.65	90-07	Fleetborough1071½LevelBest122hd[D]Mr-Kll1126	Forced wide	6
4Aug41- 5Sar	fst	1	:231 :464 1:113 1:373	3↑ ⒻHandicap 2030	2	1	16	14	1½	25	Robertson A	118	wb	1.95	88-14	War Hazard1045Level Best118hdRosetown1221	Tired badly	6
5Jly41- 6Del	my	1 1/16	:233 :48 1:141 1:49	3↑ ⒻNew Castle H 13k	5	10	1218	1320	1331	1322	Wall N	114	w	*2.35	52-28	DottedSwiss1143BalaOrmont1161½FairyChant1262		13
	Fractious start,unseated rider,refused to extend																	
12Jun41- 6Del	fst	1⅛	:474 1:12 1:372 1:494	ⒻDel Oaks 8.8k	1	2	23	24	25	315	Robertson A	119	wb	*1.15	91-08	Tangled1139Misty Isle1196Level Best1194		5
	Fractious start,broke through gate,returned bleeding from mouth																	
31May41- 4Bel	fst	1⅜	:49 1:13 1:381 2:173	ⒻC C A Oaks 13k	1	1	11½	14	12	1nk	Robertson A	121	wb	*.45	83-12	Level Best121nkDark Discovery1212Nasca121	Just lasted	3
26May41- 6Bel	fst	1 1/16	:24 :474 1:133 1:444	3↑ ⒻHandicap 2035	4	2	2nk	2hd	13	11½	Hanford I	110	wb	*.60	87-16	Level Best1101½Laatokka1046Bala Ormont112½	Easily	5
3May41- 6Pim	fst	1 1/16	:232 :472 1:122 1:453	ⒻPim Oaks 12k	5	2	11	1hd	2hd	31¾	Hanford I	121	wb	*.60	90-13	Cis Marion121noDark Discovery1211¾Level Best1213½	Tired	8
2Nov40- 4Emp	hy	5¾f	:224 :463 1:10	ⒻAutumn Day 8.9k	4	5	52½	41	11	12	Robertson A	119	wb	*.40	87-22	Level Best1192Dark Imp1102Strange Device1191¾	Easily	7
12Oct40- 6Kee	fst	6f	:224 :461 1:112	ⒻSpecial Event 6.2k	4	5	11½	12	1½	12	Longden J	119	wb	*.30	95-10	Level Best1192Valdina Myth1192½Meggy1193	Handily	9
5Oct40- 5Lrl	fst	6f	:223 :463 1:121	Richard Johnson 8.2k	6	2	2½	1½	12½	14	Robertson A	116	wb	*1.10	93-19	Level Best1164Madigama113.5¾Misty Isle1191	Going away	9
21Sep40- 4Aqu	fst	6½f	:222 :453 1:101 1:17	Jr Champion 12k	2	2	22	23	22	22¼	Robertson A	115	wb	3.95	- -	King Cole1182¼Level Best1152Nasca115nk	Second best	7
14Sep40- 5HdG	fst	6f	:231 :47 1:112	Eastern Shore H 13k	8	1	2½	12½	1½	2no	Shelhamer A	122	wb	*.90	96-10	LittleBens116noLvlBst1221½Portr'sCp1201¾	Tired in drive	9
2Sep40- 6Nar	sly	6f	:23 :461 1:112	Old Colony 10k	1	4	1hd	1hd	11½	15	Shelhamer A	114	wb	*2.50	94-16	LevelBest1145KingCole114.5nkLittleBens1153¾	Easily best	10
17Aug40- 6Sar	fst	6f	:224 :47 1:12	ⒻSpinaway 10k	1	2	1hd	1hd	11	34½	James B	119	wb	*.65	87-09	Nasca1163Tangled1161½Level Best1191½	Faltered	6
6Aug40- 5Sar	fst	5½f	:223 :46 1:051	[R]Sar Sales 2.8k	4	1	2hd	1hd	1hd	11¾	James B	119	wb	*.55	95-07	Level Best1191¾Cuantos1222Omission122½	Going away	7
4Jly40- 5Emp	my	5¾f	:223 :462 1:091	ⒻDemoiselle 8.1k	6	5	12	14	15	18¼	James B	115	wb	5.40	91-14	Level Best1158¼Strange Device122¾Tangled1192	Much best	13
22Jun40- 4Del	fst	5½f	:224 :463 1:071	Alw 1000	7	3	2½	1½	1nk	11	Peters M	112	wb	*1.10	96-08	Level Best1121Sky Lane115hdSnarler1182½	Drew out	7
13Jun40- 1Del	fst	5f	:23 :463 1:00	ⒻMd Sp Wt	6	3	32¾	45	2½	12	Peters M	116	wb	*1.25	96-10	LevelBest1162CisMarion116½GranoSaltis116hd	Going away	12

PAST PERFORMANCES: 1940's 101

Mar-Kell

b. f. 1939, by Blenheim II (Blandford)–Nellie Flag, by American Flag — Lifetime record: 53 17 17 3 $84,365

Own.– Calumet Farm
Br.– Calumet Farm (Ky)
Tr.– B.A. Jones

14Nov44- 4Pim fst 6f :224 :462 1:113 4↑ Alw 3500 5 5 34 46 34 33¾ Dodson D 116wb 2.05 91-18 Sophocles1163½Charitabl116nkMr-Kll1161½ Unable to close 5
12Oct44- 6Lrl fst 1⅛ :472 1:123 1:40 1:531 3↑ Ⓕ Queen Isabella H 11k 1 6 615 715 715 716½ Westrope J 118wb *.15e 65-23 Twilight Tear1265Good Morning1182Legend Bearer1083½ 8
Broke sluggishly,no rally
3Oct44- 6Bel fst 1½ :491 1:131 2:051 2:311 3↑ Ⓕ Ladies H 16k 1 2 21 31½ 54½ 510¼ Arcaro E 126wb 2.30 72-15 Donitas First1154Letmenow1121½Moon Maiden1134 Tired 5
6Sep44- 6Was sly 1 :24 :48 1:132 1:392 3↑ Ⓕ Modesty H 16k 1 8 57 610 718 719 Smith FA 117wb *1.90 62-24 Gold Princess1103Night Shadow1121Happy Issue1126 8
Gave way suddenly
19Aug44- 6Was fst 1⅛ :462 1:11 1:362 1:501 3↑ Ⓕ Beverly H 29k 5 12 107¾ 98¾ 53½ 2¾ McCreary C 118wb *2.80 96-09 TrafficCourt115¾Mar-Kell118½Silvestr1041½ Finished fast 12
28Jly44- 6Was fst 6f :23 :461 1:11 3↑ Ⓕ Handicap 5000 1 3 52¼ 52½ 2hd 2nk Grohs O 116wb 4.10 96-13 GoldPrincess109nkMar-Kell1163TrafficCourt1161 Held well 7
15Jly44- 5Was fst 7f :234 :472 1:111 1:233 3↑ Ⓕ Handicap 3500 6 4 32 31½ 23 35 Haas L 120wb 4.70 93-11 Burgoo Maid1093Traffic Court1162Mar-Kell120½ 6
Saved ground,faltered
8Jly44- 6Was fst 1 :231 :463 1:113 1:363 3↑ Ⓕ Arl Matron H 16k 6 5 54 54½ 76¾ 610½ Smith FA 122wb *2.10 84-08 HarrietSue103½TrafficCourt1121½HppyIssu1144 No response 7
24Jun44- 6Was fst 1 :233 :471 1:113 1:361 3↑ Equipoise Mile H 12k 2 4 52¼ 810 812 816 Smith FA 110wb *.70e 81-07 Sun Again127¾Georgie Drum113nkAnticlimax1042½ Outrun 9
1Jun44- 6Bel fst 1⁄16 :23 :454 1:11 1:432 3↑ Ⓕ Top Flight H 11k 7 8 86¾ 54¾ 23 2¾ McCreary C 126wb *1.60 93-10 Boojiana106¾Mar-Kell1263Silvestra112½ Driving 10
22May44- 7Bel fst 1⁄16 :463 1:121 1:374 1:443 3↑ Ⓕ Handicap 4965 4 6 69 66¾ 43½ 2nk McCreary C 120wb *.90 88-15 Anthemion108nkMar-Kell1204Moon Maiden1121 Belated rally 8
19May44- 6Bel fst 6f :231 :462 1:104 3↑ Handicap 4390 2 4 52½ 42¼ 44½ 33¾ McCreary C 117wb 9.45 92-14 Bossuet125¾Brownie1133Mar-Kell117nk Late gain 5
2May44- 5Pim fst 1⁄16 :24 :481 1:13 1:452 3↑ Philadelphia H 17k 5 5 54½ 53¼ 52 21 McCreary C 113wb 5.85 90-16 Rounders1201Mar-Kell113nkFour Freedoms119½ Driving 5
27Apr44- 5Pim my 1⁄16 :241 :484 1:144 1:482 3↑ Gittings H 8.4k 1 2 2hd 44 45 413½ McCreary C 114wb *.30e 62-39 Sun Again1241Famous Victory101½Tola Rose10912 Tired 4
20Apr44- 7Pim gd 1 70 :242 :483 1:141 1:452 4↑ Alw 3000 6 2 1½ 13 13 16 McCreary C 115wb *.55 84-20 Mar-Kell1156In Question1124Homeward Bound1141 Easily 6
13Apr44- 5Pim gd 6f :223 :47 1:132 4↑ Alw 2500 4 4 43½ 34 33 26 Smith FA 117wb *.75 80-25 Sollure1126Mar-Kell1174Homeward Bound116¾ No match 5
18Mar44- 6TrP fst 1⅛ :471 1:111 1:363 1:491 3↑ Coral Gables H 5.5k 6 3 32 21½ 21½ 22 McCreary C 115wb *.60e 97-05 Marriage1202Mar-Kell1153Shot Put1052 Bid,no match 6
6Mar44- 5TrP fst 6f :222 :45 1:10 4↑ Alw 2000 3 7 76 43 2nk 1¾ McCreary C 117wb *.90e 100-11 Mar-Kell117¾Adroit106½Sparkling Maid1021 Saved ground 8
7Feb44- 7Hia fst 6½f :232 :471 1:121 1:19 4↑ Alw 3500 5 4 31½ 43 44 45 Thompson B 117wb *.25e 79-29 Sun Again119½Harvard Square113¾Silvestra1083¾ Evenly 6
27Jan44- 3Hia fst 7f :233 :471 1:122 1:254 4↑ Ⓕ Alw 3000 3 1 1½ 12 13 1½ Thompson B 124wb *.25 83-24 Mar-Kell124½WisMoss1135FddlrsBt1125 Eased up,urged late 5
22Jan44- 5Hia fst 7f :234 :472 1:124 1:26 3↑ Ⓕ Evening H 5.8k 3 5 52½ 41½ 32 11½ Thompson B 126wb *1.35 82-20 Mar-Kell1261½Silvestra1121½Pig Tails1101 Impeded turn 7
5Oct43- 6Bel fst 1½ :483 1:134 2:05 2:314 3↑ Ⓕ Ladies H 16k 3 3 33½ 43½ 46½ 48¾ Thompson B 126wb *1.35 70-17 Stefanita1161½Vagrancy1236Dark Discovery1061¼ No threat 7
18Sep43- 6Aqu fst 1⅛ :474 1:132 1:383 1:513 3↑ Ⓕ Beldame H 28k 7 6 74¾ 64 31½ 11 Thompson B 126wb 4.00 89-14 Mar-Kell1261Stefanita1162Vagrancy122½ Driving 11
8Sep43- 6Aqu sly 1⁄16 :24 :481 1:132 1:44 3↑ Ⓕ Alw 5300 1 2 2nk 2nk 2nk 21½ Thompson B 118wb *.50 92-14 GoodMorning1011½Mar-Kell1182Brttny10110 Bid,drifted out 5
21Aug43- 6Was fst 1⅛ :474 1:112 1:374 1:51 3↑ Ⓕ Beverly H 11k 1 5 45 33½ 32¼ 2nk Smith FA 125wb *.70 93-11 Askmenow115nkMar-Kell1251¼Burgoo Maid1092½ Wide 8
12Aug43- 6Was sl 7f :231 :473 1:131 1:272 3↑ Ⓕ Modesty H 6.2k 2 9 75¾ 56½ 25 2nk Eads W 125wb *.90 79-33 Burgoo Maid111nkMar-Kell1256Jerry Lee109nk 10
Away slowly,wide,just missed
31Jly43- 6Was fst 1¼ :484 1:131 1:374 2:033 3↑ Arlington H 58k 9 7 85¾ 86¼ 78½ 810¼ Eads W 110wb 5.80 82-12 Marriage1201Thumbs Up118noAnticlimax1134 Never a factor 10
10Jly43- 6Was fst 1 :232 :464 1:123 1:381 3↑ Ⓕ Arl Matron H 12k 7 9 84¾ 85¼ 22 2nk Eads W 126wb *.90 87-17 Askmenow109nkMar-Kll1262½Pomayya1181 Getting to winner 10
30Jun43- 6Was fst 7f :23 :464 1:113 1:242 3↑ Ⓕ Cinderella H 6.3k 10 8 93½ 51½ 1½ 1½ Eads W 122wb *.80 94-17 Mar-Kell122½Hometown106¾Askmenow1103 Driving 10
22Jun43- 6Was gd 1 :241 :474 1:13 1:373 4↑ Alw 2500 2 2 23 22 2hd 11½ Smith FA 105wb *.50e 89-17 Mar-Kell1052½King'sAbbey110¾Whrlwy1221½ Much in reserve 7
3Jun43- 6Bel fst 1⁄16 :233 :47 1:12 1:442 3↑ Ⓕ Top Flight H 6.4k 2 5 54 21 11½ 12 Thompson B 122wb 2.10 89-17 Mar-Kell1222YarrowMaid1102Stefanita1061½ Easing up late 6
29May43- 5Bel fst 6f-WC 1:104 3↑ Roseben H 6.7k 4 6 63½ 72¾ 62¼ Eads W 114wb 3.15 90-11 Some Chance105hdMettlesome108½Salto1041½ No mishap 7
14May43- 6Bel my 1 :232 :47 1:12 1:374 3↑ Ⓕ Alw 3000 4 4 43½ 22 11 18 Thompson B 110wb 3.35 85-23 Mar-Kell1108Vagrancy1226Opera Singer101nk Easily 8
10Apr43- 6CD sl 6f :234 :473 1:13 3↑ Phoenix H 3.6k 8 1 44½ 43½ 43 21½ Eads W 113wb *1.40 86-26 MssDogwood1131½Mr-Kll1132ThrClovrs105nk Driving,no match 8
20Mar43- 4OP fst 6f :23 :47 1:12 3↑ Handicap 1500 5 1 36½ 36 3½ 11 Eads W 117wb *.40 91-17 Mar-Kell1171Chipamink1032Alohort1163 Stumbled start 5
9Mar43- 6FG fst 6f :223 :46 1:11 3↑ Mardi Gras H 5k 8 6 74 73¾ 42½ 21¼ Eads W 112wb 3.90 97-16 Riverland1241¼Mar-Kell1121½Signator1202½ Saved ground 8
4Mar43- 6FG fst 6f :241 :473 1:121 4↑ Ⓕ Alw 2500 2 3 2hd 1hd 1hd 1no Eads W 115wb *.60 92-12 Mar-Kell115noPig Tails1152½Taunt107¾ Driving 4
22Feb43- 6FG my 6f :234 :473 1:13 4↑ Washington's Bday H 5k 8 5 53 42 2½ 1no Eads W 110wb *2.20 91-23 Mar-Kell110noPompion1173Marriage115nk Driving 8
4Feb43- 6FG fst 6f :231 :463 1:12 4↑ Alw 1500 5 4 43 42½ 3½ 11½ Eads W 113wb *1.40e 96-14 Mar-Kell1131½Pig Tails1191½Augury1151¾ Drew away 9
7Nov42- 5Pim fst 1⁄16 :234 :473 1:121 1:442 3↑ Ⓕ Handicap 1300 3 3 21½ 21½ 22 22½ Keiper P 120wb *1.65 93-13 Star Copy1192½Mar-Kell1203½Night Glow1043½ 2nd best 5
29Oct42- 6Pim fst 1⁄16 :243 :491 1:124 1:44 3↑ Ⓕ Lady Baltimore H 3.1k 4 4 43½ 43½ 3½ 2nk Eads W 113wb 3.70 98-12 StarCopy110nkMar-Kell1132NghtGlow1025 Getting to winner 5
23Oct42- 6Lrl sl 6f :23 :464 1:132 3↑ Alw 2000 3 6 45 64¾ 55¼ 66¾ Claggett H 103wb *.65e 80-26 Quien Es115hdJay Jay1082½Sassy Lady106.5hd Saved ground 8
8Oct42- 4Bel fst 6f :224 :461 1:11 3↑ Ⓕ Handicap 2560 7 6 66 55 41¼ 21 Woolf G 116wb 2.25e 94-12 Yarrow Maid1121Mar-Kell1164Bostoff1091 Bore in 7
30May42- 7Bel fst 7f :232 :463 1:112 1:233 3↑ Ⓕ Handicap 2525 1 2 1hd 1hd 2hd 31½ Eads W 112wb 3.55 90-07 Fleetborough1071½Level Best122hdⒹMar-Kell1126 6
Disqualified
29Apr42- 5CD fst 6f :233 :472 1:124 3↑ Alw 1000 2 4 21 2hd 2½ 1nk Eads W 109wb *.70 89-13 Mar-Kell109nkJack Twink1156Sea Tack1112 Impeded str 6
23Apr42- 7Kee fst 6f :224 :462 1:122 3↑ Alw 1000 1 5 21 22 23 1no Eads W 110wb 2.20 90-12 Mar-Kell110noEquator114nkPet109no Driving 8
20Sep41- 7Bel fst 6f :221 :46 1:113 Ⓕ Matron 20k 15 - - - - - Eads W 119 w 5.10 - - Petrify1192Light Lady119noFicklebush110½ 15
Broke from outside stalls,left at post
16Aug41- 5Sar my 6f :23 :472 1:133 Ⓕ Spinaway 9.8k 5 4 43½ 33 41½ 11 Eads W 113 w 5.40 84-22 Mar-Kell1131Equipet1131Petrify122½ Driving 8
8Aug41- 6Sar fst 5½f :224 :463 1:062 Ⓕ Schuylerville 6k 1 9 72¾ 75½ 62¾ 22 Roberts P 113 w *1.65 89-12 RompingHome1132Mr-Kll113½PonyBallt1192 Impeded,gamely 15
6Aug41- 4Sar fst 5½f :232 :473 1:063 Ⓕ Md Sp Wt 2 1 1hd 11 13 16 Roberts P 116 w 4.25 90-13 Mar-Kell1166Waygal1161½Frilled116½ Speed in reserve 14
1Aug41- 4Sar fst 5½f :231 :473 1:07 Ⓕ Md Sp Wt 2 5 21½ 23 33½ 44¼ Eads W 116 w 6.60 84-15 Allghny1164Wygl116hdHDddl116nk Close quarters turn,hung 10
23Jly41- 4AP sl 5½f :232 :484 1:014 1:082 Alw 1200 7 7 74½ 73½ 76 64¾ Eads W 110 w 10.80 74-23 K. Dorko113¾Emolument1151½Kirwin113½ No threat 7
16Jly41- 4AP fst 5½f :231 :471 :593 1:063 Ⓕ Alw 1200 3 8 77 56 512 511¼ Shelhamer A 113 w *.90e 77-17 Questvive111noKy. Flash1163Fate116nk Never a factor 8

Market Wise

b. c. 1938, by Brokers Tip (Black Toney)–On Hand, by On Watch — Lifetime record: 53 19 7 10 $222,140

Own.– Louis Tufano
Br.– Estate of Cary T. Grayson (Va)
Tr.– G.W. Carroll

18Sep43- 6Nar fst 1³⁄16 :472 1:12 1:372 1:552 3↑ Nar Spl H 32k 9 8 88¼ 85 32¼ 1hd Longden J 124wb *3.30 98-15 MarktWise124hdAirMastr1004ThumbsUp1222½ Pulled up lame 9
11Sep43- 6Aqu fst 1⁄16 :48 1:12 1:363 1:492 3↑ Edgemere H 17k 1 5 26 35 33 33½ Longden J 126wb *2.15 96-11 Apache120½ShutOut1233MarketWise1262 Saved ground,hung 6
10Jly43- 5Jam fst 1³⁄16 :472 1:12 1:372 1:561 3↑ Butler H 33k 6 9 98½ 99¾ 48 37 Westrope J 127wb *1.85 99-15 Thumbs Up1163Apache1154Market Wise1271 Belated rally 9
5Jly43- 7Suf sly 1⅛ :472 1:122 1:383 1:52 3↑ Mass H 58k 3 6 48 46½ 31 11 Nodarse V 126wb *1.20 81-18 Market Wise1261Salto1031Don Bingo1141½ Driving 6
26Jun43- 6Aqu fst 1¼ :481 1:132 1:383 2:032 3↑ Brooklyn H 33k 9 7 86 42 31½ 21½ Nodarse V 128wb 3.35 88-12 Devil Diver1231½Market Wise128¾Don Bingo1133 Gamely 9
21Jun43- 6Aqu fst 1⅛ :483 1:132 1:382 1:51 3↑ Alw 5000 2 3 36 33 21 21½ Nodarse V 123wb 1.70 90-15 Shut Out1221½Market Wise1237Attention114 Bid,hung 3
12Jun43- 6Aqu fst 7f :23 :461 1:112 1:24 3↑ Carter H 9.7k 7 9 910 914 92¼ 62¾ Nodarse V 122wb 8.60 92-12 Devil Diver126hdMarriage1181Doublrab118nk Some gain 10
31May43- 6Bel fst 1¼ :47 1:111 1:361 2:012 3↑ Suburban H 38k 12 12 155 54¼ 52¼ 22 Eads W 128wb 3.40 91-12 Don Bingo1042ⒹMarket Wise1282½Attention121hd Driving 17
Disqualified for bearing over on rival
25May43- 6Bel fst 1⅛ :46 1:10 1:361 1:493 3↑ Handicap 3050 6 6 67½ 65¼ 51 1hd Grohs O 126wb 5.00 93-14 Market Wise126hdBoysy1121Soldier Song102hd 7
Between leaders,driving
15May43- 6Bel fst 1 :23 :463 1:103 1:363 3↑ Metropolitan H 14k 6 11 1112 1111 1011 78 Nodarse V 126wb 13.85 83-16 Devil Diver1171¼Marriage116¾Thumbs Up1172 Late rush 11
30May42- 6Bel fst 1¼ :481 1:123 1:371 2:014 3↑ Suburban H 38k 8 7 72 41¼ 11½ 12 James B 124wb 4.20 91-07 Market Wise1242Whirlaway1291½Attention1243 Driving 11

16May42- 6Bel	fst 1	:23 :452 1:103 1:362	3↑ Metropolitan H 14k	3 10 911 97½ 97¼ 31¾	James B	125wb	7.85	91-07	Attention1261½Pictor120nkMarket Wise1251	Fast finish	12
9May42- 5Jam	my 1⅛	:473 1:13 1:39 1:52	3↑ Grey Lag H 18k	5 9 815 85½ 44 23↓	Zufelt F	125wb	*2.30	85-14	Marriage109[DH]Market Wise125[DH]Boysy1132	Closed fast	11
7Mar42- 6Hia	fst 1¼	:47 1:122 1:374 2:051	3↑ Widener H 67k	15 16 1512 1314 114¼ 105	Eads W	125wb	2.40	78-17	The Rhymer111hdBest Seller112hdOlympus107nk	Lacked room	17
28Feb42- 5Hia	fst 1⅛	:462 1:112 1:364 1:493	4↑ Sp Wt 2500	4 8 53 31 3½ 11½	Eads W	120wb	3.45	93-14	Market Wise1201½Attention120½War Relic120nk	Ridden out	9
21Feb42- 6Hia	gd 1⅛	:472 1:12 1:38 1:504	3↑ McLennan H 15k	2 11 117¾ 97½ 42½ 1½	Eads W	124wb	4.45e	87-14	Market Wise124½Gramps1141Get Off1161½	Drawing away	15
28Jan42- 6Hia	fst 6½f	:23 :472 1:123 1:192	3↑ Handicap 1600	5 7 714 713 74½ 32½	Eads W	124wb	*2.25	79-21	Zacatine1041½Big Ben1151Market Wise1243	Fast finish	7
	Worked mile in 1:41										
14Jan42- 5Hia	fst 7f	:23 :463 1:113 1:243	4↑ Alw 1500	7 6 611 69 64½ 42¾	Robertson A	117 w	*.85	86-14	Allessandro1141Aboyne109nkLlanero1091½	Outside,gamely	9
13Nov41- 6Pim	fst 1⅝	:48 1:393 2:042 2:431	3↑ Governor Bowie H 12k	8 8 611 35½ 1nk 11½	Eads W	124wb	*1.30	106-09	MarketWise1241½BestSeller101.51½NelliBly1094	Going away	8
30Oct41- 8Pim	fst 1 3/16	:492 1:14 1:393 1:584	3↑ Pim Spl 10k	1 2 23 23 1hd 1hd	Eads W	120wb	-	89-07	Market Wise120hdHaltal126	Hard drive	2
16Oct41- 5Jam	fst 1⅝	:512 1:424 2:073 2:46	3↑ Gallant Fox H 16k	1 2 32 11½ 14 16	Eads W	119wb	*1.40	85-22	MarktWise1196DarkDiscovr1004ShotPut1222½	Much the best	6
4Oct41- 7Bel	fst 2¼	:483 2:304 2:564 3:47	3↑ New York H 58k	4 1 515 2½ 21 22	James B	118wb	*1.25	107-11	Fenelon1192Market Wise1186Corydon1094	Second best	11
27Sep41- 5Bel	fst 2	:492 2:284 2:55 3:204	3↑ J C Gold Cup 10k	4 3 32½ 32 2hd 1no	James B	114wb	4.45	105-09	Market Wise114noWhirlaway1148Fenelon12512	Hard drive	4
	Geldings not eligible										
20Sep41- 6HdG	fst 1 1/16	:233 :48 1:122 1:454	Potomac H 11k	2 7 56½ 64½ 34 21½	Woolf G	120wb	*1.60	87-18	Boston Man1091½Market Wise1203Cape Cod113½	Closed fast	10
6Sep41- 6Aqu	fst 1⅛	:483 1:123 1:372 1:50	3↑ Edgemere H 11k	4 4 53½ 52 31 11½	Eads W	112wb	5.00	102-07	MarktWise1121½RoyalMan1091½Foxbrough1261¾	Going away	7
1Sep41- 6Aqu	fst 1 1/16	:242 :481 1:122 1:433	3↑ Aqueduct H 11k	5 6 55½ 55½ 42½ 33½	Arcaro E	114wb	3.95	92-12	Ponty1052Foxbrough1261½Market Wise1142½	Closed well	6
9Aug41- 6Rkm	fst 1⅛	:48 1:122 1:374 1:502	3↑ Rkm Park H 6.2k	2 3 2½ 1nk 1½ 12	Howell R	115wb	*.80	97-16	MrktWise1152WarBeauty1022¾TragicEndng1054½	Going away	5
2Aug41- 6Rkm	fst 1 1/16	:232 :464 1:113 1:44	3↑ Granite State H 6.7k	7 5 54 43½ 3¾ 31¾	Taylor WL	116wb	*2.30	94-14	Tragic Ending102¾CapeCod1091Market Wise1162¾	Weakened	9
16Jly41- 7Suf	fst 1⅛	:463 1:111 1:354 1:483	3↑ Mass H 67k	7 9 74¼ 53¾ 44½ 46½	Donoso R	111wb	4.70	94-13	War Relic102¾Foxbrough1223½Royal Man1062¼	No mishap	9
4Jly41- 7Suf	fst 1 3/16	:473 1:12 1:38 1:563	Yankee H 31k	9 6 44¾ 52 2hd 21	Donoso R	121wb	*2.30	97-13	OurBoots1221MarktWise1212¾RobertMorris1211¾	Weakened	9
21Jun41- 5Aqu	fst 1¼	:49 1:132 1:383 2:032	Dwyer 11k	2 2 33 32½ 21½ 21¼	James B	122wb	10.60	97-08	Whirlaway1261¼Market Wise1222½Robert Morris11912		4
	Altered course,second best										
17Jun41- 5Aqu	fst 1 1/16	:25 :49 1:132 1:45	3↑ Handicap 2065	4 2 2hd 11½ 11½ 11½	Eads W	115wb	2.80	89-11	Market Wise1151½Choppy Sea110½Devil's Crag109½	Driving	8
23May41- 6Bel	fst 1⅛	:463 1:11 1:362 1:49	Peter Pan H 10k	1 7 79 711 66 511¼	Meade D	119wb	4.95	86-17	RobertMorrs1176BrghtGllnt1105KngCol124hd	Close quarters	7
13May41- 5Bel	fst 7f	:23 :463 1:104 1:242	Alw 2000	2 6 613 67½ 58½ 47½	Meade D	126wb	6.70	80-14	AirBrigade1154SheriffCulkin113½MondyLunch1163	No mishap	6
3May41- 7CD	fst 1¼	:463 1:113 1:372 2:012	Ky Derby 73k	7 5 612 66 53¾ 38¼	Anderson I	126wb	19.10	94-08	Whirlaway1268Staretor126nkMarket Wise1262	Late speed	11
26Apr41- 5Jam	fst 1 1/16	:231 :471 1:123 1:453	Wood Memorial 23k	1 8 76½ 64¾ 31½ 1no	Meade D	120wb	8.30	85-16	MarketWise120noCuriousCoin1201½KingCole1205	Hard drive	9
12Apr41- 4Jam	fst 6f	:232 :47 1:12	Alw 2000	4 4 66¼ 56¾ 45¼ 32½	Meade D	113wb	4.00	89-11	Zacatine113hdKansas1132½Market Wise1134	Closed fast	6
5Apr41- 4TrP	gd 6f	:221 :472 1:111	Alw 1000	5 8 89¼ 810 87½ 99¾	Eads W	115wb	*2.30	84-14	Silvestra105.51Ponty1154Bad Cold1071	Dull effort	9
20Feb41- 5Hia	fst 7f	:223 :452 1:112 1:242	Alw 1400	5 3 36 24 22 11½	Arcaro E	120wb	*1.55	91-15	Market Wise1201½Blue Lily1061Maepeace1114	Going away	7
13Feb41- 6Hia	gd 1⅛	:472 1:12 1:37 1:503	Alw 1400	5 2 2½ 1½ 15 13	Eads W	113wb	*1.60	88-11	Market Wise1133Jacopus1132Clarksville1082½	In hand	7
1Feb41- 6Hia	fst 7f	:224 :453 1:10 1:222	Bahamas H 7k	6 13 1214 1114 611 513	Anderson I	114wb	13.55	88-09	Dispose1182Curious Coin1105Battle Colors1213	Off slowly	15
17Jan41- 5Hia	my 7f	:231 :463 1:122 1:253	Alw 1400	7 6 54½ 44 33 33½	Eads W	117wb	2.35	81-26	Clarksville113hdBattleColors1113½MrktWs1176	Closed well	7
11Jan41- 6Hia	gd 6f	:23 :462 1:113	Hialeah 6.5k	8 10 119 106 62¼ 31½	Eads W	116wb	6.25	89-18	Zacatine116hdBattleColors1161½MarketWis1165	Closed fast	12
4Jan41- 6TrP	fst 1 70	:23 :471 1:121 1:421	Alw 1000	1 5 51¾ 1½ 13 15	Eads W	111wb	*2.15	98-08	Market Wise1115Version1131Take Wing1114	Going away	10
28Dec40- 4TrP	hy 6f	:23 :471 1:142	Alw 1000	9 1 23 21 14 15	Eads W	116wb	38.80	78-29	Market Wise1165Version1161Ponty116no	Easily	9
20Dec40- 4TrP	fst 6f	:224 :46 1:114	Alw 1000	2 8 89 86¼ 811 89½	Anderson I	114wb	31.95	81-14	Zacatine1141½Isolde1112Cape Cod1171	Outrun	10
25Oct40- 2Emp	fst 1 70	:233 :474 1:133 1:451	Md 1750	8 4 41 22 1nk 11½	Anderson I	114wb	43.55	84-13	Market Wise1141½Kahyrite114¾Port Alibi1144	Going away	13
16Oct40- 1Jam	fst 6f	:231 :47 1:13	©Md 1750	12 10 87¼ 1216 1016 715	Westrope J	114wb	110.15	72-16	Okabbit1181¼Rancho's Boy1103¼Dandy Fox1182½	Outrun	14
	Previously owned by Brookmeade Stable;previously trained by H. Fontaine										
19Sep40- 2Aqu	fst 6f	:23 :47 1:121	Md 1500	14 9 116½ 1115 87¾ 1013½	Robertson A	111 w	30.05	82-05	RemoteControl1111GranoSaltis1136CynicMiss1083¼	Outrun	14
13Sep40- 1Aqu	fst 6f	:23 :471 1:14	Md 1500	2 2 96 58 55¼ 64	Robertson A	111 w	61.00	83-09	Battle Won106½Outgo114noCynic Miss108½	No mishap	14
19Aug40- 2Sar	sly 6f	:23 :471 1:13	Clm 2500	16 14 1612 1614 168 1714¼	Robertson A	112 w	*1.30f	73-11	Yankee Party1123½Etruscan112½Family Doc112½	Outrun	18
2Aug40- 4Sar	fst 5½f	:224 :464 1:053	Alw 1200	8 12 1010 109¾ 1112 1312¾	Fels B	112 w	81.45e	82-13	Swing and Sway1163½Neutrality116½Thrift Shop116½	Outrun	13
29Jly40- 2Sar	fst 5½f	:223 :461 1:061	©Md Sp Wt	19 21 2118 2121 2122 2021	Robertson A	117 w	6.80f	71-08	MondyLnch1172Maerunway117½PeepShow1171	Raced greenly	21

Mercator

b. g. 1939, by Annapolis (Man o' War)–Ponova, by Pommern

Lifetime record: 46 11 10 9 $64,957

Own.– W.H. Lipscomb
Br.– Thomas H. Somerville (Va)
Tr.– W.G. Jones

18Aug49- 3Sar	hy *2	S'Chase	4:292	3↑ Alw 2500	7 1 58½ - - -	Leonard W	146wb	*1.25e	- -	Kipper14350Oak Bulger1513Bannock Laddie14415		8
	Tired,bolted off course											
11Jun46- 5Aqu	fst *2½	S'Chase	4:511	4↑ Hitchcock H 11k	3 1 1½ 1nk 32½ 32¼	Leonard W	156wb	*.90	- -	Delhi Dan133¾War Battle1391½Mercator15614	Tired	5
4Jun46- 5Bel	fst *2	S'Chase	3:541	4↑ Lion Heart H 9.2k	6 1 14 1hd 21½ 23½	Leonard W	156wb	*1.60	- -	Burma Road1523½Mercator1563Floating Isle1492½	Bobbled	8
28May46- 5Bel	hy *2½	S'Chase	4:581	4↑ Meadowbrook H 11k	4 1 110 18 13 13	Leonard W	150wb	2.65	- -	Mercator1503Beneksar1347Burma Road1521	In hand	8
22May46- 5Bel	fst *2	S'Chase	3:493	4↑ Corinthian H 9.4k	11 1 11 - - -	Leonard W	154 w	*1.80	- -	Burma Road1461Navigate1422War Battle1436	Fell at 8th	12
10May46- 5Bel	fst *2	S'Chase	3:45	4↑ International H 8.6k	5 1 15 11½ 32½ 33½	Leonard W	155wb	*1.65	- -	Fleettown1351Annotator1362½Mrctor1557	Bobbled 8th,tired	6
28Nov45- 5Pim	sly 2½	S'Chase	5:252	4↑ Manly H 12k	8 2 23 521 515 531	Leonard W	153wb	2.90e	- -	PursuitPlane1325BurmaRoad13912GreekFlag1384	Tired badly	10
21Nov45- 5Pim	sl *2	S'Chase	3:544	3↑ Battleship H 12k	5 1 2hd 46 412 518	Leonard W	159wb	*1.25	- -	Elkridge146noNavigate1368Cadd1465	Dropped back after 1m	7
14Nov45- 3Pim	fst 2	S'Chase	3:502	3↑ Handicap 5000	6 2 63½ 37 33½ 32¾	Leonard W	160wb	*1.45	- -	Cosey130¾Floating Isle1492Mercator1602	Good try	7
6Nov45- 5Bel	fst *3	S'Chase	5:50	4↑ Temple Gwathmey H 15k	1 1 1hd - - -	Leonard W	160wb	*1.05e	- -	Caddie1396Refugio1304Floating Isle1493	Fell 12th	8
31Oct45- 5Pim	fst 2	S'Chase	3:501	4↑ J Spencer H (Div 2) 11k	5 1 13 15 13 16	Leonard W	153wb	*1.20	- -	Mercator1536Floating Isle1525Lieut. Well1345	Handily	7
17Oct45- 3Lrl	fst *2½	S'Chase	5:001	4↑ Chevy Chase H 8.7k	2 2 12 12 13 16	Leonard W	145wb	*1.75	- -	Mercator1456Shotlo1303½Floating Isle15150	Easily	6
12Oct45- 3Lrl	fst *2	S'Chase	3:54	3↑ Butler H 6.4k	4 2 1hd 33 413 421	Leonard W	147wb	*1.35	- -	Great Flare1302Floating Isle15115Bill Coffman1334		9
	Bobbled 10th,tired											
3Oct45- 5Bel	fst *3	S'Chase	5:48	4↑ Grand National H 18k	3 1 14 11½ 12 15	Owen W	142wb	2.85e	- -	Mercator1425Caddie139¾Raylywn1426	Easily	12
26Sep45- 5Bel	fst *2½	S'Chase	4:484	4↑ Brook H 9.3k	2 2 11 - - -	Leonard W	143wb	*.95e	- -	Raylywn1376Rouge Dragon1552Elkridge148no	Fell at 12th	10
11Sep45- 5Aqu	my *2½	S'Chase	4:511	4↑ Glendale H 8.6k	3 1 13 14 2hd 2nk	Leonard W	143wb	2.90	- -	FloatingIsle150nkMercator1437SoldrSong1403	Bobbled last	5
4Sep45- 5Aqu	fst *2	S'Chase	3:42	3↑ Harbor Hill H 6k	2 2 110 14 1hd 1½	Leonard W	140wb	3.80	- -	Mrctor140½Elkrdg1533FlotngIsl1512½	Bobbled several fences	7
1Sep45- 3Bel	fst *2	S'Chase	3:503	4↑ Alw 3000	3 1 12 16 130 150	Leonard W	152wb	2.45	- -	Mercator15250Similar1374Invader137	Speed on flat	5
25Aug45- 3Bel	sl *2	S'Chase	3:542	3↑ Alw 3000	6 1 12 1nk 11 12	Harrison JS	139wb	*1.20	- -	Mercator1392Blue Funk1302½Parma1385	Jumped well	9
10Aug45- 3Bel	fst *2	S'Chase	3:491	4↑ Shillelah 6.1k	3 1 32 21½ 33 32	McGovern J	137wb	*1.10e	- -	Raylywn1361Rouge Dragon1521Mercator1376	Hung	10
6Aug45- 3Bel	hy *2	S'Chase	4:084	4↑ Alw 3000	14 1 18 1hd 1hd 2hd	McGovern J	137wb	9.10	- -	BrothrJons139hdMrctor1373BoojumII149nk	Swerved final ⅛	14
27Jun45- 3Del	fst *2	S'Chase	3:503	4↑ Georgetown H 12k	2 1 11 42 35½ 47	McGovern J	137wb	*1.50e	- -	Iron Shot150½Rouge Dragon1596Elkridge159½	Weakened	8
18Jun45- 5Bel	fst *2	S'Chase	3:484	4↑ Corinthian H 5.7k	5 2 13 1nk 2½ 23	Leonard W	138wb	*2.65	- -	Floating Isle1423Mercator1387Chesapeake1381	No match	8
12Jun45- 5Bel	fst *2	S'Chase	3:49	4↑ CL Appleton 5.7k	6 1 21 3¾ 24 36	Leonard W	139wb	3.10	- -	Elkridge158hdFloatingIsl1496Mrctor13910	Bad landing 4th	8
19Aug44- 3Bel	fst *2	S'Chase	3:49	3↑ Alw 3000	4 2 - - - -	Jennings E	140 w	*1.25	- -	Gay Venture1382Bill Coffman1474Frederic II1474	Fell	6
11Aug44- 5Bel	fst *2	S'Chase	3:48	4↑ Shillelah 5.7k	2 3 11½ 1½ 21 21½	Leonard W	141wb	5.45	- -	Elkridge1461½Mercator1417Floating Isle13510	No mishap	7
4Aug44- 3Bel	fst *2	S'Chase	3:491	4↑ Handicap 3000	8 4 45½ 510 53¾ 54¾	Leonard W	149wb	4.20	- -	Elkrdg1541¼FrdrcII1401½BurmRod1382	Bad landing 5th,tired	10
28Jun44- 4Del	fst *2½	S'Chase	4:504	4↑ Indian River H 7.5k	2 3 31½ 58 37½ 39	Harrison JS	141wb	2.90e	- -	Rouge Dragon1612Caddie1437Mercator14110	Early speed	6

31May44- 5Bel fst *2½ S'Chase 4:52 4↑ Meadow Brook H 7k 1 1 1hd 412 629 644½ Owen W 143wb 7.60 - - Iron Shot1593½Brother Jones1616Knight's Quest1473 6
Bad landing 4th,tired
20May44- 3Bel fst *2 S'Chase 3:492 4↑ Alw 2500 1 3 41½ 31½ 22 24 Owen W 150 w *.95 - - Frederic II1544Mercator1501½Simoon1383 Bobbled several 7
10May44- 3Pim fst 2 S'Chase 3:502 4↑ Handicap 3000 6 3 21 2½ 21½ 22½ Owen W 157 w *.70 - - Mad Policy1412½Mercator1573Circus13920 Bobbled 6
5May44- 5Pim fst 2 S'Chase 3:511 4↑ J Spencer H 12k 1 3 23 21 41 21½ Harrison JS 144 w *1.10e - - Rouge Dragon1571½Mercator144nkCaddie1481½ Gamely 10
20Nov43- 3Mtp fst *2½ S'Chase 5:47 4↑ Noel Laing H 1.4k 7 - - - - - Morlan M 145 w 4.00 - - Iron Shot1544Corrigan155½Bank Note1466 Fell 8
8Nov43- 5Pim my 2½ S'Chase 5:093 4↑ Manly H 9.1k 6 1 32¾ 2nk 45½ 315¼ Clements HW 139 w *1.95e - - Iron Shot146nkCaddie13915Mercator1393 No mishap 6
1Nov43- 5Pim fst 2 S'Chase 3:571 3↑ Battleship H 6.9k 10 1 1nk 11½ 21 31½ Clements HW 139wb *1.30e - - Knight's Quest1411Invader144½Mercator1392 Driving 10
26Oct43- 5Pim sly 2½ S'Chase 5:181 4↑ Chevy Chase H 9.3k 7 2 2hd 21½ 425 423¾ Harrison JS 137 w 3.00 - - Uncle Seaweed137¾Caddie13820Invader1453 Nothing left 7
16Oct43- 3Pim sl 2 S'Chase 4:043 3↑ Alw 1500 1 2 22½ 13 112 112 Harrison JS 150 w *1.25 - - Mercator15012Mad Policy14015Parma14620 Driving 5
5Oct43- 3Bel fst *2 S'Chase 3:524 3↑ Alw 1800 1 3 32 41¾ 32½ 1hd Harrison JS 144wb *1.80 - - Mercator144hdGreek Flag1484The Beak14620 Driving 5
Previously owned by Mrs W.G. Jones
9Aug43- 3Bel fst *2 S'Chase 3:49 3↑ Sp Wt 1500 2 1 12 11½ 11 11½ Jennings E 147wb *1.50e - - Mercator1471½YankeeChance148nkGrekFlg13720 Drifting out 6
Previously owned by Montpelier
29Jly43- 3Bel gd *2 S'Chase 3:504 4↑ Alw 1500 5 1 11½ 32 37 311 Jennings E 147 w 4.40 - - Delhi Dan1538Yankee Chance1483Mercator1472 Tired 6
10Jun43- 3Aqu gd *1½ Hurdles 2:45 3↑ Handicap 1500 12 9 111 67 813 1028 Owen W 138 w 3.50e - - GuineaClub1364GalleyBoy142½TopMilk143½ Never a factor 12
3Jun43- 3Bel fst *2 S'Chase 4:00 4↑ Alw 1500 2 1 11½ 12 23 24 Harrison JS 139 w 3.60 - - SilverBirch1344Merctor1395Cortsno14720 Bad landing 12th 7
21Nov42- 1Mtp fst *1½ Hurdles 3:033 3↑ Alw 500 7 5 2½ 16 110 110 Jennings E 137 w - - - Mercator13710Walloper14315Matsonia1388 Easily 7
12Nov42- 3Bel fst *2 S'Chase 4:09 3↑ OMdClm 1200 6 3 35 - - - Owen W 130 w *.85 - - WoodKing1445Fieldfare1404Ffty-Ffty135150 Lost rider 7th 6
Previously trained by S.L. Burch
5Nov42- 3Bel fst *2 S'Chase 4:032 3↑ OClm 1200 4 4 45¾ 2hd 1nk 22 Owen W 130 w 4.20 - - Equirita1422Merctor13010Sfght14015 Bid,bore in,faltered 5

14Jly41- 3Emp fst 5½f :223 :461 1:061 ©Md Sp Wt 6 5 57½ 513 611 614½ Schmidl A 116 w 35.80 80-10 Toujour1165Hard Blast116hdYar1163 No mishap 9
Ran under the name Ponap

Mioland

b. c. 1937, by Mio d'Arezzo (Laland)–Iolanda, by Vespasian **Lifetime record: 50 18 10 6 $244,270**

Own.– C.S. Howard
Br.– H.W. Ray (Ore)
Tr.– J.H. Stotler

2Aug43- 6Bel fst 1⅛ :464 1:112 1:364 1:494 3↑ Handicap 3080 3 3 21 1½ 1nk 1no Atkinson T 117wb 2.65 92-16 Mioland117noCorydon114nkRoyal Nap1125 Hard pressured 6
Previously trained by T. Smith
14Jly43- 6Jam fst 1⅛ :48 1:13 1:383 1:513 3↑ Handicap 3550 5 4 47 54¼ 45¼ 33½ Shelhamer A 112wb 8.85 86-15 FirstFiddle1221½Lochinvar1182Mioland112no Belated rally 5
26Jun43- 6Aqu fst 1¼ :481 1:132 1:383 2:032 3↑ Brooklyn H 33k 1 2 43 66½ 78¼ 716¼ Atkinson T 112wb 33.80 74-12 Devil Diver1231½Market Wise128¾Don Bingo1133 No mishap 9
14Jun43- 6Aqu fst 1⅛ :483 1:134 1:393 1:522 3↑ Handicap 3025 2 4 45½ 45 47 47½ Shelhamer A 117wb 3.40 77-17 Pomayya1122Lochinvr1171½SoldrSong1125 Dropped back,wide 4
31May43- 6Bel fst 1¼ :47 1:111 1:361 2:012 3↑ Suburban H 38k 4 9 168 107 128¾ 1210½ Shelhamer A 119wb 52.75 82-12 DonBingo1042[D]MarketWis1282½Attnton121hd Never a factor 17
1May43- 6Pim fst 1 3/16 :471 1:113 1:372 1:562 3↑ Dixie H 23k 1 4 43½ 56 76¾ 77¼ Wright WD 122wb 8.40 94-13 Riverland123¾Attention123noAnticlimax1134 7
Outrun,unwilling to extend
24Apr43- 5Jam fst 1 1/16 :242 :481 1:131 1:442 3↑ Excelsior H 12k 9 9 96¾ 1012 1017 1019¾ Robertson A 121wb 16.75 71-15 Riverland1245Minee-Mo1082½Marriage121no Never a factor 11
27Mar43- 7FG fst 1⅛ :472 1:114 1:364 1:493 3↑ American H 10k 4 5 53½ 43½ 21½ 2no Shelhamer A 118wb 3.40e 105-12 Marriage117noMioland1182½Rounders1263 6
Saved ground,getting to winner
13Mar43- 6FG fst 1 1/16 :24 :474 1:12 1:44 3↑ Fort Jackson H 5k 2 3 45 43 33 33 Haskell L 119wb 3.00e 96-15 Riverland123noValdina Orphan1253Mioland1194 No excuse 5
27Feb43- 7FG fst 1 1/16 :234 :462 1:112 1:434 3↑ New Orleans H 27k 4 9 99¾ 98¼ 910 42¾ Haskell L 120wb 11.20e 99-09 Marriage1151½Rounders124½Moscow II108¾ Fast finish 10
18Feb43- 5FG fst 1 1/16 :252 :494 1:144 1:48 4↑ Alw 1000 2 2 2hd 1hd 1hd 1hd Haskell L 124wb *.30 81-15 [D]Mioland124hdBriton115noPaprboy1106 Bothered rival str 4
Disqualified and placed second
6May42- 6Pim fst 1 3/16 :472 1:114 1:374 1:57 3↑ Dixie H 25k 4 2 67¾ 66¼ 41¼ 31¼ Haas L 126 w 7.95 97-12 Whirlaway128¾Attention124½Mioland126hd Held well 8
25Apr42- 5HdG fst 1 1/16 :241 :482 1:13 1:452 3↑ Philadelphia H 11k 5 5 55 31 1½ 2no Shelhamer A 124wb *1.55 91-21 Challedon122noMolnd1241½CpCod1123 Forced wide,hung late 7
10Apr42- 6TrP fst 1⅛ :47 1:104 1:36 1:49 3↑ Tropical H 11k 4 6 31 2½ 2nk 2nk Haas L 129wb *.75e 104-10 Sir Marlboro109nkMioland129½Our Boots1196 Driving 8
21Mar42- 6TrP fst 1⅛ :471 1:113 1:361 1:492 3↑ Coral Gables H 8.7k 2 5 31½ 11 14 14 Haas L 125wb *2.25 102-10 Mioland1254Signator1041½Llanero102hd Easily 10
7Mar42- 6Hia fst 1¼ :47 1:122 1:374 2:051 3↑ Widener H 67k 16 8 55½ 31½ 61 83½ Haas L 128wb 6.05e 79-17 The Rhymer111hdBest Seller112hdOlympus107nk Faltered 17
28Feb42- 5Hia fst 1⅛ :462 1:112 1:364 1:493 4↑ Sp Wt 2500 2 9 84¾ 62½ 43½ 42¼ Haas L 122 w *2.10e 91-14 Market Wise1201½Attention120½War Relic120nk Forced wide 9
20Feb42- 4Hia sly 1⅛ :473 1:122 1:38 1:511 4↑ Alw 1500 5 3 33 2½ 1½ 11¾ Haas L 124wb 2.35e 85-22 Mioland1241¾Sir Marlboro1123Porter's Cap1221 Drew away 5
26Jly41- 7Hol fst 1⅝ :473 1:382 2:042 2:442 3↑ Sunset H 27k 9 3 2½ 13 1hd 2no Haas L 128wb *.60 - - King Torch105noMioland1281Wing and Wing105hd Weakened 9
19Jly41- 7Hol fst 1¼ :46 1:104 1:361 2:023 3↑ Hol Gold Cup 88k 6 5 74¼ 33 34½ 32½ Haas L 130wb *.80e 94-06 BigPbbl119nkPprboy982¼Molnd1303½ Strong drive,held well 13
4Jly41- 7Hol fst 1⅛ :462 1:104 1:364 1:492 3↑ American H 22k 1 5 54½ 41¼ 11½ 1no Haas L 126wb 5.40 98-09 Mioland126noWoof Woof1141Big Pebble117½ Driving 10
30May41- 6Bel fst 1¼ :473 1:123 1:371 2:023 3↑ Suburban H 35k 4 3 52¾ 52¼ 2nk 56 Haas L 127wb *1.15 81-16 Your Chance1141¼Hash119nkShot Put1102½ Stopped 9
20May41- 6Bel fst 1 1/16 :234 :463 1:113 1:433 3↑ Alw 2500 5 1 23 22 21½ 22¼ Haas L 127 w 3.00 91-12 Whirlaway1082¼Mioland127nkHash1203 Weakened 5
7May41- 6Pim fst 1 3/16 :481 1:121 1:381 1:582 3↑ Dixie H 25k 1 5 42 64 31 2hd Haas L 129wb *.95 91-18 Haltal110hdMioland129¾Dit110no Just missed 10
8Mar41- 6SA fst 1½ :471 1:121 2:03 2:291 3↑ S Juan Capistrano H 61k 16 4 2nk 11 11 13 Haas L 130wb *2.30 106-09 Mioland1303Gen'l Manager1074Barrancosa1063 Easily best 17
1Mar41- 6SA sly 1¼ :47 1:121 1:383 2:052 3↑ S Anita H 124k 11 8 96½ 32½ 21½ 2nk Haas L 124wb *1.00e 79-29 Bay View108nkMioland1244Bolingbroke1062 Just missed 16
22Feb41- 6SA sl 1 1/16 :234 :473 1:121 1:452 3↑ San Antonio H 12k 6 6 35 35 34½ 1no Haas L 128wb *1.80 85-23 Mioland128noHysterical1111Bay View1051 Just up 11
8Feb41- 6SA sl 7f :23 :463 1:113 1:242 3↑ San Carlos H 13k 3 6 31½ 33 35 44 Haas L 130wb *.90 86-26 Gen'lManager1104Viscounty116noHysterical118no No mishap 12
11Jan41- 6SA my 1⅛ :472 1:123 1:382 1:513 3↑ San Pasqual H 12k 8 8 36 2hd 12 14 Haas L 130wb *1.10 86-22 Mioland1304Gen'lManager1123ValdinaGroom1005 Easily best 9
1Jan41- 6SA hy 1 :232 :472 1:131 1:393 3↑ New Year H 12k 4 7 65 3nk 11 1nk Haas L 126wb *1.60 80-31 Mioland126nkGen'l Manager1095Sweepida1192½ Hard drive 8
2Nov40- 5Emp hy 1 3/16 :48 1:13 1:393 2:001 3↑ Westchester H 22k 1 2 52¾ 35 1nk 1¾ Haas L 119wb *1.05 86-22 Mioland119¾Foxbrough1106Hash1223 Drew out 8
8Oct40- 5Jam fst 1 1/16 :234 :472 1:124 1:453 3↑ Handicap 2520 2 5 510 32 1nk 12¾ Arcaro E 126wb *.80 85-13 Mioland1262¾Gen'lManagr1121¼KsrofAudly1074½ Going away 5
26Sep40- 6Bel fst 1 :234 :474 1:113 1:371 Jerome H 9k 3 - - - - - Vedder RL 125wb *1.10 - - Roman1212Weigh Anchor112nkTola Rose1164 5
Stumbled after start,lost rider
21Sep40- 5HdG fst 1 1/16 :232 :472 1:122 1:444 Potomac H 11k 4 6 51½ 1hd 11½ 14 Bierman C 124wb *.95 94-15 Mioland1244Roncat100¾Guerrilla1081¼ Going away 8
10Aug40- 6Was sly 1¼ :493 1:143 1:394 2:054 American Derby 59k 3 3 11½ 11 11 13 Adams J 123wb 6.10 81-29 Mioland1233Sirocco1264Weigh Anchor1183½ Going away 5
20Jly40- 7Hol fst 1¼ :462 1:112 1:374 2:033 Hol Derby 27k 2 4 55½ 45 43½ 43¾ Wall N 118wb *1.00 91-08 Big Flash1141¼Weigh Anchor114hdSweepida1222½ No excuse 11
13Jly40- 6Hol fst 1⅛ :464 1:112 1:381 1:511 Alw 2500 4 5 46½ 55 3½ 12 Pollard J 126wb *2.10 93-05 Mioland1262Weigh Anchor119¾Woof Woof119½ Going away 7
11May40- 6Pim fst 1 3/16 :47 1:12 1:384 1:583 Preakness 70k 7 4 79 62¾ 32 23 Balaski L 126wb 9.70 87-15 Bimelech1263Mioland1261½Gallahadion1262 Closed fast 9
4May40- 7CD fst 1¼ :48 1:124 1:383 2:05 Ky Derby 72k 3 3 53 54¼ 43 42½ Balaski L 126wb 6.40 81-14 Gallahadion1261½Bimelech126noDit1261 No mishap 8
9Mar40- 6SA fst 1 1/16 :224 :463 1:113 1:451 S Juan Capistrano H 13k 5 7 76½ 32 22½ 11¼ Adams J 117wb *3.00 86-14 Mioland1171¼Weigh Anchor1152½Sweepida1221 Driving 14
22Feb40- 6SA fst 1⅛ :463 1:112 1:374 1:513 S Anita Derby 61k 2 16 1512 99¾ 613½ 42¼ Pollard J 120wb 13.30 84-16 Sweepida1201¼Royal Crusader1201Weigh Anchor120hd 17
Closed strongly
10Feb40- 6SA fst 1 :222 :462 1:112 1:384 San Vicente H 15k 9 9 86½ 1112 1317 137¼ Adams J 120wb 5.80 77-14 Gallahadion1131Sweepida107hdExarch113½ Outrun 19
Previously owned by Hawthorn Stable;previously trained by H.C. Fear
27Jan40- 5SA fst 1 :223 :461 1:112 1:38 Alw 1500 8 3 2hd 2hd 1hd 12½ Dew E 114wb 10.10 88-12 Mioland1142½Gallahadion1061The Gob108½ Easily best 10
18Jan40- 6SA fst 6f :222 :454 1:112 Handicap 2000 5 6 51½ 55 47 44¾ Dew E 112wb 8.00 87-12 Millfang1081½Destrer1063½Little Cartago103hd No mishap 7
1Jan40- 4SA fst 6f :221 :454 1:112 Alw 1500 7 1 42 46 55¾ 36 Dew E 112wb 20.00 86-16 Augury108noCamp Verde1166Mioland1124 Closed well 7
28Oct39- 7BM fst 1 :233 :471 1:12 1:383 Handicap 2000 6 3 31 33 34 1no Dew E 111wb 12.60e 87-17 Mioland111noBig Ben119¾Sweepida1141 Just up 9

19Oct39- 5BM	fst 6f	:23 :462 1:112	Alw 800	4 3 33 45 36½ 28	Dew E	112wb	*.90e	84-17	Augury1158Mioland1125Wee Toney112¾	Second best 7
10Oct39- 6BM	fst 6f	:23 :464 1:121	Alw 800	8 1 3½ 2hd 1hd 13½	Dew E	114wb	5.40	88-20	Mioland1143½Brother Higher1172Shervill1092	Going away 8
24Aug39- 2Lga	fst 5f	:232 :473 1:00	Md Alw 400	4 3 2½ 1hd 1½ 14	Sena T	116wb	*.50	91-12	Mioland1164Black Haw1032½Lacona1111½	Drew away 8
12Aug39- 4Lga	fst 5f	:231 :471 1:003	Md Alw 500	8 7 44 43½ 32 3hd	Merritt N	113wb	2.40	88-15	HelenI.113noIdaB.110noMiolnd113hd	Greenly,finished fast 9

Miss Request

b. f. 1945, by Requested (Questionnaire)–Throttle Wide, by Flying Heels — **Lifetime record: 56 12 6 5 $202,730**

Own.– Mrs B.F. Whitaker
Br.– B.F. Whitaker (Ky)
Tr.– J.P. Conway

25May50- 7Bel	fst 7f	:23 :461 1:104 1:232 3↑	Handicap 4620	4 13 147 146 1511 1517¾	Guerin E	114wb	18.20	75-07	Navy Chief1141High Trend1131Colosal119½	No factor 15
4Feb50- 6SA	fst 1⅛	:471 1:114 1:372 1:501 4↑	Handicap 5000	7 4 55½ 811 913 919	Brooks S	111wb	12.70	73-14	Safe Arrival116½Top's Boy117noBut Why Not1182½	Tired 9
25Jan50- 7SA	fst 1	:223 :461 1:112 1:373 4↑	Handicap 5000	1 3 67½ 711 711 711	Porch G	113wb	16.05	78-17	Fervent1201¼Knockdown1201¼Autocrat1111½	No factor 8
14Jan50- 7SA	my 1⅛	:472 1:121 1:393 1:524 3↑	ⒻS Margarita H 59k	1 5 55½ 69½ 79 816	Arcaro E	117wb	5.00	63-21	Two Lea1262Gaffery1182½But Why Not1163½	Disliked going 8
5Jan50- 7SA	fst 7f	:224 :46 1:11 1:233 4↑	ⒻHandicap 10000	6 5 53 44½ 65½ 77¼	Porch G	118 w	17.35	84-18	Two Lea122nkGaffery1162Sweet Dream1161½	Tired 10
29Dec49- 7SA	fst 6f	:232 :47 1:111 3↑	ⒻAlw 5000	2 6 55 58½ 69¼ 610	Porch G	119 w	12.10	81-21	Two Lea119hdSweet Dream1161½But Why Not1114	Tired 7
22Oct49- 6Jam	fst 1 1/16	:233 :471 1:121 1:451 3↑	ⒻComely H 29k	5 3 45½ 45 44½ 74¼	Arcaro E	121wb	*1.70	83-17	Lithe1071¼But Why Not1162Gaffery116no	No rally 12
8Oct49- 6Bel	fst 2	:501 2:323 2:573 3:224 3↑	J C Gold Cup 54k	1 4 27 2½ 33 34	Arcaro E	121wb	5.80	86-12	Ponder1172½Flying Missel1241½Miss Request1215	Hung 6
3Oct49- 6Bel	fst 1½	:482 1:131 2:033 2:294 3↑	ⒻLadies H 35k	4 5 53 1½ 11½ 2no	Arcaro E	119wb	3.90	89-14	Gaffery114noMiss Request119nkAdile1151½	Just missed 12
17Sep49- 6Aqu	fst 1⅛	:48 1:124 1:384 1:524 3↑	ⒻBeldame H 72k	14 5 57½ 22 2hd 11	Arcaro E	113 w	6.20	83-17	MissRequest1131[D]Harmonica1121¼Plunder108hd	Drew clear 18
8Sep49- 6Aqu	sly 1 1/16	:241 :482 1:134 1:463 3↑	ⒻHandicap 4550	4 4 31½ 3½ 2hd 53½	Arcaro E	115 w	*1.35	77-16	Gaffery1162½Loraine108noPail of Water1081	Tired 6
17Aug49- 6Sar	sly 1⅛	:483 1:131 1:392 1:522 3↑	ⒻDiana H 11k	7 2 52¼ 35 44½ 413	Glisson G	115 w	*1.50	75-19	Spats1068Adile115½Gaffery1154	Raced wide,tired 7
9Aug49- 6Sar	fst 1⅛	:482 1:13 1:374 1:502 3↑	Handicap 4070	3 2 21½ 2hd 2hd 2hd	Atkinson T	114 w	6.40	98-11	Stunts120hdMiss Request1141½Arise112no	Game effort 7
16Jly49- 6Jam	fst 1 3/16	:472 1:122 1:372 1:571 3↑	Butler H 58k	3 3 54 52¾ 912 1018	Atkinson T	106 w	15.30	72-14	Conniver112noPalestinian1143Stunts1051	Went wide,quit 10
2Jly49- 6Aqu	fst 1¼	:484 1:13 1:372 2:024 3↑	Brooklyn H 58k	6 4 21 1½ 42½ 95½	Delahoussaye J	108 w	19.15	87-14	Assault122¾Vulcan's Forge129nkFlying Missel117¾	Tired 10
29Jun49- 5Aqu	fst 1 1/16	:244 :49 1:134 1:453 3↑	ⒻHandicap 5025	1 3 32½ 31½ 11 13½	Arcaro E	122 w	*1.45	86-14	Miss Request1223½Quibble1115My Emma115no	Handily 5
18Jun49- 6Del	sly 1 1/16	:241 :483 1:133 1:462 3↑	ⒻNew Castle H 29k	3 2 34 35 35 59	Delahoussaye J	115 w	5.10	72-28	Allie's Pal1143½Paddleduck1194Dobodura1101½	Tired 5
14Jun49- 6Aqu	fst 6f	:231 :472 1:133 3↑	ⒻHandicap 5035	2 3 46½ 33½ 31½ 1½	Atkinson T	120 w	2.55	84-28	Miss Request120½Quibble114hdSweet Dream12614	Driving 4
2Jun49- 6Bel	fst 1	:232 :464 1:121 1:381 3↑	ⒻHandicap 5035	1 1 12 2hd 23 36	Arcaro E	119 w	*1.00	77-16	My Emma1104½Back Talk1061½Miss Request1198	Weakened 5
26May49- 6Bel	fst 1	:231 :463 1:12 1:381 3↑	ⒻHandicap 5060	1 7 65½ 69 56½ 58	Arcaro E	122 w	2.95	75-20	Paddleduck1161½Allie's Pal1164Gay Mood1061½	No factor 7
5May49- 6Jam	fst 1 1/16	:25 :484 1:13 1:444 3↑	ⒻFirenze H 28k	3 5 97¼ 915 916 918	Erickson C	118 w	6.20	71-18	But Why Not1162Allie's Pal111½Conniver1263	Quit 9
1Apr49- 6Jam	fst 6f	:223 :47 1:122 3↑	Paumonok H 21k	4 9 911 77 87¾ 85¾	Scurlock O	116 w	*2.35e	83-20	Rippey1251Energetic1102My Request130¾	No factor 13
12Mar49- 7FG	fst 1 1/16	:233 :47 1:12 1:442 3↑	New Orleans H 29k	10 4 53¼ 67 44 35	Picou C	113 w	*.60e	92-11	My Request1254Isigny1051Miss Request1131	Forced wide 11
5Mar49- 7FG	fst 1⅛	:474 1:12 1:381 1:504 3↑	LeCompte H 11k	3 4 66 812 811 815	Picou C	115 w	*.50e	79-11	[DH]CaillouRouge105[DH]MyRequest1236Rabies1151	Done early 8
26Feb49- 7FG	sly 1 1/16	:243 :49 1:17 1:514 3↑	Handicap 3500	3 3 47 813 816 816	Erickson C	120 w	*1.50	44-34	Rabies113hdIsigny1074½Caillou Rouge1062	Quit 9
27Oct48- 6Jam	fst 1 1/16	:242 :48 1:13 1:45 3↑	ⒻComely H 29k	9 4 43¼ 31¼ 1½ 21¼	Atkinson T	120 w	*1.60e	87-25	Conniver1231¼Miss Request1205Carolyn A.1182	Weakened 10
9Oct48- 6Jam	fst 1 3/16	:481 1:121 1:38 1:572	Emp City H 57k	3 3 32½ 21½ 11½ 11	Scurlock O	118 w	3.65	89-14	Miss Request1181Quarter Pole1152Noble Hero1161½	Driving 9
28Sep48- 6Bel	fst 1½	:473 1:122 2:04 2:30 3↑	ⒻLadies H 58k	6 3 21 1nk 12 14	Atkinson T	114 w	7.50	88-14	Miss Request1144Gallorette1211Honeymoon1231	Easily 9
17Sep48- 6Bel	fst 1	:231 :462 1:112 1:364 3↑	ⒻHandicap 10090	5 1 11 1nk 11½ 12	Atkinson T	109 w	*3.45e	90-18	Miss Request1092Inheritance1084Carolyn A.1133	Easily 9
25Aug48- 6Sar	fst 1¼	:481 1:13 1:39 2:06	ⒻAlabama 24k	3 2 46½ 33 4¾ 43¼	Arcaro E	122 w	6.85	75-19	Compliance112nkAlablue1083Play Tag108hd	Hung 11
6Aug48- 6Sar	sly 7f	:232 :471 1:122 1:254	ⒻTest 9.2k	4 7 63 87½ 97 914	LeBlanc C	124 w	9.95	73-23	Alablue1144Paddleduck1111½Mackinaw121hd	Outrun 9
5Jly48- 5Del	fst 1⅛	:484 1:123 1:372 1:502	ⒻDel Oaks 27k	4 1 11 1hd 1hd 1½	LeBlanc C	113 w	10.15	97-06	Miss Request113½Mackinaw1191½Scattered119hd	Driving 6
26Jun48- 5Aqu	fst 1 1/16	:243 :48 1:124 1:46	Handicap 5545	5 2 3¾ 33 31¾ 22½	LeBlanc C	111 w	7.00	81-18	ThreeRings1112½MissRequest1111SafeArrvl1223	Closed fast 6
11Jun48- 6Bel	fst 1 1/16	:23 :46 1:113 1:443	Handicap 5550	6 4 45½ 46½ 34 55¾	LeBlanc C	116 w	*2.30	82-18	Lucky Devil1103The Dervish1191½Ghost Run1131	Tired 7
27May48- 4Bel	gd 1	:231 :461 1:12 1:383	ⒻAlw 5000	6 3 3½ 3½ 1nk 12½	LeBlanc C	114 w	*2.25	81-24	Miss Request1142½White Lady1134Beausy1111	Going away 9
18May48- 5Bel	sly 7f	:23 :472 1:13 1:262	ⒻAlw 6000	10 5 67 77¾ 79 88½	LeBlanc C	110 w	11.75	69-22	Alablue111nkSweet Dream1131½Mackinaw1171	Outrun 11
10May48- 5Jam	fst 1 1/16	:24 :48 1:13 1:47	ⒻAlw 6000	3 3 35½ 33½ 21 31¼	LeBlanc C	111 w	14.70	77-20	Compliance1101¼Scattered110hdMiss Request1112	No mishap 8
28Apr48- 5Jam	fst 6f	:23 :463 1:132	ⒻPrioress 24k	5 7 86¼ 95¼ 87 86	Scurlock O	112 w	38.85	78-19	Itsabet116½Picnic Lunch1162Alablue113½	No factor 14
10Apr48- 3Jam	fst 6f	:232 :472 1:133	ⒻAlw 4500	8 7 52 2hd 1hd 1hd	LeBlanc C	117 w	11.70	83-22	Miss Request117hdAlablue1134Past Eight1131½	Hard drive 9
1Apr48- 4Jam	sly 5½f	:232 :482 1:061	Alw 4500	5 4 33 21½ 1nk 32½	LeBlanc C	117 w	7.40	84-18	Mr. Ace1221Jimikin1221½Miss Request1172	Tired 6
4Mar48- 6FG	hy 6f	:24 :483 1:154	ⒻAlw 1600	6 1 22½ 22½ 2½ 11¼	LeBlanc C	116 w	*.50	74-37	Miss Request1161¼Osculation1132Run Sally1065	Going away 7
20Feb48- 5FG	fst 6f	:23 :46 1:113	Alw 1500	1 4 56 57 59 611	Moon F	114 w	7.10	84-14	Monte's Ace1163Back Talk114¾Riverlane1192	Outrun 8
14Feb48- 5FG	hy 6f	:243 :492 1:162	Alw 1800	6 1 56½ 31½ 21½ 22½	Guerin E	115 w	4.90	68-47	Shy Guy1222½Miss Request115½Dad1191¾	Went well 6
22Jan48- 6FG	hy 6f	:24 :504 1:172	ⒻAlw 1400	5 2 21 2½ 13 16	Guerin E	115 w	3.80	66-48	Miss Request1156Queen Hairan1182Beaukiss1085	Easily 9
10Jan48- 4FG	gd 6f	:223 :463 1:121	Alw 1600	7 6 64 67¾ 64½ 67¼	Guerin E	114wb	26.90	85-17	Cotton Joe1142½Safety First119nkEternal Bomb1192	Outrun 7
6Nov47- 5Jam	sly 6f	:232 :47 1:13	ⒻAlw 4000	5 8 67 64 74½ 58	Wilson HB	116wb	20.05	78-19	Vashti1162½Wicki Wicki1161Sweet Dream1164	No mishaps 9
27Oct47- 4Jam	fst 6f	:23 :463 1:121	ⒻAlw 4000	7 7 52¾ 43½ 65 46¼	Wilson HB	114 w	24.65	84-16	Past Eight1141Vashti1145Wicki Wicki114nk	No mishap 12
15Oct47- 3Jam	fst 6f	:23 :47 1:124	ⒻAlw 4000	7 4 53 54 56¾ 58	Scurlock O	116 w	10.40	79-17	SlumberSong1093PastEight116hdSweetDream1163	No mishap 8
2Oct47- 4Bel	fst 6f-WC	:23 :462 1:12	ⒻAlw 4000	7 3 4½ 62¾ 65¾	Scurlock O	114 w	19.45	75-19	Watermill119½Cunning Miss1141¼Supply Line114½	Tired 9
26Sep47- 5Bel	fst 6f-WC	:224 :453 1:102	Alw 4000	10 19 188¾ 2212 2215½	Arcaro E	114 w	14.70	73-17	Final Touch1171¼Salmagundi111½Frankly1172	Outrun 24
20Sep47- 1Aqu	fst 5½f	:233 :473 :592 1:062	Alw 4000	7 8 41¼ 2½ 2hd 2½	Scurlock O	114 w	6.80	91-12	King'sBowl117½MissRequest1141John'sDate117no	Weakened 8
12Sep47- 4Aqu	fst 5½f	:232 :472 1:001 1:07	ⒻMd Sp Wt	12 5 3½ 1nk 1nk 1hd	Scurlock O	116 w	8.90	89-18	Miss Request116hdNo Fiddling1163Heath Fire1162	Driving 12
12Aug47- 5Sar	fst 5½f	:221 :46 :583 1:063	ⒻMd Sp Wt	2 2 22 24 23 97½	Adams J	115 w	24.05	76-13	Dusty Legs1151Vaudeville1151½Bluehaze1151	Faltered 17
4Aug47- 1Sar	fst 5½f	:223 :462 :593 1:053	ⒻMd Sp Wt	9 3 2nk 22 44¾ 48	Arcaro E	115 w	*2.40	81-08	Inheritance1153½Obedient1152Golden Apple1082½	Stopped 12
22Jly47- 3Jam	sly 5½f	:23 :471 :594 1:064	ⒻMd Sp Wt	12 11 62¾ 67 66¼ 610¾	Arcaro E	115 w	9.30	73-21	One Bell1154In Love115¾Crimson Flash1151½	Slow start 12
16Jly47- 4Jam	sly 5½f	:232 :471 1:071	ⒻMd Sp Wt	3 3 2nk 23 57 67¼	Arcaro E	115 w	4.15	75-16	Hirta1151Sun Tavy1153Swing Trot115hd	Early speed 12

Myrtle Charm

b. f. 1946, by Alsab (Good Goods)–Crepe Myrtle, by Equipoise — **Lifetime record: 8 5 1 0 $81,830**

Own.– Maine Chance Farm
Br.– Brownell & Leslie Combs II (Ky)
Tr.– T. Smith

26Jly50- 6AP	fst 1	:23 :454 1:093 1:344 3↑	ⒻArl Matron H 22k	6 2 11 1½ 35½ 815¾	Lasswell G	124 w	*.80	82-10	Lithe1084Wistful118¾Evanstep1073½	Gave way badly 10
1Jly50- 7AP	fst 6f	:222 :444 1:10 3↑	ⒻModesty 21k	5 5 1hd 12 15 16	Lasswell G	121 w	*.70	96-09	Myrtle Charm1216Alsab's Day121hdFamous Shake102½	Easily 6
24May50- 6Bel	fst 6f-WC	:222 :444 1:09 3↑	Roseben H 12k	4 3 41¾ 4¾ 51½ 51¾	Lasswell G	121 w	*1.25	94-07	Olympia130nkWine List1101Royal Governor122hd	No excuse 9
8May50- 5Bel	fst 6f	:223 :46 1:112 4↑	Alw 4000	8 2 12 13 14 16½	Lasswell G	108 w	*1.40	93-17	Myrtle Charm1086½Magic Words115¾Energetic1105	Easily 8
	Previously trained by J.W. Smith									
25Sep48- 5Bel	fst 6½f-W	:22 :441 1:081 1:143	Futurity 113k	8 3 4¾ 32 2½	Atkinson T	123 w	*.75	98-03	BluePeter126½MyrtleCharm1237SportPage118½	Good effort 12
	Geldings not eligible									
18Sep48- 5Bel	fst 6f-WC	:222 :453 1:103	ⒻMatron 49k	6 1 11½ 13 13½	Atkinson T	119 w	*.45	88-13	Myrtle Charm1193½Stole1152Lithe1152	Easily 14
17Aug48- 6Sar	fst 6f	:224 :454 1:113	ⒻSpinaway 20k	12 4 3nk 12 15 112	Skoronski A	111 w	*1.50	90-14	Myrtle Charm11112Lady Dorimar1111½Gaffery1152	Easily 12
9Aug48- 3Was	fst 5½f	:23 :453 :581 1:044	ⒻMd Sp Wt	1 3 13 13 15 18	Skoronski A	119 w	*1.70	96-19	Myrtle Charm1198Modernistic1194Patmigirl1196	Easily 12

Our Boots

dk. b. c. 1938, by Bull Dog (Teddy)–Maid of Arches, by Wardenofthemarches **Lifetime record: 32 9 3 7 $126,152**

Own.– Woodvale Farm
Br.– Coldstream Stud (Ky)
Tr.– S. Judge

16Jun43- 8Aqu	fst 1⅛	:473 1:131 1:392 1:521	4↑ Handicap 3085	5	4	410	57¾	33½	1no	McCreary C	122	w	*1.20	86-13	OurBoots122noPlantagent1104Wllr1097	Up in final strides	6
31May43- 6Bel	fst 1¼	:47 1:111 1:361 2:012	3↑ Suburban H 38k	17	7	41¼	138½	138¾	1314½	Young S	110	w	35.15	78-12	Don Bingo1042[D]Market Wise1282½Attention121hd	Tired	17
22May43- 7Bel	my 1 1/16	:23 :472 1:122 1:443	3↑ Handicap 3585	7	6	611	65½	31¼	11	McCreary C	122	w	*2.25	88-21	Our Boots1221Copperman1093Wait a Bit1134	Driving	7
17May43- 6Bel	fst 7f	:23 :461 1:11 1:241	4↑ Handicap 2110	8	9	95¾	97	76	31¾	Bierman C	119	w	11.40	87-16	Bright Willie1261Dandy Fox106¾Our Boots119no		12
	Bore out far turn,finished well																
8May43- 5Jam	fst 1⅛	:472 1:121 1:374 1:503	3↑ Grey Lag H 19k	2	8	912	913	813	814	Lindberg H	110	w	25.30	81-12	Boysy114nkAhamo106nkTolaRose1124	Shuffled back 1st turn	11
23Sep42- 6Bel	fst 1 1/16	:232 :461 1:104 1:423	3↑ Handicap 2530	2	4	47	44	53	2no	Bierman C	122	w	*1.80	98-09	Staretor110noOurBoots1221½Paperboy1021¾	Outside,driving	6
12Sep42- 6Aqu	fst 1⅛	:472 1:113 1:37 1:493	3↑ Edgemere H 11k	1	2	36	42½	41½	32	Bierman C	116	w	7.10	97-08	The Rhymer114½Pictor1171½Our Boots116no	Driving	6
20Aug42- 5Sar	fst 6f	:23 :463 1:114	3↑ Alw 1500	1	2	11	1hd	33	34½	Arcaro E	117	w	11.15	88-15	Mettlesome1131½Fairaris1143Our Boots117nk	Saved ground	5
30May42- 6Bel	fst 1¼	:481 1:123 1:371 2:014	3↑ Suburban H 38k	11	2	2hd	2hd	67½	812	Wright WD	114	w	34.25	79-07	Market Wise1242Whirlaway1291½Attention1243	Pace,tired	11
22May42- 6Bel	fst 6f	:222 :454 1:104	3↑ Handicap 2545	1	3	68¼	68½	66¼	54½	Wright WD	121	wb	15.55	91-09	Ocean Blue116hdBay View1093Parasing118no	Good finish	6
9May42- 5Jam	my 1⅛	:473 1:13 1:39 1:52	3↑ Grey Lag H 18k	10	6	614	75¼	88¼	917	Robertson A	118	w	7.70	71-14	Marriage1093[DH]Market Wise125[DH]Boysy1132	Outrun	11
10Apr42- 6TrP	fst 1⅛	:47 1:104 1:36 1:49	3↑ Tropical H 11k	2	4	52¾	32½	3¾	3¾	Wright WD	119	w	3.60	103-10	Sir Marlboro109nkMioland129½Our Boots1196	Saved ground	8
27Mar42- 6TrP	fst 1 70	:231 :464 1:111 1:423	4↑ Alw 1200	1	4	1hd	11½	13	13	Wright WD	120	w	*.70	93-14	Our Boots1203Sir Marlboro1153½Porter's Cap1204	Handily	5
21Mar42- 6TrP	fst 1⅛	:471 1:113 1:361 1:492	3↑ Coral Gables H 8.7k	6	10	63	54	66½	45½	McCreary C	120	w	2.75	96-10	Mioland1254Signator1041½Llanero102hd	Away slowly	10
7Mar42- 6Hia	fst 1¼	:47 1:122 1:374 2:051	3↑ Widener H 67k	2	3	98¾	94¾	92¾	4½	McCreary C	121	w	12.75	82-17	TheRhymer111hdBestSeller112hdOlympus107nk	Strong finish	17
21Feb42- 6Hia	gd 1⅛	:472 1:12 1:38 1:504	3↑ McLennan H 15k	6	5	85¾	87	86¾	43	McCreary C	121	w	10.75	84-14	Market Wise124½Gramps1141Get Off1161½	Went wide	15
7Feb42- 7Hia	fst 7f	:231 :463 1:113 1:24	4↑ Alw 1500	3	7	714	615	510	49¼	McCreary C	122	w	11.75	83-13	SheriffCulkin1052Challedon1241¼WarRelic1226	Off slowly	7
1Nov41- 5Emp	sly 1 3/16	:474 1:124 1:393 1:594	3↑ Westchester H 28k	4	7	47	32½	34¼	43½	McCreary C	115	w	*2.05	84-18	Gramps1051¾Tola Rose107nkBoysy1131½	Impeded	8
25Oct41- 4Emp	fst 5¾f	:224 :461 1:074	2↑ Handicap 2530	3	5	65½	68	56	45½	McCreary C	126	w	*1.95	92-08	NightEditor1121½DailyDelvry1122½FrstFddl1021½	No excuse	6
26Jly41- 6AP	fst 1¼	:491 1:132 1:372 2:024	Classic 57k	6	2	11½	33	69¾	616	Robertson A	126	w	4.40	76-17	Attention1211½Whirlaway1266Bushwhacker1213½	Tired	6
12Jly41- 5Emp	fst 1⅛	:483 1:122 1:372 1:50	Emp City H 12k	2	2	2½	2nk	2½	2hd	Donoso R	124	w	*.55	105-05	SwingandSway114hdOurBoots1245Omission1173	Just missed	8
4Jly41- 7Suf	fst 1 3/16	:473 1:12 1:38 1:563	Yankee H 31k	1	1	75¾	74	3nk	11	McCreary C	122	w	3.60	98-13	OurBoots1221MarketWise1212¾RobertMorris1211¾	Drew out	9
10May41- 6Pim	gd 1 3/16	:472 1:123 1:391 1:584	Preakness 66k	8	6	41½	51¼	36½	37½	McCreary C	126	w	3.85	81-12	Whirlaway1265½King Cole1262Our Boots126nk	Closed well	8
3May41- 7CD	fst 1¼	:463 1:113 1:372 2:012	Ky Derby 73k	10	9	47	79	89¼	814¼	McCreary C	126	w	3.90	88-08	Whirlaway1268Staretor126nkMarket Wise1262	No mishap	11
24Apr41- 6Kee	my 1⅛	:474 1:12 1:38 1:511	Blue Grass 15k	4	1	2hd	2hd	12	16	McCreary C	123	w	1.60	91-20	Our Boots1236Whirlaway12315Valdina Paul1213	Ridden out	4
19Apr41- 5Kee	fst 6f	:23 :462 1:121	Alw 1200	2	4	46½	45½	32	11	McCreary C	122	w	*.70	91-19	Our Boots1221Smacked1133My Bill1131	Drew out	5
2Nov40- 6Pim	hy 1 1/16	:233 :48 1:142 1:494	Pim Futurity 38k	1	2	32½	31	2hd	2no	Bierman C	119	w	4.75	71-33	Bold Irishman122noOur Boots1195Whirlaway1221½	Game try	8
	Geldings not eligible																
19Oct40- 6Kee	fst 6f	:223 :454 1:111	Breeders' Futurity 12k	2	2	21	31	41¼	31	Westrope J	122	w	*1.40	95-13	Whirlaway1221BluePair119noOurBoots122hd	Close quarters	5
28Sep40- 7Bel	fst 6½f-WC	1:153	Futurity 81k	3	3	73¼	65½	4¾	11¾	Arcaro E	119	w	6.10	95-05	Our Boots1191¾King Cole1221½Whirlaway1262½	Going away	14
	Geldings not eligible																
24Sep40- 6Bel	fst 6f-WC	1:103	Alw 1500	2	3	21	52¾	11	13½	Bierman C	111	w	14.45	94-06	Our Boots1113½Springwood111hdNew World1201	Going away	10
	Previously trained by C. Porter																
23Jly40- 4AP	fst 5½f	:231 :462 :584 1:051	©Alw 1000	2	3	33½	32½	42	31½	Arcaro E	116	w	*1.20	93-15	Swell Chance116nkSwain1111½Our Boots1161	No excuse	7
12Jun40- 4Aqu	fst 5f	:223 :462 :594	©Md Sp Wt	5	3	2hd	12	12	14	Anderson I	117	w	2.40	- -	Our Boots1174Good Turn1171½Poppadeets1171¾	Going away	10

Painted Veil

b. f. 1938, by Blue Larkspur (Black Servant)–Killashandra, by Ambassador IV **Lifetime record: 34 11 6 8 $39,205**

Own.– L.B. Mayer
Br.– L. Combs, Trustee (Ky)
Tr.– G. Philpot

15Jly42- 6AP	sly 1	:232 :471 1:122 1:382	3↑ ⒻArl Matron H 13k	11	5	77½	812	813	813¼	Balaski L	122	w	*3.30	67-27	Blue Delight1103Emolument102¾Inscolassie1053		13
	Broke down after race																
30May42- 6Bel	fst 1¼	:481 1:123 1:371 2:014	3↑ Suburban H 38k	2	9	51½	54¼	77½	79	Bierman C	112	w	24.55	82-07	Market Wise1242Whirlaway1291½Attention1243	Outrun	11
25May42- 6Bel	fst 1	:234 :472 1:121 1:37	3↑ ⒻHandicap 3070	7	7	85¾	85½	51¼	2hd	Westrope J	122	w	*1.35e	90-12	War Hazard118hdPainted Veil122¾Rosetown119½	Just missed	11
15May42- 6Bel	fst 1	:231 :461 1:12 1:383	3↑ ⒻAlw 3000	7	6	56	55	2hd	12	Westrope J	120	w	*1.55e	82-13	Painted Veil1202Pomayya120hdChallomine1092	Going away	12
5May42- 5Jam	fst 1 1/16	:25 :491 1:134 1:443	3↑ ⒻHandicap 3020	3	2	23	23	21	1½	Westrope J	121	w	*.75	90-14	Painted Veil121½Pomayya1226Loveday1123	Driving	5
28Apr42- 4Jam	fst 6f	:231 :47 1:122	3↑ ⒻHandicap 2525	4	4	43	42½	41¾	1hd	Westrope J	116	w	2.80	90-12	PaintedVeil116hdAugury1262½Fleetborough104hd	Hard drive	4
17Apr42- 5Jam	fst 6f	:231 :464 1:114	3↑ ⒻHandicap 2045	8	6	54½	42½	33½	33¼	Westrope J	115	w	7.60	90-14	Augury1223Sun Ginger108nkPainted Veil1152	Good effort	9
19Jly41- 5Hol	fst 1	:232 :471 1:12 1:37	Salopian H 5k	1	3	34½	32	22½	21¼	Westrope J	116	w	*.90	95-06	BuckhornCreek1161¼PaintdVeil1165VanGrov1173½	No excuse	5
12Jly41- 7Hol	fst 1¼	:462 1:112 1:364 2:031	Hol Derby 28k	2	3	55½	62¼	63¾	62¼	Westrope J	113	w	5.40	92-07	Staretor1151Porter's Cap122nkPaperboy114no	No mishap	8
28Jun41- 7Hol	fst 1 1/16	:23 :464 1:112 1:432	3↑ ⒻVanity H 10k	4	4	46	34	3nk	1¾	Westrope J	113	w	3.00e	98-03	Painted Veil113¾Cute Trick1141African Queen109¾	Driving	7
14Jun41- 7Hol	fst 7f	:222 :452 1:103 1:232	3↑ ⒻSequoia H 10k	5	4	51½	31	1hd	12½	Westrope J	110	w	1.80e	98-08	Painted Veil1102½Augury1241Omelet1145	Handily	7
31May41- 7Hol	fst 7f	:224 :454 1:103 1:233	Will Rogers H 11k	6	2	31	43½	46½	31½	Westrope J	114	w	4.60	95-07	BattleColors1241½StrongArm113hdPaintdVl1141	Good effort	9
24May41- 4Hol	fst 6f	:224 :46 1:104	Handicap 2500	1	2	21½	33	39	35¼	Westrope J	116	w	2.80	92-10	StrongArm111nkBattleColors1225PaintedVl1164	Closed well	8
	Previously trained by C. Van Dusen																
10Mar41- 6SA	fst 1 1/16	:23 :464 1:114 1:443	Allied Charities H 13k	4	3	32	1½	2hd	1hd	Wall N	106	w	7.20	89-14	Painted Veil106hdStaretor1146Valdina Groom1143		10
	Strong handling,gamely																
4Mar41- 7SA	sly 1	:233 :474 1:134 1:403	Alw 1510	1	2	21	11	2½	21	Wall N	109	w	*1.70	74-24	BuckhornCreek1141PaintedVeil1093KantrRun108nk	Held well	6
28Feb41- 6SA	sly 1 1/16	:234 :481 1:131 1:464	Alw 2510	4	2	1hd	33	35½	21	Wall N	103	w	4.40	77-19	Staretor1081PaintedVeil103¾ValdinaGroom112¾	Closed fast	6
22Feb41- 5SA	sl 6f	:223 :464 1:132	Handicap 2510	5	5	36	34½	34	2hd	Neves R	107	w	4.70e	82-23	Madigama118hdPaintedVeil107¾Trnsnt109hd	Closed strongly	10
18Feb41- 6SA	sl 7f	:232 :472 1:14 1:271	Alw 1510	1	2	1hd	1½	1hd	31	Neves R	109	w	10.60	75-26	ValdinaGroom114¾KantarRun108nkPaintedVeil1096	Held well	6
23Jan41- 5SA	gd 6f	:224 :464 1:12	Handicap 2500	4	4	23	44½	45½	35¼	Wall N	104	w	11.50	84-17	GoodTurn1185CuteTrick113nkPaintedVeil104hd	Closed well	5
23Nov40- 7BM	fst 1 1/16	:233 :474 1:122 1:453	Salinas H 5.6k	3	2	43½	59½	611	58½	Neves R	115	w	*.70e	73-20	Rackatack1091¼Isometric1067Beret Basque106nk	No excuse	9
14Nov40- 5BM	fst 6f	:224 :463 1:122	Alw 900	5	3	21½	21	2½	13½	Rodriguez E	111	w	*.30e	87-19	Painted Veil1113½Wild Oats1121Singida106hd	Easily best	7
19Oct40- 7BM	fst 6f	:224 :462 1:111	Marvelous Marin H 2.2k	2	6	21	31	21½	25	Neves R	114	w	*2.00e	88-17	Appeasement1165Painted Veil1141Ira Pan116hd	Second best	8
3Aug40- 4Hol	fst 6f	:23 :462 1:12	Alw 5000	5	7	62¼	42½	55¼	34	Rodriguez E	115	w	19.30	90-06	LadyBos'n1152½LegendCall1141½PaintedVl115hd	Closed fast	7
22Jly40- 4Hol	fst 5½f	:231 :47 :591 1:054	Alw 1200	6	6	53¾	53¼	56	48	Rodriguez E	112	w	4.20	92-09	Strong Arm1181½Over Drive1124½Labeled Win1122	Outrun	7
13Jly40- 3Hol	fst 6f	:23 :463 1:121	ⒻAlw 1500	3	4	21	21½	22½	45	Rodriguez E	115	w	*.90	88-05	LadyBos'n1114½PersianHeels108½GoldenChance109no	Tired	6
6Jly40- 7Hol	fst 6f	:224 :454 1:113	Starlet 11k	2	13	106	55¼	68¾	710	Rodriguez E	115	w	7.00	86-10	FlyingChoice1157LadyBos'n115noTinPanAlley122½	Outrun	16
14Jun40- 5Hol	fst 5½f	:23 :464 :593 1:06	ⒻAlw 1200	4	2	24	22	21	14	Rodriguez E	114	w	*1.50	99-12	Painted Veil1144Tex Hygro1112Rio Macaw1143½	Easily	6
2May40- 6Tan	fst 5f	:23 :47 1:00	Alw 1000	4	1	2hd	1hd	1½	11	Merritt N	108	w	*1.30e	95-14	PaintedVeil1081LongHouse108hdIraPan111hd	Drawing away	7
13Apr40- 6Tan	fst 5f	:232 :481 1:012	A B Spreckels H 3k	10	9	82	55	45	43½	Rodriguez E	110	w	*1.20e	84-16	Rackatack1101Ira Pan112hdStrong Arm1142½	Wide	13
30Mar40- 5Tan	my 4½f	:233 :482 :55	ⒻTan Debutante 2.9k	5	7		78	79½	3nk	Longden J	113	w	3.90e	91-09	Rackatack107hdDollBaby112hdPantdVl1136	Finished fastest	12
	Previously trained by S. Judge																
28Feb40- 5Hia	fst 3f	:22 :331	Hia Juv Champ 3.5k	5	3			51½	42	Donoso R	116		3.80	- -	Maemante1141½Double Call117noRed Mantilla119½		9
	Traffic,finished fast																

22Feb40- 3Hia	fst 3f	:221 :331	Dinner (Div 1) 1.5k	10 5 33½ 3¾	Donoso R	119 w	3.90	--	Rock Wren116nkDouble Call114½Painted Veil1193	Held well 16
6Feb40- 1Hia	fst 3f	:221 :341	ⒻAlw 800	1 2 2½ 1hd	Donoso R	119 w	1.80	--	PaintdVeil119hdMaegay1221Maemante119½	Impeded,swerved 9
31Jan40- 1Hia	fst 3f	:221 :332	ⒻMd Sp Wt	8 4 3½ 11¼	Donoso R	117 w	16.10	--	Painted Veil1171¼Puro Oro1171½Belmar Arra1171½	Driving 14

Pavot

br. c. 1942, by Case Ace (Teddy)–Coquelicot, by Man o' War — **Lifetime record: 32 14 6 2 $373,365**

Own.– Walter M. Jeffords
Br.– Walter M. Jeffords Sr (Ky)
Tr.– O. White

10May47- 6Bel	fst 1	:23 :464 1:112 1:372 3↑	Metropolitan H 30k	4 4 42 44½ 33½ 53¾	Adams J	124 w	3.50	83-15	Stymie1241Brown Mogul1131Gallorette1161½	No mishap 12
24Apr47- 5HdG	fst 6f	:222 :46 1:102 3↑	Alw 5000	4 7 64¼ 45 31½ 24	Snider A	128 w	*.70	96-15	Air Patrol1204Pavot1281Alexis116no	Close quarters 7
26Oct46- 5Jam	fst 1⅝	:462 1:373 2:03 2:424 3↑	Gallant Fox H 85k	2 2 47½ 44 511 618½	Arcaro E	125 w	7.25	82-11	Stymie1262½Rico Monte1162Assault1148	Tired 11
5Oct46- 6Bel	fst 2	:491 2:302 2:543 3:223 3↑	J C Gold Cup 27k	3 1 21 2½ 11 15	Arcaro E	124 w	3.40	91-12	Pavot1245Stymie1245Rico Monte12450	Easily 4
Geldings not eligible										
25Sep46- 6Bel	fst 1½	:493 1:143 2:032 2:292 3↑	Manhattan H 28k	4 2 2nk 11 2½ 2¾	Arcaro E	121 w	3.20	90-13	Stymie126¾Pavot1213[DH]Flareback1131	Good effort 8
14Sep46- 6Nar	fst 1 3/16	:46 1:102 1:36 1:543 3↑	Nar Spl 38k	3 1 34 33½ 33½ 23½	Arcaro E	123 w	7.30	98-16	Lucky Draw1233½Pavot123nkArmed1305	Went well 4
24Aug46- 6Sar	fst 1¼	:46 1:101 1:362 2:013 3↑	Saratoga H 33k	1 1 38 37 45½ 411¾	Kirkland A	126 w	4.15	89-02	Lucky Draw121¾Polynesian1134Stymie1257	Weakened 5
5Aug46- 6Sar	fst 1	:23 :461 1:111 1:363 3↑	Wilson 24k	10 4 33 31¾ 21 1nk	Kirkland A	126 w	8.70	98-08	Pavot126nkGallorette121nkLarky Day112hd	Hard drive 11
13Jly46- 5Jam	fst 1 3/16	:47 1:111 1:361 1:551 3↑	Butler H 57k	2 1 1hd 1½ 3½ 53¼	Kirkland A	127 w	3.25	101-08	Lucky Draw105hdGallorette1161½Stymie126¾	Tired 9
4Jly46- 6Suf	fst 1⅛	:473 1:123 1:373 1:494 3↑	Mass H 66k	8 5 3nk 2nk 11½ 12¼	Kirkland A	120 w	2.70	92-13	Pavot1202¼Dinner Party1131½Gallorette1192¾	Handily 11
15Jun46- 6Del	gd 1¼	:473 1:122 1:38 2:041 3↑	Sussex H 29k	1 1 1hd 12½ 12½ 12	Snellings A	115 w	5.70e	94-16	Pavot1152Gallorette1131Stymie1262	In hand 8
29May46- 6Del	fst 6f	:223 :46 1:113 3↑	Wilmington H 9.4k	5 7 63½ 41½ 32 41½	Longden J	119wb	*1.50	92-16	Brookfield1231Goodrob107hdHappyBuckie116½	Slow to start 7
22May46- 6Bel	fst 6f-WC	:221 :454 1:084 3↑	Roseben H 12k	6 9 82½ 51¾ 43½ 34	Longden J	118wb	12.15	93-11	Polynesian1264Flood Town106hdPavot118¾	Closed well 9
6May46- 6Bel	fst 6f-WC	:232 :471 1:13 3↑	Toboggan H 16k	4 3 4½ 3¾ 57½ 510	Arcaro E	125 w	3.45	66-22	Polynesian124hdCassis1134King Dorsett1172	No mishap 7
25Apr46- 6HdG	my 6f	:23 :464 1:14 4↑	Alw 3500	1 4 21 22 2½ 12	Snellings A	120wb	*.85	83-36	Pavot1202Quarter Moon1202Hasteville1205	Ridden out 4
Daily Racing Form time, 1:13 3/5										
22Sep45- 6Bel	fst 1⅝	:471 1:374 2:043 2:433	Lawrence Realizatn 28k	6 3 21½ 11 89¾ 1025	Arcaro E	126wb	*1.55e	61-14	Poto'Luck1261¼ChiefBarker108½Michaelo1082	Stopped badly 11
18Sep45- 6Bel	sly 1	:223 :45 1:094 1:371	Jerome H 18k	7 5 58½ 57¾ 34¼ 34½	Arcaro E	125wb	*2.10	83-20	Buzfuz115½Greek Warrior1144Pavot1251	Steady gain 11
15Aug45- 6Bel	fst 1¼	:491 1:124 1:372 2:021 3↑	Whitney 17k	5 1 21½ 36 23 24	Snider A	117 w	1.55e	85-17	Trymenow1034Pavot1173Stymie1262	No match 6
11Aug45- 6Bel	fst 1¼	:462 1:102 1:361 2:024	Travers 33k	4 3 12 12 1½ 46½	Snider A	126wb	*.85	79-16	Adonis1102BurningDream1104SirFrancis116½	Quit final⅛ 7
21Jly45- 5Jam	fst 1 3/16	:472 1:112 1:37 1:564	Empire City 57k	1 1 14 12 2nk 2¾	Snider A	126wb	*2.65e	95-08	Gallorette116¾Pavot1263Post Graduate1163	No mishap 11
14Jly45- 5Aqu	fst 1¼	:481 1:13 1:393 2:051	Dwyer 56k	2 2 11½ 46½ 612 626	Arcaro E	126wb	*.80	55-18	Wildlife116noGallorette116½Esteem11610	Quit after 5f 6
23Jun45- 6Bel	fst 1½	:47 1:122 2:041 2:301	Belmont 70k	7 4 43 12 14 15	Arcaro E	126wb	2.10	87-13	Pavot1265Wildlife1261¾Jeep126½	Driving 8
Geldings not eligible										
16Jun45- 6Pim	fst 1 3/16	:471 1:122 1:384 1:584	Preakness 83k	1 2 42½ 43 41½ 55	Woolf G	126 w	*1.35	83-08	Polynesin1262½HoopJr.126nkDrbyDpp126nk	Bothered stretch 9
6Jun45- 6Bel	gd 1	:233 :472 1:13 1:394	Withers 27k	5 5 53 32 31¼ 2½	Woolf G	126 w	*.20	74-22	Polynesian126½Pavot1262King Dorsett1261	Led,hung 8
Geldings not eligible										
30Sep44- 4Bel	fst 6½f-W	:22 :441 1:09 1:153	Futurity 68k	9 1 74¾ 52¼ 12	Woolf G	126 w	*.70	94-04	Pavot1262Alexis119nkErrard1191	Easily 15
Geldings not eligible										
2Sep44- 4Bel	fst 6½f	:223 :461 1:184	Hopeful 58k	5 5 3nk 1nk 11½ 1½	Woolf G	126 w	*.30	86-15	Pavot126½Esteem122½Great Power1142½	Tired,held 8
19Aug44- 4Bel	fst 6f	:23 :464 1:114	Grand Union Hotel 19k	4 5 31¾ 32 3¾ 12½	Woolf G	126 w	*.25	91-13	Pavot1262½Great Power114nkBymeabond114hd	Bothered str 5
12Aug44- 4Bel	fst 6f-WC	:224 :452 1:093	Sar Spl 4.9k	1 3 3¾ 1½ 11¾	Woolf G	122 w	*.35	98-07	Pavot1221¾Plebiscite1227Jeep1224	Drew away 4
5Aug44- 4Bel	fst 6f	:224 :463 1:121	U S Hotel 20k	8 3 2nk 2nk 1½ 12½	Woolf G	126 w	*.70	89-14	Pavot1262½Esteem122nkWar Jeep1222	Mild restraint late 10
22Jly44- 6Suf	fst 5½f	:23 :453 1:053	Mayflower 35k	4 5 31 2½ 11½ 12½	Woolf G	119 w	*1.70	95-12	Pavot1192½Alabama119noLady's Reward1071	Easily 10
4Jly44- 5Del	fst 5½f	:222 :452 :58 1:042	©Christiana 7.5k	7 4 22 2hd 12 12	Dodson D	116 w	*.60	105-05	Pavot1162Hillyer Court1162Alexis116½	Easily 7
26Jun44- 1Del	fst 5½f	:223 :46 :584 1:051	Md Sp Wt	5 2 22 21 13 18	Knapp L	117 w	*.70	101-08	Pavot1178Brides Biscuit1142Guard Ship1141	Galloping 6

Petrify

ch. f. 1939, by Identify (Man o' War)–Sag Rock, by Rock Man — **Lifetime record: 11 6 1 1 $41,085**

Own.– A.G. Vanderbilt
Br.– Alfred G. Vanderbilt (Md)
Tr.– L. McCoy

11Jun43- 5Aqu	fst 7f	:23 :463 1:12 1:25 3↑	ⒻHandicap 2560	2 3 52½ 65¼ 53 77½	Wright WD	118wb	7.10	82-17	Yarrow Maid122no[DH]Night Glow112[DH]War Hazard1163	9
Shuffled back on turn										
25May43- 5Bel	fst 6f	:223 :454 1:12 4↑	Handicap 2030	4 2 1hd 21 23 68¾	Wright WD	115wb	16.85	81-14	Vain Prince114nkAriel Lad1171½Colchis1143	Quit 7
25Oct41- 5Lrl	fst 1 1/16	:232 :473 1:123 1:471	ⒻSelima 28k	4 10 118 1111 1114 1115¾	Donoso R	122wb	*2.00	65-17	Ficklebush1073½HardBaked114½Vagrncy1142	Showed nothing 11
11Oct41- 6Kee	fst 6f	:224 :463 1:114	ⒻSpecial Event 5.8k	3 3 23 23 23 23	Donoso R	119 w	*.60	90-14	Miss Dogwood1193Petrify1194Sis Baker1192	No threat 6
Worked mile in 1:41 2/5										
20Sep41- 7Bel	fst 6f	:221 :46 1:113	ⒻMatron 20k	13 3 32½ 32 2½ 12	Donoso R	119 w	3.65	92-13	Petrify1192LightLady119noFicklbush110½	Speed in reserve 15
3Sep41- 6Aqu	fst 6f	:231 :472 1:13	ⒻAlw 3000	7 3 41¾ 56¾ 52 12	Donoso R	122 w	*1.30	89-12	Petrify1222Last Sou110nkTaunt1072	Drifted out 7
16Aug41- 5Sar	my 6f	:23 :472 1:133	ⒻSpinaway 9.8k	2 2 22 43 31½ 32	Donoso R	122 w	*.80	82-22	Mar-Kell1131Equipet1131Petrify122½	Driving 8
Previously trained by A. Holberg										
5Jly41- 6AP	fst 6f	:232 :47 1:123	ⒻArl Lassie 25k	1 2 11 1½ 12 16	Donoso R	117 w	*1.00	84-19	Petrify1176Lotopoise117noCourt Manners1174	7
Ridden out,drifting out late;previously trained by L. McCoy										
24Jun41- 3Aqu	fst 5½f	:23 :463 1:054	Alw 1500	1 1 1½ 1nk 2hd 1hd	Donoso R	113 w	3.20	98-12	Petrify113hdBen Gray1162Court Manners109hd	Hard drive 5
11Jan41- 1SA	my 3f	:224 :341	Alw 1500	1 2 13 11½	James B	117 w	*.60	--	Petrify1171½Hooks1203Sagittal117no	Bore in,driving 9
7Jan41- 1SA	fst 3f	:22 :332	ⒻMd Sp Wt	14 1 1½ 12	James B	117 w	*1.30	--	Petrify1172Bold Lucy1173Chiquita Mia1172	Easily 16

Phalanx

b. c. 1944, by Pilate (Friar Rock)–Jacola, by Jacopo — **Lifetime record: 41 13 7 10 $409,235**

Own.– C.V. Whitney
Br.– Abram S. Hewitt (Va)
Tr.– S.E. Veitch

2Jly49- 6Aqu	fst 1¼	:484 1:13 1:372 2:024 3↑	Brooklyn H 58k	9 8 85¾ 98 96¼ 63½	Gilbert J	123wb	7.65	89-14	Assault122¾Vulcan'sForge129nkFlyingMissel117¾	No menace 10
25Jun49- 6Del	fst 1¼	:482 1:124 1:373 2:02 3↑	Sussex H 28k	6 6 68¾ 63 66½ 58½	Gilbert J	126 w	*.65	91-10	Flying Missel1105Chains1101Rose Beam1152	Dull effort 6
14Jun49- 6Del	fst 1 1/16	:231 :462 1:12 1:451 4↑	Alw 3500	1 5 48 1hd 1½ 13	Gilbert J	123 w	1.85e	87-15	Phalanx1233Mother1101½Rose Beam1142	Easily 6
13Nov48- 6Jam	fst 1 3/16	:484 1:13 1:38 1:58 3↑	Butler H 85k	1 7 613 77½ 63 21½	Clark S	126wb	*2.50	84-20	Donor1171½Phalanx1261Better Self121½	Closed fast 9
6Nov48- 6Jam	fst 2⅛	:50 2:352 3:023 3:354 3↑	Daingerfield H 29k	4 5 419 418 23 1¾	Clark S	129 w	*.80	88-23	Phalanx129¾Flying Missel1024Donor117½	Drew out 10
30Oct48- 6Jam	fst 1 3/16	:48 1:123 1:38 1:574 3↑	Westchester H 57k	1 8 813 89¾ 54½ 31¼	Clark S	126 w	*1.05	86-22	Better Self1191War Trophy110nkPhalanx126no	Closed fast 8
16Oct48- 7Bel	fst 1⅝	:48 1:381 2:034 2:424 3↑	Gold Cup 111k	1 6 815 59 34½ 22	Donoso R	126 w	10.80	88-19	Citation1192Phalanx1265Carolyn A.1232½	Closed fast 9
Geldings not eligible										
12Oct48- 6Jam	fst 1 1/16	:24 :471 1:12 1:444 3↑	Questionnaire H 29k	11 8 99 64½ 52½ 64	Clark S	126 w	*3.20	85-18	Donor115noCarolyn A.111½Bug Juice1082	No excuse 11
2Oct48- 6Bel	fst 2	:48 2:294 2:562 3:213 3↑	J C Gold Cup 108k	3 5 521 311 28 27	Clark S	124 w	6.35	89-09	Citation1177Phalanx12412Beauchef124hd	Closed well 7
Geldings not eligible										

Date/Race	Track	Dist	Fractions	Race	Running line	Jockey	Wt/Eq	Odds	Figs	Top finishers	Comment	Field
21Sep48-6Bel	fst	1 1/16	:232 :463 1:113 1:44 3↑	Alw 7500	2 8 820 816 87¼ 46¾	Clark S	122 w	*1.75e	84-14	ThreeRings105 1¼Airosa102 1½BrightSword1224	Finished fast	8
11Oct47-6Bel	fst	2¼	:473 2:314 3:482 3↑	New York H 109k	4 6 613 47½ 34¼ 35	Guerin E	116wb	2.55	88-11	Rico Monte126noTalon1225Phalanx1167	Stumbled at start	6
4Oct47-6Bel	fst	2	:494 2:293 2:553 3:213 3↑	J C Gold Cup 26k	2 3 31½ 3nk 2hd 1no	Donoso R	117wb	1.50	96-12	Phalanx117noTalon12412Stymie124	Just up	3
29Sep47-6Bel	fst	1⅝	:482 1:382 2:033 2:424	Lawrence Realizatn 28k	1 4 43 33½ 22 2hd	Donoso R	126wb	*1.40	90-14	Cosmic Bomb114hdPhalanx1262Snow Goose1155	Game try	6
6Sep47-6Aqu	gd	1⅛	:483 1:123 1:38 1:511	Discovery H 28k	3 7 76¾ 76½ 62¾ 31	Donoso R	128wb	*1.60	90-13	Cosmic Bomb126noDouble Jay1151Phalanx1281	Closed fast	9
23Aug47-7Was	fst	1¼	:472 1:111 1:35 2:003	American Derby 93k	2 4 410 36½ 36 36¼	Donoso R	126wb	*.90	96-07	Fervent118nkCosmic Bomb1186Phalanx12610	No excuse	4
16Aug47-5Sar	sly	1¼	:511 1:16 1:411 2:061	Travers 28k	1 2 21½ 21½ 1hd 2no	Donoso R	128wb	*.55	77-20	Young Peter124noPhalanx1282½Colonel O'F122	Game try	3
19Jly47-6Bel	sly	1⅝	:483 1:39 2:042 2:423 3↑	Gold Cup 109k	3 7 724 611 43¾ 45¼	Donoso R	112wb	4.60	86-14	Stymie126nkNatchez1264Assault1261	No mishap	7
				Geldings not eligible								
5Jly47-5Jam	fst	1 3/16	:483 1:13 1:39 1:574	Empire City 56k	7 7 78½ 75¼ 4¾ 12¼	Donoso R	126wb	*.70	87-15	Phalanx1262¼But Why Not111½Harmonica116hd	Going away	7
30Jun47-5Jam	fst	1 1/16	:25 :481 1:123 1:452	Alw 7500	2 5 55¼ 23 2hd 12½	Donoso R	126wb	*.45	86-16	Phalanx1262½Tailspin1171Our Tommy1139	Cleverly	5
14Jun47-6Aqu	fst	1¼	:474 1:13 1:391 2:054	Dwyer 58k	6 9 711 64¾ 31 1nk	Donoso R	126wb	*.85	78-16	Phalanx126nkBut Why Not1117Brabancon1161½	Hard drive	9
31May47-6Bel	fst	1½	:50 1:152 2:051 2:292	Belmont 113k	7 9 74 31¾ 1nk 15	Donoso R	126wb	2.30e	91-09	Phalanx1265Tide Rips1262Tailspin1261½	Easily	9
				Geldings not eligible								
24May47-6Bel	fst	1⅛	:461 1:112 1:371 1:503	Peter Pan H 18k	7 9 73¼ 51 52½ 32	Arcaro E	126wb	*.90	86-19	Tailspin1091Brabancon1171Phalanx126hd	Closed fast	11
10May47-6Pim	fst	1 3/16	:471 1:121 1:391 1:59	Preakness 133k	8 10 97½ 76¼ 55 33¾	Arcaro E	126wb	*1.10	83-20	Faultless1261¼On Trust1262½Phalanx1261¼	Closed fast	11
3May47-7CD	sl	1¼	:49 1:142 1:402 2:064	Ky Derby 109k	8 13 1314 53 52¾ 2hd	Arcaro E	126wb	*2.00	73-23	Jet Pilot126hdPhalanx126hdFaultless1261	Sluggish start	13
19Apr47-5Jam	fst	1 1/16	:23 :47 1:114 1:434	Wood Mem (Div 1) 45k	8 8 73 43½ 21 11½	Arcaro E	126wb	*.95	94-10	Phalanx1261½Carolyn A.1211½Owners Choice1268	Drew out	10
12Apr47-5Jam	fst	1 1/16	:242 :482 1:122 1:444	Exp Free H 21k	3 8 85½ 83½ 54¼ 31¼	Arcaro E	122wb	3.00	88-10	CornishKnight110nkSecnav1061Phalanx122hd	Close quarters	9
13Nov46-6Pim	fst	1 1/16	:232 :471 1:122 1:454	Walden 33k	2 11 107 - - -	Donoso R	119wb	3.10	- -	Fervent116hdFaultless1133Royal Governor1167		11
				Ran up on heels of rival,lost rider								
2Nov46-4Jam	fst	1 70	:233 :473 1:133 1:424	Ardsley H 24k	6 7 72½ 22 21½ 12	Luther T	117wb	*.90e	90-12	Phalanx1172Brabancon1131Nathaniel1094	Ridden out	8
29Oct46-5Jam	fst	1 1/16	:24 :48 1:122 1:454	Remsen H 25k	8 8 86¾ 65¼ 41¼ 1¾	Donoso R	117wb	5.10	84-15	Phalanx117¾Tavistock116hdDonor1266	Lugged in final ⅛	8
23Oct46-4Jam	fst	1 1/16	:24 :48 1:133 1:454	Alw 5000	5 4 11 11½ 11½ 1nk	Arcaro E	119wb	*.55	84-19	Phalanx119nkDinnrHour1198Lndr1222	Drifted out,just held	5
12Oct46-5Bel	sly	1	:23 :454 1:111 1:372	Champagne 27k	6 9 77¾ 56½ 32¼ 2½	Schmidl A	110wb	6.60e	86-14	Donor116½Phalanx110nkJet Pilot1194	Closed well	11
7Oct46-7Bel	fst	1	:231 :464 1:12 1:374	Alw 5000	6 5 55 53 32½ 31¾	Schmidl A	119 w	1.40	83-16	Flashco116nkTavistock1191½Phalanx1192	Good finish	9
14Sep46-5Aqu	fst	6½f	:234 :48 1:131 1:194	Cowdin 31k	4 10 96¾ 76¾ 73 42½	Wilson HB	110wb	10.85e	83-13	CosmcBomb126nkColonelO'F122¾Brbncon1171½	Finished well	11
31Aug46-4Sar	fst	6½f	:222 :451 1:101 1:17	Hopeful 57k	7 9 117¼ 1011 56¾ 53½	James B	114wb	9.15e	96-00	BlueBorder122no[D]CsmcBmb1262GrndAdmrl1261	Closed well	11
				Placed fourth through disqualification								
27Aug46-6Sar	fst	6f	:224 :46 1:11	Alw 4000	4 5 54¼ 53¼ 42½ 3nk	James B	111wb	*1.70	97-06	Brabancon116noJohnnyDimick111nkPhlnx1112	Finish fastest	5
17Aug46-4Sar	my	6f	:232 :472 1:132	Sar Spl 6.5k	4 3 55 56¾ 43¼ 43½	James B	122wb	2.95e	81-21	GrandAdmrl1221LoyalLegion1221½KhyberPss1221	No menace	5
20Jly46-5Jam	fst	6f	:23 :463 1:113	©East View 51k	11 9 74½ 61¾ 63 33	Miller P	115wb	9.65	90-11	Grand Admiral1151I Will1192Phalanx115½	Close quarters	11
13Jly46-4Jam	fst	6f	:233 :472 1:113	Alw 5000	1 5 56 56 4¾ 11½	Miller P	106wb	3.75	93-08	Phalanx1061½Brabancon1182Owners Choice1153	Drew away	5
22May46-4Bel	fst	5f-WC	:223 :454 :584	Alw 4000	7 6 73¾ 62 4¾	Kirkland A	116 w	*1.25	85-11	Fiddlers Three116½Our Tommy116nkNathaniel111no		10
				Close quarters early								
18May46-4Bel	fst	5f-WC	:222 :45 :573	Juvenile 14k	6 12 92½ 96 97¾	Givens C	117wb	*1.00e	84-06	EternalWar1223FirstFlight1191CornshKnght113no	No factor	12
4May46-1Jam	fst	5f	:23 :47 1:001	Md Sp Wt	4 4 45¼ 33 22 1¾	Givens C	116 w	9.75	89-10	Phalanx116¾Ben Lewis1162Green Dragon1164	Driving	7

Platter

ch. c. 1941, by Pilate (Friar Rock)–Lets Dine, by Jack High — **Lifetime record: 10 2 3 2 $60,930**

Own.– George D. Widener
Br.– George D. Widener (Ky)
Tr.– W.F. Mulholland

Date/Race	Track	Dist	Fractions	Race	Running line	Jockey	Wt/Eq	Odds	Figs	Top finishers	Comment	Field
3Jun44-6Bel	fst	1½	:48 1:131 2:05 2:321	Belmont 72k	7 7 58 43½ 56½ 513½	Longden J	126wb	1.90e	63-16	Bounding Home126½Pensive1268Bull Dandy1264		7
				Hung,pulled up lame;Geldings not eligible								
13May44-6Pim	fst	1 3/16	:481 1:131 1:392 1:591	Preakness 77k	3 4 21½ 22 2½ 2¾	Longden J	126wb	3.05	85-15	Pensive126¾Platter1262Stir Up1264½	Driving	7
6May44-4Jam	fst	6f	:224 :462 1:112	Alw 4000	3 6 65¼ 47 31½ 21¼	Longden J	126wb	*1.80	94-10	Rodney Stone1161¼Platter1262½Bull Dandy1165		9
				Fast finish,worked mile in 1:41 2/5								
12Nov43-6Pim	fst	1 1/16	:234 :483 1:133 1:483	Walden 13k	4 7 65½ 57¼ 43½ 1½	McCreary C	122wb	*2.20e	75-23	Platter122½Royal Prince119nkDirector J.E.1161	Driving	9
3Nov43-6Pim	my	1 1/16	:232 :48 1:141 1:473	Pim Futurity 38k	8 3 36½ 31 2½ 1½	McCreary C	119wb	*1.85	80-30	Platter119½By Jimminy1198Smolensko1222	Just up	8
				Geldings not eligible								
23Oct43-5Jam	fst	1 70	:243 :482 1:132 1:442	Ardsley H (Div 1) 11k	1 1 21 2½ 21 33	McCreary C	112wb	4.25	79-17	Weyamoke1083Pukka Gin126hdPlatter112no	Bore out	10
9Oct43-4Bel	fst	1	:233 :464 1:12 1:381	Champagne 13k	6 1 2hd 52½ 54½ 57	McCreary C	106wb	4.05	76-17	Pukka Gin1131Pressure1065Pensive1101	Pace,tired	12
2Oct43-4Bel	sly	6½f-W	:231 :461 1:111 1:174	Futurity 68k	2 6 4¾ 63½ 32¼	McCreary C	114wb	9.50	81-17	Occupy1261¼Rodney Stone1221Platter1142	Fast finish	11
				Geldings not eligible								
28Sep43-5Bel	fst	6f-WC	:223 :45 1:10	Alw 5000	15 4 76 46½ 42¾	McCreary C	111wb	3.00e	93-09	Tambo111¾Rodney Stone1191Black Badge1191	Good finish	16
23Sep43-4Bel	fst	6f-WC	:231 :462 1:114	Md Sp Wt	3 2 4nk 33½ 2½	McCreary C	116wb	3.25	86-14	Plasma116½Platter1161½Bounding Home1161	Greenly	13

Polynesian

br. c. 1942, by Unbreakable (Sickle)–Black Polly, by Polymelian — **Lifetime record: 58 27 10 10 $310,410**

Own.– Elmendorf Farm
Br.– Elmendorf Farm Inc (Ky)
Tr.– M.H. Dixon

Date/Race	Track	Dist	Fractions	Race	Running line	Jockey	Wt/Eq	Odds	Figs	Top finishers	Comment	Field
1Nov47-5Pim	fst	6f	:224 :464 1:124 2↑	Janney H 9k	2 4 21½ 2hd 1½ 11	Snider A	134wb	*.40	89-24	Polynesian1341The Doge1222Sea Snack1162	Good effort	5
22Sep47-5Bel	sly	6f	:231 :463 1:11 3↑	Alw 6500	3 4 22 1hd 11½ 12½	Arcaro E	126wb	*.85	95-15	Polynesian1262½Armed1308Ensueno11430	Easily	4
25Aug47-6GS	fst	6f	:222 :452 1:094 3↑	Camden H 11k	5 4 52 2½ 12 15	Balzaretti W	129wb	*.40	102-06	Polynesian1295Air Patrol123nkThe Doge1191¼	Easily	6
26Jly47-5Mth	fst	1¼	:473 1:12 1:363 2:011 3↑	Mth Park H 29k	5 3 21½ 21 23 48½	Wright WD	127wb	2.15	94-02	Round View1127Talon1121½Gallorette119hd	Weakened	6
16Jly47-6Mth	fst	1⅛	:473 1:113 1:373 1:503 3↑	Omnibus H 12k	4 2 2½ 1½ 11 1½	Wright WD	129wb	*1.95	102-11	Polynesian129½Round View1144Flash Burn111nk	Driving	7
28Jun47-6Mth	fst	1 1/16	:242 :472 1:111 1:433 3↑	Long Branch H 12k	6 2 11 11 12 1no	Wright WD	129wb	*.75	104-08	Polynesian129noFlash Burn1093½Jeep1102	Hard drive	6
21Jun47-5Mth	fst	6f	:222 :451 1:102 3↑	Oceanport H 11k	7 6 2hd 12 15 12½	Wright WD	134wb	*.45	99-09	Polynesian1342½Misleader1051Gallant Bull104½	Easily	7
30May47-5Del	fst	6f	:221 :453 1:104 3↑	Wilmington H 11k	2 4 44 3½ 1½ 13	Snider A	132wb	*.80	98-14	Polynesian1323Sea Snack1102Rippey112¾	Going away	5
26May47-5Atl	fst	6f	:223 :46 1:11 3↑	Atl City Inaugural H 12k	4 4 21 4¾ 1½ 12½	Arcaro E	130wb	*.95	91-16	Polynesian1302½AirPatrol120nkLighthouse1051½	Going away	8
21May47-6Bel	my	6f-WC	:22 :45 1:10 3↑	Roseben H 17k	2 6 53¼ 42¼ 46 46	Arcaro E	132wb	*2.10	85-13	Inroc1133½Fighting Frank1251½Brown Mogul1161	Tired	7
5May47-6Bel	my	6f-WC	:221 :451 1:11 3↑	Toboggan H 24k	9 3 42½ 53½ 2nk 31¼	Arcaro E	134wb	*2.45	85-10	Buzfuz121¾Degage114½Polynesian134½	Tired	13
26Apr47-5Jam	fst	1 1/16	:24 :473 1:114 1:44 3↑	Excelsior H 22k	5 3 31 2½ 22 25	Arcaro E	126wb	*.95	88-10	Coincidence1155Polynesian126½Lets Dance1121	Weakened	8
19Apr47-4Jam	fst	6f	:23 :46 1:112 3↑	Handicap 6525	5 5 42¾ 33 3¾ 11¾	Arcaro E	130wb	*.70	94-10	Polynesian1301¾Buzfuz1201¼Tidy Bid1032	Drew out	5
5Apr47-5Jam	sly	6f	:223 :46 1:111 3↑	Paumonok H 22k	5 6 64¾ 41½ 21 2hd	Arcaro E	130wb	*2.00	95-14	FightingFrank125hdPolynesn130¾KngDorstt1202	Just missed	9
				Previously raced in name of Mrs P.A.B. Widener								
8Nov46-6Pim	fst	1 3/16	:473 1:122 1:391 1:591 3↑	Riggs H 30k	5 5 33½ 31 1hd 1½	Snider A	124wb	*1.45	86-21	Polynesian124½RoundView1111FlshBurn1061½	Under pressure	8
2Nov46-5Jam	fst	1 70	:23 :464 1:114 1:421 3↑	Scarsdale H 18k	9 5 45 33¼ 31¼ 11½	Snider A	126wb	3.25	93-12	Polynsn1261½FrstFddl1151Buzfuz1171	Drew clear under urging	10
26Oct46-6GS	sly	1⅛	:464 1:112 1:373 1:503 3↑	Trenton H 64k	6 1 11 1hd 2½ 2nk	Snider A	123wb	7.90	92-19	Turbine115nkPolynesian123½Man o' Glory1162	Gamely	12
19Oct46-6Lrl	fst	1¼	:47 1:12 1:381 2:03 3↑	Washington H 28k	1 1 11½ 1hd 2hd 31¾	Kirkland A	119wb	*1.40	93-16	Seven Hearts1191Megogo105¾Polynesian119½	Faltered late	6
15Oct46-7Bel	fst	1	:233 :461 1:103 1:363 2↑	Turf & Field H 10k	2 1 11½ 11½ 14 1¾	Arcaro E	126 w	*.95	91-19	Polynesian126¾Coincidence123nkBridlFlowr1158	Ridden out	4

20Oct46- 6Bel fst 7f :224 :461 1:111 1:234 2↑ Vosburgh H 19k 8 3 2hd 1hd 3nk 36½ Arcaro E 130wb *1.50 84-19 Coincidence118 2½Alexis109 4Polynesian130½ Faltered 11
16Sep46- 5Atl fst 6f :22 :442 1:091 3↑ Pageant H 11k 2 5 21½ 1hd 11½ 16 Arcaro E 126wb *.45 108-06 Polynesian126 6ThreeDots118 1½TheDoge118hd Speed to spare 6
9Sep46- 6Aqu fst 7f :223 :45 1:10 1:232 3↑ Bay Shore H 18k 4 5 41¼ 21½ 21 31¾ Arcaro E 130wb *2.10 93-18 Gallorette124nkKing Dorsett120 1½Polynesian130 1 Hung 9
24Aug46- 6Sar fst 1¼ :46 1:101 1:362 2:013 3↑ Saratoga H 33k 3 2 12 13 2½ 2¾ Arcaro E 113wb 4.80 100-02 Lucky Draw121¾Polynesian113 4Stymie125 7 Gamely 5
15Aug46- 6Sar fst 1 3/16 :47 1:112 1:362 1:552 3↑ Merchants & Cits H 18k 1 2 11½ 11½ 2hd 21½ Snider A 112wb 6.30 99-06 Lucky Draw117 1½Polynesian112 1Trymenow111 15 Held well 8
10Aug46- 6Sar my 1¼ :50 1:154 1:394 2:072 3↑ Whitney 28k 4 3 21 21 35 414 Wright WD 117wb 4.70 58-22 Stymie120 2Mahout103 2Trymenow112 10 Flattened out 5
5Aug46- 6Sar fst 1 :23 :461 1:111 1:363 3↑ Wilson 24k 3 2 21½ 2nk 11 4½ Wright WD 117wb *2.75 97-08 Pavot126nkGallorette121nkLarky Day112hd Hung 11
4Jly46- 6Mth fst 6f :221 :444 1:103 3↑ Rumson H 13k 5 8 41½ 31 1½ 11¼ Wright WD 130wb *1.55 - - Polynesian130 1¼Brookfield123½New Moon114 3½ Driving 9
24Jun46- 5Jam fst 6f :224 :452 1:102 3↑ Fleetwing H 12k 2 3 53½ 42 31½ 31 Wright WD 132wb *1.20 98-11 Scholarship106 1FloodTown110noPolynesin132 3 Traffic,hung 8
8Jun46- 5Del fst 6f :214 :45 1:102 3↑ Handicap 5000 8 5 21½ 2hd 12 12¼ Wright WD 126wb *2.00 100-11 Polynesian126 2½Brookfield126 1¼New Moon116 5 Ridden out 8
30May46- 6Bel fst 1¼ :482 1:123 1:373 2:02 3↑ Suburban H 60k 11 1 21½ 21 53¼ 1015¼ Wright WD 115wb 21.40 75-16 Armed130 2½Reply Paid110noStymie123 1 Quit badly 11
22May46- 6Bel fst 6f-WC :221 :454 1:084 3↑ Roseben H 12k 9 4 2nk 1hd 11 14 Wright WD 126wb 3.45 97-11 Polynesian126 4FloodTown106hdPavot118¾ Drew clear easily 9
11May46- 6Bel fst 1 :224 :451 1:104 1:37 3↑ Metropolitan H 31k 8 3 2hd 1½ 1hd 97¼ Wright WD 126 w 16.00 82-14 Gallorette110noSirde124noFirst Fiddle126½ Quit badly 14
6May46- 6Bel fst 6f-WC :232 :471 1:13 3↑ Toboggan H 16k 5 1 1hd 1nk 1½ 1hd Wright WD 124 w 6.15 76-22 Polynesin124hdCsss113 4KngDorstt117 2 Drifted out,driving 7
27Apr46- 4Jam sly 6f :23 :46 1:121 3↑ Handicap 6020 3 1 32 33 31½ 33¼ Wright WD 123 w 4.60 87-16 Buzfuz126 1½Scholarship114 1¾Polynesn123 10 Some late gain 4
17Nov45- 6Pim gd 1 3/16 :493 1:142 1:391 1:584 3↑ Pim Spl 25k 3 4 12½ 11 25 68½ Wright WD 120 w 12.75 79-20 Armed126 4First Fiddle126 2Stymie126 1¼ Weakened 7
14Nov45- 5Pim fst 6f :223 :464 1:123 3↑ Handicap 5000 3 3 2½ 2hd 1hd 1hd Wright WD 122 w *1.40 90-23 Polynesian122hdBritish Buddy113nkFirst Son109 4 Driving 5
6Nov45- 6Bel fst 1 :23 :454 1:11 1:373 2↑ Turf & Field Cup H 10k 6 5 53¼ 21 12 2no Jemas N 122 w 2.40 86-20 TexMartin104noPolynesian122 3GreekWarrior121 1¼ Weak ride 7
27Oct45- 7Pim fst 1 1/16 :241 :482 1:131 1:453 3↑ Handicap 3500 6 1 11 1½ 1hd 2½ Jemas N 126 w *1.65 89-17 Salvo120½Polynesin126 2HRolls115hd Saved ground,2nd best 7
22Oct45- 6Pim fst 6f :221 :453 1:11 3↑ Ritchie H (Div 1) 12k 7 5 55 43½ 21½ 24½ Young S 123 w *.95 93-10 New Moon118 4½Polynesian123 2Kopla116½ No match 9
17Oct45- 6Lrl fst 6f :223 :462 1:121 3↑ Handicap 5000 3 4 33 21½ 11 2no Gilbert J 122 w *1.70 93-19 The Doge114noPolynesian122 1½New Moon117 1 Gave way late 8
3Oct45- 3Bel fst 6f-WC :224 :46 1:121 3↑ Handicap 4970 3 3 11 14 13½ Wright WD 124 w 2.60 80-21 Polynesian124 3½Saguaro105 2½Occupy122 4 Easily 4
18Sep45- 6Bel sly 1 :223 :45 1:094 1:371 Jerome H 18k 8 4 36 35½ 45¼ 913¼ Wright WD 126 w 8.35 75-20 Buzfuz115½Greek Warrior114 4Pavot125 1 Quit badly 11
15Aug45- 5Bel fst 6f-WC :223 :453 1:102 Saranac H 4.9k 1 2 2hd 4½ 1½ 11¾ Wright WD 126 w *2.70 89-13 Polynesian126 1¾Alabama123 1¼Buzfuz126 1 Ridden out 6
10Jly45- 5Aqu fst 1 1/16 :243 :482 1:132 1:454 Shevlin 11k 3 1 21 32 31¾ 511½ Wright WD 126 w *1.60 73-16 Wildlife108 6Coincidence111 2½Trymenow110 2 9
Eased back when outrun
16Jun45- 6Pim fst 1 3/16 :471 1:122 1:384 1:584 Preakness 83k 7 4 11 11½ 1½ 12½ Wright WD 126 w 12.00 88-08 Polynesian126 2½HoopJr.126nkDarbyDieppe126nk Ridden out 9
6Jun45- 6Bel gd 1 :233 :472 1:13 1:394 Withers 27k 7 2 21½ 21 2nk 1½ Wright WD 126 w 13.90 75-22 Polynesian126½Pavot126 2King Dorsett126 1 Came on again 8
Geldings not eligible
30May45- 6Jam fst 1 1/16 :24 :47 1:113 1:45 Wood Mem (Div 2) 27k 9 3 31½ 22 23 49 Balz'etti W 126 w 5.00 79-16 Hoop Jr.126 2½Alexis126 1½Sir Francis126 5 Hung 9
21May45- 5Jam fst 6f :23 :46 1:113 Exp Free H 8.6k 1 3 32½ 2½ 2½ 33¾ Balz'etti W 119 w 22.65 90-14 Jeep112 1¾Greek Warrior111 2Polynesian119 1½ Faltered 13
13Nov44- 6Pim fst 1 70 :23 :471 1:131 1:44 Endurance H (Div 2) 12k 7 2 11½ 11½ 11 2½ Meade D 118 w *1.25 90-18 HailVictory110½Polynesn118 2½Bymbond113 5 Drifted out str 7
6Nov44- 6Pim fst 6f :223 :463 1:122 Sagamore (Div 2) 9.4k 1 2 11 11 11 11½ Meade D 113 w *1.55 91-19 Polynesian113 1½Kewey Dee119hdThe Doge116hd Wide,driving 8
3Oct44- 4Bel fst 7f :231 :47 1:121 1:25 ©Alw 3000 6 1 11 11 1½ 1hd Meade D 119 w *1.90 85-15 Polynesian119hdUnconditional116 3Wildlife116 2 Driving 13
22Sep44- 6Bel fst 6f-WC :231 :462 1:113 Alw 3000 7 4 3½ 2hd 11¼ Meade D 116 w *1.70 83-20 Polynesian116 1¼SpartanNoble116noSolPrt116 1 Drawing away 9
29Aug44- 5Bel fst 6f :23 :464 1:122 Alw 3500 8 5 31 3½ 3nk 1hd Meade D 111 w 2.60 88-13 Polynesian111hdGreatPower111 2Chckrhll119 1½ Bothered str 12
22Aug44- 5Bel fst 6f :223 :463 1:122 Alw 3000 3 4 43½ 44 32½ 32½ Adair R 111 w 4.45 85-17 Bobanet117hdForward117 2½Polynesian111 2 Driving 12
16Aug44- 4Bel fst 5½f-W :23 :454 1:041 ©Md Sp Wt 1 8 61½ 31½ 12½ Adair R 116 w 4.30f 93-07 Polynesian116 2½Ship Call116 4Baron Jack116 1 Driving 27
4May44- 6Pim fst 4½f :231 :474 :543 Ral Parr 7.9k 2 5 3½ 31½ 43 Scocca D 114 w 12.20 87-10 Alabama117hdDon Chance119 1Flying Bridge122 2 Tired 5
29Apr44- 5Pim gd 4½f :234 :482 :543 Alw 2000 3 5 56½ 33 33 Scocca D 112 w 9.65 87-10 Alabama112 3KeweyDee111noPolynesn112 6 Taken up backstr 7
25Apr44- 4Pim hy 4½f :24 :502 :572 ©Md Sp Wt 4 3 32 31 34 Arduini R 113 w 42.70 72-24 KeweyDee118 3Potsey118 1Polynsn113 1 Close quarters,gamely 12

Rouge Dragon

ch. g. 1938, by Annapolis (Man o' War)–Pimento II, by Pommern **Lifetime record: 59 25 9 3 $111,255**
Own.– M.A. Cushman
Br.– Mrs Marion du Pont Scott (Va)
Tr.– W.G. Jones

3Oct46- 5Bel fst *3 S'Chase 5:484 4↑ Grand National H 30k 10 2 - - - - Leonard W 161 w 6.30 - - Elkridge151 4Burma Road162 2Refugio134 3 Fell at 8th 10
26Sep46- 5Bel fst *2½ S'Chase 4:494 4↑ Brook H 19k 6 1 2½ 32 1027 925 Leonard W 163 w 2.05 - - Burma Road156 2½Caddie142noGreat Flare138 5 Tired badly 11
30Aug46- 5Sar fst *2½ S'Chase 5:082 4↑ Sar H 8.4k 2 1 115 110 4 4 Leonard W 164 w *.55 - - Replica II137 10Raylywyn135 4Beneksar134 4
Tired,fell at final fence,remounted and ridden to finish in time limit
23Aug46- 5Sar fst *2 S'Chase 4:114 3↑ Beverwyck H 5.7k 1 1 13 11½ 12 11 Leonard W 162 w *1.10 - - RougeDragon162 1WarBattle144 2½BoojumII139 12 Ridden out 4
3Jly46- 3Del fst *2½ S'Chase 4:463 4↑ Indian River H 12k 2 1 12 15 13 13½ Leonard W 157 w *1.15 - - Rouge Dragon157 3½Delhi Dan137 4½Elkridge149 2½ Easily 6
27Jun46- 3Del fst *2 S'Chase 3:483 4↑ Georgetown H 12k 3 1 16 14 13 13½ Leonard W 152 w *1.35 - - Rouge Dragon152 3½Elkridge149 8Beneksar136 6 6
Swerved before last fence
12Jun46- 2Del my *2 S'Chase 3:594 4↑ Alw 3500 2 2 26 14 22 24 Leonard W 156 w *.80 - - Beneksar141 4Rouge Dragon156 3Boojum II156 50 No match 4
16May46- 5Bel fst *2 S'Chase 3:524 4↑ C L Appleton 8.8k 5 3 315 34 48¼ 412½ Fife M 149 w *1.05 - - BurmaRoad139 5FloatingIsl151 7WrBttl152½ Slow start,tired 6
8May46- 5Pim fst *2 S'Chase 3:511 4↑ Jervis Spencer H 11k 2 4 32 35½ 11½ 12 Leonard W 153 w *1.00 - - Rouge Dragon153 2Delhi Dan137 1¼Navigate143 8 8
Bobbled 10th,ridden out
30Apr46- 3Pim fst *2 S'Chase 3:513 4↑ Alw 3500 2 2 13 14 18 110 Leonard W 152 w 2.85 - - Rouge Dragon152 10Soldier Song152¾Delhi Dan143 6 Easily 10
28Nov45- 5Pim sly 2½ S'Chase 5:252 4↑ Manly H 12k 10 3 48½ - - - Passmore F 150wb 2.90e - - PursuitPlane132 5BurmaRoad139 12GkFlg138 4 Lost rider 13th 10
6Nov45- 5Bel fst *3 S'Chase 5:50 4↑ Temple Gwathmey H 15k 8 3 36 11 26 413 Owen W 151wb *1.05e - - Caddie139 6Refugio130 4FloatingIsl149 3 Weakened final ¼ 8
31Oct45- 4Pim fst 2 S'Chase 3:494 4↑ J Spencer H (Div 1) 11k 8 3 37½ 31½ 36 34½ Leonard W 154 w *1.30 - - BoojumII141 2Raylywyn144 2½RougeDragn154½ Bad landing 9th 8
3Oct45- 5Bel fst *3 S'Chase 5:48 4↑ Grand National H 18k 2 2 35 55½ 625 631¾ Leonard W 153 w 2.85e - - Mercator142 5Caddie139¾Raylywn142 6 12
Poor landings,not persevered with
26Sep45- 5Bel fst *2½ S'Chase 4:484 4↑ Brook H 9.3k 1 1 21 23 24 26 Roberts E 155 w *.95e - - Raylywn137 6Rouge Dragon155 2Elkridge148no 10
Bothered by riderless horse
31Aug45- 5Bel fst *2½ S'Chase 4:51 4↑ Saratoga H 9.1k 7 3 2hd 11½ 1nk 1nk Roberts E 152 w 3.20 - - RougeDragn152nkSoldierSong139noBurmaRoad141hd Gamely 9
17Aug45- 4Bel fst *2 S'Chase 3:45 3↑ North American H 16k 2 8 67½ 812 915 812¼ Leonard W 157 w *2.40 - - Floating Isle149nkChesapeake136½Elkridge158 1 No factor 10
10Aug45- 3Bel fst *2 S'Chase 3:491 4↑ Shillelah 6.1k 10 2 2hd 11½ 21½ 21 Leonard W 152 w *1.10e - - Raylywn136 1Rouge Dragon152 1Mercator137 6 Driving 10
27Jun45- 3Del fst *2 S'Chase 3:503 4↑ Georgetown H 12k 4 2 21 11 11½ 2½ Owen W 159 w *1.50e - - Iron Shot150½Rouge Dragon159 6Elkridge159½ Held gamely 8
24Nov44- 5Pim fst 2½ S'Chase 4:56 4↑ Manly H 12k 7 2 23 24 24 2½ Leonard W 160 w *1.25 - - Royal Archer138½Rouge Dragon160 6Invader132 1 Gamely 9
17Nov44- 5Pim fst 2 S'Chase 3:493 3↑ Battleship H 10k 8 3 36 2hd 2hd 21 Leonard W 162 w *2.20 - - Ahmisk144 1RougeDragn162 7BoojumII140 4 Led between calls 9
6Nov44- 5Bel fst *3 S'Chase 5:57 4↑ Temple Gwathmey H 15k 2 2 37 21 21½ 42 Leonard W 163 w *1.75 - - Burma Road139 1¾Parma135hdAhmisk143nk Swerved,faltered 7
4Oct44- 5Bel fst *3 S'Chase 5:541 4↑ Grand National H 16k 5 2 11½ 12 11½ 2hd Leonard W 164 w 4.05 - - BurmaRoad136hdRougeDrgn164 7Elkridge167 8 Jumped poorly 6
27Sep44- 5Bel fst *2½ S'Chase 4:552 4↑ Brook H 8.8k 3 1 1½ 11½ 12 13 Leonard W 160 w *2.35 - - RougeDrgn160 3BurmaRoad136 5GrekFlg134 1½ Speed to spare 9
1Sep44- 5Bel fst *2½ S'Chase 4:491 4↑ Saratoga H 8.5k 3 4 43½ 42¾ 410½ 413 Leonard W 164 w 1.95 - - Elkridge155 8Brdlspur132 1Invdr140 4 Bad landing 9th,tired 5
25Aug44- 5Bel fst *2 S'Chase 3:481 3↑ Beverwyck H 5.9k 4 3 22 13 11½ 11¼ Leonard W 161 w 3.95 - - RougeDragon161 1¼Knight'sQuest142 2½Redlands137 15 Driving 7
18Aug44- 3Bel my *2 S'Chase 3:49 3↑ North American H 5.8k 4 3 413 49½ - - Leonard W 162 w *1.45 - - Ossabaw134¾Redlands136 1½Knght'sQust145 8 Lost rider 11th 7
28Jun44- 4Del fst *2½ S'Chase 4:504 4↑ Indian River H 7.5k 4 4 45½ 35 11½ 12 Leonard W 161 w 2.90e - - Rouge Dragon161 2Caddie143 7Mercator141 10 Swerved 6
21Jun44- 4Del fst *2 S'Chase 3:513 4↑ Georgetown H 7.9k 1 4 33 46½ 32½ 1nk Owen W 158 w 6.45 - - RougeDragon158nkKnight'sQuest144 6MadPolicy138 2 Driving 6
3Jun44- 3Bel fst *2 Hurdles 3:494 3↑ Alw 2500 2 6 514 513 726 725¼ Owen W 158 w *1.05 - - Raylywn147nkThe Beak140 2Yankee Chance155 5 Dull 8
16May44- 5Bel fst *2 S'Chase 3:493 4↑ CL Appleton 4.6k 2 4 46 417 414 420 Owen W 161 w *.70 - - IronShot158 6GreekFlag144 2TheBeak141 12 Bad landing 8th 5

5May44- 5Pim	fst	2	S'Chase	3:511	4↑ J Spencer H 12k	2 2 34 43 1½ 11½	Owen W	157 w	*1.10e	--	Rouge Dragon1571½Mercator144nkCaddie1481½	Driving	10
22Apr44- 3Pim	fst	2	S'Chase	4:011	4↑ Handicap 2000	5 2 1½ 12 1½ 1¾	Owen W	153 w	*.70	--	Rouge Dragon153¾Greek Flag1383Good Chance1425	Driving	5
20Nov43- 5Mtp	fst	1¾	Hurdles	3:374	3↑ Alw 500	2 1 1 14 16 17	Harrison JS	162 w	*.30	--	Rouge Dragon1627Rollo1576Sander135		3
8Nov43- 5Pim	my	2½	S'Chase	5:093	4↑ Manly H 9.1k	2 4 43¾ 614 643 649¾	Harrison JS	154 w	*1.95e	--	Iron Shot146nkCaddie13915Mercator1393	Showed nothing	6
18Oct43- 5Pim	gd	2	S'Chase	3:56	3↑ Gov Ogle H 6.6k	9 4 56 65 25 11	Harrison JS	153 w	*1.45	--	RougeDrgon1531Cdd1376GrkFlg1373	Bad landing 6th,driving	9
29Sep43- 3Bel	fst	*2½	S'Chase	4:50	4↑ Brook H 6.6k	8 1 12 21½ 32½ 13	Harrison JS	147 w	*2.65	--	Rouge Dragon1473Knight's Quest140noBank Note1381	Easily	10
28Aug43- 3Bel	gd	1½	Hurdles	2:521	3↑ Alw 2300	1 3 31 31 46 47	Harrison JS	153 w	*1.25	--	BoojumII153hdGulliverII1383Kennebunk1354	Weak handling	5
18Aug43- 3Bel	fst	*2	S'Chase	3:463	3↑ Beverwyck H 4.1k	1 2 33 1½ 1hd 1½	Harrison JS	145 w	12.30	--	Rouge Dragon145½Iron Shot1458Brother Jones1471½	Gamely	10
31Jly43- 3Bel	fst	*2	S'Chase	3:464	4↑ Handicap 2075	5 1 12 21½ 33¼ 34½	Lacy H	149 w	3.75	--	Replica II1421½Iron Shot1523Rouge Dragon1497	Tired	6
3Jly43- 4Det	fst	*2	S'Chase	4:032	4↑ Handicap 5000	1 3 21½ 2½ 11 12½	Harrison JS	144 w	2.00e	--	RougeDragn1442½Bavarian1373½Ossabaw1386	Speed to spare	6
9Jun43- 3Aqu	my	*2	S'Chase	3:511	4↑ Lion Heart H 3.8k	2 8 79½ 78 89½ 610½	Harrison JS	145 w	7.00	--	Knight's Quest1452Invader150noIron Shot1474	No mishap	9
25May43- 3Bel	fst	*2	S'Chase	3:521	4↑ Corinthian H 3.9k	8 2 32 2hd 57½ 514¼	Harrison JS	148 w	4.35	--	Invader145nkBrother Jones1394Boojum II1385	Bore in 3rd	8
18May43- 5Bel	fst	*2	S'Chase	3:494	4↑ CL Appleton 3.9k	4 3 36 21½ 11 13	Harrison JS	144 w	3.35	--	Rouge Dragon1443Knight's Quest1492½Redlands1523		8
	Swerved at final fence												
24Apr43- 3Pim	fst	2	S'Chase	4:111	4↑ Alw 1500	3 2 11½ 14 112 112	Harrison JS	146 w	3.45	--	Rouge Dragon14612Ossabaw1483Frederic II1501½		7
	Swerved at several fences,eased up late												
19Apr43- 1Pim	my	2	S'Chase	4:224	4↑ Clm 2000	2 1 11½ 15 11½ 15	Harrison JS	146 w	2.80	--	RougeDragon1465Alcadl13515StrollngOn1525	Speed to spare	7
	Previously owned by Montpelier												
21Nov42- 5Mtp	fst	1¾	Hurdles	3:331	3↑ Alw 500	1 3 35 34½ 26 28	Harrison JS	153 w	-	--	Enterprise1398RougeDragon1538Ossabaw15710	Strong finish	4
14Oct42- 3Lrl	sl	*2	S'Chase	4:183	3↑ Governor Ogle H 4.4k	1 1 1hd 35 424 428	Penrod J	135wb	2.50	--	Elkridge1488Redlands1398Strolling On13312	Tired quickly	5
7Oct42- 3Bel	fst	*3	S'Chase	6:051	4↑ Grand National H 17k	2 3 32 48¼ 632 666	Penrod J	136 w	11.20	--	Cottsmor1557Cupd13430IronShot1391	Bad landing 15th,tired	9
23Sep42- 3Bel	fst	*2	S'Chase	3:483	3↑ Broad Hollow H 3.9k	2 1 1½ 1nk 31½ 38½	Slate F	137 w	3.65	--	Elkrdg1453½LovlyNght1525RougDrgn1372½	Bobbled 8th,hung	5
29Aug42- 3Sar	fst	*2	S'Chase	4:16	3↑ Alw 1200	4 4 42 77¾ 2½ 12½	Clements HW	139 w	*1.15	--	Rouge Dragon1392½Nayr1391Cortesano1522		7
	Shuffled back 10th,easily												
1Nov41- 3Pim	hy	*2	S'Chase	4:101	3↑ Alw 1000	2 3 23 12 110 110	Jennings E	134 w	*1.75	--	RougeDragon134.510WarPort1461½Millrac1488	Eased up late	8
16Oct41- 2Lrl	fst	*2	S'Chase	3:54	3↑ Alw 1000	2 1 18 112 18 16	Jennings E	135 w	2.50	--	Rouge Dragon1356Bagpipe1451Frederic II1433		6
	Swerved at several jumps												
21Aug41- 1Sar	fst	*2	S'Chase	4:202	3↑ Alw 1200	2 1 13 110 16 110	Jennings E	138 w	*.65e	--	Rouge Dragon13810Pico Blanco II1498Sir Wick135hd	Easily	7
9Aug41- 1Sar	fst	*2	S'Chase	4:18	3↑ Alw 1500	5 1 12 15 11 2hd	Jennings E	135 w	2.70	--	Buck Langhorne137hdRouge Dragon1352½Archery136100		6
	Bad landing last,recovered												
14Jun41- 2PiR	fst	*1½	Hurdles	3:111	3↑ Alw 600	3 1 11½ 14 14 15	Jennings E	135 w	33.60	--	RgeDrgn1355KingCob14510NorthSea13515	Never threatened	8
	Previously trained by S.L. Burch												
26Jun40- 1Del	my	5½f	:232 :471	1:081	©Md Sp Wt	1 7 65¾ 79½ 1012 810	Driscoll D	118wb	124.85	81-29	Cavalier118nkZacorel1183Fantastical1181½	No excuse	11
20Jun40- 5Del	fst	5½f	:231 :472	1:074	Alw 1000	4 5 65¼ 68¾ 69¼ 69¾	Driscoll D	111wb	33.10	83-13	Overdrawn1134Miss Brideaux114nkDon Orlan115½	Trailed	6
8Jun40- 1Del	fst	5f	:232 :471	1:003	Md Sp Wt	5 10 1012 1011 1117 1121	Driscoll D	116 w	47.20	72-07	Curious Coin1161½Fitzedward116½Primarily1162½	Outrun	11

Royal Governor

ch. g. 1944, by Pilate (Friar Rock)–Feathers, by John P. Grier

Lifetime record: 135 28 15 18 $360,900

Own.– Mrs J.R.H. Thouron

Br.– Abram S. Hewitt (Va)

Tr.– J.E. Ryan

8Jun55- 6Del	sly	1 1/16	:233 :473 1:132	1:47	3↑ Alw 5000	3 5 59½ 57 59 58	Westrope J	117 w	11.80	68-22	Resilnt103noRustcBlly1172SnorCot1053	Trailed throughout	5
28May55- 7Del	fst	1 1/16	:233 :471 1:112	1:434	4↑ Alw 5000	4 6 64½ 37 38 310	Glassner G	119 w	4.80	82-12	RusticBilly1195Browse1065RoyalGovernor1193	Evenly late	6
26May55- 7Bel	hd	1⅜Ⓣ		2:181	3↑ Handicap 7500	3 7 56 44¼ 46 33¾	Bailey PJ	116 w	7.25	92-04	AlcibiadesII116nkDeepRvrII1153½RoylGovrnor116nk	Rallied	8
17May55- 7Bel	fst	1 1/16	:24 :471 1:113	1:423	4↑ Alw 6000	1 3 38 415 519 516	Westrope J	119 w	18.25	82-13	Chief Fanelli1163Dear Brutus1164Capeador1194	Outrun	6
9Apr55- 7Jam	fst	6f	:232 :463	1:11	3↑ Handicap 6000	8 8 813 815 819 816	Westrope J	113 w	35.20	76-17	Squared Away1222½Cyclotron116¾This Side1137	Trailed	8
3Mar55- 8Hia	fm	1⅛Ⓣ		1:511	4↑ Alw 4500	6 6 68 44 41½ 1hd	Brooks S	118 w	*1.80	93-07	RoyalGovernor118hdSickl'sSound105hdSmBrook109hd	Driving	7
25Feb55- 5Hia	fm	1 3/16Ⓣ		1:564	4↑ Alw 7500	5 5 53½ 53½ 54 44	Brooks S	110 w	6.35	89-07	Social Outcast1242Maharajah121hdKaster1212	No menace	5
21Feb55- 7Hia	fm	1⅛Ⓣ		1:513	4↑ Alw 5000	1 5 44 32 21½ 21¼	Guerin E	116 w	2.75	90-09	Potpourri1151¼Royal Governor116nkDead Duck115¾	Gamely	5
10Feb55- 7Hia	fm	1 1/16Ⓣ		1:441	4↑ Alw 6000	1 6 54 53 34 53¼	Atkinson T	109 w	24.35	92-05	Mister Black121¾Kaster1212Abbe Sting118½	Gave way late	12
3Feb55- 8Hia	hd	1⅛Ⓣ		1:502	4↑ Alw 5000	4 12 1112 88 76½ 77¾	Atkinson T	110 w	18.45	89-03	Kaster121½Lebanon Lad1042Assuan110nk	Never a menace	12
25Jan55- 7Hia	hd	1⅛Ⓣ		1:502	4↑ Alw 6000	3 9 810 74 44 57½	Nichols J	121 w	16.00	89-03	Cascunez1213½Assuan1121Lebanon Lad1093	No mishap	9
21Jan55- 6Hia	fst	7f	:234 :47 1:114	1:243	4↑ Alw 4500	1 8 86¾ 75¾ 43½ 43½	Nichols J	121 w	22.70	83-18	Helfast118noFull Flight1241Fife and Drum1212½	Late gain	8
21Oct54- 7Bel	fst	1 1/16	:232 :464 1:114	1:434	4↑ Alw 5000	2 4 76¾ 78¼ 79½ 711½	Westrope J	120 w	35.75	80-15	FlyWheel1143SpinningTop110hdDr.Stanley1111	Done early	9
16Oct54- 7Lrl	fm	*1⅛Ⓣ		1:51	3↑ Turf Cup H 25k	13 2 63¾ 106½ 1113 1117	Scurlock D	112wb	26.80	70-13	Stan1262½News Again1112½Tritium1142	Tired badly	13
8Oct54- 6Bel	fm	1⅜Ⓣ		2:181	3↑ Alw 10000	2 3 24 22 32½ 43¾	Westrope J	119 w	7.30	92-04	Blood Test113½Aria Viva1131¾Nitribois1141½	Tired late	8
29Sep54- 6Bel	fm	1⅜Ⓣ		2:174	3↑ Lion d'Or H 15k	10 9 912 711 56½ 69¾	Westrope J	115 w	4.55e	88-02	Kaster122½Cascunuez1081¾Tritium1142	Dropped far back	13
22Sep54- 6Bel	gd	6f-WC	:224 :461	1:111	2↑ Fall Highweight H 25k	1 14 149¾ 1412 1010 1212	Westrope J	113 w	34.80f	73-21	Pet Bully1361½Dutch Lane1171½Dark Peter125½	No speed	14
15Sep54- 6Atl	fm	1⅛Ⓣ	:473 1:124 1:382	1:51	3↑ ⓇAmerican Bred 30k	3 9 96¼ 95¾ 79 64½	Westrope J	118 w	7.10e	83-13	Brush Burn122¾Closed Door1221County Clare1221	Rallied	10
	Restricted to horses foaled within the continental United States												
9Sep54- 6Aqu	fst	6f	:231 :471	1:114	3↑ Handicap 6045	2 6 88¾ 79¾ 79½ 711	Westrope J	113 w	55.90	82-15	CopperKettle119hdBrdly1222Ruthrd1172	Raced far off pace	8
25Aug54- 7Sar	fst	1	:242 :471 1:122	1:373	3↑ Handicap 5050	3 9 67½ 77½ 821 922	Eccard R	111 w	40.05	67-18	Crash Dive1222Trusting1124½Bradley1151	Void of speed	9
12Jun54- 7Bel	hd	1⅜Ⓣ		2:172	3↑ Handicap 15085	11 12 1110 105¾ 108¼ 93½	Westrope J	121 w	9.80	--	Kaster121½Williamsburg107hdPicador116no	Never a menace	13
31May54- 6Del	fst	1 1/16	:233 :471 1:112	1:432	3↑ Brandywine H 24k	5 8 95¾ 99¾ 812 713	Green B	115 w	7.80	81-17	Cold Command116nkFirst Aid1136Better Goods1091	Outrun	10
22May54- 5Bel	sf	1⅜Ⓣ		2:211	3↑ Handicap 10045	4 4 2hd 1hd 11 1nk	Westrope J	122 w	*1.30	--	RoyalGovernor122nkTurgueneff1111½OutPoint113nk	Driving	7
10May54- 7Bel	sf	7fⓉ		1:31	3↑ Handicap 7555	3 5 55¼ 54½ 1½ 11½	Westrope J	117 w	5.25	--	RoyalGovernor1171½Kaster1224JamiK.1131½	Increasing lead	8
1May54- 5Bel	fm	7fⓉ		1:242	4↑ Alw 7500	1 8 87¾ 88½ 43½ 32	Atkinson T	119 w	7.80	--	Kaster1191½Pcdor112½RoylGovrnor1192½	Closed ground fast	10
27Apr54- 6Bel	fst	1	:223 :454 1:103	1:37	3↑ Eight Thirty H 15k	3 14 1512 119¼ 915 117	Westrope J	114 w	33.20	82-19	OpenShow119nkGoldenGloves114½JamieK.111¾	Never a factor	15
19Apr54- 5Jam	fst	1 1/16	:243 :483 1:133	1:452	4↑ Alw 5000	4 6 65¼ 44½ 24 33½	Westrope J	122 w	5.15	81-18	War Command1123Lafourche119½Royal Governor1221½	Hung	7
14Apr54- 5Jam	fst	6f	:233 :464	1:113	3↑ Handicap 6045	2 1 66 66 63½ 54¼	Westrope J	113 w	13.90	85-18	ColdCommand1231Hilarious1262½Armageddn115½	Late spurt	7
3Mar54- 7Hia	hd	1½Ⓣ		2:284	3↑ Hia Turf H 64k	10 4 64½ 129¾ 1216 1218	Stout J	114 w	3.90e	82-00	Picador1062½Royal Vale126½Parnassus1202	Done early	12
25Feb54- 7Hia	hd	1 3/16Ⓣ		1:56	4↑ Alw 6000	4 3 32½ 2hd 1hd 2½	Westrope J	112 w	4.15	96-03	IcebergII121½RoyalGovernor112½CombatBoots1124	Held well	6
17Feb54- 7Hia	hd	1 3/16Ⓣ		1:552	3↑ Bougainvillea H 33k	7 9 98 86¼ 1213 1113	Westrope J	113 w	*2.65e	93-00	Parnassus1113½Picador105½Abbe Sting116½	Dull effort	12
12Feb54- 7Hia	hd	1 1/16Ⓣ		1:431	4↑ Alw 6000	1 4 42 32 21 1nk	Westrope J	112 w	3.10	100-00	Royal Governor112nkMackville1122Parnassus1163	Driving	10
6Feb54- 5Hia	fst	6f	:222 :452	1:101	4↑ Alw 5000	4 7 79¼ 67½ 67¼ 56¾	Westrope J	118 w	19.50	90-11	Hyphasis1183Jet Master112¾Eatontown1131	No mishap	8
30Jan54- 8Hia	fst	7f	:23 :462 1:113	1:242	4↑ Alw 4500	3 6 66 53½ 51¾ 63	Stout J	118 w	7.45	85-12	Brown Booter1131½Ceremonious109hdSlim1071	No mishap	7
	Previously raced in name of Mrs E. duPont Weir												
4Nov53- 6Jam	fst	6f	:231 :46	1:113	3↑ Sport Page H 22k	2 1 89½ 98½ 88¼ 86	Westrope J	112 w	15.55	83-21	White Skies1301¼Hilarious114hdJoe Jones107¾	No threat	9
31Oct53- 6Lrl	fst	*1⅛Ⓣ		1:511	3↑ Turf Cup H (Div 1) 23k	1 5 64¼ 65¼ 32½ 21	Guerin E	120 w	3.90	85-15	Sunglow1141RoyalGovrnr1202FreshMeadow1101	Good effort	10
17Oct53- 6Jam	fst	1⅛	:472 1:113 1:37	1:501	3↑ Grey Lag H 62k	5 7 88¾ 1516 1529 1531	Westrope J	116 w	23.00	64-21	Find1154Dictar119¾Olympic113no	Dull form	15
7Oct53- 7Atl	gd	5½fⓉ	:221 :453	1:052	3↑ Absecon Island H 11k	9 7 88¼ 72¾ 52½ 52½	Westrope J	118 w	8.00	90-14	Algasir1182Roaming119½Blue Rhymer113no	Blocked late	10
26Sep53- 6Atl	fst	1 3/16Ⓣ	:473 1:12 1:362	1:554	3↑ U Nations H 60k	2 4 45 52½ 52½ 31½	Stout J	118 w	*.60e	111-00	IcebergII1201¼BrushBrun118nkRoyalGovernor118½	Blocked	8
16Sep53- 6Atl	fst	1⅛Ⓣ	:47 1:111 1:364	1:50	3↑ ⓇAmerican Bred 30k	8 4 31 11½ 11½ 1nk	Westrope J	122 w	8.30	93-06	RoyalGovernor122nkTheEagl1221½Potpourr122no	Hard drive	9
	Restricted to horses foaled within the continental United States												

Date	Track	Dist	Fractions	Race	PP	St	1C	2C	Str	Fin	Jockey	Wt	Med	Odds	Spd	Top Finishers	Comment	Field
5Sep53- 7Atl	fst	1 1/16Ⓣ	:232 :464 1:11 1:433	3↑ Atl City Turf H 23k	9	8	76½	65¾	63	2¾	Stout J	109	w	14.30	101-00	SaddleTramp107¾RoylGovrnor109¾IcbrgII119nk	Sharp effort	10
22Aug53- 6Atl	fst	1Ⓣ	:232 :47 1:112 1:371	3↑ Boardwalk H (Div 1) 18k	6	7	72¾	33	3½	45¾	Contreras J	112	w	50.40	89-04	Sunglow1083½Armageddon1211½Potpourri114¾	Weakened	10
14Aug53- 5Sar	fst	1⅛	:48 1:123 1:381 1:522	3↑ Alw 4500	2	4	57½	68	614	617	Westrope J	113	w	17.05	71-18	CombatBoots1134Bassanio1105Sickl'sSound109no	Done early	6
4Aug53- 7Sar	fst	6f	:23 :461 1:123	3↑ Alw 4000	1	10	1016	1017	914	108¼	Westrope J	113	w	16.25	77-17	Kaster118nkMr. Midnight106¾Caesar Did1103	No threat	11
22Jly53- 6Jam	fst	1 1/16	:252 :494 1:14 1:451	4↑ Alw 5000	5	4	44	42½	34	45½	Westrope J	118	w	3.35	80-15	Mully S.1181¼Begorra1183½Dawn Flight113¾	No rally	5
3Jly53- 7Del	sl	1 1/16	:234 :474 1:124 1:47	3↑ Alw 5000	1	4	45½	47	410	410	Westrope J	111	wb	3.55	66-25	G.R. Petersen1201½Promptness1086Fred R.1202½	No menace	6
27Jun53- 7Del	fst	6f	:223 :461 1:111	4↑ Alw 5000	3	5	46½	42½	42	52½	Westrope J	112	wb	*1.75	86-07	Banta112noPotpourri119nkSteak Bone115¾	No rally	6
16Nov51- 7Pim	sl	1 3/16	:472 1:112 1:372 1:572	3↑ Pim Spl 15k	2	4	31½	22	412	419	Bierman C	126	wb	*.80e	74-26	Bryan G.1265County Delight12612Call Over1262¼	No rally	4
12Nov51- 6Jam	fst	6f	:231 :454 1:111	2↑ Autumn Day H 17k	5	8	53	42¼	54	73¼	Boulmetis S	114	wb	6.35	88-20	Tea-Maker115½Guillotine126¾Delegate120hd	No rally	9
5Nov51- 6Jam	fst	1 1/16	:25 :482 1:123 1:443	3↑ Handicap 5065	1	6	44½	52¾	33	43	Guerin E	122	wb	*1.20	86-17	[D]All at Once108hdTed M.1152½Lambent112½	Tired	8
	Placed third through disqualification																	
27Oct51- 5Jam	fst	5½f	:23 :461 1:044	3↑ Handicap 5040	4	4	72¾	63¾	51¾	11¼	Guerin E	122	wb	5.95	94-15	Royal Governor1221¼Pictus117nkVigorous1181½	Driving	7
17Oct51- 5Bel	fst	1	:24 :471 1:112 1:364	3↑ Handicap 5050	2	1	2hd	2½	2hd	3¾	Guerin E	116	wb	4.80	89-15	Nullify106hdMiche122¾Royal Governor1162	Game effort	6
28Sep51- 7Atl	fst	6f	:23 :462 1:113	3↑ Alw 4500	7	4	66½	66	65¾	44¾	Servis J	119	w	1.90	82-19	Passemson112¾Mahoon117½Woodford Sir1143½	No rally	8
24Sep51- 6Bel	fst	6f-WC	:222 :443 1:09	2↑ Fall Highweight H 25k	3	12		156¼	165	125½	Combest N	128	w	*4.85f	90-07	Guillotine134noSquared Away1262Ferd128no	Outrun	18
3Sep51- 7Was	fst	1	:222 :443 1:09 1:343	3↑ Wash Park H 159k	14	7	1211	1212	119¼	117¾	Baird RL	116	w	8.50e	89-07	Curandero115noOilCapitol1161½CountyDlght1231½	No factor	19
25Aug51- 7Was	fst	1 3/16Ⓣ	:474 1:364 1:544	3↑ Meadowland H 55k	5	7	57	65	811	910	Gorman D	120	w	4.80	90-07	Volcanic1281½Cuore1131½Mr. Fox111no	No factor	9
8Aug51- 6Sar	my	6f	:234 :464 1:113	3↑ Handicap 4035	2	3	33	33½	32½	24½	Servis J	121	w	3.65	85-21	NorthernStar1124½RoylGovrnr121noMgcWords1158	Went well	4
4Jly51- 7AP	fst	1⅛Ⓣ	:47 1:112 1:361 1:491	3↑ Stars & Stripes H 60k	7	8	64¾	31½	11	11	Arcaro E	115	w	6.80	100-07	Royal Governor1151Volcanic1243½Miche1162	Driving	17
20Jun51- 5Del	fst	1 1/16	:23 :463 1:113 1:442	3↑ Alw 4000	4	6	56½	53½	54	45	Nichols J	122	wb	2.10	86-10	Bit o' Fate1171½Loyal Legion1221Arcave1162½	Tired	6
9Jun51- 5Del	fst	1¼	:472 1:12 1:37 2:02	3↑ Sussex H 28k	4	2	1hd	34	47½	511	Nichols J	116	wb	5.75	89-14	Cochise1243½Bit o' Fate1084½Post Card1161	Tired	6
5Jun51- 6Del	my	6f	:232 :474 1:13	4↑ Alw 3500	1	2	45	43	32	2½	Nichols J	126	wb	*.80	85-28	LoyalLegion117½RoyalGovrnr1262½LedngHom1125	No excuse	6
29May51- 6Del	gd	6f	:224 :462 1:113	3↑ Wilmington H 12k	5	6	610	57½	45	31	Nichols J	115	wb	4.50	92-20	CallOver1151Tea-Maker125hdRoyalGovernor115nk	Late rush	6
24May51- 4Bel	gd	6f	:222 :453 1:102	3↑ Handicap 4545	4	5	511	57	55	55¾	Nichols J	122	wb	2.60	91-10	SingingStep119nkAri'sMona1042MghtyQust1171½	Dull effort	6
18May51- 7Bel	fst	6f	:222 :451 1:101	4↑ Alw 4500	3	3	63¾	53½	32½	32	Guerin E	115	wb	*1.30	97-05	Sagittrus1141¼Extngushr114¾RoylGovrnor1151¼	Closed well	7
3Nov50- 6Pim	fst	1 3/16	:493 1:14 1:393 1:583	3↑ Pim Spl 15k	1	2	22	21	44	48¾	Scurlock O	126	wb	*1.70	78-19	One Hitter1262½Chicle II1261¼Abstract1265	Tired	4
27Oct50- 6Lrl	fst	6f	:224 :464 1:113	3↑ Alw 4000	7	2	55¼	43¼	41¾	11	McLean P	122	wb	*1.80	89-19	Royal Governor1221Flying Weather1191Magnet1161	Drew out	7
25Sep50- 6Bel	fst	7f	:223 :453 1:102 1:23	2↑ Vosburgh H 18k	2	11	1110	106¾	44½	55¼	Guerin E	118	wb	6.75	90-15	Tea-Maker1181¼More Sun106½Piet124nk	Closed gap	12
18Sep50- 6Bel	fst	6f-WC	:221 :443 1:084	2↑ Fall Highweight H 25k	7	14		132½	123	32¼	Guerin E	129	wb	8.85	95-06	Arise1332Delegate128nkRoyal Governor129½	Finished well	14
19Aug50- 6Sar	my	1¼	:483 1:132 1:383 2:053	3↑ Saratoga H 29k	4	7	89½	56½	47	69¼	Arcaro E	115	w	5.85	71-21	Better Self1141Greek Ship1101Arise1183½	Tired	9
11Aug50- 6Sar	fst	7f	:23 :462 1:11 1:233	3↑ American Legion H 9.5k	13	6	32	23	32	66	McLean P	118	w	8.90	92-13	Arise1152Guillotine118nkLoser Weeper1191½	Faltered	13
15Jly50- 6Jam	fst	1 3/16	:473 1:121 1:364 1:55	3↑ Butler H 58k	2	2	811	87¾	43½	32	Boland W	118	w	9.80	99-11	[D]Three Rings1201½Loser Weeper118½Royal Governor118½		10
	Placed second through disqualification																	
4Jly50- 6Aqu	fst	1¼	:474 1:121 1:371 2:03	3↑ Brooklyn H 59k	10	7	57	56	54¼	43¾	Guerin E	118	w	6.90	88-12	MyRequest1191¼DoublBrandy1151½HypocritII1031	No mishap	10
1Jly50- 6Aqu	fst	7f	:224 :453 1:102 1:231	3↑ Carter H 24k	3	9	98¼	98¾	97¾	86¼	Rogers C	121	w	8.00	90-10	Guillotine109¾Noble Impulse1141Hyphasis1081	Dull try	10
17Jun50- 5Del	fst	1¼	:474 1:122 1:373 2:03	3↑ Sussex H 30k	3	4	66½	42¼	41½	3¾	Rogers C	118	w	3.90	94-14	Cochise125¾Curandero112hdRoylGovrnor1182	Close quarters	7
14Jun50- 5Del	sly	1 1/16	:244 :492 1:142 1:451	3↑ Alw 3000	2	4	43½	3½	11	13	Rogers C	120	w	*.35	87-20	Royal Governor1203Taran1145Algasir1178	Easily	4
24May50- 6Bel	fst	6f-WC	:222 :444 1:09	3↑ Roseben H 12k	3	9	97¾	85¼	63	31¼	Guerin E	122	wb	10.35	95-07	Olympia130nkWine List1101Royal Governor122hd	Great rush	9
20May50- 6Bel	sly	1	:23 :452 1:102 1:363	3↑ Metropolitan H 31k	1	7	76¾	65¾	64½	64½	Rogers C	119	wb	11.25	86-13	Greek Ship106½Piet121¾Cochise1211¼	No rally	11
13May50- 6Pim	fst	1 3/16	:484 1:12 1:364 1:561	3↑ Dixie H 26k	9	1	11½	1½	22	46¼	Rogers C	118	wb	4.20	93-13	Loser Weeper1085Double Brandy110¾Going Away106½	Outrun	9
29Apr50- 6Jam	gd	1 3/16	:473 1:12 1:372 1:57	3↑ Gallant Fox H 60k	3	3	41½	43	23	52	Rogers C	120	wb	9.15	89-14	BetterSelf1161¼ChicleII120hdLoserWeeper109nk	Weakened	13
8Apr50- 6Jam	fst	1 1/16	:241 :473 1:112 1:434	3↑ Excelsior H 24k	1	6	75¾	74½	75	97½	Rogers C	122	w	4.00	86-10	Arise1161½Olympia1261½Delegate1191	Close quarters	10
1Apr50- 6Jam	fst	6f	:222 :461 1:104	3↑ Paumonok H 30k	2	13	139	128¼	84½	98½	Rogers C	126	w	7.30	88-14	Olympia1241¼Arise118½Delegate1223	No factor	15
25Feb50- 6Hia	sl	1¼	:48 1:122 1:382 2:06	3↑ Widener H 61k	5	2	36½	35	22	1nk	Rogers C	118	w	2.95	75-27	Royal Governor118nkArise1096Going Away1104	Hard drive	6
11Feb50- 6Hia	fst	1⅛	:463 1:111 1:37 1:501	3↑ McLennan H 33k	10	8	106¾	64¼	44	21	Rogers C	116	w	14.75	86-17	ThreeRings1171RoyalGovernor1161Coaltown1321	Stout rally	11
3Dec49- 6Bow	fst	1 3/16	:48 1:123 1:383 1:582	3↑ Bryan & O'Hara H 21k	6	4	51¾	62¾	1112	1114	Lynch J	124	w	2.50	81-10	Double Brandy1111½Oriole108noSeaward1132½	Dull effort	11
19Nov49- 6Bow	fst	1 1/16	:241 :482 1:132 1:452	2↑ T K Lynch Mem H 12k	12	9	109¾	96½	57½	45½	Errico C	125	w	*1.20	88-10	Cochise113½Seaward1135Manchac109no	Forced back	13
12Nov49- 6Jam	fst	1 3/16	:471 1:113 1:37 1:564	3↑ Westchester H 29k	8	5	56½	77¾	21	3nk	Scurlock O	123	w	3.20	92-17	ThreeRings116nkDelegate120hdRoyalGovernor1235	Game try	11
26Oct49- 6Jam	sly	1 1/16	:243 :48 1:122 1:452	3↑ Questionnaire H 23k	7	6	66½	44	1hd	11	Guerin E	118	w	3.60	86-17	Royal Governor1181Donor120½Vulcan's Forge125¾	Driving	8
15Oct49- 6Jam	fst	1 1/16	:242 :48 1:124 1:442	3↑ Grey Lag H 29k	7	5	45	31½	1½	11	Scurlock O	114	w	15.25	91-16	Royal Governor1141Three Rings116hdCapot121nk	Driving	12
12Oct49- 6Jam	fst	6f	:224 :461 1:111	3↑ Interborough H 17k	6	9	108	105¾	1½	11	Guerin E	119	w	9.50	95-15	Royal Governor1191Delegate122noPipette1121½	Driving	10
3Oct49- 6GS	fst	6f	:222 :453 1:10	3↑ Princeton H 12k	4	6	86	76½	78½	56½	Lynch J	118	w	10.20	91-16	RoyalBlood1165CarraraMarble1181Rippy124½	Close quarters	12
19Sep49- 6Bel	fst	6f-WC	:23 :461 1:12	2↑ Fall Highweight H 24k	12	4		73¼	31½	1hd	Guerin E	129	w	8.70	81-16	RoyalGovernor129hdRoyalBlood132nkTea-Maker127¾	Driving	13
3Sep49- 6Aqu	fst	1 1/16	:243 :482 1:123 1:46	3↑ Aqueduct H 23k	5	4	42½	42½	52¼	84½	Lynch J	114	w	12.10	79-19	Wine List114½[D]Loser Weeper114¾Riverlane107½	Tired	14
23Aug49- 6Sar	fst	6f	:223 :463 1:11	3↑ Handicap 4060	1	7	75½	54	51¼	41	Arcaro E	118	w	3.00	92-11	Wine List115hdBlue Border115nkRoyal Blood114¾	Blocked	10
18Aug49- 5Sar	sly	6f	:231 :471 1:122	3↑ Handicap 4035	1	2	32	21	2½	2nk	Glisson G	119	w	3.80	86-21	WhirlingFox112nkRoyalGovrnor1198Mngohck1262	Good effort	5
	Daily Racing Form time,1:11 4/5																	
12Aug49- 6Sar	sly	7f	:234 :464 1:113 1:252	3↑ American Legion H 9.2k	7	6	75½	67½	44½	43½	McLean P	118	w	5.20	85-18	Manyunk119hdWhirling Fox1102Big If1101½	Raced wide	8
	Daily Racing Form time,1:26 1/5																	
18Jun49- 6Mth	fst	1	:23 :461 1:111 1:373	3↑ Salvator Mile 13k	2	5	67½	54	32	33	McLean P	119	w	*1.90	104-08	Istan1142High Trend1121Royal Governor1191½	Hung	14
30May49- 5Del	fst	1 1/16	:232 :464 1:104 1:424	3↑ Brandywine H 12k	4	3	32	2hd	13	15	McLean P	115	w	2.55	99-14	RoyalGovernor1155Coincidence109nkMarchonsII112hd	Easily	8
28May49- 6Del	fst	6f	:222 :452 1:103	3↑ Wilmington H 12k	4	6	62½	52¼	21	1½	McLean P	113	w	3.85	99-12	Royal Governor113½Piet1151Royal Blood1151½	Driving	10
14May49- 6GS	fst	6f	:221 :451 1:093	3↑ Camden H 17k	1	8	95½	85¾	52¼	43	McLean P	113	w	10.80	98-08	Ocean Brief120noMacbeth1113Buzfuz121no	Late foot	10
6May49- 6Bel	fst	6f-WC	:224 :451 1:092	3↑ Toboggan H 24k	7	5	84¼	41½	31½	52½	Adams J	114	w	6.25	91-05	Rippey1291½Pipette108¾Up Beat120no	Swerved	11
28Apr49- 6HdG	fst	1 70	:24 :483 1:134 1:421	4↑ Alw 3500	6	4	45¼	31	11	11¼	McLean P	116	w	*.40	97-13	Royal Governor1161¼Hash Night11010Leamour115½	Cleverly	6
20Apr49- 6HdG	fst	6f	:224 :46 1:113	3↑ Philadelphia H 12k	8	2	85¾	53¼	31	2nk	McLean P	114	w	*3.10	93-14	PepWell112nkRoyalGovrnor114.5hdFultlss119no	Just missed	10
9Apr49- 7Jam	fst	6f	:23 :462 1:121	4↑ Handicap 5055	9	5	69	44½	11½	12	Guerin E	121	w	3.55	90-18	Royal Governor1212Master Mind1134Up Beat1181	Driving	9
1Apr49- 6Jam	fst	6f	:223 :47 1:122	3↑ Paumonok H 21k	5	6	88½	66	98¼	96	Guerin E	115	w	13.90	83-20	Rippey1251Energetic1102My Request130¾	Outrun	13
26Feb49- 7Hia	fst	1¼	:472 1:112 1:363 2:02	3↑ Widener H 60k	4	5	59	33	64¾	69¾	McLean P	111	w	15.85	85-10	Coaltown1232Shy Guy120½Faultless117¾	Quit	6
21Feb49- 5Hia	fst	6f	:22 :45 1:103	4↑ Alw 3500	4	4	66¾	54	41	3½	McLean P	118	w	7.00	94-16	BlueBorder121noLoriot114½RoyalGovernor118hd	Stout rally	8
12Nov48- 5Pim	fst	1 1/16	:233 :471 1:112 1:422	3↑ Alw 5000	2	5	54¼	4¾	2½	11½	McLean P	114	w	3.80	106-09	RoyalGovrnr1141½LoserWeeper1034Camargo115nk	Drew out	6
2Nov48- 6Pim	fst	6f	:223 :452 1:104	2↑ Janney H 9.2k	2	4	65½	58½	46	44	Basile M	110	w	5.90	93-09	Istan117½Lookout Son1093Lanlast112½	Stumbled	7
16Oct48- 5Bel	fst	6f	:23 :464 1:12	3↑ Handicap 6040	4	4	74¼	77¼	75¼	87	Permane R	111	w	5.00	83-19	Buzfuz1221½Blue Border120½Knockdown120½	Outrun	8
4Oct48- 6Jam	fst	6f	:233 :471 1:121	3↑ Fleetwing H 29k	3	2	106¾	108¼	5½	2hd	Permane R	106	w	25.75	90-19	Buzfuz115hdRoyalGovernor106½FirstFlght126no	Closed fast	10
29Sep48- 5Bel	fst	6f	:23 :464 1:122	4↑ Alw 4500	4	3	41¾	21	3nk	11	Atkinson T	117	w	*.45	88-14	Royal Governor1171Ben Lewis115noSonadora1101½	Drew out	6
3Sep48- 7Aqu	fst	6f	:241 :481 1:131	3↑ Alw 4000	1	1	42	43¼	3½	11¼	Guerin E	124	w	*2.90	86-24	Royal Governor1241¼Nassau1181½Dutel1072	Driving	9
12Aug48- 7Sar	gd	6f	:24 :472 1:122	4↑ Alw 4000	3	2	41¾	52½	41¼	25	Guerin E	114	w	2.85	81-22	Pipette1085Royal Governor1141¾Repand1131	Inside turn	8
29May48- 5Del	fst	6f	:223 :46 1:113	3↑ Wilmington H 13k	9	5	73¼	62½	65	97¼	Allgaier H	110	wb	9.65f	87-09	Itsabet113[DH]Phar Mon1142½[DH]Mity Me1121	Outrun	14
8May48- 5GS	gd	1	:233 :47 1:121 1:392	3↑ Valley Forge H 20k	10	5	45½	88¼	97¾	1010	Allgaier H	110	w	21.20	80-18	Rampart109nkRippey121¾Senoril110nk	Quit	10
24Apr48- 6HdG	gd	6f	:224 :46 1:113	3↑ Harford H 12k	4	5	57	55	55½	78	Mora H	110	w	4.10	85-28	Loyal Legion1202Daily Dip104hdLittle Harp1121½	Outrun	8
17Apr48- 5Jam	fst	1 1/16	:243 :482 1:132 1:46	3↑ Excelsior H 29k	6	5	65½	52¾	42¼	57¼	Atkinson T	114	w	4.05	76-20	Knockdown114¾Double Jay1252½Stymie1284	No mishap	9
1Apr48- 5Jam	sly	6f	:23 :462 1:114	3↑ Paumonok H 35k	5	2	54	32½	22	23½	Atkinson T	112	w	6.15	88-18	BetterSlf1123½RoylGovrnor1122LtsDnc113hd	Close quarters	13

17May47- 5HdG	fst 1 1/8	:472 1:122 1:373 1:503	Potomac 11k	1 4 43 42 55 511 1/4	Saunders W	120 w	*.90	85-13	Loyal Legion1176Mityme1172Camargo1123	No excuse	5
6May47- 6Pim	fst 1 1/16	:231 :47 1:122 1:471	Survivor 9.8k	2 9 810 64 3/4 43 3hd	Saunders W	116 w	*.80	82-20	Mityme116noLoyalLgon113noRoylGovrnor1161 1/2	Strong finish	9
26Apr47- 6HdG	fst 1 1/16	:231 :47 1:12 1:444	Chesapeake 38k	12 11 117 1/4 43 1/2 41 1/4 32 1/4	Saunders W	119 w	*2.20	90-13	BulletProof115.52Secnav114nkRoylGovrnor1192	Closed fast	14
19Apr47- 5HdG	fst 6f	:224 :462 1:103	Chesapeake Trial 12k	5 3 94 3/4 85 1/4 52 3/4 11	Saunders W	122 w	4.30	99-08	Royal Governor1221Tavistock1141Mityme1181 1/2	Drew out	10
13Nov46- 6Pim	fst 1 1/16	:232 :471 1:122 1:454	Walden 33k	6 8 63 3/4 44 1/4 32 1/2 33	Atkinson T	116 w	4.40	86-20	Frvnt116hdFultlss1133RoylGovrnor1167	Shuffled first turn	11
5Nov46- 6Pim	fst 6f	:23 :47 1:122	Sagamore 12k	8 4 2 1/2 21 1hd 1no	Atkinson T	116 w	5.70	91-17	Royal Governor116noBastogne113 3/4Faultless1141 1/2	Driving	8
23Oct46- 6Lrl	gd 1 1/16	:233 :474 1:142 1:472	SL Jenkins 9.8k	5 6 42 1/2 21 11 11 3/4	Atkinson T	118 w	*.80	80-22	Royal Governor1181 3/4Golden Bull1137Lovely Imp115no		10
	Impeded,much best										
14Oct46- 5Bel	fst 6f-WC	:224 :451 1:094	Handicap 5570	3 1 31 1/2 3nk 1hd	Atkinson T	122 w	*.95	92-06	Royal Governor122hdMr. John1102Lighthouse113 3/4	Driving	5
5Oct46- 6Lrl	fst 6f	:23 :471 1:12	Richard Johnson 9.3k	3 6 62 1/4 63 1/2 64 22	Kirk C	122 w	*1.40	92-09	Repand1152RoyalGovernr1221 1/2LovelyImp116hd	Belated rush	8
7Sep46- 4Aqu	fst 6f	:222 :462 1:123	Babylon H 12k	2 2 42 1/4 43 1/4 31 1/2 11	Guerin E	114 w	3.10	89-14	Royal Governor1141Brabancon1111 1/2Miss Disco109 3/4	Driving	6
2Sep46- 5GS	fst 6f	:222 :461 1:112	©William Penn 13k	7 5 62 1/4 44 33 1/2 43 3/4	Mehrtens W	119 w	4.05	90-14	Jobstown117hdWar Glance1173 1/2Cellophane117hd	No rally	11
24Aug46- 4Sar	fst 6f	:222 :453 1:093	Grand Union Hotel 20k	1 4 51 1/2 44 42 1/4 48	Arcaro E	118 w	21.35	96-02	Blue Border110noI Will1266Grand Admiral1262	Good try	9
20Jly46- 5Jam	fst 6f	:23 :463 1:113	©East View 51k	10 5 41 1/4 51 1/4 51 1/2 75 1/2	Lynch J	119 w	12.50	87-11	Grand Admiral1151I Will1192Phalanx115 1/2	Bore over	11
4Jly46- 6Del	fst 5 1/2f	:221 :461 1:052	Dover 12k	13 3 41 21 1/2 24 14	Lynch J	116 w	7.15	95-10	RoylGovrnor1164BnLws116nkBulltProof1161 1/2	Speed to spare	13
22Jun46- 5Del	sl 5 1/2f	:231 :481 1:072	©Christiana 11k	3 1 2hd 2hd 2 1/2 21	Mehrtens W	116 w	*2.15	84-27	Mityme1131Royal Governor11610Vacance116no	Second best	7
8Jun46- 3Del	fst 5f	:221 :47 1:001	Alw 3000	1 2 4 3/4 23 23 43 1/4	Snider A	112 w	*.50e	86-11	Mesl1142Raol122nkPenny Reward1121	Speed,crowded	7
1Jun46- 1Del	fst 5f	:223 :464 :593	©Md Sp Wt	6 2 21 1 1/2 13 14 1/2	Snellings A	118 w	*1.75	92-10	Royal Governor1184 1/2Stepinthedark1182Big Dub111nk	Easily	9

Speculate

br. g. 1936, by Westwick (Ultimus)–Virginia T., by Royal Canopy

Lifetime record: 18 4 7 1 $22,700

Own.– Bayard Sharp
Br.– P.M. Walker (Va)
Tr.– W. Passmore

4Aug43- 3Bel	fst *2	S'Chase 3:482 4↑	Shillelah 3.9k	6 5 520 55 3/4 310 39 1/2	Miller P	132 w	10.40	--	Delhi Dan1502 1/2Elkridge1507Speculate1326	Pulled up lame	10
3Jly43- 4Det	fst *2	S'Chase 4:032 4↑	Handicap 5000	6 5 416 412 415 412	Miller P	140wb	*1.10e	--	Rouge Dragon1442 1/2Bavarian1373 1/2Ossabaw1386		6
	Slow start,never a menace,stirrup irons broken after last										
14Aug42- 1Sar	fst *2	S'Chase 4:193 3↑	North American H 3.3k	3 4 313 - - -	Passmore W	145wb	*1.30	--	Elkridge1467The Beak1431Iron Shot143100	Pulled up lame	5
22Oct41- 2Lrl	fst *2 1/2	S'Chase 5:062 4↑	Chevy Chase H 6.3k	4 3 39 1/2 311 - -	Roby T	147wb	*.65	--	War Lance13315Fay Cottage1375Brother Jones138	Ran out	5
3Oct41- 4Bel	sly *3	S'Chase 5:583 4↑	Grand National H 17k	2 4 310 21 1/2 14 16	Roby T	142wb	3.70	--	Speculate1426Sussex1481LondonTown15430	As rider pleased	7
26Sep41- 4Bel	fst *2 1/2	S'Chase 4:461 4↑	Brook H 6.3k	5 6 316 38 21 1/2 21	Roby T	142wb	6.00	--	Sussex1441Speculate14215Corrigan1455	Driving	6
11Sep41- 1Aqu	fst *2 1/2	S'Chase 5:53 4↑	Glendale H 5.8k	4 4 410 49 1hd 2hd	Roby T	140wb	1.30	--	ByDn139hdSpcult1402Sussx14815	Bad landings 16th & 17th	4
4Sep41- 1Aqu	fst *2	S'Chase 3:451 3↑	Harbor Hill H 3.7k	3 4 54 1/4 47 22 22 1/2	Roby T	141wb	3.45	--	Bath1332 1/2Speculate1416Sussex1492	Finished well	5
23Aug41- 1Sar	fst *2	S'Chase 4:12 3↑	Alw 1500	1 5 59 1/4 52 1/4 23 24	Roby T	152wb	*1.05	--	Corrigan1424Speculate1528Invader1321 1/2	Bad landing last	7
8Aug41- 1Sar	fst *2	S'Chase 4:132 4↑	Shillelah 3.5k	5 5 45 1/2 22 13 16	Roby T	143wb	*.75	--	Speclte1436WingedHoofs13015TheBeak1374	Rated,drew away	5
28Jly41- 1Sar	gd *2	S'Chase 4:20 4↑	Alw 1200	2 4 418 22 13 14	Roby T	146wb	*1.70	--	Speculate1464Beach Maiden1324Golden Oak14712		6
	Gained rapidly,speed to spare;Previously owned and trained by S.J. Holloway										
7Nov40- 3Pim	fst 2	S'Chase 3:563 3↑	Alw 1000	1 5 45 1/2 35 - -	Cruz H	138 w	4.50	--	Arch Hero1356Chuckatuck14040Wrackonite140	Fell at 14th	6
21Oct40- 2Lrl	hy *2	S'Chase 4:044 3↑	Sp Wt 1000	9 5 35 1/2 11 18 18	Cruz H	137 w	*1.80	--	Speculate1378DonRoberto1411 1/2Farford13120	Speed to spare	10
14Oct40- 2Lrl	fst *2	S'Chase 3:542 3↑	Sp Wt 1000	6 8 815 48 24 22 1/2	Zajkowski J	134 w	5.50e	--	Simoon1482 1/2Speculate1344Millrace1446	Good finish	8
3Jun40- 1Bel	fst *2	S'Chase 3:51 4↑	Sp Wt 1200	2 6 514 516 38 1/2 210	Roby T	142 w	3.40	--	FrozenNorth14910Spculate1424GameRunnr14240	Second best	8
23May40- 4Bel	sly *2	S'Chase 3:572 4↑	Spring Maiden 4.9k	13 11 48 1/2 34 3 1/2 49	Clements HW	144 w	4.10e	--	Massa1372Fay Cottage1552Star Bramble1445		16
	Sent into contention,quit										
13May40- 2Bel	fst *2	S'Chase 3:503 4↑	Sp Wt 1200	4 4 46 43 21 21 1/2	Walker G	142 w	5.60	--	Kellsboro1471 1/2Speculate1425Game Runner14720		5
	Determined effort,no match										
6May40- 3Pim	fst 2	S'Chase 4:013 4↑	Sp Wt 1000	7 - - - - -	Zajkowski J	135 w	3.00e	--	Blanket1404Kosan14910Mr. Chips1542	Lost rider 3rd	9

Star Pilot

br. c. 1943, by Sickle (Phalaris)–Floradora, by Bull Dog

Lifetime record: 17 6 4 2 $187,885

Own.– Maine Chance Farm
Br.– Coldstream Stud (Ky)
Tr.– J.W. Smith

2Mar48- 8Hia	fst 1 1/8	:462 1:112 1:372 1:502 4↑	Alw 4000	3 4 53 52 1/2 57 58 3/4	Dodson D	120 w	*2.85	80-14	Respingo1261 1/2PtrolPont1091 1/4FrsAr1013 1/2	Hard ridden,tired	10
18Feb48- 5Hia	fst 6f	:222 :454 1:103 4↑	Alw 3500	4 4 65 64 1/4 66 59 1/2	Jessop JD	108wb	*1.30	85-11	EagleEye1162 1/2YankeeHill111nkBordeaux1144 1/2	Lacked rally	7
14Feb48- 5Hia	fst 7f	:233 :47 1:113 1:234 4↑	Alw 5000	3 2 21 1/2 31 1/2 32 1/2 37	Snider A	116wb	10.30	86-10	Assault128hdRampart1097Star Pilot1169	Weakened	4
23Feb46- 7SA	fst 1 1/8	:46 1:111 1:372 1:503	S A Derby 109k	3 4 44 22 22 21 3/4	Kirkland A	122 w	*.50e	89-08	Knockdown1221 3/4Star Pilot1223 1/2Honeymoon1172 1/2	Went well	5
15Feb46- 7SA	fst 1	:221 :453 1:104 1:37	Ⓡ Alw 10000	2 3 35 1/2 35 1/2 25 26	Kirkland A	122 w	*.40e	87-15	Knockdown1226Star Pilot1223Hie Heel117 1/2	Held well	6
	Previously trained by R. Waldron										
24Nov45- 5Pim	gd 1 1/16	:233 :481 1:13 1:474	Pim Futurity 43k	4 2 2 1/2 12 12 11 1/4	Kirkland A	122 w	2.75e	79-24	StarPilot1221 1/4BillyBumps119nkColonyBoy1171 1/2	Ridden out	8
	Geldings not eligible;Previously trained by T. Smith										
31Oct45- 5Jam	fst 1 70	:233 :472 1:122 1:441	Ardsley H 16k	6 1 1hd 2nk 2hd 1hd	Kirkland A	126 w	2.45	83-16	StarPilot126hdMisleader1121 3/4MarineVctory1245	Hard drive	8
20Oct45- 4Jam	fst 1 1/16	:242 :482 1:132 1:454	Alw 7500	5 5 54 3/4 43 1/2 37 38 1/2	Kirkland A	122 w	*.55e	75-13	LordBoswell1195MightyStory1193 1/2StarPilot1221 3/4	Went well	10
3Oct45- 4Bel	fst 1	:233 :47 1:123 1:391	Champagne 20k	10 1 1hd 22 23 25	Kirkland A	122 w	*.80e	73-24	Marine Victory1165Star Pilot1221 1/2Mahout106nk	No match	10
29Sep45- 4Bel	gd 6 1/2f-W	:221 :451 1:103 1:171	Futurity 65k	9 1 42 42 1/2 11	Kirkland A	126 w	*.70e	86-14	Star Pilot1261Athene1161Mighty Story1192	Driving	11
	Geldings not eligible										
12Sep45- 6Aqu	fst 6 1/2f	:231 :464 1:122 1:18	Cowdin 31k	12 8 73 3/4 77 3/4 64 1/2 75 3/4	Kirkland A	126 w	4.75e	89-14	Knockdown1141 1/2Revoked1261Southern Pride1201 1/2	No threat	13
1Sep45- 4Bel	fst 6 1/2f-W	:223 :452 1:101 1:163	Hopeful 62k	10 7 71 3/4 31 12 1/4	Kirkland A	112 w	20.35	89-09	Star Pilot1122 1/4Inroc1121 1/2Revoked126nk	Drew clear	14
25Aug45- 5Bel	fst 6f-WC	:224 :454 1:114	Grand Union Hotel 21k	2 4 73 1/4 63 1/4 21 1/2	Wright WD	113 w	5.50	80-17	Manipur1121 1/2Star Pilot113nkOur Bully112 1/2	Finished well	9
28Jly45- 6Was	sly 6f	:224 :462 1:12	Arl Futurity 70k	11 6 3 1/2 512 612 68 3/4	Grohs O	122 w	7.20e	81-19	SpySng1225Knockdown1222 1/2MightyStory122no	Dropped back	11
6Jly45- 5Was	fst 5f	:232 :48 1:001	Alw 2500	3 1 12 12 13 14	Adams J	115 w	*.80	95-21	Star Pilot1154Instanter1104Fly Off1151	Saved ground	7
23Jun45- 4Bel	fst 5f-WC	:222 :454 :583	Nat'l Stallion 16k	2 4 52 3/4 52 3/4 510 1/4	Adams J	122 w	*.70e	77-12	Enfilade119nkHarvey's Pal1227Forgetmenow1192 1/2	Outrun	5
15Jun45- 4Bel	fst 4 1/2f-W	:224 :46 :521	©Md Sp Wt	5 1 2 1/2 12 13	Adams J	116 w	*2.05	94-06	Star Pilot1163Allier116noMist o' Gold1162	Easily	13

Stefanita

b. f. 1940, by Questionnaire (Sting)–Stefana, by Stefan the Great
Own.– G.D. Widener
Br.– George D. Widener (Ky)
Tr.– W.F. Mulholland

Lifetime record: 27 8 7 4 $72,360

1Jly44-6Aqu	fst	1¼	:483 1:132 1:39 2:024	3↑ Brooklyn H 57k	7	4	11½	11	55	77½	Longden J	110wb	9.20	85-11	Four Freedoms116nkWait a Bit116noFirst Fiddle1265		9
Daily Racing Form time,2:03 3/5																	
16Jun44-5Aqu	fst	1 1/16	:243 :48 1:131 1:464	3↑ ⒻHandicap 4725	2	3	22	22	22	22½	Longden J	126wb	*.60	77-17	Good Morning1072½Stefanita1267Night Glow111		3
Fractious post,no match																	
1Jun44-6Bel	fst	1 1/16	:23 :454 1:11 1:432	3↑ ⒻTop Flight H 11k	2	7	65¼	64¾	64¼	44¼	Longden J	124wb	10.50	90-10	Boojiana106¾Mar-Kell1263Silvestra112½	Evenly	10
22May44-7Bel	fst	1 1/16	:463 1:121 1:374 1:443	3↑ ⒻHandicap 4965	8	8	89¼	77¼	810	811	Longden J	122wb	2.95	77-15	Anthemion108nkMar-Kll1204MoonMaiden1121	Never a factor	8
13Nov43-6Pim	fst	1 3/16	:484 1:141 1:402 2:00	3↑ Bryan & O'Hara H 19k	8	5	21	22	1½	1nk	McCreary C	117wb	3.30	82-31	Stefanita117nkAlsab1223Son of Peace1131	Driving	9
5Nov43-6Pim	fst	1 1/16	:24 :484 1:14 1:47	3↑ ⒻLady Baltimore H 5.9k	3	2	21½	21	21½	11¼	McCreary C	120wb	*.40	83-24	Stefanita1201¼Barbara Childs1164Ok Sugar953	Driving	5
5Oct43-6Bel	fst	1½	:483 1:134 2:05 2:314	3↑ ⒻLadies H 16k	7	2	22	3½	1½	11½	McCreary C	116wb	3.40	79-17	Stefanita1161½Vagrancy1236Dark Discovery1061¼	Handily	7
18Sep43-6Aqu	fst	1⅛	:474 1:132 1:383 1:513	3↑ ⒻBeldame H 28k	4	5	22	21	11	21	McCreary C	116wb	*2.90	88-14	Mar-Kell1261Stefanita1162Vagrancy122½	No match	11
28Aug43-6Nar	fst	1 1/16	:242 :482 1:133 1:46	ⒻNew England Oaks 11k	3	2	2½	2nk	1½	1¼	McCreary C	118wb	*.60	87-15	Stefanita1181¼Anthemion116½Best Risk1148	Ridden out	5
4Aug43-6Bel	fst	1¼	:471 1:121 1:381 2:042	ⒻAlabama 17k	3	1	11	11	11½	11¾	McCreary C	117wb	*.95	78-15	Stefanita1171¾Askmenow12420Tack Room114	Driving	3
30Jly43-6Bel	gd	7f	:23 :464 1:121 1:251	ⒻTest 6.5k	11	8	64	41¼	41¼	12	McCreary C	117wb	5.30	84-16	Stefanita1172Best Risk108hdGood Morning120no	Handily	11
30Jun43-5Jam	gd	1 1/16	:251 :491 1:134 1:462	3↑ ⒻHandicap 5120	2	2	22	22	22	21½	McCreary C	110wb	2.50	79-22	Night Glow1081½Stefanita1104Vagrancy12810	Belated rally	4
23Jun43-6Aqu	fst	1 1/16	:242 :492 1:15 1:481	ⒻGazelle 6.5k	6	5	53½	53¼	62½	2hd	McCreary C	118wb	2.25	73-19	Anthemion112hdStefanita1181½LegendBrr112no	Impeded turn	10
3Jun43-6Bel	fst	1 1/16	:233 :47 1:12 1:442	3↑ ⒻTop Flight H 6.4k	4	1	12	11	21½	34	McCreary C	106wb	9.70	85-17	Mar-Kell1222YarrowMaid1102Stfnt1061½	Saved ground,tired	6
29May43-7Bel	fst	1	:234 :472 1:131 1:392	3↑ ⒻHandicap 2550	3	5	55	32	31½	45½	McCreary C	114 w	*1.30	71-21	YarrowMaid1171BestRisk1112½MoonMdn1202	Inside,no threat	10
19May43-6Bel	sly	1	:232 :472 1:121 1:383	ⒻAcorn 14k	4	9	75¼	44	33½	33½	McCreary C	121 w	4.80e	77-20	Nellie L.1212La Reigh1211½Stefanita1211	Impeded early	13
10May43-5Bel	fst	6f	:223 :46 1:112	ⒻAlw 2000	4	10	105	54¼	47¼	21	McCreary C	113 w	8.80	92-10	SparklingMaid1101Stefanita113noDearJudy108½	Fast finish	12
1Oct42-5Bel	fst	6f-WC	:231 :46 1:111	ⒻAlw 2000	8	8	2½	51¼	51¾	65¾	Breen J	113 w	4.20	85-09	ClacketyClack113½NowMandy1131Navigatng1131½	Speed,tired	9
26Sep42-4Bel	fst	6f-WC	:222 :45 1:091	ⒻMatron 12k	7	18	138½	176¼	1611	1211½	Breen J	119 w	7.55	89-00	GoodMorning1091Askmnow1141½Navigtng1142	Never a factor	20
21Sep42-7Bel	fst	6f-WC	:224 :46 1:11	ⒻAlw 2000	9	3	41½	1hd	1hd	2hd	Breen J	119 w	22.85	92-06	Samaritan111hdStefanita119nkCape May1111	Hell well	13
14Sep42-4HdG	fst	6f	:23 :463 1:123	Alw 1500	4	8	75	42¼	75¼	58½	Mann W	112wb	*1.70	81-18	Hasteville1102½RoyalFlush1102BarKeep1154	Wide into str	9
27Jun42-6Del	my	5f	:224 :471 1:01	ⒻPolly Drummond 8.4k	3	5	57	56½	55½	43½	Peters M	122wb	4.30e	86-19	Fair Weather1221½La Reigh122hdParachutist1132	Wide	8
17Jun42-4Aqu	fst	5½f	:223 :46 1:054	ⒻAstoria 7.4k	2	1	31½	31½	3½	11	Breen J	113wb	*1.10e	98-06	Stefanita1131Shannon1131½Witchwater1132	Driving	7
4Jun42-5Bel	fst	5f-WC	:581	Alw 1500	6	2	2hd	3nk	31	31½	Breen J	108wb	*.70	87-11	SlideRule1111½TotalVictory111noStefanita1083	No mishap	7
28May42-4Bel	fst	5f-WC	:583	ⒻAlw 1500	4	2	2½	2nk	1nk	2½	Breen J	115wb	*.30	86-13	Now Mandy115½Stefanita1154Blois1105	Hung	6
16May42-1Bel	fst	5f	:23 :471 :591	ⒻMd Sp Wt	2	2	1hd	1hd	11	12½	Breen J	116wb	*1.40	95-07	Stefanita1162½Spartiate116noShannon1163	Going away	9
11May42-4Bel	fst	4½f-WC	:522	ⒻFashion 9.6k	11	4		3½	42½	33½	Breen J	111wb	*3.60e	89-07	Pomrose116½Driven Snow1163Stefanita1111	Went well	12

Stymie

ch. c. 1941, by Equestrian (Equipoise)–Stop Watch, by On Watch
Own.– Mrs E.D. Jacobs
Br.– Max Hirsch (Tex)
Tr.– Hirsch Jacobs

Lifetime record: 131 35 33 28 $918,485

1Oct49-6Bel	fst	2¼	:474 2:312 2:58 3:511	3↑ New York H 29k	8	8	814	42½	21½	23½	McCreary C	122 w	2.40	75-11	Dnr1263½Stym1222½Chains110hd	Circled field,flattened out late	8
24Sep49-6Bel	fst	1½	:49 1:13 2:022 2:28	3↑ Manhattan H 29k	6	5	78	712	68¼	48¾	Woodhouse H	118 w	4.35	89-13	Donor118¾My Request1258Stunts114hd	Blocked	7
19Sep49-5Bel	fst	1	:242 :474 1:124 1:371	3↑ Alw 5000	3	4	46½	45	33	32½	McCreary C	126 w	2.75	85-19	Stunts1212Three Rings121½Stymie1265	Some gain	5
15Sep49-6Aqu	fst	1 1/16	:25 :482 1:123 1:452	3↑ Alw 4000	5	6	66½	68¼	54	34	Woodhouse H	122 w	6.35	83-17	Quarter Pole1223Brick1051Stymie122hd	Some gain	8
10Sep49-6Aqu	fst	1⅛	:473 1:12 1:37 1:504	3↑ Edgemere H 22k	6	7	811	79¾	914	914	Woodhouse H	119 w	7.10	79-16	My Request1193Stunts115¾Assault124½	No factor	9
24Jly48-6Mth	gd	1¼	:471 1:121 1:374 2:031	3↑ Monmouth H 29k	6	7	711	65¾	47	412	Permane R	129 w	*.70	78-19	Tide Rips1086Vertigo II1093½Bug Juice1082	Lame	7
17Jly48-6Aqu	fst	1¼	:502 1:16 1:404 2:054	3↑ Brooklyn H 57k	4	6	59¼	46	3½	33	Permane R	130 w	*.95	75-21	Conniver114hdGallorette1193Stymie1302	Saved ground,hung	6
3Jly48-5Del	fst	1¼	:471 1:112 1:361 2:02	3↑ Sussex H 30k	4	7	711	31	1hd	11½	Permane R	130 w	*.70	102-10	Stymie1301½Rampart1131Tide Rips109nk	Very wide	8
26Jun48-6Aqu	fst	1 1/16	:251 :493 1:133 1:452	3↑ Aqueduct H 28k	3	5	66½	55¼	3¾	1hd	Permane R	130 w	*1.05	87-18	Stymie130hdConniver1173½Double Jay1262½	Driving	7
17Jun48-6Aqu	fst	1 1/16	:241 :48 1:123 1:443	3↑ Queens County H 22k	3	6	617	69¼	44	22	Permane R	132 w	*.85	89-16	Knockdown1132Stymie132½Gasparilla1072½	Bore in	6
31May48-6Bel	sly	1¼	:483 1:13 1:372 2:03	3↑ Suburban H 57k	1	6	611	47½	35¼	21¾	McCreary C	128 w	*.90	83-22	Harmonica1091¾Stymie1283Colosal1175	Good finish	6
26May48-6Bel	sly	1⅛	:491 1:123 1:371 1:494	4↑ Alw 7500	1	3	39½	33	1nk	12	McCreary C	122 w	*.35	92-21	Stymie1222Vertigo II1141½Tide Rips106	In hand late	3
22May48-6Bel	fst	1	:233 :463 1:112 1:364	3↑ Metropolitan H 30k	9	9	914	912	65½	1¾	McCreary C	126 w	5.10	90-14	Stymie126¾Colosal1171½Rippey1241½	Late rush	9
15May48-5Jam	fst	1 3/16	:48 1:122 1:373 1:571	3↑ Gallant Fox H 87k	10	10	1021	1015	62½	54½	McCreary C	126 w	*1.40	85-15	Faultless118hdFervent125½Gallorette1173½	Fast finish	10
8May48-6Pim	sl	1 3/16	:49 1:141 1:404 2:013	3↑ Dixie H 31k	6	9	916	913	33	21½	McCreary C	127 w	3.30	72-41	Fervent1211½Stymie1272½Incline107no	No match	9
17Apr48-5Jam	fst	1 1/16	:243 :482 1:132 1:46	3↑ Excelsior H 29k	7	6	55¼	42½	32	33¼	McCreary C	128 w	2.10e	80-20	Knockdown114¾Double Jay1252½Stymie1284	Faltered	9
1Nov47-5Jam	gd	1 1/16	:24 :472 1:121 1:443	3↑ Scarsdale H 30k	5	12	1220	128	78½	67½	McCreary C	130 w	*1.85	82-17	WithPleasure1292Gallorette119½DoubleJy1182	Reared start	12
25Oct47-5Jam	fst	1⅝	:50 1:41 2:053 2:442	3↑ Gallant Fox H 83k	7	8	915	44	11	11¾	McCreary C	125 w	2.50	92-13	Stymie1251¾Talon1253½Miss Grillo117no	Wide,driving	9
11Oct47-6Bel	fst	2¼	:473 2:314 3:482	3↑ New York H 109k	2	5	513	57¾	45¼	412	McCreary C	125 w	2.10	81-11	Rico Monte126noTalon1225Phalanx1167	Tired badly	6
4Oct47-6Bel	fst	2	:494 2:293 2:553 3:213	3↑ J C Gold Cup 26k	1	1	1hd	2hd	38	312	McCreary C	124 w	*.65	84-12	Phalanx117noTalon12412Stymie124	Flattened out	3
27Sep47-7Bel	fst	1½	:494 1:15 2:042 2:294	3↑ Manhattan H 28k	5	5	33	42¼	21½	21½	McCreary C	132 w	*.75	87-10	Rico Monte1231½Stymie1322½Talon1166	Finished well	6
13Sep47-6Aqu	fst	1⅛	:502 1:143 1:392 1:522	3↑ Edgemere H 27k	1	4	46	43¼	31½	21½	McCreary C	134 w	*.70	83-13	Elpis1141½Stymie1341Bridal Flower1131½	Finished well	4
1Sep47-6Aqu	fst	1 1/16	:242 :474 1:124 1:442	3↑ Aqueduct H 29k	11	11	1112	73½	41¾	1½	McCreary C	132 w	*2.10	92-13	Stymie132½Gallorette122hdElpis1144	Finished fast	11
9Aug47-6Sar	fst	1¼	:491 1:133 1:393 2:023	3↑ Whitney 27k	2	3	38	34½	33¼	31½	McCreary C	126 w	*.45	93-09	Rico Monte113hdGallorette1121½Stymie126	Late rush	3
30Jly47-7Suf	fst	1⅛	:47 1:123 1:37 1:50	3↑ Mass H 61k	1	7	713	77	32	11½	McCreary C	128 w	*.30	91-14	Stymie1281½Elpis111nkBlue Yonder1111¾	Drew off easily	7
19Jly47-6Bel	sly	1⅝	:483 1:39 2:042 2:423	3↑ Gold Cup 109k	4	6	522	58½	31¾	1nk	McCreary C	126 w	4.75	91-14	Stymie126nkNatchez1264Assault1261	Fast finish	7
Geldings not eligible																	
12Jly47-5Jam	fst	1 3/16	:49 1:134 1:381 1:563	3↑ Butler H 54k	4	5	58	57½	3nk	2hd	Permane R	126 w	2.65	93-09	Assault135hdStymie1261¾Gallorette117nk	Led briefly	5
5Jly47-6Del	fst	1¼	:473 1:112 1:362 2:022	3↑ Sussex H 29k	3	6	412	36	22	13	McCreary C	128 w	*.65	103-14	Stymie1283Natchez1251½Round View1128	Handily	7
28Jun47-5Jam	fst	1 1/16	:24 :472 1:12 1:44	3↑ Questionnaire H 27k	5	6	67¼	4¾	1½	12	Permane R	125 w	*1.05	93-12	Stymie1252Brown Mogul1142Concordian113no	Fast finish	6
21Jun47-6Aqu	fst	1¼	:472 1:121 1:38 2:033	3↑ Brooklyn H 55k	1	3	515	59½	32	23	James B	124 w	2.60	86-14	Assault1333Stymie1244Larky Day1101	Blocked turn	5
2Jun47-6Aqu	fst	1 1/16	:242 :482 1:123 1:452	3↑ Queens County H 21k	2	6	57	45½	21	2nk	James B	128 w	*1.20	87-19	Gallorette119nkStymie128noMangoneo1046	Hung	6
30May47-6Bel	fst	1¼	:472 1:114 1:364 2:014	3↑ Suburban H 57k	3	5	511	48½	35½	410	James B	126 w	1.95	81-09	Assault1302Natchez1207Talon1131	Flattened out late	7
10May47-6Bel	fst	1	:23 :464 1:112 1:372	3↑ Metropolitan H 30k	6	12	1213	1211	86½	11	James B	124 w	*2.30	87-15	Stymie1241Brown Mogul1131Gallorette1161½	Wide,late rush	12
3May47-5Jam	fst	1⅛	:47 1:112 1:363 1:494	3↑ Grey Lag H 46k	8	7	78¾	51¾	51¼	42½	James B	126 w	2.20	96-13	Assault128nkLetsDance110nkCoincdnc1202	Forced wide,hung	8
Daily Racing Form time,1:49 1/5																	
30Apr47-4Jam	fst	6f	:231 :462 1:104	3↑ Handicap 6535	5	7	712	712	78¾	57½	James B	126 w	3.15	89-14	BrownMogl1143¾Inroc118¾FlsMov1123	Left,worked 7f in 1:27	7
1Nov46-6Pim	fst	1 3/16	:481 1:132 1:39 1:57	3↑ Pim Spl 25k	1	4	418	417	21	26	James B	126 w	*.70	91-16	Assault1206Stymie1263Bridal Flower117½	No match	4
26Oct46-5Jam	fst	1⅝	:462 1:373 2:03 2:424	3↑ Gallant Fox H 85k	8	10	1015	21	15	12½	James B	126 w	5.15	101-11	Stymie1262½Rico Monte1162Assault1148	In hand late	11
12Oct46-6Bel	sly	2¼	:493 2:343 2:591 3:511	3↑ New York H 58k	6	5	43¾	1½	11	11¼	James B	128 w	*1.10	79-14	Stymie1281¼Rico Monte1212Athenia10910	Ridden out	9
5Oct46-6Bel	fst	2	:491 2:302 2:543 3:223	3↑ J C Gold Cup 27k	4	4	11	1½	21	25	James B	124 w	*.30	86-12	Pavot1245Stymie1245Rico Monte12450	No match	4
Geldings not eligible																	
25Sep46-6Bel	fst	1½	:493 1:143 2:032 2:292	3↑ Manhattan H 28k	6	5	42¾	21	1½	1¾	James B	126 w	*1.10	91-13	Stymie126¾Pavot1213[DH]Flareback1131	Driving	8

Date	Cond	Dist	Fractions	Race	Running line	Jockey	Wt	Odds	Speed	Top finishers	Comment	Fld
14Sep46- 6Aqu	fst	1⅛	:474 1:13 1:38 1:502	3↑ Edgemere H 28k	2 8 52¾ 31¾ 2hd 11½	James B	121 w	*1.50	95-13	Stymie1211½Gallorett1231¼KngDorstt1156	Drew away easily	8
31Aug46- 6Sar	fst	1¾	:514 2:013 2:381 3:072	3↑ Sar Cup 5.9k	1 1 1 1 1 1	James B	126 w	-	--	Stymie126	Walkover	1
Geldings not eligible,private time												
24Aug46- 6Sar	fst	1¼	:46 1:101 1:362 2:013	3↑ Saratoga H 33k	2 5 518 48½ 32½ 34¾	James B	125 w	2.15	96-02	Lucky Draw121¾Polynesian1134Stymie1257	No menace	5
19Aug46- 6Sar	sly	1	:25 :493 1:14 1:39	3↑ Alw 6650	2 3 35 22 2nk 2¾	James B	119 w	1.45	85-20	King Dorsett119¾Stymie1195Gallorette121	Driving	3
10Aug46- 6Sar	my	1¼	:50 1:154 1:394 2:072	3↑ Whitney 28k	5 4 45¼ 11 13 12	James B	120 w	*.55	72-22	Stymie1202Mahout1032Trymenow11210	Wide	5
5Aug46- 6Sar	fst	1	:23 :461 1:111 1:363	3↑ Wilson 24k	9 8 813 74¼ 64 5¾	Woodhouse H	120 w	5.05	97-08	Pavot126nkGallorette121nkLarky Day112hd	Finished well	11
20Jly46- 6Mth	fst	1¼	:464 1:112 1:361 2:014	3↑ Monmouth H 32k	6 7 714 46 22½ 26	Permane R	126 w	*.75	--	Lucky Draw1116Stymie1262½Aonbarr1006	Second best	8
13Jly46- 5Jam	fst	1 3/16	:47 1:111 1:361 1:551	3↑ Butler H 57k	7 9 914 78½ 51¾ 31½	Permane R	126 w	*1.15	102-08	LuckyDraw105hdGallortt1161½Stym126¾	Blocked,fast finish	9
22Jun46- 6Aqu	fst	1¼	:48 1:131 1:393 2:05	3↑ Brooklyn H 58k	7 8 812 53½ 2½ 2nk	Woodhouse H	128 w	*.65	82-24	Gallorette118nkStymie1284½BurningDream110½	Saved ground	8
15Jun46- 6Del	gd	1¼	:473 1:122 1:38 2:041	3↑ Sussex H 29k	8 8 813 56 45½ 33	Woodhouse H	126 w	*.65	91-16	Pavot1152Gallorette1131Stymie1262	Insufficient rally	8
30May46- 6Bel	fst	1¼	:482 1:123 1:373 2:02	3↑ Suburban H 60k	3 11 1120 97 63¾ 32½	Permane R	123 w	3.45	87-16	Armed1302½Reply Paid110noStymie1231	Closed well	11
10May46- 6Pim	fst	1 3/16	:494 1:141 1:384 1:582	3↑ Dixie H 34k	5 5 56¼ 54½ 23 23½	Permane R	124 w	1.85	86-23	Armed1303½Stymie1242½Trymenow1172	No match	6
4May46- 5Jam	fst	1⅛	:462 1:12 1:37 1:493	3↑ Grey Lag H 35k	2 7 614 44 2hd 12	Woodhouse H	127 w	*2.10	100-10	Stymie1272BoundingHom1053½FghtngStp1261¾	Speed to spare	7
23Apr46- 5Jam	fst	1 1/16	:25 :491 1:123 1:431	4↑ Alw 8000	1 4 44 23 22 22½	Permane R	121 w	*.40	94-13	Snow Boots1132½Stymie1215King Dorsett1145	No threat	4
18Apr46- 5Jam	fst	1 1/16	:242 :481 1:12 1:431	4↑ Alw 7500	3 4 35 1hd 11½ 12½	Permane R	114 w	1.95	97-13	Stym1142½FghtngStp11912OlympcZnth1145¼	Speed in reserve	4
Daily Racing Form time,1:43 3/5												
30Nov45- 7Pim	hy	2½	:532 2:442 3:394 4:351	3↑ Pim Cup H 28k	4 3 45½ 46 16 18	Permane R	128 w	*1.90	25-53	Stymie1288Poto'Luck1282Trymenow1202½	Drew out last ⅛	6
24Nov45- 6Pim	gd	1 3/16	:481 1:131 1:401 2:00	3↑ Riggs H 30k	5 10 1017 912 3½ 1nk	Permane R	123 w	3.05	83-24	Stymie123nkFirstFiddl1261¼BrtshBuddy1151¼	Circled field	10
17Nov45- 6Pim	gd	1 3/16	:493 1:142 1:391 1:584	3↑ Pim Spl 25k	6 7 77¾ 67 35 36	Permane R	126 w	4.10	82-20	Armed1264First Fiddle1262Stymie1261¼	Saved ground	7
3Nov45- 5Jam	fst	1 3/16	:48 1:113 1:371 1:564	3↑ Westchester H 56k	10 10 1014 1012 33 1hd	Permane R	125 w	3.75	96-10	Stym125hdBuzfuz1162OlympcZnth1172	Close quarters str turn	10
13Oct45- 5Jam	fst	1⅝	:49 1:403 2:052 2:443	3↑ Gallant Fox H 56k	3 3 1211 94¾ 64¼ 63¾	Permane R	126 w	*1.30	88-14	ReplyPaid1081Trymenow113hdOlympicZenith116nk	No threat	12
6Oct45- 5Jam	sly	1 1/16	:233 :473 1:12 1:432	3↑ Continental H 16k	5 7 712 33 2hd 15	Permane R	122 w	4.65	96-09	Stym1225ChiefBarker1143BoundingHom1122	Speed to spare	7
Daily Racing Form time, 1:44												
27Sep45- 6Bel	fst	2	:541 2:372 3:02 3:272	3↑ J C Gold Cup 27k	2 1 32 58 510 36	Permane R	125 w	2.15	61-18	Pot o' Luck114noEurasian1256Stymie1256		6
Geldings not eligible												
1Sep45- 6Bel	fst	1 3/16	:46 1:113 1:37 1:561	3↑ Merchants & Cits H 17k	2 6 619 520 46 36½	Permane R	126 w	*1.00e	87-13	Coronal110½Olympic Zenith1176Stymie1263	Closed fast	6
25Aug45- 6Bel	fst	1¾	:50 2:072 2:321 2:58	3↑ Sar Cup 27k	2 4 47½ 43¼ 13 13	Longden J	126 w	*.75	93-12	Stymie1263OlympicZnth126hdBnkrupt12612	Speed in reserve	4
Geldings not eligible												
18Aug45- 6Bel	fst	1¼	:463 1:104 1:364 2:024	3↑ Saratoga H 54k	7 10 1025 96 52 66	Permane R	126 w	2.40e	80-13	OlympicZenith1082FirstFiddle124nkArlFlght100¾	No menace	10
15Aug45- 6Bel	fst	1¼	:491 1:124 1:372 2:021	3↑ Whitney 17k	2 6 68¼ 513 47½ 37	Permane R	126 w	*1.45	82-17	Trymenow1034Pavot1173Stymie1262	Outrun	6
28Jly45- 5Jam	gd	1 3/16	:47 1:122 1:373 1:563	3↑ Butler H 56k	6 9 922 820 2nk 11	Permane R	121 w	2.40e	97-12	Stymie1211First Fiddle1202½Rounders1212	Driving	9
16Jly45- 5Jam	my	1 1/16	:24 :48 1:132 1:432	3↑ Yonkers H 11k	1 5 57 52¼ 31 21¾	Permane R	122wb	3.30	94-15	Wait a Bit1171¾Stymie1221½Olympic Zenith1144	Driving	6
4Jly45- 5Bel	fst	1¼	:464 1:104 1:363 2:021	3↑ Brooklyn H 56k	6 9 912 85¼ 43 11¼	Permane R	116 w	6.40e	89-12	Stymie1161¼Devil Diver1322½Olympic Zenith1102	Drew away	9
25Jun45- 5Aqu	fst	1 1/16	:24 :47 1:122 1:453	3↑ Queens County H 11k	7 7 721 619 47½ 22	Arcaro E	120 w	*1.00e	84-17	Olympic Zenith1082Stymie1203Haile1061	No match	7
16Jun45- 6Bel	fst	1¼	:502 1:142 1:39 2:04	3↑ Suburban H 52k	3 3 41¾ 46½ 33½ 22	Permane R	119 w	2.90	78-15	DevilDiver1322Stymie119nkOlympicZenith1061½	Fast finish	4
2Jun45- 5Jam	fst	1⅛	:48 1:123 1:383 1:494	3↑ Grey Lag H 15k	4 4 411 46¼ 21½ 1½	Permane R	121 w	3.40	99-10	Stymie121½Alex Barth1267Bounding Home114½	Fast finish	5
29May45- 5Jam	fst	1 1/16	:232 :473 1:123 1:443	4↑ Handicap 3965	3 4 45½ 42¼ 11½ 13½	Adams J	119 w	*.90	90-20	Stymie1193½Transformer1101½Eye for Eye1103	Saved ground	4
22May45- 6Jam	fst	1 1/16	:242 :48 1:13 1:454	4↑ Alw 4000	2 3 36 31¾ 2hd 2nk	Mills B	108wb	2.60	84-14	Great Rush114nkStymie1081¼Rounders114hd	Dwelt at start	4
Daily Racing Form time, 1:46 1/5												
25Nov44- 6Pim	fst	2½	:503 2:371 3:282 4:201	3↑ Pim Cup H 29k	2 5 2hd 41½ 25 311½	Kirkland A	109wb	9.50	145-05	Megogo10810Bolingbroke1261½Stymie109nk	Impeded	7
20Nov44- 6Pim	gd	1 3/16	:49 1:141 1:401 1:584	3↑ Riggs H 28k	5 6 52½ 43 32½ 35	Kirkland A	108wb	9.85	84-20	Seven Hearts1262Bon Jour1203Stymie1082	Bid,tired	6
15Nov44- 5Bel	fst	1	:23 :461 1:113 1:381	2↑ Victory H 10k	6 9 99¾ 64½ 41 73½	Wright WD	119wb	6.30	79-17	DoraDear106noGrntRc1141½FrstDrft112no	Saved ground,quit	11
4Nov44- 5Jam	fst	1 3/16	:48 1:132 1:39 1:58	3↑ Westchester H 34k	3 10 1019 1010 41¼ 34	Permane R	109wb	8.50	86-13	Seven Hearts1243½Good Morning109½Stymie1091	Away poorly	10
28Oct44- 6Lrl	fst	1¼	:484 1:133 1:393 2:06	3↑ Washington H 27k	5 5 45½ 57 56 610¼	Clark S	115wb	7.45	70-25	Megogo1101Bon Jour1262Harford1071¼	Flattened out	6
21Oct44- 5Jam	sly	1⅝	:483 1:391 2:051 2:46	3↑ Gallant Fox H 55k	3 10 1019 44½ 31 34	Wright WD	112wb	11.00	81-15	Some Chance1161Pyracanth1053Stymie1121	Bid,hung	10
16Oct44- 5Jam	fst	1 1/16	:233 :474 1:12 1:44	Handicap 7470	2 8 88¼ 44½ 1½ 12	Permane R	114wb	5.60	93-16	Stymie1142Saguaro1105Autocrat1145	Drew away	9
13Oct44- 6Jam	sly	1 1/16	:234 :48 1:123 1:45	Alw 3500	8 6 55½ 45½ 33½ 23	Mills B	112wb	2.10	85-18	Alory1123Stym112nkAutocrt1145	Sluggish early,finished well	9
10Oct44- 6Jam	fst	1 1/16	:24 :483 1:124 1:45	Handicap 3500	3 8 52¾ 42 3nk 2½	Wright WD	115wb	*2.35	87-14	Autocrat118½Stymie1152½Go Chicago109½	Closed well	9
2Oct44- 7Bel	fst	1 1/16	:241 :473 1:121 1:434	3↑ Alw 3500	1 4 41¼ 32 31½ 31½	Mills B	109wb	*1.90	90-14	Victory Drive116½Autocrat1141Stymie1095	Hung	5
28Sep44- 8Bel	fst	1 1/16	:231 :461 1:112 1:441	Alw 3500	4 8 810 66½ 65½ 45½	Mills B	115wb	*3.00	84-16	Saguaro1205Markobob116½Paddle109hd	Steady gain	9
18Sep44- 7Bel	fst	1 1/16	:232 :464 1:104 1:423	Alw 3500	5 5 56 58½ 59½ 616½	Zufelt F	117wb	4.85	81-12	Good Thing1084Pukka Gin1111½Letmenow1087	Hard urged	7
5Sep44- 5Aqu	fst	6f	:232 :471 1:124	Alw 3500	6 7 78 69½ 65 56¼	Zufelt F	116wb	6.10	82-22	FoxBrownie1121½JeanMiracle1211½SmartSheila1081¼	Evenly	9
24Jun44- 6Aqu	fst	1¼	:463 1:12 1:38 2:032	Dwyer 56k	2 9 820 815 611 816½	Stout J	110wb	13.40	73-15	By Jimminy1144Stir Up1205Lucky Draw1201	Never a factor	9
17Jun44- 6Aqu	fst	1 1/16	:24 :474 1:132 1:452	Shevlin 12k	9 10 98¼ 77¼ 43 34	Stout J	108wb	11.30	83-15	By Jimminy1164Stir Up122hdStymie1085	Swerved str	12
12Jun44- 6Aqu	fst	7f	:23 :46 1:11 1:224	Handicap 4980	3 5 512 512 46½ 39	Stout J	116wb	6.45	89-16	By Jimminy1163Lucky Draw1266Stymie1161½	Finished well	5
Daily Racing Form Time,1:23 1/5												
13May44- 6Pim	fst	1 3/16	:481 1:131 1:392 1:591	Preakness 77k	5 7 715 713 65½ 612¼	Roberts P	126wb	23.30	74-15	Pensive126¾Platter1262Stir Up1264½	Never a factor	7
29Apr44- 7Pim	gd	1 1/16	:233 :482 1:134 1:461	Chesapeake 31k	6 5 54½ 42 42½ 47½	Jemas N	114wb	3.30	79-24	Gramps Image114noPensive1163½Gay Bit1144	Saved ground	8
22Apr44- 5Jam	fst	1 1/16	:24 :482 1:124 1:441	Wood Mem (Div 1) 28k	2 8 78½ 52¾ 22 23	Stout J	126wb	8.45	89-14	Stir Up1263Stymie1261Autocrat1262½	Gamely	8
18Apr44- 5Jam	fst	1 70	:241 :483 1:13 1:433	Alw 5000	1 6 43½ 2hd 13 14	Stout J	113wb	3.55	86-14	Stymie1134Olympic Zenith1203Fire Sticky103nk	Easily	9
11Apr44- 5Jam	fst	1 1/16	:242 :50 1:142 1:46	3↑ Handicap 4970	2 4 42 3¾ 2½ 25	Longden J	110wb	*1.10	78-17	Grey Wing1165Stymie1101¼Sugar Ration1026	Hung	4
4Mar44- 7Hia	fst	1⅛	:474 1:131 1:391 1:523	Alw 5000	2 9 98½ 65½ 22 1hd	Adams J	116wb	5.00	78-21	Stym116hdFireSticky1033SideBoy1108	Impeded rivals,just up	9
26Feb44- 5Hia	fst	1⅛	:472 1:12 1:39 1:522	Flamingo 20k	2 9 76½ 46½ 43 35	Atkinson T	118wb	19.80	74-21	Stir Up1181Skytracer1184Stymie1183	Closed well	11
19Feb44- 6Hia	fst	1⅛	:471 1:121 1:39 1:532	Alw 5000	6 6 55¼ 46 36 35¾	Atkinson T	114wb	9.45	68-22	Director J.E.1181¾Good Bid1074Stymie1141	Away slowly	6
3Feb44- 5Hia	fst	7f	:233 :47 1:123 1:26	Alw 3000	7 5 58½ 55½ 42 31¾	Adams J	116wb	5.70	80-27	Black Badge1241½Bud Grey104nkStymie1163	Fast finish	7
29Jan44- 5Hia	fst	7f	:233 :473 1:123 1:253	Bahamas H 6.3k	5 8 73½ 73¾ 76¼ 78	Brooks S	118wb	5.10	76-15	Ariel Flight1091½Good Bid122nkFreezout1122	Tired	10
25Jan44- 4Hia	fst	6f	:234 :473 1:131	Alw 3000	5 7 76¾ 77¾ 64¾ 65	Permane R	111wb	*1.35	78-25	Jimmie107nkFire Sticky1081½Valdina Malden107nk	Outrun	7
8Jan44- 5Hia	fst	6f	:231 :472 1:133	Hialeah 6.2k	7 8 76 72½ 3nk 42	Atkinson T	120wb	3.00	79-21	Black Badge120hdGood Bid1142Brief Sigh116no	Hung	11
1Jan44- 3TrP	fst	6f	:23 :472 1:123	Alw 1200	4 7 45 34 2½ 2¾	Atkinson T	120wb	2.25	86-12	Skytracer112.5¾Stymie1201Aloraye1082	Bid,hung	8
10Nov43- 5Jam	sl	1 1/16	:241 :482 1:133 1:454	Handicap 5190	1 6 76¾ 2hd 14 15	Brooks S	120wb	*2.05	84-21	Stymie1205Peppy Miss1101½Doggone105no	Easily	7
6Nov43- 5Pim	fst	1 70	:232 :471 1:133 1:454	T K Lynch Mem H 10k	3 8 87¾ 31½ 2hd 3nk	Jemas N	112 w	3.80	82-23	Royal Prince120nkThe Man113hdStymie1124	Circled field	10
1Nov43- 5Jam	gd	6f	:23 :462 1:124	Handicap 5240	6 8 813 76 41¼ 3nk	Brooks S	115wb	4.10	88-20	SweepingTime116hdArielGame109hdStymie115hd	Wide,gamely	8
23Oct43- 6Jam	fst	1 70	:234 :474 1:13 1:434	Ardsley H (Div 2) 11k	5 8 85¾ 32½ 21 21	Lindberg H	108wb	4.25	84-17	Bel Reigh1111Stymie108hdRodney Stone1226	Bid,2nd best	10
20Oct43- 4Jam	fst	1 70	:241 :48 1:132 1:453	Alw 5000	10 10 54¾ 22 2nk 23	Permane R	106wb	7.75	73-19	Weyanoke1143Stymie1065Broadcloth114½	Hung	14
12Oct43- 4Jam	fst	6f	:231 :471 1:123	Alw 5000	14 13 116½ 109 55 1no	Permane R	106wb	7.40f	89-13	Stymie106noSweeping Time1111Aloraye115hd	Driving	14
7Oct43- 5Bel	fst	1	:234 :472 1:131 1:384	Alw 2500	8 8 85¼ 42 3½ 44½	Kirkland A	111wb	6.40	75-17	Broadcloth1162Surrogate1161½Wild Rice1161	Impeded early	12
22Sep43- 5Bel	fst	6f-WC	:223 :452 1:101	©Alw 2500	2 13 136½ 85½ 74¼	Kirkland A	106wb	19.20	91-09	PukkaGin1151½Dustman114hdProfessorLee115hd	Good finish	14
16Sep43- 6Aqu	fst	6f	:23 :463 1:122	©Alw 2300	12 13 105½ 73¾ 42 11½	Kirkland A	111wb	6.95f	90-11	Stymie1111½Tumult1111Spheric1161	Driving	14
11Sep43- 5Aqu	fst	6f	:223 :461 1:12	Alw 2500	6 8 811 66½ 67½ 57¼	Brooks S	111wb	18.40	85-11	Que Hora1151½Black Badge1222½Ravenala118¾	Broke slowly	8
1Sep43- 4Aqu	fst	6f	:232 :47 1:122	Clm 5000	5 8 75½ 64¼ 46½ 46½	Atkinson T	116wb	2.35	83-11	Peppy Miss1145Seeing Eye119hdReimburseme1131½		8
Broke slowly,bore out badly entering stretch												

28Aug43- 1Bel	gd 6f-WC	:223 :462	1:12	Clm 5000	4 8 64 42 3hd	Brooks S	116wb	*2.25	86-10	WestwoodBelle112hdP.T.Boat108noStymie1163	Broke slowly	9
26Aug43- 5Bel	fst 6f-WC	:224 :454	1:102	Alw 2300	8 7 5¾ 73 77	McCreary C	116wb	10.25	87-10	Messari1131½Stir Up1163Late City1161	Swerved start	14
20Aug43- 1Bel	fst 6f-WC	:224 :462	1:12	Clm 5000	10 3 41¼ 3½ 2¾	Brooks S	116wb	*3.35	85-12	Seeing Eye116¾Stymie1161½Plucky Raider119hd	No mishap	10
18Aug43- 1Bel	fst 6f-WC	:232 :472	1:121	©MCl 3000	2 4 32 15 15	McCreary C	115wb	*2.15	85-18	Stymie1155HurricaneYank1121ChangeHr117hd	Speed to spare	14
11Aug43- 4Bel	fst 6f-WC	:23 :462	1:12	Clm 3500	9 5 52 41¼ 31½	Brooks S	111wb	5.50	84-14	Plucky Raider1161½Westwood Belle116hdStymie1113	Driving	9
5Aug43- 5Bel	fst 5½f-W	:23 :461	1:051	©Md Sp Wt	12 14 155 126¾ 1911½	Brooks S	115wb	11.40	76-11	Smolensko115½Triplicate1151½Good Bid115½	No factor	22
28Jly43- 1Bel	gd 5½f-W	:231 :463	1:054	©MCl 4000	8 11 94 84¾ 76¼	Gilbert J	116wb	*2.60	79-14	Late City1161½Super Marines1143Lou-Bre116hd	No menace	19
23Jly43- 3Jam	gd 5½f	:233 :48	1:074	©Md Sp Wt	4 5 99¼ 79¼ 65¼ 53½	Atkinson T	116wb	*1.90	77-19	Clansman1161½ReturnCall111½HayaTnty116no	Close quarters	12
28Jun43- 3Jam	fst 5½f	:23 :463	1:062	©Md Sp Wt	13 7 55 57 42½ 44¾	Brooks S	116wb	2.10	83-16	BoyKnight116nkCaptainsAide1161½Stronghold1163	No threat	14
25Jun43- 2Aqu	fst 5½f	:233 :473	1:062	Clm 5000	2 2 23 21 2nk 2nk	Atkinson T	111wb	*1.60	93-16	Sweeping Time116nkStymie1115Shamokin1161	Driving	5
21Jun43- 4Aqu	fst 5½f	:232 :48	1:071	©Md Sp Wt	5 1 53 44½ 31½ 21	Brooks S	116wb	1.80	88-15	Morani1161Stymi1162Hoodoo1162	Slow to start,good finish	8
17Jun43- 1Aqu	fst 5½f	:233 :473	1:07	Clm 5000	7 7 43¼ 32 31½ 24	Atkinson T	111wb	2.80	86-19	Chance Mate1164Stymie1112All Talk116½	Driving	7
12Jun43- 1Aqu	fst 5f	:234 :483	1:013	MCl 3500	8 7 66½ 53½ 31½ 2nk	Rienzi D	108wb	*1.90	88-12	More Wine111nkStymie1082Lady Eli110hd	Gamely	10
8Jun43- 1Aqu	my 5½f	:24 :491 1:021	1:08	MCl 2000	12 11 2nk 2hd 61¾ 21½	Rienzi D	111wb	8.05	83-13	Powdered Milk1111½Stymie1111½Omaloo1105		12
	Rushed up,bore out turn,came on again											
2Jun43- 1Bel	my 5f-WC		1:021	MCl 1500-c	5 10 91¾ 74 74½	Garza I	116wb	19.25	64-31	Assailant1161Free Dutch116½Little Dottie113½	Evenly	14
	Claimed from King Ranch,Trainer M. Hirsch											
29May43- 1Bel	fst 5f-WC		:583	©Md Sp Wt	1 12 1212 1222 1116½	Garza I	116wb	77.65	70-11	Stir Up116¾Rodney Stone1168Home Flight116hd	No factor	12
7May43- 1Jam	fst 5f	:233 :481	1:013	Clm 2500	7 7 55 44 43½ 78	Garza I	111wb	30.95	74-18	Sirlette108½Docdonough1164Magic Heels113hd	No threat	9

Trough Hill

b. g. 1942, by Tourist II (Son-in-Law)–Rollicking Princess, by Royal Canopy

Lifetime record: 40 12 10 8 $106,955

Own.– Mrs S.C. Clark Jr

Br.– Henry W. Frost Jr (Va)

Tr.– J.T. Skinner

11Nov50- 4Mid	fst *2½	S'Chase	4:183	4↑ Manly H 4.9k	3 4 42¼ 43½ 44½ 59	Field T	160ws	-	--	IseeYou1372½BannerWvs1331½HmptonRods1522	Disliked going	6
1Nov50- 5Lrl	fst *2	S'Chase	3:552	4↑ Chevy Chase H 9k	1 6 629 523 412 37	Harris H	153ws	*.90e	--	Hot1425Monkey Wrench1342Trough Hill153no	Belated rally	7
6Oct50- 5Bel	fst *3	S'Chase	5:422	4↑ Grand National H 23k	3 4 31½ 11 2hd 12½	Harris H	150ws	1.85e	--	TroughHill1502¼Oedipus1534PontiusPilate1502½	Going away	9
29Sep50- 5Bel	fst *2½	S'Chase	4:46	4↑ Brook H 15k	5 3 21 21 22 21½	Harris H	151 w	*1.70	--	Oedipus1491¼TroughHill1515½TouristList1361	Game effort	8
22Sep50- 5Bel	sf *2	S'Chase	3:482	3↑ Broad Hollow H 11k	1 5 513 510 43½ 32½	Harris H	150ws	5.10e	--	Oedipus1471¼Elkridge1521¼Trough Hill1505	Sharp effort	10
11May50- 5Bel	fst *2	S'Chase	3:511	4↑ International H 8.7k	5 3 31½ - - -	Field T	154ws	2.85	--	The Heir1481Adaptable143¾His Boots1502½	Fell at 9th	5
10Nov49- 5Pim	fst *2½	S'Chase	4:482	4↑ Manly H 8.2k	5 2 2hd 3½ 26 28	Harris H	156ws	*1.20e	--	HisBoots1458TroughHill1566AmericanWay1526	Bad landing	5
3Nov49- 5Pim	gd *2	S'Chase	3:554	3↑ Battleship H 8.4k	3 5 412 11½ 16 110	Field T	154ws	4.90	--	Trough Hill15410Fleettown14620Luan Casca13910	Easily	7
20Oct49- 5Lrl	fst *2½	S'Chase	4:452	4↑ Chevy Chase H 11k	6 3 34 55 45 43	Adams FD	156ws	1.60e	--	LockandKey1401¼HisBoots145nkAmrcnWy1521½	Close quarters	6
7Oct49- 6Bel	fst *3	S'Chase	5:483	4↑ Grand National H 22k	5 3 36 31½ 23 22½	Molony M	158ws	*1.20e	--	His Boots1412½Trough Hill1588Tourist List1462	Went well	7
29Sep49- 5Bel	sl *2½	S'Chase	4:521	4↑ Brook H 15k	7 6 36 32½ 11 110	Molony M	153ws	4.35e	--	TroughHill15310AmericanWay1511½HisBoots1429	Ridden out	8
22Sep49- 4Bel	fst *2	S'Chase	3:44	3↑ Broad Hollow H 11k	3 4 314 28 25 36¾	Field T	152ws	3.55e	--	Sun Bath1496Hampton Roads141¾Trough Hill1522	Weakened	7
1Jly49- 5Del	fst *2½	S'Chase	4:453	4↑ Indian River H 12k	4 4 - - - -	Field T	153ws	2.10	--	Elkridge1563SunBth1361¼TourstLst14820	Lost rider at 5th	5
9Jun49- 4Bel	fst *2½	S'Chase	4:433	4↑ Meadow Brook H 11k	5 3 311 21½ 15 22	Field T	151ws	*1.25	--	Elkridge1472Trough Hill1518Rank1404	Tired badly	7
2Jun49- 4Bel	fst *2	S'Chase	3:44	4↑ Corinthian H 9.4k	5 3 22 1hd 13 16	Harris H	147ws	4.35e	--	Trough Hill1476Elkridge149hdAmerican Way1463½	Easily	10
12May49- 5Bel	fst *2	S'Chase	3:504	4↑ International H 9k	6 6 - - - -	Field T	147 w	3.60	--	Homogenize1396Fleettown1498Lieut. Well14514	Fell 4th	7
20Nov48- 3Mtp	hy *2½	S'Chase	5:043	4↑ Noel Laing H 3.2k	1 4 41¾ 31½ 21 21½	Field T	156 w	-	--	Adaptable1531½TroughHill15610TouristList15550	No excuse	5
13Nov48- 4Mid	sl *2½	S'Chase	4:443	4↑ Handicap 2335	2 1 15 18 15 15	Field T	157 w	-e	--	Trough Hill1575Adaptable1561½Gunboats1341	In hand	4
28Oct48- 5Lrl	fst *2½	S'Chase	4:474	4↑ Chevy Chase H 18k	7 5 423 46½ 35½ 35	Field T	147ws	*1.50e	--	American Way1481Sun Bath1354Trough Hill1475	Went well	8
21Oct48- 5Lrl	fst *2	S'Chase	3:551	3↑ Governor Ogle H 12k	7 6 65¼ 57½ 46 46½	Peoples C	147ws	1.70e	--	Homogenize1342½Point Bleu1463Genancoke1431	No mishap	7
1Oct48- 5Bel	gd *3	S'Chase	5:50	4↑ Grand Nat'l H 31k	1 4 35 2½ 21 33	Field T	147ws	*2.30e	--	AmericanWay1441TouristList1502TroughHill1476	No mishap	14
23Sep48- 5Bel	fst *2½	S'Chase	4:471	4↑ Brook H 19k	11 7 43½ 33¼ 11½ 12	Field T	142ws	3.45e	--	Trough Hill1422Elkridge1561½American Way1432	Easily	11
9Sep48- 5Aqu	fst *2½	S'Chase	4:54	4↑ Glendale H 11k	1 1 1½ 11 13 17	Field T	139 w	2.35	--	Trough Hill1397Big Wrack1322½Navigate140	Easily	4
2Sep48- 5Aqu	fst *2	S'Chase	3:444	3↑ Harbor Hill H 11k	1 6 55¾ 43½ 53¾ 55¼	Field T	142ws	7.00e	--	Tourist List145¾Big Wrack1312½Sun Bath1411	Faltered	9
12May48- 5Pim	fst 2	S'Chase	3:471	4↑ Jervis Spencer H 12k	6 4 516 521 520 525	Field T	148ws	*1.10e	--	Lieut. Well1441½Canford13812Adaptable1501½	No excuse	7
17Apr48- 6War	fst *2	S'Chase	4:293	4↑ Handicap 1330	2 2 13 18 17 110	Field T	162 w	-	--	Trough Hill16210Tourist List1412Bail Me Out135	Easily	4
22Nov47- 3Mtp	fst *2½	S'Chase	5:53	4↑ Noel Laing H 3.2k	4 3 24 25 25 26	Field T	155 w	-	--	TouristList1506TroughHill1558Adptbl16310	Best of others	6
15Nov47- 5Mid	my *2½	S'Chase	4:453	4↑ Handicap 2370	2 2 11½ 21 22 34½	Field T	157 w	-	--	LittleSammie1462½ChanceBullet1402TroughHll1572	Weakened	5
29Oct47- 5Lrl	gd *2½	S'Chase	4:542	4↑ Chevy Chase H 18k	5 4 34½ 26 210 315½	Field T	147 w	*2.00	--	Sun Bath13915Elkridge154½Trough Hill1478	Weakened	7
17Oct47- 6Lrl	fst *2	S'Chase	3:52	3↑ Butler H 11k	2 3 39 34 1hd 1hd	Field T	141 w	*1.30	--	Trough Hill141hdSun Bath1372½Allier13750	Hard drive	5
2Oct47- 5Bel	fst *3	S'Chase	5:413	4↑ Grand National 29k	4 5 46¼ 311 23 3nk	Field T	139 w	3.95	--	Adaptable147hdWar Battle163nkTrough Hill1394	Game try	8
17Sep47- 5Aqu	fst *2½	S'Chase	4:571	4↑ Glendale H 11k	7 5 42¼ 21 21 22	Field T	139 w	*2.35	--	Elkridge1612Trough Hill1392Delhi Dan1385	Weakened	7
11Sep47- 3Aqu	fst *2¼	S'Chase	4:204	4↑ Handicap 4535	3 2 23 2nk 14 16	Field T	138 w	2.90	--	Trough Hill1366Delhi Dan14120Refugio149	Easily	4
	Previously owned by Mrs W. Bromley											
29May47- 5Del	fst *2	S'Chase	4:03	4↑ Tom Roby 13k	3 7 64¾ 54 58½ 617¾	Field T	157 w	2.50e	--	American Way14912Tourist Pride1351½Tourist List1462		10
	Never a threat											
8May47- 4Pim	fst *2	S'Chase	3:582	4↑ Spring Maiden 7.3k	6 1 21 112 120 125	Field T	148 w	6.80	--	Trough Hill14825Allier13515Lady Janice15040	Easily	9
30Apr47- 3Pim	fst *2	S'Chase	3:54	4↑ Alw 3500	1 3 11½ 16 23½ 26	Field T	150wb	*.70e	--	TheHeir1396TroughHill1503Gnncok14712	Fenced poorly 14th	7
12Apr47- 5Mid	fst *2	S'Chase	3:54	4↑ Alw 540	1 1 13½ 15 18 112	Field T	141 w	-	--	TroughHill14112TouristIndex13025Benevolent143500	Easily	5
16Nov46- 3Mid	fst *2	S'Chase	3:544	3↑ Alw 1010	5 2 23 26 - -	Peoples C	134 w	-	--	Genncoke13712Big Wrack134noCpassRose13530	Lost rider 10th	8
6Nov46- 3Pim	fst *2	S'Chase	4:014	3↑ Md Sp Wt	1 2 31½ 26 11 21½	Bland W	147 w	3.15e	--	Boston Boy1481½Trough Hill147hdArmy Power145200		11
	Bobbled 11th,tired											
1Oct46- 3Bel	fst *2	S'Chase	3:59	3↑ Md Sp Wt	5 3 312 314 24 28	Land WD	146 w	*1.70e	--	Last Rock1468Trough Hill1463Phalanger1436	Outrun	8

Twilight Tear

b. f. 1941, by Bull Lea (Bull Dog)–Lady Lark, by Blue Larkspur

Lifetime record: 24 18 2 2 $202,165

Own.– Calumet Farm

Br.– Calumet Farm (Ky)

Tr.– B.A. Jones

28Aug45- 6Was	fst 6f	:221 :452	1:102	3↑ Alw 5000	3 1 21½ 24 47½ -	Dodson D	117 w	1.80	--	FightingDon1103Occupy1165MyTetRambler1111½	Bled,eased	5
1Nov44- 7Pim	fst 1 3/16	:481 1:122 1:372	1:563	3↑ Pim Spl 25k	2 1 13 14 14 16	Dodson D	117 w	*.65	99-12	Twilight Tear1176Devil Diver12610Megogo120	Galloping	3
21Oct44- 6Lrl	my 1¼	:481 1:14 1:414	2:083	Maryland H 16k	4 1 11 23 46½ 415½	Dodson D	130 w	*.15e	51-40	Dare Me1097Miss Keeneland1102½Aera1066	Quit badly	6
12Oct44- 6Lrl	fst 1⅛	:472 1:123 1:40	1:531	3↑ ⒻQueen Isabella H 11k	4 1 16 16 15 15	Dodson D	126 w	*.15e	82-23	Twilight Tear1265Good Morning1182Legend Bearer1083½		8
	Never extended											
2Oct44- 5Bel	fst 5½f-W	:224 :452	1:032	3↑ ⒻHandicap 3480	3 1 2hd 1½ 12½	Arcaro E	126 w	*.40e	97-08	Twilight Tear1262½Tellmenow118¾Cocopet1145		5
	Bore out,impeded runner-up str											
8Aug44- 6Bel	fst 1¼	:471 1:112 1:372	2:033	ⒻAlabama 23k	1 1 1½ 11 11½ 2¾	Haas L	126 w	*.05	81-14	Vienna114¾Twilight Tear1265Thread o' Gold1171¼	Faltered	4
22Jly44- 6Was	fst 1¼	:48 1:12 1:372	2:033	Classic 79k	1 1 11 12 13 12	Haas L	114 w	*.10e	92-08	TwlghtTr1142OldKntuck1194½Pnsv1265	Saved ground,handily	5
17Jly44- 3Was	fst 1	:233 :471 1:112	1:361	Alw 5000	2 1 12 12 13 11¼	Haas L	117 w	-e	97-11	Twilight Tear1171¼Pensive1222Appleknocker1101	Easily	4
	Nonwagering event											

6Jly44- 6Was	fst 7f	:23 :453 1:093 1:223	Skokie H 11k	5	2	11	12	13	11½	Haas L	121	w	*.30e	103-10	TwilightTear1211½Sirde1142½ChallengM1065	Speed to spare	7
28Jun44- 6Was	fst 6f	:222 :453 1:103	ⒻPrincess Doreen 11k	1	2	21	22½	2hd	11½	McCreary C	121	w	*.40	98-09	TwilightTear1211½BellSong1106HrrtSu114nk	Altered course	6
27May44- 6Bel	gd 1⅜	:481 1:133 1:40 2:21	ⒻC C A Oaks 17k	1	1	12	13	13	14	McCreary C	121	w	*.10	66-27	Twilight Tear1214Dare Me1213Plucky Maud1212	Easily	6
17May44- 6Bel	fst 1	:233 :464 1:112 1:37	ⒻAcorn 14k	9	4	42	21	11½	12½	McCreary C	121	w	*.20	89-13	TwilightTear1212½Whirlabout1216Evrgt1211	Speed to spare	10
10May44- 6Pim	fst 1 1/16	:234 :48 1:123 1:451	ⒻPim Oaks 18k	5	1	11½	11	11½	13	McCreary C	121	w	*.30	92-19	Twilight Tear1213Plucky Maud1213Everget1215	In hand	5
3May44- 6Pim	fst 6f	:221 :453 1:113	Rennert H 7k	10	3	22	2½	13	11½	McCreary C	118	w	*.40e	95-17	TwilightTear1181½Glctc1083IdlGft112.52	As rider pleased	10
25Apr44- 6Pim	sl 6f	:224 :474 1:14	Alw 4000	3	2	2hd	11	1½	11¼	McCreary C	117	w	*.50e	83-35	TwilghtTr1171¼GrampsImage1145Jimmie1146	Rated,drew away	5
17Mar44- 5TrP	sly 6f	:221 :453 1:122	ⒻAlw 1800	5	3	37	36½	2¼	13	McCreary C	118	w	*.30	88-29	Twilight Tear1183Lassie Sue1201½Cuban Bomb1062	Handily	7
10Mar44- 6TrP	fst 6f	:23 :464 1:114	Alw 1800	7	1	11	11	14	12	McCreary C	117	w	*.25	91-16	Twilight Tear1172Comenow1192½Surrogate122nk	Easily	7
29Feb44- 6Hia	fst 6f	:23 :462 1:121 3↑	Leap Year H 5k	4	5	42¼	3½	31	32	Smith FA	101	w	9.00	86-23	Mettlesome1161Adulator1121Twilight Tear101hd	Held well	8
8Nov43- 6Pim	sly 1 70	:241 :49 1:153 1:472	ⒻAlw 5000	4	1	15	12	11	12¼	Thompson B	120	w	*.50e	74-28	Twilight Tear1202¼Miss Keeneland1208Red Wonder11110		5
	Speed in reserve																
27Oct43- 6Pim	my 1 1/16	:234 :481 1:14 1:482	ⒻSelima 24k	5	3	11	11½	1nk	21	Thompson B	119	w	*1.20e	75-27	MissKeeneland1111TwilightTr1191½Whrlbout1226	No match	8
20Oct43- 5Pim	fst 1 70	:241 :49 1:143 1:454	ⒻAlw 2500	6	1	11½	12	11	12	Thompson B	115	w	*.40e	82-21	TwilightTear1152MissKenlnd1096MyMlch1061	Speed to spare	6
16Oct43- 7Pim	sly 6f	:23 :481 1:153	ⒻAlw 2500	1	4	1nk	2hd	2hd	32½	Smith FA	117	w	*1.05e	72-21	Red Wonder111noCountess Wise1142½Twilight Tear117nk		8
	Used in pace,lost ground																
3Jly43- 6Was	fst 6f	:224 :464 1:131	ⒻArl Lassie 34k	3	6	22	22	13	12½	Jemas N	113	w	*1.00e	85-14	TwilightTear1132½MissKeeneland1132MusicHall1104	Easily	15
25Jun43- 1Was	fst 5½f	:224 :473 1:003 1:073	ⒻMd Sp Wt	6	5	68½	45	21	1¾	Eads W	115	w	*1.60	87-17	Twilight Tear115¾Letmenow1151Durazna1153		12
	Slow into stride,drawing clear																

Vagrancy

dk. b. f. 1939, by Sir Gallahad III (Teddy)–Valkyr, by Man o' War

Lifetime record: 42 15 8 8 $102,480

Own.– Belair Stud

Br.– Belair Stud (Ky)

Tr.– J. Fitzsimmons

9Oct43- 6Bel	fst 2¼	:504 2:343 2:594 3:521 3↑	New York H 28k	6	4	45¼	23	31½	33	Stout J	112	wb	4.85	71-17	Bolngbrok1241½FryMnhurst1161½Vgrncy11212	Challenged,tired	6
5Oct43- 6Bel	fst 1½	:483 1:134 2:05 2:314 3↑	ⒻLadies H 16k	2	4	43½	2½	2½	21½	Stout J	123	wb	4.10	77-17	Stefanita1161½Vagrancy1236Dark Discovery1061¼	Driving	7
18Sep43- 6Aqu	fst 1⅛	:474 1:132 1:383 1:513 3↑	ⒻBeldame H 28k	9	7	86¼	75½	42½	33	Gilbert J	122	wb	9.10	86-14	Mar-Kell1261Stefanita1162Vagrancy122½	Closed well	11
28Aug43- 6GS	sl 1⅛	:474 1:132 1:391 1:524 3↑	Trenton H 13k	5	5	59½	47	46	56¾	Stout J	109	w	2.95	78-29	Aonbarr113nkWith Regards1182Boysy1134	No threat	7
25Aug43- 6Bel	fst 1⅛	:463 1:111 1:364 1:50 3↑	ⒻDiana H 5.8k	4	4	44½	33	41¼	21	Stout J	126	wb	*1.30	90-10	Bonnet Ann1131Vagrancy126nkNight Glow1121	Wide	5
20Aug43- 7Bel	fst 1	:233 :463 1:111 1:36 3↑	Alw 3000	5	2	21	2½	2hd	21¾	Stout J	108	wb	3.65	92-14	FamousVictory1051¾Vagrancy108nkFirstFiddle1201	Bid,hung	7
30Jun43- 5Jam	gd 1 1/16	:251 :491 1:134 1:462 3↑	ⒻHandicap 5120	1	3	33½	33½	35	35½	Stout J	128	wb	*.95	75-22	Night Glow1081½Stefanita1104Vagrancy12810	Tired	4
26Jun43- 6Aqu	fst 1¼	:481 1:132 1:383 2:032 3↑	Brooklyn H 33k	7	9	911	89¾	89¾	819¼	Stout J	110	wb	23.30	71-12	DevilDiver1231½MarketWise128¾DonBngo1133	Stumbled start	9
19Jun43- 7Aqu	fst 1⅛	:491 1:132 1:391 1:52 4↑	Handicap 3535	1	4	42¼	43	31	3½	Stout J	117	wb	4.30e	86-12	Lochinvar115hdDon Bingo122½Vagrancy1177	Rated,gamely	5
31May43- 6Bel	fst 1¼	:47 1:111 1:361 2:012 3↑	Suburban H 38k	2	5	103¾	127½	107½	109	Durando C	112	wb	34.90	84-12	DonBingo1042[D]MarketWise1282½Attention121hd	No threat	17
24May43- 6Bel	fst 1	:232 :464 1:121 1:374 3↑	ⒻHandicap 3025	3	4	42¼	11	11½	12	Longden J	126	wb	*.65	85-19	Vagrancy1262Too Timely1072½Waygal1021½	Very wide	5
14May43- 6Bel	my 1	:232 :47 1:12 1:374 3↑	ⒻAlw 3000	5	7	65	44	34	28	Longden J	122	wb	*.55	77-23	Mar-Kell1108Vagrancy1226Opera Singer101nk	No match	8
7May43- 5Jam	fst 1 1/16	:241 :474 1:131 1:46 3↑	ⒻHandicap 5025	2	3	31½	31	2½	2¾	Malley T	126	wb	*1.40	82-18	Pomayya122¾Vagrancy1267What Not981½	Trapped,gamely	6
	Previously trained by G. Tappen																
24Oct42- 6Lrl	fst 1¼	:473 1:122 1:383 2:032 3↑	Washington H 19k	9	5	2hd	55	69¾	714	Stout J	108	wb	9.20	79-20	Whirlaway130½Thumbs Up1102Riverland1185	Quit badly	9
17Oct42- 6Lrl	sl 1¼	:474 1:124 1:392 2:062	Maryland H 8.8k	1	2	56	57	46	47½	Stout J	117	wb	*.65	70-28	Thumbs Up113hdIncoming1112½Equinox1045	Disliked going	7
12Oct42- 6Lrl	fst 1⅛	:473 1:122 1:381 1:51 3↑	ⒻQueen Isabella H 6.1k	1	4	4¾	1½	12	13	Stout J	126	wb	*.50	93-12	Vagrancy1263Lotopoise1022Rosetown1224	Much in reserve	6
	Previously trained by J. Fitzsimmons																
6Oct42- 6Bel	gd 1½	:481 1:133 2:054 2:311 3↑	ⒻLadies H 16k	4	1	411	21	11	11¼	Stout J	126	wb	*1.40	86-13	Vagrancy1261¼Dark Discovery1081¼Loveday1175	Ridden out	10
29Sep42- 7Bel	fst 1⅝	:484 1:393 2:043 2:42	Lawrence Realizatn 11k	1	3	47½	32¼	1nk	23½	Stout J	115	wb	5.00e	90-08	Alsab1263½Vagrancy1153Trierarch110nk	Bore in final ⅛	5
19Sep42- 6Aqu	sly 1⅛	:472 1:121 1:373 1:50 3↑	ⒻBeldame H 17k	9	2	1½	14	14	14•	Stout J	119	wb	*2.15	97-06	[DH]Vgrncy119[DH]Brrncos1164Rostown126hd	Drifted out,tiring	10
29Aug42- 6Nar	fst 1 1/16	:23 :462 1:12 1:443	ⒻNew England Oaks 12k	1	5	54¼	44½	21½	2¾	Stout J	121	wb	*.80	93-14	Spiral Pass116¾Vagrancy1213Ubiquitous1166	In trouble	9
7Aug42- 5Sar	fst 1¼	:473 1:121 1:381 2:051	ⒻAlabama 10k	2	2	24	23	21½	2½	Stout J	126	wb	*.30	82-13	[D]Bonnet Ann114½Vagrancy126hdSmiles114	Impeded	3
	Placed first through disqualification																
31Jly42- 5Sar	sly 7f	:231 :471 1:122 1:26	ⒻTest 3.4k	5	4	42	31½	21	1hd	Stout J	123	wb	*.55	86-17	Vagrancy123hdTaunt113¾Smiles1132½	Hard drive	6
11Jly42- 5Emp	fst 1 3/16	:474 1:123 1:364 1:56	Emp City H 28k	2	3	32	42	45½	45¾	Malley T	114	wb	*1.50e	101-07	Apache1143Lochinvar1162½Col. Teddy115nk	No mishap	7
4Jly42- 5Emp	fst 1 3/16	:48 1:122 1:374 1:564 3↑	Butler H 33k	2	4	31½	31½	32¼	43¾	McCreary C	100	wb	4.20	99-07	Tola Rose1032½Whirlaway132nkSwing and Sway1121	Faltered	7
24Jun42- 6Aqu	fst 1 1/16	:232 :472 1:124 1:45	ⒻGazelle 6.5k	5	3	35	22	12	14	Stout J	126	wb	*.50	89-10	Vagrancy1264Smiles112nkMackerel1121½	Drew away	7
18Jun42- 6Aqu	fst 1 1/16	:242 :48 1:123 1:443	ⒻAlw 3500	3	3	32½	13	13	15	Stout J	121	wb	*1.25	91-09	Vagrancy1215Lotopoise1081Smiles108nk	Much the best	6
11Jun42- 6Del	gd 1⅛	:481 1:13 1:394 1:54	ⒻDel Oaks 10k	4	3	32	23	1hd	1no	Malley T	119	wb	1.95	79-19	Vagrancy119noWaygal1104Bostoff1103	Hard drive	6
27May42- 6Bel	fst 1½	:51 1:17 2:071 2:313	ⒻCCA Oaks 20k	6	3	1½	11½	11½	12	Malley T	121	wb	*.60	84-11	Vagrancy1212Mackerel1214Copperette1213	In hand	6
20May42- 6Bel	fst 1	:232 :46 1:11 1:381	ⒻAcorn 14k	1	6	44½	57	56½	21½	Malley T	121	wb	*2.20	82-11	Zaca Rosa1211½Vagrancy121nkBonnet Ann1211	Closed fast	15
15May42- 6Bel	fst 1	:231 :461 1:12 1:383 3↑	ⒻAlw 3000	10	9	66	66	86¾	76¼	Malley T	108	wb	4.30	76-13	Painted Veil1202Pomayya120hdChallomine1092	Outrun	12
2May42- 6Pim	fst 1 1/16	:231 :471 1:121 1:453	ⒻPim Oaks 12k	2	3	31½	22	2½	1½	Malley T	121	wb	*1.95	92-07	Vagrancy121½Chiquita Mia1217Bonnet Ann1211	Driving	7
25Apr42- 2Jam	fst 6f	:23 :462 1:114	ⒻAlw 1500	2	6	74¾	42½	11½	12½	Malley T	113	wb	7.80e	93-10	Vagrancy1132½Smiles1131½Draeh1083½	Going away	13
21Apr42- 5Jam	fst 1 1/16	:232 :471 1:122 1:453	Alw 2500	7	6	611	66½	48	510	Stout J	108	wb	3.60	75-17	Air Current113noK. Dorko1136Blue Gino1082	No mishap	7
15Apr42- 4Jam	fst 6f	:23 :462 1:12	ⒻAlw 2000	3	5	58½	58½	48½	34¾	Stout J	110	wb	2.80	87-12	Taunt115¾War Melody1104Vagrancy110hd	Closed fast	5
	Previously trained by G. Tappen																
25Oct41- 5Lrl	fst 1 1/16	:232 :473 1:123 1:471	ⒻSelima 28k	10	4	31¼	32	22	34	Deering J	114	wb	2.45e	77-17	Ficklebush1073½Hard Baked114½Vagrancy1142	Tired	11
18Oct41- 4Lrl	fst 1 70	:233 :474 1:132 1:45	ⒻAlw 1200	5	2	11	11	12	12	Deering J	113	wb	*1.05	84-16	Vagrancy1132Last Sou1092Umbril10812	Ridden out	6
13Oct41- 4Lrl	fst 1 70	:233 :48 1:134 1:452	ⒻAlw 1500	2	4	42¼	31½	1½	12	Deering J	111	wb	2.75	82-19	Vagrancy1112Seaway103noUmbril1065	Going away	8
9Oct41- 4Lrl	fst 6f	:224 :47 1:122	Alw 1200	3	6	44¼	42	42½	32	Deering J	111	wb	8.65	90-18	Bless Me1141½Tomluta117½Vagrancy1114	Closed well	6
	Previously trained by J. Fitzsimmons																
20Sep41- 7Bel	fst 6f	:221 :46 1:113	ⒻMatron 20k	11	11	1311	1212	109½	911	Stout J	115	wb	19.30	81-13	Petrify1192Light Lady119noFicklebush110½	Outrun	15
12Sep41- 5Aqu	fst 6f	:23 :464 1:13	ⒻAlw 1500	8	9	84¾	63¾	44	3½	Stout J	116	wb	6.00	88-12	Smiles113nkLast Sou113nkVagrancy1161	Strong finish	9
1Sep41- 4Aqu	fst 5½f	:232 :474 1:071	ⒻMd Sp Wt	6	5	31¾	2½	21	1½	Stout J	116	wb	7.55	91-12	Vagrancy116½Waygal1164Jezara116hd	Driving	7
23Aug41- 3Sar	fst 6f	:231 :472 1:14	ⒻAlw 1200	3	10	109¾	915	89½	78	Stout J	110	wb	32.65	74-19	Court Manners115noBig Meal1151½Spiral Pass1151	Outrun	10

War Battle

b. g. 1941, by Battleship (Man o' War)–Ponova, by Pommern **Lifetime record: 49 11 10 8 $88,360**

Own.– K. Miller
Br.– Leslie B. Gray
Tr.– K. Miller

Date	Cond	Dist	Surface / Fractions	Time	Race	Running line	Jockey	Wt	Odds	Spd	Company line	Comment	Starters
3Oct51- 4Lig	hd	*2	S'Chase	4:101	3↑ Alw 2500	7 4 55¾ 58¾ 511 514	Field K	140wb	-	--	Allflor1472½Politician140½Friese1353	Never a factor	9
27Aug51- 3Sar	fst	*2	S'Chase	4:14	3↑ Alw 3500	2 3 326 422 530 533	Carter E	146wb	4.65	--	Fulton14012Patrol14614Short Circuit1401	Jumped poorly	5
22Aug51- 3Sar	sl	*2	S'Chase	4:292	3↑ Alw 4000	6 3 24 12 312 323½	Riles S	138wb	19.95	--	Elyacin1331½Phiblant15022War Battle13815	Quit	7
15Aug51- 3Sar	gd	*2	S'Chase	4:151	4↑ Clm 3000	1 7 74 45½ 616 622	Carter E	137wb	7.70	--	Kipper1523My Good Man1474Trepid1412½	Tired	9
16Jun49- 4Aqu	fst	*2½	S'Chase	4:564	4↑ Hitchcock H 11k	4 4 47 310 620 624	Smithwick P	151wb	3.35	--	Homogenize142½Rank1401Navigate143½	Lame	6
25May49- 5Bel	fst	*2	S'Chase	3:531	4↑ Alw 4500	4 4 613 514 412 411	Rich J	150wb	7.50	--	Floating Isle1401½Genancoke1402Galactic1407	No mishap	6
19May49- 4Bel	fst	*2	S'Chase	3:434	4↑ C L Appleton 9.5k	11 2 1126 1029 942 976	Rich J	146wb	4.70	--	Navigate138½Point Bleu1422½Galactic1382½	Quit	11
10May49- 3Bel	my	*2	S'Chase	4:023	4↑ Alw 4500	2 1 14 1hd 716 725	Rich J	152wb	*1.70	--	Floating Isle1466Navigate1462Point Bleu1461½	Quit	7
			Daily Racing Form time,4:05 3/5										
23Jun48- 3Aqu	my	*2	S'Chase	4:04	4↑ Alw 4500	3 1 110 110 110 17	Bosley J III	152wb	*1.30	--	War Battle1527Big Wrack13740Fred Havecker134	Easily	5
17Jun48- 1Del	sl	*2	S'Chase	3:552	4↑ Alw 4000	4 1 2hd 13 16 18	Bosley J III	155wb	2.15	--	WarBattle1558AmericanWay1516Lieut.Well155¾	Ridden out	5
27May48- 5Bel	gd	*2	S'Chase	3:491	4↑ C L Appleton 11k	1 2 31¾ 36½ 38 310	Bosley J III	155wb	2.40	--	TheHeir1352Fleettown1468WarBattle15510	Bad landing 8th	5
23Oct47- 6Lrl	fst	*2	S'Chase	3:502	3↑ Governor Ogle H 12k	1 3 410 420 421 415	Miller R	164wb	3.40	--	Genancoke1415Sun Bath139noAdaptable15010	Outrun	6
8Oct47- 5Bel	fst	*2	S'Chase	3:45	3↑ Broad Hollow H 18k	4 1 12 21 32½ 32½	McGovern J	165wb	*.75	--	Hampton Roads1382Genancoke140½War Battle165½	Tired	4
2Oct47- 5Bel	fst	*3	S'Chase	5:413	4↑ Grand National 29k	2 2 12 110 13 2hd	McGovern J	163wb	*1.05e	--	Adaptable147hdWarBattle163nkTroughHill1394	Tired badly	8
25Sep47- 5Bel	my	*2½	S'Chase	4:521	4↑ Brook H 18k	9 2 13 11½ 311 413	Brown N	164wb	*1.55	--	Adaptable1408Delhi Dan1384Floating Isle1501	Weak ride	9
26Jly47- 6Jam	fst	1 1/16	:243 :491 1:141	1:483	3↑ Md Sp Wt	6 10 915 812 57½ 43	Wilson HB	120wb	3.40	67-14	DeepTexas1132Capt.Dorsett113hdWinterWndII1131	Late foot	10
12Jun47- 5Aqu	fst	*2½	S'Chase	4:573	4↑ Hitchcock H 10k	3 2 39 11½ 110 115	Brown N	162wb	*.65e	--	War Battle16215Copper Beech1335Floating Isle140	Easily	4
28May47- 5Bel	fst	*2½	S'Chase	4:464	4↑ Meadow Brook 17k	1 1 12 1nk 13 112	Brown N	156wb	*1.15e	--	War Battle15612Fleettown14112Floating Isle147no	Easily	6
22May47- 5Bel	sl	*2	S'Chase	4:071	4↑ Corinthian H 11k	4 3 34½ 46½ 37 32	Roberts E	156wb	5.70	--	Boojum II1431Raylywn1391War Battle15620		7
			Bothered by riderless horse										
9May47- 5Bel	fst	*2	S'Chase	3:504	4↑ International H 11k	1 1 1nk 1½ 22 26	Passmore WJ	156wb	.95	--	Boojum II1386War Battle1561½Hidalgo13720	Saved ground	5
12Nov46- 5Pim	fst	2½	S'Chase	4:482	4↑ Manly H 17k	6 2 26 21½ 12 18	Passmore W	148wb	2.85	--	WarBattle1488GalleyBoy1395TouristList13512	Bobbled 15th	6
5Nov46- 5Pim	fst	2	S'Chase	3:512	3↑ Battleship H 11k	6 4 31 33 3½ 21½	Passmore W	148wb	*.90e	--	GalleyBoy1321½WarBattle1481¼TouristList1351	Second best	6
15Oct46- 6Bel	fst	*3	S'Chase	5:422	4↑ Temple Gwathmey H 21k	1 1 120 115 115 130	Passmore W	138wb	*1.35e	--	WarBattle13830Elkridge1582½Chesapeak1403	Speed to spare	5
9Oct46- 5Bel	fst	*2	S'Chase	3:493	3↑ Broad Hollow H 11k	5 1 15 11 23 33	Mason G	145wb	4.75	--	Lieut. Well1372Greek Flag1311War Battle1455		7
			Bobbled several fences										
28Sep46- 3Bel	fst	*2	S'Chase	3:502	3↑ Alw 5000	5 3 34 21 21½ 21	Adams FD	143wb	*.60	--	Tourist List1441War Battle1435Cosey1464	Hard urged	5
6Sep46- 5Aqu	fst	*2	S'Chase	3:432	3↑ Harbor Hill H 11k	5 7 77½ 56 611 613¼	Adams FD	151wb	*1.25	--	[D]Chesapeake1321Navigate150nkKnight'sQust1488	No mishap	7
23Aug46- 5Sar	fst	*2	S'Chase	4:114	3↑ Beverwyck H 5.7k	3 3 45¼ 32½ 22 21	Adams FD	144wb	2.75	--	RougeDragon1621WarBattle1442½BoojumII13912	Bobbled 1st	4
8Aug46- 5Sar	gd	*2	S'Chase	4:15	4↑ Shillelah 5.6k	4 2 2½ 11 1½ 2no	Bauman A	147wb	*1.80	--	Tetrol138noWar Battle14725Beneksar1441½	Bothered early	5
26Jun46- 2Del	fst	*2	S'Chase	3:51	4↑ Alw 3500	3 4 33½ 33½ 34 36¼	Marzani D	141 w	*.90	--	Boojum II1532¼Gala Reigh1374War Battle1412½	Bobbled 9th	4
22Jun46- 3Aqu	fst	*2	S'Chase	3:421	4↑ Handicap 4500	2 4 33½ 37 21½ 2nk	Marzani D	146 w	*1.35e	--	Elkridge155nkWar Battle1461Lancastrian1402	Fast finish	5
11Jun46- 5Aqu	fst	*2½	S'Chase	4:511	4↑ Hitchcock H 11k	5 3 41 31¼ 21½ 2¾	Bauman A	139 w	6.55	--	Delhi Dan133¾War Battle1391½Mercator15614	Saved ground	5
8Jun46- 3Bel	fst	*1¾	Hurdles	3:222	3↑ Alw 4000	7 4 32 32 22 21½	Bauman A	153 w	*1.10e	--	H Hour1371½War Battle1532Yankee Chance138nk	Driving	8
28May46- 5Bel	hy	*2½	S'Chase	4:581	4↑ Meadowbrook H 11k	3 2 210 314 413 616	Bauman A	142 w	8.10	--	Mercator1503Beneksar1347Burma Road1521	No factor	8
22May46- 5Bel	fst	*2	S'Chase	3:493	4↑ Corinthian H 9.4k	3 7 32 2½ 22 33	Bauman A	143 w	12.15	--	Burma Road1461Navigate1422War Battle1436	Held well	12
16May46- 5Bel	fst	*2	S'Chase	3:524	4↑ C L Appleton 8.8k	1 2 1hd 2hd 35¼ 312	Adams FD	152 w	2.40	--	Burma Road1395Floating Isle1517War Battle152½	Tired	6
6May46- 3Bel	fst	1½	Hurdles	2:503	4↑ Alw 4000	1 2 42¼ 32 12 12½	Jennings E	155 w	2.55	--	War Battle1552½Mat1392Gala Reigh1434	Drew away	6
28Nov45- 5Pim	sly	2½	S'Chase	5:252	4↑ Manly H 12k	2 1 13 21 617 632	Banks D	142 w	2.85e	--	PursuitPlane1325BurmaRoad13912GeekFlag1384	Speed,tired	10
14Nov45- 3Pim	fst	2	S'Chase	3:502	3↑ Handicap 5000	1 5 21 - - -	Adams FD	142wsb	20.95	--	Cosey130¾Floating Isle1492Mercator1602	Lost rider 11th	7
3Oct45- 5Bel	fst	*3	S'Chase	5:48	4↑ Grand National H 18k	9 - - - - -	Adams FD	139wsb	4.30	--	Mercator1425Caddie139¾Raylywn1426	Fell	12
24Aug45- 5Bel	sl	*2	S'Chase	3:494	3↑ Beverwyck H 5.9k	5 1 13 12 1hd 12	Adams FD	135wsb	*1.45e	--	War Battle1352Boojum II1373Floating Isle15210	Drew away	7
17Aug45- 4Bel	fst	*2	S'Chase	3:45	3↑ North American H 16k	9 2 21½ 2nk 31¼ 63¼	Adams FD	136wb	3.85e	--	FloatingIsle149nkChesapeake136½Elkrdg1581	Bobbled,tired	10
17Nov44- 5Pim	fst	2	S'Chase	3:493	3↑ Battleship H 10k	6 - - - - -	Owen W	135wsb	3.15	--	Ahmisk1441Rouge Dragon1627Boojum II1404	Lost rider 4th	9
1Nov44- 3Pim	fst	2	S'Chase	3:58	3↑ Alw 2500	1 1 1½ 16 14 110	Owen W	135wsb	*1.15	--	War Battle13510Floating Isle1471Refugio1464	In hand	9
29Sep44- 3Bel	fst	*1¾	Hurdles	3:27	3↑ Alw 2500	5 3 43¼ 31½ 12 11½	Roberts E	136wsb	*1.30	--	War Battle1361½Peat Moss1494Beneksar1472½	Mild drive	5
18Sep44- 3Bel	fst	*1½	Hurdles	2:53	3↑ Alw 2500	6 6 43 32 2hd 2½	Roberts E	136wb	3.15	--	GreyHood137½WarBattl13612ArrvonTm1462	Bid,faltered late	7
31Aug44- 3Bel	fst	*1½	Hurdles	2:522	Md Sp Wt	2 6 56 48 12 14	Harrison JS	146 w	9.25	--	War Battle1464Cosey1454Persepolis1453	Easily	7
			Previously owned by Petard Stable;previously trained by J. Bosley Jr										
21Aug44- 3Bel	fst	*1½	Hurdles	2:502	3↑ Md Sp Wt	6 11 1010 915 916 721	Jennings E	135 w	28.50	--	[D]Longchamp II1516Lieut. Well1352Quonset1384	No factor	12
15Aug44- 3Bel	fst	*1½	Hurdles	2:49	3↑ OMdClm 2000	7 10 917 621 619¼ 515½	Jennings E	137 w	75.10	--	Nordmeer152½Navigate1374Longchamp II1525	Collided 9th	10
7Aug44- 3Bel	fst	*1½	Hurdles	2:53	3↑ OMdClm 2000	4 2 615 533 527 628¾	McGovern J	137 w	21.55	--	Wolfberry140¾Nordmeer1525Night Porter1523	No mishap	8

War Plumage

br. f. 1936, by On Watch (Colin)–War Feathers, by Man o' War **Lifetime record: 16 3 3 1 $48,600**

Own.– J.C. Brady
Br.– Howard Oots (Ky)
Tr.– H. Wells

Date	Cond	Dist	Fractions	Time	Race	Running line	Jockey	Wt	Odds	Spd	Company line	Comment	Starters
5Nov40- 6Pim	fst	1 3/16	:481 1:121 1:384	1:593	3↑ Riggs H 13k	10 4 65 56½ 64¾ 68	Craig A	110wb	43.40	77-21	Rough Pass1053Burning Star113½War Beauty1011½		10
			Saved ground,faltered										
26Oct40- 5Lrl	fst	1¼	:472 1:124 1:382	2:05	3↑ Washington H 19k	5 5 78¼ 85½ 711 710	Craig A	111 w	11.70	75-24	Can't Wait120½True Call105¾Burning Star113¾	Outrun	8
1Oct40- 6Bel	fst	1½	:471 1:124 2:05	2:30	3↑ ⒻLadies H 17k	1 9 812 53 109¼ 1016¾	Wall N	126 w	9.00	75-12	Salaminia115½Pretty Pet1141Fairy Chant1232¾	Tired	12
21Sep40- 5Aqu	fst	1⅛	:472 1:12 1:372	1:504	3↑ ⒻBeldame H 19k	10 12 1518 128 109½ 1112	Wall N	126 w	7.35	90-02	Fairy Chant1191¼Dotted Swiss1141Dolly Val1212½	Impeded	16
2Sep40- 6Was	fst	1¼	:494 1:144 1:391	2:04	3↑ Wash Park H 31k	3 3 1½ 2½ 1hd 11	Wall N	110 w	6.80e	90-14	War Plumage110¾Viscounty1183Burning Star1094	Hard drive	6
26Aug40- 6Was	my	1⅛	:512 1:16 1:422	1:561	3↑ Alw 1500	2 3 23 23 47 413	Snider A	113 w	*1.10e	56-40	Viscounty1224Shot Put1144Yale O'Nine1145	Close quarters	4
2Mar40- 6SA	fst	1¼	:471 1:111 1:36	2:011	3↑ S Anita H 121k	9 7 1110 83 88¾ 54½	Neves R	107 w	26.80	96-11	Seabiscuit1301½Kayak II1291Whichcee1141½	Close quarters	13
3Feb40- 6SA	my	1 1/16	:24 :474 1:124	1:464	3↑ ⒻS Margarita H 12k	5 4 411 48 712 815	Dotter R	122 w	*2.30	63-26	Fairy Chant1033½Omelet1101½Sweet Nancy1082	Tired	10
9Sep39- 5Aqu	fst	1 1/16	:233 :462 1:103	1:43	3↑ ⒻBeldame H 13k	17 10 117 159¾ 51¾ 53¼	Wall N	121 w	*2.20	95-03	NellieBly102noUnerring1203BalOrmont115hd	Close quarters	18
14Aug39- 5Sar	gd	1¼	:49 1:133 1:393	2:05	ⒻAlabama 12k	4 1 42½ 11½ 1hd 11½	Peters M	124 w	3.50	84-19	War Plumage1241½Bass Wood11110Hostility1242	Going away	9
17Jun39- 6Del	fst	1⅛	:482 1:132 1:392	1:523	ⒻDel Oaks 5.4k	3 4 23 21 2hd 22	Dotter R	119 w	*.45	95-09	Wise Lady1102War Plumage1193Alms11915	Weakened	5
7Jun39- 5Bel	fst	1⅜	:473 1:123 1:38	2:164	ⒻC C A Oaks 14k	8 2 46¼ 2hd 15 17	Wall N	116 w	2.60	87-16	War Plumage1167Hostility121½Wise Lady1212	Easily	9
17Sep38- 5HdG	fst	6f	:232 :464	1:124	Eastern Shore H 15k	5 11 128 127¼ 98¼ 94¼	Gilbert J	113 w	*2.00e	85-14	TimeAlone1091SweetNancy110hdT.M.Dorsett112½	Off slowly	15
17Aug38- 5Nar	my	5½f	:223 :462	1:064	ⒻJeanne d'Arc 7.4k	5 10 94¾ 85¼ 43½ 33½	Dotter R	108 w	10.45	87-24	SmartCrack1073HeatherTime119½WarPlumge1081	Closed fast	13
25Jun38- 4Del	fst	5f	:222 :47	1:002	ⒻPolly Drummond 7k	3 5 64¾ 65½ 44 2hd	Dotter R	110 w	14.00	94-08	Bud'sBell113hdWarPlumage1101Soldierette1131	Just missed	10
18Jun38- 3Del	fst	5f	:23 :464	1:002	Alw 1000	7 6 31½ 21 21 22	Dotter R	109 w	11.10	92-10	Post Luck1112War Plumage1092Oak Apple1141½	Swerved	7

Whirlaway

ch. c. 1938, by Blenheim II (Blandford)–Dustwhirl, by Sweep

Own.– Calumet Farm
Br.– Calumet Farm (Ky)
Tr.– B.A. Jones

Lifetime record: 60 32 15 9 $561,161

26Jun43- 6Was	fst	1	$:22^1$ $:44^3$ $1{:}10^2$ $1{:}37$	3↑	Equipoise Mile H 13k	11	12	10^{15}	8^{15}	6^4	$5^{5\frac14}$	Eads W	126wb	*1.30	88-11	Best Seller113^{hd}Thumbs Up113$^{1\frac14}$Some Chance109^3		12
	Saved ground,pulled up sore																	
22Jun43- 6Was	gd	1	$:24^1$ $:47^4$ $1{:}13$ $1{:}37^3$	4↑	Alw 2500	6	5	6^{11}	$5^{7\frac12}$	4^5	$3^{3\frac14}$	Eads W	122wb	*.50e	86-17	Mar-Kell105$^{2\frac12}$King'sAbby110$^{\frac34}$Whrlwy122$^{1\frac12}$	Hand ridden late	7
12Dec42- 7FG	sl	1⅛	$:49$ $1{:}14^2$ $1{:}40$ $1{:}53$	3↑	Louisiana H 17k	4	8	$8^{6\frac14}$	$4^{2\frac12}$	$3^{1\frac12}$	$1^{1\frac12}$	Eads W	130wb	*.60	89-18	Whirlaway130$^{1\frac12}$Heartman120^{3}Riverland124^{nk}	Saved ground	8
11Nov42- 6Pim	sl	1⅝	$:50^1$ $1{:}42^1$ $2{:}07^2$ $2{:}48^1$	3↑	Governor Bowie H 11k	3	4	4^3	1^2	1^3	1^3	Eads W	129wb	*.35	75-24	Whirlaway129^{3}Dark Discovery106^{hd}Equifox109.5^8	Easily	4
3Nov42- 6Pim	my	$1\frac{3}{16}$	$:50^2$ $1{:}15^3$ $1{:}41^1$ $1{:}59^4$	3↑	Riggs H 12k	5	5	$4^{4\frac12}$	5^5	3^2	$2^{2\frac12}$	Woolf G	130wb	*.45	81-22	Riverland116$^{2\frac12}$Whirlaway130$^{\frac34}$Pictor109$^{\frac34}$		6
	Taken back,lost ground str turn																	
28Oct42- 7Pim	fst	$1\frac{3}{16}$	$:55^1$ $1{:}20^3$ $1{:}46^4$ $2{:}05^2$	3↑	Pim Spl 10k	1	1	1	1	1	1	Woolf G	126wb	-	--	Whirlaway126	Galloping	1
24Oct42- 6Lrl	fst	1¼	$:47^3$ $1{:}12^2$ $1{:}38^3$ $2{:}03^2$	3↑	Washington H 19k	6	9	8^{13}	$3^{1\frac12}$	2^{hd}	$1^{\frac12}$	Woolf G	130wb	*.65	93-20	Whirlawy130$^{\frac12}$ThumbsUp110^{2}Rvrlnd118^5	Carried wide,driving	9
10Oct42- 6Bel	fst	2¼	$:49$ $2{:}29^2$ $2{:}54^2$ $3{:}47^1$	3↑	New York H 30k	3	8	$1^{\frac12}$	1^1	1^{hd}	$3^{1\frac14}$	Westrope J	130wb	*1.05	98-07	Alsab121^{hd}Obash106$^{1\frac14}$Whirlaway130^5	Tired last ⅛	12
3Oct42- 6Bel	fst	2	$:52^3$ $2{:}32$ $2{:}56^2$ $3{:}21^3$	3↑	J C Gold Cup 27k	2	3	$3^{3\frac12}$	3^{nk}	$2^{1\frac12}$	$1^{\frac34}$	Woolf G	124wb	*.55	96-05	Whirlaway124$^{\frac34}$Alsab117^{8}Bolingbroke124^{15}	Drawing away	4
	Geldings not eligible																	
26Sep42- 6Bel	fst	1½	$:48^1$ $1{:}12^3$ $2{:}02^3$ $2{:}27^3$	3↑	Manhattan H 11k	7	7	8^{13}	6^4	3^1	$2^{1\frac12}$	Westrope J	132wb	*.70	102-04	Bolingbroke115$^{1\frac12}$Whirlaway132^{2}King's Abbey111$^{2\frac12}$	Wide	8
19Sep42- 7Nar	fst	$1\frac{3}{16}$	$:50^2$ $1{:}14^1$ $1{:}38^3$ $1{:}56^2$	3↑	Match Race 25k	1	2	$2^{1\frac12}$	2^2	2^1	2no	Woolf G	126wb	*.30	93-11	Alsab119^{no}Whirlaway126	Wearing down winner	2
12Sep42- 6Nar	gd	$1\frac{3}{16}$	$:46^2$ $1{:}11$ $1{:}36^3$ $1{:}56^2$	3↑	Nar Spl H 31k	4	7	7^{17}	7^{12}	2^1	1^2	Woolf G	130wb	*.40	93-17	Whirlaway130^{2}Boysy112$^{\frac34}$Valdina Orphan114^1	Ridden out	7
29Aug42- 6GS	fst	1⅛	$:48^3$ $1{:}12^2$ $1{:}37^4$ $1{:}50^4$	3↑	Trenton H 12k	2	4	1^{hd}	1^1	$1^{\frac12}$	1^1	Eads W	130wb	*.30	--	Whirlaway130^{1}Rosetown111^{no}Aonbarr117^6		4
	Drifted out turn,drew away when straightened																	
1Aug42- 6AP	sly	1¼	$:49^4$ $1{:}13^3$ $1{:}38$ $2{:}04$	3↑	Arlington H 29k	5	5	$4^{3\frac12}$	$2^{\frac12}$	$2^{\frac12}$	$2^{3\frac12}$	Arcaro E	130wb	*.30	82-17	Rounders103$^{3\frac12}$Whirlaway130^{8}Strtor104^6	Lost ground,tired	5
15Jly42- 7Suf	fst	1⅛	$:46^3$ $1{:}11^2$ $1{:}36$ $1{:}48^1$	3↑	Mass H 61k	7	7	7^{10}	4^4	1^{hd}	$1^{2\frac14}$	Woolf G	130wb	*1.00	102-11	Whirlaway130$^{2\frac14}$Rounders108^{1}Attention122^4	Driving	7
4Jly42- 5Emp	fst	$1\frac{3}{16}$	$:48$ $1{:}12^2$ $1{:}37^4$ $1{:}56^4$	3↑	Butler H 33k	5	7	7^{13}	7^9	$4^{3\frac14}$	$2^{2\frac12}$	Woolf G	132wb	*.75	100-07	Tola Rose103$^{2\frac12}$Whirlaway132^{nk}Swing and Sway112^1		7
	Blocked start,outside,fast finish																	
27Jun42- 6Aqu	fst	1¼	$:49$ $1{:}13$ $1{:}38$ $2{:}02^2$	3↑	Brooklyn H 34k	4	8	$7^{6\frac34}$	$6^{4\frac34}$	$4^{2\frac34}$	$1^{1\frac34}$	Woolf G	128wb	*.45	103-05	Whirlaway128$^{1\frac34}$Swing and Sway110$^{1\frac12}$Attention122^{hd}	Driving	8
22Jun42- 6Aqu	fst	1⅛	$:48$ $1{:}13$ $1{:}37^2$ $1{:}49^2$	3↑	Alw 3500	1	4	$3^{5\frac12}$	3^3	$3^{1\frac34}$	1no	Woolf G	122 w	*.30	103-09	Whirlaway122^{no}Attention117$^{2\frac12}$Swing and Sway113^{no}		5
	Hard drive,drifting out																	
13Jun42- 6Aqu	fst	7f	$:22^3$ $:45^1$ $1{:}09^4$ $1{:}23$	3↑	Carter H 9.8k	9	9	9^{17}	9^{13}	$9^{6\frac34}$	$3^{\frac34}$	Haas L	130wb	*2.30	99-08	Doublrab120^{hd}SwingandSway112$^{\frac34}$Whirlaway130$^{1\frac12}$	Fast finish	9
30May42- 6Bel	fst	1¼	$:48^1$ $1{:}12^3$ $1{:}37^1$ $2{:}01^4$	3↑	Suburban H 38k	5	11	11^{12}	$9^{6\frac34}$	4^3	2^2	Arcaro E	129wb	*1.00	89-07	Market Wise124^{2}Whirlaway129$^{1\frac12}$Attention124^3	Wide	11
6May42- 6Pim	fst	$1\frac{3}{16}$	$:47^2$ $1{:}11^4$ $1{:}37^4$ $1{:}57$	3↑	Dixie H 25k	3	8	8^{17}	8^{12}	$5^{1\frac34}$	$1^{\frac34}$	Arcaro E	128 w	*1.65	98-12	Whirlaway128$^{\frac34}$Attention124$^{\frac12}$Mioland126^{hd}	Drawing clear	8
25Apr42- 6CD	fst	$1\frac{1}{16}$	$:24$ $:47^3$ $1{:}12^2$ $1{:}44^4$	3↑	Clark H 3k	3	4	$3^{7\frac12}$	3^5	2^3	1^{hd}	Eads W	127wb	*.10	96-11	Whirlaway127^{hd}Aonbarr115$^{8\frac12}$Fairmond110$^{1\frac14}$	Wide	5
15Apr42- 5Kee	fst	6f	$:23^2$ $:47^1$ $1{:}12^1$	3↑	Handicap 1500	2	8	$7^{6\frac12}$	$5^{5\frac34}$	5^3	$2^{\frac12}$	Craig A	126wb	*.50e	90-18	Sun Again109$^{\frac12}$Whirlaway126^{nk}Harvard Square119^{hd}		8
	Drifted out,getting to winner																	
9Apr42- 5Kee	my	6f	$:23^4$ $:48$ $1{:}13^2$	3↑	Phoenix H 3.4k	3	4	$5^{2\frac12}$	$5^{3\frac12}$	3^1	2^{hd}	Craig A	128wb	*.60e	85-26	DevilDivr113.5^{hd}Whrlwy128$^{1\frac12}$SunAgn112^2	Getting to winner	5
27Sep41- 5Bel	fst	2	$:49^2$ $2{:}28^4$ $2{:}55$ $3{:}20^4$	3↑	J C Gold Cup 10k	2	4	2^1	2^1	1^{hd}	2no	Robertson A	114wb	*.35	105-09	MarketWise114^{no}Whirlaway114^{8}Fenelon125^{12}	Clear lead str	4
	Geldings not eligible																	
20Sep41- 5Bel	fst	1⅝	$:49$ $1{:}38^1$ $2{:}03^4$ $2{:}44^1$		Lawrence Realizatn 26k	4	2	2^{hd}	1^5	1^6	1^8	Robertson A	126wb	*.20	83-13	Whirlaway126^{8}Alaking112^{5}Time Counts112^6	Eased up late	4
	Geldings not eligible																	
13Sep41- 6Nar	fst	$1\frac{3}{16}$	$:50^1$ $1{:}14^3$ $1{:}39$ $1{:}57^1$	3↑	Nar Spl H 29k	2	4	$4^{6\frac12}$	$3^{2\frac12}$	2^4	$2^{4\frac12}$	Robertson A	118wb	*.40	84-14	War Relic107$^{4\frac12}$Whirlaway118^{1}Equifox112$^{1\frac12}$	Driving	4
23Aug41- 7Was	fst	1¼	$:49$ $1{:}13$ $1{:}38^2$ $2{:}04$		American Derby 59k	4	4	2^1	1^1	$1^{1\frac12}$	$1^{2\frac34}$	Robertson A	126wb	*.20	90-08	Whirlaway126$^{2\frac34}$Bushwhacker121$^{3\frac12}$Delray118$^{\frac34}$	Speed to spare	5
16Aug41- 6Sar	my	1¼	$:49$ $1{:}13^2$ $1{:}39^3$ $2{:}05^4$		Travers 21k	1	2	3^{11}	3^8	$3^{2\frac12}$	$1^{3\frac34}$	Robertson A	130wb	*.15	80-22	Whirlaway130$^{3\frac34}$Fairymant112$^{2\frac12}$Lord Kitchener112	Easily	3
6Aug41- 6Sar	fst	1	$:24$ $:48$ $1{:}12^2$ $1{:}38$		Saranac H 4.8k	4	5	5^6	$4^{1\frac14}$	$4^{\frac12}$	1no	Robertson A	130wb	*.65	91-13	Whirlaway130^{no}WarRlc117$^{\frac34}$Omsson112$^{1\frac12}$	Drifted out,just up	5
26Jly41- 6AP	fst	1¼	$:49^1$ $1{:}13^2$ $1{:}37^2$ $2{:}02^4$		Classic 57k	4	6	6^6	2^{hd}	2^{hd}	$2^{1\frac12}$	Shelhamer A	126wb	*.40	90-17	Attention121$^{1\frac12}$Whirlaway126^{6}Bushwhacker121$^{3\frac12}$		6
	Away slowly,forced wide last ½,tired																	
15Jly41- 6AP	fst	1⅛	$:49^2$ $1{:}13^1$ $1{:}38$ $1{:}50^3$		Special Event 5k	2	2	1^2	$1^{2\frac12}$	1^1	$1^{2\frac12}$	Eads W	120wb	*.10	94-13	Whirlaway120$^{2\frac12}$Daily Trouble112^{2}To a Tee112$^{\frac12}$		4
	Bore out str turn,drew away when straightened																	
21Jun41- 5Aqu	fst	1¼	$:49$ $1{:}13^2$ $1{:}38^3$ $2{:}03^2$		Dwyer 11k	3	4	$4^{4\frac12}$	$1^{1\frac12}$	$1^{1\frac12}$	$1^{1\frac14}$	Arcaro E	126wb	*.20	98-08	Whirlaway126$^{1\frac14}$Market Wise122$^{2\frac12}$Robert Morris119^{12}		4
	Came over turn,drifted out str,speed to spare																	
7Jun41- 6Bel	fst	1½	$:49^4$ $1{:}13^4$ $2{:}05$ $2{:}31$		Belmont 48k	3	3	$3^{1\frac12}$	1^3	1^2	$1^{2\frac12}$	Arcaro E	126wb	*.25	87-15	Whirlwy126$^{2\frac12}$RobertMorrs126^{5}YnkChnc126^5	Speed to spare	4
20May41- 6Bel	fst	$1\frac{1}{16}$	$:23^4$ $:46^3$ $1{:}11^3$ $1{:}43^3$	3↑	Alw 2500	3	4	3^5	$4^{2\frac12}$	$1^{1\frac12}$	$1^{2\frac14}$	Eads W	108wb	*.75	93-12	Whirlaway108$^{2\frac14}$Miolnd127^{nk}Hsh120^3	Drifting out final ⅛	5
10May41- 6Pim	gd	$1\frac{3}{16}$	$:47^2$ $1{:}12^3$ $1{:}39^1$ $1{:}58^4$		Preakness 66k	1	8	8^9	7^3	1^5	$1^{5\frac12}$	Arcaro E	126wb	*1.15	89-12	Whirlaway126$^{5\frac12}$KingCole126^{2}OurBoots126^{nk}	Speed to spare	8
3May41- 7CD	fst	1¼	$:46^3$ $1{:}11^3$ $1{:}37^2$ $2{:}01^2$		Ky Derby 73k	4	6	8^{16}	4^2	1^3	1^8	Arcaro E	126wb	*2.90	102-08	Whirlaway126^{8}Staretor126^{nk}Market Wise126^2	Blocked early	11
29Apr41- 7CD	fst	1	$:23^2$ $:46^2$ $1{:}11^1$ $1{:}36^3$		Derby Trial 2.9k	6	5	5^5	$1^{\frac12}$	2^1	$2^{\frac34}$	Eads W	118wb	*.60	95-12	Blue Pair115$^{\frac34}$Whirlaway118^{8}Cadmium110^6		6
	Worked 10f in 2:07 2/5																	
24Apr41- 6Kee	my	1⅛	$:47^4$ $1{:}12$ $1{:}38$ $1{:}51^1$		Blue Grass 15k	2	2	1^{hd}	1^{hd}	2^2	2^6	Eads W	123wb	*.50	85-20	OurBoots123^{6}Whirlwy123^{15}VldnPul121^3	Bore out turn,tired	4
11Apr41- 5Kee	fst	6f	$:22^3$ $:46^2$ $1{:}11^3$		Handicap 1500	1	4	4^7	3^5	3^1	1^{nk}	Eads W	120wb	*1.00	94-17	Whirlaway120^{nk}Blue Pair116^{3}My Bill105^3	Drawing away	5
28Mar41- 5TrP	fst	5½f	$:22^4$ $:46^1$ $1{:}04^3$		Alw 1200	4	4	$5^{3\frac34}$	$4^{4\frac12}$	$3^{1\frac12}$	1^{nk}	Vedder RL	118wb	2.50	97-09	Whirlaway118^{nk}Zacatn118^{no}BluLly107^5	Forced wide,just up	6
22Mar41- 4TrP	my	6f	$:23^3$ $:47^3$ $1{:}11^4$		Alw 1200	1	5	4^6	$3^{1\frac12}$	2^{hd}	$3^{1\frac34}$	James B	118wb	*.85	89-12	Little Beans118^{1}Ponty118$^{\frac34}$Whirlaway118^2	Hung	6
18Feb41- 5Hia	fst	7f	$:23^2$ $:47$ $1{:}11^2$ $1{:}23^1$		Alw 1500	2	4	4^6	3^2	3^1	3^5	James B	122wb	*.30	92-12	Agricole110^{2}Cadmium110^{3}Whirlaway122^6	Impeded,hung	5
8Feb41- 4Hia	gd	6f	$:22^2$ $:45^1$ $1{:}11^3$		Alw 1500	5	5	$5^{7\frac34}$	$5^{7\frac12}$	$3^{3\frac12}$	1^{hd}	Eads W	117wb	*.65	91-13	Whirlaway117^{hd}Signator110^{3}Blue Twink108^2	Bore out str	5
14Nov40- 6Pim	sly	$1\frac{1}{16}$	$:23^2$ $:48^3$ $1{:}16$ $1{:}52^1$		Walden 10k	8	7	$3^{1\frac12}$	2^1	1^3	1^4	Woolf G	122wb	*1.50	59-54	Whirlaway122^{4}Magnificent113^{2}Stimady116^2	Easily	8
2Nov40- 6Pim	hy	$1\frac{1}{16}$	$:23^3$ $:48$ $1{:}14^2$ $1{:}49^4$		Pim Futurity 38k	8	5	$5^{3\frac12}$	2^1	$3^{2\frac12}$	3^5	Longden J	122wb	*1.60	66-33	BoldIrshmn122^{no}OurBts119^{5}Whrlwy122$^{1\frac12}$	Bore out both turns	8
	Geldings not eligible																	
19Oct40- 6Kee	fst	6f	$:22^3$ $:45^4$ $1{:}11^1$		Breeders' Futurity 12k	5	5	5^3	$4^{1\frac12}$	2^{hd}	1^1	Longden J	122wb	1.50	96-13	Whirlaway122^{1}Blue Pair119^{no}Our Boots122^{hd}	Drew away	5
8Oct40- 5Kee	fst	6f	$:22^3$ $:46$ $1{:}11^1$		Alw 1000	2	6	6^{10}	$6^{6\frac14}$	4^{nk}	1^2	Longden J	122wb	*1.40e	96-10	Whirlaway122^{2}Blue Pair122^{3}Valdina Groom114^{hd}	Handily	8
28Sep40- 7Bel	fst	6½f-WC	$1{:}15^3$		Futurity 81k	11	5	$11^{7\frac14}$	$4^{1\frac12}$	3^{nk}	$3^{3\frac14}$	Longden J	126wb	2.85	92-05	Our Boots119$^{1\frac34}$King Cole122$^{1\frac12}$Whirlaway126$^{2\frac12}$	Blocked str	14
	Geldings not eligible																	
24Sep40- 6Bel	fst	6f-WC	$1{:}10^3$		Alw 1500	8	1	$9^{7\frac14}$	3^{nk}	5^3	5^6	Longden J	123wb	*1.30	88-06	Our Boots111$^{3\frac12}$Springwood111^{hd}New World120^1		10
	Swerved,impeded,hung late																	
31Aug40- 5Sar	my	6½f	$:23$ $:46^3$ $1{:}11^4$ $1{:}18$		Hopeful 43k	3	4	$4^{5\frac34}$	4^4	$2^{\frac12}$	1^1	Longden J	122wb	*.65	95-13	Whirlaway122^{1}Attention126^{5}Hy-Cop116$^{1\frac34}$	Very wide	4
24Aug40- 5Sar	fst	6f	$:23$ $:47$ $1{:}11$		Grand Union Hotel 11k	1	6	$6^{5\frac14}$	$5^{2\frac34}$	3^2	$2^{1\frac12}$	Longden J	122wb	*1.20	95-09	New World117$^{1\frac12}$Whirlaway122$^{2\frac14}$Hy-Cop116$^{1\frac14}$	Close quarters	6
10Aug40- 5Sar	fst	6f	$:22^2$ $:46$ $1{:}11^1$		Sar Spl 9.7k	4	8	8^9	8^9	5^6	$1^{1\frac12}$	Longden J	122wb	*1.95	96-10	Whirlaway122$^{1\frac12}$New World122^{3}Good Turn122^2		8
	Close quarters start,wide																	
3Aug40- 5Sar	fst	6f	$:22^3$ $:46^4$ $1{:}11^4$		U S Hotel 12k	7	10	$10^{9\frac12}$	9^7	$5^{4\frac14}$	2^{nk}	Longden J	116wb	14.00	93-09	Attention122^{nk}Whirlaway116^{4}Twnkppy113^2	Finished fastest	10
27Jly40- 6AP	my	6f	$:23^4$ $:48$ $1{:}00^4$ $1{:}13^4$		Arl Futurity 44k	3	12	11^5	$6^{3\frac14}$	$4^{1\frac12}$	$3^{5\frac12}$	Longden J	117wb	9.40	72-28	Swain117$^{5\frac12}$ValdinaGroom117^{no}Whirlaway117$^{\frac34}$	Close quarters	12
20Jly40- 5AP	fst	5½f	$:23$ $:46^1$ $:58^4$ $1{:}05^1$		Alw 1200	1	7	$7^{6\frac12}$	$5^{6\frac12}$	$5^{2\frac12}$	4^4	Richard J	117 w	3.90	91-13	MistyIsle119$^{2\frac14}$BayouCook117$^{1\frac12}$FlyingStrk114^{nk}	Blocked str	7
6Jly40- 6AP	fst	5½f	$:23$ $:46^1$ $:58^1$ $1{:}04^4$		Hyde Park 7.2k	2	10	11^{10}	11^{16}	$8^{9\frac14}$	$4^{7\frac12}$	Clark S	117 w	3.40	89-12	MistyIsl114$^{2\frac14}$DKlb117$^{2\frac14}$Cuntos117^3	Closed well when clear	13
2Jly40- 5AP	fst	5½f	$:23$ $:46^2$ $:59$ $1{:}05^2$		Alw 1000	10	7	$4^{4\frac12}$	4^3	2^1	1^1	Clark S	111 w	3.40	94-16	Whirlway111^{1}De Kalb118$^{3\frac12}$Valdina Groom116^1	Drawing away	10
25Jun40- 4AP	fst	5½f	$:22^2$ $:45^4$ $:58^3$ $1{:}05^2$		©Alw 1000	5	5	5^7	3^{11}	3^9	$3^{3\frac34}$	Clark S	111 w	2.90	90-16	My Bill116^{3}Swain116$^{\frac34}$Whirlaway111^8	Bold late rally	7
3Jun40- 3LF	fst	5f	$:23$ $:47^1$ $1{:}01^4$		Md Sp Wt	10	5	$3^{1\frac12}$	$5^{6\frac12}$	$4^{4\frac12}$	1no	Richard J	116 w	*1.50e	86-20	Whirlaway116^{no}BeauBrannon116^{1}VldnSr113^{nk}	Bore out badly	11

Wistful

ch. f. 1946, by Sun Again (Sun Teddy)–Easy Lass, by Blenheim II
Own.– Calumet Farm
Br.– Calumet Farm (Ky)
Tr.– H.A. Jones

Lifetime record: 51 13 6 10 $213,060

18Oct52- 9BM	fst 1 1/16	:234 :471 1:11 1:413	3↑ Children's Hospital H 23k	7	9	912	911	97¼	85¾	Baird RL	110 w	*1.35e	96-09	Two Lea112½Moonrush1151½Grantor1202½	No factor	10
4Oct52- 9BM	fst 1	:231 :462 1:104 1:363	3↑ Ⓕ San Mateo H 11k	5	6	67½	612	45½	3¾	Baird RL	117 w	*.85e	96-11	Two Lea127½Danae115nkWistful117½	Wide,closed well	7
1Sep52- 8Dmr	fst 1⅛	:454 1:094 1:344 1:472	3↑ Del Mar H 26k	5	8	911	96¼	54½	44¾	Moreno H	110wb	10.05	100-05	Grantor1131¾Stormy Cloud1081½Moonrush1171½	Stretch gain	11
20Aug52- 7Dmr	fst 6f	:223 :454 1:101	3↑ Handicap 4000	7	8	812	713	78½	66¾	Moreno H	113wb	17.95	90-11	Boner1202Gustaf1091½Bullfighter114nk	No factor	8
19Jly52- 7Hol	fst 1⅝	:48 1:371 2:03 2:414	3↑ Sunset H 54k	4	5	69	63¼	52¾	33¾	Moreno H	112wb	5.80	91-10	Great Circle112nkStormy Cloud1083½Wistful1121¼	Wide	8
12Jly52- 7Hol	fst 1¼	:461 1:103 1:351 2:001	3↑ Hol Gold Cup 137k	5	10	1114	1214	1117	1013	Shoemaker W	108wb	*1.55e	85-07	Two Lea113½Cyclotron1003Sturdy One1063½	No factor	12
28Jun52- 7Hol	fst 1 1/16	:224 :454 1:101 1:421	3↑ Inglewood H 28k	7	6	613	67½	64¼	63¾	Pearson B	115wb	*1.35e	93-08	SturdyOn1111StormyCloud105nkAdmrlDrk1162	Close quarters	7
14Jun52- 7Hol	fst 1 1/16	:231 :461 1:11 1:432	3↑ Ⓕ Vanity H 28k	4	8	79½	77½	56	21¼	Shoemaker W	112 w	*.35e	90-11	Two Lea1221¼Wistful1121¾Jennie Lee117¾	Driving	8
6Jun52- 7Hol	fst 1	:223 :453 1:101 1:361	4↑ Ⓕ Alw 10000	4	7	513	57	33	1nk	Moreno H	109wb	*.75	94-11	Wistful109nkWorn Out112noMiss Traffic1062¼	Wide	7
31May52- 7Hol	fst 7f	:222 :45 1:092 1:213	3↑ Ⓕ Milady H 28k	8	11	116½	76¼	69	59	Neves R	112wb	*.75e	92-10	A Gleam1122½Two Lea1176Spanish Cream124no	No factor	11
22May52- 7Hol	fst 6f	:221 :451 :572 1:094	4↑ Handicap 10000	2	9	912	88¼	86¾	84¾	Moreno H	109wb	36.85	92-07	Ruth Lily109noLast Round1102Reighs Bull117no	No factor	9
3May52- 7GG	fst 6f	:221 :444 1:093	3↑ Handicap 7500	6	6	610	613	613	610	Pierson NL	112wb	20.00	83-14	Warcos1092AdmirlDrake116nkBridlRngs113¾	Showed nothing	6
16Apr52- 7GG	fst 6f	:22 :443 1:091	3↑ Ⓕ Handicap 5000	4	6	620	619	614	67½	Pierson NL	120wb	10.45	87-14	GreatDream111hdRuthLily1182SpeclTouch1291	Strong finish	6
10Apr52- 7GG	my 6f	:223 :453 1:114	3↑ Ⓕ Alw 3250	3	9	916	916	912	69½	Pierson NL	120 w	*2.30e	72-25	Frigid1152Great Dream1182Island Lass1182½	Outrun	9
22Sep51- 6Aqu	fst 1⅛	:482 1:122 1:382 1:52	3↑ Ⓕ Beldame 67k	6	10	85¼	74¾	94¾	97	Brooks S	126wb	3.70	78-14	Thelma Burger1102Bed o' Roses124½Kiss Me Kate119nk		14
	Wide,failed to respond															
14Sep51- 6Aqu	fst 1 1/16	:241 :474 1:13 1:444	3↑ Ⓕ Alw 5000	5	7	717	614	57½	36¼	Brooks S	121wb	2.25	84-16	Red Camelia1101¼Vulcania1125Wistful121hd	Late effort	7
29Aug51- 7Was	fst 1	:222 :45 1:094 1:354	3↑ Ⓕ Beverly H 28k	6	10	1013	911	54	11¼	Brooks S	126wb	*1.70e	90-13	Wistful1261¼War Talk1141¼Lithe1241	Driving	10
	Previously trained by B.A. Jones															
11Aug51- 7Was	fst 1⅛	:464 1:102 1:36 1:483	3↑ Whirlaway 27k	6	8	812	67½	52¼	1¾	Brooks S	111wb	3.80	98-06	Wistful111¾Oil Capitol116hdCurandero1161½	Just up	8
7Aug51- 6Was	hy 7f	:23 :463 1:114 1:253	4↑ Alw 4000	2	6	613	68½	46½	32	Brooks S	119 w	6.00	77-30	Yellmantown1131½Cacomo112½Wistful1191½	Closed fast	7
21Jly51- 5AP	fst 7f	:223 :452 1:092 1:224	3↑ Ⓕ Alw 5000	6	7	714	713	611	57¾	Dodson D	122wb	*1.90e	88-08	Jennie Lee1112Lithe1182¾Countess In1122	No speed	7
3May51- 7CD	fst 1 1/16	:243 :482 1:123 1:44	3↑ Clark H 11k	6	6	612	57½	33	1hd	Dodson D	116wb	*2.20	98-11	Wistful116hdShy Guy113noJohns Joy1201½	Just up	6
28Apr51- 7CD	fst 7f	:223 :453 1:091 1:224	3↑ Churchill Downs H 12k	7	8	812	87¾	77¾	65¾	Dodson D	118wb	*1.70	96-10	Johns Joy118hdRoman Bath1183½Mr. Trouble115¾	No excuse	8
21Apr51- 6Kee	fst 1 1/16	:233 :472 1:123 1:45	3↑ Ben Ali H 12k	5	5	54	1½	13	16	Dodson D	112wb	2.30	89-18	Wistful1126Counterpoint1053½Little Imp110¾	Easily	5
17Apr51- 5Kee	fst 6½f	:23 :471 1:124 1:194	3↑ Handicap 3500	4	9	912	912	86¾	85½	Dodson D	118wb	*1.40e	82-18	Cacomo113nkLady Alice110½Tidy Sum1152	Sluggish	9
	Previously trained by H.A. Jones															
20Feb51- 7SA	fst 1	:222 :46 1:112 1:363	4↑ Handicap 6000	3	7	79	63½	44	2nk	Brooks S	115wb	*2.40	93-15	Precession119nkWistful115½Renown112nk	Slow start	7
12Feb51- 7SA	fst 7f	:221 :45 1:093 1:22	4↑ Handicap 7500	11	10	1012	109¾	1012	109¾	Smith FA	111wb	*2.35e	85-10	Bullreigh Jr.1211Be Fleet1021Star Fiddle122½	Outrun	11
1Feb51- 7SA	fst 1 1/16	:234 :473 1:113 1:422	4↑ Handicap 7500	5	4	44	53½	42	31	Brooks S	111wb	7.90	95-10	Vino Fino109½Bullreigh Jr.115½Wistful111hd	Impeded	6
20Jan51- 7SA	fst 1⅛	:461 1:11 1:361 1:483	3↑ Ⓕ S Margarita H 60k	7	5	67½	78	610	612	Arcaro E	120 w	3.20e	86-16	Special Touch1141Bewitch1221¼Bed o' Roses1251½	Bore out	8
2Dec50- 7Hol	fst 1⅛	:47 1:111 1:362 1:492	3↑ Ⓕ Vanity H 30k	9	9	911	86¾	65¼	33¼	Glisson G	125 w	2.65e	91-11	Next Move1282¼Bewitch1241Wistful125½	Off slowly	9
14Nov50- 7Hol	my 1	:24 :481 1:134 1:401	3↑ Alw 4000	2	7	714	78½	59	57¾	Glisson G	111 w	*.60e	68-29	Theory1131¼Terry Bargello108½Ohsodry1062½	No excuse	8
4Oct50- 6Bel	fst 1½	:491 1:133 2:034 2:292	3↑ Ⓕ Ladies H 29k	7	8	912	99½	37	35½	Brooks S	124 w	2.35	85-11	Next Move1205½My Celeste106hdWistful1241¼	Closed well	12
16Sep50- 6Aqu	fst 1⅛	:473 1:12 1:37 1:501	3↑ Ⓕ Beldame H 66k	12	11	1113	911	59	33¼	Brooks S	125 w	3.20	91-15	Next Move1162¼September1081Wistful1252¼	Closed fast	12
9Sep50- 6Aqu	fst 1⅛	:474 1:114 1:363 1:492	3↑ Edgemere H 23k	2	7	75¼	77¼	45½	22½	Dodson D	114 w	6.60e	95-09	Three Rings1212½Wistful114½My Request1262	Lost ground	11
30Aug50- 6Was	fst 1⅛	:473 1:12 1:373 1:501	3↑ Ⓕ Beverly H 27k	5	8	88¼	57¼	32	21¾	Brooks S	128 w	*1.20	88-16	Lithe1201¾Wistful1281½Include1041	No excuse	9
16Aug50- 6Was	fst 7f	:22 :45 1:084 1:22	3↑ Ⓕ Misty Isle H 22k	2	10	107¾	97¼	96¾	54	Brooks S	123 w	*1.20	93-09	Miss Highbrow1091¼Stole1032¼Lithe118½	Off slowly	10
9Aug50- 7Was	fst 7f	:221 :444 1:092 1:22	3↑ Clang H 22k	5	9	86¼	97¾	62¾	11	Brooks S	113 w	8.10	97-11	Wistful1131Laico1161¼Lithe113nk	Drew out	11
26Jly50- 6AP	fst 1	:23 :454 1:093 1:344	3↑ Ⓕ Arl Matron H 22k	4	9	911	94¼	55¾	24	Brooks S	118 w	5.30	94-10	Lithe1084Wistful118¾Evanstep1073½	Finished fast	10
24Jun50- 6AP	my 6f	:232 :47 1:131	3↑ Alw 3500	7	3	62¼	55¾	77¾	78¼	Roser G	112 w	9.60	72-22	ShyGuy122½RomanBath1085½WhirlingDough110nk	Went wide	8
20Jly49- 6AP	fst 1	:23 :46 1:102 1:37	Ⓕ Cleopatra H 26k	2	6	64¼	56	46½	32¼	Scurlock O	121 w	*.60e	85-15	Two Lea1222Lithe108nkWistful1212	Closed well	6
28May49- 6Bel	fst 1⅜	:491 1:144 1:41 2:193	Ⓕ C C A Oaks 66k	2	14	138½	63¾	1½	1½	Brooks S	121 w	*.75	73-18	Wistful121½Adile12110Jazz Baby1211	Hard drive	14
13May49- 6Pim	fst 1 1/16	:23 :463 1:111 1:442	Ⓕ Pim Oaks 14k	7	10	107	22	1hd	1¾	Brooks S	121 w	*1.00	90-16	Wistful121¾Imacomin1214Admired121no	Ridden out	12
	Previously trained by B.A. Jones															
6May49- 6CD	fst 1 1/16	:24 :48 1:133 1:472	Ⓕ Ky Oaks 30k	8	8	75¼	53½	12	14½	Glisson G	116 w	1.40	83-15	Wistful1164½TheFatLady116nkLadyDorimar1166	Going away	10
30Apr49- 5CD	fst 1	:224 :463 1:112 1:38	Ⓕ Alw 2500	4	8	65	69½	23	11½	Glisson G*	108 w	*1.30	89-14	Wistful1081½Lady Dorimar1098Pella1085	Drew out	11
16Apr49- 6Kee	gd 6f	:23 :473 1:133	Ⓕ Ashland 13k	4	9	96¾	98¼	66	24	LoTurco A	115 w	2.80	80-18	Tall Weeds1154Wistful1153½Warsick115½	Belated speed	10
	Previously trained by H.A. Jones															
14Feb49- 4Hia	fst 7f	:232 :463 1:114 1:241	Ⓕ Alw 3500	2	5	62½	21	2nk	14	Nelson E	112 w	2.60	91-14	Wistful1124Bea Right1144¼Error1091	Drew out	6
31Jan49- 4Hia	fst 6f	:222 :452 1:104	Ⓕ Alw 3500	2	9	86¾	86	57¼	34	Nelson E	114 w	*1.45e	90-12	Cheesecloth1104Duke's Gal110noWistful1142	Slow start	10
27Jan49- 5Hia	fst 7f	:23 :46 1:113 1:242	Ⓕ Alw 4000	3	5	41½	31	2no	12	Nelson E	107 w	4.35	90-13	Wistful1072Solid Trick1095Dizzy Whirl1042	Going away	9
19Jan49- 5Hia	fst 6f	:224 :46 1:112	Ⓕ Alw 3500	8	9	107¾	98	911	714	Pierson NL	112 w	4.60	77-14	Too Sunny1152¼Sub1077½Solid Trick1092	Impeded	11
15Jan49- 4TrP	fst 6f	:223 :462 1:123	Alw 2000	8	7	75¾	47	47	49¼	Pierson NL	115 w	*.75	75-17	Abstract1181¼Winged1207Midchannel1111	No excuse	9
29Oct48- 2Pim	fst 6f	:23 :47 1:122	Ⓕ Md Sp Wt	10	3	2hd	11	12	16	Pierson NL	118 w	*.60	91-10	Wistful1186Best Blue1181Wily118½	Easily	12
30Sep48- 5Bel	sly 5½f-W	:222 :454 1:044	Ⓕ Md Sp Wt	11			52¼	65	86¼	Woodhouse H	116 w	8.00	84-10	Roguish Mood116½Zana1161Error1161½	No factor	17
	Start obscured by mist															

GHOSTS AND LEGENDS

THE 1950'S

by Joe Hirsch

IN ANY CONSIDERATION OF THE outstanding Thoroughbred stars of the 1950's, two dates are significant.

The first is May 2, 1953, and the site is Churchill Downs. An arresting gray colt named Native Dancer, the nation's first four-legged television star, comes to the 79th Kentucky Derby undefeated in 11 starts. If he can win the Derby and then complete a sweep of the Triple Crown classics in the Preakness and Belmont Stakes, he will have passed major obstacles on his way to a rare perfect record and will be hailed as a superstar of the century.

The second date is August 31, 1955, and the site is Washington Park in suburban Chicago. Two of the greatest 3-year-olds of the era, Nashua and Swaps, are to meet in one of the most celebrated match races in American history. Swaps upset Nashua in the 81st Kentucky Derby. Nashua won the Preakness and Belmont Stakes, and added the Dwyer and the Arlington Classic to his list of victories. Swaps returned to his native California following the Kentucky Derby and scored brilliantly in three stakes at Hollywood Park: the Will Rogers; the Californian, against older horses; and the Westerner. He then underlined his versatility by

capturing the American Derby on the grass at Washington Park.

The nation was divided in its admiration for the two colts, largely along geographical lines, and with each succeeding victory following their Derby confrontation, demands for a match race in the best

Only a terrible trip in the 1953 Kentucky Derby kept the handsome gray Native Dancer from an undefeated career. The head loss to Dark Star was the only blemish on his 22-race record.

traditions of the American turf grew louder. Chicago, in the heart of mid-America, and at that time the home of the best summer racing in the country, was an ideal neutral ground. Ben Lindheimer, chairman of Arlington and Washington Parks, was a willing host and announced the details in mid-July.

Derby Day, 1953, and it appeared there really were 100,000 people at the ancient Downs, as announced each year, regardless of the count. Alfred Gwynne Vanderbilt's Native Dancer, the handsome gray son of Polynesian from Geisha, by Discovery, had been a popular 2-year-old champion, winner of all nine of his starts, including four stakes victories at Saratoga. Coming out at 3, he made light work of a division of the Gotham and the Wood Memorial at Jamaica, and was considered a standout in the Derby, which drew only 11 starters. He and his stablemate, Social Outcast, were hammered down to 7-10.

Second choice was Eddie Arcaro and the horse he happened to be riding, Correspondent, at 3-1. Royal Bay Gem was third choice at 7-1, and among the others, all longshots, was the Cain Hoy Stable colt Dark Star, at almost 25-1. He won 3 of 6 starts at 2 but hadn't done anything noteworthy until he scored in the Derby Trial four days before the Run for the Roses, with the familiar Eric Guerin, Native Dancer's regular rider, in the saddle.

Dark Star, under Henry Moreno, set the pace, the first half-mile in a sensible 47⅗ seconds. Let the footnotes of the chart, as called by *Daily Racing Form*'s senior trackman, Don Fair, tell the rest of the story. "Native Dancer, roughed at the first turn by Money Broker [45-1], was eased back to secure racing room, raced wide during the run to the upper turn, then saved ground entering the stretch and finished strongly, but could not overtake the winner, although probably best."

The margin at the wire was a head.

It was one of the most fateful decisions in the long and colorful history of the Derby, not so much for what occurred at the time as for what followed.

Native Dancer picked up where he left off, winning them all. Two weeks after the Derby, he won the Withers Mile at Belmont Park by four lengths. The following weekend he won the Preakness, in which Dark Star bowed a tendon, ending his racing career.

He won the Belmont, the Dwyer, the Arlington Classic by nine lengths, the Travers by 5½, the American Derby. There was great anticipation of a meeting that fall between Native Dancer, king of the 3-year-olds, and the great Tom Fool, undefeated in the handicap ranks and emperor of older horses in the United States. But it wasn't to be. "The Dancer" didn't race at all following his American Derby score on August 22, trainer Bill Winfrey citing a stone bruise as the reason the colt was on the shelf.

On holiday all winter, Native Dancer returned to action as a 4-year-old on May 7, 1954, at Belmont Park. Coming from off the pace, as he did through much of his career, he made light work of the field of crack sprinters, which included the stakes-winning Laffango. That race served as his prep for the Metropolitan Mile, eight days later.

Carrying top weight of 130 pounds, the Dancer knew his finest hour in winning that Met Mile. Conceding 13 pounds to Greentree Stable's Straight Face, he appeared hopelessly beaten at the three-eighths pole. Guerin was asking him to run but was receiving a muted response. But then Native Dancer kicked in, and his final quarter, according to *Daily Racing Form*'s Evan Shipman, was one of the greatest ever seen in this country. As late as the furlong pole, the Dancer was still nearly four lengths behind Straight Face, Ted Atkinson up. Flying now on the outside, he got up in the final stride to score by a neck, to the repeated cheers of the 38,090 on hand.

It was a brilliant piece of racing, and the exact measurements were provided several weeks later when Straight Face came back to win the Suburban. Meanwhile, Winfrey was having problems again with the gray's soundness. The trainer and his staff worked hard, and by mid-August Native Dancer was ready for a seven-furlong overnight handicap at Saratoga. Under 137 pounds, he won easily in what was to have tuned him up for the mile-and-three-quarter Saratoga Cup. His people were considering a trip to France that fall for the Prix de l'Arc de Triomphe.

It wasn't to be. Vanderbilt broke the news a few days later with his terse memorandum: "N D N G." Racing was stunned over the retirement of its greatest star, and the full impact of his glorious record struck a responsive chord. Though he'd made only three starts that season, he was an overwhelming choice as Horse of the Year. He was also acclaimed as one of the greats of his era, and more than a few writers speculated that but for the one unfortunate incident in the Kentucky Derby, "the Gray Ghost of Sagamore" deserved ranking with the best of the best.

Nashua and Swaps, forever linked in racing history like Affirmed and Alydar, were exceptional individuals, and as different from each other as two horses can be.

Nashua, by Nasrullah out of Segula, by Johnstown, may have been the soundest horse ever bred in this country. A big, strapping bay full of muscles, he inherited the fiery disposition of his legendary sire plus the fierce talent associated with that marvelous source of bloodstock. He was 2-year-old champion with 6 wins and 2 seconds from 8 starts, and was Horse of the Year as well as champion of his division at 3.

There are many stories illustrating Nashua's physical resources. In preparation for the Arlington Classic, which was to be his last start prior to the match race, jockey Eddie Arcaro flew out to Chicago to work him on a Monday morning. Nashua was full of himself and Arcaro was not at his sharpest that day, for the big colt broke the American record with his ebullient five furlongs in 56⅕. Five days later, his edge somewhat blunted by the severe work, Nashua was forced to a hard drive to beat Traffic Judge. Almost any other horse would have bounced like a flat tire.

Swaps, by Khaled out of Iron Reward, by Beau Pere, was an eye-catching chestnut colt, full of balance and quality and the easy grace we have come to associate with the champion athlete. By training he was highly disciplined, but that did not rein in his remarkable ability. When he retired to stud at the end of the 1956 season, he held five world records. An inauspicious 2-year-old with 2 wins from 5 starts, he blossomed at 3 and reached his best form at 4 when he was handicap champion and Horse of the Year.

Swaps's self-control became a matter of national discussion after his victory in the American Derby at Washington Park, 11 days prior to the match race. A large crowd gathered at trackside as the field left the paddock and walked onto the racing strip. They wanted to see the horse who had won the Kentucky Derby and who would soon have a showdown with the mighty Nashua. As the field paraded, Bill Shoemaker guided Swaps to the outer rail, where a group of children stood with their parents. Swaps walked up to a young girl who, at Shoemaker's invitation, hesitantly stretched out a small hand and stroked the colt's nose. Swaps stood like a statue.

Three or four more times during the post parade, Shoe took Swaps to the rail to interact with the crowd, which had never seen anything like it before, and loved it. When Swaps finally broke

The cantankerous Nashua finally exacted revenge for his Kentucky Derby loss to Swaps by defeating the colt from California by 6 ½ lengths in a celebrated match race at Washington Park.

away in a gallop to warm up for the American Derby, he received a warm ovation. He received another after his successful grass debut in the American Derby. Second in the mile-and-three-sixteenths test was Traffic Judge, who had been second to Nashua in the Arlington Classic.

It was noted earlier that Nashua and Swaps were contrasting individuals. The same was true of their interests.

Investment banker William Woodward Jr., owner of Nashua, was the gracious son of a giant in American racing. His father, William Woodward Sr., was chairman of The Jockey Club for 20 years, raced such outstanding horses as Gallant Fox and Omaha, the Triple Crown winners of 1930 and 1935, and was the breeder of Nashua. Rex Ellsworth, owner of Swaps, built a sizable racing and breeding operation in Chino, California, in part with funds borrowed from the Mormon Church, of which he was a member.

Sunny Jim Fitzsimmons, the trainer of Nashua, was one of the most popular and successful horsemen in the annals of American racing. A one-time jockey and jockey's agent, he saddled his first winner in 1900, and had two Triple Crown winners to his credit, Gallant Fox and Omaha. Meshach Tenney, the trainer of Swaps, had been a close friend and associate of Rex Ellsworth's since boyhood. He assisted Ellsworth in his cattle operation and then became his trainer when Ellsworth began to concentrate on Thoroughbreds.

The Nashua-Swaps match at Washington Park received a formidable publicity campaign, not unlike the ones preceding a heavyweight championship bout. The nation's press responded, covering every detail of the preparations and every comment of the principals.

Almost every detail. Swaps had a chronic foot problem, originally triggered by a stone bruise. The condition flared during the weeks leading up to the Santa Anita Derby, but Tenney, who did his own blacksmith work, cut away a portion of the frog, packed it with medication, and covered the area with a pad. Swaps wasn't at his absolute best for the Santa Anita Derby because Tenney was forced to limit his training. But the competition was moderate and Swaps could and did win on his class.

When the foot problem recurred the week of the match race, Ellsworth and Tenney approached Ben Lindheimer and requested a postponement. Lindheimer explained why this was impossible at such a late hour and an agreement was reached to keep quiet about the foot condition.

Even Bill Shoemaker wasn't told, for fear the news might subconsciously affect his riding of Swaps.

Evan Shipman described the match race in the 1956 edition of The American Racing Manual: "There was nothing complicated about it. As the doors opened, Arcaro, yelling like a banshee and wielding his whip with all his strength, shot Nashua to the front, while Swaps, away on the outside, veered farther out toward the outside rail. Nashua was in front as they passed the stand, and he was to be in front for the entire distance, Swaps making repeated thrusts at him, all of them falling short."

Nashua won by 6½ lengths but it was obvious Shoemaker never asked Swaps for anything during the final furlong, once he saw the cause was lost. The winner's time of 2:04⅕ for 1¼ miles on a "good" track was accomplished with fractions of 23, 46, 1:10⅖, 1:37⅗, and 1:50⅗.

Swaps's connections announced he was through for the rest of the season, but Nashua returned to his base in New York to meet older horses for the first time in the Sysonby Stakes at Belmont Park. Though opposed by the likes of Helioscope, High Gun, and Jet Action, Nashua was the favorite at 65 cents to the dollar.

Rain fell all afternoon and the track was sloppy for the Sysonby. High Gun, who had won the Met Mile and the Brooklyn, and lost the Suburban by a head to Helioscope while carrying 133 pounds, came off the pace under Bill Boland to win by a head in one of the finest performances of his career. Jet Action was second, and Nashua, a trifle dull after his experience in Chicago and the severe preparation that preceded the match race, finished third.

Nashua concluded his memorable 3-year-old season with an easy triumph by five lengths in the two-mile Jockey Club Gold Cup, contested on a sloppy track. Plans were being drawn up for a winter racing campaign when they were interrupted by news of a shocking tragedy.

William Woodward Jr., the owner of Nashua, was accidentally shot to death at his home on Long Island by his wife, who mistook him for a burglar.

A dispersal of the Woodward Thoroughbred holdings by sealed bids was quickly organized and a syndicate headed by Leslie Combs II acquired Nashua on a bid of slightly more than $1,250,000. Combs asked Sunny Jim Fitzsimmons to stay on as trainer and continue his plans for Nashua's 4-year-old campaign.

Nashua was to make his first start of 1956 in Hialeah's prestigious Widener Handicap in mid-February. He hadn't run since mid-October, so he needed some training and he got it. A week before the Widener, "Mr. Fitz" vanned him to Tropical

Park and, with Ted Atkinson up – Arcaro was in California – Nashua worked the full Widener distance of a mile and a quarter in 2:01⅗. Under Arcaro, and carrying top weight of 127 pounds, Nashua came back to win the Widener by a head from Social Outcast, timed in 2:02. In other words, he went faster in his workout than in his race.

Nashua ran 10 times that season, at distances from seven furlongs to two miles, winning six. Immensely talented, he was not always the most generous of horses, the inheritance of the willful blood of his sire, Nasrullah. Arcaro wouldn't let him get away with too much, but he outweighed "the Master" by 1,100 pounds and there were times when he had his way.

His best race at 4 may have been the Suburban, in which he carried 128 pounds and ran a mile and a quarter in 2:00⅗, beating as good a handicap horse as Dedicate while spotting him 17 pounds.

Despite numerous physical problems, the game Swaps compiled a long list of records, including world marks at a mile, a mile and 70 yards, and a mile and a sixteenth.

He ended his racing career with a second tally in the Jockey Club Gold Cup, giving him an overall record of 22 wins and 4 seconds from 30 starts. He was some piece of work.

Swaps also raced 10 times at 4 and had a brilliant campaign, cut short by injury.

He set a world record of 1:39⅗ for a mile and 70 yards in winning the Broward Handicap at Gulfstream Park under 130 pounds.

He set a world record of 1:33⅕ for a mile in winning the Argonaut Handicap at Hollywood Park under 128 pounds.

He set a world record of 1:39 for a mile and a sixteenth in winning the Inglewood Handicap at Hollywood, carrying 130 pounds.

He set a track record of 1:58⅗ for a mile and a quarter in winning the Hollywood Gold Cup under 130 pounds.

He set a world record of 2:38⅕ for a mile and five furlongs in winning the Sunset Handicap at Hollywood, carrying 130 pounds.

He set a track record of 1:33⅖ for a mile in winning the Washington Park Handicap under 130 pounds.

He equaled the world record of 1:46⅘ for a mile and an eighth in winning the American Handicap at Hollywood under 130 pounds.

Swaps was flown to Atlantic City for the United Nations Handicap on the grass, but his chronic foot problem arose again and he was scratched the day of the race. Vanned to Garden State Park, he resumed training and his people indicated that he would oppose Nashua again in the Jockey Club Gold Cup. But galloping one morning at the south Jersey track, he fractured a bone in his left hind leg and his life was threatened.

Sunny Jim Fitzsimmons sent a special sling from Belmont Park and Swaps literally hung from a rafter over his stall. He had to be lowered and raised every 45 minutes for circulatory reasons, and trainer Mesh Tenney sat by his side to pull on the ropes for the first 36 hours.

Swaps, a good patient, handled the uncomfortable routine with aplomb and was saved for stud.

▪ ▪ ▪

One of the decade's brightest stars was the great handicap champion and Horse of the Year for 1953, Greentree Stable's Tom Fool. Indeed, his undefeated 4-year-old season, when he went 10 for 10 and won important stakes while carrying as much as 136 pounds, was so brilliant that some respected observers of the racing scene list him as one of the best of his era.

Tom Fool, by Menow out of Gaga, by Bull Dog, was 2-year-old champion of 1951 with a record of 5 victories and 2 seconds from 7 starts. It was his 3-year-old campaign, and his failure to contest the classics, that was the one questionable chapter in his career. Had he been as successful at 3 as he was at 2 and 4, he undoubtedly would be ranked with the superstars of the century.

Trained by John Gaver and ridden in all 30 of his starts by Ted Atkinson, Tom Fool made his debut at Saratoga on August 13, 1951, and as a 2-1 favorite, won smartly by four lengths after coming off the pace.

He then won the Sanford and the Grand Union Stakes but finished second in the Hopeful, the major juvenile feature of the meeting, with Cousin the winner. Later that fall he wrapped up the divisional title with victories in the Futurity at Belmont Park and the East View at Jamaica.

After a restful winter in Aiken, South Carolina, Tom Fool was aimed at the classics. His first start at 3 was in a prep for the Wood Memorial at Jamaica, which he won, beating Primate and Cousin. Favored in the Wood Memorial, he went to the front near the furlong pole but was unable to hold off the strong finish by Master Fiddle, who won by a neck.

In the wake of the Wood Memorial, Tom Fool developed a cough and was sidelined throughout the Triple Crown races.

After a conclusive victory in the Wilson Mile at Saratoga, he was established as a solid favorite for the Travers. He went to the front early, appeared to be comfortable on a sloppy track, but tired in the drive and finished third behind One Count and Armageddon. He concluded the campaign with three races at Jamaica, beating Battlefield by a nose in the Grey Lag, losing to Battlefield by a nose in the Westchester, and winning the Empire City under 128 pounds while conceding 19 pounds to runner-up Marcador.

Tom Fool began his signature season by winning a 5½-furlong sprint at Jamaica in late April. He underlined his high quality by capturing the six-furlong Joe Palmer Handicap under 130 pounds and conceding 16 pounds to the fine sprinter Tea-Maker, who was second. Good as he was in the Joe Palmer, however, he was even better four days later in the Metropolitan Mile. Favored at 1-2, he was always prominent despite top weight of 130 pounds, took command on the turn, and stood a hard drive gamely to win by half a length from the classy Royal Vale, to whom he was conceding three pounds.

A week later, in the traditional Suburban Handicap, Tom Fool went off as a slight favorite at 2-1 over Royal Vale, with a good deal of support showing for the Walter Jeffords entry of One Count,

Horse of the Year in 1952, and Kiss Me Kate, 3-year-old filly champion of 1951.

Carrying 128 pounds, Tom Fool went to the front at the start and remained there. Royal Vale, under 124 pounds, tested him severely through the final furlong but missed by a nose after a mile and a quarter in 2:00⅗ that touched off one of the most sustained ovations ever heard at Belmont Park.

From the mile and a quarter of the Suburban, Tom Fool successfully dropped back to the seven furlongs of the Carter Handicap at Aqueduct. Under 135 pounds, the highest weight ever carried to victory in the sprint, he equaled the track record of 1:22 while conceding 13 pounds to the tough old speedster Squared Away.

Two weeks later it was back to 10 furlongs for the Brooklyn Handicap, for which Tom Fool was assigned 136 pounds. Favored at 1-4, he was on the lead most of the way in a paceless race (the half went in 48⅗ seconds), built an advantage of some three lengths, and was eased as he passed the winning post with a margin of a length and a half on Golden Gloves, who carried 110 pounds. Tom Fool became the first horse to sweep the Handicap Triple Crown – the Metropolitan Mile, the Suburban, and the Brooklyn – since Whisk Broom II in 1913.

The Brooklyn victory touched off a nationwide tribute to a great horse in terms significant to racing. In his final four starts he never had more than two opponents, and no wagering was permitted on the Wilson Mile and the Whitney at Saratoga, the Sysonby at Belmont, and the Pimlico Special. He left like the champion he was, winning at Pimlico by eight lengths and setting a track record of 1:55⅗ for the mile and three-sixteenths.

Greentree Stable's Tom Fool raced through one of the great campaigns in Thoroughbred history, winning all 10 of his starts in 1953, including the Handicap Triple Crown, while carrying as much as 136 pounds.

A pair of 3-year-olds who fashioned outstanding records as contemporaries, one on the dirt and the other principally on the grass, were Bold Ruler and Round Table. Bold Ruler has come down history's highway as one of the fastest horses ever to race in America. Round Table is hailed as one of the finest turf horses of the century and a good but not great horse on dirt.

Both Bold Ruler and Round Table were foaled at Claiborne Farm near Paris, Kentucky. Bold Ruler, by Nasrullah out of Miss Disco, by Discovery, was bred and owned by Mrs. Henry Carnegie Phipps's Wheatley Stable, whose trainer was Sunny Jim Fitzsimmons, dean of American horsemen. Round Table was bred and originally owned by A. B. "Bull" Hancock Jr. of Claiborne Farm. The Princequillo colt out of Knight's Daughter, by Sir Cosmo, was raced as a 2-year-old by Claiborne under trainer Moody Jolley. He was sold privately, early in his 3-year-old season, for a reported $175,000 to Travis Kerr, an Oklahoma oilman and brother of United States Senator Robert Kerr of Oklahoma. Kerr's horses were trained by Willie Molter, one of California's most successful horsemen.

Bold Ruler and Round Table were foals of 1954, and with such contemporaries as Gallant Man, Gen. Duke, Iron Liege, and Federal Hill, were involved in what is widely recognized as the finest 3-year-old campaign in American racing history.

Bold Ruler began his glittering career with three victories at Jamaica's spring meeting, including an in-hand tally by more than three lengths in the Youthful Stakes. He also won the Juvenile at Belmont but was "tailed" in the starting gate, wrenching his back severely. While recuperating in his stall, he hit his near hock against a wall, injuring himself to the extent that he could not run at Saratoga.

He resumed racing in September, won the Futurity under Eddie Arcaro, and was the 2-1 favorite in a field of 19 for the Garden State Stakes at Cherry Hill, New Jersey. With Arcaro suspended, Ted Atkinson deputized and stalked the pace-setting outsider, Jaunty John, who promptly stopped leaving the half-mile pole. By the time Bold Ruler got straightened out, the race was over and Barbizon, who raced on the outside most of the way under Bill Hartack, got up to win by a desperate nose over Federal Hill.

Arcaro was back on Bold Ruler for the Remsen at Jamaica but the outcome wasn't much different. The spirited Bold Ruler reared at the break, then was checked on the first turn in heavy traffic. He was done for the day, with the victory going to the stretch-running Ambehaving.

Bold Ruler made his 3-year-old debut in Hialeah's seven-furlong Bahamas on January 30, 1957. With Ted Atkinson aboard, he shot to the front out of the gate, led all the way to win by 4½ lengths, and equaled the track record of 1:22. Gen. Duke, a top Calumet Farm prospect, was second, and Federal Hill was third in a field of 11.

The 3-year-old racing that winter was the most brilliant Florida has known, before or since. Bold Ruler's smashing score in the Bahamas made him a standout choice at 2-5 in the nine-furlong Everglades in mid-February. Once again he went to the front out of the gate. He got the first half-mile in a reasonable 46⅖ seconds, but couldn't quite hold off the acceleration of Gen. Duke, who won by a

Bold Ruler was the best of the class of 1957, possibly the finest 3-year-old crop ever. He capped his Horse of the Year resume by defeating Gallant Man and Round Table in the three-horse Trenton Handicap.

head while in receipt of 12 pounds from the favorite. Gen. Duke, timed in 1:47⅖, missed the track record by a fifth of a second, with Bill Hartack up. Iron Liege, of whom we will hear more, finished third as an entry with the winner.

That set the stage for the Flamingo. Bold Ruler, with Eddie Arcaro on hand from California, was the 1-2 favorite. He was always prominent through a lively half-mile in 45⅖, opened an advantage of two lengths at the furlong pole, and was all out to prevail by a neck over Gen. Duke at level weights, setting a track record of 1:47 for the nine furlongs. Iron Liege was third.

Four weeks after the Flamingo, Gulfstream's Florida Derby drew a field of five, with Bold Ruler favored at 3-5. This was a brilliant piece of racing, as Gen. Duke, a particularly handsome bay colt by Bull Lea out of Wistful, took the track from Bold Ruler, fastest of the fast. Hartack then throttled back to a half-mile in 46⅖ seconds.

This was a match race between two extraordinary colts, and at the furlong pole, after a mile in 1:34⅗, Bold Ruler was in front by a head. But Gen. Duke, named for the Civil War hero, wasn't through. He accelerated, won by a conclusive length and a half, and set a world record for nine furlongs of 1:46⅘. Iron Liege was third again, just a head behind Bold Ruler.

Sent to New York, Bold Ruler continued to train aggressively for Mr. Fitz and ran another corking race in the Wood Memorial at Jamaica. He was favored at 1-2 and went to the front at the start. Arcaro slowed the pace to a half in 48 seconds, virtually assuring himself a victory, but it turned out to be tougher than expected.

Gallant Man, an import who had been seasoned in the 3-year-old racing at Hialeah, put up a whale of a fight through the stretch and Bold Ruler was hard-pressed to score by a nose in a track-record 1:48⅘ for nine furlongs. Promised Land, a stretch-runner, was third.

The 1957 Kentucky Derby, for depth of quality and dramatic nature of its story line, has been called the greatest of all Runs for the Roses. Gen.

Gallant Man was denied the 1957 Kentucky Derby when Bill Shoemaker misjudged the finish line, but gained retribution in the Belmont with an eight-length victory in 2:26 ⅗, an American record for a mile and a half. He also won the Travers during a championship-quality season.

Duke, the Florida Derby winner, raced at Keeneland as a prep and bobbled. He went lame at Churchill Downs during Derby Week and was scratched from the Derby, leaving Calumet represented by Iron Liege at 8-1.

Federal Hill, as usual, set the pace, and it was realistic, with a first half-mile in 47 seconds. Bold Ruler and Iron Liege stalked together, a length and a half back, with Round Table fourth and Gallant Man well back in the field of nine. After a mile in 1:36⅘, Federal Hill was still in front but Iron Liege, showing strength, was at the leader's side. Bold Ruler and Round Table followed closely and Gallant Man was moving rapidly past horses.

Iron Liege took command straightening into the long stretch. Federal Hill, still second, was tiring, while Gallant Man, Round Table, and Bold Ruler were closely grouped. Gallant Man, finishing with determination, took aim at Iron Liege and appeared to be abreast in the final sixteenth when his rider, Bill Shoemaker, misjudged the finish and rose prematurely in the irons. Shoe quickly realized his error and began to ride his horse again, but the chance of a lifetime was lost, Iron Liege prevailing by a nose. Gallant Man was almost three lengths ahead of Round Table, and Bold Ruler was fourth.

Ralph Lowe, owner of Gallant Man, had dreamed that the rider of his horse would stand in the irons prematurely and at dinner, the night before the Derby, related his dream to Shoemaker.

"Well, Ralph, now that we've heard about it, you don't have to worry," Shoe said.

With Gallant Man and Round Table absent, Iron Liege was a narrow favorite in the Preakness over Bold Ruler. However, Bold Ruler's people decided to make use of his speed. He outran Federal Hill for the early lead and then remained in front the rest of the way to win by two lengths from Iron Liege.

Iron Liege passed the Belmont Stakes but Gallant Man returned to action, accompanied by a pacemaker, Bold Nero. Bold Ruler was the slight favorite at 85 cents to the dollar, and repeated his Preakness strategy of going to the front. Prompted by Bold Nero, he went the first six furlongs in 1:10⅖, Gallant Man well back in fourth.

Leaving the half-mile pole, Gallant Man began to move up. He had the lead entering the stretch, gradually drew out, and won by eight lengths, setting an American record for a mile and a half of 2:26⅗. Inside Tract, the runner-up, had four lengths on Bold Ruler, who found the trip beyond his scope.

Given the summer off after a strenuous classics campaign, Bold Ruler prepped smartly and then was an easy six-length winner of the Jerome Mile at Belmont on a sloppy track. He had the lead in the Woodward, found the mile and a quarter too far for him, and finished third. But he came back to beat older horses on a sloppy track in the seven-furlong Vosburgh, just missing a track record with his 1:21⅖.

He also won the Queens County at Jamaica and the Benjamin Franklin at Garden State Park, both at a mile and a sixteenth. He carried 136 pounds in the New Jersey race and won by 12 lengths on a sloppy track he loved.

Bold Ruler concluded his 3-year-old campaign in sensational fashion, beating Gallant Man and Round Table in the three-horse Trenton Handicap at Garden State. He led all the way on an off track, and got the mile and a quarter in 2:01⅗. He was later voted Horse of the Year.

He spent the winter season in Florida but did not race and began his 4-year-old campaign with consecutive victories in Belmont Park's six-furlong Toboggan and seven-furlong Carter, coming off the pace in both races, and carrying 133 and 135 pounds, respectively. He made the pace in the Metropolitan Mile under 135 pounds but tired to finish second to Gallant Man, who carried 130 pounds and won by two lengths.

His next race was the Stymie Handicap at nine furlongs, which he won easily by five lengths under 133 pounds. Bold Ruler ran one of his greatest races to capture Belmont's Suburban Handicap on July 4, 1958. Always well placed under Eddie Arcaro, he carried 134 pounds and stood a long drive with great courage to score by a nose over hard-hitting Clem, who was in receipt of 25 pounds.

Later that month he was shipped to Monmouth Park for another stakes at a mile and a quarter, the Monmouth Handicap. Carrying 134 pounds, he beat Sharpsburg by three-quarters of a length, conceding 21 pounds. One week later, he ran in the Brooklyn Handicap, and despite his top weight of 136 pounds, was favored at 2-5. He had a rough trip and finished seventh in a field of eight.

The next day, trainer Jim Fitzsimmons announced that Bold Ruler had run his last race. Mr. Fitz revealed that Bold Ruler had been bothered all season by a splintered cannon bone, which was now threatening a tendon. Despite the injury, he continued to perform with skill and courage. Fitzsimmons later would say Bold Ruler was one of his three greatest horses, together with Nashua and Gallant Fox.

Round Table's career was remarkable for success and durability. He won 43 races, an incredible achievement, from 66 starts, and finished in the money 56 times.

He began racing in February of his 2-year-old season, going three furlongs at Hialeah. After being bumped at the start, he finished fourth under Steve

Brooks, beaten two lengths. He made 10 starts in all that season, winning five times, and displayed a measure of quality with his tally in the Breeders' Futurity at Keeneland.

As he began his 3-year-old campaign, Round Table came under the scrutiny of several prospective buyers, and in February he was sold to Travis Kerr. Kerr's trainer, Willie Molter, flew Round Table to California for the Santa Anita Derby and he was installed as the 13-10 favorite. With the veteran Johnny Longden up for the first time, Round Table went to the front at the furlong pole but couldn't hold the lead on a slow track. He was beaten a head and a nose by Sir William, with Swirling Abbey second.

Round Table went to San Francisco to win the Bay Meadows Derby and then traveled to Lexington, Kentucky, to post a six-length victory in Keeneland's Blue Grass Stakes, setting a track record of 1:47⅗ for the nine furlongs with Ralph Neves up. Well backed in the Kentucky Derby, he finished third.

Returning to the West Coast, Round Table finished second to Social Climber in the Californian and then won five consecutive stakes at Hollywood Park. Four of the stakes were for 3-year-olds and the competition was moderate. But Round Table made an impression when he beat older horses in the Hollywood Gold Cup. Equaling the track record of 1:58⅖ for the mile and a quarter under Bill Shoemaker, he won by more than three lengths from Porterhouse, who carried 119 pounds and was conceding 10 pounds to the favorite.

Once Hollywood's meeting was completed, Round Table was sent to Washington Park for the American Derby on the turf. He had never raced on grass and a betless exhibition was arranged 11 days prior to the country's oldest derby. Round Table won smoothly from just off the pace, then led all the way, as even-money favorite, to win the American Derby by four lengths from Kentucky Derby winner Iron Liege.

His reputation growing with every race, Round Table headed east for Atlantic City's prestigious United Nations Handicap. Favored at 7-10 despite his assignment of 118 pounds, he stumbled at the start and lost position but gamely gained the lead and battled the classy Tudor Era, prevailing by a nose.

The versatile Round Table won three straight grass titles, and was also handicap champion and Horse of the Year in 1958. He retired in 1959 as the richest Thoroughbred in history.

Round Table returned to Chicago to win the Hawthorne Gold Cup by three lengths. With Bill Harmatz up, and favored at 7-10, he was always prominent under 121 pounds and finished strongly to beat the Midwest ace Swoon's Son, who carried 128 pounds. His outstanding 3-year-old campaign was marred when he finished third in the three-horse field for the Trenton Handicap at Garden State Park.

Resuming at Santa Anita in late December, Round Table raced in top form, running off a string of eight consecutive victories. The highlight was his Santa Anita Handicap triumph under 130 pounds, when he set a track record of 1:59⅗ for the mile and a quarter while beating Terrang and

Sword Dancer narrowly lost to Tomy Lee in a controversial running of the Derby, but became the runaway 3-year-old champion and Horse of the Year in 1959 with victories in the Belmont and Travers in his own division, and the Monmouth Handicap, Woodward, and Jockey Club Gold Cup against older horses.

Porterhouse with concessions of 11 and 10 pounds, respectively. Later that month he flew to Florida to win the Gulfstream Park Handicap by four lengths under 130 pounds.

The remainder of his busy 4-year-old campaign had mixed success. Heavily favored in the Californian Stakes at Hollywood Park, for example, he finished second to Seaneen under 130 pounds while conceding 21 pounds to the winner. In a similar race at Arlington Park, he was upset by Bernbergoo in the Warren Wright Memorial, carrying 130 pounds to Bernbergoo's 109. He was also the beaten favorite in the Equipoise Mile, when Swoon's Son beat Bardstown in an outstanding piece of racing.

Round Table captured the Arlington Handicap on the turf, beating Clem while conceding 21 pounds, but in the Washington Park Handicap on the dirt, with the same weight spread, Clem won by more than three lengths. Clem was to prove a troublesome opponent on other occasions as well. He upset Round Table in the United Nations Handicap by half a length with a 17-pound concession, and won the Woodward at level weights when the sloppy track at Belmont proved a problem for Round Table.

He salvaged some glory with a victory in the Hawthorne Gold Cup, setting a track record of 1:59⅗ for the mile and a quarter while beating Swoon's Son, to whom he conceded three pounds.

Round Table's durability was underlined by the 14 starts he made in his final season of 1959. Carrying as much as 134 pounds, he alternated victory and defeat until midsummer when he put together three impressive triumphs in the Arlington Handicap, the Washington Park Handicap, and the United Nations. He set track records in the first two events but was particularly impressive in the United Nations, winning under 136 pounds.

His last victory came that fall in the Manhattan Handicap at Aqueduct when he beat Bald Eagle while spotting that good horse 10 pounds, 132 to 122, at a mile and five furlongs on the grass. Three weeks later he returned for the Jockey Club Gold

Calumet Farm's Tim Tam, winner of the 1958 Kentucky Derby and Preakness, lost his bid to sweep the Triple Crown when he fractured a sesamoid at the quarter pole in the Belmont. Courageously, he carried on to finish second.

Cup at two miles, but was unable to handle the 3-year-old Sword Dancer, who won by seven lengths. Round Table's retirement was announced and he left the racing scene as the world's leading money-winner with earnings of $1,749,869.

Sword Dancer and Tim Tam rose to prominence late in the decade, largely on the basis of what they accomplished as 3-year-olds. Both displayed unusual talent, but Sword Dancer was able to do it over an entire season and was voted Horse of the Year in 1959. Tim Tam, the Kentucky Derby and Preakness winner of 1958, broke down in a Belmont Stakes many believe he would have won, ending his racing career. He was forced to settle for divisional honors.

Sword Dancer, by Sunglow out of Highland Fling, by By Jimminy, was owned and bred by the Brookmeade Stable of auto heiress Isabel Dodge Sloane. He showed promise at 2, winning the Mayflower Stakes at Suffolk Downs and finishing third in the Garden State, but he also disappointed on occasion and was slow to come to hand for trainer Elliott Burch.

Sword Dancer took his time in developing at 3. He didn't race at Hialeah, but his second to Easy Spur in the Florida Derby at Gulfstream earned him a bid at the classics, and in many respects his Kentucky Derby was memorable. He turned into the stretch on even terms with Tomy Lee, who was known for his irregular patterns in the drive.

Through the long stretch at Churchill Downs, Sword Dancer and Tomy Lee bumped, several times, with Sword Dancer the aggressor. Near the finish, Sword Dancer, under Bill Boland, came in again to bump Tomy Lee. The latter, tiring badly because he couldn't change leads, was thrown onto a fresh lead. He accelerated and won by a nose under Bill Shoemaker.

Sword Dancer was sailing along in the Preakness, in excellent position behind the leader, when Royal Orbit came sweeping by to upset. Royal Orbit won by four lengths and is credited with one of the most impressive finishes in classic history. With four weeks between the Preakness and the Belmont, Elliott Burch decided to give Sword Dancer a shot at the Metropolitan Mile. He won easily by 3¼ lengths.

Favored in the Belmont Stakes, Sword Dancer reveled in the sloppy going, and beat Bagdad and Royal Orbit in 2:28⅔ for the mile and a half. After the Belmont, Sword Dancer raced outside his division most of the way. He won the Monmouth Handicap, was second in the Brooklyn, and finished the campaign with three victories that earned him signal honors. He won the Travers at Saratoga to nail down the 3-year-old title and proceeded to beat older horses in a highly competitive Woodward and in the Jockey Club Gold Cup, the latter a tour de force with a winning margin of seven lengths.

Sword Dancer wasn't as effective as a 4-year-old of 1960 but ran two outstanding races toward the end of his career. With only one prep race on the grass, he put in a big effort to finish second to T.V. Lark in the United Nations at Atlantic City while conceding seven pounds. He also won the Woodward for the second time, beating Dotted Swiss and Bald Eagle.

Tim Tam, by champion Tom Fool out of champion Two Lea, owned and bred by Calumet Farm, was one of the most professional racehorses of his time. He never won by big margins but compiled a sparkling record of 10 wins from 14 starts. He was out of the money only once.

A late developer, Tim Tam made only one start as a 2-year-old, finishing fourth on a sloppy track at Garden State Park. Trainer Jimmy Jones had high hopes for him, however, and Tim Tam got a lot of seasoning from that one race.

With Bill Hartack up, he won his first two starts in Miami as he turned 3. He then had a couple of educational outings with the veteran Ovie Scurlock aboard before winning the Everglades at Hialeah with Hartack up. From that race on he was unbeatable.

He won the Flamingo on a celebrated disqualification after being bothered in the drive by Jewel's Reward, then captured the Fountain of Youth and Florida Derby at Gulfstream. He lost his rider at the start of Derby Week at Churchill Downs when Hartack broke a leg in the gate on a fractious 2-year-old, and was replaced by Ismael "Milo" Valenzuela.

The track was exceptionally muddy for the Kentucky Derby but Tim Tam won, beating Lincoln Road in 2:05 for the mile and a quarter. He had an easier time of it winning the Preakness from the same opponent, and looked like a winner in the Belmont when he suddenly swerved in the stretch. Losing momentum, he finished second to Cavan and pulled up lame. It was learned later that he shattered a sesamoid, forcing his retirement.

CHAMPIONS

PAST PERFORMANCES

THE 1950'S

•1950•
•2-Year-Old Male *Battlefield* •2-Year-Old Filly *Aunt Jinny* •3-Year-Old Male *Hill Prince*
•3-Year-Old Filly *Next Move* •Handicap Horse *Noor* •Handicap Mare *Two Lea*
•Sprinter *Sheilas Reward* •Steeplechase *Oedipus*
•**HORSE OF THE YEAR** Hill Prince

•1951•
•2-Year-Old Male *Tom Fool* •2-Year-Old Filly *Rose Jet* •3-Year-Old Male *Counterpoint*
•3-Year-Old Filly *Kiss Me Kate* •Handicap Horse *Hill Prince* •Handicap Mare *Bed o' Roses*
•Sprinter *Sheilas Reward* •Steeplechase *Oedipus*
•**HORSE OF THE YEAR** Counterpoint

•1952•
•2-Year-Old Male *Native Dancer* •2-Year-Old Filly *Sweet Patootie* •3-Year-Old Male *One Count*
•3-Year-Old Filly *Real Delight* •Handicap Horse *Crafty Admiral* •Handicap Mare *Real Delight, Next Move (TRA)*
•Sprinter *Tea-Maker* •Steeplechase *Jam, Oedipus (TRA)*
•**HORSE OF THE YEAR** One Count, Native Dancer (TRA)

•1953•
•2-Year-Old Male *Porterhouse* •2-Year-Old Filly *Evening Out* •3-Year-Old Male *Native Dancer*
•3-Year-Old Filly *Grecian Queen* •Handicap Horse *Tom Fool* •Handicap Mare *Sickle's Image*
•Grass Horse *Iceberg II* •Sprinter *Tom Fool* •Steeplechase *The Mast*
•**HORSE OF THE YEAR** Tom Fool

•1954•
•2-Year-Old Male *Nashua* •2-Year-Old Filly *High Voltage* •3-Year-Old Male *High Gun*
•3-Year-Old Filly *Parlo* •Handicap Horse *Native Dancer* •Handicap Mare *Parlo, Lavender Hill (TRA)*
•Grass Horse *Stan* •Sprinter *White Skies* •Steeplechase *King Commander*
•**HORSE OF THE YEAR** Native Dancer, Dedicate (TRA)

•1955•
•2-Year-Old Male *Needles* •2-Year-Old Filly *Doubledogdare, Nasrina (TRA)* •3-Year-Old Male *Nashua*
•3-Year-Old Filly *Misty Morn* •Handicap Horse *High Gun* •Handicap Mare *Misty Morn*
•Grass Horse *St. Vincent* •Sprinter *Berseem* •Steeplechase *Neji*
•**HORSE OF THE YEAR** Nashua

•1956•
•2-Year-Old Male *Barbizon* •2-Year-Old Filly *Leallah, Romanita (TRA)* •3-Year-Old Male *Needles*
•3-Year-Old Filly *Doubledogdare* •Handicap Horse *Swaps* •Handicap Mare *Blue Sparkler*
•Grass Horse *Career Boy* •Sprinter *Decathlon* •Steeplechase *Shipboard*
•**HORSE OF THE YEAR** Swaps

•1957•
•2-Year-Old Male *Nadir, Jewel's Reward (TRA)* •2-Year-Old Filly *Idun* •3-Year-Old Male *Bold Ruler*
•3-Year-Old Filly *Bayou* •Handicap Horse *Dedicate* •Handicap Mare *Pucker Up*
•Grass Horse *Round Table* •Sprinter *Decathlon* •Steeplechase *Neji*
•**HORSE OF THE YEAR** Bold Ruler

•1958•
•2-Year-Old Male *First Landing* •2-Year-Old Filly *Quill* •3-Year-Old Male *Tim Tam* •3-Year-Old Filly *Idun*
•Handicap Horse *Round Table* •Handicap Mare *Bornastar* •Grass Horse *Round Table*
•Sprinter *Bold Ruler* •Steeplechase *Neji*
•**HORSE OF THE YEAR** Round Table

•1959•
•2-Year-Old Male *Warfare* •2-Year-Old Filly *My Dear Girl* •3-Year-Old Male *Sword Dancer*
•3-Year-Old Filly *Royal Native, Silver Spoon (TRA)* •Handicap Horse *Sword Dancer, Round Table (TRA)*
•Handicap Mare *Tempted* •Grass Horse *Round Table* •Sprinter *Intentionally* •Steeplechase *Ancestor*
•**HORSE OF THE YEAR** Sword Dancer

Ancestor

b. g. 1949, by Challedon (Challenger II)–Bloodroot, by Blue Larkspur
Own.– Mrs Ogden Phipps
Br.– Ogden Phipps (Ky)
Tr.– D.M. Smithwick

Lifetime record: 101 26 14 13 $237,956

```
13Oct59- 5Aqu  hd *2½   S'Chase  4:47³ 4♠ Brook H 19k          1 1  1³   1²   1³   1¹½  Smithwick AP 162  s  *.70e  --      Ancestor162¹½Sun Dog137¹½Fairfax152nk        Driving 7
10Oct59- 5Aqu  fm *2    S'Chase  3:51  4♠ Broad Hollow H 16k   2 1  1²½  1hd  1¹½  1hd  Smithwick AP 160 sb 4.10e  --      Ancstor160hdDrubn138²SunDog138¹²            Jumped well,hard drive 9
11Sep59- 6Bel  hd *2½   S'Chase  4:41  4♠ Temple Gwathmey H 56k 6 3  2³½  99¾  949  966  Smithwick AP 168  w  3.40e  --      MuguetII152¹½Darubini134nkIdealView135⁴     Bad landing 9th 9
 3Sep59- 5Bel  sf *2⅛   S'Chase  4:08  4♠ C L Appleton Mem H 11k 1 1 2¹  3¹²  3⁸   3⁷   Smithwick AP 166  s  *1.30  --      Policeman Day150⁴Antonino137³Ancestor166⁸  Speed,tired 5
21Aug59- 5Sar  fm *2½   S'Chase  5:03  4♠ Saratoga H 19k       3 1  1¹   2²   4¹6  449  Smithwick AP 161  s  2.45e  --      Independence161⁹Fairfax149³⁰BasilBee152¹⁰   Used up early 5

13Jun58- 5Del  fm *2    S'Chase  3:39⁴ 4♠ Georgetown H 10k     3 1  1³   1³   1²   1¹½  Smithwick AP 169  w  *.60e  --      Ancestor169¹½Arywa149nkCarthage130⁶         Under steady drive 6
 5Jun58- 6Bel  fm *2½   S'Chase  4:44  4♠ Meadow Brook H 13k   5 1  1³   1⁴   1¹   1¹½  Smithwick AP 165  w  1.65   --      Ancestor165¹½Arywa147¹²Independenc156nk     Held clear lead 6
27May58- 6Bel  fm *2⅛   S'Chase  4:04³ 4♠ International H 11k   2 1  1³   2²   1¹   1³   Smithwick AP 162  w  2.45   --      Ancestor162³Rythminhm147¹⁴PnShot143²½      Under brisk drive 12
16Oct57- 6Bel  fm *2½   S'Chase  4:42² 4♠ Temple Gwathmey H 57k 11 2 1hd  1³   2³   2⁷   Murphy J     160  w  *.80e  --      Neji173⁷Ancestor160¹Shipboard164¹½          Used up setting pace 12
26Sep57- 5Bel  fm *2½   S'Chase  4:45¹ 4♠ Brook H 22k          2 1  1¹   1¹½  6⁶   5¹⁶  Murphy J     161  w  1.65e  --      Neji164²¾Independence151¹⁰Rythminhm148no    Set pace,tired 10
19Sep57- 6Bel  fm *2⅛   S'Chase  4:01  3♠ Broad Hollow H 17k   3 1  7⁸   45¹½ 611  621  Smithwick AP 162  w  2.95   --      Indepndnce148⁸Morpheus138²½Shipboard162³    Bobbled jump 7
12Sep57- 5Bel  fm *2⅛   S'Chase  3:57³ 3♠ Harbor Hill H 17k    7 1  1²   1²   1²   1²   Smithwick AP 158  w  *1.65e --      Ancestor158²Independence148⁶His Boots131nk  Ridden out 9
29Aug57- 5Sar  fm *2    S'Chase  5:12¹ 4♠ Saratoga H 22k       2 1  1²   1²   3⁵   310¹ Smithwick AP 157  w  *1.80  --      Shipboard154¹Independence146¹⁰Ancstor157¹³  Speed,tired 6
15Aug57- 5Sar  fm *2    S'Chase  4:14  4♠ Beverwyck H 17k      3 1  1¹   1⁶   1¹⁰  1¹⁴  Smithwick AP 152  w  5.85   --      Ancestor152¹⁴Shipbord163½Morphus143¹⁸       Speed in reserve 6
 2Aug57- 5Mth  fm *2    Hurdles  3:56  3♠ Midsummer H 15k      3 3  3³½  7⁷   811  78¼  Smithwick AP 153  w  4.50e  --      Ideal View141¹Great Tom141²½Rythminhm148nk  Early speed 10
19Jly57- 3Mth  fm *1⅜   Hurdles  3:19⁴ 3♠ Alw 4000            10 3  4²½  56¹½ 610  612  Smithwick AP 162  w  4.30   --      Marso153¹½MyLastTry130³½MossGreen142hd      Some early foot 11
27Jun57- 3Del  fm *1⅜   Hurdles  3:28⁴ 3♠ Alw 4000             1 2  41²  3⁹   311  39¼  Smithwick AP 157  w  *2.20  --      Fairshot140¼IdealView140⁹Ancstor157¹½       No apparent mishap 5
```

Previously trained by G.H. Bostwick

```
17Oct56- 6Bel  fm *2½   S'Chase  4:42  4♠ Temple Gwathmey H 58k 2 1  1¹   1¹   1⁶   1¹⁸  Adams FD    149  w  6.05   --      Ancestor149¹⁸Shipboard168²Morpheus142²½     Ridden out 12
27Sep56- 5Bel  sf *2½   S'Chase  4:43³ 4♠ Brook H 17k          8 2  2⁷   2⁶   5²⁰  5³⁴  McDonald RS 153  w  *2.10e --      Morpheus130⁷Pine Shot132³Sundowner140¹²     Used up early 9
20Sep56- 5Bel  fm *2    S'Chase  3:47  3♠ Broad Hollow H 11k   4 4  3²   5⁵   5⁸½  611  Adams FD    157  w  *1.50e --      Shipboard164nkBasilia131²Bavari154²         Early factor,tired 8
13Sep56- 5Bel  fm *2    S'Chase  3:43³ 3♠ Harbor Hill H 11k    8 1  1¹½  1hd  1²   1²½  Adams FD    153  w  3.45e  --      Ancestor153²½Bavar153¹½MghtyMo144¹³         Hard ridden,drew out 8
30Aug56- 5Sar  sf *2½   S'Chase  5:16² 4♠ Saratoga H 11k       4 3  5⁵½  5⁵½  5⁷½  513  Adams FD    155  w  *2.30  --      Mighty Mo138²½Carthage143²Basilia130hd      Showed nothing 6
16Aug56- 5Sar  hd *2½   S'Chase  4:11³ 4♠ Beverwyck H 8.8k     1 3  3³½  3³   3⁶   311  Adams FD    155  w  3.55   --      Bavaria146⁹Crthg137²Ancstor155²             Bobbled badly 10th jump 7

29Jly55- 5Bel  fm *1¾   Hurdles  3:20  3♠ Midsummer H 17k      3 1  41¼  87¼  815  716  Adams FD    149  w  *1.40  --      DearBrutus139noCarafar151¹½PrinceRegent157hd Used early 8
 1Jly55- 3Del  fm *2    S'Chase  4:42² 4♠ Indian River H 10k   1 1  1¹   1hd  2¹½  2nk  Adams FD    154  w  *.80   --      Beaupre142nkAncestor154nkBilling Bear133¹²  Came again 6
24Jun55- 0Del  sf *2    S'Chase  3:56  4♠ Georgetown H 10k     3 3  3⁶   3⁶   2²   1nk  Adams FD    148  w  -      --      Ancestor148nkCovetd140³Shpbord162³½         Jumped well,just up 5
```

Special event - no wagering

```
14Jun55- 3Aqu  fm *2    S'Chase  3:48¹ 4♠ Aqu Spring Maiden 9.7k 3 2 3½  32½  47½  48¼  Adams FD    162  w  *.45   --      Bavaria148³BeauSir138⁴½AnotherHyacinth155¾  Bobbled 7th 5
26May55- 6Bel  hd *2½   S'Chase  3:41³ 4♠ Bel Spring Maiden 9.7k 3 1 1hd 2³   2⁴   2²½  Adams FD    162  w  *1.10e --      Carafar153¹Ancestor162⁴⁰PrinceGloriux155½  Gaining fast 9
21May55- 6Bel  hd *2½   S'Chase  4:32⁴ 4♠ International 21k     9 2  2³⁹  37½  212  215  Adams FD    155  w  3.10e  --      Nej150¹⁵Ancstor155¹⁸Hyvn155¹⁸              Early foot,no late threat 10
 5May55- 6Bel  fm *2    S'Chase  3:41² 4♠ C L Appleton Mem 9.1k 8 2  2⁵   2⁴   1¹   13½  Adams FD    134  w  *1.60  --      Ancestr134³½King Commander162⁸River Jordan134⁴ Handily 8
28Apr55- 5Bel  fm *2    S'Chase  3:47  4♠ Alw 4500             7 1  1¹   2¹½  2½   1²   Adams FD    137  w  *1.45  --      Ancestor137²PrinceGlorieux130¹²CammellLaird142⁵ Driving 8
 2Apr55- 7Cam  fm *1Ⓣ            1:40  3♠ Alw 500              1 1  1⁴   1¹½  1nk  1nk  Hobales J   142wb  -    --      Ancestor142²½Hardrada151¹½Xapcourt138⁰      Going away 5
21Oct54- 3Bel  fm *2    Hurdles  3:44² 3♠ NY Turf Writers H 11k 2 2 2¹   2¹   1¹   1¹½  Hobales J   147  w  2.65   --      Ancestor147¹Khumbaba136¹½River Jordan149¹½  Drew clear 9
13Oct54- 3Bel  fm *1¾   Hurdles  3:13³ 3♠ Alw 4200             3 2  2³   2³   2hd  1¹   Hobales J   141  w  4.30   --      Ancestor141¹Eole III141¹Brechin137¼         Under hard drive 5
30Sep54- 3Bel  fm *2    Hurdles  3:43³ 3♠ Rouge Dragon H 11k   3 1  1¹½  1¹½  1⁴   1²½  Adams FD    136  w  3.55e  --      Ancestor136²½Hyvania147¹Khumbaba137³        Under a drive 8
24Sep54- 3Bel  fm *1¾   Hurdles  3:15  3♠ Alw 4000             5 5  4⁹½  49   210  210  Field K     140 ws *1.45e --      River Jordan140²Ancestor140²Brechin131¹⁰   Mild rally 6
16Jly54- 3Mth  fm *1¾   Hurdles  3:19⁴ 3♠ National Maiden 7.4k 3 3  73¼  53¾  4⁹   4¹⁶  Field K     159 ws *.70e  --      Neji157⁴Rythminhim149⁸Bombez132⁴            Done very early 9
 6Jly54- 4Aqu  fst 1¹⁄₁₆ :24 :48 1:13 1:44⁴ 4♠ Alw 5000       6 6  78¾  79¼  722  726  Glassner G  113  w  15.65  64-15   Bicarb116¹South Point108⁷Bradley114²½       Never a contender 7
 1Jly54- 6Aqu  fst 1¹⁄₁₆ :24² :48 1:12³ 1:46¹ 3♠ Handicap 7530 1 1  1¹½  1hd  2¹   45¼  Atkinson T  110  w  6.55   78-19   Resilient119¹Impulsivo118nkG.R. Petersen110⁴½ Tired 5
25Jun54- 3Aqu  hd *1½   Hurdles  2:45⁴ 3♠ Alw 3700             6 3  34¹  31½  1²   1²   Adams FD    152  w  1.70   --      Ancestor152³BillingBer142¹½FourtoGo142hd    Fully extended 9
18Jun54- 5Mth  fm 1Ⓣ            1:39¹ 3♠ Alw 5000            12 4  41¼  76¼  1116 1015 Hanford I   113wb 17.80e 75-10   IcebergII118³BobsAlibi109noGoingAway109¾   Gave way early 12
12Jun54- 7Bel  hd 1⅜Ⓣ           2:17² 3♠ Handicap 15085       6 2  3²   42¼  12¹⁰ 138¼ Roser G     109wb 52.30  --      Kaster121¹½Williamsburg107nkPicdor116no     Early speed,quit 13
 4Jun54- 3Bel  fm *1½   Hurdles  3:12⁴ 3♠ Alw 3700             9 1  1¹½  3½   38½  315¼ Adams FD    149wb 3.25   --      Sea Term130nkPar Amour134¹⁵Ancestor149¾     Tired gradually 9
17May54- 5Bel  fm *1¾   Hurdles  3:15  3♠ National Maiden 7.4k 10 12 1²   1¹   3½   45   Adams FD    154wb *1.35e --      Neji137⁴Rythminhim150²½Corinthian139no      Gave way badly 13
11May54- 3Bel  sf *1¾   Hurdles  3:24  3♠ Alw 4000             4 3  41½  5³   513  511  Adams FD    152  w  1.35   --      Out Point147⁴Sea Term131noOneida152¾        Unable to keep up 10
27Apr54- 3Bel  fm *1½   Hurdles  2:47  3♠ Sp Wt 3700          2 4  41½  2¹½  11½  1²   Adams FD    147  w  *.90   --      Ancestor147²Rythminhm142¹Altus135⁷         Drew out when ready 14
 3Apr54- 1Cam  hd 1½    Hurdles  2:42⁴ 3♠ Md Sp Wt             3 3  2¹   1½   1¾   1²   Adams FD    148  w  -      --      Ancestor148²Coit148²½Salt142³              Driving 8
24Mar54- 0Aik  5½f            1:09³                                                  1                       --      AncestorNeji
```

Previously owned by O. Phipps; previously trained by J. Fitzsimmons

```
10Oct53- 6Bel  fst 1    :23¹ :46³ 1:12¹ 1:37⁴ 3♠ Handicap 7575  9 4 64¾  713  712  812  Atkinson T  118  w  6.10   73-19   AgainII112¹½Inseparable109noCommonCause115¹ Done early 9
 8Sep53- 6Aqu  fst 1¹⁄₁₆ :24² :48 1:13¹ 1:45³ 3♠ Handicap 7565 4 4  45½  5⁸   613  610  Wall N      120wb 2.05   76-18   Timely Reward120³₄Nothirdchance108½Chello106⁴½ Tired 7
 3Sep53- 6Aqu  fst 1¹⁄₁₆ :48 1:12² 1:38¹ 1:52³ 3♠ Handicap 7535 5 1  11   1hd  23½  2¹   Wall N      122wb *.90e  81-17   G.R. Petersen120¹Ancestor122¹Assignment118½ Closed well 7
31Aug53- 6Aqu  fst 1⅛   :24³ :48 1:12 1:44³ 3♠ Aqueduct H 28k   8 2  22½  43½  56½  45   Wall N      109wb 15.60  86-17   First Aid120²Combat Boots117¹½Elixir113⁴    No mishap 8
25Aug53- 6Sar  fst 1⅛   :48¹ 1:12³ 1:39 1:52² 3♠ Handicap 5030  4 2  21½  2hd  1hd  1nk  Wall N      118wb 4.30   88-19   Ancestor118nkFreedomBell110⁴Sckl'sSound115³½ Hard drive 5
20Aug53- 6Sar  fst 1⅛   :48³ 1:13² 1:39² 1:53² 3♠ Alw 5000      8 2  21½  46   612  66¾  Wall N      117wb *1.25e 76-20   G.R. Petersen120noSickle's Sound105²Mameluke117¹½ Quit 9
17Aug53- 6Sar  fst 7f   :23 :46 1:12 1:25 3♠ American Legion H 11k 1 5 77½ 811 812 89  Atkinson T  112  w  10.20  81-23   Eatontown122¹½Kaster120¹½Acefull115hd        No speed 8
27Jun53- 6Aqu  fst 7f   :22 :44³ 1:09² 1:22 3♠ Carter H 59k      3 7 77   710  812  810  Wall N      108wb 31.90  90-09   Tom Fool135²Squared Away122²½Eatontown113¼ No factor 9
20Jun53- 6Aqu  fst 1¹⁄₁₆ :24 :47 1:11² 1:44¹ 3♠ Queens County H 29k 4 1 11½ 1½ 43 54½   Wall N      104wb 16.85  89-11   Flaunt105½Indian Land114²½Count Turf110nk   Used early 10
10Jun53- 7Suf  fst 1¼   :46² 1:10³ 1:35 2:02¹ 3♠ Mass H 61k      1 2 2¹   3¾   56¾  67¼  Wall N      103wb 28.80  89-12   Royal Vale125½Larry Ellis113¹½Count Turf107¹¼ Weakened 11
 5Jun53- 6Bel  fst 1    :46² 1:11¹ 1:37¹ 1:50¹ 3♠ Handicap 7555  6 1 1½  1½   2¹   34½  Wall N      116wb 8.00   83-12   Arcave122²¼One Hitter126²½Ancestor116¹½     Used up 6
26May53- 7Bel  fst 1    :23¹ :45⁴ 1:10¹ 1:36⁴ 4♠ Alw 5000        8 2 21   22½  32½  3³   Atkinson T  122wb 6.10   86-18   Kaster115½Byrn G.118³Ancestor122⁴          Hard urged 8
20May53- 6Bel  fst 1⅛   :45⁴ 1:10⁴ 1:37 1:50⁴ 3♠ Handicap 7555   4 1 1²  2½   3³   3⁵   Guerin E    119wb 2.50   80-19   Arcave120³¼Gloriette105¹½Ancestor119nk      Tired in drive 9
14May53- 6Bel  fst 1⅛   :45⁴ 1:10⁴ 1:37 1:50² 3♠ Handicap 7565   4 4 33½ 31½  2⁴   23½  Guerin E    119  w  *1.50  83-16   Arcave111³½Ancestor119²Anchor Man110¹       Lacked rally 9
 9May53- 7Pim  gd 1⅛    :47¹ 1:13³ 1:38³ 1:51⁴ 3♠ Dixie H 29k     5 1 1³  31½  43   44½  Wall N      105wb 12.80  90-22   RoyalVale120¹ColdCommand115²½CraftyAdmrl126nk Faltered 6
 4May53- 6Jam  gd 1⅛    :48 1:12¹ 1:37³ 1:51 3♠ Handicap 7560     8 2 22½ 22½  32½  2²½  Atkinson T  116wb 2.50   89-14   Swoop122¹Ancestor116³Anchor Man110⁴         Good try 9
25Apr53- 6Bow  fst 1¹⁄₁₆ :23³ :47³ 1:12² 1:44⁴ 3♠ Bowie H 23k     6 1 11  1¹   2²   2²½  Atkinson T  112wb 14.10  94-16   Royal Vale116²½Ancestor112¹½Post Card115⁴  Good effort 6
21Apr53- 6Jam  fst 1¹⁄₁₆ :23⁴ :47 1:12 1:45¹ 3♠ Handicap 10160    4 1 2hd 2½   2hd  74¾  Atkinson T  107wb 9.65   81-19   One Count126¹¾Assignment111noFlaunt106hd    Quit 11
 8Apr53- 5Jam  gd 1¼    :24 :48 1:24¹ 1:44 3♠ Handicap 6045        5 2 2³  23¾  34¾  47   Guerin E    117wb 2.35   85-16   Assignment112¹½King Jolie118⁴Royal Vale120¹½ Weakened 5
14Feb53- 5Hia  fst 7f   :23 :46 1:11¹ 1:24² 4♠ Alw 5000           7 3 2¹  2¹   2¹   1¹½  Atkinson T  122  w  2.75e  98-14   Ancestor122¹½MannGlory120½True Pattern110²  Driving 9
10Feb53- 8Hia  fst 7f   :23¹ :46¹ 1:10¹ 1:23⁴ 4♠ Alw 4500         4 4 45½ 5⁷   67½  6⁹   Stout J     122wb 20.00  82-13   BlinkerLight116½ChatNoirII115¹½Eatontown110² Done early 8
28Jan53- 7Hia  fst 7f   :22⁴ :46 1:11¹ 1:24² 3♠ Palm Beach H 20k   9 7 75¾ 88¾  12¹³ 12¹¹ Roberts P   109wb 28.85e 77-20   OilCapitol107nkBattlefield123½NimbleFox114¹½ No menace 14
30Dec52- 7TrP  fst 1¹⁄₁₆ :23³ :47 1:12² 1:43⁴ 3♠ Alw 3500          9 4 43½ 54¼  68½  77½  Cole S      109wb *2.50  85-12   Topside118¹Blinker Light117³½Lancaster Lady108²½ Tired 9
25Dec52- 7TrP  fst 1⅛   :46² 1:11 1:37 1:50³ 3♠ Christmas H 11k     3 6 6⁶½ 5⁷   5⁵   55½  Cole S      112wb 5.65e  82-18   Crystal Boot120²½Elixir115½Recline119hd    No factor 10
17Dec52- 7TrP  fst 1⅛   :23 :46² 1:11⁴ 1:43³ 3♠ Hurricane H 8.9k    2 3 3¹  42½  6⁷   6⁶   Stout J     112wb 6.60   88-13   Libba113½Chombro110hdRecline117²            Weakened 11
13Dec52- 6TrP  fst 6f   :22⁴ :45³ 1:10³ 3♠ Alw 3000               5 6 74  75½  9⁸   95½  Stout J     119wb 2.85   88-13   Elixir115nkWhiffenpoof115½Seaflash112¹½     No factor 10
```

Ancestor (continued)

Date-Track	Cond Dist	Times	Race	Running	Jockey	Wt	Odds	Spd	Result	Comment
17Sep52-6Bel	fst 1	:232 :471 1:122 1:37	Jerome H 24k	6 7 63¾ 53½ 813 920	GormanD	113wb	17.20	69-26	Tom Fool1207Marcador111nkMark-Ye-Well1301½	Quit 10
6Sep52-6Aqu	fst 1⅛	:474 1:121 1:38 1:504	Discovery H 28k	9 1 16 14 13 12½	Atkinson T	107wb	10.00e	91-17	Ancestor1072½Flaunt107nkMarcador111	Driving 10
2Sep52-7Bel	fst 7f	:231:46 1:103 1:233	Handicap 7535	4 2 1hd 3½ 63½ 612	Wall N	113wb	4.75	80-13	Flaunt110nkCold Command114nkWhither1128	Close quarters 6
23Aug52-7Sar	fst 1	:233 :471 1:123 1:393	Alw 5000	2 1 12 13 12 1½	Wall N	116wb	2.85	79-17	Ancestor116½Cold Command1223Anchor Man113¾	Driving 9
13Aug52-7Sar	my 1	:233:471 1:123 1:401 3↑	Alw 4000	4 6 53½ 43 52¼ 76¾	Wall N	118wb	*3.25	69-25	Nilufer110noTop Spring1175½Danger Ahead115nk	Weakened 10
4Aug52-7Sar	fst 1	:24 :473 1:13 1:393	Alw 4000	2 3 3nk 2½ 12 2nk	Wall N	122wb	3.95	79-20	Cold Commnd122nkAncstr1223Common Cause1221	Held well 7
1Aug52-6Jam	fst 1 1/16	:25 :483 1:131 1:451 3↑	Alw 5000	4 3 1½ 14 14 17	Wall N	115wb	4.10	86-21	Ancestor1157Flaunt1152Big Print1091½	Easily 6
25Jly52-6Jam	fst 1 1/16	:242:482 1:14 1:454 3↑	Alw 5000	4 4 65 64 65 59¾	Wall N	114wb	4.20	73-21	Turks Cap1082¾Begorra1084Roman Law1112	Poor start 6
19Jly52-7Jam	fst 1 1/16	:24 :473 1:124 1:46 3↑	Alw 4500	7 4 42½ 1hd 21 41½	Nichols J	116wb	*2.15e	80-19	FlamingPrince1161½ClosedSeson113noTurksCp110no	Bore out 12
26Jun52-6Aqu	fst 6f	:223:462 1:103	Rippey H 10k	4 6 64 65¾ 74¾ 79	Wall N	104wb	7.30	90-15	Hitex120hdTom Fool1262Duke Fanelli1022	Outrun 8
17Jun52-5Aqu	fst 6f	:222:46 1:111	Alw 4000	5 2 42 42½ 31 32½	Gorman D	119wb	*1.45	93-12	Rae's Reward119½Giorgetti1192Ancestor1192	Hung 6
14Jun52-3Aqu	fst 6f	:231:46 1:112	Alw 4000	7 1 41¼ 43 2hd 1	Guerin E	120wb	*2.15e	95-11	Ancestor1202Thymus1203Jet a Dandy1203½	Drew out 11
9Jun52-5Bel	sly 7f	:221:454 1:12 1:254	Alw 4000	3 5 55½ 45¼ 45 33½	Gorman D	120wb	6.85	77-20	Second Look1153Model Quest115½Ancestor120nk	Went well 12
5Jun52-7Bel	sly 7f	:224:46 1:104 1:233	Alw 4000	8 3 33 32½ 33 33	Boland W	117wb	4.55	89-08	Giorgetti1141¾Roaming1171¼Ancestor1173½	No rally 8
20May52-6Bel	sly 1	:23 :461 1:114 1:373	Handicap 10070	2 1 1hd 1hd 64¾ 813	Stuart K	105wb	40.30	73-20	Quiet Step1113Cold Command1111Old Ironsides1123½	Tired 8
16May52-7Bel	fst 6f	:224:464 1:113	Alw 4000	4 4 42½ 42½ 33 33½	Arcaro E	118wb	3.70	87-16	King Jolie1182½Requisition1181Ancestor118½	Lacked rally 4
28Apr52-5Jam	sly 1 1/16	:24 :49 1:14 1:463	Alw 4500	7 1 11 12 2½ 21½	Gorman D	117wb	2.90	77-22	Swoop1171¾Ancestor1177Top Bet1171½	Faltered 7
23Apr52-5Jam	fst 1 1/16	:243:482 1:132 1:462	Alw 4500	6 4 41¼ 21½ 2hd 43¾	Gorman D	114wb	*4.75e	78-19	Roaring Bull1133Flaunt1161¾Referee1131½	Weakened 9
19Apr52-4Jam	fst 6f	:233:472 1:121	Alw 4000	2 2 63 65½ 52½ 43	Gorman D	117wb	*.65e	85-14	Imurguy1121¼Swoop114noColonel Hoop1151½	Held well 13
10Apr52-4Jam	fst 6f	:23 1:122 3↑	Md Sp Wt	1 1 3nk 3nk 2hd 1	Shoemaker W	116wb	*.90	85-14	Ancestor1163¾Hypalong1211Runner-Up1162½	Handily 11
5Apr52-4Jam	sly 6f	:24 :48 1:132 3↑	Md Sp Wt	3 3 1½ 2hd 21 21½	Shoemaker W	116wb	*1.25	79-18	Armagh1161¼Ancestor1163¼Jolie Boy116no	Good effort 5
3Mar52-1Hia	fst 6f	:222:452 1:11	Ⓕ Md Sp Wt	7 7 74¾ 66½ 66½ 55¾	Stuart K	122wb	*2.10	86-08	Suggested1223½StopandThink122nkBobsAlibi1221½	No excuse 11
19Feb52-3Hia	fst 7f	:232:464 1:114 1:25	Ⓕ Md Sp Wt	8 1 12 1hd 2½ 21½	Rodriquez E	122wb	*1.35	83-18	Sandtop1221½Ancestor1223Cellini1202	No excuse 12
15Feb52-4Hia	fst 7f	:224:46 1:122 1:252	Md Sp Wt	5 2 21 21½ 11½ 2no	Stuart K	122wb	3.20e	85-17	Top Bet122noAncestor1224Snow Man1222½	Faltered 12
9Feb52-6Hia	fst 7f	:224:46 1:112 1:243	Alw 4000	6 4 53¾ 32 23 33	Stuart K	114wb	21.80	86-07	Blue Square1171Dinewisely1122Ancestor1141½	Lacked rally 7
9Oct51-5Bel	fst 6f-WC:223:453	1:104	Ⓕ Md Sp Wt	4 1 62¾ 66¾ 62¾	Gorman D	118wb	*1.95e	84-13	AncientCity1181DeepRiver118nkGoldenGloves118no	No rally 16
10Oct51-5Bel	fst 6f-WC:223:45	1:092	Sp Wt 5000	13 8 118¼ 1313 1317	Stuart K	118	25.45f	77-11	Hill Gail1184Tom Fool118nkBaybrook1182	Showed little 16
26Sep51-5Bel	fst 6f-WC:222:45	1:101	Ⓕ Md Sp Wt	25 11 84 116¾ 84¾	Combest J	118	11.75e	85-10	Hitex1183½Point Fortune113noChello118no	Closed ground 27

Aunt Jinny

ch. f. 1948, by Heliopolis (Hyperion)–Gaga, by Bull Dog
Own.– D.A. Headley
Br.– Duval A. Headley (Ky)
Tr.– M. Calvert

Lifetime record: 30 5 4 3 $106,020

Date-Track	Cond Dist	Times	Race	Running	Jockey	Wt	Odds	Spd	Result	Comment
25Feb52-7SA	fst 6f	:224:46 1:11 4↑	Ⓕ Alw 5000	5 1 96½ 75¾ 64¾ 45	Adams J	111 w	9.55	85-15	Great Dream1141Fleet Rings1092Miss Traffic1112	10
Dropped back,made up ground										
15Feb52-6SA	fst 7f	:222:46 1:103 1:233 4↑	Ⓕ Alw 5000	2 6 94¾ 99¾ 712 69¾	Adams J	110	13.35	77-17	Lyceum1072½Fast Reward1142Dashing By1153	Outrun 12
6Feb52-7SA	fst 6f	:223:451 1:103 4↑	Ⓕ Los Cerritos H 18k	11 2 95 1191 1211 1211	Adams J	108	96.85	81-14	Sickle's Image1201½A Gleam1152½Frigid105½	Forced wide 13
26Jan52-7SA	fst 1⅛	:47 1:114 1:381 1:512 3↑	Ⓢ Margarita H 62k	8 11 108½ 108¼ 1417 1415	Trent H	105	77.60	69-19	Bed o' Roses1291Next Move1301½Toto105½	No speed 14
11Jan52-7SA	fst 6f	:221:45 1:09 4↑	Alw 7500	4 3 68 815 1019 916	York R	112 w	43.65	84-13	To Market1141¼Reighs Bull1135Vigorous115¾	Outrun 10
Previously trained by D.A. Headley										
20Oct51-7GS	fst 1 1/16	:231:462 1:113 1:433 3↑	Ⓕ Vineland H 31k	6 15 1514 1491 1517 1411	Woodhouse H	110 w	34.90	81-15	Bedo'Roses1263½Valadium109noDixieFlyer107½	Slow start 15
26Sep51-6Bel	fst 1	:23 :46 1:104 1:361	Ⓕ Jerome H 24k	4 9 94½ 99¾ 128½ 1291	Woodhouse H	107	44.05	84-14	Alerted115nkMandingo1023Hall of Fame1281	Quit 12
22Sep51-6Aqu	fst 1⅛	:482 1:122 1:382 1:52 3↑	Ⓕ Beldame 67k	5 8 1310 1412 1416 1419	Woodhouse H	111 w	16.20	66-14	Thelma Burger1102Bed o' Roses1243½Kiss Me Kate119nk	Quit 14
29Aug51-6Sar	fst 1¼	:484 1:131 1:382 2:053	Ⓕ Alabama 22k	5 3 44½ 42½ 34 310	Woodhouse H	122 w	3.60	70-18	Kiss Me Kate1268Vulcania1162Aunt Jinny122no	No rally 5
1Aug51-6Was	fst 1	:23 :46 1:10 1:35	Ⓕ Misty Isle H 22k	10 3 21½ 21½ 1½ 11½	Woodhouse H	122 w	4.20	95-06	AuntJinny1221½DickieSue115nkWillYouDance111½	Driving 10
14Jly51-7AP	fst 1	:224:452 1:094 1:361 3↑	Ⓕ Arl Matron H 72k	10 2 2hd 11 11½ 21½	Woodhouse H	107	37.10	89-08	Sickle's Image1201Aunt Jinny1075War Talk109¾	Gave way 13
30Jun51-7AP	fst 6f	:224 1:104 3↑	Ⓕ Modesty H 24k	7 15 1517 1616 1615 1612	Wall N	111 w	34.20	80-08	Sickle's Image120¾Asphalt1052½TwoRainbows104nk	No factor 17
20Jun51-6AP	sl 6f	:224:454 1:121	Ⓕ Cleopatra 16k	1 2 75½ 89½ 99¾ 863	Wall N	118	23.20	78-18	Sickle'sImage1151½JennieLee1153¾Fleetertthan111½	Outrun 10
4May51-7CD	fst 1 1/16	:24 :482 1:133 1:453	Ⓕ Ky Oaks 31k	6 5 863 1191 1219 1117	Baird RL	116	9.30	73-14	How1152Astro1102½Sickle's Image1211½	Tired 14
14Apr51-6AP	sl 6f	:234:494 1:121	Ⓕ Ashland 22k	6 4 79½ 98 981 1hd	Baird RL	121 w	3.10	41-31	Sickle'sImage121nkJulitsNurs1181½How1152	Disliked going 6
11Nov50-6Pim	fst 1 1/16	:233:464 1:12 1:471	Ⓕ Marguerite 35k	8 4 21 1hd 11½ 21½	Wall N	116 w	*.90	72-19	CarolinaQueen1191AuntJnny1162½TwoRnbws114hd	Weakened 8
28Oct50-6Lrl	fst 1 1/16	:23 :471 1:122 1:462	Ⓕ Selima 49k	7 3 2hd 1hd 1hd 1hd	Wall N	122 w	*1.30	82-18	Aunt Jinny122hdVulcania119nkRose Fern1192	All out 9
21Oct50-6Jam	fst 1 1/16	:232:47 1:121 1:454	Ⓕ Demoiselle 48k	3 1 1hd 11 15 13	Wall N	116 w	12.65	83-14	Aunt Jinny1163Vulcania1192½Rose Fern1191½	Easily 8
29Sep50-6Bel	fst 6f-WC:22 :443	1:092	Ⓕ Alw 3500	5 6 73 44 4 2hd	Brooks S	119 w	10.35	94-10	BettyLamar114hdAuntJinny1192½SweetTalk1191½	Stout try 12
23Sep50-6Bel	fst 6f-WC:223:453	1:12	Ⓕ Matron 50k	9 9 911 919 926	Brooks S	119	11.95	55-22	Atalanta1193½Ruddy1191Sungari119½	Outrun 9
26Aug50-3Was	fst 5½f	:222:454 :581 1:044	Ⓕ Alw 3000	2 3 2hd 1hd 1½ 1nk	Baird RL	115 w	*1.30	96-07	Aunt Jinny115nkPetasus1153Native Valor115½	Driving 7
15Aug50-4Was	fst 5½f	:223:453 :584 1:044	Ⓕ Md Sp Wt	6 1 1hd 11 15 15	Baird RL	115 w	10.40	96-08	Aunt Jinny119nkDusty Vixen115nkLittle Cindy1152½	Easily 12
4Aug50-5Was	fst 5½f	:223:46 :574 1:042	Ⓕ Md Sp Wt	5 1 21 55½ 12 37½	Baird RL	115 w	10.50	90-07	Sickle'sImage1156½TheGhizeh1151AuntJnny1153	Lost ground 12
27Jly50-5AP	fst 6f	:222:443	1:104	Ⓕ Pollyanna 18k	12 7 54 56½ 781 811	Baird RL	112.5 w	42.00	81-11	Flyamanita1133¾HastyRequest1132Sckl'sImg1141½	No mishap 14
18Jly50-5AP	hy 5½f	:232:483 1:013 1:09	Ⓕ Md Sp Wt	10 10 85¾ 55½ 76½ 44	Baird RL	115wb	6.60	71-34	RomanMiss1151Fleetertha1151½Sckl'sImg115½	Lost ground 12
8Jly50-7AP	fst 6f	:222:454	1:12	Ⓕ Arl Lassie 55k	7 5 41½ 52¼ 45½ 47	Baird RL	114wb	69.80	79-18	ShawneeSquaw1193½RedCrss1191¼HastyRqst1192½	No mishap 11
3Jly50-4AP	fst 5½f	:222:461 :592 1:061	Ⓕ Md Sp Wt	5 2 1½ 12 12 13	Baird RL	115wb	11.70	86-11	On Velvet1121½Kissable1153¾Aunt Jinny115no	Drifted out 12
25May50-2Det	hy 5f	:234:502	1:041	Ⓕ Curtain Up 6.2k	8 5 56½ 66½ 64¼ 410	Combest J	110wb	*1.70e	- -	Sweet Pick1104Copperstone1142½Rule-One1143½	Raced wide 8
19May50-4CD	fst 5f	:23 :462	:591	Ⓕ Md Sp Wt	1 2 1½ 1hd 2hd 21½	Gonzalez MN	115wb	8.40	96-09	Miss Mim Jr1151½Aunt Jinny1152½Sweet Pick1153¼	Gave way 12
26Apr50-1Kee	fst *4f	:23	:471	Ⓕ Md Sp Wt	5 11 1112 119¼ 98¼	Gonzalez MN	115wb	4.50f	84-11	MyMom115nkSweetPick1151½DoubleWing115nk	Raced greenly 12

Barbizon

dkb. c. 1954, by Polynesian (Unbreakable)–Good Blood, by Bull Lea
Own.– W.L. Jones Jr
Br.– Calumet Farm (Ky)
Tr.– M. Jolley

Lifetime record: 21 7 4 2 $199,460

Date-Track	Cond Dist	Times	Race	Running	Jockey	Wt	Odds	Spd	Result	Comment
17Jan58-7Hia	fst 6f	:222:453 1:102 3↑	Royal Poinciana H 25k	13 13 128 108¾ 1012 128½	Martin B	119 w	10.20	84-16	Encore115¾Iron Liege124nkSonny Dan118¾	Broke tardily 13
1Jan58-7TrP	fst 6f	:22 :443 1:093 3↑	New Year's H 11k	4 8 77 77½ 66½ 43¾	Martin B	120 w	8.95	93-12	Pine Echo119½Sonny Dan1201Missile1162¼	Best stride late 8
Previously owned by Calumet Farm;previously trained by H.A. Jones										
29Oct57-6GS	fst 6f	:22 :45 1:102	Alw 5500	6 5 66¾ 46 3½ 2½	Hartack W	122 w	*.90	91-16	Jet Colonel1221Barbizon1222½Joe Price122nk	No excuse 8
18Oct57-6GS	sly 6f	:222:453 1:11	Alw 5500	5 6 68 42½ 32 22	Hartack W	122 w	*.60	87-22	Irish Whistler1102Barbizon1221Incaseofire1182	Hung 7
12Oct57-4GS	fst 6f	:222:443 1:094 3↑	Alw 5000	6 6 66 42½ 23 23	Cook WM	114 w	*1.70	92-11	Barbizon1142Flight History1241½Polly's Jet1141¼	Drew out 7
13Jly57-8AP	sl 1	:224:463 1:102 1:363	Arl Classic 151k	7 7 711 79¼ 67¼ 69	Erb D	120 w	*.70e	80-20	Clem1171½IronLiege1231¾Mantu117hd	Appeared in poor form 7
29Jun57-8AP	gd 7f	:23 :452 1:112 1:243	L Armour Mem 22k	2 7 52 63¾ 77¼ 88	Martin RJ	120wb	*1.50e	79-17	Iron Liege126hdGreek Game1232Manteau120no	No mishap 8
20Jun57-6AP	fst 6f	:222:443 1:094	Alw 10000	3 2 46 36 33 31½	Hartack W	123wb	3.10	93-09	GreekGame1261½Jet Colonel117nkBarbizon1238	Closing fast 4
8Jun57-7Del	sly 1⅛	:464 1:12 1:383 1:513	Leonard Richards 50k	9 5 42½ 711 77¾ 57½	Hartack W	119wb	*2.30	75-23	Lucky Dip1141¼Field of Honor1141Gama1141	No mishaps 9
1Jun57-7Del	fst 1 1/16	:23 :462 1:111 1:443	Kent 35k	6 2 91 32 57 816	Gorman D	126wb	*1.80	72-16	LuckyDip1141¼Inswept120½Assmblymn1124	Early speed,tired 10
25May57-7GS	fst 1⅛	:462 1:103 1:352 1:48	Jersey 62k	6 2 9¾ 87¾ 911 911	Scurlock O	122 w	*.60e	85-12	IronLiege126noClem1188WeTrust111½	Hard urged,no factor 11

21May57- 6GS	my	1 1/16	:24 :471 1:12 1:45	Alw 10000	1	1	1½	13	13½	11½	Scurlock O	121 w	*.30	85-16	Barbizon1211½Gam1182WTrust11412	Taken in hand late part	4
20Mar57- 7GP	sly	1 1/16	:232 :464 1:113 1:44	Fountain of Youth 18k	6	8	75	63½	56½	511	Scurlock O	122 w	*.20e	79-16	Gen. Duke1191½Iron Liege1131¼Better Bee113hd	No mishap	10
13Mar57- 7GP	fst	6½f	:223 :451 1:094 1:16	Hutcheson 12k	9	3	3nk	2hd	1hd	2no	Hartack W	122 w	*.45e	99-10	JetColonl119noBrbzon1225WTrust1141¾	Just failed to hold	9
5Mar57- 6GP	fst	6f	:222 :452 1:094	Alw 6000	9	10	108¾	97¾	58½	35¾	Hartack W	126 w	*1.20	90-11	JetColonel1132¾Encore1103Barbizon126no	Best stride late	11
27Oct56- 7GS	gd	1 1/16	:221 :454 1:12 1:444	Garden State 319k	15	12	98¼	66	35	1no	Hartack W	122 w	6.60e	86-18	Barbizon122noFederal Hill122nkAmarullah1223	Just up	19
20Oct56- 6GS	fst	1 1/16	:232 :461 1:111 1:45	Alw 10000	4	5	58	33½	21½	2¾	Hartack W	117 w	*1.20	84-19	Federal Hill120¾Barbizon1171½Clem1226	Made bid,tiring	8
12Oct56- 6GS	fst	1	:222 :452 1:104 1:374	Alw 7500	2	6	68½	35	1hd	11	Hartack W	117 w	1.60	95-12	Barbizon1171Prince Khaled1174Sonny Dan120hd	Easy score	8
8Oct56- 4Bel	fst	6f-WC	:224 :453 1:103	Alw 4500	3	5		63¾	51¾	11½	Arcaro E	119 w	*.90	86-14	Brbzon1191½PopCorn113hdBkht113½	Appeared green,drew out	11
27Sep56- 4Bel	fst	6f	:222 :454 1:12	Alw 4000	5	4	22½	22½	11½	12	Arcaro E	116 w	*.75	89-13	Barbizon1162PopCorn116nkBor1133	Swerved late,easy score	5
15Sep56- 5Bel	fst	6f-WC	:222 :452 1:093	©Md Sp Wt	1	6		73¾	32	1¾	Arcaro E	118 w	*2.15	91-10	Barbizon118¾FullStage1183½ManPowr1181½	Under hard drive	14

Battlefield

ch. c. 1948, by War Relic (Man o' War)–Dark Display, by Display **Lifetime record: 44 22 14 2 $474,727**

Own.– G.D. Widener
Br.– John A. Bell Jr (Ky)
Tr.– W.F. Mulholland

14Mar53- 7GP	fst	1¼	:454 1:10 1:344 2:004 3↑	Gulf Park H 59k	9	8	55½	32	2½	2nk	Schmidl A	125wb	2.65	95-14	CraftyAdmiral128nkBattlefield1256Dult1141	Hung in drive	11
7Mar53- 7GP	fst	1⅛	:47 1:112 1:36 1:484 3↑	Appleton H 17k	5	6	65½	44	3½	1hd	Schmidl A	122wb	*1.05	100-11	Battlefield122hdGolden Gloves1081½Mandingo1061	Just up	8
21Feb53- 7Hia	fst	1¼	:462 1:103 1:363 2:024 3↑	Widener H 130k	5	4	43	31½	11	3nk	Schmidl A	123wb	4.10	91-09	Oil Capitol114hdAlerted126hdBattlefield1231½	Held well	8
16Feb53- 6Hia	fst	1⅛	:471 1:112 1:363 1:491 4↑	Alw 6000	2	4	33½	3½	2hd	1hd	Schmidl A	122wb	*1.05	90-16	Battlefield122hdAlerted1222½BlinkerLight1063	Ridden out	6
12Feb53- 7Hia	fst	7f	:224 :454 1:104 1:232 4↑	Alw 4500	1	5	55	33½	2½	1nk	Schmidl A	124wb	*.50	93-13	Battlefield124nkPost Card1093½Corfel111nk	Ridden out	8
28Jan53- 7Hia	fst	7f	:224 :46 1:111 1:242 3↑	Palm Beach H 20k	3	11	107½	65¾	41¼	2nk	Schmidl A	123wb	*2.10	88-20	OilCapitol107nkBattlefield123½NimblFox1141½	Just missed	14
24Jan53- 6Hia	my	6f	:231 :472 1:13 4↑	Alw 5000	2	1	53½	21½	1½	2nk	Schmidl A	123wb	*1.20	83-32	Ken120nkBattlefield1231½Mandingo1174	Faltered	7
1Nov52- 6Jam	fst	1⅛	:484 1:13 1:374 1:501 3↑	Westchester H 56k	7	3	21	11	1½	1no	Schmidl A	123wb	3.85	95-18	Battlefield123noTom Fool1251Alerted1251¼	Held gamely	9
18Oct52- 6Jam	fst	1⅛	:471 1:11 1:354 1:492 3↑	Grey Lag H 60k	3	5	31	1hd	2hd	2no	Schmidl A	118wb	10.05	99-16	Tom Fool119noBattlefield118nkAlerted1211¼	Sharp effort	11
11Oct52- 7GS	fst	1⅛	:464 1:113 1:372 1:503 3↑	Quaker City H 29k	1	3	36	43¼	47½	57¾	Arcaro E	122wb	*1.20	81-18	General Staff1172½Alerted1223Mandingo1082	Impeded	10
27Sep52- 7Bel	fst	1½	:501 1:144 2:05 2:304 3↑	Manhattan H 34k	6	1	1hd	1hd	33½	78¾	Arcaro E	120wb	*1.70	75-16	Lone Eagle1073½Combat Boots110½One Hitter1173	Tired	8
20Sep52- 6Bel	sly	1⅛	:452 1:10 1:352 1:482 3↑	New York H 29k	4	4	32½	31½	2½	1hd	Arcaro E	118wb	3.15	97-08	Battlefield118hdGeneralStff1131¼CombtBoots1093½	Driving	7
16Sep52- 5Bel	fst	6f	:231 :471 1:12 4↑	Alw 4000	8	6	42¼	32	2hd	11½	Green B	120wb	*1.50	89-20	Battlefld1201½Mohammedan1141½Assgnmnt112hd	Drew clear	8
8Sep52- 6Aqu	fst	7f	:223 :451 1:102 1:24 3↑	Bay Shore H 17k	6	6	86	99	107½	119½	Green B	126 w	8.55	80-20	Next Move1151First Glance111nkSquared Away1202	Outrun	12
15Aug52- 6Sar	sl	7f	:231 :463 1:12 1:253 3↑	American Legion H 9k	5	3	3½	42	43½	48¼	Green B	126 w	*1.70	79-25	Tea-Maker118¾FirstGlance1091½NorthernStar1196	Weakened	6
8Aug52- 6Sar	fst	6f	:232 :47 1:114 3↑	Handicap 5035	1	5	57¼	55½	45½	53¼	Green B	126 w	*1.20	86-23	Squared Away1221¼Elixir1071First Glance1101	Poor start	5
30May52- 6Bel	fst	1¼	:463 1:102 1:353 2:02 3↑	Suburban H 60k	1	8	813	47	45¼	77	Arcaro E	124 w	*1.50	83-12	One Hitter112nkCrafty Admiral1132Mameluke1161	Tired	10
17May52- 6Bel	fst	1	:23 :454 1:104 1:362 3↑	Metropolitan H 36k	11	8	64¼	5¾	12	2½	Scurlock O	125 w	*1.50	91-14	Mameluke112½Battlefield1251½One Hitter1131	Weakened	11
6May52- 6Bel	fst	6f	:221 :454 1:10 3↑	Handicap 6055	8	7	65¾	55½	2½	2½	Arcaro E	126 w	*1.40	98-14	FirstGlance109½Bttlfld1262½NorthrnStr1142½	Began slowly	8
8Sep51- 6Aqu	fst	1⅛	:474 1:123 1:371 1:502	Discovery H 22k	1	4	43	21	2hd	2hd	Arcaro E	126 w	*.90	93-17	Alerted114hdBattlefield1263½Vulcania1082	Wide,missed	8
18Aug51- 6Sar	gd	1¼	:492 1:141 1:40 2:061	Travers 22k	1	1	3½	1hd	1hd	1¾	Arcaro E	123 w	*.20	77-17	Battlefield123¾Yildiz1264½Big Stretch1143½	Driving	4
		Geldings not eligible															
4Aug51- 6Mth	fst	1¼	:48 1:123 1:373 2:032	Choice 28k	4	1	34½	2hd	11	11¼	Arcaro E	126 w	*.70	89-17	Battlefield1261¼UncleMilti11815GoldnTrnd1145	Ridden out	4
21Jly51- 7AP	fst	1¼	:464 1:111 1:354 2:031	Arl Classic 81k	6	6	54½	2hd	12	2nk	Arcaro E	123 w	*1.50	89-08	Hall of Fame120nkBattlefield1232Ruhe120nk	Just failed	13
7Jly51- 6Aqu	fst	1¼	:481 1:123 1:383 2:042	Dwyer 57k	10	5	32	1hd	1hd	1½	Arcaro E	121 w	1.60	85-16	Battlefield121½Alerted1112½Hull Down1111½	All out	10
30Jun51- 6Aqu	sly	1 1/16	:242 :481 1:122 1:433	Shevlin 22k	2	2	2hd	1hd	2hd	1no	Scurlock O	123 w	*.70	96-16	Battlefield123noAlerted11210Mully S.1122	Just up	7
16Jun51- 6Bel	fst	1½	:494 1:141 2:031 2:29	Belmont 118k	5	6	83½	22	22	24	Arcaro E	126 w	*1.85	89-08	Counterpoint1264Battlefield1261½BattlMorn1269	No excuse	9
		Geldings not eligible															
9Jun51- 6Bel	fst	1⅛	:461 1:102 1:351 1:474	Peter Pan H 24k	3	6	66¾	55	34	22¾	Arcaro E	123 w	*.85	99-10	Counterpoint1142¾Battlefield1232¼HallofFm113¾	No excuse	9
26May51- 6Bel	fst	1	:224 :452 1:094 1:354	Withers 29k	7	4	21	21	2hd	1hd	Arcaro E	126 w	*.70	95-12	Battlefield126hdJumbo1265Nullify1264	All out	7
		Geldings not eligible															
22May51- 5Bel	fst	6f	:223 :454 1:101	Alw 4000	2	7	1hd	1½	11½	11	Arcaro E	126 w	*.60	99-15	Battlefield1261Nullify1121¼General Staff1134	Handily	7
16May51- 6Bel	fst	7f	:22 :45 1:093 1:222	Swift 12k	4	4	46	22	21	21¼	Arcaro E	126 w	*.85	97-11	Jumbo1261¼Battlefield1265½Iliad1263½	No excuse	9
9Apr51- 6Jam	fst	6f	:23 :46 1:101	Alw 5000	5	4	33	22½	31	24½	Arcaro E	123 w	*1.35	91-13	Uncle Miltie1174½Battlefield123½Nullify123nk	No excuse	7
30Sep50- 6Bel	fst	6½f-W	:22 :442 1:09 1:152	Futurity 106k	10	5		61	21	1no	Arcaro E	122wb	*.95	95-05	Battlefld122noBgStrtch1223½Rough'nTumbl122no	Ridden out	14
		Geldings not eligible															
25Sep50- 5Bel	fst	6f-WC	:223 :452 1:104	Sp Wt 5000	10	3		1hd	11	1¾	Arcaro E	118wb	*1.10	87-13	Battlefield118¾Pet Bully118½Rough 'n Tumble1182	Handily	11
26Aug50- 6Sar	fst	6½f	:231 :464 1:114 1:18	Hopeful 58k	2	4	41¼	41¼	1½	11½	Guerin E	122wb	*1.30e	95-11	Battlefield1221½Battle Morn1223½Big Stretch1221	Handily	10
12Aug50- 4Sar	fst	6f	:224 :462 1:111	Sar Spl 11k	2	3	1½	11½	11½	1¾	Arcaro E	122 w	*1.00	92-11	Battlefield122¾NorthernStar1222½BattleMorn1221½	Handily	6
26Jly50- 6Mth	fst	6f	:223 :453 1:104	Sapling 14k	8	1	22	2½	1½	11½	Arcaro E	122 w	*1.10	94-10	Battlefield1221½UncleMiltie1151LordPutnm1226	Ridden out	8
12Jly50- 6Jam	sl	6f	:231 :454 1:11	East View 50k	1	1	2hd	3nk	2hd	43	Arcaro E	122 w	*1.15	89-12	Win or Lose117½Nullify1222½Iliad119no	Weakened	9
		Awarded third purse money															
28Jun50- 6Aqu	fst	6f	:224 :461 1:104	Great American 18k	8	2	21½	21	2½	2hd	Arcaro E	126 w	*.70	98-15	SilverWings117hdBattlefield1265Nullify117no	Just missed	10
14Jun50- 6Aqu	fst	5½f	:223 :463 1:05	©Tremont 13k	7	2	31½	2hd	2½	11½	Arcaro E	126 w	*1.95	99-15	Battlefield1261½Patch1171Nullify117¾	Ridden out	10
17May50- 6Bel	fst	5f-WC	:221 :45 :572	Juvenile 15k	3	4		41	2hd	21½	Arcaro E	122 w	*.60	91-06	Liberty Rab1221½Battlefield1222Remove1191½	No excuse	9
5May50- 6Jam	my	5f	:23 :473 :594	Youthful (Div 2) 12k	8	2	2hd	2½	1½	11	Arcaro E	122 w	*.75	91-17	Battlefield1221Count Turf1229Liberty Rab122¾	Drew clear	10
28Apr50- 5Jam	sly	5f	:23 :473 1:003	Alw 4000	6	5	42½	2hd	1hd	12	Arcaro E	122 w	*.75	87-18	Battlefield1222Faneli'sAlley1162PointChcot116no	Handily	6
1Mar50- 5Hia	fst	3f	:213 :324	Juvenile (Div 1) 15k	3	1			1½	1½	Picou C	117	2.40	- -	Battlefield117½FairSelf1142½KingWilson117no	Hard drive	13
21Feb50- 1Hia	fst	3f	:221 :333	Md Sp Wt	13	2			1½	1½	Picou C	122 b	*1.30f	- -	Battlefield122½Propeller122hdChallcote1223	Ridden out	14

Bayou

ch. f. 1954, by Hill Prince (Princequillo)–Bourtai, by Stimulus **Lifetime record: 32 7 8 4 $143,759**

Own.– Claiborne Farm
Br.– Claiborne Farm (Ky)
Tr.– M. Jolley

14Jly58- 7AP	fst	6f	:224 :452 1:102 4↑	Alw 2750	5	2	74¾	74¾	44	33	Cook LC	119 w	11.00	89-13	Dark Toga1071¾Arcandy1181¼Bayou1191		8
		Came strongly final furlong															
1Feb58- 4Hia	fst	7f	:232 :464 1:12 1:243 4↑	ⒻAlw 7500	2	5	32½	32	3nk	2½	Grant H	121 w	*1.25	86-14	Pardala113½Bayou121¾LadyElliott1123	In a bit close late	8
18Jan58- 8Hia	fst	6f	:223 :453 1:102 4↑	ⒻAlw 7500	6	8	8¾	89	78¼	48	Ruane J5	116 w	3.75	85-11	Beautillon1124½Amort1183Ambulnc112½	Passed tired horses	12
24Oct57- 6Kee	gd	1⅛	:463 1:111 1:361 1:491 3↑	ⒻSpinster 76k	1	4	46½	43½	34	45¼	Ussery R	119 w	4.40	86-12	Bornastar1232½PuckerUp1231¾Serchng1231	Well placed,hung	6
		Open to 3-, 4- and 5-year-olds															
7Oct57- 7Bel	sly	1	:231 :461 1:11 1:37 3↑	ⒻMaskette H 29k	9	3	45½	33	2½	1½	Ussery R	118 w	5.75	89-14	Bayou118½Rare Treat116hdPink Velvet1134	Fully extended	9
11Sep57- 7Bel	fst	1 1/16	:232 :462 1:112 1:431	ⒻGazelle H 30k	5	12	117¼	83¾	3nk	11½	Arcaro E	120 w	6.95	92-12	Bayou1201½EveningTime118noPinkVlvt116½	Rated,going away	13
28Aug57- 7Sar	fst	1¼	:481 1:134 1:392 2:062	ⒻAlabama 29k	1	1	41¼	72¼	51¾	511	Ussery R	121 w	4.15	65-23	Here and There1133Snow White1133Outer Space1212	Tired	11
14Aug57- 7Sar	fst	7f	:224 :46 1:11 1:242	ⒻTest 23k	5	6	914	88¾	66	44½	Ussery R	124 w	9.75	88-17	MissBlueJay1181½OuterSpace121hdSnowWhite1153	Late bid	10
27Jly57- 6Mth	fst	1⅛	:48 1:112 1:371 1:501	ⒻMth Oaks 59k	8	7	88	87½	76¾	64½	Anderson P	121 w	*3.10	89-13	Romanita117noEveningTime1211MarketBaskt121nk	No excuse	10
29Jun57- 7Del	fst	1¼	:463 1:11 1:372 2:05 3↑	ⒻDelaware H 164k	3	4	49½	66	86½	146½	Nelson E	111 w	10.20	70-22	PrincessTuria119½PuckerUp1171LittlePache119nk	No speed	19
22Jun57- 7Bel	fst	1⅜	:484 1:131 1:381 2:163	ⒻC C A Oaks 70k	7	7	72¾	41½	2hd	2¾	Arcaro E	121 w	*.65	87-14	Willamette121¾Bayou1215½Woodlawn1211½	Led between calls	10

15Jun57- 7Del	fst	1⅛	:474 1:114 1:383 1:513	ⒻDel Oaks 51k	9	3	32½	21	1hd	1¾	Hartack W	119 w	*.80	82-18	Bayou119¾PillowTalk1191Mrbll1134½	Drew out,clever score	9
3Jun57- 7Bel	fst	1	:223 :45 1:103 1:37	ⒻAcorn 36k	11	6	66¾	1½	11½	13	Ussery R	121 w	4.30	89-12	Bayou1213Teleran121nkHereandThere1211	Under mild urging	17
24May57- 7Jam	gd	1 1/16	:233 :464 1:12 1:452	ⒻAlw 7500	2	5	34½	31	11½	12½	Ussery R	113 w	3.40	83-17	Bayou1132½Capelet1172½Willamette1111	Kept to pressure	7
25Apr57- 5Kee	fst	6f	:222 :45 1:094	Alw 3500	4	2	51¾	41¼	11½	17	Hartack W	115 w	2.10e	97-02	Byou1157Ezgo1204SlghtGo1141½	Drew far away,mildly urged	7
19Apr57- 6Kee	fst	7f	:224 :46 1:103 1:224	Alw 3500	7	1	31½	75	54	47	Church K	112 w	8.80	91-06	Manteau1135BooneBlaze1201DixieDoge1201	Fell back early	10
12Feb57- 7Hia	fst	1⅛	:473 1:121 1:372 1:502	ⒻAlw 5000	6	5	44	41½	24	21	Brooks S	112 w	*.85	83-18	TooTooFussy1101Bayou1126RoyalRespect1123½	Closed fast	7
26Jan57- 4Hia	fst	6f	:222 :461 1:113	ⒻAlw 4500	2	8	85¼	67½	57¼	34	Brooks S	121 w	2.55	83-14	Iberia1213½Adormidr116½Byou1212½	Found best stride late	12
19Jan57- 6Hia	fst	6f	:22 :452 1:103	ⒻAlw 6000	11	1	33½	34	32	2nk	Cook LC	109 w	8.05	92-09	Jerilynn109nkBayou1092MagicSpll1092	Reached lead,necked	12
10Jan57- 6TrP	fst	6f	:222 :454 1:112	ⒻAlw 2700	7	5	87¼	76½	68	44¾	Brooks S	117 w	2.90	85-10	WorthSaving117nkSandysJoy1151GrannyAnnie1123½	Rallied	12
6Nov56- 4CD	my	6f	:231 :47 1:134	ⒻMd Sp Wt	1	3	33½	32½	2½	12¼	Brooks S	118 w	*2.20	79-20	Bayou1182¼CityBll1183½Lblch1184½	Going away under drive	12
18Oct56- 4Kee	fst	6f	:224 :46 1:111	ⒻMd Sp Wt	9	8	66½	45½	33½	26	Brooks S	116 w	1.90	88-04	Miss Fleetwood1166Bayou1162½Can't Tell1163½	Next best	12
13Oct56- 6Kee	fst	*7f	1:27	ⒻAlcibiades 41k	1	3	21½	49	59½	510	Broussard R	119 w	3.90e	88-11	Leallah1192½Bluebility119noNantua1194½	Failed to stay	6
7Aug56- 3Was	fst	6f	:223 :462 1:124	ⒻMd Sp Wt	3	1	44½	37	35	22	Brooks S	116wb	2.40	79-17	Susette1162Bayou1162ScotchButy116½	Strong stretch rally	12
31Jly56- 1Was	fst	5½f	:223 :453 :584 1:05	ⒻMd Sp Wt	6	2	31½	45	45	23	Brooks S	116wb	3.00	90-12	PontchieGal1163Bayou116hdStymieDir1112¼	Came again late	12
18Jly56- 3AP	fst	5½f	:232 :472 :594 1:062	ⒻMd Sp Wt	5	2	62¾	44½	45	43¼	Brooks S	118wb	4.00	83-14	Bluebility118hdWherewuzuat118noTherapy1183¼	Went well	12
12Jly56- 4AP	fst	5½f	:23 :46 :59 1:053	ⒻMd Sp Wt	3	2	31½	34	37½	35	Brooks S	116wb	2.10	85-13	Alabama Charm1162½Marnerleen1162½Bayou1162¼	No excuse	12
28Jun56- 1AP	fst	5½f	:232 :48 1:002 1:07	ⒻMd Sp Wt	2	2	1hd	1hd	2hd	2nk	Brooks S	118wb	4.70	83-11	SlaveDancer118nkBayou1181¼PontchiGl1183¼	Very sharp try	12
14Jun56- 4Was	fst	5f	:223 :47 1:002	ⒻMd Sp Wt	11	10	66½	54½	52¼	41	Brooks S	118wb	3.70	83-14	Jestress118½Ray's Delight118nkPontchie Gal113nk	Rallied	12
21May56- 3Was	fst	5f	:222 :454 :584	ⒻMd Sp Wt	3	3	32½	34½	47½	410¼	Brooks S	118 w	4.80	82-15	SpringTune1186DaisyCrockett1183½PrincessEllen118¾	Tired	10
28Apr56- 3CD	fst	4½f	:23 :46 :533	ⒻMd Sp Wt	12	9		1012	1012	89¾	Brooks S	117 w	3.00	82-08	Piccalilli1172½DuntreathGift1172JenO'F1172½	Forced wide	12
14Apr56- 4Kee	sly	*4f	:502	ⒻAlw 3500	6	4		65½	55	35	Brooks S	112 w	3.70	90-05	Lori-El1135Rdruth118hdByou1121	Hard urged,raced greenly	7

Bed o' Roses

b. f. 1947, by Rosemont (The Porter)–Good Thing, by Discovery

Lifetime record: 46 18 8 6 $383,925

Own.– Alfred G. Vanderbilt

Br.– Alfred G. Vanderbilt (Cal)

Tr.– W.C. Winfrey

1Mar52- 7SA	my	1¼	:452 1:104 1:354 2:01	3↑ S Anita H 141k	5	8	88	87¼	67¾	48	Guerin E	114wb	4.30e	87-16	DIntnt1111Mch1154½BFlt1142½	Improved position,no menace	15
16Feb52- 7SA	fst	1⅛	:463 1:104 1:364 1:494	3↑ San Antonio H 29k	2	9	78	88¼	84¼	31	Shoemaker W	120wb	*2.30	91-16	Phil D.117noIntent1181Bed o' Roses1201	Slow start	11
26Jan52- 7SA	fst	1⅛	:47 1:114 1:381 1:512	3↑ ⒻS Margarita H 62k	5	8	75¾	42½	22	11	Shoemaker W	129wb	*.90e	84-19	Bed o' Roses1291Next Move1301½Toto105½	Mild urging	14
10Nov51- 6Jam	fst	1 3/16	:474 1:121 1:374 1:564	3↑ Butler H 60k	1	7	97¼	97¾	51¾	41¾	Guerin E	115wb	3.40	90-18	OilCapitol1081½ThreeRings114hdCountyDelight124nk	Hung	12
6Nov51- 6Jam	fst	1 1/16	:25 :484 1:133 1:443	3↑ ⒻComely H 28k	7	8	88	41¾	1½	11½	Guerin E	127wb	*1.25	89-19	Bed o' Roses1271½Nothirdchance1121¾Regal1112	Driving	8
27Oct51- 6Jam	fst	1⅛	:464 1:11 1:361 1:491	3↑ Westchester H 30k	11	9	811	89¾	610	37¼	Guerin E	116wb	3.75	95-15	BryanG.1175½CountyDelight1241¾Bedo'Ross1161	Forced wide	11
20Oct51- 7GS	fst	1 1/16	:231 :462 1:113 1:433	3↑ ⒻVineland H 31k	3	8	87¼	72¾	21½	13½	Guerin E	126wb	*2.40	92-15	Bed o' Roses1263½Valadium109noDixie Flyer107½	Easily	15
10Oct51- 6Bel	fst	1½	:483 1:132 2:04 2:301	3↑ ⒻLadies H 30k	13	14	1314	85¼	32½	21¼	Guerin E	126wb	5.35	86-15	Marta1111¼Bed o' Roses1263½Kiss Me Kate120½	Good effort	14
22Sep51- 6Aqu	fst	1⅛	:482 1:122 1:382 1:52	3↑ ⒻBeldame 67k	4	5	62¾	42	2hd	22	Guerin E	124wb	6.65	83-14	ThelmaBurger1102Bdo'Roses124½KssMKt119nk	Wide,faltered	14
14Sep51- 6Aqu	fst	1 1/16	:241 :474 1:13 1:444	3↑ ⒻAlw 5000	6	6	616	715	712	712	Guerin E	118wb	*1.60	78-16	Red Camelia1101¼Vulcania1125Wistful121hd	Dull effort	7
27Aug51- 5Sar	fst	6f	:23 :464 1:12	4↑ Alw 3500	5	1	33	33½	1½	1¾	Guerin E	119wb	*1.10	88-22	Bed o' Roses119¾Early Heath1091All at Once1243	Easily	6
3Feb51- 7SA	fst	1¼	:451 1:093 1:351 2:002	Maturity 205k	2	6	57½	32½	2½	31¾	Combest N	110wb	*.90e	96-08	GreatCircle1151¾Lotowhit116hdBdo'Ross1103½	Blocked,lame	11
20Jan51- 7SA	fst	1⅛	:461 1:11 1:361 1:483	3↑ ⒻS Margarita H 60k	1	8	79½	56	44	32¼	Combest N	125wb	*.55e	96-16	SpecialTouch1141Bewitch1221¼Bedo'Roses1251½	Closed fast	8
29Dec50- 7SA	fst	7f	:221 :45 1:092 1:213	3↑ ⒻAnita Chiquita H 15k	7	6	66½	45	21	11	Guerin E	123wb	1.45	101-07	Bedo'Roses1231SpecialTouch1213½SomeGal1071½	Ridden out	8
16Dec50- 7Hol	fst	1⅛	:462 1:103 1:36 1:483	3↑ Sunset H 58k	4	7	613	76¼	54½	63	Combest N	110wb	3.90e	95-12	HillPrince128¾NextMove1141½GreatCircle109nk	Late foot	10
9Dec50- 6Hol	fst	1	:222 :453 1:103 1:353	3↑ Handicap 5000	8	6	66¼	42	1½	12½	Guerin E	118wb	2.60e	99-09	Bed o' Roses1182½Stone Age1101¼Manyunk1201	Drew out	8
2Dec50- 7Hol	fst	1⅛	:47 1:111 1:362 1:492	3↑ ⒻVanity H 30k	6	8	89¾	76¾	45	65¼	Combest N	123wb	*.50e	89-11	Next Move1282¼Bewitch1241Wistful125½	Hung	9
25Nov50- 6Hol	fst	7f	:222 :45 1:092 1:22	3↑ Handicap 7500	9	8	96½	74½	54½	52¾	Guerin E	120wb	*.70e	96-07	Manyunk115nkChutney1081½Stone Age112½	Slow start	9
27Sep50- 6Bel	fst	1⅝	:473 1:362 2:023 2:423	Lawrence Realizatn 22k	4	6	69	31	13	14½	Combest N	107wb	3.20	91-12	Bed o' Roses1074½Greek Ship1183Theory1101¼	Easily	7
16Sep50- 6Aqu	fst	1⅛	:473 1:12 1:37 1:501	3↑ ⒻBeldame H 66k	7	10	912	67	712	88¼	Guerin E	119 w	*1.20e	86-15	Next Move1162¼September1081Wistful1252¼	Dull effort	12
11Sep50- 6Aqu	sly	6f	:234 :473 1:12	3↑ ⒻAlw 4000	4	5	56¼	54	2hd	12½	Guerin E	118 w	*1.25	92-19	Bed o' Roses1182½Leading Home108nkBaby Comet1034	Easily	5
12Aug50- 6Sar	fst	1¼	:473 1:121 1:374 2:03	Travers 23k	5	2	47	34	31	23	Combest N	109 w	*1.35	90-11	Lights Up1103Bed o' Roses1093Passemson1101	Went well	9
15Jly50- 7AP	fst	1¼	:47 1:112 1:353 2:014	Arl Classic 77k	4	8	67¼	31½	2hd	2no	Combest N	110 w	7.40	96-07	Greek Song120noBed o' Roses1101¼Your Host1268	Game try	10
3Jly50- 6Aqu	fst	1 1/16	:232 :47 1:12 1:433	ⒻGazelle 22k	4	6	44½	22	22	21	Scurlock O	116 w	*.25e	95-11	Next Move1211Bed o' Roses1165Renew112¾	In hand	7
27Jun50- 5Aqu	fst	7f	:241 :482 1:122 1:25	ⒻAlw 4000	3	3	33½	33½	11	11¼	Guerin E	121 w	*.50	87-16	Bedo'Roses1211¼MissDegree108noOurPatrice1081½	Easily	4
8Nov49- 6Jam	fst	1 1/16	:24 :47 1:12 1:454	ⒻDemoiselle 56k	5	7	79	45	2hd	11½	Guerin E	116 w	*.50e	84-19	Bedo'Roses1161½NextMove1195RarePerfume1166	Ridden out	12
29Oct49- 6Pim	my	1 1/16	:231 :47 1:122 1:454	ⒻMarguerite 36k	4	5	59	22	2½	14	Guerin E	116 w	*.40	81-20	Bed o' Roses1164Striking1192½Fais Do Do1194	Easily	7
22Oct49- 6Lrl	fst	1 1/16	:23 :473 1:133 1:454	ⒻSelima 52k	8	4	32	3nk	13	17	Guerin E	116 w	*.40	88-19	Bed o' Roses1167Striking1191Busanda1191¼	Easily	9
17Oct49- 6Lrl	fst	1 1/16	:231 :474 1:141 1:452	ⒻAlw 3500	2	3	21½	2½	11	13	Guerin E	122 w	1.90	90-23	Bed o' Roses1223Striking1163½Flying Mane10610	Easily	7
1Oct49- 5Bel	fst	6½f-W	:22 :442 1:09 1:153	Futurity 112k	2	16		1611	1516	117½	Woodhouse H	119 w	8.05e	86-06	Guillotine122¾Theory1222The Diver1222½	Off slowly	17
	Geldings not eligible																
24Sep49- 4Bel	fst	6f-WC	:222 :454 1:111	ⒻMatron 52k	3	8		75	3½	1½	Guerin E	119 w	3.75	85-15	Bed o' Roses119½Fais Do Do119nkStriking1194	Driving	9
20Sep49- 5Bel	fst	5½f-W	:23 :462 1:06	ⒻAlw 4000	5	9		32½	33½	3hd	Scurlock O	122 w	1.80e	84-16	Fais Do Do114noNext Move116hdBed o' Roses1223	Game try	13
16Aug49- 6Sar	fst	6f	:224 :453 1:112	ⒻSpinaway 19k	1	6	32	31½	3½	41½	Guerin E	119wb	10.05	89-13	SundayEvening1111Strikng115nkFsDoDo111nk	Dwelt at start	6
10Aug49- 6Sar	fst	5½f	:222 :454 1:052	ⒻSchuylerville 10k	1	9	95¾	84½	53¼	65	Guerin E	122wb	15.00	85-11	Striking1152½Sunday Evening112½Nazma115½	Off slowly	12
23Jly49- 5Det	fst	6f	:224 :461 1:122	ⒻTomboy 32k	5	7	22½	43½	44½	54¾	Gorman D	121wb	*2.10	81-15	Here'sHoping1102½HighFreqncy1152DinhRos109nk	Weakened	12
9Jly49- 6AP	my	6f	:224 :464 1:153	ⒻArl Lassie 56k	12	12	96¾	76¼	48	3½	Jessop JD	119wb	6.00	67-34	DuchessPeg119hdBabyComet119½Bdo'Ross1196	Strong finish	13
4Jly49- 6Mth	fst	5½f	:23 :482 1:002 1:072	ⒻColleen (Div 2) 12k	1	2	2hd	11	12	12½	Guerin E	119wb	*1.00	87-14	Bedo'Roses1192½SickleFlight1122½WiseCutie1142	Easily	9
18Jun49- 5Aqu	fst	5½f	:232 :47 1:07	ⒻAstoria 13k	2	8	54	45½	24	24½	Guerin E	122wb	*1.35	84-24	BabyComet1194½Bedo'Roses1222½Dentifrice114nk	Went well	10
4Jun49- 5Del	fst	5f	:222 :462 :583	ⒻP Drmmnd (Div 2) 13k	2	4	32	31½	21½	21¾	Gilbert J	122wb	*.45	95-13	Bridal Shower1131¾Bed o' Roses1228Jaleen1102	No excuse	9
28May49- 5GS	fst	5f	:223 :47 :592	ⒻRancocas 14k	2	3	32½	32	32½	1nk	Gilbert J	122wb	*1.40	96-12	Bed o' Roses122nkChloe1173½Bridal Shower117no	Drew out	13
25May49- 6Bel	fst	5f-WC	:23 :462 :592	ⒻNat'l Stallion 24k	3	1		15	16	13	Guerin E	119wb	*.85	83-20	Bedo'Roses1193SetAside119½ThreeandTwo114	Ridden out	4
20May49- 5Bel	fst	5f-WC	:222 :453 :582	ⒻAlw 4000	2	6	1½	51¾	43	42¼	Guerin E	115 w	2.25	86-07	Wise Cutie115¾Puff119hdRare Perfume1151½	No mishap	10
7May49- 4Bel	fst	4½f-W	:214 :451 :512	ⒻFashion 13k	6	1		33	33	2hd	Guerin E	115 w	*1.70	97-09	RarePerfume110hdBdo'Ross115nkHghFrquncy1143	Just missed	7
29Apr49- 3Jam	fst	5f	:232 :472 1:003	ⒻMd Sp Wt	6	6	11½	13	14	13	Guerin E	116 w	*1.95	87-16	Bedo'Roses1163RunningStory1161Stefanella116nk	In hand	12
20Apr49- 6Jam	fst	5f	:223 :47 1:00	ⒻRosedale 13k	11	11	77¾	510	512	812	Guerin E	115 w	8.75	78-17	Baby Comet1143½Rare Perfume1106Abbie Co114hd	Weakened	11
	Previously trained by L. McCoy																
16Feb49- 1SA	fst	3f	:221 :333	ⒻMd Sp Wt	6	12			106¾	56½	Gilbert J	115 w	*1.25	--	Prince'sBd1152½Bullrmmbr1151½RoylSnt115½	Close quarters	13

140 CHAMPIONS

Berseem

dkb. c. 1950, by Bernborough (Emborough)–Little Priss, by Sweep All

Own.– A. Hirschberg

Br.– Charles T. Fisher (Ky)

Tr.– R. Cornell

Lifetime record: 60 21 11 5 $189,525

31May56- 7Hol	fst	6f	:221 :45 :57 1:09	4↑	Handicap 12000	2	2	11	1½	2½	42¼	Shoemaker W	122wb	*.90	97-09	Scent118hdOne Ton Tony1142Karim115hd		8
	Saved ground,weakened																	
12May56- 4Hol	fst	6f	:222 :45 :57 1:092	4↑	Alw 7500	2	4	11½	12	11½	21½	Shoemaker W	117wb	*.65	95-11	Spring Count1121½Berseem1174½Poona II117no		5
	Rushed to front,outrun late																	
12Sep55- 7BM	fst	6f	:221 :45 1:094	3↑	Autumn H 11k	4	1	11¼	11½	11½	1¾	Longden J	126wb	2.10	98-14	Berseem126¾MisterGus124nkTheCharactr111¾	Cleverly rated	6
25Jly55- 7Hol	fst	6f	:22 :443 :564 1:091	3↑	Los Angeles H 28k	8	3	31	3nk	1hd	42½	Shoemaker W	126wb	*1.55	95-10	Karim112¾History Book1101¼The Character109½	Weakened	9
25Jun55- 7Hol	fst	1 1/16	:224 :452 1:093 1:404	3↑	Inglewood H 27k	7	3	11	1hd	42	45	Longden J	118wb	6.70	93-06	Determine124hdMisterGus114½Aldon1174½	Set pace,gave way	7
18Jun55- 7Hol	fst	7f	:214 :44 1:082 1:211	3↑	Lakes &Flowers H 28k	8	1	12	14	13	21¾	Shoemaker W	126wb	*1.65	92-09	Porterhouse1161¾Bersem126noAldon119no	Could not hold on	10
13May55- 7Hol	fst	6f	:22 :444 1:09	3↑	Hol Premiere H 28k	7	4	51¾	31	22	22¼	Shoemaker W	128wb	*.95	98-11	El Drag1122¼Berseem128½Porterhouse1191	Finished gamely	9
9Mar55- 7SA	fst	1 1/16	:233 :454 1:10 1:42	3↑	S Barbara H 28k	6	1	11	12	12	11½	Longden J	120wb	3.10	94-12	Berseem1201½Joe Jones1174Dawn Lark107½	Going away	10
2Mar55- 7SA	fst	7f	:22 :442 1:091 1:221	3↑	C J Fitzgerald H 22k	6	2	2½	1½	11	2hd	Shoemaker W	130wb	*.85	92-13	Karim114hdBerseem130hdFabulist1104¾	Barely missed	7
22Feb55- 5SA	fst	6f	:221 :443 1:091	3↑	Handicap 7500	1	2	1½	1½	11	13½	Shoemaker W	128wb	2.35	99-12	Berseem1283½Karim114noHour Regards1192¾	Drew clear	6
12Feb55- 5SA	fst	6f	:222 :444 1:09	4↑	Handicap 6000	1	4	2hd	1hd	1hd	11½	Shoemaker W	125wb	*.70	100-08	Bersm1251½OneTonTony1084½DonMcCoy1103½	Under urging	8
2Feb55- 7SA	fst	7f	:222 :452 1:101 1:222	3↑	San Carlos H 23k	11	2	2½	32½	1113	1112	Westrope J	122wb	3.45	79-16	Porterhouse115¾Imbros1301¾Encono1142	Stopped badly	11
28Dec54- 7SA	fst	6f	:22 :442 1:09	3↑	Palos Verdes H 23k	7	2	32	32	32½	2¾	Shoemaker W	124wb	*1.85	99-08	Imbros128¾Berseem1241¾Hour Regards110no	Game try	13
1Nov54- 7GG	fst	6f	:214 :443 1:09	3↑	Handicap 5000	3	2	31	21½	21	11¾	Shoemaker W	122wb	1.30	96-15	Berseem1221¾LeftyJms1062¾Imbros1261½	Drew clear handily	5
25Sep54- 8Tan	fst	6f	:223 :452 1:094	3↑	Penninsula H 16k	7	1	11½	13	1hd	1nk	Longden J	124wb	*1.20	102-08	Berseem124nkDuke's Lea1152¼Stranglehold1263½	Hard drive	7
9Sep54-11Sac	fst	1 1/16	:234 :464 1:112 1:422	3↑	Governor's H 16k	2	2	11½	13	14	14	Shoemaker W	127wb	*.50	100-08	Berseem1274Scotch Port107hdSilverado1192½	Drew out	5
2Sep54-10Sac	fst	1 70	:224 :454 1:111 1:424	3↑	Handicap 5620	3	3	1½	14	14	22	Phillippi J	125wb	*.45	89-11	Silver Ado1142Berseem1252½Chanlea1133	Gave way	7
27Aug54- 7Dmr	fst	6f	:221 :45 1:092	3↑	Handicap 7500	4	3	2½	13	12	12½	Shoemaker W	120wb	*1.15	99-09	Berseem1202½Big Noise110¾Gesticulator108¾	Won handily	6
	Previously trained by F.E. Childs																	
19Jun54- 7Hol	fst	7f	:214 :441 1:083 1:211	3↑	Lakes &Flowers H 28k	3	7	75½	74¾	77½	98½	Harmatz W	110wb	8.35	92-06	Curragh King107¾Imbros1283By Zeus1153	No factor	10
12Jun54- 7Hol	fst	1 1/16	:224 :453 1:093 1:41	3↑	Californian 121k	6	6	56½	54½	49	48¾	Harmatz W	114wb	35.20	94-06	Imbros1181Determine1151¾High Scud1146	Wide	9
26May54- 7Hol	fst	7f	:222 :444 1:091 1:213	3↑	Handicap 15000	5	3	32	31	43	44¼	Scurlock O	114wb	6.60	95-10	High Scud109½Kingly110nkImbros1303½	Held well	7
14May54- 7Hol	fst	6f	:22 :45 :571 1:091	3↑	Hol Premiere H 27k	5	5	63¾	33	43½	44¾	Scurlock O	119wb	6.85	95-00	Stranglehold115¾Imbros1323½Big Noise110½	Evenly	7
8May54- 8BM	fst	6f	:214 :442 1:093	3↑	Children's Hospital H 28k	6	2	46	45½	74¾	73¾	Harmatz W	122wb	*2.10	95-10	Kingly109½Stranglehold1162¼GoldenAbby109½	Flattened out	9
1May54- 8BM	fst	1⅛	:462 1:104 1:354 1:483	3↑	W P Kyne H 100k	5	2	31½	63¾	89½	79¼	Harmatz W	118wb	7.90	93-10	Imbros127½Fleet Bird1214Trusting109hd	Gave way after 5f	12
24Apr54- 8BM	fst	1	:224 :451 1:094 1:352	3↑	GJ Knight H 23k	8	6	43½	33½	47	66½	Harmatz W	121wb	5.30	94-09	Imbros1242½Stranglehold111¾Correspondent113hd	Gave way	11
17Apr54- 7BM	fst	1	:232 :463 1:111 1:354	3↑	Handicap 7500	1	2	31½	2½	2½	1no	Harmatz W	118wb	3.25	99-09	Berseem118noImbros1233½High Scud112¾	Driving	6
27Mar54- 8BM	gd	1 1/16	:233 :471 1:113 1:434	3↑	Bay Meadows H 28k	2	3	32½	3nk	43	44	Harmatz W	121wb	*1.30	85-18	Dcort'd113noCyclotron1171½Southrlngton1112½	Saved ground	8
3Mar54- 7SA	fst	7f	:221 :45 1:091 1:214	3↑	C J Fitzgerald H 22k	2	5	32	12	14	13½	Harmatz W	123wb	5.65	96-10	Berseem1233½Woodchck1221¼Joe Jones1172½		7
	Saved ground,ridden out																	
27Feb54- 7SA	fst	1¼	:453 1:094 1:343 2:003	3↑	S Anita H 140k	4	7	118	1616	1625	1421	Arcaro E	115wb	7.80	76-06	Rejectd1181¼Imbros1202¾Cyclotron1161¾	Taken up 1st turn	17
20Feb54- 6SA	fst	1 1/16	:231 :462 1:102 1:421	4↑	Handicap 10000	7	5	53½	32	1½	1no	Harmatz W	114wb	6.50	97-06	Bersem114noCyclotron1152½Lffngo1113	Bore out final turn	9
12Feb54- 7SA	fst	6f	:222 :451 1:092	3↑	Lincoln's Bday H 22k	8	3	73¾	74¾	77	42¾	Longden J	120wb	3.60	95-09	Imbros1281Woodchuck122nkCyclotron1211½	Forced wide	8
4Feb54- 7SA	fst	6f	:221 :451 1:09	3↑	Handicap 7500	1	6	42½	42¼	31	31½	Shoemaker W	118wb	*1.55	98-07	Imbros1241¼Hill Gail120nkBerseem1183½	Broke slowly	6
2Jan54- 7SA	fst	7f	:224 :45 1:084 1:203		Malibu Sequet 28k	5	2	2½	1hd	1hd	2no	Shoemaker W	114wb	*1.45	102-06	Imbros118noBerseem1144½Joe Jones1151	Just missed	7
29Dec53- 7SA	fst	6f	:222 :443 1:09		Alw 10000	1	9	1½	12	13	12½	Shoemaker W	114wb	*1.70	100-07	Berseem1142½Ali's Gem1222Chanlea118hd	Handily	11
12Dec53- 9BM	fst	1	:224 :454 1:101 1:362		Children's Hospital H 16k	1	4	43½	3nk	11½	11	Harmatz W	120wb	5.00	95-08	Berseem1201Golden Abbey113noResistance1111½	Driving	6
26Nov53- 9BM	sl	6f	:224 :46 1:103		San Jose H 11k	7	1	52¼	31	1hd	22	Harmatz W	120 w	4.55	92-18	Imbros1222Berseem1203Golden Abbey110no	Weakened	8
23Oct53- 7GG	fst	1 1/16	:231 :461 1:101 1:421		Handicap 3500	3	3	2hd	11½	15	12¼	Shoemaker W	118wb	2.15	94-14	Berseem1182¼Postillion107noSix Fifteen114nk	Handily	7
17Oct53- 8GG	fst	1 1/16	:224 :454 1:10 1:421		Oakland H 29k	3	1	11	2hd	33½	56	Shoemaker W	116wb	5.20e	88-12	Rejected116nkHistory Book1115Golden Abbey111½	Gave way	14
10Oct53- 8GG	gd	1	:23 :46 1:104 1:362	3↑	GG Mile H 28k	4	1	11	87¾	813	821	Pearson B	111wb	14.70	65-20	[D]Fleet Bird1221¼Goose Khal1251¾High Scud1134	Quit	8
28Sep53- 7GG	fst	6f	:222 :444 1:084	3↑	Handicap 6000	3	1	2hd	1½	13	2nk	York R	113wb	1.55	97-13	Cyclotron119nkBerseem1132½Ali's Gem116nk	Just failed	6
19Sep53- 8GG	fst	6f	:214 :442 1:084		Berkley H 17k	4	3	2½	2½	11½	11½	Shoemaker W	117wb	*.60	97-09	Berseem1171½Karim1132¾Six Fifteen1131¾	Ridden out	8
10Sep53- 7Dmr	fst	1	:231 :462 1:11 1:362		[R]Adios H 11k	4	2	2hd	12	12	12¼	Shoemaker W	115wb	*1.15	94-12	Berseem1152¼Last Wave1081½Karim1173½	Driving	6
2Sep53- 7Dmr	fst	1	:231 :462 1:103 1:36		Handicap 7500	6	3	41	43¼	64¼	64¾	Glisson G	118wb	5.85	91-11	OverandUndr110½SmartBarbara1182¼Krm114nk	Wide,weakened	6
	Previously owned by Dixiana;previously trained by J.C. Hodgins																	
11Jly53- 7AP	fst	1	:222 :451 1:084 1:344		Handicap 7500	2	5	41½	3nk	22	3½	Arcaro E	114wb	4.70	97-06	Precious Stone107½Dr.Stanley113hdBerseem1141	Held well	9
4Jly53- 7AP	fst	7f	:221 :45 1:093 1:22		W Wright Mem 30k	2	9	137	1415	1218	1215	Heckmann J	116 w	8.90e	85-06	Van Crosby1163Sir Mango1205Platan116½	No factor	18
26Jun53- 7AP	gd	6f	:223 :454 1:111	3↑	Alw 5000	5	6	54	55	45	34¾	Erb D	118 w	4.60	85-18	Van Crosby1183½Blaze1101¼Berseem1183	Driving	7
30May53- 7Haw	fst	1⅛	:473 1:122 1:382 1:521		Peabody Mem 57k	5	3	32½	23	23	65	Heckmann J	121 w	6.50e	80-16	Royal Bay Gem1261Platan121¾Sir Mango1231	Bid,tired	10
2May53- 6CD	fst	7f	:224 :451 1:101 1:231		Alw 6000	7	5	56½	33½	2hd	11	Arcaro E	115 w	*1.50	97-09	Berseem1151Platan1153Sir Mango1156		8
28Apr53- 7CD	fst	1	:224 :452 1:101 1:36		Derby Trial 15k	9	7	78	57½	86	711	Arcaro E	114 w	*2.70e	86-14	Dark Star1154Money Broker1182¾Spy Defense112no	Wide	14
11Apr53- 5Kee	fst	6f	:23 :464 1:12		Alw 3250	8	1	74¼	31½	12	14	Arcaro E	117 w	*.60	92-10	Berseem1174Jim Brier1112¼Blenriam114¾	Going away	9
11Feb53- 5FG	fst	6f	:224 :463 1:122		Alw 2500	2	4	33	21½	11	11	Keene H	116 w	*1.40	91-22	Berseem1161Paytu1196Star Request1131	Driving	9
1Nov52- 6CD	fst	1	:224 :46 1:11 1:372		Ky Jockey Club 47k	5	2	22½	34	34½	35½	Heckmann J	116 w	1.30e	84-15	Straight Face1224½Spy Defense1161Berseem1165	Weakened	7
25Oct52- 4Kee	fst	6f	:224 :463 1:112		Alw 3000	8	1	32½	32	11½	18	Heckmann J	120 w	*1.70	95-11	Berseem1208Uncle Tom114noBull Skin120nk	Easily	8
22Sep52- 5Haw	fst	6f	:224 :454 1:114		©Alw 4000	4	5	53¼	23	22	22½	Erb D	115 w	*.90	86-17	Scriptwriter1152½Berseem1155New Stream1121¼	Raced wide	9
10Sep52- 1Haw	fst	6f	:223 :454 1:11		©Md Sp Wt	9	5	21	11½	14	18	Erb D	118 w	*2.30	94-07	Berseem1188Coherence118¾Blended1182	In hand	12
20Aug52- 1Was	gd	6f	:23 :472 1:134		©Md Alw 3500	7	2	45	36½	38	613	Erb D	118 w	*1.50	64-24	American Pluck118hdRico Vino1188Pipe of Peace1181¾	Quit	10
6Aug52- 1Was	fst	5½f	:224 :462 :583 1:044		©Md Sp Wt	4	3	63¼	22	23	23	Brooks S	118 w	4.30	91-12	Nero Fiddled1183Berseem1181Ricacho1183	Held well	12
30Jly52- 1Was	fst	5½f	:224 :453 :572 1:041		©Md Sp Wt	1	2	44	46	35½	34	Brooks S	118 w	5.30	93-06	Van Crosby1134Nero Fiddled118hdBerseem1182½	No rally	12
23Jly52- 3AP	hy	5½f	:233 :482 1:022 1:092		©Md Sp Wt	8	6	66¾	69½	914	916	Brooks S	118 w	*2.30	57-28	Preposterous118½VanCrosby1183½Sampan1182	Disliked going	10
12Jly52- 1AP	fst	5½f	:224 :464 :584 1:054		Md Sp Wt	3	8	64¼	75¼	77¾	54¾	Brooks S	118 w	5.00	86-16	Bob Away118noTime to Khal1083Hardhack118½	No mishap	10

Blue Sparkler

ch. f. 1952, by Knave High (Jack High)–Blue Tiara, by Opera Hat — **Lifetime record: 22 11 7 0 $198,625**

Own.– Woodland Farm
Br.– Woodland Farm (NJ)
Tr.– Harry Wells

22Sep56- 7Bel	fst	1⅛	:452 1:101 1:363 1:50	3↑ ⒻBeldame H 66k	11	1	12	12	2½	4¾	Scurlock O	126wb	4.85	88-13	Levee115½Amoret114hdSerchng123nk	Held well under impost	14
8Sep56- 9Ran	fst	1⅛	:461 1:094 1:341 1:471	3↑ Buckeye H 46k	7	1	11½	1½	1hd	2¾	Scurlock O	120wb	3.30	103-06	Bardstown118¾Blue Sparkler1204Paper Tiger115¾	Gamely	12
25Aug56- 7Atl	fst	7f	:22 :442 1:084 1:223	3↑ Longport H 24k	4	2	3nk	1½	2½	21½	Scurlock O	124wb	*2.80	91-18	Bardstown1191½Blue Sparkler1246Skipper Bill122½	Gamely	13
11Aug56- 7Atl	fst	1⅛	:48 1:114 1:364 1:494	3↑ Atl City H 100k	1	1	11½	12	11½	1½	Boulmetis S	113wb	8.70	89-18	BlueSparkler113½SkipperBill115noFind1194	Roused sharply	7
1Aug56- 7Jam	fst	6f	:224 :453 1:11	3↑ ⒻChamplain H 23k	5	3	31	2½	11	12½	Scurlock O	125wb	*1.90	92-16	[D]BlueSparkler1252½Gandharva1182BlueBanner122hd	Bore in	13
	Disqualified and placed second																
21Jly56- 7Jam	sly	1 1/16	:233 :471 1:12 1:43	3↑ ⒻBellerose H 27k	4	1	12½	11½	2½	22½	Scurlock O	125wb	*1.35	94-12	Parlo1212½BlueSprklr1251¾Mnotck119hd	Made pace,gave way	7
7Jly56- 6Mth	sl	1 1/16	:232 :474 1:114 1:443	3↑ ⒻMolly Pitcher H 28k	1	1	12	16	16	18	Scurlock O	120wb	*2.00	92-20	Blue Sparkler1208Rico Reto1171Another World1102½	Easily	9
30Jun56- 7Del	fst	1¼	:451 1:101 1:362 2:03	3↑ ⒻDelaware H 156k	13	1	13	2hd	2½	75¼	Scurlock O	118wb	9.30	82-14	FlowerBowl1122Manotick122¾OpenSesame113hd	Speed,tired	15
16Jun56- 6Mth	fst	6f	:212 :433 1:091	3↑ ⒻRegret H 22k	8	4	1hd	12½	13	12	Scurlock O	119wb	*1.50	99-06	BlueSparklr1192Jimminetty114¾PromptImpulse115¾	Driving	9
22May56- 7GS	fst	6f	:22 :444 1:093	4↑ ⒻAlw 7500	7	7	31½	13	13	11	Scurlock O	110wb	4.70	96-10	BlueSprklr1101MizClementn121¾PromptImpuls1191	Handily	9
6Aug55- 6Mth	fst	1⅛	:47 1:112 1:371 1:503	ⒻMth Oaks 61k	3	1	15	2hd	2hd	2nk	Lasswell G	121wb	12.50	93-18	Misty Morn121nkBlue Sparkler1217Manotick121¾	Sharp try	11
20Jly55- 6Mth	fst	6f	:212 :441 1:102	ⒻMiss Woodford 25k	4	6	31½	2hd	1½	1nk	Lasswell G	118wb	7.40	93-13	Blue Sparkler118nkGandharva121½Sometime Thing1211½	Held	13
6Jly55- 6Mth	fst	6f	:214 :444 1:101	ⒻAlw 6000	6	5	1½	1½	13	13	Lasswell G	118wb	*1.20	94-13	Blue Sparkler1183Wagon Drill1151½Miss Misty1152	Easily	10
30Jun55- 6Mth	fst	6f	:213 :443 1:103	Alw 5000	5	2	21½	2hd	1hd	2½	Lasswell G	119wb	6.60e	91-08	WreckMaster118½BlueSparkler1192Indicative1121½	Faltered	8
30May55- 7GS	gd	6f	:222 :451 1:103	ⒻBetsy Ross 31k	7	8	74¾	68½	812	79	Lasswell G	121 w	13.20	82-17	Gandharva1212Sometime Thing1211½Myrtle's Jet1214	Tired	14
14May55- 7Pim	sly	1 1/16	:223 :462 1:114 1:461	ⒻBlack-Eyed Susan 26k	4	4	42½	55½	814	916	Lasswell G	121 w	10.00	63-22	HighVoltage1211BlessPat1213HenParty121hd	Had early foot	9
5May55- 7GS	fst	6f	:221 :452 1:113	Alw 5000	5	1	3½	1½	12	1½	Lasswell G	117 w	*.60	90-14	BlueSparkler117½WindsorKing1121½Ellen'sSpy117¾	Driving	8
27Oct54- 7GS	fst	6f	:222 :454 1:114	ⓈNJ Breeders' 11k	3	2	42½	32½	1hd	11	Lasswell G	119 w	1.70e	89-15	[D]Blue Sparkler1191Bunny's Babe122nkDerry1112½	Bore in	7
	Disqualified and placed second																
12Oct54- 7GS	fst	1 70	:223 :462 1:12 1:442	ⒻWanda 33k	2	1	11½	12	2hd	2nk	Lasswell G	114 w	*2.50	82-16	[D]BlueBanner113nkBlueSparklr114½MyBluSky1092½	Game try	15
	Placed first through disqualification																
29Sep54- 7Atl	fst	6f	:223 :45 1:094	ⓈHome Bred H 11k	1	8	3½	22	21	1hd	Lasswell G	113 w	*1.40e	96-10	Blue Sparkler113hdDecimal1093Sorceress1151½	Hard urged	9
14Sep54- 5Atl	fst	6f	:221 :45 1:111	ⒻAlw 3500	7	8	77¾	34½	23	11¼	Lasswell G	114 w	2.80	89-12	Blue Sparkler1141¼Sue Pat110hdPrincess Kiss119¾	Easily	9
30Aug54- 3Atl	fst	6f	:23 :46 1:102	ⒻMd Sp Wt	10	10	72¼	32	33	1¾	Lasswell G	119 w	15.00e	93-09	Blue Sparkler119¾Hello Mom119¾Linda's Dream1196	Driving	12

Bold Ruler

dkb. c. 1954, by Nasrullah (Nearco)–Miss Disco, by Discovery — **Lifetime record: 33 23 4 2 $764,204**

Own.– Wheatley Stable
Br.– Wheatley Stable (Ky)
Tr.– J. Fitzsimmons

26Jly58- 6Jam	fst	1 3/16	:471 1:114 1:37 1:553	3↑ Brooklyn H 57k	1	3	37½	51½	78	715	Arcaro E	136wb	*.40	83-15	Cohoes1101[D]Shrpsburg1146½ThrdBrothr110hd	Tired,roughed	8
19Jly58- 6Mth	fst	1¼	:48 1:12 1:362 2:013	3↑ Monmouth H 110k	1	1	11½	1hd	1½	1¾	Arcaro E	134wb	*.30	98-20	BoldRuler134¾Sharpsburg1136Bll'sSkyBoy105¾	Well in hand	6
4Jly58- 6Bel	fst	1¼	:471 1:103 1:351 2:01	3↑ Suburban H 83k	1	3	3nk	11	12	1no	Arcaro E	134wb	*.50	95-11	BoldRuler134noClm1091½ThrdBrothr1101¼	Strong drive,held	8
25Jun58- 6Bel	fst	1⅛	:473 1:111 1:352 1:482	3↑ Stymie H 28k	3	1	12½	12½	16	15	Arcaro E	133wb	*.40	94-18	BoldRuler1335AdmiralVee112¾PopCorn1081¼	Speed to spare	7
14Jun58- 7Bel	fst	1	:231 :461 1:103 1:353	3↑ Metropolitan H 58k	1	1	12	11	11½	22	Arcaro E	135wb	*.95	94-13	GallantMan1302BoldRuler1351½Clm114nk	Tired under impost	10
30May58- 7Bel	fst	7f	:223 :453 1:101 1:223	3↑ Carter H 58k	3	1	41¼	31	11½	11½	Arcaro E	135wb	*.80	94-17	BoldRuler1351½TickTock1131½GllntMn128no	Briskly handled	9
17May58- 7Bel	fst	6f-WC	:22 :443 1:09	3↑ Toboggan H 29k	2	2		3nk	2½	1½	Arcaro E	133wb	*.40	94-08	BoldRuler133½Clem1172TickTock1163	Under strong handling	10
9Nov57- 7GS	gd	1¼	:471 1:111 1:364 2:013	3↑ Trenton H 82k	1	1	18	13½	13	12¼	Arcaro E	122wb	1.60	97-14	BoldRuler1222¼GallantMan1248½RoundTable124	Ridden out	3
2Nov57- 7GS	sly	1 1/16	:231 :462 1:11 1:441	Benjamin Franklin H 27k	4	1	19	111	114	112	Arcaro E	136wb	*.20	89-20	BoldRuler13612Sarno1096JetColonel1132½	Breezing all way	4
19Oct57- 7Jam	fst	1 1/16	:234 :463 1:103 1:424	3↑ Queens County H 28k	1	1	14	16	16	12½	Arcaro E	133wb	*.25	96-15	Bold Ruler1332½Promised Land1113½Greek Spy114½	Eased up	6
9Oct57- 7Bel	sly	7f	:223 :45 1:084 1:212	2↑ Vosburgh H 23k	3	1	2hd	11½	15	19	Arcaro E	130wb	*.40	103-09	BoldRulr1309TckTock117½St.AmourII1141¾	Fast pace,in hand	8
28Sep57- 7Bel	fst	1¼	:471 1:11 1:36 2:01	3↑ Woodward 106k	2	2	21	11	2½	33½	Arcaro E	120wb	2.15	91-13	Dedicate1261½GallantMn1202BoldRulr120hd	Took lead,tired	4
14Sep57- 7Bel	sly	1	:23 :454 1:094 1:35	Jerome H 29k	6	3	3½	11	13	16	Arcaro E	130wb	*.20e	99-07	BoldRuler1306Bureaucracy1131¼WingedMercury1062	In hand	6
9Sep57- 7Bel	fst	6f	:222 :453 1:101	Handicap 15000	1	2	2hd	1hd	14	15½	Arcaro E	128wb	*.85	98-13	BoldRuler1285½GreekGame1215Egotistcl115nk	Scored easily	8
15Jun57- 6Bel	fst	1½	:464 1:102 2:012 2:263	Belmont 113k	1	1	13	1hd	21½	312	Arcaro E	126wb	*.85	93-07	GallantMan1268InsideTract1264BoldRuler1269	Tired badly	6
18May57- 7Pim	fst	1 3/16	:462 1:103 1:363 1:561	Preakness 113k	5	1	11	11½	12	12	Arcaro E	126wb	1.40	92-13	BoldRuler1262IronLiege126nkInsideTrct1262¼	Well handled	7
13May57- 0Pim	fst	1 1/16	:231 :464 1:11 1:433	Alw 6000	3	2	12	1hd	1hd	11	Arcaro E	124wb	-	92-16	Bold Ruler1241Inswept12012Convoy117	No difficulty	3
	Special event between 7th and 8th races - No wagering																
4May57- 7CD	fst	1¼	:47 1:112 1:364 2:021	Ky Derby 152k	7	2	32	31½	51¼	45¾	Arcaro E	126 w	*1.20	90-12	IronLiege126noGallantMan1262¾RoundTable1263	No excuse	9
20Apr57- 7Jam	fst	1⅛	:48 1:12 1:361 1:484	Wood Memorial 59k	2	1	1½	1hd	2hd	1no	Arcaro E	126 w	*.50	102-10	BoldRuler126noGallantMan1266PromisedLand1262¼	Just up	7
30Mar57- 7GP	fst	1⅛	:462 1:102 1:343 1:464	Fla Derby 123k	1	2	21	21	1hd	21½	Arcaro E	122 w	*.60	107-06	Gen.Duk1221½BoldRulr122hdIronLg1182¼	Reached lead,tired	5
2Mar57- 7Hia	fst	1⅛	:452 1:102 1:342 1:47	Flamingo 131k	2	3	21	11½	12	1nk	Arcaro E	122 w	*.50	101-07	BoldRuler122nkGen.Duke1222¾IronLiege12212	Held gamely	7
16Feb57- 7Hia	fst	1⅛	:462 1:102 1:343 1:472	Everglades 30k	4	1	11½	11½	11	2hd	Arcaro E	126 w	*.40	99-10	Gen.Duke114hdBoldRuler1266IronLg1171¾	Strong try,headed	7
30Jan57- 7Hia	fst	7f	:223 :45 1:091 1:22	Bahamas 26k	2	3	12	11½	14	14½	Atkinson T	126 w	3.85e	100-11	BoldRuler1264½Gen.Duke1142FederalHll1261¼	Scored easily	11
6Nov56- 7Jam	fst	1 1/16	:24 :48 1:13 1:453	©Remsen 96k	5	8	87¼	89	1019	-	Arcaro E	122 w	*.60	- -	Ambhavng1222½Missle1221½Finlandia122nk	Poor start,blocked	11
	Geldings not eligible																
27Oct56- 7GS	gd	1 1/16	:221 :454 1:12 1:444	Garden State 319k	1	3	33	1724	1734	1724	Atkinson T	122 w	*2.10	62-18	Barbizon122noFederalHill122nkAmrullh1223	Stumbled early	19
13Oct56- 7Bel	fst	6½-WC	:214 :442 1:083 1:151	Futurity 124k	8	2		22	13	12¼	Arcaro E	122 w	*1.25	96-04	BoldRuler1222¼GreekGame122noAmrullh122nk	Under pressure	13
	Geldings not eligible																
5Oct56- 6Bel	fst	6f-WC	:22 :442 1:083	Sp Wt 7500	7	4		2hd	1hd	1½	Guerin E	118 w	*.90	96-04	BoldRuler118½Missile1182½Mqult118½	Under strong pressure	9
24Sep56- 6Bel	sly	6f-WC	:223 :453 1:101	Alw 5000	1	3		2hd	2hd	21¼	Arcaro E	122 w	*.95e	87-19	Nashville1161¼Bold Ruler1221½Bureaucracy113nk	Bore out	6
6Jun56- 7Bel	fst	5f-WC	:22 :441 :56	Juvenile 33k	1	1		21½	21½	11	Arcaro E	122 w	*.60e	99-05	Bold Ruler1221King Hairan1225Supernatural1225	In hand	8
24May56- 6Bel	fst	5f-WC	:221 :451 :571	Alw 5000	7	4		2hd	1½	1nk	Arcaro E	122 w	*.55e	93-13	Bold Ruler122nkKing Hairan1227Bureaucracy1195	All out	9
2May56- 7Jam	fst	5f	:23 :463 :594	©Youthful 17k	8	6	41	2hd	1hd	13½	Atkinson T	122 w	*1.00e	91-19	Bold Ruler1223½Red Cadet1221½Encore1223½	Well in hand	10
19Apr56- 5Jam	fst	5f	:223 :47 1:00	Alw 4000	4	2	2hd	2hd	2hd	11	Atkinson T	118 w	3.15	90-20	Bold Ruler1181Red Cadet1181¾Missile1181½	Ridden out	8
9Apr56- 4Jam	gd	5f	:232 :474 1:002	©Md Sp Wt	2	3	21½	2hd	11½	13½	Atkinson T	118 w	*1.55	88-15	BoldRuler1183½WolfBadge118½ScotchRoyal1182	Easy score	6

Bornastar

dkb. f. 1953, by Alibhai (Hyperion)–Farmerette, by Sickle — **Lifetime record: 43 19 7 2 $270,178**

Own.– J.G. Brown
Br.– Shawnee Farm (Ky)
Tr.– W.G. Sparks

21Sep59- 7Aqu	fst	1	:223 :45 1:094 1:36	3↑ ⒻMaskette H 29k	5	6	62¾	53	33	32¾	Arcaro E	119	8.70	- -	Idun1191¼Temptd1261½Bornstr1192	Raced evenly in stretch	10
2Sep59- 7Bel	sly	7f	:22 :443 1:092 1:223	3↑ ⒻVagrancy H 29k	10	6	75¾	76¼	65¾	47	Church K	122	4.45	87-16	DandyBlitzen1131HoneysGem1185Idun1121	Drifted out turn	12
19Aug59- 5AP	fst	7f	:224 :453 1:102 1:231	3↑ ⒻAlw 5000	7	2	43½	32½	1hd	12½	Church K	111	*.70	92-12	Bornastar1112½LaPlume109¾Aesthetic1115	Under mild drive	7
15Aug59- 8AP	my	1⅛	:48 1:123 1:392 1:53	3↑ ⒻArl Matron H 57k	11	9	99	711	715	69¼	Church K	122	3.50	68-19	WiggleII1163HoneysGem1183½BornRich111¾	No real threat	12
25Jly59- 6Del	fst	1¼	:462 1:111 1:37 2:033	3↑ ⒻDelaware H 155k	1	5	57	42½	43	43¾	Church K	124	3.40	80-18	Endine117½Polamby114¾Tempted1192½	Well placed,no rally	11
18Jly59- 6Del	fst	1 1/16	:231 :464 1:112 1:433	3↑ ⒻNew Castle 35k	3	3	32½	21½	33	22¾	Church K	126	4.90	90-18	Tempted1162¾Bornstr126½Chstos112no	Showed a good effort	10

Date-Race	Cond	Dist	Fractions	Race	PP	St	1c	2c	Str	Fin	Jockey	Wt	Eq	Odds	Spd	Top Finishers	Comment	Fld
20Jun59- 8Was	fst	1	:22 :442 1:084 1:34	3↑ ⒻBeverly H 58k	2	4	63½	33	43	42¼	Church K	126		*.80	95-05	HoneysGem115hdIndianMd1092MllyK.108hd	Lacked room early	14
3Jun59- 7Was	fst	6f	:222 :444 1:092	3↑ ⒻAlw 4000	4	4	53¼	54½	21	11¼	Church K	118		*.80	98-05	Bornastar1181¼Tinkalero116¾Betty Linn1132¼	Won in hand	5
1Nov58- 7GS	fst	1⅛	:47 1:113 1:38 1:503	3↑ ⒻVineland H 58k	9	5	53	2½	1½	1¾	Church K	124	w	*2.10	84-23	Bornastar124¾RareTreat1121¾AGlittr1213	Under hard drive	10
23Oct58- 6Kee	fst	1⅛	:473 1:113 1:361 1:492	3↑ ⒻSpinster 73k	3	2	2½	12	12	15	Church K	123	w	*.30	90-19	Bornstr1235MoonGlory1193¼Woodlwn1231½	Very handy score	8
16Oct58- 6Kee	fst	*7f	1:261	3↑ ⒻAlw 5000	4	4	33½	21½	1hd	11¼	Church K	119	w	*.20	97-13	Bornastr1191¼BugBrush1162HstyDoll1132¼	Very handy score	6
27Sep58- 7CD	fst	1 1/16	:24 :473 1:112 1:423	3↑ Alw 6500	1	4	34	1hd	11	12	Church K	119	w	*.60	105-08	Bornastar1192Dru Away1182Praised110¾	Going away	8
20Sep58- 8CD	sly	1	:232 :463 1:114 1:371	3↑ ⒻFalls City H 22k	8	3	2hd	1½	14	16	Church K	122	w	*.70	89-16	Bornastar1226LittlPch1131¼Woodlwn1111¼	As rider pleased	9
13Sep58- 7CD	fst	6f	:223 :453 1:102	3↑ ⒻAlw 5000	6	5	66½	63¼	11	12	Church K	118	w	*1.10	96-10	Bornastar1182Gerts Image114¾Woodlawn112nk	Easily best	9
26Jly58- 6Del	fst	1¼	:464 1:111 1:361 2:03	3↑ ⒻDelaware H 160k	1	11	88¼	89¼	68	109¾	Church K	121	w	5.70	77-12	Endine111noDottedLn1161Woodlwn1081	Showed a dull effort	16
19Jly58- 6Del	fst	1 1/16	:231 :462 1:104 1:441	3↑ ⒻNew Castle 38k	9	4	32½	32	45½	88	Church K	126	w	*1.70	82-17	Alanesian1123Mlle.Dianne112¾Endin112½	Failed to respond	15
10Jly58- 6Del	fst	6f	:222 :454 1:11	4↑ ⒻAlw 4500	1	5	41½	42¼	42	2½	Church K	121	w	*.80	89-15	PuckerUp121½Bornastr1212½Slx118hd	Blocked early,rallied	6
7Jun58- 8Was	fst	1	:222 :451 1:10 1:354	3↑ ⒻBeverly H 58k	14	2	21½	23	1hd	12½	Church K	121	w	2.80	88-16	Bornastar1212½PuckerUp1221¼Burdett104¾	Under mild drive	14
2Jun58- 7Was	sl	6f	:23 :463 1:113	3↑ ⒻAlw 5000	5	3	21½	22	1hd	12	Church K	117	w	5.00	87-29	Bornastar1172PuckerUp1216BonniA.108nk	Under hand urging	6
24Oct57- 6Kee	gd	1⅛	:463 1:111 1:361 1:491	3↑ ⒻSpinster 76k	3	3	35	1½	12	12½	Church K	123	w	9.40	91-12	Bornastar1232½PuckrUp1231¾Srchng1231	Under steady drive	6
17Oct57- 0Kee	sly	*7f	1:272	3↑ ⒻAlw 5000	3	2	311	38	24	21½	Borgem'ke R	120	w	-	89-13	Pucker Up1261½Bornastar1204Beautillion117¾	Late speed	4
	Special race - Run between 4th and 5th races. No wagering																	
2Oct57- 7Haw	fst	6½f	:222 :453 1:11 1:174	3↑ ⒻYo Tambien H 17k	1	6	33	23	21½	11¼	Hartack W	119	w	*.50	91-15	Bornastar1191¼LadyLarue110hdFightingJury1111	Going away	9
21Aug57- 8Was	fst	1⅛	:47 1:112 1:363 1:492	3↑ ⒻBeverly H 28k	1	1	2hd	1½	21	34½	Church K	110	w	2.50	89-12	DottedLine1124½ⒹLadySwords108hdBornastar1101¼	Impeded	13
	Placed second through disqualification																	
14Aug57- 8Was	gd	7f	:221 :45 1:094 1:222	3↑ ⒻAlw 7500	5	2	23	21	11½	15	Hartack W	117	w	2.30	93-15	Bornastar1175Beautillion1173Amoret1154	Drew away easily	9
1Aug57- 8Was	fst	6f	:22 :45 1:102	3↑ ⒻAlw 4500	7	8	77	76½	53½	1nk	Hartack W	118	w	*2.10	93-11	Bornstr118nkFghtngJury107hdGunFly118hd	Up in final stride	8
24Jly57- 8AP	sl	1	:23 :453 1:103 1:37	3↑ ⒻArl Matron H 57k	6	6	76½	55¼	24	22	Church K	111	w	66.10f	85-18	Pucker Up1202Bornastar1114½Lady Swords1084	Strong rally	13
17Jly57- 7AP	sf	5½fⓉ	:23 :464 :591 1:052	3↑ Alw 4000	6	4	55½	54½	74¾	55¼	Borgemenke R	115	w	9.90	87-15	Springhead1111Apple Bay1171½Dark Toga117nk	No mishap	7
1Jly57- 8AP	fm	5½fⓉ	:23 :453 :583 1:044	3↑ ⒻAlw 10000	2	8	31½	31	31	1nk	Heckmann J	116	w	17.80	95-05	Bornastar116nkDale'sDelight113nkViciAdmirl1161½	Just up	8
25Jun57- 8AP	fm	5½fⓉ	:221 :451 :573 1:033	3↑ Alw 5000	7	6	76¾	65½	66¾	66¾	Hartack W	113	w	20.80	94-08	Craigwood1132½KingBruceII119½VagabondKing1193¼	No speed	8
29Apr57- 7CD	fst	6f	:23 :461 1:112	4↑ ⒻAlw 5000	4	7	64	63½	66½	57¼	Carstens W	115	w	4.90	84-17	Brujari107¾MryH.1063Commrgo1091½	Never a serious threat	7
25Apr57- 7Kee	fst	6f	:22 :444 1:093	4↑ Alw 3750	3	3	2hd	1hd	73¾	86½	Hartack W	114	w	*2.10	91-02	FirstLap119nkInvalidate1191½Brujari107hd	Speed 4f,tired	8
18Apr57- 3Kee	gd	6f	:231 :462 1:12	4↑ ⒻAlw 5000	5	-	-	-	-	-	Hartack W	117	w	*1.30	- -	Windsail1174½Mauvernn1122Attc117hd	Stumbled,threw rider	5
14Nov56- 7CD	fst	1	:231 :46 1:11 1:373	Alw 7500	8	5	55½	53½	3½	1½	Carstens W	116	w	2.80	87-22	Bornastar116½Greek Sword111nkInvalidate1191½	Hard drive	8
9Nov56- 7CD	fst	7f	:231 :46 1:104 1:24	Alw 5000	4	2	3nk	21	22½	22½	Carstens W	116	w	24.10	90-15	JovialJove1222½Bornastar1163½OurHoliday1191	Closed well	11
3Nov56- 4CD	fst	1 1/16	:25 :491 1:141 1:461	Alw 4000	1	7	714	66½	42	21¼	Brooks S	117	w	4.30	86-14	Mr.BobW.1121¼Bornstr117nkOurHoldy1206	Strong stretch bid	7
29Oct56- 4CD	gd	6½f	:232 :473 1:13 1:193	Alw 4000	4	2	32	41½	2½	11½	Brooks S	119	w	*.40	83-15	Bornastar1191½Persian Poet1125Draw Near1161½	Drew clear	6
19Oct56- 7Kee	fst	6f	:221 :45 1:101	Alw 4000	5	4	53	43½	55	66½	Brooks S	114	w	8.40	92-05	VayaConDios1173½Outfielder117¾Brujari109no	Factor,tired	8
9Oct56- 3Kee	fst	*7f	1:27	Alw 4000	1	6	1hd	21½	2hd	31	Brooks S	114	w	4.60	97-07	Homeplac117nkOutfldr117¾Bornstr1143½	Showed good effort	7
31Aug56- 6Was	sl	6f	:224 :454 1:111	ⒻAlw 6000	5	5	63½	43½	55½	67¼	Adams J	116	w	9.20	82-23	Little Pache1161Beautillion1165Judy Rullah116nk	Tired	7
18Aug56- 7Was	sly	7f	:23 :474 1:13 1:261	Alw 4500	7	2	32	21	1hd	12	Hartack W	115	w	4.10	74-23	Bornastar1152Peter Parent1201½Whatitoldyou1205	Driving	7
11Aug56- 5Was	fst	6f	:223 :461 1:11	3↑ Alw 4000	6	7	53¾	31½	42½	44	Heckmann J	113	w	*1.50	86-14	GallantRunner121¾Letmego1102HowBlue1181¼	Wide,no rally	7
	Open to 3- and 4-year-olds																	
3Aug56- 3Was	fst	6f	:223 :46 1:11	Md Sp Wt	5	4	2hd	2hd	1hd	12	Hartack W	115	w	*1.80	90-13	Bornastar1152Summer Breeze1151Flutter1158	Handy score	8
28Jly56- 6AP	fst	6f	:23 :453 1:103	Alw 5000	5	7	53	53¼	510	49½	Popara A	110.5	w	33.40	81-16	Tropic King1173Key Biscayne117½Ambiorun1176	Wide turn	10

Career Boy

dk br. c. 1953, by Phalanx (Pilate)–Swanky, by Mahmoud

Lifetime record: 32 8 5 4 $254,661

Own.– C.V. Whitney
Br.– C.V. Whitney (Ky)
Tr.– S.E. Veitch

Date-Race	Cond	Dist	Fractions	Race	PP	St	1c	2c	Str	Fin	Jockey	Wt	Eq	Odds	Spd	Top Finishers	Comment	Fld
6Oct57♦ Longchamp(Fr)	yl	*1½ⓉRH	2:332	3↑ Prix de l'Arc de Triomphe Stk250000						18	Boulmetis S	132		18.00		Oroso132½Denisy1192½Balbo1224	Toward rear throughout.Tanerko 6th	24
14Sep57- 7Atl	fm	1 3/16Ⓣ	:473 1:12 1:372 1:561	3↑ U Nations H 100k	9	7	93¼	72½	44½	44	Boulmetis S	123	wb	8.80	94-02	Round Table118noTudor Era1122Find1222	Threat,weakened	11
9Sep57- 7Atl	sf	1Ⓣ	:244 :483 1:134 1:402	3↑ Alw 4500	7	7	68½	58	35½	31¾	Batchellor L	119	wb	*1.30	77-21	Akbar Khan1191½Old Roman117nkCareer Boy1191½		7
	Forced wide first turn																	
24Aug57- 7Sar	fst	1¼	:48 1:123 1:382 2:043	3↑ Saratoga H 58k	1	6	54	63	31½	32½	Boulmetis S	118	wb	6.20	82-17	Reneged1131RicciTavi1161½CarrBoy1184	No apparent excuse	10
16Aug57- 7Sar	fst	7f	:222 :46 1:122 1:25	3↑ American Legion H 25k	1	15	1213	1110	95	76	Boulmetis S	124	wb	12.90	84-19	RicciTavi1221Nan'sMink1133½ⒹNashville117hd	Off slowly	15
13Jly57- 6Mth	fst	1¼	:463 1:104 1:354 2:014	3↑ Monmouth H 113k	3	9	98¾	67¼	68½	67	Boulmetis S	119	wb	5.00	90-13	Dedicate1243½ThirdBrother119¾Rockcastl109¾	Bumped start	9
4Jly57- 7Bel	fst	1¼	:471 1:11 1:363 2:023	3↑ Suburban H 85k	4	4	46	67	86½	75¾	Boulmetis S	122	wb	7.80	81-13	TrafficJudge124hdLoftyPeak118nkDedicate1262½	No mishap	11
27Jun57- 7Bel	fst	1⅛	:462 1:103 1:354 1:484	3↑ Handicap 10000	2	3	35½	45	57½	56	Boulmetis S	124	wb	*1.85	89-13	BeamRider113noCountrmnd1142Mr.Al L.1142	Early foot,tired	5
7Oct56♦ Longchamp(Fr)	hy	*1½ⓉRH	2:344	3↑ Prix de l'Arc de Triomphe Stk160000						48	Arcaro E	122		21.00e		Ribot1326Talgo1222Tanerko122no	Rated in 8th,finished well,just missed 3rd.Oroso 6th	20
15Sep56- 7Atl	fm	1 3/16Ⓣ	:472 1:12 1:38 1:561	3↑ U Nations H 100k	7	7	54½	52½	52½	11	Boulmetis S	116	wb	4.80e	98-02	CrrBoy1161Fnd117hdMstrGus119hd	Well rated,strong finish	9
1Sep56- 7Atl	fm	1Ⓣ	:242 :48 1:123 1:39	Ventnor Turf H 31k	2	6	89½	66	78	53¼	Choquette J	124	w	*2.30	83-14	KingGrail115¾Sol-Hi112hdSunnngdl1132	Closed ground late	10
20Aug56- 6Sar	fst	1	:242 :483 1:123 1:38	Handicap 6000	1	5	57½	33½	32½	1hd	Arcaro E	122	w	*.95	87-17	CareerBoy122hdQuarterdeck113hdJeanBaptiste112½	Just up	5
16Jun56- 6Bel	fst	1½	:472 1:114 2:024 2:294	Belmont 119k	6	5	514	27	33	2nk	Guerin E	126	wb	3.60e	89-12	Needles126nkCrrBoy1261½Fbus126hd	Missed in strong rally	8
	Geldings not eligible																	
26May56- 7GS	fst	1⅛	:471 1:104 1:353 1:484	Jersey 62k	5	10	1012	88½	65½	32¼	Guerin E	118	wb	5.00	91-14	Fabius1262Kingmakr111nkCrrBoy118hd	Strong stretch rally	10
5May56- 7CD	fst	1¼	:471 1:113 1:364 2:032	Ky Derby 167k	2	15	1312	109	85	65	Guerin E	126	wb	4.90e	85-08	Needles126¾Fabius1261½Come on Red126¾	Sluggish early	17
26Apr56- 6Kee	sl	1⅛	:474 1:121 1:363 1:51	Blue Grass 33k	3	6	66½	43½	21½	2¾	Guerin E	126	wb	*.40e	89-17	TobyB.121¾CareerBoy1263¼ReapingRght126nk	Gaining slowly	7
11Apr56- 7Jam	fst	1 1/16	:242 :484 1:134 1:453	Gotham 29k	7	9	811	57	32	13	Guerin E	122	wb	*1.15	84-21	CareerBoy1223JeanBaptiste122nkNail1265	Drew out handily	9
4Apr56- 7Jam	fst	6f	:24 :474 1:12	Alw 6000	3	2	64¾	65½	2½	21½	Guerin E	126	wb	*.55	85-16	WillofAllah1141½CareerBoy1263BeauFond1152½	No excuse	7
29Oct55- 7GS	fst	1 1/16	:231 :461 1:104 1:423	Garden State 282k	8	10	88¾	55	21½	2no	Guerin E	122	wb	4.50	97-07	Prince John122noCareer Boy1221Needles1224½	Just missed	12
22Oct55- 6GS	fst	1 1/16	:231 :461 1:102 1:423	Alw 10000	4	6	75½	54	2hd	1½	Guerin E	120	wb	2.10e	97-10	CareerBoy120½GunShot112nkEsp1143½	Well rated,hard drive	7
8Oct55- 6Bel	sly	6½f-W	:221 :451 1:10 1:164	Futurity 125k	11	12		92¾	85¼	64½	Guerin E	122	wb	*2.80e	83-12	Nail1221¼HeadMan122¾Polly'sJt1221	Appeared to hang late	15
	Geldings not eligible																	
30Sep55- 6Bel	fst	6f-WC	:214 :441 1:09	Sp Wt 10000	1	3		78¼	56	1no	Guerin E	118	wb	*1.15e	94-11	CareerBoy118noNoorsaga118¾Polly'sJet1183¾	Strong finish	8
27Aug55- 6Sar	fst	6½f	:23 :47 1:12 1:181	Hopeful 71k	7	9	910	85	24	23½	Woodhouse H	122	wb	3.15e	90-19	Needles1223½Career Boy1226Jean Baptiste1221	Closed well	9
20Aug55- 4Sar	fst	6f	:224 :463 1:122	Grand Union Hotel 26k	7	8	811	86½	33	11¾	Woodhouse H	122	wb	*3.70e	86-19	CareerBoy1221¾Nan'sMink114½HeadMan1221½	Steadily clear	8
13Aug55- 4Sar	sly	6f	:23 :46 1:112	Sar Spl 15k	1	3	511	49½	412	49½	Woodhouse H	122	wb	3.15e	81-19	Polly'sJet1221½Reneged1225Noorsag1223	Hard urged,outrun	5
6Aug55- 6Sar	fst	6f	:23 :464 1:122	U S Hotel 26k	5	8	99¾	75½	54	1½	Woodhouse H	114	wb	*1.60e	86-18	CareerBy114½CanadianChamp118hdHeadMan1141¼	Hard drive	10
1Aug55- 2Sar	fst	5½f	:233 :473 :594 1:062	©Md Sp Wt	8	8	62¾	31½	1hd	13½	Woodhouse H	118	wb	*1.60	85-18	CareerBoy1183½Thunderstruck1182½DansChoice118½	Driving	14
6Jly55- 6Aqu	fst	6f	:23 :47 1:12	Great American 18k	2	7	58½	510	510	54¾	Arcaro E	114	wb	12.15	87-17	GetthereJck1221½Rngd1141Bob-o-Bob114nk	Impeded at start	7
20Jun55- 4Aqu	fst	5½f	:24 :472 :594 1:062	©Md Sp Wt	8	9	72¼	86¾	58	42½	Arcaro E	118	w	3.00	89-15	Wild Chorus1181Inkyank118hdTarquitana1181½	Closed a gap	11
14Jun55- 5Aqu	fst	5½f	:233 :474 1:001 1:071	©Md Sp Wt	10	10	96½	85½	44½	41¼	Arcaro E	118	w	*1.90	87-18	Network118nkFoldingMon1181BlackEmperor118no	Good rally	12
4Jun55- 4Bel	fst	5f-WC	:224 :452 :573	©Md Sp Wt	4	8		82	63¾	32¼	Picou C	118	w	6.10e	89-09	Pester1181½Born Mighty118¾Career Boy118hd	Strong finish	12
20May55- 5Bel	fst	4½f-W	:222 :444 :504	©Md Sp Wt	3	10		96¾	36½	56	Picou C	118	w	7.25e	89-08	Postal1183Reneged1182FoldingMon118nk	Rallied,then tired	14

Counterpoint

ch. c. 1948, by Count Fleet (Reigh Count)–Jabot, by Sickle — **Lifetime record: 21 10 3 1 $284,575**

Own.– C.V. Whitney
Br.– C.V. Whitney (Ky)
Tr.– S.E. Veitch

9Aug52- 6Sar	fst 1¼	:48 1:131 1:39 2:053 3↑	Whitney 23k	2 5 39 2½ 12 13½	Gorman D	123 w	*.45	80-19	Counterpoint1233½Mandingo1141One Hitter126½		6
	Veered in start,drew away										
29Jly52- 4Mth	fst 1 1/16	:233 :471 1:12 1:45 3↑	Alw 5000	1 2 24 2hd 14 13½	Gorman D	124 w	*.40	92-15	Counterpoint1243½Go Between112noPilaster1242½	Easily	4
2Feb52- 7SA	fst 1¼	:47 1:111 1:362 2:024	Maturity 183k	4 5 47 65½ 69½ 64¾	Gorman D	126 w	*.50	81-13	Intent113nkGold Capitol1141Black Douglas1131	No excuse	9
19Jan52- 6SA	my 1 1/16	:23 :463 1:114 1:451	San Fernando 23k	2 7 611 57 32½ 1no	Gorman D	118 w	*.65	82-21	Counterpoint118noPhil D.115 1½Intent1146	Just up	9
3Nov51- 6Jam	sly 1 3/16	:473 1:121 1:381 1:583	Emp City H 59k	13 11 129¾ 116 4¾ 11½	Gorman D	130 w	*2.45	83-17	Counterpoint1301½HallofFame1241¾Audtng1111	Driving,wide	13
20Oct51- 6Jam	fst 1⅝	:502 1:40 2:044 2:424 3↑	Emp Gold Cup 53k	2 3 44 2hd 1hd 11¼	Gorman D	119 w	2.15	100-14	Counterpoint1191¼HillPrinc1264½HullDown11912	Ridden out	4
	Geldings not eligible										
13Oct51- 6Bel	fst 2	:493 2:302 2:56 3:213 3↑	J C Gold Cup 53k	2 3 21½ 21 2½ 1hd	Gorman D	117 w	4.35	96-11	Counterpoint117hdHillPrince12410KissMeKate1142½	Just up	5
3Oct51- 6Bel	fst 1⅝	:484 1:401 2:051 2:432	Lawrence Realizatn 22k	4 4 31 11 13 11¼	Gorman D	126 w	*1.35	87-13	Counterpoint1261¼Saxony1108Alerted1142	Easily	6
26Sep51- 6Bel	fst 1	:23 :46 1:104 1:361	Jerome H 24k	7 8 52¾ 43¼ 32 44½	Gorman D	124 w	8.35	89-14	Alerted115nkMandingo1023Hall of Fame1281	Faltered	12
7Jly51- 6Aqu	fst 1¼	:481 1:123 1:383 2:042	Dwyer 57k	9 9 87½ 105 109¼ 913	Gorman D	126 w	*1.55	72-16	Battlefield121½Alerted1112½Hull Down1111½	Dull effort	10
16Jun51- 6Bel	fst 1½	:494 1:141 2:031 2:29	Belmont 118k	2 4 2hd 12 12 14	Gorman D	126 w	5.15e	93-08	Counterpoint1264Battlefield1261½BttlMorn1269	Ridden out	9
	Geldings not eligible										
9Jun51- 6Bel	fst 1⅛	:461 1:102 1:351 1:474	Peter Pan H 24k	7 3 22 2½ 13 12¾	Gorman D	114 w	15.75	102-10	Counterpoint1142¾Battlefield1232¼HallofFame113¾	Handily	9
26May51- 6Bel	fst 1	:224 :452 1:094 1:354	Withers 29k	5 7 77 78½ 711 512	Adair R	126wb	10.80	83-12	Battlefield126hdJumbo1265Nullify1264	Dull try	7
	Geldings not eligible										
19May51- 6Pim	fst 1 3/16	:474 1:112 1:372 1:562	Preakness 110k	7 6 62¼ 52¼ 23 27	Adair R	126wb	25.80	91-14	Bold1267Counterpoint126¾Alerted1264	Went well	8
5May51- 7CD	fst 1¼	:472 1:122 1:372 2:023	Ky Derby 126k	2 7 86¾ 1212 1114 1112	Gorman D	126 w	5.90e	82-09	Count Turf1264Royal Mustang126hdRuhe1262½	Tired	20
26Apr51- 7Kee	my 1⅛	:49 1:142 1:403 1:541	Blue Grass (Div 2) 29k	4 2 31 42 32½ 41¾	Dodson D	121 w	7.70	73-27	[D]Sonic123noRuhe123nkRoyal Mustang1211½	Impeded	6
	Placed third through disqualification										
21Apr51- 6Kee	fst 1 1/16	:233 :472 1:123 1:45 3↑	Ben Ali H 12k	1 1 12 2½ 23 26	Knapp EJ	105 w	*.50e	83-18	Wistful1126Counterpoint1053½Little Imp110¾	Weakened	5
14Apr51- 7Kee	sl 6f	:243 :502 1:17	Alw 2500	4 4 31 12½ 14 18	Church K	112 w	*1.10	67-31	Counterpoint1128Baluster1113Fighting Back1161½	Easily	6
23Mar51- 5GP	fst 6f	:223 :452 1:113	Md Sp Wt	4 8 54 45 51¾ 42	Church K	120 w	*1.65	85-11	Hurry-Skurry120¾Kentario1201Changeaway120nk	Off slowly	11
26Sep50- 5Bel	fst 6f-WC	:224 :453 1:104	©Md Sp Wt	5 10 106½ 77¼ 55¼	Dodson D	118 w	*1.25e	82-14	Heliowise1184Galhampden118½Basically118½	No excuse	14
20Sep50- 5Bel	fst 5½f-W	:222 :45 1:031	©Md Sp Wt	15 6 61¼ 4nk 24	Dodson D	118 w	9.15e	94-02	BlueHelmet1184Counterpoint118hdFoxeyLad1183	Closed well	27

Crafty Admiral

b. c. 1948, by Fighting Fox (Sir Gallahad III)–Admiral's Lady, by War Admiral — **Lifetime record: 39 18 6 4 $499,200**

Own.– Charfran Stable
Br.– Harry F. Guggenheim (Ky)
Tr.– R.B. Odom

11Nov53- 7Lrl	sf *1½Ⓣ	2:36 3↑	D C Int'l 65k	9 1 2hd 109½ 1022 1028	Boland W	126wb	*2.20	46-29	Worden II1266Iceberg II1263Sunglow126½	Flattened out	10
31Oct53- 6Jam	fst 1⅝	:50 1:404 2:06 2:433 3↑	Gold Cup 80k	5 1 12 12½ 16 110	Boland W	126wb	*1.00	96-21	Crafty Admiral12610Common Cause126nkAlerted1261½	Easily	7
24Oct53- 6Jam	fst 1⅛	:471 1:111 1:363 1:493 3↑	Westchester H 56k	3 1 1½ 1hd 12 21	Arcaro E	128wb	*1.15	97-17	Cold Command1121CraftyAdmirl1284Jampol1121½	No excuse	8
17Oct53- 7Haw	fst 1¼	:461 1:102 1:343 2:003 3↑	Haw Gold Cup H 106k	6 2 24 24 46½ 58½	Arcaro E	128wb	*.50	95-08	Sub Fleet1153Smoke Screen1141Indian Hemp1092	No excuse	7
3Oct53- 7Atl	fst 1⅛	:47 1:112 1:362 1:493 3↑	Olympic H 28k	6 2 22½ 22 1hd 11¼	Scurlock D	128wb	*.50	96-11	Crafty Admiral1281¼Tuscany1217Count Cavour1041¼	In hand	7
26Sep53- 7Bel	fst 1⅛	:46 1:102 1:354 1:484 3↑	New York H 29k	5 1 12 11½ 14 14	Arcaro E	125wb	2.45	95-15	Crafty Admiral1254Flaunt1051½Jampol113¾	In hand	9
15Aug53- 6Was	fst 7f	:223 :453 1:103 1:231 3↑	Clang H 22k	4 6 41¾ 45 69½ 810	Church K	125wb	4.10	80-16	Cyclotron1162Van Crosby1102Eljay1121	Done early	12
9May53- 7Pim	gd 1⅛	:471 1:123 1:383 1:514 3↑	Dixie H 29k	4 2 23 2hd 32 34¼	Arcaro E	126wb	*1.20	91-22	RoyalVale1201¾ColdCommnd1152½CrftyAdmrl126nk	Gave way	6
2May53- 6Jam	my 1 3/16	:474 1:113 1:362 1:552 3↑	Gallant Fox H 71k	6 1 1½ 22½ 24 43	Church K	129wb	*1.05	96-14	Royal Vale1151½Cold Command1151½One Count129no	Tired	6
14Mar53- 7GP	fst 1¼	:454 1:10 1:344 2:004 3↑	Gulf Park H 59k	3 2 22 2hd 1½ 1nk	Church K	128wb	*1.95	95-14	Crafty Admiral128nkBattlefield1256Dulat1141	Hard drive	11
21Feb53- 7Hia	fst 1¼	:462 1:103 1:363 2:024 3↑	Widener H 130k	3 2 11 1hd 21 65¼	Church K	131wb	3.50	86-09	OilCapitol114hdAlerted126hdBattlefld1231½	Flattened out	8
7Feb53- 7Hia	my 1⅛	:473 1:124 1:391 1:532 3↑	McLennan H 64k	7 1 12 12 13 13½	Church K	129wb	3.30	69-34	Crafty Admiral1293½Oil Capitol115¾Ken1171	Ridden out	7
24Jan53- 7Hia	my 1⅛	:483 1:133 1:40 1:534 3↑	Royal Palm H 17k	3 1 13 11½ 12 12½	Church K	126wb	*.35	67-32	Crafty Admiral1262½Gushing Oil10715Topside1062½	Easily	5
15Jan53- 7TrP	fst 1⅛	:464 1:112 1:371 1:492 3↑	Tropical H 65k	8 2 2½ 21½ 23 33	Church K	128wb	*1.70	91-19	Spartan Valor1261½How1061½Crafty Admiral1282	No excuse	12
4Oct52- 6Bel	fst 2	:514 2:332 2:584 3:241 3↑	J C Gold Cup 79k	2 2 11 34½ 311 317	Guerin E	124wb	2.15	66-15	OneCount1172Mark-Ye-Wll11715CrftyAdmrl1245	Tired,sulked	4
	Geldings not eligible										
1Sep52- 7Was	sly 1	:231 :462 1:104 1:364 3↑	Wash Park H 172k	4 2 2½ 11½ 12½ 12	Guerin E	128 w	2.70	85-15	CraftyAdmiral1282ToMarket1231Sickle'sImage110nk	Handily	10
16Aug52- 7Was	my 1 3/16	:49 1:141 1:402 1:583 3↑	Whirlaway H 44k	2 1 13 11½ 13 13	Arcaro E	126wb	*.70	93-23	Crafty Admiral1263Oil Capitol1168Ruhe1132	Easily	8
2Aug52- 6Jam	sly 1 3/16	:48 1:12 1:38 1:572 3↑	Merchants & Cits H 28k	4 1 11½ 1½ 11 11½	Guerin E	126wb	*1.65	89-18	CraftyAdmirl1261½CombatBoots1126Mandingo1042½	In hand	8
12Jly52- 6Aqu	fst 1¼	:47 1:113 1:37 2:014 3↑	Brooklyn H 59k	4 1 11 13 14 16	Guerin E	116wb	*2.70	98-14	CraftyAdmirl1166CountyDelight122½ToMarket1194½	In hand	11
4Jly52- 6Aqu	fst 7f	:221 :443 1:09 1:22 3↑	Carter H 29k	3 2 22 22 22 22	Gorman D	120wb	3.05	100-09	NorthernStar1152CraftyAdmiral1202½ToMrkt123no	Held well	10
30May52- 6Bel	fst 1¼	:463 1:102 1:353 2:02 3↑	Suburban H 60k	2 1 14 16 14 2nk	Errico C	113wb	13.75	90-12	One Hitter112nkCrafty Admiral1132Mameluke1161	Tired	10
24May52- 7GS	fst 1⅛	:471 1:12 1:372 1:503 3↑	T J Healey H 24k	2 1 11½ 1hd 2hd 2½	Errico C	116wb	4.70	88-13	Alerted116½Crafty Admiral1161½Joey Boy112½	Good effort	9
17May52- 6Bel	fst 1	:23 :454 1:104 1:362 3↑	Metropolitan H 36k	10 4 2hd 1½ 32 65	Errico C	117 w	3.30	87-14	Mameluke112½Battlefield1251½One Hitter1131	Weakened	11
29Apr52- 6Bel	gd 6f-WC	:221 :443 1:091 3↑	Toboggan H 23k	5 3 3½ 31 2½	Errico C	118wb	*2.05	94-05	DarkPeter108½CraftyAdmiral1182½Tea-Mkr1202	Gaining fast	8
8Mar52- 7GP	fst 1¼	:462 1:103 1:35 2:01 3↑	Gulf Park H 28k	5 1 12 12 15 1nk	Errico C	114wb	5.55	94-07	Crafty Admiral114nkAlerted114½Why Not Now1132	Impeded	10
16Feb52- 6Hia	fst 7f	:224 :452 1:10 1:232 4↑	Alw 5000	5 2 2½ 1hd 12 1nk	Errico C	119 w	*.75	95-16	CraftyAdmiral119nkYildiz1222½Eatontown1161	Driving hard	10
30Jan52- 6Hia	gd 1⅛	:49 1:14 1:39 1:514 4↑	Alw 4500	2 1 11 12 12 1¾	Errico C	108 w	*1.15	79-25	CraftyAdmrl108¾ToyFox10710WhyNotNow1192	Never headed	6
23Jan52- 7Hia	fst 7f	:223 :444 1:091 1:22 3↑	Palm Beach H 13k	7 2 22 2hd 11 12	Errico C	107 w	10.70	102-12	CraftyAdmiral1072Woodchuck1163OilCapitol1122	Drew clear	10
17Jan52- 7Hia	fst 6f	:221 :452 1:10 3↑	Hia Inaugural H 13k	7 9 63 53¼ 65¾ 44½	Basile M	109 w	20.85	93-12	Spartan Valor121hdJumbo1182Woodchuck1192½	No mishap	14
2Jan52- 6TrP	fst 6f	:223 :452 1:102 4↑	Alw 3000	5 6 31½ 2½ 1½ 11½	Basile M	110 w	4.15	95-12	CraftyAdmiral1101½BullyBoy120nkTeaneckFlash1102	Driving	10
	Previously owned by H.A. Grant;previously trained by H. Hughes										
7Aug51- 5Sar	fst 6f	:231 :464 1:123	Alw 3500	7 6 3nk 3½ 63 66¼	Green B	113wb	23.45	79-17	Dulat1131¼Yildiz121nkWho Dini103nk	Gave way	7
	Previously trained by B.B. Williams										
14Nov50- 5Jam	fst 6f	:223 :462 1:12	Alw 3500	2 4 42¼ 53¾ 31½ 32	Mehrtens W	116 w	2.05	85-17	Who Dini116noTenure1162Crafty Admiral1163	Went well	7
1Nov50- 6Jam	fst 1 1/16	:24 :472 1:12 1:434	Wakefield H 18k	7 1 11 32 33 511	Mehrtens W	112 w	19.75	82-15	Uncle Miltie1265Oats1061Royal Mustang113nk	Tired	11
18Oct50- 6Jam	fst 6f	:223 :453 1:111	Remsen H 12k	3 3 63 97½ 1013 87½	Mehrtens W	119 w	3.60	83-15	Repetoire1121½Rough 'n Tumble120noPictus1182	No menace	12
12Oct50- 5Jam	sly 5½f	:23 :47 1:061	Alw 4000	6 3 12 12 13 13½	Mehrtens W	119 w	*.70	87-18	CraftyAdmiral1193½AllIsWell116½GrayMatter114½	Easily	6
5Aug50- 4Sar	sly 6f	:23 :464 1:13	U S Hotel 19k	5 2 2hd 2hd 2½ 2½	Mehrtens W	114 w	2.25	82-19	NorthernStar118½CraftyAdmrl1143½Pltoon1092½	Good effort	5
26Jly50- 6Jam	fst 5½f	:223 :462 1:053	Alw 3000	7 4 13 11 13 14	Mehrtens W	118 w	*1.10	90-16	CraftyAdmiral1184FirstRepeater1151½BlueSpeed1183	Easily	7
13Jly50- 4Jam	fst 5f	:224 :454 :59	©Md Sp Wt	3 2 21½ 21½ 2hd 12	Mehrtens W	118 w	4.75	95-12	Crafty Admiral1182Tripoli118nkBob Considine1181	Handily	12
7Jly50- 4Jam	fst 5f	:223 :47 :592	©Md Sp Wt	8 10 74¼ 57½ 33½ 42	Atkinson T	118 w	6.10	91-14	Aware118½Tripoli1181Motif118½	Went well	12

Decathlon

b. c. 1953, by Olympia (Heliopolis)–Dog Blessed, by Bull Dog — **Lifetime record: 42 25 8 1 $269,530**

Own.– River Divide Farm
Br.– Nuckols Brothers (Ky)
Tr.– R.T. Shepp

30Oct57- 7GS	fst 6f	:214 :441 1:093	3↑ Princeton H 22k	7	1	1½	13	12½	1nk	Lawless R	133wb	*.40	96-15	Decathlon133nkNan's Mink1121¼Itobe1162½	Taken in hand	7
5Oct57- 7Suf	fst 6f	:221 :451 1:11	2↑ John Alden H 28k	9	3	2hd	1hd	11½	14	Hartack W	133wb	*.60	93-21	DH Lord Jeep111 DH Decathln1334Venomous114½	Hung,lasted	10
21Sep57- 7Atl	fst 7f	:22 :434 1:082 1:213	3↑ Longport H 22k	4	1	12	13	13	11½	Lawless R	132wb	*.40	98-09	Decathlon1321½Manteau1132½SkipperBll1153	Stumbled start	4
19Aug57- 7Atl	sf 5½f(T)	:232 :47 :59 1:051	3↑ Alw 4500	5	1	13	15	14	11	Lawless R	113wb	*.40	93-07	Decathlon1131Tudor Era1133½Leap Tide1116	Taken in hand	8
27Jly57- 7Nar	fst 6f	:221 :451 1:103	3↑ Bristol H 20k	2	2	2hd	21½	21½	21	Lawless R	134wb	*.30	92-18	Oclirock1061Decathlon1341PineEcho115nk	Hit rail on turn	6
10Jly57- 6Mth	fst 6f	:22 :45 1:092	3↑ Rumson H 16k	1	2	13	14	13	12½	Lawless R	133wb	*.40	98-14	Decathlon1332½Nahoodah1231Nan'sMnk1112½	In hand all way	5
11Jun57- 6Mth	fst 6f	:212 :433 1:082	3↑ Oceanport H 16k	7	1	12	11	11	1¾	Hartack W	130wb	*.60	103-07	Decathlon130¾Itobe1162½Nahodah1225	Under a clever ride	7
17Jan57- 7Hia	fst 6f	:213 :442 1:092	3↑ Hia Inaugural H 27k	12	1	1hd	1½	1½	11¾	Hartack W	135wb	*.75	98-09	Decathlon1351¾I Appeal1171½Eiffel Blue112hd	Easily best	16
1Jan57- 7TrP	fst 6f	:214 :443 1:092	3↑ New Years H 11k	5	1	1½	12	12	11¼	Hartack W	133wb	*.30	100-07	Decathlon1331¼GrayPhantom1131NewTrend1141½	Easily best	8
15Dec56- 7TrP	fst 6f	:22 :443 1:092	3↑ Coral Gables H 11k	5	1	11½	12	12½	12½	Hartack W	130wb	*.45	100-13	Decathlon1302½Flight History1134Supreme Joy111nk	Easily	11
28Nov56- 7TrP	fst 5½f	:214 :442 :563 1:031	3↑ Inaugural H (Div 1) 11k	5	3	12½	13	14	14½	Hartack W	126wb	*.35	100-11	Decathlon1264½Apollo110nkWar Age112¾	Much the best	10
31Oct56- 7GS	sly 6f	:221 :444 1:102	3↑ Princeton H 25k	3	5	3½	22	2½	2hd	Martin GR	126wb	*2.20	92-17	Decimal112hdDecathlon1262½Impromptu1182		14
	Stumbled start,steadied															
18Oct56- 7Jam	sly 6f	:224 :453 1:104	2↑ Sport Page H 24k	1	2	12	12	12	2¾	Martin GR	126wb	*2.10	92-15	JoeJones125¾Decathlon126½HistoryBook111nk	Used in pace	13
25Aug56- 7Rkm	fst 6f	:213 :44 1:093	Rkm Spl 15k	4	2	21½	2hd	1hd	1½	Martin GR	129wb	*.50	100-08	Decathlon129½LordJep1091¼Tournur105½	Under strong drive	9
6Aug56- 6Mth	sly 6f	:22 :451 1:101	3↑ Rumson H 17k	2	2	11	2½	33	45½	Martin GR	121wb	*1.10	88-20	Impromptu113noStar Rover1205Admiral Vee111½	Speed,tired	7
23Jly56- 7Jam	fst 6f	:224 :453 1:103	3↑ Wilson H 23k	3	3	12½	11½	12	2no	Martin GR	119wb	*1.60	94-17	Ambrgrs107noDcthlon119noMr.Turf1091½	Set pace,nosed out	10
23Jun56- 6Mth	fst 6f	:212 :44 1:091	Select H 23k	4	1	1½	12	12	12½	Martin GR	126wb	*1.20	99-07	Dcthlon1262½Itob114noMr.Ptrck119nk	Good lead,ridden out	8
12Jun56- 7Mth	fst 6f	:213 :44 1:092	3↑ Oceanport H (Div 2) 17k	3	3	11	1½	11	1½	Martin GR	116wb	*.80	98-04	Decathlon116½IAppeal113nkRoyalBrr1081¼	Under long drive	10
29May56- 7GS	fst 6f	:222 :444 1:10	Alw 10000	1	1	11½	11	11½	11¼	Martin GR	124wb	*.60	94-13	Decathlon1241¼Itobe111hdManorWis1183½	Under clever ride	6
5May56- 7GS	fst 6f	:213 :441 1:094	Del Valley 30k	8	1	11	1½	11	21	Martin GR	124wb	*1.40	94-13	Mr.Patrick1151Decathlon1241Nan'sMink115¾	Speed,faltered	10
14Apr56- 7Bow	fst 6f	:224 :46 1:111	Gov Gold Cup 34k	7	1	11	12	1½	2hd	Martin GR	124wb	*.60	95-15	Besomer112hdDecathln1248Kingmakr1121½	Headed,no excuse	7
17Mar56- 7GP	fst 6½f	:222 :45 1:094 1:154	Alw 6000	4	1	12	13	11½	1nk	Martin GR	122wb	*.50	100-08	Decathlon122nkReaping Right1225Massai1082	Tiring,lasted	8
7Mar56- 7GP	fst 6½f	:22 :443 1:092 1:16	Hutcheson 12k	4	2	11½	13	13	15	Martin GR	122wb	*.75	99-11	Decathlon1225Busher Fantasy1222Getthere Jack122½	Easily	6
27Feb56- 7Hia	fst 6f	:22 :442 1:094	Alw 10000	7	1	12	13	14	14	Martin GR	122wb	2.30	98-11	Decathlon1224GetthereJack1221½WhittledyCut1113½	Easily	8
1Feb56- 7Hia	gd 7f	:224 :462 1:112 1:244	Bahamas 27k	15	1	11	2hd	35	411	Martin GR	126wb	12.75	75-31	EiffelBlue1144DarkCharger1187GunShot114hd	Early speed	15
21Jan56- 7Hia	sly 6f	:221 :46 1:122	©Hibiscus 23k	2	3	1hd	13	12	1no	Martin GR	122wb	1.90	85-20	Decathlon122noLibertySun112nkComeonRed1145	Just lasted	6
24Dec55- 7TrP	fst 6f	:221 :444 1:103	Dade County H 8.3k	1	4	11½	12	13	14	Martin GR	126wb	*.70	94-08	Decathlon1264Dark Toga114noLoose Lip1121	Well in hand	6
3Dec55- 7TrP	fst 5½f	:214 :45 :57 1:033	De Soto H 8.8k	2	4	12	11½	12	13	Martin GR	122wb	3.25	98-11	Decathlon1223Phar Wind1151½Hoop Band119½	Ridden out	10
22Oct55- 7Suf	fst 1 70	:23 :464 1:123 1:433	Mayflower 30k	3	1	13	11½	31	85¾	Martin GR	122wb	11.70	81-18	Countermnd116¾CombstonII116noAkboy1161	Much used early	14
8Oct55- 6Bel	sly 6½f-W	:221 :451 1:10 1:164	Futurity 125k	5	5		115¾	1418	1523	Martin GR	122 w	14.65f	65-12	Nail1221¼Head Man122¾Polly's Jet1221	Dropped back early	15
	Geldings not eligible															
1Oct55- 7Atl	sf 1(T)	:233 :471 1:123 1:392	Abescon Island 31k	8	1	11	1hd	65½	89½	Martin GR	121 w	20.90	74-16	HappyNewYear110¾CombustionII113¾Espea1131½	Speed,tired	11
22Sep55- 6Atl	fm 5½f(T)	:224 :461 :59 1:05	Alw 4000	6	1	2hd	32	46	37	Hartack W	116wb	*1.80	87-06	Nahodah1162ErrardPrince1145Decathlon116nk	Used up early	8
10Sep55- 7Atl	fst 7f	:213 :441 1:09 1:23	Worlds Playground 30k	6	4	33	53½	610	815	Martin GR	122wb	11.70	76-11	BusherFantasy110¾Espea112nkNeedls1222½	Brief foot,tired	9
3Sep55- 5Atl	fst 6f	:223 :46 1:12	Alw 4500	7	1	2½	1hd	2hd	2¾	Culmone J	124wb	1.80	84-18	Pylades112¾Decthlon1243BuFond1165	Tried to bear in late	7
27Aug55- 6Sar	fst 6½f	:23 :47 1:12 1:181	Hopeful 71k	4	6	2hd	2½	912	919	Martin G	122wb	9.05	75-19	Needles1223½Career Boy1226Jean Baptiste1221	Early speed	9
20Aug55- 4Sar	fst 6f	:224 :463 1:122	Grand Union Hotel 26k	6	6	44½	32	64½	64	Martin G	122wb	*1.35	82-19	CareerBoy1221¾Nan'sMink114½HedMn1221½	Stumbled at start	8
8Aug55- 6Mth	gd 6f	:214 :453 1:103	Sapling 37k	1	3	2½	21½	3nk	22	Martin GR	124wb	2.70	90-22	Needles1162Decathlon1241¼Polly's Jet1245	Closed well	6
4Jly55- 6Mth	fst 5½f	:213 :451 1:04	©Tyro 21k	5	1	12	12	12	1¾	Martin GR	122wb	2.70	104-11	Decathlon122¾Nan'sMink1152BuFond1151½	Under brisk drive	8
25Jun55- 7Nar	fst 5½f	:233 :462 :59 1:054	Nar Nursery 11k	1	5	1½	11	1½	1hd	Martin GR	117wb	*.30	93-17	Decathlon117hdOur Pleasure1122¼Impressed1143½	Held on	5
28May55- 7Suf	fst 5f	:222 :454 :581	Bay State Kindrgrtn 11k	6	1	1hd	11	12	11½	Martin GR	117wb	2.00	101-10	Decathlon1171½DarkCharger1174½GetthereJack1221	Driving	8
14May55- 4Suf	fst 4½f	:224 :462 :523	Alw 3000	5	9		11½	1hd	1¾	Martin GR	119wb	*.50	102-00	Decathlon119¾The River1193Frosty Mr.1191½	Driving clear	10
5May55- 4Suf	fst 4½f	:23 :462 :532	Md Sp Wt	5	4		11½	11½	12	Martin GR	118wb	*1.60	98-02	Decathlon1182Suave1183SpiceRound118½	Scored very easily	8

Dedicate

b. c. 1952, by Princequillo (Prince Rose)–Dini, by John P. Grier — **Lifetime record: 43 12 9 5 $533,200**

Own.– Jan Burke
Br.– Mrs Edward G. Burke (Ky)
Tr.– G.C. Winfrey

2Nov57- 0GS	sly 1 1/16	:242 :481 1:124 1:442	3↑ Alw 5575	2	2	21	1½	1½	12	Hartack W	126wb	-	88-20	Dedicate1262OleTravis11610WiseMargin114	Placed to drive	3
	Special race - Run between 6th and 7th races. No wagering															
28Sep57- 7Bel	fst 1¼	:471 1:11 1:36 2:01	3↑ Woodward 106k	1	4	44	42	1½	11½	Hartack W	126wb	3.80	95-13	Dedicate1261½GallantMan1202BoldRuler120hd	Strong drive	4
18Sep57- 7Bel	fst 1⅛	:463 1:10 1:342 1:471	3↑ Nassau County H 28k	3	2	21	2hd	2½	2nk	Arcaro E	126wb	3.35	103-11	Gallant Man121nkDedicate1261Reneged121nk	Impeded mildly	7
24Aug57- 7Sar	fst 1¼	:48 1:123 1:382 2:043	3↑ Saratoga H 58k	10	7	77½	73½	53	58	Boland W	127wb	*1.20	77-17	Reneged1131RicciTavi1161½CrrBoy1184	Bore out in stretch	10
10Aug57- 7Atl	fst 1 3/16	:472 1:112 1:361 1:544	3↑ Atl City H 100k	8	4	42	2hd	11½	13	Arcaro E	126wb	*.60	114-09	[D]Dedicate1263RoyalBeconII1121½Hlfst112½	Crowded horses	8
	Disqualified and placed last,track record disallowed															
13Jly57- 6Mth	fst 1¼	:463 1:104 1:354 2:014	3↑ Monmouth H 113k	7	3	21½	2hd	12	13½	Arcaro E	124wb	*.90	97-13	Dedicate1243½Third Brother119¾Rockcastle109¾	Mild drive	9
4Jly57- 7Bel	fst 1¼	:471 1:11 1:363 2:023	3↑ Suburban H 85k	3	3	33½	33½	31½	3nk	Boland W	126wb	*4.15	87-13	TrafficJudge124hdLoftyPeak118nkDedict1262½	Impeded late	11
8Jun57- 7Bel	fst 1	:223 :452 1:103 1:36	3↑ Metropolitan H 62k	9	10	74½	42½	2hd	2¾	Boland W	126wb	4.00	93-11	Traffic Judge118¾Dedicate1261Greek Spy1141¼	Led briefly	17
30May57- 7Bel	fst 7f	:221 :452 1:101 1:23	3↑ Carter H 58k	5	7	75¼	3½	1½	2hd	Boland W	126wb	6.40	95-13	Portersville111hdDdct126nkJutlnd1123	Led briefly,headed	11
30Mar57- 7Bow	fst 1 1/16	:244 :484 1:123 1:443	3↑ J B Campbell H 111k	6	3	3½	2hd	11	1no	Boland W	124wb	*1.10	90-18	Dedicate124noThird Brother118¾Akbar Khan111¾	Hard drive	8
16Mar57- 7Bow	fst 1 1/16	:242 :481 1:121 1:442	3↑ Bowie H 27k	3	4	41½	2hd	1½	2no	Cutshaw O	124wb	*1.40	91-14	ThirdBrother116noDedicate1242½PaperTiger117¾	Held well	7
15Feb57- 7Hia	fst 6f	:224 :454 1:101	4↑ Alw 7500	1	6	52¼	62¾	63¼	63	Guerin E	126wb	6.90	91-12	AdmiralVee114nkCanadianChamp1221SkipprBill118hd	Evenly	7
12Nov56- 7Lrl	sf *1½(T)	2:39	3↑ D C Int'l 100k	4	8	76¼	77½	412	517	Boland W	126wb	*2.80	37-40	MasterBoing1225MisterGus1267PrinceCortauld1265	Crowded	10
3Nov56- 7Jam	sly 1⅝	:492 1:382 2:032 2:413	3↑ Gallant Fox H 84k	7	2	1½	32	32	33	Boland W	126wb	5.25	101-14	Summer Tan1241Midafternoon1182Dedicate1261¼	Held well	10
13Oct56- 8Haw	fst 1¼	:47 1:111 1:362 2:022	3↑ Haw Gold Cup H 129k	6	3	3nk	2hd	1hd	1hd	Boland W	120wb	*1.80	91-16	Dedicate120hdSummerTan1194Fnd1195	Held on in hard drive	8
15Sep56- 7Atl	fm 1 3/16(T)	:472 1:12 1:38 1:561	3↑ U Nations H 100k	5	3	31½	31½	41½	41¼	Boland W	116wb	3.80	97-02	CareerBoy1161Find117hdMisterGus119hd	In close quarters	9
25Aug56- 6Sar	fst 1¼	:483 1:132 1:383 2:041	3↑ Saratoga H 57k	7	3	31	2hd	11	2hd	Boland W	123wb	*1.00	87-18	PaperTiger109hdDedicat1237Fnd1192½	Bore in badly,headed	9
18Aug56- 6Sar	fst 1⅛	:472 1:112 1:364 1:494	3↑ Whitney 46k	7	4	2hd	1hd	13	14	Boland W	116wb	*2.00	101-14	Dedicate1164Summer Tan1204½Paper Tiger112½	Easy score	8
4Aug56- 7Jam	fst 1 3/16	:474 1:12 1:37 1:554	3↑ Brooklyn H 55k	4	1	1½	1hd	3½	1hd	Arcaro E	114wb	*1.75	97-16	Dedicate114hdMidftrnoon116hdFnd1192¼	Came again,just up	8
4Jly56- 7Bel	fst 1¼	:463 1:101 1:35 2:004	3↑ Suburban H 83k	3	1	1hd	1hd	1½	21¼	Woodhouse H	111wb	18.20	95-10	Nashua1281¼Ddct1112¼Subhdr1125	Bobbled at 1⅛,swerved	8
21May56- 5Bel	fst 6f	:231 :463 1:102	4↑ Alw 5000	2	3	53	31½	21½	22½	Boland W	120wb	*1.10	94-12	Blessbull1142½Dedicate1204Dark Peter1171¾	Bore in badly	6
15May56- 6Bel	fst 6f	:224 :461 1:103	4↑ Alw 5000	3	5	66½	35	36	36	Boland W	120wb	*.65	90-13	Dark Ruler1173½White Knight1202½Dedicate1202	No excuse	7
4May56- 7Jam	fst 6f	:234 :461 1:111	4↑ Alw 5000	7	4	11	11	11	2no	Boland W	124wb	*.85	91-20	White Knight113noDedicate1246Goulash113no	Just failed	9
1Oct55- 6Bel	sly 1⅛	:472 1:12 1:361 1:481	3↑ Woodward H 58k	2	1	12	12	32	34	Boland W	110wb	8.85	94-11	TrafficJudge118hdPaperTigr1074Ddct110hd	Made early pace	7
24Sep55- 7Bel	sly 1	:222 :444 1:093 1:351	Jerome H 30k	8	4	44½	34	45	44¼	Bailey PJ	122wb	5.70	94-10	Traffic Judge1261¼Star Rover121noImpromptu1183	Evenly	13
6Sep55- 6Aqu	fst 6f	:23 :462 1:11	3↑ Alw 5000	8	6	33½	22½	11	1nk	Boland W	119wb	*1.10	97-16	[D]Dedicate119nkCrash Dive1176Brother Tex1132½	Bore out	8
	Disqualified															

PAST PERFORMANCES: THE 1950'S 145

16Jly55- 7AP	fst 1	:231 :453 1:093 1:351	Arl Classic 148k	5 4	32½	36	512	68½	Boulmetis S	120wb	7.60	87-10	Nashu126½TrffcJudg1201¼Impromptu1204	Early factor,tired	7
9Jly55- 6AP	hy 7f	:23 :46 1:11 1:234	Alw 7500	4 3	2½	2½	2½	25	Hartack W	124wb	*1.30	86-25	SpeedRouser1185Dedicate124nkHoneysAlibi1245	Tired late	8
14May55- 7GS	fst 1⅛	:454 1:094 1:351 1:481	Jersey 62k	9 3	21	1hd	1hd	1nk	Boulmetis S	118wb	3.20	101-07	Dedict118nkSrtog1186Smmy1131½	Held gamely in long drive	12
7May55- 7GS	fst 6f	:22 :443 1:093	Del Valley 31k	9 1	74¼	45	31	1½	Boulmetis S	115wb	8.20	100-05	Dedicate115½Informant1131½Craigwood1121	Strong finish	12
14Apr55- 6Jam	my 1 1/16	:24 :483 1:133 1:464	Alw 5000	4 3	21	1½	11	11½	Boland W	113wb	2.30	78-18	Dedicate1131½Simmy117nkDoorPriz1153½	Under brisk urging	6
9Apr55- 5Jam	fst 6f	:233 :473 1:114	Alw 4000	10 2	2½	2½	12	14	Boland W	115wb	2.60	88-17	Dedicate1154Dobey Doc115½Taratara1104½	Speed to spare	12
2Apr55- 3Jam	fst 6f	:232 :47 1:133	3↑ Md Sp Wt	7 3	1hd	1½	15	14½	Boland W	114wb	3.60	79-18	Dedicate1144½Reclaim114¾Skysweeper109nk	Easy score	14
2Mar55- 4SA	fst 6f	:222 :453 1:111	Alw 4500	5 9	106¾	118½	109¾	88	Boland W	113wb	7.40	81-13	Bangborough1201¾Nasrulline107½Jungle Art1121¼	Outrun	12
17Feb55- 4SA	my 6f	:224 :47 1:122	Md Sp Wt	8 7	54	33	59	912	Boland W	118wb	2.85	71-24	Bangborough118hdHappy America11810Tonalea113nk	Outrun	12
1Nov54- 4Jam	my 6f	:233 :47 1:14	ⒸMd Sp Wt	2 8	52¾	52¼	11½	4¾	Guerin E	118wb	3.05	76-26	TurkishIsle118hdCavort118nkMahopc118½	Weakened in drive	14
26Oct54- 2Jam	fst 6f	:234 :47 1:131	ⒸMd Sp Wt	7 5	2½	2hd	1hd	31½	Guerin E	118wb	3.05	79-22	EverBest118½OutofReach1181Dedicate1186	Shortened stride	10
9Oct54- 2Bel	fst 7f	:23 :471 1:131 1:262	Md Sp Wt	7 5	62¾	62¼	66	44	Guerin E	118 w	4.25	74-15	FlyingFury1181½GoldenLand118½War'sHistory116hd	Evenly	14
24Sep54- 4Bel	fst 5½f-W	:224 :46 1:042	ⒸMd Sp Wt	9 3		123¾	4¾	51	Guerin E	117 w	5.25	85-14	Taratara117hdRacingFool117noHerHero117½	Tired slightly	27
18Sep54- 3Aqu	fst 6f	:232 :473 1:123	Md Sp Wt	8 4	75½	77¼	75¼	56½	Guerin E	118 w	3.00	82-10	Minute Parade1182½Silent One115½This Evening1182	Outrun	9
31Aug54- 4Aqu	sly 6f	:231 :47 1:12	ⒸMd Sp Wt	11 8	910	99	68	59	Guerin E	118 w	4.50	83-17	Adam'sApple1182HoneysAlibi1183Mr.Al L.1182	Lacked speed	11
21Aug54- 2Sar	fst 5½f	:233 :472 1:00 1:063	Md Sp Wt	12 7	87	1110	715	69¾	Guerin E	118 w	15.25f	74-17	Decimal1184Mr.Al L.118nkRacingFool1182½	Never a menace	13
14Aug54- 5Sar	fst 5½f	:23 :461 1:073	Md Sp Wt	5 12	108¼	1013	1114	1012	Guerin E	118 w	13.70	67-18	LittleDell118nk[DH]RacingFool118[DH]ModelAce118¾	Outrun	13

Doubledogdare

b. f. 1953, by Double Jay (Balladier)–Flaming Top, by Omaha **Lifetime record: 25 13 6 1 $258,206**

Own.– Claiborne Farm
Br.– Claiborne Farm (Ky)
Tr.– M. Jolley

3Nov56- 7CD	fst 1	:232 :462 1:104 1:37	3↑ ⒻFalls City H 22k	5 5	58	43	21	1¾	Brooks S	121 w	*1.10	90-14	Doubledogdare121¾Queen Hopeful1225Lycka117½	Driving	8
19Oct56- 6Kee	fst 1⅛	:461 1:103 1:361 1:491	3↑ ⒻSpinster 70k	4 9	88½	77	2hd	11¼	Heckmann J	119 w	*2.60e	99-05	Doubledogdre1191¼QueenHopful1233LdySwords1192½	Driving	14
Open to 3-, 4- and 5-year-olds															
16Oct56- 4Kee	fst 6f	:221 :444 1:091	Alw 7500	3 3	43½	34	23	21¾	Brooks S	119 w	3.20	102-04	Swoon'sSon1261¾Doubledogdare1191½JovilJov1122	Sharp try	4
10Oct56- 5Kee	fst 6f	:224 :454 1:10	3↑ Alw 7500	5 3	42	31½	2hd	11	Brooks S	120 w	*.40	100-04	Doubledogdare1201LeatherKid1182½FthfulSong113nk	Driving	5
29Aug56- 7Was	fst 1⅛	:47 1:113 1:372 1:493	3↑ ⒻBeverly H 27k	1 5	54½	32	53¾	57½	Brooks S	112wb	2.80	85-13	Amoret113nkLadySwords1071QueenHopefl1205	Well up,tired	9
8Aug56- 7Was	fst 7f	:214 :441 1:093 1:222	ⒻMisty Isle H 22k	8 3	55½	32½	21½	2hd	Brooks S	124wb	*.80e	93-11	PuckrUp116hdDoubldogdare1246CandyDsh1192½	Just missed	9
25Jly56- 7AP	fst 1	:224 :452 1:102 1:364	3↑ ⒻArl Matron H 57k	5 2	22	1hd	11	42¼	Heckmann J	114wb	2.10e	86-16	Delta119noAmoret113¾Queen Hopeful1201½	Took lead,tired	12
14Jly56- 8AP	fst 1	:23 :454 1:103 1:364	Arl Classic 158k	2 1	14	11½	12	31¾	Brooks S	112wb	8.50	86-14	Swoon'sSon1201½BenA.Jones117nkDoubledogdare112nk	Tired	8
27Jun56- 7AP	fst 1	:23 :452 1:093 1:36	ⒻCleopatra H 22k	5 3	31½	42	21	2hd	Brooks S	122 w	1.60	92-14	Princess Turia121hdDoubledogdare122hdSupple1154	Sharp	8
9Jun56- 7Bel	fst 1⅜	:49 1:124 1:381 2:163	ⒻC C A Oaks 59k	1 5	56	44	44	54	Brooks S	121 w	2.90	84-12	Levee121nkPrincessTuria121hdLadySwords1211¾	Taken wide	9
16May56- 8Was	gd 6f	:223 :46 1:11	ⒻCoronet 16k	3 8	53¼	54½	3nk	12	Brooks S	117 w	*.70	90-22	Doubledogdare1172Royal Lark1173¼Miss Ottawa1101	Easily	9
4May56- 7CD	fst 1 1/16	:242 :482 1:133 1:444	ⒻKy Oaks 30k	5 3	37	33	21	2no	Brooks S	121 w	1.60	94-14	PrincessTuria116noDoubledogdare1213½Tournure1162½	Nosed	9
28Apr56- 7CD	fst 6f	:224 :453 1:113	ⒻOaks Prep 13k	5 2	46½	45½	21	1½	Brooks S	121 w	*.40	92-10	Doubledogdare121½Princess Turia1182Ament118nk	Just up	8
19Apr56- 6Kee	fst 6f	:221 :453 1:112	ⒻAshland 19k	5 1	23	21	12	13½	Brooks S	121 w	*.40	93-13	Doubledogdare1213½GuardRail1184½WarningBell1144½	Easily	5
12Apr56- 5Kee	fst 6f	:222 :46 1:11	ⒻAlw 5000	2 5	25	32½	1½	1¾	Brooks S	121 w	*.50	95-11	Doubledogdare121¾Guard Rail1184½Supple121hd	Hard drive	6
15Oct55- 6Kee	fst 7f	:223 :453 1:111 1:241	ⒻAlcibiades 39k	1 2	12	12	13	14	Brooks S	119wb	*.30	91-10	Doubledogdare1194Ament1196½Supple1191	Speed in reserve	4
8Oct55- 6Bel	sly 6½f-W	:221 :451 1:10 1:164	Futurity 125k	12 10		51½	64	96	Arcaro E	119wb	4.85	82-12	Nail1221¼Head Man122¾Polly's Jet1221	Brief early foot	15
Geldings not eligible															
1Oct55- 4Bel	gd 6f-WC	:222 :451 1:094	ⒻMatron 60k	9 8		43½	33	11	Arcaro E	119wb	*1.30	90-10	Doubledogdare1191Glamour1191Beautillon119¾	Strong drive	18
22Sep55- 4Bel	fst 5½f-W	:223 :451 1:032	ⒻAlw 4500	2 7		5¾	11½	12	Arcaro E	119wb	*1.20	91-09	Doubledogdare1193Glamour1122½Ferocious1171	Handy score	17
22Aug55- 6Sar	fst 6f	:232 :471 1:132	ⒻSpinaway 50k	4 2	3½	1½	21	21	Nichols J	119wb	*1.00	80-22	Register1141Doubledogdare119hdAiming High1192	Gamely	6
2Jly55- 6Mth	fst 5½f	:213 :46 1:051	ⒻColleen 27k	2 14	88¾	55	2hd	13	Nichols J	119wb	*2.00	98-11	Doubledogdare1193DarkCharger1191MissErlen1121½	Driving	14
18May55- 6Bel	fst 5f-WC	:223 :452 :573	ⒻNational Stallion 30k	1 2		21	12	16	Westrope J	119wb	*1.45	91-13	Doubledogdare1196Supple1151½Catchpenny1194½	Easily best	6
27Apr55- 6Bel	sly 4½f-W	:214 :451 :512	ⒻFashion 20k	7 7		21	23½	23	Westrope J	114wb	8.70	89-13	Pretty Plunger1143Doubledogdare1144Tweetsie114no	Gamely	14
14Apr55- 4Kee	fst *4f	:50	Alw 3500	3 5		54	41	1hd	Brooks S	112wb	2.90	97-05	Doubledogdare112hdWaikiki1153All Comers1181¼	Driving	7
23Feb55- 6Hia	fst 3f	:214 :331	Hia Juvenile (Div1) 24k	12 11			96¼	53¾	Brooks S	111 w	13.60	- -	Well Marked115½Bob-o-Bob114¾Roman Whirl1171½	Rallied	17

Evening Out

br. f. 1951, by Shut Out (Equipoise)–Evening Belle, by Eight Thirty **Lifetime record: 21 11 1 4 $214,360**

Own.– Mrs G.D. Widener
Br.– Mrs George D. Widener (Ky)
Tr.– W.F. Mulholland

11Jly55- 6Jam	fst 6f	:23 :461 1:11	3↑ ⒻChamplain H 16k	8 6	41¼	21	24½	36¾	Bailey PJ	126wb	5.70	85-17	OilPainting1216Canadiana122¾EveningOut126no	Early speed	9
25Jun55- 6Del	gd 1 1/16	:232 :471 1:12 1:443	3↑ ⒻNew Castle 39k	9 9	83¼	1212	1112	1213	Westrope J	120wb	10.50	75-17	Clear Dawn1162½Open Sesame1121½Cerise Reine120hd	Outrun	15
18Jun55- 6Mth	fst 6f	:212 :441 1:094	3↑ ⒻRegret H 23k	8 7	42	3½	1½	1½	Boulmetis S	122wb	7.30	96-10	Evening Out122½Gandharva1151Another World116½	Driving	12
8Jun55- 6Bel	fst 1 1/16	:224 :451 1:094 1:414	3↑ ⒻTop Flight H 30k	4 10	108½	97	811	811	McCreary C	121 w	8.00	91-11	Parlo1263Gainsboro Girl114½Spinning Top113nk	Outrun	12
1Jun55- 6Bel	fst 7f	:23 :462 1:111 1:241	3↑ ⒻGolden Annivrsy H 20k	6 5	52¾	53½	32½	4¾	Arcaro E	122 w	2.85	88-14	Dispute114¾Parlo125hdOil Painting107no	Speed,late rally	11
17May55- 6Bel	fst 6f	:224 :461 1:11	3↑ ⒻHandicap 5000	10 5	1hd	11	14	31	Arcaro E	125wb	*1.30	93-13	RosClag112¾MissWeesie110nkEvnngOut1254½	Speedy,faltered	10
5May55- 6Bel	fst 6f	:223 :46 1:113	4↑ ⒻAlw 5000	3 5	3½	1hd	1½	1nk	Arcaro E	120wb	*1.30	91-13	EveningOut120nkDispute1171EverBright1091	Cleverly rated	6
18Aug54- 6Sar	fst 1⅛	:474 1:121 1:38 1:523	3↑ ⒻDiana H 23k	10 4	32	11	14	31½	Arcaro E	116wb	*1.30	85-19	LavenderHill1211½LaCorredora121hdEvenngOut1166	Bore out	10
7Aug54- 6Mth	fst 1⅛	:46 1:101 1:37 1:501	ⒻMth Oaks 63k	7 1	15	14	13	12	Arcaro E	117wb	*1.60	95-12	EveningOut1172ClearDawn1212½JuneFete113½	Never headed	14
28Jly54- 7Mth	fst 6f	:22 :452 1:10	ⒻMiss Woodford 24k	5 7	52½	85½	86	34	Woodhouse H	118 w	*1.10	91-11	ClearDawn1122½Parlo1211½EveningOut118hd	Good late rally	10
5Jly54- 6Del	fst 1¼	:454 1:101 1:361 2:023	3↑ ⒻNew Castle H 138k	6 1	22	24	1617	1822	Arcaro E	114 w	*2.30	67-19	GainsboroGirl1134SunshineNell1262LavenderHill111hd	Quit	20
28Jun54- 6Del	fst 1 1/16	:224 :462 1:112 1:443	3↑ ⒻAlw 10000	10 1	11	13	13	11½	Woodhouse H	104 w	*1.10	88-19	EvningOut1041½GrecianQueen1241½LaCorredora124hd	Easily	12
19Jun54- 6Aqu	fst 1 1/16	:244 :484 1:133 1:463	ⒻGazelle 30k	8 10	106½	87¼	44	21	Arcaro E	113 w	*.40	80-19	On Your Own1131Evening Out1131Fascinator1212¼	Gaining	11
14Jun54- 5Aqu	fst 7f	:23 :46 1:104 1:234	ⒻAlw 7500	4 4	44	36½	23½	11	Arcaro E	121 w	*.55	91-10	Evening Out1211On Your Own1141Happy Mood1213½	Driving	10
28Apr54- 5Bel	fst 6f	:23 :461 1:11	ⒻAlw 7500	1 4	11½	1hd	1½	1no	Arcaro E	122 w	*.45	94-12	EvnngOut122noDangrousDame1123½SottoVoce1131½	Just up	4
3Oct53- 5Bel	fst 6½f-W	:221 :451 1:092 1:16	Futurity 117k	13 4		1hd	23	55¾	Scurlock O	119 w	3.70	86-11	Porterhouse1223½Artismo122½Best Years1221¼	Tired	14
Geldings not eligible															
26Sep53- 5Bel	fst 6f-WC	:221 :452 1:102	ⒻMatron 53k	2 2		1hd	12½	11¾	Scurlock O	119 w	*.80	89-11	Evening Out1191¾Queen Hopeful1191Clear Dawn119nk	Easily	8
21Aug53- 0Sar	fst 6f	:24 :474 1:133	ⒻSpinaway 51k	2 1	11½	13½	15	18	Scurlock O	123 w	-	80-20	Evening Out1238Alines Pet111	Easily	2
No wagering															
14Aug53- 6Sar	fst 5½f	:23 :47 :59 1:052	ⒻSchuylerville 13k	3 3	1½	1½	13	14½	Scurlock O	123 w	*1.25	90-18	Evening Out1234½Riant1191Incidentally1233	Easily best	6
20May53- 6Bel	fst 5f-WC	:22 :441 :563	ⒻNational Stallion 29k	5 4		2hd	2hd	1hd	Scurlock O	119 w	*1.25	96-08	Evening Out119hdFascinator1193½Clear Dawn119nk	Driving	10
8May53- 6Bel	fst 4½f-W	:222 :452 :52	ⒻFashion 14k	7 3		21½	2½	12½	Scurlock O	114 w	17.65	89-11	EveningOut1142½WolfGal1191¼SittingDuck1191¾	Ridden out	10

First Landing

b. c. 1956, by Turn-to (Royal Charger)–Hildene, by Bubbling Over — Lifetime record: 37 19 9 2 $779,577

Own.– Meadow Stable
Br.– C.T. Chenery (Ky)
Tr.– J.H. Hayes

17Sep60- 7Atl	fm 1 3/16 Ⓣ	:463 1:12 1:372 1:57	3↑ U Nations H 100k	4 3 56 76¼ 98¼ 98½	Grant H	123 b	11.10	79-12	T.V.Lark120¼SwordDancer127¼BallyAche122hd Fell back 10
5Sep60- 7Aqu	fst 1	:232 :461 1:102 1:344	3↑ Aqueduct H 56k	4 3 52 45 44½ 43	Arcaro E	122 b	2.75	91-11	Bald Eagle130hdIntentionally125noWarhead1133 Even try 5
30Jly60- 7Aqu	sly 1¼	:471 1:12 1:38 2:03	3↑ Brooklyn H 109k	5 5 67½ 68 610 613	Boulmetis S	123 b	3.95	80-17	On-and-On118hdGrekStr1102Wltz113¼ Disliked the footing 7
16Jly60- 7Mth	fst 1¼	:47 1:111 1:362 2:024	3↑ Monmouth H 112k	9 3 42½ 44½ 33½ 11¼	Arcaro E	123 b	*1.10	92-19	FirstLanding1231¼ManassaMaulr1171½TIntShow1172½ Driving 9
4Jly60- 7Aqu	fst 1¼	:472 1:111 1:361 2:013	3↑ Suburban H 108k	1 1 1hd 1hd 1hd 2½	Ussery R	122 b	6.90	111-11	SwordDancer125½FirstLanding1221½Waltz1154½ Game effort 6
22Jun60- 8Suf	fst 1¼	:463 1:111 1:37 2:033	3↑ Mass H 56k	1 4 413 67 57½ 44¾	Shoemaker W	124 b	*.70	82-16	TalentShow1171½Polyld1163¼BttlNck107no Appeared to sulk 7
30May60- 7Aqu	fst 1	:224 :453 1:09 1:333	3↑ Metropolitan H 114k	3 8 41¼ 21½ 21 23½	Boulmetis S	123 b	4.05	104-03	Bald Eagle1283½First Landing123nkTalent Show118¾ Gamely 10
30Apr60- 7Aqu	fst 1⅛	:473 1:114 1:37 1:493	3↑ Grey Lag H 70k	7 2 21½ 22 2½ 2nk	Shoemaker W	124 b	*1.70	96-06	SwordDancer126nkFirstLanding124noWhitley1162 Sharp try 11
9Apr60- 8Lrl	fst 1⅛	:474 1:121 1:371 1:492	Lrl Maturity H 70k	3 1 1½ 1hd 1hd 1hd	Shoemaker W	124 b	1.20	123-05	FirstLandng124hdOn-and-On1226Nimmr116¾ Long,hard drive 5
27Feb60- 7SA	fst 1¼	:462 1:104 1:352 2:003	3↑ S Anita H 145k	9 8 75 72¾ 1112 1113	Arcaro E	123 b	4.10	83-11	Linmold110hdFleet Nasrullah113noAmerigo120nk No factor 12
13Feb60- 7SA	fst 1⅛	:454 1:102 1:354 1:481	3↑ San Antonio H 57k	6 7 64¾ 51½ 4¾ 22¼	Arcaro E	124 b	*2.10	89-12	Bagdad1232¼FrstLndng1242¼HowNow118no Finished strongly 11
30Jan60- 7SA	fst 1¼	:461 1:103 1:351 2:003	Maturity 166k	4 5 57 1hd 1hd 1½	Arcaro E	116 b	*2.40	96-13	First Landing116½Bagdad1182½Linmold1172 Drew out slowly 8
16Jan60- 7SA	my 1⅛	:472 1:12 1:374 1:50	San Fernando 55k	5 2 2½ 1hd 1hd 2½	Arcaro E	117 b	*.70	81-24	Kingo'Turf113½FirstLanding1175½CivicPride1135½ Gamely 7
8Jan60- 7SA	fst 1 1/16	:231 :461 1:102 1:421	Handicap 1000	4 3 32 21½ 1hd 1nk	Arcaro E	125 b	*1.00	93-14	FirstLanding125nkCivicPride1148Demobilize114no Driving 5
7Nov59- 7GS	my 1¼	:461 1:111 1:38 2:053	3↑ Trenton H 87k	8 5 43¼ 43½ 54½ 56¼	Arcaro E	123 b	*2.20	71-27	Greek Star115½Amerigo1211½Talent Show119¾ Well up,tired 9
3Nov59- 7Aqu	fst 1 3/16	:473 1:121 1:374 1:573	Roamer H 57k	5 4 33 3½ 1½ 2no	Arcaro E	123 b	2.50	- -	Polylad112noFirst Landing1236½Middle Brother1243 Nosed 9
28Oct59- 4Aqu	sl 1	:24 :471 1:122 1:383	Alw 7500	1 1 1½ 1hd 11½ 11½	Arcaro E	124 b	*.55	- -	FirstLanding1241½Polylad112hdTopChargr11220 Brisk drive 5
16Oct59- 6Aqu	fst 6f	:223 :462 1:114	Alw 5000	5 4 33½ 32 1hd 1½	Arcaro E	124 b	*.60	- -	FirstLanding124½FightinIndian120¾MoonAgain120½ Driving 7
16May59- 8Pim	fst 1 3/16	:471 1:113 1:374 1:57	Preakness 190k	2 5 34 54½ 610 916	Arcaro E	126 b	*1.60	72-17	RoyalOrbit1264SwordDancer1263Dunce1262½ Tiring,crowded 11
2May59- 7CD	fst 1¼	:473 1:113 1:36 2:021	Ky Derby 163k	3 7 88½ 44 42½ 32¼	Arcaro E	126 b	*3.60	94-06	TomyLee126noSwordDancer1262¼FirstLanding1261 Good try 17
28Apr59- 8CD	fst 1	:231 :463 1:10 1:361	Derby Trial (Div 2) 15k	3 2 32 2hd 1hd 11	Arcaro E	122	*.40	94-16	FirstLanding1221JohnBruce116¾Quantrell1161¾ Mild drive 6
18Apr59- 7Jam	fst 1⅛	:461 1:11 1:37 1:493	Wood Memorial 88k	3 2 2hd 1hd 1hd 2¾	Arcaro E	126 b	*.85	92-14	ManassaMauler126¾FirstLanding126¾OurDad1266 No excuse 8
13Apr59- 7Jam	gd 6f	:232 :464 1:101	Alw 7500	5 4 3½ 1hd 1½ 13	Arcaro E	124 b	*.35	96-07	FirstLanding1243Nimmer120¾Hilwn1111¾ Under a mild drive 6
28Feb59- 7Hia	fst 1⅛	:454 1:094 1:352 1:491	Flamingo 135k	7 4 45½ 46 36 34¾	Arcaro E	122 b	*.85	84-11	Troilus1223Open View1221¾First Landing1221¼ No excuses 10
18Feb59- 7Hia	fst 1⅛	:461 1:101 1:36 1:494	Everglades 29k	4 1 1hd 1hd 11 1nk	Arcaro E	126 b	*.20	86-17	FirstLanding126nkMoony117noRareRic120nk Long,hard drive 7
11Feb59- 6Hia	fst 7f	:224 :452 1:093 1:223	Alw 6000	6 4 41½ 32½ 23 22¾	Arcaro E	124 b	*.35	94-17	Octopus1162¾FirstLndng1242¾Moony1081¾ In close,steadied 9
Previously raced in the name of C.T. Chenery									
25Oct58- 7GS	sly 1 1/16	:222 :463 1:124 1:462	Garden State 297k	6 8 66½ 23½ 21½ 1hd	Arcaro E	122wb	*1.50	78-31	FirstLanding122hdTomyLee1222SwordDancer1223 Hard drive 13
18Oct58- 6GS	fst 1 1/16	:232 :463 1:114 1:443	Alw 10000	4 5 36 34½ 21 1¾	Arcaro E	122wb	*.30	87-17	FirstLanding122¾CraftySkipper1205PenBolro1121½ Cleverly 6
11Oct58- 7Bel	fst 1	:231 :47 1:123 1:392	Champagne 151k	7 7 3nk 1½ 11 1nk	Arcaro E	122wb	*2.00	77-21	FirstLndng122nk[D]TomyL1223Intntonlly1222 Saddle slipped 10
20Sep58- 7Bel	fst 6½-WC	:214 :443 1:082 1:143	Futurity 114k	5 4 41½ 2hd 21	Arcaro E	122wb	*.40	98-01	Intentionally1221First Landing122nkDunce1223½ No excuse 8
Geldings not eligible									
23Aug58- 6Sar	fst 6½f	:23 :463 1:11 1:174	Hopeful 57k	2 1 21½ 1hd 11½ 15½	Arcaro E	122wb	*.45	96-18	FirstLanding1225½FirstMinstr1221¾ThtLuckyDy1224½ Easily 5
6Aug58- 5Sar	fst 6f	:224 :463 1:124	Sar Spl 14k	2 1 21½ 1hd 11½ 17	Arcaro E	122wb	*.25	84-24	FirstLandng1227Plot1224½Don'tAlb122no Much the best 4
23Jly58- 6Jam	fst 5½f	:222 :453 :574 1:04	Great American 33k	1 1 1hd 1hd 1½ 1nk	Arcaro E	122 w	*.20	98-15	FirstLandng122nkAtoll11810JtFul1144½ Best in hard drive 4
17Jly58- 5Jam	fst 5½f	:232 :472 :593 1:054	Alw 5000	1 1 11 1½ 1½ 14	Arcaro E	122 w	*.20	89-23	FirstLanding1224Moony116nkBluevll1161½ Under mild drive 5
2Jun58- 6Bel	fst 5f-WC	:223 :45 :57	Juvenile 35k	10 3 2½ 21½ 11	Arcaro E	117 w	*.90	94-12	First Landing1171Watch Your Step1179Bagdad122nk Driving 10
23Apr58- 6Jam	sly 5f	:23 :463 :583	Alw 4500	2 4 53 32 32½ 11¾	Arcaro E	118 w	*.65	97-12	First Landing1181¾The Hunter118hdSteverino1189½ Driving 5
14Apr58- 4Jam	fst 5f	:223 :462 :584	©Md Sp Wt	2 4 44½ 21½ 2½ 21	Arcaro E	118 w	*.90	95-14	[D]RestlessWind1181FirstLanding1186SteveW.1186 Bore out 7
Placed first through disqualification									

Gallant Man (GB)

b. c. 1954, by Migoli (Bois Roussel)–Majideh, by Mahmoud — Lifetime record: 26 14 4 1 $510,355

Own.– R. Lowe
Br.– H.H. Aga Khan & Prince Aly Khan (GB)
Tr.– J.A. Nerud

6Sep58- 7Bel	fst 1	:23 :452 1:10 1:35	3↑ Sysonby H 28k	1 7 68½ 52¾ 53¾ 54½	Arcaro E	134 w	*.65	94-14	Cohoes116hdMisterJive1133Rengd124nk No racing room late 7
22Jly58- 7Hol	fst 1⅝	:464 1:371 2:023 2:41	3↑ Sunset H 107k	5 3 37 2hd 1½ 14	Shoemaker W	132 w	*.50	86-18	GallantMan1324EddieSchmidt1106St.Vincent111nk Eased up 6
12Jly58- 7Hol	fst 1¼	:484 1:131 1:373 2:012	3↑ Hol Gold Cup H 162k	1 5 55½ 3½ 1hd 1½	Shoemaker W	130 w	*.40	85-18	GallantMan130½EddieSchmidt1101¾Seaneen1181¼ Hard urged 5
14Jun58- 7Bel	fst 1	:231 :461 1:103 1:353	3↑ Metropolitan H 58k	9 9 88¼ 57 42 12	Shoemaker W	130 w	2.95	96-13	GallantMan1302BoldRuler1351½Clm114nk Drew clear handily 10
30May58- 7Bel	fst 7f	:223 :453 1:101 1:223	3↑ Carter H 58k	2 8 86¾ 75½ 53½ 33	Shoemaker W	128 w	3.60	91-17	BoldRuler1351½TickTock1131½GallantMan128no Closed well 9
9Nov57- 7GS	gd 1¼	:471 1:111 1:364 2:013	3↑ Trenton H 82k	3 3 311 23½ 23 22¼	Shoemaker W	124 w	*1.40	95-14	BoldRuler1222¼GallantMan1248½RoundTbl124 Gaining slowly 3
12Oct57- 5Bel	fst 2	:50 2:321 2:573 3:23	3↑ J C Gold Cup 80k	3 5 54½ 33 1hd 11	Shoemaker W	119 w	*.30	87-14	Gallant Man1191Third Brother1248Reneged12418 Going away 5
28Sep57- 7Bel	fst 1¼	:471 1:11 1:36 2:01	3↑ Woodward 106k	4 3 33½ 31½ 3½ 21½	Shoemaker W	120 w	*.65	93-13	Dedicate1261½GallantMn1202BoldRulr120hd Rated,no excuse 4
18Sep57- 7Bel	fst 1⅛	:463 1:10 1:342 1:471	3↑ Nassau County H 28k	1 4 53½ 42½ 3½ 1nk	Shoemaker W	121 w	*.65	103-11	Gallant Man121nkDedicate1261Reneged121nk Ridden out 7
17Aug57- 7Sar	fst 1¼	:49 1:14 1:39 2:04	Travers 44k	4 4 44 2hd 1hd 1½	Shoemaker W	126 w	*.15	88-17	GallantMan126½Bureaucracy1167FieldofHonor1127 Handily 5
6Aug57- 7Sar	fst 7f	:23 :454 1:111 1:243	Alw 6000	4 4 611 68½ 1hd 14	Shoemaker W	126 w	*.35	92-23	GallantMan1264LittleHermit1161¾Tenacious1191 Much best 6
15Jun57- 6Bel	fst 1½	:464 1:102 2:012 2:263	Belmont 113k	4 4 23 2hd 11½ 18	Shoemaker W	126 w	.95e	105-07	GallantMan1268InsideTract1264BoldRuler1269 Easily best 6
1Jun57- 7Bel	fst 1⅛	:472 1:113 1:361 1:482	Peter Pan H 28k	3 4 32½ 2hd 1hd 12½	Shoemaker W	124 w	*.45	97-10	GallantMan1242½PromisedLand114¾NahHiss1132½ Mild drive 6
4May57- 7CD	fst 1¼	:47 1:112 1:364 2:021	Ky Derby 152k	4 7 79½ 54 3½ 2no	Shoemaker W	126 w	3.70	96-12	IronLiege126noGllntMn1262¾RoundTbl1263 Misjudged finish 9
20Apr57- 7Jam	fst 1⅛	:48 1:12 1:361 1:484	Wood Memorial 59k	4 3 44½ 2hd 1hd 2no	Choquette J	126 w	8.00	102-10	BoldRuler126noGallantMan1266PromisedLand1262¼ Game try 7
6Apr57- 7Jam	sly 6f	:224 :452 1:11	Swift 23k	6 6 67 54½ 53¾ 41¾	Choquette J	126 w	2.80	90-15	KingHairan1261¼Missile126½Clm126hd Best stride too late 7
30Jan57- 7Hia	fst 7f	:223 :45 1:091 1:22	Bahamas 26k	8 5 78 57 58 47¾	Choquette J	123 w	*2.05	92-11	BoldRuler1264¾Gen.Duke1142FedrlHll1261¼ Only mild rally 11
19Jan57- 7Hia	fst 6f	:221 :451 1:10	©Hibiscus 26k	10 8 94¼ 64½ 53 1½	Choquette J	117 w	2.60e	95-09	GallantMan117½Missile1221½KingHairan1221½ Strong drive 13
3Jan57- 8TrP	fst 6f	:22 :452 1:092	Alw 2800	2 6 33 11½ 16 16	Choquette J	119 w	*.95	100-09	GallantMan1196Gen.Duke1132Asgard119¾ Drew to long lead 12
25Dec56- 5TrP	fst 6f	:224 :46 1:11	Alw 2800	7 6 54¼ 43½ 43 1nk	Choquette J	117 w	4.05	92-12	GallantMan117nkSundayStar114½Buddy1151¼ Cleverly ridden 9
17Oct56- 5Bel	fst 6f	:221 :454 1:101	Alw 4000	7 5 45 55½ 21½ 1¾	Ussery R	113 w	46.95	98-08	Gallant Man113¾Discernment1158Osceola115hd Driving hard 12
3Oct56- 6Bel	fst 6f-WC	:223 :453 1:102	Alw 4000	4 7 88 99 910	Choquette J	115 w	60.10	77-13	Asgard1153½Dodger1151JollyJck1151½ Showed sluggish form 12
Previously trained by G. Bloss									
11Jly56- 3Hol	fst 5½f	:222 :461 :583 1:05	Alw 5500	8 10 117½ 119½ 812 67¼	Rivera A	120 w	18.95	84-13	Golden One120½Lealito111¾Blue Torch120no Made up ground 12
13Jun56- 1Hol	fst 5f	:223 :46 :583	©Md Sp Wt	7 5 2½ 1hd 1½ 1¾	Rivera A	118 w	48.65	92-10	Gallant Man118¾Four Heels113nkGate Smasher118no Driving 12
29May56- 2Hol	fst 5f	:22 :454 :582	©Md Sp Wt	11 9 96½ 1011 811 98¾	Rivera A	118 w	75.70	84-10	Golden Notes1181½Pie Master1182½[DH] Vihiunis118 Outrun 12
18May56- 1Hol	fst 5f	:223 :463 :591	©Md Sp Wt	6 9 108¾ 1015 1015 1011	Trejos R	120 w	31.60	78-13	FuriousProfit120¾Jicky1201¼GoldnNots120nk Always outrun 11

Grecian Queen

dkb. f. 1950, by Heliopolis (Hyperion)–Qbania, by Questionnaire **Lifetime record: 53 12 8 8 $323,575**

Own.– Mrs B.F. Whitaker
Br.– Ben F. Whitaker (Ky)
Tr.– J.P. Conway

4Aug55- 3Sar fst 1 :243 :474 1:132 1:392 3↑ ⒻAlw 5000 5 3 3½ 21½ 35 39 Atkinson T 113wb 4.05 71-16 BattleWave1133HulaHula1096GrcnQun1136 Failed to respond 6
2Jly55- 6Del fst 1¼ :462 1:112 1:363 2:022 3↑ ⒻDelaware H 151k 5 9 104¾ 1112 1117 1120 Errico C 110wb 27.40f 70-17 Parlo1283Open Sesame1142Clear Dawn1191½ Broke to inside 13
25Jun55- 6Del gd 1 1/16 :232 :471 1:12 1:443 3↑ ⒻNew Castle 39k 7 11 127½ 1415 1214 1112 Errico C 116wb 34.20 76-17 Clear Dawn1162½Open Sesame1121½Cerise Reine120hd Outrun 15
16Jun55- 6Aqu fst 1 1/16 :25 :492 1:13 1:463 3↑ ⒻHandicap 7500 1 4 41½ 42½ 35 2nk Moreno H 112wb 11.40 81-19 OldBaasket113nkGrcnQueen112nkRomanWarbler1126 Necked 7
18May55- 7Bel fst 1 :234 :472 1:123 1:373 4↑ ⒻAlw 5000 3 6 77¼ 810 819 824 Broussard R 114 w 19.85 62-14 Riverina1115Carry the News1116Sweet Nell117¾ Outrun 9
2May55- 7Bel fst 7f :233 :474 1:131 1:261 4↑ ⒻAlw 4500 7 1 31½ 23 36 46½ Broussard R 112 w 9.10 72-22 Intencion115½Sweet Nell1224½Garb1111½ Speed for ⅝ 8
18Apr55- 7Jam fst 6f :232 :47 1:122 3↑ ⒻCorrectn H (Div 2) 28k 3 4 78¾ 67½ 717 712 Broussard R 111 w 40.20 73-19 BrazenBrat1191RosClag1106Trsong1161 Never in contention 9
12Apr55- 6Jam sly 6f :233 :47 1:123 4↑ ⒻAlw 4500 1 3 89 89¾ 814 713 Cole S 110 w 18.75 71-19 Crisset1122Sweet Nell121¾Murph's Deb112¾ Never close 9
30Oct54- 6Jam sly 1⅛ :474 1:131 1:394 1:532 3↑ ⒻFirenze H 35k 6 6 79½ 1113 1231 1228 Scurlock D 113 w 21.25 51-28 Parlo1257Rivern115¾SpnnngTop1101¾ Disliked sloppy going 13
12Oct54- 6Bel fst 1½ :471 1:122 2:044 2:321 3↑ ⒻLadies H 61k 8 9 86¾ 44 712 712 Shuk N 116 w 10.10 65-19 Lavender Hill1221½Ming Yellow1132½Riverina1141½ Tired 15
4Oct54- 6Bel fst 1 :231 :463 1:113 1:373 3↑ ⒻMaskette H 26k 4 3 5¾ 11¼ 12½ 2¾ Shuk N 113 w 8.65f 85-18 Ballerina106¾Grecian Queen1131½Gay Grecque1121 Tired 16
18Sep54- 6Aqu fst 1⅛ :48 1:12 1:37 1:494 3↑ ⒻBeldame H 64k 6 6 68 67½ 47½ 46¼ Shuk N 114 w 12.20 90-10 Parlo1163Open Sesame1101¾Clear Dawn1141½ Lacked a rally 9
7Sep54- 6Aqu fst 1 1/16 :253 :493 1:132 1:46 3↑ ⒻAlw 5000 4 1 11 1hd 2hd 33¼ Guerin E 122 w *1.05 81-18 Valadium118nkPetal1183GrecianQueen1226 Shortened stride 4
18Aug54- 6Sar fst 1⅛ :474 1:121 1:38 1:523 3↑ ⒻDiana H 23k 2 5 57 69½ 1017 1015 Atkinson T 120wb 7.35 72-19 Lavender Hill1211½La Corredora121hdEvening Out1166 Quit 10
6Aug54- 6Sar gd 1 :234 :473 1:123 1:384 3↑ ⒻHandicap 5045 3 2 2hd 1hd 2½ 2no Atkinson T 118wb 3.85 83-20 Petal106noGrecian Queen1183Mab's Choice114hd Outgamed 8
19Jly54- 6Jam fst 1 1/16 :241 :481 1:13 1:45 3↑ ⒻHandicap 7550 8 4 44½ 41½ 53 42¾ Guerin E 122wb 2.85 84-19 LavendrHill119¾MingYellow1161¼Nothrdchnc115¾ No excuse 8
5Jly54- 6Del fst 1¼ :454 1:101 1:361 2:023 3↑ ⒻNew Castle H 138k 12 6 78 1011 1416 1617 Green B 124wb 7.80 72-19 GainsboroGirl1134SunshineNell1262LavendrHll111hd Sulked 20
28Jun54- 6Del fst 1 1/16 :224 :462 1:112 1:443 3↑ ⒻAlw 10000 6 4 43 34½ 35 21½ Green B 124wb 19.90 86-19 EvningOut1041½GrecianQueen1241½LaCorredor124hd Gaining 12
22Jun54- 7Aqu fst 1 1/16 :25 :481 1:13 1:442 4↑ Alw 5000 7 2 21 22 38 412½ Green B 114wb 23.25 79-17 Crash Dive1145South Point1086Bicarb1161½ Tired 8
14Jun54- 6Mth fst 6f :221 :451 1:101 3↑ ⒻAlw 5000 3 6 87½ 812 814 813 Green B 118 w 11.80e 81-09 Cinda118¾Blue Rhymer1133Centenaire107¾ Never a threat 10
11May54- 5Bel gd 6f :23 :471 1:12 4↑ ⒻAlw 4500 4 4 912 910 914 911 Boland W 120 w 8.10e 78-22 Petal1081SpeedyWave1091Hadassah116nk Trailed throughout 9
15Apr54- 5Jam fst 6f :233 :48 1:123 4↑ ⒻAlw 5000 3 4 43¼ 35 45½ 34½ Woodhouse H 119 w 3.60 79-18 Outsmart1172½Petal1172GrecianQun119no Wide,lacked rally 7
1Mar54- 7Hia hy 1⅛ :492 1:154 1:433 1:574 3↑ ⒻBlack Helen H 32k 5 6 65½ 78½ 711 712 Atkinson T 123 w 4.95 35-41 GainsboroGirl109¾LavenderHill1084½Emard120½ Dull effort 10
22Feb54- 7Hia fst 7f :223 :452 1:10 1:23 3↑ ⒻColumbiana H 21k 10 7 147¾ 1516 1316 1316 Atkinson T 124 w 8.60 79-13 Fascinator1101Lavender Hill105nkAtalanta1261 No speed 16
1Feb54- 7Hia fst 6f :224 :46 1:104 4↑ ⒻAlw 5000 7 5 74¼ 86¾ 68 66 Shuk N 122 w 4.55 88-14 Emardee116noWinningStrd1184AtInt124hd Faltered in drive 8
23Jan54- 6Hia fst 6f :223 :46 1:11 4↑ Alw 5000 3 2 74¾ 85¾ 87½ 84¼ Atkinson T 117 w 3.15 89-09 Emardee105½Blenriam1131¼Armageddon112nk No threat 10
26Sep53- 6Bel fst 1 :231 :461 1:11 1:364 3↑ Sysonby 54k 3 3 31½ 22½ 36 33½ Guerin E 116 w - 86-15 Tom Fool1263Alerted126½Grecian Queen116 No excuse 3
19Sep53- 6Aqu fst 1⅛ :48 1:122 1:383 1:521 3↑ ⒻBeldame H 66k 7 3 45½ 711 911 813 Arcaro E 125 w *1.10 71-18 Atalanta1213Miss Traffic1063La Corredora119hd No excuse 12
26Aug53- 6Sar fst 1¼ :492 1:142 1:40 2:06 ⒻAlabama 27k 4 2 1hd 12½ 12 2nk Shuk N 126 w 1.20 78-23 Sabette114nkGrecianQueen1269CherryFizz109nk Game effort 5
8Aug53- 6Mth fst 1⅛ :481 1:124 1:38 1:511 ⒻMth Oaks 59k 8 3 31½ 1hd 11½ 11 Shuk N 121 w *.90 94-15 GrecianQueen1211Sabette1131¼ArabActress1212½ Ridden out 9
4Jly53- 6Del fst 1¼ :473 1:12 1:37 2:024 3↑ ⒻNew Castle H 121k 4 2 1hd 1hd 11½ 11 Atkinson T 114 w *1.50 88-14 GrecianQueen1141Devilkin1201½MyCeleste117hd Drew clear 10
24Jun53- 6Aqu fst 1 1/16 :233 :471 1:113 1:454 ⒻGazelle 30k 9 4 310 38 22 11½ Guerin E 121 w 2.80 85-17 Grecian Queen1211½Canadiana1211¾Sabette1132¾ Drew clear 10
6Jun53- 6Bel fst 1⅜ :481 1:132 1:384 2:183 ⒻC C A Oaks 63k 8 3 33½ 1hd 13½ 1no Guerin E 121 w 4.20 78-16 GrecianQueen121noSabette1212½MingYellow1213 Tiring fast 9
30May53- 6Del sly 1⅛ :47 1:113 1:374 1:503 ⒻDel Oaks 42k 5 4 47½ 210 212 313½ Boland W 119 w 5.05 78-19 Cerise Reine11912Script1101½Grecian Queen1192 No rally 8
22May53- 6Bel fst 1⅛ :471 1:122 1:39 1:52 ⒻAlw 6500 9 3 33 33½ 21 13 Woodhouse H 118 w *1.35 79-24 Grecian Queen1183Sabette1082½Milspal1093½ Easily 10
9May53- 6Bel gd 1 :231 :462 1:123 1:392 ⒻAcorn 25k 3 10 96¾ 77 64½ 69¼ Scurlock O 121 w *.90 68-24 Secret Meeting1211Wings o' Morn1213Tritium1212 Faltered 12
15Apr53- 6Jam fst 6f :232 :47 1:132 ⒻPrioress 24k 12 7 98¼ 87 42½ 12¼ Guerin E 121 w *1.40e 80-21 GrecianQueen1212¼[D]Flamenco121½Tritium121nk Ridden out 12
7Apr53- 5Jam sly 6f :243 :48 1:124 ⒻAlw 4000 5 1 3½ 3nk 2hd 1½ Guerin E 120 w *1.30 83-20 Grecian Queen120½Petal1155½Sabette1102 Hard urged 6
8Nov52- 6Pim fst 1 1/16 :232 :473 1:13 1:48 ⒻMarguerite (Div 1) 24k 9 4 54½ 53 53 1nk Guerin E 118 w *1.70 70-24 Grecian Queen118nkIs Proud121½Mi-Marigold115¾ Just up 9
29Oct52- 6Jam fst 1 1/16 :252 :491 1:131 1:463 ⒻDemoiselle 51k 5 1 11 12 12 12½ Guerin E 119 w 2.00 79-22 Grecian Queen1192½Ballerina119¾Tritium1147 Ridden out 7
8Oct52- 6Jam fst 6f :23 :46 1:122 ⒻFrizette 17k 8 3 32½ 32 32 31¾ Arcaro E 119 w 3.90 83-17 SweetPatootie1191¼PiedmontLass119½GrcnQn1191½ Impeded 8
20Sep52- 4Bel sly 6f-WC :221 :45 1:092 ⒻMatron 52k 6 8 64 63¼ 33¼ Atkinson T 119 w 14.20 91-08 Is Proud1193Aerolite119nkGrecian Queen1192 Sharp effort 9
6Sep52- 4Aqu fst 6f :232 :472 1:133 ⒻAstarita 12k 10 2 31 41¼ 31 1½ Guerin E 119 w 9.15 84-17 GrecianQueen119½PiedmontLass116½Flirtatous122hd Driving 11
20Aug52- 6Sar fst 6f :233 :47 1:131 ⒻSpinaway 21k 4 6 54 34½ 25 28 York R 119 w *2.25e 74-22 Flirtatious1198GrecianQueen1194Loto'Hony115nk No excuse 9
21Jly52- 6Jam sly 5½f 1:072 ⒻSchuylerville 13k 8 32 1¾ York R 111 w 4.45e 81-19 GrecianQueen111¾ColdHeart114noPiedmontLass1144 Driving 9
Further calls unavailable due to heavy rain
16Jly52- 5Jam fst 5½f :23 :463 1:054 ⒻAlw 5000 1 2 72¾ 96¾ 45½ 21½ York R 110 w *1.55e 87-16 Tiny Request1101½Grecian Queen110hdPiedmont Lass1162 9
Strong finish
23Jun52- 6Aqu fst 5½f :23 :464 :591 1:054 ⒻAlw 5000 3 2 2hd 31 2½ 2½ Woodhouse H 114 w 17.85 94-13 ColdHeart114½GrecianQueen1141½Equableu1142 Good effort 7
14May52- 6Bel fst 5f-WC :224 :462 :591 ⒻNational Stallion 28k 5 5 63 67 610 Boland W 119 w 30.20 73-19 Home-Made1191Appian1193Flirtatious119no Tired 9
5May52- 5Bel fst 4½f-W :223 :453 :514 ⒻAlw 4000 1 3 62¼ 55 64 Scurlock O 118 w 4.00e 86-14 Flirtatious1182¼MissNancy115¾PearlDvr118nk Bumped horse 7
22Apr52- 4Jam fst 5f :233 :472 1:00 ⒻMd Sp Wt 5 3 21 2hd 21 11½ Gorman D 116 w 3.55 90-18 GrecianQueen1161½SilverBlue1163½Arista1162½ Drew clear 10
14Apr52- 6Jam sly 5f :23 :463 :592 ⒻRosedale (Div 2) 12k 3 2 79¾ 812 89½ 78½ Boland W 114 w 29.60 84-15 Emardee116hdKitchen Maid1152½Waterline1142½ Impeded 10
4Apr52- 2Jam fst 5f :233 :472 1:001 ⒻMd Sp Wt 3 9 87¼ 68 57½ 34 Gorman D 116 w 3.30 85-15 CountssJane1094SweetGoddess111hdGrcnQn116hd Went well 10
28Feb52- 5FG fst 2f :23 ⒻMd Sp Wt 5 8 44½ 43½ Van Hook E 111 *1.10 - - Actuate1162½Ruler's Girl111nkE-Town111¾ Slow start 12

High Gun

br. c. 1951, by Heliopolis (Hyperion)–Rocket Gun, by Brazado **Lifetime record: 24 11 5 4 $486,025**

Own.– King Ranch
Br.– K.M. & W.P. Little & C.C. Boshamer (Ky)
Tr.– M. Hirsch

24Sep55- 6Bel sly 1⅛ :451 1:101 1:36 1:491 3↑ Sysonby 106k 3 5 58½ 43¾ 33 1hd Boland W 126 w 4.50 93-10 HighGun126hdJetActon1261¾Nshu1213½ Just up final stride 5
30Jly55- 7AP fm 1 3/16Ⓣ :48 1:12 1:37 1:543 3↑ Arlington H 161k 4 1 1½ 2½ 31½ 75¼ Arcaro E 130 w *2.20 101-03 Platan1173Impass110¾Mrk-Y-Wll116nk Early speed,weakened 15
23Jly55- 6Mth fst 1¼ :464 1:112 1:362 2:021 3↑ Monmouth H 83k 3 2 21¼ 21½ 22½ 21½ Arcaro E 135 w *.80 93-14 Helioscope1311½HighGn1356PunkinVn1111 Crowded at break 4
9Jly55- 6Aqu fst 1¼ :49 1:132 1:373 2:032 3↑ Brooklyn H 56k 5 1 14 14 14½ 13½ Arcaro E 132 w *.50 90-15 High Gun1323½Paper Tiger107noStraight Face11612 In hand 5
4Jly55- 6Aqu fst 7f :222 :444 1:10 1:232 3↑ Carter H 61k 3 12 129¾ 97¼ 65¾ 63½ Arcaro E 133 w *1.60 89-13 BobbyBrocato1161SocialOutcst1231Artsmo111½ Broke in air 14
30May55- 6Bel fst 1¼ :474 1:113 1:36 2:003 3↑ Suburban H 88k 9 2 2½ 2hd 1hd 2hd Arcaro E 133 w *.70 97-11 Helioscope128hdHighGun1334½Subahdar1199 Held stubbornly 9
14May55- 6Bel fst 1 :231 :461 1:104 1:353 3↑ Metropolitan H 36k 9 6 52 2hd 12½ 14½ De Spirito A 130 w *1.85 96-11 HighGun1304½Artsmo115noJoJons119no Increasing long lead 9
16Oct54- 6Bel fst 2 :501 2:342 2:594 3:254 3↑ J C Gold Cup 82k 1 1 12½ 13½ 15 13 Arcaro E 119 w *.50 75-16 HighGun1193Fisherman1191Bicarb12410 Well rated,eased up 7
Geldings not eligible
9Oct54- 4Bel fst 1½ :49 1:134 2:04 2:303 3↑ Manhattan H 35k 4 5 2hd 11½ 12 11¼ Arcaro E 123 w *.50 85-15 High Gun1231¼Subahdar110hdBicarb1162 Under brisk urging 9
27Sep54- 6Bel fst 1 :232 :463 1:11 1:363 3↑ Sysonby 28k 1 4 1hd 1hd 1½ 12 Arcaro E 121 w *1.25 91-10 High Gun1212Landlocked1261¼Sir Mango1261¾ Drew out 4
21Aug54- 7Was fst 1⅛ :47 1:111 1:36 1:494 American Derby 115k 6 7 69 57½ 34½ 22 Shoemaker W 124 w *1.30 90-13 ErrardKing1242HighGun1243½HastyRod124¾ Gaining steadily 9
17Jly54- 7AP fst 1 :222 :45 1:092 1:35 Arl Classic 161k 4 13 117¾ 76½ 45½ 32½ Guerin E 123 w 4.10 94-08 ErrardKing1202½Hloscop120noHghGun123nk Closed fast late 13
3Jly54- 6Aqu fst 1¼ :50 1:15 1:40 2:05 Dwyer 57k 5 2 2½ 2½ 1hd 11 Guerin E 126 w *.55 82-14 HighGun1261PalmTree1145PaperTgr1146 Drew clear steadily 5
12Jun54- 6Bel fst 1½ :49 1:14 2:033 2:304 Belmont 125k 5 8 811 56½ 22½ 1nk Guerin E 126 w 3.45e 84-16 High Gun126nkFisherman1265Limelight1263 Just up 13
Geldings not eligible
5Jun54- 6Bel fst 1⅛ :501 1:151 1:40 1:522 Peter Pan H 36k 6 7 76 75¼ 2½ 13 Guerin E 116 w 5.80 77-20 High Gun1163Fisherman1211¾Diving Board1161½ Drew out 7

29May54- 7GS	fst	1⅛	:472 1:114 1:372 1:513	Jersey 64k	11 9 77 44½ 44½ 32½	Hanford I	111 w	7.10	81-16	WarofRoses1111½RedHnngn1111HghGn1111½	Crowded at start	12
15May54- 7GS	fst	6f	:221 :452 1:11	Del Valley (Div 2) 35k	4 11 108½ 75¾ 65 42	Hanford I	112 w	7.10	91-15	Brsut115nkDucdFr1211Rvolt121¾	Steadied early,good rally	11
8May54- 4Bel	sly	1	:23 :461 1:111 1:363	Withers 35k	6 11 106¾ 75¾ 34½ 34	Guerin E	126 w	5.85	87-12	JetAction1262Buttevant1262HghGun126½	Slow start,rallied	11
Geldings not eligible												
3May54- 6Bel	sly	1⅛	:462 1:103 1:36 1:492	Alw 5000	2 3 31½ 2½ 22½ 23½	Guerin E	119 w	*.95	88-14	PalmTree1163½HighGun1196PaperTiger1222½	No late rally	6
24Apr54- 6Jam	fst	1⅛	:481 1:13 1:383 1:50	Wood Memorial 122k	8 4 42½ 22 44½ 37½	Guerin E	126 w	18.30	88-16	Correlation1263½Fisherman1264HghGun1263	Rider lost whip	8
Geldings not eligible. Daily Racing Form time, 1:50 4/5												
6Apr54- 5Jam	fst	1 1/16	:24 :482 1:132 1:45	Alw 4000	4 3 3½ 2½ 22 26	Guerin E	116 w	*1.10	81-15	Full Flight1136High Gun1166Pat Thompson1139	Faltered	5
7Nov53- 7Jam	sly	1 1/16	:24 :48 1:14 1:473	Alw 7500	1 4 33½ 1hd 13 13	Guerin E	116 w	3.00	74-19	High Gun1163Hobcaw Sage1123Wise Pop1123	Handily	7
24Oct53- 5GS	fst	1 1/16	:233 :473 1:13 1:464	Alw 10000	3 7 64¾ 63¾ 58½ 58	Williams WB	111 w	4.90	68-21	Passembud1152Red Hannigan1133Road-Star1112	No mishap	13
20Oct53- 4Jam	fst	5½f	:233 :474 1:064	ⒸMd Sp Wt	10 8 45 55 44 11¾	Arcaro E	118 w	5.70	84-19	High Gun1181¾Ashenden1182Surmount1182	Ridden out	11

High Voltage

gr. f. 1952, by Ambiorix (Tourbillon)–Dynamo, by Menow

Lifetime record: 45 13 5 7 $362,240

Own.– Wheatley Stable
Br.– Wheatley Stable (Ky)
Tr.– J. Fitzsimmons

1Aug56- 7Jam	fst	6f	:224 :453 1:11	3↑ⒻChamplain H 23k	9 8 1211 139½ 1112½ 76½	Atkinson T	113 w	7.65e	85-16	ⒹBlueSparkler1252½Gandharv1182BluBnnr122hd	Stride late	13
21Jly56- 7Jam	sly	1 1/16	:233 :471 1:12 1:43	3↑ⒻBellerose H 27k	7 4 34½ 56½ 510 512	Atkinson T	114 w	4.80	85-12	Parlo1212½BluSprklr1251¾Mnotck119hd	Bobbled start,tired	7
16Jly56- 7Jam	fst	6f	:23 :461 1:103	3↑ⒻHandicap 6000	5 6 64½ 53 33 32½	Cole S	118 w	3.15e	91-12	Blue Banner122hdSorceress1142½High Voltage1182	Rallied	9
7Jly56- 6Mth	sl	1 1/16	:232 :474 1:114 1:443	3↑ⒻMolly Pitcher H 28k	7 4 32½ 47½ 511 716	Moreno H	116wb	8.00	76-20	Blue Sparkler1208Rico Reto1171Another World1102½	Tired	9
30Jun56- 7Del	fst	1¼	:451 1:101 1:362 2:03	3↑ⒻDelaware H 156k	8 6 58 1111 1412 1414	Atkinson T	119wb	15.50	73-14	Flower Bowl1122Manotick122¾Open Sesame113hd	Fell back	15
16Jun56- 6Mth	fst	6f	:212 :433 1:091	3↑ⒻRegret H 22k	7 7 78¼ 714 68 43½	Culmone J	117wb	4.20e	95-06	BlueSparkler1192Jimminetty114¾PromptImpulse115¾	Rallied	9
26May56- 7Bel	fst	1 1/16	:223 :451 1:102 1:423	3↑ⒻTop Flight H 28k	4 2 33½ 55 1012 814	Arcaro E	118 w	4.40e	82-11	Searching121½Prlo1241½RcoRto107nk	Early speed,fell back	10
17May56- 7Bel	fst	1	:224 :452 1:104 1:364	4↑ⒻAlw 7500	1 2 22 24 55¾ 57¾	Atkinson T	122 w	8.45	82-18	Gandharva1101½FlowerBowl1031¾RareTreat118½	Early speed	10
9May56- 7Jam	fst	6f	:233 :47 1:113	3↑ⒻCorrection H 22k	8 8 62¼ 73¼ 87¾ 86¼	Atkinson T	120 w	5.35	83-19	Searching120¾Gandharva1191Up Betimes110nk	Wide all way	8
3May56- 6Jam	fst	6f	:233 :463 1:113	4↑ⒻAlw 6000	1 2 1hd 2hd 2½ 23	Atkinson T	122 w	*1.20	86-15	Sorceress1113High Voltage122hdManotick1222	Held on well	7
24Apr56- 7Jam	fst	1 1/16	:25 :492 1:14 1:462	3↑ⒻHandicap 10000	3 3 42 53¾ 57¼ 67¾	Atkinson T	126wb	1.80e	72-21	RareTreat1161EscaLass1055RicoReto1111	Early foot,tired	7
14Apr56- 7Jam	fst	1 1/16	:241 :473 1:121 1:431	3↑ Excelsior H 28k	7 3 34½ 78 713 819	Woodhouse H	112wb	9.50	77-15	Find116nkJoe Jones1193½Fisherman1224	Dropped back early	9
9Apr56- 7Jam	gd	5½f	:23 :46 :59 1:05	3↑ⒻHandicap 6000	6 5 34 32½ 3nk 11	Atkinson T	121wb	*1.40	93-15	High Voltage1211On the Move1143Tarquilla1072½	Driving	6
21Mar56- 7GP	fst	1 1/16	:232 :47 1:113 1:43	3↑ⒻSuwannee River H 17k	7 4 53 75¾ 1011 1011	Atkinson T	124wb	*2.25	84-10	Tremor106½FlowerBowl1062QueenHopful116hd	Factor,stopped	10
2Mar56- 7Hia	fst	1⅛	:453 1:10 1:36 1:492	3↑ⒻBlack Helen H 40k	7 2 23 22 3½ 3¾	Atkinson T	125wb	*1.55e	88-09	Clear Dawn108noMiss Arlette112¾High Voltage125hd	Gamely	12
22Feb56- 7Hia	fst	7f	:223 :451 1:092 1:221	3↑ⒻColumbiana H 25k	7 4 52¼ 43½ 47 26	Atkinson T	126wb	4.75	93-12	Myrtle's Jet1146HighVoltage126nkSometimThng126no	Rallied	12
16Feb56- 7Hia	fst	6f	:224 :461 1:102	4↑ⒻAlw 7500	1 4 21½ 31 31½ 33¾	Atkinson T	126wb	3.35	91-16	SometimeThing1213FantineBushr109¾HighVoltag1261½	Tired	7
8Nov55- 6Jam	fst	1⅛	:473 1:113 1:37 1:504	3↑ⒻFirenze H 35k	1 2 33 53¼ 78½ 79	Arcaro E	121wb	*2.15	83-15	RareTreat112½Searching118noWhiteCross1081¼	Early factor	12
31Oct55- 6Jam	gd	1 1/16	:242 :48 1:122 1:441	ⒻHandicap 10000	4 2 21 2½ 1hd 1no	Arcaro E	126wb	*1.05	91-11	HighVoltage126noTwoStars109nkRareTreat1165	Hard drive	5
22Oct55- 7GS	fst	1⅛	:453 1:10 1:353 1:481	3↑ⒻVineland H 51k	12 6 3½ 2hd 11 13	Arcaro E	117wb	2.80e	96-10	High Voltage1173Manotick1181Crisset110no	Going away	18
8Oct55- 7GS	my	1 1/16	:243 :492 1:153 1:512	ⒻJersey Belle 29k	6 2 23 21½ 1½ 2½	Higley J	121wb	4.70	52-41	RareTreat115½HighVoltage1213RicoRomance1142½	Faltered	9
3Oct55- 6Bel	fst	1	:232 :461 1:104 1:363	3↑ⒻMaskette H 25k	2 2 43½ 69 816 914	Arcaro E	117 w	*2.45	77-17	OilPainting119nkMissWeesie1045ClearDawn1161	Brief foot	12
23Sep55- 6Bel	fst	1	:231 :46 1:104 1:364	ⒻHandicap 10000	2 4 52½ 53 56½ 43	Arcaro E	122wb	*.60e	87-17	MistyMorn124¾RareTreat1122¼SweetMusic106hd	Closed well	7
9Sep55- 6Aqu	fst	1 1/16	:251 :493 1:133 1:462	3↑ⒻHandicap 10000	5 6 53¼ 42½ 53¼ 74	Arcaro E	122wb	1.95	78-20	Searching1201ClearDawn122noSilentOn108nk	Close quarters	8
24Aug55- 6Sar	gd	1¼	:484 1:142 1:394 2:054	ⒻAlabama 29k	7 4 32 44 712 712	Arcaro E	124wb	*.40e	67-22	RicoReto1133BlueBnnr114nkMstyMorn1211¼	Early foot,tired	8
2Jly55- 6Del	fst	1¼	:462 1:112 1:363 2:022	3↑ⒻDelaware H 151k	3 8 94¾ 64 57½ 46½	Cole S	116wb	10.80	83-17	Parlo1283Open Sesame1142Clear Dawn1191½	Crowded early	13
27Jun55- 6Aqu	fst	1 1/16	:241 :48 1:123 1:453	ⒻGazelle 30k	7 7 65½ 54¼ 3½ 3nk	Arcaro E	121wb	*.75e	86-15	Mnotck113hdTwoStrs113nkHghVoltg1212	Close quarters early	10
18Jun55- 6Del	fst	1⅛	:463 1:11 1:372 1:503	ⒻDel Oaks 49k	6 6 33½ 22 1hd 1nk	Arcaro E	119wb	*.50	87-13	High Voltage119nkHen Party110½Rico Romance113¾	Driving	10
8Jun55- 6Bel	fst	1 1/16	:224 :451 1:094 1:414	3↑ⒻTop Flight H 30k	2 6 75 64½ 68 78¾	Arcaro E	117wb	2.60	93-11	Parlo1263Gainsboro Girl114½Spinning Top113nk	No excuse	12
28May55- 6Bel	fst	1⅜	:472 1:114 1:372 2:173	ⒻC C A Oaks 63k	4 9 63¾ 51¼ 11 12½	Atkinson T	121wb	*.60e	83-15	High Voltage1212½Lalun1212Manotick121nk	Driving clear	11
14May55- 7Pim	sly	1 1/16	:223 :462 1:114 1:461	ⒻBlack-Eyed Susan 26k	3 3 32 2½ 2hd 11	Arcaro E	121wb	*1.30	79-22	High Voltage1211Bless Pat1213Hen Party121hd	Ridden out	9
4May55- 6Bel	fst	1	:224 :461 1:121 1:384	ⒻAcorn 31k	5 6 63½ 41 21½ 1¾	Arcaro E	121wb	*2.20	80-13	HighVoltage121¾SometimeThing1211¾HenParty121hd	Driving	14
26Apr55- 5Bel	sly	6f	:221 :453 1:111	ⒻAlw 5000	4 3 43½ 45½ 58 47	Atkinson T	121 w	3.25	86-12	Gandharva1174½Sorceress1141½TwoStrs1171¼	Evenly all way	9
2Nov54- 6Jam	sly	1 1/16	:242 :482 1:142 1:491	ⒻFrizette 53k	8 7 55½ 32 23 42½	Arcaro E	119 w	*.75	63-27	Myrtle'sJet1192HenParty119nkSorcrss119nk	Bothered,tired	9
23Oct54- 7Lrl	fst	1 1/16	:223 :454 1:113 1:45	ⒻSelima 66k	6 6 48 21 1hd 1¾	Arcaro E	119 w	*.60	89-13	High Voltage119¾Myrtle's Jet1194Misty119¾	Ridden out	9
2Oct54- 4Bel	fst	6f-WC	:213 :443 1:10	ⒻMatron 61k	13 3 93 13 13	Arcaro E	119 w	*2.10	91-09	High Voltage1193Blue Banner1192Lalun119½	Easy score	20
23Sep54- 6Bel	fst	5½f-W	:223 :454 1:041	ⒻAlw 5000	8 4 74½ 31½ 32½	Arcaro E	124 w	*1.35	84-13	BlessPat113½Errasina1162HighVoltage1242	Tired in drive	12
1Sep54- 6Aqu	fst	6f	:223 :463 1:124	ⒻAstarita 18k	9 8 96½ 87¾ 44 2no	Arcaro E	125 w	*1.60	88-14	TwoStars119noHighVoltage1252½MyBlueSky110hd	Nosed out	10
23Aug54- 6Sar	fst	6f	:224 :462 1:124	ⒻSpinaway 59k	1 6 78 77 57½ 32	Arcaro E	123 w	*1.80	82-22	Gandharva1111½My Blue Sky111½High Voltage1231	Gaining	9
3Jly54- 6Mth	fst	5½f	:213 :452 1:051	ⒻColleen 28k	8 6 57 47½ 36 1nk	Arcaro E	119 w	*2.40	98-09	High Voltage119nkMenolene1191½Sue Pat112½	Strong drive	14
19May54- 6Bel	fst	5f-WC	:214 :444 :571	ⒻNational Stallion 31k	9 4 31½ 3nk 1¾	Nichols J	119 w	3.35	93-10	High Voltage119¾Delta1191Sly Vixen119hd	Hard punished	9
28Apr54- 6Bel	fst	4½f-W	:214 :444 :511	ⒻFashion 15k	2 5 52¼ 42½ 2½	Guerin E	119 w	*1.00	92-08	Sofarsogood114½HighVoltage1191½Chapl114¾	Gaining at end	10
14Apr54- 6Jam	fst	5f	:232 :47 :592	ⒻRosedale 13k	9 6 2½ 2hd 21 12	Higley J	114 w	2.15	93-18	HighVoltage1142Guppie1141RedLetterDay1154½	Ridden out	9
10Apr54- 3Jam	fst	5f	:23 :463 :594	ⒻMd Sp Wt	4 3 31 2hd 2hd 12½	Guerin E	116 w	*1.20e	91-13	HighVoltage1162½BlessPat1163½LadyBrownie116nk	In hand	10
2Apr54- 3Jam	fst	5f	:223 :47 :594	ⒻMd Sp Wt	4 6 58 57½ 34 33	Guerin E	116 w	*2.05	88-15	SweetMusic1162½HiddnShip116½HighVoltag1163½	No excuse	10

Hill Prince

b. c. 1947, by Princequillo (Prince Rose)–Hildene, by Bubbling Over

Lifetime record: 30 17 5 4 $422,140

Own.– C.T. Chenery
Br.– C.T. Chenery (Va)
Tr.– J.H. Hayes

1Mar52- 7SA	my	1¼	:452 1:104 1:354 2:01	3↑ S Anita H 141k	4 15 1521 1011 79¾ 58¾	Arcaro E	129wb	*1.25e	86-16	ⒹIntent1111Miche1154½Be Fleet1142½		15
Moved up inside,failed to threaten												
9Feb52- 6SA	fst	1	:223 :454 1:103 1:354	3↑ San Marcos H 24k	4 10 812 35 2½ 12	Arcaro E	126wb	*.75e	97-14	Hill Prince1262Bryan G.122noBe Fleet1173½	Easily best	11
3Nov51- 7GS	sly	1⅛	:47 1:113 1:374 1:52	3↑ Trenton H 60k	4 8 814 811 48½ 45¼	Arcaro E	130wb	*.70	77-23	Call Over116hdInseparable108hdPost Card1135	No excuse	8
20Oct51- 6Jam	fst	1⅝	:502 1:40 2:044 2:424	3↑ Emp Gold Cup 53k	1 4 21 1hd 2hd 21¼	Arcaro E	126wb	*.35	99-14	Counterpoint1191¼HillPrince1264½HullDown11912	Gave way	4
Geldings not eligible												
13Oct51- 6Bel	fst	2	:493 2:302 2:56 3:213	3↑ J C Gold Cup 53k	1 1 11½ 11 1½ 2hd	Arcaro E	124wb	*.30	96-11	Counterpoint117hdHillPrince12410KssMKt1142½	Just failed	5
29Sep51- 6Bel	fst	1⅛	:464 1:114 1:363 1:49	3↑ New York H 29k	7 8 43 1½ 15 15	Arcaro E	128wb	*.80	94-15	Hill Prince1285One Hitter1171Sudan1051½	Easily	8
24Sep51- 5Bel	fst	1	:232 :461 1:102 1:352	3↑ Alw 5000	3 3 21 2½ 1hd 1¾	Arcaro E	121wb	*1.05	97-16	HillPrince121¾SheilasReward1218OneHitter1211½	Handily	4
15Sep51- 5Aqu	fst	6f	:23 :46 1:104	3↑ Handicap 4560	5 5 57½ 58 56 35½	Arcaro E	128wb	3.10	92-13	Tea-Maker1211NorthernStar1184½HillPrinc128¾	Closed well	7
16Dec50- 7Hol	fst	1⅛	:462 1:103 1:36 1:483	3↑ Sunset H 58k	6 8 713 54½ 42½ 1¾	Arcaro E	128wb	*.45	98-12	HillPrince128¾NxtMov1141½GrtCrcl109nk	Wide into stretch	10
9Dec50- 7Hol	fst	1¼	:463 1:101 1:35 1:594	3↑ Hol Gold Cup 137k	7 7 67 75¼ 55 34	Arcaro E	130wb	3.70	97-09	Noor1301Palestinian1223Hill Prince1301	Blocked,gamely	8
23Nov50- 7Hol	fst	1 1/16	:233 :47 1:104 1:414	3↑ Thanksgiving Day H 44k	8 6 63½ 53 52½ 3hd	Arcaro E	128wb	*1.05	99-07	Your Host124noPonder124hdHill Prince1282	Poor start	10
7Oct50- 6Bel	fst	2	:494 2:31 2:563 3:232	3↑ J C Gold Cup 54k	3 1 12 11½ 13 14	Arcaro E	117wb	1.25	87-13	Hill Prince1174Noor1247Adile1212	Easily best	5
Geldings not eligible												
20Sep50- 6Bel	fst	1	:224 :452 1:103 1:354	Jerome H 24k	11 13 139¾ 107¼ 41¾ 14	Arcaro E	129 w	*1.70	95-10	Hill Prince1294Greek Ship1221Navy Chief108nk	Easily	13

26Aug50- 7Was fst 1¼ :472 1:112 1:351 2:011 American Derby 78k 3 9 77 24 21 11½ Arcaro E 126wb *1.50 96-07 Hill Prince1261½All Blue1144½Your Host126nk Drew out 9
24Jun50- 6Aqu fst 1¼ :491 1:13 1:374 2:03 Dwyer 45k 5 5 12 13 11 21½ Arcaro E 121 w *.90 90-12 Greek Song1161½Hill Prince1216Lights Up1164 No excuse 5
10Jun50- 6Bel fst 1½ :482 1:123 2:021 2:283 Belmont 91k 2 7 11½ 11½ 42 74 Arcaro E 126wb *.85 91-13 Middleground1261Lights Up126½Mr. Trouble126hd Stopped 9
Geldings not eligible
30May50- 6Bel gd 1¼ :472 1:103 1:361 2:02 3↑ Suburban H 59k 5 6 1hd 2½ 32 32¾ Woodhouse H 113wb *.90 87-14 LoserWeeper115nkMyRqust1192½HllPrnc1133½ Bled 7
20May50- 6Pim sl 1 3/16 :482 1:132 1:401 1:591 Preakness 75k 1 6 31 13 11 15 Arcaro E 126wb *.70 84-23 Hill Prince1265Middleground1265Dooly1266 Ridden out 6
13May50- 6Bel fst 1 :23 :454 1:102 1:354 Withers 29k 2 6 43¼ 2hd 1½ 11½ Arcaro E 126wb *1.10 95-11 Hill Prince1261½Middleground1264Ferd1263 Handily 7
6May50- 7CD fst 1¼ :463 1:112 1:364 2:013 Ky Derby 120k 5 9 89¾ 52½ 31½ 21¼ Arcaro E 126wb 2.50 98-09 Mddlground1261¼HllPrnc126½Mr.Troubl1262¾ Close quarters 14
22Apr50- 6Jam fst 1 1/16 :24 :472 1:12 1:433 Wood Memorial 49k 5 10 44 42 1½ 12 Arcaro E 126wb *1.50 95-13 Hill Prince1262Middleground1261½Ferd126¾ Going away 11
15Apr50- 6Jam fst 1 1/16 :23 :46 1:113 1:443 Exp Free H #2 27k 10 10 813 1110 1016 920 Arcaro E 124wb *.50 70-12 Lotowhit1074½RoylCstl106½SturdyOn1061½ Stumbled,impeded 11
5Apr50- 6Jam sly 6f :223 :461 :592 1:12 Exp Free H #1 21k 6 6 611 68 34 11¼ Arcaro E 124wb *.60 91-18 Hill Prince1241¼Starecase1083Casemate116½ Going away 7
Daily Racing Form time, 1:11 3/5
14Sep49- 6Aqu sly 6½f :23 :461 1:102 1:163 Cowdin 23k 4 6 66 32½ 1½ 12½ Arcaro E 122wb *.30 102-15 Hill Prince1222½Selector1171Suleiman117no Going away 6
7Sep49- 6Aqu fst 6f :23 :463 1:123 Babylon H 13k 2 11 119¾ 88½ 41½ 12 Arcaro E 126wb *.95 89-17 Hill Prince1262Miss Degree106¾Navy Chief121¾ Drew out 11
13Aug49- 5Atl sly 6f :23 :461 1:124 World's Playground 16k 3 8 65 42½ 2hd 15 Dodson D 117wb *.40 82-21 Hill Prince1175Attention Mark1171½Cornwall114hd Easily 8
3Aug49- 4Mth sly 6f :224 :46 1:124 Alw 4000 5 7 32 31 11 11 Dodson D 116 w *.50 84-22 Hill Prince1161Jersey Queen1054Clean Broom1103 Cleverly 7
27Jly49- 5Mth fst 6f :23 :452 1:113 Sapling 13k 4 7 77 33½ 23 21 Arcaro E 115 w *.80 89-12 Casemate1221Hill Prince1154½Thorn113¾ Off poorly 7
9Jly49- 4Mth fst 5½f :22 :464 :592 1:062 Alw 4000 3 5 64¾ 31½ 2hd 12 Dodson D 113 w 2.30 92-17 Hill Prince1132Ferd1223Thorn1161½ Going away 7
2Jly49- 4Aqu fst 5½f :23 :473 1:062 Md Sp Wt 6 6 54 44½ 21 17 Arcaro E 118 w 3.55 92-14 Hill Prince1187Black Wizard1181½Pontalba113½ Easily 10

Iceberg II (Chi)

b. c. 1948, by Espadin (Full Sail)–Bellagamba, by Statuto **Lifetime record: 56 13 10 11 $165,108**
Own.– W.A. Hanger
Br.– L.C. Allende (Chi)
Tr.– Horatio A. Luro

4Jly55- 7AP fm 1⅛Ⓣ :462 1:104 1:354 1:482 3↑ Stars & Stripes H 28k 7 6 48 53 74¾ 42¾ Gorman D 117wb 14.90 97-06 Mark-Ye-Well114nkRuh1111½BluChor1171 Tight quarters str 10
21Jun55- 6AP fm 1 1/16Ⓣ :232 :463 1:12 1:433 4↑ Alw 5000 3 8 53 21½ 13 1hd Gorman D 121wb 1.80e 95-11 Iceberg II121hdKing1151¼Ruhe1121 Clear lead,tiring fast 9
11Jun55- 7Bel fm 1⅜Ⓣ 2:181 3↑ Handicap 15000 1 5 53½ 44½ 2½ 32¼ Gorman D 119wb 7.60 94-04 PrinceHill1171¾Secant111½IcebergII1191½ Made bid,tired 11
10May55- 6Pim fm 1 1/16Ⓣ 1:433 4↑ Alw 4000 6 6 56½ 58½ 58 56 Nelson E 119wb 2.10 103-00 Old Glendale1144Potpourri1191Baroda Boy112¾ Off slowly 6
2Mar55- 7Hia fm 1½Ⓣ 2:293 3↑ Hia Turf H 63k 6 10 104½ 42 32 32 Contreras J 112wb 14.35 94-00 Stan128½Capeador1181½Iceberg II112no Lacked final rally 11
16Feb55- 7Hia hd 1 3/16Ⓣ 1:56 3↑ Bougainvillea H 34k 1 6 63¾ 3½ 3nk 34 Contreras J 115wb 8.20 93-03 Cascanuez1221Kaster1213Iceberg II115½ Tired in drive 12
10Feb55- 7Hia fm 1 1/16Ⓣ 1:441 4↑ Alw 6000 9 9 106½ 64 45 43¼ Contreras J 121wb 24.95 92-05 Mister Black121¾Kaster1212Abbe Sting118½ Rallied mildly 12
19Nov54- 7Pim fm 1Ⓣ 1:403 3↑ Alw 4000 5 6 45½ Shuk N 122wb 5.10 84-07 Kaster1222Modest Pete1151½Rare Knave1172 Taken up early 7
Fog prevented other race calls
11Nov54- 7Pim fm 1½Ⓣ 2:321 3↑ Exterminator H 10k 8 3 52½ 86¼ 68½ 713 Hartack W 116wb 4.30 - - Cascanuez1144½Kaster121noBrushBurn1244 Dropped far back 10
16Oct54- 7Lrl fm *1⅛Ⓣ 1:51 3↑ Turf Cup H 25k 5 7 84¼ 64 66 68½ Contreras J 117wb 4.20 78-13 Stan1262½News Again1112½Tritium1142 Tired in drive 13
25Sep54- 6Atl fm 1 3/16Ⓣ :48 1:12 1:372 1:57 3↑ U Nations H 67k 6 5 55½ 77¾ 78¼ 74¼ Contreras J 122wb 4.90 90-06 Closed Door117hdRoyal Vale120½Kaster114¾ Dull effort 8
15Sep54- 7Atl fm 1⅛Ⓣ :48 1:38 1:511 3↑ ⓇForeign Bred 29k 1 5 53¾ 2hd 11 1¾ Contreras J 118wb *1.00e 87-13 Iceberg II118¾Royal Vale118nkBlood Test1181 Hard urged 8
Restricted to horses foaled outside the continental United States
6Sep54- 7Atl fm 1 1/16Ⓣ :231 :464 1:112 1:43 3↑ Atl City Turf H 30k 9 7 64 53½ 44 41 Contreras J 124wb 8.00 98-01 Landlocked115hdCounty Clare116noKaster1171 Closed fast 13
31Jly54- 7AP sf 1 3/16Ⓣ :462 1:112 1:382 1:57 3↑ Arlington H 156k 9 6 65 52 72¾ 107 Contreras J 121wsb 5.40e 87-12 Stan114nkBrushBurn1133½SirMngo1251½ Lacked needed rally 14
12Jly54- 7AP fst 1⅛ :482 1:113 1:37 1:493 3↑ L Armour Mem H 28k 6 2 2½ 1hd 1hd 2nk Church K 124wb 5.40 94-11 Mister Black111nkIceberg II1242½Ruhe1192 Just failed 10
5Jly54- 8AP fm 1⅛Ⓣ :47 1:112 1:363 1:492 3↑ Stars & Stripes H 28k 6 6 64¾ 32½ 22 23 Church K 123wb 6.60 92-08 Sir Mango1243Iceberg II1231Stan114no Showed game effort 12
18Jun54- 5Mth fm 1Ⓣ 1:391 3↑ Alw 5000 2 6 31 1hd 12 13 Gorman D 118wb *1.30 90-10 IcebergII1183BobsAlibi109noGoingAway109¾ Won eased up 12
5Jun54- 7Bel fst 1 :24 :481 1:134 1:391 4↑ Alw 4500 3 2 1hd 11 2½ 23½ Contreras J 120wb 5.30 74-20 Domquil1133½IcebergII1203Lafourch108no Couldn't keep up 11
3Mar54- 7Hia hd 1½Ⓣ 2:284 3↑ Hia Turf H 64k 11 7 86½ 75¼ 88 810 Contreras J 124wb *2.70e 90-00 Picador1062½Royal Vale126½Parnassus1202 Raced wide 12
25Feb54- 7Hia hd 1 3/16Ⓣ 1:56 4↑ Alw 6000 2 5 43½ 4¾ 3½ 1½ Contreras J 121wb *.75 97-03 IcebergII121½RoyalGovernor112½CombatBoots1124 Cleverly 6
20Feb54- 7Hia fst 1¼ :473 1:114 1:371 2:031 3↑ Widener H 139k 3 5 63½ 54 55½ 54 Contreras J 119wb 10.75 85-13 Landlocked116hdQuiet Step1131¼Andre117nk Lacked rally 14
6Feb54- 7Hia fst 1⅛ :454 1:102 1:362 1:49 3↑ McLennan H 72k 10 12 138½ 107¼ 139¼ 64 Contreras J 119wb 7.50 87-11 Elixir110½ⒹRoyalVale1262WiseMargin108¾ Impeded early 16
Placed fifth by disqualification
15Jan54- 7TrP fst 1⅛ :46 1:102 1:363 1:502 3↑ Tropical H 47k 7 12 1310 116¾ 44 33½ Contreras J 123wsb 14.35 85-15 Capeador1121Count Cain1052½Iceberg II123no Closed well 14
11Nov53- 7Lrl sf *1½Ⓣ 2:36 3↑ D C Int'l 65k 4 4 3½ 2hd 2hd 26 Contreras J 126wb 7.60 68-29 Worden II1266Iceberg II1263Sunglow126½ Good effort 10
31Oct53- 7Lrl fst *1⅛Ⓣ 1:512 3↑ Turf Cup H (Div 2) 23k 1 4 31 2hd 11 21½ Contreras J 126wb *1.70 83-15 County Clare1051½Iceberg II1262Ruhe119no Good effort 8
26Sep53- 6Atl fst 1 3/16Ⓣ :473 1:12 1:362 1:554 3↑ U Nations H 60k 4 5 58 31½ 11½ 11¼ Contreras J 120wb 7.10 113-00 IcebergII1201½BrushBrun118nkRoyalGovrnor118½ Drew clear 8
16Sep53- 7Atl fst 1⅛Ⓣ :47 1:112 1:361 1:492 3↑ Foreign Bred 29k 4 4 32½ 11½ 1½ 21¼ Contreras J 122 w 3.80 95-06 Royal Vale1221¼Iceberg II1223Stan1152 Game effort 8
Restricted to horses foaled outside the continental United States
5Sep53- 7Atl fst 1 1/16Ⓣ :232 :464 1:11 1:433 3↑ Atl City Turf H 23k 7 6 54½ 44½ 32 31½ Wilson HB 119wb 5.70 100-00 SaddleTramp107¾RoyalGovernor109¾IcebrgII119nk Went well 10
28Jly53- 6AP fst 1⅛ :48 1:112 1:36 1:49 3↑ Handicap 6000 3 3 13 14½ 16 16 Contreras J 120wb 4.90 97-15 Iceberg II1206Adams Off Ox1101Brush Burn1112 Easily 7
20Jly53- 6AP fst 1 1/16Ⓣ :233 :474 1:123 1:442 3↑ L Armour Mem H 29k 13 8 76 53½ 74¾ 95¾ Contreras J 120wb 8.20 85-15 Abbe Sting1142½The Eagle114nkBobs Alibi1101 Forced wide 13
4Jly53- 8AP fst 1⅛Ⓣ :47 1:11 1:36 1:482 3↑ Stars & Stripes H 28k 9 4 21½ 22 21 33¼ Contreras J 122wb 5.20 101-05 AbbeSting110nkArmageddon1183IcebergII122½ Dropped back 10
24Jun53- 7AP fst 1 1/16Ⓣ :232 :472 1:114 1:423 4↑ Alw 5000 6 7 83½ 51¾ 44 42¾ Contreras J 120wb *2.50 98-05 The Eagle114hdVantage120½Hierarch1142¼ Raced wide 10
30May53- 6Bel fst 1¼ :471 1:11 1:353 2:003 3↑ Suburban H 58k 7 3 45½ 33½ 34 49 Contreras J 109wb 18.15 88-17 Tom Fool128noRoyal Vale1247Cold Command1142 Tired 7
20May53- 7Bel fst 1⅛ :454 1:104 1:371 1:504 3↑ Handicap 7555 6 3 35 33 22½ 45¼ Contreras J 121wb 5.25 80-19 Arcave1203½Gloriette1051½Ancestor119nk Weakened 9
15May53- 6Bel sly 7f :222 :454 1:11 1:241 3↑ Handicap 6070 3 8 811 813 711 612 Contreras J 120wb 11.00 77-22 Hitex1171¼Master Fiddle115nkRae's Reward1103½ No speed 8
1May53- 8CD fst 1 :232 :471 1:112 1:37 4↑ Alw 3300 2 4 31½ 32½ 21 1hd Contreras J 120wb 4.30 92-13 Iceberg II120hdGray Challenge1083¾The Gink1145 Just up 7
14Apr53- 3Kee fst 7f :23 :462 1:113 1:241 4↑ Alw 3750 3 6 67 55 43 34 Rogers C 122wb *2.10 87-10 OldMason1111RoyalMustang1103IcebergII122¾ Strong finish 6
20Mar53- 7GP fst 1 1/16 :253 :502 1:14 1:464 4↑ Alw 5000 2 4 42 3½ 31 31¾ Gorman D 121wb 5.45 74-26 Mandingo1161¼Dry Run114½Iceberg II1215 Lacked rally 8
3Mar53- 7Hia fst 1½Ⓣ 2:284 3↑ Miami Beach H 31k 5 7 48 32½ 43½ 34½ Contreras J 122wb *1.20 96-05 Royal Vale1133Dulat1221½Iceberg II122¾ Tired 10
18Feb53- 7Hia fst 1 3/16Ⓣ 1:573 3↑ Bougainvillea H 20k 3 9 83¼ 51¾ 1hd 1¾ Contreras J 119wb 8.55 95-05 Iceberg II119¾Brush Burn123noDulat1222½ Driving 16
13Feb53- 7Hia fst 1 1/16Ⓣ 1:462 4↑ Alw 4500 6 4 32 11 12 12 Contreras J 112wb *.70 84-16 IcebergII1122Streaking1086SaddleBags1165 Driving clear 7
5Feb53- 7Hia sf 1⅛Ⓣ 1:54 4↑ Alw 5000 7 1 12 12 11 21½ Contreras J 112wb 4.30 79-19 Brush Burn1191½Iceberg II112¾Chicle II1122 Sharp effort 7
20Jan53- 7Hia fst 1⅛Ⓣ 1:522 4↑ Alw 5000 7 9 85¾ 64¼ 53½ 65 Nichols J 113wb *2.85 84-11 Dulat1073Blue Volt1081½Evicted107hd Raced wide 12
14Jan53- 7TrP fst 5½f :22 :45 :58 1:042 4↑ Alw 3200 3 10 109 913 88¾ 64½ Nichols J 114wb 79.10 89-17 DoReport1141Earmarked111nkCircusClown1112 Closed ground 10
Previously trained by Carlos Munoz Guzman
9Mar52♦ Valparaiso(Chi) fm*1 3/16ⓉLH 1:542 Clsc Casino Municipal de Vina Stk4500 21 Parodi R 119 - Paschanillo1191Iceberg II119Armadillo119 13
27Feb52♦ Valparaiso(Chi) fm*1ⓉLH 1:364 Premio Cuerpo de Bomberos Hcp700 11 Poblete A 121 *2.00 Iceberg II1211Huaraculen117½Negrina108 10
20Jan52♦ Valparaiso(Chi) fm*1½ⓉLH 2:293 Chilean Derby Stk75000 4 Flores P 128 - Fascinado1283Liberty1285Soldado128 7
6Jan52♦ Valparaiso(Chi) fm*1 3/16ⓉLH 1:544 Clasico Juan S. Jackson Stk1700 1½ Parodi R 113 *.60 Iceberg II113½Soldado1135Majestic113 6
18Nov51♦ Hipodromo(Chi) sly*1¼LH 2:054 Pr Junta Central Beneficencia Hcp1600 37 Flores P 126 Gitanita1067Maretako110hdIceberg II126 16

4Nov51♦ Hipodromo(Chi) sly *1⅛LH	1:53²	Premio Rosignol Alw500	1¹	Flores P	118	*.80	Iceberg II118¹Palay123⁶Gitanita114	7
28Oct51♦ Club Hippico(Chi) fm *1½①RH	2:30	Clasico El Ensayo Stk9200	2²¹	Parodi R	123	–	Liberty123²¹Iceberg II123²Soldado123	13
30Sep51♦ Club Hippico(Chi) fm *1¼①RH	2:02²	GP Nacional Ricardo Lyon Stk3000	3³	Orellana J	123	–	Liberty123½Fascinado110²¹Iceberg II123	13
19Aug51♦ Club Hippico(Chi) gd *1¹₁₆①RH	1:45	Polla de Potrillos Stk2500	2³	Orellana J	123	–	Laconico123³Iceberg II123½Fantasma Gris123 Soldado 6th,Liberty 11th	26
29Jly51♦ Club Hippico(Chi) sf *1①RH	1:42	Clasico Alberto Vial Infante Stk2200	1¹	Sepulveda G	120	–	Fascinado117⁷Parcoy117¹½Odin126 Laconico 5th	16
17Jun51♦ Hipodromo(Chi) my *7½fLH	1:33	Clasico Domingo 2nd Herrera Stk2000	1⁴	Giraldez C	119	–	Odin119¹Maretazo119ⁿᵏToscano119	17
18Mar51♦ Club Hippico(Chi) fst *5f①Str	1:01	Premio Centurion Mdn500	1¾	Caballero H	122	2.70	Iceberg II122¾Singo122²Dashing Lad121	11

Idun

b. f. 1955, by Royal Charger (Nearco)–Tige O'Myheart, by Bull Lea
Own.– Josephine B. Paul
Br.– Leslie Combs & John W. Hanes (Ky)
Tr.– S.W. Ward

Lifetime record: 30 17 4 4 $392,490

28Oct59- 7Aqu sl 6f	:221 :461	1:12¹ 3↑Ⓕ Interborough H 27k	7 2 2³ 2³ 2¹	2ⁿᵏ	Guerin E	124	*1.45 – –	Nushi111ⁿᵏIdun124²Cobul107½ Led between calls,no excuse 7
30Oct59- 7Aqu fst 1⅛	:471 1:12¹ 1:37 1:50¹ 3↑Ⓕ Beldame H 67k	1 2 21½ 21½ 21½	22½	Guerin E	121	4.15 – –	Tempted125²⁴Idun121ⁿᵏHigh Bid113¹ No apparent excuse 14
21Sep59- 7Aqu fst 1	:223 :45 1:09⁴ 1:36 3↑Ⓕ Maskette H 29k	9 3 41¾ 41 2ⁿᵈ	11½	Guerin E	119	8.75 – –	Idun119¹½Tempted126¹Bornastar119² Under hard drive 10
2Sep59- 7Bel fst 1⅛	:22 :463 1:09² 1:22³ 3↑Ⓕ Vagrancy H 29k	11 5 5³ 43 24	36	Ussery R	112	3.60 88-16	Dandy Blitzen113¹Honeys Gem118⁵Idun112¹ Mild bid,tired 12
10Aug59- 5Sar fst 1	:23 :461 1:10⁴ 1:36 3↑Ⓕ Handicap 7500	5 1 11 1ʰᵈ 2½	35	Ussery R	122	2.00 92-15	Tempted122⁴Polomby116⁴½Idun122²½ Tired when challenged 10
18Jly59- 6Del fst 1¹₁₆	:231 :464 1:11² 1:43³ 3↑Ⓕ New Castle 35k	7 4 5³ 3² 4³½	5³¾	Guerin E	116	4.20 90-18	Tempted116²³Bornst126¹½Chstos112ⁿᵒ Well placed,weakened 10
6Jly59- 7Bel fst 6f	:22² :454 1:11¹ 3↑Ⓕ Liberty Belle H 27k	1 5 31½ 31½ 1½	11¼	Hartack W	124	*.95 92-14	Idun124¹¼HappyPrincss115¹Polmby113½ Under a brisk drive 7
20Jun59- 7Mth fst 1¹₁₆	:23 :451 1:10³ 3↑Ⓕ Regret H 22k	8 4 46 34½ 2ʰᵈ	2¾	Hartack W	126	*1.00 88-19	Mlle.Dianne116²Idun126¹SandysJoy116³ Led between calls 8
25May59- 7Bel fst 7f	:221 :453 1:11¹ 1:24¹ 3↑Ⓕ Distaff H 28k	3 6 33½ 3² 31	1¼	Erb D	125	*1.30 84-18	HappyPrincss114¹½Mlle.Dinn115ⁿᵒIdun125¹½ Made even try 8
16May59- 7GS fst 6f	:221 :454 1:12 3↑Ⓕ Colonial H 28k	8 1 2½ 21½ 21½	11½	Hartack W	124	*1.30 84-20	Idun124¹½DandyBlitzen120¹BttyLnn113ⁿᵏ Driving,drew clear 8
3Mar59- 7Hia fst 1⅛	:461 1:10⁴ 1:37¹ 1:50¹ 3↑Ⓕ Black Helen H 40k	9 10 89½ 98 10¹²	11¹⁶	Hartack W	124	*1.45 68-17	Rosewood116²½Happy Princess110²½A Glitter122ⁿᵏ Dull try 12
11Feb59- 7Hia fst 1¹₁₆	:23 :461 1:11¹ 1:23¹ 3↑Ⓕ Columbia H 26k	3 9 2¹ 1ʰᵈ 1¹	1ⁿᵏ	Hartack W	123	*1.65 94-17	Idun123ⁿᵏWoodlawn111¹½HappyPrincss115½ Under hard drive 15
	Previously raced in the name of Mrs C.U. Bay						
8Nov58- 6Jam fst 1¹₁₆	:471 1:11⁴ 1:37² 1:56⁴ Roamer H 88k	10 4 55 31½ 41	31¾	Hartack W	119 w	*4.00 90-15	Warhead125¹GreyMonarch119½Idun119¹ Showed a good effort 14
13Oct58- 6Bel fst 1½	:48 1:12¹2:03⁴2:30² 3↑Ⓕ Ladies H 58k	7 2 24 1½ 1ʰᵈ	43½	Hartack W	122 w	2.35 77-20	Endine114¹⁴DottedLine123ⁿᵏAnnie-Lu-Sn108¹½ Used in lead 10
4Oct58- 7Bel fst 1⅛	:453 1:10 1:36 1:49² 3↑Ⓕ Beldame H 70k	3 2 3² 31½ 41	51¼	Guerin E	124 w	*1.35 88-14	OuterSpace117ⁿᵒAGlitter119ʰᵈDottedLine120ⁿᵏ No excuse 17
15Sep58- 6Bel fst 1¹₁₆	:223 :451 1:10¹ 1:43¹ Ⓕ Gazelle H 29k	7 4 2½ 11 1²	14	Hartack W	124 w	*.80 92-15	Idun124⁴Munch122ⁿᵒTmptd116½ Increasing long lead easily 10
5Sep58- 5Bel fst 1	:23 :453 1:10³ 1:36² Ⓕ Alw 7500	3 2 21½ 2ʰᵈ 1½	14	Guerin E	121 w	*.40 92-13	Idun121⁴DandyBlitzen118⁵BigFright113½ Speed in reserve 4
12Jly58- 6Del sly 1⅛	:47 1:12 1:39 1:52¹ Ⓕ Del Oaks 49k	2 1 11 11 2ʰᵈ	22½	Hartack W	119 w	*.70 77-20	BgEffort119²½Idun119³½Tmptd119½ Rated in lead,no excuse 14
5Jly58- 7Bel fst 1¹₁₆	:23 :452 1:09⁴ 1:43³ Ⓕ Mother Goose 28k	2 2 2½ 11 11½	1³	Hartack W	118 w	*.45 90-16	Idun118³Lopar112½Lea Moon113½ Going away easily 9
27Jun58- 5Bel fst 6f	:23 :461 1:11 Ⓕ Alw 5000	3 3 2½ 1² 1⁴	1⁴	Hartack W	121 w	*.25 93-11	Idun121³CountessMarcy114⁵CarlynSarah114¹½ Taken in hand 6
27May58- 7Bel fst 6f	:22² :454 1:11 Ⓕ Alw 7500	4 5 63½ 64½ 46½	47½	Erb D	118 w	*.25 85-16	AGlitter118²½AnyMorn115²CarlynSarah113³ Very wide turn 7
10May58- 6GS fst 6f	:22 :452 1:12 Ⓕ Alw 10000	3 2 1½ 11½ 15	18	Erb D	121 w	*.10 84-15	Idun121⁸Delnita118¹½Say So109 Drew far out with ease 3
30Oct57- 7Jam fst 1¹₁₆	:24 :481 1:13³ 1:46⁴ Ⓕ Frizette 89k	2 1 12½ 1² 12½	11½	Hartack W	119	*.10 76-20	Idun119¹½Lopar119ʰᵈBigFrght119¹ Scored as rider pleased 7
19Oct57- 6Bel my 1¹₁₆	:231 :463 1:11³ 1:45² Ⓕ Gardenia 144k	5 1 14 16 16	13½	Hartack W	119	*1.30 83-16	Idun119³Craftiness119½MeantWell119³ Long lead,eased up 15
12Oct57- 5GS fst 1	:23 :464 1:11² 1:37² Ⓕ Alw 10000	2 2 1ʰᵈ 2ʰᵈ 1ʰᵈ	1ⁿᵒ	Boulmetis S	121 w	*.70 95-11	Idun121ⁿᵒQuigFlame112½LocustTim112½ Loafed lead,lasted 11
21Sep57- 5Bel fst 6f-WC	:221 :45 1:09³ Ⓕ Matron 63k	12 6 2ʰᵈ 1½	1³	Hartack W	119wb	2.75 91-09	Idun119³PolyH119²Armorl119² Drew clear while ridden out 13
14Sep57- 5Bel sly 6f-WC	:214 :45 1:10 Ⓕ Alw 6000	1 5 2³ 2ʰᵈ	1ʰᵈ	Guerin E	116 w	3.40 89-13	Idun116ʰᵈArmorial111¹½Pocahonts119² Under a brisk drive 8
27Aug57- 5Sar fst 6f	:231 :472 1:14² Ⓕ Alw 4500	1 3 12½ 1½ 11½	1½	Guerin E	119 w	*.65 76-27	Idun119½Abientot116²½CourtPlantng116¹ Little speed left 5
	Daily Racing Form time,1:14						
16Aug57- 4Sar fst 5½f	:223 :47 :594 1:06³ Ⓕ Alw 3700	8 4 42¾ 2ʰᵈ 1½	13½	Guerin E	119 w	*1.70 84-19	Idun119³½Picnicking119⁶SingleStroke119² Drew out easily 11
19Jly57- 4Bel fst 5f-WC	:223 :452 :58² Ⓕ Md Sp Wt	14 1 2½ 2¹	2¾	Guerin E	115 w	*2.20 86-13	ⒹBridgework110¾Idun115ⁿᵏLament115³ Bothered repeatedly 18
	Placed first by disqualification						

Intentionally

blk. c. 1956, by Intent (War Relic)–My Recipe, by Discovery
Own.– Tartan Stable
Br.– Brookfield Farms (Ky)
Tr.– J.A. Nerud

Lifetime record: 34 18 7 2 $652,258

10Feb62- 7Hia fst 1⅛	:461 1:10² 1:35² 1:48² 3↑ Seminole H 62k	3 1 1ʰᵈ 15	18	Ycaza M	126	3.85 93-13	Intentionally126⁸Carry Back127¹Yorky120½ Much the best 10
31Jan62- 7Hia fst 7f	:22² :444 1:09² 1:22³ 3↑ Palm Beach H 33k	10 2 34 33½ 2²	11½	Ussery R	126 b	*2.60 97-11	Intentionally126¹³CarryBack124²Ambiopoise122ⁿᵏ Drew out 13
24Jan62- 8Hia fm 5½f①	1:07 4↑ Alw 6000	8 1 31½ 32½ 23	43	Hinojosa H	118	*1.05 80-23	Winonly121ʰᵈGordianKnot115¹¾CaptainKidd111²1¼ Bore in 8
	Previously owned by Brookfield Farms;previously trained by E.I. Kelly						
7Nov61- 7Aqu fst 6f	:22² :453 3↑ Sport Page H 23k	10 1 4ⁿᵏ 3½ 3½	1ʰᵈ	Ycaza M	129 b	*.95 95-14	Intentionally129ʰᵈWindy Sands112¹¼Gyro119¹½ Bore in,up 6
28Oct61- 7GS fst 1¼	:471 1:11² 1:36³ 2:03 3↑ Trenton H 84k	2 1 1½ 1ʰᵈ 1ʰᵈ	2½	Boulmetis S	124 b	4.60 89-13	Carry Back120½Intentionally124⁴¼Ambiopoise120ⁿᵏ Bumped 9
12Oct61- 6GS fst 1⅛	:481 1:12¹ 1:37 1:49³ 3↑ Quaker City H 27k	5 1 11½ 1² 1²	1²	Boulmetis S	122 b	*1.20 89-16	Intentionally122²MailOrder116²¾ChiefofChifs119⁸ Driving 5
7Oct61- 5GS fst 6f	:22 :444 1:09³ 3↑ Alw 7500	3 3 2¹ 21½ 21½	1³	Boulmetis S	119 b	*.70 97-10	Intentionally119³BeauAdmiral106¹½MailOrder122³½ Driving 8
16Sep61- 8Atl fm 1³₁₆①	:463 1:11¹ 1:37 1:56 3↑ U Nations H 100k	4 1 1ʰᵈ 11 1½	62¾	Boulmetis S	117 b	16.90 90-07	Oink119ⁿᵒTompion117²ArtMarket116ⁿᵏ Used up setting pace 12
4Sep61- 8AP gd 1	:224 :452 1:09³ 1:34³ 3↑ Wash Park H 120k	4 2 2¹ 2³ 35	57	Hartack W	120 b	5.70 93-08	ChiefofChiefs124⁴TalentShow110ⁿᵏIntentionlyⒺ Tired 11
28Aug61- 6Bel fst 7f	:224 :453 1:09² 1:22³ 3↑ Alw 6500	4 1 1² 14 14	13½	Ycaza M	117 b	*.55 94-11	Intentionally117³½Trans-Way119¹Grwol114⁴ Speed to spare 6
17Sep60- 7Atl fm 1³₁₆①	:463 1:12 1:37² 1:57 3↑ U Nations H 100k	5 1 1½ 41½ 63¼	85½	Hartack W	124 b	7.60 82-12	T.V.Lark120¹½SwordDancer127¹½BallyAche122ʰᵈ Used early 10
5Sep60- 7Aqu fst 1⅛	:232 :461 1:10² 1:34⁴ 3↑ Aqueduct H 56k	2 1 1¹ 1½ 11	2ʰᵈ	Hartack W	125 b	1.95 94-11	Bald Eagle130ʰᵈIntentionally125ⁿᵒWarhead113³ Sharp try 5
16Jly60- 8AP fst 1	:221 :443 1:08³ 1:34² 3↑ Equipoise Mile H 55k	8 4 1ʰᵈ 1³ 1⁴	1ⁿᵒ	Hartack W	126 b	*1.40 98-09	Intentionally126ⁿᵒDunce121³¹½Little Tytus113⁵ All out 8
29Jun60- 7Bel fst 6f	:223 :454 1:10³ 3↑ Toboggan H 27k	6 2 11½ 1² 13	12½	Hartack W	128 b	*.60e 94-17	Intentionally128²½RickCity122²½Vendett115ⁿᵏ Easily best 6
16Sep59- 7Aqu fst 1⅛	:471 1:12 1:37³ 1:50³ Discovery H 29k	6 4 53½ 43 34½	35½	Ycaza M	129 b	*.90 – –	MiddleBrother116³½Demobilize117²Intentionlly129ⁿᵏ Tired 10
7Sep59- 7Bel fst 1	:224 :451 1:09² 1:35² Jerome H 56k	3 1 1² 13 16	110	Ycaza M	126 b	*.75 97-15	Intentionally126¹⁰Atoll120²SevenCorners110ʰᵈ Easy score 9
25Jly59- 8AP fst 1	:224 :452 1:09² 1:35 Arl Classic 140k	5 3 3² 2² 2²⁴	32¾	Hartack W	124 b	*.40 92-13	Dunce117¹½On-and-On115¹¼Intentionally123¾ Speed,hung 7
27Jun59- 8Was fst 1	:214 :432 1:07³ 1:33¹ W Wright Mem 55k	2 1 1½ 11½ 11½	2½	Ycaza M	121 b	*.80 101-05	Intentionally121²On-and-On115¾LittleTytus109⁴¾ In hand 7
23May59- 6Bel fst 1	:221 :442 1:09¹ 1:35³ Withers 90k	11 2 2² 2½ 13	13½	Ycaza M	126 b	2.75 96-10	Intentionally126³ManassaMauler126⁴½Bagdad126¹½ Easily 13
9May59- 6Bel fst 6f	:22² :454 1:12 Del Valley Pha	1 8 3½ 1ʰᵈ 11½	11¾	Hartack W	124 b	*.60 87-22	Intentionally124¹¾CedrBrook121¹²½NsrullhSwp121¹½ Driving 8
18Apr59- 7Jam fst 1⅛	:461 1:11 1:37 1:49³ Wood Memorial 88k	6 3 31½ 31 44	47½	Shoemaker W	126 b	2.70 80-14	Manassa Mauler126¾First Landing126⁵Our Dad126⁶ Tired 8
11Apr59- 7Jam sly 1⅛	:232 :462 1:11¹ 1:43 Gotham 28k	4 2 2½ 2ʰᵈ 2¹	2²	Shoemaker W	122 b	*.85 94-10	Atoll122²Intentionally122⁵Open View114ⁿᵒ No excuses 7
6Apr59- 5Jam fst 6f	:224 :462 1:10⁴ Alw 7500	4 1 12½ 13 14	16½	Shoemaker W	124 b	*.15 93-17	Intentionally124⁶½Outgiving113¹¼ThatLuckyDay108⁶ Easily 4

Race	Cond	Dist	Type	Times	Age	Class	PP	St	1C	2C	Str	Fin	Jockey	Wt	Odds	Fig	Result	Comment	Fld
22Nov58-7Pim	fst	1 1/16		:224 :462 1:113 1:46		Pim Futurity 168k	3	2	22	13	14	11¾	Shoemaker W	122wb	*1.30	80-28	Intentionally1221¾RicoTso1223½BlckHlls1223½	Hand ridden	9
	Geldings not eligible																		
25Oct58-7GS	sly	1 1/16		:222 :463 1:124 1:462		Garden State 297k	10	4	32	33½	510	512	Nelson E	122wb	8.50	66-31	FirstLanding122hdTomyLee1222SwordDancer1223	Speed,tired	13
11Oct58-7Bel	fst	1		:231 :47 1:123 1:392		Champagne 151k	8	4	4¾	2½	32	33¼	Nelson E	122wb	9.25	74-21	FirstLandng122nk[D]TomyL1223Intntonlly1222	Roughed early	10
20Sep58-7Bel	fst	6½-WC		:214 :443 1:082 1:143		Futurity 114k	2	1		1hd	1hd	11	Shoemaker W	122 w	8.30	99-01	Intentionally1221First Landing122nkDunce1223½	Driving	8
	Geldings not eligible																		
10Sep58-7Atl	fst	7f		:214 :441 1:094 1:232		World's Playground 36k	5	1	21	2hd	13	2hd	Culmone J	122wb	5.70	89-16	Demobilize119hdIntentonlly1222½PnBolro110hd	Just failed	15
30Aug58-8AP	fst	6f		:222 :443 1:093		Wash Park Futurity 164k	7	7	62½	74¾	66¼	45¼	Valenzuela I	119 w	10.70	91-03	RestlssWind122nkWinsomeWinner1161½Demoblz1193½	Rallied	10
13Aug58-6Sar	fst	6f		:231 :472 1:13		Grand Union Hotel 34k	5	1	1hd	1hd	1hd	23¼	Arcaro E	120 w	*1.10	80-19	FirstMinister1203¼Intentionally1202½EastIndn1143½	Tired	7
26Jly58-6Mth	fst	6f		:213 :443 1:103		Sapling 58k	5	6	56	47½	36	24½	Culmone J	124 w	2.70e	84-22	WatchYourStep1144½Intntonlly124hdRstlssWnd1245½	Rallied	8
25Jun58-6Mth	fst	5½f		:22 :452 :58 1:05		©Tyro 26k	10	1	2hd	12	13	11½	Culmone J	119 w	*2.00	93-16	Intentionally1191½EasySpur1222RoyalAnthem1221½	In hand	13
14Jun58-5Mth	sl	5½f		:224 :472 1:00 1:063		Alw 5000	1	1	11½	13½	15	16	Boulmetis S	122 w	*.80	85-31	Intentionally1226Dark Look1221½Rough Tempo1225	In hand	7
29May58-4GS	fst	5f		:222 :463 :59		Alw 4500	6	2	2hd	12	14	14	Truman J	112 w	11.70	95-14	Intentionally1124WeatherProphet1172½JyJyJr.117no	Easily	10

Jam

b. g. 1947, by Impound (Sun Beau)–Cherry Orchard, by Display — **Lifetime record: 76 14 11 8 $69,585**

Own.– J.F. McHugh
Br.– Alfred G. Vanderbilt (Md)
Tr.– M.H. Dixon Jr

Race	Cond	Dist	Type	Times	Age	Class	PP	St	1C	2C	Str	Fin	Jockey	Wt	Odds	Fig	Result	Comment	Fld
22Oct55-5RB	sf	*1¼Ⓣ		2:111	3↑	Alw 400	8	7	74½	64	63¾	62½	Phelps E	134wb	-	--	Lethnot130nkMeadow Mint133½Another Hyacinth1581		9
5Oct55-3Lig	fm	*2	Hurdles	4:031	3↑	Alw 2000	4	4	35½	49½	44¾	39	Phelps E	141wb	-	--	Morpheus1321Ring o' Roses1478Jam1413	Driving	6
19Sep55-3Aqu	hd	*1¾	Hurdles	3:263	3↑	Alw 3800	3	7	77½	79	721	722¼	Phelps E	142wb	17.10	--	Morpheus134noKing Gavin1354Irish Pageant1494	Trailed	7
10Sep55-5Fai	fm	*3	S'Chase	6:061	4↑	Foxcatcher Nat'l 3.1k	5	4	453	4	4	4	Phelps E	148wb	6.95	--	Repose153hdMightyMo15320MnkeyWrnch148	Distanced,eased	5
7Sep55-3Aqu	fm	*2	Hurdles	3:453	3↑	Alw 4000	5	6	612	612	624	623	Phelps E	138wb	31.55	--	King Commander150nkThe Proff1479Good Cards142¾	Trailed	6
23Aug55-3Sar	sf	*1½	Hurdles	3:044	3↑	Alw 3500	1	6	88	83¼	75	511	McDonald RS	141wb	13.65e	--	Galatian146½Polly Pep1422Irish Pageant1346	Mild rally	11
12Aug55-3Sar	sf	*1¾	Hurdles	3:334	3↑	Alw 3500	2	2	54	74¼	717	718	Phelps E	142wb	4.95	--	Good Cards1342Irish Pageant1351Antagonizer1422	Outrun	9
6Aug55-3Sar	hd	*1½	Hurdles	2:591	3↑	Alw 3500	1	7	511	513	512	55¾	Glass J10	130wb	*1.45e	--	DearBrutus1475RiverJordan151¾Camee151hd	Never a threat	9
5Jly55-3Aqu	hd	*2	S'Chase	3:46	4↑	Alw 4000	6	3	21	39	320	319½	Phelps E	143wb	9.75	--	Beau Sir1384½Moot13815Jam14310	Jumped poorly throughout	6
16Jun55-5Aqu	fm	*2	S'Chase	3:453	4↑	Hitchcock H 10k	4	7	722	723	728	733	Phelps E	143wb	37.20	--	Fulton1322½Shipbrd1631Rythmnhm1426½	Fenced very poorly	7
2Jun55-5Bel	fm	*2½	S'Chase	4:442	4↑	Meadow Brook H 11k	1	6	647	616	-	-	Phelps E	136wb	22.00	--	Shipboard1566CurlyJo13115Nj15630	Bobbled,unseated rider	6
21May55-6Bel	hd	*2½	S'Chase	4:432	4↑	International 21k	8	9	924	829	435	451	Phelps E	155wb	64.50	--	Neji15015Ancestor15518Hyvania15518	Raced far back	10
12May55-5Bel	hd	*2	S'Chase	3:411	4↑	Corinthian H 8.9k	4	2	37	412	520	523	Phelps E	137wb	15.65	--	Shipboard1553Beaupr1363Nj1551½	Early foot,jumped poorly	6
28Apr55-3Bel	sf	*2	S'Chase	3:47	4↑	Alw 4500	5	8	611	611	617	621	Phelps E	137wb	5.60	--	Ancestor1372PrinceGlorieux13012CammellLaird1425	Outrun	8
16Apr55-3Mid	hd	*2	S'Chase	3:551	3↑	Alw 750	3	1	2½	2½	2½	23	Phelps E	145wb	-	--	Prince Glorieux1433Jam1455Virginius1458	Tired in drive	9
19Sep53-5Fai	hd	*2	S'Chase	3:513	4↑	Manly H 3.2k	1	5	74	77½	511	512	Phelps E	158wb	*1.90	--	Moot141¾Banner Waves144½Uncle Joe1385	No menace	7
12Sep53-1Fai	fst	*1⅞Ⓣ		3:263	3↑	Alw 800	1	2	22	21	21	23½	Gall'her W	155 w	-	--	Sea Term1273½Jam15515Jack Kent139	Went well	3
26Jun53-5Del	fst	*2	S'Chase	3:464	3↑	Georgetown H 12k	3	4	32½	21	514	515	Phelps E	158wb	4.50	--	The Mast148½Monkey Wrench1351Hunting Fox13612	Quit	6
19Jun53-6Bel	fst	*2¼	S'Chase	4:121	4↑	Temple Gwathmey H 16k	6	3	41¾	413	740	740	Phelps E	162wb	9.10	--	Errolford1305½Sea Legs1652Oedipus1645	Outdistanced	7
	Daily Racing Form time,4:16 2/5																		
4Jun53-5Bel	fst	*2½	S'Chase	4:421	4↑	Meadow Brook H 11k	6	5	22½	32	-	-	Phelps E	162wb	6.10	--	Sea Legs1575Oedipus1642½His Boots1462½	Hit fence	6
3Oct52-5Bel	sf	*3	S'Chase	5:44	4↑	Grand Nat'l H 28k	5	8	823	64½	515	414	Phelps E	164wb	3.10	--	Sea Legs1365The Mast1542Oedipus1657	Bobbled at jump	9
25Sep52-5Bel	fst	*2½	S'Chase	4:412	4↑	Brook H 17k	7	8	54¼	42	1hd	15	Phelps E	156wb	2.60	--	Jam1565Oedipus1631Lone Fisherman1313	Drew away	8
18Sep52-5Bel	sf	*2	S'Chase	3:391	3↑	Broad Hollow H 11k	2	7	412	45	21½	2hd	Phelps E	154wb	2.40	--	Oedipus160hdJam15420The Creek1386	Just missed	8
11Sep52-5Aqu	fst	*2	S'Chase	3:441	3↑	Harbor Hill H 11k	1	6	44	33½	36	36½	Phelps E	155wb	4.80	--	Semper Eadem1354½Hot1472½Jam1556	Bad landing 4th	6
29Aug52-5Sar	hd	*2½	S'Chase	5:064	4↑	Saratoga H 11k	4	3	38	47½	410	413	Phelps E	156wb	4.70	--	Banner Waves1362Titien II1473His Boots1518	Bobbled	6
14Aug52-5Sar	sl	*2	S'Chase	4:274	4↑	North Am H 6.3k	3	6	31½	2½	33	1½	Phelps E	152wb	2.65	--	Jam152½Navy Gun1471Flaming Comet1367	Driving	7
7Aug52-5Sar	fst	*2	S'Chase	4:11	4↑	Shillelah 5.8k	4	2	31½	22	47	412	Phelps E	153wb	*1.85	--	Oedipus1622His Boots1405Phiblant1405	Stumbled	5
27Jun52-6Del	fst	*2½	S'Chase	4:44	4↑	Indian River H 12k	3	2	23	112	120	120	Phelps E	152wb	2.55	--	Jam15220Monkey Wrench1342The Mast1616	Easily best	5
20Jun52-6Del	fst	*2	S'Chase	3:431	4↑	Georgetown H 12k	7	5	77¼	55¼	47½	25	Phelps E	151wb	10.40	--	The Mast1575Jam1511½[DH]Crooning Wind1431½	Good effort	8
11Jun52-6Bel	fst	*2¼	S'Chase	4:163	4↑	Temple Gwathmey H 16k	3	9	61½	65½	47	49	Phelps E	153wb	11.40	--	The Mast153¾Oedipus1631½Navy Gun1497	Swerved	9
29May52-5Bel	fst	*2½	S'Chase	4:431	4↑	Meadow Brook H 11k	4	6	2½	2hd	521	630	Phelps E	152wb	2.60	--	The Mast1462¼Navy Gun14815Titien II1476	Jumped poorly	8
8May52-5Bel	fst	*2	S'Chase	3:424	4↑	C L Appleton Mem 9k	6	6	69	43½	2hd	13	Phelps E	139wb	*1.00	--	Jam1393Lone Fisherman139¾The Mast143¾	Handily,drew out	6
1May52-5Bel	sf	*2	S'Chase	3:471	4↑	International H 9.3k	7	8	76	2½	13	18	Phelps E	141wb	*2.90	--	Jam1418Flaming Comet1371Palaja1418	Easily	11
19Apr52-4Mid	fst	*2	S'Chase	3:522	4↑	Handicap 2420	3	4	33½	-	-	-	Phelps E	148wb	-	--	[D]High Road1401Proceed1381½Crown Royal1381	Lost rider	8
12Apr52-3War	fst	*2	S'Chase	4:122	4↑	Alw 800	6	1	14½	19	115	117	Phelps E	142wb	-	--	Jam14217Sundance Kid1441½Trout Brook1429	Easily	7
17Nov51-6Mtp	gd	*1¾		3:08	3↑	Alw 700	2	1	13	15	18	110	Smithwick AP	151wb	-	--	Jam15110McGinty Moore148½Beaupre12922	Easily	5
10Nov51-7Pim	fst	2½		:511 3:022 4:192	3↑	Pim Cup 29k	5	4	21	48½	531	545	Culmone J	124wb	16.80	31-16	Pilaster1247Lone Eagle12415Hull Down1188	Early speed	6
17Oct51-6Bel	fst	*2	Hurdles	3:442	3↑	NY Turf Writers H 7.3k	3	5	1½	2½	47½	57	Phelps E	155 w	5.25e	--	Triomphe1432½Hyvania152½Snob Tourist144½	Tired	8
8Oct51-3Bel	sf	*1¾	Hurdles	3:171	3↑	Handicap 4545	2	3	31	21	1½	21	Phelps E	152 w	4.20	--	Hyvania1461Jam1527Quiet14712	Gave way	6
2Oct51-8Bel	fst	1 1/16		:224 :46 1:112 1:45	3↑	Alw 4000	4	6	78¾	66	76	78	Passmore WJ	113 w	15.20	78-14	Guard of Honor1141¼Mirabeau110hdSalaise120¾	Outrun	7
8Sep51-3Fai	fst	*1⅞Ⓣ		3:181	3↑	Alw 800	3	2	12	14	18	117	Phelps E	149 w	-e	--	Jam14917Scotch Wave152nkAdmiral Tan1488	Easily	7
31Aug51-3Sar	fst	*2	Hurdles	3:472	4↑	Alw 3500	4	2	2hd	11	13	12	Phelps E	145 w	2.25	--	Jam1452Salemaker131¾Navy Gun1382	Ridden out	7
18Aug51-3Sar	sl	*2	Hurdles	3:592	3↑	Handicap 5045	2	2	21	21	23	38	Phelps E	146 w	4.65	--	Quiet1426½Navy Gun1451½Jam14612	Bobbled	6
10Aug51-5Sar	sl	*1¾	Hurdles	3:353	3↑	Nat'l Maiden 8.3k	7	7	53½	63	57½	59	Phelps E	156 w	5.80	--	Fulton160½Manchon1443½Hyvania1512	Stumbled	9
27Jly51-5Mth	fst	*1¾	Hurdles	3:08	3↑	Alw 4000	7	5	31½	32½	65	46½	Phelps E	150 w	8.00	--	Fulton1501Titien II1491½Fonda1424	Weakened	7
20Jly51-7Jam	fst	1 1/16		:243 :482 1:132 1:462	3↑	Alw 4500	6	8	108½	83¼	98¼	99¼	Guerin E	115 w	23.15	71-18	Coveted113noDalpark1131Saxony1133½	Outrun	10
5Jly51-5Aqu	sf	*2	Hurdles	3:403	3↑	Forget H 11k	4	6	73½	55	612	615	Zimmerman J	144 w	4.45	--	Fulton145hdTitien II160¾Hyvania1412	Tired	7
22Jun51-5Aqu	fst	*1¾	Hurdles	3:09	3↑	Na'l Maiden 7.8k	1	4	22	44	410	414	Phelps E	151 w	2.00	--	Fulton1495Hyvania1499Stunts155nk	Bad landing 6th	4
18Jun51-3Bel	fst	*1¾	Hurdles	3:15	3↑	Handicap 4555	6	10	74¼	3½	12	13	Phelps E	140 w	7.85	--	Jam1403Quiet1344½Hyvania130½	Driving	10
28May51-5Bel	sf	*1¾	Hurdles	3:194	3↑	Nat'l Maiden 8.1k	5	6	21	2hd	1½	16	Phelps E	142 w	2.15	--	Jam1426Fulton14915Tellanrun15010	Driving	7
21May51-3Bel	fst	*1½	Hurdles	2:45	3↑	Sp Wt 3000	8	10	22	32½	32	33½	Phelps E	137 w	*2.20	--	Hyvania1421El Arabi1482½Jam1372	Bobbled 4th	11
5May51-6War	my	*1¾	Hurdles	2:573	3↑	Alw 600	3	3	2½	1hd	1no	2½	Smithwick AP	142 w	-	--	Swiggle142½Jam1424Kipper1532½	Hung	6
14Apr51-1DRn	fst	*1½	Hurdles	2:301	3↑	Alw 500	7	6	55	41½	3nk	1hd	Phelps E	135 w	-	--	Jam135hdIrish Clown1471½Wenham142hd	Hard drive	9
18Nov50-6Mtp	fst	*1¾		3:082	3↑	Alw 700	1	2	2½	2nk	1½	12	Cushman C	141 w	-	--	Jam1412Allflor142	Handily	2
10Nov50-5Pim	fst	1⅛		:474 1:123 1:39 1:521		Alw 3500	6	4	35½	35	24	36½	Catalano A	108wb	11.90	86-21	Twinkley1163Arcave1193½Jam1083	No rally	7
2Nov50-6GS	fst	1 1/16		:233 :473 1:114 1:46		Alw 4000	7	3	32½	22	22	43	Saunders W	112wb	*3.20	77-16	Twinkley108hdPendant1132½Mackle108½	Hung	8
27Oct50-5GS	fst	1 1/16		:233 :474 1:123 1:471	3↑	Alw 3000	7	4	34	33	32	2hd	Saunders W	112wb	4.00	74-19	Luremenow117hdJam112noIntrigue110no	Just missed	10
4Jly50-6Del	fst	1 1/16		:233 :471 1:121 1:444	3↑	Alw 3500	5	8	79	67¾	57½	512	Passmore WJ	112wb	3.70e	77-14	My Nell109.5½Uncle Don1169High Bracket1222	Off poorly	8
1Jly50-3Del	fst	1 1/16		:234 :482 1:141 1:452	3↑	Alw 3500	2	2	22	31	33	26	Passmore WJ	111wb	*1.40	80-14	Uncle Don1166Jam1111½The Flier1141¼	No excuse	5
	Previously owned by Mam Stable;previously trained by H.H. Goodwin																		
8Jun50-7Bel	fst	1 1/16		:232 :462 1:114 1:443		Clm 10000	5	3	36	24	23	21¼	Boland W	114wb	4.10	87-14	Oilomacy1201¼Jam114¾Persist1143½	Game try	6
31May50-4Bel	fst	1		:232 :463 1:121 1:391		Clm 8000-c	6	6	63¾	32	31½	3½	Stuart K	106wb	*2.70	77-13	Deflation116noPay Window118½Jam1062	Forced wide	7
	Claimed from Mrs L. Laurin;trainer, L. Laurin																		

25May50- 3Bel fst 1 1/16 :232 :471 1:121 1:434 Clm 7000-c 2 1 11 12 2½ 22 Atkinson T 117wb 2.20 90-07 Mr. Willie1192Jam1175½Beret1122½ Went wide 7
Claimed from Mam Stable;trainer, H.H. Goodwin
15May50- 7Bel fst 1 :231 :462 1:114 1:383 Clm 8000 3 9 86¾ 83¾ 86¼ 63¼ Boland W 114wb 20.35 78-21 AirMail120noFullMeasure109noEthelTerry116¾ Closed gap 13
Previously owned by A.G. Vanderbilt;previously trained by W.C. Winfrey
13Apr50- 8Jam fst 1 1/16 :24 :483 1:123 1:463 Clm 10000 2 6 54¾ 77½ 75¾ 56 Guerin E 115 w 5.30 74-17 HappyEast1132½PeaceMission116noEvnLatr1132½ No menace 10
7Apr50- 7Jam fst 1 1/16 :24 :48 1:132 1:462 Clm 10000 7 7 85¾ 76 710 710 Guerin E 116 w 3.70 71-20 EthelTerry1141HappyEast116noPecMsson1195 Close quarters 9
1Apr50- 7Jam fst 1 1/16 :243 :49 1:141 1:471 Clm 10000 1 4 53½ 51¾ 43¼ 21 Guerin E 116 w 12.20 76-14 Questus1161Jam116hdHappy East116½ Strong finish 9
3Mar50- 7Hia fst 1⅛ :48 1:124 1:38 1:51 Alw 3500 8 7 103½ 95¾ 77½ 86½ Dodson D 115 w 11.40 76-09 Three and Two110nkNoblest113nkHickory1151 Outrun 11
18Feb50- 3Hia fst 7f :23 :461 1:113 1:242 ©Alw 3500 8 6 75 73 75 52¼ Dodson D 122 w 5.30 88-12 Feefifofum109hdPotent1131Hickory118hd Closed gap 9
15Feb50- 3Hia fst 7f :23 :461 1:121 1:253 ©Md Sp Wt 2 3 33½ 2hd 1½ 13 Dodson D 122 w 20.30 84-17 Jam1223Johns Admiral11710pinionated1221½ Ridden out 8
7Feb50- 3Hia fst 7f :233 :47 1:122 1:252 ©Md Sp Wt 12 7 43 56¼ 68 712 Woodhouse H 122 w 55.75 73-14 Roughhouse1222Johns Admiral117noNoblest1223 No mishap 12
15Nov49- 4Pim fst 1 1/16 :241 :472 1:13 1:452 Md Sp Wt 4 7 611 613 514 419½ Martin RJ 122 w 7.60 63-14 Alfadur1158Swyndor12210Opal Blossom1221½ No mishap 10
27Oct49- 1Jam gd 6f :232 :472 1:14 ©Md 8000 10 12 117½ 1114 1117 109½ Scurlock O 122 w 9.50 71-18 DHDeflation116DHBashful Sun1136Beret113¾ Outrun 14
8Oct49- 3Lrl sl 6f :23 :474 1:134 Md Sp Wt 8 8 88¼ 77 79¾ 715 Martin RJ 120 w 9.60 70-23 PrinceDandy1206Possessive117½MiltntLdy117no Never close 9
5Oct49- 3Lrl fst 6f :233 :483 1:14 ©Md Sp Wt 5 6 96½ 67 510 513 Guerin E 122 w 2.90 71-23 Honors1222Hi-Pilate1227Djinn1222½ Raced wide 12
28Sep49- 4Lrl fst 6f :232 :482 1:144 ©Md Sp Wt 5 6 66¼ 67½ 56¼ 34¼ Martin RJ 122 w 2.90 76-21 Be Fleet122nkOpal Blossom1224Jam122no Closed fast 8
19Sep49- 4Bel fst 5½f-W :223 :454 1:052 ©Md Sp Wt 11 9 98¾ 814 68 Guerin E 118 w 17.25 79-16 Eternal City118¾Ode118nkWar King1184 Closed ground 19

King Commander

dkb. g. 1949, by Brown King (Nid d'Or)–Guinea Egg, by Cohort **Lifetime record: 67 17 15 6 $100,295**
Own.– Mrs L.R. Troiano
Br.– Mrs Joe W. Brown (Ky)
Tr.– E.E. Weymouth

15Jly58- 3Mth fm *1¾ Hurdles 3:201 4↑ Clm 4000 2 4 48 511 - - KnlsJD5 140 w 3.60 -- Caste15012Mielaison1452Curly Joe1455 Broke down 7
Previously owned by L.R. Troiano
19Sep57- 5Bel fm *2⅛ S'Chase 4:01 3↑ Broad Hollow H 17k 5 2 2hd - - - Cotter J 147 w 8.00 -- Independence1488Morpheus1382½Shipboard1623 Fell,lame 7
12Sep57- 5Bel fm *2⅛ S'Chase 3:573 3↑ Harbor Hill H 17k 3 2 22 43¾ 47 59 Cotter J 152 w 3.70 -- Ancestor1582Independence1486His Boots131nk Speed,tired 9
30Aug57- 3Sar fm *2 S'Chase 4:162 3↑ Alw 6500 2 1 12 13 12 12½ Cotter J 148 w *1.40 -- King Commander1482½Billing Bear1482½Affable14025 Easily 6
Previously trained by M.G. Walsh
7Jun56- 5Bel fm *2½ S'Chase 4:394 4↑ Meadow Brook H 17k 2 1 11½ 12 21½ 39½ Smithwick P 164 w 1.55 -- Neji1653½Carthage1366KngCmmndr1648 Brushed jumps,lame 5
24May56- 5Bel fm *2 S'Chase 3:434 4↑ International H 11k 3 1 14 13 15 17 Smithwick P 160 w *.50e -- King Commander1607Cap-a-Pie1403½Hyvania1507 Much best 6
17May56- 5Bel fm *2 S'Chase 3:44 4↑ Corinthian H 11k 3 2 1hd 1½ 1hd 23 Smithwick P 160 w *.40e -- Montadet1373King Commander1606Carthage1404 Bore out 6
7Sep55- 3Aqu fm *2 Hurdles 3:453 3↑ Alw 4000 3 1 11½ 12 11½ 1nk Smithwick P 150 w *.65 -- King Commander150nkThe Proff1479Good Cards142¾ Lasted 6
21May55- 6Bel hd *2½ S'Chase 4:432 4↑ International 21k 7 1 18 15 - - Smithwick P 155 w 2.05e -- Neji15015Ancestor15518Hyvn15518 High speed,fell at 15th 10
5May55- 5Bel fm *2 S'Chase 3:412 4↑ C L Appleton Mem 9.1k 1 4 416 36½ 21 23½ Smithwick P 162 w 2.40e -- Ancestor1343½KingCommandr1628RiverJordan1344 Swerved 8
22Oct54- 6Bel fm *2½ S'Chase 4:39 4↑ Temple Gwathmey H 16k 4 1 12 12½ 14 1¾ Smithwick P 164 w 3.00 -- King Commander164¾Neji1497Coveted13170 Driving,tiring 6
14Oct54- 5Bel fm *3 S'Chase 5:42 4↑ Grand National H 28k 7 1 11 - - - Smithwick P 164 w 2.75e -- Shipboard1522¾Coveted13122Curly Joe13310 Bobbled 16th 7
5Oct54- 5Bel fm *2½ S'Chase 4:394 4↑ Brook H 17k 2 2 12 13 13 21½ Smithwick P 161 w *1.40e -- Neji1371½KingCommndr16116Covtd13115 Tired under weight 9
16Sep54- 3Aqu sf *2 Hurdles 3:452 3↑ Bushwick H 8k 4 6 819 58½ 33 33½ Smithwick P 157 w *.90e -- Carafar1433Khumbaba134½King Commander1573 No rally 8
26Aug54- 5Sar fm *2½ S'Chase 5:002 4↑ Saratoga H 11k 2 1 11½ 11 16 19 Smithwick P 154 w 2.00 -- KingCommndr1549Shpbord14814Covtd1328 Speed in reserve 6
19Aug54- 5Sar fm *2 S'Chase 4:083 4↑ Beverwyck H 8.7k 2 1 11 12½ 16 13 Smithwick P 149 w *1.00 -- King Commndr1493MightyMo13520Imbursed1302 Ridden out 5
12Aug54- 5Sar fm *2 S'Chase 4:13 4↑ North American H 8.6k 4 4 2½ 21 2hd 2no Riles S 145 w 1.00e -- Escargot139noKing Commander1456Sun Shower1602 Hung 5
5Aug54- 5Sar sf *2 S'Chase 4:172 4↑ Shillelah H 8.8k 5 4 1½ 11½ 11½ 22 Riles S 143 w 2.45e -- Shipboard1392King Commander14320Coveted13812 Tired 7
30Jly54- 5Mth hd *1¾ Hurdles 3:19 3↑ Midsummer H 11k 5 6 46½ 32½ 2hd 2hd Riles S 152 w 2.20e -- Escargot143hdKing Commndr1522CammellLaird1457 Gamely 7
28Jun54- 5Del hd *2 S'Chase 3:47 4↑ Spring Maiden 6.8k 3 5 43 43 1½ 2½ Smithwick P 160 w *.60e -- Imbursed130½KingCommandr16012Bavaria14012 Outjumped 6
15Jun54- 5Aqu fm *2 S'Chase 3:493 4↑ Spring Maiden 6.8k 1 4 36 33½ 1hd 2hd Smithwick P 160 w *.40 -- Coveted155hdKingCommandr1602Imbursd13285 Bore in,tired 5
13May54- 5Bel fm *2 S'Chase 3:482 4↑ Spring Maiden 6.8k 3 3 45½ 3½ 110 17 Smithwick P 153 w *.95 -- KingCommnder1537IndianFire1402½Coveted15015 Easy score 5
6May54- 3Bel fm *2 S'Chase 3:482 4↑ Alw 4000 7 6 21½ 43½ 11½ 14½ Smithwick P 143 w *.55 -- KingCommndr1434½Coveted1434Carafr1352½ Handily ridden 8
29Apr54- 3Bel fm *2 S'Chase 3:462 4↑ Sp Wt 4000 10 6 411 49 11 2½ Smithwick P 148 w *1.20 -- Shipboard140½KingCmmndr14812PacificPct1482½ Weakened 11
10Oct53- 3Lig hd *2 Hurdles 3:582 3↑ Handicap 2000 7 7 79 2nk 13 15 Smithwick AP 149 w - -- King Commander1495Allflor143¾Salemaker137hd Easily 8
5Oct53- 5Bel fst *2 Hurdles 3:45 3↑ Rouge Dragon H 11k 7 5 710 47½ 22½ 2hd Smithwick P 154 w *1.60e -- Williamsburg142hdKingCommndr1543Hyvan1466 Just missed 9
28Sep53- 3Bel fst *1¾ Hurdles 3:132 3↑ Alw 4500 6 6 59½ 33½ 1½ 12½ Smithwick P 149 w 2.75e -- KingCommndr1492½Wllmsburg1402RvrJordn1494½ Ridden out 9
17Sep53- 3Aqu fst *2 Hurdles 3:421 3↑ Bushwick H 8k 5 3 327 619 11 11 Smithwick P 148 w 3.60e -- KingCommndr1481Williamsburg1392Antagonzr1531½ Driving 8
21Aug53- 5Sar hd *2 Hurdles 3:502 3↑ Lovely Night H 6.4k 2 1 11 32 36 23½ Smithwick P 149 w *1.35e -- WarRhodes1543½KingCmmndr1492½BattlWv1392½ Hard urged 8
14Aug53- 3Sar fst *1¾ Hurdles 3:302 3↑ Handicap 4085 4 5 77½ 54½ 33 21½ Smithwick P 149 w 3.35e -- War Rhodes1501½King Commander1493Knocks Twice1443½ 10
Close quarters
31Jly53- 5Mth fst *1¾ Hurdles 3:221 3↑ Midsummer H 11k 9 6 33 31½ 21 1no Smithwick P 140 w 7.60e -- KingCommandr140noMackville1485War Rhodes1472½ Just up 13
28Jly53- 3Mth fst *1½ Hurdles 2:42 3↑ Alw 3500 9 2 22 2½ 1hd 11½ Smithwick P 143 w 3.50 -- KingCommndr1431½JoeRayJr14310FleurdJo14010 Drew clear 9
2Jly53- 5Aqu fst *2 Hurdles 3:394 4↑ Forget H 11k 3 5 511 516 48 46 Cameron C 141 w 5.95e -- Williamsburg135hdEternalSon1432WarRhodes1484 Late foot 6
25Jun53- 5Aqu fst *1¾ Hurdles 3:104 3↑ Amagansett H 8.9k 5 1 12 2hd 22½ 24½ Cameron C 140 w 3.05e -- WarRhodes1424½KingCmmndr140½EtrnlSon14418 Hard ridden 6
22Jun53- 3Aqu fst *1½ Hurdles 2:441 3↑ Md Sp Wt 2 3 1½ 12 11½ 11½ Cameron C 145 w *.60 -- KingCommander1451½Imbursed1351½WatchDog1356 Driving 6
15Jun53- 3Bel sf *1½ Hurdles 2:444 3↑ Sp Wt 3700 3 9 910 78 46 2¾ Cameron C 142 w 56.55 -- Mackville142¾KngCommandr1425Rythminhim1359 Impeded 12
4Jun53- 3Bel fst 7f :231 :47 1:123 1:254 4↑ Clm 5000 2 12 139½ 1313 1320 1313 Nichols J 113wb 49.20 68-20 Demi-Heure113½Brown Dalton1172Riverlane117nk No speed 13
23May53- 2Bel sly 7f :232 :474 1:124 1:251 4↑ Clm 6500 7 6 88½ 815 822 831 Wallis G 113wb 44.70 53-13 Belton Boy119½Hoplite1262¼Evans Mountain114hd Far back 8
Previously owned by Mrs M.G. Walsh
14Oct52- 4Jam fst 1 1/16 :244 :483 1:133 1:464 Clm 5000 5 2 2hd 22 32½ 35 Nichols J 122wb 3.25 73-19 Jonskid1172½Lesliefay1172½King Commander1221 Weakened 8
9Oct52- 7Jam fst 1 1/16 :234 :48 1:132 1:452 3↑ Clm 6000 4 7 711 75½ 66¼ 45¾ Nichols J 117wb 14.50 79-21 Big Road1142Tape Reader110¾Flying Mane1123 Slow start 7
6Oct52- 7Jam fst 1 1/16 :242 :49 1:133 1:461 Clm 7500 9 7 66 64¼ 64½ 77 Nichols J 116wb 39.60 74-15 Westmeath1172Stone Saucer119nkLegate112nk Outrun 9
23Sep52- 8Bel fst 1⅛ :454 1:112 1:374 1:51 3↑ Clm 6000 5 6 65 32 44½ 511 Ploof H 105wb 8.20 73-12 Kay'sChildren1131FlyingMane114hdAttentionSir1194½ Tired 8
13Sep52- 8Aqu fst 7f :23 :472 1:133 1:263 Clm 5000-c 4 8 93¼ 97 73¾ 43 Schab H 109wb 3.60 74-17 Westmeath1193GalliesPride114hdBlueFlash108no Slow start 9
Claimed from H.M. Boshamer;trained by J.R. Hastie
4Sep52- 2Aqu fst 7f :233 :472 1:13 1:263 Clm 5000 10 12 127¼ 1210 75¼ 31¾ Anderson P 118wb 13.20 75-17 Service1131¾Grandad113noKing Commander1181½ Late rush 13
27Aug52- 8Sar fst 1⅛ :49 1:141 1:401 1:54 Clm 5000 8 5 65½ 45 44¼ 34 Hardinbrook JN 114wb 6.70 76-19 NextStop1111½WallSt.George1132½KngCmmndr114¾ No mishap 8
21Aug52- 2Sar fst 7f :232 :47 1:13 1:261 Clm 5000 14 9 63 52¾ 33 44 Hardinbrook JN 115wb 9.90 80-22 Service114½Sea Bob1141Next Stop1132½ Faltered 14
13Aug52- 2Sar my 7f :23 :464 1:124 1:273 Clm 6500 4 8 98¼ 1014 93 86½ Anderson P 119wb 78.50 70-25 Fancy Bonnet115¾Standee1163Lafourche112nk No factor 11
30Jly52- 7Jam fst 1 1/16 :25 :481 1:14 1:462 Clm 7000 4 8 89 87½ 97¾ 912 Anderson P 115wb 31.55 68-20 Harlem Maid1124La Gaulois108nkDocedoe1122½ Outrun 9
Previously owned by J.W. Brown;previously trained by J.B. Theall
12Jly52- 7Aqu fst 1 1/16 :24 :49 1:134 1:47 Clm 7000 2 7 88½ 99¼ 55 58¼ Hardinbrook JN 114wb 14.65e 71-14 FirstWing1193WingingAlong119¾HarlemMaid1173 No menace 9
2Jly52- 7Aqu fst 1 1/16 :243 :482 1:141 1:483 Clm 5000 7 4 415 55½ 31 1¾ Hardinbrook JN 111wb 2.25 71-18 KingCommndr111¾Vocabulary1091Drems108no Driving clear 7
28Jun52- 2Aqu fst 7f :233 :471 1:132 1:264 Clm 3500 9 10 106¼ 84 1½ 12½ Hardinbrook JN 109wb *3.05e 78-16 KngCmmandr1092½FrnchQurtr1091KthyMndl1131 Drew clear 11
26Jun52- 1Aqu fst 6f :231 :47 1:13 Clm 3500 5 9 75½ 89¼ 710 67 Coffman E 113wb 7.20 80-15 Muscidae1131Rachel G.1093½Query108¾ Raced wide 11
20Jun52- 2Aqu fst 7f :231 :47 1:14 1:273 Clm 3500 11 10 95¾ 96 21 2nk Hardinbrook JN 109wb 4.60 74-15 Tio Tito114nkKing Commander1092½Camouflet109nk Hung 11
28May52- 4GS fst 6f :223 :454 1:12 Clm 5000 8 7 711 814 89½ 915 Culmone J 115wb 4.20 73-15 Tiger Jay1136½Lady Like114¾Ambrose1152 Outrun 9

20May52- 2GS	sly 6f	:233 :48 1:143	Clm 5000	1 8 65 67 64½ 32¼	Permane R	115wb	5.50	73-21	UpHigh110nkBigKeis1192KingCommander1151½	Strong finish	9
10May52- 1GS	fst 6f	:221 :452 1:123	Clm 5000	11 12 1214 1112 614 56¾	Coffman E	115wb	49.80	78-11	FlyingPolly112¾BigKs1193½Hollowbrook1122	Sluggish start	12
1Apr52- 2Jam	fst 6f	:23 :47 1:123	Clm 5000	6 14 1413 149¼ 1215 1213	Coffman E	113wb	21.60	71-13	Deep River1171Inezmuch117¾Wolf Bait112nk	Outrun	14
1Mar52- 5FG	fst 6f	:231 :472 1:114	Clm 7000	1 4 54 43 45 45	Coffman E	111wb	6.40	89-11	ArizonaK114½QuickTulip1142½TopBrass1112	Close quarters	7
16Feb52- 8FG	gd 6f	:232 :472 1:124	Clm 7000	2 4 51½ 75½ 55½ 54¾	Coffman E	111wb	46.30	84-15	Mr. Michael S.114nkBalsa112nkDynastic114nk	No mishap	8
16Jan52- 6FG	fst 6f	:23 :47 1:134	Clm 6000	7 5 58 69 911 911	Coffman E	117wb	23.40	73-20	Balsa114nkLegatee1091½Odds Advance1122½	No factor	9
12Jan52- 5FG	fst 1 1/16	:242 :482 1:134 1:482 3↑	Alw 1800	5 6 66½ 45½ 56 58	Coffman E	112 w	3.10e	69-18	Gloriette1153½PointFortune1123FancyGent1121½	No menace	7
12Dec51- 1FG	fst 6f	:233 :473 1:151	Clm 5000	7 9 98 65 31½ 1nk	Coffman E	111wb	71.30	77-19	KingCommandr111nkGeorgeDavie1131½BeutfulJn1112	Just up	12
6Dec51- 7FG	fst 6f	:231 :473 1:141	Clm 6000	2 9 107¾ 1013 712 715	Coffman E	112wb	94.30	67-22	Seasoned1111½Quick Tulip1066Balsa1142	Outrun	10
24Nov51- 5FG	fst 6f	:231 :47 1:131	Alw 2000	3 7 79¼ 712 712 714	Chiapetta S	108wb	36.70	73-18	Our Challenge117hdPlunger1146Bold Sab117½	Trailed	7
20Oct51- 4GS	fst 6f	:222 :454 1:121	Alw 4500	3 9 912 911 915 913	LeBlanc C	115wb	95.40	74-15	Star Delight1142½La Gaulois117¾Saddle Tramp1122	Trailed	9
17Oct51- 2Bel	fst 6f	:224 :47 1:131	Clm 7500	14 10 86¼ 129 1321 1211	LeBlanc C	113wb	14.05f	72-15	Vantage107¾Flaunt116¾Our Dorie1131½	Outrun	14
3Oct51- 5Bel	fst 6f-WC	:223 :452 1:10	©Md Sp Wt	2 25 2615 2518 2620	LeBlanc C	118 w	71.90e	71-09	Warpath1182Golden Gloves118hdForelock1181	Outrun	26

Kiss Me Kate

ch. f. 1948, by Count Fleet (Reigh Count)–Irish Nora, by Pharamond II — **Lifetime record: 29 7 4 7 $196,505**

Own.– W.M. Jeffords
Br.– Walter M. Jeffords (Ky)
Tr.– O. White

30May53- 6Bel	fst 1¼	:471 1:11 1:353 2:003 3↑	Suburban H 58k	4 4 35 59½ 711 718	Scurlock O	112wb	2.30e	79-17	Tom Fool128noRoyal Vale1247Cold Command1142	Done early	7
5May53- 6Jam	sly 1⅛	:48 1:123 1:373 1:504 3↑	ⒻFirenze H 35k	6 6 56 41½ 1hd 13	Gorman D	126wb	*2.10	92-19	KssMeKate1263ParadngLady1232½LaCorredora123¾	Drew out	8
23Apr53- 6Jam	fst 1 1/16	:25 :481 1:121 1:443 4↑	Alw 5000	4 5 54 43½ 32 2½	Gorman D	115wb	*.70	88-21	Swoop108½Kiss Me Kate1154Deluge113½	Gaining fast	8
11Nov52- 6Pim	sl 1⅛	:49 1:133 1:394 1:522 3↑	ⒻGallorette 29k	4 6 64 52¼ 32½ 23½	Nash R	123wb	2.50	88-22	La Corredora1123½Kiss Me Kate1231Marta1173	Good effort	9
18Oct52- 7GS	fst 1 1/16	:23 :471 1:112 1:453 3↑	ⒻVineland H 49k	4 12 1214 1010 66½ 2¾	Nash R	118wb	8.00e	81-20	Sickle'sImage120¾KissMeKate118¾LilyWhit111hd	Late speed	17
1Oct52- 6Bel	fst 1½	:483 1:132 2:044 2:312 3↑	ⒻLadies H 59k	6 4 52½ 31½ 35½ 44½	Arcaro E	121wb	3.75e	76-15	How1121¼Marta1222½Enchanted Eve112¾	Faltered	11
13Sep52- 7Aqu	fst 1⅛	:474 1:121 1:38 1:51 3↑	ⒻBeldame H (Div 2) 62k	3 9 910 99¾ 86 44¾	Gorman D	122wb	10.80	85-17	Real Delight126¾Marta117½La Corredora1123½	Late foot	9
28Aug52- 6Sar	fst 1¾	:494 2:07 2:33 2:594 3↑	Sar Cup 16k	2 3 32 45 33½ 35	Guerin E	121wb	*1.05	71-20	Busanda1212½Lone Eagle1262½Kiss Me Kate1212	No rally	5
	Geldings not eligible										
19Aug52- 6Sar	fst 1⅛	:49 1:143 1:412 1:532 3↑	ⒻDiana H 11k	3 4 41½ 53 52¾ 45¾	Nash R	126wb	*.85	77-22	Busanda1111¼Nilufer106½Valadium1154	No rally	5
5Jly52- 5Del	fst 1¼	:462 1:104 1:363 2:023 3↑	ⒻNew Castle H 61k	7 2 1½ 12 13 12½	Nash R	126wb	*2.20	97-14	Kiss Me Kate1262½Renew1231¼My Celeste1131½	Cleverly	10
30May52- 6Bel	fst 1¼	:463 1:102 1:353 2:02 3↑	Suburban H 60k	4 10 1015 1013 711 43¼	Woodhouse H	107wb	16.45	87-12	One Hitter112nkCrafty Admiral1132Mameluke1161	Late foot	10
21Apr52- 6Jam	fst 1⅛	:471 1:114 1:372 1:511 3↑	ⒻFirenze H 33k	8 6 67 67 45½ 33¾	Arcaro E	123wb	*2.40	86-18	NxtMove1262ThelmaBurger1101¾KssMeKate123¾	Closed fast	9
7Apr52- 6Lrl	fst 6f	:223 :47 1:114 4↑	Alw 5000	1 4 33½ 44 55 32¼	Nash R	117wb	4.80	86-21	ⒹSenatorJoe119nkRockyHeghts1052KssMKt117hd	Closed fast	6
13Oct51- 6Bel	fst 2	:493 2:302 2:56 3:213 3↑	J C Gold Cup 53k	3 4 47½ 414 412 310	Shoemaker W	114wb	9.30	86-11	Counterpoint117hdHillPrince12410KissMKt1142½	Rough trip	5
10Oct51- 6Bel	fst 1½	:483 1:132 2:04 2:301 3↑	ⒻLadies H 30k	8 12 98½ 106 77¼ 34¾	Arcaro E	120wb	*2.45	82-15	Marta1111¼Bed o' Roses1263½Kiss Me Kate120½	Late rush	14
22Sep51- 6Aqu	fst 1⅛	:482 1:122 1:382 1:52 3↑	ⒻBeldame 67k	13 4 41¼ 31½ 51¾ 32½	Arcaro E	119wb	*1.70	82-14	ThelmaBurger1102Bedo'Roses124½KssMeKt119nk	Closed well	14
29Aug51- 6Sar	fst 1¼	:484 1:131 1:382 2:053	ⒻAlabama 22k	4 2 23 2½ 13 18	Arcaro E	126wb	*.85	80-18	Kiss Me Kate1268Vulcania1162Aunt Jinny122no	Ridden out	5
11Jly51- 6Aqu	fst 1 1/16	:241 :474 1:122 1:46	ⒻGazelle 28k	9 11 85¼ 94¾ 3½ 11½	Mehrtens W	121wb	6.00	84-14	KissMeKate1211½BootAll1121¼SpanishCream1121	Drew clear	12
30Jun51- 5Del	sly 1¼	:474 1:124 1:383 2:043 3↑	ⒻNew Castle H 60k	2 4 64½ 43 46 59	Mehrtens W	113wb	*1.95e	78-20	Busanda1262¼Leading Home109¾How1155	Tired	9
16Jun51- 5Del	fst 1⅛	:463 1:114 1:381 1:502	ⒻDel Oaks 34k	3 4 42½ 4¾ 2½ 14	Mehrtens W	119wb	*.70	93-11	Kiss Me Kate1194Signal1131Jacodema1164	Ridden out	8
2Jun51- 6Bel	fst 1⅜	:48 1:131 1:39 2:164	ⒻC C A Oaks 64k	5 13 43½ 2hd 33½ 24	Mehrtens W	121wb	*1.95	83-11	How1214Kiss Me Kate1211Jacodema1211¾	No excuse	15
23May51- 6Bel	sly 1	:224 :46 1:11 1:362	ⒻAcorn (Div 1) 24k	11 6 3nk 11½ 16 112	Mehrtens W	121wb	7.70	92-14	Kiss Me Kate12112Wisteria121¾Jacodema1211¼	Easily	12
2Apr51- 3Lrl	my 6f	:232 :482 1:13	Md Sp Wt	8 8 64 3nk 14 112	Culmone J	117wb	*1.80	82-25	Kiss Me Kate11712Baker's Wood1222No Disgrace1171	Easily	11
2Mar51- 3Hia	fst 6f	:223 :463 1:124	Md Sp Wt	3 2 85¼ 88¾ 37 33½	Boulmetis S	116 w	7.30	80-17	SylvanRock1212BleuFeatur1161½KssMKt1164	Closed steadily	11
13Feb51- 8Hia	fst 1⅛	:472 1:12 1:374 1:512	Alw 3500	9 4 76 810 89¼ 45	Boulmetis S	109 w	15.80	76-18	OldRowley115nkChallarian118¾TimelyReward1154	Closed gap	9
30Jan51- 3Hia	fst 6f	:223 :462 1:123	Md Sp Wt	8 7 98¾ 1012 69 44½	Mehrtens W	117 w	47.15	80-20	Arctic Flyer122noDictionary1224Graphic122½	Raced wide	12
31Jly50- 4Sar	fst 5½f	:224 :461 :591 1:06	ⒻMd Sp Wt	8 11 135½ 148¾ 1413 1319	Woodhouse H	116 w	19.40	68-12	Rose Fern1165½Chelsie1161Fleecy Cloud1161½	No factor	14
22Apr50- 3HdG	fst 4½f	:222 :462 :524	Alw 3500	3 6 710 67½ 68¼	Snellings A	111 w	28.80	87-14	Brazen Brat1152½Iswas118½Top Spring1221½	Outrun	7
15Apr50- 3HdG	fst 4½f	:231 :47 :533	Alw 3500	11 11 910 116½ 97¾	Snellings A	111 w	12.20	83-16	Top Spring1181½Stag118nkB Battery1181½	No factor	12

Leallah

br. f. 1954, by Nasrullah (Nearco)–Lea Lark, by Bull Lea — **Lifetime record: 20 10 2 2 $152,784**

Own.– C. Clay
Br.– Charlton Clay (Ky)
Tr.– M. Miller

10Jun58- 6Bel	sly 6f	:222 :461 1:113 3↑	ⒻHandicap 7500	2 2 2hd 2hd 31 35	Arcaro E	119 w	4.40	85-17	Mlle. Dianne1195Miss Blue Jay122hdLeallah11910		4
	Speed for half,weakened										
30May58- 7GS	fst 6f	:22 :444 1:103 3↑	ⒻColonial H 29k	2 7 83¾ 88¾ 69 95¾	Grant H	116 w	4.90	85-16	Venomous123½Fall Wind1091½Romanita116½	Always far back	12
23May58- 6Bel	fst 6f	:223 :454 1:104 4↑	ⒻAlw 5500	2 3 1½ 1½ 1hd 21½	Arcaro E	114 w	2.95	92-12	MissBlueJay1151½Leallah1141½FloralGirl1114	Used in pace	7
2Nov57- 7CD	fst 1	:224 :452 1:101 1:361 3↑	ⒻFalls City H 22k	3 1 1hd 1hd 13 14¼	Erb D	114 w	*.70e	94-10	Leallah1144¼Beautillion118¾LdyLru1112	Increasing margin	8
26Oct57- 7CD	fst 6½f	:223 :453 1:104 1:172 3↑	ⒻAlw 4500	3 7 2hd 2hd 12 13½	Heckmann J	115 w	*.60e	94-11	Leallah1153½Lebkuchen1153I Say No1151½	Increased margin	8
9Oct57- 3Kee	fst 6f	:214 :442 1:09	Alw 3750	1 1 11 13 14 12½	Erb D	117 w	*.30e	101-06	Leallah1172½Resolved120noOn-the-Ready1204	Much the best	7
1Oct57- 7Bel	fst 6f	:231 :471 1:11	ⒻAlw 6000	2 1 11 1hd 1hd 2hd	Shoemaker W	117 w	4.75	94-22	Alanesian117hdLeallah1171½Wan1116	Headed in game effort	7
2Sep57- 7Bel	fst 6f-WC	:223 :45 1:092 2↑	Fall Highweight H 29k	2 8 62¾ 75¾ 85½	Lester W	113 w	23.70	86-08	Itobe1241½Commendation116½GayWarrior117nk	Swerved early	11
21Aug57- 4Sar	fst 6f	:224 :462 1:132	ⒻAlw 4500	1 2 23 25 45 513	Ussery R	118wb	2.30	68-22	Htsu1151MgcForst1211Mrs.Hlln1188	Early factor,tired badly	5
20Jly57- 6Mth	fst 6f	:212 :44 1:101	ⒻMiss Woodford 25k	3 7 2hd 23 25 63½	Shuk N	118wb	6.60	90-15	Mrs.Hellen1121½Light'nLovely112noNilLly112no	Used early	15
15Jly57- 6Bel	fst 6f	:223 :46 1:102 3↑	ⒻAlw 5500	2 1 2½ 2½ 33½ 48½	Anderson P	115wb	3.85	88-13	FancifulMiss1143½Alanesian1153Recherche1182	Forced wide	7
2Jly57- 6Bel	fst 6f	:223 :461 1:111	ⒻAlw 5500	2 2 2½ 2hd 31 32¾	Arcaro E	122 w	1.25	90-12	Miss Blue Jay118¾Alanesian1222Leallah122	No excuse	3
13Oct56- 6Kee	fst *7f	1:27	ⒻAlcibiades 41k	5 1 11½ 14 13 12½	Boulmetis S	119 w	*.40	98-11	Leallah1192½Bluebility119noNantu1194½	Under mild urging	6
28Sep56- 4Bel	sly 6f-WC	:222 :45 1:093	ⒻAlw 6000	4 1 1hd 11 1½	Arcaro E	124 w	*1.20	91-10	Leallah124½Defilade114hdEvening Time1142½	Ridden out	6
13Aug56- 7Was	hy 6f	:23 :472 1:132	ⒻPrincess Pat 97k	2 4 23 11 2hd 46	Arcaro E	119 w	*.30	72-26	Splendored113hdRomant1163½Blublty1112½	Disliked going	8
18Jly56- 7Jam	fst 5½f	:223 :46 :581 1:043	ⒻAstoria 22k	4 2 12 12 12 1¾	Arcaro E	119 w	*.35	95-15	Leallah119¾Marullah1154MissBlueJay1191	Had to be urged	6
7Jly56- 8AP	fst 6f	:22 :443 1:113	ⒻArl Lassie 95k	2 2 2hd 11 15 14	Hartack W	119 w	*.20	86-10	Leallah1194Splendored1192½Frnk'sFlowr119½	Much the best	7
30Jun56- 6Mth	fst 5½f	:211 :443 1:04	ⒻColleen 25k	9 3 22 2hd 14 14½	Boulmetis S	114 w	*1.90	100-07	Leallah1144½Marullah1142Alpenrose1121½	Speed in reserve	12
19Jun56- 6Bel	fst 5f-WC	:22 :444 :572	Alw 4000	2 1 11½ 14 11¾	Arcaro E	113 w	*.35	92-10	Leallah1131¾Prtshr1161¾Asgrd116nk	Eased through stretch	6
11Jun56- 5Bel	fst 5f-WC	:22 :45 :573	ⒻMd Sp Wt	10 2 1½ 13 11¾	Arcaro E	115 w	*.65e	91-12	Leallah1151¾Gossamer1158Lodestone115¾	Speed in reserve	14

Misty Morn

b. f. 1952, by Princequillo (Prince Rose)–Grey Flight, by Mahmoud **Lifetime record: 42 11 6 7 $212,575**

Own.– Wheatley Stable
Br.– Wheatley Stable (Ky)
Tr.– J. Fitzsimmons

5Jun56- 7Bel	fst	1	:23 :462 1:112 1:373	4↑	Alw 6000	7 3 52¼ 55½ 69½ 67	Atkinson T	117wb	*.85	79-12	Prince Morvi114noJean's Joe1131¾Chief Fanelli1132		8
	Wide,gave way suddenly												
26May56- 7Bel	fst	1 1/16	:223 :451 1:102 1:423	3↑	ⒻTop Flight H 28k	3 5 89 75¾ 54¼ 42¼	Atkinson T	124wb	4.40e	94-11	Searching121½Parlo1241½RcoRto107nk	Best stride too late	10
22May56- 7Bel	fst	1 1/16	:241 :472 1:114 1:423	3↑	Handicap 7500	6 3 56 56½ 58½ 47¾	Arcaro E	123wb	*2.55	88-12	Midafternoon126½Woodbrook110nkMaharajah1177	Outrun	7
14May56- 6Bel	fst	1	:23 :454 1:103 1:364	4↑	Alw 6000	2 4 34½ 32 3nk 42	Arcaro E	117wb	3.00	88-14	FirstAid109½WarPiper113½LittleDell1131	Made bid,tired	7
2Mar56- 7Hia	fst	1⅛	:453 1:10 1:36 1:492	3↑	ⒻBlack Helen H 40k	2 8 1118 1113 109¾ 97½	Cole S	126wb	*1.55e	81-09	ClearDawn108noMissArlette112¾HighVoltage125hd	Dull try	12
12Nov55- 6Jam	gd	1⅝	:483 1:383 2:04 2:422	3↑	Gallant Fox H 85k	3 6 814 4½ 1½ 13	Cole S	113wb	10.65	102-13	Misty Morn1133Cavort1118Thinking Cap1163½	Drew clear	9
5Nov55- 6Jam	sly	1 3/16	:471 1:112 1:372 1:56		Roamer H 58k	7 11 1111 86¼ 79 68¾	Nichols J	116wb	10.70	87-17	Sailor1123½Cvort1112Nnc'sLd122nk	No apparent mishap	12
26Oct55- 6Suf	fst	1⅛	:473 1:112 1:371 1:502		Yankee H 58k	11 8 76 76¼ 56 54	Atkinson T	115wb	3.00	85-18	Rockcastle1131½Nance's Lad1201Speed Rouser1161½	Blocked	11
22Oct55- 7GS	fst	1⅛	:453 1:10 1:353 1:481	3↑	ⒻVineland H 51k	18 13 169¼ 1514 1211 1110	Atkinson T	124wb	2.80e	86-10	High Voltage1173Manotick1181Crisset110no	Never a factor	18
12Oct55- 6Bel	fst	1½	:482 1:132 2:051 2:312	3↑	ⒻLadies H 62k	8 9 76 32 42½ 2hd	Atkinson T	124wb	*2.25	81-17	Manotick117hdMisty Morn1241¼Countess Fleet1172	Gaining	15
30Sep55- 7Bel	fst	1⅛	:472 1:12 1:371 1:493		Handicap 10000	6 7 74¾ 51¼ 3½ 3¾	Atkinson T	122wb	*.95	90-12	Cavort113¾ThinkingCap122hdMstyMorn1221	Evenly late part	7
23Sep55- 6Bel	fst	1	:231 :46 1:104 1:364		ⒻHandicap 10000	1 7 64¼ 64½ 2½ 1¾	Atkinson T	124wb	*.60e	90-17	MstyMrn124¾RareTreat1122¼SweetMusic106hd	Won cleverly	7
24Aug55- 6Sar	gd	1¼	:484 1:142 1:394 2:054		ⒻAlabama 29k	2 3 42 33 34½ 33¼	Atkinson T	121wb	*.40e	76-22	Rico Reto1133Blue Banner114nkMisty Morn1211¼	No excuse	8
17Aug55- 6Sar	sly	1⅛	:474 1:122 1:38 1:511	3↑	ⒻDiana H 23k	5 4 43½ 31½ 1½ 11½	Atkinson T	115wb	*1.05	94-15	MistyMorn1151½CarrytheNews110½OilPainting11820	Driving	6
6Aug55- 6Mth	fst	1⅛	:47 1:112 1:371 1:503		ⒻMth Oaks 61k	8 2 25 1hd 1hd 1nk	Arcaro E	121wb	*1.10	93-18	MistyMrn121nkBlueSparkler1217Manotick121¾	Held gamely	11
23Jly55- 6Jam	fst	1 1/16	:242 :474 1:123 1:44		Saranac H 29k	3 7 712 57½ 38 23½	Woodhouse H	112wb	4.60	88-15	Saratoga1263½MistyMorn112nkNanc'sLd1232	Closed gap late	8
9Jly55- 6Mth	fst	1 1/16	:231 :47 1:114 1:452	3↑	ⒻMolly Pitcher H 30k	9 8 84¼ 3nk 1½ 1¾	Boulmetis S	112wb	*1.50	88-13	Misty Morn112¾Clear Dawn120noManotick111¾	Held gamely	12
22Jun55- 7Nar	fst	1⅛	:482 1:132 1:39 1:52		Providence 37k	3 3 36 14 1hd 11½	Atkinson T	106wb	2.80	86-19	MistyMorn1061½[D]Saratog1231¾Mr.AlL.1115	Drew out in dr.	4
17Jun55- 6Aqu	fst	7f	:232 :464 1:112 1:242		ⒻAlw 5000	5 6 62¼ 3½ 21 21	Atkinson T	118wb	*.65	87-14	TwoStrs1181MstyMorn1186Sorcrss1112½	Slow to reach stride	6
1Jun55- 6Bel	fst	7f	:23 :462 1:111 1:241	3↑	ⒻGolden Annivrsy H 20k	8 6 63¾ 77 66¼ 61	Atkinson T	113wb	*2.25	88-14	Dispute114¾Parlo125hdOilPantng107no	Wide in stretch bid	11
27May55- 6Bel	fst	1 1/16	:232 :46 1:102 1:42	3↑	ⒻHandicap 6000	3 3 34 31½ 12½ 15	Atkinson T	110wb	1.45	101-13	MistyMorn1105Talora119hdCarrytheNws1144	Drew out easily	5
20May55- 6Bel	fst	1⅛	:473 1:124 1:38 1:504		ⒻAlw 6000	8 6 83¾ 6½ 1½ 1½	Lester W	113wb	3.35e	85-15	MistyMorn113½InReserve1175Lalun1212	Well rated,driving	8
12May55- 7Bel	fst	1 1/16	:234 :473 1:123 1:44		ⒻAlw 4000	6 2 31 2½ 11 11¾	Atkinson T	114wb	4.70	91-13	Misty Morn1141¾Elenem117nkManotick1201	Fully extended	7
7May55- 4Bel	fst	1	:232 :461 1:113 1:381		Alw 4000	1 5 58 57 57 55¼	Higley J	113wb	11.20	78-14	Jabneh1192½War and Peace1161Thunder Hole1161½	Outrun	6
5Mar55- 3GP	fst	6f	:221 :464 1:123		ⒻAlw 3500	10 3 52¼ 87¾ 87¾ 87	Atkinson T	115wb	3.00	75-14	Derry1133Miss Energy1121Rare Treat1111½	Quit early	11
28Feb55- 6Hia	fst	6f	:223 :454 1:111		ⒻAlw 4500	8 6 34 44 33½ 22	Atkinson T	110wb	9.10	89-15	NimbleDoll1162MistyMorn110noWagonDrill1051	Late rally	8
22Feb55- 5Hia	fst	6f	:224 :462 1:104		ⒻAlw 4500	1 7 83¼ 912 911 710	Higley J	118wb	36.05	83-15	MissEnergy110½Vestment118hdSometimeThing1182	Far back	9
28Oct54- 6Jam	fst	6f	:233 :47 1:123		ⒻAlw 4500	3 11 1113 1115 69½ 58	Cole S	116wb	11.30	76-21	Fantan110hdHurry By1101Lalun1166	Off sluggishly	11
19Oct54- 4Bel	fst	7f	:23 :472 1:124 1:26		ⒻAlw 4000	1 10 86¼ 43 42 1hd	Guerin E	116wb	4.70e	80-19	Misty Morn116hdFantan1112Sweet Music1162½	Strong finish	13
12Oct54- 3Bel	fst	6f-WC	:223 :454 1:102		ⒻAlw 4000	8 4 2½ 31½ 32¼	Atkinson T	119wb	3.70	87-11	Myrtle'sJet1192SweetMusic119nkMistyMorn1192	Even race	11
27Sep54- 4Bel	fst	6f-WC	:221 :453 1:11		ⒻAlw 4000	1 13 168 98 98½	Cole S	119 w	11.00e	77-14	Lalun114½Minnie Moocher119nkSofarsogood1195	Outrun	18
20Sep54- 5Aqu	sly	6f	:222 :462 1:122		ⒻAlw 4000	2 4 44 45½ 54 32¼	Atkinson T	115 w	6.35	88-10	Girl Crazy1081¾Minnie Moocher115½MistyMorn115¾	Impeded	11
3Sep54- 5Aqu	fst	6f	:23 :463 1:131		ⒻAlw 4000	3 7 87¾ 76¾ 44½ 34	Atkinson T	116 w	3.10	82-19	Blue Banner1161½Sabourin1162½Misty Morn116nk	Mild rally	9
25Aug54- 4Sar	fst	6f	:223 :463 1:134		ⒻAlw 3500	3 5 55 67 89¼ 79¼	Cole S	116 w	3.65e	70-18	CarelssMiss1163PromptImpulse1121PrincssKss116hd	Outrun	12
15Jly54- 4Jam	fst	5½f	:23 :47 1:00 1:063		ⒻSp Wt 4000	4 3 66½ 66 33 22	Higley J	116 w	4.90	83-19	Chapel1162Misty Morn1163Precious Lady116hd	Good try	10
9Jly54- 4Aqu	fst	5½f	:232 :47 1:001 1:071		ⒻMd Sp Wt	8 5 42 2hd 14 13½	Higley J	116 w	*.55e	88-19	MistyMorn1163½Maebliss1165Searching1162½	Mild hand ride	12
1Jly54- 4Aqu	fst	5½f	:231 :463 :594 1:064		ⒻMd Sp Wt	1 1 1½ 21 23½ 21¼	Higley J	116 w	*.50e	89-19	Precious Lady1161¼Misty Morn1163½Searching1161½	Gaining	8
15Jun54- 4Aqu	fst	5½f	:232 :47 1:00 1:07		ⒻMd Sp Wt	2 4 31½ 44 42½ 33½	Atkinson T	116 w	1.65e	85-17	BlessPat1162FirstFlower1161½MistyMorn116nk	Mild rally	8
10Jun54- 4Bel	fst	4½f-W	:222 :451 :512		ⒻMd Sp Wt	5 11 113¼ 84¼ 73¾	Atkinson T	116 w	4.45e	88-10	Trying116½Bright Flash1162½[DH]Blue Banner116	No mishap	15
5Jun54- 3Bel	fst	5f-WC	:232 :464 :593		ⒻMd Sp Wt	4 9 95½ 812 912	Cole S	116 w	4.65e	69-19	Long Stretch116¾Audrey Lee116½Two Stars116hd	Outrun	12
20Apr54- 3Jam	fst	5f	:23 :473 1:003		ⒻMd Sp Wt	5 6 75½ 55½ 610 610	Atkinson T	116 w	3.10	77-20	Sorceress1161½FletsDlt1162½Msty1161½	Outrun all the way	8
15Apr54- 4Jam	fst	5f	:233 :473 1:00		ⒻMd Sp Wt	5 4 64¼ 78½ 47 39½	Atkinson T	116 w	4.30	80-18	Whitewash1163½Bless Pat1166Misty Morn1161		8
	Close quarters,taken up												

My Dear Girl

ch. f. 1957, by Rough'n Tumble (Free for All)–Iltis, by War Relic **Lifetime record: 20 8 4 1 $209,739**

Own.– Mrs F.A. Genter
Br.– Ocala Stud Farms Inc (Fla)
Tr.– M. Calvert

27Apr61- 7Lrl	fst	6f	:23 :47 1:121	4↑	ⒻAlw 4000	5 2 32½ 11 14 14	Hinojosa H	115	*.70	94-11	My Dear Girl1154Funny Bone1072½Effie J.112¾	Mild urging	7
12Jan61- 7SA	fst	7f	:222 :451 1:093 1:221	4↑	ⒻS Monica H (Div 2) 17k	5 7 41½ 32 33 79¾	Arcaro E	118	*1.60	82-15	SwissRoll1174½WiggleII122¾Tritom112nk	Early speed,tired	9
31Dec60- 6SA	fst	6f	:214 :45 1:101	3↑	ⒻLas Flores H 24k	1 14 117¼ 106¼ 119 2½	Arcaro E	119	6.50	92-13	Linita116½My Dear Girl119nkSwiss Roll1182¼	Closed fast	15
3Dec60- 8Pim	fst	1⅛	:48 1:123 1:384 1:524	3↑	ⒻGallorette 17k	4 1 14 14 14 3nk	Hinojosa H	117	4.80	87-25	SisterAntoine111hdLoyalLadyII114hdMyDearGirl117hd	Sharp	10
25Nov60- 8Pim	fst	6f	:232 :47 1:123	3↑	ⒻAlw 4000	6 8 54 41½ 1½ 1¾	Chambers A	115	*.80	87-21	My Dear Girl115¾Punta Gorda1181¼Funny Bone107no		8
	Slow start,driving												
11Nov60- 7GS	my	1⅛	:464 1:11 1:372 1:504	3↑	ⒻVineland H 58k	5 1 11½ 1½ 21 45¼	Sellers J	113	10.20	78-19	RoyalNative124½MakeSail118¾WiggleII1194	Used up early	9
24Oct60- 7Aqu	fst	6f	:223 :454 1:103	3↑	ⒻInterborough H 29k	13 2 31½ 21 21 22	Shoemaker W	114	9.15	90-17	WiggleII1212MyDearGirl114¾Improve114nk	Made game effort	14
8Oct60- 7GS	fst	1 1/16	:231 :463 1:11 1:433		ⒻJersey Belle 29k	9 5 32 23 26 913	Gonzalez MN	115	6.40	79-15	Undulation1127Sister Antoine1152½Vanairess115½	Tired	13
22Sep60- 8Aqu	fst	6f	:223 :451 1:10	3↑	ⒻAlw 5000	4 2 2½ 12 14 11¾	Shoemaker W	108	*1.55	97-11	MyDearGirl1081¾MissCloudy1166AliWing1091½	Scored easily	7
7Sep60- 7Aqu	fst	1	:222 :443 1:084 1:352		ⒻGazelle H (Div 2) 22k	7 4 42½ 33½ 69 1112	Gonzalez MN	118	3.70	79-11	Sarcastic115½Twinkle Twinkle119½Undulation1122	Stopped	12
30Aug60- 6Aqu	fst	7f	:223 :451 1:094 1:224		ⒻAlw 5000	8 1 11½ 12 11 2½	Gonzalez MN	114	3.00	95-10	TwinkleTwinkle114½MyDearGirl1141½SistrAnton1143½	Gamely	8
21May60- 7Aqu	fst	1	:224 :451 1:093 1:354		ⒻAcorn 59k	2 2 31 32½ 33½ 712	Arcaro E	121	3.85	85-06	Irish Jay121nkAirmans Guide1219Sister Antoine121½	Tired	13
10May60- 7Aqu	fst	6f	:222 :451 1:093		Alw 7500	5 4 2½ 21 57 511	Woodhouse H	114	8.20	93-07	Brush Fire1192½Irish Lancer119nkNew Commander1161	Tired	8
7Nov59- 7Aqu	sly	1	:232 :473 1:132 1:401		ⒻFrizette 101k	8 4 31½ 2hd 2hd 1no	Gonzalez MN	119	*.55	- -	MyDearGirl119noIrishJay1197Sarcstc1192½	Long,hard drive	11
24Oct59- 7GS	sly	1 1/16	:232 :472 1:122 1:463		ⒻGardenia 134k	5 1 12 13 12 15	Gonzalez MN	119	4.00	77-23	MyDearGirl1195BlueCrooner119nkHevnlyBody119¾	Mild drive	10
9Oct59- 6Aqu	sly	7f	:222 :45 1:102 1:24		ⒻAlw 5000	1 2 21½ 21 1hd 15	Gonzalez MN	119	1.70	- -	MyDearGirl1195EveningGlow1193OurSpecialJet116½	Easily	5
22Jly59- 8AP	fst	6f	:222 :45 1:10		ⒻArl Lassie 101k	5 3 1hd 22 3nk 2nk	Gonzalez MN	119	2.10	94-10	Monarchy119nkMy Dear Girl119nkHeavenly Body1191½	Sharp	12
3Jun59- 4Was	fst	5½f	:222 :45 :57 1:031		ⒻAlw 10000	3 4 21 3½ 13 15	Gonzalez MN	120	3.40	102-05	My Dear Girl1205Madam Regel114¾Blue Crooner114½	In hand	9
	Previously trained by G. Seabo												
25Feb59- 7Hia	fst	3f	:223 :341		ⓈFla Breeders 27k	19 1 31 12	Gonzalez MN	117	16.90	- -	My Dear Girl1172Niequest120hdAlgenib120½	Going away	25
19Feb59- 4Hia	fst	3f	:22 :333		Alw 4500	12 10 106¼ 104¾	Gonzalez MN	112	15.75f	- -	Niequest110hdRosofSrro117noCrftyKng120no	Unruly at post	13

Nadir

b. c. 1955, by Nasrullah (Nearco)–Gallita, by Challenger II — **Lifetime record: 32 11 7 8 $434,316**

Own.– Claiborne Farm
Br.– Claiborne Farm (Ky)
Tr.– M. Jolley

30May59- 6Bel	fst 1	:224:452 1:101 1:351 3↑	Metropolitan H 115k	11 10 119 1111 -	-	Arcaro E	121 b	*2.35	- -	Sword Dancer1143¼Jimmer1122¼Talent Show115no	11
	Went lame leaving backstretch										
20May59- 7Bel	fst 7f	:222:45 1:092 1:223 3↑	Carter H 58k	2 9 95½ 65½ 58	33¾	Arcaro E	122 b	*1.75	90-15	Jimmer108¾Tick Tock1223Nadir1221 Finished full of run	9
23Apr59- 5Kee	fst 6f	:224:451 1:092 4↑	Alw 3250	5 6 35 33 2½	1¾	Brooks S	122 b	*.70	98-08	Nadir122¾LitteReaper1162½Mr.Fantastic1192 Driving hard	6
18Apr59- 6Kee	sly *7f	1:263 3↑	Ben Ali H 13k	4 8 68 66¼ 46	26	Brooks S	125 b	*.70	89-16	GreekChief1136Nadir125hdGleemn1122½ Rallied for placing	8
21Feb59- 7Hia	fst 1¼	:471 1:111 1:36 2:011 3↑	Widener H 139k	1 5 54½ 2½ 2½	21¼	Hartack W	120 b	2.95	98-13	Bardstown1241¼Nadr1207DHoopBnd117¾ In close early,hung	13
7Feb59- 7Hia	gd 1⅛	:461 1:103 1:36 1:49 3↑	McLennan H 64k	4 2 1hd 13 21½	34	Hartack W	118 b	2.95	86-15	Sharpburg1164ADragonKiller114noNadir1183½ Used in pace	8
24Jan59- 7Hia	gd 1⅛	:462 1:103 1:353 1:483 3↑	Royal Palm H 33k	8 4 42¼ 2½ 21	32¼	Hartack W	120 b	*.75	90-14	Petare120¾Sharpsburg1161½Nadir1203 Made bid,then tired	12
10Jan59- 8TrP	fst 1⅛	:454 1:103 1:361 1:49 3↑	Trop Park H 67k	4 10 64 3½ 2½	31¾	Hartack W	122 b	2.55	94-13	Bardstown1261½RccTv113nkNdr1222¼ Sharp speed to stretch	14
27Sep58- 7Bel	sly 1¼	:464 1:104 1:353 2:01 3↑	Woodward 111k	4 3 31½ 2hd 2½	2½	Boland W	120wb	5.20	94-13	Clem126½Nadir1202Reneged1269 Made a sharp effort	7
17Sep58- 6Bel	fst 1⅛	:454 1:094 1:353 1:481 3↑	Nassau County H 29k	3 3 52½ 43 21½	2hd	Ycaza M	113wb	4.05	95-17	EddieSchmidt108hdNadir1132½Rengd1192¾ Led between calls	10
1Sep58- 8AP	fst 1	:223:451 1:091 1:34 3↑	Was Park H 139k	7 5 21½ 21½ 21	33¼	Ycaza M	114wb	4.00	99-02	Clem1103¼RoundTable131noNdr1146 Sharp factor to stretch	9
16Aug58- 8AP	hy 1⅛	:482 1:123 1:382 1:513	American Derby 160k	1 1 11 13 14	13¼	Ycaza M	120wb	*2.00	84-22	Nadir1203¼VictoryMorn1231¼TalentShow1201½ Much the best	11
6Aug58- 7AP	fst 1	:23 :454 1:094 1:343	Alw 10000	7 2 21½ 22 2hd	1½	Ycaza M	120wb	*2.30	99-07	Nadr120½StrongBay1232½Alhambra117½ Under strong urging	11
26Jly58- 8AP	fst 1	:224:452 1:10 1:362	Arl Classic 146k	3 9 95½ 76¼ 5¾	31	Nichols J	120wb	3.40	89-14	ADragonKiller117¾TalntShow117nkNdr120no Raced wide late	12
19Jly58- 7AP	fst 7f	:23 :454 1:10 1:223	Alw 5000	3 6 64¼ 63¼ 1hd	12½	Meaux C	113wb	3.50	95-13	Nadr1132½Olymr116½PrzHost113nk Wide stretch turn,easily	7
4Jly58- 8Was	gd 1⅛	:472 1:121 1:372 1:503	Stars & Stripes H 85k	2 8 810 811 614	716	Hartack W	122wb	2.90	72-16	Terra Firma118noLincoln Road1249Judge114½ Very dull try	9
27Jun58- 7Was	gd 7f	:224:46 1:11 1:242	Alw 4500	4 4 77¾ 710 56	32¾	Heckmann J	122wb	*.80	80-22	Prize Host1221¾Olymar1221Nadir1221¼ Closed full of run	7
14Jun58- 6Mth	sl 6f	:223:471 1:124	Select H 24k	6 13 97½ 53½ 1hd	1no	Nichols J	126wb	4.60	78-31	Nadir126noStrongRuler1206Hubcap122no Best in long drive	13
29Apr58- 7CD	sl 1	:23 :463 1:13 1:393	Derby Trial 16k	2 5 65¾ 22 32	43½	Heckmann J	122 w	3.40	73-29	Tim Tam122nkEbony Pearl1161¼Flamingo1122 Well placed	8
18Apr58- 6Kee	fst 7f	:232:452 1:093 1:221	Alw 4500	4 4 32½ 32 1hd	2½	Heckmann J	119 w	3.80	100-10	TimTam122½Nadir119nkHillsdl113hd Reached lead,sharp try	8
11Apr58- 0Kee	sly 6f	:224:453 1:103	©Alw 4500	3 4 47½ 35 34½	34½	Heckmann J	119 w	-	87-18	Benedicto1162RomanBow1162½Nadir11912 Urged,no rally	4
	Special race run before the first race										
1Mar58- 7Hia	fst 1⅛	:464 1:11 1:361 1:484	Flamingo 135k	9 3 31 2½ 44	47¼	Brooks S	122wb	3.25	84-11	DJewl'sReward122hdTimTam1223¾TalntShow1223½ Faltered	9
22Feb58- 6Hia	fst 1$\frac{1}{16}$	:223:453 1:10 1:424	Alw 7500	8 9 65 53¾ 23	23	Hartack W	126 w	*.80	97-12	SirRobby1093Ndr1262¾NshtAmool117hd Couldn't reach winner	11
14Feb58- 7Hia	fst 7f	:223:454 1:104 1:234	Alw 5000	5 8 65½ 43 1hd	12½	Hartack W	124 w	*.50	91-18	Nadir1242½FourFivs114¾Ambtwxt1071½ Drew clear with ease	8
26Oct57- 7GS	fst 1$\frac{1}{16}$	:23 :462 1:11 1:441	Garden State 277k	5 3 2hd 13 11	12	Hartack W	122wb	3.90	89-16	Nadir1222TerraFirma122noRosTrlls1221 Well rated,driving	13
19Oct57- 6GS	my 1$\frac{1}{16}$	:224:461 1:111 1:44	Alw 10000	7 5 55 34 31	11½♦	Brooks S	117wb	3.40	90-16	DHMusicMnFox120DHNdir1171½Yemen1122 Up for dead-heat	10
12Oct57- 7Bel	fst 1	:231:461 1:112 1:373	Champagne 156k	12 7 55 66 64½	56¼	Ussery R	122wb	5.00	80-14	Jewel'sReward122nkMistyFlight1221½RoseTrlls122½ Swerved	12
28Sep57- 5Bel	fst 6½-WC	:222:444 1:093 1:161	Futurity 114k	5 5 73½ 63¾	53	Hartack W	122wb	2.25	88-09	Jester1221MstyFlght1221¼Alhmbr122nk Swerved,lost chance	9
	Geldings not eligible										
16Sep57- 7Bel	fst 6½-WC	:22 :453 1:111 1:173	Cowdin 37k	12 11 87 64¾ 32	2hd	Arcaro E	117wb	*2.45e	92-13	Jewel'sReward124hdNadr1171¼Jstr117½ Headed in sharp try	13
6Sep57- 6Bel	fst 6f	:222:461 1:12	Alw 6000	3 8 77 65½ 42½	1hd	Arcaro E	119wb	*1.25	89-12	Nadir119hdFletFt1193UnclRlph115¾ Sluggish start,just up	8
13Aug57- 5Sar	fst 5½f	:231:464 :594 1:062	Alw 4000	2 3 42 31½ 2½	1nk	Anderson P	118wb	*.65	85-21	Nadir118nkGrandMogul1121Etok1101½ Under very hard drive	8
5Aug57- 4Sar	gd 5½f	:232:47 1:01 1:073	©Md Sp Wt	1 2 21½ 22 11½	16	Anderson P	118wb	2.80	79-22	Nadir1186Surinam118nkLeader118nk Going away with ease	12

Nashua

b. c. 1952, by Nasrullah (Nearco)–Segula, by Johnstown — **Lifetime record: 30 22 4 1 $1,288,565**

Own.–Leslie Combs II
Br.– Belair Stud Inc (Ky)
Tr.– J. Fitzsimmons

13Oct56- 6Bel	fst 2	:491 2:282 2:541 3:202 3↑	J C Gold Cup 54k	1 1 1½ 2hd 11½	12¼	Arcaro E	124wb	*.75	102-09	Nashua1242¼Rily1191¾ThrdBrothr1194 Kept to strong drive	7
29Sep56- 7Bel	gd 1¼	:47 1:112 1:371 2:03 3↑	Woodward 80k	1 2 1hd 3nk 31½	22½	Arcaro E	126wb	*.30	82-12	Mister Gus1262½Nashua126½Jet Action12620 No excuse	4
14Jly56- 6Mth	my 1¼	:46 1:11 1:364 2:024 3↑	Monmouth H 114k	7 1 14 14 14	13½	Arcaro E	129wb	*.30	92-20	Nashua1293½Mr. First1105Mielleux1071 Speed in reserve	8
4Jly56- 7Bel	fst 1¼	:463 1:101 1:35 2:004 3↑	Suburban H 83k	4 2 2hd 2hd 2½	11½	Arcaro E	128wb	*1.20	96-10	Nashua1281½Dedicat1112½Subhdr1125 Well rated,going away	8
30Jun56- 7Bel	fst 7f	:221:452 1:102 1:231 3↑	Carter H 58k	3 6 44½ 65 62¾	73½	Arcaro E	130 w	*1.10	90-12	Red Hannigan1141½Switch On119½Artismo111¾ Well up,hung	10
30May56- 7Bel	fst 1	:224:451 1:094 1:35 3↑	Metropolitan H 55k	7 1 32½ 42½ 53	4¾	Arcaro E	130 w	*.65	98-09	Midaftrnoon111hdSwtchOn113½Fnd116nk Came again too late	7
19May56- 7GS	fst 1⅛	:463 1:111 1:362 1:491 3↑	Camden H 33k	4 1 11 1½ 11	12	Arcaro E	129 w	*.40	91-10	Nashua1292Fisherman1201½Mielleux1102 Very handy score	5
5May56- 7Jam	fst 1⅛	:49 1:13 1:38 1:503 3↑	Grey Lag H 55k	6 3 2hd 1hd 1hd	1hd	Atkinson T	128 w	*.95	93-17	Nashua128hdFind118hdFisherman1201¾ Almost fell at start	7
17Mar56- 8GP	fst 1¼	:47 1:113 1:36 2:003 3↑	Gulf Park H 112k	6 5 43½ 53½ 56	57	Arcaro E	129 w	*.70	89-08	Sailor1191¾Mielleux1101Find116¾ Wide both turns,tired	7
18Feb56- 8Hia	fst 1¼	:463 1:104 1:353 2:02 3↑	Widener H 129k	9 3 41¾ 2½ 2hd	1hd	Arcaro E	127 w	*.40	95-11	Nashua127hdSocilOutcst121hdSlor119nk Under strong drive	9
	Previously owned by Belair Stud										
15Oct55- 6Bel	sly 2	:494 2:321 2:583 3:244 3↑	J C Gold Cup 79k	3 2 1½ 11 13½	15	Arcaro E	119 w	*.25	80-14	Nashua1195Thinking Cap11915Mark's Puzzle1198 Easy score	5
24Sep55- 6Bel	sly 1⅛	:451 1:101 1:36 1:491 3↑	Sysonby 106k	5 1 41½ 3nk 22	31¾	Arcaro E	121 w	*.65	91-10	HighGun126hdJetActn1261¾Nshu1213½ Weakened when urged	5
31Aug55- 7Was	gd 1¼	:46 1:102 1:373 2:041	WP Match 100k	1 1 1½ 11½ 12	16½	Arcaro E	126 w	1.20	81-17	Nashua1266½Swaps126 Drew far out to handy score	2
16Jly55- 7AP	fst 1	:231:453 1:093 1:351	Arl Classic 148k	2 2 22 24 21	1½	Arcaro E	126 w	*.30	96-10	Nashua126½Traffic Judge1201¼Impromptu1204 Under a drive	7
2Jly55- 0Aqu	fst 1¼	:493 1:134 1:382 2:034	Dwyer 55k	3 1 1½ 11½ 11½	15	Arcaro E	126 w	-	88-15	Nashua1265Saratoga12240Mainlander114 Easing up late	3
	Run as special event with no wagering										
11Jun55- 6Bel	fst 1½	:49 1:133 2:042 2:29	Belmont 119k	5 2 1hd 12½ 16	19	Arcaro E	126 w	*.15	93-12	Nashua1269Blazing Count1265½Portersville1266 A romp	8
	Geldings not eligible										
28May55- 7Pim	fst 1$\frac{3}{16}$	:471 1:11 1:353 1:543	Preakness 116k	5 4 42½ 2hd 1hd	11	Arcaro E	126 w	*.30	106-08	Nashua1261Saratoga1267TrafficJudg126nk Rated,mild drive	8
7May55- 7CD	fst 1¼	:472 1:122 1:37 2:014	Ky Derby 152k	5 3 31 2½ 2½	21½	Arcaro E	126 w	*1.30	96-12	Swaps1261½Nashua1266½Summer Tan1264 Good bid,no excuse	10
23Apr55- 6Jam	fst 1⅛	:471 1:111 1:363 1:503	Wood Memorial 111k	4 2 21½ 22 21½	1nk	Atkinson T	126 w	1.10	93-17	Nashua126nkSummer Tan12625Simmy1266 Sensational score	5
26Mar55- 7GP	sly 1⅛	:463 1:122 1:391 1:531	Fla Derby 148k	1 5 56½ 22½ 2½	1nk	Arcaro E	122 w	*.95	78-26	Nashua122nkBlueLem1132¼FirstCabin1131 Unruly,hard urged	9
26Feb55- 7Hia	fst 1⅛	:462 1:113 1:371 1:493	Flamingo 141k	2 2 1hd 1hd 1hd	11½	Arcaro E	122 w	*.70	88-12	Nashua1221½Saratoga1224½CupMan1227 Drifted out in drive	12
21Feb55- 0Hia	fst 1$\frac{1}{16}$	:231:47 1:114 1:441	Alw 7500	2 2 3nk 2hd 1½	11½	Arcaro E	126wb	-	94-11	Nshua1261½Munchausen1172HappyMemries1142½ Unruly late	4
	Special event run between 2nd and 3rd races - No wagering										
9Oct54- 6Bel	fst 6½f-W	:222:451 1:092 1:153	Futurity 112k	6 4 21 1½	1hd	Arcaro E	122wb	*.65	94-06	Nshua122hdSummrTan122¾RoylCoinage1227 Held on gamely	7
	Geldings not eligible										
1Oct54- 6Bel	fst 6f-WC	:22 :442 1:081	Sp Wt 10000	4 2 4¾ 2hd	11	Arcaro E	118wb	*1.05	100-00	Nashua1181Royal Coinage1185Pyrenees1181½ Clever score	7
21Sep54- 6Aqu	fst 6½f	:223:451 1:092 1:16	Cowdin 30k	9 1 2hd 4¾ 41½	21½	Arcaro E	124wb	*1.25	101-12	SummerTn1201½Nshua124¾Bunny'sBabe1201½ Mildly impeded	10
28Aug54- 6Sar	fst 6½f	:23 :464 1:111 1:174	Hopeful 78k	4 1 1½ 1hd 11	1nk	Arcaro E	122wb	*.55e	96-18	Nashua122nkSummrTan1221½Pyrens1221½ Well rated,held on	8
21Aug54- 4Sar	fst 6f	:23 :463 :592 1:122	Grand Union Hotel 27k	5 2 23 1hd 12	11¾	Arcaro E	122 w	2.75e	86-17	Nashua1221¾Pyrens1152½ModlAc1143½ Won in clever fashion	6
19May54- 7GS	fst 5f	:221:454 :583	Cherry Hill 20k	3 5 2½ 22 21½	2nk	Higley J	119 w	3.80	98-13	RoyalNote122nkNashua1195Menolen1191½ Unruly all the way	11
12May54- 6Bel	fst 5f-WC	:221:453 :58	Juvenile 15k	1 2 1hd 2½	1½	Arcaro E	117 w	3.00e	89-18	Nshua117½SummerTn1228Lugh1172 Scored under clever ride	8
5May54- 4Bel	fst 4½f-W	:222:462 :523	©Md Sp Wt	14 9 8½ 11½	13	Higley J	118 w	8.50e	86-14	Nashua1183Retract118½Danger Quest118no Won in hand	21

Native Dancer

gr. c. 1950, by Polynesian (Unbreakable)–Geisha, by Discovery — **Lifetime record: 22 21 1 0 $785,240**
Own.– A.G. Vanderbilt
Br.– Alfred G. Vanderbilt (Ky)
Tr.– W.C. Winfrey

16Aug54- 0Sar sly 7f :233 :472 1:12 1:244 3↑ Handicap 5025 2 3 22½ 22 18 19 Guerin E 137 w - 91-19 Native Dancer1379First Glance1194½Gigantic107 Easily 3
15May54- 6Bel fst 1 :231 :46 1:101 1:351 3↑ Metropolitan H 39k 3 8 77¾ 57 23½ 1nk Guerin E 130 w *.25 98-11 Native Dancer130nkStraight Face1176Jamie K.1102 Just up 9
7May54- 6Bel fst 6f :224 :463 1:114 3↑ Alw 15000 4 3 42 31 12 11¼ Guerin E 126 w *.15 90-15 Native Dancer1261¼Laffango121nkImpasse114nk Easily best 7
22Aug53- 7Was fst 1⅛ :462 1:103 1:352 1:482 American Derby 112k 4 7 711 45½ 41¾ 12 Arcaro E 128 w *.20e 99-11 NativeDancr1282Landlocked1201¼PrecousSton1143 Drew out 8
15Aug53- 6Sar fst 1¼ :494 1:14 1:393 2:053 Travers 27k 1 3 31 21½ 11 15½ Guerin E 126 w *.05 80-20 NativeDancer1265½Dictar1202½GuardianII1141 Easily best 5
Geldings not eligible
18Jly53- 7AP hy 1 :232 :471 1:114 1:38 Arl Classic 154k 4 6 67 34 13 19 Guerin E 126 w *.70 82-25 NativeDancer1269SirMango120hdVanCrosby1202 Easily best 8
4Jly53- 6Aqu fst 1¼ :494 1:14 1:392 2:051 Dwyer 56k 3 4 33½ 11½ 12½ 11¾ Guerin E 126 w *.05 81-17 NativeDancer1261¾[D]Dictar1142GuardnII1144 Much the best 5
13Jun53- 6Bel fst 1½ :501 1:15 2:041 2:283 Belmont 118k 5 4 32½ 2hd 1hd 1nk Guerin E 126 w *.45 95-11 NativeDancr126nkJamieK.12610RoylByGm1264½ Held gamely 6
Geldings not eligible
23May53- 7Pim fst 1 3/16 :47 1:114 1:382 1:574 Preakness 113k 4 3 33 2hd 1hd 1nk Guerin E 126 w *.20 91-19 NativeDancer126nkJamieK.1266RoyalBayGem1262 Hard drive 7
16May53- 6Bel fst 1 :234 :471 1:113 1:361 Withers 32k 3 2 2½ 1½ 12½ 14 Guerin E 126 w *.05 93-12 Native Dancer1264Invigorator1262½Real Brother126 Easily 3
Geldings not eligible
2May53- 7CD fst 1¼ :474 1:121 1:363 2:02 Ky Derby 118k 6 8 42½ 42½ 21½ 2hd Guerin E 126 w *.70e 97-09 DarkStar126hdNativeDancer1265Invgortor1262 Roughed,wide 11
25Apr53- 6Jam fst 1⅛ :50 1:133 1:371 1:503 Wood Memorial 123k 4 2 31 2hd 1½ 14½ Guerin E 126 w *.10e 93-12 NativeDancer1264½TahitianKing126hdInvigortor1263 Easily 7
Geldings not eligible
18Apr53- 6Jam fst 1 1/16 :242 :49 1:134 1:441 Gotham (Div 1) 35k 8 4 62¾ 41¼ 2hd 12 Guerin E 120 w *.15 91-10 NatveDancr1202MagicLmp1203Sckl'sSound1201¼ Ridden out 9
22Oct52- 6Jam fst 1 1/16 :242 :48 1:123 1:441 ©East View 56k 1 4 46 33 1½ 11½ Guerin E 122 w *.20 91-15 Native Dancer1221½Laffango1229Teds Jeep1221½ Ridden out 6
Geldings not eligible
27Sep52- 6Bel fst 6½f-W :214 :442 1:082 1:142 Futurity 107k 8 6 54 2½ 12¼ Guerin E 122 w *.35 100-05 NativeDancer1222¼TahitianKing1224DarkStr1223 Ridden out 10
Geldings not eligible
22Sep52- 5Bel fst 6f-WC :22 :443 1:093 Sp Wt 5000 6 6 53 12 11¼ Guerin E 118 w *.40 93-07 NativeDancer1181¼TahitianKing1182¼Reprimnd118hd In hand 8
30Aug52- 6Sar fst 6½f :233 :48 1:123 1:184 Hopeful 62k 4 1 62¾ 52½ 2hd 12 Guerin E 122 w *.25 91-19 Native Dancer1222Tiger Skin1222Platan1221 Handily 7
23Aug52- 4Sar fst 6f :224 :462 1:111 Grand Union Hotel 20k 1 2 31 1½ 11½ 13½ Guerin E 126 w *.55 92-17 NativeDancer1263½Laffango1222½TahitianKing1225½ In hand 5
16Aug52- 4Sar sly 6f :231 :464 1:131 Sar Spl 17k 4 2 42½ 42 11 13½ Guerin E 122 w *.70 82-22 NativeDancr1223½DocWalkr1224SouthPont1223½ Ridden out 8
4Aug52- 6Sar fst 5½f :231 :47 :593 1:06 Flash 10k 6 4 31 31 1½ 12¼ Guerin E 122 w *.80 87-20 Native Dancer1222¼Tiger Skin1142Bradley122no Easily 7
23Apr52- 6Jam fst 5f :223 :463 :592 ©Youthful 14k 4 2 21 2hd 13 16 Guerin E 117 w *.90 93-19 NativeDancr1176Tribe1221½[DH]Mr.Mdnght1171 Much the best 12
19Apr52- 2Jam fst 5f :23 :47 :593 Md Sp Wt 9 7 42 42 1½ 14½ Guerin E 118 w *1.40 92-16 Native Dancer1184½Putney118nkKhan118hd Drew out easily 9

Needles

b. c. 1953, by Ponder (Pensive)–Noodle Soup, by Jack High — **Lifetime record: 21 11 3 3 $600,355**
Own.– D.–H. Stable
Br.– W.E. Leach (Fla)
Tr.– H.L. Fontaine

6Apr57- 7GP fst 1 1/16 :23 :462 1:102 1:42 3↑ Fort Lauderdale H 28k 5 9 920 88½ 45½ 12 Erb D 126 w *.65 100-10 Needles1262Tussle Patch110nkGrand Canyon107½ In hand 9
23Mar57- 7GP fst 1¼ :464 1:111 1:351 2:002 3↑ Gulf Park H 126k 5 7 66½ 63¼ 33 31½ Erb D 126 w 1.60 95-09 Bardstown130½Fabius1231Needles1264 Very wide,game try 7
11Mar57- 7GP fst 6½f :222 :452 1:094 1:16 4↑ Handicap 6000 8 8 88 61½ 41¼ 2no Erb D 126 w 4.15 99-13 Admiral Vee119noNeedles1264Nan's Mink110no Gaining fast 8
18Aug56- 8Was sf 1 3/16Ⓣ :472 1:123 1:394 1:591 American Derby 159k 2 8 812 65 64½ 52¾ Erb D 126 w *1.10 74-23 Swoon'sSon122¾TheWarrior1161¾TobyB.116nk Disliked grass 8
4Aug56- 7Was fm 6fⓉ :221 :444 1:094 3↑ Handicap 10000 8 8 812 814 814 86¼ Erb D 120 w 6.30 95-06 BurntChild1131SuthernAccent110nkHutchson1111½ Late foot 8
16Jun56- 6Bel fst 1½ :472 1:114 2:024 2:294 Belmont 119k 3 8 717 47½ 21½ 1nk Erb D 126 w *.65 89-12 Needles126nkCareer Boy1261½Fabius126hd All out to hold 8
Geldings not eligible
19May56- 7Pim fst 1 3/16 :472 1:12 1:38 1:582 Preakness 132k 6 9 914 55½ 34 21¾ Erb D 126 w *.60 79-19 Fabius1261¾Needls1261NoRgrts1265½ Rallied from far back 9
5May56- 7CD fst 1¼ :471 1:113 1:364 2:032 Ky Derby 167k 1 16 1615 74½ 2hd 1¾ Erb D 126 w *1.60 90-08 Needles126¾Fabius1261½ComeonRed126¾ Going away in drive 17
24Mar56- 8GP fst 1⅛ :462 1:112 1:353 1:483 Florida Derby 145k 13 13 129¾ 95¼ 42 1¾ Erb D 117 w *1.70 101-09 Needles117¾CountChic1191¾PintorL113½ Under strong drive 14
25Feb56- 8Hia fst 1⅛ :453 1:101 1:362 1:492 Flamingo 148k 3 12 117 74½ 1hd 12¾ Erb D 117 w 2.60 89-11 Needles1172¾GolfAce1221¾Fabus1222½ Drew out,mild urging 15
6Feb56- 7Hia fst 7f :23 :453 1:094 1:224 Alw 10000 3 6 66¾ 66¾ 44½ 25 Erb D 119 w 3.30 91-17 CallMeLucky1125Needles119nkBeuFond1211½ Strong late bid 6
29Oct55- 7GS fst 1 1/16 :231 :461 1:104 1:423 Garden State 282k 6 11 1111 76¾ 31½ 31 Choquette J 122 w *1.70 96-07 PrinceJohn122noCareerBoy1221Needles1224½ Hung slightly 12
15Oct55- 5GS sly 1 :223 :46 1:111 1:371 Alw 7500 6 8 711 21½ 12½ 12 Choquette J 122 w *.70 101-15 Needles1222Nahodah1151Singer1133 Rated early,easy score 8
10Sep55- 7Atl fst 7f :213 :441 1:09 1:23 Worlds Playground 30k 7 7 78 43½ 42 31 Arcaro E 122 w *.40 90-11 BusherFantsy110¾Esp112nkNdls1222½ Raced outside,gaining 9
27Aug55- 6Sar fst 6½f :23 :47 1:12 1:181 Hopeful 71k 6 4 77¼ 54 14 13½ Choquette J 122 w 3.25 94-19 Needles1223½Career Boy1226Jean Baptiste1221 Mild drive 9
8Aug55- 6Mth gd 6f :214 :453 1:103 Sapling 37k 2 5 48 43 1hd 12 Choquette J 116 w 6.80 92-22 Needles1162Decathlon1241¼Polly's Jet1245 Drew clear 6
4Jly55- 6Mth fst 5½f :213 :451 1:04 ©Tyro 21k 7 7 52¾ 42½ 45 44¼ Choquette J 115 w *2.30 100-11 Decathln122¾Nan'sMink1152BeauFond1151½ Impeded on turn 8
22Jun55- 7Mth fst 5f :214 :46 :583 Alw 4500 1 5 53¾ 43½ 2½ 11 Choquette J 113 w *1.20 99-07 Needles1131But First1193Nan's Mink1191 Drew out in hand 9
20Apr55- 4GP fst 4½f :222 :454 :522 Alw 4000 5 6 31½ 2hd 13 Choquette J 111 w *.75 101-00 Needles1113Tolna Rose113hdRite-Step1193½ 10
Steadied early,speed in reserve
5Apr55- 5GP fst 4½f :224 :454 :524 GP Juvenile 18k 11 10 98½ 56 42¾ Choquette J 113 w 2.25 96-01 GetthereJack1221¼Swoon'sSon110½FlyngTddy1101 Poor start 11
29Mar55- 3GP fst 4½f :232 :47 :53 [S]Md Sp Wt 2 2 11 13 15 Choquette J 120 w *1.15 98-02 Needles1205Game o' Hearts1175Elrusa1173 Scored easily 12

Neji

ch. g. 1950, by Hunters Moon IV (Foxhunter)–Accra, by Annapolis — **Lifetime record: 49 17 11 9 $270,834**
Own.– Mrs Ogden Phipps
Br.– Mrs Marion duPont Scott (GB)
Tr.– D.M. Smithwick

29Sep60- 5Bel fm *2½ S'Chase 4:421 4↑ Brook H 19k 2 7 711 44 520 529 Smithwick AP 159 s *1.65 -- Benguala1436Independence1593½Cartagena1503½ No excuse 7
15Sep60- 5Aqu fm *2 S'Chase 3:531 4↑ Broad Hollow H 16k 1 5 67½ 69 44 44¾ Smithwick AP 162 sb *.55 -- Gridiron1362SunDog148¾Benguala1502 Bad landing 7th,sore 6
1Sep60- 5Aqu fm *2 S'Chase 3:493 4↑ Harbor Hill H 10k 2 5 58 43½ 23 21½ Smithwick AP 164 sb *1.35e -- Cartagena1431½Neji1642BasilB13310 Made game late effort 6
21Feb59♦ Leopardstn(Ire) yl *3LH 6:28 6↑ Leopardstown Handicap Chase Hcp3000 6 Smithwick AP 168 b 4.50 Zonda1361¼NicAtkins1335Top Twenty136 12
Rated in midpack,weakened 4 out
5Feb59♦ Hurst Park(GB) gd 3 6:373 5↑ Morden Handicap Chase Hcp1500 31½ Smithwick AP 175 b 4.00 Lochroe1751Arthur Cox140½Neji17515 7
Toward rear,midrally when blundered 2 out,gaining late
29Jan59♦ Gowran Park(Ire) fm *3 1/16 RH 7:121 5↑ Thyestes Handicap Chase Hcp2000 5 Smithwick AP 168 b 10.00 Slippery Serpent1436Zonda1334Mr. What157 13
Toward rear,mild late gain
22Oct58- 6Bel fm *2½ S'Chase 4:453 4↑ Temple Gwathmey H 55k 6 5 77 67 3½ 2hd Smithwick AP 176wsb *.95e -- Bengual147hdNj1764½Trboots135nk Led between calls,tired 8
9Oct58- 5Bel hd *3⅛ S'Chase 6:06 4↑ Grand National H 28k 5 5 57 56½ 1hd 12½ Smithwick AP 173wsb *1.15e -- Neji1732½Rythmnhm1474½Drubn130hd Bad landings,much best 9
30Sep58- 5Bel sf *2½ S'Chase 4:474 4↑ Brook H 14k 7 6 77 45½ 32½ 33¾ Smithwick AP 175wsb *1.30e -- Beguala1433½Independence154nkNeji17510 In close late 7
31Jly58- 5Mth fm *2 Hurdles 3:544 3↑ Midsummer H 22k 1 2 35 34 24 35 Smithwick AP 175wsb *.50 -- Cloonroughan1565My Last Try140hdNeji1753½ Swerved,tired 7
18Jly58- 3Mth fm *1¾ Hurdles 3:151 3↑ Alw 4000 5 5 68 33½ 1½ 1½ Smithwick AP 162wsb *1.10e -- Neji162½Cloonroughan1565½Ragtime Cowboy130¾ Driving 11
16Oct57- 6Bel fm *2½ S'Chase 4:422 4↑ Temple Gwathmey H 57k 7 6 63 31½ 13 17 Smithwick AP 173wsb *.80e -- Neji1737Ancestor1601Shpbord1641½ Jumped superbly,easily 12
8Oct57- 5Bel sf *3⅛ S'Chase 6:151 4↑ Grand National H 32k 3 4 416 35 1½ 16 Smithwick AP 168wsb *.80e -- Neji1686Independence1501¾His Boots132nk Ridden out 5

Race	Cond	Dist	Type	Time	Race	Calls	Fin	Jockey	Wt	Odds	Fig	Top three	Comment	Fld
26Sep57-5Bel	fm	*2½	S'Chase	4:451	4↑ Brook H 22k	7 7 79 31 11½	12¾	Smithwick AP	164wb	1.65e	--	Neji164¾Independnc15110Rythmnhm148no	Going away easily	10
12Sep57-5Bel	fm	*2⅛	S'Chase	3:573	3↑ Harbor Hill H 17k	2 3 43 56½ 58½	48¼	Murphy J	163wb	*1.65e	--	Ancestor1582Independence1486HsBoots131nk	Bobbled at 7th	9
Previously trained by G.H. Bostwick														
3Aug56-5Mth	fm	*2	Hurdles	3:533	3↑ Midsummer H 22k	1 2 25 33½ 24	22½	Adams FD	164wsb	*1.00	--	FlyingFury1432½Neji1644PolicemanDay1503	Came back lame	5
20Jly56-3Mth	fm	*1¾	Hurdles	3:21	3↑ Alw 4000	4 4 33 41 21½	21¼	Adams FD	162 ws	*.40e	--	Flying Fury1341¼Neji1622Songai1593½	Showed good effort	10
29Jun56-7Del	fm	*2½	S'Chase	4:462	4↑ Indian River H 10k	8 7 31 56½ 24	1no	Adams FD	168wsb	*1.50e	--	Neji168noCarthag136¾Cst1501	Strongly handled,up in time	11
15Jun56-7Del	fm	*2	S'Chase	3:37	4↑ Georgetown H 10k	4 6 46 45½ 38	33½	Adams FD	169wsb	*.40e	--	Ringo'Roses1432Carafar1521½Nj1692½	Rallied under impost	6
7Jun56-5Bel	fm	*2½	S'Chase	4:394	4↑ Meadow Brook H 17k	1 3 36½ 32½ 11½	13½	Adams FD	165wb	*1.00	--	Nji1653½Carthage1366KingCommander1648	Drew out in hand	5
26May56-3Bel	fm	1⅜Ⓣ		2:173	3↑ Handicap 7500	3 6 79½ 66 44	2½	Atkinson T	115wb	3.95	98-01	LovelyWave110½Nj115hdKstr125no	Between horses,sharp try	7
21Oct55-6Bel	sf	*2½	S'Chase	4:553	4↑ Temple Gwathmey H 57k	6 3 21 53½ 24	1¾	Adams FD	167wsb	3.40e	--	Neji167¾Rhythmnhm1497HsBoots1371½	Well rated,going away	11
13Oct55-5Bel	fm	*3	S'Chase	5:542	4↑ Grand National H 28k	6 4 21 42 2½	1hd	Adams FD	163wsb	2.45e	--	Nj163hdRhythmnhm14615HsBoots1351½	Impeded late,recovered	8
4Oct55-5Bel	fm	*2½	S'Chase	4:462	4↑ Brook H 17k	4 6 56½ 43½ 22	12	Adams FD	159wsb	*.85e	--	Neji1592Rythminhim1453Hyvania13620	Drew out when urged	7
22Sep55-5Bel	fm	*2	S'Chase	3:463	3↑ Broad Hollow H 11k	4 3 42½ 44 46	22	Adams FD	157wb	4.10	--	Shipboard1582Nj1571½Rhythmnhm145½	Guided wide,sharp try	4
2Jun55-5Bel	fm	*2½	S'Chase	4:442	4↑ Meadow Brook H 11k	6 3 432 43½ 324	321	Adams FD	156wb	1.60	--	Shpbord1566CurlyJo13115Nj15630	Rated early,no late foot	6
21May55-6Bel	hd	*2½	S'Chase	4:432	4↑ International 21k	5 4 28 25 112	115	Schulhofer FS	150wb	3.10e	--	Neji15015Ancestor15518Hyvania15518	Increasing long lead	10
12May55-5Bel	hd	*2	S'Chase	3:411	4↑ Corinthian H 8.9k	5 4 59 513 412	36	Adams FD	155wb	*.90	--	Shipboard1553Beaupre1363Neji1551½	Some early foot	6
2May55-3Bel	fm	*1¾	Hurdles	3:153	3↑ Alw 4200	4 4 33½ 41 21	1hd	Adams FD	155wb	*1.40	--	Neji155hdPermain1326Secnt13625	Tried to bear in,just up	6
22Oct54-6Bel	fm	*2½	S'Chase	4:39	4↑ Temple Gwathmey H 16k	6 4 54½ 59 24	2¾	Adams FD	149wb	2.25	--	King Commander164¾Neji1497Coveted13170	Gaining fast	6
14Oct54-5Bel	fm	*3	S'Chase	5:42	4↑ Grand National H 28k	1 - - - -	-	Adams FD	149wb	1.95	--	Shipboard1522½Coveted13122CurlyJo13310	Fell at 8th jump	7
5Oct54-5Bel	fm	*2½	S'Chase	4:394	4↑ Brook H 17k	8 7 712 68 23	11½	Adams FD	137wb	2.55	--	Neji1371½King Commander16116Coveted13115	Going away	9
23Sep54-5Bel	fm	*2	S'Chase	3:44	3↑ Broad Hollow H 11k	1 1 32 22½ 22	22	Adams FD	137wb	2.70	--	Shipboard1542Nej13718Covtd13645	Unable to menace winner	5
6Sep54-7Atl	fm	1 1/16Ⓣ		:231 :464 1:112 1:43	3↑ Atl City Turf H 30k	13 10 128½ 1212 1216	1213	Passmore WJ	114wb	11.90f	86-01	Landlocked115hdCounty Clare116noKaster1171	No speed	13
20Aug54-5Sar	fm	*2	Hurdles	3:482	3↑ Lovely Night H 6.5k	2 4 39½ 34½ 32	33½	Adams FD	152wb	*1.10e	--	Carafar139hdCammell Laird1443½Neji1523	Tired when urged	7
6Aug54-5Sar	fm	*1¾	Hurdles	3:292	3↑ National Mdn 7.4k	2 4 32½ 32 11½	12	Adams FD	161wb	*.60	--	Neji1612Heureux II1554Oneida1552	Gradually drew clear	5
16Jly54-3Mth	fm	*1¾	Hurdles	3:194	3↑ National Maiden 7.4k	6 7 31 2hd 1hd	14	Adams FD	157wb	*.70e	--	Neji1574Rythminhim1498Bombez1324	Drew out with ease	8
1Jly54-5Aqu	hd	*2	Hurdles	3:40	4↑ Forget H 11k	1 5 510 45½ 21	21	Adams FD	142wb	1.35e	--	Hyvania1501Neji1422½Williamsburg1561½	Good late speed	7
24Jun54-5Aqu	fm	*1¾	Hurdles	3:13	3↑ Amagansett H 9k	1 3 48 35½ 31	32½	Adams FD	144wb	3.15e	--	Williamsburg1511Hyvania1481½Nej14410	Insufficient rally	7
18Jun54-5Mth	fm	1Ⓣ		1:391	3↑ Alw 5000	10 9 74 86¾ 59	43¾	Roser G	109wb	17.80e	86-10	Iceberg II1183Bobs Alibi109noGoing Away109¾	Forced wide	12
10Jun54-3Bel	hd	*2	Hurdles	3:443	4↑ Handicap 4255	4 5 43½ 57 32½	2½	Adams FD	140wb	*.50e	--	Hyvania143½Neji1403½Democles1331	Gaining on winner	8
2Jun54-6Bel	fm	1⅜Ⓣ		2:172	3↑ Handicap 10050	6 5 48 75 66½	76	Adams J	113wb	4.35	--	Kaster119hdOut Point1163½Bicarb108½	Forced to take up	8
26May54-3Bel	fm	*1¾	Hurdles	3:134	3↑ Alw 3700	6 5 53½ 31½ 2½	13½	Adams FD	142wb	*1.20	--	Neji1423½Fulton1482½Sea Term1322	Drew clear in hand	9
17May54-5Bel	fm	*1¾	Hurdles	3:15	3↑ National Maiden 7.4k	5 3 31 1½ 12	14	Field K	137wb	*1.35e	--	Neji1374Rythminhim1502½Corinthian139no	Under mild drive	13
4May54-3Bel	sf	*1½	Hurdles	2:501	3↑ Sp Wt 3700	3 6 62½ 66½ 38	23½	Adams FD	142 w	5.05	--	Oneida1473½Neji1421½Cam14725	Reserved early,closed fast	10
29Apr54-3Bel	fm	*2	S'Chase	3:462	4↑ Sp Wt 4000	1 7 923 838 754	754	Adams FD	140 w	6.75	--	Shipboard140½KingCommndr14812PacificPact1482½	Bobbled	11
3Apr54-6Cam	hd	*1½	Hurdles	2:382	3↑ Alw 700	3 5 55 44 34½	32½	Field K	130 w	-	- --	Rythminhim1391Fiddlers Choice1491½Neji1308	Mild rally	5
24Mar54-0Aik		5½f		1:093			2				--	AncestorNeji		
6Nov53-3Jam	gd	6f		:25 :49 1:161	3↑ Md Sp Wt	4 5 42 34½ 48½	410½	Nichols J	120 w	1.90	56-27	Fleet Count115¾Black Saint1207Quisas1172½	Off slowly	5
24Oct53-1RB	fst	*6fⓉ		1:22	2↑ Alw 300	1 4 65¾ 65¾ 55	48½	Mergler M	141 w		--	Tico Tico1633Tommy Tiddler1541½Brushless1514	No mishap	14

Next Move

br. f. 1947, by Bull Lea (Bull Dog)–Now What, by Chance Play
Own.– A.G. Vanderbilt
Br.– Alfred G. Vanderbilt (Md)
Tr.– W.C. Winfrey

Lifetime record: 46 17 11 3 $398,550

Race	Cond	Dist	Type	Time	Race	Calls	Fin	Jockey	Wt	Odds	Fig	Top three	Comment	Fld
18Oct52-7GS	fst	1 1/16		:23 :471 1:112 1:453	3↑ ⒻVineland H 49k	12 10 1013 89¾ 78	62¾	Guerin E	126 w	*2.20	79-20	Sickle's Image120¾Kiss Me Kate118¾Lily White111hd	Closed well,no threat	17
1Oct52-6Bel	fst	1½		:483 1:132 2:044 2:312	3↑ ⒻLadies H 59k	3 2 2hd 41¾ 1014	1121	Guerin E	129 w	*2.10	60-15	How1121¼Marta1222½Enchanted Eve112¾	Quit	11
13Sep52-6Aqu	fst	1⅛		:48 1:124 1:38 1:51	3↑ ⒻBeldame H (Div 1) 62k	1 4 42 41¾ 11	13	Guerin E	125 w	*1.30	90-17	Next Move1253Renew1171½Nilufer106nk	Easily	10
8Sep52-6Aqu	fst	7f		:223 :451 1:102 1:24	3↑ Bay Shore H 17k	9 9 96¼ 74 53¼	11	Guerin E	115 w	4.40e	90-20	NextMove1151FirstGlance111nkSquardAwy1202	Driving clear	12
4Jun52-6Bel	fst	1 1/16		:221 :45 1:103 1:434	3↑ ⒻTop Flight H 24k	8 3 34 56½ 89	814	York R	129wb	2.95	78-15	Renew115¾Valadium1152Blue Moon1111½	Bore in	9
17May52-6Bel	fst	1		:23 :454 1:104 1:362	3↑ Metropolitan H 36k	1 1 1hd 3½ 98½	1011	Guerin E	114 w	20.95	81-14	Mameluke112½Battlefield1251½One Hitter1131	Quit badly	11
26Apr52-6Jam	my	1 3/16		:461 1:103 1:364 1:561	3↑ Gallant Fox H 69k	3 7 1014 109¼ 1018	1020	Guerin E	115wb	10.10	75-18	Spartan Valor1292Alerted1101¾Auditing112¾	Outclassed	10
21Apr52-6Jam	fst	1⅛		:471 1:114 1:372 1:511	3↑ ⒻFirenze H 33k	1 1 12 11½ 14	12	Guerin E	126wb	2.95	90-18	NxtMove1262ThelmaBurgr1101¾KissMeKate123¾	Ridden out	9
1Mar52-7SA	my	1¼		:452 1:104 1:354 2:01	3↑ S Anita H 141k	11 5 64½ 77 1120	1117	Shoemaker W	114wb	4.30e	78-16	[D]Intent1111Miche1154½Be Fleet1142½	Tired	15
22Feb52-7SA	fst	7f		:222 :444 1:094 1:222	3↑ Wash Birthday H 11k	9 3 31½ 53½ 89½	87¾	Guerin E	126wb	*2.05	85-15	Pet Bully112¾Interpretation113¾Guillotine126nk	Stopped	9
26Jan52-7SA	fst	1⅛		:47 1:114 1:381 1:512	3↑ ⒻS Margarita H 62k	3 1 13 12 12	21	Guerin E	130wb	*.90e	83-19	Bed o' Roses1291Next Move1301½Toto105½	Held well	14
12Jan52-6SA	sly	1		:224 :463 1:121 1:391	3↑ ⒻS Maria H 23k	3 3 22 21½ 21½	22½	Guerin E	128wb	*1.25	77-22	Special Touch1212½Next Move1282½Blue Cloth108nk	Impeded	8
28Dec51-7SA	fst	6f		:221 :451 1:094	3↑ ⒻLas Flores H 18k	10 2 3½ 2hd 1hd	11	Guerin E	124wb	2.60	96-08	NextMove1241SpecialTouch122nkSickl'sImg1173½	Ridden out	13
5May51-6Jam	fst	1⅛		:473 1:12 1:382 1:503	3↑ ⒻFirenze H 34k	9 10 64½ 22 3½	31½	Guerin E	126wb	*.90	93-12	Renew112noThelma Berger1091½Next Move126½	Impeded	12
25Apr51-6Jam	fst	6f		:223 :46 1:112	3↑ ⒻCorrection H 17k	2 8 63½ 105 74½	42¼	Guerin E	128wb	*1.85	88-12	GrowingUp1101DarkFavorite1121MssDgr111hd	Stumbled early	14
3Mar51-7SA	gd	1¼		:462 1:11 1:364 2:023	3↑ S Anita H 135k	5 2 32 22 2½	2nk	Guerin E	116wb	4.30	87-24	Moonrush114nkNext Move1162¾Sudan111hd	Just missed	14
17Feb51-7SA	fst	1⅛		:453 1:101 1:363 1:492	3↑ San Antonio H 68k	2 3 33½ 2hd 11	3¾	Guerin E	119wb	4.20	93-17	All Blue111¾Sudan109hdNext Move119½	Weakened	16
3Feb51-7SA	fst	1¼		:451 1:093 1:351 2:002	Maturity 205k	8 2 21 12 31	67	Guerin E	121wb	*.90e	91-08	Great Circle1151¾Lotowhite116hdBed o' Roses1103½	Tired	11
20Jan51-7SA	fst	1⅛		:461 1:11 1:361 1:483	3↑ ⒻS Margarita H 60k	2 2 21½ 21½ 32	43¾	Guerin E	130wb	*.55e	94-16	SpecialTouch1141Bewitch1221½Bedo'Roses1251½	No excuse	8
16Dec50-7Hol	fst	1⅛		:462 1:103 1:36 1:483	3↑ Sunset H 58k	3 1 11½ 12 11½	2¾	Guerin E	114wb	3.90e	97-12	HillPrince128¾NextMove1141½GreatCircle109nk	Game effort	10
9Dec50-7Hol	fst	1¼		:463 1:101 1:35 1:594	3↑ Hol Gold Cup 137k	6 3 12 11½ 2½	45	Guerin E	116wb	10.35	96-09	Noor1301Palestinian1223Hill Prince1301	Tired	8
2Dec50-7Hol	fst	1⅛		:47 1:111 1:362 1:492	3↑ ⒻVanity H 30k	3 1 12 12 13	12¼	Guerin E	128wb	*.50e	94-11	Next Move1282½Bewitch1241Wistful125½	Easing up	9
25Nov50-7Hol	fst	1 1/16		:224 :46 1:102 1:423	ⒻCinderella 29k	1 2 2hd 11½ 12	13	Guerin E	126wb	*.45	95-07	Next Move1263Special Touch1232½Fair Regards1141	Easily	8
11Nov50-7Hol	fst	1 1/16		:231 :463 1:103 1:423	3↑ ⓈGolden St Brdrs' H 29k	2 2 1hd 2½ 22	21¼	Guerin E	118wb	2.35	94-12	Your Host1241¼Next Move118½On Trust1131½	Sharp try	7
4Oct50-6Bel	fst	1½		:491 1:133 2:034 2:292	3↑ ⒻLadies H 29k	6 4 21 15 16	15½	Guerin E	120wb	*2.15	91-11	Next Move1205½My Celeste106hdWistful1241¼	Easily	12
16Sep50-6Aqu	fst	1⅛		:473 1:12 1:37 1:501	3↑ ⒻBeldame H 66k	2 1 13 12 15	12¼	Combest N	116wb	*1.20e	94-15	Next Move1162¼September1081Wistful1252¼	Easily	12
28Aug50-6Aqu	fst	1⅛		:471 1:113 1:353 1:49	Discovery H 22k	6 4 43½ 32 56½	513	Guerin E	114wb	*.50	89-08	Sunglow113hdSteel Blue1064Bit o' Fate1047	Tired badly	9
23Aug50-6Sar	fst	1¼		:483 1:13 1:384 2:042	ⒻAlabama 23k	5 4 2hd 12½ 13	2nk	Guerin E	126wb	*.70	86-15	Busanda108nkNext Move126hdAntagonism1083	Weak ride	7
12Jly50-6AP	fst	1		:222 :442 1:08 1:344	ⒻCleopatra H 22k	3 6 55 56¼ 54½	32	Guerin E	126wb	*1.40	96-04	Here's Hoping1151Siama1171Next Move126nk	Closed fast	11
3Jly50-6Aqu	fst	1 1/16		:232 :47 1:12 1:433	ⒻGazelle 22k	2 2 13 12 12	11	Guerin E	121wb	*.25e	96-11	Next Move1211Bed o' Roses1165Renew112¾	Easily	7
24Jun50-5Del	fst	1⅛		:463 1:104 1:363 1:492	ⒻDel Oaks 33k	2 4 31½ 13 14	15	Guerin E	119wb	*.65	95-08	Next Move1195Busanda1104½Include1101¼	Easily	10
27May50-6Bel	fst	1⅜		:472 1:112 1:362 2:154	ⒻC C A Oaks 62k	3 6 73¼ 55 1hd	11	Guerin E	121wb	*1.30	92-11	Next Move1211Aegina1164Busanda1212½	Handily	8
22May50-6Bel	fst	1 1/16		:222 :451 1:101 1:44	ⒻAlw 5000	3 1 11 11 13	11	Guerin E	122wb	2.05	91-14	Next Move1221Busanda1105Sunday Evening116½	Ridden out	8
10May50-6Bel	fst	1		:224 :461 1:113 1:371	ⒻAcorn 18k	6 4 33½ 31 2½	21¾	Guerin E	121 w	*.30	86-16	Siama1211¾Next Move1214Honey's Gal121no	Forced wide	8
3May50-6Jam	sly	6f		:231 :47 1:121	ⒻPrioress 17k	9 8 62 11 13	18	Guerin E	115 w	*.85	90-22	Next Move1158Honey's Gal116nkMiss Degree1121½	Easily	9
22Apr50-6Jam	fst	1 1/16		:24 :472 1:12 1:433	Wood Memorial 49k	7 1 11 11 2½	44½	Guerin E	121 w	5.35	91-13	Hill Prince1262Middleground1261½Ferd126¾	Weakened	11
13Apr50-6Jam	fst	6f		:23 :471 1:122	ⒻAlw 4500	5 3 1hd 11½ 14	15½	Guerin E	115 w	*.25	89-17	Next Move1155½Abbie Co1104Navy Bean1103	Easily	8

8Apr50- 5Jam	fst	6f	:224 :461	1:111	ⒻAlw 3500	4	2	11½	12	13	14	Guerin E	116 w	*.55	95-10	Next Move1164Countess Molly1133½La Nappe1137	Easily	7
8Nov49- 6Jam	fst	1$\frac{1}{16}$	:24 :47 1:12	1:454	ⒻDemoiselle 56k	8	3	34	22½	3½	21½	Scurlock O	119 w	*.50e	82-19	Bedo'Roses1161½NextMove1195RarePerfume1166	Good effort	12
3Nov49- 5Jam	gd	6f	:233 :471	1:122	ⒻAlw 4000	4	5	31½	21½	21½	2¾	Scurlock O	110 w	2.75	88-15	Rare Perfume122¾Next Move1104[D]Nazma1111½	Sharp effort	8
19Oct49- 6Jam	fst	6f	:23 :464	1:121	ⒻAutumn Day 12k	11	7	64	33	23	24	Guerin E	115 w	6.80	86-17	Rare Perfume1194Next Move1154½Nazma112½	Went well	13
20Sep49- 5Bel	fst	5½f-W	:23 :462	1:06	ⒻAlw 4000	13	3		2½	1½	2no	Guerin E	116 w	1.80e	84-16	Fais Do Do114noNext Move116hdBed o' Roses1223	Game try	13
5Sep49- 4Aqu	fst	5½f	:23 :474 1:001	1:064	ⒻAlw 3500	1	2	12	13	12	15	Guerin E	116 w	*1.20	90-17	Next Move1165Light Upon1162Blue Heart116no	Easily	8
5Jly49- 5Jam	fst	5f	:23 :462	1:01	ⒻMd Sp Wt	10	6	13	15	15	12½	Guerin E	116 w	8.35	85-20	NextMove1162½Sailor'sChoice116noSweeptheSky1164	In hand	12
4Jun49- 2Bel	fst	5f-WC	:222 :451	:58	ⒻMd Sp Wt	8	1		2hd	52½	66	Guerin E	116 w	4.30	84-09	Mislead1161Sailors Choice1162La Nappe1161	Tired	9
16May49- 4Bel	fst	4½f-W	:221 :45	:511	ⒻMd Sp Wt	7	8		4¾	45	108½	Guerin E	116 w	*2.70	89-03	Fais Do Do1165Light Upon116hdOur Patrice1161	Stopped	17

Noor (Ire)

br. c. 1945, by Nasrullah (Nearco)–Queen of Baghdad, by Bahram — **Lifetime record: 31 12 6 6 $394,863**

Own.– Estate of C.S. Howard
Br.– H.H. Aga Khan (Ire)
Tr.– B. Parke

9Dec50- 7Hol	fst	1¼	:463 1:101 1:35	1:594	3↑ Hol Gold Cup 137k	8	8	79	64¾	32½	11	Longden J	130wb	*.70	101-09	Noor1301Palestinian1223HillPrinc1301	Rated,drawing away	8
1Dec50- 7Hol	fst	1⅛	:48 1:114 1:361	1:48	3↑ Alw 5000	4	4	42¼	2½	13	17	Longden J	124wb	*.75	101-11	Noor1247Palestinian1201Assault1121	Much best	5
7Oct50- 6Bel	fst	2	:494 2:31 2:563	3:232	3↑ J C Gold Cup 54k	4	2	22	21½	23	24	Longden J	124wb	*.65	83-13	Hill Prince1174Noor1247Adile1212	No excuse	5
	Geldings not eligible																	
23Sep50- 6Bel	fst	1½	:473 1:123 2:031	2:291	3↑ Manhattan H 29k	3	10	615	52¾	2½	2nk	Longden J	128wb	*.65	92-15	One Hitter110nkNoor1282Ponder1261¼	Slow start	10
18Sep50- 7Bel	fst	1$\frac{1}{16}$	:231 :462 1:111	1:424	3↑ Handicap 5035	3	4	45½	43¼	43	21¼	Longden J	128wb	*.95	96-15	One Hitter1071¼Noor1281½Sky Miracle1022½	Not punished	5
22Jly50- 7Hol	fst	1¼	:481 1:122 1:361	2:001	3↑ American H 55k	4	5	59	3nk	3nk	1½	Longden J	132wb	*.35	99-05	Noor132½Dharan1004Frankly107no	Driving	5
24Jun50- 8GG	fst	1¼	:451 1:091 1:34	1:581	3↑ Golden Gate H 57k	4	5	515	27	22	13	Longden J	127wb	*.70	108-12	Noor1273Citation1261On Trust1032½	Drew out	5
17Jun50- 8GG	fst	1⅛	:463 1:093 1:344	1:464	3↑ Forty-Niners H 10k	4	5	54½	42¼	2hd	1nk	Longden J	123wb	1.80	104-08	Noor123nkCitation1283Roman In1112	Hard drive	5
	Previously raced in name of C.S. Howard																	
4Mar50- 7SA	fst	1¾	:474 2:023 2:271	2:524	3↑ S Juan Capistrano H 64k	4	7	64½	2hd	2hd	1no	Longden J	117wb	3.40	127-06	Noor117noCitation13012½Mocopo107hd	Hard drive	8
25Feb50- 7SA	fst	1¼	:462 1:11 1:351	2:00	3↑ S Anita H 135k	3	10	96¾	21	2hd	11¼	Longden J	110wb	6.40	106-11	Noor1101¼Citation1321Two Lea113nk	Drew clear	11
11Feb50- 7SA	gd	1⅛	:471 1:113 1:372	1:501	3↑ San Antonio H 60k	1	8	79½	64	42	31½	Longden J	114wb	5.15	90-17	Ponder1281Citation130½Noor114¾	Late rush	9
7Jan50- 7SA	fst	1$\frac{1}{16}$	:232 :471 1:114	1:434	3↑ San Pasqual H 67k	4	11	107¼	63¾	24	21	Longden J	112wb	6.45	88-17	Solidarity1211Noor1123Ponder1253	Off slowly	14
31Dec49- 7SA	fst	7f	:214 :444 1:102	1:232	3↑ San Carlos H 65k	8	9	69½	79	75	51¾	Neves R	109wb	21.20	90-19	Manyunk114nkStar Reward1201Miche116hd	Late rush	12
17Dec49- 8Tan	my	1⅛	:473 1:122 1:39	1:514	3↑ San Francisco H 16k	9	9	89½	66	31½	2hd	Longden J	115wb	4.40	95-20	Huon Kid107hdNoor115noMocopo1091	Gaining fast	9
3Dec49- 8Tan	fst	1¼	:464 1:113 1:362	2:021	3↑ Tanforan H 28k	1	6	611	56	45	34½	James B	115wb	5.35	98-03	Miche1152Johns Joy1202½Noor1151½	Raced wide	9
24Nov49- 8Tan	fst	1$\frac{1}{16}$	:233 :473 1:12	1:44	3↑ Marchbank H 12k	9	6	53¼	42¼	31½	3½	James B	115wb	4.80	99-09	Oration108hdGolden Glory108½Noor115hd	Game effort	11
4Nov49- 7Tan	fst	6f	:224 :454	1:113	3↑ Alw 3000	4	5	610	59½	68¼	42¾	James B	120 w	2.25e	94-12	ThreeRivers1141Frankly1141¼FastandFair117½	Closed fast	7
14Oct49- 6BM	fst	6f	:223 :454	1:104	3↑ Alw 3000	4	7	36	23	1hd	1no	James B	117 w	7.95	94-11	Noor117noFrankly1202¾See-Tee-See1201½	Hard drive	7
	Previously trained by Frank Butters																	

28Sep48♦ Newmarket(GB)	fm 1¼Ⓣ Str	2:072	Great Foal Stakes Alw3900	11½	Richards G	133	*.50	Noor1331½Pretexte12110Cotswold119 Tracked leader,led 150y out,ridden out	3
11Sep48♦ Doncaster(GB)	fm *1¾Ⓣ LH	3:083	St Leger Stakes Stk94000	8	Richards G	126	8.00	Black Tarquin1261½Alycidon1265Solar Slipper1262 Prominent to 3f out,weakened	14
31Jly48♦ Epsom(GB)	fm 1½Ⓣ LH	2:401 3↑	Diomed Stakes Stk16400	16	Richards G	116	*.15	Noor1166Straight Play116 Led throughout,drew clear 2f out	2
16Jly48♦ Sandown(GB)	gd 1¼Ⓣ RH	2:101 3↑	Eclipse Stakes Stk40900	3nk	Johnstone W	114	*2.50	Petition133noSayajirao136nkNoor114¾ Led to 170y out,came again near line	8
5Jun48♦ Epsom(GB)	gd 1½Ⓣ LH	2:40	Epsom Derby Stk80300	35½	Weston T	126	22.00	My Love1261½Royal Drake1264Noor1261 Slowly away,well behind after 4f,midpack 3f out,up for 3rd	32
28Apr48♦ Newmarket(GB)	fm 1Ⓣ Str	1:354	2000 Guineas Stakes Stk86700	9	Beary M	126	50.00	My Babu126hdThe Cobbler1264Pride of India1262 Never a factor	18
12Nov47♦ Windsor(GB)	fm 5fⓉ Str	1:001	Riverside Nursery Handicap Hcp3300	7	Richards G	120	*2.00	Red brae100noRossini1171½Hidden Valley110½ Chased leaders,never threatened	19
30Oct47♦ Newmarket(GB)	fm 6fⓉ Str	1:161	Bretby Nursery Handicap Hcp3900	1nk	Richards G	125	*3.30	Noor125nkWilliam the Lion113½Nursery Rhyme110nk Slowly away,bumped early,rallied to lead 100y out,driving	11
13Sep47♦ Doncaster(GB)	gd 6fⓉ Str	1:15	Bradgate Park Nursery Handicap Hcp4700	13	Richards G	119	5.50	Noor1193Lake Placid112¾Rodin126¾ Sharp run 2f out,soon led,drew clear final furlong	8
21Aug47♦ Newmarket(GB)	fm 6fⓉ Str	1:163	Elveden Stakes Alw5900	43¾	Richards G	123	12.50	Ottoman128nkMistress Ann1251½Rear Admiral1322 Led for 4f,gradually weakened	5
29Jly47♦ Goodwood(GB)	fm 6fⓉ Str	1:134	New Ham Foal Stakes Alw7000	44¼	Johnstone W	114	10.00	Pride of India1141½Ottoman119¾Howdah1192 Lost touch 1½f out	8
4Jun47♦ Epsom(GB)	fm 6fⓉ LH	1:10	Woodcote Stakes Alw15500	35	Richards G	116	3.50	Lerins1215Fair Friar116noNoor1164 Prominent,faded 1f out.Lerins later renamed My Babu	6
3May47♦ Birmingham(GB)	gd 5fⓉ Str	1:034	Compton Wynyates Plate Alw2100	23	Johnstone W	124	6.00	Minster Lovell1243Noor1245Sicklejas1218 Toward rear,finished well without threatening	6

Oedipus

br. g. 1946, by Blue Larkspur (Black Servant)–Be Like Mom, by Sickle — **Lifetime record: 58 14 12 9 $132,405**

Own.– Mrs O. Phipps
Br.– Idle Hour Stock Farm Co (Ky)
Tr.– G.H Bostwick

2Sep54- 3Aqu	sf	*2	S'Chase	3:523	4↑ Alw 4000	6	3	32	32½	22	21¾	Adams FD	145	w	2.85	--	MightyMo1481¾Oedips14510MonkeyWrench1455	Second best	6
28Aug54- 3Sar	fm	*1¾	Hurdles	3:24	3↑ Alw 3500	6	2	2½	66½	618	620	Adams FD	145	w	5.20	--	Curly Joe1394Heureux II1492½Cammell Laird144nk	Gave way	7
5Aug54- 5Sar	sf	*2	S'Chase	4:172	4↑ Shillelah H 8.8k	4	2	31	412	429	434	Adams FD	145	w	3.95	--	Shipboard1392King Commander14320Coveted13812	Tired	7
18Jun54- 3Aqu	hd	*1¾	Hurdles	3:12	4↑ Alw 4000	9	5	21½	31½	411	610¾	Adams FD	144	w	*1.45	--	Cammell Laird1426Curly Joe1321½Corinthien1322½	Quit	9
29May54- 7Pur	fm	*6fⓉ		1:15	3↑ Alw 400	5	3	62¾	62¾	63¾	65½	Adams FD	141	w	2.65e	--	Nairn1372½Escargot141½Beau Broke131½	Never a menace	7
13Aug53- 5Sar	fst	*2	S'Chase	4:093	4↑ North Am H 8.8k	2	2	22	25	611	617	Adams FD	159	w	1.95	--	The Mast1444Sundowner1432½Virginius1341½	Quit early	6
6Aug53- 5Sar	fst	*2	S'Chase	4:10	4↑ Shillelah H 8.9k	6	1	11½	2½	33	34	Adams FD	160	w	*1.95	--	Sun Shower1321Sundowner1393Oedipus1604	Used early	7
19Jun53- 6Bel	fst	*2¼	S'Chase	4:121	4↑ Temple Gwathmey H 16k	5	2	21½	35	35½	37½	Adams FD	164	w	3.20	--	Errolford1305½Sea Legs1652Oedipus1645	No rally	7
	Daily Racing Form time,4:16 2/5																		
4Jun53- 5Bel	fst	*2½	S'Chase	4:421	4↑ Meadow Brook H 11k	2	1	12½	1hd	24	25	Adams FD	164	w	*1.20	--	Sea Legs1575Oedipus1642½His Boots1462½	No rally	6
14May53- 5Bel	fst	*2	S'Chase	3:453	4↑ C L Appleton Mem 8.9k	6	1	14	11	12	11½	Adams FD	158	w	1.90	--	Oedipus1581½His Boots1422The Mast1447	Hard drive	6
3Oct52- 5Bel	sf	*3	S'Chase	5:44	4↑ Grand Nat'l H 28k	3	3	45½	33	37	37	Foot A	165	w	*2.60	--	Sea Legs1365The Mast1542Oedipus1657	No rally	9
25Sep52- 5Bel	fst	*2½	S'Chase	4:412	4↑ Brook H 17k	3	3	31	21	31	25	Foot A	163	w	*2.50	--	Jam1565Oedipus1631Lone Fisherman1313	Impeded	8
18Sep52- 5Bel	sf	*2	S'Chase	3:391	3↑ Broad Hollow H 11k	4	3	32	2½	11½	1hd	Foot A	160	w	2.60	--	Oedipus160hdJam15420The Creek1386	Just lasted	8
11Sep52- 5Aqu	fst	*2	S'Chase	3:441	3↑ Harbor Hill H 11k	5	2	22	44	49	412½	Foot A	162	w	2.45	--	Semper Eadem1354Hot1472½Jam1556	Bad landing last	6

21Aug52- 5Sar	fst	*2	S'Chase	4:091	4↑ Beverwyck H 9k	2	3	32	31½	513	514	Foot A	165 w	*1.00e	--	His Boots1448Titien II1451Hot1461½	Tired 7
7Aug52- 5Sar	fst	*2	S'Chase	4:11	4↑ Shillelah 5.8k	2	1	11½	12	12	12	Foot A	162 w	2.05	--	Oedipus1622His Boots1405Phiblant1405	All out 5
3Jly52- 5Aqu	fst	*2	S'Chase	3:461	4↑ Hitchcock H 11k	5	5	55	53½	44	35	Foot A	162 w	*.90	--	Hot1442His Boots1433Oedipus1621½	No excuse 6
20Jun52- 6Del	fst	*2	S'Chase	3:431	4↑ Georgetown H 12k	2	2	21	42¼	35½	58	Foot A	164 w	*1.65e	--	The Mast1575Jam1511½DHCrooning Wind1431½	Weakened 8
11Jun52- 6Bel	fst	*2¼	S'Chase	4:163	4↑ Temple Gwathmey H 16k	4	2	2½	11	1hd	2¾	Foot A	163 w	*1.90	--	The Mast153¾Oedipus1631¼Navy Gun1497	Weakened 9
12Oct51- 5Bel	sf	*3	S'Chase	5:501	4↑ Grand National H 24k	2	2	21	2½	11	11½	Foot A	165 w	*1.80	--	Oedipus1651½Navy Gun1402½Banner Waves14045	All out 10
4Oct51- 5Bel	fst	*2½	S'Chase	4:45	4↑ Brook H 16k	1	1	11½	11½	13	13	Foot A	161wb	*2.00	--	Oedipus1613Palaja1387Lone Fisherman148nk	Easily 12
27Sep51- 5Bel	fst	*2	S'Chase	3:43	3↑ Broad Hollow H 12k	11	1	22	24	12	17	Foot A	158 w	3.95	--	Oedipus1587Palaja1342Genancoke1412½	Easily 11
6Sep51- 5Aqu	fst	*2	S'Chase	3:47	3↑ Harbor Hill H 11k	4	4	46	53½	3nk	42¾•	Smithwick P	159 w	*1.95	--	Boom Boom1452Genancoke140¾Tourist List134hd	Blocked 8
30Aug51- 5Sar	fst	*2½	S'Chase	5:053	4↑ Saratoga H 11k	2	2	2½	21	26	38¼	Adams FD	159 w	*1.50	--	Hampton Roads1408Lone Fisherman147nkOedipus15925	7
	Bad landing 10th																
23Aug51- 5Sar	sf	*2	S'Chase	4:192	3↑ Beverwyck H 8.9k	1	1	13	12	11½	13	Adams FD	155 w	*1.40	--	Oedipus1553Hampton Roads13913Boom Boom1452	Easily 7
9Aug51- 5Sar	sf	*2	S'Chase	4:164	3↑ Shillelah 6.1k	2	1	12	11½	3½	33½	Adams FD	154 w	*1.10	--	Banner Waves1341½Extra Points1372Oedipus1542	Tired 5
12Jly51- 5Aqu	hd	*2	S'Chase	3:441	4↑ Hitchcock 11k	3	2	36	36½	52¾	56	Adams FD	157 w	*1.00	--	Genncoke1352¼DLarky Day147nkSemprEadem140½	Impeded 7
	Placed fourth through disqualification																
27Jun51- 5Del	fst	*2	S'Chase	3:404	4↑ Georgetown H 12k	4	3	35½	46½	26	24	Smiley J	158 w	*1.75	--	Crooning Wind1304Oedipus15812Genancoke1373	No rally 6
7Jun51- 5Bel	fst	*2	S'Chase	3:432	4↑ Corinthian H 8.7k	2	1	15	12	11	1¾	Smiley J	156 w	*.85	--	Oedipus156¾Lone Fisherman14812Elkridge1501	Driving 4
18May51- 5Bel	fst	*2	S'Chase	3:42	4↑ International H 9k	7	2	21	11½	1hd	24	Smiley J	154 w	2.40	--	Pontius Pilate1524Oedipus1547Elkridge1493½	Held well 7
11Oct50- 6Bel	fst	*2¼	S'Chase	4:182	4↑ Temple Gwathmey H 11k	3	1	1½	21½	23	210	Molony T	153 w	*.45	--	TouristList13810Oedipus1536AmericanWay1454	Bad landing 5
6Oct50- 5Bel	fst	*3	S'Chase	5:422	4↑ Grand National H 23k	4	3	41½	21	1hd	22¼	Molony T	153 w	3.45	--	Trough Hill1502¼Oedipus1534Pontius Pilate1502½	Weakened 9
29Sep50- 5Bel	fst	*2½	S'Chase	4:46	4↑ Brook H 15k	2	1	11	11	12	11¼	Adams FD	149 w	3.15	--	Oedipus1491¼Trough Hill1515½Tourist List1361	Easily 8
22Sep50- 5Bel	sf	*2	S'Chase	3:482	3↑ Broad Hollow H 11k	9	2	25	23	12	11¼	Williams CH	147 w	17.45	--	Oedipus1471¼Elkridge1521¼Trough Hill1505	Ridden out 10
7Sep50- 5Aqu	fst	*2	Hurdles	3:381	3↑ Bushwick H 11k	1	4	73¾	78½	819	816	McDonald RS	152 w	5.10	--	Scare Play1431½Larky Day1531¼Bengal1324	Close quarters 9
25Aug50- 5Sar	fst	*2½	S'Chase	5:082	4↑ Saratoga H 11k	6	3	33½	43½	36	39	Field T	147 w	3.35	--	Elkridge1503Lone Fisherman1356Oedipus147nk	Fair effort 6
18Aug50- 5Sar	fst	*2	S'Chase	4:082	3↑ Beverwyck H 9.1k	3	1	12	12	28	215	Field T	143 w	3.40	--	Pontius Pilate13815Oedipus14313Elkridge14640	Gave way 6
10Aug50- 5Sar	fst	*2	S'Chase	4:094	3↑ North American H 6.4k	3	1	1½	1hd	47½	414	McDonald RS	143 w	2.40	--	TheHeir143nkHamptnRoads14510Scuttlman1354	Bad landing 6
3Aug50- 5Sar	fst	*2	S'Chase	4:102	3↑ Shillelah 6.6k	2	3	3nk	2hd	15	16	Smiley J	135 w	5.35	--	Oedipus1356His Boots15216Repose136hd	Easily 10
27Jun50- 5Del	fst	*2	S'Chase	3:524	4↑ Spring Maiden 7.3k	8	-	-	-	-	-	Smiley J	154 w	*2.05	--	Port Raider15010Whirl Along1426Tolbiac1506	Fell at 1st 8
19Jun50- 4Aqu	sf	*2	S'Chase	3:422	4↑ Spring Maiden 7.3k	1	1	11½	11½	12	12	Smiley J	147 w	*1.35	--	Oedipus1472PortRaider15035LoneFisherman15025	Ridden out 7
13Jun50- 3Aqu	fst	*2	S'Chase	3:461	4↑ Alw 3500	2	1	13	16	110	120	Smiley J	137 w	2.90	--	Oedipus13720Le Buis Fleuri147nkPort Raider1475½	Easily 7
31May50- 3Bel	fst	*1½	Hurdles	2:463	3↑ 3500	10	1	14	14	22	39½	Smiley J	142 w	4.15	--	Enon1504½Proceed1425Oedipus14220	Weakened 12
22May50- 3Bel	fst	*1½	Hurdles	2:454	3↑ Alw 3500	3	6	51¼	33	37¼	512	Smiley J	134 w	5.15e	--	Rialto1561½Uncle Sam13110Macanudo143nk	Tired 11
10May50- 3Bel	fst	*2	S'Chase	3:50	4↑ Sp Wt 3500	8	2	1228	-	-	-	Smiley J	142 w	4.00	--	LoneFishrmn1424SeaLegs14210WhattaKnight1361½	Ran out 14
11Oct49- 3Bel	fst	*1½	Hurdles	2:463	3↑ Alw 3000	9	6	512	25	21½	21½	Smiley J	139 w	9.55	--	Silver Bridge1391½Oedipus139½Half Hour1505	Good effort 14
5Oct49- 3Bel	fst	*1½	Hurdles	2:461	3↑ Alw 3500	3	7	68¼	48½	31½	22	Molony T	132 w	7.90	--	SilverBridge1322Oedipus1322½MonkyWrnch13910	Closed well 11
27Sep49- 3Bel	fst	*2	Hurdles	3:463	3↑ Handicap 4045	4	2	35	11	63½	511	Field T	133 w	*2.05e	--	NewRule1381Skyscraper1502½LeBuisFlur145½	Close quarters 9
	Daily Racing Form time,3:47 4/5																
20Sep49- 4Bel	fst	6f	:232 :473	1:122	3↑ Md Sp Wt	10	12	1111	1111	811	716	Renick J	119 w	24.35	72-17	Challadroit1195GoodEnding1192½HickoryLea124no	No mishap 14
9Sep49- 3Aqu	sl	*1½	Hurdles	2:573	3↑ Alw 3000	1	1	1½	1½	21½	32	Adams FD	136 w	*1.35	--	Monkey Wrench1481Firebet1501Oedipus1364	Close quarters 8
30Aug49- 3Aqu	fst	*1½	Hurdles	2:52	3↑ Md Sp Wt	7	1	11	11½	1hd	11	Adams FD	136 w	*1.35	--	Oedipus1361North Branch1314½Alphabetical1323½	Driving 8
25Aug49- 3Sar	fst	*1½	Hurdles	3:082	3↑ Md Sp Wt	1	2	36	611	32½	22	Smiley J	137 w	11.00	--	Titien II1372Oedipus1371½The Viceroy1502½	Closed well 9
	Previously owned by O. Phipps;previously trained by J. Fitzsimmons																
29Jly48- 3Jam	fst	5½f	:232 :472 :592	1:063	©Md Sp Wt	8	9	109¼	106½	108¾	1015	Combest N	116wb	114.80	70-20	Dry Fly116nkBlue Dart1164Fireagain116nk	Trailed 10
9Jun48- 4Bel	fst	5f-WC	:223 :452	:572	©Md Sp Wt	6	13		156¾	168¾	1511	Guerin E	116wb	42.60e	82-09	Prince Quest116¾Halt116½Kibosh116¾	Outrun 17
22May48- 4Bel	fst	5f-WC	:232 :47	:591	Alw 5000	3	3		64	66¾	612	Jessop JD	111wb	10.00e	72-14	Capot1111½Mirabeau1146Amarillo Kid1131½	Outrun 6
29Apr48- 3Jam	fst	5f	:232 :482	1:012	©Md Sp Wt	6	5	67¼	78	77¾	67½	Guerin E	116wb	33.90	75-21	Transfluent116noSwords Town1162Good Egg116nk	No factor 11
24Apr48- 3Jam	fst	5f	:232 :473	1:01	Md Sp Wt	6	5	811	84½	99¾	913	Guerin E	116 w	31.20	72-18	BlueCounselor1163BlueThanks1161½Dsconsolt1161	No factor 12
19Apr48- 3Jam	fst	5f	:23 :472	1:003	©Md Sp Wt	9	5	56	712	610	814	Guerin E	116 w	5.70e	73-17	Ennobled1164Good Egg1165Blue Thanks116¾	Outrun 10

One Count

dk br. c. 1949, by Count Fleet (Reigh Count)–Ace Card, by Case Ace

Lifetime record: 23 9 3 3 $245,625

Own.– Mrs W.M. Jeffords

Br.– Walter M. Jeffords (Ky)

Tr.– O. White

27Jun53- 6Del	fst	1¼	:452 1:092 1:344	2:002	3↑ Sussex H 28k	5	5	510	43½	45½	44¼	Gorman D	127 w	2.85e	104-07	Royal Vale130nkPost Card1133Risque Rouge1111	Faltered 5
30May53- 6Bel	fst	1¼	:471 1:11 1:353	2:003	3↑ Suburban H 58k	5	6	56¾	48½	56¼	510	Gorman D	126 w	2.30e	87-17	Tom Fool128noRoyal Vale1247Cold Command1142	Tired 7
2May53- 6Jam	my	1 3/16	:474 1:113 1:362	1:552	3↑ Gallant Fox H 71k	3	4	46	44½	35	33	Gorman D	129 w	2.35	96-14	RoyalVale1151½ColdCommand1151½OneCount129no	No excuse 6
21Apr53- 6Jam	fst	1 1/16	:234 :47 1:12	1:451	3↑ Handicap 10160	7	9	88¾	51¼	31	11¾	Gorman D	126 w	*2.15	86-19	One Count1261¾Assignment111noFlaunt106hd	Driving clear 11
7Feb53- 7Hia	my	1⅛	:473 1:124 1:391	1:532	3↑ McLennan H 64k	1	4	45½	46	68½	613	Gorman D	126 w	3.45	56-34	Crafty Admiral1293½Oil Capitol115¾Ken1171	Tired 7
25Oct52- 6Jam	fst	1⅝	:494 1:401 2:051	2:44	3↑ Gold Cup 79k	4	4	3½	16	18	19	Gorman D	119 w	*.60	94-15	One Count1199Alerted1261½Lafourche1191	Easily 6
	Geldings not eligible																
4Oct52- 6Bel	fst	2	:514 2:332 2:584	3:241	3↑ J C Gold Cup 79k	4	3	21	14	13	12	Gorman D	117 w	3.80	83-15	OneCount1172Mark-Ye-Well11715CraftyAdmiral1245	Driving 4
	Geldings not eligible																
24Sep52- 6Bel	fst	1⅝	:482 1:38 2:031	2:42	Lawrence Realizatn 29k	5	6	55½	31	24	24	Guerin E	126 w	1.60	90-15	Mark-Ye-Well1184One Count1265Marcador1143½	Hard urged 7
16Aug52- 6Sar	sly	1¼	:493 1:144 1:401	2:072	Travers 23k	3	5	54½	43	11	13	Guerin E	126 w	4.10	71-22	One Count1263Armageddon1231Tom Fool114¾	In hand 8
	Geldings not eligible																
7Jun52- 6Bel	fst	1½	:483 1:134 2:042	2:301	Belmont 118k	3	3	2hd	1hd	11½	12½	Arcaro E	126 w	12.80	88-14	OneCnt1262½BlueMan12610Armagddn1266	Swerved,drew out 6
17May52- 6Pim	fst	1 3/16	:472 1:12 1:38	1:572	Preakness 113k	1	4	32½	32½	43	36	Arcaro E	126 w	8.10	87-13	Blue Man1263½Jampol1262½One Count126½	No rally 10
10May52- 6Bel	fst	1	:224 :453 1:11	1:37	Withers 31k	5	7	75¾	64¼	34½	23½	Atkinson T	126 w	2.95	85-14	Armageddon1263½One Count1264Primate126¾	Closed well 9
	Geldings not eligible																
7May52- 5Bel	fst	1 1/16	:231 :464 1:122	1:44	Alw 5000	5	6	53¼	21	13	18	Gorman D	117 w	3.10	91-16	One Count1178Brechin109noGrover B.1221	Easily,drew out 8
15Apr52- 7Lrl	my	1	:232 :47 1:13	1:392	Alw 4000	2	4	32	21	21	21½	Hanford I	119wb	1.80	86-23	ComtedeGrasse1161½OneCnt1197OceanBreeze1104	No excuse 5
29Mar52- 6Lrl	fst	6f	:224 :47	1:122	Cherry Blossom 9k	4	7	84½	77½	79	77	Hanford I	115wb	20.60	78-20	Cinda1163½Pintor118noOrco121hd	No factor 9
1Mar52- 6Hia	fst	1⅛	:462 1:113 1:37	1:50	Flamingo (Div 1) 66k	8	10	104	87½	913	914	Stout J	117wb	8.05	72-09	Blue Man1173½Jampol120¾DTop Bet111¾	No factor 11
20Feb52- 7Hia	fst	1⅛	:46 1:11 1:374	1:521	Everglades H 13k	7	7	79	68	65	51	Boulmetis S	114wb	4.45	74-18	OneThrow110nkMasterFiddle123nkCandlWood122hd	Late rush 13
13Feb52- 5Hia	fst	7f	:224 :453 1:11	1:242	Alw 3500	9	2	2hd	2½	2½	1hd	Boulmetis S	122wb	*1.90	90-14	One Count122hdImurguy1111½Blenomar1146	Unruly,up 11
30Jan52- 4Hia	sl	6f	:234 :482	1:15	Alw 3500	3	6	31	21½	21½	3nk	Boulmetis S	122wb	2.45	73-28	Why Not119nkNimble Fox116hdOne Count1223	Closed well 10
22Jan52- 4Hia	fst	7f	:224 :462 1:114	1:244	©Alw 3000	1	3	31½	2½	11	11¼	Boulmetis S	122wb	2.65	88-13	One Count1221¼Sandtop1164½Outback1221½	Drew clear 9
24Oct51- 2GS	fst	1 70	:233 :474 1:131	1:443	Md Sp Wt	12	3	21	1½	11	1½	Boulmetis S	119 w	*2.40	84-16	One Count119½Cobber1195High Petal1163	Driving 12
3Oct51- 5Bel	fst	6f-WC	:223 :452	1:10	©Md Sp Wt	16	13		125¾	65¼	97	Shoemaker W	118 w	8.85f	84-09	Warpath1182Golden Gloves118hdForelock1181	No menace 26
26Sep51- 5Bel	fst	6f-WC	:222 :45	1:101	©Md Sp Wt	19	23		2715	2115	189¼	Guerin E	118 w	27.30	81-10	Hitex1183½Point Fortune113noChello118no	Slow start 27

Parlo

ch. f. 1951, by Heliopolis (Hyperion)–Fairy Palace, by Pilate

Lifetime record: 34 8 6 3 $309,240

Own.– Foxcatcher Farms

Br.– William duPont Jr (Va)

Tr.– R.E. Handlen

12Oct56-7Bel	fst	1½	:473	1:113	2:034	2:294	3↑	ⒻLadies H 58k	11	1	14	41¼	108¾	1112	Westrope J	116	w	10.55	77-13	FlowerBowl1161¾DottedLn111hdBrghtstStrt107nk	Used early	12
1Oct56-7Bel	fst	1	:224	:461	1:112	1:37	3↑	ⒻMaskette H 29k	5	4	41½	32½	33½	43¼	Guerin E	117	w	4.60	86-15	Searching123½HappyPrincess1072PuckerUp112¾	Raced evenly	11
22Sep56-7Bel	fst	1⅛	:452	1:101	1:363	1:50	3↑	ⒻBeldame H 66k	1	2	22	22	31	73	Guerin E	120	w	9.80	86-13	Levee115½Amoret114hdSearching123nk	Well placed,no rally	14
5Sep56-7Bel	fst	7f	:222	:452	1:103	1:232	3↑	ⒻVagrancy H 23k	4	7	65¾	66½	912	1011	Guerin E	125	w	*2.15	82-11	MizClementine125hdSearching1252½HappyPrincess1103	Dull	10
22Aug56-6Sar	fst	1⅛	:482	1:13	1:383	1:52	3↑	ⒻDiana H 28k	4	1	11	43½	914	923	Guerin E	125	w	*1.30	67-18	Searching1222RicoReto113¾BlueBanner1172	Saddle slipped	9
21Jly56-7Jam	sly	1 1/16	:233	:471	1:12	1:43	3↑	ⒻBellerose H 27k	5	2	22½	21½	1½	12½	Guerin E	121	w	4.25	97-12	Parlo1212½Blue Sparkler1251¾Manotick119hd	Drawing clear	7
30Jun56-7Del	fst	1¼	:451	1:101	1:362	2:03	3↑	ⒻDelaware H 156k	4	2	23	3nk	105¼	128½	Anderson P	124	w	7.20	78-14	FlowrBowl1122Mantick122¾OpenSesame113hd	Speed,stopped	15
23Jun56-7Del	gd	1 1/16	:231	:463	1:113	1:44	3↑	ⒻNew Castle 37k	6	7	88½	75¼	1211	1211	Guerin E	120	w	*2.40	80-19	Miz Clementine1162½Searching1201½Myrtle's Jet116½	Tired	12
26May56-7Bel	fst	1 1/16	:223	:451	1:102	1:423	3↑	ⒻTop Flight H 28k	1	3	22	12	1hd	2½	Anderson P	124	w	6.05	95-11	Searchng121½Prlo1241½RcoRto107nk	Held well under weight	10
15May56-6Bel	fst	6f	:224	:461		1:103	4↑	Alw 5000	4	6	56	67	610	512	Guerin E	115	w	3.85	84-13	DarkRuler1173½WhiteKnight1202½Dedicate1202	Dull effort	7
8Nov55-6Jam	fst	1⅛	:473	1:113	1:37	1:504	3↑	ⒻFirenze H 35k	10	3	22	1hd	43	57¾	Guerin E	126	w	3.80	84-15	RareTreat112½Searching118noWhiteCross1081¼	Led briefly	12
22Oct55-7GS	fst	1⅛	:453	1:10	1:353	1:481	3↑	ⒻVineland H 51k	3	5	1hd	1hd	21	64¾	Guerin E	128	w	*1.90	91-10	HighVoltage1173Manotck1181Crsst110no	Tired under impost	18
3Sep55-6Aqu	fst	7f	:23	:463	1:112	1:233	3↑	ⒻVagrancy H (Div 1) 28k	5	5	75¾	64½	3½	32½	Bailey PJ	129	w	*1.05	89-16	Searching1111½BluBnnr1141Prlo1291¾	Led briefly,faltered	11
20Aug55-6Sar	fst	1¼	:491	1:132	1:39	2:042	3↑	Saratoga H 55k	3	1	1½	3½	36½	312	Arcaro E	121	w	*.95e	74-19	Social Outcast1253Red Hannigan1069Parlo1212½	Tired late	5
2Jly55-6Del	fst	1¼	:462	1:112	1:363	2:022	3↑	ⒻDelaware H 151k	10	5	2½	1½	16	13	Guerin E	128	w	*1.00	90-17	Parlo1283Open Sesame1142Clear Dawn1191½	Speed to spare	13
8Jun55-6Bel	fst	1 1/16	:224	:451	1:094	1:414	3↑	ⒻTop Flight H 30k	9	4	52½	31½	11	13	Guerin E	126	w	*2.05	102-11	Parlo1263Gainsboro Girl114½Spinning Top113nk	Drew out	12
1Jun55-6Bel	fst	7f	:23	:462	1:111	1:241	3↑	ⒻGolden Annivrsy H 20k	1	1	1½	21½	2hd	2¾	Guerin E	125	w	4.75	88-14	Dispute114¾Parlo125hdOilPntng107no	Good speed,held well	11
30Oct54-6Jam	sly	1⅛	:474	1:131	1:394	1:532	3↑	ⒻFirenze H 35k	1	1	12	11	16	17	Atkinson T	125	w	*1.70	79-28	Parlo1257Riverina115¾Spinning Top1101¾	Much the best	13
18Sep54-6Aqu	fst	1⅛	:48	1:12	1:37	1:494	3↑	ⒻBeldame H 64k	9	2	11	12½	14	13	Guerin E	116	w	5.00	96-10	Parlo1163Open Sesame1101¾Clear Dawn1141½	Mild hand ride	9
25Aug54-6Sar	fst	1¼	:481	1:13	1:394	2:06		ⒻAlabama 29k	5	1	15	13	15	11½	Arcaro E	121	w	9.30	78-18	Parlo1211½Moonsight1119Open Sesame1113	Long lead,tiring	10
7Aug54-6Mth	fst	1⅛	:46	1:101	1:37	1:501		ⒻMth Oaks 63k	6	5	57¼	610	69½	910	Nash R	121	w	9.20	85-12	Evening Out1172Clear Dawn1212½June Fete113½	Done early	14
28Jly54-7Mth	fst	6f	:22	:452		1:10		ⒻMiss Woodford 24k	6	5	63½	53	32½	22½	Nash R	121	w	20.10	92-11	ClearDwn1122½Prlo1211½EvnngOut118hd	Rallied for placing	10
5Jly54-6Del	fst	1¼	:454	1:101	1:361	2:023	3↑	ⒻNew Castle H 138k	8	3	33½	46	47½	79¼	Nash R	113	w	18.80	80-19	GainsboroGirl1134SunshineNell1262LavenderHll111hd	Tired	20
26Jun54-6Del	fst	1⅛	:471	1:114	1:381	1:512		ⒻDel Oaks 47k	5	4	1hd	13	13	1¾	Westrope J	113	w	21.50	83-16	Parlo113¾OpenSesm1135O'Alson119½	Clear lead,held gamely	13
4Jun54-6Del	fst	6f	:222	:454		1:12		ⒻAlw 4000	5	1	2hd	1½	1hd	21¼	Westrope J	119	wb	*1.60	84-15	Greek Lady1191¼Parlo1191½Level Rippey1161	No excuse	8
12May54-7GS	gd	6f	:223	:454		1:123		ⒻBetsy Ross 38k	11	4	1hd	13	22	33½	Hartack W	111	wb	13.50f	81-19	OnYourOwn1141½Jenjy1212Prlo1111	Set early pace,weakened	16
1May54-3Bel	fst	6f	:23	:471		1:123		ⒻAlw 4000	6	3	53¾	42½	65¼	41	Catalano A	109	wb	*2.70	85-16	GayGreeting109noOldBaaskt1181Indn115no	Rallied too late	9
14Nov53-7Lrl	fst	1 1/16	:232	:47	1:132	1:462		ⒻSelima 57k	4	1	12	1hd	910	914	Boland W	116	wb	3.90	68-22	Small Favor1161Queen Hopeful119hdClear Dawn119½	Quit	11
28Oct53-6Jam	sly	1 1/16	:24	:48	1:124	1:462		ⒻDemoiselle 72k	2	1	12½	11	21½	23½	Boland W	119	wb	12.65	76-21	O'Alison1193½Parlo1194½Case Goods1192½	Faltered	12
17Oct53-4Jam	fst	6f	:24	:473		1:133		ⒻFrizette 19k	11	7	74¾	106	98½	45½	Scurlock D	110	wb	44.80	73-21	IndianLegend110noCaseGoods1193SmallFavr1152½	No mishap	14
18Sep53-5Aqu	fst	5½f	:23	:473	1:001	1:071		ⒻMd Sp Wt	10	7	52¼	11½	16	16	Guerin E	116	wb	*2.00	88-17	Parlo1166Errorless1162½The Tormentil111hd	Easily	12
18Jun53-4Bel	fst	4½f-W	:222	:453		:514		ⒻMd Sp Wt	6	5		3nk	74¼	108	Peters M	116	wb	*1.55	82-10	Talora116hdSunrise Siren116nkThe Tormentil1161	Tired	17
11Jun53-4Bel	fst	4½f-W	:222	:452		:513		ⒻMd Sp Wt	11	5		3½	2hd	21¼	Peters M	116	wb	10.10	90-12	Mainsail1161¼Parlo116¾Boda1161¼	Lacked rally	12
3Jun53-4Bel	fst	4½f-W	:223	:453		:514		ⒻMd Sp Wt	3	10		116	86¾	87	Peters M	116	w	13.30	83-11	Blue Eyes1162½Bonnie Black116hdBunty B.116nk	No mishap	13

Porterhouse

br. c. 1951, by Endeavour II (British Empire)–Red Stamp, by Bimelech

Lifetime record: 70 19 8 12 $519,460

Own.– Llangollen Farm

Br.– Mrs M.E. Person (Ky)

Tr.– Charles Whittingham

4Jly58-7Hol	fst	1⅛	:471	1:11	1:36	1:482	3↑	American H 54k	7	7	77½	79¼	611	57½	Shoemaker W	116	wb	*1.80e	84-16	HowNow1221¼Seaneen116¾EddieSchmdt1203	Never a contender	7
21Jun58-7Hol	fst	1 1/16	:231	:462	1:102	1:413	3↑	Inglewood H 54k	3	8	811	77	68¼	46½	Shoemaker W	118	wb	*1.45e	80-16	EddieSchmidt117noHowNw1223¼SoclClimbr1173¼	No menace	8
31May58-7Hol	fst	5½f	:22	:454	:572	1:033	3↑	Hol Express H 27k	8	9	912	98½	78½	63¾	Longden J	124	wb	*2.70	90-15	HowNow1191½BettyRose113noGoldenNotes114hd	Full of run	9
10Mar58-7SA	fst	1 1/16	:23	:461	1:102	1:42	3↑	San Bernardino H 28k	6	7	76	73	51¼	2hd	Arcaro E	123	wb	*1.75e	94-11	Terrang125hdPorterhouse123½Seann1151¾	Getting to winner	7
1Mar58-7SA	fst	1¼	:452	1:093	1:343	1:594	3↑	S Anita H 135k	5	7	69	56½	47½	36	Arcaro E	120	wb	13.95	95-09	RoundTable1302½Terrang1193½Porterhous1202	Mild late bid	9
15Feb58-7SA	fst	1⅛	:462	1:101	1:343	1:464	3↑	San Antonio H 56k	1	9	99½	99¾	78¼	45½	Arcaro E	118	wb	6.90	97-11	RoundTable1303½MysticEye1081½PromisedLand116½	Late bid	9
1Feb58-6SA	fst	1 1/16	:231	:463	1:11	1:412	3↑	San Pasqual H 27k	2	8	711	41½	32	3½	Longden J	125	wb	*.90e	96-10	Terrang122½Fnd121hdPortrhous1254	Made strong late rally	8
4Jan58-7SA	fst	7f	:221	:444	1:091	1:221	3↑	San Carlos H 60k	9	14	1410	1410	128	2no	Taniguchi G	126	wb	*1.45e	92-11	Seaneen114noPorterhouse126nkMysticEye114½	Closed boldly	14
26Oct57-6Jam	fst	6f	:232	:47		1:112	3↑	Sheepshead Bay H 15k	4	11	1115	1110	117¾	99¼	Valenzuela I	126	wb	7.85	81-17	ByJeepers107nkBunny'sBabe108½AdmiralVee1211	Dull form	11
28Sep57-6Bel	fst	6f	:224	:461		1:104	3↑	Handicap 10000	2	9	99¾	99¾	98¼	86½	Arcaro E	130	wb	*2.10e	88-13	Hastego1161¼Cohoes1201¾Belmont Breeze111hd	Away slowly	9
23Jly57-7Hol	fst	1⅝	:473	1:364	2:014	2:40	3↑	Sunset H 112k	8	6	66½	42¼	33	33¾	Longden J	122	wb	*2.00	87-15	Find119hdEddieSchmidt1093¾Portrhous122nk	Went wide late	10
13Jly57-7Hol	fst	1¼	:452	1:091	1:334	1:583	3↑	Hol Gold Cup H 162k	11	9	95½	44	34½	23¼	Longden J	119	wb	4.40	97-15	Round Table1093¼Porterhouse1192Find1187	Best of others	11
26Jun57-6Hol	fst	7f	:22	:442	1:084	1:211	3↑	Alw 20000	1	4	45½	31	12	16	Longden J	126	wb	*.60	94-17	Porterhouse1266LiberalArt1081¼ElKhobr1187	Drew out fast	4
13Jun57-7Hol	fst	5½f	:213	:442	:563	1:022	3↑	Hol Express H 23k	9	12	115½	95¾	46	12½	Longden J	125	wb	3.60e	104-17	Porterhouse1262½FlightHistory1121½LibrlArt1091¼	Driving	12
25May57-7Hol	fst	1 1/16	:222	:451	1:093	1:402	3↑	Californian 116k	6	12	1012	109	918	817	Longden J	119	wb	*1.20e	76-20	SocialClmbr1191½RoundTbl1054½Fnd119nk	Failed to respond	12
18May57-7Hol	fst	7f	:221	:444	1:09	1:204	3↑	Los Angeles H 55k	3	8	63¼	41½	3nk	15	Longden J	123	wb	*1.25e	96-12	Porterhouse1235Flight History1101Corn Husker119¾	Easily	9
9May57-7Hol	fst	6f	:214	:443	:564	1:09	3↑	Hol Premiere H 28k	9	10	108¾	88½	53¾	31½	Longden J	124	wb	*2.05e	97-13	Find123¾SocialClimbr118¾Portrhous1242½	Best stride late	10
6Mar57-7SA	fst	1 1/16	:23	:462	1:103	1:42	3↑	S Barbara H 28k	5	6	69	54½	44	43½	Arcaro E	123	wb	2.95e	90-11	Pylades1072½Terrang124½Duc de Fer120½	Mild late rally	7
27Feb57-7SA	fst	7f	:22	:444	1:091	1:22	3↑	C J Fitzgerald H 22k	1	10	1012	85¾	78¼	67¼	Arcaro E	126	wb	3.60	86-14	Duc de Fer1201¾Travertine115noTerrang126½	No mishap	10
5Jan57-7SA	gd	1 1/16	:232	:47	1:111	1:421	4↑	San Pasqual H 27k	5	6	67¾	66½	55	33	Arcaro E	126	wb	*2.05	90-14	BattleDance110nkHoneysAlibi1202¾Porterhous1262¼	Rallied	7
26Dec56-7SA	fst	6f	:224	:45		1:101	3↑	Palos Verdes H 22k	8	8	88½	85¾	34	11¼	Arcaro E	125	wb	*2.50	94-18	Porterhouse1251¼JohniMk119noScnt1191¾	Under mild urging	8
8Oct56-7Bel	fst	7f	:224	:462	1:11	1:233	2↑	Vosburgh H 24k	6	12	1210	97¼	87½	64¾	Valenzuela I	123	wb	19.15	87-16	SummerTan1241½JoeJones121½LeBeauPrince121nk	Late rally	15
15Sep56-7Bel	fst	1	:224	:453	1:094	1:351	3↑	Sysonby H 28k	2	4	44	51¼	811	99¼	Valenzuela A	117	wb	3.90	89-08	Jet Action114hdAdmiral Vee1091Midafternoon116nk	Tired	10
3Sep56-7Bel	fst	6f-WC	:22	:442		1:09	2↑	Fall Highweight H 30k	4	16		1411	126¾	84	Westrope J	137	wb	5.30	90-09	Impromptu127½Decimal122nkGayWarrior1141½	Closed ground	16
28Jly56-8AP	fm	1 3/16 Ⓣ	:463	1:103	1:361	1:541	3↑	Arlington H 154k	1	9	1016	1011	1011	99¼	Erb D	118	wb	*2.70e	93-06	Mister Gus1181Summer Tan1221¼Sir Tribal1221	No mishap	12
14Jly56-8Hol	fst	1¼	:452	1:09	1:331	1:583	3↑	Hol Gold Cup H 162k	2	4	57½	47	38	33¼	Westrope J	119	wb	*5.45e	102-05	Swaps1302MisterGus1171¼Porterhous1192¼	Finished stoutly	7
7Jly56-7Hol	fst	6f	:222	:451	:571	1:09	3↑	Lakes &Flowers H 27k	7	5	63¼	53½	33	11½	Valenzuela I	124	wb	*1.70	99-13	Portrhous1241½Scnt120hdMoolhBux1202¼	Driving,drew clear	7
9Jun56-7Hol	fst	1	:222	:451	1:084	1:331	3↑	Argonaut H 52k	4	4	43	46½	48	37¼	Valenzuela I	119	wb	9.95	101-07	Swaps1281¼BobbyBrocato1236Porterhous1192¾	Finished well	6
26May56-7Hol	fst	1 1/16	:23	:453	1:092	1:404	3↑	Californian 109k	4	3	34½	33½	23	1hd	Valenzuela I	118	wb	13.35e	98-11	Porterhous118hdSwps1275MstrGus1181¾	Up in final strides	6
11May56-7Hol	fst	6f	:22	:444	:57	1:091	3↑	Hol Premiere H 28k	5	11	84	64¾	53¾	2½	Longden J	118	wb	*2.15e	97-10	Cyclotron112½Porterhouse1181OnTonTony1121¼	Gaining fast	12
7Mar56-7SA	fst	1 1/16	:224	:46	1:102	1:43	3↑	S Barbara H 27k	4	6	44½	52½	32	1¾	Arcaro E	116	wb	2.10	89-17	Porterhouse116¾Colonel Mack113½Cyclotron1097	Drew clear	6
29Feb56-7SA	fst	7f	:221	:444	1:092	1:222	3↑	C J Fitzgerald H 23k	2	9	94½	115¾	58½	33½	Arcaro E	124	wb	*2.55	87-14	ColonelMack1131½Cyclotron1122Porterhous124nk	Late rally	11
11Feb56-7SA	fst	1⅛	:47	1:111	1:363	1:49	3↑	San Antonio H 59k	11	10	1012	911	812	77½	Arcaro E	117	wb	4.75e	88-16	MisterGus120nkHoneysAlibi116noBobbyBrocato1246½	Outrun	13
1Feb56-7SA	fst	7f	:222	:45	1:102	1:224	3↑	San Carlos H 23k	6	3	54¾	53¾	42¼	11	Arcaro E	119	wb	*1.80	89-17	Porterhouse1191Karm1102¼HckoryStck109hd	Just up,driving	10
10Jan56-7SA	fst	6f	:223	:453		1:101	4↑	Alw 7500	3	8	76	65¼	53¾	1nk	Arcaro E	124	wb	3.05	94-12	Porterhouse124nkDuece Admiral1081¼Steven Mc1131	Just up	8
26Dec55-7SA	sl	6f	:222	:454		1:104	3↑	Palos Verdes H 23k	3	8	53¾	68	89¾	1214	Arcaro E	120	w	6.65	77-15	History Book1131Karim1155Hour Regards1112	Stopped badly	12
16Jly55-7Hol	fst	1¼	:452	1:092	1:341	1:593	3↑	Hol Gold Cup H 137k	4	3	34	55	611	613	Neves R	122	wb	2.50e	88-06	Rejected118noAlidon116¾Determine1264	Done early	6
4Jly55-8Hol	fst	1⅛	:463	1:10	1:342	1:463	3↑	American H 53k	3	2	21½	42½	53	43	Neves R	114	wb	1.50e	104-06	Alidon116noMisterGus1141¼Rejectd1181¾	Lacked late rally	6

18Jun55- 7Hol fst 7f :214 :44 1:082 1:211 3↑ Lakes &Flowers H 28k 4 7 43½ 35 23 11¾ Longden J 116wb 3.40 94-09 Porterhouse116 1¾Berseem126noAlidon119no Saved ground 10
28May55- 7Hol fst 1 :22 :443 1:093 1:344 3↑ Argonaut H 55k 4 5 58¼ 52¼ 65½ 64¾ Neves R 114wb 3.55e 96-09 Alidon113¾Mister Gus116nkRejected118¾ Gave way 9
21May55- 6Hol fst 7f :222 :443 1:081 1:20 3↑ Handicap 15000 1 3 2½ 32 23 24½ Valenzuela I 115wb 7.35 101-06 ElDrag1154½Porterhouse115hdDetermine1283¾ No late speed 7
13May55- 7Hol fst 6f :22 :444 1:09 3↑ Hol Premiere H 28k 4 7 62¼ 51½ 33 32¾ Neves R 119wb 5.70 97-11 El Drag1122¼Berseem128½Porterhouse1191 Closed ground 9
13Apr55- 7GG fst 6f :223 :452 1:092 3↑ Handicap 5000 4 3 22 22 23 32¼ Longden J 118wb *1.50 92-14 Scent1111¼Poona II1231Porterhouse1181¾ Held on well 5
9Mar55- 7SA fst 1 1/16 :233 :454 1:10 1:42 3↑ S Barbara H 28k 1 10 109 109 79 69½ Boland W 120wb 3.95 84-12 Berseem1201½Joe Jones1174Dawn Lark107½ Dull effort 10
26Feb55- 7SA gd 1¼ :46 1:102 1:363 2:03 3↑ S Anita H 149k 6 2 1hd 1hd 21 33¼ Boland W 112wb 19.80e 82-19 PoonaII1132½JoeJones117¾Porterhouse1121¼ Held on gamely 15
16Feb55- 6SA sly 1 1/16 :233 :472 1:123 1:451 4↑ Alw 7500 2 3 21 2½ 21½ 37½ Boland W 118wb *1.55 70-22 MyChief1124½DoubleReigh1153Porterhouse1183½ Weak rally 7
2Feb55- 7SA fst 7f :222 :452 1:101 1:222 3↑ San Carlos H 23k 4 4 44½ 56 31½ 1¾ Arcaro E 115wb 3.30e 91-16 Porterhouse115¾Imbros1301¾Encono1142 Hard drive 11
25Jan55- 6SA fst 6f :214 :442 1:091 4↑ Alw 5000 7 4 32½ 32 22 2nk Arcaro E 121 w *1.15 99-13 Hour Regards115nkPorterhouse121¾Karim1181½ Game try 8
14Jan55- 6SA fst 6f :22 :443 1:09 4↑ Alw 6000 5 6 31½ 23 21½ 1¾ Arcaro E 114 w *1.00 100-11 Porterhouse114¾Hour Regards1173½Fleet Khal109½ Drew out 12
28Dec54- 7SA fst 6f :22 :442 1:09 3↑ Palos Verdes H 23k 9 9 911 99½ 89 53 Boland W 115 w 13.20 97-08 Imbros128¾Bersm1241¾Hour Regards110no Impeded,bore in 13
27Oct54- 6Jam fst 6f :23 :454 1:114 3↑ Interborough H 30k 9 8 107¼ 1211 1615 1610 Boland W 111 w 21.85 78-23 Laffango116noDark Peter119nkSquared Away120¾ No threat 17
18Oct54- 5Bel fst 1 1/16 :24 :474 1:13 1:443 Alw 5000 2 2 2hd 1hd 1hd 22 Boland W 120 w *.60 86-17 Bill Cane1152Porterhouse1205Dan Giddings1096 Tired 6
11Oct54- 6Bel fst 7f :221 :452 1:11 1:234 2↑ Vosburgh H 25k 7 8 84¼ 75½ 63¼ 42¼ Boland W 112 w 17.15 89-16 JoeJones1162PetBully134nkHyphasis111hd Rallied too late 12
22Sep54- 6Bel gd 6f-WC :224 :461 1:111 2↑ Fall Highweight H 25k 3 10 125¼ 75¼ 64½ 56 Boland W 122 w 8.60 79-21 PetBully1361½DutchLane1171½DarkPeter125½ Lacked a rally 14
10Jly54- 6Mth fst 1 1/16 :231 :461 1:104 1:434 Lamplighter H 25k 11 12 1213 128¾ 127¾ 106¾ Nichols J 122wb 11.40e 89-10 Artismo120nkCoastal Light111nkPelouse105½ Dull effort 12
3Jly54- 6Aqu fst 1¼ :50 1:15 1:40 2:05 Dwyer 57k 4 3 33 45 46½ 412 Boland W 114wb 6.65 70-14 High Gun1261Palm Tree1145Paper Tiger1146 No late foot 5
28Jun54- 5Aqu fst 1 1/16 :24 :481 1:144 1:473 Alw 7500 4 3 43½ 53½ 44 35¾ Boland W 113 w 4.10 70-23 [D]PalmTree1131¾PaperTgr1134Portrhous1132½ No late rally 6
Placed second through disqualification
21Jun54- 6Aqu fst 7f :222 :45 1:102 1:233 Shevlin 31k 2 8 75¾ 44 87¼ 88½ Boland W 116wb *2.05e 83-18 QuickLunch111nkRevolt111½DucdeFr111¾ No apparent mishap 13
12Jun54- 6Bel fst 1½ :49 1:14 2:033 2:304 Belmont 125k 9 2 32½ 33½ 610 917 Boland W 126wb 9.30 67-16 High Gun126nkFisherman1265Limelight1263 Quit badly 13
Geldings not eligible
5Jun54- 6Bel fst 1⅛ :501 1:151 1:40 1:522 Peter Pan H 36k 4 3 31½ 32 64½ 67¼ Boland W 126wb *1.30 70-20 HighGun1163Fisherman1211¾DvngBord1161½ Early foot,tired 7
15May54- 5Bel fst 6f :223 :453 1:111 3↑ Handicap 6070 7 7 54½ 55¾ 43½ 1hd Boland W 114wb *1.40 93-11 Porterhouse114hdHilarious1221¼Caesar Did1131 Just up 9
24Feb54- 5SA fst 6f :214 :443 1:091 Alw 6000 1 6 55 33½ 2hd 13 Boland W 122 w *1.05 99-09 Porterhouse1223Rolyat1113½Musselshell114no Drew clear 8
17Oct53- 6Pim fst 1 1/16 :23 :464 1:104 1:451 Pim Futurity 72k 4 4 37 313 416 524 Boland W 122wb *.40e 60-19 Errard King1228War Doings1226Nirgal Lad1197 Poor start 5
Geldings not eligible
3Oct53- 5Bel fst 6½f-W :221 :451 1:092 1:16 Futurity 117k 14 3 2hd 13 13¼ Boland W 122wb 7.05 92-11 Porterhouse1223¼Artismo122½Best Years1221¼ Easily 14
Geldings not eligible
28Sep53- 5Bel fst 6f-WC :221 :45 1:101 Sp Wt 10000 2 11 43 21½ 1hd Boland W 118wb 9.35 90-10 Porterhouse118hdBy Jeepers1181½Athenian118no Hard drive 13
15Aug53- 4Sar fst 6f :224 :462 1:124 Sar Spl 17k 4 3 31½ 22 11 1½ Guerin E 122 w *1.30 84-20 [D]Porterhouse122½Turn-to1224½Permian1222¼ Bore in 5
Disqualified and placed last
24Jun53- 5Del fst 5½f :214 :46 1:051 ©Christiana 15k 2 5 21½ 23 2½ 11¼ Boland W 125 w 4.75 96-13 Prtrhouse1251¼WarofRoses113noTroyWght1161¼ Drew clear 8
10Jun53- 6Bel fst 5f-WC :222 :451 :574 ©Nat'l Stallion 30k 4 3 22 1hd 1nk Boland W 117wb 5.45 90-11 Porterhouse117nkBest Years122½Catspaw1221 Hard drive 8
Geldings not eligible
2Jun53- 4Bel fst 4½f-W :223 :454 :52 ©Md Sp Wt 14 5 72¾ 1½ 13 Boland W 118 w 3.55f 89-14 Porterhouse1183Affrighted1183First Watch113¾ Drew clear 22
23May53- 4Bel sly 5f-WC :23 :47 1:002 ©Md Sp Wt 7 12 127¾ 1011 75¾ Westrope J 118 w 18.40 71-22 Coreopsis1181½Landscaping118nkBlue Skies118¾ No speed 16

Pucker Up

b. f. 1953, by Olympia (Heliopolis)–Lou Lea, by Bull Lea **Lifetime record: 32 16 8 4 $304,585**

Own.– Mrs A.L. Rice
Br.– Danada Farm (Ky)
Tr.– J.P. Conway

19Jly58- 6Del fst 1 1/16 :231 :462 1:104 1:441 3↑ ⒻNew Castle 38k 14 3 42½ 44 1313 1413½ Brooks S 126wb 8.50 76-17 Alanesian1123Mlle.Dianne112¾Endin112½ Stopped to a walk 15
10Jly58- 6Del fst 6f :222 :454 1:11 4↑ ⒻAlw 4500 5 6 31 3nk 1hd 1½ Brooks S 121wb 1.50 90-15 PuckerUp121½Bornastar1212½Slx118hd Under a strong drive 6
28Jun58- 7Del fst 6f :221 :45 1:094 4↑ Alw 6000 3 3 12 2hd 2hd 22½ Brooks S 119wb *1.20 93-13 Besomer1182½Pucker Up1191½Ricci Tavi1241 Went wide late 7
7Jun58- 8Was fst 1 :222 :451 1:10 1:354 3↑ ⒻBeverly H 58k 13 1 11½ 13 2hd 22½ Grant H 122wb *2.10 85-16 Bornastar1212½PuckerUp1221¼Burdett104¾ Clear lead,tired 14
2Jun58- 7Was sl 6f :23 :463 1:113 3↑ ⒻAlw 5000 4 1 11½ 12 2hd 22 Burr C 121wb *.80 85-29 Bornastar1172PuckerUp1216BonnieA.108nk Used up in pace 6
12May58- 7GS fst 6f :222 :454 1:104 4↑ Alw 6000 6 2 1hd 1hd 11½ 12 Grant H 112wb *1.20 90-16 PuckerUp1122Irate1103½SundayPtch107nk Under mild urging 8
5Mar58- 7GP fst 6f :221 :45 1:10 3↑ Armed H 11k 8 4 2hd 1hd 22 53 Erb D 118wb *1.95 92-10 JovialJove114noGrekGm114noAron1142½ Used vying for lead 13
24Feb58- 7Hia fst 6f :221 :452 1:112 4↑ ⒻAlw 7500 5 3 3nk 2½ 1hd 2½ Erb D 118wb *.70 87-14 HappyPrincess115½PuckerUp118¾Scansion1121½ Game effort 8
24Oct57- 6Kee gd 1⅛ :463 1:111 1:361 1:491 3↑ ⒻSpinster 76k 2 2 22 2½ 22 22½ Shoemaker W 123wb *.40e 88-12 Bornastar1232½Pucker Up1231¾Searching1231 No excuse 6
Open to 3-, 4- and 5-year-olds
17Oct57- 0Kee sly *7f 1:272 3↑ ⒻAlw 5000 1 1 16 14 14 11½ Heckmann J 126wb - 91-13 Pucker Up1261½Bornastar1204Beautillion117¾ In hand 4
Special race - Run between 4th and 5th races. No wagering
21Sep57- 7Bel fst 1⅛ :45 1:093 1:36 1:492 3↑ ⒻBeldame H 69k 4 2 22 31½ 21½ 1nk Shoemaker W 125wb *1.90 92-13 PuckerUp125nkPlotter119nkGayLf1041 Wide on turn,just up 16
2Sep57- 8Was fst 1 :222 :45 1:094 1:344 3↑ Wash Park H 117k 8 1 11½ 13 11½ 13 Shoemaker W 111wb 5.10 93-15 Pucker Up1113Find122½Swoon's Son130½ Good lead all way 9
24Jly57- 8AP sl 1 :23 :453 1:103 1:37 3↑ ⒻArl Matron H 57k 13 2 11 15 14 12 Shoemaker W 120wb 1.70 87-18 Pucker Up1202Bornastar1114½Lady Swords1084 Mild urging 13
29Jun57- 7Del fst 1¼ :463 1:11 1:372 2:05 3↑ ⒻDelaware H 164k 1 1 16 12 1½ 2½ Shoemaker W 117wb *3.70 76-22 Princess Turia119½Pucker Up1171Little Pache119nk Gamely 19
6Jun57- 7Hol fst 1 :222 :45 1:091 1:343 3↑ ⒻHandicap 15000 2 1 13 14 16 16 Shoemaker W 122wb *.90 93-13 PuckerUp1226SunnyGal105noTripleJay1162 Speed in reserve 8
21May57- 7Hol fst 6f :221 :444 :563 1:091 3↑ ⒻMilady H 21k 3 2 21½ 21½ 21 2nk Taniguchi G 120wb *.80 98-19 Coverit118nkPucker Up1207Myrtle1071 Very strong finish 6
10May57- 7Hol fst 6f :221 :451 :57 1:084 3↑ ⒻHandicap 12000 6 5 3½ 2½ 2½ 2¾ York R 118wb 2.50e 99-09 MissTodd122¾PuckerUp1186½Beautillion116½ Held on gamely 9
27Mar57- 7GP fst 1 1/16 :232 :464 1:111 1:422 3↑ ⒻSuwannee River H 28k 8 3 1hd 11 31 33¼ Arcaro E 114wb *1.60e 95-12 Estacion1091¾Amort1211½PuckrUp114hd Bore out when urged 9
13Feb57- 7Hia fst 7f :224 :452 1:102 1:231 3↑ ⒻColumbiana H 24k 9 5 11½ 12 2½ 34¼ Atkinson T 119wb *.70e 90-15 Amoret116nkQuenHopful1194PuckrUp119nk Early speed,tired 10
6Feb57- 7Hia fst 6f :214 :45 1:093 4↑ ⒻAlw 7500 6 2 1hd 1hd 12 12½ Atkinson T 109wb 3.60 97-11 PckrUp1092½Amoret1132½SupremJoy112½ Cleared with ease 10
18Jan57- 8Hia fst 6f :222 :454 1:104 4↑ ⒻAlw 10000 6 2 41 31½ 43 74½ Martin RJ 118wb *1.75 86-12 Myrtle'sJet118½Glamour1181¼OlympiaDell118nk Speed,tired 11
12Oct56- 7GS fst 1 1/16 :24 :47 1:102 1:422 ⒻJersey Belle 29k 6 1 13 110 111 112 Anderson P 118wb 6.00 98-12 PuckerUp11812LittlePache115hdPrincessTuria1211 Eased up 8
1Oct56- 7Bel fst 1 :224 :461 1:112 1:37 3↑ ⒻMaskette H 29k 7 3 31½ 21 22 32½ Arcaro E 112wb 5.25 86-15 Searching123½HappyPrincess1072PckrUp112¾ Raced evenly 11
19Sep56- 6Bel fst 6f :222 :46 1:113 3↑ ⒻHandicap 7500 3 3 11½ 13 13 12 Arcaro E 118wb *.90 91-14 PuckerUp1182Tarquilla1162Equableu114no Speed in reserve 11
8Aug56- 7Was fst 7f :214 :441 1:093 1:222 ⒻMisty Isle H 22k 7 1 2½ 2½ 11½ 1hd Erb D 116wb 3.10e 93-11 PuckrUp116hdDoubledogdare1246CandyDsh1192½ Just lasted 9
18Jly56- 6AP fm 5½f(T) :223 :453 :58 1:042 Alw 6000 1 6 11 2hd 11 1¾• Erb D 113wb 2.00 97-06 [DH]PckrUp113[DH]TobyB.120¾Tommy'sJt1141½ All out to last 7
15Jun56- 6Bel fst 6f :233 :46 1:11 ⒻAlw 4500 6 4 13½ 12 1½ 1½ Arcaro E 119wb *1.30 94-14 PuckerUp119½Recherche115¾Bolette1196 Well rated,driving 7
30May56- 5Bel fst 7f :222 :453 1:104 1:241 ⒻAlw 4000 3 2 12 13 13 11½ Arcaro E 119wb *2.00 89-09 PuckerUp1191½FlyingTrapeze1134½PalaceDancr1141½ Driving 9
18May56- 6Bel fst 6f :223 :461 1:113 ⒻAlw 4000 13 4 1hd 2hd 12 11½ Arcaro E 114wb 2.35 91-13 Pucker Up1141½Flying Trapeze1133½Tweetsie1121 All out 13
10May56- 6Jam fst 6f :23 :463 1:123 ⒻAlw 4000 1 3 2hd 31½ 32½ 34¼ Arcaro E 115wb *1.95 80-21 HideOut116¾EthelWalker1163½PuckerUp1158 Blocked early 8
11Oct55- 5Bel fst 6f-WC :22 :45 1:102 ⒻMd Sp Wt 6 1 12 12½ 17 Guerin E 115wb *1.55 87-13 PuckerUp1157Dupatta115nkStolenHour1152¾ Drew out easily 10
28Sep55- 5Bel sly 6f-WC :224 :46 1:121 ⒻMd Sp Wt 2 5 21 3½ 45¼ Moreno H 115 w 11.15 73-22 Countess Tina115¾Navira1151Tug Boat1153½ Speed,tired 18

Quill

ch. f. 1956, by Princequillo (Prince Rose)–Quick Touch, by Count Fleet

Lifetime record: 26 14 4 2 $382,041

Own.– R.N. Webster
Br.– R.N. Webster (Ky)
Tr.– L. Laurin

29Jly61- 6Del	gd 1¼	:46 1:11 1:362 2:022 3↑	ⒻDelaware H 159k	9 8 1011 89¼ 714 916	Ussery R	123	b	4.70	74-20	AirmansGuide1213½RoyalNative120nkTrtom1182½ Poor effort	12
22Jly61- 6Del	fst 1 1/16	:231 :47 1:113 1:434 3↑	ⒻNew Castle 38k	11 9 1411 1312 1116 1112	Leonard J	120	b	*2.70	78-21	Airmans Guide1166Tritoma1201¾Mountain Glory1121 Dull	15
8Jly61- 6Aqu	fst 1	:224 :453 1:102 1:354 3↑	ⒻAlw 6500	5 3 51¾ 32 2½ 1¾	Ussery R	118	b	*1.10	89-13	Quill118¾Rash Statement1184½Stretch Drive1181½ Driving	7
26Jun61- 6Bel	fm 7fⓉ	:232 :47 1:114 1:244 3↑	ⒻAlw 5000	4 7 89 53½ 21 1¾	Ussery R	114	b	*2.00	88-14	Quill114¾Shuett106¾Pocosb1151½ Won easily,returned sore	8
14Jun61- 7Bel	fst 7f	:222 :453 1:103 1:233 3↑	ⒻVagrancy H 24k	6 12 65¼ 1412 149½ 147	Ussery R	123	b	10.25	82-15	Sun Glint116noUndulation116½Refute113hd Bore out late	14
3Jun61- 6Bel	fst 6f	:222 :454 1:102 4↑	ⒻAlw 10000	8 9 912 913 911 814	Ussery R	123	b	3.05	81-13	Improve1144Refute1143¼Repetitious114nk Slow start,wide	9
22Aug60- 7Sar	fst 1⅛	:471 1:113 1:374 1:512 3↑	ⒻDiana H 38k	1 3 410 47½ 33½ 27	Ussery R	128	b	*.55	81-14	Tempted1247Quill1281¾Aesthetic1121 Showed a game effort	5
30Jly60- 6Del	sly 1¼	:461 1:103 1:364 2:022 3↑	ⒻDelaware H 146k	7 4 48½ 11½ 15 19	Ussery R	125	b	5.90	90-15	Quill1259RoyalNative1291¼GeecheeLou110¾ Drew out easily	8
23Jly60- 6Del	fst 1 1/16	:23 :46 1:102 1:431 3↑	ⒻNew Castle 35k	4 5 47 44½ 43½ 11¼	Ussery R	120	b	*1.60	95-11	Quill1201¼IndnMd1201¾Tmptd1262¼ Under very strong drive	8
9Jly60- 7Mth	fst 1 1/16	:224 :461 1:11 1:434 3↑	ⒻMolly Pitcher H 28k	6 9 66½ 42 43½ 24	Ussery R	122	b	3.50	82-17	Royal Native1274Quill1221¾Miss Orestes114½ Held on well	10
2Jly60- 8Mth	fst 1 1/16	:232 :47 1:111 1:434 4↑	Alw 6000	2 2 1½ 11 11 13½	Blum W	116	b	*.70	86-15	Quill1163½Ideology1155Alsvider1152 Speed to spare	7
4Jun60- 7Bel	fst 1 1/16	:223 :452 1:102 1:43 3↑	ⒻTop Flight H 56k	2 2 21½ 41¾ 33 21½	Ycaza M	123	b	3.25	87-15	RoyalNatv1261½Qull123¾BugBrush1202 Showed a game effort	10
16May60- 7Aqu	fst 1	:241 :482 1:134 1:384 4↑	ⒻAlw 7500	8 3 31½ 32 1½ 13½	Ycaza M	114	b	*.65	82-14	Quill1143½Meticulous1222Starlet Miss1081½ Much the best	8
11Jly59- 6Del	gd 1⅛	:48 1:132 1:383 1:513	ⒻDel Oaks 47k	8 3 44 45½ 57 510	Ussery R	119	b	4.20	72-21	Resaca1192SilverSpoon119½IndianMaid1194 Gave way early	9
20Jun59- 6Bel	fst 1¼	:461 1:104 1:363 2:022	ⒻC C A Oaks 91k	7 1 2½ 21 22 2½	Bailey PJ	121	b	*.25	87-11	Resaca121½Quill12114Czarina1215 Came again in stretch	8
3Jun59- 7Bel	fst 1⅛	:46 1:103 1:361 1:492	ⒻMother Goose 28k	5 3 33 1hd 13 13½	Bailey PJ	124	b	*.45	89-09	Quill1243½Toluene1181½GeecheeLou112¾ Drew out with ease	8
16May59- 7Bel	fst 1	:231 :463 1:12 1:373	ⒻAcorn 59k	2 5 32½ 31 11 16½	Ussery R	121	b	*1.85	86-16	Quill1216½Cobul1211½HopeIsEtrnl121½ Drew away with ease	12
7May59- 7Jam	fst 1 1/16	:241 :482 1:13 1:444	ⒻAlw 1000	5 5 44½ 44½ 44 44¾	Bailey PJ	120	b	1.60	81-17	ShirleyJones114noCobul114¾HighBid1144 Made even effort	7
18Oct58- 7GS	fst 1 1/16	:224 :463 1:114 1:451	ⒻGardenia 135k	7 7 59 23 1hd 1½	Bailey PJ	119	wb	2.20	84-17	Quill119½Resaca1141¼Ruwenzori119hd Under light urging	12
11Oct58- 6GS	fst 1	:231 :464 1:131 1:404	ⒻAlw 10000	3 6 32½ 32 1½ 11½	Bailey PJ	121	wb	*.70	78-23	Quill1211½[D]Canario1141¼JmsonWd114¾ Kept to mild urging	10
13Sep58- 6Bel	fst 6f-WC	:221 :451 1:10	ⒻMatron 64k	9 7 51¾ 11½ 13¾	Bailey PJ	119	wb	3.60	89-15	Quill1193¾RichTradition1192Lvlx1192¾ Drew out with ease	9
5Sep58- 6Bel	fst 6f-WC	:224 :453 1:092	ⒻAlw 5000	2 8 87 43 11	Bailey PJ	111	wb	11.35	92-13	Quill1111MommyDear1191½Recit1124½ Under strong handling	11
22Aug58- 6Sar	fst 6f	:231 :47 1:124	ⒻSpinaway 43k	7 8 99 87½ 53½ 33½	Anderson P	119	wb	11.00	80-21	RichTradition1191½Recite1192Quill1191¾ Best stride late	10
4Aug58- 6Sar	fst 5½f	:23 :473 1:004 1:073	ⒻSchuylerville 18k	9 7 54½ 76 44½ 33¼	Arcaro E	116	wb	*1.70	76-24	RichTradition1162LadyBeGood1221¼Quill1161¼ Forced wide	11
22Jly58- 4Jam	fst 5½f	:23 :471 :59 1:051	ⒻAlw 4200	3 4 32 31½ 1½ 11¼	Arcaro E	116	wb	2.25	92-14	Quill1161¼SitThisOut1163JimsonWeed119¾ Going away	6
11Jly58- 3Jam	fst 5½f	:231 :471 :591 1:053	ⒻMd Sp Wt	9 4 2½ 2½ 2½ 11½	Raia J	115	wb	58.20	90-15	Quill1151½CalaisDover1159AtS1153 Drew clear under drive	9

Real Delight

b. f. 1949, by Bull Lea (Bull Dog)–Blue Delight, by Blue Larkspur

Lifetime record: 15 12 1 0 $261,822

Own.– Calumet Farm
Br.– Calumet Farm (Ky)
Tr.– B.A. Jones

15Aug53- 8Was	fst 1⅛Ⓣ	:482 1:12 1:364 1:493 3↑	Grassland H 28k	11 4 52¼ 56¼ 1019 1113	Arcaro E	122	w	*1.20	84-13	Stan110½Brush Burn1143Vantage115no Wide,quit	11
29Jly53- 7AP	fst 1	:23 :453 1:091 1:352 3↑	ⒻArl Matron H 43k	5 5 32½ 32½ 1hd 11¾	Arcaro E	124	w	*.90	95-13	RealDelight1241¾Fulvous107nkBellaFigura1192 Ridden out	7
18Jly53- 6AP	fst 5½fⓉ	:222 :46 :58 1:043 4↑	Alw 4500	5 9 79½ 78½ 511 47¾	Arcaro E	114	w	*1.20	90-02	Le Monde112hdJo Pilot1114½Recover1093¼ Off slowly	9
13Sep52- 7Aqu	fst 1⅛	:474 1:121 1:38 1:51 3↑	ⒻBeldame H (Div 2) 62k	8 5 54 43 22 1¾	Arcaro E	126	w	*.60	90-17	Real Delight126¾Marta117½La Corredora1123½ Driving,wide	9
2Aug52- 7Was	fst 1	:221 :452 1:093 1:344 3↑	ⒻBeverly H 27k	6 6 63 42½ 21 1hd	Arcaro E	129	w	*.80	95-07	Real Delight129hdAesthete1052Sickle's Image1212 Driving	9
16Jly52- 7AP	fst 1	:23 :454 1:094 1:353 3↑	ⒻModesty H 46k	12 9 85¼ 55 2½ 1hd	Arcaro E	126	w	*.70	94-08	RealDelight126hdSickle'sImage1173½DickieSu1111½ Just up	12
5Jly52- 7AP	fst 1	:222 :452 1:103 1:363	ⒻArl Matron 52k	7 6 65¼ 41½ 12 12½	Arcaro E	126	w	*.40	89-13	RealDelight1262½BellaFigura1122½WhirlaLea1133 In hand	8
16Jun52- 6AP	fst 6f	:222 :45 1:101	ⒻCleopatra 17k	7 6 54½ 33 22 1¾	Arcaro E	121	w	*.40	95-12	RealDelight121¾Recover1152½BellaFigura1123½ Ridden out	10
24May52- 6Bel	fst 1⅜	:483 1:131 1:384 2:174	ⒻC C A Oaks 63k	4 3 11 12 14 12½	Arcaro E	121	w	*.30	82-17	Real Delight1212½Lily White1211½Sufie1214 Easily	10
10May52- 6Pim	fst 1⅛	:492 1:14 1:391 1:514	ⒻBlack-Eyed Susan 24k	3 1 1½ 13 14 14½	Arcaro E	121	w	*.30	95-16	RealDelight1214½Dinewisely121hdParadingLady1216 Easily	5
2May52- 7CD	fst 1 1/16	:232 :473 1:13 1:452	ⒻKy Oaks 31k	5 6 52¾ 32½ 1½ 11¾	Arcaro E	121	w	*.50	91-13	Real Delight1211¾Whirla Lea116¾Big Mo1163 In hand	15
23Apr52- 5Kee	fst 6½f	:223 :454 1:101 1:164	Alw 3000	8 2 52 42 33½ 2hd	Devine D	110	w	*.70	99-06	WhiteSkies117hdRealDelight1104½ShagTails117¾ Late speed	10
12Apr52- 7Kee	fst 6f	:231 :464 1:114	ⒻAshland (Div 2) 14k	6 1 22 2½ 1½ 15	Arcaro E	114	w	*.40	93-12	Real Delight1145Ave1153Level Sands1153 Easily,drew out	7
	Previously trained by H.A .Jones										
22Feb52- 4SA	fst 1	:232 :471 1:12 1:374	ⒻOClm 7500	2 1 11½ 12 14 16	Arcaro E	117	w	*.50	87-15	RealDelight1176NuncaNunca117hdAbbeyGirl1135 Much best	8
8Feb52- 2SA	fst 7f	:223 :454 1:12 1:25	ⒻOMd 7500	9 2 1½ 12 14 16	Brooks S	119	w	*2.20	80-16	Real Delight1196Blue Norka1192½Sea Cap1191 Easily best	12

Rose Jet

br. f. 1949, by Jet Pilot (Blenheim II)–Knots of Roses, by War Admiral

Lifetime record: 11 5 1 2 $132,485

Own.– Maine Chance Farm
Br.– Maine Chance Farm (Ky)
Tr.– J.H. Hayes

8Aug52- 7Sar	fst 6f	:23 :471 1:124	ⒻAlw 4000	7 2 21 1hd 31½ 43½	Woodhouse H	116	w	4.35	80-23	Hadassah111hdNilufer1193Knot Hole109½ Gave way	9
8Jly52- 6Aqu	fst 6f	:224 :453 1:104 3↑	ⒻHandicap 7550	6 4 53 610 612 616	Shuk N	113	w	6.70	82-15	Sunshine Nell114nkJacodema1222½Boot All1143 Outrun	6
	Previously trained by W. Booth										
12Nov51- 7Pim	fst 1 1/16	:233 :472 1:124 1:464	ⒻMarguerite 36k	1 1 1½ 1hd 1hd 35¼	Woodhouse H	116	w	*.40	71-19	No Score1162¼Knot Hole1193Rose Jet116¾ Gave way	7
31Oct51- 6Jam	fst 1 1/16	:241 :481 1:13 1:461	ⒻDemoiselle 50k	7 1 12 11½ 1hd 1¾	Woodhouse H	116	w	*1.80	81-19	Rose Jet116¾Papoose1193½No Score1192 Driving	8
13Oct51- 6Lrl	fst 1 1/16	:23 :48 1:141 1:47	ⒻSelima 50k	2 1 1hd 11½ 1hd 1hd	Guerin E	115	w	*1.40	79-22	Rose Jet115hdFaberose1194½Knot Hole119nk All out	8
29Sep51- 4Bel	fst 6f-WC	:223 :453 1:111	ⒻMatron 56k	14 4 21 1½ 12½	Woodhouse H	119	w	9.15e	85-15	Rose Jet1192½Knot Hole119no[DH]Landmark119hd Drew out	17
5Sep51- 6Aqu	fst 6f	:224 :462 1:123	ⒻAstarita 13k	9 2 2hd 31½ 2hd 31½	Guerin E	119	w	2.30	87-17	Place Card111½Landmark1101Rose Jet1192 Faltered	13
22Aug51- 6Sar	my 6f	:224 :463 1:131	ⒻSpinaway 21k	2 3 2hd 1hd 11 2nk	Guerin E	119	w	*1.05	82-16	Blue Case119nkRose Jet1192Recess1151 Faltered	7
15Aug51- 6Sar	fst 5½f	:224 :461 :593 1:061	ⒻSchuylerville 11k	1 1 1½ 1½ 11 13	Guerin E	115	w	9.25	86-18	Rose Jet1153Star-Enfin122noLandmark113hd Going away	12
9Aug51- 6Sar	gd 5½f	:23 :47 1:002 1:072	ⒻAlw 3500	5 6 73¾ 53¼ 62¾ 63¼	Atkinson T	110	w	2.50	77-18	Level Sands1101¼Strings105hdStar Delight113hd No menace	8
	Previously trained by M. Parke										
18Jly51- 5Jam	fst 5f	:23 :461 :594	ⒻMd Sp Wt	10 4 11 11 11½ 11½	Guerin E	116	w	8.15	91-16	RoseJet1161½GunMoll1163½DustyDarlin1161½ Driving,wide	10

Round Table

b. c. 1954, by Princequillo (Prince Rose)–Knight's Daughter, by Sir Cosmo — **Lifetime record: 66 43 8 5 $1,749,869**

Own.– Kerr Stable
Br.– Claiborne Farm (Ky)
Tr.– W. Molter

Date-Race	Trk	Dist	Fractions	Race	PP	St	1st	2nd	Str	Fin	Jockey	Wt	Odds	Spd	Top finishers	Comment	Fld
31Oct59- 7Aqu	fst	2	:463 2:284 2:55 3:221	3↑ J C Gold Cup 110k	1	2	24	2½	36	27	Bailey PJ	124 b	1.70	--	Sword Dancr1197RoundTable1241¼Tudor Era1242¼	No match	8
10Oct59- 7Aqu	fst	1⅝	:491 1:392 2:041 2:423	3↑ Manhattan H 58k	4	4	41½	31½	1hd	11	Shoemaker W	132 b	*1.55	--	RoundTable1321BaldEagle1221½Coloneast1122	Brisk urging	11
26Sep59- 7Aqu	fst	1¼	:491 1:141 1:40 2:042	3↑ Woodward 109k	3	2	2½	2hd	31½	31¾	Shoemaker W	126 b	*.70	--	SwordDancer120hdHillsdale1261¾RoundTable1265	No excuse	4
19Sep59- 7Atl	fm	1 3/16Ⓣ	:472 1:114 1:363 1:551	3↑ U Nations H 100k	6	2	23	2½	11	11¼	Shoemaker W	136 b	*.80	97-03	RoundTable1361¼Noureddin1173½Li'lFella1201½	Mild urging	10
7Sep59- 8AP	fst	1⅛	:47 1:103 1:35 1:471	3↑ Wash Park H 122k	2	5	56¾	43½	13	16½	Shoemaker W	132 b	*.70	106-04	RoundTable1326½Dunce114¾BelluChf112hd	Under mild urging	6
22Aug59- 8AP	fm	1 3/16Ⓣ	:463 1:102 1:352 1:532	3↑ Arlington H 125k	1	3	34	11	12½	1hd	Shoemaker W	132 b	*.80e	104-02	RndTable132hdManassas112nkNoureddin1092	Strong urging	9
15Aug59- 4AP	sf	1⅛Ⓣ	:484 1:132 1:392 1:514	3↑ Handicap 10000	5	2	21½	21	2hd	1nk	Shoemaker W	132 b	*.80	83-17	RndTable132nkTudorEra1151¾TerraFirma1101½	Hand ridden	5
8Aug59- 8AP	sl	1	:23 :46 1:112 1:37	3↑ Equipoise Mile H 56k	1	7	66¼	68½	36	35	Shoemaker W	132 b	*.90	80-23	BetterBee1151BelleauChief1144RoundTable1322¼	Slow start	10
4Jly59- 8Was	fm	1⅛Ⓣ	:47 1:103 1:35 1:471	3↑ Stars & Stripes H 85k	4	2	22	22	12	13¼	Shoemaker W	132 b	*.70	107-00	RndTable1323¼Noureddn110nkTudorEr117½	Scored cleverly	9
25Jun59- 0Was	fm	1 1/16Ⓣ	:242 :473 1:12 1:423	4↑ Exhibition 4k	3	1	16	110	110	110	Brooks S	b	-	97-07	Round Table010On the Job01Martini II03¼	Speed to spare	4
	Special exhibition purse run between 3rd and 4th races. No weights assigned. No wagering																
13Jun59- 8Was	fst	1	:222 :444 1:091 1:332	3↑ Citation H 56k	2	4	44	41¼	2hd	1nk	Brooks S	130 b	*.90	100-06	RoundTable130nkEtonian1043¼Charli'sSong1122¼	Bore in,up	11
23Feb59- 7SA	sf	1½Ⓣ	:474 1:132 2:062 2:322	3↑ Wash Birthday H 60k	9	5	2½	97¼	1524	1630	Shoemaker W	134 b	*.50e	35-35	Hakuchikar109nkAnsdo1103¾Aorng1071¼	Cut front left heel	16
24Jan59- 7SA	fm	1¼Ⓣ	:453 1:094 1:334 1:582	3↑ San Marcos H 28k	5	1	12½	12	15	15	Shoemaker W	132 b	*.55e	102-00	RndTable1325EddieSchmidt1161AndrewAln115¾	Won in hand	8
3Jan59- 7SA	fst	7f	:224 :45 1:092 1:214	3↑ San Carlos H 56k	4	5	31	2hd	2½	2hd	Shoemaker W	132 b	*1.80	94-12	Hillsdale115hdRoundTable1322¼EddiSchmdt112¾	Closed fast	10
11Oct58- 8Haw	fst	1¼	:463 1:102 1:352 1:594	3↑ Haw Gold Cup H 123k	6	2	21¼	12	12	12¼	Shoemaker W	126wb	*.70	102-02	RndTable1262¼Swoon'sSon1232Ekb113nk	Good lead in hand	6
27Sep58- 7Bel	sly	1¼	:464 1:104 1:353 2:01	3↑ Woodward 111k	1	1	2hd	43½	59½	517	Arcaro E	126wb	*.80	78-13	Clem126½Nadir1202Reneged1269	Had speed 6f,tired	7
13Sep58- 7Atl	fm	1 3/16Ⓣ	:472 1:112 1:362 1:543	3↑ U Nations H 100k	2	4	54	22	21	2½	Valenzuela I	130wb	*.60	105-00	Clem113½Round Table1303Combustion II115¾	No excuse	12
8Sep58- 7Atl	fm	1 1/16Ⓣ	:231 :461 1:112 1:433	3↑ Alw 5000	4	3	33	21½	1hd	12	Shoemaker W	128wb	*.30	95-05	RoundTabl1282St.Vncnt113nkRfty115hd	Eased final strides	7
1Sep58- 8AP	fst	1	:223 :451 1:091 1:34	3↑ Was Park H 139k	3	8	74¾	44½	34	23¼	Shoemaker W	131wb	*2.00e	99-02	Clem1103¼Round Table131noNadir1146	Rallying strongly	9
23Aug58- 8AP	fm	1 3/16Ⓣ	:47 1:11 1:36 1:542	3↑ Arlington H 85k	3	4	43	2hd	1hd	12¼	Shoemaker W	130wb	*.90	99-09	RoundTable1302¼Clem109¾St.Vincent1111½	Drew away easily	8
9Aug58- 8AP	fst	1	:24 :463 1:101 1:344	3↑ Equipoise Mile H 133k	1	8	87	87¼	88½	54	Shoemaker W	131wb	*.90	94-11	Swoon'sSon129½Bardstown122½IndianCrk107½	In close early	10
19Jly58- 8AP	fm	1⅛Ⓣ	:481 1:12 1:363 1:482	3↑ Laurance Armour H 87k	1	3	42½	41½	21½	1no	Hartack W	130wb	*.70e	100-07	RndTable130noClem1103¼HoopBnd1182	Blocked off,just up	10
12Jly58- 8AP	fst	1⅛	:47 1:104 1:354 1:483	3↑ W Wright Mem H 85k	4	5	52¼	1hd	12	2hd	Longden J	130wb	*.30	99-10	Bernburgoo109hdRoundTable1302¼ShnPc1085	Good lead,tired	8
28Jun58- 8Was	fm	1 3/16Ⓣ	:464 1:104 1:362 1:544	3↑ Arch Ward H 56k	3	3	21½	21	11½	12½	Shoemaker W	129wb	*.30e	99-01	RoundTable1292½TallChiefII1152¼Aysha1062¼	Scored easily	9
20Jun58- 0Was	fm	1 1/16Ⓣ	:243 :49 1:141 1:464	3↑ Alw 6000	3	3	33	2hd	11½	12	Valenzuela I	122wb	-	76-31	Round Table1222Bernburgoo1143Black Patch114¾	Easily	5
	Special event run between 3rd and 4th races. No wagering																
7Jun58- 7Hol	fst	1	:231 :461 1:101 1:343	3↑ Argonaut H 53k	2	5	55½	33	32	1no	Shoemaker W	132wb	*.70	93-24	Round Table132noHow Now1165¾Seaneen1203	Up in time	6
24May58- 7Hol	fst	1 1/16	:233 :47 1:104 1:41	3↑ Californian 108k	1	3	34½	32	23	24¼	Shoemaker W	130wb	*.15	86-14	Seaneen1094¼RoundTable1303Terrng1154½	Failed to respond	5
11May58-10AC	gd	1 1/16	:23 :46 1:112 1:411	3↑ Caliente H 51k	2	3	43½	2hd	13½	19¼	Shoemaker W	126 w	*.10	105-15	RoundTable1269¼WarMarshall1051LikeMagic108¾	Easy score	10
22Mar58- 7GP	fst	1¼	:471 1:11 1:352 1:594	3↑ Gulf Park H 110k	4	3	37½	22	1½	14	Shoemaker W	130wb	*.20	100-12	RoundTable1304Meeting111nkOligrchy1112	Speed in reserve	6
14Mar58- 7GP	fst	1 1/16	:232 :462 1:103 1:413	4↑ Alw 10000	4	3	35	21½	1½	13½	Harmatz W	128wb	*.25	102-11	RoundTable1283½Meeting11111Bureaucracy1092½	Easily best	6
1Mar58- 7SA	fst	1¼	:452 1:093 1:343 1:594	3↑ S Anita H 135k	9	3	42	2hd	1½	12½	Shoemaker W	130wb	*.15	101-09	RoundTable1302½Terrang1193½Porterhous1202	Under a drive	9
15Feb58- 7SA	fst	1⅛	:462 1:101 1:343 1:464	3↑ San Antonio H 56k	3	6	42½	1hd	12	13½	Shoemaker W	130wb	*.45	103-11	Round Table1303½Mystic Eye1081½Promised Land116½	Easily	9
25Jan58- 7SA	fst	1¼	:472 1:113 1:362 2:014	S Anita Maturity 156k	5	1	13	11½	13	14½	Harmatz W	126wb	*.20	91-18	Rnd Table1264½Seaneen117¾Promised Land1252¾	Easing up	6
11Jan58- 7SA	fst	1 1/16	:24 :471 1:111 1:421	San Fernando 27k	3	1	13	14	16	14¼	Shoemaker W	130wb	*.25	93-13	RndTable1304¼TheSearcher114½Seaneen124hd	Eased at end	6
28Dec57- 7SA	fst	7f	:231 :454 1:094 1:22	Malibu Sequet 28k	4	6	53	31½	1½	1hd	Shoemaker W	130wb	*.15e	93-11	RoundTable130hdSeaneen1143¼MystcEy122nk	Brisk hand ride	8
9Nov57- 7GS	gd	1¼	:471 1:111 1:364 2:013	3↑ Trenton H 82k	2	2	28	33½	35	310¾	Harmatz W	124wb	1.70	86-14	BoldRuler1222¼GallantMan1248½RoundTable124	Tired badly	3
1Nov57- 0GS	sly	1 70	:23 :472 1:123 1:413	Alw 6000	1	2	21½	1½	15	18	Shoemaker W	126wb	-	89-16	RoundTble1268CommdreCurt11111HoosierHony108	Breezing	3
	Special race run between the 4th and 5th races. No wagering																
12Oct57- 8Haw	fst	1¼	:461 1:103 1:351 2:001	3↑ Haw Gold Cup H 126k	1	2	21½	2hd	1hd	13	Harmatz W	121wb	*.70	102-08	RndTbl1213Swoon'sSon1282½Fnd1192½	Drew clear with ease	6
4Oct57- 0Haw	fst	1 1/16	:232 :472 1:114 1:434	Alw 5000	2	1	11½	13	14	17	Shoemaker W	126wb	-	93-18	Round Table1267Hundred Grand1116Mr. Donmar1111½	Easily	4
	Special race run between the 8th and 9th races. No wagering																
14Sep57- 7Atl	fm	1 3/16Ⓣ	:473 1:12 1:372 1:561	3↑ U Nations H 100k	11	4	1hd	2hd	1hd	1no	Shoemaker W	118wb	*.70	98-02	RoundTable118noTudorEra1122Find1222	Stumbled st.,gamely	11
31Aug57- 8Was	fm	1 3/16Ⓣ	:473 1:114 1:37 1:55	American Derby 145k	8	1	11½	13	13	14	Shoemaker W	126wb	*1.00	98-12	Round Table1264Iron Liege1263½Ekaba1202	Very easy score	8
20Aug57- 0Was	fm	1 1/16Ⓣ	:25 :49 1:13 1:433	Alw 5000	4	1	2½	21½	21	11¼	Shoemaker W	124wb	-	92-08	RoundTable1241¼Ekaba113.52¼MartiniII11215	An easy score	4
	Exhibition race run before 1st race. No wagering																
20Jly57- 7Hol	fst	1¼	:454 1:094 1:344 2:003	Westerner 115k	8	5	31	13	15	12	Shoemaker W	129wb	*.15	90-12	RoundTable1292Irisher110noJoePrice1187	Eased at the end	8
13Jly57- 7Hol	fst	1¼	:452 1:091 1:334 1:583	3↑ Hol Gold Cup H 162k	8	4	2hd	11½	14	13¼	Shoemaker W	109wb	*1.40	100-15	Round Table1093¼Porterhouse1192Find1187	Drew out	11
6Jly57- 7Hol	fst	1⅛	:461 1:102 1:351 1:474	Cinema H 47k	1	2	1½	1hd	14	14	Shoemaker W	130wb	*.20	95-14	RoundTable1304JoePrice1142¾Seanen1092¾	Speed in reserve	7
15Jun57- 7Hol	fst	1 1/16	:231 :46 1:10 1:41	El Dorado H 37k	5	3	21	1½	14	17	Taniguchi G	126wb	*.25	90-16	Round Table1267Joe Price1154Playtown107hd	Easy score	6
30May57- 7Hol	fst	1	:222 :452 1:093 1:342	©Will Rogers 28k	9	1	42½	2hd	13	13½	Neves R	122wb	*.45	94-11	RoundTable1223½JoePrice1182¾Mqult1111¼	Driving,bore out	9
25May57- 7Hol	fst	1 1/16	:222 :451 1:093 1:402	3↑ Californian 116k	4	4	43½	2hd	2½	21½	Neves R	105wb	2.85	91-20	SocialClmbr1191½RoundTbl1054½Fnd119nk	Led between calls	12
4May57- 7CD	fst	1¼	:47 1:112 1:364 2:021	Ky Derby 152k	3	4	43½	42	41	32¾	Neves R	126wb	3.60	93-12	IronLiege126noGallantMan1262¾RoundTable1263	Held well	9
25Apr57- 6Kee	fst	1⅛	:48 1:11 1:343 1:472	Blue Grass 31k	1	1	11½	11½	12½	16	Neves R	126wb	*1.00	108-02	Round Table1266One-Eyed King1212Manteau1211¼	Much best	6
6Apr57- 8BM	fst	1 1/16	:224 :462 1:102 1:413	BM Derby 52k	3	2	12	11	13	14½	Neves R	122wb	1.80	96-13	Round Table1224½Swirling Abbey1226Irisher1221¼	Easily	6
11Mar57- 7SA	hy	1 1/16	:241 :484 1:144 1:491	San Bernardino H 28k	9	2	21½	21½	22	58½	Longden J	122wb	*.65e	49-34	LightningJack112¾MysticEye1113¼RoyalHeir1151	Faltered	9
2Mar57- 7SA	sl	1⅛	:474 1:132 1:414 1:541	S Anita Derby 98k	11	3	33½	22	1hd	3hd	Longden J	118wb	*1.30e	70-30	SirWilliam118hdSwirlingAbbey118noRoundTabl1182½	Ran out	13
	Previously trained by M. Jolley																
16Feb57- 8Hia	fst	7f	:224 :451 1:092 1:222	Alw 5000	6	1	14	16	16	16	Brooks S	126wb	7.05	98-10	Round Table1266Lucky Dip1142½Jet Colonel1235	Much best	9
	Previously owned by Claiborne Farm																
9Feb57- 5Hia	fst	1 1/16	:232 :47 1:112 1:424	Alw 10000	6	5	64	65¾	68½	611	Brooks S	113wb	6.45	90-15	IronLiege1142¼Gen.Duke112hdMssl1244	Could not keep pace	7
19Jan57- 7Hia	fst	6f	:221 :451 1:10	©Hibiscus 26k	7	3	3½	118	118	1010	Brooks S	122 w	10.60	85-09	Gallant Man117½Missile1221½King Hairan1221½	Speed,tired	13
3Nov56- 6CD	fst	7f	:232 :464 1:113 1:25	Alw 7500	9	4	127¾	139¾	136¼	87¼	Brooks S	122 w	*1.00	81-14	Charlie'sSong113nkSrPutnm107nkEkb113hd	Wide most of way	14
20Oct56- 6Kee	fst	*7f	1:264	Breeders' Futurity 66k	4	7	75¼	76½	32	1½	Brooks S	122 w	2.50	99-04	RoundTable122½Missile1221Tranquil122¾	Under brisk drive	10
11Oct56- 5Kee	fst	6f	:224 :454 1:101	©Alw 5000	2	1	23	21½	21½	11½	Brooks S	119 w	*.40	99-08	RoundTable1191½DixieDudley1163CardinalSin1161½	Handily	5
6Aug56- 7Was	fst	6f	:222 :452 1:102	George Woolf Mem 18k	6	-	-	-	-	-	Brooks S	120 w	2.10	--	Smart Phil114hdJet Colonel1175Federal Hill1144		9
	Stumbled leaving gate,lost rider																
21Jly56- 8AP	sly	6f	:223 :46 1:121	Arl Futurity 140k	3	3	32	44½	410	46½	Brooks S	122 w	6.50	76-30	GreekGame1225JetColonel122¾Etonian117¾	Fell back early	7
4Jly56- 7AP	gd	5½f	:221 :454 :59 1:053	Hyde Park 22k	3	5	45¼	47½	310	25	Brooks S	122 w	2.10	85-19	GreekGame1225RoundTable122nkJetColonel118½	Closed fast	8
28Jun56- 3AP	fst	5f	:222 :454 :583	Alw 3500	1	1	4nk	2hd	11½	12	Brooks S	118 w	*.90	97-11	Round Table1182Jet Colonel1181½Kid Jr.1202	Ridden out	6
25Apr56- 6Kee	fst	*4f	:493	Lafayette 20k	1	1		11	1hd	1½	Brooks S	117 w	3.80	99-02	Round Table117½Jet Colonel117hdChookoss1172	Hard urged	9
14Apr56- 3Kee	sly	*4f	:503	Md Sp Wt	1	1		11	11	12½	Brooks S	118 w	*1.20	94-05	Round Table1182½Pandean1188Yonshu113no	Under mild drive	8
24Feb56- 3Hia	fst	3f	:214 :332	Alw 5000	7	5			43	42	Brooks S	116 w	14.50	--	Myla111½OlympiaJet119½LuckyMistake1161	Bumped at start	14

Sheilas Reward

b. c. 1947, by Reaping Reward (Sickle)–Smart Sheila, by Jamestown

Lifetime record: 33 13 12 3 $119,020

Own.– Mrs L. Lazare
Br.– Mrs Louis Lazare (Ky)
Tr.– Charles Feltner

25Jun52- 6Mth	fst	6f	:223 :46	1:104	3↑ Rumson H 18k	2	7	72½	63½	53¼	43¾	Hanford I	124wb	*1.40	90-16	Northern Star1122½Senator Joe115¾War King105½		7
	Wide into stretch,pulled up lame																	
13Jun52- 6Aqu	fst	6f	:23 :463	1:112	3↑ Handicap 7530	4	3	31	2hd	1½	2no	Gorman D	126wb	*1.10	95-14	Delegate118noSheilas Reward1261¼Heap Big Chief1052		5
	Gave way grudgingly;Previously trained by E. Jacobs																	
29Sep51- 6Bel	fst	1⅛	:464 1:114 1:363	1:49	3↑ New York H 29k	4	1	11	2½	25	47½	Gorman D	119wb	4.20	86-15	Hill Prince1285One Hitter1171Sudan1051½	Weakened	8
24Sep51- 5Bel	fst	1	:232 :461 1:102	1:352	3↑ Alw 5000	2	1	11	1½	2hd	2¾	Gorman D	121wb	1.35	96-16	HillPrince121¾SheilasReward1218OneHitter1211½	Gave way	4
10Sep51- 6Aqu	fst	7f	:222 :451 1:101	1:232	3↑ Bay Shore H 18k	11	6	52½	32	2½	1½	Gorman D	126wb	5.85	95-15	SheilasReward126½Guillotine117¾BrynG.123nk	Driving,wide	12
14Jly51- 6Aqu	fst	1¼	:47 1:112 1:364	2:032	3↑ Brooklyn H 57k	5	1	15	15	11½	21	Gorman D	117wb	15.85	89-12	Palestinian1221SheilasRwrd1171¼CountyDlght1244	Weakened	9
10Jly51- 6Aqu	fst	1 1/16	:24 :473 1:113	1:444	3↑ Alw 7500	5	1	2hd	2½	21	32½	Gorman D	116wb	*1.85	87-13	GreekShip1201¾Palestinian120¾ShelsRwrd116no	Drifted out	6
30Jun51- 6Mth	my	1 1/16	:233 :473 1:123	1:464	3↑ Long Branch H 12k	1	1	12	11½	11½	13	Gorman D	118wb	*.90	83-29	Sheilas Reward1183Chains106½Ferd1181¼	Driving	6
23Jun51- 6Aqu	sly	1 1/16	:234 :47 1:111	1:443	3↑ Queens County H 22k	6	1	14	15	13	12	Scurlock O	113wb	2.60	91-12	Sheilas Reward1132Lights Up1212Piet1223	Driving	7
20Jun51- 6Mth	fst	6f	:22 :443	1:094	4↑ Alw 5000	6	3	1½	13	15	18	Gorman D	124wb	*.90	99-08	Sheilas Reward1248Play Toy115hdThe Pincher1242	Easily	6
16Jun51- 7Mth	gd	6f	:223 :454	1:114	4↑ Alw 5000	6	6	54	41¾	31½	2hd	Fernandez F	124wb	*1.70	89-15	JessLinthicum115hdSheilasRwrd1241T-Mkr1242¼	Just missed	8
14May51- 6Bel	fst	6f-WC	:222 :444	1:092	3↑ Toboggan H 24k	3	8		112	114	94½	Arcaro E	122wb	*2.55	89-06	Hyphasis110noTea-Maker1231Casemate1191	Blocked	14
7May51- 6Jam	fst	6f	:23 :461	1:111	3↑ Jamaica H 17k	4	4	2½	2hd	1hd	31½	Arcaro E	124wb	*1.45	89-15	[D]Tea-Maker121½Piet1241Sheilas Reward1242¼	Weakened	7
	Placed second through disqualification																	
1May51- 6Jam	fst	6f	:23 :462	1:11	3↑ Handicap 5030	1	4	2hd	1hd	2hd	21	Atkinson T	124wb	*.75	91-13	Piet1201Sheilas Reward124hdTea-Maker1216	No excuse	6
25Oct50- 6Jam	gd	6f	:23 :46	1:111	2↑ New Rochelle H 17k	11	9	73¼	51¾	21½	21	Arcaro E	124wb	2.65	90-19	MagicWords1131SheilasRewrd124¾Tea-Mkr1252	Good effort	12
12Oct50- 6Jam	sly	6f	:23 :46	1:12	3↑ Interborough H 17k	2	6	75	75¾	43½	1¾	Arcaro E	120wb	*2.55	87-18	SheilasRwrd120¾MgcWords112½WsconsnBoy109nk	Going away	10
3Oct50- 6GS	fst	6f	:222 :45	1:094	3↑ Alw 5000	3	6	43½	66	33	3¾	Fernandez F	122wb	*.60	98-08	EagleRiver112¾AirAttack116hdShlsRwrd122no	Strong finish	10
25Sep50- 6Bel	fst	7f	:223 :453 1:102	1:23	2↑ Vosburgh H 18k	8	5	61¾	41¾	21½	42	Arcaro E	116wb	*2.20	93-15	Tea-Maker1181¼More Sun106½Piet124nk	Faltered	12
18Sep50- 6Bel	fst	6f-WC	:221 :443	1:084	2↑ Fall Highweight H 25k	11	2		2hd	21	75¼	Combest N	135wb	*2.35	92-06	Arise1332Delegate128nkRoyal Governor129½	Tired	14
13Sep50- 5Aqu	sl	6f	:232 :464	1:114	3↑ Handicap 4k	3	1	21	1½	12	14	Arcaro E	122wb	*.80	93-16	Sheilas Reward1224Scipio1112Jacks Town102hd	Easily	5
5Jly50- 6Jam	fst	6f	:224 :453	1:092	3↑ Fleetwing H 22k	7	5	31½	21	21	1hd	Fernandez F	116wb	4.50	104-06	Sheilas Reward116hdGuillotine1156Capot1281	Just up	9
24Jun50- 6Mth	fst	6f	:222 :45	1:094	Select H 12k	5	5	41¾	41¼	1hd	1¾	Fernandez F	116wb	4.20	99-06	Sheilas Reward116¾Hyphasis1122½Fabricate1123	Going away	7
20Jun50- 6Mth	fst	6f	:222 :453	1:11	Alw 4000	5	4	3nk	12	16	17	Fernandez F	124wb	*.50	93-16	Sheilas Reward1247Call Over1181½East Indies121hd	Easily	8
16Jun50- 6Mth	gd	6f	:22 :444	1:101	Alw 6000	3	5	33	2½	22	21½	Stout J	116wb	*1.70	95-10	Casemate1261½Sheilas Reward1166Tea Deb1211	Drifted wide	9
31May50- 5Bel	fst	6f	:22 :451	1:102	Alw 5000	4	5	43¼	21	21½	2¾	Arcaro E	114wb	*1.05	97-13	Guillotine120¾Sheilas Reward1146Detective1131	No excuse	6
27May50- 5Bel	fst	6f	:221 :452	1:103	Alw 4000	6	6	52¼	4¾	1½	11½	Arcaro E	120wb	*.95	97-11	SheilasReward1201½AdmiralDrake1184½ErlyHth111hd	Handily	7
17May50- 4Bel	fst	7f	:222 :453 1:112	1:25	Alw 4000	3	2	1hd	11½	13	11½	Arcaro E	116wb	*.50	85-17	SheilasReward1161½ThasianHero1164KeepRight111no	Easily	10
8May50- 6Bel	fst	7f	:223 :46 1:114	1:244	Swift 12k	8	3	31½	49½	2hd	22½	Rogers C	126wb	32.90	83-17	Ferd1262½SheilasReward126½AdmiralsPrd126hd	Sharp effort	12
3May50- 4Jam	sly	6f	:232 :472	1:124	©Alw 3500	8	3	2hd	12	15	14	Arcaro E	117wb	*.85	87-22	Sheilas Reward1174Erosion123½Teddies Imp120½	Easily	8
28Apr50- 7Jam	sly	6f	:233 :464	1:114	3↑ Sp Wt 3500	6	6	1½	1½	11	2no	Nichols J	116wb	2.55	92-18	RoyalCastle116noSheilsRwrd1165Promptnss1162	Just missed	7
24Apr50- 5Jam	fst	6f	:23 :461	1:113	Alw 3500	8	5	31	21	21	23½	Nichols J	118wb	7.15	89-15	CurtainRaiser1133½SheilsRwrd1183½CupKng1181	Forced wide	9
	Previously trained by T.H. Heard Jr																	
10Sep49- 6Atl	fst	6f	:231 :462	1:131	Alw 3500	6	2	3nk	21	31	34	J'n WL	120wb	4.20	76-21	ThasianHro1202½Conqurnt1201½ShlsRwrd1202½	Weakened,sore	8
31Aug49- 3Atl	fst	6f	:223 :462	1:143	Md Sp Wt	9	1	14	14	11½	1½	Lewis F	113wb	6.00	73-23	Sheilas Reward113½Invariant1172Bambi Lynne120½	Driving	9

Shipboard

ch. g. 1950, by Battleship (Man o' War)–Sea Borne, by Annapolis

Lifetime record: 41 15 6 4 $151,415

Own.– Montpelier
Br.– Mrs Marion duPont Scott (Ky)
Tr.– R.G. Woolf

6Aug59- 5Sar	fm	*2	S'Chase	4:103	4↑ Beverwyck H 16k	2	6	-	-	-	-	Woolfe RG Jr	152	9.70	- -	Frfx1442½Indpndnc1627HghBhn1502	Bad landing at 3rd,fell	6
26Jun59- 5Del	fm	*2½	S'Chase	4:372	4↑ Indian River H 10k	6	7	59	45	-	-	Foot A	153	7.30	- -	MugutII14315Goky1332½Drubn141hd	Unseated rider 15th jump	8
12Jun59- 5Del	fm	*2⅛	S'Chase	4:004	4↑ Georgetown H 10k	3	7	419	38	1½	31	Foot A	154	8.20	- -	Darubini135noIndependence1631Shipboard1544½	Bore out	7
23May59- 6Pur	fm	*1¾Ⓣ		3:023	3↑ Alw 600	2	2	3½	22½	21	2hd	Land H	149	1.65	- -	HighlandLight149hdShipboard1494½CarolinaHlls1498	Missed	4
14May59- 5Bel	sf	*2⅛	S'Chase	4:062	4↑ International H 16k	2	4	616	624	624	626	Foot A	161	6.55	- -	BasilBee1514½Independnc162hdChmbourg1407	Jumped poorly	6
5Jun58- 5Bel	fm	*2½	S'Chase	4:44	4↑ Meadow Brook H 13k	1	5	615	615	613	615	Woolfe R Jr	160 w	3.40	- -	Ancestor1651½Arywa14712Independnc156nk	Trailed far back	6
27May58- 5Bel	fm	*2⅛	S'Chase	4:043	4↑ International H 11k	4	5	513	-	-	-	Foot A	159wb	*1.50	- -	Ancestor162¾Rythminhim14714Pine Shot1432½		6
	Bad landing at 9th,fell																	
21May58- 3Bel	fm	*2⅛	S'Chase	4:151	4↑ Alw 5000	5	5	612	26	-	-	Woolfe RG Jr	158 w	*.85	- -	Pine Shot1467Out of Reach143nkBavaria14319		6
	Bad landing at 12th,lost rider																	
16Oct57- 6Bel	fm	*2½	S'Chase	4:422	4↑ Temple Gwathmey H 57k	1	9	31	41½	44	38	Foot A	164wsb	4.05e	- -	Neji1737Ancestor1601Shpbord1641½	Showed very good effort	12
8Oct57- 5Bel	sf	*3⅛	S'Chase	6:151	4↑ Grand National H 32k	1	5	519	24	48½	48	Foot A	163 w	2.75	- -	Neji1686Independence1501¾His Boots132nk	Made bid,tired	5
19Sep57- 5Bel	fm	*2⅛	S'Chase	4:01	3↑ Broad Hollow H 17k	7	7	46	55½	34	310½	Foot A	162 w	*1.65	- -	Independence1488Morpheus1382½Shipboard1623	Lost irons	7
29Aug57- 5Sar	fm	*2½	S'Chase	5:121	4↑ Saratoga H 22k	6	6	56½	33½	23	1nk	Foot A	161 w	2.05	- -	Shipboard161nkIndependence14610Ancestor15713	Hard drive	6
15Aug57- 5Sar	fm	*2	S'Chase	4:14	4↑ Beverwyck H 17k	1	5	37	312	210	214	Foot A	163 w	2.10	- -	Ancstr15214Shpbrd1633½Morphus14318	Couldn't reach winner	6
28Jun57- 7Del	fm	*2½	S'Chase	4:403	4↑ Indian River H 10k	1	8	624	79	24	23½	Smithwick P	164 w	*3.00e	- -	Rhythminhim1423½Shipboard1644½Carafar147½	Game effort	14
14Jun57- 5Del	hd	*2	S'Chase	3:353	4↑ Georgetown H 10k	5	8	814	852	732	736	Foot A	164 w	*1.50	- -	Morpheus1393½Carafar1477PineShot1372½	Refused to extend	8
17Oct56- 6Bel	fm	*2½	S'Chase	4:42	4↑ Temple Gwathmey H 58k	9	6	69	69½	417	218	Foot A	168 w	*.90	- -	Ancestor14918Shipbord1682Morphus1422½	Passed tired ones	12
8Oct56- 5Bel	fm	*3	S'Chase	5:501	4↑ Grand National H 28k	7	5	415	24	15	112	Foot A	164 w	*1.45	- -	Shipboard16412Glencannon13312HisBoots1341	Much the best	8
20Sep56- 5Bel	sf	*2	S'Chase	3:47	3↑ Broad Hollow H 11k	5	6	42	22	12	1nk	Foot A	164 w	2.15e	- -	Shipboard164nkBasilia1301½Bavaria1542	Held on gamely	8
21Oct55- 6Bel	sf	*2½	S'Chase	4:553	4↑ Temple Gwathmey H 57k	8	11	85¾	42	-	-	Foot A	166 w	*1.70	- -	Neji167¾Rhythminhim1497His Boots1371½		11
	Bobbled at 15th jump,fell																	
13Oct55- 5Bel	fm	*3	S'Chase	5:542	4↑ Grand National H 28k	1	8	66	32	-	-	Foot A	165 w	*1.20	- -	Neji163hdRhythminhim14615His Boots1351½		8
	Went through 17th hedge,fell																	
22Sep55- 5Bel	fm	*2	S'Chase	3:463	3↑ Broad Hollow H 11k	1	4	31½	1½	11	12	Foot A	158 w	*.80	- -	Shipbrd1582Nj1571½Rhythmnhm145½	Won under mild urging	4
25Aug55- 5Sar	fm	*2½	S'Chase	5:063	4↑ Saratoga H 11k	1	3	35½	23½	12½	12	Foot A	160 w	1.75	- -	Shipboard1602Palaja13112½BillingBear132½	Held good lead	5
24Jun55- 0Del	sf	*2	S'Chase	3:56	4↑ Georgetown H 10k	4	5	410	47½	32½	33¼	Foot A	162 w	-	- -	Ancestor148nkCoveted1403Shpbord1623½	Tired under impost	5
	Special event - no wagering																	
16Jun55- 5Aqu	fm	*2	S'Chase	3:453	4↑ Hitchcock H 10k	6	5	35	32	33	22½	Foot A	163 w	*.90	- -	Fulton1322½Shipboard1631Rythminhim1426½	Very game try	7
2Jun55- 5Bel	fm	*2½	S'Chase	4:442	4↑ Meadow Brook H 11k	5	5	330	3nk	14	16	Foot A	156 w	*.60e	- -	Shipboard1566Curly Joe13115Neji15630	Taken in hand	6
21May55- 6Bel	hd	*2½	S'Chase	4:432	4↑ International 21k	4	8	514	48½	-	-	Foot A	150 w	*1.50	- -	Neji15015Ancstor15518Hyvn15518	Threw rider at 15th jump	10
12May55- 5Bel	hd	*2	S'Chase	3:411	4↑ Corinthian H 8.9k	1	6	47	33½	11½	13	Foot A	155 w	1.15e	- -	Shipboard1553Beaupre1363Nej1551½	Bobbled jump,recovered	6
22Oct54- 6Bel	fm	*2½	S'Chase	4:39	4↑ Temple Gwathmey H 16k	1	5	44	33½	-	-	Foot A	151 w	*1.20e	- -	King Commander164¾Neji1497Coveted13170		6
	Stumbled 13th jump,lost rider																	
14Oct54- 5Bel	fm	*3	S'Chase	5:42	4↑ Grand National H 28k	5	6	43	12	13½	12½	Foot A	152 w	*1.25e	- -	Shipboard1522¾Covtd13122CurlyJo13310	Under brisk urging	7

Date	Cond	Dist	Fractions	Race	PP	St	1st	2nd	Str	Fin	Jockey	Wt	Eq	Odds	Spd	Finishers	Comment	Fld
23Sep54- 5Bel	fm	*2	S'Chase 3:44	3↑ Broad Hollow H 11k	4	4	1½	12¼	12	12	Foot A	154	w	1.80	--	Shipboard1542Neji13718Covtd13645	Held lead under urging	5
26Aug54- 5Sar	fm	*2½	S'Chase 5:002	4↑ Saratoga H 11k	5	5	49	35	26	29	Foot A	148	w	*1.25	--	KingCommndr1549Shpbrd14814Covtd1328	Bobbled 8th jump	6
5Aug54- 5Sar	sf	*2	S'Chase 4:172	4↑ Shillelah H 8.8k	7	5	2½	21½	21½	12	Foot A	139	w	*1.35	--	Shipboard1392King Commander14320Coveted13812	Drew out	7
21Jun54- 5Del	hd	*2	S'Chase 3:434	4↑ Tom Roby 12k	1	7	55½	2½	13	14	Foot A	149	w	*2.60	--	Shipboard1494Imbursed130hdCammell Laird1434½	Ridden out	7
21May54- 3Bel	sf	*2	S'Chase 3:56	4↑ Alw 4000	3	3	11½	11½	13	12½	Foot A	145	w	*.85	--	Shipboard1452½Cherwell14520Moot14060	Fully extended	6
13May54- 5Bel	fm	*2	S'Chase 3:482	4↑ Spring Maiden 6.8k	5	4	33	1½	-	-	Foot A	145	w	1.40	--	KingCommander1537IndianFire1402½Covtd15015	Fell at 11th	5
29Apr54- 3Bel	fm	*2	S'Chase 3:462	4↑ Sp Wt 4000	8	5	23	22	21	1½	Foot A	140	w	6.20	--	Shipbrd140½KingCommander14812PacificPact1482½	Driving	11
28Sep53- 3Bel	fst	*1¾	Hurdles 3:132	3↑ Alw 4500	8	9	917	818	719	515	Foot A	132	w	10.10	--	KingCommndr1492½Willimsburg1402RvrJordn1494½	Sluggish	9
25Sep53- 3Bel	fst	*1½	Hurdles 2:43	3↑ Alw 4000	6	6	43½	-	-	-	Foot A	134	w	*2.30e	--	BattlWv1423½Allflor145nkIndnFr1343½	Stumbled,lost rider	11
17Jun53- 3Bel	fst	*1½	Hurdles 2:47	Md 4000	5	8	11	1½	21	11¾	Woolfe RG Jr	140	w	*1.65e	--	Shipboard1401¾Indian Fire1453½Watch Dog1351½	Going away	9
4Apr53- 7Cam	fst	1Ⓣ	1:42	3↑ Alw 400	4	1	1¾	1nk	1nk	11	Woolfe RG Jr	134	w	-	--	Shipboard1341Deadeye1401¾Rewing140nk	Wide,driving	4
21Mar53- 1SoP	fst	*6fⓉ	1:124	3↑ Alw 400	2	4	54¼	57¼	59	49½	Woolfe RG Jr	132	w	-	--	ExtraPoints1433½Escarp1474QueerWednsday1402	No menace	5

Sickle's Image

lt br. f. 1948, by Sickletoy (Sickle)–Ariel Image, by Ariel

Lifetime record: 73 27 13 16 $413,275

Own.– C. Hartwick
Br.– Clarence Hartwick (Ky)
Tr.– C. Hartwick

Date	Cond	Dist	Fractions	Race	PP	St	1st	2nd	Str	Fin	Jockey	Wt	Eq	Odds	Spd	Finishers	Comment	Fld
1Sep54- 7Was	fst	1	:222:443 1:094 1:352	3↑ ⒻBeverly H 28k	10	5	32	33	1217	1222¾	Swain C	121	w	7.20	69-14	Good Call113noVixen Fixit108noLavender Hill1241½		12
Appeared slightly lame after pulling up																		
4Aug54- 7Was	fst	7f	:231:463 1:114 1:244	3↑ Clang H 23k	9	3	44	33½	41	2nk	Fisk B	116	w	7.00	82-12	Precious Stone114nkSickle's Image116½Hi Billee112¾		12
Gamely,forced in late																		
28Jly54- 7AP	gd	1	:222:453 1:102 1:363	3↑ ⒻArl Matron H 34k	8	7	78¾	1013	1113	1120	Fisk B	124	w	4.70	69-14	LavenderHill1153¼VixenFixit1053RosemaryB.111nk	Outrun	12
20Jly54- 6AP	fst	7f	:232:464 1:121 1:251	3↑ ⒻAlw 5000	4	3	21	3½	1hd	52½	Fisk B	122	w	*.80	81-16	Intencion111hdLillal1222Mimi Mine114hd	Tired suddenly	6
10Jly54- 8AP	fst	6f	:22 :45 1:10	3↑ ⒻModesty H 23k	5	3	22	2½	13	12½	Dodson D	118	w	8.30	94-13	Sickle'sImage1182½MimiMine1122½VixenFixit103nk	Driving	13
5Jly54- 7Det	fst	1	:233:472 1:123 1:384	3↑ ⒻTomboy 8.5k	1	3	31½	32	32	32½	Baird RL	122	w	*1.60	88-15	Rosemary B.1061¾Eternal Frolic102¾Sickle's Image122¾		7
Could not rally																		
26Jun54- 6Det	sl	6f	:232:472 1:123	3↑ Alw 2300	4	2	43	46	47	411	Swain C	120	w	2.70	74-25	Epic King1197Fiddle1192½Nocallula1141½	Poor effort	6
19Jun54- 7Det	gd	6f	:231:471 1:124	3↑ ⒻRose Leaves 11k	2	5	31	32½	4¾	65½	Fisk B	122	w	*1.50	78-14	Sharbot110nkSunTanGal1102¼TaskFleet108nk	Tired in drive	8
31Oct53- 6CD	fst	1	:223:452 1:114 1:363	3↑ ⒻFalls City H 11k	9	5	67	79	56	912	Fisk B	123	w	*1.30	82-13	GalaFete1173Cajole1072¾BelleRebelle1061½	Gave way,sore	15
20Oct53- 5Kee	fst	6f	:221:454 1:102	3↑ ⒻAlw 4000	4	5	45	46½	44	33¼	Fisk B	122	w	*1.40	97-08	Flyamanita110nkGalaFete1183Sickle'sImage1222¼	Sluggish	5
7Oct53- 7Haw	sl	6½f	:231:461 1:122 1:19	3↑ ⒻYo Tambien H 16k	3	5	24	25	21½	21	Fisk B	124	w	1.50	84-27	Gala Fete1171Sickle's Image124½Good Call111.51	Weakened	6
14Sep53- 6Haw	fst	6½f	:231:462 1:103 1:171	3↑ Martie Flynn H 10k	7	2	2hd	1hd	1hd	1½	Fisk B	119	w	*1.50	94-18	Sickle'sImag119½CoffMony1111¼Mon-Phro1133	Driving clear	7
7Sep53- 7Was	gd	1	:221:454 1:104 1:364	3↑ Wash Park H 165k	13	2	42	43½	13	1½	Cook WM	106	w	24.00	85-16	Sickle's Image106½Ruhe1163¼Indian Hemp1142	Hard drive	13
28Aug53- 7Atl	fst	7f	:221:444 1:092 1:23	3↑ Alw 6000	3	1	1hd	2hd	1½	11½	Headley O	109	w	*.90	--	Sickle'sImage1091½Halter121½WinningStrid1104	Ridden out	8
20Aug53- 5Atl	fst	6f	:223:461 1:113	3↑ ⒻAlw 5000	4	3	42	2hd	12	15	Headley O	112	w	*.60	87-18	Sickl'sImge1125BlueRhymer1174MssShdow115hd	Easy score	7
15Aug53- 7Atl	fst	7f	:221:452 1:093 1:232	3↑ ⒻMermaid H 18k	2	5	52	53½	43	43¼	Fisk B	118	w	5.60	--	Atalanta1191¼GayGrecque1191WinningStrd1101	Lacked rally	10
29Jly53- 7AP	fst	1	:23 :453 1:091 1:352	3↑ ⒻArl Matron H 43k	7	4	55	46	45	75¼	Fisk B	116	w	6.50	90-13	Real Delight1241¾Fulvous107nkBella Figura1192	Faltered	7
23Jly53- 6AP	fst	1	:23 :462 1:102 1:354	3↑ Handicap 10000	1	4	45½	32½	33	32½	Church K	110	w	3.60	90-16	SubFleet1201¼Jampol1111¼Sickle'sImag1101	Close quarters	8
15Jly53- 6AP	fst	6f	:223:453 1:102	4↑ Alw 4500	3	3	31	44	41½	1¾	Fisk B	112	w	*2.20	92-13	Sickle'sImage112¾Futuramatic120nkAirMail114½	Hard urged	9
8Jly53- 7AP	fst	6f	:214:444 1:101	3↑ ⒻModesty H 17k	9	3	88¼	89¼	84¾	75	Fisk B	118	w	7.10	88-13	BellaFigura1172GalaFete116¾Night-Phara109.5hd	No threat	12
26Jun53- 6Det	sl	6f	:231:471 1:131	3↑ Alw 3000	2	4	23	32	2½	21¾	Fisk B	117	w	2.30	80-29	BlackBantam1131¾Sckle'sImge1171HotPenny111hd	Game try	8
29Nov52- 5Bow	fst	6f	:23 :463 1:114	2↑ Handicap 6045	8	5	74½	76	63¾	32	Gorman D	126	w	*1.10	--	Nullify1071Nimble Fox1071Sickle's Image126¾	Closed well	8
11Nov52- 6Pim	sl	1⅛	:49 1:133 1:394 1:522	3↑ ⒻGallorette 29k	1	2	2hd	1hd	53½	913	Fisk B	123	w	*2.40	79-22	La Corredora1123½Kiss Me Kate1231Marta1173	Stopped	9
1Nov52- 5Pim	fst	6f	:221:453 1:104	3↑ Alw 5000	4	1	31	2½	2½	1hd	Gorman D	121	w	*1.70	97-21	Sickle's Image121hdHi Billee1212½Prop115½	Cleverly	6
18Oct52- 7GS	fst	1 1/16	:23 :471 1:112 1:453	3↑ ⒻVineland H 49k	2	3	33½	1hd	1hd	1¾	Fisk B	120	w	5.00e	82-20	Sickle'sImage120¾KissMeKate118¾LilyWhit111hd	Hard drive	17
13Oct52- 6Jam	fst	6f	:232:46 1:111	2↑ ⒻCorrection H 24k	6	6	41¾	83¼	53	31½	Fisk B	122	w	*1.80e	89-21	QuizSong1101½Landmark116noSickl'sImg122¾	Close quarters	12
8Oct52- 7Haw	fst	6½f	:222:452 1:093 1:16	3↑ ⒻRegret H 11k	4	1	42	52½	1hd	2no	Fisk B	120	w	*.50	102-13	RomanMiss114noSickle'sImge1203½OurRequst1121½	Faltered	6
17Sep52- 7Haw	fst	6f	:222:451 1:093	3↑ Billings H 11k	5	3	52¼	54½	44¼	24½	Adams J	112	w	*1.20	96-09	AndyB.W.1194½Sickle'sImage112noUnbridld109¾	Closed fast	7
6Sep52- 7Haw	fst	6½f	:222:451 1:092 1:16	3↑ Midwest H 18k	4	6	2½	42¼	34	35¼	Fisk B	114	w	*2.40	97-09	Sabaean1122¼Eljay1143Sickle's Image1141½	No excuse	11
1Sep52- 7Was	sly	1	:231:462 1:104 1:364	3↑ Wash Park H 172k	9	3	53¼	33½	22½	33	Fisk B	110	w	11.90	82-15	CraftyAdmiral1282ToMarket1231Sickle'sImag110nk	Faltered	10
26Aug52- 7Was	fst	7f	:222:442 1:083 1:211	3↑ Alw 7500	1	2	21½	31½	21½	1hd	Church K	108	w	3.30	101-09	Sickle'sImag108hdSprtnVlor1233Cyclotron1112	Held gamely	6
13Aug52- 6Was	fst	6f	:222:452 1:093	3↑ Handicap 5000	1	2	4¼	47½	45	32	Arcaro E	115	w	*.90	96-08	Andy B.W.122½Sun David1171¼Sickle's Image115½	No excuse	6
2Aug52- 7Was	fst	1	:221:452 1:093 1:344	3↑ ⒻBeverly H 27k	4	4	31	32	31½	32	Fisk B	121	w	2.60	93-07	Real Delight129hdAesthete1052Sickle's Image1212	Blocked	9
28Jly52- 4Was	fst	6f	:221:453 1:092	3↑ ⒻAlw 4500	6	2	33	23	1hd	11¼	Arcaro E	119	w	*.40	99-08	Sickle's Image1191¼Flyamanita1131Gala Fete1072	Driving	6
16Jly52- 7AP	fst	1	:23 :454 1:094 1:353	3↑ ⒻModesty H 46k	5	3	33	34	1½	2hd	Fisk B	117	w	8.80	94-08	RealDelight126hdSickle'sImg1173½DckSu1111½	Sharp effort	12
2Jly52- 6Aqu	fst	6f	:23 :461 1:111	3↑ ⒻBridal Flower H 10k	8	5	105	74¾	53	32	Fisk B	122	w	*2.15e	94-18	Jacodema1151½SunshinNll110½Sckl'sImg122nk	Strong finish	13
28Jun52- 6Aqu	fst	1 1/16	:25 :49 1:131 1:45	3↑ ⒻVagrancy H 28k	1	1	3nk	22	1½	42¼	Fisk B	115	w	4.95	87-16	Marta117noRenew118¾Valadium1151½	Weakened	8
21Jun52- 7Mth	fst	6f	:214:451 1:112	3↑ ⒻRegret H (Div 2) 17k	2	1	22	21½	2hd	21	Fisk B	122	w	3.10	90-16	DixieFlyer1131Sickle'sImag1221Bob'sBtty1102	Good effort	9
7Jun52- 7Det	fst	6f	:23 :462 1:11	3↑ Alw 5000	2	3	31½	42½	31	22¼	Armstrong S	121	w	*.40	91-14	Pur Sang1202¼Sickle's Image1211¼Radical1132	Good effort	5
30May52- 7Det	fst	6f	:224:46 1:104	3↑ F M Alger Mem 7.5k	4	3	1hd	11	12	12	Fisk B	115	w	*1.10	94-15	Sickle's Image1152Dixie Flyer113nkBully Boy1101	Driving	8
23May52- 7Det	my	6f	:242:48 1:142	3↑ Alw 3500	1	4	1½	21	2hd	35¼	Fisk B	115	w	*1.50	71-30	DixieFlyer1121¾BatedBreath1143½Sickle'sImg1152	Faltered	7
22Feb52- 7SA	fst	7f	:222:444 1:094 1:222	3↑ Wash Birthday H 11k	4	7	64¼	74¾	43	62¾	Arcaro E	113	w	3.90	90-15	PetBully112¾Interpretation113¾Guillotn126nk	Even effort	9
12Feb52- 7SA	fst	6f	:22 :443 1:094	3↑ Lincoln's BD H 17k	8	3	43	45	33	2no	Westrope J	112	w	6.35	96-17	Guillotine126noSickle'sImg112nkRghsBull1211½	Raced wide	8
6Feb52- 7SA	fst	6f	:223:451 1:103	3↑ ⒻLos Cerritos H 18k	3	4	3nk	2hd	13	11½	Arcaro E	120	w	2.15	92-14	Sickle's Image1201½A Gleam1121½Frigid105½	Handily	13
12Jan52- 6SA	sly	1	:224:463 1:121 1:391	3↑ ⒻS Maria H 23k	6	5	56	33½	34½	58¾	Fisk B	116	w	5.50	71-22	Special Touch1212½Next Move1282½Blue Cloth108nk	Tired	8
5Jan52- 7SA	fst	7f	:221:45 1:101 1:23	Malibu Sequet 30k	15	2	2hd	64¼	72¾	96½	Fisk B	114	w	15.40	83-14	Phil D.118noIntent1152Black Douglas110½	Tired	15
28Dec51- 7SA	fst	6f	:221:451 1:094	3↑ ⒻLas Flores H 18k	2	9	62¾	41¾	31½	31¼	Fisk B	117	w	5.55	95-08	NextMove1241SpeclTouch122nkSckl'sImg1173½	Good effort	13
17Nov51- 5CD	gd	6f	:223:453 1:111	3↑ Alw 2500	2	5	31½	34¼	44	35	Fisk B	115	w	*1.00	89-16	DixieFlyer1084Ari'sMona1121Sickle'sImage115no	No rally	10
8Aug51- 6HP	fst	6f	:223:461 1:114	Alw 3000	7	1	53	11	11	12	Fisk B	121	w	*.40	97-13	Sickle'sImage1212Badger1141½Ted Yochum114nk	Going away	7
14Jly51- 7AP	fst	1	:224:452 1:094 1:361	3↑ ⒻArl Matron H 72k	8	9	64½	43	22½	11½	Fisk B	120	w	3.80	91-08	Sickle'sImage1201½Aunt Jinny1075WarTalk109¾	Drew away	13
30Jun51- 7AP	fst	6f	:224:452 1:104	3↑ ⒻModesty H 24k	14	6	89	65	33½	1¾	Swain C	120	w	6.10	92-08	Sickle'sImge120¾Asphalt1052½TwoRanbows104nk	Hard drive	17
27Jun51- 6AP	fst	7f	:23 :452 1:11 1:24	Warren Wright Mem 24k	12	5	55	58	23	43¼	Fisk B	113	w	6.50	87-13	Jumbo114¾Ruhe1182½Bernwood114hd	Good effort	17
20Jun51- 6AP	sl	6f	:224:454 1:121	ⒻCleopatra 16k	7	4	4¾	43	11½	11½	Fisk B	115	w	*3.10	85-18	Sickle'sImage1151½JennieLee1151¾Fleeterthan111½	Driving	10
13Jun51- 7Was	fst	6f	:222:452 1:104	ⒻAlw 5000	2	1	31½	21½	13	11¼	Swain C	121	w	*1.80	92-13	Sickle'sImage1211¼LadyIndian1091½RomanMiss1091	Driving	10
19May51- 7CD	fst	6½f	:232:464 1:113 1:174	ⒻAlw 5000	3	4	42	41½	3nk	21¼	Swain C	121	w	*1.10	91-12	Jennie Lee1171¼Sickle's Image1212½Lyceum109no	No excuse	7
4May51- 7CD	fst	1 1/16	:24 :482 1:133 1:453	ⒻKy Oaks 31k	8	3	32	32½	43½	35¼	Fisk B	121	w	5.70	85-14	How1162¾Astro1102½Sickle's Image1211½	Went well	14
28Apr51- 6CD	fst	6½f	:223:453 1:10 1:163	ⒻAlw 2500	2	3	44	33½	1hd	1nk	Swain C	121	w	*1.10	98-10	Sickle's Image121nkRuddy1183½Biddy Bid1151½	All out	7
14Apr51- 6Kee	sl	6f	:234:494 1:18	ⒻAshland 13k	3	1	2hd	21	11½	1nk	Fisk B	121	w	*2.00	62-31	Sickle's Image121nkJuliets Nurse1181½How1152	All out	9
6Apr51- 5Jam	fst	5½f	:222:452 1:043	ⒻAlw 4500	7	3	2½	2hd	12½	12	Fisk B	115	w	*1.80	95-13	Sickle'sImage1152FairSelf115nkSweetTalk115½	Ridden out	7
31Mar51- 6LD	gd	5f	:224:464 1:001	3↑ Alw 1800	8	2	1hd	11	1½	11	Spinale J	104	w	*.30	90-17	Sickle's Image1041Klimie112noBeaming Light115½	Driving	9
10Feb51- 7SA	fst	7f	:223:451 1:103 1:232	ⒻS Susana 65k	11	2	1hd	12½	1hd	31½	Fisk B	121	w	*1.80	86-15	ⒹSweetTlk115noRuthLly1151½Sckl'sImg121½	Close quarters	11
Placed second through disqualification																		

19Jan51- 7SA	gd 6f	:222 :453 1:103	Alw 5000	2 3 2hd 2hd 1hd 22	Smith FA	117	w	2.65	92-19	Phil D.1222Sickle's Image117½Rough'n Tumble118¾	Hung	8
24Nov50- 7Hol	fst 6f	:221 :45 1:10	Ⓕ Lassie 33k	9 11 11 11¼	Fisk B	112	w	*.90	96-10	Sickle's Image1121¼Ruth Lily1073½Worn Out1083	Driving	10
Fog prevented other calls												
17Nov50- 7Hol	fst 6f	:223 :454 1:103	Ⓕ Alw 5000	3 3 1½ 12 12 12½	Fisk B	116	w	3.55	93-13	Sickle'sImage1162½WornOut1164½HaughtyMiss112nk	In hand	10
23Sep50- 6Nar	fst 6f	:221 :451 1:12	J H Connors Mem 9.3k	2 3 1nk 1½ 11½ 1¾	Fisk B	112	w	*1.40	91-16	Sickle's Image112¾Loridale1092½Fair Game115½	Driving	8
16Sep50- 4Nar	fst 6f	:222 :452 1:113	Alw 2600	7 3 11 12 12 11½	Fisk B	112	w	3.70	93-12	Sickle's Image1121½Blue Roxy1071½Swift Swiv1224	Driving	8
9Sep50- 6Nar	fst 6f	:222 :452 1:111	Ⓕ Jeanne D'Arc 6.7k	5 10 1010 811 79½ 78	Fisk B	111	w	4.40	87-09	Jacodema1162½BettyLamr1051½DollFoot1071½	Sluggish start	11
30Aug50- 6Aqu	fst 6f	:23 :462 1:12	Ⓕ Astarita 12k	4 2 2hd 2hd 31½ 69	Fisk B	113	w	3.50	83-11	Jacodema113½Self Assurance116noRuddy1161	Close quarters	11
24Aug50- 7Sar	fst 5½f	:222 :453 :59 1:054	Ⓕ Alw 3000	6 3 1hd 1hd 11 14½	Fisk B	113	w	2.65	88-12	Sickle's Image1134½Tides1131¼Toto113no	Easily	8
10Aug50- 6HP	fst 6f	:234 :471 1:122	Alw 2200	8 4 1hd 1hd 21½ 23½	Arcaro E	117	w	*.60	92-09	PurSang1173½Sickle'sImage1171½PsychicLad1116	Weakened	8
4Aug50- 5Was	fst 5½f	:223 :46 :574 1:042	Ⓕ Md Sp Wt	10 6 2hd 13 15 16½	MacAndrew D	115	w	*1.00	98-07	Sickle's Image1156½The Ghizeh1151Aunt Jinny1153	Easily	12
27Jly50- 6AP	fst 6f	:222 :443 1:104	Ⓕ Pollyanna 18k	13 2 11 21 23 35¾	MacAndrew D	114	w	5.60	86-11	Flyamanita1133¾HastyRequest1132Sckl'sImg1141½	Weakened	14
18Jly50- 5AP	hy 5½f	:232 :483 1:013 1:09	Ⓕ Md Sp Wt	12 6 2hd 12 15 32½	MacAndrew D	115	w	4.60	72-34	RomanMiss1151Fleeterthan1151½Sickle'sImg1151½	Gave way	12

Silver Spoon

ch. f. 1956, by Citation (Bull Lea)–Silver Fog, by Mahmoud

Lifetime record: 27 13 3 4 $313,930

Own.– C.V. Whitney
Br.– C.V. Whitney (Ky)
Tr.– J.J. Greely Jr

14Oct60- 6Kee	fst *7f	1:26	3↑ Ⓕ Alw 7500	5 2 31 3nk 42 57	Rotz JL	121		5.50	90-11	Indian Maid118¾Royal Native1212¼Chance Gauge1061½	Tired	8
Open to 3-, 4- and 5-year-olds												
1Oct60- 7Bel	fst 1⅛	:461 1:11 1:362 1:492	3↑ Ⓕ Beldame 91k	1 5 41¾ 62¾ 45 46	Shoemaker W	123		4.25	83-16	Berlo1192Royal Native1231Make Sail1193	In close on turn	9
Previously trained by R.L. Wheeler												
13Aug60- 8AP	fst 1⅛	:48 1:12 1:371 1:502	3↑ Ⓕ Arl Matron H 56k	2 5 54 52½ 21 31½	Shoemaker W	128		*1.40	82-07	RoyalNative128hdWoodlawn1101½SlvrSpoon1281	Reared start	11
5Aug60- 5AP	sl 1	:223 :463 1:124 1:393	3↑ Ⓕ Alw 5000	5 4 32½ 22 22 2no	Shoemaker W	128		*.50	72-30	WeeFleet111noSilverSpoon1283¾Isk1082¼	Getting to winner	6
2Jly60- 7Hol	fst 1⅛	:454 1:094 1:354 1:49	3↑ Ⓕ Vanity H 38k	5 3 2hd 13 12 1¾	Longden J	130		*.70	89-13	SilvrSpoon130¾Tritoma1072¾HonysGm118nk	Wide,hard drive	6
16Jun60- 7Hol	fst 1	:22 :444 1:092 1:344	3↑ Ⓕ Milady H 22k	2 2 24 2hd 12 12¾	Shoemaker W	126		*.70	92-10	SilverSpn1262¾HoneysGem1204LPlum110¾	Drew out handily	7
28May60- 7Hol	fst 1 1/16	:23 :454 1:092 1:403	3↑ Californian 111k	4 4 21½ 23 32½ 45¾	Valenzuela I	118		5.40	86-10	FleetNsrullah1192½EddieSchmidt1131¾Bagdd1231½	Weakened	7
24May60- 7Hol	fst 6f	:212 :434 :56 1:082	3↑ Ⓕ Sequoia H 16k	6 7 65½ 65½ 34 23¼	Shoemaker W	127		*.60	98-09	LiberalLady1173¼SilverSpoon127½SweetJune1093¼	Rallied	9
18May60- 6Hol	fst 6f	:222 :452 :571 1:091	4↑ Alw 10000	1 5 3½ 32½ 34 32¼	Shoemaker W	117		*.90	94-12	Revel113¾LittlMoon1221½SlvrSpoon1176½	In close,steadied	5
27Feb60- 7SA	fst 1¼	:462 1:104 1:352 2:003	3↑ S Anita H 145k	11 3 42½ 41¼ 54 52½	Valenzuela I	120		5.10	93-11	Linmold110hdFleet Nasrullah113noAmerigo120nk	Evenly	12
6Feb60- 7SA	fst 1⅛	:463 1:102 1:36 1:484	4↑ Ⓕ S Margarita H 57k	10 4 3½ 1½ 11 11¾	Arcaro E	130		*.90	88-12	Silver Spoon1301¾Indian Maid1162Narva1131	Under urging	12
21Jan60- 7SA	fst 1 1/16	:23 :46 1:103 1:423	4↑ Ⓕ S Maria H 28k	10 3 1hd 1½ 1½ 11¾	Arcaro E	127		*.90	91-12	SilverSpoon1271¾LaPlume111nkIndianMaid1161½	Drew clear	10
12Jan60- 7SA	gd 7f	:23 :454 1:103 1:23	4↑ Ⓕ S Monica H 22k	5 2 41½ 3nk 3nk 12	Arcaro E	124		*1.40	88-22	Silver Spoon1242Margaretta121¾Indian Maid120nk	Driving	8
1Jan60- 6SA	fst 6f	:22 :444 1:093	4↑ Ⓕ Las Flores H 23k	5 3 84 64½ 67 44¾	Arcaro E	125		*.80	91-11	Margaretta1172½Khalita115noIndian Maid1202¼	Lacked room	9
18Aug59- 6Sar	fst 7f	:221 :45 1:102 1:24	Ⓕ Alw 5000	4 4 47 47 57 511	Boland W	124		1.90	84-17	MommyDear1155MissBlueGem1121Recite1213	Lacked response	5
1Aug59- 7Mth	fst 1⅛	:471 1:111 1:37 1:503	Ⓕ Mth Oaks 55k	3 3 22 33½ 35½ 36	Boland W	121		*.40	85-18	RoyalNative1133½IndianMaid1172½SilverSpoon1214½	Tired	6
24Jly59- 6Mth	gd 1 1/16	:233 :474 1:121 1:444	Ⓕ Alw 7500	5 3 32½ 3nk 2hd 11	Boland W	126		*.70	81-25	SilverSpoon1261IndianMaid118¾RoyalNative1121½	Driving	5
11Jly59- 6Del	gd 1⅛	:48 1:132 1:383 1:513	Ⓕ Del Oaks 47k	5 2 22 1hd 1hd 22	Boland W	119		*.40	80-21	Resaca1192Silver Spoon119½Indian Maid1194	No excuse	9
13Jun59- 7Hol	fst 1⅛	:453 1:092 1:344 1:473	Cinema H 52k	4 5 53 21½ 12¼ 14¾	Boland W	120		2.20	96-08	Silver Spoon1204¾Friar Roach1112¼Civic Pride105½	Easily	8
2May59- 7CD	fst 1¼	:473 1:113 1:36 2:021	Ky Derby 163k	4 9 99 32 32 53¼	York R	121		10.80	93-06	TomyLee126noSwordDancer1262¼FirstLanding1261	Bid,tired	17
25Apr59- 7CD	fst 7f	:23 :452 1:094 1:221	Alw 5000	4 3 3nk 2hd 3½ 32½	York R	117		*1.20	96-14	Sword Dancer1221Easy Spur1221½Silver Spoon1172	In close	5
7Mar59- 7SA	fst 1⅛	:453 1:092 1:354 1:49	S Anita Derby 147k	6 3 31 21 1hd 12½	York R	113		*1.50	89-14	SilverSpoon1132½RoyalOrbit1182½FightinIndn118hd	Driving	10
18Feb59- 7SA	fst 1 1/16	:23 :462 1:11 1:414	Ⓕ S Susana 22k	5 2 2hd 1½ 15 110½	York R	117		*.65	95-13	Silver Spoon11710½Miss Uppity1172Bitter Feud110½	Easily	9
28Jan59- 7SA	fst 6½f	:22 :45 1:102 1:17	Ⓕ S Ynez 17k	11 4 42 41½ 1hd 11¼	York R	116		*.80	93-15	SilverSpoon1161¼GunBox116¾PardalLassie113¾	Handy score	13
7Jan59- 7SA	fst 6½f	:22 :45 1:102 1:17	Ⓕ La Centinela 18k	2 7 53 32½ 12 12¼	York R	119		*.70	93-16	SilverSpoon1192¼BitterFeud1191¾SybilBrand119hd	Easily	14
30Dec58- 5SA	fst 6f	:221 :45 1:093	Ⓕ Alw 4500	10 5 21½ 23 2hd 13¼	York R	115	w	3.80	97-12	SilverSpoon1153¼Satina1152PardalLassie1153½	Easily best	12
Previously trained by S.E. Veitch												
23Sep58- 3Bel	fst 6f-WC	:223 :454 1:10	Ⓕ Md 8000	11 3 2½ 2½ 16	Nelson E	118	w	18.35	89-11	SilverSpoon1186LynchMary113nkBasqu1121½	Drew out easily	28

St. Vincent (GB)

ch. g. 1951, by Ocean Swell (Blue Peter)–Light of Day, by Hyperion

Lifetime record: 72 17 7 6 $228,280

Own.– J. Gheen
Br.– Lady Irwin (GB)
Tr.– B.R. Roberts

10Sep60- 7Dmr	fm 1Ⓣ	:24 :48 1:13 1:382	3↑ Handicap 4000	6 6 63¼ 52¾ 3nk 1no	Lanoway G	113		*1.40	--	St.Vincent113noBalsarrochBoy1091½Queen'sWy1041½	Driving	6
27Aug60- 9Dmr	fm 7½fⓉ	1:324	3↑ Clm 5000-c	2 5 53 52½ 42 2nk	Lanoway G	122		*.80	--	PurePitch114nkSt.Vincent122¾BigJak1141½	Strong late bid	7
Claimed from Mr & Mrs A.T. Cattani;trainer, J. Nicholson												
22Aug60- 4Dmr	fst 1Ⓣ	:24 :483 1:133 1:40	3↑ Clm 4000	1 5 53½ 42 1hd 12	Lanoway G	120		*.70	--	St.Vincent1202SanDiego1121¾Lesur1171½	Wide into stretch	7
10Aug60- 9Dmr	fm 7½fⓉ	1:33	3↑ Clm 5000	5 6 66 41¼ 31½ 1nk	Lanoway G	119		5.40	--	St. Vincent119nkNet Man1112¼April1091¼	Driving	8
5Aug60- 8Dmr	fst 1 1/16	:233 :473 1:114 1:43	3↑ Clm 3500	6 7 715 78¼ 64¾ 33½	Burns E	117		4.60	82-00	Amarillo Speed112¾Peter Potter1122¾St. Vincent1171¼		7
Closed ground outside												
29Jly60- 8Dmr	fst 1 1/16	:24 :474 1:113 1:424	3↑ Clm 4000	1 7 611 68 69 69	Neves R	120		4.30	78-08	Baccarat1122¼Tribal Chief112noAmblingorix1204	No threat	7
23Jly60- 8Hol	fst 1 1/16	1:44	4↑ Clm 4000	10 11 1110 97¼ 3nk 1no	Neves R	117		23.90	75-15	St. Vincent117noNoration120¾Paint Brush1142½	Just up	12
9Jly60- 4Hol	fst 1¼	:471 1:12 1:363 2:021	4↑ Clm 4000	3 8 79¾ 64¼ 48½ 56¾	Burns E	117		5.80	75-12	Talktalk1141½Tribal Chief1141Easy Four1204½	Hung	8
4Jly60- 2Hol	fst 1 1/16	:234 :464 1:112 1:432	4↑ Clm 6000	5 7 76 64¾ 62½ 54½	Lanoway G	119		12.40	73-13	Butcher Boy1161¼Blue G.116nkAsombroso1081½	No factor	7
23Jun60- 8Hol	fst 1½	:474 1:131 2:04 2:30	4↑ Clm-c 2500	2 7 69½ 12 12 13¼	Longden J	114		2.70	95-11	St.Vincent1143¼LookOutII117¾NightHawk1111½	Going away	8
Claimed from Mr & Mrs R. Godfrey,trainer V. Longden												
11Jun60- 3Hol	12 1⅛	:47 1:114 1:364 1:494	4↑ Clm 3000	5 9 107½ 84½ 711 711	Longden J	116		6.20	74-09	Telyar1195½Good Start1162High Drawer119½	No factor	12
27May60- 8Hol	fst 1⅛	:472 1:12 1:374 1:502	4↑ Clm 4000	4 12 1215 77 53 44½	Longden J	117		16.10	77-13	Sassy Sea109½Sayacieux114½Phantom Ace1143½		12
20May60- 8Hol	fst 1 1/16	:233 :47 1:111 1:42	4↑ Clm 7000	2 6 710 613 617 619	Longden J	116		12.70	66-00	Hello Junedear1141¼Tranquilizer1165Selling Fast1223¾		7
10Mar60- 7SA	fm *1¾Ⓣ	2:474	3↑ S Juan Capistrano H 119k	10 17 1514 1617 1312 1115	Trejos R	108		17.00f	73-14	Amerigo122noKing o' Turf1156½Aorangi109no	No factor	17
3Mar60- 8SA	sf *1¾Ⓣ	2:57	4↑ Handicap 10000	2 12 1216 1217 107¼ 44½	Shoemaker W	126		*3.10	47-48	NiteShift1171¾LeBeau114nkLastRow1212½	Best stride late	13
18Feb60- 6SA	fm 1½Ⓣ	:46 1:102 2:033 2:282	4↑ Handicap 7500	13 14 1312 31½ 2½ 13½	Shoemaker W	120		*1.80	85-15	St.Vincent1203½Castlestone117½LockOutII1112½	Going away	14
4Feb60- 4SA	sf 1½Ⓣ	:473 1:14 2:071 2:352	4↑ Handicap 6000	11 10 108¾ 31 31½ 73	Longden J	119		*2.80	47-50	GoodStart112½LastRow119¾TheSands1121½	Bold rally,tired	14
22Jan60- 8SA	fst 1⅛	:463 1:114 1:38 1:504	4↑ Clm 5000	3 10 85 62¾ 52 3½	Longden J	117		5.20	77-16	Flagg'sBandit115½OverdrivII115hdSt.Vncnt1172	Slow start	11
9Jan60- 8SA	fst 1⅛	:471 1:113 1:37 1:50	4↑ OClm 8000	4 10 1012 67 712 611	Longden J	116		9.60	71-11	LandofHope114¾WearandTr1163¼FlyingSouth1161½	No speed	10
Previously owned by Alberta Ranches Ltd-Gardiner												
21Feb59- 5SA	sly 1 1/16	:234 :472 1:12 1:441	4↑ Alw 10000	6 7 66¼ 54½ 55½ 56¼	Longden J	120		14.20	77-12	Solid Son113nkNew Shift1133½Prophetic1111½	No factor	7
10Feb59- 7SA	sf 1½Ⓣ	:48 1:133 2:06 2:314	3↑ San Luis Rey H 28k	9 10 1011 1115 1129 1128	Longden J	113	b	11.30	40-32	Infntry1133LookoutPont1122¼Whttoldyou118¾	Disliked going	11
28Jan59- 6SA	fm 1¼Ⓣ	:453 1:103 1:353 2:011	4↑ OClm 12500	2 10 99¾ 62 2hd 1no	Longden J	113		*1.40	88-12	St.Vincent113noAorangi1223LookoutPoint113nk	Hard drive	12
16Jan59- 7SA	fm 1¼Ⓣ	:463 1:114 1:36 2:004	4↑ Alw 10000	4 9 89¼ 84¼ 52½ 54½	Longden J	113		9.45	85-10	Andrew Alan1181¾Hakuchikara113noMacBern1181¼	Bid,tired	12
1Jan59- 7SA	fm 1¼Ⓣ	:462 1:112 1:351 2:002	4↑ San Gabriel H 28k	9 8 87 65 89 710	Longden J	122	w	4.10	82-08	MacBern1132¼Andrew Alan1161Hakuchikara1191¼	No factor	9
26Dec58- 6SA	fm 1⅛Ⓣ	:464 1:104 1:354 1:474	3↑ Alw 7500	10 10 914 97¾ 65¼ 55¾	Longden J	113	w	3.30e	92-02	AnxiousMomnt1162¾Hakuchikara1133TllChfII119hd	Good try	10

25Oct58- 7WO sf 1⅝Ⓣ 2:462 3↑ Can Championship 60k 8 10 1118 1222 1226 1226 Contrada G 126 w 14.40 - - JackKetch126hdMahan1264AndrwAln121hd Showed very little 12

20Sep58- 6Bel sf 1⅜Ⓣ :50 1:152 1:401 2:182 3↑ Handicap 10000 8 4 44 55½ 64¼ 65 Ycaza M 120 w 6.15 84-11 LangtonBreeze1172¼Sam1111Rfty122no Raced without mishap 10

13Sep58- 7Atl fm 1 3/16Ⓣ :472 1:112 1:362 1:543 3↑ U Nations H 100k 7 12 1211 105½ 813 88 Harmatz W 114 w 13.20 98-00 Clem113½RoundTabl1303CombustonII115¾ Failed to threaten 12

8Sep58- 7Atl fm 1 1/16Ⓣ :231 :461 1:112 1:433 3↑ Alw 5000 5 7 714 69½ 65¼ 22 Ycaza M 113 w 7.40 93-05 RoundTable1282St.Vncnt113nkRfty115hd Strong stretch bid 7

23Aug58- 8AP fm 1 3/16Ⓣ :47 1:11 1:36 1:542 3↑ Arlington H 85k 7 7 710 76¼ 55½ 33 Longden J 111 w 32.80 96-09 RoundTable1302¼Clm109¾St.Vncnt1111½ Off slowly,game try 8

22Jly58- 7Hol fst 1⅝ :464 1:371 2:023 2:41 3↑ Sunset H 107k 3 4 415 47¼ 37½ 310 Longden J 111 w 13.65 76-18 GallantMan1324EddieSchmidt1106St.Vncnt111nk Never close 6

16Jly58- 7Hol fst 1 1/16 :232 :464 1:113 1:44 4↑ Alw 10000 7 8 712 54½ 47 43¾ Longden J 112 w 1.85 71-19 Timloch1121¾FathersRisk1121¼LglCrss115¾ Slow start,wide 8

8Jly58- 5Hol fst 1 :23 :462 1:111 1:363 4↑ Alw 10000 7 8 78½ 66¼ 56½ 53¾ Longden J 112 w 10.45 79-19 Barely Nothing1121½Timloch112¾Khliesas1101¼ No factor 9

2Jly58- 7Hol fst 1 1/16 :233 :472 1:12 1:434 4↑ Alw 7500 2 9 911 86½ 815 815 Longden J 114 w 10.55 61-20 Cino114noRevolt1203¾LightnngJck114nk Raced far off pace 9

27Jly57- 8AP fm 1 3/16Ⓣ :481 1:122 1:373 1:552 3↑ Arlington H 125k 7 11 84¾ 72¾ 44 34½ Longden J 120 w 14.80 89-04 Manasss1212Swoon'sSon1282½St.Vncnt120no Stride too late 14

1Jun57- 8Was sf 1⅛Ⓣ :473 1:122 1:39 1:512 3↑ Continental Turf H 28k 3 10 1114 1213 1110 1010 Gilligan L 121 w 4.10 76-14 Bernburgoo1091½Sunningdale112nkBlue Choir1131¾ Weak try 13

11May57- 7Pim hd 1⅜Ⓣ :49 1:143 1:393 2:161 3↑ Dixie H 28k 5 10 53½ 52¾ 52¼ 43 Longden J 125 w *1.50 93-04 Akbar Khan1131¼Jabneh1201¼Blue Choir116½ Made bid,hung 10

27Apr57- 8BM fst 1⅛ :454 1:101 1:353 1:48 3↑ W P Kyne Mem H 115k 2 14 1416 1313 77 73 Longden J 118 w 5.55 96-10 PibeCarlos110hdEddieSchmidt112½CountChic115no Rallied 15

9Mar57- 7SA sf *1¾Ⓣ :452 2:03 2:29 2:55 3↑ S Juan Capistrano H 115k 4 9 85¾ 4nk 42¼ 68¼ Longden J 125 w *2.20 51-41 Corn Husker116hdSpinney1142½Infantry1111¼ Bid,weakened 13

22Feb57- 7SA fm 1½Ⓣ :47 1:111 2:004 2:261 3↑ Wash Birthday H 29k 7 10 69 42½ 12 14½ Longden J 121 w *2.40 96-04 St.Vincent1214½PrinceofGreine1111½MastrBong124¾ Handily 13

12Feb57- 7SA fm 1½Ⓣ :484 1:123 2:03 2:273 4↑ San Luis Rey H 28k 8 9 64½ 31½ 57 44 Longden J 122 w 3.70 85-11 Posadas113nkInfantry1141½Prince of Greine1102½ Bore out 11

2Feb57- 5SA fst 7f :22 :444 1:092 1:221 4↑ Alw 6000 7 6 818 812 816 711 Longden J 113 w 5.55 81-12 Starover1152½HowNow113noMizban1131½ Never close to pace 8

30May55- 6Bel fst 1¼ :474 1:113 1:36 2:003 3↑ Suburban H 88k 4 7 610 712 717 718 Longden J 126 w 13.70 79-11 Helioscope128hdHighGun1334½Subahdr1199 Never formidable 9

21May55- 7Pim fm 1⅜Ⓣ 2:152 3↑ Dixie H 31k 6 7 78 2hd 13 12½ James B 126 w *1.10 125-00 St. Vincent1262½Kaster120noMaharajah1131 Ridden out 8

16May55- 6Pim fm 1 1/16Ⓣ 1:434 3↑ Alw 4500 5 5 56 22 2hd 1½ James B 124 w 1.60 108-00 St.Vincent124½OldGlendale1133Martha'sWave1073 Driving 6

2Apr55- 7GP fst 1 1/16 :243 :48 1:112 1:432 3↑ Fort Lauderdale H 7.5k 9 9 913 87¾ 84¾ 21¼ Adams J 121 w *1.45 92-12 TwoFisted1091¼St.Vincent1211BadConduct110nk Closed fast 9

5Mar55- 7SA fm *1¾Ⓣ 2:464 3↑ S Juan Capistrano H 115k 13 8 52¼ 41½ 31½ 1½ Longden J 123 w *2.60 127-00 St. Vincent123½Determine126½Gigantic1103¼ Hard drive 13

22Feb55- 7SA fm 1½Ⓣ :463 1:11 2:01 2:252 3↑ Wash Birthday H 29k 4 11 93½ 4¾ 3nk 13½ Longden J 122 w *2.55e 103-00 St. Vincent1223½Alidon1133Kings Mutiny1083½ Going away 13

19Feb55- 5SA fm *6½fⓉ 1:16 4↑ Alw 7500 10 7 74½ 73½ 2½ 41¼ Longden J 121 w 5.55 93-06 Allied118½Pajone113nkScent122½ Hung 11

29Jan55- 6SA fm 1¼Ⓣ :454 1:101 1:344 2:00 4↑ San Gabriel H 31k 5 14 85¼ 74½ 45½ 1hd Longden J 116 w 7.25 100-00 St.Vincent116hdStaroftheForest122noNovrullh119¾ Just up 19

22Jan55- 7SA sf 1¼Ⓣ 2:034 4↑ San Marcos H 29k 6 5 65½ 53½ 41½ 73¾ Longden J 113 w 12.90 77-19 Great Captain1102¼Poona II124noHigh Scud115nk Taken up 10

29Dec54- 6SA fm 1⅛Ⓣ :45 1:09 1:344 1:472 3↑ Alw 10000 12 11 1016 912 58½ 36½ Pearson B 110 w 22.65 101-00 PoonaII1083BlueTrumpeter1093½St.Vincnt1101½ Closed fast 12

24Nov54- 6GG fst 1 :23 :462 1:112 1:364 Alw 3500 5 5 62¼ 52¼ 1hd 12¼ Taniguchi G 110 w 8.70 84-18 St.Vincent1102¼KingsMutiny1145ShowMeFirst1201 Driving 7

13Nov54- 6GG my 6f :233 :48 1:131 Alw 3000 6 7 64¼ 63¾ 56 58 Longden J 114 w 3.75 67-39 DoubleReigh1192½TheHoop1142Toro-San109hd Lacked speed 7

27Oct54- 6Tan fst 6f :223 :452 1:094 3↑ Alw 3000 1 6 68¼ 47½ 35 25 Longden J 113 w 9.10 97-06 Sahib1195St. Vincent1131½Swell109½ Wide,good finish 6

20Oct54- 7Tan fst 6f :224 :454 1:102 Alw 3000 4 8 74 54 56½ 54¼ Longden J 114 w 13.65 95-08 MajrSpeed116½TheCharactr1222½TheHoop109½ Broke slowly 8

20Jly54- 7Hol fst 1 1/16 :232 :463 1:11 1:422 El Dorado H 22k 6 8 75 76½ 611 67¾ Longden J 111 w 21.35 88-08 WarTryst1161½HobcawSag1093MusslshlI1122½ Never a factor 9

10Jly54- 5Hol fst 1 :231 :463 1:104 1:353 Alw 10000 5 5 31½ 3nk 45 46¼ Longden J 113 w 8.60 91-08 Musselshll114hdWrTryst119¾IndnRd1172¼ Bid turn,weakened 7

5Jly54- 6Hol fst 1 1/16 :234 :472 1:113 1:422 Alw 6000 9 9 82¾ 83 99¼ 912 Longden J 114 w 9.10 84-08 Musselshell109hdHobcawSge1143½SprngCount120no No factor 9

29Jun54- 6Hol fst 6f :22 :451 :572 1:101 3↑ Alw 7500 2 5 46½ 44½ 43½ 52¾ Neves R 111 w 15.95 92-08 ZePippin1171¼Endorser1221½Ove'randUnder122no No factor 6

1May54- 6BM fst 1 :232 :463 1:113 1:37 Handicap 4000 6 3 2hd 2½ 44 55 Longden J 120 w *.85 88-10 Bright Liberty1131Tchaikowski109½Larks Music1162 6
Flattened out drive

10Apr54- 7BM fst 1 :23 :46 1:111 1:364 Handicap 5000 5 7 67½ 64½ 41½ 21¼ Longden J 113 w 15.40 93-11 Indian Red1101¼St. Vincent1132½Leterna105¾ Closed well 8

27Mar54- 6BM gd 6f :223 :462 1:11 Alw 4000 3 8 63 87¼ 811 813 Balaski L 114 w *1.45e 79-18 Arrogate119nkBrighterDays1082½ZeBull1133 Showed nothing 8

6Mar54- 4SA fst 6f :222 :452 1:101 Alw 6000 5 6 85¼ 88¾ 811 88¼ Longden J 114 w 3.60e 86-07 Affrighted111½Knockmealdown112noZee Bull1141¼ No factor 8
Previously trained by George Colling

24Oct53♦ Doncaster(GB) gd 7fⓉStr 1:282 Allendale Plate Alw1700 14 Smith D 133 *1.85 St. Vincent1334By Thunder!126½Potential1192 23
Tracked leaders,led over 1f out,quickly clear

7Oct53♦ York(GB) fm6fⓉStr 1:144 Leyburn Stakes Alw2600 44 Smith D 133 *1.00 Swallow Dive1173Byzantium124noComatose 11
Whipped round start,trailed,finished well

12Sep53♦ Doncaster(GB) yl 1ⓉStr 1:394 Prince of Wales's Nursery Hcp Hcp9400 16 Smith D 111 4.50 St. Vincent1116No Worry118¾No Peace1103 20
Prominent,led 1½f out,drew clear 1f out

5Aug53♦ Yarmouth(GB) yl 6fⓉStr 1:13 Cliff Park Stakes Alw2300 67¼ Smith D 130 12.00 Sea Swan1353Carrion1202Birikorus123hd 22
Raced in midpack,evenly late;Race for maidens at time of entry

25Jly53♦ Doncaster(GB) gd 6fⓉStr 1:161 Cantley Plate Alw1700 11½ Smith D 119 2.00 St. Vincent1191½Joe's Ginger1192Sensitive1194 15
Close up,led 1f out,driving;Race for maidens at time of entry

27Jun53♦ Doncaster(GB) fm5fⓉStr :592 Lonsdale Foal Stakes Alw6900 2nk Smith D 115 4.50 Holiday Date127nkSt. Vincent1153Gondola112 4
Tracked leaders,bid 1f out,always held by winner

12Jun53♦ Thirsk(GB) gd 5fⓉStr 1:021 Carlton Miniott Maiden Stakes Mdn1400 21½ Smith D 123 2.50 Brittle1231½St. Vincent123¾Don Quixote1231 21
Prominent,bid 1f out,not good enough

16Apr53♦ Newmarket(GB) gd 5fⓉStr 1:022 Bartlow Stakes Alw2300 Unp Brown LG5 121 16.50 Sybil's Niece1231½Sir Vincent1261½Princely Gift1264
Never a factor;Race for maidens at time of entry

Stan (GB)

b. g. 1950, by Kingsway (Fairway)–Final Sweep, by Brumeaux **Lifetime record: 40 18 2 4 $248,989**

Own.– Hasty House Farms
Br.– J. Sharp (GB)
Tr.– H. Trotsek

13Feb61- 9Hia fm 1 1/16Ⓣ 1:431 4↑ Clm 12000 1 12 1226 1112 99¼ 713 Adams JR 115 *2.60 86-04 Mozart1161½FranciscoII1164½RhinIndr1115 Pulled up lame 12

1Feb61- 4Hia fm 1 1/16Ⓣ 1:45 4↑ Clm 9000 2 12 1219 810 46½ 11¼ Adams JR 114 8.15 90-10 Stan1141¼Billy Bluejay117noSunningdale1144½ Going away 12

2Nov60- 7WO sf 1 1/16Ⓣ :244 :484 1:152 1:483 3↑ Clm 6000 7 6 65 53½ 2nk 13 Adams JR 115 *.85 69-31 Stan1153Detan1182½West Four11010¾ Drew out with ease 7

20Oct60- 8WO fm 1 1/16Ⓣ :231 :461 1:114 1:434 3↑ Clm 7500 7 9 88¼ 65¾ 31 4nk Adams JR 115 *1.15 93-07 Mr.Rooster113noRoyalBorder112noPercyYats114hd No excuse 9

13Oct60- 7WO fm 1Ⓣ :224 :461 1:122 1:364 3↑ Clm 6000 10 11 108 64½ 2½ 2no Adams JR 115 4.65 95-05 BrownPanther110noStan1153¼Culpepper120½ Strong late bid 12

22Oct59- 7WO fm 1Ⓣ 1:373 3↑ Clm 7500 4 7 89½ 54 2hd 1no Anyon E 120 *1.20 107-00 Stan120noSwallowswift111½John Berry1172¼ Hard drive 12

14Sep59- 6Haw fm 1Ⓣ 1:374 4↑ OClm 5000 4 6 65½ 21 11½ 13 Sellers J 117 *.70 87-13 Stan1173Painted Porch1142Last Impulse114no Easily 7

1Sep59- 9AP fm 1 1/16Ⓣ :233 :471 1:123 1:434 3↑ Clm 5000 9 7 59 32½ 12 13½ Sellers J 109 *1.90 90-16 Stan1093½Last Impulse111hdIrish Spark105nk Easily 9

8Aug59- 4AP sf 1 1/16Ⓣ :232 :472 1:132 1:463 3↑ Clm 8000 1 7 613 68 55½ 33¾ Sellers J 113 *1.30 72-21 Amy's Pet1141½Iskai1142¼Stan1132 Best stride too late 7

21Jly59- 8AP fm 1 1/16Ⓣ :24 :48 1:123 1:442 3↑ Clm 14500 3 7 712 78½ 65½ 41¾ Sellers J 111 *1.90 85-13 Yunlay114hdPripoly1091Camlbck114¾ Going strongly at end 8

14Jly59- 9AP fm 5½fⓉ :223 :46 :58 1:05 4↑ Clm 8500 4 10 910 911 99½ 62½ Sellers J 114 18.90 90-06 O'McSmith114nkMusicSuprme114½RessaBob102nk Closed gap 10

2Mar55- 7Hia fm 1½Ⓣ 2:293 3↑ Hia Turf H 63k 3 10 1112 96¾ 63¼ 1½ Adams J 128 w 7.45 96-00 Stan128½Capeador1181½Iceberg II112no Circled field 11

19Feb55- 7Hia fst 1¼ :48 1:12 1:363 2:022 3↑ Widener H 132k 1 7 76¼ 78¼ 67 55¼ Nelson E 116 w 2.95e 88-12 Hasty Road122nkCapeador1192¾Social Outcast126¾ No rally 10

12Feb55- 6Hia fst 1⅛ :463 1:111 1:363 1:494 4↑ Alw 7500 10 10 1016 1014 78¼ 67½ Nelson E 123 w *1.00e 79-15 HastyRoad1201½CeriseReine115½Mahrjh117hd Sluggish early 10

5Feb55- 3Hia fst 7f :224 :454 1:111 1:241 4↑ Alw 4500 4 7 714 77½ 23 11½ Nelson E 124 w 10.85 89-14 Stan1241½King'sEvidenc1095PmpsButy106¾ Impressive score 7

16Oct54- 7Lrl fm *1⅛Ⓣ 1:51 3↑ Turf Cup H 25k 6 12 119 95¾ 41 12½ Nelson E 126 w *2.00 87-13 Stan1262½News Again1112½Tritium1142 Easily,drew out 13

28Aug54- 7Was sf 1 3/16Ⓣ :482 1:132 1:412 2:002 3↑ Meadowland H 55k 2 7 711 611 24 15 Nelson E 120 w *1.70e 72-38 Stan1205CountyClare1111BrushBurn118½ Drew clear easily 10

31Jly54- 7AP sf 1 3/16Ⓣ :462 1:112 1:382 1:57 3↑ Arlington H 156k 2 10 1011 76½ 61¼ 1nk Nelson E 114 w 5.40e 94-12 Stan114nkBrush Burn1133½Sir Mango1251½ 14
Saved ground,going away

5Jly54- 8AP fm 1⅛Ⓣ :47 1:112 1:363 1:492 3↑ Stars & Stripes H 28k 9 10 1212 1211 1012 34 Nelson E 114 w 10.90e 91-08 SirMango124¾IcebergII1231Stan114no Closed fast in drive 12
25Jun54- 7AP fm 1 1/16Ⓣ :242 :483 1:12 1:434 4↑ Alw 5000 3 6 710 613 513 54¼ Adams J 111 w 2.70 90-12 TheEagle114¾BlueDar117¼Lordl120¾ Outrun early,rallied 8
17Feb54- 7Hia hd 1 3/16Ⓣ 1:552 3↑ Bougainvillea H 33k 4 10 119½ 106½ 58 56 Adams J 113 w 7.65 100-00 Parnassus111¾Picador105½Abbe Sting116½ Late rally 12
10Feb54- 6Hia hd 1 1/16Ⓣ 1:44 4↑ Alw 5000 6 9 99¾ 66¾ 45½ 31 Adams J 114 w 4.70 95-04 Brown Booter114½Picador101½Stan114no Closed gamely 12
22Jan54- 7Hia fst 7f :231 :46 1:103 1:232 4↑ Alw 5000 10 7 88¼ 912 917 814 Rotz J 111 w 18.20e 79-18 Hyphasis1182Impasse114¾Brown Booter1104 Outrun 10
31Oct53- 6Lrl fst *1⅛Ⓣ 1:511 3↑ Turf Cup H (Div 1) 23k 10 8 109½ 1011 711 55 Adams J 111 w 8.50 81-15 Sunglow1141RoyalGovernor1202FreshMeadow1101 Mild rally 10
26Oct53- 7Lrl fst 1 :24 :472 1:132 1:392 Alw 5000 2 1 31 68 715 817 Adams J 122 w 3.30 71-16 Smart Choice1161County Clare1104Tattletown1192 Stopped 9
26Sep53- 6Atl fst 1 3/16Ⓣ :473 1:12 1:362 1:554 3↑ U Nations H 60k 3 6 612 66½ 74½ 77¾ Adams J 112 w 9.80 105-00 IcebergII1201¼BrushBrun118nkRoyalGovernor118½ Crowded 8
16Sep53- 7Atl fst 1⅛Ⓣ :47 1:112 1:361 1:492 3↑ Foreign Bred 29k 2 3 43½ 44 34½ 34¼ Adams J 115 w 4.90 92-06 Royal Vale122¼Iceberg II1223Stan1152 No rally 8
Restricted to horses foaled outside the continental United States
29Aug53- 7Was fst 1 3/16Ⓣ :473 1:121 1:381 1:57 3↑ Meadowland H 57k 3 8 89½ 97 96¼ 42 Arcaro E 118 w *1.50e 87-16 Brush Burn118hdRuhe121½Jampol1181½ Late speed 13
22Aug53- 7Was fst 1⅛ :462 1:103 1:352 1:482 American Derby 112k 5 8 610 610 68 58¾ Adams J 117 w 7.40e 90-11 NativeDancr1282Landlocked1201¼PrcousSton1143 No factor 8
15Aug53- 8Was fst 1⅛Ⓣ :482 1:12 1:364 1:493 3↑ Grassland H 28k 7 6 73¾ 77¾ 57 1½ Adams J 110 w 7.50 97-13 Stan110½Brush Burn1143Vantage115no Driving clear 11
27Jly53- 6AP fst 1 1/16Ⓣ :224 :46 1:11 1:432 Handicap 10000 4 4 46 33½ 1hd 2½ Adams J 120 w *1.80e 95-08 Guy109½Stan1201¼Dubuque109nk Held well 9
16Jly53- 6AP fst 5½fⓉ :222 :462 :583 1:044 Alw 4500 9 10 83¼ 64¾ 53¼ 1nk Adams J 110 w 8.70 97-12 Stan110nk[DH]Smackover120[DH]Warless1101¼ Just up 10
Previously trained by Willie Stephenson
14Oct52♦ Newmarket(GB) gd 6fⓉStr 1:15 2↑ Challenge Stakes Stk3400 46 Parnell R 105 4.00 Agitator1291Lady Sophia1265Fleeting Storm116hd 4
Trailed throughout
21Aug52♦ York(GB) fm 6fⓉStr 1:112 Gimcrack Stakes Stk16800 49½ Parnell R 126 8.00 Bebe Grande1231½Whistler1264Libator1234 10
Outrun early,mild late gain
25Jly52♦ Hurst Park(GB) gd 6fⓉStr 1:143 Greensleeves Stakes Alw2200 11½ Parnell R 123 *1.50 Stan1231½Brolly125¾My Brazil116nk 10
Toward rear,rallied to lead 1f out,driving
11Jun52♦ Beverley(GB) fm 5fⓉStr 1:043 Bishop Burton Stakes Alw1400 15 Parnell R5 131 *.15 Stan1315Full Blown1196Lindy119½ 5
Rated in last,rallied to lead over 1f out,quickly clear
30May52♦ Stockton(GB) fm 6fⓉStr 1:16 Summer Stakes Alw1700 14 Parnell R5 129 *.15 Stan1294Swallow Falls1195Monocello119 4
24May52♦ Beverley(GB) fm 5fⓉStr 1:033 Leconfield Stakes Alw1600 15 Parnell R5 126 *.90 Stan1265Jetty1264Knuckles136 9
20May52♦ Wolvrhmptn(GB) gd 5fⓉStr 1:023 Ironbridge Plate Alw1700 11½ Parnell R 129 *1.60 Stan1291½Khandi Star1193Persian Sound119 9
15Apr52♦ Newmarket(GB) gd 5fⓉStr 1:023 Ashley Stakes Alw2300 15 Parnell R5 118 8.00 Stan1185Sediment1203Amsheer122 21
Open to maidens at time of entry

Swaps

ch. c. 1952, by Khaled (Hyperion)–Iron Reward, by Beau Pere **Lifetime record: 25 19 2 2 $848,900**

Own.– R.C. Ellsworth
Br.– Rex C. Ellsworth (Cal)
Tr.– M.A. Tenney

3Sep56- 8Was fst 1 :221 :441 1:074 1:332 3↑ Wash Park H 142k 5 3 22 1½ 13 12 Shoemaker W 130 w *.40 102-13 Swaps1302Summer Tan1152Sea o Erin1123 Well in hand late 6
25Aug56- 8Was fm 1 3/16Ⓣ :47 1:103 1:362 1:55 3↑ Arch Ward Mem H 54k 7 2 3½ 2hd 31 76¼ Shoemaker W 130 w *.30 92-02 Mahan114½SirTribal1161¾PrincMorv113hd Well up,no excuse 8
25Jly56- 7Hol fst 1⅝ :463 1:361 2:003 2:381 3↑ Sunset H 110k 5 1 11½ 11½ 16 14¼ Shoemaker W 130 w *.10 112-08 Swaps1304¼Honeys Alibi1081Blue Volt1083 Eased up late 9
14Jly56- 8Hol fst 1¼ :452 1:09 1:331 1:583 3↑ Hol Gold Cup H 162k 3 1 22 1hd 14 12 Shoemaker W 130 w *.15 105-05 Swaps1302MisterGus1171¼Porterhouse1192¼ Eased at finish 7
4Jly56- 8Hol fst 1⅛ :462 1:092 1:34 1:464 3↑ American H 103k 3 3 34½ 3nk 13 11¾ Shoemaker W 130 w *.20 100-12 Swaps1301¾MstrGus1116BobbyBrocto1158 Eased final stages 5
23Jun56- 7Hol fst 1 1/16 :231 :46 1:09 1:39 3↑ Inglewood H 52k 5 3 21½ 1hd 13 12¾ Shoemaker W 130 w *.30 107-06 Swaps1302¾MisterGus1152BobbyBrocto1217 Eased final 16th 7
9Jun56- 7Hol fst 1 :222 :451 1:084 1:331 3↑ Argonaut H 52k 1 1 11 1½ 12 11¼ Shoemaker W 128 w *.20 108-07 Swaps1281¼Bobby Brocato1236Porterhouse1192¾ In hand 6
26May56- 7Hol fst 1 1/16 :23 :453 1:092 1:404 3↑ Californian 109k 6 4 21½ 1½ 13 2hd Shoemaker W 127 w *.35 98-11 Porterhse118hdSwaps1275MistrGus1181¾ Eased by mistake 6
14Apr56- 7GP fst 1 70 :23 :453 1:092 1:393 3↑ Broward H 25k 4 2 22 11½ 13 12¼ Shoemaker W 130 w *.30 105-09 Swaps1302¼Gldr1055OurGob114no Never to a drive,eased up 8
17Feb56- 7SA fst 1 1/16 :224 :462 1:103 1:43 4↑ Handicap 15000 7 4 42 1hd 1hd 11¾ Shoemaker W 127 w *.70 89-15 Swaps1271¾Bobby Brocato124nkArrogate1159 Strong finish 7
31Aug55- 7Was gd 1¼ :46 1:102 1:373 2:041 WP Match 100k 2 2 21 21½ 22 26½ Shoemaker W 126 w *.30 74-17 Nashua1266½Swaps126 Wide on stretch turn,tired,swerved 2
20Aug55- 7Was fm 1 3/16Ⓣ :472 1:114 1:354 1:543 American Derby 146k 5 1 11 11½ 13 11 Shoemaker W 126 w *.20 101-05 Swaps1261Traffic Judge1194Parador1131½ Very handy score 6
9Jly55- 7Hol fst 1¼ :463 1:102 1:344 2:003 Westerner 57k 1 1 11½ 12 110 16 Shoemaker W 126 w *.05 96-11 Swaps1266Fabulous Vegas1171Jean's Joe1203½ Eased up 5
11Jun55- 7Hol fst 1 1/16 :231 :46 1:10 1:402 3↑ Californian 109k 1 1 22 21 11 11¼ Erb D 115 w *.65 103-06 Swaps1151¼Detrmine126½MistrGus1173 In hand throughout 6
30May55- 6Hol fst 1 :222 :452 1:101 1:35 ©Will Rogers 27k 3 3 21½ 1hd 13 112 Shoemaker W 126 w *.15e 100-07 Swaps12612Bequeath122noMr.Sullivan1183 Drew out in hand 6
7May55- 7CD fst 1¼ :472 1:122 1:37 2:014 Ky Derby 152k 8 1 11 1½ 1½ 11½ Shoemaker W 126 w 2.80 98-12 Swps1261½Nshua1266½SummrTn1264 Drew clear when urged 10
30Apr55- 6CD fst 6f :23 :462 1:101 Alw 5000 1 3 12½ 12 14 18½ Shoemaker W 123 w *.30 99-13 Swaps1238½TrimDestiny115¾Styrunnr1104½ Speed in reserve 5
19Feb55- 7SA fst 1⅛ :454 1:103 1:37 1:50 SA Derby 137k 12 3 31 13 11 1½ Longden J 118 w 3.60e 91-14 Swaps118½Jean'sJoe1183½BlueRuler1183 Went wide,driving 14
19Jan55- 7SA my 7f :214 :45 1:103 1:24 San Vicente 22k 1 5 56½ 21 12 13½ Shoemaker W 116 w 4.40e 83-25 Swaps1163½Trentonian120hdJean'sJoe1146 Speed in reserve 8
30Dec54- 6SA fst 6f :221 :451 1:10 Alw 6000 5 5 2hd 21 2hd 1no Shoemaker W 118 w 5.25 95-11 Swaps118noBeau Busher1131¾Battle Dance118½ Strong drive 12
8Jly54- 6Hol fst 5½f :221 :453 :581 1:044 ©CS Howard 29k 1 5 63½ 65¼ 58 58¾ Burton J 118 w 9.95e 85-12 ColonlMack114¾Mr.Sullivan1221BackHo1181 Showed nothing 6
22Jun54- 7Hol fst 5f :221 :454 :582 ©Haggin 24k 9 7 83¾ 73 31½ 32 Burton J 122 w 6.40e 92-13 Mr. Sullivan114½Back Hoe1221½Swaps1221¾ Good effort 10
10Jun54- 7Hol fst 5f :221 :46 :582 ©June Juv 16k 5 5 42½ 32 1½ 12½ Burton J 116 w 4.70 94-10 Swaps1162½Trentonian1192Noir116nk Drew out 7
3Jun54- 7Hol fst 5f :221 :452 :58 Westchester 16k 2 5 42½ 53½ 51¾ 32¼ Burton J 116 w 7.25 94-11 Back Hoe1191¼Trentonian1191Swaps116½ Failed to rally 7
20May54- 2Hol fst 5f :222 :454 :582 ©Md Sp Wt 9 5 2hd 2hd 1hd 13 Burton J 120 w 12.60 94-12 Swaps1203Irish Cheer1203½Battle Dance1201½ Won handily 11

Sweet Patootie

dkb. f. 1950, by Alquest (Questionnaire)–Sweet Woman, by Roman **Lifetime record: 21 8 4 1 $64,327**

Own.– Mrs E.E.D. Shaffer
Br.– Coldstream Stud Inc (Ky)
Tr.– H.H. Battle

28Jan54- 6Hia fst 6f :23 :463 1:11 4↑ ⒻAlw 4500 4 1 1½ 1½ 2hd 54¾ Erb D 117 w 1.95 88-19 Missou1111¼La Perouse1072Centenaire1101½ Faltered 10
22Jan54- 6Hia fst 6f :222 :46 1:112 4↑ ⒻAlw 4500 6 3 2½ 11 11 51¾ Rotz J 109 w 5.30 89-18 Pampas Beauty110nkMissou1111Fulvous114no Faltered 11
20Jun53- 7Det fst 6f :222 :451 1:103 3↑ ⒻRose Leaves 11k 13 1 44½ 68 57 1311 Madden D 110 w 12.70 84-09 Lilly Valenti1111Peu-a-Peu1111½Amabala981 Outrun 13
12Jun53- 6Det fst 6f :222 :453 1:103 3↑ Alw 3500 9 2 2½ 3½ 43½ 45¼ Madden D 110 w 2.50 90-14 ShagTails1101BlackBantam1112ElaineRuth1062¼ No mishap 10
2May53- 6CD fst 7f :224 :451 1:101 1:231 Alw 6000 1 2 32 45½ 76½ 616 Madden D 118 w 3.20 81-09 Berseem1151Platan1153Sir Mango1156 Sore 8
15Apr53- 6Kee fst 6f :224 :47 1:121 ⒻAshland 22k 4 3 12 12 12 31¼ Madden D 121 w 8.60 90-14 CeriseReine1151Bubbley118nkSweetPatootie1212½ Faltered 10
9Apr53- 5Kee fst 6f :222 :452 1:11 ⒻAlw 4000 7 4 1½ 3nk 34 89 Madden D 121 w 4.70 88-10 Task Fleet1152¼Bubbley1213Cerise Reine115¾ Early foot 10
4Feb53- 7Hia sl 7f :233 :481 1:143 1:282 3↑ ⒻColumbiana H 20k 7 3 21 22 32½ 712 Atkinson T 106 w 3.10 56-40 Sunny Dale114¾Emardee1057La Corredora122¾ Tired,swerved 15
21Jan53- 7Hia fst 6f :222 :46 1:11 ⒻJasmine 19k 5 2 2hd 42½ 68¼ 1013 Atkinson T 121 w *.90 80-19 Emardee1183GoodCall1132BiddyJane121½ Stumbled at start 13
18Oct52- 6Kee fst 7f :223 :46 1:112 1:233 ⒻAlcibiades 27k 4 1 11½ 12 11½ 12 Armstrong S 119 w *1.10 94-12 Sweet Patootie1192Good Call1193Aerolite119hd Driving 12
8Oct52- 6Jam fst 6f :23 :46 1:122 ⒻFrizette 17k 5 2 2½ 1hd 11 11¼ Atkinson T 119 w *1.50 85-17 SweetPatootie1191¼PiedmontLass119½GrecnQn1191½ All out 8
17Sep52- 7Atl fst 6f :221 :451 1:114 ⒻMargate H 11k 6 7 32 1hd 1½ 2no Armstrong S 127 w *.70 86-17 PiedmontLass111noSweetPatoot1272½RtsBst1111 Just failed 9
1Sep52- 6Nar fst 6f :222 :453 1:113 ⒻJeanne D'Arc 11k 7 1 1½ 13 19 17 Armstrong S 116 w *.50 93-13 Sweet Patootie1167Air Town105½I'm Marie111¾ Easily best 8
23Aug52- 7Atl fst 6f :224 :46 1:121 Longport H 12k 10 1 11½ 13 15 14 Armstrong S 117 w *.70 84-17 Sweet Patootie1174Prince Dare113½Late Model1091 Easily 11
16Aug52- 3Atl sly 6f :222 :45 1:113 Alw 4500 1 1 12 13 14 15 Armstrong S 113 w 3.50 87-20 Sweet Patootie1135Dinner Winner116½Mr. Jones1101 Easily 8

12Jly52- 7Det	fst 5f	:222 :461 :583		ⒻAlw 7500	6 1 12 12½ 13 14	Sisto R	113	w	2.70	100-11	Sweet Patootie1134Task Fleet1081Pegnpat1132¼	Easily	6
7Jun52- 7Haw	fst 5f	:224 :454 :59		ⒻMiss America 12k	3 1 1hd 2hd 2hd 22½	Johnson WL	119	w	4.90	97-13	BiddyJane1222½SwtPatootie1193ArabActress1191¼	Impeded	13
31May52- 4Det	fst 4½f	:23 :473 :534		Alw 2000	6 1 13 14 16	Cook LC	114	w	*.70	92-14	Sweet Patootie1146Full Circle1091¼Caboose1172	Easily	7
29Apr52- 3CD	fst 4½f	:23 :462 :53		Alw 2000	4 4 52¾ 31½ 2hd	Garner W	115	w	3.30	95-14	CelticPlay115hdSweetPtoot115¾Suprm'sBub1183	Just missed	7
2Apr52- 4GP	fst 3f	:213 :324		Alw 2600	5 2 2½ 21	Scurlock D	109	w	*1.70	- -	AriGold1041SweetPatootie1094CountTwenty107½	No excuse	8
25Mar52- 3GP	fst 3f	:222 :34		ⒻMd Sp Wt	4 4 2hd 12	Scurlock D	118	w	3.55	- -	Sweet Patootie1182Eddie Sue1182½Nalaca1141	Drew away	14

Sword Dancer

ch. c. 1956, by Sunglow (Sun Again)–Highland Fling, by By Jimminy **Lifetime record: 39 15 7 4 $829,610**

Own.– Brookmeade Stable
Br.– Brookmeade Stable (Va)
Tr.– E. Burch

22Oct60- 7Bel	sf 1½Ⓣ	:50 1:162 2:08 2:331	3↑	Man o' War 110k	8 6 711 53½ 55 36¼	Arcaro E	126	b	*1.40	74-20	Harmonizing1262¼Bald Eagle1264Sword Dancer126nk	Bore in	8
24Sep60- 7Aqu	fst 1¼	:472 1:111 1:354 2:011	3↑	Woodward 112k	2 6 68 53½ 3½ 11½	Arcaro E	126	b	3.15	102-08	SwordDancer1261½DottedSwiss1262½BaldEagle1261	Driving	7
17Sep60- 7Atl	fm 1 3/16Ⓣ	:463 1:12 1:372 1:57	3↑	U Nations H 100k	1 10 1015 87¼ 73¼ 21¼	Arcaro E	127	b	4.40	87-12	T.V.Lark1201¼SwordDancer1271¼BallyAche122hd	Strong bid	10
20Aug60- 8AP	sf 1 3/16Ⓣ	:482 1:132 1:39 1:583	3↑	Arlington H 55k	8 5 67½ 87¼ 64¼ 63	Arcaro E	126	b	3.20	71-26	One-EyedKing1181KingGrail109hdMartiniII109no	Late foot	8
30Jly60- 7Aqu	sly 1¼	:471 1:12 1:38 2:03	3↑	Brooklyn H 109k	3 7 711 56 55¼ 55¾	Arcaro E	127	b	2.00	87-17	On-and-On118hdGreek Star1102Waltz1131¼	Began sluggishly	7
4Jly60- 7Aqu	fst 1¼	:472 1:111 1:361 2:013	3↑	Suburban H 108k	5 6 65¾ 43 3½ 1½	Arcaro E	125	b	2.95	112-11	SwordDancr125½FirstLanding1221½Wltz1154½	Crowded early	6
30May60- 7Aqu	fst 1	:224 :453 1:09 1:333	3↑	Metropolitan H 114k	2 10 106¼ 85½ 78¼ 44½	Arcaro E	127	b	3.35	103-03	BaldEagle1283½FirstLanding123nkTalentShow118¾	Rallied	10
30Apr60- 7Aqu	fst 1⅛	:473 1:114 1:37 1:493	3↑	Grey Lag H 70k	9 10 107¾ 53¼ 1½ 1nk	Arcaro E	126	b	2.65	96-06	SwordDancer126nkFirstLanding124noWhitley1162	Hard drive	11
19Mar60- 7GP	gd 1¼	:473 1:122 1:362 2:011	3↑	Gulf Park H 112k	8 8 89½ 56 56½ 45¾	Arcaro E	127	b	2.55	87-05	Bald Eagle126¾Amerigo1233On-and-On1212	Had no mishaps	8
5Mar60- 6GP	fst 1 1/16	:231 :454 1:103 1:414		Alw 4000	2 6 35 11 12½ 12¼	Hartack W	117	b	*.35	99-08	SwordDancer1172¼Don'tAlibi1114½SixShooter1111½	In hand	8
20Feb60- 7Hia	fst 1¼	:464 1:101 1:351 1:593	3↑	Widener H 126k	8 5 56½ 83¼ 77½ 78¾	Arcaro E	129	b	1.95e	98-07	Bald Eagle123¾On-and-On1191½Talent Show118½	Dull effort	8
1Feb60- 6Hia	fst 7f	:232 :46 1:103 1:231	4↑	Alw 5000	6 5 56 58 45½ 43¾	Arcaro E	126	b	*.25e	90-15	Petare112noMaster Palynch1122½Big Effort1071¼	No mishap	6
	Previously trained by J.E. Burch												
31Oct59- 7Aqu	fst 2	:463 2:284 2:55 3:221	3↑	J C Gold Cup 110k	8 4 47 31½ 13 17	Arcaro E	119	b	*1.25	- -	SwordDancr1197RoundTable1241¼TudorEra1242¼	Easy score	8
26Sep59- 7Aqu	fst 1¼	:491 1:141 1:40 2:042	3↑	Woodward 109k	4 3 33 31 2hd 1hd	Arcaro E	120	b	2.90	- -	SwordDancer120hdHillsdale1261¾RoundTable1265	Hard drive	4
22Aug59- 6Sar	fst 1¼	:48 1:121 1:372 2:041		Travers 81k	2 4 47 32 31 1½	Ycaza M	126	b	*.95	87-18	Sword Dancer126½Middle Brother1121¾Nimmer1124	Driving	5
1Aug59- 6Jam	fst 1 3/16	:473 1:122 1:374 1:562	3↑	Brooklyn H 113k	4 5 613 83¾ 51¼ 2¾	Shoemaker W	124	b	*1.05	93-15	Babu112¾Sword Dancer124hdAmerigo1173		10
	Unruly post,swerved start												
25Jly59- 7Mth	sl 1¼	:471 1:123 1:391 2:05	3↑	Monmouth H 113k	4 7 67½ 61¼ 1hd 12	Shoemaker W	120	b	*.60	81-32	SwordDancer1202Amerigo1161½Talent Show1242½	Drew clear	10
13Jun59- 7Bel	sly 1½	:463 1:104 2:024 2:282		Belmont 145k	8 7 715 21 2hd 1¾	Shoemaker W	126	b	*1.65	91-10	Sword Dancer126¾Bagdad12612Royal Orbit12615	Brisk drive	9
30May59- 6Bel	fst 1	:224 :452 1:101 1:351	3↑	Metropolitan H 115k	5 9 75 42 21 13¼	Shoemaker W	114	b	2.50e	98-12	SwordDncr1143¼Jimmer1122¼TlntShow115no	Speed to spare	11
16May59- 8Pim	fst 1 3/16	:471 1:113 1:374 1:57		Preakness 190k	7 6 56 2hd 22 24	Shoemaker W	126	b	1.70	84-17	RoyalOrbit1264SwordDancer1263Dunce1262½	Best of others	11
2May59- 7CD	fst 1¼	:473 1:113 1:36 2:021		Ky Derby 163k	14 4 43 1½ 1hd 2no	Boland W	126	b	8.80	96-06	Tomy Lee126noSword Dancer1262¼First Landing1261	Bore in	17
25Apr59- 7CD	fst 7f	:23 :452 1:094 1:221		Alw 5000	1 5 1hd 1hd 1½ 11	Shoemaker W	122	b	3.60	99-14	Sword Dancer1221Easy Spur1221½Silver Spoon1172	Driving	5
4Apr59- 7GP	fst 1⅛	:463 1:094 1:344 1:471		Florida Derby 116k	9 2 2½ 13 12 2¾	Boulmetis S	122	b	3.90	97-10	Easy Spur122¾SwordDancer1229Master Palynch1221	Gamely	9
24Mar59- 7GP	fst 1 70	:233 :472 1:112 1:41		Alw 3800	3 3 2½ 1½ 13 12	Boulmetis S	118	b	1.70	93-14	SwordDancer1182NobleSel1083Dunce1142½	Speed in reserve	8
11Mar59- 7GP	fst 6½f	:221 :443 1:093 1:16		Hutcheson 12k	5 9 76¾ 56 54½ 54	Boulmetis S	122		5.25	91-14	Easy Spur1222½Pointer114½Octopus122nk	In close in drive	9
11Nov58- 6Jam	fst 1 1/16	:24 :472 1:12 1:443		Remsen 28k	4 5 75 73 74¾ 46½	Guerin E	117	wb	*1.00	80-21	Atoll1174½RicoTso114hdDrrck1142	In close on backstretch	7
25Oct58- 7GS	sly 1 1/16	:222 :463 1:124 1:462		Garden State 297k	2 9 87¼ 47 33½ 32	Guerin E	122	wb	11.40	76-31	First Landing122hdTomyLee1222SwordDancer1223	Game try	13
18Oct58- 8Suf	fst 1 70	:221 :451 1:114 1:424		Mayflower 30k	14 11 1113 65 11½ 14½	Mercier N	116	wb	13.00	91-19	SwordDancer1164½Atoll1191¾OpenView1191½	Speed to spare	14
7Oct58- 5Bel	fst 6f	:223 :463 1:122		Alw 4200	2 3 31½ 21 21 1nk	Kay M5	112	wb	3.55	86-20	SwordDancer112nkSirSalonga1155Principality1171½	Just up	14
27Sep58- 3Bel	sly 7f	:222 :453 1:111 1:241		Alw 4200	2 4 43¼ 54 32 32¼	Nelson E	118	wb	5.30	84-13	Hoist Away118nkMatinal1152Sword Dancer118¾	Held on well	13
10Sep58- 7Atl	fst 7f	:214 :441 1:094 1:232		World's Playground 36k	3 10 83½ 107 77 42¾	Choquette J	111	wb	82.70	86-16	Demobilize119hdIntentionlly1222½PnBolro110hd	Closed gap	15
23Aug58- 2Sar	fst 6f	:231 :474 1:133		©Md Sp Wt	4 5 52½ 53 2½ 11¾	Boland W	118	wb	*1.15	80-18	Sword Dancer1181¾Time Off1182½Nimmer1183½	Going away	12
15Aug58- 4Sar	fst 5½f	:23 :472 1:001 1:064		©Md Sp Wt	2 3 22½ 21½ 22 21½	Nelson E	118	wb	2.20	81-22	Landing1181½SwordDancer11812TimOff1181½	Easily 2nd best	9
26Jly58- 4Del	fst 5½f	:22 :462 :582 1:053		Md Sp Wt	4 7 54½ 45½ 34½ 21½	Grant H	119	wb	*3.40	92-12	CarolinaJoy1191½SwordDancer1192Harlegh1192½	Fast finish	13
12Jly58- 4Del	fst 5½f	:222 :47 :592 1:052		©Md Sp Wt	5 3 21 21 21 32½	Anderson P	119	wb	4.20	92-12	Genian1192½Troilus119hdSwordDancr1196	Forced pace,tired	8
4Jly58- 4Bel	fst 5½f	:23 :471 1:00 1:062		©Md Sp Wt	9 9 64½ 72¾ 43½ 43	Boulmetis S	118	wb	6.25	87-11	Matinal118¾MoonAge118nkLakeErie1182	Forced wide on turn	10
23Jun58- 3Bel	fst 5f-WC	:223 :45 :57		©Md Sp Wt	9 10 1013 109 67	Lovato F	118	wb	7.85f	87-06	Benbecul118nkJtFul1184½Occultd115nk	Slow finding stride	20
10Jun58- 7Bel	sly 5f-WC	:222 :443 :57		©Md Sp Wt	11 10 1014 1012 1020	Kay M5	113	w	38.20	74-08	RestlssWind1186TroubldTms1181½BostonTprty118½	No speed	11
28Feb58- 3Hia	fst 3f	:223 :333		©Md Sp Wt	8 5 77¼ 46½	Boulmetis S	120	w	12.35	- -	Wizardo'Waxah1202JerseyAdmiral1204½JetEra120no	Rallied	14

Tea-Maker

dkb. g. 1943, by Only One (Lucullite)–Tea Leaves, by Pharamond II **Lifetime record: 115 29 23 16 $211,530**

Own.– F.A. Clark
Br.– Mrs F. A. Clark (Ky)
Tr.– J.D. Byers

25Sep53- 5Bel	fst 6f	:223 :462 1:113	4↑	Alw 5000	5 2 1½ 1hd 1hd 1no	Gorman D	118	w	*2.30	91-15	Tea-Makr118noThisSd106hdColdCmmnd1182¼	Held on gamely	12
7Sep53- 6Aqu	fst 7f	:224 :454 1:11 1:234	3↑	Bay Shore H 22k	2 2 24 48½ 619 717	Hanford I	120	w	7.10	74-17	Squared Away1302Eatontown1203Elixir1122½	Done early	9
2Sep53- 5Aqu	fst 6f	:224 :46 1:11	3↑	Fayette H 10k	1 1 56 56¾ 44 33	Woodhouse H	121	w	4.35	94-14	DarkPeter1221½WheatState1071½Tea-Makr1214½	Closed well	7
24Aug53- 6Sar	fst 6f	:23 :472 1:121	3↑	Handicap 4575	6 2 23½ 2½ 1½ 2hd	Green B	123	w	*2.55	87-21	Hilarious118hdTea-Maker1232Sandtop116nk	Held gamely	10
15Jly53- 6Jam	fst 6f	:231 :462 1:11	3↑	Fleetwing H 22k	6 2 32½ 21½ 22 2nk	Woodhouse H	117	w	4.40	92-15	Eatntown118nkTea-Makr117hdSquaredAwy1304½	Just missed	7
27Jun53- 6Aqu	fst 6f	:22 :443 1:092 1:22	3↑	Carter H 59k	2 2 44½ 35 55½ 66¼	Woodhouse H	117	w	19.55	94-09	Tom Fool1352Squared Away1222¼Eatontown1131¼	Tired	9
20Jun53- 5Aqu	fst 6f	:224 :461 1:11	3↑	Handicap 7545	5 3 34½ 35½ 33½ 43¾	Woodhouse H	123	w	2.95	93-11	Eatontown114½DarkPeter1211½FrstGlnc1181¾	Tired in drive	7
10Jun53- 5Bel	fst 6f	:23 :463 1:104	4↑	Alw 4500	7 1 41¾ 4¾ 1hd 1¾	O'Brien C	121	w	*1.20	95-19	Tea-Maker121¾Primate1134½Bit o' Fate108½	Drew out	7
2Jun53- 6Del	gd 6f	:224 :462 1:123	4↑	Alw 4000	5 4 32½ 31½ 1hd 1nk	Boman D	121	w	*.40	82-24	Tea-Maker121nkRuthred1212Yildiz126hd	Cleverly	5
27May53- 6Bel	fst 6f-WC	:214 :443 1:101	3↑	Roseben H 23k	3 8 62¾ 66 42¾	Woodhouse H	119	w	6.05	87-09	SquaredAway1241¼DarkPeter1221½Sagittarius115hd	Swerved	9
19May53- 6Bel	fst 6f	:223 :462 1:113	3↑	Joe Palmer H 15k	6 4 32 41¾ 33 21½	Woodhouse H	114	w	7.30	89-27	Tom Fool1301½Tea-Makr1141½Dark Peter121¾	Closed gamely	7
6May53- 6Bel	gd 6f-WC	:221 :444 1:10	3↑	Toboggan H 30k	1 1 96½ 88¼ 74½	Woodhouse H	118	w	7.70	86-12	Tuscany122noHyphasis116½Dark Peter122nk	No menace	9
25Apr53- 5Jam	fst 5½f	:23 :461 :582 1:041	3↑	Handicap 7560	4 5 43½ 44 48 47¾	Woodhouse H	123	w	4.70	89-12	Tom Fool1282½Do Report1162¼Earmarked1143	Raced wide	5
11Nov52- 6Jam	fst 6f	:223 :454 1:11	2↑	Autumn Day H 22k	5 3 32 44 42½ 31¼	Woodhouse H	126	w	*1.95	91-16	Squared Away119¾Delegate119½Tea-Maker1261½	Closed well	7
20Oct52- 6Jam	fst 6f	:224 :453 1:104	2↑	New Rochelle H 22k	4 4 42 42¼ 32 21½	Woodhouse H	126	w	*2.75	91-20	Delegate1141½Tea-Maker126¾War King1111½	Good effort	9
6Oct52- 6Jam	fst 6f	:23 :46 1:11	2↑	Interborough H 23k	2 2 73¾ 85 53¼ 2½	Gorman D	124	w	3.80	91-15	Squared Away118½Tea-Makr124noTrue Pattern1061¼	Gaining	11
27Sep52- 4Bel	fst 5½f-W	:22 :444 1:032	2↑	Handicap 6045	8 7 63¾ 4nk 1no	Woodhouse H	130	w	*1.15	91-05	Tea-Maker130noTruePattern115hdTwoRainbows1062	Just up	9
22Sep52- 6Bel	fst 7f	:223 :454 1:111 1:234	2↑	Vosburgh H 23k	6 6 61¾ 4¾ 1hd 21½	Woodhouse H	123	w	4.05	89-19	Parading Lady1051½Tea-Maker1232Cyclotron110nk	Held well	8
15Sep52- 6Bel	fst 6f-WC	:22 :441 1:082	2↑	Fall Highweight H 24k	10 8 4nk 2hd 2½	Woodhouse H	140	w	13.00	98-03	Hitex130½Tea-Maker140½Papoose117nk	Good effort	15
8Sep52- 6Aqu	fst 7f	:223 :451 1:102 1:24	3↑	Bay Shore H 17k	10 5 33 34 23 53¼	Woodhouse H	123	w	6.65	87-20	NextMove1151FirstGlance111nkSquaredAway1202	No excuse	12
23Aug52- 5Sar	fst 5½f	:23 :46 :582 1:051	3↑	Handicap 5045	6 1 2½ 21½ 2½ 11	Woodhouse H	122	w	4.10	91-17	Tea-Makr1221FirstGlance111½SquardAway126hd	Drew clear	7
15Aug52- 6Sar	sl 7f	:231 :463 1:12 1:253	3↑	American Legion H 9k	4 1 1½ 1hd 1½ 1¾	Woodhouse H	118	w	4.60	87-25	Tea-Maker118¾First Glance1091½Northern Star1196	Driving	6
8Aug52- 6Sar	fst 6f	:232 :47 1:114	3↑	Handicap 5035	2 1 41¼ 45 56 43¼	Woodhouse H	119	w	4.65	86-23	Squared Away1221¼Elixir1071First Glance1101	Raced wide	5
16Jly52- 6Jam	fst 6f	:23 :454 1:101	3↑	Fleetwing H 21k	5 1 21 21 21 1¾	Woodhouse H	114	w	8.45	96-16	Tea-Maker114¾Squared Away1202½Arise1221	Driving	6

4Jly52- 6Aqu	fst	7f	:221 :443 1:09 1:22	3↑ Carter H 29k	7	9	97½	97½	1016	1013	Scurlock O	115	w	15.90	89-09	NorthernStar1152CraftyAdmiral1202½ToMarket123no	Outrun	10
21Jun52- 5Aqu	fst	6f	:222 :452 1:102	3↑ Handicap 7540	3	2	34½	36	25	25	Gorman D	121	w	3.45	95-11	Squared Away1225Tea-Maker121noDelegate1201½	Impeded	4
14Jun52- 6Mth	fst	6f	:221 :45 1:112	3↑ Oceanport H 17k	8	5	41¼	75¼	76¾	77¾	Gorman D	120	w	*2.30	83-21	GeneralStaff1122HiBillee112nkNorthernStar113hd	Faltered	8
7Jun52- 5Bel	fst	6f	:223 :461 1:104	3↑ Handicap 7540	2	2	3nk	3½	2½	31¼	Gorman D	121	w	3.05	94-14	First Glance112¾Delegate113½Tea-Maker121no	Held well	7
29May52- 5Del	fst	6f	:222 :453 1:103	3↑ Wilmington H 12k	5	2	2hd	1hd	13	13	Gorman D	121	w	6.00	98-11	Tea-Maker1213Jet Master113hdSenator Joe119½	Ridden out	8
21May52- 6Bel	sl	6f-WC	:223 :462 1:124	3↑ Roseben H 17k	1	1		32½	76¼	67¾	Gorman D	120	w	6.40	69-23	DarkPeter1133NorthernStar112noSquaredAwy118½	Quit early	7
29Apr52- 6Bel	gd	6f-WC	:221 :443 1:091	3↑ Toboggan H 23k	8	1		2hd	21	33	Gorman D	120	w	5.10	92-05	Dark Peter108½Crafty Admiral1182½Tea-Maker1202	Faltered	8
16Apr52- 6Jam	gd	6f	:23 :46 1:111	3↑ Jamaica H 17k	4	1	1½	1hd	13	12½	Woodhouse H	112	w	10.20	91-15	Tea-Maker1122½Northern Star115noDelegate1142	In hand	9
11Apr52- 6Jam	fst	6f	:23 :46 1:113	3↑ Mettlesome H 7.9k	6	2	1½	2hd	2hd	31	Gorman D	115	w	4.20	88-21	Delegate111hdBryan G.1261Tea-Maker1153	Held well	8
1Apr52- 6Jam	fst	6f	:222 :453 1:094	3↑ Paumonok H 29k	9	3	41¾	63½	46¼	88¾	Gorman D	116	w	11.55	89-13	Woodchuck1193½Squared Away116½[D]Jumbo116¾	Tired	11
12Nov51- 6Jam	fst	6f	:231 :454 1:111	2↑ Autumn Day H 17k	2	1	31½	32	32	1½	Porch G	115	w	10.45	91-20	Tea-Maker115½Guillotine126¾Delegate120hd	Driving	9
3Nov51- 7Jam	sly	6f	:222 :452 1:121	3↑ Handicap 5065	6	4	45	34½	33½	41	Scurlock O	117	w	4.90	85-17	Assignment105noDelegate119½Atalanta104½	No excuse	7
19Oct51- 6Jam	fst	6f	:223 :452 1:101	2↑ New Rochelle H 17k	6	2	31½	31	42	43½	Gorman D	118	w	6.15	92-15	Squared Away1151½Delegate116½Guillotine1261½	Faltered	12
10Oct51- 5Bel	fst	5½f-W	:22 :441 1:013	3↑ Handicap 4565	2	2		51½	32	33¾	Gorman D	123	w	6.85	102-00	Delegate1133Guillotine132¾Tea-Maker123nk	No mishap	8
1Oct51- 6Bel	fst	7f	:221 :453 1:103 1:231	2↑ Vosburgh H 18k	13	4	42	3nk	1½	53	Gorman D	120	w	15.20	91-17	[D]Miche109½War King108¾Bryan G.122nk	Faltered	13
			Placed fourth through disqualification															
24Sep51- 6Bel	fst	6f-WC	:222 :443 1:09	2↑ Fall Highweight H 25k	9	16		134¼	113¼	115¼	Riles S	134	w	13.45	91-07	Guillotine134noSquared Away1262Ferd128no	Showed little	18
15Sep51- 5Aqu	fst	6f	:23 :46 1:104	3↑ Handicap 4560	3	3	11	11½	11½	11	Gorman D	121	w	2.70	98-13	Tea-Maker1211Northern Star1184½Hill Prince128¾	All out	7
10Sep51- 6Aqu	fst	7f	:222 :451 1:101 1:232	3↑ Bay Shore H 18k	9	7	96¼	74½	72¼	63½	Mehrtens W	121	w	7.05	91-15	Sheilas Reward126½Guillotine117¾Bryan G.123nk	No mishap	12
17Aug51- 6Sar	my	7f	:231 :461 1:114 1:252	3↑ American Legion H 9.3k	8	2	2hd	2hd	2½	2¾	Mehrtens W	120	w	6.45	87-19	[D]War King109¾Tea-Maker1201[D]More Sun113hd	Impeded	10
			Placed first through disqualification															
6Aug51- 7Sar	fst	1	:241 :48 1:13 1:384	3↑ Alw 4000	3	5	42	3½	3nk	41½	Passmore WJ	119	w	2.45	81-18	Blue Hills113½Combat Boots1051Charleston113no	Weakened	6
18Jly51- 6Jam	fst	6f	:231 :462 1:112	3↑ Fleetwing H 22k	7	6	41½	41½	1hd	2hd	Mehrtens W	122	w	6.75	90-16	More Sun110hdTea-Maker1221½Arise1301½	Just failed	9
11Jly51- 7Aqu	fst	6f	:224 :454 1:111	3↑ Handicap 5035	3	6	51¾	63¼	42¾	42¼	Mehrtens W	126	w	4.40	94-14	Repetoire118hdJessLinthcum1182¼MghtyQust112no	No mishap	6
4Jly51- 6Aqu	fst	7f	:223 :452 1:101 1:232	3↑ Carter H 23k	9	7	79	66½	43½	64½	Scurlock O	122	w	4.75	90-17	Arise1221More Sun1081¼Piet1231	Stumbled at start	9
29Jun51- 6Aqu	sly	6f	:23 :461 1:104	3↑ Handicap 5050	4	2	32	32	32	32¾	Mehrtens W	124	w	4.15	95-14	Bryan G.1182½Magic Words116nkTea-Maker1241	Mild rally	6
16Jun51- 7Mth	gd	6f	:223 :454 1:114	4↑ Alw 5000	8	5	44	51¾	43	31	Flutie E	124	w	2.00	88-15	JessLinthicum115hdSheilasRwrd1241T-Mkr1242¼	Good effort	8
6Jun51- 6Bel	fst	6f-WC	:222 :444 1:084	3↑ Roseben H 12k	4	8		73¾	2½	3nk	Arcaro E	126	w	*1.70	97-04	Delegate111nkMiche116noTea-Maker126¾	Crowded early	10
29May51- 6Del	gd	6f	:224 :462 1:113	3↑ Wilmington H 12k	2	5	42½	3½	32	21	Arcaro E	125	w	*.95	92-20	CallOver1151Tea-Maker125hdRoyalGovrnor115nk	Forced wide	6
14May51- 6Bel	fst	6f-WC	:222 :444 1:092	3↑ Toboggan H 24k	11	2		2hd	1hd	2no	Mehrtens W	123	w	3.45	94-06	Hyphasis110noTea-Maker1231Casemate1191	Just missed	14
7May51- 6Jam	fst	6f	:23 :461 1:111	3↑ Jamaica H 17k	6	2	42½	4¾	2hd	1½	Mehrtens W	121	w	5.35	91-15	[D]Tea-Maker121½Piet1241SheilasRwrd1242¼	Driving,bore in	7
			Disqualified															
1May51- 6Jam	fst	6f	:23 :462 1:11	3↑ Handicap 5030	5	2	1hd	2hd	1hd	31	Mehrtens W	121	w	2.90	91-13	Piet1201Sheilas Reward124hdTea-Maker1216	Good effort	6
			Previously owned by Mrs S.C. Clark Jr															
25Oct50- 6Jam	gd	6f	:23 :46 1:111	2↑ New Rochelle H 17k	5	10	116	94½	52½	31¾	Mehrtens W	125	w	4.20	89-19	MagicWords1131SheilasRewrd124¾Tea-Makr1252	Closed fast	12
12Oct50- 6Jam	sly	6f	:23 :46 1:12	3↑ Interborough H 17k	6	2	65	65¾	55	51½	Robertson J	126	w	4.10	85-18	SheilsRwrd120¾MgcWords112½WsconsnBoy109nk	Forced wide	10
			Previously owned by Mrs F.A. Clark															
25Sep50- 6Bel	fst	7f	:223 :453 1:102 1:23	2↑ Vosburgh H 18k	5	2	11	11½	11½	11¼	Robertson J	118	w	6.60	95-15	Tea-Maker1181¼More Sun106½Piet124nk	Easily	12
18Sep50- 6Bel	fst	6f-WC	:221 :443 1:084	2↑ Fall Highweight H 25k	2	11		112	102¼	42¾	Robertson J	134	w	6.25	94-06	Arise1332Delegate128nkRoyal Governor129½	Finished well	14
2Sep50- 6Aqu	fst	7f	:224 :452 1:10 1:231	3↑ Bay Shore H 18k	2	2	2hd	21	11	21	Mehrtens W	117	w	*2.25e	95-09	Piet1201Tea-Maker1171¼Arise1211½	No excuse	14
15Aug50- 5Sar	fst	6f	:223 :453 1:101	3↑ Handicap 3565	7	4	41¼	62¾	3½	11	Woodhouse H	122	w	*1.60	97-09	Tea-Maker1221Sagittarius1172½Marabout113nk	Driving	9
7Aug50- 6Sar	fst	1	:241 :481 1:13 1:38	4↑ Alw 4000	6	2	2½	2hd	2hd	31½	Guerin E	116	w	*.75	85-17	The Mater108½Pibroch1131Tea-Maker1164½	No rally	6
3Aug50- 4Sar	fst	6f	:23 :461 1:111	3↑ Handicap 4050	1	1	11	11½	11	13	Guerin E	120	w	*1.55	92-13	Tea-Maker1203Marabout1163Mount Marcy1231½	Going away	6
15Jly50- 5Jam	fst	6f	:231 :462 1:11	3↑ Handicap 4565	7	6	51¾	42	31	1hd	Guerin E	122	w	2.55	92-11	Tea-Maker122hdSagittarius118nkWhirling Fox1151	Just up	10
28Jun50- 6Del	fst	6f	:223 :453 1:11	3↑ Alw 4000	2	4	3nk	11	13	13	Robertson J	117	w	*.60	96-09	Tea-Maker1173Rare Mineral115hdLittle Harp1171	Easily	7
17Jun50- 6Del	fst	6f	:224 :462 1:112	4↑ Alw 4000	2	4	2hd	1hd	11	11½	Culmone J	114	w	*1.80	94-14	[D]Tea-Maker1141½Larn1171½LttlHrp1141½	Impeded rival str	6
			Disqualified															
13Jun50- 6Del	fst	6f	:224 :454 1:102	4↑ Alw 3000	5	1	1½	1½	11	11	Robertson J	116	w	4.25	99-13	Tea-Maker1161Fleeting Star120nkLaran1191	Driving	6
9Jun50- 5Del	fst	1 1/16	:234 :473 1:12 1:433	4↑ Alw 3500	1	1	12	1hd	21	23	Culmone J	115	w	2.60	92-12	Curandero1193Tea-Maker115hdSlam Bang1163½	Weakened	7
30May50- 4Del	sl	6f	:23 :471 1:132	4↑ Alw 3500	3	4	32	21	1½	1¾	Culmone J	112	w	3.30	84-19	Tea-Maker112¾Lucky Ned115¾Noble Impulse1243	Driving	5
2Nov49- 6Jam	sly	6f	:232 :462 1:112	2↑ New Rochelle H 17k	1	1	73¾	85¼	76½	66¼	Passmore WJ	110	w	15.70	88-19	Delegate1226Better Self124noLithe109no	Never close	8
26Oct49- 6Jam	sly	1 1/16	:243 :48 1:122 1:452	3↑ Questionnaire H 23k	6	4	45	67½	810	814	Passmore WJ	109	w	10.70	72-17	Royal Governor1181Donor120½Vulcan's Forge125¾	Tired	8
20Oct49- 6Jam	fst	1 1/16	:244 :48 1:122 1:443	3↑ Handicap 5030	2	3	33½	46½	49	59½	Passmore WJ	122	w	4.10	80-16	Our John Wm.1163Dart By1161½Wine List1193½	Tired	6
10Oct49- 6Lrl	fst	1 1/16	:232 :474 1:134 1:462	2↑ Laurel 8.6k	1	2	22	2hd	2hd	2nk	Passmore WJ	114	w	*.60e	85-18	Alfoxie108nkTea-Maker1141Gasparilla1152	Game try	7
24Sep49- 6Lrl	fst	6f	:224 :463 1:112	3↑ Capitol H 8.7k	9	2	42¼	31½	32½	2no	Passmore WJ	117	w	*2.60	97-17	Irisen115noTea-Maker117½Big Story1092	Just missed	9
19Sep49- 6Bel	fst	6f-WC	:23 :461 1:12	2↑ Fall Highweight H 24k	8	3		1hd	2hd	3nk	Passmore WJ	127	w	16.05	81-16	RoyalGovernr129hdRoyalBlood132nkTea-Makr127¾	Lost iron	13
15Sep49- 6Aqu	fst	1 1/16	:25 :482 1:123 1:452	3↑ Alw 4000	6	2	31	21	31	54¾	Passmore WJ	117	w	3.55	82-17	Quarter Pole1223Brick1051Stymie122hd	Weakened	8
5Sep49- 5Aqu	fst	6f	:231 :462 1:111	3↑ Handicap 4045	5	4	65½	67½	34½	34¼	Passmore WJ	116	w	3.20	92-17	Royal Blood1154Mangohick122nkTea-Maker1164	Faltered	7
29Aug49- 6Aqu	sly	7f	:233 :47 1:121 1:25	3↑ Bay Shore H 18k	13	7	107	106¾	52¼	2½	Passmore WJ	113	w	19.65	86-17	Loser Weeper116½Tea-Maker1131½Rippey121nk	Held gamely	15
23Aug49- 6Sar	fst	6f	:223 :463 1:11	3↑ Handicap 4060	7	4	63½	74½	62¾	52	Passmore WJ	114	w	5.70	91-11	WineList115hdBlueBorder115nkRoyalBlood114¾	Raced wide	10
12Aug49- 6Sar	sly	7f	:234 :464 1:113 1:252	3↑ American Legion H 9.2k	4	7	65	56	55	55½	Passmore WJ	116	w	8.20	83-18	Manyunk119hdWhirling Fox1102Big If1101½	Even effort	8
			Daily Racing Form time,1:26 1/5															
9Aug49- 5Sar	fst	6f	:223 :453 1:111	4↑ Handicap 3565	4	3	53¾	54½	2hd	1hd	Passmore WJ	120	w	4.55	92-11	Tea-Maker120hdPipette1162Our John Wm.115nk	Hard drive	8
4Aug49- 6Sar	gd	6f	:23 :464 1:12	3↑ Handicap 4045	3	3	32	22	2hd	2¾	Passmore WJ	119	w	*1.30e	87-18	Arise113¾Tea-Maker1192Algasir1084	Weakened	5
21Jly49- 6Jam	fst	1⅛	:481 1:13 1:392 1:522	3↑ Handicap 4535	1	2	21	2½	21	24½	Passmore WJ	122	w	2.10	81-20	Stunts1144½Tea-Maker1222½Prefect1191½	Forced wide	5
16Jly49- 5Jam	fst	6f	:232 :462 1:112	3↑ Handicap 5050	1	1	55	55½	56½	41½	Passmore WJ	115	w	2.60	92-14	EagleEye111hdMyRequest1261¼BluBordr112hd	Closed stoutly	5
9Jly49- 5Jam	fst	6f	:232 :46 1:112	3↑ Handicap 5065	10	8	43½	41¼	1hd	11¼	Passmore WJ	111	w	5.80	94-16	Tea-Maker1111¼Stunts1041My Request126½	Drew out	10
4Jly49- 5Jam	fst	1 1/16	:241 :48 1:123 1:454	3↑ Handicap 5040	5	4	31½	32	3½	2nk	Passmore WJ	119	w	2.50	84-17	Prefect112nkTea-Maker1191¼Coincidence112hd	Just missed	6
25Jun49- 5Aqu	fst	7f	:231 :462 1:12 1:251	3↑ Carter H 29k	5	4	56	43½	41½	41½	Passmore WJ	111	w	19.05	84-26	Better Self126nkRippey123½High Trend107¾	No mishap	9
18Jun49- 6Mth	fst	1	:23 :461 1:111 1:373	3↑ Salvator Mile 13k	14	6	46	43½	65	87¾	Passmore WJ	112	w	8.50	99-08	Istan1142High Trend1121Royal Governor1191½	Faltered	14
7Jun49- 6Bel	fst	7f	:231 :47 1:114 1:241	4↑ Alw 4500	7	2	1hd	1hd	1½	2hd	Passmore WJ	122	w	*1.20	89-19	Bug Juice117hdTea-Maker1226Hyblaze115¾	Game try	8
3Jun49- 6Bel	fst	6f	:22 :452 1:11	4↑ Alw 4000	5	4	34	23	1hd	16	Passmore WJ	113	w	3.50	95-14	Tea-Maker1136Thwarted114nkEagle Eye113½	Easily	11
30May49- 6Bel	fst	1¼	:48 1:123 1:38 2:03	3↑ Suburban H 61k	3	7	21	42½	68	711	Passmore WJ	106	w	23.80	74-17	Vulcan'sForge1242½ButWhyNot1174FlyingMissel108½	Quit	13
20May49- 7Bel	sly	1	:222 :453 1:104 1:384	4↑ Alw 4000	5	2	23	23	23	1hd	Passmore WJ	114	w	3.60	80-19	Tea-Maker114hdUp Beat122hdThwarted114½	Hard drive	10
14May49- 6Bel	fst	1	:23 :461 1:11 1:362	3↑ Metropolitan H 30k	8	6	53	42½	22	42¾	Passmore WJ	107	w	10.95	89-15	LosrWeepr1051½Vulcan'sForg126nkBtWhyNt1191	Weakened	10
6May49- 6Bel	fst	6f-WC	:224 :451 1:092	3↑ Toboggan H 24k	6	8	54	84¾	86¼	73	Passmore WJ	110	w	17.30	91-05	Rippey1291½Pipette108¾Up Beat120no	No factor	11
30Apr49- 5Jam	fst	6f	:23 :46 1:112	3↑ Handicap 5040	2	3	34½	37	25	34¾	Arcaro E	117	w	3.95	89-13	Up Beat1224½Make-Up Man108nkTea-Maker117¾	Went well	7
12Nov48- 6Jam	fst	1 1/16	:243 :483 1:143 1:452	3↑ Handicap 5035	7	2	2hd	2½	2nk	2½	Rustia W	122	w	*2.20	85-25	Caifero111½Tea-Maker1223Rinaldo107½	Weakened	7
5Nov48- 6Pim	my	2 1/16	:53 2:402 3:061 3:392	3↑ Exterminator H 11k	4	2	45	411	413	426	Passmore WJ	114	w	10.40	83-30	Pilaster126nkPetrol Point1026Miss Grillo12020	Outrun	4
30Oct48- 7Pim	fst	1¾	:473 2:033 2:291 2:553	3↑ Governor Bowie H 12k	3	2	36	3½	38	311	Passmore WJ	120	w	2.60	119-00	Pilaster1242½Natural1048Tea-Maker1204	Went well	7
23Oct48- 5Jam	fst	5½f	:231 :47 1:052	3↑ Handicap 6030	5	5	44	32½	33	21¼	Passmore WJ	111	w	4.60	90-22	Grey Flight1151¼Tea-Maker1111½Buzfuz1262	Good effort	5
19Oct48- 6Jam	fst	6f	:232 :471 1:121	3↑ Handicap 4565	8	8	74	52¼	4½	11	Passmore WJ	120	w	11.05	90-22	Tea-Maker1201Energetic114hdNathaniel1211	Driving	9

14Oct48- 7Jam	fst 1 1/16	:244 :483 1:134 1:464	4↑ Alw 5000	3 6 52½ 52 1hd 1nk	Passmore WJ	118 w	3.55	79-22	Tea-Maker118nkCencerro1121¼Ned Luck112½	Driving	9
9Oct48- 7Jam	fst 1⅛	:483 1:131 1:382 1:512	3↑ Handicap 5055	3 3 3nk 11 2½ 44¼	Anderson P	114 w	6.30	87-14	Bright Sword1211¼Campos1131Frere Jacques1222	Faltered	10
6Oct48- 5Jam	fst 6f	:24 :481 1:13	4↑ Alw 4000	6 2 2hd 1nk 11 11½	Rustia W	119 w	30.85	86-22	Tea-Makr1191½Flying Weather1221Winter Wheat1152	Easily	12
1Oct48- 6Bel	sly 1½	:494 1:151 2:06 2:313	3↑ Handicap 6055	7 3 54 74½ 812 818	James B	118 w	5.75	62-22	Frere Jacques122noMy Emma111hdCampos1141½	No mishap	8
21Sep48- 7Bel	fst 1⅛	:472 1:12 1:37 1:494	3↑ Handicap 5080	3 3 21 41¼ 2hd 43½	Passmore WJ	108 w	16.20	88-14	War Trophy115hdQuarter Pole1153Star Reward126½	Hung	8
16Sep48- 8Bel	fst 1½	:481 1:124 2:04 2:313	3↑ Alw 5000	1 4 511 33 2½ 11	Passmore WJ	109 w	6.20	80-14	Tea-Maker1091Happiness106¾Ready Jack1064	Driving	8
8Sep48- 5Aqu	fst 7f	:25 :483 1:142 1:273	4↑ Alw 4000	3 5 42½ 43 31 11¼	Passmore WJ	106 w	17.70	74-31	Tea-Maker1061¼Liberty Road111hdNed Luck1111	Driving	7
30Aug48- 3Aqu	fst *1¾	Hurdles 3:104	3↑ Alw 4000	7 4 416 523 628 641	Mong'o T	130 ws	11.80e	--	Deep Sea Tale1393Coeur1316Frere Markette1441½	Impeded	7
11Aug48- 5Sar	fst 7f	:233 :47 1:123 1:27	3↑ Md Sp Wt	10 3 52¼ 42¼ 21 11	Passmore WJ	117 w	50.65	81-21	Tea-Maker1171Brass Band1173¼Harbor1173	Driving	10
6Aug48- 5Sar	sl *1¾	Hurdles 3:332	3↑ National Maiden 7.8k	3 2 25 210 240 250	Mong'o T	143 ws	4.65	--	Lock and Key14650Tea-Maker14330Jordan1301½	Outrun	5
7Jly48- 3Aqu	gd *1½	Hurdles 2:473	3↑ Md Sp Wt	11 4 67½ 911 720 728	Mon'lo T	141 ws	28.40	--	DeepSeaTale1325LionRampant1483½TopKnot137nk	No factor	11
28Jun48- 5Del	fst *1¾	Hurdles 3:051	3↑ National Maiden 7.9k	6 4 - - - -	Peoples C	150 ws	12.55	--	Lock and Key1437Rank1567Charioteer1352		6
	Broken equipment,pulled up										
22Jun48- 1Del	fst *1¾	Hurdles 3:084	3↑ Alw 3500	1 13 79¾ 79 718 822	Peoples C	145 ws	7.20	--	Lock and Key1301½Todmorden1371¼Mr. Man1426	Outrun	13
19Jun48- 8Del	my 6f	:231 :481 1:142	4↑ Alw 5000	4 5 54¼ 42 55 46½	Passmore WJ	110 w	32.10	73-31	Tacaro Briar1202½Meetmenow1101½Pujante1202½	No mishap	7
27Mar48- 7Cam	fst *1½	Hurdles 2:45	3↑ Alw 800	2 5 55½ - - -	Dodson S	140 w	-	--	GoldenRsk156hdNghtLgnd148hdEscondrjo1344	Lost rider 6th	6
13Mar48- 2Cam	fst *1½	Hurdles 2:414	4↑ Alw	5 7 713 - - -	Seidler W	136 w	-	--	NightLegend153hdDeferment1364TheBoyn1466	Lost rider 4th	8

Tempted

ch. f. 1955, by Half Crown (Hyperion)–Enchanted Eve, by Lovely Night

Lifetime record: 45 18 4 9 $330,760

Own.– Mooring Stable
Br.– Christiana Stables (Ky)
Tr.– H.S. Clark

29Oct60- 8Nar	fst 1 3/16	:463 1:12 1:38 1:572	3↑ Nar Spl H 29k	2 2 22 11 1hd 33	Nelson E	114	5.20	83-25	Reinzi1111½Polylad1191½Tempted1142	Set fast pace,tired	12
12Oct60- 7Bel	fst 1½	:471 1:114 2:042 2:303	3↑ ⒻLadies H 59k	4 1 13 11½ 23 86¼	Nelson E	121	6.05	74-15	Berlo1242½Woodlawn112½Who's Ahead105½	Used in pace	13
1Oct60- 7Bel	fst 1⅛	:461 1:11 1:362 1:492	3↑ ⒻBeldame 91k	8 1 3nk 31½ 88 88¾	Nelson E	123	*2.50	80-16	Berlo1192RoyalNative1231MakeSal1193	Early speed,stopped	9
21Sep60- 7Aqu	fst 1	:23 :453 1:102 1:353	3↑ ⒻMaskette H 30k	1 6 64¼ 53¼ 5¾ 1nk	Nelson E	126	*2.20	90-13	Tempted126nkMakeSail118½Craftinss108no	Swerved start,up	12
22Aug60- 7Sar	fst 1⅛	:471 1:113 1:374 1:512	3↑ ⒻDiana H 38k	3 2 23 21½ 11½ 17	Nelson E	124	3.75	88-14	Tempted1247Quill1281¾Aesthetc1121	Going away easily	5
12Aug60- 7Sar	fst 7f	:222 :45 1:102 1:231	3↑ Handicap 1000	10 1 33½ 88 106½ 108	Nelson E	118	9.35	90-15	Four Lane117½Seven Corners116½Tick Tock1204	Brief speed	10
30Jly60- 6Del	sly 1¼	:461 1:103 1:364 2:022	3↑ ⒻDelaware H 146k	2 1 15 31½ 59 716	Nelson E	125	5.00	74-15	Quill1259RoyalNative1291¼GeecheLou110¾	Early foot,tired	8
23Jly60- 6Del	fst 1 1/16	:23 :46 1:102 1:431	3↑ ⒻNew Castle 35k	8 1 12 1½ 21 33	Nelson E	126	3.30e	92-11	Quill1201¼IndianMad1201¾Tmptd1262¼	Set pace,tired badly	8
9Jly60- 7Mth	fst 1 1/16	:224 :461 1:11 1:434	3↑ ⒻMolly Pitcher H 28k	3 2 2hd 2hd 33½ 46¼	Nelson E	127	4.80	80-17	RoyalNative1274Quill1221¾MissOrestes114½	Well up,tired	10
2Jly60- 7Mth	fst 6f	:213 :443 1:10	3↑ Rumson H 28k	8 2 67 65¾ 54½ 35½	Nelson E	119	*2.10	86-15	Alhambra1183¼SevenCornrs1122¼Temptd119¾	Wide last turn	8
30May60- 4Del	fst 6f	:222 :454 1:104	4↑ ⒻAlw 6500	2 1 1hd 13 13 12½	Nelson E	123	*.30	91-13	Tempted1232½Wedlock1142NoraDars1146	Scored well in hand	6
17May60- 7GS	fst 6f	:22 :451 1:11	4↑ ⒻAlw 7500	1 1 33 36½ 33 22	Nelson E	115	*.30	87-17	WindRose1212Tmptd1151½MissRoyl115½	Wide upper stretch	6
12Oct59- 7Aqu	fst 1 5/16	:472 1:111 1:362 2:09	3↑ ⒻLadies H 57k	5 1 11½ 12 12 12¾	Nelson E	128	*.85e	--	Tempted1282¾High Bid1121Big Effort1151½	Saved ground	8
3Oct59- 7Aqu	fst 1⅛	:474 1:121 1:37 1:501	3↑ ⒻBeldame H 67k	3 1 11½ 11½ 11½ 12½	Nelson E	125	*1.75e	--	Tempted1252½Idun121nkHigh Bid1131	Drew away,mild urging	14
21Sep59- 7Aqu	fst 1	:223 :45 1:094 1:36	3↑ ⒻMaskette H 29k	1 4 3nk 2hd 1hd 21¼	Bailey PJ	126	*2.20	--	Idun1191¼Temptd1261½Bornstr1192	Off sluggishly,game try	10
17Aug59- 6Sar	fst 1⅛	:471 1:111 1:364 1:502	3↑ ⒻDiana H 56k	2 1 11 12 13 15½	Nelson E	122	*2.30	97-15	Tempted1225½Polamby1162½SparMaid110hd	Speed in reserve	9
10Aug59- 5Sar	fst 1	:23 :461 1:104 1:36	3↑ ⒻHandicap 7500	1 2 21 2hd 1½ 1½	Nelson E	122	*.90e	97-15	Temptd122½Polamby1164½Idun1222½	Forced pace,hard drive	5
25Jly59- 6Del	fst 1¼	:462 1:111 1:37 2:033	3↑ ⒻDelaware H 155k	5 2 21½ 11 2½ 31¼	Nelson E	119	*3.20e	83-18	Endine117½Polamby114¾Tmptd1192½	Made very game effort	11
18Jly59- 6Del	fst 1 1/16	:231 :464 1:112 1:433	3↑ ⒻNew Castle 35k	2 1 12 11½ 11½ 12¾	Nelson E	116	4.50e	93-18	Tempted1162¾Bornastar126½Chstos112no	Under a mild drive	10
11Jly59- 5Del	gd 1 1/16	:232 :47 1:121 1:443	3↑ ⒻAlw 10000	2 1 13 13 13 12	Ussery R	115	*.90e	88-21	Tempted1152Chistosa1132½MissOrsts118¾	Well rated,easily	9
30Jun59- 7Del	fst 6f	:222 :453 1:111	4↑ Alw 6000	5 3 33½ 33½ 4¾ 11¼	Batcheller L	117	*.40	89-17	Tempted1171¼Amplitud112nkStyrunnr122no	Under mild drive	6
8Jun59- 7Bel	fst 1 1/16	:223 :451 1:102 1:424	3↑ ⒻTop Flight H 27k	2 2 1½ 1½ 23 37	Ussery R	118	2.40e	87-13	Big Effort1235½Endine1181½Tempted1181½	Tired badly	7
25May59- 7Bel	fst 7f	:221 :453 1:111 1:241	3↑ ⒻDistaff H 28k	1 2 22½ 22 21 42¾	Nelson E	120	2.85	83-18	HappyPrincess1141½Mlle.Dianne115noIdun1251¼	Speed,tired	8
13May59- 5GS	sly 6f	:224 :463 1:112	4↑ ⒻAlw 5500	3 5 2hd 1hd 12 18	Kirk J5	111	*.70	87-21	Tempted1118DanceCard1183½BonnieA.110nk	Drew out easily	7
5May59- 7GS	fst 6f	:223 :462 1:12	4↑ ⒻAlw 6000	11 2 3nk 21½ 2½ 11½	Kirk J5	110	4.50	84-22	Tempted1101½BattleHill1182½MissOrestes115hd	Drew clear	12
4Nov58- 7GS	sl 1 1/16	:24 :474 1:112 1:45	ⒻJersey Belle 28k	1 1 1hd 1½ 11½ 1¾	Nelson E	121 w	6.70	85-24	Tempted121¾Lopar115noPointPleasant112hd	Long,hard drive	9
13Oct58- 6Bel	fst 1½	:48 1:121 2:034 2:302	3↑ ⒻLadies H 58k	8 1 14 2½ 611 714	Ussery R	114 w	7.35e	67-20	Endine1141¾Dotted Line123nkAnnie-Lu-San1081½	Led,tired	10
4Oct58- 7Bel	fst 1⅛	:453 1:10 1:36 1:492	3↑ ⒻBeldame H 70k	2 1 11½ 11 3½ 61½	Ussery R	114 w	7.90e	87-14	OuterSpace117noAGlitter119hdDottedLin120nk	Used in pace	17
24Sep58- 6Bel	fst 1	:222 :452 1:102 1:363	3↑ ⒻMaskette H 29k	11 2 2½ 11½ 12 12½	Ussery R	113 w	5.10e	91-19	Tempted1132½Alanesian1231¾Annie-Lu-San1112	Ridden out	12
15Sep58- 6Bel	fst 1 1/16	:223 :451 1:101 1:431	ⒻGazelle H 29k	2 1 1½ 21 22 34½	Nelson E	116 w	11.55	87-15	Idun1244½Munch122noTempted116¾	Led pace for 4f,tired	10
27Aug58- 6Sar	fst 1¼	:474 1:13 1:384 2:054	ⒻAlabama 29k	9 1 12 1hd 1hd 11½	Ussery R	113 w	6.50	79-24	Temptd1131½SprMd1133Lopr1141	Drew clear in strong drive	11
20Aug58- 4Sar	fst 1⅛	:473 1:123 1:383 1:531	ⒻAlw 5000	4 1 1½ 1½ 1½ 2nk	Nelson E	116 w	3.65	83-20	A Glitter122nkTempted1165Daumay1192	Made a sharp effort	5
15Aug58- 6Sar	fst 7f	:224 :454 1:113 1:254	ⒻTest 25k	13 7 84¼ 87½ 1013 79	Nelson E	115 w	*4.00	77-22	AnyMorn1151¾DandyBlitzen115¾Armorial1151½	Bore out late	17
26Jly58- 6Del	fst 1¼	:464 1:111 1:361 2:03	3↑ ⒻDelaware H 160k	10 2 21 12 1hd 42	Chambers A	106 w	11.00e	85-12	Endine111noDotted Line1161Woodlawn1081	Speed to stretch	16
12Jly58- 6Del	sly 1⅛	:47 1:12 1:39 1:521	ⒻDel Oaks 49k	8 2 21 21 34 35¾	Nelson E	119 w	11.50	73-20	Big Effort1192¼Idun1193½Tempted119½	Forced pace,tired	9
30Jun58- 5Del	fst 1	:24 :472 1:112 1:371	ⒻAlw 4000	2 3 2hd 1hd 13 13½	Nelson E	118 w	*.70	100-11	Tempted1183½Locust Time1153Bokaris1104	Speed in reserve	5
21Jun58- 7Bel	sly 1⅜	:48 1:124 1:393 2:20	ⒻC C A Oaks 71k	2 6 53½ 63¼ 811 818	Nelson E	121 w	9.90	53-21	A Glitter121½Spar Maid1219Craftiness1214	Speed,stopped	12
12Jun58- 6Bel	fst 1⅛	:461 1:111 1:374 1:511	ⒻAlw 10000	6 2 1½ 21 21 2½	Nelson E	114 w	18.90	79-17	AGlitter117½Tempted1141¾Lopr1113	Coming again at finish	13
31May58- 8Del	fst 6f	:22 :451 1:112	3↑ ⒻAlw 5000	5 10 47½ 410 46½ 32	Nelson E	114 w	*2.80e	86-12	Mumtaz1182TooHasty118noTemptd1141½	Best stride too late	12
14May58- 7Pim	fst 1 1/16	:233 :473 1:123 1:463	ⒻBlack-Eyed Susan 23k	1 2 21 54½ 53¾ 54½	Nelson E	121 w	6.10	72-22	Daumay121hdMovitave1213½StaySmooch121¾	Early foot,tired	8
5May58- 6Pim	sly 6f	:223 :47 1:133	Alw 4000	8 6 42 34 31½ 32¾	Kirkland A	119 w	*1.60e	79-23	Staysail1121½Alstar1181¼Tmptd1191¼	Raced without mishap	8
23Nov57- 5Pim	gd 1 70	:23 :463 1:114 1:441	Alw 4500	7 5 58½ 58¾ 59½ 56¼	Nelson E	116 w	2.20	82-15	FrankZero1131¼PoliceCll1161½CountDown110hd	Lacked rally	9
9Nov57- 7Nar	gd 1 1/16	:234 :474 1:123 1:474	ⒻJeanne d'Arc 16k	5 4 45½ 21 11 13½	Nelson E	109 w	7.00	72-23	Tmptd1093½TwoCentStamp105½Slon116½	Under light urging	9
16Oct57- 4Bel	fst 7f	:224 :472 1:141 1:271	ⒻMd Sp Wt	6 11 53½ 41 2hd 14½	Nelson E	115 w	4.25e	74-18	Tempted1154½Colic1151½Redone1154½	Kept to mild pressure	14
10Oct57- 5Bel	gd 6f-WC	:23 :47 1:132	ⒻMd Sp Wt	18 14 72¾ 71¾ 157¼	Nelson E	115 w	5.85e	65-28	Doricharger115nkIntent One1151Beguiling115hd	Fell back	21

The Mast

blk. g. 1947, by Annapolis (Man o' War)–Claddagh, by Alcazar

Lifetime record: 36 10 4 7 $103,400

Own.– Mrs J.R.H. Thouron
Br.– Mrs James E. Ryan (Pa)
Tr.– J.E. Ryan

25Jun54- 6Del	hd *2	S'Chase 3:45	4↑ Georgetown H 12k	1 - - - - -	McDonald RS	153wsb	*.60	--	SunShower1555Sundowner1403½TouristList1345	Fell at 1st	6
17Jun54- 5Aqu	hd *2	S'Chase 3:471	4↑ Hitchcock H 11k	5 1 12½ 12½ 18 112	McDonald RS	150wsb	*1.20	--	ThMast15012SunShower1572BannrWaves1321½	Scored easily	5
3Jun54- 5Bel	hd *2½	S'Chase 4:391	4↑ Meadow Brook H 11k	5 2 22 15 - -	McDonald RS	154wsb	2.65	--	Sun Shower1551½Beaupre1324Sundowner14425		7
	Bobbled last jump,fell										
27May54- 5Bel	fm *2	S'Chase 3:412	4↑ Corinthian H 8.9k	5 6 68½ 56 314 314¾	McDonald RS	156wsb	2.65	--	ExtraPoints1622¾SunShower15212TheMast1563	Lacked rally	7
8May54- 6Bel	sf *2	S'Chase 3:562	4↑ International 22k	3 4 32½ 22 210 218	McDonald RS	153wsb	*2.25	--	ExtraPoints15318TheMast15320HisBoots1531¾	Bobbled badly	13
26Apr54- 3Bel	fm *2	S'Chase 3:432	4↑ Alw 4500	4 3 42½ 23 24 27	McDonald RS	157 w	*2.25e	--	ExtraPoints1397ThMst1575Sundownr1451	Weakened in drive	10
	Previously raced in name of Mrs E. duPont Weir										
9Oct53- 5Bel	fst *3	S'Chase 5:451	4↑ Grand Nat'l H 29k	3 4 35½ 24½ 23 22½	McDonald RS	160wsb	2.30	--	His Boots1412½The Mast16018Mighty Mo1325	Good effort	11

1Oct53- 5Bel	fst *2½	S'Chase 4:463	4↑ Brook H 17k	4	3	34½	32½	13	1hd	McDonald RS	157wsb	*2.50	- -	The Mast157hdHis Boots14012Sundowner1511	Just lasted 9
24Sep53- 5Bel	fst *2	S'Chase 3:454	3↑ Broad Hollow H 11k	5	1	22½	2½	2½	1hd	McDonald RS	155wsb	3.10	- -	The Mast155hdSundowner1502½Mighty Mo1312	Just up 7
13Aug53- 5Sar	fst *2	S'Chase 4:093	4↑ North Am H 8.8k	3	1	36	49	11½	14	McDonald RS	144wsb	10.85	- -	The Mast1444Sundowner1432½Virginius1341½	Handily 6
6Aug53- 5Sar	fst *2	S'Chase 4:10	4↑ Shillelah H 8.9k	4	4	714	717	728	727	McDonald RS	148 w	4.40	- -	Sun Shower1321Sundowner1393Oedipus1604	Quit early 7
3Jly53- 5Del	fst *2½	S'Chase 4:512	4↑ Indian River H 12k	4	4	32	48½	45	47	McDonald RS	151 w	*1.75	- -	Monkey Wrench1351Tourist List136hdCherwell1346	No rally 5
26Jun53- 5Del	fst *2	S'Chase 3:464	3↑ Georgetown H 12k	5	2	21½	33	12	1½	McDonald RS	148 w	3.95	- -	TheMast148½MonkeyWrench1351HuntingFox13612	Hard drive 6
19Jun53- 6Bel	fst *2¼	S'Chase 4:121	4↑ Temple Gwathmey H 16k	7	6	69¼	513	414	515	McDonald RS	155 w	22.75	- -	Errolford1305½Sea Legs1652Oedipus1645	No factor 7
	Daily Racing Form time,4:16 2/5														
4Jun53- 5Bel	fst *2½	S'Chase 4:421	4↑ Meadow Brook H 11k	5	3	55	-	-	-	McDonald RS	154 w	9.45	- -	SeaLegs1575Oedipus1642½HisBoots1462½	Hit obstacle,fell 6
21May53- 5Bel	fst *2	S'Chase 3:471	4↑ Corinthian H 8.8k	2	3	512	513	-	-	McDonald RS	156 w	2.80	- -	Sea Legs149½Hot1445His Boots14625	Bobbled,fell 5
14May53- 5Bel	fst *2	S'Chase 3:453	4↑ C L Appleton Mem 8.9k	4	4	47½	32½	34½	33½	Garr'anT	144 w	*1.20e	- -	Oedipus1581½His Boots1422The Mast1447	No excuse 6
7May53- 5Bel	sl *2	S'Chase 3:581	4↑ Int'l H 8.8k	5	5	518	710	36½	33¼	McDonald RS	156 w	2.10	- -	Sea Legs1442½Hunting Fox133¾The Mast15613	Closed fast 7
3Oct52- 5Bel	sf *3	S'Chase 5:44	4↑ Grand Nat'l H 28k	7	5	514	43½	23	25	Smithwick P	154 w	3.15	- -	Sea Legs1365The Mast1542Oedipus1657	Faltered 9
11Sep52- 5Aqu	fst *2	S'Chase 3:441	3↑ Harbor Hill H 11k	2	5	64¼	65½	510	514	Smithwick P	157 w	3.70	- -	Semper Eadem1354Hot1472½Jam1556	No factor 6
29Aug52- 5Sar	hd *2½	S'Chase 5:064	4↑ Saratoga H 11k	2	4	512	512	514	518	Smithwick P	158 w	2.55	- -	Banner Waves1362Titien II1473His Boots1518	No factor 6
27Jun52- 6Del	fst *2½	S'Chase 4:44	4↑ Indian River H 12k	2	1	13	318	322	322	Smithwick P	161 w	*.55e	- -	Jam15220Monkey Wrench1342The Mast1616	Fenced poorly 5
20Jun52- 6Del	fst *2	S'Chase 3:431	4↑ Georgetown H 12k	5	4	51¾	32	15	15	Smithwick P	157 w	3.20	- -	The Mast1575Jam1511½[DH]Crooning Wind1431½	Easily 8
11Jun52- 6Bel	fst *2¼	S'Chase 4:163	4↑ Temple Gwathmey H 16k	9	4	4¾	31	2hd	1¾	Smithwick P	153 w	3.00	- -	The Mast153¾Oedipus1631¼Navy Gun1497	Hard urged 9
29May52- 5Bel	fst *2½	S'Chase 4:431	4↑ Meadow Brook H 11k	3	8	67½	47	11	12¼	Smithwick P	146 w	8.50	- -	The Mast1462¼Navy Gun14815Titien II1476	All out 8
8May52- 5Bel	fst *2	S'Chase 3:424	4↑ C L Appleton Mem 9k	1	4	21½	32½	43½	33¾	Smithwick P	143 w	3.10	- -	Jam1393Lone Fisherman139¾The Mast143¾	Jumped poorly 6
1May52- 5Bel	sf *2	S'Chase 3:471	4↑ International H 9.3k	5	7	-	-	-	-	Smithwick P	144 w	3.50	- -	Jam1418Flaming Comet1371Palaja1418	Fell 11
18Jun51- 6Del	fst *2	S'Chase 3:453	4↑ Tom Roby 14k	4	4	31	16	18	115	Snyder J	133 w	4.95	- -	The Mast13315Proceed1484Extra Points1486	Driving 10
31May51- 5Bel	fst *2	S'Chase 3:443	4↑ Spring Maiden 7.2k	7	5	32	-	-	-	Snyder J	133 w	3.60e	- -	Boom Boom150¾Cicas14015Night Patrol14014	Fell 13
25May51- 3Bel	fst *2	S'Chase 3:484	4↑ Alw 4000	1	1	15	1hd	21	32¼	Snyder J	130 w	2.60	- -	IrishEaster1491¼SyracuseLad1331TheMst13012	Bobbled last 13
21Jun50- 1Del	gd *1¾	Hurdles 3:051	3↑ Alw 3000	1	1	14	14	-	-	Snyder J	130 w	1.95	- -	Spleen1302Easter Vigil14110Alphabetical13510	7
	Rank early,left course														
13Jun50- 1Del	fst *1¾	Hurdles 3:012	3↑ Alw 3000	6	3	35½	2hd	2hd	12	Coleman R	131.5 w	2.10e	- -	The Mast131.52Sauchiehall13010Easter Vigil14215	Handily 6
2Jun50- 2Del	fst 6f	:23 :471 1:142	Md Sp Wt	2	11	93½	77	78	65½	Rogers C	120wb	23.45	73-22	Hindi1201Extra Early1201½Dr. Cricket120no	Rough trip 14
24May50- 7Bel	fst 1	:233 :47 1:122 1:381	3↑ Md Sp Wt	9	4	41¾	66	818	922	Hettinger G	115wb	19.75	61-15	Demon115¾Hyvania1156On the Mark1121½	Done early 10
9May50- 3Bel	fst *1½	Hurdles 2:481	3↑ Sp Wt 3000	10	11	117¾	78½	54	44½	Snyder J	130 w	28.35	- -	Wunderprinz145hdBoom Boom1502½Rialto1502	Finished well 14
14Jun49- 1Del	fst 5½f	:223 :471 1:064	Md 6500	4	7	73¾	75½	46½	35½	Snyder J	111wb	7.85	82-15	Icy Stare1153½Make Hay1162The Mast111hd	Closed fast 14

Tim Tam

dkb. c. 1955, by Tom Fool (Menow)–Two Lea, by Bull Lea

Lifetime record: 14 10 1 2 $467,475

Own.– Calumet Farm
Br.– Calumet Farm (Ky)
Tr.– H.A. Jones

7Jun58- 7Bel	fst 1½	:482 1:133 2:041 2:301	Belmont 114k	7	7	69½	21	21½	26	Valenzuela I	126 w	*.15	76-17	Cavan1266TimTam1265½Flamingo126¾	8
	Swerved often,finished lame														
17May58- 8Pim	fst 1 3/16	:464 1:113 1:374 1:571	Preakness 133k	8	9	710	21½	1½	11½	Valenzuela I	126 w	*1.10	87-15	TimTam1261½LincolnRoad1263½GoneFishin'126no	Ridden out 12
3May58- 7CD	my 1¼	:473 1:131 1:382 2:05	Ky Derby 160k	2	8	811	45½	22	1½	Valenzuela I	126 w	2.10	82-17	Tim Tam126½Lincoln Road126½Noureddin1266	Fully extended 14
29Apr58- 7CD	sl 1	:23 :463 1:13 1:393	Derby Trial 16k	1	6	55½	65¼	52½	1nk	Valenzuela I	122 w	*.60	77-29	Tim Tam122nkEbony Pearl1161¼Flamingo1122	Forced wide 8
18Apr58- 6Kee	fst 7f	:232 :452 1:093 1:221	Alw 4500	8	3	44	43½	3nk	1½	Hartack W	122wb	*.60	101-10	TimTam122½Nadr119nkHllsdl113hd	Under confident handling 8
29Mar58- 7GP	fst 1⅛	:463 1:113 1:362 1:491	Florida Derby 119k	5	7	47½	36	22	1½	Hartack W	122 w	*.35	88-16	TimTam122½LincolnRoad1187GreyMonarch1221½	Strong drive 11
19Mar58- 7GP	fst 1 1/16	:233 :463 1:104 1:424	Fountain of Youth 16k	2	9	65¾	55	2hd	12	Hartack W	122 w	*.65	96-10	TimTam1222GreyMonarch119hdLi'lFella1221	Speed to spare 10
1Mar58- 7Hia	fst 1⅛	:464 1:11 1:361 1:484	Flamingo 135k	6	6	52½	51½	2hd	2hd	Hartack W	122 w	*1.50	91-11	[D]Jewel'sRewrd122hdTmTam1223¾TalentShow1223½	Bumped 9
	Placed first through disqualification														
15Feb58- 7Hia	gd 1⅛	:454 1:112 1:364 1:512	Everglades 31k	1	8	67	43	1hd	11¼	Hartack W	114 w	*.70e	78-20	Tim Tam1141¼Kentucky Pride1176Liberty Ruler114¾	Easily 9
5Feb58- 7Hia	fst 7f	:22 :443 1:091 1:224	Bahamas 25k	11	7	913	79	54½	3½	Scurlock O	114 w	*.50e	95-10	Olymar123½KntuckyPride117noTmTm114½	Rallied on outside 11
28Jan58- 7Hia	fst 6f	:222 :452 1:104	Alw 5000	8	7	711	611	38	35¼	Scurlock O	119 w	*.25e	86-19	KntuckyPride1192½Yemen1162¾TmTm1195	Strong in stretch 10
22Jan58- 8Hia	my 7f	:234 :47 1:12 1:251	Alw 5000	6	4	31½	32	1½	1½	Hartack W	122 w	*.45	84-24	TimTm122½BeauDaumier1142½BigFreeze1175	Stout restraint 9
17Jan58- 6Hia	fst 6f	:223 :454 1:111	Alw 5000	6	3	2hd	1½	12	12¾	Hartack W	112 w	*.65	89-16	Tim Tam1122¾Field Trophy110½Best of Show1061¾	Easily 8
18Oct57- 3GS	sly 6f	:222 :462 1:122	Md Sp Wt	8	12	810	74¾	44½	44¼	Hartack W	118 w	*.80	78-22	Royal Warrior1181¼Vengeance1183Wait for It118hd	12
	Broke slowly,made up ground														

Tom Fool

b. c. 1949, by Menow (Pharamond II)–Gaga, by Bull Dog

Lifetime record: 30 21 7 1 $570,165

Own.– Greentree Stable
Br.– Duval A. Headley (Ky)
Tr.– J.M. Gaver

24Oct53- 7Pim	fst 1 3/16	:474 1:114 1:371 1:554	3↑ Pim Spl 50k	1	1	13	15	16	18	Atkinson T	126 w	-	101-20	Tom Fool1268Navy Page120noAlerted126	Much the best 3
	No wagering														
26Sep53- 6Bel	fst 1	:231 :461 1:11 1:364	3↑ Sysonby 54k	2	1	11	12½	16	13	Atkinson T	126 w	-	90-15	Tom Fool1263Alerted126½Grecian Queen116	Under restraint 3
	No wagering														
8Aug53- 7Sar	fst 1¼	:49 1:13 1:382 2:052	3↑ Whitney 27k	1	2	22	12	14	13½	Atkinson T	126 w	-	81-20	Tom Fool1263½Combat Boots114	Very much the best 2
	No wagering														
4Aug53- 6Sar	fst 1	:232 :462 1:111 1:371	3↑ Wilson 16k	1	1	11	12½	16	18	Atkinson T	126 w	-	91-17	Tom Fool1268Indian Land117	No competition here 2
	No wagering														
11Jly53- 6Aqu	fst 1¼	:483 1:132 1:38 2:042	3↑ Brooklyn H 56k	3	2	2hd	13½	13	11½	Atkinson T	136 w	*.25	85-13	Tom Fool1361½Golden Gloves1107High Scud109no	Easing up 5
27Jun53- 6Aqu	fst 7f	:22 :443 1:092 1:22	3↑ Carter H 59k	5	5	56	45	21½	12	Atkinson T	135 w	*.65	100-09	Tom Fool1352Squared Away1222¼Eatontown1131¼	Easily best 9
30May53- 6Bel	fst 1¼	:471 1:11 1:353 2:003	3↑ Suburban H 58k	1	1	13	13	11	1no	Atkinson T	128 w	*2.05	97-17	Tom Fool128noRoyal Vale1247Cold Command1142	Hard drive 7
23May53- 6Bel	gd 1	:223 :46 1:111 1:354	3↑ Metropolitan H 36k	3	2	22½	1½	11½	1½	Atkinson T	130 w	*.50	95-13	Tom Fool130½Royal Vale1278½Intent1251½	Driving,bore in 7
19May53- 6Bel	fst 6f	:223 :462 1:113	3↑ Joe Palmer H 15k	4	3	21½	2hd	12½	11½	Atkinson T	130 w	*.70	91-27	Tom Fool1301½Tea-Maker1141½Dark Peter121¾	Eased up 7
25Apr53- 5Jam	fst 5½f	:23 :461 :582 1:041	3↑ Handicap 7560	1	1	33	33½	2½	12½	Atkinson T	128 w	*.95	97-12	Tom Fool1282½Do Report1162¼Earmarked1143	Ridden out 5
8Nov52- 6Jam	fst 1 3/16	:47 1:112 1:381 1:58	Empire City H 55k	4	1	1½	1hd	1½	1hd	Atkinson T	128 w	*.65	86-23	Tom Fool128hdMarcador1092Roaring Bull1051½	Hard drive 8
1Nov52- 6Jam	fst 1⅛	:484 1:13 1:374 1:501	3↑ Westchester H 56k	3	2	31	31	2½	2no	Atkinson T	125 w	*1.75	95-18	Battlefield123noTomFool1251Alerted1251¼	Blocked,gaining 9
18Oct52- 6Jam	fst 1⅛	:471 1:11 1:354 1:492	3↑ Grey Lag H 60k	10	2	1hd	2hd	1hd	1no	Atkinson T	119wb	*1.40e	99-16	Tom Fool119noBattlefield118nkAlerted1211¼	Hard drive 11
11Oct52- 6Jam	fst 1 3/16	:472 1:11 1:361 1:554	Roamer H 47k	7	5	42	31½	21	22	Atkinson T	126 w	*.75	95-14	Quiet Step1112Tom Fool1261Risque Rouge105¾	No excuse 9
30Sep52- 6Bel	fst 1	:232 :463 1:114 1:362	3↑ Sysonby H 15k	7	3	31½	3½	12	11¼	Atkinson T	126 w	*1.10	92-18	Tom Fool1261¼Alerted1183Greek Ship1181¼	Easily 8
17Sep52- 6Bel	fst 1	:232 :471 1:122 1:37	Jerome H 24k	5	2	21½	21½	14	17	Atkinson T	120 w	2.80	89-26	Tom Fool1207Marcador111nkMark-Ye-Well1301½	Hard drive 10
16Aug52- 6Sar	sly 1¼	:493 1:144 1:401 2:072	Travers 23k	4	1	11	11½	21	34	Atkinson T	114 w	*1.55	67-22	OneCount1263Armageddon1231TomFl114¾	Wide,weakened 8
	Geldings not eligible														
11Aug52- 6Sar	sl 1⅛	:482 1:13 1:383 1:532	Alw 5000	3	2	21	2½	1hd	2no	Atkinson T	117 w	*.80	83-22	CountFlame117noTomFool117½GoldnGloves117½	Just missed 7

5Aug52- 6Sar	sly 1		:232 :47 1:123 1:392 3↑	Wilson 16k	1 3 37 22 12	14½	Atkinson T	106	w	*.25e	80-25	TomFool1064½NorthernStar1201ColonyDate1148	Drew clear 4
14Jly52- 6AP	fst 7f		:232 :452 1:10 1:223	Alw 6000	4 1 2hd 31 33½	44	Atkinson T	124	w	*.90	93-11	High Scud118½Mark-Ye-Well118½Eljay1183	Weakened 5
26Jun52- 6Aqu	fst 6f		:223 :462 1:103	Rippey H 10k	3 4 41½ 52¾ 2hd	2hd	Atkinson T	126	w	*1.00	99-15	Hitex120hdTom Fool1262Duke Fanelli1022	Hung 8
19Apr52- 6Jam	fst 1⅛		:48 1:12 1:383 1:522	Wood Memorial 63k	2 1 2hd 22½ 1hd	2nk	Atkinson T	126	w	*1.65	84-16	Master Fiddle126nkTom Fool126½Pintor126½	Just failed 14
7Apr52- 6Jam	fst 6f		:232 :464 1:121	Alw 10000	1 5 1½ 1hd 11	1nk	Atkinson T	120	w	*.80	86-20	Tom Fool120nkPrimate117nkCousin1202	Won cleverly 6
24Oct51- 6Jam	sly 1 1/16		:242 :48 1:131 1:451	©East View 53k	4 3 45½ 42 1hd	1nk	Atkinson T	122	w	*.65	86-15	Tom Fool122nkPut Out122nkRisque Rouge122¾	Hard drive 6
6Oct51- 6Bel	fst 6½f-W		:221 :451 1:101 1:171	Futurity 111k	7 4 41¼ 1nk	11¾	Atkinson T	122	w	5.75	86-14	Tom Fool1221¾Primate1221Jet's Date122hd	Driving 10
	Geldings not eligible												
1Oct51- 5Bel	fst 6f-WC		:223 :45 1:092	Sp Wt 5000	3 1 31½ 31½	24	Atkinson T	118	w	*1.90	90-11	Hill Gail1184Tom Fool118nkBaybrook1182	Bothered early 16
1Sep51- 6Sar	gd 6½f		:233 :472 1:123 1:191	Hopeful 62k	2 4 31 1hd 1hd	21¼	Atkinson T	122	w	*.75e	88-20	Cousin1221¼Tom Fool122nkHannibal12212	No excuse 6
25Aug51- 4Sar	fst 6f		:224 :463 1:114	Grand Union Hotel 21k	4 3 32 32 1hd	11	Atkinson T	122	w	2.05	89-16	Tom Fool1221Cousin126¾Jet Master1261¼	Driving 5
20Aug51- 6Sar	fst 6f		:231 :47 1:123	Sanford 11k	6 3 21 21 1½	12¼	Atkinson T	113	w	*.90	85-18	Tom Fool1132¼First Refusal1163½Secant1082½	Easily 8
13Aug51- 5Sar	fst 5½f		:232 :47 :593 1:062	©Md Sp Wt	8 7 52 43½ 11	14	Atkinson T	118	w	*2.00	85-17	Tom Fool1184Handsome Teddy1181Warpath1181	Easily 12

Two Lea

b. f. 1946, by Bull Lea (Bull Dog)–Two Bob, by The Porter

Lifetime record: 26 15 6 3 $309,250

Own.– Calumet Farm
Br.– Calumet Farm (Ky)
Tr.– H.A. Jones

25Oct52- 9BM	fst 1¼		:474 1:111 1:36 2:013 3↑	Bay Meadows H 56k	1 2 45½ 42½ 31	2½	Moreno H	126	w	*.70	114-04	Moonrush115½Two Lea1261Grantor118hd	Finished gamely 8
18Oct52- 9BM	fst 1 1/16		:234 :471 1:11 1:413 3↑	Children's Hospitl H 23k	4 5 55½ 43½ 1½	1½	Moreno H	122	w	*1.35e	102-09	Two Lea122½Moonrush1151½Grantor1202½	Wide,driving 10
4Oct52- 9BM	fst 1		:231 :462 1:104 1:363 3↑	ⒻSan Mateo H 11k	7 4 33½ 34 1hd	1½	Moreno H	127	w	*.85e	97-11	Two Lea127½Danae115nkWistful117½	Saved ground 7
12Jly52- 7Hol	fst 1¼		:461 1:103 1:351 2:001 3↑	Hol Gold Cup 137k	7 2 43 21 1hd	1½	Moreno H	113	w	*1.55e	98-07	Two Lea113½Cyclotron1003Sturdy One1083½	Driving 12
5Jly52- 6Hol	fst 6f		:222 :452 :574 1:10 3↑	ⒻRamona H 22k	8 3 83 83 41½	11	Moreno H	125	w	*2.25e	96-07	TwoLea1251[DH]PrincessLygia113[DH]RuthLly1141	Wide into str 8
28Jun52- 7Hol	fst 1 1/16		:224 :454 1:101 1:421 3↑	Inglewood H 28k	4 4 46 43½ 23	43¼	Moreno H	122	w	*1.35e	94-08	SturdyOne1111StormyCloud105nkAdmrlDrk1162	Saved ground 7
14Jun52- 7Hol	fst 1 1/16		:231 :461 1:11 1:432 3↑	ⒻVanity H 28k	5 4 34½ 32½ 13	11¼	Moreno H	122	w	*.35e	91-11	Two Lea1221¼Wistful1121¾Jennie Lee117¾	Saved ground 8
31May52- 7Hol	fst 7f		:222 :45 1:092 1:213 3↑	ⒻMilady H 28k	10 6 53¾ 53¼ 21	22½	Moreno H	117	w	*.75e	98-10	A Gleam1122½Two Lea1176Spanish Cream124no	Second best 11
24May52- 4Hol	fst 6f		:222 :453 :574 1:10 4↑	Alw 5000	1 5 53½ 62¼ 2hd	2nk	Moreno H	113	w	*.75e	96-07	Jennie Lee108nkTwo Lea1132½Akimbo1182	Closed well 7
14May52- 7Hol	fst 6f		:22 :444 :572 1:102 4↑	ⒻAlw 10000	1 6 66¾ 66¾ 32	11¼	Shoemaker W	112	w	*.90	94-09	Two Lea1121¼La Franza106nkJennie Lee113hd	Wide,bore in 8
2May52- 7GG	fst 6f		:222 :444 1:092 3↑	Alw 4000	7 6 53 53½ 74½	55¼	Pierson NL	112	w	*1.35e	89-13	Mohammedan1193Witch-English1221Jennie Lee109¾	9
	Close quarters												
15Jly50- 6AP	fst 6f		:224 :45 1:094 3↑	Handicap 4000	5 4 44 32½ 22	2½	Brooks S	122	w	*.80e	96-07	Porter'sBroom115½TwoLea1225OceanDrive1171	Forced wide 6
25Feb50- 7SA	fst 1¼		:462 1:11 1:351 2:00 3↑	S Anita H 135k	1 2 11½ 11 1hd	32¼	Gilbert J	113	w	*.35e	104-11	Noor1101¼Citation1321Two Lea113nk	Game try 11
28Jan50- 7SA	fst 1¼		:472 1:122 1:37 2:022	Maturity 122k	4 2 11 1½ 1hd	21	Arcaro E	116	w	*.50e	93-10	Ponder1261Two Lea1165Mocopo1121½	Easing up 9
14Jan50- 7SA	my 1⅛		:472 1:121 1:393 1:524 3↑	ⒻS Margarita H 59k	2 4 32 2½ 11	12	Brooks S	126	w	*1.75	79-21	Two Lea1262Gaffery1182½But Why Not1163½	Driving 8
5Jan50- 7SA	fst 7f		:224 :46 1:11 1:233 4↑	ⒻHandicap 10000	1 2 31 21½ 1hd	1nk	Brooks S	122	w	*.55	91-18	Two Lea122nkGaffery1162Sweet Dream1161½	Held gamely 10
29Dec49- 7SA	fst 6f		:232 :47 1:111 3↑	ⒻAlw 5000	6 5 44 33½ 32	1hd	Brooks S	119	w	*.85	91-21	Two Lea119hdSweet Dream1161½But Why Not1114	Just up 7
17Aug49- 6Was	fst 7f		:212 :443 1:083 1:214	ⒻArtful 22k	4 7 72¾ 23 2½	11½	Brooks S	124	w	*.50	101-07	Two Lea1241½Imacomin1121½Stole1071½	Drew out 7
20Jly49- 6AP	fst 1		:23 :46 1:102 1:37	ⒻCleopatra H 26k	1 1 11 14 15	12	Brooks S	122	w	*.60e	87-15	Two Lea1222Lithe108nkWistful1212	Eased up 6
2Jly49- 6AP	fst 6f		:222 :45 1:10 3↑	ⒻModesty 28k	6 6 41½ 43¼ 33½	2½	Brooks S	111	w	*1.40e	96-10	No Strings101½Two Lea1112Dandilly1081	Strong finish 10
22Jun49- 6AP	fst 6f		:223 :452 1:094	ⒻPrincess Doreen 23k	2 8 31 31 2hd	11¼	Brooks S	111	w	3.30	98-11	Two Lea1111¼No Strings1118Alsab's Day1211	Driving 11
28May49- 4Bel	fst 6f		:231 :471 1:12	ⒻAlw 4000	1 3 42 31½ 1½	1¾	Brooks S	113	w	*1.10	90-18	Two Lea113¾Lady Dorimar1134Black Chiffon1103	Drew out 11
20Apr49- 5HdG	fst 6f		:231 :462 1:122	Alw 3000	6 8 63½ 51¾ 32	1no	Brooks S	114	w	*1.40	89-14	Two Lea114noGambler1142Magna Charta117hd	Hard drive 10
17Sep48- 4Bel	fst 6f-WC		:222 :453 1:102	ⒻMd Sp Wt	12 5 21 2hd	14	Pierson NL	116	w	*.80e	89-12	Two Lea1164Ochita1161½Boomdeay1164	Easily 15
13Sep48- 4Bel	fst 5½f-W		:224 :454 1:043	ⒻMd Sp Wt	13 8 125 51¾	3¾	Pierson NL	116	w	*2.15	90-05	Wild Pitch116nkParting Shot111½Two Lea1161½	Bore out 26
25Aug48- 3Was	fst 5½f		:23 :463 :594 1:064	ⒻMd Sp Wt	6 9 1011 108¼ 65½	31	Pierson NL	116	w	*1.50	85-11	Top Hope1161Pella116hdTwo Lea1162	No excuse 12

Warfare

gr. c. 1957, by Determine (Alibhai)–War Whisk, by War Glory

Lifetime record: 16 7 2 4 $414,445

Own.– Bellehurst Stable
Br.– C.H. Jones & Sons (Cal)
Tr.– W.C. Winfrey

26Mar60- 7Aqu	fst 6f		:221 :451 1:093	Swift 27k	5 1 63½ 54 2½	11½	Arcaro E	126	b	*.40	104-03	Warfare1261½Francis S.126¾Greek Page126nk	Mild urging 8
	Previously trained by H. Ross												
6Jan60- 6SA	fst 6f		:223 :46 1:101	Alw 10000	8 3 41½ 21 2hd	2nk	Valenzuela I	124	b	*.90	93-13	T.V. Lark124nkWarfare1241½Tompion120¾	Made game effort 8
31Oct59- 7GS	sly 1 1/16		:23 :46 1:10 1:424	Garden State 283k	2 5 41¾ 21 2hd	1½	Valenzuela I	122	b	*1.20	96-15	Warfare122½BllyAch1224Tompon122hd	Best under hard drive 10
17Oct59- 7Aqu	fst 1		:223 :451 1:094 1:351	Champagne 230k	8 4 31½ 3½ 1½	11	Valenzuela I	122	b	2.05	- -	Wrfare1221Tompon1225½BllyAch1224	Well rated,going away 10
5Oct59- 7Aqu	fst 7f		:222 :451 1:10 1:223	Cowdin 70k	6 5 43½ 42½ 11	12½	Valenzuela I	117	b	10.50	- -	Warfare1172½VitalForc124nkBllyAch1241¾	Under mild drive 12
28Sep59- 7Aqu	fst 6½f		:221 :451 1:104 1:173	Alw 5000	4 6 43¼ 33½ 32½	21½	Bauer R	119	b	5.00	- -	Four Lane1161½Warfare1193Ira Eaker1161½	Sharp effort 12
12Sep59- 7Dmr	fst 6f		:221 :442 1:093	Dmr Futurity 86k	6 9 84¼ 84¾ 57½	3¾	Valenzuela I	119	b	*1.90e	95-10	Azure'sOrphan116¾Salatom116noWarfr119hd	Gaining rapidly 11
4Sep59- 7Dmr	fst 6f		:222 :45 1:093	Alw 7500	5 2 41¾ 41¼ 11½	11	Valenzuela I	122	b	*2.20	96-09	Warfare1221Noble Noor1223¼Fay's Night Out1192¾	Driving 8
22Aug59- 8Dmr	fst 6f		:214 :444 1:092	Alw 5000	9 4 76 88¼ 89¼	88	Campas R	112	b	*1.80	89-11	BrightTiny1161¼Fay'sNightOut119½Azure'sOrphan122½	Wide 9
18Jly59- 7Hol	fst 6f		:214 :444 :571 1:10	Hol Juv Champ 163k	12 3 84½ 84 53¾	31½	Maese A	122	b	5.30e	91-11	NobleNoor113½Tompion1161Wrfare122nk	Strong stretch bid 15
9Jly59- 7Hol	fst 5½f		:221 :444 :57 1:03	©C S Howard H 30k	8 1 63¼ 53½ 22	1½	Maese A	114	b	20.10	97-09	Wrfare114½NewPolicy1142¾Hdmstr1142¼	Under strong drive 9
18Jun59- 7Hol	fst 5f		:22 :45 :57	©Haggin 23k	5 7 76¾ 87¾ 67	65¾	Maese A	119		12.20	92-14	Psyche's First1224½T.V. Lark119noTompion122nk	No excuse 8
4Jun59- 7Hol	fst 5f		:221 :453 :573	©Westchester 18k	1 1 3½ 22 21½	31½	Valenzuela I	122		4.25	93-15	BritishRoman122¾NewPolicy122¾Wrfar1223½	Held on gamely 9
23May59- 1Hol	fst 5f		:221 :453 :573	Md Sp Wt	6 2 2hd 1hd 11	13¾	Shoemaker W	120		*1.70	95-09	Warfare1203¾Pierica120¾Jimbo Rose120¾	Drew out easily 10
16May59- 1Hol	fst 5f		:222 :453 :574	Md Sp Wt	6 6 43¼ 35 37	37	Neves R	118		3.25	87-14	Temple1182Noble Noor1185Warfare1182	Evenly in drive 10
9May59- 2Hol	fst 5f		:221 :454 :582	Md Sp Wt	8 6 55 56½ 42	41¼	Taniguchi G	118		13.05	90-11	Nagea118¾British Roman118½Temple118hd	Some late foot 12

White Skies

ch. c. 1949, by Sun Again (Sun Teddy)–Milk Dipper, by Milkman
Own.– W.M. Wickham
Br.– Charles Nuckols & Sons (Ky)
Tr.– T. Root

Lifetime record: 37 20 8 4 $246,025

25Apr55- 6Bel	fst 6f-WC	$:22^1$ $:44^3$	$1{:}08^4$	3↑ Toboggan H 28k	1	1		$5^{1\frac14}$	$2^{\frac12}$	3^{nk}	Guerin E	132wb	*.85	95-08	Sailor106^{no}Bobby Brocato116^{hd}White Skies132^6		7
	Failed to respond sufficiently																
1Apr55- 6Jam	fst 6f	$:22^4$:46	$1{:}10^3$	3↑ Paumonok H 29k	8	5	$4^{\frac34}$	2^{hd}	1^{hd}	3^1	Arcaro E	130wb	*.70	93-19	BobbyBrocato113^1Blessbull119^{no}WhiteSkies$130^{8\frac12}$	Faltered	12
5Jly54- 6Aqu	fst 7f	$:22^3$ $:45^2$ $1{:}09^3$	$1{:}23^3$	3↑ Carter H 62k	6	3	3^1	$1^{\frac12}$	$1^{2\frac12}$	$1^{1\frac12}$	Stout J	133wb	*1.85	92-17	White Skies$133^{1\frac12}$First Aid115^{nk}Royal Vale$126^{\frac12}$	Driving	13
12Jun54- 6Mth	fst 6f	$:21^3$ $:44^2$	1:09	3↑ Oceanport H 18k	7	3	3^3	2^2	2^2	$2^{2\frac12}$	Stout J	136wb	*.60	100-06	Master Ace$106^{2\frac12}$White Skies$136^{1\frac34}$Eatontown113^3	Hung late	9
22May54- 6Bel	fst 7f	$:22^2$ $:45^2$ $1{:}09^4$	$1{:}22^2$	3↑ Roseben H 34k	12	2	2^{hd}	1^2	1^3	$1^{\frac12}$	Stout J	135wb	*1.15	98-13	WhiteSkies$135^{\frac12}$[DH]Impasse115[DH]FirstAid$113^{4\frac12}$	Tiring,lasted	13
26Apr54- 6Bel	fst 6f-WC	$:22^2$ $:45^1$	$1{:}09^1$	3↑ Toboggan H 30k	2	1		1^{hd}	2^{hd}	$1^{2\frac14}$	Arcaro E	132wb	*.85	95-07	WhiteSkies$132^{2\frac14}$CaesarDid109^{hd}Hilarious120^1	Handy score	8
1Apr54- 6Jam	fst 6f	:23 $:45^3$	$1{:}10^4$	3↑ Paumonok H 30k	2	1	$1^{\frac12}$	$1^{1\frac12}$	1^{hd}	1no	Arcaro E	130wb	*.75	93-16	WhiteSks130^{no}Laffango$115^{2\frac12}$ColdCommand$116^{\frac34}$	Just lasted	10
	Daily Racing Form time, 1:10 1/5																
10Mar54- 5GP	my $5\frac12$f	:23 :47 1:00	$1{:}06^3$	4↑ Handicap 5000	4	6	4^2	3^1	1^2	1^4	Stout J	128wb	*1.50	84-33	WhiteSkies128^4Ruthred$114^{1\frac12}$HeartFlash$107^{1\frac14}$	Much the best	7
4Nov53- 6Jam	fst 6f	$:23^1$:46	$1{:}11^3$	3↑ Sport Page H 22k	3	3	$2^{\frac12}$	2^{hd}	$1^{\frac12}$	$1^{1\frac14}$	Stout J	130wb	*1.60	89-21	White Skies$130^{1\frac14}$Hilarious114^{hd}Joe Jones$107^{\frac34}$	Drew clear	9
24Oct53- 7GS	fst 6f	$:22^1$ $:45^2$	$1{:}11^2$	3↑ Princeton H 23k	2	5	4^2	4^1	3^3	$4^{4\frac14}$	Stout J	128wb	*.50	87-21	[DH]Hyphsis110[DH][D]CandlWood$118^{3\frac12}$SkipprBll$111^{\frac34}$	Weakened	6
19Oct53- 6Jam	fst 6f	:23 $:45^4$	1:11	2↑ New Rochelle H 22k	6	3	$1^{\frac12}$	$1^{2\frac12}$	$1^{2\frac12}$	$1^{2\frac34}$	Stout J	128wb	*2.15	92-17	White Skies$128^{2\frac34}$Hilarious$110^{\frac12}$Do Report$113^{2\frac12}$	Ridden out	10
12Oct53- 6Jam	fst 6f	:23 $:46^2$	$1{:}11^3$	3↑ Interborough H 23k	1	1	$1^{1\frac12}$	1^{hd}	1^1	1^{hd}	Stout J	126wb	*1.25	89-20	White Skies126^{hd}Do Report$112^{\frac34}$Hilarious$110^{1\frac12}$	Just lasted	9
25Sep53- 6Atl	fst 7f	$:22^1$ $:44^4$ $1{:}09^3$	1:23	4↑ T.R.A. 21k	1	1	$1^{1\frac12}$	1^5	1^5	1^5	Boulmetis S	118wb	1.80	98-18	White Skies118^5Tuscany$126^{1\frac12}$Candle Wood$110^{2\frac12}$	Easily	5
19Sep53- 4Atl	fst 7f	$:22^2$ $:45^2$ 1:10	$1{:}22^3$	3↑ Alw 4500	1	1	1^2	1^4	1^6	1^9	Stout J	122wb	*.60	- -	WhitSkies122^9BrazenBrat$119^{\frac12}$Mohammedan119^5	Easily best	6
10Sep53- 7Atl	fst 6f	$:22^1$ $:45^2$	$1{:}10^1$	3↑ King Neptune H 17k	5	7	$6^{4\frac14}$	$4^{3\frac12}$	4^3	$3^{2\frac12}$	Stout J	116wb	*1.10	91-15	BlueRhymr$104^{1\frac12}$Roaming119^1WhiteSkies$116^{\frac34}$	Unruly in gate	7
31Aug53- 5Atl	fst 6f	$:22^2$ $:45^2$	$1{:}10^1$	3↑ Alw 5000	4	2	$3^{2\frac12}$	1^1	1^6	1^5	Wilson HB	109wb	*.40	94-16	White Skies109^5Topside$109^{1\frac12}$Influence118^4	Easily	6
26Aug53- 6Atl	fst 6f	$:22^1$ $:45^2$	1:11	3↑ Alw 5000	11	7	5^6	$3^{3\frac12}$	$3^{1\frac12}$	$2^{1\frac14}$	LeBlanc R	111wb	2.60	89-21	LateModl$112^{1\frac14}$WhteSkies111^{nk}CongoKing$116^{1\frac12}$	Forced wide	11
1Nov52- 7GS	fst 6f	:22 $:44^4$	$1{:}10^4$	3↑ Princeton H 22k	3	2	$2^{1\frac12}$	$2^{1\frac12}$	1^{hd}	$1^{\frac34}$	Stout J	116wb	3.80	94-21	White Skies$116^{\frac34}$General Staff124^{hd}Pet Bully120^{nk}	Driving	6
24Oct52- 7GS	fst 6f	$:22^1$ $:45^1$	1:11	3↑ Alw 5000	7	2	2^2	2^{hd}	1^2	2no	Wilson HB	118wb	2.90	93-20	Pet Bully122^{no}White Skies$118^{\frac34}$Occupancy112^2	Just missed	7
7Oct52- 6GS	fst 6f	$:22^1$ $:45^2$	1:11	3↑ Fall Inaugural 7.5k	7	2	$2^{1\frac12}$	3^2	$3^{\frac12}$	2^2	Stout J	115wb	*1.40	91-17	Mohammedn111^2White Skies115^{nk}Pet Bully124^1	Good effort	7
10Sep52- 7Atl	fst 6f	$:22^1$:45	$1{:}09^1$	3↑ Boardwalk H 16k	3	5	2^1	$2^{\frac12}$	$2^{\frac12}$	$2^{\frac12}$	Stout J	117wb	*1.40e	98-12	Dominave$100^{\frac12}$White Skies117^1Senator Joe120^{hd}	Good effort	7
6Sep52- 7Atl	fst 1Ⓣ	:23 $:46^2$ $1{:}11^2$	$1{:}37^2$	Philadelphia Turf H 18k	9	5	5^3	2^{hd}	2^{hd}	$4^{2\frac12}$	Culmone J	121wb	*2.00	102-00	Faga-La104^{no}Decapolis108^{no}HandsmeTeddy$121^{2\frac12}$	Weakened	11
30Aug52- 6Atl	fst 1Ⓣ	$:23^2$ $:46^2$ $1{:}11^1$	$1{:}36^1$	Alw 5000	3	1	2^{hd}	1^1	1^1	2no	Stout J	121wb	*.90	111-00	BobsAlibi114^{no}WhiteSks121^{nk}HndsomTddy124^{hd}	Just missed	10
11Aug52- 6Atl	gd 6f	$:22^3$ $:45^3$	$1{:}11^4$	Pageant H 11k	4	3	3^{nk}	1^{hd}	1^3	$1^{2\frac12}$	Stout J	118wb	*.90	86-25	WhiteSks$118^{2\frac12}$HandsomeTeddy111^1Hannbl126^4	Clever score	7
4Aug52- 6Mth	fst 6f	$:22^3$ $:45^3$	$1{:}10^4$	Alw 5000	3	2	2^2	$1^{\frac12}$	1^3	1^7	Stout J	121wb	*.60	94-21	White Skies121^7Jeannie C.$119^{4\frac12}$Congo King121^2	Easily	8
19Jly52- 3Mth	fst 6f	$:22^3$ $:45^3$	$1{:}11^1$	3↑ Alw 5000	5	3	2^{hd}	1^1	1^3	1^1	Roberts P	105wb	*1.70	92-16	White Skies105^1Blue Kay$110^{\frac12}$Whiffenpoof$115^{\frac34}$	Driving	5
15Jly52- 6Jam	fst 6f	$:22^4$ $:45^4$	$1{:}11^2$	Handicap 10045	1	2	$4^{2\frac12}$	4^2	$2^{1\frac12}$	$2^{1\frac14}$	Rodriguez E	120wb	3.60	89-15	TruePattern$107^{1\frac14}$WhiteSkies120^2HeapBigChf114^{nk}	Held well	7
5Jly52- 6Mth	fst 6f	:23 $:46^1$	$1{:}12^2$	Select H 20k	5	9	$9^{5\frac34}$	7^6	$4^{1\frac34}$	$3^{\frac34}$	Stout J	114wb	2.40e	85-15	Hannibal$122^{\frac12}$Congo King105^{nk}White Skies114^{nk}	Closed well	14
24Jun52- 7Mth	gd 6f	$:22^3$ $:45^3$	$1{:}11^3$	Alw 5000	5	5	$2^{\frac12}$	$1^{1\frac12}$	1^4	1^5	Stout J	115wb	*1.50	90-17	White Skies115^5Rae's Reward115^{hd}Thymus115^3	Ridden out	8
23Apr52- 5Kee	fst $6\frac12$f	$:22^3$ $:45^4$ $1{:}10^1$	$1{:}16^4$	Alw 3000	2	6	$2^{\frac12}$	1^1	1^3	1^{hd}	Porch G	117wb	3.80	99-06	White Skies117^{hd}Real Delight$110^{4\frac12}$Shag Tails$117^{\frac34}$	Driving	10
18Apr52- 5Kee	fst 7f	$:22^3$ $:45^3$ $1{:}10^4$	1:24	Alw 5000	2	5	$4^{1\frac12}$	$2^{1\frac12}$	2^2	$5^{4\frac34}$	Grohs O	111wb	9.70e	87-19	ColdCommand110^{hd}HillGail121^{nk}GushingOil$118^{1\frac12}$	Weakened	8
10Apr52- 5Kee	fst 6f	$:22^3$ $:46^2$	$1{:}11^3$	Alw 3000	3	5	4^2	$3^{\frac12}$	1^3	1^5	Porch G	116wb	*1.40	94-13	White Skies116^5Eljay$120^{1\frac12}$Cullerton115^1	Easily	7
31Mar52- 7GP	fst 7f	$:23^2$:47 1:11	$1{:}24^3$	Alw 3000	10	2	$2^{\frac12}$	2^{hd}	$1^{\frac12}$	$2^{\frac12}$	Rodriquez E	119wb	3.20e	89-14	ShortSupply$111^{\frac12}$WhiteSkies119^{nk}Fg-L102^4	Shortened stride	10
19Mar52- 5GP	fst 6f	$:22^3$ $:45^3$	$1{:}11^1$	Alw 2600	5	6	$2^{1\frac12}$	$2^{1\frac12}$	$2^{\frac12}$	1^3	Rodriquez E	117wb	8.30e	89-16	White Skies117^3San-Jo$112^{1\frac12}$Colonel Hoop117^2	Driving	12
2Nov51- 2Pim	sly 6f	$:22^3$:47	$1{:}14^2$	©Md Sp Wt	1	2	2^{hd}	1^2	1^3	$1^{\frac34}$	Richardson HL	110wb	*2.30	79-26	White Skies$110^{\frac34}$Charles117^2Bit o' Whiz$117^{3\frac12}$	Driving	11
7Jly51- 2AP	fst $5\frac12$f	$:22^2$ $:45^3$ $:58^2$	$1{:}04^4$	Md Sp Wt	6	5	4^3	$3^{3\frac12}$	3^3	$8^{9\frac12}$	Richardson HL	111wb	46.70	86-06	Seasn'sBest$115^{3\frac12}$Espino'sImage118^1GushngOl118^4	Gave way	12
27Jun51- 2AP	fst 5f	$:22^4$ $:46^3$	$1{:}00^2$	©Md Sp Wt	5	11	$8^{8\frac34}$	8^6	$8^{4\frac14}$	$7^{6\frac34}$	Richardson HL	111 w	27.90	81-13	QuickSolution118^3AceCaptain118^{hd}OldPat$118^{1\frac12}$	No threat	11

BOOM TIME

THE 1960'S

by Dave Litfin

THOROUGHBRED RACING ROARED into the 1960's gaining in popularity with every stride, as large and enthusiastic crowds poured themselves and their considerable betting dollars into racetracks from coast to coast.

Aqueduct, which had been completely rebuilt in 1959, reopened to an eager crowd of 42,473 that wagered $3.4 million, and the place was jammed with a record 73,435 fans when Gun Bow won the Metropolitan Handicap on Memorial Day in 1964. Monmouth Park, the picturesque track near the Jersey shore, closed its record-breaking 1962 meeting with a throng of 43,591. Arlington Park regularly drew 30,000 to 40,000 people on weekends. In the West, Santa Anita and Hollywood Park hosted midweek crowds of 25,000, a figure that often doubled on Saturdays.

Racing's inexorable rise to prominence in the landscape of American sports was the synergistic by-product of three fortuitous geographical and economic factors. First, Nevada was the only state that offered casino gambling, and a trip to that remote desert locale, even in the dawn of the space age, remained highly impractical for the great majority of Americans with an inclination to bet their money. Second, there was no such thing as off-track betting, except through illegal bookmakers, many of whom were under close scrutiny in the aftermath of the Kefauver hearings on organized crime. And third, other states were slow to follow New Hampshire's lead when, in 1964, it became the first state in modern times to institute a lottery.

In short, racing was pretty much the only game in town, and it responded to this idyllic state of affairs with steady year-to-year gains on all fronts.

In 1963, total wagering handle rocketed past the $3 billion mark for the first time, as 38,093,417 fans filled the stands and a total of $99,553,769 was distributed in purses. This represented gains of 4 percent in crowds, 5 percent in handle, and 7 percent in purses over 1962 – which had been a record-breaking year as well.

"He would be a brash prophet who would suggest Thoroughbred racing has realized its maximum potential volume of business," wrote *Daily Racing Form* columnist Charles Hatton in his "Review of 1963 Races" for The American Racing Manual. "It continues to grow in public favor, and the trend is toward ever-lengthening seasons in the 24 racing states."

But above and beyond its favorable economic circumstances and convenient access to the nation's

$2 bettors, racing prospered through the 1960's thanks to an improbable sequence of captivating champions who stretched from one end of the decade to the other.

From his appearance and early racing record, few could have guessed that an insignificant-looking gelding bred and owned by Mrs. Richard C. duPont's Bohemia Stable would come to epitomize the qualities of courage and consistency universally admired by horsemen and horseplayers.

Kelso, whom Mrs. duPont named after her friend Kelso Everett, was a dark bay with no conspicuous markings except for a small patch of white hair on his right jowl, where he was bitten as a yearling. Although he was by no means imposing in stature at just over 15 hands as a 3-year-old, and slightly over 16 hands when fully mature, "Kelly" possessed extraordinary propulsive muscling across his hips and hindquarters ("These are outsize and recall a souped-up Ford," Hatton described), and had an efficient low-to-the-ground stride that gave him enough speed to win at six furlongs as well as the stamina to win at two miles. His one Achilles' heel was a trick stifle, which

Kelso's record of five consecutive Horse of the Year titles, from 1960 through 1964, may never be broken. Despite the inflation in purses following his retirement, the gelding's earnings record of $1,977,896 would stand for 15 years.

made his connections reluctant to start him on yielding turf.

Kelso's sire was Your Host, a California speedball who was beaten as the heavy favorite in the 1950 Kentucky Derby. Following an accident in which he suffered a broken shoulder and crushed femur, injuries that nearly cost him his life (and would have, had his insurer, Lloyds of London, not insisted on trying to save him for stud duty), Your Host had a decent career as a stallion, but he would have been all but forgotten were it not for Kelso, whose dam was the stakes-placed Maid of Flight.

"Maid of Flight was a nice filly," recalled Mrs. duPont, whose 900-acre Woodstock Farm is located along the banks of the Bohemia River in Chesapeake City, Maryland. "I owned a few shares in Your Host. I'd seen him race and was very fond of him. Since I had a few seasons to him and since he was close by in New Jersey, I decided to send Maid of Flight to him for her first breeding." The foal Maid of Flight dropped in April 1957 at Claiborne Farm near Paris, Kentucky, was Kelso.

Depending on which reference source is consulted, Kelso was either gelded as a yearling by the farm manager, or as a 2-year-old by Dr. John Lee, who trained him for the first three races of his career in September 1959, or the following winter by Carl Hanford, who handled him for the 60 subsequent starts that are now part of racing lore. Whatever the circumstances, it proved to be a fortuitous decision. In 1960 the late-blooming gelding captured the first of his unbelievable five straight Horse of the Year titles, despite the fact that he did not make his debut as a 3-year-old until two weeks after the Triple Crown races were over.

After winning a pair of allowance events by a combined 22 lengths, Kelso was a nonthreatening eighth making his stakes debut in the Arlington Classic. Two races after that, however, he teamed up with Eddie Arcaro, and the duo did not lose again for more than a year. Underneath "The Master," Kelso won the Choice, the Jerome, the Discovery Handicap, the Hawthorne Gold Cup, and the Jockey Club Gold Cup, a streak that made him the first horse in 37 years to be named 3-year-old champion without winning a Triple Crown race.

Kelso returned as a 4-year-old with an allowance win at Aqueduct on May 19, 1961, and 11 days later he carried 130 pounds in the Metropolitan Handicap. Things didn't look good for the even-money favorite as he lagged behind in the early going and remained far back in seventh position at the quarter pole.

"He had absolutely no shot at the head of the stretch, and I didn't give him too much chance at the eighth pole," Hanford told *Daily Racing Form's* Joe Hirsch on the eve of Kelso's retirement several years later. "But he bulled his way between horses somehow, and got up to win under 130 pounds. I'll never forget it as long as I live."

Kelso completed a sweep of the 1961 Handicap Triple Crown by winning the Suburban and Brooklyn Handicaps in July, and overwhelmed his opposition that autumn winning the Woodward and the Jockey Club Gold Cup by a combined 13 lengths. He closed out his second straight Horse of the Year campaign with a runner-up finish in the Washington, D.C., International, in which he made his grass debut and was finally caught by the year's champion turf horse, T. V. Lark , after setting all the pace.

That would be the first of Kelso's three straight seconds in the D.C. International – he finally won it in 1964 – and it would also be his last race under an aging Arcaro.

After going without a stakes victory through the first eight months of 1962, Kelso received a switch from the soft-handed Bill Shoemaker to the incredibly strong Ismael "Milo" Valenzuela, who, it was said, could hold a starving elephant an inch away from a bale of hay. They went together like hand and glove. Valenzuela rode Kelso 35 times and the pair came away with 22 victories, none more electrifying than the Aqueduct Handicap on Labor Day, September 7, 1964, when Kelso beat his archrival, Gun Bow, by three-quarters of a length.

"The weather was salubrious, a confection of clear skies and 75 degrees, and an enthusiastic throng of 65,066 New Yorkers came out to the Jamaica Bay course to see the sport," Hatton described. "They saw one of the most exciting and dramatic races ever witnessed at any of the three Aqueducts . . . There have been richer events but artistically it has rarely if ever been surpassed within the memory of the oldest racing man."

Gun Bow was the heavy favorite at 55 cents to the dollar, and Kelso was 2-1, having been defeated in five previous stakes starts as a 7-year-old. Gun Bow broke from the rail and went right to the lead, with Kelso stalking close behind. At the quarter pole Kelso began to inch nearer, and many of those who had bet against him suddenly switched allegiances and began shouting, "Come on, Kelso! Go get him, Kelly!"

"The din reverberated, rocking and crashing throughout all five levels of the immense Big A stands and lawns," Hatton continued. "It was like the brink of Niagara, deafening and almost terrifying. Go get him Kelso did . . . The sirocco of sound continued unabated as the field pulled up and Kelso jogged casually back to unsaddle. Perfect strangers thumped one another on the back . . . and there was a continuous roar of applause that did not end until Kelso disappeared from view."

Old-timers recall that ovation as perhaps the longest and loudest ever at a New York track, where the hard-boiled railbirds are not known to dispense their appreciation casually. The New York fans had grown to adore Kelso like no other horse before or since, and Kelso loved them back.

"Whenever we went onto the track he would always walk with the outrider," remembered Valenzuela. "But he would always stop in front of the grandstand and let the other horses keep going. He would stand by himself and look up into the grandstand. It seemed like he wanted to salute the people. He'd stick his ears up, like he knew the applause was for him."

Never before had a horse been so good for so many seasons. Kelso retired with 39 wins from 63 starts, and set an earnings record of $1,977,896 that stood for 15 years. All told, he won 30 stakes races, 13 of them while carrying at least 130 pounds, and set seven track or course records, including a phenomenal clocking of 2:23⅘ for 1½ miles in the 1964 running of the D.C. International. Along that long and winding road, it is safe to say that Kelso beat more good horses than any other Thoroughbred of the 20th century, a list that includes the likes of Gun Bow, Carry Back, Bald Eagle, Tompion, Never Bend, Beau Purple, Quadrangle, and Roman Brother, to name just a few.

Kelso retired to a life of hunting and hacking through the woods on his owner's farm, and made occasional appearances for racing research and charities. A couple of days after leading the post parade for the 1983 Jockey Club Gold Cup along with two other venerable geldings, Forego and John Henry, Kelso died of colic at Woodstock Farm at the age of 26.

Of all the hallowed prose written about Kelso over the course of his distinguished career, no one summed things up more appropriately or more succinctly than Joe Hirsch when he wrote, "Once upon a time there was a horse named Kelso. But only once."

Though Kelso dominated the sport for five straight years, the first half of the 1960's was graced with a number of other exceptionally talented Thoroughbreds who staged many memorable events.

The champion 3-year-old of 1961 was Carry Back, a colt of unlikely lineage who for two seasons did more to merchandise and promote racing to the masses than any horse since Native Dancer.

"The People's Horse," as Carry Back was known, was bred, owned, and trained by the irrepressible Jack Price, a former manufacturer of jet-engine parts in Cleveland, who was in the process of blowing his retirement nest egg in racing until this once-in-a-lifetime stroke of outrageous fortune came along.

As legend has it, Price took over the ownership of an obscure mare named Joppy for $150 as partial payment for an overdue board bill at his small Ohio farm, and kicked in another $150 to close the deal. Then, for a modest $400 fee, he bred his new acquisition to the equally obscure Saggy – a horse who had been the only colt to beat Citation at 3 – and the

Lowdown on French Trainers; Price Hails Diligent Blacksmith

The following report is written exclusively for The Morning Telegraph by Jack Price, owner-trainer-breeder of Carry Back, America's hope in the Arc de Triomphe at Longchamp on October 7.

▼

by Jack Price

PARIS, Oct. 3.—I suppose you are wondering why, after I ended my last column with "finis," you are hearing from me again. The reason is when J. S. P. arrived here Monday, he asked me to continue. As an added inducement he increased my pay check by two zeros. So here goes.

Monday evening we went to a cocktail party given by the Bert Taylors at the Tour d'Argent. Everyone important connected with the French turf was invited. We met many owners and public trainers. Their problems are about what they are at home. It is easier to make a profit on the operation of a racing stable here. A public trainer will charge between $5 and $7 per day per horse. All shipping expenses are paid by the Jockey Club. The purses for an average card are high in relationship to the cost of operation. They can do this because of off the course betting. It was an interesting evening, because it gave us a chance to get the views not only of the Calumets and Cain Hoys of Europe but also the views of the trainers and owners of small stables.

Tuesday morning CB galloped about two miles and acted wonderful. Promptly at 9 that morning, the Jockey Club vet and a blacksmith arrived to make CB's shoes conform to French style. They couldn't speak English and as our interpreter, Whitney Tower, was not there, it was very hard to communicate. When the blacksmith tried to file the toes off Carry Back's shoes it was impossible, as the tips were steel and his rasp made no impression.

Used Set of Shoes Brought from States

They suggested pulling his shoes off and grinding down the toes on a wheel. An alternative would be to put on a new set of French plates on him. We objected because I was reluctant for a strange blacksmith to work on him. Things were at an impasse. Finally I decided to take a chance with their blacksmith, but instead of reworking our old shoes, we used a set of new ones which we had brought along with us. The toes were ground off and the blocks behind were rounded under our supervision. The old shoes were then removed and the new ones were tacked on.

The blacksmith was good and as he worked my doubts about his ability to do this job vanished. When he was through the horse was taken out of his stall and walked around for a few minutes. I was completely satisfied. Now the question was—how could he handle the turf Wednesday morning in shoes with no toes?

Tuesday night it rained hard for hours and the turf was soft. Wednesday morning at 7.30 CB walked on the track, galloped perfectly and blew out a quarter of a mile in preparation for his final three-quarter work on Thursday. Mike said he went as good as he ever did. Tomorrow, his work will be timed by the Teletimer from the 1,200-meter pole. This is approximately three quarters of a mile.

With all our doubts about his shoes dissipated and his condition, in my opinion, as good as it ever was, the only question in my mind is: will he be able to negotiate the 1 1-2 miles distance.

PADDOCK PATTER: Saw a horse run in bell boots in front at St. Cloud here. The stands were built in 1955. They have a glass-enclosed dining room and a board in the infield that gives the results and mutuels, but no odds . . . Blacksmith's here clip off the clinched nail ends on a horse's hoof and pull every nail they can pry off the shoe with a thin flat tool. Blacksmiths in America jerk the shoe off with nippers without bothering to remove the nails . . . Our rooting section is beginning to arrive in force, and Joe Hirsch will take over in that department.

The modestly bred Carry Back was "the People's Horse" and reigned during the 1961 classics, winning the Kentucky Derby and Preakness. His owner, Jack Price, kept a journal — published in Daily Racing Form — *chronicling Carry Back's trip to Paris for the Prix de l'Arc de Triomphe.*

mysterious forces of nature somehow combined to create this uncommonly tough competitor.

"He changed the whole course of my life," admitted Price, who campaigned the stretch-running Carry Back through an ambitious 3-year-old schedule of 16 starts, which included hard-fought wins in the Kentucky Derby and the Preakness from out of the clouds, and photo-finish victories in the Flamingo, the Florida Derby, and the Jerome.

As a 4-year-old, Carry Back became just the fourth millionaire in American racing – joining Round Table, Nashua, and Citation – when he won the Metropolitan Handicap at the expense of, among others, Kelso, who would eventually surpass them all atop the earnings list.

Jack and Katherine Price were nothing if not sporting, and in the fall of 1962 they traveled to Paris with Carry Back to take a shot in the Prix de l'Arc de Triomphe. This was an extremely rare and bold move in those days, when transatlantic shipping was a daunting challenge for even the most experienced and well-heeled owner.

Their quixotic quest captured the imagination of Carry Back fans everywhere, and Price was enlisted by *Daily Racing Form* to write a daily diary during the trip. After Carry Back finished a very respectable 10th in the 24-horse field, beaten less than six lengths for all the marbles, Price was philosophical in his final entry: "Are we sorry we came? No. We set out to prove that a good American horse could compete favorably with the best in Europe on their own grounds and on their own terms . . . We didn't get the money, but we proved our point."

The 3-year-olds of 1962 were not an outstanding crop per se, but there was an element of high drama to their class, with photo finishes determining the winners of the Wood Memorial, Jersey Derby, Florida Derby, Preakness, Belmont Stakes, and, most notably, the Travers.

The Travers pitted Jaipur, winner of the Gotham, Withers, and Belmont, against the well-traveled Ridan, who was the pride of the West Coast.

On some afternoons Jaipur didn't have it, but on others he responded like a genuine champion. Such was the case on August 16, 1962, when he hooked up with Ridan in a gut-wrenching struggle through every desperate yard of the prestigious 1¼-mile Travers.

Jaipur prevailed by a nose to cement his 3-year-old championship, but proved no match for Kelso when next tried against older handicap horses in the Woodward. He never won another race.

Somewhat surprisingly, neither Kelso nor Carry Back was the richest American horse of 1962. That distinction went to the 2-year-old champion colt, Never Bend, trained by Woody Stephens. Never Bend reeled off consecutive wins in the Futurity, the Cowdin, and the Champagne Stakes en route to amassing a bankroll of $402,969 for Capt. Harry F. Guggenheim's Cain Hoy Stable.

Guggenheim, who had secured Stephens as his private trainer toward the end of 1956, customarily sent a couple of yearlings to Europe each year, and they were trained in England by Cecil Boyd-Rochfort, who also had horses for Queen Elizabeth. The best of them was Bald Eagle, who showed flashes of ability marked by inconsistency at Epsom and Ascot. In despair, Boyd-Rochfort sent him back to America in the fall of his 3-year-old season with the comment "Not very genuine."

Stephens and Guggenheim gave Bald Eagle almost a full year to acclimate, and their patience was rewarded with nine stakes wins, including back-to-back runnings of the Washington, D.C., International, and the title of handicap champion in 1960. At Christmas that year, Captain Guggenheim sent Stephens a turkey, and a bonus check for $75,000.

While Kelso was in the process of becoming the world's richest Thoroughbred, a bay filly named Cicada won championships at ages 2, 3 and 4, accumulating total earnings of $783,674, a record among females at the time. Cicada won 23 of 42 lifetime starts, and was trained and raced harder than the average filly, to prevent her from kicking down the proverbial barn for want of something to do.

Shortly after World War II, Bull Lea, who topped the list of leading stallions in the United States five

Northern Dancer won the Kentucky Derby in record time and then took the Preakness, but couldn't stay the mile-and-a-half distance of the Belmont. The diminutive bay went on to become one of the most influential sires of all time.

times, would have been the choice as Sire of the Century, and years later, both Nasrullah and his son Bold Ruler were immensely influential at stud.

But as the millennium approached, Northern Dancer was widely regarded as the most productive and important sire of the 20th century. And to think that Edward P. Taylor's Canadian homebred was passed over when offered for $25,000 at a Windfields Farm yearling sale!

Taylor had a unique method of convincing buyers that he was not keeping his best yearlings for himself: He placed what he considered a fair price on each member of his yearling crop, then held a private sale at the farm. Each horse was offered at the price until half of the yearlings had been sold. Taylor retained those unsold, and in 1962 that group included Northern Dancer.

It is easy to understand the lack of enthusiasm among yearling buyers, because Northern Dancer was a late foal and a bit of a runt, standing barely over 15 hands when fully grown. But he did have a 73-inch girth, comparable to that of a much larger horse, and that ample girth gave him plenty of heart and lung room. Northern Dancer also had exceptional balance, and these qualities may have

been the catalysts for his relatively brief but brilliant 10-month tenure on the racetrack.

"He has a stride that looks two sizes too big for him, but it is perfectly controlled, like something they do at the Bolshoi Ballet," Hatton noted.

As a 2-year-old, Northern Dancer won 5 of 7 starts in Canada to establish himself as the best of his division there, and then invaded Aqueduct in November, where he dismantled Futurity Stakes winner Bupers in an allowance race. Northern Dancer concluded his campaign with an easy wire-to-wire triumph in the Remsen just nine days later, but had developed a quarter crack.

The standard procedure at the time was to cut out the crack, send the colt to the farm for the winter, and bring him back to the races in the spring after the crack had finally grown out. Such a course of action would have meant missing the Kentucky Derby, however. Northern Dancer's trainer, Horatio Luro, had read about the work of California-based blacksmith Bill Bane, who had developed a vulcanized patch for quarter cracks. Luro persuaded E. P. Taylor to let him try the patch, and Northern Dancer went to Florida that winter for training and racing.

After winning the Flamingo and the Florida Derby, the small but feisty Northern Dancer went to Keeneland for the Blue Grass, which he won by a well-measured half-length. This set him up perfectly to run the race of his life in the 1964 renewal of the Kentucky Derby, which was exactly what it took to repel the hulking Hill Rise by a neck in the record time of two minutes flat.

Northern Dancer then took the Preakness by 2¼ lengths, but failed in his bid to become the first Triple Crown winner since Citation, fading to third as the 4-5 favorite in the Belmont Stakes behind Quadrangle and Roman Brother (who, a year later, would become the first horse other than Kelso to be named Horse of the Year in the 1960's).

"He fought on gallantly but just couldn't handle that mile and a half," remarked Bill Hartack, who rode Northern Dancer in his final five races. "In fact, I think the most unusual thing about Northern Dancer was that he got a mile and a quarter."

Just two weeks after the Belmont, Northern Dancer returned to Canada and rebounded to win the Queen's Plate easily, but he bowed a tendon shortly thereafter and was retired. In a prescient observation in The American Racing Manual, Charles Hatton wrote of the 3-year-old champion, "It will be disappointing if racing's loss does not prove the stud's gain, as he is a colt of impeccable breeding and demonstrable class."

Of Northern Dancer's racing career, Luro said he most remembered the bay colt's gameness. "He never needed the whip to give his best, just the simple encouragement of a little tap on his shoulder," explained the Argentinean known as the Grand Senor.

"He refused to be punished. Once, in a prep for the Kentucky Derby, the jockey disobeyed my orders and whipped him. To show his disapproval, Northern Dancer wouldn't let me take him to the track for a week. How intelligent he was!" (Northern Dancer's personal preference aside, the Derby was still the Derby, and the chart says that the colt "prevailed under strong left-handed whipping" by Hartack.)

Initially, Northern Dancer's stud fee was $10,000. From his seven sales yearlings in 1967, his

Stamped with an impeccable pedigree, 1966 Horse of the Year Buckpasser was a star in a stellar era that included Dr. Fager and Damascus.

first crop, there were seven starters, seven winners, and five stakes winners. In all, there were 21 foals in Northern Dancer's first crop, with 18 starters, 16 winners, and 10 stakes winners.

By 1980, those fortunate enough to send a mare to Northern Dancer paid upward of $100,000 . . . without a guarantee. By 1982 he commanded a stud fee of $250,000, and breeders were rumored during the boom years of the mid-1980's to have paid as much as $1 million to send him their mares.

Unlike Bull Lea, Nasrullah, and Bold Ruler, who were kept under tight control by their owners, Northern Dancer was commercially available, and so he was the first dominant sire with plenty of offspring out there for anyone with enough money to buy them. At the 1983 Keeneland summer yearling sale, a colt by Northern Dancer sent shock waves through the industry when he was sold for $10,200,000. At that time, the Keeneland auction board had only seven numbers. An eighth digit was added after that sale, in order to accommodate the unprecedented demand from buyers around the world.

In 1981, when Northern Dancer was 20, an offer of $40 million was made for his purchase. It was turned down by the 32-person syndicate that stood the horse at Windfields Farm in Maryland.

As successful as his progeny were as racehorses – he sired 146 stakes winners – Northern Dancer's most indelible mark on the breed was his potency as a sire of great sires, such as Lyphard, Nijinsky II, Nureyev, Danzig, The Minstrel, Sadler's Wells, Storm Bird, Vice Regent, and Be My Guest.

Charles Taylor, who took over the Windfields operation in 1981, was interviewed shortly after Northern Dancer was put down in November 1990 at the age of 29.

"Of all my father's accomplishments in racing and breeding, I believe he was most proud of having established the Northern Dancer sire line," Taylor said. "Everyone talks about him being small and stocky, which was true, but to me it was the intelligence through the eye – the look of eagles and all that – that is the thing that remains, the way he carried himself like a champion. I only really remember Northern Dancer as the stallion in the paddock, when he thought all the mares arriving were for him."

Ogden Phipps will surely go down as one of the greatest breeders of the 20th century. Phipps bred and raced more than 100 stakes winners, beginning with 1936 Withers winner White Cockade, and he campaigned such luminaries as Easy Goer and the undefeated Personal Ensign. But many students of the turf feel that Buckpasser was infinitely the best horse ever bred by the former chairman of The Jockey Club.

By 1953 Horse of the Year Tom Fool and out of Busanda, Buckpasser was a great-grandson of the immortal broodmare La Troienne, and wasted little time running roughshod over the 2-year-old class of 1965 for trainer Bill Winfrey.

Winfrey retired after guiding Buckpasser to 9 wins from 11 starts, and record 2-year-old earn-ings of $568,096. After racing greenly and finish-ing a fast-closing fourth in his career debut at Aqueduct on May 13, Buckpasser did not lose again until the Futurity, when he finished second on an off track.

Winfrey, who had succeeded one of the sport's legends, Sunny Jim Fitzsimmons, as the Phippses' trainer, noted that Buckpasser was "a bit of a loafer at times, especially in the mornings, but he is deter-mined in the afternoons."

Buckpasser was given over to Eddie Neloy and put away for the year after winning the Champagne, in order to prepare for the 3-year-old classics. He was held in such high regard during the winter of 1966 that Hialeah management, fear-ing a huge minus pool, refused to allow betting when he ran in the Flamingo, which in that era was the most prestigious of all the stakes races on the path to the Kentucky Derby. Despite drawing a fairly large nine-horse field, the race was run as a betless exhibition and dubbed by the press as the

Damascus clinched the 1967 Horse of the Year award with a powerhouse 10-length victory over Buckpasser and Dr. Fager in the Woodward.

"Chicken Flamingo," with Buckpasser coming again in deep stretch to prevail by a nose.

While training toward the Florida Derby, Buckpasser developed a quarter crack that kept him out of the Triple Crown events. He returned to win an allowance sprint at Aqueduct in early June, and then ran the table, winning nine straight stakes to secure titles as champion 3-year-old, champion handicap horse, and Horse of the Year in 1966. In so doing, Buckpasser – who regularly ran coupled with a "rabbit" in order to ensure sufficient early pace for his late run – set a world record for a mile, winning the Arlington Classic in 1:32⅗. He became the youngest millionaire in racing history, with earnings of $1,218,874 after two seasons of racing.

Recurring quarter cracks and the onset of arthritis in his right fore hoof and pastern compromised Buckpasser's effectiveness as a 4-year-old in 1967, but he still managed victories in the San Fernando Stakes, the Metropolitan Handicap, and the Suburban Handicap. In the latter, he shouldered 133 pounds and appeared beaten in midstretch when fourth, still four lengths from the leaders, but responded to Braulio Baeza's insistent urging and was up in the final strides to edge Ring Twice, while conceding 22 pounds to that rival.

After being upset by the Allen Jerkens-trained Handsome Boy in the Brooklyn Handicap 18 days later, Buckpasser was sidelined for two months due to his infirmities, and it was uncertain whether he would make the Woodward Stakes, in which he would face the crack 3-year-olds Damascus and Dr. Fager.

The 14th running of the Woodward Stakes on September 30, 1967, aroused more interest than any race since the match between Swaps and Nashua a dozen years earlier, and represented a changing of the guard.

Defending Horse of the Year Buckpasser had been out of action since midsummer, but he was installed as the slight favorite at 8-5 over Damascus and Dr. Fager, who were co-second choices at 9-5. Buckpasser and Damascus brought along their respective rabbits, Great Power and Hedevar, to go after the speedy but headstrong Dr. Fager through the opening fractions.

Tom Ainslie, the dean of handicapping authors, recounted the Woodward in The Handicapper's Handbook: "Dr. Fager wilted after running the legs off Hedevar. Meanwhile, Shoemaker let Damascus dawdle twelve to fifteen lengths behind the pace. And when he asked the colt for some run, he got the most sensational burst of speed I have ever seen. Poor Buckpasser tried to come on in the stretch but was not the Buckpasser of old and had all he could do to beat the fading Dr. Fager for second money. The old Buckpasser would have made it close, but under today's weights would have been by no means a cinch to win. The Damascus of the late summer of 1967 was a horse for the ages."

The Woodward was Buckpasser's final race. He was syndicated for stud duty at the unprecedented rate of $4,800,000 for 32 shares, and would eventually become one of the most influential broodmare sires of all time.

While the Woodward marked the end of Buckpasser's career, it put the stamp of greatness on Damascus, who was a unanimous choice as 1967 Horse of the Year after also taking the Preakness, Belmont, Dwyer, American Derby, Travers, and Jockey Club Gold Cup, and finishing second by a nose when tried on turf in the D.C. International.

All in all, Damascus made 16 starts as a 3-year-old and won a dozen times, amassing what was then a single-season earnings record of $817,941.

Damascus is on most lists of all-time greats, but his star might have burned brighter still had he not finished third as the favorite in the Kentucky Derby. Under humid conditions, Damascus washed out and became a nervous wreck while being saddled.

"When he started pinning his ears and kicking his back legs up, I knew we were in trouble," said Bill Shoemaker, who was aboard for 17 of the colt's 21 career wins. "I went to work on him like crazy, but he was completely out of sorts. That was absolutely the most disappointed I have ever been in the outcome of a race."

Damascus atoned, however, coming within two noses of winning 11 straight to close out the year, including an incredible 22-length tour de force in

Dr. Fager closed out his career with a track-record-setting performance in the Vosburgh under 139 pounds. Two starts back, he had set a world record for a flat mile that would last for 29 years.

CHAMPIONS

the Travers. A crowd of 28,576, at the time the second-largest gathering in Saratoga's history, saw the race, which was run in the slop after overnight rains and another downpour that fell just before post time.

The crowd would have been larger had the weather been better – and if Dr. Fager had been running. He had been pointing for the Travers, but a viral infection two weeks earlier had briefly forced him out of training.

The rivalry between Damascus and Dr. Fager began in the Gotham Stakes on April 15, 1967, when 50,522 screaming fans filled Aqueduct to the rafters.

Dr. Fager had won 4 of 5 starts as a 2-year-old, his only loss coming to divisional champion Successor when he was rank early and unable to hold on to a three-length lead in midstretch of the Champagne. The Gotham marked his seasonal debut, while Damascus, who was riding a five-race winning streak, had already taken both his starts at 3, including an impressive score in the Bay Shore three weeks earlier.

"I did want to give him a prep before the Gotham but I couldn't get one," explained John Nerud, who trained the Tartan Farm homebred. "Everyone said I was crazy to run against Damascus first time out, but I just told them to come to the races." At the finish, it was Dr. Fager by a half-length.

As 4-year-olds, Damascus and Dr. Fager met twice more. They first hooked up in the Suburban at Aqueduct on July 4, 1968, and 54,336 fans turned out to watch Dr. Fager, under 132 pounds, repulse every challenge from Damascus. He drew away to a two-length victory over Bold Hour, equaling the track record of 1:59⅗ for 1¼ miles, as Damascus finished third. Sixteen days later, they were back at it in the Brooklyn, in which Dr. Fager carried 135 pounds to Damascus's 130. More importantly, Hedevar was also in the race. Damascus was able to sit back and then unleash a powerful move that carried him to a 2½-length victory in 1:59⅕, breaking the track record equaled by Dr. Fager in the Suburban.

Damascus won twice more that summer, but suffered a career-ending bowed tendon as the favorite in the Jockey Club Gold Cup and was retired to stud by his owner and breeder, Mrs. Edith W. Bancroft.

Following the Brooklyn, in which he had been somewhat rank under rating tactics behind Damascus's rabbit, Dr. Fager was given a looser rein by Braulio Baeza and responded to win the Whitney by eight lengths under 132 pounds. Next, he broke Buckpasser's world record for a mile, winning the Washington Park Handicap at Arlington in 1:32⅕ while carrying 134 pounds. To show his versatility, Dr. Fager then spotted the formidable turf runner Advocator 22 pounds and outdueled him through the stretch when tried on grass for the first (and only) time in the United Nations Handicap at Atlantic City.

Dr. Fager's final race came in the Vosburgh Handicap on November 2, 1968. In an awe-inspiring exhibition of sheer unbridled speed, Dr. Fager,

Native Diver was a headstrong sprinter early in his career, but added another dimension later on, winning the 10-furlong Hollywood Gold Cup from 1965 through 1967. He died of enterotoxemia just nine days after winning the 1967 Del Mar Handicap.

as Bill Nack later wrote in Sports Illustrated, "blew around Aqueduct like a malevolent wind" and stormed through the seven furlongs in a track-record 1:20⅕ while carrying a staggering 139 pounds. The time would remain the benchmark at that track for more than three decades.

After that phenomenal performance, Nerud observed, "He is the best horse I've ever been around . . . He has gone a distance, sprinted, been on the grass and carried weight. Any horse who looks him in the eye is dead. No one horse ever beat Dr. Fager doing anything."

As the story goes, the office staff of William L. McKnight's Tartan Farm chipped in to buy a cheap claimer as a birthday present for the boss. After failing to get their first choice, their alternative gift selection was a mare named Aspidistra, who had managed just two wins from 14 starts, and who could not, in the words of Charles Hatton, "beat a fat man kicking a barrel up a hill."

Nevertheless, Aspidistra produced a pair of champions for Tartan: the freakishly fast and hot-blooded speed demon Dr. Fager, and Ta Wee, who was the sprint champion of 1969 and 1970.

After losing the first two legs of the Triple Crown to Majestic Prince, Arts and Letters was dominant the remainder of the 1969 season, taking the Belmont, Jim Dandy, Travers, Woodward, and Jockey Club Gold Cup.

Ta Wee (Sioux for "beautiful girl") won 13 of 17 starts during her two-season run as the top sprinter in the land, including back-to-back renewals of the Fall Highweight. A tremendous weight carrier, she had a massive set of hips and hindquarters that enabled her to successfully carry 142 pounds in her final race, the Interborough Handicap.

In terms of the dynamically and often violently changing American culture, the 1960's didn't really become "the sixties" until the latter half of the decade, and during those turbulent times racing, too, had to deal with the tragic and untimely losses of some of its leading figures.

Trained by Buster Millerick, Native Diver was as revered on the West Coast as his Eastern counterpart, Kelso, had been in New York. The gritty gelding won 3 of 5 races as a 2-year-old in 1961, and then ran at least 10 times during each of the next six years, winning 37 of 81 starts all told.

Native Diver first came to prominence as a headstrong sprinter with a tendency to bear out around the turn, and tied a world record by running seven furlongs in 1:20 flat in the Los Angeles Handicap. He proved to be more than a one-dimensional sprinter with maturity, winning three straight Hollywood Gold Cups from 1965-67. The 1967 Gold Cup was his penultimate outing, and pushed the 8-year-old's earnings past the $1 million plateau.

Native Diver went out a winner in the Del Mar Handicap on September 4, 1967, but died suddenly just nine days later from enterotoxemia, a breakdown of the intestinal tract. The beloved warhorse was buried at Hollywood Park, which had been the stage for so many of his triumphs.

Like Carry Back, the filly Dark Mirage came from humble beginnings. Obtained for the paltry sum of $6,000 at a Keeneland yearling sale by Lloyd Miller, she was a relative pipsqueak, standing slightly over 14 hands and weighing a bit more than 700 pounds soaking wet.

During her 2-year-old campaign, anyone who thought Dark Mirage would become the first filly to sweep New York's Filly Triple Crown must have kept it to himself for fear of being laughed off the track, because she won just twice from 15 starts. But by the end of her 3-year-old season in 1968, it was obvious there wasn't another in the division who could so much as warm her up.

After a fourth-place finish in her seasonal debut, Dark Mirage ripped off nine straight wins, including the Acorn, Mother Goose, and Coaching Club American Oaks by an aggregate 28 lengths.

Dark Mirage won the Delaware Oaks at the end of July, but was sidelined the remainder of the year by a foot injury that kept her out of the Alabama, as well as preventing a possible confrontation with colts in the fall. Said rival trainer Max Hirsch at the time, "I'm not at all sure that little filly can't beat any of them – Dr. Fager, Damascus, any of them – at a mile and a half, scale weights."

Dark Mirage returned in February 1969 to win her 10th consecutive race, carrying 126 pounds in the Santa Maria Handicap at Santa Anita. In her next start, she carried 130 pounds in the Santa Margarita. Bumped hard at the break, Dark Mirage hesitated and then jumped a cellophane wrapper that had blown onto the track. She was retired after it was discovered she had dislocated a sesamoid in the right front ankle, near the area of her original injury the preceding year.

She never recovered. Her left foreleg wobbled from the additional weight while her right leg was in a cast. After emergency surgery in July 1970, the "Tiny Tigress" with the big heart was put down.

Dr. Timothy Leary encouraged America's youth to turn on, tune in, and drop out in the sixties, and Thoroughbred racing endured a major drug scandal of its own when Dancer's Image finished first in the 1968 Kentucky Derby by a length and a half over Forward Pass. Three days later, a public announcement was made that postrace testing of Dancer's Image had come up positive for the then-prohibited analgesic Butazolidin.

A long legal battle ensued. The stewards awarded the winner's share to Forward Pass, but did not technically disqualify Dancer's Image, because Kentucky racing rules at the time stated only that any horse showing up positive for a derivative of phenylbutazone "shall not participate in the purse distribution."

Later in 1968, a two-week hearing by the Kentucky State Racing Commission upheld the stewards' ruling. At Churchill Downs, Forward Pass's name came down as the Derby winner, and later the names of both horses went up. The purse-distribution decision was appealed by Peter Fuller, owner of Dancer's Image, and nearly two years later the commission's ruling was overturned. The racing commission, in turn, then appealed to the Kentucky Court of Appeals, which awarded first-place money to Forward Pass on April 28, 1972 – nearly four years after the disputed Run for the Roses.

In the May 8, 1972, issue of The Blood-Horse magazine, Kent Hollingsworth wrote, "The purse finally having been distributed, there remains of the Dancer's Image case an unresolved quiddity . . . which will forever plague quiz-show contestants and anyone else ever asked: Who won the 1968 Kentucky Derby? Dancer's Image finished first, was never disqualified from first, but was denied any part of the purse; Forward Pass finished second, has never been declared the official winner but received first money."

In terms of total domination, few campaigns can match that of Arts and Letters in 1969. After being beaten in photo finishes by Majestic Prince in the Kentucky Derby and the Preakness, Paul Mellon's homebred chestnut ruined that rival's bid to become the first undefeated Triple Crown winner, easily thrashing him in the Belmont Stakes by 5 ½ lengths.

The Rokeby Stable colt towered over his opposition during the remainder of the year, winning the Jim Dandy by 10 lengths, the Travers by 6½, the Woodward by two, and the two-mile Jockey Club Gold Cup by 14.

Arts and Letters was on the smallish side at just over 15 hands, and although he was not a flashy horse to look at, he ran with the kind of grim determination that gave credence to famed breeder Federico Tesio's assertion that "a horse runs with his legs and resists with his heart."

As the 1960's came to a close, America scarcely resembled what it had been at the beginning of the decade. A fledgling space program had developed to the point where Neil Armstrong and Buzz Aldrin set foot on the moon in July 1969. A few months later, a hapless expansion team that had established a record for futility by losing 120 games in its debut season of 1962 became the Miracle Mets, after a thoroughly implausible World Series victory over the heavily favored Baltimore Orioles.

By the autumn of 1969, political assassinations, race riots, and anti-Vietnam War protests had exacted a heavy toll on the American psyche, inexorably wearing off the last remaining vestiges of the nation's innocence.

Significant upheaval loomed on the horizon for racing as well. As a new decade of uncertainty dawned, offtrack betting, lotteries, and casinos would provide increasingly sterner competition for America's betting dollar.

The game, and all its many players, would never again be quite the same.

CHAMPIONS

PAST PERFORMANCES

THE 1960'S

•1960•
•2-YEAR-OLD MALE *Hail to Reason* •2-YEAR-OLD FILLY *Bowl of Flowers* •3-YEAR-OLD MALE *Kelso*
•3-YEAR-OLD FILLY *Berlo* •HANDICAP HORSE *Bald Eagle* •HANDICAP MARE *Royal Native* •STEEPLECHASE *Benguala*
•**HORSE OF THE YEAR** Kelso

•1961•
•2-YEAR-OLD MALE *Crimson Satan* •2-YEAR-OLD FILLY *Cicada* •3-YEAR-OLD MALE *Carry Back*
•3-YEAR-OLD FILLY *Bowl of Flowers* •HANDICAP HORSE *Kelso* •HANDICAP MARE *Airmans Guide*
•GRASS HORSE *T.V. Lark* •STEEPLECHASE *Peal*
•**HORSE OF THE YEAR** Kelso

•1962•
•2-YEAR-OLD MALE *Never Bend* •2-YEAR-OLD FILLY *Smart Deb* •3-YEAR-OLD MALE *Jaipur*
•3-YEAR-OLD FILLY *Cicada* •HANDICAP HORSE *Kelso* •HANDICAP MARE *Primonetta* •STEEPLECHASE *Barnabys Bluff*
•**HORSE OF THE YEAR** Kelso

•1963•
•2-YEAR-OLD MALE *Hurry to Market* •2-YEAR-OLD FILLY *Tosmah, Castle Forbes (TRA)* •3-YEAR-OLD MALE *Chateaugay*
•3-YEAR-OLD FILLY *Lamb Chop* •HANDICAP HORSE *Kelso* •HANDICAP MARE *Cicada*
•GRASS HORSE *Mongo* •STEEPLECHASE *Amber Diver*
•**HORSE OF THE YEAR** Kelso

•1964•
•2-YEAR-OLD MALE *Bold Lad* •2-YEAR-OLD FILLY *Queen Empress* •3-YEAR-OLD MALE *Northern Dancer*
•3-YEAR-OLD FILLY *Tosmah* •HANDICAP HORSE *Kelso* •HANDICAP MARE *Tosmah, Old Hat (TRA)*
•STEEPLECHASE *Bel Nouvel*
•**HORSE OF THE YEAR** Kelso

•1965•
•2-YEAR-OLD MALE *Buckpasser* •2-YEAR-OLD FILLY *Moccasin* •3-YEAR-OLD MALE *Tom Rolfe*
•3-YEAR-OLD FILLY *What a Treat* •HANDICAP HORSE *Roman Brother* •HANDICAP MARE *Old Hat* •GRASS HORSE *Parka*
•SPRINTER *Affectionately* •STEEPLECHASE *Bon Nouvel*
•**HORSE OF THE YEAR** Roman Brother, Moccasin (TRA)

•1966•
•2-YEAR-OLD MALE *Successor* •2-YEAR-OLD FILLY *Regal Gleam* •3-YEAR-OLD MALE *Buckpasser*
•3-YEAR-OLD FILLY *Lady Pitt* •HANDICAP HORSE *Buckpasser Bold Bidder (TRA)*
•HANDICAP MARE *Open Fire, Summer Scandal (TRA)* •GRASS HORSE *Assagai* •SPRINTER *Impressive*
•STEEPLECHASE *Mako, Tuscalee (TRA)*
•**HORSE OF THE YEAR** Buckpasser

•1967•
•2-YEAR-OLD MALE *Vitriolic* •2-YEAR-OLD FILLY *Queen of the Stage* •3-YEAR-OLD MALE *Damascus*
•3-YEAR-OLD FILLY *Furl Sail, Gamely (TRA)* •HANDICAP HORSE *Damascus, Buckpasser (TRA)*
•HANDICAP MARE *Straight Deal* •GRASS HORSE *Fort Marcy* •SPRINTER *Dr. Fager* •STEEPLECHASE *Quick Pitch*
•**HORSE OF THE YEAR** Damascus

•1968•
•2-YEAR-OLD MALE *Top Knight* •2-YEAR-OLD FILLY *Gallant Bloom, Process Shot (TRA)*
•3-YEAR-OLD MALE *Stage Door Johnny* •3-YEAR-OLD FILLY *Dark Mirage* •HANDICAP HORSE *Dr. Fager*
•HANDICAP MARE *Gamely* •GRASS HORSE *Dr. Fager* •SPRINTER *Dr. Fager* •STEEPLECHASE *Bon Nouvel*
•**HORSE OF THE YEAR** Dr. Fager

•1969•
•2-YEAR-OLD MALE *Silent Screen* •2-YEAR-OLD FILLY *Fast Attack, Tudor Queen (TRA)*
•3-YEAR-OLD MALE *Arts and Letters* •3-YEAR-OLD FILLY *Gallant Bloom*
•HANDICAP HORSE *Arts and Letters, Nodouble (TRA)* •HANDICAP MARE *Gallant Bloom, Gamely (TRA)*
•GRASS HORSE *Hawaii* •SPRINTER *Ta Wee* •STEEPLECHASE *L'Escargot*
•**HORSE OF THE YEAR** Arts and Letters

Affectionately

dkb. f. 1960, by Swaps (Khaled)–Searching, by War Admiral

Own.– Mrs E.D. Jacobs

Br.– Bieber–Jacobs Stable (Ky)

Tr.– H. Jacobs

Lifetime record: 52 28 8 6 $546,660

1Nov65-7Aqu	fst 6f	:224 :453 1:102 3↑	Sport Page H 28k	6 1 2hd 1hd 1½ 2¾	Blum W	127	b	*1.10	90-21	Ornamento112¾Affectionately127¾R. Thomas119no	Gamely 8
14Oct65-6Kee	fst *7f	1:27 3↑	ⒻAlw 10000	2 2 1hd 1hd 2hd 1¾	Blum W	121	b	-	88-16	Affectionately121¾Star Maggie1151 2Basking11811	Driving 4
27Sep65-7Aqu	fst 1⅛	:463 1:104 1:36 1:491 3↑	ⒻBeldame 82k	1 1 1½ 1hd 31½ 53	Blum W	123	b	2.10e	87-19	WhataTreat118noSteeplJll123½StrghtDl1181½	Swerved start 6
20Sep65-7Aqu	fst 1	:223 :444 1:084 1:351 3↑	ⒻMaskette H 28k	8 1 1½ 1hd 1hd 2no	Blum W	128	b	2.90e	92-16	Tosmah128noAffectionately1283Straight Deal113½	Sharp 9
5Jly65-7Aqu	fst 1¼	:463 1:111 1:36 2:01 3↑	Suburban H 108k	7 3 42½ 46½ 512 625	Valenzuela I	119	b	8.95	68-14	Pia Star1171½Smart1198Tenacle1144	Drifted out late 7
26Jun65-7Aqu	fst 7f	:221 :443 1:091 1:23 3↑	ⒻVagrancy H 58k	1 1 1½ 12 16 1hd	Blum W	137	b	*1.05e	91-13	Affectionately137hdSoughtAftr1113½FcthFcts1191½	All out 13
9Jun65-7Aqu	fst 6f	:214 :442 1:092 3↑	ⒻLiberty Belle H 28k	4 1 11½ 13 16 16	Blum W	132	b	*.50	96-15	Affectionately1326Songster1123Petite Rouge109½	Easily 8
31May65-7Aqu	fst 1	:222 :442 1:081 1:342 3↑	Metropolitan H 111k	5 1 11 11 2hd 33¼	Valenzuela I	121	b	4.55	93-16	GunBow130nkChieftain1173Affectionately1214½	Game effort 8
22May65-7Aqu	fst 1⅛	:47 1:111 1:362 1:494 3↑	ⒻTop Flight H 57k	5 1 13 13 15 18	Blum W	120	b	3.90e	87-20	Affectionately1208Steeple Jill123½Old Hat127¾	Easily 10
19May65-7Aqu	fst 7f	:221 :441 1:084 1:222 3↑	Roseben H 28k	2 2 1½ 23 23 34½	Blum W	127	b	*.60	89-17	National1162Chieftain122½Affectionately1272½	Bid,tired 7
21Apr65-7Aqu	fst 6f	:22 :442 1:092 3↑	Toboggan H 27k	3 1 1½ 13 16 15	Blum W	124	b	*1.45	96-16	Affectionately1245Chieftain1263½ExclusivNshu1152	Easily 8
14Apr65-7Aqu	fst 7f	:231 :461 1:103 1:24 3↑	ⒻDistaff H 27k	7 1 1½ 12½ 14 13	Blum W	128	b	*.70	86-21	Affectionately1283Treachery115hdPetticoat113hd	Easily 7
31Mar65-7Aqu	fst 6f	:23 :461 1:11 3↑	ⒻCorrection H 27k	7 1 12 12 13 12	Baeza B	125	b	*.75	88-24	Affectionately1252FacetheFacts123½ChopHouse122nk	Easily 7
23Jan65-7SA	fst 1 1/16	:231 :46 1:102 1:424 4↑	ⒻS Maria H 29k	8 1 1½ 1hd 1hd 21	Shoemaker W	122	b	3.40e	88-11	Batteur1191Affectionately1221½CuriousClover118no	Gamely 9
12Jan65-8SA	fst 7f	:222 :451 1:093 1:222 4↑	ⒻS Monica H (Div 2) 19k	1 4 2hd 21 24 23½	Shoemaker W	126	b	*1.20e	87-16	Chop House1203½Affectionately126nkBatteur118hd	Gamely 10
31Dec64-8SA	fst 6f	:221 :451 :573 1:10 3↑	ⒻLas Flores H 24k	4 2 2½ 1hd 1hd 13↓	Shoemaker W	125	b	*.90	92-17	[DH]Affectiontly125[DH]ChopHous1193CurousClovr120½	Driving 10
11Nov64-7Aqu	fst 7f	:221 :45 1:091 1:22 3↑	Vosburgh H 28k	7 5 22 2½ 13 11	Grant H	120	b	*2.05e	96-17	Affectionately1201RdGr1132Bonjour114nk	Strongly handled 9
2Nov64-7Aqu	fst 6f	:222 :451 1:102 3↑	Sport Page H 28k	8 3 1½ 1hd 12 11½	Shoemaker W	117	b	*1.75e	91-16	Affectionately1171½Red Gar1132Macedonia1162½	Easily 11
21Oct64-7Aqu	gd 6f	:214 :45 1:103 3↑	ⒻInterborough H 27k	4 2 32 21½ 1½ 12	Shoemaker W	124	b	*1.60	90-16	Affectionately1242Ballet Rose110¾Charspiv1164	Easily 6
13Oct64-7Aqu	fst 6f	:221 :451 1:094 3↑	ⒻAlw 10000	5 1 22 2hd 11 12	Shoemaker W	123	b	*.35	94-14	Affectionately1232Gold Frame1083Steeple Jill1142	Easily 5
30Jly64-7Aqu	fst 6f	:222 :452 1:10 3↑	ⒻHandicap 10000	1 2 11½ 11 12½ 11½	Chambers W	124	b	3.60	93-18	Affectionately1241½ChopHouse120½LookMa1133	Brisk drive 6
1Jly64-7Aqu	fst 6f	:213 :443 1:101 3↑	ⒻLiberty Belle H 27k	2 3 3nk 32½ 812 815	Ussery R	123	b	4.65	77-17	Tosmah1202LookMa1101½LizzieTsh111no	Early speed,stopped 8
10Jun64-7Aqu	fst 7f	:221 :443 1:101 1:234 3↑	ⒻVagrancy H 28k	7 2 12 1½ 1½ 41¼	Chambers W	122	b	6.20	86-18	NoResisting112nkOilRoyalty1251LookMa110no	Used in pace 10
2Jun64-7Aqu	fst 6f	:222 :452 1:102 3↑	ⒻHandicap 8500	3 1 12 13 13 12	Chambers W	122	b	*.90	91-16	Affectionately1222SparklingSiren113nkPmsEgo1215	Handily 8
29May64-7Aqu	fst 7f	:223 :453 1:103 1:232 3↑	ⒻAlw 10000	3 3 12 12 12 22	Venezia M7	116	b	*1.05	87-17	Colonia1162Affectionately1162No Resisting1161	Gamely 10
16May64-7GS	fst 6f	:214 :443 1:101 3↑	ⒻColonial H 29k	6 5 1hd 21½ 45 44¾	Grimm PI	123	b	3.30	88-18	Tosmah1151½LookMa1103LatinWalk111nk	Tired under impost 11
1Apr64-7Aqu	fst 6f	:221 :453 1:104 3↑	ⒻCorrection H 29k	2 2 11 12½ 11½ 12½	Chambers W	121	b	4.25	89-19	Affectionately1212½DecimalCoinag111noChrspv1204	Driving 12
24Feb64-7SA	fst 7f	:214 :443 1:093 1:224 4↑	ⒻS Monica H 24k	7 5 1½ 1½ 32 125¾	Ycaza M	118	b	*3.40	83-14	ChopHouse116hdSundayDoll1111½JazzQueen112¾	Early foot 16
17Feb64-6SA	fst 6f	:22 :45 :57 1:093 4↑	ⒻAlw 7500	3 3 21 2½ 21 21	Valenzuela I	120	b	*1.90	95-13	Kea1171Affectionately1201½Sunday Doll1172½	Game effort 8
17Jan64-7SA	fst 6f	:221 :451 :574 1:103 4↑	ⒻAlw 10000	5 2 2hd 1hd 31 75½	Valenzuela I	120	b	*1.60	85-17	Hi Rated120¾Bloomer Girl1131Savaii1141	Used up early 11
5Nov63-7Aqu	fst 6f	:214 :442 1:10 3↑	ⒻInterborough H 23k	9 1 2hd 21 1½ 11½	Valenzuela I	116	b	*2.15	93-16	Affectionately1161½Charspiv114½[D]Smart Deb1211	Driving 12
17Oct63-6Aqu	fst 6½f	:221 :444 1:101 1:17 3↑	ⒻAlw 7500	6 1 1½ 14 14 12	Valenzuela I	114	b	*.70e	95-17	Affectionately1142Speedwell111¾GrenupTm114hd	Mild drive 9
7Oct63-6Aqu	fst 6f	:221 :452 1:102 3↑	ⒻAlw 7500	5 1 12 11½ 13 2hd	Valenzuela I	114	b	*1.70	91-15	Tamarona116hdAffectionately1142Royal Babs1141	Sharp 6
29Jly63-6Sar	fst 6f	:214 :451 1:101 3↑	ⒻAlw 6000	9 1 12½ 11½ 11 31¼	Gomez A	114	b	*2.15	96-11	Sailor'sHunch113½WindyMiss120¾Affectionately1142	Tired 9
29Jun63-7Aqu	sly 6f	:22 :452 1:103 3↑	ⒻLiberty Belle H 27k	2 3 31½ 32½ 65¾ 612	Ycaza M	112	b	3.45	80-13	MahMoola1125Bramalea120¾King'sStory112¾	Bore out,tired 6
24May63-7Aqu	fm 1 1/16Ⓣ	1:424 3↑	ⒻAlw 10000	1 1 11½ 1hd 2½ 53¾	Adams L	111		4.90	90-06	Errcountess1181¼Speedwell1102My Portrait121hd	Tired 8
18May63-7Aqu	sly 1	:222 :453 1:111 1:371	ⒻAcorn 60k	3 1 2½ 2hd 914 1125	Adams L	121		6.15	57-17	SpicyLiving1213½Nalee121½LambChop1213	Early speed,tired 12
25Apr63-7Aqu	fst 6f	:23 :47 1:113 3↑	ⒻAlw 10000	2 1 11 11 12 11½	Shoemaker W	105		*.65	87-17	Affectionately1051½Windy Miss122noSome Song1221½	Easily 8
19Apr63-6Aqu	fst 6f	:221 :453 1:104 3↑	ⒻAlw 7500	2 3 21½ 11 11½ 11½	Valenzuela I	114		*.30	91-15	Affectiontly1141½RumBottlBy1112Wlson'sB.W.116no	Driving 7
19Oct62-7GS	fst 1	:223 :454 1:104 1:372	ⒻAlw 10000	10 1 12½ 1½ 21 37	Baeza B	121	b	4.20e	88-20	Wise Nurse1122Smart Deb1215Affectionately1212½	Tired 11
6Oct62-7Bel	sly 1	:223 :453 1:111 1:38	ⒻFrizette 110k	7 2 2hd 2hd 2hd 33¼	Valenzuela I	119	b	3.20e	81-15	PamsEgo1191½Fool'sPlay1191¾Affectionately1194	Weakened 10
8Sep62-7Aqu	fst 6f	:213 :442 1:094	ⒻMatron 102k	6 2 2hd 2hd 22½ 35½	Valenzuela I	119	b	*.65	90-11	SmartDeb1191½FashionVerdict1194Affectionately1193	Tired 9
22Aug62-7Sar	fst 6f	:221 :45 1:102	ⒻSpinaway 79k	8 1 11½ 11½ 11½ 11¼	Valenzuela I	119	b	*.30	96-12	Affectionately1191¼Nalee1192½Rare Exchange1192	Driving 9
28Jly62-8Mth	fst 6f	:212 :441 1:10	ⒻSorority 100k	9 1 12 15 14 15	Valenzuela I	119	b	*.30	92-16	Affectionately1195Fashion Verdict119¾Nalee1192½	Easily 9
16Jly62-7Aqu	fst 5½f	:22 :451 1:043	ⒻAstoria 28k	6 1 1½ 12 13 12½	Baeza B	123	b	*.65	96-10	Affectionatly1232½NoRsstng120¾Kng'sStory1172	Mild drive 9
27Jun62-7Mth	fst 5½f	:213 :462 1:051	ⒻColleen 23k	2 7 51½ 53¼ 3½ 22½	Baeza B	119		*.60	88-20	NoResisting1122½Affectiontly1195Nl1122	Blocked ⅛ pole 11
18Jun62-5Bel	fst 5½f	:221 :461 1:051	ⒻNational Stallion 37k	2 2 32 21 1½ 13	Baeza B	119		*.15	95-15	Affectionately1193Charspiv1142½No Resisting119¾	Easily 5
2Jun62-5Del	fst 5f	:221 :463 :59	ⒻPolly Drummond 23k	8 1 1hd 2hd 1hd 11	Valenzuela I	122		*.70	94-22	Affectionately1221Bold Princess1134Nalee1091½	Driving 8
16May62-7Aqu	fst 5f	:22 :454 :584	ⒻFashion 22k	2 2 1½ 1½ 12 12	Baeza B	116		*.35	96-16	Affectionately1162FashonVrdct116nkPrncssBbu116½	Handily 7
9May62-5Aqu	fst 5f	:23 :463 :583	ⒻAlw 5000	5 3 43 21½ 11½ 12½	Baeza B	120		*.75	97-12	Affectionately1202½FashionVerdct1201½PmsEgo1172½	Easily 6
28Apr62-4Aqu	fst 5f	:22 :462 :591	ⒻAlw 4500	1 1 11 11 11½ 17	Baeza B	117		*1.30	94-10	Affectionately1177Mardoll115noTamanrasset1201½	Easily 7
17Jan62-3SA	fst 3f	:22 :331	ⒻMd Sp Wt	1 3 13 11½	Baeza B	115		4.30	- -	Affectionately1151½Snickersnee115noDelhiMad1152	Driving 14

Airmans Guide

b. f. 1957, by One Count (Count Fleet)–Navigating, by Hard Tack

Own.– H.A. Grant

Br.– W.P. Little (Ky)

Tr.– B.B. Williams

Lifetime record: 20 13 2 2 $315,673

19Oct61-6Kee	sly 1⅛	:464 1:103 1:36 1:491 3↑	ⒻSpinster 84k	1 1 1½ 2½ 22 42¾	Grant H	123	b	*.70	88-11	BowlofFlowers119¾Primonetta1191TimesTwo1191	No excuse 7
12Oct61-6Kee	fst *7f	1:25 3↑	ⒻAlw 7500	3 2 21½ 31½ 2hd 12	Grant H	121	b	*.40	102-09	Airmans Guide1212Indian Maid115¾Flavia1093½	In hand 5
23Sep61-7Bel	fst 1⅛	:463 1:11 1:361 1:492 3↑	ⒻBeldame 96k	5 2 21 2½ 1½ 1¾	Grant H	123	b	3.65	89-18	Airmans Guide123¾Craftiness1232½Primonetta1185½	Driving 12
29Jly61-6Del	gd 1¼	:46 1:11 1:362 2:022 3↑	ⒻDelaware H 159k	10 2 23 14 14 13½	Grant H	121	b	*2.40	90-20	Airmans Guide1213½Royal Native120nkTritoma1182½	Easily 12
22Jly61-6Del	fst 1 1/16	:231 :47 1:113 1:434 3↑	ⒻNew Castle 38k	6 1 1hd 11½ 16 16	Grant H	116	b	10.90	90-21	Airmans Guide1166Tritoma1201¾Mountain Glory1121	Easily 15
8Jly61-7Mth	fst 1 1/16	:23 :454 1:102 1:431 3↑	ⒻMolly Pitcher H 30k	9 1 11½ 2hd 3½ 105¾	Blum W	124	b	*2.20	83-12	ShirleyJones1212¼SecretHonor114noChalvedele112nk	Tired 16
21Jun61-7Mth	fst 6f	:213 :44 1:094 3↑	ⒻRegret H 24k	11 2 53¾ 1hd 11½ 11¼	Blum W	121	b	*2.30	93-12	Airmans Guide1211¼Craftiness1121½Staretta1221¼	Cleverly 12
20May61-7GS	fst 6f	:22 :451 1:101 3↑	ⒻColonial H 28k	2 4 31 42 21½ 3hd	Blum W	119	b	*1.80	90-15	Staretta117hdCoupd'etat117noAirmansGuide1191½	Sharp try 9
29Mar61-7GP	fst 7f	:221 :45 1:092 1:222 3↑	ⒻSuwannee River H 16k	8 2 41 3nk 11½ 11¾	Hartack W	120	b	*1.15	101-13	AirmansGuide1201¾ShirleyJones1193¼IndianMd119hd	In hand 8
22Mar61-6GP	gd 6f	:224 :453 1:104 3↑	ⒻAlw 5000	2 3 32 32 12 14½	Hartack W	113	b	*1.65	90-17	AirmansGuide1134½PrimFlower1171½Coupd'etat1232	Easily 8
21May60-7Aqu	fst 1	:224 :451 1:093 1:354	ⒻAcorn 59k	1 1 11 11½ 1½ 2nk	Blum W	121	b	6.25	97-06	IrishJay121nkAirmansGuide1219SisterAntoine121½	Bore out 13
14May60-8Pim	gd 1 1/16	:241 :474 1:13 1:461	ⒻBlack-Eyed Susan 23k	2 1 11½ 1hd 2hd 1¾	Harmatz W	121	b	1.70	79-20	Airmans Guide121¾Chalvedele1213Warlike12112	Driving 4
6May60-7CD	fst 1 1/16	:231 :464 1:12 1:441	ⒻKy Oaks 40k	2 1 1hd 1hd 3nk 33¼	Hartack W	116	b	*1.40	89-15	Make Sail116nkQuaze1163Airmans Guide1162½	Used in pace 8
16Apr60-6Kee	fst 6f	:222 :453 1:101	ⒻAshland 26k	10 6 11 11½ 11 21	Hartack W	121	b	*1.90	93-10	Tingle1121AirmansGuide1211MakeSail118nk	Held on gamely 12
26Nov59-8Pim	gd 1 1/16	:233 :472 1:122 1:463	ⒻMarguerite 39k	8 1 11½ 12 11½ 13½	Hartack W	119	b	*.30	77-29	AirmansGuide1193½[D]Improve119nkFlowerBonnet1196	Easily 8
21Nov59-6Pim	fst 1 1/16	:244 :482 1:131 1:461	Alw 3500	6 1 14 11½ 12 13	Nichols J	117	b	4.40	79-17	AirmnsGuide1173WiseShip1142½CountChuck1151¼	Mild drive 7
23Oct59-4Kee	fst 6½f	:222 :45 1:093 1:162	ⒻAlw 4000	1 6 1hd 11½ 12 11¼	Hartack W	119	b	2.70	100-13	AirmansGuide1191¼Bolerita1165½HastyDancer1164½	Driving 6
26Aug59-8AP	fst 6f	:22 :444 1:094	ⒻPrincess Pat 104k	3 11 75½ 88¼ 711 714	Nichols J	116	b	4.80	81-11	HeavenlyBody1161¾Pierpontella1162RashStatmnt1161½	Tired 11
2May59-5CD	fst 5f	:222 :452 :583	ⒻDebutante 14k	4 5 2hd 2hd 13 12	Gross E	119		4.40	99-06	AirmansGuide1192GreekTop1192¼Sandy'sSisW.1192	Driving 10
18Apr59-4Kee	sly *4f	:492	Md Sp Wt	10 4 1½ 16 16	Gross E	115		12.20	95-06	Airmans Guide1156April Five1155Natural Bid1181	Easily 12

Amber Diver

b. g. 1954, by Ambiorix (Tourbillon)–Marapania, by Devil Diver
Own.– Mrs S.C. Clark Jr
Br.– Belair Stud (Ky)
Tr.– S. Watters Jr

Lifetime record: 103 27 23 18 $240,725

30Oct64- 6Aqu	fm 3		S'Chase	5:394	4↑ Temple Gwathmey H 55k	4	2	21	1½	110	120	Aitcheson J	157		4.35	--	Amber Diver15720Aquitania1351Bon Nouvel162½	In hand	7
20Oct64- 5Aqu	sf 3		S'Chase	5:401	4↑ Grand National H 28k	6	3	26	28	220	220	Aitcheson J	156		2.75	--	BonNouvl15620AmbrDiver1566BamptonCastle140hd	Bobbled	8
17Sep64- 5Aqu	fm 2		S'Chase	3:402	4↑ Broad Hollow H 16k	6	3	23	24	-	-	Murphy J	158		*1.95	--	BonNouvl1462Tuscror1492½Nutlus1465	Stumbled at 12th,fell	6
27Aug64- 5Sar	hd 2½		S'Chase	4:364	4↑ Saratoga H 19k	4	-	-	-	-	-	Murphy J	158		*.75	--	Nautilus13512Tuscarora15060Rao Raja142	Bobbled 3rd jump	4
7Aug64- 5Sar	hd 2 1/16		S'Chase	3:48	4↑ Beverwyck H 16k	7	2	32	1hd	1hd	2½	Murphy J	160		*1.55	--	Nautilus131½Amber Diver16020Tuscarora154no	Just failed	7
11Jun64- 5Aqu	fm 2½		S'Chase	4:343	4↑ Meadow Brook H 19k	1	3	39	34	2½	22½	Murphy J	164		1.80	--	RaoRaja1382½AmberDiver16440StrollingSquar13110	2nd best	5
25Oct63- 6Aqu	hd *3		S'Chase	5:373	4↑ Temple Gwathmey H 55k	4	2	21½	11	12	12¼	Aitcheson J	164		*1.60	--	AmberDiver1642¼TheSport158nkTuscarora16330	Brisk urging	7
15Oct63- 5Aqu	hd *3		S'Chase	5:371	4↑ Grand National H 27k	3	1	11¼	1hd	31¼	22	Murphy J	163		*.95e	--	Tuscarora1602AmbrDiver163nkThSport15810	Bothered often	8
1Oct63- 5Aqu	fm *2½		S'Chase	4:371	4↑ Brook H 20k	8	2	24	23	112	120	Murphy J	155		12.55e	--	AmberDiver15520TheSport1583½Tuscror161nk	Speed to spare	9
12Sep63- 5Aqu	fm *2		S'Chase	3:421	4↑ Broad Hollow H 16k	5	4	46½	49	414	318¼	Murphy J	160		3.35	--	TheSport1453½BrnabysBluff16015[DH]BadgeofHonor151	Tired	5
22Aug63- 5Sar	fm 2½		S'Chase	4:38	4↑ Sar H 19k	1	4	36	42¼	37	410¼	Murphy J	161		3.50	--	Tuscarora1518BadgeofHonr1482Shntyboat145nk	Bobbled 10th	5
2Aug63- 5Sar	sf 2 1/16		S'Chase	3:473	4↑ Beverwyck H 17k	1	2	26	2½	21½	23	Murphy J	161		3.20	--	BadgeofHonor1433AmbrDvr1612½BarnbysBluff16430	Gamely	6
5Jly63- 3Del	fm *2½		S'Chase	4:361	4↑ Indian River H 10k	5	1	12	11	13	13½	Murphy J	152		2.30e	--	AmbrDiver1523½BarnabysBluff16310BeckysShip1402	Handily	6
25Jun63- 3Del	fm *2⅛		S'Chase	4:01	4↑ Georgetown H 10k	1	3	13	12	13	12½	Murphy J	148		4.10	--	AmberDiver1482½BarnabysBluff1641BeckysShip1414	Easily	7
17Jun63- 3Del	fm *2⅛		S'Chase	4:032	4↑ Tom Roby 10k	2	5	2½	13	12	11	Murphy J	143		*1.40	--	Amber Diver1431Red Circle1454Shantyboat13810	Driving	5
23May63- 5Aqu	fm *2		S'Chase	3:47	4↑ Hitchcock 11k	4	5	21	2hd	31½	36	Murphy J	155		2.65	--	Bimeland1314½Kampina1511½AmberDiver1552½	Bold bid,tired	5
4May63- 3War	hd *2		S'Chase	4:33	4↑ Alw 3000	4	3	2nk	1hd	1nk	1½	Murphy J	158		-	--	Amber Diver158½Welstead1435Bampton Castle1522½	Driving	5
20Apr63- 3Mid	fm *2		S'Chase	3:50	4↑ Handicap 2000	2	2	21	1½	12	12	Murphy J	157		-	--	Amber Diver1572Royal Vision1484Half Baked1331	Driving	4
13Apr63- 3Mid	fm *2		S'Chase	3:50	4↑ Langley Mem Cup 2k	4	4	32	2½	12	1¾	Murphy J	148		-	--	Amber Diver148¾Royal Vision151½Hustle15110	Driving hard	6
10Nov62- 4Mid	sf *2½		S'Chase	4:292	4↑ Alw 1200	7	4	46½	-	-	-	Murphy J	154		-	--	BamptonCastle1568BugleCallII1627HlfBkd1403	Bobbled,fell	9
				Previously owned by F.A. Clark;previously trained by F.T. Bellhouse															
27Oct62- 7Lrl	fm 1(T)			1:373	3↑ Alw 10000	6	6	54½	98¼	95¾	96½	Church K	112		26.60	78-18	Parka111nkGaelicLad1181½CalltheWitness116hd	Fell back	10
18Oct62- 3Bel	hd *1⅞		Hurdles	3:24	3↑ Alw 4200	4	4	33½	31½	57½	59½	Cartwright R	144		*2.20	--	Kantikoy135¾Shantyboat1524Ramshorn Creek137¾	Tired	7
11Oct62- 5Bel	sf *2½		Hurdles	4:392	4↑ Rouge Dragon H 11k	9	5	611	610	1020	1030	Cartwright R	160		4.95	--	BabyPrince1402½EstecoII1404½Palladio148hd	Far off pace	10
1Oct62- 6Bel	fm 7f(T)			:23 :461 1:10 1:221	3↑ Alw 7500	5	2	2hd	1hd	2hd	54½	Nelson E	114		21.80	95-00	ShieldBearer1241¼TheAxeII1141CalltheWitness1141½	Tired	9
12Jun62- 5Bel	sf *2½		S'Chase	4:47	4↑ Meadow Brook H 19k	6	4	48½	43	210	214	Cartwright R	152		*2.05	--	Blackmail15014Amber Diver152½Brannagh1394½	No excuse	6
1Jun62- 7Bel	hd 7f(T)			1:222	3↑ Alw 10000	6	8	55½	54½	52¼	53	Adams L	117		6.35	96-01	ShieldBearr1191Narokan1171¼Chich114nk	Even performance	10
26May62- 4Pur	fm *1(T)			1:443	3↑ Alw 500	4	2	11	1½	11½	11½	Foot A	158		*.95	--	AmberDiver1581½PierCapponi145nkNavalTreaty1401½	Handily	9
26Apr62- 8Lrl	fst 7f			:231 :463 1:113 1:24	4↑ Alw 4000	2	4	42½	33	22	22½	Church K	119		*2.10	99-09	Klinkhouse1122½Amber Diver1193Maniquest112½	Game try	7
13Apr62- 8Lrl	my 7f			:224 :462 1:124 1:26	4↑ Alw 4000	4	5	61¾	51¾	3nk	1hd	Church K	113		16.10	92-17	AmberDiver113hdPolynesinBully1151½RosTrlls1132½	Driving	8
27Oct61- 6Aqu	hd *2½		S'Chase	4:354	4↑ Temple Gwathmey H 55k	3	3	3½	-	-	-	Foot A	149		3.95	--	Peal16114NavalTreaty1392Chufquen1413	Bobbled,lost rider	8
19Oct61- 3Aqu	hd *2		S'Chase	3:482	4↑ Alw 4200	1	1	1½	1½	1hd	13½	Foot A	148		*1.80	--	AmberDiver1483½Negocio1511½BasilBe1418	Under mild drive	7
10Oct61- 5Aqu	fm *2½		Hurdles	4:343	4↑ Rouge Dragon H 11k	6	4	2½	11½	11	1¾	Foot A	156		4.60	--	Amber Diver156¾Blackmail1354Pocosaba1496	Hard ridden	7
4Oct61- 4Lig	fm *2		S'Chase	4:10	4↑ Alw 3000	8	4	1hd	25	36	311	Jackson E	145		-	--	Seroul1396Sir Patsy1454½Amber Diver14515	Well up,tired	8
7Sep61- 3Bel	hd *1⅞		Hurdles	3:20	3↑ Handicap 5000	2	3	22	45	413	532	Cartwright R	155		2.10	--	Swing Fever1484Seroul14520Gallant Tonto1146	Bobbled 6th	5
24Aug61- 5Sar	sf 2 1/16		Hurdles	3:444	4↑ Lovely Night H 11k	4	2	22	21½	11½	15	Cartwright R	150		2.10	--	Amber Diver1505Gallant Tonto1452½Seroul1518	Drew out	6
11Aug61- 5Sar	hd *2		Hurdles	3:351	4↑ Sar Natl Hurdle 11k	3	2	25	1hd	12	12½	Cartwright R	154		*2.05	--	AmberDiver1542½Seroul16215Blackml15020	Under mild drive	5
5Aug61- 3Sar	fm *1⅞		Hurdles	3:212	3↑ Alw 4200	4	3	22	22½	34½	49	Schulhofer F	140		*1.25	--	GallantTonto140nkGreekBrother1505¾AfterSupper1373	Tired	6
27May61- 3Pur	sf *2		Hurdles	4:24	4↑ Handicap 1500	1	3	3¾	21	24	26	Foot A	155		*1.05	--	December1396Amber Diver15515Gridiron15015	Made good try	5
2May61- 3Lrl	fm *1¾		Hurdles	3:112	4↑ Handicap 4000	6	2	44½	24	51½	43½	Cartwright R	154		2.30	--	Palladio153nkMoon Rock140nkMe Broke1363	No excuse	8
21Apr61- 3Lrl	fm *1⅝		Hurdles	3:002	3↑ Alw 3500	8	3	22	1hd	2hd	2½	Cartwright R	152		*1.00	--	Praesepe140½Amber Diver1524Me Broke14010	Wide,bumped	11
1Apr61- 5Cam	fm *2		S'Chase	3:244	4↑ Springdale Cup 1.2k	2	2	2¾	11½	2nk	1no	Cartwright R	142		-	--	AmbrDvr142noRomo15415Antonno1482	Lost lead,came again	4
10Nov60- 8Lrl	sly 6f			:223 :464 1:113	3↑ Alw 3500	2	5	65	63¼	63¾	56	Korte K	116	b	6.90	91-14	SevnCornrs1131¾Bonus1191¼ColdCut117hd	No serious threat	6
2Nov60- 8Lrl	gd 6f			:224 :47 1:114	4↑ Alw 4000	4	4	34	2hd	1hd	1no	Korte K	110	b	*2.20	96-11	Amber Diver110noOld Timer110noEastern Hobo1162	All out	6
11Oct60- 6Bel	hd 7f(T)			:233 :473 1:114 1:242	3↑ Alw 5000	1	7	42½	65	54½	66½	Arcaro E	114	b	5.90	83-11	[DH]Pilot119[DH]CalltheWitness1141CivicGuard1184½	Tired	14
3Oct60- 8Bel	fm 7f(T)			:234 :463 1:103 1:232	3↑ Handicap 6000	1	5	55½	58	1210	1212	Arcaro E	114	b	8.45	83-05	ShieldBearer117½Eurasia1161½Alhambra1172½	Fell far back	12
18Aug60- 7Sar	fst 1			:231 :463 1:11 1:372	3↑ Alw 6000	5	3	32	31½	41	43	Arcaro E	113	b	3.65	87-16	Best Brother1161¾Careless John101¾Lone Wolf113½	Tired	8
1Aug60- 8Sar	fst 1			:23 :46 1:101 1:354	3↑ Alw 6000	10	1	11½	13	21½	34½	Moreno H	113	b	3.50	93-12	Warhead1164½Derrick116noAmberDivr113½	Used setting pace	10
25Jun60- 5Bel	fm 7f(T)			:233 :463 1:111 1:234	3↑ Handicap 6000	1	10	52¼	32	41½	43¼	Moreno H	119		4.95	92-05	MysticII124nkVendetta119noEurs1163	Well placed,no rally	10
18Jun60- 5Bel	fst 6f			:221 :45 1:104	3↑ Alw 5000	6	6	46	46	33	3hd	Woodhouse H	114		12.40	93-09	Bumpy Road114hdOutgiving117noAmber Diver114¾	Sharp try	8
6Jun60- 6Bel	fm 7f(T)			:232 :463 1:101 1:222	3↑ Handicap 6000	5	3	42½	54	55	43	Arcaro E	119		3.70	99-00	Shield Bearer119¾Dunce124nkGeneral Arthur1162	Even race	8
26May60- 7Aqu	fst 1⅛			:49 1:133 1:391 1:513	4↑ Alw 7500	2	2	2½	1hd	41	46	Boulmetis S	113		2.95	80-09	Derrick1141½Nasomo1193½Prnc'sGm1131	Swerved in at break	6
7May60- 8Pim	fm 1⅛(T)			:474 1:114 1:364 1:501	3↑ Riggs H 17k	8	3	3½	31½	2½	3nk	Korte K	116		7.60	100-03	Troubadour II108hdCrasher109hdAmber Diver116¾	Held well	12
26Apr60- 8Lrl	fst 1			:23 :47 1:114 1:372	4↑ Alw 4000	5	4	43½	32	31	1no	Korte K	113		*1.70	109-02	AmbrDvr113no[DH]CyprianCat116[DH]LordGregor115hd	Driving	8
19Nov59- 7Pim	fst 1 1/16			:242 :48 1:121 1:451	3↑ Alw 4000	6	1	13	15	16	13½	Korte K	113		*1.00	84-20	AmberDiver1133½WiseGuy113hdPrincipado1112	Scored easily	7
2Nov59- 7Lrl	fst 6f			:23 :464 1:122	3↑ Alw 4000	7	3	31½	21	2½	21	Nichols J	116		*1.40	--	Eastern Hobo1161Amber Diver1163Liberty Sun1111¼	Gamely	7
24Oct59- 4Aqu	sly 6f			:222 :453 1:104	3↑ Handicap 5000	3	2	53½	55½	53½	52¾	Boland W	123		4.40	--	Saci114hdMissile1182Commndton112¾	Bore out into stretch	7
9Oct59- 7Aqu	sly 6f			:222 :452 1:102	3↑ Handicap 7500	2	5	56	56½	43¼	31½	Burr C	109		24.60	--	TickTock124hdDiscard1151½AmberDiver109½	Best foot late	7
25Sep59- 7Aqu	fst 1⅛			:481 1:124 1:38 1:504	3↑ Handicap 7500	5	3	33½	32	44½	68½	Boland W	113		13.20	--	Demobilize1161½Reinzi1103GreekStr1161	Well placed,tired	6
11Sep59- 7Bel	hd 7f(T)			:231 :461 1:11 1:23	3↑ Handicap 7500	11	6	85¾	75½	41	2nk	Arcaro E	121		5.20	99-01	ShieldBearer122nkAmberDiver121hdVegeo112½	Sharp effort	12
19Aug59- 5Sar	fst 1			:24 :471 1:114 1:371	3↑ Handicap 6000	5	3	31½	21	21½	23½	Arcaro E	122		2.30	87-16	ShieldBearer1133½AmberDiver122¾Nivrag117hd	Held gamely	5
8Aug59- 6Sar	fst 1⅛			:481 1:13 1:393 1:53	4↑ Whitney H 58k	5	2	2½	2½	3½	54¾	Nelson E	110		16.05	79-23	Plon114hdAmrgo1122½VllgIdot112hd	Forced wide turn,tired	10
3Aug59- 7Sar	fst 1			:24 :482 1:131 1:383	3↑ Alw 6000	1	1	1hd	13	12½	1¾	Arcaro E	114		4.20	84-21	AmberDiver114¾Ambehaving1133½Plion1221	Under hard drive	6
4Jly59- 7Mth	fm 1(T)			:231 :474 1:114 1:374	3↑ Longfellow H 24k	2	4	32	33	25	36¼	Cook WM	118		33.90	91-03	Li'l Fella1216Fairfield113nkAmber Diver118no	No excuse	11
24Jun59- 7Bel	fm 1⅜(T)			:483 1:123 1:37 2:143	3↑ Bowling Green H 29k	2	2	1hd	54¾	88¼	1013	Sorrentino M	117		7.10	91-00	BllHop116nkKngGrl1093½PopCorn1204	Lost whip after break	11
13Jun59- 6Bel	sf 7f(T)			:234 :47 1:123 1:254	3↑ Handicap 10000	3	3	44	44½	46	34½	Arcaro E	118		*1.80	80-15	CombustionII1191BaldEagle1153½AmberDiver1182	Bore out	6
3Jun59- 6Bel	fst 7f			:224 :454 1:102 1:23	3↑ Alw 6000	4	2	21	2hd	1hd	2nk	Arcaro E	117		*1.55	92-09	CombustionII117nkAmbrDivr1171LittleHermt1175½	Brushed	6
26May59- 7Bel	fm 7f(T)			:23 :462 1:102 1:224	3↑ Alw 6000	6	3	2½	21½	3½	42	Nelson E	117		7.95	98-00	Pantene114hdTenacious124noAmbergris1172	Speed,tired	12
9May59- 8Pim	fm 1⅜(T)			:482 1:143 1:39 2:152	3↑ Dixie H 29k	9	6	53	915	913	918	Nelson E	118		13.00	82-00	One-EyedKing1201Olgrchy1162½MystcII110¾	Fell back early	9
27Apr59- 7Jam	fst 6f			:224 :453 1:101	4↑ Alw 10000	3	6	68¼	67	59	56¾	Nelson E	117		32.75	89-15	TickTock120noWarhead124hdItob113¾	Never a strong factor	7
1Nov58- 7Lrl	fm *1⅛(T)			1:474	3↑ Turf Cup 24k	2	1	2hd	3nk	4nk	64½	Guerin E	114	w	6.40	92-09	TudorEra1222¼Mahan118hdPntn1141½	Speed to stretch,tired	12
4Oct58- 6Bel	fm 7f(T)			:231 :47 1:113 1:242	3↑ Handicap 6000	5	2	2½	2hd	2½	11	Valenzuela A	121	w	5.65	93-07	Amber Diver1211St. Amour121¾Pantene1171½	Driving clear	10
20Sep58- 6Bel	sf 1⅜(T)			:50 1:152 1:401 2:182	3↑ Handicap 10000	7	5	55	2½	32	43¼	Valenzuela A	121	w	4.70	86-11	LangtonBreeze1172¼Saim1111Rfty122no	Made bold bid,tired	10
8Sep58- 6Bel	sf 1⅜(T)			:48 1:141 1:40 2:172	3↑ Handicap 10000	1	6	64	2hd	1½	1nk	Valenzuela A	119	w	4.35	94-06	Amber Diver119nkPop Corn1181Jabneh116¾	Fully extended	10
30Aug58- 7Atl	sf 1⅛(T)			:483 1:131 1:39 1:522	3↑ Olympic H 28k	3	3	21½	21	21½	23	Valenzuela A	114	w	8.10	78-19	Tudor Era1173Amber Diver1146One-Eyed King114¾	Good try	8
16Aug58- 4Sar	fst 1			:24 :473 1:13 1:394	3↑ Handicap 5000	3	3	43½	21	4¾	32¾	Arcaro E	118	w	*1.00	75-22	Tenacious1141¾Ambergris1171Amber Diver1182	Bid,tired	6
9Aug58- 7Sar	gd 1⅛			:483 1:133 1:392 1:524	3↑ Handicap 6000	4	2	21	2½	1½	11¾	Boland W	114	w	3.15	85-20	Amber Diver1141¾Go Lightly1225Tenacious115¾	Going away	6

16Jly58- 5Jam	fst 1 1/16	:25 :49 1:124 1:442 4 ↑	Alw 6000	4 2 22 23 23 21½	Arcaro E	113	w	5.20	86-17	Cohoes1101½Amber Diver113½Ambergris1082½	Closing fast 6
4Jly58- 7Bel	fm 7f(T)	:23 :464 1:112 1:24 3 ↑	Alw 5000	10 3 43 41 2½ 14	Arcaro E	115	w	5.15	- -	Amber Diver1154Saci1182½Gray Phantom1181½	Ridden out 10
14Jun58- 6Bel	fst 6f	:224 :462 1:104 4 ↑	Alw 6000	6 6 54 44½ 47 46¾	Arcaro E	116	w	3.15	87-13	Commendation1162¼GayWarrior1161Craigwood1203½	No rally 7
31May58- 6Bel	fm 7f(T)	:23 :46 1:111 1:231 4 ↑	Alw 5500	8 3 36 33 3nk 34	Arcaro E	114	w	*1.90	- -	CombustionII1171Cavort1173AmbrDivr1141½	Stumbled late 8
28Apr58- 7Jam	sly 6f	:232 :462 1:103 3 ↑	Alw 7500	4 5 2½ 2½ 21½ 22¼	Woodhouse H	111	w	9.95	92-12	Hastego1222¼Amber Diver1112¾Pylades109nk	Good effort 6
21Nov57- 7Jam	fst 1 1/16	:243 :482 1:13 1:443	Alw 7500	3 2 2½ 3nk 21½ 36½	Atkinson T	111	w	*2.85	80-20	RoscoeManey1125MondayMrning1061½AmbrDivr111nk	Tired 7
9Nov57- 8Jam	sly 1 1/16	:241 :473 1:12 1:441	Alw 5500	7 5 54 31 21½ 34¾	Atkinson T	113	w	*1.20	84-17	FourFathoms1224½TheHorseFar116nkAmbrDvr1133½	Poor start 7
29Oct57- 7Jam	fst 6f	:223 :454 1:112	Alw 6000	2 4 47½ 47 46½ 2nk	Arcaro E	117	w	4.60	90-21	Missile117nkAmber Diver1172Red Cadet1173	Sharp try 9
15Oct57- 7Bel	fst 1	:232 :462 1:114 1:37 3 ↑	Alw 5000	1 2 23 21 1½ 23	Atkinson T	115	wb	*1.60	86-17	JazzAge1153AmberDiver1155CannonFir1122½	Late lead,tired 6
7Oct57- 5Bel	sly 7f	:23 :46 1:111 1:241	Alw 4500	4 3 2½ 1½ 12 12	Arcaro E	117	w	*1.20	89-14	AmbrDivr1172MondayMorning1081½Salor'sKnot1142	Driving 7
28Sep57- 4Bel	fst 1	:24 :471 1:122 1:372 3 ↑	Alw 5000	5 4 3½ 41½ 31 3nk	Woodhouse H	118	w	*1.60	87-13	JazzAge115noSausg106nkAmbrDvr1181½	Drifted wide on turn 7
31Aug57- 6Sar	fst 1	:234 :474 1:13 1:384	Alw 5000	2 2 1hd 11½ 11½ 2no	Woodhouse H	120	w	*1.95	83-17	PrinceWilly113noAmberDiver1204CannonFire113½	Nosed out 6
24Aug57- 8Sar	fst 1	:233 :471 1:122 1:383 3 ↑	Alw 4500	4 3 32 22 2hd 24	Woodhouse H	112	wb	*2.55	80-17	Patlarkit1224Amber Diver1123Sid's Gambol1121½	No excuse 8
12Aug57- 5Sar	fst 1	:232 :47 1:122 1:383	Alw 4200	1 2 2hd 1hd 11 11½	Woodhouse H	114	w	2.35	84-20	AmberDiver1141½PrinceWilly1092Trac1142½	Drew clear late 7
27Jly57- 6Bel	fst 1 1/16	:231 :46 1:104 1:43 3 ↑	Alw 5000	6 4 42½ 54 23 3½	Atkinson T	108	wb	7.30	93-11	Jesper110nkPromethean115nkAmber Diver1086	Late foot 7
17Jly57- 3Bel	fst 6f	:23 :471 1:13	Md Sp Wt	8 9 85 41 2hd 11	Woodhouse H	120	w	4.90	84-12	AmberDiver1201Avenge1151Winged Mercury1206	Going away 14
2Jly57- 2Bel	fst 6f	:224 :47 1:123 3 ↑	Md Sp Wt	10 6 56½ 55½ 43 45¼	Broussard R	118	w	*2.60	81-12	BetterBeGay1184½Avenge118¾IndinTruc124hd	Made bid,tired 11
12Jun57- 5Bel	fst 7f	:23 :464 1:123 1:254 3 ↑	Md Sp Wt	1 4 31½ 33½ 54½ 44¼	Woodhouse H	116	w	*.95	77-12	Charlies Alibi116hdHung Up111hdApostle1164	Dull effort 9
	Previously trained by G.H. Bostwick										
16Oct56- 2Bel	fst 6f	:222 :461 1:112	©Md Sp Wt	12 9 54 45 47 35½	Woodhouse H	118	w	4.75	86-11	Slaipner1184Teno'Clock1181½AmberDiver118½	Closing well 14
4Oct56- 6Bel	sly 6f-WC	:22 :453 1:101	©Md Sp Wt	9 5 64¾ 32½ 32	Woodhouse H	118	w	5.55	86-12	Double X.1182Tenacious118noAmber Diver1181½	Good effort 23
25Aug56- 5Sar	fst 6f	:23 :464 1:123	Sanford 17k	8 10 119¾ 1111 1011 812	Westrope J	111	w	35.50	73-18	Thin Ice116nkClem1165Bora116hd	Far off pace 12
20Aug56- 4Sar	fst 5½f	:232 :47 :592 1:06	©Md Sp Wt	3 4 12 11½ 2hd 34	Arcaro E	118	wb	3.20	83-17	Lucky Dip1182Miquelet1182Amber Diver1183	Set pace,tired 14
6Aug56- 2Sar	fst 5½f	:232 :474 :591 1:06	©Md Sp Wt	12 7 41½ 33 24 411	Arcaro E	118	wb	*2.65	76-18	Discernment1186AlmondHill118½LuckyDip1184½	Speed,tired 13
16Jun56- 3Bel	fst 5f-WC	:222 :452 :574	Md Sp Wt	11 5 41¼ 2½ 2hd	Arcaro E	118	w	*.70	90-10	Gavel113hdAmbrDvr1183Plytown1181½	Wearing down winner 15
7Jun56- 6Bel	fst 5f-WC	:221 :451 :571	©Md Sp Wt	19 3 21½ 2½ 21½	Woodhouse H	118	w	3.30	91-11	Dodger1181½AmberDiver118nkIrishWhistler1186	Held gamely
30May56- 3Bel	fst 5f-WC	:222 :453 :58	©Md Sp Wt	4 6 33 23 21¼	Woodhouse H	118	w	15.65	88-11	FourFathoms1181¼AmberDiver1182½Easy1182	Very sharp try 13
17May56- 4Bel	fst 4½-WC	:223 :453 :514	©Md Sp Wt	15 5 64½ 812 712	Arcaro E	118	w	5.35	78-10	Roommate1181½Dodger118nkThinIc1187	Fell back very early 16

Arts and Letters

ch. c. 1966, by Ribot (Tenerani)–All Beautiful, by Battlefield
Own.– Rokeby Stable
Br.– Paul Mellon (Va)
Tr.– Elliott Burch

Lifetime record: 23 11 6 1 $632,404

16May70- 8Hol	fst 1 1/16	:232 :462 1:101 1:401 3 ↑	Californian 112k	2 7 78½ 76½ 69½ 610	Baeza B	124		*.60	84-12	Baffle1135Figonero1241¼Nodouble130hd	Steadied 8
25Apr70- 7Aqu	fst 1⅛	:46 1:10 1:352 1:482 3 ↑	Grey Lag H 84k	2 6 711 56½ 35 1½	Baeza B	128		*1.10	94-18	ArtsandLetters128½NeverBow1192GaelicDancer117nk	Driving 9
28Mar70- 7Aqu	fst 1	:223 :444 1:084 1:341 4 ↑	Westchester 57k	2 5 514 68½ 47 47¼	Baeza B	130		*.30	89-19	Dewan119¾Gaelic Dancer1146Gleaming Light117½	No excuses 7
25Oct69- 7Aqu	fst 2	:511 2:293 2:544 3:222 3 ↑	J C Gold Cup 106k	1 3 2hd 18 110 114	Baeza B	119		*.30	84-14	Arts and Letters11914Nodouble1249Harem Lady121	Easily 4
27Sep69- 7Bel	fst 1¼	:481 1:121 1:363 2:01 3 ↑	Woodward 106k	1 4 32 21 1½ 12	Baeza B	120		*.30	95-17	ArtsandLetters1202Nodouble1261½Verbatim1268	Ridden out 4
16Aug69- 6Sar	fst 1¼	:48 1:113 1:364 2:013	Travers 106k	5 4 43½ 31 12 16½	Baeza B	126		*.20	100-06	Arts and Letters1266½Dike120¾Distray114nk	Easy score 5
8Aug69- 7Sar	fst 1	:241 :47 1:111 1:36	Jim Dandy 27k	1 3 33 11 14 110	Baeza B	126		*.10	94-13	ArtsandLetters12610GleamingLight1191½Mr.Mag1145	Easily 4
7Jun69- 8Bel	fst 1½	:51 1:161 2:042 2:284	Belmont 147k	1 2 23 11½ 13 15½	Baeza B	126		1.70	89-12	ArtsandLetters1265½MajesticPrince1262Dike1263½	Easily 6
30May69- 7Aqu	fst 1	:224 :453 1:10 1:34 3 ↑	Metropolitan H 116k	8 10 88 33½ 1hd 12½	Cruguet J	111		*1.50	97-22	ArtsandLetters1112½Nodouble1293½Promise1191	Mild drive 11
17May69- 8Pim	fst 1 3/16	:464 1:112 1:37 1:553	Preakness 182k	6 6 68¾ 53½ 21 2hd	Baeza B	126		5.00	95-17	MajesticPrinc126hdArtsndLttrs1264JyRy1264	Brushed start 8
3May69- 8CD	fst 1¼	:48 1:122 1:373 2:014	Ky Derby 155k	3 2 42½ 1½ 2½ 2nk	Baeza B	126		4.40	91-11	MajesticPrince126nkArtsandLetters126½Dike12610	Gamely 8
24Apr69- 6Kee	fst 1⅛	:48 1:112 1:353 1:474	Blue Grass 31k	6 2 13 17 18 115	Shoemaker W	126		*.30	98-17	ArtsandLetters12615TrafficMark1262Mr.Concdnc1233	Easily 6
29Mar69- 9GP	fst 1⅛	:482 1:12 1:361 1:482	Florida Derby 121k	5 4 43 42¾ 23 25	Shoemaker W	122		3.10	87-13	Top Knight1225Arts and Letters1222½Al Hattab1221	Gamely 5
19Mar69- 9GP	fst 1 1/16	:243 :484 1:122 1:423	Fountain of Youth 22k	5 5 56 34½ 33½ 22	Shoemaker W	119		*.50	93-17	AlHattab1222ArtsandLetters119¾AdMajora1224	Slow early 5
4Mar69- 8Hia	fst 1⅛	:462 1:103 1:352 1:474	Flamingo 146k	2 2 22 1hd 1hd 22	Cruguet J	122		2.10	94-15	TopKnight1222ArtsandLetters122½BeauBrummel122¾	Gamely 12
19Feb69- 8Hia	fst 1⅛	:47 1:114 1:363 1:493	Everglades 32k	11 8 77¼ 33 13 13	Cruguet J	112		9.00	87-21	Arts and Letters1123Top Knight1222Al Hattab119½	Driving 12
25Jan69- 6Hia	fst 7f	:224 :453 1:093 1:223	©Alw 5500	4 6 54½ 45 36 36	Cruguet J	119		3.50	89-16	Ack Ack1173Distinctive1193Arts and Letters1193	Evenly 9
2Nov68- 8Lrl	fst 1 1/16	:233 :464 1:12 1:44	Pim Lrl Futurity 182k	7 4 34 22 32 41¼	Velasquez J	122		2.80	96-11	King Emperor122hdDike1221Mr. Leader122nk	Lacked rally 8
15Oct68- 6Bel	fst 1	:232 :47 1:114 1:362	Alw 7500	9 2 2½ 12 13 12½	Velasquez J	122		*1.90	92-18	Arts and Letters1222½Hydrologist1222½King of the Castle122¾	9
	Easily										
25Sep68- 5Bel	fst 7f	:224 :461 1:113 1:241	Md Sp Wt	9 8 63 33 1hd 13½	Velasquez J	122		*3.00	86-19	ArtsandLetters1223½Hydrologist122½WldctHlls1223	In hand 12
18Sep68- 1Bel	fst 6f	:221 :453 1:111	Md Sp Wt	2 3 33 21½ 2½ 23	Velasquez J	122		3.70	86-13	KingoftheSea1223ArtsandLettrs122½ElephntWlk122¾	Gamely 14
11Sep68- 4Aqu	sly 6f	:22 :452 1:122	©Md Sp Wt	6 9 57½ 57 45½ 44¾	Turcotte R	122		*2.00	76-21	Royal Tom122¾Full of Gin1192½Izaak1221½	Mild late rally 12
9Aug68- 5Sar	fst 5½f	:222 :461 :583 1:044	©Md Sp Wt	1 4 3½ 21 33½ 47	Pincay L Jr	122		5.10	86-09	DixieGus122hdCharlestonHarbor1222BeauBrummel1225	Tired 12

Assagai

dkbbr. c. 1963, by Warfare (Determine)–Primary II, by Petition
Own.– Cragwood Stable
Br.– Robin F. Scully (Ky)
Tr.– M. Miller

Lifetime record: 31 11 7 2 $357,074

21Oct67- 7Aqu	fm 1⅝(T)	2:424 3 ↑	Man o' War 116k	8 11 913 75¼ 65½ 43	Shoemaker W	126	b	*1.10e	77-20	RuffledFeathrs121hdFortMarcy121noHndsomBoy1263	Rallied 13
2Oct67- 7Aqu	fm 1 3/16(T)	1:544 3 ↑	Long Island H (Div 2) 23k	3 2 21½ 3½ 3nk 1¾	Baeza B	126		*.80	96-04	Assagai126¾Fast Count1091½Kentucky Kin113½	Driving 9
20Sep67- 8Atl	fm 1 3/16(T)	1:54 3 ↑	U Nations H 100k	4 6 55½ 66½ 54 2nk	Baeza B	122	b	*2.40	102-05	Flit-To110nkAssagai122no[D]MundenPont115hd	Strong finish 8
25Aug67- 7Sar	fm 1⅝(T)	2:392 3 ↑	Seneca H 29k	1 1 1½ 12 1hd 2nk	Baeza B	126	b	*1.40	96-07	Paoluccio109nkAssagai126¾Isokh1111½	Gamely under impost 11
9Aug67- 7Sar	fm 1 1/16(T)	1:402 3 ↑	B Baruch H (Div 2) 23k	7 4 33 32 3nk 2¾	Rotz JL	126	b	2.10	97-02	Fort Marcy117¾Assagai1263Paoluccio1121	Finished gamely 7
24Jly67- 8Hol	fm 1½(T)	:494 1:142 2:031 2:274 3 ↑	Sunset H 108k	1 5 56½ 53½ 56 56¼	Adams L	126		4.00	- -	Hill Clown109¾Pretense1293Niarkos121½	Wide on turns 6
2Jly67♦ Saint-Cloud(Fr)	fm*1 9/16(T)LH	2:423 3 ↑	Grand Prix de Saint-Cloud Stk180000	44½	Baeza B	134		9.00		Taneb134noNelcius1342½Taj Dewan1192	8
										Led,soon well clear,headed 2f out,one-paced late	
17Jun67- 7Aqu	hd 1⅝(T)	2:412 3 ↑	Bowling Green H 55k	4 3 23 23 24 21½	Adams L	127		2.10	85-13	Poker1121½Assagai1273Buckpasser135½	Best of others 5
30May67- 8AP	sf 1⅛(T)	:49 1:14 1:39 1:512 3 ↑	Round Table H 43k	8 6 67 54½ 42¼ 1½	Adams L	124		*.50	84-23	Assagai124½Auteuil1111Voluntario III113hd	Up in time 8
20May67- 8Aqu	fm 1 1/16(T)	1:421 3 ↑	Alw 15000	6 6 68¼ 66 4¾ 1nk	Adams L	123		2.40	95-05	Assagai123nkIrish Rebellion1002Flit-To120¾	In close,up 10
26Nov66- 7Aqu	fst 1⅝	:474 1:382 2:034 2:423 3 ↑	Gallant Fox H 58k	11 4 4¾ 814 815 817	Adams L	119		5.40	75-20	Munden Point1132¾Yonder1124Moontrip114½	Tired 11
11Nov66- 7Lrl	fm 1½(T)	:494 1:142 2:284 3 ↑	D C Int'l 150k	6 2 23 2½ 21½ 33½	Adams L	120		*1.70	71-18	Behistoun1202½Aniline1271¼Assagai1201	Game try,weakened 10
22Oct66- 7Aqu	fm 1⅝(T)	2:443 3 ↑	Man o' War 112k	7 2 2½ 21 2hd 1¾	Adams L	121		*1.90	71-29	Assagai121¾Gallup Poll1215Knightly Manner126nk	All out 9
17Sep66- 8Atl	fm 1 3/16(T)	1:583 3 ↑	U Nations H 100k	9 6 72¾ 74½ 43 1hd	Adams L	118		*2.30	79-24	Assagai118hdGingerFizz1141¼Toulore118¾	Up final strides 12
3Sep66- 8Atl	fm 1⅛(T)	1:482 3 ↑	Kelly-Olympic H 35k	10 4 31 41¾ 2hd 2no	Adams L	120		*1.20	93-13	Ginger Fizz115noAssagai1201¼Imasmartee123¾	In close 12
10Aug66- 7Sar	fm 1 1/16(T)	1:40 3 ↑	Bernard Baruch H 30k	6 5 511 53½ 3½ 13	Adams L	115		*3.10	105-00	Assagai1153GingerFizz114¾NorthernDeamon113no	Mild drive 10
30Jly66- 7Aqu	fm 1⅛(T)	1:49 3 ↑	Tidal H 59k	8 4 43 52¾ 33 1½	Adams L	109		4.40	90-15	Assagai109½Canal1132½Moontrip1151½	Up in final yards 11
29Jun66- 8Mth	fm 1(T)	1:381	Long Branch 23k	9 9 85½ 52½ 31½ 14	Brumfield D	116		7.70	94-13	Assagai1164Social Song120½Tequillo1181½	Mild drive 13

14Jun66- 8Mth fst 1 1/16⊗ :233 :472 1:12 1:442 Alw 6000 4 2 33 44 34 43½ Brumfield D 119 4.10 79-18 Deck Hand119½Arabian Spy1173Tequillo116no Lacked rally 7
2Jun66- 6Aqu fm 1 1/16Ⓣ 1:413 3↑ Alw 6500 8 2 25 22 12 13½ Blum W 113 12.30 98-02 Assagai1133½SeaCastle1145Hnbj1201½ Drew clear with ease 10
25May66- 8Aqu fst 1⅛ :461 1:103 1:362 1:493 3↑ Alw 6500 5 3 46½ 56½ 46 59 Blum W 113 11.10 79-13 Highest Honors113½Buffle1123½Bushfighter1132½ No mishap 7
7May66- 6Aqu fst 6f :22 :453 1:112 3↑ Alw 5500 6 6 87¼ 65½ 52¾ 1nk Blum W 113 6.30e 86-17 Assagai113nkPitchMan106hdDey Sovereign113nk Up in time 11
13Apr66- 5Kee sly 6f :222 :463 1:122 ©Md Sp Wt 4 3 3½ 1½ 13 12 Adams L 122 3.80 81-18 Assagai1222Puppeteer1177Dominar1222 Under pressure 10
27Nov65- 4Aqu sly 1 :224 :463 1:121 1:39 Md Sp Wt 10 3 3nk 1½ 11½ 2¾ Venezia M 122 4.20e 72-25 HighestHonors122¾Assagai1223½ProspectStret117½ 2nd best 11
20Nov65- 1Aqu fst 1 :233 :464 1:122 1:401 ©Md Sp Wt 5 3 41½ 32 23 44¾ Blum W 122 b 4.00 62-20 Tequillo1171½Squadron E.1222½Paddyland122¾ Speed,tired 10
13Nov65- 3Aqu fst 1 :233 :472 1:13 1:391 ©Md Sp Wt 8 5 62¼ 63 44 31¾ Venezia M 122 b 5.90 70-22 Earldom122¾Mask of Play1221Assagai1221 Finished fast 9
6Nov65- 4Aqu fst 1 :233 :463 1:113 1:374 Md Sp Wt 5 8 76½ 62¾ 51¾ 42¾ Sellers J 122 b 10.20 76-17 Poker122noEarldom1222AmeriPlot122¾ Only mild late rally 12
2Nov65- 4Aqu fst 6f :231 :464 1:12 ©Md Sp Wt 3 8 78½ 711 511 28 Blum W 122 b 7.20 75-18 Nashwood1228Assagai1221Exhibitionist122½ Closed well 14
26Oct65- 5Aqu fst 6f :223 :454 1:13 Md Sp Wt 7 9 109¾ 1016 1015 1115 Blum W 122 b 3.00 63-18 Draeh's Folly122nkNashwood1226Pilot Major122½ Bore out 14
19Oct65- 1Aqu fst 6f :223 :463 1:123 ©Md Sp Wt 8 9 86¼ 85¾ 55 43 Blum W 122 4.70 77-18 Clarinetist122nkSpaceCitation122¾Draeh'sFolly1222 Wide 10
12Jly65- 4Aqu fst 5½f :223 :46 :581 1:043 ©Md Sp Wt 5 7 78½ 69 56 55¾ Boland W 122 48.90 84-10 Amberoid1221Draeh's Folly1221Bobillard1223 No mishap 12

Bald Eagle

b. c. 1955, by Nasrullah (Nearco)–Siama, by Tiger **Lifetime record: 29 12 5 4 $692,922**
Own.– Cain Hoy Stable
Br.– Harry F. Guggenheim (Ky)
Tr.– Woodford C. Stephens

11Nov60- 7Lrl fm 1½Ⓣ :473 1:113 2:33 3↑ D C Int'l 100k 2 1 15 110 16 12 Ycaza M 126 *1.70 75-25 BaldEagle1262Harmonizing1261Zabeg1251¼ Under mild drive 11
29Oct60- 7Aqu sly 2 :472 2:29 2:54 3:192 3↑ J C Gold Cup 109k 4 7 717 43½ 37 313½ Ycaza M 124 2.50e 100-16 Kelso1193½DonPoggio12410BldEgl12415 Lacked needed rally 8
22Oct60- 7Bel sf 1½Ⓣ :50 1:162 2:08 2:331 3↑ Man o' War 110k 7 3 35½ 43 23 22¼ Ycaza M 126 *1.40e 78-20 Harmonizing1262¼BaldEagle1264SwordDancer126nk In close 8
24Sep60- 7Aqu fst 1¼ :472 1:111 1:354 2:011 3↑ Woodward 112k 6 5 31½ 22 42 33 Ycaza M 126 b *.90 99-08 Sword Dancer1261½Dotted Swiss1262½Bald Eagle1261 Hung 7
5Sep60- 7Aqu fst 1 :232 :461 1:102 1:344 3↑ Aqueduct H 56k 3 4 41½ 22 31½ 1hd Ycaza M 130 *1.30 94-11 Bald Eagle130hdIntentionally125noWarhead1133 Just up 5
30Jly60- 7Aqu sly 1¼ :471 1:12 1:38 2:03 3↑ Brooklyn H 109k 2 6 56½ 43 43¼ 43¼ Ycaza M 130 *1.65 90-17 On-and-On118hdGreekStar1102Waltz1131¼ Failed to respond 7
4Jly60- 7Aqu fst 1¼ :472 1:111 1:361 2:013 3↑ Suburban H 108k 4 5 53¾ 33 44½ 46½ Hartack W 133 *.70 105-11 SwordDancer125½FirstLandng1221½Wltz1154½ Impeded early 6
30May60- 7Aqu fst 1 :224 :453 1:09 1:333 3↑ Metropolitan H 114k 8 4 62¾ 32½ 11 13½ Ycaza M 128 *1.95 108-03 Bald Eagle1283½First Landing123nkTalent Show118¾ Easily 10
19Mar60- 7GP gd 1¼ :473 1:122 1:362 2:011 3↑ Gulf Park H 112k 1 6 78 44 32½ 1¾ Ycaza M 126 *1.25 93-05 Bald Eagle126¾Amerigo1233On-and-On1212 Blocked,driving 8
20Feb60- 7Hia fst 1¼ :464 1:101 1:351 1:593 3↑ Widener H 126k 2 6 66¾ 42¼ 1½ 1¾ Ycaza M 123 *1.35 107-07 Bald Eagle123¾On-and-On1191½Talent Show118½ Mild urging 8
6Feb60- 7Hia gd 1⅛ :46 1:101 1:354 1:484 3↑ McLennan H 64k 4 7 74¾ 65¼ 32 2nk Ycaza M 124 *1.55 91-12 On-and-On120nkBldEgl1243TudorEr1201¼ Hung final strides 9
21Nov59- 7Aqu fst 1⅝ :484 1:383 2:033 2:41 3↑ Gallant Fox H 85k 4 6 64¼ 31½ 1hd 11¾ Ycaza M 126 *1.15 - - BaldEagl1261¾Whodunt1123½Whtly114no In close,mild drive 10
11Nov59- 7Lrl fm 1½Ⓣ :47 1:113 2:014 2:28 3↑ D C Int'l 100k 6 2 21 15 14 12½ Ycaza M 126 3.60 - - BaldEagle1262½MidnightSun1224½TudorEra1268 Easily best 12
24Oct59- 6Aqu sf 1½Ⓣ :51 1:182 2:102 2:404 3↑ Man o' War (Div 1) 112k 1 6 64½ 33¼ 35 42¼ Ycaza M 126 2.25 - - Dotted Line1111¼Amerigo121¾Prince Willy112nk No mishaps 10
10Oct59- 7Aqu fst 1⅝ :491 1:392 2:041 2:423 3↑ Manhattan H 58k 3 7 64½ 43½ 41¾ 21 Ycaza M 122 2.45 - - RndTable1321BaldEagle1221½Coloneast1122 Closed gamely 11
14Sep59- 7Aqu fst 1 :23 :46 1:111 1:362 3↑ Aqueduct H 59k 6 9 84 83¾ 41¼ 2¾ Ycaza M 122 5.75 - - Hillsdale132¾BaldEagle1221TickTock119nk In close,sharp 12
15Aug59- 6Sar fst 1¼ :473 1:113 1:361 2:03 3↑ Saratoga H 57k 2 3 33½ 42½ 42½ 1nk Ycaza M 120 *1.40 93-12 BaldEagle120nkGreyMonarch1111¾Amerigo1142 Taken out,up 7
1Aug59- 6Jam fst 1 3/16 :473 1:122 1:374 1:562 3↑ Brooklyn H 113k 6 6 59½ 41½ 41¼ 43¾ Ycaza M 123 4.05 90-15 Babu112¾SwordDncr124hdAmrgo1173 In close,turn & drive 10
4Jly59- 6Bel fst 1¼ :463 1:101 1:354 2:013 3↑ Suburban H 111k 5 9 67½ 53 3nk 11½ Ycaza M 119 3.95 92-13 BaldEgl1191½TlntShow1255½Plon1191 Taken wide,mild drive 10
24Jun59- 8Suf fst 1¼ :473 1:123 1:37 2:022 3↑ Mass H 84k 4 6 54 74¾ 42 31 Ycaza M 112 10.60 92-17 [D]DayCourt115nkAirPilot116¾BldEgl1121¾ Impeded in drive 8
13Jun59- 6Bel sf 7fⓉ :234 :47 1:123 1:254 3↑ Handicap 10000 4 5 13 13 12 21 Ycaza M 115 3.30 84-15 CombustionII1191BaldEagle1153½AmberDiver1182 No excuse 6
17Feb59- 9Hia fm 1 1/16Ⓣ 1:443 4↑ Alw 5000 4 6 45 46½ 47 46 Anderson P 124 *3.15 87-09 Little Hermit124hdSaferris1153Royal Float1103 No excuse 9
15Oct58- 6Bel fm 7fⓉ :23 :462 1:111 1:24 Handicap 7500 5 10 66 64 73 76 Shoemaker W 124wb *2.00 90-04 Phaeton120½Washington109½Rickover109nk Sluggish start 10
Previously trained by Cecil Boyd-Rochfort
17Jun58♦ Ascot(GB) fm 1ⓉRH 1:432 St. James Palace Stakes Stk24100 33 Carr W 126 3.30 Major Portion1262Guersillus1261Bald Eagle1262 5
Tracked in 4th,lacked rally
4Jun58♦ Epsom(GB) gd 1½ⓉLH 2:411 Epsom Derby Stk95600 12 Carr W 126 7.00 Hard Ridden1265Paddy's Point1261½Nagami126hd
Sweating,tracked in 4th,weakened over 3f out
21May58♦ York(GB) gd *1 5/16ⓉLH 2:234 Dante Stakes Stk15200 11½ Carr W 126 *1.10 Bald Eagle1261½Carbon Copy1262The Mongoose126nk 7
Rated in 5th,led over 1f out,ridden out
30Apr58♦ Newmarket(GB) gd 1ⓉStr 1:392 2000 Guineas Stakes Stk65200 79 Carr WH 126 *1.75 Pall Mall126½Major Portion1263Nagami126hd 14
In touch to halfway,ridden and faded 2f out
17Apr58♦ Newmarket(GB) gd 1ⓉStr 1:43 Craven Stakes Stk3400 11 Carr WH 130 3.50 Bald Eagle1301Nagami1303Pinched1304 6
Led 2f out,hard ridden to maintain edge
11Oct57♦ Ascot(GB) gd 6fⓉStr 1:181 Duke of Edinburgh Stakes Mdn8000 11 Carr W 119 *1.20 Bald Eagle1191Barleycroft129½Teynham1206 8
Rated toward rear,rallied to lead 150y out,handily;For maidens at closing,three weeks previous

Barnabys Bluff

b. g. 1958, by Cyclotron (Pensive)–Ophelia Rose, by Pavot **Lifetime record: 28 11 7 2 $124,346**
Own.– G.H. Bostwick
Br.– G.H. Bostwick (Ky)
Tr.– G.H. Bostwick

1Oct63- 5Aqu fm *2½ S'Chase 4:371 4↑ Brook H 20k 6 4 37 37 - - McDonald RS 160 sb *1.30e - - AmbrDvr15520ThSport1583½Tuscror161nk Fell 14th,destroyed 9
12Sep63- 5Aqu fm *2 S'Chase 3:421 4↑ Broad Hollow H 16k 1 1 21½ 33 21½ 23¼ Walsh T 160 sb 2.45 - - TheSport1453½BarnabysBluff16015[DH]BadgeofHnr151 Gamely 5
5Sep63- 3Aqu hd *2 Hurdles 3:35 3↑ Handicap 6000 1 4 48 412 417 423 Walsh T 162 *1.30 - - ExhbtA.1544ThSport1431Knghtsboro14718 Tired under impost 5
2Aug63- 5Sar sf 2 1/16 S'Chase 3:473 4↑ Beverwyck H 17k 5 5 59½ 34½ 34½ 35½ Walsh T 164 2.35 - - Badge of Honor1433Amber Diver1612½Barnabys Bluff16430 6
Bad landing 1st
5Jly63- 3Del fm *2½ S'Chase 4:361 4↑ Indian River H 10k 2 3 34 21 23 23½ Walsh T 163 *.90 - - AmbrDivr1523½BarnabysBluff16310BeckysShip1402 Bobbled 6
25Jun63- 3Del fm *2⅛ S'Chase 4:01 4↑ Georgetown H 10k 5 6 43½ 33 33½ 22½ Walsh T 164 *1.50 - - AmberDiver1482½BarnabysBluff1641BeckysShip1414 Gamely 7
26Oct62- 6Bel sf *2½ S'Chase 4:503 4↑ Temple Gwathmey H 55k 4 2 22 11 11 110 Walsh T 157 *1.05 - - BarnabysBluff15710BugleCallII1363½PocktRockt1366 Easily 7
16Oct62- 5Bel fm *3⅛ S'Chase 5:523 4↑ Grand National H 28k 6 3 35 21½ 11½ 11¾ Walsh T 153 *1.70 - - BarnbysBluff1531¾PocketRocket1328BeckysShp1422 Driving 9
4Oct62- 5Bel fm *2½ S'Chase 4:371 4↑ Brook H 19k 5 3 46 2½ 12 16 Walsh T 148 2.95 - - Barnabys Bluff1486Kampina1461Blackmail1575 Easily 5
20Sep62- 5Aqu fm *2 S'Chase 3:453 4↑ C L Appleton Mem H 11k 2 3 36 34 34½ 23 Walsh T 152 2.95 - - Kampina1403Barnabys Bluff1526Beckys Ship1478 Bobbled 6
18Aug62- 3Sar fm 2 1/16 Hurdles 3:474 4↑ Handicap 6000 8 6 65¼ 34 43½ 36¾ Cartwright R 154 3.05e - - GuardianAngel153¾BabyPrince1396BrnbysBlff154no Bobbled 8
11Aug62- 3Sar sf *2 1/16 S'Chase 3:55 4↑ Handicap 6000 5 5 44½ - - - Schulhofer F 151 *1.00 - - Naval Treaty1451¾Julep Time1365Bugle Call II1374 7
Bobbled,lost rider
31Jly62- 3Sar sf 2 1/16 S'Chase 3:512 4↑ OClm 7000 1 4 2½ 11 13 17 Schulhofer F 138 *1.05 - - Barnabys Bluff1387Shantyboat1431½Julep Time14510 Easily 7
25Jly62- 5Mth sf *2 Hurdles 4:094 3↑ Midsummer H 22k 1 - - - - - Thompson J 150 5.80 - - Hunter's Rock1445Miracle Moose1497The Sport14720 8
Ran out,left course
18Jly62- 3Mth fm *1¾ Hurdles 3:20 3↑ Alw 4000 9 3 37½ 1½ 1hd 2½ Thompson JW 147 *2.20 - - Gem Ruby147½BarnbysBluff1472Miracle Moose1471¼ Gamely 9
22Jun62- 4Del sf 1Ⓣ 1:411 3↑ Md Sp Wt 3 3 23 22 2½ 1¾ Shuk N 122 *1.10 76-27 BarnabysBluff122¾PeaceJohn1121Grape1141½ Strong urging 10
7Jun62- 5Bel fm *2 Hurdles 3:43 4↑ Bushwick H 11k 5 3 2hd 21½ 56 59¼ Cartwright R 151 *1.65 - - The Sport1391¼Prince Fearless1302½Hunter's Rock1481½ 6
Saddle slipped
27Oct61- 3Aqu hd *1⅞ Hurdles 3:213 LE Stoddard Jr 11k 4 2 31½ 11 12 1nk Schulhofer F 145 *.65 - - BarnabysBluff145nkHunter'sRock1405½Shntybot1404 Driving 7

28Sep61- 5Bel	fm *1⅞	Hurdles	3:21²		Elkridge 16k	1 2 34½ 1hd 11½ 11¼	Schulhofer F	145	*1.00	--	BarnabysBluff1451¼Hunter'sRock14010Shntybot1366	Driving	6
17Aug61- 5Sar	hd *1⅝	Hurdles	2:51⁴		Promise 13k	5 6 43½ 2½ 1½ 11½	Cartwright R	145	2.20	--	Barnabys Bluff1451½Hunter's Rock142½Nizam13818	Drew out	6
26Jly61- 5Mth	fm *2	Hurdles	3:53³	3↑	Midsummer H 22k	1 2 11½ 31½ 35 -	Cartwright R	136	2.50	--	LandoftheFree149nkNala15510BeModrt149nk	Lost rider last	9
14Jly61- 3Mth	sf *1¾	Hurdles	3:23¹	3↑	Alw 4000	4 2 2hd 1½ 13 16	Cartwright R	135	2.50	--	BarnbysBlff1356BeModerate1515½GrekBrothr1474½	Handily	7
27Jun61- 4Bel	fst 1⅛	:47² 1:12 1:37	1:49⁴	3↑	Md Sp Wt	5 2 2½ 2½ 21½ 23½	Arcaro E	115	*1.80	83-12	Narwhal1233½Barnabys Bluff1154Del Wells1157	Speed,tired	8
15Jun61- 5Bel	fm *1½	Hurdles	2:44²		Annapolis 11k	5 2 1½ 1hd 12 15	Cartwright R	145	*.45	--	BarnabysBluff1455AndNow1371¼BlackChallenger1451	Easily	8
2Jun61- 7Del	fm 1Ⓣ		1:38³		Alw 4500	3 4 53¾ 54 25 21½	Shuk N	110	4.20	87-11	MicheLea1141½BarnabysBluff1104RebelFire117nk	Slow start	9
23May61- 3Aqu	fm *1½	Hurdles	2:43²		Md Sp Wt	6 2 1hd 1hd 110 125	Cartwright R	145	*1.80	--	BarnabysBlff14525BlackChallengr1451¼AndNow145no	Easily	9
8May61- 3Aqu	sf *1⅝	Hurdles	2:56	3↑	Sp Wt 3700	8 9 912 815 69 47½	Cartwright R	133	39.45	--	Ben Arthur1521Kampina1372½Mantegna1524	Some late foot	11
7Jly60- 6Aqu	fst 5½f	:22³ :46⁴ :59²	1:06⁴		©Md Sp Wt	1 5 98½ 917 915 914	Leonard J	118	10.65	71-16	Jet Request118noRudolph1182MainMark1181½	Raced greenly	9

Benguala

b. g. 1954, by Annapolis (Man o' War)–Bennu, by Heliopolis **Lifetime record: 26 9 1 4 $133,775**

Own.– Montpelier
Br.– Mrs Marion duPont Scott (Va)
Tr.– R.G. Woolf

3Aug61- 5Sar	fm 2 1/16	S'Chase	2:50	4↑	Beverwyck H 16k	7 4 419 69 - -	Foot A	154	2.45	--	Tuscarora1487Bugle Call II130¾Negocio139hd	Fell at 11th	7
13Jun61- 5Bel	hd *2½	S'Chase	4:39	4↑	Meadow Brook H 18k	1 6 69 53½ 35 35½	Foot A	161	2.95	--	Muguet II163noTuscarora1445½Benguala1618	Bobbled 12th	6
1Jun61- 5Bel	hd *2⅛	S'Chase	3:56¹	4↑	International H 16k	4 6 615 617 613 413	Woolf R Jr	160	2.70e	--	Nala155hdMuguet II1606Peal1427	Never a threat	6
21Oct60- 6Bel	sf *2½	S'Chase	4:46²	4↑	Temple Gwathmey H 56k	4 5 530 43 21½ 13	Foot A	160	3.35	--	Benguala1603Chufquen13810Sun Dog1603	Going away	9
11Oct60- 5Bel	hd *3⅛	S'Chase	5:54¹	4↑	Grand National H 27k	5 5 46 36 315 323	Foot A	156	*1.15	--	Sun Dog14515Cartagena1458Benguala15650	Well up,tired	5
29Sep60- 5Bel	fm *2½	S'Chase	4:42¹	4↑	Brook H 19k	4 5 48 32½ 12 16	Foot A	148	5.40	--	Benguala1486Independence1593½Cartagena1503½	Easily best	7
15Sep60- 5Aqu	fm *2	S'Chase	3:53¹	4↑	Broad Hollow H 16k	5 6 56½ 58½ 33½ 32¾	Foot A	150	8.00	--	Gridiron1362Sun Dog148¾Benguala1502	Swerved,late rally	6
19Aug60- 5Sar	hd *2⅝	S'Chase	5:05⁴	4↑	Saratoga H 19k	6 6 410 33½ 46 46½	Mahoney J	151	11.45	--	MuguetII1605Hustle1431½Indepndnc160hd	Bobbled 1st hedge	7
4Aug60- 5Sar	fm *2¼	S'Chase	4:09⁴	4↑	Beverwyck H 16k	2 4 58½ 33 416 422	Foot A	151	*1.60	--	Muguet II1555Sun Dog14714Basil Bee1343	Bad landing 10th	7
30Jun60- 5Bel	hd *2½	S'Chase	4:41⁴	4↑	Meadow Brook H 19k	7 7 77½ 23 1½ 1no	Foot A	148	7.35	--	Benguala148noChambourg15530NarcissusII1366	Swerved late	8
16Jun60- 5Bel	sf *2⅛	S'Chase	3:57	4↑	International H 17k	3 6 811 513 717 728	Foot A	155	6.80	--	Chambourg1478Amateur1468Fairfax152hd	No serious threat	11
6Jun60- 3Bel	fm *2⅛	S'Chase	3:58²	4↑	Alw 5000	8 8 711 54¼ 31½ 1¾	Foot A	140	*1.35	--	Benguala140¾Hunter's Lad1323½Fairfax1601	Briskly urged	8
13Oct59- 5Aqu	hd *2½	S'Chase	4:47³	4↑	Brook H 19k	6 3 64 45 45 43¼	Foot A	156	7.00	--	Ancestor1621½Sun Dog1371½Fairfax152nk	Even effort	7
1Oct59- 5Aqu	fm *2	S'Chase	3:51	4↑	Broad Hollow H 16k	6 7 711 69¾ 615 622	Foot A	162	4.25	--	Ancestor160hdDarubini1382Sun Dog13812	Never a contender	9
11Sep59- 6Bel	hd *2½	S'Chase	4:41	4↑	Temple Gwathmey H 56k	9 1 1½ 77¾ 846 863	Foot A	158	3.10	--	MuguetII1521¾Darubini134nkIdealView1354	Much used early	9
22Oct58- 6Bel	fm *2½	S'Chase	4:45³	4↑	Temple Gwathmey H 55k	4 2 21 21½ 1½ 1hd	Foot A	147 w	2.30	--	Benguala147hdNeji1764½Trboots135nk	Lost lead,came again	8
30Sep58- 5Bel	sf *2½	S'Chase	4:47⁴	4↑	Brook H 14k	2 1 12½ 11 12 13½	Foot A	143 w	10.15	--	Beguala1433½Independence154nkNeji17510	Speed in reserve	7
21Aug58- 5Sar	fm *2½	S'Chase	5:16¹	4↑	Saratoga H 14k	2 3 24 26 2hd 12½	Foot A	139 w	5.55	--	Benguala1392½Carthage133hdDarubin1408	Well rated,easily	5
8Aug58- 3Sar	sf *2	S'Chase	4:18	4↑	Alw 5000	6 4 48½ 2½ 24 28	Foot A	139 w	3.50	--	Rythminhim1458Benguala1391½Tremere1409	Best of others	7
31Jly58- 3Sar	fm *2	S'Chase	4:15³	4↑	Alw 4200	4 3 37 35 11½ 13	Foot A	136 w	2.70	--	Benguala1363Eastcor1503½Darubini14810	Mild drive	6
20Jun58- 5Del	sf *2	S'Chase	3:42²	4↑	Spring Maiden 9.8k	2 4 24 516 520 420	Foot A	142 w	6.10	--	Arywa1582Blen More1533Prince Nam15115	Bad landing 6th	6
9Oct57- 3Bel	sf *1½	Hurdles	2:47		Alw 5000	6 4 47½ 48½ 513 521	Foot A	135 w	4.60e	--	My Last Try1351Sun Dog1308Tombigbee1322	Fell back early	8
3Oct57- 3Bel	fm *1⅞	Hurdles	3:23³	3↑	Alw 5500	6 5 513 623 631 653	Foot A	131wb	6.05	--	Nizam'sPet1387BestGift1438PatrickBegorra1353	No speed	6
8Aug57- 5Sar	fm *1⅝	Hurdles	3:08⁴		Promise 11k	3 3 2hd 21 33 33½	Foot A	140wb	*1.20e	--	PatrickBegorra1352MyLastTry1301½Benguala1408	No excuse	10
11Jly57- 3Mth	fm *1½	Hurdles	2:46⁴		Md Sp Wt	2 3 21½ 21 1hd 1½	Foot A	145 w	1.80e	--	Benguala145½RomanRequest14010SeaChart1384	Strong drive	6
30Mar57- 7Cam	fm *1Ⓣ		1:40¹	3↑	Alw 500	2 4 43¾ 42 43 56½	Foot A	132 w	-	--	MuguetII1382SquareDanceII1452½BarodaBoy1481½	No excuse	6

Berlo

br. f. 1957, by Heliopolis (Hyperion)–Faberose, by Rosemont **Lifetime record: 14 8 0 2 $208,186**

Own.– Foxcatcher Farm
Br.– W. duPont Jr (Ky)
Tr.– E.A. Christmas

23Sep61- 7Bel	fst 1⅛	:46³ 1:11 1:36¹	1:49²	3↑	ⒻBeldame 96k	2 12 1211 115¾ 67 48¾	Guerin E	123	3.20	80-18	AirmansGuide123¾Craftiness1232½Primontt1185½	Slow start	12
6Sep61- 7Bel	fst 1	:22² :45 1:09²	1:36¹	3↑	ⒻMaskette H 28k	7 9 913 89 86¾ 44½	Guerin E	126	*1.10	88-13	Teacation1161Shimmy Dancer1061½Craftiness1202	No excuse	9
29Aug61- 7Bel	fst 7f	:23 :46² 1:11	1:24	3↑	ⒻAlw 10000	8 7 810 87¼ 75¼ 41½	Guerin E	123	*.60	85-15	Staretta109nkGreatDame112nkMssCloudy1141	Swerved in dr.	8
	Previously trained by R.E. Handlen												
12Oct60- 7Bel	fst 1½	:47¹ 1:11⁴ 2:04²	2:30³	3↑	ⒻLadies H 59k	9 8 715 33½ 13 12½	Guerin E	124	*1.05	80-15	Berlo1242½Woodlawn112½Who's Ahead105½	Speed to spare	13
1Oct60- 7Bel	fst 1⅛	:46¹ 1:11 1:36²	1:49²	3↑	ⒻBeldame 91k	6 9 96¾ 73¼ 12 12	Guerin E	119	4.05	89-16	Berlo1192Royal Native1231Make Sail1193	Slow start,clear	9
7Sep60- 6Aqu	fst 1	:22¹ :44² 1:10	1:35⁴		ⒻGazelle H (Div 1) 22k	12 12 1111 72¾ 13 12½	Guerin E	122	*1.80	89-11	Berlo1222½SisterAntoin1131FunnyBon109hd	Drew out easily	12
23Jly60- 7Mth	fst 1⅛	:47² 1:11² 1:36⁴	1:49²		ⒻMth Oaks 57k	7 8 87½ 95¾ 65¾ 46¼	Guerin E	121	*1.20	91-14	Teacation1131¼Refute1172Rash Statement1213	No mishap	9
16Jly60- 6Del	fst 1⅛	:47¹ 1:11³ 1:38	1:50³		ⒻDel Oaks 64k	7 10 75½ 64¼ 31½ 32	Guerin E	121	*.70	85-14	Rash Statement1212Sarcastic115noBerlo1212	Wide bid,hung	12
25Jun60- 7Bel	fst 1¼	:48³ 1:13² 1:38³	2:04¹		ⒻC C A Oaks 86k	4 7 3nk 21 1½ 1¾	Guerin E	121	*.45	79-13	Berlo121¾Sarcastic1213½Rash Statement1212½	Brisk urging	8
8Jun60- 7Bel	fst 1⅛	:45² 1:10² 1:36⁴	1:50		ⒻMother Goose 29k	9 7 84¼ 41½ 1hd 13½	Guerin E	114	2.20	86-17	Berlo1143½Chalvedele1112½MakeSal1212	Had speed to spare	11
2Jun60- 7Bel	fst 6f	:22³ :46¹	1:11³		ⒻAlw 5000	3 8 109½ 53½ 3½ 16	Guerin E	115	*2.00	89-14	Berlo1156All Wing115nkRash Statement121½	Speed to spare	12
18May60- 6Aqu	gd 6f	:23¹ :47	1:11⁴		ⒻAlw 4500	3 5 43¼ 32½ 11 11¼	Guerin E	116	1.95	93-11	Berlo1161¼Princess Rousse;1201Holly Beach1204	Handily	5
15Oct59- 6Aqu	gd 6f	:23¹ :48¹	1:14¹		ⒻMd Sp Wt	4 9 64½ 41½ 12 12½	Guerin E	115	*1.10	--	Brlo1152½CtchM115nkHulLou115¾	Bumped stretch,mild drive	9
8Oct59- 6Aqu	fst 7f	:23 :46² 1:12	1:25²		ⒻMd Sp Wt	1 11 42¼ 42½ 22 31½	Guerin E	115	3.60	--	Kathy Kim115¾Four Cent Stamp115¾Berlo1152½	Off poorly	11

Bold Lad

ch. c. 1962, by Bold Ruler (Nasrullah)–Misty Morn, by Princequillo **Lifetime record: 19 14 2 1 $516,465**

Own.– Wheatley Stable
Br.– Wheatley Stable (Ky)
Tr.– E.A. Neloy

4Jly66- 7Aqu	fst 1¼	:47⁴ 1:11⁴ 1:37	2:02	3↑	Suburban H 110k	1 1 3nk 45½ 56½ 610	Baeza B	135 b	*1.40	78-21	Buffle1103Pluck1132Paoluccio1081½	Tired under impost	9
30May66- 7Aqu	fst 1	:22¹ :44 1:08	1:34¹	3↑	Metropolitan H 115k	2 6 44 34 22 12½	Baeza B	132 b	*.70e	97-13	Bold Lad1322½Hedevar1132½Tio Viejo115no	Going away	11
18May66- 7Aqu	fst 7f	:22¹ :44⁴ 1:09²	1:21⁴	3↑	Roseben H 28k	3 6 44½ 43½ 1hd 13	Baeza B	126 b	*.50	97-15	Bold Lad1263Davis II118hdHoist Bar117¾	Drew out easily	7
6May66- 7Aqu	fst 7f	:22³ :44⁴ 1:09	1:22¹	4↑	Alw 10000	5 1 15 16 16 14	Knapp K	119 b	*.50	95-18	Bold Lad1194A. Deck1195Off the Top117½	Easily the best	7
30Apr66- 7GS	sly 6f	:22⁴ :46⁴	1:12³	4↑	Alw 6500	3 2 2hd 1½ 1½ 1hd	Knapp K	113 b	*.40	81-32	BoldLad113hdBugler11312Cosmo122hd	Under long,hard drive	6
	Previously trained by W.C. Winfrey												
1May65- 7CD	fst 1¼	:47¹ 1:11⁴ 1:37	2:01¹		Ky Derby 154k	3 5 65 54 1012 1012	Hartack W	126 b	*2.00	82-05	Lucky Debonair126nkDapper Dan1262Tom Rolfe1261	Tired	11
27Apr65- 7CD	fst 1	:22³ :45⁴ 1:10	1:35¹		Derby Trial 15k	2 2 21 13 14 14	Hartack W	122 b	*.30	97-16	Bold Lad1224Carpenter's Rule1166Bugler1164	Well in hand	5
17Apr65- 7Aqu	fst 1⅛	:45⁴ 1:09³ 1:36	1:50¹		Wood Memorial 92k	7 2 24 24 22½ 31¼	Ycaza M	126 b	*.50e	84-18	FlagRasr126nkHltoAll1261BoldLd126½	Lacked late response	11
3Apr65- 6Aqu	fst 6f	:22⁴ :46²	1:10³	3↑	Alw 8500	3 3 31½ 3½ 1½ 13	Baeza B	114 b	*.25	90-19	BoldLad1143PackTrip1152½ExclusiveNashu1242½	Easily best	5
17Oct64- 7Aqu	sly 1	:22⁴ :46¹ 1:11	1:36²		Champagne 176k	1 2 21½ 11½ 16 17	Baeza B	122 b	*.25	86-21	Bold Lad1227Royal Gunner1224½Philately122½	Easy score	6
26Sep64- 7Aqu	fst 6½f	:22 :45 1:09³	1:16		Futurity 138k	5 4 44½ 42 1hd 11¼	Baeza B	122 b	*.20	100-10	BoldLad1221¼NativeCharger1222¼TomRolfe1225½	Drew clear	5
29Aug64- 6Sar	fst 6½f	:22² :45¹ 1:09¹	1:15³		Hopeful 111k	4 2 22 12 14 17	Baeza B	122 b	*.30e	102-07	Bold Lad1227Native Charger1222Time Tested1223½	Easily	5
8Aug64- 8Mth	fst 6f	:21⁴ :44³	1:09²		Sapling 102k	8 2 42 41 1hd 1½	Baeza B	122 b	*.70e	95-15	BoldLad122½NativeCharger1223Sadair1228	Long,hard drive	9

1Aug64- 6Mth	fst	6f		:22 :444 1:093		Alw 6000	3	4	23	24	2½	12	Baeza B	122	b	*.70	94-15	BoldLad1222NativeCharger1222¼Sadr12210	Shown whip,clear	6
8Jly64- 7Aqu	sly	5½f		:222 :46 :592 1:061		Tremont 37k	5	4	42½	43½	32½	1½	Ycaza M	122	b	2.70	82-23	Bold Lad122½Joust1142Turn to Reason114no	Brisk handling	9
22Jun64- 7Aqu	fst	5½f		:22 :45 :572 1:04		©National Stallion 28k	2	4	32½	22	21½	1½	Baeza B	122	b	2.45	93-16	BoldLad122½Tanistair1172TurntoReason1175	Strong urging	4
16Jun64- 6Aqu	fst	5f		:223 :462 :584		Alw 5000	2	5	41½	43	33	21½	Baeza B	122	b	5.55	89-19	Groton1221½BoldLad1222½OnHolidy1222½	Drifted final turn	6
8Jun64- 4Aqu	sly	5f		:222 :464 1:00		©Md Sp Wt	8	5	33½	33½	21½	1¾	Ussery R	122		*.85	85-19	Bold Lad122¾Casque1224The Jouster1225	Strong handling	8
26May64- 4Aqu	fst	5f		:223 :464 :594		©Md Sp Wt	9	7	86¼	53½	22	21	Ussery R	122		*2.70	85-16	IndiaInk1221BoldLad122¾Egocentrical1222	Extremely wide	10

Bon Nouvel

b. g. 1960, by Duc de Fer (Spy Song)–Good News, by Happy Argo

Own.– Mrs Theodora A. Randolph

Br.– Dr Archibald C. Randolph (Va)

Tr.– D.M. Smithwick

Lifetime record: 51 16 11 7 $176,149

25Oct68- 6Bel	sf	3⅛	S'Chase	6:02	4↑	Temple Gwathmey H 55k	8	1	15	34½	628	-	Aitcheson J Jr	161		*.80e	- -	China Run1401½Apollon1462Gentle Boy13620	Lame,eased	8
15Oct68- 5Bel	fm	2½	S'Chase	4:421	4↑	Brook H 19k	7	1	120	11	1½	2hd	Aitcheson J Jr	161		*1.90e	- -	Roublet153hdBonNouvel16113ChinaRun13714	Failed to last	8
1Oct68- 5Bel	hd	2⅛	S'Chase	3:533	4↑	Broad Hollow H 16k	6	1	15	13	12	21	Aitcheson J Jr	162	b	*1.20e	- -	Exhibit A.1451Bon Nouvel16218Flying Artist1462½	Gamely	6
14Sep68- 4Fai	fm	*1¼Ⓣ		2:084	3↑	Alw 1200	11	1	1nk	1½	2¾	411	Aitcheson J Jr	140	b	*1.00	- -	Charlie Wright133½Molterer1401½Aiken Road1409	No excuse	11
22Aug68- 5Sar	sf	2½	S'Chase	4:421	4↑	Saratoga H 21k	1	1	15	16	1hd	24	Aitcheson J Jr	165		2.00	- -	Apollon1444Bon Nouvel1654Roublet155nk	Poor landing 16th	4
2Aug68- 5Sar	fm	2 1/16	S'Chase	3:513	4↑	Beverwyck H 16k	2	1	11½	12	13	12½	Aitcheson J Jr	154		*.30	- -	Bon Nouvel1542½Sky Epic13514Appollon1491½	Ridden out	4
29Jly68- 3Sar	sf	2 1/16	S'Chase	3:564	4↑	OClm 10000	7	1	13	14	18	118	Aitcheson J	155		*.70	- -	Bon Nouvel15518Atamisqui143¾China Run1321	Easily best	8
28Jun68♦ Auteuil(Fr)	fm	*2⅝		5:04	5↑	Prix des Drags Steeplechase Stk17000						26	Robinson W	132		15.00		Vin Sec1326Bon Nouvel1326Pontage1322	Led,soon well clear,headed approaching last,second best	
23Jun68♦ Auteuil(Fr)	sf	*4 1/16		7:59	5↑	Grand Steeple-Chase d'Paris Stk68000						-	Small D Jr	141		19.00e		Haroue1418Parandero14120Philae1412½	With leaders,fell at 6th	14
31May68- 5Bel	fm	2⅛	S'Chase	4:024	4↑	Hitchcock H 11k	4	2	2½	14	12	33	Aitcheson J Jr	159		*.70e	- -	Roublet152½Teana1412½Bon Nouvel15940	Fenced poorly	7
23May68- 5Bel	fm	2½	S'Chase	4:471	4↑	Meadow Brook H 18k	4	1	14	-	-	-	Aitcheson J	157		*.40e	- -	Sun Game1412½Irish Hammer146	Overjumped 6th	5
4May68- 4War	fm	*2	S'Chase	4:401	4↑	Alw 2200	6	5	210	16	115	120	Aitcheson J Jr	154		-	- -	Bon Nouvel15420Greek Myth1421½Enquest1353	Handily	7
20Apr68- 5Mid	hd	*2	S'Chase	3:481	4↑	Clark Cup 5.5k	3	2	2¾	1½	2hd	2½	Aitcheson J	140		-	- -	Tuscalee160½Bon Nouvel140noGaddo1404½	Held on willingly	7
13Apr68- 3Mid	fm	*2	S'Chase	4:492	4↑	W C Langly Mem Cup 2.2k	6	4	2nk	12	11	12	Aitcheson J	142		-	- -	Bon Nouvel1422Gaddo1379Hustle1421½	Steady drive	6
6Apr68- 3DRn	fm	*1⅝	Hurdles	2:443	3↑	Alw 1000	5	3	31½	3¾	3¾	1½	Aitcheson J Jr	143		-	- -	Bon Nouvel143½Lucent147¾Shod Over1381½	Driving	5
7May66- 7War	fm	*1¼Ⓣ		2:343	3↑	Alw 500	3	2	12	12	12½	14½	Smithwick AP	147	s	-	- -	Bon Nouvel1474½Aquitania140½Brandon Hill1303	Mild drive	10
23Apr66- 6Mid	sf	*1¼Ⓣ		2:173	3↑	Alw 200	7	-				813	Walsh T	149	s	-	- -	PrinceBective1391½LazyRiver1381½EarlyFind1434	No threat	12
	Dense fog																			
29Oct65- 6Aqu	hd	3	S'Chase	5:334	4↑	Temple Gwathmey H 54k	3	1	16	16	120	130	Walsh T	170	s	*.30e	- -	Bon Nouvel17030Lucentaur13415Mako14650	Outclassed field	6
5Oct65- 5Aqu	hd	2½	S'Chase	4:363	4↑	Brook H 20k	2	1	13	15	12	11	Walsh T	169	s	*.30e	- -	Bon Nouvel1691Mako1423Sun Game14350	Good handling	5
16Sep65- 5Aqu	hd	2 1/16	S'Chase	3:432	4↑	Broad Hollow H 16k	6	1	13	15	16	18	Walsh T	162	s	*.90e	- -	Bon Nouvel1628The Sport15410Impeach137¾	Much the best	6
26Aug65- 5Sar	fm	2½	S'Chase	4:333	4↑	Saratoga H 22k	2	1	18	12	1½	22	Walsh T	160	s	2.20e	- -	TheSport1482BonNouvel1605SunGame1463	Bobbled,2nd best	6
21Aug65- 3Sar	fm	2 1/16	S'Chase	3:411	4↑	Handicap 7500	6	1	12	23	47	419½	Smithwick AP	156	s	*1.40e	- -	Nashandy1465Magic Technique1452½Niksar13712	Used up	7
5Aug65- 8Sar	fm	1⅛Ⓣ		1:483	3↑	Alw 6000	1	1	1½	33	89	1116	Blum W	115		13.50	74-00	Lancastrian1102Winklepicker1124Ali Baba II115½	Used up	14
17Jly65- 5Del	hd	1 1/16Ⓣ		1:453	3↑	Alw 4000	6	5	65½	77¼	76¾	78¾	Turcotte R	122		*2.60e	67-24	ⒹScambio122nkIsland Stream1093½Cannelton1101	Steadied	9
30Oct64- 6Aqu	fm	3	S'Chase	5:394	4↑	Temple Gwathmey H 55k	7	1	11	2½	210	321	Smithwick AP	162	s	*.30e	- -	Amber Diver15720Aquitania1351Bon Nouvel162½	Gave way	7
20Oct64- 5Aqu	sf	3	S'Chase	5:401	4↑	Grand National H 28k	3	1	16	18	120	120	Smithwick AP	156	s	*.70e	- -	BonNouvel15620AmberDiver1566BamptonCastle140hd	Easily	8
6Oct64- 5Aqu	fm	2½	S'Chase	4:401	4↑	Brook H 19k	7	1	16	115	120	112	Smithwick AP	152	s	*1.15e	- -	Bon Nouvel15212Tuscarora1562Pocket Rocket137¾	Easily	8
17Sep64- 5Aqu	fm	2	S'Chase	3:402	4↑	Broad Hollow H 16k	4	1	13	14	14	12	Smithwick AP	146	s	*1.95	- -	Bon Nouvel1462Tuscarora1492½Nautilus1465	Ridden out	6
3Sep64- 5Aqu	fm	2	S'Chase	3:43	4↑	Harbor Hill H 11k	7	2	18	112	112	112	Smithwick AP	148	s	*1.15	- -	Bon Nouvel14812Arctic Flow1352Hustle1491	Easily best	8
26Aug64- 3Sar	hd	2 1/16	S'Chase	3:46	4↑	Alw 5000	3	2	1½	16	18	125	Hruska J	135	s	*1.10e	- -	Bon Nouvel13525Half Baked1365El Moro1504	Easily best	8
8Aug64- 3Sar	hd	1⅞	Hurdles	3:211	3↑	Alw 5500	8	1	11	12	1hd	23	Smithwick AP	143	s	4.25	- -	Our Jeep1483Bon Nouvel143hdLumiere1341	Game try	9
29Jly64- 5Mth	fm	*2	Hurdles	3:544	3↑	Midsummer H 17k	11	5	23	21½	23	36¼	Smithwick AP	142	s	20.10	- -	IntheCloset152nkExhibitA.1656BonNouvel142no	Game try	11
17Jly64- 3Mth	fm	*1¾	Hurdles	3:263	3↑	Alw 4000	2	6	23	12	2hd	24	Smithwick AP	143	s	9.80e	- -	Rapidan1474Bon Nouvel14310Hermod1482	Set pace,gamely	10
20May64- 3Aqu	hd	1⅝	Hurdles	2:521	3↑	Alw 5000	6	5	610	614	719	725	Smithwick AP	143	s	12.20	- -	AtomCloud1504PrinceBective1442IntheCloset1478	No speed	8
7May64- 5Aqu	fm	2	S'Chase	3:484	4↑	Aqu Spring 14k	10	- -	-	-	-	-	Smithwick AP	143	s	20.20	- -	RamshornCreek1483RapidPlay1414Mildor14314	In close,fell	11
18Apr64- 4Mid	fm	*2	S'Chase	3:52	4↑	Piedmont Cup H 2.3k	6	6	21	22	34½	38½	Hruska J	137	b	-	- -	War Union II1478Fortification135½Bon Nouvel137¾	Tired	8
11Apr64- 3Mid	fm	*2	S'Chase	3:581	4↑	WC Langley Mem Cup 2.1k	2	3	11	311	38	212	Hruska J	141	sb	-	- -	Cher Man13812Bon Nouvel141½Seroval151	Set pace,gamely	3
30Nov63- 5Pim	sl	6f		:24 :481 1:01 1:134		Alw 4000	7	2	21	31½	54½	66¾	Turcotte R	119		2.90	74-25	Romay1161¼North Channel116½Evil Dick1161	Speed,tired	8
23Nov63- 7Pim	sly	6f		:231 :47 1:002 1:143		Alw 4000	8	2	52¼	44½	34	22	Torres O	113		4.30	75-23	Big Little Man1142Bon Nouvel113¾Evil Dick1165	Gamely	9
14Nov63- 5Pim	fst	6f		:24 :48 1:01 1:141		Md Sp Wt	11	2	31	11	11½	11½	Torres O	120		5.10	79-19	Bon Nouvel1201½Turning Point1201Mono Boy120nk	All out	12
9Nov63- 5Lrl	gd	6f		:231 :474 1:133	3↑	Alw 4000	1	5	96½	919	919	926	Torres O	110		14.00	61-24	LansingLane1227SecondMortgage1151FnfnlTulp1221½	Trailed	9
17Oct63- 3Aqu	sf	*1⅝	Hurdles	2:583	3↑	O Clm 7500	8	6	23	11	13	1¾	Smithwick AP	147	s	2.80e	- -	BonNvl147¾HoistHimAboard142¾ⒹAtomCloud1572½	Driving	8
11Oct63- 3Aqu	hd	1⅝	Hurdles	2:512	3↑	O Clm 5000	9	6	23	1½	311	323	Smithwick AP	145	s	*2.40e	- -	Fort Riley1408Cassorbit14015Bon Nouvel145½	Used in lead	11
13Sep63- 3Aqu	sf	*1⅝	Hurdles	2:571		O Md 7500	2	1	1½	21	1hd	36½	Smithwick AP	145	s	*2.20	- -	EarlyFind137½Roi-a-Dan1386BonNouvl14512	Used up in pace	8
30Aug63- 3Aqu	fm	*1⅝	Hurdles	2:503		O Md 7500	2	4	46	42	31½	2¾	Smithwick AP	145	s	9.85	- -	Lumiere145¾BonNouvl1451JohnCano1452½	Finished strongly	10
7Aug63- 1Sar	fst	1⅛		:472 1:124 1:392 1:524	3↑	Md Sp Wt	7	2	64¾	97	76½	815	Gustines H	117		54.00	66-13	War Lord1171¾Nacelle1172Mac Brathar117¾	Fell back early	9
30Jly63- 8Sar	gd	1⅛		:481 1:134 1:403 1:534	3↑	Md Sp Wt	10	10	119¾	1111	1112	1019	Sorrentino M	115		13.05	57-20	Watch Word1152½Deer Falls110nkMacBrathar1153½	Far back	11
2Jly63- 3Del	fm	1 1/16Ⓣ		1:434	3↑	Md Sp Wt	7	1	11½	42	47½	49¾	Cox N	114		16.50	83-05	GallantChiefII1134SidlingSam1084RockyThumb1131¾	Tired	12
21Jun63- 8Aqu	fst	6f		:224 :471 1:12		Md Sp Wt	2	9	910	98½	911	911	Cox N	122		25.95	74-14	BrownJay122noFriendlyPeople1221½SeekndFnd1221	No factor	10
8Jun63- 2Del	sly	6f		:224 :463 1:13	3↑	Md Sp Wt	7	8	118	96¾	68¾	35	Cox N	114		7.80	75-17	Hallatnan1133½Procrastination1081½BonNouvl114hd	Rallied	12
25May63- 7Pur	fm	*7fⓉ		1:29	3↑	Alw 400	3	5	57½	514	59	44½	Cox N	133	s	*1.70e	- -	AngusBear148noPeacockThroneII1484½Sagvel143hd	No excuse	6

Bowl of Flowers

ch. f. 1958, by Sailor (Eight Thirty)–Flower Bowl, by Alibhai

Lifetime record: 16 10 3 3 $398,504

Own.– Brookmeade Stable
Br.– Brookmeade Stable (Ky)
Tr.– E. Burch

11Nov61- 7Aqu	fst	1 3/16	:48 1:121 1:371 1:564		Roamer H 56k	6	5	53	33½	32½	3hd	Rotz JL	121	b	3.45	95-13	Sherluck126noHittingAway120noBowlofFlowers121 2¼	Gamely	9
19Oct61- 6Kee	sly	1⅛	:464 1:103 1:36 1:491	3↑	ⒻSpinster 84k	3	7	57½	54	32½	1¾	Arcaro E	119	b	4.40	91-11	Bowl of Flowers119¾Primonetta1191Times Two1191	Driving	7
Open to 3-,4- and 5-year-olds																			
26Sep61- 7Bel	fst	1 1/16	:231 :47 1:114 1:434	3↑	ⒻAlw 7500	6	9	88¼	67	34½	32¾	Arcaro E	115		*.65	82-22	RoseO'Neill1132Siesta118¾BowlofFlowrs1155	Returned sore	10
5Aug61- 6Sar	fst	1¼	:481 1:121 1:371 2:031		ⒻAlabama 54k	5	5	57½	65	52½	36	Arcaro E	124		*.55	86-10	Primonetta1215MightyFair1141BowlofFlowers124hd	Bore out	6
24Jun61- 7Bel	fst	1¼	:483 1:124 1:374 2:031		ⒻC C A Oaks 116k	1	6	4¾	2hd	12	15½	Arcaro E	121		*.45	84-13	BowlofFlowers1215½Funloving1215MightyFair121 2¼	Easily	6
10Jun61- 7Bel	fst	1⅛	:473 1:122 1:373 1:503		ⒻMother Goose 87k	5	7	67	42½	23	2hd	Arcaro E	121		*.80	83-18	Funloving117hdBowlofFlowers121 1¼MightyFair117 1¼	Gaining	8
20May61- 7Aqu	fst	1	:233 :47 1:112 1:372		ⒻAcorn 57k	3	7	54	42½	41½	1¾	Arcaro E	121		*.25	81-18	BowlofFlowers121¾BlackDarter121noSevnThrty121nk	Driving	7
4May61- 7Aqu	fst	7f	:231 :462 1:104 1:232		Handicap 10000	1	1	43	31	1½	12	Arcaro E	121		*.30	93-12	BowlofFlowers1212UpScope117 2¼BraveAlly113 2¾	Easily best	5
12Nov60- 7Aqu	fst	1	:222 :444 1:094 1:353		ⒻFrizette 106k	4	10	97	85½	1½	13	Arcaro E	119		*.70e	90-13	BowlofFlowers1193CounterCall119 1¾GoodMove1192	Easily	12
22Oct60- 7GS	fst	1 1/16	:23 :464 1:114 1:46		ⒻGardenia 153k	4	13	1116	99¼	53½	1½	Shoemaker W	119		*.70e	80-19	BowlofFlowrs119½AnglSpeed1191PromnntLdy119 1½	Taken up	13
15Oct60- 6GS	fst	1	:224 :462 1:12 1:381		ⒻAlw 10000	7	7	65¼	1½	11½	13½	Boulmetis S	121		*1.70	91-16	BowlofFlowers121 3½AngelSpeed116 2½MyPortrait1181	Easily	11
7Oct60- 7Bel	fst	7f	:231 :472 1:123 1:251		ⒻAlw 15000	10	6	910	76¾	2½	15	Arcaro E	116		*.80	81-24	Bowl of Flowers1165Dewali116nkMaggie James107nk	Easily	11
29Sep60- 6Bel	fst	6f	:222 :462 1:114		ⒻAlw 4500	4	12	1211	76	32½	2hd	Arcaro E	119		*1.60	88-16	Dewali116hdBowlofFlowers119nkPlayTm1166	Slow start,wide	13
20Jun60- 7Bel	fst	5½f	:222 :46 :58 1:041		ⒻNational Stallion 37k	7	8	56½	44	21½	1no	Ycaza M	114		2.70	101-11	BowlofFlowers114noShuette1148EasternPrincss119½	Driving	8
26May60- 6Aqu	fst	5f	:224 :464 :592		ⒻMd Sp Wt	6	8	54½	32½	11	13	Arcaro E	115		*1.05	- -	Bowl of Flowers1153Chuckaway1155Cargreen1153	Easily	9
13May60- 3Aqu	fst	5f	:224 :463 :59		ⒻMd Sp Wt	4	7	98½	911	610	26	Arcaro E	115		6.50	- -	Shuette1156BowlofFlowers1151BlesstheBride115½	Greenly	9

Buckpasser

b. c. 1963, by Tom Fool (Menow)–Busanda, by War Admiral

Lifetime record: 31 25 4 1 $1,462,014

Own.– O. Phipps
Br.– Ogden Phipps (Ky)
Tr.– E.A. Neloy

30Sep67- 7Aqu	fst	1¼	:451 1:091 1:353 2:003	3↑	Woodward 107k	6	6	614	33½	38	210	Baeza B	126	b	*1.60e	85-15	Damascus12010Buckpasser126½Dr. Fager12013	Good try	6
22Jly67- 7Aqu	fst	1¼	:462 1:094 1:342 2:001	3↑	Brooklyn H 106k	3	3	33	23	25	28	Baeza B	136	b	*.70	89-11	Handsome Boy1168Bckpassr136 4½Mr. Right113 3½	No excuse	5
4Jly67- 7Aqu	fst	1¼	:474 1:114 1:363 2:021	3↑	Suburban H 109k	1	5	65	44	44	1½	Baeza B	133	b	*.50	87-17	Buckpasser133½RingTwice111 2½Yondr109 1½	Up final strides	7
17Jun67- 7Aqu	hd	1⅝Ⓣ	2:412	3↑	Bowling Green H 55k	3	4	47½	46½	35	34½	Baeza B	135	b	*.40e	82-13	Poker112 1½Assagai1273Buckpasser135½	Failed to respond	5
30May67- 7Aqu	fst	1	:232 :454 1:10 1:343	3↑	Metropolitan H 109k	5	3	32	34½	21	11¼	Baeza B	130	b	*.30	95-13	Buckpasser130 1¼Yonder108 4½Impressive1131	Scored easily	6
14Jan67- 8SA	fst	1⅛	:462 1:103 1:354 1:481		San Fernando 56k	3	3	37½	44½	32½	11½	Baeza B	124	b	*.30	91-12	Buckpasser124 1½FleetHost121¾Pretens118hd	With authority	6
31Dec66- 6SA	fst	7f	:223 :451 1:093 1:22		Malibu 29k	2	9	76½	54½	21	1¾	Baeza B	126	b	*.40	93-15	Buckpasser126¾Drin1201KingsFvor117 1½	Slow start,driving	9
29Oct66- 7Aqu	fst	2	:494 2:333 3:261	3↑	J C Gold Cup 110k	1	4	44½	1hd	11	11¾	Baeza B	119	b	*.30e	65-21	Buckpasser119 1¾Niarkos124½O'Hara1248	Drew out handling	7
19Oct66- 7Aqu	sly	1⅝	:492 1:423 2:071 2:441		Lawrence Realizatn 54k	4	5	44½	33½	32½	12½	Baeza B	126	b	*.20e	84-19	Buckpasser126 2½Ring Twice116½Poker11612	Going away	5
1Oct66- 7Aqu	sly	1¼	:47 1:114 1:373 2:024	3↑	Woodward 112k	4	6	64½	31½	1hd	1¾	Baeza B	121	b	*.90e	84-24	Buckpasser121¾Royal Gunner126¾Buffle1215	Ridden out	9
20Aug66- 6Sar	fst	1¼	:472 1:112 1:362 2:013		Travers 82k	6	5	512	43½	21	1¾	Baeza B	126	b	*.30e	100-10	Buckpssr126¾Ambrod123 3½Buffl120no	Under strong handling	6
6Aug66- 8AP	fst	1⅛	:464 1:103 1:354 1:47		American Derby 129k	9	5	59½	68	42	1nk	Baeza B	128	b	*.60e	101-09	Buckpasser128nkJolly Jet1161Advocator1163	Driving	9
23Jly66- 7Aqu	fst	1¼	:483 1:122 1:364 2:014	3↑	Brooklyn H 107k	2	2	22½	21½	1hd	1hd	Baeza B	120	b	*.60	89-16	Buckpasser120hdBuffle1135Pluck1132	Faltered,came again	5
9Jly66- 8AP	fst	1⅛	:473 1:112 1:363 1:491		Chicagoan 103k	3	3	33	2½	1hd	1¾	Baeza B	123	b	*.30	90-18	Buckpasser123¾Whisper Jet114nkAbe's Hope1167	Mild drive	5
25Jun66- 8AP	fst	1	:221 :433 1:064 1:323		Arl Classic H 108k	4	6	79	59	34	1¾	Baeza B	125	b	*.70e	103-04	Buckpasser125 1¾CremeDelaCreme123¾HeJr.116nk	Ridden out	8
18Jun66- 8Del	fst	1⅛	:463 1:10 1:364 1:492		Leonard Richards 41k	2	4	47	48½	2hd	1¾	Baeza B	126	b	*.30e	90-14	Buckpasser126¾Buffle114¾Deck Hand1144	Under hand urging	6
4Jun66- 6Aqu	fst	6f	:222 :451 1:091	3↑	Alw 8500	5	3	22	1hd	1hd	12	Baeza B	115	b	*.40	97-14	Buckpasser1152Tim'sStingry1152Undrstudy121nk	Mild drive	7
3Mar66- 0Hia	fst	1⅛	:462 1:104 1:363 1:50		Flamingo 136k	4	3	34	32	2½	1no	Shoemaker W	122	b	-	85-18	Buckpasser122noAbe'sHope122 2¼BlueSkyer122 2½	Came again	9
Run between 7th and 8th races. No wagering																			
23Feb66- 8Hia	fst	1⅛	:452 1:09 1:343 1:474		Everglades 30k	6	2	23	21	2hd	1hd	Shoemaker W	122	b	*.20e	96-12	Buckpasser122hdStupendous115¾Abe's Hope1154	Swerved	8
14Feb66- 0Hia	fst	7f	:224 :45 1:084 1:214		Alw 5000	1	5	514	512	46	24½	Shoemaker W	124	b	-e	95-13	Impressive122 4½Buckpasser124 1½Stupendous113nk	Rallied	5
Exhibition race run between 7th and 8th races. No wagering;Previously trained by W.C. Winfrey																			
16Oct65- 7Aqu	fst	1	:223 :453 1:104 1:362		Champagne 223k	1	7	54½	54½	1½	14	Baeza B	122	b	*.90e	86-20	Buckpasser1224Our Michael122½Advocator122 1½	Easily	9
25Sep65- 7Aqu	gd	6½f	:23 :462 1:104 1:171		Futurity 151k	7	6	41¾	21	21	2½	Baeza B	122	b	*.70	93-20	PricelessGem119½Buckpassr12210ⒹAdvoctor1223	No excuse	9
11Sep65- 8AP	fst	7f	:223 :452 1:102 1:23		Arl-Wash Futurity 335k	8	8	66½	56¼	14	1½	Baeza B	122	b	*.80	92-15	Buckpasser122½Fathers Image1222Flame Tree122no	Driving	10
28Aug65- 6Sar	fst	6½f	:22 :444 1:093 1:16		Hopeful 110k	7	7	42½	31½	3nk	12½	Baeza B	122	b	*.30e	98-08	Buckpasser122 2½Impressive122¾Indulto122 2½	Going away	7
7Aug65- 8Mth	fst	6f	:22 :45 1:103		Sapling 112k	1	7	63¾	33½	33	1½	Baeza B	122	b	1.90	89-21	Buckpasser122½Quinta122 1½OurMichael1225	Left at post,up	7
30Jly65- 7Mth	fst	5½f	:221 :454 1:04		Alw 5000	3	5	42	33	11	17	Baeza B	122	b	*.90	97-19	Buckpasser1227Model Fool116¾Gary Dear1193	Drew far out	6
7Jly65- 7Aqu	fst	5½f	:221 :45 :572 1:034		Tremont 34k	3	6	66½	42½	2½	1nk	Baeza B	118	b	*.70	94-13	Buckpasser118nkSpringDouble118 2½Hospitalty118no	Driving	6
28Jun65- 7Aqu	fst	5½f	:222 :452 :58 1:043		©National Stallion 32k	3	5	59	47	34	15♦	Baeza B	122	b	*1.00	90-15	DH Hospitality117 DH Buckpassr1225KentuckyKn117no	Just up	6
8Jun65- 6Aqu	fst	5½f	:223 :461 :583 1:05		Alw 5500	7	5	55	52½	2½	11½	Baeza B	122		*1.90	88-21	Buckpassr122 1½KentuckyKin122 2½BanderaBeau1194	Driving	9
29May65- 3Aqu	sly	5f	:23 :471 1:00		©Md Sp Wt	7	5	43	42	2½	12	Baeza B	122		*1.25	85-20	Buckpasser1222Exhibitionist122 2½Clique1224	Easy score	8
13May65- 4Aqu	fst	5½f	:231 :482 1:003 1:07		©Md Sp Wt	8	10	66	57	55	41¼	Baeza B	122		5.30	77-26	LonelyGambler122½HndsmeBy122noMaskofPlay117¾	Greenly	10

Carry Back

br. c. 1958, by Saggy (Swing and Sway)–Joppy, by Star Blen

Lifetime record: 61 21 11 11 $1,241,165

Own.– Dorchester Farm Stable
Br.– J.A. Price (Fla)
Tr.– J.A. Price

2Nov63- 8GS	my	1¼	:464 1:111 1:361 2:014	3↑	Trenton H 59k	2	6	44½	12	12	12½	Sellers J	119		7.00	96-22	Carry Back119 2½Mongo1242Smart1166	Kept to brisk drive	10
9Oct63- 7Aqu	fst	1½	:47 1:114 2:024 2:28	3↑	Manhattan H 58k	7	9	810	64½	1116	1116	Rotz JL	125		5.50	95-18	Smart114 2½Will I Rule112noGarwol1112	Made move,stopped	12
28Sep63- 7Aqu	fst	1¼	:473 1:114 1:362 2:004	3↑	Woodward 108k	4	4	45½	45½	49½	411	Rotz JL	126		8.75	85-13	Kelso126 3½Never Bend120 1½Crimson Satan1266	Even effort	5
14Sep63- 8Atl	fm	1 3/16Ⓣ	1:551	3↑	U Nations H 125k	10	6	53½	42	51¼	32¾	Grant H	127		*2.60	94-03	Mongo1242Never Bend118¾Carry Back127 1½	Made fair try	10
Daily Racing Form time,1:54 2/5																			
7Sep63- 6Atl	fm	1 1/16Ⓣ	1:423	3↑	Alw 7500	2	3	2hd	1½	14	16	Grant H	116		*1.80	98-02	CarryBack1166PrinceO'Pilsen1183FatCat114 1½	Ridden out	7
17Aug63- 7Ran	fst	1⅛	:471 1:113 1:364 1:49	3↑	Buckeye H 33k	2	3	26	25	23	25	Rotz JL	126		*1.80	86-13	Gushing Wind1145CarryBack126 2¾Loyal Son116 1½	Wide,hung	8
12Nov62- 7Lrl	sf	1½Ⓣ	:471 1:112 2:031 2:281	3↑	D C Int'l 125k	6	4	42	21	31½	36	Rotz JL	126		4.50	84-20	MatchII128 1½Kelso126 4½CarryBck1265	Good early bid,tired	13
3Nov62- 7GS	sly	1¼	:471 1:121 1:382 2:053	3↑	Trenton H 86k	3	8	712	34	22	2no	Rotz JL	129		*1.20	77-29	Mongo118noCarryBck129 4½Snstvo116¾	Impeded st.,sharp try	8
27Oct62- 7Bel	sf	1½Ⓣ	2:283	3↑	Man o' War 114k	5	8	77	43	57½	512	Rotz JL	126		9.25	91-11	BeauPurple1262Kelso126 6½TheAxII126 1¼	Early bid,weakened	12
7Oct62♦ Longchamp(Fr)	fm	*1½ⓉRH	2:304	3↑	Prix de l'Arc de Triomphe Stk285000						105¾	Breasley A	132		5.50		Soltikoff1221Monade119nkVal de Loir122no		24
Wide throughout in midpack,one-paced last quarter.Exbury 6th																			
3Sep62- 7Aqu	fst	1⅛	:473 1:111 1:36 1:484	3↑	Aqueduct 106k	2	3	31	2hd	3½	41	Rotz JL	128		*.75	97-09	Crozier114½Guadalcanal114hdRidan123½	Speed,hung late	4
28Aug62- 5Aqu	sly	1	:231 :463 1:114 1:373	3↑	Handicap 10000	4	2	1hd	13	18	18	Rotz JL	133		1.00	80-23	CarryBack1338NickelBoy1151Djeddar11610	As rider pleased	4
4Aug62- 6Sar	fst	1⅛	:47 1:11 1:36 1:50	4↑	Whitney 57k	1	5	58½	45	2hd	12	Sellers J	130		*1.60	95-09	Carry Back1302Crozier1114Garwol110no	Under brisk urging	10
21Jly62- 7Aqu	fst	1¼	:471 1:10 1:342 2:00	3↑	Brooklyn H 109k	4	8	811	66	66¼	45	Rotz JL	127		*.85	101-05	BuPurpl116 3½Grwol106noPolyld114 1½	In close,loose band's	8
14Jly62- 8Mth	fst	1¼	:46 1:10 1:344 2:002	3↑	Monmouth H 109k	4	6	67	33	1hd	13	Rotz JL	124		3.50	104-14	Carry Back1243Kelso130¾Beau Purple117½	Kept to drive	6

4Jly62- 7Aqu	fst	1¼	:484 1:124 1:363 2:003	3↑ Suburban H 105k	3 4 47½ 45 45½ 47¼	Rotz JL	126	1.85	96-08	BeauPurple1152½Klso1323½Grwol1091¼	Bore in late,checked	4
30May62- 7Aqu	fst	1	:221 :44 1:08 1:333	3↑ Metropolitan H 111k	3 7 79½ 77¼ 35 12½	Rotz JL	123	4.90	100-08	CarryBack1232½MerryRuler120½RullahRed1114½	Easily best	9
28Apr62- 7Aqu	fst	1⅛	:463 1:101 1:36 1:49	3↑ Grey Lag H 85k	10 8 816 89½ 53½ 22½	Ycaza M	125	*1.10	94-10	Ambiopoise1152½Carry Back125½Beau Prince115nk	Game try	10
20Apr62- 7Aqu	fst	1	:224 :454 1:102 1:351	4↑ Alw 10000	2 7 77¾ 54 11½ 15	Ycaza M	126	*.70	92-13	CarryBack1265Garwol117nkGuadalcanal1171¼	Speed to spare	8
17Mar62- 7GP	fst	1¼	:454 1:101 1:36 2:013	3↑ Gulf Park H 112k	3 9 815 53¾ 43½ 32	Ycaza M	126	*1.25	89-13	[D]Yorky121nkJayFox1121¾CarryBack1261	Wide late,gaining	9
3Mar62- 9FG	fst	1⅛	:47 1:113 1:374 1:503	3↑ New Orleans H 64k	8 9 912 67 52½ 33¼	Sellers J	129	*.70	91-14	Yorktown1131½Hillsborough1131¾Carry Back1293½	Late bid	12
24Feb62- 7Hia	fst	1¼	:46 1:101 1:36 2:02	3↑ Widener H 134k	7 10 1015 99¾ 55 2nk	Sellers J	127	*1.10	88-12	Yorky120nkCarryBack1273Ambopos121nk	Blocked,fast finish	12
10Feb62- 7Hia	fst	1⅛	:461 1:102 1:352 1:482	3↑ Seminole H 62k	9 7 812 711 56¼ 28	Sellers J	127	*.75	85-13	Intentionally1268Carry Back127½Yorky120½	Closed gamely	10
31Jan62- 7Hia	fst	7f	:222 :444 1:092 1:223	3↑ Palm Beach H 33k	12 6 1113 1014 68½ 21¾	Sellers J	124	3.15	95-11	Intentionally1261¾CarryBack1242Ambiopois122nk	Sharp try	13
28Oct61- 7GS	fst	1¼	:471 1:112 1:363 2:03	3↑ Trenton H 84k	8 6 67 41¾ 31 1½	Sellers J	120	*3.00	90-13	Carry Back120½Intentionally1241¼Ambiopoise120nk	Driving	8
11Oct61- 7Aqu	fst	1⅝	:471 1:38 2:04 2:434	Lawrence Realizatn 54k	1 4 46 33 36 39¼	Sellers J	123	*.55	82-18	Sherlck1231¼Ambiopoise1208CarryBck1234½	Came back sore	6
30Sep61- 7Bel	fst	1¼	:461 1:10 1:344 2:00	3↑ Woodward 109k	1 5 56 43½ 47 38½	Sellers J	120	4.00	91-13	Klso1268DivineComedy126½CarryBck120nk	Raced on outside	5
16Sep61- 8Atl	fm	1 3/16Ⓣ	:463 1:111 1:37 1:56	3↑ U Nations H 100k	5 10 910 74¼ 65 73¾	Sellers J	123	*1.20	89-07	Oink119noTompion1172Art Market116nk	No apparent excuse	12
2Sep61- 7Bel	fst	1	:223 :451 1:094 1:36	Jerome H 57k	9 7 88 87¼ 61¾ 1hd	Sellers J	128	*1.95	94-15	CarryBack128hdGarwol111hdBeauPrnc126nk	Up final strides	9
26Aug61- 7Atl	my	7f	:224 :453 1:11 1:243	3↑ Alw 6000	4 7 78 56¼ 53¼ 1nk	Sellers J	117	*1.00	80-21	CarryBack117nkRareRice114noAbatn1072	Needed mild urging	7
3Jun61- 7Bel	fst	1½	:483 1:133 2:041 2:291	Belmont 148k	2 6 77 77½ 713 715	Sellers J	126	*.45	72-13	Sherluck1262¼Globemaster1262½Guadlcnl1264	Returned sore	9
20May61- 8Pim	fst	1 3/16	:481 1:121 1:38 1:573	Preakness 178k	4 8 915 66 24 1¾	Sellers J	126	*1.00	85-22	CarryBack126¾Globemaster1264Crozir126½	Under hard drive	9
6May61- 7CD	gd	1¼	:473 1:112 1:361 2:04	Ky Derby 163k	14 11 1118 613 44½ 1¾	Sellers J	126	*2.50	87-14	CarryBack126¾Crozier1262BassClf1262¼	Under strong drive	15
22Apr61- 7Aqu	fst	1⅛	:47 1:112 1:364 1:501	Wood Memorial 86k	6 6 610 47 34 23¼	Sellers J	126	*.95	88-16	Globemaster1263¼Carry Back1266Ambiopoise126hd	Rallied	7
1Apr61- 7GP	sly	1⅛	:462 1:102 1:361 1:484	Florida Derby 115k	5 7 713 41½ 32 1hd	Sellers J	122	*1.60	90-16	CarryBack122hdCrozier1223¼BeauPrinc1224	Brushed,driving	8
22Mar61- 7GP	gd	1 1/16	:234 :473 1:113 1:431	Fountain of Youth 17k	1 6 712 59 36 33	Sellers J	122	*1.50	89-17	BeauPrince114noCrozier1223CrryBck1223	Wide late,rallied	7
25Feb61- 7Hia	fst	1⅛	:463 1:113 1:372 1:503	Flamingo 129k	3 5 44 32 21½ 1hd	Sellers J	122	*.65	82-19	Carry Back122hdCrozier1228Your Bill1221¾	Forced wide	7
15Feb61- 7Hia	fst	1⅛	:46 1:104 1:37 1:503	Everglades 32k	5 8 711 65¼ 43 1½	Sellers J	126	*.65	82-17	CarryBack116½Sherluck114hd[D]Crozier126¾	Bore in,driving	11
8Feb61- 6Hia	fst	1 1/16	:223 :461 1:112 1:443	Alw 7500	3 5 57½ 21½ 14 12	Sellers J	124	*.90	80-21	CarryBack1242TryCash1103Bookcliffe1103½	Speed to spare	10
1Feb61- 7Hia	fst	7f	:224 :453 1:102 1:234	Bahamas 29k	3 8 74¼ 66 64½ 45¼	Sellers J	126	2.75	86-19	Vapor Whirl117nkCrozier1263½Nashua Blue1141½	In close	8
8Nov60- 7Aqu	fst	1	:222 :443 1:094 1:362	Remsen 35k	5 8 99¾ 77 54½ 1½	Sellers J	120	*1.35	86-16	CarryBack120½VaporWhirl111nkAmbiopoise1132½	Hard drive	13
29Oct60- 7GS	sly	1 1/16	:23 :464 1:124 1:462	Garden State 287k	5 14 1010 73¼ 12½ 13½	Sellers J	122	8.20	78-23	Carry Back1223½Ambiopoise1221¼Guadalcanal1221¼	Easily	15
22Oct60- 6GS	fst	1 1/16	:234 :47 1:114 1:452	Alw 10000	7 9 89¼ 67½ 55 5¾	Sellers J	120	7.80	82-19	Intensive115noItsaGreatDay120hdGuadalcanl111hd	Bore out	10
15Oct60- 7Bel	fst	1	:223 :454 1:102 1:353	Champagne 183k	1 8 810 89½ 811 913	Hartack W	122	*1.95	83-12	RovingMinstrel122noGarwol1222Bronzrullh122no	Poor start	9
3Oct60- 7Bel	fst	7f	:222 :46 1:111 1:24	Cowdin 96k	6 7 76¾ 65 33½ 11½	Hartack W	114	6.30	87-17	Carry Back1141½Globemaster117nkGarwol114½	Brisk urging	14
10Sep60- 7Atl	fst	7f	:222 :45 1:101 1:223	Worlds Playground 135k	6 9 109 73½ 63¾ 44½	Culmone J	122	32.90	85-13	HailtoReason1224½ItsaGreatDay122noRossSea122no	Bumped	13
31Aug60- 7Atl	fst	6f	:22 :451 1:101	Seashore 26k	5 4 107 95¾ 85¾ 56½	Lawless R	114	4.00	87-12	Itsa Great Day1223½Inbalance111¾Cross King114nk	Rallied	15
6Aug60- 7Mth	fst	6f	:214 :444 1:102	Sapling 136k	2 15 127¾ 85¾ 65 33	Lawless R	122	26.70	87-17	HailtoReason122½He'saPistol1222½CarryBack122nk	Game try	18
30Jly60- 5Del	sly	5½f	:212 :452 :58 1:042	Dover 24k	11 7 53¾ 45½ 34 21¾	Lawless R	116	*2.90	98-15	KiscoKid1161¾CarryBack1161¾NashuaBlue1163	Closed well	12
20Jly60- 7Aqu	fst	5½f	:23 :464 :59 1:05	Great American 29k	3 3 1hd 3nk 21½ 32	Lawless R	117	6.60	92-15	HailtoReason1242Bronzerullah117hdCarryBck117hd	Bore out	12
4Jly60- 5Del	fst	5½f	:214 :453 :573 1:041	©Christiana 23k	4 4 1hd 1hd 11 2½	Lawless R	116	8.00	100-10	ItsaGreatDay125½CarryBack116½CoveredBridge1163	Sharp	9
22Jun60- 7Mth	fst	5½f	:214 :451 :574 1:043	©Tyro 26k	11 7 86¾ 65¾ 32½ 33	Lawless R	115	24.00f	92-12	Chinchilla111½Song of Wine1152½Carry Back1151¾	Game try	14
10Jun60- 6Mth	fst	5½f	:23 :464 :593 1:053	Alw 5000	4 7 73 61¾ 76½ 56½	Blum W	122	4.90	83-14	Globemaster1222NobleMaestro114½GoldenSixts1221	Bore out	8
18May60- 7GS	sly	5f	:224 :473 :594	Cherry Hill 19k	4 10 107½ 88½ 78¾ 1019	Hartack W	116	*1.90	72-23	IronRail11310SongofWine1132½Reltv114hd	Very dull effort	15
18Apr60- 5GP	fst	5f	:222 :452 :573	Alw 5000	4 2 2hd 1hd 1hd 1½	Hartack W	114	*2.35	107-07	CarryBack114½[D]IronRail1183SongofWn1161½	Fully extended	8
13Apr60- 3GP	fst	4½f	:221 :452 :513	Alw 3000	1 10 65 65 21¼	Hartack W	114	*1.50	100-00	Editorialist1161¼Carry Back1141Glad116hd	Off slowly	12
17Mar60- 5GP	fst	3f	:214 :332	Alw 5000	9 9 44½ 42½	Thornburg B	113	40.40	- -	Opus115hdIronRail1151[D]LittleTumbler1121½	Mild late bid	14
	Placed third through disqualification											
24Feb60- 7Hia	gd	3f	:22 :334	[S]Hialeah Breeders 24k	17 6 62¼ 21¾	Hartack W	120	7.05	- -	MyOldFlame1171¾CarryBack120hdJultt117hd	Finished gamely	18
10Feb60- 3Hia	fst	3f	:221 :334	Alw 3500	4 3 34 43½	Layton JR	114	15.85	- -	Fading Sky1152New Pepi118¾Mt. Hope118¾	No late response	8
3Feb60- 3Hia	fst	3f	:221 :34	[S]Md Sp Wt	14 2 21 1nk	Layton JR	118	*1.75f	- -	CarryBack118nkKalmia1151½Milndr118½	Under a brisk drive	14
29Jan60- 3Hia	fst	3f	:221 :333	©Md Sp Wt	6 12 89 109¼	Layton JR	114	4.10	- -	Opus1184Agapanthus1183Milander113nk	Crowded back early	12

Chateaugay

ch. c. 1960, by Swaps (Khaled)–Banquet Bell, by Polynesian

Lifetime record: 24 11 4 2 $360,722

Own.– Darby Dan Farm

Br.– John W. Galbreath (Ky)

Tr.– J.P. Conway

20Feb65- 8Hia	fst	1¼	:464 1:111 1:371 2:033	3↑ Widener H 135k	11 7 914 109¾ 712 716	Baeza B	120	7.40	64-15	PrimordialII118½HotDust1124YourAlibha1131	Showed little	12
6Feb65- 8Hia	fst	1⅛	:471 1:113 1:372 1:504	3↑ Seminole H 65k	4 2 49 69 55 87¾	Baeza B	124	3.80	73-22	Sunstruck119noPiave114nkPointduJour1161½	Fell far back	13
23Jan65- 8Hia	fst	7f	:23 :453 1:101 1:231	3↑ Royal Palm H 30k	5 7 78 77¾ 66¼ 58½	Broussard R	126	*1.40	84-19	Sunstruck1185Rainy Lake1181¾Morry E.116½	Carried wide	8
16Jan65- 9Hia	fst	7f	:233 :462 1:11 1:234	4↑ Alw 6500	2 9 43½ 45 33 1nk	Baeza B	117	*.80	90-20	Chateaugy117nkKnightlyMannr117¾Bbngton119no	Hand ride	9
6Aug64- 6Sar	fst	7f	:23 :46 1:104 1:231	3↑ Alw 8500	1 5 68 67 33 11	Baeza B	124	*1.00e	94-14	Chateaugay1241Decidedly124nkMatch Wits1086	Handy score	7
20May64- 7Aqu	fst	7f	:231 :464 1:113 1:242	3↑ Roseben H 29k	6 4 95¼ 96¾ 44 2¾	Baeza B	124	*3.10	83-25	Bonjour112¾Chateaugay1242½Red Gar112¾	Wide,game effort	10
2May64- 7Aqu	fst	7f	:223 :451 1:09 1:213	3↑ Carter H 57k	11 1 109½ 913 813 812	Baeza B	126	3.65	86-13	Ahoy1332Red Gar112½Gun Bow1261	Never a serious threat	11
16Oct63- 9Suf	fst	1⅛	:464 1:103 1:36 1:49	Yankee H 58k	7 7 815 8711 57 44¾	Baeza B	127	2.30	91-13	NeverBend1264DeanCarl123½QuestLink117nk	Mild late bid	9
2Oct63- 7Aqu	fst	1⅝	:491 1:401 2:04 2:42	Lawrence Realizatn 56k	2 2 43 57½ 411 410	Baeza B	126	*.70	85-13	DeanCarl1203¾B.Major120nkMasterDennis1166	No excuse	9
14Sep63- 7Aqu	fst	1	:233 :47 1:113 1:36	Jerome H 57k	7 5 42½ 21 21 1½	Baeza B	128	*1.35	88-13	Chateaugay128½Accordant117½Outing Class123½	Driving	7
5Sep63- 7Aqu	fst	7f	:234 :47 1:111 1:232	Handicap 10000	5 2 53 54¾ 41½ 11	Baeza B	130	*.40	89-18	Chateaugay1301Tropical Breeze1152½Time Step1111	Easily	5
17Aug63- 6Sar	fst	1¼	:472 1:111 1:36 2:022	Travers 81k	4 5 56 44 43½ 32½	Baeza B	126	1.75	93-08	Crewman1201½Hot Dust1141Chateaugay1262½	Bore in stretch	6
13Jly63- 7Aqu	fst	1¼	:47 1:111 1:354 2:013	Dwyer H 85k	9 8 814 75¾ 55½ 31½	Baeza B	129	*.80e	90-08	Outing Class1221Tenacle108½Chateaugay129no	Closed fast	10
8Jun63- 7Aqu	fst	1½	:492 1:143 2:044 2:301	Belmont 145k	5 4 45 32½ 1½ 12½	Baeza B	126	4.50	- -	Chateaugay1262½Candy Spots1261Choker1264	Scored easily	7
18May63- 8Pim	fst	1 3/16	:472 1:113 1:37 1:561	Preakness 180k	4 6 68½ 43 21½ 23½	Baeza B	126	2.90	88-12	Candy Spots1263½Chteaugay1264½NeverBend1262¼	Game try	8
4May63- 7CD	fst	1¼	:462 1:10 1:352 2:014	Ky Derby 151k	1 6 610 43 11 11¼	Baeza B	126	9.40	93-08	Chateaugay1261¼Never Bend126nkCandy Spots1264¾	Driving	9
25Apr63- 6Kee	fst	1⅛	:462 1:103 1:353 1:48	Blue Grass 30k	1 2 32½ 42 1hd 1hd	Baeza B	121	*1.30	97-12	Chateaugay121hdGet Around1213½Lemon Twist121½		10
	Overcame trouble											
10Apr63- 7Kee	fst	1 1/16	:234 :472 1:111 1:431	Alw 4500	5 1 12 12 11 1¾	Ycaza M	120	*.30	98-08	Chateaugay120¾Sleuth Hound1122½Bowl Along11411	Easily	5
23Feb63- 5Hia	fst	7f	:231 :46 1:103 1:233	Alw 5000	6 3 34 22½ 11 1¾	Grant H	115	2.90	91-18	Chateaugay115¾Pack Trip1153½Bally Squire1154	All out	9
24Nov62- 8Pim	gd	1 1/16	:251 :494 1:144 1:47	Pim Futurity 117k	7 9 72 1hd 2½ 41¼	Grant H	122	5.80	74-22	RightProud122nkDeltaJudge122nkMastrDennis122¾	Swerved	9
17Nov62- 6Pim	fst	6f	:232 :47 :592 1:114	Alw 4000	8 4 21 2hd 1hd 1hd	Ferraro R5	113	*.70	91-20	Chateaugy113hdSirGay1185TheSmoochr1113	Strong urging	11
3Nov62- 5Aqu	sly	1	:24 :48 1:123 1:373	Alw 5000	1 1 11 1hd 21 21½	Shoemaker W	122	*.60	78-18	RoylAscot1191½Chateaugay12214RaritanValley1192½	Gamely	6
25Oct62- 4Bel	fst	7f	:224 :461 1:11 1:234	©Md Sp Wt	11 2 12 11½ 12½ 16	Baeza B	122	*.90	88-16	Chateaugy1226HoistHimAboard1226½FredmFghtr1222	Easily	14
17Oct62- 1Bel	fst	6f	:224 :462 1:111	©Md Sp Wt	6 5 53½ 42 24 22½	Baeza B	122	*1.20	88-11	Might and Main1222½Chateaugay1221¾RunningBowline1221½		14
	Gamely											

Cicada

b. f. 1959, by Bryan G. (Blenheim II)–Satsuma, by Bossuet
Own.– Meadow Stable
Br.– Meadow Stud Inc (Ky)
Tr.– J.H. Hayes

Lifetime record: 42 23 8 6 $783,674

15Oct64-8GS	fst	6f	:221 :451 1:10	3↑ Alw 5000	6 8 76¼ 65½ 52½ 43¼	Shoemaker W	110		*.90	91-12	Relative1131½Ed'sScholr113nkRhwn1221½ No stretch threat 8
27Jly63-7Del	fst	1¼	:464 1:131 1:374 2:04	3↑ ⒻDelaware H 172k	5 7 74½ 54 31½ 2½	Shoemaker W	128		*1.80	81-20	Waltz Song116½Cicada128noTable Mate1231¼ Saddle slipped 10
6Jly63-7Aqu	fm	1$\frac{1}{16}$Ⓣ	1:422	3↑ ⒻSheepshead Bay H 28k	3 6 2½ 11 12½ 1nk	Adams L	128		*1.45	96-04	Cicada128nkNubile1091DollIn1171½ Hard drive,just lasted 7
12Jun63-7Aqu	fst	7f	:224 :461 1:101 1:224	3↑ ⒻVagrancy H 21k	2 5 32½ 2hd 12 13½	Adams L	127		*.70	92-13	Cicada1273½Bramalea120½My Portrait1144 Speed to spare 5
25May63-7Aqu	fst	1⅛	:473 1:111 1:354 1:483	3↑ ⒻTop Flight H 55k	4 3 32 3nk 34½ 37	Adams L	128		*1.45	91-09	FirmPolicy1254½Tamarona1112½Cicd128¾ Drifted out,tiring 7
17Apr63-7Aqu	fst	7f	:221 :442 1:09 1:213	3↑ ⒻDistaff H 22k	7 1 34½ 34 1½ 14	Shoemaker W	125		*.85	98-10	Cicada1254Pocosaba119½Royal Patrice120nk Ridden out 7
27Mar63-8GP	fst	7f	:224 :46 1:102 1:231	3↑ ⒻSuwannee River H 16k	4 6 68¼ 33½ 22½ 21¼	Shoemaker W	126		*.50	95-18	OldHat1171¼Cicad1264½Coupd'Ett1111½ In close early,wide 6
27Feb63-8Hia	fst	1⅛	:464 1:111 1:362 1:492	4↑ ⒻBlack Helen H 47k	4 4 46 33½ 34½ 58½	Rotz JL	126		*.45	79-14	Pocosaba117hdOldHat1155MissMarcela1142¾ Pulled up sore 8
13Feb63-8Hia	gd	7f	:23 :453 1:104 1:234	3↑ ⒻColumbiana H 30k	6 4 45 33½ 1½ 11¾	Rotz JL	125		*1.30	90-16	Cicada1251¾RoyalPatrice121½OldHt1151½ Drew clear easily 7
3Nov62-7Aqu	sly	1$\frac{5}{16}$	:47 1:122 1:383 2:103	3↑ ⒻLadies H 57k	2 1 11½ 13 2½ 54¾	Shoemaker W	122		*1.80	87-18	Royal Patrice1141Waltz Song1152¾Oil Royalty1131 Tired 10
20Oct62-7GS	fst	1⅛	:491 1:132 1:383 1:504	3↑ ⒻVineland H 57k	4 4 31½ 41½ 51¼ 44¾	Shoemaker W	123		*.70	78-15	Tamarona110hdShirlyJones1262¼LincolnCntr1122½ Stumbled 7
13Oct62-7GS	fst	1$\frac{1}{16}$	:234 :474 1:121 1:451	ⒻJersey Belle 27k	1 3 3½ 2½ 11 15½	Valenzuela I	121		*.30	84-20	Cicada1215½LincolnCenter112hdRareStamp1153½ Clear score 6
22Sep62-7Aqu	fst	1⅛	:463 1:103 1:354 1:481	3↑ ⒻBeldame 87k	5 9 62¼ 41½ 11 11½	Shoemaker W	118		3.95	101-06	Cicada1181½ShirlyJons1232¼FrmPolcy1181½ Strong pressure 13
18Aug62-6Sar	fst	1¼	:472 1:11 1:352 2:013	Travers 82k	5 5 45½ 53¾ 64¼ 76¾	Ussery R	118		10.05	93-07	Jaipur126noRidan1261Military Plume114¾ Bore in at start 7
11Aug62-6Sar	my	1¼	:48 1:13 1:384 2:06	ⒻAlabama 57k	8 2 1½ 11 2½ 35¼	Ussery R	124		*.80	73-21	Firm Policy1211¾Lincoln Center1143½Cicada124nk Gave way 9
28Jly62-6Del	fst	1¼	:474 1:113 1:363 2:023	3↑ ⒻDelaware H 141k	2 2 2½ 13 11 2hd	Shoemaker W	114		3.80	89-21	Seven Thirty120hdCicada1147Bramalea1151¼ Failed to last 9
14Jly62-6Del	fst	1⅛	:472 1:121 1:391 1:52	ⒻDel Oaks 57k	1 2 1hd 1hd 32½ 34	Baeza B	121		*.50	73-20	NorthSouthGal1181½Bramalea1212½Cicada1212¼ Speed,tired 4
23Jun62-7Bel	fst	1¼	:471 1:111 1:362 2:023	ⒻC C A Oaks 120k	4 3 3½ 3nk 2hd 2½	Shoemaker W	121		*.45	86-13	Bramalea121½Cicad121noFrmPolcy1212 Hung final sixteenth 9
2Jun62-7Bel	fst	1⅛	:462 1:111 1:37 1:50	ⒻMother Goose 86k	6 1 15 14 11 11	Shoemaker W	121		*.85	86-15	Cicada1211FirmPolicy1214RoyalPatrice121½ Briskly ridden 6
19May62-7Aqu	fst	1	:223 :443 1:094 1:353	ⒻAcorn 58k	5 3 33 1hd 11 11½	Shoemaker W	121		*.25	90-10	Cicada1211½Tamarona121½Upswpt121½ Drifted in,ridden out 8
4May62-8CD	sly	1$\frac{1}{16}$	:234 :47 1:114 1:443	ⒻKy Oaks 42k	1 4 4¾ 11 13 13	Shoemaker W	121		*.10	89-18	Cicada1213Flaming Page1162¾Fortunate Isle1166 Easily 6
28Apr62-8CD	fst	7f	:222 :45 1:092 1:221	ⒻOaks Prep 16k	5 8 64½ 43 1hd 14	Shoemaker W	121		*.30	99-09	Cicada1214Dinner Partner1153Summer Sea118nk Handy score 12
31Mar62-7GP	fst	1⅛	:463 1:104 1:37 1:502	Florida Derby 125k	1 2 11 14 2½ 2no	Shoemaker W	117		2.45	82-17	Ridan122noCicada1176Admiral'sVoyag122hd Bore out,gamely 11
20Mar62-7GP	fst	6f	:221 :452 1:101	3↑ ⒻAlw 4000	3 4 56 31½ 11 13½	Shoemaker W	113		*.35	93-13	Ccada1133½Coupd'Etat117½PrimFlower1172½ Speed to spare 7
14Feb62-7Hia	fst	7f	:224 :451 1:094 1:23	3↑ ⒻColumbiana H 33k	8 7 54¼ 32½ 23 23	Valenzuela I	112		*.65	92-12	Smashing Gail1163Cicada1121½Seven Thirty1152 Game try 13
7Feb62-6Hia	fst	6f	:22 :45 1:101	3↑ ⒻAlw 5500	2 9 53½ 54 21½ 12¾	Shoemaker W	108		*.75	94-13	Cicada1082¾SevnThirty1153DreamOn114nk Stumbled,in hand 11
21Oct61-7GS	sly	1$\frac{1}{16}$	:23 :471 1:13 1:444	ⒻGardenia 161k	7 6 51¼ 16 16 110	Shoemaker W	122		*1.00	86-20	Cicada12210Narola1191¼Tamarona1198 Drew clear,eased up 8
7Oct61-7Aqu	fst	1	:233 :462 1:111 1:364	ⒻFrizette 121k	6 3 3½ 2hd 12 1½	Shoemaker W	119		*.65e	84-17	Cicada119½FirmPolicy1193½JazzQueen1192 Under hard drive 7
25Sep61-7Bel	fst	7f	:223 :461 1:112 1:242	ⒻAstarita 30k	6 10 85½ 83½ 4¾ 1hd	Shoemaker W	122		*.85	85-18	Cicada122hdFirmPolicy1162JzzQun112hd Slow start,driving 12
9Sep61-7Bel	fst	6f	:223 :46 1:103	ⒻMatron 98k	3 3 31½ 3nk 1½ 13½	Shoemaker W	119		*1.35	94-14	Cicada1193½Jazz Queen1191Pontivy1193 Drew out with ease 9
23Aug61-7Sar	fst	6f	:231 :463 1:12	ⒻSpinaway 80k	6 5 52 52½ 1½ 1nk	Valenzuela I	119		*.60e	88-12	Cicada119nkPontivy1193JazzQuen119¾ Saved ground,driving 8
7Aug61-7Sar	fst	6f	:222 :452 1:11	ⒻSchuylerville 29k	6 4 44 2½ 12 11½	Adams L	119		6.15	93-07	Cicada1191½BatterUp1222Bramale116¾ Kept to brisk urging 10
17Jly61-7Aqu	fst	5½f	:214 :451 :572 1:034	ⒻAstoria 27k	4 3 33½ 32 22 34½	Valenzuela I	113		2.85	95-12	Polylady1174½BatterUp123noCicad1231 Made bid,then tired 6
28Jun61-7Mth	fst	5½f	:213 :451 :574 1:04	ⒻColleen 24k	7 5 63 42 2hd 21	Valenzuela I	119		*1.30	97-18	BatterUp1191Cicada1196Pontivy1142¾ Bold rally,hung late 11
19Jun61-7Bel	fst	5½f	:223 :461 :583 1:052	ⒻNat'l Stallion 30k	3 3 21 21 2hd 11½	Valenzuela I	119		4.75e	94-20	Cicada1191½BatterUp1194JazzQueen1191 Going away,driving 8
10Jun61-5Del	gd	5f	:22 :462 :591	ⒻPolly Drummond 24k	3 1 1hd 1hd 2hd 21¾	Corle RE	122		2.80	91-21	Broadway1131¾Cicada122¾Miss Summer Time1131¼ Game try 9
30May61-5Del	fst	5f	:221 :463 :593	ⒻBlue Hen 11k	1 4 1hd 11 14 15½	Nelson E	116		3.90	91-22	Ccada1165½DodgeM114noFlshbck1101½ Going away with ease 12
25May61-6Aqu	fst	5f	:23 :47 :594	ⒻAlw 5000	5 4 2½ 2hd 11 13	Valenzuela I	116		*.35	91-19	Cicada1163Fingerling1121½Go on Green1125 Speed to spare 7
17May61-7Aqu	fst	5f	:224 :462 :584	ⒻFashion 24k	3 4 31½ 21½ 32 33¾	Valenzuela I	116		4.70	92-15	LaurelMae1163½StrBolt116nkCcd1161¾ Swerved late,brushed 9
17Mar61-3GP	fst	3f	:22 :332	Alw 5000	8 5 2hd 1no	Hinojosa H	112		6.45	- -	Cicada112noPryann115nkPortofMecc1121 Best in hard drive 14
10Mar61-3GP	fst	3f	:213 :324	Alw 3000	5 3 2½ 3¾	Ussery R	117		*1.90	- -	Mlle.Tessa112½GutterBall117nkCcd1173 Hung final strides 14
23Feb61-3Hia	fst	3f	:222 :34	ⒻMd Sp Wt	13 6 1½ 14¼	Ussery R	117		*1.15f	- -	Cicada1174¼AthensMiss117noSecretPort117¾ Bumped,in hand 14

Crimson Satan

ch. c. 1959, by Spy Song (Balladier)–Papila, by Requiebro
Own.– Crimson King Farm
Br.– Crimson King Farm (Ky)
Tr.– G.R. Potter

Lifetime record: 58 18 9 9 $796,077

24Oct64-8Haw	fst	1¼	:472 1:112 1:363 2:013	3↑ Gold Cup H 126k	4 9 86¾ 99¼ 913 813	Gargan D	120	b	10.30	75-13	GoingAbroad1202½Interceptd118½OldnTimes1231¾ No speed 9
3Oct64-6Kee	fst	1$\frac{1}{16}$	:233 :464 1:103 1:42	3↑ Fayette H 28k	4 9 98¼ 78¾ 814 821	Hinojosa H	120		3.90	75-12	Swoonen113½City Line1194Lemon Twist116¾ Raced far back 10
19Sep64-8Det	sly	1$\frac{1}{16}$	:23 :471 1:14 1:49	3↑ Mich 1$\frac{1}{16}$ H 72k	4 12 1221 1113 1023 1122	Hinojosa H	125	b	*2.80	36-34	DH GoingAbroad120 DH Tibaldo112nkCloseBy1152½ Fractious 12
12Sep64-9Det	fst	1$\frac{1}{16}$	:23 :464 1:112 1:442	3↑ Handicap 15000	7 10 1021 913 - -	Hinojosa H	126	b	*.60	- -	CityLine121¾Swoonen115½Tibaldo1141½ Unruly gate,bore in 10
Sulked											
5Sep64-9Det	fst	6f	:213 :442 1:092	3↑ Handicap 7500	6 7 712 66 42½ 12½	Hinojosa H	122	b	*.70	99-10	CrimsnSatan1222½YouLookCute109nkRedEff1205 Easy score 7
19Aug64-7Det	fst	6f	:22 :444 1:103	3↑ Alw 3000	1 9 54 21 2hd 34½	Gargan D	122	b	*1.50	88-16	MissMaru1091½LoriJ.1103CrimsonSatan122½ Bold bid,tired 9
21Jan64-7SA	gd	1$\frac{1}{16}$	:231 :464 1:114 1:442	4↑ San Pasqual H 28k	6 7 55 52½ 52¾ 55	Pierce D	126	b	*1.60	77-26	OldenTimes120¾DocJocoy118hdDonutKing1134 Wide on turn 8
15Jan64-7SA	fst	1$\frac{1}{16}$	:231 :462 1:104 1:422	4↑ Alw 10000	8 7 43 2hd 1hd 12	Pierce D	124	b	*2.20	92-11	Crimson Satan1242Pirate Cove121¾Aldershot118½ Driving 8
4Jan64-8SA	fst	7f	:221 :444 1:092 1:22	4↑ San Carlos H 59k	6 8 75 42 63¾ 811	Chambers W	123	b	11.10	82-14	Admiral'sVoyage1242Cyrano126¾NativeDiver125½ Fell back 8
2Nov63-8GS	my	1¼	:464 1:111 1:361 2:014	3↑ Trenton H 59k	10 10 108¼ 54½ 49 513	Shoemaker W	122	b	*3.30	83-22	Carry Back1192½Mongo1242Smart1166 Bold bid,weakened 10
19Oct63-8Haw	sl	1¼	:463 1:11 1:373 2:034	3↑ Haw Gold Cup H 127k	8 9 913 75½ 78½ 67	Shoemaker W	120	b	*1.10	70-17	AdmiralVic1221½DonutKing115½Pipr'sSon1103 Dismal effort 10
28Sep63-7Aqu	fst	1¼	:473 1:114 1:362 2:004	3↑ Woodward 108k	1 5 56½ 32½ 33½ 35	Hinojosa H	126	b	10.00	91-13	Kelso1263½NeverBend1201½CrimsonSatan1266 Bold bid,hung 5
14Sep63-8Atl	fm	1$\frac{3}{16}$Ⓣ	1:551	3↑ U Nations H 125k	5 10 109¼ 96¼ 94½ 87	Hinojosa H	125	b	9.30	90-03	Mongo1242Never Bend118¾Carry Back1271½ Failed to rally 10
Daily Racing Form time,1:54 2/5											
2Sep63-7Aqu	fst	1⅛	:49 1:124 1:371 1:494	3↑ Aqueduct 110k	3 8 89 66½ 45 25½	Hinojosa H	129	b	6.00	86-17	Kelso1345½Crimson Satan129hdGarwol116no Finished gamely 8
24Aug63-8AP	my	1⅛	:47 1:111 1:364 1:493	3↑ Wash Park H 113k	6 10 1016 911 33 12	Hinojosa H	126	b	*2.40	88-19	CrimsonSatan1262Piper'sSon110nkB.Major1174¼ Dwelt,wide 10
13Jly63-8Hol	fst	1¼	:45 1:09 1:333 1:593	3↑ Hol Gold Cup H 162k	3 9 914 62¼ 99¼ 1016	Hinojosa H	125	b	*.80	79-14	Cadz1111½Aldrshot1103OlympdKng111¾ Appeared unruly turn 10
22Jun63-9Det	fst	1$\frac{1}{16}$	:224 :453 1:103 1:403	3↑ Mich 1$\frac{1}{16}$ H 58k	9 10 96½ 61¼ 1½ 15½	Hinojosa H	128	b	*2.30	106-09	Crimson Satan1285½Decidedly117nkGreek Money1143 Easily 10
5Jun63-9Suf	fst	1¼	:461 1:101 1:351 2:011	3↑ Mass H 59k	1 10 914 11 1½ 12½	Hinojosa H	124	b	*2.10	99-12	CrimsnSatn1242½Admrl'sVoyg1253SunrsCounty120no Driving 11
30May63-7Aqu	fst	1	:223 :451 1:10 1:35	3↑ Metropolitan H 115k	3 11 118¾ 86½ 55 44	Hinojosa H	123	b	4.30	89-10	Cyrano1131½George Barton1142Sunrise County121½ Bore in 12
27Apr63-7Aqu	fst	1⅛	:482 1:111 1:361 1:50	3↑ Grey Lag H 84k	4 6 42 1hd 12 21¼	Gomez A	123	b	3.25	90-18	SunriseCounty1181¼CrimsnSatan1231½Decidedly120¾ Sulked 9
23Mar63-8Bow	fst	1$\frac{1}{16}$	:242 :481 1:12 1:43	3↑ J B Campbell H 109k	1 6 69½ 57¾ 34½ 2¾	Hinojosa H	124	b	6.70	97-15	Kelso131¾Crimson Satan124hdGushing Wind1166 Late rush 6
9Mar63-7SA	fm	*1¾Ⓣ	2:481	3↑ S Juan Capistrano H 115k	6 4 11½ 2hd 89½ 1217	Hinojosa H	125	b	*2.90	69-15	Pardao119nkJuanro114nkRablero119½ Early speed,stopped 13
23Feb63-7SA	fst	1¼	:462 1:103 1:352 2:004	3↑ S Anita H 145k	9 11 106½ 32 34½ 25½•	Hinojosa H	125	b	*.90	89-13	Crozier1225½ DH Game108 DH CrimsonSatan1253¼ Evenly late 14
9Feb63-7SA	sly	1⅛	:472 1:114 1:374 1:51	4↑ San Antonio H 58k	2 5 51¾ 12 13 21	Hinojosa H	127	b	*1.30	76-21	Physician1171CrimsonSatan1279¼Gam1072½ Clear lead,tired 6
26Jan63-7SA	fst	1¼	:464 1:113 1:352 2:003	C H Strub 137k	6 14 147½ 13 18 15¾	Hinojosa H	118	b	*.70	96-10	CrimsonSatan1185¾PirateCove1142Dr.Kacy112nk Easily best 16
12Jan63-7SA	fst	1⅛	:453 1:093 1:344 1:471	San Fernando 58k	12 7 49½ 2½ 2½ 1nk	Hinojosa H	117	b	1.70	96-12	CrimsonSatan117nkNativeDiver12010PirateCove1142 Driving 14
5Jan63-7SA	fst	7f	:214 :442 1:084 1:211	4↑ San Carlos H 61k	4 10 911 97¾ 87¾ 46	Hinojosa H	121	b	20.60	91-12	Crozier1241¼OldenTimes125noNativeDiver1254¾ Mild rally 10
17Nov62-8CD	gd	1⅛	:482 1:13 1:372 1:50	3↑ Clark H 27k	3 7 64½ 55 1½ 11¼	Hinojosa H	121	b	*1.80	92-18	CrimsonSatan1211¼TumbleTurbie116hdBassClef1173 Driving 8

10Sep62-8AP	sf 1 3/16 (T)	:484 1:121 1:382 1:583 3↑	Arlington H 57k	10	11	89	75¾	73¾	21	Gomez A	122 b	*1.40	73-24	El Bandito1151Crimson Satan122nkRablero109no	Slow start	13
1Sep62-8AP	fm 1 1/16 (T)	:231 :463 1:11 1:42	Laurance Armour H 33k	6	7	52¼	2hd	12	12½	Gomez A	123 b	3.40	99-04	CrimsnSatn1232½TumbleTurbi1091½GshngWnd1221¼	Driving	10
18Aug62-8Tdn	fst 1⅛	:461 1:102 1:351 1:48 3↑	Buckeye H 29k	10	9	88	51	32½	36¼	Baldwin R	121 b	*1.20	94-10	GushngWind1181½BlackBeard1114¾CrmsnStn1213	No excuse	10
11Aug62-8Tdn	fst 1 1/16	:232 :47 1:112 1:423 3↑	Handicap 7500	3	6	59	32½	31½	1nk	Baldwin R	119 b	*1.10	102-12	Crimson Satan119nkMysticMountain1092½Touch Bar112½	Bore in,up	6
1Aug62-8Mth	fst 1 1/16	:232 :472 1:104 1:42	Choice 56k	3	5	53½	54	44½	35¼	Ycaza M	118 b	2.90	90-16	Jaipur1264½Cyane126¾Crimson Satan118¾	Forced wide late	8
14Jly62-7Aqu	fst 1¼	:471 1:104 1:36 2:013	Dwyer H 84k	1	6	32	11½	3½	47½	Gilligan L	125 b	*1.30	90-11	Cyane116¾Flying Johnnie1114Noble Jay1192¾	Bore out turn	9
23Jun62-6Del	fst 1⅛	:473 1:112 1:374 1:504	Leonard Richards 42k	1	5	32½	2hd	12	11¼	Gilligan L	122 b	*.80	83-20	Crimson Satan1221¼Noble Jay1193½Cyane1194½	Handy score	6
	Disqualified from purse money															
9Jun62-7Bel	fst 1½	:482 1:121 2:021 2:284	Belmont 153k	1	4	33	31	3½	31¼	Ycaza M	126 b	3.80	88-11	Jaipur126noAdmiral'sVoyage1261¼CrimsonSatn1266½	Bore in	8
30May62-8GS	fst 1⅛	:47 1:102 1:354 1:49	Jersey Derby 130k	6	6	52	3nk	1hd	1no	Gilligan L	126 b	10.10	92-14	[D]CrimsonSatan126noJaipur126noAdmiral'sVoyg1261	Bore in	12
	Disqualified and placed third															
19May62-8Pim	fst 1 3/16	:474 1:114 1:37 1:561	Preakness 188k	7	6	63¾	62¼	58	712	Phelps B	126 b	13.80	80-13	Greek Money126noRidan1265½RomanLine1261¾	No mishap	11
5May62-7CD	fst 1¼	:454 1:101 1:351 2:002	Ky Derby 162k	11	14	1418	1012	64¾	66¼	Phelps B	126 b	21.50	99-06	Decidedly1262¼RomanLin126nkRdn126nk	Bumped at the start	15
26Apr62-6Kee	fst 1⅛	:473 1:111 1:354 1:473	Blue Grass 33k	6	8	68	54¼	42½	58½	Phelps B	126 b	2.50	90-10	Ridan1264Decidedly1212¼Roman Line1262¼	Wide stretch bid	9
7Apr62-7Kee	fst 6f	:222 :453 1:102	Alw 5000	4	7	57	22½	12	15	Phelps B	122 b	*.70	92-14	CrimsnSatan1225LeeTown1192¼LoilRoil1163	Scored handily	8
3Mar62-7Hia	fst 1⅛	:452 1:094 1:353 1:49	Flamingo 136k	10	10	1019	1015	912	715	Shoemaker W	122 b	2.80	75-09	[D]SunriseCounty1221½Prego122nkRidan1224½	Showed nothing	10
21Feb62-7Hia	fst 1⅛	:46 1:101 1:353 1:482	Everglades 30k	8	9	914	78	614	516	Shoemaker W	126 b	2.30	77-14	SirGaylord1264¾Decidedly1143[D]Ridan126½	Stumbled start	9
7Feb62-7Hia	fst 7f	:223 :452 1:092 1:22	Bahamas 30k	3	8	813	78¾	34½	35	Shoemaker W	126 b	3.80	95-13	SirGaylord1261¾Ridan1263¼CrimsonSatan1266	Bold bid,hung	8
30Jan62-7Hia	fst 6f	:223 :453 1:092	Alw 6000	7	9	75¾	32	2hd	2¾	Gilligan L	122 b	3.50	97-14	SirGaylord122¾CrimsonSatan1221½FloridnBy1107	Mild drive	11
18Nov61-8Pim	gd 1 1/16	:24 :474 1:13 1:462	Pim Futurity 116k	7	7	75¼	2½	12	15	Shoemaker W	122 b	*.30	78-21	CrimsonSatan1225GreenTicket122nkEndymion1221	Mild drive	7
4Nov61-7GS	fst 1 1/16	:232 :47 1:112 1:441	Garden State 301k	5	11	85¾	43½	13	12½	Shoemaker W	122 b	*1.30	89-15	CrimsnSatn1222½DonutKng122noOby1228	Under brisk drive	11
28Oct61-5GS	fst 1 1/16	:242 :48 1:121 1:441	Alw 10000	2	4	31½	31	1hd	17	Shoemaker W	122 b	*1.10	89-13	Crimson Satan1227Pinsetter112nkDecidedly1123	Easy score	12
14Oct61-7Aqu	fst 1	:231 :462 1:111 1:36	Champagne 206k	8	10	8¾	54	43½	42	Phelps B	122 b	6.85	85-16	DonutKing122hdJaipur1222SirGaylord122no	Stride too late	10
7Oct61-8Haw	fst 1 1/16	:224 :46 1:111 1:431	Haw Juv (Div 2) 18k	3	9	713	45	15	16	Phelps B	114 b	*.90	91-13	Crimson Satan1146Treasury Note1141½Affray1145	Easily	9
30Sep61-7Haw	sly 1 1/16	:231 :472 1:132 1:472	Alw 5000	10	8	56	2hd	16	16	Phelps B	113 b	4.30	70-25	Crimson Satan1136Dogeola1137Neck Bones113nk	Hard urged	11
22Sep61-6Haw	fst 6½f	:222 :451 1:101 1:172	Alw 6000	1	9	43½	33½	2½	2nk	Carstens W	114 b	*1.20	87-21	Renade113nkCrimsonSatn114noCraftyActor1131½	Slow start	9
13Sep61-8Haw	sl 6f	:222 :462 1:13	©Alw 10000	3	8	64	32	31	22	Carstens W	122 b	7.20	80-26	LoilRoil1132CrimsonSatan1221PutOff116¾	Game effort	8
21Jun61-8AP	fst 5½f	:223 :46 :581 1:042	Hyde Park 17k	8	6	51¼	3½	46	69¼	Carstens W	122 b	28.20	86-16	Ridan1226GreenHornet119noPortofMecca119no	Well up,tired	8
14Jun61-6Was	fst 5½f	:222 :451 :572 1:032	Alw 5000	5	6	52¾	21½	33½	38	Carstens W	122 b	5.40	90-13	Ridan1176Obey1142Crimson Satan1223	Well placed,tired	7
26Apr61-6Kee	fst *4f	:49	Lafayette 15k	6	7		42½	1½	11¾	Carstens W	117 b	2.10	97-07	CrimsnSatn1171¾MikeG.1176JettingHome117hd	Handy score	7
18Apr61-3Kee	gd *4f	:492	Md Sp Wt	4	3		33½	22	1¾	Carstens W	120 b	*1.40	95-06	Crimson Satan120¾Tom Turkey1205Dusty Guy1207	Driving	7
11Apr61-2Kee	gd *4f	:50	©Md Sp Wt	3	5		3nk	21½	3¾	Carstens W	119 b	*2.00	91-09	I'mforMore119¾Uppercut119hdCrimsonSatan1193½	Game try	12

Damascus

b. c. 1964, by Sword Dancer (Sunglow)–Kerala, by My Babu — Lifetime record: 32 21 7 3 $1,176,781

Own.– Mrs Edith W. Bancroft
Br.– Mrs Thomas Bancroft (Ky)
Tr.– F.Y. Whiteley Jr

26Oct68-7Bel	gd 2	:502 2:313 3:224 3↑	J C Gold Cup 109k	1	3	48	612	624	637	Adams L	124	*1.30	48-16	QuickenTree1241¼FunnyFllow1193½Chmpon1193	Bowed tendon	6
28Sep68-7Bel	fst 1¼	:472 1:113 1:37 2:03 3↑	Woodward 106k	3	2	1hd	1hd	1hd	2no	Baeza B	126	*.10	85-16	Mr. Right126noDamascus1267Grace Born12616	Just failed	4
14Sep68-9Det	fst 1⅛	:471 1:111 1:361 1:49 3↑	Mich 1⅛ H 123k	1	9	1014	79½	66¾	22¾	Baeza B	133	*.30e	93-19	Nodouble1112¾Dmscs133hdMstyRun1092¼	Very wide stretch	12
2Sep68-7Aqu	fst 1⅛	:47 1:11 1:354 1:482 3↑	Aqueduct 108k	4	3	35	33	2½	11½	Baeza B	134	*.40	94-13	Damascus1341½More Scents1148Fort Drum1143	Going away	6
10Aug68-8Del	fst 1 1/16	:24 :484 1:123 1:433 3↑	W Du Pont H 53k	4	5	31	2hd	1hd	12	Baeza B	134	*.20	91-20	Damascus1342BigRockCandy113¾CharlesElliott11010	Driving	5
20Jly68-7Aqu	fst 1¼	:454 1:092 1:343 1:591 3↑	Brooklyn H 109k	2	5	511	2½	1½	12½	Ycaza M	130	1.40e	102-13	Damascus1302½Dr. Fager1353Mr. Right114hd	Won going away	7
13Jly68-8Mth	fst 1¼	:48 1:121 1:371 2:03 3↑	AL Haskell H 111k	6	6	68	33	21	31½	Ycaza M	131	*.60	85-16	BoldHour1161½Mr.Rght114nkDmscus1315	Stumbled after start	8
4Jly68-7Aqu	fst 1¼	:482 1:11 1:343 1:593 3↑	Suburban H 107k	1	2	2½	2hd	22	35	Ycaza M	133	1.40	95-11	Dr. Fager1322Bold Hour1163Damascus1333½	Failed to rally	5
17Jun68-5Del	fst 1 70	:234 :473 1:114 1:402 4↑	Alw 10000	3	3	24	2hd	11	13¾	Ycaza M	124	*.10	98-16	Damascus1243¾LighttheFuse1196ClassicWork120nk	Handily	5
10Feb68-8SA	sl 1¼	:482 1:131 1:382 2:04	C H Strub 118k	1	5	57	1½	1hd	2hd	Turcotte R	126	*.20	78-22	Most Host114hdDamscs12610Ruken117½	Gave way gradually	6
20Jan68-6SA	fst 1⅛	:49 1:13 1:371 1:484	San Fernando 56k	4	2	2½	1hd	11	12	Shoemaker W	126	*.10	88-12	Damascs1262Most Host113hdRuken1204½	Won drawing clear	6
6Jan68-8SA	fst 7f	:223 :45 1:09 1:211	Malibu 45k	4	1	32½	3½	1½	12½	Shoemaker W	126	*.40	97-15	Damascus1262½Rising Market120nkRuken1231	Handily	8
11Nov67-7Lrl	fm 1½ (T)	:491 1:14 2:03 2:27 3↑	D C Int'l 150k	2	4	43½	3½	2hd	2no	Shoemaker W	120	*.60	84-13	FortMarcy120noDmascus1202½TobinBronze1272½	Just failed	9
28Oct67-7Aqu	fst 2	:494 2:302 2:554 3:201 3↑	J C Gold Cup 106k	1	2	22	2hd	14	14½	Shoemaker W	119	*.30	95-12	Dmascus1194½HandsomBoy1247½Successr1196½	Handy score	4
30Sep67-7Aqu	fst 1¼	:451 1:091 1:353 2:003 3↑	Woodward 107k	5	5	512	1½	15	110	Shoemaker W	120	1.80e	95-15	Damascus12010Buckpasser126½Dr. Fager12013	Easy score	6
4Sep67-7Aqu	fst 1⅛	:482 1:121 1:361 1:481 3↑	Aqueduct 106k	3	3	34	32	1hd	12	Shoemaker W	125	*.30	95-14	Damascus1252Ring Twice119½Straight Deal1166	Handily	5
19Aug67-6Sar	sly 1¼	:454 1:11 1:364 2:013	Travers 80k	4	3	316	16	110	122	Shoemaker W	126	*.20	100-10	Damascus12622Reason to Hail1207Tumiga1175	Won eased up	4
5Aug67-8AP	fst 1⅛	:46 1:101 1:343 1:464	American Derby 120k	2	6	612	66¼	14	17	Shoemaker W	126	*.80	101-16	Damascus1267InReality1203FavorableTurn1121½	Ridden out	7
15Jly67-7Aqu	sly 1¼	:473 1:12 1:374 2:03	Dwyer H 83k	6	9	912	21	1hd	1¾	Shoemaker W	128	*.50	83-18	Damascus128¾FavorableTurn1122½BlastingChrg116hd	Driving	9
8Jly67-8Del	fst 1 1/16	:234 :471 1:104 1:421 3↑	W Du Pont Jr H 54k	4	5	58	43	21	2no	Shoemaker W	121	*.20	98-12	Exceedingly113noDamascus1214Flag Raiser1145	Hung	5
17Jun67-8Del	fst 1⅛	:47 1:113 1:37 1:491	Leonard Richards 41k	4	4	32½	1½	1hd	13¼	Turcotte R	126	*.10	91-13	Damascus1263¼Misty Cloud1191½Favorable Turn1192½	Easily	6
3Jun67-8Aqu	fst 1½	:47 1:122 2:023 2:284	Belmont 148k	1	6	59½	31	2hd	12½	Shoemaker W	126	*.80	87-15	Dmascus1262½CoolReception126½GentlmanJams1261	In hand	9
20May67-8Pim	fst 1 3/16	:462 1:104 1:364 1:551	Preakness 194k	2	9	811	86	13½	12¼	Shoemaker W	126	*1.80e	97-11	Damascus1262¼In Reality1264Proud Clarion126¾	Ridden out	10
6May67-7CD	fst 1¼	:463 1:104 1:36 2:003	Ky Derby 162k	2	6	44	41½	32	34	Shoemaker W	126	*1.70	93-07	ProudClarion1261BarbsDelight1263Damascus1261¼	Bid,hung	14
22Apr67-7Aqu	fst 1⅛	:462 1:104 1:363 1:493	Wood Memorial 112k	4	3	45	42	11	16	Shoemaker W	126	*.70	88-16	Damascus1266Gala Performance1263Dawn Glory1261½	Easily	9
15Apr67-7Aqu	fst 1	:233 :461 1:102 1:351	Gotham 57k	9	2	23	2hd	1hd	2½	Shoemaker W	122	*1.30	91-14	Dr. Fager122½Damascus1225Reason to Hail1147	Game try	9
25Mar67-7Aqu	my 7f	:224 :464 1:124 1:254	Bay Shore 28k	1	4	46	45½	22	12½	Shoemaker W	115	2.40	77-35	Damascus1152½Disciplinarian1171½Nhoc'sBullt1103	Driving	7
11Mar67-7Pim	fst 6f	:233 :472 1:121	Alw 5000	8	3	31½	42	53¼	1hd	Shuk N	122	*.60	89-16	Dmascus122hdSolar Bomb1221½Last Cry119½	Bumped late,up	8
30Nov66-7Aqu	gd 1	:231 :46 1:112 1:37	Remsen 30k	2	3	2hd	32	4¾	11½	Shoemaker W	117	*1.30	83-22	Damascus1171½NativeGuile117½ReflectedGlory119¾	Driving	14
29Oct66-3Lrl	fst 7f	:224 :462 1:121 1:251	©Alw 4000	2	1	1½	12	19	112	Shoemaker W	119	*.40	93-16	Damascus11912Joxer1153½Roman Away1172½	Scored in hand	7
12Oct66-5Aqu	fst 7f	:23 :462 1:12 1:243	©Md Sp Wt	8	1	11	11	14	18	Shoemaker W	122	*.90	83-18	Damascus1228Winslow Homer1225Gun Mount1221	Easily	14
28Sep66-4Aqu	fst 7f	:223 :46 1:113 1:243	©Md Sp Wt	11	9	76	77½	32½	22½	Shoemaker W	122	*2.60	80-19	Comprador1222½Damascus122¾Air Rights1221	Game try	14

Dark Mirage

dkbbr. f. 1965, by Persian Road II (Persian Gulf)–Home by Dark, by Hill Prince — Lifetime record: 27 12 3 2 $362,788

Own.– L.I. Miller
Br.– Duval A. Headley (Ky)
Tr.– E.W. King

Date / Race	Trk	Dist	Fractions	Race	Positions	Jockey	Wt	Eq	Odds	Figs	Top finishers	Comment	Fld
1Mar69- 8SA	sl	1⅛	:482 1:131 1:393 1:53 4↑	ⒻS Margarita H 100k	5 5 - - - - -	Belmonte E	130		*.70	- -	Princessnesian125noGuest Room116 1¾Sinking Spring113¾		9
Roughed at start,ducked out turn,broke down													
12Feb69- 8SA	fst	1 1/16	:232 :47 1:111 1:43 4↑	ⒻS Maria H 33k	2 3 41¾ 51¾ 4¾ 1nk	Belmonte E	126		*1.00	88-17	DarkMirage126nkDesertLaw115noSinkingSpring1122	Driving	7
27Jly68- 0Del	fst	1⅛	:473 1:114 1:374 1:502	ⒻDel Oaks 57k	2 3 36 22½ 2hd 12	Ycaza M	121		-	85-20	Dark Mirage1212Sale Day1148Singing Rain1172	Mild drive	4
Exhibition race,run between 7th and 8th races - No wagering													
4Jly68- 8Mth	fst	1⅛	:471 1:121 1:382 1:512	ⒻMth Oaks 54k	3 4 43 2hd 1½ 14	Ycaza M	121		*.20	87-22	Dark Mirage1214Singing Rain1185Guest Room117hd	Easily	6
22Jun68- 7Bel	fst	1¼	:482 1:121 1:364 2:014	ⒻC C A Oaks 116k	4 3 21 13 16 112	Ycaza M	121		*.10	91-15	Dark Mirage12112Gay Matelda1216Syrian Sea1211¼	Easily	6
8Jun68- 7Bel	fst	1⅛	:452 1:101 1:36 1:492	ⒻMother Goose 85k	5 5 55½ 41½ 12½ 110	Ycaza M	121		*.20	89-15	Dark Mirage12110Guest Room121nkParida1211	Easy score	6
25May68- 7Bel	fst	1	:224 :46 1:102 1:344	ⒻAcorn 60k	2 4 42 21 1½ 16	Ycaza M	121		*1.30	100-11	Dark Mirage1216Another Nell121nkGay Matelda1212½	Easily	12
3May68- 8CD	fst	1 1/16	:243 :48 1:123 1:443	ⒻKy Oaks 63k	4 9 86½ 54½ 2½ 14½	Ycaza M	121		*1.20	89-17	DarkMirge1214½MissRibot121½LadyTramp1213½	Handy score	14
27Apr68- 8CD	fst	7f	:23 :463 1:114 1:243	ⒻLa Troienne 16k	10 8 68 55 21 13	Ycaza M	121		2.70	84-18	Dark Mirage1213Lady Tramp1211Yes Sir1182	Ridden out	12
3Apr68- 7Aqu	fst	6f	:221 :451 1:104	ⒻPrioress 27k	5 3 66 42 21½ 11	Cordero A Jr	121		6.00	89-17	Dark Mirage1211Guest Room121nkPleasantness1213	Driving	6
22Mar68- 6Aqu	fst	1	:233 :47 1:11 1:362 3↑	ⒻAlw 12000	7 1 11½ 13 16 19	Turcotte R	112		*1.00	86-23	Dark Mirage1129Castaneye1118Wild Beauty1132	Easily best	7
15Mar68- 7Aqu	gd	6f	:224 :46 1:104	ⒻAlw 15000	1 5 55½ 55 46½ 47½	Turcotte R	114		13.60	81-21	Pleasantness1184CockeyMiss1182LucretiBor1181½	No threat	5
7Dec67- 7Aqu	fst	7f	:233 :471 1:122 1:252	ⒻAlw 15000	6 3 63¾ 43 21 2½	Turcotte R	116		3.30	78-25	APleasantSort115½DarkMirage116¾Teddy'sTrue1192	Sharp	8
30Nov67- 7Aqu	fst	6f	:222 :453 1:101	ⒻAlw 15000	9 10 1011 1014 914 611	Ycaza M	116		4.70	81-18	GuestRoom1166½Teddy'sTrue1161½TwiceCited1161	No speed	11
22Nov67- 7Aqu	fst	1	:233 :47 1:121 1:38	ⒻAlw 15000	2 5 52¾ 3nk 1hd 2hd	Ycaza M	115		5.60	78-22	Good Game116hdDark Mirage115nkA Pleasant Sort1129	Sharp	6
11Nov67- 8GS	fst	1 1/16	:234 :472 1:12 1:454	ⒻGardenia 187k	8 11 1012 883 65½ 52½	Gavidia W	119		112.70	73-21	Gay Matelda119noGo Go Windy119noPleasantness1191½	Wide	11
1Nov67- 7GS	fst	1 70	:224 :482 1:112 1:423	ⒻAlw 10000	2 6 65¼ 813 88¼ 57½	Ycaza M	115		13.00	73-23	Pleasantness112noObeah1137Amadancer112hd	Showed little	8
25Oct67- 6Aqu	fst	7f	:221 :45 1:101 1:231	ⒻAlw 10000	4 8 66 65 44½ 34	Ruane J	114	b	18.20	86-12	Yes Sir1163Allie's Serenade1121Dark Mirage1141½	Rallied	8
14Oct67- 6Kee	fst	*7f	1:28	ⒻAlcibiades 50k	2 9 33½ 45 1118 1118	Grubb L	119	b	34.60	65-19	Lady Tramp1195Sweet Tooth119¾Walk My Lady1191¼	Tired	12
27Sep67- 7Aqu	fst	7f	:214 :44 1:093 1:223	ⒻAstarita 29k	7 3 44½ 33 77½ 712	Ruane J	116	b	18.00	81-13	SyrianSea1194GoodGame116½DawnofTomorrw1121¾	Fell back	10
16Sep67- 8CD	fst	7f	:223 :454 1:104 1:234	ⒻGolden Rod 62k	13 7 910 46 43½ 43¾	Ruane J	113		22.80	84-13	Shenow1191Moss1131¼Lady Tramp1161½	Stride late	13
9Sep67- 7Aqu	fst	6f	:221 :452 1:10	ⒻMatron 104k	1 7 63¾ 67 67½ 612	Ruane J	119		16.50	81-16	QueenoftheStag1194GayMatlda119¾SyrianSea1193	No threat	7
12Aug67- 4Sar	fst	6f	:22 :453 1:121	ⒻAlw 7000	2 12 54 56 31 11	Ruane J	119		4.30	87-11	Dark Mirage1191Someday109½Sassy Piece113nk	Drew clear	12
2Aug67- 6Sar	fst	5½f	:223 :461 :582 1:043	ⒻMd Sp Wt	7 3 31 2½ 1½ 14	Ruane J	119		5.20	94-08	Dark Mirage1194Chenille119noBest in Show1191	Easy score	11
26Jly67- 3Aqu	gd	5½f	:222 :454 :581 1:044	ⒻMd Sp Wt	10 7 66¾ 611 36½ 36¾	Caceres A	119		4.20	82-15	Ave Valeque1196Terri Tyker119¾Dark Mirage1196	Fair try	12
19Jly67- 3Aqu	fst	5½f	:221 :46 :584 1:052	ⒻMd Sp Wt	7 11 73¼ 64½ 64¾ 22½	Caceres A	119		101.00	83-13	FullofLaughs1092½DarkMirage1192½EsteNoche119hd	Sharp	12
14Jly67- 4Mth	fst	5½f	:222 :462 :593 1:063	ⒻMd Sp Wt	5 6 77 69 57 67¼	Brumfield D	117		21.50	77-19	TwiceCitd1171½WalkMyLdy1171BwamznLdy1173½	No threat	11

Dr. Fager

b. c. 1964, by Rough'n Tumble (Free for All)–Aspidistra, by Better Self — Lifetime record: 22 18 2 1 $1,002,642

Own.– Tartan Stable
Br.– Tartan Farms (Fla)
Tr.– John A. Nerud

Date / Race	Trk	Dist	Fractions	Race	Positions	Jockey	Wt	Eq	Odds	Figs	Top finishers	Comment	Fld
2Nov68- 7Aqu	fst	7f	:221 :434 1:074 1:201 3↑	Vosburgh H 57k	3 4 1hd 1hd 13 16	Baeza B	139		*.30	105-12	Dr.Fager1396Kissin'George1276JmJ.125hd	Under mild drive	7
11Sep68- 8Atl	fm	1 3/16Ⓣ	:484 1:123 1:364 1:551 3↑	U Nations H 100k	6 1 1hd 2hd 1hd 1nk	Baeza B	134		*.80	94-10	Dr.Fgr134nkAdvoctor1121¼FortMrcy1181¼	Under stiff drive	9
24Aug68- 8AP	fst	1	:224 :44 1:073 1:321 3↑	Washington Park H 112k	9 6 2hd 1½ 13 110	Baeza B	134		*.30	102-10	Dr. Fager13410Racing Room1161½Info1121	Easily best	10
3Aug68- 6Sar	fst	1⅛	:471 1:113 1:363 1:484 3↑	Whitney 53k	2 1 1½ 13 13 18	Baeza B	132		*.05	97-12	Dr. Fager1328Spoon Bait1141Fort Drum11415	Much the best	4
20Jly68- 7Aqu	fst	1¼	:454 1:092 1:343 1:591 3↑	Brooklyn H 109k	3 2 21½ 1½ 2½ 22½	Baeza B	135		*.60	99-13	Damascus1302½Dr.Fager1353Mr.Right114hd	Rank early going	7
4Jly68- 7Aqu	fst	1¼	:482 1:11 1:343 1:593 3↑	Suburban H 107k	3 1 1½ 1hd 12 12	Baeza B	132		*.80	100-11	Dr.Fager1322BoldHour1163Damascus1333½	Under mild drive	5
18May68- 8Hol	fst	1 1/16	:222 :45 1:083 1:404 3↑	Californian 119k	11 4 2½ 1½ 14 13	Baeza B	130		*1.20	91-13	Dr. Fager1303Gamely1161Rising Market1211½	Much the best	14
4May68- 7Aqu	fst	7f	:222 :45 1:084 1:212 3↑	Roseben H 54k	5 1 1½ 11 13 13	Rotz JL	130		*.20	99-17	Dr. Fager1303Tumiga1213Diplomat Way121¾	Won eased up	5
7Nov67- 7Aqu	fst	7f	:222 :451 1:093 1:213 3↑	Vosburgh H 57k	6 8 52½ 2hd 1hd 14½	Baeza B	128		*.20e	98-16	Dr. Fager1284½Jim J.1151½R. Thomas1223	Wide,easily best	9
21Oct67- 8Haw	fst	1¼	:461 1:101 1:351 2:011 3↑	Haw Gold Cup H 121k	1 1 1½ 1hd 11½ 12½	Baeza B	123		*.30	90-12	Dr.Fagr1232½WhisprJt1141¼Pontmnow1081¼	Without urging	7
30Sep67- 7Aqu	fst	1¼	:451 1:091 1:353 2:003 3↑	Woodward 107k	2 1 1hd 2½ 25 310½	Boland W	120		1.80	84-15	Damascus12010Buckpasser126½Dr. Fager12013	Faltered	6
2Sep67- 8Rkm	fst	1¼	:463 1:11 1:351 1:594	NH Sweep Classic 265k	1 1 1½ 2hd 2hd 11¼	Baeza B	120		*.20	115-17	Dr.Fager1201¼InReality1269BarbsDelight1152¾	Mild drive	5
15Jly67- 9Rkm	fst	1⅛	:462 1:101 1:353 1:481	Rkm Spl 85k	5 1 16½ 13½ 13½ 14¼	Baeza B	124		*.10	105-15	Dr.Fager1244¼ReasontoHail1214¾JackofAllTrds1128¼	Easily	7
24Jun67- 8AP	sly	1	:224 :45 1:102 1:36	AP Classic 106k	1 3 3nk 13 16 110	Baeza B	120		*.40	83-25	Dr.Fagr12010LightningOrphan1161¾DiplomatWay1187	Easily	6
30May67- 7GS	fst	1⅛	:47 1:103 1:353 1:48	Jersey Derby 119k	4 1 1½ 12 13 16½	Ycaza M	126		*.30	97-14	ⒹDr.Fager1266½InReality1268AirRghts12612	Crowded field	4
Disqualified and placed fourth													
13May67- 7Aqu	fst	1	:223 :441 1:08 1:334	Withers 58k	8 4 21 2hd 11½ 16	Baeza B	126		*.80	99-16	Dr. Fager1266Tumiga1265Reason to Hail1265	Easy score	8
15Apr67- 7Aqu	fst	1	:233 :461 1:102 1:351	Gotham 57k	5 4 33 3nk 2hd 1½	Ycaza M	122		*1.30e	92-14	Dr. Fager122½Damascus1225Reason to Hail1147	Driving	9
15Oct66- 7Aqu	fst	1	:222 :444 1:092 1:35	Champagne 208k	7 4 3½ 1hd 13 21	Shoemaker W	122		*1.00	92-14	Successor1221Dr. Fager1224Proviso1224	Rank early,failed	10
5Oct66- 7Aqu	gd	7f	:224 :46 1:113 1:244	Cowdin 88k	1 10 31 32 21½ 1¾	Shoemaker W	117		*.80	82-22	Dr.Fager117¾InRlty1171½Succssor1172½	Slow start,driving	10
10Sep66- 8Atl	fst	7f	:223 :452 1:103 1:231	World's Playground 28k	3 6 1hd 1½ 14 112	Ycaza M	115		*.90	87-24	Dr. Fager11512Glengary1153½Pointsman115hd	Much the best	11
13Aug66- 4Sar	fst	6f	:223 :462 1:102	Alw 5500	5 5 21½ 22 12 18	Hidalgo D5	117		*.90	96-09	Dr. Fager1178Bandera Road1172Quaker City1152	Easily	8
15Jly66- 3Aqu	fst	5½f	:224 :464 :59 1:05	©Md Sp Wt	8 8 83 21 11½ 17	Hidalgo D5	117		10.80	88-20	Dr. Fager1177Lift Off1224Rising Market122½	Easily best	11

Fast Attack

b. f. 1967, by Your Alibhai (Alibhai)–Fusilade, by Phalanx — Lifetime record: 29 7 4 5 $184,205

Own.– Har-Bar Ranch
Br.– Elcee-H Breeding Farms Inc (Ky)
Tr.– Harry Wells

Date / Race	Trk	Dist	Fractions	Race	Positions	Jockey	Wt	Eq	Odds	Figs	Top finishers	Comment	Fld
11Nov70- 8GS	sly	1 1/16	:232 :463 1:112 1:444	ⒻJersey Belle H 29k	2 5 43½ 26 32 2½	Blum W	118	b	5.10	80-21	Predictabl115½FstAttck1183I'mforMm1104	Rallied,no match	10
3Nov70- 8GS	fst	1 70	:222 :452 1:102 1:411	ⒻPrinceton H (Div 2) 24k	2 5 34 33 32 22	Blum W	120	b	*1.00	86-23	PeacefulUnion1122FastAttack120hdI'mforMama1105	Gamely	10
26Oct70- 7GS	fst	1 70	:23 :463 1:112 1:412	ⒻAlw 8000	2 2 2hd 13 14 17	Blum W	118	b	*.70	87-17	Fast Attack1187Imsodear112½Private Parking113no	Easily	9
19Oct70- 8GS	fst	1⅛	:462 1:103 1:362 1:491 3↑	ⒻVineland H 59k	2 4 33 74½ 73¼ 73½	Blum W	113		11.20	87-12	CathyHoney113¾DarkEmerld1111DedictdtoSu116no	No mishap	10
3Oct70- 8Atl	fst	1 3/16	:47 1:111 1:364 1:562 3↑	ⒻMatchmaker 50k	5 7 67¾ 68 78½ 69½	Patterson G	114		6.10e	84-15	Dedicated toSue1131½ColdComfort1085ⒹHelenJennings115no		10
No factor													
23Sep70- 8Atl	fst	1⅛	:484 1:13 1:381 1:503 3↑	ⒻAlw 8000	4 7 64 41¾ 32½ 21¾	Patterson G	109		2.40e	83-20	OfficeQueen1191¾FastAttack1091HelenJennings1233	Gamely	9
5Sep70- 7Bel	fst	1⅛	:471 1:121 1:374 1:504	ⒻGazelle H 58k	7 7 65¼ 55½ 65¼ 53	Vasquez J	117		11.40	77-14	MissileBelle120nkPredictable114nkFnfrluch1221	No mishap	10
28Aug70- 8Atl	fst	1 1/16	:233 :472 1:113 1:441 3↑	ⒻAlw 8000	5 6 33 3½ 1hd 1nk	Blum W	112		*.70	86-19	FastAttack112nkDeb'sDarling113nkPrizeStudnt1136	Driving	8
15Aug70- 6Sar	fst	1¼	:481 1:122 1:373 2:034	ⒻAlabama 59k	2 8 88½ 66½ 55½ 43¾	Thornburg B	118		11.10	85-10	Fanfreluche1181½Hunnemannia1142Office Queen124½	Rallied	12
8Aug70- 7Lib	fst	1 1/16	:232 :464 1:112 1:44	ⒻCotillion H 57k	2 6 52½ 41½ 21½ 31	Hole M	116		8.10	85-07	Office Queen123½Ellen Girl117½Fast Attack1162½	Good try	10
27Jly70- 8Mth	fst	6f	:214 :444 1:103 3↑	ⒻAlw 10000	4 7 67 65¾ 55¾ 66	Thornburg B	114		3.10	83-13	PrizeStudent1141½Destny'sTwst115hdFnulHll1154	No threat	7
29May70- 7Bel	fst	1⅛	:444 1:101 1:361 1:494	ⒻMother Goose 119k	5 7 65 73½ 65½ 47¾	Thornburg B	121	b	22.80	79-14	OfficeQueen121¾CathyHoney1212MissileBelle1215	No threat	16
16May70- 7Aqu	fst	1	:224 :453 1:101 1:36	ⒻAcorn (Div 2) 56k	2 5 43 41½ 23 34	Thornburg B	121	b	3.70	83-14	CathyHoney1212MissileBelle1212FastAttack121½	Weakened	12
7May70- 7Aqu	fst	7f	:23 :463 1:112 1:233 3↑	ⒻAlw 15000	3 4 32 21½ 3nk 2nk	Thornburg B	113	b	*1.80	83-22	Native Partner123nkFast Attack113½Meritus1084	Sharp	8

29Apr70- 8GS	fst 6f	:22 :444 1:104	ⒻAlw 12000	5 5 45½ 45 42½ 31	Thornburg B	118 b	2.10	89-15	BoxtheCompass115hdLadySadie1181FastAttack1184 Gamely 6
8Nov69- 8GS	gd 1 1/16	:231 :474 1:124 1:461	ⒻGardenia 200k	10 5 52½ 32 41½ 1hd	Thornburg B	119 b	7.90	74-26	Fast Attack119hdSunny Sal119hdOffice Queen119hd Driving 11
29Oct69- 8GS	fst 1 70	:23 :464 1:122 1:43	ⒻAlw 10000	3 4 46½ 32½ 2hd 1nk	Thornburg B	114 b	12.00	79-22	Fast Attack114nkMeritus1155Hail Hail112½ Up in time 10
20Oct69- 7GS	fst 6f	:221 :453 1:12	ⒻAlw 6500	10 1 32 34½ 2hd 1½	Thornburg B	113 b	5.90	84-20	FastAttack113½LostLagoon1123ExclusiveDancer1124 Driving 12
1Oct69- 6Atl	fst 7f	:223 :453 1:103 1:233	ⒻAlw 4500	4 7 63 52¼ 1hd 1nk	Cardone E	114 b	5.10	85-17	Fast Attack114nkSweet Mist1162Bundestag118hd Driving 10
24Sep69- 7Atl	fst 6f	:222 :453 1:11	ⒻAlw 4500	5 9 62¼ 77½ 43¼ 33	Cardone E	114 b	16.60	84-16	Out in Space116noSweet Mist1163Fast Attack1143 Rallied 11
17Sep69- 5Atl	fst 6f	:214 :45 1:112	ⒻAlw 4500	10 4 53 74¼ 54¾ 42¼	Cardone E	114	24.70	83-16	CleverWitch112hdVirginiaCrckr118¾NotNotc1161½ No mishap 11
27Aug69- 7Atl	fst 6f	:222 :454 1:113	ⒻAlw 5000	9 8 97½ 69¼ 68¾ 512	Maple E	114	8.30	72-16	Craim Check1181Canaveral1148Lost Lagoon116¾ No factor 12
13Aug69- 6Atl	fst 6f	:222 :454 1:113	ⒻAlw 5000	3 6 51½ 55½ 54¾ 44¾	Maple E	114	18.50	79-20	Scamtan1203½Office Queen120¾Sure to Show114½ Even race 8
6Aug69- 6Mth	fst 5½f	:222 :463 :592 1:061	ⒻAlw 7000	4 6 55½ 56½ 57 55½	Maple E	114	22.40	80-19	Dowitcher1162¾Sure to Show1161½Stepolina1161 No threat 8
30Jly69- 4Mth	gd 5½f	:224 :47 1:00 1:063	ⒻAlw 7000	3 7 711 714 66 57	Cardone E	114	19.40	77-17	VelocityQueen1162½CutiePaula116¾CramChck1162¾ No factor 7
	Previously trained by W. Gateman								
22Mar69- 3FG	fst 4½f	:233 :482 :55	Alw 2600	9 7 41¼ 54½ 32½	Mora G	117	7.00	86-12	GoTwistGo117¾MissDuplicate1171½FastAttack1171 Rallied 9
12Mar69- 9FG	gd 4½f	:232 :481 :55	ⒻDebutante (Div 2) 7.1k	3 3 54½ 33½ 42½	Nichols J	119	3.90	85-12	Guadarequest1191½MissDuplicate119noNobleIntrgu1191 Hung 10
22Feb69- 3FG	sl 3f	:231 :35	Alw 2800	5 9 67½ 53¼	Nichols J	117	3.20	- -	Mr.MikeM.117½Guadarequest117nkMudBnkSlly1142½ Late foot 10
12Feb69- 3FG	fst 3f	:232 :344	Md Sp Wt	1 1 11½ 12	Suire L	115	*1.50	- -	Fast Attack1152Skylight Star115½Arky Twist118nk Driving 10

Furl Sail

b. f. 1964, by Revoked (Blue Larkspur)–Windsail, by Count Fleet

Lifetime record: 34 17 2 3 $273,759

Own.– Mrs E.K. Thomas
Br.– Mrs E.K. Thomas (Ky)
Tr.– J. Winans

22Aug68- 8Atl	fst 7f	:221 :443 1:092 1:222 3↑	ⒻAlw 7000	6 3 63 51¼ 43 42¼	Broussard R	119	2.90	89-15	Gay Sailorette118nkRegal Hostess117¾Telepathy1171¼ 7
	Nothing for drive								
9Aug68- 8Atl	fst 6f⊗	:22 :442 1:10 3↑	Kng Nptune H (Div 2) 14k	2 5 33 59½ 57 57¾	Cusimano G	115	5.40	84-16	Chicot1153½Kaskaskia1141Bowler King115nk Through early 7
20Jly68- 8Del	fst 1 1/16	:232 :472 1:112 1:44 3↑	ⒻNew Castle 38k	3 1 2hd 22 67¾ 1012	Phelps B	117	12.40	77-24	PluckyPan1144SereneQueen1201LadyDiplomat1141½ Used up 12
10Jly68- 8Del	fm 1Ⓣ	1:382 3↑	ⒻAlw 7000	1 1 52¼ 86 710 712	Goldberg L5	116	*1.90	71-15	Inge109nkRhubarb1212I Be Dandy1111½ Bolted first turn 8
24Jun68- 7Bel	fst 7f	:222 :451 1:10 1:223 3↑	ⒻVagrancy H 28k	4 2 41½ 21 58 512	Rotz JL	123	12.60	82-15	Mac'sSparkler121nkPluckyPan1122½AmerigoLady1218 Tired 7
12Jun68- 8Mth	sly 6f	:213 :443 1:102 3↑	ⒻRegret H 22k	3 3 51¾ 53 43½ 54¼	Passmore WJ	125	2.40	86-16	Codorniz1181½JustKidding115hdRglHostss1121½ No response 7
22May68- 7Bel	fst 6f	:222 :453 1:10 3↑	ⒻLiberty Belle H 28k	7 5 11 1hd 1hd 1hd	Ycaza M	123	3.40	97-14	FurlSail123hdJustKidding115noMac'sSparkler122¾ Driving 8
4May68- 8GS	fst 6f	:22 :454 1:103 3↑	ⒻColonial H 28k	2 6 32 64 54½ 56¾	Vasquez J	126	*.60	84-19	Telepathy1111PluckyPan112nkGreenGlad1122½ Showed little 7
11Apr68- 6Kee	fst 6f	:213 :444 :57 1:10 3↑	ⒻAlw 7500	4 5 23 22 13 13	Brumfield D	121	*.60	93-11	Furl Sail1213La Contessa1123½Edswinner1101 Easy score 8
15Nov67- 8GS	fst 1 1/16	:234 :474 1:123 1:453	ⒻJersey Belle H 29k	5 1 2hd 23 34 35	Velasquez J	124	*.70	72-27	Sumtex115hdTreacherous1125FurlSl1244 Bore in repeatedly 9
26Oct67- 6Kee	fst 1⅛	:474 1:114 1:37 1:491 3↑	ⒻSpinster 61k	5 1 11 1hd 3nk 34¼	Richard D	119	1.70	87-18	StraightDeal123nkⒹAmerigo'sLady1194FurlSal1193 Impeded 6
	Placed second through disqualification								
19Oct67- 6Kee	fst *7f	1:262 3↑	ⒻAlw 10000	1 3 1½ 2hd 12 15	Richard D	118	*.50	91-19	FurlSail1185FineThanks112½LadySwaps1182½ Scored handily 6
10Oct67- 7Kee	fst 6f	:221 :453 :573 1:10 3↑	ⒻAlw 7500	2 1 11½ 11½ 12 13	Richard D	120	*.60	93-17	Furl Sail1203Lady Swaps1232Silver Bright1212½ Handily 5
23Sep67- 8CD	fst 1	:221 :443 1:094 1:36 3↑	ⒻFalls City H 29k	5 1 11½ 12 34½ 711	Knapp K	120	*.70	82-12	Amerigo Lady1165Gusher113½Likely Swap113¾ Used in lead 13
12Jly67- 8Del	gd 1 70	:231 :462 1:12 1:431	ⒻRosenna 18k	5 1 2hd 2½ 41¾ 37	Broussard R	121	*.40	77-18	ⒹLewiston1114½IBeDandy1142½FurlSal1212½ Had no excuses 5
24Jun67- 7Aqu	gd 1¼	:473 1:121 1:374 2:032	ⒻC C A Oaks 131k	7 1 1½ 2hd 34 416	Vasquez J	121	*.70	65-18	Quillo Queen1217Muse1211½Pepperwood1217½ Hard used,sore 10
10Jun67- 7Aqu	fst 1⅛	:47 1:104 1:361 1:493	ⒻMother Goose 97k	7 1 14 14 15 13	Vasquez J	121	*.70	88-12	Furl Sail1213Quillo Queen121noMuse1214½ Speed to spare 11
27May67- 7Aqu	fst 1	:22 :442 1:091 1:353	ⒻAcorn 68k	5 3 2½ 12 16 13	Vasquez J	121	*3.00	90-15	Furl Sail1213Quillo Queen1212½Pepperwood1213 Mild drive 17
20May67- 8GS	gd 6f	:214 :452 1:113	ⒻBetsy Ross H 29k	9 1 64½ 31½ 31½ 11½	Velasquez J	124	3.40	86-20	Furl Sail1241½Rhubarb1241½Lori Mac1155 Going away 10
5May67- 8CD	fst 1 1/16	:234 :464 1:113 1:44	ⒻKy Oaks 60k	2 3 33 33 2hd 32¾	Shoemaker W	121	*.70	89-14	NancyJr.1211¼GaySailorette1211½FurlSail1212 No excuse 8
29Apr67- 8CD	fst 7f	:224 :454 1:10 1:232	ⒻLa Troienne 16k	7 1 32½ 21½ 12 14	Shoemaker W	121	*.40	90-12	Furl Sail1214Overstreet1181¼Gay Sailorette1151 Handily 8
15Apr67- 6Kee	fst 6f	:214 :444 :57 1:092	ⒻAshland 29k	7 1 41 2hd 1½ 2½	Brumfield D	118	2.70	95-12	Dun-Cee115½Furl Sail1184½Woozem1214 Made game effort 7
8Apr67- 7Kee	fst 6f	:221 :453 :58 1:102	ⒻAlw 10000	6 2 31 2hd 11½ 13	Brumfield D	118	*1.10	91-15	Furl Sail1183Fish House1213Dun-Cee1151½ Driving clear 8
11Mar67- 9FG	fst 1 1/16	:233 :464 1:122 1:451	ⒻFG Oaks 17k	3 2 2½ 1½ 13 14	Lopez JR	121 b	*.30	89-12	Furl Sail1214Nancy Jr.1183Filly Folly1153 Mild drive 7
3Mar67- 9FG	fst 1 40	:23 :461 1:122 1:414	ⒻAlw 5000	5 3 21½ 2½ 13 18	Lopez JR	122	*.40	86-13	Furl Sail1228Needle Cushion112noPlessis112nk Easily 7
4Feb67- 9FG	fst 6f	:221 :463 1:113	ⒻThelma 13k	5 2 21 1½ 13 14½	Lopez JR	119	*1.10	93-13	FurlSail1194½Shenan1173½SunelsGirl112½ Drew out easily 11
6Jly66- 8Mth	fst 5½f	:221 :452 :581 1:044	ⒻColleen 18k	11 8 62½ 86¾ 67¾ 69¼	Nichols J	119	5.30	84-18	Rhubarb1146Momma Pierre1141½Betoken119hd No late rally 14
20Jun66- 3AP	fst 5½f	:212 :442 :57 1:034	ⒻMademoiselle 21k	1 3 1hd 2hd 2½ 12	Nichols J	119	5.50	98-06	FurlSail1192Techr'sArt113¾Woozm11910 Vigorously handled 4
7May66- 5CD	fst 5f	:23 :461 :591	ⒻDebutante 19k	2 1 11 1hd 11½ 12	Shoemaker W	122	2.50	94-09	FurlSail1222PoppingMary119½YourIt114hd Under pressure 7
26Apr66- 6Kee	sly 4½f	:224 :461 :523	ⒻBewitch (Div 2) 12k	2 2 2hd 1hd 12	Fires E	114	*1.60	96-03	Furl Sail1142Idle Dreamer1197Ritanita1141¼ Drew clear 7
16Apr66- 4Kee	fst 4½f	:224 :46 :521	Alw 4500	3 1 11½ 13 16	Fires E	112	13.50	98-06	Furl Sail1126Crimson Beau119hdHe's Bowin1195 Ridden out 8
2Mar66- 8FG	fst 4f	:234 :482	ⒻDebutante 9.2k	3 7 87½ 119½ 129	Holmes D	119	*2.50	81-10	MissMaryM.1221½RomanWick119noPrimPrime119¾ Dull effort 13
21Feb66- 6FG	fst 4f	:234 :483	ⒻAlw 2800	6 6 41½ 42 42¼	Holmes D	119	*.90	86-11	MissMaryM.115nkRomanWick1171½WeepingHeart106¾ Wide 9
2Feb66- 3FG	hy 4f	:241 :504	ⒻMd Alw 2000	1 1 11½ 13 14½	Holmes D	120	*.60	78-22	Furl Sail1204½Jo-L-Liz1202½Traveling Light1202 Easily 7

Gallant Bloom

b. f. 1966, by Gallant Man (Migoli)–Multiflora, by Beau Max

Lifetime record: 22 16 1 1 $535,739

Own.– King Ranch
Br.– King Ranch (Ky)
Tr.– W.J. Hirsch

4Jly70- 7Aqu	fst 1¼	:482 1:12 1:361 2:011 3↑	Suburban H 110k	2 6 42½ 42½ 711 711	Rotz JL	119 b	3.50	79-12	Barometer1112½Verbatim1163Hitchcock1133 Fell back 8
22Jun70- 7Bel	sly 1⅛	:46 1:10 1:344 1:464 3↑	Nassau County 27k	5 4 52¼ 31½ 47½ 316	Rotz JL	121 b	2.10	86-15	Reviewer1144Dewan12312Gallant Bloom121nk In close 5
28Feb70- 8SA	sly 1⅛	:47 1:112 1:371 1:503 4↑	ⒻS Margrta Inv'l H 100k	7 4 32 2hd 11½ 12	Rotz JL	129 b	*.80	79-17	GallntBloom1292Commissary1176TippingTime1172½ Handily 8
17Feb70- 8SA	fst 1 1/16	:231 :463 1:111 1:421 4↑	ⒻS Maria H 34k	8 4 43 2½ 1hd 1no	Rotz JL	126 b	*.50	92-11	GallntBloom126noCommissry1165½LuzDlSol1141¼ Hard drive 8
24Oct69- 0Kee	fst 1⅛	:483 1:12 1:37 1:484 3↑	ⒻSpinster 57k	2 2 32½ 22 13 12	Rotz JL	119 b	-	93-17	GallantBloom1192MissRibot1232½SaleDay123nk Well in hand 4
	Exhibition race,no wagering								
4Oct69- 8Atl	fst 1 3/16	:48 1:112 1:363 1:552 3↑	ⒻMatchmaker 50k	7 3 31½ 11½ 14 17	Rotz JL	117 b	1.60	99-15	Gallant Bloom1177Gamely1231½Singing Rain1183 Easily 7
30Aug69- 7Bel	fst 1⅛	:462 1:102 1:352 1:49	ⒻGazelle H 53k	2 4 32 21½ 12 13½	Rotz JL	127 b	1.50	91-12	Gallant Bloom1273½Pit Bunny1163Shuvee1271½ Going away 5
26Jly69- 8Del	gd 1⅛	:464 1:122 1:384 1:511	ⒻDel Oaks 59k	4 3 44 21 2hd 21¼	Rotz JL	121 b	*.70	81-23	ⒹPitBunny1121¼GallntBlm12112WhiteXmass1113¼ Impeded 7
	Placed first through disqualification								
19Jly69- 8Mth	fst 1⅛	:472 1:121 1:38 1:504	ⒻMonmouth Oaks 54k	4 2 21½ 1½ 13 112	Baeza B	121 b	*1.40	90-16	GallantBloom12112HailtoPatsy1183AroundthHorn111½ Easily 6
4Jly69- 8Mth	fst 1 70	:223 :454 1:101 1:42	ⒻPost-Deb 27k	1 2 21 1hd 1hd 1½	Rotz JL	117 b	1.50	91-12	Gallant Bloom117½Process Shot117½Golden Or1172½ Driving 6
25Jun69- 5Mth	sly 1 70	:231 :474 1:131 1:431	ⒻAlw 12000	3 2 32 2hd 1hd 12	Rotz JL	119 b	*.30	85-22	Gallant Bloom1192Golden Or1144½Excited11312 Easily 5
28May69- 7Aqu	fst 6f	:212 :443 1:102 3↑	ⒻLiberty Belle H 28k	1 1 11½ 13 15 1no	Belmonte E	114 b	*1.70	91-13	GallntBlm114noClmsFryGold1164Incommuncdo115nk Driving 8
	Previously trained by M. Hirsch								
9Nov68- 8GS	sl 1 1/16	:23 :474 1:13 1:454	ⒻGardenia 183k	3 4 31 1hd 11½ 11¼	Rotz JL	119 b	1.90	76-28	GallantBloom1191¼Shuvee11915Let'sBeGay119nk Hard drive 7
30Oct68- 8GS	fst 1 70	:221 :452 1:102 1:432	ⒻAlw 10000	4 6 66¾ 42¼ 3½ 12¼	Rotz JL	112 b	*.50	77-22	GallantBloom1122¼DeartoAll112nkHailtoYou1121½ Drew out 8
5Oct68- 7Bel	fst 1	:23 :463 1:112 1:37	ⒻFrizette 130k	11 1 13 13 13 2nk	Rotz JL	119 b	*.80	89-13	Shuvee119nkGallantBloom1193Dihl1194 Just failed to last 11
7Sep68- 7Aqu	fst 6f	:23 :453 1:102	ⒻMatron 100k	2 1 13 14 18 19	Belmonte E	119 b	4.40	91-18	Gallant Bloom1199Irradiate1192Queen's Double119¾ Easily 6
30Aug68- 6Aqu	fst 6f	:222 :46 1:112	ⒻAlw 12000	3 1 2hd 12 15 13	Carmean C10	106 b	7.50	86-20	Gallant Bloom1063Shuvee1143Prefer1161 Something left 7

21Aug68- 7Sar	gd	6f	:214 :454 1:112	ⒻSpinaway 80k	1 3 11½ 21½ 813 818	Toro F	119	b	32.40	73-10	Queen's Double119¾Show Off119½Fillypasser1194	Stopped	10
20Jly68- 8Mth	fst	6f	:22 :453 1:11	ⒻSorority 100k	8 1 52 813 820 823	Rotz JL	119	b	6.60	64-17	Big Advance11910Alert Princess119¾White Xmass1193	Tired	8
10Jly68- 4Mth	fst	5½f	:224 :462 :583 1:05	ⒻAlw 6000	5 1 22 21½ 25 511	Rotz JL	121		*.40	81-15	Big Advance1198Li'l Puss117noGolden Or121½	Tired badly	5
26Jun68- 7Bel	fst	5½f	:224 :462 :581 1:041	ⒻNational Stallion 36k	1 2 11½ 11½ 1½ 11¼	Rotz JL	119		*.60	100-12	Gallant Bloom1191¼Golden Or1143Tatallah1198	Hard urged	4
19Jun68- 5Bel	fst	5½f	:223 :462 :584 1:051	ⒻMd Sp Wt	4 5 21 1½ 13 19	Toro F	119		2.00	95-17	GallntBlm1199WithThisRing1192Repercusson1191½	Easily	10
2Mar68- 0Pal	fst	2f	:25	ⒻTrial	- - 11				-	--	Gallant Bloom1Rasberry SherbethdTurned Onhd		5
	Palmetto trials,Columbia S.C. No purse,no wagering												

Gamely

b. f. 1964, by Bold Ruler (Nasrullah)–Gambetta, by My Babu — **Lifetime record: 41 16 9 6 $574,961**

Own.– W.H. Perry
Br.– Claiborne Farm (Ky)
Tr.– J.W. Maloney

1Nov69- 7Aqu	fst	7f	:221 :442 1:083 1:213	3↑ Vosburgh H 58k	7 7 95½ 96¾ 95½ 82½	Belmonte E	119		6.60	90-13	Ta Wee123hd[DH]Plucky Lucky116[DH]Rising Market120½	Wide	11
4Oct69- 8Atl	fst	1 3/16	:48 1:112 1:363 1:552	3↑ ⒻMatchmaker 50k	3 1 1hd 21½ 24 27	Pincay L Jr	123		*1.10	92-15	Gallant Bloom1177Gamely1231½Singing Rain1183	Gamely	7
13Sep69- 7Bel	fst	1⅛	:462 1:103 1:36 1:491	3↑ ⒻBeldame 81k	4 2 11½ 13 13 13	Pincay L Jr	123		*.40	90-16	Gamely1233Amerigo Lady1233½Shuvee1182	Under mild drive	5
18Aug69- 7Sar	fst	1⅛	:474 1:114 1:364 1:493	3↑ ⒻDiana H 44k	1 1 13 11½ 13 12½	Belmonte E	127		*.40e	93-14	Gamely1272½Obeah118½Amerigo Lady1231½	Under mild drive	5
7Aug69- 7Sar	fst	1	:24 :472 1:121 1:373	3↑ Alw 15000	5 1 11 11½ 11½ 12½	Velasquez J	111		*.50	86-14	Gamely1112½Prevailing1095EneasII1183	Won without urging	6
28Jun69- 8Hol	fst	1⅛	:464 1:103 1:354 1:481	3↑ ⒻVanity H 81k	8 8 84¾ 52½ 3nk 21½	Harris W	128		*.90e	89-17	DesrtLaw1191½Gmly128noAmrgoLdy125¾	Mate won,held on	11
7Jun69- 8Hol	fst	1⅛	:463 1:101 1:341 1:463	3↑ Inglewood H 55k	4 4 33 21 34 44	Harris W	117		2.20e	95-13	RisingMarkt1202½Dwn1141½Rvt114hd	Made bold bid,weakened	9
17May69- 8Hol	fst	1 1/16	:23 :454 1:094 1:402	3↑ Californian 120k	7 8 98¼ 63½ 65½ 87¼	Harris W	119		*3.20e	86-07	Nodoubl1272½RisngMarket1211LondonJet112¾	Checked turn	14
29Apr69- 8Hol	fst	7f	:223 :45 1:084 1:21	3↑ ⒻWilshire H 22k	3 4 32 32 22 1¾	Harris W	128		*.50e	95-14	Gamely128¾TimetoLeave1232¾IndianLoveCall1201½	Driving	6
20Mar69- 8SA	fm	1¼Ⓣ	:451 1:09 1:332 1:581	4↑ ⒻS Barbara H 57k	12 3 33 22½ 25 39½	Harris W	129		*.80e	91-00	Pink Pigeon1236Desert Law1173½Gamely1292	Bid,tired	12
8Mar69- 8SA	fst	1¼	:46 1:10 1:351 2:014	4↑ S Anita H 145k	14 7 75½ 63 22 21½	Harris W	122		7.00e	87-13	Nodouble1221½Gamely122noQuicken Tree1261	Game effort	16
8Feb69- 8SA	sl	1 1/16	:234 :472 1:123 1:453	4↑ San Pasqual H 46k	5 5 44 52¾ 74 67½	Harris W	125		*2.10	67-28	KingsFavr1162½MostHost1181½JimmyPeanuts112no	Weakened	8
21Jan69- 8SA	my	7f	:223 :452 1:102 1:233	4↑ ⒻS Monica H 22k	5 3 21½ 22 2½ 1¾	Harris W	127		*.70e	85-26	Gamely127¾Time to Leave1246Guest Room1152½	Ridden out	5
29Oct68- 8GS	fst	1 1/16	:241 :472 1:113 1:431	3↑ Alw 8000	4 3 23 34½ 45 43	Grant H	119		*1.10	86-19	BigRockCandy114hdKing'sPalace114½PetitDuc1152½	No rally	9
14Sep68- 7Aqu	fst	1⅛	:473 1:121 1:371 1:493	3↑ ⒻBeldame 81k	2 1 14 11½ 2hd 1no	Pincay L Jr	123		*.70	88-14	Gamely123noPolitely123nkAmrgoLdy1235	Came again,just up	5
19Aug68- 7Sar	fst	1⅛	:471 1:113 1:37 1:493	3↑ ⒻDiana H 28k	7 4 26 23 11 1nk	Belmonte E	130		3.30e	93-14	[D]Gamely130nkGreen Glade1102Mount Regina118¾	Swerved	10
	Disqualified and placed second												
12Aug68- 6Sar	fst	1	:23 :451 1:10 1:361	3↑ ⒻHandicap 15000	2 3 44 31 14 1½	Belmonte E	132		1.70e	93-12	Gamely132½Green Glade1121½Swiss Cheese1139	Driving	8
13Jly68- 8Hol	fst	1¼	:45 1:09 1:343 1:594	3↑ Gold Cup H 162k	8 4 49 52½ 75½ 72¾	Harris W	120		*.90e	91-11	Princssnesian117nkRacngRoom1121QucknTr119hd	No excuse	11
29Jun68- 8Hol	fst	1⅛	:464 1:103 1:351 1:473	3↑ ⒻVanity H 79k	8 5 11½ 11 12½ 1¾	Harris W	131		*.30e	94-08	Gamely131¾Princessnesian1282DsrtLw1151	Drifted out,held	7
8Jun68- 8Hol	fst	1⅛	:464 1:101 1:35 1:471	3↑ Inglewood H 57k	3 1 42 2½ 1hd 1no	Harris W	119		2.90	96-04	Gamely119noRisingMarket1202HillShn1181	Under hard drive	12
18May68- 8Hol	fst	1 1/16	:222 :45 1:083 1:404	3↑ Californian 119k	3 9 67 53½ 24 23	Harris W	116		10.80	88-13	Dr.Fager1303Gamely1161RisingMrkt1211½	Rallied well late	14
1May68- 8Hol	fst	7f	:222 :443 1:084 1:21	3↑ ⒻWilshire H 23k	6 2 31½ 31½ 1hd 13½	Harris W	125		*1.00e	95-10	Gmly1253½Romanticism119hdNevadMrg1143	Drew out easily	8
2Apr68- 8SA	yl	1⅛Ⓣ	:481 1:114 1:362 1:49	4↑ San Bernardino H 28k	4 4 31 11½ 1hd 33¼	Lambert J	118	b	2.00	85-12	Tiltable113nkModel Fool1193Gamely1182	Led,tired	6
2Mar68- 6SA	fm	*1¼Ⓣ	:471 1:13 1:374 2:022	4↑ ⒻS Barbara H (Div 1) 42k	6 7 76 2hd 1½ 21½	Ycaza M	128	b	*1.80	--	Amerigo'sFancy1181½Gmely1285LadyPitt1151½	Wide,bore in	9
17Feb68- 8SA	fst	1⅛	:463 1:104 1:354 1:49	4↑ ⒻS Margarita H 100k	6 6 44½ 21½ 1½ 1no	Ycaza M	125	b	*1.30e	87-11	Gmly125noPrincessnesian1203AmergoLdy123hd	Bore out,up	12
27Jan68- 8SA	gd	1 1/16	:223 :46 1:112 1:434	4↑ ⒻS Maria H 36k	4 6 53 3½ 1½ 1¾	Ycaza M	122	b	*1.40e	84-14	Gamely122¾Princessnesian117noMoog1102	Hard drive	12
9Jan68- 8SA	fst	7f	:22 :443 1:102 1:23	4↑ ⒻS Monica H 25k	7 12 99½ 86½ 54½ 33	Shoemaker W	122	b	*2.00e	85-20	Amerigo Lady1182Amerigo's Fancy1171Gamely1223	Rallied	13
14Oct67- 8GS	fst	1⅛	:482 1:123 1:384 1:511	3↑ ⒻVineland H 56k	1 2 21½ 21 1hd 33¼	Shoemaker W	117	b	2.60	78-23	StraightDeal122nkPolitly1203Gmly1173½	Steadied,weakened	7
30Sep67- 8Atl	fst	1 3/16	:46 1:101 1:341 1:551	3↑ ⒻMatchmaker 50k	5 2 23 1hd 1½ 3¾	Velasquez J	114	b	4.80	104-15	Politely118¾StraightDel123hdGmly1143	Propped under whip	13
16Sep67- 7Aqu	fst	1⅛	:49 1:132 1:372 1:494	3↑ ⒻBeldame 81k	1 6 54½ 54¾ 45 32¾	Ycaza M	118	b	4.50	84-16	Mac'sSparkler123nkTripleBrook1232½Gamely1182½	In close	6
2Sep67- 7Aqu	fst	1⅛	:49 1:124 1:381 1:502	ⒻGazelle H 59k	1 3 52½ 31½ 3nk 43¼	Shoemaker W	123	b	*.80	81-16	Sweet Folly1122½Treacherous116¾Swiss Cheese115hd	Hung	13
12Aug67- 6Sar	fst	1¼	:47 1:113 1:373 2:031	ⒻAlabama 60k	9 5 23 2½ 1hd 12	Shoemaker W	118	b	*.90e	92-11	Gamely1182Treacherous1144Muse1141½	Under mild drive	13
3Aug67- 7Sar	fst	7f	:223 :452 1:093 1:214	ⒻTest (Div 1) 23k	7 3 53 41½ 1½ 16	Belmonte E	121	b	4.80	101-07	Gamely1216Wageko1153Just Kidding121¾	Drew out easily	8
20Jly67- 8Hol	fst	1⅛	:463 1:101 1:354 1:491	ⒻHol Oaks 55k	2 2 2½ 1½ 11½ 2½	Shoemaker W	121	b	2.50e	85-15	Amerigo Lady112½Gamely1211½Princessnesian113no	Bore out	10
3Jly67- 8Hol	fst	1 1/16	:23 :454 1:10 1:422	ⒻPrincess 33k	8 5 53 21 12½ 12¼	Shoemaker W	112	b	2.70	83-13	Gamely1122¼Forgiving1213½Fish House118hd	Kept to drive	9
23Jun67- 6Hol	fst	7f	:222 :444 1:093 1:222	ⒻAlw 10000	4 8 73¼ 41½ 65 42½	Lambert J	113	b	*2.00	85-16	Amerigo Lady115½Fish House1131Francine M.1151	Bad start	8
13Jun67- 8Hol	fst	1	:223 :46 1:104 1:363	ⒻHoneymoon 28k	9 8 87¼ 52½ 52¾ 52¾	Blum W	114		3.10e	80-18	SpinnngAround1121½AmrigoLdy114hdNatveHoney118¾	Hung	11
25May67- 8Hol	fst	7f	:214 :441 1:092 1:221	ⒻRailbird 29k	10 9 62¾ 4¾ 32 21½	Blum W	113		3.00	87-14	Forgiving1181½Gamely113½FrncnM.113hd	Finished willingly	14
11May67- 8Hol	fst	6f	:22 :451 :574 1:103	ⒻGoose Girl 23k	3 7 63¼ 62¾ 21½ 51¾	Blum W	113		*1.00e	86-18	Forgiving118nkLouisador115¾Ellen Gruder115no	Bid,hung	11
9Mar67- 4SA	fst	1 1/16	:231 :463 1:112 1:434	ⒻMd Sp Wt	8 4 32½ 22 2hd 1nk	Shoemaker W	115		*.80	84-13	Gamely115nkScoop Time1155Deerfleet1155	Up in time	11
23Feb67- 2SA	fst	6f	:22 :451 :573 1:101	ⒻMd Sp Wt	11 10 53 33½ 23 23¼	Shoemaker W	115		*1.20	88-11	Pooncarie1153¼Gamely1151½Partheny115½	Off slowly,gamely	12

Gun Bow

b. c. 1960, by Gun Shot (Hyperion)–Ribbons and Bows, by War Admiral — **Lifetime record: 42 17 8 4 $798,722**

Own.– Gedney Farm
Br.– Maine Chance Farm (Ky)
Tr.– E.A. Neloy

5Jly65- 7Aqu	fst	1¼	:463 1:111 1:36 2:01	3↑ Suburban H 108k	1 7 717 715 618 522	Blum W	131	b	*1.10	71-14	Pia Star1171½Smart1198Tenacle1144	Attempted to bear out	7
23Jun65- 9Suf	fst	1¼	:471 1:112 1:362 2:013	3↑ Mass H 55k	2 2 1hd 1hd 2hd 2no	Blum W	131	b	*.30	97-17	Smart117noGun Bow1315Tenacle1174½	Held on determinedly	6
31May65- 7Aqu	fst	1	:222 :442 1:081 1:342	3↑ Metropolitan H 111k	8 2 31 41 31 1nk	Blum W	130	b	*.90	96-16	GunBow130nkChieftain1173Affctontly1214½	Strong handling	8
24May65- 6Aqu	fst	6f	:222 :452 1:102	3↑ Alw 10000	6 4 53½ 54½ 52 2hd	Blum W	119	b	*.35	91-19	Malicious119hdGun Bow1191Dark King119nk	Trapped,gaining	7
27Mar65- 9GP	fst	1¼	:47 1:112 1:372 2:042	3↑ Gulf Park H 111k	8 1 1½ 21½ 2½ 31½	Blum W	130	b	*.60	75-15	Ampose112¾Tronado1121¾GnBow130hd	Held well under impost	8
13Mar65- 9GP	fst	1⅛	:473 1:112 1:37 1:50	3↑ Donn H 56k	4 1 11 1½ 12 13	Blum W	127	b	*.70	84-18	Gun Bow1273Temper108½Lt. Stevens119¾	Wide turn,driving	6
27Feb65- 8SA	fst	1¼	:453 1:093 1:351 2:003	3↑ S Anita H 145k	1 1 1hd 2hd 56¼ 47½	Ycaza M	131	b	*1.00	88-10	HillRise1201½CandySpots127hdGeorgeRoyal1146	Used early	8
13Feb65- 8SA	fst	1⅛	:453 1:093 1:35 1:474	4↑ San Antonio H 57k	4 1 12 11 11 1¾	Ycaza M	129	b	2.30	93-11	Gun Bow129¾Candy Spots127nkGeorge Royal1132	Mild urging	8
11Nov64- 7Lrl	hd	1½Ⓣ	:464 1:102 2:00 2:234	3↑ D C Int'l 150k	1 1 14 2½ 23 24½	Blum W	126	b	1.50	107-00	Kelso1264½Gun Bow1269Aniline1223½	Tried to bear out	8
24Oct64- 7Aqu	fm	1⅝Ⓣ	2:424	3↑ Man o' War 111k	7 2 1hd 1hd 21½ 2¾	Blum W	126		*.75	85-14	TurboJetII126¾GunBow1262½KnightlyManner1211	Game try	9
3Oct64- 7Aqu	gd	1¼	:481 1:121 1:371 2:022	3↑ Woodward 108k	2 1 11½ 1hd 2hd 1no	Blum W	126	b	1.45	86-22	GnBow126noKlso1264Quadrangle12125	Extreme hand urging	5
7Sep64- 7Aqu	fst	1⅛	:463 1:104 1:353 1:483	3↑ Aqueduct 107k	5 1 15 11½ 2½ 2¾	Blum W	128	b	*.55	97-16	Kelso128¾Gun Bow1286Saidam1194½	Clear lead,second best	5
22Aug64- 8AP	sly	1⅛	:463 1:104 1:373 1:51	3↑ Washington H 114k	1 1 12 12½ 1hd 12	Blum W	132	b	*.70	81-16	GunBow1322LemonTwist111hdGoingAbroad1141½	Ridden out	12
8Aug64- 6Sar	fst	1⅛	:471 1:104 1:361 1:491	4↑ Whitney 54k	4 1 12 12½ 13 110	Blum W	130	b	*.90	99-10	Gun Bow13010Mongo1303Delta Judge1113½	Speed in reserve	4
25Jly64- 7Aqu	fst	1¼	:461 1:101 1:35 1:593	3↑ Brooklyn H 110k	3 1 12 12 14 112	Blum W	122	b	11.30	102-12	Gun Bow12212Olden Times122noSunrise Flight113hd	Easily	8
18Jly64- 8Mth	fst	1¼	:451 1:101 1:353 2:014	3↑ Monmouth H 107k	2 1 14 1hd 2½ 34¾	Blum W	124	b	4.90	88-17	Mongo127nkKelso1304½Gun Bow12418	Set fast pace,hung	5
2May64- 7Aqu	fst	7f	:223 :451 1:09 1:213	3↑ Carter H 57k	1 9 32½ 32½ 32½ 32½	Guerin E	126	b	3.35e	95-13	Ahoy1332Red Gar112½Gun Bow1261	Well placed,game finish	11
25Apr64- 7Aqu	fst	1⅛	:463 1:102 1:352 1:482	3↑ Grey Lag H 82k	6 2 3nk 21 44½ 58	Shoemaker W	128	b	*1.65	91-16	Saidam1144Mongo128½Bonjour1122½	Well up,tired	7
21Mar64- 9GP	sly	1¼	:454 1:101 1:354 2:014	3↑ Gulf Park H 116k	5 2 1½ 13 13 11¼	Shoemaker W	125	b	*.80	90-15	GunBow1251¼[D]AdmiralVic1244½Garwol1131	Fully extended	11
7Mar64- 8Bow	fst	1 1/16	:24 :473 1:122 1:444	3↑ J B Campbell H 109k	5 1 12 2¼ 2¼ 2no	Shoemaker W	126	b	*1.30	89-20	Mongo126noGun Bow1261Uppercut1145	Nosed in sharp effort	7
22Feb64- 7SA	fst	1¼	:443 1:091 1:351 2:01	3↑ S Anita H 147k	18 4 32½ 21½ 58 79	Shoemaker W	130	b	*1.10	85-10	Mr.Consistency120¾DocJocoy1171½Cyrano1251	Steadied late	18
8Feb64- 7SA	fst	1⅛	:452 1:092 1:342 1:472	4↑ San Antonio H 58k	5 2 21 12 14 14	Shoemaker W	125	b	*.90	95-12	Gun Bow1254Cyrano1243Quita Dude114no	Scored easily	7
25Jan64- 7SA	fst	1¼	:451 1:091 1:34 1:594	C H Strub 132k	1 2 21 110 115 112	Shoemaker W	117	b	*2.00	100-10	Gun Bow11712Rocky Link114noWin-Em-All11310	Easily best	13

15Jan64- 8SA fst 1⅛ :46 1:10 1:35 1:474 S Fernando (Div 2) 43k 3 1 1½ 13 13 15½ Shoemaker W 114 b 9.50 93-11 GnBow1145½LambChop1153Win-Em-All111hd Much the best 9
Previously owned by Maine Chance Farm; previously trained by A. Scotti
30Nov63- 7Aqu my 1 :222 :442 1:094 1:352 3↑ Queens County H 29k 4 1 11 4½ 711 714 Brooks S 113 b *1.60e 77-22 Uppercut1142½Tropical Breeze1111½Get Around1212½ Tired 11
16Nov63- 7Aqu fst 1⅝ :471 1:382 2:033 2:43 3↑ Gallant Fox H 87k 3 2 2½ 2hd 107¼ 1114 Guerin E 115 b 17.65 76-15 SunriseFlight112noB.Major1151½MasterDennis1123 Stopped 12
8Nov63- 7Nar my 1 3/16 :473 1:123 1:393 1:584 3↑ Nar Spl H 26k 2 1 12¼ 12 14¼ 113 Brooks S 114 b *2.20 79-35 GnBow11413GridIronHero1119HalfBreed1135 Scored in hand 6
30Oct63- 8GS fst 1 1/16 :233 :47 1:113 1:443 B Franklin H 28k 2 1 1¼ 11¼ 1hd 2nk Brooks S 114 b 10.60 87-22 BigRaff113nkGunBow1141QuestLnk1161½ Just failed to last 8
26Oct63- 5GS fst 6f :223 :46 1:112 3↑ Alw 6000 4 5 1hd 3¼ 2hd 11 Shoemaker W 119 b 3.70 87-14 GnBow1191JetsPat115½Outriggr115¾ Came again,hard drive 7
9Oct63- 9Suf fst 6f :22 :442 1:093 Suf Downs 28k 5 8 74¼ 76¼ 1115 119 Boland W 115 b 14.60 89-11 Rockity1171¾Indian Relic115½Time Step117¾ Fell far back 11
20Sep63- 8Aqu fst 7f :223 :452 1:102 1:232 3↑ Alw 6500 5 1 1hd 1hd 12 12 Sellers J 113 b *1.30 89-17 GunBow1132FlyingSniper1135½MannJack1031 Kept to drive 6
10Sep63- 8Aqu fst 1 :223 :45 1:093 1:352 Alw 7500 4 1 1hd 1¼ 21 26 Sellers J 115 b 10.00 85-15 Going Around1156Gun Bow1152½President Jim1221½ Gamely 7
Previously trained by G.T. Poole
23Aug63- 5Sar fst 6f :221 :451 1:094 Handicap 6500 1 5 21 31¼ 46 56½ Ussery R 114 b *1.65 92-10 BigEnd1163Ornamnto1222Chshr1121½ Prompted pace,used up 5
10Aug63- 4Sar fst 6f :223 :454 1:104 3↑ Alw 4500 2 3 21 2hd 13 15 Baeza B 114 b 17.00 94-11 GnBow1145DoubleDouble1191½MannJack1142 Much the best 9
2Jly63- 8Aqu fst 1⅛ :462 1:111 1:363 1:493 Alw 6500 6 3 33 66 613 614 Ycaza M 117 b 5.65 79-11 Cabelery1172DareSay115¾Tenacle1151 Speed for 4 furlongs 6
22Jun63- 7Tdn fst 1 1/16 :223 :461 1:112 1:442 Ohio Derby 31k 3 4 76 1319 1311 1320 Boulmetis S 111 b 5.20 71-15 LemonTwist120¾TheBaron110hdGrandStand1132 Never close 15
30May63- 6GS gd 6f :224 :461 1:104 3↑ Alw 5000 1 5 2hd 14 16 110 Shoemaker W 111 b 1.50 90-14 GnBw11110Kiboko1142½LadyPonderos1153 As rider pleased 7
24May63- 6Aqu fst 7f :224 :453 1:10 1:224 Alw 5000 9 7 73 21 53 44¾ Rotz JL 122 b 19.60 87-11 Going Around122¾Tenacle1192½Much Motion1171½ Bid,tired 9
9May63- 6Aqu fst 7f :224 :452 1:094 1:221 Alw 4500 4 5 43½ 21½ 44½ 410½ Rotz JL 122 b 13.60 84-09 Jimmy Cannon1173Going Around122½Tenacle1197 Used up 8
25Mar63- 3GP fst 1 1/16 :243 :483 1:131 1:454 3↑ Md Sp Wt 3 2 12 13 12 13 Blum W 113 b 2.10 79-19 Gun Bow1133Salt Box113¾New Democracy1138 Ridden out 8
7Mar63- 4GP fst 7f :232 :471 1:123 1:254 Md Alw 3000 3 5 52¼ 45 36 36 Rotz JL 121 2.70 77-21 Brenner Pass1183Lotus Petal1163Gun Bow12117 Evenly late 10
27Feb63- 3Hia fst 6f :222 :453 1:11 ©Md Sp Wt 5 10 45 47 58½ 411 Hartack W 119 5.45 78-14 Dancing Dervish1194¾Brenner Pass1193½Royal Jay1192¾ 11
Sluggish start

Hail to Reason

br. c. 1958, by Turn–to (Royal Charger)–Nothirdchance, by Blue Swords **Lifetime record: 18 9 2 2 $328,434**

Own.– Patrice Jacobs
Br.– Bieber–Jacobs Stable (Ky)
Tr.– H. Jacobs

10Sep60- 7Atl fst 7f :222 :45 1:101 1:223 Worlds Playground 135k 3 8 85 62½ 12 14½ Ussery R 122 b *.90 90-13 HailtoReason1224½ItsaGreatDay122noRossSea122no Easily 13
27Aug60- 6Sar fst 6½f :221 :45 1:092 1:16 Hopeful 119k 11 1 54 31½ 14 110 Ussery R 122 b *1.30 104-08 HailtoReason12210Bronzerullah1222½Chinchill1222½ Easily 11
17Aug60- 7Sar fst 6f :223 :454 1:113 Sar Spl 35k 7 8 63½ 43½ 44½ 67½ Ussery R 126 b *1.10 82-15 Bronzerullah1164Ambiopoise116nkChinchilla1191 Bore out 11
6Aug60- 7Mth fst 6f :214 :444 1:102 Sapling 136k 7 9 73¾ 53½ 2½ 1½ Ussery R 122 b *1.50 90-17 HailtoReason122½He'saPistol1222½CarryBack122nk Driving 18
1Aug60- 7Sar fst 6f :224 :46 1:11 Sanford 36k 1 3 21½ 11½ 14 16 Ussery R 124 b *.45 93-12 Hail to Reason1246Busher's Beauty1146½Apple114no Easily 7
20Jly60- 7Aqu fst 5½f :23 :464 :59 1:05 Great American 29k 9 6 41 1hd 11½ 12 Ussery R 124 b *1.75 94-15 HailtoReason1242Bronzerullah117hdCarryBack117hd Driving 12
6Jly60- 7Aqu fst 5½f :222 :46 :582 1:05 Tremont 37k 7 9 54 1hd 13 13 Ussery R 118 b 3.75 94-17 HailtoReason1183Bronzerullh1182¾NshuBlu114hd Mild drive 10
22Jun60- 7Mth fst 5½f :214 :451 :574 1:043 ©Tyro 26k 2 12 107¾ 98¾ 64 55½ Ussery R 122 b 5.10 89-12 Chinchilla111½Song of Wine1152½Carry Back1151¾ Mild bid 14
25May60- 7Aqu sly 5f :222 :452 :58 Juvenile 37k 8 7 53½ 65¼ 33½ 32½ Ussery R 122 b 5.50 -- Iron Rail1221½Globemaster1171Hail to Reason1221½ Wide 9
11May60- 7Aqu fst 5f :223 :46 :583 Youthful 17k 2 1 42½ 42½ 31½ 1¾ Ussery R 122 b *1.65 -- HailtoReason122¾Garwol1221½Opus1222 Under a hard drive 9
3May60- 5Aqu fst 5f :221 :46 :584 Alw 4500 2 1 11½ 12 14 15 Ycaza M 118 b *1.00 -- Hail to Reason1185Stan the Man118¾Ambiopoise1182 Easily 8
15Apr60- 6Aqu fst 5f :224 :46 :581 Alw 4500 4 5 31½ 3½ 31 31¾ Shoemaker W 118 b *.40 -- King's Song118noGarwol1181¾Hail to Reason1189 No excuse 7
4Apr60- 5Aqu fst 5f :223 :453 :581 ©Md Sp Wt 3 - 16 19 Ussery R 118 b *.50 -- Hail to Reason1189Mixed Deal1184½Right Note118½ Easily 6
Foggy
31Mar60- 5Aqu my 5f :223 :462 :591 ©Md Sp Wt 10 9 52¼ 3½ 21½ 21¾ York R 118 b *1.20e -- No Dance1181¾Hail to Reason118nkCumatara1181 Slow start 10
26Mar60- 4Aqu fst 5f :223 :462 :584 ©Md Sp Wt 2 3 33 21 22 22 Woodhouse H 118 b 7.00 -- Stan the Man1182Hail to Reason1184Meison1184 Game try 7
21Mar60- 5Aqu fst 5f :231 :474 1:001 ©Md Sp Wt 7 6 77¾ 79½ 79¾ 68½ Shoemaker W 118 5.00 -- Garwol1181Stan the Man1181No Dance1184 Raced greenly 9
11Feb60- 1SA fst 3f :222 :333 ©Md Sp Wt 7 12 137¼ 138¼ Shoemaker W 118 10.50 -- Hi-Daddy-O118hdHustlBubbl1181¾TranqulVc1181½ No speed 14
21Jan60- 1SA fst 3f :221 :333 ©Md Sp Wt 7 10 1212 1213 Harmatz W 118 22.80 -- DouglasC.118hdMr.Turk118½RodeoHand118hd Always far back 14

Hawaii (SAf)

b. c. 1964, by Utrillo II (Toulouse Lautrec)–Ethane, by Mehrali **Lifetime record: 28 21 2 3 $326,963**

Own.– Cragwood Stable
Br.– A.L. Dell (SAf)
Tr.– M. Miller

11Nov69- 7Lrl fm 1½Ⓣ :50 1:141 2:27 3↑ D C Int'l 150k 5 4 42½ 2½ 31½ 21¼ Velasquez J 127 *1.20 83-16 Karabas1271¼Hawaii127½Czar Alexander12712 Game try 7
18Oct69- 7Bel fm 1½Ⓣ 2:271 3↑ Man o' War 113k 6 4 411 31½ 3nk 12¼ Velasquez J 126 *1.10 101-11 Hawaii1262¼North Flight1211¼Fort Marcy1261¼ Going away 9
20Sep69- 8Atl hd 1½Ⓣ :472 1:123 2:03 2:274 3↑ Sunrise H 55k 5 5 516 53¾ 1½ 11¼ Velasquez J 126 *.70 97-09 Hawaii1261¼Ruffled Feathers1154Balustrade114no Drew out 8
10Sep69- 8Atl sf 1 3/16Ⓣ :493 1:144 1:41 2:003 3↑ U Nations H Inv'l 125k 9 8 64¾ 23 21½ 1½ Velasquez J 124 *1.70 67-33 Hawaii124½North Flight1177Fort Marcy1303 Hard drive 10
30Aug69- 8Atl hd 1⅛Ⓣ :501 1:14 1:38 1:501 3↑ Kelly-Olympic H 34k 9 9 97¼ 105¼ 85¾ 3¾ Baeza B 124 *2.30 84-19 Fort Marcy128½Balustrade116nkHawaii124¾ No excuse 10
6Aug69- 7Sar fm 1 1/16Ⓣ 1:42 3↑ B Baruch H (Div 2) 23k 7 5 45½ 3½ 2hd 14 Ycaza M 122 *1.00 90-10 Hawaii1224Rhinelander II113hdMara Lark1131 Easily 8
26Jly69- 7Aqu sf 1⅛Ⓣ 1:551 3↑ Tidal H 58k 4 5 64¼ 65½ 33 31½ Baeza B 123 *1.20 57-47 Fort Marcy126½Baitman1101Hawaii1233 Lacked final rally 8
4Jly69- 8AP fm 1⅛Ⓣ :484 1:122 1:372 1:494 3↑ Stars & Stripes H 57k 4 3 43½ 53½ 44 1¾ Ycaza M 118 *1.50 92-11 Hawaii118¾Great Cohoes1144Quilche1121¼ Under drive 15
17Jun69- 7Bel fst 1 :233 :47 1:12 1:363 3↑ Alw 15000 7 8 86½ 73 63¾ 66¾ Ycaza M 117 *.70 84-20 Sly Bird1171Mr. Right119nkTrade In1171 Trapped,no rally 8
3Jun69- 7Bel sf 7fⓉ 1:234 3↑ Alw 15000 2 9 72¾ 32 12 17 Ycaza M 115 *1.90 89-20 Hawaii1157Baitman1152½Rixdal119no Speed to spare 10
Previously trained by George Azzie
10Oct68♦ Turffontein(SAf) hy 6½fⓉRH 1:25 3↑ Spring Champion Stakes Stk3700 12½ Rhodes R 126 *.15 Hawaii1262½Cuff Link1281½Villan128½ 9
14Aug68♦ Greyville(SAf) hy 1¼ⓉRH 2:141 3↑ Champion Stakes Stk1500 2nk Rhodes R 125 *.60 William Penn130nkHawaii1254½Smash and Grab1304 4
27Jly68♦ Clairwood(SAf) fm 1⅛ⓉLH 1:494 3↑ Winter Handicap Stk9000 12½ Rhodes R 123 *1.25 Hawaii1232½Peter Beware1201½Anglesea1031 12
6Jly68♦ Greyville(SAf) gd 1 5/16ⓉRH 2:094 3↑ Rothmans July Handicap Stk15000 43 Rhodes R 122 *1.50 Chimboreaa106½William Penn1321½Smash and Grab1221 19
8Jun68♦ Greyville(SAf) fm 1ⓉRH 1:374 South African Guineas Stk9000 12¾ Rhodes R 126 *.25 Hawaii1262¾Westra126½Tarma1212¼ 9
25May68♦ Clairwood(SAf) fm 6fⓉLH 1:102 Clairwood Anniversary Plate Alw2100 13¾ Rhodes R 132 *.20 Hawaii1323¾Double Eagle1201¾Fountainhead120hd 10
3Feb68♦ Milnerton(SAf) sf 1ⓉLH 1:39 Cape Mellow-Wood Guineas Stk Alw14000 12 Rhodes R 126 *.50 Hawaii1262Syracuse1261½Tarma123nk 10
20Jan68♦ Kenilworth(SAf) sf 7fⓉLH 1:284 Guineas Trial Stakes Stk Alw1200 12½ Rhodes R 128 *.40 Hawaii1282½Luna Base1232Master Bidder128hd 7
2Dec67♦ Benoni(SAf) sf 1ⓉLH 1:42 Royal Reserve Guineas Stk2500 1 Rhodes R 117 Hawaii117Court CraftSend Me
25Nov67♦ Turffontein(SAf) sf 5½fⓉStr 1:082 3↑ Chairmans Handicap Stk4500 1 Rhodes R 106 Hawaii106King's MenPat Me Quick

10Oct67♦ Turffontein(SAf)	yl 1ⓉRH	1:401	Derby Trial Stakes Stk1200	1	Rhodes R	126	Hawaii126Star Flame126Bill Bailey126
30Sep67♦ Turffontein(SAf)	sf 5½fⓉStr	1:08	Turffontein Sprint Alw800	1	Rhodes R	127	Hawaii127EnjoymentKarroo Dust
22Jly67♦ Clairwood(SAf)	fm6fⓉLH	1:103	Margate Handicap Hcp1000	1	Rhodes R	120	Hawaii120IntenseifYoung David
5Jly67♦ Greyville(SAf)	gd 7fⓉRH	1:252	Champion Nursery Stakes Stk1200	3	Rhodes R	121	Master Builder121Macaw121Hawaii121
27May67♦ Greyville(SAf)	gd 6fⓉRH	1:131	African Breeders Plate Stk3000	1	Rhodes R	124	Hawaii124MacawSend Me
28Jan67♦ Benoni(SAf)	fm5fⓉStr	:573	East Rand Juvenile Stakes Stk1200	1	Rhodes R	119	Hawaii119EdmundoEnjoyment
26Dec66♦ Turffontein(SAf)	gd 5½fⓉStr	1:083	Pepsi-Cola Cup Stk2100	1	Rhodes R	126	Hawaii126Prussian PrideLobito
12Nov66♦ Benoni(SAf)	fm4fⓉStr	:47	Maiden Juvenile Plate Mdn600	1	Rhodes R	119	Hawaii119Court Craft119Off Parade119

Hurry to Market

b. c. 1961, by To Market (Market Wise)–Hasty Girl, by Princequillo — **Lifetime record: 7 3 2 2 $204,129**

Own.– Wilson & Mrs Hull Jr
Br.– Miss Louise Clements (Ky)
Tr.– D. Erb

8Feb65- 8FG	hy 6f	:231 :474	1:133	4↑ Alw 3000	5	4	41½	21	21	2¾	Heckmann J	115 b	*.40	82-23	Little Lu108¾Hurry to Market1151¼Morning Cast114¾		5
	Bid,tired,stumbled repeatedly final furlong																
9Nov63- 8GS	my 1 1/16	:232 :471 1:12	1:451	Garden State 317k	3	3	2½	1hd	1hd	11	Cook WM	122 b	9.20	84-21	HrrytoMarket1221RomnBrothr1223¼Ishkoodah1221	Driving	14
1Nov63- 8GS	sly 1	:23 :462 1:114	1:384	Alw 10000	3	2	2hd	11½	11½	11½	Cook WM	113 b	25.60	88-21	HrrytoMarkt1131½RomanBrothr120½Susn'sGnt1203	Driving	8
5Oct63- 8Haw	fst 1 1/16	:224 :462 1:11	1:434	Haw Juvenile 30k	2	9	83¾	34½	44½	37¾	Brumfield D	112	3.70	80-12	CountTario114¾Ishkoodah1107HurrytoMarket1121	Even try	14
27Sep63- 8Haw	fst 6f	:22 :451	1:101	©Alw 10000	3	2	44½	46½	33½	21	Brumfield D	110	8.40	95-12	Flamisan1191HrrytoMrkt1101¼CountTro116½	Gaining at end	7
19Sep63- 6Haw	fst 6f	:223 :461	1:121	Alw 3800	4	6	51½	42	31½	31½	Brumfield D	121	*2.30	84-17	MyPridenJoy1111½Ivalinda118noHrrytoMrkt1212¼	No excuse	8
10Sep63- 3Haw	fst 6f	:222 :461	1:114	Md Sp Wt	7	6	44	32	11	11½	Brumfield D	120	*2.00	88-09	HrrytoMrkt1201½MyPridnJoy1211MssDwnUndr1173	Driving	12

Impressive

dkbbr. c. 1963, by Court Martial (Fair Trial)–High Voltage, by Ambiorix — **Lifetime record: 41 13 6 5 $266,346**

Own.– Little M. Farm
Br.– Ogden Phipps & Wheatley Stable (Ky)
Tr.– W.A. Kelley

21Oct67- 6Aqu	fst 6f	:221 :453	1:103	3↑ Alw 15000	7	2	3nk	3½	54	68	Turcotte R	117 b	*1.50	82-16	Wyoming Wildcat1213Hoist Bar1172½Alslad121¾	Weakened	8
7Oct67- 8Atl	fst 7f	:221 :443 1:091	1:21	3↑ Atl City H 28k	8	1	4¾	55½	52¾	712	Broussard R	120 b	*3.60	86-15	FlagRaiser1233SpringDouble1197FullofFun119nk	No rally	10
3Oct67- 8Atl	fst 6f	:22 :442	1:091	3↑ Alw 5500	1	3	1hd	11½	13	15	Broussard R	122 b	*.80	96-15	Impressive1225Fearless Lee1222½Swoonland119½	Easily	8
16Sep67- 6Aqu	fst 6f	:222 :46	1:102	3↑ Alw 15000	3	3	31½	33	41¾	34	Turcotte R	115 b	*1.30	87-16	Successor1133GoldenButtons1191Impressive115hd	No excuse	8
12Jly67- 8Mth	fst 6f	:214 :443	1:101	3↑ Rumson H 23k	3	2	21	31½	32½	105¼	Knapp K	123 b	2.60	86-17	In Reality1173½Country Friend118½Quinta118no	Weakened	13
3Jun67- 7Aqu	fst 6f	:223 :453	1:094	3↑ Alw 15000	5	1	2hd	2½	2½	2no	Turcotte R	124 b	*1.10	94-15	BuzOn115noImpressiv124½Aforthought1192	Brushed in drive	9
30May67- 7Aqu	fst 1	:232 :454 1:10	1:343	3↑ Metropolitan H 109k	4	1	1½	11½	11	35¾	Turcotte R	113 b	15.40	89-13	Buckpasser1301¼Yonder1084½Impressive1131	Used in pace	6
17May67- 7Aqu	fst 7f	:221 :441 1:09	1:221	3↑ Roseben H 27k	6	1	2½	1hd	2½	33¼	Turcotte R	121 b	3.20	92-16	Indulto113¾Our Michael1192½Impressive121no	Drifted out	7
22Apr67- 8GS	fst 6f	:214 :45	1:102	3↑ Cherry Hill H 28k	8	6	43	3nk	3½	53	Turcotte R	124 b	3.10	89-20	OurMichael118noCanHeRun1121¾Irongate1111	Lacked rally	8
12Apr67- 7Aqu	fst 6f	:223 :454	1:101	3↑ Toboggan H 28k	1	1	1½	1hd	1hd	44	Turcotte R	126 b	*2.60	88-21	Advocator1182½BoldandBrv117noBupy1121½	Faltered stretch	9
11Mar67- 8Pim	gd 6f	:224 :461	1:111	3↑ Old Line H 27k	1	3	1hd	3½	33½	67¾	Turcotte R	126 b	*.70	86-14	SubCall1174½HansomHarve120noFaultlssLight1132½	Stopped	7
18Feb67- 9Hia	fst 6f	:213 :441	1:093	4↑ Alw 8000	8	1	1hd	1hd	12	11¼	Knapp K	124 b	2.30	96-09	Impressive1241¼FleetAdmiral112¾CountryFrind113½	Driving	8
25Jan67- 8Hia	fst 7f	:221 :443 1:10	1:231	3↑ Royal Palm H 31k	2	3	1hd	32½	1021	1027	Turcotte R	126 b	4.30	66-15	Bold and Brave116nkBold Tactics1141Quinta116no	Tired	10
11Nov66- 7Aqu	sly 7f	:223 :452 1:10	1:224	3↑ Vosburgh H 57k	9	1	41½	43½	1020	1034	Turcotte R	127 b	5.50	58-17	GallntRomeo1233DavisII1222½FlagRasr121nk	Stopped badly	10
31Oct66- 7Aqu	fst 6f	:221 :444	1:094	3↑ Sport Page H 27k	1	2	1½	1½	11	1½	Turcotte R	126 b	*1.20	94-17	Impressive126½Vitencamps1102Hoist Bar1131½	Driving	8
12Oct66- 8GS	fst 6f	:214 :444	1:093	Quaker City H 29k	7	1	2hd	2½	1½	11¾	Ussery R	126 b	3.10	96-16	Impressive1261¾Our Michael117½Pretense1131	Drew out	11
15Sep66- 7Aqu	gd 1	:222 :454 1:12	1:38	Jerome H 58k	5	1	14	2½	914	928	Blum W	117 b	3.50	50-30	BldandBrave1151½Understandng1078OurMichl1161½	Stopped	9
5Sep66- 8Atl	hd 1Ⓣ		1:352	Ventnor H 30k	7	3	1hd	1hd	11½	63½	Knapp K	117 b	*1.30	90-08	Poker113nkWarCensor116¾SpringDouble1142	Tired suddenly	13
29Aug66- 7Aqu	fst 6f	:222 :444	1:102	3↑ Fall Highweight H 28k	2	1	1½	14	16	13	Knapp K	132 b	*2.80	91-13	Impressive1323Brooklyn Bridge128noHoist Bar1232½	Easily	10
12Aug66- 7Sar	gd 1	:232 :46 1:11	1:37	Jim Dandy 28k	2	1	11	21½	44	58	Baeza B	117 b	*1.00	81-16	Indulto1192½Imam114½Federalist Boy1143½	Gave way badly	7
23Jly66- 8Mth	fst 1 1/16	:233 :464 1:104	1:442	Choice 57k	6	2	11	11½	11½	2no	Knapp K	122 b	*1.40	83-17	Tequillo111noImpressive122nkTurnforHom111hd	Just failed	10
	Previously owned by O. Phipps;previously trained by E.A. Neloy																
25Jun66- 8AP	fst 1	:221 :433 1:064	1:323	Arl Classic H 108k	8	1	12	14	12½	42¾	Knapp K	120 b	*.70e	100-04	Buckpassr1251¾Creme DelaCreme123¾He Jr.116nk	Mate won	8
17Jun66- 8AP	fst 7f	:22 :44 1:081	1:211	Handicap 25000	1	7	41½	22	12	14½	Knapp K	124 b	*1.00	99-08	Impressive1244½JungleBoy1121¼BetterSea1162¼	Handy score	9
23Apr66- 7Aqu	fst 1⅛	:464 1:104 1:362	1:493	Wood Memorial 114k	9	2	1hd	1hd	76½	1116	Knapp K	126 b	*2.20	72-14	Amberoid1262Advocator126noBuffle1262½	Stumbled late	11
16Apr66- 7Aqu	fst 1	:224 :451 1:084	1:343	Gotham 59k	1	3	1½	1½	11½	2¾	Knapp K	118 b	1.90e	94-14	Stupendous114¾Impressive118¾Handsome Boy118hd	2nd best	11
26Mar66- 7Aqu	fst 7f	:223 :444 1:09	1:224	Bay Shore 28k	5	1	2hd	1hd	2hd	23	Knapp K	128 b	*.60	89-19	Quinta1143Impressive128noBuffle1132½	Crowded,held on	8
14Mar66- 7Aqu	fst 6f	:221 :452	1:102	Swift 28k	2	2	31½	1½	14½	17	Knapp K	126 b	*.50	91-21	Impressive1267Quinta126noKeenKuttr1261½	Easily the best	8
26Feb66- 8Pim	sly 6f	:23 :462	1:123	Pimlico H 27k	6	2	2hd	1hd	11½	13	Knapp K	126 b	*.70	87-24	Impressive1263Quinta120½Sandoval115½	Much the best	8
14Feb66- 0Hia	fst 7f	:224 :45 1:084	1:214	Alw 5000	2	2	13	12	14	14½	Knapp K	122 b	-e	100-13	Impressive1224½Buckpasser1241½Stupendous113nk	Driving	5
	Exhibition race run between 6th and 7th races. No wagering																
2Feb66- 8Hia	fst 7f	:224 :453 1:103	1:233	Bahamas 29k	6	3	12	13	1½	24	Knapp K	118 b	3.80	87-18	Graustark1204Impressive1184½Fleet Admiral1161	2nd best	7
22Jan66- 8Hia	fst 7f	:223 :452 1:111	1:244	Hibiscus 33k	3	2	2½	11	13	12¾	Knapp K	117 b	7.20	85-25	Impressive1172¾Needle Him115hdGunflint1152½	Easily best	14
	Previously trained by W.C. Winfrey																
16Oct65- 7Aqu	fst 1	:223 :453 1:104	1:362	Champagne 223k	9	1	11½	1hd	75¼	713	Ycaza M	122 b	*.90e	73-20	Buckpasser1224Our Michael122½Advocator1221½	Used up	9
6Oct65- 7Aqu	fst 7f	:221 :444 1:102	1:233	Cowdin 78k	6	5	53	52¾	32½	41¾	Baeza B	117 b	8.50	86-22	Advocator114hdFathers Image116¾Our Michael1241	Good try	12
29Sep65- 5Aqu	fst 7f	:224 :451 1:102	1:233	Alw 10000	7	2	3nk	1hd	1hd	43¼	Baeza B	124 b	2.20	85-16	FrancisU.119noHospitality1223FlameTree124nk	Wide,tired	7
28Aug65- 6Sar	fst 6½f	:22 :444 1:093	1:16	Hopeful 110k	6	2	2hd	1½	1hd	22½	Ussery R	122 b	*.30e	95-08	Buckpasser1222½Impressive122¾Indulto1222½	Held gamely	7
16Aug65- 7Sar	fst 6f	:221 :453	1:101	Sar Spl 35k	2	3	21	31	11½	11½	Baeza B	114 b	2.60e	97-11	Impressive1141½Flame Tree1245½Irish Ruler1141	Driving	8
9Aug65- 7Sar	my 5½f	:221 :454 :581	1:043	Sanford 36875	2	1	11	1hd	3nk	32¾	Baeza B	115 b	2.50e	91-12	Flame Tree120¾Spring Double1152Impressive115nk	Fair try	8
2Aug65- 7Sar	fst 5½f	:22 :453 :572	1:033	Flash 25k	3	11	84½	52	2½	34	Baeza B	116 b	*1.60	95-09	Indulto1164Amberoid113hdImpressive1161½	Bold bid,hung	12
19Jun65- 4Aqu	fst 5½f	:222 :454 :574	1:041	Alw 5500	2	3	1hd	11½	13	13½	Baeza B	122 b	2.25	92-16	Impressive1223½Francis U.1224Bandera Beau1192	Easily	9
10Jun65- 3Aqu	fst 5f	:223 :463	:591	©Md Sp Wt	10	6	2½	11	1½	14	Baeza B	122 b	10.45	89-18	Impressive1224Total Talent122½Hospitality1223	Easily	10
1Jun65- 4Aqu	fst 5f	:224 :463	:592	©Md Sp Wt	9	10	99½	98	910	911	Baeza B	122	12.40	77-21	RingingAppeal1152Devil'sTattoo122¾TotalTlnt1223	Greenly	10

Jaipur

dkb. c. 1959, by Nasrullah (Nearco)–Rare Perfume, by Eight Thirty — **Lifetime record: 19 10 6 0 $618,926**

Own.– G.D. Widener
Br.– Erdenheim Farms Co (Ky)
Tr.– W.F. Mulholland

9Feb63- 7Hia	fst 1⅛	:462 1:104 1:354 1:484	3↑ Seminole H 58k	2 2 2hd 1½ 33½ 48¾	Adams L	127		4.90	82-19	Kelso1282¾Ridan1292½Sensitivo1153½	Bumped at start,used	6
30Jan63- 8Hia	fst 7f	:233 :46 1:101 1:224	3↑ Palm Beach H 29k	3 3 1hd 21 31½ 23¾	Sellers J	127		4.70	91-16	Ridan1273¾Jaipur127¾MerryRulr1171	Attempted to bear out	5
10Nov62- 7Aqu	sly 1 3/16	:48 1:12 1:371 1:561	Roamer H 57k	8 2 11 2hd 2hd 21	Valenzuela I	126		*.95	97-13	DeadAhead1171Jaipur1262¼SunriseFlight112nk	Held gamely	9
12Oct62- 7Bel	fst 1½	:464 1:122 2:023 2:282	3↑ Manhattan H 58k	5 1 2hd 43 57 611	Shoemaker W	122	b	*.80	80-16	Tutankhamen1112Sensitivo115¾Windy Sands1161	Fell back	9
29Sep62- 7Aqu	gd 1¼	:471 1:113 1:37 2:031	3↑ Woodward 115k	7 2 26 34 23 24½	Shoemaker W	120	b	2.45	79-17	Kelso1264½Jaipur1206½Guadalcnl1261½	Swerved in at start	8
18Aug62- 6Sar	fst 1¼	:472 1:11 1:352 2:013	Travers 82k	2 2 2hd 1hd 1hd 1no	Shoemaker W	126	b	*.65	100-07	Jaipur126noRidan1261Military Plume114¾	Under hard drive	7
1Aug62- 8Mth	fst 1 1/16	:232 :472 1:104 1:42	Choice 56k	6 2 21 21½ 1½ 14½	Shoemaker W	126	b	*.90	95-16	Jaipur1264½Cyane126¾Crimson Satan118¾	Drew out easily	8
9Jun62- 7Bel	fst 1½	:482 1:121 2:021 2:284	Belmont 153k	4 2 22 2½ 2½ 1no	Shoemaker W	126	b	*2.85	89-11	Jaipur126noAdmiral's Voyage1261¼CrimsonSatn1266½	Just up	8
30May62- 8GS	fst 1⅛	:47 1:102 1:354 1:49	Jersey Derby 130k	11 1 1hd 1hd 2hd 2no	Adams L	126	b	3.10	92-14	[D]CrimsnSatn126noJaipur126noAdmiral's Voyg1261	Impeded	12
	Placed first through disqualification											
19May62- 8Pim	fst 1 3/16	:474 1:114 1:37 1:561	Preakness 188k	3 1 1hd 72¾ 913 1019	Ussery R	126		*2.70	73-13	GreekMoney126noRidan1265½RomnLine1261¾	Speed,stopped	11
12May62- 7Aqu	fst 1	:223 :454 1:10 1:353	Withers 58k	2 2 21½ 22 2hd 11	Shoemaker W	126		*.75	90-13	Jaipur1261GreenTicket126¾Cyrano126no	Well rated,in hand	7
7Apr62- 7Aqu	sly 1	:22 :442 1:092 1:37	Gotham 58k	8 4 43 31 1hd 11½	Shoemaker W	122		*1.15	83-20	Jaipur1221½SunriseCounty1182½Sdluck1142	Easily the best	8
14Oct61- 7Aqu	fst 1	:231 :462 1:111 1:36	Champagne 206k	2 2 1hd 1hd 1hd 2hd	Arcaro E	122		*1.10e	88-16	DonutKing122hdJaipur1222SirGaylord122no	Held on gamely	10
2Oct61- 7Bel	fst 7f	:221 :451 1:10 1:223	Cowdin 80k	11 6 62¼ 62½ 31½ 1½	Arcaro E	124		*1.05e	94-12	Jaipur124½Obey117nkSirGylord1241½	Up in final sixteenth	12
16Sep61- 7Bel	fst 6½f	:222 :452 1:103 1:171	Futurity 138k	1 2 1½ 1hd 2hd 2nk	Arcaro E	122	b	1.30	94-16	Cyane122nkJaipur122hdSirGaylord1226	Made a sharp effort	5
26Aug61- 6Sar	sly 6½f	:22 :45 1:094 1:162	Hopeful 117k	7 3 33½ 2½ 11 16	Arcaro E	122	b	3.10	98-14	Jaipur1226SuKaWa1225SirGylord1223½	Speed in reserve	9
16Aug61- 7Sar	fst 6f	:223 :454 1:10	Sar Spl 38k	5 2 21 2hd 21 22	Arcaro E	120		*.90	96-12	Battle Joined1142Jaipur1206Cavalanche1144	Game try	6
31Jly61- 7Sar	sly 5½f	:222 :451 :58 1:041	Flash 29k	7 6 1hd 1½ 12½ 13¾	Arcaro E	113		*.75e	96-09	Jaipur1133¾SunriseCounty1193½SeaSprt119nk	Scored easily	10
19Jly61- 5Aqu	fst 5½f	:224 :461 :581 1:043	©Md Sp Wt	4 2 1½ 1hd 14 16	Arcaro E	118		*.90	96-10	Jaipur1186RoyalLevee1183BreezyLane1182	Drew out easily	10

Kelso

dkbbr. g. 1957, by Your Host (Alibhai)–Maid of Flight, by Count Fleet — **Lifetime record: 63 39 12 2 $1,977,896**

Own.– Bohemia Stable
Br.– Mrs Richard C. duPont (Ky)
Tr.– C.H. Hanford

2Mar66- 9Hia	fst 6f	:222 :444 1:10	4↑ Alw 10000	8 3 87¾ 89¾ 77¾ 44½	Boland W	113	3.30	89-13	DavusII119hdTimeTested1191CountryFrind1133½	Closed well	8
22Sep65- 7Aqu	fst 1¼	:473 1:12 1:364 2:024	3↑ Stymie H 27k	6 4 45½ 1½ 16 18	Valenzuela I	128	*.30	84-17	Kelso1288[D]O'Har107¾Ky.Ponr110¾	With complete authority	6
6Sep65- 7Aqu	fst 1⅛	:481 1:121 1:363 1:49	3↑ Aqueduct 108k	7 5 510 56 48 49	Valenzuela I	130	*1.00	82-14	Malicious1163Pluck116noRmnBrothr1216	Lacked any response	7
7Aug65- 6Sar	fst 1⅛	:471 1:111 1:364 1:494	4↑ Whitney 54k	3 4 44 45 22½ 1no	Valenzuela I	130	*1.20	96-08	Kelso130noMalicious1146PiaStar127nk	Up in final strides	5
24Jly65- 7Aqu	fst 1¼	:47 1:102 1:35 2:003	3↑ Brooklyn H 107k	1 5 56½ 43½ 33½ 34	Valenzuela I	132	*1.20	91-10	PiaStar1212RomnBrothr1212Kelso1321½	Hung under impost	5
10Jly65- 8Del	fst 1 1/16	:241 :482 1:122 1:422	3↑ Diamond State H 21k	2 2 21½ 2½ 1½ 13¼	Valenzuela I	130	*.30	97-13	Kelso1303¼Kilmoray1093Big Brigade114no	Going away	4
29Jun65- 8Mth	fst 6f	:222 :454 1:111	4↑ Alw 5000	8 3 56 86¾ 54¼ 3½	Boland W	122	*.50	85-23	Cachto117noCommunqu122½Klso122hd	Showed strong late bid	8
11Nov64- 7Lrl	hd 1½Ⓣ	:464 1:102 2:00 2:234	3↑ D C Int'l 150k	5 2 24 1½ 13 14½	Valenzuela I	126	*1.20	112-00	Kelso1264½Gun Bow1269Aniline1223½	Drew out handily	8
31Oct64- 7Aqu	fst 2	:484 2:533 3:191	3↑ J C Gold Cup 108k	2 5 43 11½ 14 15½	Valenzuela I	124	*.45	101-14	Kelso1245½Roman Brother1196Quadrangle11916	Easy score	6
3Oct64- 7Aqu	gd 1¼	:481 1:121 1:371 2:022	3↑ Woodward 108k	3 2 21½ 2hd 1hd 2no	Valenzuela I	126	*.95	86-22	Gun Bow126noKelso1264Quadrangle12125	Bore in slightly	5
7Sep64- 7Aqu	fst 1⅛	:463 1:104 1:353 1:483	3↑ Aqueduct 107k	3 2 25 21½ 1½ 1¾	Valenzuela I	128	2.20	98-16	Klso128¾GnBow1286Sadm1194½	Responded to strong urging	5
27Aug64- 7Sar	hd 1⅛Ⓣ	1:463	3↑ Alw 9500	4 2 22½ 2hd 1½ 12½	Valenzuela I	118	*.30	102-00	Klso1182½Knghtsboro1161½RockyThumb1205	Scored in hand	8
25Jly64- 7Aqu	fst 1¼	:461 1:101 1:35 1:593	3↑ Brooklyn H 110k	5 6 69 58½ 610 514	Valenzuela I	130	*.85	88-12	GnBow12212OldnTimes122noSunriseFlght113hd	Bumped gate	8
18Jly64- 8Mth	fst 1¼	:451 1:101 1:353 2:014	3↑ Monmouth H 107k	1 5 56 43¼ 3½ 2nk	Valenzuela I	130	*.60	93-17	Mngo127nkKlso1304½GunBow12418	Hung through late stages	5
4Jly64- 7Aqu	fst 1¼	:472 1:112 1:364 2:014	3↑ Suburban H 110k	6 4 34 32 31½ 2hd	Valenzuela I	131	*1.35	91-17	Iron Peg116hdKelso1314Olden Times128¾	Getting to winner	8
25Jun64- 7Aqu	fst 1⅛	:483 1:124 1:371 1:50	3↑ Handicap 15000	5 4 43½ 21½ 11½ 11¼	Valenzuela I	136	*.55	91-15	Kelso1361¼TropicalBreeze114½SunrisFlght12110	Mild drive	5
6Jun64- 8Hol	fst 1 1/16	:224 :461 1:102 1:413	3↑ Californian 115k	3 5 65 75¼ 78¾ 68	Valenzuela I	127	*1.40	79-14	Mustard Plaster1111½Mr. Consistency1231½ColordoKing1232½		10
	Impeded										
23May64- 8Hol	fst 7f	:214 :44 1:084 1:212	3↑ Los Angeles H 55k	9 1 713 98½ 913 89¼	Valenzuela I	130	*1.70	84-13	Cyrano124hdQuitaDude1142Admiral's Voyag121no	Dull effort	9
11Nov63- 7Lrl	fm 1½Ⓣ	:483 1:133 2:033 2:272	3↑ D C Int'l 150k	8 4 41½ 21 2½ 2½	Valenzuela I	126	*.50	93-14	Mongo126½Klso12612Nyrcos1223	Sluggish start,game effort	10
19Oct63- 7Aqu	fst 2	:482 2:30 2:551 3:22	3↑ J C Gold Cup 108k	1 4 2hd 12 16 14	Valenzuela I	124	*.15	87-14	Kelso1244Guadalcanal1245Garwol1243½	Speed in reserve	7
28Sep63- 7Aqu	fst 1¼	:473 1:114 1:362 2:004	3↑ Woodward 108k	2 3 34 2½ 1½ 13½	Valenzuela I	126	*.25	96-13	Kelso1263½NeverBend1201½CrimsonSatn1266	Speed to spare	5
2Sep63- 7Aqu	fst 1⅛	:49 1:124 1:371 1:494	3↑ Aqueduct 110k	7 3 41½ 31 12 15½	Valenzuela I	134	*.70	92-17	Kelso1345½CrimsonSatan129hdGrwol116no	Under mild urging	8
3Aug63- 6Sar	fst 1⅛	:48 1:12 1:372 1:502	4↑ Whitney 55k	2 4 42½ 42½ 11 12½	Valenzuela I	130	*.35	93-14	Kelso1302½Saidam1111Sunrise County117hd	Easily the best	7
4Jly63- 7Aqu	fst 1¼	:484 1:131 1:381 2:014	3↑ Suburban H 108k	7 3 33 31½ 11½ 11¼	Valenzuela I	133	*.45	91-13	Kelso1331¼Saidam1111½Garwol1121	Retained a safe margin	7
19Jun63- 7Aqu	fst 1⅛	:474 1:113 1:36 1:484	3↑ Nassau County 27k	3 3 31½ 31 12 11½	Valenzuela I	132	*.30	97-07	Kelso1321½Lnvn114noPolyld1143	Cleverly rated,easy score	5
23Mar63- 8Bow	fst 1 1/16	:242 :481 1:12 1:43	3↑ J B Campbell H 109k	5 5 44½ 33 21½ 1¾	Valenzuela I	131	*.80	98-15	Kelso131¾Crimson Satan124hdGushing Wind1166	Hard drive	6
16Mar63- 8GP	fst 1¼	:482 1:121 1:372 2:031	3↑ Gulf Park H 110k	2 2 1½ 12 12 13¼	Valenzuela I	130	*.20	83-20	Kelso1303¼Sensitivo1129Jay Fox113½	Speed in reserve	6
23Feb63- 7Hia	fst 1¼	:483 1:122 1:364 2:014	3↑ Widener H 128k	5 3 54½ 42½ 23 22¼	Valenzuela I	131	*.45	87-18	Beau Purple1252¼Kelso1313Heroshogala1104	Best of others	9
9Feb63- 7Hia	fst 1⅛	:462 1:104 1:354 1:484	3↑ Seminole H 58k	1 4 47½ 42 12 12¾	Valenzuela I	128	2.35	91-19	Kelso1282¾Ridan1292½Senstvo1153½	Rallied wide,drew away	6
30Jan63- 8Hia	fst 7f	:233 :46 1:101 1:224	3↑ Palm Beach H 29k	4 2 2hd 32 43½ 45½	Valenzuela I	128	2.45	89-16	Ridan1273¾Jaipur127¾MerryRulr1171	Broke in stride,tired	5
1Dec62- 8GS	fst 1½	:493 1:15 2:051 2:301	3↑ Gov's Plate 54k	2 1 1hd 13 13 15	Valenzuela I	129	*.40	105-20	Kelso1295Bass Clef1175Polylad1178	Drew away with ease	5
12Nov62- 7Lrl	sf 1½Ⓣ	:471 1:112 2:031 2:281	3↑ D C Int'l 125k	3 2 2hd 11 1hd 21½	Valenzuela I	126	2.10	88-20	MatchII1281½Kelso1264½CarryBack1265	Easily best of rest	13
27Oct62- 7Bel	sf 1½Ⓣ	2:283	3↑ Man o' War 114k	12 5 43 21½ 22 22	Valenzuela I	126	*1.05	101-11	BeauPurple1262Klso1266½ThAxII1261¼	Finished very gamely	12
20Oct62- 7Bel	fst 2	:483 2:282 2:532 3:194	3↑ J C Gold Cup 108k	3 2 32 12 18 110	Valenzuela I	124	*.25	103-08	Kelso12410Guadalcanal1242Nickel Boy1241½	Easily best	6
29Sep62- 7Aqu	gd 1¼	:471 1:113 1:37 2:031	3↑ Woodward 115k	5 3 38½ 13 13 14½	Valenzuela I	126	*.90	84-17	Kelso1264½Jaipur1206½Guadlcnl1261½	Won as rider pleased	8
19Sep62- 7Aqu	fst 1¼	:48 1:12 1:362 2:004	3↑ Stymie H 29k	2 3 34½ 11½ 13 12½	Valenzuela I	128	*1.25	96-14	Klso1282½Plyld114hdTutnkhmn110hd	With complete authority	11
8Sep62- 7Atl	fm 1 1/16Ⓣ	1:431	3↑ Alw 6000	2 1 2hd 11½ 1½ 41¾	Pierce D	113	*.40	93-05	CalltheWitness113nkArtMarket113hdWindySands1131½	Tired	7
22Aug62- 6Sar	fm 1 1/16Ⓣ	1:414	3↑ Alw 5000	3 4 41¾ 2½ 1½ 11½	Valenzuela I	124	*.25	97-03	Kelso1241½CalltheWitness1175FountainHill1172	Mild drive	7
14Jly62- 8Mth	fst 1¼	:46 1:10 1:344 2:002	3↑ Monmouth H 109k	5 4 45½ 44 42½ 23	Shoemaker W	130	*.80	101-14	Carry Back1243Kelso130¾Beau Purple117½	In close turn	6
4Jly62- 7Aqu	fst 1¼	:484 1:124 1:363 2:003	3↑ Suburban H 105k	4 3 36 22 22 22½	Shoemaker W	132	*.65	100-08	BeauPurpl1152½Klso1323½Grwol1091¼	Couldn't reach winner	4
16Jun62- 3Bel	fst 1	:241 :472 1:113 1:353	3↑ Alw 7500	2 4 42 22 2hd 12¼	Shoemaker W	117	*.25	96-14	Klso1172¼Grwol1153½RosNt117½	Rated early,drew out easily	6
30May62- 7Aqu	fst 1	:221 :44 1:08 1:333	3↑ Metropolitan H 111k	2 6 69 56½ 510 68¼	Shoemaker W	133	*.60	92-08	CarryBack1232½MerryRuler120½RullahRed1114½	Dull effort	9
11Nov61- 7Lrl	fm 1½Ⓣ	:483 2:013 2:261	3↑ D C Int'l 100k	6 1 1½ 1hd 2hd 2¾	Arcaro E	126	*.40	108-01	T.V.Lrk126¾Klso12612Prnupcl12610	Made very sharp effort	8
21Oct61- 7Aqu	fst 2	:494 2:35 3:004 3:254	3↑ J C Gold Cup 105k	3 2 22 13 14 15	Arcaro E	124	*.10	68-25	Kelso1245Hillsborough1248Peace Isle12430	Easily best	4
30Sep61- 7Bel	fst 1¼	:461 1:10 1:344 2:00	3↑ Woodward 109k	5 3 21½ 2hd 13 18	Arcaro E	126	*.50	100-13	Kelso1268Divine Comedy126½Carry Back120nk	Much the best	5
4Sep61- 8AP	gd 1	:224 :452 1:093 1:343	3↑ Wash Park H 120k	8 9 106½ 67 47 45¾	Arcaro E	132	*.70	94-08	ChiefofChiefs1124¾TalentShow110nkRunforNurse112¾	Boxed	11
22Jly61- 7Aqu	fst 1¼	:462 1:101 1:36 2:013	3↑ Brooklyn H 112k	7 4 316 35½ 31½ 11¼	Arcaro E	136	*.50	98-10	Klso1361¼DvnComdy118noYorky122hd	Under strong handling	10
4Jly61- 7Aqu	fst 1¼	:482 1:122 1:373 2:02	3↑ Suburban H 111k	7 4 43½ 3nk 12 15	Arcaro E	133	*.60	96-13	Kelso1335NickelBoy112nkTalentShow110hd	Speed in reserve	10
17Jun61- 7Bel	fst 1⅛	:454 1:102 1:351 1:48	4↑ Whitney 56k	5 3 33½ 11 2hd 2hd	Arcaro E	130	*.45	96-12	[D]Our Hope111hdKelso1305Reinzi114hd	Roughed repeatedly	7
	Placed first through disqualification										
30May61- 7Aqu	fst 1	:23 :46 1:102 1:353	3↑ Metropolitan H 114k	9 8 85¼ 76¼ 44 1nk	Arcaro E	130	*1.05	90-16	Kelso130nkAllHands1173SweetWillim1084	Altered course,up	10

19May61- 7Aqu	fst 7f	:23 :461 1:11 1:24	4↑ Alw 10000	7	6	54½	31½	2hd	11½	Arcaro E	124		*.35	90-17	Kelso1241½Gyro115nkLongGoneJohn121½	Drew out with ease	8
29Oct60- 7Aqu	sly 2	:472 2:29 2:54 3:192	3↑ J C Gold Cup 109k	8	3	313	2½	11	13½	Arcaro E	119		*.80	114-16	Kelso1193½Don Poggio12410Bald Eagle12415	Speed to spare	8
15Oct60- 8Haw	my 1¼	:464 1:113 1:364 2:02	3↑ Haw Gold Cup H 144k	4	6	41½	12	13	16	Arcaro E	117		*2.20	86-21	Kelso1176Heroshogala119½On-and-On1221¾	Speed to spare	9
28Sep60- 7Bel	fst 1⅝	:472 1:372 2:021 2:404	Lawrence Realizatn 56k	1	4	42½	11	14	14½	Arcaro E	120		*.50	100-14	Kelso1204½Tompion1231½ToothandNal1165½	Speed in reserve	8
14Sep60- 7Aqu	fst 1⅛	:463 1:102 1:354 1:482	Discovery H 28k	2	6	43½	42	1½	11¼	Arcaro E	124		*1.20	102-14	Kelso1241¼CarelssJohn1161½CountAmbr116½	Swerved,driving	8
3Sep60- 7Aqu	fst 1	:223 :452 1:10 1:344	Jerome H 59k	7	9	95¼	53	32½	1hd	Arcaro E	121		2.65	94-13	Kelso121hdCarelessJohn1162½FourLan1192½	Long,hard drive	13
3Aug60- 7Mth	fst 1 1/16	:224 :46 1:093 1:411	Choice 56k	7	2	21	11	16	17	Hartack W	114		3.90	99-18	Klso1147CarelessJohn114¾CountAmber1143½	Speed to spare	8
23Jly60- 8AP	fst 1	:223 :452 1:103 1:361	Arl Classic 135k	5	10	75¼	97¾	77½	87½	Brooks S	117		3.90	81-13	T.V. Lark120¾John William1232½Venetian Way1231	Dull try	12
16Jly60- 5Aqu	fst 1	:23 :451 1:09 1:341	Alw 4500	4	1	1½	13	110	112	Blum W	117		*1.30	97-10	Kelso11712DoubleDly120noAugustSun109nk	As rider pleased	8
22Jun60- 5Mth	fst 6f	:214 :45 1:10	Alw 4500	6	3	43½	31	13	110	Hartack W	117		*1.00	92-12	Kelso11710Burnt Clover1172½Gordian Knot1171½	Ridden out	8
	Previously trained by J.M. Lee																
23Sep59- 3Atl	fst 7f	:22 :442 1:093 1:23	©Alw 3600	3	5	2hd	1hd	2hd	2¾	Blum W	117		*1.90	87-11	WindySands117¾Klso1172WeGuarantee1172½	Made good try	8
14Sep59- 4Atl	fst 6f	:231 :462 1:112	©Alw 3400	6	4	42¼	42½	43½	21½	Block J	117		4.40	86-18	DressUp1201½Kelso1171¾DuskyRam117nk	Rallied for placing	7
4Sep59- 2Atl	gd 6f	:232 :471 1:134	©Md Sp Wt	7	8	72¼	66	45	11¼	Block J	120		6.00	76-23	Kelso1201¼Crafty Master120¾Adapt1201	Under a hard drive	12

Lady Pitt

ch. f. 1963, by Sword Dancer (Sunglow)–Rock Drill, by Whirlaway
Own.– Golden Triangle Stable
Br.– John W. Greathouse (Ky)
Tr.– S. DiMauro

Lifetime record: 47 10 14 5 $413,382

19Mar68- 8SA	fst 1 1/16	:24 :472 1:113 1:43	4↑ ⒻOneonta H (Div 2) 15k	5	6	611	610	611	614	Ycaza M	120	b	3.30	74-13	Lucky Spot1165Sculptured115noCourageously1201		6
	Steadied at break,lame																
2Mar68- 6SA	fm *1¼	:471 1:13 1:374 2:022	4↑ ⒻS Barbara H (Div 1) 42k	1	3	32½	1hd	32½	36½	Pincay L Jr	115	b	9.00	- -	Amerigo'sFancy1181½Gamely1285LadyPitt1151½	Speed,tired	9
17Feb68- 8SA	fst 1⅛	:463 1:104 1:354 1:49	4↑ ⒻS Margarita H 100k	3	10	1212	119	79	812	Sellers J	116		8.90	75-11	Gamely125noPrincessnesian1203Amerigo Lady123hd	No speed	12
9Feb68- 8SA	sly 7f	:222 :454 1:113 1:244	4↑ ⒻS Paula H 24k	9	6	910	87½	64	21½	Ycaza M	116		14.70	77-23	Sharp Curve1151½Lady Pitt1161¼My Thel108½	Closed fast	10
27Jan68- 8SA	gd 1 1/16	:223 :46 1:112 1:434	4↑ ⒻS Maria H 36k	7	10	1114	72¾	98	912	Lambert J	117		12.10	72-14	Gamely122¾Princessnesian117noMoog1102	Never close	12
28Dec67- 8SA	fst 6f	:22 :45 :571 1:093	3↑ ⒻLas Flores H 24k	4	9	920	917	917	816	Blum W	118		10.00	78-14	SharpCurve1143NevadaMarga118hdPggy'sWorld1092½	Dull try	9
23Nov67- 7Aqu	sly 1⅛	:473 1:13 1:394 1:53	3↑ ⒻFirenze H 57k	4	7	917	1019	1028	1034	Blum W	115		10.80	37-32	Politely1216GreenGlade1141¼Princessnesian1112	No threat	10
9Nov67- 7Aqu	fst 1	:231 :461 1:11 1:363	3↑ ⒻAlw 15000	6	4	33	21½	1½	1¾	Cordero A Jr	118		*.80	85-19	Lady Pitt118¾Narova1091Regal Gleam1201	Long hard drive	7
4Nov67- 7Aqu	my 1¼	:493 1:141 1:393 2:043	3↑ ⒻLadies H 58k	10	2	21½	3½	43	97¾	Cordero A Jr	116		7.00	67-22	SweetFolly1142½HaremLady1081½Muse106nk	Speed to stretch	12
24Oct67- 7Aqu	fst 1	:233 :461 1:101 1:352	3↑ ⒻAlw 15000	7	3	32	31	3½	1nk	Cordero A Jr	116		4.40	91-17	Lady Pitt116nkRomanticism118¾Encanta118½	Up in time	8
14Oct67- 8GS	fst 1⅛	:482 1:123 1:384 1:511	3↑ ⒻVineland H 56k	7	3	36½	46½	66¼	614	Baltazar C	116	b	14.00	67-23	Straight Deal122nkPolitely1203Gamely1173½	Factor,tired	7
30Sep67- 8Atl	fst 1 3/16	:46 1:101 1:341 1:551	3↑ ⒻMatchmaker 50k	11	8	911	1013	1019	925	Woodhouse H	118	b	8.70e	80-15	Politely118¾StraightDeal123hdGamely1143	Not a contender	13
16Sep67- 7Aqu	fst 1⅛	:49 1:132 1:372 1:494	3↑ ⒻBeldame 81k	2	3	33	33	34	55¼	Ussery R	123	b	5.20	82-16	Mac'sSparklr123nkTripleBrook1232½Gamely1182½	Weakened	6
6Sep67- 7Aqu	fst 1	:23 :453 1:10 1:353	3↑ ⒻMaskette H 28k	8	6	68½	68	57	33¾	Baeza B	115	b	3.70	86-18	Politely115¾Triple Brook1173Lady Pitt115nk	Closed well	9
21Aug67- 7Sar	gd 1⅛	:474 1:123 1:37 1:493	3↑ ⒻDiana H 28k	5	3	33	2½	33½	45¾	Baeza B	118	b	3.00	90-11	PridesProfile114nkStraightDeal1273Malhoa1112½	Bid,tired	9
7Aug67- 6Sar	fst 1	:232 :46 1:103 1:362	3↑ ⒻAlw 15000	8	3	42	42	3nk	23	Rotz JL	114	b	4.10	89-15	ReluctantPearl1163LadyPitt1143BelledeNuit120nk	Gamely	9
29Jly67- 6Aqu	fst 1	:222 :443 1:09 1:344	3↑ Alw 15000	5	2	37	45	67½	68¼	Rotz JL	113	b	5.30	86-14	Command Performer109nkAczay108¾Beau Apple113nk	Tired	7
5Nov66- 7Aqu	fst 1¼	:481 1:122 1:371 2:022	3↑ ⒻLadies H 56k	7	7	711	76½	67½	54½	Broussard R	120	b	*1.70	81-13	Destro115noStraightDeal1183MissDickey109hd	Dull effort	8
15Oct66- 8GS	fst 1⅛	:474 1:112 1:361 1:49	3↑ ⒻVineland H 58k	11	6	66¾	44½	44½	1¾	Broussard R	118	b	3.20	92-15	Lady Pitt118¾Juanita1122½Mac's Sparkler112no	Hard drive	11
17Sep66- 7Aqu	fst 1⅛	:47 1:111 1:361 1:492	3↑ ⒻBeldame 85k	2	3	36	36	25	38½	Rotz JL	118	b	3.60	80-18	Summer Scandal1238Straight Deal123½Lady Pitt1182	Hung	10
3Sep66- 7Aqu	fst 1⅛	:473 1:131 1:39 1:522	ⒻGazelle H 55k	1	3	34½	3½	13	2nk	Blum W	124	b	*1.20	74-22	PridesProfile113nkLadyPitt1246SwingingMood1204	Missed	7
13Aug66- 6Sar	fst 1¼	:472 1:12 1:38 2:041	ⒻAlabama 56k	4	5	34	1½	1½	1nk	Blum W	124	b	*1.20	87-09	[D]LadyPitt124nkNatashka1216PridesProfile1141½	Bore in	6
	Disqualified and placed second																
23Jly66- 8Del	fst 1⅛	:463 1:103 1:364 1:494	ⒻDel Oaks 63k	1	2	23½	2hd	13	15	Blum W	121	b	*1.70	88-14	LadyPitt1215HlponWy114hdMssSpn114no	Drifted out,handily	11
4Jly66- 8Mth	fst 1⅛	:462 1:111 1:374 1:512	ⒻMth Oaks 57k	5	11	1116	1011	84½	42½	Blum W	121	b	*1.90	84-15	Natashka1161½Indian Sunlite118¾Justakiss118nk	Late rush	11
25Jun66- 7Aqu	fst 1¼	:472 1:12 1:382 2:05	ⒻC C A Oaks 119k	5	5	57½	1hd	1hd	1¾	Blum W	121	b	*1.70	73-17	LadyPitt121¾[D]GentleRain121nkPridesProfile1218	Driving	10
11Jun66- 7Aqu	fst 1⅛	:472 1:12 1:371 1:502	ⒻMother Goose 87k	9	5	44½	43¼	1½	11¼	Blum W	121	b	7.20	84-15	LadyPitt1211¼MarkingTime121½PridesProfile1212½	Driving	9
28May66- 7Aqu	sly 1	:224 :452 1:102 1:36	ⒻAcorn 59k	2	7	55	47	63	45	Blum W	121	b	9.50	83-18	MarkngTime1212½AroundtheRoses1212Moccasin121½	No rally	11
6May66- 8CD	fst 1 1/16	:234 :472 1:121 1:444	ⒻKy Oaks 60k	9	1	715	712	76¾	31½	Baeza B	121	b	*2.00	86-14	NativeStreet121hd[D]Justakiss1211½LadyPitt121nk	Rallied	10
	Placed second through disqualification																
15Apr66- 7Aqu	fst 1	:223 :45 1:092 1:352	ⒻAlw 10000	5	5	510	32½	2½	12	Baeza B	114	b	*1.10	91-15	Lady Pitt1142Ego Twist1186Be Suspicious1151½	Going away	6
9Mar66- 9GP	fst 1 1/16	:241 :482 1:123 1:432	ⒻOrchid 16k	1	4	45½	44½	22½	2hd	Baeza B	114	b	2.00	91-12	Chalina114hdLady Pitt1141¼Native Street1185	Fast finish	6
26Feb66- 5Hia	fst 1⅛	:48 1:123 1:384 1:514	ⒻAlw 6000	7	6	55½	42	2hd	2½	Adams L	113	b	*.90	75-22	Boiseana115½Lady Pitt1132¼Our Dear Ruth1074	Just failed	8
9Feb66- 8Hia	fst 7f	:224 :452 1:10 1:23	ⒻMimosa 35k	8	7	811	88¼	68	48	Adams L	114		3.60	86-15	Destro1127MyBossLady112hdNativeStreet1211	Broke slowly	8
19Jan66- 7Hia	fst 6f	:221 :454 1:113	ⒻJasmine (Div 1) 20k	2	7	87¼	78½	68½	22	Adams L	116		3.40	84-22	IndianSunlite1162LadyPitt116nkOurDearRuth1121½	Rallied	9
27Nov65- 8Pim	gd 1 1/16	:233 :471 1:113 1:454	ⒻMarguerite 73k	5	8	76¼	54¼	55½	45½	Blum W	119		*1.20	75-18	SwiftLady119¾PridesProfile1193½IndianSunlite1191¼	Wide	8
17Nov65- 7Aqu	fst 1	:224 :454 1:112 1:381	ⒻDemoiselle 30k	5	5	63	44	23	2nk	Velasquez J	116		*1.40	77-27	IndianSunlite114nkLadyPitt1162¾PridesProfile1161	Sharp	12
6Nov65- 8GS	fst 1 1/16	:234 :471 1:121 1:442	ⒻGardenia 183k	6	5	510	55¼	32	22½	Velasquez J	119		10.60	80-21	Moccasin1192½Lady Pitt119½Prides Profile119nk	Good try	9
9Oct65- 7Aqu	fst 1	:224 :461 1:103 1:36	ⒻFrizette 122k	1	6	32	23	23	21½	Turcotte R	119		6.90	86-17	Priceless Gem1191½Lady Pitt1195Swift Lady1191	Game try	7
29Sep65- 7Aqu	fst 7f	:222 :45 1:10 1:23	ⒻAstarita (Div 2) 23k	4	9	912	711	33	15•	Turcotte R	116		8.20	91-16	[DH] Prides Profile119[DH] Lady Pitt1165Destro1164	Driving	9
21Sep65- 7Aqu	fst 6f	:221 :45 1:094	ⒻAlw 10000	1	8	85½	46	39	310	Turcotte R	116		17.30	84-18	PricelessGem1168LadyDiplomat1192LadyPitt1164	No threat	12
2Sep65- 7Aqu	fst 6f	:224 :47 1:121	ⒻAlw 10000	7	6	64½	32	2½	21¾	Blum W	116		3.70	80-26	Hula Girl1191¾Lady Pitt116¾My Boss Lady1145	Good effort	8
18Aug65- 7Sar	gd 6f	:221 :454 1:113	ⒻAdirondack 25k	14	11	116¾	108¾	73½	64½	Ussery R	114		7.20	85-13	LadyDulcinea114nkLovelyGypsy1201½PridesProfile1232	Wide	14
4Aug65- 6Sar	fst 5½f	:22 :454 :582 1:05	ⒻSchuylrville (Div 1) 23k	3	2	65¾	65	33½	24½	Blum W	116		2.40	87-13	PridesProfile1164½LadyPitt1161½NeverinPrs1194	Wide late	7
31Jly65- 8Mth	fst 6f	:212 :45 1:102	ⒻSorority 124k	10	10	1112	1113	912	918	Blum W	119		8.10	72-17	NatveStrt1196ShimmrngGold1147LovlyGypsy119¾	No speed	15
14Jly65- 7Aqu	fst 5½f	:213 :444 :572 1:041	ⒻAstoria 30k	2	8	86¼	87½	56½	33½	Blum W	117		8.10	88-16	Native Street1172½Lyvette1171Lady Pitt1171	Late rush	10
21Jun65- 6Aqu	fst 5½f	:221 :46 :591 1:06	ⒻAlw 5500	2	3	41½	41	2hd	13	Blum W	119		*.90	83-17	Lady Pitt1193Amerala1192Sweety Kid119¾	Drew out easily	7
5Jun65- 4Aqu	fst 5f	:222 :454 :583	ⒻAlw 5500	1	2	1hd	1½	2hd	2no	Turcotte R	119		*2.75	92-13	ChokePont115noLdyPtt11910Aurous1142	Showed sharp effort	8
14May65- 4Aqu	fst 5f	:231 :474 1:003	ⒻMd Sp Wt	3	9	915	79	32	13½	Blum W	119		3.70	82-21	Lady Pitt1193½Zatullah119hdBoiseana119nk	Going away	9

Lamb Chop

ch. f. 1960, by Bold Ruler (Nasrullah)–Sheepsfoot, by Count Fleet
Own.– W.H. Perry
Br.– Claiborne Farm (Ky)
Tr.– J.W. Maloney

Lifetime record: 23 12 5 4 $324,032

25Jan64- 7SA	fst 1¼	:451 1:091 1:34 1:594	C H Strub 132k	2 11 1211 - - -	Ycaza M	120	2.40	- -	Gun Bow11712Rocky Link114noWin-Em-All11310	13
	Broke down,destroyed									
15Jan64- 8SA	fst 1⅛	:46 1:10 1:35 1:474	S Fernando (Div 2) 43k	4 4 21½ 23 23 25½	Ycaza M	115	*.90	87-11	GnBow1145½LmbChop1153Win-Em-All111hd Held on gamely	9
28Nov63- 7Aqu	fst 1⅛	:463 1:114 1:364 1:494 3↑	ⒻFirenze H 27k	1 2 26 1½ 13 12	Ycaza M	126	*.30	92-14	LambChop1262WaltzSong1234DupageLady1084 Handy score	6
5Nov63- 8GS	fst $1\frac{1}{16}$	:23 :462 1:102 1:413	ⒻJersey Belle 29k	6 2 25 15 18 112	Ycaza M	123	*.50	102-14	LmbChp12312ProdanaNeviesta114hdGoofed121¾ Easy score	9
17Oct63- 6Kee	fst 1⅛	:484 1:122 1:362 1:482 3↑	ⒻSpinster 69k	5 2 21 12½ 15 111	Ycaza M	119	-	95-09	LambChop11911ElevenKeys1192½LaughingBreeze1193 Easily	5
	Open to 3-, 4- and 5-year-olds									
10Oct63- 6Kee	fst *7f	:213 :442 1:082 1:243 3↑	ⒻAlw 10000	5 3 34½ 32½ 1½ 12½	Ycaza M	118	*.50	102-12	LambChop1182½Abrogate1123Bonnie'sGrl1063½ Kept to drive	5
19Sep63- 7Aqu	gd 1⅛	:491 1:132 1:383 1:51 3↑	ⒻBeldame 87k	12 5 52 63 2hd 2no	Baeza B	118	*1.15	86-17	Oil Royalty123noLambChop1182SmartDeb1182½ Nosed,sharp	13
11Sep63- 7Aqu	fst 1⅛	:474 1:113 1:37 1:50	ⒻGazelle H 29k	12 6 63 52 1½ 11¾	Baeza B	125	3.35	91-13	LmbChop1251¾DelhiMaid119nkSmartDb1232½ Clear under dr.	12
10Aug63- 6Sar	fst 1¼	:472 1:113 1:38 2:041	ⒻAlabama 57k	5 6 64¾ 62¼ 21½ 2no	Baeza B	124	*.45e	87-11	Tona114noLmbChop1242½ProdanaNeviesta1144½ Forced wide	9
1Aug63- 7Sar	sly 7f	:222 :46 1:114 1:25	ⒻTest (Div 2) 17k	7 3 66 64½ 31 21	Ycaza M	124	*1.50	84-21	Barbwolf1151Lamb Chop1244No Resisting121½ Bore out late	8
6Jly63- 8Mth	fst 1⅛	:48 1:122 1:373 1:513	ⒻMth Oaks 56k	1 7 52½ 31 1hd 1hd	Grant H	118	*2.30	86-16	Lamb Chop118hdSpicy Living1211Smart Deb1183 Hard drive	8
22Jun63- 7Aqu	fst 1¼	:472 1:111 1:37 2:024	ⒻC C A Oaks 120k	2 3 43 2hd 1½ 13½	Gustines H	121	4.15	86-12	LambChop1213½SpicyLiving1211½SmartDeb121¾ Ridden out	10
1Jun63- 7Aqu	fst 1⅛	:481 1:123 1:372 1:502	ⒻMother Goose 91k	11 10 97½ 95¼ 44½ 32½	Rotz JL	121	4.30e	86-11	SpicyLiving121noSmartDeb1212½LambChop121nk Closed fast	14
18May63- 7Aqu	sly 1	:222 :453 1:111 1:371	ⒻAcorn 60k	10 7 84½ 52½ 33½ 34	Rotz JL	121	4.10	78-17	SpicyLiving1213½Nalee121½LambChop1213 Finished gamely	12
24Apr63- 7Aqu	fst 7f	:232 :464 1:113 1:242	ⒻComely (Div 2) 17k	4 2 3nk 32 1hd 11½	Baeza B	118	4.30	84-17	LambChop1181½SpicyLivng1121Fool'sPly1151¼ Driving clear	7
14Feb63- 7SA	my $1\frac{1}{16}$	:224 :462 1:122 1:462	ⒻS Susana 27k	5 7 46 41½ 32 1½	Ycaza M	115	2.20	72-24	LmbChp115½Nalee115½CurousClovr1144¾ Vigorous handling	7
24Jan63- 7SA	fst 6½f	:221 :453 1:101 1:162	ⒻS Ynez 22k	5 9 72¾ 82½ 77½ 25	Ycaza M	117	*2.00	90-12	Nalee1175LambChop117noDelhiMad111nk Rallied for placing	9
3Jan63- 7SA	fst 6½f	:221 :45 1:10 1:162	ⒻⓇLa Centinela 18k	12 9 104 95¾ 35 11¼	Ycaza M	119	*2.50	95-15	LmbChp1191¼JoLarTay119noCuriousClover1195½ Hard drive	14
28Dec62- 7SA	fst 6f	:223 :454 1:11	ⒻAlw 10000	12 1 73¼ 63¾ 62¼ 31¾	Ycaza M	113	*1.30	87-15	[DH] Lanabu115[DH] Nalee1151¾Lamb Chop113½ Slow to settle	12
10Nov62- 8Lrl	sly $1\frac{1}{16}$	:231 :473 1:13 1:464	ⒻSelima 55k	3 4 1hd 43½ 55½ 55¾	Hartack W	119	3.30	79-17	Fool's Play1191Gay Serenade1194Smart Deb119½ Fell back	5
2Nov62- 6Aqu	fst 7f	:224 :454 1:102 1:232	ⒻAlw 5000	6 2 35½ 36½ 32 31	Shoemaker W	116	*1.15	88-19	Charspiv116½PortofCall114½LmbChp116nk Wide backstretch	7
1Sep62- 6Aqu	fst 6f	:221 :452 1:11	ⒻAlw 4500	1 4 41½ 31½ 31 1½	Ycaza M	119	2.50	90-11	Lamb Chop119½Rare Exchange119½Main Swap1125 Hand ride	10
21Aug62- 5Sar	fst 6f	:223 :46 1:113	ⒻMd Sp Wt	10 4 34 31½ 13 11½	Sellers J	118	*1.00	90-10	Lamb Chop1181½Wise Nurse1184½Blue Blur1184½ Ridden out	10

L'Escargot (GB)

ch. g. 1963, by Escart III (Turmoil II)–What a Daisy, by Grand Inquisitor
Own.– Powhatan
Br.– Mrs B. O'Neill (GB)
Tr.– Dan L. Moore

Lifetime record: 57 14 15 7 $212,214

23Sep75♦ Listowel(Ire)	gd 3LH	6:081 6↑	Kerry National Hcp Chase Hcp4000	2hd	Carberry T	168	12.00	Black Mac145hdL'Escargot1684Double 'Em133½	11
5Apr75♦ Aintree(GB)	gd 4½LH	9:31 7↑	Grand National Handicap Chase Stk105000	115	Carberry T	157	6.50	L'Escargot15715Red Rum1688Spanish Steps14312 Blundered at 7th,dueled 4 out,led after last	31
12Mar75♦ Cheltenham(GB)	hy 2LH	4:163 6↑	Two Mile Champion Chase Stk12500	523	Carberry T	168	20.00	Lough Inagh1683Royal Relief1687Skymas1686 Never a factor	8
22Feb75♦ Leopardstwn(Ire)	hy 3LH	6:393 6↑	Leopardstown Handicap Chase Hcp7500	8	Ennis M	144	16.00	Highway View1331½Lean Forward1532Argent1485	9
7Nov74♦ Thurles(Ire)	gd 3RH	6:302 6↑	Morlony Cup Chase Hcp1900	6	Carberry P	170	5.00	Our Albert1333Mr Baggins1422½Gothic Arch1294	8
24Oct74♦ Punchstwn(Ire)	yl 2½RH	5:503 7↑	Free Handicap Chase Hcp2500	39½♦	Carberry T	151	6.00	Lough Inagh1441½Hillhead IV1348[DH]Argent146 Finished in dead-heat for 3rd	7
15Apr74♦ Fairyhouse(Ire)	gd 3½RH	7:50 6↑	Irish Grand National Hcp Chase Stk25000	25	Carberry T	148	4.00	Colebridge1565L'Escargot148noHighway View1348	10
30Mar74♦ Aintree(GB)	gd 4½LH	9:201 7↑	Grand National Handicap Chase Stk78000	27	Carberry T	167	8.50	Red Rum1687L'Escargot167noCharles Dickens1408 6th halfway,bid 2 out,held by winner	42
14Mar74♦ Cheltenham(GB)	sf 2LH	4:214 6↑	Cathcart Challenge Cup Chase Alw5000	24	Carberry T	157	10.00	Soothsayer1574L'Escargot1576Clever Scot1572 Tracked leaders,bid 3 out,held by winner	7
23Feb74♦ Leopardstwn(Ire)	sf 3LH	6:411 6↑	Leopardstown Handicap Chase Hcp7200	6	Carberry T	160	16.00	Lean Forward155¾Ormond King1476Inkslinger1696	8
1Feb74♦ Sandown(GB)	yl $3\frac{1}{16}$RH	6:331 6↑	Gainsborough Chase Alw4500	45½	Carberry T	154	*2.50	Kilvulgan1493Titus Oates149hdInto View1632½ Tracked leaders,one-paced from 2 out	6
29Dec73♦ Punchstwn(Ire)	hy 2½RH	5:58 4↑	Morgiana Hurdle Alw4200	38	Carberry T	158	3.00	Yenisei168noFlashy Boy1638L'Escargot1581½	6
25Sep73♦ Listowel(Ire)	yl 3LH	6:291 6↑	Kerry National Hcp Chase Hcp2500	-	Carberry T	168	*1.75	Pearl of Montreal1333Cottage Time1264Rough Silk133 Fell	5
23Apr73♦ Fairyhouse(Ire)	fm 3½RH	6:541 6↑	Irish Grand National Hcp Chase Stk27000	8	Moore ALT	163	9.00	Tartan Ace1338Skymas14310Sea Brief160½	14
31Mar73♦ Aintree(GB)	fm 4½LH	9:014 7↑	Grand National Hcp Chase Stk80000	325¾	Carberry T	168	11.00	Red Rum145¾Crisp16825L'Escargot16812 17th halfway,13th 7 out,3rd 3 out,no chance with first two	38
15Mar73♦ Cheltenham(GB)	gd *3¼LH	6:371 6↑	Cheltenham Gold Cup Chase Stk45000	411	Carberry T	168	20.00	The Dikler168noPendil1686Charlie Potheen1685 Progress 5 out,weakened 2 out	8
17Feb73♦ Leopardstwn(Ire)	sf 3LH	6:281 6↑	Leopardstown Handicap Chase Hcp7800	7	Carberry T	168	6.00	Sea Brief1554Lockyersleigh1332½Argent1652	8
30Dec72♦ Punchstwn(Ire)	sf 2½RH	5:172 4↑	Morgiana Hurdle Alw2700	2no	Carberry T	151	*2.50	Lockyersleigh151noL'Escargot1514Cart It1448	13
29Nov72♦ Haydock(GB)	gd 3LH	6:141 6↑	Sundew Chase Alw3900	1no	Carberry T	161	*.90	L'Escargot161noSpanish Steps16130The Laird166 With leader to 3 out,dueled 1 out,led near line	4
8Nov72♦ Punchstwn(Ire)	gd 3RH	6:403 6↑	Donaghmore Handicap Chase Hcp1900	24	Carberry T	172	2.00	Sea Brief1524L'Escargot1725Highway View14510	5
28Oct72♦ Aintree(GB)	fm $2\frac{15}{16}$LH	5:571 6↑	Grand National Trial Hcp Chase Stk15000	212	Carberry T	171	*4.50	Glenkiln14012L'Escargot1714Gyleburn1491½ Unhurried in 8th,progress under pressure 3 out,second best	11
26Sep72♦ Listowel(Ire)	fm 3LH	7:162 6↑	Kerry National Hcp Chase Hcp3000	2½	Carberry T	175	*2.50	Culla Hill127½L'Escargot175½Clover Prince1335	5
27Apr72♦ Punchstwn(Ire)	fm $3\frac{1}{16}$RH	6:231 6↑	Guinness Handicap Chase Hcp5000	-	Moore ALT	169	8.00	Alaska Fort1412Colebridge1524Beggar's Way1336 Pulled up	11
8Apr72♦ Aintree(GB)	sf 4½LH	10:082 7↑	Grand National Hcp Chase Stk75000	57	Carberry T	168	*8.50	Well to Do1412Gay Trip1633[DH]Black Secret156	42

16Mar72♦ Cheltenham(GB)	sf *3¼LH		7:18	6↑ Cheltenham Gold Cup Chase Stk35000		$4^{7\frac{3}{4}}$	Carberry T	168	4.00		Glencaraig Lady$168^{\frac{3}{4}}$Royal Toss168^{hd}The Dikler168^{7} Prominent,balked and hit 3rd,one-paced from 2 out	12
5Feb72♦ Leopardstwn(Ire)	hy 3LH		6:15^{1}	6↑ Foxrock Cup Hcp Chase Hcp2000		2^{4}	Carberry T	175	*.80		Esban134^{4}L'Escargot175	3
27Dec71♦ Kempton(GB)	gd 3RH		6:12^{4}	6↑ King George VI Chase Stk11800		4^{8}	Carberry T	168	6.00		The Dikler$161^{1\frac{1}{2}}$Spanish Steps168^{7}Titus Oakes$168^{\frac{1}{2}}$ Progress at 10th,one-paced from 2 out	10
27Nov71♦ Newbury(GB)	gd *3¼LH		6:37^{2}	6↑ Hennessy Gold Cup Hcp Chase Stk19000		6^{38}	Carberry T	175	10.00		Bighorn151^{6}Young Ash Leaf156^{2}Saggart's Choice142^{25} Blundered at 4th,always well behind	13
3Nov71♦ Fairyhouse(Ire)	gd 3RH		7:07^{1}	6↑ Donaghmore Handicap Chase Hcp2000		-	Carberry T	175	6.00		Veuve139^{5}Proud Tarquin160^{2}Alectryon133 Fell	5
12Apr71♦ Fairyhouse(Ire)	gd 3¼RH		7:19^{1}	6↑ Irish Grand National Hcp Chase Stk29000		$3^{2\frac{1}{4}}$	Carberry T	175	8.00		King's Sprite$139^{1\frac{1}{2}}$Proud Tarquin$155^{\frac{3}{4}}$L'Escargot175	19
18Mar71♦ Cheltenham(GB)	hy *3¼LH		8:00^{3}	6↑ Cheltenham Gold Cup Chase Stk25000		1^{10}	Carberry T	168	*3.50		L'Escargot168^{10}Leap Frog168^{15}The Dikler168 Chased leader from 12th,left in lead 21st,all out	8
20Feb71♦ Leopardstwn(Ire)	yl 3LH		6:29	6↑ Leopardstown Handicap Chase Hcp6700		3^{4}	Carberry T	170	12.00		Macroney133^{6}King's Sprite137^{3}L'Escargot170	10
9Jan71♦ Punchstwn(Ire)	sf 3RH		7:05^{3}	6↑ Rathside Chase Alw2700		-	Carberry T	168	*1.75		French Tan164^{12}No Other160^{5}Proud Tarquin160 Lost rider	6
28Dec70♦ Fairyhouse(Ire)	hy 2RH		4:08^{4}	4↑ Sweeps Hurdle Stk31000		4	Carberry T	162	4.00		Persian War168^{8}Lockyersleigh162^{6}Inishmaan160	11
14Nov70- 4Cam	sf $2\frac{13}{16}$	S'Chase	5:20	4↑ Colonial Cup 100k	- 11 10^{10} $4^{1\frac{1}{2}}$ $4^{7\frac{1}{2}}$	4^{9}	Carberry T	160	-	--	Top Bid$160^{1\frac{1}{2}}$Shadow Brook$160^{1\frac{1}{2}}$Jaunty158^{6}	22
19Mar70♦ Cheltenham(GB)	gd *3¼LH		6:47^{2}	6↑ Cheltenham Gold Cup Chase Stk25300		$1^{1\frac{1}{2}}$	Carberry T	168	33.00		L'Escargot$168^{1\frac{1}{2}}$French Tan168^{10}Spanish Steps168^{6} Progress from 6 out,led run-in,all out	12
21Feb70♦ Navan(Ire)	hy 3LH		6:36^{2}	6↑ Leopardstown Hcp Chase Hcp8200		2^{15}	Carberry T	167	*1.50		King Vulgan145^{15}L'Escargot167^{1}Plume142^{5}	9
17Jan70♦ Haydock(GB)	sf 2½LH		5:05^{3}	6↑ World Premier Chase Final Stk14000		1^{2}	Carberry T	154	*2.25		L'Escargot154^{2}East Bound159^{nk}Young Ash Leaf154^{15} Always close up,led 1 out,ridden out	17
26Dec69♦ Fairyhouse(Ire)	yl 2¼RH		4:49^{4}	5↑ Paddock Handicap Chase Hcp2000		1^{3}	Carberry T	171	2.75		L'Escargot171^{3}Garrynagree162^{12}Dead Beat133^{6}	6
15Nov69♦ Punchstwn(Ire)	gd 2½RH		5:24^{4}	5↑ Sandymount Chase Alw3200		2^{10}	Carberry T	164	*.80		East Bound143^{10}L'Escargot164^{20}Arthur McAlinden159^{10}	11
17Oct69- 6Bel	fm 3	S'Chase	5:40^{3}	4↑ Temple Gwathmey H 58k	10 5 3^{5} 2^{3} $2^{\frac{1}{2}}$	3^{3}	Carberry T	152	*2.30	--	Somaten132^{3}LakeDelaware148^{no}L'Escargot152^{1} Bobbled 18th	12
3Jun69- 5Bel	sf 2½	S'Chase	4:52^{3}	4↑ Meadow Brook H 23k	4 6 $4^{4\frac{1}{2}}$ $2^{1\frac{1}{2}}$ 2^{hd}	1^{hd}	Carberry T	148	5.40	--	L'Escargot148^{hd}Rural Riot$139^{\frac{1}{2}}$Wanderlure147^{8} Driving	12
12May69♦ Leopardstwn(Ire)	sf 2¼LH		4:53^{1}	5↑ Woodbine Chase Alw2000		1^{8}	Carberry T	166	*.50		L'Escargot166^{8}Twigairy163^{20}Struell Park166^{10}	5
1May69♦ Punchstwn(Ire)	gd 2RH		4:17	5↑ Colliers Chase Alw2200		1^{6}	Carberry T	158	*.65		L'Escargot158^{6}Twigairy163^{8}Devon Fair153^{6}	5
7Apr69♦ Fairyhouse(Ire)	gd 2¼RH		4:45	5↑ Power Gold Cup Chase Alw3600		2^{10}	Coonan R	159	3.00		Kinloch Brae171^{10}L'Escargot159^{12}Straight Fort171^{4}	8
19Mar69♦ Cheltenham(GB)	hy 2⅛LH		4:41^{4}	5↑ Champion Hurdle Stk25000		$4^{10\frac{1}{2}}$	Carberry T	168	6.50		Persian War168^{4}Drumikill$138^{2\frac{1}{2}}$Privy Seal166^{4} Chased leader from 4th,one-paced after 7th	17
22Feb69♦ Leopardstwn(Ire)	hy 2LH		4:33^{2}	5↑ Scalp Hurdle Alw2800		1^{12}	Carberry T	168	4.50		L'Escargot168^{12}Muir168^{8}Caro Bello165^{4}	10
11Jan69♦ Leopardstwn(Ire)	hy 2LH		4:30^{4}	5↑ Ticknock Handicap Hurdle Hcp1200		$3^{4\frac{1}{4}}$	Carberry T	166	3.00		French Excuse142^{4}Casque131^{nk}L'Escargot$166^{1\frac{1}{2}}$	8
28Dec68♦ Leopardstwn(Ire)	sf 2⅜LH		5:01^{4}	5↑ Tower Handicap Hurdle Hcp2600		6	Carberry T	168	5.00		San-Feliu$145^{2\frac{1}{2}}$Shan La128^{3}Ladyfort148^{8}	8
22May68♦ Down Royal(Ire)	gd 2RH		3:44^{3}	4↑ Carling Black Label Novice Hurdle Alw1700		$2^{1\frac{1}{2}}$	Carberry T	167	*.80		Ispahan$141^{1\frac{1}{2}}$L'Escargot167^{hd}French Alliance$149^{2\frac{1}{2}}$	9
30Apr68♦ Punchstwn(Ire)	yl 2RH		3:56^{4}	5↑ Irish Champion Novice Hurdle Stk4000		4^{12}	Carberry T	167	3.00		Ebony King157^{2}King Candy153^{4}French Tan168^{6}	12
19Mar68♦ Cheltenham(GB)	fm 2⅛LH		4:09^{1}	5↑ Gloucestershire Hurdle Alw4000		1^{6}	Carberry T	172			L'Escargot172^{6}Pick Me Up164^{15}King Penny$174^{\frac{1}{2}}$ Led throughout,ridden out	11
2Mar68♦ Naas(Ire)	gd 2⅛LH		4:22^{1}	4↑ Oberstown Hurdle Alw3200		1^{4}	Carberry P	152	10.00		L'Escargot152^{4}Golden Scene147^{3}Murpep145^{2}	13
14Oct67♦ Naas(Ire)	sf 2⅛ⓉLH		4:26^{2}	4↑ Rathangan INH Flat Race (Amateurs) Alw1600		1^{2}	Hanbury B	170	3.50		L'Escargot170^{2}Honest Injun$170^{2\frac{1}{2}}$[D]Plutarch170^{1}	17
27Apr67♦ Punchstwn(Ire)	gd 2ⓉRH		3:41^{2}	4↑ Cooltrim Plate Alw1600		2^{3}	Hanbury B	167	2.50		Garrynagree162^{3}L'Escargot167^{6}Fulmar170^{3}	13
25Mar67♦ PhoenixPark(Ire)	gd 2ⓉRH		3:47^{3}	4↑ Ashbourne INH Flat Race (Amateurs) Alw1200		2^{1}	Hanbury B	165	6.00		Irish National155^{1}L'Escargot165^{3}Chamac$165^{\frac{1}{2}}$	16
15Feb67♦ Navan(Ire)	sf 2ⓉLH		4:18^{2}	Grattan Cup (Amateur Riders) Mdn700		1^{5}	Hanbury B^{5}	156	14.30		L'Escargot156^{5}Garrynagree156^{15}Nostra161^{6}	22

Mako

dkb. g. 1960, by Tulyar (Tehran)–Puccoon, by Bull Lea

Own.– Mrs Ogden Phipps

Br.– Ogden Phipps & Wheatley Stable (Ky)

Tr.– D.M. Smithwick

Lifetime record: 75 18 13 12 $162,373

25Oct68- 6Bel	sf 3⅛	S'Chase	6:02	4↑ Temple Gwathmey H 55k	6	3	3^{9}	7^{10}	-	-	Mahoney J	155	s	*.80e	--	ChinRun$140^{1\frac{1}{2}}$Apollon146^{2}GntlBoy136^{20} Unseated rider 17th	8
15Oct68- 5Bel	fm 2½	S'Chase	4:42^{1}	4↑ Brook H 19k	2	2	6^{25}	6^{14}	4^{25}	5^{30}	Mahoney J	159	s	*1.90e	--	Roublet153^{hd}BonNouvel161^{13}ChinaRun137^{14} Far off leaders	8
1Oct68- 5Bel	hd 2⅛	S'Chase	3:53^{3}	4↑ Broad Hollow H 16k	3	2	2^{5}	3^{4}	6^{16}	6^{32}	Armstrong R	162	s	*1.20e	--	Exhibit A.145^{1}Bon Nouvel162^{18}Flying Artist$146^{2\frac{1}{2}}$ Tired	6
14Sep68- 7Fai	fm *1⅞	Hurdles	3:24^{3}	3↑ Handicap 3000	5	5	$4^{6\frac{1}{4}}$	$5^{9\frac{3}{4}}$	5^{19}	5^{24}	Aitcheson J Jr	165		*1.30	--	Farmers Lot148^{5}Bold Beggar148^{6}Shod Over140^{8} Dull	5
7Sep68- 4Fai	fm *1¼Ⓣ		2:09	3↑ Alw 1200	5	3	3^{6}	$3^{5\frac{3}{4}}$	$3^{3\frac{1}{4}}$	$1^{\frac{3}{4}}$	O'Brien L	142		*1.70e	--	Mako$142^{\frac{3}{4}}$Gaelic Prince142^{2}Semaforo$139^{2\frac{1}{2}}$ Driving	17
27Oct67- 6Aqu	sf 3	S'Chase	5:46^{3}	4↑ Temple Gwathmey H 55k	4	4	$4^{4\frac{1}{2}}$	4^{8}	4^{29}	4^{29}	Aitcheson J Jr	168	s	*.80e	--	Bampton Castle147^{17}Lumiere135^{7}Irish Hammer142^{5} Evenly	7
17Oct67- 5Aqu	fm 2½	S'Chase	4:40^{3}	4↑ Brook H 19k	1	3	3^{10}	3^{19}	3^{3}	$3^{4\frac{1}{4}}$	Aitcheson J	170	s	*.60e	--	BragadoII$139^{3\frac{1}{2}}$IrishHammer$139^{\frac{3}{4}}$Mko$170^{4\frac{1}{2}}$ Poor landing last	5
3Oct67- 5Aqu	fm $2\frac{1}{16}$	S'Chase	3:47^{2}	4↑ Broad Hollow H 16k	5	3	$3^{2\frac{1}{2}}$	3^{9}	1^{hd}	1^{3}	Aitcheson J	166	s	*.30e	--	Mako166^{3}Golpista$152^{3\frac{3}{4}}$Irish Hammer$138^{\frac{1}{2}}$ Drew out easily	5
25Sep67- 3Aqu	fm $2\frac{1}{16}$	S'Chase	3:48^{1}	4↑ Harbor Hill H 10k	2	3	3^{4}	2^{1}	1^{4}	1^{12}	Aitcheson J	164	s	2.10e	--	Mako164^{12}HoistHimAboard$146^{1\frac{1}{2}}$BragadoII$140^{1\frac{1}{2}}$ Easily best	7
9Sep67- 2Fai	fm *$1\frac{1}{16}$Ⓣ		2:00^{4}	3↑ Alw 1200	17	8	7^{7}	$6^{5\frac{1}{2}}$	5^{2}	2^{nk}	Aitcheson J Jr	141	s	*1.00e	--	Mighty Stroke143^{nk}Mako141^{hd}Kyrenia138^{1} Strong late rush	17
24Aug67- 5Sar	fm 2½	S'Chase	4:46^{4}	4↑ Saratoga H 20k	1	1	1^{5}	1^{8}	$3^{3\frac{1}{2}}$	$3^{13\frac{1}{2}}$	Aitcheson J	163	s	*1.00	--	Spooky Joe$149^{4\frac{1}{2}}$Lumiere136^{9}Mako163 Long lead,weakened	4
4Aug67- 5Sar	gd $2\frac{1}{16}$	S'Chase	3:49^{3}	4↑ Beverwyck H 16k	2	2	1^{hd}	1^{3}	$1^{\frac{1}{2}}$	$2^{2\frac{1}{2}}$	Aitcheson J Jr	165	s	*1.00	--	Spooky Joe$144^{2\frac{1}{2}}$Mako165^{10}Lumiere142^{hd} Tired under impost	5
2Jun67- 5Aqu	fm 3	S'Chase	5:39^{2}	4↑ Grand National H 39k	5	-	-	-	-	-	O'Brien L	164	s	*.70e	--	Golpista146^{6}General Tingle143^{hd}Bampton Castle146^{3}	8

Bobbled 2nd,lost rider

18May67- 5Aqu fm 2½ S'Chase 4:391 4↑ Meadow Brook H 22k 2 5 33 33 14 18 O'Brien L 160 *1.50e -- Mako1608Golpista1443Tuscalee160nk Speed to spare 10
13May67- 1Mal fm *1¾Ⓣ 3:202 4↑ Alw 1000 9 7 55½ 31½ 3½ 2¾ Aitcheson J Jr 149 s -e -- Pardor149¾Mako149½Tout Royal149½ Showed game effort 10
22Apr67- 6Mid hd *1¼Ⓣ 2:152 3↑ Alw 200 2 4 1hd 1hd 33½ 54½ O'Brien L 152 -e -- Double Easter1491½Irish Hammer146¾Taut Ship1502 Tired 12
28Oct66- 6Aqu fm 3 S'Chase 5:424 4↑ Temple Gwathmey H 54k 3 1 16 110 21 39 Walsh T 168 s *.50e -- Lumiere1338Bampton Castle1471Mako1687 Fenced poorly 6
4Oct66- 5Aqu sf 2½ S'Chase 4:451 4↑ Brook H 20k 6 2 23 23 310 415 Walsh T 171 *.70e -- General Tingle1497Tails1322Hoist Him Aboard1506 Bobbled 8
25Aug66- 5Sar fm 2½ S'Chase 4:373 4↑ Saratoga H 21k 1 1 31 13 13 18 Walsh T 166 s *.60 -- Mako1668RuralRiot13514GeneralTingle155 Drew out easily 4
5Aug66- 5Sar fm 2 1/16 S'Chase 3:463 4↑ Beverwyck H 16k 2 1 23 23 11½ 13 Walsh T 163 s *.80 -- Mako1633SurugaBay1431½KingsCrek149 Drew out easily flat 5
6Jun66- 5Aqu fm 2½ S'Chase 4:403 4↑ Meadow Brook H 21k 2 1 1hd 11 14 18 Walsh T 158 s *.80e -- Mako1588Tails13410Gramatam1352½ Speed to spare 5
28May66- 5Pur sf *1⅛Ⓣ 2:092 3↑ Alw 600 5 1 12½ 18 16 18 Smithwick AP 148 s *.60e -- Mko1488MarchKing1571½CombinedOperation1531 Under drive 6
11May66- 3Aqu fm 2 1/16 S'Chase 3:512 4↑ Alw 7500 6 5 618 511 38 39½ Walsh T 158 s *.60e -- The Sport1586Lucentaur1433½Mako15810 Fair effort 7
3May66- 9Pim gd 1 1/16 :242 :484 1:134 1:474 4↑ Alw 7000 2 4 44 78 716 812 Lee T 113 3.70e 59-15 Protected112¾RainSong1121½DarkRuana111¾ Fell back early 11
23Apr66- 6Mid sf *1¼Ⓣ 2:173 3↑ Alw 200 12 - 710 Smithwick AP 152 -e -- PrinceBective1391½LazyRiver1381½EarlyFind1434 No threat 12
Dense fog
16Apr66- 5Mid fm *6fⓉ 1:15 3↑ Alw 200 15 11 108¾ 1010 98 89 Smithwick AP 155 s -e -- Win'sStar1431InthePrime139½BigTulyar155½ Raced far back 15
29Oct65- 6Aqu hd 3 S'Chase 5:334 4↑ Temple Gwathmey H 54k 5 4 312 314 330 345 Smithwick AP 146 s *.30e -- Bon Nouvel17030Lucentaur13415Mako14650 Mate to winner 6
19Oct65- 5Aqu hd 3 S'Chase 5:383 4↑ Grand National H 27k 1 3 2½ 1½ 15 14 Walsh T 142 s *.50e -- Mako1424Lucentaur13315The Sport159½ Kept under urging 6
5Oct65- 5Aqu hd 2½ S'Chase 4:363 4↑ Brook H 20k 3 2 23 25 22 21 Smithwick AP 142 s *.30e -- Bon Nouvel1691Mako1423Sun Game14350 Bad landing 11th 5
18Sep65- 5Fai hd *2 S'Chase 3:573 3↑ Manly H 10k 3 2 2nk 2¾ 2½ 22½ Smithwick AP 153 s *1.00 -- Lucentaur1442½Mako1534½Navy Blue14210 Best of others 6
2Sep65- 5Aqu fm 2 1/16 S'Chase 3:49 4↑ Harbor Hill H 11k 5 5 53 21½ 12 14 Smithwick AP 145 s *1.90e -- Mako1454Risky1434Lucentaur1404 Won with something left 7
23Aug65- 3Sar fm 2 1/16 S'Chase 3:464 4↑ O Clm 6500 1 3 32 23 11½ 13½ Smithwick AP 147 s 5.30 -- Mako1473½Risky1478Sea Smoke1436 Fenced well,easily best 9
14Aug65- 3Sar sf 1⅞ Hurdles 3:24 3↑ Alw 5500 1 3 2½ 2½ 39 422½ Smithwick AP 148 sb 9.30 -- Risky15516SummitSlep1432½OldStr1324 Prominent until 9th 8
28Jly65- 5Mth fm *2 Hurdles 4:07 3↑ Midsummer H 17k 9 1 1hd - - - Smithwick AP 141 sb 15.30 -- Gentles Pride150½Sacred River1422½My Passion1474 10
Used early,outdistanced
19Jly65- 5Del fm 1 1/16Ⓣ 1:442 3↑ Clm 14000 5 4 31½ 52¼ 44½ 56¾ Valenzuela A 114 b 21.20 75-16 Triumvirate112¾Ali Baba II1111½Local Gossip1184½ Tired 6
9Jly65- 3Mth fm *1¾ Hurdles 3:22 3↑ Alw 4000 5 3 2½ 23 4¾ 313½ Smithwick AP 148 sb 3.20e -- Tuscalee15412JumpingJuptr1421½Mko1482½ Held for placing 11
5Jly65- 7Del fst 6f :224 :462 1:112 3↑ Alw 4500 3 7 711 814 812 814 Valenzuela A 112 b 42.10 74-18 Snow House1193½Communique122hdHelioroad108½ No speed 8
2Jun65- 3Aqu fm 2 1/16 S'Chase 3:544 4↑ Alw 5500 2 3 35 35 511 514 Smithwick AP 147 sb 2.90e -- KingsCreek1483½OrkhanBoy1392½Lucentur1301½ Poor landing 8
20May65- 5Aqu fm 2 S'Chase 3:411 4↑ Hitchcock H 11k 3 1 2hd 53 628 635 Smithwick AP 155 sb 1.90e -- Golpista1514RaoRaja1543½NavyBlu154no Landed poorly late 7
6May65- 5Aqu fm 2 S'Chase 3:431 4↑ Aqu Spring 14k 6 1 14 12 1hd 2nk Smithwick AP 151 5.20 -- Gramatam148nkMako1512Navy Blue1542 Bobbled,missed 9
30Apr65- 9Pim fm 1 1/16Ⓣ :243 :481 1:123 1:443 4↑ Alw 5000 1 1 31 613 813 819 Corle RE 119 27.80 73-08 Hyperborean113¾Triumvirate1154Zapata1192½ Tired 9
17Apr65- 6Mid fm *1¼Ⓣ 2:19 3↑ Alw 200 9 1 11 1nk 12 11½ Smithwick AP 149 s -e -- Mako1491½Bonus Pot152½Sun Game146¾ Kept to drive 11
7Nov64- 4Mtp fm *2 S'Chase 3:573 3↑ Alw 1200 2 1 1¾ 2¾ 2no 1no Smithwick AP 149 s -e -- Mako149noPocketRocket143nkSkyJinks1394 Up final strides 7
29Oct64- 6Aqu fm 2½ S'Chase 4:34 4↑ NY Turf Writers H 18k 1 2 38 21½ 39½ 218 Smithwick AP 145 s 14.60e -- Sun Game13918Mako1451½Exhibit A.1606 Bad landing 11th 9
23Oct64- 3Aqu sf 1⅝ Hurdles 2:534 3↑ Alw 6000 1 4 31½ 2½ 11 21½ Smithwick AP 151 s 13.60 -- Navy Blue1511½Mako1511Sun Game1512 Game effort 9
15Oct64- 5Aqu hd 2½ S'Chase 4:313 4↑ Rouge Dragon H 11k 1 6 68½ 613 624 634 Smithwick AP 144 sb 10.35 -- Gramatam1391MonarcaII145hdExhibitA.1635 Never a factor 8
24Sep64- 5Aqu hd 2 S'Chase 3:431 4↑ C L Appleton Mem H 11k 8 4 415 23 53½ 66¼ Smithwick AP 145 sb 2.65e -- BeModerate1442Hustle1531RedCircle139¾ Poor landing last 8
19Sep64- 3Fai hd *2 S'Chase 4:023 3↑ Handicap 3000 1 5 56¼ 2hd 13 13½ Smithwick AP 148 s *1.30 -- Mako1433½Half Baked144½Greek King II137¾ Ridden out 5
12Sep64- 2Fai hd 1 1/16Ⓣ 1:483 3↑ Alw 1200 9 6 42¾ 42¾ 42¼ 45¾ Smithwick AP 148 s 2.30e -- LightofDevon1483KingsWild141hdPocketRocket1482¾ Evenly 14
2May64- 5War sf *2 S'Chase 5:143 4↑ Sp Wt 800 4 2 2hd 11 16 12½ Smithwick AP 144 s -e -- Mako1442½What a Boy15330Eugarie148 Kept to hard drive 5
24Oct63- 3Aqu hd *1⅞ Hurdles 3:22 L E Stoddard Jr H 14k 2 5 59½ 52 74¾ 66 Smithwick AP 147 s 3.80e -- Fort Riley139hdTask Force1453½Vesuvius1371 Rough trip 9
4Oct63- 3Aqu fm *1⅝ Hurdles 2:543 Alw 4500 1 4 2hd 11 11½ 22 Smithwick AP 145 sb *.50e -- Marigny1452Mako1452Vesuvius1457 Clear lead,tired 8
26Sep63- 5Aqu fm *1⅞ Hurdles 3:223 Elkridge H 13k 5 4 34½ 3½ 1hd 3nk Smithwick AP 148 sb 2.20 -- Citizenship137hdLumiere136hdMako1482½ Led,gamely 7
16Sep63- 3Aqu sf *1⅝ Hurdles 2:554 3↑ Alw 4300 7 2 32 31½ 1½ 21 Smithwick AP 143 s 2.35 -- Task Force1381Mako1431Prosecutor153¾ Used reaching lead 7
15Aug63- 5Sar fm 1⅝ Hurdles 2:51 Promise H 13k 4 4 48½ 24 24 28 Smithwick AP 143 s 3.65 -- WillIRule1498Mko1436TskForc13712 Bad landing 3rd,gamely 7
3Aug63- 8Sar fm 1 1/16Ⓣ 1:414 3↑ Alw 4700 3 7 87½ 86 55 46 Combest J 111 35.80 91-03 UnclePercy1153½TeleJr.111½SyltII1192 Failed to threaten 11
23Jly63- 3Mth fm *1½ Hurdles 2:46 3↑ Alw 3500 2 3 42 32 33 34¾ Smithwick AP 142 s *1.90 -- RapidAddition1433RamshornCreek1481¾Mko1427 No excuse 8
3Jly63- 3Del fm *1½ Hurdles 2:474 O Md 5000 5 6 44 1hd 1½ 11½ Smithwick AP 145 s *.70 -- Mako1451½Task Force1453½Miller Street14510 Easily best 8
18Jun63- 5Aqu fm *1⅝ Hurdles 2:483 Annapolis 11k 5 6 57½ 25 22 23 Smithwick AP 140 s 18.95 -- Will I Rule1453Mako1408Lumiere1378 Bore in 5th 7
8Jun63- 6Aqu sf 1 1/16Ⓣ 1:451 Handicap 7500 4 3 33½ 79 715 723 Sorrentino M 112 b 2.60e 59-18 TheIbex1243MarlinBay1181Cabelry113nk Dropped back early 7
29May63- 7Aqu sly 1 :223 :454 1:113 1:39 3↑ Alw 7500 5 6 69 65½ 55 57¼ Errico C 107 23.35 66-18 FirstBreak1081¼JimmyCannon112noAncientAttc1161 No speed 6
23May63- 6Aqu fst 6f :223 :454 1:102 Alw 5000 1 7 108¾ 811 617 616 Boland W 117 89.70 77-13 MatchWits1177½MarlinBay117noWaterTwister122½ No speed 10
23Apr63- 7Lrl fst 6f :224 :464 1:113 Alw 4500 4 2 66¾ 613 618 619 Chambers W 112 3.10 77-07 Fairfab1122½Cycloreen1073Short Nail1124 Couldn't stay 7
29Nov62- 7Pim fst 1 1/16 :243 :482 1:134 1:471 Alw 3500 3 4 46 24 1hd 12 Chambers W 122 7.80 74-23 Mako1222Knocklofty122nkPrinceo'Pilsen1223 Kept driving 8
17Nov62- 6Pim fst 6f :232 :47 :592 1:114 Alw 4000 10 9 105 1012 711 711 Broussard R 122 9.80 80-20 Chateaugay113hdSirGay1185TheSmoochr1113 Showed nothing 11
5Nov62- 1Lrl sly 7f :233 :49 1:153 1:283 Md Sp Wt 8 5 52½ 31 1hd 1nk Broussard R 118 3.40 77-18 Mako118nkTeleJr.1182½Scopelk118nk Kept under hard drive 11
Previously owned by O. Phipps; previously trained by J. Fitzsimmons
9Oct62- 6Bel fst 6f :22 :45 1:11 ©Md Sp Wt 8 8 610 613 617 610 Ruane J 122 10.40 82-13 Crewman1225Might and Main1222½Rolling Sea1221 Far back 10
4Oct62- 4Bel fst 6f :221 :46 1:104 ©Md Sp Wt 5 6 56 64¼ 76½ 812 Sellers J 122 b 4.15 81-15 NoRobbery1226PartyDancer1221¼JohnCanoe122nk Fell back 9
29Sep62- 4Aqu gd 7f :224 :462 1:111 1:243 Md Sp Wt 14 3 63½ 44 37 616 Shoemaker W 122 b *3.00 68-17 CoolPrince1228Dowdeley-Dow1221½Reap theWind1226 Tired 14
21Sep62- 6Aqu fst 7f :223 :46 1:111 1:24 ©Md Sp Wt 3 12 64¼ 65¼ 36 37½ Sellers J 122 b 3.50 79-12 SirGay1222½Macedonia1225Mako1222 Rallied insufficiently 14
15Sep62- 1Aqu fst 7f :233 :471 1:123 1:253 Md Sp Wt 7 6 2hd 2hd 2hd 3¾ Sellers J 122 b *3.10 78-13 HonorBlue117½Tempr122nkMko1225½ Forced pace,weakened 14
15Jun62- 4Bel gd 5½f :234 :48 1:07 ©Md Sp Wt 4 5 2hd 2hd 2hd 21½ Woodhouse H 122 b *2.25 84-18 MonsieurDavid1221½Mako1221HonorBlu122no Held lead,tired 10
23Apr62- 3Aqu fst 5f :232 :474 1:001 ©Md Sp Wt 2 9 44 42½ 35½ 39¼ Woodhouse H 122 3.35 80-22 Cheshire1221¼RoyalTurn1228Mako122¾ Well placed,no rally 10
17Apr62- 3Aqu fst 5f :224 :474 1:011 ©Md Sp Wt 10 9 811 611 54 32¼ Woodhouse H 122 8.00 82-26 President Jim1221Prosperous1221¼Mako122¾ Good late bid 10
9Apr62- 3Aqu gd 5f :223 :463 :592 ©Md Sp Wt 2 4 95¾ 44 55½ 55¼ Woodhouse H 122 *2.40 88-16 The Beadle1222¼Prosperous1222Marching Song122½ Green 10

Moccasin

ch. f. 1963, by Nantallah (Nasrullah)–Rough Shod II, by Gold Bridge **Lifetime record: 21 11 2 4 $388,075**

Own.– Claiborne Farm
Br.– Claiborne Farm (Ky)
Tr.– H. Trotsek

17Jun67- 9AP sly 1 :222 :451 1:103 1:37 3↑ Equipose Mile 43k 2 4 47½ 44¼ 69 59½ Fires E 115 2.20 68-29 Renewed Vigor1111½Estreno II1111½Errante II1144½ 7
Flattened out in drive
24May67- 8AP fst 7f :231 :46 1:103 1:23 3↑ ⒻFour Winds H 21k 4 6 45 67¼ 45½ 31 Fires E 121 b *1.10 89-17 MssMoon120hdMstySwords1111Mccsn1215 Wide,strong finish 7
22Apr67- 6Kee fst 1 1/16 :241 :473 1:114 1:45 3↑ Ben Ali H 23k 3 2 21½ 2hd 32 31¼ Fires E 116 b *1.30 80-17 FrancisU.119nkSwiftRuler1201Moccsn1161½ Lacked response 6
8Apr67- 6Kee fst 6f :213 :451 :571 1:093 3↑ Phoenix H 23k 1 6 43½ 22 2hd 11 Knapp K 114 b 3.30 95-15 Mccsn1141CountryFrnd1144¼GlbrtB.114hd Wore down leader 7
25Feb67- 8Bow fst 7f :223 :442 1:084 1:214 3↑ ⒻBarbara Fritchie H 59k 5 8 4nk 32 3½ 2nk Broussard R 120 b *.60 104-05 Holly-O117nkMccsn1202½LdyDplmt1112¾ Bobbled leaving gate 13
15Feb67- 8Hia fst 7f :23 :452 1:10 1:23 3↑ ⒻColumbiana H 33k 4 3 1½ 15 13 2hd Hartack W 117 b *2.40 94-16 Mac'sSparkler115hdMoccasin1171½StraightDeal122½ Failed 14
6Feb67- 9Hia fst 6f :22 :444 1:103 4↑ Alw 5500 3 8 52¼ 65¼ 46 31¾ Baeza B 114 b *1.00 89-14 FleetAdmiral116¾GoldenButtons1131Moccasin114¾ Steadied 12
4Aug66- 8Sar fst 7f :223 :45 1:10 1:232 ⒻTest (Div 2) 24k 8 2 2hd 23 22 11½ Baeza B 118 b *.90 93-13 Moccasin1181½Native Street1242Politely112¾ Going away 10
25Jun66- 7Aqu fst 1¼ :472 1:12 1:382 2:05 ⒻC C A Oaks 119k 2 2 22 42¼ 55 59¼ Broussard R 121 b 2.40 64-17 LadyPitt121¾DGentleRain121nkPridesProfile1218 Weakened 10
28May66- 7Aqu sly 1 :224 :452 1:102 1:36 ⒻAcorn 59k 7 4 22 21 2hd 34½ Broussard R 121 b *1.40 83-18 Marking Time1212½Around the Roses1212Moccasin121½ Tired 11

17May66- 7Aqu fst 6f :222 :453 1:102 Alw 10000 5 5 21½ 21 1hd 11½ Baeza B 112 b *1.10 91-19 Moccasin1121½Imam1151Bold Tactics115nk Bore out,handily 6
16Apr66- 6Kee fst 6f :213 :45 1:10 ⒻAshland 30k 3 9 54½ 66½ 66½ 66¼ Adams L 121 *.30 87-12 Justakiss121nkPridsProfl1211½ChmpgnWomn1182 Away slowly 9
9Apr66- 7Kee fst 6f :214 :452 1:101 ⒻAlw 10000 6 5 67½ 66½ 55 41¾ Adams L 121 *.20 90-14 Stealaway115¾Dutch Maid110hdJustakiss1211 6
In close entering stretch
6Nov65- 8GS fst 1 1/16 :234 :471 1:121 1:442 ⒻGardenia 183k 7 3 35 31 11½ 12½ Adams L 119 *.30 83-21 Moccasin1192½Lady Pitt119½Prides Profile119nk Cleverly 9
23Oct65- 0Lrl fst 1 1/16 :244 :491 1:144 1:454 ⒻSelima 93k 1 1 12 13 14½ 15 Adams L 119 - 88-15 Moccasin1195SwiftLady119½Drryll114¾ Scored well in hand 5
Run between 6th and 7th races. No wagering
16Oct65- 6Kee fst *7f 1:254 ⒻAlcibiades 37k 2 3 1½ 14 18 115 Adams L 119 - 94-16 Moccasin11915Chalina119noHurry Star11920 Speed to spare 4
No wagering
9Oct65- 4Kee fst 6½f :23 :463 1:113 1:18 ⒻAlw 7500 1 7 76 43¼ 1hd 13 Adams L 119 *.10 88-14 Moccasin1193Fanrullah1074½Strawshy1071½ Drew out easily 7
11Sep65- 7Aqu fst 6f :223 :464 1:113 ⒻMatron 108k 3 2 2½ 2hd 14 16 Adams L 119 *.40 85-20 Moccasin1196Lyvette1192Shimmering Gold1191 Easily 12
25Aug65- 7Sar fst 6f :22 :451 1:11 ⒻSpinaway 76k 7 1 2hd 11 14 13½ Adams L 119 *.30 93-10 Moccasin1193½Swift Lady119noForefoot119hd Much the best 7
17Aug65- 6Sar fst 5½f :214 :452 :573 1:04 ⒻAlw 5500 1 3 1½ 11 15 18 Adams L 119 *.30 97-11 Moccasin1198IndianSunlite1196RoyalTantrm1193½ Galloping 7
6Aug65- 4Sar fst 5½f :221 :46 :58 1:042 ⒻMd Sp Wt 9 2 11½ 11½ 14 18 Adams L 119 7.90 95-13 Moccasin1198Lady Dulcinea1196Ultra Quest1192 Easily 12

Mongo

ch. c. 1959, by Royal Charger (Nearco)–Accra, by Annapolis
Lifetime record: 46 22 10 4 $820,766
Own.– Montpelier
Br.– Mrs Marion duPont Scott (Va)
Tr.– F.A. Bonsal

11Nov64- 8GS fst 1¼ :464 1:11 1:352 2:00 3↑ Trenton H 59k 6 6 66½ 2hd 1hd 1½ Chambers W 125 3.00e 105-10 Mongo125½Drill Site112½Sunrise Flight1171¼ Hard drive 8
29Oct64- 5GS fst 1 1/16 :241 :474 1:111 1:421 4↑ Alw 5500 1 2 22 2½ 1hd 1hd Chambers W 116 *.70 97-13 Mongo116hdDrill Site113nkSunrise Flight1166 All out 6
10Oct64- 7Atl fm 1 1/16Ⓣ 1:444 3↑ Boardwalk H 29k 3 5 52¾ 64½ 67¼ 49 Chambers W 127 *.70e 78-18 Turbo Jet II1181½Cool Prince1133Indoctrinate1154½ Tired 7
19Sep64- 8Atl sf 1 3/16Ⓣ 1:574 3↑ U Nations H 125k 7 6 53½ 75½ 99 96¾ Chambers W 130 *1.90e 77-21 WesternWarrior114¾Parka121hdTurboJetII116nk Fell back 10
22Aug64- 8Atl fst 1 3/16 :484 1:122 1:373 1:561 3↑ Atl City H 33k 4 4 44 48 513 522 Chambers W 133 *.90 78-16 Inbalance1146Cool Prince1136Invigor113½ Sluggish,wide 6
8Aug64- 6Sar fst 1⅛ :471 1:104 1:361 1:491 4↑ Whitney 54k 2 4 33 43½ 33½ 210 Chambers W 130 2.05 89-10 Gun Bow13010Mongo1303Delta Judge1113½ Bested the others 4
18Jly64- 8Mth fst 1¼ :451 1:101 1:353 2:014 3↑ Monmouth H 107k 5 4 46 2hd 1½ 1nk Chambers W 127 5.40 93-17 Mongo127nkKelso1304½Gun Bow12418 Drifted out slightly 5
27Jun64- 0Del fst 1 1/16 :242 :474 1:114 1:434 3↑ Diamond State H 22k 4 2 22½ 2hd 11½ 11½ Chambers W 127 - 90-17 Mngo1271½BoldCmmndr1107ShootLuke1091½ Much the best 4
Special event run between 7th and 8th races - No wagering
25Apr64- 7Aqu fst 1⅛ :463 1:102 1:352 1:482 3↑ Grey Lag H 82k 5 4 45¼ 43½ 24 24 Chambers W 128 3.20 95-16 Saidam1144Mongo128½Bonjour1122½ Finished willingly 7
11Apr64- 7Aqu fst 1⅛ :48 1:12 1:371 1:50 3↑ Excelsior H 27k 1 2 23 31 53 53¾ Chambers W 129 *1.20 87-17 Uppercut1123Rocky Link116hdMorry E.115nk In close,tired 6
7Mar64- 8Bow fst 1 1/16 :24 :473 1:122 1:444 3↑ J B Campbell H 109k 2 6 53¼ 1½ 1½ 1no Rotz JL 126 *1.30 89-20 Mongo126noGun Bow1261Uppercut1145 Drifted wide,lasted 7
22Feb64- 8Hia sly 1¼ :47 1:111 1:363 2:011 3↑ Widener H 130k 2 3 46½ 11 11 1hd Chambers W 125 *2.80 92-18 Mongo125hdSunriseFlight1192AdmrlVc1255 In close,driving 10
8Feb64- 8Hia sl 1⅛ :464 1:113 1:364 1:494 3↑ Seminole H 61k 8 4 54¼ 31½ 22 53 Chambers W 125 *1.20 83-20 [DH]TopGallnt112[DH]AdmirlVic1241SunrsFlght1191¾ Bold bid 9
1Feb64- 0Hia fst 7f :233 :463 1:224 Sp Wt 1 1 11½ 12 11 12½ Chambers W 118 - -- Mongo1182½DoctorHank1153½Tollwy1156 Drifted out,in hand 4
Exhibition race - No purse,no wagering. Not to be considered as a race start
11Nov63- 7Lrl fm 1½Ⓣ :483 1:133 2:033 2:272 3↑ D C Int'l 150k 9 1 1hd 11 1½ 1½ Chambers W 126 3.80 94-14 Mongo126½Kelso12612Nyrcos1223 Under long,hard drive 10
2Nov63- 8GS my 1¼ :464 1:111 1:361 2:014 3↑ Trenton H 59k 4 3 34½ 22 22 22½ Chambers W 124 3.60 93-22 Carry Back1192½Mongo1242Smart1166 Showed good effort 10
19Oct63- 8GS fst 1 1/16 :233 :47 1:112 1:424 3↑ Quaker City H 27k 3 3 34½ 33 33 34¼ Hartack W 127 *.80 92-14 Saidam1131Inbalance1143¼Mongo127nk Lacked late response 5
14Sep63- 8Atl fm 1 3/16Ⓣ 1:551 3↑ U Nations H 125k 2 2 43 31 2hd 12 Chambers W 124 4.90 97-03 Mngo1242NeverBnd118¾CarryBack1271½ Came outside,clear 10
Daily Racing Form time,1:54 2/5
31Aug63- 8Atl fm 1⅛Ⓣ 1:48 3↑ Kelly-Olympic H 35k 10 3 42 43 43¼ 1no Chambers W 124 *2.50 103-00 Mongo124noBronze Babu1201½Parka116¾ Up in final strides 10
17Aug63- 8Atl fst 1⅛ :471 1:11 1:352 1:481 3↑ Atl City H 28k 3 5 514 36½ 33½ 32¾ Chambers W 125 *.90 94-12 DnCrl1092Inblnc113¾Mongo1259 Lacked sufficient response 7
20Jly63- 7Aqu sly 1¼ :472 1:111 1:354 2:013 3↑ Brooklyn H 112k 3 4 33 32 31½ 52¼ Burr C 126 2.75 90-11 Cyrano113noSunrise County1161¼Lanvin108½ In close,tired 10
13Jly63- 8Mth fst 1¼ :473 1:12 1:363 2:02 3↑ Monmouth H 111k 2 4 42½ 32 1hd 21½ Gilligan L 126 *2.30 90-16 Decidedly1201½Mongo1262½Guadalcanl113¾ Short lead,tired 9
29Jun63- 7Del fst 1 1/16 :233 :47 1:113 1:431 3↑ Diamond State H 22k 5 4 43 32 2hd 1¾ Gilligan L 126 *.70 93-20 Mongo126¾FortheRoad1142½Polylad115nk Under a mild drive 6
12Jun63- 8Mth fst 1 :233 :464 1:113 1:364 3↑ Salvator Mile 17k 2 3 2½ 2hd 1hd 2nk Gilligan L 126 *.50 89-17 Dedimoud118nkMngo1263½Narokn1144 Stumbled start,failed 6
25May63- 8GS fst 1⅛ :482 1:121 1:371 1:501 3↑ Camden H 28k 2 1 11 11½ 13 12½ Gilligan L 126 *.90 86-14 Mongo1262½Military Plume1111¾Endymion1133 Mild urging 6
11May63- 7GS gd 1 70 :223 :461 1:113 1:43 3↑ Valley Forge H 27k 1 2 23 22½ 21 3½ Gilligan L 127 *.50 81-22 Manassa Mauler113½Guadalcanal113hdMongo127¾ No excuse 6
23Mar63- 8Bow fst 1 1/16 :242 :481 1:12 1:43 3↑ J B Campbell H 109k 6 3 34 47½ 49½ 46¾ Burr C 128 1.60 91-15 Kelso131¾Crimson Satan124hdGushing Wind1166 Forced up 6
9Mar63- 8Bow fst 1 1/16 :241 :483 1:13 1:444 3↑ Bowie H 26k 5 2 2¾ 2hd 1hd 13½ Burr C 126 *.30 89-23 Mngo1263½WarCouncil1154½FruitShppr106½ Drew out easily 5
22Nov62- 7GS my 1⅛ :474 1:121 1:381 1:512 3↑ Pilgrim H 55k 1 1 1½ 12½ 13 15 Burr C 120 *.90 80-29 Mongo1205Garwol1096Dedimoud1143 Going away with ease 6
3Nov62- 7GS sly 1¼ :471 1:121 1:382 2:053 3↑ Trenton H 86k 6 2 2½ 13 12 1no Burr C 118 5.40 77-29 Mongo118noCarryBck1294½Snstvo116¾ Best under hard drive 8
17Oct62- 7Bel hd 1⅜Ⓣ 2:131 3↑ Knickerbocker H 30k 5 3 32 31½ 11 2¾ Burr C 120 5.45 103-00 TheAxeII120¾Mongo1201½IrishDandy112½ Clear lead,tired 12
15Sep62- 8Atl fm 1 3/16Ⓣ 1:563 3↑ U Nations H 100k 5 6 41¾ 1hd 1hd 1nk Burr C 117 8.70 90-10 Mongo117nkT.V.Lark123½WiseShip1232 Hard ridden to hold 12
1Sep62- 7Aqu fst 1 :224 :453 1:09 1:343 Jerome H 58k 8 4 42 41¾ 45 65½ Burr C 121 *2.70 89-11 Black Beard1143Fauve109½Dedimoud116½ Well up,tired 12
11Aug62- 8Atl sf 1 1/16Ⓣ 1:441 Ventnor Turf H 30k 13 2 21½ 12 18 110 Burr C 122 8.30 90-10 Mngo12210NobleJy122hdOurTwg1141 Scored with great ease 14
25Jly62- 7Aqu fst 1 :224 :443 1:082 1:341 Lexington H 29k 5 2 32 31½ 11 1nk Burr C 118 3.05 97-10 Mngo118nkDedmoud1172½InForc1172 Drifted out,hard drive 8
7Jly62- 7Del fst 1 :234 :47 1:112 1:37 Alw 6500 4 2 12 13 15 18 Burr C 114 3.20 91-17 Mongo1148Cyane120¾Water Hole114nk Long lead,easily best 7
18Jun62- 7Del fst 6f :224 :462 1:114 Alw 5000 1 3 32 53 33 23 Burr C 116 2.80 83-25 FortheRoad1163Mngo1161WaterHol1161½ Shuffled back turn 9
23Apr62- 7Lrl fst 6f :23 :472 1:122 Alw 4000 2 2 46 43½ 2hd 1¾ Chambers A 120 1.70 93-17 Mongo120¾In Force1173Nemrac1172½ Under strong handling 6
6Apr62- 7Lrl fst 6f :23 :47 1:113 Alw 4000 5 8 62¾ 53 22 11 Korte K 112 3.10 97-16 Mongo1121Bullfinch1191Nip o' Brandy1226 Won going away 9
4Nov61- 4Lrl fst 7f :231 :464 1:122 1:243 Alw 3200 5 3 52 4¾ 22 23 Lee T 114 *2.20 96-09 WillofIron1123Mngo1142¼DicksPet1145 Showed good effort 7
27Oct61- 7Lrl fst 6f :224 :48 1:133 Alw 3000 4 6 74¼ 61¾ 31½ 1¾ Lee T 113 *.80 87-15 Mngo113¾Astounded1132GetSomeMre1143½ Long,hard drive 10
14Oct61- 3GS sly 6f :23 :47 1:121 Alw 4000 4 3 51¾ 43 23 23½ Lee T 113 *1.60 79-20 PaddedCll1173½Mngo1135Dck'sPt1173½ Rallied,then evenly 8
27Sep61- 5Atl fst 7f :223 :452 1:10 1:222 Alw 3600 7 5 2½ 21 23 31¾ Lee T 109 *1.40 89-10 BrownBulldog116¾Nipo'Brndy1151Mongo109nk Lacked a rally 8
12Sep61- 5Atl fst 6f :221 :45 1:094 Alw 3800 3 5 56¼ 56 34½ 43¾ Lee T 110 *1.50 92-12 SweetEvenin'1132LadyDame1161¼InForce119½ Mild bid,hung 7
2Sep61- 4Atl fst 6f :221 :453 1:102 Alw 3600 5 1 31½ 2½ 2nk Lee T 119 4.10 93-07 Senator119nkMongo1191¼Proud Fox1143 Very sharp effort 8
31May61- 5Del fst 5f :22 :463 :592 Alw 4000 8 6 53¾ 68 57½ 55¾ Lee T 120 *.50 86-23 Princegret1201PostExchange1201GetSomeMor1201¾ No excuse 8
18May61- 5Pim fst 5f :23 :471 1:00 Md Sp Wt 4 3 11 14 16 110 Lee T 118 *.60 95-18 Mongo11810Reinav1182½Black Blazer118nk Easily best 6

Native Diver

br. g. 1959, by Imbros (Polynesian)–Fleet Diver, by Devil Diver
Own.– Mr & Mrs L.K. Shapiro
Br.– Mr & Mrs L.K. Shapiro (Cal)
Tr.– M.E. Millerick

Lifetime record: 81 37 7 12 $1,026,500

Date/Race	Cond	Dist	Fractions	Race	Running line	Jockey	Wt	Eqp	Odds	Figures	Finishers	Comment	Field
4Sep67- 8Dmr	fst	1⅛	:452 1:092 1:342 1:463	3↑ Del Mar H 43k	3 1 12 12 13 13½	Lambert J	130		*.50	100-14	NativeDiver1303½SharpDecline1093½QuickenTre117½	Handily	9
15Jly67- 8Hol	fst	1¼	:454 1:092 1:34 1:584	3↑ Hol Gold Cup H 162k	2 1 14 11 12 15	Lambert J	123		4.80	99-17	Native Diver1235Pretense131¾Biggs1174	Drew out easily	5
4Jly67- 8Hol	fst	1⅛	:452 1:093 1:341 1:47	3↑ American H 54k	6 1 13 11½ 23½ 24¼	Lambert J	123		3.90	93-15	Pretense1314¼Native Diver123¾Biggs1171¾	Held on gamely	8
17Jun67- 8Hol	fm	1 1/16Ⓣ	:221 :46 1:093 1:394	3↑ Inglewood H (Div 2) 44k	6 2 2hd 68½ 715 722	Lambert J	124		2.90	- -	Pretense1284½Biggs1171½AureliusII1114	Early speed,tired	7
3Jun67- 8Hol	fst	1 1/16	:23 :453 1:093 1:413	3↑ Californian 119k	12 4 43 87½ 1313 1317	Pierce D	127		*1.90	70-14	Biggs112¾Make Money1123¾Pretense130hd	Raced wide	14
20May67- 8Hol	fst	7f	:221 :442 1:084 1:21	3↑ Los Angeles H 54k	8 1 11½ 11 1½ 11½	Lambert J	128		*.90	95-16	NativeDivr1281½Shbson1112¼Chclro1142	Under steady drive	8
10May67- 8Hol	fst	6f	:22 :444 :564 1:091	3↑ Premiere H 27k	7 1 31½ 32 43½ 33¾	Lambert J	131		*1.30	91-10	FleetDiscovery1102Chiclero1151¾NativeDivr1312½	No rally	7
18Mar67- 8GG	fst	1	:224 :45 1:094 1:351	3↑ San Fran Mile H 16k	7 1 11½ 1½ 1½ 1hd	Lambert J	133		*.60	92-15	NativeDiver133hdPerris1134½TrplTux113no	Strong handling	8
11Mar67- 8GG	sly	6f	:214 :442 :57 1:092	3↑ Albany H 11k	2 4 1½ 1½ 1½ 11½	Lambert J	130		*.40	92-19	NativeDiver1301½TripleTux113hdChclro117hd	Driving clear	8
25Feb67- 8SA	fst	1¼	:454 1:10 1:352 2:004	3↑ S Anita H 145k	4 1 13½ 2hd 22 23	Pierce D	125		4.70	91-11	Pretense1183Native Diver125¾O'Hara1131½	Held gamely	9
11Feb67- 8SA	fst	1⅛	:45 1:092 1:351 1:483	4↑ San Antonio H 57k	2 1 12 1hd 23 35¼	Lambert J	128		*1.00	84-12	Pretense1212Drin1193¼NatvDvr1282	Set pace on loose rein	8
26Jan67- 8SA	gd	1 1/16	:23 :46 1:103 1:43	4↑ San Pasqual H 27k	3 1 1hd 2hd 32½ 34	Lambert J	132		*.70	84-21	Pretense1184Aurelius II114hdNative Diver1322	No excuse	5
7Jan67- 8SA	fst	7f	:22 :442 1:091 1:22	4↑ San Carlos H 62k	5 1 12 12½ 14 14	Lambert J	128		*2.20	93-15	NativeDiver1284HoistBar1152Pretense118½	Speed to spare	13
25Jly66- 8Hol	fst	1⅝	:454 1:361 2:022 2:402	3↑ Sunset H 85k	6 1 14 32 59 619	Lambert J	130		*1.60	70-16	O'Hara1132Rehabilitate1061½SilkHt1093	Set pace 6f,tired	11
16Jly66- 8Hol	fst	1¼	:451 1:091 1:341 2:00	3↑ Hol Gold Cup H 162k	7 1 12 13 15 14¾	Lambert J	126		*1.40	93-19	NativeDiver1264¾O'Hara112nkTravelOrb1188	Speed to spare	10
4Jly66- 8Hol	fst	1⅛	:452 1:092 1:35 1:474	3↑ American H 56k	7 1 12 13 11 2¾	Mahorney W	128		*1.10	92-16	TravelOrb118¾NativeDiver1284RealGoodDeal1122½	Stubborn	12
18Jun66- 8Hol	fst	1 1/16	:223 :452 1:094 1:413	3↑ Inglewood H 58k	2 1 12 12 13½ 16	Lambert J	125		*2.00	87-18	Native Diver1256Sledge1151Tronado113¾	Under mild drive	14
4Jun66- 8Hol	fst	1 1/16	:223 :453 1:094 1:414	3↑ Californian 120k	7 5 129¾ 1411 1412 1415	Lambert J	127		2.50	71-14	Travel Orb1121Make Money1121½Sledge1121¼	Bore out turns	14
21May66- 8Hol	fst	7f	:214 :44 1:084 1:213	3↑ Los Angeles H 54k	6 3 3½ 31 41½ 41½	Lambert J	128		*.80	90-15	Nasharco1131Pelegrn116nkAurlusII111nk	Hung under impost	8
11May66- 8Hol	fst	6f	:221 :45 :571 1:101	3↑ Premiere H 28k	7 1 41¼ 63 78½ 74¼	Lambert J	130		*.60	86-20	Sledg115noChclro110nkRlGoodDl116½	Forced wide,no chance	9
9Mar66- 7SA	fst	1 1/16	:224 :453 1:093 1:403	3↑ San Bernardino H 27k	5 1 12½ 11½ 11½ 12½	Lambert J	130		*.50e	100-10	Native Diver1302½Real Good Deal1169Prairie Schooner1141	Mild drive	5
26Feb66- 8SA	fst	1¼	:452 1:094 1:35 2:001	3↑ S Anita H 145k	2 1 12 2½ 3nk 32	Lambert J	126		6.10	96-12	Lucky Debonair1241Cupid1171Native Diver126nk	Gamely	13
12Feb66- 8SA	fst	1⅛	:452 1:092 1:343 1:47	4↑ San Antonio H 56k	5 1 12 1hd 43 45	Lambert J	128		2.20	92-14	HillRise125½Terry'sSecret1222½BoldBidder1252	Weakened	6
25Jan66- 8SA	fst	1 1/16	:224 :453 1:094 1:41	4↑ San Pasqual H 28k	3 1 14 11½ 11½ 1hd	Lambert J	128		*1.60	98-15	NativeDiver128hdCupid118nkIsleofGrc1191¼	Lasted,driving	10
8Jan66- 8SA	fst	7f	:22 :443 1:091 1:22	4↑ San Carlos H 61k	7 6 2½ 44½ 1010 109½	Lambert J	132		*1.20	83-15	Cupid1152HillRise126noQuitDud115no	Lost action,bore out	12
28Dec65- 7SA	fst	6f	:213 :442 :563 1:09	3↑ Palos Verdes H 22k	6 1 1½ 11 1½ 1nk	Lambert J	129		*.50	97-13	Native Diver129nkIsle of Greece1141Sledge1211	Driving	6
6Sep65- 8AP	fst	1	:223 :451 1:094 1:351	3↑ Wash Park H 113k	8 1 2hd 33 32½ 62½	Lambert J	128		*2.00	90-11	Take Over110noChieftain126noGallant Romeo1201	Weakened	11
7Aug65- 7Dmr	fst	1 1/16	:221 :45 1:09 1:40	3↑ San Diego H 22k	4 1 13 11½ 12 13½	Lambert J	131		*.30	100-11	NativeDiver1313½NearcoBlue1104½Carang111¾	Much the best	8
17Jly65- 8Hol	fst	1¼	:444 1:084 1:341 2:001	3↑ Hol Gold Cup H 162k	3 1 16 13 14 15	Lambert J	124		*1.20	92-13	NativeDiver1245Babington1141½HllRs1212	As rider pleased	7
5Jly65- 8Hol	fst	1⅛	:45 1:09 1:342 1:471	3↑ American H 53k	1 1 16 12 14 12	Lambert J	125		3.90	96-11	NativeDiver1252Trondo1181¼HllRs122¾	Scored well in hand	6
22May65- 8Hol	fst	7f	:221 :44 1:074 1:20	3↑ Los Angeles H 55k	3 3 11½ 1hd 1hd 1nk	Lambert J	126		1.90	100-13	NativeDiver126nkVikngSprt1266Trondo115¾	Long,hard drive	9
12May65- 8Hol	fst	6f	:214 :441 :561 1:082	3↑ Premiere H 27k	6 3 3nk 2½ 31½ 34	Lambert J	127		*1.40	95-10	VikingSpirit1233Perris1131NtvDvr127hd	Forced pace,tired	8
27Mar65- 8GG	my	1	:222 :453 1:104 1:364	3↑ San Fran Mile H 15k	1 1 13 1½ 1hd 22½	Lambert J	128		*.50	81-24	Viking Spirit1192½Native Diver1286Honored Sir113½	Bore out stretch	5
13Mar65- 8GG	my	6f	:214 :453 :58 1:11	3↑ Albany H 10k	2 4 33½ 2hd 2½ 1hd	Lambert J	129		*.50	85-26	NativeDivr129hdWarHelmt1162Emphl'sLodg1174½	Hard drive	6
9Jan65- 8SA	fst	7f	:214 :44 1:084 1:212	4↑ San Carlos H 58k	5 1 14 13 12 13½	Lambert J	126		1.90	96-12	Native Diver1263½Candy Spots125½Bonjour1144	Mild urging	9
26Dec64- 6SA	gd	6f	:22 :451 :573 1:101	3↑ Palos Verdes H 23k	1 3 12 11½ 11½ 12½	Lambert J	125		2.40	91-25	NativeDiver1252½VikingSpirit1202Sledge125nk	Mild drive	7
7Nov64- 8BM	fst	6f	:22 :442 :563 1:083	3↑ Redwood City H 10k	2 3 12 13 13 15	Lambert J	127		*1.00	99-12	Native Diver1275Testum1233¾Clavo114no	Drew out at will	7
8Aug64- 8Dmr	fst	1 1/16	:22 :443 1:09 1:414	3↑ San Diego H 22k	5 2 11½ 13 13 14	Lambert J	122		*.70	91-15	NativeDiver1224FinalCommand1094½DrillSite117no	Easily	8
18Jly64- 8Hol	fst	1¼	:443 1:084 1:342 2:002	3↑ Hol Gold Cup H 162k	9 1 15 11 2hd 32	Lambert J	117		28.50	89-13	ColoradoKing1182MustardPlastr119hdNtvDvr1174	Weakened	11
4Jly64- 8Hol	fst	1⅛	:451 1:093 1:342 1:462	3↑ American H 55k	5 1 11 2hd 34½ 513	Lambert J	120		6.70	88-15	ColoradoKing1198MustardPlaster1202VikingSpirt1112½	Used	9
20Jun64- 8Hol	fst	1 1/16	:23 :453 1:093 1:413	3↑ Inglewood H 55k	6 1 13 12 13 1¾	Lambert J	116		12.40	87-15	NativeDiver116¾MustrdPlstr1181½Mr.Consstncy1242	Driving	9
6Jun64- 8Hol	fst	1 1/16	:224 :461 1:102 1:413	3↑ Californian 115k	8 1 11½ 1hd 31½ 811	Moreno P	115		11.70	76-14	Mustard Plaster1111½Mr. Consistency1231½ColordoKing1232½	Took up final ⅛	10
18May64- 8GG	fst	1⅛	:46 1:10 1:353 1:481	3↑ Oakland H 29k	6 2 11½ 11½ 11 1nk	Valenzuela I	122		*.40	93-16	NativeDiver122nkEscadal1055½Jim'sPurchase1111	Hand ride	7
25Apr64- 8GG	fst	1 1/16	:224 :452 1:092 1:421	3↑ W G Gilmore H 22k	9 1 12 11½ 13 1nk	Lambert J	120		*1.60	93-15	Native Diver120nkUpper Half1112½Drill Site116¾	Driving	10
11Apr64- 8GG	fst	6f	:22 :444 :571 1:092	3↑ Sacramento H 10k	4 3 2½ 23 23 31	Lambert J	123		*1.10	92-17	Mustard Plaster119nkDouble Lea119¾Native Diver1231	Not enough late	5
28Mar64- 8GG	fst	1	:222 :444 1:09 1:344	3↑ S Fran Mile H (Div 2) 12k	6 2 2½ 2hd 11½ 3½	Lambert J	123		*1.40	93-11	MustardPlaster115nkUpperHlf110nkNtvDvr1233	Used in pace	8
14Mar64- 8GG	fst	6f	:213 :44 :561 1:084	3↑ Albany H 10k	5 4 41½ 45½ 57½ 43¾	Lambert J	126		*1.30	92-14	Double Lea1192½Clavo1111¼Sledge123no	Wide,fast finish	5
8Feb64- 7SA	fst	1⅛	:452 1:092 1:342 1:472	4↑ San Antonio H 58k	7 1 11 37 410 613	Longden J	119		13.80	82-12	Gun Bow1254Cyrano1243Quita Dude114no	Gave way	7
21Jan64- 7SA	gd	1 1/16	:231 :464 1:114 1:442	4↑ San Pasqual H 28k	8 1 13 11 3½ 65½	Church K	123		3.70	76-26	OldenTimes120¾DocJocoy118hdDonutKing1134	In close late	8
4Jan64- 8SA	fst	7f	:221 :444 1:092 1:22	4↑ San Carlos H 59k	5 5 11 1hd 2hd 32¾	Pierce D	125		6.60	90-14	Admiral's Voyage1242Cyrano126¾Native Diver125½	Weakened	8
21Dec63- 8GG	my	1 1/16	:231 :463 1:112 1:444	3↑ Golden Gate H 21k	1 1 16 16 16 11¾	Shoemaker W	130		*.60	80-35	NativeDiver1301¾FriendlyFried1124¾Ol'Bleu104¾	In hand	6
7Dec63- 8GG	fst	1	:23 :46 1:093 1:351	3↑ San Fran Mile H 15k	5 2 11½ 12 14 14½	Shoemaker W	125		*.60	92-20	NativeDiver1254½MoreMegaton1181¼ArofInt1153½	Easy score	8
26Oct63- 8Tan	fst	1 1/16	:221 :444 1:093 1:42	3↑ Tanforan H 22k	5 3 1hd 1hd 2½ 65½	Volzke M	126		*.40	95-10	Mill'sTurk109nkIc1132RoylTowr1081½	Tired last sixteenth	9
5Oct63- 8Tan	fst	1 1/16	:224 :453 1:092 1:413	3↑ Westlake H 10k	5 1 11½ 15 18 112	Lambert J	123		*1.20	103-14	NativeDivr12312Four-and-Twnty124noMll'sTurk1111½	Easily	7
2Sep63- 8Dmr	fst	1⅛	:443 1:083 1:341 1:47	3↑ Del Mar H 33k	10 1 1½ 32 46½ 77	Neves R	124		*3.20	91-12	Mr.Consistency116hdRapido1162Mr.Wag1131½	Speed 6f,tired	11
17Aug63- 7Dmr	fst	6f	:213 :441 :562 1:083	3↑ Bing Crosby H 15k	5 6 64½ 64¼ 66½ 67¾	Neves R	125		*.90	88-13	Sledge117½Testum1191GallntHost1145	Showed a dull effort	6
3Aug63- 7Dmr	fst	1 1/16	:223 :453 1:092 1:403	3↑ San Diego H 22k	4 1 11½ 11½ 12 11½	Neves R	123		*1.20	97-13	NativeDiver1231½RobRoyIII117½PirateCove119½	Handy score	8
13Jly63- 8Hol	fst	1¼	:45 1:09 1:333 1:593	3↑ Hol Gold Cup H 162k	1 1 11½ 1½ 1hd 45¼	Neves R	121		7.30	90-14	Cadiz1111½Aldrshot1103OlympdKng111¾	Made all pace,tired	10
4Jly63- 8Hol	fst	1⅛	:451 1:093 1:351 1:481	3↑ American H 57k	3 1 1hd 21½ 33½ 75¼	Neves R	122		*1.90	87-12	Dr. Kacy114½Admiral's Voyage1231½[DH]Mr. Consistency1131¼	No excuse	12
15Jun63- 8Hol	fst	1 1/16	:224 :453 1:094 1:421	3↑ Inglewood H 54k	3 1 11 11½ 14 14¼	Neves R	121		3.50	84-12	NativeDiver1214¼PiratCov1153¼Aldrshot1141	Much the best	8
6Jun63- 8Hol	fst	6f	:214 :442 :563 1:084	3↑ Coronado H 16k	4 6 52¼ 44 33½ 23¾	Neves R	124		3.30	93-13	WindySea1193¾NativDvr124hdMr.Wg115½	Altered course turn	7
9May63- 8Hol	fst	6f	:214 :442 :564 1:092	3↑ Hol Premiere H 22k	8 6 52¼ 65¼ 76¾ 66	Neves R	125		*.70	88-13	Winonly1211¾Kisco Kid112½Double Lea115½	Very wide turn	8
29Jan63- 7SA	fst	1 1/16	:223 :453 1:101 1:421	4↑ San Pasqual H 27k	3 1 12 1½ 22 22¾	Neves R	125		*.90	90-15	OldenTimes1252¾NativeDiver1251½Physicn117nk	Held gamely	6
12Jan63- 7SA	fst	1⅛	:453 1:093 1:344 1:471	San Fernando 58k	13 4 18 1½ 1½ 2nk	Shoemaker W	120		*1.40	96-12	CrimsonSatan117nkNativeDiver12010PirateCove1142	Gamely	14
5Jan63- 7SA	fst	7f	:214 :442 1:084 1:211	4↑ San Carlos H 61k	10 1 12 11½ 11 31¼	Neves R	125		*2.40	96-12	Crozier1241¼Olden Times125noNative Diver1254¾	Weakened	10
29Dec62- 6SA	fst	7f	:22 :443 1:09 1:213	Malibu 29k	12 2 13 16 15 16¼	Neves R	117		*.70	95-15	NativeDvr1176¼GrdIronHro1214½Humoso1141½	Speed to spare	13
8Dec62- 8BM	fst	1 1/16	:222 :451 1:092 1:42	San Jose H 16k	1 1 11½ 11 13 12	Neves R	122		*1.10	94-15	NativeDiver1222Raiko112nkRoyalAttack124hd	Scored easily	8
10Nov62- 8BM	fst	6f	:214 :442 :562 1:083	3↑ Salinas H 10k	6 3 11 12 13 15	Neves R	119	b	*.80	100-16	NativeDiver1195Aeroflint118hdMr.Wag1184	Set pace,easily	7
3Nov62- 8BM	fst	6f	:214 :44 1:082	Hillsdale H 10k	7 1 11 12 13 15½	Neves R	120		*1.30	101-15	NativeDiver1205½BoldCorporal1195Jesse'sInvdr114½	Easily	8
11Aug62- 6Dmr	fst	5½f	:22 :45 :564 1:024	3↑ Handicap 5000	5 2 41¾ 41½ 66 57½	Spraker L	114		2.70	97-08	Henrijan115¾Ann's Knight1181½Rob Bob1121¼	Well up,tired	7
28Jly62- 7Dmr	fst	6f	:214 :442 :563 1:09	Oceanside H 16k	5 3 31½ 43 46 43¾	Neves R	123		2.10	93-06	Doc Jocoy126nkTestum120¾Private World1172¾	Raced evenly	8
19Jly62- 7Hol	fst	6f	:214 :443 :563 1:084	3↑ Lakes & Flowers H 27k	5 2 1hd 31 45½ 34¾	Neves R	113		4.00	92-11	WalletLifter1112¾Ann'sKnight1192NativeDvr113½	Wide turn	9

6Jly62-7Hol	fst	6f	:214 :443 :563 1:09	3↑ Alw 12000	2 3 2hd 3½ 4½ 5¾	Neves R	115	*1.60	93-14	CrazyKid1131½LittleJuan116¾Testum112¾	Bore out,weakened	7
8Jun62-6Hol	fst	7f	:22 :441 1:09 1:214	Alw 8500	8 2 12 1½ 13 14½	Neves R	120	*2.40e	91-14	NativeDiver1204½CalgryBrook114hdWldy1112½	Much the best	12
30May62-7Hol	fst	1	:222 :451 1:093 1:343	©Will Rogers (Div 2) 27k	6 1 1½ 2½ 67½ 614	Neves R	120	6.90	79-11	PrinceofPlnty1142RoyalAttack126½DocJocoy1234½	Gave way	8
12May62-7Hol	fst	6f	:214 :442 :563 1:091	©Debonair 29k	5 5 1hd 1hd 2hd 1no	Neves R	112	*1.40	95-13	Native Diver112noPrince of Plenty1123Black Sheep116hd		12
Led again late												
30Dec61-7SA	fst	1 1/16	:23 :462 1:113 1:443	[S]Cal Br Champ 64k	5 2 21 21½ 47 49¾	Neves R	118	1.60	71-14	Najin1182½BoldCorporl1181¾IndnBlood1185½	Wide,weakened	6
16Dec61-8Tan	fst	1 1/16	:224 :46 1:102 1:433	San Bruno H 16k	7 2 21 24 23 36¼	Neves R	122	*.30	87-16	Indian Blood1202½Poland China1133¾Native Diver1222½		7
Weakened final 1/8												
25Nov61-8Tan	sly	6f	:222 :45 :573 1:102	El Camino H 10k	7 6 11½ 14 18 16¼	Volzke M	120	*.30	94-19	NativeDiver1206¼Turalea1131¼IndianBlood1222	Plenty left	8
7Nov61-8Tan	fst	6f	:221 :443 :571 1:10	Alw 2500	7 3 13 18 112 110	Neves R	114	*.20	96-18	NativeDiver11410NightsGlory1103½Nov'sBoo1144½	In hand	7
27Sep61-4BM	fst	6f	:221 :451 :572 1:094	Md Sp Wt	7 2 12 11½ 15 17½	Neves R	118	*1.50	94-13	Native Diver1187½El Peco1183½Crafty Pupil118hd	Easily	9

Never Bend

dkb. c. 1960, by Nasrullah (Nearco)–Lalun, by Djeddah

Own.– Cain Hoy Stable

Br.– Harry F. Guggenheim (Ky)

Tr.– W.C. Stephens

Lifetime record: 23 13 4 4 $641,524

2Nov63-7Aqu	sf	1 5/8 (T)	2:453	3↑ Man o' War 113k	8 1 12 36 716 1030	Ycaza M	122	4.00	42-28	TheAxeII1265WillIRule1222½Guadalcanal1262½	Speed,tired	11
16Oct63-9Suf	fst	1 1/8	:464 1:103 1:36 1:49	Yankee H 58k	9 1 11 11 12 14	Ycaza M	126	*2.20	96-13	NeverBend1264DeanCarl123½QuestLink117nk	Kept to drive	9
7Oct63-7Aqu	fm	1 3/16 (T)	1:543	3↑ Long Island H 29k	3 2 2½ 2hd 1hd 32¼	Ycaza M	120	*1.10	95-03	DavidK.113nkTheAxeII1262NeverBend1202	Short lead,tired	10
28Sep63-7Aqu	fst	1¼	:473 1:114 1:362 2:004	3↑ Woodward 108k	3 1 13 1½ 2½ 23½	Shoemaker W	120	4.85	92-13	Kelso1263½Never Bend1201½Crimson Satan1266	Game effort	5
14Sep63-8Atl	fm	1 3/16 (T)	1:551	3↑ U Nations H 125k	3 1 11 11 1hd 22	Ycaza M	118	5.70	95-03	Mongo1242Never Bend118¾Carry Back1271½	Set pace,gamely	10
Daily Racing Form time,1:54 2/5												
27Aug63-7Aqu	fst	1	:231 :461 1:102 1:35	Handicap 10000	6 4 41½ 3½ 12 13½	Ycaza M	130	*.50	93-20	NeverBend1303½MasterDennis1152½RollingSe110½	Mild drive	6
17Aug63-6Sar	fst	1¼	:472 1:111 1:36 2:022	Travers 81k	2 1 11 1hd 33 611	Ycaza M	126	2.95	85-08	Crewmn1201½HotDust1141Chateaugy1262½	Used setting pace	6
2Aug63-7Sar	my	1	:234 :471 1:12 1:373	Alw 7500	2 1 11 11 12 11¾	Ycaza M	126	*.40	89-18	NevrBnd1261¾HenrytheEighth114noMasterDnns1141½	Easily	5
18May63-8Pim	fst	1 3/16	:472 1:113 1:37 1:561	Preakness 180k	5 1 11½ 1½ 33 38	Ycaza M	126	1.80	84-12	CandySpots1263½Chateaugay1264½NevrBnd1262¼	Weakened	8
4May63-7CD	fst	1¼	:462 1:10 1:352 2:014	Ky Derby 151k	6 1 11 11 21 21¼	Ycaza M	126	3.10	92-08	Chateaugay1261¼NeverBend126nkCandySpots1264¾	Gamely	9
26Apr63-8CD	fst	7f	:23 :453 1:094 1:222	Alw 7500	2 2 1hd 13 14 18	Ycaza M	122	-	98-16	Never Bend1228Space Skates1193½Book Full1101	Ridden out	4
Nonwagering event												
19Apr63-6Kee	fst	7f	:222 :451 1:10 1:224	Alw 10000	3 5 55 43½ 11 11	Ycaza M	122	-e	94-09	NeverBnd1221BlazeStarr110nkRunnngBowln1132¼	Mild drive	5
Nonwagering event												
2Mar63-7Hia	fst	1 1/8	:47 1:11 1:36 1:492	Flamingo 135k	5 1 13 12 14 15	Ycaza M	122	*.35	88-16	NeverBnd1225KingToots1222RoylAscot1221¼	Kept to urging	10
18Feb63-0Hia	my	7f	:233 :464 1:241	Special Weight	4 1 1hd 11 15 114	Ycaza M	122		88-17	NevrBnd12214MyCount1105½Dog'sFool1104	Drew out easily	4
Exhibition. Run between 6th and 7th races. No purse,no wagering. Not to be considered as a race start												
10Nov62-7GS	sly	1 1/16	:24 :48 1:122 1:44	Garden State 273k	3 2 21½ 42 33 39	Ycaza M	122	*.50	81-23	Crewmn1226InthePocket1223NverBnd122¾	Lacked response	7
2Nov62-7GS	fst	1 1/16	:232 :472 1:122 1:441	Alw 10000	2 3 41½ 31½ 13 15	Ycaza M	122	*.40	89-23	Never Bend1225Right Proud112noIn the Pocket1132½	Easily	14
13Oct62-7Bel	fst	1	:232 :461 1:11 1:354	Champagne 189k	4 1 1½ 11½ 14 18	Ycaza M	122	*.45	95-15	Never Bend1228Master Dennis122¾Outing Class122hd	Easily	7
1Oct62-7Bel	fst	7f	:221 :453 1:103 1:231	Cowdin 71k	8 12 86½ 64 1hd 13	Ycaza M	124	*.90	91-13	NeverBend1243ValiantSkol1171¼RockyLnk1142	Reared,easily	13
15Sep62-7Aqu	fst	6½f	:221 :452 1:103 1:171	Futurity 152k	9 7 41¾ 31½ 1½ 11¾	Shoemaker W	122	*1.15	97-13	NeverBnd1221¾OutingClss1222½PckTrp122hd	Scored handily	13
8Sep62-8AP	fst	7f	:221 :443 1:093 1:214	Arl-Wash Futurity 357k	3 3 42½ 33 1hd 2½	Ycaza M	122	*1.10	97-09	Candy Spots122½Never Bend1226Rash Prince122½	Bore in	13
31Aug62-8AP	fst	6f	:22 :443 1:092	Alw 10000	7 9 54 54½ 32½ 11½	Ycaza M	115	*.80	97-08	NeverBend1151½AimnFire1152½RashPrince120½	Clear at end	10
4Aug62-8Mth	fst	6f	:211 :44 1:103	Sapling 108k	1 4 1hd 2hd 1hd 31	Ycaza M	122	*.90	88-14	DeltaJudge122½Bonjour122½NeverBend1225	Hard used,tired	9
16Jly62-8Mth	fst	6f	:213 :444 1:101	Alw 4500	4 2 13 15 18 18	Ycaza M	120	*.30	91-21	NevrBnd1208SumDumKid120½MonsieurDavid1209	Mild drive	7
30Jun62-3Bel	fst	5½f	:224 :454 1:043	Md Sp Wt	3 3 11½ 13 16 18	Ycaza M	122	*.95	98-12	Never Bend1228Master Dennis1225Dare Say122nk	Easy score	9

Nodouble

ch. c. 1965, by Noholme II (Star Kingdom)–Abla-Jay, by Double Jay

Own.– Verna Lea Farm

Br.– Gene Goff (Ark)

Tr.– J.B. Sonnier

Lifetime record: 42 13 11 5 $846,749

24Oct70-7Aqu	fst	7f	:222 :443 1:09 1:212	3↑ Vosburgh H 59k	6 6 63¾ 74¾ 74 52¼	Tejeira J	126	3.30	92-15	Best Turn115hdTrue North115noOcean Bar1132	Lacked rally	11
20Jun70-9Det	fst	1 1/8	:46 1:092 1:344 1:472	3↑ Mich 1 1/8 126k	1 1 47½ 49 69¼ 57½	Tejeira J	127	*1.10	92-19	FastHilarious116noFigonero1192¼PleasurSkr1115	No excuse	9
30May70-7Bel	fst	1	:223 :45 1:092 1:343	3↑ Metropolitan H 114k	1 3 33 31½ 31½ 1hd	Tejeira J	126	5.80	101-11	Nodouble126hdReviewer1233Dewan122¾	Last strides	10
16May70-8Hol	fst	1 1/16	:232 :462 1:101 1:401	3↑ Californian 112k	5 4 44 31 46 36¼	Pineda A	130	5.00	88-12	Baffle1135Figonero1241¼Nodouble130hd	No rally	8
21Mar70-9GP	fst	1¼	:48 1:123 1:38 2:04	3↑ Gulf Park H 123k	3 6 76¾ 2hd 46 58¼	Tejeira J	127	2.30	70-17	Snow Sporting1182½Twogundan1152½Al Hattab1142	Bumped	9
7Mar70-8SA	fst	1¼	:451 1:092 1:341 1:593	4↑ S Anita H 145k	3 5 88½ 94¾ 95¾ 87¾	Tejeira J	130	*1.20	92-05	QuickenTree118¾FiddleIsle1193½FieldMstr1141¾	No excuse	12
7Feb70-8SA	fst	1 1/16	:222 :451 1:092 1:402	4↑ San Pasqual H 46k	5 5 57½ 2½ 1½ 12	Tejeira J	128	*.70	101-07	Nodouble1282Field Master116¾Dewan120hd	Drew clear	9
25Oct69-7Aqu	fst	2	:511 2:293 2:544 3:222	3↑ J C Gold Cup 106k	2 2 1hd 28 210 214	Belmonte E	124	2.90	70-14	Arts and Letters11914Nodouble1249Harem Lady121	Gamely	4
18Oct69-8Haw	fst	1¼	:462 1:102 1:351 1:594	3↑ Haw Gold Cup H 123k	5 3 47¼ 2½ 11½ 14	Belmonte E	125	*.90	97-07	Nodouble1254Vif111hdVerbatim1241¼	Mild drive	7
27Sep69-7Bel	fst	1¼	:481 1:121 1:363 2:01	3↑ Woodward 106k	4 1 11 11 2½ 22	Belmonte E	126	2.60	93-17	ArtsandLetters1202Nodouble1261½Verbatim1268	Drifted out	4
1Sep69-7Bel	fst	1 1/8	:464 1:103 1:353 1:482	3↑ Governor Nicolls 109k	4 3 21½ 21½ 31½ 43½	Belmonte E	126	*.50	90-17	Verbatim121½Rising Market1171Tropic King II1142	Tired	7
19Jly69-7Aqu	fst	1¼	:464 1:103 1:353 2:002	3↑ Brooklyn H 109k	7 2 1½ 12 11 11½	Belmonte E	127	*1.50	94-14	Nodouble1271½Verbatim1201Dike114hd	Drifted,going away	7
12Jly69-8Hol	fst	1¼	:462 1:101 1:341 1:584	3↑ Hol Gold Cup H 162k	4 4 34 32 41¾ 21	Belmonte E	129	*.90	98-12	Figonero1151Nodouble129hdPoleax118hd	Held on willingly	6
30May69-7Aqu	fst	1	:224 :453 1:10 1:34	3↑ Metropolitan H 116k	6 4 56 54½ 32 22½	Belmonte E	129	8.80	94-22	Arts and Letters1112½Nodouble1293½Promise1191	Gamely	11
17May69-8Hol	fst	1 1/16	:23 :454 1:094 1:402	3↑ Californian 120k	12 6 45½ 41 1½ 12½	Belmonte E	127	4.00	93-08	Nodouble1272½RisingMarkt1211LondonJt112¾	Drawing clear	14
22Mar69-9GP	fst	1¼	:471 1:113 1:36 2:012	3↑ Gulfstream H 126k	9 1 11 11 1½ 2no	Belmonte E	125	2.70	92-10	CourtRecess108noNodbl1252¼TropcKngII1162¾	Raced wide	9
8Mar69-8SA	fst	1¼	:46 1:10 1:351 2:014	4↑ S Anita H 145k	12 6 43 1½ 12 11½	Belmonte E	122	4.30	89-13	Nodouble1221½Gamely122noQuicken Tree1261	Drew clear	16
1Feb69-8SA	fst	1¼	:46 1:104 1:362 2:02	C H Strub 126k	3 7 65¾ 1½ 1½ 1no	Pincay L Jr	123	3.10	88-15	[D]Nodouble123noDignitas1159½Cavamore1173½	Drifted out	10
Disqualified and placed second												
18Jan69-8SA	sl	1 1/8	:46 1:10 1:353 1:49	San Fernando 59k	1 3 55 57 511 514	Pincay L Jr	123	*2.40	73-17	Cavamore1134½Dignitas117hdDewan1204½	In close,tired	10
9Nov68-7Aqu	fst	1 3/16	:474 1:114 1:37 1:553	Roamer H 56k	7 7 97¾ 89½ 819 826	Heath M	125	3.90e	71-17	Funny Fellow120nkDraft Card1152Iron Ruler1262	Bled	9
19Oct68-8Haw	fst	1¼	:472 1:103 1:352 1:591	3↑ Gold Cup H 132k	3 2 21½ 3½ 1hd 11	Heath M	117	4.40	100-07	Nodouble1171Cabildo120noIrish Dude112no	Under pressure	10
14Sep68-9Det	fst	1 1/8	:471 1:111 1:361 1:49	3↑ Mich 1 1/8 H 123k	11 3 35 22 1½ 12¾	Heath M	111	17.60	96-19	Nodouble1112¾Damascus133hdMisty Run1092¼	Clear at end	12
3Aug68-8AP	fst	1 1/8	:473 1:11 1:36 1:484	American Derby 115k	4 1 12 1½ 2hd 24½	Pincay L Jr	116 b	17.20	85-08	ForwardPass1234½Ndouble116noPoleax1201½	Bore out badly	6
6Jly68-8AP	fm	1 (T)	:232 :461 1:113 1:372	Nashua H 34k	9 2 21 21 22 43½	Marquez CH	117 b	6.50	88-09	TeVega1162PaintRock110nkRelntlssPursuit1131¼	Weakened	11
22Jun68-8AP	fst	1	:23 :454 1:103 1:36	Arl Classic 108k	2 5 2hd 41½ 45 47¾	Blum W	118	13.00	75-16	ExclusivNativ113¾IronRulr1162GoodInvstmnt1165	Weakened	8
30May68-8GS	fst	1 1/8	:471 1:11 1:362 1:49	Jersey Derby 134k	7 3 34 46 57½ 712	Grant H	126	7.40	80-18	OutoftheWay1262½Captain'sGig126nkIronRuler1264	Swerved	10
18May68-8Pim	fst	1 3/16	:471 1:11 1:373 1:564	Preakness 195k	1 2 2½ 1hd 35 48	McKeever W	126	16.80	81-15	ForwrdPass1266OutoftheWay126hd[D]Dncr'sImg1262	Impeded	10
Placed third through disqualification												
6Apr68-9OP	fst	1 1/8	:462 1:103 1:373 1:50	Ark Derby 58k	6 5 43 33 2hd 11	McKeever W	116	*2.50e	93-16	Nodouble1161Te Vega1191½Etony1191½	Strong drive	10
25Mar68-8OP	fst	1 70	:232 :463 1:12 1:411	Alw 7500	6 2 32 2½ 1½ 1½	McKeever W5	112	*2.10e	90-15	Nodouble112½TeVega1225SailorsSong1162	Under hard drive	9
4Mar68-7OP	fst	6f	:22 :46 1:111	[S]Alw 6000	9 1 65½ 44½ 2hd 1½	McKeever W5	114	*.60e	89-16	Nodouble114½Loud Singer1196Pass 'Em Up1163	Driving hard	9
30Oct67-8Spt	sly	6½f	:221 :453 1:112 1:183	Land of Lincoln 22k	6 3 611 46 45½ 52½	Fleming W	116	6.80	83-19	Felony118noForeign Comet1141¼Gadget Man1201	No mishap	10

14Oct67- 9Det	fst 1 70	:221 :454 1:102 1:413	Graduation 21k	5 3 2hd 1½ 33 34¾	Maple E	110		4.10e	86-18	Strate Stuff1221¾Mial Spencer1193Nodouble1105	Weakened	10
29Sep67- 8Haw	sl 6½f	:224 :47 1:123 1:193	©To Market (Div 2) 11k	3 2 2hd 2hd 32 33¼	Lopez JR	110		4.70	73-24	Irish Chief111nkLifelike1223Nodouble1101½	Speed,tired	7
9Sep67- 7AP	fst 7f	:224 :46 1:112 1:234	Futurity (Div 1) 185k	7 1 11½ 1hd 67½ 715	Whited D	122	b	38.00	71-22	T.V. Commercial1223¾Gin-Rob1224½Royal Cap122¾	Used up	9
1Sep67- 7Det	fst 6f	:224 :46 1:112	Alw 3000	7 1 15 16 16 18	Whited DE	115	b	*.90	83-27	Nodouble1158GateCrasher1181CompanyMan1152	Ridden out	7
12Aug67- 6Det	fst 6f	:231 :46 1:113	Alw 3000	8 1 33 22 22 22½	Anderson JR	116	b	3.10	79-17	KeyRulla1202½Nodoubl1166RoyalHrbor1202¼	Held on gamely	8
15Jly67- 8HP	fst 6½f	:221 :47 1:131 1:194	Freshman Derby 22k	4 8 77¾ 75 52½ 22¼	Green FF	111	b	32.80	80-21	MialSpencer1122¼Nodoubl111nkCarbbnLn117hd	Gaining fast	9
8Jly67- 7HP	fst 6f	:233 :47 1:131	Freshman Trial 11k	6 5 2½ 2½ 23 44½	Lawless R	113	b	4.90	83-20	KntuckySherry1122¼RoyalHrbor1121PortDggr1121¼	Weakened	6
23Jun67- 4HP	gd 6f	:24 :481 1:153	Alw 3200	7 4 42½ 31½ 21½ 21¼	Lawless R	118		*1.40	75-27	DandyDodo1151¼Nodouble1181¾GreekBaron1184	Held gamely	10
3Jun67- 6Tdn	fst 5½f	:22 :46 :59 1:053	©Heritage 7.7k	5 3 32½ 32 21½ 32¼	Rincon R	110		2.30	89-15	BeaucoupD'Argent110¾CaribbeanLin1141½Nodoubl1105	Gamely	5
24May67- 5HP	fst 4f	:223 :464	Alw 3600	8 1 31½ 21½ 2nk	Zakoor W	117		5.20	94-11	CaribbeanLine122nkNodouble1173HarkthHrld1222½	Sharp try	8
4May67- 3HP	sl 4f	:25 :524	Md 7500	3 10 42½ 45½ 13½	Rincon R	118		8.30	64-26	Nodouble1183½Gold Rags115noFiela1151¼	Drew clear at end	10

Northern Dancer

b. c. 1961, by Nearctic (Nearco)–Natalma, by Native Dancer **Lifetime record: 18 14 2 2 $580,806**

Own.– Windfields Farm
Br.– E.P. Taylor (Can)
Tr.– H.A. Luro

20Jun64- 7WO	fst 1¼	:474 1:123 1:364 2:021	®Queen's Plate 74k	1 7 85 1½ 14 17½	Hartack W	126	b	*.15	98-08	NorthernDancer1267½Langcrest1264½GrandGrcon1261¼	Easily	8
6Jun64- 7Aqu	fst 1½	:49 1:144 2:04 2:282	Belmont 154k	2 5 52¾ 31 2½ 36	Hartack W	126	b	*.80	92-10	Quadrangle1262RomanBrothr1264NorthrnDncr126½	Bid,tired	8
16May64- 8Pim	fst 1 3/16	:482 1:122 1:373 1:564	Preakness 176k	4 3 33 1½ 13 12¼	Hartack W	126	b	2.10	89-14	NorthernDancer1262¼TheScoundrel126hdHillRis126½	Driving	6
2May64- 7CD	fst 1¼	:46 1:103 1:36 2:00	Ky Derby 156k	7 7 64½ 1hd 12 1nk	Hartack W	126	b	3.40	102-05	NorthernDancer126nkHillRise1263¼ThScoundrl126no	Driving	12
23Apr64- 6Kee	fst 1⅛	:501 1:141 1:382 1:494	Blue Grass 29k	5 2 2hd 2hd 1hd 1½	Hartack W	126	b	*.20	88-11	NorthernDncr126½AllnAdr1214½RoylShuck121nk	Well in hand	5
4Apr64- 8GP	fst 1⅛	:473 1:121 1:38 1:504	Florida Derby 116k	1 2 23 22 1½ 11	Shoemaker W	122	b	*.30	80-16	NorthrnDancr1221ThScoundrl1222½DndyK.1222¼	Ridden out	8
28Mar64- 7GP	fst 7f	:22 :443 1:093 1:222	Alw 6000	2 5 31½ 2hd 13 14	Ycaza M	122	b	*.40	100-14	NorthrnDancr1224ThScoundrl1142¾TroyOurBoy1203	Handily	7
3Mar64- 8Hia	fst 1⅛	:453 1:092 1:343 1:474	Flamingo 138k	9 2 21½ 21 11 12	Shoemaker W	122	b	*1.00	96-16	NorthrnDncr1222Mr.Brck1228Qudrngl1226	Lugged in,driving	11
24Feb64- 0Hia	gd 7f	:231 :461 1:104 1:232	Sp Wt	1 3 1½ 1½ 13 17	Shoemaker W	118	b	-	92-17	Northern Dancer1187Chieftain1182½Trader118		3
	Exhibition event,no purse,no wagering											
10Feb64- 7Hia	fst 6f	:224 :453 1:102	Alw 7000	2 7 55½ 32½ 31½ 32	Ussery R	122	b	1.40	90-17	Chieftan122hdMom'sRqust1132NrthrnDncr1225	Bumped start	7
27Nov63- 7Aqu	fst 1	:233 :461 1:102 1:353	Remsen 28k	3 1 11½ 11½ 13 12	Ycaza M	124	b	*.25	90-17	Northern Dancer1242Lord Date1123Repeating1171	Handily	6
18Nov63- 7Aqu	fst 1	:23 :451 1:103 1:36	Alw 10000	5 4 45½ 41½ 14 18	Ycaza M	124	b	2.60	88-16	NorthernDancer1248Bupers1241½SaVet1164½	Easily the best	6
6Nov63- 7Grd	my 7f	:231 :472 1:141 1:273	®Carleton 8.7k	2 3 21 2hd 1nk 12½	Fitzsimmons J	122	b	*.30	84-28	NorthrnDancr1222½NorthernFlght1151Wnk113hd	Going away	6
12Oct63- 6WO	fst 1⅛	:464 1:112 1:383 1:51	®Coronation Fut 46k	10 7 41½ 11½ 13 16¼	Turcotte R	122	b	*1.00e	88-16	NorthernDancr1226¼JammdLovly122½Prlou1222¼	Easily best	15
7Oct63- 5WO	fst 1 70	:224 :461 1:11 1:42	®Alw 2900	4 2 35½ 2½ 1hd 11	Turcotte R	122	b	*.45	95-18	Northern Dancer1221Northern Flight11726Fast Answer1123¼		6
	Mild drive											
28Sep63- 6WO	fm 1 1/16 Ⓣ	:224 :464 1:12 1:453	®Cup & Saucer 42k	5 1 2hd 1hd 2hd 2¾	Turcotte R	124	b	*1.60e	84-13	GrandGarcon113¾NrthrnDncr1241JammdLovly1191½	Gamely	16
	Previously trained by T.P. Fleming											
24Aug63- 6FE	sf 1Ⓣ	:24 :482 1:142 1:432	Summer 20k	1 1 1hd 13 12½ 11¼	Bohenko P	115	b	*1.65e	66-27	NorthrnDancr1151½SlitherngSm1153½Wndlshm112no	Driving	7
17Aug63- 6FE	fst 6½f	:231 :464 1:122 1:19	Vandal 9.6k	5 3 2hd 12½ 2nk 24	Bohenko P	108	b	6.55	84-12	RamblinRod1224NrthrnDncr1092½BrocktonBoy1151¼	2nd best	11
2Aug63- 3FE	fst 5½f	:231 :472 1:061	®Md Sp Wt	7 2 21 1nk 11 16¾	Turcotte R5	113		*.95	92-13	NorthernDncr1136¾Ncub1187½Fbson1182	Drawing away easily	8

Old Hat

b. f. 1959, by Boston Doge (The Doge)–Fine Feathers, by Double Jay **Lifetime record: 80 35 18 9 $556,401**

Own.– S. Conrad
Br.– W.A. Nelson (Ky)
Tr.– C.C. Norman

2Dec66- 9TrP	fst 6f	:221 :451 1:09	4↑ Alw 5000	1 1 22½ 2½ 11½ 14¾	Sellers J	116		1.80	97-11	Old Hat1164¾Yucatan1193¼Valiant Bull1224½	Mild drive	8
27Oct66- 6Kee	fst 1⅛	:464 1:103 1:371 1:502	3↑ ⒻSpinster 58k	4 2 2hd 32 2hd 21¼	Church K	123		4.60	84-21	OpenFire1231¼OldHat1231½SummerScandal1236	Game effort	5
20Oct66- 6Kee	sl *7f	:222 :453 1:101 1:263	3↑ ⒻAlw 10000	3 1 21½ 23 21½ 24¾	Church K	121		1.70	85-27	SummrScandal1214¾OldHat1211½Maestrina1099	Second best	5
1Oct66- 8Det	gd 1 1/16	:24 :472 1:113 1:443	3↑ ⒻSweet Patootie 27k	1 2 2½ 2hd 1½ 11½	Church K	118		*1.10	80-21	Old Hat1181½Out Talk1071½Treasure Chest1154	Game effort	8
24Sep66- 8CD	fst 1	:23 :454 1:101 1:35	3↑ ⒻFalls City H 27k	8 1 1hd 1hd 2½ 1nk	Church K	116		3.80	98-14	OldHat116nkⒹMac'sSparklr1172½NaidniDm1102¾	Came again	9
17Sep66- 7CD	fst 7f	:23 :454 1:10 1:224	3↑ ⒻAlw 5000	2 2 21 32 21 21¼	Church K	111		3.50	92-12	MarrythePrince1211¼OldHat1117TurfTalk1143¼	Game effort	7
7Sep66- 8AP	fst 1	:223 :452 1:103 1:353	3↑ ⒻBewitch H 20k	7 8 66 56 58½ 310	Valenzuela I	118		*2.70	78-13	Marry the Prince1201Cologne1129Old Hat1181¼	Rallied	11
20Aug66- 8AP	fm 1⅛Ⓣ	:472 1:113 1:362 1:483	3↑ ⒻMatron H 55k	7 2 2½ 42¾ 69½ 912	Brumfield D	122		5.10	86-11	Swinging Mood1126Margarethen1241Amerivan114nk	Stopped	9
5Aug66- 7AP	fst 6f	:221 :451 1:094	3↑ ⒻAlw 6000	6 6 45½ 55½ 56½ 66	Fires E	113		*.80	88-17	Codorniz1222May's Guide1221¼Country Maid119hd	Dull try	7
23Jly66- 6Del	fst 6f	:221 :452 1:111	3↑ ⒻAlw 5000	6 2 63¾ 68 56½ 3¾	Leonard J	121		*.70	88-14	TurfTalk113¾FlaminHat121noOldHt121no	Made strong finish	7
21Oct65- 6Kee	sly 1⅛	:462 1:102 1:362 1:501	3↑ ⒻSpinster 58k	3 4 49 39 36 43	Gallimore R	123		*.40	83-23	StarMaggie1233Swoonalong123hdFairwayFun119no	No excuse	5
9Oct65- 6Kee	fst 1 1/16	:24 :481 1:114 1:424	3↑ Fayette H 28k	2 1 51¾ 52¾ 41½ 1nk	Gallimore R	119		*1.30	92-14	OldHat119nkLt.Stevens122hdBigBrgd116nk	Up final strides	9
18Sep65- 8Det	fst 1⅛	:471 1:113 1:364 1:492	3↑ Mich 1⅛ H 91k	5 6 73¾ 31 1hd 1½	Gallimore R	115		5.50	94-18	OldHat115½RomanBrother118¾TakeOver114½	Long,hard drive	11
21Aug65- 8AP	fst 1⅛	:482 1:12 1:372 1:494	3↑ ⒻMatron H 78k	2 3 46½ 46½ 24 1¾	Gallimore R	126		1.90	87-17	Old Hat126¾Swoonalong1222¼Miss Cavandish125¾	Just up	6
12Aug65- 8AP	fst 1	:231 :452 1:092 1:343	3↑ ⒻHandicap 15000	5 2 22 2½ 13 21	Gallimore R	124		*.50	95-12	Miss Cavandish1211Old Hat1246Yes Please115½	Failed	5
8Jun65- 7Del	fst 6f	:221 :453 1:101	4↑ ⒻAlw 6000	7 1 32½ 1hd 13 16	Thornburg B	121		*.40	94-10	Old Hat1216Crown Silver1181Jeune Occupy115no	Easily	7
22May65- 7Aqu	fst 1⅛	:47 1:111 1:362 1:494	3↑ ⒻTop Flight H 57k	4 2 23 23 35½ 38½	Brumfield D	127		*2.55	78-20	Affectionately1208SteepleJill123½OldHat127¾	No response	10
6May65- 7CD	fst 7f	:23 :452 1:092 1:22	4↑ ⒻAlw 4500	6 1 22 21½ 1½ 12	Gallimore R	123		*.30	97-14	Old Hat1232Abrograte1185Alecee1182½	Scored well in hand	7
31Mar65- 9GP	fst 7f	:221 :444 1:101 1:23	3↑ ⒻSuwannee River H 21k	3 3 44½ 31 11½ 13¼	Brumfield D	125		*.40	97-15	OldHat1253¼Abrogate1121½MoneytoBurn1101¼	Much the best	6
20Mar65- 9GP	fst 7f	:222 :45 1:103 1:234	3↑ Appleton H 16k	1 5 45½ 47 2hd 2nk	Thornburg B	122		*1.10	93-14	Ampose115nkOld Hat1221¼Editorialist115nk	Gave sharp try	7
24Feb65- 8Hia	fst 1⅛	:473 1:113 1:364 1:494	3↑ ⒻBlack Helen H 60k	5 5 52¼ 32 11 1¾	Brumfield D	125		*.90	86-10	Old Hat125¾Steeple Jill116½Windsor Lady1133	Brisk drive	9
27Jan65- 8Hia	fst 7f	:232 :46 1:104 1:24	3↑ ⒻColumbiana H 31k	10 1 41½ 53½ 22 1¾	Brumfield D	124		5.30	89-19	Old Hat124¾Miami Mood1111½Steeple Jill118½	Up in time	10
7Nov64- 8CD	fst 1	:223 :45 1:094 1:353	3↑ ⒻFalls City H 29k	13 3 33½ 31 2hd 1¾	Brumfield D	128		*.60	95-15	Old Hat128¾De Cathy113¾Abrogate1173	Under hard drive	13
2Nov64- 7CD	fst 7f	:231 :46 1:10 1:222	3↑ ⒻAlw 7500	1 4 31½ 32 12½ 12½	Brumfield D	124		*.30	95-16	Old Hat1242½Godessa116½Tirata1163¼	Easily best	8
15Oct64- 6Kee	fst 1⅛	:474 1:113 1:361 1:482	3↑ ⒻSpinster 58k	5 2 21 21 1½ 11	Brumfield D	123		1.40	95-15	Old Hat1231Miss Cavandish119nkTime for Bed1192½	Driving	5
8Oct64- 6Kee	fst *7f	1:263	3↑ ⒻAlw 10000	4 1 3½ 22 12 12¼	Brumfield D	118		*.50	90-17	Old Hat1182¼Oil Royalty121nkBatteur1182½	Scored in hand	8
26Sep64- 7Atl	fm 1 1/16 Ⓣ	1:432	3↑ ⒻMargate H (Div 1) 29k	9 3 34 108¾ 105¾ 44¼	Thornburg B	119		*3.10	90-04	Snow Scene II1152Batteur112nkIsaduchess1162	Came again	11
5Sep64- 7Aqu	fst 1	:23 :454 1:103 1:363	3↑ ⒻMaskette H 30k	2 3 33½ 35 36 26	Thornburg B	117		4.90	79-21	Tosmah1236Old Hat1172Snow Scene II1132	Finished gamely	13
15Aug64- 8AP	fst 1⅛	:47 1:11 1:362 1:492	3↑ ⒻMatron H 81k	1 4 45 47 23 2½	Thornburg B	116		3.70	88-14	Tosmah117½Old Hat116½Nubile111½	Finished full of run	10
1Aug64- 7Del	fst 1¼	:48 1:124 1:381 2:04	3↑ ⒻDelaware H 121k	1 1 11 2hd 12¼ 11¼	Thornburg B	113		17.00	82-20	Old Hat1131¼Miss Cavandish1151¼Waltz Song116¾	Driving	12
18Jly64- 7Del	fst 1 1/16	:233 :472 1:114 1:442	3↑ ⒻNew Castle 37k	1 1 11½ 13 13 21¼	Thornburg B	110		4.90	86-24	Snow Scene II1071¼Old Hat1102½Spicy Living1242	Game try	9
11Jly64- 6Del	fst 1	:231 :462 1:114 1:383	4↑ ⒻAlw 7500	1 1 13½ 15 15 13	Thornburg B	112		*.90	83-21	Old Hat1123Tona1182½Colonia1158	Bobbled,handily	7
1Jly64- 8Mth	fst 1 1/16	:224 :46 1:102 1:431	3↑ ⒻMolly Pitcher H 29k	12 2 32 2½ 11 32	Zakoor W	119		10.20	87-16	SpicyLiving124noSnowSceneII1122OldHat119½	Used in lead	13
13Jun64- 7Mth	fst 6f	:222 :452 1:101	3↑ ⒻAlw 7500	8 1 4¾ 21 21 11¼	Chambers W	121		3.40	91-13	Old Hat1211¼Cyclopavia1155½Fair Summer1211	Going away	8
7May64- 7CD	sl 6f	:22 :451 1:111	4↑ Alw 5000	2 1 2½ 1½ 12 11	Brumfield D	112		*.70	90-18	Old Hat1121Ambarmar1202Boone Co.1101½	Kept to pressure	7
27Apr64- 6CD	my 6f	:22 :46 1:13	3↑ ⒻAlw 5000	6 4 52½ 41¼ 31¼ 2hd	Brumfield D	114		*.30	81-24	Maiden'sLove113hdOldHat114¾Godessa1112	Missed,sharp try	6
1Apr64- 9GP	fst 7f	:222 :45 1:10 1:23	3↑ ⒻSuwannee River H 16k	1 1 2½ 32½ 46 54½	Brumfield D	118		2.60	92-17	Smart Deb1232Lady Karachi1161Yes Please1111½	Tired	8
26Mar64- 7GP	fst 6f	:222 :452 1:11	4↑ ⒻAlw 4200	2 1 1hd 11½ 12 11½	Brumfield D	113		*.80	89-17	OldHat1131½Suntanned1161LuckyViola1151½	Scored in hand	7

Date	Track	Dist	Fractions	Race	Positions	Jockey	Wt	Odds	Speed-Var	Top three finishers	Comment	Field
6Jly63-8AP	fst	1	:23 :452 1:10 1:361	3↑ Ⓕ Beverly H 32k	5 4 4 4½ 4 4½ 5 5½ 66	Hartack W	123	*1.00	82-12	Patrol Woman117½Hushaby118½My Portrait1163½	No excuse	7
31May63-8Was	fst	6f	:214 :444 1:093	4↑ Ⓕ Four Winds 16k	7 1 3 2 2 2 1½ 13	Grant H	118	*.60	97-07	Old Hat1183Hushaby1152¼Alecee1151¾	Drew clear in hand	7
16May63-7CD	sly	6f	:23 :462 1:104	4↑ Ⓕ Alw 4000	2 2 2½ 1 1½ 13 17	Vasquez J	121	*.40	92-22	OldHat1217Venture118¾Cynthia'sReward114hd	Scored easily	7
27Mar63-8GP	fst	7f	:224 :46 1:102 1:223	3↑ Ⓕ Suwannee River H 16k	1 1 2 2 2½ 1 2½ 1 1¼	Grant H	117	3.35	96-18	OldHat1171¼Cicad1264½Coupd'Ett1111½	Wide,fully extended	6
16Mar63-7GP	fst	6f	:224 :461 1:114	4↑ Ⓕ Alw 4200	4 1 41 4 3½ 3 1½ 11	Grant H	118	*.65	85-20	OldHat1181Retirement116noCoupd'Etat1143	Long,hard drive	6
27Feb63-8Hia	fst	1⅛	:464 1:111 1:362 1:492	4↑ Ⓕ Black Helen H 47k	2 1 13 12 1½ 2hd	Grant H	115	8.85	88-14	Pocosaba117hdOldHat1155MissMarcela1142¾	Failed to last	8
13Feb63-8Hia	gd	7f	:23 :453 1:104 1:234	3↑ Ⓕ Columbiana H 30k	4 3 5 5½ 711 5 3½ 3 2¼	Grant H	115	5.75	88-16	Cicada1251¾RoyalPatrice121½OldHat1151½	Closed very well	7
7Feb63-8Hia	gd	6f	:222 :454 1:104	4↑ Ⓕ Alw 5500	7 3 3 2 21 1 1½ 1 3¾	Hartack W	119	*1.15	90-18	OldHat1193¾LuckyViola1151½Hushaby1172½	Speed in reserve	10
22Jan63-8Hia	fst	6f	:221 :451 1:10	4↑ Ⓕ Alw 6000	1 4 33 3 3½ 43 4 3½	Rotz JL	112	8.45	90-17	PatrolWoman1111¾Coupd'Etat1181¾RedBll112no	Fairly eveny	9
15Nov62-7CD	fst	7f	:221 :443 1:092 1:222	3↑ Ⓕ Alw 5000	3 4 54 4 3½ 11 2½	Nono R	114	*1.70	97-10	Fortunate Isle114½Old Hat114¾Myway1082	Clear lead,tired	8
3Nov62-8CD	fst	1	:224 :451 1:094 1:353	3↑ Ⓕ Falls City H 22k	7 3 5 5¼ 36 22 22	Nono R	113	16.50	93-12	Primonetta1262Old Hat1131¼Fortunate Isle1103	Game try	9
29Oct62-7CD	sly	6f	:224 :464 1:114	Ⓕ Alw 5000	3 3 43 4 1½ 2½ 1¾	Miller S5	111	*.80	87-25	OldHat111¾RecklessDriver1194½Babyo'Mine1083½	Driving	7
19Oct62-8Haw	fst	6f	:222 :451 1:101	3↑ Ⓕ Alw 4500	6 2 31 22 1hd 1 1¾	Hartack W	116	*1.20	96-12	OldHat1161¾Cynthia'sReward1123½MissOffset107hd	Driving	8
10Oct62-8Haw	fst	6½f	:221 :453 1:103 1:164	3↑ Ⓕ Yo Tambien H 18k	7 1 22 11 2½ 2½	Moreno H	116	5.20	89-20	NarkiSong114½OldHat1166FoolishYouth1161½	Sharp effort	10
3Oct62-8Haw	gd	6½f	:222 :452 1:113 1:164	Handicap 10000	6 1 3 2½ 35 34 3 4½	Skoronski A	115	4.00	85-22	Boston Sailor114½Mighty Fennec1194Old Hat1156	No rally	7
29Sep62-7Haw	fst	6f	:221 :452 1:111	Ⓕ Alw 5000	1 3 3 2½ 4 2¼ 4 1½ 11	Hartack W	116	*1.20	90-14	Becky Ann106hdCherry Laurel1151Old Hat116nk	No excuses	11
21Sep62-7Haw	fst	6½f	:221 :451 1:093 1:161	3↑ Ⓕ Alw 4500	2 4 4 3½ 2½ 3nk 31	Burton J	115	*1.60	92-13	Gerts Image114nkFoolish Image108¾Old Hat1152½	Bid,tired	6
13Sep62-8Haw	fst	6f	:221 :451 1:094	3↑ Ⓕ Alw 4500	7 1 21 1hd 2½ 2¾	Skoronski A	111	2.60	97-10	Gerts Image111¾Old Hat1115Cherry Laurel113nk	Game try	7
29Aug62-6AP	fst	6½f	:224 :453 1:101 1:163	Ⓕ Alw 5000	7 3 22 2hd 2½ 1no	Skoronski A	116	2.90	93-08	OldHat116noCherryDear1183¼CherryLaurel1182	Up in time	8
25Aug62-7AP	my	6½f	:232 :464 1:113 1:18	Alw 4500	6 2 22 11 14 1 4¾	Burton J	108	8.30	86-24	OldHat1084¾MghtyFnnc1172½BostonSlor1172¼	Speed to spare	8
11Aug62-8AP	fst	1⅛	:462 1:11 1:36 1:484	Ⓕ Pucker Up 61k	4 3 3 3½ 3 1½ 45 5 7¾	Phelps B	112	27.20	84-07	RoyalPatrice1121Polylady1143¼DnnrPrtnr1153¼	No response	10
2Aug62-8AP	fst	1	:224 :453 1:11 1:363	Ⓕ Alw 6000	7 2 1hd 2hd 2hd 2¾	Phelps B	114	23.00	85-13	Venture111¾Old Hat114noHushaby1141¾	Gamely	8
26Jly62-7AP	fst	6f	:22 :451 1:101	3↑ Ⓕ Alw 4500	8 5 5 6½ 5 5¾ 68 5 6½	Ruybali J	105	4.00	86-13	Windy Miss1081¾Star Bolt1151½Foolish Youth115nk	Outrun	9
7Jly62-8AP	fst	1	:224 :454 1:103 1:372	Ⓕ Misty Isle 27k	6 6 98 69 712 5 9¾	Phelps B	113	17.60	73-16	DinnerPartnr1143¼ChrryLurl1131RodMd1103½	Never a factor	9
21Jun62-8AP	fst	6f	:22 :452 1:103	Ⓕ Alw 5000	2 4 34 3 2½ 4nk 21	Phelps B	115	4.40	90-10	Rudoma1131Old Hat115½Painful1151	Finished strongly	7
6Jun62-8Was	fst	7f	:221 :444 1:094 1:224	Ⓕ Cleopatra 17k	6 4 3 4½ 36 35 4 5¼	Phelps B	113	15.70	86-12	CherryLaurel1094Venture109nkDinnerPartner1181	No excuse	12
23May62-8Was	fst	6f	:221 :453 1:101	Ⓕ Cinderella 17k	4 3 4¾ 4 1½ 5 2¾ 7 3¾	Sorenson B	112	9.00	88-16	Dinner Partner114hdRudoma115¾Venture109½	Used in pace	9
5May62-4CD	fst	6f	:221 :45 1:101	Alw 3500	6 1 2hd 12 12 12	Lucas WD	108	4.30	95-06	Old Hat1082Overton Lane1132¼Prince Dale1112½	Drew clear	7
21Apr62-7Kee	fst	6½f	:223 :454 1:102 1:164	Ⓕ Alw 3750	1 5 33 33 2hd 1 1½	Grant H	116	*1.60	94-08	OldHt1161½Narola1192½NoCommnt119¾	Brushed,going away	9
11Apr62-7Kee	my	6f	:223 :462 1:104	Ⓕ Alw 3500	3 3 21 21 2hd 1no	Grant H	116	*1.50	90-14	Old Hat116noPrincess Revoked1167Hushaby1164	Up in time	6
16Mar62-7OP	fst	6f	:221 :464 1:121	Alw 3000	4 9 1014 6 5¼ 32 2 2½	Campbell RJ	112	6.80	85-20	PrncssBng1092½OldHt112nkDurndl111½	Crowded leaving gate	12
5Mar62-7OP	fst	6f	:223 :463 1:113	Alw 3200	6 3 4 2½ 69 715 714	Cook WM	109	9.30	77-14	Battle Ground114nkThe Nutts111nkNice W.1071¼		8
				Taken up repeatedly;Previously owned by Breckenridge Stable								
6Nov61-6CD	gd	6f	:224 :463 1:112	Ⓕ Alw 3200	8 1 2½ 1½ 2 1½ 2 2¼	Phelps B	113	*2.30	87-18	Venture1102¼Old Hat1132½Dinner Partner1101¼	Gamely	9
30Oct61-4CD	fst	6f	:221 :452 1:112	Ⓕ Alw 3000	1 1 1 1½ 12 1hd 1½	Phelps B	116	6.60	89-16	OldHat116½Venture1093½LuckyViola116¾	Under strong ride	7
2Oct61-6Haw	hy	6f	:222 :464 1:132	Alw 3200	1 1 15 13 1½ 11	Phelps B	115	15.30	80-29	Old Hat1151Times Roman1187Wa-Wa Cy1165	Kept to drive	8
18Sep61-5Haw	fst	6f	:222 :461 1:12	Ⓕ Alw 3500	6 7 43 54 3 3½ 31	Gilligan L	117	10.20	86-16	[D]Narola108nkJet Strauss106¾[D]Old Hat117hd	Bore out	12
				Disqualified and placed fifth								
8Sep61-6Haw	fst	6f	:222 :46 1:112	Ⓕ Alw 4000	8 1 1hd 4 2½ 53 4 5¼	Chambers W	111	18.10	85-11	Lucky Viola109¾Dorark1092Saba Saba1122½	Used early	8
23Aug61-3AP	fst	6f	:224 :453 1:103	Ⓕ Alw 4000	1 3 5 1¼ 6 8½ 6 9½ 3 9¼	Heckmann J	118	16.90	82-11	WindyMiss1187OurJosi1182¼OldHt118nk	Passed tired horses	8
15Aug61-4AP	fst	6f	:23 :451 1:114	Ⓕ Md Sp Wt	12 1 1 1½ 13 13 1hd	Heckmann J	115	22.70	85-11	OldHat115hdHushaby1154Cynthia'sReward115nk	Just lasted	12
10Aug61-5AP	fst	6f	:232 :46 1:104	Ⓕ Md Sp Wt	5 10 12 8¾ 1111 815 615	Heckmann J	117	33.90	75-09	Matsu1173Dulaturee1172½Salvia1173½	Never in contention	12
20May61-1CD	fst	5f	:231 :464 :594	Ⓕ Md Sp Wt	9 8 78 73 7 5¼ 8 6¼	Cook WM	117	10.40	87-09	Imply117½Lady Oil C.117noPurple Star117¾	No factor	12
13May61-2CD	fst	5f	:224 :463 :594	Ⓕ Md Sp Wt	1 5 6 7½ 710 68 8 8½	Cook WM	117	4.70	84-06	Mc Mc Lake1171¾Shot Rock1171½Princess Bang1121		12
				Never in contention								

Open Fire

ro. f. 1961, by Cochise (Boswell)–Lucy Lufton, by Nimbus

Lifetime record: 30 13 6 5 $227,329

Own.– Brandywine Stable
Br.– Renappi Corp. (Va)
Tr.– V.W. Raines

Date	Track	Dist	Fractions	Race	Positions	Jockey	Wt	Odds	Speed-Var	Top three finishers	Comment	Field
27Oct66-6Kee	fst	1⅛	:464 1:103 1:371 1:502	3↑ Ⓕ Spinster 58k	1 1 1hd 2½ 3nk 1 1¼	Baeza B	123	1.90	85-21	OpnFire1231¼OldHat1231¼SummerScandl1236	Drawing clear	5
10Oct66-7Kee	fst	6f	:22 :451 :572 1:103	3↑ Ⓕ Alw 7500	1 5 57 45 2 2½ 1 1½	Brumfield D	123	*1.00	90-19	OpenFire1231½BearGrass115¾MarrythePrinc1212½	Mild drive	5
17Sep66-7Aqu	fst	1⅛	:47 1:111 1:361 1:492	3↑ Ⓕ Beldame 85k	5 4 48 49 4 6½ 411	Baeza B	123	*1.50	78-18	SummerScandal1238StraightDeal123½LadyPitt1182	No rally	10
22Aug66-7Sar	sly	1⅛	:471 1:11 1:354 1:484	3↑ Ⓕ Diana H 28k	4 2 1hd 14 14 110	Lovato F	117	*1.40	101-17	OpenFire11710ReluctantPearl1081¾Mac'sSparklr1131	Easily	8
30Jly66-8Del	fst	1¼	:462 1:102 1:351 2:002	3↑ Ⓕ Delaware H 122k	4 4 45 1 3½ 1 4½ 15	Lovato F	110	4.30	100-15	Open Fire1105Treachery1102Discipline1193½	Handy score	13
16Jly66-8Del	fst	1 1/16	:234 :472 1:104 1:423	3↑ Ⓕ New Castle 36k	5 3 31 1 2½ 13 14	Lovato F	107	7.90	96-15	Open Fire1074Queen Empress1131Ho Ho108¾	Hand urging	9
29Jun66-8Del	fst	1 70	:223 :462 1:12 1:424	3↑ Ⓕ Alw 4500	1 3 3½ 1 2½ 2hd 2nk	Rogers C	121	*1.30	86-19	HoHo112nkOpnFire1211½PeakPerformance1154	Game effort	7
7Jun66-8Del	fst	6f	:222 :46 1:113	3↑ Ⓕ Alw 6000	8 1 1hd 1 1½ 1 2½	Rogers C	121	*.80	87-17	Open Fire1212½Shiralee112hdHo Ho1111	Under mild urging	8
21May66-8GS	fst	6f	:22 :453 1:10	3↑ Ⓕ Colonial H 28k	3 1 52 7 3½ 7 4¼ 7 4¼	Rogers C	121	34.90	90-18	Tosmah1251½Wild Note1161Cohasset114no	Never a threat	8
19Apr66-8Bow	fst	6f	:231 :471 1:123	4↑ Ⓕ Alw 5500	7 2 6 3¼ 4 2¼ 41 12	Rogers C	112	*1.00e	84-20	Open Fire1122Sharon Market112noUpturn112nk	Handy score	8
20Nov65-8Pim	fst	1⅛	:473 1:123 1:394 1:531	3↑ Ⓕ Gallorette 30k	9 5 5 4½ 32 3 3½ 4 5¾	Ruane J	117	5.10	79-19	Gold Digger1142½Gallarush1113Lovejoy114nk	Well up,tired	14
12Nov65-4Aqu	fst	1	:223 :461 1:111 1:374	3↑ Alw 7500	3 3 3 1½ 21 23 3 1¾	Ruane J	119	9.40	77-21	BalletRose1191½SkyWonder119nkOpenFir1191½	No excuse	5
18Oct65-7Aqu	fst	6f	:22 :451 1:103	3↑ Ⓕ Interborough H 27k	6 6 55 54 23 24	Rotz JL	113	6.60	86-19	Ballet Rose1144Open Fire1132Good Jane114hd	Held gamely	8
9Oct65-8Atl	fst	7f	:222 :45 1:10 1:233	3↑ Ⓕ Parkway H 24k	2 4 2 1½ 46 4 6½ 4 7½	Valenzuela A	114	7.10	77-13	Juanita1155Mighty Happy1152½Lovejoy114no	Well up,tired	11
28Sep65-7Aqu	fst	7f	:222 :45 1:092 1:231	3↑ Ⓕ Alw 10000	3 5 31 2½ 11 13	Rotz JL	121	3.70	90-17	Open Fire1213Good Jane121¾Crown Silver1161	Ridden out	7
20Sep65-7Aqu	fst	1	:223 :444 1:084 1:351	3↑ Ⓕ Maskette H 28k	2 5 5 6½ 59 711 8 9¾	Rotz JL	113	25.80	82-16	Tosmah128noAffectionately1283Straight Deal113½	Tired	9
6Sep65-3Aqu	fst	7f	:224 :46 1:111 1:241	3↑ Ⓕ Alw 8500	3 4 2hd 1 1½ 1 1½ 1no	Rotz JL	120	*1.20	85-14	OpenFire120noSceree1092½HemandHaw1163	Long,hard drive	6
28Aug65-8Sar	fst	6f	:222 :454 1:104	3↑ Ⓕ Alw 7500	1 2 1hd 1½ 2hd 2 2½	Rotz JL	120	*1.90	91-08	Silwall1182½OpenFire1201HmndHw1163½	Set fast pace,tired	6
19Aug65-6Sar	sly	7f	:23 :462 1:114 1:243	3↑ Ⓕ Alw 6500	5 4 53 3 1½ 1hd 1 2½	Rotz JL	116	*1.70	87-15	OpnFire1162½GeeJudge118nkMissDicky1186	Drew clear wide	7
10Jly65-6Del	fst	6f	:222 :454 1:11	3↑ Ⓕ Alw 4200	4 5 76 5 4½ 45 2 3½	Nelson E	113	4.40	86-13	MakeaWish1123½OpenFire121nkSouthsideMiss1084	Rallied	8
14Nov64-8Pim	fst	1⅛	:471 1:112 1:374 1:511	3↑ Ⓕ Gallorette 29k	6 2 21 1 2½ 2hd 2no	Ruane J	111	19.40	95-16	Gay Serenade117noOpenFire1112MyCard117½	Made game try	11
31Oct64-8GS	fst	1 1/16	:231 :461 1:10 1:414	Ⓕ Jersey Belle 28k	4 3 55 510 6 8¼ 3 9¾	Chambers W	112	10.50	89-14	Tosmah1241¾SteepleJill1148OpenFire112hd	No real threat	7
23Oct64-8GS	fst	1 70	:223 :461 1:11 1:41	Ⓕ Alw 5500	3 4 43 811 713 613	Grant H	120	*2.70	79-16	MyCard1123GoldnHostss112½Lovjoy1183	Impeded backstr	8
6Oct64-6Aqu	fst	7f	:222 :451 1:10 1:231	3↑ Ⓕ Alw 6500	7 3 42 33 33 3 3¾	Rotz JL	117	*.65	86-17	Gold Frame108¾Hilly1113Open Fire117¾	Forced out early	7
21Sep64-6Aqu	fst	6f	:224 :454 1:104	3↑ Ⓕ Alw 8500	2 4 3nk 4 3½ 3 3½ 21	Rotz JL	114	2.30	88-16	Songster1081OpenFire114hdPetiteRouge1133	Finished well	6
8Sep64-6Aqu	fst	1	:233 :464 1:114 1:374	3↑ Ⓕ Alw 6500	6 3 3½ 3½ 11 11	Rotz JL	114	*.25	79-20	Open Fire1141Kisco Gal1071½Sun Tartan1122	Strong urging	6
27Aug64-6Sar	fst	7f	:223 :451 1:093 1:222	3↑ Ⓕ Alw 5500	10 1 2½ 1 1½ 14 110	Rotz JL	113	*1.00	98-11	OpnFire11310SnugglUp1124[DH]KnwnQuantty117½	Easy score	10
19Aug64-6Sar	fst	6f	:222 :454 1:12	3↑ Ⓕ Alw 5000	4 3 43 3 4½ 4 2½ 3 1½	Pierce D	113	2.45	86-13	Tudor Emblem118½Snuggle Up1111Open Fire1131	Closed well	9
2Jly63-5Del	fst	5½f	:222 :464 1:051	Ⓕ Md Sp Wt	8 1 21 1 1½ 16 110	Ward D5	112	*1.20	95-17	OpnFire11210Ambering1171LakeCampo1171¾	Drew out easily	12
19Jun63-5Del	fst	5f	:224 :47 :59	Ⓕ Md Sp Wt	10 7 5¾ 3nk 32 3 1¾	Ward D5	112	*2.20	92-14	MyCard1171½Ambring117nkOpnFr1125	Lacked late response	12

Parka

br. g. 1958, by Arctic Prince (Prince Chevalier)–Manchon, by Blenheim II
Own.– Pelican Stable
Br.– Mrs Marion duPont Scott (Va)
Tr.– W.A. Croll Jr

Lifetime record: 93 27 14 18 $446,236

4Oct65- 7Aqu	hd	1 3/16Ⓣ		1:543	3↑	Long Island H 29k	10	3	21	1½	1½	11	Blum W	125		*1.40	97-03	Parka1251Or et Argent116½Polar Sea1201½	Long,hard drive	10
18Sep65- 8Atl	fm	1 3/16Ⓣ		1:542	3↑	U Nations H 125k	1	5	62	51¼	4¾	1nk	Blum W	119		*1.80	101-06	Parka119nkHillRis1185Chftn122no	Blocked,driving outside	10
4Sep65- 8Atl	hd	1⅛Ⓣ		1:473	3↑	Kelly-Olympic H 35k	3	4	31	22	22	13	Blum W	118		*1.50	98-05	Parka1183Indoctrinate1141Twice as Gay1143½	Drew out	10
21Aug65- 8Atl	fm	1 1/16Ⓣ		1:413	3↑	Philadelphia Turf H 29k	4	5	54½	32½	24	23½	Patterson G	119		3.00	95-08	TurboJetII1243½Parka119¾TwiceasGay1144½	Best of others	7
14Aug65- 7Atl	fm	1Ⓣ		1:35	3↑	Alw 4500	7	6	67½	62¼	33½	22	Witmer R5	114		4.50	94-05	TurboJetII1212Parka114½Baitman1231¼	Finished very fast	7
27Feb65- 8Hia	fm	1½Ⓣ		2:291	3↑	Hia Turf Cup H 97k	6	6	78	41½	46	63¼	Rotz JL	123		*1.90	90-06	HotDust114hdYourAlibhai113nkKnightlyMnnr1152½	Weakened	12
19Feb65- 8Hia	fm	1 1/16Ⓣ		1:432	4↑	Alw 7000	2	4	53¼	44	1hd	1hd	Rotz JL	122		*1.50	88-12	Parka122hdSuspicous1193½ChfGronmo113nk	Under hard drive	9
30Jan65- 8Hia	fm	1 3/16Ⓣ		1:534	3↑	Bougainvillea H 34k	3	6	68	43½	2hd	1¾	Rotz JL	122		*1.90	100-04	Parka122¾Western Warrior118¾Your Alibhai1121½	Driving	14
22Jan65- 8Hia	fm	1 1/16Ⓣ		1:413	4↑	Alw 7500	11	4	510	47	411	36	Rotz JL	119		*1.70	91-08	Lucky Turn1163Your Alibhai1133Parka1192	Even effort	11
3Nov64- 7Aqu	fm	1 3/16Ⓣ		1:561	3↑	Knickerbocker H 29k	10	3	31½	42½	42	42½	Blum W	124		*2.40	86-11	ThirdMartini115nkGrandApplause108nkWillIRule1162	Wide	11
24Oct64- 7Aqu	fm	1⅝Ⓣ		2:424	3↑	Man o' War 111k	8	4	46	41½	78	813¾	Rotz JL	126		6.95	72-14	TurboJetII126¾GunBow1262½KnightlyManner1211	Bid,tired	9
7Oct64- 7Aqu	fm	1 3/16Ⓣ		1:544	3↑	Long Island H 28k	4	3	36	33	1½	12½	Blum W	123		3.25	96-04	Parka1232½CedarKey1261WillIRule112nk	Drew clear easily	7
19Sep64- 8Atl	sf	1 3/16Ⓣ		1:574	3↑	U Nations H 125k	3	9	74	64½	55½	2¾	Blum W	121		10.10	83-21	WesternWarrior114¾Parka121hdTurboJetII116nk	Fast finish	10
5Sep64- 8Atl	fm	1⅛Ⓣ		1:471	3↑	Kelly-Olympic H 35k	6	4	45	48	66	74	French D	122		5.70	100-01	TurboJetII111¾Indoctinate1101¼ColoradoKing126nk	Tired	9
15Aug64- 8Atl	fm	1 1/16Ⓣ		1:42	3↑	Philadelphia Turf H 29k	2	4	41	41½	52¼	1¾	Blum W	121		3.30	101-04	Parka121¾CoolPrince113noTurboJetII112no	Long,hard drive	9
1Aug64- 8AP	fm	1 3/16Ⓣ	:474 1:12 1:373	1:554	3↑	Arlington H 56k	5	3	33	31½	11	2hd	Blum W	118		4.70	88-07	MasterDennis112hdParka1181¼Carteret1164½	Failed to last	10
4Jly64- 8AP	fm	1⅛Ⓣ	:471 1:111 1:362	1:483	3↑	Stars & Stripes H 46k	7	6	65½	64¾	45	41¾	DeSpirito A	119		*3.10	96-04	SpanishFort1121¼IrishDandy110½RobRoyIII106hd	Rallied	13
27Jun64- 8Mth	fm	1 1/16Ⓣ		1:432	3↑	Longfellow H 22k	5	4	55¼	56	32½	1no	DeSpirito A	120		*2.10	98-04	Parka120noWesternWarrior121¾RedDog112hd	Up final stride	7
20Jun64- 7Mth	fm	1Ⓣ		1:372	3↑	Alw 7500	3	5	716	78	74¾	2¾	DeSpirito A	124		*.90e	97-03	Jalico110¾Parka1243Jet Clipper110hd	Wide for the drive	9
10Jun64- 7Mth	fm	1Ⓣ		1:384	3↑	Tercentnry H (Div 1) 17k	5	6	53½	23	33	2no	DeSpirito A	119		*1.00	91-17	Lucky Turn114noParka1193Fan Jet1115	Getting to winner	9
30May64- 7Del	fm	1 1/16Ⓣ		1:404	3↑	Brandywine H (Div 2) 18k	8	8	88¾	65½	33½	22½	Culmone J	119		*2.00	97-03	Red Dog1082½Parka119nkGreek Money1152	Closed very fast	8
16May64- 9Suf	fm	*1 1/16Ⓣ		1:453	3↑	B Tckrmn Jr H (Div 2) 17k	3	6	63¾	73¼	53½	31	Nelson E	120		2.70	95-04	WesternWarrior119noMarlinBay1191Parka120nk	Wide stretch	9
2May64- 8Pim	sf	1 1/16Ⓣ	:253 :503 1:163	1:50	3↑	Riggs H 18k	6	6	75¼	63¼	42½	42	Turcotte R	120		*1.40	63-35	Mr. Steu114noDedimoud1121Grand Applause1081	Closed fast	11
28Mar64- 9GP	fm	1½Ⓣ	:47 1:11 2:004	2:26	3↑	Donn H 59k	7	6	713	32½	23	22¼	Chambers W	119		3.70e	97-05	CedarKey1222¼Parka119noSuspicious1151¼	Held for placing	13
18Mar64- 9GP	fm	1 1/16Ⓣ	:221 :454 1:101	1:412	3↑	Green Valley H 17k	7	8	917	1010	99½	52¼	Chambers W	120		*1.50	96-03	PolarSea112hdCaptain'sCross113¾Molino115nk	Settled late	10
29Feb64- 8Hia	fm	1½Ⓣ		2:283	3↑	Hia Turf Cup H 98k	7	6	43½	53	66½	813	Chambers W	121		*1.60	83-07	Cartert1153½RoylAscot1131¼HotDust1141¼	Early foot,tired	13
20Feb64- 8Hia	fm	1⅛Ⓣ		1:484	4↑	Alw 7500	8	7	715	811	56	2hd	Chambers W	121		3.60	103-04	IrishDandy112hdParka121no[D]Finklehoffe1151¼	Wide,missed	9
1Feb64- 8Hia	fm	1 3/16Ⓣ		1:534	3↑	Bougainvillea H 34k	1	7	817	89½	63¼	1nk	Chambers W	120		6.50	107-00	Parka120nkSunrise Flight1201½Hot Dust120nk	Up near wire	14
24Jan64- 7Hia	fm	1 1/16Ⓣ		1:421	4↑	Alw 10000	4	5	59	69¼	47	42	Adams L	115		*2.00	98-04	Charablanc1121¼WldCard112hdHrdRockMn112¾	Finished well	11
17Jan64- 7Hia	fm	1 1/16Ⓣ		1:432	4↑	Alw 7000	8	9	77½	33	2½	11¾	Adams L	119		4.70	94-09	Prka1191¾WesternWarrior1152½HardRockMn1151	With ease	12
28Nov63- 8Pim	fm	1½Ⓣ	:473 1:131 2:044	2:321	3↑	Dixie H 62k	2	6	611	57	46	31	Chambers W	119		3.20	93-14	CedarKey1101Mr.Steu112noParka1194	Finished full of run	12
2Nov63- 8Lrl	sf	1⅛Ⓣ		1:51	3↑	Lrl Turf Cup H 24k	12	8	97½	73¼	3nk	2no	Blum W	117		2.50	82-18	[D]Intercepted116noParka1171SalesmanPrior109nk	Bothered	13
Placed first through disqualification																				
23Oct63- 5Aqu	fm	1 3/16Ⓣ		1:551	3↑	Knickerbckr H (Div 1) 21k	7	2	22	22	22	1½	Shoemaker W	110		*2.20	94-03	Parka110½CedarKy1122½Thygold1101½	Under strong handling	8
18Oct63- 7GS	fst	1 1/16	:234 :48 1:12	1:431	3↑	Alw 5500	5	7	73¾	67	712	714	Adams L	119		8.10	80-16	GypsyBaron118nkWhyLie1192MorryE.1158	Never a contender	7
7Oct63- 7Aqu	fm	1 3/16Ⓣ		1:543	3↑	Long Island H 29k	7	7	88	75½	75¼	55¾	Nelson E	112		13.80	91-03	DavidK.113nkTheAxelI1262NeverBend1202	Never prominent	10
21Sep63- 8Atl	sf	1 3/16Ⓣ		1:472	3↑	Boardwalk H 29k	1	4	43½	43½	34	33¾	Grant H	116		3.60	70-26	Bronze Babu120¾Marlin Bay1133Parka1162	Lacked a rally	7
31Aug63- 8Atl	fm	1⅛Ⓣ		1:48	3↑	Kelly-Olympic H 35k	6	5	52½	53½	64¾	31½	Grant H	116		7.80	101-00	Mngo124noBronzeBabu1201½Parka116¾	Lacked sufficient bid	10
24Aug63- 8Atl	sf	1 1/16Ⓣ		1:45	3↑	Philadelphia Turf H 30k	4	7	813	812	88¼	66¼	Grant H	118		*3.20	80-14	Sunrise County116hdDedimoud1151¼Hitting Away1132	Dull	10
12Aug63- 7Atl	fm	1 1/16Ⓣ		1:43	4↑	Alw 6000	7	4	511	44	41½	12	Grant H	122		*1.00	96-04	Parka1222Fat Cat122½Dedimoud1182	Kept to mild drive	7
31Jly63- 8Mth	fm	1 1/16Ⓣ		1:442	3↑	Longfellow H 34k	1	6	611	56	46	12	Grant H	116		5.80	93-07	Parka1162Inbalance1141¼Charabanc110¾	Clear under drive	9
4Jly63- 7Del	fm	1Ⓣ		1:354	3↑	Alw 10000	7	7	79	75	55	32¼	Culmone J	117		3.50	101-02	Bronze Babu1241¼Charabanc1101Parka1171½	Wide in rally	8
21Jun63- 7Aqu	fm	1 1/16Ⓣ		1:414	3↑	Alw 10000	6	6	53½	32	3hd	2½	Adams L	120		5.55	98-01	TheAxelI123½Parka1202½MarlinBay111hd	Stretch bid,hung	8
31May63- 7Mth	fm	1 1/16Ⓣ		1:463	4↑	Alw 10000	5	10	810	66	2hd	11¼	Monacelli E	116		3.90	82-20	Parka1161¼Pollingfold1122General Arthur1141	Drew out	12
17May63- 8GS	fst	1 1/16	:241 :481 1:122	1:444	4↑	Alw 6500	1	6	41½	76½	89½	78½	Monacelli E	117		6.10	77-19	Inbalance119½Military Plume1132¾Fat Cat1171	Fell back	8
4May63- 8Pim	fm	1 1/16Ⓣ	:253 :491 1:13	1:442	3↑	Riggs H 16k	5	4	31½	42½	42½	44¼	Monacelli E	111		4.80	89-12	BronzeBabu126nkShieldBearer1181½WarCouncil1182½	Tired	5
17Apr63- 8GP	fm	1 1/16Ⓣ	:23 :464 1:111	1:422	4↑	Alw 4000	6	3	32½	1hd	11	12	Monacelli E	114		*1.70	93-07	Prka1142ErinVale1143WiseCommand1162¼	Drew out handily	11
6Apr63- 7GP	fm	1Ⓣ	:232 :472 1:112	1:364	4↑	Alw 4000	3	4	65	85¾	43½	2¾	Grant H	116		*.70	93-13	Tinte109¾Parka1161½Bewildroom1142	Getting to winner	9
23Mar63- 8GP	fm	1½Ⓣ	:481 1:12 2:012	2:26	3↑	Donn H 41k	3	4	41	21	22	34½	Grant H	115		13.55	95-00	Tutankhamen1242½ElLoco1121¾Park1151¼	Extended bid,tired	12
13Mar63- 8GP	fm	1 1/16Ⓣ	:231 :462 1:101	1:411	3↑	Green Valley H 17k	8	3	48½	56½	45	45	Grant H	116		5.80	94-06	Tutankhamen122½El Loco1112½Carteret1162	Lacked a rally	9
2Mar63- 8Hia	fm	1 1/16Ⓣ		1:431	4↑	Alw 6500	2	6	711	87¾	54	33¼	Grant H	117		*1.75	92-05	Moderado1082AugustSun1151½Prk1171¾	Best stride too late	10
18Feb63- 8Hia	my	1⅛⊗	:463 1:114 1:372	1:50	4↑	Alw 6000	5	6	616	59	55½	49¾	Grant H	117		3.30	75-17	JayFox116½BelowDeck1148FilisteoII1171¼	Never prominent	7
31Jan63- 8Hia	fm	5½fⓉ		1:052	4↑	Alw 6000	12	9	119	1011	78¾	42¼	Grant H	124		10.60	88-14	[D]SwiftSands119nkAlwaysAlive1091¼ByInvitton119¾	Rallied	12
3Nov62- 8Lrl	sf	1⅛Ⓣ		1:552	3↑	Lrl Turf Cup H 23k	9	8	87¾	84¼	76¾	32½	Ferraro R	116		13.10	59-38	BronzeBabu1191¼WiseShip1241½Prk1161½	Best foot too late	10
27Oct62- 7Lrl	fm	1Ⓣ		1:373	3↑	Alw 10000	1	5	43	31½	3nk	1nk	Ferraro R5	111		5.20	85-18	Parka111nkGaelicLad1181½CalltheWitness116hd	Up in time	10
20Oct62- 6GS	fst	6f	:222 :452	1:094	4↑	Alw 7000	4	7	710	713	710	511	Grant H	119		9.10	84-15	Tilmar1194½St.Tropez1193½Intervener122nk	Never a factor	8
22Sep62- 8Atl	fst	1 1/16	:233 :463 1:103	1:414	3↑	Boardwalk H 28k	3	4	4¾	43¼	57	68	Lynch J	111		32.30	90-13	Ambiopoise116½Hellenic Hero113¾Towson111nk	Tired	8
15Sep62- 6Atl	fst	7f	:23 :451 1:092	1:214	3↑	Alw 4500	32	4	44	8½	46	47½	Lynch J	113		6.40	86-15	HellenicHero122noTilmar1161½NobleJay1186	Lacked a rally	6
1Sep62- 8Atl	fm	1⅛Ⓣ		1:50	3↑	Kelly-Olympic H 35k	8	4	43¼	33½	34½	32	Lynch J	111		25.60	91-07	WiseShip124½HittingAway1241½Park111½	Finished willingly	11
25Aug62- 8Atl	fm	1 1/16Ⓣ		1:422	3↑	Philadelphia Turf H 29k	1	7	69½	68	74¼	56¼	Brooks S	113		7.00	93-01	T.V.Lark1202HellenicHero111¾LoyalLadyII108½	In close	8
Placed fourth through disqualification																				
8Aug62- 7Sar	sf	1 1/16Ⓣ		1:421	3↑	Bernard Baruch H 28k	2	5	59½	66	43	53¼	Grant H	118		7.25	92-15	HittingAway1221¼WiseShip126nkNiksar111nk	Mild bid,tired	7
7Jly62- 8Mth	fm	1Ⓣ		1:391	3↑	Longfellow H 29k	6	5	55	5¾	21½	21½	Gilligan L	118		9.80	87-11	RoyalRecord1151½Parka1181¾Inbalance117no	Held on gamely	11
27Jun62- 6Mth	sf	1 1/16Ⓣ		1:491	3↑	Alw 6000	5	4	33½	22	2hd	1hd	Gilligan L	117		7.70	69-35	Parka117hdInblnc117noMrryRulr1227	Best under hard drive	6
16Jun62- 6Mth	sf	1Ⓣ		1:411	3↑	Alw 6000	1	6	63	53¼	3½	1¾	Grant H	116		*2.20	79-29	Parka116¾August Sun1247Green Hornet1131¼	Strong drive	8
6Jun62- 5Mth	fm	1Ⓣ		1:372	4↑	Alw 5000	2	7	67¼	44	41¾	31	Barrow T	119		4.90	97-04	Li'lFella1221RoyalRaton115noPrk119no	Blocked midstretch	7
22May62- 7GS	fst	1 1/16	:242 :48 1:122	1:442	4↑	Alw 10000	6	4	56½	42¼	53½	55¾	Grant H	119		2.70	82-15	TryCash1162½Fngo116½L'lBuddy1102½	Showed an even effort	8
8May62- 7GS	fst	1 1/16	:24 :473 1:113	1:434	4↑	Alw 10000	5	5	52¼	54¾	23	21½	Grant H	122		5.10	89-15	Snow Dune1221½Parka122noClaret II1161¼	Gaining at end	8
24Apr62- 7GP	fm	1 1/16Ⓣ	:23 :462 1:103	1:414	4↑	Alw 3800	9	4	33½	42	2hd	32	Scurlock O	118		*1.70	94-10	HisLegend1161½HyPrince115¾Parka1182	Bold bid,then tired	9
14Apr62- 7GP	fst	1⅛	:463 1:122 1:383	1:511	3↑	Pan American H 20k	5	5	34	3nk	22	57¾	Hartack W	115	b	8.20	70-15	Shirley Jones1212½Aeroflint1183Deton1091½	Well up,tired	10
7Apr62- 7GP	fst	1 1/16	:24 :472 1:114	1:443	3↑	Fort Lauderdale H 15k	6	3	2hd	3½	53	56¾	Monacelli E	113	b	6.85	78-19	Cactus Tom1191Aeroflint118¾Trans-Way1221	Speed,tired	8
14Mar62- 7GP	fm	1 1/16Ⓣ	:223 :454 1:094	1:41	3↑	Green Valley H 17k	4	3	33	33	1hd	3¾	Monacelli E	109	b	12.95	99-00	Eurasia122hdNasomo112¾Parka109no	Stretch lead,weakened	9
8Mar62- 8GP	fm	1Ⓣ	:231 :47 1:114	1:364	3↑	Alw 4200	5	2	41½	3nk	1½	1nk	Grant H	118	b	2.70	94-06	Parka118nkWise Command120¾Tapis1221	Under hard drive	10
12Feb62- 7Hia	fm	1 1/16Ⓣ		1:451	4↑	Alw 5000	8	6	64½	32½	1hd	11½	Grant H	116	b	3.55	85-15	Parka1161½MissJ.G.107½RoylRdrss1121¾	Driving,drew clear	12
30Jan62- 8Hia	fst	7f	:231 :46 1:103	1:232	4↑	Alw 5000	11	2	97	99½	57	52¾	Grant H	120	b	5.20	90-14	The Tongan116½Whitechapel1141¾Misty Day118½	Late gain	12
6Jan62- 8TrP	fst	1 1/16	:231 :46 1:094	1:423	3↑	Orange Bwl H (Div 2) 15k	7	4	43	43	32	42½	Monacelli E	111	b	7.95	86-14	Eurasia119½BeauPrince1242Trans-Wy114no	Made even effort	9
25Dec61- 8TrP	fst	1 1/16	:224 :46 1:104	1:44	3↑	Christmas H 11k	4	5	54	53	41½	5¾	Monacelli E	111	b	64.15	81-27	Humane Leader113½Eurasia120noLevel Flight114nk	Evenly	11
2Dec61- 8TrP	fst	1 70	:221 :453 1:112	1:42	3↑	City of Miami H 11k	8	7	76¼	55½	56	66¼	Monacelli E	112	b	9.40	81-13	Eurasia1181½Pointer1141½ImWilling113no	Made even effort	14

25Nov61- 5TrP	fst 6f	:221 :454 1:104	Alw 3000	4 8 89 66 45 42	Grant H	122	b	*1.25	86-21	Cyclobob113¾CountRose1191¼Troa116no	Passed tired horses	10
10Nov61- 7GS	fst 1 70	:232 :471 1:122 1:43	Alw 6000	4 7 52½ 42½ 42 33	Grant H	122	b	3.80	79-26	Earful111noSho Lea1163Parka122¾	Dwelt at the start	8
26Oct61- 7GS	fst 1	:24 :48 1:13 1:373	Alw 10000	7 5 42 3nk 13 12	Grant H	119	b	2.90	94-24	Parka1192Sho Lea1197Sunshine Cake1111½	Kept to pressure	7
19Oct61- 7GS	fst 1 70	:23 :463 1:12 1:43	Alw 10000	9 5 53 85½ 1010 1010	Sellers J	116	b	*2.70	72-16	JayFox1221½Earful1122NobleTurn1141¼	Made a dull effort	11
13Oct61- 7GS	fst 1	:231 :461 1:104 1:374	Alw 10000	9 2 11½ 11 12 2no	Sellers J	116	b	*2.50	93-17	HellenicHero119noParka116nkNobleTurn1094	Failed to last	12
26Sep61- 6Atl	fst 7f	:222 :45 1:092 1:214	Clm 13000	3 2 12 13 16 18	Sellers J	120	b	*1.70	94-11	Parka1208GoldenSixties1182¼EnglishSole115no	Mild drive	8
11Sep61- 6Atl	fst 6f	:221 :444 1:092	Clm c-10000	4 2 32 32 31 1hd	Lee T	116	b	*2.10	98-08	Parka116hdLangleyFiver1141½PhlLppy1144	Up final strides	7
	Claimed from W.A. Leiser,F.A. Bonsal trainer											
19Aug61- 7Atl	fst 7f	:223 :45 1:092 1:22	Alw 4500	8 5 31 54 54½ 65½	Lee T	114	b	35.40	87-11	Relative121hdCovered Bridge1141¼Somali Bird1143½	Tired	9
12Aug61- 6Atl	fst 6f	:214 :451 1:102	Alw 4200	1 7 59 67½ 76 76	Lee T	116	b	19.20	87-11	Relative1161St. Tropez116DHLong Distance1102	No factor	8
27Jly61- 8Del	fm 1 1/16Ⓣ	1:443	3↑ Alw 5000	1 2 2hd 1hd 2hd 11¾	Lee T	114	b	1.50	89-11	Parka1141¾Why Lie1224Almitra117¾	Under long,hard drive	7
13Jly61- 4Del	sly 1 1/16	:234 :474 1:121 1:461	Alw 4000	2 1 1hd 11 2hd 31¼	Lee T	116	b	7.40	77-20	BraxtonBragg116¾RainDance116½Park116no	Drifted out late	6
7Jly61- 4Del	fst 6f	:224 :462 1:112	Alw 5000	5 3 53½ 54½ 59 57½	Lee T	108		8.80	80-21	RestlessCloud1171¼BraxtonBragg1121¼GlencoeKid1175	Tired	7
14Jun61- 5Del	fm 1Ⓣ	1:391	Alw 5000	2 2 25 37 35½ 33¼	Lee T	116		4.50	83-14	World Record1162½Kowtow116¾Parka1162½	Mild late rally	9
6Jun61- 5Del	fst 6f	:221 :454 1:113	Alw 4500	8 4 53½ 55 31 31½	Lee T	122		6.40	85-19	Arstar122nkAffectiont1171¼Prk122nk	Best stride too late	12
20May61- 6Pim	fst 6f	:233 :472 1:133	Alw 3000	6 2 43½ 33½ 1hd 13	Lee T	116		*1.40	82-22	Parka1163Mart1163FndM1131½	Mildly urged,increasing lead	7
16May61- 7Pim	fst 6f	:233 :463 1:13	Alw 4000	4 3 31½ 38 36 33	Choquette J	113		2.90	82-22	PhilLippy1131¾LookofEagles1081¼Park1136	Stride too late	7
2May61- 5Lrl	gd 6f	:23 :473 1:133	©Md Sp Wt	7 1 1hd 1½ 11½ 11½	Choquette J	118		*1.80e	87-12	Parka1181½DHInitiator118DHWait Again1184	Kept driving	9

Peal

b. g. 1956, by Hunters Moon IV (Foxhunter)–Golden Bells, by Swing and Sway — **Lifetime record: 12 4 5 2 $73,707**

Own.– H.A. Love
Br.– Harry A. Love (Md)
Tr.– C.V.B. Cushman Jr

27Oct61- 6Aqu	hd *2½	S'Chase	4:354	4↑ Temple Gwathmey H 55k	1 2 2½ 38½ 18 114	Aitcheson J Jr	161	*1.55	--	Peal16114NavalTreaty1392Chufquen1413	Had speed to spare	8
17Oct61- 5Aqu	hd *3	S'Chase	5:402	4↑ Grand National H 28k	2 2 22 1½ 2½ 2½	Aitcheson J Jr	159	*2.20	--	Independence138½Peal1598Naval Treaty1386	Jumped well	8
3Oct61- 5Bel	sf *2½	S'Chase	4:484	4↑ Brook H 19k	6 3 35 43½ 21 2¾	Aitcheson J Jr	158	2.95	--	NavalTreaty133¾Peal1588Chufqun1412	Bore out final drive	7
14Sep61- 5Bel	hd *2⅛	S'Chase	3:52	4↑ Broad Hollow H 16k	5 2 23 23 11 14½	Aitcheson J Jr	147	2.90	--	Peal1474½Negocio13210Hustl13418	Going away,mildly urged	6
7Jly61- 3Del	fm *2½	S'Chase	4:403	4↑ Indian River H 10k	4 1 1½ 12 15 17	Aitcheson J Jr	146	*.70e	--	Peal1467Arywa138noBugleCllII1427	Well rated,easily best	7
19Jun61- 3Del	fm *2⅛	S'Chase	4:014	4↑ Tom Roby 10k	5 3 411 2hd 21½ 12½	Aitcheson J Jr	141	5.40	--	Pl1412½Juvntus1334BuglCllII14612	Fenced well,drew clear	7
1Jun61- 5Bel	hd *2⅛	S'Chase	3:561	4↑ International H 16k	2 1 23 33 36 36	Aitcheson J Jr	142	5.05	--	Nala155hdMuguet II1606Peal1427	Forced to check slightly	6
22May61- 3Aqu	fm *2	S'Chase	3:54	4↑ Alw 4500	1 7 2½ 23 23 2½	Aitcheson J Jr	137	*1.15e	--	RealFncy147½Pl137½BslB14230	Slow start,bad landing 12th	8
9May61- 3Aqu	sf *2	S'Chase	3:53	4↑ Sp Wt 4200	6 5 53½ 34½ 11½ 21	Riles S	152	27.55	--	OurJeep1431Peal152hdNavalTrety1438	Led briefly,game try	9
9Jun60- 5Bel	fm *2⅛	S'Chase	3:57	4↑ Bel Spring 13k	4 1 12 - - -	Walsh T	142	18.55	--	Hustle151hdAmateur15614Cartagena1461½		8
	Stumbled 8th fence,lost rider											
1Jun60- 3Bel	hd *2⅛	S'Chase	3:563	4↑ Sp Wt 4500	9 1 11½ 2½ 37½ 312	Walsh T	145	7.55e	--	Amateur1547Black Andy1455Peal1456	Set early pace,tired	9
23Apr60- 5Mid	hd *2	S'Chase	3:51	4↑ Alw 600	2 4 411 2½ 22 28	Aitcheson J Jr	139	-	--	Doural1438Peal13910Rhythm Master141	Made game try	5

Primonetta

ch. f. 1958, by Swaps (Khaled)–Banquet Bell, by Polynesian — **Lifetime record: 25 17 2 2 $306,690**

Own.– Darby Dan Farm
Br.– John W. Galbreath (Ky)
Tr.– J.P. Conway

3Nov62- 8CD	fst 1	:224 :451 1:094 1:353	3↑ ⒻFalls City H 22k	4 2 23 22 12 12	Baird RL	126	*.60	95-12	Primonetta1262Old Hat1131¼Fortunate Isle1103	Easy score	9
18Oct62- 6Kee	fst 1⅛	:46 1:101 1:36 1:482	3↑ ⒻSpinster 73k	6 3 34 21 11 11	Shoemaker W	123	*.60e	95-12	Primonetta1231Royal Patrice119hdFirm Policy1191	Driving	7
	Open to 3-, 4- and 5-year-olds										
11Oct62- 6Kee	fst *7f	1:251	3↑ ⒻAlw 10000	2 1 32½ 24 2hd 13½	Lynch J	118	*.90	99-13	Primonetta1183½Times Two112nkCyclopavia1046	Easily best	4
22Sep62- 7Aqu	fst 1⅛	:463 1:103 1:354 1:481	3↑ ⒻBeldame 87k	2 1 1hd 1hd 21 45¼	Baeza B	123	*2.80e	96-06	Cicada1181½ShirleyJones1232¼FirmPolcy1181½	Used in pace	13
10Sep62- 7Aqu	fst 6f	:22 :444 1:094	3↑ ⒻHandicap 10000	1 4 41¾ 43½ 3nk 11½	Valenzuela I	125	*1.35	96-10	Primonetta1251½Staretta119nkReally Sumthin1121½	Easily	8
29Aug62- 7Aqu	my 6½f	:224 :461 1:111 1:174	3↑ ⒻHandicap 10000	6 2 1hd 2½ 22 35¼	Valenzuela I	126	*.90	89-19	Play Time1204Linita1231¼Primonetta126½	Used up early	7
28Jly62- 6Del	fst 1¼	:474 1:113 1:363 2:023	3↑ ⒻDelaware H 141k	4 1 1½ 33½ 36 48¼	Baeza B	124	*1.50e	81-21	SevenThirty120hdCicada1147Bramalea1151¼	Hard used early	9
4Jly62- 8Mth	fst 1 1/16	:232 :463 1:103 1:422	3↑ ⒻMolly Pitcher H 27k	5 1 11 11 11 12	Baeza B	126	*.50	93-11	Primonetta1262ShirleyJones123½Dremflowr1124½	Mild drive	6
20Jun62- 7Mth	fst 6f	:22 :444 1:091	3↑ ⒻRegret H 22k	4 1 1hd 1hd 11½ 12½	Baeza B	124	*.40	96-13	Primonetta1242½Coup d'etat1131¼Cup of Tea112¾	In hand	5
12Jun62- 7Bel	sly 6f	:222 :452 1:094	3↑ ⒻAlw 6500	3 1 11½ 13 16 110	Baeza B	114	*.25	98-16	Primonetta11410Shuett118¾Whspy1145	Long lead,easy score	4
23Nov61- 7Aqu	fst 1	:223 :453 1:11 1:363	3↑ ⒻFirenze H 28k	5 2 2½ 1hd 42 66½	Ycaza M	123	*.80	78-18	Oil Royalty109¾Frimanaha113¾Seven Thirty1164	Used up	8
19Oct61- 6Kee	sly 1⅛	:464 1:103 1:36 1:491	3↑ ⒻSpinster 84k	7 2 2½ 1½ 12 2¾	Shoemaker W	119	4.30	90-11	Bowl of Flowers119¾Primonetta1191Times Two1191	Gamely	7
	Open to 3-,4- and 5-year-olds										
23Sep61- 7Bel	fst 1⅛	:463 1:11 1:361 1:492	3↑ ⒻBeldame 96k	4 1 11 1½ 2½ 33¼	Shoemaker W	118	*3.10	86-18	Airmans Guide123¾Craftiness1232½Primonetta1185½	Tired	12
13Sep61- 7Bel	fst 1⅛	:463 1:11 1:361 1:49	ⒻGazelle H 28k	2 4 2hd 1hd 53¼ 59½	Shoemaker W	126	*.55	81-16	Shimmy Dancer1122½My Portrait120noFunloving1226	Tired	11
5Aug61- 6Sar	fst 1¼	:481 1:121 1:371 2:031	ⒻAlabama 54k	2 1 11 11½ 1½ 15	Shoemaker W	121	2.45	92-10	Primonetta1215MightyFar1141BowlofFlowrs124hd	Mild drive	6
22Jly61- 6Mth	fst 1⅛	:474 1:111 1:361 1:484	ⒻMth Oaks 56k	3 2 1hd 1hd 1hd 2nk	Rogers C	121	*.70	100-15	My Portrait121nkPrimonetta1217Funloving1212	Sharp try	9
15Jly61- 6Del	gd 1⅛	:48 1:123 1:383 1:511	ⒻDel Oaks 59k	3 1 12 11 1½ 1no	Shoemaker W	121	*.50	81-27	Primonetta121noMighty Fair1214Funloving1214	All out	6
3Jly61- 7Mth	fst 6f	:221 :451 1:101	ⒻMiss Woodford 22k	5 2 13 13 13 14½	Grant H	121	*.40	91-15	Primonetta1214½HighlandLass112nkAnglSpd1131¾	Mild drive	7
12Jun61- 7Mth	fst 6f	:211 :434 1:082	3↑ ⒻAlw 6000	4 2 34 34 13 13½	Grant H	115	*.70	100-12	Primonetta1153½ShirleyJones1157GrenTrunk1153	Mild drive	7
12Apr61- 7Aqu	fst 6f	:22 :451 1:103	ⒻPrioress 24k	8 2 31½ 21½ 11 11½	Hartack W	121	*.35	92-12	Primonetta1211½Apatontheback1211¼MightyFair1211	Handily	10
4Apr61- 7Aqu	fst 6f	:23 :47 1:12	ⒻAlw 10000	3 3 1hd 11 113 13¼	Hartack W	123	*.30	85-20	Primonetta1233¼Apatontheback1233½Vivandiere1121	Easily	5
26Nov60- 8Pim	fst 1 1/16	:251 :483 1:124 1:462	ⒻMarguerite 37k	3 1 12 13 14 15	Hartack W	119	*1.00	78-27	Primonetta1195Plum Cake11910Rice Shower1195	Easy score	5
15Nov60- 7Aqu	fst 6f	:222 :46 1:112	ⒻAlw 5000	4 1 11 11½ 12 11	Hartack W	119	*.35	88-19	Primnetta1191Marwol1125Short Span1154	Was kept driving	5
28Oct60- 6Aqu	fst 6f	:224 :47 1:113	ⒻAlw 4500	6 1 1hd 1hd 11 12½	Arcaro E	119	*1.10	87-20	Primonetta1192½Shimmy Dancer1161M'selle Mill1162	Easily	13
13Sep60- 4Aqu	fst 6f	:221 :454 1:111	ⒻMd Sp Wt	4 1 11½ 12 11½ 1¾	Arcaro E	115	4.70	91-12	Primonetta115¾TinyRoyal1152CounterCall115nk	Brisk ride	10

Queen Empress

b. f. 1962, by Bold Ruler (Nasrullah)–Irish Jay, by Double Jay — **Lifetime record: 33 15 10 4 $431,419**

Own.– Wheatley Stable
Br.– Wheatley Stable (Ky)
Tr.– E.A. Neloy

26Oct66- 7Aqu	fm 1 1/16Ⓣ	1:44	3↑ ⒻNew York H (Div 2) 23k	7 3 3nk 22 920 935½	Baeza B	120 b	5.70	50-13	Swinging Mood1192Short Fall112noWhat a Treat121¾		9
	Early speed,sulked										
17Oct66- 7Aqu	fst 6f	:222:453 1:102	3↑ ⒻInterborough H 27k	2 3 64 64 44½ 25	Baeza B	123 b	6.00	86-19	NativeStreet1185QueenEmpress1232Codorniz1181½	In close	6
16Jly66- 8Del	fst 1 1/16	:234:472 1:104 1:423	3↑ ⒻNew Castle 36k	1 2 2hd 22½ 23 24	Baeza B	113 b	*1.10	92-15	Open Fire1074Queen Empress1131Ho Ho108¾	No excuse	9
29Jun66- 7Aqu	fst 7f	:232:46 1:102 1:231	3↑ ⒻVagrancy H 27k	2 2 1hd 1½ 12 12½	Baeza B	123 b	*.20	90-17	QnEmpress1232½PetiteRouge1133½MountRegina113½	Easily	4
8Jun66- 7Aqu	fst 6f	:221:444 1:093	3↑ ⒻLiberty Belle H 27k	6 4 43 32½ 21 2no	Baeza B	122 b	*1.50	95-12	TripleBrook113noQnEmprss1225Cohsst115¾	Altered course	8
21May66- 8GS	fst 6f	:22 :453 1:10	3↑ ⒻColonial H 28k	4 4 41 41½ 5¾ 42½	Knapp K	122 b	3.70	91-18	Tosmah1251½WildNote1161Cohsst114no	Lacked late response	8
27Apr66- 7Aqu	fst 1	:24 :464 1:11 1:354	3↑ ⒻBed o' Roses H 27k	1 1 1½ 1hd 2hd 33	Blum W	123 b	3.20	86-18	StraightDeal1171½WhtaTreat1261½QnEmprss123nk	Weakened	7
18Apr66- 7Aqu	fst 7f	:223:452 1:094 1:222	3↑ ⒻDistaff H 27k	6 2 33 21½ 1hd 2nk	Baeza B	123 b	*.60	94-17	SailorPrincess111nkQueenEmprss1232½Pttcot112no	Bore out	7
9Apr66- 8Bow	fst 7f	:223:45 1:102 1:232	3↑ ⒻBarbara Fritchie H 59k	3 5 31½ 31½ 2hd 21	Knapp K	123 b	3.30	95-14	Tosmah1211Queen Emprss1231½Privileged111nk	Game effort	12
30Mar66- 7Aqu	fst 6f	:221:453 1:111	3↑ ⒻCorrection H 28k	3 4 52½ 32 2hd 12	Knapp K	122 b	*.80	87-20	QnEmpress1222Adorable1122½Admrng1151¾	Loafing,roused	8
2Mar66- 8Hia	fst 1⅛	:47 1:11 1:372 1:502	3↑ ⒻBlack Helen H 62k	5 1 1½ 11 32 42¾	Baeza B	117 b	8.00	80-13	WhataTreat1201¾AlondraII110hdTosmah1151	Set pace,tired	11
16Feb66- 8Hia	fst 7f	:231:453 1:103 1:231	3↑ ⒻColumbiana H 30k	4 1 1½ 1½ 1hd 33	Baeza B	120 b	2.20e	90-17	Gold Digger112½Tosmah1172½Queen Empress1201	Lead,tired	9
8Feb66- 8Hia	fst 7f	:232:454 1:101 1:232	4↑ ⒻAlw 8000	7 1 2½ 2½ 21½ 1no	Baeza B	113 b	*.90	92-13	Queen Empress113noTosmah113nkWhat a Treat1193	Driving	7
1Feb66- 8Hia	fst 6f	:221:46 1:113	4↑ ⒻAlw 6000	6 1 31 1½ 12 12½	Baeza B	115 b	*.40	86-23	QueenEmpress1152½MeetMeLater112¾DeCathy113hd	In hand	7
	Previously trained by W.C. Winfrey										
14Aug65- 6Sar	fst 1¼	:471 1:112 1:364 2:033	ⒻAlabama 63k	13 4 31 75 1726 1736	Baeza B	118 b	6.20e	54-06	WhataTreat118nk[D]Discipline1182Terentia114½	Brief speed	18
12Aug65- 7Sar	fst 7f	:221:443 1:094 1:231	ⒻHandicap 10000	2 5 23 22 2hd 1no	Baeza B	123 b	*.90	94-12	QnEmprss123noTwoofAkind114½ValiantQueen121no	Lasted	8
5Aug65- 7Sar	fst 7f	:222:45 1:094 1:23	ⒻTest (Div 2) 23k	1 4 21½ 2½ 1½ 21½	Baeza B	118 b	*.70	93-12	Cestrum1121½Queen Empress118½Ground Control1212	Failed	9
26Jly65- 7Aqu	fst 6f	:214:45 1:10	3↑ ⒻAlw 10000	1 2 21 21½ 1hd 13	Baeza B	111 b	*.70	93-13	Queen Empress1113Petite Rouge1161Ballet Rose1204	Easily	4
20Jly65- 8Mth	fst 6f	:22 :45 1:112	ⒻAlw 5000	6 3 1½ 13 11 1½	Grant H	121 b	*.60	85-19	Queen Empress121½Bacasiwo1137Street Show118no	Driving	8
7Nov64- 8GS	fst 1 1/16	:232:47 1:112 1:44	ⒻGardenia 188k	2 1 11 1½ 3nk 1nk	Shoemaker W	119 b	*1.00e	88-13	Queen Empress119nkMarshua119noDiscipline1191¾	Driving	13
24Oct64- 8Lrl	fst 1 1/16	:232:464 1:122 1:441	ⒻSelima 96k	5 3 21 21 21 2nk	Shoemaker W	122 b	*.40e	96-10	Marshua119nkQueen Empress122nkDiscipline1194½	Failed	7
10Oct64- 7Aqu	fst 1	:224:453 1:11 1:372	ⒻFrizette 124k	3 3 36½ 24½ 1½ 11	Shoemaker W	119 b	*.90e	81-18	QueenEmpress1191[D]Marshua119¾MoneytoBurn1192½	Easily	8
30Sep64- 7Aqu	my 7f	:224:462 1:124 1:263	ⒻAstarita 30k	9 4 3½ 11½ 1hd 1no	Valenzuela I	122	*2.20	73-31	[D]QueenEmpress122noIDeceive1192½Admiring1222	Bore out	12
	Disqualified and placed second										
23Sep64- 6Aqu	fst 6½f	:222:452 1:102 1:17	ⒻAlw 9500	2 3 31 32½ 21 2hd	Shoemaker W	122 b	*.85	95-13	LayAft116hdQueenEmpress122noMarshua1225	Steadied,sharp	6
26Aug64- 7Sar	fst 6f	:213:442 1:104	ⒻSpinaway 81k	4 4 32½ 22½ 24 31	Ycaza M	119 b	*1.05	93-08	Candalita1191Marshua119hdQnEmprss1191	Swerved backstr.	6
19Aug64- 7Sar	fst 6f	:22 :45 1:104	ⒻAdirondack 24k	1 8 21½ 22 23 22½	Ycaza M	123 b	*.90	91-13	Candalita1142½Queen Empress1233Marshua123¾	No excuse	9
1Aug64- 8Mth	fst 6f	:22 :443 1:093	ⒻSorority 100k	2 3 42 41 32 34½	Baeza B	119 b	*1.20	89-15	BoldExperience1192½Rhodie1192QnEmpress1195	No excuse	7
15Jly64- 8Mth	fst 5½f	:213:45 1:04	ⒻColleen 17k	2 5 32 2hd 11½ 1¾	Baeza B	119 b	1.30	97-15	QueenEmprss119¾BoldExperience1198Centrvll114nk	Driving	9
29Jun64- 7Aqu	fst 5½f	:222:453 :574 1:041	ⒻAstoria 28k	7 4 32½ 31½ 21½ 1hd	Baeza B	123 b	*.55	92-16	Queen Empress123hdMarshua1175First Offence1173½	Driving	8
15Jun64- 7Aqu	fst 5½f	:223:461 :584 1:054	ⒻNational Stallion 26k	4 4 3½ 31½ 13 12	Baeza B	119	*.35	84-17	QueenEmpress1192Adorabl1142ClrRock1191	Tried to bear in	5
13May64- 7Aqu	fst 5f	:22 :453 :581	ⒻFashion 23k	6 6 45½ 46½ 33½ 1nk	Baeza B	116	4.05	94-18	QueenEmpress116nkBoldExperience1166Privilgd1122	Driving	7
5May64- 6Aqu	fst 5f	:224:461 :583	ⒻAlw 7500	7 7 45 43½ 31 1½	Baeza B	116	*.75e	92-15	QueenEmpress116½Discipline1162½NativPrncss1161½	Driving	8
29Apr64- 3Aqu	sly 5f	:23 :471 :593	ⒻMd Sp Wt	6 3 2hd 1hd 12 1¾	Ussery R	119	2.70e	87-25	Queen Empress119¾Privileged1195½Small Voice1192	Easily	10

Queen of the Stage

b. f. 1965, by Bold Ruler (Nasrullah)–Broadway, by Hasty Road — **Lifetime record: 14 9 2 1 $316,515**

Own.– O. Phipps
Br.– Ogden Phipps (Ky)
Tr.– E.A. Neloy

21Jan69- 8Hia	fst 6f	:22 :45 1:092	4↑ ⒻAlw 7000	1 5 1½ 2½ 24 37¾	Baeza B	118	*.60	89-15	TooBald1157ClemsFairyGold121¾QnoftheStg118¾	Gave way	9
24Oct68- 7Bel	fst 6f	:23 :46 1:101	3↑ ⒻAlw 15000	3 2 11 1hd 13 11¼	Baeza B	120	*.20	94-16	QnoftheStge1201¼QueenVkng1132½GustRoom1133½	Handily	8
14Oct68- 7Bel	fst 6f	:22 :443 1:094	3↑ ⒻInterborough H 27k	1 3 11½ 14 12 2nk	Baeza B	119 b	*2.20	96-16	Romanticism117nkQnoftheStg1192½JustKddng1175	Gamely	7
5Oct68- 8Atl	fst 1 3/16	:472 1:111 1:364 1:551	3↑ ⒻMatchmaker 50k	1 1 1hd 1hd 33½ 815	Baeza B	114	*2.90	85-12	Politely1234½GreenGlade115¾AmerigoLady1182	Used in pace	11
25Sep68- 8Atl	fst 1 1/16	:233:464 1:102 1:42	3↑ Alw 7500	4 1 11½ 11 1hd 1hd	Baltazar C	111	*.90	97-11	[D]QueenoftheStage111hdBig Rock Candy1135NavyAdmirl114nk		8
	Disqualified and placed second										
13Sep68- 7Aqu	fst 6f	:223:462 1:104	3↑ ⒻAlw 15000	7 1 11½ 12 12 11½	Baeza B	112	*.90	89-19	Queen of the Stage1121½Just Kidding1164Indian LoveCall116½		7
	Driving										
28Oct67- 8Lrl	fst 1 1/16	:232:463 1:124 1:442	ⒻSelima 109k	5 3 43 44½ 411 418¼	Baeza B	122	*.40	77-17	SyrianSea1192GayMatelda1193½SingingRain11913	No excuse	6
7Oct67- 7Aqu	fst 1	:23 :454 1:101 1:352	ⒻFrizette 114k	7 2 2hd 2½ 1½ 1¾	Baeza B	119	*.40e	91-12	Queen of the Stage119¾Gay Matelda1191Obeah119½	Driving	7
9Sep67- 7Aqu	fst 6f	:221:452 1:10	ⒻMatron 104k	4 1 21 21 12 14	Baeza B	119	*.30	93-16	QueenoftheStage1194GayMatelda119¾SyrianSea1193	Easily	7
23Aug67- 7Sar	fst 6f	:222:453 1:101	ⒻSpinaway 80k	9 1 1hd 1½ 1½ 1½	Baeza B	119	*.80	97-11	QueenoftheStg119½DreamPath1194½GayMtelda119no	Driving	9
29Jly67- 8Mth	fst 6f	:221:45 1:10	ⒻSorority 103k	2 2 1½ 11 1½ 1½	Baeza B	119	*.30	92-17	QnoftheStge119½CockeyMiss119noGayMatelda1196	Driving	7
12Jly67- 7Aqu	fst 5½f	:222:453 :572 1:033	ⒻAstoria 27k	2 1 1½ 11½ 13 16	Baeza B	117	*.30	95-13	QueenoftheStag1176GayMatelda120½Zoomalong1172	Easily	4
5Jly67- 6Aqu	gd 5½f	:223:463 :583 1:05	ⒻAlw 10000	7 7 3nk 11½ 14 17	Baeza B	116	*.50	88-21	QueenoftheStge1167CopperCanyon107noWiggins1166	Easily	7
10May67- 5Aqu	fst 5f	:224:464 :59	ⒻMd Sp Wt	2 1 1hd 1hd 12 19	Baeza B	119	*1.70	90-21	QueenoftheStge1199MickBQuick119½FunnyMiss1193½	Easily	10

Quick Pitch

ch. g. 1960, by Charlevoix (Princequillo)–The Ghizeh, by Questionnaire — **Lifetime record: 66 23 13 6 $229,217**

Own.– F.P. Ryan
Br.– F.P. Ryan (Ky)
Tr.– E.B. Ryan

24Oct68- 6Bel	fm 2½	Hurdles 4:351	4↑ NY Turf Writers Cup 19k	5 1 1hd 1hd 512 621	Mahoney J	164	*.90	--	LeCerisier1381½BoldBeggar1564LakeDelawar1455	Done early	9
11Oct68- 3Bel	fm 2⅛	Hurdles 3:53	4↑ Alw 10000	7 1 13 1½ 2½ 22	Mahoney J	155	*.90	--	BoldBeggar1512QuickPitch1558NationalAnthem1434	Gamely	7
14Sep67- 5Aqu	hd 2½	Hurdles 4:302	4↑ Rouge Dragon H 11k	5 1 13 13 112 116	Mahoney J	172	*.40	--	Quick Pitch17216Gay Sparkle1372Brandon Hill131hd	Easily	6
18Aug67- 3Sar	hd 2 1/16	Hurdles 3:382	4↑ Lovely Night H 12k	3 1 11 15 110 118	Mahoney J	170	1.40	--	QuickPitch17018Roublet15025Lumiere1363	As rider pleased	7
26Jly67- 5Mth	fm *2	Hurdles 4:033	3↑ Midsummer H 16k	6 1 1hd 12 13 13	Mahoney JA	166	*.80	--	Quick Pitch1663Amble Up138¾My Chap1489	Kept to urging	9
27Jun67- 3Del	fm *1¾	Hurdles 3:31	3↑ Holly Tree H 7.9k	3 1 13 125 18 16	Armstrong RO	164	*.60	--	Quick Pitch1646My Chap15317Calanthe1336	Easily the best	6
1Jun67- 5Aqu	fm 2 1/16	Hurdles 3:402	4↑ Bushwick H 11k	1 1 16 16 16 13	Armstrong R	157	*1.10	--	Quick Pitch1573Bowzen1442Sandhill Flight148no	Easily	10
24May67- 3Aqu	fm 2 1/16	Hurdles 3:374	4↑ Land Boy H 8.5k	3 2 21½ 16 18 12	Armstrong R	151	2.00	--	Quick Pitch1512Market Center1333Go Lloyd Go1466	Easily	9
15May67- 3Aqu	fm 1⅞	Hurdles 3:224	4↑ Alw 7000	3 2 22 2hd 33½ 38	Armstrong R	151	3.10	--	SandhillFlight1445BoldBeggr1513QuickPtch15110	Weakened	8
27Oct66- 6Aqu	fm 2½	Hurdles 4:341	4↑ NY Turf Writers H 18k	2 6 22 21½ 21 32	Biger P	154	2.20	--	Spooky Joe151noMy Chap1542Quick Pitch1542½	Hung at end	10
10Oct66- 3Aqu	fm 1⅞	Hurdles 3:254	3↑ OClm 7500	4 2 2½ 2½ 16 13½	Biger P	155	*1.20	--	Quick Pitch1553½Iambic1454Arenque1401	Scored in hand	9
12Sep66- 7Aqu	fm 1⅝Ⓣ	2:412	3↑ Brighton Beach H 30k	1 1 1½ 1118 1128 1138	Combest J	117 b	*2.00	49-13	KnightlyManner116¾GallupPoll110noFastCount1137	Stopped	11
3Sep66- 7FE	sf 1⅜Ⓣ	:513 1:182 1:433 2:234	3↑ Niagara H 29k	2 1 11½ 1nk 21 21¾	Combest J	123 b	*.50	64-34	Orbiter1181¾QuckPtch123nkBluSol11025	No apparent excuse	4
26Aug66- 7Sar	fm 1⅝Ⓣ	2:411	3↑ Seneca H 29k	5 1 13 11 1hd 24½	Combest J	125 b	4.70	82-17	Paoluccio1124½QuickPitch1253Dunderhd105nk	Couldn't last	8
19Aug66- 7Sar	fm 1⅛Ⓣ	1:474	3↑ Alw 10000	2 1 13 12 13 11½	Combest J	123 b	5.20	94-06	Quick Pitch1231½Ginger Fizz1182Imam1114	Ridden out	6

10Aug66- 7Sar	fm	1 1/16Ⓣ		1:40	3↑ Bernard Baruch H 30k	5	4	45	2½	2hd	43¾	Combest J	115	b	16.70	101-00	Assagai1153Ginger Fizz114¾Northern Deamon113no	Faltered 10
30Jly66- 7FE	fm	1Ⓣ	:233 :471 1:114	1:372	3↑ Fair Play 12k	7	6	32½	1nk	12½	1½	McComb S	119	b	2.25	96-07	QuickPitch119½VictorianEra1234¾GoodOldMort1182¾	Driving 8
19Jly66- 8Mth	fm	1 1/16Ⓣ		1:45	4↑ Alw 6000	5	2	1hd	11½	2hd	1no	Brumfield D	113	b	3.40	90-10	Quick Pitch113noLeonine1061½Silverado II1132	Hard drive 8
12Jly66- 7Aqu	hd	1⅛Ⓣ		1:474	3↑ Handicap 10000	2	3	41	35	411	417½	Combest J	119	b	8.80	78-04	Flag1174½Canal11810Bonny Star1073	Early speed,tired 6
2Jly66- 8Del	hd	1⅜Ⓣ		2:133	3↑ Sussex H 30k	6	1	11½	24	49	717	Combest J	117	b	12.00	77-12	Portsmouth1162½Knightly Manner1173½Prolijo1143½	Used up 13
20Jun66- 8Del	fm	1 1/16Ⓣ		1:441	4↑ Alw 5000	7	1	2½	43¼	510	517	Combest J	122	b	*.70	66-21	Rucapequen113¾DoubleWarrnt1133Brochazo1145½	No excuse 7
11Jun66- 7Del	sf	1 1/16Ⓣ		1:441	3↑ Alw 7500	4	3	34½	22	2½	2¾	Rogers C	119	b	4.80	82-25	Lucky Tom119¾Quick Pitch1192Portsmouth1196	Sharp 7
4Jun66- 6Aqu	fst	6f	:222 :451	1:091	3↑ Alw 8500	2	6	58	58	511	713	Combest J	117	b	55.80	84-14	Buckpasser1152Tim'sStingray1152Understudy121nk	No speed 7
23Oct65- 7WO	sf	1⅝Ⓣ	:523 1:514	3:052	3↑ Can Championship 60k	7	2	2½	611	516	535	Combest J	126	b	2.00	- -	GeorgeRoyal123½BraveLad1265¾Ribot'sFling1218¾	Stopped 11
11Oct65- 7WO	sf	1¼Ⓣ	:503 1:171 1:432	2:111	3↑ Jockey Club Cup H 18k	7	1	11	11	11	12¼	Combest J	126	b	*1.85	58-49	QuickPitch1262¼Bandangn1152BluSol112hd	Kept to pressure 8
25Sep65- 8Aqu	sf	1⅛Ⓣ		1:501	3↑ Handicap 10000	1	1	1½	1hd	2½	33	Combest J	124	b	5.60	81-16	Master Dennis115noKentucky Jug1143Quick Pitch1244	Tired 7
15Sep65- 7Aqu	fm	1⅝Ⓣ		2:434	3↑ Brighton Beach H 28k	4	3	1½	2hd	22	36	Combest J	120	b	3.30	75-19	KnightlyMannr1146BraveLad110noQckPtch1204½	Weakened 8
4Sep65- 7FE	fm	1⅜Ⓣ	:473 1:13 1:392	2:20	3↑ Niagara H 30k	2	1	1nk	14	14	1hd	Combest J	120	b	*.60	85-15	QuckPtch120hdBluSol1113¾UnclBlu1133¼	Rated early,lasted 9
27Aug65- 7Sar	fm	1⅝Ⓣ		2:40	3↑ Seneca H 28k	8	1	13	14	1½	2hd	Combest J	119	b	8.60	93-06	Nashandy115hdQuickPitch1198Flg1191	Set pace,held gamely 8
11Aug65- 7Sar	sf	1 1/16Ⓣ		1:423	3↑ Bernard Baruch H 29k	10	3	2hd	12	11½	1no	Combest J	111	b	8.00	92-08	Quick Pitch111noFlag1142Circus1131	Hard ridden to last 10
31Jly65- 7Aqu	fm	1⅛Ⓣ		1:492	3↑ Tidal H 58k	9	5	35	21	2½	42¾	Valenzuela A	113	b	10.60	85-16	OretArgent115nkPursr1122TurboJtII130½	Bold bid,weakened 9
21Jly65- 8Del	fm	1Ⓣ		1:362	3↑ Alw 4500	6	4	46	52¾	32	35	Combest J	122	b	*1.50	89-09	Captain's Cross1222Uncle Perry1223Quick Pitch1222	Hung 8
3Jly65- 8Del	hd	1⅜Ⓣ		2:122	3↑ Sussex H 29k	9	3	32	11½	12	21¾	Combest J	115	b	17.60	105-07	CoolPrince1141¾QuickPitch1158Captain'sCross1121	Sharp 11
21Jun65- 7Del	hd	1 1/16Ⓣ		1:423	4↑ Alw 5000	6	2	2hd	2hd	21½	46¾	Lee T	122	b	3.00	84-09	Captain'sCross1164FederlMan1132Sorpsso113¾	Forced wide 7
8Jun65- 8Del	fm	1Ⓣ		1:38	4↑ Alw 4500	5	2	1½	13	13½	13½	Lee T	119	b	*.80	86-18	Quick Pitch1193½Henbaj1134Bray Head1132½	Easy score 6
29May65- 8Del	fm	1 1/16Ⓣ		1:423	3↑ Brandywine H 24k	4	1	21½	33	58	813	Combest J	116	b	12.00	78-09	Baitman1153Western Warrior123½Lucky Turn1155	Crowded 10
15May65- 6Aqu	fst	6f	:222 :452	1:104	3↑ Alw 8500	1	7	67¼	811	813	817	Combest J	117	b	34.50	72-20	CornishPrince107noExclusiveNashu1212½Chokr1174	Far back 8
31Oct64- 8Lrl	fm	1Ⓣ	:223 :452 1:094	1:342	3↑ Maryland H 23k	7	2	21	2hd	42½	54	Grant H	117		3.20	97-05	TwiceasGay113noCoolPrince112hdCachito1112	Speed,tired 11
27Oct64- 7Aqu	fm	1 1/16Ⓣ		1:424	3↑ Handicap 10000	9	2	2hd	11	13	2nk	Ycaza M	122	b	*2.55	92-08	YourAlibhai113nkQuickPitch1221GrandApplause1164	Failed 9
17Oct64- 8Aqu	sf	1⅛Ⓣ		1:532	3↑ Handicap 10000	7	2	1½	11	75¼	815	Ycaza M	119	b	6.10	53-32	WillIRule1171TomCat1171MeanCold111½	Early speed,tired 9
29Sep64- 7Aqu	sly	1⅛⊗	:47 1:13 1:401	1:542	3↑ Handicap 12000	3	1	14	14½	32½	58¾	Ycaza M	122	b	*1.25e	60-27	Polizonte1181RockyThmb118nkBraveLad1126	Bore out badly 6
14Sep64- 7Aqu	sf	1⅝Ⓣ		2:433	3↑ Brighton Beach H 28k	2	2	2½	21	711	721	Grant H	122	b	2.20	61-18	Jalico1123Endymion1152½Weatherbeaten107½	Speed,stopped 8
28Aug64- 7Sar	hd	1⅝Ⓣ		2:383	3↑ Seneca H 29k	7	1	13	12½	1½	1nk	Grant H	117	b	2.95	106-00	ⒹQuickPitch117nkTheIbex1105WillIRul1143	Swerved inside 8
	Disqualified and placed second																	
12Aug64- 7Sar	fm	1 1/16Ⓣ		1:422	3↑ Bernard Baruch H 30k	5	3	35½	32½	22	23	Grant H	117	b	5.05	91-06	Western Warrior1193Quick Pitch117¾Endymion1092	Gamely 12
4Aug64- 7Sar	hd	1 1/16Ⓣ		1:41	3↑ Alw 10000	10	3	33½	31½	2½	1nk	Grant H	120	b	2.40e	101-00	QuckPtch120nkTomCt120hdEndymon1141½	Up in final strides 11
18Jly64- 6Del	fm	1Ⓣ		1:353	3↑ Handicap 10000	2	3	1½	12	12½	13	Thornburg B	122	b	*2.60	101-07	QuickPitch1223GreekForm113hdBlueThor1101	Scored easily 8
11Jly64- 7Del	fm	1⅜Ⓣ		2:134	3↑ Sussex H 27k	1	1	11½	12	33	57¾	Thornburg B	118	b	5.80	92-00	RedDog1112¼ⒹGrkForm1101½LaughAloud1112	Used up early 7
30Jun64- 7Del	fm	1 1/16Ⓣ		1:42	4↑ Alw 6000	3	1	15	14½	14	12½	Lee T	116	b	2.50	94-06	Quick Pitch1162½Egg Hunt1034Blue Thor1061	Much the best 8
16Jun64- 7Del	fm	1 1/16Ⓣ		1:424	4↑ Alw 5000	1	2	2½	1½	1½	1nk	Lee T	110		4.40	90-10	QuickPitch110nkChicoco110hdInterven114¾	Long,hard drive 7
8Jun64- 7Del	fst	1	:24 :481 1:133	1:392	4↑ Alw 6000	2	1	12	34½	47	510¾	Turcotte R	124		9.90	68-23	GreekMoney1241¾Mi Rey110¾GypsyBaron1178	Used up early 8
23May64- 6Aqu	fst	6f	:223 :454	1:111	3↑ Alw 7500	5	5	33½	42½	68	611	Combest J	115		15.35	76-14	Narokan117½Humorismo115hdMacedonia1212	Well up,tired 6
30Oct63- 7Aqu	hd	1 1/16Ⓣ		1:431	3↑ Handicap 10000	3	1	21½	2½	65½	611	Sellers J	119	b	2.45	79-10	WesternWarrior1221JetClipper1131MarlinBay117hd	Stopped 6
19Oct63- 7WO	fm	1⅝Ⓣ	:484 1:374	2:41	3↑ Can Champ 60k	3	1	1hd	78¼	822	828	Ycaza M	121		5.10	78-00	TheAxeII1264¼HardRockMn1263½BronzeBabu1265¾	Bore out 9
2Oct63- 7Aqu	fst	1⅝	:491 1:401 2:04	2:42	Lawrence Realizatn 56k	7	4	32	35	816	817	Hartack W	120		18.45	78-13	DeanCarl1203¾B.Major120nkMastrDnns1166	Early foot,tired 9
9Sep63- 7Aqu	fm	1⅝Ⓣ		2:40	3↑ Brighton Beach H 28k	6	1	1hd	2½	12	1nk	Ycaza M	113		4.85	100-00	QuickPitch113nkDavidK.1142½WillIRule111½	All out,lasted 9
23Aug63- 7Sar	fm	1⅝Ⓣ		2:394	3↑ Sar Cup 28k	1	2	22	1hd	11	2nk	Sellers J	110	b	*2.65	106-00	WillIRule107nkQuickPitch1101DavidK.1193	Failed to last 9
15Aug63- 7Sar	fm	1⅛Ⓣ		1:474	3↑ Handicap 7500	2	3	34	31	1½	2nk	Gilligan L	111		5.20	96-04	TheAxeII129nkQuickPitch1113DavdK.1151½	Clearly 2nd best 6
8Aug63- 8Sar	gd	1	:234 :464 1:113	1:374	3↑ Alw 5000	4	2	21	2hd	1hd	11½	Gilligan L	111		2.90	88-12	QuickPitch1111½LuckyTurn1143DoctorHankK.115¾	Handily 7
1Aug63- 8Sar	sly	1⊗	:234 :471 1:12	1:383	3↑ Alw 5000	3	2	22	21	21	21½	Adams L	112		4.90	82-21	Cabelry1121½QckPitch1125TomCat1143	Showed game effort 7
24Jly63- 7Del	fm	1Ⓣ		1:354	Handicap 7500	1	4	41½	43	32	2hd	Carrozzella M	110		9.80	103-00	WildCard119hdQckPtch1103InWar1173½	Lacked room,sharp 7
5Jly63- 6Del	fst	6f	:23 :463	1:12	Alw 4500	5	3	31½	21½	2hd	13½	Vasquez J	118		*1.70	85-24	QuickPitch1183½ShiftyShekl1183¾Frnk'sNod113¾	Mild drive 7
24Jun63- 6Del	fst	6f	:223 :46	1:121	Alw 4500	3	7	81½	73½	77¼	62½	Nelson E	122		*1.20	81-21	Aesop'sAble1151¼Redgauntlet1181ShiftyShkl122hd	In close 8
23May63- 6Aqu	fst	6f	:223 :454	1:102	Alw 5000	8	10	96¾	911	814	819	Ycaza M	117		*1.05	74-13	MatchWits1177½MarlinBay117noWatrTwister122½	Slow start 10
8May63- 6Aqu	fst	6f	:221 :45	1:101	Alw 5000	6	2	21½	22	42¾	33½	Ycaza M	115		5.75	90-08	Stearic1171O'Calaway1152½QuickPtch1152	Drifted out turn 8
20Oct62- 5Kee	fst	6½f	:224 :46 1:102	1:164	Alw 3250	8	4	11	12	13	12½	Nichols J	119		*.70	94-11	QuickPitch1192½NeverWrong1191½BigJoe1193½	Mild urging 9
13Oct62- 3Kee	fst	7f	:231 :461 1:11	1:233	©Md Sp Wt	9	5	41½	1hd	13	18	Nichols J	120		8.10	90-12	Quick Pitch1208Telethon120¾Putoquill120¾	Easy score 10

Regal Gleam

dkbbr. f. 1964, by Hail to Reason (Turn-to)–Miz Carol, by Stymie

Lifetime record: 32 8 2 4 $246,793

Own.– Patrice Jacobs

Br.– Bieber–Jacobs Stable (Ky)

Tr.– Hirsch Jacobs

9Nov67- 7Aqu	fst	1	:231 :461 1:11	1:363	3↑ ⒻAlw 15000	2	1	11	11½	2½	31¾	Belmonte E	120	b	3.70	83-19	Lady Pitt118¾Narova1091Regal Gleam1201	Led,weakened 7
4Nov67- 8GS	gd	1 70	:23 :483 1:114	1:434	ⒻPrinceton H 30k	3	5	3nk	41½	77	99¾	Blum W	115	b	5.50	65-24	GreenGlade113¾Sumtex116½FarestNan1121½	Early bid,tired 12
27Oct67- 7Aqu	fst	6f	:222 :451	1:104	3↑ ⒻAlw 15000	2	3	34	23	1hd	11	Belmonte E	117	b	2.70	89-15	Regal Gleam1171Cestrum123¾Fennel1182½	Drew clear 9
16Oct67- 7Aqu	fst	6f	:22 :444	1:093	3↑ ⒻInterborough H 28k	5	5	57	78¼	79½	46¼	Belmonte E	113	b	7.10	89-16	Recall113nkCodorniz1173Romanticism1233	Changed course 9
29Sep67- 7Aqu	sly	6f	:22 :45	1:11	3↑ ⒻAlw 15000	6	5	43½	34½	23	11¾	Belmonte E	114	b	2.40	88-20	DHRegalGleam114DHAmeriBll1161¾CourtCrcut1124½	Driving 8
21Sep67- 7Aqu	hd	1 1/16Ⓣ		1:424	3↑ ⒻAlw 15000	7	4	3nk	2hd	31	76	Shoemaker W	111	b	*2.10	86-08	SwimtoMe1161½I'mAllReady116noSpire1111½	Well up,tired 9
15Sep67- 7Aqu	fst	6f	:232 :471	1:114	3↑ ⒻAlw 15000	10	4	51½	2½	1hd	11½	Belmonte E	111	b	*2.10	84-19	Regal Gleam1111½Cestrum120noAmeri Belle114nk	Drew clear 10
6Sep67- 7Aqu	fst	1	:23 :453 1:10	1:353	3↑ ⒻMaskette H 28k	4	2	2½	2hd	21½	44	Belmonte E	110	b	16.40	86-18	Politely115¾Triple Brook1173Lady Pitt115nk	Weakened 9
19Aug67- 5Sar	sly	6f	:221 :452	1:102	ⒻAlw 15000	4	7	66¾	54	45	36¼	Ycaza M	115	b	7.70	90-10	PlumPlum1145½Wageko114¾ReglGleam1151½	Evenly in drive 7
20Jly67- 8Hol	fst	1⅛	:463 1:101 1:354	1:491	ⒻHol Oaks 55k	5	3	31	32½	79	68	Pineda A	115	b	7.20	78-15	AmerigoLady112½Gamely1211½Princssnesn113no	Speed,tired 10
10Jly67- 7Aqu	fm	1 1/16Ⓣ		1:434	3↑ ⒻAlw 15000	7	2	2hd	2hd	2½	41¾	Belmonte E	114	b	*2.30	85-13	Encanta116½Bubbles O'Tudor118¾Fatal Step118½	Weakened 7
5Jly67- 7Aqu	gd	6f	:222 :461	1:112	ⒻHandicap 15000	7	1	64½	63¾	45½	32	Belmonte E	116	b	8.70	84-21	Abifaith1161Rhubarb1241Regal Gleam116hd	Wide turn 7
17Jun67- 8Mth	fst	1 70	:231 :463 1:113	1:432	ⒻPost-Deb 29k	7	5	66¼	912	914	611	Knapp K	118	b	*2.00	73-18	T.V.'sPrincss1121¾Amhrst1122¼FortyMrry's1121¼	No threat 10
10Jun67- 7Aqu	fst	1⅛	:47 1:104 1:361	1:493	ⒻMother Goose 97k	1	2	24	24	25	47½	Cordero A Jr	121	b	23.20	80-12	FurlSail1213QuilloQueen121noMuse1214½	Well placed,tired 11
27May67- 7Aqu	fst	1	:22 :442 1:091	1:353	ⒻAcorn 68k	14	4	55	35	57	88½	Cardone E	121	b	19.40	81-15	Furl Sail1213Quillo Queen121½Pepperwood1213	Tired 17
10May67- 7Aqu	fst	7f	:222 :454 1:111	1:25	ⒻComely 29k	7	8	76	711	813	88¼	Cordero A Jr	121	b	8.40	73-21	Gala Honors113¾Just Kidding118nkLake Chelan1161	Tired 11
26Apr67- 7Aqu	fst	6f	:221 :451	1:103	ⒻPrioress 28k	5	4	64½	78½	713	613	Ycaza M	121	b	*1.30	77-17	Just Kidding1214Great Era121½Lake Chelan121nk	Wide 7
13Apr67- 7Aqu	fst	6f	:224 :46	1:111	ⒻHandicap 12000	6	4	42½	42	2hd	2no	Ussery R	124	b	7.50	87-16	Recall118noRegal Gleam1242½Lake Chelan113nk	Just missed 8
18Jan67- 8Hia	fst	6f	:214 :444	1:094	ⒻJasmine 32k	8	4	65½	710	815	814	Ycaza M	121	b	13.00	81-12	Woozem1166Quillo Queen115nkIrish County116nk	Far back 10
5Nov66- 8Lrl	fst	1 1/16	:232 :472 1:131	1:452	ⒻSelima 125k	9	3	42	42¼	31½	1½	Ycaza M	122	b	5.30	90-14	Regal Gleam122½Quillo Queen1192Thong1191	Hard drive 14
22Oct66- 8GS	fst	1 1/16	:231 :461 1:103	1:443	ⒻGardenia 196k	7	5	65	58½	87¾	75½	Cordero A Jr	119	b	12.20	76-20	Pepperwood119hdFish House1191¾Woozem119¾	No mishap 14
8Oct66- 7Aqu	fst	1	:224 :452 1:102	1:372	ⒻFrizette 132k	8	2	1½	11½	1hd	1hd	Ycaza M	119	b	16.10	81-17	RglGleam119hdIrishCounty1194½Pepprwood1192	Came again 8
28Sep66- 7Aqu	fst	7f	:221 :451 1:11	1:242	ⒻAstarita 29k	4	7	811	99	87½	66	Shoemaker W	119		6.40	78-19	IrishCounty1161Pepperwood116nkGreenGlade1164	No speed 10
10Sep66- 7Aqu	fst	6f	:224 :462	1:124	ⒻMatron 110k	3	4	21½	22½	23	3hd	Cardone E	119		8.00e	79-23	Swiss Cheese119hdGreat Era119noRegal Gleam1198	Game try 9

Date/Race	Cond	Dist	Fractions	Race	PP	St	1st	2nd	Str	Fin	Jockey	Wt	Odds	Figs	Top Finishers	Comment	Field
24Aug66- 7Sar	gd	6f	:221 :454 1:12	(F)Spinaway 78k	5	1	44	77	613	612	Knapp K	119	6.30	76-17	Silver True119¾Great Era1192½Shirley Heights119no	Wide	7
6Jly66- 8Mth	fst	5½f	:221 :452 :581 1:044	(F)Colleen 18k	6	1	83¼	76¾	89¾	811	Thornburg B	119	9.00	82-18	Rhubarb1146Momma Pierre1141½Betoken119hd	Not a factor	14
25Jun66- 8Del	fst	5½f	:213 :462 1:053	(F)Blue Hen 24k	6	2	43½	51¾	2hd	1no	Thornburg B	119	15.30	92-18	RegalGleam119noFamilyGallry1112½NorthstTrds1112	Just up	11
30May66- 8Del	fst	6f	:221 :47 1:001	(F)P Drummnd (Div 2) 18k	8	7	64½	73½	78½	74¾	Valenzuela A	116	6.40	83-22	Tota Nell113¾Sentica113nkIntriguing113½	Never close	9
17May66- 5Aqu	fst	5f	:23 :463 :59	(F)Alw 5500	5	3	33	31½	1½	13	Blum W	119	3.00	90-19	Regal Gleam1193Tainted Lady1196Effayeff119no	With ease	6
11May66- 5Aqu	fst	5f	:223 :471 1:003	(F)Md Sp Wt	2	1	32½	33½	3nk	11½	Blum W	119	3.60e	82-19	Regal Gleam1191½Henrietta1192½Euphorbia1191	Driving	10
20Apr66- 3Aqu	fst	5f	:224 :464 :59	(F)Md Sp Wt	2	2	2hd	31	77½	714	Knapp K	119	3.00	76-16	GreatEra1198GreekSong'sGet119noCurrentEvent119hd	Tired	10
13Apr66- 3Aqu	fst	5f	:23 :463 :591	(F)Md Sp Wt	2	4	44	34½	34	2¾	Knapp K	119	4.10	88-16	Lake Chelan119¾Regal Gleam1195Euphorbia1192½	Game try	10

Roman Brother

b. g. 1961, by Third Brother (Princequillo)–Roman Zephyr, by Roman

Lifetime record: 42 16 10 5 $943,473

Own.– Harbor View Farm
Br.– Ocala Stud Farms Inc (Fla)
Tr.– B. Parke

Date/Race	Cond	Dist	Fractions	Race	PP	St	1st	2nd	Str	Fin	Jockey	Wt	Odds	Figs	Top Finishers	Comment	Field
5Feb66- 8Hia	fst	1⅛	:472 1:112 1:37 1:50	3↑ Seminole H 61k	9	7	711	712	58	45¾	Baeza B	126	*.50	79-23	Convex1164¼Selari112½Pia Star1181	Mild rally,no threat	9
25Jan66- 8Hia	fst	7f	:23 :46 1:113 1:241	4↑ Alw 8000	7	1	58½	35½	2hd	1½	Baeza B	123	*.70	88-18	Roman Brother123½Selari1145Sunstruck1142	Mild urging	7
11Nov65- 7Lrl	fm	1½(T)	:493 1:134 2:281	3↑ D C Int'l 150k	1	1	2hd	1½	2hd	31¼	Baeza B	127	*1.40	77-16	Diatome120noCarvin II1201¼Roman Brother127no	Held well	7
30Oct65- 7Aqu	fst	2	:47 2:293 2:554 3:223	3↑ J C Gold Cup 110k	2	4	33½	12	16	15	Baeza B	124	*.20	83-21	Roman Brother1245Barenjenal1244Brave Lad1243	Easily	7
12Oct65- 7Aqu	gd	1⅝	:48 1:381 2:431	3↑ Manhattan H 56k	2	3	34	13	15	18	Baeza B	125	*.60	89-16	RomanBrother1258HillRise119¾KnightlyManner1144	Easily	8
2Oct65- 7Aqu	fst	1¼	:46 1:104 1:363 2:014	3↑ Woodward 109k	5	4	36	11	15	110	Baeza B	126	*1.80	89-18	Roman Brother12610Royal Gunner1211½Malicious126½	Easily	6
18Sep65- 8Det	fst	1⅛	:471 1:113 1:364 1:492	3↑ Mich 1⅛ H 91k	2	5	43	83¾	43	2½	Baeza B	118	*1.80	93-18	OldHat115½RomanBrother118¾TakeOver114½	Gaining at end	11
6Sep65- 7Aqu	fst	1⅛	:481 1:121 1:363 1:49	3↑ Aqueduct 108k	3	3	35	32½	33	33	Baeza B	121	3.10	88-14	Malicious1163Pluck116noRoman Brother1216	Bore out turn	7
23Aug65- 8Sar	fst	1	:232 :461 1:111 1:36	3↑ Alw 8500	2	3	34½	2½	11½	16	Baeza B	123	*.30	97-12	Roman Brother1236Reely Beeg1162Spoon Bait1131½	Easily	5
11Aug65- 7Sar	sf	1 1/16(T)	1:423	3↑ Bernard Baruch H 29k	4	5	55½	43½	55½	55	Baeza B	123	*1.60	87-08	Quick Pitch111noFlag1142Circus1131	No apparent excuse	10
24Jly65- 7Aqu	fst	1¼	:47 1:102 1:35 2:003	3↑ Brooklyn H 107k	4	4	43½	33	23	22	Baeza B	121	2.80	93-10	PiaStar1212RomanBrother1212Kelso1321½	Game,drifted out	5
10Jly65- 6Aqu	fst	1	:224 :451 1:092 1:342	3↑ Alw 10000	1	4	35	11½	13	15	Baeza B	115	*.80	96-13	Roman Brother1155Riot Squad1172½Africanus119¾	Easily	6
26Jun65- 6Aqu	fst	6f	:222 :453 1:101	3↑ Alw 8500	6	4	66	62¾	43½	42¾	Baeza B	121	*3.00	89-13	Near Man117½Kilmoray1112R. Thomas117nk	Mild late bid	8
6Feb65- 8Hia	fst	1⅛	:471 1:113 1:372 1:504	3↑ Seminole H 65k	9	7	712	59	76¾	74¾	Rotz JL	124	4.30	76-22	Sunstruck119noPiave114nkPointduJour1161½	No late rally	13
16Jan65- 8SA	fst	1⅛	:47 1:11 1:36 1:482	San Fernando 61k	4	8	86½	94¾	1012	911	Ycaza M	126	3.50e	79-14	Hill Rise1232Pelegrin114½Canadian B.113no	No mishap	12
2Jan65- 8SA	fst	7f	:221 :442 1:092 1:22	Malibu 30k	9	1	96½	96½	93½	105	Ycaza M	126	*1.80	88-09	PowerofDestiny112½Maker'sMark113noHillRis122hd	Dull try	10
31Oct64- 7Aqu	fst	2	:484 2:533 3:191	3↑ J C Gold Cup 108k	6	3	31½	21½	24	25½	Shoemaker W	119	3.35	95-14	Kelso1245½Roman Brother1196Quadrangle11916	Went well	6
14Oct64- 7Aqu	fst	1⅝	:53 1:443 2:083 2:45	Lawrence Realizatn 54k	4	5	54½	21	42	2nk	Alvarez F	123	2.05	80-18	Quadrangl126nkRomnBrothr123¾KnightlyMnnr1161	Checked	5
28Sep64- 7Aqu	fst	1⅛	:481 1:122 1:364 1:49	Discovery H 27k	3	3	3nk	42	42½	1no	Alvarez F	125	*1.25	96-13	RomanBrother125noLt.Stevens113¾TwiceasGay109¾	Driving	6
12Sep64- 9Rkm	fst	1 3/16	:462 1:102 1:362 1:554	N H Sweepstakes 144k	9	10	99	65½	21	1½	Alvarez F	123	*.90	106-12	RomanBrother123½KnightlyManner1161¼Purser114nk	Driving	11
29Aug64- 8AP	fst	1¼	:473 1:114 1:364 2:012	American Derby 134k	10	7	76½	41½	2hd	11	Alvarez F	122	*2.30	97-15	Roman Brother1221Lt. Stevens1165Close By1205	Drew out	10
8Aug64- 8AP	fst	1	:23 :454 1:104 1:361	Arl Classic 114k	8	9	96¾	55½	44½	43¾	Alvarez F	122	*2.00	84-19	Tosmah1152½Lt. Stevens118noClose By1201¼	No excuse	10
11Jly64- 7Aqu	fst	1¼	:474 1:111 1:36 2:012	Dwyer H 81k	4	4	47	33½	34	36¼	Alvarez F	124	3.60	87-12	Quadrangle126nkMalicious1206RomanBrother1246	Even race	6
27Jun64- 8AP	fst	1⅛	:454 1:094 1:352 1:48	Chicagoan 115k	9	5	55½	31	21½	23	Alvarez F	123	*.80	93-13	DandyK.1143RomanBrother1238CapSize120hd	No excuse	11
6Jun64- 7Aqu	fst	1½	:49 1:144 2:04 2:282	Belmont 154k	7	6	63¾	31	31	22	Alvarez F	126	8.35	96-10	Quadrangle1262RomnBrothr1264NorthrnDancr126½	Gamely	8
30May64- 7GS	fst	1⅛	:473 1:114 1:37 1:493	Jersey Derby 125k	8	5	42¼	11	12	13	Alvarez F	126	3.30	89-20	Roman Brother1263Mr. Brick1263National1261½	Hard drive	8
16May64- 8Pim	fst	1 3/16	:482 1:122 1:373 1:564	Preakness 176k	2	6	64	56	56¼	55¾	Chambers W	126	25.40	83-14	NorthernDancr1262¼TheScoundrel126hdHllRs126½	No factor	6
2May64- 7CD	fst	1¼	:46 1:103 1:36 2:00	Ky Derby 156k	12	9	98¼	63¾	45½	43½	Chambers W	126	30.60	98-05	NorthernDancer126nkHillRis1263¼ThScoundrl126no	In close	12
28Apr64- 7CD	gd	1	:23 :452 1:10 1:351	Derby Trial 16k	3	5	34½	32½	1½	22¼	Chambers W	122	3.70	95-14	HillRise1222¼RomanBrother1222¼[D]He'saGem1223	Led,tired	7
18Apr64- 7Aqu	fst	1⅛	:463 1:111 1:362 1:491	Wood Memorial 89k	5	5	56	43	31½	32¼	Chambers W	126	4.30	93-15	Quadrangle126½Mr. Brick1261¾Roman Brother1264½	Evenly	9
4Apr64- 8GP	fst	1⅛	:473 1:121 1:38 1:504	Florida Derby 116k	3	4	45½	44½	43¼	45¾	Ycaza M	122	7.30	74-16	NorthernDancer1221TheScoundrel1222½DandyK.1222¼	Evenly	8
25Mar64- 9GP	fst	1 1/16	:232 :464 1:112 1:444	Fountain of Youth 18k	1	4	45	33	11	21	Ycaza M	122	*.70	83-17	Dandy K.1121Roman Brother1222½Saltville1111	Held well	9
3Mar64- 8Hia	fst	1⅛	:453 1:092 1:343 1:474	Flamingo 138k	3	7	717	614	613	516♦	Ussery R	122	2.30	80-16	Northern Dancer1222Mr. Brick1228Quadrangle1226	In close	11
19Feb64- 8Hia	gd	1⅛	:47 1:114 1:381 1:514	Everglades 30k	6	6	611	44½	23	1hd	Ycaza M	122	*.50	76-25	RomanBrother122hdMr.Brick1226Journalist1193	Bore in,up	8
5Feb64- 8Hia	fst	7f	:224 :451 1:102 1:231	Bahamas 34k	11	2	76¼	55½	11½	13½	Ycaza M	123	*1.80	93-18	RomanBrother1233½[D]Mr.Brick123¾Journlst1201½	Mild drive	13
29Jan64- 7Hia	fst	7f	:224 :452 1:101 1:232	Alw 7000	2	7	57½	35	34	32¾	Ycaza M	122	*.40	89-11	Delirium1172¼High Finance114½Roman Brother1222	Rallied	8
9Nov63- 8GS	my	1 1/16	:232 :471 1:12 1:451	Garden State 317k	1	4	41½	3nk	2hd	21	Rotz JL	122	*1.50	83-21	HurrytoMarkt1221RomanBrothr1223¼Ishkoodah1221	Bore in	14
1Nov63- 8GS	sly	1	:23 :462 1:114 1:384	Alw 10000	8	6	44½	33	21½	21½	Rotz JL	120	*.80	86-21	HurrytoMarkt1131½RomnBrthr120½Susn'sGnt1203	Poor start	8
12Oct63- 7Aqu	fst	1	:23 :46 1:121 1:38	Champagne 212k	9	7	54¼	31½	12	14½	Rotz JL	122	*.95e	78-18	Roman Brother1224½Traffic1221Bupers122½	Drew out easily	11
7Oct63- 5Aqu	fst	7f	:222 :444 1:092 1:223	Alw 7500	3	2	23	21	1½	13	Rotz JL	115	*.65e	93-15	Roman Brother1153Prexy1154Irvkup115nk	Speed in reserve	7
28Sep63- 5Aqu	fst	6½f	:222 :46 1:111 1:173	Alw 5000	3	10	107½	96¾	31½	13½	Rotz JL	117	*3.50	92-13	RomanBrothr1173½ShadyPlanet117½ScotchTune115nk	Easily	14
25Jly63- 5Aqu	fst	5½f	:223 :462 :583 1:044	©Md Sp Wt	9	8	76½	54	2½	1hd	Rotz JL	122	5.35	95-12	Roman Brother122hdMartyr1225Emblematic1224	Driving	10

Royal Native

ch. f. 1956, by Royal Charger (Nearco)–Native Gal, by Sir Gallahad III

Lifetime record: 49 18 13 3 $422,769

Own.– W.B McDonald Jr
Br.– R.W. McIlvain (Ky)
Tr.– P.F. Gacicia

Date/Race	Cond	Dist	Fractions	Race	PP	St	1st	2nd	Str	Fin	Jockey	Wt	Odds	Figs	Top Finishers	Comment	Field
23Sep61- 7Bel	fst	1⅛	:463 1:11 1:361 1:492	3↑ (F)Beldame 96k	1	11	1111	128¼	1011	812	Boland W	123	33.70	77-18	AirmansGuide123¾Craftinss1232½Prmontt1185½	Broke slowly	12
11Sep61- 8Atl	fm	1⅛(T)	:464 1:102 1:351 1:483	3↑ (F)Miss America H 29k	10	3	34	45	611	99½	Boland W	119	7.20	90-00	Sarcastic120nkLoyalLadyII1113½ShirleyJones1262½	Stopped	10
23Aug61- 8AP	fst	1⅛	:463 1:103 1:354 1:48	3↑ (F)Arl Matron H 46k	8	11	1110	1111	911	89¼	Hartack W	120	6.80	87-11	ShirleyJones1241½CallCard1103Equifun111nk	Impeded early	11
7Aug61- 8Atl	fm	1 1/16(T)	:24 :473 1:12 1:43	3↑ (F)Margate H 23k	4	6	67	31½	31	21	Grant H	119	*2.00	95-04	Sarcastic1151RoyalNative1193½Lint1162½	Made game effort	12
29Jly61- 6Del	gd	1¼	:46 1:11 1:362 2:022	3↑ (F)Delaware H 159k	3	10	810	46	24	23½	Adams L	120	9.20	86-20	AirmansGuide1213½RoyalNative120nkTritoma1182½	Game try	12
22Jly61- 6Del	fst	1 1/16	:231 :47 1:113 1:434	3↑ (F)New Castle 38k	9	13	119	87¼	713	59½	Adams L	120	14.50	80-21	AirmansGuide1166Tritoma1201¾MountainGlory1121	Sluggish	15
13Jly61- 6Del	sly	1	:231 :462 1:113 1:374	3↑ (F)Alw 7500	3	5	512	713	69¾	68	Adams L	121	*1.70	79-20	Perizade1212½Tritoma1181Solid Thought1151	Dull effort	8
30Jun61- 7Mth	fst	1 70	:222 :454 1:104 1:401	3↑ (F)Alw 10000	2	4	56	56	57	46¾	Korte K	111 b	*1.30	106-11	ShirleyJones1155DottyKirsten1121LoylLdyII115¾	No factor	8
14Jun61- 7Bel	fst	7f	:222 :453 1:103 1:233	3↑ (F)Vagrancy H 24k	2	13	129¼	96¾	32½	4½	Adams L	123	10.50	88-15	SunGlint116noUndulation116½Refute113hd	Closed very well	14
3Jun61- 6Bel	fst	6f	:222 :454 1:102	4↑ (F)Alw 10000	7	6	56½	79	78	612	Rotz JL	123	*3.00	83-13	Improve1144Refute1143¼Repetitious114nk	Wide on turn	9
20May61- 7GS	fst	6f	:22 :451 1:104	3↑ (F)Colonial H 28k	4	9	97½	87¾	79¾	66¾	Korte K	126	4.10	83-15	Staretta117hdCoupd'etat117noAirmansGuide1191½	No mishap	9
11Nov60- 7GS	my	1⅛	:464 1:11 1:372 1:504	3↑ (F)Vineland H 58k	3	6	67	34½	33½	1½	Hartack W	124	*1.70	83-19	Royal Native124½Make Sail118¾Wiggle II1194	Up in time	9
21Oct60- 6Kee	fst	1⅛	:482 1:13 1:371 1:493	3↑ (F)Spinster 87k	4	2	2hd	2hd	3½	33	Hartack W	123	*.40	86-24	RashStatement119¾IndianMaid1232¼RoyalNative1234	Tired	6
	Open to 3-, 4- and 5-year-olds																
14Oct60- 6Kee	fst	*7f	1:26	3↑ (F)Alw 7500	6	3	52½	41¾	21	2¾	Hartack W	121	*.50	96-11	IndianMaid118¾RoyalNative1212¼ChanceGauge1061½	Rallied	8
	Open to 3-, 4- and 5-year-olds																
1Oct60- 7Bel	fst	1⅛	:461 1:11 1:362 1:492	3↑ (F)Beldame 91k	3	3	2hd	11½	22	22	Hartack W	123	2.70	87-16	Berlo1192RoyalNative1231MakeSal1193	Used vying for lead	9
17Sep60- 7Atl	fm	1 3/16(T)	:463 1:12 1:372 1:57	3↑ U Nations H 100k	8	5	66¼	107¾	1011	1013	Harmatz W	118	10.30	75-12	T.V.Lark1201¼SwordDancer1271¼BallyAche122hd	Fell back	10
10Sep60- 0Atl	sf	1 1/16(T)	:232 :481 1:131 1:454	3↑ Alw 5000	1	4	41	2½	2½	2½	Hartack W	118	-	81-18	Bally Ache116½Royal Native1188Exaltado1182	In close	4
	Exhibition race - run between 5th and 6th races. No wagering																
13Aug60- 8AP	fst	1⅛	:48 1:12 1:371 1:502	3↑ (F)Arl Matron H 56k	10	4	31½	21	11	1hd	Hartack W	128	2.20	84-07	Royal Native128hdWoodlawn1101½Silver Spoon1281	Driving	11

30Jly60- 6Del	sly	1¼	:461 1:103 1:364 2:022	3↑ ⒻDelaware H 146k	6	3	36½	21½	25	29	Hartack W	129		*.90	81-15	Quill1259Royal Native1291¼Geechee Lou110¾	Had no mishap	8
9Jly60- 7Mth	fst	1 1/16	:224 :461 1:11 1:434	3↑ ⒻMolly Pitcher H 28k	2	5	42½	31	13	14	Hartack W	127		*1.00	86-17	RoyalNative1274Quill1221¾MissOrestes114½	Much the best	10
4Jun60- 7Bel	fst	1 1/16	:223 :452 1:102 1:43	3↑ ⒻTop Flight H 56k	7	7	62¾	21½	1hd	11½	Hartack W	126		*1.45	89-15	RoyalNative1261½Quill123¾BugBrush1202	Drew clear in hand	10
28May60- 7GS	fst	6f	:221 :452 1:102	3↑ ⒻColonial H 27k	6	5	55	54	5¾	11½	Hartack W	126		*.70	92-13	RoyalNative1261½BugBrush1231¼Tinkalero118nk	Drew clear	6
7May60- 7Aqu	fst	1	:234 :463 1:11 1:362	3↑ ⒻBed o' Roses H 27k	7	2	1½	1½	11	2nk	Moreno H	128		1.60	94-08	Chistosa106nkRoyal Native1281½Craftiness110¾	Game try	7
30Mar60- 7GP	fst	1 1/16	:233 :462 1:101 1:42	3↑ ⒻSuwannee River H 16k	1	2	1hd	13	13	13	Hartack W	130		*.25	98-11	RoylNative1303MeadowsMiss1071½Woodlawn1102	Easy score	6
	Previously owned by P.L. Grissom; previously trained by K. Noe Sr																	
2Mar60- 7Hia	fst	1⅛	:461 1:101 1:36 1:49	3↑ ⒻBlack Helen H 47k	1	3	33	2½	11½	13¾	Hartack W	126		*.55	90-15	RoyalNative1263¾HappyPrincess1123½Woodlawn1101¾	Easily	9
24Feb60- 6Hia	gd	7f	:223 :444 1:09 1:222	4↑ ⒻAlw 6000	5	4	510	511	49½	27	Brooks S	124		*.45	91-16	MommyDear1127RoylNative124½StarletMiss1111½	No excuse	6
10Feb60- 7Hia	fst	7f	:223 :444 1:10 1:224	3↑ ⒻColumbiana H 25k	2	9	63¼	51¼	2½	14½	Hartack W	122		*1.95	96-12	Royal Native1224½Starlet Miss110¾Mommy Dear1181¾	Easily	12
2Feb60- 8Hia	fm	5½f Ⓣ	1:051	4↑ Alw 5000	1	7	53½	710	66½	54	Hartack W	116		*.70	88-09	UpandComingII112½Alarullah1121¼WarEagle1182	Rough trip	8
22Jan60- 7Hia	fst	6f	:224 :46 1:10	4↑ Alw 6000	1	3	2hd	1½	2hd	1nk	Hartack W	116		4.45	95-18	RoylNatve116nkKentuckyPride1152½TalntShow1185	Gamely	6
3Nov59- 7GS	fst	1 1/16	:234 :47 1:103 1:423	ⒻJersey Belle 27k	5	2	1hd	1½	21	25	Hartack W	121		*.90	92-17	HighBid1215RoylNative1212½GeecheLou115nk	Impeded,tired	7
23Oct59- 6Kee	fst	1⅛	:47 1:11 1:362 1:492	3↑ ⒻSpinster 81k	5	2	2½	11	11	11	Hartack W	119		*.30	90-13	Royal Native1191Aesthetic119½Tacking119nk	Under drive	6
	Open to 3-, 4- and 5-year-olds																	
16Oct59- 6Kee	fst	*7f	1:254	3↑ ⒻAlw 7500	4	4	21	1hd	1½	11¼	Hartack W	117		*.40	99-16	RoyalNative1171¼Lindaway1061Natal106nk	Drew away easily	7
	Open to 3-, 4- and 5-year-olds																	
26Sep59- 7Atl	fm	1 1/16 Ⓣ	:231 :472 1:122 1:45	ⒻPageant H 30k	15	2	1hd	12	15	11¼	Hartack W	122		*.70	88-12	RoyalNative1221¼SunsetGlow1133LoyalLadyII1112	Cleverly	15
21Sep59- 7Atl	fm	1 Ⓣ	:234 :472 1:112 1:362	ⒻAlw 4500	1	1	12	13	16	16	Hartack W	118		*.30	99-01	RylNative1186[DH]SybilBrand118[DH]DanceandPly1052½	Easily	6
9Sep59- 6Bel	fst	1	:223 :451 1:10 1:364	ⒻGazelle (Div 1) 22k	4	1	1½	1½	1½	21	Culmone J	121		*.90	89-14	SunsetGlow1081RoyalNative121¾HighBid1182½	Just missed	10
31Aug59- 7Atl	fst	7f	:223 :443 1:092 1:221	ⒻAlw 4500	5	2	2hd	1½	1½	12	Hartack W	121		*.60	92-17	RoyalNative1212Kit'sPet1142SybilBrand1194½	Easy score	8
1Aug59- 7Mth	fst	1⅛	:471 1:111 1:37 1:503	ⒻMth Oaks 55k	5	1	12	12	12½	13½	Culmone J	113		6.70	91-18	RoyalNative1133½IndianMaid1172½SilverSpoon1214½	Driving	6
24Jly59- 6Mth	gd	1 1/16	:233 :474 1:121 1:444	ⒻAlw 7500	2	1	11½	1hd	3nk	31¾	Boulmetis S	112		3.70	79-25	Silver Spoon1261Indian Maid118¾Royal Native1121½	Tiring	5
14Jly59- 5Mth	sly	6f	:22 :452 1:103	ⒻAlw 5000	5	2	1½	13	13	110	Culmone J	115		*.60	89-22	RoyalNative11510RulingBeauty114½TimetoSell1124	Easily	5
8Jly59- 7Mth	fst	6f	:214 :44 1:09	ⒻMiss Woodford 24k	3	4	31½	23	26	25	Culmone J	114		10.90	92-17	Recite1155RoyalNative1147½MissQuick1152	Best of others	11
27Jun59- 5Mth	fst	6f	:221 :454 1:114	ⒻAlw 5000	2	5	41½	33	11	16	Culmone J	117		*1.30	83-18	Royal Native1176Portulaca1143½Heliotrope II114no	Easily	8
23Jun59- 7Mth	fst	6f	:222 :461 1:11	ⒻAlw 6000	3	3	21	1½	11	2½	Hartack W	121		2.30	86-18	Lastborn118½RoyalNative1213Starn'Garter1189	No excuse	6
17Jun59- 6Mth	fst	6f	:221 :454 1:113	Alw 5000	9	5	57½	610	57	46	Gilligan L	117		5.50	78-21	MinstrelShowII1221½RoyalHome1222JohnDoe1222½	Rallied	10
28May59- 6GS	fst	6f	:222 :46 1:122	ⒻAlw 4000	4	6	54	45	44½	35¾	Boulmetis S	110		*.60	76-16	RomanRevel1105PatsyKelly114¾RoyalNative110nk	No excuse	9
20May59- 6GS	fst	6f	:22 :45 1:113	ⒻAlw 10000	9	1	22	25	25	46¼	Gilligan L	110		19.00	80-18	MissQuick1041¼MissRoyal1213½MerryHll1211½	Used up early	9
	Previously owned by Walmac Farm; previously trained by M.M. Greene																	
30Jly58- 7Mth	sl	6f	:214 :454 1:132	ⒻSorority 23k	2	8	78½	69	58	23½	Culmone J	114	w	37.90	71-31	MommyDear1123½RoyalNative114nkFlyingJosie1142	Rallied	9
5Jly58- 6Mth	fst	5½f	:221 :462 :592 1:053	ⒻColleen 24k	2	5	54½	58	79½	66½	Culmone J	114	w	35.40	83-19	LadyBeGood119¾LawdyClaudy1192SybilBrand112¾	No excuse	10
9Jun58- 6Bel	sly	5f-WC	:222 :45 :572	ⒻNational Stallion 30k	2	6		911	78	55¾	Hartack W	119	w	11.35	86-11	LadyBeGood1191Aesthetic1191½SitThisOut1143	Late foot	11
13May58- 5GS	fst	5f	:231 :48 1:003	ⒻMd Sp Wt	8	7	21½	21½	1hd	11½	Grant H	115	w	*2.30	87-20	RoyalNative1151½AnnsiePie1151½PalmLeaves115nk	Handily	10

Silent Screen

ch. c. 1967, by Prince John (Princequillo)–Prayer Bell, by Better Self — **Lifetime record: 18 7 2 4 $514,388**

Own.– Elberon Farm
Br.– D.R. Noviello & A. Vespo (NY)
Tr.– J.B. Bond

10Mar71- 7GP	fst	6f	:214 :44 1:09	4↑ Alw 7000	5	5	23	32½	34	33	Vasquez J	112	b	*.70	96-08	Royal Comedian113½Insubordination1222½Silent Screen1122		9
	Failed to respond																	
27Feb71- 7Hia	fst	6f	:221 :45 1:101	4↑ Alw 10000	9	5	44	33	42½	41½	Rotz JL	122	b	*2.40	91-21	HardWork116noBestTurn122hdSmellingSalts1191½	No rally	10
16Jan71- 8Hia	fst	6f	:222 :452 1:10	3↑ Super Bowl H 31k	10	10	57½	35	47	64	Rotz JL	122	b	1.90	90-10	LionSleeps1241½TrueNorth111nkSpottdLn1142	Swerved start	10
1Aug70- 7Lib	gd	1 1/16	:241 :472 1:11 1:424	Minuteman H 55k	4	6	54	24	514	618	Rotz JL	123	b	*.50	74-11	WellMannerd1208Rollckng1192TumblnHll1113½	Bobbled start	6
27Jun70- 7Bel	sly	1	:23 :461 1:104 1:36	Saranac H 56k	3	3	33	21	11½	13½	Rotz JL	123	b	*1.40	94-15	Silent Screen1233½Aggressively112½Naskra117hd	Handily	6
30May70- 8GS	fst	1⅛	:462 1:102 1:352 1:481	Jersey Derby 128k	8	3	31½	1½	1hd	33¾	Rotz JL	126	b	3.20	92-10	Prsonality1261¼CornoffthCob1262½SlntScrn1262¾	Weakened	8
16May70- 8Pim	fst	1 3/16	:464 1:104 1:363 1:561	Preakness 203k	3	3	11	11½	1hd	33¼	Rotz JL	126	b	4.20	89-16	Personality126nkMyDadGeorge1263SilntScrn1262	Weakened	14
2May70- 9CD	gd	1¼	:464 1:12 1:372 2:032	Ky Derby 170k	6	6	37	11	21½	56½	Rotz JL	126		5.70	76-16	DustCmmndr1265MyDdGrg126½HghEchln126hd	Bumped start	17
18Apr70- 7Aqu	fst	1⅛	:472 1:114 1:364 1:492	Wood Memorial 117k	10	2	2½	2hd	2hd	2¾	Shoemaker W	126		*1.10	88-19	Personality126¾SilentScreen126hdDelawarChf1262	Steadied	14
4Apr70- 7Aqu	fst	1	:23 :453 1:101 1:361	Gotham 58k	1	2	2½	2hd	31	3½	Rotz JL	126		1.70	85-20	NativeRoyalty114hdDelawareChif114¾SlntScrn1262	No rally	8
3Mar70- 8Hia	fst	1⅛	:452 1:093 1:353 1:483	Flamingo 161k	5	3	35	31½	57½	812	Rotz JL	122		*.60	80-14	MyDadGrge122noCornoffthCob1223BurdAln1222	Unruly turn	13
4Feb70- 8Hia	fst	7f	:232 :461 1:101 1:23	Bahamas 32k	8	4	43	22	23	1hd	Rotz JL	122		*1.90	93-16	SilentScreen122hdGeorgeLewis1224½RstlssRtrt1151	Driving	10
5Nov69- 8GS	fst	1 70	:233 :481 1:131 1:431	Alw 15000	8	2	2½	1hd	1hd	1½	Rotz JL	120		*.40	78-25	Silent Screen120½My Dad George1121Forum1122	Tight hold	8
11Oct69- 7Bel	fst	1	:23 :454 1:104 1:371	Champagne 188k	11	6	4¾	3nk	11	11	Rotz JL	122		*.90	88-19	Silent Screen1221Brave Emperor1221Toasted1221½	Driving	11
1Oct69- 7Bel	fst	7f	:222 :454 1:104 1:234	Cowdin 77k	1	6	33	3½	11	1½	Rotz JL	124		*.40	88-16	SilentScreen124½WigOut114hdInsubordination1241½	Driving	8
6Sep69- 8AP	fst	7f	:221 :45 1:094 1:223	Arl Wash Futurity 366k	7	6	42½	11½	14	18	Rotz JL	122		4.20	89-21	SilentScreen1228Insubordination1221½WindyTid122¾	Easily	12
8Aug69- 4Sar	fst	6f	:222 :454 1:103	ⒸMd Sp Wt	3	1	13	13	16	114	Rotz JL	122		3.10	95-13	SilentScreen12214BraveEmperor1222½PrinceTurn122½	Easily	12
1Aug69- 4Sar	fst	6f	:224 :471 1:121	ⒸMd Sp Wt	8	6	54	44	2hd	21	Turcotte R	122		5.40	86-13	Sun Cross1221Silent Screen1221Many Pinnacles1224	Gamely	12

Smart Deb

b. f. 1960, by Dedicate (Princequillo)–Demree, by Revoked — **Lifetime record: 37 16 4 8 $383,766**

Own.– Mrs R.L. Reineman
Br.– Russell L. Reineman (Ky)
Tr.– A.N. Winick

15Aug64- 8AP	fst	1⅛	:47 1:11 1:362 1:492	3↑ ⒻMatron H 81k	5	3	33	35	46½	56½	Hartack W	119		3.90	82-14	Tosmah117½Old Hat116½Nubile111½	Could not keep pace	10
29Jly64- 8AP	fst	1	:232 :464 1:121 1:374	3↑ ⒻBeverly H 22k	1	4	32	31½	2hd	2¾	Hartack W	124		*2.30	79-22	StarMaggie119¾SmartDb1241½Alc1192¼	Carried wide stretch	11
10Jun64- 7Aqu	fst	7f	:221 :443 1:101 1:234	3↑ ⒻVagrancy H 28k	3	4	22	32½	56	74¼	Ussery R	124		*1.95	83-18	NoResisting112nkOilRoyalty1251LookMa110no	Speed,tired	10
23May64- 7Aqu	fst	1⅛	:473 1:12 1:373 1:504	3↑ ⒻTop Flight H 57k	9	1	14	12	11	31	Ussery R	122		4.05	86-14	Oil Royalty122½Tona114½Smart Deb1221	Set pace,weakened	10
29Apr64- 7Aqu	sly	1	:231 :464 1:114 1:374	3↑ ⒻBd o'Ross H (Div 2) 21k	7	2	1hd	1hd	3½	33¼	Hartack W	127		*2.20	76-25	Beauful1102PamsEgo1221½SmrtDb1274	Used up setting pace	7
15Apr64- 7Aqu	my	7f	:224 :46 1:114 1:251	3↑ ⒻDistaff H (Div 2) 21k	7	1	31	31	1hd	1¾	Hartack W	125		*1.60	80-22	SmrtDb125¾PamsEgo1211½DecimalCoinage1102½	Hard drive	7
1Apr64- 9GP	fst	7f	:222 :45 1:10 1:23	3↑ ⒻSuwannee River H 16k	3	3	1½	1½	11½	12	Blum W	123		*.90	97-17	Smart Deb1232Lady Karachi1161Yes Please1111½	In hand	8
26Feb64- 8Hia	fst	1⅛	:473 1:12 1:372 1:503	3↑ ⒻBlack Helen H 60k	4	3	32	42¾	43½	46	Hartack W	122		*1.70	76-18	PrincessArle1121PatrolWoman1132½Tona1152½	Well up,tired	9
29Jan64- 8Hia	fst	7f	:224 :452 1:101 1:232	3↑ ⒻColumbiana H 31k	9	1	33½	21½	1hd	1no	Hartack W	123		*.90	92-11	SmartDeb123noYesPlease1122½LatinWlk113nk	Fully extended	10
21Jan64- 8Hia	fst	6f	:221 :451 1:094	4↑ ⒻAlw 10000	1	3	2½	1½	13	13½	Hartack W	119		*.60	95-13	SmartDeb1193½Alecee1152LuckyViola113¾	Drew out handily	7
5Nov63- 7Aqu	fst	6f	:214 :442 1:10	3↑ ⒻInterborough H 23k	2	4	75¼	76½	44½	32	Hartack W	121		3.30	91-16	Affectionately1161½Charspiv114½[D]SmartDeb1211	Bore out	12
	Disqualified and placed last																	
12Oct63- 8GS	fst	1⅛	:481 1:122 1:381 1:51	3↑ ⒻVineland H 58k	2	2	32	3nk	1hd	42¾	Hartack W	121		*2.00	79-20	Oil Royalty118noMy Portrait1122¾Tamarona110no	Led,tired	10
5Oct63- 7GS	fst	1 1/16	:241 :48 1:123 1:444	3↑ ⒻAlw 6000	2	2	1hd	1hd	11	1nk	Hartack W	116		*.70	86-13	Smart Deb116nkTona1131½Suiti113¾	Lost whip,hand ride	9
19Sep63- 7Aqu	gd	1⅛	:491 1:132 1:383 1:51	3↑ ⒻBeldame 87k	10	4	31	3½	1hd	32	Hartack W	118		6.85	84-17	Oil Royalty123noLamb Chop1182Smart Deb1182½	Led,tired	13
11Sep63- 7Aqu	fst	1⅛	:474 1:113 1:37 1:50	ⒻGazelle H 29k	11	5	41½	3½	3½	32	Hartack W	123		4.70	89-13	LambChop1251¾DelhiMaid119nkSmartDeb1232½	Hung in drive	12
17Aug63- 8AP	fst	1⅛	:462 1:104 1:364 1:50	3↑ ⒻArl Matron H 83k	1	1	32	3½	12	1nk	Hartack W	116		4.60	86-16	Smart Deb116nkSolabar1131½Nubile1142	Fully extended	14
7Aug63- 8AP	fst	7f	:223 :454 1:111 1:234	3↑ ⒻBeaugay H 17k	2	6	43	22	1hd	1½	Hartack W	118		3.00	88-18	SmartDeb118½Nubile1111¾OilRoyalty113½	Kept to pressure	11

31Jly63- 8AP	fst 1⅛	:463 1:112 1:364 1:494	ⒻPucker Up H 56k	1 2 41½ 42½ 69 613	Ussery R	126		*2.00	74-15	VitaminShot110nkDelhiMd1193Solbr1143½	Early speed,tired	11
6Jly63- 8Mth	fst 1⅛	:48 1:122 1:373 1:513	ⒻMth Oaks 56k	3 2 2½ 2hd 2hd 31	Ussery R	118		3.90	85-16	Lamb Chop118hdSpicy Living1211Smart Deb1183	Speed,tired	8
22Jun63- 7Aqu	fst 1¼	:472 1:111 1:37 2:024	ⒻC C A Oaks 120k	1 1 11½ 1hd 31 35	Ussery R	121		3.30	81-12	LambChop1213½SpicyLiving1211½SmartDeb121¾	Drifted out	10
1Jun63- 7Aqu	fst 1⅛	:481 1:123 1:372 1:502	ⒻMother Goose 91k	12 1 1½ 11½ 21 2no	Baeza B	121		3.75	89-11	SpicyLiving121noSmartDeb1212½LambChop121nk	Came again	14
18May63- 7Aqu	sly 1	:222 :453 1:111 1:371	ⒻAcorn 60k	4 3 31½ 63¾ 1116 1023	Ussery R	121	b	*2.50	59-17	SpicyLiving1213½Nalee121½LambChop1213	Early speed,tired	12
10May63- 7Aqu	fst 7f	:222 :453 1:101 1:23	ⒻAlw 10000	4 3 31 11 1½ 12	Ussery R	121		*.65	91-09	SmartDeb1212FashionVerdict1161½Fool'sPlay1181½	In hand	6
5Apr63- 7GP	fst 6f	:222 :452 1:10	Alw 3800	3 2 32 11½ 14 18	Grant H	115		*.30	94-15	Smart Deb1158The Baron1161Rustlin Raymond108¾		8
	Bolted to outside rail final furlong,pulled up											
17Nov62- 8Pim	fst 1 1/16	:241 :481 1:131 1:453	ⒻMarguerite 44k	6 2 1hd 1½ 21 33¾	Ussery R	119		*1.10	78-20	WiseNurse1193½Nalee119nkSmrtDb1192	Well rated,weakened	8
10Nov62- 8Lrl	sly 1 1/16	:231 :473 1:13 1:464	ⒻSelima 55k	2 1 3nk 21½ 33 35	Ussery R	119		*1.20	80-17	Fool's Play1191Gay Serenade1194Smart Deb119½	No excuse	5
27Oct62- 7GS	gd 1 1/16	:242 :482 1:123 1:462	ⒻGardenia 159k	3 1 12 11½ 2½ 2½	Ycaza M	119		*1.20	77-24	MainSwap119½SmartDeb1193Nale1195	Bolted to outside turn	9
19Oct62- 7GS	fst 1	:223 :454 1:104 1:372	ⒻAlw 10000	7 2 22½ 2½ 11 22	Shoemaker W	121	b	*2.10e	93-20	Wise Nurse1222Smart Deb1215Affectionately1212½	Propped	11
6Oct62- 7Bel	sly 1	:223 :453 1:111 1:38	ⒻFrizette 110k	5 1 1hd 1hd 32 68	Shoemaker W	119		*.70e	76-15	PamsEgo1191½Fool'sPlay1191¾Affectionately1194	Gave way	10
26Sep62- 7Aqu	fst 7f	:221 :444 1:094 1:23	ⒻAstarita 29k	1 4 1½ 1hd 11 13	Shoemaker W	122		*.50	92-11	[D]SmrtDb1223MainSwap112nkPamsEgo1193	Bore out badly	10
	Disqualified and placed last											
8Sep62- 7Aqu	fst 6f	:213 :442 1:094	ⒻMatron 102k	2 1 1hd 1hd 12½ 11½	Ussery R	119		2.80	96-11	SmartDeb1191½FashionVerdict1194Affectiontly1193	In hand	9
29Aug62- 8AP	fst 6½f	:222 :45 1:094 1:161	ⒻArl Lassie 67k	6 2 12 12 12 13¼	Ycaza M	119		*1.10e	95-08	Smart Deb1193¼Honey Bunny119¾Fast Luck1192½	Ridden out	10
15Aug62- 8AP	fst 6f	:214 :443 1:091	ⒻPrincess Pat 25k	9 1 1hd 1hd 3nk 1nk	Ycaza M	119		1.80e	98-13	SmartDeb119nkPoonetta1071½HoneyBunny1191½	Came again	11
18Jly62- 8AP	sl 5½f	:231 :471 1:002 1:073	ⒻMademoiselle 17k	9 3 2hd 1hd 13 1nk	Hartack W	119		*.50	79-28	Smart Deb119nkVitamin Shot1162½Eleven Keys1101½	All out	10
27Jun62- 8AP	fst 5½f	:224 :452 :58 1:042	ⒻMiss Chicago 17k	2 1 1hd 1½ 1½ 14	Hartack W	116		*.60	95-12	SmrtDb1164RoyalEscapade113hdVitmnShot116no	Mild drive	9
5Jun62- 5Was	fst 5f	:221 :45 :574	ⒻAlw 4000	4 4 3hd 11 14 13	Hartack W	119		*1.20	97-10	SmartDeb1193Burnsy119hdQuickChange119nk	Speed to spare	6
19Jan62- 3Hia	fst 3f	:22 :331	ⒻMd Sp Wt	4 3 21 1hd	Blum W	115		7.05	- -	Smart Deb115hdEnglish Nannie1152Speedwell115½	Driving	14

Stage Door Johnny

ch. c. 1965, by Prince John (Princequillo)–Peroxide Blonde, by Ballymoss **Lifetime record: 8 5 2 1 $223,965**

Own.– Greentree Stable
Br.– Greentree Stud Inc (Ky)
Tr.– J.M. Gaver

13Jly68- 7Aqu	fst 1¼	:494 1:13 1:37 2:013	Dwyer H 81k	6 6 43 43½ 2hd 12	Gustines H	129		*.40	90-09	StgeDoorJhnny1292OutoftheWy123noChompion110½	Driving	6
29Jun68- 7Bel	fst 1	:23 :454 1:102 1:352	Saranac H 55k	2 4 44½ 43½ 2½ 11¼	Gustines H	126		*.70	97-15	StgeDoorJhnny1261¼OutofthWy1242½IronRulr1221½	Driving	5
1Jun68- 8Bel	fst 1½	:482 1:122 2:022 2:271	Belmont 161k	7 7 67½ 21½ 1hd 11¼	Gustines H	126		4.40	97-10	StgeDoorJhnny1261¼ForwardPss12612CllMPrnc1265	Driving	9
23May68- 7Bel	fst 1⅛	:463 1:111 1:361 1:482	Alw 15000	3 5 53½ 11 11 14	Gustines H	116		2.10	94-17	StgeDoorJhnny1164DraftCard1181Ardoise118no	Ridden out	8
8May68- 1Aqu	fst 1	:23 :453 1:102 1:351 3↑	Md Sp Wt	3 7 53 64¾ 1½ 16	Gustines H	114		*.50	92-11	StgeDoorJohnny1146Nageire1146SpaceCowboy115¾	Driving	9
17Apr68- 1Aqu	fst 1	:23 :46 1:104 1:37	Md Sp Wt	2 8 31½ 34½	Gustines H	122		3.50	78-17	JadeAmicol1222OakSpring1222½StagDoorJhnny1223	In close	9
6Sep67- 5Aqu	fst 6f	:224 :47 1:123	ⒸMd Sp Wt	9 10 118½ 86¼ 53 2½	Gustines H	122		*1.50	79-18	Grimaldi122½Stage Door Johnny122¾Forever122hd	Rallied	14
22Aug67- 1Sar	fst 5½f	:221 :461 :591 1:061	ⒸMd Sp Wt	9 11 76 55½ 23 21	Gustines H	122		*2.10	85-13	DreamLanding1221StgeDoorJhnny1225Esteban122½	Greenly	12

Straight Deal

b. f. 1962, by Hail to Reason (Turn-to)–No Fiddling, by King Cole **Lifetime record: 99 21 21 9 $733,020**

Own.– Mrs Ethel D. Jacobs
Br.– Bieber-Jacobs Stable (Ky)
Tr.– H. Jacobs

5Feb69- 6Hia	fm 1 1/16Ⓣ	1:424 4↑	ⒻAlw 7500	9 10 1117 1215 1216 1011¼	Ussery R	118	b	3.10	80-08	Crystal Palace115½Spire1122½Treacherous1121	Outrun	12
27Jan69- 8Hia	fst 7f⊗	:224 :444 1:091 1:221 4↑	ⒻAlw 7000	2 8 819 825 518 211	Ussery R	119	b	4.00	86-18	TooBald11311StraightDeal1193Femtastc1163	Best of others	8
23Jan69- 8Hia	fm 1 1/16Ⓣ	1:444 4↑	ⒻAlw 7500	3 6 68½ 57 43 22½	Ussery R	116	b	3.20	78-18	KlassyPoppy1122½StraightDeal1162Mrs.Petrkn1122½	Rallied	9
28Nov68- 7Aqu	fst 1⅛	:472 1:121 1:363 1:493 3↑	ⒻFirenze H 58k	9 6 78¾ 54½ 54¾ 42½	Pincay L Jr	112	b	4.80e	85-16	Politely1312½Obeah112noSerene Queen114no	Bold bid,hung	11
20Nov68- 7Aqu	fst 1	:241 :472 1:122 1:371 3↑	ⒻAlw 15000	3 3 31 2½ 1hd 12½	Velasquez J	118	b	2.10	81-21	StraightDeal1182½GuestRoom1201WildBeauty115¾	Mild drive	6
2Nov68- 8GS	fst 1⅛	:47 1:111 1:371 1:494 3↑	ⒻVineland H 58k	5 9 99¾ 35 52¾ 42	Kallai P	113	b	15.00	86-22	Politely1261½Serene Queen116½Another Nell116no	Rallied	10
17Oct68- 7Bel	fst 1	:224 :453 1:103 1:362 3↑	ⒻAlw 15000	6 6 69½ 56 34½ 3¾	Velasquez J	116	b	2.20	91-11	NatureII116nkClemsFairyGold116½StraightDeal116½	Wide	7
27Sep68- 7Bel	fst 1	:233 :464 1:11 1:354 3↑	Alw 15000	11 10 87¼ 912 712 711	Velasquez J	115	b	12.60	84-19	Trade In116¾Verbatim111½Misty Run113¾	No factor	11
20Sep68- 7Bel	fm 1⅜Ⓣ	2:151 3↑	ⒻAlw 15000	3 4 31 31½ 32½ 56½	Rotz JL	123	b	6.70	83-10	Harem Lady1232Gay Matelda118½Raison D'Etre1162½	Tired	9
14Sep68- 7Aqu	fst 1⅛	:473 1:121 1:371 1:493 3↑	ⒻBeldame 81k	4 5 410 44 53¾ 45¼	Vasquez J	123	b	12.80	83-14	Gamely123noPolitely123nkAmerigo Lady1235	Lacked a rally	5
4Sep68- 7Aqu	fst 1	:223 :452 1:102 1:362 3↑	ⒻMaskette H 29k	7 9 89¾ 98¼ 76 44½	Toro F	115	b	4.90	80-22	AmergoLdy120noSereneQueen1142GreenGlade1122½	In close	10
16Aug68- 8Sar	fst 1	:231 :463 1:111 1:364 3↑	ⒻAlw 15000	1 7 66½ 54 32½ 11½	Toro F	116	b	2.30	90-11	StraightDeal1161½TwiceCited113hdSyrianSea1113	Driving	8
3Aug68- 8Del	fst 1¼	:471 1:112 1:37 2:024 3↑	ⒻDelaware H 117k	4 9 910 46 48 47¼	Toro F	116	b	8.50	81-19	Politely1262¾PluckyPan1171½Treacherous1133	Rallied,hung	9
20Jly68- 8Del	fst 1 1/16	:232 :472 1:112 1:44 3↑	ⒻNew Castle 38k	11 11 1012 1013 78¾ 67	Cruguet J	117	b	8.60	82-24	Plucky Pan1144Serene Queen1201Lady Diplomat1141½	Hung	12
6Jly68- 7Aqu	fm 1 3/16Ⓣ	1:552 3↑	ⒻShpshdBay H(Div 2) 46k	6 2 11½ 1½ 45 67¾	Ussery R	118	b	6.90	85-09	Politely125noMount Regina1153Treacherous1142	Tired	9
29Jun68- 8Mth	fst 1 1/16	:232 :47 1:12 1:45 3↑	ⒻMolly Pitcher H 39k	7 9 916 79¼ 59 52	Grant H	120	b	3.60	78-21	Politely1221¼Mac'sSparkler123¾GreenGlade114no	Late foot	9
19Jun68- 5Mth	fst 1 70	:233 :473 1:124 1:432 3↑	ⒻAlw 15000	2 6 611 51¼ 3nk 2no	Grant H	118	b	*1.00	84-18	SereneQueen118noStraightDeal1182½LaContss1162	No excuse	6
18May68- 7Aqu	fst 1⅛	:471 1:112 1:364 1:49 3↑	ⒻTop Flight H 58k	9 7 710 86½ 74¾ 76¾	Belmonte E	122	b	5.30	84-11	AmerigoLady119nk[D]Politely1212SereneQueen1111½	No rally	11
4May68- 8Pim	fst 1 1/16	:233 :472 1:121 1:444 3↑	ⒻGallorette H 33k	5 8 87¾ 75½ 52½ 2½	Marquez CH	122	b	*1.30	85-18	Serene Queen109½Straight Deal122½Politely1221	Wide turn	8
27Apr68- 7Aqu	fst 1⅛	:461 1:101 1:354 1:484 3↑	Grey Lag H 85k	1 9 1011 87½ 62¾ 53½	Marquez CH	113	b	13.30	88-14	BoldHour113¾[D]DiplomatWay1222FortMarcy118no	Late bid	10
20Apr68- 8Bow	fst 1 1/16	:231 :464 1:11 1:42 3↑	J B Campbell H 111k	6 7 74¼ 66¼ 55¼ 54½	Blum W	115	b	7.70	98-08	In Reality1221Barbs Delight117½Peter Piper1172	No rally	7
6Apr68- 7Aqu	fst 1⅛	:453 1:093 1:35 1:48 3↑	Excelsior H 55k	5 6 617 69½ 36½ 26½	Belmonte E	115	b	2.60	89-14	Peter Piper1126½Straight Deal1154Grace Born1124	Rallied	7
30Mar68- 8Bow	fst 7f	:224 :451 1:09 1:214 3↑	ⒻBarbara Fritchie H 58k	10 9 1014 916 57½ 26	Belmonte E	122	b	8.40	90-12	Too Bald1186Straight Deal122¾Treacherous121¾	Rallied	10
13Mar68- 9GP	fm 1Ⓣ	:224 :461 1:111 1:354 3↑	ⒻOrchid H 23k	2 14 1425 1418 1420 1414	Grant H	124	b	*1.80	80-09	Chriscinca109nkRing Francis1093Farest Nan1133	No speed	14
2Mar68- 5Hia	fst 7f	:224 :451 1:092 1:22 4↑	Alw 10000	4 8 816 812 89¼ 36¼	Belmonte E	112	b	7.20	93-11	Jim J.1191¼Bold Tactics1165Straight Deal1122	Rallied	8
4Nov67- 7Aqu	my 1¼	:493 1:141 1:393 2:043 3↑	ⒻLadies H 58k	5 3 32 41½ 73¾ 55¼	Grant H	126	b	*2.30	70-22	SweetFolly1142½HaremLdy1081½Muse106nk	Lacked room late	12
26Oct67- 6Kee	fst 1⅛	:474 1:114 1:37 1:491 3↑	ⒻSpinster 61k	1 6 68½ 66 2hd 1nk	Grant H	123	b	*.80	91-18	StraightDel123nk[D]Amrgo'sLdy1194FurlSl1193	Reared start	6
14Oct67- 8GS	fst 1⅛	:482 1:123 1:384 1:511 3↑	ⒻVineland H 56k	6 7 714 57 3nk 1nk	Grant H	122	b	*1.60	81-23	Straight Deal122nkPolitely1203Gamely1173½	Stiff drive	7
30Sep67- 8Atl	fst 1 3/16	:46 1:101 1:341 1:551 3↑	ⒻMatchmaker 50k	1 10 811 57¾ 46½ 2¾	Cordero A Jr	123	b	*2.00	104-15	Politely118¾StraightDeal123hdGmly1143	Hung under impost	13
16Sep67- 7Aqu	fst 1⅛	:49 1:132 1:372 1:494 3↑	ⒻBeldame 81k	5 4 44½ 44½ 56½ 45¼	Cordero A Jr	123	b	*.70	82-16	Mac'sSparkler123nkTripleBrook1232½Gamely1182½	No excuse	6
4Sep67- 7Aqu	fst 1⅛	:482 1:121 1:361 1:481 3↑	Aqueduct 106k	5 4 47 45 31½ 32½	Cordero A Jr	116	b	6.30	92-14	Damascus1252Ring Twice119½Straight Deal1166	Bore out	5
21Aug67- 7Sar	gd 1⅛	:474 1:123 1:37 1:493 3↑	ⒻDiana H 28k	3 5 56½ 52¼ 23 2nk	Ussery R	127	b	*1.30	96-11	Prides Profile114nkStraight Deal1273Malhoa1112½	Brushed	9
5Aug67- 6Sar	fst 1⅛	:47 1:11 1:352 1:481 4↑	Whitney 56k	7 7 814 78 33 31	Ussery R	116	b	3.80e	102-06	Stupendous114nkRing Twice114¾Straight Deal1164	Rallied	8
29Jly67- 8Del	fst 1¼	:471 1:114 1:37 2:021 3↑	ⒻDelaware H 118k	4 4 46½ 2hd 12 11¾	Ussery R	125	b	*2.60	91-20	Straight Deal1251¾Malhoa112¾Miss Spin1141½	Mild drive	10
8Jly67- 7Aqu	fm 1 3/16Ⓣ	1:544 3↑	ⒻSheepshead Bay H 57k	3 7 65½ 63¼ 52 55	Ussery R	124	b	2.70	91-04	Indian Sunlite1183½Mount Regina117nkAmerivan1191	Hung	10
1Jly67- 8Mth	fst 1 1/16	:234 :471 1:114 1:444 3↑	ⒻMolly Pitcher H 38k	2 6 710 73¾ 63¾ 22¾	Ussery R	126	b	*1.00	78-17	Politely1152¾StraightDeal1261IndianSunlite1173½	Gaining	7
21Jun67- 7Aqu	gd 7f	:222 :451 1:101 1:234 3↑	ⒻVagrancy H 27k	3 6 619 622 616 611	Ussery R	127	b	2.60	76-21	Triple Brook116½Mac's Sparkler1213Cestrum1112½	Impeded	6
7Jun67- 7Aqu	hd 1 3/16Ⓣ	1:55 3↑	Edgemere H 30k	10 5 58 76¼ 45 73¾	Ussery R	115	b	3.80	91-05	GingerFizz117nkChinatowner1143HandsomeBoy111no	In close	14
20May67- 7Aqu	fst 1⅛	:48 1:114 1:37 1:493 3↑	ⒻTop Flight H 55k	2 4 42½ 53 1hd 1¾	Cordero A Jr	126	b	2.40	88-14	Straight Deal126¾Mac's Sparkler1224Malhoa112¾	Driving	7
12May67- 7Aqu	sl 1	:234 :471 1:121 1:371 3↑	ⒻHandicap 15000	4 6 65 44½ 1½ 1¾	Ussery R	126	b	*1.70	82-26	StraightDeal126¾Mac'sSparklr1234ShmmrngGold1133	Driving	8
6May67- 8Pim	fst 1 1/16	:233 :472 1:113 1:423 3↑	ⒻGallorette H 33k	3 8 88¼ 78½ 56 24	Nelson E	126	b	*2.10	93-14	LadyDiplomat1124StraightDeal126hdIndnSunlt117nk	Rallied	9
25Apr67- 7Aqu	sl 1	:241 :474 1:124 1:373 3↑	ⒻBed o' Roses H 28k	1 8 811 42½ 4¾ 12½	Ussery R	122	b	3.30	80-28	StraightDeal1222½IndianSunlite116hdKerens110hd	Drew out	9

17Apr67- 7Aqu	sly	7f	:233 :464 1:113 1:241	3↑ ⒻDistaff H 27k	3	3	710	715	711	59	Ussery R	123	b	2.00	76-23	Cologne1131Lady Diplomat1142Miss Moona1226	Far back	7
15Mar67- 9GP	fm	1Ⓣ	:232 :464 1:111 1:351	3↑ ⒻOrchid H (Div 2) 22k	4	9	78¾	32	21	1½	Velasquez J	122		*.50	98-03	Straight Deal122½Cologne1116Pollen1172½	Up in time	10
1Mar67- 8Hia	fst	1⅛	:47 1:11 1:36 1:483	3↑ ⒻBlack Helen H 65k	10	6	53½	22	2hd	2hd	Ussery R	122	b	*1.20	92-13	Mac's Sparkler117hdStraight Deal1222Malhoa1162¾	Gamely	13
15Feb67- 8Hia	fst	7f	:23 :452 1:10 1:23	3↑ ⒻColumbiana H 33k	5	12	1314	1216	78¼	31½	Ussery R	122	b	3.50	92-16	Mac'sSparkler115hdMoccasin1171½StraightDeal122½	Rallied	14
20Jan67- 8Hia	sl	7f⊗	:241 :481 1:131 1:253	4↑ ⒻAlw 7000	7	3	89	75½	45	1¾	Ussery R	118	b	*1.10	81-19	StraightDeal118¾TradeMrk1151Srols1121¾	Up final strides	8
24Nov66- 7Aqu	fst	1⅛	:473 1:114 1:37 1:493	3↑ ⒻFirenze H 56k	7	8	813	89½	34	12¼	Ussery R	118	b	3.30	88-21	StraightDeal1182¼Mac'sSparkler113¾BelldNut1121½	Driving	8
5Nov66- 7Aqu	fst	1¼	:481 1:122 1:371 2:022	3↑ ⒻLadies H 56k	5	4	23	2½	1½	2no	Ussery R	118	b	4.40	86-13	Destro115noStraightDeal1183MissDickey109hd	Sharp,missed	8
26Oct66- 5Aqu	fm	1 1/16Ⓣ	1:432	3↑ ⒻNew York H (Div 1) 23k	4	6	45½	46½	46½	45¼	Ussery R	122	b	3.10	84-13	IndianSunlite115nkNativeStret119noMountRgn1205	Bore out	9
15Oct66- 8GS	fst	1⅛	:474 1:112 1:361 1:49	3↑ ⒻVineland H 58k	6	7	88¾	67	56½	43¼	Ussery R	121	b	*2.00	89-15	LadyPitt118¾Juanita1122½Mac'sSparklr112no	Belated rally	11
17Sep66- 7Aqu	fst	1⅛	:47 1:111 1:361 1:492	3↑ ⒻBeldame 85k	8	7	713	613	57	28	Ussery R	123	b	11.30	81-18	SummerScandal1238StraightDeal123½LadyPitt1182	Rallied	10
7Sep66- 7Aqu	fst	1	:233 :463 1:114 1:374	3↑ ⒻMaskette H 28k	7	6	56	23	26	26	Ussery R	119	b	3.80	73-30	SummerScandal1236StraightDeal119noTrechry1112½	Fair try	9
9Jly66- 7Aqu	hd	1 3/16Ⓣ	1:552	3↑ ⒻSheepshead Bay H 57k	5	3	31½	32	1hd	1½	Blum W	122	b	*3.40e	93-13	StraightDeal122½MountRegina120hdTreachery111hd	Driving	10
2Jly66- 8Mth	fst	1 1/16	:233 :47 1:112 1:433	3↑ ⒻMolly Pitcher H 38k	5	6	55½	43½	24	2nk	Brumfield D	120	b	6.20	87-15	Discipline117nkStraight Deal1203½Lovejoy1122	Sharp try	8
18Jun66- 7Aqu	hd	1⅝Ⓣ	2:384	3↑ Bowling Green H 59k	11	8	1117	1211	1113	1115	Ussery R	115	b	19.30	91-00	Moontrip112hdFlag113½Knightly Manner116¾	Unruly post	12
11Jun66- 8Aqu	fm	1 3/16Ⓣ	1:543	3↑ Handicap 8500	8	4	33½	43	52¼	53	Shoemaker W	116	b	4.40	94-03	ChosunVictory113¾WhiteBearLake1131Rochefort112½	Tired	11
21May66- 7Aqu	fst	1⅛	:472 1:112 1:361 1:492	3↑ ⒻTop Flight H 55k	6	2	25	23	26	310	Ussery R	119	b	*1.70e	79-15	Summer Scandal1175Malhoa1135Straight Deal119¾	Tired	7
27Apr66- 7Aqu	fst	1	:24 :464 1:11 1:354	3↑ ⒻBed o' Roses H 27k	2	3	33½	31½	3½	11½	Ussery R	117	b	4.90e	89-18	StraightDeal1171½WhataTreat1261½QuenEmprss123nk	Driving	7
18Apr66- 7Aqu	fst	7f	:223 :452 1:094 1:222	3↑ ⒻDistaff H 27k	2	6	611	77½	63½	42¾	Shoemaker W	119	b	3.90e	91-17	SailorPrincess111nkQueenEmprss1232½Pttcot112no	Bore out	7
9Apr66- 8Bow	fst	7f	:223 :45 1:102 1:232	3↑ ⒻBarbara Fritchie H 59k	11	2	85¼	66¾	53¼	42¾	Sellers J	120	b	7.00e	93-14	Tosmah1211Queen Empress1231½Privileged111nk	Stride late	12
12Mar66- 8SA	fm	*1¾Ⓣ	2:484	3↑ S Juan Capistrano H 125k	3	5	47	73½	74½	68	Gustines H	116	b	17.80	75-17	George Royal118noPlaque115½Tom Cat1141½	Well up,tired	9
24Feb66- 8SA	fm	1¼Ⓣ	:444 1:091 1:34 1:584	4↑ ⒻS Barbara H 46k	13	8	89½	31	11½	12½	Shoemaker W	122	b	4.80e	98-02	StraightDeal1222½MissRincon1071½Petticoat113no	Driving	13
16Feb66- 8SA	fm	1⅛Ⓣ	:472 1:12 1:37 1:491	4↑ ⒻHandicap 15000	6	9	812	811	810	89	Shoemaker W	125	b	4.80	78-13	Curious Clover1162Pollen1202½Miss Rincon108½	Wide	12
5Feb66- 8SA	fst	1⅛	:47 1:11 1:361 1:483	4↑ ⒻS Margarita H 61k	9	6	75½	32½	32½	1nk	Shoemaker W	121	b	2.50e	89-12	StraightDeal121nkPollen1192Batteur124no	Long,hard drive	12
22Jan66- 7SA	fst	1 1/16	:223 :45 1:10 1:422	4↑ ⒻS Maria H 31k	7	8	816	85½	52	2½	Shoemaker W	121	b	3.40e	90-11	PoonaQueen119½StraightDeal121nkGallarush112hd	Sharp try	14
11Jan66- 8SA	fst	7f	:22 :443 1:10 1:223	4↑ ⒻS Monica H 26k	14	9	912	915	1010	55¼	Shoemaker W	112	b	3.70e	85-15	Batteur1231½Terentia1193½Jalousie II117hd	Mild bid	14
28Dec65- 8SA	fst	6f	:221 :451 :573 1:10	3↑ ⒻLas Flores H 26k	3	13	137¾	129¼	78	74	Church K	122	b	*2.40e	88-13	Poona Queen117¾Respected116nkFairway Fun116nk	No threat	14
25Nov65- 7Aqu	gd	1⅛	:48 1:124 1:384 1:521	3↑ ⒻFirenze H 55k	3	4	43	2hd	1½	21¾	Sellers J	118	b	*.70e	73-26	SailorPrincess1111¾StrghtDl118nkPttcot1143½	Second best	7
6Nov65- 7Aqu	fst	1¼	:49 1:132 1:381 2:033	3↑ ⒻLadies H 55k	3	6	55½	41	11	13	Sellers J	114	b	4.20	80-17	StraightDeal1143SteepleJill1262½YesPles109no	Mild drive	7
27Oct65- 7Aqu	fm	1 1/16Ⓣ	1:423	3↑ ⒻNew York H (Div 2) 23k	2	3	31½	32	33	34½	Sellers J	116	b	4.40	88-07	Batteur123½GoodJane1104StraightDeal1161½	Held on gamely	9
16Oct65- 8GS	fst	1⅛	:48 1:12 1:371 1:494	3↑ ⒻVineland H 56k	3	2	24	43	44½	43½	Velasquez J	115	b	9.20	84-21	Steeple Jill1232Cordially113½Tosmah1221	Even race	8
7Oct65- 7Aqu	fst	1	:231 :461 1:104 1:364	ⒻAlw 10000	4	5	54½	54	21	11½	Sellers J	118	b	1.50	84-20	StraightDeal1181½Terentia1181EdieB.M.1202	Slightly best	6
27Sep65- 7Aqu	fst	1⅛	:463 1:104 1:36 1:491	3↑ ⒻBeldame 82k	6	4	44	52¾	42	3½	Sellers J	118	b	2.10e	89-19	WhataTreat118noSteepleJill123½StraightDeal1181½	Blocked	6
20Sep65- 7Aqu	fst	1	:223 :444 1:084 1:351	3↑ ⒻMaskette H 28k	1	6	46	35	33	33	Sellers J	113	b	2.90e	89-16	Tosmah128noAffectionately1283Straight Deal113½	Gamely	9
4Sep65- 7Aqu	fst	1⅛	:473 1:122 1:381 1:512	ⒻGazelle H 59k	1	6	77	74¾	41½	42½	Cordero A	117	b	4.80	76-20	WhataTreat123½Terentia118½Discipline1181½	In close,hung	13
23Aug65- 7Sar	fst	1⅛	:464 1:11 1:364 1:493	3↑ ⒻDiana H 28k	1	3	33	21	1hd	2hd	Sellers J	113	b	18.50	97-12	SteepleJill126hdStraightDel113½HoHo109no	Very sharp try	8
14Aug65- 6Sar	fst	1¼	:471 1:112 1:364 2:033	ⒻAlabama 63k	9	11	116	96	85½	78	Sellers S	121	b	20.70	82-06	WhataTreat118nk[D]Discipline1182Terentia114½	No mishap	18
22Jly65- 8Hol	fst	1⅛	:47 1:11 1:37 1:494	ⒻHol Oaks 56k	6	9	97	52¼	31½	12½	Sellers J	112	b	12.30	83-16	StraightDeal1122½SeaEagle1122½GalaHost1183½	Handy score	11
5Jly65- 8Mth	fst	1⅛	:464 1:11 1:372 1:503	ⒻMth Oaks 57k	4	9	813	815	79¾	69½	Vasquez J	112	b	13.90	81-19	Summer Scandal1126Terentia116¾Marshua118¾	Slow start	10
23Jun65- 8Mth	fst	1 70	:223 :461 1:114 1:433	ⒻPost-Deb (Div 2) 23k	9	7	78¼	64¼	43½	2no	Turcotte R	112	b	13.90	83-19	Desert Love118noStraight Deal1121Cestrum1123	Sharp try	12
12Jun65- 7Aqu	fst	1¼	:481 1:121 1:37 2:023	ⒻC C A Oaks 129k	7	10	99½	96¼	811	817	Boland W	121	b	26.60	68-14	Marshua1212½What a Treat1216Terentia1212½	Never close	10
29May65- 7Aqu	sly	1⅛	:482 1:123 1:513	ⒻMother Goose 97k	10	6	53	54½	45	44	Belmonte E	121	b	24.50f	74-20	Cordially121noWhat a Treat1211Up Oars1213	No late rally	12
25May65- 6Aqu	fst	6f	:221 :453 1:12	3↑ ⒻAlw 6500	11	8	87	76	51¾	2no	Boland W	115	b	12.45	83-19	Think Quick112noStraight Deal115½Ruth Fogel118½	Gaining	12
15May65- 7Aqu	fst	1	:222 :45 1:101 1:371	ⒻAcorn 58k	2	5	55½	45½	57½	68¼	Blum W	121	b	65.55	74-20	GroundControl121nkMarshua121noUpOars1213	Wide final ⅜	10
22Apr65- 8Aqu	fst	6f	:231 :463 1:113	3↑ ⒻAlw 6500	1	6	52	43½	55	45½	Blum W	113	b	8.10	79-18	Png113½IcCrnvl1151½RuthFogl1153½	Crowded early,no rally	8
16Apr65- 8Aqu	gd	7f	:233 :471 1:122 1:243	3↑ ⒻAlw 6000	6	6	62	51¼	2½	1nk	Blum W	112	b	6.80	83-23	StraightDeal112nkGroundControl1134RingaBell1101	Driving	7
8Apr65- 7Aqu	fst	6f	:223 :454 1:111	3↑ ⒻAlw 7500	4	6	63¾	53½	66½	54½	Alvarez F	110	b	11.95	82-20	Self-Supporting118hdIceCrnvl1201½SpnshBrz1131½	In close	9
27Jan65- 7Hia	fst	7f	:23 :46 1:113 1:253	ⒻAlw 6000	5	6	66¼	49	48½	55½	Turcotte R	116	b	3.00	75-19	Taunoa1083½LovelyHanna113hdSpecialT.113½	Never a factor	7
20Jan65- 9Hia	fst	6f	:223 :461 1:11	ⒻJasmine (Div 2) 20k	8	8	97	76¾	67	56	Turcotte R	112	b	8.10	83-15	OpenHearing1123¾SpecialT.113hdMagcRy1142	Sluggish start	9
4Jan65- 8TrP	fst	6f	:222 :453 1:111	ⒻAlw 3200	11	2	33	64½	88	97¼	Ussery R	121	b	3.50	79-14	Amerivan116hdSpecialT.1211SuzanneMarie121hd	Raced wide	11
10Dec64- 7Aqu	fst	7f	:223 :452 1:101 1:23	Alw 10000	5	1	55½	33	24	2½	Venezia M5	109	b	2.05	90-14	WazaOurs122½StraightDl1095Mr.Kish1173	Finished gamely	5
23Nov64- 6Aqu	fst	6f	:222 :461 1:12	ⒻAlw 5500	2	6	52	63¼	2hd	12½	Turcotte R	119	b	6.10	83-24	StraightDeal1192½Respected1191½WellHeeld1162	Mild drive	9
18Nov64- 7Aqu	fst	1	:234 :471 1:132 1:391	ⒻDemoiselle 28k	8	1	11	1hd	63¼	77½	Gustines H	112	b	19.65e	64-26	Discipline1132Lay Aft115¾Cordially1121	Used up early	8
12Oct64- 5Aqu	fst	6½f	:221 :443 1:094 1:163	ⒻAlw 5000	1	6	66½	77½	68	57¼	Valenzuela I	119		9.00	90-07	TwoofAkind119½LuckyFlight1142Equiria113¾	Raced evenly	7
7Oct64- 5Aqu	fst	6f	:231 :471 1:12	ⒻMd Sp Wt	5	6	62¾	43½	2½	13	Turcotte R	119	b	13.50f	83-17	Straight Deal1193Holli Dawn119¾Wee Lassie1192½	Driving	14
2Oct64- 4Aqu	sly	7f	:224 :471 1:142 1:284	ⒻMd Sp Wt	7	9	85¾	812	711	78¼	Alvarez F	119	b	55.90	54-31	EncoreUne119½CmpassRose119½SheetHome119nk	No threat	11
25Sep64- 5Aqu	fst	6f	:223 :463 1:12	ⒻMd Sp Wt	13	8	115	1415	1421	1422	Connolley R	119		72.15f	61-18	Bebopper1191½Up Oars1196Mount Regina119½	Far off pace	14
8Sep64- 5Aqu	fst	6f	:223 :46 1:111	ⒻMd Sp Wt	9	13	139¾	1219	1020	820	Tartaglia J10	109		11.40e	67-20	Meripats1198Titania1192Be Reasonable114hd	Slow start	14

Successor

b. c. 1964, by Bold Ruler (Nasrullah)–Misty Morn, by Princequillo

Lifetime record: 25 7 6 6 $532,254

Own.– Wheatley Stable

Br.– Wheatley Stable (Ky)

Tr.– E.A. Neloy

3Feb68- 8Hia	fst	1⅛	:454 1:092 1:342 1:471	3↑ Seminole H 65k	5	7	713	715	511	511¾	Baeza B	117	b	2.60	87-14	Favorable Turn1118Rixdal1112In Reality121nk	Outrun	12
26Jan68- 9Hia	fst	7f	:234 :463 1:104 1:231	4↑ Alw 7000	3	6	64½	45	42¼	11½	Baeza B	119	b	*.70	93-17	Successor1191½Angelico114¾Gaylord'sFeather113nk	Driving	9
20Jan68- 9Hia	fst	7f	:231 :463 1:111 1:233	4↑ Alw 6500	2	5	46	54½	53½	41¼	Baeza B	119	b	*.50	90-14	JohnJacob113½RenewedVigor113nkRoyalSpeed113½	In close	12
18Nov67- 7Aqu	fst	1⅛	:463 1:103 1:361 1:493	3↑ Queens County H 55k	3	6	610	67	46½	31½	Shoemaker W	116	b	2.30	86-14	Mr. Right115½Proud Clarion1251Successor1161	Bore in	6
11Nov67- 7Aqu	fst	1 3/16	:471 1:11 1:36 1:55	Roamer H 56k	5	6	2hd	1½	1hd	24	Boland W	118	b	3.00	100-11	Proud Clarion1224Successor1183½Royal Speed1123	Faltered	8
28Oct67- 7Aqu	fst	2	:494 2:302 2:554 3:201	3↑ J C Gold Cup 106k	4	3	35	34	34	312	Boland W	119	b	6.60	83-12	Damascus1194½Handsome Boy1247½Sccssr1196½	No mishap	4
18Oct67- 7Aqu	sly	1⅝	:48 1:402 2:061 2:443	Lawrence Realizatn 54k	6	2	22½	11½	1hd	1nk	Baeza B	116	b	*.70	82-23	Successr116nkGentlemnJms1169IrshRbllon11610	Hard urged	6
9Oct67- 7Aqu	fst	1⅛	:464 1:104 1:353 1:483	Discovery H 28k	8	7	75¾	66½	33	2¾	Baeza B	119	b	*1.00	92-16	BoldHour119¾Successr1192½GalaPrformnc11810	Closed fast	9
26Sep67- 7Aqu	fst	1	:223 :444 1:083 1:343	3↑ Alw 15000	7	6	64¾	64	52¾	31½	Baeza B	112		*.80	93-11	Indulto1201¼Flag Raiser123nkSuccessor112hd	Closed fast	8
16Sep67- 6Aqu	fst	6f	:222 :46 1:102	3↑ Alw 15000	1	7	53¾	54	3nk	13	Boland W	113		1.50	91-16	Successor1133Golden Buttons1191Impressive115hd	Easily	8
4Sep67- 6Aqu	fst	6f	:22 :45 1:093	3↑ Alw 15000	1	6	611	69	39½	35¾	Baeza B	113		3.10	89-14	Jim J.115¾Mr. Washington1205Successor11310	Stride late	6
20May67- 6Aqu	fst	6f	:221 :452 1:093	3↑ Alw 12000	8	6	74½	65½	67½	67½	Ycaza M	116	b	1.70	87-14	Aforthought1151½BrooklynBrdg1153Voygr105no	No response	8
6May67- 7CD	fst	1¼	:463 1:104 1:36 2:003	Ky Derby 162k	6	10	1013	1213	68¼	68	Baeza B	126	b	4.60	89-07	ProudClarion1261BarbsDelight1263Dmascs1261¼	No mishap	14
27Apr67- 6Kee	fst	1⅛	:472 1:111 1:363 1:493	Blue Grass 31k	1	5	64¾	68½	57	48¼	Broussard R	126	b	*.60	81-17	DiplomatWy1261½ProudClrion1216GentlmnJms126¾	In close	9
15Apr67- 7Kee	fst	7f	:224 :451 1:10 1:22	Alw 7500	6	1	42½	35	32½	2no	Baeza B	122	b	*.70	98-12	Ruken122noSuccessor1226Balouf113no	Bold late rally	7
13Mar67- 7Aqu	fst	6f	:222 :452 1:092	Swift 27k	2	4	45½	58½	48½	47¾	Baeza B	126	b	*.50	88-18	SoloLanding1265½SunGala126¾FlyingTackle1261½	No excuse	5
12Nov66- 8GS	sly	1 1/16	:232 :472 1:121 1:441	Garden State 314k	1	5	56	45	31½	13	Baeza B	122	b	*2.30	84-29	Successor1223Bold Hour1226Proviso122¾	Scored easily	12
29Oct66- 8Lrl	fst	1 1/16	:232 :472 1:133 1:454	Pim Futurity 194k	6	3	43	43½	21½	2nk	Shoemaker W	122	b	*.50e	88-16	In Reality122nkSuccessor1222Proviso1224	Bore in,gaining	9
15Oct66- 7Aqu	fst	1	:222 :444 1:092 1:35	Champagne 208k	6	6	54½	42¼	23	11	Baeza B	122	b	3.10e	93-14	Successor1221Dr. Fager1224Proviso1224	Won going away	10

5Oct66- 7Aqu	gd	7f	:224 :46 1:113 1:244	Cowdin 88k	4 7 94¼ 87¾ 44	32¼	Baeza B	117	b	2.30	80-22	Dr.Fager117¾InRealty1171½Succssor1172½	In close,rallied	10
24Sep66- 7Aqu	fst	6½f	:224 :46 1:11 1:173	Futurity 147k	7 7 75¼ 74¼ 34	2½	Baeza B	122	b	1.50e	91-18	Bold Hour122½Successor1223½Pinnacle1222	Finished fast	7
20Jly66- 7Aqu	fst	5½f	:231 :463 :582 1:042	Great American 27k	3 1 51¼ 42½ 33	3¾	Baeza B	124	b	*.70	90-23	Native Prince124nkHermogenes120½Successor1246	Bore in	6
6Jly66- 7Aqu	fst	5½f	:221 :452 :574 1:041	Tremont 36k	4 3 42 42 3nk	1nk	Baeza B	114	b	*.90	92-20	Successor114nkBold Hour1143Favorable Turn1141½	Driving	6
24Jun66- 3Aqu	fst	5½f	:233 :471 :592 1:06	©Md Sp Wt	2 1 1½ 13 16	16	Baeza B	122	b	*.10	83-21	Successor1226Richroband1222½Celebration1222	Easily	9
10Jun66- 5Aqu	fst	5f	:222 :454 :58	Md Sp Wt	5 6 34 33 31	2nk	Baeza B	122	b	*.90	95-16	Bold Hour122nkSuccessor1228Bracer122no	Gave sharp try	8

T.V. Lark

b. c. 1957, by Indian Hemp (Nasrullah)–Miss Larksfly, by Heelfly

Lifetime record: 72 19 13 6 $902,194

Own.– P.W. Madden
Br.– Dr W.D. Lucas (Cal)
Tr.– P.K. Parker

22Nov62- 8Pim	sf	1½(T)	:504 1:183 2:141 2:422 3↑	Dixie H 63k	12 13 1519 1216 912	811¼	Sellers J	122		7.00	32-57	WiseShip123¾SunshineCak1081¼ElBnddo118nk	Never a factor	15
27Oct62- 7Bel	sf	1½(T)	2:283 3↑	Man o' War 114k	6 6 87½ 89¼ 719	822	Sellers J	126		6.70	81-11	Beau Purple1262Kelso1266½The Axe II1261¼		12
Failed to respond in drive														
17Oct62- 7Bel	hd	1⅜(T)	2:131 3↑	Knickerbocker H 30k	1 6 66½ 95¼ 63¼	63¼	Ycaza M	123		*1.55	101-00	TheAxeII120¾Mngo1201½IrishDandy112½	No apparent excuse	12
8Oct62- 5Bel	fm	1⅜(T)	2:153 3↑	Long Island H (Div 1) 22k	5 4 21½ 43 32	2¾	Gomez A	124		2.95	91-09	TheAxeII117¾T.V.Lark1242½ShieldBearer1181	Game effort	10
29Sep62- 7Aqu	gd	1¼	:471 1:113 1:37 2:031 3↑	Woodward 115k	3 4 616 815 816	816	Gomez A	126		18.60	68-17	Kelso1264½Jaipur1206½Guadlcnl1261½	Dropped far off pace	8
15Sep62- 8Atl	fm	1 3/16(T)	1:563 3↑	U Nations H 100k	1 10 85¼ 83½ 62¼	2nk	Gomez A	123		7.00	90-10	Mongo117nkT.V.Lark123½WiseShip1232	Fast finish outside	12
1Sep62- 8Atl	fm	1⅛(T)	1:50 3↑	Kelly-Olympic H 35k	4 9 109¾ 108¼ 810	85¼	Longden J	124		*1.70	88-07	WiseShip124½HittngAwy1241½Parka111½	No apparent mishap	11
25Aug62- 8Atl	fm	1 1/16(T)	1:422 3↑	Philadelphia Turf H 29k	2 6 813 78 43¼	12	Grant H	120		*1.90	99-01	T.V.Lark1202HellenicHero111¾LoyalLadyII108½	Cleverly	8
23Jly62- 7Hol	fst	1⅝	:464 1:361 2:012 2:393 3↑	Sunset H 88k	2 11 108¾ 75¼ 45½	47¾	Valenzuela A	120		7.10	85-12	ProveIt129noWindySnds1126NotblII1071¾	Lacked room,wide	14
14Jly62- 8Hol	fst	1¼	:45 1:093 1:344 2:00 3↑	Hol Gold Cup H 162k	11 12 1216 95¼ 79	712	Neves R	125		5.50	81-14	Prove It1253¼Windy Sands111½Cadiz1175		12
Failed to threaten seriously														
4Jly62- 8Hol	fst	1⅛	:46 1:092 1:342 1:473 3↑	American H 55k	9 6 812 78¾ 87¾	54¾	Sellers J	123		3.10	90-16	ProveIt124nkWindySands1131¼Harpi1103¼	Wide stretch turn	9
16Jun62- 7Hol	fst	1 1/16	:223 :451 1:09 1:41 3↑	Inglewood H 55k	1 8 79¼ 77 76½	65	Longden J	126		4.50	85-14	ProveIt122¾SeOrbt112nkRblro109no	Saved ground,late gain	10
30May62- 8Was	fm	1 1/16(T)	:24 :472 1:112 1:431 3↑	Round Table H 32k	5 8 714 712 45	21¼	Ycaza M	126		1.90	93-11	PorvenirII1161¼T.V.Lark1261¼RunforNurse118nk	Wide bid	8
10May62- 7Aqu	fst	1⅛	:464 1:112 1:364 1:492 3↑	Sun Forward H 20k	4 5 512 510 48½	610	Sellers J	127		2.45	85-18	BeauPurple1181½Eurasia1156RuffWeather1081½	Never close	7
1May62- 7Aqu	sf	1 1/16(T)	1:501 3↑	Alw 10000	3 1 21 21½ 2hd	1¾	Sellers J	124		*.65	57-39	T.V. Lark124¾Juanro1141½John William1196	Hard ridden	8
21Apr62- 8Lrl	fm	1⅛(T)	1:474 3↑	Laurel H 28k	3 2 31½ 31½ 34	24½	Longden J	127		*.40	97-00	BronzBbu1174½T.V.Lrk127¾Polrty109nk	Evenly through stretch	9
30Jan62- 7SA	fst	1⅛	:462 1:104 1:361 1:482 4↑	[S]S Catalina H 27k	3 7 73¼ 72¼ 23	2no	Longden J	127		*1.10	90-12	New Policy118noT.V. Lark12710Dress Up1142¾	Just missed	7
11Nov61- 7Lrl	fm	1½(T)	:483 2:013 2:261 3↑	D C Int'l 100k	4 2 2½ 2hd 1hd	1¾	Longden J	126		3.60	109-01	T.V.Lark126¾Klso12612Prnupcl12610	Under long,hard drive	8
25Oct61- 7Aqu	hd	1⅝(T)	2:40 3↑	Knickerbocker H 29k	10 7 77½ 43 31½	1no	Longden J	119		6.45	110-00	T.V.Lark119noNasomo113¾WiseShip120¾	Up in final stride	11
14Oct61- 8Haw	gd	1¼	:471 1:112 1:372 2:023 3↑	Haw Gold Cup H 127k	9 6 68 1½ 11½	1½	Longden J	113	b	7.90	83-17	T.V.Lark113½Heroshogala1097RunforNurse119no	Hard drive	9
29Sep61- 7Haw	sf	1 3/16(T)	:483 1:143 1:402 2:013 3↑	Handicap 10000	5 3 36 42½ 33½	33	Meaux C	112		2.60	79-25	Tudorich1213GetLucky107hdT.V.Lrk112hd	Raced wide,evenly	9
Previously owned by C.R. Mac Stable Inc														
9Sep61- 8Haw	fm	1(T)	:23 :47 1:112 1:371 3↑	Chicago H 30k	2 8 109 1014 714	57¾	Meaux C	112		13.80	82-17	Tudorich1122¾NoholmeII1144RunforNurse116nk	Mild rally	13
4Sep61- 8AP	gd	1	:224 :452 1:093 1:343 3↑	Wash Park H 120k	6 11 1115 1115 1117	1115	Solomone M	114		21.60	85-08	ChiefofChiefs1124¾TlntShow110nkRunforNurs112¾	No factor	11
24Aug61- 8AP	fst	1	:232 :46 1:10 1:343 3↑	Wash Park Preview H 15k	6 9 97¼ 108¼ 99¼	78¾	Shoemaker W	120		*1.20	91-11	Currock1151RomanColonel1141¼WillYe1151¾	Showed dull try	11
9Aug61- 8AP	fst	6½f	:223 :444 1:084 1:151 3↑	Myrtlewood H 16k	8 7 118¾ 1111 1010	88½	Shoemaker W	120		5.50	91-09	JohnWilliam1121½VitalForce1142RunforNurs1221¼	No factor	11
27May61- 7Hol	fst	1 1/16	:231 :461 1:094 1:402 3↑	Californian 112k	7 8 75½ 75½ 66	47	Longden J	123		2.10	86-12	First Balcony1154¼Prove It1271½Sea Orbit1151¼	Dull try	8
20May61- 7Hol	fst	7f	:22 :441 1:083 1:211 3↑	Los Angeles H 55k	5 8 86¾ 75½ 53¼	1nk	Longden J	121		*2.30	94-11	T.V.Lark121nkNewPolicy117nkFirstBalcony1113	Up in time	9
10May61- 7Hol	fst	6f	:22 :443 :562 1:084 3↑	Hol Premiere H 22k	9 10 97½ 95¾ 85¼	42½	Longden J	125		10.40	94-13	Revel1261¼Finnegan118½Henrijan117¾	Best stride too late	10
11Mar61- 7SA	fm	*1¾(T)	2:48 3↑	S Juan Capistrano H 113k	4 9 108¾ 71¾ 62¾	44	Arcaro E	122		4.00	83-11	Don'tAlibi118noPrinceBlessed116½NotableII1063½	Mild bid	11
22Feb61- 7SA	fm	1½(T)	:462 1:10 2:002 2:26 3↑	Wash Birthday H 45k	4 5 58 51¾ 41¾	32¼	Arcaro E	124		*2.40	95-03	GeecheeLou1171½Don'tAlibi120¾T.V.Lrk124no	Good late bid	9
11Feb61- 7SA	fst	1⅛	:452 1:092 1:353 1:483 3↑	San Antonio H 57k	2 10 1115 1112 117¾	96	Arcaro E	124		5.40	83-12	AmericanComet113½HowNow1161½GreyEagle113½	Dull effort	11
2Feb61- 7SA	fst	1⅛	:461 1:104 1:361 1:49 4↑	[S]S Catalina H 27k	5 5 56 53½ 44	1¾	Arcaro E	124		*1.20	87-15	T.V.Lark124¾AmericanComet1142FreeCopy1131¾	Hard urged	6
28Jan61- 7SA	fst	1¼	:461 1:103 1:353 2:01	Maturity 167k	4 7 76½ 52½ 52¾	67¼	Arcaro E	126		3.30	87-13	Prove It1164½Prince Blessed113noGrey Eagle113½	No rally	7
14Jan61- 7SA	fst	1⅛	:464 1:11 1:354 1:473	San Fernando 54k	6 6 54½ 63¼ 44½	58½	Sellers J	126		1.90	85-11	ProveIt113½Tmpion1236PrinceBlssd1131¼	Appeared to hang	6
7Jan61- 7SA	fst	7f	:22 :443 1:092 1:221 4↑	San Carlos H 58k	12 5 1210 107¾ 85¾	21	Sellers J	125		*1.60	91-11	FirstBalcony1111T.V.Lark125nkOleFols120¾	Strong finish	12
26Dec60- 7SA	fst	6f	:214 :442 1:092 3↑	Palos Verdes H 23k	6 12 148¼ 95¾ 73½	41¾	Sellers J	123		4.70	95-10	Ole Fols117nkHenrijan114¾Finnegan118¾	Best stride late	14
15Oct60- 8Haw	my	1¼	:464 1:113 1:364 2:02 3↑	Haw Gold Cup H 144k	5 9 911 913 815	827	Sellers J	121		3.00	59-21	Kelso1176Heroshogala119½On-and-On1221¾	Disliked footing	9
8Oct60- 8Haw	fst	1⅛	:473 1:113 1:352 1:48 3↑	Handicap 10000	2 3 52¼ 64¼ 3½	2no	Sellers J	123		1.80	98-06	Hymnt115noT.V.Lrk1235RgolttoII110no	Bore in through drive	6
24Sep60- 7Aqu	fst	1¼	:472 1:111 1:354 2:011 3↑	Woodward 112k	7 7 710 78½ 79	615	Sellers J	120		4.35	87-08	SwordDancer1261½DottedSwiss1262½BaldEagle1261	Dull try	7
17Sep60- 7Atl	fm	1 3/16(T)	:463 1:12 1:372 1:57 3↑	U Nations H 100k	10 9 913 66 41½	11¼	Sellers J	120		8.30	88-12	T.V.Lark1201¼SwordDancer1271¼BllyAch122hd	Driving clear	10
5Sep60- 8AP	fst	1	:23 :452 1:092 1:341 3↑	Wash Park H 122k	1 8 98½ 74½ 52¾	1hd	Sellers J	116		*2.30	99-05	T.V.Lark116hdDottedSwiss1231¼TalentShow1181½	Up in time	9
27Aug60- 8AP	fst	1⅛	:461 1:102 1:35 1:471	American Derby 118k	8 4 33 2hd 11½	13½	Sellers J	123		*1.60	100-05	T.V. Lark1233½New Policy1202Heroshogala1111½	Ridden out	8
15Aug60- 7AP	fst	1	:23 :452 1:094 1:344	Alw 1000	2 4 44½ 31½ 1hd	1nk	Sellers J	126		2.30	96-09	T.V.Lark126nkNewPolicy1233BoldLrk1134½	Very handy score	7
23Jly60- 8AP	fst	1	:223 :452 1:103 1:361	Arl Classic 135k	12 3 32 42¼ 1hd	1¾	Sellers J	120		16.70	89-13	T.V. Lark120¾John William1232½Venetian Way1231	Driving	12
9Jly60- 7Hol	fst	1¼	:444 1:084 1:344 2:012	Hol Derby 114k	8 9 97¾ 73 41½	22	Harmatz W	122		2.20	84-12	Tempstuous1102T.V.Lrk1222BlankCheck1111	Much trouble	9
25Jun60- 7Hol	fst	1⅛	:46 1:093 1:341 1:463	Cinema H 57k	12 11 104¾ 85¾ 59½	38	Harmatz W	126		*1.80	93-06	NewPolicy1231½Tmpstuous1136½T.V.Lrk126½	From far back	13
11Jun60- 7Hol	fst	1 1/16	:231 :454 1:093 1:411	Argonaut 38k	10 7 76½ 53½ 4nk	11¾	Harmatz W	120		4.60e	89-09	T.V.Lrk1201¾Henrijan114¾NewPolcy123¾	Under mild urging	10
21May60- 8Pim	fst	1 3/16	:484 1:132 1:382 1:573	Preakness 175k	2 6 56 69¼ 69	69½	Harmatz W	126		15.30	75-22	BallyAche1264VictoriaPark1261¾CelticAsh1262¼	No factor	6
14May60- 7Pim	gd	1 1/16	:233 :463 1:111 1:442	Alw 5000	2 7 612 59½ 58½	48	Harmatz W	122		5.60	80-20	BallyAche1224DivineComedy112hdCelticAsh1104	No factor	7
23Apr60- 8BM	fst	1⅛	:464 1:112 1:362 1:49	Cal Derby 44k	1 3 61¼ 52¼ 46	53¾	Maese A	120		*.70	90-13	NobleNoor120hdHenrjn113¾GntGuy1122½	Bore out in stretch	8
Previously trained by W. Molter														
2Apr60- 8BM	fst	1 1/16	:224 :452 1:094 1:412	Tropicana 22k	6 6 79 32 1hd	11½	Maese A	118		2.90	97-08	T.V.Lark1181½FlowLine1183¼FirstBalcony1143¼	Ridden out	7
25Mar60- 7BM	fst	1 1/16	:224 :454 1:101 1:432	Alw 5000	3 1 59½ 33 21	1½	Maese A	118		2.00e	87-15	T.V.Lrk118½FlowLin1224Tmpstuous1102	Impeded,going away	6
5Mar60- 7SA	fst	1⅛	:453 1:10 1:351 1:474	S Anita Derby 130k	4 6 45½ 52¼ 46	57¾	Barrow T	118		8.60e	85-13	Tompion1184John William1183¼Eagle Admiral118½	Evenly	9
20Feb60- 7SA	fst	1 1/16	:223 :461 1:101 1:422	San Felipe H 58k	10 8 63¼ 78½ 45½	23½	Barrow T	120		13.00e	88-13	FlowLine1183½T.V.Lrk120½JohnWllm1211¼	Finished strongly	13
12Feb60- 7SA	fst	1 1/16	:244 :473 1:113 1:422	[S]Cal Br Champ 67k	1 2 1hd 2hd 21½	32¾	Valenzuela I	118		3.30	89-13	NwPolcy1181½NoblNoor1181¼T.V.Lrk118no	Weakened slightly	5
27Jan60- 7SA	fst	7f	:221 :45 1:093 1:22	San Vicente H 23k	7 3 61¼ 52½ 43½	31	Longden J	120		8.70	92-12	JohnWilliam114½NewPolicy120½T.V.Lrk1201½	Gained ground	9
14Jan60- 7SA	sly	6½f	:222 :451 1:093 1:154	San Miguel 22k	5 2 2hd 2hd 23	34¾	Longden J	126		2.80	94-14	NewPolicy118nkTompion1264½T.V.Lark126hd	Held on gamely	5
6Jan60- 6SA	fst	6f	:223 :46 1:101	Alw 10000	2 4 31½ 42½ 3½	1nk	Longden J	124		5.50	93-13	T.V. Lark124nkWarfare1241½Tompion120¾	Up final strides	8
26Dec59- 7SA	fst	7f	:223 :452 1:094 1:224	[S]Cal Breeders' Trial 27k	1 1 3nk 2hd 1hd	1¾	Shoemaker W	118		4.30	89-13	T.V. Lark118¾Noble Noor1183¼Fighting Hodge1181¼	Driving	5
Previously trained by P.F. Miller														
31Oct59- 7GS	sly	1 1/16	:23 :46 1:10 1:424	Garden State 283k	9 7 77¼ 76½ 79¼	712	Maese A	122	b	44.70	84-15	Warfare122½BallyAche1224Tompon122hd	Never close to pace	10
24Oct59- 5GS	sly	1 1/16	:233 :481 1:132 1:471	Alw 10000	5 3 2hd 21½ 23	27	Maese A	120	b	10.80	67-23	BourbonPrince1137T.V.Lark120noKeenation1106½	Went well	7
10Oct59- 8Haw	hy	1 1/16	:231 :471 1:132 1:503	Haw Juvenile H 42k	2 2 11 11 22	47	Maese A	120	b	5.80	52-41	JiveMusic114hdTonyGrff1131Ntgo1226	Set early pace,tired	13
29Sep59- 7Haw	hy	6f	:231 :464 1:134	Alw 3200	2 3 2½ 2½ 2hd	2½	Maese A	120	b	*1.30	77-33	GoodJoy116½T.V.Lark12010GrandTotal1132	Wide,sharp try	8
5Sep59- 8AP	fst	6½f	:222 :443 1:092 1:154	Wash Park Futurity 184k	1 7 56½ 610 77	99	Maese A	122		18.90	92-09	Venetian Way119½Bally Ache1193Lurullah119¾	Fell back	12
24Aug59- 8AP	sl	6f	:223 :462 1:114	Prairie State 18k	5 11 69 712 915	914	Maese A	122		6.10	71-26	VenetianWay1164Winonly116¾Lurullh116¾	Forced back early	11
1Aug59- 8AP	gd	6f	:222 :46 1:122	Arl Futurity 212k	2 6 32½ 46½ 45	1nk	Maese A	122		33.00f	82-22	T.V.Lark122nkBallyAche122noLurullh1221¼	Up final stride	20

Date / Race	Cond	Dist	Fractions / Time	Race	PP	St	1st	2nd	Str	Fin	Jockey	Wt	Eq	Odds	Speed	Top Finishers	Comment	Field
18Jly59- 7Hol	fst	6f	:214 :444 :571 1:10	Hol Juv Champ 163k	1	10	95½	129½	1414	1310	Pederson G	113		32.20	83-11	NobleNoor113½Tompion1161Warfare122nk	Raced far off pace	15
9Jly59- 7Hol	fst	5½f	:221 :444 :57 1:03	©C S Howard H 30k	7	2	1hd	21	33½	45½	Pederson G	114		5.80	91-09	Warfare114½NwPolicy1142¾Hedmstr1142¼	Weakened in drive	9
18Jun59- 7Hol	fst	5f	:22 :45 :57	©Haggin 23k	8	4	32½	34½	45½	24½	Pederson G	119		10.05	93-14	Psyche'sFirst1224½T.V.Lark119noTompion122nk	Raced wide	8
4Jun59- 7Hol	fst	5f	:221 :453 :573	©Westchester 18k	3	5	53¾	63¼	45	45	Boland W	122		9.85	90-15	BritishRoman122¾NewPolicy122¾Warfar1223½	Even effort	9
4Mar59- 1SA	fst	3f	:22 :332	©[S]Md Sp Wt	6	1			1½	1¾	Longden J	118		*1.20	--	T.V.Lark118¾Azure'sOrphan118noFay'sNghtOut118no	Driving	14
20Feb59- 1SA	fst	3f	:212 :322	©[S]Md Sp Wt	6	8			36½	25½	Longden J	118		8.75	--	Truly Truckle1185½T.V. Lark118½College Boy1185	Good try	14

Tom Rolfe

b. c. 1962, by Ribot (Tenerani)–Pocahontas, by Roman

Lifetime record: 32 16 5 5 $671,297

Own.– Powhatan

Br.– R. Guest (Ky)

Tr.– F.Y. Whiteley Jr

Date / Race	Cond	Dist	Fractions / Time	Race	PP	St	1st	2nd	Str	Fin	Jockey	Wt	Eq	Odds	Speed	Top Finishers	Comment	Field
11Nov66- 7Lrl	fm	1½Ⓣ	:494 1:142 2:284	3↑ D C Int'l 150k	5	6	78½	88½	78½	68¾	Shoemaker W	127		4.30	66-18	Behistoun1202¼Aniline1271¼Assagai1201	No serious threat	10
29Oct66- 7Lrl	fm	*1⅛Ⓣ	1:54	3↑ Alw 6500	5	7	55½	44	2½	1½	Shoemaker W	123		*.30	86-17	TomRolfe123½AlSirat1121FanJet1131½	Bobbled,hard ridden	7
1Oct66- 7Aqu	sly	1¼	:47 1:114 1:373 2:024	3↑ Woodward 112k	2	8	89¼	66¼	58	46½	Shoemaker W	126		4.20	77-24	Buckpasser121¾Royal Gunner126¾Buffle1215	Mild bid	9
17Sep66- 8Det	fst	1⅛	:461 1:103 1:373 1:49	3↑ Mich 1⅛ H 114k	1	8	77¼	61¼	31	23½	Shoemaker W	127		*.70	92-13	Stanislas1093½TomRolfe1271¾Selari1101½	In close,brushed	11
5Sep66- 7Aqu	fst	1⅛	:474 1:124 1:384 1:521	3↑ Aqueduct H 114k	8	10	1012	108½	611	1nk	Shoemaker W	127		*2.40	75-25	TomRolf127nkPluck114½BgRockCndy110hd	Up in final strides	11
27Aug66- 8AP	fst	1	:224 :442 1:08 1:324	3↑ Was Park H 109k	2	6	713	79	57	23½	Shoemaker W	128		*.50	98-07	BoldBidder1203½TomRolfe128hdTronado117nk	Sluggish start	7
17Aug66- 0AP	fst	7f	:23 :452 1:09 1:21	3↑ Alw 3000	2	2	21	21	1hd	11½	Shoemaker W	123		-	100-09	Tom Rolfe1231½Tronado123	With complete authority	2
Exhibition race run between 5th and 6th races. No wagering																		
3Aug66- 8Mth	fst	1	:242 :472 1:111 1:37	3↑ Salvator Mile H 27k	4	6	64¾	65½	54¼	1¾	Shoemaker W	126		*.40	88-19	Tom Rolfe126¾Steel Pike113nkTwin Teddy1121	Mild drive	6
23Jly66- 7Mth	fst	6f	:213 :442 1:10	4↑ Alw 6000	3	7	811	611	55¾	21¼	Shuk N	119		2.20e	91-17	VagabondPrinc1131¼TomRolf1192½Pollux119nk	Strong finish	9
3Oct65♦ Longchamp(Fr)	gd	*1½ⓉRH	2:352	3↑ Prix de l'Arc de Triomphe Stk325000						616¾	Shoemaker W	122		8.00		Sea Bird1226Reliance1225Diatome122nk	7th early,4th halfway,weakened 2f out.Anilin 5th	20
13Sep65- 8AP	fst	1¼	:48 1:112 1:361 2:003	American Derby 128k	1	2	1½	11½	1½	12½	Shoemaker W	126		*.40	101-09	TomRlfe1262½RoyalGunner1121¾Mr.Pak1123¼	Scored in hand	5
28Aug65- 8AP	fst	1	:232 :453 1:101 1:344	Arl Classic 107k	2	6	612	58	3½	1nk	Shoemaker W	124		*.30	95-13	Tom Rolfe124nkRoyal Gunner1183¾Sum Up1181½	Driving	7
7Aug65- 8AP	fst	1⅛	:47 1:104 1:35 1:472	Chicagoan 110k	3	2	25	1½	12	14	Shoemaker W	123		*.30	99-07	TomRlfe1234Gummo1205PreciousGift11410	Drew out easily	6
17Jly65- 8AP	gd	1	:224 :454 1:111 1:361	Citation H 53k	5	6	612	32½	11½	13½	Shoemaker W	126		*.50	85-16	TmRlfe1263½Mr.Clown110½PassthWord1165	Drew out easily	6
5Jun65- 7Aqu	fst	1½	:473 1:132 2:032 2:282	Belmont 147k	7	4	46	32	2½	2nk	Turcotte R	126		2.05	89-13	Hail to All126nkTom Rolfe1261First Family126¾	Game try	8
15May65- 8Pim	fst	1 3/16	:46 1:103 1:37 1:561	Preakness 180k	6	5	59	52¾	11½	1nk	Turcotte R	126		3.60	92-15	TomRlfe126nkDapperDan1264HaltoAll126nk	Long,hard drive	9
1May65- 7CD	fst	1¼	:471 1:114 1:37 2:011	Ky Derby 154k	9	7	54	42½	33	32¼	Turcotte R	126		5.60	92-05	Lucky Debonair126nkDapperDan1262TomRolfe1261	Game try	11
24Apr65- 7CD	fst	7f	:224 :46 1:10 1:224	Alw 6000	6	4	66½	3½	11½	11¾	Turcotte R	122		2.50	93-13	Tom Rolfe1221¾Native Charger1221¼Narushua1131	In hand	7
10Apr65- 9Lrl	gd	1 1/16	:231 :471 1:131 1:45	Chesapeake 34k	2	8	85½	32½	2½	12¾	Turcotte R	119		*1.20	92-16	TomRlfe1192¾IsleofGreece1193RepublcnWy1131½	Mild drive	8
3Apr65- 8Lrl	fst	1	:231 :463 1:122 1:383	Alw 7500	4	7	52½	2hd	1½	11	Ferraro R	121		*1.10	90-16	TomRolfe1211UncleWillieM.1182AppleCore1122½	Mild drive	7
24Mar65- 7Aqu	gd	7f	:223 :453 1:102 1:233	Bay Shore 29k	1	7	76¼	55	49	39½	Shoemaker W	120		*1.20	78-24	FlagRaiser1145½TurntoRson1114TomRolf1202	Sluggish start	7
3Mar65- 7Bow	fst	6f	:23 :47 1:122	Alw 6000	7	4	43½	55½	31½	1nk	Turcotte R	122		*.40	85-22	TomRolfe122nkIndeedIDo1191¼GreySpot1161¼	Clever score	7
5Oct64- 7Aqu	fst	7f	:224 :46 1:11 1:234	Cowdin 67k	8	5	63¾	62	1hd	12½	Turcotte R	114		12.80	87-21	TomRolfe1142½Sadair1241RoyalGunnr1176	Wide into stretch	8
26Sep64- 7Aqu	fst	6½f	:22 :45 1:093 1:16	Futurity 138k	4	5	56	56	44½	33½	Shoemaker W	122		18.90	96-10	BoldLad1221¼NativeCharger1222¼TomRolfe1225½	Late rally	5
12Sep64- 8AP	fst	7f	:223 :452 1:103 1:232	Arl-Wash Futurity 349k	7	12	128¾	1113	611	58½	Turcotte R	122		10.50	81-12	Sadair1222¼Umbrella Fella1222¼Royal Gunner1222½	Wide	14
26Aug64- 8AP	fst	6½f	:224 :453 1:104 1:171	©Fut Trial 56k	7	8	911	811	66½	44	Turcotte R	114		24.80e	86-15	RoyalGunner116nkI'mNashville1162½UmbrllFll1201¼	Rallied	10
15Aug64- 4AP	fst	6f	:221 :46 1:104	Alw 5000	1	5	35½	36	35	47	Turcotte R	119		3.20	82-14	Hempen1163½Olympia Tiger1163½My Lark111hd	Well up,tired	7
27Jun64- 3Del	fst	5½f	:224 :474 1:064	Alw 4000	6	4	62¼	75	52¾	11½	Turcotte R	115		*.70	87-17	TomRolfe1151½EvilWeevil1151WazaOurs1151½	Clear at wire	8
13Jun64- 7Del	fst	5½f	:22 :454 1:043	©Christiana 25k	11	10	86¾	57	511	35½	Turcotte R	116		5.50e	92-15	Shannon Run116½Time Tested1195Tom Rolfe1163½	Late bid	11
6Jun64- 3Del	fst	5f	:231 :48 1:002	Md Sp Wt	6	4	44	42	22½	13	Turcotte R	120		*2.30	87-21	TomRolfe1203ReasonablyFair1201½Amiri1204	Scored easily	8
12May64- 3Pim	fst	5f	:234 :474 1:01	©Md Sp Wt	2	3	51¼	511	37	22	Carrozella M	120		*1.40	88-24	ArtTheft1202TomRolfe1201BigRockCandy1204	Closed fast	9
27Apr64- 3Pim	fst	5f	:242 :483 1:013	©Md Sp Wt	11	8	63½	47½	34½	31¾	Ferraro R	120		*1.70	85-18	Cosimo1201Art Theft120¾Tom Rolfe1202	Finished very fast	11

Top Knight

ch. c. 1966, by Vertex (The Rhymer)–Ran–Tan, by Summer Tan

Lifetime record: 46 11 6 8 $545,685

Own.– Ardwin Farm

Br.– Steven B. Wilson (Fla)

Tr.– G.W. Taylor

Date / Race	Cond	Dist	Fractions / Time	Race	PP	St	1st	2nd	Str	Fin	Jockey	Wt	Eq	Odds	Speed	Top Finishers	Comment	Field
9Aug75- 8Nar	fst	6f	:222 :453 1:11	3↑ Alw 4800	5	3	42	48	411	511½	Lapensee M	120	b	9.00	79-21	El Arish119½Admiral's Notion1098Sadye's Reveler1141		5
4Aug75- 8Nar	fst	5½f	:224 :453 :573 1:041	3↑ Alw 4800	5	7	614	614½	715	79	Thomason WG	116	b	9.20	92-11	Measurator1126Divorce Trial116hdMore Cricket116½		7
4Jly75-11Suf	fst	1 70	:23 :462 1:113 1:43	4↑ Alw 7000	4	3	48	57½	57¾	45	Greco T	111	b	16.90	80-21	Megotreat1161Brilliant Mist116noAm Siam1224	No threat	8
14Jun75- 7LD	sly	1	:223 :472 1:133 1:421	3↑ Handicap 7500	8	5	510	512	57½	59	Greco T	108	b	12.40	64-26	BarleyLane112nkCountofWinloc123nkHarpyEgl1158	No factor	8
31May75- 8LD	fst	7f	:233 :474 1:14 1:272	3↑ Alw 5000	5	3	57½	67	64¼	32¾	Greco T5	111	b	*1.60	75-17	DocHoss114nkPunchoutCowboy1092½TopKnight111nk	Rallied	6
24May75- 8LD	fst	7f	:233 :47 1:131 1:261	3↑ Alw 5000	5	4	510	613	410	46	Greco T5	111	b	*1.10	78-21	Megotreat1143Misty Plumage122½Motor Ting1142½	Dull	6
10May75- 7LD	fst	7f	:233 :472 1:132 1:264	3↑ Alw 4800	2	1	33	32	12	17	Greco T5	109	b	5.20	81-26	TpKnight1097EarlyRythm116¾KentuckyTip1191½	Drew clear	9
23Apr75- 8Suf	fst	1 70	:24 :474 1:124 1:44	4↑ Alw 5500	4	4	57½	59½	48	47¾	Marchese P	114	b	9.40	72-25	JimmyMcDaniel1222¾TakonII1121¾NygeiaRoad1123¼	No mishap	6
10Mar75- 8Suf	fst	6f	:222 :451 1:103	4↑ Alw 5000	2	7	712	713	711	67	Marchese P	113	b	9.80	81-23	Bobby More1131¼Grey Corner119½Spicer Brook1161¼	Outrun	7
20Feb75- 8LD	fst	7f	:251 :50 1:184 1:33	4↑ Alw 3700	3	2	3½	46½	55¾	3½	Marchese P	114	b	*2.00	49-45	MommaPhenie114½Lacewood114noTpKnight114nk	Closed well	6
1Feb75- 8LD	fst	7½f	:222 :483 1:154 1:364	4↑ Alw 3700	4	5	513	59	46½	313	Marchese P	114	b	*1.20	56-33	Harpy Eagle119½Bold Kip11912Top Knight1147	No threat	6
17Jan75- 8LD	fr	7f	:23 :462 1:124 1:263	4↑ Alw 3800	6	2	47	414	34	21	Marchese P	114	b	2.00	81-21	Megotreat1221Top Knight114nkBold Kip1152	Gamely	6
7Dec74- 8LD	fst	7½f	:224 :481 1:15 1:37	3↑ Alw 3500	4	5	616	714	58¾	33¼	Marchese P	114	b	*1.50	65-33	Motor Ting114¾Dennis Beau1142½Top Knight1142¼	Rallied	7
29Nov74- 7LD	fst	5f	:224 :473 1:003	3↑ Alw 3800	5	10	1010	1014	911	85¼	Marchese P	114	b	4.70	79-24	Hi Ole Man1131¾[D]Sir Eagle1101½Pooja115½	No factor	10
Previously owned by Estate of S.B. Wilson																		
3Jun73- 9Suf	fst	6f	:221 :443 1:102	3↑ Handicap 9000	3	7	77½	710	511	45	Capalbo P	114	b	12.90	84-15	ReneDepot1203LatestThing1121¾CashonDelivry113nk	Rallied	7
19May73- 7LD	fst	1	:224 :463 1:114 1:394	3↑ Handicap 7500	2	3	45½	47½	47	54½	Martin RJ	115	b	2.10	80-24	ImmediateJoy1121RiskyAlibhai120½RunningBear1241	Tired	7
5May73- 7LD	fst	7½f	:223 :463 1:121 1:33	3↑ Handicap 7500	6	4	21	2hd	1hd	31	Martin RJ	116	b	3.00	87-22	Ahira113¾Running Bear124nkTop Knight1161¼	Weakened	7
28Apr73- 7LD	sly	1	:231 :473 1:123 1:403	3↑ Alw 5000	5	2	23½	24	46½	522	Martin RJ	116	b	*1.00	59-30	ImmediateJoy114hdMotorTing1148CircusFle1147	Early speed	6
3Mar73- 7Bow	fst	1 1/16	:231 :463 1:104 1:424	3↑ J B Cmpbll H (Div 1)-G2	10	9	911	911	1116	1121	Martin RJ	112	b	13.70	73-16	Vertee1163¾Amber Hawk112½Favorecidian1152½	Far back	12
24Feb73- 7Bow	fst	7f	:231 :46 1:11 1:242	4↑ Alw 10000	7	3	54	56	56½	62½	Martin RJ	119	b	3.50	80-24	Mister Diz112¾[D]Stomp and Go119hdSunny Lad119¾	Wide	8
10Feb73- 6Bow	fst	1 1/16	:233 :47 1:112 1:431	3↑ Handicap 12000	7	4	31½	2hd	14	13½	Martin RJ	113	b	6.80	92-16	TopKnight1133½HighTrapper1072¾JetaBit1072¾	Ridden out	7
27Jan73- 6Bow	sly	1 1/16	:234 :471 1:114 1:434	4↑ Alw 12000	4	3	24	24	25	48¼	Martin RJ	114	b	4.00	81-22	Delay1198Festive Mood117nkNative Heir119no	Tired	7
20Jan73- 7Bow	gd	1 1/16	:244 :49 1:141 1:473	4↑ Alw 12000	4	5	2hd	2½	1½	31¾	Martin RJ	119	b	2.60	68-28	EllensReason1191MajstcRod119¾TpKnght1191¼	Drifted wide	9
2Jan73- 6Bow	gd	6f	:223 :461 1:12	3↑ S Maryland H (Div 1) 16k	5	5	59	64½	52½	42½	DeSpirito A	114	b	4.40	80-30	Penholder114hdSunny Lad1111Burning On1101½	Evenly	6
2Dec72- 8LD	gd	7f	:24 :481 1:152 1:29	3↑ Alw 4000	6	5	513	511	45½	11½	DeSpirito A	116	b	*.30	70-36	Top Knight1161½Mediate122hdEd n Mert1161½	Driving	6
23Nov72- 8LD	fst	7f	:241 :48 1:132 1:263	3↑ Alw 4000	6	3	11½	12½	15	19½	DeSpirito A	114	b	*.80	82-23	Top Knight1149½Mediate1222Hard Joe1143	Ridden out	7
10Nov72- 7LD	fst	5f	:223 :464 :592	3↑ Alw 4000	5	3	35	38	36	24	DeSpirito A	114	b	*1.50	86-27	Dream Bar1134Top Knight1142Hannibob1162	Gamely	7
9Jly72- 7Suf	fst	6f	:222 :451 1:102	3↑ Alw 4000	4	5	57½	711	813	89¼	Miller W	114	b	*.40	80-18	GoodProfit1142WindonTid1171½NorthrnPrd1142½	Dull effort	8
2Jly72- 7Suf	fst	6f	:22 :451 1:104	4↑ Alw 4200	2	2	33	2hd	1hd	21	Miller W	115	b	2.10	86-14	Black Pond1191Top Knight1155Funbun Star1121½	Gamely	6
3Jun72- 7Suf	fst	6f	:22 :442 1:10	4↑ Alw 4500	5	7	55½	56½	48	610	Carrozella M	112	b	*1.20	81-14	Black Pond122¾Not Boistrous1224½Last Dance1221½	Bled	8
Previously trained by R. Metcalf																		

5Jly69- 8Mth	fst	1 1/16	:234 :472 1:111 1:42	Lamplighter H 27k	4 6 69½ 611 67½ 411	Ycaza M	125	b	*.90	84-22	AlHattab1244PrimeFool113noMr.Leadr1137 Dull performance 7
17May69- 8Pim	fst	1 3/16	:464 1:112 1:37 1:553	Preakness 182k	1 3 44¼ 31 44 48	Ycaza M	126	b	2.90	87-17	Majestic Prince126hdArts and Letters1264Jay Ray1264 8
			Bore out start								
3May69- 8CD	fst	1¼	:48 1:122 1:373 2:014	Ky Derby 155k	1 3 22 45½ 511 513	Ycaza M	126	b	2.30	78-11	MajesticPrince126nkArtsandLetters126½Dike12610 Gave way 8
29Mar69- 9GP	fst	1⅛	:482 1:12 1:361 1:482	Florida Derby 121k	1 2 2½ 2hd 13 15	Ycaza M	122	b	*1.10	92-13	TopKnight1225ArtsandLetters1222½AlHattab1221 Handily 5
			Previously owned by S.B. Wilson								
4Mar69- 8Hia	fst	1⅛	:462 1:103 1:352 1:474	Flamingo 146k	5 3 32½ 31 2hd 12	Ycaza M	122	b	*1.40	96-15	TpKnight1222ArtsandLetters122½BeauBrummel122¾ Driving 12
19Feb69- 8Hia	fst	1⅛	:47 1:114 1:363 1:493	Everglades 32k	4 4 43¼ 43½ 34½ 23	Rotz JL	122	b	*1.50	84-21	ArtsandLettrs1123TpKnight1222AlHattab119½ Ducked out 12
5Feb69- 8Hia	fst	7f	:223 :452 1:102 1:224	Bahamas (Div 2) 25k	1 8 69½ 610 32½ 1½	Ycaza M	122	b	2.20	94-14	[D]Top Knight122½Fast Hilarious1173King of the Castle113hd 9
			Disqualified and placed third								
16Nov68- 8GS	fst	1 1/16	:233 :473 1:12 1:443	Garden State 312k	3 6 66¼ 66¼ 45½ 31¾	Ycaza M	122	b	*.40	80-20	BeauBrumml1221¾Stretchapoint122noTpKnight1222 Rallied 10
12Oct68- 7Bel	fst	1	:23 :46 1:102 1:351	Champagne 170k	2 2 22 1hd 11 13½	Ycaza M	122	b	.80	98-14	TpKnight1223½BeauBrumml1221½KngEmprr12220 Mild drive 4
21Sep68- 7Bel	fst	6½f	:23 :461 1:10 1:161	Futurity 142k	1 6 41½ 31 12 16	Ycaza M	122	b	*.60	99-14	Top Knight1226True North122½Never Confuse1223½ Easily 6
24Aug68- 6Sar	fst	6½f	:23 :453 1:094 1:16	Hopeful 123k	11 4 42 53 2hd 12½	Ycaza M	122	b	2.90	98-06	TopKnight1222½Reviewer1224Bushido1221½ Won going away 11
10Aug68- 2Sar	fst	5½f	:222 :453 :573 1:034	Alw 7000	4 1 31 1hd 13 16	Ycaza M	119	b	*1.90	98-07	Top Knight1196Flagstaff1221½Never Confuse122no Easily 11
27Jly68- 8Mth	fst	6f	:214 :444 1:102	Sapling 114k	6 10 1013 1014 85¾ 65¾	Gustines H	122	b	3.40	84-15	Reviewer1222Night Invader122noAl Hattab122nk No threat 10
1Jly68- 7Aqu	fst	5½f	:221 :453 :572 1:031	Tremont 33k	3 3 42½ 31½ 21½ 2no	Baeza B	114	b	1.60	97-08	Buck Run114noTop Knight1148Virginia Delegate114¾ Sharp 5
14Jun68- 4Bel	sly	5½f	:224 :46 :574 1:04	©Md Sp Wt	8 5 12 13 16 115	Gustines H	122	b	*2.70	101-10	TopKnight12215BorninaTrunk1221VirginiaDelgt1222½ Easily 10
3Jun68- 5Mth	fst	5f	:231 :473 1:00	©Md Sp Wt	8 11 1010 65¾ 55 22½	Kassen D	118	b	7.80	87-14	Dot Ed's Bluesky1182½Top Knight118hdFunny Business1182½ 12
			Gamely								

Tosmah

b. f. 1961, by Tim Tam (Tom Fool)–Cosmah, by Cosmic Bomb

Own.– Briardale Farm

Br.– Eugene Mori (Ky)

Tr.– J.W. Mergler

Lifetime record: 39 23 6 2 $612,591

2Jly66- 8Mth	fst	1 1/16	:233 :47 1:112 1:433 3↑	ⒻMolly Pitcher H 38k	3 3 31½ 31½ 34½ 68¾	Boulmetis S	127	b	*.80	78-15	Discipline117nkStraightDeal1203½Lovejoy1122 Lost action 8
18Jun66- 8AP	fst	1	:223 :443 1:081 1:331 3↑	Equipoise Mile H 55k	5 2 22 23 22½ 2¾	Boulmetis S	119	b	4.40	99-11	Hedevar116¾Tosmah1192½Bold Bidder12410 Wide in rally 11
30May66- 7Aqu	fst	1	:221 :44 1:08 1:341 3↑	Metropolitan H 115k	5 5 55 56½ 88 89½	Boulmetis S	121	b	6.60	87-13	Bold Lad1322½Hedevar1132½Tio Viejo115no Never a threat 11
21May66- 8GS	fst	6f	:22 :453 1:10 3↑	ⒻColonial H 28k	5 8 86¾ 63 2hd 11½	Boulmetis S	125	b	*.90	94-18	Tosmah1251½WildNote1161Cohasst114no With something left 8
16Apr66- 8Bow	fst	1 1/16	:24 :482 1:123 1:442 3↑	J B Campbell H 114k	5 2 2½ 2hd 2hd 1no	Boulmetis S	118	b	9.10	91-20	Tsmh118noJustAbout1161¼Trondo1161¾ Well ridden to prevail 10
9Apr66- 8Bow	fst	7f	:223 :45 1:102 1:232 3↑	ⒻBarbara Fritchie H 59k	10 1 41½ 41½ 3nk 11	Boulmetis S	121	b	4.10	96-14	Tosmah12111Queen Empress1231½Privileged111nk Handily 12
2Mar66- 8Hia	fst	1⅛	:47 1:11 1:372 1:502 3↑	ⒻBlack Helen H 62k	9 7 76½ 64 21½ 31¾	Ussery R	115	b	2.80	81-13	WhataTreat1201¾AlondraII110hdTosmah1151 Hung in drive 11
16Feb66- 8Hia	fst	7f	:231 :453 1:103 1:231 3↑	ⒻColumbiana H 30k	5 4 63½ 53½ 2hd 2½	Ussery R	117	b	*1.50	92-17	Gold Digger112½Tosmah1172½Queen Empress1201 Game try 9
8Feb66- 8Hia	fst	7f	:232 :454 1:101 1:232 4↑	ⒻAlw 8000	2 4 1½ 1½ 11½ 2no	Boulmetis S	113	b	2.40	92-13	Queen Empress113noTosmah113nkWhat a Treat1193 Game try 7
17Jan66- 9Hia	fst	6f	:221 :452 1:103 3↑	RylPnciana H (Div 2) 20k	5 7 75¾ 56 611 88¼	Boulmetis S	120	b	2.80	83-18	TimeTested121noBayPhantom1174SkyWonder113no Dull 9
6Nov65- 6GS	fst	6f	:224 :452 1:10 4↑	Alw 5500	3 3 1hd 1hd 11½ 14	Boulmetis S	119	b	*.40	94-21	Tosmh1194Receptiv113¾Communqu1162½ Handy winner 6
16Oct65- 8GS	fst	1⅛	:48 1:12 1:371 1:494 3↑	ⒻVineland H 56k	4 1 14 12 1½ 32½	Boulmetis S	122	b	2.00	85-21	Steeple Jill1232Cordially113½Tosmah1221 Weakened late 8
9Oct65- 8Atl	fst	7f	:222 :45 1:10 1:233 3↑	ⒻParkway H 24k	5 10 911 912 610 57½	Boulmetis S	134	b	*1.10	77-13	Juanita1155Mighty Happy1152½Lovejoy114no Dwelt at start 11
27Sep65- 7Aqu	fst	1⅛	:463 1:104 1:36 1:491 3↑	ⒻBeldame 82k	2 3 31 2hd 52½ 65	Boulmetis S	123	b	*1.10	85-19	What a Treat118noSteeple Jill123½Straight Deal1181½ 6
			Bumped start,rushed up wide,tired,swerved stretch								
20Sep65- 7Aqu	fst	1	:223 :444 1:084 1:351 3↑	ⒻMaskette H 28k	3 2 2½ 2hd 2hd 1no	Boulmetis S	128	b	*.80	92-16	Tosmah128noAffectionately1283Straight Deal113½ All out 9
9Sep65- 8Atl	fst	7f	:222 :451 1:092 1:22 3↑	ⒻAlw 4000	4 4 11½ 15 18 19	Boulmetis S	117	b	*.40	93-16	Tosmah1179I Deceive1132Road to Romance1173½ Eased up 8
27Jan65- 8Hia	fst	7f	:232 :46 1:104 1:24 3↑	ⒻColumbiana H 31k	8 6 31 22 44½ 65½	Boulmetis S	128	b	*.80	83-19	OldHat124¾MiamiMood1111½SteeplJll118½ Gave way stretch 10
31Oct64- 8GS	fst	1 1/16	:231 :461 1:10 1:414	ⒻJersey Belle 28k	1 1 12 14 12 11¾	Boulmetis S	124	b	*.30	99-14	Tosmah1241¾SteepleJill1148OpenFire112hd Cleverly ridden 7
17Oct64- 8GS	sly	1⅛	:472 1:121 1:39 1:523 3↑	ⒻVineland H 57k	2 1 13 14 14 2hd	Boulmetis S	126	b	*.40	74-32	Tona113hdTosmah1264Star Maggie1152½ Tired under impost 7
12Oct64- 8GS	fst	6f	:213 :441 1:084	Quaker City H 30k	12 11 95 54 1½ 12¾	Boulmetis S	124	b	*1.10	100-04	Tosmah1242¾Reely Beeg115hdVastland1101¾ Ridden out 14
16Sep64- 7Aqu	fst	1⅛	:474 1:112 1:361 1:493 3↑	ⒻBeldame 81k	2 2 11 16 16 14	Boulmetis S	118	b	*.50	93-13	Tosmah1184Miss Cavandish11810Castle Forbes1182½ Easily 5
5Sep64- 7Aqu	fst	1	:23 :454 1:103 1:363 3↑	ⒻMaskette H 30k	8 2 2½ 2hd 13 16	Boulmetis S	123	b	*.75	85-21	Tosmah1236Old Hat1172Snow Scene II1132 Speed in reserve 13
15Aug64- 8AP	fst	1⅛	:47 1:11 1:362 1:492 3↑	ⒻMatron H 81k	10 2 2hd 13 13 1½	Boulmetis S	117	b	*2.40	89-14	Tosmah117½Old Hat116½Nubile111½ Kept to a hard drive 10
8Aug64- 8AP	fst	1	:23 :454 1:104 1:361	Arl Classic 114k	5 1 3nk 14 14 12½	Boulmetis S	115	b	7.90	88-19	Tosmah1152½Lt.Stevens118noCloseBy1201¼ Drew out easily 10
25Jly64- 8AP	sl	7f	:224 :46 1:12 1:244	Warren Wright H 34k	2 6 1hd 1½ 2hd 21¼	Boulmetis S	118	b	*1.60	82-24	Cap Size1241¼Tosmah1183Pollux1143½ Set pace,game effort 11
1Jly64- 7Aqu	fst	6f	:213 :443 1:101 3↑	ⒻLiberty Belle H 27k	3 4 2hd 11 13 12	Boulmetis S	120	b	*.35	92-17	Tosmah1202Look Ma1101½Lizzie Tish111no Was ridden out 8
24Jun64- 8Mth	sly	6f	:22 :45 1:102	ⒻMiss Woodford 16k	6 1 1hd 12 14 14½	Boulmetis S	121	b	*.30	90-20	Tosmah1214½FlaminHat1182Silwall1154 Long lead,galloping 6
17Jun64- 7Mth	fst	6f	:221 :444 1:091	ⒻAlw 7500	6 1 11 12 16 110	Boulmetis S	124	b	*.50	96-16	Tosmah12410Redpoll1214Flamin Hat121nk Eased up at end 6
16May64- 7GS	fst	6f	:214 :443 1:101 3↑	ⒻColonial H 29k	4 7 3nk 11½ 13 11½	Boulmetis S	115	b	*1.70	93-18	Tosmah1151½LookMa1103LatinWalk111nk Under a mild drive 11
2May64- 8GS	fst	6f	:22 :45 1:103	ⒻBetsy Ross 29k	6 4 2hd 12½ 11 2½	Boulmetis S	121	b	*1.20	90-18	Nilene Wonder116½Tosmah121¾Ironshire1161½ Game effort 11
25Apr64- 6GS	fst	6f	:222 :452 1:11	ⒻAlw 5500	4 4 2hd 1hd 2½ 41½	Boulmetis S	121	b	*.40	87-13	Grey Sibling121½Silwall113noRedpoll1211 Used up in lead 7
26Oct63- 8GS	fst	1 1/16	:231 :463 1:111 1:452	ⒻGardenia 168k	9 5 1hd 1hd 21½ 86½	Boulmetis S	122	b	*1.60	76-14	CastlForbs119hdBlueNorthr119noMssCvndsh119hd Impeded 15
18Oct63- 8GS	fst	1	:223 :452 1:10 1:363	ⒻAlw 10000	4 1 14 12 1½ 1hd	Boulmetis S	119	b	*.50	99-16	Tosmah119hdBlueNorther1172¾CastlForbs116¾ Kept to drive 9
5Oct63- 7Aqu	fst	1	:222 :444 1:091 1:36	ⒻFrizette 119k	3 1 12½ 13 14 11	Boulmetis	119	b	*.45	88-13	Tosmah1191Beautiful Day119hdCastle Forbes1192½ Driving 10
25Sep63- 7Aqu	fst	7f	:22 :442 1:091 1:23	ⒻAstarita (Div 2) 22k	8 2 2hd 1½ 16 15	Boulmetis S	119	b	*1.40	91-12	Tosmah1195Beautiful Day119hdTeo Pepi1162 Bore in,easily 9
18Sep63- 8Atl	sly	6f	:223 :462 1:123	ⒻMermaid 17k	9 1 1hd 15 14 110	Boulmetis S	116	b	*.40	79-33	Tosmah11610MyCard113¾LaughingJudy1101 Speed in reserve 9
27Aug63- 5Atl	fst	6f	:221 :452 1:104	ⒻAlw 4500	5 2 1½ 14 14 15	Boulmetis S	117	b	*.90	88-18	Tsmh1175First Orbit117½Wendy's Watch1194 Won eased up 6
8Aug63- 5Atl	fst	6f	:222 :454 1:114	ⒻAlw 4000	4 6 2½ 14 15 13	Boulmetis S	121	b	*.90	83-22	Tosmah1213Cadabra1178Really Trying1171¼ Scored eased up 9
26Jly63- 5Mth	fst	5½f	:22 :452 1:054	ⒻMd Sp Wt	5 4 1hd 11½ 14 13½	Boulmetis S	117	b	*1.50	88-14	Tosmah1173½Lovejoy1171½Isaduchess1172 Speed in reserve 9

Vitriolic

b. c. 1965, by Bold Ruler (Nasrullah)–Sarcastic, by Ambiorix

Own.– O. Phipps

Br.– Ogden Phipps (Ky)

Tr.– E.A. Neloy

Lifetime record: 21 9 4 2 $453,558

30May69- 7Aqu	fst	1	:224 :453 1:10 1:34 3↑	Metropolitan H 116k	10 7 99 86½ 79 711½	Baeza B	119	b	3.70	85-22	Arts and Letters1112½Nodouble1293½Promise1191 11
			In close,no response								
13May69- 7Aqu	fst	1	:233 :461 1:103 1:353 3↑	Alw 15000	7 8 75½ 42 13 12	Belmonte E	117	b	*1.00	89-15	Vitriolic1172Best Turn1092Virginia Delegate1093 Driving 8
7May69- 6Aqu	fst	6f	:221 :454 1:102 3↑	Alw 12000	6 6 69 45½ 3½ 12	Belmonte E	119	b	3.50	91-13	Vitriolic1192VelvetFlash1191½Call a Cop1211½ Handy score 8
20Feb69- 8Hia	fst	1⅛	:483 1:122 1:372 1:494 4↑	Alw 7000	5 2 42½ 45 35 68½	Baeza B	113	b	*1.70	77-19	San Roque1137Futura Bold116noSubpet1171 Finished early 8
4Feb69- 7Hia	fst	6f	:222 :452 1:094 4↑	Alw 8000	5 7 812 79½ 711 66¼	Baeza B	113	b	*1.50	89-17	Advance Party1123More Scents112noAir King II1141½ 8
			Finished well,worked extra ¼								
25Jan69- 9Hia	fst	7f	:231 :452 1:10 1:223 4↑	Alw 7500	9 3 75¼ 68 55½ 44½	Baeza B	115	b	*1.30	90-16	PalaisdeGlace115hdPerfectTan1173Mr.Brogann1151½ Rallied 10
21Feb68- 8Hia	fst	1⅛	:452 1:091 1:351 1:49	Everglades 30k	3 7 718 713 58 43¼	Baeza B	122	b	*.60	87-14	ForwrdPass117hdWiseExchang112nkMastrBold1153 Bumped 8
12Feb68- 8Hia	fst	7f	:224 :45 1:093 1:222	Alw 6500	3 7 78¾ 68 21½ 11	Baeza B	122	b	*1.10	97-07	Vitriolic1221Master Bold119nkIron Ruler1193½ Going away 8
4Nov67- 8Lrl	gd	1 1/16	:231 :463 1:124 1:451	Pim-Lrl Futurity 180k	4 6 78¾ 65½ 1hd 13	Baeza B	122	b	*.60e	91-15	Vitriolic1223T.V.Commercil1222[D]FmlyFun1222½ Mild drive 7
14Oct67- 7Aqu	fst	1	:231 :451 1:09 1:343	Champagne 179k	5 5 511 57½ 34½ 12	Baeza B	122	b	1.50	95-11	Vitriolic1222Iron Ruler1224½Captain's Gig1222½ In hand 5
5Oct67- 7Aqu	fst	7f	:224 :452 1:092 1:213	Cowdin 71k	1 6 52½ 53¼ 32 23	Baeza B	124	b	*.80	95-14	Iron Ruler1173Vitriolic1241¾Family Fun1141 No excuse 6

23Sep67- 7Aqu	fst	6½f	:223 :454 1:093 1:154	Futurity 146k	3	6	54½	55	33½	23	Baeza B	122	*.70	98-13	Captain'sGig1223Vitriolic122¾ExclusiveNatv1225½	Rallied	6
9Sep67- 8AP	fst	7f	:224 :454 1:112 1:24	Arl Wash Fut (Div 2) 185k	7	8	817	810	1hd	13½	Shoemaker W	122	*1.30	85-22	Vitriolic1223½ExclusvNtv1224½[D]CourtRcss1221	Ridden out	9
30Aug67- 8AP	fst	6½f	:232 :471 1:123 1:184	©Fut Trial (Div 2) 21k	5	9	812	74¾	21½	1½	Ussery R	122	*1.70	81-22	Vitriolic122½Frosty Dear1135Royal Cap113nk	Cleverly	9
16Aug67- 7Sar	fst	6f	:221 :45 1:102	Sar Spl 35k	3	7	813	66	42½	1no	Baeza B	114	5.30	96-08	Vitriolic114noExclusiveNative122nkPappaStev1143	Driving	9
7Aug67- 7Sar	fst	5½f	:221 :45 :571 1:033	Sanford 34k	5	6	57	36	34½	24	Ussery R	116	2.50	95-15	ExclusiveNative1154Vitriolic116¾ForwardPss12010	Rallied	6
31Jly67- 7Sar	fst	5½f	:222 :453 :574 1:041	Flash 23k	4	4	55	53½	42	31½	Gustines H	113	3.10	94-12	ForwardPass114noPappaSteve1151½Vitriolc1131	Closed fast	7
22Jly67- 3Aqu	fst	5½f	:222 :46 :582 1:05	©Md Sp Wt	3	4	58	43½	21	15	Gustines H	122	*.70	88-11	Vitriolic1225ChathamCenter1221½MaterilWtnss112no	Easily	11
17Jly67- 5Aqu	gd	5f	:224 :463 :593	Md Sp Wt	7	8	85½	77	52¾	2½	Baeza B	122	*1.50	86-15	NotBoistrous112½Vitriolic122hdArmorBearer1224½	In close	10
27Jun67- 3Aqu	fst	5½f	:222 :462 :59 1:053	©Md Sp Wt	2	11	119½	98½	43	31	Belmonte E	122	8.00	84-18	Skookum122½Noted Scholar122½Vitriolic1222½	Closed well	12
13May67- 3Aqu	fst	5f	:224 :464 :592	Md Sp Wt	2	9	98¾	1014	813	713	Baeza B	122	*2.60	75-16	Ben Ben122nkFavorable Path1222½Count Flip1223	Greenly	10

What a Treat

dkb. f. 1962, by Tudor Minstrel (Owen Tudor)–Rare Treat, by Stymie

Lifetime record: 30 11 5 4 $321,608

Own.– G.D. Widener

Br.– Erdenheim Farms Co (Ky)

Tr.– S.E. Veitch

24Nov66- 7Aqu	fst	1⅛	:473 1:114 1:37 1:493 3↑	ⒻFirenze H 56k	1	4	35	44	44	54½	Rotz JL	118	2.70e	83-21	StraightDeal1182¼Mac'sSparkler113¾BlldNut1121½	No rally	8
5Nov66- 7Aqu	fst	1¼	:481 1:122 1:371 2:022 3↑	ⒻLadies H 56k	2	1	13	1½	2½	43	Rotz JL	121	4.40e	83-13	Destro115noStraightDeal1183MissDcky109hd	Tired abruptly	8
26Oct66- 7Aqu	fm	1 1/16Ⓣ	1:44 3↑	ⒻNew York H (Div 2) 23k	5	6	76¼	86¼	53½	32	Rotz JL	121	*1.10e	84-13	SwingingMood1192ShortFall112noWhataTreat121¾	Rallied	9
7Sep66- 7Aqu	fst	1	:233 :463 1:114 1:374 3↑	ⒻMaskette H 28k	3	3	35	36	714	715	Rotz JL	123	2.90	64-30	SummerScandal1236StraightDeal119noTreachery1112½	Tired	9
22Aug66- 7Sar	sly	1⅛	:471 1:11 1:354 1:484 3↑	ⒻDiana H 28k	7	3	32	45	57½	513	Rotz JL	124	3.00	88-17	OpenFire11710ReluctantPearl1081¾Mac'sSparkler1131	Tired	8
1Aug66- 8Sar	fm	1 1/16Ⓣ	1:403 3↑	Alw 8500	9	5	511	23	12	11½	Rotz JL	113	2.80	102-00	What a Treat1131½Sky Wonder1051½Berry II1152½	Forced very wide,driving	10
20Jly66- 7Mth	fst	1 1/16	:233 :474 1:123 1:444 4↑	ⒻAlw 6000	4	4	41½	31	1hd	32½	Rotz JL	122	1.70	78-19	MissDickey1151½Lovejoy1151WhataTreat1223½	Raced outside	6
27Apr66- 7Aqu	fst	1	:24 :464 1:11 1:354 3↑	ⒻBed o' Roses H 27k	5	2	2½	2hd	1hd	21½	Rotz JL	126	*1.60e	87-18	StraightDeal1171½WhataTreat1261½QunEmprss123nk	2nd best	7
14Apr66- 7Aqu	fst	6f	:222 :452 1:102 4↑	ⒻAlw 10000	2	7	76	62¾	2hd	11	Rotz JL	118	*.80	91-17	WhataTrt1181Samarta116noTheonia1163	Going away at end	8
2Mar66- 8Hia	fst	1⅛	:47 1:11 1:372 1:502 3↑	ⒻBlack Helen H 62k	6	4	43	32	11½	11¾	Rotz JL	120	*1.60e	83-13	WhataTreat1201¾AlondraII110hdTosmh1151	Drew off readily	11
16Feb66- 8Hia	fst	7f	:231 :453 1:103 1:231 3↑	ⒻColumbiana H 30k	8	3	41½	3½	3nk	44	Rotz JL	120	2.10	89-17	Gold Digger112½Tosmah1172½QueenEmprss1201	Speed,tired	9
8Feb66- 8Hia	fst	7f	:232 :454 1:101 1:232 4↑	ⒻAlw 8000	6	3	42½	33	32	3nk	Rotz JL	119	3.90	92-13	Queen Empress113noTosmah113nkWhat a Treat1193	Gaining	7
26Jan66- 9Hia	sly	7f	:23 :454 1:104 1:232 4↑	ⒻAlw 8000	1	6	32	44½	67¼	712	Rotz JL	119	*1.60	80-17	Discipline1131¾Silwall1132½Sailor Princess1112	Gave way	8
27Sep65- 7Aqu	fst	1⅛	:463 1:104 1:36 1:491 3↑	ⒻBeldame 82k	3	2	2½	3nk	11	1no	Rotz JL	118	2.30e	90-19	WhataTreat118noSteepleJill123½StraightDeal1181½	Driving	6
4Sep65- 7Aqu	fst	1⅛	:473 1:122 1:381 1:512	ⒻGazelle H 59k	8	7	56½	42½	1½	1½	Rotz JL	123	*3.50e	79-20	WhataTreat123½Terentia118½Discipline1181½	Strong drive	13
14Aug65- 6Sar	fst	1¼	:471 1:112 1:364 2:033	ⒻAlabama 63k	4	10	106	32	3½	1nk	Rotz JL	118	*2.80e	90-06	What a Treat118nk[D]Discipline1182Terentia114½	Driving	18
5Aug65- 7Sar	fst	7f	:222 :45 1:094 1:23	ⒻTest (Div 2) 23k	2	6	52¾	53¾	43	44	Rotz JL	124	4.30	91-12	Cestrum1121½QnEmprss118½GroundControl1212	No response	9
12Jun65- 7Aqu	fst	1¼	:481 1:121 1:37 2:023	ⒻC C A Oaks 129k	1	4	43½	21½	21	22½	Rotz JL	121	3.50	82-14	Marshua1212½WhataTreat1216Terenti1212½	Clearly 2nd best	10
29May65- 7Aqu	sly	1⅛	:482 1:123 1:513	ⒻMother Goose 97k	7	4	42½	2hd	11	2no	Rotz JL	121	4.50	78-20	Cordially121noWhataTreat1211UpOars1213	Held on gamely	12
15May65- 7Aqu	fst	1	:222 :45 1:101 1:371	ⒻAcorn 58k	8	7	811	56½	32	43¼	Baeza B	121	*.95	79-20	GroundControl121nkMarshua121noUpOars1213	Bold bid,hung	10
16Apr65- 7Aqu	gd	7f	:232 :47 1:114 1:243	ⒻComely 27k	1	3	2½	1½	12	12	Rotz JL	118	*.35	83-23	What a Treat1182Equiria1135Adorable112¾	Easily the best	5
7Apr65- 7Aqu	fst	6f	:222 :46 1:102	ⒻPrioress 27k	1	4	31½	32	12	16	Rotz JL	121	2.95	91-17	WhataTreat1216Admiring1213Adorabl1216	Going away easily	6
10Feb65- 8Hia	fst	1⅛	:471 1:122 1:39 1:531	ⒻMimosa 35k	4	4	44½	22	14	11	Rotz JL	112	*.60	69-21	WhataTreat1121VassarGrad1124¾Amerivan1144½	Mild drive	9
27Jan65- 6Hia	fst	6f	:221 :454 1:121	ⒻAlw 4500	6	8	911	811	65¼	11½	Freed M5	111	*.90	83-19	WhataTreat1111½CanoeBrook116½NativPrincss1162	Cleverly	11
20Jan65- 8Hia	fst	6f	:222 :46 1:113	ⒻJasmine (Div 1) 20k	1	8	63½	42	32	2½	Rotz JL	112	4.90	85-15	WildNote114½WhataTreat1121¾FourUnits1123	Closed fast	10
29Sep64- 5Aqu	sly	7f	:224 :463 1:113 1:243	ⒻAlw 5500	8	4	31½	21½	23	25	Sorrentino M	119	2.60	78-27	Privileged1145WhtaTreat11910Ping1111½	Made game effort	8
12Sep64- 7Aqu	sl	6f	:222 :46 1:13	ⒻMatron 102k	10	6	45½	48	58½	55¾	Sorrentino M	119	13.00	72-27	Candalita1191Admiring1192½Gold Digger119nk	No mishap	10
2Sep64- 5Aqu	fst	6f	:223 :463 1:123	ⒻMd Sp Wt	2	3	42½	44	22½	1nk	Sorrentino M	119	*1.25	80-23	What a Treat119nkMerispats1195Titania1192½	Driving hard	13
19Aug64- 7Sar	fst	6f	:22 :45 1:104	ⒻAdirondack 24k	2	9	54	46	58½	58¼	Ruane J	111	12.95	86-13	Candalita1142½QueenEmpress1233Marshu123¾	Off sluggishly	9
5Aug64- 7Sar	fst	5½f	:222 :461 :581 1:044	ⒻSchuylerville 30k	2	5	62¼	75	45½	34½	Ruane J	112	12.40	88-13	Marshua1162Candalita1162½What a Treat1121	Mild late bid	12

RETURN OF THE CROWN

THE 1970'S

by Jay Hovdey

I T COULDN'T HAVE BEEN THE CULTURE. Nothing worth a damn could have come from a world oozing with the evil juju spawned by Vietnam, Watergate, gas lines, and disco. Big, bad hair was everywhere. The attorney general was going to jail. And forget about what passed as fashion. Polyester was the fabric of choice.

The sporting scene was just as much to blame. There were the quaintly anarchic Oakland A's, with their handlebar mustaches and wretched color schemes. Too weird, you say? Then take the fascist Dodgers or the autocratic Yanks, or shift gears completely and lie down with the dull Steelers, saved only by the occasional diving Swann.

These were the 1970's in America. Forgive us those trespasses. If honesty were the only policy, a rational mind would draw a line through the entire decade and pretend it all happened in a bad dream, induced by constant exposure to Bob Hope specials and the Fonz.

But there was a silver lining. There was a saving grace. With very few exceptions, through nearly every month of every year for 10 solid calendars, there was something extraordinary going on in the world of Thoroughbred racing. It was a giddy era of excess and excellence, the likes of which never will be seen again.

Okay, sure, the sixties were swell with that gang of Dr. Fager, Damascus, Buckpasser, and Kelso. And the fifties were worth a swoon or two over Native Dancer, Tom Fool, Swaps, and Nashua. But then came the morning of January 1, 1980, when the survivors of the 1970's awoke with thick tongues, heads throbbing, and still dizzy from the residue of guilty pleasures. A decade was born, a decade had died, and they looked back in wonder at what had just transpired.

"Whoa. What was that?"

It was nothing less than amazing.

The natural world pays very little attention to the artificial confines of the Roman calendar. Just because it was January did not mean that something was on the boil. In fact, the first organic moment of transcendent significance during the decade occurred just past midnight on March 30, 1970, when a chestnut colt by Bold Ruler emerged from the womb of Princequillo's daughter Somethingroyal at The Meadow, owned by Christopher Chenery, near the northern Virginia town of Doswell.

The birth of Secretariat at decade's dawn set the theme. It would require something very special to penetrate the consciousness to follow. Mere champions and run-of-the-mill classic winners need not apply. Older horses had Forego for inspiration. Young fillies could dream of growing up like Ruffian. And if young colts were intimidated by Secretariat's lofty image, they were no less daunted by the public works of Seattle Slew, Affirmed, and Spectacular Bid.

To that end, the artistic climax of the 1970's came on October 6, 1979, when the 4-year-old Affirmed defeated the 3-year-old Spectacular Bid in the Jockey Club Gold Cup at Belmont Park. The race was the perfect summation, as Affirmed handled his younger opponent by three-quarters of a length and then handed him the torch. The decade closed as it had opened, with a chestnut champion leading the way, his white beacon of a star and stripe illuminating the best parts of the game.

Affirmed, thankfully, was allowed to do what Secretariat was not: enhance his reputation beyond his accomplishments as a 3-year-old. The death of Christopher Chenery in January 1973 forced his heirs, led by Penny Chenery Tweedy, to syndicate Secretariat as a stallion in order to pay estate taxes. They were committed to his retirement at the end of the year. As a result, Uncle Sam was paid off, and history was cheated out of a 4-year-old Secretariat roaming the land, raising the bar higher and higher with each indelible stride.

Of course, by the time Secretariat completed his two seasons of 21 starts, 16 wins, three seconds, one third, $1,316,808 in earnings, the 1973 Triple Crown, and Horse of the Year in both 1972 and 1973, it was safe to say that he had nothing left to prove.

The argument was true, but it was also beside the point.

"There was an unwritten guarantee of high drama whenever he sported the blue and white

In a moment etched in time, jockey Ron Turcotte turns to the infield Teletimer to see that Secretariat has shattered the world record for a mile and a half, winning the 1973 Belmont Stakes by 31 lengths in 2:24.

Chenery blocks," wrote Charles Hatton in the 1973 edition of *The American Racing Manual.*

The Nielson ratings of Secretariat's 1973 Kentucky Derby – accomplished in a race-record 1:59⅖ by 2½ lengths over the relentless Sham – was a 16.5. The Preakness earned a 14.9, and Secretariat rewarded his loyal viewers with a move on the first turn that redefined explosive Thoroughbred power. For the Belmont, as Secretariat attempted to become the first Triple Crown winner since Citation in 1948, the ratings jumped to 17.5, representing more than 11 million homes.

Each giddy, festive atmosphere of a Secretariat appearance was laced with the tensions surrounding an animal who had been syndicated for a world-record amount of $6,080,000 at the beginning of his 3-year-old season. When Secretariat ran, *Time, Newsweek,* and *Sports Illustrated* paid serious attention, as they did with cover stories the week before he went forth to win the Belmont Stakes by 31 lengths.

The date was June 9, 1973, a bright spring day on Long Island, when Secretariat utterly justified every superlative ever hurled his way, every gallon of ink spilled in his praise, every roll of newsprint that recorded his story. He ran his first of 12 furlongs in 12⅕ seconds, accompanied by his shadow, Sham. They ran the next furlong in 11⅖, banking around the long Belmont turn. After a half-mile in 46⅕ – insane by all standards – Sham was done and Secretariat was in a race of his own.

By the time the Big Horse was over a dozen lengths clear around the final turn, the mellow tenor of Belmont announcer Chic Anderson had reached a fevered aria pitch. "He is moving like a tremendous machine!" Anderson proclaimed, unable to hide his glee. The machine continued unabated, a runaway train, and did not stop until Ron Turcotte stood in the irons to admire the final time on the infield tote board: a mile and one-half in 2:24, a world record on dirt.

It may be hard to believe, but there was no anticlimax to Secretariat. The end of his time on stage was marked by two surprising defeats – in the Whitney Stakes at Saratoga (he had a temperature) and the Woodward Stakes at Belmont (he was undertrained). But those blips retreated under the bright glare of his victory in the inaugural Marlboro Cup over his accomplished stablemate, Riva Ridge. And they disappeared completely when Secretariat concluded his career by racing on the grass and winning both the Man o' War Stakes at Belmont and then, as a tribute to trainer Lucien Laurin's homeland, the Canadian International Championship at Woodbine in Toronto.

As the Secretariat story rose and crested, the greatest sportswriters of the age weighed in. There was Red Smith, Jim Murray, Hatton, of course, and Bill Nack, whose biography, *Big Red of Meadow Stable,* told the tale from foal to finish.

Writing in *Newsweek* magazine, as Secretariat stood on the threshold of his Triple Crown, Pete Axthelm captured both the moment and the meaning in a simple handful of words: "If there is urgency in every 26-foot stride that Secretariat takes," Axthelm wrote, "there is also a rich, meandering history behind him; it is a tale of hope and vision, painstaking work and superb performance under pressure – all the elements that contribute to the fascination and beauty of the sport of racing."

In the wake of Secretariat's retirement, the game was threatened with a dire letdown. It could have been 1965 all over again, when the five-year reign of Kelso ended with a dull thud, and nothing of consequence emerged to fill the void.

But then, toward the end of 1973, a giant gelding won both the Roamer and Discovery Handicaps at Aqueduct. At the beginning of 1974, he took the Donn, the Gulfstream Park, and the Widener Handicaps in a sunny procession. A white puff of smoke appeared from the rooftop of the game. The line of succession would hold.

Forego was from the outstanding 1970 crop of 24,361 North American foals registered by The Jockey Club. In addition to Secretariat, Sham, and Forego, they grew up to be Dahlia (champion grass horse of 1975), Desert Vixen (champion 3-year-old filly of 1973 and older female of 1974), Cafe Prince (champion steeplechase horse of 1977 and '78), Shecky Greene (champion sprinter as a 3-year-old in

1973), Allez France (European champion and winner of the Prix de l'Arc de Triomphe), Ancient Title (winner of the Hollywood Gold Cup, the Whitney Handicap, and 18 other stakes), and Mr. Prospector, who enhanced his brief, brilliant career on the track by leaving an everlasting mark as a stallion.

Born on April 30, 1970, at Claiborne Farm in Kentucky, Forego was the son of the Argentine superstar Forli and the 12-year-old mare Lady Golconda, a daughter of 1954 Preakness Stakes winner Hasty Road. To stem the tide of his inordinate growth, he was gelded; and good thing, too, because his chronically troubled left front ankle was not designed to hold up under Forego's tremendous size. How big was he? In the fall of 1974, William H. Rudy of *The Blood-Horse* asked Dr. Manuel Gilman of the New York Racing Association to compare the dimensions of Forego and Secretariat.

"I can't compare him to anything," Gilman said of Forego. "No other good horse that I've ever seen has such measurements."

According to Gilman, Forego girthed 77 inches. Secretariat girthed 76. From his withers to the point

Three-time Horse of the Year Forego won Grade 1 races from 7 furlongs to 1½ miles. The oversized gelding was a champion at 7 despite numerous nagging injuries, and retired in 1978 as the second-leading money earner of all time.

of the shoulder, Forego was 31 inches, while Secretariat was 28½. In terms of length, from point of shoulder to buttocks, Gilman's tape stretched 74 inches – more than six feet! Secretariat was 69½ inches. And on the scale, Forego weighed 1,225 pounds. Secretariat, at the end of his career, weighed 1,154.

Of course, size does not matter in a racehorse unless he can pick it up and move it quickly. Though he was slow to assemble his act at age 3, Forego eventually flourished into a versatile entertainer, winning major races at 7, 8, 8½, 9, 9½, 10, and 12 furlongs. Between his victory in the Donn at the beginning of 1974 at Gulfstream Park, through the Marlboro Cup on October 2, 1976, at Belmont Park, Forego raced 30 times. He won 20, finished second four times, third four times, and fourth in the other two. There were 24 handicaps during that stretch; Forego's average assignment was 131 pounds. Of the eight handicaps he lost, he conceded 24, 22, 20, and 15 pounds to four of the horses who beat him.

Accordingly, Forego was voted Horse of the Year in 1974, 1975, and 1976. In 40 years of keeping track, only Kelso was honored more than twice. The comparisons were predictable and received with modesty by Martha Gerry, Forego's owner, and Sherrill Ward, who trained the champion during his first three campaigns.

"I don't say he's a better horse than Secretariat or Man o' War or Citation," Ward told writer Ed Comerford for *The Horseman's Journal* at the end of the 1975 season. "I can't say he's as good a gelding as Kelso, because he hasn't had the length of time to express that. But outside of Kelso, I'd measure him up to any gelding that I ever saw. I have to wonder what he would have been if he'd been sound."

Forego's unsoundness was legendary, and well documented. The enlarged sesamoid on the outside of his front left ankle created problems both fore and aft. In early 1975 he was temporarily stopped by a filling in his right hind ankle. Toward the end of 1975 the left hind flared up, but he raced on, winning the Woodward Stakes over champion Wajima and Belmont Stakes winner Avatar. Not

Nearly coal-black and more physically imposing than most colts, Ruffian was peerless and unrelenting on the racetrack.

long after that race, the left front ankle filled. His season was finished.

Ward retired at the end of 1975, suffering from a bad heart and an arthritic hip. Eddie Hayward, the trainer who beat Native Dancer with Dark Star in the 1953 Kentucky Derby, had been helping Ward with the stable. But Mrs. Gerry decided to place Forego and the rest of her small string in the hands of Frank Whiteley, the man who had trained Damascus, Tom Rolfe, and Ruffian.

Getting Forego was a mixed blessing. Whiteley could hardly do better than Ward, but he could certainly do worse.

"I just got hardheaded and thought I'd give it a try," Whiteley said. "I had nothing to lose. But when I got him he didn't have but one sound leg."

Somehow, Whiteley held Forego together through another 2½ years, 17 starts, and 11 wins. How did he do it?

"The grace of the good Lord and three hours a day on that hose," Whiteley said.

Without a doubt, Forego's best race during the Whiteley years was the 1976 Marlboro Cup, in which he carried 137 pounds on a sloppy, slippery Belmont main track before getting up to beat Honest Pleasure, winner of the '76 Travers and

champion 2-year-old colt of 1975. The margin was a very short head.

There was another race, however, that defined the impact of Forego in equally vivid terms. It was an unassuming seven-furlong allowance race designed to comfortably launch his 1977 season on May 23 at Belmont Park. Of course, he won. Bill Shoemaker was riding Forego by then, and he remembered the moment in an interview with William Leggett of *Sports Illustrated*.

"There was no betting allowed at the track that day because of a mutuel clerks' strike," Shoemaker said. "But 7,500 people showed up. It seemed everyone was down by the walking ring before the race looking at Forego. The clapping was tremendous. They just seemed to want to say thanks for all the great races he's given them."

By the summer of 1978, Forego had developed ringbone in his right hind ankle. After watching her champion beat one horse in the Suburban Handicap on July 4 at Belmont, Mrs. Gerry announced his retirement. And while his earnings of $1,938,957 fell just short of Kelso's all-time mark, on the day he retired, Forego would have won in a close ballot for the title of America's greatest gelding, with additional apologies to Old Rosebud, Exterminator, and Armed.

As the Forego saga unfolded, a filly appeared in a parallel universe.

When Ruffian was first displayed for public consideration on May 22, 1974, her purpose on this earth quickly became apparent. She was meant to reveal, once and for all, how big, how beautiful, and how fast a Thoroughbred racehorse could be, and how the combination could be deadly when taken to Ruffian's physical extremes.

The daughter of Reviewer was nearly coal black and larger than most colts. The source of her power was obvious, emanating from large hindquarters, an Olympian reach, and a chest that housed two huge, fuel-injected lungs. Her speed, however, came from a pure, natural-born action of such honeyed grace that she made even the violence of racing seem balletic and civilized.

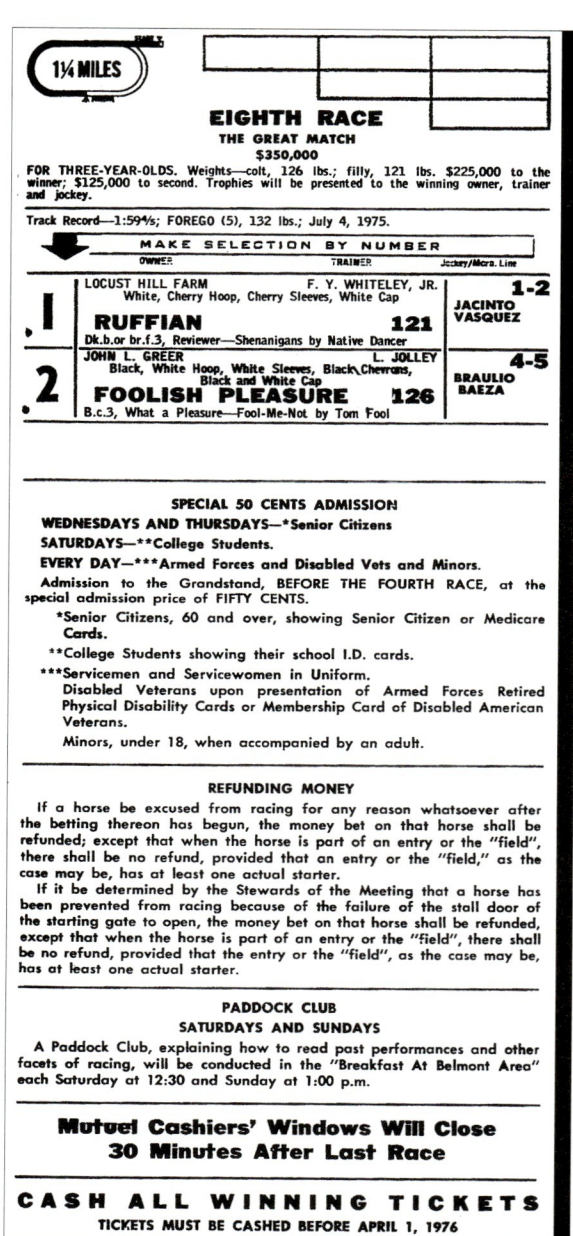

The Great Match Race between Ruffian and Kentucky Derby winner Foolish Pleasure was a spectacle replete with campaign-style buttons for the filly and the colt.

During 1974, Ruffian sliced through her 2-year-old filly rivals with merciless ease. It was five starts, five wins, and the only horse who was within earshot at the end of a race was Hot n Nasty, Dan Lasater's little flash, in the Sorority Stakes at Monmouth Park. Ruffian won the Spinaway Stakes at Saratoga by nearly 13 lengths, and she was preparing for the same type of assault on the September 26 Frizette Stakes when a hairline fracture was detected in her right hind leg. Were it not for Forego, Ruffian might have been the 1974 Horse of the Year.

In 1975, Ruffian picked up where she left off for trainer Frank Whiteley and the Locust Hill Farm of Mr. and Mrs. Stuart Janney. After an allowance win at Aqueduct in April, she won the Comely Stakes and the Acorn Stakes, then the Mother Goose and the Coaching Club American Oaks. There was really nothing left for her to do, at least among her own age and sex.

Then came the match race with Kentucky Derby winner Foolish Pleasure on July 6, 1975, an event partly inspired by the corny hype over the Billie Jean King-Bobby Riggs "Battle of the Sexes" in tennis, not to mention the nascent movement for women's rights and the success of Virginia Slims cigarettes ("You've come a long way, baby").

On July 4, at the start of that unforgettable holiday weekend, Forego carried 132 pounds to win the Brooklyn Handicap at a mile and one-quarter in a Belmont track record of 1:59⅗. Then the old champ stepped aside to make way for the match, which by then had become a media phenomenon, complete with campaign buttons, a network broadcast, and a Belmont Park crowd of 50,764.

Amid all this, there was still a testing 1¼-mile race to run. Leading up to the match, Foolish Pleasure was trained for speed by LeRoy Jolley. The tough little colt responded by seizing the lead at the start. Ruffian reacted almost too quickly to the challenge. She ducked inward slightly, straightened her course, and then rushed up to thrust her head in front. They went the first quarter, brushing against each other, in 22⅕ seconds.

The mad pace continued into the second quarter-mile, with the filly on the inside. It was at about the three-furlong mark that her right front ankle gave

The Ogden Phipps-owned Numbered Account was freakishly fast as a 2-year-old, easily winning the division title in 1971.

way, shattering the sesamoids and rupturing the supporting soft tissue structure of tendons and ligaments. By the time her jockey, Jacinto Vasquez, could get reined to a stop, she had driven the tip of the splintered cannon bone into the sandy Belmont ground.

Ruffian died as she had lived, wild-eyed and slave to no man. She survived the surgery, but in thrashing around during postoperative recovery she ripped loose the cast on her lower leg and spoiled the work of the surgeons. In later years, there would be recovery systems that might have saved her. History is full of such regrets. It was early on the morning of July 7 that Stuart Janney told the attending veterinarians that the great filly should suffer no more. Ruffian was euthanized, and with her a corner of racing was darkened forever.

Ruffian rendered the decade's other champion 3-year-old fillies pale and wan. Those who came before were quickly forgotten. Those who came after could never hope to meet such expectations. Still, they tried.

Office Queen, the champion 3-year-old filly of 1970, started 19 times that year, earning her title for persistence as much as for her victories in the Black-Eyed Susan and Mother Goose. The daughter of Fair Ruler cost just $8,500 as a 2-year-old, and she is usually lost in the shuffle, barely a scene-setter for a procession of vibrant divisional champs that included Turkish Trousers (1971), Susan's Girl (1972), Desert Vixen (1973), and Chris Evert (1974) before Ruffian.

Revidere, coming along in 1976, was certainly no slouch, and there was something comforting in the fact that she was by Reviewer and trained by Frank Whiteley's son, David.

Yet Revidere was very much her own filly. She was a tall, lanky chestnut whose debut was delayed until the spring of her 3-year-old season by growth spurts and tender ankles. Wasting no time, she promptly won her first seven starts before finishing second to that year's older female champion, Proud Delta, in the Beldame Stakes.

Revidere's next race was her best. And, for those who like their racing laced with sweet irony, it occurred in the first running of the Ruffian Stakes at Belmont Park on October 9, 1976. Revidere won by 14 lengths with Jacinto Vasquez in the saddle.

For the remainder of the decade, the 3-year-old scene was colored primarily in the devil's-red and blue of Calumet Farm and the fawn brown of the Galbreath family's Darby Dan Farm.

Calumet's Our Mims, a daughter of Herbager, won all the right races for trainer John Veitch in 1977, taking the Fantasy Stakes, the Coaching Club American Oaks, the Alabama Stakes, and finally the Delaware Handicap by a nose over the older filly Mississippi Mud. She outpolled Darby Dan's Cum Laude Laurie, who beat older mares in the fall but lost twice to Our Mims.

Calumet took a brief intermission in 1978 while Tempest Queen took charge for Darby Dan and trainer Lou Rondinello. The daughter of Graustark raced 13 times, from January to October, and clinched the championship by beating her elders in the Spinster Stakes at Keeneland.

Two days after Tempest Queen won the Spinster, John Veitch unveiled a 2-year-old Calumet filly named Davona Dale in a maiden race at Belmont Park. Over the next nine months the daughter of Best Turn established herself as the breakaway leader of the division, winning 8 of her first 10 starts, including the Kentucky Oaks, the Black-Eyed Susan, and the trio of major springtime races for 3-year-old fillies in New York – the Acorn, Mother Goose, and Coaching Club American Oaks.

The specter of Ruffian hung over the 2-year-old filly division as well as the 3-year-olds. As good as they were, none could ever hope to match her blinding speed and raw power.

Of the 2-year-old filly champions who came before Ruffian, Forward Gal (1970) won 7 of 13 starts, Numbered Account (1971) was the fastest by far, and the Canadian La Prevoyante (1972) was a national heroine. All three of them won the Frizette at Belmont Park. Talking Picture (1973) lost the Frizette, but by then she was already the queen of Saratoga, having become the first to sweep the Schuylerville, Adirondack, and Spinaway Stakes at the upstate New York track.

Dearly Precious, by Dr. Fager, did her best to follow Ruffian's example by winning eight straight races and the championship in 1975. Sensational started quietly for trainer Woody Stephens in 1976, then came on like a champ to win the Frizette and the Selima Stakes at the end of the season. To her credit, Sensational did not wear out until she had made 44 starts over three full campaigns.

Lakeville Miss could have been claimed for $25,000 at Belmont in June 1977, but there were no takers. Safely back home in the stable of Jose Martin, the big, rawboned filly got the message and developed into a monster, eventually running off four straight major stakes at the end of the year to take the championship.

The decade ended democratically for the best of the 2-year-old fillies. Candy Eclair, a graceful gray daughter of Northern Jove, dominated so-so company on the mid-Atlantic circuit in a perfect 1978 season of five starts. Eclipse Award voters allowed her a share of the championship with It's in the Air, a daughter of Mr. Prospector who had five wins and three seconds in eight starts, with stakes victories in Chicago and Los Angeles. There was a suspicion, however, that the best of the bunch might have been the Secretariat filly Terlingua, who defeated males in California and won more money than either of the co-champions.

Smart Angle did nearly everything right in 1979, winning 6 of 9 starts and the Spinaway, Matron, Frizette, and Selima Stakes along the way for Woody Stephens. Waiting in the wings, however, were her undefeated classmates, Genuine Risk and Bold 'n Determined, both poised to take the generation into a new decade.

There were certain races in the 1970's that spoke for the entire era. They were contests of immediate consequence and lasting significance. The memory cheats, plays tricks, and teases with time, but the following events were foolproof:

San Juan Capistrano Handicap, April 4, 1970, at Santa Anita Park

Fort Marcy straddled the decades like that grumpy old man who never left the neighborhood. He was there in the 1960's, defeating Damascus in a thriller at the 1967 Washington, D.C., International, and he was still there at the dawn of the 1970's, winning his second grass championship and his first and only title as Horse of the Year.

Although he was once offered for $77,000 in a paddock sale, by the age of 6 in 1970 Fort Marcy had become an indispensable mercenary. There was nowhere he would not ship for trainer Elliott Burch to carry the colors of his owner and breeder, Paul Mellon. As the 1970 season began, the gelded son of Amerigo had started 54 times at 10 different tracks. His best was yet to come.

Fort Marcy's Horse of the Year campaign started in balmy Florida, detoured through a snowy New York spring, and concluded on a damp autumn afternoon at Laurel when he won his second D.C. International to wrap up the year on three straight major wins. He was playing in a tough division, too, full of old pros and fellow travelers, among them Hitchcock, Red Reality, Vent du Nord, and the great filly Drumtop. And to win the ultimate honor, he had to outpoll the Preakness winner, Personality, whose 18 starts for the Hirsch Jacobs family also included victories in the Woodward Stakes, Jersey Derby, Jim Dandy, and Wood Memorial.

Out west, where Fort Marcy appreciated the firm Southern California ground, the competition was just as rough. All the heavy hitters were present and accounted for in the 1970 San Juan Capistrano, and the result may have been the best grass race of the entire decade.

At the end of the 1¾ miles, Fiddle Isle, under 125 pounds, and Quicken Tree, carrying 124, finished in a dead heat. Fort Marcy, at 124, finished a nose behind those two (it was more like an eyelash), while Hitchcock was only a neck farther back in fourth.

For Fort Marcy, it was one of the best races of a career that finally ended on September 4, 1971, in his 75th start, with 21 wins and earnings of $1,109,791. On that day he finished third in the Kelly-Olympic Handicap at Atlantic City, beaten less than a length by his stablemate Run the Gantlet. Perhaps inspired by such proximity to the old king of the Mellon shed row, Run the Gantlet proceeded to win the United Nations Handicap, the Man o' War Stakes, and the Washington, D.C., International to claim a grass championship of his own.

Match Race, June 17, 1972, at Hollywood Park

It can be argued, without fear of serious contradiction, that the early part of the 1970's produced the century's greatest collection of fillies and mares.

The champions of the era included Shuvee ("massive in all directions," wrote Charles Hatton), twice the winner of the Jockey Club Gold Cup and champion in 1970 and 1971; Numbered Account, a freak at age 2 in 1971 and still one of the best at 3; the petite Chou Croute, the weight-packing sprint champ of 1972 who was dangerous going long; Susan's Girl, the durable three-time champion who retired as the richest member of her sex; Turkish Trousers, so good she did not need to leave California to win her title in 1971; and Desert Vixen, the two-time champ who equaled the Belmont record of 1:46⅕ for nine furlongs in the 1973 Beldame Stakes.

Desert Vixen was upstaged less than an hour later by Secretariat's world-record clocking of 1:45⅖ in the inaugural Marlboro Cup. And while the Marlboro had the effect of rendering the Beldame but a footnote to history, Desert Vixen's victory over a field that included Susan's Girl, Poker Night, Summer Guest, and Convenience was perhaps the finest moment of a career that could brag of 13 wins in 28 starts, including eight in a row in 1973, all by daylight margins.

In terms of sheer depth of quality, the West Coast counterpart to the '73 Beldame was the 1972 Santa Margarita Invitational. Turkish Trousers, the reigning champ of her generation, defeated her fellow 4-year-old Convenience by a head, with the older Typecast just a neck behind in third and Street Dancer a head back in fourth. Manta and Minstrel Miss – both major stakes winners on grass – came home fifth and sixth, certainly no embarrassment under the circumstances.

These mares clawed at each other all through 1972. But the two that emerged at the top were Typecast, a classically constructed daughter of Prince John who was owned by Fletcher Jones, and Convenience, Leonard Lavin's daughter of Fleet Nasrullah who was built like a powerful flying wedge.

Convenience was the speed, Typecast the stayer – even though she had defeated Turkish Trousers at seven furlongs in January 1972. When Convenience

Cougar II, with his high action and distinctive long tail, was a star for trainer Charlie Whittingham on both grass and dirt. His greatest moment on the main track came in his victory in the 1973 Big 'Cap.

beat Typecast by a half-length while getting five pounds in the Vanity Handicap at Hollywood Park on June 3, Jones thought his mare got the worst of the trip and the weights. After a week's worth of negotiations, Jones and Lavin each put up $100,000 (with a $50,000 sweetener from the track) for a nine-furlong match race at level weights on June 17. At a quarter of a million dollars, it was at the time the richest match in history.

Shoemaker rode Typecast for trainer Tommy Doyle, but it was Jerry Lambert and Convenience who carried out the strategy of trainer W. L. Proctor to perfection. They took the lead and then drifted wide, forcing Shoemaker to make his run inside through the stretch with Typecast. Convenience, who battled with a sinus infection in the days before the race, ran with an extended right blinker. With Typecast on the inside, Convenience could not be ambushed. Typecast closed furiously through the last 50 yards, but to no avail. Convenience won by a head.

One week after the match race, Typecast defeated males in Hollywood's Invitational Turf Handicap. She later added the Sunset Handicap and the Man o' War Stakes, also against the boys, to secure honors as the best older female of 1972.

SANTA ANITA HANDICAP, MARCH 10, 1973, AT SANTA ANITA PARK

Charlie Whittingham had so many good older male horses in the 1970's it was almost unfair. There were plenty of times he would saddle two, three, even four horses in major stakes. He liked to say, with a twinkle in his eye and a dash of military flair, "We've got 'em surrounded."

Two of his older boys were champions – Ack Ack and Cougar II – and several others could have been were it not for the presence of their stablemates. In 1970, Whittingham won six grass stakes with Fiddle Isle. In 1971, he won seven races with Ack Ack, ranging from 5½ to 10 furlongs, on both dirt and turf, which was good enough for the Eclipse

Award voters to choose him as their Horse of the Year, best older male, and champion sprinter.

Quack, a big, backward young horse, blossomed by the summer of 1972 to beat his elders in the Hollywood Gold Cup and equaled the world record for 1¼ miles in the process. Kennedy Road also won a Hollywood Gold Cup, plus three other stakes and the honor of Canadian Horse of the Year. And then there was Cougar II, the high-stepping, long-tailed Chilean owned by Mary Jones, who won six stakes in 1971, four in 1972, when he was North American grass champion, and three more stakes in 1973.

For all his zeal on the grass, Cougar's name remains strongly linked to the main track through the 1973 Santa Anita Handicap. He had just turned 7. He had not run since November 11, a period of four months. He would be carrying top weight of 126 pounds and switching to Laffit Pincay Jr., since Bill Shoemaker had broken a bone in his hand that winter.

Whittingham put the miles to Cougar, working him long and hard. "I'd rather run a horse than work 'em, because they can get sour, and you can get one hurt just as easy working as running," Whittingham said. "But I didn't want the racing secretary piling the weight on this horse. The only thing I could do was work him up to the Handicap."

The race played out under gray skies to a crowd of 59,625. Kennedy Road got loose in the stretch and nearly stole the show. But Cougar, knees reaching to the clouds and long tail flying, thrust home to win by a nose, survived a claim of foul for drifting in, and topped the one-two finish for Whittingham.

KENTUCKY DERBY, MAY 4, 1974, AT CHURCHILL DOWNS

Whitney Tower, witness to a considerable amount of racing history, described the scene of 163,628 people at the 100th Kentucky Derby as something that sounded like a cross between Woodstock and the 1968 Democratic Convention.

Canonero II, the mystery horse and winner of the 1971 Kentucky Derby, drew 82,694 fans to fill cavernous Belmont Park, where he failed in his bid to win the Triple Crown. Not at his physical best, he finished fourth to Pass Catcher in the Belmont Stakes.

"Police were helpless to prevent the mob from breaking through barriers and crowding against the rails," Tower wrote in *Sports Illustrated,* "and an effort to remove an army of stripped-to-the-waist youths from the top of one of the tote boards ended in abashed failure. Bands played, streakers streaked, one of them to the point of such exhaustion that she finished the day by jumping into an infield fountain, and nearly everyone had a good time."

Angel Cordero Jr. and Woody Stephens had a very good time, as it turned out, when the record field of 23 parted like the Red Sea for John Olin's Cannonade to put them forever in the heart of Derby lore. But the centennial Derby was less a legitimate horse race than a gaudy festival of American excess. It was not necessary for Cannonade to do anything else for the rest of his life. He would always be the answer to the question, Who won the 100th Derby?

As it turned out, Cannonade was soon upstaged by Darby Dan Farm's Little Current. The chestnut son of Sea-Bird finished fifth in the rough-and-tumble Derby, coming from far, far back (he actually got the magic "23" in *Daily Racing Form's* first point of call).

In the more sensible 13-horse Preakness field and nine-horse Belmont field, however, Little

Current's powerful stretch kick was unobstructed. He won both races by seven lengths, with Cannonade finishing third in each. Little Current's two legs of the Triple Crown were enough to earn the 3-year-old championship of 1974, despite the fact that he lost his next three races and was retired with a chipped ankle.

The voters were not nearly so kind to Riva Ridge. In 1972, before Secretariat was a household name, Riva Ridge carried the colors of Meadow Stable to victories in the Blue Grass Stakes, Kentucky Derby, and Belmont Stakes and then traveled to California to win the Hollywood Derby under 129 pounds, giving 14 to the runner-up, Bicker.

By the time the Hollywood race was run, the son of First Landing had been a star for a solid year. At age 2 he won 7 of 9 races to be acclaimed champion among males. His first six months of 1972 were every bit as impressive, with the exception of his fourth-place finish on a sloppy track in the Preakness.

In the meantime, Paul Mellon's Key to the Mint overcame an injured stifle during his winter in Florida to finish third in the Preakness and fourth in the Belmont. The son of Graustark then unfurled a remarkable three months, defeating the older Autobiography in the Brooklyn Handicap, the Whitney Handicap, and the Woodward Stakes, and handling the remnants of his 3-year-old peers in the Travers.

Even though Autobiography later put the Mellon colt in his place, winning the Jockey Club Gold Cup by 15 lengths, Key to the Mint's late-season display was enough to erase the memory of Riva Ridge in the minds of the voters.

It should be noted that in Autobiography, Key to the Mint was not facing one of the better older champions of the decade. The son of Sky High II was, however, a horse of some drama. Owned by Sigmund Sommer and trained by Frank "Pancho" Martin, Autobiography started 19 times as a 4-year-old in 1972 at six different tracks. His record included only four outright wins, a dead heat in the San Fernando Stakes at Santa Anita, and a disqualification from victory in the Gallant Fox Handicap at the end of the year. His reputation for durability proved ephemeral, however, when he suffered a fatal breakdown at Santa Anita the following winter.

Canonero II and Bold Forbes injected welcome Latin American flair into the 3-year-old adventures of the 1970's. They both nearly seized the Triple Crown, failed gallantly, and were later rewarded with divisional championships.

Canonero was the mystery horse of 1971, arriving at Churchill Downs with an odd batch of past-performance lines from Venezuela, a couple of losses the previous summer at Del Mar, and connections who were hard-pressed to communicate in English, let alone the local Kentucky patois. So Canonero did all the talking, winning the Derby by 3¾ lengths and then the Preakness by a length and a half. A crowd of 82,694 crammed Belmont Park for a chance to watch Canonero win the Triple Crown, but he was not in the best physical shape for the race and trailed home a sad fourth to Pass Catcher.

Bold Forbes, owned by Esteban Tizol of Puerto Rico and trained by Lazaro Sosa Barrera, led Honest Pleasure and seven others on a wild chase in the 1976 Kentucky Derby to win by a length. In the subsequent Preakness, Honest Pleasure was sent after Bold Forbes from the start. After six furlongs neither colt had much left to resist the finishing kick of Elocutionist, but at least Bold Forbes stuck around for third.

Honest Pleasure wisely stayed home for the Belmont, which gave Bold Forbes and Angel Cordero free rein. While the son of Irish Castle was far from a classic stayer, he had the courage to lead all the way and win by a rapidly diminishing neck in a three-way photo finish with longshots MacKenzie Bridge and Great Contractor.

NATIONAL THOROUGHBRED CHAMPIONSHIP, NOVEMBER 1, 1975, AT SANTA ANITA PARK

Forego was supposed to headline the field of major stakes winners gathering at the Oak Tree meet for a $350,000 purse and a juicy spot on network TV. Sadly, Forego's ankles flared up to bring his season to an end.

That left Charlie Whittingham licking his chops. He won the 1¼-mile main-track race with the Argentine mare Dulcia, who closed from last place to beat Royal Glint (winner of the 1976 Santa Anita Handicap), Tizna (two-time winner of the Santa Margarita), and such also-rans as Holding Pattern (the Travers winner), L'Enjoleur (the Queen's Plate winner), Ancient Title (at the peak of his game), and Forceten, who defeated Belmont Stakes winner Avatar in the Swaps Stakes that summer. Allez France, the queen of Europe, also made the race but shipped poorly and finished an uncharacteristic last.

Still, it was a treat for Americans just to see a mare like Allez France under silks. The National Thoroughbred Championship lasted only one more running (Whittingham won it again) and then disappeared. Nine years later the concept was resurrected under a different name, but the inspiration was the same. In 1984, they called it the Breeders' Cup Classic.

SUBURBAN HANDICAP, JULY 5, 1976, AT BELMONT PARK

Foolish Pleasure spent the last half of his career living in the shadow of his match race with Ruffian, as if it were his fault.

In fact, the streamlined son of What a Pleasure had been a credit to his generation from the start, when he reeled off nine straight wins and 11 victories in his first 12 races. He was the overwhelming choice as champion 2-year-old of 1974. At age 3 in 1975 he won the Flamingo, the Wood Memorial, and the Kentucky Derby, and suffered second by just a length in the Preakness and by a neck in the Belmont. Furthermore, LeRoy Jolley had him ready to run the race of his life on the day Ruffian broke down.

That same year, Bold Ruler's son Wajima came along late to take the Monmouth Invitational and the Travers, and then shaded Foolish Pleasure by a head in the Governor Stakes at Belmont Park while getting 10 pounds. In the subsequent Marlboro Cup, Foolish Pleasure ran the first bad race of his life and finished a distant fifth. Up ahead, it was Wajima again, this time defeating Forego by a head (while getting 10 pounds). The coffin was nailed shut. Wajima was voted champion 3-year-old over Foolish Pleasure.

As a 4-year-old, Foolish Pleasure won 4 of 8 starts, including the Donn Handicap under 129 pounds. But he was never better than he was for the 1976 Suburban Handicap at Belmont Park.

There were only four in the field for that 90th Suburban. The bad news was obvious. One of them

The pint-sized Ta Wee not only was able to beat males, but also did it carrying a heavy load. The two-time sprint champ won the 1970 Fall Highweight Handicap under 140 pounds.

was Forego, age 6 and fresh from victories in the Metropolitan and the Nassau County Handicaps. Foolish Pleasure got nine pounds from the old champ, 134 to 125. His rider, Eddie Maple, tried to steal away and slow things down. Forego stayed close, though, and so did Lord Rebeau, winner of the Roseben Handicap. They came together at the finish, with Foolish Pleasure obscured on the inside but a nose in front of the mountainous Forego. Between them, in a champion sandwich, Lord Rebeau was a nose behind Forego.

HOLLYWOOD GOLD CUP, JUNE 18, 1977, AT HOLLYWOOD PARK

Walter Vosburgh, the legendary racing secretary and weight lifter, once got caught saying, "When the fillies can beat the colts, depend upon it – the colts are a bad lot." Of course, he died long before the man-bashers of the 1970's came along.

More appropriate to the spirit of the era was this from Angel Penna Sr., by way of writer Patrick Robinson from *Decade of Champions*: "Most women are a lot braver than most men in terms of pain, which a racehorse endures at the height of battle," Penna said. "They are innately more stoic than we. The secret is to make them want to do their best for you. A great one will not let you down."

Cascapedia was a great one in a grand decade for the success of mares against males. And even though she never beat the colts, she certainly put the fear of God in them. Laffit Pincay had to ride Crystal Water like a demon to edge Don Pierce and Cascapedia by a neck in the 1977 Hollywood Gold Cup. With turf star Caucasus lapped on in third, the Gold Cup was considered the best race of the year.

The daughter of Chieftain, owned by B. J. Ridder, also finished third to Ancient Title in the Del Mar Handicap (ahead of Crystal Water and Pay Tribute) to give her final 1977 record a championship sheen for trainer Gordon Campbell.

Before Cascapedia, Shuvee set the tone for her sisters of the seventies with her twin killing in the Jockey Club Gold Cups of 1970 and '71 – four miles

in total. While Shuvee enjoyed long strolls, blink and you missed the best of the female sprinters. They were particularly anti-male, and no less than four of them were champions in open competition:

Ta Wee, a two-time sprint champ, was the rapid yin to Shuvee's slow-burning yang. Nearing the end of her career, she carried 140 pounds to beat Distinctive in the 1970 Fall Highweight Handicap, her second straight win in the Belmont event. She actually picked up two pounds for her next race, the Interborough, and won.

Chou Croute ("sauerkraut" in French, or "inedible cabbage" in English) beat the boys in the 1972 Fall Highweight and the Fayette Handicap en route to her title. When not otherwise occupied, she dusted fillies for fun.

My Juliet, as fast as her old man, Gallant Romeo, won 24 races in 36 starts and the 1976 sprint title. To clinch her championship she beat Bold Forbes wire to wire and on the square in the premier sprint of the New York fall season, the – what's this! – Vosburgh Stakes.

What a Summer picked up where My Juliet left off, winning her 1977 sprint championship by taking the Fall Highweight under 134 pounds. The daughter of What Luck also won in California and nearly bagged the 10-furlong Beldame, losing to Cum Laude Laurie by three-quarters of a length.

Mr. Vosburgh's philosophy was strained further by the exploits of fillies and mares in mixed grass competition during the decade, with the imported Dahlia, Waya, and Trillion leading the way.

Dahlia was a Kentucky-bred daughter of Vaguely Noble, trained by Maurice Zilber and owned by Nelson Bunker Hunt. Author Patrick Robinson called her "a capricious little hussy" who lost far more often than she won. Robinson was fair, however, pointing out that "she tended to make her biggest efforts when the stakes were highest."

Dahlia first descended upon North America as a 3-year-old in 1973 to win the Washington, D.C., International. Back in Europe the following year, she continued to thrash top males like On My Way, Highclere, and Snow Knight (later an American grass champion) in the Coronation Cup, King

Affirmed and Alydar's memorable series of battles reached its zenith in the 1978 Belmont, with Affirmed (inside) desperately getting a head in front at the wire to complete his sweep of the Triple Crown.

George VI and Queen Elizabeth Diamond Stakes, and Benson and Hedges Gold Cup.

In the fall of 1974, Dahlia returned to North America to win the Man o' War Stakes and the Canadian International Championship. She could not be denied the title.

(Two years later, Hunt and Zilber won the North American grass championship again with their 3-year-old colt Youth, a son of Ack Ack who won the Prix du Jockey-Club in France and then crossed the pond to take the Canadian International and Washington, D.C., International.)

Waya, a French filly trained by Angel Penna for Daniel Wildenstein, was arguably the best grass horse of either sex in North America in 1978 when she won the Diana and Flower Bowl Handicaps against mares and the Man o' War and Turf Classic against males. She split two decisions with Mac Diarmida, a 3-year-old colt trained by Scotty Schulhofer who began the year as a maiden and ended up winning the Canadian International and Washington, D.C., International. He was voted champion.

But the Eclipse Award committee felt a pang of guilt. Without admitting it directly, they were thinking of Waya when they created a new category for a female grass champion in 1979.

At the end of 1978, Waya was sold to Peter Brant for $1 million (Wildenstein was, after all, in the business of moving fine art) and went to work for David Whiteley. She never missed a beat, winning two major races on the Santa Anita grass to open the 1979 campaign. After that, Whiteley expanded Waya's horizons to the dirt and was rewarded with four stakes wins, including the Saratoga Cup over the previous year's female champion, Late Bloomer, and assorted males.

By the end of the season, there were championships to go all around. Bowl Game, Greentree Stable's male version of Late Bloomer, got the male grass award after beating Waya 2 out of 3. Trillion, a stalwart of the European scene, finished second in four major North American fall races and was given the female grass title. And Waya herself was honored with the best older filly or mare title, when everyone knew she had been that all along.

BELMONT STAKES, JUNE 10, 1978, AT BELMONT PARK

The final plot line of the 1970's began to unspool in June 1977. By the middle of the month, the cast was established and the drama was set in motion. Only the various endings remained in doubt.

On June 2, 1977, over the historic downs at Epsom, England, Nelson Bunker Hunt's Exceller won the Coronation Cup to mark the first victory of his 4-year-old campaign.

On June 11, Seattle Slew won the 109th Belmont Stakes by four lengths to sweep the Triple Crown and remain undefeated in nine starts.

On June 15, also at Belmont Park, a bright chestnut colt named Affirmed won the Youthful Stakes at 5½ furlongs in his second start, with a dark chestnut colt named Alydar finishing fifth making his debut. Alydar had been favored at 9-5.

During the ensuing 12 months, Affirmed and Alydar would face each other eight more times. Each time, the stakes were higher. And each time

Triple Crown winner Seattle Slew (LEFT) may have given his finest effort in defeat, nearly coming back to beat Exceller in the 1978 Jockey Club Gold Cup despite setting a blistering early pace.

The older, more seasoned Affirmed (LEFT) was not quite ready to abdicate his position as the reigning star of Thoroughbred racing when he met 3-year-old sensation Spectacular Bid (CENTER) in the 1979 Jockey Club Gold Cup. In a battle for Horse of the Year, Affirmed defeated his younger rival by three-quarters of a length.

the two chestnuts came away with a larger piece of the historical pie. Woody Stephens, who tried to beat them with Believe It, called Affirmed and Alydar "the greatest act horse racing has ever had," then added, "I hope it never ends."

Affirmed was bred and owned by Louis and Patrice Wolfson's Harbor View Farm and trained by Lazaro Barrera. Alydar was bred and owned by Admiral and Mrs. Gene Markey's Calumet Farm. He was trained by John Veitch, the son of Hall of Famer Sylvester Veitch.

In their six meetings in 1977, Affirmed beat Alydar four times. Still, the 2-year-old title went right down to the wire in the Laurel Futurity on October 29. They banged away at each other for the last half of the 1 1/16 miles before Affirmed finally won by a neck. Star de Naskra, a fine colt who went on to be sprint champion of 1979, finished 10 lengths behind the feuding chestnuts in third.

The Laurel Futurity was a vivid preview of the 1978 Triple Crown. Affirmed beat Alydar by 1½ lengths in the Kentucky Derby on a day that Alydar

protested the texture of the track. Apparently, Pimlico was more to his taste, but the result was the same – Affirmed by a neck. The only thing that stood between Affirmed and the Triple Crown was the mile and one-half of the Belmont Stakes. And Alydar.

Veitch decided to take the blinkers off his colt for the Belmont and told Jorge Velasquez to take the race to Affirmed. Barrera was worried that Affirmed had lost weight, but he was confident his champion could sustain one more round against Alydar. Steve Cauthen, Affirmed's 18-year-old jockey, remained cool and calm in the face of the Triple Crown fuss.

"I knew that Alydar would come up and we would fight it out," Cauthen told William Leggett of *Sports Illustrated*. "I didn't think we'd have to fight it out for a mile, but with Affirmed and Alydar it always seems to turn out that they fight for every inch."

In fact, the Belmont came down to just a few of those precious inches. Locked together, eight red legs churning as if attached to a single desperate beast, Affirmed and Alydar hit the wire as one . . . almost. Alydar ran a better race without those blinkers, but it was Cauthen's surprising left-handed whip applied to Affirmed's side deep in the stretch that might have made the difference. The difference was a head.

Jockey Club Gold Cup, October 14, 1978, at Belmont Park

While Affirmed and Alydar tested each other to the brink and left no lingering questions of their quality, Seattle Slew labored in a comparative vacuum. There was nothing for him to be measured against.

At age 2 in 1976, the son of Bold Reasoning was left dangling without competition in three dazzling starts, climaxed by a 9¾-length win in the Champagne Stakes. Other 2-year-old male champions had more extensive records – Rockhill Native won three major New York stakes in 1979 and was disqualified from a fourth, while Protagonist won the Champagne, the Laurel Futurity, and a division of the Cowdin in 1973 – but few had Seattle Slew's knack for the dramatic.

Indeed, if he had an antecedent, it was Hoist the Flag, the 2-year-old male champ of 1970. Under the guidance of Sid Watters, Hoist the Flag ran four times between September 11 and October 10 and finished first by daylight on each occasion, although he lost the Champagne Stakes in the stewards' stand. Voters ignored the decision.

Hoist the Flag fractured an ankle after winning his first two races at age 3. Thank goodness, Seattle Slew remained sound through his memorable Triple Crown, which turned out to be a textbook piece of training by the young William Turner Jr. in his first crack at the classics. Ridden by Jean Cruguet, Seattle Slew won the Derby by 1¾ lengths after a flat-footed start, then took the Preakness by a geared-down length and a quarter before his coronation in the Belmont. He was the first horse to emerge undefeated from the Triple Crown.

Events off the track were almost as interesting as on, given the cast of characters that included

Washington lumberman Mickey Taylor; his wife, Karen; and Jim and Sally Hill of New York and Kentucky. Jim Hill was a practicing racetrack vet.

Hill's hidden ownership got the "Slew Crew" in dutch later on, when both Dr. Hill and Seattle Slew were barred from racing for six months at the end of 1977. At that point it was moot, since Seattle Slew had been put away for the year after his first defeat, a fourth-place finish to J.O. Tobin in the Swaps Stakes at Hollywood Park. At the end of 1977, Turner was fired and Doug Peterson was hired to train Seattle Slew at age 4. But before he had the pleasure of saddling the champion, Peterson had to nurse the tempestuous colt through a viral infection and high fever that nearly spelled the end of the fairy tale.

Seattle Slew returned in May 1978 with a cautious win in allowance company (among the beaten that day was Gallant Bob, the nearly forgotten sprint champion of 1975). Seattle Slew was given another soft allowance spot in August, after which he was tested in the Paterson Handicap at The Meadowlands. His narrow loss to Dr. Patches looked better down the road, when Dr. Patches was accorded a share of the 1978 sprint championship with the same J.O. Tobin who had beaten Seattle Slew in the Swaps.

In the meantime, Exceller had long since ended his stellar European career and was a full-fledged member of Charlie Whittingham's California stable. He won five stakes out west, including the Hollywood Gold Cup over Santa Anita Handicap winner Vigors. Whittingham thought he had the Horse of the Year in the making, so he packed up Exceller and Bill Shoemaker and took the show on the road.

Seattle Slew proved he was back in top form by dusting off the younger Affirmed in the Marlboro Cup on September 16, just 11 days after the Paterson. It was the first time two Triple Crown winners had met. Two weeks later, Seattle Slew was introduced to Exceller in the Woodward Stakes and paid him very little mind, winning by four while controlling all the pace.

The deciding race would be the Jockey Club Gold Cup on October 14: Affirmed, Seattle Slew, and Exceller for all the marbles. It was a testing mile and a half, played out in mud and cold rain. Seattle Slew set off with the lead, but he was surprisingly joined by Affirmed, who was out of Cauthen's control. It was the wrong day for the saddle to slip.

Affirmed did not last long, but he pressed Seattle Slew hard enough to give Shoemaker hope. Starting from far back, smeared with Belmont mud, Shoemaker and Exceller began to eat into Seattle Slew's long lead. They caught him on the turn, and with a furlong to go Exceller was clearly ahead on all cards. Then, from deep within his unforgiving soul, Seattle Slew fought back under Angel Cordero to make it a contest to the finish. Exceller won by a nose, but Seattle Slew got all the headlines.

JOCKEY CLUB GOLD CUP, OCTOBER 6, 1979, AT BELMONT PARK

The precedent had been set by Seattle Slew. Triple Crown winners should be Horse of the Year. The voters agreed in 1978 and anointed Affirmed with the honor. Seattle Slew was given the older male title for his late-season heroics, which seemingly left the grass championship to Exceller as a fitting consolation prize. Five of his seven 1978 stakes victories were on the California turf.

But when the ballots were counted, the grass title went to Mac Diarmida.

"Dumbest thing I ever heard of," said Whittingham, almost, since a few expletives required careful deletion.

Seattle Slew was retired and neither Alydar nor Exceller was ever the same, leaving the 1979 season a sitting duck for bigger, stronger, and apparently more cagey Affirmed, who was freshly syndicated for $14.4 million. After two uninspired January losses under Cauthen, however, Barrera bounced his young rider and added Laffit Pincay to the mix.

Affirmed responded by winning the Strub Stakes (before a crowd of 50,220), the Santa Anita Handicap (66,477 came out), the Californian, and the Hollywood Gold Cup (48,884 in the house), then continued uninterrupted in New York to take

a little allowance prep for the Marlboro Cup.

Barrera drew a line in the sand at 131 pounds for Affirmed's Marlboro Cup assignment. Belmont's racing secretary, Lenny Hale, responded with 133. Barrera, exercising both his option and his sense of indignation, announced that Affirmed would pass the race to await the weight-for-age Woodward Stakes, which he won without serious bother.

In Affirmed's absence, Spectacular Bid stepped up to beat fellow 3-year-olds General Assembly and Coastal with arrogant ease. General Assembly had won the Travers by 15 lengths; Coastal had spoiled Spectacular Bid's attempt to win the Triple Crown in June. The score between them would never be even, but the Marlboro helped.

Laboring in the long shadow of Affirmed, Spectacular Bid possessed enough presence to hold his own. His motormouth trainer, the Maryland kingpin Buddy Delp, proclaimed his "Bid" the best horse ever to look through a bridle. Spectacular Bid did his best to back that up with a run of 12 straight wins from September 1978 through his powerful Preakness triumph by 5½ lengths. He won the Derby by 2¾.

Still, the jury was out – and leaning toward conviction – unless Spectacular Bid could beat Affirmed on the square, under weights determined by age, not the handicapper. He got his chance in the Jockey Club Gold Cup on October 6, 1979. A Belmont Park crowd of 36,187 came for the show. No one went home disappointed.

Affirmed and Pincay set the tone of the race and the pace from the start. Spectacular Bid and Shoemaker pressed them down the long Belmont backstretch, while Coastal and Gallant Best stayed out of the way. Suddenly, Spectacular Bid lost his concentration. Shoemaker said the colt spit the bit. Affirmed and Coastal moved to the quarter pole on nearly even terms, yet spread far apart. Pincay, on the outside, was still in control.

That's when something clicked in Spectacular Bid, and the race was on again. The great 3-year-old tested the great 4-year-old through the final three-sixteenths of a mile. Affirmed held the advantage, but Spectacular Bid refused to yield. The wire approached.

"The gray colt got his head inside Affirmed's flanks, perhaps to the girth," Joe Hirsch wrote in his *American Racing Manual* review. "But no one passes Affirmed in the stretch, as Alydar had discovered the season before. Spectacular Bid kept trying and Affirmed produced enough effort to hold him safe." Safe by three-quarters of a length.

"He lost fair and square," Barrera said of the vanquished. "Spectacular Bid had his chance with Affirmed. He got five pounds. He got Shoemaker. And he got beat."

And so the decade ended, though certainly not with a whimper. Affirmed retired with his second straight title as Horse of the Year. Spectacular Bid went to California to follow in the footsteps of the handsome red colt from Harbor View Farm. The calendar turned, but the memories have lingered, paying frequent visits to those 10 unforgettable years.

Champions

⚬◦⚬

Past Performances

The 1970's

•1970•
•2-Year-Old Male *Hoist the Flag* •2-Year-Old Filly *Forward Gal* •3-Year-Old Male *Personality*
•3-Year-Old Filly *Office Queen, Fanfreluche (TRA)* •Handicap Horse *Fort Marcy, Nodouble (TRA)*
•Handicap Mare *Shuvee* Grass •Horse *Fort Marcy* •Sprinter *Ta Wee* •Steeplechase *Top Bid*
•**HORSE OF THE YEAR** Fort Marcy, Personality (TRA)

•1971•
•2-Year-Old Male *Riva Ridge* •2-Year-Old Filly *Numbered Account* •3-Year-Old Male *Canonero II*
•3-Year-Old Filly *Turkish Trousers* •Handicap Horse *Ack Ack* •Handicap Mare *Shuvee* Grass
•Horse *Run the Gauntlet* •Sprinter *Ack Ack* •Steeplechase *Shadow Brook*
•**HORSE OF THE YEAR** Ack Ack

•1972•
•2-Year-Old Male *Secretariat* •2-Year-Old Filly *La Prevoyante* •3-Year-Old Male *Key to the Mint*
•3-Year-Old Filly *Susan's Girl* •Handicap Horse *Autobiography* •Handicap Mare *Typecast*
•Grass Horse *Cougar II* •Sprinter *Chou Croute* •Steeplechase *Soothsayer*
•**HORSE OF THE YEAR** Secretariat

•1973•
•2-Year-Old Male *Protagonist* •2-Year-Old Filly *Talking Picture* •3-Year-Old Male *Secretariat*
•3-Year-Old Filly *Desert Vixen* •Handicap Horse *Riva Ridge* •Handicap Mare *Susan's Girl*
•Grass Horse *Secretariat* •Sprinter *Shecky Greene* •Steeplechase *Athenian Idol*
•**HORSE OF THE YEAR** Secretariat

•1974•
•2-Year-Old Male *Foolish Pleasure* •2-Year-Old Filly *Ruffian* •3-Year-Old Male *Little Current*
•3-Year-Old Filly *Chris Evert* •Handicap Horse *Forego* •Handicap Mare *Desert Vixen* •Grass Horse *Dahlia*
•Sprinter *Forego* •Steeplechase *Gran Kan*
•**HORSE OF THE YEAR** Forego

•1975•
•2-Year-Old Male *Honest Pleasure* •2-Year-Old Filly *Dearly Precious* •3-Year-Old Male *Wajima*
•3-Year-Old Filly *Ruffian* •Handicap Horse *Forego* •Handicap Mare *Susan's Girl* •Grass Horse *Snow Knight*
•Sprinter *Gallant Bob* •Steeplechase *Life's Illusion*
•**HORSE OF THE YEAR** Forego

•1976•
•2-Year-Old Male *Seattle Slew* •2-Year-Old Filly *Sensational* •3-Year-Old Male *Bold Forbes*
•3-Year-Old Filly *Revidere* •Handicap Horse *Forego* •Handicap Mare *Proud Delta* •Grass Horse *Youth*
•Sprinter *My Juliet* •Steeplechase *Straight and True*
•**HORSE OF THE YEAR** Forego

•1977•
•2-Year-Old Male *Affirmed* •2-Year-Old Filly *Lakeville Miss* •3-Year-Old Male *Seattle Slew*
•3-Year-Old Filly *Our Mims* •Handicap Horse *Forego* •Handicap Mare *Cascapedia* •Grass Horse *Johnny D.*
•Sprinter *What a Summer* •Steeplechase *Cafe Prince*
•**HORSE OF THE YEAR** Seattle Slew

•1978•
•2-Year-Old Male *Spectacular Bid* •2-Year-Old Filly *Candy Eclair, It's in the Air* •3-Year-Old Male *Affirmed*
•3-Year-Old Filly *Tempest Queen* •Handicap Horse *Seattle Slew* •Handicap Mare *Late Bloomer*
•Grass Horse *Mac Diarmida* •Sprinter *Dr. Patches, J.O. Tobin* •Steeplechase *Cafe Prince*
•**HORSE OF THE YEAR** Affirmed

•1979•
•2-Year-Old Male *Rockhill Native* •2-Year-Old Filly *Smart Angle* •3-Year-Old Male *Spectacular Bid*
•3-Year-Old Filly *Davona Dale* •Handicap Horse *Affirmed* •Handicap Mare *Waya*
•Grass Horse *Bowl Game (M) Trillion (F)* •Sprinter *Star de Naskra* •Steeplechase *Martie's Anger*
•**HORSE OF THE YEAR** Affirmed

Ack Ack

b. c. 1966, by Battle Joined (Armageddon)–Fast Turn, by Turn-to **Lifetime record: 27 19 6 0 $636,641**

Own.– Forked Lightning Ranch
Br.– H.F. Guggenheim (Ky)
Tr.– Charles Whittingham

17Jly71- 8Hol	fst 1¼	:45^2 1:09 1:34^1 1:59^4	3↑ Gold Cup Inv'l H 175k	7	1	1^3	1^4	1^6	1^{3¾}	Shoemaker W	134	*.30	94-10	Ack Ack134^{3¾}Comtal111^{1}Manta117^2	Ridden out	8
5Jly71- 8Hol	fm 1⅛Ⓣ	:46^3 1:10^3 1:35 1:47^1	3↑ American H 79k	5	1	1^{1½}	1^{1½}	1^5	1^4	Shoemaker W	130	*.60	101-09	Ack Ack130^{4}Divide and Rule121^{6}Figonero119^1	Easily	7
17Jun71- 8Hol	fst 5½f	:22 :44^3 :56^2 1:02^3	3↑ Hol Express H 33k	2	5	3^{2½}	3^2	2^½	1^3	Shoemaker W	130	*.40	99-14	Ack Ack130^{3}Pitching Wedge109^{no}Galea Pass113^{nk}	Easily	7
13Mar71- 8SA	sl 1¼	:46^4 1:11^1 1:37 2:03	4↑ S Anita H 145k	3	1	1^{hd}	1^4	1^6	1^{1½}	Shoemaker W	130	*.80	83-22	Ack Ack130^{1½}Cougar II125^{4}The Field109^{1¼}	Driving	10
27Feb71- 8SA	fst 1⅛	:46 1:09^3 1:34^2 1:47	4↑ San Antonio 88k	8	1	1^{2½}	1^{2½}	1^4	1^{3¼}	Shoemaker W	124	*1.00	97-11	Ack Ack124^{3¼}Good Manners115^{1½}Hanalei Bay117^{1½}	Handily	11
6Feb71- 8SA	fst 1$\frac{1}{16}$	:22^4 :45^3 1:09^3 1:41^2	4↑ San Pasqual H 55k	5	1	1^4	1^4	1^2	1^{¾}	Shoemaker W	129	*.90	95-07	AckAck129^{¾}DelawareChief118^{¾}Figonro121^½	Stumbled,driving	8
Previously owned by Cain Hoy Stable																
16Jan71- 8SA	gd 7f	:22^2 :44^3 1:08^2 1:21	4↑ San Carlos H 56k	6	2	2^½	2^1	1^2	1^{1¾}	Shoemaker W	126	*1.20	98-13	AckAck126^{1¾}JungleSavage120^{8}KingofCricket119^{hd}	Driving	7
2Jan71- 8SA	gd 6f	:21^3 :44 :56^1 1:08^3	3↑ Palos Verdes H 32k	1	4	1^{hd}	2^2	3^1	2^{3½}	Shoemaker W	129	*.80	95-11	JungleSavage117^{3½}AckAck129^{¾}KingofCricket119^6	Held well	5
6Oct70- 6SA	fm *6½fⓉ	:22^3 :45 1:06^4 1:13	2↑ Autumn Days H 21k	2	1	1^{1½}	1^2	1^{3½}	1^{1½}	Shoemaker W	128	*.30	94-06	AckAck128^{1½}FleetSurprise117^{10}BargainDay115^{12}	Mild drive	4
12Sep70- 6Dmr	fst 5½f	:21^3 :44^2 1:02^1	3↑ Alw 8500	1	4	1^½	1^3	1^4	1^5	Shoemaker W	124	*.70	103-12	Ack Ack124^{5}Fleet Surprise116^{¾}Derby Day Boy114^3	Driving	6
2May70- 8Hol	fst 7f	:22^1 :44^1 1:08^1 1:20^3	3↑ Los Angeles H 53k	6	5	1^½	1^{hd}	1^½	2no	Pierce D	126	*.60	97-11	[D]RightorWrong114^{no}AckAck126^{4½}Baffle123^1	Impeded late	6
Placed first through disqualification																
24Apr70- 8Hol	fst 6f	:21^4 :44^1 :56^1 1:08^3	4↑ Handicap 15000	2	8	2^{hd}	1^½	1^{2½}	1^2	Shoemaker W	123	*.70	98-13	Ack Ack123^{2}First Mate122^{no}Fleet Surprise117^½	Driving	8
10Apr70- 8Hol	fst 6f	:22 :44^3 :56^3 1:08^4	3↑ Premiere H 33k	1	4	3^{1½}	4^2	4^{1½}	4^{3¼}	Shoemaker W	124	2.30	94-11	First Mate118^{2¾}Right or Wrong114^{nk}Baffle124^{nk}	Blocked	7
Previously trained by F.A. Bonsal																
21Jun69- 8AP	fst 1	:22^3 :45 1:09^2 1:34^2	Arl Classic 111k	7	3	3^3	1^{hd}	1^4	1^{4½}	Baeza B	120	*1.60	89-15	AckAck120^{4½}KingoftheCastl120^{1¼}FstHlrous120^{nk}	Mild drive	10
30May69- 8GS	fst 1⅛	:45^4 1:09^4 1:35^2 1:48	Jersey Derby 137k	6	2	1^{hd}	1^{hd}	1^{hd}	2^{2½}	Ycaza M	126	*3.30	94-16	Al Hattab126^{2½}Ack Ack126^{½}Rooney's Shield126^{1½}	Weakened	10
21May69- 8GS	fst 1$\frac{1}{16}$	:23^3 :47^1 1:11^2 1:43^3	Alw 12000	3	3	3^{1½}	2^1	2^3	2^½	Ycaza M	122	*.50	86-19	Night Invader119^{½}Ack Ack122^{¾}Ad Majora119^{3½}	Game effort	6
10May69- 7Aqu	fst 1	:22^3 :45 1:09 1:34^4	Withers 58k	8	3	3^1	2^{hd}	2^{hd}	2^{¾}	Ycaza M	126	*.50	92-14	[D]GleamingLight126^{¾}AckAck126^{hd}Tyrant126^{nk}	Bothered late	8
Placed first through disqualification																
29Apr69- 8CD	fst 1	:22^1 :45 1:09 1:34^2	Derby Trial 16k	4	3	3^3	1^3	1^5	1^7	Ycaza M	122	*.30	101-16	Ack Ack122^{7}Indian Emerald122^{½}Fleet Allied122^3	Handily	7
18Apr69- 6Kee	sly 7f	:22^4 :45^2 1:10 1:22^4	Alw 10000	1	2	1^½	1^3	1^6	1^{12}	Ycaza M	121	*.30	94-20	Ack Ack121^{12}Tripsville112^{2¾}Sheik of Bagdad112^{11}	Handily	4
5Apr69- 7Kee	fst 6f	:22 :44^4 :57^2 1:10^1	Alw 7500	6	5	2^{1½}	1^{hd}	1^2	2^{¾}	Brumfield D	119	*.60	91-14	WalkingStick115^{¾}AckAck119^{2¼}Viceregal122^5	Couldn't last	7
19Feb69- 8Hia	fst 1⅛	:47 1:11^4 1:36^3 1:49^3	Everglades 32k	3	2	3^{nk}	1^2	2^3	4^{5½}	Ycaza M	115	7.30	81-21	Arts and Letters112^{3}Top Knight122^{2}Al Hattab119^½	Tired	12
5Feb69- 7Hia	fst 7f	:23^3 :46 1:10^1 1:22^3	Bahamas (Div 1) 24k	7	3	2^1	2^½	1^{hd}	1^{hd}	Ycaza M	115	*.80	95-14	Ack Ack115^{hd}Al Hattab119^{2}Curette117^{nk}	Bore out,lasted	8
25Jan69- 6Hia	fst 7f	:22^4 :45^3 1:09^3 1:22^3	©Alw 5500	6	3	3^1	2^{hd}	1^2	1^3	Ycaza M	117	*.70	95-16	Ack Ack117^{3}Distinctive119^{3}Arts and Letters119^3	Handily	9
17Jan69- 5Hia	fst 6f	:22 :45 1:09^3	©Alw 5000	2	3	1^3	1^2	1^3	1^6	Ycaza M	119	3.30	96-15	Ack Ack119^{6}Next Beauty116^{1¾}Banquet Circuit119^4	Driving	12
Previously trained by W.W. Stephens																
23Oct68- 5Bel	fst 7f	:23^1 :46^3 1:11^1 1:24	Alw 7000	2	4	1^{1½}	1^1	1^{1½}	2^{hd}	Rotz JL	122	3.10	87-13	IFoundGold115^{hd}AckAck122^{no}KingoftheCastle122^½	Missed	8
10Oct68- 5Bel	fst 6f	:22^2 :46 1:11^2	©Md Sp Wt	12	7	4^1	3^{nk}	1^{hd}	1no	Ycaza M	122	*1.50	88-17	Ack Ack122^{no}Izaak122^{2½}Alaskan Reindeer122^5	Hard drive	14
2Oct68- 3Bel	fst 6f	:22^2 :45^4 1:11	©Md Sp Wt	12	6	3^{1½}	3^{1½}	2^{hd}	2^{¾}	Ycaza M	122	*2.50	89-13	Nephew122^{¾}Ack Ack122^{1½}Banquet Circuit122^{1½}	Good effort	14

Affirmed

ch. c. 1975, by Exclusive Native (Raise a Native)–Won't Tell You, by Crafty Admiral **Lifetime record: 29 22 5 1 $2,393,818**

Own.– Harbor View Farm
Br.– Harbor View Farm (Fla)
Tr.– Lazaro S. Barrera

6Oct79- 8Bel	fst 1½	:49 1:13^1 2:02^2 2:27^2	3↑ J C Gold Cup-G1	3	2	1^½	1^{hd}	1^½	1^{¾}	Pincay L Jr	126	*.60	83-21	Affirmed126^{¾}Spectacular Bid121^{3}Coastal121^{31}	Driving	4
22Sep79- 8Bel	sly 1¼	:47^3 1:11^4 1:36^1 2:01^3	3↑ Woodward-G1	2	2	2^4	1^½	1^3	1^{2½}	Pincay L Jr	126	*.40	92-15	Affirmed126^{2½}Coastal120^{3¾}Czaravich120^{8½}	Ridden out	5
29Aug79- 0Bel	sly 1	:22^2 :45 1:09^2 1:34	3↑ Alw 30000	3	1	1^½	1^1	1^2	1^6	Pincay L Jr	122	-	98-15	Affirmed122^{6}Island Sultan115^{14}Prefontaine117	Ridden out	3
No wagering. Exhibition race run between 7th and 8th races																
24Jun79- 8Hol	fst 1¼	:45^3 1:09^3 1:34^1 1:58^2	3↑ Hol Gold Cup-G1	1	2	1^{hd}	1^{hd}	1^{hd}	1^{¾}	Pincay L Jr	132	*.30	99-13	Affirmed132^{¾}Sirlad120^{4}Text119^5	Driving	10
20May79- 8Hol	fst 1$\frac{1}{16}$	:22^2 :44^4 1:09^1 1:41^1	3↑ Californian-G1	2	1	1^1	1^1	1^2	1^5	Pincay L Jr	130	*.30	89-16	Affirmed130^{5}Syncopate114^{4}Harry's Love117^{¾}	Driving	8
4Mar79- 8SA	fst 1¼	:46^2 1:10^1 1:34^1 1:58^3	4↑ S Anita H-G1	3	2	2^1	1^{1½}	1^4	1^{4½}	Pincay L Jr	128	*1.30	103-09	Affirmed128^{4½}Tiller127^3[DH]PaintedWagon115	Speed to spare	8
4Feb79- 8SA	gd 1¼	:47 1:10^4 1:35^3 2:01	C H Strub-G1	8	2	3^1	1^1	1^2	1^{10}	Pincay L Jr	126	*.90	91-17	Affirmed126^{10}Johnny's Image115^{4}Quip115^7	Handily	9
20Jan79- 8SA	gd 1⅛	:45^3 1:09^3 1:35 1:48	San Fernando-G2	4	3	4^{9½}	5^{7½}	3^{3½}	2^{2¾}	Cauthen S	126	*.50	88-14	Radar Ahead123^{2¾}Affirmed126^{nk}Little Reb120^4	Drifted out	8
7Jan79- 8SA	fst 7f	:22^2 :45 1:08^3 1:21	Malibu-G2	2	1	3^2	3^{2½}	3^{2½}	3^{2¼}	Cauthen S	126	*.30	96-13	LittleReb120^{2¼}RadarAhed123^{hd}Affrmd126^3	Hemmed in to str	5
14Oct78- 8Bel	sly 1½	:45^1 1:09^2 2:01^4 2:27^1	3↑ J C Gold Cup-G1	2	2	2^{hd}	3^7	4^{15}	5^{18¾}	Cauthen S	121	2.20e	65-13	Exceller126^{no}Seattle Slew126^{14}Great Contractor126^{4¾}		6
Saddle slipped																
16Sep78- 8Bel	fst 1⅛	:47 1:10^1 1:33^1 1:45^4	3↑ Marlboro Cup H-G1	1	2	2^{2½}	2^{2½}	2^3	2^3	Cauthen S	124	*.50	95-12	SeattleSlew128^{3}Affirmed124^{5}NastyandBold118^4	No excuse	6
19Aug78- 8Sar	fst 1¼	:48 1:11^3 1:36^4 2:02	Travers-G1	3	2	2^{hd}	1^{1½}	1^2	1^{1¾}	Pincay L Jr	126	*.70	91-14	[D]Affirmed126^{1¾}Alydar126^{3¾}NastyandBold126^{15}	Came over	4
Disqualified and placed second																
8Aug78- 8Sar	gd 1⅛	:46^3 1:10^1 1:35 1:47^4	Jim Dandy-G3	4	2	2^8	2^7	2^4	1^½	Cauthen S	128	*.05	96-04	Affirmed128^{½}SensitivePrince119^{20}Addison114^{6½}	Going away	5
10Jun78- 8Bel	fst 1½	:50 1:14 2:01^3 2:26^4	Belmont-G1	3	1	1^1	1^{hd}	1^{hd}	1^{hd}	Cauthen S	126	*.60	86-11	Affirmed126^{hd}Alydar126^{13}Darby Creek Road126^{7¾}	Driving	5
20May78- 8Pim	fst 1$\frac{3}{16}$	:47^3 1:11^4 1:36^1 1:54^2	Preakness-G1	6	2	1^1	1^1	1^½	1^{nk}	Cauthen S	126	*.50	98-12	Affirmed126^{nk}Alydar126^{7½}Believe It126^{2½}	Brisk handling	7
6May78- 8CD	fst 1¼	:45^3 1:10^4 1:35^4 2:01^1	Ky Derby-G1	2	2	3^{5½}	2^{hd}	1^2	1^{1½}	Cauthen S	126	1.80	91-12	Affirmed126^{1½}Alydar126^{1¼}Believe It126^{4¼}	Fully extended	11
16Apr78- 8Hol	fst 1⅛	:45 1:09^2 1:35 1:48^1	Hol Derby-G1	2	1	1^{hd}	1^1	1^{2½}	1^2	Cauthen S	122	*.30	91-17	Affirmed122^{2}Think Snow122^{3}Radar Ahead122^2	Driving	9
2Apr78- 8SA	fst 1⅛	:45^4 1:09^4 1:35^3 1:48	S Anita Derby-G1	7	2	1^1	1^{1½}	1^{3½}	1^8	Pincay L Jr	120	*.30	92-16	Affirmed120^{8}Balzac120^{1}Think Snow120^{2½}	Handily	12
18Mar78- 8SA	fst 1$\frac{1}{16}$	:24^1 :48^2 1:12 1:42^3	San Felipe-G2	4	2	2^1	2^{hd}	1^{hd}	1^2	Cauthen S	126	*.30	89-17	Affirmed126^{2}Chance Dancer117^{6}Tampoy118^{1½}	Driving	6
8Mar78- 6SA	fst 6½f	:21^3 :44^2 1:09 1:15^3	Alw 30000	4	1	4^{3½}	1^{1½}	1^4	1^5	Cauthen S	124	*.20	92-16	Affirmed124^{5}Spotted Charger114^{½}Don F.114^{hd}	Easily	5
29Oct77- 8Lrl	fst 1$\frac{1}{16}$	:24 :48^4 1:13^3 1:44^1	Lrl Futurity-G1	3	2	2^1	2^{hd}	1^{hd}	1^{nk}	Cauthen S	122	1.40	92-27	Affirmed122^{nk}Alydar122^{10}StardeNskr122^{27}	Long,hard drive	4
15Oct77- 6Bel	my 1	:24^2 :48^1 1:12^2 1:36^3	Champagne-G1	5	3	3^2	1^{hd}	1^½	2^{1¼}	Cauthen S	122	*1.20	84-17	Alydar122^{1¼}Affirmed122^{1¼}Darby Creek Road122^{1½}	2nd best	6
10Sep77- 8Bel	gd 7f	:23^3 :46^3 1:09^4 1:21^3	Futurity-G1	2	2	2^½	1^{hd}	2^{hd}	1no	Cauthen S	122	*1.20	94-10	Affirmed122^{no}Alydar122^{11}NastyandBold122^{hd}	Strong drive	5
27Aug77- 8Sar	fst 6½f	:22^4 :45^1 1:09^1 1:15^2	Hopeful-G1	4	1	3^2	2^{hd}	1^{hd}	1^½	Cauthen S	122	2.30	98-11	Affirmed122^{½}Alydar122^{2½}RegalandRoyal122^{hd}	Good handling	5
17Aug77- 8Sar	fst 6f	:21^4 :44^3 1:09^3	Sanford-G2	3	2	3^{5½}	4^3	2^½	1^{2¾}	Cauthen S	124	*1.30	92-15	Affirmed124^{2¾}TltUp122^{hd}JtDplomcy124^{nk}	Driving,very wide	6
23Jly77- 5Hol	fst 6f	:21^3 :44^2 :56^2 1:09^1	Juv Champ (Div 1) 104k	6	3	1^{hd}	1^½	1^4	1^7	Pincay L Jr	122	*.40	93-15	Affirmed122^{7}He's Dewan122^{6}Esops Foibles122^{¾}	Easily	8
6Jly77- 8Bel	fst 5½f	:22^2 :45^4 :57^2 1:03^3	Great American 36k	1	1	1^1	2^{hd}	2^{1½}	2^{3½}	Cordero A Jr	122	4.60	93-16	Alydar117^{3½}Affirmed122^{2}Going Investor122^4	No match	7
15Jun77- 8Bel	fst 5½f	:22^2 :45^3 :58^2 1:05	©Youthful 37k	1	1	2^½	2^½	1^{hd}	1^{nk}	Cordero A Jr	119	3.40	90-17	Affirmed119^{nk}Wood Native119^{½}Sensitive Nose119^{2½}	Driving	11
24May77- 4Bel	fst 5½f	:23 :47^2 :59^3 1:06	Md Sp Wt	10	1	1^½	1^{1½}	1^2	1^{4½}	Gonzalez B	117	14.30	85-21	Affirmed117^{4½}Innocuous122^{3½}Gymnast122^2	Ridden out	10

Alydar

ch. c. 1975, by Raise a Native (Native Dancer)–Sweet Tooth, by On-and-On

Lifetime record: 26 14 9 1 $957,195

Own.– Calumet Farm
Br.– Calumet Farm (Ky)
Tr.– John M. Veitch

Date–Track	Cond/Dist	Fractions	Race	Running Line	Jockey	Wt	Odds	Spd	Top Finishers	Comment
4Jly79- 8Bel	fst 1¼	:492 1:133 1:371 2:013 3↑	Suburban H-G1	4 3 36½ 2nd 3½ 31½	Fell J	126	*.60	91-16	StateDinner118½MistrBr120¾Alydr126½	Weakened 5
17Jun79- 8Bel	sly 1⅛	:46 1:09 1:333 1:463 3↑	Nassau County H-G3	1 2 21½ 2½ 11½ 13¾	Fell J	124	*.40	94-06	Alydar1243¾Nasty and Bold11614Sorry Lookin113	In hand 3
28May79- 8Bel	fst 1	:224 :45 1:091 1:34 3↑	Metropolitan H-G1	9 3 3½ 32 66½ 612	Velasquez J	126	*.40	86-16	State Dinner1153Dr. Patches1183½Sorry Lookin113½	Tired 9
5May79- 8Aqu	fst 7f	:224 :451 1:091 1:214 3↑	Carter H-G2	2 3 35½ 38½ 36 2nk	Velasquez J	126	1.50	92-25	StardeNaskra122nkAlydr128½SnstvPrnc1266½	Finished fast 6
13Apr79- 9OP	fst 1 1/16	:241 :481 1:13 1:433 4↑	Oaklawn H-G2	2 5 3nk 2½ 3½ 2no	Velasquez J	127	*.30	90-19	SanJuanHill114noAlydar127¾ALettrtoHrry1257	Lost the nod 7
31Mar79- 5Hia	fst 7f	:233 :462 1:103 1:222 4↑	Alw 13000	5 2 31½ 3½ 12 17	Velasquez J	114	*.10	91-17	Alydar1147Fort Prevel1224Jachal II1091½	Much the best 6
19Aug78- 8Sar	fst 1¼	:48 1:113 1:364 2:02	Travers-G1	4 4 32 21½ 22 21¾	Velaquez J	126	1.00	89-14	[D]Affirmed126½Alydar126¾Nasty and Bold12615	Taken up 4

Placed first through disqualification

Date–Track	Cond/Dist	Fractions	Race	Running Line	Jockey	Wt	Odds	Spd	Top Finishers	Comment
5Aug78- 8Sar	fst 1⅛	:463 1:102 1:351 1:472 3↑	Whitney H-G2	9 7 613 45½ 14 110	Velasquez J	123	*.70	98-09	Alydar12310Buckaroo112hdFather Hogan114nk	Hand ride 9
22Jly78- 8AP	fst 1¼	:474 1:111 1:353 2:002	Arl Classic-G2	3 3 23½ 15 18 113	Fell J	126	*.05	95-19	Alydar12613ChiefofDixieland1141GordieH.1145	Much best 5
10Jun78- 8Bel	fst 1½	:50 1:14 2:013 2:264	Belmont-G1	2 3 21 2nd 2nd 2nk	Velasquez J	126	1.10	86-11	Affirmed126hdAlydar126½Darby Creek Road1267¾	Game try 5
20May78- 8Pim	fst 1 3/16	:473 1:114 1:361 1:542	Preakness-G1	3 6 65½ 42 2½ 2nk	Velasquez J	126 b	1.80	98-12	Affirmed126hdAlydar126¾Believe It1264½	Game effort 7
6May78- 8CD	fst 1¼	:453 1:104 1:354 2:011	Ky Derby-G1	10 9 917 44½ 34 21½	Velasquez J	126 b	*1.20	89-12	Affirmed126½Alydar126½Believe It1264¼	Closed fast 11
27Apr78- 7Kee	gd 1⅛	:471 1:112 1:372 1:493	Blue Grass-G1	9 6 611 47 16 113	Velasquez J	121 b	*.10	89-19	Alydar12113Raymond Earl121noGo Forth1211¾	Ridden out 9
1Apr78- 9GP	fst 1⅛	:471 1:111 1:352 1:47	Florida Derby-G1	6 4 21 1½ 1hd 12	Velasquez J	122 b	*.20	99-10	Alydar1222Believe It1227½Dr. Valeri122nk	Handily 7
4Mar78- 9Hia	fst 1⅛	:453 1:094 1:35 1:47	Flamingo-G1	6 6 65 31 12 14½	Velasquez J	122 b	*.90e	97-05	Alydar12242NoonTimeSpender1221Dr. Valeri122nk	Ridden out 8
11Feb78- 5Hia	fst 7f	:234 :464 1:103 1:221	Alw 14000	5 8 54 53½ 2nd 12	Velasquez J	122 b	*.30	92-13	Alydr1222NoonTimeSpendr1195½LaVoyagus109nk	Ridden out 8
26Nov77- 8Aqu	sly 1⅛	:471 1:112 1:351 1:474	Remsen-G2	5 4 49 45½ 35 22	Velasquez J	122 b	*.60	94-13	Believe It1222Alydar1221½Quadratic1166	2nd best 5
29Oct77- 8Lrl	fst 1 1/16	:24 :484 1:133 1:441	Lrl Futurity-G1	1 3 31 1hd 2nd 2nk	Velasquez J	122 b	*.40	92-27	Affirmed122nkAlydr12210StrdNskr12227	Steadied,sharp try 4
15Oct77- 6Bel	my 1	:242 :481 1:122 1:363	Champagne-G1	1 5 42 52¾ 41½ 11½	Velasquez J	122 b	1.50	85-17	Alydar1221½Affirmed1221¼DarbyCreekRoad1221½	Ridden out 6
10Sep77- 8Bel	gd 7f	:233 :463 1:094 1:213	Futurity-G1	1 5 32½ 2hd 1hd 2no	Maple E	122 b	1.50	94-10	Affirmd122noAlydr12211NstyndBold122hd	Short lead, missed 5
27Aug77- 8Sar	fst 6½f	:224 :451 1:091 1:152	Hopeful-G1	1 4 44 4¾ 2hd 2½	Maple E	122 b	*1.00	97-11	Affirmed1222½Alydar1222½RegalandRoyl122nk	Steadied early 5
13Aug77- 8Mth	sly 6f	:222 :453 1:103	Sapling-G1	4 5 34 23 2hd 12½	Maple E	122 b	*.60	87-17	Alydr1222½NoonTimeSpendr1224½DominantRulr122no	Easily 5
27Jly77- 8Bel	fst 1	:23 :457 1:10	Tremont 36k	4 4 33 31½ 11 11½	Maple E	124	*.40	92-16	Alydar1241½Believe It1173¾Jet Diplomacy1245½	Ridden out 7
6Jly77- 8Bel	fst 5½f	:222 :454 :572 1:033	Great American 36k	7 7 42½ 1hd 11½ 13½	Maple E	117	*.80	95-16	Alydar117¾Affirmed1222Going Investor1224	Ridden out 7
24Jun77- 4Bel	fst 5½f	:224 :461 :581 1:041	Md Sp Wt	9 8 63¾ 1hd 12 16¾	Maple E	122	*2.10	94-20	Alydar1226¾Believe It1221Sauce Boat1173½	Handily 10
15Jun77- 8Bel	fst 5½f	:222 :453 :582 1:05	©Youthful 37k	7 9 912 911 510 55	Maple E	115	*1.80	85-17	Affirmed119nkWoodNative119½SenstvNos1192½	In close turn 11

Ancient Title

dkbbr. g. 1970, by Gummo (Fleet Nasrullah)–Hi Little Gal, by Bar le Duc

Lifetime record: 57 24 11 9 $1,252,791

Own.– Kirkland Stable
Br.– Mr & Mrs William Kirkland (Cal)
Tr.– Keith L. Stucki

Date–Track	Cond/Dist	Fractions	Race	Running Line	Jockey	Wt	Odds	Spd	Top Finishers	Comment
19Aug78- 8Dmr	fst 1 1/16	:224 :461 1:101 1:401 3↑	San Diego H 43k	6 2 21 55½ 512 -	Shoemaker W	125 b	*.30	--	Vic's Magic1167Mr. Redoy1197Clout1172½	Lame 6
30Jly78- 7Dmr	fst 6f	:214 :441 :56 1:081 3↑	Alw 17000	2 4 32½ 2½ 1hd 2½	Shoemaker W	117 b	*.40	97-11	AncientTitle1172½SeLeTe1148StainedGlass1144	Drew out 6
19Feb78- 8SA	fst 1⅛	:453 1:093 1:342 1:461 4↑	San Antonio-G1	2 2 2½ 1½ 21½ 27	Shoemaker W	120 b	2.20	94-12	Vigors1217Ancient Title1203½Double Discount1167	7

No match for winner

Date–Track	Cond/Dist	Fractions	Race	Running Line	Jockey	Wt	Odds	Spd	Top Finishers	Comment
29Jan78- 8SA	fst 1 1/16	:231 :461 1:094 1:401 4↑	San Pasqual H-G2	4 1 12½ 11 1½ 11½	McHargue DG	124 b	1.80	101-09	Ancient Title1241½Mark's Place120nkDouble Discount12017	4

Broke slowly

Date–Track	Cond/Dist	Fractions	Race	Running Line	Jockey	Wt	Odds	Spd	Top Finishers	Comment
23Oct77- 8SA	fm 1½Ⓣ	:471 1:113 2:013 2:262 3↑	Oak Tree Inv'l-G1	3 2 11 2hd 2hd 3nk	McHargue DG	126 b	6.30	83-17	Crystal Water126nkVigors126noAncient Title1261½	Gamely 10
9Oct77- 8SA	fm 1¼Ⓣ	:444 1:084 1:332 1:572 3↑	C F Burke H-G2	3 2 2½ 1hd 22 56½	McHargue DG	127 b	*1.80	95-00	DoubleDiscount1161NoTurning1183½Vigors1204	Faltered late 8
5Sep77- 8Dmr	fst *1⅛	:443 1:081 1:323 1:552 3↑	Del Mar H-G2	7 1 12½ 13 15 15	McHargue DG	123 b	8.50	106-08	AncientTitle1235PaintedWagon1183Cascapedia1171	In hand 9
29Aug77- 8Dmr	fm 1Ⓣ	:233 :473 1:114 1:36 3↑	Alw 14000	4 1 1½ 1hd 11½ 12½	Pierce D	120 b	*.70	95-06	AncientTitle1202½Chindo117noChil the Kite1207	Handily 6
17Jly77- 8Hol	fst 1¼	:223 :454 1:092 1:41 3↑	Citation H 82k	1 4 41½ 42 53½ 42½	Hawley S	124 b	*.90	87-16	PaintdWagon11711½Legndrio III1141½PayTribute1183	Bore out 7
18Jun77- 8Hol	fst 1¼	:451 1:09 1:334 2:00 3↑	Hol Gold Cup H-G1	10 7 52¾ 44 44 45½	Hawley S	125 b	6.50	86-13	CrystalWater129nkCascapedia116noCaucasus1245	Wide,hung 12
5Jun77- 8Hol	fst 1⅛	:46 1:093 1:344 1:473 3↑	Bel Air H-G2	5 3 1hd 2hd 2hd 1no	Hawley S	124 b	*1.10	94-14	Ancient Title124noRajab1146Legendario III115no	Hard drive 6
22May77- 8Hol	fst 1¼	:222 :452 1:091 1:41 3↑	Californian-G1	3 6 64½ 33 34 1½	Hawley S	123 b	5.30	88-14	CrystalWater128hdMark's Plc1212½AncntTtl1238	Evenly late 6
6Mar77- 8SA	fst 1¼	:452 1:093 1:341 1:591 4↑	S Anita H-G1	2 7 76½ 76 1112 1113	Hawley S	125 b	3.90	89-14	CrystalWater122hdFaliraki1144½KingPellnor1305½	No speed 11
20Feb77- 8SA	fst 1⅛	:463 1:101 1:35 1:474 4↑	San Antonio-G1	2 2 1hd 1½ 2½ 11	Hawley S	119 b	*2.80	93-14	AncntTtle1191DoubleDiscnt1151½Propernts1143	Going away 10
29Jan77- 8SA	fst 1 1/16	:231 :462 1:101 1:41 4↑	San Pasqual H-G2	6 4 2½ 53 63¾ 56¼	Hawley S	125	*2.10	91-12	Uniformity117¾Distant Land1161Pisistrato117¾	8

Weakened final quarter

Date–Track	Cond/Dist	Fractions	Race	Running Line	Jockey	Wt	Odds	Spd	Top Finishers	Comment
28Dec76- 8SA	fst 6f	:214 :441 :56 1:083 2↑	Palos Verdes H 47k	11 3 63½ 33½ 34 33½	Cordero A Jr	126	3.00	92-12	Maheras119½Sure Fire1163Ancient Title1263½	Mild rally 13
4Jly76- 8Hol	fm 1⅛Ⓣ	:474 1:113 1:352 1:48 3↑	American H-G2	2 4 45 43 41½ 53½	Hawley S	126 b	2.60	92-09	KingPellinore1213RiotinParis123¾Caucasus120hd	Weakened 7
20Jun76- 8Hol	fst 1¼	:454 1:10 1:343 1:584 3↑	Hol Gold Cup H-G1	5 6 79½ 52½ 65 91¾	Hawley S	127 b	*1.70	88-09	Pay Tribute1173¾Avatar1232Riot in Paris123¾	8

Little speed,lacked rally

Date–Track	Cond/Dist	Fractions	Race	Running Line	Jockey	Wt	Odds	Spd	Top Finishers	Comment
23May76- 8Hol	fst 1 1/16	:231 :464 1:094 1:411 3↑	Californian-G1	1 5 55½ 42 32 1hd	Hawley S	127 b	*.80	89-14	AncientTitle127hdPayTrbut1174AustnMttlr116no	Off slowly 7
8May76- 8Hol	fst 1	:23 :454 1:094 1:343 3↑	Caballero H-G3	1 5 55 41¾ 2hd 1½	Hawley S	128 b	1.40	93-15	AncientTitle128½BigDestiny1183½PayTribut1203	Wide rally 5
7Mar76- 8SA	fst 1¼	:452 1:093 1:342 2:002 4↑	S Anita H-G1	9 3 74 43 21½ 2no	Hawley S	124 b	9.30	96-11	Royal Glint124noAncient Title1241½Lightning Mandate1206½	15
22Feb76- 8SA	fst 1⅛	:471 1:111 1:353 1:481 4↑	San Antonio-G1	10 5 66 54½ 1010 1010	Hawley S	126 b	3.90	81-13	LightningMandate1182DancingPapa117½MessngrofSong1222¾	10

Fractious in gate,bore out on turn

Date–Track	Cond/Dist	Fractions	Race	Running Line	Jockey	Wt	Odds	Spd	Top Finishers	Comment
1Nov75- 5SA	fst 1¼	:462 1:102 1:35 2:01 3↑	Nat'l Champ Inv'l 350k	5 5 75½ 32 74¾ 75¾	Pincay L Jr	124 b	*2.20	87-15	Dulcia117nkRoyal Glint1202½Tizna118½	Wide,tired 11
13Sep75- 8Bel	fst 1¼	:471 1:104 1:352 2:00 3↑	Marlboro Cup Inv'l H-G1	2 4 21½ 11½ 32 37½	Pincay L Jr	126 b	9.00	91-11	Wajima119hdForego1297½Ancient Title126¾	Tired 7
1Sep75- 8Bel	fst 1⅛	:452 1:09 1:341 1:471 3↑	Governor-G1	5 3 34½ 23 21 32	Hawley S	130 b	10.30	89-18	Wajima115hdFoolish Pleasure1252Ancient Title130¾	10

Long drive,weakened

Date–Track	Cond/Dist	Fractions	Race	Running Line	Jockey	Wt	Odds	Spd	Top Finishers	Comment
2Aug75- 8Sar	fst 1⅛	:462 1:101 1:352 1:481 3↑	Whitney H-G2	6 1 1½ 1½ 1hd 1nk	Hawley S	128 b	3.50	94-07	Ancient Title1281½Group Plan1153Arbees Boy1184	Best 7
4Jly75- 8Hol	fm 1⅛Ⓣ	:50 1:134 1:373 1:493 3↑	American H (Div 2)-G2	6 2 21 3nk 21½ 31	Pincay L Jr	128 b	*1.50	87-11	Montmartre1151TopCrowd115hdAncntTtl128hd	Broke slowly 9
21Jun75- 8Hol	fst 1¼	:47 1:103 1:344 1:591 3↑	Hol Gold Cup Inv'l H-G1	4 1 11½ 12½ 14 14½	Pincay L Jr	124 b	*1.40	95-15	Ancient Title1254½Big Band115½El Tarta1152¾	Much best 7
26May75- 8Hol	fst 1 1/16	:231 :461 1:092 1:401 3↑	Californian-G1	5 2 32 2½ 1hd 1hd	Pincay L Jr	126 b	*1.30	94-10	AncientTitle126hdBigBand1174½Century'sEnvoy1173	Driving 10
10May75- 8Hol	fst 1	:222 :45 1:083 1:334 3↑	Caballero H 55k	6 6 74 21 22½ 23½	Pincay L Jr	126 b	*1.20	94-10	June's Love1163½Ancient Title126½Big Band1193	Hung 9
23Feb75- 8SA	fst 1 1/16	:454 1:09 1:34 1:464 4↑	San Antonio-G1	1 3 34 33 32½ 32½	Pincay L Jr	128 b	*1.60	96-10	Cheriepe1202½FirstBack117nkAncientTitle1282	No excuse 5
19Jan75- 8SA	fst 7f	:212 :432 1:08 1:211 4↑	San Carlos H-G2	1 8 44½ 31½ 1½ 1¾	Pincay L Jr	128 b	*1.00	97-12	AncientTitl128¾[DH]HudsnCounty116[DH]BhKy117nk	Off slowly 12
26Dec74- 8SA	fst 6f	:221 :444 :562 1:084 2↑	Palos Verdes H-G3	4 4 21½ 2hd 1½ 11½	Pincay L Jr	126 b	*1.10	95-15	Ancient Title126½Princely Native116½King of theBlues113hd	8

Drew clear under urging

Date–Track	Cond/Dist	Fractions	Race	Running Line	Jockey	Wt	Odds	Spd	Top Finishers	Comment
23May74- 8Hol	fst 1¼	:471 1:112 1:353 1:594 3↑	Hol Gold Cup Inv'l H-G1	7 3 34 1hd 21½ 22½	Pincay L Jr	125 b	1.50	89-14	TreeofKnowldge1152¼AncntTtl125hdWrHm114¾	Bid,weakened 10
27May74- 8Hol	fst 1⅛	:231 :462 1:092 1:401 3↑	Californian-G1	8 3 22 2hd 1½ 21½	Grant H	126 b	*1.80	93-16	Quack1261¼Ancient Title126¾Woodland Pines120hd	No match 9
11May74- 8Hol	fst 7f	:222 :45 1:082 1:202 3↑	Los Angeles H-G2	8 2 2½ 2½ 1nk 1nk	Pincay L Jr	126 b	*2.00	97-14	AncientTtl126nkWoodlndPns1182SoftVictory118nk	Hard urged 8
14Apr74- 8Hol	fm 1 1/16Ⓣ	:223 :464 1:102 1:404 3↑	Lakeside H-G2	6 2 2½ 2½ 54 52¾	Pincay L Jr	126 b	*1.40	93-06	Matun120hdVisualizer1151Dancing Papa1161	Rank,faltered 7

10Mar74- 8SA sl 1¼ :473 1:12 1:372 2:033 4↑ S Anita H-G1 1 3 2½ 21 23 24½ Pincay L Jr 125 b 2.60 75-26 PrinceDantan1194½AncientTitle125½BigSpruce1225 Good try 11
9Feb74- 8SA fst 1¼ :464 1:111 1:352 2:004 C H Strub-G1 7 1 11½ 12 13½ 13 Pincay L Jr 121 b 1.40 94-15 AncientTitle1213DancngPp1161PrncDntn1151 In full stride 9
26Jan74- 8SA fst 1⅛ :464 1:102 1:344 1:473 San Fernando-G2 6 1 12½ 13½ 16 13½ Pincay L Jr 120 b 4.30 94-14 Ancient Title1203½Linda's Chief1233½Mariache II114½ 7
Ridden out
12Jan74- 8SA gd 7f :221 :443 1:093 1:224 Malibu-G2 2 2 1hd 13½ 16 13 Toro F 120 b 2.20 89-15 Ancient Title1203Linda's Chief126½Dancing Papa1204 7
Opened lead on turn
27Dec73- 8SA fst 6f :214 :442 :563 1:09 2↑ Palos Verdes H-G3 1 5 32½ 41½ 3½ 33 Pincay L Jr 122 b *1.20 93-13 Woodland Pines1151Tragic Isle1172Ancient Title1222 Hung 8
19May73- 8Hol fm 1Ⓣ :222 :46 1:102 1:353 ©Will Rogers H-G2 2 3 35 44½ 11 21¾ Toro F 124 b 3.10 90-11 Groshawk1231¾AncntTtl124nkDHMugPntr1131¾ Led,no match 10
28Apr73- 8Hol fst 7f :214 :434 1:08 1:21 Inglewood-G2 8 1 33 2½ 1½ 1hd Toro F 122 b *1.10 94-13 Ancient Title122hdGroshawk1223¾Pontoise1146 Driving 8
31Mar73- 8SA fst 1⅛ :46 1:094 1:343 1:47 S Anita Derby-G1 4 2 1hd 11½ 33 48 Toro F 120 b 13.60 89-12 Sham1202½Linda'sChief1202¼OutoftheEast1203¼ Wide,tired 6
17Mar73- 8SA fst 1 1/16 :224 :46 1:10 1:414 San Felipe H-G2 1 1 12 11 2½ 23 Toro F 120 b 15.50 90-13 Linda'sChief1263AncientTitl1201¾OutofthEst1153 No match 9
1Mar73- 8SA fst 1 :223 :451 1:092 1:334 San Jacinto-G2 3 1 2hd 1hd 21 25 Toro F 122 b 2.30 96-12 Linda'sChief1225AncientTitle1221¼Aljamin1155½ No match 7
1Feb73- 8SA fst 7f :22 :442 1:083 1:21 San Vicente-G3 3 4 12 12 1½ 1nk Toro F 122 b 2.70 98-16 Ancient Title122nkLinda's Chief1227Out of the East114hd 9
Going away
18Jan73- 8SA sly 6f :214 :451 :581 1:112 San Miguel-G3 3 6 42 41 2hd 23½ Toro F 120 b 2.20 80-24 Linda'sChief1203½AncientTtl1201PlntyofStyl117½ No match 7
30Dec72- 8SA fst 7f :214 :441 1:091 1:222 ⓈCal Br Champ 61k 5 2 3½ 1½ 11½ 14¾ Toro F 117 b 1.50 91-10 AncientTitle1174¾RiverLad114¾PlentyofStyle115nk Handily 8
18Oct72- 8SA fst 7f :214 :434 1:074 1:204 Sunny Slope 28k 3 3 2hd 11 12½ 13 Grant H 121 b 7.40 99-14 Ancient Title1213Groshawk1241¼Autry1192½ In full stride 9
25Aug72- 7Dmr fst 6f :214 :442 :563 1:09 De Anza 20k 4 2 2hd 2hd 22½ 32½ Harris W 117 b 3.00 91-10 Lucky Mike1192Bottle Brush115½Ancient Title1172½ Tired 5
11Aug72- 7Dmr fst 6f :214 :441 :563 1:091 ⓈCTBA 16k 2 5 1½ 13½ 13½ 18 Harris W 116 b 1.50 93-14 AncientTitle1168BoldBlcony116noRsHgh1211¾ Much the best 7
22Jly72- 8Hol fst 6f :212 :434 :561 1:092 Hol Juv Ch 140k 7 6 53 44½ 55 84½ Valenzuela I 122 b 8.70 87-11 BoldLiz1191DocMarcus122¾DLuckyMike122hd Speed,tired 11
14Jly72- 7Hol fst 5½f :211 :442 :564 1:03 Alw 6500 4 7 34 3nk 1½ 15 Grant H 120 b 7.30 97-14 Ancient Title1205Crocation1201Rotarian120¾ Going away 10
7Jly72- 3Hol fst 5½f :22 :452 :573 1:04 ©Md Sp Wt 3 6 2hd 1hd 21 1hd Pincay L Jr 118 b *.60 92-12 AncntTtl118hdSpnLghtnng1187Nbu118nk Up in final strides 12
15Jun72- 3Hol fst 5f :22 :45 :571 ©Md Sp Wt 7 3 31 2½ 23 26 Palomino J 118 b 9.20 91-15 Lucky Mike1186Ancient Title1182½Nabu1184 Bid turn,hung 12

Athenian Idol

ch. g. 1968, by Alcibiades II (Alycidon)–Dottys Dream, by Francis S. **Lifetime record: 22 6 2 4 $36,530**
Own.– W.L. Pape
Br.– Harbor View Farm (Ky)
Tr.– J. Sheppard

30Mar74- 4Cam fm *2 S'Chase 4:191 4↑ Carolina Cup 10k 4 4 - - - - O'Brien M 155 -e -- Breaking Dawn1391Metello1535½Winigo15099 Fell 6
16Mar74- 4AtH fm *2 S'Chase 3:522 4↑ Alw 10000 1 5 510 43½ 21 31¼ O'Brien M 154 - -- Metello147¾Juac Hollow157½Athenian Idol1546 5
17Nov73- 2Cam fm 2 3/16 S'Chase 5:214 4↑ Colonial Cup 50k 2 12 1115 1112 921 41¼ Fishback J 147 -e -- LuckyBoyIII149noSoothsayr162noDremMgc1531¼ Closed fast 15
27Oct73- 6FH fm *2Ⓣ 3:414 3↑ Alw 1000 3 4 53¼ 24 2½ 15 Sheppard J 168 - -- Athenian Idol1685Minaccia1654Noble Spirit1632 Drew out 7
6Oct73- 4Lig fm *2½ S'Chase 5:032 4↑ Temple Gwathmey H 25k 1 8 88½ 86½ 3¾ 11¼ Fishback J 140 -e -- Athenian Idol1401¼Soothsayer1628Top Bid1572 Driving 8
23Aug73- 9Sar fm 2 1/16 Hurdles 3:424 4↑ Handicap 10000 7 6 57 58½ 16 110 Fishback J 140 5.00 -- Athenian Idol14010Jive145nkManchu Prince1395 Ridden out 8
15Aug73- 9Sar gd 2 1/16 Hurdles 3:532 4↑ Alw 7500 3 3 53½ 57 38½ 27½ Fishback J 145 2.50 -- Jive1427½Athenian Idol1451¼Hipocampo1481 Second best 6
9Aug73- 9Sar fm 1⅞ Hurdles 3:24 4↑ Clm 7000 5 5 45½ 2½ 18 110 Fishback J 138 *1.50 -- Athenian Idol13810Star of Vertex1381½Christmas Cheer1419 6
Ridden out
1Aug73- 9Sar fm 1⅞ Hurdles 3:24 4↑ Clm 7000 7 6 512 26 22 43 O'Brien M 150 *3.30e -- Tater Pie1441Manchu Prince1411¼Seven Trips156¾ Tired 9
11Jly73- 6Del sly 5f :222 :463 :584 4↑ Clm 7500 3 4 67½ 79¼ 611 68½ Lee T 114 b 17.60 86-17 Harbor King1143¼Gray Idol1172½Joes Battlecry1121 Outrun 8
6Jun73- 4Del fm *1½ Hurdles 2:411 3↑ Clm 8000 2 7 913 94½ 44½ 57¼ Achuff W5 148 *2.40 -- Seven Trips150¾Antigua Star1474¾Star of Vertex137hd 10
Bobbled third jump
9May73- 5Fai fm *1⅞ Hurdles 3:211 4↑ Alw 3000 5 4 45 22½ 314 322 O'Brien L 155 s 2.90 -- Babamist14710CastlebarII15212AthenianIdol155¾ Weakened 5
21Apr73- 3Clm fm *1¾ Hurdles 3:26 3↑ Alw 4000 5 4 41¾ 1¾ 21½ 32¼ Brittle C III 148 s - -- Monsieur Ledocteur1482BreakingDawn148nkAthenian Idl1481½ 6
Weakened
7Apr73- 2Try sf *1½ Hurdles 2:401 3↑ Alw 1800 4 3 32½ 22½ 12 11½ O'Brien M 155 s - -- AthenianIdl1551½PineyCreek136MonsiurLdoctur150 Driving 4
24Mar73- 1Aik fm *1½ Hurdles 2:41 3↑ Alw 2500 1 9 64½ 32½ 21 24 O'Brien M 155 s -- Monsieur Ledocteur1504Athenian Idol1551½Jay's Trouble1368 9
Game try
17Mar73- 2AtH gd *1½ Hurdles 3:062 3↑ Alw 1750 6 6 54 1½ 12 12 O'Brien M 155 s -- Athenian Idol1552Mr. Moody1456Cup Hunt1483 Driving 7
Previously owned by J. Sheppard
23Sep71- 3Bel sf 1⅞ Hurdles 3:284 Elkridge H 19k 7 11 - - - - Skiffington T Jr 135 41.60 -- Winigo1508JuacHollow1404ManchuPrince1414 Poor landing 11
27Aug71- 9Sar sf 1⅝ Hurdles 3:082 3↑ Alw 6500 10 9 98½ 63¾ 711 97¾ O'Brien M 141 *2.30 -- ManchuPrince141½BrkngDwn141½GlrousCmbt1421¼ Bobbled 10
12Aug71- 9Sar fm 1⅝ Hurdles 2:574 3↑ Alw 6500 7 6 77½ 1hd 11 1hd Skiffington T Jr5 136 14.90 -- DAthnnIdl136hdArmyHtch1414½GlorousCombt1452 Bore out 8
Disqualified and placed third
28Jun71- 3Del fm 1 1/16Ⓣ :231 :471 1:123 1:453 3↑ Md Sp Wt 4 7 65½ 75¾ 68 510 Lee T 113 38.60 66-25 IrishTenor1242¾Chrisaway113nkForwardDrive1135 No factor 9
31May71- 4Del my 6f :223 :46 1:123 3↑ Md 7000 11 10 79 1015 1014 99¾ Lee T 110 47.30 72-18 SummrPlanning1101Villad'Est108¾NoonFlowr109½ No factor 12
17Nov70- 1Lrl gd 7f :232 :483 1:153 1:282 Md 5000 9 11 84¾ 66 813 821 Lee T 120 9.90 48-24 CallAssistant1129TedsGlow117½SharpDoer1202½ No factor 12

Autobiography

ch. c. 1968, by Sky High II (Star Kingdom)–King's Story, by Bold Ruler **Lifetime record: 36 10 11 4 $385,909**
Own.– S. Sommer
Br.– Wheatley Stable (Ky)
Tr.– F. Martin

19Feb73- 8SA fst 1½ :471 1:121 2:012 2:271 4↑ San Luis Obispo H-G2 3 7 712 - - - Belmonte E 126 b *.70e -- Queen'sHustlr1127ChinaSilk1151¼RvrBuoy1171½ Broke down 9
3Feb73- 8SA sly 1 1/16 :234 :464 1:102 1:414 4↑ San Pasqual H-G2 1 6 611½ 57 48½ 39¼ Belmonte E 125 b *1.50 84-12 Single Agent1193½Kennedy Road1195¾Autobiography1252 6
Passed tired horses
2Dec72- 7Aqu fst 1⅝ :463 1:37 2:022 2:41 3↑ Gallant Fox H 56k 2 5 510 31 12½ 1¾ Cordero A Jr 128 b *.60 100-10 DAutobiography128¾CraftyKhal117nkRulbyRson1139 Bore in 7
Disqualified and placed second
28Oct72- 7Aqu fst 2 :474 2:281 2:541 3:212 3↑ J C Gold Cup 113k 7 1 12 110 114 115 Cordero A Jr 124 b 2.10e 89-17 Autobiography12415KeytotheMnt1193RivaRidge11910 Easily 7
20Oct72- 7Aqu my 1⅛ :48 1:123 1:372 1:494 3↑ Alw 15000 2 4 34 2hd 1hd 12 Cordero A Jr 119 b 1.50 87-20 Autbiography1192CnonroII119nkRulbyRson1163½ Ridden out 6
30Sep72- 7Bel sly 1½ :47 1:112 2:012 2:282 3↑ Woodward 115k 8 10 1012 49 410 34¼ Cordero A Jr 126 b 6.10e 87-14 Key to the Mint1191¼DSummer Guest1163Autobiography1262 10
Placed second through disqualification
16Sep72- 7Det fst 1⅛ :47 1:11 1:36 1:491 3↑ Mich 1⅛ H (Div 1) 78k 4 5 79 78¾ 45 34¼ Cordero A Jr 119 b *1.20 87-16 King's Bishop116¾Figonero1103½Autobiography1194 Rallied 9
4Sep72- 7Bel fst 1⅛ :47 1:111 1:354 1:481 3↑ Governor 118k 4 5 31½ 11 11½ 2hd Cordero A Jr 120 b 4.30e 93-12 Loud114hdAutobiography1202Hitchcock120½ Sharp 12
26Aug72- 8Lib sly 1¼ :471 1:114 1:371 2:024 3↑ Hobson H 100k 7 2 32 23 22 24¼ Cordero A Jr 121 b *1.10e 91-20 West Coast Scout1204¼Autbiogrphy1213StaroftheNorth1131¼ 7
Gamely
5Aug72- 7Sar fst 1⅛ :474 1:112 1:362 1:491 3↑ Whitney 57k 8 7 75¼ 42 45 45¾ Belmonte E 120 b 5.20 89-12 Key to the Mint1132Tunex1173Loud117¾ Rallied 8
22Jly72- 7Aqu fst 1¼ :472 1:102 1:35 2:00 3↑ Suburban H 113k 8 7 65 74½ 53½ 42¾ Velasquez J 126 b *1.50e 93-10 Hitchcock1132WestCoastScout120nkNaskra110½ Raced wide 8
8Jly72- 7Aqu fst 1 3/16 :484 1:12 1:362 1:544 3↑ Brooklyn H 118k 1 7 95 74½ 33 22 Cordero A Jr 122 b 5.30 98-09 Key to the Mint1122Autobiography1223WestCoastScout1141½ 12
Closed well
28Jun72- 7Aqu fst 7f :223 :443 1:084 1:211 3↑ Nassau County H 28k 6 4 44 45 52 51½ Cordero A Jr 121 b 3.00 93-11 TowzieTyke114¾WstCoastScout116hdSilverMllt116½ Impeded 8
Placed fourth through disqualification
19Jun72- 7Aqu sly 6f :221 :451 1:091 3↑ Gravesend H 27k 3 5 59 58½ 58½ 57¼ Cordero A Jr 123 b 2.20 90-09 SilverMallet115nkCloseDcson1112½Rollckng1212½ No factor 5

15Apr72- 7Aqu fst 1⅛ :49 1:12⁴1:36⁴1:49 3↑ Excelsior H 58k 10 4 2¹ 3ⁿᵏ 1ʰᵈ 1¹½ Cordero A Jr 123 b *2.80e 91-10 Autobiogrphy123¹½NatvRoylty115ʰᵈUrgntMssg119ʰᵈ Driving 11
1Apr72- 7Aqu fst 1 :22³:44² 1:08³1:34¹ 3↑ Westchester H 57k 2 7 6⁷¼ 5⁴ 1ʰᵈ 1¹ Cordero A Jr 119 b 3.90e 96-15 Autobiography119⁴Tunx118ⁿᵏNtvRoylty118ⁿᵏ Bore in,driving 11
12Feb72- 8SA fst 1¼ :45¹1:09¹1:34³2:00² C H Strub 130k 10 7 6⁹½ 5²³½ 5⁴ 6⁵½ Belmonte E 118 b 4.00e 90-11 Unconscious121½TriplBnd118³GoodCounsl116ⁿᵏ Lacked rally 11
29Jan72- 8SA fst 1⅛ :46 1:09⁴1:34⁴1:47¹ San Fernando 89k 1 6 6⁶½ 5³ 3¹ 1ⁿᵏ↓ Belmonte E 117 b 4.40e 96-07 DH Autobiography117 DH Triple Bend117ⁿᵏGood Counsel117ⁿᵒ 12
Bumped,driving
19Jan72- 8SA fst 1¹⁄₁₆ :24¹:48¹ 1:11³1:41⁴ 4↑ Alw 15000 1 6 6⁵½ 6⁶ 5⁵ 3⁴½ Pincay L Jr 120 b *.90 89-13 TripleBnd122³¾GoodCounsl117¾Autobogrphy120ⁿᵏ Late rally 6
8Jan72- 6SA fst 7f :21³:43³ 1:08²1:21 Malibu (Div 1) 46k 4 7 5⁵½ 5⁸½ 3³ 2ⁿᵒ Pincay L Jr 117 b *1.40 98-08 KfarTov115ⁿᵒAutbiogrphy117⁷Dplomtc Agnt117¼ Just missed 7
1Jan72- 4SA fst 6f :21²:44 :56² 1:09¹ Alw 15000 5 5 6⁵¾ 6⁹¼ 4⁶½ 4²½ Pincay L Jr 122 b *2.00 93-10 Wing Out122½Kfar Tov118ⁿᵏSingle Agent118¹½ Wide turn 6
1Dec71- 7Aqu fst 1⅛ :47³1:12⁴1:38¹1:50² Discovery H 34k 1 9 9⁵ 5²½ 1ʰᵈ 1⁴½ Pincay L Jr 115 b 2.30 84-27 Autobiography115⁴½Minsky114²BoonetheGret109³ Ridden out 11
23Nov71- 7Aqu fst 1⅛ :47⁴1:12²1:37³1:50 4↑ Alw 10000 6 6 6¹² 5⁷ 2½ 1ʰᵈ Ussery R 115 b *1.00 86-26 Autobiography115ʰᵈNight Patrol113⁷Fair Test113½ Driving 6
2Nov71- 5Aqu fst 6f :22⁴:46¹ 1:09³ 3↑ Alw 10000 1 7 7⁶½ 6¹ 2ʰᵈ 1⁴ Ussery R 117 b *.80e 95-11 Autobiography117⁴LittleDixBay117⁷¼Accohick117³½ Driving 7
18Oct71- 6Aqu fst 6f :22⁴:46 1:10 3↑ Alw 12000 7 4 6³¾ 4³¾ 3¹ 2ⁿᵒ Ussery R 117 b 6.50 93-18 Smelling Salts115ⁿᵒAutobiography117ʰᵈEver On121³ Sharp 8
Previously owned by O.M. Phipps;previously trained by R. Laurin
3Sep71- 7Bel fst 1⅛ :48 1:12 1:36⁴1:49¹ 3↑ Alw 14000 2 4 4⁴½ 5⁵½ 5⁶¾ 5⁶½ Baltazar C 112 6.70 81-17 Joans Bo113ⁿᵏShadyside111ⁿᵒLaminate116¹¼ No rally 7
26Aug71- 5Sar fst 7f :22³:44² 1:10³1:22³ 3↑ Alw 10000 5 5 8⁶³ 8⁶½ 8⁷⅓ 3³ Baltazar C 119 b 5.80 87-12 Riot119¹Bell Bird1119²¼Arctarus114³½ No threat 8
7Aug71- 4Sar fst 7f :22⁴:46¹ 1:11 1:23³ 3↑ Alw 10000 5 5 7⁶½ 8³⅓ 6³½ 6⁴³ Cruguet J 119 b *2.90 86-11 Wig Out119²Bazoom124ʰᵈShadyside116½ No excuse 9
21Jly71- 5Aqu fst 7f :22¹:45¹ 1:10¹1:22⁴ 3↑ Alw 10000 8 7 4⁶ 4¹ 2ʰᵈ 1ʰᵈ Baltazar C 114 b *.90 87-15 Autobiography114⁴SilverShield112²¼AdobeEd112¹ Driving 10
5Jly71- 5Aqu fst 6f :22¹:45³ 1:10²3↑ Alw 10000 5 9 7¹² 7⁶ 4⁴½ 2½ Cruguet J 114 b 6.30 90-17 Ellen'sVoyage105½Autobiogrphy114¼SlThrough117ⁿᵏ Gamely 9
10Jun71- 6Bel fst 1 :23²:46⁴ 1:11³1:36³ 3↑ Alw 10000 3 8 6⁶½ 6³½ 3²½ 2½ Baeza B 113 b *2.10 88-19 BoldCrusadr114²Autobiogrphy113²TrnqultyBs114ⁿᵏ Gaining 10
3Jun71- 7Bel fst 1⅛ :24¹:48 1:13¹1:45¹3↑ Alw 13000 4 5 3ⁿᵏ 4¹¾ 3³ 3¹½ Baeza B 113 b *1.00 76-22 Spread the Word112¾Tranquility Base114³½Autobiography113³ 8
Wide turn;Previously trained by E.A. Neloy
18May71- 6Aqu fst 1⅛ :47⁴1:12 1:38 1:50³ 3↑ Alw 14000 3 8 8⁷ 6⁵¾ 4² 2²½ Venezia M 108 b 4.90 80-19 EpicJourney113²½Autbiogrphy108¹¼PncumRpns118⁵ Blocked 9
11May71- 8Aqu yl 1¹⁄₁₆ T 1:45² 3↑ Alw 13000 10 8 9⁸½ 7¹⁰ 6⁸ 5⁴ Baeza B 113 b *.80 80-19 Miannus110½Rough Place110³Bulgari113² No excuse 10
28Apr71- 1Aqu fst 7f :22³:46¹ 1:12¹1:25½ 4↑ Md Sp Wt 5 7 8¹³ 8⁸¾ 4²½ 1³½ Baeza B 113 b *.90 75-23 Autobiography113³½Buckner112ⁿᵏT.V.Replay112² Mild drive 9
Previously owned by Wheatley Stable
5Jun70- 5Bel sly 5½f :23³:48¹ 1:00³1:07 3 3 5⁴ 3²½ 3³ 2² Baeza B 122 b 5.00 83-18 AmberDuke122²Autobiography122ʰᵈGreatQuest122⁵ Gamely 9

Bold Forbes

dkbbr. c. 1973, by Irish Castle (Bold Ruler)–Comely Nell, by Commodore M.   Lifetime record: 18 13 1 4 $523,035
Own.– E.R. Tizol
Br.– Eaton Farms Inc & Red Bull Stable (Ky)
Tr.– Lazaro S. Barrera

30Oct76- 8Aqu fst 7f :22³:44³ 1:08³1:21⁴ 3↑ Vosburgh H-G2 4 3 2½ 2¹ 2³½ 2² Cordero A Jr 126 b *.50 90-16 MyJuliet120²D BoldForbes126¹It'sFrezng113²½ Bore in,out 6
Disqualified and placed third
19Oct76- 8Bel fst 6f :22¹:44⁴ 1:09² 3↑ Alw 30000 4 3 2½ 2ʰᵈ 1¹ 1¹½ Cordero A Jr 119 b *.40 95-14 BoldForbes119¹½QuietLittlTbl119³½McCorkl117ⁿᵒ Ridden out 6
5Jun76- 7Bel fst 1½ :47 1:11¹2:01⁴2:29 Belmont-G1 8 1 1⁶ 1⁶ 1⁶ 1ⁿᵏ Cordero A Jr 126 b *.90 75-15 Bold Forbes126ⁿᵏMcKenzieBridge126ⁿᵏGreatContractor126⁸½ 10
Bore out,lasted
15May76- 8Pim fst 1¹⁄₁₆ :45 1:09 1:35¹1:55 Preakness-G1 4 1 1² 1² 2ʰᵈ 3⁴ Cordero A Jr 126 b 1.10e 91-11 Elocutonst126¾PlythRd126½BoldForbs126³ Drifted,swerved 6
1May76- 8CD fst 1¼ :45⁴1:10²1:35³2:01³ Ky Derby-G1 2 1 1⁵ 1½ 1½ 1¹ Cordero A Jr 126 b 3.00 89-11 Bold Forbes126¹Honest Pleasure126³½Elocutionist126¹¼ 9
Drifted,driving
17Apr76- 8Aqu fst 1⅛ :46 1:09⁴1:34²1:47² Wood Memorial-G1 5 2 1³ 11½ 1⁴ 1⁴¾ Cordero A Jr 126 b *.40 98-11 BoldForbes126⁴¾OntheSly126ⁿᵏSonkisser126¹½ Ridden out 7
20Mar76- 8Aqu fst 7f :22¹:44 1:08¹1:20⁴ Bay Shore-G3 7 2 2ʰᵈ 1² 1⁷ 1⁷¾ Cordero A Jr 119 b 1.70 97-17 Bold Forbes119⁷¾Eustace121½Full Out124¹½ Kept driving 8
28Feb76- 8SA fst 1 :23³:45³ 1:09³1:35 San Jacinto-G3 5 1 1² 1¹⁴ 1⁴ 1⁴³ Pincay L Jr 117 b 2.10 94-12 BoldForbes117³Grandaries114⁴StainedGlss122ⁿᵏ Mild drive 7
14Feb76- 8SA fst 7f :22 :44³ 1:09 1:21⁴ San Vicente-G3 7 3 1ʰᵈ 3½ 1²½ 3³¾ Pincay L Jr 119 b *1.70 93-11 ThermalEnergy117½StaindGlss122ⁿᵏBoldForbs119½ Wide turn 7
24Jan76- 8SA fst 6f :22¹:45 :57 1:09³ San Miguel 33k 2 4 2½ 2² 2½ 2ⁿᵒ Pincay L Jr 120 b *1.30 91-12 SureFire114ⁿᵒBoldForbes120½RestlessRestless122ⁿᵏ Gamely 6
31Dec75- 4SA fst 5½f :21⁴:44² 1:03 ©Alw 16000 1 3 1½ 2½ 2ʰᵈ 3⁵ Pincay L Jr 122 b *.30 94-14 Sure Fire114ⁿᵒBeau Talent114⁵Bold Forbes120⁷ Weakened 5
3Aug75- 8Sar fst 6f :22⁴:44¹ 1:09⁴ Sar Spl-G2 5 1 1² 1⁸ 1¹⁰ 1¹⁰ Velasquez J 120 b *.10 91-13 BoldForbes120⁸FamilyDoctor117ʰᵈGentleKng120³ Handily 5
23Jly75- 8Bel fst 6f :22²:45² 1:09² Tremont 26k 2 2 1½ 1² 1⁴ 1⁵ Pincay L Jr 120 b 1.70 96-16 BoldForbes120⁵IronBit114⁹PeerlessMcGrath114¹³ Handily 5
Previously trained by R. Cruz
15Jun75- 7PR fst 6f :22²:45⁴ 1:10³ Dia Padres 2 2 1² 1⁴ 1⁵ 1¹³ Hiraldo JF 118 b *.15 101-17 Bold Forbes118¹³Lovely Jay118³El Gallo118³¾ Easily 4
4Jun75- 4PR fst 6f :23 :45³ 1:11² Alw 3 1 1² 1³½ 1⁵ 1⁸ Hiraldo JF 114 b *.25e 97-11 BoldForbes114⁸LovelyJay116⁷½AnotherBeauty113ʰᵈ Easily 10
25Apr75- 1PR fst 5f :22 :45³ :59¹ Alw 3 1 1⁴ 1⁵ 1⁶ 1⁸½ Hiraldo JF 116 b *.15 95-20 BoldForbes116⁸½LovelyJay113⁶½AnotherBeauty113⁷ Easily 5
11Apr75- 1PR fst 5f :22 :45³ :58⁴ Alw 4 1 1⁵ 1⁵ 1⁵ 1¹⁵ Hiraldo JF 115 b *.30 97-20 Bold Forbes115⁵Lovely Jay116¹¹Eternal Day115⁶½ Easily 5
12Mar75- 1PR fst 5f :22 :45⁴ :59² Md Sp Wt 2 1 1⁵ 1⁶ 1⁸ 1¹⁷ Hiraldo JF 116 b 35.00 94-20 BoldForbes116¹⁷MyDad'sBrandy116²½Ruben Jl.116¹¼ Easily 8

Bowl Game

b. g. 1974, by Tom Rolfe (Ribot)–Around the Roses, by Round Table   Lifetime record: 23 11 6 5 $907,083
Own.– Greentree Stable
Br.– Greentree Stud Inc (Ky)
Tr.– John M. Gaver Jr

15Jun80- 7Bel fm 1¹⁄₁₆ :22²:45 1:08²1:40 3↑ Alw 35000 7 7 7¹⁸ 6¹⁵½ 6⁸¾ 2⁵½ Velasquez J 122 *1.10 90-10 Told117⁵½BowlGame122ʰᵈScythnGold119ⁿᵒ Finished strongly 7
10Nov79- 8Lrl sf 1½ :57³1:25²2:23²2:51 3↑ D C Int'l-G1 7 3 2¹½ 2¹ 2ʰᵈ 1³½ Velasquez J 127 3.60 -- Bowl Game127¾Trillion124ⁿᵒLe Marmot120⁸ Driving 8
27Oct79- 8Aqu fm 1½ T :48¹1:14 2:04⁴2:28¹ 3↑ Turf Classic-G1 2 3 3¹² 2² 2²½ 1ⁿᵏ Velasquez J 126 2.80 120-00 Bowl Game126ⁿᵏTrillion123ⁿᵏNative Courier126⁴¾ Driving 7
8Oct79- 8Bel sf 1⅜ T :51²1:17 1:42 2:19 3↑ Man o' War-G1 3 3 3⁶ 3²½ 2⁴ 1ʰᵈ Velasquez J 126 2.60 67-38 Bowl Game126ʰᵈNative Courier126¹¹Czaravich121²¾ Driving 4
1Sep79- 8AP fm 1½ T :48 1:13 2:06¹2:32¹ 3↑ Arlington H-G2 9 10 10²⁴ 4⁷ 1¹ 1⁴½ Velasquez J 126 *.70 78-28 BowlGame124¹½YoungBob110⁸Liveinthesunshine105½ Drew out 14
21Jly79- 8Bel fst 1¼ :50³1:15 2:03³2:28⁴ 3↑ Brooklyn H-G2 2 3 4²½ 3⁴½ 3¹½ 2½ Velasquez J 119 5.10 75-24 TheLiberlMember114³½BwlGme119ʰᵈStateDinnr123²¾ Gamely 5
1Jly79- 8Bel fm 1⅜ T :48³1:13¹1:37⁴2:13¹ 3↑ Tidal H-G2 2 2 2ʰᵈ 3ⁿᵏ 1¹ 2ʰᵈ Velasquez J 125 *.70 103-11 Gldn Rsve109ʰᵈBowl Game125ⁿᵏScthn Gold110¹½ Didn't last 5
16Jun79- 8Bel fm 1⅜ T :48 1:12 1:35²2:11²3↑ Bowling Green H-G2 3 4 4⁹½ 6⁷½ 2²½ 3⁴ Velasquez J 123 5.20 108-01 Overskate117⁴Waya125ʰᵈBowl Game123¹½ Gave way 7
14Apr79-11Hia hd 1 T 2:26³ 3↑ Hia Turf Cup H-G2 7 6 6⁴½ 3½ 2½ 1¹ Cordero A Jr 114 2.90 98-10 BowlGame114²NobleDancer111³⁰⁵GreatSound111ʰᵈ Driving 7
4Apr79- 9Hia fm *1⅛ T :22²:45 1:46² 4↑ Alw 20000 5 5 5⁸½ 5³½ 4³½ 3⁵½ Velasquez J 114 *1.20 97-08 That's a Nice114⁴½Fed Funds114¹Bowl Game114½ Bumped 7
22Mar79- 9Hia fm 1 :23 :46² 1:10³4↑ Alw 13000 1 8 7⁴¾ 7⁶½ 5⁷½ 5¹⁰ Velasquez J 114 *.80 80-18 NorthCourse119⁴GetPermsson122½Robb'sChrm119⁴½ Slow st. 8
17Apr78- 8Bel fm 1⅜ T :48²1:12¹1:36¹2:12²3↑ Bowling Green H-G2 2 7 7¹¹ 7⁶½ 5³ 3³¾ Velasquez J 124 *1.20 97-10 Tiller117²½Proud Arion111¹½Bowl Game124⅜ Rallied 10
29May78- 8Hol fm 1½ T :47²1:11²2:01²2:25⁴ 3↑ Hol Inv'l H-G1 10 8 10¹¹ 4² 3²½ 2²½ Velasquez J 123 3.00 96-04 Exceller127²½Bowl Game123½Noble Dancer126³½ Rallied 12
13May78- 8Pim fm 1½ T :48 1:14⁴2:07²2:32³ 3↑ Dixie H (Div 2)-G2 6 4 5⁸ 4¹² 1⁶ 1ⁿᵏ Velasquez J 126 *.40 70-29 Bowl Game126ⁿᵏOilfield110³½Trumpeter Swan110ʰᵈ Handily 9
15Apr78- 9GP fm 1½ T :49⁴1:15²2:06¹2:30¹ 3↑ Pan American H-G2 7 7 6⁶ 9⁶ 2ʰᵈ 1¹½ Velasquez J 117 *1.00 73-22 Bowl Game117¹½That's a Nice116½Court Open112⅜ Driving 10
25Mar78- 9GP fst 1¼ :46 1:10¹1:35²2:00³ 3↑ Gulf Park H-G1 9 7 8¹⁰ 3¹ 2ʰᵈ 1² Velasquez J 112 4.10 94-21 BowlGme112²TrueStatement108¹½SilverSers126⁵ Drew clear 11
4Mar78- 8Hia fst 1⅛ :47³1:11³1:36²1:48³ 4↑ Alw 11000 6 8 8⁶½ 5³¾ 1² 1⁵½ Velasquez J 114 *.40 89-05 BowlGame114⁵½Roy Roy122⁹Turra Murra119⁴½ Easily 8
24Feb78- 8Hia yl 1⅛ T 1:52 4↑ Alw 9000 3 10 10⁹³8⁵¾ 4²½ 1³ Velasquez J 116 *.70 75-30 BowlGame114³Tabatex114¹½In All Sincerity114¹½ Handily 10
15Feb78- 3Hia fst 7f :23²:46² 1:11³1:24¹ Md Sp Wt 5 11 10¹¹8⁸½ 1² 1³ Velasquez J 122 *.40 85-20 BowlGme122³Czar'sRansom122²½Yestertime122¹ Drew clear 11
3Feb78- 3Hia fst 6f :22⁴:46¹ 1:11 Md Sp Wt 3 10 11¹⁸¹⁰ 5⁶ 2½ Velasquez J 122 *.30 87-18 Darkest Hour122½Bowl Game122²³Dr. Joe F.122¹ Gaining 12
19Jan78- 3Hia sly 6f :21⁴:45 1:09² Md Sp Wt 4 7 10¹¹7¹⁰ 4⁶ 2⁴ Velasquez J 122 *2.30 92-14 NorthernDictatr122⁴BowlGame122²DressExtra122⁶ 2nd best 12
Previously trained by John M. Gaver
20Aug77- 1Sar fst 6f :22¹:45⁴ 1:10⁴3↑ Md Sp Wt 1 9 6⁵½ 7⁷ 6⁷ 3⁹ Cauthen S 117 4.70 77-10 Roger W.117⁶½Sun Flame117²⁷½Bowl Game117½ Raced wide 9
11Aug77- 1Sar sly 6f :22 :44⁴ 1:10⁴ Md Sp Wt 8 5 4⁵ 4¹¹ 4⁸ 3⁹½ Cauthen S 117 3.90e 80-12 ThePrnc'sPants122⁸½CmAwyWthMe117¹½BwlGme117¹½ Evenly 8

Cafe Prince

b. g. 1970, by Creme Dela Creme (Olympia)–Princess Blair, by Blue Prince — Lifetime record: 52 18 5 4 $228,238

Own.– Augustin Stable
Br.– Verne H. Winchell (Cal)
Tr.– Jonathan E. Sheppard

Race	Cond	Dist	Type	Fractions	Class	Running line	Jockey	Wt	Odds	Figs	Top three	Comment	Field
1Nov80- 3Mtp	fm	*2½	S'Chase	4:41	4↑ Noel Laing H 5.4k	2 4 41¾ 35 518 633¾	Cushman J	157	-	--	Owhata Chief158½Down First15715Pala Mountain1456		6
18Oct80- 5RB	fm	*2	S'Chase	3:44	3↑ Metcalf Mem 7k	1 5 3¾ 1nk 11 11¾	Cushman J	158	-e	--	Cafe Prince1581¾Quixotic1461Wasted Trip140½	Driving	7
9Oct80- 6Bel	fm	2	S'Chase	3:554	3↑ Alw 25000	2 4 512 512 417 420¼	Cushman J	157	3.00	--	Cookie1412½CocontCreek14913PalMountn1424¾	Outrun early	7
27Sep80- 5Fx	fm	*2⅝	S'Chase	5:034	4↑ Handicap 20000	2 2 2¾ 11½ 1¾ 21	Cushman J	155	-	--	Down First1531Cafe Prince1556Blue Nearco1349		4
13Sep80- 6Lig	hd	*2(T)		3:40	3↑ Alw 2500	8 1 18 112 14 112	Sheppard J	168	-	--	CafePrince16812WaterTable16216PrivateGry1688	Ridden out	9
22Aug80- 6Sar	fm	2 1/16	S'Chase	3:422	3↑ Handicap 25000	1 4 - - - -	Champion R	158	7.90	--	Popular Hero1381Too Few Stripes130¾Romeo Lima1452½	Fell	7
14Aug80- 6Sar	fm	2⅜	S'Chase	4:141	4↑ NY Turf Writers H 43k	6 5 11½ 734 - -	Champion R	161	1.20e	--	Zaccio1571¼Running Comment1422¼Leaping Frog152¼	Eased	7
1Aug80- 8Del	fm	1 1/16(T)		:234 :48 1:122 1:46	3↑ Alw 7000	9 7 711 812 69¼ 512	Dufton E	117	7.20	62-30	Lightning Lead1176½Freon1152Dr. Williams1053	No factor	9
10Nov79- 6Uni	yl	*2(T)		3:45	3↑ Alw 1000	2 2 34½ 415 46 424	Strawbridge G Jr	168	-	--	Town and Country1685Quixotic1644Ruysch16815	Tired	9
3Oct79- 6Lig	sf	*2	S'Chase	4:321	4↑ Rolling Rock Cup 17k	1 2 2½ - - -	Small D Jr	166	-	--	HappyIntellctual1492¼FirControl15010Beauhill138	Pulled up	5
23Aug79- 6Sar	fm	2⅜	S'Chase	4:174	4↑ NY Turf Writers H 21k	2 4 47½ 64¼ 615 636	Quanbeck A Jr	167	*.40e	--	Leaping Frog1598¾Tan Jay1506½Canadian Regent143hd	Tired	6
3Aug79- 6Sar	fm	2 1/16	S'Chase	3:411	4↑ Lovely Night H 21k	3 3 23 13 11½ 12¾	Fishback J	164	*.40e	--	CafePrince1642¾LeapingFrog1613¾Mrt'sAngr1555	Ridden out	7
13Jly79- 3Del	fm	*2¼	S'Chase	4:162	4↑ Handicap 10000	1 5 - - - -	Fishback J	165	*1.20	--	Martie'sAnger1521¼DeuxCoup159½StraightandTrue1457	Fell	5
12May79- 7Fai	fm	*2 3/16	S'Chase	4:112	4↑ Handicap 10000	1 - - - - -	Fishback J	164	*1.10	--	DeuxCoup1552¾StraightandTrue1481LoveIn1425	Lost rider	7
28Apr79- 5Fx	gd	*1(T)		1:473	3↑ Alw 2000	6 9 924 718 1nk 1nk	Fishback J	145	-	--	CafePrince145nkDeuxCoup1442StatelyPrince137nk	Driving	11
18Nov78- 4Cam	fm	2¾	S'Chase	5:102	4↑ Colonial Cup 100k	1 7 513 28 2¾ 32	Fishback J	162	-	--	GrandCnyon1622DeuxCoup155hdCfePrnc16217	Bid,weakened	10
20Oct78- 6Bel	fm	2⅝	S'Chase	4:52	4↑ Temple Gwathmey H 36k	2 1 1½ 2hd 1½ 24	Fishback J	167	*.70	--	FireControl1464CafePrince167noPopularHero1398¾	2nd best	6
7Oct78- 4Lig	yl	*2½	S'Chase	5:224	4↑ Int'l Gold Cup H 25k	2 1 14 110 112 114	Fishback J	163	-	--	CafePrince16314Crg'sCornr14315PopulrHro14112	Ridden out	6
23Sep78- 7Fai	fm	*2½	S'Chase	4:574	4↑ Grand National H 10k	1 1 11 1½ 14 13	Fishback J	158	*.70	--	CafePrince1583LeapingFrog155hdHappyIntllctul155	In hand	5
16Sep78- 4Fai	fm	*1 5/16(T)		2:173	3↑ Alw 1000	2 8 88½ 712 51½ 32¾	Fishback J	145	*1.60	--	PopularHero152noHappyIntellectul1412¾CfPrnc1455	Rallied	10
26Nov77- 4Cam	fm	2¾	S'Chase	5:223	4↑ Colonial Cup 100k	1 6 66¾ 36 21½ 15½	Fishback J	162	-e	--	Cafe Prince1625½Bel Iman1518Leaping Frog1464½	Handily	12
29Oct77- 6FH	yl	*2 5/16	S'Chase	5:19	4↑ Handicap 10000	2 7 52¼ 33 1½ 1hd	Fishback J	155	-e	--	Cafe Prince155hdBel Iman1451Fire Control143½	Lasted	8
14Oct77- 6Bel	sf	2⅝	S'Chase	5:161	4↑ Temple Gwathmey H 36k	2 6 32½ 2½ 622 629	Fishback J	159	*1.00	--	Bel Iman14010Deux Coup1493¾Leaping Frog1428	Stopped	6
8Oct77- 4Lig	sf	*2½	S'Chase	5:311	4↑ Int'l Gold Cup H 25k	1 7 512 115 112 118	Fishback J	155	-	--	CafePrnce15518ItsGoodforYou1377MichaelsMad13710	Easily	8
5Oct77- 7Lig	yl	*7f(T)		1:361	3↑ Alw 2500	2 8 83½ 63¾ 3¾ 2½	Fishback J	143	-e	--	Down First155½Cafe Prince1431½Jacasaba140¾	Rallied	13
25Aug77- 6Sar	fm	2⅜	S'Chase	4:184	4↑ NY Turf Writers H 21k	8 4 421 65 33½ 58	Fishback J	158	3.10	--	HappyIntellectual152¾NvlPrson143hdCsmyor1505½	Bid,tired	8
15Aug77- 4Sar	fm	2 1/16	S'Chase	3:453	4↑ Alw 12500	2 5 37 31½ 11½ 15	Fishback J	156	*.90e	--	CafePrince1565SunnyIce1302¾LeapingFrog14510	Ridden out	9
5Aug77- 6Sar	fm	2 1/16	S'Chase	3:441	4↑ Lovely Night H 21k	6 3 411 511 45½ 46¾	Fishback J	157	3.40	--	Life'sIlluson1603¼Csmyor149½HppyIntllctul1543	No mishap	6
23Jly77- 3Del	fm	2⅜	S'Chase	4:38	4↑ Indian River H 13k	7 7 73¼ 65¼ 35 36½	Fishback J	158	*.80e	--	Jacasaba1422½Salvo1414Cafe Prince158½	Rallied	7
16Jly77- 4Del	fm	1 1/16(T)		:233 :471 1:12 1:431	3↑ Clm 40000	2 3 34 34½ 45½ 414	Castaneda K	119	2.40	74-10	Famous Jim1177Ensilage117¾Jamison1176	Lacked rally	4
15Nov75- 4Cam	fm	2 13/16	S'Chase	5:301	4↑ Colonial Cup 50k	7 7 125¾ 67 41 13	Washer D	160	-e	--	Cafe Prince1603Augustus Bay162½Soothsayer162½	Handily	18
25Oct75- 6FH	sf	*2 5/16	S'Chase	4:45	4↑ Handicap 10000	4 8 712 77½ 3½ 21½	Fishback J	160	-e	--	Life'sIllusion1511½CafePrinc160½TllAwrd150½	Closed well	8
4Oct75- 4Lig	yl	*2½	S'Chase	5:211	4↑ Temple Gwathmey 25k	3 5 53 38½ 36 315¾	Fishback J	151	-e	--	HappyIntellectual149¾SpeedKills14715CafePrinc1516	Tired	7
13Sep75- 5Fai	fm	*2 3/16	S'Chase	4:07	3↑ Handicap 3500	9 8 57½ 33 1½ 11½	Fishback J	158	*.90e	--	Cafe Prince1581½County Wicklow1402Winigo143¾	Driving	10
2Aug74- 6Sar	fm	2 1/16	S'Chase	3:443	4↑ Lovely Night H 22k	4 9 78 11 16 12¾	Fishback J	145	9.70e	--	CfePrince1452¾GranKan1603JuacHollow1548	Speed to spare	10
18Jly74- 6Del	fm	1 1/16(T)		:233 :463 1:103 1:432	4↑ Alw 5500	3 5 412 47½ 45 5½	McCarron G	119	5.00	86-15	MistrYouEssay113nkBuffloRun112nkJucHollow107hd	Closing	6
10Jly74- 4Mth	fm	1 1/16(T)		:24 :482 1:123 1:431	3↑ Alw 7500	8 3 54 42 57½ 616	Tichenor W	120	14.30	77-11	PamperedJabneh124noMr.Darby12011FlyngWedge124½	Tired	8
25Jun74- 4Del	fst	1 1/16		:231 :472 1:122 1:442	4↑ Alw 5500	7 5 510 511 615 718	McCarron G	119	7.00	69-18	PlayEveryDay1125MistrYouEssy1143½CryStrt1071½	No factor	8
8Jun74- 8Del	fm	*2½	S'Chase	4:323	4↑ Indian River H 13k	11 7 65 43 64¾ 822	Fishback J	146	4.60	--	Gran Kan1581Metello153hdLucky Boy III1552¾	Tired	11
25May74- 5Del	fm	1(T)		:234 :481 1:134 1:391	3↑ Md Sp Wt	12 5 53½ 32½ 11½ 15	McCarron G	122	4.10e	79-24	Cafe Prince1225Bronze Image122noIdle Gossip1155	Handily	12
11May74- 1Fai	fm	*7f(T)		1:262	3↑ Alw 1000	5 2 28 210 412 618	O'Brien L	149	*1.40e	--	SunMeeting15213CitizenX.155nkUnexpectedVstor1552½	Tired	15
17Nov73- 4Cam	fm	*2	Hurdles	3:463	3↑ Handicap 5000	2 6 55 2½ 1½ 12½	O'Brien M	150	-	--	Cafe Prince1502½Gun Gold142½Plumsted1391½	Easily	6
27Oct73- 4FH	fm	*2	Hurdles	4:051	3↑ SK Martin H 10k	1 3 1½ 16 11½ 11½	O'Brien M	136 s	-	--	CafePrince1361½JuacHollow1623½SummerCrop14210	Driving	6
6Oct73- 1Lig	fm	*1¾	Hurdles	3:181	3↑ Alw 4000	4 5 119¾ 45½ 21 14	O'Brien M	143	-	--	Cafe Prince1434Remagen145½Jacasaba1524½	Drew out	13
17Sep73- 2Bel	fst	1⅛⊗		:47 1:111 1:371 1:504	3↑ Md Sp Wt	5 7 77 712 715 716	Maple E	116	13.60	61-14	Walther F.1161Tonk1161½Vehement116hd	No factor	7
14Aug73- 9Sar	fm	1⅝	Hurdles	2:552	3↑ Md 10000	4 4 54 26 1½ 16½	Fishback J	139	*1.50	--	Cafe Prince1396½Tarrative1363National Park15316	Handily	8
7Aug73- 9Sar	fm	1⅞	Hurdles	3:222	3↑ Md Sp Wt	5 5 78½ 25 24 26½	Fishback J	138	5.00e	--	Bailar1546½CafePrince1388½NationalPark1542½	Second best	8
16May73- 1Pim	fst	6f		:231 :471 1:132	3↑ Md 10500	9 7 105½ 85¾ 75¼ 65¼	Lee T	115	20.00	74-18	FeudingClan1152PassingFlght115noPlttrnsh1171¼	No threat	12
2May73- 3Pim	fst	6f		:232 :47 1:123	3↑ Md Sp Wt	4 7 75¼ 95 76¼ 58¾	Black AS	114 b	19.90	75-17	Gallant Hitter1141¾Impressive Imp1143Raza114½	Outrun	12
16Apr73- 2Pim	fst	6f		:231 :472 1:14	3↑ Md 10500	1 5 43½ 33 2½ 84¼	Lee T	114 b	11.70	72-24	Robert'sDay117noRathcool1142¼VillrsLd114no	Speed,tired	11
1Dec72- 3Lrl	my	6f		:221 :454 1:112	Md Sp Wt	8 8 812 814 822 819	Lee T	120 b	7.90	74-14	DoublEdgeSword1203Startahemp120½ThEqulzr1205	No factor	8
10Aug72- 3Del	fst	5½f		:224 :473 1:001 1:063	Md Sp Wt	2 5 53 64¼ 615 615	Lee T	120	5.20	70-19	SecurityGuard1201¼CosmicTraffic1203VllrsLd1204	No speed	6

Candy Eclair

gr. f. 1976, by Northern Jove (Northern Dancer)–Candy's Best, by Candy Spots — Lifetime record: 23 15 4 1 $403,845

Own.– Mrs H.D. Paxson
Br.– Mrs Henry D. Paxson (Ky)
Tr.– Mary Edens

Race	Cond	Dist	Fractions	Class	Running line	Jockey	Wt	Odds	Figs	Top three	Comment	Field
3Dec80- 8Aqu	fst	6f[•]	:223 :462 1:111	3↑ (F)Petrify H 56k	9 2 51½ 2½ 32 31	Solomone M	124	*1.20	87-21	SoftColrs1141TheWheelTurns113noCndyEclr124nk	Weakened	9
11Nov80- 8Aqu	fst	7f	:24 :482 1:131 1:253	3↑ (F)First Flight H 56k	5 3 1hd 1½ 4¾ 53¾	Brumfield D	126	*.90	69-30	SamartaDancer1121½Jedina1151½Damask Fan112¾	Weakened	9
18Oct80- 8Aqu	fst	7f	:223 :443 1:084 1:212	3↑ Vosburgh-G1	8 1 2½ 2½ 53½ 86¼	Bailey JD	123	13.90	88-12	PluggdNickle123½JaklinKlugman1231Dav'sFrnd126¾	Used up	9
8Oct80- 8Bel	fst	6f	:221 :452 1:103	3↑ Boojum H 57k	8 7 31 31½ 52 22¼	Bailey JD	124	10.40	87-22	Double Zeus1202¼Candy Eclair124hdKing's Fashion123no		9
Altered course												
24Sep80- 8Bel	fst	6f	:223 :453 1:103	3↑ (F)Grey Flight H 55k	5 1 2hd 3nk 11 12¾	Bailey JD	125	*1.30	89-20	Candy Eclair1252¾[D]The Wheel Turns113nkMongo Queen114¾		8
Ridden out												
10Aug80- 9Del	fst	6f	:213 :44 1:094	3↑ (F)Endine H 45k	1 5 1hd 2½ 1hd 1¾	Bailey JD	126	*.50	96-10	CndyEclr126¾[D]SheCan'tMiss112¾WondrousMe108no	Driving	9
23Jly80- 8Bel	my	7f	:221 :451 1:10 1:223	3↑ (F)Imperatrice H 55k	5 3 2hd 1hd 21½ 23½	Bailey JD	124	*1.70	85-22	Alada1173½Candy Eclair1242Pradera1153	2nd best	6
2Jly80- 8Mth	fm	5f(T)	:22 :444 :571	3↑ (F)Alw 16000	7 1 4nk 1hd 11 15	Bailey JD	122	*.40	97-03	CndyEclair1225CavyCakes1151½ThalieDncr115no	Ridden out	8
15Jun80- 5Bel	fst	6f	:232 :471 1:11	3↑ (F)Alw 32000	2 1 11 11 13 11	Bailey JD	119	*.40	87-17	CandyEclair1191Pradera1191¾SpanishFake1192½	Ridden out	5
31May80- 8Mth	fst	6f	:214 :441 1:093	3↑ (F)Regret H 33k	6 2 1hd 1½ 11½ 11½	Bailey JD	125	*.40	92-13	CndyEclr1251½GrcnVctry1121¼CornshQueen1163	Ridden out	7
23May80- 7Mth	fst	6f	:213 :442 1:10	4↑ (F)Alw 16000	6 1 2hd 1hd 11½ 15	Bailey JD	122	*.70	90-16	Candy Eclair1225Cornish Queen1221¼Hill Billy Dancer118½		7
Ridden out												
1Apr80- 8GP	sly	6f	:222 :453 1:102	4↑ (F)Alw 14000	7 2 12 11½ 11 11¼	Solomone M	114	*.40	87-20	Candy Eclair1141¼Guimauve1171¼Dungarven1191	In hand	8
2Jun79- 8Mth	fst	6f	:212 :441 1:094	(F)Miss Woodford 27k	2 5 1½ 1½ 1½ 21	Black AS	123	*.60	90-20	DropMeANote1151CndyEclr123¾Restanbegon1192	No excuse	7
4May79- 8CD	sly	1 1/16	:241 :48 1:134 1:471	(F)Ky Oaks-G1	6 1 14 11 2hd 47	Black AS	121	3.00	65-30	Davona Dale1214½Himalayan1212Prize Spot121½	Wide,tired	6
21Apr79- 7Kee	fst	*7f	1:27	(F)Ashland-G2	3 4 11 1½ 1hd 11½	Black AS	121	*.30	88-13	CndyEclr1211½Hmlyn1141¼CountssNorth1151¾	Bumped,driving	7
Previously trained by S. Allen King Jr												
28Feb79- 0GP	fst	7f	:221 :442 1:083 1:21	(F)Bonnie Miss 27k	4 2 11½ 1½ 1½ 2¾	Black AS	122	-	98-17	DavonaDale122¾CandyEclair12220ProveMeSpecial1142	Failed	4
Run between 7th and 8th races - No wagering												

14Feb79- 9GP	fst 6f	:22 :441 1:083	ⒻShirley Jones 28k	4 1 14 15 14	11¾	Black AS	122	*.50	96-16	CandyEclair1221¾DavonaDale1228DropMeaNote1141	Handily	4
3Feb79- 9GP	fst 6f	:213 :441 1:101	ⒻAlw 20000	5 2 11½ 13 14	12½	Black AS	117	*.10	88-10	CndyEclair1172½PrecociousLss1141¼FeuD'Artfc114nk	Easily	6
21Oct78- 8Lrl	fst 1$\frac{1}{16}$	:233 :471 1:13 1:453	ⒻSelima-G1	4 1 11 11½ 11½	11½	Black AS	119	2.10	85-24	CndyEclr1191½WhisprFleet1191½DropMeANote11913	Driving	7
30Sep78- 8Atl	fst 7f	:214 :442 1:101 1:221	ⒻMermaid 75k	2 2 11½ 12 13	12	Black AS	117	*.90e	91-16	Candy Eclair1172Salem Ho113nkWhisper Fleet1211½	Easily	7
2Sep78- 6Atl	fst 6f	:213 :442 1:10	ⒻBrigantine 21k	4 4 1½ 11 12	16	Black AS	113	2.10e	92-19	CandyEclair1136[D]SalemHo113½MaybetheBest114no	Easily	11
23Aug78- 6Mth	fst 6f	:221 :452 1:104	ⒻAlw 9000	1 3 11 1½ 12½	15	Black AS	117	*1.30	86-17	Candy Eclair1175Bedtime Toy1171Gentle Touch117¾	Easily	6
5Jly78- 5Mth	fst 5f	:221 :462 :592	ⒻMd Sp Wt	7 4 42½ 32 32½	1nk	Black AS	117	7.40	89-23	CandyEclair117nkDropMeANote1175OurRuler117nk	Just up	8

Canonero II

b. c. 1968, by Pretendre (Doutelle)–Dixieland II, by Nantallah

Lifetime record: 23 9 3 4 $361,006

Own.– King Ranch
Br.– Edward B. Benjamin (Ky)
Tr.– W.J. Hirsch

20Oct72- 7Aqu	my 1⅛	:48 1:123 1:372 1:494 3↑	Alw 15000	3 2 22 1hd 2hd	22	Avila G	119 b	*.90	85-20	Autobiogrphy1192CnonroII119nkRulbyRson1163½	Held place	6
20Sep72- 7Bel	fst 1⅛	:461 1:093 1:332 1:461 3↑	Stymie H 28k	5 3 32 2hd 1½	15	Avila G	110 b	5.50	103-07	Canonero II1105Riva Ridge1236Loud115½	Brisk handling	5
1Sep72- 6Bel	fst 1$\frac{1}{16}$	:231 :452 1:091 1:412 3↑	Alw 12000	8 2 11 15 1½	55¼	Avila G	114	*1.50	91-12	HolyLand115¾RulebyReason1201½UrgentMessage1201½	Tired	9
12Aug72- 5Sar	fst 7f	:224 :452 1:092 1:222 3↑	Alw 15000	2 6 68 35 36½	26	Gustines H	115	2.80	89-11	Onion1106Canonero II115½Sportique1161½	Gamely	6
29Jly72- 7Aqu	hd 1$\frac{3}{16}$Ⓣ	:48 1:112 1:353 1:54 3↑	Tidal H 59k	4 7 79 74¾ 1011	99	Rotz JL	117 b	7.10	91-02	Droll Role1211½Twist the Axe111½Tentam108¾	No factor	10
19Jly72- 6Aqu	fm 1$\frac{1}{16}$Ⓣ	:234 :471 1:103 1:412 3↑	Alw 15000	3 5 44½ 42½ 84¼	66	Rotz JL	113	5.00	90-06	Maraschino II1121½Apollo Nine1121Gleaming121hd	Gave way	8
29May72- 7Bel	fst 1	:224 :451 1:094 1:352 3↑	Metropolitan H 118k	7 8 95¼ 108¼ 1010	89½	Rotz JL	123	2.70	85-13	Executionr119nkBoldReasoning1231¼PecCorps113½	In close	11
20May72- 7Bel	sly 7f	:22 :442 1:091 1:222 3↑	Carter H 57k	5 7 814 711 46½	24¾	Rotz JL	121	4.20	90-09	Leematt1164¾CanoneroII121¾NativeRoylty121¾	Wide,rallied	8
Previously owned by E. de Caibet;previously trained by J. Arias												
5Jun71- 8Bel	fst 1½	:481 1:122 2:03 2:302	Belmont 162k	7 1 12½ 21½ 25	44½	Avila G	126	*.70	76-15	PassCatchr126¾JimFrench1263½BoldReason126nk	Weakened	13
15May71- 8Pim	fst 1$\frac{3}{16}$	:47 1:102 1:35 1:54	Preakness 189k	9 2 2hd 2hd 1hd	11½	Avila G	126	*3.40	103-09	CanoneroII1261½EasternFleet1264½JimFrench126no	Driving	11
1May71- 9CD	fst 1¼	:464 1:113 1:361 2:031	Ky Derby 188k	12 16 1820 42½ 13	13¾	Avila G	126	8.70f	84-13	CanoneroII1263¾JimFrench1262BoldReason126nk	Ridden out	20
10Apr71♦ Rinconada(Ven)	fst*1⅛LH	1:544 3↑	Free Hcp (Series 4a-5a) Hcp3500		33¾	Guzman RD	112	*.40		Mon Chanson1122¼Golden Flake1191½Canonero II1121¾	Tracked in 3rd,lacked rally	11
4Apr71♦ Rinconada(Ven)	fst6½fLH	1:171 3↑	Free Hcp (Series 5a) Hcp3300		16½	Guzman RD	110	*.80		Canonero II1106½Fast Track1102¼Mi Rebano106½	Well placed in 3rd,led 1½ f out,easily	14
21Mar71♦ Rinconada(Ven)	fst*6½fLH	1:164	Free Hcp (Series 6a) Hcp3200		1½	Avila G	126	*1.20		Canonero II126½Latour1083½Carven1102	Midpack,strong late run,led near line	11
14Mar71♦ Rinconada(Ven)	fst* 6½fLH	1:174	Free Hcp (Series 6a) Hcp3200		35	Avila G	126	4.20		Mi Rebano1153King River1172Canonero II126hd	Rated in 7th,finished well	12
7Mar71♦ Rinconada(Ven)	fst*1¼LH	2:032	Free Hcp (Series 8a) Hcp2800		12½	Avila G	115	*1.40		Canonero II1152½Neverest1103½Paupero1081¼	Led final furlong,quickly clear	14
14Feb71♦ Rinconada(Ven)	fst*1LH	1:411	Free Hcp (Series 6a) Hcp3200		34¼	Contreras JE	112			Rienda Suelta1144¼Harmattan114hdCanonero II1121¼	Tracked leader,weakened late	12
7Feb71♦ Rinconada(Ven)	fst*1¼LH	2:061	Clasico Prensa Nacional Stk15800		11	Cruz JE	105			Yves114nkEjemplo127nkOutsville1234¾	Never a factor	12
9Jan71♦ Rinconada(Ven)	my*7fLH	1:262	Free Hcp (Series 7a) Hcp3000		15¼	Contreras JE	110			Canonero II1105¼Silver Spray1163Fast Track1103¼	Always close up,led 2f out,easily clear	14
17Dec70♦ Rinconada(Ven)	fst*6fLH	1:124	Free Hcp (Series 8a) Hcp2800		11	Contreras JE	112			Canonero II1101Grass Paddock1102¼Florencio1123¼	Tracked in 3rd,led 1f out,ridden out	14
12Sep70- 7Dmr	fst 6f	:213 :441 :561 1:084	Dmr Futurity 108k	5 5 64 77 77	57¾	Ferrer I	116	10.90	87-12	June Darling1192Kfar Tov1193Bold Joey1162	Not a factor	9
5Sep70- 6Dmr	fst 6f	:214 :444 :572 1:10	ⒸAlw 5500	3 9 89¼ 84½ 44	31½	Ferrer I	120	21.50	87-14	King Cross1171½Serenader114hdCanonero II1203	Rallied	9
8Aug70♦ Rinconada(Ven)	fst*6fLH	1:13	Free Hcp (Series 9a) Hcp2600		16½	Contreras JE	110	12.60e		Canonero II1106½Comenve106½Gramal115½	Rallied to lead 1f out,drew clear final 16th	13

Cascapedia

b. f. 1973, by Chieftain (Bold Ruler)–Princess Ribot, by Ribot

Lifetime record: 19 10 4 2 $324,921

Own.– Bernard J. Ridder
Br.– Raymond R. Guest (Ky)
Tr.– Gordon C. Campbell

24Sep77- 8Bel	sly 1⅛	:46 1:111 1:374 1:521 3↑	ⒻRuffian H-G1	11 2 43 31½ 2hd	31	Hawley S	128 b	3.90	65-25	CumLaudeLaurie114½MssissippMd123½Cscpd1281¼	Very wide	12
5Sep77- 8Dmr	fst *1¼	:443 1:081 1:323 1:552 3↑	Del Mar H-G2	6 7 711 56½ 37½	38	Hawley S	117 b	3.00	98-08	AncientTitle1235PaintedWagon1183Cascapedia1171	Rallied	9
10Jly77- 8Hol	fst 1⅛	:463 1:103 1:35 1:473 3↑	ⒻVanity H-G1	6 5 55 43 3½	1no	Hawley S	129 b	*1.10	94-17	Cascapedia129noBastonera II1221¼Swingtime1174	Driving	9
18Jun77- 8Hol	fst 1¼	:451 1:09 1:334 2:00 3↑	Hol Gold Cup H-G1	8 10 98¼ 33 21	2nk	Pierce D	116 b	3.80	91-13	CrystalWater129nkCascapedia116noCaucasus1245	Forced out	12
4Jun77- 8Hol	fst 1$\frac{1}{16}$	:224 :461 1:10 1:404 3↑	ⒻMilady H-G2	3 5 44 31 1½	13	Hawley S	126 b	*1.50	91-15	Cascapedia1263Rocky Trip1152Just a Kick1182	Easily	6
21May77- 8Hol	fm 1$\frac{1}{16}$Ⓣ	:221 :451 1:102 1:404 3↑	ⒻHawthorne H 44k	8 3 312 1hd 1½	12¾	Hawley S	123 b	*1.40e	95-07	Cascapedia1232¾BastoneraII124¾StarBall121nk	Mild drive	10
12May77- 8Hol	gd 1⅛	:471 1:111 1:361 1:483 4↑	ⒻAlw 30000	4 3 2½ 1hd 12	15	Hawley S	117 b	*.70	89-21	Cascapedia1175Woodsome114nkUp to Juliet1196	Easily	5
29Apr77- 6Hol	fm 1$\frac{1}{16}$Ⓣ	:233 :48 1:114 1:42 4↑	ⒻAlw 25000	5 5 31 3½ 11	12½	Hawley S	114 b	*.70	89-13	Cascapedia1142½Katonka1152Mia Amore122nk	Handily	5
16Apr77- 8Hol	fm 1⅛Ⓣ	:492 1:141 1:382 1:493 3↑	ⒻGamely H-G2	1 6 65½ 41½ 31½	2nk	Hawley S	118 b	4.40	88-15	HailHilarious123nkCascapedia1183Swingtim119no	Wide turn	6
10Apr77- 6SA	fst 1	:223 :452 1:093 1:352 4↑	Alw 30000	6 7 79½ 66½ 67½	43½	Hawley S	109 b	*2.60	88-14	Branford Court116noThe Keed Himself1141½Announcer1182	Rallied	7
25Mar77- 8SA	sl 6½f⊗	:214 :444 1:10 1:163 4↑	ⒻAlw 20000	7 2 55 54 23½	12¾	Hawley S	114 b	*2.10	90-22	Cascapedia1142¾DearRita1145SassyGaelic1223¾	Drew clear	7
26Jun76- 8Hol	fst 1⅛	:474 1:114 1:36 1:482	ⒻHol Oaks-G2	1 7 84¾ 95½ 66	54¼	Shoemaker W	121 b	4.00	86-14	Answer1211¾Franmari1162I Going115¾	Blocked,no late run	9
12Jun76- 8Hol	fst 1$\frac{1}{16}$	:231 :462 1:104 1:413	ⒻPrincess-G3	1 2 2hd 2½ 31	56¾	Shoemaker W	122 b	1.40	80-16	HalHlrous1191½Answr1193GoMrch1162	Stumbled start,rushed	7
29May76- 8Hol	fm 1$\frac{1}{16}$Ⓣ	:23 :47 1:113 1:421	ⒻHoneymoon H-G3	8 3 2½ 1½ 12	12½	Shoemaker W	121 b	*.80e	88-14	Cascapedia1212½GoMarch117¾DreamofSprng118no	Full stride	10
13May76- 7Hol	fst 1$\frac{1}{16}$	:233 :464 1:111 1:421	ⒻAlw 15000	3 2 2½ 1hd 12	12½	Lambert J	116 b	*.40	84-15	Cascapedia1162½Go March1182Franmari12112	Driving	7
28Apr76- 8Hol	fm 1Ⓣ	:23 :471 1:113 1:354	ⒻSenorita 34k	5 7 107½ 106¾ 55	2½	Lambert J	115 b	2.60	90-20	NowPending117½Cscapdia1153QueentoB119no	Troubled trip	11
6Apr76- 8SA	fm *6½fⓉ	:212 :44 1:071 1:133	ⒻLa Habra 34k	9 2 42 66½ 35	23½	Lambert J	115 b	*1.90	87-11	Dancing Femme1143½Cascapedia115nkDoc Shah's Siren1176	No threat to winner	9
26Mar76- 7SA	fst 6f	:221 :452 :574 1:10	ⒻAlw 14000	3 8 31 42 22	1½	Lambert J	120 b	*1.00	89-19	Cascapedia120½Grecian Honey1145Spyjara118hd	Slow strt,saved ground	9
7Mar76- 3SA	fst 6f	:22 :452 :58 1:103	ⒻMd Sp Wt	4 6 21½ 2hd 1½	13	Lambert J	117 b	*.70	86-11	Cascapedia1173Jaunting1171Shamar1173½	Slow start,easily	8

Chou Croute

b. f. 1968, by Lt. Stevens (Nantallah)–Witherite, by Ky. Colonel
Lifetime record: 28 18 2 3 $284,661
Own.– Folsom Farm and Jones Jr
Br.– E.V. Benjamin III & William G. Clark (Ky)
Tr.– B. Dunham

3Mar73- 8SA	fst	1⅛	:463 1:101 1:352 1:474	4↑ (F)S Margarita Inv'l H-G1	7 1 1½ 21 77½ 717¾	Rotz JL	123	4.90	75-11	Susan'sGirl1273Convenience123¾MinstrlMss115½	Gave way	8
17Feb73- 8SA	fst	1 1/16	:234 :473 1:114 1:42	4↑ (F)S Maria H-G2	6 1 11 1½ 4¾ 68½	Rotz JL	128	*1.10	83-11	Susan'sGirl125½Conveninc1233HllCrcus119hd	Faltered late	6
16Jan73- 8SA	sly	7f	:221 :444 1:101 1:233	4↑ (F)S Monica H-G2	2 1 2hd 11 16 114	Rotz JL	128	*1.00	85-25	Chou Croute12814Generous Portion114nkMinstrel Miss1155	Won as rider pleased	7
28Dec72- 8SA	fst	6f	:221 :452 :571 1:091	2↑ (F)Las Flores H 35k	3 4 41¾ 51¼ 22½ 1¾	Rotz JL	126	*.80	95-19	Chou Croute126¾Generous Portion1151¼Minstrel Miss1145	Relaxed late,going away	10
27Oct72- 6Kee	fst	1⅛	:452 1:101 1:35 1:472	3↑ (F)Spinster 59k	7 3 35 1½ 12 22¼	Rotz JL	123	*.90e	98-15	NumbrdAccnt1192¼ChouCrout1231½BrlyEvn1198	2nd best	7
7Oct72- 6Kee	fst	1 1/16	:231 :461 1:103 1:44	3↑ Fayette H 29k	9 8 79¼ 33 21 1nk	Rotz JL	123	*.70	86-16	ChouCroute123nkSensitiveMusic1171½Chateuvr114nk	Just up	12
9Sep72- 7Bel	fst	1⅛	:46 1:102 1:35 1:472	3↑ (F)Beldame 112k	8 5 44½ 21 11 32	Rotz JL	123	4.40	95-06	Susan's Girl1181Summer Guest1181Chou Croute1233¼	Weakened late	9
28Aug72- 7Bel	fst	6f	:223 :454 1:10	3↑ Fall Highweight 28k	1 3 63 73¾ 31 12	Rotz JL	131	9.80	94-12	ChouCroute1312Icecapade135nk[DH]SaxnyWarr1321½	Driving	10
13Aug72- 8Del	fst	1¼	:464 1:104 1:352 2:003	3↑ (F)Delaware H 114k	4 2 22½ 54½ 47½ 48	Kotenko R	126	3.80	91-09	BlessingAngelica1143¼Grafitt113¾NumbrdAccount1154	Tired	8
5Aug72- 8Lib	fst	1 1/16	:231 :462 1:104 1:431	3↑ (F)Susquehanna H 55k	5 2 22 13 14 18	Kotenko R	124	2.30	90-18	ChouCroute1248Grafitti1152¼AlmaNorth1175	Crowded,easily	6
22Jly72- 8Mth	fm	1⅛(T)	:46 1:10 1:36 1:483	3↑ (F)Margate H (Div 2) 35k	1 3 34 54½ 68 718	Kotenko R	123	2.40	79-04	Tanagra114nkSydneys Nurse1167Ziba Blue112nk	Tired	7
8Jly72- 8Mth	fst	1 1/16	:224 :454 1:103 1:434	3↑ (F)Molly Pitcher H 45k	6 3 34 2½ 11½ 2½	Kotenko R	124	*1.90	85-18	OutinSpace113½ChouCroute1244½SecrtRetreat1122½	Gamely	10
28Jun72- 8Mth	fst	6f	:214 :443 1:102	3↑ (F)Regret H 28k	8 3 1hd 1hd 3nk 33¾	Kotenko R	128	*1.00	86-20	Lucky Traveler1103Secret Retreat111¾Chou Croute1281¼	Stumbled start	8
29May72- 7Bel	fst	1	:224 :451 1:094 1:352	3↑ Metropolitan H 118k	1 3 31½ 2½ 75¼ 910	Kotenko R	114	8.80	85-13	Executionr119nkBoldReasoning1231¼PeacCorps113½	Used up	11
15May72- 7Bel	fst	7f	:222 :444 1:09 1:222	3↑ (F)Vagrancy H 29k	7 1 1hd 11 13 14	Kotenko R	124	*1.30	95-08	Chou Croute1244Cyamome1141¼Wire Chief113¾	Easily	10
5May72- 7Aqu	fst	6f	:231 :47 1:102	4↑ (F)Alw 15000	7 3 52¼ 2hd 1hd 1no	Kotenko R	121	*.40	91-19	Chou Croute121noSea Saga1213Royal Signal1214	Driving	7
19Apr72- 6Kee	fst	6½f	:223 :454 1:103 1:172	4↑ (F)Alw 6500	4 2 1½ 16 17 17	Kotenko R	121	*.10	91-21	ChouCroute1217PickaNurse117½Jessie'sGirl1142½	Easily	6
1Jan72- 9TrP	fst	6f	:22 :442 1:09	3↑ (F)New Years H 30k	9 6 21½ 2½ 1½ 12	Kotenko R	123	*1.10	93-20	Chou Croute1232Magnabid1181Royal Signal1201¼	Easily	14
16Dec71- 8FG	fst	6f	:214 :451 1:101	Alw 4500	6 5 43 32 31½ 11½	Kotenko R	116	*.40e	97-13	Chou Croute1161½Honey Jay1222Ronnie1096	Ridden out	9
29Oct71- 6Kee	fst	1⅛	:463 1:102 1:354 1:49	3↑ (F)Spinster 63k	1 1 11 12 11 12½	Kotenko R	119	4.00	92-18	Chou Croute1192½Viewpoise119½Alma North119½	Driving	9
22Oct71- 6Kee	fst	*7f	1:27	3↑ (F)Alw 10000	3 3 1½ 11 12 11½	Kotenko R	110	*.30	88-19	Chou Croute1101½Viewpoise1136Secret Retreat1126	Driving	5
13Oct71- 6Kee	fst	6f	:222 :453 :57 1:084	(F)Alw 7500	3 4 12 12 14 110	Kotenko R	118	*.90	98-15	Chou Croute11810Misty Gem1211Family Way121hd	Easily	10
4Sep71- 6Rkm	fst	6f	:22 :443 1:10	3↑ (F)Alw 7500	7 3 2hd 14 14½ 16	Kotenko R	111	*.70	94-12	ChouCroute1116MusicalAnnie1153¾FlemishPrncss1151	Easily	9
19May71- 6Aks	my	5½f	:232 :462 :59 1:054	(F)Alw 6000	7 5 32½ 3½ 1½ 14	Jones K	112	*1.40	81-20	Chou Croute1124Cornish Sister11515Pelani1202	Easily	8
27Jan71- 8Hia	fst	6f	:222 :46 1:112	(F)Jasmine (Div 1) 25k	7 3 42½ 21½ 22½ 33	Kassen D	114	2.90	84-18	Pas de Nom1142½You All112½Chou Croute114½	Bid,bled	8
18Jan71- 6Hia	fst	6f	:221 :462 1:101	(F)Alw 10000	1 6 32½ 1½ 11½ 11½↓	Tauzin L	112	*1.80	93-12	[DH]ChouCrout112[DH]RosemntBw1181¼WireChief1121	Driving	9
29Dec70- 9FG	sly	6f	:224 :462 1:104	Alw 2800	6 1 11½ 12 15 111	Tauzin L	116	3.20	95-20	ChouCroute11611ToelessTom1193½TaniasMagic111nk	Easily	8
17Dec70- 6FG	fst	6f	:214 :46 1:121	(F)Alw 3000	3 8 13 12½ 12 1nk	Tauzin L	113	*.70e	88-13	ChouCroute113nkTaniasMagic110nkCruline115¾	Just lasted	9

Chris Evert

ch. f. 1971, by Swoon's Son (The Doge)–Miss Carmie, by T.V. Lark
Lifetime record: 15 10 2 2 $679,475
Own.– C. Rosen
Br.– Echo Valley Horse Farm (Ky)
Tr.– J.A. Trovato

1Mar75- 8SA	fst	1⅛	:454 1:103 1:36 1:483	4↑ (F)S Margarita H-G1	5 3 33 31 85 87¼	Velasquez J	127 b	*1.40	82-13	Tizna1201½Susan'sGirl123½GayStyle125no	Faded gradually	12
1Feb75- 8SA	fst	1 1/16	:23 :46 1:094 1:41	(F)La Canada 57k	2 3 1½ 1hd 1½ 1no	Velasquez J	128 b	*1.30	97-09	Chris Evert128noMercy Dee1161¾Lucky Spell1196	Driving	7
31Dec74- 8Aqu	fst	6f	:222 :45 1:102	(F)Conniver 25k	2 2 45 55½ 55½ 1½	Velasquez J	122 b	*.90	91-12	ChrisEvert122½Superstitious1161¼Knny'sChoc1131¼	Wide,up	5
17Aug74- 8Sar	sly	1¼	:473 1:12 1:382 2:051	Travers-G1	6 3 2hd 1½ 21 34½	Velasquez J	121 b	1.90	74-16	HoldingPattrn121hdLttlCurrnt1264½ChrsEvrt1212½	Weakened	11
10Aug74- 8Sar	fst	1¼	:474 1:114 1:363 2:023	(F)Alabama-G1	3 2 21 21½ 21½ 2nk	Velasquez J	121 b	*.50	92-14	QuazeQuilt121nkChrisEvert1215FiestaLibre1152½	Game try	8
20Jly74- 6Hol	fst	1¼	:443 1:084 1:35 2:02	(F)Match Race 350k	2 1 1½ 112 125 150	Velasquez J	121 b	.70	81-11	Chris Evert12150Miss Musket121	Galloping	2
22Jun74- 8Bel	fst	1½	:484 1:133 2:032 2:284	(F)C C A Oaks-G1	1 2 1½ 1hd 11½ 13½	Velasquez J	121 b	*.90	76-16	ChrisEvert1213½FiestaLibre121½MaudMullr12110	Going away	10
1Jun74- 8Bel	sly	1⅛	:454 1:102 1:353 1:483	(F)Mother Goose-G1	14 3 32 21½ 1hd 1½	Velasquez J	121 b	2.80	84-13	Chris Evert121½Maud Muller1215Quaze Quilt1211¾	Driving	14
11May74- 8Aqu	fst	1	:23 :452 1:093 1:36	(F)Acorn (Div 2)-G1	1 2 52¼ 43 31½ 1¾	Velasquez J	121 b	*1.80	87-17	Chris Evert121¾Clear Copy121Fiesta Libre121hd	Driving	9
1May74- 8Aqu	fst	7f	:224 :46 1:111 1:242	(F)Comely-G3	10 4 74¾ 66¼ 67½ 34½	Velasquez J	118 b	*2.00	74-22	Clear Copy113hdShy Dawn1184½Chris Evert1181	Rallied	10
14Nov73- 8Aqu	fst	1	:232 :462 1:11 1:362	(F)Demoiselle-G3	11 2 2hd 2hd 11 11¼	Pincay L Jr	121 b	*.90	85-18	Chris Evert1211¼Ambalero1161¼Khaled's Kaper1162	Driving	11
3Nov73- 8CD	fst	7f	:231 :464 1:124 1:251	(F)Golden Rod-G3	2 9 911 913 43½ 11¼	Pincay L Jr	116 b	*1.30e	81-27	Chris Evert1161¼Bundler1198Kiss Me Darlin1168	Driving	13
6Oct73- 7Bel	fst	1	:232 :464 1:112 1:362	(F)Frizette-G1	11 9 72¾ 31½ 41 2½	Castaneda M	121 b	6.20	85-13	Bundler121½ChrisEvert121nkI'maPleasure1211	Reared start	14
2Oct73- 6Bel	fst	6f	:222 :452 1:101	(F)Alw 9000	10 7 52½ 44½ 3½ 12¾	Pincay L Jr	120 b	3.10	92-15	ChrisEvert1202¾[D]Sympathetc120½FlshngLdy118½	Ridden out	10
Previously owned by Robish Stable												
14Sep73- 3Bel	fst	6f	:223 :454 1:11	(F)Md Sp Wt	10 6 31½ 32 2½ 11¾	Pincay L Jr	120 b	3.50	88-11	ChrisEvert1201¾MaudMuller1202½MamaKali1201½	Ridden out	13

Cougar II (Chi)

dkbbr. c. 1966, by Tale of Two Cities (Tehran)–Cindy Lou, by Madara
Lifetime record: 50 20 7 17 $1,162,725
Own.– Mary F. Jones
Br.– Haras General Cruz (Chi)
Tr.– Charles Whittingham

29Sep73- 7Bel	sly	1½	:50 1:132 2:014 2:254	3↑ Woodward-G1	4 5 55 44¼ 49½ 315½	Shoemaker W	126	2.90	75-15	Prove Out1264½Secretariat11911Cougar II126½	Even try	5
15Sep73- 7Bel	fst	1⅛	:453 1:091 1:33 1:452	3↑ Marlboro Cup Inv'l H 250k	2 7 79¼ 78¾ 38 35½	Shoemaker W	126	4.00e	98-07	Secretariat1243½RivaRidg1272CougrII1266½	Altered course	7
23Jly73- 8Hol	fm	1½(T)	:484 1:123 2:012 2:26	3↑ Sunset H-G1	4 5 56¼ 21 2hd 11	Shoemaker W	128	*.90e	98-08	Cougar II1281Life Cycle1201½Rock Bath114½	Ridden out	7
24Jun73- 8Hol	fst	1¼	:451 1:09 1:341 1:592	3↑ Hol Gold Cup Inv'l-G1	4 6 617 613 56 35	Pincay L Jr	128	*1.30	89-16	Kennedy Road120noQuack1275Cougar II1281¾	Rallied	6
27May73- 8Hol	fm	1½(T)	:474 1:121 2:004 2:253	3↑ Hol Inv'l H-G1	2 7 713 64½ 34½ 31½	Shoemaker W	130	*.80	98-05	Life Cycle1151¼Wing Out118nkCougar II1303½	Late bid	10
5May73- 8Hol	fm	1⅜(T)	2:132	3↑ Century H-G1	3 7 74½ 42 11 13½	Shoemaker W	127	*1.00	91-11	Cougar II1273½Wing Out1183¼Life Cycle1171	Handily	11
7Apr73- 8SA	fm	1¾(T)	:483 2:011 2:241 2:462	4↑ S Juan Capistrano H-G1	6 7 77 66 55¼ 3¾	Shoemaker W	127	*.60	95-08	Queen's Hustler115hdBig Spruce119¾Cougar II1272	Rallied	7
24Mar73- 8SA	yl	1½(T)	:474 1:123 2:03 2:273	4↑ San Luis Rey-G1	5 4 33 75½ 56½ 313	Pincay L Jr	126	*.30	64-23	BgSpruc12610Ccro'sCourt1263CougrII126nk	Disliked footing	10
10Mar73- 8SA	fst	1¼	:462 1:101 1:35 2:00	4↑ S Anita H-G1	10 8 65½ 31 2½ 1no	Pincay L Jr	126	*1.50	98-11	Cougar II126noKennedy Road1194Cabin110nk	Drifted in,up	10
1Nov72- 8SA	fm	1½(T)	:494 1:142 2:023 2:271	3↑ Oak Tree Inv'l 100k	7 8 86½ 44 31 12	Shoemaker W	126	*.30	79-21	Cougar II1262Queen's Hustler122nkBicker122¾	Driving	10
14Oct72- 8Hol	fm	1¼(T)	:464 1:104 1:351 2:001	3↑ C F Burke H 57k	5 10 1017 72 31 11¼	Pierce D	128	*.80	89-11	Cougar II1281¼Kentuckian1103Tetrack114nk	Handy score	11
24Jun72- 8Hol	fm	1½(T)	:481 1:113 2:012 2:254	3↑ Inv'l Turf H 125k	2 7 76¾ 2hd 1½ 31½	Shoemaker W	129	*.40	97-08	Typecast117nkViolonor1101¼Cougar II1296½	Drifted in	9
20May72- 8Hol	fst	1 1/16	:224 :444 1:081 1:391	3↑ Californian 133k	6 6 616 47 31½ 12¾	Shoemaker W	127	*.40	99-12	CougarII1272¾KennedyRoad1198MilesTyson1182¼	Going away	6
29Apr72- 8Hol	fm	1⅜(T)	2:11	3↑ Century H 106k	1 5 59 42 14 14¾	Shoemaker W	126	*.90	103-09	Cougar II1264¾Unconscious1231¾Star Envoy118no	Driving	8
8Apr72- 8SA	fm	*1¾(T)	:48 1:594 2:231 2:453	4↑ S Juan Capistrano H 125k	9 7 510 1hd 11 2¾	Shoemaker W	127	*.60	98-03	Practicante118¾Cougar II1273¼Nor II1201¼	No excuse	9
11Mar72- 8SA	fst	1¼	:47 1:10 1:343 2:00	4↑ S Anita H 170k	2 4 47 34 31½ 2hd	Shoemaker W	126	*.90	98-10	Triple Bend119hdCougar II1261¼Unconscious1277	Sharp	7
26Feb72- 8SA	fst	1⅛	:46 1:101 1:351 1:472	4↑ San Antonio 86k	3 8 613 67¼ 44 35	Shoemaker W	128	*.60	90-11	Unconscious123noTriple Bend1175Cougar II1281	Mild rally	9
5Feb72- 8SA	fst	1 1/16	:232 :462 1:102 1:411	4↑ San Pasqual H 57k	8 7 68 64¾ 54½ 21½	Shoemaker W	128 b	*.50	94-08	Western Welcome1151½Cougar II128noStar of Kuwait1141½	Blocked,rallied	8

31Oct71- 8SA fm 1½Ⓣ :451 1:091 1:592 2:243 3↑ Oak Tree Inv'l 100k 8 9 813 12½ 15 15 Shoemaker W 126 *.40 92-08 CougarII1265VgsVc1214¼Mnt1238 Wide rally,hand ride late 10
2Oct71- 7Bel fst 1¼ :461 1:10 1:35 2:002 3↑ Woodward 113k 6 5 48 22 13 15 Shoemaker W 126 4.10 98-13 ⒹCougarII1265WestCoastScout121nkTinajro121no Ducked in 10
Disqualified and placed third
18Sep71- 8Atl sf 1 3/16Ⓣ :492 1:151 1:423 2:02 3↑ U Nations H 100k 10 11 1120 1018 1013 621 Shoemaker W 126 *2.50 39-48 RuntheGantlet117½TwicWorthy1184½Chompon1166 Taken back 11
26Jly71- 8Hol fm 2Ⓣ :48 2:29 2:54 3:191 3↑ Sunset H 138k 5 9 714 1hd 11 2½ Shoemaker W 130 *.70 93-12 OvertheCounter114½CougarII1301Typecast1102½ Lugged in 12
26Jun71- 8Hol fm 1½Ⓣ :471 1:11 2:012 2:262 3↑ Inv'l Turf H 125k 5 7 719 59 34 1nk Shoemaker W 127 *1.30 96-12 CougarII127nkFortMarcy1251½DivideandRule1215 Driving 8
22May71- 8Hol fst 1 1/16 :224 :454 1:094 1:411 3↑ Californian 138k 9 10 1012 65½ 22½ 11¼ Shoemaker W 124 *1.10 89-17 CougarII1241¼MasterHand1124¾FleetSurprise1182½ Driving 11
1May71- 8Hol fm 1⅜Ⓣ 2:132 3↑ Century H 108k 2 8 812 53½ 54 41 Shoemaker W 128 *.60 90-13 Big Shot II111hdⒹThe Field113¾Drumtop117nk Rallied 11
Placed third through disqualification
10Apr71- 8SA fm *1¾Ⓣ :481 2:012 2:241 2:461 4↑ S Juan Capistrano H 125k 2 6 610 53¼ 3½ 13 Shoemaker W 126 1.90 96-07 Cougar II1263ⒹFort Marcy1273¼Try Sheep1142¾ Driving 7
13Mar71- 8SA sl 1¼ :464 1:111 1:37 2:03 4↑ S Anita H 145k 1 5 69½ 78½ 46½ 21½ Pincay L Jr 125 3.80 81-22 Ack Ack1301½Cougar II1254The Field1091¼ Gamely 10
20Feb71- 8SA yl 1½Ⓣ :49 1:133 2:024 2:291 4↑ San Luis Obispo H 65k 5 2 21 31 2hd 2½ Shoemaker W 127 4.00 68-22 Daryl's Joy128½Cougar II127noOnandaga1103 Gamely 7
23Jan71- 8SA fm 1¼Ⓣ :474 1:133 1:374 2:02 4↑ San Marcos H 43k 3 1 1½ 11½ 14 16 Shoemaker W 124 *.90 80-17 CougarII1246StaunchEagle1151½SuertealCobre114hd Handily 7
1Jan71- 8SA yl 1⅛Ⓣ :482 1:131 1:384 1:523 4↑ San Gabriel H 34k 3 8 84½ 77 51¾ 11¼ Shoemaker W 120 *2.30 66-34 CougrII1201¼SurtlCobr111¾TryShp112hd Hard urged,gamely 10
31Oct70- 8SA fm 1½Ⓣ :493 1:144 2:032 2:261 3↑ Oak Tree 108k 2 5 54 42 52¾ 34¼ Toro F 126 b *.30 84-14 Daryl's Joy126nkFiddle Isle1264Cougar II126½ Outside 6
17Oct70- 7Bel sf 1½Ⓣ 2:334 3↑ Man o' War 116k 9 5 54 1016 1027 1025 Shoemaker W 126 6.50 39-40 Fort Marcy1261¾Loud1214½Drumtop123nk Disliked going 10
7Oct70- 7Bel fm 1⅜Ⓣ 2:143 3↑ Manhattan H 62k 4 2 2½ 32 33½ 3¾ Shoemaker W 119 2.10 92-09 ShelterBay113½Loud115nkCougrII1191¼ Saved ground,gamely 13
7Sep70- 7Dmr fm 1⅜Ⓣ :491 1:151 1:391 2:152 3↑ Del Mar H 55k 6 4 45½ 33 32 2hd Toro F 120 5.10 117-02 Daryl's Joy123hdCougar II120noContratodos1103 6
Checked,finished well;Previously owned by Perla de Chico Stud;previously trained by G.A. Riley
22Aug70- 7Dmr fst *1¼ :452 1:10 1:35 1:58 3↑ Cabrillo H 21k 4 5 54¼ 42 1hd 1no Toro F 117 5.40e - - Cougar II117noQuicken Tree124¾Over the Counter1171½ 7
Between horses
8Aug70- 7Dmr fm 1⅛Ⓣ :483 1:123 1:363 1:49 3↑ Escondido H 22k 8 3 32 42½ 2hd 11¾ Toro F 114 6.80e 102-04 Cougar II1141¾Neurologo120½California114nk Drew away 8
1Aug70- 6Dmr fm 1 1/16Ⓣ :221 :461 1:11 1:421 3↑ Alw 8000 5 5 56 41 52¼ 44 Ramos W 112 16.30 98-03 Over the Counter1203Fleet Surprise1201Neurologo117no 6
Lost ground on turn
25Jly70- 6Dmr fst 6f :22 :45 :573 1:10 3↑ Alw 6000 8 6 87 88¼ 85½ 66½ Ramos W 113 35.90 82-09 GrecoTime113½SandCanyon113nkTraffcBt113¾ Never a factor 8
Previously trained by Alvaro Breque
23May70♦ Hipodromo(Chi) fst*1½LH 2:292 Chilean St. Leger Stk7500 4 Azocar S 123 - Burnakoff1232½Exotico1232Morro de Avico123 6
9May70♦ Hipodromo(Chi) gd *1¼LH 2:042 3↑ Clsc Republica del Paraguay-Hcp Stk2000 1¾ Azocar S 128 4.90 Cougar II128¾Antupillan107hdPimpolla1122½ 12
29Mar70♦ Valparaiso(Chi) fm*1 3/16ⓉLH 1:542 3↑ Cl Municipal de Vina del Mar-Hcp Stk5000 11½ Salinas J 117 3.00 Cougar II1171½Sisal119nkGuantanamera1281 12
Burnakoff (108) 4th
8Mar70♦ Valparaiso(Chi) fm*1 3/16ⓉLH 1:552 Clasico Thompson Matthews Stk2000 11½ Astorga C 114 *.90 Cougar II1141½Camotillo1172Burnakoff119½ 5
1Feb70♦ Valparaiso(Chi) fm*1½ⓉLH 2:29 Chilean Derby Stk10000 3 Salinas J 128 - Exotico128Burnakoff128Cougar II128 17
Pimentero 5th,Sisal 7th
11Jan70♦ Valparaiso(Chi) fm*1 3/16ⓉLH 1:564 Clasico Juan S. Jackson Stk5000 31¼ Salinas J 112 - Trinera112½Campomar112¾Cougar II112¾ 12
Sisal 4th,Burnakoff 7th,Gran Kan 11th
13Dec69♦ Hipodromo(Chi) gd *1 3/16LH 1:58 3↑ Pr Inst Nacl Hipodrm Venezuela Hcp2000 33¾ Salinas J 106 - Le Petit Navire1143½Huinche119nkCougar II1063 7
29Nov69♦ Hipodromo(Chi) gd *1 3/18LH 2:172 3↑ Gran Premio Hipodromo Chile Stk2900 52½ Azocar S 115 - A Go Go115hdAlifar128½Sisal115¾ 16
Burnakoff 4th,Huinche 6th,Pimentero 7th
1Nov69♦ Hipodromo(Chi) fst*7½fLH 1:302 3↑ Premio Sabella Hcp700 17 Salinas J 112 *1.50 Cougar II1127Economist115hdPuerte Varas110¾ 15
22Jun69♦ Club Hippico(Chi) sf *1ⓉRH 1:411 Premio Zanzibar Mdn650 12½ Salinas J 121 7.40 Cougar II1212½Crepuicuio1212Exotico121¾ 10
Pimentero 6th
4Jun69♦ Club Hippico(Chi) fm*6½fⓉRH 1:17 Premio Ujiji Mdn650 31¾ Salinas J 121 - Sabrosito1221¾Que Pasa121hdCougar II1211 14
11May69♦ Club Hippico(Chi) sf *5½fⓉStr 1:101 Premio Oropel Mdn650 34½ Azocar S 121 - Napotigre1211½Abaneio1213Cougar II121no 15

Dahlia

ch. f. 1970, by Vaguely Noble (Vienna)–Charming Alibi, by Honeys Alibi **Lifetime record: 48 15 3 7 $1,543,139**
Own.– N.B. Hunt
Br.– N.B. Hunt (Ky)
Tr.– Charles Whittingham

30Oct76- 8SA fm 1⅛Ⓣ :474 1:122 1:362 1:483 3↑ ⒻLas Palmas H-G3 1 12 1216 128½ 96¼ 73½ Castaneda M 124 6.90 82-14 Vagabonda118¾Bastonera II1221½Accra II115hd Outrun 12
24Oct76- 8SA sf 1½Ⓣ :482 1:134 2:061 2:312 3↑ Oak Tree Inv'l-G1 9 3 13 75 715 727 Pincay L Jr 123 *.50e 31-42 KingPellinore126nkRoyalDerbyII126nkL'Heureux121hd Wide 9
11Oct76- 8Bel sf 1½Ⓣ :493 1:153 2:05 2:311 3↑ Man o' War-G1 10 5 53½ 95¼ 85½ 83 Shoemaker W 123 4.80 65-33 Effervescing1211½Banghi121hdⒹCrackle121no No excuse 13
26Jly76- 8Hol fm 1½Ⓣ :483 1:122 2:014 2:262 3↑ Sunset H-G1 10 2 12 2hd 75½ 713 Shoemaker W 121 *.70e 83-14 Caucasus121noKingPellinore1243½RiotinPars1231¾ Faltered 10
11Jly76- 8Hol fst 1⅛ :463 1:104 1:354 1:48 3↑ ⒻVanity H-G1 11 8 43 62¾ 74½ 55¾ Shoemaker W 127 *3.00 86-11 MissToshiba120hdBastoneraII1213½BoldBaby1152 Slow start 11
20Jun76- 8Hol fst 1¼ :454 1:10 1:343 1:584 3↑ Hol Gold Cup H-G1 4 2 24 2hd 42 46 Shoemaker W 121 2.40e 91-09 Pay Tribute1173¼Avatar1232Riot in Paris123¾ Weakened 8
31May76- 8Hol fm 1½Ⓣ :491 1:132 2:014 2:264 3↑ Hol Inv'l H-G1 2 6 42½ 12 1½ 1½ Shoemaker W 117 *4.30 94-11 Dahlia117½Caucasus1194PasstheGlass121hd Bumped,driving 12
13May76- 8Hol fm 1⅛Ⓣ :481 1:12 1:37 1:492 4↑ Alw 25000 3 8 912 75½ 51½ 1½ Shoemaker W 111 *1.00 89-14 Dahlia111½Caucasus1161Ameri Flyer121nk Driving 10
25Apr76- 8Hol fm 1⅜Ⓣ :481 1:132 1:374 2:143 3↑ Century H-G1 3 5 75 98¾ 74¾ 31 Lambert J 117 8.50 81-16 Winds of Thought115hdPass the Glass1191Dahlia117no 9
Blocked,taken up
10Apr76- 8Hol fm 1⅛Ⓣ :50 1:141 1:38 1:502 3↑ ⒻGamely H 53k 5 5 57 57 46 44 Hawley S 123 4.90 80-15 Katonka1213Fascinating Girl117noTizna1261 No mishap 5
21Mar76- 8SA fm 1¼Ⓣ :462 1:11 2:001 2:244 4↑ San Luis Rey-G1 4 5 54 64½ 76¼ 78¾ Hawley S 121 4.70 82-08 Avatar126hdⒹGa Hai126¾Top Crowd1261 Showed nothing 7
7Mar76- 8SA fst 1¼ :452 1:093 1:342 2:002 4↑ S Anita H-G1 1 14 1212 1420 1012 913 Grant H 120 19.10 83-11 RoyalGlint124noAncientTtl1241¼LghtnngMndt1206½ Dull try 15
31Jan76- 8SA fst 1 1/16 :241 :474 1:113 1:412 4↑ ⒻS Maria H-G2 4 4 32½ 43½ 43½ 47½ Shoemaker W 126 3.70 87-14 GayStyle127noRaiseYourSkirts1206Tizna1271½ Drifted out 9
Previously trained by Maurice Zilber
8Nov75- 7Lrl yl 1½Ⓣ :494 1:152 2:062 2:311 3↑ D C Int'l-G1 7 6 38½ 815 821 827 Saint-Martin Y 124 2.50e 36-37 Nobiliary117¾ComtessedeLoir1243OnMyWayII1272 Bid,tired 9
26Oct75- 7WO fm 1⅝Ⓣ :501 1:392 2:431 3↑ Can Int'l-G1 4 10 911 84½ 54 42 Hawley S 123 *1.95 82-16 Snow Knight126½Comtesse de Loir1231½Crny's Point126hd 11
Wide late
5Oct75♦ Longchamp(Fr) sf 1½ⓉRH 2:333 3↑ Prix de l'Arc de Triomphe-G1 Stk380000 15 Navarro N 129 8.70e Star Appeal1323On My Way1322½Comtesse de Loir1291½ 24
Midpack,heels clipped from behind 3f out,never recovered
21Sep75♦ Longchamp(Fr) sf *1¼ⓉRH 2:092 3↑ Prix du Prince d'Orange-G3 Stk35200 3¾ Navarro N 129 *2.20 Kasteel118½Ramirez132nkDahlia1291½ 10
Rated toward rear,bid 1½f out,hung
31Aug75♦ Deauville(Fr) gd *1 11/16ⓉRH 2:57 3↑ Grand Prix de Deauville-G2 Stk85000 31¾ Piggott L 131 3.00 ⒹDuke of Marmalade1261½L'Ensorceleur131nkDahlia1312 18
Rated in 10th,bid 2f out,3rd 1f out.Placed 2nd via DQ
19Aug75♦ York(GB) gd *1 5/16ⓉLH 2:092 3↑ Benson & Hedges Gold Cup-G1 Stk140000 11½ Piggott L 130 3.50 Dahlia1301½Card King1335Star Appeal1334 6
Led throughout,met challenge 2f out,held well
26Jly75♦ Ascot(GB) gd 1½ⓉRH 2:264 3↑ King George VI & Queen Eliz Stakes-G1 Stk265000 35½ Piggott L 130 6.00 Grundy119½Bustino1305Dahlia1301½ 11
Tracked in 4th,one-paced last quarter

6Jly75♦ Saint-Cloud(Fr) gd *1½ⓉLH 2:38 3↑ Grand Prix de Saint-Cloud-G1 Stk204000 | 56¾ Piggott L 133 6.00 | Un Kopeck134½Ashmore134nkOn My Way1363 11 | Unhurried in 7th,bid 2f out,one-paced last quarter

15Jun75♦ San Siro(Ity) fm*1½ⓉRH 2:273 3↑ Gran Premio di Milano-G1 Stk124000 | 64¼ Navarro N 131 1.70e | Star Appeal132¾Duke of Marmalade132¾ⒹUn Kopeck132¾ 11 | Never a factor

19May75♦ Saint-Cloud(Fr) gd *1½ⓉLH 2:331 3↑ Prix Jean de Chaudenay-G2 Stk85500 | 911 Lequeux A 133 4.20 | Ashmore1302Battle Song128½Un Kopeck1341½ 15 | Raced in midpack,outfinished

4May75♦ Longchamp(Fr) gd *1 5/16ⓉRH 2:12 4↑ Prix Ganay-G1 Stk136000 | 68½ Piggott L 124 6.00 | Allez France1244Card King1281½Comtesse de Loir1241 6 | Toward rear throughout

9Nov74- 5Lrl fm 1½Ⓣ :514 1:171 2:062 2:293 3↑ D C Int'l-G1 | 3 7 87¾ 67 53½ 31½ Piggott L 124 *.60 69-29 | Admetus127¾Desert Vixen124¾Dahlia1241¾ Rallied,wide 9

27Oct74- 7WO fm 1⅝Ⓣ :471 1:373 2:40 3↑ Can Int'l-G2 | 9 7 721 64¾ 1hd 11 Piggott L 123 *.45 105-05 | Dahlia1231Big Spruce1261½Carney's Point126hd Ridden out 9

12Oct74- 8Bel fm 1½Ⓣ :484 1:134 2:024 2:263 3↑ Man o' War-G1 | 5 7 78 52¼ 12 12 Turcotte R 123 *2.40 91-10 | Dhlia1232CraftyKhale126hdLondnCompany126no Ridden out 13

15Sep74♦ Longchamp(Fr) gd *1¼ⓉRH 2:052 3↑ Prix de Prince d'Orange-G3 Stk27000 | 3½ Piggott L 129 *.30 | On My Way126nkToujours Pret126nkDahlia1272 7 | Rated at rear,bid 2f out,hung

20Aug74♦ York(GB) gd *1 5/16ⓉLH 2:092 3↑ Benson & Hedges Gold Cup-G1 Stk120000 | 12½ Piggott L 130 *.50 | Dahlia1302½Imperial Prince1221½Snow Knight122nk 9 | Rated in 6th,rallied to lead over 1f out,drew clear

27Jly74♦ Ascot(GB) gd 1½ⓉRH 2:33 3↑ King George VI & Queen Eliz Stakes-G1 Stk258000 | 12½ Piggott L 130 *1.85 | Dahlia1301½Highclere1261Dankaro129 10 | Tracked in 5th,led over 1f out,quickly clear

7Jly74♦ Saint-Cloud(Fr) gd *1 9/16ⓉLH 2:392 3↑ Grand Prix de Saint-Cloud-G1 Stk152000 | 1nk St. Martin Y 129 *2.60 | Dahlia129nkOn My Way134nkDirect Flight1361 11 | Led virtually throughout,met challenge 1f out,gamely

6Jun74♦ Epsom(GB) gd 1½ⓉLH 2:362 4↑ Coronation Cup-G1 Stk36000 | 34½ Pyers WB 123 *1.50 | Buoy1261½Tennyson1263Dahlia1235 5 | Raced in last,mild bid 3f out,one-paced last quarter

5May74♦ Longchamp(Fr) hy *1 5/16ⓉRH 2:231 4↑ Prix Ganay-G1 Stk105000 | 515 Pyers WB 124 3.70 | Allez France1245Tennyson1284Gombos1284 10 | Trailed to 2f out,passed tired ones

15Apr74♦ Longchamp(Fr) fm*1¼ⓉRH 2:113 4↑ Prix d'Harcourt-G2 Stk51300 | 46½ Pyers WB 127 3.20 | Allez France1273Ksar1261½Mister Sic Top1302 9 | Unhurried in last,mild late gain

10Nov73- 7Lrl yl 1½Ⓣ :511 1:164 2:073 2:314 3↑ D C Int'l-G1 | 4 8 88½ 53½ 42 13¼ Pyers W 118 4.60 60-40 | Dahlia1183¼BigSpruce1271ScottishRifle1271¾ Brisk urging 8

5Oct73♦ Longchamp(Fr) yl *1½ⓉRH 2:354 3↑ Prix de l'Arc de Triomphe-G1 Stk306000 | 1619 Pyers WB 119 8.00 | Rheingold1322½Allez France1194Hard to Beat1322 27 | Progress 4f out,soon weakened.San San 12th

23Sep73♦ Longchamp(Fr) sf *1½ⓉRH 2:432 ⒻPrix Vermeille-G1 Stk153000 | 56½ Pyers WB 128 *.90 | Allez France1282Hurry Harriet1282½El Mina1282 13 | Rated in 6th,brief bid 2f out,returned lame

9Sep73♦ Longchamp(Fr) gd *1⅜ⓉRH 2:282 Prix Niel-G3 Stk30600 | 1½ Pyers WB 127 *.90 | Dahlia127½Tennyson130¾Dom Luc1235 5 | Well placed in 3rd,led 1f out,driving

28Jly73♦ Ascot(GB) gd 1½ⓉRH 2:302 3↑ King George & Queen Elizabeth Stakes-G1 Stk253000 | 16 Pyers WB 116 10.00 | Dahlia1166Rheingold1332Our Mirage133nk 12 | Rated in 6th,rallied to lead 1½f out,easily clear

21Jly73♦ TheCurragh(Ire) gd 1½ⓉRH 2:434 ⒻIrish Oaks-G1 Stk70000 | 13 Pyers WB 126 8.00 | Dahlia1263Mysterious1264Hurry Harriet126hd 12 | Rated in midpack,rallied to lead 1f out,drew clear

10Jun73♦ Chantilly(Fr) yl *1 5/16ⓉRH 2:072 ⒻPrix de Diane (French Oaks)-G1 Stk178000 | 22½ Pyers WB 128 4.50 | Allez France1282½Dahlia1284Virunga128hd 25 | Rated in midpack,finished well without threatening

20May73♦ Longchamp(Fr) sf *1¼ⓉRH 2:102 ⒻPrix Saint-Alary-G1 Stk89200 | 11½ Pyers WB 123 5.40 | Dahlia1231½Virunga1231½Kashara1231 11 | Rated in 7th,rallied to lead 100y out,going away

29Apr73♦ Longchamp(Fr) sf *1ⓉRH 1:443 ⒻPoule d'Essai des Pouliches-G1 Stk76500 | 32¾ Pyers WB 128 6.50 | Allez France1282½Princess Arjumand128nkDahlia128nk 11 | Tracked in 4th,mild bid 2f out,outfinished

8Apr73♦ Longchamp(Fr) fm*1ⓉRH 1:401 ⒻPrix de la Grotte-G3 Stk25500 | 1¾ Pyers WB 128 7.30 | Dahlia128¾Gay Style128nkMidou1282½ 11 | Rated toward rear,rallied to lead near line

26Oct72♦ Longchamp(Fr) gd *1ⓉRH 1:443 ⒻPrix des Reservoirs Stk22400 | 21 Piggott L 126 15.00 | Begara1231Dahlia1262Calba1231 11 | Rated in 5th,rallied to lead over 1f out,headed 100y out

10Sep72♦ Longchamp(Fr) sf *5fⓉStr 1:024 Prix d'Arenberg-G3 Stk32000 | 55 Piggott L 121 | Enitram1282Senantes1211Challenge1211½ 6 | Tracked in 4th,lacked rally

22Aug72♦ Deauville(Fr) yl *6½fⓉStr 1:184 ⒻPrix du Calvados Stk20000 | 58 Piggott L 126 | Fiery Diplomat1261½Cannabis1213Sorata1212 9 | Rated toward rear,passed tired ones

6Aug72♦ Deauville(Fr) sf *5fⓉStr :591 Prix Yacowlef (for first-time strs) Stk22300 | 12 Piggott L 120 | Dahlia1202Challenge1232Ruling1231½ 7 | Rated in 5th,rallied to lead 150y out,quickly clear

Davona Dale

b. f. 1976, by Best Turn (Turn-to)–Royal Entrance, by Tim Tam

Own.– Calumet Farm

Br.– Calumet Farm (Ky)

Tr.– John M. Veitch

Lifetime record: 18 11 2 1 $641,612

10Sep80- 8Bel fst 1 :232 :461 1:104 1:352 3↑ ⒻMaskette-G1 | 3 3 33 41¼ 44½ 47¼ Velasquez J 123 *1.20 84-22 | Bold'nDetrmind122noGnuineRsk1186¾LovSgn120½ Weakened 5

8Aug80- 8Sar fst 7f :22 :441 1:091 1:221 3↑ ⒻBallerina-G3 | 2 4 44 3nk 4¾ 11 Velasquez J 119 1.80 91-15 | DavonaDale1191MistyGallor124noIt'snthAr1191¾ Ridden out 4

26Jly80- 5Bel fst 6f :224 :46 1:101 3↑ ⒻAlw 32000 | 5 4 32½ 32½ 32½ 31¾ Velasquez J 122 *.70 89-16 | Cornish Queen1151½Damask Fan109nkDavona Dale1226 Wide 7

12Sep79- 8Bel fst 1 :23 :453 1:093 1:344 3↑ ⒻMaskette-G2 | 3 2 31 41½ 44½ 43½ Velasquez J 122 2.30 90-20 | Blitey112nkIt'sintheAir122noPearlNecklace1253¼ Weakened 5

18Aug79- 8Sar sly 1¼ :473 1:111 1:354 2:00 Travers-G1 | 5 4 32½ 514 517 428¾ Velasquez J 121 *2.70 72-16 | GeneralAssembly12615Smarten12611PrivtAccount1262¾ Tired 7

11Aug79- 8Sar fst 1¼ :49 1:124 1:364 2:012 ⒻAlabama-G1 | 2 2 2½ 21½ 23 21½ Velasquez J 121 *.30 92-13 | It'sintheAir1211½DvnaDale1213¾MairzyDoates1212¼ Gamely 5

30Jun79- 8Bel fst 1½ :491 1:133 2:034 2:30 ⒻC C A Oaks-G1 | 5 5 31½ 12 16 18 Velasquez J 121 *.10 70-24 | Davona Dale1218Plankton121½Croquis12114 Ridden out 5

10Jun79- 8Bel fst 1⅛ :453 1:10 1:354 1:484 ⒻMother Goose-G1 | 5 3 11 11½ 14 110 Velasquez J 121 *.20 83-23 | Davona Dale12110Eloquent1214¾Plankton1211 Ridden out 6

26May79- 8Bel fst 1 :223 :452 1:102 1:36 ⒻAcorn-G1 | 6 3 42½ 2hd 1hd 12¼ Velasquez J 121 *.30 88-25 | Davona Dale1212¼Eloquent1217¾Plankton1212¼ Ridden out 8

18May79- 8Pim fst 1 1/16 :231 :464 1:113 1:423 ⒻBlack-Eyed Susan-G2 | 2 1 11 11 12½ 14¼ Velasquez J 121 *.10 92-21 | DvonaDale1214¼Phoebe'sDonky1183½Plnkton1214 Ridden out 6

4May79- 8CD sly 1 1/16 :241 :48 1:134 1:471 ⒻKy Oaks-G1 | 5 5 45½ 31½ 1hd 14½ Velasquez J 121 *.40 72-30 | Davona Dale1214½Himalayan1212Prize Spot121½ Ridden out 6

7Apr79- 9OP fst 1 1/16 :231 :463 1:113 1:442 ⒻFantasy-G1 | 3 5 45 2hd 1hd 12½ Velasquez J 121 *1.10 86-21 | Davona Dale1212½Cline1213½Very Special Lady1106 7
Stumbled st.,clear

17Mar79- 9FG fst 1 1/16 :24 :48 1:133 1:45 ⒻDebutante 59k | 3 3 2½ 2hd 11½ 17 Velasquez J 121 *.30 87-21 | DvonaDale1217JustaReflcton118nkOthrSho1152¼ Ridden out 11

28Feb79- 0GP fst 7f :221 :442 1:083 1:21 ⒻBonnie Miss 27k | 3 4 21½ 2½ 2½ 1¾ Velasquez J 122 - 99-17 | DavonaDale122¾CandyEclair12220ProveMeSpecil1142 Driving 4
Run between 7th and 8th races - No wagering

14Feb79- 9GP fst 6f :22 :441 1:083 ⒻShirley Jones 28k | 2 3 34½ 25 24 21¾ Velasquez J 122 2.70 94-16 | CandyEclair1221¾DavonaDale1228DropMeANote1141 Gamely 4

13Jan79- 9Crc fst 1 1/16 :232 :48 1:124 1:441 Trop Park Derby-G3 | 12 5 52¼ 44 46 45 Velasquez J 114 *1.30 93-12 | Bishop's Choice111½Lot o' Gold1192Smarten1192½ No rally 12

30Nov78- 6Med sly 6f :22 :453 1:111 ⒻHolly 54k | 7 7 84¾ 43½ 1hd 11½ Velasquez J 115 *1.10 89-22 | Davona Dale1151½Wondrous Me1183Aunt Hattie1123 Driving 11

23Oct78- 9Bel fst 6f :232 :461 1:102 ⒻMd Sp Wt | 8 12 63 31½ 2½ 11¼ Velasquez J 119 *1.50 90-14 | DavonaDale1191¼Clfd'Argnt11910ConstntTlk1191 Ridden out 12

Dearly Precious

dkbbr. f. 1973, by Dr. Fager (Rough'n Tumble)–Imsodear, by Chieftain

Lifetime record: 16 12 2 0 $370,465

Own.– R.E. Bailey
Br.– Mrs Jean R. Pancoast (Fla)
Tr.– S. DiMauro

11Jly76- 8Aqu	fst 6f	:214 :442 1:091	ⓕDark Mirage 42k	3 3 31½ 1hd 11½ 12½	Maple E	116	*.40	97-11	Dearly Precious116 2½Doc Shah's Siren1141Old Goat114 3¾ Pulled up lame		5
4Jun76- 8Bel	fst 1⅛	:442 1:084 1:351 1:484	ⓕMother Goose-G1	1 1 1½ 22 512 522	Velasquez J	121	1.20	61-16	GirlinLove1211¼OptimisticGl12111AncntFbls1216¾	Bore out	5
22May76- 8Bel	fst 1	:24 :47 1:111 1:354	ⓕAcorn-G1	4 1 11 11½ 12 12¼	Velasquez J	121	2.20	89-15	Dearly Precious1212¼Optimistic Gal121nkTell Me All121nk Ridden out		8
14May76- 8Pim	fst 1$\frac{1}{16}$	:234 :464 1:104 1:422	ⓕBlack-Eyed Susan-G2	4 2 22 1hd 2hd 2no	Velasquez J	121	*.80	93-14	WhatSmmr111noDrlyPrcous1215Artfully1141	Bore out early	10
5May76- 8Bel	fst 7f	:223 :453 1:101 1:231	ⓕComely-G3	3 1 1½ 11 1hd 2½	Baeza B	121	*.30	85-24	TellMeAll113½DearlyPrecious1215¾Worthyan11310	No excuse	5
26Apr76- 8Aqu	fst 6f	:233 :454 1:094	ⓕPrioress 36k	2 1 11½ 11½ 11 12	Baeza B	121	*.20	94-14	Dearly Precious1212Old Goat1188¼Answer1181¼	Handy score	4
3Apr76- 8Pim	fst 6f	:231 :462 1:112	ⓕFlirtation 28k	4 1 1½ 14 14 112	Hole M	119	*.20	89-20	Dearly Precious11912NineThrills116½Dad's Thrill113½ Swerved,handily		8
6Sep75- 8AP	fst 6f	:22 :451 :574 1:111	ⓕArl Wash Lassie-G3	10 1 32½ 12 13½ 14	Hole M	119	*.40	87-21	Dearly Precious1194Free Journey1192Head Spy119no	Easily	12
22Aug75- 8Sar	fst 6f	:233 :454 1:103	ⓕSpinaway-G1	4 4 1½ 12 12 11	Hole M	120	*.50	87-17	Dearly Precious1201Optimistic Gal120 1¾Quintas Vicki120½ Ridden out		6
26Jly75- 8Mth	fst 6f	:221 :452 1:102	ⓕSorority-G1	2 2 2hd 1½ 11 12¼	Hole M	119	*1.10	88-17	Dearly Precious1192¼Optimistic Gal1197Totie Fields1193½ Drew clear		6
13Jly75- 8Bel	sly 5½f	:222 :452 :574 1:041	ⓕAstoria 27k	3 1 1hd 1hd 11½ 12¾	Hole M	118	*1.00	94-15	DearlyPrcious1182¾OldGoat115½FreJournry115no	Ridden out	7
28Jun75- 8Mth	fst 5½f	:22 :451 :573 1:041	ⓕColleen 27k	1 4 33½ 3nk 11½ 14	Hole M	121	1.40	96-18	DearlyPrecious12140ldGoat1174BellsandBlades1177	Driving	7
15Jun75- 8Bel	fst 5½f	:222 :454 :582 1:052	ⓕFashion 28k	6 3 1½ 1½ 11½ 12½	Hole M	117	*.90	88-13	DrlyPrecious1172½HoneyPot117nkQuntsVck1172	Ridden out	8
25May75- 8Del	fst 5½f	:224 :473 1:002 1:064	ⓕPolly Drummond 23k	4 3 21 12 11 13	Hole M	115	1.70	84-26	DrlyPrecious1153HayPatcher1152½MimiRos1152	Ridden out	5
22Apr75- 4Aqu	fst 5f	:223 :453 :573	ⓕMd Sp Wt	1 1 11½ 11½ 16 19½	Hole M	115	11.80	97-13	DrlyPrcs1159½Angl'sCommnd115½Htton'sRos1102½	Handily	6
15Apr75- 4Aqu	fst 5f	:221 :46 :59	ⓕMd Sp Wt	5 5 512 512 513 58¼	Baeza B	115	6.40	82-16	Pleasant Tune1151½Xalapa Sunrise1151½Artful Woman1101¾ Broke slowly		5

Desert Vixen

dkbbr. f. 1970, by In Reality (Intentionally)–Desert Trial, by Moslem Chief

Lifetime record: 28 13 6 3 $421,538

Own.– H.T. Mangurian Jr
Br.– Mrs Vanderbilt Adams (Fla)
Tr.– T.F. Root Sr

21Jan75- 9Hia	fst 6f	:221 :452 1:093 4↑	ⓕAlw 10000	2 12 83¾ 96 77 65¼	Long JS7	114	*.80	90-15	BirdIsland1121¼Clandenita1212WingedWishs1141½	No threat	12
9Nov74- 5Lrl	fm 1½Ⓣ	:514 1:171 2:062 2:293 3↑	D C Int'l-G1	6 1 12½ 12½ 12 2¾	Turcotte R	124	5.50	70-29	Admetus127¾Desert Vixen124¾Dahlia1241¾	Gamely	9
26Oct74- 7Kee	fst 1⅛	:48 1:113 1:36 1:482 3↑	ⓕSpinster-G1	5 2 2hd 3½ 2½ 2hd	Pincay L Jr	123	*.40	95-17	Summer Guest123hdDesert Vixen1231½Coraggioso1231½	Hung	5
14Oct74- 8Atl	fst 1$\frac{3}{16}$	:482 1:121 1:364 1:551 3↑	ⓕMatchmaker-G1	7 4 21 2hd 13 13¾	Pincay L Jr	123	*.30	100-10	Desert Vixen1233¾Coraggioso115hdTwixt1231¾	Handily	9
21Sep74- 8Bel	sly 1⅛	:452 1:093 1:341 1:463 3↑	ⓕBeldame-G1	3 1 1½ 1½ 14 112	Pincay L Jr	123	*1.30	94-11	Desert Vixen12312Poker Night1236Tizna1232	Ridden out	9
11Sep74- 8Bel	fst 1	:223 :444 1:094 1:343 3↑	ⓕMaskette H-G2	1 3 23 2½ 1½ 11¼	Pincay L Jr	120	6.80	95-13	DesertVixn1201¼PonteVeccho118½PokrNght1163½ Disqualified from purse money	Hard drive	12
29Aug74- 8Bel	fst 6½f	:223 :451 1:091 1:152 3↑	ⓕAlw 20000	6 1 1hd 21 3½ 21¾	Long JS7	115	*.70	97-06	Full of Hope1161¾Desert Vixen1153North of Venus1134½ Best of others		6
22Aug74- 6Sar	fst 6f	:214 :443 1:094 3↑	Alw 20000	1 3 45½ 45 42 11¼	Long JS	103	*2.60	91-15	Desert Vixen1031¼Tambac114nkTarboosh1131¾	Going away	8
15Jun74- 6Bel	fst 6f	:222 :451 1:102 3↑	ⓕAlw 25000	3 1 21½ 24 47½ 48	Velasquez J	114	*1.80	83-14	IEncompass1141½HonorableMiss1144¼SongTitle1142¼	Tired	6
30May74- 8Bel	fst 7f	:224 :453 1:094 1:223 3↑	ⓕAlw 25000	5 1 22 42 69 614	Velasquez J	124	*1.40	75-14	PonteVcchio1151Flo'sPleasure112½LadyLove1181¾	Gave way	7
23May74- 8Bel	fst 7f	:222 :45 1:091 1:214 4↑	ⓕAlw 15000	1 3 22 23 32 34	Velasquez J	118	*.40	89-13	Flightoletti1123½IEncompss107½DsrtVxn11813	Lacked rally	5
13May74- 8Bel	fst 7f	:222 :45 1:094 1:222 3↑	ⓕVagrancy H-G3	7 6 63¾ 118¼ 1313 129¼	Velasquez J	129	*1.40	81-14	Coraggioso119noPonte Vecchio114no[D]Wanda112½ Placed 11th through disqualification	Dull try	14
15Sep73- 6Bel	fst 1⅛	:462 1:10 1:34 1:461 3↑	ⓕBeldame-G1	5 1 11½ 12 16 18½	Velasquez J	118	*.80	100-07	DesertVixen1188½PokerNight1183Susan'sGrl123¾	Ridden out	7
3Sep73- 7Bel	fst 1⅛	:454 1:094 1:344 1:472	ⓕGazelle H-G2	3 1 11 11½ 16 16	Velasquez J	126	*.90	94-10	DesertVixen1266BagofTunes1171¼PokerNight1204½	In hand	7
11Aug73- 7Sar	sly 1¼	:47 1:113 1:373 2:041	ⓕAlabama-G1	7 2 12½ 110 18 18	Velasquez J	119	*.50	84-18	DesrtVixn1198BagofTunes1197½SummerFestvl1167½	Handily	9
1Aug73- 7Sar	fst 7f	:223 :451 1:10 1:23	ⓕTest (Div 1)-G2	1 3 21½ 21 13 12½	Velasquez J	121	*1.00	92-13	DesertVixen1212½FullofHope118¾Clandenita1184	Ridden out	5
15Jly73- 8Del	sly 1⅛	:462 1:111 1:371 1:491	ⓕDel Oaks-G1	6 2 1hd 11 13 16	Velasquez J	121	*.90	91-17	DsertVixn1216BagofTunes1212¼LadiesAgremnt1126	Driving	10
4Jly73- 8Mth	fst 1⅛	:481 1:112 1:361 1:49	ⓕMth Oaks-G1	3 1 2hd 11½ 12 16	Hole M	114	2.80	95-10	DesertVixn1146LadiesAgreement1114LadyLove111hd	Driving	11
23Jun73- 8Mth	gd 1 70	:46 1:102 1:401	ⓕPost-Deb (Div 2)-G3	4 2 2½ 14 13 12	Hole M	113	*2.20	100-13	Desert Vixen1132Lilac Hill1159Lady Barbizon1136	Driving	10
14Jun73- 6Bel	fst 6f	:223 :452 1:084 3↑	ⓕAlw 10000	5 2 1hd 1½ 13 16	Velasquez J	114	*.70	100-04	DesertVixen1146FullofHope1142Hairbrush1101½	Ridden out	7
4Jun73- 8Mth	fst 6f	:214 :451 1:10	ⓕMiss Woodford-G3	6 4 56 33½ 34½ 2¾	Velasquez J	115	*1.70	91-13	ShakeaLeg119¾DesertVixen1155NaturalSound121¾	Gaining	9
25May73- 6Bel	sly 6f	:222 :46 1:10 3↑	ⓕAlw 9000	5 4 1½ 12 15 18	Velasquez J	112	*.70	94-16	DesertVixen1128MagcStory11210Proptously113no Previously owned by T.F. Root Sr;previously trained by T.F. Root Jr	Ridden out	8
15May73- 6Bel	fst 6f	:221 :443 1:093	ⓕAlw 8500	1 5 44 46 33½ 2¾	Velasquez J	118	3.00	95-04	Mulready118¾Desert Vixen118hdFull of Hope1213 Previously owned by H.T. Mangurian Jr	Gamely	8
23Nov72- 7Aqu	fst 1	:223 :452 1:102 1:373	ⓕDemoiselle 30k	11 8 67 58½ 410 43½	Velasquez J	114	4.30	75-26	Protest114¾Flightoletti1161¼Rose Chapeau1151½	Rallied	14
14Nov72- 5Aqu	sly 7f	:224 :464 1:122 1:254	ⓕAlw 10000	6 3 65½ 86½ 66¾ 34	Velasquez J	112	2.60	68-22	Yalobi112noFamous Tale1174Desert Vixen112hd	Rallied	8
27Oct72- 2Aqu	fst 6½f	:221 :46 1:112 1:18	ⓕMd Sp Wt	12 2 76 42½ 11½ 16	Velasquez J	120	*1.10	88-20	Desert Vixen1206Sumba1201Effeffvee1203	Ridden out	14
19Oct72- 3Aqu	sly 6f	:223 :464 1:121	ⓕMd Sp Wt	9 6 68 79 57½ 34½	Pincay L Jr	120	*2.20	77-20	NorthBroadwy1152GlamourPard1202½DsrtVxn1203	Mild rally	14
28Sep72- 3Bel	fst 6f	:222 :46 1:113	ⓕMd Sp Wt	9 10 109½ 78 45 2nk	Pincay L Jr	119	2.80	86-15	Flightoletti119nkDsrtVxn1191½GlmourPrd1192½	Lacked room	12

Dr. Patches

ch. g. 1974, by Dr. Fager (Rough'n Tumble)–Expectancy, by Intentionally

Lifetime record: 47 17 14 3 $737,612

Own.– Tartan Stable
Br.– Tartan Farms (Fla)
Tr.– Jan H. Nerud

13May82- 8Aqu	fst 1	:23 :451 1:091 1:343 4↑	Alw 35000	2 4 34 32½ 31½ 1½	Cordero A Jr	115	3.70	93-17	Dr.Patches115½AndMore1153½ManStm1101½	Wide into stretch	6
3May82- 7Aqu	fst 6f	:231 :461 1:103 4↑	Alw 32000	4 5 54¾ 56½ 67½ 66¼	Cordero A Jr	115	3.80	82-24	Birthday Song119nkAnd More1152Waj. Jr.1192¾	Raced wide	7
17Apr82- 7Aqu	fst 6f	:22 :443 1:101 4↑	Alw 32000	6 5 510 612 68¾ 55¼	Cordero A Jr	115	4.90	85-23	Gratification1152¼FeathersLad1151½BrthdySong117¾	Outrun	7
30May81- 6Bel	fst 7f	:232 :46 1:10 1:222 3↑	Handicap 32000	4 5 32½ 32 33 33¾	Cordero A Jr	118	3.00	86-17	Rise Jim1222½Ring of Light1201¼Dr. Patches118nk	Evenly	6
15May81- 8Bel	fst 7f	:231 :462 1:102 1:233 4↑	Alw 32000	3 5 65 54 59½ 67½	Cordero A Jr	122	2.40e	76-19	Rivalero122¾Winter's Tale122hdTax Holiday1053	Outrun	6
1Nov80- 8Aqu	fst 1⅛	:483 1:131 1:372 1:501 3↑	Stuyvesant H-G3	5 5 42 32 27 26	Cordero A Jr	115	1.80	78-25	PluggedNickle1226Dr.Patches1152¾RngofLght116hd	2nd best	10
16Oct80- 5Med	fst 1¼	:471 1:11 1:352 2:002 3↑	Med Cup H-G2	4 4 42½ 22½ 26 26	Cordero A Jr	116	3.50	98-12	Tunerup1176Dr.Patches1168DewanKeys115no	Best of others	12
24Sep80- 7Med	fst 1$\frac{1}{16}$	:24 :472 1:114 1:431 3↑	Alw 25000	4 5 54½ 31½ 2hd 11	Cordero A Jr	115	*.20	93-18	Dr.Patches1151RoylHrrchy1123Mjsty'sWorld1159	Ridden out	7
27Aug80- 8Bel	fst 1	:224 :452 1:10 1:35 3↑	Forego H 85k	2 2 1hd 1½ 2hd 2½	Cordero A Jr	114	*.50	92-17	Tanthem114½Dr. Patches1146¾Hold Your Tricks116¾	Gamely	7
2Aug80- 8Sar	fst 1⅛	:46 1:093 1:351 1:481 3↑	Whitney-G1	1 4 43½ 31½ 2hd 2½	Cordero A Jr	114	4.40	93-10	State Dinner120½Dr. Patches114½Czaravich1232½	Gamely	8
20Jly80- 8Bel	fst 7f	:23 :453 1:092 1:221 3↑	Tom Fool-G3	2 4 33½ 44½ 33½ 23	Hernandez R	119	4.30	88-16	PluggedNickle1213Dr.Patches1191½Isell1191¼	Gained place	6
5Jly80- 7Bel	fst 1⅛	:461 1:101 1:35 1:48 3↑	Alw 35000	3 6 63¾ 2½ 11½ 1hd	Cordero A Jr	115	*.70	87-17	Dr.Patches115hdBigBulldozer1152¼ThinSlice119nk	Driving	7

16Jun80- 5Bel	fst 6f	:223 :452 1:092	3↑ Alw 32000	2 2 44 45 43½ 42¾	Cordero A Jr	122	*.90	92-15	J.P.Brother1091¾NiceCtch112½DoublZus115½	Altered course	6
30May80- 8Bel	fst 7f	:23 :461 1:10 1:221	3↑ Alw 32000	5 1 21 2½ 11 11¾	Cordero A Jr	117	*1.10	91-20	Dr. Patches1171¾Frejus121nkTanthem11710	Ridden out	5
16May80- 8Aqu	fst 6f	:222 :443 1:092	4↑ Alw 32000	5 6 42½ 43½ 33 31¾	Cordero A Jr	119	1.70	94-16	King'sFashion1191¾PrinceAndrew119noDr.Ptches1192½	Wide	6
3Nov79- 8Aqu	sly 1⅛	:474 1:122 1:372 1:502	3↑ Stuyvesant H-G3	4 3 42 41 45¼ 53¼	Cordero A Jr	122	*1.30	80-23	MusicofTime114noWhataGent111hdDewanKys1122	Lacked rally	6
27Oct79- 7Aqu	fst 1	:224 :454 1:104 1:36	3↑ Alw 27000	5 3 33 11 14 16½	Cordero A Jr	115	*.40	86-22	Dr.Patches1156½DewanKeys115hdTimtheTiger1142	Ridden out	6
20Oct79- 8Aqu	fst 7f	:223 :444 1:083 1:21	3↑ Vosburgh-G1	2 3 52 53¼ 41½ 22	Cordero A Jr	126	11.90	94-15	GeneralAssmbly1232Dr.Ptchs126¾Syncopt1262¼	Wide stretch	6
10Oct79- 8Bel	sly 6f	:221 :451 1:101	3↑ Boojum H 53k	4 4 44½ 69 68½ 410¾	Cordero A Jr	118	1.90	80-26	Syncopate1183¾King's Fashion1197Tilt Up116no	No threat	6
19Sep79- 6Med	fst 6f	:224 :462 1:111	3↑ Alw 25000	5 3 43 32 1hd 12½	Cordero A Jr	115	*.40	89-23	Dr.Patches1152½Wm.Withers117noNoHouseCll1173	Ridden out	7
20Jun79- 6Bel	fst 7f	:222 :444 1:09 1:22	3↑ Celanese Cup H 80k	3 3 22 22 44½ 35¼	Cordero A Jr	118	*1.10	87-17	[D]StardeNaskra1264NorthCourse1121¼Dr.Ptchs118½	Weakened	4
	Placed second through disqualification										
28May79- 8Bel	fst 1	:224 :45 1:091 1:34	3↑ Metropolitan H-G1	3 1 1½ 11½ 112 23	Cordero A Jr	118	6.60	95-16	State Dinner1153Dr. Patches1183¼Sorry Lookin1131½	Tired	9
19May79- 8Aqu	sly 7f	:222 :45 1:09 1:214	3↑ Roseben H 54k	2 4 32½ 33½ 55¼ 54½	Venezia M	120	4.80	87-14	NiceCatch1141¼RomanMissile1142½Kng'sFshon115nk	Weakened	9
5May79- 8Aqu	fst 7f	:224 :451 1:091 1:214	3↑ Carter H-G2	5 2 67½ 515 622 619	Venezia M	122	9.60	73-25	StardeNaskra122nkAlydar1263¾SensitivePrince1266¾	Outrun	6
	Previously trained by John A. Nerud										
2Nov78- 6Med	fst 1¼	:482 1:12 1:362 2:013	3↑ Med Cup H-G2	7 3 3½ 1½ 11½ 14	Cordero A Jr	119	*.40	105-12	Dr.Patches1194DoTellGeorge1146Niteange1155	Kept driving	7
22Oct78- 8Bel	fst 7f	:221 :442 1:082 1:21	3↑ Vosburgh H-G2	2 5 43½ 42½ 2½ 1¾	Cordero A Jr	117	*1.30	97-13	Dr.Patches117¾WhataSummer1243¾SorryLookin1095	Driving	8
22Sep78- 6Bel	fst 7f	:223 :45 1:084 1:211	3↑ Celanese Cup H 52k	2 2 1½ 2hd 2hd 2no	Cordero A Jr	117	*.50	96-15	Buckfinder119noDr.Patches1172¾WarmFront113	Just missed	3
5Sep78- 6Med	fst 1⅛	:46 1:094 1:35 1:48	3↑ Paterson H-G3	9 2 23½ 21½ 2½ 1nk	Cordero A Jr	114	4.70	93-13	Dr.Patches114nkSeattleSlew1282¼It'sFreezing1125	Driving	10
	Previously trained by D. Wayne Lukas										
26Aug78- 7Sar	fst 6f	:223 :452 1:083	3↑ Alw 25000	4 3 1½ 11½ 13 16½	Cordero A Jr	122	*1.10	97-12	Dr.Patches1226½Bartendr'sPrd115½SorryLookn1141¾	Driving	7
23Jly78- 7Hol	fst 1	:223 :451 1:092 1:341	3↑ Alw 30000	5 4 48½ 43½ 1hd 13	Pincay L Jr	120	*.40	95-11	Dr. Patches1203Transcription1141Farnesio1141½	Easily	6
9Jly78- 8Hol	fst 1 1/16	:223 :451 1:092 1:401	3↑ Citation H-G3	1 3 35½ 3½ 1hd 2¾	Cordero A Jr	116	4.10	93-14	Effervescing120¾Dr. Patches1161½Text1222¾	Swerved early	6
	Previously trained by John A. Nerud										
19Jun78- 8Bel	fst 7f	:233 :462 1:094 1:213	3↑ Alw 25000	3 1 1hd 1hd 11 2nk	Cordero A Jr	122	1.80	94-12	Forego122nkDr. Patches1227Gabe Benzur1152	Held gamely	4
1Jun78- 8Bel	fst 1	:224 :45 1:09 1:333	3↑ Alw 25000	7 6 44 41½ 21½ 1nk	Cordero A Jr	117	2.60	100-11	Dr. Patches117nkVencedor1193½It's Freezing1195¼	Driving	7
12May78- 8Aqu	gd 1 1/16Ⓣ	:232 :48 1:122 1:433	4↑ Handicap 25000	4 5 56 67½ 69½ 613	Venezia M	111	8.70	75-12	Cinteelo1181½True Colors118½All the More113hd	Outrun	6
1May78- 8Aqu	fst 6f	:224 :462 1:104	4↑ Alw 25000	3 1 2hd 43 46 38	Vasquez J	122	3.00	81-24	Prefontaine1221GabeBenzur1227Dr.Patches122hd	Weakened	5
26Oct77- 7Aqu	fst 1	:233 :463 1:103 1:341	3↑ Alw 20000	1 3 1hd 1½ 1½ 1½	Cordero A Jr	114	1.40	95-17	Dr.Ptchs114½Buckfndr1149¾LghtnngBob1177¼	Strong handling	5
17Oct77- 7Aqu	sly 1⊗	:232 :46 1:101 1:343	3↑ Alw 18000	2 3 2½ 2½ 2hd 12	Cordero A Jr	114	*1.80	93-18	Dr. Patches1142Bold Palette1141¼Liberal1177	Ridden out	6
5Oct77- 6Bel	fst 6f	:221 :452 1:104	3↑ Alw 13000	4 7 53 44½ 24 1¾	Cordero A Jr	119	*.80	88-14	Dr. Patches119¾Super Pleasure1163Tiresome1191	Driving	8
13Sep77- 6Bel	fst 6f	:224 :454 1:101	3↑ Alw 11000	4 2 2½ 2½ 2hd 12	Cordero A Jr	113	1.60	91-24	Dr. Patches1132Topsider1132¾Jungle Jim1156¼	Drew clear	8
25Aug77- 7Sar	fst 6f	:22 :451 1:101	3↑ Alw 11000	4 3 41½ 54 52½ 47¼	Vasquez J	112	*1.20	82-21	PeakTop1122¼JungleJim1144¾IroquoisTribe117nk	No excuse	9
27Jun77- 8Bel	fst 1	:23 :452 1:101 1:351	Saranac-G2	8 5 31½ 3nk 2hd 42	Vasquez J	114	9.60	90-17	Bailjumper1141¼LynnDavis114¾GiftofKings114no	Weakened	9
20Jun77- 6Bel	fst 6f	:224 :462 1:101	3↑ Alw 12000	8 4 2½ 21 2hd 2no	Vasquez J	111	*1.10e	91-18	Doctr'sOrdrs114noDr.Ptchs1112½PumpknMoonshn1144¾	Sharp	11
3Jun77- 7Bel	fst 6f	:224 :46 1:101	3↑ Alw 12000	7 3 32 32½ 32½ 2nk	Vasquez J	112	*1.40	91-20	Intercontinent114nkDr. Patches1122Preferred Position1111¾		7
	Finished well										
19May77- 6Aqu	sly 1	:231 :461 1:103 1:362	Alw 13000	6 2 2½ 25 47½ 48	Venezia M	115	7.50	76-12	LeadngScorer1102½LynnDavis122hdJhnnyD.1155½	Weakened	8
2May77- 6Aqu	fst 6f	:223 :454 1:102	3↑ Alw 12000	1 5 43 43 52¼ 52	Vasquez J	112	*2.00e	89-15	Solly114hdBartender'sPride104¾HostilePlanet119hd	Tired	7
23Apr77- 4Aqu	fst 6f[•]	:222 :454 1:101	3↑ Md Sp Wt	10 2 33 2hd 1hd 12¾	Vasquez J	112	*.90	96-05	Dr.Patches1122¾LeadingScorer1077¼SunFlame113hd	Driving	12
11Apr77- 4Aqu	fst 6f[•]	:222 :46 1:111	3↑ Md Sp Wt	8 3 1hd 21½ 22½ 23	Vasquez J	112	5.50	88-13	Spirit Level1123Dr. Patches1121First Gang1125	Gamely	11

Exceller

b. c. 1973, by Vaguely Noble (Vienna)–Too Bald, by Bald Eagle
Own.– Belair Stud & Hunt
Br.– Mrs Charles W. Engelhard (Ky)
Tr.– Charles Whittingham

Lifetime record: 33 15 5 6 $1,654,003

29Apr79- 8Hol	fm 1⅜Ⓣ	:481 1:13 1:371 2:132	3↑ Century H-G1	6 10 1011 53 33½ 33	Hawley S	127	*.70	85-10	StateDinner1122StarSpngld1221Excllr1271¼	Pulled up lame	10
8Apr79- 8SA	fm *1¾Ⓣ	:48 2:03 2:273 2:48	4↑ S Juan Capistrano H-G1	6 7 716 42 1½ 2¾	Shoemaker W	127	1.50	86-12	Tiller126¾Exceller127¾Noble Dancer II1281½	Weakened	11
18Mar79- 8SA	gd 1½Ⓣ	:484 1:152 2:08 2:343	4↑ San Luis Rey-G1	2 7 715 76½ 614 629	Shoemaker W	126	*.90	- -	NobleDancrII1262½Tllr1264GoodLord1261¾	Disliked footing	7
4Mar79- 8SA	fst 1¼	:462 1:101 1:341 1:583	4↑ S Anita H-G1	4 8 812 710 47½ 37½↓	Shoemaker W	127	2.40	95-09	Affirmed1284½Tiller1273[DH]PaintedWgon115	Blocked,rallied	8
	Previously owned by N.B. Hunt										
5Nov78- 8SA	fm 1½Ⓣ	:472 1:104 1:591 2:243	3↑ Oak Tree Inv'l-G1	6 7 615 310 35½ 11	Shoemaker W	126	*.30	92-11	Exceller1261StarofErinII1263¾[DH]GoodLord126	Going away	9
14Oct78- 8Bel	sly 1½	:451 1:092 2:014 2:271	3↑ J C Gold Cup-G1	5 5 522 2hd 1½ 1no	Shoemaker W	126	3.80	84-13	Exceller126noSeattle Slew12614Great Contractor1264¾		6
	Drifted,lasted										
30Sep78- 8Bel	fst 1¼	:473 1:104 1:351 2:00	3↑ Woodward-G1	3 3 22 22½ 22½ 24	Shoemaker W	126	1.90	105-12	SeattleSlew1264Exceller1266¾It'sFreezing126no	No match	5
24Jly78- 8Hol	fm 1½Ⓣ	:492 1:14 2:03 2:27	3↑ Sunset H-G1	2 7 79 32 2½ 11¼	Shoemaker W	130	*.40e	93-13	Exceller1301¼Diagramatic1221¾Effervescing1221½	Driving	8
25Jun78- 8Hol	fst 1¼	:452 1:091 1:333 1:591	3↑ Hol Gold Cup H-G1	7 7 716 611 43½ 1nk	Shoemaker W	128	1.20e	95-16	Exceller128nkText118hdVigors1294	Just up	7
29May78- 8Hol	fm 1½Ⓣ	:472 1:112 2:012 2:254	3↑ Hol Inv'l H-G1	7 12 1213 2hd 11½ 12½	Shoemaker W	127	*2.40	99-04	Exceller1272½Bowl Game123½Noble Dancer II1263½	In hand	12
30Apr78- 8Hol	fm 1⅜Ⓣ	:482 1:133 1:372 2:13	3↑ Century H-G1	4 9 64¼ 41 35 53¼	Pierce D	128	*1.20	87-08	Landscapr115hdStrSpngld1171½NoTurnng1161½	Wide all way	9
9Apr78- 8SA	sf *1¾Ⓣ	:472 2:031 2:282 2:51	4↑ S Juan Capistrano H-G1	11 6 54½ 32 32 1nk	Shoemaker W	126	*1.30	72-28	Exceller126nkNoble Dancer II1251½Xmas Box115nk	Driving	11
19Mar78- 8SA	fm 1½Ⓣ	:463 1:104 1:593 2:24	4↑ San Luis Rey-G1	7 6 611 64¼ 41½ 41	Shoemaker W	126	*1.40	94-11	Noble Dancer II126nkProperantes126¾Text126hd	Blocked	7
8Mar78- 8SA	fst 1¼	:473 1:112 1:36 2:011	4↑ Arcadia H-G3	5 5 36 2½ 11½ 11¼	Shoemaker W	126	*1.60	90-16	Exceller1261¼Soldier's Lark1131¼Tacitus1154	Much best	6
	Previously trained by Maurice Zilber										
19Nov77- 8Aqu	sf 1½Ⓣ	:51 1:154 2:06 2:331	3↑ Turf Classic 200k	1 1 1hd 58 711 722	Piggott L	126	3.00	- -	JohnnyD.1223¾MajesticLight126¾Crow126nk	Finished early	9
5Nov77- 8Lrl	sf 1½Ⓣ	:553 1:204 2:154 2:42	3↑ D C Int'l-G1	6 7 87¾ 47½ 311 316½	Cordero A Jr	127	*1.50	42-41	Johnny D.1202½Majestic Light12714Exceller1273	No threat	8
23Oct77- 7WO	sf 1⅝Ⓣ	:511 1:443 2:522	3↑ Can Int'l-G1	8 10 812 53¼ 31½ 11	Cordero A Jr	126	*1.20e	38-44	Exceller1261Majestic Light1263½Johnny D.1183	Ridden out	12
8Oct77- 8Bel	gd 1½Ⓣ	:474 1:121 2:031 2:273	3↑ Man o' War-G1	3 9 914 42½ 52¼ 24½	Cordero A Jr	126	*1.60e	81-13	MjstcLght1264½Excllr126noJohnnyD.121¾	Brushed,alt course	11
23Jly77♦ Ascot(GB)	gd 1½ⓉRH	2:302	3↑ King George & Queen Eliz-G1 Stk230000	31½	Head F	133	5.50		The Minstrel120noOrange Bay1331½Exceller1333		11
	Raced in midpack,finished well but held by first two										
3Jly77♦ Saint-Cloud(Fr)	gd *1 9/16ⓉLH	2:324	3↑ Grand Prix de St Cloud-G1 Stk230000	1nk	Head F	134	*1.20e		Exceller134nkRiboboy134½Iron Duke1342		10
	Trailed to 2f out,sharp run to lead late.Crow 4th,Tip Moss 6th										
2Jun77♦ Epsom(GB)	gd 1½ⓉLH	2:364	4↑ Coronation Cup-G1 Stk47600	1nk	Dubroeucq G	126	*1.60		Exceller126nkQuiet Fling1233Smuggler1266		6
	Well placed in 4th,bid 1½f out,up near line										
1May77♦ Longchamp(Fr)	gd *1 5/16ⓉRH	2:11	4↑ Prix Ganay-G1 Stk122000	2½	Dubroeucq G	128	6.20		Arctic Tern128½Exceller128nkInfra Green124½		12
	Rated in 9th,late run,up for 2nd.Tip Moss 4th,Crow 7th										
17Mar77♦ Saint-Cloud(Fr)	hy *1¼ⓉLH	2:172	4↑ Prix Exbury-G3 Stk31000	48¾	Dubroeucq G	130	*1.50		Cheraw126¾Citoyen1302Kasteel1306		7
	Never a factor.Far North 6th										
3Oct76♦ Longchamp(Fr)	hy *1½ⓉRH	2:392	3↑ Prix de l'Arc de Triomphe-G1 Stk412000	19	Dubroeucq G	123	*2.00e		Ivanjica1272Crow1233Youth123nk		20
	Tracked in 5th,weakened 2f out.Noble Dancer 4th,Pawneese 11th										
12Sep76♦ Longchamp(Fr)	sf *1 15/16ⓉRH	3:334	Prix Royal-Oak-G1 Stk191000	14	Dubroeucq G	128	*.20		Exceller1284Sir Montaya128½Adam van Vianen1285		7
	Well placed in 3rd,led 2½f out,drew clear in hand										
27Jun76♦ Longchamp(Fr)	gd *1 15/16ⓉRH	3:202	Grand Prix de Paris-G1 Stk340000	14	St Martin Y	123	*.40		Exceller1234Secret Man1231½Caron1234		9
	Unhurried in 5th,rallied to lead 1f out,going away										

6Jun76♦	Chantilly(Fr)	yl *1½ⓉRH 2:284	Prix du Lys-G3 Stk43500	16	Dubroeucq G	128	*1.90	Exceller1286Brouhaha128nkCaron1281½	Well placed in 3rd,led 1½f out,drew clear	8
19May76♦	Evry(Fr)	sf *1¼ⓉLH 2:074	Prix Matchem (Listed) Stk23400	12½	Dubroeucq G	124	*.40	Exceller1242½Lithidan1211½Dauphin du Roi124½	Close up,led 3f out,held well	6
2May76♦	Longchamp(Fr)	gd *1 5/16ⓉRH 2:132	Prix de Suresnes (Listed) Stk23400	21	Dubroeucq G	121	*2.00	Malacate1261Exceller1212Bizantus121hd	Tracked in 4th,bid 1½f out,outfinished	8
19Oct75♦	Longchamp(Fr)	sf *1¼ⓉRH 2:151	Prix de Conde-G3 Stk42500	32¾	St Martin Y	123	*1.75	French Friend1232½Djeban123nkExceller1236	Tracked in 4th,brief bid 2f out,one-paced final furlong	9
1Oct75♦	Evry(Fr)	sf *1ⓉLH 1:473	Prix Herod (Listed) Stk17600	1hd	Navarro N	128	*2.00	ⒹExceller128hdHappy Tim1211½Chateau Country1215	Bid 2f out,drifted in 1f out,dueled,prevailed. Disqualified and placed third for impeding Chateau Country	7
15Sep75♦	Evry(Fr)	yl *1⅛ⓉLH 1:532	Prix de Blois Mdn11700	1nk	Navarro N	128	4.50	Exceller128nkAppassionato1286Skylab1281½	Rated in 6th,rallied to lead near line	12
10Aug75♦	Deauville(Fr)	gd *7½fⓉRH 1:312	Prix de Touques Mdn13600	88	Navarro N	123	6.00	Malacate1232½Carvello123nkSalud1231½	Never a factor	12

Foolish Pleasure

b. c. 1972, by What a Pleasure (Bold Ruler)–Fool-Me-Not, by Tom Fool **Lifetime record: 26 16 4 3 $1,216,705**

Own.– J.L. Greer
Br.– Waldemar Farms Inc (Fla)
Tr.– Leroy Jolley

7Aug76- 8AP	fst 1⅛	:452 1:092 1:344 1:473 3↑	Golden Inv'l H 125k	4 2 21 2½ 12 13½	Fires E	125	*.30	96-19	FoolishPleasr1253½Proponnt1082½FstvMood1152	Going away	6
24Jly76- 8Aqu	fst 1¼	:464 1:111 1:362 2:011 3↑	Brooklyn H-G1	3 3 43 34½ 34 36½	Maple E	126	3.70	83-14	Forego1342Lord Rebeau1144½Foolish Pleasure126no	Bore in	8
5Jly76- 8Aqu	fst 1 3/16	:474 1:112 1:361 1:552 3↑	Suburban H-G1	4 1 11½ 11½ 11 1no	Maple E	125	2.80	85-15	Foolish Pleasure125noForego134noLord Rebeau1164¼	Lasted	4
20Jun76- 8Hol	fst 1¼	:454 1:10 1:343 1:584 3↑	Hol Gold Cup H-G1	1 7 69½ 74½ 76 56½	Pincay L Jr	126	1.80	90-09	Pay Tribute1173¼Avatar1232Riot in Paris123¾	Checked	8
6Jun76- 8Hol	fst 1⅛	:462 1:102 1:35 1:471 3↑	Bel Air H-G2	2 4 33 42½ 42 33¾	Pincay L Jr	128	*.70	92-13	Riot in Paris122¾Pay Tribute1183Foolish Pleasure1282		5
	Altered course										
27Mar76- 9GP	fm 1 1/16Ⓣ	:231 :464 1:094 1:401 3↑	Can Turf H-G3	3 3 21½ 22 32½ 84¼	Baeza B	129	*.60	99-02	StepForwrd117¾LordHenham112hdConesaba1131½	No excuse	9
6Mar76- 9GP	fst 7f	:22 :443 1:091 1:212 3↑	Donn H-G2	2 7 43 63¾ 1½ 13½	Baeza B	129	*.30	97-17	FoolishPlsre1293½PackerCaptain114¾HomJrom112¾	Easily	10
4Feb76- 7Hia	fst 7f	:23 :454 1:101 1:222 4↑	Alw 10000	4 3 42¼ 43 1hd 17	Baeza B	119	*.30	93-16	Foolish Pleasure1197Dashboard1171Orders117nk	Easy score	7
10Oct75- 8Bel	fst 1 1/16	:24 :464 1:11 1:413 3↑	Alw 20000	6 2 21½ 11½ 1hd 2no	Cordero A Jr	120	*.20	94-21	Stonewalk126noFoolishPlsur12010FrstSlc117no	Just missed	6
13Sep75- 8Bel	fst 1¼	:472 1:104 1:352 2:00 3↑	Marlboro Cup Inv'l H-G1	4 5 54 66½ 66¼ 510	Cordero A Jr	121	2.80	89-11	Wajima119hdForego1297½Ancient Title126¾	No response	7
1Sep75- 8Bel	fst 1⅛	:452 1:09 1:341 1:471 3↑	Governor-G1	6 4 45½ 33 11 2hd	Cordero A Jr	125	3.60	91-18	Wajima115hdFoolishPlsur1252AncntTtl130¾	Held stubbornly	10
6Jly75- 8Bel	fst 1¼	:443 1:083 1:352 2:024	Match Race 350k	2 2 1 1 1 1	Baeza B	126	.90	86-11	Foolish Pleasure126	Galloping	2
7Jun75- 7Bel	fst 1½	:48 1:122 2:02 2:281	Belmont-G1	2 6 67 43½ 32½ 2nk	Vasquez J	126	*1.30	79-18	Avatar126nkFoolishPleasure1263½MstrDrby1264	Closed fast	9
17May75- 8Pim	fst 1 3/16	:471 1:113 1:361 1:562	Preakness-G1	4 7 76 52¾ 23 21	Vasquez J	126	*1.20	87-18	MasterDerby1261FoolshPlsur1261Dbolo1261½	Altered course	10
3May75- 8CD	fst 1¼	:452 1:103 1:36 2:02	Ky Derby-G1	3 11 812 43½ 2½ 11¾	Vasquez J	126	*1.90	87-11	Foolish Pleasure1261¾Avatar1262½Diabolo1262½	Ridden out	15
19Apr75- 8Aqu	fst 1⅛	:463 1:103 1:352 1:484	Wood Memorial-G1	15 4 43½ 31½ 22 1hd	Vasquez J	126	*.50	91-12	Foolish Pleasure126hdBombay Duck1261Media1264¾	Driving	15
29Mar75- 9GP	fst 1⅛	:472 1:12 1:38 1:502	Florida Derby-G1	2 3 33½ 31 2½ 33½	Vasquez J	122	*.20	78-17	PrinceThouArt1183¼SylvnPlace118nkFoolishPlsur1227	Hung	9
1Mar75- 9Hia	fst 1⅛	:462 1:104 1:361 1:482	Flamingo-G1	2 7 64¼ 43½ 12 11¾	Vasquez J	122	*.40	90-13	FoolishPleasre1221¾PrinceThouArt1223Somethngfblous1222½		10
	Bore in,clear										
12Feb75- 0Hia	fst 7f	:231 :453 1:092 1:212	Alw 7600	2 2 24 25 11 14¼	Vasquez J	122	-	98-15	FoolishPleasure1224¼Ambassador'sImage114½CircleHme119		3
	Exhibition race - no wagering										
5Oct74- 8Bel	fst 1	:233 :463 1:11 1:36	Champagne-G1	9 3 31½ 13 17 16	Vasquez J	122	*.30	88-12	FlishPleasre1226HarvardMn1221¾Rmhorn1221¾	Ridden out	9
25Sep74- 8Bel	fst 7f	:23 :462 1:102 1:223	Cowdin-G2	7 6 42½ 31½ 12 16½	Vasquez J	121	*.90	89-14	Foolish Pleasure1216½Our Talisman1135¾CardinalGeorge1131¼		11
	Ridden out										
24Aug74- 8Sar	fst 6½f	:214 :442 1:092 1:16	Hopeful (Div 2)-G1	1 5 32½ 32 2½ 13¾	Baeza B	121	*1.10	96-13	FoolishPleasr1213¾GrkAnswr1211¾OurTlsmn121½	Drew clear	8
10Aug74- 8Mth	gd 6f	:22 :45 1:102	Sapling-G1	13 3 43½ 42½ 1hd 11¾	Vasquez J	122	*2.30	88-19	Foolish Pleasure1221¾The BagelPrince1224½BombayDuck1222		15
	Drew clear										
24Jly74- 8Aqu	fst 6f	:221 :453 1:104	Tremont-G3	4 5 22½ 21½ 2hd 1nk	Baltazar C	120	*1.10	89-12	FoolishPlsre120nkWhataSktch1141¼RcksJt115½	Bumped,up	9
27May74- 6Del	gd 5½f	:223 :471 :593 1:053	Dover (Div 1)-G3	5 4 3nk 12 15 110	Baltazar C	116	*1.00	90-24	FoolishPleasre11610Jimbosanda1122ⒹRamahorn1161	Easily	7
4Apr74- 3Hia	fst 5f	:223 :461 :59	©Md Sp Wt	8 9 42 11½ 13 14½	Baltazar C	120	*1.40	94-18	FoolishPlsure1204½SwingLbrSwng120hdTrKng1201½	Handily	11

Forego

b. g. 1970, by Forli (Aristophanes)–Lady Golconda, by Hasty Road **Lifetime record: 57 34 9 7 $1,938,957**

Own.– Lazy F Ranch
Br.– Lazy F Ranch (Ky)
Tr.– Frank Y. Whiteley Jr

4Jly78- 8Bel	sly 1¼	:483 1:123 1:37 2:014 3↑	Suburban H-G1	3 5 43½ 68½ 611 514	Shoemaker W	132	*.90	89-13	Upper Nile1131½Nearly on Time1092¼Great Contractor1143		6
	Tired after ¾										
19Jun78- 8Bel	fst 7f	:233 :462 1:094 1:213 3↑	Alw 25000	4 4 41½ 31½ 31½ 1nk	Shoemaker W	122	*.30	94-12	Forego122nkDr. Patches1227Gabe Benzur1152	Ridden out	4
17Sep77- 8Bel	sly 1⅛	:453 1:101 1:352 1:48 3↑	Woodward H-G1	3 8 79½ 44 4¾ 11½	Shoemaker W	133	*1.90	87-18	Forego1331½SilverSeries114nkGrtContrctor115nk	Ridden out	10
6Aug77- 8Sar	sly 1⅛	:463 1:103 1:361 1:492 3↑	Whitney H-G2	7 6 712 716 716 718	Shoemaker W	136	*.80	70-16	Nearly on Time1034½American History1124¾Dancing Gun112¾		7
	Disliked going										
23Jly77- 8Bel	fst 1½	:49 1:124 2:023 2:261 3↑	Brooklyn H-G1	12 6 2hd 21½ 25 211	Shoemaker W	137	*.70	78-17	GreatContractr11211Forego137nkAmrcnHstory112¾	Held 2nd	13
4Jly77- 8Bel	fst 1¼	:472 1:113 1:373 2:03 3↑	Suburban H-G1	4 3 36½ 45 42 2nk	Shoemaker W	138	*.30	84-16	QuietLittleTable114nkForego138nkNearlyonTm104¾	Bore out	6
13Jun77- 8Bel	fst 1⅛	:471 1:111 1:354 1:481 3↑	Nassau County H-G3	3 5 54 51¼ 4¾ 1½	Shoemaker W	136	*.05	86-21	Forego136½Co Host110nkNorcliffe117½	Easily	7
30May77- 8Bel	fst 1	:23 :451 1:101 1:344 3↑	Metropolitan H-G1	10 10 1014 86½ 2hd 12	Shoemaker W	133	*.50	94-14	Forego1332Co Host1112Full Out1151½	Handily	12
23May77- 6Bel	fst 7f	:242 :47 1:11 1:224 4↑	Alw 25000	2 3 31 32 2hd 1½	Shoemaker W	122	*.05	88-17	Forego122½Dance Spell1147Sawbones1092	Ridden out	5
2Oct76- 8Bel	sly 1¼	:472 1:104 1:35 2:00 3↑	Marlboro Cup H-G1	10 4 86¼ 67½ 44 1hd	Shoemaker W	137	*1.10	99-11	Forego137hdHonestPleasure1191FthrHogn1102¾	Wide,just up	11
18Sep76- 8Bel	fst 1⅛	:453 1:091 1:332 1:454 3↑	Woodward H-G1	2 7 76 76½ 42½ 11¼	Shoemaker W	135	*1.10	98-10	Forgo1351¼DanceSpell1152¾ⒹⒽHonstPleasur121	Ridden out	10
21Aug76- 8Mth	fst 1¼	:472 1:112 1:354 2:003 3↑	AL Haskell H-G1	7 5 33 22 21 31	Vasquez J	136	*.60	98-12	Hatchet Man1121Intrepid Hero119hdForego1366	Forced wide	8
24Jly76- 8Aqu	fst 1¼	:464 1:111 1:362 2:011 3↑	Brooklyn H-G1	4 6 68½ 21½ 2hd 12	Gustines H	134	*.70	90-14	Forego1342LordRebeau1144½FoolishPleasur126no	Ridden out	8
5Jly76- 8Aqu	fst 1 3/16	:474 1:112 1:361 1:552 3↑	Suburban H-G1	2 3 32½ 21½ 31½ 2no	Gustines H	134	*.40	85-15	Foolish Pleasure125noForego134noLord Rebeau1164¼	Gamely	4
13Jun76- 8Bel	fst 1⅛	:472 1:112 1:362 1:483 3↑	Nassau County H-G3	1 4 42½ 32 1hd 12¾	Vasquez J	132	*.80	84-22	Forego1322¾El Pitirre1152¾Hatchet Man1142	Easily	5
31May76- 8Bel	fst 1	:231 :453 1:092 1:344 3↑	Metropolitan H-G1	4 5 54½ 44 41½ 1hd	Gustines H	130	*1.10	94-16	Forego130hdMaster Derby1261¼Lord Rebeau1192¼		6
	Sluggish,just up										
20May76- 8Bel	fst 7f	:234 :464 1:10 1:22 4↑	Alw 25000	2 2 41½ 3½ 1hd 11¼	Gustines H	126	*.30	92-18	Forego1261¼Wishing Stone1196½Tiempazo III119½	Easily	4
	Previously trained by S.W. Ward										
27Sep75- 8Bel	fst 1½	:493 1:132 2:023 2:271 3↑	Woodward-G1	6 3 3½ 1hd 1hd 11¾	Gustines H	126	*.90	84-19	Forego1261¾Wajima11911Group Plan126¾	Drew clear	6
13Sep75- 8Bel	fst 1¼	:472 1:104 1:352 2:00 3↑	Marlboro Cup Inv'l H-G1	3 7 76 32 1hd 2hd	Gustines H	129	*1.40	99-11	Wajima119hdForego1297½Ancient Title126¾	Bore out,missed	7
1Sep75- 8Bel	fst 1⅛	:452 1:09 1:341 1:471 3↑	Governor-G1	8 8 710 88¾ 54½ 42¾	Gustines H	134	*2.00	88-18	Wajima115hdFoolishPleasure1252AncntTtl130¾	Wide stretch	10
19Jly75- 8Bel	fst 1½	:484 1:132 2:024 2:274 3↑	Suburban H-G1	3 6 69½ 42½ 3½ 1hd	Gustines H	134	*.60	81-18	Forego134hdArbees Boy1182¼Loud1147	Just up	7

Date	Cond	Dist	Fractions	Age	Race	PP	St	1st	2nd	Str	Fin	Jockey	Wt	Odds	Speed	Top Finishers	Comment	Field
4Jly75- 8Bel	fst	1¼	:463 1:101 1:344 1:594	3↑	Brooklyn H-G1	2	5	412	31½	1hd	11½	Gustines H	132	*.70	101-07	Frgo1321½MonetryPrncpl109noStopthMusc1215¾	Ridden out	8
26May75- 8Aqu	fst	1	:231 :453 1:084 1:333	3↑	Metropolitan H-G1	3	7	75¼	64¾	34	31	Gustines H	136	*.90	97-11	GoldandMyrrh121¾StoptheMusic124nkForego1363½	Rallied	7
17May75- 8Aqu	fst	7f	:223 :444 1:091 1:213	3↑	Carter H-G2	5	10	811	87¾	22	1hd	Gustines H	134	*.90	93-11	Forego134hdStop the Music1232½Orders1141¼	Brisk drive	10
15Feb75- 9Hia	fst	1¼	:463 1:102 1:35 2:014	3↑	Widener H-G1	5	9	813	45½	1hd	11¼	Gustines H	131	*.70	89-11	Forego1311¼Hat Full1111¼Gold and Myrrh115nk	Ridden out	9
1Feb75- 9Hia	fst	1⅛	:47 1:103 1:343 1:471	3↑	Seminole H-G2	5	8	85	32	2½	1¾	Gustines H	129	*.80	96-09	Forego129¾Mr. Door1151Lord Rebeau1152½	Ridden out	8
9Nov74- 8Aqu	fst	2	:493 2:304 2:56 3:211	3↑	J C Gold Cup-G1	2	8	42½	1hd	12½	12½	Gustines H	124	*.70	90-15	Forego1242½Copte124¾Group Plan1243¼	Ridden out	8
19Oct74- 8Aqu	fst	7f	:223 :452 1:094 1:213	3↑	Vosburgh H-G2	4	10	99½	77½	21	13½	Gustines H	131	*2.20	93-10	Forgo1313½StoptheMusic118noPrinceDantn1191¾	Ridden out	12
28Sep74- 8Bel	fst	1½	:49 1:132 2:022 2:272	3↑	Woodward-G1	5	10	1017	84¼	42	1nk	Gustines H	126	*2.30	83-13	Forego126nkArbees Boy1261¾Group Plan1262½	Driving	11
14Sep74- 8Bel	sly	1⅛	:46 1:102 1:343 1:463	3↑	Marlboro Cup H 250k	2	9	810	72¾	34½	34	Gustines H	126	2.70	90-12	Big Spruce1202¾Arbees Boy1191¼Forego126½	No final rally	10
2Sep74- 8Bel	fst	1⅛	:452 1:092 1:34 1:461	3↑	Governor-G1	10	8	812	65	57	45¼	Gustines H	128	*1.60	91-09	Big Spruce1182½Arbees Boy1211½Plunk1211¼	Wide	10
20Jly74- 8Aqu	fst	1¼	:472 1:111 1:361 2:012	3↑	Suburban H-G1	6	6	512	46½	44½	31½	Gustines H	131	*1.40	87-12	True Knight1271½Plunk114hdForego1312½	Rallied	10
4Jly74- 8Aqu	fst	1 3/16	:463 1:102 1:354 1:544	3↑	Brooklyn H-G1	6	6	615	48	2hd	1¾	Gustines H	129	*.40	88-14	Forego129¾BillyComeLately1142ArbeesBoy1166	Ridden out	7
26Jun74- 8Aqu	fst	7f	:223 :444 1:084 1:211	3↑	Nassau County H-G3	2	6	612	612	56½	2½	Gustines H	132	*.70	94-10	Timeless Moment112½Forego132½North Sea1142½	Fast finish	6
27May74- 8Bel	fst	1	:222 :443 1:09 1:342	3↑	Metropolitan H-G1	2	6	47½	2hd	11½	22	Gustines H	134	*1.30	94-11	Arbees Boy1122Forego134½Timeless Moment109hd	Gamely	8
18May74- 8Bel	fst	7f	:221 :45 1:092 1:221	3↑	Carter H-G2	7	8	89	63½	11½	12¼	Gustines H	129	*1.40	91-13	Forego1292¼Mr.Prospector1241TimelessMoment1132¾	Easily	8
23Mar74- 9Hia	fst	1¼	:471 1:11 1:354 2:011	3↑	Widener H-G1	5	5	58½	1½	11½	11	Gustines H	129	*.80	92-12	Forego1291True Knight1242Play the Field114no	Driving	7
23Feb74- 9GP	fst	1¼	:464 1:104 1:354 1:594	3↑	Gulf Park H-G2	2	4	413	22	1hd	1½	Gustines H	127	1.40	98-14	Forego127½True Knight1236Golden Don1183	Ridden out	6
9Feb74- 9GP	fst	1⅛	:471 1:112 1:362 1:483	3↑	Donn H-G3	2	4	35	32½	21	1no	Gustines H	125	*.70	91-19	Forego125noTrue Knight123½Proud and Bold122nk	Just up	5
8Dec73- 8Aqu	fst	1⅛	:454 1:10 1:35 1:471		Discovery H-G3	6	5	37	34	11½	1¾	Gustines H	127	*.60	100-13	Forego127¾MyGallant1225[D]KeytotheKingdom1131	Driving	7
24Nov73- 8Aqu	fst	1 3/16	:462 1:11 1:36 1:543		Roamer H-G2	9	4	514	32½	13	15	Gustines H	123	*2.10	89-13	Forego1235My Gallant1212½Twice a Prince1141	Handily	10
10Nov73- 6Aqu	fst	7f	:233 :463 1:102 1:223	3↑	Alw 12000	2	5	35½	36	34	34	Gustines H	122	*.90	84-22	North Sea1152¾Tap the Tree1141¼Forego1223½	Evenly	5
20Oct73- 8Aqu	fst	1	:233 :46 1:094 1:34		Jerome H-G2	7	6	63½	32½	2hd	2hd	Gustines H	124	2.20	97-14	Step Nicely118hdForego1243Linda's Chief1261¾	Gamely	10
8Oct73- 5Bel	fst	1	:234 :461 1:093 1:333	3↑	Alw 20000	3	3	31	1½	12½	15½	Gustines H	120	*1.60	100-07	Forego1205½Rule by Reason114noRoyal Owl12010	Ridden out	5
15Sep73- 8Bel	fst	1 1/16	:232 :462 1:102 1:402		Alw 20000	6	4	41½	1hd	13	12½	Gustines H	116	2.10	101-07	Forego1162½Arbees Boy1132Matinee Idol1133	Driving	8
1Sep73- 4Bel	fst	7f	:214 :442 1:091 1:221		Alw 20000	1	6	49½	25	13	1hd	Gustines H	113	*.60	91-10	Forego113hdCutlass113¾Jazziness116nk	Driving	6
24Aug73- 5Sar	fst	7f	:224 :451 1:083 1:21	3↑	Alw 12000	5	4	56½	56	47½	37¼	Anderson P	116	*.60	95-10	Prove Out1126½Cutlass109¾Forego1161¼	No excuse	6
9Jun73- 7Bel	fst	1 1/16	:232 :46 1:101 1:404		Alw 20000	4	5	53¼	12	17	19	Gustines H	111	*1.00	99-05	Forego1119AdaptiveAce114noIllberightbck114no	Ridden out	10
30May73- 7Bel	fst	1	:231 :45 1:091 1:344		Withers-G2	3	5	56	45	43½	35	Anderson P	126	8.00	93-17	Lnda'sChief1263StoptheMusc1262Forgo126½	Between horses	6
5May73- 9CD	fst	1¼	:472 1:114 1:361 1:592		Ky Derby-G1	9	9	912	66	46½	411	Anderson P	126	28.60	92-10	Secretariat1262½Sham1268OurNative126½	Hit rail far turn	13
26Apr73- 6Kee	fst	1⅛	:463 1:11 1:37 1:493		Blue Grass-G1	5	6	611	52½	52¾	55	Anderson P	117	*2.60	84-18	My Gallant117hdOur Native1233½[DH]Warbucks117	No rally	9
31Mar73- 9GP	fst	1⅛	:471 1:102 1:342 1:472		Florida Derby-G1	6	4	56	33	23	23	Anderson P	118	*2.30	94-06	Royal and Regal1222Forego1181¼Restless Jet122hd	Gamely	8
24Mar73- 3GP	fst	7f	:221 :444 1:092 1:213		Alw 6500	1	8	65	53	11	12	Anderson P	119	*.30	96-12	Forego1192Cades Cove114noMalicious Music1143½	Driving	8
7Mar73- 9GP	fst	7f	:221 :443 1:082 1:204		Hutcheson-G3	1	7	56¾	37	24	23¼	Anderson P	116	2.40	97-10	Shecky Greene1223¼Forego1169Leo's Pisces1124½		7
	Away sluggishly																	
10Feb73- 4Hia	fst	6f	:214 :452 1:094		Alw 6500	5	4	45½	32½	11	12½	Anderson P	122	*.60	95-18	Forego1222½Borage1152½Paternity1174	Easily	8
29Jan73- 1Hia	fst	6f	:222 :46 1:102		©Md Sp Wt	4	1	22	1hd	1½	18	Anderson P	122	*1.30	92-16	Forego1228Jonata1222Barclay Jet122½	Easily	11
17Jan73- 1Hia	fst	7f	:232 :461 1:11 1:233		©Md Sp Wt	9	11	97¼	89	79½	47	Anderson P	122	10.30	82-04	BuffaloLark1223¾TwoHarbrs1222CommandrLiz1221¼	Bumped	12

Fort Marcy

b. g. 1964, by Amerigo (Nearco)–Key Bridge, by Princequillo

Lifetime record: 75 21 18 14 $1,109,791

Own.– Rokeby Stable

Br.– Paul Mellon (Va)

Tr.– E. Burch

Date	Cond	Dist	Fractions	Age	Race	PP	St	1st	2nd	Str	Fin	Jockey	Wt	Eq	Odds	Speed	Top Finishers	Comment	Field
4Sep71- 8Atl	fm	1⅛Ⓣ	:492 1:121 1:362 1:483	3↑	Kelly-Olympic H 33k	8	6	68	56	53½	3¾	Velasquez J	126	b	*1.30e	92-11	Run the Gantlet115¾Charlie's Luck110noFort Marcy126hd		8
	Strong finish																		
5Jly71- 7Aqu	fst	1¼	:48 1:121 1:371 2:021	3↑	Suburban H 115k	3	9	88¾	127½	109¾	1010	Velasquez J	120	b	8.10	75-17	Twice Worthy116½Ejemplo1143Tunex117hd	No factor	13
26Jun71- 8Hol	fm	1½Ⓣ	:471 1:11 2:012 2:262	3↑	Inv'l Turf H 125k	6	4	414	25	22	2nk	Lambert J	125	b	4.20	101-12	CougarII127nkFortMarcy1251½DvdndRul1215	Drifted,rallied	8
12Jun71- 7Bel	hd	1½Ⓣ	2:252	3↑	Bowling Green H 56k	5	4	55½	31	3nk	21¾	Turcotte R	128	b	*1.50	104-00	Drumtop1241¾Fort Marcy128noPracticante1151½	Bore in	7
8May71- 8Pim	sf	1½Ⓣ	:501 1:17 2:083 2:341	3↑	Dixie H 56k	4	3	35	22	15	16	Turcotte R	126	b	*.70	66-34	[D]FortMarcy1266Chompion1193½TudorReward1143½	Brushed	5
	Disqualified and placed fourth																		
10Apr71- 8SA	fm	*1¾Ⓣ	:481 2:012 2:241 2:461	4↑	S Juan Capistrano H 125k	4	5	59	3nk	1½	23	Velasquez J	127	b	*1.00	93-07	Cougar II1263[D]Fort Marcy1273¼Try Sheep1142¾	Bore out	7
	Disqualified and placed sixth																		
27Feb71- 8Hia	hd	1½Ⓣ	2:264	3↑	Hia Turf Cup H 143k	8	1	1hd	11½	1hd	31¾	Velasquez J	128	b	*.70	100-03	Drumtop119hdThe Pruner1131¾Fort Marcy128¾	Drifted badly	13
13Feb71- 8Hia	hd	1 3/16Ⓣ	1:54	3↑	Bougnvillea H (Div 1) 48k	3	4	414	57½	23	2hd	Velasquez J	126	b	*1.10	99-01	Shelter Bay117hdFort Marcy1262Stop Time1111½	Gamely	10
11Nov70- 7Lrl	sf	1½Ⓣ	:511 1:172 2:151 2:424	3↑	Wash Int'l Inv'l 150k	9	4	41	12	1½	11	Velasquez J	127	b	*1.10	--	Fort Marcy1271Miss Dan II1175Bacuco127no	Fully extended	10
17Oct70- 7Bel	sf	1½Ⓣ	2:334	3↑	Man o' War 116k	5	4	43	11½	15	11¾	Velasquez J	126	b	*.70	64-40	Fort Marcy1261¾Loud1214½Drumtop123nk	Mild drive	10
16Sep70- 8Atl	fm	1 3/16Ⓣ	:473 1:121 1:374 1:56	3↑	U Nations Inv'l H 125k	7	5	58	42	11½	15	Velasquez J	125	b	*1.50	90-10	Fort Marcy1255Fiddle Isle1271Mr. Leader119nk	Mild drive	10
5Sep70- 8Atl	fm	1⅛Ⓣ	:474 1:112 1:36 1:482	3↑	Kelly-Olympic H 41k	13	11	108¾	95¼	43¼	2no	Velasquez J	126	b	*2.10	94-09	Red Reality115noFort Marcy1261Mister Diz1163	Missed	13
21Aug70- 7Sar	fst	1	:24 :464 1:104 1:351	3↑	Alw 15000	5	2	21½	31	31½	31½	Velasquez J	120	b	6.10	96-08	True North116nkMaster Hand1161¼Fort Marcy1201	Good try	7
20Jun70- 8Hol	fm	1½Ⓣ	:481 1:121 2:013 2:253	3↑	Hol Inv'l H 100k	5	3	35	32½	21½	2nk	Velasquez J	126	b	*1.60e	105-10	FiddleIsle128nkFortMrcy1263Govrnor'sPrty1121¼	Sharp try	9
13Jun70- 7Bel	fm	1½Ⓣ	2:263	3↑	Bowling Green H 57k	5	2	28	25	11	1½	Velasquez J	127	b	*1.50	103-13	Fort Marcy127½Drumtop1201½Hitchcock118¾	Driving	7
9May70- 8Pim	fm	1½Ⓣ	:483 1:134 2:022 2:272	3↑	Dixie H 57k	6	4	45	32	2hd	13½	Velasquez J	124	b	*1.30	108-01	FortMarcy1243½WarCensor112½JungleCove114nk	Mild drive	10
25Apr70- 8Hol	fm	1⅜Ⓣ	2:113	3↑	Century H 80k	2	5	54½	53	32½	2no	Velasquez J	123	b	3.70	108-08	Quilche115noFort Marcy123½Pinjara1201¼	Hemmed in	9
4Apr70- 8SA	fm	*1¾Ⓣ	:471 2:001 2:24 2:462	4↑	S Juan Capistrano H 125k	3	4	46½	53	3½	3no	Velasquez J	124	b	8.50	95-05	[DH] Fiddle Isle125[DH] Quicken Tree124noFort Marcy124nk		11
	Squeezed																		
18Mar70- 7Aqu	fst	1	:233 :463 1:103 1:351	4↑	Alw 15000	8	4			2½	2no	Velasquez J	116	b	6.90	91-17	Hydrologist120noFortMarcy116noSpiralStaircas1183½	Sharp	9
	View of race obscured by snow																		
14Feb70- 9Hia	fm	1 3/16Ⓣ	1:534	3↑	Bougnvillea H (Div 2) 46k	6	8	713	55½	54½	43¾	Marquez CH	123	b	3.20	96-05	Vent du Nord122noHitchcock1151¼Jungle Cove1142½	Rallied	10
21Jan70- 9Hia	fm	1 1/16Ⓣ	1:424	4↑	Alw 8000	11	8	78¼	53	65½	74¾	Ycaza M	116	b	*1.10	86-07	[D]HighHat113¾ElegantHeir1131½VirginiaBron108¾	No threat	12
29Nov69- 7Aqu	fst	1	:223 :443 1:084 1:342	3↑	Stuyvesant H 60k	5	11	1115	1112	1012	65	Velasquez J	120	b	15.50	90-14	King Emperor1162¼Dewan1161¼Jaikyl112nk	No early foot	11
18Oct69- 7Bel	fm	1½Ⓣ	2:271	3↑	Man o' War 113k	2	3	36½	51¾	41¼	33½	Ycaza M	126	b	2.30	97-11	Hawaii1262¼North Flight1211¼Fort Marcy1261¼		9
	Hung under impost																		
10Sep69- 8Atl	sf	1 3/16Ⓣ	:493 1:144 1:41 2:003	3↑	U Nations H Inv'l 125k	7	7	74¾	76½	35½	37½	Ycaza M	130	b	2.30	59-33	Hawaii124½North Flight1177Fort Marcy1303	Close quarters	10
30Aug69- 8Atl	hd	1⅛Ⓣ	:501 1:14 1:38 1:501	3↑	Kelly-Olympic H 34k	7	7	74¾	31½	31½	1½	Ycaza M	128	b	*2.30	85-19	Fort Marcy128½Balustrade116nkHawaii124¾	Driving	10
26Jly69- 7Aqu	sf	1⅛Ⓣ	1:551	3↑	Tidal H 58k	3	6	53¼	32	2hd	1½	Ycaza M	126	b	2.60	59-47	Fort Marcy126½Baitman1101Hawaii1233	Under hard drive	8
4Jly69- 7Aqu	gd	1¼	:512 1:161 1:404 2:044	3↑	Suburban H 107k	5	5	42½	53½	56½	511	Velasquez J	121	b	7.10	61-31	Mr. Right117hdDike114nkChompion1113	Off sluggishly	5
21Jun69- 8Hol	fm	1½Ⓣ	:47 1:12 2:022 2:271	3↑	Hol Turf Inv'l H 100k	7	7	99	2½	11½	1no	Ycaza M	124	b	*1.20	97-11	FortMrcy124noPoleax1173CourtFool115hd	Lasted under drive	12
2Jun69- 7Bel	yl	1⅜Ⓣ	2:19	3↑	Edgemere H 29k	3	3	33½	1hd	2½	32	Ycaza M	126	b	*2.20	69-29	Majetta1142Liaison114hdFort Marcy1261	In close stretch	8
5Apr69- 8SA	fm	*1¾Ⓣ	:464 1:593 2:251 2:472	4↑	S Juan Capistrano H 125k	10	4	512	42½	21½	22¾	Ycaza M	124	b	5.10	87-07	Petrone1222¾FortMarcy1241½Rivet115nk	Finished willingly	10
22Mar69- 9GP	fst	1¼	:471 1:113 1:36 2:012	3↑	Gulfstream H 126k	8	7	714	711	79	45	Maple E	121	b	13.90	87-10	CourtRcss108noNodoubl1252¼TropcKngII1162¾	Not a threat	9
22Feb69- 8Hia	fst	1¼	:482 1:12 1:37 2:031	3↑	Widener H 137k	9	8	79½	66¾	68½	63¼	Cruguet J	124	b	5.80	79-26	Yumbel112hdFunnyFellw121noMr.Brognn113¾	Never a threat	11
15Feb69- 8Hia	sf	1 3/16Ⓣ	2:03	3↑	Bougainvillea H 68k	3	4	44½	21½	2hd	1hd	Ycaza M	124	b	3.20	54-46	Fort Marcy124hdTaneb115¾Blanquette II1164	Just up	14

4Feb69- 8Hia	fm	1⅛Ⓣ	1:491	4↑ Alw 8000	6	3	22	13	12	11¼	Ycaza M	119	b	*.80	94-10	FortMarcy1191¼Taneb1133Hibernin113hd	Complete authority	8
11Nov68- 7Lrl	sf	1½Ⓣ	:521 1:18 2:122 2:371	3↑ D C Int'l 150k	8	3	3½	1hd	2hd	3¾	Ycaza M	127	b	3.80	32-59	Sir Ivor120¾Czar Alexander120noFort Marcy1271¼	Tired	8
19Oct68- 7Bel	sf	1½Ⓣ	2:304	3↑ Man o' War 116k	6	6	66½	1½	2½	23½	Ycaza M	126	b	3.10	85-11	Czar Alexander1213½Fort Marcy1264½Advocator1284½	Gamely	12
30Sep68- 5Bel	hd	1⅜Ⓣ	2:144	3↑ Long Island H (Div 1) 23k	2	7	52	31	55	69	Velasquez J	125	b	*1.10	83-15	Ruth'sRullah112¾RffledFethrs1183CzrAlxndr1152½	Roughed	9
11Sep68- 8Atl	fm	1 3/16Ⓣ	:484 1:123 1:364 1:551	3↑ U Nations H 100k	2	4	55¼	54¼	33	31½	Velasquez J	118	b	3.20	92-10	Dr.Fgr134nkAdvoctor1121¼FortMrcy1181¼	Finished willingly	9
31Aug68- 8Atl	hd	1⅛Ⓣ	:474 1:111 1:34 1:48	3↑ Kelly-Olympic H 33k	2	6	65	2hd	1hd	2nk	Velasquez J	124	b	*.60	96-04	ShootingChant112nkFortMarcy1242½Advocator1162	Bumped	6
22Jly68- 8Hol	fm	1½Ⓣ	:472 1:103 2:013 2:263	3↑ Sunset H 118k	6	5	58¼	2hd	12	1no	Pincay L Jr	122	b	*3.40	106-11	Fort Marcy122noQuicken Tree122½Fiddle Isle1085	Lasted	15
4Jly68- 8AP	fm	1⅛Ⓣ	:48 1:114 1:37 1:503	3↑ Strs & Strps H (Div 2) 44k	3	3	36	14	14	11	Marquez CH	119	b	*1.00	88-13	FortMarcy1191TheKnackII1105NashuaPilot1141¼	Hard drive	7
19Jun68- 8Suf	fst	1¼	:473 1:112 1:362 2:024	3↑ Mass H 61k	6	6	66	54½	53¾	41¼	Ycaza M	116	b	*2.20	90-17	Out of the Way112½Big Rock Candy114noKing's Palace114¾		11
	Checked																	
12Jun68- 7Bel	sly	1⅛	:472 1:114 1:362 1:49	3↑ Nassau County 27k	4	3	33½	32½	2½	2¾	Ycaza M	114	b	*.50	90-14	Primo Richard103¾Fort Marcy1142½Ardoise1054	Game effort	5
27Apr68- 7Aqu	fst	1⅛	:461 1:101 1:354 1:484	3↑ Grey Lag H 85k	10	5	56	44	73¾	32¾	Velasquez J	118	b	*3.20	89-14	BoldHour113¾[D]DiplomatWay1222FortMarcy118no	Impeded	10
	Placed second through disqualification																	
6Apr68- 6Aqu	fst	1	:224 :453 1:094 1:352	4↑ Alw 15000	9	9	79	65	3nk	11¾	Velasquez J	116	b	2.20	91-14	Fort Marcy1161¾Rogo111nkBeaupy116hd	Drew out easily	11
23Mar68- 8GP	fm	1Ⓣ	:24 :474 1:112 1:351	4↑ Alw 4500	2	2	22½	23	23	21¼	Baeza B	122	b	*.60	96-13	QuiteanAccent1091¼FortMarcy1224Hardihood1194½	Gaining	8
14Mar68- 9GP	fm	1 1/16Ⓣ	:23 :471 1:113 1:42	4↑ Alw 5000	6	7	75	33	32	2no	Velasquez J	119		*.50	94-13	New SongII113noFort Marcy1192½Tequillo1197		7
	Steadied,just missed																	
11Nov67- 7Lrl	fm	1½Ⓣ	:491 1:14 2:03 2:27	3↑ D C Int'l 150k	6	3	33	1hd	1hd	1no	Ycaza M	120	b	8.20	84-13	FortMrcy120noDamascus1202½TobinBronze1272½	Hard drive	9
21Oct67- 7Aqu	fm	1⅝Ⓣ	2:424	3↑ Man o' War 116k	10	4	46½	53¼	2hd	2hd	Pincay L Jr	121	b	4.10	80-20	RuffledFeathrs121hdFortMrcy121noHandsmeBoy1263	Sharp	13
7Oct67- 8Aqu	fm	1 1/16Ⓣ	1:414	3↑ Alw 15000	4	4	410	44½	31	3½	Turcotte R	119	b	*.80	96-03	Mystic Lad118nkFlag118nkFort Marcy1193	Wide,closed fast	10
20Sep67- 8Atl	fm	1 3/16Ⓣ	1:54	3↑ U Nations H 100k	1	3	45	33½	21	4nk	Velasquez J	115	b	4.70	102-05	Flit-To110nkAssagai122no[D]MundnPont115hd	Checked sharply	8
	Placed third through disqualification																	
4Sep67- 8AP	fm	1 3/16Ⓣ	:462 1:104 1:364 1:55	3↑ B Lindheimer H 118k	15	12	1118	1110	89¾	66¼	Turcotte R	119	b	3.10	86-09	FusilierBoy1144½Ramsinga110noCarteret1101¼	In close early	15
9Aug67- 7Sar	fm	1 1/16Ⓣ	1:402	3↑ B Baruch H (Div 2) 23k	2	6	66	55½	2hd	1¾	Turcotte R	117	b	*1.30	98-02	FortMarcy117¾Assagai1263Paoluccio1121	Under brisk drive	7
29Jly67- 7Aqu	sf	1⅛Ⓣ	1:521	3↑ Tidal H 57k	8	4	41½	2hd	1hd	13	Turcotte R	111	b	2.50	74-27	Fort Marcy1113Dunderhead1102Flit-To113nk	Mild drive	9
8Jly67- 8AP	fm	1 1/16Ⓣ	:231 :461 1:103 1:414	Nashua H 54k	9	3	37	311	11	14½	Pincay L Jr	118	b	4.60	100-05	FrtMrcy1184½DiplomatWay1192BlastingCharg122nk	In hand	11
28Jun67- 8Mth	fm	1Ⓣ	1:373	Long Branch H (Div 2) 22k	2	4	52	51¼	31	12	Velasquez J	116	b	3.40	97-07	FortMarcy1162RoyalMalabar124hdJean-Pierre118no	Driving	9
10Jun67- 7Mth	fm	1Ⓣ	:23 :471 1:11 1:362	3↑ Spring H (Div 1) 23k	3	10	1010	1016	913	69	Velasquez J	110	b	6.80	94-00	Lucky Turn118noModel Fool1156Green Felt1162	Hit hedge	10
3Jun67- 6Aqu	hd	1 1/16Ⓣ	1:412	3↑ Alw 9000	5	8	816	74½	21½	13	Cordero A Jr	109	b	*1.80	99-01	FortMarcy1093RoyalComedian1143Vis-a-Vis1231	Ridden out	10
25May67- 6Aqu	sl	1⅛	:492 1:141 1:383 1:51	3↑ Alw 9000	1	3	66½	67	37	34½	Cordero A Jr	110	b	4.40	76-24	Prinkipo1132½Royal Comedian1132Fort Marcy1102	Rallied	8
30Mar67- 7Aqu	sl	1	:234 :472 1:122 1:382	3↑ Alw 7000	4	3	32½	23	23	32½	Gustines H	110	b	4.70	73-33	Primo Theo1152Tom Poker121½Fort Marcy1107	Held well	6
25Mar67- 8Aqu	my	6f	:231 :482 1:14	3↑ Alw 6500	4	4	57½	511	410	45½	Ycaza M	115	b	3.60	67-35	MisterPitt'sKid1132½DandySteal1123Disembark121no	Wide	7
3Mar67- 7Hia	fm	1 1/16Ⓣ	1:43	Alw 6000	11	6	710	75½	33	2hd	Ycaza M	114	b	40.20	90-14	Royal Malabar118hdFort Marcy114½More Skies1123½	Sharp	11
15Feb67- 7Hia	fm	*1 1/16Ⓣ	1:444	Alw 7000	2	6	64	1011	915	913	Ycaza M	112		12.40	73-20	High Hat1132Royal Malabar118nkRoyal Esteem1121	Tired	11
4Feb67- 3Hia	fst	7f	:231 :462 1:121 1:251	ⒸAlw 4500	7	4	64¾	43½	41½	11	Ycaza M	118		3.30	83-13	Fort Marcy1181Sun Stream1181½Keene Terra1181½	Driving	12
17Jan67- 4Hia	gd	6f	:221 :453 1:103	ⒸAlw 4500	7	3	66½	69¾	48½	49¼	Ycaza M	118		23.50	82-13	Balouf1166Bold Monarch1181¼Wedgedale1162	No mishap	10
26Nov66- 5Aqu	gd	6f	:222 :47 1:114	Alw 5500	2	7	910	87	811	815	Blum W	119	b	6.30	69-20	Light the Fuse122noMisty Cloud1152½Osage1223	Far back	9
5Nov66- 5Aqu	fst	6f	:213 :443 1:111	Alw 5500	4	7	78¾	611	66½	73½	Fires E	119	b	34.60	83-13	Flying Tackle1221½Comfrey115noFort Drum115½	No factor	10
8Oct66- 6Aqu	fst	7f	:224 :453 1:111 1:241	Alw 5500	4	9	119¾	1111	85¾	811	Blum W	122	b	9.00	74-17	Major Art1223Unexpected117¾Proviso1223½	Never close	14
1Oct66- 5Aqu	sly	7f	:231 :47 1:131 1:261	Alw 5500	12	1	79¼	77¾	79¼	24	Blum W	122	b	3.80	71-24	IrishRebellion1174FortMarcy122noGalaPrformnc122½	Gamely	12
21Sep66- 4Aqu	sly	6f	:231 :472 1:13	Md Sp Wt	4	3	52¼	41¼	11½	14	Blum W	122	b	*1.50	78-24	Fort Marcy1224Quiet Town1221½George Arnold122½	Easily	8
7Sep66- 5Aqu	fst	6f	:224 :48 1:132	Md Sp Wt	14	1	24	21	21	45¾	Blum W	122	b	*1.80e	70-30	Proviso1222½DownatMory's122nkIrishRebellion1223	Tired	14
27Aug66- 1Sar	fst	6f	:224 :471 1:132	Md Sp Wt	3	9	84¾	107½	1115	1116	Baeza B	122		7.10	65-08	Twist of Time1224½Prime Motive1221½Court Service122hd		14
	Roughed																	
29Jly66- 4Aqu	fst	5½f	:23 :471 :592 1:054	ⒸMd Sp Wt	10	6	84¾	41½	23	25	Belmonte E	122		3.20	79-17	OneGem1225FortMarcy1221RisingMarket122½	Wide stretch	11
22Jly66- 5Aqu	fst	5½f	:222 :46 :59 1:054	ⒸMd Sp Wt	4	6	108¾	1010	68	34½	Belmonte E	122		19.80	79-19	Monitor1224½Duke Cannon122hdFort Marcy1221½	Stride late	12
14May66- 4Aqu	fst	5f	:223 :462 :59	ⒸMd Sp Wt	2	7	716	78¾	712	716	Gustines H	122		26.30	74-13	GreatPower1223½BoldAmbition122¾BeauApple1226	Far back	8

Forward Gal

ch. f. 1968, by Native Charger (Native Dancer)–Forward Thrust, by Jet Action

Lifetime record: 26 12 4 6 $439,933

Own.– Aisco Stable

Br.– A.I. Savin (Fla)

Tr.– W.A. Croll Jr

19Oct71- 8GS	fm	1Ⓣ	1:38	ⒻPrinceton H (Div 2) 23k	1	1	11	11½	21	21¾	Rotz JL	126	b	*1.20	81-15	CanterburyTale1151¾ForwardGal126noWireChif1125	Faltered	7
19Sep71- 8Del	gd	1⅛	:461 1:103 1:373 1:504	ⒻDel Oaks 59k	8	2	22	21	3nk	32¼	Hole M	121	b	2.60	81-20	Lauries Dancer1212¼Secret Retreat114hdForward Gal121nk		8
	Lacked rally																	
4Sep71- 7Bel	fst	1⅛	:463 1:102 1:352 1:483	ⒻGazelle H 56k	3	1	1hd	1½	14	13	Hole M	122	b	2.60	91-12	ForwrdGl1223OurCherAmour1181½AlmNorth1232½	Mild drive	8
14Aug71- 7Sar	fst	1¼	:474 1:12 1:371 2:03	ⒻAlabama 53k	3	3	25	23	31½	36	Hole M	121	b	*2.60	84-05	LauriesDancer1183AlmaNorth1183FrwrdGl1211½	Weakened	11
5Aug71- 7Sar	gd	7f	:221 :45 1:11 1:234	ⒻTest 35k	3	6	41½	52½	42½	32½	Hole M	124	b	*1.40	87-20	Lucky Traveler1152Tibb115½Forward Gal1241½	Lacked rally	12
17Jly71- 8Lib	fst	1 1/16	:224 :454 1:102 1:433	ⒻCotillion H 55k	7	2	33	33½	32½	21	Hole M	123	b	*.90	87-17	Alma North1161Forward Gal1234Miss Pat R.110no	Gaining	7
5Jly71- 8Mth	fst	1⅛	:463 1:104 1:361 1:491	ⒻMth Oaks 57k	1	2	2hd	11½	13	14¾	Hole M	119	b	5.20	96-08	ForwardGl1194¾AlmaNorth1141ForNoReason112½	Mild drive	11
26Jun71- 8Mth	fst	1 70	:224 :46 1:102 1:404	ⒻPost-Deb (Div 2) 22k	1	3	51¾	65½	56½	42¾	Hole M	117	b	*1.10	94-12	Cyamome117¾Isafloridan113noSilent Beauty1192	In close	8
29May71- 7Bel	fst	1⅛	:454 1:102 1:364 1:501	ⒻMother Goose 89k	4	4	31½	3½	11	33¼	Velasquez J	121	b	*1.50	80-19	Deceit121¾Grafitti1212½Forward Gal1213	Weakened	9
15May71- 7Aqu	fst	1	:232 :463 1:11 1:363	ⒻAcorn 64k	8	2	2½	1½	21	3¾	Hole M	121	b	*.40	83-22	Deceit121½Sea Saga121nkForward Gal1212	No excuses	9
5May71- 7Aqu	fst	7f	:224 :454 1:101 1:232	ⒻComely 34k	7	1	21	1½	13	14	Hole M	121	b	*.40	84-25	Forward Gal1214Sea Saga1182Deceit115½	Mild drive	8
24Apr71- 8GS	fst	6f	:22 :45 1:102	ⒻBetsy Ross H 29k	7	1	63½	41¾	1½	12½	Hole M	126	b	*.40	92-14	Forward Gal1262½Sea Saga1202Alma North1121	Driving	10
17Apr71- 4GS	fst	6f	:22 :452 1:101	ⒻAlw 12000	6	1	2hd	12	15	16	Hole M	121	b	*.30	93-13	ForwrdGal1216AlmaNorth1151½SwoonsSymbol1135	Handily	6
7Nov70- 8GS	fst	1 1/16	:234 :473 1:114 1:45	ⒻGardenia 188k	6	2	2hd	1hd	1½	31	Ianelli F	119	b	*1.50	79-15	Eggy119¾Rosemont Bow119nkForward Gal1193	Weakened	9
12Oct70- 7Bel	fst	1	:222 :45 1:10 1:363	ⒻFrizette 125k	3	2	21	14	16	13½	Velasquez J	119	b	*.80	90-16	ForwrdGal1193½Isafloridan1197MakeMLugh119hd	Mild drive	11
5Oct70- 5Bel	fst	6½f	:221 :454 1:102 1:17	ⒻAlw 15000	3	3	2½	1hd	13	13	Velasquez J	122	b	*1.00	95-10	ForwardGal1223BlessingAngelic1161¼Exorbtnt11610	Handily	9
26Aug70- 7Sar	fst	6f	:221 :453 1:104	ⒻSpinaway 84k	6	2	1hd	1hd	1hd	11	Ianelli F	119	b	2.80	92-14	Forward Gal1191Patelin1192½Deceit119¾	Mild drive	11
17Aug70- 7Sar	fst	6f	:22 :453 1:104	ⒻAdirondack 29k	2	3	2½	2½	2½	21½	Ianelli F	122	b	2.60	90-16	Dutiful1141½Forward Gal122½Patelin1224½	Game try	9
25Jly70- 8Mth	fst	6f	:213 :443 1:113	ⒻSorority 105k	1	6	42¼	34½	34½	12	Ianelli F	119	b	12.00	84-22	Forward Gal1192Unity Hall1191Deceit1192	Driving	12
18Jly70- 6Lib	fst	5½f	:213 :452 1:04	ⒻSchuykill (Div 1) 22k	9	8	65½	33½	32	1½	Ianelli F	115	b	*1.80	100-05	Forward Gal115½Hot Gravey1154Native Game1136	Driving	9
24Jun70- 7Bel	fst	5½f	:224 :462 :583 1:05	ⒻNational Stallion 31k	3	4	33	32½	46½	48	Blum W	119	b	5.10	87-14	UnityHall1193½BidHigh1194½CarolineG.114hd	Factor,tired	7
10Jun70- 8Mth	fst	5½f	:22 :454 :59 1:054	ⒻColleen 24k	8	7	74¾	32	35	23	Ianelli F	114	b	5.80	85-17	Deceit1193Forward Gal114nkCaroline G.1133	Gamely	12
3Jun70- 6Mth	fst	5f	:221 :454 :583	ⒻAlw 6000	3	9	1½	11½	15	19	Blum W	116	b	18.30	97-13	ForwardGl1169TigerCoed1161½SchoolBoard114no	Ridden out	11
29Apr70- 4GS	fst	5f	:222 :463 :594	ⒻMd Sp Wt	7	1	2½	23	21	1¾	Blum W	115	b	*1.50	89-15	Forward Gal115¾Lady Herald1151½Reunion1151	Driving	12
22Apr70- 3GS	fst	5f	:222 :471 :592	ⒻMd Sp Wt	2	5	2hd	1hd	2hd	45	Blum W	115	b	3.00	86-17	MurielsDream115hdTelly1153WindsofDestiny1152	Weakened	9
26Mar70- 3GP	sly	5f	:222 :471 1:00	Md Sp Wt	3	4	2hd	32	48	511	Blum W	118		3.30	77-16	HarrodsGreek1115QueenofArts1083LadiesAuxiliry118½	Tired	12

Gallant Bob

dkbbr. g. 1972, by Gallant Romeo (Gallant Man)–Wisp O'Will, by New Policy **Lifetime record: 77 23 11 8 $489,992**

Own.– R.P. Horton
Br.– J.L. Homan (Ky)
Tr.– Floyd M. Tolle

2Dec79- 7Pen	fst 6f	:223 :462 :582 1:122	3↑ Alw 7200	7	5	63½	52½	53½	41	Lloyd JS	113		8.10	81-25	Musical Mickey115½Jiva Coolit113½Coastal Call116hd	9
	Not enough final furlong															
16Nov79- 8Key	fst 6f	:224 :462 1:122	3↑ Alw 12000	6	3	54¾	79	78½	76¾	Zook DJ	115		16.90	73-31	BoldPhantm116¾LuckyFling1131RedWhitenGreen1142 Outrun	7
4Nov79- 7Pen	sf 1Ⓣ	1:393	3↑ Alw 7800	7	1	12	11	1hd	23½	Lloyd JS	113		10.50	68-32	Confort1083½GallantBob113nkFrostyHonor1132 Second best	7
29Sep79- 8Tim	fst 4f	:222 :463	3↑ Handicap 8000	1	6		66½	69	63	Hernandez RZ	110		12.60	90-07	Bee Country113½B.F.'s Sailingman1151Elbuort122no Outrun	6
1Sep79- 7Tim	fst 4f	:224 :462	3↑ Alw 6500	6	4		43½	45	54¾	Torre MJ	113		8.20	89-09	Bold and Lucky122¾Light Tiger1131Royal Re Re1162 Tired	6
	Previously trained by D. Michael Smithwick															
9Aug79- 4Sar	fm 2 1/16	S'Chase 3:47	3↑ Md Sp Wt	9	1	32	-	-	-	Aitcheson J Jr	156	s	2.90	- -	BronzeCelt1519¾AcademicFreedom1491½Mozambique1492 Fell	11
	Previously trained by J.D. Marquette															
17Mar79- 7Key	fst 6f	:224 :462 1:103	4↑ Alw 12000	1	3	1½	42	714	715	Ruane J	112	b	13.10	74-23	Spunky112¾No No Jim118noPegasus Pete1183½ Tired	7
25Feb79- 7Key	my 7f	:232 :464 1:124 1:26	4↑ Alw 12000	5	2	1hd	54	816	821	Walford J	113		10.10	56-30	GreatCombnation114noPgasusPete1181½NevrRetreat1051½ Tired	9
19Jan79- 8Key	fst 6f	:222 :453 1:103	4↑ Alw 12000	2	6	64½	54¼	76	74¼	Solomon G	116		8.80	85-17	DoubleCraps115½Spunky115½GreatCombinaton117hd No factor	7
29Dec78- 8Key	fst 7f	:222 :45 1:102 1:232	3↑ Alw 12000	2	6	32½	34	44¼	65¾	Walford J	116		10.00	84-17	Eastern Monarch1161½Hickory Cap1154Spunky117no Tired	9
17Dec78- 7Key	fst 6f	:23 :474 1:132	3↑ Alw 12000	7	8	87	88	76¼	57¼	Black AS	114		4.70	68-31	Ornithologist1133Ten Ten110hdGovernor's Pardon1143½	9
	Sluggish early															
3Dec78- 8Key	fst 6f	:224 :46 1:111	3↑ Alw 12000	3	6	55½	57½	69½	510	Pagano SR	112		4.70	76-25	PistolWhite1132EightDominoes1227FloatingPrm113nk Evenly	8
24Jly78- 8Bel	fst 1	:23 :452 1:092 1:334	3↑ Handicap 25000	5	1	1hd	55	915	917	Velez RI	109		29.80	82-09	Vencedor1163¼Proud Arion1131¼Life's Hope1223½ Used up	9
6Jly78- 8Bel	fst 6f	:222 :452 1:092	3↑ Alw 25000	6	4	45	56½	58	58¾	Turcotte R	119		16.90	86-19	Buckfinder1192½Myriad1193¾Dan Black115¾ No excuse	6
3Jun78- 7Mth	fst 6f	:214 :443 1:092	4↑ Alw 12000	1	4	1hd	33	49	612	MacBeth D	113		6.50	81-24	White Rammer1173Taylor's Falls1172Buena Shore1224 Tired	7
23May78- 8Key	fst 6f	:222 :451 1:093	4↑ Alw 15000	2	6	41¼	31½	21½	21¼	Mucciolo J	117		*1.50	93-13	BearerBond1121¼GllntBb1172Tmothy'sChmp112hd Slow start	6
	Disqualified from purse money															
14May78- 7Aqu	sly 7f	:224 :453 1:101 1:224	4↑ Alw 25000	6	1	1½	21½	412	414½	Borden DA	115		14.00	72-26	Seattle Slew1228¼Proud Arion1191¼Capulet's Song1155	6
	Used up															
29Apr78- 7Key	fst 6f	:222 :453 1:093	4↑ Alw 15000	8	4	86¾	65¼	99¾	913	Tejeira J	121		2.90	81-12	Loaded or Busted121½Thunder O'Shay115½Big Z.1154 Outrun	9
9Apr78- 7Key	fst 6f	:223 :463 1:112	4↑ Alw 16000	4	4	65½	52	54	54	Tejeira J	119		*2.20	81-24	CruiseonIn122hdKohoutek119¾TripleRevers1143 Lacked room	6
25Mar78- 7Key	fst 6f	:23 :462 1:112	4↑ Alw 14000	4	1	41½	21	21	12½	Black AS	113		*1.60	85-31	Gallant Bob1132½Insubordinate Lad1161½Mighty Steve1154	5
	Driving															
10Mar78- 8Key	fst 6f	:224 :461 1:111	4↑ Alw 14000	4	4	1hd	31	44½	57	Edwards JW	114		3.60	79-29	Mug Hunter1164Kohoutek119hdJiva Coolit1191½ Tired	6
26Feb78- 8Key	fst 6f	:231 :47 1:13	4↑ Alw 13000	2	7	52½	62¾	75¾	53½	Edwards JW	114		5.10	73-34	Kohoutek1191¼Ragtime Cowboy Joe1121Insubordinate Lad114nk	7
	Off slowly															
4Oct77- 6Med	fst 6f	:224 :454 1:11	3↑ Alw 25000	6	3	41¼	66¾	79	78¾	Black AS	119		*1.00	81-19	Kohoutek1172Godolphin122noThird World1152 Brief speed	7
10Sep77- 8Key	fst 7f	:224 :451 1:102 1:232	3↑ Independence H 27k	1	2	11	2hd	21½	2½	Black AS	115		2.20	91-23	Ferrous114½GallantBob1155RagtimeCowboyJoe113hd Gamely	6
1Sep77- 8Mth	fst 6f	:213 :44 1:091	3↑ Handicap 25000	3	2	1hd	32½	33	33¼	MacBeth D	119		2.90	91-17	SeetheU.S.A.1182½Godolphin108¾GallantBob1192 Held show	6
30Jly77- 5Mth	my 6f	:224 :462 1:102	3↑ Handicap 15000	3	4	3½	31½	21½	22	MacBeth D	120		*1.50	86-23	SeetheU.S.A.1152GallantBb1208ChfTmnco11920 Second best	4
16Jly77- 8Key	fst 6½f	:22 :442 1:081 1:143	3↑ Neshaminy H 27k	4	3	2½	31½	45½	47½	Tejeira J	117		3.80	96-16	My Juliet1211½Raise a King1193½Silver Hope1202½ Tired	4
6Jly77- 8Key	fst 6f	:221 :451 1:093	3↑ Alw 10000	4	5	32	2hd	1hd	1½	Tejeira J	119		2.00	94-15	GallantBb119½ChiefTamanaco1193½WingSouth1161¾ Driving	6
18Jun77- 8Bow	fst 6f	:221 :44 :57 1:09	3↑ Terrapin H 27k	5	6	54	35½	45½	34¾	Edwards JW	117		4.60	90-14	Raise a King1163½Whatsyourpleasure1171¼Gallant Bob117no	7
	Steadied															
9Jun77- 8Bel	sly 1⊗	:23 :454 1:11 1:363	3↑ Alw 25000	5	1	13	2hd	33	46	Edwards JW	117		2.30	79-23	Star of the Sea1151½El Pitirre110½Dan Black1174 Tired	5
1Jun77- 8Key	fst 6f	:22 :443 1:094	3↑ Garrison H 27k	1	4	2hd	42½	57½	59¾	Edwards JW	118		*.40	83-23	ChiefTamanaco114½Bereber1122½RealTerror1135¼ Done early	5
7May77- 8Aqu	fst 7f	:221 :45 1:093 1:221	3↑ Carter H (Div 2)-G2	2	4	21½	21½	42¼	33¼	Edwards JW	116		6.50	87-17	SoyNumeroUno1262½Barrera119¾GallantBob116hd Weakened	6
20Apr77- 8Aqu	fst 6f⊡	:221 :452 1:102	4↑ Alw 25000	4	2	2½	2½	1hd	2½	Edwards JW	122		*1.00	94-14	QuietLittleTable122½GallantBob122½Dr.Emil1151¼ Weakened	6
12Apr77- 8GS	fst 6f	:221 :451 1:102	4↑ Alw 15000	2	3	2hd	2hd	12	11	Edwards JW	119		2.70	91-22	GallantBob1191MovingCloud1191½DeltaLegacy1121¼ Driving	8
6Oct76- 8Bel	fst 6f	:224 :453 1:083	3↑ Boojum H 38k	7	7	2hd	4nk	96½	98	Arellano J	122		8.70	91-08	SoyNumeroUno1182½It'sFreezing1121¼QueenCityLd112¾ Tired	9
25Sep76- 8Atl	fst 7f	:22 :44 1:074 1:202	3↑ Atl City H 31k	5	3	1hd	2hd	69	612	Arellano J	124		*1.30	89-01	Our Hero1204½Packer Captain115noMexican General115hd	8
	Squeezed back															
17Sep76- 8Bel	sly 1	:222 :444 1:093 1:353	3↑ Alw 25000	2	1	11½	2hd	2hd	2nk	Arellano J	115		*1.10	90-15	Nalees Knight122nkGallant Bob115½Blue Times1191¼	6
	Sharp effort															
7Sep76- 8Bel	fst 6f	:224 :451 1:084	3↑ Alw 30000	8	4	11	11	11	11¼	Arellano J	115		3.60	98-12	Gallant Bob1151¼It's Freezing1192¼Relent122no Driving	8
30Aug76- 8Bel	fst 6f	:223 :454 1:10	3↑ Fall Hwt H (Div 2)-G2	6	8	86¾	1010	910	813	Gallitano G	140		13.50	79-18	HonorableMiss1301¼Lachesis1261¾RushingMan129nk Dull try	10
11Aug76- 7Mth	fst 6f	:213 :44 1:082	3↑ Alw 11000	2	3	2½	21½	31½	43	Arellano J	122		*.70	95-13	See the U.S.A.119¾That Wing117nkPompini1222 Weakened	5
18Jly76- 8Del	fst 6f	:214 :444 1:094	3↑ Hannibal H 28k	3	4	1hd	3½	42	75½	Arellano J	125		*1.90	90-20	SilverHope119½NorthCall119nkNoteofVictory1171½ Gave way	11
3May76- 8Haw	fst 6f	:212 :441 1:082	3↑ Midwest H 45k	3	5	41½	22½	33½	410	Gallitano G	128		*.70	94-08	Marluel'sTroy1108NativeDrone113noSilvrDoctor1122¼ Tired	7
16Apr76- 8Aqu	fst 6f	:22 :45 1:094	3↑ Gravesend H 44k	1	5	1hd	1hd	2½	31	Brumfield D	128		*2.50	93-18	Christopher R.131¾Mac Corkle115nkGallant Bob128nk Tired	8
3Apr76- 7Kee	fst 6f	:22 :443 :564 1:082	3↑ Phoenix H 28k	7	3	22	22	1½	15	Brumfield D	126		*1.10	100-18	Gallant Bob1265Real Value120¾Amerrico1152½ Drew clear	12
27Mar76- 8Pim	fst 6f	:231 :453 1:104	3↑ J E Hoover H 27k	2	5	2½	2hd	22½	2½	Edwards JW	128		2.90	91-20	ChristopherR.130½GallntBob128¾NorthCll1222¾ Drifted out	5
13Mar76- 8Aqu	sly 6f	:213 :452 1:101	3↑ Toboggan H 57k	11	1	31½	2hd	3nk	36¾	Gallitano G	129		3.50	85-19	Due Diligence1114¾Pompini1132Gallant Bob129¾ Bothered	11
16Feb76- 8Aqu	fst 7f	:222 :451 1:093 1:223	3↑ Sporting Plate H 38k	6	2	1hd	1hd	3½	83¼	Gallitano G	130		*1.90	85-25	ChristophrR.124½NorthCll110hdDoublEdgSword115hd Stopped	8
10Jan76- 8Key	fst 6f	:214 :443 1:084	4↑ Bensalem H 27k	2	6	32	33½	35	37	Gallitano G	131		*.60	91-14	DukeTom1157Rosinate110noGallantBob131no Stumbled badly	6
3Jan76- 8Aqu	sly 6f	:22 :451 1:104	3↑ Paumonok H-G3	5	3	1hd	1hd	1hd	1hd	Gallitano G	129		*2.00	89-18	GallantBob129hdOurHero1133½HoleinthePants113no Driving	8
27Dec75- 8Key	my 6f	:224 :462 1:114	3↑ Squires H 27k	1	3	1½	1½	1½	1½	Gallitano G	127		*.70	83-31	Gallant Bob127½Admiral Jim1124½Plain Pete1163½ Driving	7
1Dec75- 8Aqu	fst 6f	:222 :452 1:093	Sword Dancer H 46k	6	1	1hd	2hd	2½	1hd	Gallitano G	126		*1.80	95-14	GallantBob126hdOurHero1132DueDilgnc113¾ Long,hard drive	9
22Nov75- 8Key	gd 6f	:221 :451 1:093	Flintlock 27k	3	2	2½	1½	1½	11½	Gallitano G	119		*.60	93-20	GallntBb1191½BearerBond112¾BumpyLndng112¾ Drew clear	8
4Oct75- 8Key	fst 6½f	:22 :444 1:10 1:163	Penn Treaty 27k	3	1	3½	21	11½	12	Gallitano G	119		*.40	94-14	Gallant Bob1192Talc1192Real Value1174 Ridden out	6
6Sep75- 8Key	fst 7f	:214 :441 1:103 1:24	Philmont H 27k	7	2	31	32	2hd	13	Gallitano G	129		*1.20	89-22	Gallant Bob1293Talc1181¼Ascetic118½ Drew clear	9
13Aug75- 8Mth	fst 6f	:204 :434 1:092	Select H 27k	5	2	27	23½	2½	11¼	Gallitano G	129		*2.00	93-17	Gallant Bob1291¼Talc1202Red Cross1173 Driving	7
5Jly75- 8Bow	fst 6f	:223 :454 1:102	Annapolis H 27k	5	3	2hd	11½	13	13½	Gallitano G	127		*.40	91-17	Gallant Bob1273½French Whistler1141¼Starta Victory1082¼	6
	Ridden out															
21Jun75- 8AP	fst 7f	:22 :443 1:10 1:232	Olympia H 33k	5	1	1hd	1½	12	11	Gallitano G	124		4.40	85-21	Gallant Bob1241Doug118noCountry Boy Jim1211 Driving	11
1Jun75- 8Del	fst 1 1/16	:23 :462 1:12 1:461	Rosemont 29k	5	1	1hd	1hd	56	512	Gallitano G	117		*1.50	66-19	Grey Beret1126Dr's Enjoy Dollars114¾Resound112nk Tired	10
24May75- 8Del	fst 6f	:214 :45 1:111	Kelso H 27k	4	2	2hd	2hd	2hd	1½	Gallitano G	124		*.90	89-21	Gallant Bob124½Bold Gun121nkReal Value1211½ All out	7
22Mar75- 8Pim	fst 6f	:224 :461 :584 1:111	Hirsch Jacobs 28k	8	3	3½	2hd	11	2hd	Gallitano G	122		*1.10	90-15	Bombay Duck122hdGallant Bob1224Ben S.116nk Just missed	9
15Mar75- 8Aqu	sly 7f	:223 :453 1:104 1:234	Bay Shore (Div 2)-G3	8	1	2hd	2hd	1½	3¾	Gallitano G	119		*2.70	81-21	Lefty113noTass113¾Gallant Bob119nk Weakened	8
1Mar75- 8Aqu	fst 6f	:214 :452 1:094	Swift-G3	9	2	1hd	11	2½	33½	Gallitano G	117		3.00	90-16	Singh1143½Laramie Trail114noGallant Bob117¾ Weakened	10
22Feb75- 8Key	fst 7f	:221 :45 1:11 1:253	Patriot-G3	1	3	13	16	18	110	Gallitano G	119		*.40	81-29	GallntBb11910WickdPark1172½Methdioxya1221½ Ridden out	11
15Feb75- 8GS	gd 6f	:221 :454 1:11	Zev 26k	6	1	1hd	13	15	19	Gallitano G	122		*.40	88-30	GallantBob1229LuckyLeaf1161½FamousTrial1161 Ridden out	7
1Feb75- 8Bow	gd 6f	:224 :463 1:12	W P Burch 27k	6	3	13	15	15	14½	Gallitano G	124		*.90	83-28	GallntBob1244½PendulumSam1163KingofFools1161¼ Driving	6

25Jan75- 8Key	sly 6f	:222 :461	1:132	Sentinel 27k	6	1	1½	1hd	1½	12	Gallitano G	119	*.90	75-33	Gallant Bob1192Sgt. Hunt1176Sneaky Win1121¾	Ridden out	7
1Jan75- 8GS	sly 6f	:222 :46	1:11	Fairmount Park 26k	4	3	11	14	15	19	Gallitano G	122	5.10	88-38	GallantBob1229Sgt.Hunt1222OnPoundStrlng117nk	Ridden out	10
14Dec74- 8Key	fst 1 1/16	:23 :463 1:111	1:421	Heritage-G3	7	2	3nk	1hd	45	513	Gallitano G	118	20.80	- -	Circle Home1243Singh1154Master Derby1213	Tired	10
28Nov74- 8GS	fst 6f	:23 :471	1:131	Autumn Harvest 26k	6	5	2hd	1½	1hd	2nk	Gallitano G	122	11.20	77-34	Sgt. Hunt118nkGallant Bob1221Impatient Fool1166½	Gamely	12
15Nov74- 8Key	fst 6f	:22 :452	1:112	Alw 7000	1	5	32	55	56	58	Knapp K	119	1.50	- -	Dr. Frank B.1112¼North Call1193½Go Super116nk	Tired	5
6Nov74- 8CD	sly 7f	:224 :46 1:114	1:252	Alw 12500	8	4	1hd	13	22	78½	Gallitano G	117	5.50	71-29	MasterDerby1221¾WaywardRed114¾Ruggle'sFerry115hd	Tired	11
19Oct74- 8Bow	fst 7f	:222 :45 1:104	1:244	©Marlboro Nursery 30k	10	3	12½	12	2hd	1¾	Gallitano G	113	8.40	81-24	GallntBb113¾GreekAnswer1192¾ParvaHasta1133	Hard drive	10
9Oct74- 7Kee	fst 6f	:221 :443 :564	1:093	Alw 6500	3	1	11	12	11	21½	Melancon L	115	2.30	92-12	RugglesFerry1151½GallntBb1152PackerCaptain1181	Gamely	6
31Aug74- 8Lib	fst 6f	:213 :444	1:114	Kindergarten-G3	11	2	12	13	14	2½	Melancon L	112	5.10	85-19	Master Derby121½Gallant Bob112noTalc113½	Gamely	14
22Aug74- 8Lib	sly 6f	:224 :461	1:112	Alw 5500	6	3	11	13	16	110	Melancon L	112	2.40	88-25	Gallant Bob11210Go Super1152½Spanish Indian1162	Easily	7
6Aug74- 6Lib	fst 5½f	:222 :462	1:051	Alw 5500	2	3	1½	2hd	2hd	22	Brumfield D	115	13.10	92-19	BuddyBoots1152GllntBb11510WhataFiasco1153	Second best	6
15Jly74- 3Lib	fst 5½f	:224 :481	1:08	Md Clm 12500	10	6	2hd	11½	1½	11¼	Fantini P	120	46.40	80-25	Gallant Bob1201¼Lil Fairy1202½Shiney Walker1205	Driving	11

Gran Kan (Chi)

dkbbr. c. 1966, by Licencioso (L'Oriflamme)–Klapp, by Espace Vital

Lifetime record: 43 16 5 8 $103,650

Own.– Mrs F. Ambrose Clark

Br.– Haras El Huerton (Chi)

Tr.– C. Furr

15Nov75- 4Cam	fm 2 13/16	S'Chase	5:301 4↑	Colonial Cup 50k	17	17	158	78½	911	613	O'Brien L	162	-	- -	CafePrince1603AugustusBay162½Soothsayr162½	Never close	18
1Nov75- 3Mtp	fm *2½	S'Chase	4:413 4↑	Noel Laing H 5.6k	10	9	97½	84¾	42	34	O'Brien L	155	-	- -	Soothsayer158hdAugustus Bay1514Gran Kan1551½		10
13Sep75- 7Fai	fm *2½	S'Chase	5:02 4↑	Grand National H 12k	3	9	84	3nk	21½	25½	O'Brien L	155	6.10	- -	Augustus Bay1475½Gran Kan1551½Happy Intellectual1465		9
21Aug75- 4Sar	fm 2⅜	S'Chase	4:201 4↑	NY Turf Writers H 22k	8	4	2hd	25	33½	46¼	O'Brien L	158	*1.70	- -	Life'sIllusion145nkSoothsayr160½ArcticJoe1485½	Gave way	9
1Aug75- 6Sar	fm 2 1/16	S'Chase	3:401 4↑	Lovely Night H 22k	6	2	26	26	23	2½	O'Brien L	158	2.70	- -	Life'sIllusion143½GranKan15810Anthropologst1388¾	Gamely	8
15Jly75- 8Bow	my 1 1/16	:232 :472 1:13	1:452 3↑	Alw 7000	1	6	618	614	510	59¼	Stone C	118	12.50	72-18	Fantastex1113½SealedLips1182¼LandofRhythm1212½	Outrun	6
16Nov74- 4Cam	fm 2 13/16	S'Chase	5:24 4↑	Colonial Cup 50k	1	3	63¼	51¾	53¼	515	Twyman N	162	-	- -	Augustus Bay1428Tarratine1432John U1535	Fell back	11
2Nov74- 3Mtp	fm *2½	S'Chase	4:353 4↑	Noel Laing H 5.3k	5	2	21½	22	2½	32½	O'Brien L	163	-	- -	Speed Kills1502John U151½Gran Kan1638	Weakened	5
5Oct74- 4Lig	sf *2½	S'Chase	5:212 4↑	Gold Cup H 25k	7	7	46	55¼	22	28	O'Brien L	166	-	- -	Arctic Joe1398Gran Kan1664Breaking Dawn1371	Went well	8
14Sep74- 7Fai	sf *2½	S'Chase	5:203 4↑	Grand National H 12k	1	2	42	1½	12½	13½	O'Brien L	162	*.80	- -	Gran Kan1623½Tall Award140nkJohn U1523½	Driving	5
2Aug74- 6Sar	fm 2 1/16	S'Chase	3:443 4↑	Lovely Night H 22k	10	4	43½	21	26	22¾	O'Brien L	160	*1.70	- -	Cafe Prince1452¾Gran Kan1603Juac Hollow1548	Gamely	10
8Jun74- 8Del	fm *2½	S'Chase	4:323 4↑	Indian River H 13k	2	4	54	21½	2hd	11	O'Brien L	158	*1.70	- -	Gran Kan1581Metello153hdLucky Boy III1552¾	Driving	11
4May74- 3War	fm *2	S'Chase	4:212 4↑	Handicap 10000	2	2	22½	11½	12	14½	O'Brien L	153 s	-	- -	Gran Kan1534½Wustenchef1563Metello1572½	Ridden out	6
	Previously trained by S. Watters Jr																
21Apr74- 7Mid	fm *1¼Ⓣ		2:171 3↑	Alw 1000	1	1	12	12	11½	1½	O'Brien L	145	-	- -	Gran Kan145½Machu Picchu1292Mod Man1451½	Driving	16
16Sep72- 5Fai	fm *2½	Hurdles	4:514 4↑	Handicap 10000	3	4	64¼	22	1nk	12½	Skiffington T	158	*2.00	- -	Gran Kan1582½Perigo14216Speed Kills1413	Drew clear	8
9Sep72- 2Fai	fm *1 5/16Ⓣ		2:074 3↑	Alw 1200	2	7	78¼	69½	410	38	Watters E3	153	*1.00	- -	Jaunty1426Mystic's Desire1422Gran Kan153no	Rallied	9
23Aug72- 7Sar	hd 1⅝Ⓣ	:482 1:363 2:01	2:374 3↑	Seneca H 30k	4	12	1221	1011	89½	810	Ruane J	111	6.80e	94-04	Red Reality113¾Acclimitization114¾[D]Larceny Kid1133		12
	Steadied at start																
17Aug72- 3Sar	fm 2 1/16	Hurdles	3:421 4↑	Lovely Night H 22k	1	5	2½	2hd	32½	33¼	O'Brien M	157 s	*.50e	- -	ShadowBrook163¾Dream Magic1522½GrnKan1574	Weakened	8
11Jly72- 4Mth	fm *2 1/16	Hurdles	4:094 4↑	Midsummer H 16k	3	1	1½	2hd	22	18	O'Brien L	158	2.40	- -	Gran Kan1588Dream Magic1446Ghost Charger145hd	Driving	10
9Jun72- 9Del	fm *2½	Hurdles	4:291 4↑	Indian River H 13k	1	3	34	2hd	14	14	O'Brien M	148 b	2.70e	- -	Gran Kan1484Dualamar1415El Martirio1403½	Ridden out	9
3Jun72- 2Mid	hd *1¼Ⓣ		2:131 3↑	Sp Wt 600	11	9	97¼	63½	3¾	15	Watters E	158	-	- -	Gran Kan1585Still in All1432½Favori1451½	In hand	11
27May72- 3Mid	fm *1Ⓣ		1:342 3↑	Alw 500	5	2	1nk	1hd	2nk	12½	Watters E	152	-	- -	Gran Kan1522½Port Manech1423La Strega1524	Driving	11
20Nov71- 5Cam	fm *2	S'Chase	3:41 4↑	Alw 5000	1	3	36	2½	1hd	11½	Skiffington T Jr	155	-	- -	Gran Kan1551½Dualamar140hdTuscalee1511	Driving	14
6Nov71- 4Mtp	sf *2	S'Chase	4:122 3↑	Alw 2000	6	4	32¼	31½	45½	48¼	Skiffington T Jr	155	-	- -	Inkslinger1492½Bookbinder140¾Dream Magic1455	Weakened	12
14Oct71- 5Bel	sf 2⅝	Hurdles	4:554 4↑	NY Turf Writers H 33k	6	4	64	53	721	717	Skiffington T Jr	150 s	9.40	- -	Soothsayer1533Predominio1413Wustenchef1623½	Bobbled	8
7Oct71- 9Bel	fm 1⅞	Hurdles	3:212 4↑	Alw 9500	6	4	34½	32	2½	11½	Skiffington T Jr5	147 s	6.70	- -	Gran Kan1471½John U1423Persian Honour1464	Driving	9
23Aug71- 9Sar	fm 2 1/16	Hurdles	3:441 4↑	Alw 9500	7	3	36	1hd	2hd	31	Skiffington T Jr5	149 s	4.80	- -	Shadow II132¾Dream Magic137nkGran Kan1494	Good try	8
11Aug71- 9Sar	fm 2 1/16	Hurdles	4:454 4↑	Alw 7000	4	2	21½	17	18	112	Skiffington T Jr5	143 s	8.90	- -	GranKan14312PortManech147nkDuchessofMalfi1353½	Easily	11
12Jly71- 9Aqu	fm 1⅞	Hurdles	3:222 4↑	Sp Wt 6800	7	3	31½	41½	611	613	Skiffington T Jr5	147 s	2.80	- -	Blue Runner1452½Big Red Rocket152½Jive1456	Tired	8
29Jun71- 3Aqu	fm 1⅞	Hurdles	3:232 4↑	Alw 7000	2	4	21½	1½	23	32¼	Skiffington T Jr5	142 s	*.80e	- -	Jus' Behaving1471Blue Runner1401¼Gran Kan1429	Held well	10
21Jun71- 4Mth	fm *1¾	Hurdles	3:26 4↑	Alw 5500	7	5	42½	53½	512	311½	Skiffington T Jr5	147 s	5.40e	- -	Misty Forsome1476½Flying Bee1475Gran Kan1471	Driving	10
	Previously trained by Guillermo Sarmiento																

5Jun70♦	Hipodromo(Chi) fst *1¼LH	2:034 3↑	Clsc Universidad Catolica-Hcp Stk1200	9	Toro L	119	-	Love Me1101¾Good Look1281¼Mariscal1191¼	10
21May70♦	Club Hippico(Chi) fm *1ⓉRH	1:362 3↑	Premio Your Highness Hcp1000	11½	Toro L	112	7.20	Gran Kan1121½Barthou1071½Droguel1191½	7
25Apr70♦	Hipodromo(Chi) gd *7½fLH	1:31 3↑	Premio Jockey Club de Arequipa Hcp1100	12¼	Jorquera G	121	7.20	Gran Kan1212¼Germinal1062½Equino1194	13
19Apr70♦	Club Hippico(Chi) fm *6½fⓉRH	1:163 3↑	Premio Quemarropa Hcp1500	6	Sepulveda C	119	-	Zante106hdPercal114½Meritorio112hd	12
1Feb70♦	Valparaiso(Chi) fm *1ⓉLH	1:38 3↑	Premio Andres G. Scott Hcp1500	8	Astorga C	116	-	Notable114hdParlas126noPuro Oro1142½	8
11Jan70♦	Valparaiso(Chi) fm *1 3/16ⓉLH	1:564	Clasico Juan S. Jackson Stk5000	11	Azocar S	112	-	Trinera112½Campomar112¾Cougar II112¾	12
26Oct69♦	Club Hippico(Chi) fm *1½ⓉRH	2:261	Clasico El Ensayo Stk5000	54¾	Munoz D	123	-	Vagabundo1231Aristocratico123¾Exotico1232½	11
								Good Look 6th	
31Aug69♦	Club Hippico(Chi) fm *1 1/16ⓉRH	1:404	Polla de Potrillos Stk6000	85¾	Salinas J	123	-	Vagabundo123½Bien Machito1231Aristocratico1232½	19
								Exotico 4th	
10Aug69♦	Club Hippico(Chi) sf *1ⓉRH	1:401	Clasico Alberto Vial Infante Stk3500	32¾	Astorga C	121	-	Pimentero121¾Oro Es Triunfo1212Gran Kan121½	15
29Jun69♦	Hipodromo(Chi) gd *7½fLH	1:34	Premio All Serene Alw1200	23	Ulloa P	121	-	Aristocratico1123Gran Kan121hdTribuno113¾	10
27Apr69♦	Club Hippico(Chi) fm *6½fⓉRH	1:18	Premio Japon Alw1200	1hd	Astorga C	115	6.40	Gran Kan115hdBriquet1131Dagafiante1122½	9
5Apr69♦	Club Hippico(Chi) fm *5fⓉStr	1:00	Premio Fez Mdn600	1nk	Astorga C	121	9.80	Gran Kan121nkCamaro1172Dagafiante1172	10

Hoist the Flag

b. c. 1968, by Tom Rolfe (Ribot)–Wavy Navy, by War Admiral — Lifetime record: 6 5 0 0 $78,145

Own.– Mrs S.C. Clark Jr
Br.– John M. Schiff (Ky)
Tr.– S. Watters Jr

20Mar71- 7Aqu	fst 7f	:22 :443 1:09 1:21	Bay Shore 34k	6	3	21	2½	14	17	Cruguet J	126	*.30	96-17	Hoist the Flag1267Droll Role117nkJim French121½	Easily	9
12Mar71- 8Bow	fst 6f	:232 :471 1:103	Alw 9500	2	4	11	13	16	115	Cruguet J	122	*.10	93-05	HoisttheFlag12215TotheMan119½Backslidng1191	Drew clear	5
10Oct70- 7Bel	fst 1	:22 :443 1:092 1:352	Champagne 205k	10	3	33	1½	12	13	Cruguet J	122	*.80	96-13	[D]HoisttheFlag1223LimttoRson1223Arctrus122¼	Caused jam	16
Disqualified and placed last																
1Oct70- 7Bel	fst 7f	:221 :451 1:10 1:222	Cowdin 65k	12	12	99	5½	2½	1¾	Cruguet J	115	*1.70	95-13	HoisttheFlag1151¾LimittoReason1154Executonr117¾	Handily	12
23Sep70- 6Bel	fst 6½f	:223 :461 1:102 1:162	Alw 8500	2	9	1½	1hd	1½	15	Cruguet J	122	*.70	98-12	HoisttheFlag1225BoldSkipper1137EastrnFlt1221	Mild drive	9
11Sep70- 2Bel	gd 6f	:224 :461 1:11	Md Sp Wt	7	11	53½	21	1hd	12½	Cruguet J	122	3.20	90-14	HoisttheFlag1222½Ogontz122¾SitintheCorner1226	Driving	11

Honest Pleasure

dkbbr. c. 1973, by What a Pleasure (Bold Ruler)–Tularia, by Tulyar — Lifetime record: 25 12 6 2 $839,997

Own.– B.R. Firestone
Br.– Waldemar Farms Inc (Fla)
Tr.– Leroy Jolley

20Aug77- 8Mth	fst 1¼	:47 1:11 1:352 2:002 3↑	AL Haskell H-G1	2	1	1½	54	58½	615½	Solomone M	123	2.30	84-19	Majestic Light1248Capital Idea1084½Peppy Addy116¾		6
Done after a mile																
3Aug77- 5Sar	fst 7f	:223 :442 1:09 1:22 3↑	Alw 25000	5	2	2½	1hd	1½	2½	Vasquez J	117	*.40	94-13	El Portugues119½Honest Pleasure1171¾Piamem119¾	Gamely	6
16Apr77- 7Kee	fst 1$\frac{1}{16}$	:23 :452 1:093 1:422 3↑	Ben Ali H-G3	1	1	12	14½	12	1½	Perret C	124	*.60	94-16	HonestPleasure124½IncaRoca1182PackerCaptan113no	Driving	9
23Mar77- 9Hia	fm 1$\frac{1}{16}$Ⓣ	1:402 4↑	Alw 10000	1	2	2hd	2½	23	55¼	Perret C	122	*.80	91-09	AllFriends1221Improviser1222½QuickDecision1171	Faltered	11
6Nov76- 8SA	fst 1¼	:454 1:094 1:35 2:00 3↑	Champions Inv'l H 350k	2	1	11½	1hd	33	87¾	Perret C	121	2.30	90-09	KngPellinore126noL'Heureux1181¾FestivMood1154	Weakened	10
25Oct76- 8Aqu	fst 1	:223 :45 1:084 1:34	Jamaica H 55k	6	3	31½	21½	42½	43¼	Perret C	125	*.60	93-13	Dance Spell119¾Cojak119½Quiet Little Table1142	Weakened	9
2Oct76- 8Bel	sly 1¼	:472 1:104 1:35 2:00 3↑	Marlboro Cup H-G1	4	1	11½	12½	11½	2hd	Perret C	119	2.80	99-11	Forego137hdHonestPlesur1191FthrHogn110¾	Failed to last	11
18Sep76- 8Bel	fst 1⅛	:453 1:091 1:332 1:454 3↑	Woodward H-G1	1	1	11½	11	3½	34	Perret C	121	2.10	94-10	Forego1351½DanceSpell1152¾[DH]HnstPleasre121	Weakened	10
21Aug76- 6Sar	fst 1¼	:463 1:102 1:35 2:001	Travers-G1	4	1	16	12	13	14	Perret C	126	2.10	104-12	HonestPleasure1264Romeo1261½DanceSpell1263	Ridden out	8
7Aug76- 8Mth	fst 1⅛	:46 1:10 1:343 1:47	Mth Inv'l H-G1	4	2	21½	11½	2½	36	Perret C	126	*1.10	99-08	MajesticLight1226Appassionato113noHonestPlesr126½	Hung	10
27Jly76- 8Mth	fst 1$\frac{1}{16}$	:232 :46 1:10 1:411 3↑	Alw 13000	1	1	13½	11½	2hd	21½	Baeza B	115	*.10	97-13	Peppy Addy1191½Honest Pleasure1157Lee Gary1171½	Hung	6
15May76- 8Pim	fst 1$\frac{3}{16}$	:45 1:09 1:351 1:55	Preakness-G1	6	2	22	22	42	57¼	Baeza B	126	*.90	88-11	Elocutionist1263½Play the Red126½Bold Forbes1263		6
Brushed,drifted in																
1May76- 8CD	fst 1¼	:454 1:102 1:353 2:013	Ky Derby-G1	5	2	25	2½	2½	21	Baeza B	126	*.40	88-11	BoldForbes1261HonestPlsr1263¼Elocutonst1261¼	No excuse	9
22Apr76- 7Kee	fst 1⅛	:48 1:123 1:372 1:492	Blue Grass-G1	2	1	14	15	12	11½	Baeza B	121	*.10	90-15	HnstPleasre1211½CertanRomo1213IncRoc1212¼	Ridden out	7
3Apr76- 9GP	fst 1⅛	:464 1:103 1:351 1:474	Florida Derby-G1	3	1	13	13	13	13	Baeza B	122	*.05	95-14	Honest Pleasure1223Great Contractor1222½Proud Birdie1222		6
Speed in reserve																
28Feb76- 9Hia	fst 1⅛	:454 1:09 1:334 1:464	Flamingo-G1	7	1	12	18	18	111	Baeza B	122	*.30	98-06	HonestPleasre12211IncaRoca122no[D]Togus1221½	Easy score	8
11Feb76- 0Hia	fst 7f	:23 :452 1:093 1:222	Alw 10000	4	2	11	14	110	114	Baeza B	122	-	93-18	HonestPleasure12214ParcForillon115½ImprovIt11516	Easily	4
Exhibition race - No wagering																
1Nov75- 8Lrl	fst 1$\frac{1}{16}$	:23 :454 1:103 1:424	Lrl Futurity-G1	3	1	11	13	11½	12½	Baeza B	122	*.20	99-14	Honest Pleasure1222½Whatsyourpleasure1223½DanceSpll1228		7
Ridden out																
18Oct75- 8Bel	sly 1	:222 :45 1:101 1:362	Champagne-G1	9	2	1½	11½	15	17	Baeza B	122	*1.20	86-17	Honest Pleasure1227Dance Spell1222½Whatsyourpleasure122½		14
Ridden out																
8Oct75- 8Bel	fst 7f	:224 :452 1:094 1:223	Cowdin-G2	7	1	13	14	15	18	Baeza B	121	2.80	89-18	Honest Pleasure1218Whatsyourpleasure116hdUncle Gene1132		7
Mild drive																
13Sep75- 8AP	fst 6½f	:222 :452 1:113 1:182	©Arl Wash Futurity-G1	4	8	85½	72½	2hd	1nk	McHargue DG	122	5.00	83-21	Honest Pleasure122nkKhyber King122nkRule The Ridge1221½		19
Hard drive																
3Sep75- 5Bel	fst 6f	:23 :462 1:101	Alw 9000	3	2	11	12	12½	16	Baeza B	120	*.20	91-17	Honest Pleasure1206Pastry120¾Bakor1204	Ridden out	7
25Aug75- 5Bel	fst 6f	:223 :46 1:101	Alw 9000	2	3	31	2½	1½	2¾	Baeza B	120	*1.20	90-12	TurnandCount120¾HonstPleasre1204BeauTalnt120no	Gamely	8
21Jun75- 3Bel	fst 5½f	:223 :46 :574 1:04	©Md Sp Wt	6	7	23	2½	12	15½	Vasquez J	118	*.80	95-12	HonestPlsure1185½DanceSpell118¾TtonRng118¾	Ridden out	10
4Jun75- 3Bel	fst 5½f	:224 :461 :581 1:042	©Md Sp Wt	2	4	2hd	2hd	2½	2½	Vasquez J	118	*.90	92-11	RomanticLead118½HonstPlsur118nkFmlyDoctr1185½	Gamely	10

It's In the Air

b. f. 1976, by Mr. Prospector (Raise a Native)–A Wind Is Rising, by Francis S. — Lifetime record: 43 16 9 6 $892,339

Own.– Due Process Stable
Br.– Happy Valley Farm (Fla)
Tr.– Reynaldo H. Nobles

11Oct81- 9Suf	fst 1$\frac{1}{16}$	:233 :472 1:12 1:442 3↑	ⒻHannah Dustin H 52k	2	1	2½	76	715	722½	Skinner K	123	10.90	64-26	WeberCityMiss1266AngeGal114½WaterDance116½	Brief speed	8
30Sep81- 6Med	fst 6f	:221 :45 1:102 3↑	ⒻHandicap 25000	4	6	78¾	712	715	510	Lopez C	121	3.00	81-20	Delta Crisis1123Larla120noFavorite Prospect1124½		7
Outrun,worked mile in 1:40 3/5																
4Jly81- 9Mth	sly 1$\frac{1}{16}$	:234 :471 1:112 1:44 3↑	ⒻMolly Pitcher H-G2	6	3	23	47½	617	626	Tejeira J	114	8.60	59-24	Weber City Miss1192Jameela1186Wistful1212	Tired	6
24Jun81- 8Mth	fst 1$\frac{1}{16}$	:241 :474 1:12 1:46 3↑	ⒻAlw 17000	1	1	1½	11	12	1½	Tejeira J	124	*1.40	75-20	It'sintheAir124½DanceTroupe1181¼ReallyMean1185	Driving	6
7Jun81- 8Bel	fst 1⅛	:464 1:112 1:363 1:494 3↑	ⒻHempstead H-G2	5	5	52¾	45¼	410	417¾	Asmussen CB	115	5.30	60-20	Wistful119hdChain Bracelet1236½Love Sign11512	Tired	5
25May81- 8Mth	fm 1Ⓣ	:234 :47 1:112 1:37 3↑	ⒻAlw 17000	7	5	44	21½	21½	11½	Velez JA Jr7	110	*1.00	90-10	It'sintheAir1101½LadyLobbyist1155Earlham108½	Drew clear	7
7May81- 8Mth	fst 1	:242 :482 1:124 1:374 3↑	ⒻAlw 16000	3	3	32	11	12½	15¼	Velez JA Jr7	110	*.30	84-16	It'sintheAir1105¼SistrRosmund115¾FlshDoubl108hd	Driving	5
26Apr81- 8Aqu	fst 1⅛	:461 1:102 1:362 1:493 3↑	ⒻTop Flight H-G1	5	3	36½	37	48½	49¾	Asmussen CB	118	4.90	77-23	ChainBracelet1151¾LadyOakley1155WbrCtyMss1183	No threat	5
8Apr81- 9OP	fst 1$\frac{1}{16}$	:233 :462 1:111 1:441 4↑	ⒻApple Blossom H-G2	4	2	2½	42¼	69	69¾	Lopez C	120	7.00	77-20	Bold 'n Determined124hdLa Bonzo1113¼Karla's Enough1193½		7
Early speed																
21Mar81- 8Aqu	fst 7f	:232 :47 1:123 1:252 3↑	ⒻDistaff H-G3	8	1	53	31	21½	2hd	Asmussen CB	120	*2.30	74-35	LadyOakley114hdIt'sintheAir1205½Lovin'Lass1102	Gamely	8
7Mar81- 9Bow	fst 7f	:222 :443 1:093 1:23 3↑	ⒻBarbara Fritchie H-G3	4	7	74¾	76¾	79½	611	Lopez C	123	*1.40	79-24	Skipat1247½Whispy'sLass114¾SecretEmotion113hd	No mishap	8
Previously owned by Harbor View Farm;previously trained by Lazaro Barrera																
11Jan81- 7SA	fst 6f	:213 :441 :564 1:093 4↑	ⒻAlw 32000	3	7	54	55½	31	1nk	Pincay L Jr	121	*.90	91-17	It'sintheAir121nkBackatTwo1135½ProudestBee1132¼	Just up	7
8Nov80- 8Aqu	fst 1¼	:474 1:114 1:372 2:03 3↑	ⒻLadies H-G1	4	3	21½	42½	42	46	Pincay L Jr	118	1.60	75-22	Planktn119noSugarandSpice114noWebrCtyMss1196	Gave way	6
11Oct80- 8Bel	fst 1¼	:47 1:114 1:37 2:024 3↑	ⒻBeldame-G1	1	1	2hd	35½	39	310½	Pincay L Jr	123	3.20	75-17	LoveSign1184MistyGallore1236½It'sintheAir1238½	Tired	4
27Sep80- 8Bel	fst 1⅛	:48 1:122 1:364 1:491 3↑	ⒻRuffian H-G1	5	1	1½	1½	3nk	3nk	Fell J	118	4.00e	81-19	GenuineRisk118noMistyGllor124nkIt'snthAr1185¾	Held well	6
2Sep80- 6Med	sly 1⅛	:46 1:103 1:362 1:493 3↑	ⒻLong Look H-G2	1	2	22	2½	21	22	Fell J	119	2.60	83-18	MistyGallore1232It'sintheAir1195Poppycock112¾	Steadied	6
8Aug80- 8Sar	fst 7f	:22 :441 1:091 1:221 3↑	ⒻBallerina-G3	4	1	31	1hd	3½	31	McHargue DG	119	*1.30	90-15	DavonaDale1191MistyGallore124noIt'sinthAir1191¾	Weakened	4
13Jly80- 8Hol	fst 1⅛	:453 1:091 1:341 1:47 3↑	ⒻVanity H-G1	6	6	66½	31½	3½	13¾	Pincay L Jr	120	*2.10	97-12	It's in the Air1203¾Conveniently111nkImage of Reality119nk		7
Drew clear																
31May80- 8Hol	fst 1$\frac{1}{16}$	:224 :453 1:091 1:401 3↑	ⒻMilady H-G2	5	4	42½	35	23	23¼	Pincay L Jr	122	*1.10	91-14	Image of Reality1173¼It's in the Air1221¼Fondre1137		5
Best of others																
14May80- 8Hol	fst 7f	:212 :432 1:071 1:193 3↑	ⒻSilver Spoon H 54k	5	7	85¼	76¼	68¼	45½	Pincay L Jr	123	*1.30	95-14	Splendid Girl1174½Fondre115½Celine114½	Mild bid	9
24Feb80- 8SA	fst 1⅛	:462 1:103 1:36 1:482 4↑	ⒻS Margarita H-G1	1	5	42½	52¼	3½	44	Pincay L Jr	124	*1.90	83-11	Glorious Song1202The Very One116noKankam1252	Checked	11
10Feb80- 8SA	fst 1⅛	:452 1:093 1:35 1:473	ⒻLa Canada-G1	6	4	45½	42	44½	35¾	Pincay L Jr	125	*.80	85-09	GloriousSong1181¾PrizSpot1194It'snthAr1251	Trapped late	7

Date	Cond	Dist	Fractions	Race	PP	St	1C	2C	Str	Fin	Jockey	Wt	Odds	Figs	Top Finishers	Comment	Fld
26Jan80-8SA	fst	1 1/16	:224 :453 1:093 1:411	(F)El Encino-G3	7	6	66½	63¾	52½	11¼	Pincay L Jr	124	*2.60	95-09	It'sintheAir1241¼PrizeSpot121¼[D]Terlingua121¼	Driving	8
16Jan80-8SA	gd	1⅛	:472 1:12 1:372 1:50 4↑	(F)San Gorgonio H 66k	7	3	2hd	2½	611	724	Pincay L Jr	125	*1.30	55-23	Miss Magnetic11115Maytide1121¼Persona113½	Tired	9
13Oct79-8Bel	sly	1¼	:473 1:124 1:39 2:061 3↑	(F)Beldame-G1	4	1	21	78½	59	511	Pincay L Jr	118	*.40	58-27	Waya1233Fourdrinier1184Kit's Double1231¼	Tired	7
29Sep79-8Bel	fst	1⅛	:474 1:12 1:351 1:472 3↑	(F)Ruffian H-G1	4	1	11	12½	12½	14	Pincay L Jr	122	3.00	90-12	It's in the Air1224Bliteу1135Waya126	Ridden out	4
12Sep79-8Bel	fst	1	:23 :453 1:093 1:344 3↑	(F)Maskette-G2	5	1	1½	2hd	2hd	2nk	Shoemaker W	122	2.40	94-20	Blitey112nkIt'sintheAir122noPearlNecklace1253¼	Game try	5
26Aug79-9Del	gd	1⅛	:482 1:122 1:372 1:492	(F)Del Oaks-G1	1	1	1½	2hd	11½	15	Shoemaker W	122	*.30	90-14	It's in the Air1225Jameela1151Himalayan114½	In hand	6
11Aug79-8Sar	fst	1¼	:49 1:124 1:364 2:012	(F)Alabama-G1	4	1	1½	11½	13	11½	Fell J	121	3.10	94-13	It'sintheAir1211½DavonaDale1213¾MairzyDots1212¼	Driving	5
4Aug79-5Sar	fst	6f	:221 :45 1:091 3↑	(F)Alw 27000	5	2	11	13	15	18	Fell J	117	*.40	94-12	It'sintheAir1178EnglishTrifle108¾LucyBelle1052¾	Handily	7
15Jly79-8Hol	fst	1⅛	:453 1:094 1:344 1:472 3↑	(F)Vanity H-G1	1	2	22½	1hd	1½	1nk	Shoemaker W	113	*.90	95-12	It'sintheAir113nkCountryQueen121hdInnuendo1169	Driving	8
7Jly79-8Hol	fst	1⅛	:454 1:101 1:353 1:481	(F)Hol Oaks-G1	2	3	21	21	2hd	2hd	Shoemaker W	121	*1.10	91-14	PrizeSpot121hdIt'sintheAir1216VarietyQueen1241	Sharp	7
2Jun79-8Hol	fst	1 1/16	:221 :443 1:092 1:411 3↑	(F)Milady H-G2	4	2	23½	2hd	1½	2½	Shoemaker W	112	2.30	88-14	Innuendo115½It'sintheAir112½CountryQueen1213½	Failed	9
11Mar79-8SA	fst	1 1/16	:222 :451 1:092 1:413	(F)S Susana-G1	7	4	43	32	35½	39	Pincay L Jr	117	1.90e	84-12	Caline1151Terlingua1158It's in the Air117hd	Checked	8
24Feb79-8SA	fst	7f	:22 :442 1:082 1:211	(F)S Ynez-G3	4	5	44	21½	33½	36	Delahoussaye E	121	*1.20	91-12	Terlingua1214Caline1192It's in the Air1213¼	Weakened	5
22Oct78-8SA	fst	1 1/16	:223 :461 1:101 1:411	(F)Oak Leaf-G2	1	2	21½	2½	2hd	11½	Delahoussaye E	115	1.60	95-11	It's in the Air1151½Caline11512Spiffy Laree115¾	Handily	8
20Oct78-8Bel	fst	1	:23 :452 1:094 1:352	(F)Frizette-G1	4	5	62¼	43	22½	25	Delahoussaye E	119	6.80	86-14	Golferette1195It'sintheAr1197½Trlngu119¾	Best of others	7
Previously owned by J. Frankel;previously trained by Lou Goldfine																	
9Sep78-8AP	fst	6f	:221 :451 :571 1:093	(F)Arl-Wash Lassie-G2	8	1	73¾	63¾	1hd	14	Delahoussaye E	119	5.40	95-06	It'sintheAir1194AngelIsland119¾Bequa1191¼	Ridden out	8
9Aug78-8AP	fst	6f	:221 :464 :582 1:104	(F)Mademoiselle 22k	8	8	65½	44½	1½	13	Delahoussaye E	115	4.60	89-18	It'sintheAir1153SplittheTab1156AngelIsland122hd	Handily	10
19Jly78-7AP	fst	5½f	:222 :453 :573 1:04	(F)Alw 7500	3	3	31	11	14	17	Sibille R	117	*1.30	95-15	It'sintheAir1177Buddy'sAngel117nkMiniWig1202	Easily	6
26Jun78-5AP	sly	5f	:22 :453 :582	(F)Alw 8500	6	4	47	45½	33	21½	Sibille R	117	*1.20	92-16	JustaReflection1171½It'sintheAr1172GrdnGlovs1177	Gamely	6
20Jun78-6AP	gd	5f	:23 :47 :593	(F)Md Sp Wt	6	2	1½	1½	11	17	Sibille R	118	*.40	88-24	It'sintheAir1187DancingChant1189KlipKlop1182	Ridden out	6
12Jun78-3AP	fst	5f	:231 :47 :593	(F)Md Sp Wt	9	7	31	2hd	2hd	2hd	Sibille R	119	2.70	88-22	Justa Reflection119hdIt's in the Air1197Bye119nk	Gamely	9

J.O. Tobin

dkbbr. c. 1974, by Never Bend (Nasrullah)–Hill Shade, by Hillary

Lifetime record: 21 12 2 2 $659,416

Own.– G.A. Pope Jr
Br.– George A. Pope Jr (Md)
Tr.– Lazaro S. Barrera

Date	Cond	Dist	Fractions	Race	PP	St	1C	2C	Str	Fin	Jockey	Wt	Odds	Figs	Top Finishers	Comment	Fld
8Sep78-8Bel	fm	7f(T)	:223 :451 1:093 1:22 3↑	Alw 30000	3	5	2hd	2hd	23½	47¼	Cauthen S	122	*.40	87-11	Tiller122hdArachnoid122hdQuick Card1157	Broke in air	5
5Aug78-8Sar	fst	1⅛	:463 1:102 1:351 1:472 3↑	Whitney H-G2	8	4	34½	2hd	35½	611	Fell J	128	2.80	87-09	Alydar12310Buckaroo112hdFathrHogn114nk	Squeezed,drifted	9
23Jly78-8Bel	fst	7f	:221 :443 1:08 1:204 3↑	Tom Fool H 43k	8	5	11½	12	14	16½	Fell J	129	*1.30	98-15	J.O.Tobin1296½WhiteRammer119noIt'sFreezing116½	Handily	8
25Jun78-8Hol	fst	1¼	:452 1:091 1:333 1:591 3↑	Hol Gold Cup H-G1	1	1	13½	16	11½	44¼	Cauthen S	128	1.20e	91-16	Exceller128nkText118hdVigors1294	Drifted out,turn	7
14May78-8Hol	fst	1 1/16	:222 :452 1:092 1:41 3↑	Californian-G1	4	3	32½	1½	11½	12½	Cauthen S	126	*.50	90-20	J.O.Tobin1262½Replant1201½Cox'sRidge1271¼	Steady drive	6
22Apr78-8Hol	fst	7f	:214 :451 1:083 1:212 3↑	Los Angeles H-G2	3	3	21½	1½	11½	13½	Cauthen S	130	*.30	92-17	J.O. Tobin1303½Maheras125½Drapier1215	Going away	4
12Apr78-8Hol	fst	1 1/16	:224 :452 1:091 1:412 3↑	Premiere H 53k	3	1	12½	14	16	17	Cauthen S	125	*1.10	88-16	J.O. Tobin1257Mr. Redoy1211Miami Sun115¾	Speed to spare	5
25Mar78-8SA	fm	1⅛(T)	:462 1:102 1:344 1:474 4↑	San Bernardino H-G2	2	2	21½	1½	1hd	1¾	Cauthen S	123	*.50	88-12	J.O. Tobin123¾Henschel1151½Riot in Paris1194	Driving	6
5Feb78-8SA	sl	1¼	:454 1:093 1:343 2:01	C H Strub-G1	8	1	12½	14	12	34½	Cauthen S	122	*1.00	86-14	Mr. Redoy1162½Text1212J.O. Tobin1223	Drifted out	9
15Jan78-8SA	sl	1⅛	:453 1:10 1:353 1:492	San Fernando-G2	4	1	12	13	21	22	Cauthen S	123	*.30	83-17	Text1202J.O. Tobin123¾Centennial Pride1141	Drifted out	5
1Jan78-8SA	sl	7f	:221 :444 1:092 1:23	Malibu-G2	5	2	12	13	14	15½	Cauthen S	123	*.70	88-29	J.O. Tobin1235½Bad 'n Big1206Eagle Ki1142	Easily	9
Previously trained by John H. Adams																	
17Sep77-8Bel	sly	1⅛	:453 1:101 1:352 1:48 3↑	Woodward H-G1	2	1	21	2½	53¾	58½	McHargue DG	121	2.60	78-18	Forego1331½SilverSeries114nkGreatContractor115nk	Tired	10
3Jly77-8Hol	fst	1¼	:452 1:091 1:333 1:583	Swaps-G1	4	1	11½	15	18	18	Shoemaker W	120	3.10	98-11	J.O. Tobin1208Affiliate117noText1208	Scored in hand	7
25Jun77-6Hol	fm	1⅛(T)	:47 1:11 1:344 1:47 3↑	Alw 22000	6	2	22	11	12	13	Shoemaker W	107	*.30	101-15	J.O. Tobin1073Riverside Sam1183½Niebo1172	Handily	6
21May77-8Pim	fst	1 3/16	:453 1:094 1:344 1:542	Preakness-G1	6	7	812	57	45½	55½	Shoemaker W	126	6.50	92-10	Seattle Slew1261½Iron Constitution1262Run Dusty Run1261¼		9
Broke in air																	
30Apr77-8Hol	fm	1(T)	:232 :463 1:103 1:342	Coronado H 44k	3	4	34	32	21	12	Shoemaker W	124	*.80	98-05	J.O.Tobin1242Bad'nBig1172HighlandLight1182	Mild drive	8
17Mar77-0SA	gd	6f	:214 :443 :571 1:10	Alw 20000	1	4	33½	21	2½	2¾	Shoemaker W	122	-	88-16	Incredibly Lucky115¾J.O. Tobin1223Important Reason11720		4
Off poorly;Exhibition race - No wagering. Previously trained by Noel Murless																	
10Oct76♦ Longchamp(Fr)	sf	*1(T)RH	1:443	Gran Criterium-G1 Stk182000						34	Piggott L	123	1.20		Blushing Groom1234Amyntor123hdJ.O. Tobin1233		10
Progress into 2nd 1½f out,lost 2nd near line																	
8Sep76♦ Doncaster(GB)	gd	7f(T)Str	1:274	Champagne Stakes-G2 Stk28500						14	Piggott L	126	*.45		J.O. Tobin1264Durtal1237Ampulla1232½		6
Rated at rear,sharp run to lead 1f out,quickly clear																	
28Jly76♦ Goodwood(GB)	fm	6f(T)Str	1:122	Richmond Stakes-G2 Stk39500						11½	Piggott L	123	*.70		J.O. Tobin1231½Prior's Walk123hdTchypous1235		5
Rated in 5th,smooth progress to lead 1½f out,handily																	
8Jly76♦ Newmarket(GB)	gd	6f(T)Str	1:141	Fulbourn Maiden Stakes Mdn5400						12½	Piggott L	126	*1.50		J.O. Tobin1262½Chain of Reasoning1264Daring March126¾		14
Rallied to lead 1½f out,easily																	

Johnny D.

b. g. 1974, by Stage Door Johnny (Prince John)–Dusk, by Olden Times

Lifetime record: 18 7 2 6 $371,256

Own.– Dana S. Bray Jr
Br.– Peggy Augustus (Va)
Tr.– Michael Kay

Date	Cond	Dist	Fractions	Race	PP	St	1C	2C	Str	Fin	Jockey	Wt	Odds	Figs	Top Finishers	Comment	Fld
3Aug81-7Sar	fm	1[T]	:242 :483 1:122 1:362 3↑	Alw 35000	3	8	52½	41½	74¾	97¼	Hernandez R	115	*2.40	87-10	NatvCourr1151¼Gttor115hdMortlFrnds115¾	No late response	9
19Nov77-8Aqu	sf	1½(T)	:51 1:154 2:06 2:331 3↑	Turf Classic 200k	4	2	2hd	1hd	1½	13¾	Cauthen S	122	3.60	- -	Johnny D.1223¾Majestic Light126¾Crow126nk	Drew out	9
5Nov77-8Lrl	sf	1½(T)	:553 1:204 2:154 2:32 3↑	D C Int'l-G1	5	6	1hd	16	15	12½	Cauthen S	120	10.00	59-41	JohnnyD.1202½MajesticLight12714Exceller1273	Ridden out	8
23Oct77-7WO	sf	1⅝(T)	:511 1:443 2:522 3↑	Can Int'l-G1	6	4	53½	2hd	21	34½	Velasquez J	118	14.30	33-44	Exceller1261Majestic Light1263½Johnny D.1183	Weakened	12
8Oct77-8Bel	gd	1½(T)	:474 1:121 2:031 2:273 3↑	Man o' War-G1	2	8	811	31½	41¾	34½	Velasquez J	121	5.40	81-13	Majestic Light1264½Exceller126noJohnny D.121¾	Good try	11
17Sep77-6Bel	sly	1½(X)	:48 1:131 2:034 2:291	Lawrence Realization-G2	3	5	42½	33½	310	314	Cordero A Jr	117	*1.20	60-18	Zinov11711Poor Man's Bluff1172½Johnny D.1171	Rallied	8
16Aug77-8Sar	fm	1 1/16(T)	:241 :474 1:114 1:42 3↑	Handicap 25000	3	4	33	21½	2hd	1½	Cordero A Jr	112	*.50	87-11	Johnny D.112½Dominion116nkRuthie's Native1132¼	Driving	7
30Jly77-8Bel	fm	1 1/16(T)	:231 :461 1:103 1:41	Lexington H (Div 2)-G2	4	3	32½	11½	16	19½	Cordero A Jr	113	*1.40	95-05	JohnnyD.1139½[D]TrueColors117nkForwardChrgr1171¼	Handily	6
4Jly77-7Bel	fm	1 1/16(T)	:231 :464 1:102 1:41 3↑	Alw 15000	7	5	2½	1hd	12	15	Cordero A Jr	115	*.70	95-05	JohnnyD.1155WinterWind1121¾KendallDrive119½	Ridden out	8
22Jun77-7Bel	fm	1 1/16(T)	:232 :473 1:11 1:412 3↑	Alw 13000	2	6	2½	2½	2hd	1½	Velasquez J	114	*2.30	93-07	JohnnyD.114½ShowtheFlag1129½HonorableGuest113no	Driving	9
1Jun77-8Bel	fst	1⅛	:471 1:12 1:364 1:491	Peter Pan 54k	8	4	51¾	3½	67	69	Montoya D	114	14.10	72-27	Spirit Level114hdSanhedrin1142Lynn Davis1141¼	Bid,tired	9
19May77-6Aqu	sly	1	:231 :461 1:103 1:362	Alw 13000	3	8	85½	67¾	37	32½	Velasquez J	115	*1.70	81-12	LeadingScorer1102½LynnDavis122hdJohnnyD.1155½	Rallied	8
2May77-6Aqu	fst	6f	:223 :454 1:102 3↑	Alw 12000	2	6	77½	66½	63¼	41	Velasquez J	112	3.50	90-15	Solly114hdBartender's Pride104¾Hostile Planet119hd	Wide	7
Previously owned by Dana S. Bray;previously trained by Thomas J. Kelly																	
12Feb77-7GP	fst	1 1/16	:234 :482 1:121 1:433	Alw 7000	7	8	2hd	11½	2hd	21	Perret C	122	3.70	82-17	Coined Silver1171Johnny D.1224½Court Open1171	Gamely	12
5Feb77-7GP	fst	1 1/16	:234 :474 1:121 1:431	Alw 7000	2	9	95½	85¾	56¼	35¼	Perret C	122	4.80	80-18	Baldski114¾Cornucopian1144½Johnny D.1222	Rallied	11
Previously trained by M. Kay																	
20Dec76-6Aqu	fst	1 70[•]	:242 :49 1:142 1:443	(C)Md Sp Wt	1	3	34	2hd	11	15	Velasquez J	122	*.70	- -	JohnnyD.1225SeetheWorld1224Portraiture1172	Ridden out	7
11Dec76-4Aqu	fst	6f[•]	:232 :472 1:121	(C)Md Sp Wt	3	4	41½	44½	24	22¼	Velasquez J	122	2.90	- -	Coffee1222¼Johnny D.1224¾Portraiture1221¼	Gamely	7
Previously trained by Mack Miller																	
25Nov76-3Aqu	fst	6f	:22 :461 1:114	(C)Md 40000	6	7	711	710	45	32	Velasquez J	122	2.70	82-18	DewanndOnly118½PpBrownng1201½JhnnyD.122½	Finished fast	10

Key to the Mint

b. c. 1969, by Graustark (Ribot)–Key Bridge, by Princequillo — **Lifetime record: 29 14 4 3 $576,016**

Own.– Rokeby Stable
Br.– Paul Mellon (Va)
Tr.– Elliott Burch

27Sep73- 8Atl	fm 1 3/16(T)	:473 1:111 1:36 1:543	3↑ U Nations H-G1	6 3 2hd 31 43 1110¼	Baeza B	124	b	3.30	87-08	Tentam1234StarEnvoy1161¼ReturntoRlty113hd	Stopped badly	12
15Sep73- 7Bel	fst 1⅛	:453 1:091 1:33 1:452	3↑ Marl Cup Inv'l H 250k	1 6 65¼ 67¾ 713 717	Baeza B	126	b	3.50	87-07	Secretariat1243½Riva Ridge1272Cougar II1266½	Dull try	7
21Jly73- 7Aqu	sly 1¼	:462 1:10 1:351 2:004	3↑ Suburban H-G1	1 1 1½ 13 16 11¾	Baeza B	126	b	*.70	92-16	KeytotheMint1261¾TrueKnight1186CloudyDawn113hd	Driving	6
4Jly73- 7Aqu	fst 1 3/16	:462 1:092 1:333 1:522	3↑ Brooklyn H-G1	6 2 2½ 2hd 31 45½	Baeza B	128	b	*1.60	104-07	Riva Ridge127hdTrue Knight1172Tentam1193½	Hard to rate	7
22Jun73- 7Aqu	sly 1⅛	:464 1:111 1:36 1:484	3↑ Alw 20000	2 2 1hd 11½ 12½ 12	Baeza B	126	b	*.20	92-16	KytotheMnt1262RulebyReason112hdCloudyDawn1149	Easily	4
28May73- 7Bel	sly 1	:223 :444 1:091 1:35	3↑ Metropolitan-G1	8 4 32½ 32 31½ 21¼	Vasquez J	127	b	*1.40	92-16	Tentam1161¼KeytotheMint127hdKing'sBishop1186	Wide	8
14Apr73- 7Aqu	fst 1⅛	:462 1:093 1:342 1:474	3↑ Excelsior H-G2	1 1 2hd 1hd 11 12	Turcotte R	126	b	*.90	97-13	KeytotheMint1262King'sBishop115hdNorthSe1207	Ridden out	5
28Oct72- 7Aqu	fst 2	:474 2:281 2:541 3:212	3↑ J C Gold Cup 113k	1 4 22 210 214 215	Baeza B	119	b	*1.00	74-17	Autobiography12415KeytotheMnt1193RvRdg11910	2nd best	7
30Sep72- 7Bel	sly 1½	:47 1:112 2:012 2:282	3↑ Woodward 115k	3 1 2½ 1hd 13 11¼	Baeza B	119	b	1.70e	91-14	KytothMnt1191¼[D]SummrGust1163Autobogrphy1262	Driving	10
19Aug72- 7Sar	fst 1¼	:453 1:093 1:352 2:011	Travers 111k	6 3 35 23 2hd 11	Baeza B	117	b	*.50	99-07	KeytotheMint1171Tentam114½TrueKnight1145	Brisk urging	7
5Aug72- 7Sar	fst 1⅛	:474 1:112 1:362 1:491	3↑ Whitney 57k	1 3 1½ 1½ 13 12	Baeza B	113	b	*.80	95-12	Key to the Mint1132Tunex1173Loud117¾	Ridden out	8
8Jly72- 7Aqu	fst 1 3/16	:484 1:12 1:362 1:544	3↑ Brooklyn H 118k	11 1 1½ 1½ 13 12	Baeza B	112	b	5.20	100-09	Key to the Mint1122Autobiography1223WestCoastScout1141½	Hard drive	12
10Jun72- 8Bel	fst 1½	:48 1:12 2:021 2:28	Belmont 155k	6 4 3½ 23 48 412¾	Baeza B	126	b	3.80	80-08	RivaRidge1267Ruritn126¾CloudyDwn1265	Brushed first turn	10
31May72- 7Bel	fst 1	:231 :46 1:10 1:344	Withers 59k	2 4 42 1½ 11½ 11	Baeza B	126	b	*1.70	98-16	Key to the Mint1261Icecapade1265½Zulu Tom126¾	Driving	10
20May72- 8Pim	sly 1 3/16	:47 1:11 1:362 1:553	Preakness 187k	3 3 21½ 32 34½ 35¾	Baeza B	126	b	4.20	86-18	BeeBeeBee1261½NoLeHace1264½KytotheMnt126nk	Weakened	7
13May72- 6Pim	fst 1 1/16	:233 :47 1:11 1:424	Alw 12000	3 4 41 41 13 12½	Woodhouse R	119	b	1.30	96-13	KeytotheMint1192½Ladiga1141½SmilingJack1121½	Driving	5
2May72- 8CD	gd 1	:23 :454 1:102 1:361	Derby Trial 22k	3 2 21 12 15 12½	Baeza B	122	b	2.30e	88-20	KeytotheMint1222½NoLeHace1227Dr.Neale1162½	Driving	12
15Mar72- 8Hia	fst 6f	:214 :442 1:10	Alw 8000	5 12 1230 1244 1242 1242	Baeza B	122	b	*1.60	52-18	Over Arranged1156Second Bar1156Nose for Money1152	Went down behind at start, came back sore	12
3Mar72- 9Hia	fst 7f	:214 :434 1:082 1:212	Bahamas 34k	6 4 54½ 57 48 410½	Baeza B	115		*1.20e	90-12	NewProspct112hdHldYourPeace11910SecndBar115½	Bumped	10
26Nov71- 7Aqu	gd 1	:22 :443 1:103 1:363	Remsen 35k	10 8 76¼ 61¾ 2hd 1½	Baeza B	119	b	*.80	84-19	KytotheMint119½DetermindCosmc1193½TrffcCp1173	Driving	12
13Nov71- 8GS	fst 1 1/16	:232 :47 1:113 1:433	Garden State 293k	3 2 23 2½ 2hd 32¾	Rotz JL	122	b	5.20	84-19	RivaRidge1222½Freetex122nkKeytotheMint1221¾	Swerved in	8
6Nov71- 5Aqu	fst 7f	:22 :442 1:093 1:223	Alw 8500	5 2 33 32½ 12½ 12	Rotz JL	119	b	*.60	88-16	KytotheMnt1192NoLeHace1223FollwtheLeadr117hd	Handily	8
20Oct71- 7GS	fst 1 70	:224 :464 1:113 1:424	Alw 6500	7 7 5¾ 1hd 11 1nk	Rotz JL	118		*.60	80-18	[D]KeytotheMnt118nkDeterminedCsmc118½AndrewFeeney118½	Disqualified and placed fourth	8
29Sep71- 7Bel	fst 7f	:222 :453 1:111 1:241	Cowdin 68k	4 2 62½ 22 2½ 2no	Rotz JL	115		8.70	86-20	Loquacious Don115noKey to the Mint1152Mr. Paul B.1153	Carried wide	9
18Sep71- 7Bel	sly 6½f	:22 :451 1:094 1:163	Futurity 153k	3 3 21½ 1hd 44 55½	Rotz JL	122		13.10	91-11	RivaRdge1221½ChvrnFlight122½HldYourPeace1222	Gave way	8
4Sep71- 5Bel	fst 6f	:23 :47 1:114	Alw 9500	2 4 11 1½ 11 1½	Turcotte R	119		3.20	86-12	KytotheMint119½SearchforGold1172PrinceAdgo1173	Driving	12
17Jly71- 6Aqu	fst 5½f	:221 :454 :583 1:05	Alw 10000	5 4 32½ 1hd 1½ 32½	Rotz JL	122		*1.20	85-15	BeeBeeBee1191LuckyBidder1221½KytothMnt1223	Weakened	11
7Jly71- 5Aqu	fst 5½f	:222 :461 :583 1:05	©Md Sp Wt	5 4 32 1½ 11 12	Rotz JL	122		*1.30	88-16	KeytotheMint1222FloorShow1221½DrumFire1224	Mild drive	10
23Jun71- 2Bel	fst 5½f	:223 :461 :582 1:05	©Md Sp Wt	5 1 2½ 1hd 22 25½	Rotz JL	122		*.90	89-15	RivaRdge1225½KeytotheMint1223½Cndyvll122hd	Second best	8

La Prevoyante

b. f. 1970, by Buckpasser (Tom Fool)–Arctic Dancer, by Nearctic — **Lifetime record: 39 25 5 3 $572,417**

Own.– J.L. Levesque
Br.– J. Louis Levesque (Can)
Tr.– J. Starr

28Dec74- 9Crc	fm 1 1/16(T)	:224 :463 1:103 1:43	3↑ ⒻMiss Florida H 30k	5 1 17 14 2hd 85¾	Rogers C	121	b	*1.30	87-05	Tommy's Girl115no[D]Gems and Roses1161Lizabeth Action113¾	Faltered	11
7Dec74- 8Crc	fst 6f	:224 :462 1:13	3↑ ⒻAlw 7500	1 2 1hd 1hd 2½ 2¾	Rogers C	122	b	*.80	87-20	Tastybit122¾La Prevoyante1221½La Noticia104½	Gamely	7
14Oct74- 7WO	sly 6f	:22 :451 1:111	3↑ Nearctic H 17k	4 3 3½ 43½ 43 44½	Leblanc JB	123	b	*.95	82-20	HnryTudr1212DontAskMeThat118hdParkRomeo1132½	No rally	6
11Sep74- 8Bel	fst 1	:223 :444 1:094 1:343	3↑ ⒻMaskette H-G2	4 1 13 1½ 914 1126	Turcotte R	121	b	3.20	69-13	DesertVixen1201½PonteVecchio118½PokerNight1163½	Tired	12
17Aug74- 7Sar	sly 6f	:214 :444 1:103	3↑ Alw 25000	5 4 2hd 1hd 1hd 1nk	Turcotte R	116	b	*.80	87-16	La Prevoyante116nkLonetree1185Piamem114hd	Driving	8
8Aug74- 8Sar	fst 6f	:221 :443 1:09	3↑ ⒻAlw 25000	1 2 1½ 1½ 14 17	Turcotte R	112	b	*.30	95-12	LaPrevoyante1127Clandent120noSpclGoddss109no	Ridden out	5
1Aug74- 7Sar	fst 6f	:22 :443 1:082	3↑ ⒻAlw 20000	5 1 1½ 14 15 17¾	Turcotte R	115	b	*.60	98-12	LaPrevoyante1157¾FullofHope1175½JavaMoon1214½	Handily	6
30Jun74- 7WO	sf 1 1/16(T)	:241 :492 1:152 1:514	3↑ ⒻⓇCanadian 17k	6 1 14½ 13 1hd 36	Castaneda M	124	b	*.60	39-52	Hildesheim1174½MusketeerMiss1241½LaPrvynt1242	Gave way	6
22Jun74- 9WO	sl 7f	:23 :454 1:111 1:242	3↑ ⒻAlw 5800	3 2 1½ 13½ 17 111½	Hawley S	121	b	*.20	88-25	LaPrevoyante12111½TwoRings1171¼Victorianette1112	Easily	7
12Jun74- 7WO	fm *1(T)	:233 :474 1:121 1:392	3↑ ⒻHandicap 7500	6 2 12 15 13½ 13	Hawley S	123	b	*.85	76-00	LaPrevoyante1233LeveeLuck117noHildeshem1161½	Mild drive	10
26May74- 6WO	fst 7f	:232 :453 1:094 1:22	3↑ ⒻSeaway 17k	7 2 1hd 12½ 11 22½	Leblanc JB	121	b	1.30	97-11	MissRebound1242½LaPrevoyante1216Hildshm114½	2nd best	8
13May74- 8Bel	fst 7f	:222 :45 1:094 1:222	3↑ ⒻVagrancy H-G3	12 1 2hd 2hd 1212 1311	Turcotte R	124	b	3.50	79-14	Coraggioso119noPonte Vecchio114no[D]Wanda112½	Stopped; Placed 12th through disqualification	14
19Apr74- 9Hia	fst 6f	:222 :45 1:09	4↑ ⒻAlw 6000	6 1 1hd 13 15 19	Rivera MA	122	b	*.80	98-18	La Prevoyante1229True Pitch1222½Aloha Miss1131	Easily	7
31Oct73- 6Lrl	gd 6f	:223 :454 1:102	ⒻAlw 7500	5 2 2hd 2hd 1hd 11¼	Leblanc JB	122	b	*.20	97-13	LaPrvoynte1221¼ReginaMars1222NturlSound1193	Hand ride	5
20Oct73- 6WO	fst 6f	:221 :453 1:10	ⒻAlw 5100	1 4 2hd 11 11½ 14	Leblanc JB	119		*.20	95-16	LaPrvoyant1194GlamourPrd1175EmrldLndng121½	Ridden out	5
6Oct73- 7WO	fm 1¼(T)	:462 1:124 1:401 2:072	ⒻⓇWonder Where 22k	8 1 1½ 56 613 624	Grubb R	123	b	*1.25	46-22	[D]SquareAngel123noMusketeerMss1135½SharpQull118¾	Tired	8
28Sep73- 9WO	fm *1 1/16(T)	:23 :484 1:133 1:473	ⒻAlw 5300	4 1 11 12½ 12½ 2no	Leblanc JB	121	b	*1.30	75-12	LadyShooter116noLaPrvoynt1212¾Vctorntt1166½	Just missed	6
14Sep73- 6WO	fst 6f	:223 :462 1:094	ⒻAlw 4800	2 3 1hd 13 15 16½	Leblanc JB	118	b	*.35	96-16	LaPrvyante1186½GlamourParade1164LadyShootr120½	Easily	6
21Jly73- 7FE	fst 6½f	:221 :443 1:101 1:164	Friar Rock 11k	8 3 31 22 31 31¾	Leblanc JB	119	b	*.55	93-16	Symmetric1181¼ShakeaLeg121½LaPrvoynte1192½	Weakened	8
30Jun73- 6WO	sl 1¼	:471 1:131 1:41 2:08	ⓇQueen's Plate 124k	15 2 2hd 2hd 23 810	Leblanc JB	121	b	*1.40	56-31	RoyalChocolte1265½Sinister Purpose126nkMyArchieBald1261	No excuse	17
23Jun73- 7WO	fst 1⅛	:453 1:092 1:484	ⒻⓇCanadian Oaks 60k	5 1 19 112 2hd 32	LeBlanc JB	121	b	*.05	97-13	Square Angel1211½Impressive Lady121½La Prevoyante12112	Speed,tired	9
16Jun73- 8BB	sly 1⅛	:47 1:133 1:402 1:54	ⓇQuebec Derby 50k	4 1 15 11½ 1½ 12½	LeBlanc JB	121	b	*.25e	79-34	La Prevoyante1212½Victorian Prince1265LeesandDregges1265	Driving	6
27May73- 8BB	fst 6f	:23 :46 1:104	ⒻVille-Marie 11k	1 4 1½ 11½ 12½ 18	LeBlanc JO	122	b	*.05	100-13	LaPrevoyante1228JamRuler1153EmeraldLanding1172	Easily	5
4May73- 8CD	fst 1 1/16	:24 :471 1:113 1:441	ⒻKy Oaks-G2	2 1 13 14 11½ 25	LeBlanc JO	121	b	*.80	82-15	BagofTunes1215LaPrvoyante1211½Coraggso121hd	No excuse	13
28Apr73- 8CD	fst 7f	:23 :454 1:103 1:234	ⒻLa Troienne 21k	5 3 14 15 11 1no	LeBlanc JO	121	b	*.20	88-16	La Prevoyante121hdOld Goldie1151½Coraggioso1182½	Lasted	8
7Apr73- 7Kee	sly 6f	:22 :451 :574 1:103	ⒻAlw 10000	3 8 32 2hd 1hd 13½	LeBlanc JO	124	b	*.20	89-21	LaPrvoyante1243½ALittleLovin1121DancingBnd1141	Handily	10
5Mar73- 5GP	fst 6f	:22 :442 1:084	ⒻAlw 8500	6 5 33 21½ 22 23	LeBlanc JO	122	b	*.20	97-07	BoldMemory1173LaPrvynte1222½OperFn107¾	Brushed start	8
11Nov72- 8GS	fst 1 1/16	:23 :462 1:114 1:472	ⒻGardenia 190k	5 1 15 18 18 11¾	LeBlanc JO	119	b	*.30	68-26	LaPrevoynte1191¾NorthBroadwy119hdFnTunng1191½	Driving	11
28Oct72- 6Lrl	sly 1 1/16	:23 :46 1:121 1:462	ⒻSelima 121k	2 2 1½ 15 110 114	LeBlanc JO	122	b	*.10	81-14	LaPrvoynte12214Naive1193FamousTale1193½	Much the best; Run on Selima-Futurity course	4
7Oct72- 7Bel	sly 1	:222 :453 1:104 1:372	ⒻFrizette 114k	8 1 13 15 15 12	LeBlanc JO	121	b	*.30	85-14	LaPrevynte1212CamAxe1212½FineTuning1212	Never headed	8
23Sep72- 7Bel	fst 7f	:222 :451 1:101 1:233	ⒻMatron 104k	4 1 2hd 11 19 17½	LeBlanc JO	119	b	*.20	89-13	LaPrvoyant1197½UpAbov1198½Corggoso119hd	Speed to spare	4
9Sep72- 7WO	sl 1 1/16	:232 :464 1:114 1:472	ⒻⓇPrin Elizabeth 24k	4 1 12½ 110 17 17½	LeBlanc JO	119	b	*.20	75-28	La Prevoyante1197½Cailey Jane1195Buh Buh Buh Bold1197	Much the best	8

25Aug72- 7Sar	gd 6f	:214 :451 1:104	ⒻSpinaway 58k	8 3 41 11½ 14 13	LeBlanc JO	120	b	*.40	92-08	LaPrvoyant1203PrincessDoubleday1201Behrm120nk	Handily	10
2Aug72- 7Sar	fst 6f	:222 :46 1:112	ⒻSchuylerville 29k	6 2 2hd 12 15 15½	LeBlanc JO	119	b	*1.90	89-14	LaPrvoyante1195½Sparkalark1163½SwetSop1161½	Ridden out	12
22Jly72- 7FE	fst 6½f	:223 :454 1:111 1:174	ⓇColin 12k	4 6 31½ 2hd 14 15	LeBlanc JO	121	b	*.55	90-14	LaPrevoyante1215ZacaSpirt114nkQun'sSplndour1174¼	Easily	10
9Jly72- 0BB	fst 6f	:231 :461 1:112	ⓇFleur de Lys 14k	1 2 12 15 15 19¾	LeBlanc JO	117	b	-	97-16	La Prevoyante1179¾First I Like112	Easily	2
	No wagering											
2Jly72- 7WO	fst 6f	:221 :461 1:111	ⒻMy Dear 12k	5 1 1hd 12 12 11¼	LeBlanc JO	112	b	*.45	89-17	LaPrevoyante1121¼LadyShooter11510SeaAria1092	Mild drive	7
10Jun72- 4WO	fm 5fⓉ	:221 :47 1:00	ⓇAlw 4000	2 2 2hd 2hd 1hd 13	LeBlanc JO	119	b	*.50	- -	La Prevoyante1193Queen's Splendour1223½Dr. Rowland12210		6
	Ridden out											
31May72- 2WO	gd 5½f	:23 :464 1:062	ⒻⓇMd Sp Wt	2 5 14 17 17 18½	LeBlanc JO	119	b	*.80e	88-22	LaPrevoyante1198½CaileyJane1191½NewProvider1191¼	Easily	9

Lakeville Miss

dkbbr. f. 1975, by Rainy Lake (Royal Charger)–Hew, by Blue Prince — **Lifetime record: 14 7 4 1 $371,582**

Own.– Randolph Weinsler
Br.– Randolph Weinsler (Ky)
Tr.– Jose Martin

1Jly78- 8Bel	fst 1½	:464 1:112 2:023 2:292	ⒻC C A Oaks-G1	2 3 36½ 2½ 1½ 16	Hernandez R	121		4.60	73-16	LakvilleMss1216Caesar'sWsh1214TmpstQn1215	Ridden out	5
11Jun78- 8Bel	fst 1⅛	:451 1:09 1:342 1:473	ⒻMother Goose-G1	8 5 58 35 2½ 22	Hernandez R	121		8.80	87-15	Caesr'sWsh1212LakvlleMss1211½TempstQueen121hd	Gamely	8
27May78- 8Bel	fst 1	:224 :45 1:094 1:352	ⒻAcorn-G1	5 5 56 2hd 21½ 21¾	Hernandez R	121		4.40	89-17	Tempest Queen1211¾Lakeville Miss121nkWhite Star Line1211¾		6
	Game try											
5May78- 8CD	gd 1 1/16	:24 :463 1:113 1:451	ⒻKy Oaks-G1	7 9 88¼ 73¾ 57 68¼	Hernandez R	121		3.50	74-15	WhiteStarLine1212Grnzn1212½BoldRndzvous1212¼	Slow early	11
15Apr78- 8Key	fst 7f	:234 :472 1:131 1:26	ⒻConstitution 58k	2 12 87½ 73½ 11½ 14	Hernandez R	121		*.50	79-25	LakevilleMiss1214Paradigmatic112¾LaNijinska1125	Easily	12
1Apr78- 8Pim	fst 6f	:233 :463 :584 1:12	ⒻFlirtation 32k	4 5 52½ 34 34 2¾	Hernandez R	119		*.40	85-19	Dance of the Grebe116¾LakevlleMiss1191½Marston's Mill1132		5
	Steadied											
19Nov77- 6Aqu	fst 1⅛	:471 1:114 1:38 1:503	ⒻDemoiselle-G2	2 6 44 32½ 24 26¾	Hernandez R	121		*.80	75-18	Caesar'sWish1166¾LakevillMss1212¾IslndKss1141¾	2nd best	7
22Oct77- 8Lrl	fst 1 1/16	:233 :464 1:12 1:452	ⒻSelima-G1	4 7 46½ 33 2½ 11	Hernandez R	122		*.50	86-16	Lakeville Miss1221L'Alezane1222¼ⒹLa Voyageuse1191¼		7
	Steadied,dr.											
1Oct77- 6Bel	fst 1	:233 :45 1:101 1:361	ⒻFrizette-G1	5 6 45½ 1½ 13 15	Hernandez R	119		*1.30	87-14	Lakeville Miss1195Misgivings1192Itsamaza119¾	Ridden out	8
21Sep77- 8Bel	my 7f	:23 :46 1:101 1:224	ⒻMatron-G1	5 5 84¾ 55 21 1nk	Hernandez R	119		2.60	88-21	Lakeville Miss119nkStub1196¾Akita119¾	Driving	10
5Sep77- 6Bel	fst 6½f	:223 :461 1:112 1:174	ⒻAstarita-G3	1 5 43½ 53 1hd 1¾	Hernandez R	112		5.90	87-17	LakvlleMss112¾Sherry Peppers1163¾Temperamental Pet112nk		6
	Driving											
26Aug77- 8Sar	fst 6f	:222 :454 1:104	ⒻSpinaway-G1	6 3 1hd 3½ 52 54¼	Hernandez R	119		9.80	82-15	Sherry Peppers119½Akita119noStub1192¾	Used early	8
1Aug77- 8Sar	fst 6f	:223 :461 1:114	ⒻSchuylerville-G3	4 7 73½ 63¼ 43½ 3nk	Hernandez R	114		18.80	81-20	L'Alezane121noAkita121nkLakevilleMss1143½	Strong finish	8
30Jun77- 4Bel	fst 5½f	:23 :47 :593 1:061	ⒻMd 25000	5 7 33 22 1½ 14	Hernandez R	119		2.40	84-19	Lakeville Miss1194Irish Rising1126¾Hypsipyle119¾	Easily	9

Late Bloomer

b. f. 1974, by Stage Door Johnny (Prince John)–Dunce Cap II, by Tom Fool — **Lifetime record: 24 11 5 5 $512,040**

Own.– Greentree Stable
Br.– Greentree Stud Inc (Ky)
Tr.– John M. Gaver Jr

28Jly79- 8Bel	fm 1¼Ⓣ	:491 1:13 1:373 2:013	3↑ⒻSheepshead Bay H-G2	4 7 711 84¼ 41 2no	Velasquez J	123		4.50	86-09	Terpsichorist117noLate Bloomer1232¾Warfever110nk	Missed	10
23Jun79- 8Bel	fm 1 1/16Ⓣ	:234 :472 1:104 1:411	3↑ⒻNew York H-G3	4 4 42½ 64 64 51½	Velasquez J	124		*.80	88-07	LaSoufriere111½NavajoPrincss118hdEmrldHll120¾	No excuse	8
3Jun79- 6Bel	sly 1¼	:494 1:14 1:391 2:041	3↑ Sar Cup H 109k	6 3 31½ 21 2hd 2no	Velasquez J	119		1.20	76-30	Waya125noLate Bloomer1194¾Sten1101¼	Missed	6
21Apr79-11Hia	fst 1⅛	:464 1:113 1:371 1:502	3↑ⒻBlack Helen H-G2	3 4 38 26 2hd 1½	Velasquez J	123		*.20	80-22	LateBloomr123½TimeforPlesur11510Exctbl12216	Ridden out	5
11Apr79- 9OP	my 1 70	:232 :464 1:121 1:43	4↑ⒻApple Blossom H-G2	5 7 99¾ 77¾ 54½ 42¾	Velasquez J	124		*.50	78-27	MissBaja1131¾Kit'sDouble114noNavajoPrincss1211	No rally	10
30Mar79- 9Hia	fst 7f	:231 :461 1:112 1:241	4↑ⒻAlw 13000	5 7 63½ 55¼ 1hd 17½	Velasquez J	114		*.40	82-23	LateBloomer1147½HuggleDuggle114noIrishAgate1223½	Easily	7
9Oct78- 8Bel	fst 1¼	:49 1:131 1:374 2:021	3↑ⒻBeldame-G1	3 3 21½ 2½ 1hd 11¼	Velasquez J	123		*.90	89-15	LateBlmr1231½PearlNcklace1234CmLdLaurie12312	Handily	4
23Sep78- 8Bel	fst 1⅛	:462 1:094 1:343 1:47	3↑ⒻRuffian H-G1	5 7 64½ 45 2hd 11½	Velasquez J	122		3.10	92-15	LateBlmr1221½PearlNecklc1244TmpstQueen1172½	Ridden out	9
3Sep78- 9Del	fst 1¼	:483 1:13 1:371 2:021	3↑ⒻDelaware H-G1	7 5 43½ 41¼ 1hd 1no	Velasquez J	119		*2.30	91-12	LateBlmr119noDottie'sDoll1171CmLaudLaurie119no	Driving	9
15Jly78- 8Bel	gd 1¼Ⓣ	:471 1:113 1:354 2:01	3↑ⒻSheepshead Bay H-G2	8 10 1017 89½ 55 1hd	Velasquez J	118		*2.10	89-11	Late Bloomer118hdWaya115nkPearl Necklace1241¼	Driving	11
24Jun78- 8Bel	fm 1 1/16Ⓣ	:243 :474 1:11 1:411	3↑ⒻNew York H (Div 2)-G3	5 6 54 53½ 4¾ 12¾	Velasquez J	115		2.50	90-09	Late Bloomer1152¾Island Kiss1081½Fia1131½	Drew clear	9
30May78- 8Bel	fm 1 1/16Ⓣ	:241 :473 1:111 1:413	3↑ⒻGarden City H 58k	5 4 54 53½ 21½ 1½	Velasquez J	113		*1.90	88-10	LateBlmr113½PearlNcklc1212HugglDuggl114hd	Ridden out	11
10May78- 8Aqu	gd 1	:24 :47 1:12 1:374	4↑ⒻHandicap 25000	4 3 32 3½ 11 12	Maple E	115		*.80	77-19	ⒹLateBloomer1152Nanticious1135GypsyClown113no	Bore in	5
	Disqualified and placed second											
8Apr78- 9GP	fm 1 1/16Ⓣ	:224 :453 1:091 1:41	3↑ⒻOrchid H-G3	10 4 47½ 42½ 52¼ 2½	Maple E	113		3.20	95-03	TimeforPleasure115½LateBloomr113nkRichSoil116½	Gamely	11
15Mar78- 9GP	fm 1Ⓣ	:233 :47 1:11 1:353	3↑ⒻSuwannee River H 32k	3 5 64½ 64¼ 42¼ 3½	Maple E	113		4.80	91-11	Len'sDetermined119nkWhataSummr122nkLtBlmr1131	Rallied	9
3Mar78- 7Hia	sly 6f	:223 :452 1:091	4↑ⒻAlw 12000	8 2 54¾ 45½ 43½ 34	Maple E	114		*1.90	93-16	Gladiolus1141Dear Paris1123Late Bloomer1141½	Fair try	8
	Previously trained by John M. Gaver											
15Oct77- 2Bel	sly 1 1/16⊗	:241 :482 1:133 1:444	3↑ⒻAlw 15000	7 2 21½ 2hd 12½ 14½	Cauthen S	119		*2.00	78-17	LatBloomr1194½AlphaDelta1193½EqulHonor114¾	Ridden out	7
4Oct77- 5Bel	yl 1 1/16Ⓣ	:244 :491 1:143 1:453	3↑ⒻAlw 13000	2 4 54 31 12½ 14	Cauthen S	114		*2.20	68-28	Late Bloomer1144La Fabelle1147¾Swiss114nk	Handily	8
2Sep77- 7Bel	fst 7f	:23 :461 1:103 1:231	3↑ⒻAlw 11000	4 6 56 46½ 47½ 36¾	Cauthen S	119		*1.80	79-21	CarryItHigh1131¾MenageaTrois1155LateBloomer118nk	Wide	8
23Aug77- 9Sar	fst 7f	:223 :454 1:104 1:232	3↑ⒻMd Sp Wt	9 2 65 73¼ 3½ 13¾	Cauthen S	117		*1.20	88-13	LateBloomr1173¾Misconduct1172¼ConGame117¾	Ridden out	12
4Aug77- 1Sar	fst 6f	:22 :451 1:10	3↑ⒻMd Sp Wt	11 2 74½ 118¼ 78½ 34	Gonzalez B	117		4.80	86-13	MenageaTrois1173¼ConGame117¾LateBlmr117hd	Closed well	14
25Sep76- 4Bel	fst 6f	:222 :452 1:102	ⒻMd Sp Wt	5 3 55½ 47 33½ 32¼	Gustines H	119		2.90	88-12	SmileEvenThrough1192¼Flying Buttress119hdLate Blmr1192½		7
	Rallied											
11Sep76- 3Bel	fst 6f	:223 :46 1:11	ⒻMd Sp Wt	1 2 3nk 1hd 1½ 2½	Gustines H	119		4.70	86-14	Splendid Size119½Late Bloomer119½Kennelot1191¼	Gamely	11
17Aug76- 1Sar	fst 6f	:23 :47 1:113	ⒻMd Sp Wt	6 5 52½ 43½ 46½ 49	Gustines H	119		*2.20	73-14	Shufleur1193½RomanGroundr1191½FlyngAbov1194	No response	7

Life's Illusion

b. f. 1971, by Mystic II (Relic)–Dark Mile, by Black Tarquin — **Lifetime record: 34 13 6 1 $96,828**

Own.– Mrs Virginia G. Van Alen
Br.– Virginia Guest (Md)
Tr.– P.R. Fout

25Aug77- 6Sar	fm 2⅜	S'Chase 4:184	4↑ NY Turf Writers Cup H 21k	3 7 624 86 714 714¾	Quanbeck A Jr	163		*1.20	- -	HappyIntellectual152¾NvlPrson143hdCsmyor1505½	Bid,tired	8
5Aug77- 6Sar	fm 2 1/16	S'Chase 3:441	4↑ Lovely Night H 21k	3 2 15 15 13 13¼	Quanbeck A Jr	160		*1.50	- -	Life'sIllusion1603¼Casamyor149½HppyIntllctul1543	Easily	6
7Jly77- 4Bel	fm 2	S'Chase 3:38	4↑ Handicap 10000	6 1 116 114 14 14½	Quanbeck A Jr	157		4.50	- -	Life's Magic1574½Casamayor149¾Down First1385	Easily	7
22Jun77- 5Mth	fm *2¼	S'Chase 4:224	4↑ Midsummer H 16k	2 1 3nk - - -	Fout DP	158		4.80	- -	TallAwrd142½BreakngDawn1391¼Casamayor1502	Left course	8
4Jun77- 7Fai	hd *2½	S'Chase 5:051	4↑ Handicap 10000	5 3 - - - -	Fout DP	157		5.10	- -	TanJay1544¾HappyIntellectual1603BrkngDwn14020	Pulled up	5
30May77- 8Fai	hd *1 5/16Ⓣ	2:133	3↑ Alw 1000	4 6 620 52¾ 42¾ 47	Fout DP3	138		*1.20	- -	Germanicus1531Sun Meeting1465½Plumsted146½	No rally	8
27Nov76- 4Cam	fm 2¾	S'Chase 5:122	4↑ Colonial Cup 100k	12 1 14 2½ 76¼ 710	Fout DP7	150		-	- -	GrandCnyon162½FireControl1622½Crag'sCornr160no	Used up	16
28Sep76- 4Mth	fm *2¼	S'Chase 4:262	4↑ Midsummer H 15k	1 2 2½ 12½ 13 13¾	Skiffington T Jr	160		1.90	- -	Life's Illusion1603¾Montpellier139noCrag's Corner1433½		6
	Unruly,driving											
18Sep76- 7Fai	fm *2½	S'Chase 4:571	4↑ Grand National H 15k	7 4 52 1½ 32 36¼	Skiffington T Jr	161		2.80	- -	StraightandTrue1546¼HappyIntellectual157hdLfe'sIllusn1612¾		7
	Tired											
26Aug76- 6Sar	fm 2⅜	S'Chase 4:192	4↑ NY Turf Writers Cup H 22k	6 2 2½ 11½ 2½ 2¾	Skiffington T Jr	160		*1.50	- -	Happy Intellectual152¾Life's Illusn1602½StraightandTrue155½		7
	Gamely											

17Jly76- 7Del fm *2⅜ S'Chase 4:34² 4♦ Indian River 13k 8 - - - - - Fout DP 160 *1.60 -- StraightandTrue151²¾Crag'sCorner136²CloverOver135⁴ Fell 8
25Jun76- 4Del fm *2¹⁄₁₆ S'Chase 3:56⁴ 4♦ Handicap 8000 1 2 1¹ 1⁴ 11½ 1² Fout DP 156 3.20 -- Life'sIllusion156²Straight and True152⁷ [DH]Deux Coup145 9
Ridden out
16Jun76- 7Bel fm 1¹⁄₁₆ :23¹:46² 1:10³1:41¹ 3♦ ⒻAlw 12000 7 6 7³½ 7⁶¾ 7⁸ 7⁹½ Maple E 119 10.10 85-11 StudentLeadr115⁴½Fiddling122⅔PlaceDuphn115¹½ No factor 8
6Jun76- 7Bel gd 1¹⁄₁₆ :24¹:48² 1:13²1:46³ 4♦ Alw 6500 1 6 5³ 5³¾ 4⁶ 2² Pilar H 107 3.00 69-29 PimmsCup112²Lif'sIlluson107²BlznWondr112⁶ Bobbled start 6
15May76- 4Mal hd *2 Handicap 7500 4 5 1² - - - Fishback J 158 -- -- [DH]Castlebar II142[DH D]Tall Award145⁴Juggernaut II143⁸ 5
Left course
8May76- 6Fai fm *2⅛ S'Chase 4:09⁴ 4♦ Handicap 7500 4 1 1³ 1⁴ 2ʰᵈ 21½ Fishback J 158 - -- LondonGrove148¹³Life'sIllusion158⁴½AgesAgo147³³ Tired 5
15Nov75- 4Cam fm 2⅝ S'Chase 5:30¹ 4♦ Colonial Cup 50k 2 15 13⁶½ 14¹⁹ 10⁴½ 8²⁴ Quanbeck A Jr 148 -e -- Cafe Prince160³Augustus Bay162½Soothsayer162½ Outrun 18
Previously raced in name of Virginia Guest
25Oct75- 6FH sf *2⅝ S'Chase 4:45 4♦ Handicap 10000 2 3 2⁴ 21½ 1½ 11½ Quanbeck A Jr 151 -e -- Life'sIllusion151¹½CafePrince160½TallAward150½ Driving 8
1Oct75- 7Lig yl *7f Ⓣ 1:35² 3♦ Alw 2500 7 7 107¾ 77⅜ 42¼ 1ʰᵈ Quanbeck A Jr 145 -- -- Life'sIllusion145ʰᵈTor'sRib145ⁿᵏRdGrsshoppr149½ Driving 19
13Sep75- 7Fai fm *2⅝ S'Chase 5:02 4♦ Grand National H 12k 6 4 6⁶ 6¹ 6⁶ 6¹⁷ Quanbeck A Jr 148 2.90e -- AugustusBay151¹GranKan155¹½HppyIntllctul146⁵ No threat 9
21Aug75- 4Sar fm 2⅜ S'Chase 4:20¹ 4♦ NY Turf Writers Cup H 22k 5 5 4² 1⁵ 11½ 1ⁿᵏ Quanbeck A Jr 148 2.50e -- Life'sIllusion145ⁿᵏSoothsayer160½ArcticJoe148⁵½ Driving 8
1Aug75- 6Sar fm 2¹⁄₁₆ S'Chase 3:40¹ 4♦ Lovely Night H 22k 8 1 1⁶ 1⁶ 1³ 1½ Quanbeck A Jr 143 *1.80e -- Life'sIllusion143½GranKn158¹⁰Anthropologst138⁸¾ Driving 8
24Jun75- 4Mth fm *2⅛ S'Chase 4:22¹ 4♦ Midsummer H 16k 5 3 34½ 9¹⁹ - - Quanbeck A Jr 145 4.30e -- Chrisaway148¹⁰ArcticJo154ⁿᵏJzbll'sMn150⁴ Saddle slipped 9
17May75- 4Mal fm *2 S'Chase 3:53² 4♦ Handicap 6000 6 2 1² 12½ 1² 1³ Quanbeck A Jr 148 - -- Life'sIllusion148³CastlebarII155⁴Shameca142⁸ Ridden out 6
3May75- 3War fm *2 S'Chase 4:36 4♦ Handicap 10000 5 1 11½ 1⁴ 21½ 2⁵ Quanbeck A Jr 144 - -- Jezabell'sMan143⁵Life'sIllusion144⁸BlueShore154³ Tired 7
19Apr75- 4Clm fm *2 S'Chase 3:43¹ 4♦ Handicap 10000 7 2 1⁸ 1¹⁰ 1¹⁵ 1¹² Quanbeck A Jr 138 - -- Life'sIllusion138¹²Afilador145½AlvaroII147⁸ Ridden out 7
29Mar75- 2Cam fm 7f Ⓣ 1:33² 3♦ Md Sp Wt 4 6 5³ 4³ 2½ 1² Quanbeck A Jr 145 - -- Life's Illusion145²Paulgail133¹Kasai150³ Driving 9
22Mar75- 4Sar gd *1⅞ S'Chase 3:44 4♦ Handicap 7500 1 5 2½ 2ʰᵈ 41½ 6⁵ Quanbeck A Jr 142 - -- Tall Award155½Ballet Master148³Sun Sign144¹ Tired 7
16Dec74- 7Aqu sly 1⅛ :49 1:14²1:38²1:50⁴ 3♦ Alw 15000 8 6 68½ 7¹⁸ 8²² 7²² Smith RC 109 13.90 59-21 All Our Hopes117¹½Dicey117²Crag's Corner117⁶ Outrun 8
16Nov74- 2Cam fm *2 S'Chase 3:46² Handicap 5000 6 3 1½ 1ʰᵈ 2ʰᵈ 1ʰᵈ Quanbeck A Jr 142 b -- Life'sIllusion142ʰᵈEarlCardigan144⁶Fortssmo152²½ Just up 8
2Oct74- 1Lig sf *1⅝ S'Chase 3:35² 3♦ Md Sp Wt 3 - - - - 1⁶ Quanbeck A Jr 130 - -- Life'sIllusion130⁶CountyFrost133⁴SunMeeting148½ Handily 14
Further race positions unavailable due to weather conditions
21Sep74- 2Mid fm *1⅞ S'Chase 3:36⁴ 3♦ Md Sp Wt 4 5 2² 32½ 32¼ 2² Quanbeck A Jr 136 -e -- Muller143²Life's Illusion136½Dunshaughlin153³ Sharp 14
7Sep74- 5Fai fm *1¾ S'Chase 3:31⁴ 3♦ Md Sp Wt 12 9 75¾ 62¾ 41¾ 2³ Quanbeck A Jr 132 8.00f -- Fortissimo140³Life'sIllusion132¹Gumersindo153²½ Gamely 14
19Sep74- 4Sar gd 1⅝ S'Chase 2:57² 3♦ Md Sp Wt 3 7 6⁷ 73⁴ 64⁸ 44⁷ Quanbeck A 135 16.10 -- MachuPicchu138¹⁵UpLikeThunder138²²Darnley138¹⁰ Rallied 7

Little Current

ch. c. 1971, by Sea–Bird (Dan Cupid)–Luiana, by My Babu
Own.– Darby Dan Farm
Br.– John W. Galbreath (Ky)
Tr.– T.L. Rondinello
Lifetime record: 16 4 3 1 $354,704

31Aug74- 8Bel sf 1½ Ⓣ :49 1:15³2:08⁴2:35 Lawrence Realizatn-G2 1 4 5⁵ 6¹¹ 6¹³ 6¹⁹ Rivera MA 126 *.60 30-51 Prod117³½PrinceofReason117¹½TheScotsmn117ⁿᵏ No excuse 7
17Aug74- 8Sar sly 1¼ :47³1:12 1:38²2:05¹ Travers-G1 8 10 9¹³ 76¼ 4⁴ 2ʰᵈ Rivera MA 126 *1.00 79-16 Holding Pattern121ʰᵈLittle Current126⁴Chris Evert121²¼ 11
Just missed
3Aug74- 8Mth fst 1⅛ :46³1:10³1:36¹1:49⁴ Mth Inv'l H-G1 6 9 9¹⁸ 8¹³ 34¼ 2ⁿᵒ Rivera MA 127 *1.00 91-11 Holding Pattern117ⁿᵒLittle Current127³Better Arbitor119¾ 10
Just missed
8Jun74- 8Bel fst 1½ :49³1:14 2:04¹2:29¹ Belmont-G1 2 8 8¹² 4⁵ 1¹ 1⁷ Rivera MA 126 *1.50 74-11 LittleCurrent126⁷JollyJohu126ⁿᵒCannonade126³ Drew clear 9
18May74- 8Pim gd 1³⁄₁₆ :47 1:10³1:36²1:54³ Preakness-G1 2 12 12¹¹ 10⁵ 3¹ 1⁷ Rivera MA 126 13.10 97-09 LittleCurrent126⁷NeapolitnWy126¹Cnnond126² Steady drive 13
4May74- 8CD fst 1¼ :46³1:11⁴1:38³2:04 Ky Derby-G1 10 23 21²² 17¹⁸ 7¹³ 56¼ Ussery R 126 22.60 70-15 Cannonade126²¼HudsonCounty126³¼Agitate126² Closed gap 23
25Apr74- 6Kee fst 1⅛ :46³1:10³1:36³1:49¹ Blue Grass-G1 7 13 12¹³ 4³ 42¼ 44¼ Rivera MA 114 5.40 87-15 Judger123⁴BigLatch117ʰᵈGold and Myrrh114ʰᵈ Rallied 14
30Mar74- 9Hia fst 1⅛ :47²1:11 1:36²1:49 Flamingo-G1 2 9 9¹⁰ 69½ 77¾ 44¼ Cordero A Jr 122 6.30e 82-16 Bushongo122²Hasty Flyer122¹Judger121⁵ Lacked room 10
20Mar74- 9Hia fst 1⅛ :46 1:10¹1:36 1:49¹ Everglades-G2 9 9 9¹² 6⁹ 3¹ 1² Cordero A Jr 113 3.50 86-17 Little Current113½Bushongo112ʰᵈHasty Flyer117² Driving 11
4Mar74- 9GP fst 1⅛ :46²1:11¹1:36¹1:49 Florida Derby-G1 12 14 15²³ 13¹¹ 7¹¹ 56¾ Cordero A Jr 118 11.80 82-11 Judger118³Cannonade122⁵Buck's Bid118ⁿᵏ Bumped 16
20Feb74- 9GP fst 1¹⁄₁₆ :23 :45³1:09⁴1:42² Fountain of Youth-G3 1 14 14²⁵ 11¹⁷ 11¹¹ 64¼ Cordero A Jr 113 8.70 85-18 GreenGambados112¾Judger115²½Eric'sChamp112½ Stride late 15
6Feb74- 9GP fst 7f :22¹:44³1:09³1:22² Hutcheson-G3 6 13 13¹⁷ 12¹⁶ 75¼ 42¾ Cordero A Jr 112 21.10 89-16 Frankie Adams114²³[DH]Judger110[DH]Training Table113ʰᵈ 13
Belated rally
5Dec73- 3Aqu fst 7f :22⁴:45³1:10 1:22³ Md Sp Wt 11 2 107½ 64¾ 3½ 11¾ Cordero A Jr 122 *1.70 88-11 LittleCurrnt121¹½Rube the Great122²SplittingHeadache122ʰᵈ 12
Drew out
24Nov73- 2Aqu fst 6f :22²:45³ 1:11 ©Md Sp Wt 10 11 87½ 6⁷ 4⁵ 22¾ Cordero A Jr 122 5.40 85-13 Nile Delta122²½Little Current122⁴Whoa Boy122¹ Bore in 14
8Aug73- 2Sar fst 5½f :22³:46²:59²1:06¹ ©Md Sp Wt 1 5 21½ 2² 44½ 54¾ Cordero A Jr 119 b *2.20 81-13 Ding Dong Bell119ⁿᵏLea's Pass119ⁿᵏBuck Hill119¹¼ Tired 9
21Jly73- 2Aqu fst 6f :23 :46¹ 1:11² ©Md Sp Wt 4 9 1½ 11½ 1¹ 3½ Cordero A Jr 118 b 3.00 85-14 Monsieur Lafitte118¹Third Cavalry118ⁿᵒLittle Current118ⁿᵏ 10
Weakened

Mac Diarmida

dkbbr. c. 1975, by Minnesota Mac (Rough'n Tumble)–Flying Tammie, by Tim Tam
Own.– J.M. Torsney
Br.– John H. Hartigan (Fla)
Tr.– Flint Schulhofer
Lifetime record: 16 12 0 2 $503,184

4Nov78- 8Lrl fm 1½ Ⓣ :50 1:14¹2:03³2:27 3♦ D C Int'l-G1 7 6 53½ 4² 2ʰᵈ 1ʰᵈ Cruguet J 120 4.90 84-16 Mac Diarmida120ʰᵈTiller127³Waya124¹½ Poor start 8
22Oct78- 7WO fm 1⅝ Ⓣ :49⁴1:39¹ 2:41¹ 3♦ Can Int'l-G1 8 3 2²½ 2½ 1¹ 1¹ Cruguet J 118 *1.25 94-05 Mac Diarmida118¹Dom Alaric126½Amazer115²¼ Drew clear 10
7Oct78- 8Bel yl 1⅜ Ⓣ :49²1:14 1:38²2:16¹ 3♦ Man o' War-G1 5 2 2½ 1¹ 2½ 34½ Cruguet J 121 2.00 76-19 Waya124¹½Tiller126²½Mac Diarmida121⁴ Used reaching lead 5
17Oct78- 8Bel gd 1⅜ Ⓣ :48³1:13¹2:01²2:27¹ Lawrence Realizatn-G2 7 2 2¹ 2½ 1½ 13½ Cruguet J 123 *.50 88-11 MacDiarmida123³½NatveCourier114⁶½Robn'sSong114³ Easily 9
4Sep78- 8AP fm 1¼ Ⓣ :48⁴1:14²2:05 2:29⁴ Secretariat-G2 1 4 3½ 1¹ 1¹ 1³ Cruguet J 126 *.60 90-10 MacDiarmda120³AprilAxe120⁴½TheLiberalMmbr114⁴¼ In hand 11
29Jly78- 8Bel fm 1 Ⓣ :23³:46 1:10³1:41 Lexington H-G2 4 4 3³ 2² 2ʰᵈ 1ʰᵈ Cruguet J 126 *1.00 91-11 MacDiarmda120³John Henry112⁴½Ashikaga110ʰᵈ In time 9
16Jly78- 9Del fm 1¹⁄₁₆ Ⓣ :23⁴:48 1:13³1:46⁴ Leonard Richards-G3 7 7 5⁶ 3¹½ 1½ 1³ Cruguet J 122 *.30 70-30 MacDiarmda122³Prince Misko122½StrngProposl113¹½ Handily 10
29May78- 8Mth sf 1 Ⓣ :24⁴:49³ 1:15³1:42¹ Long Branch-G3 6 6 4⁶ 3ⁿᵏ 1³ 1⁵ Cruguet J 124 *.50 64-36 MacDrmida124⁵NoonTimeSpender118²½MorningFrolic116ⁿᵒ 8
In hand
22May78- 8Mth fm 1⅛ Ⓣ :24³:48 1:13¹1:38⁴ 3♦ Alw 15000 9 8 5⁵ 22½ 1ʰᵈ 13½ Cruguet J 122 *.60 81-19 Mac Diarmida122³½Prince Misko117⁴Silent Cal114⁵ Handily 9
22Apr78- 9GP fm 1¹⁄₁₆ Ⓣ :23¹:47 1:11 1:41² Golden Grass H 32k 9 6 6³ 52½ 1¹ 13½ Cruguet J 121 *1.50 94-08 MacDiarmida121³½DoubleAl118¹½PrinceMisko118ⁿᵏ Handily 9
17Mar78- 5GP fm *1¹⁄₁₆ Ⓣ 1:45¹ Alw 8500 5 5 43½ 3¹ 11½ 1² Cruguet J 112 *.70 81-22 Mac Diarmida112²Rough Sea114³½Fidelius114¹¹ Easily 7
15Feb78- 7Hia fm *1⅛ Ⓣ 1:49¹ Alw 9000 3 4 41½ 2² 1⁴ 12½ Cruguet J 114 *.90 89-16 Mac Drmida114²½HurricaneDennis114⁴ContinentalCousin117² 10
Handily
1Feb78- 3Hia fst 1⅛ 1:49 Md Sp Wt 2 8 6⁵ 52½ 1ʰᵈ 1⁵ Cruguet J 120 5.80 90-05 MacDrmida120⁵FreetheSpirit120³½NovelNotion120² Handily 10
18Jan78- 3Hia fst 6f :22 :45 1:09² Md Sp Wt 7 9 86½ 8¹¹ 7¹¹ 8¹⁵ Fell J 120 5.20 81-13 GrayWillowsAce120²WindThmUp120²SilntSunrise120⁴ Outrun 12
15Oct77- 3Bel sly 6f :23 :46² 1:10³ Md Sp Wt 8 4 43½ 4⁷ 49½ 6¹⁵ Adams L 122 3.30 74-17 Shindig122⁴½Bold Voyager122⁸Reason Not122²¼ Tired 9
10Oct77- 3Bel fst 6f :22¹:46¹ 1:12² ©Md Sp Wt 10 7 46½ 4⁶ 3³ 3² Adams L 122 18.80 78-14 CloudForest122ʰᵈCalligraphy122²MacDiarmida122⁴ Good try 12

Martie's Anger

b. g. 1975, by Spring Double (Double Jay)–Martie's Mad, by Martins Rullah — **Lifetime record: 49 15 8 9 $196,990**

Own.– W.L. Pape
Br.– Pape & Sheppard (Pa)
Tr.– Jonathan E. Sheppard

17Sep83- 5Lig	fm *2½	S'Chase	5:194 4↑	Int'l Gold Cup 30k	1 3 2½ 727 - -	Cushman J	149		-	--	SugarBee1451FabulousTim1494SpoutngCrqu1425	Outrun,eased	7
14Sep83- 6Lig	fm *7fⓉ		1:324 3↑	Alw 1000	10 1173 74½ 63 68	Cushman J	144		-	--	Joe Mac142½Mysterious Arthur1511½Mc Adam1422½		12
28May83- 5Pro	gd *3	Hurdles	5:583 4↑	Hard Scuffle H 30k	2 3 47½ - - -	Houghton B	151		-	--	Double Reefed1541¾Census1484The Hall of Famer1405	Eased	7
30Apr83- 5Fx	fm *2¼	S'Chase	4:061 3↑	Alw 10000	6 4 44¼ 1hd 2nk 22½	Cushman J	154		-	--	StoneyCreekBoy1382½Martie'sAnger154nkBalkanChief142¾		6
16Apr83- 6SoP	fm *1Ⓣ		1:45 3↑	Alw 1000	5 9 86½ 52 56¾ 56	Cushman J	142		-	--	Caraquet142¾Mc Adam142nkNo Picnic1423		10
2Apr83- 5Cam	gd *2⅛	S'Chase	4:223 4↑	Carolina Cup H 16k	2 4 48½ 411 43¼ 38¾	Stickley M	149		-	--	Hypertrophic1356Turtle Head1442¾Martie's Anger14910		4
22Jly81- 8Del	fm 5fⓉ	:222 :461	:583 3↑	Alw 11000	2 7 711 712 711 77½	Dufton E	117	b	6.40e	86-15	Galaxy Road112½ⒹAmbitious Ruler1121½Never Rome1172½		8
	Previously trained by Tim Forster												
17Mar81♦ Cheltenham(GB)	hy 2LH		4:112 5↑	Champion Hurdle Stk87500	11	Davies BR	168		100.00		Sea Pigeon1681½Pollardstown168nkDaring Run1687	Progress from 5th,bid 6th,weakened 2 out	13
26Feb81♦ Wincanton(GB)	yl 2RH		3:482 5↑	Kingwell Pattern Hurdle Stk11500	514	Davies BR	156		25.00		Jugador161hdGay George166hdHeighlin1664	Chased leader from third last,weakened approaching last	11
	Previously trained by Jonathan Sheppard												
16Nov80- 4Cam	fm 2¾	S'Chase	5:322 4↑	Colonial Cup Int 50k	2 5 32½ 1¾ 1nk 3½	Quanbeck A Jr	160		-	--	Sailor'sClue151noCorribChieftain162½Martie'sAnger1601¼		9
4Nov80- 8Aqu	sf 1⅜Ⓣ	:51 1:18 1:44	2:233 3↑	Knickrbckr H (Div 2)-G3	5 2 21 1hd 2hd 45	Hernandez R	114	b	5.90	48-43	LobsangII1113MatchtheHatch1152KingCrimson111no	Weakened	7
10Oct80- 6Bel	fm 2⅝	S'Chase	4:544 4↑	Temple Gwathmey H 43k	3 1 2hd 2½ 2hd 21½	Quanbeck A Jr	158		4.20e	--	LeapingFrog1481½Martie'sAnger1581½BlueNrco1331½	Bobbled	7
13Sep80- 4Lig	hd *2½	S'Chase	5:041 4↑	Gold Cup H 30k	2 2 32¾ 34 11 11	Quanbeck A Jr	156		-	--	Martie's Anger1561Leaping Frog1506Running Comment1448		5
14Aug80- 6Sar	fm 2⅜	S'Chase	4:141 4↑	NY Turf Writers H 43k	3 6 610 39 44 45¾	Quanbeck A Jr	159		1.20e	--	Zaccio1571¼Running Comment1422¼Leaping Frog1522¼		7
1Aug80- 6Sar	gd 2 1/16	S'Chase	3:451 4↑	Lovely Night H 43k	1 3 1½ 1½ 1½ 21¾	Quanbeck A Jr	160		1.60e	--	Zaccio1551¾Martie'sAnger1601¾LeapingFrog1531¼	Bothered	8
3Jly80- 8Bel	fm 1½Ⓣ	:50 1:16 2:054	2:303 3↑	Handicap 25000	8 4 41½ 13 1½ 11½	Hernandez R	124	b	*.90e	71-24	Martie'sAngr1241½PopularHero1156McAdam118¾	Ridden out	9
12Jun80- 6Atl	fm *1 1/16Ⓣ	:243 :494 1:133	1:46 3↑	Alw 8000	4 3 3nk 12½ 12½ 12	Dufton E	114	b	*1.30	87-13	Martie's Anger1142Millden1142½Second Paw1144	Driving	6
24May80- 5Pro	gd *3	S'Chase	5:514 4↑	Hard Scuffle 20k	3 1 1½ 1½ 11 11¼	Quanbeck A Jr	151		-	--	Martie's Anger1511¼Zaccio1405Leaping Frog15616	Driving	5
17May80- 4Mal	fm *2	S'Chase	3:44 4↑	National Hunt Cup 7.5k	3 1 1½ 11 1nk 1nk	Quanbeck A Jr	159		-	--	Martie's Anger159nkObstacle147¾Popular Hero14512		4
27Apr80- 4Lex	yl *2½	S'Chase	5:121 4↑	Pillar 17k	3 - - - - -	Quanbeck A Jr	160		-	--	Zacco148hdDddyDumplng15018Schollr15412	Refused to break	5
12Apr80- 3SoP	fm *2¼	S'Chase	4:211 4↑	Sandhills Cup 15k	1 2 2nk 21 4¾ 21	Quanbeck A Jr	158		-e	--	Archange d'Or1431Martie's Anger158noZaccio155¾	Sharp	7
5Apr80- 3AtH	fm *2	S'Chase	3:501 4↑	Atlanta Cup 15k	1 3 38 21 2½ 2no	Quanbeck A Jr	159		-	--	Winigo139noMartie's Anger1591½Archange d'Or140	Sharp	3
29Mar80- 4Cam	gd *2⅛	S'Chase	4:104 4↑	Handicap 12500	3 7 79 711 46½ 48½	Quanbeck A Jr	160		-	--	Zaccio1526Popular Hero1441Tan Jay1581½	No menace	7
18Nov79- 4Cam	fm 2¾	S'Chase	5:214 4↑	Colonial Cup 50k	4 6 65 32 3½ 1½	Quanbeck A Jr	151		-	--	Martie'sAnger151½LeapingFrog1621¼Quixotic1511¼	Driving	9
27Oct79- 5FH	gd *2 5/16	S'Chase	5:082 4↑	Handicap 12000	6 4 33 21 3½ 2½	Quanbeck A Jr	152		-	--	Parson'sWaiting140½Mrt'sAngr152¾DownFrst15515	Sharp try	6
12Oct79- 6Bel	sf 2⅝	S'Chase	5:12 4↑	Temple Gwathmey H 36k	3 7 67½ 59½ 310 313¼	Quanbeck A Jr	152		*.90e	--	DownFirst14713Parson'sWatng137nkMrt'sAngr1523½	Mild bid	7
20Sep79- 8Med	fm 1 1/16Ⓣ	:231 :464 1:102	1:42 3↑	Alw 16000	8 8 813 76¾ 45 11½	Hernandez R	122	b	*2.70	92-05	Martie'sAnger1221½AgateBay113½Mr.KnowItAll112½	Driving	9
27Aug79- 2Sar	sf 1 1/16Ⓣ	:234 :481 1:134	1:46 3↑	Alw 17000	1 6 52½ 42 1½ 16	Hernandez R	117	b	20.60	67-29	Mrtie'sAngr1176Slammer1172¾NorthernTrt1121	Ridden out	10
20Aug79- 1Sar	gd 1½Ⓣ	:49 1:132 2:041	2:291 3↑	Alw 17000	4 3 35 45 33 36½	Venezia M	117	b	10.30	--	BeauJohnny117½Mr.Justice1176Mrtie'sAngr1178¼	Weakened	8
3Aug79- 6Sar	fm 2 1/16	S'Chase	3:411 4↑	Lovely Night H 21k	2 5 55½ 33 32 36½	Quanbeck A Jr	155		*.40e	--	CfePrince1642¾LeapingFrog1613¾Marti'sAngr1555	Weakened	7
13Jly79- 3Del	fm *2¼	S'Chase	4:162 4↑	Handicap 10000	5 3 36 24 22 11¼	Quanbeck A Jr	152		4.10	--	Martie'sAngr1521¼DeuxCoup159½StraightndTru1457	Driving	5
7Jly79- 1Atl	fst 6f	:223 :461	1:113 3↑	Alw 6500	3 6 815 813 813 716	Walford J	120	b	5.00	68-19	Tom's Luck1205Capt. Ridiculous1142Satan's Reign1162		8
	Altered course												
26May79- 2Pro	fm *2	S'Chase	3:314 4↑	Alw 15000	2 4 41 1nk 11 1½	Quanbeck A Jr	155		-	--	Martie's Anger155½Winigo1424Tall Award163nk	Driving	9
7Apr79- 4AtH	fm *2	S'Chase	3:51 4↑	Atlanta Cup H 12k	2 5 57 34¼ 2nk 1hd	Quanbeck A Jr	149		-	--	Martie'sAngr149hdWinigo1382½DaddyDumpling13510	Just up	5
31Mar79- 3Cam	fm *2	S'Chase	3:412 4↑	Alw 6000	2 2 32¼ 12½ 1nk 12½	Quanbeck A Jr	146		-	--	Martie'sAngr1462½Underhanded1506Prson'sWtng144	Driving	4
18Nov78- 1Cam	fm *2	S'Chase	3:421	Handicap 7500	5 4 35½ 1nk 1nk 11¼	Quanbeck A Jr	152		-	--	Martie'sAnger1521¼BananaSplit1454½LoveIn15013	Driving	8
28Oct78- 3FH	fm *2 1/16	S'Chase	3:554 3↑	Alw 5000	1 9 89½ 514 - -	Carrier RN Jr	138		-	--	BitterEnder145noParson'sWatng1442PumpknP156½	Lost rider	9
4Oct78- 2Lig	gd *1⅞	S'Chase	3:40 3↑	Md Sp Wt	4 5 52½ 21 11½ 15	Quanbeck A Jr	140		-	--	Martie'sAngr1405Curazao1555BroadwayReviwr15330	In hand	7
21Sep78- 7Atl	fst 6f	:22 :451	1:101 3↑	Alw 6500	3 6 65½ 43½ 34 33½	Castaneda K	118	b	*1.80	87-18	Familyholdback1153Pokeberry119½Martie'sAngr1187	Rallied	6
9Sep78- 6Atl	fm 5½fⓉ	:222 :462	1:041 3↑	Alw 6500	2 6 66 51¾ 41¾ 21	Castaneda K	116	b	10.70	91-07	I Am Sure1181Martie's Anger1167Pokeberry1204	Gamely	7
4Sep78- 9Bel	fm 1 1/16Ⓣ	:232 :462 1:104	1:42 3↑	Alw 15000	3 4 43½ 64¼ 912 916	Santiago A	113	b	39.20	70-12	CapePlayhous1136Robin'sSong118nkOneCutAbove1172¾	Tired	10
22Aug78- 6Sar	fst 6f	:221 :452	1:103 3↑	Alw 13000	2 3 48½ 49½ 410 39½	Santiago A	113	b	11.20	77-20	King's Fashion1143½Alra1176Martie's Anger1132	Evenly	5
14Aug78- 5Sar	fst 7f	:221 :444 1:093	1:231 3↑	Alw 13000	10 8 98 88 67¼ 34½	Santiago A	117	b	36.40	84-13	WayStation1171½Williamstown1173Marti'sAngr117nk	Rallied	11
8Aug78- 5Sar	my 1⅛	:472 1:12 1:374	1:503 3↑	Alw 14000	4 3 32 2hd 41½ 56¾	Santiago A	113	b	10.50	75-18	SilverThrone117hdMightHaveBn1122¾SuddnThw1131½	Weakened	8
28Jly78- 7Atl	fst 6f	:22 :452	1:103 3↑	Alw 6500	2 8 810 87¼ 67¼ 21¼	Castaneda K	114	b	4.30	88-16	Holiday Crossing1161¼Martie's Anger1144½Tom's Luck114hd		9
	Wide stretch												
7Jly78- 1Atl	fst 6f	:221 :453	1:121 3↑	Md Sp Wt	3 5 66½ 67½ 66½ 1½	Pilar H	116	b	4.70	81-24	Martie's Anger116½TV Pruner116½Reshone116½	Driving	9
21Jun78- 2Atl	fm 1Ⓣ	:232 :471 1:111	1:372 3↑	Md Sp Wt	7 8 97½ 67½ 512 57½	Castaneda K	115		*2.60	76-23	Oil Barrel1151Million1221½Jack Frost1223	Wide	11
10Jun78- 2Atl	fst 6f	:221 :462	1:122 3↑	Md Sp Wt	4 7 77¾ 77 46½ 33	Castaneda K	116		27.70	77-20	BayPhoto1162½Richiejim111½Marti'sAngr1163	Belated rally	10
29May78- 1Fai	fm *7fⓉ		1:253 3↑	Md Sp Wt	10 11 139½ 83¼ 64½ 49½	Quanbeck A Jr	142		11.20	--	Little Catworth1551½Mystan1425Loveable Fizz1473	Rallied	15

My Juliet

dkbbr. f. 1972, by Gallant Romeo (Gallant Man)–My Bupers, by Bupers — **Lifetime record: 36 24 4 2 $548,859**

Own.– G. Weasel Jr
Br.– J.R. Bettersworth (Ky)
Tr.– Eugene Euster

24Sep77- 8Bel	sly 1⅛	:46 1:111 1:374	1:521 3↑	ⒻRuffian H-G1	12 1 1hd 11 3½ 65½	Black AS	127		*3.50	60-25	CumLaudeLaurie114½MississippiMd123½Cscpd1281¼	Gave way	12
3Sep77-10Det	fst 1⅛	:46 1:102 1:361	1:482 3↑	Mich 1⅛ H-G2	1 1 12 11½ 12 1¾	Black AS	112		5.20	95-26	My Juliet112¾Strike Me Lucky1102½On the Sly1162	Driving	10
7Aug77- 8Del	fst 6f	:22 :442	1:093 3↑	ⒻEndine H 27k	2 2 21 11 11½ 11¾	Black AS	127		*.20	97-12	My Juliet1271¾Debby's Turn1151¾Catabias1135	Easily	4
16Jly77- 8Key	fst 6½f	:22 :442 1:081	1:143 3↑	Neshaminy H 27k	1 1 1½ 11½ 12 11½	Black AS	104		*.80	104-16	My Juliet1211½Raise a King1193½Silver Hope1202½	Driving	4
21Jun77- 8Bel	fst 6f	:222 :454	1:094 3↑	ⒻAlw 25000	1 4 11 12 12 1½	Black AS	117		*.40	93-16	My Juliet117½Ivory Wand1157Artfully1101	Mild drive	6
5Feb77- 8SA	fst 1 1/16	:231 :462 1:102	1:42 4↑	ⒻS Maria H-G2	1 1 12 11 11½ 54¼	Black AS	123		5.20	88-12	HailHilarious122hdSwingtime1201¼BastonrII1262¾	Bore out	10
16Jan77- 8SA	fst 7f	:22 :441 1:082	1:213 4↑	San Carlos H-G2	1 4 31½ 2½ 11 22	Black AS	123		*1.30	93-11	Uniformity1152MyJulit123nkMssngrofSong1222¾	Drifted out	7
1Jan77- 8SA	gd 6f	:214 :443 :57	1:101 4↑	ⒻLas Flores H 44k	5 1 1hd 1½ 1½ 11	Black AS	128		*.90	88-17	My Juliet1281Just a Kick121½Juliana F.115nk	Driving	7
30Oct76- 8Aqu	fst 7f	:223 :443 1:083	1:214 3↑	Vosburgh H-G2	5 1 1½ 11 13½ 12	Black AS	120		9.10	92-16	MyJuliet1202ⒹBoldForbes1261It'sFreezng1132½	Ridden out	6
23Oct76- 8Key	fst 6½f	:222 :451 1:094	1:163 3↑	ⒻDoylestown H 27k	1 1 11 12 16 12	Black AS	125		*.30	94-19	My Juliet1252Kudara1114Point of Balance1082	Easily	5
11Oct76- 8Mth	fst 6f	:221 :452	1:103 3↑	ⒻTa Wee H 28k	9 1 11 12 14 12¼	Black AS	127		*.90	87-24	My Juliet1272¼Regal Rumor1171¼Four Bells1142	In hand	9
1Oct76- 8Key	sly 6f	:222 :453	1:102 3↑	ⒻAlw 9500	2 5 1½ 11½ 11½ 1½	Black AS	122		*.50	90-22	My Juliet122½Foxy J.G.1159Boss of the House117nk	Easily	6
3May76- 8Bel	fst 7f	:223 :452 1:093	1:22 3↑	ⒻVagrancy H-G3	1 3 21 21 11 11¼	Velasquez J	127		*.70	92-17	My Juliet1271¼Shy Dawn1191¾Kudara1161¾	Drew clear	5
17Apr76- 8Pim	fm 1 1/16Ⓣ	:24 :473 1:112	1:421 3↑	ⒻGallorette H (Div 2)-G3	2 1 2hd 64 813 830	Passmore WJ	127		*2.60	70-00	Deesse du Val119nkSummertime Promise1173½Jbot114nk		9
	Bobbled												
31Mar76- 8Aqu	fst 7f	:231 :46 1:093	1:214 4↑	ⒻHandicap 25000	4 1 11½ 12 12 11½	Velasquez J	126		*.50	92-15	My Juliet1261½Let Me Linger1161¼Land Girl114¾	Easily	5
10Jan76- 8SA	fst 7f	:22 :443 1:083	1:211	Malibu-G2	1 4 1½ 1½ 12½ 33	McHargue DG	115		6.10	94-15	Forceten1231¼MssengrofSong1201¾MyJuliet1153	Weakened	8

10Dec75- 8Aqu my 1 :224 :453 1:103 1:353 ⒻNext Move H 56k 3 1 1hd 1½ 13 1¾ McHargue DG 125 *1.50 88-19 MyJuliet1251¾Channelett117nkSprngIsHr1136¼ Brisk urging 7
15Nov75- 8Lrl fst 1 :23 :454 1:111 1:364 ⒻAnne Arundel H 33k 5 1 11 12 12 1½ McHargue DG 123 *.70 89-20 My Juliet1231½Funny Cat1142½Gala Lil1191½ Driving 6
1Nov75- 8Mth fst 1 70 :231 :46 1:101 1:402 ⒻSea Bright H 28k 2 1 24 2hd 11 42½ Turcotte R L 125 *.80 93-16 Funny Cat1111Vivacious Meg115¾Jolly Song114¾ Weakened 10
18Oct75- 8Mth sly 6f :214 :444 1:104 ⒻFair Haven H 27k 1 1 11 1½ 13½ 1½ Turcotte RL 123 *.80 86-24 MyJuliet1231½-ingMiss1152BeyondReasoning1162 Easily 7
Previously trained by L.G. Ripley
16Aug75- 8Key sly 1 1/16 :224 :454 1:103 1:433 ⒻCotillion-G2 3 2 25 1½ 12 1nk Brumfield D 116 *2.00 86-18 My Juliet116nkHot n Nasty1164¼Gala Lil1182 Driving 7
30Jly75- 8Sar fst 7f :223 :451 1:091 1:22 ⒻTest (Div 2)-G3 5 1 11½ 11½ 12 12½ Velasquez J 116 *1.20 95-14 MyJuliet1162½SlipScreen113hd[D]FltVctrss113nk Ridden out 7
Previously trained by S.A. Long
28Jun75- 7Aks fst 1 1/16 :223 :46 1:102 1:43 Omaha Gold Cup 106k 11 1 1½ 11 1hd 22 Hill A 119 7.50 89-12 Gray Bar1142My Juliet119nkMaster Derby1261 Game try 11
20Jun75- 7Aks fst 6f :212 :443 1:111 ⒻPrincess 20k 5 1 2½ 22 2hd 1½ Hill A 121 *.70 81-24 My Juliet1211½The Rage1182Bold and Modest1181½ Driving 6
7Jun75- 8CD fst 7f :23 :454 1:104 1:24 ⒻDogwood 23k 6 1 11½ 11½ 11½ 12½ Hill A 121 *.80 87-14 My Juliet1212½Snow Doll1181¾Hope She Does1184¼ In hand 9
29May75- 8Mth fst 6f :203 :43 1:09 ⒻMiss Woodford 28k 12 1 1hd 13½ 1hd 54 Hill A 121 *2.00 91-08 Stulcer119hdA Charm115noStream Across1192 Hard used 12
16May75- 8Pim fst 1 1/16 :234 :473 1:123 1:44 ⒻBlack-Eyed Susan-G3 5 1 13 12 14 14 Hill A 116 14.10 85-24 My Juliet1164Gala Lil1141¾Funalon1213 In hand 6
2May75- 8CD fst 1 1/16 :232 :463 1:12 1:443 ⒻKy Oaks-G2 10 2 13 12 1½ 45¼ Hill A 121 29.10 80-20 Sun and Snow121nkFunalon1214½Funny Cat121½ Weakened 11
26Apr75- 8CD fst 7f :233 :463 1:114 1:253 ⒻLa Troienne 21k 2 2 12 11 21½ 34 Hill A 121 1.70 75-21 High Estimate121½Hoso1213½My Juliet1211½ Weakened 6
12Apr75- 7Kee fst *7f 1:263 ⒻAshland-G3 6 1 12 11 11½ 2hd Hill A 116 *1.30 90-17 SunandSnow116hdMyJuliet1163½RedCross1143 Just failed 8
5Apr75- 6Kee fst 6f :211 :433 :563 1:103 ⒻAlw 12500 1 3 11½ 12 11½ 12 Hill A 123 3.20 89-17 My Juliet1232Red Cross1142½Sun and Snow1203½ Hard drive 8
28Nov74- 8CD fst 7f :231 :461 1:104 1:233 ⒻPocahontas 24k 9 1 13 11 1½ 1¾ Hill A 121 *1.10 89-21 My Juliet121¾Channelette1158Yale Coed1213½ Handily 12
Previously owned by R.R. Ladd
20Nov74- 8CD fst 6f :214 :452 :572 1:111 ⒻAlw 10000 1 2 14 13 14 14 Hill A 116 4.30 90-20 My Juliet1164Miss Cabildo1161¼Yale Coed119nk Easily 7
23Oct74- 7Spt fst 6f :224 :464 1:124 Alw 7500 4 4 13½ 11½ 12 13 Hill A 112 *1.40 87-15 MyJuliet1123TudorPoint1132¾GeneralDiplomat119hd Driving 7
16Oct74- 3Haw fst 6f :222 :46 1:102 Md Sp Wt 7 3 11½ 13 13 16 Hill A 120 14.80 94-13 My Juliet1206Pink Paint120noSherburne1207 Easily 9
Previously trained by R.R. Ladd
2Apr74- 3Fon fst 4f :473 ⒻMd Sp Wt 5 3 1½ 1hd 2hd Orona W 115 9.40 91-09 Bold and Modest115hdMy Juliet1152Political Party1187½ 10

Numbered Account

b. f. 1969, by Buckpasser (Tom Fool)–Intriguing, by Swaps **Lifetime record: 22 14 3 2 $607,048**
Own.– O. Phipps
Br.– Ogden Phipps (Ky)
Tr.– R. Laurin

14May73- 7Bel fst 7f :23 :462 1:101 1:223 3↑ ⒻVagrancy H-G3 7 8 52¾ 62¼ 2hd 2nk Vasquez J 120 b *1.20 94-08 Krislin113nkNumbered Account120½Fairway Flyer115nk 8
Bold finish,just missed
28Apr73- 7Aqu gd 1⅛ :473 1:111 1:354 1:481 3↑ ⒻTop Flight H-G1 5 5 53 53¾ 48½ 48½ Pincay L Jr 121 b 1.90 86-14 Poker Night1104Summer Guest123hdRoba Bella1134½ Tired 7
18Apr73- 7Aqu fst 1 :232 :452 1:10 1:352 3↑ ⒻBed o' Roses H-G2 3 5 611 56½ 34 21½ Pincay L Jr 123 b *.30 88-15 PokerNight1081½NumberedAccount123½Ferly1144 No excuse 6
6Apr73- 7Aqu fst 6f :222 :454 1:094 3↑ ⒻAlw 15000 3 2 45½ 32 12 16 Vasquez J 121 b *.30 94-16 NumbrdAccnt1216PasdNom112noPop'sPck113hd Ridden out 6
27Oct72- 6Kee fst 1⅛ :452 1:101 1:35 1:472 3↑ ⒻSpinster 59k 2 5 511 55½ 22 12¼ Pincay L Jr 119 b 2.50 100-15 NumberedAccnt1192¼ChouCroute1231½BarlyEvn1198 Handily 7
9Oct72- 8Atl fst 1 3/16 :464 1:104 1:373 1:573 3↑ ⒻMatchmaker 50k 8 8 611 58½ 31½ 2½ Pincay L Jr 115 b *1.70 87-22 [D]AlmaNrth115½NumbrdAccount115½Honstous1105 In close 8
Placed first through disqualification
9Sep72- 7Bel fst 1⅛ :46 1:102 1:35 1:472 3↑ ⒻBeldame 112k 2 6 66¼ 31½ 42½ 55¼ Cordero A Jr 118 b 3.90 92-06 Susan'sGirl1181SummerGust1181ChouCrout1233¼ Speed,tired 9
30Aug72- 7Bel fst 1 :23 :454 1:10 1:353 3↑ ⒻMaskette H 27k 3 4 32½ 11 13½ 1¾ Cordero A Jr 115 b *.50 94-11 NumbrdAccnt115¾Mnt1121Aldncr114½ Stumbled start,driving 4
13Aug72- 8Del fst 1¼ :464 1:104 1:352 2:003 3↑ ⒻDelaware H 114k 7 3 33 21½ 23 34 Cordero A Jr 115 b *.90 95-09 BlessngAnglica1143¼Grftt113¾NumbrdAccnt1154 Weakened 8
31Jly72- 7Sar fst 7f :232 :461 1:103 1:234 ⒻTest 27k 3 3 34½ 2½ 1½ 11 Vasquez J 121 b *.60 88-13 Numbered Account1211LightHearted118¾CandidCathrne1211½ 6
Driving
3May72- 7Aqu fst 7f :23 :452 1:09 1:213 ⒻComely 27k 2 5 57½ 57½ 35 2no Baeza B 121 b *.20 93-15 Staceyd'Ette115noNumberedAccnt1211¼CandidCathrne1184½ 5
Bore in
19Apr72- 7Aqu fst 6f :22 :451 1:10 ⒻPrioress 27k 2 4 54 11 13 12½ Baeza B 121 b *.10 93-14 NumbrdAccount1212½MindyMalone121¾IMove1211½ Handily 6
13Nov71- 8GS fst 1 1/16 :232 :47 1:113 1:433 Garden State 293k 4 7 44½ 46½ 42 44½ Baeza B 119 b 2.30 82-19 Riva Ridge1222½Freetex122nkKey to the Mint1221¾ Evenly 8
6Nov71- 8GS gd 1 1/16 :234 :474 1:13 1:454 ⒻGardenia 184k 7 7 76 25 2hd 12¾ Baeza B 119 b *.30 76-28 Numbered Account1192¾Susan'sGirl1196CatmousamRoad1196 11
Ridden out
23Oct71- 0Lrl fst 1 1/16 :24 :481 1:13 1:442 ⒻSelima 124k 4 3 2hd 1½ 14 16 Baeza B 122 b -e 91-17 NumberedAccount1226Susceptible119noFarwyFlyr1199 Easily 5
No wagering
11Oct71- 7Bel fst 1 :231 :461 1:104 1:353 ⒻFrizette 135k 1 4 41 13 16 17 Baeza B 119 b *.40 95-16 NumbrdAccount1197Susan'sGirl1195BarlyEvn11920 Handily 4
25Sep71- 7Bel fst 6f :222 :46 1:102 ⒻMatron 105k 2 6 44 21 13 16½ Baeza B 119 b *.20e 95-16 NumbrdAccnt1196½StppngHgh119½Informtv119nk Mild drive 6
25Aug71- 7Sar fst 6f :221 :451 1:094 ⒻSpinaway 87k 3 5 35½ 32½ 21½ 12½ Baltazar C 119 *1.10 97-12 Numbrd Account1192½Rondeau1191½Debby Deb1192 Driving 7
16Aug71- 7Sar fst 6f :222 :454 1:101 ⒻAdirondack 34k 8 6 62½ 3nk 31 31½ Baltazar C 122 *.90 93-12 DebbyDeb1141½DancePartner114noNmberdAccnt122nk Wide 9
4Aug71- 7Sar my 6f :22 :462 1:123 ⒻSchuylerville 33k 3 3 35 32½ 2½ 11 Baeza B 119 *.20 83-17 Numbered Account1191Bendara1145Vichy1146 Mild drive 4
Previously trained by E.A. Neloy
19May71- 7Aqu fst 5f :22 :452 :572 ⒻFashion 33k 1 5 59½ 57½ 34 13 Baeza B 116 *.60 98-15 Numbered Account1163Rondeau116hdBendara1168 Driving 7
14May71- 3Aqu fst 5f :23 :461 :581 ⒻMd Sp Wt 1 2 21½ 2½ 14 110 Baeza B 119 *.30e 94-24 NumbrdAccnt11910BrendaBeauty1191MdmRoyl119½ Handily 9

Office Queen

dkbbr. f. 1967, by Fair Ruler (Nasrullah)–Determine Gal, by Determine **Lifetime record: 39 16 6 8 $385,689**
Own.– S.A. Calder
Br.– Ocala Stud Farms Inc (Fla)
Tr.– B. Lepman

10Jly71- 8Mth fst 1 1/16 :23 :454 1:102 1:424 3↑ ⒻMolly Pitcher 46k 2 5 57½ 45½ 46½ 513 Baltazar C 123 *2.30e 78-16 DoubleDlta1218½CathyHoney118noPeacfulUnon1132 No rally 13
26Jun71- 6Lib fst 1 :224 :462 1:103 1:36 3↑ ⒻWhtemrsh H (Div 1) 22k 1 1 1hd 21 33½ 35 Rivera M 126 *1.40 93-12 DoubleDelta1181½Glenary1143½Office Queen1262 Weakened 9
4Jun71- 8Mth fm 1 1/16Ⓣ :232 :47 1:113 1:432 4↑ ⒻAlw 12000 5 2 2hd 1½ 13 32 Blum W 122 *1.10 95-08 Evening Bag1172Ziba Blue117hdOffice Queen122¾ Weakened 10
22May71- 7Aqu fst 1⅛ :471 1:122 1:37 1:493 3↑ ⒻTop Flight H 53k 1 2 2hd 3½ 21 32 Baltazar C 127 3.40 86-17 Shuvee127¾Cathy Honey1181¼Office Queen1277 No mishap 5
28Apr71- 7Aqu fst 1 :232 :464 1:113 1:364 3↑ ⒻBed o' Roses H 32k 3 1 1½ 1½ 11½ 12 Baltazar C 125 6.30 83-23 Office Queen1252Shuvee1273Royal Fillet1103½ Handily 6
17Apr71- 8Bow fst 7f :23 :46 1:11 1:233 3↑ ⒻBarbara Fritchie H 59k 4 6 72¾ 85½ 75¼ 65½ Broussard R 126 *1.20e 81-23 Cold Comfort1142¼Take Warning110½Double Delta117nk Dull 10
10Apr71- 7Bow fst 6f :221 :451 1:112 3↑ ⒻAlw 10000 9 1 53 52 3nk 11½ Broussard R 123 2.90 89-23 OfficeQueen1231½ProcessShot1232Sally'sTruce1161 Driving 9
24Mar71- 9GP fm 1 1/16Ⓣ :223 :453 1:094 1:413 3↑ ⒻOrchid H 46k 10 3 34½ 31½ 1hd 64¼ Cordero A Jr 124 *2.10 92-10 Swoon'sFlowr1152½StolnBase115¾ToterBack1121 Weakened 10
3Mar71- 7Hia hd 1⅛Ⓣ 1:482 4↑ ⒻAlw 12000 5 1 11 1hd 2½ 1½ Baltazar C 121 2.80 96-06 OfficeQn121½TopRound1182½SignoftheTimes112no Driving 8
9Feb71- 8Hia fst 6f :222 :461 1:103 4↑ ⒻAlw 10000 2 3 41½ 22 2½ 1¾ Baltazar C 113 *1.00 91-17 OfficeQn113¾RomanConsort113½DorothyJon1131½ Cleverly 8
19Oct70- 8GS fst 1⅛ :462 1:103 1:362 1:491 3↑ ⒻVineland H 59k 9 3 43½ 31 3nk 62½ Baltazar C 119 3.80 88-12 CathyHney113¾DarkEmrld1111DedicatdtoSu116no Weakened 10
3Oct70- 8Atl fst 1 3/16 :47 1:111 1:364 1:562 3↑ ⒻMatchmaker 50k 2 4 46½ 55 45 46½ Baltazar C 121 *2.70 87-15 DedicatedtoSue1131½ColdComfort1085[D]Helen Jennings115no 10
Placed third through disqualification
23Sep70- 8Atl fst 1⅛ :484 1:13 1:381 1:503 3↑ ⒻAlw 8000 6 3 3½ 2hd 1½ 11¾ Baltazar C 119 *1.00 85-20 OfficeQueen1191¾FastAttack1091HelenJennings1233 Handily 9
29Aug70- 8Atl fm 1 1/16Ⓣ :24 :481 1:123 1:444 ⒻPageant H (Div 2) 22k 8 4 3½ 2hd 1hd 4nk Blum W 123 *1.40 82-17 ApplePrincess112noToterBack111noSweetMist115hd Faltered 8
15Aug70- 6Sar fst 1¼ :481 1:122 1:373 2:034 ⒻAlabama 59k 7 4 44½ 32 23 33¼ Rotz JL 124 4.10 86-10 Fanfrelche1181¼Hunnemannia1142OfficeQn124½ Weakened 12
8Aug70- 7Lib fst 1 1/16 :232 :464 1:112 1:44 ⒻCotillion H 57k 1 2 21 11 11½ 1½ Rotz JL 123 *1.00 86-07 Office Queen123½Ellen Girl117½Fast Attack1162½ Driving 10
25Jly70- 8Del fst 1⅛ :453 1:10 1:363 1:494 ⒻDel Oaks 60k 11 7 78 85¼ 62¼ 21¾ Marquez CH 121 *1.00 86-11 VirgniaCrackr1111¾OffcQn121½LumnousLgoon1111 Roughed 12
11Jly70- 8Mth fst 1⅛ :464 1:111 1:37 1:502 ⒻMth Oaks 57k 7 4 65¼ 31 1hd 31½ Marquez CH 121 *2.30 90-17 Kilts n Kapers116½Sweet Mist1141Office Queen1214 Wide 9

(Office Queen — continued)

Date-Race	Cond/Dist	Fractions	Race	Running Line	Jockey	Wt	Odds	SR	Top Finishers	Comment Fld
27Jun70- 8Mth	gd 1 70	:24 :48² 1:12⁴ 1:42²	(F)Post-Deb (Div 2) 22k	2 2 1½ 1³ 1³ 1²	Marquez CH	119	*.50	89-20	OfficeQn119²PowdrMountn113⁶Shp'sChnnl113½ Mild drive 8
20Jun70- 7Bel	fst 1¼	:46³ 1:11³ 1:38 2:03⁴	(F)C C A Oaks 133k	7 1 1⁸ 1³ 3⁴ 4¹⁰	Marquez CH	121	2.60	71-17	MissileBelle121¹CathyHoney121⁷KiltsnKprs121² Rank early 7
29May70- 8Bel	fst 1⅛	:44⁴ 1:10¹ 1:36¹ 1:49⁴	(F)Mother Goose 119k	3 2 2¹ ½ 1² 1½	Marquez CH	121	6.30	87-14	OfficeQueen121²CathyHoney121²MissileBelle121⁵ Driving 16
15May70- 8Pim	fst 1¹⁄₁₆	:23² :47 1:11¹ 1:43⁴	(F)Black-Eyed Susan 34k	9 2 2½ 2½ 1ʰᵈ	Marquez CH	118	*2.70	91-11	OfficQun118ʰᵈPrncssRoycrft116²½ArtstsProof116¹½ Just up 11
6May70- 7Aqu	fst 7f	:22⁴ :46¹ 1:11 1:24	(F)Comely (Div 2) 23k	6 1 1ʰᵈ 2ʰᵈ 2¹ 2¹	Marquez CH	118	*1.40	88-17	Royal Signal118¹⁰Office Queen118¹½Luci Tee112³½ Gamely 8
20Apr70- 8GS	sly 6f	:22⁴ :46 1:11¹	(F)B Ross H (Div 2) 22k	5 2 2½ 3²½ 3¹½ 1ʰᵈ	Marquez CH	124	*1.00	88-17	OfficeQueen124ʰᵈLadySadie115³DelayedDelvry113ⁿᵒ Driving 7
7Apr70- 6GP	fst 6f	:22³ :46¹ 1:11⁴	(F)Alw 7500	2 2 1ʰᵈ 1¹½ 1³ 1³	Perret C	122	*.50	85-19	Office Queen122³Dorothy Jean107¹Lady Sadie117ⁿᵒ Handily 7
12Mar70- 8SA	fst 1¹⁄₁₆	:23¹ :46³ 1:10³ 1:42¹	(F)S Susana 45k	5 3 4²½ 4²½ 4⁴½ 5⁶³½	Rotz JL	115	3.00	85-12	OpenngBd115³½CthyHony115³½Turn'nTurnAbt115½ No mishap 11
23Feb70- 8Hia	fst 7f	:23² :46² 1:10³ 1:24	(S)Fla Breeders H 31k	5 3 3²½ 3²½ 3²	Rotz JL	122	*1.30	88-12	Joe Namath110ⁿᵒOffice Queen122ⁿᵏIron Warrior118²¾ Missed 9
28Jan70- 8Hia	fst 7f	:23 :45³ 1:10⁴ 1:23⁴	(F)Mimosa 35k	4 6 2ʰᵈ 1½ 1³ 1⁸	Rotz JL	116	*1.40	89-18	Office Queen116⁸Devilish Angel114¾Tsip115ⁿᵏ In hand 16
17Jan70- 8Hia	sly 6f	:22³ :46 1:11¹	(F)Jasmine (Div 2) 25k	6 5 3¹½ 3¹ 1½ 1²	Rotz JL	116	*2.00	88-14	OfficeQueen116²Attil'sHony114ⁿᵏDvlshAngl114ⁿᵏ Lost whip 8
8Nov69- 8GS	gd 1¹⁄₁₆	:23¹ :47⁴ 1:12⁴ 1:46¹	(F)Gardenia 200k	4 1 1ʰᵈ 1ʰᵈ 2ʰᵈ	Baltazar C	119	11.90	74-26	Fast Attack119ʰᵈSunny Sail114⁵Office Queen119ʰᵈ Gamely 11
25Oct69- 8Lrl	fst 1¹⁄₁₆	:23 :46² 1:11⁴ 1:43¹	(F)Selima 122k	9 1 1ʰᵈ 1½ 1½ 2⁴	Baltazar C	119	3.40	94-09	Predictable119⁴Office Queen119½Sweet Mist119¹½ Weakened 11
11Oct69- 8Atl	fst 7f	:22² :45² 1:10⁴ 1:24¹	(F)Mermaid 29k	6 5 1ʰᵈ 1ʰᵈ 1¹½ 1²	Marquez CH	114	4.50ᵉ	82-18	Office Queen114²Sweet Mist113ʰᵈBundestag112³ Driving 11
20Aug69- 5Atl	sly 6f	:22³ :46³ 1:11⁴	(F)Alw 5000	4 3 1ʰᵈ 1ʰᵈ 1⁴ 1⁷	Marquez CH	120	*1.10	83-22	OfficeQn120⁷Boatswain'sMate118½PromisYou114ⁿᵒ Easily 9
13Aug69- 6Atl	fst 6f	:22² :45⁴ 1:11⁴	(F)Alw 5000	5 4 3¹ 4²½ 2³ 2³½	Broussard R	120	*1.00ᵉ	80-21	Scamtan120³½OfficeQueen120³SuretoShow114½ Held gamely 8
6Aug69- 6Mth	fst 5½f	:22² :46² :59² 1:06¹	(F)Alw 7000	7 3 3²½ 3³ 3² 4⁵½	Marquez CH	119	*.80	81-19	Dowitcher116²¾Sure to Show116¹½Stepolina116¹ Tired 11
25Jly69- 5Mth	gd 5½f	:22³ :46² :59³ 1:06¹	(F)Md Sp Wt	4 1 3ⁿᵏ 3⁴ 2¹½ 1⁴½	Marquez CH	117	1.90	86-24	OfficeQn117⁴½PleasureGame117⁶RoughJad117² Ridden out 9
	Previously trained by R.N. Guerini								
28Feb69- 3Hia	fst 3f	:22³ :34¹	(F)Md Sp Wt	3 4 1½ 2¹	Saumell F	116	8.10	— —	Bushel Basket116¹⁰Office Queen116¹½Karen H.116ⁿᵒ Gamely 14
18Feb69- 3Hia	fst 3f	:22 :33¹	(F)Md Sp Wt	1 6 2¹½ 3³½	Saumell F	116	26.30	— —	Canaveral116¹½Sun Lover116²Office Queen116ⁿᵒ Gamely 14
11Feb69- 3Hia	fst 3f	:22¹ :33³	(F)Md Sp Wt	7 7 7⁷¼ 6⁴¼	Saumell F	116	24.90	— —	Bzz-Bzz116¹Karen H.116ⁿᵏMulberry Bush116¹ No mishaps 13

Our Mims

b. f. 1974, by Herbager (Vandale)–Sweet Tooth, by On-and-On
Own.– Calumet Farm
Br.– Calumet Farm (Ky)
Tr.– John M. Veitch

Lifetime record: 18 6 6 1 $368,034

Date-Race	Cond/Dist	Fractions	Race	Running Line	Jockey	Wt	Odds	SR	Top Finishers	Comment Fld
4Jly78- 7Bel	sly 7f	:22⁴ :46 1:11³ 1:25	3↑(F)Alw 30000	3 4 3²½ 3⁶ 2¹ 1²½	Velasquez J	122	*.30	77-13	Our Mims122²½Mimi Rose115½Sans Arc115²¾ Drew off 5
4Sep77- 8Del	fst 1¼	:48² 1:12¹ 1:37 2:01	3↑(F)Delaware H-G1	3 5 5⁸ 3²½ 3² 1ⁿᵒ	Velasquez J	117	*1.60	97-12	OurMims117ⁿᵒMississippiMud124²½Dottie'sDoll118⁸ Driving 5
13Aug77- 8Sar	fst 1¼	:49² 1:13² 1:37² 2:03	(F)Alabama-G1	11 4 4³ 3¹ 7² 1ⁿᵏ	Velasquez J	121	5.70	86-13	OurMims121ⁿᵏSensationl121¹CumLaudeLaurie121ʰᵈ Driving 11
23Jly77- 8Bel	fst 1½	:49 1:12⁴ 2:02³ 2:26¹	3↑(F)Brooklyn H-G1	7 7 1ʰᵈ 7⁶½ 6¹² 6¹⁸	Velasquez J	110	8.80	71-17	GreatContractr112¹⁴Forego137ʰᵈAmrcnHistory112³ Weakened 13
2Jly77- 8Bel	fst 1¼	:47⁴ 1:11⁴ 2:03³ 2:29²	(F)C C A Oaks-G1	3 7 7¹⁵ 1½ 1³ 1²½	Velasquez J	121	8.80	73-18	Our Mims121²½Road Princess121½Fia121ʰᵈ Driving 12
11Jun77- 6Bel	my 1⅛	:46¹ 1:11 1:36¹ 1:48⁴	(F)Mother Goose-G1	2 5 5³½ 3³ 6⁵½ 6⁸½	Vasquez J	121 b	14.80	75-17	RoadPrncss121¹Mrs.Wrrn121²½CmLdLaurie121ⁿᵏ Weakened 16
28May77- 8Bel	fst 1	:23¹ :46² 1:11² 1:36⁴	(F)Acorn-G1	3 3 3¹½ 4² 3³½ 4⁴¾	Vasquez J	121 b	9.00	79-22	BringouttheBand121³½YourPlaceorMine121¹½Mrs.Warrn121ⁿᵒ 11
	Weakened								
6May77- 8CD	fst 1¹⁄₁₆	:23³ :46⁴ 1:11 1:43³	(F)Ky Oaks-G2	1 7 6⁶½ 5⁴ 6⁵½ 2²½	Turcotte R	121 b	6.70	87-17	SweetAlliance121²½OurMms121¹Mrs.Wrrn121¹½ Finished well 12
23Apr77- 7Kee	sly *7f	1:26⁴	(F)Ashland-G3	6 5 3⁴ 3⁵½ 4⁴ 3⁸½	Turcotte R	118 b	4.30	80-19	SoundofSummer118⁴½Mrs.Warren121⁴OurMims118³ Evenly 9
26Mar77- 9OP	fst 1¹⁄₁₆	:23 :46³ 1:12 1:45	(F)Fantasy-G2	15 4 3³ 3²½ 2¹ 1ⁿᵒ	Brumfield D	112 b	8.60	83-20	OurMims112ⁿᵒSweetAlliance118ʰᵈMeteorDancer110⁶ Driving 15
10Mar77- 7Bel	fst 7f	:23³ :46² 1:10¹ 1:22³	(F)Alw 5500	7 11 6¹½ 3½ 1ʰᵈ 1⁴	Brumfield D	114 b	*2.10	92-14	OurMims114⁴ⒹLikelyExchange114²½LaLonja114³ Mild drive 12
20Nov76- 8Aqu	fst 1⅛	:46⁴ 1:12 1:37⁴ 1:50⁴	(F)Demoiselle-G2	7 4 4³½ 4¹ 2¹½ 2ⁿᵒ	Maple E	113	12.80	81-17	BringouttheBand116ⁿᵒOurMims113ʰᵏRoadPrincss112ⁿᵏ Sharp 12
8Nov76- 8Aqu	fst 1	:24¹ :48¹ 1:13² 1:39³	(F)Tempted 37k	6 3 4³½ 3³½ 2⁴ 2³	Maple E	113	17.10	65-27	PearlNcklace114³OurMims113³RoadPrncss113ⁿᵒ Second best 10
23Oct76- 1Bel	fst 1	:23¹ :47² 1:12³	(F)Md Sp Wt	3 5 3³ 4⁴ 2⁵	Vasquez J	119	*.60	74-18	Bagiorix119⁵OurMms119¹½AffctionateOne119ⁿᵒ Second best 7
16Jun76- 8Bel	fst 5½f	:22³ :46² :59 1:05²	(F)Fashion 38k	1 5 6⁶ 5⁶ 4⁵ 2³	Vasquez J	113	5.90	83-21	Drama Critic113²¾Sly Grin119ⁿᵏOur Mims113ⁿᵏ Rallied 7
	Disqualified from purse money								
4Jun76- 3Bel	fst 5½f	:23¹ :45⁴ :58³ 1:05²	(F)Md Sp Wt	9 7 5²¼ 4⁴ 4³½ 2³	Turcotte R	119	7.10	87-16	Tickle My Toes119³OurMims119¹½BonnieEmpress119¹½ Wide 10
17May76- 4Bel	fst 5½f	:23 :46³ :59 1:05¹	(F)Md Sp Wt	4 5 4²½ 5⁴½ 4⁴½ 4⁵	Velasquez J	119	*2.20	84-14	Miss Medurable119¹Din119¹½Spontaneous119²¼ Weakened 8
	Previously trained by R. Cornell								
9Apr76- 3GP	fst 5f	:23¹ :48¹ 1:01	(F)Md Sp Wt	4 11 9⁵ 8⁸½ 7⁶¼ 2³	Castaneda M	119	3.00	80-25	SaxonyMiss119¾OurMims119ⁿᵒBrookward119½ Sluggish early 11

Personality

b. c. 1967, by Hail to Reason (Turn-to)–Affectionately, by Swaps
Own.– Ethel D. Jacobs
Br.– Bieber–Jacobs Stable (Ky)
Tr.– J.W. Jacobs

Lifetime record: 25 8 4 2 $462,603

Date-Race	Cond/Dist	Fractions	Race	Running Line	Jockey	Wt	Odds	SR	Top Finishers	Comment Fld
31May71- 7Bel	fst 1	:22¹ :44³ 1:09² 1:35⁴	3↑Metropolitan H 121k	15 7 8⁸½ 12¹⁷ 11¹³ 11¹¹½	Woodhouse R	125 b	7.90	83-10	Tunex113ⁿᵒProtanto112¹KnightnArmor114ʰᵈ Fell back early 17
22May71- 6Aqu	fst 6f	:22² :45³ 1:09⁴	3↑Alw 15000	1 8 8¹²½ 2¹³ 1⁸¹⁵ 5⁹½	Belmonte E	117 b	2.20	84-17	Duck Dance115⁷Prize Silver119¹½Happy Harmony115ʰᵈ 8
	Passed tired horses								
10Apr71- 7Aqu	fst 1⅛	:45⁴ 1:11¹ 1:38 1:50⁴	3↑Excelsior H 57k	5 5 5⁹¾ 5¹½ 2ʰᵈ 2¹½	Belmonte E	126	*2.30	80-23	Loud116¹½Personality126ⁿᵒKnight in Armor110³ No match 9
3Apr71- 8Bow	fst 1¹⁄₁₆	:23² :47¹ 1:12¹ 1:44³	3↑J B Campbell H 115k	8 6 10⁹ 9¹¹ 8¹¹ 6⁸½	Belmonte E	125	*1.10	76-24	Bushido114¹½Never Bow120¹¹True North120⁵ Brushed 10
13Mar71- 7Aqu	fst 6f	:22¹ :45 1:09⁴	3↑Paumonok H 33k	2 7 6⁷¾ 6⁵½ 5²½ 3ⁿᵏ	Belmonte E	125	*2.10	94-17	Forum112ⁿᵒEstimator Dave111ⁿᵏPersonality125¹½ Wide 8
29Jan71- 7Hia	fst 7f	:23³ :46² 1:10 1:23¹	3↑Alw 10000	7 3 3¹ 2³ 2² 2²½	Belmonte E	122	*.60	90-17	GleamingLight119²Personality122⁴Coaltown126¹¼ Bore out 8
30Oct70- 7Bel	fst 1¼	:46² 1:10¹ 1:35² 2:01⁴	3↑Woodward 109k	4 1 1¹ 1½ 1¹½ 1ⁿᵒ	Belmonte E	121 b	*1.20	91-08	Personlity121ⁿᵒⒹⒹHydrologist126ⒹⒹTwogundn126⁴½ Driving 7
21Sep70- 7Bel	fst 1¼	:46⁴ 1:10³ 1:35² 2:00⁴	3↑Stymie H 27k	4 2 2³ 1ʰᵈ 1½ 2¹½	Belmonte E	120 b	2.60	95-12	Hydrologist119½Personality120¹Judgable117¹ Gamely 5
7Sep70- 7Bel	fst 1⅛	:45² 1:09¹ 1:34³ 1:48	3↑Gov Nicolls 116k	4 8 9⁸½ 10⁷½ 6⁶½ 5²½	Belmonte E	123	*2.90	92-09	Distinctive119½Hydrologist117½Plymouth110ⁿᵒ No threat 13
22Aug70- 6Sar	fst 1¼	:47 1:10³ 1:35⁴ 2:01	3↑Travers 112k	2 3 2¹½ 2¹½ 3¹ 4²	Pincay L Jr	126	2.10ᵉ	101-07	Loud114ⁿᵏJudgable117¹½Plymouth114ʰᵈ Weakened 9
14Aug70- 7Sar	fst 1¼	:23 :45³ 1:10² 1:35⁴	3↑Jim Dandy 30k	1 2 1½ 1½ 1ʰᵈ 1ⁿᵒ	Pincay L Jr	126 b	*.70	95-11	Personality126ⁿᵒLoud114³Plymouth114⁴ Driving 8
24Jly70- 7Aqu	fst 7f	:22³ :44² 1:09 1:22²	3↑Alw 15000	4 2 2³ 2⁶ 2⁶ 2ⁿᵏ	Belmonte E	117	*.80	89-15	BoldFavorite119ⁿᵏPrsonlty117ʰᵈBllBolnd107ⁿᵏ Just missed 5
30May70- 8GS	fst 1⅛	:46² 1:10² 1:35² 1:48¹	Jersey Derby 128k	4 5 5¹³½ 3½ 3ⁿᵏ 1¹½	Belmonte E	126	*1.20ᵉ	96-10	Personality126¹½CornoftheCob126²½SlntScrn126²¾ Driving 8
16May70- 9Pim	fst 1¹⁄₁₆	:46¹ 1:10⁴ 1:36³ 1:56¹	Preakness 203k	2 5 6⁵ 4⁵¼ 3ⁿᵏ 1ⁿᵏ	Belmonte E	126	4.50ᵉ	92-16	Personality126ⁿᵏMyDadGeorge126³SilentScreen126² Driving 14
2May70- 9CD	gd 1¼	:46¹ 1:12 1:37² 2:03²	Ky Derby 170k	16 7 9¹⁴ 9⁸½ 8¹⁴ 8¹²	Belmonte E	126	4.90ᵉ	71-16	DustCommanr126⁴MyDadGeorge126¹¼HghEchln126ⁿᵏ No threat 17
18Apr70- 8Aqu	fst 1⅛	:47² 1:11⁴ 1:36⁴ 1:49²	Wood Memorial 117k	8 5 3¹ 3ⁿᵏ 1ʰᵈ 1¹³	Belmonte E	126	3.10ᵉ	89-18	Personality126²SilentScreen126⁶DelawareChf126² Driving 14
11Apr70- 6Aqu	fst 7f	:22³ :45² 1:10³ 1:23¹	Alw 9000	9 9 8¹¹ 6⁴¼ 1² 1⁵	Belmonte E	122	*2.30	85-18	Personality122⁵TallFellow108ⁿᵏPrimeVenture117ⁿᵏ Easily 10
4Apr70- 4Aqu	fst 1	:23 :45³ 1:10¹ 1:36¹	Gotham 58k	5 3 3¹½ 3¹ 4⁴ 4²¾	Belmonte E	114 b	4.40ᵉ	83-20	NativeRoyalty114ʰᵈDelawareChief114⁵SilentScrn126² Tired 8
21Mar70- 7Aqu	gd 1	:23² :46⁴ 1:12 1:24¹	Bay Shore 29k	9 1 10⁶²9⁵¼ 6⁵½ 4⁹½	Belmonte E	112 b	3.00	70-25	SunnyTim117⁴NativeRoyalty110³DelawareChif111²½ In close 10
3Mar70- 8Hia	fst 1⅛	:45² 1:09³ 1:35³ 1:48³	Flamingo 161k	13 4 4¹⁰ 5⁵½ 4⁵½ 4⁵	Belmonte E	122	4.60ᵉ	87-14	My Dad George122ⁿᵒCorn off the Cob122³Burd Alane122² 13
	Finished well								
18Feb70- 8Hia	fst 1⅛	:46³ 1:11 1:36¹ 1:48⁴	Everglades 33k	4 10 11¹⁶ 10¹² 6⁶ 4⁵¾	Belmonte E	113	3.00	85-15	Naskra115⁴Burd Alane112ⁿᵏMy Dad George117¹½ In close 13
9Feb70- 4Hia	fst 1⅛	:46³ 1:11 1:35¹ 1:44¹	Alw 6000	6 8 8¹³ 9¹² 3¹ 1³½	Belmonte E	122	*1.50	87-16	Personality122³½Grandiose122ⁿᵏBell Bird117ⁿᵒ Handily 9
3Feb70- 4Hia	sly 6f	:22² :46¹ 1:11	(C)Md Sp Wt	5 3 2½ 2ʰᵈ 1⁴ 1⁶	Belmonte E	119	*1.20	89-15	Personality119⁶Air Song119⁴Bird of Thoria119¹ Easily 10
	Previously trained by H. Jacobs								
26Jan70- 4Hia	fst 6f	:22¹ :45³ 1:11	(C)Md Sp Wt	3 7 7⁸½ 7⁹ 5⁷½ 3³½	Cordero A Jr	119	4.40	85-13	Summer Air119²Elated Prince119¹½Personality119⁴ Rallied 12
31Oct69- 1Aqu	fst 6f	:22² :45³ 1:10²	Md Sp Wt	3 8 9⁶½ 8⁸¼ 8¹² 9¹³	Venezia M	122	5.60	78-14	KeepitfrmGeorge117⁶BonniTm122ʰᵈHtHolmr122¹½ Off slowly 14

Protagonist

ch. c. 1971, by Prince John (Princequillo)–Hornpipe II, by Hornbeam
Own.– Elmendorf Farm
Br.– Elmendorf Farm (Ky)
Tr.– J.P. Campo

Lifetime record: 10 4 1 0 $203,995

27Apr74- 7CD	fst	7f	:22^3 :45^3 1:11^1 1:23^4	Stepping Stone Purse 10k	10	9	10^{17}	11^{18}	12^{25}	12^{20}	Santiago A	122	b	6.40	68-22	Cannonade122^{2}J.R.'s Pet122½Destroyer122^4	Outrun	13
6Apr74- 8Aqu	sly	1	:23^2 :45^4 1:10^3 1:35^1	Gotham (Div 2)-G2	6	8	8^{11}	$8^{9\frac{1}{4}}$	7^{12}	8^{16}	Santiago A	124	b	*1.50	75-15	Rube the Great119$^{4\frac{1}{2}}$Hosiery116^{nk}Cumulo Nimbus116½		8
	Disliked slop																	
16Mar74- 8Aqu	sly	7f	:22 :44^1 1:09 1:22^3	Bay Shore-G3	2	11	11^{15}	10^{15}	8^{13}	$4^{8\frac{1}{4}}$	Santiago A	124	b	*1.90	80-11	HdsnCounty113$^{1\frac{3}{4}}$FrankiAdms119$^{5\frac{3}{4}}$InstdofRoss116¾	Rallied	11
3Nov73- 8Lrl	fst	1$\frac{1}{16}$	:23^2 :46^2 1:12 1:43^1	Lrl Futurity-G1	5	4	4^{10}	4^3	1^2	1^3	Santiago A	122	b	*.70	97-12	Protagnist122^{3}HastyFlyer122$^{3\frac{1}{2}}$PrncofRson122¾	Going away	5
13Oct73- 8Bel	fst	1	:23^2 :46^4 1:11^1 1:36	Champagne (Div 2)-G1	4	6	$7^{3\frac{1}{4}}$	$7^{1\frac{3}{4}}$	$5^{2\frac{1}{4}}$	1^{nk}	Santiago A	122	b	2.70	88-15	Protagonist122^{nk}PrinceofReason122^{1}Cannonad122^{hd}	Driving	10
26Sep73- 6Bel	fst	7f	:22^3 :45^2 1:10^1 1:23	Cowdin (Div 1)-G2	10	10	11^{11}	$10^{9\frac{3}{4}}$	5^3	$1^{1\frac{1}{4}}$	Santiago A	113	b	3.50	87-11	Protagonist113$^{1\frac{1}{4}}$Hosiery113½Stonewalk113$^{2\frac{1}{4}}$	Going away	12
12Sep73- 7Bel	fst	6½f	:23 :46^2 1:10^3 1:17	Futurity-G1	3	9	$10^{9\frac{1}{4}}$	$7^{5\frac{3}{4}}$	$5^{3\frac{1}{2}}$	3^3	Santiago A	122	b	7.40e	88-10	Wedge Shot122^3[D]Judger122^{hd}Protagonist122^1	Bumped	10
	Placed second by disqualification																	
24Aug73- 3Sar	fst	7f	:23^1 :46^1 1:11^1 1:23^4	ⒸMd Sp Wt	2	6	$6^{7\frac{1}{2}}$	5^6	2^3	1^2	Santiago A	119	b	5.70	88-10	Protgonist119^{2}DeterminedKing119¾TheScotsmn119^3	Driving	6
11Aug73- 2Sar	fst	6f	:22^3 :46 1:11	ⒸMd Sp Wt	8	3	$5^{2\frac{1}{4}}$	$4^{3\frac{1}{4}}$	$4^{4\frac{1}{2}}$	$4^{6\frac{1}{2}}$	Santiago A	119	b	5.70	78-12	Take By Storm119$^{6\frac{1}{2}}$Hilo119^{no}The Scotsman119^{hd}	Evenly	12
31Jly73- 1Sar	fst	6f	:23 :47 1:11^3	ⒸMd Sp Wt	2	11	$8^{6\frac{1}{4}}$	8^7	6^8	$6^{7\frac{3}{4}}$	Santiago A	119		12.10	74-16	PrinceofReasn119^{nk}TakebyStorm119^{nk}L'sPss119^3	No factor	11

Proud Delta

dkbbr. f. 1972, by Delta Judge (Traffic Judge)–Loving Sister, by Olympia
Own.– Montpelier
Br.– Danada Farm (Ky)
Tr.– Peter M. Howe

Lifetime record: 31 12 6 1 $387,761

4Jly77- 8Mth	fst	1$\frac{1}{16}$	:23 :46^1 1:09^4 1:41^4	3↑ ⒻMolly Pitcher H-G2	11	4	$5^{3\frac{1}{4}}$	2^3	3^4	2^4	Velasquez J	123		*2.40	92-09	Dottie'sDoll113^{4}ProudDelta123¾MississippiMud115¾	Gamely	11
4Jun77- 8Bel	fst	1⅛	:47^2 1:12 1:36^3 1:49^1	3↑ ⒻHempstead H-G2	4	1	$1^{\frac{1}{2}}$	3^{nk}	$3^{3\frac{1}{2}}$	$5^{7\frac{3}{4}}$	Cordero A Jr	124		*1.30	73-18	Pacific Princess112¾Mississippi Mud114$^{2\frac{3}{4}}$Fleet Victress113^{nk}		10
	No excuse																	
30Apr77- 8Aqu	fst	1⅛	:47 1:11 1:36^3 1:49^4	3↑ ⒻTop Flight H-G1	3	4	$4^{3\frac{1}{2}}$	2^{hd}	2^{hd}	2no	Velasquez J	124		*.70	86-13	Shawi111^{no}Proud Delta124^{hd}Mississippi Mud114^{no}	Missed	9
8Apr77- 8Aqu	fst	1$\frac{1}{16}$⊡	:23 :47^3 1:13 1:45^4	3↑ ⒻBed o' Roses H-G3	1	2	$1^{\frac{1}{2}}$	1^{hd}	2^{hd}	$2^{1\frac{3}{4}}$	Maple E	125		*1.30	87-19	Shawi109$^{1\frac{3}{4}}$Proud Delta125^{no}Secret Lanvin111^1	Gamely	8
13Nov76- 8Aqu	fst	1¼	:48^2 1:12^3 1:37^1 2:01^2	3↑ ⒻLadies H-G1	3	1	$1^{1\frac{1}{2}}$	$1^{\frac{1}{2}}$	1^{hd}	2no	Velasquez J	125		*1.50	89-19	Bastonera II122^{no}Proud Delta125^{7}Sugar Plum Time114¾		9
	Stumbled start																	
9Oct76- 8Bel	sly	1¼	:46^2 1:10 1:35^3 2:01	3↑ ⒻRuffian 132k	1	3	$3^{1\frac{1}{2}}$	4^{14}	5^{19}	5^{28}	Velasquez J	123		3.00	66-17	Revidere118^{14}BastonrII123^{2}OptmstcGl118$^{2\frac{1}{2}}$	Disliked going	5
25Sep76- 8Bel	fst	1⅛	:46^1 1:10^1 1:34^1 1:46^4	3↑ ⒻBeldame-G1	8	1	1^1	1^1	$1^{2\frac{1}{2}}$	1^3	Velasquez J	123		5.50	93-12	ProudDelta123^{3}Revidere118½BastoneraII123^{hd}	Never headed	8
15Sep76- 8Bel	fst	1	:22^4 :45 1:09^1 1:34	3↑ ⒻMaskette H (Div 2)-G2	1	4	2^{hd}	3^1	$3^{\frac{1}{2}}$	4^3	Velasquez J	124		3.30	95-10	Sugar Plum Time111½Pacific Princess110^{no}FleetVictrss115$^{2\frac{1}{2}}$		9
	Weakened																	
11Jly76- 8Hol	fst	1⅛	:46^3 1:10^4 1:35^4 1:48	3↑ ⒻVanity H-G1	7	2	2^1	10^{12}	10^{21}	10^{26}	Grant H	122		6.40	66-11	Miss Toshiba120^{hd}Bastonera II121$^{3\frac{1}{2}}$Bold Baby115^2	Stopped	11
3Jly76- 8Mth	sly	1$\frac{1}{16}$	:23^2 :47^2 1:13 1:46	3↑ ⒻMolly Pitcher H-G2	2	1	$1^{\frac{1}{2}}$	$2^{1\frac{1}{2}}$	$7^{4\frac{1}{4}}$	$7^{8\frac{1}{2}}$	Velasquez J	126		*1.30	66-30	GardnVerse112¾SpringIsHere111¾VodkaTm112$^{1\frac{1}{4}}$	Speed,tired	8
29May76- 8Bel	fst	1⅛	:45^3 1:09^4 1:35^1 1:48^2	3↑ ⒻHempstead H-G2	3	1	$1^{1\frac{1}{2}}$	$1^{\frac{1}{2}}$	$1^{1\frac{1}{2}}$	$1^{\frac{3}{4}}$	Velasquez J	124		*1.20	85-19	ProudDelta124¾GardenVerse111$^{5\frac{1}{4}}$LetMeLinger114$^{2\frac{1}{2}}$	Driving	8
16May76- 8Bel	fst	1	:23 :45^2 1:09^3 1:35	3↑ ⒻShuvee H 56k	5	-		$1^{\frac{1}{2}}$	1^3	$1^{4\frac{1}{4}}$	Velasquez J	122		3.70	93-17	Proud Delta122$^{4\frac{1}{4}}$Snooze108^{hd}Let Me Linger115^4	Mild drive	8
	Obscured by fog																	
24Apr76- 8Aqu	fst	1⅛	:47 1:11^1 1:36 1:49	3↑ ⒻTop Flight H-G1	4	3	$3^{2\frac{1}{2}}$	3^1	$3^{\frac{1}{2}}$	$1^{\frac{3}{4}}$	Velasquez J	120		5.00	90-13	ProudDelta120¾LetMeLinger116^{hd}SpringIsHere108¾	Driving	7
7Apr76- 8Aqu	fst	1	:24 :47^2 1:11^2 1:35^2	3↑ ⒻBed o' Roses H-G3	3	4	1^{hd}	$3^{2\frac{1}{2}}$	$5^{4\frac{3}{4}}$	$5^{8\frac{1}{2}}$	Gustines H	122		5.80	80-17	Imminence115^{2}Spring Is Here108$^{1\frac{1}{4}}$Land Girl114^{nk}	Gave way	9
28Feb76- 8Aqu	fst	1⅛	:47^3 1:12^2 1:36^4 1:49^2	3↑ ⒻNext Move H 80k	8	2	$2^{1\frac{1}{2}}$	2^3	2^{10}	4^{13}	Velasquez J	124		*2.30	75-22	YesDearMaggy119^{13}Pass aGlance115^{hd}MaryQueenofscts119^{nk}		8
	Weakened																	
11Feb76- 8Aqu	fst	1⅛	:48^3 1:13 1:38 1:50^3	3↑ ⒻRare Treat H 37k	2	1	1^2	1^{hd}	1^3	$1^{2\frac{3}{4}}$	Velasquez J	121		*1.20	82-24	ProudDelta121$^{2\frac{3}{4}}$MaryQueenofscots120$^{1\frac{1}{4}}$PettLuc111^{nk}	Easily	6
24Jan76- 8Aqu	fst	1	:24 :47^3 1:12^3 1:37^2	3↑ ⒻAffectionately H 57k	6	4	$3^{1\frac{1}{2}}$	2^{hd}	1^3	$1^{1\frac{3}{4}}$	Velasquez J	114		6.30	79-21	PrdDlta114$^{1\frac{3}{4}}$MaryQueenofscots119^{no}ShyDawn119¾	Driving	10
10Jan76- 8Aqu	fst	6f	:22^1 :46^1 1:11^4	3↑ ⒻInterborough H 57k	5	8	$4^{3\frac{1}{2}}$	$6^{2\frac{1}{4}}$	$5^{3\frac{1}{2}}$	$7^{3\frac{1}{2}}$	Cordero A Jr	114		4.30	80-21	Donetta115^{nk}Foolish Polly118$^{1\frac{1}{4}}$Misinform113½	Impeded	10
	Placed sixth through disqualification																	
15Nov75- 8Aqu	fst	1¼	:50^3 1:14^2 1:38^3 2:03^3	3↑ ⒻLadies H-G1	2	4	$3^{1\frac{1}{2}}$	$5^{2\frac{3}{4}}$	$5^{6\frac{1}{2}}$	$6^{5\frac{1}{2}}$	Gustines H	114		15.30	72-15	Tizna124^{nk}Pass a Glance113^{nk}Susan's Girl126^2	Tired	8
30Oct75- 8Bel	fst	1$\frac{1}{16}$	:23^3 :46^2 1:11^1 1:42^4	3↑ ⒻAlw 12000	2	1	1^{hd}	1^{hd}	1^{hd}	$1^{\frac{1}{2}}$	Gustines H	118		*1.90	88-17	PrdDlt118½SpunkyPrncss116^{no}Immnnc118^4	Long,hard drive	7
	Previously owned by Ada Rice;previously trained by F. Catrone																	
5Oct75- 8Bel	fst	1	:23^1 :45^1 1:10^2 1:35^4	ⒻⓇSuffolk County H 46k	9	10	11^{11}	$7^{7\frac{3}{4}}$	2^3	$1^{\frac{1}{2}}$	Bracciale V Jr	112		8.20	89-19	ProudDelta112½SlipScreen115$^{7\frac{3}{4}}$Imminence112^{nk}	Hard drive	11
8Sep75- 8Bel	fst	7f	:22^4 :45^4 1:10^2 1:23	3↑ ⒻAlw 20000	3	5	5^5	4^4	2^2	2^{hd}	Velasquez J	111		2.00	87-19	FleetVictress113^{hd}ProudDelta111^{15}Remd109^2	Strong finish	5
17Aug75- 5Sar	fst	6½f	:22^3 :45^3 1:10^1 1:16^4	3↑ ⒻAlw 20000	7	1	$6^{4\frac{1}{2}}$	$4^{3\frac{1}{2}}$	$3^{4\frac{1}{2}}$	2^4	Velasquez J	114		5.00	87-17	A Charm107^{4}Proud Delta114¾Land Girl116$^{5\frac{1}{2}}$	Wide turn	7
1Aug75- 8Sar	fst	6f	:22^2 :45^2 1:10^1	3↑ ⒻAlw 15000	2	4	4^3	$3^{1\frac{1}{2}}$	2^{hd}	1^{nk}	Velasquez J	112		6.90	89-14	Proud Delta112^{nk}Lady Portia114^{6}Lisa A. J.116¾	Driving	5
20Jly75- 5Bel	fm	1$\frac{1}{16}$Ⓣ	:23^1 :46^4 1:10^3 1:42^1	3↑ ⒻAlw 15000	10	7	$10^{7\frac{1}{4}}$	$10^{7\frac{3}{4}}$	10^{16}	10^{16}	Shoemaker W	111		12.60	74-11	FleetVictress113$^{2\frac{1}{4}}$HighestTrump112¾TallyRound116¾	Outrun	10
28Jun75- 7Bel	fst	6f	:22^3 :45^4 1:10^2	3↑ ⒻAlw 15000	2	2	5^3	5^3	$5^{2\frac{1}{2}}$	$5^{2\frac{1}{2}}$	Baeza B	114		2.80	88-11	Misinform112^{no}InnrCommnd116^{nk}FletVctrss116^2	No mishap	7
13Jun75- 7Bel	fst	1⅛	:46^1 1:10^2 1:35^3 1:48^3	3↑ ⒻAlw 15000	3	2	$2^{1\frac{1}{2}}$	$4^{1\frac{1}{4}}$	$4^{4\frac{1}{2}}$	$3^{8\frac{1}{2}}$	Baeza B	113		2.60	75-11	Land Girl113^{no}Footsie111$^{8\frac{1}{2}}$Proud Delta113$^{1\frac{1}{2}}$	Weakened	6
27May75- 7Aqu	fst	6f	:22^2 :45^3 1:10^4	ⒻAlw 11000	7	7	6^4	4^3	$2^{\frac{1}{2}}$	$1^{\frac{3}{4}}$	Baeza B	114		*2.10	89-14	Proud Delta114¾Illiterate106^{3}Piece of Luck113¾	Driving	7
30Apr75- 8Aqu	fst	7f	:22^4 :45 1:08^4 1:21^1	ⒻComely-G3	2	4	$3^{2\frac{1}{2}}$	3^4	3^8	4^{12}	Maple E	113		25.30	83-16	Ruffian113$^{7\frac{3}{4}}$Aunt Jin113$^{2\frac{1}{2}}$Point in Time113^2	Tired	5
9Apr75- 6Aqu	fst	1	:24^1 :47^3 1:12^1 1:37^4	ⒻAlw 10000	6	5	$5^{3\frac{1}{4}}$	2^3	2^2	$1^{3\frac{1}{4}}$	Maple E	119		4.10	77-20	ProudDlta119$^{3\frac{1}{4}}$RoamngFancy114$^{6\frac{1}{2}}$Decantr119$^{4\frac{1}{2}}$	Ridden out	6
24Mar75- 4Aqu	fst	6f	:23 :46^3 1:11^3	ⒻMd Sp Wt	5	4	3^2	3^2	2^{hd}	1no	Maple E	121		4.00	85-13	ProudDlta121^{no}Imminence116$^{1\frac{1}{2}}$Barny'sBby121$^{1\frac{1}{4}}$	Hard drive	5

Revidere

ch. f. 1973, by Reviewer (Bold Ruler)–Quillesian, by Princequillo
Own.– W. Haggin Perry
Br.– Claiborne Farm (Ky)
Tr.– David A. Whiteley

Lifetime record: 11 8 2 1 $330,019

4Jly77- 6Bel	fst	7f	:23^1 :46^3 1:11^1 1:23^2	3↑ Alw 25000	2	6	$1^{1\frac{1}{2}}$	1^{hd}	1^{hd}	$2^{\frac{1}{2}}$	Cordero A Jr	117		*.60	84-16	WisePhilip117½Revidere112$^{1\frac{1}{4}}$AmericanHistory117$^{2\frac{1}{4}}$	Gamely	7
23Oct76- 8Bel	fst	1½	:50^1 1:14^2 2:04 2:28^4	3↑ J C Gold Cup-G1	1	1	$1^{1\frac{1}{2}}$	1^1	$2^{\frac{1}{2}}$	$3^{2\frac{3}{4}}$	Vasquez J	118		*.90	73-18	GreatCntractr121$^{1\frac{1}{4}}$Appassionato121$^{1\frac{1}{2}}$Rvdr118$^{3\frac{3}{4}}$	Weakened	10
9Oct76- 8Bel	sly	1¼	:46^2 1:10 1:35^3 2:01	3↑ ⒻRuffian 132k	3	2	$2^{\frac{1}{2}}$	1^4	1^9	1^{14}	Vasquez J	118		*1.70	94-17	Revidere118^{14}Bastonera II123^{2}Optimistic Gal118$^{2\frac{1}{2}}$	Urging	5
25Sep76- 8Bel	fst	1⅛	:46^1 1:10^1 1:34^1 1:46^4	3↑ ⒻBeldame-G1	3	4	2^1	3^1	$3^{3\frac{1}{2}}$	2^3	Shoemaker W	118		*.90	90-12	ProudDelta123^{3}Revidere118½BastonerII123^{hd}	Finished well	8
4Sep76- 8Bel	fst	1⅛	:46^3 1:10^1 1:35 1:47^4	ⒻGazelle H-G2	1	2	2^3	2^3	2^2	$1^{1\frac{1}{2}}$	Cordero A Jr	124		*.60	88-15	Revidere124$^{1\frac{1}{2}}$PacificPrncss112^{9}AncntFbls112^{15}	Ridden out	5
5Jly76- 8Mth	fst	1⅛	:48 1:12^2 1:37^4 1:50^3	ⒻMth Oaks-G1	7	2	2^1	$1^{\frac{1}{2}}$	2^{hd}	1^{hd}	Vasquez J	121		*.60	87-17	Revidere121^{hd}Javamine112^{6}Quacker114^{nk}	Came again	8
26Jun76- 7Bel	fst	1½	:48^2 1:13^3 2:03^1 2:28^2	ⒻC C A Oaks-G1	5	2	$2^{\frac{1}{2}}$	$1^{\frac{1}{2}}$	2^{hd}	$1^{\frac{1}{2}}$	Vasquez J	121		2.40	78-13	Revidere121½OptimisticGal121$^{8\frac{1}{2}}$NoDuplicat121½	Came again	10
12Jun76- 8Key	fst	1$\frac{1}{16}$	:23^1 :47^4 1:12^2 1:44	ⒻCotillion-G2	3	2	1^{hd}	1^{hd}	$1^{1\frac{1}{2}}$	1^4	Vasquez J	118		*.60	84-18	Revidere118^{4}Critical Miss116$^{1\frac{1}{2}}$Hay Patcher116^1	Handily	8
11May76- 7Bel	fst	1$\frac{1}{16}$	:23^1 :46 1:10^4 1:43^1	3↑ ⒻAlw 15000	7	1	$2^{\frac{1}{2}}$	1^{hd}	1^2	1^3	Vasquez J	114		1.20	86-20	Revidere114^{3}Cohabitation114^{nk}Amata119$^{1\frac{1}{4}}$	Brisk drive	7
22Apr76- 7Aqu	fst	1	:22^4 :46 1:10^3 1:35^1	ⒻAlw 15000	7	2	$2^{\frac{1}{2}}$	1^2	$1^{1\frac{1}{2}}$	$1^{2\frac{3}{4}}$	Vasquez J	114		*1.20	90-14	Revidere114$^{2\frac{3}{4}}$Perl114^{4}Ten Cents a Dance109^5	Mild drive	7
5Apr76- 3Aqu	fst	7f	:23^2 :47^1 1:12^2 1:25	3↑ ⒻMd Sp Wt	8	5	2^1	$2^{\frac{1}{2}}$	$1^{1\frac{1}{2}}$	$1^{7\frac{1}{2}}$	Vasquez J	112		*.50	76-18	Revidere112$^{7\frac{1}{2}}$HowPleasing113^{2}YoungatHeart112^7	Ridden out	8

Riva Ridge

b. c. 1969, by First Landing (Turn-to)–Iberia, by Heliopolis **Lifetime record: 30 17 3 1 $1,111,347**

Own.– Meadow Stable
Br.– Meadow Stud Inc (Ky)
Tr.– Lucien Laurin

27Oct73- 7Aqu	fst 2	:472 2:293 2:551 3:20	3↑ J C Gold Cup-G1	3 2	21½	611	627	633	Maple E	124	b	*.50	63-18	Prove Out1244¾Loud12413Twice a Prince119½	Gave way	6
15Oct73- 8Aqu	fst 1⅛	:471 1:102 1:342 1:47	3↑ Stuyvesant H-G2	8 3	43	21½	13	13	Maple E	130	b	*.70	101-09	Riva Ridge1303Forage1161¾True Knight122no	Drew clear	9
15Sep73- 7Bel	fst 1⅛	:453 1:091 1:33 1:452	3↑ Marl Cup Inv'l H 250k	6 2	2hd	1½	22	23½	Maple E	127	b	*.40e	100-07	Secretariat1243½RivaRidge1272CougarII1266½	Held gamely	7
21Aug73- 7Sar	fst 1⅛	:461 1:10 1:354 1:491	3↑ Alw 15000	4 2	21½	1½	14	1½	Turcotte R	126	b	*.20	95-16	Riva Ridge126½Halo1126Rule by Reason112¾	All out	6
1Aug73- 5Sar	fm 1 1/16Ⓣ	:232 :463 1:094 1:40	3↑ Alw 15000	1 1	2hd	2hd	11	21¼	Turcotte R	124	b	*.50	96-06	WichitaOil1131¼RivaRidge124nkGlemng124no	Held for place	7
4Jly73- 7Aqu	fst 1 3/16	:462 1:092 1:333 1:522	3↑ Brooklyn H-G1	3 3	33½	33	1hd	1hd	Turcotte R	127	b	1.80	110-07	Riva Ridge127hdTrue Knight1172Tentam1193½	Driving	7
17Jun73- 9Suf	fst 1⅛	:473 1:11 1:36 1:481	3↑ Mass H-G2	5 1	11	12½	13	13¾	Turcotte R	125	b	*.40	100-14	Riva Ridge1253¾Crafty Khale1121½Loud1131	Ridden out	7
28May73- 7Bel	sly 1	:223 :444 1:091 1:35	3↑ Metropolitan-G1	2 5	58	58½	511	716¾	Turcotte R	127	b	2.30	80-16	Tentam1161¼Key to the Mint127hdKing's Bishop1186	Wide	8
12May73- 3Aqu	fst 6f	:222 :452 1:084	4↑ Alw 12000	1 4	21½	12	14	14	Turcotte R	121	b	*.30	99-09	RivaRidge1214DreamofKings1142SilverMallt1122	Ridden out	5
11Nov72- 7Lrl	sf 1½Ⓣ	:484 1:152 2:121 2:384	3↑ International 150k	8 1	2hd	519	626	638	Velasquez J	120	b	4.20	- -	Droll Role1274Parnell1279Steel Pulse1201	Bobbled early	9
28Oct72- 7Aqu	fst 2	:474 2:281 2:541 3:212	3↑ J C Gold Cup 113k	3 3	32	317	320	318	Velasquez J	119	b	2.10	71-17	Autobiography12415KeytotheMint1193RivaRidge11910	Tired	7
30Sep72- 7Bel	sly 1½	:47 1:112 2:012 2:282	3↑ Woodward 115k	5 2	1½	2hd	23	46¼	Turcotte R	119	b	*1.40	85-14	KytotheMnt1191¼ⒹSmmrGst1163Autobogrphy1262	Gave way	10
20Sep72- 7Bel	fst 1⅛	:461 1:093 1:332 1:461	3↑ Stymie H 28k	1 1	1½	1hd	2½	25	Turcotte R	123	b	*.70	98-07	Canonero II1105Riva Ridge1236Loud115½	Held willingly	5
5Aug72- 8Mth	fst 1⅛	:474 1:113 1:364 1:50	Mth Inv'l H 100k	3 3	2hd	2hd	23	46	Turcotte R	126	b	*.30	84-16	Freetex1171¼King's Bishop1153½Cloudy Dawn1171¼	Bid,hung	8
1Jly72- 8Hol	fst 1¼	:462 1:102 1:342 1:593	Hol Derby 109k	4 1	11½	1hd	11½	1nk	Turcotte R	129	b	*.60	95-16	Riva Ridge129nkBicker114½Finalista120½	Driving	8
10Jun72- 8Bel	fst 1½	:48 1:12 2:021 2:28	Belmont 155k	1 1	1½	13	17	17	Turcotte R	126	b	*1.60	93-08	Riva Ridge1267Ruritania126¾Cloudy Dawn1265	Handy score	10
20May72- 8Pim	sly 1 3/16	:47 1:11 1:362 1:553	Preakness 187k	2 4	42½	22	24	46	Turcotte R	126	b	*.30	86-18	BeeBeeBee1261¼NoLeHace1264½KytotheMnt126nk	No excuse	7
6May72- 9CD	fst 1¼	:473 1:114 1:36 2:014	Ky Derby 182k	9 1	11½	11½	13	13¼	Turcotte R	126	b	*1.50	91-11	RvaRdge1263¼NoLeHc1263½HldYourPc1263½	Scored in hand	16
27Apr72- 6Kee	fst 1⅛	:461 1:111 1:364 1:493	Blue Grass 49k	11 3	33	11	1hd	14	Turcotte R	126	b	*.30	89-21	RivaRidge1264SensitiveMusc1213ThurloSqur121¾	Mild drive	11
1Apr72- 9Hia	sly 1⅛	:453 1:10 1:362 1:494	Everglades 66k	1 3	33	31	41¾	45¾	Turcotte R	122	b	*.70	80-15	Head of the River112¾Hold Your Peace1224New Prospect1191		6
	Checked final eighth															
22Mar72- 9Hia	fst 7f	:224 :444 1:093 1:224	Hibiscus 33k	6 2	42½	22	11	12¼	Turcotte R	122	b	*.60	94-26	Riva Ridge1222¼New Prospect115nkSecond Bar1154½	In hand	8
13Nov71- 8GS	fst 1 1/16	:232 :47 1:113 1:433	Garden State 293k	5 4	34	32½	1hd	12½	Turcotte R	122	b	*1.00	87-19	Riva Ridge1222½Freetex122nkKey to the Mint1221¾	Driving	8
30Oct71- 6Lrl	fst 1 1/16	:231 :462 1:114 1:432	Pim-Lrl Futurity 144k	3 4	33	22	15	111	Turcotte R	122	b	*.10	96-24	Riva Ridge12211Festive Mood122¾Drum Fire1222	Handily	5
9Oct71- 7Bel	fst 1	:231 :452 1:10 1:362	Champagne 195k	7 1	11	11½	14	17	Turcotte R	122	b	*1.40	91-20	Riva Ridge1227Chevron Flight1223½Head of the River1221½		7
	Ridden out															
18Sep71- 7Bel	sly 6½f	:22 :451 1:094 1:163	Futurity 153k	8 2	31½	2hd	12	11½	Turcotte R	122	b	3.60	97-11	RvaRidge1221½ChevronFlght122½HoldYourPc1222	Mild drive	8
2Aug71- 7Sar	gd 6f	:214 :453 1:094	Flash 34k	6 3	21	1½	13	12½	Turcotte R	116	b	4.50	97-14	RvaRidge1162½LoquacousDon1135RstYourCs1192½	Mild drive	9
21Jly71- 7Aqu	fst 5½f	:213 :451 :574 1:042	Great American 35k	3 1	2hd	44½	54½	86¾	Baltazar C	117	b	*1.30	84-15	Chevron Flight120¾Plum Bold1244Chauffeur124no	Steadied	10
9Jly71- 6Aqu	fst 5½f	:214 :451 :573 1:041	Alw 10000	3 1	1hd	1hd	11½	14	Baltazar C	122	b	*2.20	92-17	RivaRidge1224BigBluffer1221LuckyBidder1222	Mild drive	8
23Jun71- 2Bel	fst 5½f	:223 :461 :582 1:05	©Md Sp Wt	2 2	1½	2hd	12	15½	Baltazar C	122	b	2.00	95-15	RivaRidge1225½KeytotheMint1223½Candyvll122hd	Mild drive	8
9Jun71- 4Bel	fst 5½f	:231 :464 :584 1:05	©Md Sp Wt	7 8	86½	811	815	716	Baltazar C	122		2.30	79-12	SearchforGld1227TheGenerl1223½CryingtoRun1222	Bumped	10

Rockhill Native

ch. g. 1977, by Our Native (Exclusive Native)–Beanery, by Cavan **Lifetime record: 17 10 2 3 $465,382**

Own.– H.A. Oak
Br.– Dr E.W. Thomas & Carolaine Farm (Ky)
Tr.– Herbert K. Stevens

7Jun80- 8Bel	my 1½	:501 1:151 2:04 2:294	Belmont-G1	7 6	2hd	1½	3½	33½	Oldham J	126		12.80	67-17	TemprnceHll1262GenuinRsk1211½RockhllNtv1262	Weakened	10
3May80- 8CD	fst 1¼	:48 1:124 1:373 2:02	Ky Derby-G1	6 2	11½	21½	46½	56	Oldham J	126		*2.10	81-11	GnuineRsk1211Rumbo1261JaklnKlgmn1264	Swerved,checked	13
24Apr80- 7Kee	fst 1⅛	:473 1:111 1:363 1:50	Blue Grass-G1	4 1	11½	11½	12	12	Oldham J	121		*.50	87-18	RockhillNtive1212SuprMomnt121nkGoldStg121nk	Ridden out	11
15Apr80- 7Kee	gd 1 1/16	:241 :483 1:123 1:432	Alw 24860	1 1	11	13½	15	16¾	Oldham J	118		*.30	89-19	RckhillNative1186¾HzrdDuk112hdRy'sWord121nk	Ridden out	6
5Mar80-10Hia	fst 1⅛	:454 1:104 1:37 1:511	Flamingo-G1	8 4	49½	43½	24	36	Oldham J	122		*1.40	70-26	Suprbity1226KoluctooBy122noRockhllNtv1223½	Forced wide	10
20Feb80- 9Hia	fst 1⅛	:451 1:092 1:351 1:49	Everglades 49k	5 3	35	32	1½	11¼	Oldham J	122		3.30	87-16	RockhillNative1221¼IrishTowr1142½InlndVoygr112½	Driving	8
6Feb80- 9Hia	fst 7f	:23 :451 1:092 1:223	Bahamas 36k	5 2	3½	33	26	312	Oldham J	122		*.30	78-20	IrishTowr11712Ry'sWord117nkRockhllNtv1223	Brushed early	6
23Jan80- 5Hia	fst 6f	:222 :46 1:11	Alw 15000	6 3	34	2hd	12	11¼	Oldham J	122		*.10	88-21	RockhillNative1221¼SpeedyProspct1155SlvrShrs1151	Easily	6
14Oct79- 8Bel	my 1	:23 :463 1:122 1:381	Champagne-G1	6 2	11	12	11½	21¾	Oldham J	122		*.20	75-25	Joanie'sChief1221¾RockhllNtv1222Googolplx1224¼	Weakened	8
30Sep79- 8Bel	sly 7f	:223 :461 1:101 1:233	Cowdin-G2	5 4	45½	21	14	16	Oldham J	122		*.30	84-24	RckhillNtv1226KoluctooBy115noSonofDodo1172	Ridden out	6
15Sep79- 8Bel	fst 7f	:222 :451 1:092 1:22	Futurity-G1	7 1	21½	22	14	14	Oldham J	122		*.20	92-11	Rockhill Native1224Sportful1224¼Gold Stage1221½	Handily	8
25Aug79- 8Sar	fst 6½f	:221 :444 1:093 1:161	Hopeful-G1	2 9	22	2hd	12	16½	Oldham J	122		*1.10	94-12	ⒹRockhillNatv1226½J.P.Brothr122¾GoldStg1221¼	Came over	12
	Disqualified and placed sixth															
11Aug79- 9Mth	fst 6f	:214 :443 1:084	Sapling-G1	7 2	32	21	1½	13	Oldham J	122		2.70	96-10	RockhillNative1223AntiqueGold1227GoldStg1223	Ridden out	7
31Jly79- 9Mth	fst 5½f	:221 :45 1:03	Tyro 26k	2 3	33	37½	36½	22	Oldham J	122		6.30	100-11	AntiqueGold1182RockhillNativ1225½IrshTowr122nk	2nd best	4
30Jun79- 8CD	fst 5½f	:223 :463 :59 1:051	Jefferson Cup 29k	2 6	44	3nk	11	12	Oldham J	122		*.50	97-10	RockhillNative1222EarlofOdss1225½Egg'sDynmt122½	Driving	9
19Jun79- 7CD	fst 5f	:224 :46 :582	Alw 10860	4 4	2½	2hd	1½	13	Oldham J	122		*.90	97-15	Rockhill Native1223Varga115hdEgg's Dynamite1153	Easily	7
2Jun79- 3CD	fst 5f	:231 :463 :591	Md Sp Wt	6 5	11	11	12	14	Oldham J	122		*2.50	93-15	Rockhill Native1224Real Emperor122hdBoom Boom Billy1224		7
	Ridden out															

Ruffian

dkbbr. f. 1972, by Reviewer (Bold Ruler)–Shenanigans, by Native Dancer **Lifetime record: 11 10 0 0 $313,429**

Own.– Locust Hill Farm
Br.– Mr & Mrs Stuart S. Janney Jr (Ky)
Tr.– F.Y. Whiteley Jr

6Jly75- 8Bel	fst 1¼	:443 1:083 1:352 2:024	Match Race 350k	1 1	-	-	-	-	Vasquez J	121		*.40	- -	Foolish Pleasure126	Broke down	2
21Jun75- 8Bel	fst 1½	:49 1:132 2:031 2:274	ⒻC C A Oaks-G1	5 1	14	11½	13	12¾	Vasquez J	121		*.05	81-12	Ruffn1212¾EqulChng1219LtMLngr1212¼	Confidently ridden	7
31May75- 8Aqu	fst 1⅛	:473 1:113 1:353 1:474	ⒻMother Goose-G1	6 1	11¾	12	18	113½	Vasquez J	121		*.10	96-07	Rffian12113½SweetOldGirl1212SunandSnow1212½	Easy score	7
10May75- 8Aqu	fst 1	:232 :453 1:093 1:342	ⒻAcorn-G1	3 1	11	13	17	18¼	Vasquez J	121		*.10	94-08	Ruffian1218¼Somethingregal121noGallantTrial1211	In hand	7
30Apr75- 8Aqu	fst 7f	:224 :45 1:084 1:211	ⒻComely-G3	3 5	11	11½	16	17¾	Vasquez J	113		*.05	95-16	Ruffian1137¾AuntJin1132½PointnTm1132	Slow start,handily	5
14Apr75- 8Aqu	fst 6f	:23 :454 1:092	ⒻAlw 20000	2 3	11	1½	12	14¾	Vasquez J	122		*.10	96-17	Ruffian1224¾SirIvor'sSorrow113hdChannelette1132	Easily	5
23Aug74- 8Sar	fst 6f	:221 :444 1:083	ⒻSpinaway-G1	2 1	12	13	17	112¾	Bracciale V Jr	120		*.20	97-10	Ruffian12012¾LaughingBridge1201½ScottshMlody1205	Easily	4
27Jly74- 8Mth	fst 6f	:213 :441 1:09	ⒻSorority-G1	3 3	1½	1hd	1½	12¼	Vasquez J	119		*.30	95-15	Ruffian1192¼Hot n Nasty11922Stream Across1194	Driving	4
10Jly74- 8Aqu	fst 5½f	:214 :442 :562 1:024	ⒻAstoria-G3	2 2	11	13	16	19	Bracciale V Jr	118		*.10	99-15	Ruffian1189Laughing Bridge11512Our Dancing Girl1153¼		4
	Speed to spare															
12Jun74- 8Bel	fst 5½f	:222 :451 :57 1:03	ⒻFashion-G3	3 4	11½	11½	14	16¾	Vasquez J	117		*.40	100-12	Ruffian1176¾Copernica11713Jan Verzal117nk	Ridden out	6
22May74- 3Bel	fst 5½f	:221 :45 :57 1:03	ⒻMd Sp Wt	9 8	13	15	18	115	Vasquez J	116		4.20	100-15	Ruffian11615Suzest1135Garden Quad116½	Ridden out	10

Run the Gantlet

b. c. 1968, by Tom Rolfe (Ribot)–First Feather, by First Landing — **Lifetime record: 21 9 4 1 $559,079**

Own.– Rokeby Stable
Br.– Paul Mellon (Va)
Tr.– Elliott Burch

3Jun72- 7Bel fm 1½Ⓣ :491 1:134 2:022 2:274 3↑ Bowling Green H 56k 4 4 46 31 12 13 Woodhouse R 121 b 2.20 88-08 Run the Gantlet1213Kling Kling112noOnandaga114½ Driving 7
13May72- 8Pim yl 1½Ⓣ :502 1:153 2:043 2:30 3↑ Dixie H 59k 1 5 42½ 33 37½ 47½ Woodhouse R 123 b *1.10 79-16 Onandaga1103Star Envoy1164New Alibhai112½ Lacked rally 9
25Mar72- 9Hia fst 1¼ :461 1:103 1:362 2:022 3↑ Widener H 144k 2 9 713 1115 1015 910 Woodhouse R 123 b 4.90e 76-16 GoodCounsl111noHisMajesty1146UrgntMssg121nk No speed 13
18Mar72- 9Hia fm 1 3/16Ⓣ 1:523 3↑ Bougainvillea H 73k 9 10 1013 1193⁄4 1193⁄4 109¼ Woodhouse R 125 b *1.60 95-01 Star Envoy1112Bagdads Rocket107nkDouble Entry113no Dull 14
25Oct71- 7Lrl sf 1½Ⓣ :532 1:214 2:204 2:503 3↑ D C Int'l 150k 2 3 2½ 12 14 16 Woodhouse R 120 b *.80 -- RuntheGantlet1206IrishBall1209Chompion12716 Ridden out 9
16Oct71- 7Bel sf 1½Ⓣ :513 1:172 2:064 2:331 3↑ Man o' War 112k 1 4 46 3½ 1hd 12¼ Woodhouse R 121 b *.90 61-39 RntheGantlet1212¼Gleaming121hdPractcnt126hd Ridden out 8
18Sep71- 8Atl sf 1 3/16Ⓣ :492 1:151 1:423 2:02 3↑ U Nations H 100k 4 6 57½ 34 1½ 11½ Woodhouse R 117 b 3.20 60-48 RntheGantlet1171½TwiceWorthy1184½Chompion1166 Driving 11
4Sep71- 8Atl fm 1⅛Ⓣ :492 1:121 1:362 1:483 3↑ Kelly-Olympic H 33k 5 2 43 43 31 1¾ Woodhouse R 115 b *1.30e 93-11 RuntheGantlet115¾Charli'sLuck110noFortMrcy126hd Driving 8
31Jly71- 7Aqu sf 1⅛Ⓣ :474 1:124 1:383 1:513 3↑ Tidal H 61k 2 7 64½ 45½ 23 14 Woodhouse R 109 b 10.00 77-23 RuntheGntlt1094RoylHrmony110hdOnthTrck1122 Drew clear 11
13Jly71- 7Aqu fm 1 1/16Ⓣ :232 :472 1:113 1:432 3↑ Alw 13000 8 6 612 53 41 2nk Rotz JL 113 b *1.30 86-15 Hope Eternal115nkRun the Gantlet113nkEvasive Action118hd 8
Slow start
26Jun71- 7Bel fst 1 :232 :461 1:102 1:344 Saranac 56k 2 6 65 41½ 54¾ 56½ Rotz JL 121 2.30e 92-08 Salem121nkFarewell Party1175½Highbinder114½ Bid,tired 7
5Jun71- 7Bel fm 1 1/16Ⓣ 1:404 3↑ Alw 15000 1 8 86¼ 54¾ 52½ 25½ Rotz J 113 b 3.10 92-06 Gleaming1135½RntheGantlt1132RoughPlace113hd Wide turn 9
20May71- 7Aqu fst 1 :231 :461 1:104 1:361 3↑ Alw 15000 7 4 43½ 22 61¼ 76¼ Rotz J 113 b *.60 80-21 SoleMio1132SilverMallet110hdBoldSkipper110½ Bid,tired 9
10May71- 6Aqu gd 6f :222 :454 1:103 3↑ Alw 11000 5 6 65½ 43¼ 3½ 13 Rotz JL 113 b 4.30 90-16 RuntheGantlet1133Plotting1101RsYourGlss110nk Mild drive 7
14Nov70- 8GS gd 1 1/16 :224 :463 1:113 1:45 Garden State 352k 9 8 85½ 51¼ 21 1hd Rotz JL 122 b 9.40 80-21 Run the Gantlet122hdExecutioner122½Ruffinal1221 Driving 15
4Nov70- 5GS my 1 70 :231 :47 1:122 1:422 Alw 8000 7 8 76¼ 32½ 2hd 2nk Rotz JL 116 b *2.30 82-26 Ruffinal116nkRuntheGantlet1167BigBarracuda114½ Gamely 9
26Oct70- 2Aqu fst 1 :24 :472 1:113 1:36 Md Sp Wt 9 5 42 2½ 1hd 11½ Tejeira J 122 b 3.40 87-15 RntheGantlt1221½FareYouWell1222HeadMt122nk Mild drive 11
17Oct70- 1Bel gd 1 :232 :464 1:122 1:382 Md Sp Wt 12 5 54 22 23 22 Tejeira J 122 b 6.20e 79-15 DrollRol1172RunthGntlt1227Woodchoppr'sBll122no 2nd best 13
14Aug70- 1Sar fst 6f :223 :46 1:112 Md Sp Wt 13 7 710 1010 812 88½ Pincay L Jr 122 12.90 80-11 Raja Baba1222Sound Thinking1222Gran Bid1222 Rank 13
17Jly70- 3Aqu fst 5½f :231 :474 :593 1:052 Md Sp Wt 6 7 74 64½ 34 37½ Ussery R 122 6.40 78-15 GreatGuffaw1224HardyLife1223½RuntheGantlet122no Wide 11
8May70- 3Aqu fst 5f :231 :47 :592 Md Sp Wt 5 8 1011 89 613 49¼ Velasquez J 122 15.00 79-16 Good Behaving122nkTinsel Time1228Poppadums1221 Greenly 10

Seattle Slew

dkbbr. c. 1974, by Bold Reasoning (Boldnesian)–My Charmer, by Poker — **Lifetime record: 17 14 2 0 $1,208,726**

Own.– Tayhill Stable
Br.– B.S. Castleman (Ky)
Tr.– Douglas Peterson

11Nov78- 8Aqu fst 1⅛ :464 1:10 1:342 1:472 3↑ Stuyvesant H-G3 1 1 11½ 13 13 13¼ Cordero A Jr 134 *.10 98-12 SeattleSlew1343¼JumpingHill1152¾WisePhlp113½ Ridden out 5
14Oct78- 8Bel sly 1½ :451 1:092 2:014 2:271 3↑ J C Gold Cup-G1 1 1 1hd 1hd 2½ 2no Cordero A Jr 126 *.60 84-13 Exceller126noSeattleSlew12614GrtContrctor1264¾ Bore out 6
30Sep78- 8Bel fst 1¼ :473 1:104 1:351 2:00 3↑ Woodward-G1 5 1 12 12½ 12½ 14 Cordero A Jr 126 *.30 109-12 SeattleSlew1264Exceller1266¾It'sFreezng126no Ridden out 5
16Sep78- 8Bel fst 1⅛ :47 1:101 1:333 1:454 3↑ Marlboro Cup H-G1 4 1 12½ 12½ 13 13 Cordero A Jr 128 2.10 98-12 Seattle Slew1283Affirmed1245Nasty and Bold1184 Driving 6
Previously owned by Karen L. Taylor
5Sep78- 6Med fst 1⅛ :46 1:094 1:35 1:48 3↑ Paterson H-G3 10 1 13½ 11½ 1½ 2nk Cruguet J 128 *.20 93-13 Dr.Patches114nkSeattleSlew1282¼It'sFrzng1125 Drifted in 10
12Aug78- 7Sar sly 7f :22 :444 1:091 1:213 3↑ Alw 25000 5 2 11 15 14 16 Cruguet J 119 *.10 97-18 SeattleSlew1196ProudBirdie1152¾CapitalIdea11516 Handily 5
14May78- 7Aqu sly 7f :224 :453 1:101 1:224 4↑ Alw 25000 3 3 2½ 11½ 17 18¼ Cruguet J 122 *.10 87-26 SeattleSlew1228¼ProudArion1191¼Capult'sSong1155 Handily 6
Previously trained by William Turner Jr
3Jly77- 8Hol fst 1¼ :452 1:091 1:333 1:583 Swaps-G1 2 2 32 36 411 416 Cruguet J 126 *.20 82-11 J.O. Tobin1208Affiliate117noText1208 Steadied,bore in 7
11Jun77- 8Bel my 1½ :482 1:14 2:034 2:293 Belmont-G1 5 1 1½ 14 13½ 14 Cruguet J 126 *.40 72-17 SeattleSlw1264RunDstyRun1262Sanhedrn1262¼ Handy score 8
21May77- 8Pim fst 1 3/16 :453 1:094 1:344 1:542 Preakness-G1 8 2 1hd 2½ 13 11½ Cruguet J 126 *.40 98-10 Seattle Slew12611½Iron Constitution1262Run Dusty Run1261¼ 9
Drew clear
7May77- 8CD fst 1¼ :454 1:103 1:36 2:021 Ky Derby-G1 4 2 2hd 1hd 13 11¾ Cruguet J 126 *.50 86-12 SeattleSlew1261¾RunDstyRn126nkSanhdrn1263¼ Ridden out 15
23Apr77- 8Aqu fst 1⅛ :474 1:121 1:363 1:494 Wood Memorial-G1 6 1 1hd 11½ 16 13¼ Cruguet J 126 *.10 87-13 Seattle Slew1263¼Sanhedrin1264½Catalan126hd Handily 7
26Mar77- 9Hia fst 1⅛ :451 1:09 1:34 1:472 Flamingo-G1 4 1 11½ 16 16 14 Cruguet J 122 *.20 95-15 SeattleSlew1224Gboul122nkFortPrvl1224½ Speed in reserve 13
9Mar77- 9Hia fst 7f :221 :44 1:08 1:203 Alw 7000 2 6 1hd 12 14 19 Cruguet J 117 *.10 102-10 SeattleSlw1179WhitRammr1223½SmashingNatv1192½ Easily 8
16Oct76- 8Bel fst 1 :232 :46 1:10 1:342 Champagne-G1 3 1 12 12 13 19¾ Cruguet J 122 *1.30 96-13 SeattleSlw1229¾FortheMoment1221¼SltoRom1223 Easy score 10
5Oct76- 7Bel fst 7f :223 :454 1:092 1:22 Alw 11000 1 8 11½ 11 13 13½ Cruguet J 122 *.40 92-13 SeattleSlew1223½CruiseonIn1196Lancer'sPrid1172½ Handily 8
20Sep76- 5Bel fst 6f :222 :452 1:101 Md Sp Wt 8 10 11½ 12 15 15 Cruguet J 122 *2.60 91-12 Seattle Slew1225Proud Arion122½Prince Andrew1222 Easily 12

Secretariat

ch. c. 1970, by Bold Ruler (Nasrullah)–Somethingroyal, by Princequillo — **Lifetime record: 21 16 3 1 $1,316,808**

Own.– Meadow Stable
Br.– Meadow Stud Inc (Va)
Tr.– L. Laurin

28Oct73- 8WO fm 1⅝Ⓣ :472 1:373 2:414 3↑ Can Int'l-G2 12 2 21½ 15 112 16½ Maple E 117 b *.20 96-04 Secretariat1176½BigSpruce1261½GoldenDon117¾ Ridden out 12
8Oct73- 7Bel fm 1½Ⓣ :47 1:113 2:00 2:244 3↑ Man o' War-G1 3 1 13 11½ 13 15 Turcotte R 121 b *.50 103-01 Secretariat1215Tentam1267½Big Spruce126½ Ridden out 7
29Sep73- 7Bel sly 1½ :50 1:132 2:014 2:254 3↑ Woodward-G1 5 2 2½ 1hd 21½ 24½ Turcotte R 119 b *.30 86-15 ProveOut1264½Secretariat11911CougarII126½ Best of rest 5
15Sep73- 7Bel fst 1⅛ :453 1:091 1:33 1:452 3↑ Marl Cup Inv'l H 250k 7 5 51¼ 3½ 12 13½ Turcotte R 124 b *.40e 104-07 Secretariat1243½Riva Ridge1272Cougar II1266½ Ridden out 7
4Aug73- 7Sar fst 1⅛ :474 1:11 1:36 1:491 3↑ Whitney H-G2 3 4 31 2½ 2hd 21 Turcotte R 119 b *.10 94-15 Onion1191Secretariat119½Rule by Reason1192 Weakened 5
30Jun73- 8AP fst 1⅛ :48 1:111 1:35 1:47 Invitational 125k 4 1 13 12½ 16 19 Turcotte R 126 b *.05 99-17 Secretariat1269My Gallant120nkOur Native12017 Easily 4
9Jun73- 8Bel fst 1½ :461 1:094 1:59 2:24 Belmont-G1 1 1 1hd 120 128 131 Turcotte R 126 b *.10 113-05 Secretariat12631TwiceaPrince126½MyGllnt12613 Ridden out 5
19May73- 8Pim fst 1 3/16 :481 1:112 1:353 1:542 Preakness-G1 3 4 1½ 12½ 12½ 12½ Turcotte R 126 b *.30 98-13 Secretariat1262½Sham1268Our Native1261 Handily 6
Daily Racing Form time 1:53 2/5
5May73- 9CD fst 1¼ :472 1:114 1:361 1:592 Ky Derby-G1 10 11 69½ 2½ 1½ 12½ Turcotte R 126 b *1.50e 103-10 Secretariat1262½Sham1268Our Native126½ Handily 13
21Apr73- 7Aqu fst 1⅛ :481 1:121 1:364 1:494 Wood Memorial-G1 6 7 66 55½ 45½ 34 Turcotte R 126 b *.30e 83-17 Angle Light126hdSham1264Secretariat126½ Wide,hung 8
7Apr73- 7Aqu fst 1 :231 :451 1:083 1:332 Gotham-G2 3 3 1hd 12 1½ 13 Turcotte R 126 b *.10 100-08 Secretariat1263ChampagneCharl11710Flush1172½ Ridden out 6
17Mar73- 7Aqu sly 7f :221 :444 1:10 1:231 Bay Shore-G3 4 5 56 53 1hd 14½ Turcotte R 126 b *.20 85-17 Secretarit1264½ChmpgnChrl1182½Impcunous126no Mild drive 6
18Nov72- 8GS fst 1 1/16 :241 :472 1:12 1:442 Garden State 298k 6 6 46¼ 33 11½ 13½ Turcotte R 122 b *.10e 83-23 Secretariat1223½Angle Light122½Step Nicely122¾ Handily 6
28Oct72- 7Lrl sly 1 1/16 :224 :454 1:112 1:424 Lrl Futurity 133k 5 6 510 53 15 18 Turcotte R 122 b *.10e 99-14 Secretariat1228Stop the Music1228Angle Light1221 Easily 6
14Oct72- 7Bel fst 1 :224 :451 1:094 1:35 Champagne 146k 4 11 98½ 53½ 1½ 12 Turcotte R 122 b *.70e 97-12 [D]Secretariat1222StoptheMusic1222StepNicly1221½ Bore in 12
Disqualified and placed second
16Sep72- 7Bel fst 6½f :223 :453 1:10 1:162 Futurity 144k 4 5 65½ 53½ 12 11¾ Turcotte R 122 b *.20 98-09 Secretariat1221¾StoptheMusic1225SwiftCourr1222½ Handily 7
26Aug72- 7Sar fst 6½f :224 :463 1:094 1:161 Hopeful 86k 8 8 96½ 1hd 14 15 Turcotte R 121 b *.30 97-12 Secretariat1215FlighttoGlory121nkStopthMusc1212 Handily 9
16Aug72- 7Sar fst 6f :224 :461 1:10 Sanford 27k 2 5 54 41 1½ 13 Turcotte R 121 b 1.50 96-14 Secretariat1213Lnd'sChf1216NorthstrDncr1213½ Ridden out 5
31Jly72- 4Sar fst 6f :231 :462 1:104 Alw 9000 4 7 73¾ 3½ 1hd 11½ Turcotte R 118 b *.40 92-13 Secretariat1181½Russ Miron1187Joe Iz1182½ Ridden out 7
15Jly72- 4Aqu fst 6f :221 :452 1:103 ©Md Sp Wt 8 11 66½ 43 1½ 16 Feliciano P5 113 b *1.30 90-14 Secretariat1136Master Achiever118¾Be on It1184 Handily 11
4Jly72- 2Aqu fst 5½f :222 :461 :584 1:05 ©Md Sp Wt 2 11 107 108¾ 75½ 41¼ Feliciano P5 113 b *3.10 87-11 Herbull118nkMaster Achiever1181Fleet 'n Royal118no 12
Impeded,rallied

Sensational

dkbbr. f. 1974, by Hoist the Flag (Tom Rolfe)–Meritus, by Bold Ruler **Lifetime record: 44 9 9 9 $496,395**

Own.– Mill House
Br.– Mill House (Ky)
Tr.– Woodford C. Stephens

15Nov78- 8Aqu	fst	1	:234 :471 1:12 1:372	3↑ (F)Alw 30000	8 6 62½ 89¼ 87¾ 56	Cauthen S	115	b	7.70	73-23	Casquette115½Negotiator1104TgrHrt122no	No late response	9
4Nov78- 8Aqu	fst	1¼	:461 1:11 1:363 2:022	3↑ (F)Ladies H-G1	2 4 410 1015 1019 1016	Venezia M	113	b	25.60	68-18	IdaDelia1142¼WaterMalone1221¼CumLaudLur1151¼	Early foot	11
24Oct78- 6Med	fst	1 1/16	:242 :474 1:112 1:423	3↑ (F)Long Look H 54k	11 9 97 98¼ 812 714	Venezia M	115	b	3.50e	84-13	WaterMalone120hdQueenLib1208TigerHeart1152	Stumbled st.	11
1Oct78- 8Bel	fm	1¼[T]	:482 1:12 1:37 2:003	3↑ (F)Flower Bowl H 54k	3 1 1½ 32 56 58½	Velasquez J	113	b	3.90	82-10	Waya120¾Magnificence1084¾Leave Me Alone1081	Used up	7
23Sep78- 8Bel	fst	1⅛	:462 1:094 1:343 1:47	3↑ (F)Ruffian H-G1	4 3 33 34½ 47 611	Cauthen S	115	b	10.90	81-15	LateBloomr1221½PearlNecklace1244TempestQuen1172½	Tired	9
10Sep78- 8Bel	fst	1	:23 :453 1:092 1:334	3↑ (F)Maskette H-G2	5 3 45½ 36 39 37¾	Cauthen S	117	b	2.90	91-17	Pearl Necklace123¾Ida Delia1137Sensational117hd	Wide	5
3Jun78- 8Hol	fst	1 1/16	:224 :46 1:102 1:414	3↑ (F)Milady H-G2	7 3 21 31 32 32	Pincay L Jr	121	b	3.50	84-18	TaisezVous1271¾DramaCritiz118nkSensational121nk	Evenly	8
20May78- 8Hol	fm	1 1/16(T)	:221 :454 1:101 1:414	3↑ (F)Hawthorne H 45k	4 4 31 1hd 11 1½	Pincay L Jr	119	b	2.80	90-09	Sensational119½Up to Juliet1142¼Grand Luxe1172	Driving	10
11May78- 7Hol	fm	1 1/16(T)	:223 :47 1:11 1:421	4↑ (F)Alw 35000	6 4 31 32½ 23 3½	Pincay L Jr	116	b	*1.00	87-14	DramaCrtc116nkSoundofSmmr118nkSnstonl116no	Good effort	6
27Apr78- 8Hol	fm	1 1/16(T)	:233 :48 1:113 1:414	4↑ (F)Alw 30000	4 2 2½ 2½ 21 2hd	McCarron CJ	114	b	*1.40	90-10	Glenaris114hdSensational114½UptoJuliet119hd	Just missed	7
15Apr78- 6Hol	sly	1⅛	:464 1:103 1:351 1:481	3↑ (F)Gamely H (Div 1)-G2	3 4 43 41½ 41½ 2hd	Cauthen S	120	b	*1.20	91-12	Lucie Manet119hdSensational1202Glenaris1131	Bumped	7
26Mar78- 8SA	fm	1¼(T)	:471 1:114 1:36 2:003	4↑ (F)S Barbara H-G1	4 2 21½ 21½ 31½ 31	Cauthen S	120	b	3.70	83-15	Kittyluck1161Countess Fager117noSensational120no	Hung	9
16Mar78- 8SA	fm	1⅛(T)	:473 1:111 1:352 1:474	4↑ (F)Alw 35000	1 1 12 1½ 12 1no	Cauthen S	119	b	*1.40	88-12	[D]Sensational119noUptoJuliet1122½Glenrs1121	Drifted out	6
	Disqualified and placed second												
26Feb78- 8SA	fst	1⅛	:46 1:102 1:354 1:49	4↑ (F)S Margarita Inv H-G1	5 5 24 21 21 21½	Cauthen S	118	b	8.10	85-16	TaisezVous1201½Sensational1182MerryLdyIII1144½	Good try	11
16Feb78- 8SA	fst	1 1/16	:23 :462 1:101 1:414	4↑ (F)Alw 35000	4 3 33 22 22 21¼	Cauthen S	117	b	*.70	92-14	SoundofSummer1151¼Senstnl1174MrryLdyIII1148	No excuse	5
10Feb78- 8SA	my	6½f	:221 :454 1:111 1:173	4↑ (F)Alw 25000	8 5 55 44 32½ 1¾	Cauthen S	116	b	*1.50	82-25	Sensational116¾Don's Music1132Tumble Along119½	Handily	8
19Nov77- 6Med	fst	1¼	:494 1:142 1:384 2:034	3↑ (F)Long Look H 105k	1 1 11 1½ 2½ 25	Venezia M	114	b	*1.40	89-19	Dottie's Doll1145Sensational1144¾Charming Story1153½		6
	Faltered late												
5Nov77- 8Aqu	fst	1¼	:473 1:122 1:373 2:024	3↑ (F)Ladies H-G1	8 6 57 2½ 11 12¾	Venezia M	110	b	12.90	82-14	Sensatonl1102¾Dott'sDoll114¾ChrmngStory116no	Ridden out	8
24Oct77- 8Aqu	gd	1 1/16(T)	:234 :481 1:121 1:434	3↑ (F)Long Island H-G3	6 4 21½ 21½ 65½ 77¾	Venezia M	113	b	8.90	79-13	PearlNecklace1231¼Javamine121hdLeaveMeAlone113¾	Tired	7
15Oct77- 5Bel	my	1⊗	:231 :462 1:11 1:363	3↑ (F)Gallant Bloom H 25k	4 3 21½ 31 34½ 34	Venezia M	118	b	5.80	81-17	Pearl Necklace1212¾Nijana1221¼Sensational118nk	Evenly	6
7Oct77- 6Med	fm	1 1/16(T)	:231 :471 1:12 1:441	3↑ (F)Alw 25000	2 5 52¼ 62¾ 43 53½	Wallis T	111	b	*1.20	87-09	MascaradaII115nkLikelyDouble1153Becky'sHoney115nk	Tired	9
24Sep77- 8Bel	sly	1⅛	:46 1:111 1:374 1:521	3↑ (F)Ruffian H-G1	8 6 57 611 916 915	Maple E	115	b	12.00	51-25	CumLaudeLaurie114½MississippiMud123½Cascaped1281¼	Tired	12
3Sep77- 8Bel	my	1⅛	:464 1:11 1:352 1:48	(F)Gazelle H-G2	4 2 22 21 23½ 22¾	Wallis T	120	b	*1.60	84-14	PearlNecklace1112¾Sensational120½RoadPrincss118¾	Gamely	5
13Aug77- 8Sar	fst	1¼	:492 1:132 1:372 2:03	(F)Alabama-G1	1 1 12 11 1hd 2nk	Wallis T	121	b	29.70	86-13	OurMims121nkSensatnl1211¾CumLaudeLaurie121hd	Gamely	11
3Aug77- 8Sar	fst	7f	:221 :451 1:092 1:222	(F)Test (Div 2)-G3	7 1 68½ 65½ 48 45¼	Wallis T	121	b	3.80	88-13	NorthernSea121¾Northernette1212FlyngAbov1142½	No mishap	8
16Jly77- 8Mth	fst	1⅛	:464 1:103 1:36 1:493	(F)Mth Oaks-G1	4 - - - - -	Wallis T	119	b	*2.20	- -	Small Raja1214¾Herecomesthebride1171¼Suede Shoe1142		8
	Stumbled start,lost rider												
2Jly77- 8Bel	fst	1½	:474 1:114 2:033 2:292	(F)C C A Oaks-G1	4 9 917 118½ 910 712	Wallis T	121	b	9.80	61-18	Our Mims1212½Road Princess121½Fia121hd	Bumped,wide	12
25Jun77- 8Mth	fst	1 70	:221 :452 1:104 1:43	(F)Post-Deb-G3	3 6 68½ 43½ 21 15½	Wallis T	117	b	3.40	83-19	Sensational1175½Raise Old Glory1135Hagany113nk	Easily	6
11Jun77- 6Bel	my	1⅛	:461 1:11 1:361 1:484	(F)Mother Goose-G1	14 13 1511 1412 1214 1115	Velasquez J	121		14.20	68-17	RoadPrincess1211¾Mrs.Warren1212¾CumLaudeLur121nk	Outrun	16
6May77- 8CD	fst	1 1/16	:233 :464 1:11 1:433	(F)Ky Oaks-G2	2 4 43½ 32 33 67¼	Velasquez J	121	b	2.60e	83-17	SweetAlliance1212½OurMims1211Mrs.Warrn1211¼	Weakened	12
23Apr77- 7Kee	sly	*7f	1:264	(F)Ashland-G3	1 4 78 612 57 411½	Velasquez J	121	b	3.70e	77-19	SoundofSummer1184½Mrs.Warren1214OurMims1183	No rally	9
30Mar77- 9Hia	fst	7f	:222 :45 1:093 1:23	(F)Hibiscus 30k	3 8 86¾ 68 45½ 31	Velasquez J	122	b	*.80	87-17	NeedaDime114½GrandLuxe114½Sensational1222	Belated rally	8
19Mar77- 3Hia	fst	6f	:22 :444 1:101	(F)Alw 10000	5 3 46 45½ 43½ 31	Wallis T	121	b	*.80	91-14	GrandLuxe118hdNoble Madame1181Sensationl121no	Gaining	7
23Oct76- 8Lrl	fst	1 1/16	:224 :452 1:11 1:434	(F)Selima-G1	4 5 57 42 1hd 13½	Velasquez J	122	b	*.90	94-13	Sensationl1223½NorthernSe1192Dbby'sTurn1191	Ridden out	6
4Oct76- 8Bel	fst	1	:224 :453 1:101 1:361	(F)Frizette-G1	2 4 21½ 21½ 2½ 11½	Velasquez J	119	b	10.40	87-18	Sensational1191½Northern Sea1193Mrs. Warren1198	Driving	7
22Sep76- 8Bel	fst	7f	:232 :472 1:121 1:243	(F)Matron-G1	7 1 74½ 62¾ 613 516	Shoemaker W	119	b	3.50	63-17	Mrs. Warren1196½Negotiator1193½Resolver119½	No mishap	7
6Sep76- 6Bel	fst	6½f	:231 :463 1:11 1:172	(F)Astarita-G3	3 4 42½ 4¾ 1hd 11¼	Cordero A Jr	112	b	*1.50	89-14	Sensational1121¼TickleMyToes1123¾SpyFlg1122½	Ridden out	7
27Aug76- 8Sar	fst	6f	:22 :45 1:102	(F)Spinaway-G1	5 5 65½ 65½ 33½ 33½	Cordero A Jr	119	b	4.60e	84-10	Mrs. Warren1193Exerene119½Sensational1192	Rallied	10
16Aug76- 8Sar	fst	6f	:221 :453 1:111	(F)Adirondack-G3	2 2 42½ 42½ 56½ 57¾	Wallis T	116	b	*.90e	76-18	HarvestGirl1142BonnieEmpress114½DramaCritic1191¼	Tired	7
31Jly76- 8Mth	fst	6f	:213 :444 1:104	(F)Sorority-G1	10 1 75½ 45½ 42½ 21¼	Wallis T	119	b	15.50	85-17	Squander1191¼Sensational119¾Miss Cigarette119nk	Wide	11
7Jly76- 8Mth	sly	5½f	:222 :473 1:012 1:09	(F)Colleen (Div 2) 22k	5 8 811 79 56½ 1½	Wallis T	115	b	5.10	72-35	Sensational115½Intrepid Way115½Drama Critic1212	Driving	8
28Jun76- 4Bel	fst	5½f	:223 :462 :584 1:051	(F)Md Sp Wt	4 2 52¾ 52½ 1½ 11½	Wallis T	119	b	5.50	89-12	Snsationl1191½SpyFlag1193¾YourPlcorMn1141¾	Ridden out	9
13Jun76- 4Bel	fst	5½f	:224 :464 :593 1:061	(F)Md Sp Wt	4 2 43 43¼ 43½ 31½	Maple E	119		3.70	82-22	Squander119¾Harvest Girl119¾Sensational119nk	Hung	10
4Jun76- 5Bel	fst	5½f	:23 :463 :59 1:053	(F)Md Sp Wt	4 4 53¼ 76¾ 76½ 45¼	Maple E	119		*1.30	82-16	Din119hdDrama Critic1191¾Squander1193½	No excuse	10

Shadow Brook

b. g. 1964, by Cohoes (Mahmoud)–Chanteur Star, by Chanteur II **Lifetime record: 78 20 13 15 $307,057**

Own.– S.C.Clark Jr
Br.– Elmendorf Farm (Ky)
Tr.– S. Watters Jr

3Aug73- 5Sar	gd	2 1/16	Hurdles 3:44	4↑ Lovely Night H 22k	6 5 511 44½ 417 413½	O'Brien L	156	s	2.00	- -	JuacHollow1504Wustenchef1558½StillinAll1401	No factor	7
26Jun73- 4Mth	fm	*2 1/16	Hurdles 4:13	4↑ Mid Summer H 16k	2 3 37½ 44½ 36½ 37	O'Brien L	161	s	*1.20	- -	DreamMagic1521JuacHollow1486ShadowBrook16118	No rally	8
9Jun73-10Del	fm	*2⅛	Hurdles 4:332	4↑ Indian River H 13k	3 4 54¾ 21½ 15 2no	O'Brien L	160		*1.10	- -	Breaking Dawn138noShadow Brook16012Master Irish II1418		7
	Just missed												
30May73- 6Bel	fst	7f	:223 :453 1:101 1:223	3↑ Alw 15000	4 1 54½ 78½ 714 618	Vasquez J	112	b	27.60	76-17	DndeeMrmalad1183½ZuluTm1184CurousCours1182	No factor	7
18Nov72- 3Cam	fm	2 13/16	S'Chase 5:234	4↑ Colonial Cup 100k	- 4 31½ 31½ 3¾ 32¾	O'Brien L	160		-	- -	Soothsayer1582½Inkslinger158¼Shadow Brook160nk		16
4Nov72- 5Lrl	gd	1 1/16⊗	:232 :471 1:132 1:454	3↑ Alw 7000	1 3 32 41¼ 46 56½	Passmore WJ	117	b	*1.60	- -	ConvoyII1123¼MajesticRoad1092¾BurdosII112no	Early speed	7
7Oct72- 4Lig	sf	*2½	S'Chase 5:192	4↑ Temple Gwathmey H 30k	7 5 33¾ 34¾ 23 37¾	O'Brien L	163	s	-	- -	Soothsayer1627Speed Kills143¾Shadow Brook16310	Evenly	12
20Sep72- 5Bel	gd	1 1/16(T)	:242 :48 1:121 1:44	3↑ Alw 15000	1 1 1½ 3½ 2½ 25	Rotz JL	114	b	3.80	77-18	Rocky Mount1165Shadow Brook114nkExotico1139	Gamely	6
23Aug72- 7Sar	hd	1⅝(T)	:482 1:363 2:01 2:374	3↑ Seneca H 30k	1 1 11½ 33 57 912	Rotz JL	114	b	6.80e	92-04	RedReality113¾Acclimitization114¾[D]LarcnyKd1133	Used up	12
17Aug72- 3Sar	fm	2 1/16	Hurdles 3:421	4↑ Lovely Night H 22k	6 2 1½ 1hd 11 1¾	O'Brien L	163	s	*.50e	- -	Shadow Brook163¾Dream Magic1522½Gran Kan1574	Driving	8
9Aug72- 8Sar	fm	1 1/16(T)	:231 :454 1:092 1:40	3↑ Clm 50000	2 4 65 77 46 27	Cordero A Jr	116	b	4.70	90-05	Nevado1167Shadow Brook116nkJogging118½	Gamely	10
20Nov71- 2Cam	fm	2 13/16	S'Chase 5:17	4↑ Colonial Cup 10k	4 6 86¾ 59 55 411¼	O'Brien L	160	s	-	- -	Inkslinger149nkSoothsayer1498Top Bid1603	Evenly	15
5Nov71- 7Aqu	sf	1 1/16[T]	:234 :494 1:15 1:482	3↑ Alw 11000	9 2 2½ 2hd 2½ 3hd	Rotz JL	118	b	*2.10	69-31	Chartino116hdHeyGoodLookin116noShadowBrook1181	Sharp	10
15Oct71- 3Bel	yl	3	S'Chase 5:47	4↑ Gwathmey H 55k	3 7 33 33 16 15½	Fishback J	163	s	*.80e	- -	Shadow Brook1635½Amerind1414½Top Bid160¾	Handily	9
28Sep71- 3Bel	yl	2⅝	S'Chase 4:571	4↑ Brook H 33k	2 3 24 22 13 12¼	O'Brien L	159	s	*.70e	- -	Shadow Brook1592¼Amarind135nkTingle Creek1536	Driving	8
26Aug71- 3Sar	fm	2½	S'Chase 4:372	4↑ Grand National H 40k	2 1 37 2½ 13 112	O'Brien L	155	s	*1.10e	- -	Shadow Brook15512Top Bid1635Madagascar1421	Driving	7
12Aug71- 3Sar	fm	2 1/16	Hurdles 3:433	4↑ Lovely Night H 22k	2 2 21½ 1½ 1½ 1nk	O'Brien L	156	s	1.50e	- -	Shadow Brook156nkSoothsayer1398Inkslinger1502½	Driving	7
22Jly71- 3Aqu	fm	2½	Hurdles 4:351	4↑ Meadow Brook 22k	4 1 45½ 34½ 23 23	O'Brien L	154	s	1.60e	- -	Wustenchef1543ShadwBrk1544Madagascr14020	Second best	7
17Jly71- 8Aqu	fm	1 1/16(T)	:233 :462 1:103 1:422	3↑ Alw 20000	2 2 2½ 2½ 1hd 11	Rotz J	114	b	5.60	91-07	ShdwBrk1141PasstheDrink114nkHandsomeKd1183½	Driving	6
5Jly71- 6Aqu	fm	1 1/16(T)	:23 :461 1:103 1:423	3↑ Alw 20000	7 10 1016 1011 107 94½	Cruguet J	116	b	14.90	85-14	Elephant Walk116nkOur Cadet120½Naskra111no	Reared	11
11Jun71- 7Bel	fst	7f	:224 :453 1:102 1:23	3↑ Alw 20000	4 5 711 612 615 622	Cruguet J	119	b	11.50	70-15	TwiceWorthy1191½PrizeSilver1214LimttoRsn1128½	No speed	7
4Jun71- 5Bel	fm	7f(T)	1:222	3↑ Alw 15000	1 5 32 55½ 42 32¼	Cruguet J	117	b	5.70	94-09	Shah Abbas1171¼Decies II1171Shadow Brook117¾	Rallied	9
25May71- 5Bel	fm	7f(T)	1:222	3↑ Alw 15000	10 1 65 55½ 54½ 44	Cruguet J	117	b	11.50	92-08	Our Cadet1191Shah Abbas1173Wilkinson121no	Steadied turn	10
14Nov70- 4Cam	sf	*2 13/16	S'Chase 5:20	4↑ Colonial Cup 100k	- 10 99½ 3¾ 12 21½	O'Brien L	160	s	-e	- -	Top Bid1601½Shadow Brook1601½Jaunty1586	Gamely	22
29Oct70- 7Aqu	yl	1 1/16(T)	1:461	3↑ Alw 15000	3 2 42 41½ 51¼ 43½	Cruguet J	116	b	5.50	68-28	Tampa Trouble1162½Perplejo116½Perpetual II116½	Blocked	7

Date	Cond	Dist	Fractions	Race	PP	St	1st	2nd	Str	Fin	Jockey	Wt	Eq	Odds	Speed	Top finishers	Comment	Field
15Oct70- 5Bel	sf	2½	Hurdles 4:491	4↑ NY Trf Writrs Cup H 24k	7	2	32½	55½	414	310	O'Brien L	155	s	2.30e	--	ElMartirio139noWustenchef15110ShadowBrook1551	Fair try	10
6Oct70- 3Bel	fm	1⅞	Hurdles 3:261	3↑ Handicap 14000	4	1	31½	2½	11½	11½	O'Brien L	153	s	*1.30	--	ShadowBrk1531½Wustenchef1497Hipocampo1384½	Mild drive	6
21Sep70- 3Bel	fm	2 1/16	Hurdles 3:414	4↑ Alw 10000	1	1	1½	2½	1½	12½	O'Brien L	153	s	*.60	--	Shadow Brook1532½Taku1506Amarind14414	Under drive	7
10Sep70- 4Bel	sf	2½	Hurdles 4:414	4↑ Rouge Dragon H 17k	5	5	54½	2½	26	29	O'Brien L	152	s	*.80	--	Wustenchef1439ShadowBrk152¾StarofVertex13018	2nd best	7
3Sep70- 3Bel	hd	1⅞	Hurdles 3:20	4↑ Sp Wt 7200	9	3	38	2hd	112	120	O'Brien L	152	s	2.50	--	ShadowBrk15220ShotandShell1458Jus'Behaving145¾	Easily	10
12Aug70- 6Sar	hd	1 1/16Ⓣ	1:392	3↑ B Baruch H (Div 1) 24k	7	2	43	66½	714	716	Cruguet J	109	b	26.60	87-02	BigShotII111¾ShelterBay111¾PleasantHarbour112hd	Tired	9
30Jly70- 7Aqu	fm	1 1/16Ⓣ	1:45	3↑ Alw 15000	2	3	44	54	57½	55	Cruguet J	120	b	7.70	73-22	NeverConfuse116¾Mr.Clinch123nkRhinelanderII1202½	Tired	6
9Jly70- 7Aqu	fm	1 1/16Ⓣ	1:432	3↑ Alw 15000	6	4	55	52½	53	54½	Cruguet J	123	b	7.30	81-14	Red Reality120nkSailstone1092½Thai Silk113nk	No threat	8
4Jly70- 5Aqu	fst	7f	:22 :442 1:084 1:212	3↑ Alw 15000	6	1	811	916	918	916	Gustines H	121	b	31.90	78-12	TrueNrth1212¼TowzieTyke1153½GleamngLght119no	Far back	9
25Jun70- 7Bel	fm	1 1/16Ⓣ	1:422	3↑ Alw 15000	4	4	58	75¼	54¾	58¼	Cruguet J	120	b	9.30	82-13	Mr. Leader120nkZarco123noRed Reality1204½	No room	8
6Jun70- 6Bel	sly	7f	:23 :463 1:112 1:241	3↑ Alw 15000	6	1	63	76	55½	69	Cruguet J	119	b	16.20	77-20	Buck Run119hdBarometer1192½Noble Victory1195	No mishap	8
30May70- 8Bel	fm	1 1/16Ⓣ	1:422	3↑ Alw 15000	2	2	2½	22	2½	1nk	Cruguet J	116	b	8.70	90-16	Shadow Brook116nkJungle Cove1181Afan1131½	Driving	7
23May70- 3Aqu	fst	6f	:223 :451 1:10	3↑ Alw 15000	1	4	55	57½	47	47	Cruguet J	119	b	28.70	86-13	Verbatim117noPrize Silver1041Grey Slacks1136	No mishap	6
22Nov69- 7Aqu	fst	1⅝	:494 1:40 2:05 2:423	3↑ Gallant Fox H 59k	5	5	88	1113	1127	1129	Cruguet J	112	b	60.70	63-16	ShipLeave111noHydrologist117hdQuickenTree1163	Far back	11
13Nov69- 7Aqu	gd	1	:232 :461 1:11 1:354	3↑ Alw 15000	6	2	53¼	41½	32	33¾	Cruguet J	118	b	12.80	84-20	Barometer1161¾Rixdal1142Shadow Brook118½	Weakened late	7
28Oct69- 7Aqu	fst	1	:233 :463 1:112 1:351	3↑ Alw 15000	5	3	47	65¾	67	512	Cordero A Jr	123	b	12.40	79-22	Hydrologist1195Rixdal116hdFlagstaff1123	Fell back	9
18Oct69- 6Bel	fst	1 1/16	:242 :48 1:123 1:43	3↑ Alw 15000	3	2	11	1hd	2hd	1hd	Cruguet J	118	b	4.10	89-17	Shadow Brook118hdRixdal116½Flagstaff1124	Driving	7
30Sep69- 7Bel	fst	1 1/16	:233 :463 1:111 1:423	3↑ Alw 15000	1	1	11	1½	1½	2no	Turcotte R	118	b	19.80	91-19	FourFingers118noShadowBrook1185BoldHour116hd	Sharp try	8
20Sep69- 6Bel	hd	1 1/16Ⓣ	1:402	3↑ Alw 15000	6	4	43	75¼	76	65½	Cruguet J	118	b	3.60	--	Loiret II116¾Dike1111½Rhinelander II120hd	Brief factor	8
13Sep69- 8Bel	fm	1 1/16Ⓣ	1:43	3↑ Alw 15000	8	1	21½	2hd	1hd	2no	Cruguet J	118	b	5.10	--	Swoonland118noShadw Brook1183Hydronaut116½	Nosed out	8
22Aug69- 7Sar	hd	1⅝Ⓣ	2:401	3↑ Seneca H 29k	6	6	46	89½	810	714	Cruguet J	112	b	14.20	78-12	Harem Lady1126Larceny Kid116nkNashandy1121¼	Fell back	10
7Aug69- 9Sar	fm	1 1/16Ⓣ	1:422	3↑ Alw 15000	6	4	48	48½	44½	37	Cruguet J	123	b	*1.90	81-12	Tradesman116noLoiretII1187ShadwBrook1231½	No response	6
29Jly69- 7Sar	sf	1 1/16Ⓣ	1:434	3↑ Alw 15000	4	2	24	22	31	2no	Cruguet J	118	b	*1.40	81-18	BurningBridges110noShadwBrook1183RobotIII116¾	Gaining	6
11Jly69- 7Aqu	sf	1⅛Ⓣ	1:542	3↑ Alw 15000	3	2	21½	22	2½	1nk	Cruguet J	116	b	*1.20	63-37	Shadow Brook116nkLoiret II118½[D]Mara Lark1202	Driving	4
28Jun69- 5Bel	fm	7fⓉ	1:222	3↑ Alw 15000	2	3	22	21½	2½	1nk	Cruguet J	117	b	4.60	96-16	ShdowBrook117nkBaitman119nkPasstheBrandy1191½	Driving	7
20Jun69- 6Bel	yl	7fⓉ	1:23	3↑ Alw 15000	2	4	42½	34	11	11½	Cruguet J	117	b	4.00	93-06	Shadow Brook1171½Util1172½Brunch1071	Brisk urging	6
14Jun69- 6Bel	hd	7fⓉ	1:222	3↑ Alw 15000	11	1	3nk	1½	4¾	63¾	Cruguet J	117	b	5.10	92-08	Otomano II1171½Hespero117hdHigh Tribute117½	Speed,tired	12
30May69- 6Aqu	fm	1 1/16Ⓣ	1:423	3↑ Alw 15000	6	5	57	54	52½	32	Cruguet J	117	b	5.30	88-12	Rhinelander II1171Denegri1171Shadow Brook1172	Rallied	8
19May69- 6Aqu	fst	7f	:22 :441 1:10 1:234	3↑ Alw 15000	2	5	26	48	55½	52	Cruguet J	118	b	18.70	80-14	AlleyFighter118noCallaCop1181FlyingTackle118nk	In close	8
8Jun68- 7Del	fm	1 1/16Ⓣ	1:422	3↑ Alw 10000	2	2	24	32	33½	31½	Passmore WJ	119	b	*2.40	90-08	Robot III113½Lucky Turn1191Shadow Brook119½	No excuses	6
1Jun68- 8Del	sf	1 1/16Ⓣ	1:45	3↑ Brandywine H 30k	6	4	66½	33	51¾	74¾	Passmore WJ	112	b	7.60	74-21	Birthday Card1091¾Spoon Bait1121¼Tornum1121	Tired	13
11May68- 7Pim	fst	6f	:231 :462 1:113	3↑ Alw 8500	7	3	45½	44	1hd	2no	Cordero A Jr	112	b	3.20	92-17	BigRockCandy115noShdwBrk1121¼GreatWhitWy122½	Gamely	7
29Apr68- 7Pim	sf	5fⓉ	:223 :461 :584	4↑ Alw 7500	3	4	65	510	48	32½	Passmore WJ	117	b	7.00e	92-15	Road at Sea1171½Sikkim1171½Shadow Brook1172	Stride late	9
25Nov67- 7Lrl	fm	1 1/16Ⓣ	1:424	3↑ Laurel H (Div 1) 17k	4	3	42	42½	3nk	1hd	Passmore WJ	111	b	7.70	92-07	ShadowBrook111hdGreenFelt115noAttheHelm1081½	Driving	8
16Nov67- 8Lrl	fst	1	:233 :473 1:122 1:371	3↑ Alw 6000	6	4	3½	2½	1hd	1¾	Passmore WJ	112	b	4.60	95-17	ShadowBrook112¾LighttheFuse1125GayFlight1121½	Driving	8
8Nov67- 8Lrl	fm	*1Ⓣ	:234 :472 1:131 1:394	Alw 6000	4	5	43½	32	1½	11½	Passmore WJ	112	b	*2.40	91-09	ShadowBrk1121½EnglishMuffn1221Mystc'sDsr115hd	Driving	8
11Oct67- 6Aqu	my	1⊗	:232 :463 1:112 1:362	3↑ Alw 12000	2	1	2hd	2½	49	34¾	Turcotte R	112	b	*1.70	81-19	Ski Lift123¾Hornbeam1124Shadow Brook1124½	Used early	7
27Sep67- 8Aqu	fm	1 1/16Ⓣ	1:431	3↑ Alw 12000	3	4	31¼	32	62	43¾	Turcotte R	111	b	7.80	86-10	RoyalComedian113¾RoylConcert1181Hornbeam1132	In close	8
18Sep67- 7Aqu	fst	7f	:224 :453 1:10 1:23	3↑ Alw 15000	8	1	64½	68½	78½	55¼	Turcotte R	115	b	19.60	86-15	Prinkipo113¾FirstandFinest1201¾MajorArt1132	No threat	9
17Aug67- 8Sar	fst	7f	:223 :451 1:091 1:214	3↑ Alw 10000	2	5	68¼	69	45½	511	Cordero A Jr	116	b	2.70	90-09	PeterPiper1178MisterPitt'sKid1122MjorArt112nk	No threat	6
31Jly67- 6Sar	fst	7f	:222 :453 1:104 1:233	3↑ Alw 10000	4	6	612	54½	43	23½	Cordero A Jr	117	b	17.30	88-12	High Tribute1173½Shadow Brook1173Tanrackin1124	Rallied	8
22Jly67- 6Del	fst	6f	:22 :45 1:104	3↑ Alw 5000	6	8	88¼	78½	710	78¾	Lee T	111	b	4.90	82-18	VikingDancer1111¾LittltoDo111nkLghtthFus1142½	No factor	8
12Jly67- 7Del	gd	6f	:22 :453 1:114	3↑ Alw 4500	9	7	65¾	66	54½	1½	Lee T	108	b	3.00	86-18	ShadowBrook108½CrownedKing112noGayFlight1122½	Driving	9
21Jun67- 7Del	sf	1Ⓣ	1:382	3↑ Alw 5500	3	2	2½	1hd	2½	2hd	Lee T	114	b	*2.50	83-17	Mystic'sDesire114hdShadowBrook1141¼BleVert124nk	Gamely	9
30May67- 5Del	fst	6f	:222 :463 1:121	Alw 4500	3	6	67¼	43	3nk	11	Lee T	122	b	*1.30e	84-19	Shadow Brook1221Stitches1193Tangelo122no	Drew clear	8
12May67- 7Pim	fst	5f⊗	:224 :464 :591	3↑ Alw 5000	8	7	87½	75¼	62¼	31½	Lee T	113	b	2.70	96-15	LittletoDo1081ComeonGeorge112½ShadwBrk1131½	Gaining	12
25Nov66- 7Lrl	fst	7f	:222 :461 1:121 1:254	Alw 5000	8	2	37	25	23	3hd	Cruguet J	117	b	7.30	90-18	GalaPerformance122noIrishStil122noShdwBrook1173	Gamely	9
18Nov66- 7Lrl	fm	*1Ⓣ	:232 :471 1:14 1:41	Alw 5500	3	4	49	35½	33	21½	Cruguet J	117	b	5.80	83-15	ShootingChant1171½ShdwBrk117½GalaPerfrmnc1224	Game	12
7Nov66- 4Lrl	fst	6f	:232 :48 1:134	©Md Sp Wt	10	5	52¾	44½	32	12½	Cruguet J	118	b	*1.20	83-18	[DH]ShdwBrook118[DH]GrandTodd1182½TigersTune1181	Driving	12
12Oct66- 3Aqu	fst	7f	:23 :463 1:13 1:252	©Md Sp Wt	8	3	63¾	56½	33½	33½	Turcotte R	122	b	4.10	75-18	Shah1221½Quiet Town1222Shadow Brook1224	Made fair try	14
28Sep66- 4Aqu	fst	7f	:223 :46 1:113 1:243	©Md Sp Wt	4	3	64½	56½	43	44¼	Turcotte R	122	b	30.10	79-19	Comprador1222½Damascus122¾Air Rights1221	Even race	14
14Sep66- 4Aqu	gd	6f	:223 :464 1:123	©Md Sp Wt	3	7	66	78½	75½	612	Blum W	122		28.50	68-23	Hornbeam1226Quaich1221½Court Service122hd	Showed little	10
27Aug66- 1Sar	fst	6f	:224 :471 1:132	Md Sp Wt	12	4	32	84½	812	812	Turcotte R	122		42.70	69-08	TwistofTime1224½PrimeMotive1221½CourtServc122hd	Swerved	14

Shecky Greene

b. c. 1970, by Noholme II (Star Kingdom)–Lester's Pride, by Model Cadet

Lifetime record: 29 15 4 1 $317,654

Own.– J. Kellman
Br.– Joseph Kellman (Fla)
Tr.– L.M. Goldfine

Date	Cond	Dist	Fractions	Race	PP	St	1st	2nd	Str	Fin	Jockey	Wt	Eq	Odds	Speed	Top finishers	Comment	Field
26Jun74- 8Aqu	fst	7f	:223 :444 1:084 1:211	3↑ Nassau County H-G3	5	3	2hd	22	46	69½	Perret C	126	b	9.20	85-10	Timeless Moment112½Forego132½North Sea1142½	Gave way	6
20Jun74- 8Mth	fm	1 1/16Ⓣ	:243 :482 1:114 1:423	4↑ Alw 12000	1	1	2½	2hd	2hd	41½	Perret C	115	b	*1.20	95-08	DownAmng118hdBigRedL.1131BldStatemnt113nk	Weakened	6
8Jun74- 7Mth	fst	6f	:221 :443 1:092	3↑ Alw 10000	2	2	1hd	12	12	1¾	Perret C	124	b	*.80	93-17	Shecky Greene124¾Alehouse114noHome Jerome114¾	Driving	8
1Jun74- 7Mth	gd	6f	:222 :452 1:104	4↑ Alw 10000	6	2	2hd	1hd	1hd	33¾	Perret C	119	b	*.40	85-26	ProprBostonian116¾TwinTime119noShckyGrn1191¼	Bore out	8
16Feb74- 5GP	fst	6f	:213 :44 1:092	4↑ Alw 10000	8	1	22	11½	12	12	Turcotte R	122	b	*.30	92-16	ShckyGrn1222HomeJerome1122TrggrHppy112hd	Ridden out	8
2Feb74- 0GP	fst	7f	:222 :442 1:091 1:222	3↑ Sprint Champ H 41k	3	2	2½	1hd	1hd	22	Cordero A Jr	127	b	-	90-17	Cheriepe1152SheckyGreen1273GyPrr1127	Tired under impost	4
			Exhibition race run between 5th and 6th races - No wagering															
19Jan74- 9GP	fst	6f	:214 :443 1:091	3↑ Renaissance H 31k	5	1	42	32	22	2¾	Cordero A Jr	129	b	*.90	92-17	Lonetree119¾ShckyGreene129½Cherip1162	Bumped after st.	8
22Oct73- 8Aqu	fst	7f	:223 :444 1:084 1:211	3↑ Vosburgh H-G2	5	2	1hd	1½	21½	44¼	Baeza B	126	b	*1.40	91-16	Aljamin118noHighbinder1153TimelssMomnt1121¼	No excuse	8
3Oct73- 7Bel	fst	6f	:223 :451 1:092	3↑ Fall Highweight H-G3	9	3	83	64½	31½	21¼	Perret C	137	b	3.80	95-12	King's Bishop1291¼Shecky Greene137noAljamin1253	Wide	10
15Sep73- 8Bow	gd	6f	:23 :453 1:102	3↑ Patuxent H 28k	5	2	11	11	12	11½	Perret C	126	b	*1.00	91-17	SheckyGreene1261¼King'sBshop1181½PlsurCstl1082¼	Driving	9
5Aug73- 8Del	fst	6f	:443 1:094	Kelso H-G3	7	1	33	31½	3½	11¾	Perret C	128	b	*.70	96-14	ShckyGreene1281¾CarCounty1161½LttlBgChf1193	Drew clear	7
28Jly73- 8Haw	fst	6½f	:22 :451 1:092 1:161	3↑ Midwest H 28k	7	1	31	3½	12	14½	Perret C	119	b	*.40	92-11	Shecky Greene1194½Iterate1132Makambo115¾	Easily	8
18Jly73- 8Mth	fst	6f	:214 :44 1:084	Select H-G3	5	2	3nk	2hd	1hd	1½	Perret C	126	b	*1.60	96-14	SheckyGrne126½TimelessMoment1201¼BigBand1154	Driving	7
16Jun73- 9Tdn	gd	1⅛	:461 1:103 1:364 1:501	Ohio Derby-G3	8	4	35½	34	1116	1122	Perret C	122	b	7.80	67-14	OurNative1221½HeartsofLLttuc1123ArbsBoy115nk	Speed,tired	12
30May73- 7Bel	fst	1	:231 :45 1:091 1:334	Withers-G2	4	2	21	21½	21½	45½	Cordero A Jr	126	b	7.30	92-17	Linda'sChief1263StopthMusc1262Forgo126½	Bore in on turn	6
5May73- 9CD	fst	1¼	:472 1:114 1:361 1:592	Ky Derby-G1	11	1	13	32	57	616	Adams L	126	b	5.70e	87-10	Secretariat1262½Sham1268Our Native126½	Used in pace	13
28Apr73- 7CD	fst	7f	:224 :444 1:092 1:23	Alw 10000	6	2	12	12½	12½	15	Blum W	122	b	*.50	92-16	SheckyGreene1225RestlessJet122nkCrCounty1194	Mild drive	7
7Apr73- 9OP	gd	1⅛	:462 1:11 1:372 1:493	Ark Derby-G2	7	2	2½	3nk	88¼	1016	Baeza B	126	b	*.90	79-13	Impecunious1262Vodk1231¾Wrbucks1233½	Brushed first turn	10
21Mar73- 9GP	sl	1 1/16	:242 :48 1:114 1:434	Fountain of Youth-G3	3	2	23	21	11	11	Baeza B	122	b	*1.10	84-23	SheckyGreene1221TwiceaPrince117½MyGallant1122½	Driving	6
7Mar73- 9GP	fst	7f	:221 :443 1:082 1:204	Hutcheson-G3	2	3	3½	12	14	13¼	Baeza B	122	b	*.30	100-10	Shecky Greene1223¼Forego1169Leo's Pisces1124½	Easily	7
21Feb73- 9Hia	fst	7f	:231 :46 1:10 1:223	[S]Fla Breeders' H 30k	6	2	12	11½	12½	11¾	Baeza B	127		*.70	94-14	SheckyGreene1271¾StepNicely1164½JmDuncn115no	Ridden out	6
14Feb73- 7Hia	fst	6f	:214 :442 1:083	Alw 8000	1	2	2hd	11½	15	18	Baeza B	122		*2.10	101-13	SheckyGreene1228AssagaiJr115¾StepNicely1153	Ridden out	8
18Nov72- 8CD	fst	1	:223 :451 1:104 1:353	Ky Jockey Club 59k	5	2	21	62¼	818	831	Marquez C	122	b	1.90e	60-20	Puntilla1169Golden Don116nkAnnihilate 'Em1228	Tired	8
8Nov72- 8CD	sl	7f	:223 :45 1:10 1:234	Alw 10000	4	2	1½	11	11½	2nk	Marquez C	122	b	*.50	88-22	Annihilate'Em112nkShckyGreen1229TonitheCt1133	Swerved	10

4Oct72- 7Bel	fst 7f	:221 :444 1:093 1:223	Cowdin 54k	3 5 52¼ 64¾ 54½ 56¼	Marquez CH	121 b	3.80	88-11	StepNicely1152StoptheMusic1212Linda'sChief1151½	Checked	12
12Aug72- 8AP	fst 6f	:223 :46 :58 1:102	Futurity 186k	10 2 43 1½ 15 19	Marquez C	122 b	*.40e	91-16	SheckyGrn1229SunnySouth1221¼Slor'sNghtOut1224	In hand	12
26Jly72- 8AP	sly 5½f	:222 :462 :584 1:051	©Arch Ward 28k	3 5 42 32 13 12	Marquez C	117 b	*1.00	89-26	ShckyGreene1172DeadlyDream1155SunnySouth122½	Driving	12
8Jly72- 6AP	fst 5½f	:222 :444 :564 1:031	Alw 5400	6 1 3½ 18 17 19	Marquez C	115 b	*.30	99-09	ShckyGreene1159StrongSide118hdBacktoJack1152¼	Easily	8
15Jun72- 7AP	fst 5f	:22 :453 :571	Md Sp Wt	6 2 14 15 17 111	Marquez C	118 b	5.90	100-15	SheckyGrne11811HandsomDplomt1185IrshDoubt118hd	Easily	8

Shuvee

ch. f. 1966, by Nashua (Nasrullah)–Levee, by Hill Prince **Lifetime record: 44 16 10 6 $890,445**

Own.– Mrs W. Stone
Br.– Whitney Stone (Va)
Tr.– W.C. Freeman

30Oct71- 7Aqu	fst 2	:482 2:30 2:552 3:202 3↑	J C Gold Cup 111k	6 4 2½ 11½ 15 17	Velasquez J	121	*1.30	94-16	Shuvee1217Paraje1242Loud1248	Ridden out	7
11Oct71- 8Atl	gd 1 3/16	:482 1:113 1:364 1:564 3↑	ⒻMatchmaker 50k	6 5 45½ 56½ 31 4¾	Turcotte R	118	*1.30	91-12	Deceit113hdSea Saga114hdDouble Delta125½	No excuse	8
2Oct71- 7Bel	fst 1¼	:461 1:10 1:35 2:002 3↑	Woodward 113k	7 4 510 69 69 69	Turcotte R	123	3.70	89-13	DCougarII1265WestCoastScout121nkTinajro121no	No threat	10
11Sep71- 7Bel	sly 1⅛	:453 1:093 1:351 1:483 3↑	ⒻBeldame 82k	2 6 46½ 26 24 2½	Baeza B	123	*.70	90-12	Double Delta123½Shuvee12310Cathy Honey1231½	Second best	7
23Aug71- 7Sar	fst 1⅛	:50 1:141 1:382 1:503 3↑	ⒻDiana H 44k	5 3 31½ 21 21 1nk	Turcotte R	128	*1.10	88-11	Shuvee128nkDouble Delta1265½Cathy Honey116nk	Hard drive	5
7Aug71- 7Sar	fst 1⅛	:473 1:114 1:364 1:492 3↑	Whitney 60k	13 9 108½ 116¼ 66 33	Turcotte R	116	*4.10	91-11	Protanto117hdPeace Corps1143Shuvee116nk	Rallied wide	14
22May71- 7Aqu	fst 1⅛	:471 1:122 1:37 1:493 3↑	ⒻTop Flight H 53k	5 3 31½ 1½ 11 1¾	Turcotte R	127	*.70e	88-17	Shuvee127¾Cathy Honey1181¼Office Queen1277	Driving	5
28Apr71- 7Aqu	fst 1	:232 :464 1:113 1:364 3↑	ⒻBed o' Roses H 32k	2 4 42½ 42 21½ 22	Turcotte R	127	*.60	81-23	Office Queen1252Shuvee1273Royal Fillet1103½	Gamely	6
15Apr71- 7Aqu	fst 6f	:23 :462 1:103 3↑	Alw 20000	6 1 53½ 67 68 25	Baeza B	116	*1.60e	85-25	SummerAir1195Shvee116nkPrimeVenture1211½	Finished well	9
31Oct70- 7Aqu	fst 2	:503 2:302 2:554 3:213 3↑	J C Gold Cup 108k	4 1 1½ 1hd 12½ 12	Turcotte R	121	2.90	88-16	Shuvee1212Loud1191¼Hydrologist1243¾	Mild urging	5
3Oct70- 7Bel	fst 1¼	:462 1:101 1:353 2:014 3↑	Woodward 109k	2 4 46 41½ 55½ 57¾	Turcotte R	123	7.70	83-08	Personality121nkDHHydrologst126DHTwogundn1264½	Hit rail	7
12Sep70- 7Bel	fst 1⅛	:454 1:10 1:351 1:48 3↑	ⒻBeldame 83k	2 2 25 23 11 11	Turcotte R	123	*1.30e	94-14	Shuvee1231Obeah1231¼Cold Comfort1182½	Brisk drive	7
24Aug70- 7Sar	sly 1⅛	:464 1:112 1:371 1:493 3↑	ⒻDiana H 49k	4 6 76¾ 43 21 1no	Turcotte R	120	3.50	93-15	Shuvee120noDark Emerald1094Native Partner1121	Driving	12
8Jly70- 8Mth	fst 1 1/16	:232 :463 1:111 1:44 3↑	ⒻMolly Pitcher 44k	4 3 58¼ 67½ 66½ 56	Baeza B	123	*.70	79-13	DoublRippl112¾WhataDream1151Deb'sDarlng1144	No excuse	9
10Jun70- 7Bel	fst 7f	:222 :452 1:102 1:234 3↑	ⒻVagrancy H 28k	2 4 511 611 611 510	Baeza B	123	2.00	78-15	Process Shot1272½Powder Mountain104¾Native Partner1106	No response	6
23May70- 7Aqu	fst 1⅛	:481 1:114 1:362 1:483 3↑	ⒻTop Flight H 57k	2 1 1hd 1½ 1½ 14	Baeza B	120	2.40	93-13	Shuvee1204Singing Rain1227Swiss Cheese110¾	Handily	10
2May70- 8Pim	fst 1 1/16	:233 :464 1:11 1:433 3↑	ⒻGallorette H 32k	5 6 67 56½ 27 28	Davidson J	122	*1.20	84-13	SingingRain1198Shuvee1223½MissFallRiver1091½	No excuse	7
25Apr70- 8Aqu	fst 1	:24 :464 1:11 1:352 3↑	Alw 15000	6 5 75¼ 53 42 43¼	Davidson J	113	*3.30	87-18	GleamngSword1161¾ShinngSword1181½Bromtr120hd	No rally	9
8Apr70- 7Aqu	fst 7f	:23 :452 1:10 1:224 3↑	ⒻDistaff H 27k	2 5 510 512 613 615	Davidson J	123	7.50	72-20	ProcssShot1261¾TaWee1342DedctdtoSu115hd	Never a factor	6
27Nov69- 7Aqu	fst 1⅛	:492 1:134 1:381 1:50 3↑	ⒻFirenze H 56k	1 1 2½ 42 21 2¾	Davidson J	122	*1.40	85-19	Amerigo Lady121¾Shuvee1221½Obeah120½	Finished willingly	8
11Nov69- 7Aqu	gd 1¼	:473 1:121 1:38 2:03 3↑	ⒻLadies H 58k	7 3 612 43 3½ 11¼	Davidson J	117	*2.80	81-22	Shuvee1171¼AmrigoLdy1211¼Obeh1212½	Blocked,hard drive	11
1Nov69- 7Aqu	fst 7f	:221 :442 1:083 1:213 3↑	Vosburgh H 58k	3 10 119 1012 85½ 61¾	Turcotte R	114	14.90	91-13	TaWee123hdDHPlckyLucky116DHRisingMarkt120½	Late bid	11
13Sep69- 7Bel	fst 1⅛	:462 1:103 1:36 1:491 3↑	ⒻBeldame 81k	3 4 48½ 46 37 36½	Davidson J	118	3.00	83-16	Gamely1233Amerigo Lady1233½Shuvee1182	Finished willing	5
30Aug69- 7Bel	fst 1⅛	:462 1:102 1:352 1:49	ⒻGazelle H 53k	1 5 57 56½ 47 36½	Davidson J	127	*1.10	84-12	Gallant Bloom1273½Pit Bunny1163Shuvee1271½	No excuse	5
9Aug69- 6Sar	gd 1¼	:483 1:131 1:392 2:062	ⒻAlabama 54k	2 4 46 31½ 11½ 14	Davidson J	124	*1.00	76-15	Shuvee1244PitBunny114½HailtoPatsy1182	Easily the best	5
26Jly69- 8Del	gd 1⅛	:464 1:122 1:384 1:511	ⒻDel Oaks 59k	7 5 68½ 56½ 411 417	Davidson J	121	1.60	64-23	DPitBunny1121¼GallantBlm12112WhitXmss1113¼	No excuse	7
12Jly69- 7Lib	fst 1 1/16	:231 :47 1:104 1:431	ⒻCotillion H 55k	3 6 54¾ 53¼ 3½ 1nk	Davidson J	124	*.40	- -	Shuvee124nkClass Is Out1133Secret Verdict1142	Just up	7
21Jun69- 7Bel	fst 1¼	:462 1:103 1:363 2:031	ⒻC C A Oaks 119k	4 5 511 44½ 1hd 13	Davidson J	121	*.30	84-17	Shuvee1213Hail to Patsy1211½Secret Verdict1211½	Easily	7
31May69- 7Aqu	fst 1⅛	:474 1:123 1:38 1:501	ⒻMother Goose 87k	1 4 511 55½ 22 12½	Davidson J	121	*1.10	85-17	Shuvee1212½HailtoPatsy1212½RestlssTorndo1214	Ridden out	6
17May69- 7Aqu	fst 1	:223 :443 1:091 1:353	ⒻAcorn 59k	7 5 58½ 36 2hd 1¾	Davidson J	121	*.80	89-14	Shuvee121¾Hail to Patsy1213Big Advance121nk	Mild drive	9
7May69- 7Aqu	fst 7f	:222 :451 1:092 1:223	ⒻComely 28k	3 6 66 45 23 2hd	Davidson J	121	2.90	88-13	TaWee118hdShuvee1215HastyHitter118hd	Getting to winner	6
9Nov68- 8GS	sl 1 1/16	:23 :474 1:13 1:454	ⒻGardenia 183k	5 7 52½ 2hd 21½ 21¼	Davidson J	119	*1.00	75-28	Gallant Bloom1191¼Shuvee11915Let's Be Gay119nk	Game try	7
26Oct68- 0Lrl	fst 1 1/16	:23 :463 1:123 1:444	ⒻSelima 108k	4 5 47 23½ 2hd 1nk	Turcotte R	122	-	93-17	Shuvee122nkProcess Shot1196Queen's Double11940	Driving	5
			Exhibition race run between 7th and 8th races-No wagering								
5Oct68- 7Bel	fst 1	:23 :463 1:112 1:37	ⒻFrizette 130k	7 8 99½ 76 23 1nk	Davidson J	119	4.50e	89-13	Shuvee119nkGallant Bloom1193Dihela1194	Up final strides	11
23Sep68- 7Bel	fst 7f	:223 :46 1:104 1:241	ⒻAstarita (Div 2) 23k	3 6 56½ 65½ 74¾ 31½	Davidson J	112	10.80	85-17	Dihela1121Imbibe116nkShuvee1122	Found stride late	8
14Sep68- 4Aqu	fst 6f	:223 :461 1:114	ⒻAlw 7000	3 10 107½ 97 64¼ 21¼	Davidson J	119	*2.70	83-14	Gunite1081¼Shuvee119¾Plane119hd	In close,rallied	12
30Aug68- 6Aqu	fst 6f	:222 :46 1:112	ⒻAlw 12000	1 7 711 69½ 25 23	Baeza B	114	6.40	83-20	Gallant Bloom1063Shuvee1143Prefer1161	Finished strongly	7
20Aug68- 5Sar	fst 6f	:221 :462 1:114	ⒻMd Sp Wt	13 11 98 98¼ 2½ 14	Baeza B	119	3.70	89-09	Shuvee1194Table D'Hote119½Ambranded1192½	Easily best	14
13Aug68- 5Sar	fst 5½f	:221 :454 :573 1:04	ⒻMd Sp Wt	4 7 87¼ 1012 613 512	Gustines H	119	4.20	85-11	Ta Wee1196Drip Spring1192Socializing1192½	No mishap	12
3Aug68- 1Sar	fst 5½f	:224 :471 :592 1:054	ⒻMd Sp Wt	7 4 41½ 52¾ 31½ 31½	Baeza B	119 b	*1.40	86-12	Pashamin119noElizabeth'sDancr1161½Shuvee1195	No mishap	10
25Jly68- 5Aqu	gd 5½f	:222 :462 :584 1:051	ⒻMd Sp Wt	8 8 63½ 74¾ 33½ 23	Baeza B	119 b	*2.50	84-18	French Bread1193Shuvee1194Keep a Secret1191	Rallied	9
5Jun68- 4Bel	fst 5½f	:231 :47 :591 1:053	ⒻMd Sp Wt	9 8 52 52 43½ 35¾	Davidson J	119 b	*1.70	87-15	Golden Or119¾Go to Bed1195Shuvee119¾	Raced wide late	10
22May68- 4Bel	fst 5½f	:23 :462 :584 1:052	ⒻMd Sp Wt	4 7 34 33 45 42¼	Davidson J	119	*2.50	92-14	Fillypasser119hdFoolish Miss119nkTudor Home1192	Hung	10
8May68- 4Aqu	fst 5f	:222 :461 :59	ⒻMd Sp Wt	5 8 87¾ 69½ 56½ 47¾	Davidson J	119	*1.90	82-11	Gunite1194Miss Georgene119¾Most Welcome1193	No threat	10

Smart Angle

b. f. 1977, by Quadrangle (Cohoes)–Smartaire, by Quibu **Lifetime record: 17 7 4 1 $414,217**

Own.– Ryehill Farm
Br.– Ryehill Farm (Md)
Tr.– Woodford C. Stephens

24Jan81- 8GP	sly 6f	:221 :454 1:11 4↑	ⒻAlw 20000	3 2 1½ 1hd 3½ 59¼	Maple E	115 b	*2.30	75-20	Lacey1175Nice and Sharp1172Sober Jig1151	Faltered	10
12Jan81- 9GP	fm *1Ⓣ	1:373 4↑	ⒻAlw 25000	7 1 13 2½ 57½ 713	Maple E	115	*2.40	80-19	SoloHaina1177LaSoufriere119hdDoingItMyWy122½	Gave way	8
18Dec80- 8Crc	fst 6f	:222 :46 1:113 3↑	ⒻAlw 13000	9 1 42 44½ 811 914	Maple E	118	*.80	80-16	Migdalia C.1133Lacey118nkClassy Witch1146½	Fell back	9
16May80- 8Pim	fst 1 1/16	:232 :464 1:111 1:442	ⒻBlack-Eyed Susan-G2	7 2 22 31½ 34 65	Maple S	121	*.90	78-17	WeberCityMiss1182¼Bishop'sRing1111ChampagnStr114½	Tired	8
5Apr80- 9OP	fst 1 1/16	:231 :464 1:114 1:451	ⒻFantasy-G1	7 4 52¼ 34½ 513 728	Maple S	121	1.40	54-20	Bold 'nDetermind1212¼Satin Ribera1154Honest and True1187	Gave way	7
22Mar80- 9FG	fst 1 1/16	:241 :473 1:121 1:442	ⒻFG Oaks 56k	7 1 11½ 11½ 11½ 2hd	Maple S	121	*.20	90-15	Honest and True118hdSmartAngle121½LadyTaurianPeace1184	Just failed	8
3Mar80- 9Hia	fst 1⅛	:474 1:122 1:38 1:51	ⒻPoinsettia-G3	1 1 16 17 16 17	Maple S	122	*.40	77-23	SrtAngle1227SweetAudrey114½BrownSt.Belle11414	Easily	5
13Feb80- 9Hia	fst 7f	:231 :454 1:103 1:24	ⒻHibiscus 36k	4 2 1hd 2½ 1½ 2no	Maple S	122	*.40	83-14	BrownSt.Belle112noSmrtAngle1222½SweetAudry1172½	Failed	6
17Nov79- 8Aqu	fst 1⅛	:481 1:131 1:383 1:511	ⒻDemoiselle-G2	2 3 51½ 61¾ 1hd 2no	Maple S	121	*1.10	79-21	GenuineRisk116noSmartAngle1216¾SprucePine1123¾	Bore in	7
20Oct79- 9Pim	fst 1 1/16	:232 :471 1:114 1:451	ⒻSelima-G1	4 2 23 22 11½ 12	Maple S	122	*.50	79-18	SmartAngle1222ParExcellance122½StretBllt1193	Ridden out	6
7Oct79- 8Bel	fst 1	:233 :47 1:123 1:381	ⒻFrizette-G1	8 4 32 11 1hd 11¾	Maple S	119	2.90	77-20	Smart Angle1191¾Royal Suite11911Hardship1195	Driving	11
24Sep79- 8Bel	fst 7f	:231 :462 1:103 1:234	ⒻMatron-G1	3 1 1hd 11 1hd 1½	Maple S	119	8.00	83-22	SmartAngle119½RoyalSuite1193¾NuitD'Amour1193¾	Driving	5
10Sep79- 8Bel	fst 6½f	:224 :461 1:104 1:171	ⒻAstarita-G3	6 1 3½ 3½ 21½ 33¼	Maple S	116	*1.40	87-20	Royal Suite1142¾Andrea F.112½Smart Angle1161½	Weakened	6
26Aug79- 8Sar	fst 6f	:213 :45 1:103	ⒻSpinaway-G1	1 2 24 2½ 12 11½	Maple S	119	*.80	87-12	SmrtAngle1191½JetRating1193½MarthonGrl119hd	Ridden out	6
13Aug79- 8Sar	my 6f	:214 :452 1:11	ⒻAdirondack-G3	1 3 2hd 1hd 1hd 1nk	Maple S	119	3.90	85-14	Smart Angle119nkLucky My Way1141½Andrea F.1142	Driving	9
28Jly79- 7Bow	fst 5½f	:214 :452 :581 1:05	ⒻⓈLuck Penny 32k	4 4 33 36½ 33½ 1nk	Maple S	114	1.30	94-17	Smart Angle114nkHail to Ambition1153Salem's Nymph1229	Driving	5
12Jly79- 4Bel	fst 5½f	:22 :453 :582 1:051	ⒻMd Sp Wt	4 2 1hd 1hd 1hd 2hd	Maple E	117	2.00	89-14	RioRita117hdSmartAngle1171¾DamaskFan1171	Stubborn try	10

Snow Knight (GB)

ch. c. 1971, by Firestreak (Pardal)–Snow Blossom, by Flush Royal — Lifetime record: 22 9 5 2 $532,427

Own.– Windfields Farm
Br.– J.A.C. Lilley (GB)
Tr.– M. Miller

8Nov75- 7Lrl yl 1½Ⓣ :494 1:152 2:062 2:311 3↑ D C Int'l-G1 5 3 59½ 52¾ 611 612 Velasquez J 127 *2.10 51-37 Nobiliary117¾Comtesse de Loir1243On My Way II1272 9
Bobbled backstretch
26Oct75- 7WO fm 1⅝Ⓣ :501 1:392 2:431 3↑ Can Int'l-G1 11 6 66 31 12 1½ Velasquez J 126 3.70 84-16 Snow Knight126½Comtesse de Loir1231½Carney's Point126hd 11
Ridden out
11Oct75- 8Bel gd 1½Ⓣ :493 1:15 2:05 2:291 3↑ Man o' War-G1 8 5 53½ 31½ 3½ 21¾ Velasquez J 126 *1.00 76-22 ⒹOneontheAisle1211¾SnowKnight1261Drollry126nk Bothered 8
Placed first through disqualification
1Oct75- 8Bel gd 1⅜Ⓣ :483 1:133 1:38 2:161 3↑ Manhattan H (Div 2)-G2 5 7 74¾ 4¾ 1hd 1¾ Velasquez J 123 *1.00e 84-17 Snow Knight123¾Shady Character1131¼One on the Aisle114 2½ 8
Driving
17Sep75- 8Bel fm 1¼Ⓣ :48 1:121 1:364 2:01 3↑ Brightn Bch H (Div 2) 43k 5 2 32½ 1½ 13 11¼ Baeza B 121 *1.80e 95-08 Snow Knight1211¼Drollery111nkGolden Don126 2½ Driving 9
20Aug75- 8Sar fm 1⅝Ⓣ 2:42 3↑ Seneca H-G3 6 1 11 1½ 12 11½ Velasquez J 118 *2.00e 79-21 Snow Knight1181½Golden Don126½Drollery1113 Mild drive 8
26Jly75- 7Atl gd 1 3/16Ⓣ :49 1:13 1:392 1:57 3↑ U Nations H-G1 7 6 713 912 914 915 Barrera C 118 3.80 70-26 RoyalGlint1203½Stonewalk1205½R.TomCan116hd Unruly start 9
10Jly75- 6Bel gd 1 1/16Ⓣ :24 :464 1:11 1:424 3↑ Alw 20000 2 6 68½ 53½ 42½ 2no Velasquez J 122 *1.00 87-13 Harbor Pilot116noSnow Knight1221¾Branford Court1161 7
Circled horses
18Jun75- 6Bel gd 1 1/16Ⓣ :233 :471 1:114 1:433 3↑ Alw 15000 4 3 33 32½ 1½ 11 Velasquez J 116 *.90 83-17 SnowKnight1161TelexNumber1132¾Ladd113hd Blocked,easily 6
Previously trained by J. Bentley
27Oct74- 7WO fm 1⅝Ⓣ :471 1:373 2:40 3↑ Can Int'l-G2 5 1 18 12 64¼ 810 Hawley S 117 b 12.90 95-05 Dahlia1231Big Spruce1261½Carney's Point126hd Used early 9
19Oct74- 7WO fm 1¼Ⓣ :48 1:124 1:38 2:03 3↑ Jockey Club Cup H 17k 8 3 21 2hd 3nk 65½ Rogers C 123 *.90 86-09 Carney's Point120noGood Port1142½Olmedo112¾ Tired 8
12Oct74- 6WO fm *1 1/16Ⓣ :251 :51 1:161 1:463 3↑ Alw 6500 3 1 11½ 11½ 1hd 2no Hawley S 117 *.65 71-22 Carney's Point126noSnow Knight1172¾Good Port123¾ Missed 5
Previously trained by P. Nelson
20Aug74♦ York(GB) gd *1 5/16ⓉLH 2:092 3↑ Benson & Hedges Gold Cup-G1 Stk120000 34 Taylor B 122 14.00 Dahlia1302½Imperial Prince1221½Snow Knight122nk 9
Tracked in 3rd,one-paced last quarter
27Jly74♦ Ascot(GB) gd 1½ⓉRH 2:33 3↑ King George VI & Queen Eliz Stk245000 69 Taylor B 119 5.50 Dahlia1302½Highclere1161Dankaro119 10
Tracked leader,led over 2f out,weakened 1½f out
5Jun74♦ Epsom(GB) fm 1½ⓉLH 2:35 Epsom Derby Stk267000 12 Taylor B 126 50.00 Snow Knight1262Imperial Prince1261Giacometti126nk 18
Led over 6f out,held well
11May74♦ Lingfield(GB) gd 1½ⓉLH 2:394 Derby Trial Stakes Stk23200 32½ Taylor B 126 2.25 Bustino1261Sin y Sin1261½Snow Knight1262½ 7
Trailed to 4f out,bid 2f out,one-paced final furlong
27Apr74♦ Sandown(GB) gd 1¼ⓉRH 2:094 Classic Trial Stakes Stk8700 2½ Taylor B 126 *1.75 Bustino121½Snow Knight126¾Understudy1261½ 9
Led,hard ridden over 1f out,headed 100y out,gamely
27Oct73♦ Doncaster(GB) yl 1ⓉLH 1:432 Observer Gold Cup Stk90000 821 Hide E 126 8.00 Apalachee1262Mississipian12610Alpine Nephew126¾ 10
Tracked in 5th,weakened 3f out
12Sep73♦ Doncaster(GB) gd 7fⓉStr 1:28 Champagne Stakes Stk22000 2no Taylor B 126 10.00 Giacometti126noSnow Knight1262Pitcairn1262½ 8
Drifted throughout,rallied 1f out,just missed
14Jly73♦ Newbury(GB) gd 7fⓉStr 1:313 Donnington Castle Stakes Alw4000 15 Taylor B 123 *1.10 Snow Knight1235Red Trooper1191Teasing1191½ 13
Led 2½f out,drew clear final furlong
5Jly73♦ Newmarket(GB) gd 7fⓉStr 1:31 Limekilns Plate Alw2900 2¾ Moore G 123 *.50 Meon Hill119¾0Snow Knight1232½Charente1191½ 8
Led to 100y out,gave way grudgingly
1Jun73♦ Kempton(GB) gd 6fⓉStr 1:141 Rivermead Maiden Plate Mdn1700 11½ Moore G 126 16.00 Snow Knight1261½Galindo1265Ballylickey120½ 16
Led over 2f out,driving

Soothsayer

dkbbr. g. 1967, by Mystic II (Relic)–Sagoma, by Saratoga — Lifetime record: 36 13 13 3 $217,119

Own.– Montpelier
Br.– Mrs Marion duPont Scott (Va)
Tr.– Toby Balding

11Nov76♦ Wincanton(GB) gd 2⅝RH 5:211 6↑ Badger Beer Handicap Chase Hcp5400 318 Linley R 174 12.00 Zeta's Son1616Go-Over16112Soothsayer1741½ 14
Behind to 12th,bid 2 out,finished well
23Oct76♦ Newbury(GB) yl 2½LH 5:123 6↑ Hermitage Chase Alw6700 4 Linley R 160 6.50 Game Spirit1601Bula164Lean Forward1608 4
Chased in 3rd,behind from 13th,distanced
Previously trained by P.M. Howe
15Nov75- 4Cam fm 2 13/16 S'Chase 5:301 4↑ Colonial Cup 50k 9 11 105¼ 89½ 51½ 33½ Aitcheson J Jr 162 -e -- Cafe Prince1603Augustus Bay162½Soothsayer162½ Rallied 18
1Nov75- 3Mtp fm *2½ S'Chase 4:413 4↑ Noel Laing H 5.6k 9 5 75½ 72¾ 1½ 1hd Aitcheson J Jr 158 s -- Soothsayer158hdAugustus Bay1514Gran Kan1551½ All out 10
13Sep75- 7Fai fm *2½ S'Chase 5:02 4↑ Grand National H 12k 2 3 31½ 5¾ 42½ 412 Aitcheson J Jr 161 *1.20 -- AugustusBay1475½GranKan1551½HappyIntellectual1465 Tired 9
21Aug75- 4Sar fm 2⅜ S'Chase 4:201 4↑ NY Trf Wrtrs Cup H 22k 7 6 65½ 310 21½ 2nk Aitcheson J Jr 160 s 3.20 -- Life's Illusion145nkSoothsayer160½Arctic Joe1485½ Sharp 9
Previously trained by Fred Winter
13Mar75♦ Cheltenhm(GB) hy *3¼LH 7:512 7↑ Cheltenham Gold Cup Chase Stk54000 26 Pitman R 168 28.00 Ten Up1686Soothsayer168½Bula16812 8
Progress 13th,bid 2 out,mistake last,up for 2nd
12Feb75♦ Ascot(GB) hy 3RH 6:503 7↑ Whitbread Trial Hcp Chase Hcp9300 225 Francome J 167 6.50 Ten Up16025Soothsayer167¾Glanford Brigg1615 8
Tracked leaders,led 16th and 17th,mistakes and weakened 18th
16Jan75♦ Wincanton(GB) sf 2⅝RH 5:514 7↑ John Bull Chase Alw3400 130 Francome J 168 *.55 Soothsayer16830Game Spirit168 2
Jumped well,led throughout,left clear 14th
26Dec74♦ Kempton(GB) sf 3RH 6:212 7↑ King George VI Chase Stk21000 38¾ Francome J 157 4.50 Captain Christy1688Pendil168¾Soothsayer15710 6
Tracked leaders,ones paced from 3 out
30Nov74♦ Sandown(GB) yl 2RH 4:00 6↑ Benson & Hedges Gold Cup Chase Stk13000 - Francome J 162 *1.35 Dorless1444Tingle Creek174½Amarind1541½ 10
3rd when fell at 6th
9Nov74♦ Cheltenhm(GB) yl 2½LH 5:15 6↑ Mackeson Gold Cup Hcp Chase Stk14700 28 Francome J 168 6.00 Bruslee1478Soothsayer1682½High Ken1495 11
Progress from 11th,led 2 out,headed after last,one-paced
30Oct74♦ Ascot(GB) gd 2RH 4:01 6↑ Dunkirk Handicap Chase Hcp3700 21½ Francome J 169 *1.00 Golden Sol1471½Soothsayer1691½Well Oiled1476 6
Rated toward rear,bid approaching last,finished well
14Mar74♦ Cheltenhm(GB) sf 2LH 4:214 6↑ Cathcart Challenge Cup Chase Stk5000 14 Pitman R 157 *1.35 Soothsayer1574L'Escargot1576Clever Scot1572 7
Led approaching second last,comfortably
Previously trained by P.M. Howe
17Nov73- 2Cam fm 2 13/16 S'Chase 5:214 4↑ Colonial Cup 50k 14 5 68 67 33 2no Aitcheson J Jr 162 s - -- LuckyBoyIII149noSthsayr162noDremMgc1531¼ Just missed 15
3Nov73- 3Mtp fm 2½ S'Chase 4:44 4↑ Noel Laing H 5k 3 7 55¼ 63¼ 2nk 21½ Aitcheson J Jr 165 s - -- LuckyBoyIII1471½Sthsayer16510BrkngDwn140¾ Second best 7
6Oct73- 4Lig fm *2½ S'Chase 5:032 4↑ Temple Gwathmey H 25k 5 7 77½ 42 2nk 21¼ Aitcheson J Jr 162 - -- Athenian Idol1401¼Soothsayer1628Top Bid1572 Sharp try 8
3Oct73- 7Lig gd *7fⓉ 1:304 3↑ Alw 2000 14 14 119½ 98 95½ 109 Aitcheson J Jr 155 - -- Loch Lomond II1582Mod Man1431½Dot to Dot131nk No factor 15
18Nov72- 3Cam fm 2 13/16 S'Chase 5:234 4↑ Colonial Cup 100k 4 14 85¼ 21 1½ 12½ Aitcheson J Jr 158 -e -- Soothsayer1582½Inkslinger158¾Shadow Brook160nk Driving 16
7Oct72- 4Lig sf *2½ S'Chase 5:192 4↑ Temple Gwathmey H 30k 3 10 911 78¾ 13 17 Aitcheson J Jr 162 -e -- Soothsayr1627SpeedKills143¾ShadwBrook16310 Ridden out 12

Date	Track/Cond	Dist/Time	Race	Running	Jockey	Wt	Odds	Speed	Finish	Comment	Field
4Oct72-6Lig	fm *7f ⊤	1:34 3↑ Alw	8 7 5³ 32¾ 1nk 1²	Aitcheson J Jr	155	s -e --	Soothsayer155²Jaunty146½Emerald Isle145nk	Driving 12
16Sep72-1Fai	fm *7f ⊤	1:25 13↑ Alw 1000	2 2 75½ 62½ 43 1no	Aitcheson J Jr	152	s *1.30 --	Soothsayer152noDetangle1376Tudor Winds1491	Hard drive 14
20Nov71-2Cam	fm 2⅛	S'Chase 5:17 4↑ Colonial Cup 10k	2 5 4³↑ 4 2 2nk	Fishback J	149	-e --	Inkslinger149nkSoothsayer1498Top Bid1603	Unruly early 15
6Nov71-2Mtp	fst *1	1:35² 3↑ Alw 600	5 5 31½ 2½ 1½ 11½	Fishback J	149	-e --	Soothsayer1491Sail Master142³Eagle's Top1421¾	Drew out 11
14Oct71-5Bel	sf 2⅝	Hurdles 4:55⁴ 4↑ NY Trf Wrtrs Cup H 33k	5 6 3² 21½ 16 1³	Fishback J	153	2.10 --	Soothsayer153³Predominio141³Wustenchef162³½	Easily 8
14Sep71-3Bel	sf 2⅝	Hurdles 5:03⁴ 4↑ Broad Hollow H 22k	4 5 36½ 15 118 117	Fishback J	143	*1.40e --	Soothsayer14317Inkslinger1516DremMgc1388	With authority 6
12Aug71-3Sar	fm 2⅛	Hurdles 3:43³ 4↑ Lovely Night H 22k	5 7 54½ 2½ 2½ 2nk	Brittle C III	139	8.60 --	Shadow Brook156nkSoothsayer1398Inkslinger1502½	2nd best 7
5Aug71-9Sar	fm 1⅞	Hurdles 3:24² 4↑ Alw 12000	7 8 716 2² 1½ 12½	Brittle C III	144	*1.60e --	Soothsayer1442½Shadow II135noDream Magic1411	Easily 8
2Jun71-4Del	yl *2⅛	Hurdles 3:54⁴ 4↑ Tom Roby 10k	4 11 107 68¾ 57¼ 510	Brittle C III	133	11.70 --	ExplodeII142³Balustrd143²½PortMnch133³	Poor landing 9th 13
22May71-7Fai	fm *1⅞	Hurdles 3:40² 4↑ Alw 1800	1 6 86½ 64¼ 64¼ 63½	Brittle C III	145	2.90e --	Alegar131noProfile1442½Uldimeo141¾	No threat 13
14Nov70-3Cam	fm *2	2:41³ Governors H 10k	- 8 65¼ 41 32 2²	Brittle C III	137	-e --	Inkslinger149²Soothsayer1374½Shadow II132⁴	Gamely 8
15Oct70-3Bel	sf 2	Hurdles 3:47⁴ LE Stoddard Jr H 17k	1 9 81³ 42½ 21 2³	Brittle C III	139	5.60e --	Inkslinger1483Soothsayer1394½EasternPromise1351½	Gamely 9
30Sep70-3Bel	yl 1⅞	Hurdles 3:26⁴ 3↑ Sp Wt 7500	6 10 911 34½ 1½ 12½	Brittle C III	134	4.80e --	Soothsayer1342½TresurHuntIII154⁴BluRunnr134²	Mild drive 12
19Sep70-5Fai	hd *1¾	Hurdles 3:10¹ 3↑ Md Sp Wt	5 1 5³ 31½ 14 112	Brittle C III⁵	133	s *1.10 --	Soothsayer13312Favori152¹⁵Marine Band1428	Handily 7
11Sep70-9Fai	sf 1¾	3:13³ OClm 10000	8 8 710 36 23 26	Brittle C III⁵	140	12.50e --	Summer Crop1456Soothsayr1409Colosso You13818	Steadied 10
23May70-9Fai	sf *7f ⊤	1:28 3↑ Md Sp Wt	10 10 64¾ 69¾ 65¾ 510	Brittle C III	140	3.00 --	Dream Magic136²Othello140²Troponi154¹	No threat 13

Spectacular Bid

gr. c. 1976, by Bold Bidder (Bold Ruler)–Spectacular, by Promised Land
Own.– Hawksworth Farm
Br.– Mmes Gilmour & Jason (Ky)
Tr.– Grover G. Delp

Lifetime record: 30 26 2 1 $2,781,608

Date	Track/Cond	Dist/Time	Race	Running	Jockey	Wt	Odds	Speed	Finish	Comment	Field
20Sep80-0Bel	fst 1¼	:50² 1:14¹ 1:38¹ 2:02² 3↑ Woodward-G1	1 1 1 1 1 1	Shoemaker W	126	88-21	Spectacular Bid126	In hand 1
	Walkover,run between 7th and 8th race - Walkover,no wagering								
16Aug80-9Mth	fst 1⅛	:46⁴ 1:11¹ 1:35³ 1:48 3↑ AL Haskell H-G1	5 7 65½ 5¾ 1½ 11¾	Shoemaker W	132	*.10 95-15	SpectacularBd132¹¾Glorious Song117¹¼The Cool Virginian112⁴ 8
	Ridden out								
19Jly80-8AP	fst 1⅛	:46¹ 1:09⁴ 1:34 1:46¹ 3↑ Wash Park-G3	4 4 44 2nd 14 110	Shoemaker W	130	*.05 103-17	SpectacularBid130¹⁰HoldYourTrcks119⁸Archtct119¹½ Easily 6
8Jun80-8Hol	fst 1⅛	:45 1:08⁴ 1:33¹ 1:45⁴ 3↑ Californian-G1	3 3 31½ 11 16 14¼	Shoemaker W	130	*.05 103-05	SpectacularBid130⁴¼PaintKng115³¾CroBmbno118⁸ Easy score 7
18May80-8Hol	fst 1⅛	:22³ :45² 1:08⁴ 1:40² 3↑ Mervyn LeRoy H-G2	1 5 42 2nd,13½ 17	Shoemaker W	130	*.20 93-18	SpectacularBd132⁷Peregrintor119³Beau'sEgl121² Ridden out 6
2Mar80-8SA	sly 1¼	:48³ 1:12² 1:36⁴ 2:00³ 4↑ S Anita H-G1	5 2 22½ 1hd 1½ 15	Shoemaker W	130	*.30 90-18	SpctaclarBid130⁵Flyng'Pstr1238Beau'sEgl121² Ridden out 5
3Feb80-8SA	fst 1¼	:44³ 1:08² 1:32⁴ 1:57⁴ C H Strub-G1	3 4 29 2nd 13 13¼	Shoemaker W	126	*.30 104-08	SpectacularBid126³¼FlyingPaster1219Vldz122¼ Handy score 4
19Jan80-8SA	gd 1⅛	:46² 1:11 1:35³ 1:48 San Fernando-G2	1 3 33½ 1hd 1½ 11½	Shoemaker W	126	*.05 89-19	SpectacularBid126¹½FlyingPstr216¹⁵Rlunch120³³ Drew clear 4
5Jan80-8SA	fst 7f	:22¹ :44² 1:08 1:20 Malibu-G2	3 4 52½ 41 1½ 15	Shoemaker W	126	*.30 103-10	SpectacularBid126⁵FlyingPastr1231½Ros'sSvll117no Easily 5
18Oct79-6Med	fst 1¼	:47⁴ 1:12 1:36²2:01¹ 3↑ Med Cup H-G2	1 3 33 1½ 1½ 12¾	Shoemaker W	126	*.10 102-14	SpectacularBid126³Smarten 120hdValdez121¹¹ Drew out 5
6Oct79-8Bel	fst 1¼	:49 1:13¹2:02²2:27²3↑ J C Gold Cup-G1	2 3 2½ 31 2½ 2³	Shoemaker W	121	1.40 82-21	Affirmed126¾Spectacular Bid1213Coastal121³¹ Gamely 4
8Sep79-8Bel	fst 1⅛	:47² 1:11 1:34¹ 1:46³ 3↑ Marlboro Cup H-G1	5 3 1hd 1½ 13 15	Shoemaker W	124	*.50 94-17	SpectacularBid124⁵GenrlAssmbly1200¾½Costl122¾ Ridden out 5
26Aug79-7Del	gd 1¹⁄₁₆	:23 :46³ 1:11¹1:41³ Alw 18000	3 3 21½ 16 112 117	Shoemaker W	122	*.05 101-14	SpectacularBd12217ArmadaStrik1127NotSoProud1126 Easily 5
9Jun79-8Bel	fst 1½	:47³ 1:11¹2:02²2:27¹ Belmont-G1	3 2 1½ 13 2½ 3³	Franklin RJ	126	*.30 73-17	Coastal126³¼Golden Act126nkSpectacular Bid126⁹¼ Tired 8
19May79-8Pim	gd 1¹⁄₁₆	:46⁴ 1:10³ 1:35 1:54¹ Preakness-G1	2 4 45 1hd 16 15½	Franklin RJ	126	*.10 99-09	SpctacularBd126⁵½GoldenAct1264ScrnKng126⁵¼ Ridden out 5
5May79-8CD	fst 1¼	:47² 1:12²1:37³2:02² Ky Derby-G1	3 7 610 2nd 11½ 12¾	Franklin RJ	126	*.60 85-14	SpectacularBid126²¾GnrlAssmbly126³GoldnAct126¹¾ Driving 10
26Apr79-7Kee	fst 1⅛	:46³ 1:10³ 1:36¹ 1:50 Blue Grass-G1	4 4 1hd 12 15½ 17	Franklin RJ	121	*.05 87-20	Spectacular Bid121⁷Lot o' Gold121⁸Bishop's Choice121¹⁰ 4
	Easily best								
24Mar79-10Hia	fst 1⅛	:46 1:09³ 1:35¹ 1:48² Flamingo-G1	8 3 1½ 18 110 112	Franklin RJ	122	*.05 90-16	Spectacular Bid122¹²Strike the Min118³Sir Ivor Again122hd 8
	Ridden out								
6Mar79-11GP	fst 1⅛	:47⁴ 1:11⁴ 1:36³ 1:48⁴ Florida Derby-G1	5 5 47½ 3½ 11½ 14½	Franklin RJ	122	*.05 90-14	Spectacular Bd124²¼Lot o' Gold122¾Fantasy 'n Reality123³ 7
	Four wide,clear								
19Feb79-9GP	fst 1¹⁄₁₆	:24 :47² 1:10⁴ 1:41¹ Fountain of Youth-G3	2 3 1hd 13 14 18½	Franklin RJ	122	*.10 95-12	SpectacularBid122⁸½Lot o'Gold117¹Bishop's Choice122¹ 6
	Ridden out								
7Feb79-9GP	fst 7f	:22⁴ :44⁴ 1:08⁴ 1:21² SpectacularBid123²¾Lot o' Gold114⁷½Northern Prospect114³½ 4	1 2 2hd 22 13 13¾	Franklin RJ	122	*.05 97-22		
	In hand								
11Nov78-8Key	fst 1¹⁄₁₆	:22⁴ :46² 1:10³ 1:42 Heritage-G2	6 5 55 1hd 13 16	Franklin RJ	122	*.10 94-13	SpctacularBid122⁶SunWatcher112³¾Terrfc.Son117no Handily 7
28Oct78-8Lrl	fst 1¹⁄₁₆	:23⁴ :46⁴ 1:11 1:41³ Lrl Futurity-G1	2 1 11½ 1½ 14 18½	Franklin RJ	122	*.90 105-14	SpectacularBd122⁸½General Assembly122¹²Clever Trick123²½ 4
	Driving								
19Oct78-6Med	fst 1¹⁄₁₆	:23² :46² 1:11¹ 1:43¹ Young America-G1	5 3 2hd 2½ 2hd 1nk	Velasquez J	122	*.30 95-14	SpectclrBid122nkStrikeYourColrs119hdInstrumntLanding1134 9
	Driving								
8Oct78-8Bel	fst 1	:23¹ :46 1:10¹ 1:34⁴ Champagne-G1	1 2 11 12½ 14 12¾	Velasquez J	122	2.40 94-19	SpectclrBid122²¾GeneralAssembly122⁵½Crest of theWave122¾ 6
	Ridden out								
23Sep78-8Atl	gd 7f	:22 :44³ 1:09 1:20⁴ World's Playground-G3	3 3 1½ 12 16 115	Franklin RJ	114	5.20 98-25	SpctaculrBid114¹⁵CrstofthWv124¼½GrotonHgh118½ Driving 7
20Aug78-9Del	fst 6f	:22² :46 :58 1:10⁴ Dover 34k	2 4 43 53¾ 44 22½	Franklin RJ	112	*1.00 88-13	StrikeYourColors112²½SpectacularBid112⁵½Spy Charger122¹ 7
	2nd best								
2Aug78-8Mth	sly 5½f	:22⁴ :46¹ :59 1:04⁴ Tyro (Div 2) 27k	6 8 816 812 610 46¾	Franklin RJ	118	*1.70 86-22	GrotonHigh122²½GreatBoon116nkOurGry1164 Very wide early 8
22Jly78-5Pim	fst 5½f	:22³ :46¹ :58¹ 1:04¹ Alw 6500	3 4 31 1hd 13 18	Franklin RJ⁵	115	*.30 100-17	SpectacularBid115⁸SilentNative1209DoublePrd114¹ Driving 5
30Jun78-3Pim	fst 5½f	:22³ :46³ :58² 1:04³ Md Sp Wt	5 4 1½ 11½ 12½ 13¼	Franklin RJ⁵	115	6.30 98-15	Spectacular Bid115³¼Strike Your Colors120⁴Instant Love1124 11
	Drew out								

Star de Naskra

dkbbr. c. 1975, by Naskra (Nasram)–Candle Star, by Clandestine
Own.– C.J. Lancaster
Br.– Carlyle J. Lancaster (Md)
Tr.– Richard D. Ferris

Lifetime record: 36 15 10 4 $587,391

Date	Track/Cond	Dist/Time	Race	Running	Jockey	Wt	Odds	Speed	Finish	Comment	Field
20Oct79-8Aqu	fst 7f	:22³ :44⁴ 1:08³ 1:21 3↑ Vosburgh-G1	6 5 41½ 1hd 21 45	Fell J	126	2.80 91-15	GeneralAssmbly123²Dr.Patches126¾Syncopat126²¼ Gave way 6
8Sep79-8Bel	fst 1⅛	:47² 1:11 1:34¹1:46³ 3↑ Marlboro Cup H-G1	4 1 41 43½ 65¾ 68	Fell J	124	8.60 86-17	SpctaculrBid124⁵GeneralAssmbly1200¾Costl122¼ Weakened 6
4Aug79-8Sar	fst 1⅛	:48¹1:10⁴1:35 1:47³ 3↑ Whitney-G2	2 1 1½ 1hd 1hd 1¾	Fell J	120	*1.10 97-12	StardeNskra120¾Cos'xRidge117½TheLiberlMmbr120½ Driving 6
14Jly79-8Aks	fst 1⅛	:47 1:11¹1:35¹1:48² 3↑ Cornhusker H 164k	4 4 42 1½ 14 18½	Fell J	125	*1.80 95-14	Star de Naskra125⁸½Prince Majestic119¼Quiet Jay117nk 13
	Bumped,easily								
20Jun79-6Bel	fst 7f	:22² :44⁴ 1:09 1:22 Celanese Cup H 80k	1 2 32½ 32 11½ 14	Fell J	126	1.40 92-17	Ⓓ StardeNaskr126⁴NorthCours112¹½Dr.Ptchs118½ Drifted in 4
	Disqualified and placed fourth								
9Jun79-5Bel	fst 1¹⁄₁₆	:23⁴ :46³ 1:10³ 1:34³ 3↑ Alw 27000	2 2 1½ 1hd 13 16¼	Fell J	115	*.90 95-17	StardeNaskra115⁶¼DarbyCreekRoad1154QuietLittleTable1179 6
	Ridden out								
5May79-8Aqu	fst 7f	:22⁴ :45¹ 1:09¹1:21⁴ 3↑ Carter H-G2	3 4 1½ 1½ 15 1nk	Fell J	122	7.70 92-25	StardeNaskra122nkAlydar126³Sensitive Prince126⁶¾ Lasted 6
22Apr79-8Aqu	fst 6f	:21³ :45 1:09¹3↑ Bold Ruler 80k	5 1 42¾ 11 15 15	Fell J	119	*1.70 97-11	StrdeNaskra119⁵Vencdor126¹¾BgJohnTylor119¹¼ Ridden out 8
31Mar79-7Bow	fst 6f	:22 :44² :55³ 1:08⁴ 4↑ Alw 19000	1 4 2² 2hd 11 12¾	Miceli M	112	*.60 96-18	StardeNaskra112²¾IronDerby112⁴½Parnis11212 Ridden out 6
1Jan79-8Bow	sly 1¹⁄₁₆	:23³ :47² 1:12² 1:43⁴3↑ Resolution H 55k	4 5 37 51¾ 43½ 47	Passmore WJ	122	2.40 80-22	Frejus109hdCortan1142½Chati124⁴½ No mishap 6

7Dec78- 6Med gd 1 1/16 :234 :471 1:112 1:434 Winter Quarters H 53k 7 7 75½ 52¼ 33½ 21¼ Maple E 121 *2.10 91-19 SilentCal1181¼StrdNskr1211¼MornngFrolc1151¼ Drifted out 7
18Nov78- 8Lrl fst 1 :224 :453 1:11 1:373 Japan Racing Assn H 44k 5 2 31½ 2hd 2hd 22 Kupfer T 122 b *.80 83-20 Silent Cal1152Star de Naskra1225Morning Frolic1143 Wide 6
1Nov78- 8Aqu fst 6f :23 :453 1:092 3↑ Alw 30000 1 2 1hd 1hd 1½ 1½ Maple E 120 b 7.30 96-14 StrdeNskra120½WarmFront1193NearlyOnTime1154¾ Driving 5
7Oct78- 8Bow fst 1⅛ :472 1:11 1:362 1:50 Governor's Cup H 108k 5 3 3½ 31½ 37 312½ Moyers L 118 b 11.50 82-21 NastyandBld1232½Dave'sFriend12010StardeNskr11820 Tired 5
16Sep78- 6Bow fst 1 1/16 :242 :492 1:141 1:45 3↑ Alw 16000 6 3 2½ 2½ 1½ 1¾ Kupfer T5 107 *.20 81-26 Star de Naskra107¾Gala Forecast1144Combat Patrol1174 6
Ridden out
4Sep78- 8Del fst 1 1/16 :233 :471 1:112 1:432 Rosemont 33k 5 4 43½ 31 23 24½ Passmore WJ 122 *.50 87-17 SilentCal1124½StardeNaskra1222Fredd'sFlsh1123 No excuse 8
5Aug78- 8Mth sly 1⅛ :47 1:123 1:393 1:531 Mth Inv'l H-G1 1 4 55½ 43½ 66½ 67 Moyers L 116 3.20 62-31 DeltaFlag112¾Dave'sFriend1202½SpecialHonr1182¾ No rally 7
22Jly78- 8Pim fst 1⅛ :46 1:101 1:352 1:482 Marylander H 56k 5 3 35½ 35 21½ 21 Moyers L 119 3.70 101-17 Dave'sFriend1171StardeNaskra1196SensitvPrnc1225 Brushed 5
1Jly78- 8AP sly 1¼ :462 1:111 1:364 2:032 American Derby-G2 13 8 41½ 22 21½ 25 Moyers L 114 *1.90 75-29 NastyandBold1145StrdeNskra1147BeauSham1147 Second best 13
18Jun78-10Tdn fst 1⅛ :46 1:10 1:351 1:474 Ohio Derby-G2 5 3 4¾ 4¾ 41¾ 31½ Moyers L 120 8.60 99-04 SpecialHonor115½Batonnier1221StardeNaskra1201 Rallied 10
28May78- 8Bel fst 1⅛ :451 1:092 1:35 1:48 Peter Pan-G3 8 5 44 42½ 46 38½ Moyers L 123 3.90 78-16 Bckaroo1143½DarbyCreekRoad1175StrdeNskr123nk Mild bid 8
14May78- 8Aqu sly 1 :23 :46 1:11 1:364 Withers-G2 3 4 32 22 24 24¾ Moyers L 126 *1.60 77-26 Junction1264¾StardeNaskra1261½Buckaroo126½ Second best 8
24Apr78- 8Aqu fst 1 :234 :462 1:104 1:363 Alw 25000 5 5 42 41 1½ 15½ Moyers L 122 *1.30 83-20 StardeNaskra1225½ShelterHalf1221¾NeverMind1193 In hand 5
8Apr78- 8Key fst 6f :232 :464 1:11 Penn Treaty 27k 3 4 31½ 3nk 1½ 12 Moyers L 122 *.90 87-27 Star de Naskra1222Pirateer1221¼Al Battah1228 Driving 6
25Mar78- 8Pim fst 6f :231 :461 :58 1:11 Hirsch Jacobs 33k 8 9 62½ 34½ 34½ 22½ Moyers L 122 3.30 88-18 ShelterHalf1192½StardeNskr1222¼GamePrnc1161½ 2nd best 9
10Dec77- 6Med fst 6f :223 :453 1:094 Giant Step 53k 8 3 2hd 2hd 31½ 45½ Turcotte RL 122 *1.80 90-06 MomboJumbo1193JustRightClassi1152AlBattah119½ Gave way 8
11Nov77- 8Lrl gd 7f :231 :47 1:122 1:251 Ⓢ Senatorial 30k 6 1 2hd 2½ 22 21 Bracciale V Jr 122 *.30 84-29 TenTen1171StardeNaskra1228M.A.'sDate122nk Carried wide 6
29Oct77- 8Lrl fst 1 1/16 :24 :484 1:133 1:441 Lrl Futurity-G1 4 1 11 3½ 35 310 Bracciale V Jr 122 11.90 82-27 Affirmed122nkAlydar12210Star de Naskra12227 Speed,tired 4
15Oct77- 8Bow fst 7f :224 :452 1:102 1:241 ©Marl Nursery 28k 2 6 53¾ 3½ 11 11 Bracciale V Jr 122 *.60 84-22 StardeNaskra1221PeacefulCountry113½Isella1137 Driving 7
24Sep77- 8AP sly 6½f :221 :444 1:10 1:163 ©Arl Wash Futurity-G1 14 1 42½ 43½ 65 56¾ Bracciale V Jr 122 6.60 85-18 Sauce Boat1222Gonquin1223½Forever Casting122¾ Wide 14
3Sep77- 8Tim fst *6½f :224 :47 1:124 1:173 Tim Futurity 58k 1 2 1hd 2hd 11 14¾ Turcotte RL 122 2.00 96-12 StrdeNaskra1224¾ForeverCastng1227MsWrrnt1192 Drew away 4
21Aug77- 9Del fst 6f :221 :454 1:111 Dover 30k 5 2 41½ 2hd 12 12¾ Bracciale V Jr 114 *1.30 89-15 StrdeNskr1142¾MomboJumbo113¾ⒹFmousCzr1121¾ Ridden out 8
11Aug77- 7Del fst 6f :214 :453 1:103 Alw 12000 3 7 55½ 52¼ 1hd 2hd Bracciale V Jr 120 2.30 92-14 ForevrCasting120hdStrdeNskr1207BombyExprss1151¼ Sharp 7
16Jly77- 8Bow fst 5½f :223 :461 :581 1:041 Ⓢ Playpen 27k 7 5 2½ 2½ 1hd 2¾ Bracciale V Jr 115 *.70 97-20 Quadratic113¾StardeNaskra1154SilkorSatin1133½ Gamely 7
29Jun77- 7Bow fst 5f :224 :462 :584 Ⓢ Alw 9000 6 1 13½ 11½ 12½ 13 Kurtz J 120 *1.20 96-21 StrdeNskra1203MarineCorpTom1172½TenTn1202½ Ridden out 6
14Jun77- 3Bow fst 5f :231 :463 :59 Ⓢ Md Sp Wt 1 6 21 1hd 2½ 13½ Bracciale V Jr 120 6.30 95-18 Star de Naskra1203½Silk or Satin1201Combat Fatigue113hd 8
Handily

Straight and True

dkbbr. g. 1970, by Never Bend (Nasrullah)–Polly Girl, by Prince Bio
Own.– Mrs O. Phipps
Br.– Mrs Ogden Phipps (Ky)
Tr.– D.M. Smithwick

Lifetime record: 74 12 9 9 $78,689

13Aug79- 4Sar yl 2 1/16 S'Chase 3:463 3↑ Alw 12500 1 3 31 - - - Martin W 151 b 10.70 -- PopulrHero1454¾CanadianRegent1484TanJy15122 Broke down 7
3Aug79- 6Sar fm 2 1/16 S'Chase 3:411 4↑ Lovely Night H 21k 1 1 13 54¼ 619 632 Martin W 144 sb 6.80 -- CafePrince1642¾LeapingFrog1613¾Martie'sAnger1555 Tired 7
13Jly79- 3Del fm *2¼ S'Chase 4:162 4↑ Handicap 10000 4 1 16 14 12 31¾ Martin WS 145 sb 13.20 -- Martie'sAnger1521½DeuxCoup159½StrghtndTru1457 Lost iron 5
25Jun79- 4Atl fm *1Ⓣ :24 :481 1:131 1:391 3↑ Alw 7500 10 2 21 1011 1015 916 Moseley JW 119 b 28.40 75-14 Great Cloud114hdBeau Rascal119½New Look119¾ Stopped 10
2Jun79- 7Fai gd *2 3/16 S'Chase 4:14 4↑ Handicap 6000 4 4 2¾ 74¼ 613 522¼ Martin W 150 sb 1.60 -- Beauhill142nkPopular Hero1497½Orotund14611 Tired 8
26May79- 2Pro fm *2 S'Chase 3:314 4↑ Alw 15000 3 3 62½ 63 65¾ 513 Martin W 158 b - -- Martie's Anger155½Winigo1424Tall Award163nk No rally 9
12May79- 7Fai fm *2 3/16 S'Chase 4:112 4↑ Handicap 10000 6 2 15 1nk 31½ 22¾ Martin W 148 sb 5.60 -- Deux Coup1552¾Straight and True1481Love In1425 Sharp 7
5May79- 3War fm *2⅛ S'Chase 4:421 4↑ Alw 6000 3 2 22 24 2¾ 1no Martin W 153 sb - -- StraightandTrue153noElVientoII1392½Saramyst131 Just up 3
28Apr79- 4Fx gd *2¼ S'Chase 4:274 4↑ Foxfield Cup H 12k 4 3 2½ 39 220 225 Martin W 154 sb - -- Tall Award15825Straight and True154 Tired 4
22Apr79- 4Mid fm *2 S'Chase 4:02 4↑ Alw 8500 4 1 11¾ 12½ 2hd 2nk Martin W 156 sb - -- FireControl156nkStraightandTrue156hdOwhatChf15920 Sharp 4
4Nov78- 3Mtp fm *2½ S'Chase 4:394 4↑ N Laing H 5.4k 5 1 13 32½ 49½ 514 Quanbeck A Jr 146 - -- Deux Coup153nkFire Control1553Curazao14510 Tired 7
20Oct78- 6Bel fm 2⅝ S'Chase 4:52 4↑ Temple Gwathmey H 36k 4 3 42 615 634 636 Cushman J 147 7.30e -- FireControl1464CafePrince167noPopulrHro1398¾ Done early 6
4Oct78- 6Lig gd *2 S'Chase 4:142 4↑ Handicap 12500 1 3 32¾ - - - Martin WS 149 - -- Owhata Chief153¾Leaping Frog15914Don Panta150 Fell 4
16Sep78- 7Fai fm *2 3/16 S'Chase 4:102 4↑ Handicap 5000 4 3 32 31½ 310 315½ Martin WS 152 sb *1.60 -- OwhtaChief1483½DonPanta14912StrghtndTru15210 No excuse 6
9Sep78- 4Fx hd *2¼ S'Chase 4:133 3↑ Alw 7500 3 2 1½ 13 1nk 2nk Martin WS5 148 sb - -- Leaping Frog156nkStraight and True14812Don Panta156½ 5
14Aug78- 4Sar gd 2⅛ S'Chase 3:572 4↑ Alw 12500 1 3 2hd 53½ 59 517 Martin WS5 150 sb *1.10 -- Emory Jay1402Jive1526½Jacasaba1553¾ Tired after 7th 5
4Aug78- 6Sar sf 2 1/16 S'Chase 3:524 4↑ Lovely Night H 21k 1 3 33 33½ 33½ 32¾ Martin WS 147 b 3.70 -- LeapingFrog1532¾UnAdios137noStrghtndTru1476¼ No mishap 6
22Jly78- 3Del fm 2¼ S'Chase 4:184 4↑ Alw 10000 5 1 13 1hd 1½ 2½ Martin WS5 147 b 2.70 -- LeapingFrog152½StraightandTrue1473½Jacasaba1436 Gamely 6
10Jly78- 6Atl sly 1 1/16 :23 :46 1:104 1:44 3↑ Alw 7500 3 6 815 818 617 519 Pagano SR 112 b 9.60 66-27 ThouFool1071½RoamFree1194WilmingtonFlask1196 No rally 8
21Jun78- 4Mth gd *2¼ S'Chase 4:291 4↑ Midsummer H 15k 6 4 39 23 31 5¾ Martin W 147 sb *1.60 -- Deux Coup153noDon Panta146nkLeaping Frog148no Hung 7
10Jun78- 7Fai fm *2 3/16 S'Chase 4:122 4↑ Handicap 7500 4 3 43¾ 41 2nk 1¾ Martin W 144 sb 1.70 -- Straight and True144¾Deux Coup1547¾Tall Award1462 6
29May78- 7Fai fm *2 3/16 S'Chase 4:144 4↑ Alw 6000 6 3 16 11½ 11 13½ Martin W7 146 sb 2.40 -- StraightandTrue1463½CanadianRegent14711Slvo1504½ Easily 6
20May78- 4Mal sf *2 S'Chase 3:554 4↑ Handicap 7500 3 3 45¼ 44¼ 35½ 2hd Martin B 138 sb - -- ⒹTallAward145hdStraightandTrue1382ElVientoII1446 Sharp 4
Placed first through disqualification
6May78- 6War yl *2⅛ S'Chase 4:403 4↑ Alw 2500 7 1 14 12 215 222 Smithwick D 163 sb - -- ElVientoII16322StraightandTrue1632½Mr.Jam1656 Tired 8
29Apr78- 4SH fm *1⅞ S'Chase 3:423 4↑ Alw 3500 2 2 35 3½ 311 34½ Martin W10 134 sb - -- CanadianRegent1474ElVientoII137½StraightndTru1345 Tired 5
23Apr78- 4Mid fm *2 S'Chase 3:593 4↑ Alw 3500 4 1 22 212 315 312 Martin W10 138 sb - -- FrenchHollow1568FireControl1504StraightndTru13815 Tired 6
15Oct77- 4Mid gd *2½ S'Chase 4:383 4↑ Alw 1500 8 4 75½ 814 825 733 Aitcheson J Jr 158 b - -- DonPanta1561½ManchuPrinc1382½SunSign143½ Fell far back 9
8Oct77- 4Lig sf *2½ S'Chase 5:311 4↑ Int'l Gold Cup H 25k 3 1 18 830 659 678 Martin W 157 b -e -- CafePrince15518ItsGoodforYou1377MichaelsMd13710 Stopped 8
1Oct77- 4Fax fm *2¼ S'Chase 4:221 3↑ Alw 2500 1 4 413 37 310 414 Aitcheson J Jr 155 b - -- Afilador1562Aunt Sheila15010Orotund1482 4
17Sep77- 5Fai fm *1 5/16Ⓣ 2:15 3↑ Alw 1000 3 4 56 52½ 88½ 916 Skiffington T Jr 150 b 3.10 -- Farnisky1505Corning Day1401¾Michael's Mad140½ No speed 10
10Sep77- 4Fai fm *1 5/16 S'Chase 2:19 3↑ Alw 1000 2 7 64¾ 52 44¾ 48 Aitcheson J Jr 147 s 2.70 -- Deux Coup1402½Corning Day1403½Winigo1372 10
24Aug77- 8Del gd 1 1/16⊗ :24 :481 1:131 1:454 3↑ Alw 7000 3 4 68½ 722 731 736¾ Canessa J 117 b 21.30 43-21 HafPro1172½JohnAlden1135Admiral'sPppy1137 Through early 7
2Aug77- 8Tim fst 1 1/16 :24 :48 1:141 1:463 3↑ Alw 4200 1 2 41¾ 57½ 513 520 Passmore WJ 114 b 5.30 68-11 Sport News114½Uncle Baby1141½Hey Look1096 Tired 5
3Jly77- 5Pen fst 6f :224 :464 1:094 4↑ Alw 5000 1 6 612 622 623 631 Smith DD 113 b 6.90 66-13 HickoryCap1197½Peggy'sPrince1131½AvalonBech1133½ Outrun 6
27Nov76- 4Cam fm 2¾ S'Chase 5:122 4↑ Colonial Cup 100k 1 14 1226 - - - Fishback J 162 -e -- GrandCanyon162½FireControl1622½Crag'sCorner160no Bled 16
6Nov76- 3Uni fm *2Ⓣ 3:35 3↑ Alw 1000 7 2 43½ 3nk 31½ - McKnight HT Jr 173 - -- Paginai15526DnMiguelII1681OneDy'sFrdom1611 Left course 15
22Oct76- 6Bel sf 2⅝ S'Chase 5:023 4↑ Temple Gwathmey H 36k 1 2 23 31 612 712 Fishback J 162 b *1.00e -- FireControl144hdCrag'sCorner1412¼ArcticJoe1514 Stopped 7
6Oct76- 6Lig gd *2 S'Chase 4:15 4↑ Rolling Rock Hunt H 12k 1 1 11½ 2½ 1½ 11½ Fishback J 162 -e -- StrghtandTrue1621½ManchuPrinc135hdTllAwrd142½ Driving 7
18Sep76- 7Fai fm *2½ S'Chase 4:571 4↑ Grand National H 15k 4 6 2½ 3½ 11 16¼ Fishback J 154 b *1.30e -- StrghtndTrue1546¼HappyIntellectual157hdLife'sIllusion1612¾ 7
In hand
11Sep76- 8Fai hd *1 5/16Ⓣ 2:134 3↑ Alw 1200 2 2 22½ 11 1nk 13½ Rowland J 147 b *.40 -- StraightandTrue1473½RulngLine149noGermncus1423 In hand 8
26Aug76- 6Sar fm 2⅜ S'Chase 4:192 4↑ NY Turf Writers H 22k 5 3 42½ 46 35½ 33¼ Fishback J 155 b 1.70e -- HappyIntellectual152¾Life'sIllusion1602½Strght andTrue155½ 7
Evenly
6Aug76- 6Sar fm 2 1/16 S'Chase 3:49 4↑ Lovely Night H 22k 2 6 65½ 32 33 45 Fishback J 158 b *.90e -- Crag'sCorner1401¼Deux Coup1421¼Casamayor1482½ Bobbled 7
30Jly76- 8Tim fst 1 :24 :474 1:132 1:403 3↑ Alw 4400 5 4 610 512 512 59¼ Rowland J 112 b 2.30 79-15 JohnnieScott1121¾Prdful1123½Bully'sBunny1121½ No factor 6
17Jly76- 7Del fm *2⅜ S'Chase 4:342 4↑ Indian River H 13k 7 4 2hd 12 110 12¾ Fishback J 151 b 2.90 -- StraightandTrue1512¾Crag'sCornr1362ClovrOvr1354 Handily 8
8Jly76- 9Del fst 1 70 :243 :49 1:133 1:43 3↑ Alw 6000 2 1 11½ 2hd 31 31¾ Rowland J 118 b 13.00 80-14 RoyalJete112¾Exploring1201StraightandTrue1183 Weakened 7
25Jun76- 4Del fm *2 1/16 S'Chase 3:564 4↑ Handicap 8000 9 1 21 24 21½ 22 Fishback J 152 b 2.30 -- Life's Illusion1562Straight and True1527ⒹⒽDeux Coup145 9

Second best

Date	Track	Cond	Dist	Time	Race	Pos	Jockey	Wt	Odds	SR	Finish	Comment
23Jun76- 8Pim	fst 5f	:22 :45	:57¹ 4↑Clm 30000	6 6 6¹³ 6¹³ 6²²	6¹⁹	Rowland J	114 b	53.60	80-17	Kintla'sFolly114¹JivaCoolt114noOxfordFlght119⁴½	Trailed 6
11Jun76- 4Del	fm *2⅛	S'Chase	3:50⁴ 4↑Alw 7000	6 5 35½ 32 23	22½	Fishback J	160 b	2.80		DeuxCoup140²⅟StrghtndTru160⁷Juggrnut114812	Swerved in 7
30May76- 4Del	yl *2⅛	S'Chase	3:46¹ 4↑Alw 7000	1 2 2² 2½ 15	14¾	Fishback J	155 b	11.50		StrghtndTru155⁴⅟DuxCoup143⁷Juggrnut11510¼	Ridden out 8
8May76- 6Fai	fm *2⅛	S'Chase	4:09⁴ 4↑Handicap 7500	2 4 5¹⁴ 4¹² 5¹⁷	5⁴²	Aitcheson J Jr	138 sb	-		LondonGrove148¹³⅟Life'sIlluson158⁴⅟AgsAgo147³³	No threat 5
26Apr76- 8Pim	fm 1¼⊤	:23⁴:46⁴ 1:11³1:44³ 4↑Alw 8000	2 8 10²³ 10²⁸ 10²²	10¹⁹	Rowland J	115 b	17.50	69-11	Romus119noRoyal Romany115noLast Hail119²¾	Outrun 10
11Apr76- 6Mid	fm *1⅛⊤	2:17⁴ 3↑Alw 500	2 7 66 3⁸ 4¹³	3²	Aitcheson J Jr	155 b	-		SpittinImage155hdBabeen150²StraightandTrue155½	Evenly 10
15Nov75- 4Cam	fm 2⅛	S'Chase	5:30¹ 4↑Colonial Cup 50k	4 18 16⁷½ 16²¹ 14⁷¼	15⁴⁴	Carberry T	160	-e		Cafe Prince160³Augustus Bay162½Soothsayer162½	Outrun 19
1Nov75- 4Mtp	fm *2	S'Chase	4:25¹ 3↑Alw 2000	9 9 86½ 74½ 3²	2⁴	Elser C	156	-e		Tor'sLib136⁴StraightandTrue156¼Afilador156²	Closed well 19
18Oct75- 4RB	sf *2	S'Chase	5:37⁴ 3↑Alw 3500	3 5 47 3¹⁰ -	-	Elser C	155	-		CltcSongIII155¹²Jy'sTroubl142¹⁰Strtch II155¹⁸	Pulled up 6
11Oct75- 5Mid	yl *1⅟₁₆	2:30² 3↑Alw 500	4 6 73 12 11½	1³	Rowland JP	141 sb	-e		Straight and True141²¼Bacara150⁶Sabinus159½	Driving 10
4Oct75- 6Lig	yl *7f⊤	1:35¹ 3↑Alw 2500	12 12⁸⁴ 78½ 7¹⁰	410½	Rowland J	136 b	-e		Fortissimo143⁶Gumersindo143¹½Pilot Himself146³	Late bid 14
10Oct75- 7Lig	yl *7f⊤	1:35² 3↑Alw 2500	2 2 14⁹½ 11¹⁰ 106	7²½	Rowland JP⁷	136	-e		Life's Illusion145hdTor's Rib145nkRed Grasshopper149½	19

Previously trained by Pierre Head

22Jun75♦ Auteuil(Fr)	hy *2⅛	4:22 5↑Prix Arthur O'Connor Chase Alw15700	-	Chirol M	139	19.00	Mister Magoo132½Lift134⁸Bergerac139²	15
							Fell at 2nd.Tingle Creek 7th	
27May75♦ Enghien(Fr)	gd *2¼	4:34¹ 5↑Prix du Puy-de-Dome Chase Alw21700	79¾	Chirol M	136 b	25.00	Celtic Air136⁴Tofano136½Romati141¹½	9
							Well placed in 4th,weakened approaching second last	
4May75♦ Compiegne(Fr)	gd *2¹³⁄₁₆LH	4:50 5↑Prix de la Heronniere Chase Alw4600	1½	Chirol M	136	3.10	Straight and True136½Rayure150²⁰Fort d'Ivry141²⁰	5
							Tracked in 3rd,dueled 1 out,gamely prevailed	
13Apr75♦ Strasbourg(Fr)	sf *2⅛RH	-	5↑Prix de l'Ami Fritz Chase Alw3000	11	Bonni F	141	*.80	Straight and True141¹Donner141½Vickywyn141	10
							Always close up,led at last,held well.Time not taken	
22Oct74♦ Enghien(Fr)	hy *1¹⁄₁₆LH	3:49	Prix de la Scarpe Hurdle Hcp11600	10	Lautier R	136	5.50	Voldic145nkKamarjaan156⁸Typhor141³	15
							Never a factor	
12Aug74♦ Clairefntaine(Fr)	gd *1⅞RH	3:40¹ 4↑Prix du Golf Hurdle Alw9400	5¹⁴½	Lautier R	136	3.50	Lord David145⁴Debil136²Dark Lessly136⁶	11
							Tracked in 4th,faded from 2 out	
23Jly74♦ Evry(Fr)	gd *1⅛⊤LH	1:53³ 4↑Prix Incertitude (Div 2) Hcp5100	7⁶	Gibert A	133	-	Dark Lessly121¹Flabel122²Golden Calf127½	15
							Raced in mid-pack throughout	
22Jun74♦ Saint-Cloud(Fr)	gd *1¼⊤LH	2:09⁴ 4↑Prix de Castillon Hcp7700	5¾	Gibert A	113	-	Les Capucins120nkA Cappella112nkExpertease123hd	16
							Rated toward rear,gaining late	
26May74♦ Longchamp(Fr)	gd *1⁵⁄₁₆⊤RH	2:14³ 4↑Prix des Batignolles Hcp7700	12	Gibert A	110	-	Tetouan114¹Novart117hdBrio Khan121³	13
							Never a factor	
31Mar74♦ Auteuil(Fr)	hy *1⅞LH	4:02	Prix Santo Pietro Hurdle Mdn (FT)11600	3²⁵	Lautier R	136	6.00	Way Away137²⁰The Kid136⁵Straight and True136²½	9
							Settled in 5th,bid after 3rd last,no chance with first two	
7Nov73♦ Saint-Cloud(Fr)	hy *1¼LH	2:20²	Prix de Lude Mdn8500	9	Gibert A	123	-	Lourenco Marques123³Bayazid123¹½Miribi123³	9
							Toward rear throughout	
11Oct73♦ Evry(Fr)	sf *1⅛⊤LH	2:38²	Prix d'Annency Hcp10200	42¼	Gibert A	113	-	Gingko Biloba116¹Verine101¹½Grand Canal123nk	14
							Wide 7th,finished well without threatening	
24Sep73♦ Maisns-Lfftte(Fr)	sf *1⊤RH	1:43⁴	Prix du Tage Hcp7600	8	Florin A	117	-	Penrod120nkScarlet Sun100nkMeriadeck116¹	15
							Never a factor	
23Jly73♦ Maisns-Lfftte(Fr)	sf *1⁵⁄₁₆⊤RH	2:22⁴	Prix Montmartin Mdn7600	10	Gibert A	123	-	Copper123²Extravagant123hdCantador123⁴	11
							Toward rear throughout	
7Jun73♦ Chantilly(Fr)	gd *1³⁄₈⊤RH	2:18⁴	Prix de Montgeroult Mdn7600	5²¾	Gibert A	123	-	Veld123nkRibot Lad116²Winterthur117no	19
							Rated in 10th,mild late gain	
14May73♦ Saint-Cloud(Fr)	sf *1⁵⁄₁₆⊤LH	2:22⁴	Prix Isard II Mdn (FT)7600	9	Gibert A	123	-	Florapal121³Valaze123nkNoumay123nk	14
							Never a factor	

Susan's Girl

b. f. 1969, by Quadrangle (Cohoes)—Quaze, by Quibu

Own.– F.W. Hooper Jr
Br.– F.W. Hooper Jr (Fla)
Tr.– L.R. Fenstermaker

Lifetime record: 63 29 14 11 $1,251,667

24Nov75- 8Aqu	fst 1	:23⁴:47³ 1:12²1:37 3↑⒡Berlo H 59k	2 2 2¹ 1hd 1hd	3²	Baeza B	126	*1.20	79-16	CostlyDream115¹³⁄₄LandGirl113nkSusan'sGirl126¹	Weakened 11
15Nov75- 8Aqu	fst 1⅛	:50³ 1:14² 1:38³ 2:03³ 3↑⒡Ladies H-G1	8 1 2¹ 2² 33	3½	Pincay L Jr	126	*1.40	77-15	Tizna124nkPass a Glance113nkSusan's Girl126²	Weakened 8
25Oct75- 7Kee	fst 1⅛	:47⁴1:12 1:37 1:49⁴ 3↑⒡Spinster-G1	7 2 2hd 1hd 1hd	3½	Pincay L Jr	123	*.30e	88-15	Susan'sGirl123¾FlamaArdient119½CostlyDrm123⁴	Hard drive 7
16Oct75- 7Kee	gd *7f	1:28²3↑⒡Alw 15000	7 2 22½ 33½ 32	1nk	Nichols J	122	*.30e	81-18	Susan'sGirl122nkCostlyDream114¾MoonGlitter111⁸	Driving 7
20Sep75- 8Bel	sly 1⅛	:46⁴1:11¹1:36 1:48² 3↑⒡Beldame-G1	9 1 1½ 1hd 1hd	1nk	Baeza B	123	*.70	85-14	Susan'sGirl123nkTizna123¹¾PssGlnc123⁴	Lost lead,driving 9
10Sep75- 8Bel	fst 1	:23³:46² 1:10³1:35¹3↑⒡Maskette H-G2	1 3 3½ 32 33	33½	Broussard R	128	*1.60	88-18	LetMeLinger117noHonorbIMss121¾Ssn'sGrl128⁵½	No excuse 8
10Aug75- 8Del	fst 1¼	:49 1:13 1:37²2:01⁴3↑⒡Delaware H-G1	5 2 2¹ 11½ 11½	1¾	Broussard R	125	*.40	93-16	Susan'sGirl125²¾Pass a Glance116noRaisela117¹½	Handily 6
28Jly75- 8Atl	fst 1¾	:47³1:10³1:35¹1:54¹3↑⒡Matchmaker-G1	4 2 4¹½ 32½ 11	13¼	Broussard R	121	*2.30	105-05	Susan'sGirl121³¼AuntJin114⁵¼PinkTights114¾	Ridden out 6

Previously trained by R.L. Smith

6Jly75- 8Hol	fst 1⅛	:46 1:09⁴1:34⁴1:47²3↑⒡Vanity H-G1	1 1 2½ 2hd 1½	2¾	Pincay L Jr	123	*2.60	94-13	Dulcia118¾Susan's Girl123²¾La Zanzara120½	Gamely 11
22Jun75- 8Hol	fm 1⅛⊤	:47¹1:11¹1:36 1:48³3↑⒡Wilshire H-G3	6 6 75½ 52½ 31½	2hd	Pincay L Jr	123	*1.50e	93-12	Tizna123hdSusan's Girl123¹¾Dulcia120¹½	Gamely 10
31May75- 8Hol	fst 1¼	:23³:47 1:10⁴1:42 3↑⒡Milady H-G2	4 2 2½ 3½ 53	43½	Pincay L Jr	125	*1.80	81-11	Modus Vivendi121¾Tizna124nkMercy Dee111²½	Lacked rally 9
10May75- 8Hol	fst 1	:22²:45 1:08³1:33⁴3↑⒡Caballero H 55k	7 8 95½ 85½ 6¹¹	6¹³	Toro F	116	6.00	84-10	June's Love116³¾Ancient Title126²¾Big Band119³	Dull try 9
26Apr75- 8Hol	fm 1⅛⊤	:46 1:10²1:35²1:48 3↑⒡Long Beach H-G2	3 4 46½ 32½ 1hd	1½	Tejeira J	124	2.20	96-05	Susan's Girl124½Bold Ballet118³Dulcia121¹½	Driving 6

Previously trained by J.L. Newman

| 2Apr75- 8OP | fst 1 70 | :22¹:46¹ 1:11⁴1:42²4↑⒡Apple Blossom H 61k | 12 4 3² 1½ 12½ | 13½ | Nichols J | 124 | *.90 | 84-22 | Susan's Girl124³½Truchas116nkMatuta114¹½ | Handily 12 |

Previously trained by R.L. Smith

1Mar75- 8SA	fst 1⅛	:45⁴1:10³1:36 1:48³4↑⒡S Margarita H-G1	9 4 44½ 51³⁄₄ 21	21½	Pincay L Jr	123	3.50e	87-13	Tizna120¹½Susan's Girl123½Gay Style125no	Good try 12
16Feb75- 8SA	fst 1⅛	:24¹:48¹ 1:12¹1:42 4↑⒡S Maria H-G2	1 1 31½ 3½ 32½	32	Hawley S	124	3.00e	90-14	Gay Style122¾Tizna120¹¼Susan's Girl124²	Weakened 8
18Jan75- 8SA	fst 7f	:22 :44² 1:08⁴1:21²4↑⒡S Monica H-G2	1 1 75½ 65 54¼	2½	Hawley S	125	4.40e	95-12	SisterFleet115¾Susan'sGirl125nkModus Vivendi123¹	Gamely 13
27Dec74- 8SA	fst 1	:24¹:47² 1:11¹1:35³3↑Alw 20000	1 1 3¹ 34 34½	35½	Pincay L Jr	117	1.40	86-15	Nantwice119nkTreeofKnowledge115⁵Ssn'sGrl117²	Bad start 4

Previously trained by T.W. Kelley

| 9Nov74- 8CD | fst 1 | :23³:47² 1:12³1:37²3↑⒡Falls City H-G3 | 8 2 23½ 2hd 11½ | 1no | Gavidia W | 126 | *.70e | 82-19 | Susan'sGirl126noCrystalStone114¾EnchntdNtv112¹½ | All out 9 |
| 30Oct74- 8CD | fst 7f | :23²:46³ 1:11 1:24¹3↑⒡Alw 12500 | 8 3 33½ 34 2hd | 1½ | Gavidia W | 114 | *1.10 | 86-22 | Susan'sGirl114¾GallantDvll121²¼DogtoothVolt121³ | Driving 9 |

Previously trained by C.R. Parke

16Feb74- 8SA	fst 1¹⁄₁₆	:23²:46⁴ 1:11¹1:42⁴4↑⒡S Maria H-G2	1 3 44½ 65½ 56	52¾	Baeza B	128	*.80	85-14	Convenience121¹½Tizna117nkTallahto119½	Mild bid 8
2Feb74- 8SA	fst 1¹⁄₁₆	:23³:47¹ 1:10⁴1:41²4↑⒡San Pasqual H-G2	1 1 2½ 42 3½	3³	Baeza B	119	*1.30e	92-12	Tri Jet121hdForage121³Susan's Girl119³	Weakened 10
19Jan74- 8SA	gd 7f	:22²:45³ 1:10³1:24 4↑⒡S Monica H-G2	1 1 44 5⁶ 45	2½	Baeza B	123	*2.30	92-12	Tizna116½Susan's Girl127¹Impressive Style119⁴	Gamely 7
27Oct73- 6Kee	fst 1⅛	:47 1:10³1:36 1:48⁴3↑⒡Spinster-G1	2 2 21½ 21 1½	11	Pincay L Jr	123	*.70	93-13	Susan's Girl123¹Light Hearted123¹Coragioso123½	Driving 8
8Oct73- 8Atl	fst 1⅛	:47 1:11 1:36¹1:55¹3↑⒡Matchmaker-G1	5 3 37 55½ 43	31½	Baeza B	125	*1.20	99-13	AlmaNorth118¹½Light Hearted121noSusan's Girl125²	Good try 8
15Sep73- 6Bel	fst 1⅛	:46²1:10 1:34 1:46¹3↑⒡Beldame-G1	2 3 42½ 56½ 49½	3¹²	Pincay L Jr	123	2.60	88-07	Desert Vixen118⁸½Poker Night118³Susan's Girl123¾	7

Passed tired ones;Previously trained by J.W. Russell

12Aug73- 8Del	fst 1¼	:463 1:104 1:354 2:003	3↑ ⒻDelaware H-G1	6 5	514 44 21 1nk	Pincay L Jr	127		*1.40	99-10	Susn'sGirl127nkSummrGuest1225½LightHeartd1254	Driving 6
4Aug73- 8Lib	fst 1 1/16	:232 :47 1:113 1:433	3↑ ⒻSusquehanna H-G2	5 5	47 44 1hd 13½	Pincay L Jr	125		*.50	88-24	Susan's Girl1253½Twixt1184½Knightly Belle1131¼	Handily 6
7Jly73- 8Hol	fst 1⅛	:454 1:094 1:35 1:474	3↑ ⒻVanity H-G1	1 3	34½ 35½ 42½ 31¾	Pincay L Jr	127		1.40	91-09	Convenience121½MinstrelMiss1211¼Susan'sGrl127½	Bid,hung 8
2Jun73- 8Hol	fst 1 1/16	:231 :464 1:11 1:414	3↑ ⒻMilady H-G2	6 4	2½ 1½ 2½ 21	Pincay L Jr	128		*.90e	85-17	Minstrel Miss1181Susan's Girl1281Pallisima1153	Gamely 6
5May73- 8Hol	fm 1⅜Ⓣ	2:132	3↑ Century H-G1	9 1	11½ 1½ 21 47¾	Rotz JL	119		5.10	80-11	Cougar II1273½Wing Out1183¼Life Cycle1171	Weakened 11
21Apr73- 8Hol	fm 1⅛Ⓣ	:46 1:10 1:344 1:473	3↑ ⒻLong Beach H-G2	8 6	612 69½ 54 2hd	Pincay L Jr	130		*1.70	98-05	BirdBoots115hdSusan'sGirl130¾HillCrcus1201½	Just missed 9
22Mar73- 8SA	fst 1¼⊗	:502 1:15 1:393 2:033	4↑ ⒻS Barbara H-G1	1 1	11½ 11½ 12 14¾	Pincay L Jr	129		*.30	80-15	Susan'sGirl1294¾VeiledDesire1102½GrayMirag1124½	Driving 5
3Mar73- 8SA	fst 1⅛	:463 1:101 1:352 1:474	4↑ ⒻS Margarita Inv'l H-G1	8 2	32 44 31½ 13	Pincay L Jr	127		2.50	93-11	Susan'sGirl1273Convenience1232¾MnstrlMss115½	Drew clear 8
17Feb73- 8SA	fst 1 1/16	:234 :473 1:114 1:42	4↑ ⒻS Maria H-G2	2 2	21 2½ 2hd 1½	Pincay L Jr	125		2.60	92-11	Susan'sGirl125½Convnnc1233HllCrcus119hd	Swerved,driving 6
27Jan73- 8SA	fst 1⅛	:453 1:094 1:352 1:481	San Fernando-G2	3 5	55½ 54 56 54¼	Tejada V	118		2.80e	87-12	Bicker1201½Royal Owl1201½Commoner114¾	No rally 14
6Jan73- 8SA	fst 7f	:214 :442 1:084 1:212	Malibu-G2	1 1	64½ 64 51¼ 55	Tejada V	121		*1.10e	91-11	Bicker117hdRoyal Owl120½Tri Jet1171½	In close 13
9Sep72- 7Bel	fst 1⅛	:46 1:102 1:35 1:472	3↑ ⒻBeldame 112k	3 4	24 42 21 11	Pincay L Jr	118		3.30	97-06	Susan's Girl1181Summer Guest1181Chou Croute1233¼	9
	Bore out,driving											
2Sep72- 7Bel	fst 1⅛	:461 1:10 1:351 1:48	ⒻGazelle H 55k	1 2	25 25 1hd 11½	Pincay L Jr	124		*1.10	94-09	Susan's Girl1241½Honestous1125Light Hearted1215	Driving 7
29Jly72- 8Lib	fst 1 1/16	:231 :464 1:113 1:441	ⒻCotillion H 59k	5 3	31½ 21½ 11 14½	Tejada V	125		*1.10	85-22	Susan'sGirl1254½GrotonMiss1193Honestous1154	Ridden out 13
20Jly72- 8Hol	fst 1⅛	:462 1:102 1:353 1:483	ⒻHol Oaks 64k	2 4	55½ 41¾ 33 31¾	Tejeira J	124		*.40	87-15	Pallsm1121¼Brt'sTryst112½Susn'sGrl1243½	Checked,rallied 7
29Jun72- 8Hol	fm 1 1/16Ⓣ	:241 :483 1:14 1:433	ⒻPrincess 33k	2 2	24 2hd 31 2hd	Tejada V	121		*1.10	81-19	Le Cle121hdSusan's Girl121¾Ground Song1171¼	Just missed 7
17Jun72- 7Bel	sly 1½	:491 1:132 2:031 2:292	ⒻC C A Oaks 110k	3 1	1hd 32 34½ 38	Tejada V	121	b	*.90	78-09	Summer Guest1214Wanda1214Susan's Girl1216	Gave way 8
27May72- 7Bel	fst 1⅛	:462 1:102 1:353 1:482	ⒻMother Goose 84k	4 3	22 21½ 21 2nk	Tejada V	121	b	*.40	92-10	Wanda121nkSusan's Girl1216Summer Guest1211½	Sharp 8
13May72- 7Aqu	fst 1	:232 :454 1:093 1:343	ⒻAcorn 56k	2 2	21½ 1½ 12 12½	Tejada V	121	b	*.70	94-11	Susan's Girl1212½Wanda1213Stacey d'Ette1213	Handily 7
5May72- 8CD	fst 1 1/16	:241 :481 1:122 1:441	ⒻKy Oaks 61k	7 4	31½ 1½ 13 11	Tejada V	121	b	*.30	87-16	Susan'sGirl1211BarelyEven1211¾FairwayFlyer1212½	Handily 7
29Apr72- 8CD	fst 7f	:224 :46 1:104 1:234	ⒻLa Troienne 21k	8 2	44½ 42½ 11 11¾	Tejada V	121	b	*1.10	88-17	Susan'sGirl1211¾BarelyEven1216HempensSong121hd	Easily 8
9Mar72- 8SA	fst 1 1/16	:23 :46 1:102 1:43	ⒻS Susana 54k	3 3	31 1hd 1½ 13½	Tejada V	115	b	*.30	87-15	Susan'sGirl1153½Dumpty'sDream1156Chargerett115¾	Handily 7
24Feb72- 8SA	fst 7f	:22 :443 1:091 1:214	ⒻS Ynez 47k	5 1	53½ 21½ 2½ 13¼	Tejada V	118	b	*1.10	94-13	Susan'sGirl1183¼Foreseer115noImpressiveStyle1186	Easily 10
20Jan72- 8SA	fst 6f	:214 :443 :562 1:083	ⒻPasadena 34k	7 2	32½ 3½ 1½ 1¾	Tejada V	118	b	*1.60e	98-10	Susan's Girl118¾Sumatra113noBrenda Beauty1212½	Driving 7
25Nov71- 8Lib	sly 1 70	:23 :473 1:134 1:434	ⒻVillager 27k	2 1	11½ 12½ 14 18	Hinojosa H	119	b	*.70	86-27	Susan'sGirl1198RoyalKin11412TurbulentMiss1125	Handily 7
17Nov71- 7Aqu	fst 1	:231 :452 1:10 1:354	ⒻDemoiselle 36k	2 4	34 34½ 25 22	Pincay L Jr	119	b	*.50	86-16	DresdenDoll1142Susan'sGrl1194BrndButy1221	Belated rally 14
6Nov71- 8GS	gd 1 1/16	:234 :474 1:13 1:454	ⒻGardenia 184k	2 2	21 15 1hd 22¾	Blum W	119	b	7.70	73-28	NumberedAccnt1192¾Susan'sGirl1196Catmousam Road1196	11
	Second best											
27Oct71- 7GS	my 1 70	:232 :48 1:131 1:441	ⒻAlw 10000	3 6	53½ 32 23 22½	Velasquez J	112	b	*.50	70-33	BoldRoyal1132½Susan'sGirl1123TurbulentMss1142	Willingly 9
11Oct71- 7Bel	fst 1	:231 :461 1:104 1:353	ⒻFrizette 135k	2 3	3½ 23 26 27	Velasquez J	119	b	4.70	88-16	NmberdAccnt1197Susan'sGirl1195BarelyEvn11920	Gamely 4
4Oct71- 3Bel	fst 7f	:222 :454 1:104 1:24	ⒻAlw 12000	7 1	32½ 2hd 14 15	Velasquez J	123	b	2.40e	87-18	Susan'sGirl1235BoldRoyal116hdBrendaButy1234½	Mild drive 8
15Sep71- 7Bel	fst 7f	:221 :452 1:104 1:232	ⒻAstarita 35k	7 2	1111 106 72¾ 43¼	Velasquez J	122		4.30	87-12	BarelyEven1193MissGunflint116noBrdgtO'Brck112nk	Rallied 11
	Previously trained by J.E. Picou											
16Aug71- 7Sar	fst 6f	:222 :454 1:101	ⒻAdirondack 34k	3 2	76½ 41¾ 41½ 52	Velasquez J	122	b	8.60	93-12	DebbyDeb1141½DancePrtnr114noNumbrdAccnt122nk	No rally 9
7Aug71- 8Lib	fst 6f	:221 :46 1:113	ⒻSignature 58k	2 8	75¾ 63¾ 2hd 15	Brumfield D	118	b	*.90e	87-16	Susan'sGirl1185HempensSong1183CastleFlower1121	Driving 8
24Jly71- 6Aqu	fst 5½f	:22 :46 :582 1:044	ⒻAlw 10000	5 3	42 42 1½ 15	Velasquez J	119	b	*1.20	89-15	Susan'sGirl1195RoyalStatut119¾Stcyd'Ett114hd	Mild drive 10
9Jly71- 4Aqu	fst 5½f	:22 :461 :583 1:044	ⒻMd Sp Wt	3 1	62¾ 63¾ 2hd 14	Velasquez J	119	b	4.20	89-17	Susan'sGirl1194EarlyTide119nkPlsntFlght1191½	Mild drive 8
18Jun71- 3Bel	fst 5½f	:223 :47 :592 1:061	ⒻMd Sp Wt	4 2	33½ 34½ 23 2½	Velasquez J	119	b	21.40	88-20	Bold Example119½Susan's Girl1194Dandy Duchess1191½	10
	Rallied,finished strongly											
4Jun71- 2Bel	fst 5½f	:233 :474 :593 1:054	ⒻMd Sp Wt	3 1	31 77 69 410¼	Velasquez J	119		8.80	81-15	BrendaBeauty119nkChildofGrace1198SingleLine1192	Tired 8

Ta Wee

dkbbr. f. 1966, by Intentionally (Intent)–Aspidistra, by Better Self — **Lifetime record: 21 15 2 1 $284,941**

Own.– Tartan Stable
Br.– Tartan Farms (Fla)
Tr.– F.S. Schulhofer

5Oct70- 7Bel	fst 6f	:221 :451 1:10	3↑ ⒻInterborough H 21k	2 3	1½ 11 15 1¾	Rotz JL	142		*.60	95-10	Ta Wee142¾Hasty Hitter1132½Kushka1121	Handily 5
31Aug70- 7Bel	fst 6f	:231 :461 1:102	3↑ Fall Highweight H 28k	3 3	32 31½ 1hd 1nk	Rotz JL	140		*1.50e	93-19	Ta Wee140nkTowzie Tyke121nkDistinctive1344	Safe margin 9
29Jly70- 7Aqu	fst 6f	:22 :443 1:084	3↑ Gravesend H 28k	6 5	64½ 23 23 24	Rotz JL	134		*2.10	95-12	Distinctive1144Ta Wee134hdTyrant121nk	Gamely 9
17Jun70- 8Mth	fst 6f	:213 :443 1:10	3↑ ⒻRegret H 28k	2 5	2hd 1½ 12 1½	Rotz JL	136		*.60	92-15	Ta Wee136½Golden Or1133Deb's Darling114½	Driving 8
1Jun70- 7Bel	fst 6f	:221 :444 1:10	3↑ ⒻHempstead H 28k	5 3	2hd 11½ 13 13½	Rotz JL	132		*1.20	95-11	Ta Wee1323½Process Shot1271Grey Slacks1112	Easy score 8
8Apr70- 7Aqu	fst 7f	:23 :452 1:10 1:224	3↑ ⒻDistaff H 27k	4 3	21 2hd 1½ 21¾	Rotz JL	134		*1.40	85-20	ProcssSht1261¾TaWee1342DedicatdtoSu115hd	Tired-impost 6
27Mar70- 7Aqu	gd 6f	:223 :462 1:112	3↑ ⒻCorrection H 27k	1 5	1½ 11½ 13 1nk	Rotz JL	131		*.50	86-26	Ta Wee131nkTaken Aback1144Dedicated to Sue1171	Lasted 7
1Nov69- 7Aqu	fst 7f	:221 :442 1:083 1:213	3↑ Vosburgh H 58k	6 5	31 1hd 1hd 1hd	Rotz JL	123		*1.70	93-13	TaWee123hd[DH]PluckyLucky116[DH]RisingMarket120½	Driving 11
15Oct69- 7Bel	fst 6f	:222 :46 1:093	3↑ ⒻInterborough H 27k	5 4	21 11 12 13½	Rotz JL	124		*.50	97-16	Ta Wee1243½Dedicated to Sue1144½Grey Slacks118nk	Easily 7
11Sep69- 7Bel	yl 1 1/16Ⓣ	1:45	3↑ ⒻAlw 15000	2 2	23 21 11½ 42¾	Rotz JL	119		1.60	- -	PersianIntrigue118¾DesertLaw1182OlympianIdle116hd	Tired 8
25Aug69- 7Bel	fst 6f	:213 :454 1:101	3↑ Fall Highweight H 28k	9 5	4¾ 2½ 1hd 1¾	Rotz JL	130		*1.50e	94-17	TaWee130¾KngEmperr1311Gaylord'sFeathr1292½	Hard drive 9
	Previously trained by J.A. Nerud											
31Jly69- 7Sar	fst 7f	:223 :444 1:111 1:233	ⒻTest 27k	1 3	12 16 13 11	Belmonte E	124		*.30	91-16	Ta Wee1241French Bread1158½Bold Tribute1121½	Driving 6
31May69- 8Mth	fst 6f	:212 :434 1:083	ⒻMiss Woodford 29k	11 8	1½ 12 15 17	Belmonte E	121		*.60	99-13	Ta Wee1217Imbibe1156Script Girl115hd	As rider pleased 12
7May69- 7Aqu	fst 7f	:222 :451 1:092 1:223	ⒻComely 28k	2 5	32½ 1½ 13 1hd	Belmonte E	118		*.40	88-13	TaWee118hdShuvee1215HstyHttr118hd	Stumbled start,lasted 6
3Apr69- 7Aqu	fst 6f	:221 :444 1:092	ⒻPrioress 28k	1 9	22 22 2hd 13	Rotz JL	121		2.90	96-15	Ta Wee1213Frances Flower1214Juliet121½	Handy score 9
29Jan69- 8Hia	fst 7f	:224 :453 1:102 1:232	ⒻMimosa 34k	13 8	54¼ 43½ 22 33½	Rotz JL	114		*1.30	87-15	NuttyDonut1122Queen'sDouble1211½TaWee114hd	Weakened 13
18Jan69- 8Hia	fst 6f	:221 :451 1:102	ⒻJasmine (Div 2) 27k	2 4	11 1½ 11½ 13	Rotz JL	113		3.40	92-12	Ta Wee1133Spring Sunshine1215Imbibe1121½	Scored handily 12
7Sep68- 4Aqu	fst 6f	:231 :471 1:121	ⒻAlw 7000	9 9	43½ 22 1½ 12	Rotz JL	119		*1.50	82-18	TaWee1192Dihela1131½DorisWhite1166	Scored well in hand 10
21Aug68- 7Sar	gd 6f	:214 :454 1:112	ⒻSpinaway 80k	7 2	21½ 11½ 1hd 46¼	Rotz JL	119		*1.10	85-10	Queen's Double1191¾Show Off119½Fillypasser1194	Tired 10
13Aug68- 5Sar	fst 5½f	:221 :454 :573 1:04	ⒻMd Sp Wt	2 10	1½ 13 16 16	Rotz JL	119		*.80	97-11	Ta Wee1196Drip Spring1192Socializing1192½	Easily best 12
30Jly68- 4Sar	fst 5½f	:221 :461 :584 1:052	ⒻMd Sp Wt	1 10	13 11 2½ 44	Rotz JL	119		*1.90	86-17	Queen's Double1193Hasty Hitter119noIrradiate1191	Tired 12

Talking Picture

dkbbr. f. 1971, by Speak John (Prince John)–Poster Girl, by Nasrullah — **Lifetime record: 15 6 2 3 $178,643**

Own.– Elmendorf Farm
Br.– Elmendorf Farm (Ky)
Tr.– J.P. Campo

11May74- 8Aqu	fst 1	:23 :452 1:093 1:36	ⒻAcorn (Div 2)-G1	9 8	85½ 67½ 64 52¾	Turcotte R	121		2.60	84-17	ChrisEvert121¾ClearCopy1211FiestaLibre121hd	Mild rally 9
22Apr74- 8Aqu	fst 6f	:222 :444 1:101	ⒻPrioress-G3	3 9	98¾ 67½ 45½ 3¾	Turcotte R	115		3.90	91-14	Clear Copy115noHeartful118¾Talking Picture1153¼	Rallied 12
18Feb74- 9GP	fst 7f	:221 :45 1:093 1:223	ⒻBonnie Miss 35k	3 10	1010 1111 1111 94¾	Turcotte R	122		*1.90	86-17	City Girl112¾Maud Muller112½Double Bend1121	No factor 12
30Jan74- 9GP	fst 6f	:221 :453 1:11	ⒻPromise (Div 2) 26k	10 2	89½ 55 22 1½	Turcotte R	119		*1.10	84-22	TalkingPicture119½CityGirl1122½DoubleBend1122	Driving 10
27Oct73- 8Lrl	fst 1 1/16	:231 :461 1:111 1:424	ⒻSelima-G1	6 7	68 55 33 33	Venezia M	119		*1.20	96-12	Dancealot119¾I'maPleasure1192¼TlkngPctur1193½	No excuse 9
6Oct73- 7Bel	fst 1	:232 :464 1:112 1:362	ⒻFrizette-G1	2 11	84¾ 83¾ 74½ 53¾	Turcotte R	121		*1.80	82-13	Bundler121½Chris Evert121nkI'm a Pleasure1211	Rallied 14
19Sep73- 7Bel	fst 7f	:224 :46 1:104 1:231	ⒻMatron-G1	2 6	87 83¾ 31½ 1hd	Turcotte R	119		*.70	86-11	Talking Picture119hdDancealot119nkRaisela119nk	Driving 9
24Aug73- 7Sar	fst 6f	:223 :461 1:10	ⒻSpinaway-G1	6 8	94¾ 52½ 1½ 12½	Turcotte R	120		*1.90e	90-10	TalkingPicture1202½SpecialTeam1203Raisela1202½	Driving 10
13Aug73- 7Sar	fst 6f	:22 :452 1:11	ⒻAdirondack-G2	5 8	86¾ 65½ 25 1hd	Baeza B	120		5.80	85-15	TalkingPicture120hdInHotPursuit1204½Bedknob1202	Driving 10

30Jly73- 7Sar fst 6f :221 :453 1:104 ⒻSchuylerville-G2 9 1 74½ 55 43½ 1no Baeza B 116 4.50 86-14 Talking Picture116noImajoy1162Celestial Lights1192 Driving 10
14Jly73- 8Hol fst 6f :22 :444 :57 1:093 ⒻLassie-G2 8 13 115¾ 87¾ 89½ 88 Rotz JL 119 3.20 83-14 Special Goddess1191Calaki119¾Fleet Peach119nk Dull try 13
3Jly73- 3Aqu fst 5½f :221 :444 :564 1:03 ⒻAlw 9500 4 3 43½ 35½ 26 24½ Baeza B 118 *.80 93-11 What Brilliance1184½Talking Picture1188I'm a Pleasure1182 5
Second best
13Jun73- 7Bel sly 5½f :221 :451 :571 1:031 ⒻFashion-G3 5 8 713 711 511 311¼ Baeza B 117 3.50e 88-09 InHotPursuit11710Provincial1171¼TlkngPctur1172½ Rallied 8
4Jun73- 5Bel fst 5½f :23 :462 :58 1:04 ⒻAlw 10000 1 6 85½ 63½ 33½ 22 Baeza B 117 2.70 97-07 In Hot Pursuit1172Talking Picture117¾Nice to Have1174½ 8
Second best
15May73- 3Bel fst 5½f :23 :462 :582 1:043 ⒻMd Sp Wt 5 7 62½ 41 2½ 14 Baeza B 116 *2.60 96-04 Talking Picture1164Shy Dawn1162Graziella1161 Ridden out 10

Tempest Queen

b. f. 1975, by Graustark (Ribot)–Queen's Paradise, by Summer Tan **Lifetime record: 19 8 3 4 $289,219**
Own.– Darby Dan Farm
Br.– Mrs J.W. Galbreath (Ky)
Tr.– Thomas Rondinello

21Mar79-11Hia fst 7f :213 :441 1:091 1:221 3↑ ⒻPoinciana H 32k 3 6 35½ 79 911 913½ Velasquez J 123 *.80 78-18 FrostySkater119¾NavajoPrincess1221Excitabl1124 Stopped 9
7Mar79-10Hia fst 7f :23 :452 1:101 1:23 4↑ ⒻAlw 15000 8 2 31½ 33 3½ 11¼ Velasquez J 122 *.90 88-14 TempestQn1221¼IrishAgate119½Whatsupbaby114nk Driving 10
17Feb79- 9GP fst 7f :221 :444 1:09 1:211 4↑ ⒻAlw 20000 7 4 52½ 65½ 58½ 611 Velasquez J 122 *.60 87-13 Hagany117noFrostySkater1144½SharpBelle1141 No response 8
21Oct78- 7Kee fst 1⅛ :464 1:103 1:362 1:49 3↑ ⒻSpinster-G1 3 1 11 12 11 11¾ Velasquez J 119 8.40 92-14 TempstQueen1191¾Northerntt123hdLklyExchng123hd Driving 10
23Sep78- 8Bel fst 1⅛ :462 1:094 1:343 1:47 3↑ ⒻRuffian H-G1 6 2 21 2½ 33 35½ Venezia M 117 18.10 86-15 LateBloomr1221½PearlNcklace1244TmpstQn1172½ Weakened 9
2Sep78- 8Bel my 1⅛ :462 1:11 1:364 1:494 ⒻGazelle H-G2 4 1 11½ 11½ 14 15½ Velasquez J 117 1.60 78-21 TmpstQueen1175½Lulubo1164¾Terpschorst1135¾ Ridden out 5
12Aug78- 8Sar sly 1¼ :47 1:121 1:381 2:04 ⒻAlabama-G1 5 2 21 2hd 32½ 310 Velasquez J 121 4.50 71-18 WhiteStarLine1211½SummerFlng1218½TmpstQn1217 Bid,tired 6
2Aug78- 7Sar fst 7f :221 :45 1:092 1:212 ⒻTest (Div 1)-G2 2 6 63¼ 74½ 55 46¾ Velasquez J 124 *2.50 91-10 WhiteStarLine1211½SilknDlght1143¼Zrld1142 No room early 8
1Jly78- 8Bel fst 1½ :464 1:112 2:023 2:292 ⒻC C A Oaks-G1 5 2 21½ 32 35½ 310 Velasquez J 121 4.40 63-16 LakevilleMiss1216Caesar'sWish1214TmpstQn1215 Weakened 5
11Jun78- 8Bel fst 1⅛ :451 1:09 1:342 1:473 ⒻMother Goose-G1 2 2 23 23 32½ 33½ Velasquez J 121 1.90 85-15 Caesar'sWish1212LakevilleMss1211½TmpstQn121hd Weakened 8
27May78- 8Bel fst 1 :224 :45 1:094 1:352 ⒻAcorn-G1 1 1 23 1hd 11½ 11¾ Velasquez J 121 4.90 91-17 TempstQueen1211¾Lakeville Miss121nkWhite Star Line1211¾ 6
Ridden out
13May78- 8Aqu fst 7f :224 :451 1:094 1:23 ⒻComely-G3 3 5 2hd 2hd 21½ 23 Turcotte R 118 *1.40 83-21 Mashteen1133TempstQn1181½Mucchin1133 Altered course 6
30Apr78- 8Aqu fst 6f :23 :464 1:112 ⒻPrioress 42k 1 5 11½ 11½ 13 12½ Velasquez J 118 *.30 86-20 TempestQueen1182½SweetJoyce112nkSilverIce1154½ Handily 5
22Feb78- 9Hia gd 1⅛ :471 1:114 1:37 1:50 ⒻPoinsettia-G3 5 6 32 2hd 11 11½ Velasquez J 113 2.00 82-18 Tempest Queen1131½Jevalin1142L'Alezane122nk Ridden out 9
30Jan78-10Hia fst 7f :223 :46 1:102 1:231 ⒻAlw 8500 1 7 24 21½ 12 12 Velasquez J 114 *.60 87-20 TempestQn1142Mucchina1154½MakeItKnown1173½ Driving 10
17Jan78- 3Hia fst 6f :214 :45 1:094 ⒻMd Sp Wt 11 2 21½ 32 1hd 14 Velasquez J 119 *.90 94-11 TempstQueen1194Marci Lynn1191Ericka Downs1196 In hand 11
2Dec77- 5Aqu sly 6f :222 :46 1:103 ⒻMd Sp Wt 5 1 1½ 1hd 1hd 2nk Cordero A Jr 119 3.50 90-18 IvyRoad119nkTempestQueen1194¾MissBaja1195 Just failed 9
16Nov77- 4Aqu fst 6f :223 :462 1:112 ⒻMd Sp Wt 9 5 2½ 1hd 1hd 2hd Velasquez J 119 5.70 86-19 Idmon112hdTempest Queen1192¾Miss Ivor1194 Gamely 9
1Nov77- 2Aqu fst 6f :224 :462 1:121 ⒻMd Sp Wt 13 14 129¼ 1211 710 66¾ Velasquez J 119 28.20 75-18 AllforAmy1192¾Tara'sTheme119nkMissIvor1192¾ Off slowly 14

Top Bid

b. g. 1964, by Olympia (Heliopolis)–High Bid, by To Market **Lifetime record: 74 25 9 11 $310,128**
Own.– Mrs O. Phipps
Br.– Wheatley Stable (Ky)
Tr.– D.M. Smithwick

17Nov73- 2Cam fm 2 13/16 S'Chase 5:214 4↑ Colonial Cup 50k 5 10 - - - - McDonald RS 158 -e - - LuckyBoyIII149noSthsyer162noDreamMgc1531¼ Broke down 15
11Nov73- 6Mid fm *1¼Ⓣ 2:19 3↑ Alw 300 9 - 39¾ Brittle C III 153 s -e - - Still In All1438Sabinus1401¾Top Bid1533 Hung 16
Further running positions unavailable due to weather conditions
27Oct73- 5FH fm *1½Ⓣ 2:294 3↑ Alw 1500 7 2 3¾ 35½ 31 11½ Brittle C III 142 s - - Top Bid1421½Tor's Lib149¾Honest Crook1494 Driving 8
6Oct73- 4Lig fm *2½ S'Chase 5:032 4↑ Temple Gwathmey H 25k 4 1 11 1½ 1nk 39¼ Brittle C III 157 -e - - Athenian Idol1401¼Soothsayer1628Top Bid1572 Weakened 8
3Oct73- 6Lig gd *2 S'Chase 4:102 4↑ Handicap 10000 1 3 11½ 12 1½ 33¼ Aitcheson J Jr 162 - - [D]Perigo150nkJuac Hollow1603Top Bid1622 In close 10
Placed second by disqualification
15Sep73- 6Fai fm *2½ Hurdles 5:211 4↑ Grand National H 12k 2 2 16 13 12½ 11¼ Aitcheson J Jr 152 s 2.70 - - Top Bid1521¼Summer Crop1395Dream Magic1532 Driving 6
8Sep73- 6Fai hd *2⅛ Hurdles 4:133 4↑ Alw 4850 1 2 32½ 1¾ 11 11¼ Aitcheson J Jr 158 s 5.00 - - Top Bid1581¼Wustenchef1585Castlebar II1501 Driving 4
24Aug73- 9Sar fm 1⅞ Hurdles 3:231 4↑ OClm 6000 7 5 55½ 24 21½ 1hd Aitcheson J Jr 154 s *2.20 - - Top Bid154hdTarratine133¾Hipocampo1476 Driving 7
8Aug73- 9Sar fm 2 Hurdles 3:372 4↑ OClm 8000 6 3 322 316 46 - Aitcheson J Jr 155 s 2.60 - - Hipocampo1391¾ManchuPrinc1396FarmrsLot1422 Lost rider 8
3Aug73- 5Sar gd 2 1/16 Hurdles 3:44 4↑ Lovely Night H 22k 3 3 49 611 625 521 Aitcheson J Jr 149 s 6.60e - - Juac Hollow1504Wustenchef1558½Still in All1401 Tired 7
22Jly73- 6Del sf 1Ⓣ :232 :473 1:121 1:39 3↑ Alw 8500 8 4 65¼ 715 716 726 Cooke C 118 24.50 54-31 Mr. Clinch120nkLeematt1224Away Satan1181 Tired 8
18Nov72- 3Cam fm 2 13/16 S'Chase 5:234 4↑ Colonial Cup 100k 7 2 74¾ 3½ 41 43 Brittle C III 160 - - - Soothsayr1582½Inkslinger158¼ShadowBrook160nk Weakened 16
4Nov72- 5Mtp fm *2 Hurdles 4:253 3↑ Alw 1500 3 3 25 2nk 25 26 Brittle C III 143 s -e - - Summer Crop1436Top Bid1432½Arctic Joe15110 Best of rest 8
28Oct72- 4FH sf *2 Hurdles 4:12 3↑ Handicap 10000 9 1 11½ 56¼ 63¾ 58 Brittle C III 157 s - - - Persian Honour145½Americus1391Dream Magic1505 Tired 11
21Oct72- 4RB fm *2 S'Chase 4:093 4↑ Alw 3500 3 2 21½ 23 44¼ 35½ Gregory T 143 -e - - Profile1431½Americus1464Top Bid143¾ Tired 8
7Oct72- 6Lig sf *7fⓉ 1:374 3↑ Alw 1500 12 1 1¾ 1nk 2no 44½ Brittle C III 155 s - - - Perpetual II1581½Dream Magic143½Powdermill1432½ Tired 12
Previously trained by Pierre Head
25Aug72◆ Clairefontaine(Fr) gd *2 11/16 5:14 4↑ Grand Steeple-Chase de Deauville Stk18800 310¼ Lautier R 156 8.00 Mr. So and So145nkBelpic14710Top Bid156½ 20
Tracked leaders,led 2 out,headed 1 out,outfinished
8Aug72◆ Clairefontaine(Fr) gd *2⅜ 4:46 4↑ Prix Leopold d'Orsetti Hcp Hcp15000 11 Lautier R 158 6.00 Kind Tady14315Mini Chief134½Malefine145½ 17
Rated in midpack,bid 3 out,weakened after second last
9Jly72◆ Auteuil(Fr) gd *2 3/16 4:22 51 Prix Palamede Alw15400 24 Dreux T 137 *2.20 Pique Puce1454Top Bid1362½Mehryvan1471½ 15
Tracked in 4th,2nd 2 out,outfinished
18Jun72◆ Auteuil(Fr) gd *2⅛ 4:12 51 Prix Arthur O'Connor Alw15400 99 Lautier R 154 3.00 Bengalien1362Mistonette1413Franc Ryk1452 13
Rated in 6th,brief effort 3 out,weakened
Previously trained by D.M. Smithwick
27Nov71- 8Lrl gd 1¼⊗ :47 1:121 1:39 2:044 3↑ Lrl Turf Cup 28k 2 1 32½ 617 639 649 Nelson E 115 b 4.50 42-20 CrackRulr1161½FreshAlibha11310SrMtthw1094½ Early speed 6
20Nov71- 2Cam fm 2 13/16 S'Chase 5:17 4↑ Colonial Cup 10k 3 11 75¾ 813 68 38¼ Aitcheson J Jr 160 s -e - - Inkslinger149nkSoothsayer1498Top Bid1603 Rallied 15
6Nov71- 3Mtp sf *2½ S'Chase 4:493 4↑ Noel Laing H 5.6k 4 8 87¼ 811 716 821½ Aitcheson J Jr 165 s - - - TingleCreek1548TheCritter143nkAttribution144nk No factor 9
15Oct71- 3Bel yl 3 S'Chase 5:47 4↑ Gwathmey H 55k 1 4 65½ 43 515 310 Aitcheson J Jr 160 s 4.10 - - Shadow Brook1635½Amerind1414½Top Bid160¾ Bobbled 9
28Sep71- 3Bel yl 2⅝ S'Chase 4:571 4↑ Brook H 33k 5 7 713 59½ 413 513 Aitcheson J Jr 162 s 1.60 - - Shadow Brook1592¼Amarind135nkTingle Creek1536 Bobbled 8
18Sep71- 8Fai fm *1 5/16Ⓣ 2:202 3↑ Alw 1200 8 7 66¾ 55 21 13 Aitcheson J Jr 153 s *.50 - - Top Bid1533Mystic's Desire1476Pelham II1404½ Handily 8
11Sep71- 2Fai fm *1 5/16Ⓣ 2:122 3↑ Alw 1200 2 13 1413 97¼ 87 14 Aitcheson J Jr 142 s *1.00e - - TopBid1424BrandyPrinceII156½Mystic'sDesr142¾ Mild drive 14
26Aug71- 3Sar fm 2½ S'Chase 4:372 4↑ Grand National H 40k 5 4 24 31 23 212 Aitcheson J Jr 163 s 2.40 - - Shadow Brook15512Top Bid1635Madagascar1421 2nd best 7
12Aug71- 3Sar fm 2 1/16 Hurdles 3:433 4↑ Lovely Night H 22k 6 6 64¾ 54 410 511 Aitcheson J Jr 162 s *1.30e - - Shadow Brook156nkSoothsayer1398Inkslinger1502½ Tired 7
14Nov70- 4Cam sf *2 13/16 S'Chase 5:20 4↑ Colonial Cup 100k - 8 66¼ 74 35 11½ Aitcheson J Jr 160 -e - - Top Bid1601½Shadow Brook1601½Jaunty1586 Driving 22
16Oct70- 5Bel sf 3 S'Chase 5:522 4↑ Temple Gwathmey H 55k 6 4 312 31½ 13 14 Aitcheson J Jr 156 2.10 - - Top Bid1564Duke Cannon1329Tingle Creek1467 Handy score 7
17Sep70- 4Bel fm 2½ S'Chase 4:37 4↑ Broad Hollow H 17k 9 3 513 49 21½ 26 Aitcheson J Jr 155 *1.50e - - TingleCreek1396TopBid1554½DukeCannon13215 Bobbled 12th 10
1Sep70- 4Bel fm 2 S'Chase 3:412 4↑ International H 16k 4 4 47 44 1½ 1½ Aitcheson J Jr 152 *.90e - - Top Bid152½Lost Lamb135hdVocalist1429 Hard drive 6
20Aug70- 6Sar hd 2 1/16 S'Chase 3:444 4↑ Saratoga H 18k 4 3 23 2½ 16 19 Aitcheson J Jr 146 s *1.60e - - Top Bid1469The Critter1342½Teana1412 Easy score 7
13Aug70- 6Sar hd 2 1/16 Hurdles 3:434 4↑ Lovely Night H 17k 3 1 1½ 21 1½ 21½ Aitcheson J Jr 150 3.00 - - Metello1411½Top Bid1502½Augustus Bay1482½ Game try 9
29Jly70- 4Mth fm *2 1/16 Hurdles 4:03 4↑ Midsummer H 16k 2 3 42½ 1hd 1hd 53¼ Aitcheson J Jr 150 *2.00 - - Encarnado136nkAtrevido1402Predominio144no Weakened 7
28Aug69- 3Bel fm 2 Hurdles 3:372 3↑ Alw 12000 8 5 33 21½ 3½ 65 Aitcheson J Jr 153 *1.40e - - Lake Delaware156½Bold Beggar150½Attribution153¾ Tired 8

6Aug69- 3Sar gd 2 1/16 S'Chase 3:48⁴ 4↑ Alw 8500 2 6 46½ 1½ 11 13 Aitcheson J Jr 143 *.80 -- Top Bid1433Yale Fence14715Brandon Hill1555 Mild drive 9
23Jly69- 5Mth sf *2 1/16 Hurdles 4:25 1 4↑ Midsummer H 16k 1 2 25 28 417 474 Aitcheson J Jr 154 *1.50 -- Nashandy15610CarillonII14116LakeDelaware15548 Poor form 4
3Jly69- 3Del hd *2⅛ Hurdles 4:00 1 3↑ Holly Tree H 10k 2 3 44½ 21 24 24½ Aitcheson J Jr 156 *.70 -- Lake Delaware1494½Top Bid156hdBonavena153 2¼ Very unruly 6
5Jun69- 5Bel fm 2 1/16 Hurdles 3:43 2 4↑ Bushwick H 18k 3 2 34½ 34½ 15 12 Aitcheson J Jr 149 4.10 -- Top Bid1492National Anthem15412Kurrewa1413 Won in hand 10
26May69- 3Aqu fm 1⅞ Hurdles 3:23 2 4↑ Alw 10000 7 3 322 23 53½ 511 Aitcheson J Jr 152 *.80 -- Hipocampo146hdLakeDelaware1463¼NtionlAnthm1523 Tired 7
10May69- 2Mal sf *1¾Ⓣ 3:13 2 4↑ Alw 10000 9 8 55½ 31¾ 2nk 13 Aitcheson J Jr 150 -e -- Top Bid1503Pembroke1431½Astrographer1505 Driving 10
3May69- 5War hd *2 S'Chase 4:47 1 4↑ Sp Wt 1200 6 4 34½ 33½ 28 210 Aitcheson J Jr 153 -e -- Vocalist15310Top Bid1536Aiken Road1533 Fair try 7
19Apr69- 7Mid sf *1¼Ⓣ 2:20 3 3↑ Alw 2000 4 6 31½ 2½ 1½ 11 Aitcheson J Jr 149 s -e -- Top Bid1491Greek Myth1494Long Valley1551½ Driving 13
8Aug68- 5Sar sf 2 1/16 Hurdles 3:41 2 4↑ Sar National 11k 8 6 11½ 28 615 642 Aitcheson J Jr 156 *.80 -- NationalAnthem13630YaleFenc158noCountrySttng149no Tired 8
16Jly68- 3Mth fm *1¾ Hurdles 3:24 4 3↑ Alw 6000 2 5 42½ 32½ 1hd 33¼ Aitcheson J Jr 147 *.90 -- Tuscalee151¾Mrlgo1482½TopBd1473½ Bad landing final jump 7
4Jun68- 5Bel fm 2⅛ Hurdles 3:56 3 4↑ Bushwick H 11k 3 3 31½ 11 11 12 Aitcheson J Jr 150 *1.60 -- Top Bid1502Lake Delaware1387Miralgo1542½ Easy score 6
28May68- 3Bel fm 2⅛ Hurdles 4:02 1 4↑ Alw 9000 4 2 2½ 45 1hd 11 Aitcheson J Jr 142 *1.20 -- Top Bid1421Miralgo1542Crannog1401½ Under hard drive 6
9May68- 5Aqu fm 1⅞ Hurdles 3:25 1 4↑ Aqu National 11k 4 3 32½ 23 11½ 1¾ Aitcheson J Jr 142 *.50 -- TopBid142¾Daufuskie1511½Lucnt1524½ Stumbled 10th,lasted 10
6May68- 3Aqu fm 1⅞ Hurdles 3:28 2 4↑ Alw 7500 7 1 11½ 12 13 18 Aitcheson J Jr 143 *1.20 -- Top Bid1438Ringling154½Out of Print1543 Easily best 8
13Apr68- 1Mid fm *1½ Hurdles 2:47 1 3↑ Md Sp Wt 11 7 96½ 32½ 2½ 13 Aitcheson J Jr 145 -e -- Top Bid1453Chippendale1451Arnold W.137½ Drew out easily 14
Previously owned by Wheatley Stable;previously trained by E.A. Neloy
15Aug67- 7Sar fst 6f :22 4 :45 2 1:09 4 Alw 15000 3 4 65½ 68½ 68 614 Baeza B 118 b 3.50 85-10 JimJ.1143RoadatSea1204½FlyingTackle1141½ Trailed field 6
7Jly67- 7Aqu fm 1 1/16Ⓣ 1:43 Alw 15000 5 5 66 65 57 57 Baeza B 120 b 2.10 84-09 Irish Rebellion116noMake It116½Fort Drum1164 Wide 6
28Jun67- 7Mth fm 1Ⓣ 1:38 1 Long Branch (Div 1) 22k 3 2 1hd 11 3½ 21¼ Gustines H 120 b 5.40 93-07 Blasting Charge1201¼Top Bid120nkMake It112hd Gamely 8
3Jun67- 8Del fst 1 1/16 :23 :46 1:10 2 1:42 4 Kent 31k 12 11 136¼ 1313 1314 1215 Nelson E 120 b 10.60 80-17 Galaerfrmance1204Mr.Scipio114½MstyCloud120nk No speed 14
8May67- 8Pim gd 1 1/16⊗ :23 :45 4 1:10 1 1:44 Woodlawn 29k 4 5 55 44 1hd 1hd Nelson E 116 b *3.70 90-18 TopBid116hdCharlsEllott113hdCltcAr116hd Strong pressure 10
29Apr67- 4Aqu fst 7f :23 2 :47 1 1:12 1 1:25 1 Alw 12000 6 2 1hd 1hd 11 1hd Belmonte E 120 b 7.30 80-18 Top Bid120hdYorkville1182½Bologna Gellis1183 Hard drive 6
18Mar67- 9FG fst 1⅛ :47 4 1:11 3 1:37 1 1:50 La Derby 54k 9 6 64 74 61¾ 64½ Anderson P 118 3.60 89-07 AsktheFare115hdDiplomtWy126½GrndPremr1202½ No mishap 10
4Mar67- 8SA fst 1⅛ :45 3 1:10 3 1:37 1:49 4 SA Derby 139k 11 7 54 62¾ 53¾ 67 Mahorney W 118 b 3.70e 76-16 Ruken1181½Tumble Wind1181½Sand Devil118½ No mishap 13
22Feb67- 8SA fst 1 1/16 :23 :46 4 1:11 1:42 4 San Felipe H 62k 1 8 109¼ 76 63½ 4nk Mahorney W 118 b 3.90e 89-12 Rising Market118noRuken117nkField Master113no Rallied 13
8Feb67- 8SA fst 1 1/16 :23 3 :47 1:11 1:42 3 Alw 10000 5 4 31 1½ 11½ 1½ Mahorney W 117 b 24.80 90-15 Top Bid117½Dr. Isby1176Ruken120½ Under hard drive 8
2Feb67- 8SA fst 1 1/16 :22 4 :46 1 1:10 4 1:43 3 ⓇS Catalina 24k 5 1 11½ 1hd 42 79½ Blum W 118 b 6.70 75-18 Serve Notice118½ⒹBeau Alibi118nkNechako1181½ Used up 9
12Jan67- 5SA fst 7f :22 3 :45 1 1:10 1:23 Alw 7500 3 7 1hd 11½ 13 1nk Blum W 115 b *2.40 88-15 TopBid115nkServeNotice1202½GentlemansGame120 2½ Lasted 7
26Dec66- 5SA fst 6f :22 1 :45 3 :57 3 1:09 4 Alw 7000 1 12 118½ 109¾ 97½ 912 Baeza B 116 b 3.70 81-14 RisingMarket114noSandDevil1184Bradleyvill116½ No factor 12
17Oct66- 4Aqu fst 6½f :23 :46 2 1:11 1 1:17 2 Alw 6000 1 7 74¾ 76¼ 57½ 59 Baeza B 116 b *.80 84-19 JackofAllTrades1136ReflectedGlory1132StampAct119¾ Wide 7
27Sep66- 7Aqu fst 6½f :23 1 :46 2 1:11 1:17 4 Alw 10000 6 2 32½ 62 66 68 Baeza B 119 b 3.40 83-21 Wilbur Clark1221½Racing Room1191½Gordorigo1191 In close 6
10Sep66- 8AP fst 7f :22 3 :45 2 1:10 1 1:22 3 Arl-Wash Futurity 367k 4 12 118¾ 63½ 78¼ 917 Adams L 122 b 9.70 75-13 DiplomtWy122hdWilbrClrk1227LghtnngOrphn122¾ Crowded 15
27Aug66- 6Sar fst 6½f :22 2 :45 3 1:10 3 1:17 1 Hopeful 107k 4 3 46 45½ 35 31¾ Adams L 122 b *.10e 90-08 BoldHour122 1¾GrtPowr122hdTopBd122 6½ Drifted out stretch 5
17Aug66- 7Sar fst 6f :22 1 :45 1 1:10 3 Sar Spl 33k 6 5 66 77½ 47½ 37¾ Baeza B 114 b 9.20 87-14 Favorable Turn1167Bold Hour120¾Top Bid114hd Rallied 7
8Aug66- 7Sar fst 5½f :22 4 :46 1 :58 3 1:05 Sanford 34k 3 4 42 32 33 35 Baeza B 115 b 2.00 87-13 Yorkville1152SrWnzlot1153TopBd115¾ Swerved into stretch 5
13Jly66- 6Aqu fst 5½f :22 :45 4 :58 2 1:05 Alw 5500 7 5 2hd 2hd 2hd 12 Knapp K 122 b *.90 88-17 TopBid1222QuakerCity1172½Voyager1192½ Speed in reserve 8
1Jly66- 5Aqu fst 5½f :22 2 :46 2 :59 1:05 3 ⒸMd Sp Wt 8 4 21 1hd 13 16 Baeza B 122 b *.90 85-19 TopBid1226GayLordFlynn122¾Seance117nk Easily the best 12
17Jun66- 5Aqu fst 5½f :22 1 :46 :58 4 1:05 3 ⒸMd Sp Wt 6 7 32½ 57 59 312 Baeza B 122 3.30 73-22 FavorableTurn12212LiftOff122noTopBid122no Bumped rail 12

Trillion

b. f. 1974, by Hail to Reason (Turn-to)–Margarethen, by Tulyar
Lifetime record: 32 9 14 3 $954,672
Own.–Stephenson & Hunt
Br.– N.B. Hunt (Ky)
Tr.– Maurice Zilber

10Nov79- 8Lrl sf 1½Ⓣ :57 3 1:25 2 2:23 2 2:51 3↑ D C Int'l-G1 5 2 32½ 51¾ 1hd 2¾ Fell J 124 7.70 -- Bowl Game127¾Trillion124noLe Marmot1208 Hung 8
4Nov79- 8SA fm 1½Ⓣ :45 4 1:10 2:01 1 2:25 2 3↑ Oak Tree Inv'l-G1 5 4 510 53½ 53 21¾ Shoemaker W 123 *.90 86-12 Balzac1261¾Trillion1231Silver Eagle126½ Gamely 9
Previously owned by E. Stephenson
27Oct79- 8Aqu fm 1½Ⓣ :48 1 1:14 2:04 4 2:28 1 3↑ Turf Classic-G1 7 2 27 44 33 2nk Shoemaker W 123 4.40 120-00 Bowl Game126nkTrillion123nkNative Courier1264¾ 7
Steadied,in close
21Oct79- 8WO sf 1⅝Ⓣ :49 3 1:41 2 2:48 3 3↑ Can Int'l-G1 7 4 43½ 2hd 1hd 2nk Shoemaker W 123 3.20 57-42 Golden Act118nkTrillion1232½Gain1187 Sharp try 10
7Oct79♦ Longchamp(Fr) gd *1½ⓉRH 2:28 4 3↑ Prix de l'Arc de Triomphe-G1 Stk382000 58¼ Piggott L 127 16.00 Three Troikas1203Le Marmot1231Troy123nk 22
Tracked in 4th,effort 3f out,beaten when bumped 1f out
16Sep79♦ Longchamp(Fr) fm *1¼ⓉRH 2:03 3 3↑ Prix du Prince d'Orange-G3 Stk44600 2½ Lequeux A 127 2.50 Rusticaro126½Trillion127hdNorthern Baby1212 8
Tracked leader,slight lead 3f to 1f out,dueled,outgamed
9Sep79♦ Longchamp(Fr) gd *1½ⓉRH 2:35 4 4↑ Prix Foy-G3 Stk44600 21½ Lequeux A 124 2.50 Pevero1231½Trillion124½Gay Mecene1301 6
Led for 2f,tracked leader,led again 2f out,headed 100y out
15Aug79♦ Deauville(Fr) fm *1¼ⓉRH 2:01 4↑ Prix Gontaut-Biron-G3 Stk44600 22 Lequeux A 129 *.70 Rusticaro1282Trillion129noStrong Gale1232 9
Well placed in 3rd,led 2f to 150y out,second best
1Jly79♦ Saint-Cloud(Fr) gd *1 9/16ⓉLH 2:33 2 3↑ Grand Prix de Saint-Cloud-G1 Stk191000 710½ Lequeux A 131 7.30 Gay Mecene1344Ela-Mana-Mou1211Gain121nk 13
Rated toward rear,passed tired ones
Placed sixth through disqualification
24Jun79♦ Longchamp(Fr) gd *1⅛ⓉRH 1:51 3 3↑ Prix d'Ispahan-G1 Stk127000 35 Piggott L 129 .90 Irish River1215Opus Dei132hdⒹTrillion1291½ 8
Led,clear 2½f out,headed 1f out,drifted left;
Disqualified and placed 5th
27May79♦ Longchamp(Fr) sf *1 3/16ⓉRH 2:10 3 4↑ Prix Dollar-G2 Stk79000 12½ Piggott L 129 *.60 Trillion1292½Pevero123½Talis Filius123¾ 7
Led throughout,drew clear 2f out,handily.Rusticaro 7th
29Apr79♦ Longchamp(Fr) sf *1 5/16ⓉRH 2:17 1 4↑ Prix Ganay-G1 Stk127000 21½ Piggott L 124 *.60 Frere Basile1281½Trillion124hdPevero1283 8
Led for 2f,settled in 4th,lacked room on rail,up for second
1Apr79♦ Longchamp(Fr) hy *1¼ⓉRH 2:19 4 4↑ Prix d'Harcourt-G2 Stk80000 12 Piggott L 127 *1.10 Trillion1272Fatusael1281Frere Basile1284 11
Led throughout,finished strongly
4Nov78- 8Lrl fm 1½Ⓣ :50 1:14 1 2:03 3 2:27 3↑ D C Int'l-G1 6 3 31 52¼ 73½ 44½ Hawley S 124 *1.90 79-16 Mac Diarmida120hdTiller1273Waya1241½ Wide late 8
21Oct78- 8Bel fm 1½Ⓣ :49 1:13 3 2:03 2:26 4 3↑ Turf Classic-G1 2 2 21½ 2½ 3nk 3nk Shoemaker W 123 3.50 90-09 Waya123noTiller126nkTrillion1231¾ Held gamely 6
8Oct78♦ Cologne(Ger) gd *1½ⓉRH 2:30 2 3↑ Preis von Europa-G1 Stk260000 32½ Piggott L 128 *1.80 Aden119½Tip Moss1282Trillion128hd 14
Tracked in 3rd,lacked rally.Strong Gale 4th
1Oct78♦ Longchamp(Fr) sf *1½ⓉRH 2:36 3↑ Prix de l'Arc de Triomphe-G1 Stk382000 22 Shoemaker W 127 16.00 Alleged1302Trillion1272Dancing Maid120¾ 18
Tracked leaders,2nd 2f out,chased winner home.Gay Mecene 8th
10Sep78♦ Longchamp(Fr) gd *1⅜ⓉRH 2:17 4↑ Prix Foy-G3 Stk38200 12 Piggott L 127 *1.80 Trillion1272Monseigneur128noDom Alaric1304 7
Led throughout,handily
22Jly78♦ Ascot(GB) fm 1½ⓉRH 2:30 2 3↑ King George VI & Queen Eliz-G1 Stk290000 1221 Piggott L 130 7.00 Ile de Bourbon1201½HawaiianSound120nkMountcontour1331½ 13
Never a factor
2Jly78♦ Saint-Cloud(Fr) gd *1 9/16ⓉLH 2:41 3 3↑ Grand Prix de Saint-Cloud-G1 Stk195000 21 Piggott L 131 *2.00 Guadanini1341Trillion1311½Noir et Or1211 9
Tracked in 3rd,dueled 1½f out,outfinished
25Jun78♦ Longchamp(Fr) yl *1⅛ⓉRH 1:53 4 3↑ Prix d'Ispahan-G1 Stk136000 22 Piggott L 129 *1.50 Carwhite1322Trillion129¾Gairloch132nk 10
Led,clear 1f out,headed 100y out,saved 2nd.Kenmare 6th

28May78♦ Longchamp(Fr)	fm*1 3/16Ⓣ RH 1:594 4↑	Prix Dollar-G2 Stk85000	1nk	Piggott L	129	*1.50	Trillion129nkCarwhite129¾Monseigneur1292½ Led throughout,held gamely.Tip Moss 5th	7
15May78♦ Saint-Cloud(Fr)	sf *1½Ⓣ LH 2:422 3↑	Prix Jean de Chaudenay-G2 Stk85000	3nk	Piggott L	131	*2.00	Guadanini130hdDom Alaric130hdTrillion1312 Tracked leader,led 3f out,dueled 150y out,just failed	11
30Apr78♦ Longchamp(Fr)	sf *1 5/16Ⓣ RH 2:181 4↑	Prix Ganay-G1 Stk131000	13	Piggott L	124	5.90	Trillion1243Monseigneur128¾Sirlad128hd Led virtually throughout,ridden clear.Carwhite 5th	8
2Apr78♦ Longchamp(Fr)	hy *1¼Ⓣ RH 2:152 4↑	Prix d'Harcourt-G2 Stk65800	2nk	Piggott L	122	*1.30e	Monseigneur128nkTrillion1222½Carwhite1282½ Tracked entrymate in 2nd,led halfway,dueled 1½f out,gamely	8
							Previously trained by Francois Mathet	
30Oct77♦ Longchamp(Fr)	sf *1 15/16Ⓣ RH 3:283	Prix Royal-Oak-G1 Stk95600	21½	Badel A	124	4.00	Rex Magna1281½Trillion124½Dunfermline1244 Rated in midpack,rallied to lead 1½f out,headed 100y out	13
9Oct77♦ Longchamp(Fr)	sf *1 9/16Ⓣ RH 2:444	Prix de Royalleiu-G3 Stk40800	14	Badel A	123	*.50	Trillion1234Paix Armee1202½Proud Event1231½ Tracked leader,led 2f out,easily clear	9
18Sep77♦ Longchamp(Fr)	fm*1½Ⓣ RH 2:302	ⒻPrix Vermeille-G1 Stk204000	63½	Dubroeucq G	128	*2.00	Kamicia1281½Royal Hive128nkFabuleux Jane128hd Tracked in 5th,led 2f out,drifted left,headed 1f out,faded	18
30Jly77♦ Evry(Fr)	sf *1½Ⓣ LH 2:404	ⒻPrix de Minerve-G3 Stk25500	16	Dubroeucq G	126	*.30	Trillion1266Beronaire119nkSwiss1193 Led virtually throughout,clear 2f out,in a canter	7
12Jun77♦ Chantilly(Fr)	sf *1 5/16Ⓣ RH 2:104	ⒻPrix de Diane-G1 Stk220000	2hd	Dubroeucq G	128	5.00	Madelia128hdTrillion1282½Fabuleux Jane128¾ Led or dueled,led 3f to 1f out,came again near line	13
27May77♦ Longchamp(Fr)	gd*1½Ⓣ RH 2:324	ⒻPrix des Tuileries Stk20000	15	Dubroeucq G	123	5.70	Trillion1235Lestelle123nkKelso's Niece123nk Led throughout,unchallenged	13
19Mar77♦ Saint-Cloud(Fr)	hy *1¼Ⓣ LH 2:27	ⒻPrix Perruche Bleue Mdn (FT)9900	1¾	Dubroeucq G	123	*1.30	Trillion123¾Angelotte123½Lyanta1238 Tracked leader,led 2f out,held well	7

Turkish Trousers

dkbbr. f. 1968, by Bagdad (Double Jay)–Nas-Mahal, by Nasrullah **Lifetime record: 18 12 1 2 $308,225**

Own.– Mrs H.B. Keck
Br.– Howard B. Keck (Ky)
Tr.– Charles Whittingham

3Jun72- 8Hol	fst 1⅛	:464 1:102 1:351 1:472 3↑	ⒻVanity H 105k	8	2	31½	31	31	41¾	Shoemaker W	123	1.80	93-08	Convenience121½Typecst126¾StreetDncr115½	Weakened late	9
18May72- 8Hol	fst 1	:224 :461 1:094 1:341 3↑	ⒻMilady H 44k	7	5	2½	21	34½	712	Shoemaker W	125	*1.80	83-16	Typecast1236Balcony's Babe114noConvenience122½	Checked	9
4Mar72- 8SA	fst 1⅛	:461 1:101 1:351 1:474 4↑	ⒻS Margarita Inv'l 10k	6	4	42	42	31	1hd	Shoemaker W	125	1.70	93-09	TurkishTrousers125hdConvenience118nkTypcst124hd	Driving	12
19Feb72- 8SA	fst 1 1/16	:224 :454 1:094 1:411 4↑	ⒻS Maria H 57k	8	3	32	32	12½	1½	Shoemaker W	123	2.90	96-10	Turkish Trousers126½Typecast1264¼Street Dancer1231¼	Drifted,driving	8
9Feb72- 8SA	fst 7f	:213 :441 1:083 1:211 4↑	ⒻS Barbara Cy Fair H 20k	2	4	32½	31½	21½	35½	Shoemaker W	126	*.60	91-15	Conveninc1192¾StrtDncr1232¾TurkshTrousrs1264	Mild rally	7
18Jan72- 8SA	fst 7f	:213 :44 1:084 1:212 4↑	ⒻS Monica H 47k	9	5	22½	32½	21	23	Shoemaker W	126	*.90	93-10	Typecast1233TurkishTrousrs126¾GoddssSpcl1144	Drifted in	10
25Aug71- 7Dmr	fm 1⅛Ⓣ	:484 1:132 1:374 1:50	ⒻDmr Oaks 26k	3	1	1½	1½	1½	11¾	Shoemaker W	124	*.30	95-05	TurkishTrousers1241¾Aladancr117noShlfTlkr1181¾	Drew out	5
22Jly71- 8Hol	fst 1⅛	:464 1:103 1:351 1:474	ⒻHol Oaks 64k	8	2	21	2½	21½	1nk	Shoemaker W	124	*.40	93-14	TurkishTrousers124nkConvennc1156Blcony'sBb1153½	Driving	8
2Jly71- 8Hol	fm 1 1/16Ⓣ	:224 :463 1:11 1:414	ⒻPrincess 33k	8	3	32	3½	22½	1¾	Shoemaker W	121	*.60	90-10	TurkishTrousers121¾Conveninc1152Blcony'sBb1151¼	Driving	10
3Jun71- 8Hol	fst 1 1/16	:231 :461 1:103 1:422	ⒻHoneymoon 33k	1	3	21½	2hd	1½	13	Shoemaker W	121	*.50	83-14	TurkshTrousrs1213Convenience115noMiaMood1141½	Driving	9
18May71- 8Hol	fst 7f	:22 :442 1:09 1:214	ⒻRailbird 28k	6	4	55	43½	23	1¾	Shoemaker W	121	*.70	91-16	TurkshTrousrs121¾Convennc1152CountssMrkt115hd	Driving	9
27Apr71- 8Hol	fm 1Ⓣ	:224 :462 1:103 1:354	ⒻSenorita (Div 2) 32k	2	4	45	54	31	12	Shoemaker W	118	*.90	91-12	TurkishTrousers1182Aladancer118hdLadyofRome112nk	Easily	6
11Mar71- 8SA	fst 1 1/16	:234 :472 1:112 1:424	ⒻS Susana 54k	1	1	2hd	2hd	1hd	1¾	Shoemaker W	115	*.80	88-16	TurkishTrousrs115¾GenrousPorton1156SposSpd1152	Driving	9
18Feb71- 8SA	fst 7f	:213 :443 1:101 1:233	ⒻS Ynez 33k	5	6	55	32½	2½	13¾	Shoemaker W	112	*1.40	85-16	TurkishTrousers1123¾UllaBritta1151¼SaposSpd1143	Driving	7
9Feb71- 8SA	fst 1 1/16	:24 :484 1:131 1:431	ⒻS Ysabel 28k	8	3	3½	31	32	3¾	Shoemaker W	116	*.60	85-11	Balcony'sBabe116¾Aldncr116noTrkshTrousrs1162	No excuse	8
22Jan71- 7SA	fst 1	:23 :463 1:103 1:354	ⒻAlw 7000	1	4	3½	32½	13	15	Rosales R	115	2.20	95-15	Turkish Trousers1155Hollywood Gossip115nkShelfTalker115nk	Handily	10
7Jan71- 8SA	fst 6½f	:22 :451 1:10 1:162	ⒻLa Centinela 29k	6	8	72¼	62¼	32	41¾	Rosales R	118	*2.50	89-11	CrowningGlory118hdWicked Firy1181Hollywood Gossip113¾	No excuse	11
30Dec70- 5SA	fst 6f	:22 :452 :573 1:094	ⒻMd Sp Wt	10	8	62¾	2½	2½	12½	Shoemaker W	115	3.40	93-11	Turkish Trousers1152½At Twilight110nkGrecian Times1156	Rushed into contention,won convincingly	12

Typecast

b. f. 1966, by Prince John (Princequillo)–Journalette, by Summer Tan **Lifetime record: 57 21 12 9 $535,567**

Own.– Westerly Stud
Br.– Nuckols Bros. (Ky)
Tr.– A.T. Doyle

9Oct72- 7Bel	sf 1½Ⓣ	:48 1:14 2:054 2:314 3↑	Man o' War 117k	1	10	119½	2½	1½	1¾	Cordero A Jr	123	b	*2.30	68-33	Typecast123¾Ruritania1214½Droll Role1261	Driving	11
27Sep72- 6Bel	fm 1⅜Ⓣ	:492 1:134 1:373 2:133 3↑	Manhattan H (Div 1) 46k	5	4	54½	44½	24	22	Pincay L Jr	122	b	4.60	96-06	Star Envoy1162Typecast1223½Exotico111½	Raced wide	10
9Sep72- 7Bel	fst 1⅛	:46 1:102 1:35 1:472 3↑	ⒻBeldame 112k	1	3	34	52½	77	68¼	Sellers J	123	b	5.90	89-06	Susn'sGirl1181SummerGust1181ChouCrout1233¼	Speed,tired	9
24Jly72- 8Hol	fm 2Ⓣ	:481 2:291 2:54 3:203 3↑	Sunset H 135k	4	3	47	53½	31½	1hd	Sellers J	120	b	3.20	87-16	Typecast120hdOver the Counter112nkViolonor114hd	Driving	10
8Jly72- 8Hol	fm 1⅜Ⓣ	2:131 3↑	ⒻBeverly Hills H 64k	8	6	515	55	69½	310	Lambert J	127	b	*1.10	79-13	Hill Circus11510Manta116hdTypecast127nk	Rallied	8
24Jun72- 8Hol	fm 1½Ⓣ	:481 1:113 2:012 2:254 3↑	Inv'l Turf H 125k	6	6	66½	31	2½	1nk	Lambert J	117	b	5.70	99-08	Typecast117nkViolonor1101¼Cougar II1296½	Driving	9
17Jun72- 7Hol	fst 1⅛	:462 1:10 1:35 1:473 4↑	ⒻMatch Race 250k	1	2	2nk	21½	22	2hd	Shoemaker W	120	b	*.40	94-14	Convenience120hdTypecast120	Closed fast	2
3Jun72- 8Hol	fst 1⅛	:464 1:102 1:351 1:472 3↑	ⒻVanity H 105k	1	5	64½	52½	41½	2½	Tejada V	126	b	*1.40	94-08	Convenience121½Typecast126¾Street Dancer115½	Gamely	9
18May72- 8Hol	fst 1	:224 :461 1:094 1:341 3↑	ⒻMilady H 44k	9	7	62½	41½	21½	16	Tejada V	123	b	4.50	95-16	Typecast1236Balcony's Babe114noConvenience122½	Driving	9
22Apr72- 8Hol	fm 1 1/16Ⓣ	:221 :454 1:102 1:411 3↑	ⒻLong Beach H 55k	5	6	511	32½	21½	1¾	Tejada V	122	b	1.90	93-09	Typecast122¾Balcony's Babe1163Manta1231½	Driving	8
21Mar72- 8SA	fm 1¼Ⓣ	:443 1:082 1:324 1:583 4↑	ⒻS Barbara H 65k	5	3	312	37½	57	-	Belmonte E	124	b	*1.10	- -	Hail the Grey1122Manta1255Street Dancer1181	Bled	7
4Mar72- 8SA	fst 1⅛	:461 1:101 1:351 1:474 4↑	ⒻS Margarita Inv'l 10k	1	7	75	63	54	3nk	Pincay L Jr	124	b	*1.40e	93-09	TurkishTrousers125hdConvnnc118nkTypcst124hd	Closed fast	12
19Feb72- 8SA	fst 1 1/16	:224 :454 1:094 1:411 4↑	ⒻS Maria H 57k	1	4	44½	54½	22½	2½	Pincay L Jr	126	b	*1.20	95-10	TurkishTrousers126½Typecast1264¼StreetDncr1231¼	Rallied	8
18Jan72- 8SA	fst 7f	:213 :44 1:084 1:212 4↑	ⒻS Monica H 47k	5	7	99	911	54½	13	Pincay L Jr	123	b	3.50	96-10	Typecast1233TurkishTrousers126¾GoddessSpecl1144	Driving	10
25Oct71- 8SA	yl 1⅛Ⓣ	:481 1:124 1:364 1:494 3↑	ⒻLas Palmas H 32k	1	5	44½	2½	15	16	Shoemaker W	126	b	*.50	80-20	Typecast1266Hail the Grey1161Aladancer1191½	Easily	6
14Oct71- 7SA	fm 1⅛Ⓣ	:47 1:112 1:352 1:471 3↑	ⒻAlw 12000	6	4	45	22	14	16	Shoemaker W	123	b	*.30	93-07	Typecast1236Boughs o' Holly1172½Dating1152¼	Easily	6
7Aug71- 7Dmr	fm 1⅛Ⓣ	:483 1:122 1:361 1:484 3↑	ⒻRamona H 27k	9	7	78½	67	56½	21½	Shoemaker W	116	b	2.90	99-02	StreetDancer1141½Typecst116½Mnt1301¾	Wide,finished fast	9
26Jly71- 8Hol	fm 2Ⓣ	:48 2:29 2:54 3:191 3↑	Sunset H 138k	7	11	1218	74¼	34	31½	Alvarez F	110	b	38.60	92-12	Over the Counter114½Cougar II1301Typecast1102½	Rallied	12
10Jly71- 8Hol	fm 1⅜Ⓣ	2:121 3↑	ⒻBeverly Hills H 66k	10	7	54½	32½	33½	23½	Shoemaker W	116	b	3.20	94-09	Manta1273½Typecast116¾Hail the Grey1074	Lacked rally	11
2Jly71- 7Hol	fm 1Ⓣ	:23 :464 1:104 1:351 3↑	ⒻHandicap 14000	3	5	53½	52½	31½	1nk	Shoemaker W	120	b	*1.40	94-8	Typecast120nkStreet Dancer1161½Mizzle1162	Driving	9
19Jun71- 7Hol	fm 1Ⓣ	:231 :463 1:101 1:353 4↑	ⒻAlw 12000	7	7	710	69½	55¼	1½	Shoemaker W	117	b	*2.30	92-13	Typecast117½Hi Q.1202¼Sallarina120½	Driving	8
	Previously trained by M. Lipton																
17Apr71- 7Hol	fm 1 1/16Ⓣ	:224 :462 1:104 1:423 3↑	ⒻLong Bch H (Div 1) 55k	5	9	914	89	53	53½	Lambert J	114	b	5.80	82-16	Tipping Time1152Blow Up II110¾Beja117no	Rallied	9
6Apr71- 8SA	fm 1⅛Ⓣ	:473 1:113 1:352 1:481 4↑	ⒻS Ana H 32k	8	5	55½	76½	89	88¾	Pincay L Jr	121	b	5.30	79-12	Mizzle1141¼Tipping Time1201¼Sight to See110½	No speed	8
27Feb71- 8GG	gd 1 1/16	:224 :464 1:12 1:443 3↑	ⒻGolden Poppy H 27k	4	8	89	815	716	713½	Grant H	123	b	*1.60	67-23	HiQ.1172¼IrishTryst1101SchatzP111nk	Never in contention	8
2Feb71- 8SA	fst 1 1/16	:231 :462 1:103 1:43 4↑	ⒻOneonta H 29k	11	11	1111	96½	31½	1¾	Pincay L Jr	122	b	*1.60	87-12	Typecast122¾Belle o' Belgium1141¾Loved1193¼	Driving	11

Date	Cond	Dist	Fractions	Race	Running line	Jockey	Wt	Eq	Odds	Speed	Top three finishers	Comment
22Jan71- 8SA	fm	1⅛Ⓣ	:234 :484 1:132 1:504	4↑ ⒻAlw 12000	1 1 31 52½ 11½ 11¼	Pincay L Jr	120	b	*1.40	75-25	Typecast1201¼SlvrGoblt1164½ThorolyBlu119¾	Outside rally 12
15Jan71- 8SA	hy	1 1/16	:25 :494 1:151 1:48	4↑ ⒻAlw 10000	6 3 21 3½ 1½ 14	Pincay L Jr	120	b	*.90	62-36	Typecast1204DustyEys1151ScrltLrkspur1186	Speed to spare 6
26Nov70- 8BM	my	1 1/16	:232 :471 1:12 1:443	3↑ ⒻThnksgvng Day H 22k	3 10 82¾ 66½ 35 22	Toro F	122	b	*1.30	74-24	TalestoTell1162Typecast1221½ThFrstDy1142¾	Finished fast 11
28Oct70- 8SA	fm	1⅛Ⓣ	:454 1:101 1:341 1:463	3↑ ⒻLas Palmas H 32k	1 3 46½ 53½ 57 56	Sellers J	117	b	4.00	90-04	Manta1254Beja119½Thoroly Blue115½	Hung 8
11Sep70- 7Dmr	fm	1 1/16Ⓣ	:231 :48 1:12 1:432	3↑ ⒻAlw 8500	6 5 43½ 33 41½ 11½	Lambert J	118	b	*.60	96-13	Typecast1181½[D]Dress Me Up111¾Sony Gay1132	6
	Saved ground,checked											
2Sep70- 7Dmr	fm	1 1/16Ⓣ	:224 :462 1:11 1:43	3↑ ⒻOsunitas 16k	4 8 813 88¾ 66½ 3½	Lambert J	118		*.70	97-05	QueenJanine118nkDressMeUp111nkTypcst1182	Finished well 11
24Aug70- 8Dmr	fm	1 1/16Ⓣ	:231 :47 1:111 1:423	3↑ ⒻHandicap 8500	2 6 68¼ 55½ 1½ 18	Lambert J	122	b	*1.70	100-04	Typcst1228MssLrksvll112hdWndyMm117hd	Drew off quickly 6
14Aug70- 6Dmr	fm	1 1/16Ⓣ	:233 :473 1:111 1:423	3↑ ⒻAlw 8000	2 3 23½ 22½ 21½ 12	Lambert J	117	b	5.80	100-01	Typecst1172Chatupv1141¼Boughso'Holly1172½	Bumped start 6
17Jly70- 7Aqu	fst	1	:223 :444 1:092 1:35	3↑ ⒻAlw 15000	3 3 2½ 32½ 913 915	Baltazar C	120	b	9.00	77-15	RoyalFillet1161½TaknAback118½NativePartner1166	Stopped 9
6Jun70- 8GG	fst	1 1/16	:23 :461 1:101 1:431	3↑ ⒻSn Juan Bautista H 21k	6 6 64 41½ 32½ 2¾	Gonzalez JT	118	b	*2.80	87-17	Windy Mama117¾Typecast1181½Flying Dot1161½	Game try 10
26May70- 5Hol	fm	1Ⓣ	:233 :473 1:113 1:363	4↑ ⒻAlw 10000	4 5 61¾ 42½ 31½ 1nk	Pincay L Jr	117	b	3.10	88-10	Typecast117nkBelleo'Belgium1172Lover'sQurrl114½	Driving 7
7May70- 7Hol	fm	1 1/16Ⓣ	:234 :482 1:13 1:431	4↑ ⒻAlw 12000	5 5 55½ 64½ 64½ 56	Pierce D	120	b	6.70	77-17	Luz del Sol1201Fairfleet II1142Hi Q.1171¾	Even try 8
18Apr70- 8Hol	fm	1 1/16Ⓣ	:232 :47 1:102 1:41	3↑ ⒻLong Beach H 46k	8 14 139¾ 137¾ 149¼ 1410	Alvarez F	111	b	17.20	84-08	TippingTime115¾PatteeCnyon120nkSchatziPi1151¼	Far back 15
8Apr70- 5SA	fst	1 1/16	:231 :463 1:11 1:423	4↑ ⒻAlw 15000	4 4 36 32½ 1½ 11	Pincay L Jr	114	b	2.50	90-09	Typecast1141Hi Q.1203Dumptys Lady1162¾	Driving 6
26Mar70- 7SA	fst	1⅛Ⓣ	:473 1:113 1:362 1:481	4↑ ⒻAlw 15000	4 4 41½ 42 22 22½	Pierce D	114	b	4.00	85-12	Boughs o' Holly1162½Typecast1142¾Riva1161¾	Second best 8
18Mar70- 5SA	fst	1 1/16	:232 :47 1:113 1:432	4↑ ⒻAlw 10000	5 4 46 43 43 32	Pierce D	118	b	2.60	84-13	Hi Q.1182I've Bin Spotted120hdTypecast118¾	No rally 6
6Mar70- 7SA	fst	1 1/16	:231 :463 1:104 1:422	4↑ ⒻAlw 9000	6 5 63¾ 63 43½ 33¾	Pierce D	116	b	2.60	87-07	Gay Year120hdDumptys Lady1163¾Typecast1164¼	Closed well 6
28Feb70- 8SA	sly	1⅛	:47 1:112 1:371 1:503	4↑ ⒻS Margrta Inv'l H 100k	2 7 75½ 76½ 615 616	Alvarez F	110	b	29.20	63-17	GallantBlm1292Commissary1176TippingTime1172½	No speed 8
6Feb70- 4SA	fst	1 1/16	:232 :47 1:113 1:434	4↑ ⒻAlw 6500	1 1 13 12½ 1½ 1¾	Pierce D	119	b	1.80	84-12	Typecast119¾Queen Janine1196Make Me Yours1134	Driving 6
17Jly69- 8Hol	fst	1⅛	:463 1:103 1:35 1:472	ⒻHol Oaks 54k	7 8 86 65 57 57½	Pineda A	113	b	8.10	87-11	TippngTime121noCommissary1181¼YnezQn1145	Even effort 8
9Jly69- 7Hol	fm	1Ⓣ	:223 :461 1:111 1:363	ⒻAlw 7500	4 7 79½ 74½ 33 31½	Pineda A	120	b	*1.80	86-13	Sallarina117hdSeric1141½Typcst1204	Best stride too late 7
2Jly69- 8Hol	fm	1 1/16Ⓣ	:231 :461 1:103 1:412	ⒻPrincess 27k	8 9 912 85¼ 54½ 56½	Alvarez F	112	b	5.10	85-08	Tipping Time1155Ynez Queen114hdMarjorie's Theme1211¼	9
	Never a threat											
20Jun69- 4Hol	fm	1 1/16Ⓣ	:232 :481 1:123 1:434	ⒻAlw 7000	3 7 65½ 41¾ 11 13	Lambert J	117	b	*1.70	80-13	Typecast1173Tasu1203Queen Janine1141½	Wide rally 7
3Jun69- 5Hol	fst	1	:223 :453 1:103 1:362	ⒻAlw 7500	4 10 109 56½ 32½ 3½	Lambert J	117	b	4.10	83-17	Caper Mate115noFar Piece117½Typecast1178	Bid,not enough 10
16May69- 6Hol	fst	1 1/16	:231 :462 1:104 1:43	ⒻAlw 7000	1 4 42½ 43 32 23	Rosales R5	115	b	2.90	77-14	Marjorie'sTheme1173Typecst115½FarPiec1204	Saved ground 10
2May69- 5Hol	fst	1 1/16	:23 :462 1:11 1:43	ⒻAlw 7500	7 10 1011 85½ 43½ 23	Rosales R5	115	b	4.20	77-13	TippingTime1203Typecast115¾Mrjor'sThm1173	Outside rally 11
18Apr69- 8Hol	fst	1	:231 :462 1:104 1:362	ⒻAlw 8500	6 8 77½ 74½ 65½ 32½	Pierce D	117	b	5.60	81-18	Marjorie's Girl117½Snap Hance1092Typecast117nk	Wide 8
7Apr69- 4SA	gd	1 1/16	:24 :484 1:14 1:462	ⒻAlw 7500	3 2 22½ 44½ 34 22½	Rosales R5	108		6.70	68-22	Sallarina1162½Typecst1081½MagicCsmnts1154	Saved ground 6
3Apr69- 6SA	fst	6f	:221 :454 :582 1:111	ⒻAlw 6500	8 3 108 109 79½ 68½	Trevino S	118		51.60	77-20	Mrjorie'sGirl115½Marjori'sThm115½TppngTm1183	No factor 12
20Mar69- 2SA	fst	6f	:221 :453 :581 1:112	ⒻAlw 6000	9 2 86½ 910 89 810	Pineda A	118		1.90	75-17	BelleMere118hdMarjorie'sGirl1104Sallrn113½	Lacked speed 9
6Mar69- 2SA	fst	6f	:224 :463 :592 1:12	ⒻAlw 5000	6 12 1011 1011 89 57¼	Pineda A	118		4.90	75-16	HappyMomnt1183HazelA.115¾WindyMama1183	Took up start 12
26Feb69- 4SA	sl	6f	:222 :464 1:00 1:133	ⒻMd Sp Wt	4 9 65 55 23 11¼	Pineda A	116		2.50	74-24	Typecast1161¼DoubleGoGo1151QueenNaleika1154	Slow start 9

Wajima

b. c. 1972, by Bold Ruler (Nasrullah)–Iskra, by Le Haar

Lifetime record: 16 9 5 0 $537,838

Own.– East-West Stable
Br.– Claiborne Farm (Ky)
Tr.– S. DiMauro

Date	Cond	Dist	Fractions	Race	Running line	Jockey	Wt	Eq	Odds	Speed	Top three finishers	Comment
25Oct75- 8Bel	sly	2	:494 2:32 2:57 3:231	3↑ J C Gold Cup-G1	4 2 2hd 1hd 2hd 2nk	Baeza B	119		*.30	83-15	Group Plan124nkWajima11910Outdoors1241¼	Fought gamely 4
27Sep75- 8Bel	fst	1½	:493 1:132 2:023 2:271	3↑ Woodward-G1	5 2 2½ 2hd 2hd 21¾	Baeza B	119		1.10	82-19	Forego1261¾Wajima11911Group Plan126¾	Steadied late 6
13Sep75- 8Bel	fst	1¼	:472 1:104 1:352 2:00	3↑ Marl Cup Inv'l H-G1	1 6 64½ 42½ 2hd 1hd	Baeza B	119		4.70	99-11	Wajima119hdForego1297½Ancient Title126¾	Bumped,driving 7
1Sep75- 8Bel	fst	1⅛	:452 1:09 1:341 1:471	3↑ Governor-G1	1 5 56½ 55¼ 31½ 1hd	Baeza B	115		2.70	91-18	Wajima115hdFoolishPleasure1252AncientTitle130¾	Driving 10
16Aug75- 7Sar	fst	1¼	:483 1:123 1:37 2:02	Travers-G1	5 2 21½ 11 15 110	Baeza B	126		*.90	95-14	Wajima12610Media1263¾Prince Thou Art1262	Ridden out 5
2Aug75- 8Mth	fst	1⅛	:462 1:102 1:361 1:493	Mth Inv'l H-G1	2 5 64¾ 52½ 32½ 1nk	Baeza B	118		*.70	92-18	Wajima118nkIntrepid Hero1152My Friend Gus1161¼	Driving 8
19Jly75- 8Bow	fst	1⅛	:473 1:114 1:364 1:49	Marylander H 57k	6 2 3½ 11 13 18	Baeza B	116		*.30	102-11	Wajima1168Logical1139Pimms Cup109¾	Brushed,ridden out 7
12Jly75- 8Bel	sly	1⅛	:453 1:093 1:35 1:482	Dwyer H-G2	6 7 63½ 44 35½ 23	Baeza B	118		*.90	82-16	Valid Appeal1103Wajima1184Hunka Papa1163	Raced wide 8
29Jun75- 8Bel	fst	1	:232 :464 1:104 1:344	Saranac-G2	5 4 63 84 42½ 2hd	Baeza B	114		*1.30	94-12	Bravest Roman114hdWajima1143¾Valid Appeal114no	Gaining 9
21Jun75- 6Bel	fst	1	:223 :453 1:10 1:351	Alw 20000	4 2 21½ 3½ 1hd 1½	Baeza B	113		*.80	92-12	Wajima113½Bravest Roman1163Packer Captain1132	Driving 5
11Jun75- 6Bel	fst	6½f	:224 :46 1:101 1:161	3↑ Alw 15000	7 5 53½ 52½ 31 13½	Baeza B	113		2.30	95-17	Wajima1133½Townsand116noSailors Watch1201¼	Ridden out 7
29Jan75- 9Hia	fst	7f	:222 :444 1:09 1:22	Bahamas 33k	2 10 78½ 712 69½ 55	Baeza B	115		*1.10	90-14	Ascetic1151½Ellora1152½Sylvan Place113¾	No excuse 11
2Nov74- 8Lrl	fst	1 1/16	:233 :464 1:114 1:423	Lrl Futurity-G1	3 3 22 32 31½ 21	Baeza B	122		3.60	99-13	L'Enjoleur1221Wajima1221¾Bombay Duck1223¾	Good try 9
19Oct74- 7Kee	fst	*7f	1:254	Breeders' Futurity-G3	6 5 76¼ 1011 78¼ 46¼	Baeza B	122		1.80	88-15	PackerCaptain1221½MasterDrby1224RugglesFerry122¾	Wide 11
5Oct74- 5Bel	fst	6f	:224 :462 1:11	Alw 9500	9 8 87½ 54 2½ 13½	Baeza B	121		*.60	88-12	Wajima1213½Pride of Pan Gil1193Doug119nk	Handily 10
	Previously owned by H.I. Snyder											
21Sep74- 3Bel	fst	6f	:223 :462 1:101	©Md Sp Wt	5 5 52¼ 31 2hd 1nk	Baeza B	121		*.60	92-12	Wajima121nkTumeko1215¼Rue de Rivoli1218½	Driving 6

Waya (Fr)

b. f. 1974, by Faraway Son (Ambiopoise)–War Path, by Blue Prince

Lifetime record: 29 14 6 4 $822,816

Own.– P. Brant
Br.– Dayton Ltd (Fr)
Tr.– David A. Whiteley

Date	Cond	Dist	Fractions	Race	Running line	Jockey	Wt	Eq	Odds	Speed	Top three finishers	Comment
10Nov79- 8Lrl	sf	1½Ⓣ	:573 1:252 2:232 2:51	3↑ D C Int'l-G1	8 7 42½ 64¼ 78¼ 616	Asmussen CB	124		19.30	- -	Bowl Game127¾Trillion124noLe Marmot1208	Tired 8
27Oct79- 8Aqu	fm	1½Ⓣ	:481 1:14 2:044 2:281	3↑ Turf Classic-G1	3 4 618 68½ 69½ 67¾	Asmussen CB	123		4.50	112-00	BowlGame126nkTrillion123nkNativeCourier1264¾	Fell back 7
13Oct79- 8Bel	sly	1¼	:473 1:124 1:39 2:061	3↑ ⒻBeldame-G1	5 7 714 43½ 22 13	Asmussen CB	123		3.00e	69-27	Waya1233Fourdrinier1184Kit's Double1231¼	Ridden out 7
29Sep79- 8Bel	fst	1⅛	:474 1:12 1:351 1:472	3↑ ⒻRuffian H-G1	2 4 35 37½ 311 39	Velasquez J	126		2.30	81-12	It's in the Air1224Blitey1135Waya126	Evenly 4
10Sep79- 7Bel	fm	1 1/16Ⓣ	:24 :47 1:11 1:414	3↑ Alw 30000	1 4 48½ 33 22 32½	Cordero A Jr	119		*.50	84-17	John Henry1172Silent Cal117½Waya119no	Hung 4
28Jly79- 8Bel	fm	1¼[T]	:491 1:13 1:373 2:013	3↑ ⒻSheepshead Bay H-G2	10 10 1013 107¼ 85 74¾	Shoemaker W	130		*2.00	81-09	Terpsichorist117noLate Bloomer1232¾Warfever110nk	Outrun 10
16Jun79- 8Bel	fm	1⅜[T]	:48 1:12 1:352 2:112	3↑ Bowling Green H-G2	4 5 512 57 53½ 24	Cordero A Jr	125		*.80	108-01	Overskate1174Waya125hdBowl Game1231¾	Rallied 7
3Jun79- 6Bel	sly	1¼	:494 1:14 1:391 2:041	3↑ Sar Cup H 109k	5 6 69 31 1hd 1no	Cordero A Jr	125		*.90	76-30	Waya125noLate Bloomer1194¾Sten1101¼	Driving 6
28Apr79- 8Aqu	sly	1⅛	:48 1:122 1:374 1:504	3↑ ⒻTop Flight H-G1	2 8 717 57½ 22 1nk	Cordero A Jr	128		*1.60	81-17	Waya128nkPearl Necklace1207Island Kiss1121	Driving 8
25Mar79- 8SA	yl	1¼Ⓣ	:462 1:104 1:354 2:01	4↑ ⒻS Barbara H-G1	2 7 713 53 31½ 11¼	Cordero A Jr	131		*.70	82-18	Waya1311¼Petron's Love1171Island Kiss1113	Easily 8
14Mar79- 8SA	sf	1⅛Ⓣ	:47 1:11 1:36 1:481	4↑ ⒻSanta Ana H 65k	1 10 1011 86¼ 31 13½	Cordero A Jr	127		*1.00	86-14	Waya1273½Amazer123¾Shua115hd	Easily 10
10Feb79- 8SA	sf	1¼Ⓣ	:484 1:123 1:364 2:033	4↑ Arcadia H-G3	8 7 78¾ 45 32½ 21¾	Cordero A Jr	123		*1.80	67-25	Fluorescent Light1211¾Waya123nkAs de Copas1181	Gamely 9
	Previously owned by D. Wildenstein;previously trained by Angel Penna											
4Nov78- 8Lrl	fm	1½Ⓣ	:50 1:141 2:033 2:27	3↑ D C Int'l-G1	8 8 811 73¼ 51½ 33	Cordero A Jr	124		2.90	81-16	Mac Diarmida120hdTiller1273Waya1241½	Lacked room 8
21Oct78- 8Bel	fm	1½Ⓣ	:49 1:133 2:03 2:264	3↑ Turf Classic-G1	6 5 57 41½ 1hd 1no	Cordero A Jr	123		*1.60	90-09	Waya123noTiller126nkTrillion1231¾	Long hard drive 6
7Oct78- 8Bel	yl	1⅜Ⓣ	:492 1:14 1:382 2:161	3↑ Man o' War-G1	4 4 47 42 31 11¾	Cordero A Jr	123		6.60	81-19	Waya1231¾Tiller1262¾Mac Diarmida1214	Driving clear 5
1Oct78- 8Bel	fm	1¼[T]	:482 1:12 1:37 2:003	3↑ ⒻFlower Bowl H 54k	2 6 78 43 22½ 1¾	Cordero A Jr	120		*.50	91-10	Waya120¾Magnificnce1084¾Leave Me Alone1081	Going away 7
21Aug78- 8Sar	fm	1⅛Ⓣ	:45 1:091 1:332 1:452	3↑ ⒻDiana H-G2	7 8 711 54 1hd 12¾	Cordero A Jr	115		2.40	100-00	Waya1152¾Pearl Necklace1254Fia110½	Ridden out 12
15Jly78- 8Bel	gd	1¼[T]	:471 1:113 1:354 2:01	3↑ ⒻSheepshead Bay H-G2	6 8 711 46 32½ 2hd	Cordero A Jr	115		2.80	89-11	Late Bloomer118hdWaya115nkPearl Necklace1241¼	Sharp 11
24Jun78- 6Bel	fm	1 1/16Ⓣ	:231 :46 1:10 1:40	3↑ ⒻNew York H (Div 1)-G3	3 5 56½ 33½ 25 23	Cordero A Jr	116		*.90	93-09	Pearl Necklace1223Waya116hdDottie's Doll1182	Good try 7

15Jun78- 8Bel fm 1 1/16Ⓣ :23 :454 1:093 1:41 3↑ ⒻAlw 25000 7 6 55 21½ 1½ 12 Velasquez J 117 *.70 91-15 Waya1172Maria's Baby1171½Magnificence117½ Handily 7
7Jun78- 8Bel fm 1 1/16[T] :233 :481 1:12 1:431 3↑ ⒻAlw 20000 1 8 89 73 11½ 12½ Cordero A Jr 117 *1.20 88-08 Waya1172½Milina117nkMake It Known1123¼ Handily 8
2Oct77♦ Longchamp(Fr) gd *1⅛ⓉRH 1:532 3↑ ⒻPrix de l'Opera-G2 Stk63500 1hd St-Martin Y 121 *1.10e Waya121hdBeaune1211Silk Slipper121½ 12
Rated in last,rallied to lead near line
18Sep77♦ Longchamp(Fr) fm *1¼ⓉRH 2:041 3↑ Prix du Prince d'Orange-G3 Stk42000 32 St-Martin Y 119 7.00 Carwhite126hdGairloch1212Waya119nk 11
Trailed to 1½f out,sharp late run,up for 3rd.Tip Moss 6th
4Sep77♦ Longchamp(Fr) gd *1ⓉRH 1:411 3↑ Prix du Rond-Point-G3 Stk42200 62½ St-Martin Y 120 3.00 Pharly128½River Dane122nkMonseigneur1211½ 7
Chased leaders throughout,never threatened
7Aug77♦ Deauville(Fr) gd *1ⓉStr 1:373 3↑ ⒻPrix d'Astarte-G3 Stk42200 42½ St-Martin Y 128 *2.20 Sanedtki128¾Hartebeest1281Silk Slipper121¾ 13
Rated in 6th,mild bid over 1f out,evenly late
13Jly77♦ Evry(Fr) gd *1⅛ⓉLH 1:522 ⒻPrix Chloe-G3 Stk33100 2hd St-Martin Y 128 *.80 Lillan128hdWaya128¾Dekeleia128¾ 11
Rallied toward rear,finished fast,just failed
26Jun77♦ Longchamp(Fr) gd *1¼ⓉRH 2:062 ⒻPrix de Malleret-G3 Stk51000 2hd St-Martin Y 123 *.60 Les Saintes Claires123hdWaya1231½Kamicia123hd 9
Tracked in 5th,led 1f out,dueled late,outgamed
12Jun77♦ Chantilly(Fr) sf *1 5/16ⓉRH 2:111 ⒻPrix de Royaumont-G3 Stk41900 11 St-Martin Y 128 3.30 Waya1281Kalkeen128½Kelso's Niece128¾ 13
Rated at rear,long drive to lead final strides
30May77♦ Saint-Cloud(Fr) gd *1ⓉLH 1:433 ⒻPrix de la Croix St. Jacques Mdn (FT)13000 16 St-Martin Y 123 *1.40 Waya1236Sonabie123½Come Gailly123½ 11
Tracked in 3rd,led over 1f out,easily clear

What a Summer

gr. f. 1973, by What Luck (Bold Ruler)–Summer Classic, by Summer Tan
Lifetime record: 31 18 6 3 $479,161
Own.– Mrs B.R. Firestone
Br.– Milton Polinger (Md)
Tr.– Leroy Jolley

26Nov78- 8Aqu fst 6f :221 :451 1:101 3↑ Sport Page H 54k 6 1 3nk 31 21½ 2nk Fell J 124 *.70 92-20 Topsider109nkWhat a Summer1241¼Affiliate118²¼ Sharp 6
19Nov78- 8Aqu fst 7f :222 :45 1:091 1:221 3↑ ⒻFirst Flight H 42k 2 3 2hd 11½ 13 11½ Fell J 126 *.50 90-17 WhtaSmmr1261½FlyingAbove1201¾Mrs.Wrrn1132 Ridden out 5
22Oct78- 8Bel fst 7f :221 :442 1:082 1:21 3↑ Vosburgh H-G2 6 3 32 21 1½ 2¾ Fell J 124 5.90 96-13 Dr.Patches117¾WhataSummr1243¾SorryLookin1095 Gamely 8
21Sep78- 6Med fst 6f :221 :46 1:101 3↑ ⒻEgret H 54k 3 6 31 32 22½ 31¾ Cordero A Jr 127 *.70 92-19 Dainty Dotsie127½Gladiolus1161¼What a Summer1271½ Wide 9
28Aug78- 8Bel sly 6f :22 :45 1:092 3↑ Fall Highweight H-G2 5 3 11½ 14 12 11¾ Cordero A Jr 134 *.90 95-14 WhtaSmmr1341¾Buckfindr1298WhiteRmmr1281¼ Ridden out 5
8Jly78- 8Hol fst 6½f :212 :431 1:074 1:141 3↑ ⒻSilver Spoon H 42k 6 1 2½ 1½ 1½ 1¾ Shoemaker W 126 *.50 99-14 What a Summer126¾Eximious1144Dallas Deb1145 Driving 6
17Jun78- 6Bel fst 6f :221 :45 1:09 3↑ ⒻHandicap 30000 3 1 11 11½ 14 16 Cordero A Jr 126 *.50 97-12 What a Summer1266Gladiolus1191½Flying Above1101 Easily 4
29May78- 8Bel fst 1 :223 :45 1:091 1:343 3↑ Metropolitan H-G1 8 6 63 42 41½ 42¾ Perret C 120 12.90 92-16 Cox'sRidge130¾Buckfinder112½QuietLittlTbl1181½ No rally 9
7May78- 8Aqu my 7f :221 :441 1:082 1:214 3↑ ⒻVagrancy H-G3 1 3 32 22½ 22 21¾ Vasquez J 127 *1.60 90-13 Dainty Dotsie1241¾What a Summer1273Navajo Princess110½ 6
No match
8Apr78- 9GP fm 1 1/16Ⓣ :224 :453 1:091 1:41 3↑ ⒻOrchid H-G3 1 1 15 11½ 1hd 41¼ Solomone M 122 *1.20 95-03 TimeforPleasure115½LateBloomr113nkRichSoil116½ Bore out 11
15Mar78- 9GP fm 1Ⓣ :233 :47 1:11 1:353 3↑ ⒻSuwannee River H 32k 2 1 11 1hd 1hd 2nk Solomone M 122 1.90 92-11 Len'sDetermind119nkWhtaSmmr122nkLatBlmr1131 Bore out 9
4Feb78- 7Hia fst 7f :224 :454 1:101 1:221 4↑ ⒻAlw 16000 8 1 11½ 13 12 11½ Solomone M 122 *.60 92-10 WhataSummr1221½CumLaudeLaurie1227Plain and Fancy114¾ 8
Ridden out
22Oct77- 7Kee fst 1⅛ :461 1:102 1:36 1:482 3↑ ⒻSpinster-G1 10 1 11½ 11 2hd 45¼ Vasquez J 123 3.00 90-17 CumLaudeLaurie1191MssissippiMd1233¾IvoryWnd123½ Tired 10
10Oct77- 8Bel gd 1¼ :482 1:131 1:373 2:014 3↑ ⒻBeldame-G1 2 1 12½ 11½ 11 2¾ Vasquez J 123 3.30 89-13 CumLdLaurie118¾WhtaSmmr1231½ChrmngStory118½ Gamely 7
13Sep77- 8Bel fst 1 :24 :47 1:112 1:372 3↑ ⒻMaskette H-G2 7 1 11 1½ 1½ 1hd Vasquez J 126 *.80 81-24 WhataSummer126hdCrabGrass114nkHarvestGirl1113 Lasted 8
29Aug77- 8Bel fst 6f :22 :452 1:10 3↑ Fall Highweight H-G2 12 3 54½ 42 1hd 12 Vasquez J 134 8.00 92-19 What a Summer1342BroadwayForli123½Piamem129nk Driving 12
4Aug77- 8Sar fst 6f :221 :45 1:09 3↑ ⒻHandicap 25000 5 4 52½ 41½ 1hd 13½ Vasquez J 125 *1.60 95-13 WhataSmmr1253½Artfully112½QuintasVicki1121¼ Ridden out 9
9Jly77- 8Hol fst 6½f :214 :441 1:083 1:15 3↑ ⒻSilver Spoon H 43k 5 3 2½ 11½ 12 12 Shoemaker W 122 3.10 95-14 What a Summer1222RegalRumor1242SingBack113nk Driving 7
4Jun77- 8Mth fst 6f :203 :453 1:093 3↑ ⒻRegret H 27k 1 7 12½ 2hd 23½ 36 Perret C 123 b *.90 86-16 Cast the Die1164½IvoryWand1181½What a Summer123½ Wide 8
2May77- 8Aqu fst 6f :214 :451 1:102 3↑ ⒻGrey Flight H 42k 1 4 1½ 1hd 2hd 31¾ Maple E 126 b *.70 89-15 Sylvan'sGirl112¾ShyDawn1201WhataSummr1261¼ Weakened 6
23Apr77- 6Aqu fst 6f[•] :221 :453 1:104 4↑ ⒻHandicap 25000 1 5 11 14 15 11¾ Black AS 123 b *.70 95-05 What a Summer1231¾Moontee1112Sylvan's Girl114¾ Easily 6
23Mar77- 8Aqu my 6f[•] :221 :454 1:113 3↑ ⒻDistaff H-G3 1 5 14 17 15 12½ Maple E 118 b *.60 91-15 WhataSummer1182½SecretLanvin112nkShyDawn1204 Driving 5
Previously owned by Estate of M. Polinger;previously trained by Grover G. Delp
27Dec76- 8Lrl fst 1 :222 :444 1:102 1:362 3↑ Ⓕ[S]All Brandy H 30k 4 1 14 13 34 97¾ McCarron CJ 123 b *.50 83-16 Gala Lil1222Avum1123Shark's Jaws113½ Saddle slipped 10
Previously owned by M. Polinger
11Dec76- 8Lrl fst 1 :23 :461 1:114 1:381 ⒻAnne Arundel H 27k 2 1 14½ 16 15 13¼ McCarron CJ 122 b *.30 82-22 What a Summer1223¼Turn the Guns1141¼Avum114½ Driving 7
23Nov76- 8Lrl fst 1 :223 :443 1:102 1:361 Ⓕ[S]Alw 15000 3 1 17 15 17 14¾ McCarron CJ 122 b *.20 92-17 What aSummr1224¾Avum1173Body Snatcher1175 Ridden out 7
30Oct76- 8Key fst 1 1/16 :232 :472 1:112 1:441 ⒻHeirloom 34k 1 1 11½ 2½ 2hd 21¾ McCarron CJ 116 *.80 81-24 Forlana1181¾WhtSmmr1162½MsssppMd1165 Weakened late 9
21Oct76- 8Bow fst 7f :224 :453 1:10 1:23 3↑ ⒻAlw 8500 5 3 11 11½ 13½ 13 McCarron CJ 113 *.50 90-21 WhataSmmr1133[D]ChesapeakeBugeye1191Avum1196 Driving 9
14May76- 8Pim fst 1 1/16 :234 :464 1:104 1:422 ⒻBlack-Eyed Susan-G2 2 1 12 2hd 1hd 1no McCarron CJ 111 3.30e 93-14 WhataSummer111noDearlyPrecious1215Artfully1141 Driving 10
7May76- 5Pim fst 6f :223 :453 1:102 ⒻAlw 7500 1 4 1½ 13 13½ 15 McCarron CJ 117 *.20 94-16 What a Summer1175Avum1171¼Miss Berta1173½ Handily 6
26Apr76- 7Pim fst 6f :231 :463 1:122 ⒻAlw 7000 7 3 3nk 14 16 15 McCarron CJ 112 *.40 84-23 WhataSmmr1125Hillybob1143¾TurntheGuns112¾ Ridden out 8
10Apr76- 9Pim fst 6f :232 :464 1:122 3↑ ⒻMd Sp Wt 7 3 2½ 12 15 18 McCarron CJ 114 *1.40 84-22 What a Summer1148Bold Folly1145Hap's Easter1141 Easily 12

Youth

b. c. 1973, by Ack Ack (Battle Joined)–Gazala II, by Dark Star
Lifetime record: 11 8 1 1 $687,624
Own.– N.B. Hunt
Br.– N.B. Hunt (Md)
Tr.– Maurice Zilber

6Nov76- 8Lrl sf 1½Ⓣ :531 1:201 2:184 2:461 3↑ D C Int'l-G1 1 5 45 31½ 13 110 Hawley S 120 *1.80 - - Youth12010On My Way II127noIvanjica1246 Ridden out 8
23Oct76- 8WO sf 1⅝Ⓣ :49 1:423 2:48 3↑ Can Int'l-G1 5 8 814 3nk 13 14 Hawley S 117 *.95 60-35 Youth1174Improviser1267Effervscng1171½ As rider pleased 11
3Oct76♦ Longchamp(Fr) sf *1½ⓉRH 2:392 3↑ Arc de Triomphe-G1 Stk412000 35 Pyers WB 123 *2.00e Ivanjica1272Crow1233Youth123nk 20
Well up throughout
5Sep76♦ Longchamp(Fr) gd *1⅜ⓉRH 2:22 Prix Niel-G3 Stk51000 1¾ Piggott L 130 *.80 Youth130¾Arctic Tern1262½Malacate1304 5
Led throughout,met challenge 1f out,held well
24Jly76♦ Ascot(GB) fm 1½ⓉRH 2:291 3↑ K George & Q Elizabeth-G1 Stk290000 911 Head F 120 *1.85 Pawneese1171Bruni133noOrange Bay133¾ 10
Tracked in 4th,wide turn 2½f out,weakened
6Jun76♦ Chantilly(Fr) gd *1½ⓉRH 2:272 Prix du Jockey-Club-G1 Stk386000 13 Head F 128 *1.90e Youth1283Twig Moss128¾Malacate1281½ 18
Tracked in 5th,led 2f out,clear 1f out,driving
16May76♦ Longchamp(Fr) gd *1 5/16ⓉRH 2:133 Prix Lupin-G1 Stk212000 1¾ Head F 128 *.40e Youth128¾Arctic Tern1281Empery1284 12
Well placed in 3rd,led 1½f out,held well
19Apr76♦ Longchamp(Fr) gd *1 5/16ⓉRH 2:094 Prix Daru-G2 Stk85000 14 Head F 128 *1.70 Youth1284Danestic1281½French Scandal128½ 10
Tracked in 4th,led 2f out,drew clear 1f out.Far North 8th
4Apr76♦ Longchamp(Fr) sf *1 5/16ⓉRH 2:203 Prix Greffulhe-G2 Stk86000 11½ Head F 128 4.20 Youth1281½Velino1281½Yule Log1281½ 9
Rated in 5th,strong late run to lead 70y out,going away
4Oct75♦ Longchamp(Fr) sf *1⅛ⓉRH 1:574 Prix Saint Roman-G3 Stk42500 22½ Navarro N 123 3.25 Far North1232½Youth1232½Ydja123¾ 9
Tracked in 4th,bid 2f out,second best
14Sep75♦ Longchamp(Fr) sf *1ⓉRH 1:463 Prix de Fontenoy Mdn (FT)15600 11½ Navarro N 123 5.90 Youth1231½Chateau Country123½Three Hlfs1231½ 7
Tracked in 3rd,led 1½f out,drew clear,handily

THE CUP IS BORN

THE 1980'S

by Steven Crist

HERE IS NO ARGUMENT that the last minute of the twentieth century commenced at 11:59 p.m. on December 31, 1999. There can be little more dispute that the last minute of championship racing as practiced in the United States for the bulk of that century commenced at 11:14 a.m., Pacific time, on November 10, 1984.

That was the minute that it took 10 2-year-olds to be loaded into the starting gate at Hollywood Park for the inaugural Breeders' Cup Juvenile, the opener on a card featuring seven rich new races. The revolutionary attempt to create a single showcase day of championship-deciding events was at last a reality, with the nation's top 2-year-olds moving into position and the stars of six other divisions assembled in one barn area for the biggest afternoon ever.

And yet, the moment was surreal. It wasn't just that the 64,254 on hand were rubbing the sleep from their eyes, unaccustomed to being at a racetrack before noon, much less seeing a Grade 1 race with the sun still in the east. The whole proposition of assembling the world's best runners at one track for a single day of title matches even now seemed a fantasy. Would the event really work and last more than a year? Would a sport whose highest awards had for decades been decided in ancient and storied fixtures suddenly convert to a one-day showdown for honors and riches?

The decade's first Horse of the Year was its best.

At the end of the 1970's, Spectacular Bid was ranked below that starry era's foremost champions on the basis of his 3-year-old campaign in 1979. He had been a fine colt, but on the heels of Seattle Slew's and Affirmed's Triple Crowns in the two preceding seasons, his failure to complete the sweep made him the exception rather than the norm. Nor did it help that trainer Bud Delp boasted that "Bid" was "the best horse ever to look through a bridle," and blamed his Belmont Stakes failure on the implausible notion that the colt had stepped on a safety pin.

In 1980, though, Delp gave Spectacular Bid the opportunity to prove he belonged with Affirmed and Seattle Slew, and Bid took it, mounting the most dominant 4-year-old campaign since Tom Fool a quarter-century earlier and achieving more in his post-Triple Crown career than Secretariat, Seattle Slew, or Affirmed.

Spectacular Bid swept the Strub Series at Santa Anita like no horse before him, stretching from a

Emblematic of Spectacular Bid's overwhelming dominance of the 1980 racing season was his unopposed victory in the Woodward.

blazing 1:20 for seven furlongs in the Malibu to a record 1:57⅗ for 10 furlongs in the Strub, leaving solid handicap rivals such as Flying Paster in his wake. He then ripped off five straight victories under 130 pounds or more, winning the Santa Anita Handicap and Hollywood's Mervyn LeRoy Handicap and Californian Stakes before heading east to take the Washington Park Stakes at Arlington and the Haskell at Monmouth.

After eight straight victories by a combined 37¾ lengths, he had scared off all comers. On September 20 at Belmont Park, he completed his career with a walkover, racing the mile and a quarter of the Woodward unopposed in 2:02⅖ to the cheers of a crowd acknowledging one of the greatest.

Bid would prove to be the last of his kind in the century, not just in terms of quality, but in form as well. After a decade in which one champion after another had come up through the same ranks – juvenile honors, Triple Crown bids, fall battles at Belmont Park – Spectacular Bid was the last to play strictly by those rules as the eighties spun off into new ways of creating and campaigning for Eclipse Awards. As it turned out, he would be the last 2-year-old male champion in the century to win the Kentucky Derby or the divisional title at 3.

Seven of the 10 Kentucky Derbies in the 1970's were won by the favorite. After Spectacular Bid, favorites lost the century's remaining 20 Derbies, and the 1980 rendition was not even won by a colt or gelding.

Genuine Risk won her first six starts against fillies, then tried colts in the Wood Memorial. She finished third, beaten 1½ lengths by eventual Derby second choice Plugged Nickle. Trainer LeRoy Jolley was not inclined to take on colts again, but owners Bert and Diana Firestone persisted. Sent off at 13-1, Genuine Risk swept to the lead entering the stretch and held off the closers to become the first filly to win the Derby since Regret in 1915.

Her next start turned out to be the decade's most controversial race. Santa Anita Derby victor Codex, who had not been nominated to the Kentucky Derby by his then little-known trainer, D. Wayne Lukas, made a winning move to grab the lead turning for home in the Preakness. His jockey, Angel Cordero Jr., a fierce competitor who took every available edge, forced Genuine Risk wide as she ranged up outside him. Codex was the better horse, and the incident did not affect the race's outcome, but the idea of the storybook filly Derby winner being muscled and intimidated by Cordero and a colt became an inflammatory image, and the Firestones appealed the outcome to the Maryland Racing Commission. After a hearing only slightly less carnivalesque than the Scopes Monkey Trial, the result stood.

Over a muddy track in the Belmont, 50-1 shot Temperence Hill ran down the filly as Codex faded to seventh. Temperence Hill turned out not to be a fluke, winning the Travers, Jockey Club Gold Cup, and Super Derby to take the 3-year-old title. Genuine Risk received 3-year-old filly honors, her Derby outweighing her loss to the higher-weighted Bold 'n Determined in the Maskette.

The runner-up in the Gold Cup that year also received an Eclipse Award. John Henry was the nation's top grass horse that season, and with 53 starts under his girth seemed in the twilight of a remarkable career, but he was just getting warmed up to become the decade's most enduring star.

Obscurely bred (by the Michigan-based sire Ole Bob Bowers), sold three times for pittances early in his career, racing for purses as low as $2,400 at Evangeline Downs, John Henry was seemingly transformed when he made his first start on the grass at Belmont Park in June 1978, winning by 14 lengths under a $35,000 claiming price. Over the next two years the bay gelding became a frequent gutty winner of grass stakes, and reached the level of champion in 1980 with eight victories in graded events, including the San Juan Capistrano and Oak Tree Invitational. An ornery, scrappy sort, John Henry would reign as a blue-collar hero for the first half of the decade, prompting memories of Kelso and Forego as he returned with triumphs at advancing age year after year.

As a 6-year-old in 1981, John Henry took it to the next level, scoring dramatic photo-finish victories

The cantankerous and game John Henry was the pre-eminent horse during the first half of the decade, winning Horse of the Year titles in 1981 and 1984. Early in his career, the gelding raced for purses as low as $2,400.

on both grass and dirt. He notched his first Grade 1 on the dirt when he won the Santa Anita Handicap in March. In August, Arlington Park offered the sport's first seven-digit purse to entice entrants to its new international grass event, the Arlington Million, and John Henry ensured its status as an instant classic with a heart-stopping nose victory. Returning to the dirt, he won the Jockey Club Gold Cup by a head, then switched coasts and footing again to take the Oak Tree Invitational by a neck.

He was an easy selection as champion older horse, grass horse, and Horse of the Year over Pleasant Colony, who won the first two legs of the Triple Crown and the Woodward but sputtered in the Belmont, Travers, and Marlboro.

A filly winning the Derby, an ex-claimer grass gelding winning Horse of the Year – this was not your typical decade of champions. The 1982 season

continued the oddball trend. Gato Del Sol, a loping California stretch-runner, won a weak Kentucky Derby at 21-1, then chagrined traditionalists by skipping the Preakness because trainer Eddie Gregson thought his colt was better suited to a longer rest and the longer distance of the Belmont. It seemed that even the Triple Crown was no longer sacred. The Preakness was heisted by wire-to-wire winner Aloma's Ruler, and then a new face appeared on the sophomore scene: Conquistador Cielo, a speedy but somewhat brittle colt who had been withheld from the Derby and Preakness by trainer Woody Stephens, whipped the best older horses around, winning the Metropolitan Mile by 7¼ lengths in a sizzling 1:33.

That was on a Monday and the Belmont was on Saturday, so no one took Stephens too seriously when he said he was thinking about wheeling the colt right back. Stephens loved the way Conquistador bounced out of the race, jogged him the wrong way over the Belmont track the rest of the week, and didn't mind when the weatherman called for rain on the weekend. Breaking from the outside post in a field of 11 over a sloppy track, Conquistador Cielo went to the lead and forgot to stop, swamping Gato Del Sol by 14 widening lengths.

The appearance of dazzling displays of first speed in the Met and then stamina in the Belmont impressed no one more than the breeding community, which snapped up stallion shares over the next sixty days at a record $910,000 apiece. Conquistador Cielo won his next two starts with ease, if not brilliance, taking the Dwyer and the Jim Dandy, then faced Gato Del Sol and Aloma's Ruler in a Travers that seemed like a fourth leg of the Triple Crown. Over a dry track at 10 furlongs, Conquistador – who appeared on the track wearing

front bandages for the first time – never shook loose early and then tired late, settling for third behind longshot Runaway Groom and Aloma's Ruler.

Conquistador Cielo never raced again, but he had done enough in a week to be the Horse of the Year. John Henry was back as a 7-year-old but won only 1 of 6 starts, while two horses tried and failed to match his 1981 campaign: Lemhi Gold, the champion older horse, won the Jockey Club Gold Cup and Marlboro Cup on dirt but then ran off the board in the Oak Tree Invitational. Perrault, the grass champion, won the Hollywood Gold Cup and the second Arlington Million but pulled up with a career-ending injury in the Marlboro.

It was a star-crossed year all around. Timely Writer, one of the early favorites for the Kentucky Derby, was euthanized after suffering a fatal injury in the Jockey Club Gold Cup. Landaluce, the champion 2-year-old filly, evoked legitimate com-

Conquistador Cielo had plenty of speed and could carry it over a distance. Just five days after winning the Met Mile in 1:33, he took the Belmont Stakes wire to wire by 14 lengths.

parisons to Ruffian, winning all five of her starts by a combined 46½ lengths, but contracted an infection in November and died in trainer Lukas's arms. Roving Boy, that year's champion 2-year-old, did not race again for 10 months and then broke down past the finish line in his second start back as a 3-year-old.

The 1983 Horse of the Year announcement was one of the few to carry some real suspense. It was a year of brief runs by specialists. The 3-year-olds had taken turns beating one another through the classics, then Slew o' Gold put together a championship campaign in the fall, winning the Woodward and the Jockey Club Gold Cup. Bates Motel had been a runaway leader of the older horses but then lost his last three starts of the year.

It came down to a 2-year-old and a grass filly. Woody Stephens, who had won his second straight Belmont with Caveat, unveiled a gritty son of Seattle Slew named Swale early in the summer,

After winning the Arc de Triomphe, Europe's most prestigious race, the French filly All Along made a unique run through North America's top fall turf races and was named 1983's Horse of the Year.

then waited until August to showcase Devil's Bag, a flashy Halo colt with a world of speed. Winner of all five of his starts, Devil's Bag set stakes records of 1:21⅖ in the Cowdin and 1:34⅕ in the Champagne, then stretched out to win the Laurel Futurity in another romp as if he might be racing's next great one. No 2-year-old since Secretariat had been Horse of the Year, but perhaps this was a worthy successor.

When the envelope was opened, though, 1983's top honor went to All Along, whose campaign broke all the rules. The 4-year-old French-bred filly lost her first three starts of the year in France, then began an astounding six-week international run: Victories over males in the Prix de l'Arc de Triomphe in Paris, the Rothmans International at Woodbine in Canada, the Turf Classic at Aqueduct, and the Washington, D.C., International at Laurel.

Critics carped that her three North American victories came over yielding grass in races that were run from 5 to 10 seconds off the course records, but no horse had put together such a transcontinental assault before. Her award illustrated how quickly the sport was changing. Grass racing already was thriving, helped by John Henry and the popularity of the Arlington Million, and All Along's success added an element of international possibilities that would take full flower a year later with the Breeders' Cup.

The 1984 season had more than its share of drama even before that inaugural Cup, most of it provided by Stephens's 3-year-olds. Devil's Bag, whose $36 million syndication had been announced in December, whistled through his season debut in February but then, before a record Hialeah crowd that had gathered for a coronation, tired and finished a shocking fourth in the Flamingo. He won his next two starts around one turn but was never the same and was retired to stud.

In the meantime, Swale proved to be the one who could carry his speed. He alternated victories and losses in seven starts, losing three times at odds-on but winning the Hutcheson, the Florida Derby, and the Kentucky Derby. After dropping the

Preakness to Gate Dancer, he gave Stephens his third straight Belmont Stakes victory. A week later, the trainer was heading off on a fishing vacation when he got a phone call from the stable: While cooling out after a routine gallop, Swale had keeled over, dead from an apparent heart attack.

The summer and fall leading up to the Breeders' Cup belonged to a pair of returning champions. John Henry, as good as ever at 9, wrapped up his fourth grass title, winning all six of his turf starts from May to October including a one-time sponsor's bonus of $500,000 for sweeping the Arlington Million, Turf Classic, and inaugural Ballantine's Classic at The Meadowlands. The only question was which Breeders' Cup race the old man would contest: the $2 million Breeders' Cup Turf or the $3 million Classic on dirt. The latter event would have meant facing Slew o' Gold, who had come back with a vengeance at 4 and swept through the Whitney, Woodward, Marlboro, and Jockey Club Gold Cup.

Shortly after pre-entries were taken, however, a strained ligament sent John Henry to the sidelines, and Slew o' Gold was expected to be the star of the afternoon. As the fields began taking shape for the new races, it seemed that everyone wanted to be a part of history.

The seven races roughly corresponded to the sport's divisions, except that there was no race for 3-year-olds, who by season's end were expected to race their elders anyway. There was the Juvenile for 2-year-old colts and geldings, the Juvenile Fillies for 2-year-old fillies, the Sprint for sprinters, the Distaff for fillies and mares 3 and up, the Turf for grass horses of both sexes, and the Classic for 3-year-olds and up. The oddball event was the Mile, a grass race clearly designed to attract Europeans.

First up was the Juvenile. Chief's Crown, New York's best 2-year-old, had cruised through the traditional Saratoga and Belmont tests but then skipped the Champagne in order to get a race in California under his belt in Santa Anita's Norfolk.

The Breeders' Cup ushered in a new era of racing in the United States. The first day of championship events ended with a rodeo finish, resulting in an upset by 31-1 Wild Again (INSIDE) in the Classic.

He proved clearly best in the Juvenile as the 3-5 favorite, winning the race and the 2-year-old title by acclamation. It turned out to be quite a key race: Tank's Prospect, the runner-up, would come back to win the 1985 Preakness for the burgeoning Lukas outfit, while Spend a Buck, who finished third, would win the 1985 Derby as well as turn the sport on its ear. The Breeders' Cup era had begun with a formful and title-making note.

The rest of the afternoon was a scriptwriter's dream, a blend of improbable outsiders and convincing performances that either clearly sealed championships or threw them up for grabs. It all came down to the Classic, where Slew o' Gold found himself playing bumper cars in deep stretch between Gate Dancer and the 31-1 shot Wild Again. Slew o' Gold, who ended up third, was elevated to second on the disqualification of Gate Dancer, and the previously unsung Wild Again had won history's richest race. The outcome was not enough to keep Slew o' Gold from being named champion older male, but in a different photo finish he dropped the Horse of the Year title to John Henry.

While few could summon the bile to be unkind to the ageless and lovable John Henry, Slew o' Gold's backers had every right to feel cheated that the rules had changed. Before the Breeders' Cup, there had been no question that Slew o' Gold was the best horse in training, going undefeated in 1984 despite being troubled by quarter cracks. Had he not run, voters would have been left only with the memory of his perfect season; instead, he was being penalized for contesting the Classic and losing it through no fault of his own. The message was clear: Unless you had a championship utterly and unquestionably sewn up, you were expected to show up for the new Super Bowl – and you had better win.

Racing now had a year-end national event that the sport's promoters hoped could grow in popu-

Spend a Buck ran the field off its feet in the 1985 Kentucky Derby. His connections then broke standard by pursuing a $2 million bonus offered by Garden State Park instead of trying for the Triple Crown.

CHAMPIONS

larity and prestige to match what had been its lone marquee events, the Triple Crown races for 3-year-olds in the spring. Only six months later, though, the hallowed Triple Crown came under assault from an unlikely pair: the third-place finisher in the inaugural Breeders' Cup Juvenile and a maverick securities salesman who had purchased Garden State Park in Cherry Hill, New Jersey.

The 1985 classic season began conventionally enough, as Chief's Crown returned from his Breeders' Cup Juvenile triumph to rip through the Swale Stakes at Gulfstream, the Flamingo at Hialeah, and the Blue Grass at Keeneland. He looked like a legitimate 6-5 shot for the Derby, a race that probably was decided at the start when front-running Wood Memorial winner Eternal Prince broke slowly. That left Spend a Buck loose on the lead over a fast and speed-favoring track. Six in front after six furlongs in 1:09⅗, he just kept going. Chief's Crown tried to make a run at him turning for home but couldn't come close and ended up third behind the rallying Stephan's Odyssey, whom he had beaten in the Flamingo.

Spend a Buck's winning margin was an impressive 5¼ lengths and his time of 2:00⅕ was the third-fastest in history behind Secretariat's 1:59⅖ and Northern Dancer's 2:00. He would have been a heavy Preakness favorite, but for the second time in just four years, the Derby winner was not headed to Pimlico.

Spend a Buck had begun his 3-year-old campaign with a mediocre third in Aqueduct's Bay Shore, then headed away from the top classic prospects to run in two new rich events at Garden State Park, which had just reopened for the first time in eight years after being nearly destroyed by fire. The track had been purchased and transformed into a modern showplace by Robert Brennan, who tried to draw attention to his inaugural meeting's Derby preps by putting up a $2 million bonus for any horse who could take the Cherry Hill Mile and the Garden State Stakes, then win the Kentucky Derby and the $1 million Jersey Derby. That sounded like a 100-1 shot, but now Spend a Buck was three-quarters of the way there.

His connections had already decided their horse was not cut out to handle a mile and a half at Belmont, so they had no Triple Crown to bid for and more than two million reasons to return to Garden State instead of going to Pimlico. Traditionalists wailed, but the Preakness was run in his absence. Chief's Crown was even money and ran well, but was nipped at the wire by Tank's Prospect in track-record time.

Spend a Buck was 1-20 to complete his Garden State bonus nine days later in the Jersey Derby, but he had to gut it out. Never able to get clear early, he barely held off a stretch-long challenge from a Woody Stephens-trained gelding named Creme Fraiche to win by a neck. Twelve days later, with Spend a Buck spending the day in his stall, Creme Fraiche ran down barnmate Stephan's Odyssey to give Stephens an astounding fourth straight Belmont victory as Chief's Crown faded to third as the favorite.

Spend a Buck raced only twice more, staying in New Jersey to run second in the Haskell behind Skip Trial and then scoring his lone victory over older horses, edging Carr de Naskra in the Monmouth Invitational before being retired to stud. In a year filled with strong performers, no one else could put together quite a solid enough second season to unseat him. Chief's Crown regained his winning ways in the Travers and the Marlboro but then ran fourth in the second Breeders' Cup Classic, which was won by fellow 3-year-old Proud Truth. Mom's Command swept the Filly Triple Crown and the Alabama but barely held her own division title as 3-year-old Lady's Secret, who had beaten Mom's Command in the Test, swept her elders in that fall's Maskette, Ruffian, and Beldame. Lady's Secret then finished second to a fellow Lukas trainee, 4-year-old Life's Magic, in the Breeders' Cup Distaff. Vanlandingham took the Suburban and the Jockey Club Gold Cup on dirt and the D.C. International on turf, but failures elsewhere, including the Breeders' Cup Classic, left him with only the older-horse title.

Spend a Buck galloped to an easy Horse of the Year award, meaning that for the second time in as many runnings, a horse who had skipped the Breeders' Cup entirely had won the sport's highest honor. The Cup races, held at Aqueduct, did decide many of that year's titles, however: Eclipse Awards went to the winners of both grass races, Cozzene and the filly Pebbles; Distaff winner Life's Magic; Sprint winner Precisionist; and the 2-year-old Tasso.

Spend a Buck's unorthodox championship season blazed no lasting trails. Within a decade, he had proven a bust at stud, Brennan was out of racing due to securities violations, the Jersey Derby was a grass race, and Garden State offered racing of little importance. His challenge to the Triple Crown, however, galvanized the hosts of those three races to band together, forming Triple Crown Productions to promote and market the series and offer bonus money of its own to keep horses from ever again straying from the classic path.

The 1986 Triple Crown was never in danger of being swept but offered some individual milestones. In the Derby, 73-year-old Hall of Fame trainer Charlie Whittingham and 54-year-old Hall of Fame rider Bill Shoemaker teamed for a last-to-first victory with Ferdinand. In the Preakness, eventual 3-year-old champion Snow Chief rebounded from an 11th-place finish as the Derby favorite to win by four. As for the Belmont, who else? Danzig Connection took to a sloppy track and gave Woody Stephens a fifth consecutive Belmont, a record sure to stand, and to boggle the mind and the odds, for ages.

The 1986 season, however, belonged to a pair of very different 4-year-olds: the front-running gray filly Lady's Secret and the stretch-running brown colt Turkoman. In the end, a record number of Eclipse Award voters, unwilling to compare apples and oranges, split their Horse of the Year ballots.

Lady's Secret gained the nickname Iron Lady as she made 15 starts for Lukas in 1986 from coast to coast. Having run out of fillies to conquer after early-season triumphs in the El Encino, La Canada, Santa Margarita, and Shuvee, she tried males in the Met Mile and ran third. A brief return to her division was followed by three more Grade 1 races

against males, and she finished third in the Iselin, second in the Woodward, and won the Whitney. Then she went back to trouncing her own, sweeping the Maskette-Ruffian-Beldame series a second time under weights of up to 129 pounds before winning the Breeders' Cup Distaff under a hand ride.

Turkoman won the Widener, the Oaklawn Handicap, and the Marlboro Cup and was flying at the finish of the races he lost. With a little more luck he might have rounded out his season with two additional victories, but instead ran second to Creme Fraiche in a paceless Jockey Club Gold Cup and second again to Skywalker in the Classic after circling very wide from 16 lengths back over an inside-speed-favoring track. Those decisions tipped the scales to Lady's Secret, who had finished a neck in front of Turkoman when both were beaten in the Met Mile. She became Lukas's first Horse of the Year and joined Twilight Tear in 1944, Busher in 1945, and All Along in 1983 as the only fillies to win that prize.

Lady's Secret became just the fourth female to be elected Horse of the Year after a prolific and highly successful 1986 campaign.

Ferdinand, the 1986 Derby winner, got off to a slow start as a 4-year-old, but finished with a rush, nailing down Horse of the Year with a narrow victory over Alysheba in the Breeders' Cup Classic.

Turkoman was retired at year's end and Lady's Secret came back the worse for wear, winning only a pair of allowances from five starts. In 1987, a 4-year-old again was Horse of the Year, but the power resided in the 3-year-olds, a crop memorable for its talent and for its extreme depth.

After a chaotic spring of confusing prep races, Alysheba came into the Derby with a career record of just 1 for 10, but stormed to a three-quarter-length victory over Bet Twice at 8-1. He edged that same colt by half a length in the Preakness, setting up the first possible Triple Crown since Pleasant Colony's attempt in 1981. Most of the prerace speculation focused not on whether 3-for-12 Alysheba was the next Secretariat, but on drug policy. Alysheba had been racing on the antibleeding medication Lasix, which over the past decade had been legalized in most racing jurisdictions. It was pro-

hibited in New York, however, where concerns lingered over the drug's ability to flush other evidence from a horse's system.

For whatever reason, the Belmont wasn't Alysheba's day. In a stunning reversal, Bet Twice romped to a 14-length triumph while Alysheba finished fourth, beaten a nose and a neck for second by Cryptoclearance and Gulch.

Alysheba and Bet Twice renewed their rivalry in the Haskell, where Bet Twice evened the score with a neck victory. They headed for Saratoga and the Travers, but waiting for them was Java Gold, who had looked like something special winning the Remsen at 2 before missing the classics with a virus. Since returning, he had defeated older horses twice, most recently in Saratoga's Whitney Handicap. The Travers track came up a wet one and Java Gold relished it, circling a field that included eight Grade 1 winners to beat Cryptoclearance by two lengths, with Polish Navy third, Bet Twice fourth, and Alysheba a distant sixth.

Java Gold then took the Marlboro and might have stolen the Horse of the Year title had he won his next start, but he suffered a season-ending broken foot during the Jockey Club Gold Cup, finishing second to 5-year-old Creme Fraiche.

The season came down to a faceoff in the Breeders' Cup Classic between the last two Derby winners. Ferdinand had lost 8 of his first 9 starts after the 1986 Derby but then hit stride halfway through his 4-year-old campaign, winning the Hollywood Gold Cup, Cabrillo, and Goodwood in succession. Alysheba had followed his Travers debacle with an easy victory in the Super Derby at Louisiana Downs.

In a rousing finish that lived up to its billing, Ferdinand got the jump and then held off Alysheba by a nose through a furious drive to win the race

and the Horse of the Year and older-horse titles. Alysheba's gallant effort earned him the 3-year-old honors over Java Gold and Bet Twice, and several other Breeders' Cup winners cemented their championships with Cup triumphs: Epitome (2-year-old filly), Sacahuista (3-year-old filly), Theatrical (turf male), and Miesque (turf female).

The Cup was now the final arbiter of titles, and would be again in the 1988 season, an unforgettable year capped by a Breeders' Cup that many still call the most dramatic day of racing they have ever seen.

Forty Niner, a compact chestnut who did enough for trainer Stephens as a 2-year-old in 1987 to win the juvenile championship without running in the Breeders' Cup, was a solid early favorite for the 1988 Triple Crown races. In both the Florida Derby and the Lexington Stakes, however, the Mr. Prospector colt surrendered the lead in the stretch, fueling doubts about his ability to last 10 furlongs. Meanwhile, out west, an unusual rival emerged

In what many consider to be the most thrilling moment in racing history, Personal Ensign (OUTSIDE), in her 13th and final career start, nips Derby winner Winning Colors at the wire of the 1988 Breeders' Cup Distaff, making her the first major horse in 80 years to retire undefeated.

CHAMPIONS

from the Lukas stable: Winning Colors, an Amazonian roan filly, clobbered her peers by eight lengths in the Santa Anita Oaks, then handled the boys just as easily, winning the Santa Anita Derby on the lead by 7½.

When the gates opened at Churchill Downs, Winning Colors shot to the lead again with Forty Niner tracking her in second. Turning for home, she was sailing along three in front while Forty Niner, still being conserved for the drive, had fallen back to fifth. He rallied furiously in the stretch, making up almost seven lengths, but fell a neck short of catching the filly. The big Secretariat colt Risen Star, who had run down Forty Niner in the Lexington, was a fast-closing third after a wide trip.

Lukas had his first Derby, and Stephens was determined not to let Winning Colors loose on the lead again. In the Preakness, Forty Niner was hustled to the front and stayed there for six furlongs, with the filly just a head behind. The early battle cost both horses any chance and set the table for Risen Star to come flying to a clear victory as Winning Colors tired to third and Forty Niner faded to seventh. For the Belmont, Forty Niner went to the sidelines, Winning Colors went to the lead but stopped after less than a mile, and Risen Star racked up the fastest time and widest margin since his sire's as he galloped home a 14¾-length winner.

It would be Risen Star's final race, but Forty Niner reemerged in the summer to win the Haskell and Travers in a pair of photos over another Mr. Prospector colt, Seeking the Gold, who represented the resurgent Ogden Phipps stable and its young trainer, Shug McGaughey. The Phippses had begun incorporating more speed influences into their breeding program and in the summer of 1988 saw it come to fruition with Seeking the Gold, the 2-year-old colt Easy Goer, and the 4-year-old filly Personal Ensign.

Easy Goer lost his debut by a neck but then quickly stamped himself as a special 2-year-old. A chestnut son of Alydar and the champion mare Relaxing, he would settle early and then unleash spectacular moves around the turn, a particularly effective style at sweeping Belmont Park, where he scored stunning victories in the Cowdin and the Champagne.

Personal Ensign, by Private Account, won her only two starts at 2, including the Frizette, then fractured a rear pastern shortly before the 1986 Breeders' Cup and was sidelined nearly a year. She returned at 3 with screws in her ankle and won all four of her starts, including the Beldame. When she began her 4-year-old campaign with daylight victories in the Shuvee, Hempstead, and Molly Pitcher, fans noticed she was now 9 for 9 and turf writers began hitting the history books to find the last comparable undefeated racehorse. There had been none since Colin, 15 for 15 in 1907-08.

Personal Ensign made it 10 for 10 trying males, running down Gulch to win a three-horse Whitney. A sterner test came in the Maskette, where a rested Winning Colors opened a clear lead, but Personal Ensign was up in time to win by three-quarters of a length. She then ran her record to 12 for 12 with a romp at 1-10 in the Beldame.

It would have been an outstanding season even without the star of the handicap division. Alysheba was a much better colt at 4 and proved it by winning the Strub and then edging Ferdinand in the Santa Anita Handicap and the San Bernardino. He followed defeats in the Pimlico Special and Hollywood Gold Cup with a rousing score over Bet Twice and Gulch in the Iselin, then came back to New York. His sporting owners, Clarence and Dorothy Scharbauer, decided to silence those who said Alysheba could not win east of the Hudson without his usual Lasix and took him off the medication for the Woodward, where he threaded his way through traffic to nail Forty Niner by a neck.

The 1988 Breeders' Cup was the first held at Churchill Downs, and despite damp and chilly weather drew a crowd of 71,237. They were in for a memorable day. Gulch, so often overshadowed by the strong 3-year-old class of '87, rallied powerfully to win the Sprint, earning that division's title. Miesque became the first repeater in Cup history, again coming over from France to take the Mile with a flourish. Open Mind led a 1-2-3 finish by

With darkness about to fall, Alysheba holds off a late run from Seeking the Gold to win the 1988 Breeders' Cup Classic. The victory put Alysheba at the top of the list of Thoroughbred money winners.

Lukas trainees in the Juvenile Fillies. Easy Goer failed to catch Is It True on a muddy track he never picked up, but would still be champion at year's end.

The day came down to the Distaff and the Classic. In the Maskette rematch everyone had been waiting for, between a Derby-winning filly and an unbeaten 4-year-old making what had been announced as her final career start, Winning Colors came onto the track breathing fire and quickly opened a clear lead; Personal Ensign seemed to be slipping and sliding in the slop and was eight lengths back after six furlongs. Turning for home, her task seemed hopeless. She was still four lengths behind with a furlong to go, but somehow Personal Ensign kicked into high gear and began slashing into the lead, lunging at the wire to remain undefeated by a nose.

The skies were nearly dark when post time arrived for the Classic. Alysheba now had to win to ensure Horse of the Year honors over Personal Ensign, while Forty Niner had one last chance to unseat the retired Risen Star for the 3-year-old title. Waquoit led down the backstretch and Forty Niner made his move but was gunned into the worst going at the rail and fell back after stepping on a soft spot. Alysheba launched his bid on the turn and hauled in Waquoit, but now Seeking the Gold was flying down the center of the track. Those two battled to the wire and Alysheba prevailed by half a length, nailing down top honors and running his bankroll to a record $6,679,242.

The decade ended with a season dominated by its best rivalry. Like Affirmed and Alydar 11 years earlier, Sunday Silence and Easy Goer were not only inches apart, but also miles ahead of their contemporaries.

Easy Goer came back bigger and better at 3, winning the Swale by nearly nine lengths and then roaring to a 13-length Gotham victory with a mile in 1:32⅖, the fastest ever by a 3-year-old. A workmanlike three-length Wood Memorial triumph seemed to prime him perfectly for Kentucky.

On the other coast, a challenger emerged. Having waited 26 years between Derby starters, Charlie Whittingham was back three years after Ferdinand, with a colt named Sunday Silence who came from just off the pace to win the Santa Anita Derby by 11.

The two arrived in Louisville as the favorites and as a study in complementary contrasts. They had grown up eight miles apart in the Bluegrass on the farms of two brothers. Easy Goer, with his regal pedigree, had been foaled at Seth Hancock's Claiborne Farm while Sunday Silence had been born and raised at renegade elder brother Arthur's

Stone Farm. Easy Goer had run all but one of his races in New York, while Sunday Silence had not left California. Easy Goer, an enormous chestnut, was the classic pride of the Eastern establishment while the slender, raven-coated Sunday Silence carried the banner of California, which was on a Derby roll with Ferdinand, Alysheba, and Winning Colors.

The Derby looked like Affirmed and Alydar all over again, as the nimbler Sunday Silence sliced to the lead in upper stretch and Easy Goer came with too little too late, barely edging stablemate Awe Inspiring for second. For Easy Goer's downhearted fans, it felt like the previous November, and not just because the Derby Day temperature – the coldest on record – dipped to 43 degrees; for a second time, their champion had seemed not to fire his usual powerful shot over the muddy track. McGaughey wondered whether his colt simply didn't relish Churchill Downs, scene of his only other defeat since his debut.

The Preakness two weeks later ended with a breathtaking stretch duel. This time Easy Goer was sharper, and moved outside the Lukas-trained Houston to seize a brief lead before Sunday Silence joined him. Easy Goer dropped to the inside and seemed sure to blow by, but the two colts matched strides every step of the way, and it was Sunday Silence by a nose at the wire. Had Sunday Silence proved his superiority or had the wide-running Easy Goer fallen into a trap in tight quarters?

Sunday Silence was finally favored in the Belmont, and this time it wasn't close. He made a nice move after a mile to take the lead between calls, but Easy Goer was on his home court and the extra distance was going to work to his advantage. He swept by his nemesis in upper stretch and ran off by himself, scoring by eight lengths in a brilliant 2:26, the second-fastest Belmont ever.

This race seemed like the true bill, and Easy Goer's excuses in the prior two legs suddenly sounded more plausible. Sunday Silence's stock dropped when he lost the Swaps in his next start to the unheralded Prized. Meanwhile, Easy Goer became the toast of racing in the months ahead,

*The epic rivalry between Sunday Silence and Easy Goer was at its most dramatic in the 1989 Preakness. The multi-staged battle ended with Sunday Silence (*LEFT*) a desperate nose in front.*

running off consecutive victories in the Whitney, Travers, Woodward, and Jockey Club Gold Cup. Sunday Silence returned with an easy but otherwise uninspiring victory in the Super Derby. So despite Sunday Silence's 2-1 lead in matchups, the two colts headed for Breeders' Cup VI at Gulfstream Park in the same roles they had played in the spring classics: Easy Goer the odds-on favorite, Sunday Silence the outsider with something to prove.

Easy Goer broke slowly and fell far behind as Sunday Silence stalked in third behind Slew City Slew and Blushing John, the latter a Pimlico Special and Hollywood Gold Cup winner who would be named champion older horse at year's end. Turning for home, Easy Goer was 4½ lengths back, and was basically no closer when Sunday Silence finally collared Blushing John with a furlong to go.

Pat Day, determined to beat Sunday Silence by nailing him with a single rush rather than engaging in a Preakness-like duel, finally turned his colt loose but it was too late. Gaining with every massive stride, Easy Goer fell a neck short and Sunday Silence dug in for his third victory in four meetings.

In the absence of either, the other would have been a dominant Triple Crown winner with only history as a benchmark. Instead, each proved the other's greatness and provided superb drama in the process.

Nine years earlier, on a September afternoon at Belmont Park, Spectacular Bid had capped his career alone and unchallenged. Now that kind of solitary triumph seemed inconceivable. The Breeders' Cup had created a new theater of war, and the last, epic battle between Sunday Silence and Easy Goer was a fitting finale to the decade.

CHAMPIONS

PAST PERFORMANCES

THE 1980'S

•1980•
•2-Year-Old Male *Lord Avie* •2-Year-Old Filly *Heavenly Cause* •3-Year-Old Male *Temperence Hill*
•3-Year-Old Filly *Genuine Risk* •Handicap Horse *Spectacular Bid* •Handicap Mare *Glorious Song*
•Grass Horse *John Henry (M) Just a Game II (F)* •Sprinter *Plugged Nickle* •Steeplechase *Zaccio*
•**HORSE OF THE YEAR** Spectacular Bid

•1981•
•2-Year-Old Male *Deputy Minister* •2-Year-Old Filly *Before Dawn* •3-Year-Old Male *Pleasant Colony*
•3-Year-Old Filly *Wayward Lass* •Handicap Horse *John Henry* •Handicap Mare *Relaxing*
•Grass Horse *John Henry (M) De La Rose (F)* •Sprinter *Guilty Conscience* •Steeplechase *Zaccio*
•**HORSE OF THE YEAR** John Henry

•1982•
•2-Year-Old Male *Roving Boy* •2-Year-Old Filly *Landaluce* •3-Year-Old Male *Conquistador Cielo*
•3-Year-Old Filly *Christmas Past* •Handicap Horse *Lemhi Gold* •Handicap Mare *Track Robbery*
•Grass Horse *Perrault (M) April Run (F)* •Sprinter *Gold Beauty* •Steeplechase *Zaccio*
•**HORSE OF THE YEAR** Conquistador Cielo

•1983•
•2-Year-Old Male *Devil's Bag* •2-Year-Old Filly *Althea* •3-Year-Old Male *Slew o' Gold*
•3-Year-Old Filly *Heartlight No. One* •Handicap Horse *Bates Motel* •Handicap Mare *Ambassador of Luck*
•Grass Horse *John Henry (M) All Along (F)* •Sprinter *Chinook Pass* •Steeplechase *Flatterer*
•**HORSE OF THE YEAR** All Along

•1984•
•2-Year-Old Male *Chief's Crown* •2-Year-Old Filly *Outstandingly* •3-Year-Old Male *Swale*
•3-Year-Old Filly *Life's Magic* •Handicap Horse *Slew o' Gold* •Handicap Mare *Princess Rooney*
•Grass Horse *John Henry (M) Royal Heroine (F)* •Sprinter *Eillo* •Steeplechase *Flatterer*
•**HORSE OF THE YEAR** John Henry

•1985•
•2-Year-Old Male *Tasso* •2-Year-Old Filly *Family Style* •3-Year-Old Male *Spend a Buck*
•3-Year-Old Filly *Mom's Command* •Handicap Horse *Vanlandingham* •Handicap Mare *Life's Magic*
•Grass Horse *Cozzene (M) Pebbles (F)* •Sprinter *Precisionist* •Steeplechase *Flatterer*
•**HORSE OF THE YEAR** Spend a Buck

•1986•
•2-Year-Old Male *Capote* •2-Year-Old Filly *Brave Raj* •3-Year-Old Male *Snow Chief*
•3-Year-Old Filly *Tiffany Lass* •Handicap Horse *Turkoman* •Handicap Mare *Lady's Secret*
•Grass Horse *Manila (M) Estrapade (F)* •Sprinter *Smile* •Steeplechase *Flatterer*
•**HORSE OF THE YEAR** Lady's Secret

•1987•
•2-Year-Old Male *Forty Niner* •2-Year-Old Filly *Epitome* •3-Year-Old Male *Alysheba*
•3-Year-Old Filly *Sacahuista* •Handicap Horse *Ferdinand* •Handicap Mare *North Sider*
•Grass Horse *Theatrical (M) Miesque (F)* •Sprinter *Groovy* •Steeplechase *Inlander*
•**HORSE OF THE YEAR** Ferdinand

•1988•
•2-Year-Old Male *Easy Goer* •2-Year-Old Filly *Open Mind* •3-Year-Old Male *Risen Star*
•3-Year-Old Filly *Winning Colors* •Handicap Horse *Alysheba* •Handicap Mare *Personal Ensign*
•Grass Horse *Sunshine Forever (M) Miesque (F)* •Sprinter *Gulch* •Steeplechase *Jimmy Lorenzo*
•**HORSE OF THE YEAR** Alysheba

•1989•
•2-Year-Old Male *Rhythm* •2-Year-Old Filly *Go for Wand* •3-Year-Old Male *Sunday Silence*
•3-Year-Old Filly *Open Mind* •Handicap Horse *Blushing John* •Handicap Mare *Bayakoa*
•Grass Horse *Steinlen (M) Brown Bess (F)* •Sprinter *Safely Kept* •Steeplechase *Highland Bud*
•**HORSE OF THE YEAR** Sunday Silence

All Along (Fr)

b. f. 1979, by Targowice (Round Table)–Agujita, by Vieux Manoir

Lifetime record: 21 9 4 2 $3,015,764

Own.– D. Wildenstein
Br.– Dayton Ltd (Fr)
Tr.– Patrick L. Biancone

10Nov84-6Hol	fm 1½Ⓣ	:491 1:131 2:011 2:251	3↑ BC Turf-G1	7 7 73¼ 1½ 11	2nk	Cordero A Jr	123	3.20	94-00	Lashkari122nkAllAlong123½Ram122½ Failed to hold winner	11
21Oct84-7WO	gd 1⅝Ⓣ	:491 1:391 2:044 2:424	3↑ Rothmans Int'l-G1	5 8 812 63¾ 34	42½	Swinburn WR	123	*.75	84-15	Majesty'sPrince1262JckSld126noEsprtduNord126nk Bid,hung	9
7Oct84♦ Longchamp(Fr)	sf *1½ⓉRH	2:39	3↑ Prix de l'Arc de Triomphe-G1 Stk550000		38	Swinburn WR	127	2.90e		Sagace1302Northern Trick1206All Along127¾ Progress into 7th 2½f out,mild late gain.Sadler's Wells 8th	22
22Sep84-8Bel	fm 1½Ⓣ	:484 1:13 2:013 2:251	3↑ Turf Classic-G1	1 4 43 32½ 33	44¼	Swinburn WR	123	1.80	94-10	JohnHenry126nkWin1264Majesty's Prince126hd Flattened out	6
12Nov83-8Lrl	yl 1½Ⓣ	:514 1:173 2:084 2:35	3↑ DC Int'l-G1	6 6 52½ 13½ 16	13¼	Swinburn WR	124	*.40	44-56	AllAlong1243¼WelshTerm1272¾Majsty'sPrnc127hd Ridden out	8
29Oct83-8Aqu	yl 1½Ⓣ	:494 1:144 2:09 2:34	3↑ Turf Classic-G1	10 3 36½ 2hd 14	18¾	Swinburn WR	123	*.90	71-29	AllAlong1238¾ThunderPuddles1261½ErinsIsl1261 Ridden out	10
16Oct83-9WO	yl 1⅝Ⓣ	:511 1:42 2:45	3↑ Rothmans Int'l-G1	5 10 811 42½ 11½	12	Swinburn WR	123	*1.65	75-25	AllAlong1232ThundrPuddls126¾Mjsty'sPrnc126nk Drew clear	11
2Oct83♦ Longchamp(Fr)	fm*1½ⓉRH	2:28	3↑ Prix de l'Arc de Triomphe-G1 Stk635000		11	Swinburn WR	127	17.30e		All Along1271Sun Princess120nkLuth Enchantee120no Rated in midpack,rail bid 2f out,led 100y out. Time Charter 4th	26
11Sep83♦ Longchamp(Fr)	sf *1½ⓉRH	2:403	3↑ Prix Foy-G3 Stk39600		2¾	Head F	120	6.00		Time Charter127¾All Along120½Great Substence1262 Rated in 7th,lacked room 2f out,angled out,gaining late	11
3Jly83♦ Saint-Cloud(Fr)	gd *1 9/16ⓉLH	2:344	3↑ Grand Prix de Saint-Cloud-G1 Stk276000		77¾	Starkey G	131	5.75		Diamond Shoal134¾Lancastrian134¾Zalataia129¾ Tracked in 3rd,weakened 1½f out,bled.Lemhi Gold 4th	9
12Jun83♦ Chantilly(Fr)	fm*1½ⓉRH	2:242	4↑ La Coupe-G3 Stk44200		32¾	Starkey G	127	*1.20		Zalataia1242Flower Prince123¾All Along1276 Tracked leader,led 2f out,headed and faded 150y out	8
28Nov82♦ Tokyo(Jpn)	fm*1½ⓉLH	2:27	3↑ Japan Cup-G1 Stk940000		2nk	Moore GW	117	5.20		Half Iced121nkAll Along117nkApril Run1211 Closed well	15
3Oct82♦ Longchamp(Fr)	sf *1½ⓉRH	2:37	3↑ Arc de Triomphe-G1 Stk637000		1521	Starkey G	120	17.00		Akiyda120hdArdross130½Awaasif120hd Raced in midpack to 3f out,weakened quickly	17
12Sep82♦ Longchamp(Fr)	fm*1½ⓉRH	2:293	ⒻPrix Vermeille-G1 Stk191000		11½	Starkey G	128	7.30		All Along1281½Akiyda128hdGrease128¾ Tracked in 3rd,led 2½f out,ridden out.Zalataia 6th	13
14Jly82♦ Saint-Cloud(Fr)	gd *1 9/16ⓉLH	2:463	3↑ Prix Maurice de Nieuil-G2 Stk95600		1½	Gorli S	113	5.20		All Along113½No Attention1283Arc d'Or1282 Close up,led 1f out,held well	12
13Jun82♦ Chantilly(Fr)	sf *1 5/16ⓉRH	2:164	ⒻPrix de Diane-G1 223000		55¾	Gorli S	128	13.00		Harbour1282Akiyda1282Paradise128¾ Tracked in 4th,led briefly 1½f out,weakened 170y out	14
5Jun82♦ Epsom(GB)	fm 1½ⓉLH	2:321	ⒻEnglish Oaks-G1 Stk220000		65¾	St. Martin Y	126			Time Charter1261Slightly Dangerous1261½Last Feather126¾ Toward rear,brief bid 2f out,one-paced late.Awaasif 4th	13
23May82♦ Longchamp(Fr)	sf *1¼ⓉRH	2:20	ⒻPrix Saint-Alary-G1 Stk127000		24	Gorli S	128	*.70		Harbour1284All Along1281½Perlee128nk Well placed in 3rd,led 2f to 1f out,no chance with winner	8
27Mar82♦ Saint-Cloud(Fr)	sf *1 5/16ⓉLH	2:232	ⒻPrix Penelope-G3 Stk51000		14	Gorli S	123			All Along1234Paradise1231Charmer1231 Strong run to lead 1f out,ridden clear	11
27Feb82♦ Saint-Cloud(Fr)	hy *1¼ⓉLH	2:241	ⒻPrix Mirska Alw18800		14	Gorli S	123			All Along1234Zalataia1231Magic and Magic1231 Tracked in 3rd,led 2f out,easily. Previously trained by Maurice Zilber	13
10Nov81♦ Amiens(Fr)	sf *1 50ⓉRH		ⒻPrix d'Hornoy Mdn7200		1nk	Vache S	119			DHAll Along119DHTarbelissima118nkVitilla1211 Tracked leader,dueled 1f out,gamely.Time not taken	12

Althea

ch. f. 1981, by Alydar (Raise a Native)–Courtly Dee, by Never Bend

Lifetime record: 15 8 4 0 $1,275,255

Own.– Alexander & Aykroyd & Groves
Br.– Groves-Alexander-Aykroyd (Ky)
Tr.– D. Wayne Lukas

27Jun84-8Hol	fst 7f	:214 :442 1:083 1:211	3↑ ⒻA Gleam 66k	7 2 21 21 34½	612	Valenzuela PA	116	*1.20	79-19	Lass Trump1161Pleasure Cay1165½Angel Savage1122 Tired	9
5May84-8CD	fst 1¼	:472 1:114 1:363 2:022	Ky Derby-G1	1 1 11 55 1922	1930¾	McCarron CJ	121	*2.80e	54-19	Swale1263¼Coax Me Chad1262At the Threshold126nk Tired	20
21Apr84-9OP	fst 1⅛	:463 1:101 1:352 1:464	Ark Derby-G1	10 1 11 1½ 16	17	Valenzuela PA	121	3.00	109-04	Althea1217PineCircle118noGateDancer118no Kept to drive	11
14Apr84-9OP	fst 1 1/16	:23 :463 1:104 1:411	ⒻFantasy-G1	1 6 52 31½ 1hd	2¾	Pincay L Jr	121	*.60	101-10	MyDarlingOne121¾Alth12110PrsonblLdy118¾ Poor st,drifted	6
11Mar84-8SA	fst 1 1/16	:232 :472 1:113 1:433	ⒻS Susana-G1	2 3 32 1½ 11	1¾	Pincay L Jr	117	*.60	83-18	Althea117¾PersonableLady115hdLife'sMagc1154 Proved best	5
25Feb84-8SA	fst 1	:224 :462 1:11 1:37	ⒻLas Virgenes 250k	1 5 51¾ 42 42½	1no	Pincay L Jr	124	*1.00	83-18	Althea124noVagabondGal117nkMyDarlingOn1143¼ Rough trip	6
18Dec83-8Hol	fst 1 1/16	:222 :454 1:101 1:413	Hol Futurity-G1	4 2 2½ 1hd 34	611	Pincay L Jr	118	2.80	76-14	FaliTime121½BoldT.Jay1213¼Life'sMagic1183 Led,weakened	12
27Nov83-8Hol	fst 1 1/16	:23 :464 1:112 1:43	ⒻHol Starlet-G2	6 1 11 11 11½	11½	Pincay L Jr	120	*1.20	80-20	Althea1201½Life's Magic120hdSpring Loose1202½ Driving	6
12Nov83-8SA	sly 1 1/16	:224 :463 1:113 1:442	ⒻOak Leaf-G1	1 1 11 11½ 1½	2½	Pincay L Jr	117	*.90	78-23	Life's Magic115½Althea11717Percipient115hd Game try	9
26Oct83-8SA	fst 7f	:222 :451 1:10 1:231	ⒻAnoakia-G3	2 2 2hd 2hd 2½	21¼	Pincay L Jr	123	*.10	83-20	Percipient1171¼Althea1231½Personable Lady117½ Bore out	4
14Sep83-8Dmr	fst 1	:223 :454 1:102 1:344	Dmr Futurity-G2	4 1 11 12½ 16	16½	Pincay L Jr	117	*.30	94-14	Althea1176½Juliet's Pride1154Gumboy1142½ Easy score	5
4Sep83-8Dmr	fst 1	:223 :453 1:102 1:36	ⒻDebutante-G2	4 1 110 114 114	115	Pincay L Jr	119	*.30	88-17	Althea11915Diachrony1134Victorous Joy113½ Easily	6
23Jly83-8Hol	fst 6f	:214 :441 :564 1:092	Juv Champ-G2	3 4 2hd 13 17	110	Pincay L Jr	117	2.30	90-21	Althea11710RejectedSuitor1171AutoCommander1171½ Easily	9
9Jly83-8Hol	fst 6f	:22 :444 :573 1:103	ⒻLandaluce-G2	11 1 2hd 2hd 1hd	22	Pincay L Jr	117	*.40e	82-23	Simple Magic1162Althea11713Reb's Gateau1161½ Game try	11
22Jun83-6Hol	fst 5f	:214 :443 :57	ⒻMd Sp Wt	10 1 2hd 1½ 12½	16½	Pincay L Jr	117	*.80	92-19	Althea1176½MissCamouflage116noBigPotential1165½ Driving	10

Alysheba

b. c. 1984, by Alydar (Raise a Native)–Bel Sheba, by Lt. Stevens

Lifetime record: 26 11 8 2 $6,679,242

Own.– Dorothy & Pam Scharbauer
Br.– Preston Madden (Ky)
Tr.– Jack C. Van Berg

5Nov88-10CD	my 1¼	:474 1:122 1:383 2:044	3↑ BC Classic-G1	5 4 48½ 31 1hd	1½	McCarron CJ	126		*1.50	73-20	Alyshb126½SkngthGold1225Wquot126nk Bumped start,driving	9
14Oct88-10Med	fst 1¼	:461 1:092 1:334 1:584	3↑ Med Cup H-G1	3 3 37 21 1hd	1nk	McCarron CJ	127		*.50	108-05	Alysheba127nkSlewCitySlew1166¼PleasntVrgnn114nk Driving	5
17Sep88-8Bel	fst 1¼	:473 1:111 1:35 1:592	3↑ Woodward H-G1	4 3 31 3½ 3½	1nk	McCarron CJ	126		*1.80	101-08	Alysheba126nkForty Niner119nkWaquoit1221¼ Driving	8
27Aug88-9Mth	fst 1⅛	:462 1:094 1:343 1:474	3↑ Iselin H-G1	4 5 511 45 22½	1¾	McCarron CJ	124		*1.00	95-12	Alysheba124¾Bet Twice1234Gulch1222½ Driving	6
26Jun88-8Hol	fst 1¼	:454 1:093 1:342 1:592	3↑ Hol Gold Cup H-G1	6 5 58 31½ 24	26½	McCarron CJ	126	b	*1.00	88-07	Cutlass Reality1166½Alysheba1265½Ferdinand1254 2nd best	6
14May88-8Pim	fst 1 3/16	:462 1:102 1:352 1:541	4↑ Pim Spl H 600k	2 3 32 2½ 44½	44¼	McCarron CJ	127	b	*.60	92-19	BetTwice124¾LostCode1261Cryptoclearanc1212½ Drifted str	6
17Apr88-8SA	fst 1⅛	:462 1:094 1:343 1:471	4↑ S Bernardino H-G2	1 2 21½ 1hd 2hd	1no	McCarron CJ	127	b	*.80	93-17	Alysheba127noFerdinand127hdGood Taste1133½ Driving	5
6Mar88-8SA	fst 1¼	:463 1:10 1:343 1:594	4↑ S Anita H-G1	2 3 33 1½ 11	1½	McCarron CJ	126	b	*1.00	90-13	Alysheba126½Ferdinand1272½Super Diamond1242½ Driving	4
7Feb88-8SA	fst 1¼	:453 1:094 1:351 2:002	C H Strub-G1	3 5 58½ 1hd 1hd	13	McCarron CJ	126	b	*.90	87-16	Alysheba1263Candi's Gold1178On the Line1198½ Drew out	6
21Nov87-7Hol	fst 1¼	:462 1:101 1:352 2:012	3↑ BC Classic-G1	9 9 98½ 54 41	2no	McCarron CJ	122	b	3.60	85-12	Ferdinand126noAlysheba1221¼JudgAnglucc1261½ Just missed	12
27Sep87-10LaD	fst 1¼	:47 1:112 1:362 2:031	Super Derby-G1	2 7 76½ 32½ 21	1½	McCarron CJ	126	b	*.50	85-19	Alysheba126½Candi'sGold1261½Parochil1263¼ Brushed rival	8
22Aug87-8Sar	sly 1¼	:461 1:10 1:362 2:02	Travers-G1	6 7 712 78½ 69	620¼	McCarron CJ	126	b	*2.50	70-16	JavaGold1262Cryptoclearance1266¾PolshNvy1261½ No factor	9
1Aug87-9Mth	fst 1⅛	:463 1:093 1:34 1:47	Haskell Inv'l H-G1	4 2 32½ 21 32½	2nk	McCarron CJ	126	b	1.50	99-07	BetTwice126nkAlysheba126nkLostCod12412 In close on turn	5
6Jun87-8Bel	fst 1½	:492 1:342 2:03 2:281	Belmont-G1	3 4 47 47 39	414¼	McCarron CJ	126	b	*.80	65-15	Bet Twice12614Cryptoclearance126noGulch126nk Rough trip	9
16May87-9Pim	fst 1 3/16	:471 1:113 1:364 1:554	Preakness-G1	6 6 56½ 43 2hd	1½	McCarron CJ	126	b	*2.00	88-18	Alysheba126½Bet Twice1261½Cryptoclearance1263½ Driving	9

2May87- 8CD fst 1¼ :46^2 1:11 1:36^4 2:03^2 Ky Derby-G1 3 14 13^12 3^1½ 2^1 1¾ McCarron CJ 126 b 8.40 80-09 Alysheba126¾BetTwice126^2¼AvisCopy126^nk Stumbled midstr 17
23Apr87- 7Kee fst 1⅛ :46^4 1:10^2 1:36^1 1:48^2 Blue Grass-G1 4 4 3^2 4^2½ 2^hd 1^hd McCarron CJ 121 b *.90 95-13 [D]Alysheba121^hdWar121^hdLeo Castelli121^8 Ducked out 5
Disqualified and placed third
22Mar87- 8SA gd 1 1/16 :22^4 :46^2 1:10^4 1:43 San Felipe H-G1 3 7 7^6½ 6^3½ 4¾ 2¾ Day P 120 b 3.30 85-23 CharttheStars116¾Alysheb120^2¾TmprtSl122^2½ Lugged in str 8
8Mar87- 9SA fst 1 1/16 :23^1 :46^4 1:11^2 1:43 Alw 30000 6 4 4^4½ 4^5 4^4 4^5 Day P 114 b *.70 81-15 Barb's Relic117^2¾Blanco114¾Rakaposhi114^1½ No rally 9
14Dec86- 8Hol fst 1 :22^1 :44^4 1:09^3 1:36^1 Hol Futurity-G1 12 4 4^1¾ 2^2½ 2½ 2^nk Day P 121 b 6.60e 82-18 TemperateSl121^nkAlyshb121^nkMstrfulAdvoct121^2¼ Sharp try 12
1Nov86- 1SA fst 1 1/16 :22^2 :45^4 1:10^2 1:43^4 BC Juvenile-G1 4 13 12^11 9^8¾ 7^7½ 3^2½ Shoemaker W 122 b 33.40 79-13 Capote122^1¼Qualify122^1¼Alysheba122^2¼ Angled out str 13
10Oct86- 7Kee fst 1 1/16 :23^4 :47^3 1:12^2 1:45^1 Breeders' Futurity-G2 10 4 4^1½ 3^1½ 2^hd 2¾ Brumfield D 121 b 4.30 79-18 Orono121¾Alysheba121^1¼Pledge Card121^1 Wide 10
27Sep86- 9TP gd 1 :21^3 :45 1:10^4 1:37^1 In Memoriam 120k 4 5 3^3 1½ 2^hd 2½ Brumfield D 120 b *2.30 91-07 RainbowEast120½Alysheba120^12DavidL.'sRib120^6 Game try 11
14Sep86- 3TP fst 1 1/16 :24 :48^1 1:13^1 1:46^2 Md Sp Wt 4 1 1^hd 1½ 1^3 1^8 Brumfield D 119 b *.30 78-22 Alysheba119^8Aerator119½Najor Domo119^6 Easily 12
22Aug86- 9AP fst 1 :23^2 :46^2 1:11^1 1:36^4 Md Sp Wt 9 6 6^4¾ 3^4 3^3 2^hd Day P 120 1.80 77-14 GemMaster120^hdAlysheba120^3¼Contractor'sTun120^14 Rallied 10
21Jly86- 4Hol fst 5½f :22^2 :45^4 :58^1 1:05 Md Sp Wt 2 6 4^6½ 4^7 5^6 5^4¾ Romero RP 118 2.40 84-16 FleetingJet118½BiloxiBlues118^1¼SoyAmigo118^2¾ No rally 7

Ambassador of Luck

b. f. 1979, by What Luck (Bold Ruler)–Detente, by Dark Ruler **Lifetime record: 23 14 4 3 $489,583**

Own.– Envoy Stable
Br.– C.T. Fuller (Pa)
Tr.– Mitchell C. Preger

14Sep84- 8Bel fst 7f :23^1 :46^2 1:10^3 1:23 3↑ (F)Alw 33000 4 6 2^1 2^hd 1^1½ 1¾ Graell A 115 *.60 87-18 AmbassadorofLuck115¾QuixoticLady119^2¾MadamForbes122¾ 6
Bumped,hand ride
18Aug84- 3Sar fst 6f :22^1 :45^1 1:09^4 3↑ (F)Revidere 55k 1 7 4^3 3^1½ 2^1½ 3^1½ Graell A 122 *.80 89-15 MadmForbs117^1¼OnthBnch117^nkAmbssdrofLck122¾ Weakened 7
4Sep83- 8Bel fst 1 :22^4 :45^2 1:10^1 1:36^2 3↑ (F)Maskette-G1 6 1 1^1½ 1^3 1^4 1^5 Graell A 116 *.20 83-13 AmbassadorofLuck116^5A Kiss forLuck120^hdAmCapable109^4½ 6
Ridden out
5Aug83- 8Sar fst 7f :23 :46^1 1:09^4 1:22^1 3↑ (F)Ballerina-G3 3 1 2^1½ 1^hd 1^1½ 1^1 Graell A 124 *.60 91-14 AmbassadorofLck124^1Number119^3¾BroomDance122^3 Driving 4
Previously owned by S.D. Peskoff
4Jly83- 9Mth fst 1 1/16 :24^1 :47 1:09^4 1:41^1 3↑ (F)Molly Pitcher H-G2 5 2 2^4 2^3 1½ 1^3½ Graell A 117 2.40 99-13 AmbassadorofLuck117^3½Kattegat'sPride122^1DanceNumber115^5 8
Drew off
16Jun83- 8Bel fst 7f :22^4 :45 1:09^3 1:22^1 3↑ (F)Handicap 35000 5 1 3^4½ 2^1½ 1^5 1^6 Graell A 124 *.90 91-22 AmbassadrofLck124^6SproutedRye121^2Syrnn119^5 Ridden out 5
4Jun83- 7Bel gd 6f :22 :44^3 1:08^3 3↑ (F)Alw 35000 5 2 2^1 1^hd 1^1 1^4¾ Graell A 117 1.40 99-08 AmbassdrofLck117^4¾JonesTimeMachine122^11Mrs.Roberts117^4¼ 5
Ridden out
12May83- 8Aqu fst 6f :23^2 :46^3 1:10^2 3↑ (F)Handicap 35000 5 2 1^hd 1^1½ 1^2 1^1½ Graell A 122 2.60 89-20 AmbassadorofLck122^1½VivaSec117^2½Mochil118^10 Ridden out 5
Previously trained by Flint S. Schulhofer
11Sep82- 8Bel fst 1 :22^2 :45 1:09^4 1:34^4 3↑ (F)Maskette-G1 6 5 4^1¼ 3^1 2^1½ 2^3½ Graell A 111 15.70 87-12 TooChic110^3½AmbassadorofLuck111^1AntiLib116¾ No match 8
6Sep82- 3Bel fm 1 1/16[T] :24^1 :47^2 1:11^3 1:42^1 3↑ (F)Alw 35000 3 3 3^2½ 3^1½ 3^1½ 3^1¼ Graell A 115 4.50 89-18 Norsan112^1¼MajestcNorth115^hdAmbssdorofLck115^2 Even try 7
24Aug82- 7Sar fm 1[T] :24 :47^3 1:11^3 1:36^4 3↑ (F)Alw 35000 6 2 2^1 1^hd 1^hd 3^nk Graell A 117 *2.50 92-12 Suspcous112^noSunwontshn117^nkAmbssdrofLck117¾ Weakened 7
5Aug82- 8Sar fst 7f :22^1 :45 1:09^4 1:22^4 (F)Test-G2 7 2 3^3¼ 2^1½ 2^2 2^1 Graell A 121 29.20 87-16 GoldButy116^1AmbssdrofLck121^1¾Numbr114^1¾ Best of others 12
25Jly82- 9WO fst 7f :22^1 :44^3 1:08^4 1:23 (F)Duchess 56k 1 7 5^1¾ 3^1 1^2 1¾ Graell A 123 *1.75 94-12 AmbassadorofLuck123¾ProudLou118^5Aironlass118^no Driving 8
3Jly82-10Suf fst 6f :22 :45^2 1:10^3 (F)Pinafore 31k 1 8 7^3½ 4^1½ 1^1 1^1½ Graell A 122 *1.30 88-16 AmbassdrofLck122^1½ASttusSymbol119^nkNornd112^1½ Driving 10
12Jun82-10Suf fst 6f :22^1 :45^2 1:10^2 (F)Linda 31k 6 3 2½ 1^1 1^3 1½ Graell A 122 *1.40 89-16 AmbassdorofLck122½HopfulContrct118^2Crushm116^1¾ Driving 12
Previously owned by Ransom & Peskoff;previously trained by W.M. Carrelli
17Apr82- 7Kee sly 1 1/16 :23^3 :47^3 1:12^1 1:45 (F)Ashland-G2 6 5 6^7 5^5 10^13 10^31 Day P 118 6.40e 50-21 Blush With Pride118^2¾Exclusive Love116^nkDelicate Ice113^11 10
Fell back
7Apr82- 7Kee fst *7f 1:27 (F)Alw 29940 1 4 1^1 1½ 2½ 4^5 McKnight J 120 *1.50 83-13 ExclusiveLov112^hdNoonBlloon120^2½AplchHony123^2½ Gave way 7
12Mar82- 9OP fst 6f :21^3 :45^2 1:11^2 (F)Magnolia 64k 9 5 5^5½ 3^2½ 3^1½ 2^3 Patterson G 121 *.60e 85-23 JasminJul112^3AmbssdrofLck121½SnowPlow121^3 Second best 12
Previously owned by R. Ransom
15Feb82- 9OP fst 6f :22 :46^3 1:12^1 (F)M Washington 58k 6 - 1^3½ Patterson G 115 *1.40 84-22 AmbssdorofLck115^3½Ecoled'Humanite118^2ShadMss112^2 Fog 8
31Oct81- 8Lrl fst 1 1/16 :23 :46^4 1:13^1 1:46^1 (F)Selima-G1 2 1 1^2 1^hd 1^1 2^2¼ Shoemaker W 119 3.90 75-24 SnowPlow119^2¼Ambassador ofLuck119^1ChillingThought119^6 6
Drifted out
17Oct81- 6Key fst 6f :22^1 :45^2 1:10^4 (F)Schuykill (Div 1) 22k 6 1 3^nk 1½ 1½ 1^3¾ Black AS 115 6.00 88-18 AmbassadrofLck115^3¾Delicate Ice115^hdMarshua's Lady115^hd 9
Ridden out
20Sep81- 9Lat fst 6f :22^3 :46^1 1:00 1:13^4 (F)Clipsetta (Div 2) 11k 5 2 2½ 2½ 2^1 1¾ Sayler B 114 *.40 75-29 AmbassadorofLuck114¾GoldenTry110^hdRiddles113^12 Driving 7
5Sep81- 5RD fst 5½f :22^1 :45^1 :58^1 1:05^1 (F)Md Sp Wt 4 1 1^2 1^4 1^8 1^16 Woods CR Jr 120 *1.10 89-27 AmbassdorofLck120^16SummerTimeLass120^7BestofQuiz120^4 9
Easily

April Run (Ire)

b. f. 1978, by Run the Gantlet (Tom Rolfe)–April Fancy, by No Argument **Lifetime record: 18 8 2 4 $1,092,514**

Own.– Mrs B.R. Firestone
Br.– F. Feeney (Ire)
Tr.– Francois Boutin

28Nov82♦ Tokyo(Jpn) fm*1½(T)LH 2:27 3↑ Japan Cup-G1 3½ Asmussen CB 121 1.80 Half Iced121^nkAll Along117^nkApril Run121^1 15
Stk801000 Always close up,bid 1f out,outfinished.John Henry 13th
6Nov82- 8Lrl yl 1½(T) :48^3 1:13^1 2:07 2:31 3↑ D C Int'l-G1 8 7 8^12 1^1 1^2 1^6½ Asmussen CB 124 *.70 64-36 April Run124^6½Majesty's Prince120^4½Thunder Puddles120^1½ 10
Ridden out
23Oct82- 8Aqu fm 1½(T) :50^1 1:14 2:05^2 2:29^4 3↑ Turf Classic-G1 2 5 4^6½ 4^3 1^1 1^6½ Asmussen CB 123 *1.30 92-08 AprlRn123^6½Naskra'sBreeze126^3¼BottldWtr126^4¼ Ridden out 7
3Oct82♦ Longchamp(Fr) sf *1½(T)RH 2:37 3↑ Prix de l'Arc de Triomphe-G1 4¾ Asmussen CB 127 15.00 Akiyda120^hdArdross130½Awaasif120^hd 17
Stk637000 Led briefly,soon lost place,8th 2½f out,gaining late
12Sep82♦ Longchamp(Fr) fm*1½(T)RH 2:32^1 4↑ Prix Foy-G3 1no Piggott L 120 *.50 April Run120^no[D]Mariacho123^nkNo Attention123^2 7
Stk47800 Led throughout,met challenge 1f out,very game
21Aug82♦ Deauville(Fr) gd *1 11/16(T)RH 3:01^1 3↑ (F)Prix de Pomone-G2 3^2 Moore GW 128 3.20 Zalataia119½Akiyda128^1½April Run128¾ 13
Stk63700 Midpack behind slow pace,impeded twice,finished well
2May82♦ Longchamp(Fr) gd *1 5/16(T)RH 2:09^3 4↑ Prix Ganay-G1 9^9 Piggott L 124 3.50 Bikala128½Lancastrian128^2Al Nasr128^nk 10
Stk127000 Never a factor
18Apr82♦ Longchamp(Fr) fm*1½(T)RH 2:32^2 4↑ Prix d'Hedouville (Listed) 4^1¼ Piggott L 124 *.70 Gap of Dunloe121^nkProtection Racket128^nkTwo Step121¾ 8
Stk30600 Toward rear,bid 1f out,finished well
7Nov81- 8Lrl fm 1½(T) :50^2 1:15^3 2:06^4 2:31^1 3↑ D C Int'l-G1 1 4 4^2¼ 2^hd 1½ 2^1 Paquet P 117 3.20 62-37 ProvidentialII127^1AprilRun117^3½GalaxyLibra127¾ Lost whip 10
24Oct81- 8Aqu gd 1½(T) :48^2 1:14 2:06^1 2:31^1 3↑ Turf Classic-G1 4 4 4^2½ 2^hd 1^3½ 1¾ Paquet P 118 2.60 85-15 AprlRn118¾GalxyLibra126^3TheVeryOne123^5 Bore out,driving 9
4Oct81♦ Longchamp(Fr) yl *1½(T)RH 2:35^1 3↑ Prix de l'Arc de Triomphe-G1 3¾ Paquet P 120 6.50e Gold River127¾Bikala123^noApril Run120^2 24
Stk595000 Midpack,checked 1½f out,angled out,held by first two
13Sep81♦ Longchamp(Fr) gd *1½(T)RH 2:32^4 (F)Prix Vermeille-G1 1^1½ Paquet P 128 4.80 April Run128^1½Leandra128^hdMadam Gay128^3 10
Stk208000 Tracked in 3rd,led 2f out,driving
22Aug81♦ Deauville(Fr) gd *1 11/16(T)RH 3:01^4 3↑ (F)Prix de Pomone-G3 1^5 Paquet P 123 *.50 April Run123^5Anitra'sDance123^nkTerre Froide128^1½ 8
Stk47600 Rated at rear,rallied to lead 1f out,handily
5Jly81♦ Saint-Cloud(Fr) gd *1 9/16(T)LH 2:38^4 3↑ Grand Prix de Saint-Cloud-G1 4^3¼ Paquet P 118 13.00 Akarad121^2Bikala121½Lancastrian134^nk 10
Stk240000 Well placed in 3rd,lacked rally

14Jun81♦ Chantilly(Fr)	fm *1 5/16 Ⓣ RH	2:062	ⒻPrix de Diane (French Oaks)-G1 Stk240000	34¼	Starkey G	128		4.70		Madam Gay1284Val d'Erica128nkApril Run128hd Rated in 7th,bid 2f out,up for 3rd	14
16May81♦ Saint-Cloud(Fr)	sf *1 5/16 Ⓣ LH	2:202	ⒻPrix Cleopatre-G3 Stk49300	13	Paquet P	119		2.40		April Run1193Landresse1193Leandra1191½ Led throughout,ridden clear 1f out	9
28Apr81♦ Saint-Cloud(Fr)	gd *1½ Ⓣ LH	2:342	ⒻPrix Dushka Mdn14600	16	Paquet P	126		6.80		April Run1266La Hougue126¾Heliade1202 Tracked leader,led 2f out,easily clear	17
28Mar81♦ Saint-Cloud(Fr)	hy *1¼ Ⓣ LH	2:234	ⒻPrix Dorina Mdn (FT)14000	22½	Paquet P	123		4.00		Marie d'Urcel1232½April Run1232Cariziana123nk Tracked in 3rd,bid 2f out,second best	11

Bates Motel

b. c. 1979, by Sir Ivor (Sir Gaylord)–Sunday Purchase, by T.V. Lark

Lifetime record: 19 9 1 4 $851,050

Own.– J. Getty Phillips & Riordan
Br.– Mrs G.F. Getty II (Ky)
Tr.– John H.M. Gosden

24Sep83- 8Bel	fst 1¼	:472 1:111 1:361 2:011 3↑	Marlboro Cup H-G1	5 6 66½ 23 2½ 3¾	McCarron CJ	124	b	*.80	91-17	HighlandBlade117nkSlewo'Gld119½BatesMotel1244 Weakened	9
3Sep83- 8Bel	fst 1⅛	:454 1:092 1:34 1:463 3↑	Woodward-G1	5 5 73¾ 42½ 2hd 2no	Lipham T	123	b	*.60	94-13	Slewo'Gold118noBatesMotel1235SingSing1195 Just missed	10
20Aug83- 9Mth	fst 1⅛	:463 1:101 1:343 1:471 3↑	Monmouth H-G1	6 6 67 63½ 12½ 12½	Lipham T	124	b	*.90	99-16	BatesMotel1242½IslandWhirl124nkLinkage1152½ Ridden out	9
7Aug83- 8Dmr	fst 1 1/16	:23 :46 1:103 1:41 3↑	San Diego H-G3	4 4 42½ 1hd 15 17	Lipham T	122	b	*1.10	95-18	BatesMotel1227The Wonder123hdRunaway Groom1173 Easily	6
6Mar83- 8SA	fst 1¼	:453 1:093 1:344 1:593 4↑	S Anita H-G1	13 13 911 52½ 11 12½	Lipham T	118	b	3.80	91-17	BatesMotl1182½It'sthOn123noWvrngMonrch1214½ Wide,clear	17
20Feb83- 8SA	fst 1⅛	:454 1:093 1:343 1:47 4↑	S Antonio H-G1	7 9 915 78½ 12½ 13½	Lipham T	114	b	6.20	94-13	Bates Motel1143½Time to Explode121noIt's the One1243	10
	Jostled,driving										
6Feb83- 8SA	my 1¼	:473 1:113 1:361 2:02	C H Strub-G1	3 4 43 76¾ 99¾ 1018	Lipham T	115	b	10.40	61-19	Swing Till Dawn1152Wavering Monarch1211Water Bank1172	10
	Shuffled back st										
1Jan83- 6SA	fst 1 1/16	:23 :454 1:093 1:41 4↑	Alw 35000	3 2 21½ 2½ 12 11½	Lipham T	116		2.10	96-11	BatesMotel1161½ExclusiveOne1183FightingFit1166½ Driving	5
25Nov82- 8Hol	fst 1 1/16	:224 :453 1:094 1:41	Affirmed H 85k	3 9 99¼ 78¼ 55 31¾	Lipham T	115	b	5.90	88-18	Poley118nkExclusiveEra1151½BatesMotel115hd Bobbled st.	11
17Oct82- 5SA	fst 1 1/16	:223 :454 1:094 1:413 3↑	Alw 32000	10 7 83¼ 87¼ 53½ 11	Lipham T	118	b	3.30	93-09	BatesMotel1181Pettrax116nkWestCoastNative1112½ Driving	11
6Oct82- 6SA	fst 1	:22 :443 1:092 1:342	Alw 30000	3 6 613 45½ 33½ 33	Lipham T	119	b	4.10	93-15	Jet Travel115hdPoley1173Bates Motel1193½ Lugged in	6
11Sep82-11Bmf	fst 1 1/16	:224 :46 1:102 1:413	Sophomore H 21k	4 5 54½ 43 21 1nk	Lipham T	114	b	*1.20	91-19	Bates Motel114nkPet's Dude1146Top Pole1184 Driving	8
18Aug82- 5Dmr	fst 1 1/16	:223 :452 1:101 1:414	Alw 15000	1 3 36 2½ 2hd 14	Lipham T	114	b	15.90	91-21	Bates Motel1144Penngrove1122Royal Serb1182 Driving	6
11Aug82- 5Dmr	fst 1 1/16	:224 :461 1:103 1:423	Alw 15000	5 5 64½ 75¼ 78 710	Lipham T	117	b	16.80	77-16	Poley1152Checker's Orphan115nkDurable115hd No factor	8
5Jly82- 9Hol	fm 1Ⓣ	:232 :462 1:101 1:344	Alw 21000	7 10 1020 1022 1020 1017	McCarron CJ	120		*2.30	78-06	Prosperous115nkSir Pele1202½Salty Creek117no Dull	10
31May82- 6Hol	fst 1 1/16	:224 :462 1:11 1:432 3↑	Md Sp Wt	7 3 32 22½ 13½ 18	McCarron CJ	114	b	3.40	78-19	Bates Motel1148Crimson Axe1093The Hague1173½ Easily	11
1May82- 6Hol	fst 1 1/16	:231 :464 1:114 1:432 3↑	Md Sp Wt	12 9 1010 64 56½ 43½	Sibille R	115	b	10.60	74-15	Valais114½Bruin County1242½Tree Runner114½ Wide	12
4Apr82- 3SA	fst 1 1/16	:222 :453 1:101 1:422	©Md Sp Wt	10 12 1227 1118 414 39¼	Sibille R	118	b	60.70	80-09	Donbion1183¼Chargeur1186Bates Motel118½ Stumbled start	12
28Feb82- 2SA	fst 1 1/16	:23 :462 1:104 1:43	©Md Sp Wt	8 8 1112 119¼ 612 710	McCarron CJ	118	b	23.50	76-09	Penngrove118noHatamoto1181Seventh Dwarf1184 Wide	12

Before Dawn

b. f. 1979, by Raise a Cup (Raise a Native)–Moonbeam, by Tim Tam

Lifetime record: 14 9 2 1 $432,855

Own.– Calumet Farm
Br.– Calumet Farm (Ky)
Tr.– John M. Veitch

5Aug82- 8Sar	fst 7f	:221 :45 1:094 1:224	ⒻTest-G2	8 7 95½ 75½ 1114 913	Vasquez J	121		5.10	75-16	GoldBeauty1161AmbassadrofLck1211¾Numbr1141¾ No factor	12
22May82- 8Bel	fst 1	:231 :46 1:093 1:341	ⒻAcorn-G1	1 3 42½ 65 89½ 913	Velasquez J	121		*1.60	82-11	Cupecoy's Joy1212¾Nancy Huang1213½Vestris1212¼ Tired	9
30Apr82- 8CD	fst 1⅛	:482 1:131 1:373 1:501	ⒻKy Oaks-G1	7 2 21 1½ 2hd 2¾	Velasquez J	121		*1.30	90-13	Blush With Pride121¾Before Dawn1212¼Flying Partner1216	7
	Held gamely										
3Apr82- 9OP	fst 1 1/16	:234 :481 1:143 1:47	ⒻFantasy-G1	3 2 1hd 1hd 32½ 36	Velasquez J	121		*.40	67-33	FlyingPartner1182¾SkillfulJoy1213¼BforDwn1215½ Weakened	7
27Mar82-10FG	fst 1 1/16	:24 :471 1:121 1:452	ⒻFG Oaks-G3	2 4 55 3nk 14 12½	Velasquez J	121		*.30	85-16	Before Dawn1212½Girlie1213½Linda North1181 Poor st.,dr.	7
17Feb82- 9Hia	fst 7f	:222 :45 1:094 1:23	ⒻHibiscus 36k	2 2 32½ 21½ 11½ 11	Velasquez J	122		*.10	88-21	Before Dawn1221All Manners1174First Flurry1173½ Handily	5
8Feb82- 9Hia	fst 6f	:22 :45 1:094	ⒻAlw 20000	5 1 2hd 11 14 18	Velasquez J	122		*.30	94-23	BeforeDawn1228FirstFlurry1151ExclusvLov1151¼ Ridden out	7
9Jan82- 9Hia	fst 6f	:214 :452 1:104	ⒻJasmine 37k	8 3 54 41½ 2½ 1no	Velasquez J	122		*.30	89-15	Before Dawn122noIron Queen1171¼Larida1137 Driving	9
10Oct81- 7Bel	fst 1	:233 :464 1:111 1:362	Champagne-G1	1 4 1½ 1hd 21 24¾	Velasquez J	119		*.80	81-14	Timely Writer1224¾Before Dawn1193New Discovery122nk	13
	Best of others										
19Sep81- 7Bel	my 7f	:231 :462 1:104 1:231	ⒻMatron-G1	2 3 11 11½ 13 16½	Velasquez J	119		*.40	86-13	BefreDwn1196½ArabinDncr1191¼MystclMood119¾ Ridden out	9
3Sep81- 8Bel	fst 6½f	:224 :453 1:094 1:163	ⒻAstarita-G2	2 2 2½ 11 12½ 12½	Velasquez J	119		*.10	93-19	BeforeDwn1192½BettyMoney1126½TakeLadyAnne1121 Easily	5
23Aug81- 8Sar	fst 6f	:22 :444 1:092	ⒻSpinaway-G1	7 3 31½ 11½ 15 17¾	McCarron G	119		*.80	93-12	BfreDwn1197¾BettyMoney1192½TakeLadyAnne119no Handily	10
24Jun81- 8Bel	fst 5½f	:221 :454 :574 1:041	ⒻFashion 55k	3 4 32½ 31½ 13 15¼	Velasquez J	115		*.50	94-19	Before Dawn1155¼Mystical Mood1152½Bold and Joyful1153	7
	Ridden out										
15Jun81- 6Bel	fst 5½f	:222 :454 :572 1:033	ⒻMd Sp Wt	5 3 13 13 14 16¾	Velasquez J	117		1.90	97-10	BforeDawn1176¾ChillingThought11710Spell1175 Ridden out	7

Blushing John

ch. c. 1985, by Blushing Groom (Red God)–La Griffe, by Prince John

Lifetime record: 19 9 1 2 $1,524,599

Own.– Allen E. Paulson
Br.– North Ridge Farm (Ky)
Tr.– Richard J. Lundy

4Nov89-10GP	fst 1¼	:461 1:102 1:35 2:001 3↑	BC Classic-G1	7 2 23 11½ 1hd 31¼	Cordero A Jr	126		21.50	106-01	SundaySilnce122nkEasyGoer1221BlshngJohn1269¾ Willingly	8
13Oct89- 9Med	fst 1¼	:461 1:102 1:344 2:001 3↑	Med Cup H-G1	6 6 55 64¼ 610 720	Cordero A Jr	124		*.60	73-16	MiSelecto1152MaketheMost1105¾[DH]MasterSpeaker114 Tired	8
9Sep89- 8AP	sly 1⅛	:481 1:132 1:384 1:504 3↑	Wash Park H-G2	2 1 21½ 2½ 13 17½	Day P	124		*.40	77-34	Blushing John1247½Grantley112¾Paramount Jet1131¼ Easily	5
12Aug89- 9AP	sf 1¼Ⓣ	:52 1:173 1:442 2:111 3↑	Arlington H-G1	5 1 2½ 31 519 531¾	Day P	124		*1.20	- -	UnknownQuantityII1123FrostytheSnowmn1221¾Delegnt113hd	5
	Eased stretch										
25Jun89- 8Hol	fst 1¼	:472 1:114 1:362 2:002 3↑	Hol Gold Cup H-G1	7 3 23½ 1½ 11 11	Day P	122		*1.30	90-19	Blushing John1221Sabona1163½Payant1161 Much the best	7
4Jun89- 8Hol	fst 1⅛	:462 1:101 1:344 1:464 3↑	Californian-G1	1 2 22 21 1hd 21¼	Day P	124		3.00	102-14	Sabona1151¼BlushingJohn1243½LvlyOn1181 Gave way stretch	6
13May89- 9Pim	fst 1 3/16	:462 1:10 1:342 1:531 4↑	Pim Spl H 700k	11 4 44¼ 23 2hd 12	Day P	117		7.10	101-10	BlushingJohn1172ProperRlty1181¼Grncus113½ Brushed,clear	12
15Apr89- 6OP	fst 1⅛	:47 1:111 1:361 1:49 4↑	Oaklawn H-G1	2 4 42 52¼ 54 42	Day P	119		3.10	86-21	Slew City Slew118½Stalwars113noHomebuilder1151½ Bumped	8
25Mar89- 9OP	fst 1 1/16	:243 :492 1:134 1:43 4↑	Razorback H-G2	4 5 41¼ 4nk 2hd 11½	Day P	117		4.20	86-24	Blushing John1171½Lyphard's Ridge1113Proper Reality1234	5
	Wide,ridden out										
9Mar89- 8OP	fst 1	:231 :463 1:112 1:372 4↑	Alw 25000	9 10 711 45 21½ 13	Day P	114		*1.50	85-23	Blushing John1143Flippable114hdZarbyev1146½ Wide	11
	Previously trained by Francois Boutin										
5Nov88- 7CD	gd 1Ⓣ	:233 :472 1:123 1:383 3↑	BC Mile-G1	5 8 1012 1215 1123 1030	Day P	123		2.00e	66-04	Miesque1234Steinlen126hdSimply Majestic1261¼ Outrun	12
4Sep88♦ Longchamp(Fr)	sf *1Ⓣ RH	1:403 3↑	Prix du Moulin de Longchamp-G1 Stk243000	49	Mosse G	123		8.50		Soviet Star128hdMiesque1245Gabina1204 Rated in 6th,rallied to lead 2f out,headed and weakened 1f out	7
14Jun88♦ Ascot(GB)	gd 1Ⓣ RH	1:392	St. James's Palace Stakes-G1 Stk290000	43½	Head F	126		7.50		Persian Heights1261½Raykour126½Caerwent1261½ Tracked leader,one-pace through stretch	7
29May88♦ Longchamp(Fr)	sf *1⅛ Ⓣ RH	1:54	Prix Jean Prat-G1 Stk146000	42¼	Head F	128		1.20		Lapierre1281½Fijar Tango128½Triteamtri128nk Rated at rear,7th 2½f out,5th 1f out,evenly late	9

8May88♦ Longchamp(Fr)	fm*1Ⓣ RH	1:37 1	Poule d'Essai des Poulains-G1 Stk298000	1no	Head F	128	*.60e	Blushing John128noFrench Stress128 2Tay Wharf128 1 Trailed,progress 3f out,angled out to lead 1f out,all out	10
17Apr88♦ Longchamp(Fr)	yl *1Ⓣ RH	1:41 3	Prix de Fontainebleau-G3 Stk51300	1 2	Head F	128	*1.40	Blushing John128 2Triteamtri128½Soviet Lad128hd Led throughout,quickened 2½f out,clear 1f out,ridden out	7
11Nov87♦ Saint-Cloud(Fr)	sf *1¼Ⓣ LH	2:20 3	Criterium de Saint-Cloud-G1 Stk89300	34½	Head F	123	*.70	Waki River123½Hours After123 4Blushing John123½ Unhurried in 5th,late gain to take 3rd near line	9
3Oct87♦ Longchamp(Fr)	fm*1⅛Ⓣ RH	1:51 1	Prix Saint Roman-G3 Stk47200	1 4	St Martin Y	123	*.60	Blushing John123 4Triteamtri123nkTruly Special123 1½ Rated in 4th,led over 1f out,quickly clear,handily	9
13Sep87♦ Longchamp(Fr)	gd *1Ⓣ RH	1:42	Prix de Villebon Mdn (FT)21300	1 1	Head F	123	3.60	Blushing John123 1Reve Dore123 1Lytrump123no Tracked in 3rd,led before halfway,clear over 1f out,ridden out	7

Bold 'n Determined

b. f. 1977, by Bold and Brave (Bold Ruler)–Pidi, by Determine

Lifetime record: 20 16 2 0 $949,599

Own.– Saron Stable
Br.– G.E. Layton (Ky)
Tr.– Neil Drysdale

24Apr81- 7Kee	fst 1 1/16	:24 2 :48 4 1:12 2 1:43 4 3↑	Ⓕ Bewitch 58k	2 1 1 1 1½ 1hd 1nk	Delahoussaye E	121	*.30	87-19	Bold'nDtrmind121nkLikely Exchange113 6½Save Wild Life110 4	Driving	5
8Apr81- 9OP	fst 1 1/16	:23 3 :46 2 1:11 1 1:44 1 4↑	Ⓕ Apple Blossom H-G2	3 1 1½ 1hd 1hd 1hd	Delahoussaye E	124	*.30	87-20	Bold 'n Determined124hdLa Bonzo111 3¼Karla's Enough119 3½	Fully extended	7
30Mar81- 9OP	fst 6f	:21 4 :45 2 1:10 4↑	Ⓕ Alw 30000	4 4 44½ 1 1 1 4 1 6	Maple E	113	*.30	95-20	Bld'nDtrmnd113 6RunKy.Run121 2½HmpnsSyn116 1¼	Ridden out	5
3Jan81- 8SA	fst 7f	:21 4 :44 1 1:08 4 1:21 2	Ⓕ La Brea 54k	4 1 31½ 3 2 1hd 2no	Delahoussaye E	125	*.40	93-10	Dynamite114noBold'nDetermined125 6Pachn114 2½	Just missed	5
9Nov80- 8SA	fm 1¼Ⓣ	:45 2 1:09 4 1:34 3 1:59 1 3↑	Ⓕ Yellow Ribbon Inv-G1	2 2 2 5 3 3 31½ 4 5	Delahoussaye E	119	*1.20	86-09	Kilijaro123¾Ack'sSecret123 1¼QueentoConqur123½	Weakened	10
25Oct80- 7Kee	fst 1⅛	:47 3 1:11 2 1:36 2 1:49 1 3↑	Ⓕ Spinster-G1	5 2 3 1 2hd 1hd 1nk	Delahoussaye E	119	*.30	91-20	Bold'nDetermind119nkLoveSgn119 7¼LklyExchng123¾	Driving	6
16Oct80- 7Kee	fst *7f	1:26 1 3↑	Ⓕ Alw 29750	1 5 1hd 1 1 1 2 16¾	Delahoussaye E	120	*.10	92-20	Boldn'Determined120 6¾ViteView120 1¼Shawn'sGl120 4	Handily	6
10Sep80- 8Bel	fst 1	:23 2 :46 1 1:10 4 1:35 2 3↑	Ⓕ Maskette-G1	1 2 22½ 1hd 2hd 1no	Delahoussaye E	122	10.40	91-22	Bold'nDetrmined122noGenuineRisk118 6¾LovSgn120½	Driving	5
28Jun80- 8Bel	fst 1½	:49 4 1:14 3 2:06 2 2:31 4	Ⓕ C C A Oaks-G1	2 3 2hd 1hd 3½ 1hd	Delahoussaye E	121	*1.20	61-25	Bold 'n Determind121hdErin'sWord121hdFarewell Letter121 2¼	Driving	7
8Jun80- 8Bel	sly 1⅛	:46 1 1:11 1 1:36 3 1:49 3	Ⓕ Mother Goose-G1	8 3 3 3 1½ 2hd 2hd	Delahoussaye E	121	*.50	79-23	Sugar and Spice121hdBold'nDetrmind121 8¾Erin's Word121 3½	Gamely	8
24May80- 8Bel	fst 1	:22 2 :44 4 1:09 3 1:36 4	Ⓕ Acorn-G1	7 3 2½ 1 1 1 2 12¾	Delahoussaye E	121	*.40	84-17	Bold'nDetermind121 2¾MiteyLively121 1¼Sugar andSpice121 3½	Driving	8
2May80- 8CD	fst 1 1/16	:24 2 :48 3 1:13 3 1:44 4	Ⓕ Ky Oaks-G1	2 1 1½ 1hd 11½ 11½	Delahoussaye E	121	*.60	84-18	Bold'nDetermind121 1½Mitey Lively121½Honest and True121 3	Driving	8
5Apr80- 9OP	fst 1 1/16	:23 1 :46 4 1:11 4 1:45 1	Ⓕ Fantasy-G1	3 2 1hd 1½ 11½ 12¼	Delahoussaye E	121	*1.10	82-20	Bold 'nDetermind121 2¼Satin Ribera115 4Honest and True118 7	Drew clear	7
9Mar80- 8SA	fst 1 1/16	:22 2 :45 1:09 3 1:41 1	Ⓕ S Susana-G1	6 2 2 10 2 2 3½ 1½	Delahoussaye E	115	3.50	95-10	Bold'nDetermined115½StreetBllt115nkTblHnds115 12	Just up	7
23Feb80- 8SA	fst 7f	:21 3 :44 1 1:09 2 1:22 2	Ⓕ S Ynez-G2	1 6 64½ 6 7 44½ 4 2	Delahoussaye E	121	2.10	89-14	Table Hands124hdStreet Ballet119 1¼Hazel R.119¾	Rallied	7
30Jan80- 8SA	gd 6f	:21 4 :44 4 :57 1:09 4	Ⓕ Pasadena 53k	4 1 3 2 3½ 1hd 12¼	Delahoussaye E	121	*.80	90-21	Bld'nDetrmnd121 2¼Thundrt116nkBckAtTwo115 4½	Drew clear	5
21Oct79- 8SA	gd 1 1/16	:23 :47 1:12 4 1:46 1	Ⓕ Oak Leaf-G2	7 5 53¾ 2hd 12½ 1 3	Cordero A Jr	115	1.80	70-28	Bold'nDetrmined115 3HazelR.115 1¼ArcadesAmbo115 2	Driving	8
12Oct79- 4Bel	sly 1	:23 :46 2 1:11 4 1:39 1	Ⓕ Alw 18000	5 2 21½ 2½ 1 2 1 5	Cordero A Jr	115	*1.30	72-24	Bold'nDetermind115 5Tell a Secret115½Two Cents Extra115 11	Driving	5
1Oct79- 7Med	sly 6f	:22 1 :45 4 1:11	Ⓕ Alw 14000	3 4 4 5 3 4 1hd 1 4	Cordero A Jr	114	2.70	90-16	Bld'nDetrmind114 4LoaddGun117 9SproutdRy112 1½	Drew out	7
3May79- 4Hol	fst 5f	:22 :45 3 :57 2	Ⓕ Md Sp Wt	6 1 3 2 3 1 3 2 1hd	Delahoussaye E	115	3.40	93-14	Bold'nDetrmind115hdOvrdrawnLdy115 2½AudaciousFinance115½	Driving	7

Brave Raj

dkbbr. f. 1984, by Rajab (Jaipur)–Bravest Yet, by Bravo

Lifetime record: 9 6 1 0 $933,650

Own.– Dolly Green
Br.– Dr W.S. Karutz (Fla)
Tr.– Melvin F. Stute

14Dec86- 8Hol	fst 1	:22 1 :44 4 1:09 3 1:36 1	Hol Futurity-G1	8 5 31½ 3 3 52½ 53¼	Valenzuela PA	118	*1.70	79-18	TemperateSl121nkAlyshb121nkMstrfulAdvoct121 2¼	Lugged in	12
1Nov86- 2SA	fst 1 1/16	:22 1 :45 3 1:10 1 1:43 1	Ⓕ BC Juv Fillies-G1	4 4 4 6 3 2 13½ 15½	Valenzuela PA	119	4.00	85-13	Brave Raj119 5½Tappiano119 3½Saros Brig119 1¾	Driving	12
12Oct86- 9Crc	fst 1 1/16	:24 :48 1 1:13 4 1:48 1	ⒻⓇ My Dear Girl 400k	3 2 2 1 1 4 1 4 1¾	Valenzuela PA	120	*.50	78-14	BraveRaj120¾AddedElgnc120 2½BlusCourt120 7	Drifted,lasted	13
21Sep86- 9Crc	sly 7f	:22 1 :45 3 1:11 2 1:25	ⒻⓇ Susan's Girl 75k	4 5 2½ 2 1 1 4 14½	Valenzuela PA	118	*.50	91-16	BraveRaj118 4½CarolsInhertnc118 6ApplngOn118 9½	Ridden out	9
31Aug86- 8Dmr	fst 1	:22 :45 2 1:10 1 1:35 4	Ⓕ Dmr Debutante-G2	1 3 3½ 2½ 11½ 13½	Black CA	117	*1.50	89-12	BraveRaj117 3½RoadtoHappiness113noSoftCopy115 3½	Easily	7
18Aug86- 8Dmr	fst 7f	:22 :44 3 1:09 2 1:22 3	Ⓕ Sorrento-G3	5 5 52½ 42½ 3½ 11¼	Valenzuela PA	117	*1.90	92-14	Brave Raj117 1¼Breech117 2½Footy121 1¾	Lugged in	10
6Aug86- 8Dmr	fst 6f	:21 3 :44 4 :56 4 1:10	Ⓕ Jr Miss 55k	9 9 6 3 52½ 43½ 2¾	Valenzuela PA	117	*1.60e	87-13	Footy114¾Brave Raj117hdEvil Elaine114 2½	Off in tangle	10
4Jly86- 7Hol	fst 6f	:21 2 :45 :57 1 1:10	Ⓕ Landaluce-G3	6 9 76½ 75¾ 5 8 59¾	Valenzuela PA	116	10.30	84-09	DelicateVin116 2AnythngforLov114 1½PurduQun119 5	No threat	9
Previously owned by Alben Partnership; previously trained by Ben Perkins Jr											
22May86- 5GS	fst 5f	:22 3 :46 2 :59	Ⓕ Md Sp Wt	2 1 1 3 12½ 1 5 17½	Thomas DB	116	10.00	86-22	BrveRaj116 7½Daremightythngs116 1½Wondcor116 3	Ridden out	7

Brown Bess

dbbr. f. 1982, by Petrone (Prince Taj)–Chickadee, by Windy Sands

Lifetime record: 36 16 8 6 $1,300,920

Own.– Calbourne Stable
Br.– Calbourne Farm (Cal)
Tr.– Charles J. Jenda

6Oct90- 8BM	fm *1⅛Ⓣ	:46 2 1:10 4 1:36 1 1:46 2 3↑	Ⓕ Cal Jockey Club H-G3	5 3 3 5 3 3 1 2 2nk	Kaenel JL	LB	120	*.90	98-12	Sweet Roberta115nkBrown Bess120 3Oeilladine114 4	2nd best	6
18Aug90- 8Dmr	fm 1⅛Ⓣ	:47 3 1:11 4 1:36 3 1:49 3↑	Ⓕ Ramona H-G1	5 4 4 3 5 3 64¼ 5 5	Kaenel JL	LB	122	*2.10	88-10	DoubleWedge114¾RluctntGust117 3Nkshk116no	4-wide stretch	8
16Jun90- 8GG	fm 1⅜Ⓣ	:48 2 1:13 1 1:37 4 2:15 3 3↑	Golden Gate H-G2	11 5 47½ 33½ 3 2 43½	Kaenel JL		117	*3.50	89-10	PetiteIle113 1½Valdali114 1PleasantVrty116 1	Brushed drive	11
12May90- 8GG	fm 1⅜Ⓣ	:48 3 1:14 1:38 2 2:15 3 3↑	Ⓕ Yerba Buena H 150k	3 1 1 2 1hd 2hd 31¼	Kaenel JL		124	*.70	92-09	Petite Ile118¾Double Wedge112½Brown Bess124 4	Set pace	5
31Mar90- 8SA	fm 1¼Ⓣ	:45 1:10 1:34 1:58 2 4↑	Ⓕ S Barbara H-G1	2 3 3 2 1hd 1½ 1no	Kaenel JL		123	*.70	96-09	BrwnBss123noRoyalTouch121hdDoubleWdg111 2¾	Game winner	5
11Mar90- 8SA	fm 1⅛Ⓣ	:48 1:11 3 1:35 2 1:47 4 4↑	Ⓕ S Ana H-G1	4 2 2 1 2 1 1hd 3hd	Kaenel JL		123	*1.30	86-15	Annoconnr119hdRoylTouch121noBrwnBss123 1	Strong effort	7
12Nov89- 8SA	fm 1¼Ⓣ	:45 2 1:09 1 1:33 2 1:57 3 3↑	Ⓕ Yellow Ribbon Inv'l-G1	6 7 64½ 3½ 1hd 11¾	Kaenel JL		123	4.10	108-00	BrownBess123 1¾Drby'sDughtr119½ColordoDncr119 2	Hand ride	11
7Oct89- 8BM	fm *1⅛Ⓣ	:47 1 1:11 4 1:36 3 1:47 3↑	Ⓕ Cal Jockey Club H-G3	2 3 3 2 31½ 1hd 1 1	Kaenel JL		120	*.90	95-17	Brown Bess120 1Nikishka115 2Gold Firecracker113 4	Driving	5
19Aug89- 8Dmr	fm 1⅛Ⓣ	:48 2 1:12 2 1:36 4 1:48 4 3↑	Ⓕ Ramona H-G1	5 2 2½ 2hd 2hd 1nk	Kaenel JL		117	5.00	89-11	Brown Bess117nkDaring Doone117½Galunpe118 1¼	Gamely	7
17Jun89- 8GG	fm 1⅜Ⓣ	:49 1:13 2 1:37 3 2:15 3↑	Golden Gate H-G2	2 1 1½ 1 2 11½ 32¼	Chapman TM		114	3.40	88-10	FranklyPerfect122nkPleasntVrty114 2BrwnBss114 2	Weakened	7
13May89- 8GG	fm 1⅜Ⓣ	:47 4 1:12 4 1:37 3 2:15 3 3↑	Ⓕ Yerba Buena H-G3	5 4 66½ 52½ 1 2 12¼	Kaenel JL		119	*1.50	87-20	BrownBss119 2¼Carmanetta114 4½FlttrngNws111hd	Wide rally	10
15Apr89- 8GG	fm 1⅛Ⓣ	:49 1 1:13 1 1:37 4 1:50 1 3↑	Ⓕ Countess Fager H-G3	1 6 64½ 63¾ 3 1 11½	Kaenel JL		117	2.40	97-15	Brown Bess117 1½Beat115 1Daring Doone113 1	Forced out 3/16	9
18Mar89- 8GG	sly 1 1/16⊗	:23 2 :46 3 1:10 1 1:42 2 3↑	Ⓕ Golden Poppy H-G3	1 5 73½ 54½ 3 2 22½	Kaenel JL		117	4.90	84-14	Invited Guest116 2½Brown Bess117¾Daloma116 3	Gamely	7
11Feb89- 8GG	gd 1	:23 3 :47 3 1:11 3 1:36 3 3↑	Ⓕ Princessnesian H 55k	5 1 1½ 2hd 2 3 3 10	Kaenel JL		118	*1.40	72-27	Novel Sprite114 7Lady Annabelle113 3Brown Bess118 1½	No late response	8
7Jan89- 8SA	fst 1⅛⊗	:47 1:11 1:36 1:48 4 4↑	Ⓕ San Gorgonio H-G2	1 3 32½ 41½ 6 11 516¾	Kaenel JL		118	6.90	68-14	NoReview117½Annoconnr122 2½WhiteMischifII116 1¾	Faltered	6

12Nov88- 8BM	gd	1⅛Ⓣ	:48^{1} 1:12 1:37^{2} 1:50^{2}	3↑ ⒻHillsborough H-G3	3	2	2$^{1\frac{1}{2}}$	2^{1}	1^{2}	1^{3}	Kaenel JL	116	2.90	88-14	BrownBess116^{3}Balbonella118$^{1\frac{1}{2}}$Griefnggrvton114^{2}	Hand ride	6
8Oct88- 8BM	fm	*1⅛Ⓣ	1:46^{3}	3↑ ⒻCal Jockey Club H-G3	10	2	2^{3}	2^{2}	2^{hd}	1$^{\frac{3}{4}}$	Kaenel JL	115	10.90	102-03	BrownBss115$^{\frac{3}{4}}$JungleDawn116$^{1\frac{1}{2}}$Choritzo120$^{\frac{1}{2}}$	Strong urging	10
4Sep88- 8BM	fm	1$\frac{1}{16}$Ⓣ	:23^{4} :49 1:13^{3} 1:42^{3}	3↑ ⒻTizna H 54k	3	1	1$^{\frac{1}{2}}$	1^{hd}	2^{hd}	2no	Kaenel JL	118	2.70	96-10	Davie'sLamb120^{no}BrwnBss118^{3}HollyDonna113^{2}	Just missed	7
20Aug88-11Bmf	fst	1$\frac{1}{16}$	:23 :46^{1} 1:09^{4} 1:42	3↑ ⒻLady Morvich H 32k	2	3	3$^{1\frac{1}{2}}$	2$^{\frac{1}{2}}$	1^{1}	1^{1}	Kaenel JL	120	3.20	82-16	Brown Bess120^{1}Chanango's Alibi119^{2}Stemware118^{1}		7
	Gamely under urging																
4Jly88-11Pln	fst	1$\frac{1}{16}$	:24^{4} :48^{4} 1:12^{1} 1:43^{4}	3↑ ⒻAlameda County H 32k	2	2	2^{hd}	1$^{\frac{1}{2}}$	1^{2}	2$^{\frac{1}{2}}$	Kaenel JL	120	*.90	84-16	Stemware115$^{\frac{1}{2}}$BrwnBess120^{3}Honeymoon Toast114^{2}	No match	6
4Jun88- 8GG	fm	1Ⓣ	:23^{3} :47^{3} 1:11^{4} 1:36^{2}	3↑ ⒻLakes & Flowers H 53k	6	3	3^{2}	2^{1}	1$^{1\frac{1}{2}}$	1^{2}	Baze RA	116	*1.40	85-17	Brown Bess116^{2}Chanango's Alibi115^{1}Miss Alto116^{1}	Wide	6
21May88- 8GG	fm	1Ⓣ	:23^{2} :47^{4} 1:12 1:36^{4}	3↑ Ⓕ[R]Star Ball Inv'l H 52k	8	4	3$^{1\frac{1}{2}}$	2^{hd}	1$^{\frac{1}{2}}$	1^{2}	Baze RA	116	*1.60	83-17	BrwnBess116^{2}Sovereign Answer113$^{\frac{3}{4}}$Griefnaggrevation116^{no}		9
	Restricted to horses stabled at Golden Gate Fields																
6Apr88- 8GG	fm	1$\frac{1}{16}$Ⓣ	:23^{2} :48^{4} 1:12^{3} 1:44^{1}	4↑ ⒻHandicap 24000	3	2	2^{2}	2^{1}	1^{1}	1no	Castaneda M	115	2.80	81-19	BrwnBess115^{no}MissMaiTai116$^{1\frac{1}{2}}$LurnLgh115$^{1\frac{1}{2}}$	Strong urging	5
17Mar88- 7GG	fm	1Ⓣ	:23^{1} :46^{4} 1:11^{2} 1:37^{2}	4↑ ⒻHandicap 22000	4	1	1$^{1\frac{1}{2}}$	1$^{\frac{1}{2}}$	1$^{\frac{1}{2}}$	4$^{2\frac{1}{2}}$	Castaneda M	115	5.40	77-21	Cruisin' Two Su116$^{1\frac{1}{2}}$Lauren Leigh115^{hd}Tender Force117^{1}		10
	Drifted out ⅛																
31Mar87- 8GG	fm	1Ⓣ	:23 :46^{3} 1:11^{1} 1:36	4↑ ⒻAlw 24000	4	5	5$^{3\frac{3}{4}}$	3$^{2\frac{1}{2}}$	1^{hd}	1$^{1\frac{1}{4}}$	Baze RA	115	*2.60	87-13	BrwnBss115$^{1\frac{1}{4}}$TndrForc115^{4}AbstrctEnrgy115$^{2\frac{1}{2}}$	Bumped start	8
12Mar87- 8GG	sly	1	:23^{2} :47 1:11^{3} 1:38^{4}	4↑ ⒻAlw 20000	3	3	3^{3}	3^{2}	2^{3}	2^{4}	Castaneda M	121	4.00	70-28	Pass All Hope116^{4}Brown Bess121^{2}River Char121^{1}	2nd best	7
8Feb87- 8BM	gd	1$\frac{1}{16}$Ⓣ	:23^{3} :48^{3} 1:13^{4} 1:45^{2}	4↑ ⒻPalo Alto H 55k	1	2	2$^{1\frac{1}{2}}$	1^{hd}	2^{hd}	3$^{2\frac{1}{2}}$	Castaneda M	114	4.20	73-21	RoyalRegatta120$^{\frac{1}{2}}$BrigadeSpecial113^{2}BrwnBss114^{2}	Weakened	9
17Jan87- 4BM	fm	1$\frac{1}{16}$Ⓣ	:23^{3} :48^{1} 1:13^{2} 1:45^{1}	4↑ ⒻInt'l Jockey's Cup 17k	7	3	4^{5}	1^{2}	1$^{1\frac{1}{2}}$	1^{2}	Eddery P	121	*.80	77-23	Brown Bess121^{2}Mia Rosa117^{nk}Golden Twenties117^{5}	Driving	8
14Dec86- 7BM	fst	1$\frac{1}{16}$	:22^{4} :46 1:10^{4} 1:43^{1}	3↑ ⒻAlw 17000	2	2	2^{2}	2^{1}	1^{2}	1^{4}	Castaneda M	115	3.60	76-17	Brown Bess115^{4}Bramble Dawn113$^{\frac{3}{4}}$Roberts Regal Girl115^{3}		10
	Stumbled start																
11Nov86- 6BM	fm	1Ⓣ	:23^{4} :47^{4} 1:12^{3} 1:38^{1}	3↑ ⒻAlw 20000	3	2	2^{1}	1^{hd}	1^{hd}	2no	Campbell BC	114	3.70	89-11	NobHillNative114^{no}BrownBess114^{2}GirlnBlu114^{4}	Just missed	6
22Oct86- 8BM	fm	7½fⓉ	:23^{2} :48 1:12^{3} 1:31^{3}	3↑ ⒻAlw 19000	1	1	3$^{\frac{1}{2}}$	1^{hd}	1^{hd}	2^{hd}	Campbell BC	114	4.00	86-14	Heartlifter117^{hd}Brown Bess114^{4}Soft Dawn108^{6}	Gamely	9
28Sep86- 9BM	gd	7½fⓉ	:23^{1} :46^{4} 1:11^{4} 1:30^{3}	3↑ ⒻClm 50000	3	4	4^{2}	4$^{2\frac{1}{2}}$	1^{hd}	2no	Campbell BC	114	52.60	91-08	GirlinBlue114^{no}BrownBess114$^{1\frac{1}{2}}$J.D.Canyon109^{1}	Just missed	10
10Sep86-11Bmf	fst	1	:22^{4} :46^{1} 1:10^{3} 1:36	3↑ ⒻAlw 17000	10	6	6$^{3\frac{3}{4}}$	5$^{4\frac{1}{2}}$	8^{17}	9$^{18\frac{1}{4}}$	Lamance C	118	13.00	70-22	Heartlifter114^{hd}Icy Run114^{5}Wooly Nan114$^{2\frac{1}{2}}$	Outrun	10
29Jly86- 7SR	fst	1	:22^{3} :45^{1} 1:10^{3} 1:37^{1}	3↑ ⒻMd Sp Wt	7	4	5^{2}	3^{2}	1^{hd}	1$^{1\frac{1}{2}}$	Lamance C	121	*1.90	86-17	BrownBess121$^{1\frac{1}{2}}$NorthernFey114$^{3\frac{1}{2}}$MuffettsSun114$^{\frac{1}{2}}$	Driving	8
16Jly86- 4Sol	fst	6f	:21^{4} :44^{4} :57^{2} 1:10^{2}	3↑ ⒻMd Sp Wt	8	5	5$^{4\frac{1}{2}}$	5$^{5\frac{1}{2}}$	3^{4}	3$^{2\frac{1}{2}}$	Lamance C	121	4.90	88-13	Whirling Too116^{no}Swift Victress116$^{2\frac{1}{2}}$Brown Bess121$^{1\frac{1}{2}}$		10
	Bumped start,pinched ⅝																
28Sep85- 2BM	fst	6f	:22^{4} :46 :58^{3} 1:11^{1}	3↑ Ⓕ[S]Md Sp Wt	6	7	7$^{5\frac{1}{2}}$	5$^{3\frac{1}{2}}$	5$^{3\frac{1}{2}}$	4^{5}	Lamance C	116	6.70	78-19	Donna's Terne116^{1}Manhattan Magic116$^{1\frac{1}{2}}$A Real Gasser116$^{2\frac{1}{2}}$		7
	Lacked rally																

Capote

dkbbr. c. 1984, by Seattle Slew (Bold Reasoning)–Too Bald, by Bald Eagle — **Lifetime record: 10 3 0 1 $714,470**

Own.– Beal & French Jr & Klein
Br.– North Ridge Farm (Ky)
Tr.– D. Wayne Lukas

10Oct87- 3SA	fst	6f	:21^{3} :44^{3} :56^{4} 1:09^{2}	3↑ Alw 34000	5	3	3^{2}	3^{3}	5^{8}	6$^{13\frac{1}{4}}$	McCarron CJ	114	*.80	78-17	Decore114$^{1\frac{1}{2}}$HotSauceBby115^{no}CaballodOro116^{hd}	Done early	6
2Sep87- 3Bel	fst	7f	:22^{3} :45^{2} 1:11 1:23^{4}	3↑ Alw 31000	1	1	1^{hd}	1$^{\frac{1}{2}}$	1^{hd}	4$^{3\frac{1}{2}}$	Cordero A Jr	114	*.50	79-16	Mr. Classic117^{1}Landyap113$^{1\frac{1}{4}}$Britton's Mill117$^{1\frac{1}{4}}$	Weakened	5
10Aug87- 6Sar	sly	7f	:22^{3} :45^{1} 1:09^{4} 1:22^{4}	3↑ Alw 29000	4	2	1^{hd}	1^{hd}	2^{2}	3$^{6\frac{3}{4}}$	Cordero A Jr	115	*1.70	81-19	Quick Call114$^{\frac{3}{4}}$Leo Castelli112^{6}Capote115^{7}	Weakened	6
2May87- 8CD	fst	1¼	:46^{2} 1:11 1:36^{4} 2:03^{2}	Ky Derby-G1	5	2	1$^{1\frac{1}{2}}$	10$^{5\frac{1}{4}}$	16^{23}	-	Cordero A Jr	126	6.30e	--	Alysheba126$^{\frac{3}{4}}$Bet Twice126$^{2\frac{1}{4}}$Avies Copy126^{nk}	Eased	17
18Apr87- 8Aqu	my	1⅛	:47 1:11^{3} 1:36^{2} 1:49	Wood Memorial Inv'l-G1	5	1	1^{1}	1$^{1\frac{1}{2}}$	3^{4}	4$^{7\frac{3}{4}}$	Cordero A Jr	126	*1.30	82-15	Gulch126^{hd}Gone West126^{6}Shawklit Won126$^{1\frac{3}{4}}$	Gave way	8
4Apr87- 8Aqu	sly	1	:22^{2} :44^{2} 1:08^{1} 1:34^{3}	Gotham-G2	5	1	2^{hd}	2^{2}	3$^{5\frac{1}{2}}$	4$^{9\frac{1}{2}}$	Day P	123	*1.40	83-21	Gone West114^{1}Shawklit Won114$^{8\frac{1}{2}}$Gulch123^{hd}	Weakened	9
1Nov86- 1SA	fst	1$\frac{1}{16}$	:22^{2} :45^{4} 1:10^{2} 1:43^{4}	BC Juvenile-G1	3	1	1$^{1\frac{1}{2}}$	1^{1}	1$^{2\frac{1}{2}}$	1$^{1\frac{1}{4}}$	Pincay L Jr	122	*2.40	82-13	Capote122$^{1\frac{1}{4}}$Qualify122$^{1\frac{1}{4}}$Alysheba122$^{2\frac{1}{4}}$	Driving	13
11Oct86- 8SA	fst	1$\frac{1}{16}$	:22^{3} :46^{1} 1:11 1:45^{1}	Norfolk-G1	3	1	1$^{1\frac{1}{2}}$	1$^{\frac{1}{2}}$	1$^{1\frac{1}{2}}$	1$^{1\frac{3}{4}}$	Pincay L Jr	118	3.70	75-17	Capote118$^{1\frac{3}{4}}$Gulch118$^{\frac{3}{4}}$Gold on Green118$^{2\frac{3}{4}}$	Driving	6
3Oct86- 6SA	fst	6f	:21^{4} :44^{3} :56^{3} 1:09^{2}	Md Sp Wt	1	5	1$^{2\frac{1}{2}}$	1^{5}	1^{7}	1^{11}	Pincay L Jr	118	*3.10	91-17	Cpte118^{11}WindwoodLane118$^{3\frac{1}{2}}$BooBoo'sBuckroo118^{hd}	Easily	12
1Sep86- 6Dmr	fst	6f	:22 :44^{4} :57 1:09^{4}	Md Sp Wt	8	4	3$^{\frac{1}{2}}$	3^{5}	11^{16}	11$^{21\frac{3}{4}}$	Shoemaker W	118	4.00	67-13	SpecialTrick118^{5}SwordCharger118$^{\frac{3}{4}}$CharlieZee118^{4}	Greenly	12

Chief's Crown

b. c. 1982, by Danzig (Northern Dancer)–Six Crowns, by Secretariat — **Lifetime record: 21 12 3 3 $2,191,168**

Own.– Star Crown Stable
Br.– Carl Rosen (Ky)
Tr.– Roger Laurin

2Nov85- 7Aqu	fst	1¼	:46^{4} 1:11 1:36^{2} 2:00^{4}	3↑ BC Classic-G1	5	3	4$^{4\frac{1}{2}}$	2^{hd}	3$^{2\frac{1}{2}}$	4$^{9\frac{3}{4}}$	MacBeth D	122	*1.80	82-10	ProudTruth122^{hd}GateDancr126^{4}Trkomn122$^{5\frac{3}{4}}$	Bid,weakened	8
13Oct85- 6Bel	gd	1Ⓣ	:23^{1} :46 1:10^{2} 1:36^{2}	3↑ Handicap 40000	2	4	3^{5}	3^{6}	3^{4}	1$^{2\frac{1}{2}}$	MacBeth D	125	*.70	83-25	Chief's Crown125$^{2\frac{1}{2}}$Intensify114$^{2\frac{1}{2}}$Smile116^{12}	Ridden out	5
14Sep85- 8Bel	fst	1¼	:47 1:11 1:36^{1} 2:01^{1}	3↑ Marlboro Cup H-G1	8	5	6^{4}	3$^{\frac{1}{2}}$	1$^{\frac{1}{2}}$	1^{nk}	MacBeth D	119	10.50	92-09	Chief'sCrwn119^{nk}GateDancr125$^{\frac{3}{4}}$Vanlandnghm122^{hd}	Driving	9
31Aug85- 8Bel	gd	1⅛	:46^{1} 1:10 1:34^{1} 1:46^{3}	3↑ Woodward-G1	3	4	4$^{6\frac{1}{2}}$	4$^{4\frac{1}{2}}$	3^{5}	3$^{5\frac{1}{2}}$	Pincay L Jr	121	1.90	88-10	TrackBarrn123^{4}Vanlndinghm123$^{1\frac{1}{2}}$Chf'sCrwn121$^{\frac{1}{2}}$	Weakened	6
17Aug85- 8Sar	fst	1¼	:48^{1} 1:11^{4} 1:36^{1} 2:01^{1}	Travers-G1	3	4	4$^{4\frac{1}{2}}$	3^{1}	1$^{\frac{1}{2}}$	1$^{2\frac{1}{4}}$	Cordero A Jr	126	*1.20	94-08	Chief's Crown126$^{2\frac{1}{4}}$Turkoman126^{3}Skip Trial126$^{\frac{1}{2}}$	Driving	7
3Aug85- 5Sar	fm	1[T]	:24^{3} :48^{2} 1:12^{2} 1:36^{3}	Tell 55k	4	3	5^{3}	3^{2}	2^{hd}	1$^{\frac{3}{4}}$	Cordero A Jr	122	*.70	93-09	[D]Chief'sCrwn122$^{\frac{3}{4}}$ExclusivePartnr115$^{4\frac{1}{2}}$ExplosiveDancr115^{nk}		6
	Swung out turn;Disqualified and placed fourth																
8Jun85- 8Bel	my	1½	:47 1:10^{4} 2:01^{2} 2:27	Belmont-G1	1	4	4$^{2\frac{1}{2}}$	1^{hd}	3^{2}	3^{5}	Cordero A Jr	126	*2.00	80-12	CremeFrach126$^{\frac{1}{2}}$Stphn'sOdyssy126$^{4\frac{1}{2}}$Chf'sCrwn126^{4}	Weakened	11
18May85- 8Pim	fst	1$\frac{3}{16}$	:45^{1} 1:09^{2} 1:34^{1} 1:53^{2}	Preakness-G1	3	5	4^{5}	2^{1}	1^{1}	2^{hd}	MacBeth D	126	*1.00	101-10	Tank's Prospect126^{hd}Chief's Crown126$^{2\frac{1}{2}}$Eternal Prince126^{3}		11
	Just failed																
4May85- 8CD	fst	1¼	:45^{4} 1:09^{3} 1:34^{4} 2:00^{1}	Ky Derby-G1	2	2	2^{6}	2^{6}	2^{5}	3$^{5\frac{3}{4}}$	MacBeth D	126	*1.20	90-08	Spend a Buck126$^{5\frac{1}{4}}$Stephan's Odyssey126$^{\frac{1}{2}}$Chief's Crown126^{nk}		13
	Lacked rally																
25Apr85- 7Kee	fst	1⅛	:48^{2} 1:12 1:35^{4} 1:47^{3}	Blue Grass-G1	2	1	1$^{1\frac{1}{2}}$	1^{1}	1^{3}	1$^{5\frac{1}{2}}$	MacBeth D	121	*.30	99-16	Chief'sCrwn121$^{5\frac{1}{2}}$FloatngRsrv121^{hd}BnnrBob121^{11}	Hand ride	4
30Mar85-11Hia	fst	1⅛	:48^{4} 1:12^{2} 1:36^{1} 1:48^{2}	Flamingo-G1	5	1	1^{hd}	1^{1}	1$^{2\frac{1}{2}}$	1^{1}	MacBeth D	122	1.30	90-12	[D]Chief'sCrown122^{1}ProudTruth122^{nk}Stephan's Odyssey122$^{3\frac{1}{2}}$		8
	Disqualified and placed second - reversed by Fla. board																
2Mar85-10GP	fst	7f	:22^{3} :45^{1} 1:09^{3} 1:22^{2}	Swale 51k	9	2	2^{hd}	2^{hd}	1^{1}	1$^{3\frac{1}{4}}$	MacBeth D	122	*.30	92-15	Chief'sCrwn122$^{3\frac{1}{4}}$CremeFrch117$^{3\frac{1}{2}}$ChrokFst113^{nk}	Ridden out	9
10Nov84- 1Hol	fst	1	:22^{2} :45 1:10 1:36^{1}	©BC Juvenile-G1	5	6	6$^{4\frac{3}{4}}$	3$^{2\frac{1}{2}}$	2^{1}	1$^{\frac{3}{4}}$	MacBeth D	122	*.70	--	Chief'sCrown122$^{\frac{3}{4}}$Tank'sProspect122$^{\frac{3}{4}}$SpndBck122$^{6\frac{1}{2}}$	Driving	10
27Oct84- 8SA	fst	1$\frac{1}{16}$	:23^{1} :46^{3} 1:10^{4} 1:42^{2}	Norfolk-G1	6	2	2$^{\frac{1}{2}}$	1^{hd}	1^{hd}	1$^{1\frac{1}{2}}$	MacBeth D	118	*.30	89-13	Chief'sCrwn118$^{1\frac{1}{2}}$MatthewT.Parker118^{9}VivaMx118^{hd}	Driving	6
6Oct84- 8Bel	fst	1	:22^{1} :45^{2} 1:10^{3} 1:36^{3}	Cowdin-G1	4	4	2^{1}	1^{2}	1^{3}	1^{6}	MacBeth D	122	*.50	82-17	Chief'sCrwn122^{6}BioncLght122$^{12\frac{1}{2}}$ScrptOho122$^{1\frac{1}{4}}$	Ridden out	8
15Sep84- 5Bel	sly	7f	:22^{4} :46 1:10^{2} 1:23^{1}	Futurity-G1	5	2	6^{8}	6^{4}	3^{4}	2^{1}	MacBeth D	122	*.70	85-18	SpectacularLove122^{1}Chief'sCrown122$^{3\frac{1}{4}}$Mugzy's Rullah122$^{2\frac{3}{4}}$		8
	Wide str.;Previously owned by A. Rosen																
26Aug84- 8Sar	fst	6½f	:21^{4} :44^{4} 1:09^{2} 1:16	Hopeful-G1	3	4	3$^{3\frac{1}{2}}$	3$^{\frac{1}{2}}$	1$^{\frac{1}{2}}$	1$^{3\frac{3}{4}}$	MacBeth D	122	*1.10	92-15	Chif'sCrwn122$^{3\frac{3}{4}}$TffnyIc122$^{3\frac{3}{4}}$Mugzy'sRullh122$^{\frac{1}{2}}$	Ridden out	9
3Aug84- 8Sar	fst	6f	:22^{3} :46 1:10^{1}	Sar Spl-G2	4	3	3^{3}	2^{hd}	1^{hd}	1$^{2\frac{3}{4}}$	MacBeth D	117	*2.10	89-19	Chief's Crown117$^{2\frac{3}{4}}$Do It Again Dan117^{hd}Sky Command122$^{\frac{3}{4}}$		6
	Ridden out																
5Jly84- 6Bel	fst	5½f	:22^{2} :45^{4} :58 1:04^{2}	Md Sp Wt	5	1	1^{hd}	2^{hd}	1^{1}	1^{5}	MacBeth D	118	*1.10	93-15	Chief'sCrown118^{5}DesertWar118$^{2\frac{1}{4}}$TigerBiddr118^{4}	Ridden out	9
22Jun84- 4Bel	fst	5½f	:22^{1} :46^{1} :59 1:05^{3}	Md Sp Wt	1	1	4$^{3\frac{1}{2}}$	4$^{6\frac{1}{2}}$	3$^{4\frac{1}{2}}$	2^{1}	MacBeth D	118	5.20	86-21	SecretaryGeneral118^{1}Chif'sCrown118$^{1\frac{1}{4}}$TffnyIc118^{9}	Rallied	10
13Jun84- 4Bel	fst	5f	:22^{4} :46^{2} :58^{4}	Md Sp Wt	8	8	4$^{6\frac{1}{2}}$	6^{13}	5^{13}	4$^{11\frac{1}{2}}$	Cordero A Jr	118	3.10	81-18	Don't Fool With Me118^{8}Attribute118^{nk}Mount Reality118$^{3\frac{1}{4}}$		8
	Carried out																

Chinook Pass

dkbbr. g. 1979, by Native Born (Native Dancer)–Yu Turn, by Turn–to

Lifetime record: 25 16 4 1 $480,073

Own.– Hi Yu Stable
Br.– Hi Yu Stable (Wash)
Tr.– Laurie N. Anderson

21Aug83- 9Lga	fst 1	:22 :443 1:093 1:353	3↑ Lga Mile H 182k	6 1 16 15 14 16	Pincay L Jr	125	*1.15	91-25	ChinookPass1256TravellngVctor118noErthquck119nk	In hand	14
31Jly83- 8Dmr	fst 6f	:214 :442 :561 1:083	3↑ Bing Crosby H 54k	5 1 13 15 17 18	Pincay L Jr	125	*.50	95-20	ChnkPss1258VagabondSong116 2½HaughtyButNc1152	Easily	7
23Apr83- 8SA	fst 6½f	:211 :434 1:083 1:152	4↑ San Simeon H 66k	7 1 16 15 15 14	Pincay L Jr	124	*1.30	93-16	ChnookPss1244Shanekite118 1¼Earthquack121hd	Ridden out	7
13Mar83-11TuP	fst 6f	:21 :431 :56 1:092	3↑ Phoenix Gold Cup-G3	1 4 1hd 1hd 12 53½	Pincay L Jr	126	*.40	85-19	BirthdaySong115½Dave'sFriend1211SonofDodo115 1½	Weakened	9
2Mar83- 8SA	sly 6½f	:211 :432 1:074 1:143	4↑ Potrero Grande H 64k	5 1 15 12½ 14 13½	Pincay L Jr	123	*.60	97-15	ChnookPass123 3½HaughtyButNice1154TheCaptan114no	Easily	5
			Previously trained by Bud Klokstad								
26Jan83- 8SA	gd 6½f	:214 :443 1:094 1:164	4↑ Sierra Madre H 66k	5 1 15 15 12½ 1nk	Pincay L Jr	121	*.70	75-22	ChinookPass121nkFightingFt116 1½PolcInspctor1202	Driving	7
2Jan83- 8SA	fst 7f	:221 :443 1:082 1:21	Malibu-G2	7 5 11½ 1½ 45½ 616¼	McCarron CJ	120	1.90	79-13	TimetoExplode117nkPrinceSpellbnd1235WaveringMnrch1232	Lunged at start	8
26Dec82- 8SA	fst 6f	:21 :431 :544 1:073	2↑ Palos Verdes H 67k	6 2 14 13½ 13½ 13½	Pincay L Jr	120	*1.60	100-08	ChinookPss120 3½GenralJmmy112¾Unprdctbl1222	Ridden out	8
4Dec82- 8Hol	fm 5fⓉ	:221 :441 :56	3↑ Meteor H 54k	4 4 12 12 13 13	Pincay L Jr	117	*.80	100-05	ChinookPss1173Dv'sFrnd1171FortClgry1151	Bumped,driving	7
14Nov82- 9Hol	fst 6f	:213 :441 :56 1:083	3↑ Nat Sprint Ch (Div 2) 114k	2 8 31½ 3½ 31½ 32	Shoemaker W	112	2.90	92-12	Unpredictabl120 1½RmmbrJohn120½ChnkPss112hd	Poor start	8
25Oct82-10LA	fst 6f	:21 :443 :571 1:10	3↑ Orange Coast H 26k	5 1 13 1hd 1½ 2nk	Davidson JR	114	2.90	95-16	PompeiCourt122nkChnkPss1142ToB.orNot119no	Just missed	6
25Sep82- 9Lga	my 1 1/16	:233 :463 1:122 1:46	Puget Sound H 24k	7 1 14 12 1hd 27	Frazier B	120	*.90	62-32	IronBilly1187ChinookPass120hdBabaAdhem113 1½	Little left	7
17Sep82- 9Lga	fst 5f	:212 :432 :551	3↑ Handicap 12000	4 2 12 13 15 16½	Davidson JR	113	*.25	104-14	ChnookPss113 6½MyOmen105 1½LotoCanada1172	Saved ground	6
22Aug82- 9Lga	fst 1	:221 :451 1:102 1:353	3↑ Lga Mile H-G2	5 1 1½ 1 2hd 21½	Davidson JR	113	7.95	89-20	PompeiiCrt121 1½ChinookPss113noPolcInspctor1194	Gamely	11
8Aug82- 9Lga	fst 6½f	:211 :434 1:083 1:15	3↑ Governor's H 35k	7 1 14 13 12½ 12	Baze G	118	2.15	94-15	ChinookPass1182RoyalHudson114noTilttheBlnc123no	Driving	8
25Jly82- 9Lga	fst 6f	:213 :441 :562 1:091	3↑ Speed H 29k	7 2 11½ 1½ 12 1½	Baze G	114	*1.75	90-17	ChinookPass114½Foolish Owners1173Che112 1½	Saved ground	9
5Jly82- 9Lga	fst 1	:222 :453 1:11 1:371	Seattle Slew H 28k	7 1 1hd 57 - -	Baze G	123	*2.95	- -	NightCommand121nkFabulsOmen1202SkiRacr118 1½	Distanced	14
1May82- 9Lga	fst 5½f	:213 :442 :562 1:022	Alw 12000	5 2 13½ 13 13 18	Baze G	116	*.70	100-16	Chinook Pass1168Ski Racer120 5½Fabulous Omen11413	Easily	6
10Apr82- 7PM	fst 6f	:221 :46 :581 1:11	Alw 3000	5 2 11 12 11 11	Baze G	120	*.40	92-18	ChinookPss1201LighthouseJim120 4½FamilyFox117 1½	Handily	7
20Mar82-10PM	fst 6f	:221 :45 :574 1:112	Alw 3000	2 5 13 15 15 12	Taketa J	117	*.30	90-16	ChinookPass1172FamilyFox1202UpYourIncome120½	Driving	6
30Aug81- 9Lga	fst 6½f	:213 :443 1:104 1:172	ⓈGottstein Fut 98k	5 4 1½ 12½ 1hd 1117	Loseth C	121	*1.20	65-23	Belle of Ranier1181Sarada Spy1213Long Gyland121hd	Broke slowly,rushed up,gave way str	14
12Aug81- 9Lga	fst 6f	:212 :443 :57 1:102	Stripling 24k	9 1 13½ 13 14 11½	Loseth C	121	*1.30	84-20	ChnookPss121 1½LongGylnd117noHotSummrKnght118 2½	Driving	9
11Jly81- 9Lga	gd 5½f	:22 :451 :574 1:042	©Wash Stallion 26k	8 1 12 12½ 14 14	Sorenson D	118	5.70	90-21	ChnookPss1184SrdSpy120 2½ChngT118 2½	Saved ground,easily	9
27Jun81- 4Lga	fst 5½f	:221 :453 :582 1:051	©ⓈMd Sp Wt	2 2 11½ 12 14 12	Sorenson D	120	1.95	86-18	ChinookPass1202SaradaSpy1204FlashYourWallet1201	Driving	8
20Jun81- 4Lga	sl 5½f	:22 :47 1:003 1:074	©ⓈMd Sp Wt	1 1 14 12 13 1¾	Baze MB	120	5.95	73-29	[D]ChnkPss120¾TopThought120hdHotSummrKnght120hd	Driving	7
			Disqualified and placed second								

Christmas Past

gr. f. 1979, by Grey Dawn II (Herbager)–Yule Log, by Bold Ruler

Lifetime record: 15 8 2 3 $563,670

Own.– Cynthia Phipps
Br.– Cynthia Phipps (Ky)
Tr.– Angel Penna Jr

26Feb83-10GP	fst 1¼	:481 1:131 1:373 2:023	3↑ Gulf Park H-G1	11 10 911 63¼ 3½ 1nk	Velasquez J	117	*1.30	83-19	ChristmasPast117nkCraftyProspctor115¾Rvlro120 2½	Driving	12
11Feb83- 9GP	fst 1 1/16	:24 :473 1:113 1:423	4↑ ⒻAlw 25000	8 4 44 31½ 11 15	Vasquez J	122	*.30	88-21	ChristmsPst1225Acharmer1159SheCommandum117nk	Handily	8
9Oct82- 8Bel	fst 1½	:473 1:114 2:04 2:311	3↑ J C Gold Cup-G1	7 6 619 34½ 25 36½	Vasquez J	118	7.00	57-25	Lemhi Gold126 4½Silver Supreme1262Christmas Past11817	Wide,weakened	10
26Sep82- 8Bel	fst 1⅛	:461 1:101 1:352 1:483	3↑ ⒻRuffian H-G1	8 7 74¼ 1hd 11½ 15	Vasquez J	117	2.50	84-19	ChristmsPast1175MadmosllForl112 2¼LovSgn123¾	Ridden out	8
15Sep82- 8Bel	fst 1⅛	:463 1:101 1:344 1:473	ⒻGazelle H-G2	2 6 62¾ 21 44½ 44¼	Vasquez J	123	*.70	85-14	BroomDance121nkNmbr123 2¾MdmosllForl114 1¼	Bid,weakened	7
24Jly82- 9Mth	fst 1⅛	:474 1:112 1:362 1:492	ⒻMonmouth Oaks-G2	9 6 62¼ 3½ 1½ 11¼	Vasquez J	121	*.40	88-14	ChristmasPast121 1¼Milingo119 1¼MadmosllForl112 1½	Driving	9
26Jun82- 8Bel	fst 1½	:471 1:11 2:021 2:283	ⒻC C A Oaks-G1	1 4 412 1hd 12 16	Vasquez J	121	2.50	77-20	ChristmasPast1216Cupcoy'sJoy121noFlyngPrtnr1213	Driving	10
4Jun82- 8Bel	fst 1⅛	:454 1:094 1:351 1:482	ⒻMother Goose-G1	6 5 59 47 21½ 2¾	Vasquez J	121	7.10	84-18	Cpecoy'sJoy121¾ChrstmsPst121 3¼BlushWthPrd121 4¾	Rallied	12
22May82- 8Bel	fst 1	:231 :46 1:093 1:341	ⒻAcorn-G1	9 5 53 44½ 56½ 59½	Vasquez J	121	4.30	85-11	Cupecoy's Joy121 2¾Nancy Huang121 3½Vestris121 2¼	Wide	9
24Mar82- 9GP	fst 1 1/16	:241 :474 1:114 1:441	ⒻBonnie Miss-G3	2 6 41¾ 31 11½ 13	Vasquez J	121	*.40	80-22	Christmas Past1213Norsan1131Our Darling112 1½	Ridden out	6
4Mar82- 9Hia	fst 1⅛	:481 1:121 1:363 1:492	ⒻPoinsettia-G3	6 5 31½ 21½ 11½ 16	Vasquez J	113	7.20	85-23	Christmas Past1136Larida1147Smart Heiress112½	Handily	8
1Feb82- 6Hia	fst 1 1/16	:24 :482 1:133 1:451	ⒻMd Sp Wt	6 2 2hd 13 16 111	Vasquez J	120	*.60	77-25	ChristmasPast12011Friedenau12012Saidamzelle120 2½	Easily	9
18Jan82- 4Hia	fst 6f	:222 :453 1:104	ⒻMd Sp Wt	9 10 76¼ 48½ 36½ 29	Vasquez J	120	*1.40	80-20	Artic Moss1209Christmas Past120nkPittsy1205	Bore in	12
8Oct81- 9Bel	fst 6f	:223 :461 1:123	ⒻMd Sp Wt	5 7 64¾ 53½ 34 33¼	Vasquez J	117	*1.60	76-21	Initial Encounter117 2¾PushYourLuck117½ChristmasPast117½	Rallied	12
23Sep81- 3Bel	fst 6f	:224 :462 1:12	ⒻMd Sp Wt	7 13 109½ 87¾ 54½ 32½	Vasquez J	117	8.20	78-18	Pert112nkBroom Dance117 2¼Christmas Past117¾	Rallied	13

Conquistador Cielo

b. c. 1979, by Mr. Prospector (Raise a Native)–K D Princess, by Bold Commander

Lifetime record: 13 9 0 2 $474,328

Own.– H. DeKwiatkowski
Br.– L.E. Iandoli (Fla)
Tr.– Woodford C. Stephens

21Aug82- 8Sar	fst 1¼	:462 1:103 1:354 2:023	Travers-G1	4 1 21 2hd 1hd 31¼	Maple E	126	*.40	86-14	RunawayGroom126½Aloma's Ruler126¾ConquistdrCielo126 5¾	Rank,tired	5
8Aug82- 8Sar	fst 1⅛	:463 1:104 1:354 1:483	Jim Dandy-G3	2 1 1½ 14 12 11	Maple E	128	*.10	92-14	ConquistadorCielo1281Lejoli11414NoHomeRun11417	Handily	4
5Jly82- 8Bel	fst 1⅛	:451 1:083 1:333 1:464	Dwyer-G2	1 1 11 14 15 14	Maple E	126	*.10	93-13	ConquistadorCielo1264John'sGold114 8¾Renvstd119 8¼	Easily	6
5Jun82- 8Bel	sly 1½	:471 1:12 2:031 2:281	Belmont-G1	11 2 11½ 14 110 114	Pincay L Jr	126	4.10	79-17	Conquistador Cielo12614Gato Del Sol1264Illuminate126 3¾	Wide,ridden out	11
31May82- 8Bel	fst 1	:224 :45 1:09 1:33	3↑ Metropolitan H-G1	11 1 3nk 12 15 17¼	Maple E	111	*2.00	101-12	Conquistador Cielo111 7¼Silver Buck111 2½Star Gallant111 1¼	Ridden out	14
19May82- 7Bel	fst 1	:231 :454 1:094 1:341	3↑ Alw 35000	4 1 1hd 13 17 111	Maple E	113	*.70	95-14	ConquistdorCielo11311Swinging Light119¾Bachelor Boo124 3¼	Ridden out	7
8May82- 7Pim	fst 1 1/16	:241 :473 1:113 1:441	Alw 27000	3 2 22 21 11½ 13	Maple E	112	*.50	84-20	CnquistdrCielo1123DoublNo11510SixSails112 2½	Bore in,clear	5
26Feb82- 7Hia	fst 7f	:224 :451 1:094 1:221	Alw 14000	1 7 1½ 11½ 12½ 14	Maple E	116	*.60	92-18	ConquistadorCilo1164Hostg11610MystcSqur116nk	Ridden out	7
16Feb82- 9Hia	fst 7f	:223 :443 1:10 1:23	Alw 14000	1 6 53½ 67½ 44 47¼	Maple E	116	5.60	81-17	StarGallant1164CutAway1202Rex'sProfile116 1¼	No factor	7
12Aug81- 8Sar	gd 6f	:213 :45 1:111	Sanford-G2	2 8 64½ 78 54½ 4nk	Maple E	122	3.70	84-12	Mayanesian115hdShipping Magnate115noLejoli115no	Bumped	10
3Aug81- 8Sar	fst 6f	:221 :453 1:103	Sar Spl-G2	2 6 63¾ 2hd 1hd 1½	Maple E	117	8.20	87-18	ConquistdrCielo117½Herschelwalker117 1¼Timely Writer122 1¼	Driving	10
10Jly81- 6Bel	fst 5½f	:23 :464 :59 1:05	Md Sp Wt	7 3 32 21 13 18	Saumell L	118	*1.60	90-12	Conquistador Cielo1188High Ascent1186Greers' Leader118 1½	Ridden out	9
29Jun81- 4Bel	fst 5½f	:224 :464 :593 1:062	Md Sp Wt	9 8 44¼ 53 23 3¾	Saumell L	118	4.60	82-15	AntiguaBird118¾Commodity118hdConquistdorCilo118 1½	Wide	10

Cozzene

gr. c. 1980, by Caro (Fortino II)–Ride the Trails, by Prince John — Lifetime record: 24 10 5 5 $978,152

Own.– J.A. Nerud
Br.– John A. Nerud (Fla)
Tr.– Jan H. Nerud

2Nov85- 4Aqu	fm	1Ⓣ	:224 :462 1:111 1:35	3↑	BC Mile-G1	6	3	32½	31½	2½	12¼	Guerra WA	126	3.60	101-00	Cozzene1262¼[D]PalaceMusic126noAlMamoon126no	Drew clear	14
3Oct85- 8Med	sly	1 1/16⊗	:232 :47 1:121 1:45	3↑	Cliff Hanger H-G3	6	4	52½	55½	513	616	Guerra WA	123	*1.00	62-25	LateAct117nkSilverSurfer1162½PxNobscum1167	Off sluggish	7
24Aug85- 9Mth	fm	1⅛Ⓣ	:481 1:122 1:362 1:482	3↑	Longfellow H-G2	6	4	38½	45½	1hd	12	Guerra WA	122	*.70	98-09	Cozzene1222Zoffany114¾Mourjane1173	Driving	8
11Aug85- 8Sar	fm	1⅛Ⓣ	:474 1:102 1:342 1:47	3↑	B Baruch H-G2	3	5	54	32	2hd	2nk	Guerra WA	120	2.20	92-13	Win124nkCozzene1204½Sitzmark112¾	Bore out	9
13Jly85- 9Mth	fm	1 1/16Ⓣ	:243 :48 1:113 1:422	3↑	Oceanport H-G3	8	3	35	32½	2hd	13	Guerra WA	121	*1.70	93-14	Cozzene1213StaytheCourse1193½RovingMinstrel1181	Driving	9
8Jun85- 4Bel	sly	6f	:214 :442 1:091	3↑	Jaipur 81k	3	4	35	34	33½	33¼	Cordero A Jr	117	2.40	93-12	Mt. Livermore1192¾Main Top117½Cozzene117¾	Even try	7
27May85- 7Bel	fm	7fⓉ	:223 :45 1:093 1:23	3↑	Wise Ship 56k	2	7	44	24	22½	31¾	Guerra WA	119	*.40e	87-19	Sitzmark1191Red Wing Dream119¾Cozzene1191	Off slowly	7
10May85- 8Bel	fst	6f	:221 :452 1:11	3↑	Alw 36000	7	7	56½	46	2½	11¼	Guerra WA	124	5.10	87-20	Cozzene1241¼Basket Weave124½Momento II1192½	Driving	7
10Nov84- 4Hol	fm	1Ⓣ	:223 :453 1:084 1:323	3↑	BC Mile-G1	5	3	32½	3½	1hd	31¾	Guerra WA	126	3.80	103-01	Royal Heroine1231½Star Choice126nkCzzene126nk	Weakened	10
10Oct84- 8Bel	fm	1Ⓣ	:221 :451 1:092 1:33	3↑	Alw 36000	2	3	32	11½	14	14	Guerra WA	117	*.90	100-12	Cozzene1174Sitzmark1152¾Alev1152¾	Ridden out	6
21Sep84- 8Med	fm	1 1/16Ⓣ	:233 :47 1:103 1:402	3↑	Cliff Hanger H (Div 2) 73k	6	3	31	2hd	1hd	1½	Guerra WA	115	*1.00	100-06	Cozzene115½Ayman1121¼Pin Puller1144¾	Driving	6
8Sep84- 8Bel	fm	1⅜[T]	:472 1:114 1:36 2:143	3↑	Man o' War-G1	1	4	42½	31½	2hd	31¾	Guerra WA	126	10.80	82-16	Majesty's Prince126¾Win1261Cozzene126nk	Weakened	9
12Aug84- 8Sar	fm	1⅛Ⓣ	:473 1:12 1:342 1:472	3↑	B Baruch H-G2	3	3	3½	3nk	3nk	31	Venezia M	114	3.40	89-07	Win112¾Intensify113nkCozzene114hd	Evenly	9
14Jly84- 8Atl	fm	1 3/16Ⓣ	:481 1:114 1:352 1:54	3↑	U Nations H-G1	8	4	42¼	31	23½	21½	Venezia M	114	9.70e	92-14	Hero'sHonor1231½Czzene114noWho'sforDinner110hd	Gamely	11
23Jun84- 8Mth	fm	1 1/16Ⓣ	:234 :474 1:11 1:41	3↑	Alw 19000	3	4	41	42½	3½	1¾	Swatuk B	115	2.70e	106-03	Cozzene115¾Wild Again1192Castle Guard1172	Drew clear	6
9Jun84- 6Bel	fst	6f	:221 :444 1:091	3↑	Jaipur 58k	3	10	64½	55½	68	67¾	Cordero A Jr	115	*2.00	88-10	CannnShell1152ChanBalum1152BelievetheQuen1153	In close	12
28May84- 8Bel	fst	1	:223 :444 1:084 1:34	3↑	Metropolitan H-G1	7	6	43	33	36	48¼	Venezia M	114	13.10	87-17	Fit to Fight124hdA Phenomenon1267¼Moro1161	Tired	10
10May84- 8Bel	fst	7f	:23 :454 1:091 1:211	3↑	Alw 33000	5	4	42½	32½	24½	27½	Venezia M	119	6.90	88-17	Fit to Fight1247½Cozzene1192Mugatea1191	Wide stretch	7
20Oct83- 8Med	fst	1 1/16	:232 :462 1:102 1:434		Palisades 53k	5	5	43½	32	21	2hd	Cordero A Jr	113	7.10	90-16	Bet Big114hdCozzene113½Jacque's Tip1191	Just missed	7
9Oct83- 8Bel	fst	1	:231 :46 1:093 1:34		Jamaica H-G3	8	4	53	33½	57¼	510½	Bailey JD	113	8.10	84-10	Bounding Basque1151½A Phenomenn1203Bet Big1155¾	Tired	8
5Sep83- 7Bel	fst	7f	:223 :452 1:103 1:241	3↑	Alw 27000	1	6	21½	2½	11	11¼	Cordero A Jr	115	*1.00	81-20	Cozzene1151¼DavetheDude1172EcstaticPride1131¼	Driving	9
17Aug83- 9Sar	fst	6f	:221 :45 1:093	3↑	Alw 20000	11	9	21½	2½	1hd	12¼	Cordero A Jr	112	*1.60	92-11	Czzene1122¼StopCard1145¾CglSprngs112hd	Brushed,driving	12
27Jly83- 7Sar	fst	6f	:214 :444 1:102	3↑	Alw 20000	6	9	65½	37	34	23¼	Migliore R	111	*1.90	85-13	Big McCoy1063¼Cozzene1112Spring Fever113nk	Raced wide	11
25May83- 6Bel	fst	6f	:223 :46 1:111	3↑	Md Sp Wt	3	11	53½	21½	2hd	13	Migliore R	113	*4.10	86-16	Czzene1133GallantMinded113¾BigMcCoy113no	Slow st,clear	12

Dave's Friend

b. g. 1975, by Friend's Choice (Crimson Satan)–Duc's Tina, by Duc de Fer — Lifetime record: 76 35 16 8 $1,079,915

Own.– John Franks
Br.– R.L. Beall (Md)
Tr.– Albert Toups

18Jun86- 9LaD	fst	6f	:222 :454 1:114	3↑	Alw 15000	5	2	52¼	21	32½	42¼	Trosclair AJ	114	*.70e	81-20	Wendy Tom122nkLittle Slick118hdTexas Delta1122		6
	Unable to sustain bid;Previously trained by Jack C. Van Berg																	
26Jan86- 7FG	gd	6f	:224 :47 :591 1:121	4↑	Alw 11500	1	2	11	1½	2hd	53¾	Snyder L	114	*1.30	80-26	Head Games1141Justto Satisfy You1131½Double Ready121nk		9
	Weakened in stretch																	
4Dec85- 7Aqu	fst	6f⊡	:22 :451 1:102	3↑	Alw 36000	2	6	1½	11½	11½	23	MacBeth D	115	3.50	89-18	Sonrie Jorge1153Dave's Friend115noDewan for Us1151		6
	Held place gamely;Previously trained by Frank Trosclair																	
31May85- 9LaD	fst	6f	:231 :473 1:134	3↑	Alw 14000	5	3	31½	31½	1hd	1nk	Snyder L	114	*.80e	73-39	Dave's Friend114nkEstate1152½Safe Cracker1187	Driving	6
	Previously trained by Jack C. Van Berg																	
18Apr85- 9OP	fst	6f	:213 :442 1:082	4↑	Count Fleet Sprint H 159k	9	2	21½	3nk	33	812¼	Patterson G	118	2.60e	86-20	Taylor'sSpecial1235Mt.Livermore1192¼T.H.Bend110no	Tired	10
6Apr85- 8OP	fst	6f	:223 :461 1:103	4↑	Alw 18000	6	3	11½	1½	12	21½	Snyder L	112	*1.00	85-18	Wipe'EmOut1121½Dve'sFrnd1121CheyenneChr112½	No match	7
28May84- 9Aks	fst	6f	:222 :45 1:101	3↑	Ak-Sar-Ben H 102k	9	11	1110	1111	1114	1113½	MacBeth D	124	3.60	72-28	TimelessNative1231½FivePrcnt110hdAllSoldOut1151	Trailed	11
3May84- 8CD	sly	7f	:23 :46 1:102 1:23	4↑	Churchill Downs 33k	5	5	41½	43	46	511½	Delahoussaye E	118	*.60	80-23	Habitonia118½Roman Jamboree1152Euathlos1137	Wide	5
19Apr84- 9OP	fst	6f	:212 :441 1:09	4↑	Count Fleet H 130k	2	7	43¾	33½	33	11½	Delahoussaye E	122	4.90	100-12	Dave'sFrind1221½AllSoldOut1143½LuckySlvton113hd	Driving	8
4Apr84- 5SA	fm	*6½fⓉ	:21 :431 1:071 1:14	4↑	Alw 45000	4	3	33½	32½	46	57	Pincay L Jr	117	1.70	82-17	Champagne Bid1221¾Famous Star1144Academic1191	Tired	7
21Mar84- 8SA	fst	5½f	:214 :444 :57 1:031	4↑	El Conejo H (Div 2) 50k	5	2	2½	1hd	12	21¼	Pincay L Jr	120	4.30	94-15	Night Mover1171¼Dave's Friend1201½Bara Lass1173	Gamely	7
13Nov83- 5SA	my	6f	:22 :452 :573 1:102	3↑	Alw 45000	7	1	31	21	1hd	11	McCarron CJ	117	*2.10	86-26	Dave's Friend1171Total Departure1153Hey Rob1177	Driving	7
15Oct83- 8SA	fst	6½f	:212 :441 1:091 1:16	2↑	Morvich H 65k	1	3	32	31	34	33½	Meza RQ	121	6.80	86-17	KangrooCourt119hdShanekite1203½Dave'sFrind121½	Even try	7
24Sep83-10Dar	fm	*6fⓉ	1:07	3↑	Chateaugay 16k	3	4	32	32	24	44¼	McKnight J	118	*.40	101-00	SmrtandShrp1154WndyProspct115hdCmpRobbr115hd	Weakened	6
27Aug83- 8CD	fst	6f	:214 :444 :571 1:102	3↑	Alw 13980	4	5	32	2hd	11½	13	McKnight J	122	*.20	94-11	Dave'sFrind1223RonnyTurcott112noFlyngTrophy1124	Driving	5
7Aug83-10Suf	fst	6f	:214 :443 :58 1:093	3↑	Suf Sprint H-G3	1	5	31½	44	57	58	Snyder L	123	4.80	85-18	All Sold Out110¾Let Burn1151½Gold Beauty1244	Tired	8
4Jly83- 9CD	sly	7f	:233 :462 1:094 1:231	3↑	Firecracker H 44k	2	3	11	1½	11½	2nk	Snyder L	124	*.70	91-19	ShotN'Missed121nkDave'sFrnd1245Rackensack1185½	Gamely	4
30May83- 9Aks	fst	6f	:221 :443 1:094	3↑	Ak-Sar-Ben H 116k	9	4	3½	43	32	2½	Snyder L	127	*1.00	87-25	AllSoldOut110½Dave'sFriend1271BoldRuddy112nk	Game try	13
14Apr83- 9OP	fst	6f	:22 :454 1:10	4↑	Count Fleet Sprint H 117k	8	5	31	2hd	12½	15	Snyder L	124	4.60	95-22	Dave's Friend1245General Jimmy117noLiberty Lane113no		9
	Wide,drew clear																	
13Mar83-11TuP	fst	6f	:21 :431 :56 1:092	3↑	Phoenix Gold Cup-G3	6	7	56½	56½	62¾	2½	Snyder L	121	4.20	88-19	BirthdaySong115½Dave'sFrnd1211SonofaDodo1151½	Gaining	9
26Feb83- 9OP	fst	6f	:22 :46 1:112	4↑	Handicap 50000	6	2	45	43	43	43	Snyder L	128	*.70e	85-23	Rackensack120nkPrcl1102½Sndbggr117nk	Lacked closing bid	7
19Feb83- 9OP	fst	6f	:22 :46 1:111	4↑	Handicap 50000	6	3	2hd	1hd	15	12½	Snyder L	124	*1.30	89-22	Dave'sFriend1242½LuckyPoint116½CircleofStel1164	Driving	7
6Feb83- 7SA	my	1 1/16	:231 :471 1:113 1:43	4↑	Alw 35000	4	2	31	65½	620	-	Romero RP	115	1.60	--	Red Crescent117¾Mandato1156Sari's Dreamer1115	Eased	6
15Jan83- 8SA	fst	7f	:221 :442 1:082 1:21	4↑	San Carlos H-G2	1	4	1½	11	12½	2¾	Romero RP	117	*1.50	94-10	KangrooCourt118¾Dav'sFrnd117noShnkt1184	Lacked late run	6
18Dec82- 8Hol	fst	7f	:214 :442 1:083 1:203	3↑	Yuletide H 55k	3	3	2hd	1hd	2hd	22	Romero RP	117	6.10	92-21	Time to Explode1182Dave's Friend1172Travelling Victor1141½		8
	2nd best																	
4Dec82- 8Hol	fm	5fⓉ	:221 :441 :56	3↑	Meteor H 54k	2	3	42½	33	34½	23	Black K	117	3.30	97-05	ChinookPass1173Dave'sFriend1171FortCalgry1151	No threat	7
14Nov82- 8Hol	fst	6f	:212 :433 :553 1:081	3↑	Nat Sprint Ch (Div 1) 115k	7	4	52¾	33	22	31	Shoemaker W	114	4.70	95-12	Mad Key1161Shanekite120hdDave's Friend114nk		9
	Saved ground,driffted out str																	
2Oct82- 8Haw	fst	6½f	:213 :44 1:091 1:153	3↑	Midwest H 31k	4	2	33	32½	2½	32¼	Jones K	123	*1.20	93-20	Tinsley's Hope119hdGo With the Times1122¼Dave's Frnd1231¾		7
	Wide bid,bled																	
5Sep82- 9Tdn	fst	6f	:22 :452 :574 1:102	3↑	George Lewis H 27k	5	1	1hd	12½	1½	12½	Jones K	127	*.50	92-22	Dave's Friend1272½Silahis1225½Ballacashtal117nk	Driving	6
21Aug82- 9Det	fst	6f	:212 :442 :564 1:091	3↑	Prince 15k	6	1	21	21½	21½	1½	Jones K	120	*1.00	94-14	Dave'sFriend120½Tinsley'sHope120nkSoloRide1132	All out	7
	Previously trained by Robert E. Holthus																	
16Jly82- 8Aks	fst	6f	:212 :432 1:09	3↑	Ak-Sar-Ben H 56k	6	4	2hd	2½	22	3¾	Jones K	125	*1.70	91-19	Smokite123noMadKey114¾Dave'sFrnd125hd	Lacked response	11
5Jly82- 8Aks	fst	6f	:222 :45 1:101	3↑	Alw 18000	1	4	1½	1hd	11½	1½	Jones K	122	*.80	86-21	Dave's Friend122½Smokite1222Destroy 'em1161	Driving	5
12Jun82- 9Aks	fst	6f	:212 :434 1:083	3↑	Speed 31k	6	3	1hd	1hd	2½	12	Jones K	117	*1.10	94-18	[DH]Dave's Friend117[DH]Ogataul1162Daddyal117hd	Driving	8
23May82- 3LaD	fst	6f	:221 :444 1:083	3↑	Alw 14500	3	2	11	11½	12½	14½	Snyder L	122	*.20	106-03	Dave'sFrnd1224½HiHoBlack1196YstrdysHro1176	Ridden out	5
8May82- 8LaD	fst	6f	:222 :451 1:094	3↑	Alw 14000	4	3	21½	2hd	1½	17½	Snyder L	114	*.40	100-12	Dave'sFriend1147½SpecialSpecial114nkPartout1141	Driving	10
29Apr82- 8CD	fst	7f	:23 :463 1:102 1:224	3↑	Ch Downs H (Div 2) 35k	5	3	1½	11½	22	46¾	Romero RP	121	*2.10	86-15	BayouBlack1193¼VodikaCollins1183½PrincCrmson116hd	Tired	6
	Previously trained by Louis G. Marshall																	
3Jly81- 8Bel	my	6f	:221 :45 1:09	3↑	True North H 55k	2	2	42½	64½	76¾	79	Black AS	128	2.20	88-16	Joanie's Chief1091¼Proud Appeal117nkGuiltyConscnce1133½		7
	Tired																	

7Jun81- 9Suf fst 6f :222 :452 1:103 3↑ Suf Downs H 79k 1 5 21½ 21 21½ 2no Black AS 128 *.80 88-29 RingofLight116noDave'sFriend1281¾Triocala1121½ Brushed 10

17May81- 8Bel fst 6f :223 :453 1:094 3↑ Roseben H 55k 3 2 2½ 1hd 11 42¼ Romero R 132 *1.30 91-22 RingofLight113¾GuiltyConscnce1121Convnnt114½ Weakened 8

Previously trained by Robert L. Beall

25Apr81- 7Aqu fst 6f :221 :451 1:093 3↑ Bold Ruler 80k 3 2 1hd 13 13½ 11½ Black AS 123 *.60 93-23 Dave'sFrnd1231½NaughtyJimmy1191½Fppno1192¾ Drew clear 6

15Apr81- 8Aqu fst 6f :22 :452 1:10 4↑ Alw 32000 4 1 1hd 12 14½ 1½ Black AS 122 *.10 91-23 Dave'sFrnd122½HerbWater1172½BoldVoyagr1225 Ridden out 5

Previously owned by Mrs Robert L. Beall

29Mar81- 8Aqu fst 6f :214 :442 1:092 3↑ White Skies H 54k 3 2 11 11 12 13¾ Bracciale V Jr 130 *.30 94-21 Dave'sFriend1303¾GuiltyConscience114½RarePerformer1174½ 4

Handily

13Mar81- 8Key fst 7f :221 :452 1:092 1:222 4↑ Alw 14000 4 3 34 22 21½ 1no Bracciale V Jr 119 *.20 95-28 Dave's Friend119noCheating Arthur1227King Bold Reality1197 5

Bumped st.,driving

3Jan81- 9Bow fst 6f :221 :45 :564 1:09 3↑ Southern Maryland H 42k 1 1 11 11½ 13 14¾ Bracciale V Jr 129 *.30 95-14 Dave'sFriend1294¾Gasp1132PeaceforPeace111¾ Ridden out 5

20Dec80- 6Lrl fst 1 :232 :462 1:103 1:35 3↑ Alw 18000 2 1 1½ 1½ 11 12 Bracciale V Jr 122 *.30 98-12 Dave's Friend1222Naughty Jimmy116nkGasp1224½ Ridden out 7

29Nov80- 8Aqu my 6f :214 :441 1:081 3↑ Sport Page H 57k 2 2 11 12 14 15 Bracciale V Jr 126 *1.20 102-13 Dave'sFriend1265TiltUp114nkHawkin'sSpecl1142 Ridden out 8

21Nov80- 8Lrl fst 5f :222 :444 :57 3↑ Alw 18000 8 3 1hd 1½ 12 15 Bracciale V Jr 119 *.20 101-15 Dave's Friend1195No Scruples1133Right Bank113no Handily 9

8Nov80- 5Lrl fst 6f :223 :462 :58 1:103 3↑ Alw 20000 3 2 11 11 11½ 12 Bracciale V Jr 122 *.40 93-12 Dave's Friend1222Gasp1157Hot Words1131 Driving 7

18Oct80- 8Aqu fst 7f :223 :443 1:084 1:212 3↑ Vosburgh-G1 2 4 1½ 1½ 11 31½ Bracciale V Jr 126 4.20 92-12 PluggdNickle123½JaklinKlugmn1231Dv'sFrnd126¾ Weakened 9

8Oct80- 8Bel fst 6f :221 :452 1:103 3↑ Boojum H 57k 7 3 1hd 2hd 2½ 52½ Bracciale V Jr 127 4.10 86-22 DoubleZeus1202¼CndyEclr124hdKng'sFshon123no Drifted out 9

21Jun80- 9Bow fst 6f :223 :45 :563 1:093 3↑ Terrapin H 27k 2 3 11 11½ 1hd 2½ Bracciale V Jr 128 *.50 91-19 Isella117½Dave's Friend1284Fuzzbuster1121 Drifted out 4

Previously owned by Bel-Mar Stable

17May80- 8Aqu fst 6f :22 :443 1:09 3↑ Roseben H 55k 4 1 11½ 11½ 12 11¼ Bracciale V Jr 126 *1.50 98-16 Dave'sFriend1261¼DoubleZeus118½StateDinner1181¾ Driving 7

20Apr80- 7Aqu fst 6f :214 :441 1:094 3↑ Bold Ruler 81k 1 2 11½ 12 12 12¾ Bracciale V Jr 123 4.10 94-16 Dave's Friend1232¾Tilt Up1211½Double Zeus121¾ Driving 6

5Apr80- 7Pim fst 6f :23 :453 :574 1:103 3↑ J E Hoover H 31k 4 3 21 26 37½ 312½ Bracciale V Jr 125 *.30 80-19 Isella11611AmbitiousRuler1101½Dave'sFrnd125no Lugged in 4

22Mar80- 9Pim fst 1 1/16 :24 :474 1:121 1:44 3↑ [S]Alw 25000 4 1 11 11 1½ 2¾ Bracciale V Jr 124 *.70 84-21 Red Light117¾Dave's Friend124¾T.V. Hill117¾ Weakened 7

18Feb80- 8Aqu fst 6f[•] :212 :442 1:093 3↑ Sporting Plate H 55k 5 3 21 1hd 12 12¼ Black AS 122 4.10 96-19 Dave'sFriend1222¼DoublZus1263¼BoldndStormy115no Driving 6

9Feb80- 8Bow fst 7f :23 :46 1:101 1:233 4↑ Alw 20000 2 4 11 1hd 2½ 22¼ Black AS 122 *.90 85-26 PolePosition1222¼Dave'sFrind1223¼IslndSultn1222½ Failed 5

12Jan80- 9Bow gd 6f :224 :454 :58 1:11 3↑ S Maryland H 43k 4 3 1hd 11 13 12¼ Bracciale V Jr 118 *.90 85-33 Dave's Friend1182¼Isella115¾Shelter Half118¾ Driving 8

25Nov79- 8Aqu fst 6f :22 :444 1:092 3↑ Sport Page H 54k 5 3 2hd 1hd 1hd 31¾ Black AS 119 5.10 94-21 Amadevil113nkTanthem1231½Dave's Friend119¾ Weakened 7

11Nov79- 6Aqu fst 6f :22 :443 1:093 3↑ Alw 25000 4 2 2hd 2hd 2hd 45 Bracciale V Jr 117 1.90 90-15 Tilt Up1173¼C.J.'s Boy1171Bold and Stormy117¾ Gave way 6

26May79- 8Pim my 1 1/16 :24 :48 1:114 1:46 3↑ City of Baltimore H 33k 1 1 11 2hd 24 37¾ Bracciale V Jr 124 *.30 67-27 Revivalist1151¾T.V. Hill1146Dave's Friend1244 Bore in 5

14May79- 8Pim gd 1⅛ :474 1:114 1:371 1:503 [S]Jennings H 56k 5 1 11 1½ 11 2no Bracciale V Jr 124 *.30 89-13 WhataGent111noDave'sFrnd1242½TakethePledge112hd Nosed 7

5May79- 6Pim fst 1 1/16 :233 :47 1:103 1:423 3↑ [S]Alw 25000 1 1 1½ 11 13 13¼ Bracciale V Jr 115 *.30 92-13 Dave'sFriend1153¼GalaForecast1171¼BigPunt1155 Handily 5

26Apr79- 8Pim fst 6f :231 :454 :57 1:094 4↑ Alw 19000 1 3 11 11½ 12 12½ Bracciale V Jr 119 *.40 97-17 Dave's Friend1192½Tiny Monk107½Bold Road1153 Handily 8

16Nov78- 6Med fst 6f :22 :451 1:103 Palisades H 53k 1 6 1½ 1hd 1½ 1no Bracciale V Jr 126 *.50 92-15 Dave's Friend126noTanthem1142Al Battah119nk Lasted 9

4Nov78- 7Lrl fst 6f :222 :454 :571 1:094 3↑ Handicap 20000 4 3 1½ 1½ 14 14 Bracciale V Jr 125 *.50 97-16 Dave'sFrnd1254Hmpt'sLrk1152¼SportngPowdr115hd Handily 7

7Oct78- 8Bow fst 1⅛ :472 1:11 1:362 1:50 Governor's Cup H 108k 4 1 1½ 11½ 21 22½ Bracciale V Jr 120 3.80 92-21 NastyandBold1232½Dave'sFrind12010StrdNskr11820 2nd best 5

16Sep78- 8Bow fst 1 1/16 :23 :473 1:123 1:441 [S]Chesapeake H 27k 1 1 11½ 11½ 11 1¾ Bracciale V Jr 119 *.10 85-26 Dave'sFriend119¾KingofFools1109PerfectDaddy1143 Driving 4

4Sep78- 8Bel fst 1 :222 :45 1:093 1:36 Jerome H-G2 5 1 11½ 1½ 1hd 41¼ Bracciale V Jr 119 3.40 87-14 SensitivePrince118nkDarbyCreekRoad122nkSorry Lookin112¾ 5

Ducked in

5Aug78- 8Mth sly 1⅛ :47 1:123 1:393 1:531 Mth Inv'l H-G1 3 1 11 11½ 1½ 2¾ Bracciale V Jr 120 *1.40 68-31 DeltaFlag112¾Dave'sFrnd1202½SpecilHonor1182¾ Weakened 7

22Jly78- 8Pim fst 1⅛ :46 1:101 1:352 1:482 Marylander H 56k 3 1 11½ 13 11½ 11 Bracciale V Jr 117 *1.00 102-17 Dave's Friend1171Star de Naskra1196Sensitive Prince1225 5

Bobbled,driving

11Jly78- 7Pim fst 6f :232 :461 :574 1:094 3↑ Alw 7500 3 3 11½ 11½ 13 18 Bracciale V Jr 117 *.30 97-18 Dave'sFriend1178HellorHeaven110¾Wm.Withers1216 Handily 7

27May78- 8Key fst 7f :213 :44 1:082 1:212 Patriot-G3 1 4 11½ 11½ 11½ 12 Bracciale V Jr 117 *1.00 102-13 Dave'sFriend1172FullPartner115noShelterHlf1191½ Driving 4

14May78- 8Key sly 6½f :213 :441 1:09 1:154 Alw 20000 1 6 1½ 11 14 18 Bracciale V Jr 114 1.90 94-20 Dave's Friend1148Al Battah122½Bold Conceiver1123 Easily 6

22Apr78- 5Pim fst 6f :232 :471 :59 1:112 Alw 6500 7 3 11 1½ 14 110 Bracciale V Jr 120 *.30 89-16 [D]Dave'sFriend12010SeaofDavid107nkBackBayBu1153 Bore in 7

Disqualified and placed seventh

12Apr78- 2Pim fst 6f :233 :463 1:104 3↑ Md Sp Wt 7 2 1½ 11½ 16 112 Bracciale V Jr 115 *1.30 92-19 Dave'sFriend11512BlackBeau1141¼NorthrnStndrd1093 Easily 8

De La Rose

b. f. 1978, by Nijinsky II (Northern Dancer)–Rosetta Stone, by Round Table

Lifetime record: 26 11 6 0 $544,647

Own.– H. DeKwiatkowski

Br.– Dr & Mrs R. Smiser West & Mackenzie Miller (Ky)

Tr.– Woodford C. Stephens

31Mar82- 9GP fm 1Ⓣ :24 :472 1:112 1:351 3↑ ⒻS River H (Div 2)-G3 3 6 611 67½ 77¾ 65½ Maple E 123 *.90 88-10 Tchr'sPt1141¼ShrkSong1143½Blush113hd No apparent excuse 9

5Mar82- 9Hia fm 1⅛Ⓣ 1:47 3↑ ⒻBlack Helen H-G2 3 7 77 66 43½ 42½ Maple E 124 *.60 96-09 HoneyFox123¾Endcott1131¼ShrkSong112½ Slow start,bobbled 8

15Feb82- 9Hia fm 1 1/16Ⓣ 1:423 3↑ ⒻColumbiana H 63k 8 9 98¾ 86¾ 47½ 23¾ Maple E 124 *.90 81-14 HoneyFox1213¾DeLaRose124hdShrkSong113hd Slow start,wide 10

15Nov81- 8Hol fm 1⅛Ⓣ :462 1:11 1:352 1:473 Hol Derby (Div 1)-G1 2 7 79¾ 51¾ 11 1nk Maple E 119 *.70 92-10 De La Rose119nkHigh Counsel1225Lord Trendy122hd 8

Slow start,driving

17Oct81- 9WO fm 1¼[T] :492 1:154 1:411 2:052 3↑ ⒻE P Taylor-G3 4 8 84½ 2hd 13½ 12½ Maple E 118 *.30 80-20 De La Rose1182½Sangue1182Sajama1181¼ Handily 9

12Oct81- 8Bel fm 1¼[T] :473 1:12 1:364 2:002 ⒻAthenia H-G3 6 8 89¾ 11½ 13 12¾ Maple E 125 *.90 92-11 DeLaRse1252¾NobleDamsel111¾AndoverWay1131 Ridden out 8

30Sep81- 8Bel fm 1 1/16Ⓣ :241 :473 1:114 1:42 ⒻLamb Chop H 56k 6 8 76 31 11 11¾ Maple E 123 *.50 86-20 DeLaRose1231¾AndoverWay114nkWingsofGrace113hd Driving 9

7Sep81- 8Bel fm 1¼[T] :472 1:112 1:372 2:013 3↑ ⒻFlower Bowl H-G2 5 5 518 52¾ 22 21¾ Maple E 116 *.40 84-22 Rokeby Rose1141¾De La Rose1161Euphrosyne1104 Wide 6

16Aug81- 8Sar yl 1⅛Ⓣ :474 1:124 1:372 1:503 3↑ ⒻDiana H-G2 1 5 46½ 52¼ 2½ 11¾ Maple E 114 *1.10 74-26 DeLaRose1141¾RokebyRose1153Euphrosyne112nk Ridden out 8

26Jly81- 8Bel fm 1¼[T] :473 1:122 1:354 2:001 Lexington-G2 10 10 810 2½ 21½ 21¼ Maple E 121 *.80 92-08 Acaroid1171¼De La Rose1214Wicked Will117nk 2nd best 11

27Jun81- 8Bel fst 1½ :474 1:114 2:014 2:281 ⒻC C A Oaks-G1 3 6 58½ 616 623 627 Maple E 121 *.40e 52-16 [D]RealPrize1212¼WaywardLass1212¼BannerGala12113 Outrun 6

13Jun81- 8Mth fm 1Ⓣ :24 :472 1:111 1:353 Long Branch-G3 9 7 74¼ 11½ 12½ 18½ Maple E 117 *.30 97-16 DeLaRose1178½CenturyBanker114noVictorinDoubl1143 Easily 9

31May81- 8Bel fm 1Ⓣ :23 :454 1:102 1:342 Saranac-G2 1 7 66 31½ 12½ 16½ Maple E 112 *.80e 93-10 DeLaRose1126½StageDoorKey114½ColorBearer1143 Handily 7

23May81- 6Bel fm 1Ⓣ :234 :46 1:092 1:331 Alw 35000 1 4 21½ 2½ 1hd 13¾ Maple E 112 *.60 99-11 DeLaRose1123¾ExplosiveBid1158SlvrExprss1101¾ Ridden out 7

1May81- 8CD fst 1 1/16 :25 :484 1:13 1:434 ⒻKy Oaks-G1 3 6 55½ 53 21½ 2no Day P 121 1.50e 89-17 HeavnlyCause121noDeLaRse1215WaywrdLss1213 Just missed 6

8Apr81- 7Kee fst 7f :231 :461 1:103 1:224 ⒻAlw 25780 6 5 88½ 76½ 43½ 45¾ Day P 118 *.60e 86-17 DameMysterse1212¾Bushmaid1132¼SwetRvng121¾ No factor 9

2Mar81- 9GP fst 1 1/16 :25 :492 1:133 1:442 ⒻBonnie Miss 87k 3 7 75¼ 47 47 47½ Perret C 114 3.90 71-22 DameMystrieuse1181BannerGala1135HeavnlyCs1211½ Outrun 7

11Feb81- 9GP fst 7f :223 :45 1:092 1:221 ⒻForward Gal 43k 7 9 910 89 64¼ 42 Perret C 114 9.90 91-18 DameMysterse1181¼HeavnlyCs121¾MstrsDrm113no Rallied 10

15Nov80- 8Aqu fst 1⅛ :48 1:123 1:373 1:504 ⒻDemoiselle-G1 4 6 67 64½ 21½ 2hd Maple E 116 6.80 81-20 RainbowCnnection119hdDeLaRs1166TnTnToo1162¼ Ducked in 6

29Oct80- 8Aqu gd 1⅛Ⓣ :48 1:13 1:384 1:512 ⒻMiss Grillo 55k 4 5 57 51¾ 11½ 21 Maple E 121 1.40 86-13 Smilin' Sera1181De La Rose1213¾Seaholme1183¾ Gamely 8

5Oct80- 8Bel fst 1 :241 :48 1:124 1:38 ⒻFrizette-G1 3 7 52½ 41 43 57½ Venezia M 119 11.70 70-23 HeavenlyCause1191½SweetRevnge1194½Prayrs'nPromiss119hd 8

Tired

22Sep80- 8Bel fst 7f :232 :471 1:114 1:243 ⒻMatron-G1 5 6 54½ 43½ 43 43¼ Maple E 119 6.60 76-23 Prayers'nPromises119hdHeavenlyCs1191SwtRvng1192¼ Wide 8

29Aug80- 8Bel fm 7fⓉ :23 :46 1:094 1:232 ⒻEvening Out 56k 1 6 65 42 2hd 1hd Maple E 114 *.50 87-13 DeLaRose114hdBravoNative11210PrimeProspect1132¾ Driving 7

20Aug80- 6Sar fm 1[T] :24 :484 1:134 1:381 ⒻAlw 20000 2 6 54½ 1½ 11½ 15 Maple E 114 1.80 88-16 DeLaRose1145PicturePretty109noJanJill114¾ Ridden out 10

30Jly80- 8Sar fst 6f :212 :444 1:102 ⒻSchuylerville-G3 10 11 1118 98½ 810 711 Maple E 114 *1.60 77-12 SweetRevnge114nkCompanonshp1143HvnlyCs1143 Poor start 11

11Jly80- 4Bel fst 6f :23 :48 1:12 ⒻMd Sp Wt 2 11 911 42½ 1hd 13½ Maple E 117 *.50 82-16 De La Rose1173½Bravo Native1175¾Circle Game117hd 11

Slow start,ridden out

Deputy Minister

dkbbr. c. 1979, by Vice Regent (Northern Dancer)–Mint Copy, by Bunty's Flight | **Lifetime record: 22 12 2 2 $696,964**

Own.– Due Process Stable
Br.– Centurion Farms (Can)
Tr.– Reynaldo H. Nobles

17Nov83- 8Med	fst	1¼	:47 1:104 1:361 2:022	3↑ Med Cup-G1	9	7	76¾	31	11	2nk	MacBeth D	118	5.10	90-18	Slewpy116nkDeputy Minister1181Water Bank117½	Gamely	9
5Nov83- 8Aqu	fst	1⅛	:474 1:111 1:361 1:49	3↑ Stuyvesant H-G2	1	4	43	42	22	21¼	MacBeth D	119	2.50	89-22	FittoFight1171¼DeputyMinister119hdSingSing1154	Gamely	7
22Oct83- 8Aqu	fst	7f	:221 :45 1:083 1:21	3↑ Vosburgh-G1	6	8	74½	53	44½	32¼	MacBeth D	126	4.40	94-19	APhenomenon1231¾FittoFight126½DeputyMinister1261	Wide	8
28Sep83- 7Bel	fst	1	:232 :454 1:093 1:342	3↑ Alw 40000	4	6	54	42½	22	32¼	MacBeth D	115	*1.10	91-19	FittoFight1192Reinvested115nkDeputyMinistr1152	Weakened	6
3Sep83- 8Bel	fst	1⅛	:454 1:092 1:34 1:463	3↑ Woodward-G1	8	8	84¼	63½	69	612½	MacBeth D	121	4.60	81-13	Slew o' Gold118noBates Motel1235Sing Sing1195	No factor	10
30Jly83- 8Sar	fst	1⅛	:464 1:104 1:353 1:482	3↑ Whitney H-G1	7	7	64½	63¾	64¼	42¾↓	MacBeth D	126	1.70	90-14	IslandWhirl123noBoldStyl114¾Sunny'sHlo1162	Wide stretch	9
17Jly83- 8Bel	fst	7f	:224 :453 1:093 1:221	3↑ Tom Fool-G2	5	8	85½	42¼	12½	14¾	MacBeth D	126	3.40	91-13	DeputyMinister1264¾FittoFight119noMudln126hd	Ridden out	9
12Feb83-10GP	fst	1⅛	:471 1:11 1:354 1:483	3↑ Donn H-G2	7	7	66½	31	1hd	11¼	MacBeth D	122	*1.10	89-17	DeputyMinister1221¼KeyCount1133½Rivalro1212½	Ridden out	16
29Jan83-10GP	fst	7f	:22 :444 1:10 1:224	3↑ Sprint Champ H 63k	4	9	1113	107	5½	1½	MacBeth D	122	5.50	90-20	DeputyMinister122½Wipe'EmOut1092½CenterCut118½	Driving	12
Previously owned by Due Process, Centurion Farms & Kinghaven Farms;previously trained by John Tammaro																	
21Nov82- 8Aqu	fst	6f	:222 :452 1:092	3↑ Sport Page H 57k	3	9	94¾	87¼	87½	78¼	MacBeth D	124	*1.60	86-24	Maudlin1154[D]King'sFashion117hdTopAvengr115nk	No menace	11
Previously trained by Michael Tammaro																	
28Oct82- 8WO	fst	6f	:224 :452 1:092	3↑ Alw 16000	6	1	1½	12½	16	16½	Platts R	115	*.30	96-19	DeputyMinistr1156½ToutOuRien1231½RddyRodstr1262	Easily	6
Previously trained by John Tammaro																	
24Feb82- 9Hia	fst	7f	:232 :46 1:094 1:221	Alw 25000	8	2	31½	21	44½	99	MacBeth D	122	4.70	83-19	DistinctivePro1194½D'Accord1192¼CecisLilBandt115¾	Tired	9
27Jan82- 9Hia	fst	7f	:223 :451 1:094 1:221	Bahamas 38k	5	9	76	57	55½	59½	MacBeth D	122	*1.10	82-19	Aloma'sRulr117hdDstnctvPro1174LtsDontFght1193	Steadied	9
Previously owned by Centurion Farms & Kinghaven Farms																	
5Nov81- 6Med	fst	1 1/16	:232 :471 1:113 1:443	Young America-G1	7	5	42	11	14	13	MacBeth D	122	*1.90	86-17	DeputyMinister1223LaserLight1191RealTwister1192	Driving	14
24Oct81- 8Lrl	gd	1 1/16	:233 :47 1:122 1:443	Lrl Futurity-G1	3	4	42½	1hd	11½	1no	MacBeth D	122	*1.60	85-18	DeputyMinister122noLaserLght1229[D]CgyCougr122hd	Driving	8
10Oct81- 7Bel	fst	1	:233 :464 1:111 1:362	Champagne-G1	11	6	52	41¾	44	48	Cordero A Jr	122	3.50	76-14	TimelyWritr1224¾BeforeDawn1193NewDscovry122nk	Weakened	13
Previously trained by Bill Marko																	
2Aug81- 9WO	fst	6f	:221 :462 1:111	[R]Bull Page 42k	4	7	52½	31½	1½	12½	Duffy L	122	*.30	87-17	DeputyMinstr1222½FraudSquad1152½MapleCrk1173½	Handily	7
11Jly81- 9WO	fst	6f	:222 :45 1:103	Colin 27k	2	5	2½	1hd	1hd	11½	Duffy L	122	*.15	90-15	DeputyMinister1221½RichSaul1151MapleCrk1131¼	Ridden out	6
Previously owned by Centurion Farms																	
21Jun81- 9WO	fst	5½f	:221 :454 1:044	[R]Clarendon 32k	6	1	41¾	31½	1½	14¾	Duffy L	122	*.30	93-16	DeputyMinister1224¾RichSaul1151¼RoyalFriesn1153	Handily	6
8Jun81- 8Bel	fst	5½f	:22 :453 :581 1:044	©Youthful 56k	6	5	33	31½	1½	11¼	Duffy L	122	1.50	91-19	DeputyMinistr1221¼Ringaro1224NwDscovry115hd	Ridden out	6
18May81- 9WO	fst	5f	:22 :451 :571	Victoria 28k	6	1	1½	1hd	11	13¾	Duffy L	117	*1.20	101-16	DeputyMinistr1173¾Youngship1174½RegalSton1171½	Handily	8
10May81- 4WO	fst	5f	:23 :471 :592	[R]Md Sp Wt	6	4	11½	11	14	14	Duffy L	120	2.10	90-17	DeputyMinistr1204BraveRegent1208Pck'sChoc1201¼	Handily	11

Devil's Bag

b. c. 1981, by Halo (Hail to Reason)–Ballade, by Herbager | **Lifetime record: 9 8 0 0 $445,860**

Own.– Hickory Tree Stable
Br.– E.P. Taylor (Md)
Tr.– Woodford C. Stephens

28Apr84- 8CD	fst	1	:232 :46 1:101 1:353	Derby Trial 54k	3	1	11½	12	11½	12¼	Maple E	122	*.10	91-16	Devil's Bag1222¼Biloxi Indian1225Secret Prince1222¾		5
Under steady urging																	
19Apr84- 7Kee	gd	7f	:231 :46 1:111 1:233	Alw 25860	3	2	1hd	12½	15½	115	Maple E	123	*.10	88-27	Devil'sBag12315SoVague1201½TrplSc1234	Widened with ease	5
3Mar84-11Hia	fst	1⅛	:462 1:093 1:341 1:47	Flamingo-G1	7	1	1hd	1hd	33½	47¼	Maple E	122	*.30	90-13	Time for a Change122nkDr. Carter1226Rexson's Hope1221		8
Gave way approaching stretch																	
20Feb84-10Hia	fst	7f	:23 :453 1:092 1:213	[R]Flamingo Prep 29k	2	3	22½	2½	11½	17	Maple E	122	*.05	95-16	Devil'sBg1227FrndlyBob1191¼Tumblr11511	Strong hand ride	4
29Oct83- 8Lrl	fst	1 1/16	:233 :462 1:112 1:421	Lrl Futurity-G1	3	1	1hd	15	14	15¼	Maple E	122	*.05	97-09	Devil'sBag1225¼HailBoldKing1225½Pieda'Tierre1228	Easily	5
15Oct83- 6Bel	fst	1	:23 :461 1:094 1:341	Champagne-G1	3	1	11½	13	15	16	Maple E	122	*.30	94-14	Devil'sBag1226Dr.Carter1223½OurCasey'sBoy1224½	Handily	12
28Sep83- 8Bel	fst	7f	:223 :451 1:083 1:212	Cowdin-G2	5	3	11½	12	15	13	Maple E	115	*.50	95-19	Devil'sBag1153Dr.Carter1153ExitFiveB.1153	Ridden out	9
28Aug83- 7Bel	sly	6f	:22 :452 1:103	Alw 22000	4	3	11½	14½	14½	15¼	Cruguet J	122	*.50	89-16	Devil's Bag1225¼Exit Five B.1195Spender1172½	Handily	6
20Aug83- 6Sar	fst	6f	:221 :453 1:103	Md Sp Wt	6	1	12	11½	14	17½	Maple E	118	*1.10	87-16	Devil'sBag1187½ChimesKeeper1187¼FrenchFlame118nk	Easily	9

Easy Goer

ch. c. 1986, by Alydar (Raise a Native)–Relaxing, by Buckpasser | **Lifetime record: 20 14 5 1 $4,873,770**

Own.– Ogden Phipps
Br.– Ogden Phipps (Ky)
Tr.– Claude McGaughey III

4Jly90- 8Bel	fst	1¼	:463 1:094 1:352 2:00	3↑ Suburban H-G1	1	2	2½	11½	12½	13¾	Day P	126	*.20	97-12	Easy Goer1263¾De Roche1134¾Montubio1131¾	Ridden out	7
28May90- 8Bel	fst	1	:223 :45 1:091 1:342	3↑ Metropolitan H-G1	8	6	55	43½	33½	31¾	Day P	127	*.40	95-18	Criminal Type120nkHousebuster1131½Easy Goer1273		9
Wide,mild response																	
16May90- 8Bel	sly	7f	:232 :463 1:10 1:221	3↑ Gold Stage 47k	2	2	24	21½	1½	17½	Day P	121	*.20	93-14	Easy Goer1217½Hadif11910½Yurtu12129	Ridden out	4
4Nov89-10GP	fst	1¼	:461 1:102 1:35 2:001	3↑ BC Classic-G1	1	6	611	44½	34	2nk	Day P	122	*.50	107-01	Sunday Silence122nkEasy Goer1221Blushing John1269¾		8
Finished boldly																	
7Oct89- 8Bel	fst	1½	:483 1:134 2:05 2:291	3↑ J C Gold Cup-G1	3	4	35½	11	12	14	Day P	121	*.10	74-23	EasyGoer1214Cryptoclearnc12619½ForvrSlvr126¾	Ridden out	7
16Sep89- 8Bel	my	1¼	:481 1:122 1:361 2:01	3↑ Woodward H-G1	1	4	45½	43	1hd	12	Day P	122	*.30	92-17	EasyGoer1222ItsAcedemic109¾ForeverSilver1195	Ridden out	5
19Aug89- 8Sar	fst	1¼	:464 1:103 1:353 2:004	Travers-G1	5	4	34½	21	11½	13	Day P	126	*.20	96-04	EsyGor1263ClvrTrvor1269ShyTom1265¾	Ducked in,ridden out	6
5Aug89- 8Sar	fst	1⅛	:481 1:12 1:36 1:472	3↑ Whitney H-G1	1	4	43	42½	1½	14½	Day P	119	*.30	98-12	Easy Goer1194½Forever Silver122½Cryptoclearance1224		6
Steadied,easily																	
10Jun89- 8Bel	fst	1½	:47 1:111 2:004 2:26	Belmont-G1	7	5	42½	11	14½	18	Day P	126	1.60e	90-13	EasyGoer1268SundaySilnce1261LeVoyageur12612	Ridden out	10
20May89-10Pim	fst	1 3/16	:462 1:093 1:341 1:534	Preakness-G1	2	5	54½	1hd	2hd	2no	Day P	126	*.60	98-10	Sunday Silence126noEasy Goer1265Rock Point1262		8
Broke in air,brushed																	
6May89- 8CD	my	1¼	:463 1:112 1:374 2:05	Ky Derby-G1	13	6	58	52½	63½	22½	Day P	126	*.80e	69-28	Sunday Silence1262½Easy Goer126hdAwe Inspiring126¾		15
Bothered st,rallied																	
22Apr89- 8Aqu	fst	1⅛	:483 1:132 1:382 1:503	Wood Memorial-G1	3	2	2½	2½	11	13	Day P	126	*.10	82-29	EasyGoer1263RockPoint126hdTripleBuck12611½	Ridden out	6
8Apr89- 7Aqu	fst	1	:222 :441 1:083 1:322	Gotham-G2	5	2	42¼	21½	12½	113	Day P	123	*.05	104-14	EasyGoer12313DiamndDonnie1147¼ExpnsvDcson1187½	Handily	5
4Mar89-11GP	fst	7f	:214 :443 1:10 1:221	Swale 57k	1	6	511	310	1½	18¾	Day P	122	*.30	93-18	Easy Goer1228¾Trion112nkTricky Creek1227½	Handily	6
5Nov88- 8CD	my	1 1/16	:233 :471 1:121 1:463	BC Juvenile-G1	9	7	77¾	66	23	21¼	Day P	122	*.30	74-20	IsItTrue1221¼EasyGor1228Tgl1223	Bumped st,jumped tracks	10
15Oct88- 8Bel	fst	1	:224 :453 1:10 1:344	Champagne-G1	1	2	2½	21½	11½	14	Day P	122	*.10	91-17	EasyGoer1224IsItTrue12215½IrishActor1221¼	Ridden out	4
1Oct88- 8Bel	fst	7f	:222 :453 1:104 1:233	Cowdin-G1	6	5	53½	21½	21	13	Day P	122	*.30	84-21	EasyGoer1223WinnersLaugh1221[D]IsItTrue122¾	Ridden out	6
9Sep88- 5Bel	fst	6½f	:22 :444 1:091 1:152	Alw 27000	2	4	35½	34½	11½	15½	Day P	122	*.60	98-16	Easy Goer1225½Winners Laugh1174½Icy Jr,117¾	Ridden out	6
19Aug88- 5Sar	fst	7f	:224 :453 1:101 1:223	Md Sp Wt	2	5	32	32	1hd	12½	Day P	118	*.60	89-19	EasyGoer1182½IsItTru1188MgcEgl1183¾	Steadied,ridden out	8
1Aug88- 3Bel	fst	6f	:23 :463 1:113	Md Sp Wt	4	7	53½	2½	2hd	2no	Day P	118	*1.70	81-18	Lorenzoni118noEasy Goer1185¼Tiajuana1183	Off slowly	7

Eillo

ch. c. 1980, by Mr. Prospector (Raise a Native)–Barbs Dancer, by Northern Dancer

Lifetime record: 17 12 0 1 $657,670

Own.– Crown Stable
Br.– O.A. Cohen (Fla)
Tr.– Budd Lepman

10Nov84- 3Hol	fst	6f	:222 :453 :571 1:101 3↑	BC Sprint-G1	5 2 11½ 11 12½ 1no	Perret C	126	*1.30	- -	Eillo126noCommemorate1241½Fighting Fit1262½	Driving	11
6Oct84- 8Med	fst	6f	:222 :45 1:094 3↑	Chief Pennekeck H 73k	3 1 11 12½ 14 15	Perret C	124	*.50	93-18	Eillo1245Introspective1122¼RollinonOver114nk	Ridden out	6
11Sep84- 8Key	fst	6f	:22 :443 1:084 3↑	Alw 16000	1 3 11½ 12 13 19	Perret C	120	*.20	97-19	Eillo1209Obgyn1202Good Ole Master120¾	Handily	6
21Jly84- 5Mth	sly	6f	:221 :444 1:093 3↑	Alw 17000	5 1 11½ 11½ 13 11¼	Perret C	122	*.40	92-16	Eillo1221¼Lordly Love1173¼Her Pal1153	Driving	6
19Apr84- 9OP	fst	6f	:212 :441 1:09 4↑	Count Fleet H 130k	8 2 1hd 1hd 21½ 79	Perret C	126	*1.10	91-12	Dave'sFriend1221½AllSoldOut1143½LuckySalvton113hd	Tired	8
31Mar84- 9GP	fm	1Ⓣ	:23 :462 1:10 1:35 4↑	Alw 20000	3 1 1hd 21½ 1022 1131	Perret C	115	*.90	64-09	HapesMill1221¼BlueEmmanuelle1151OutofHock122no	Tired	11
5Mar84- 9Hia	fst	7f	:231 :453 1:091 1:214 3↑	Sprint Champ H 76k	5 1 1hd 11 13 16	Perret C	125	*.30	94-23	Eillo1256Awesome Count1141Victorious1143½	Ridden out	5
10Feb84- 9Hia	fst	7f	:23 :452 1:09 1:211 4↑	Alw 20000	4 1 1½ 1½ 12½ 13	Perret C	122	*.30	97-22	Eillo1223Brother Liam122½Bill Wheeler1225	Handily	6
28Jan84- 8Hia	fst	6f	:221 :451 1:084 4↑	Kendall 22k	5 2 11 12 12½ 17	Perret C	122	*.50	99-15	Eillo1227Compo's Tempo1172Fast Reason117nk	Handily	6
9Jan84- 9Hia	fst	6f	:22 :442 1:081 3↑	Tallahassee H 37k	3 2 1½ 12½ 12½ 13	Perret C	115	2.10	102-15	Eillo1153Center Cut1165½In the Bucks111½	Drew clear	10
30Nov83- 9Crc	sly	6½f	:221 :451 1:104 1:173 3↑	Alw 17000	1 4 1½ 1½ 2½ 46½	Perret C	119	*.80	90-19	ChainLink'sDrm117hdMyMc1173½CourtousMjsty1173	Gave way	6
11Nov83- 9Crc	fst	6f	:221 :453 1:111 3↑	Handicap 25000	6 1 1hd 1½ 12 32¾	Perret C	116	*1.40	92-16	Opening Lead1102Center Cut116¾Eillo116½	Weakened	7
8Oct83- 8Bel	fst	6f	:221 :453 1:102 3↑	Fall Highweight H-G2	6 4 3½ 2½ 63½ 78	Velasquez J	130	3.80	82-19	Chas Conerly136½Singh Tu124½Let Burn1344	Tired	9
27Sep83- 8Med	fst	6f	:22 :45 1:082 3↑	Alw 20000	2 3 2hd 11½ 12 14½	Velasquez J	114	*.70	101-14	Eillo1144½KingBoldReality1106JewelrySale1171	Ridden out	7
17Sep83- 7Bel	fst	6f	:222 :454 1:104 3↑	Alw 27000	2 2 1½ 1½ 12½ 1½	Velasquez J	115	*.60	88-17	Eillo115½Nearice1134Big McCoy108no	Driving	7
31Aug83- 7Mth	gd	6f	:231 :461 1:10 3↑	Alw 11500	1 4 11½ 12½ 12½ 17	Perret C	114	*.50	90-20	Eillo1147Talc Powder1156Stoneyford106hd	Ridden out	8
26Feb83- 6GP	fst	6f	:222 :452 1:101	©Md Sp Wt	3 4 11 14 14 18	Perret C	122	*1.10	88-19	Eillo1228Silent Landing1223U.S. Flag1221	Easily	11

Epitome

b. f. 1985, by Summing (Verbatim)–Honest and True, by Mr. Leader

Lifetime record: 14 5 5 1 $631,755

Own.– J.A. Bell III
Br.– Jessica Bell Nicholson & H. Bennett Bell (Ky)
Tr.– Philip Hauswald

24Nov88- 9CD	fst	1⅛	:472 1:122 1:382 1:514 3↑	ⒻFalls City H-G3	14 10 107¼ 107¼ 42½ 22	Day P	116	3.80e	81-20	Top Corsage1212Epitome1163Lawyer Talk111hd	No threat	14
5Nov88- 6CD	my	1⅛	:474 1:12 1:381 1:52 3↑	ⒻBC Distaff-G1	1 7 810 816 813 713½	Day P	119	10.30e	68-20	PersonlEnsign123noWinnngColrs119½GoodbyHlo1195	Outrun	9
25Oct88- 7Kee	fst	1 1/16	:251 :491 1:14 1:461 3↑	ⒻAlw 28600	1 1 1hd 2½ 1hd 22	Day P	120	*.30	73-24	Stoneleigh'sHope1172Epitome1203DoItaZn112½	Led,weakened	5
8Oct88- 6Kee	fst	1 1/16	:25 :491 1:131 1:45 3↑	ⒻAlw 40600	5 5 42½ 31 1hd 11½	Romero RP	113	*.50e	81-21	Epitome1131½StillWaving1141Bstofbothworlds118no	Driving	6
17Sep88- 4Bel	fst	6f	:224 :46 1:101 3↑	ⒻAlw 30000	1 4 54½ 45 43½ 1hd	Day P	113	3.80	88-08	Epitome113hdBanbury Fair1153¼Sharpening Up1172	Driving	7
1Apr88- 9OP	fst	1 1/16	:231 :47 1:12 1:434	ⒻHoneybee 88k	1 6 76½ 54½ 24 24½	Day P	115	*.80e	77-27	LostKitty1154½Epitome1153Far'sTm1155	Jumped gate tracks	8
21Nov87- 2Hol	fst	1	:22 :44 1:09 1:362	ⒻBC Juv Fillies-G1	6 11 1114 89 36 1no	Day P	119	30.40	81-12	Epitme119noJeanneJones1192¾DremTm119hd	Up final stride	12
8Nov87- 8CD	fst	1	:221 :451 1:113 1:381	ⒻPocahontas 53k	5 9 98½ 43½ 22 12¼	Day P	114	*1.50	78-19	Epitome1142¼Darien Miss1145Cushion Cut1181¼	Driving	9
24Oct87- 8Kee	fst	1 1/16	:224 :462 1:104 1:443	ⒻAlcibiades H-G2	7 6 78¼ 65½ 34½ 22½	Smith ME	118	13.70	80-15	Terra Incognita1182½Epitome118¾Pearlie Gold1187	Rallied	8
13Oct87- 3Kee	fst	1 1/16	:233 :474 1:132 1:454	ⒻMd Sp Wt	2 7 44½ 42 11 15	Day P	120	*.90	77-13	Epitome1205Indian Riffle120¾Sincere Foolish1205	Easily	12
7Sep87- 6Bel	fst	7f	:221 :46 1:114 1:252	ⒻMd Sp Wt	3 4 54½ 53 32½ 34¾	Migliore R	117	5.00	70-19	Aquaba1171¾Dangerous Type1173Epitome1173¾	Rallied	10
13Aug87- 3Sar	fst	7f	:221 :453 1:11 1:241	ⒻMd Sp Wt	8 7 75 66 24 22½	Santos JA	117	6.20e	78-14	WinningColors1172½Epitome1174Bippus1171½	Lugged in late	11
20Jly87- 4Bel	my	5½f	:223 :462 :584 1:052	ⒻMd Sp Wt	7 9 79 89¼ 610 511¼	Romero RP	117	3.70	77-15	Truth or Dare1174Missy Valentine1171¾Towering Success1125		10
			Slow start,wide									
28Jun87- 4Bel	fst	5½f	:23 :464 :592 1:06	ⒻMd Sp Wt	4 9 811 89¼ 58 54¾	Bailey JD	117	37.90	80-19	Joe's Tammie1122¾Heavenly Halo1172Connecting Link117no		9
			Raced wide									

Estrapade

ch. f. 1980, by Vaguely Noble (Vienna)–Klepto, by No Robbery

Lifetime record: 30 12 5 5 $1,924,556

Own.– A.E. Paulson
Br.– N.B. Hunt (Ky)
Tr.– Charles Whittingham

7Dec86- 8Hol	fm	1½Ⓣ	:474 1:121 2:01 2:254 3↑	Hol Turf Cup Inv'l-G1	8 4 4¾ 54 79½ 612¼	Toro F	123	*1.20e	81-09	Alphabatim126hdDahar126nkTheatrical126½	Weakened	8
1Nov86- 6SA	fm	1½Ⓣ	:472 1:111 2:003 2:252 3↑	BC Turf-G1	5 1 12½ 11 2hd 34	Toro F	123	2.70e	84-07	Manila122nkTheatrical1263¾Estrapade123¾	Weakened	9
12Oct86- 8SA	fm	1½Ⓣ	:464 1:111 2:003 2:26 3↑	Oak Tree Inv'l-G1	6 1 11½ 12 12 12¼	Toro F	123	*.40e	85-12	Estrapade1232¼Theatrical1265½Uptown Swell126½	Driving	10
31Aug86- 8AP	fm	1¼Ⓣ	:471 1:113 1:371 2:004 3↑	Bud Arl Million-G1	7 6 64½ 1hd 11½ 15	Toro F	122	*2.10e	90-11	Estrapade1225Divulge126hdPennine Walk126½	Driving	14
9Aug86- 8Dmr	fm	1Ⓣ	:23 :461 1:104 1:342 3↑	ⒻPalomar H-G2	3 3 32 41 44½ 65¾	Toro F	124	*.90e	94-04	Aberuschka118hdSauna1183½Fran's Valentine119nk	Boxed in	9
29Jun86- 8Hol	fm	1¼Ⓣ	:464 1:104 1:341 1:59 3↑	ⒻBeverly Hills H-G2	3 2 25 11½ 11½ 1½	Toro F	122	*.90e	112-02	Estrapade122½Treizieme1151½Sauna1172¼	Driving	7
8Jun86- 8Hol	fm	1⅛Ⓣ	:461 1:10 1:334 1:454 3↑	ⒻGamely H-G1	5 3 32 31½ 31 21¾	Shoemaker W	123	*.70	101-00	La Koumia1181¾Estrapade1232¼Tax Dodge1151¼	Steadied	8
25May86- 8Hol	fm	1 1/16Ⓣ	:25 :484 1:121 1:413 3↑	ⒻWilshire H-G2	5 3 2½ 2hd 3nk 3nk	Shoemaker W	124	*.60	96-03	Outstandingly117hdLaKoumia118hdEstrapade1243½	Held well	5
30Mar86- 8SA	fm	1¼Ⓣ	:481 1:124 1:363 2:01 4↑	ⒻS Barbara H-G1	7 4 41½ 3½ 21½ 2½	Shoemaker W	124	*.80e	81-16	MountainBear119½Estrapade1243½RoyalRegatta1162¼	Gamely	8
24Nov85- 8Hol	fm	1⅛Ⓣ	:464 1:104 1:36 1:481 3↑	ⒻMatriarch Inv'l-G1	5 2 21 1hd 1hd 41¾	Shoemaker W	123	*.60e	- -	FactFinder1231Tamarinda123noPossibleMate123¾	Weakened	10
			Previously owned by Summa Stable (Lessee)									
10Nov85- 8SA	fm	1¼Ⓣ	:473 1:114 1:352 2:002 3↑	ⒻYellow Ribbon Inv'l-G1	8 3 31½ 31 11 1¾	Shoemaker W	123	*.80	85-18	Estrapade123¾Alydar's Best118½La Koumia118½	Driving	11
19Oct85- 8SA	fm	1⅛Ⓣ	:453 1:094 1:35 1:471 3↑	ⒻLas Palmas H-G2	7 4 42½ 31 13 13½	Shoemaker W	124	*1.00e	91-12	Estrapade1243½L'Attrayante118noJohnica1181¾	Driving	11
2Sep85- 8Dmr	fst	*1¼	:461 1:103 1:352 1:58 3↑	Dmr Inv'l H-G2	1 1 11 2hd 21 43¾	Delahoussaye E	117	*2.70	83-15	Barberstown117½My Habitony1181First Norman1142¼	Tired	10
14Jly85- 8Hol	fst	1⅛	:453 1:092 1:342 1:474 3↑	ⒻVanity Inv'l H-G1	4 6 611 55½ 34½ 33	Stevens G	119	2.90	107-02	DontstopThemusic118¾SaltSpring1142¼Estrapd1192½	Rallied	7
30Jun85- 8Hol	fm	1⅛Ⓣ	:482 1:123 1:362 1:481 3↑	ⒻBeverly Hills H-G2	3 2 21 21 2hd 2no	McCarron CJ	125	*.40	89-09	Johnc115noEstrpd125½L'Attrynt1184	Veered in,bumped start	5
2Jun85- 8Hol	fm	1⅛Ⓣ	:471 1:101 1:342 1:463 3↑	ⒻGamely H-G1	1 5 43½ 42 2hd 1¾	McCarron CJ	124	*.80	97-05	Estrapade124¾Johnica115½Possible Mate1162	Driving	6
21Apr85- 8SA	fm	*1¾Ⓣ	:461 2:01 2:262 2:474 4↑	S Juan Capistrano H-G1	2 2 11 11 1½ 21½	Toro F	120	1.40e	123-14	Prince True1241½Estrapade120hdSwoon117¾	Gamely	7
16Mar85- 8SA	fm	1⅛Ⓣ	:461 1:103 1:35 1:47 4↑	ⒻSanta Ana H-G1	4 3 32½ 31 13 16	Toro F	123	*2.50	92-10	Estrapade1236FactFinder119nkAirDstngu1161¼	Easily	10
24Feb85- 8SA	fst	1⅛	:46 1:10 1:35 1:48 4↑	ⒻS Margarita Inv'l H-G1	7 7 54 78½ 819 830	Toro F	123	3.10	59-16	LovlierLinda1193Mitternd1231¾Prcpnt1161½	Showed nothing	8
31Jan85- 8SA	fm	1⅛Ⓣ	:472 1:114 1:354 1:473 4↑	ⒻAlw 42000	4 5 41¾ 2hd 12½ 15½	Toro F	118	*.70	89-16	Estrapade1185½Clear Talk1135Linda's Leader1132	In hand	6
			Previously trained by Maurice Zilber									
21Oct84- 8SA	fm	1¼Ⓣ	:472 1:113 1:354 2:00 3↑	ⒻYellow Ribbon Inv'l-G1	8 6 65 32 33 33½	Lequeux A	123	20.00	83-13	Sabin1232¼Grise Mine1181¼Estrapade123hd	Bid,hung	8
7Oct84♦ Longchamp(Fr)	sf	*1½ⓉRH	2:39 3↑	Arc de Triomphe-G1 Stk550000	1530	Samani H	127	31.00		Sagace1302Northern Trick1206All Along127¾	Chased leaders,weakened halfway.Sadler's Wells 6th	22
27Sep84♦ Maisns-Lfftte(Fr)	sf	*1¼ⓉStr	2:083 3↑	La Coupe de Maisons-Laffitte-G3 Stk63000	14	Lequeux A	122	2.50e		Estrapade1224Palace Music121nkBob Back119nk	In touch,led over 1f out,drew clear 170y out.Seattle Song 4th	11
16Sep84♦ Longchamp(Fr)	sf	*1¼ⓉRH	2:143 3↑	Pr Prince d'Orange-G3 Stk62700	42½	Guignard G	122	5.20		Lovely Dancer1301½Fly Me124½Darly126nk	Midpack,bid over 1f out,gaining late,just missed 3rd	8
16May84♦ Longchamp(Fr)	yl	*1¼ⓉRH	2:152 4↑	ⒻPrix de la Pepiniere (Listed) Stk40000	13	Lequeux A	123	*.60		Estrapade1233Badinage119½Maganyos1273	Led throughout,ridden clear 1f out,going away	5
21Apr84♦ Saint-Cloud(Fr)	yl	*1 5/16 LH	2:24 4↑	ⒻPrix Corrida-G3 Stk62000	34¾	Lequeux A	126	3.00		Fly Me128¾Marie de Litz1284Estrapade1261	Rated toward rear,progress to take 3rd near line	11

24Mar84♦ Saint-Cloud(Fr) gd *1 5/16Ⓣ LH 2:23³ Ⓕ Prix Transvaal Alw30500 5 1¾ Lequeux A 120 *1.00 Sisnel121nkAborigine118½Olindo121½ 8
Rated in 7th,sharp run over 1f out,hung

11Sep83♦ Longchamp(Fr) yl *1½Ⓣ RH 2:42 Ⓕ Pr Vermeille-G1 Stk268000 2² Piggott L 128 3.20 Sharaya128²Estrapade128nkVosges128nk 12
Chased winner over 1f out,hard ridden,saved 2nd

4Sep83♦ Longchamp(Fr) gd *1½Ⓣ RH 2:38¹ 3↑ Ⓕ Prix des Tourelles Alw29000 1³ Piggott L 118 *.80 Estrapade118³Fly Me118⁴Tinorosa126² 8
Rated in 6th,rallied to lead over 1f out,soon clear,handily

6Aug83♦ Deauville(Fr) gd *1¼Ⓣ RH 2:11 Ⓕ Prix de Dives Mdn24500 1nk St Martin Y 128 3.00e Estrapade128nkDear Lorraine128²Allicance128 1½ 14
Rated at rear,wide bid 3f out,long drive to lead near line

Family Style

ch. f. 1983, by State Dinner (Buckpasser)–Sharp Kitty, by Blade — Lifetime record: 35 10 8 7 $1,537,118
Own.– Mr & Mrs Eugene V. Klein
Br.– Selective Seasons (Ky)
Tr.– D. Wayne Lukas

27Sep87- 8Bel fst 1⅛ :46² 1:09² 1:35 1:48³ 3↑ Ⓕ Ruffian H-G1 11 2 5 2½ 8 6¼ 10 9¼ 11 6½ Day P 121 *.40e 77-19 ⒹSacahuista114hdCoup de Fusil117 1¾Clabber Girl112½ 12
Finished at far turn
23Aug87- 9AP fst 1⅛ :46⁴ 1:12 1:38³ 1:52¹ 3↑ Ⓕ Arl Matron-G2 3 1 1½ 1¹ 1 2½ 1 1¼ Hawley S 123 *.30 70-30 Family Style123 1¼Royal Cielo113 2½Tide114hd Driving 7
2Aug87- 8AP fst 1 :22⁴ :45 1:09⁴ 1:35 3↑ Ⓕ Cleopatra 54k 5 2 2 2½ 1hd 1³ 1⁹ Hawley S 123 *.50 86-22 FamilyStyle123⁹LadyVernl115½MssBd115⁵ Drifted wide turn 6
18Jly87-10Aks fst 1⅛ :47¹ 1:11³ 1:37² 1:50² 3↑ Ⓕ Queen's H-G3 6 2 2¹ 2hd 2hd 2hd Doocy TT 122 *.70 85-25 SocialBusinss111hdFmlyStyl122 3½HppyHollowMss117½ Gamely 8
5Jly87-10Aks fst 1 1/16 :23 :46¹ 1:10² 1:44² 3↑ Ⓕ Bud BC 133k 4 3 2² 2³ 2¹ 2² Doocy TT 122 *1.00 79-24 Explosive Girl110²Family Style122²Turn and Dance114nk 9
Saved ground
30May87- 8Hol fst 7f :22¹ :45 1:10¹ 1:23 3↑ Ⓕ A Gleam H-G3 1 7 7 3¾ 5 4½ 5 3½ 6 5½ Stevens GL 120 7.80 83-14 Le L'Argent118¾Sari's Heroine117 3½Rare Starlet115¹ 8
Off slowly,outrun
1May87- 7CD fst 1 1/16 :24 :48 1:11³ 1:42⁴ 3↑ Ⓕ Bud BC H 154k 6 2 2¹ 3² 4⁴ 5⁶ Stevens GL 119 *.40e 88-12 Queen Alexandra117¾Infinidad116 2½I'm Sweets116 2¾ 6
Saved ground,gave way
15Apr87- 9OP fst 1 1/16 :23² :46³ 1:10¹ 1:41⁴ 4↑ Ⓕ Apple Blossom H-G1 4 3 3 2½ 3³ 2³ 2⁴ Stevens GL 120 *.30 91-18 NorthSider122⁴FamilyStyle120²QueenAlexndr119 2½ 2nd best 7
1Mar87- 8SA fst 1⅛ :45⁴ 1:10³ 1:36 1:48⁴ 4↑ Ⓕ S Margarita Inv'l H-G1 3 3 4⁴ 5 1½ 4⁴ 6 4¾ Stevens GL 120 2.40e 80-15 NorthSider117hdWinterTreasure115 1¼FrauAltiva117nk Tired 12
15Feb87- 8SA my 1⅛ :46² 1:10³ 1:36¹ 1:49³ Ⓕ La Canada-G1 2 2 2 2½ 1hd 1² 1 2½ Stevens GL 122 *1.00 81-17 FamilyStyle122 2½WinterTreasure117⁴Sr'sHron121 1¾ Driving 6
24Jan87- 8SA fst 1 1/16 :23¹ :47¹ 1:11⁴ 1:43 Ⓕ El Encino-G3 5 4 4⁵ 4⁴ 4 4½ 4 10¼ Stevens GL 122 *.80 76-18 SeldomSeenSue114⁶Miraculous117 1¾TopCorsage122 2½ Tired 6
3Jan87- 8SA fst 7f :22² :45¹ 1:10 1:22³ Ⓕ La Brea-G3 1 5 4 2¾ 4 1¾ 1¹ 1⁶ Stevens GL 122 *1.70e 87-16 Family Style122⁶Sari's Heroine119hdWinter Treasure117 1¾ 6
Finished strongly
6Dec86- 8Hol gd 1⅛ :46² 1:11² 1:36⁴ 1:50 3↑ Ⓕ Silver Belles H-G2 1 3 3 1½ 2 1½ 1² 1½ Stevens GL 115 6.70 87-13 Family Style115½Infinidad114 9½Waterside113 2¼ 7
Drifted out into str,swerved,lugged in,gamely
31Oct86- 8SA fst 1 1/16 :23¹ :46³ 1:11² 1:43¹ Ⓕ Linda Vista H-G3 8 8 8 4¾ 9 4¾ 9 9¼ 8 11¼ Delahoussaye E 121 *1.70 74-16 Marianna'sGirl114 1¼WintrTrsur118 2½FnKudos115 1¾ No rally 9
22Oct86- 8SA fst 6½f :22¹ :45² 1:09⁴ 1:16¹ 3↑ Ⓕ Cascapedia H 48k 1 5 5⁴ 5 5¼ 5⁴ 3² Delahoussaye E 117 10.50 87-23 Winter Treasure117¾Her Royalty121 1¼Family Style117 3½ 5
5 wide into str
2Aug86- 9Aks fst 1⅛ :48 1:12 1:37² 1:50³ Ⓕ Aks Oaks-G3 3 5 4 2½ 3 3½ 5⁸ 7 12¼ Baze RA 120 *.30 72-20 TrickyFingers117⁴LadyGallnt111⁴Mrnn'sGrl116hd No excuse 9
6Jly86- 9Hol fst 1⅛ :45⁴ 1:10¹ 1:34⁴ 1:47⁴ Ⓕ Hol Oaks-G1 2 2 2 2½ 2² 3⁷ 3¹¹ McCarron CJ 121 2.10 87-09 HiddenLight121⁵AnEmpress121⁶FamilyStyle121²⁰ Faltered 4
14Jun86- 8Bel fst 1⅛ :46³ 1:11¹ 1:36² 1:49³ Ⓕ Mother Goose-G1 5 4 4 5½ 3 1½ 2½ 3¹ Vasquez J 121 *.80e 78-20 LifeattheTop121½DynamicStar121½FamlyStyl121no Lugged in 8
26May86- 6GS fst 1⅛ :46⁴ 1:12 1:38³ 1:51² Ⓕ Jersey Belle 152k 3 3 4³ 3 1½ 2hd 2no Pincay L Jr 121 *.40 72-20 I'm Sweets118noFamily Style121 9½True Chompion118 6¼ 8
Bumped turn,missed
16May86- 9Pim fst 1 1/16 :22⁴ :46⁴ 1:11¹ 1:44³ Ⓕ Black-Eyed Susan-G2 1 2 2² 2 1½ 1² 1 3¼ McCarron CJ 121 *.40 81-22 Family Style121 3¼Steel Maiden121 1½Firgie's Jule121½ 8
Lugged in,driving
2May86- 9CD fst 1⅛ :46³ 1:11 1:37¹ 1:50³ Ⓕ Ky Oaks-G1 10 8 8 6½ 7 4¼ 3 1½ 3nk McCarron CJ 121 4.40e 89-14 TiffanyLass121hdLifeattheTop121nkFamlyStyl121hd Rallied 12
19Apr86- 9OP sly 1⅛ :45⁴ 1:10¹ 1:35⁴ 1:48¹ Ark Derby-G1 1 4 4² 4 1¾ 3² 3 4½ Maple S 121 2.90e 88-07 Rampage118 1½Wheatly Hall115³Family Style121³ Evenly 14
12Apr86- 9OP fst 1 1/16 :23² :47¹ 1:11³ 1:42 Ⓕ Fantasy-G1 7 6 3¹ 3¹ 3 2½ 4 4¼ McCarron CJ 121 *2.00 86-16 Tiffany Lass121 2½Lotka116²Turn and Dance112hd No rally 8
23Mar86- 8SA fst 1 1/16 :23 :46³ 1:11² 1:42² Ⓕ S Anita Oaks-G1 1 4 4³ 4 1½ 4⁵ 4⁵ Pincay L Jr 117 1.50e 84-17 HiddenLight117 1½TwilightRidge117 2¼AnEmpress117 1¼ Evenly 6
5Mar86- 9GP fst 1 1/16 :23² :47⁴ 1:12³ 1:45¹ Ⓕ Bonnie Miss-G3 3 4 3³ 3³ 3 3½ 3 3¾ Velasquez J 121 3.00 71-27 PatriciaJ.K.121 3¼Noranc121½FamilyStyle121 4½ Drifted out 11
15Dec85- 8Hol fst 1 :22 :44³ 1:09 1:34¹ Hol Futurity-G1 6 8 7⁵ 6⁹ 5 8½ 6 13¼ Pincay L Jr 118 *2.10 79-09 SnowChief121 6½ElectricBlue121noFerdinnd121nk Wide,tired 10
24Nov85- 8Aqu fst 1⅛ :49¹ 1:13³ 1:38² 1:50¹ Ⓕ Demoiselle-G1 3 5 5 3½ 5 2¾ 2hd 2nk Velasquez J 121 *.40 84-15 I'mSweets121nkFamilyStyle121nkStealKss112 4¾ Just missed 8
2Nov85- 2Aqu fst 1 :22³ :45² 1:10⁴ 1:35⁴ Ⓕ BC Juv Fillies-G1 1 6 6 3¾ 3² 2 2½ 2¹ Pincay L Jr 119 *.60e 86-10 Twilight Ridge119¹Family Style119 7¼Steal a Kiss119 3¼ 12
Bore in start
14Oct85- 8Bel fst 1 :22⁴ :46 1:11¹ 1:37¹ Ⓕ Frizette-G1 2 3 3¹ 3½ 1½ 1 1½ Pincay L Jr 119 1.20 79-19 FamilyStyle119 1½Funistrada119hdGuadery119⁶ Brisk urging 7
29Sep85- 8Bel fst 7f :23 :46⁴ 1:11² 1:24 Ⓕ Matron-G1 1 2 3 1½ 4 2½ 2³ 2nk Pincay L Jr 119 *.60 82-19 MusicalLark119nkFamilyStyle119 2½I'mSweets119no Game try 5
7Sep85- 8Haw fst 6½f :22² :45⁴ 1:11¹ 1:18 Ⓕ Arl-Wash Lassie-G1 1 6 5 3½ 6 2¾ 2hd 1² Pincay L Jr 119 *.70 83-26 Family Style119²Deep Silver119⁴Pamela Kay119² Driving 8
26Aug85- 8Sar sly 6f :22 :45³ 1:12 Ⓕ Spinaway-G1 5 5 5 6½ 5 9½ 4⁵ 1¹ MacBeth D 119 *2.30e 80-21 FamilyStyle119¹MusicalLark119hdNervousBaba119nk Driving 7
15Aug85- 8Sar fst 6f :21⁴ :44³ 1:09³ Ⓕ Adirondack-G2 5 5 2² 2 1½ 2² 2 1¾ MacBeth D 114 2.80e 90-08 NervousBaba114 1¾FamilyStyle114 4¼StealaKiss114nk Gamely 8
28Jly85- 6Bel fst 6f :22³ :46² 1:11³ Ⓕ Md Sp Wt 5 2 2hd 1¹ 1⁴ 1⁷ Velasquez J 117 *.70 84-16 FmilyStyle117⁷PasdsTros117¹NorthofDnzg117 2½ Ridden out 8
7Jly85- 6Bel fst 5½f :22³ :45⁴ :58 1:04² Ⓕ Md Sp Wt 1 1 3⁴ 3⁵ 3 6½ 3⁷ Velasquez J 117 14.40 86-16 Storm and Sunshine117 4¾Patti's Lark117 2¼Family Style117 2½ 9
Bore out stretch

Ferdinand

ch. c. 1983, by Nijinsky II (Northern Dancer)–Banja Luka, by Double Jay — Lifetime record: 29 8 9 6 $3,777,978
Own.– Mrs H.B. Keck
Br.– H.B. Keck (Ky)
Tr.– Charles Whittingham

22Oct88- 8SA fst 1⅛ :46² 1:09⁴ 1:34² 1:47¹ 3↑ Goodwood H-G3 2 4 5⁴ 6 5¼ 5 6½ 5⁷ Shoemaker W 125 *1.60 86-12 Cutlass Reality124 1¾Lively One116 1¼Stylish Winner113 3½ 8
Saved ground,no rally
26Jun88- 8Hol fst 1¼ :45⁴ 1:09³ 1:34² 1:59² 3↑ Hol Gold Cup H-G1 4 4 4⁷ 4 1¾ 3 4½ 3¹² Shoemaker W 125 2.60 83-07 Cutlass Reality116 6½Alysheba126 5½Ferdinand125⁴ 6
Bid,lacked late response
12Jun88- 8Hol fst 1⅛ :47³ 1:10⁴ 1:35 1:47³ 3↑ Californian-G1 3 4 4 1½ 4⁴ 4⁷ 4⁹ Shoemaker W 126 *.70 90-09 CutlassRelty115 2¾Gulch126 4½JudgAnglucc126 1¾ No response 4
17Apr88- 8SA fst 1⅛ :46² 1:09⁴ 1:34³ 1:47¹ 4↑ S Bernardino H-G2 3 3 3² 2hd 1hd 2no Shoemaker W 127 1.00 93-17 Alysheba127noFerdinand127hdGood Taste113 3½ Just missed 5
6Mar88- 8SA fst 1¼ :46³ 1:10 1:34³ 1:59⁴ 4↑ S Anita H-G1 4 4 4 5½ 2½ 2¹ 2½ Shoemaker W 127 1.70 89-13 Alysheba126½Ferdinnd127 2½SuperDmond124 2¼ Wide,2nd best 4
14Feb88- 8SA fst 1⅛ :45⁴ 1:10² 1:35⁴ 1:48³ 4↑ San Antonio H-G1 1 6 6¹² 5 6½ 3 5½ 2 3½ Shoemaker W 128 *.70 82-20 Judge Angelucci122 3½Ferdinand128nkCrimson Slew115 2¼ 6
Rallied,2nd best
21Nov87- 7Hol fst 1¼ :46² 1:10¹ 1:35² 2:01² 3↑ BC Classic-G1 6 7 6 4¾ 3 1½ 3½ 1no Shoemaker W 126 *1.00 85-12 Ferdinand126noAlysheba122 1¼JudgeAngelucc126 1½ Prevailed 12
7Nov87- 8SA my 1⅛ :48³ 1:13¹ 1:37³ 1:50⁴ 3↑ Goodwood H-G3 4 5 5 3½ 5² 2¹ 1¹ Shoemaker W 127 1.60 75-26 Ferdinand127¹Candi's Gold117¾Skywalker123hd Driving 5
29Aug87- 8Dmr fst 1⅛ :45³ 1:09¹ 1:34⁴ 1:47² 3↑ Cabrillo H 125k 2 3 2¹ 2hd 1hd 1² Shoemaker W 126 1.50 93-12 Ferdinnd126²SuperDiamond124 2½Nostalg'sStr116 Ridden out 3
28Jun87- 8Hol fst 1¼ :46 1:09³ 1:34³ 2:00³ 3↑ Hol Gold Cup H-G1 5 5 4² 2¹ 2½ 1 1¼ Shoemaker W 124 *.40e 89-12 Ferdinand124 1¼ⒹⒽJudge Angelucci118ⒹⒽTasso115⁴ Driving 11
7Jun87- 8Hol fst 1⅛ :46⁴ 1:10⁴ 1:35³ 1:48¹ 3↑ Californian-G1 1 7 6⁵ 5 3½ 5⁴ 4 3¾ Shoemaker W 126 *1.70 92-17 JudgeAngelucci118¹IronEyes115noSnowChief126 2¾ No rally 8
10May87- 8Hol fm 1⅛Ⓣ :49 1:12² 1:35³ 1:47 3↑ John Henry H-G1 5 2 2½ 2hd 2 1½ 3 2¼ Shoemaker W 123 1.90 91-09 Al Mamoon121¾Skip Out Front114 1½Ferdinand123no Tired 5
29Mar87- 8SA fm 1½Ⓣ :49³ 1:14³ 2:03¹ 2:27¹ 4↑ San Luis Rey-G1 2 1 1½ 2hd 3nk 4 2¼ Shoemaker W 126 *1.50 77-19 Zoffny126nkLouisLeGrnd126nkLongMick126 1¾ Broke stride 5
8Mar87- 8SA fst 1¼ :45⁴ 1:10¹ 1:35 2:00³ 4↑ S Anita H-G1 9 5 5 5¾ 1hd 1¹ 2no Shoemaker W 125 *1.30e 86-15 Broad Brush122noFerdinand125 6½Hopeful Word117nk Sharp 9

8Feb87- 8SA fst 1¼ :464 1:102 1:343 2:00 C H Strub-G1 4 2 31 2½ 21½ 2no Delahoussaye E 126 *2.00 89-14 SnowChf126noFrdnnd1264½BrodBrush1267 Bumped hard late 8
18Jan87- 8SA fst 1⅛ :482 1:121 1:363 1:49 San Fernando-G1 1 6 54 55 45 46½ Shoemaker W 123 1.30 77-19 VarietyRoad123nkBroadBrush1262¾SnowChief1263½ Checked 8
26Dec86- 8SA fst 7f :222 :444 1:09 1:213 Malibu-G2 11 10 96¼ 75¼ 41¾ 11¼ Shoemaker W 123 4.20 92-13 Ferdinand1231¼Snow Chief1261½Don B. Blue1144 Driving 12
7Jun86- 8Bel sly 1½ :474 1:124 2:04 2:294 Belmont-G1 7 5 33½ 3½ 2½ 31½ Shoemaker W 126 3.60 69-16 DanzigConnecton1261¼JohnsTrsur126nkFrdnnd1262¾ Steadied 10
17May86- 8Pim fst 1 3/16 :472 1:11 1:36 1:544 Preakness-G1 5 6 614 612 24 24 Shoemaker W 126 3.10 89-18 SnowChief1264Ferdinnd1266½BrodBrush126no Best of others 7
3May86- 8CD fst 1¼ :451 1:101 1:37 2:024 Ky Derby-G1 1 15 1620 52 11 12¼ Shoemaker W 126 17.70 83-10 Frdnnd1262¼BoldArrngmnt126¾BrodBrush126nk Bothered start 16
6Apr86- 5SA fst 1⅛ :471 1:11 1:36 1:483 S Anita Derby-G1 2 6 55 54 54½ 37 Shoemaker W 122 5.20 79-15 Snow Chief1226Icy Groom1221Ferdinand122¾ No threat 7
22Feb86- 8SA fst 1 :223 :453 1:102 1:353 San Rafael-G2 9 7 77¼ 41½ 12 2½ Shoemaker W 116 *1.90 89-16 VarietyRoad116½Ferdinand1166½JettingHom116¾ Just failed 9
29Jan86- 8SA fst 1 1/16 :23 :462 1:11 1:43 ⓇS Catalina 65k 6 7 64¾ 64½ 32 1½ Shoemaker W 114 2.20 86-15 Ferdinand114½VarietyRoad1142¾GrandAllegInc1172½ Driving 8
4Jan86- 8SA fst 1 :221 :453 1:103 1:361 ⒸⓇLos Feliz 81k 3 4 32½ 3½ 11½ 2hd Shoemaker W 114 b *.80 87-13 Badger Land117hdFerdinand1146Cut by Glass1161¼ Wide str 7
15Dec85- 8Hol fst 1 :22 :443 1:09 1:341 Hol Futurity-G1 2 9 95¾ 35½ 35½ 36½ Shoemaker W 121 b 34.40 85-09 SnowChief1216½ElectricBlue121noFerdinnd121nk Off slowly 10
Previously owned by H.B. Keck
3Nov85- 1SA fst 1 :231 :471 1:12 1:372 Md Sp Wt 1 3 32½ 11 11 12¼ Ward WA 117 b *.40 81-15 Ferdinand1172¼StarRibot1173½ImperiousSpirt1172¾ Driving 6
20Oct85- 6SA fst 1 :223 :463 1:12 1:373 Md Sp Wt 7 6 53¼ 2½ 2hd 2no Toro F 117 b *2.30 80-17 AcksLikaRuler117noFerdinand1174½Franknstrll1171¾ Bumped 10
6Oct85- 6SA fst 6f :214 :451 :573 1:101 Md Sp Wt 3 10 96 56¾ 48 311 Shoemaker W 117 b 18.70 76-16 Judge Smells1178½Our Grey Fox1172½Ferdinand1172 Outrun 12
8Sep85- 6Dmr fst 6f :223 :46 :581 1:102 Md Sp Wt 5 10 1012 1012 89½ 811½ Shoemaker W 118 b 4.30 74-08 Don B. Blue118hdEl Corazon1185½Au Bon Marche1181 Outrun 11

Flatterer

dkbbr. g. 1979, by Mo Bay (Cyane)–Horizontal, by Nade **Lifetime record: 51 24 7 5 $538,708**

Own.– W.L. Pape
Br.– Pape & Sheppard (Pa)
Tr.– Jonathan E. Sheppard

31Oct87- 5Fai fm *2⅝ S'Chase 5:151 3↑ BC Chase 250k 10 2 - - - - Dunwoody R 156 *.80 -- Gacko1568¾Inlander156½Gateshead1563¾ Pulled up 10
17Oct87- 6GrM fm *2Ⓣ 3:312 3↑ Alw 1000 2 4 32 22 22 16 Fitzgerald JM 155 - -- Flatterer1556FleetingRoy1584WhisperingGrass1551 Handily 13
9May87- 6PW fm *3 S'Chase 5:273 4↑ Iroquois Mem 100k 2 3 31¾ 15 16 14 Tomson-Jones T 168 - -- Flatterr1684SameEchelon1681¼Eremt1682 Never threatened 9
18Apr87- 5Mid sf *2⅛ S'Chase 4:243 4↑ Middleburg H 25k 1 2 22 22 32½ 36½ Thompson TL 178 - -- Gogong1503½Sailor's Dance1543Flatterer1789 No gain 5
17Mar87♦ Cheltenham(GB) 2LH 3:571 4↑ Champion Hurdle Stk101000 21½ Fishback J 168 10.00 See You Then1681½Flatterer1681Barnbrook Again1686 18
Outpaced approaching 3 out,rallied 1 out,finished well
16Nov86- 4Cam fm 2¾ S'Chase 5:124 4↑ Colonial Cup Int'l 60k 2 5 64 2hd 15 117 Fishback J 162 - -- Flatterer16217TurtleHead1621¼JeanRapier1622¾ Ridden out 9
18Oct86- 5RB fm *1½Ⓣ 2:282 3↑ Alw 1000 1 9 97½ 21 13 110 Dufton E 145 - -- Flatterer14510Rug Raiser1551Student Dancer1451 Easily 10
27Jun86♦ Auteuil(Fr) yl *3 3/16LH 6:09 5↑ Grande Course de Haies d'Auteuil Stk160000 25 Dunwoody R 141 9.50 Le Rheusois1415Flatterer1412Gacko13720 7
Tracked pacesetting winner,bid 2 out,second best
17May86- 6Mal fm *2¼ S'Chase 4:182 4↑ Nat'l Hunt Cup H 25k 5 2 32 13½ 16 17 Fishback J 176 - -- Flatterer1767Jolly Four1488Kalankoe1505 Driving 5
5Apr86- 4AtH fm *2 S'Chase 3:461 4↑ Ath Cup H 53k 6 2 11 13 11 12 Fishback J 173 - -- Flatterer1732Steve Canyon1446Chammsky15020 Driving 6
17Nov85- 4Cam fm 2¾ S'Chase 5:141 4↑ Colonial Cup 60k 2 2 22 21 2nk 12 Fishback J 162 - -- Flatterer1622Salute II1629Gateshead16211 Driving 9
19Oct85- 6Bel fm 2Ⓣ :522 2:303 2:562 3:214 3↑ NY Turf Writers H 56k 3 4 86 65½ 44 35¾ Cruguet J 118 3.40 87-20 Bobby Burns1123¾Dance Caller1212Flatterer1183½ Rallied 9
11Oct85- 6Bel fm 2⅝ S'Chase 4:511 4↑ Temple Gwathmey H 55k 2 7 715 1hd 14 12 Fishback J 170 *.60e -- Flatterer1702Gateshead1588Chammsky15217 Handily 7
27Jun85- 5Mth fm *2¼ S'Chase 4:193 4↑ Midsummer H 21k 2 3 46 2hd 12 21¾ Guessford B 170 *.60e -- Chammsky1491¾Flatterer1701¼Huallatiri1436 Second best 7
18Nov84- 4Cam fm 2¾ S'Chase 5:09 4↑ Colonial Cup 50k 2 5 53¼ 32¼ 2hd 11¼ Fishback J 160 - -- Flatterer1601¼Census16218Eremite1518 Up final stride 7
27Oct84- 7FH yl *1½Ⓣ 2:402 3↑ Alw 1500 3 4 41¾ 2hd 2hd 16 Fishback J 154 - -- Flatterer1546SmokeRise1412HeartoftheDesert140½ Easily 10
21Sep84- 6Bel fm 2½ S'Chase 4:40 4↑ Brook H 42k 4 1 21½ 13 12½ 12 Fishback J 167 *.40e -- Flatterer1672Census15621Double Reefed153 Ridden out 4
24Aug84- 6Sar yl 2⅜ S'Chase 4:22 4↑ NY Turf Writers H 43k 1 2 210 1hd 1hd 11¾ Fishback J 164 *.60e -- Flatterer1641¾Census15512½DoubleRefd15818¾ Clearly best 5
17Aug84- 7Sar fm 1 1/16Ⓣ :232 :472 1:12 1:424 3↑ Alw 36000 7 7 95½ 83¼ 76¾ 78¾ Cruguet J 115 16.30 74-17 Quick Dip1171¼Lost Canyon114nkRoman Bend115½ Outrun 9
26May84- 6Pro fm *3 S'Chase 6:081 4↑ Hard Scuffle H 35k 2 2 11 11½ 1nk 2½ Fishback J 164 - -- Census154½Flatterer16412Uncle Edwin1448 Failed 6
12May84- 5Clm fm *1¼Ⓣ 2:142 3↑ Alw 1000 3 2 2½ 1½ 1½ 12 Achuff CW 142 - -- Flatterer1422Dellersbeck1445Another Ripple1496 Driving 6
7Apr84- 4AtH fm *2 S'Chase 3:522 4↑ Delta Air H 50k 2 1 12 12 14 14 Fishback J 160 - -- Flatterer1604Census1522½TheHallofFamr143no Well in hand 9
24Mar84- 1Aik fm *1Ⓣ 1:464 3↑ Alw 1000 8 1 14 13 2hd 43¾ Wiseman B 143 - -- Beat a Path1431½Bomb1522Deify146nk 10
20Nov83- 4Cam gd *2¾ S'Chase 5:18 4↑ Colonial Cup 50k 1 9 99 41¾ 1nk 13¼ Francome J 151 - -- Flatterer1513¼Twas Ever Thus1511¾Census16011 Ridden out 12
14Oct83- 6Bel sf 2⅝ S'Chase 5:062 4↑ Temple Gwathmey H 43k 8 4 44 22½ 1½ 11¼ Francome J 154 *.30e -- Flatterer1541¼MysteriousArthur1421¾GivWhrl1454¼ Handily 8
1Oct83- 4Fx fm *2¼ S'Chase 4:16 4↑ Grand National H 15k 1 5 2nk 1½ 15 17 Cushman J 150 - -- Flatterer1507Mc Adam1405Mysterious Arthur1447 Easily 8
17Sep83- 4Lig fm *2 S'Chase 3:551 3↑ Alw 9000 1 4 22 22 11 18 Cushman J 151 - -- Flatterer1518Mc Adam141¾Hawaiki156nk Easily 6
18Aug83- 6Sar sf 2⅜ S'Chase 4:274 3↑ NY Turf Writers H 43k 5 4 713 43½ 44 410¼ Martin WS 140 *.90e -- DoubleReefed1611¼SugarBee135hdCensus1489 Jumped poorly 7
10Aug83- 6Sar fm 2 1/16 S'Chase 3:442 3↑ Alw 19000 3 3 32 42¼ 1hd 11¾ Cushman J 146 *.90 -- Flatterer1461¾Sugar Bee1498¾Hawaiki1559½ Driving 7
23Jly83- 2Bel gd 1 1/16Ⓣ :244 :484 1:13 1:451 4↑ Clm 50000 1 2 45 44¼ 34 32¼ Velasquez J 117 3.80 73-23 Millbank1082¼MagnusPater117noFlattrr117nk Steadied turn 6
13Jly83- 5Bel fm 1Ⓣ :24 :473 1:111 1:36 4↑ Clm 70000 2 6 64½ 65½ 58½ 57¾ Velasquez J 113 21.30 77-12 Cannon Royal1172Revocation113½Fan Letter108¾ No factor 9
30Apr83- 3Fx fm *2 S'Chase 3:443 3↑ Alw 6000 2 3 3¾ 2nk 2½ 2¾ Cushman J 144 - -- Bomb149¾Flatterer14415Paddy's Punch1434 8
9Apr83- 1AtH sf *2 S'Chase 4:101 3↑ Md Sp Wt 3 2 21½ 11½ 14 18 Cushman J 144 - -- Flatterer1448Bomb1497Publisher14810 Easily 6
5Dec82- 5Aqu gd 1 1/16⊡ :231 :471 1:12 1:453 Clm 45000 3 8 1012 915 917 916 Hernandez R 114 16.90 69-16 Brae Axe117¾Asticou1133¼David K.1133¼ Outrun 10
22Nov82- 1Aqu yl 1⅛Ⓣ :49 1:15 1:411 1:543 Clm 45000 4 3 35 21 33½ 32¼ Velasquez J 114 *1.60 69-27 Whale'sEye113¾PrideofSatan1171½Flatterr114nk Lacked bid 7
11Nov82- 3Aqu fm 1⅛Ⓣ :503 1:15 1:404 1:532 Clm 45000 6 4 43½ 21 3½ 2no Velasquez J 114 5.30 77-22 FourBases117noFlatterer114noWeThaPeople117¾ Just missed 8
20Oct82- 9Med fm 1Ⓣ :233 :471 1:111 1:363 Clm 45000 6 7 67¾ 63½ 64¾ 32¾ Gonzalez MA 115 3.90 88-13 Limit Position1151¼Ablantin1161½Flatterer1151¼ Rallied 8
29Sep82- 9Med fm 1Ⓣ :233 :471 1:114 1:373 Clm 45000 6 6 66½ 64¾ 22 11¼ Gonzalez MA 112 3.50 86-14 Flatterer1121¼Fair Roger1142½Papal Order113½ Drew clear 7
9Sep82- 8Med fm 1 1/16Ⓣ :232 :471 1:112 1:423 Clm 32000 3 6 64 62¼ 22½ 2½ Dufton E 116 6.60 88-07 Fire Away112½Flatterer1163Hey Kennedy1122¾ Rallied 9
30Aug82- 1Sar fm 1Ⓣ :242 :474 1:122 1:372 Clm 35000 4 4 31½ 41½ 51¼ 51¾ Samyn JL 117 b 3.00 87-09 Milieu117¾Mighty Mecca117nkSunset Mark117¾ Hung 10
23Aug82- 2Sar fm 1 1/16Ⓣ :224 :472 1:12 1:434 Clm 40000 9 8 53 31 44½ 49¾ Samyn JL 117 b 6.10 81-13 ⒹFull Concert117¾Current Pride1135¾Lucrative Way1173¼ 10
Off slowly
10Aug82- 1Sar my 1⅛ :481 1:122 1:381 1:512 Clm 50000 1 1 2hd 44 77½ 714 Velasquez J 117 b 7.00 64-16 RichButterfly1102DomandJerry107nkAncestry1172¾ Stopped 7
9Jly82- 9Bel fm 1¼Ⓣ :493 1:133 1:391 2:041 Clm 35000 2 3 21½ 42½ 73¼ 42¼ Samyn JL 113 b 8.40 71-13 SparkyRidge1171IntentionalForce1151¼Whppn115no Steadied 10
26Jun82- 7Del fm 1Ⓣ :231 :462 1:111 1:38 3↑ Alw 10000 5 4 47½ 54 42 54¼ Dufton E 110 b 6.70 81-13 HiddnCapital110½JohnnyKas119¾SwingtheBlade1123 Outrun 6
11Jun82- 8Del fm 5fⓉ :224 :464 :59 3↑ Alw 9500 6 6 63¾ 53½ 44 66½ Dufton E 110 7.70 81-15 NobleOcean1192PrincelyRulr1172½Papadopoulos1171 Outrun 7
1May82- 8Key fst 1 1/16 :232 :474 1:124 1:441 ⓈBarberry 27k 6 4 42½ 46½ 517 528 Walford J 117 b *2.30 55-23 Fabiano1178½Gray Charles1129½Once Twice11310 Tired 8
18Apr82- 7Key fst 1 70 :224 :47 1:131 1:442 ⓈAlw 15000 6 7 711 76¾ 22 1nk Dufton E 115 b 2.00 78-23 Flatterer115nkOnce Twice1155Sioux Dancer1101¼ Driving 7
2Apr82- 8Key fst 1 70 :232 :472 1:13 1:442 ⓈAlw 13000 2 1 2hd 1½ 11 13 Dufton E 114 b 4.20 78-27 Flatterer1143InGoodTime1132¼SirBrendBoy1141½ Drew clear 7
23Mar82- 5Key fst 6f :223 :464 1:133 ⓈMd Sp Wt 2 5 44 34½ 1½ 13½ Dufton E 120 b 20.50 74-24 Flatterer1203½Frisky Dan120¾Jewel's Gold115hd Drew off 9
20Feb82- 3Key gd 6f :224 :473 1:131 ⓈMd Sp Wt 7 7 714 610 512 513 Dufton E 120 5.00 63-25 CarolinaDutchmn1151½LittleSlalom1208½IcyBdg120½ Outrun 8
16Jan82- 6Aqu fst 6f⊡ :223 :461 1:114 Md Sp Wt 12 14 1416 1418 1314 1216 Miceli M 122 76.80 69-10 Let'EmHum1221IntervenngHero122noIvanLendl1221 Outrun 14

Forty Niner

ch. c. 1985, by Mr. Prospector (Raise a Native)–File, by Tom Rolfe — **Lifetime record: 19 11 5 0 $2,726,000**

Own.– Claiborne Farm
Br.– Claiborne Farm (Ky)
Tr.– Woodford C. Stephens

5Nov88-10CD my 1¼ :474 1:122 1:383 2:044 3↑ BC Classic-G1 3 5 511 84¼ 73¾ 45¾ Krone JA 122 3.70 67-20 Alysheba126½Seeking the Gold1225Waquoit126nk 9
Shied shadow 2nd turn
22Oct88-8Aqu fst 1 :223 :451 1:09 1:34 3↑ NYRA Mile H 567k 5 3 4¾ 3½ 11 1nk Fox WI Jr 121 *.40 96-18 Forty Niner121nkMawsuff1151¼Precisionist124nk All out 6
17Sep88-8Bel fst 1¼ :473 1:111 1:35 1:592 3↑ Woodward H-G1 2 2 2½ 1hd 1hd 2nk Pincay L Jr 119 2.70 101-08 Alysheba126nkForty Niner119nkWaquoit1221¼ Gamely 8
20Aug88-8Sar fst 1¼ :483 1:131 1:374 2:012 Travers-G1 5 2 1½ 1½ 12 1no McCarron CJ 126 2.20 93-09 FortyNiner126noSeekingtheGold126¾Brian'sTm1265½ Driving 6
30Jly88-9Mth fst 1⅛ :473 1:112 1:352 1:473 Haskell Inv'l H-G1 1 1 21½ 1hd 1hd 1no Pincay L Jr 126 *.80 96-10 Forty Niner126noSeeking the Gold1254Primal117½ Driving 5
16Jly88-8Mth fst 1 :231 :452 1:091 1:334 3↑ Alw 30000 4 2 22 21 12½ 17¼ Krone JA 114 *.30 104-09 Forty Niner1147¼Slew City Slew1176Blue Buckaroo1172½ 6
Won eased up
21May88-9Pim gd 1 3/16 :47 1:111 1:363 1:561 Preakness-G1 4 1 1hd 1hd 78 714¼ Day P 126 2.30 72-11 RisenStr1261½Brn'sTm1261¼WnnngColors1212½ Brushed rival 9
7May88-8CD fst 1¼ :464 1:112 1:36 2:021 Ky Derby-G1 17 2 34½ 57 34 2nk Day P 126 4.90e 86-11 WinningColors121nkFortyNiner1263RisnStr126½ Fast finish 17
16Apr88-8Kee fst 1 1/16 :24 :48 1:122 1:424 Lexington-G2 4 2 31 21½ 1½ 2hd Day P 121 *.40 92-18 RisnStr118hdFortyNnr12112Stlwrs1182 Steadied st.,gamely 5
8Apr88-8Kee fst 7f :23 :452 1:084 1:22 Lafayette 72k 7 2 42½ 3½ 11 15 Day P 121 *.50 96-21 Forty Niner1215Buoy12210Aloha Prospector1215 Ridden out 8
5Mar88-10GP fst 1⅛ :463 1:104 1:363 1:494 Florida Derby-G1 9 1 1½ 11½ 12 2nk Maple E 122 3.00 83-16 Brian'sTime118nkFortyNiner1223Notebook122nk Just missed 10
15Feb88-10GP fst 1 1/16 :232 :463 1:104 1:431 Fountain of Youth-G2 7 1 1hd 1hd 1hd 1no Maple E 122 *.80 85-21 Forty Niner122noNotebook1221Buoy1192 Driving 9
3Feb88-9GP fst 7f :214 :443 1:094 1:23 Hutcheson-G3 5 2 2hd 2½ 21½ 21 Maple E 122 *.70 88-24 PerfectSpy1141FortyNiner122½Notebook1224 Couldn't gain 7
30Oct87-8Kee fst 1 1/16 :224 :464 1:11 1:434 Breeders' Futurity-G2 2 1 21 2hd 2hd 1no Maple E 121 *.40 87-18 Forty Niner121noHey Pat1212½Sea Trek1213 Driving 7
17Oct87-8Bel fst 1 :23 :464 1:104 1:364 Champagne-G1 7 2 31½ 2hd 11½ 14¼ Maple E 122 3.30 81-20 Forty Niner1224¼Parlay Me1221¼Tejano1225½ Drew away 11
20Sep87-6Bel gd 7f :221 :452 1:093 1:223 Futurity-G1 1 2 11½ 11½ 13 13 Maple E 122 4.50 89-14 FortyNinr1223Tsarbaby1222¼CrusaderSword1224 Ridden out 5
19Aug87-8Sar sly 6f :214 :443 1:10 Sanford-G2 3 3 22 21¼ 1hd 13½ Maple E 115 6.10 90-15 Forty Niner1153½Once Wild1153Velvet Fog1155½ Driving 6
7Aug87-8Sar fst 6f :214 :45 1:101 Sar Spl-G2 2 4 1½ 2hd 31 610 Maple E 117 3.40 79-17 Crusader Sword117nkTejano1175½Endurance1194 Tired 8
17Jly87-5Bel fst 6f :222 :46 1:113 Md Sp Wt 8 4 1½ 11½ 13 13¼ Maple E 118 *1.40e 82-20 Forty Niner1183¼Dynaformer1182¾Tsarbaby1181½ Ridden out 13

Genuine Risk

ch. f. 1977, by Exclusive Native (Raise a Native)–Virtuous, by Gallant Man — **Lifetime record: 15 10 3 2 $646,587**

Own.– Mrs B.R. Firestone
Br.– Mrs G.W. Humphrey Jr (Ky)
Tr.– Leroy Jolley

10Aug81-1Sar fst 7f :224 :452 1:09 1:212 3↑ ⒻAlw 32000 3 2 1hd 11 16 18¼ Fell J 119 *.10 95-15 Genuine Risk1198¼Clown's Doll117½Samarta Dancer1193¾ 4
Ridden out mile 1:34 3/5
25May81-6Bel fm 1 1/16Ⓣ :243 :474 1:12 1:42 3↑ ⒻAlw 35000 5 2 31½ 1½ 1hd 32 MacBeth D 121 *.40 84-12 Smilin'Sera1101¾InRhythym117nkGenuineRisk121no Weakened 6
11Apr81-7Aqu fst 7f :224 :453 1:101 1:224 4↑ ⒻAlw 32000 2 4 22½ 2½ 17 19½ Vasquez J 122 *.10 87-22 GnuineRisk1229½BacktoStay1102½Justacam114nk Ridden out 5
27Sep80-8Bel fst 1⅛ :48 1:122 1:364 1:491 3↑ ⒻRuffian H-G1 1 5 3½ 31 2hd 1no Vasquez J 118 *.50 81-19 GenuineRisk118noMistyGallore124nkIt'snthAr1185¾ Driving 6
10Sep80-8Bel fst 1 :232 :461 1:104 1:352 3↑ ⒻMaskette-G1 2 4 45 31 1hd 2no Vasquez J 118 *1.20 91-22 Bold'nDetrmind122noGnunRsk1186¾LovSgn120½ Just missed 5
7Jun80-8Bel my 1½ :501 1:151 2:04 2:294 Belmont-G1 1 5 53 2½ 1hd 22 Vasquez J 121 5.10 69-17 Temperence Hill1262Genuine Risk1211½Rockhill Native1262 10
Led,gamely
17May80-9Pim fst 1 3/16 :474 1:111 1:36 1:541 Preakness-G1 5 6 44 43¼ 21 24¾ Vasquez J 121 *2.00 94-12 Codex1264¾GnuineRisk1213¼ColonelMorn1267 Bothered turn 8
3May80-8CD fst 1¼ :48 1:124 1:373 2:02 Ky Derby-G1 10 7 74¼ 11½ 12 11 Vasquez J 121 13.30 87-11 Genuine Risk1211Rumbo1261Jaklin Klugman1264 Driving 13
19Apr80-8Aqu fst 1⅛ :472 1:113 1:37 1:504 Wood Memorial-G1 3 3 32 31½ 32 31½ Vasquez J 121 8.20 79-17 PluggedNickle1261½ColnlMorn126hdGnunRsk1213¾ Game try 11
5Apr80-7Aqu gd 1 :233 :464 1:12 1:383 ⒻHandicap 35000 4 4 32 11½ 11 12¼ Vasquez J 124 *.20 73-20 GenuineRisk1242¼TellaSecret1153¼SprucPn11311 Ridden out 4
19Mar80-7GP fst 7f :22 :444 1:094 1:223 ⒻAlw 17000 3 5 44 32½ 1½ 12½ Vasquez J 113 *.40 91-20 GenuineRisk1132½SoberJig1123½PeaceBells1151½ Ridden out 6
17Nov79-8Aqu fst 1⅛ :481 1:131 1:383 1:511 ⒻDemoiselle-G2 6 4 3½ 2hd 2hd 1no Pincay L Jr 116 1.20 79-21 GenuineRisk116noSmartAngle1216¾SprucePine1123¾ Driving 7
5Nov79-8Aqu fst 1 :23 :46 1:102 1:36 ⒻTempted-G3 4 5 51¼ 11½ 12 13 Vasquez J 114 *.90 86-18 GenuineRisk1143StreetBallet117½TellScrt1144½ Ridden out 9
18Oct79-6Aqu fst 1 :233 :47 1:114 1:362 ⒻAlw 15000 6 2 21 2hd 12 17¼ Vasquez J 115 *.60 84-18 GenuineRisk1157¼GoingEast1175CintoTora1154½ Ridden out 6
30Sep79-4Bel sly 6½f :223 :452 1:112 1:18 ⒻMd Sp Wt 8 11 45 46½ 23 11¾ Vasquez J 118 *3.10 86-24 GenuineRisk1181¾RemoteRuler11813Espadrille1181¾ Driving 11

Glorious Song

b. f. 1976, by Halo (Hail to Reason)–Ballade, by Herbager — **Lifetime record: 34 17 9 1 $1,004,534**

Own.– Hunt & Stronach
Br.– E.P. Taylor (Can)
Tr.– John Cairns

13Dec81-8Hol fst 1⅛ :463 1:103 1:361 1:493 3↑ ⒻSilver Belles H 107k 1 4 54 52¼ 33½ 42¾ McCarron CJ 125 *.80 78-21 Happy Guess117hdTrack Robbery1232½Targa112hd Dull 6
22Nov81-8Hol fm 1⅛Ⓣ :473 1:114 1:352 1:47 3↑ ⒻMatriarch 221k 9 4 45½ 43½ 23 22½ McCarron CJ 123 4.90 92-08 Kilijaro1232½Glorious Song123nkBersid120½ Wide 9
31Oct81-7Kee fst 1⅛ :472 1:113 1:363 1:491 3↑ ⒻSpinster-G1 4 6 41¼ 42 22 1nk Platts R 123 2.20 91-19 Glorious Song123nkTruly Bound1196Safe Play119¾ Driving 7
11Oct81-8Bel fst 1¼ :482 1:121 1:37 2:014 3↑ ⒻBeldame-G1 4 7 32 2½ 22½ 27♦ Velasquez J 123 *1.70 84-16 LoveSign1237[DH]Jameela123[DH]GloriousSng1235½ Weakened 7
19Sep81-8Bel my 1¼ :481 1:114 1:354 2:003 3↑ Marlboro Cup H-G1 7 6 45 34 65½ 79¼ Platts R 118 23.10 88-13 NobleNashua1163¾AmbrPss1201½TmprncHll1271¼ Early speed 8
15Aug81-9Mth fst 1⅛ :46 1:092 1:342 1:472 3↑ Monmouth H-G1 5 5 66 75¼ 67 78 Platts R 119 3.10 90-09 Amber Pass1172Joanie's Chief1082Ring of Light114no 10
Unruly before start
1Jly81-9WO fst 1⅛ :463 1:104 1:36 1:48 3↑ Dominion Day H-G3 2 3 31½ 2½ 14½ 15½ Platts R 125 *.35 102-14 GloriousSong1255½DrivingHome1252½ByeByTony112hd Handily 8
26Apr81-8Hol fst 1 :224 :461 1:112 1:362 3↑ Mervyn LeRoy H-G2 6 4 53¾ 32 1hd 2nk Toro F 121 *1.70 84-21 ElevenStitches115nkGloriousSng1212¼SummrTime Guy1145½ 8
Sharp try
8Mar81-8SA fst 1¼ :452 1:092 1:341 1:592 4↑ S Anita H-G1 11 8 89¼ 66½ 57 55½ McHargue DG 119 10.30 86-11 John Henry1281King Go Go1171¼Exploded115no Wide 11
22Feb81-8SA fst 1⅛ :444 1:084 1:342 1:471 4↑ ⒻS Margarita H-G1 6 4 47 44½ 31 2nk McCarron CJ 130 *1.10 93-12 PrincessKarenda118nkGlorousSong1301¼Ack'sScrt1222 Sharp 10
31Jan81-8SA gd 1 1/16 :23 :462 1:104 1:431 4↑ ⒻS Maria H-G2 1 3 32 2hd 12½ 12 McCarron CJ 127 *.50 85-23 Glorious Song1272Track Robbery1175Miss Huntington11310 4
Eased final yards
10Jan81-8SA fst 7f :214 :434 1:074 1:201 4↑ San Carlos H-G2 1 7 75½ 63 46 46½ Hawley S 120 4.50 92-10 Flying Paster1243¼To B. or Not1232Double Discount1151¼ 8
Flattened out;Previously trained by Gerald W. Belanger Jr
6Sep80-7Bel fst 1⅛ :45 1:092 1:341 1:47 3↑ Marlboro Cup H-G1 4 7 710 63¾ 22 24½ Velasquez J 117 *1.70 87-15 Wintr'sTl1234½GlorousSng117nkJklnKlugmn1183½ Went well 8
16Aug80-9Mth fst 1⅛ :464 1:111 1:353 1:48 3↑ AL Haskell H-G1 2 5 75¾ 4nk 2½ 21¾ Velasquez J 117 6.70 93-15 Spectacular Bid1321¾GlorsSng1171¼The Cool Virginian1124 8
Drifted out,brushed
12Jly80-9WO fm 1¼Ⓣ :453 1:112 1:371 2:013 ⓇMaturity H 54k 2 4 35½ 11½ 13 13½ Leblanc JB 121 *.25 99-09 Glorious Song1213½Great State1261Nice Idea1211 Handily 6
1Jly80-7WO fst 1⅛ :48 1:114 1:364 1:501 3↑ Dominion Day H-G3 2 5 54¾ 3nk 11½ 11 Leblanc JB 123 *.30 91-13 GloriousSng1231MapleGrove1184Knight'sTurn1181½ Handily 8
15Jun80-10Det fst 1⅛ :471 1:114 1:374 1:50 3↑ Mich Mile H-G2 7 6 54¾ 34 1hd 1no Leblanc JB 117 3.10 87-25 Glorious Song117noPrince Majestic1154½Uncool1221 Lasted 7
26May80-8AP fm 1⅛Ⓣ :484 1:13 1:372 1:501 3↑ Laurance Armour H 117k 3 6 54 44 21 21 Velasquez J 118 2.80 85-16 Overskate1271GlorousSong1183YoungBob114¾ Best of others 7
26Apr80-6Aqu fst 1⅛ :472 1:114 1:364 1:493 3↑ ⒻTop Flight H-G1 2 4 511 44 1½ 11¾ Velasquez J 123 1.90e 87-19 Glorious Song1231¾Misty Gallore1261¾Blitey1172¾ Driving 7
24Feb80-8SA fst 1⅛ :462 1:103 1:36 1:482 4↑ ⒻS Margarita H-G1 3 7 75¾ 42 1hd 12 McCarron CJ 120 2.30 87-11 Glorious Song1202The Very One116noKankam1252 Drew off 11
Previously owned by F. Stronach
10Feb80-8SA fst 1⅛ :452 1:093 1:35 1:473 ⒻLa Canada-G1 2 6 56 31½ 1hd 11¾ McCarron CJ 118 3.30 91-09 GloriousSong1181¾PrizeSpot1194It'sinthAr1251 Drew clear 7
26Jan80-8SA fst 1 1/16 :224 :453 1:093 1:411 ⒻEl Encino-G3 8 7 55½ 51¾ 31 43¾ McCarron CJ 116 *2.60 91-09 It'sintheAir1241¼PrizeSpot1211¼[D]Terlingua1211¼ Impeded 8
Placed third through disqualification

6Jan80- 8SA fst 7f :214 :44 1:081 1:204 ⒻLa Brea 52k 3 3 34 32 2½ 2½ McCarron CJ 116 6.70 98-11 Terlingua121½Glorious Song1164Prize Spot1217 Gamely 4
Previously trained by F.H. Loschke
3Nov79- 7Grd fst 1¼ :501 1:16 1:411 2:084 3↑ⒻⓇMaple Leaf 34k 1 5 31 11½ 11 1¾ Leblanc J 122 *.40e 71-30 GloriousSng122¾SinstrQun1111½DncngDors1091½ Ridden out 8
20Oct79- 8WO sf 1¼Ⓣ :49 1:154 1:422 2:101 3↑ⒻNettie 70k 1 6 54 21 53¾ 410¼ Leblanc J 118 2.25 46-44 SenoritaPoquito1182¼Christy'sMnt1242½Liveinthesnshine1245½ 10
Weakened
6Oct79- 8WO sf 1⅛Ⓣ :483 1:154 1:421 2:11 ⒻⓇWonder Where 36k 12 8 84¾ 1hd 1½ 11½ Leblanc J 120 *1.75 52-48 GloriousSong1201½Fud'Artfc1202½DoublDwn1115½ Ridden out 12
23Sep79- 7WO fst 1⅛ :483 1:124 1:371 1:50 3↑ⒻⓇBelle Mahone 34k 5 5 54 21½ 1hd 12½ Leblanc JB 115 5.30 92-19 GlorsSng1152½LVoygus1258Chrsty'sMount1235½ Drew clear 7
8Sep79- 8WO fm 6½fⓉ :223 :453 1:10 1:162 ⒻⓇOnt Damsel 29k 3 2 2hd 2hd 12 1½ Leblanc JB 114 *1.65 98-08 GloriousSong114½Feud'Artifice1201SusieBggr1142½ Driving 8
18Aug79- 8FE gd 1 1/16 :23 :47 1:113 1:441 ⒻDuchess 28k 8 5 52¾ 32 32½ 22 Leblanc JB 117 4.60 88-29 Kamar1232GloriousSong117½Feud'Artifc120nk Finished well 10
10Aug79- 6FE fst 1 70 :23 :464 1:111 1:421 Ⓕ 10000 8 3 33 1hd 12 1¾ LeBlanc JB 112 8.55 92-18 Glorious Song112¾Feu d'Artifice1181¾DHRaise Your Sights1151 8
Ridden out
2Aug79- 7FE sl 6f :23 :464 1:123 ⒻHandicap 12500 4 3 2½ 1hd 42¼ 56 LeBlanc JB 119 b *.70 78-24 Your My Choice114¾Sundae Star120nkRaise Your Sights1201¾ 7
Pressed,gave way
15Jly79- 5WO sly 6f :22 :451 1:11 3↑ⒻAlw 7500 4 3 1hd 22 21½ 12 LeBlanc JB 112 *.75 88-17 GloriousSng1122CougarKittn1144½BoogieDancer1152 Wide 7
7Jly79- 6WO fst 6f :222 :45 1:094 3↑ⒻAlw 7500 2 5 1hd 12 13½ 19 LeBlanc JB 112 2.95 94-09 GloriousSong1129Hermnvll1152AlbonLdy118nk Bore out turn 9
20Nov78- 1Grd fst 7f :23 :463 1:134 1:264 ⒻⓇMd Sp Wt 5 4 2hd 1½ 11½ 13 Clark D 117 4.45 81-23 GloriousSng1173Look'nLeap117hdWicketLady1172½ Handily 12

Gold Beauty

b. f. 1979, by Mr. Prospector (Raise a Native)–Stick to Beauty, by Illustrious **Lifetime record: 12 8 2 1 $251,901**

Own.– Mrs P.B. Hofmann
Br.– Mr & Mrs P.B. Hofmann (Fla)
Tr.– William Curtis Jr

8Oct83- 8Bel fst 6f :221 :453 1:102 3↑ Fall Highweight H-G2 2 1 1hd 1½ 43 57½ Brumfield D 140 5.60 82-19 Chas Conerly136½Singh Tu124½Let Burn1344 Tired 9
11Sep83- 8Bel fst 6f :22 :451 1:103 3↑ Boojum 55k 1 1 1½ 1½ 11½ 22 Brumfield D 123 *.80 87-22 ChasConerly1182GldBeauty1233¾Shimatoree1202¼ Weakened 4
7Aug83-10Suf fst 6f :214 :443 :58 1:093 3↑ Suf Sprint H-G3 5 1 2hd 1hd 2½ 32¼ Brumfield D 124 *.70 91-18 All Sold Out110¾Let Burn1151½Gold Beauty1244 Weakened 8
26Jun83- 8Bel fst 6f :222 :451 1:102 3↑ True North H-G3 6 2 2½ 14 14 12¼ Brumfield D 121 *.70 90-24 GoldBeauty1212¼SinghTu1111¼FittoFight1132 Ridden out 8
21May83- 9Mth fst 6f :224 :453 1:093 3↑ ⒻRegret H 33k 6 1 12½ 11½ 1½ 12¾ Brumfield D 126 *.40 92-17 GldBeauty1262¾PlatnumBll1161¼SproutdRy1181¼ Ridden out 8
16Oct82- 8Aqu fst 7f :224 :454 1:104 1:234 3↑ Vosburgh-G1 5 1 11 1½ 13 31 Brumfield D 120 *.60 81-26 EngneOne126½DDukeMitchell123½GldBty1201½ Weakened 6
Placed second through disqualification
10Sep82- 8Bel fst 6f :222 :45 1:091 3↑ Fall Highweight H-G2 5 1 2hd 14 16 16 Brumfield D 126 5.20 96-20 Gold Beauty1266Engine One131nkOsorno1251 Ridden out 9
5Aug82- 8Sar fst 7f :221 :45 1:094 1:224 ⒻTest-G2 2 5 11½ 11½ 12 11 Brumfield D 116 *1.00 88-16 GldBeauty1161AmbassadorofLuck1211¾Number1141¾ Driving 12
17Jly82- 8Key fst 6f :22 :444 1:094 3↑ ⒻSpring Valley H 28k 1 4 1½ 1hd 12 15½ Brumfield D 118 *.20 93-19 GldBty1185½ATearinHerEye1143¾MadamMschf1151½ Easily 8
5Jly82- 8Key fst 6f :213 :44 1:10 ⒻRushland 28k 6 1 2½ 18 110 110 Tejeira J 114 *.20 92-15 Gold Beauty11410Lady Ann's Key114½Sparkling Savage1181¾ 7
Easy score
24Jun82- 6Mth fst 6f :214 :442 1:082 3↑ ⒻAlw 10000 5 1 13 11½ 16 112 Brumfield D 114 *.70 98-17 Gold Beauty11412Keys Special1083Satan Gal1134 Easily 7
16Feb82- 4Hia fst 6f :214 :444 1:101 ⒻMd Sp Wt 8 4 11½ 15 17 112 Brumfield D 120 4.70 92-17 Gold Beauty12012Illiana1202Tracie Elaine120½ Ridden out 12

Groovy

ch. c. 1983, by Norcliffe (Buckpasser)–Tinnitus, by Restless Wind **Lifetime record: 26 12 4 1 $1,346,956**

Own.– Prestonwood Farm
Br.– Marshall T. Robinson (Tex)
Tr.– Jose Martin

21Nov87- 1Hol fst 6f :211 :44 :554 1:084 3↑ BC Sprint-G1 1 3 3½ 21½ 23½ 24 Cordero A Jr 126 *.80 94-12 VerySbtle1214Groovy1261¾ExclusvEnough1241 Pressed pace 13
10Oct87- 7Bel fst 7f :224 :451 1:092 1:223 3↑ Vosburgh-G1 8 1 11 12½ 15 1¾ Cordero A Jr 126 *.30 89-22 Groovy126¾Moment of Hope1263Sun Master1261½ Driving 8
23Aug87- 8Sar fst 7f :22 :441 1:084 1:214 3↑ Forego H-G2 5 1 11½ 11½ 12½ 11¾ Cordero A Jr 132 *.60 93-14 Groovy1321¾Purple Mountain1131¾Sun Master1182 Driving 6
Previously owned by J.A. Ballis
18Jly87- 8Bel fst 7f :231 :454 1:092 1:222 3↑ Tom Fool-G2 5 1 12 11½ 14½ 16½ Cordero A Jr 128 *.60 90-20 Groovy1286½Sun Master121nkMoment of Hope1193 Driving 6
5Jly87- 9FL fst 6f :221 :444 1:092 3↑ Bud BC 156k 3 3 1½ 1hd 1½ 1hd Pezua JM 122 *.05 102-11 Groovy122hdPurpleMountn1192½VinnietheVipr1197 Driving 7
21Jun87- 8Bel my 6f :22 :44 1:074 3↑ True North H-G2 1 1 11½ 14 15 15¾ Cordero A Jr 123 *.20 101-10 Groovy1235¾King's Swan120nkSun Master117no Ridden out 4
6Jun87- 1Bel fst 6f :213 :44 1:082 3↑ Roseben H-G3 1 1 12½ 14 14½ 14¼ Cordero A Jr 119 *1.10 98-15 Groovy1194¼Love That Mac1182King's Swan1213½ Drew clear 6
15Nov86- 8Aqu fst 6f :213 :441 1:084 3↑ Sport Page H-G3 4 1 1½ 1hd 3½ 46½ Cordero A Jr 122 *.50 90-22 BestbyTest1125King'sSwan118hdSunMaster1171½ Weakened 7
Previously owned by Ballis & Kruckel Jr
1Nov86- 3SA fst 6f :211 :433 :554 1:082 3↑ BC Sprint-G1 9 2 31 31½ 32 44¼ Santos JA 124 *.40 92-13 Smile1261¼PineTreeLane1231¾BedsidePrmise1261¼ Weakened 9
15Oct86- 8SA fst 6f :212 :434 :554 1:081 3↑ Ancient Title H 76k 5 1 11½ 13 12½ 12 Santos JA 123 *.40 97-18 Groovy1232Rosie's K.T.1171Sun Master114½ Driving 8
1Sep86- 8Bel fst 1 :22 :44 1:082 1:34 Jerome H-G1 4 1 18 13½ 2½ 45¼ Velasquez J 124 2.50 90-14 Ogygian126hdMogambo1192Moment of Hope1113¼ Tired 5
17Aug86- 8Sar my 7f :214 :441 1:082 1:211 3↑ Forego H-G2 1 4 12 14 15 1¾ Santos JA 118 2.00 96-11 Groovy118¾Turkoman1244¾Innamorato110nk Driving 8
20Jly86- 8Bel fst 7f :221 :443 1:084 1:213 3↑ Tom Fool-G2 2 2 11½ 12½ 16 16¼ Santos JA 112 2.50 94-14 Groovy1126¼Phone Trick1266Basket Weave119nk Drew clear 5
4Jly86- 6Bel fst 6f :214 :444 1:09 Firecracker 53k 4 1 11½ 12 12½ 12¾ Velasquez J 119 *1.20 97-11 Groovy1192¾RoyalPennant1153LandingPlot122hd Drew clear 8
Previously trained by Howard Crowell
7Jun86- 7Bel sly 7f :213 :442 1:094 1:232 Riva Ridge 81k 2 1 12½ 11 22½ 48½ Day P 117 b 2.90 76-16 Ogygian1223½Wayar115hdLanding Plot1225 Weakened 5
17May86- 8Pim fst 1 3/16 :472 1:11 1:36 1:544 Preakness-G1 4 1 1½ 1hd 35½ 613¾ Perret C 126 11.10 79-18 SnowChief1264Frdinand1266½BroadBrush126no Used in pace 7
3May86- 8CD fst 1¼ :451 1:101 1:37 2:024 Ky Derby-G1 14 1 11 1515 1628 1649¾ Pincay L Jr 126 57.30 33-10 Ferdinnd1262¼BldArrangement126¾BrodBrush126nk Stopped 16
Previously trained by Petro Peters
19Apr86- 8Aqu fst 1⅛ :472 1:111 1:361 1:503 Wood Memorial-G1 2 1 11 11 21 3¾ Perret C 126 3.80 81-18 Broad Brush126½Mogambo126nkGroovy1261¼ Weakened 7
5Apr86- 8Aqu fst 1 :222 :444 1:083 1:343 Gotham-G2 8 1 11½ 13 13½ 2¾ Santos JA 114 8.70 92-18 Mogambo121¾DGroovy1141¼Tasso1231 Bore in 9
Disqualified and placed fifth
22Mar86- 7Aqu fst 7f :223 :451 1:093 1:22 Bay Shore (Div 1)-G2 6 4 21 1hd 2hd 24½ Santos JA 117 5.10 86-25 Zabaleta1144½Groovy1179½Belocolus1142 Best of rest 8
Previously owned by T. Kruckel Jr;previously trained by Kimberly Hardy
8Jan86- 9GP sly 6f :213 :444 1:114 Spectacular Bid 46k 1 4 1½ 12 12½ 1¾ Perret C 113 b *.90 80-21 Groovy113¾Kenny Lane1141¼Limited Practice1131½ Driving 6
Previously trained by John B. Adams
2Nov85- 1Aqu fst 1 :222 :452 1:104 1:361 ⒸBC Juvenile-G1 11 1 11½ 31½ 1014 1016 Murphy DJ 122 b 22.90 69-10 Tasso122noStormCt1221¾SctDncr122no Stumbled after start 13
19Oct85- 8Bel fst 1 :231 :462 1:12 1:371 Champagne-G1 1 1 12 12 23 29¾ MacBeth D 122 10.90 69-17 Mogambo1229¾Groovy122hdMr. Classic1221¾ No match 5
10Oct85- 8Med fst 1 1/16 :224 :46 1:102 1:433 Young America-G1 10 1 12 1½ 43½ 57½ MacBeth D 119 *2.00 77-15 StormCat119noDnzigCnnection122nkMogmbo1196 Weakened 12
14Sep85- 6Bel fst 7f :222 :453 1:093 1:222 Futurity-G1 6 3 1½ 1½ 22½ 29½ Murphy DJ 122 4.70 80-09 Ogygian1229½Groovy1226DHMr. Classic122 2nd best 6
2Sep85- 8Med fst 6f :222 :45 1:103 Forever Casting 28k 9 8 31½ 1hd 12½ 12½ Murphy DJ 112 7.90 89-10 Groovy1122½Hey Now Harry114nkKruckel1142½ Driving 11

Guilty Conscience

b. c. 1976, by Court Ruling (Traffic Judge)–Gracefully, by Gallant Man — Lifetime record: 41 14 8 4 $382,805

Own.– Mrs R. Davison
Br.– Mrs R. Davison (Md)
Tr.– Hubert Hine

28Nov81- 8Aqu	fst 6f	:23 :462 1:103	3↑ Sport Page H 54k	4 4 42 31½ 22½ 33½	Asmussen CB	126	*.90	85-28	WellDecoratd1172¾EnginOn116½GltyConscnc1261¼	Weakened	6
17Oct81- 8Aqu	fst 7f	:224 :454 1:093 1:22	3↑ Vosburgh-G1	6 2 42 4nk 13 13¾	Asmussen CB	126	2.90	91-23	GuiltyConscience1263¾RisJm1261WllDcortd123no	Ridden out	8
7Oct81- 8Bel	fst 6f	:224 :452 1:091	3↑ Boojum H 55k	2 5 76¼ 55½ 2hd 15	Asmussen CB	115	4.50	96-25	GuiltyCnscnce1155ImperlDlmm112nkMudln115½	Ridden out	8
26Aug81- 8Bel	fst 1	:223 :45 1:084 1:334	3↑ Forego H 83k	2 3 1hd 2hd 32 38¾	Asmussen CB	112	4.30	90-16	Fappiano119¾Herb Water1088Guilty Conscience112nk	Tired	5
29Jly81- 7Sar	sly 7f	:224 :454 1:092 1:221	3↑ Alw 32000	4 2 11½ 13 16 16¾	Asmussen CB	117	*.50	91-18	GltyCnscienc1176¾SngSng1092½DynmcMov115nk	Ridden out	6
3Jly81- 8Bel	my 6f	:221 :45 1:09	3↑ True North H 55k	1 3 65 52½ 4nk 31½	Asmussen CB	113	5.50	95-16	Joanie's Chief1091¼Proud Appeal117nkGuilty Conscience1133½	Rallied	7
6Jun81- 7Bel	fst 1	:231 :461 1:102 1:353	3↑ Alw 37000	3 3 11 13 15 15	Asmussen CB	115	*1.30	90-14	GuiltyConscience1155Joanie's Chief1171½Prince Crimson115½	Drew clear	10
17May81- 8Bel	fst 6f	:223 :453 1:094	3↑ Roseben H 55k	8 4 32 34 31 2¾	Asmussen CB	112	16.20	92-22	RingofLight113¾GuiltyConscience1121Convennt114½	Rallied	8
2May81- 8Aqu	gd 7f	:222 :451 1:094 1:23	3↑ Carter H-G2	3 3 21½ 1hd 12 2½	Lovato F Jr	111	5.60e	85-19	AmberPass114½GltyCnscienc1111Dunhm'sGft1161	Game try	7
4Apr81- 9Pim	fst 6f	:223 :45 :572 1:101	3↑ J E Hoover H 32k	3 3 52¼ 44½ 43 52½	McCauley WH	114	*1.30	92-19	NaughtyJimmy1131¼Gasp1131RexImperator112hd	No menace	7
29Mar81- 8Aqu	fst 6f	:214 :442 1:092	3↑ White Skies H 54k	1 4 33 32½ 32 23¾	Asmussen CB	114	6.30	90-21	Dave'sFriend1303¾GuiltyConscience114½Rare Performer1174½	Gained place	4
14Mar81- 8Aqu	fst 6f⊡	:231 :462 1:111	3↑ Toboggan H 53k	1 1 11½ 1hd 2½ 22½	Asmussen CB	115	2.50	85-18	Dr.Blum1232½GltyCnscnc115noDunhm'sGft1182¾	Brushed st.	4
16Feb81- 8Aqu	fst 6f⊡	:222 :45 1:091	3↑ Sporting Plate H 55k	4 1 21½ 2½ 2hd 2nk	Asmussen CB	115	4.30	98-13	Dr.Blum122nkGuiltyConscience115¾RingofLight113¾	Sharp	6
28Jan81- 8Aqu	fst 6f⊡	:221 :444 1:10	4↑ Coaltown 54k	2 4 2hd 2hd 21 43½	Asmussen CB	119	*1.20	90-20	Dr.Blum1211¾Dunham'sGift1231¾TonyMack114hd	Weakened	6
16Jan81- 8Aqu	fst 6f⊡	:223 :453 1:102	4↑ Handicap 32000	1 5 2½ 11 14 16	Asmussen CB	116	*1.70	92-24	GuiltyConscience1166BoldVoyager114noSkt1101¾	Ridden out	7
9Dec80- 8Med	fst 6f	:223 :46 1:103	3↑ Alw 25000	1 5 11½ 12½ 15 14	Asmussen CB	117	*1.20	90-22	GltyCnscience1174AmbtousRulr1175TwoPr110¾	Ridden out	9
28Nov80- 7Aqu	sly 6f	:223 :453 1:101	3↑ Alw 32000	4 4 32 2½ 1hd 11¾	Asmussen CB	119	5.30	92-17	GltyConscience1191¾TrckRwrd119nkSpyChrgr1153¾	Driving	6
5Apr80- 7Pim	fst 6f	:23 :453 :574 1:103	3↑ J E Hoover H 31k	1 4 45 49½ 49½ 412½	Adams JK	110	8.10	80-19	Isella11611AmbitiousRuler1101½Dave'sFriend125no	Trailed	4
26Mar80- 8Pim	fst 1 1/16	:23 :461 1:104 1:434	4↑ Alw 23000	7 3 32 23 511 515	Adams JK	117	2.20	71-23	Dooley's1155Grey Beret1152¼Best Man1152	Tired	7
9Feb80- 9Bow	fst 1 1/16	:233 :473 1:124 1:452	3↑ ⓈG L Stryker H 27k	2 3 33 31½ 32½ 87¼	Adams JK	115	*2.20e	72-26	Skipper'sFriend1131ThCoolVrgnn1191½T.V.Hll1141	Steadied	8
26Jan80- 5Bow	fst 7f	:223 :443 1:093 1:231	4↑ ⓈAlw 20000	4 2 21½ 31½ 43 42½	Adams JK	119	*.70	86-21	Skippr'sFriend1191¼AmbitousRulr119hdGsp1151¼	No excuse	5
22Dec79- 8Lrl	fst 1	:23 :461 1:112 1:372	ⓈE T Chewing H 32k	7 2 3nk 1½ 12 11	Adams JK	117	1.30e	86-15	GltyConscience1171TheCoolVirginian1231¼DurhamRangr1171¼	Driving	7
10Dec79- 8Lrl	fst 1	:24 :471 1:114 1:362	ⓈAlw 20000	5 1 12 12 14 17	Adams JK	113	*.80	91-23	GuiltyConscience1137StormWatch1131FunnyCap1112	Handily	6
23Nov79- 8Lrl	fst 7f	:224 :46 1:094 1:221	Capitol H 46k	10 5 3½ 21 2hd 21½	Adams JK	109	54.20	98-17	PolePosition1211½GultyCnscnc1096Buck'sChf112¾	Good try	12
12Nov79- 8Med	gd 6f	:221 :45 1:102	3↑ Alw 20000	1 4 31½ 35 34 23½	Adams JK	115	16.40	89-20	Coup de Kas1133½Guilty Conscience1151Klassy Flight110no	Up for place	8
30Oct79- 7Med	fst 6f	:221 :453 1:11	Palisades H (Div 2) 43k	8 5 64¼ 64½ 53¾ 45	Adams JK	109	67.70	85-20	Rise Jim120¾Convenient1154Pianist110nk	No factor; Awarded third purse money	9
19Oct79- 8Med	fst 6f	:23 :454 1:10	3↑ Alw 25000	6 4 61¾ 54 48 58	Adams JK	112	17.10	87-19	Amadevil1154Coupon Rate1154Team Captain122no	No threat	8
6Oct79- 6Med	fst 6f	:221 :451 1:111	3↑ Alw 20000	5 1 23 33½ 35½ 55½	Adams JK	116	5.60	83-17	Bold Bishop1152½Wm. Withers122½Sir Rossel1152	Tired	6
26Sep79- 7Med	fst 6f	:222 :452 1:103	3↑ Clm 32000	7 2 31½ 2hd 11½ 13	Adams JK	112	19.10	92-19	Guilty Conscience1123Two Pair1162Simplified1112	Driving	8
18Aug79- 8Tim	fst 4f	:222 :453	3↑ ⓈJet H 16k	5 7 96¼ 812 86	Sasser B	112	33.60	92-08	Silk or Satin1191¾Great Point1181¼Ten Ten117½	Outrun	10
7Aug79- 8Bow	fst 6f	:224 :454 :572 1:101	Alw 10000	6 4 32 2½ 23 22½	Adams JK	115	16.30	86-22	GreatPoint1202½GltyConscience1153RootieToot1122½	Wide	6
25Jly79- 8Bow	fst 7f	:224 :454 1:101 1:231	3↑ ⓈAlw 25000	5 4 44 43 45½ 56½	Adams JK	115	21.50	82-22	Side Board1173Combat Patrol1221½Great Point1151½	Tired	7
9Jly79- 8Bow	fst 6f	:223 :454 :582 1:12	Alw 9000	4 6 66¼ 46 58 68½	Iliescu A	115	7.20	71-26	J.D.May115noAnothergamblr115nkJohnVonWolfgng115¾	Tired	7
21Apr79- 8Pim	fm 1 1/16Ⓣ	:24 :481 1:132 1:454	ⓈSurvivor 32k	8 1 14½ 42 715 823	Adams JK	116	4.20e	59-17	DurhamRangr1167DoubleRefd1221¾Mon110hd	Used early pace	8
7Apr79- 8Pim	fst 6f	:232 :47 :59 1:114	Hirsch Jacobs 33k	1 5 32 42 78½ 715	Adams JK	119	3.80	73-18	BreezingOn1222½FearlssMcGuire113¾OurGary1221¼	Bore out	8
28Mar79- 8Bow	fst 7f	:233 :464 1:112 1:242	ⓈAlw 20000	6 1 14 13 15 13¼	Adams JK	117	3.20	83-25	GltyConscience1173¼ForLoveandGlory120hdDouble Reefd1171	Driving	6
16Mar79- 6Bow	fst 6f	:23 :463 :592 1:131	Alw 11000	1 3 1½ 11½ 13 11½	Adams JK	120	2.40	74-37	GltyConscience1201½Watch The Varmint1131Native Ginger1152	Driving	6
10Feb79- 3Bow	fst 6f	:223 :461 :582 1:12	Alw 10000	9 1 21 1hd 11½ 13	Adams JK	112	2.50e	80-31	GuiltyConscience1123Ransack1171Buck'sChief1151½	Driving	9
31Jan79- 8Bow	fst 6f	:223 :454 :581 1:12	Alw 10000	8 7 43 2hd 23 55	Adams JK	112	3.00e	75-26	Sugarbuck1083¾Ransack120nkTigger Too1121	Drifted out	10
5Jan79- 5Bow	fst 6f	:224 :461 :581 1:114	Md 25000	7 5 33 31½ 1hd 11¾	Adams JK	120	30.90e	81-23	GuiltyConscience1201¾Sugarbuck1151EazySwezy1204	Driving	12
24Oct78- 4Med	fst 6f	:221 :453 1:123	Md Sp Wt	8 11 1113 1116 1122 1123	Kurtz J	120	52.50	59-13	Infusive120nkPonchoSorefoot1203NevrRome1202	No threat	12

Gulch

b. c. 1984, by Mr. Prospector (Raise a Native)–Jameela, by Rambunctious — Lifetime record: 32 13 8 4 $3,095,521

Own.– P.M. Brant
Br.– Peter M. Brant (Ky)
Tr.– D. Wayne Lukas

5Nov88- 4CD	sly 6f	:21 :441 :562 1:102	3↑ BC Sprint-G1	10 5 87¼ 67 41¾ 1¾	Cordero A Jr	126	5.80e	91-20	Gulch126¾Play the King1261Afleet126½	Driving	13
9Oct88- 7Bel	my 7f	:223 :452 1:094 1:222	3↑ Vosburgh-G1	2 4 42½ 32½ 22 22¾	Cordero A Jr	126	*.50e	87-24	Mining1262¾Gulch1265½High Brite1264½	Held place	4
27Aug88- 9Mth	fst 1⅛	:462 1:094 1:343 1:474	3↑ Iselin H-G1	2 3 31 31 32½ 34¾	Cordero A Jr	122	2.40	90-12	Alysheba124¾Bet Twice1234Gulch1222½	Weakened	6
6Aug88- 8Sar	sly 1⅛	:472 1:113 1:353 1:474	3↑ Whitney H-G1	2 1 11½ 11 2hd 21½	Santos JA	124	1.80	94-12	Personal Ensign1171½Gulch12417King's Swan123	Tight turn,drifted out	3
16Jly88- 8Bel	fst 7f	:23 :461 1:101 1:222	3↑ Tom Fool-G2	1 1 2½ 2hd 2hd 2¾	Santos JA	128	*.40	89-22	King's Swan128¾Gulch1286Abject1192	Brushed late	4
12Jun88- 8Hol	fst 1⅛	:473 1:104 1:35 1:473	3↑ Californian-G1	4 2 3½ 31 21 22¾	Stevens GL	126	4.20	96-09	CutlassReality1152¾Gulch1264½JudgeAnglucc1261¾	2nd best	4
30May88- 8Bel	fst 1	:222 :444 1:084 1:343	3↑ Metropolitan H-G1	4 3 21 2hd 1½ 1½	Santos JA	125	1.40e	92-19	Gulch125½Afleet1241½Stacked Pack110¾	Driving	8
7May88- 8Aqu	fst 7f	:223 :444 1:082 1:202	3↑ Carter H-G1	3 3 1½ 1hd 1½ 11¼	Santos JA	124	2.20	99-13	Gulch1241¼Afleet1242Its Acedemic1081¾	Driving	8
16Apr88- 9OP	gd 1⅛	:463 1:103 1:351 1:47	4↑ Oaklawn H-G1	7 2 42 42¼ 22 33¾	Delahoussaye E	120	5.70	94-12	LostCode126¾Cryptoclearnc1223Gulch1204	Lacked solid bid	8
30Mar88- 8SA	fst 6½f	:214 :442 1:083 1:15	4↑ Potrero Grande H 70k	3 1 1½ 21 21½ 11¼	Delahoussaye E	123	1.20	95-18	Gulch1231¼Very Subtle1202¼Gallant Sailor111	Driving	3
18Mar88- 8SA	fst 6f	:221 :45 :564 1:084	4↑ Alw 55000	6 3 41 2hd 1hd 11¾	Delahoussaye E	116	3.10	94-18	Gulch1161¾Sebrof1183½My Gallant Game1163½	Driving; Previously trained by LeRoy Jolley	6
21Nov87- 7Hol	fst 1¼	:462 1:101 1:352 2:012	3↑ BC Classic-G1	11 8 87¾ 87½ 910 915¼	Santos JA	122	25.20	70-12	Ferdinand126noAlysheba1221¼Judge Angelucci1261½	Outrun	12
21Oct87- 8Aqu	fst 1	:224 :452 1:092 1:344	Jamaica H-G3	1 7 711 65½ 33½ 2¾	Santos JA	123	*.80	91-19	Stacked Pack110¾Gulch123¾Homebuilder1121¾	Rallied	8
20Sep87- 8Bel	gd 1¼	:482 1:123 1:364 2:01	3↑ Marlboro Cup H-G1	2 4 58 34 32 43¼	Santos JA	117	4.80	90-14	Java Gold1202¼Nostalgia's Star116nkPolish Navy117¾	Hung	5
5Sep87- 8Bel	fst 1⅛	:46 1:091 1:34 1:47	3↑ Woodward-G1	8 6 88¾ 68½ 33 2¾	Santos JA	118	5.50	91-15	Polish Navy116¾Gulch118nkCreme Fraiche1192¾	Rallied	9
22Aug87- 8Sar	sly 1¼	:461 1:10 1:362 2:02	Travers-G1	4 6 612 44 55 410¼	Santos JA	126	9.90e	80-16	JavaGold1262Cryptoclearnce1266¾PolshNvy1261½	No threat	9
8Aug87- 8Sar	fst 1⅛	:462 1:102 1:351 1:482	3↑ Whitney H-G1	1 6 58 42½ 12½ 2¾	Santos JA	117	3.40e	92-13	Java Gold113¾Gulch1172¼Broad Brush127no	Drifted out	7
6Jun87- 8Bel	fst 1½	:492 1:134 2:03 2:281	Belmont-G1	9 6 813 816 412 314	Day P	126	7.70e	65-15	Bet Twice12614Cryptoclearance126noGulch126nk	Wide str	9
25May87- 8Bel	fst 1	:223 :442 1:091 1:344	3↑ Metropolitan H-G1	9 9 811 62¼ 3nk 1nk	Day P	110	5.80	91-16	Gulch110nkKing's Swan121½Broad Brush1282	Driving	9
16May87- 9Pim	fst 1 3/16	:471 1:113 1:364 1:554	Preakness-G1	7 8 66¾ 73¾ 43½ 45½	Cordero A Jr	126	3.50	82-18	Alysheba126½BetTwice1261½Cryptoclearnce1263½	Weakened	9
2May87- 8CD	fst 1¼	:462 1:11 1:364 2:032	Ky Derby-G1	6 15 1618 126¾ 76 64¼	Shoemaker W	126	4.90e	76-09	Alysheba126¾Bet Twice1262¼Avies Copy126nk	Very wide	17

18Apr87- 8Aqu my 1⅛ :47 1:113 1:362 1:49 Wood Memorial Inv'l-G1 1 4 67½ 44½ 22½ 1hd Santos JA 126 3.60 90-15 Gulch126hdGone West1266Shawklit Won1261¾ Strong urging 8
4Apr87- 8Aqu sly 1 :222 :442 1:081 1:343 Gotham-G2 4 9 812 612 49½ 39½ Vasquez J 123 2.60 83-21 Gone West1141Shawklit Won1148½Gulch123hd Rallied 9
21Mar87- 8Aqu fst 7f :222 :453 1:101 1:231 Bay Shore-G2 3 5 63 52¾ 21½ 11 Santos JA 123 *.60 85-28 Gulch1231High Brite119nkShawklit Won1145½ Drew clear 9
28Feb87- 9Hia fst 6f :222 :451 1:101 Key West 43k 7 4 42 31 53¼ 41½ Cordero A Jr 122 b *.80 87-19 Mr. Zippity Do Dah114½Bet Twice122¾Vlid Prospect112nk 9
Lunged in air str
1Nov86- 1SA fst 1 1/16 :222 :454 1:102 1:434 BC Juvenile-G1 7 3 31½ 21 33 54¾ Cordero A Jr 122 2.60 77-13 Capote1221¼Qualify1221¼Alysheba1222¼ Bid,weakened 13
11Oct86- 8SA fst 1 1/16 :223 :461 1:11 1:451 Norfolk-G1 4 4 31½ 2½ 33 21¾ Cordero A Jr 118 *.80 73-17 Capote1181¾Gulch118¾Gold on Green1182¾ Best of rest 6
13Sep86- 7Bel fst 7f :23 :454 1:093 1:221 Futurity-G1 7 1 31 1½ 15 11¼ Cordero A Jr 122 *.20 91-11 Glch1221¼Demn'sBegone1227½CaptainVald122no Ridden out 7
23Aug86- 8Sar fst 6½f :214 :442 1:094 1:162 Hopeful-G1 3 2 22 21 12 13½ Cordero A Jr 122 *.30 90-10 Gulch1223½Persevered1227½Flying Granville122nk Driving 4
1Aug86- 8Sar fst 6f :222 :452 1:10 Sar Spl-G2 8 3 21 2½ 11½ 12½ Cordero A Jr 122 *1.00 90-17 Gulch1222½Jazzing Around1174¾Java Gold1171½ Driving 10
13Jly86- 8Bel my 6f :22 :444 1:102 Tremont-G3 5 4 32½ 1hd 11 13½ Cordero A Jr 115 *1.00 90-15 Gulch1153½Shawklit Won1171½Bucks Best11513 Ridden out 5
2Jun86- 4Bel fst 5f :23 :46 :573 Md Sp Wt 5 5 52 41 11½ 17¾ Bailey JD 118 *1.10 99-13 Gulch1187¾FlyingGranville1182½JamesOscar1182 Ridden out 7

Heartlight No. One

dkbbr. f. 1980, by Rock Talk (Rasper II)–Icantell, by Tell **Lifetime record: 7 5 1 1 $322,880**
Own.– B. Bacharach
Br.– Blue Seas Music Inc (Md)
Tr.– Pedro Marti

16Oct83- 8Bel fst 1¼ :471 1:11 1:352 2:003 3↑ ⒻBeldame-G1 4 1 12½ 2½ 2½ 2hd Pincay L Jr 118 b *.50 95-14 DanceNmbr123hdHrtlghtNo.On1188½Mochl1232½ Just missed 7
25Sep83- 8Bel fst 1⅛ :452 1:09 1:342 1:471 3↑ ⒻRuffian H-G1 5 2 2½ 2hd 1½ 11 Pincay L Jr 117 b *1.60 91-15 HrtlightNo.One1171Mochil113½TrySomthngNw1161½ Driving 12
20Aug83- 8Dmr fm 1⅛Ⓣ :474 1:12 1:372 1:501 ⒻDmr Oaks-G2 3 5 65½ 43 11 13½ Pincay L Jr 122 b *1.50 87-11 HrtlightNo.One1223½Foggy Moon1151Fabulous Notion1221¼ 10
Rough trip,driving
28Jly83- 5Dmr fm 1Ⓣ :233 :473 1:114 1:363 ⒻAlw 20000 6 3 2hd 12½ 16 16½ Pincay L Jr 120 b *.30 90-10 HrtlightNo.One1206½GoldenGrand120noSwtDn1203½ Driving 7
10Jly83- 8Hol fst 1⅛ :454 1:101 1:363 1:494 ⒻHol Oaks-G1 3 1 12½ 16 16 112 Pincay L Jr 121 b 3.60 80-21 HeartlightNo.One12112Prcptrss1212½RdyforLuck1212 Easily 7
4Jun83- 6Hol fst 6f :221 :443 :572 1:101 3↑ ⒻMd Sp Wt 1 4 2hd 13 16 17 Pincay L Jr 117 b *1.40 86-20 HeartlightNo.One1177HellionQuen1154½NclyNtv1222½ Easily 11
8Jan83- 4SA fst 6f :213 :444 :571 1:094 ⒻMd Sp Wt 5 11 109¼ 69 35 35½ Shoemaker W 117 b *2.30 83-10 Anesthesiologist1173½Taisez Too1172Heartlight No. One117¾ 12
Rallied,hung

Heavenly Cause

ro. f. 1978, by Grey Dawn II (Herbager)–Lady Dulcinea, by Nantallah **Lifetime record: 21 9 4 2 $622,481**
Own.– Ryehill Farm
Br.– Ryehill Farm (Md)
Tr.– Woodford C. Stephens

31Oct81- 7Kee fst 1⅛ :472 1:113 1:363 1:491 3↑ ⒻSpinster-G1 5 5 62¾ 53 66½ 612 Day P 119 3.30 79-19 Glorious Song123nkTruly Bound1196Safe Play119¾ Outrun 7
22Oct81- 7Kee fst 1 1/16 :243 :482 1:12 1:434 3↑ ⒻAlw 26820 1 3 22 11½ 13 14½ Day P 120 *.30 87-19 Heavenly Cause1204½Sweetest Chant1177Forever Cordial1151 4
Ridden out
26Sep81- 8Key fst 1 1/16 :234 :474 1:112 1:424 ⒻCotillion-G3 4 6 42 32½ 34 45¾ Saumell L 121 *1.40 84-20 TrulyBound1214½PukkaPrincss118nkDebonrDncr1181 Blocked 8
10Sep81- 8Bel fst 7f :222 :451 1:10 1:23 3↑ ⒻAlw 32000 4 5 59 56½ 47½ 49¼ Venezia M 118 3.30 78-16 Wayward Lass1151Highest Regard1156¾Cherokee Frolic1181½ 5
No factor
27Jun81- 8Bel fst 1½ :474 1:114 2:014 2:281 ⒻC C A Oaks-G1 4 4 42½ 45½ 412 418 Pincay L Jr 121 *.40e 61-16 DRealPrize1212½WywrdLss1212½BannerGala12113 Weakened 6
5Jun81- 8Bel fst 1⅛ :47 1:11 1:354 1:484 ⒻMother Goose-G1 1 5 42½ 42 21 2nk Pincay L Jr 121 *.70e 83-17 WaywrdLss121nkHeavnlyCause1212¾BannerGl1211¾ Bore in 8
23May81- 8Bel fst 1 :231 :46 1:094 1:351 ⒻAcorn-G1 1 5 2½ 11½ 12 13¾ Pincay L Jr 121 *.30e 92-13 HeavnlyCause1213¾Dame Mysterieuse1214Autumn Glory121½ 7
Ridden out
1May81- 8CD fst 1 1/16 :25 :484 1:13 1:434 ⒻKy Oaks-G1 4 4 41½ 1½ 11½ 1no Pincay L Jr 121 1.50e 89-17 HeavnlyCse121noDe La Rose1215WaywardLass1213 Driving 6
25Apr81- 8CD fst 7f :234 :473 1:113 1:24 ⒻLa Troienne 26k 6 6 53 1½ 11½ 15 Day P 121 *.30 87-23 HeavnlyCause1215Fiddleatune1215Roger'sTurn1212 Handily 6
4Apr81- 9OP fst 1 1/16 :233 :471 1:122 1:434 ⒻFantasy-G1 3 3 42½ 1hd 1hd 1hd Pincay L Jr 121 *1.90 89-19 HeavnlyCause121hdNell's Briquette1215¼Wayward Lass1214½ 9
Prolonged dr
2Mar81- 9GP fst 1 1/16 :25 :492 1:133 1:442 ⒻBonnie Miss 87k 1 3 32 32 34 36 Maple E 121 *.70 73-22 DameMysterieuse1181BannrGala1135HvnlyCs1211½ Weakened 7
11Feb81- 9GP fst 7f :223 :45 1:092 1:221 ⒻForward Gal 43k 6 8 42½ 53 32 21¼ Maple E 121 *1.20 92-18 DameMystrieuse1181¼HeavnlyCs121¾MstrsDrm113no Gaining 10
1Nov80- 9Lrl fst 1 1/16 :234 :472 1:122 1:432 ⒻSelima-G1 4 2 2½ 31 11½ 12¼ Pincay L Jr 122 1.60 91-14 HvnlyCause1222¼RainbowConnctn1222¼Carolina Command1223½ 6
Ridden out
23Oct80- 6Med fst 1 1/16 :231 :461 1:113 1:443 ⒻGardenia-G3 4 6 59½ 34 12½ 22 Pincay L Jr 121 *.20 84-15 CarolinaCommnd1182HvnlyCaus1218½StunnngNtv1181 Wide 7
5Oct80- 8Bel fst 1 :241 :48 1:124 1:38 ⒻFrizette-G1 2 4 32 3½ 2hd 11½ Pincay L Jr 119 5.70 78-23 HvnlyCause1191½SweetRevenge1194½Prayers'nPromises119hd 8
Driving
22Sep80- 8Bel fst 7f :232 :471 1:114 1:243 ⒻMatron-G1 3 7 34 33 1hd 2hd Pincay L Jr 119 4.90 79-23 Prayers 'n Promises119hdHeavnlyCause1191Sweet Revenge1192¼ 8
Sharp
8Sep80- 7Bow fst 7f :233 :471 1:122 1:252 ⒻMarlboro Nursery 43k 5 6 53½ 42 1½ 15 Maple E 116 2.60 78-25 HeavnlyCause1165Cavort113hdStunningNtv1141½ Drew clear 6
29Aug80- 8Bel fm 7fⓉ :23 :46 1:094 1:232 ⒻEvening Out 56k 6 5 54½ 52½ 47 412¾ Saumell L 113 4.80 74-13 De La Rose114hdBravoNtive11210PrimeProspect1132¾ Wide 7
20Aug80- 6Sar fm 1Ⓣ :24 :484 1:134 1:381 ⒻAlw 20000 8 7 87½ 65 711 717 Saumell L 114 *1.20 71-16 De La Rose1145Picture Pretty109noJan Jill114¾ Bothered 10
30Jly80- 8Sar fst 6f :212 :444 1:102 ⒻSchuylerville-G3 11 2 814 65 44½ 33¼ Saumell L 114 6.80 85-12 SweetRevenge114nkCompanionship1143HeavnlyCs1143 Wide 11
23Jly80- 4Bel sly 7f :232 :471 1:113 1:242 ⒻMd Sp Wt 7 2 74½ 31½ 14 19 Saumell L 117 4.70 80-22 HeavnlyCause1179WaywardLass1176Zimbaba1174½ Ridden out 8

Highland Bud

b. g. 1985, by Northern Baby (Northern Dancer)–Fleur d'Or, by Exclusive Native **Lifetime record: 27 10 10 3 $508,269**
Own.– Jesse M. Henley Jr
Br.– William Floyd (Ky)
Tr.– Jonathan E. Sheppard

14Nov93- 4Cam fm *2¾ S'Chase 5:074 4↑ Colonial Cup 100k 8 10 106½ - - - Dunwoody R 162 - -- DeclareYourWish1622¾Simonov1511¾LnesomeGlry1602 Lame 11
16Oct93- 10Bel sf 2⅝ S'Chase 4:532 3↑ BC Chase 250k 9 8 54½ 31 1½ 28½ Dunwoody R 156 *.70e -- Lonesome Glory1568½Highland Bud1565Mistico1564 9
Sharp try,second best
11Sep93- 6Fai fm 1¼Ⓣ 2:133 3↑ Alw 1000 1 2 31½ 31¼ 1hd 12¼ Miller B 150 *1.80 -- Highland Bud1502¼Equal Measure1442My Babys Fast1432¾ 8
10Oct92- 2Bel sf 2⅝ S'Chase 4:562 3↑ BC Chase 250k 4 6 51½ 51½ 1hd 13 Dunwoody R 156 *1.10e -- Highland Bud1563Mistico1563Sassello1468½ Driving 10
7Sep92- 10Mth fm *2¼ S'Chase 4:134 3↑ Handicap 20000 3 4 44 32 1½ 2no Miller B 154 5.40 -- Ninepins148noHighlandBud1547SummitPoint1411¼ Game try 7
29Sep91- 2Fx hd *2Ⓣ 3:134 3↑ Alw 1000 5 9 918 45 2nk 22 Guessford B 150 - -- Jive With Five1502Highland Bud1504Tower of Torture150nk 11
Blocked,driving
6Jun91- 4Bel yl 2 S'Chase 3:37 4↑ Handicap 45000 5 2 42½ 44½ 619 639 Dunwoody R 156 *.70e -- WoodyBoyWould1471½MadeNble14613LeSauvage1495½ Tired 7
11May91- 6PW sf *3 S'Chase 5:592 4↑ Iroquois H 100k 6 2 53¾ 34¾ 2½ 22 Smithwck DM Jr 168 - -- VictorianHill1682HghlndBd1687DclrYourWsh16313 Bid,hung 8
21Apr91- 2Due fm *2¼ S'Chase 4:16 4↑ Dueling Int'l 250k 5 8 47¾ 411 23 29½ Guessford B 154 22.00 -- Victorian Hill1549½Highland Bud1546¾Penascal1543 Tired 8
6Apr91- 4AtH fm *2⅛ S'Chase 3:592 4↑ Ath Cup H 100k 3 5 53 32 31¾ 33½ Guessford B 160 - -- DeclreYourWish145noChiefoftheCln1483½DHighlndBud1604½ 7
Disqualified and placed sixth;Previously trained by Jonathan E. Sheppard
7Apr90- 4AtH fm *2⅛ S'Chase 4:022 4↑ Ath Hunt Cup 100k 2 6 63¼ 35 21 2hd Guessford B 162 - -- PolrPlesur150hdDHSmmrColony156DHHghlndBd16215 Gamely 6
31Mar90- 6Cam fm *1Ⓣ 1:42 3↑ Sp Wt 1000 2 11 1011 86½ 48½ 46 Guessford B 150 - -- Morewoods1504Summer Colony1501Chief of the Clan1501 12
19Nov89- 4Cam fm *2¾ S'Chase 5:174 4↑ Colonial Cup 60k 1 3 3¾ 11½ 13 114 Dunwoody R 151 - -- Highland Bud15114Opacity1602¾Dawson1602¼ Easily 5
28Oct89- 3FH fm *2⅝ S'Chase 4:584 3↑ BC Chase 250k 1 3 34½ 2hd 17 110 Dunwoody R 146 - -- HighlandBud14610PolarPleasure15615VctornHll1464 Driving 8

8Oct89- 7Mid fm *2$\frac{1}{16}$ S'Chase 3:543 4↑ O Clm 25000 3 10 99½ 54 1½ 11¼ Guessford B 148 - -- Highland Bud148 1¼Yaw147 1Cadent148 1 Driving 10
24Sep89- 3Fx gd *2Ⓣ 3:152 3↑ Sp Wt 1000 1 1 2½ 11 12 2hd Miller B 150 - -- Uranio152hdHighland Bud150 2Delivery150 3 7
Previously trained by David Nicholson

27Apr89♦ Punchestwn(Ire) hy 2RH 4:043 Irish Champion Hurdle Stk28700 310¾ Dunwoody R 163 4.00 Royal Derbi163 10Lunulae155¾Highland Bud163 6 11
Prominent,bid 2out,never threatened.Ikdam 4th,Vayrua 5th

7Apr89♦ Aintree(GB) sf 2LH 4:244 Glenlivet Anniversary Hurdle Stk60400 25 Dunwoody R 154 *2.25 Vayrua154 5Highland Bud154hdBank View154 15 9
Rated toward rear,progress at 4th,saved 2nd

16Mar89♦ Cheltenham(GB) hy 2LH 4:184 Triumph Hurdle Stk80500 21½ Dunwoody R 154 8.00 Ikdam154 1½Highland Bud154hdDon Valentino154 2½ 27
Tracked leaders,bid over 1f out,finished well.Royal Derbi 4th

28Jan89♦ Cheltenham(GB) yl 2LH 4:14 Food Brokers Hurdle Stk18600 13 Dunwoody R 157 4.00 Highland Bud157 3Enemy Action161 8Propero154 3 6
Tracked in 3rd,led approaching last,driving

30Dec88♦ Newbury(GB) gd 2$\frac{1}{16}$LH 4:002 Wickham Hurdle Alw5000 110 Dunwoody R 154 *1.85 Highland Bud154 10Victory Gate154 4Durzi154 6 15
Close up,led at 5th,ridden clear approaching last
Previously trained by John Oxx

24Sep88♦ Down Royal(Ire) gd 1¾ⓉRH - 3↑ Ulster St Leger Alw7000 34 Hogan D 125 *.65 Husaam130 2Dublin's Coq Hardi117 2Highland Bud125 4 5
Led to 2f out,gradually faded.Time not taken

20Aug88♦ Phoenix Park(Ire) yl 1¾ⓉRH 3:03 3↑ St Leger Trial Alw6900 13 Quinton R 122 2.50 Highland Bud122 3Ard Countess131 5Allen's Mistake134nk 7
Tracked in 3rd,led over 2f out,drew clear final furlong

13Jly88♦ Down Royal(Ire) gd *1½ⓉRH - Ulster Harp Derby Alw14400 14 Quinton R 123 6.00 Highland Bud123 4Magistro128 2Montefiore123 4 4
Led throughout,drew clear final furlong.Time not taken

8Jly88♦ Gowran Park(Ire) gd 1¼ⓉRH 2:11 3↑ Dunbell Maiden (Div 2) Mdn2900 1¾ Quinton R 126 *.50 Highland Bud126¾Burrow Bard126 4John O'Dreams126 4 9
Tracked leader,led 1½f out,held well

19Sep87♦ Leopardstwn(Ire) sf 1ⓉLH 1:464 Torquay Maiden Mdn3900 34½ Hogan D 126 4.00 Clash of Ideas126 2Law Lord126 2½Highland Bud126 1½ 15
Tracked in 3rd,close 6th on rail over 2f out,3rd 1f out

29Aug87♦ The Curragh(Ire) gd 7fⓉStr 1:282 Panasonic Copier Maiden Mdn6100 2½ Hogan D 126 14.00 Gold Discovery126½Highland Bud126 1Easter King123 1½ 17
Tracked in 5th,3rd 1½f out,2nd 100y out

Inlander (GB)

b. g. 1981, by Ile de Bourbon (Nijinsky II)–Blissful Evening, by Blakeney
Own.– Dogwood Stable
Br.– Cleaboy Farms Co (GB)
Tr.– Charles Fenwick Jr

Lifetime record: 38 10 8 1 $233,148

9Apr88- 4AtH fm *2⅛ S'Chase 4:012 4↑ Atlanta Hunt Cup 100k 4 5 - - - - Morris G 158 - -- MickeyFree148nkSaffan145noPolarParalll152 1½ Fell at 6th 8
5Dec87- 4Cam fm *2¾ S'Chase 5:211 4↑ Colonial Cup 60k 1 6 54¼ 44 21 13¼ Morris GL 162 - -- Inlander162 3¼Ormus162 3Statesmanship162 2¾ Driving 8
21Nov87- 5Pmt fm *2⅜ S'Chase 4:04 4↑ Crown Royal H 40k 4 4 61½ 45 3½ 1hd Morris GL 155 - -- Inlander155hdStatesmanship152hdMckyFr148 2 Strong urging 7
31Oct87- 5Fai fm *2⅝ S'Chase 5:151 3↑ BC Chase 250k 4 10 88½ 43½ 34½ 28¾ Morris GL 156 9.40 -- Gacko156 8¾Inlander156½Gateshead156 3¾ Strong pressure 10
17Oct87- 5RB fm *2 S'Chase 3:583 4↑ Handicap 50000 1 2 23 32 42 44 Hendriks R 156 - -- PolarParallel153 1¼MickeyFree146 2TheCleverest149¾ Tired 6
Previously trained by Reg Akehurst

16Jun87♦ Ascot(GB) gd 2½ⓉRH 4:283 4↑ Ascot Handicap Hcp26700 110 Adams N 105 5.00 Inlander105 10White Mill110 4El Conquistador136no 9
Tracked in 3rd,bid 2½f out,led 2f out,easily clear

30May87♦ Kempton(GB) gd 2ⓉRH 3:261 4↑ H S Persse Memorial Handicap Hcp6700 12 Carson W 111 *2.10 Inlander111 2All Is Revealed114 2Ile de Roi131 4 9
Tracked in 3rd,led 170y out,driving

4May87♦ Haydock(GB) gd 2LH 3:463 4↑ Handicap Hurdle Hcp47700 1no Smith-Eccles S 148 4.00 Inlander148noSantopadre133hdJanus145 6 8
Rated at rear,rallied to lead on line

8Apr87♦ Ascot(GB) gd 2RH 3:572 5↑ Kestrel Handicap Hurdle Hcp11000 2¾ McKeown D7 157 *1.75 Beat the Retreat161¾Inlander157 25Kescast161 2 8
Prominent,chasing winner 2 out,finished well

21Mar87♦ Lingfield(GB) sf 2½LH 4:561 5↑ Bic Razor Gold Cup Hcp Hurdle Hcp33600 318 Smith-Eccles S 161 6.50 Tigerwood150 12Mandavi151 6Inlander161 2 15
Progress into 3rd 2 out,one-paced to line

14Mar87♦ Sandown(GB) gd 2RH 3:50 5↑ Imperial Cup Hcp Hurdle Stk27500 11 Smith-Eccles S 143 10.00 Inlander143 1Kescast146 5Timely Star154 1½ 23
Previously trained by Jeff Davies
Midpack,rallied 2 out,led 1 out,all out

4Nov86♦ Fontwell(GB) gd 2¼LH 4:411 4↑ Veuve Clicquot Hcp Hurdle Hcp7100 613½ Heaver G7 157 *2.25 Hot Handed154 1The Diplomat140 2½Paris North159 3 10
Prominent,weakened approaching second last

25Oct86♦ Doncaster(GB) yl 2¼ⓉLH 4:102 3↑ Elmfield Park Stakes Alw4300 7 Lines R3 114 11.00 Troy Fair126 1½Shah's Choice118 6La Rose Grise114¾ 11
Toward rear,bid to track leaders 4½f out,soon weakened

15Mar86♦ Lingfield(GB) yl 2½LH 5:022 5↑ Bic Razor Gold Cup Hcp Hurdle Hcp29000 12 Woods S7 133 *4.50 Inlander133 2Moon Mariner143 8Opening Bars145 2 16
Led 2 out,swerved badly right last,ridden out

8Mar86♦ Sandown(GB) gd 2RH 3:58 5↑ Imperial Cup Handicap Hurdle Stk27300 41 Woods S 133 Insular136¾Hypnosis142nkPeter Martin142no 19
Lost place at 3rd,rallied 2 out,gamely

3Feb86♦ Fontwell(GB) sf 2¼LH 4:584 5↑ Lyminster Handicap Hurdle Hcp4400 16 Lovejoy J 152 3.30 Inlander152 6Lir142 1Hal's Prince157¾ 16
Led at 5th,quickened clear 6th,ridden out

23Jan86♦ Huntingdon(GB) gd 3RH 6:06 5↑ Sapley Handicap Hurdle Hcp3400 2nk Lovejoy J 153 10.00 Jennie Pat168nkInlander153 15North West149 3 21
Midpack,progress after 6th,bid 3 out,gamely

15Jan86♦ Windsor(GB) gd 2 3:534 5↑ Weir Handicap Hurdle Hcp3000 9 Lovejoy J 161 14.00 Quite a Night156 2Batu162 2Rix Woodcock154 2 24
Never a factor

6Jan86♦ Chepstow(GB) sf 2LH 4:192 5↑ Duck Conditional Jockeys Hcp Hurdle Hcp2100 14 Heaver G4 146 5.50 Ribobelle146 2Panto Prince148 5Chemist Broker0 3 21
Toward rear throughout

26Dec85♦ Kempton(GB) sf 2RH 4:111 4↑ Boxing Day Handicap Hurdle Hcp8000 530 Lovejoy J 143 12.00 Yabis148 15The Tariahs150 7Dhofar161 4 10
Never a factor

10Dec85♦ Plumpton(GB) sf 2LH 3:49 4↑ December Handicap Hurdle Hcp3100 523 Lovejoy J 154 *2.25 Mr Key152 15Pip143 4Mighty Steel142no 10
Rated at rear,close 3rd 3 out,soon weakened

19Oct85♦ Newmarket(GB) gd 2¼ⓉRH 3:512 3↑ Cesarewitch Handicap Hcp68400 917¾ Still R 105 20.00 Kayudee113 2Jamesmead116hdBourbon Boy120½ 21
Prominent to 4f out,gradually weakened

10Sep85♦ Folkestone(GB) gd *1$\frac{15}{16}$ⓉRH 3:244 3↑ Windsor Hotel Stakes (Amateurs) Alw3300 2no Woods S5 154 5.00 Careo153noInlander154 3Cheshire House154 4 17
Toward rear,long drive halfway,strong late run,just missed

27Aug85♦ Chepstow(GB) sf 2ⓉLH 3:572 3↑ Lysaght Handicap Hcp3700 2no Bennyworth D5 163 *1.85 Carmel State143noInlander163 1½Rocas142 15 7
Dwelt,far behind,soon midpack,strong late run,just missed

10Aug85♦ Lingfield(GB) hy 2ⓉLH 3:464 4↑ Gatwick Handicap Hcp3900 2½ Adams J7 131 10.00 Neraida107½Inlander131 8New Zealand125nk 11
Midpack,bid 2f out,dueled 170y out,gamely

21Jun85♦ Ascot(GB) gd *2¾ⓉRH 5:13 4↑ Queen Alexandra Stakes (Listed) Stk22000 7 Carson W 114 25.00 Valuable Witness129 2½Ravaro124 12Real Pegus112 3 11
Tracked in 5th,weakened over 2f out

3Jun85♦ Folkestone(GB) fm *1$\frac{15}{16}$ⓉRH 3:201 4↑ Dover Handicap Hcp2600 2hd Landau G7 127 7.50 Forewarn122hdInlander127¾Puget128 2 17
Tracked leaders,bid 1f out,dueled final 16th,gamely

16Apr85♦ Fontwell(GB) sf 2¼LH 4:43 Amberley Hurdle Alw1200 14 Lovejoy J 156 *3.30 Inlander156 4Ribobelle151 8Bronski150 12 13
Prominent,led 3 out,all out

8Apr85♦ Plumpton(GB)	hy 2LH	4:094	John Hare Maiden Hurdle Mdn1000	115	Lovejoy J	152	3.50	Inlander15215Atkins1528Coldharbour Lad14810 Led at 6th,clear 2 out,mistake last,handily	8
31Jan85♦ Lingfield(GB)	hy 2LH	4:262 4↑	Haddon Novices Hurdle Alw1000	-	Jones A7	138	12.00	Pottstown1451Larry-O16212Telephone Numbers15710 Always behind,tailed off and eased before 2nd last	7
Previously trained by Henry Candy									
15Oct84♦ Sandown(GB)	yl 1¾ⓉRH	3:10	Leatherhead Stakes Alw3900	43¾	Williams T3	120	3.50	Widdicombe Fair124¾Recamier1202In the Shade1201 Midpack,ridden into lead 2f out,headed 1f out,weakened	11
2Oct84♦ Nottingham(GB)	gd 1¾ⓉLH	3:063	Nottingham Goose Fair Hcp Hcp6900	614¾	Williams T3	123	*3.00	Carnet de Danse1261½Whispering Grass1333Chatter1033 Pushed along early to keep pace,led 1½f out,soon weakened	9
26Sep84♦ Sandown(GB)	yl 1¾ⓉRH	3:052 3↑	Autumn Handicap Hcp7200	2no	Williams T5	116	9.00	Vital Boy116noInlander116½Madam Flutterbye1174 Close up,slight lead 1f out,dueled,just missed	9
18Sep84♦ Lingfield(GB)	gd 1½ⓉLH	2:39	Hartfield Stakes Alw5300	56	Matthias J	123	16.00	Luminate1231½Newsells Park130½Kafouaine1301½ Tracked leaders,weakened 2f out	14
3Aug84♦ Newmarket(GB)	gd 1½ⓉRH	2:313	Running Gap Handicap Hcp10800	49½	Williams T5	112	16.00	Crazy1312½Rynechra128noNewsells Park1177 Tracked leaders,outfinished	9
5May84♦ Newmarket(GB)	fm 1½ⓉRH	2:352	Culford Stakes Alw8200	618¼	Eddery Pat	123	5.00	Baynoun1334Face Facts12612Jerry Can133nk Never a factor	14
13Apr84♦ Newbury(GB)	gd 1⅝ⓉLH	2:242	Spring Maiden Stakes Mdn5900	44½	Matthias J	126	20.00	Spicy Story126¾Kinski1263Longboat126¾ Tracked in 3rd,dueled briefly 2f out,weakened 1f out	10
18Oct83♦ Leicester(GB)	gd 7fⓉStr	1:251	Soar Maiden Stakes (Div 2) Mdn2300	512¾	Curant R	126	14.00	Bold Patriach126¾Raami1262Triple Tower1263 Tracked leaders,weakened 2f out	18

Jimmy Lorenzo (GB)

dkbbr. g. 1982, by Our Jimmy (Tom Rolfe)–Love Beach, by Lorenzaccio
Own.– Bertram R. Firestone
Br.– J.W. Demestre (GB)
Tr.– Rodney Jenkins

Lifetime record: 37 11 3 9 $248,646

15May93- 4Mgo	gd	*2¼	Hurdles	4:082 4↑	Handicap 15000	6	5	517	510	620	639½	Newman G	154	-	--	Arctic Circle1374Dangerfield1486Billy King1481½	6
Previously trained by Jonathan E. Sheppard																	
7Sep92- 2Fai	gd	*1⅜Ⓣ		2:15 3↑	Alw 2500	6	9	917	55	511	419¼	Neilson S	154	*1.60	--	Lord of Flanders15113Greg1473¼Oslek1543	Late rally 9
16Nov91- 3Cam	fm	*2¾	S'Chase	5:14 4↑	Colonial Cup 60k	9	6	74¾	46	78	79½	Smart J	162	-	--	Moonstruck1622Made Noble1601¼Double Bill1621½	Bid,hung 10
12Oct91- 3Fai	gd	*2⅝	S'Chase	5:103 3↑	BC Chase 250k	10	10	1116	1012	1017	942¾	Smart J	156	6.40	--	MorleyStrt1569¾Declare Your Wish15615½CheeringNews146hd	12
Dull effort																	
18Aug89- 8Sar	fm	2⅜	S'Chase	4:181 4↑	NY Turf Writers H 115k	5	7	46	46	44	46¾	Scudamore P	162	1.40e	--	DoubleBill1421½UptownSwell152nkPolrPlsur1495	Rank early 7
9Jun89- 4Bel	sf	2	S'Chase	3:584 4↑	Alw 40000	3	7	55	53½	21	12	Scudamore P	155	*.60e	--	JimmyLornzo1552DuelingOak1438BrkCln139hd	Bobbled,clear 8
8Apr89- 4AtH	yl	*2⅛	S'Chase	4:212 4↑	Ath Cup H 100k	3	5	59½	48	-	-	Guessford B	162	-	--	Polar Pleasure1481¼Kesslin1508Limaton13810	Lost rider 5
1Apr89- 6Cam	fm	*1Ⓣ		1:43 3↑	Sp Wt 1000	1	11	97½	42½	12	110	Guessford B	150	-	--	Jimmy Lorenzo15010Census1501Tisa Feast150½	Ridden out 11
27Nov88- 4Cam	fm	2¾	S'Chase	5:154 4↑	Colonial Cup 60k	2	8	812	814	41¾	12¼	Smart J	162	-	--	Jimmy Lorenzo1622¼Le Sauvage1512Polar Pleasure1621	8
Under hand ride																	
29Oct88- 4Fai	fm	*2⅝	S'Chase	5:122 3↑	BC Chase 250k	10	14	117¼	2nk	1½	1¾	McCourt G	156	8.40	--	JimmyLorenzo156¾Kalankoe1531½PolarPleasure156¾	Driving 14
2Oct88- 6Mid	fm	*2	S'Chase	3:523 4↑	O Clm 25000	9	12	1214	43	1½	18	Smart J	152	-	--	Jimmy Lorenzo1528Jet Wave1567Pajarero1445	Handily 12
Previously trained by Peter Hedger																	

6Apr88♦ Ascot(GB)	gd 2RH	3:463 5↑	Kestrel Handicap Hurdle Hcp11200	31¼	Shoemark I7	157	*2.00	Convinced147¾Relekto152½Jimmy Lorenzo1576 Rated toward rear,bid 2 out,finished well	8
12Mar88♦ Sandown(GB)	gd 2RH	3:552 5↑	Imperial Cup Handicap Hurdle Stk57600	46½	Osborne J	160	20.00	Sprowston Boy151½Jimbalou1402Capa1334 Rated toward rear,bid 2 out,finished well	15
25Feb88♦ Wincanton(GB)	gd 2RH	3:423 5↑	Kingwell Hurdle Alw24100	527½	Shoemark I	156	11.00	Floyd1623Private Audience1562½Past Glories15612 Never a factor	7
1Jan88♦ Windsor(GB)	gd *2	3:59 5↑	New Year's Day Hurdle Stk42100	37	Richards M	158	4.00	Celtic Shot1586Beech Road1581Jimmy Lorenzo1584 Rated in 8th,brief bid 2 out,no late response	10
26Dec87♦ Kempton(GB)	gd 2RH	3:514 4↑	Royal Garden Htl Hcp Hurdle Hcp9700	110	Shoemark I7	154	*3.00	JimmyLrnzo15410Chasing the Dragon153½Brookmount152nk Progress 3 out,led 2 out,drew clear in hand	16
8Dec87♦ Fontwell(GB)	gd 2¼LH	4:234 4↑	Coomes Handicap Hurdle Hcp16100	32¼	Shoemark I7	152	16.00	Southernair156nkOsric1502Jimmy Lorenzo15210 Unhurried,bid over approaching last,outfinished	9
21Nov87♦ Ascot(GB)	yl 2RH	3:552 5↑	Snow Hill Handicap Hurdle Hcp17600	14	Shoemark I7	140	3.50	Jimmy Lorenzo1404Beat the Retreat165½Insular15020 Rated in 5th,led approaching last,ridden out	6
7Nov87♦ Warwick(GB)	yl 2LH	3:444 4↑	St Mary's Trial Hurdle Alw9200	43¾	Shoemark I7	159	7.00	Lashkafdal147noNebris166¾Rampallion1523 Progress 2 out,lacked finishing bid	8
19May87♦ Newtn Abbot(GB)	fm *2$\frac{1}{16}$LH	3:534 4↑	C Vicary Meml Clng Cup Hcp Hurdle Hcp5900	1½	Shoemark I7	157	4.50	Jimmy Lorenzo157½Bronze Opal14425Come on Gracie15312 Rated in last,progress 3 out,dueled 2 out,led last,gamely	7
8May87♦ Newtn Abbot(GB)	fm *2$\frac{1}{16}$LH	3:48 4↑	McEwans Export Handicap Hurdle Hcp6100	23	Shoemark I7	158	7.00	Bronze Opal1423Jimmy Lorenzo1585Redgrave Girl13910 Progress 4 out,2nd approaching last,no match.New course record	10
14Apr87♦ Exeter(GB)	sf 2⅛RH	4:263 5↑	Handicap Hurdle Hcp7100	13	Richards M	156	*3.00	Jimmy Lorenzo1563Cons Pal1446Lord Murphy1544 Rated toward rear,progress 4th,led on bit 1 out,handily	18
28Mar87♦ Newbury(GB)	hy 2$\frac{1}{16}$LH	4:114 5↑	Schweppes Handicap Hurdle Hcp16800	311½	Shoemark I7	133	20.00	Juven Light15510Ra Nova1631½Jimmy Lorenzo1333 Toward rear,progress 3 out,ridden without response 2 out	10
5Mar87♦ Lingfield(GB)	sf 2LH	4:094 5↑	Three Counties Handicap Hurdle Hcp6900	34½	Richards M	152	*2.50	Rix Woodcock1462Young Nicholas1612½Jimmy Lorenzo152½ Rated in 10th,bid 2 out,held by first two	11
6Feb87♦ Sandown(GB)	gd 2RH	3:591 5↑	Me & My Girl Handicap Hurdle Hcp6500	710¾	Richards M	148	14.00	Easter Lee1442How Now144¾Neblin1592½ Behind,progress at 3rd,bid 3 out,soon one-paced	16
24Jan87♦ Kempton(GB)	yl 2RH	4:011 5↑	Lanzarote Handicap Hurdle Hcp20100	9	Richards M	140	8.00	Stray Shot1404Record Harvest152noCool Strike1405 Never a factor	9
26Dec86♦ Kempton(GB)	sf 2RH	4:022 4↑	Haven Abroad Handicap Hurdle Hcp8000	24	Richards M	142	7.50	Yabis1614Jimmy Lorenzo1421Welsh Warrior1431½ Trailed,progress into 2nd 3 out,always held by winner	13
20Nov86♦ Kempton(GB)	yl 2RH	4:071 4↑	Fairview Homes Hcp Hurdle Hcp6000	36½	Richards M	156	10.00	Oryx Minor160½Freemason1596Jimmy Lorenzo15610 Progress 3 out,one-paced from second last	10
5Nov86♦ Newbury(GB)	gd 2$\frac{9}{16}$LH	4:581 4↑	Tom Masson Trophy Hurdle Alw7600	-	Corrigan P	152	33.00	Ibn Majed15610Ten Plus162hdMrs Muck15320 Behind when brought down at 6th	9
19Apr86♦ Stratford(GB)	yl 2LH	4:052	Tote Hurdle Alw8000	425½	Richards M	154	*2.00	Heart of Stone15012Bollin Palace15012Avebury1541½ Progress from behind halfway,never threatened	12
31Mar86♦ Huntingdon(GB)	sf 2$\frac{1}{16}$RH	4:191 4↑	EBF Miltons Handicap Hurdle Hcp4000	17	Richards M	161	*1.75	Jimmy Lorenzo1617Kingholm Quay137¾Deep Trouble13812 Rated in last,progress halfway,led over 2 out,handily	5

22Mar86♦ Newbury(GB) gd 2 1/16LH 4:052 Tote Credit Handicap Hurdle Hcp24000 35½ Richards M 151 20.00 My Dominion1492½Wantage1443Jimmy Lorenzo1511 23
Led 2 out,headed last,one-paced to line

15Jan86♦ Windsor(GB) gd 2 3:55 Rays Hurdle Alw2800 22 Richards M 157 20.00 Brunico1502Jimmy Lorenzo1578Crimson Bold150¾ 22
Toward rear,progress 3 out,angled out last,finished well

27Dec85♦ Taunton(GB) hy 2⅛RH 4:192 Holly Tree Hurdle (Div 2) Alw1200 13 Richards M 149 *3.00 Jimmy Lorenzo1493Gibbous Moon14910Sedgewell Lad15220 14
Midpack,progress 4 out,led over 2 out,ridden out

20Dec85♦ Fakenham(GB) gd *2LH 4:09 West Norfolk Hurdle Alw1200 311 Richards M 152 14.00 Boom Patrol1521Northern Hope14710Jimmy Lorenzo1521½ 15
Midpack,gained 3rd out 2 out,never reaching leaders

26Nov85♦ Newtn Abbot(GB) gd 2LH 4:062 St Just Hurdle Alw1700 37½ Richards M 154 25.00 Purple Peak1542½Christo1545Jimmy Lorenzo1546 16
Progress into 2nd before halfway,weakened after 2nd last

11Nov85♦ Plumpton(GB) gd 2LH 3:464 Cuckfield Hurdle Alw1200 619½ Richards M 147 33.00 Courageous Charger1474The Italian1476Nice Business1472 14
Never a factor

John Henry

b. g. 1975, by Ole Bob Bowers (Prince Blessed)–Once Double, by Double Jay **Lifetime record: 83 39 15 9 $6,597,947**
Own.– Dotsam Stable
Br.– Golden Chance Farm Inc (Ky)
Tr.– Ronald McAnally

13Oct84- 8Med fm 1⅜Ⓣ :464 1:11 1:351 2:13 3↑ Ballantine H 900k 4 8 89 53½ 31½ 12¾ McCarron CJ 126 *.60 100-06 JohnHnry1262¾Who'sforDinner115hdWin1201 Came out,clear 12
22Sep84- 8Bel fm 1½Ⓣ :484 1:13 2:013 2:251 3↑ Turf Classic-G1 4 1 11½ 1½ 1½ 1nk McCarron CJ 126 *1.00 98-10 JohnHnry126nkWin1264Majesty'sPrnc126hd Strong handling 6
26Aug84- 9AP fm 1¼Ⓣ :482 1:122 1:372 2:012 3↑ Bud Arl Million-G1 6 4 31½ 32 1hd 11¾ McCarron CJ 126 *1.10 87-15 JohnHenry1261¾RoyalHeroine1223GatodelSol126no Drew out 12
23Jly84- 8Hol fm 1½Ⓣ :471 1:103 1:594 2:244 3↑ Sunset H-G1 7 5 47 32 21 11 McCarron CJ 126 *1.20 96-08 JhnHnry1261LoadtheCannons1181½PairofDeuces113nk Driving 9
24Jun84- 8Hol fst 1¼ :47 1:10 1:35 2:002 3↑ Hol Gold Cup H-G1 4 4 43½ 32 32 22 McCarron CJ 125 2.60 87-20 DesertWine1222JohnHnry1251½Sari'sDreamer114nk Game try 8
28May84- 8Hol fm 1½Ⓣ :49 1:123 2:011 2:25 3↑ Hol Inv'l H-G1 1 2 31½ 31½ 3nk 1½ McCarron CJ 126 *.80 95-08 JohnHnry126½GalantVert1162¾LoadtheCannons1201¼ Driving 9
6May84- 8GG fm 1⅜Ⓣ :472 1:12 1:354 2:13 3↑ Golden Gate H-G3 6 3 34½ 22 1½ 12 McCarron CJ 125 *.50 103-09 John Henry1252Silveyville1176Lucence1166 Slow st.,clear 6
1Apr84- 8SA fm 1½Ⓣ :482 1:132 2:022 2:264 3↑ San Luis Rey-G1 4 2 21 1½ 2½ 3¾ McCarron CJ 126 1.60 80-17 Interco126nkGato del Sol126½John Henry1263½ Weakened 10
4Mar84- 8SA fst 1¼ :453 1:10 1:35 2:003 4↑ S Anita H-G1 10 7 76¼ 45 56 58 McCarron CJ 127 *2.40 78-17 Interco1212¾Journey at Sea1171½Gato del Sol1171¾ 12
Stumble after start
11Dec83- 8Hol gd 1⅜Ⓣ :494 1:153 1:40 2:163 3↑ Hol Turf Cup-G1 4 2 22½ 1½ 2hd 1½ McCarron CJ 126 *1.50 72-27 John Henry126½Zalataia1231½Palikaraki1261¼ Came again 12
13Nov83- 8SA gd 1½Ⓣ :472 1:131 2:034 2:291 3↑ Oak Tree Inv'l-G1 2 5 31 43½ 31 2½ McCarron CJ 126 *.80 68-31 Zalataia123½JohnHnry1261½LoadthCnnons1223½ Held gamely 9
15Oct83- 8Bel fst 1½ :48 1:123 2:01 2:261 3↑ J C Gold Cup-G1 7 6 53 45 55 56¾ McCarron CJ 126 2.90 82-14 Slew o'Gold1213Highland Blade126nkBounding Basque1211½ 11
Weakened
28Aug83- 9AP gd 1¼Ⓣ :503 1:154 1:413 2:042 3↑ Arl Million-G1 13 3 21 2½ 2½ 2nk McCarron CJ 126 *1.40 72-28 Tolomeo118nkJohnHenry126½Nijinsky'sSecret1262 Sharp try 14
4Jly83- 8Hol fm 1⅛Ⓣ :49 1:13 1:363 1:482 3↑ American H-G2 1 3 33 21½ 2½ 11¼ McCarron CJ 127 2.10 88-12 JohnHenry1271¼PrinceFlorimund120½Tonzarun114no Driving 8
28Nov82♦ Tokyo(Jpn) fm*1½ⓉLH 2:27 3↑ Japan Cup-G1 Stk801000 138 Shoemaker W 126 *.90 Half Iced121nkAll Along117nkApril Run1211 15
Prominent to stretch
13Nov82- 6Med gd 1¼ :473 1:121 1:37 2:012 3↑ Med Cup H-G2 2 5 37½ 44¼ 35½ 35¾ Shoemaker W 129 *1.10 89-15 Mehmet1181¼ThirtyEghtPcs1134½JhnHnry1294½ Lacked a bid 9
31Oct82- 8SA fm 1½Ⓣ :472 1:103 1:593 2:24 3↑ Oak Tree Inv'l-G1 6 4 44 21½ 2½ 12½ Shoemaker W 126 1.40 95-05 John Henry1262½Craelius1221½Regalberto1262 Drew clear 7
17Oct82- 8SA fm 1¼Ⓣ :471 1:11 1:343 1:583 3↑ C F Burke H-G2 6 3 31½ 42 42¾ 41½ Shoemaker W 129 *.80 92-06 Mehmet117hdCraelius1141½It's the One124no Evenly 7
28Mar82- 8SA fm 1½Ⓣ :462 1:102 2:00 2:24 4↑ San Luis Rey-G1 3 3 33 33 43½ 34¾ Shoemaker W 126 *.50 90-05 Perrault1263¼Exploded1261½John Henry126no Evenly 5
7Mar82- 8SA fst 1¼ :45 1:09 1:342 1:59 4↑ S Anita H-G1 9 8 913 51¼ 2½ 2no Shoemaker W 130 *1.30 94-07 [D]Perrault126noJhnHenry1303¼It'stheOne123nk Impeded end 11
Placed first by disqualification
6Dec81- 8Hol fm 1½Ⓣ :49 1:13 2:03 2:264 3↑ Hol Turf Cup 550k 5 1 12 11 3½ 42 Shoemaker W 126 *.40 84-11 Providential II126nkQueen to Conquer1231½Goldiko126nk 10
Weakened;Previously trained by Victor J. Nickerson
8Nov81- 8SA fm 1½Ⓣ :472 1:102 1:593 2:232 3↑ Oak Tree Inv'l-G1 4 3 1½ 1½ 2hd 1nk Shoemaker W 126 *.40 98-02 John Henry126nkSpence Bay1264½The Bart126no Driving 7
10Oct81- 8Bel fst 1½ :48 1:123 2:021 2:282 3↑ J C Gold Cup-G1 8 5 42½ 21 11½ 1hd Shoemaker W 126 *3.10 78-14 JohnHenry126hdPeatMoss126¾Relaxing123hd Bore in,driving 11
Previously trained by Ronald McAnally
30Aug81- 6AP sf 1¼Ⓣ :501 1:153 1:422 2:073 3↑ Arl Million 1000k 12 8 86½ 56 31 1no Shoemaker W 126 *1.10e - - John Henry126noThe Bart1262¼Madam Gay117½ Just up 12
Previously trained by Victor J. Nickerson
11Jly81- 8Bel fm 1½Ⓣ :494 1:142 2:03 2:264 3↑ Sword Dancer-G3 3 3 31½ 11 11½ 13½ Shoemaker W 126 *.30 90-13 JohnHnry1263½PassingZone1261¾PeatMoss1261¾ Ridden out 5
Previously trained by Ronald McAnally
14Jun81- 8Hol fst 1¼ :453 1:093 1:344 2:002 3↑ Hol Gold Cup H-G1 7 7 66¼ 65¾ 46½ 42¾ Pincay L Jr 130 *1.20 86-16 [D]Caterman120hdEleven Stitches1222½Super Moment117nk 10
Wide late
17May81- 8Hol fm 1½Ⓣ :511 1:151 2:04 2:274 3↑ Hol Inv'l H-G1 5 2 2½ 2½ 1½ 1¾ Pincay L Jr 130 *.40 81-12 John Henry130¾Caterman122hdGalaxy Libra118nk Driving 7
29Mar81- 8SA fm 1½Ⓣ :46 1:104 2:00 2:251 4↑ San Luis Rey-G1 1 2 21½ 22 1hd 12¼ Pincay L Jr 126 *.20 89-11 John Henry1262¼Obraztsovy1261½Fiestero126hd Easily 6
8Mar81- 8SA fst 1¼ :452 1:092 1:341 1:592 4↑ S Anita H-G1 3 7 65¼ 22 1hd 11 Pincay L Jr 128 1.90 92-11 John Henry1281King Go Go1171¼Exploded115no Driving 11
16Feb81- 8SA fm 1½Ⓣ :474 1:113 1:59 2:24 4↑ San Luis Obispo H-G2 4 1 11 11 12½ 11½ Pincay L Jr 127 *.50 95-05 John Henry1271½Galaxy Libra1195½Zor1151½ Ridden out 6
16Nov80- 8SA fm 1½Ⓣ :454 1:101 1:582 2:232 3↑ Oak Tree Inv-G1 6 5 56½ 66¾ 37½ 11½ Pincay L Jr 126 *1.50 98-02 John Henry1261½Balzac126½Bold Tropic126nk Drew clear 10
Previously trained by Victor J. Nickerson
25Oct80- 8Aqu sf 1½Ⓣ :514 1:192 2:13 2:393 3↑ Turf Classic-G1 4 1 12 23 25 38 Pincay L Jr 126 *2.00 35-57 Anifa1233Golden Act1265John Henry126nk Weakened 8
4Oct80- 8Bel fst 1½ :494 1:15 2:051 2:301 3↑ J C Gold Cup-G1 3 2 21 2½ 23 25½ Cordero A Jr 126 *.70 63-19 Temperence Hill1215½John Henry1262Ivory Hunter1263¼ 7
Best of others
7Sep80- 8Bel fm 1¼[T] :483 1:122 1:362 1:592 3↑ Brighton Beach H-G3 5 1 1hd 11½ 11½ 1nk Cordero A Jr 125 *.40 97-15 John Henry125nkPremier Ministre1174Match the Hatch1133 5
Driving
12Jly80- 8Bel fm 1½Ⓣ :47 1:111 2:01 2:251 3↑ Sword Dancer 161k 2 2 21 1½ 2hd 21¼ McHargue DG 126 *.80 97-15 Tiller1261¼John Henry1265Sten12612 Gamely 4
14Jun80- 8Bel fm 1⅜Ⓣ :473 1:113 1:352 2:131 3↑ Bowling Green H-G2 3 1 1½ 1hd 1½ 2nk McHargue DG 128 *1.80 96-15 Sten117nkJohn Henry1281Lyphard's Wish120nk Brushed 9
Previously trained by Ronald McAnally
26May80- 8Hol fm 1½Ⓣ :483 1:123 2:012 2:252 3↑ Hol Inv'l H-G1 4 1 14 12½ 1½ 1nk McHargue DG 128 *.90 93-09 John Henry128nkBalzac1201½Go West Young Man1172½ 10
Fully extended
6Apr80- 8SA fm *1¾Ⓣ :46 1:594 2:464 4↑ S Juan Capistrano H-G1 3 1 12 11½ 12 11¼ McHargue DG 126 *2.20 93-08 John Henry1261¼Fiestero114nkThe Very One113hd Driving 11
16Mar80- 8SA fm 1½Ⓣ :464 1:104 1:592 2:23 4↑ San Luis Rey-G1 3 2 21 2½ 2½ 11½ McHargue DG 126 6.90 100-00 John Henry1261½Relaunch126noSilver Eagle126no Drew out 7
23Feb80-10Hia fm 1½Ⓣ 2:292 3↑ Hia Turf Cup H-G2 10 2 31½ 11 11½ 1½ McHargue DG 122 2.30 84-22 JohnHenry122½DancingMaster1135IvoryHunter111hd Driving 10
20Jan80- 8SA fst 1¼ :47 1:113 1:364 2:013 4↑ San Marcos H-G3 2 1 11½ 11 11 12½ McHargue DG 124 *.80 85-17 John Henry1242½El Fantastico1132¼Commemorativo110nk 5
Handily
1Jan80- 8SA gd 1⅛Ⓣ :48 1:121 1:371 1:494 4↑ San Gabriel H-G3 4 2 22 21½ 2½ 1hd McHargue DG 123 *1.70 78-22 John Henry123hdSmasher1115As de Copas1173 Driving 9
8Dec79- 8BM fm 1⅛Ⓣ :471 1:111 1:363 1:493 3↑ Bay Meadows H 114k 7 5 44½ 83¾ 1hd 21¼ McHargue DG 123 2.70 103-00 Leonotis1181¼John Henry1234Capt. Don117½ Held on 14
5Nov79- 8SA fm 1⅛Ⓣ :461 1:102 1:352 1:48 3↑ HP Russell H (Div 2) 45k 5 2 11 11 12 13¼ McHargue DG 122 *.70 87-15 JohnHenry1223¼Rusty Canyon114hdLeonotis1172 Ridden out 8
14Oct79- 8SA fm 1¼Ⓣ :454 1:10 1:343 1:591 3↑ C F Burke H-G2 5 3 21½ 1hd 1hd 21¼ McHargue DG 118 3.40 90-09 Silver Eagle1151¼John Henry118½Shagbark1181¼ Gamely 9
Previously trained by Victor J. Nickerson
10Sep79- 7Bel fm 1 1/16Ⓣ :24 :47 1:11 1:414 3↑ Alw 30000 2 1 13 11½ 12 12 Santiago A 117 1.90 87-17 John Henry1172Silent Cal117½Waya119no Ridden out 4
22Aug79- 7Sar fm 1⅛Ⓣ :462 1:111 1:343 1:462 3↑ Alw 27000 3 1 11½ 11½ 11½ 12½ Santiago A 115 *1.40 95-13 John Henry1152½Told114¾Poison Ivory1224 Driving 7
29Jly79- 7Pen sly 1 1/16 :232 :471 1:114 1:443 3↑ Capital City H 33k 7 5 41½ 31 41¼ 42 Santiago A 113 2.30 81-23 Horatius118nkTanthem1121½Shy Jester115nk Hung 7

14Jly79- 8Bel fm 1 1/16Ⓣ :233 :47 1:104 1:413 3↑ Sword Dancer 57k 2 1 2hd 21 22 22½ Santiago A 119 5.70 85-11 Darby Creek Road1192½John Henry1194Poison Ivory1191¾ 8
Best of others
6Jly79- 6Atl fm 1 1/16Ⓣ :23 :462 1:102 1:411 3↑ Sunrise H 35k 2 2 21½ 1½ 1hd 22¼ McCauley WH 111 *1.50 98-09 Chati1182¼John Henry111½Fed Funds1154 Tired 11
24Jun79-10Suf fst 1⅛ :453 1:10 1:36 1:483 3↑ Mass H-G3 9 4 68¾ 84¼ 96 108½ Borden DA 108 6.90 89-21 Island Sultan110¾Western Front113½Quiet Jay1161½ Tired 13
5Jun79- 8Mth fst 1 :232 :47 1:114 1:373 4↑ Alw 18000 1 3 2hd 13 18 114 McCauley WH 119 *.90 85-23 John Henry11914Thou Fool119noM.A.'s Date1131¾ Driving 7
26May79- 6Mth fst 6f :22 :443 1:104 4↑ Alw 16000 4 4 53½ 41¾ 21½ 2½ McCauley WH 117 6.90 85-19 ReallyandTruly117½JohnHnry1171¼Kintla'sFolly1153 Gamely 7
Previously trained by Robert A. Donato
29Oct78- 6Pen fm 1 1/16Ⓣ 1:412 Chcltetwn H (Div 2) 22k 5 2 21 1½ 12 11 Broussard R 124 *.70 - - John Henry1241Scythian Gold1166½Berlin's Burning1122 7
Ridden out
15Oct78- 5SA fm 1¼Ⓣ :453 1:094 1:342 1:59 3↑ C F Burke H (Div 1)-G2 2 1 1hd 1hd 44 65 Baltazar C 117 2.80 87-08 Star of Erin II113noImproviser1152¾Mr. Redoy1181¼ Tired 9
8Oct78- 8SA fm 1⅛Ⓣ :46 1:102 1:351 1:474 Volante H-G3 6 4 42 41 31½ 3½ Baltazar C 122 *2.30 87-12 WaysideStation117noAprilAxe120½JohnHenry1222 In close 11
16Sep78- 8AP gd 1 1/16Ⓣ :241 :484 1:131 1:454 Round Table H-G3 6 1 11 13 18 112 Amy J 121 *.50 80-30 JhnHnry12112GordieH.109noBringtheMoney111no Ridden out 9
9Sep78- 5Bel fm 7fⓉ :232 :46 1:093 1:22 3↑ Alw 21000 1 1 11½ 11½ 11 11½ Amy J 113 3.60 94-09 John Henry1131½Gab Bag1174Proud Arion1171¼ Hard ridden 8
18Aug78- 7Sar fm 1 1/16Ⓣ :251 :49 1:12 1:41 3↑ Alw 23000 7 2 2½ 2hd 44 47¼ Amy J 112 5.10 85-08 Blue Baron1172¼Quip1141Stir the Embers1194 Weakened 8
8Aug78- 7Sar gd 7f :223 :444 1:081 1:202 3↑ Alw 23000 2 2 31½ 24 38 514 Santiago A 113 2.90 89-04 DarbyCreekRoad11311Liberal117¾GoldenReserve117¾ Tired 6
29Jly78- 8Bel fm 1 1/16Ⓣ :233 :46 1:103 1:41 Lexington H-G2 5 1 12½ 12 11 2hd Santiago A 112 5.90 91-11 Mac Diarmida126hdJohn Henry1124¼Ashikaga110hd Gamely 9
19Jly78- 8Bel fm 1Ⓣ :24 :473 1:104 1:351 Hill Prince H 37k 5 1 2hd 2hd 2½ 21½ Santiago A 111 3.60 92-12 DarbyCreekRd1211½JhnHnry1112ScythianGold1116 Gamely 9
1Jly78- 8Mth fm 1 1/16Ⓣ :232 :47 1:11 1:432 Lamplighter H-G3 4 2 2hd 1hd 1½ 3½ Santiago A 112 *1.50 83-16 North Course112nkHoratius114nkJohnHenry112no Weakened 9
25Jun78- 6Bel hd 1 1/16Ⓣ :232 :47 1:102 1:411 3↑ Alw 18000 2 5 62½ 52 42 1nk Santiago A 112 3.40 90-07 John Henry112nkTurn of Coin1171¾Valinsky1171¾ Driving 9
1Jun78- 7Bel fm 1 1/16Ⓣ :231 :47 1:11 1:413 Clm 35000 1 2 21 1½ 17 114 Santiago A 117 3.30 88-12 JhnHnry11714ContinentalCousin117¾CptnPeter1132¼ Driving 10
21May78- 2Aqu fst 6f :224 :471 1:123 Clm 25000 4 4 32½ 1½ 11 12½ Santiago A 117 12.30 80-27 John Henry1172½Please See Me1171½Orfanik115nk Driving 9
Previously owned and trained by H. Snowden Jr
11Apr78- 7Kee fst 6f :22 :45 :59 1:093 Alw 8500 4 4 47½ 46 48½ 49½ McKnight J 113 6.40 84-15 Johnny Blade1074½Schottis112½Jester Beau1154½ No mishap 6
Previously owned by D. Lingo & C. Madere; previously trained by Phil Marino
22Mar78- 9FG fst 6f :23 :47 1:12 Clm 25000 7 6 78 89 64¾ 34 Copling D 114 25.10 81-16 Kim's Red1142Bunny Wag1122John Henry1141 Rallied 9
22Feb78- 9FG fst 6f :223 :463 1:113 Clm 20000 11 2 98¾ 98¾ 1015 1020 Elmer D 112 b 19.10 67-19 AdriaticEditions1144Bladesville113½Kim'sRed1141 Outrun 11
15Feb78- 6FG fst 6f :22 :462 1:113 Clm 25000 5 5 85¼ 61¼ 63¾ 66¼ Guajardo A 112 b 4.90 81-19 MercrCounty1121½Gen'sLTroy1121AdrtcEdtons1141 No mishap 8
4Feb78- 6FG fst 1 40 :252 :493 1:151 1:43 Alw 7500 2 9 84¾ 83½ 53¼ 55¾ Guajardo A 112 17.10 72-23 HogTown114¾TrafficWarning114hdSmokePole1092½ No mishap 10
23Jan78- 8FG gd 1 40 :241 :473 1:131 1:424 Alw 7500 7 4 42¾ 52¾ 86¾ 86½ Guajardo A 112 22.20 72-24 CabriniGreen117½DayTimeTudor1121As in Elbow112no Tired 9
31Dec77- 9FG fst 6f :22 :46 1:121 Sugar Bowl H 50k 4 12 127¾ 127½ 1210 1114 McKnight J 113 16.80 70-21 CabriniGreen122½CouponRate113¾SpecialHonr1101¼ Outrun 12
17Dec77- 6FG gd 6f :223 :472 1:122 ©Alw 7000 1 6 64¼ 62¾ 53¾ 31¼ McKnight J 113 7.90 82-18 CabriniGreen1201¼CouponRate113hdJohnHenry113hd Rallied 12
3Dec77- 8FG fst 6f :222 :462 1:114 Alw 7000 1 7 75¾ 54 51¾ 43½ McKnight J 120 8.70 82-19 DragonTamer1171½TrafficWarnng1171¼HogTwn117¾ Rallied 11
19Nov77- 9FG fst 6f :221 :464 1:124 ©Sthern Hospitality 19k 8 12 105 63¼ 64¼ 59 Guajardo A 122 9.60 72-22 CbrniGreen1144MajesticSpiral1122½HogTown112hd Late bid 12
5Sep77-11EvD sly 6f :232 :47 1:01 1:142 Lafayette Futurity 86k 1 6 45 32½ 1hd Guajardo A 120 5.10 79-26 JohnHenry120hdLilLizaJayne1171SoundNote1203½ Driving 12
25Aug77- 7EvD gd 6f :223 :462 1:002 1:13 Sp Wt 2700 8 5 33 32 2½ Guajardo A 120 4.10 85-21 Note to Mame117½John Henry1203Tudor Luck117hd 9
6Aug77- 7EvD sly 5f :224 :483 1:001 Alw 2400 4 9 54½ 1hd 13 Guajardo A 120 3.00 82-19 John Henry1203Motor Dude1201½Bell's Chief1174 Driving 12
29Jly77- 8JnD fst *6f :233 :473 1:02 1:152 Handicap 7500 9 9 - - - - Munster L 102 3.90 - - RunLikeHeck1191CapGardnr1072HarktheLedr1102 Lost rider 9
2Jly77- 6JnD sly 5f :23 :481 1:011 Alw 4500 2 5 42 33 23 Spiehler G 116 *2.60 81-19 KindaNughty1133JhnHnry1161MossBluffKd1152 Bid,weakened 7
7Jun77- 8JnD fst 4f :22 :471 Alw 3500 4 6 59 55½ 31 Spiehler G 120 14.60 89-11 DancngMeadw109¾DancingJudge120nkJhnHnry1201 Rallied 8
20May77- 1JnD fst 4f :23 :481 Md Sp Wt 1 7 54½ 34 1no Spiehler G 120 1.70 85-15 JhnHnry120noYouSexyThing1172Ricky'sChoice112¾ Driving 8

Just a Game II (Ire)

dkbbr. f. 1976, by Tarboosh (Bagdad)–Hobby, by Falcon **Lifetime record: 28 14 4 3 $416,069**

Own.– P.M. Brant
Br.– Rathvale Stud (Ire)
Tr.– LeRoy Jolley

1Jan82- 9Crc yl *1⅛Ⓣ 1:502 3↑ ⒻLa Prvoynte (Div 2)-G3 3 1 1½ 1hd 12½ 13 Cordero A Jr 123 *.50 71-28 JustaGmeII1233SweetestChnt115nkIrshJoy1143½ Ridden out 9
22Nov81- 8Hol fm 1⅛Ⓣ :473 1:114 1:352 1:47 3↑ ⒻMatriarch 221k 3 3 34½ 23 55 77 Cordero A Jr 123 3.70 88-08 Kilijaro1232½Glorious Song123nkBersid120½ Gave way 9
13Nov81- 8Hol fm 1 1/16Ⓣ :234 :474 1:113 1:404 3↑ ⒻAlw 40000 6 1 11 11 13 11 Cordero A Jr 114 *1.10 95-05 Just a Game II1141Saison1152½Mi Quimera1143 Driving 9
Previously trained by David A. Whiteley
2Nov81- 7Aqu gd 1Ⓣ :234 :48 1:131 1:38 3↑ ⒻAlw 32000 4 1 1½ 32½ 39 316 Cordero A Jr 115 *.80 72-12 Adlibber1225StephanieLeigh12211JustaGameII1159¾ Tired 4
3Oct80- 8Bel fm 1⅜Ⓣ :51 1:15 1:393 2:152 3↑ Man o' War-G1 1 2 21 2½ 1hd 21½ Brumfield D 123 *.90 83-20 FrenchColonial1261½JstaGmeII1233¾GoldnAct126no Gamely 5
1Sep80- 8Bel fm 1¼Ⓣ :474 1:114 1:362 2:004 3↑ ⒻFlower Bowl H-G2 7 1 33½ 1½ 14 12 Brumfield D 124 *2.00 90-12 JustaGmeII1242HeyBabe114noEuphrosyne112nk Ridden out 11
17Aug80- 8Sar fm 1⅛Ⓣ :48 1:124 1:363 1:49 3↑ ⒻDiana H-G2 9 1 11 11 13 1nk Brumfield D 123 *1.60 82-18 JustaGameII123nkTheVeryOne117hdRelaxing1131¼ Driving 9
4Jly80- 8Atl fm 1 3/16Ⓣ :484 1:132 1:38 1:573 3↑ ⒻMatchmaker-G2 3 2 42½ 32½ 12 11 Brumfield D 120 *.60 79-28 JustaGmeII1201LaSoufriere115noRecordAcclam1152 Driving 10
21Jun80- 8Bel fm 1¼Ⓣ :49 1:13 1:363 2:002 3↑ ⒻNew York H-G3 5 1 1½ 11½ 14 11 Brumfield D 121 *1.10 92-11 JstaGameII1211Poppycock112hdPleaseTryHard1132¼ Driving 6
5Jun80- 8Bel fm 1Ⓣ :23 :461 1:104 1:353 3↑ ⒻAlw 35000 2 1 1hd 1½ 15 14 Brumfield D 119 *.50 87-10 Just a Game II1194Chestnut Speester117noKarin Jones115nk 6
Ridden out
5Apr80- 9GP fm 1 1/16Ⓣ :223 :461 1:101 1:402 3↑ ⒻOrchid H-G3 5 3 32½ 21 13 1¾ Brumfield D 119 *.70 99-07 JustaGmeII119¾LaSoufriere1152½LaRouquineII114hd Driving 10
12Mar80- 9GP fm 1Ⓣ :232 :471 1:103 1:351 3↑ ⒻSwnnee Rvr (Div 1) 31k 3 2 2hd 11½ 15 15 Brumfield D 117 *1.70 94-13 JustaGmeII1175LaSoufriere1134½LaVoygus120no Ridden out 10
25Feb80- 9Hia fm 1 1/16Ⓣ 1:423 4↑ ⒻAlw 16000 2 2 21 12 15 16½ Brumfield D 115 4.10 85-17 JustaGameII1156½BallGate115noLaSoufriere1154 Ridden out 7
18Feb80- 7Hia fst 6f :221 :452 1:103 4↑ ⒻAlw 14000 8 6 76½ 77 65¾ 56½ Vasquez J 115 4.40 83-20 Hill Billy Dancer1172Yoka1153Guimauve115½ No mishap 9
29Jan80- 9Hia fst 6f :22 :452 1:103 4↑ ⒻAlw 14500 5 4 31 2½ 2½ 98 Vasquez J 116 4.20 82-25 SilverOaks1161HillBllyDncr1161SstrRosmund116hd Gave way 10
Previously trained by Charles Magnier
9Jun79♦ Epsom(GB) yl 1½ⓉLH 2:433 ⒻEnglish Oaks-G1 Stk140000 1025 Shoemaker W 126 20.00 Scintillate1263Bonnie Isle1261Britannias Rule1264 14
Prominent to halfway,lost place downhill turn,weakened
2Jun79♦ Leopardstwn(Ire) gd 1⅛ⓉLH 1:582 3↑ Kilmacanogue H Hcp6600 2¾ Piggott L 131 4.00 Mississippi133¾Just a Game II131noOisin Dubh1342½ 8
Led to 2f out,dueled briefly,gave ground grudgingly
7Oct78♦ The Curragh(Ire) gd 1ⓉStr 1:424 Beresford Stakes-G2 Stk15000 1hd Carberry T 123 50.00 Just a Game II123hdSandy Creek1264Accomplice126¾ 5
Tracked in 3rd,bid 2f out,led 100y out,gamely
30Sep78♦ Phoenix Park(Ire) gd 5fⓉStr :582 Maher Nursery H Hcp6900 54¼ Coogan B 130 8.00 Feathers Lad126nkLattygar1073Sun's Image102hd 10
Toward rear,mild late gain
9Sep78♦ Phoenix Park(Ire) gd 7fⓉRH 1:21 ⒻPark Stakes-G3 Stk11200 22 Morgan J 126 10.00 Solar1262Just a Game II126hdSister Jinks1162 9
Close up,mild bid 3f out,chased winner home
23Aug78♦ York(GB) gd 6fⓉStr 1:14 ⒻLowther Stakes-G3 Stk24500 9 Carson W 123 12.00 Devon Ditty1261½Eyelet123nkGreenland Park129½ 11
Slow into stride,never a factor
12Aug78♦ Phoenix Park(Ire) gd 6fⓉStr 1:121 Naas Nursery H Hcp3700 1nk Morgan J 115 *1.50 Just a Game II115nkPitora1004Nice Client1098 8
Tracked in 3rd,drifted left 2f out,led 100y out,held gamely
7Aug78♦ Leopardstwn(Ire) gd 5fⓉStr 1:032 Newtonpark Nursery H Hcp3700 31½ Coogan B5 116 *1.35 Meeson Girl105hdConcordia1221½Just a Game II116¾ 10
Missed break,progress halfway,finished well
29Jly78♦ The Curragh(Ire) gd *6fⓉStr 1:18 Railway S-G3 Stk8600 2nk Swinburn WR 122 14.00 Solar119nkJust a Game II1226Cajolery1196 4
Dueled thoughout,very game

19Jly78♦ Naas(Ire)	fm 5f Ⓣ Str	1:001	Clane Nursery H Hcp3600	11	Morgan J	113	8.00	Just a Game II1131Nice Client103noMeeson Girl103½ Tracked in 3rd,led 150y out,driving	7
8Jly78♦ Leopardstwn(Ire)	gd 7f Ⓣ LH	1:344	Hennessy VSOP Race Alw3300	77¾	Coogan B5	114	8.00	Five Stars Final122nkHighest Regards122hdSwizzle1222½ Tracked in 3rd,weakened 1½f out	9
8Jun78♦ Lmrick Jnctn(Ire)	gd 5f Ⓣ Str	:583	Ballykisteen Maiden Mdn2200	1no	Coogan B5	118	5.00	Just a Game II118noReal Snug1234Saulest1236 Tracked leaders,rallied to lead on line	13
24May78♦ Down Royal(Ire)	fm 5f Ⓣ Str	-	W&R Barnett Ltd Maiden Mdn1300	31¼	Corr J	123	10.00	Mount Oriel126nkDallynot1231Just a Game II1232 Toward rear,finished well without threatening.Time not taken	9

Lady's Secret

gr. f. 1982, by Secretariat (Bold Ruler)–Great Lady M., by Icecapade **Lifetime record: 45 25 9 3 $3,021,425**

Own.– Mr & Mrs E.V. Klein
Br.– Robert H. Spreen (Okla)
Tr.– D. Wayne Lukas

10Aug87- 1Sar	sly 1⅛	:471 1:113 1:361 1:492 3↑	Alw 45000	2	-	-	-	-	-	McCarron CJ	117	*.30	--	Kamakura11511The Watcher1222¼Jack of Clubs1192½ Bolted	5
21Jly87- 8Mth	fst 1 1/16	:231 :462 1:11 1:432 3↑	ⒻAlw 25000	1	2	1½	13½	19	17	McCarron CJ	119	*.10	88-18	Lady'sSecret1197BriefRemarks115nkShaknBy115¾ Easy score	6
4Jly87-10Mth	fst 1 1/16	:231 :461 1:10 1:42 3↑	ⒻMolly Pitcher H-G2	3	2	21½	2½	2hd	22	McCarron CJ	125	*.30	93-10	ReelEasy1122Lady'sSecret125¾Cattonc117nk Best of others	8
13Jun87- 8Mth	sly 6f	:222 :444 1:094 3↑	ⒻAlw 25000	5	1	2hd	1½	11	13½	Cordero A Jr	122	*.30	91-14	Lady'sSecret1223½Nick'sNag1156BriefRmrks1158 Ridden out	5
14Mar87-10GP	fst 1⅛	:462 1:11 1:361 1:484 3↑	Donn H-G2	2	1	12	43	618	632½	Day P	120	*.80	55-18	LittleBoldJohn111noSkipTrl1186WsTms1174½ Fin. after ½	7
1Nov86- 5SA	fst 1¼	:461 1:10 1:344 2:011 3↑	ⒻBC Distaff-G1	5	1	14	14	14	12½	Day P	123	*.50	83-13	Lady's Secret1232½Fran's Valentine1232Outstandingly123¾ Ridden out	8
12Oct86- 8Bel	fst 1¼	:461 1:10 1:352 2:013 3↑	ⒻBeldame-G1	4	1	15	11	1½	1½	Day P	123	*.05	90-13	Lady's Secret123½Coup de Fusil1231¾Classy Cathy11823½ Drifted,ridden out	4
21Sep86- 8Bel	fst 1⅛	:454 1:093 1:341 1:464 3↑	ⒻRuffian H-G1	5	2	1½	13½	16	18	Day P	129	*.50	93-12	Lady's Secret1298Steal a Kiss1092¼Endear1196 Handily	6
6Sep86- 8Bel	fst 1	:231 :454 1:094 1:332 3↑	ⒻMaskette-G1	5	1	11	11½	14½	17	Day P	125	*.30	98-10	Lady's Secret1257Steal a Kiss1091¾Endear120no Handily	6
30Aug86- 8Bel	fst 1⅛	:453 1:092 1:334 1:46 3↑	Woodward-G1	4	1	11½	12½	2hd	24¾	Cordero A Jr	121	1.40e	92-14	Precisionist1264¾Lady'sScrt1215½PrsonlFlg1105¾ 2nd best	5
16Aug86- 9Mth	sly 1⅛	:464 1:103 1:353 1:484 3↑	Iselin H-G1	1	1	11½	1hd	1hd	33½	Day P	120	*1.20	86-16	Roo Art1172¼Precisionist1251¼Lady's Secret1206 Gave way	5
2Aug86- 8Sar	sly 1⅛	:463 1:104 1:363 1:494 3↑	Whitney H-G1	2	1	12½	13	12½	14½	Day P	119	*1.30e	86-22	Lady's Secret1194½Ends Well1163¼Fuzzy110nk Ridden out	7
5Jly86- 9Mth	fst 1 1/16	:23 :46 1:091 1:411 3↑	ⒻMolly Pitcher H-G2	4	1	1½	1½	13½	16¼	Day P	126	*.20	99-13	Lady's Secret1266¼Chaldea1142¼Key Witness1121½ Easily	8
8Jun86- 8Bel	my 1⅛	:444 1:094 1:353 1:483 3↑	ⒻHempstead H-G1	4	2	1hd	1hd	22½	26	Day P	128	*.40	78-16	Endear1156Lady's Secret1281½Ride Sally12413 2nd best	5
26May86- 8Bel	fst 1	:232 :454 1:091 1:333 3↑	Metropolitan H-G1	4	1	2hd	1hd	1½	31¼	Day P	120	5.30	96-11	Garthorn1241¼LoveThatMac117noLady'sSecrt120nk Held well	8
17May86- 8Bel	fst 1 1/16	:233 :461 1:101 1:414 3↑	ⒻShuvee H-G1	3	1	11	11	13	13½	Day P	126	*.70	93-15	Lady's Secret1263½Endear1156¼Ride Sally1251 Easy score	6
16Apr86- 9OP	fst 1 1/16	:231 :454 1:101 1:402 4↑	ⒻApple Blossom H-G1	4	1	13	1hd	2½	2nk	Velasquez J	127	*.40	99-16	LoveSmitten119nkLady'sSecret1276Sefa'sBeauty1226 Failed	7
23Feb86- 8SA	fst 1⅛	:462 1:10 1:343 1:47 4↑	ⒻS Margarita H-G1	1	1	11½	11	11½	12¾	Velasquez J	125	*1.60	94-11	Lady'sSecret1252¾Johnica1201¼DontstopThemusc1222 Easily	9
9Feb86- 8SA	fst 1⅛	:464 1:11 1:363 1:494	ⒻLa Canada-G1	3	1	1½	11½	11½	11¼	McCarron CJ	126	*.50	80-16	Lady'sSecrt1261½Shywing1194NorthSider1181¾ Hard ridden	6
18Jan86- 8SA	fst 1 1/16	:222 :452 1:093 1:414	ⒻEl Encino-G3	8	3	1½	13	12½	12	McCarron CJ	124	*.80	92-12	Ldy'sScrt1242Shywng1194ShrpAscnt119nk Lugged into stretch	10
27Dec85- 8SA	fst 7f	:222 :45 1:093 1:222	ⒻLa Brea-G3	1	3	1hd	1½	2hd	2½	McCarron CJ	124	*.80	87-16	SavannahSlew119½Lady'sSecret1243AmbraRidge1142½ Gamely Previously owned by E.V. Klein	7
2Nov85- 5Aqu	fst 1¼	:464 1:112 1:364 2:02 3↑	ⒻBC Distaff-G1	1	1	14	11	21½	26¼	Velasquez J	119	*.40e	80-10	Life's Magic1236¼Lady's Secret1193Dontstop Themusic1231¼ Ducked out start	7
13Oct85- 8Bel	fst 1¼	:454 1:102 1:36 2:033 3↑	ⒻBeldame-G1	4	1	1½	12	13	12	Velasquez J	118	*.60	80-19	Lady'sSecret1182Isayso1232¾KamikazeRick1182¼ Ridden out	5
22Sep85- 8Bel	fst 1⅛	:462 1:094 1:343 1:472 3↑	ⒻRuffian H-G1	3	1	11½	14	15	14	Velasquez J	116	*.30e	90-17	Lady's Secret1164Isayso1152¼Sintrillium118hd Ridden out	6
7Sep85- 8Bel	fst 1	:222 :444 1:091 1:344 3↑	ⒻMaskette-G1	6	1	1½	11	14	15½	Velasquez J	111	*1.00e	91-14	Lady's Secret1115½Dowery117noMrs. Revere117¾ Ridden out	8
9Aug85- 8Sar	fst 7f	:214 :441 1:091 1:223 3↑	ⒻBallerina-G2	4	3	21½	2hd	1½	1no	MacBeth D	117	*.90e	89-19	Lady'sSecret117noMrs.Revere1162¾SolarHalo116¾ Driving	9
1Aug85- 8Sar	gd 7f	:221 :444 1:09 1:213	ⒻTest-G2	9	1	42½	31½	1hd	12	Velasquez J	121	10.10	94-13	Lady'sScrt1212Mom'sCommand124nkMjstcFolly118½ Driving	10
6Jly85- 6Bel	fst 6f	:22 :451 1:111 3↑	ⒻThe Rose 54k	6	1	32	3nk	12	14¾	Velasquez J	116	*.40	86-20	Lady'sScrt1164¾FoolishIntentions115¾ProudClarioness115nk Ridden out	6
22Jun85- 9Mth	fst 6f	:221 :443 1:093 3↑	ⒻRegret H 49k	6	1	11½	11½	12½	13½	Antley CW	114	*.40	92-16	Lady'sSecret1143½FurashFolly1182Nck'sNg1202½ Ridden out	6
26May85- 5Bel	fst 6f	:222 :444 1:09	ⒻBowl of Flowers 55k	6	1	1½	1hd	14	17	Velasquez J	121	*.50	97-13	Lady'sSecrt1217RideSally114nkIndinRomnc1143 Ridden out	7
11May85- 8Bel	fst 7f	:22 :443 1:091 1:221	ⒻComely-G3	1	4	43	45	47½	411	Cordero A Jr	121	6.30	80-12	Mom'sCommnd1214½MajestcFolly1131¾ClocksScrt1214¾ Tired	9
28Apr85- 8Aqu	fst 6f	:222 :451 1:10	ⒻPrioress-G3	5	1	21	21½	21½	21¼	Velasquez J	118	*1.30	90-21	ClocksSecret1151¼Lady'sSecret1185RideSally1122 Gamely	8
16Apr85- 9OP	fst 6f	:214 :45 1:10	ⒻPrima Donna 76k	7	2	32½	3½	11½	15	Velasquez J	123	*.80	90-18	Lady'sSecret1235TakeMyPictur1232Lt.A.J.1121¾ Ridden out	9
23Feb85- 8GG	fst 6f	:213 :442 :573 1:10	ⒻVallejo 43k	1	3	11½	1½	1hd	21½	Baze RA	122	1.90	87-16	SavannahSlew1141½Ldy'sScrt1226SprtdMdm1143½ Game try	7
30Jan85- 8SA	fst 7f	:221 :444 1:094 1:232	ⒻS Ynez-G3	6	1	2hd	1hd	2hd	53¾	Valenzuela PA	122	7.40	79-17	Wising Up119¾Rascal Lass1222Reigning Countess119¾ Hung	9
12Jan85- 8BM	fst 6f	:222 :444 :572 1:101	Determine 44k	7	1	2½	1hd	2hd	2nk	Baze RA	115	*1.10	88-21	Bedside Promise113nkLady'sScrt1151½DSantaRosaPrince115no Gamely	8
5Jan85- 8BM	fst 6f	:222 :45 :573 1:10	ⒻHail Hilarious 43k	5	3	31½	1hd	13	14	Baze RA	120	*.70	89-16	Lady's Secret1204Missadoon1125Bloomer Miss115no Bumped start,wide into str	7
9Nov84- 9Hol	fst 6f	:221 :453 :58 1:111	ⒻMoccasin 61k	8	1	1hd	2½	1½	1½	McCarron CJ	120	*1.90	--	Lady's Secret120½Neshia1131Lotta Blue1173 Driving	9
20Oct84- 8SA	fst 1 1/16	:224 :454 1:102 1:423	ⒻOak Leaf-G1	6	1	13	1½	36	516¼	Sibille R	115	7.10	72-13	FolkArt1174½Pirate'sGlow1156½WaywardPirate1153½ Tired	6
8Oct84- 8SA	fst 7f	:22 :443 1:101 1:233	ⒻAnoakia-G3	11	1	12½	13½	12	3hd	Black K	120	6.10e	82-16	WaywardPirate120hdPrt'sGlow117noLdy'sScrt1201¼ Weakened	11
8Aug84- 8Dmr	fst 6f	:22 :451 :58 1:111	ⒻJunior Miss 53k	3	1	2hd	1hd	22½	46	Valenzuela PA	122	3.00e	76-21	Doon's Baby1172½Fiesta Lady1173Trunk117½ Weakened	6
23Jly84- 3Hol	fst 6f	:214 :443 :572 1:11	ⒻⓇWavy Waves 46k	5	1	1½	12	12	11½	Valenzuela PA	117	2.20	82-18	Lady's Secret1171½Full o Wisdom115½Neshia1172¼ Driving	6
7Jly84- 8Hol	fst 6f	:213 :444 :571 1:10	ⒻLandaluce-G3	13	1	2hd	22½	25	49	Valenzuela PA	116	21.40e	78-18	WindowSeat1146½RaiseaProspctor1191FulloWsdom1141½ Tired	13
2Jly84- 8Bel	fst 5½f	:214 :454 :583 1:051	ⒻAstoria 75k	4	3	1hd	1hd	21	55½	Cordero A Jr	112	2.60	83-15	Faster Than Fast1103Something113½Queen Breeze1121½ Pace between horses	9
21May84- 4Bel	fst 5f	:221 :454 :584	ⒻMd Sp Wt	1	3	11½	11½	11½	11½	Cordero A Jr	117	*1.40	93-09	DHLady'sScrt117DHBonnie's Axe1171½Launching Shot1172¼ Drifted out	8

Landaluce

dkbbr. f. 1980, by Seattle Slew (Bold Reasoning)–Strip Poker, by Bold Bidder **Lifetime record: 5 5 0 0 $372,365**

Own.– French & Beal
Br.– Spendthrift Farm & Francis Kernan (Ky)
Tr.– D. Wayne Lukas

23Oct82- 8SA	fst 1 1/16	:223 :454 1:094 1:414	ⒻOak Leaf-G1	6	3	1hd	13	14	12	Pincay L Jr	117	*.05	92-10	Landaluce1172SophisticatedGirl1158GrnjRn115½ Ridden out	7
11Oct82- 8SA	fst 7f	:222 :45 1:09 1:214	ⒻAnoakia-G3	8	2	3nk	12	18	110	Pincay L Jr	123	*.10	91-15	Landaluce12310Rare Thrill1171¼Time of Sale1202½ Easily	8
5Sep82- 8Dmr	fst 1	:223 :46 1:104 1:353	ⒻDmr Debutante-G2	4	2	2½	1hd	11½	16½	Pincay L Jr	119	*.30	90-12	Landaluce1196½IssuesN'Answers1164GranjaReina1132 Easily	6
10Jly82- 8Hol	fst 6f	:212 :434 :56 1:08	ⒻHol Lassie-G2	3	2	2½	11½	19	121	Pincay L Jr	117	*.30e	97-16	Landaluce11721Bold Out Line1151½Barzell119½ Easy score	5
3Jly82- 4Hol	fst 6f	:22 :443 :562 1:081	ⒻMd Sp Wt	6	2	11½	13	16	17	Pincay L Jr	117	*.80	96-10	Landaluce1177MidnightRapture1165MissBigWig1161½ Easily	7

Lemhi Gold

ch. c. 1978, by Vaguely Noble (Vienna)–Belle Marie, by Candy Spots
Own.– Aaron U. Jones
Br.– Aaron U. Jones (Ky)
Tr.– Olivier Douieb

Lifetime record: 22 8 3 1 $1,129,645

23Jly83♦ Ascot(GB)	gd 1½ⓉRH	2:303	3↑ King George & Queen Eliz-G1 Stk296000	823¾	Head F	133	16.00		Time Charter130¾Diamond Shoal1331Sun Princess1172	Unruly pre-start,dwelt,rushed to lead,headed 4f out,weakened	9
3Jly83♦ Saint-Cloud(Fr)	gd *1 9/16ⓉLH	2:344	3↑ Grand Prix de Saint-Cloud-G1 Stk276000	42¼	Head F	134	9.00		Diamond Shoal134¾Lancastrian134¾Zalataia129¾	Led to 1f out,faded.All Along 7th	9
29May83♦ Longchamp(Fr)	gd *1⅛ⓉRH	2:03	4↑ Prix Dollar-G2 Stk69000	79	Head F	129	2.20		Welsh Tern129nkOrofino1291Darly123½	Tracked in 3rd,weakened 1½f out	9
										Previously trained by Lazaro S. Barrera	
31Oct82- 8SA	fm 1½Ⓣ	:472 1:103 1:593 2:24	3↑ Oak Tree Inv'l-G1	4 1 1hd 33½ 43½ 57¼	McCarron CJ	126	*.90	88-05	John Henry1262½Craelius1221½Regalberto1262	Speed,tired	7
9Oct82- 8Bel	fst 1½	:473 1:114 2:04 2:311	3↑ J C Gold Cup-G1	2 3 28 14 15 14½	McCarron CJ	126	2.60	64-25	LmhiGld1264½SilverSuprm1262ChrstmsPst11817	Ridden out	10
18Sep82- 8Bel	fst 1¼	:473 1:113 1:36 2:01	3↑ Marlboro Cup H-G1	2 3 31 11 15 18¾	Vasquez J	115	7.50e	93-17	LmhiGold1158¾SilvrSupreme117¾ParofDucs1169	Ridden out	8
29Aug82- 8AP	fm 1¼Ⓣ	:462 1:101 1:35 1:584	3↑ Bud Million 1000k	5 8 85¾ 52¼ 44½ 45¼	McCarron CJ	126	3.20	120-00	Perrault1262¼Be My Native118nkMotavato1262¾	Rallied	14
7Aug82- 8Sar	fst 1⅛	:472 1:11 1:352 1:474	3↑ Whitney H-G1	1 5 47 45 56¼ 45¾	McCarron CJ	117	5.70	90-14	SilverBuck1151½Wntr'sTl119nkTpShos1134	Broke in the air	6
10Jly82- 8Bel	fm 1½Ⓣ	:491 1:132 2:014 2:26	3↑ Sword Dancer H-G2	2 1 13 1½ 1hd 1nk	McCarron CJ	126	*1.00	94-11	Lemhi Gold126nkErin's Isle1267¾Field Cat1261¾	Driving	5
31May82- 8Hol	fm 1½Ⓣ	:492 1:132 2:013 2:251	3↑ Hol Inv'l H-G1	6 3 32 3½ 1hd 22½	Guerra WA	123	*.60	91-07	Exploded1172½Lemhi Gold123¾The Bart1252½	Game try	6
18Apr82- 8SA	fm *1¾Ⓣ	:46 1:584 2:453	4↑ San Juan Cap H-G1	4 4 35½ 1hd 12½ 17	Guerra WA	121	3.10	99-06	Lemhi Gold1217Exploded1181¾Perrault1292½	Easy score	9
13Mar82- 8SA	gd 1½Ⓣ	:484 1:13 2:022 2:272	4↑ S Marino H (Div 1) 66k	4 1 12½ 12½ 15 15	Guerra WA	119	2.30	78-29	Lemhi Gold1195Exploded1191½Chancey Bidder1124¼	Easily	8
25Feb82- 8SA	fm 1⅛Ⓣ	:464 1:111 1:353 1:48	4↑ Alw 35000	8 5 42 41½ 1½ 11¼	Guerra WA	113	*1.70	87-13	Lemhi Gold1131¼Fingal's Cave1142½Essenbee1152½	Driving	10
15Feb82- 8SA	fst 1 1/16	:231 :462 1:10 1:41	4↑ ⓇEl Monte 73k	1 5 43 31½ 33½ 31¼	Guerra WA	114	3.40	95-12	Woodland Lad119½Sir Dancer115¾Lemhi Gold1141½	Evenly	10
6Feb82- 6SA	fst 1 1/16	:231 :462 1:094 1:41	4↑ Alw 25000	4 5 53½ 33½ 23½ 25½	Guerra WA	114	*.90	90-09	Shashy1155½Lemhi Gold1143½Call Me Mister117½	No match	7
29Aug81- 8Bel	fst 1	:223 :444 1:082 1:331	Jerome H-G2	11 9 108¼ 913 913 915	Velasquez J	117	11.60	87-09	Noble Nashua1203½Maudlin1123½Sing Sing1091¾	Outrun	11
15Aug81- 8Sar	sly 1¼	:463 1:112 1:372 2:034	Travers-G1	6 7 811 911 923 726	Vasquez J	126	16.80	55-20	WillowHour126hdPleasantColony1261¾LordAvie1264¼	Outrun	10
2Aug81- 8Sar	fst 1⅛	:47 1:103 1:36 1:491	Jim Dandy-G3	6 7 53 33 31½ 2½	Cordero A Jr	117	3.40	88-11	WillowHour117½LemhiGold117½SilverSupreme114¾	Steadied	8
9Jly81- 9Hol	fm 1Ⓣ	:23 :462 1:103 1:35	ⓇWestwood (Div 2) 40k	6 5 44 62¼ 4¾ 1½	McCarron CJ	114	2..50	94-09	Lemhi Gold114½Rock Softly114hdIsland Whirl115hd	Driving	7
28Mar81- 8SA	fst 1 1/16	:223 :46 1:10 1:42	San Felipe H-G2	6 5 57½ 68 711 58	Pincay L Jr	119	*1.50	83-13	Stancharry118nkSplendidSpruce116½FlyingNshu1211¾	Evenly	12
19Mar81- 7SA	fst 1	:223 :452 1:093 1:351	Alw 22000	5 5 44 44½ 46½ 49	Pincay L Jr	120	*.20	84-07	Torso1144Native Tactics1204½El Jebel109½	Lacked rally	5
8Mar81- 4SA	fst 1	:222 :461 1:11 1:353	©Md Sp Wt	6 8 54½ 31½ 14½ 114	Pincay L Jr	118	*.70	91-11	LemhiGold11814HaloReason118½AtYourPleasure1182½	Easily	8

Life's Magic

b. f. 1981, by Cox's Ridge (Best Turn)–Fire Water, by Tom Rolfe
Own.– E.V. Klein
Br.– D.C. Parrish III & Mr & Mrs D. Parrish (Ky)
Tr.– D. Wayne Lukas

Lifetime record: 32 8 11 6 $2,255,218

2Nov85- 5Aqu	fst 1¼	:464 1:112 1:364 2:02	3↑ ⒻBC Distaff-G1	6 7 710 21 11½ 16¼	Cordero A Jr	123	*.40e	86-10	Life'sMgc1236¼Ldy'sScrt1193DontstopThmusc1231¼	Drew off	7
12Oct85- 7Kee	fst 1⅛	:48 1:124 1:373 1:502	3↑ ⒻSpinster-G1	2 10 115½ 72 2½ 22½	Velasquez J	123	*2.20	82-19	DonstopThemusic1232½Life'sMgc1231¼Dowery123½	Wide rally	11
22Sep85- 8Bel	fst 1⅛	:462 1:094 1:343 1:472	3↑ ⒻRuffian H-G1	1 6 57 611 47½ 46¼	Pincay L Jr	120	*.30e	84-17	Lady's Secret1164Isayso1152¼Sintrillium118hd	Mild gain	6
24Aug85- 8Sar	fst 1¼	:474 1:113 1:362 2:02	3↑ ⒻDelaware H-G1	5 5 58 53½ 31 33	Velasquez J	122	*.90e	87-13	Basie1101½Heatherten1261½Life's Magic1222	Wide,weakened	5
3Aug85- 8Sar	fst 1⅛	:474 1:112 1:351 1:473	3↑ Whitney H-G1	5 4 45½ 44½ 45½ 46½	Velasquez J	113	7.60	90-11	TrackBarrn124½CarrdeNskr1204¼Vnlndnghm1241¾	No threat	5
20Jly85- 8Bel	fst 1½	:48 1:12 2:022 2:282	3↑ Brooklyn H-G1	7 5 57 32½ 2½ 2½	Velasquez J	114	6.50	77-22	BoundngBasque111½Life'sMgic1143¾PineCircl1151¾	Gamely	10
4Jly85- 8Bel	fst 1¼	:463 1:10 1:342 2:01	3↑ Suburban H-G1	9 7 911 47 46½ 410	Velasquez J	115	10.60	83-17	Vanlandingham1158¾Carr de Naskra120nkDramatic Desire1091	Mild response	9
9Jun85- 8Bel	gd 1⅛	:474 1:12 1:37 1:484	3↑ ⒻHempstead H-G1	4 4 45½ 42½ 21½ 24¼	Velasquez J	122	1.20	79-18	Heatherten1244¼Lif'sMgc1222¼Sf'sButy1205	Best of others	6
18May85- 8Bel	fst 1 1/16	:23 :462 1:112 1:422	3↑ ⒻShuvee H-G2	4 6 54 32 1½ 12	Velasquez J	121	3.10	90-15	Life'sMagic1212Heatherten1266½SomforAll1096¾	Drew clear	7
	Previously owned by Hatley & Klein										
17Apr85- 9OP	fst 1 1/16	:233 :472 1:104 1:421	4↑ ⒻApple Blossom H-G1	4 6 67½ 53 31½ 34	Velasquez J	123	1.80	86-19	Sefa's Beauty120noHeatherten1274Life's Magic1233½	Carried out str	7
16Mar85- 8SA	fm 1⅛Ⓣ	:461 1:103 1:35 1:47	4↑ ⒻSanta Ana H-G1	1 4 55¾ 62¾ 911 812¼	Valenzuela PA	122	4.30	80-10	Estrapade1236Fact Finder119nkAir Distingue1161¼	Tired	10
3Mar85- 8SA	fst 1¼	:454 1:091 1:342 2:003	4↑ S Anita H-G1	3 5 59½ 55½ 57 44	Valenzuela PA	117	22.40	82-14	Lord at War1251¾Greinton1201Gate Dancer1251¼	Evenly	7
10Feb85- 8SA	fst 1⅛	:462 1:102 1:354 1:484	ⒻLa Canada-G1	4 4 35 33 46 35¼	Velasquez J	126	2.00	80-15	Mitterand121¾Percipient1174½Life's Magic126½	Evenly	5
10Nov84- 5Hol	fst 1¼	:471 1:113 1:37 2:022	3↑ ⒻBC Distaff-G1	5 5 56 33 23 27	Velasquez J	119	3.50	- -	PrincessRooney1237Life'sMagic119¾Adored1232	Held place	7
21Oct84- 8Bel	fst 1¼	:473 1:112 1:37 2:031	3↑ ⒻBeldame-G1	4 2 21 1hd 1½ 13¾	Velasquez J	118	1.40	82-21	Life'sMgic1183¾MissOceana1189¾KeyDancr11818	Ridden out	4
1Sep84- 8Bel	fst 1⅛	:47 1:111 1:351 1:473	ⒻGazelle H-G1	1 2 32 41½ 32½ 32¾	Velasquez J	122	*.70	86-13	Miss Oceana1212Sintra117¾Life's Magic122hd	Weakened	5
11Aug84- 8Sar	fst 1¼	:48 1:114 1:363 2:023	ⒻAlabama-G1	2 3 21 2½ 2½ 1hd	Velasquez J	121	*.80e	87-15	Life'sMgc121hdLuckyLuckyLucky12115½ClssPly1213¾	Driving	5
21Jly84- 9Mth	sly 1⅛	:473 1:113 1:371 1:50	ⒻMth Oaks-G2	2 6 74½ 1hd 12 16½	Velasquez J	121	*.50	85-16	Life's Magic1216½Flippers1181Cassowary1124	Driving	10
7Jly84- 8Bel	sly 1½	:50 1:15 2:043 2:294	ⒻC C A Oaks-G1	3 2 24 31 21½ 21½	Velasquez J	121	*.40e	69-16	ClassPlay1211½Life'sMagc1212¼MssOcn12122	Best of others	5
16Jun84- 8Bel	fst 1⅛	:453 1:093 1:352 1:484	ⒻMother Goose-G1	1 5 55 53 11½ 13¼	Velasquez J	121	1.60	83-22	Life's Magic1213¼Miss Oceana121¾Wild Applause1214¼	Off slowly,clear	5
26May84- 8Bel	fst 1	:23 :453 1:102 1:354	ⒻAcorn-G1	3 9 89¼ 54 22½ 2nk	Velasquez J	121	2.70e	86-15	MissOceana121nkLif'sMgc1215½ProudClronss121no	Sharp try	9
5May84- 8CD	fst 1¼	:472 1:114 1:363 2:022	Ky Derby-G1	5 13 138 86¼ 88¼ 88	Brumfield D	121	*2.80e	77-19	Swale1263¼CoaxMeChad1262AttheThreshold126nk	No factor	20
8Apr84- 8SA	fst 1⅛	:452 1:10 1:36 1:49	S A Derby-G1	1 7 714 611 69½ 59	Cordero A Jr	115 b	9.20e	75-16	MightyAdversry1201¼Precisonst120nkPrncTru1202½	Checked	8
	Previously owned M.E. Hatley										
11Mar84- 8SA	fst 1 1/16	:232 :472 1:113 1:433	ⒻS Susana-G1	1 5 43 42 42 3¾	Cordero A Jr	115	2.80	82-18	Althea117¾Personable Lady115hdLife's Magic1154	Rallied	5
16Feb84- 7SA	fst 1	:23 :463 1:114 1:38	ⒻAlw 35000	6 5 53 42½ 22½ 21½	Pincay L Jr	119	*.30	76-23	VagabondGal1171½Life'sMgc1191½Dchrony119no	Wide,bumped	6
18Dec83- 8Hol	fst 1 1/16	:222 :454 1:101 1:413	Hol Futurity-G1	10 9 88½ 71½ 44½ 34	Cordero A Jr	118	10.80	83-14	FaliTime121½BoldT.Jay1213½Life'sMagic1183	Fin. strong	12
27Nov83- 8Hol	fst 1 1/16	:23 :464 1:112 1:43	ⒻHol Starlet-G2	5 5 41¼ 21 32 21½	McCarron CJ	120	2.00	78-20	Althea1201½Life's Magic120hdSpring Loose1202½	Gamely	6
12Nov83- 8SA	sly 1 1/16	:224 :463 1:113 1:442	ⒻOak Leaf-G1	5 7 44½ 21½ 2½ 1½	McCarron CJ	115	1.80	79-23	Life's Magic115½Althea11717Percipient115hd	Driving	9
5Nov83- 8SA	fst 1 1/16	:23 :464 1:113 1:441	Norfolk-G1	8 7 51¾ 42 31 2no	Pincay L Jr	117	2.00	80-20	FaliTime118noLife'sMgc117¾Artchok1182	Wide into stretch	10
10Oct83- 8Bel	fst 1	:224 :454 1:101 1:363	ⒻFrizette-G1	10 9 74¼ 32½ 32½ 2no	Cordero A Jr	119	*1.50e	82-15	Miss Oceana119noLife's Magic1192Lucky Lucky Lucky1198¾	Just missed	10
4Sep83- 8AP	fst 7f	:22 :442 1:094 1:232	ⒻArl-Wash Lassie-G1	5 11 910 812 38 23¾	Shoemaker W	119	3.40	81-22	MissOceana1193¾Life'sMgc1194BottlTop1193	Circled horses	11
25Aug83- 3Dmr	fst 6f	:221 :454 :591 1:121	ⒻAlw 17000	3 7 714 611 44 12	Pincay L Jr	117	4.00	77-22	Life's Magic1172Diachrony1184½Early Quest118¾	Driving	7

Lord Avie

b. c. 1978, by Lord Gaylord (Sir Gaylord)–Avie, by Gallant Man — Lifetime record: 16 8 4 4 $705,977

Own.– S K S Stable
Br.– Viking Farms Ltd (Ky)
Tr.– Daniel Perlsweig

15Aug81- 8Sar	sly	1¼	:463 1:112 1:372 2:034	Travers-G1	7 10 1026 68¾ 45½ 31¾	Velasquez J	126	3.90	79-20	Willow Hour126hdPleasant Colony1261¾Lord Avie1264¼	Wide	10
1Aug81- 8Mth	fst	1⅛	:473 1:104 1:352 1:482	Haskell Inv'l H-G1	5 5 55 21½ 23 25	Velasquez J	126	*.50	88-12	FiveStarFlight1195LordAv1265OrnryOdis112½	Best of others	6
14Jly81- 8Mth	fst	1 70	:233 :474 1:122 1:421 3↑	Alw 17000	3 5 513 48 22½ 12	Velasquez J	116	*.20	85-27	Lord Avie1162Bold Josh1225Corre Pronto1138	Ridden out	5
6Mar81- 9GP	fst	1⅛	:47 1:111 1:374 1:502	Florida Derby-G1	4 8 916 56¼ 1½ 14½	McCarron CJ	122	*1.00	80-17	Lord Avie1224½Akureyri122¾Linnleur1186	Ridden out	11
16Feb81- 9GP	fst	1 1/16	:241 :48 1:121 1:442	Fountain of Youth-G3	3 6 711 75¾ 41¼ 3hd	McCarron CJ	122	*.40	79-23	Akureyri119noPleasant Colony122hdLord Avie1221½	Rallied	9
4Feb81- 9GP	fst	7f	:223 :452 1:101 1:232	Hutcheson 56k	2 5 713 516 45½ 1hd	McCarron CJ	122	*.30	87-22	LordAvie122hdSpiritdBoy1141½Lnnlur1142½	Brushed,driving	7
1Nov80- 6Med	fst	1 1/16	:224 :46 1:113 1:443	Young America-G1	2 7 812 76 2½ 11½	Velasquez J	122	*.40	86-19	Lord Avie1221½Sezyou1191¼Financial Genius1193	Driving	10
12Oct80- 8Bel	fst	1	:23 :461 1:113 1:371	Champagne-G1	7 9 76¼ 64¼ 21 12¼	Velasquez J	122	3.40	82-19	Lord Avie1222¼Noble Nashua1224Sezyou1221¾	Ridden out	9
28Sep80- 8Bel	fst	7f	:224 :463 1:111 1:233	Cowdin-G2	3 7 64 21 1hd 12¼	Velasquez J	119	1.80	84-22	LordAvie1192¼Akureyri1153Dasho'Pleasure1151¾	Ridden out	7
6Sep80- 8AP	fst	7f	:221 :444 1:11 1:234	Arl Wash Futurity-G1	12 11 108¾ 68 2hd 22	Bailey JD	122 b	*2.80	81-20	WellDecoratd1222LrdAv122noFrwyPhntom122no	Bid,weakened	15
23Aug80- 8Sar	fst	6½f	:222 :453 1:103 1:17	Hopeful-G1	6 9 93¾ 72¾ 42½ 22	Bailey JD	122 b	3.20	85-17	Tap Shoes1222Lord Avie1226Well Decorated122nk	Bore in	9
9Aug80- 9Mth	fst	6f	:22 :45 1:11	Sapling-G1	2 8 76 54¼ 25 2¾	Bailey JD	122 b	3.40	84-19	TravellingMusic122¾LordAvie1225½TimelessEvent122hd	Wide	8
21Jly80- 8Bel	fst	6f	:222 :46 1:112	Tremont-G3	4 3 64¾ 67¾ 55½ 31	Bailey JD	122	4.80	84-24	GoldnDerby122hdGretProspctor1151LrdAv1223¾	Raced wide	9
7Jly80- 8Bel	fst	5½f	:224 :461 :582 1:043	Juvenile 53k	1 2 42½ 42¼ 21½ 1½	Bailey JD	115	12.20	92-16	Lord Avie115½Jiggs Alarm1159Mambo1131	Driving	5
25Jun80- 3Mth	fst	5f	:214 :454 :581	Md Sp Wt	6 4 24 22 11 1½	Bailey JD	118	*1.00	95-10	LordAvie118½ClosetheCase1188¼SteelCurtain1181¼	Driving	7
17Jun80- 6Mth	fst	5f	:22 :454 :582	Md Sp Wt	6 3 31½ 31 35 32	Bailey JD	118	17.90	92-16	TravllngMusc118noGrtProspctr1182LrdAv1185½	Came again	10

Manila

b. c. 1983, by Lyphard (Northern Dancer)–Dona Ysidra, by Le Fabuleux — Lifetime record: 18 12 5 0 $2,692,799

Own.– B.M. Shannon
Br.– E.M. Cojuangco Jr (Ky)
Tr.– Leroy Jolley

6Sep87- 8AP	fm	1¼Ⓣ	:482 1:133 1:383 2:022 3↑	Bud Arl Million-G1	3 4 43 41½ 13 11½	Cordero A Jr	126	*1.00	82-27	Manila1261½Sharrood1263¼Theatrical1263¾	Driving	8
16Aug87- 8Sar	fm	1⅛Ⓣ	:48 1:104 1:341 1:472 3↑	Bernard Baruch H-G2	3 2 2½ 2hd 1hd 2½	Vasquez J	127	*.30	89-08	Talakeno115½Manila127¾Duluth1142	Just failed	4
15Jly87- 4Atl	sf	1 3/16Ⓣ	:512 1:161 1:411 1:584 3↑	U Nations H-G1	3 2 2½ 1½ 11 12½	Vasquez J	124	*.10	69-33	Manila1242½Racing Star1153Air Display110no	Ridden out	5
1May87- 8CD	fm	1⅛Ⓣ	:49 1:122 1:363 1:484 4↑	E T Turf Classic 169k	2 2 21 2½ 12½ 13	Vasquez J	120	*.40	- -	Manila1203Vilzak1121Lieutenant's Lark1202¼	Ridden out	4
14Apr87- 7Kee	fm	1⅛Ⓣ	:461 1:104 1:361 1:482 4↑	Elkhorn 53k	5 4 43 31½ 1hd 13	Vasquez J	113	*.40e	115-00	Manila1133Lieutennt'sLrk1127½RoylTrsurr1122¼	Ridden out	7
1Nov86- 6SA	fm	1½Ⓣ	:472 1:111 2:003 2:252 3↑	BC Turf-G1	2 4 43½ 32 31½ 1nk	Santos JA	122	8.80	88-07	Manila122nkTheatrical1263¾Estrapad1232¾	Checked,just up	9
20Sep86- 8Bel	hd	1½Ⓣ	:511 1:164 2:042 2:274 3↑	Turf Classic-G1	9 3 41½ 21 2hd 1no	Santos JA	119	*.90	85-10	Manila119noDamister126nkDanger's Hour1261½	Just up	9
5Sep86- 9Med	yl	1⅜Ⓣ	:484 1:144 1:401 2:184 3↑	Ball Scotch Classic-G3	8 4 45 31 13½ 19½	Santos JA	120	*.70	71-29	Manila1209½I'm a Banker1263Fiery Celt1264½	Ridden out	9
9Aug86- 7Atl	fm	1 3/16Ⓣ	:471 1:103 1:343 1:523 3↑	U Nations H-G1	2 4 44 31 21 11¼	Santos JA	114	2.80	101-08	Manila1141¼UptownSwell116hdLieutenant'sLrk1214½	Driving	8
12Jly86- 8Bel	yl	1¼[T]	:494 1:14 1:39 2:031	Lexington-G2	5 5 74¾ 34 21½ 1no	Santos JA	126	*1.70e	78-22	Manila126noGlow1233¾Dance Card Filled1141½	Long drive	10
7Jun86- 8Hol	fm	1⅛Ⓣ	:474 1:114 1:351 1:47	Cinema H-G2	4 4 44 42 31½ 12½	Toro F	117	3.50	97-02	Manl1172½VrnonCstl1202½FullofStrs115no	Blocked,drew out	10
18May86- 8Bel	fm	1Ⓣ	:224 :453 1:093 1:343	Saranac-G2	9 8 911 87½ 55 21¾	Velasquez J	114	*.70e	90-13	Glow1141¾Manila114nkPillaster1201¼	Checked st.	11
17Apr86- 7Kee	yl	1 1/16Ⓣ	:234 :484 1:144 1:483	Forerunner 56k	6 9 53 31 22 22½	Velez RI	118	*1.10	84-13	Autobot1122½Manila1183½Glow1124¼	2nd best	10
9Apr86- 7Kee	fm	1 1/16Ⓣ	:233 :504 1:16 1:492	Alw 33510	1 3 22 2½ 14 17¼	Velez RI	111	*.90	83-17	Manila1117¼SharpGinistrelli1112½AerialDisply1123	Easily	6
18Mar86-10Hia	fst	1 1/16⊗	:232 :462 1:113 1:431	Md Sp Wt	5 2 21 11 12 18	Velez RI	119	*.40	87-16	Manila1198NudistColony11911CaptainKingwell1191	Driving	9
	Previously owned by E.M. Cojuangco Jr											
23Oct85- 6Aqu	fst	1	:241 :481 1:124 1:382	Md Sp Wt	1 7 62½ 41½ 22 21¼	Cordero A Jr	118	2.40	73-17	Fabulous Flight1181¼Manila1182½Man Up118hd	Poor start	8
21Aug85- 6Sar	fst	6f	:222 :461 1:113	Md Sp Wt	3 4 65¼ 56 45½ 22	Cordero A Jr	118	11.00	80-14	PerfectbyFar1182Manila118½RoyalDoulton1182½	Wide str.	12
3Aug85- 3Sar	fst	6f	:221 :453 1:114	Md Sp Wt	1 13 34 47 79½ 78	Cruguet J	118	8.70	73-11	RelCourg1182¼ProudWorld118hdArMco1183½	Slow start,tired	13

Miesque

b. f. 1984, by Nureyev (Northern Dancer)–Pasadoble, by Prove Out — Lifetime record: 16 12 3 1 $1,987,514

Own.– Flaxman Holdings Ltd
Br.– Flaxman Holdings Ltd (Ky)
Tr.– Francois Boutin

5Nov88- 7CD	gd	1Ⓣ	:233 :472 1:123 1:383 3↑	B C Mile-G1	8 7 67 32½ 2hd 14	Head F	123	2.00e	96-04	Miesque1234Steinlen126hdSimply Majestic1261¼	Driving	12
4Sep88♦ Longchamp(Fr)	sf	*1ⓉRH	1:403 3↑	Prix du Moulin de Longchamp-G1 Stk243000	2hd	Head F	124	*.20e		Soviet Star128hdMiesque1245Gabina1204	Tracked in 4th,rail bid 1½f out,held by winner	7
14Aug88♦ Deauville(Fr)	gd	*1ⓉStr	1:383 3↑	Prix Jacques le Marois-G1 Stk160000	11	Head F	124	*.60		Miesque1241Warning1212Gabina118no	Rated toward rear,rallied to lead 1f out,ridden out	6
29May88♦ Longchamp(Fr)	sf	*1⅛ⓉRH	1:551 4↑	Prix d'Ispahan-G1 Stk131000	1nk	Head F	124	*.20e		Miesque124nkSt Andrews1281½Jalaajel128hd	Rated in 4th,lacked room 1f out,strong run to lead late	6
21Nov87- 4Hol	fm	1Ⓣ	:231 :453 1:09 1:324 3↑	B C Mile-G1	4 5 33½ 32 12 13½	Head F	120	3.60	103-00	Miesque1203½Show Dancer126½Sonic Lady1231	Ridden out	14
26Sep87♦ Ascot(GB)	gd	1ⓉRH	1:40 3↑	Queen Elizabeth II Stakes-G1 Stk395000	22½	Cauthen S	120	*.25		Milligram1202½Miesque1205Sonic Lady123	Tracked in 3rd,ridden and drifted left 1f out,second best	5
6Sep87♦ Longchamp(Fr)	yl	*1ⓉRH	1:372 3↑	Prix du Moulin de Longchamp-G1 Stk282000	12½	Head F	120	*.10e		Miesque1202½Soviet Star1231Grecian Urn1202½	Tracked in 4th,3rd 2f out,led 2f out,drew clear 1f out	7
16Aug87♦ Deauville(Fr)	gd	*1ⓉStr	1:35 3↑	Prix Jacques le Marois-G1 Stk190000	13	Head F	118	*.70e		Miesque1183Nashmeel1182½Hadeer128½	Rated at rear,rallied to lead over 1f out,handily	9
14Jun87♦ Chantilly(Fr)	sf	*1 5/16ⓉRH	2:112	ⒻPrix de Diane (French Oaks)-G1 Stk390000	24	Head F	128	1.80e		Indian Skimmer1284Miesque128¾Masmoud1281	Never far away,4th 3f out,2nd 1f out,chased winner home	11
17May87♦ Longchamp(Fr)	sf	*1ⓉRH	1:38	ⒻPoule d'Essai des Pouliches-G1 Stk285000	12½	Head F	128	*.20e		Miesque1282½Sakura Reiko1283Libertine128hd	Rated in last,rallied to lead 150y out,going away	8
30Apr87♦ Newmarket(GB)	gd	1ⓉStr	1:382	Ⓕ1000 Guineas Stakes-G1 Stk229000	11½	Head F	126	*1.85		Miesque1261½Milligram126hdInterval1263	Rated at rear,angled out over 1f out,led 100y out,handily	14
3Apr87♦ Maisns-Lfftte(Fr)	hy	*7fⓉStr	1:332	ⒻPrix Imprudence (Listed) Stk33600	12½	Head F	128	*.30e		Miesque1282½Grecian Urn1282Musimara128nk	Well placed in 3rd,led 150y out,easily	5
5Oct86♦ Longchamp(Fr)	fm	*1ⓉRH	1:372	ⒻPrix Marcel Boussac-G1 Stk107000	1½	Head F	121 b	*1.40e		Miesque121½Milligram121nkSakura Reiko1212	Unhurried in last,strong late run to lead near line	11
21Sep86♦ Longchamp(Fr)	yl	*7fⓉRH	1:252	Prix de la Salamandre-G1 Stk113000	11½	Head F	120 b	3.60e		Miesque1201½Sakura Reiko1203Whakilyric1201	Rated at rear,sharp run to lead 170y out,driving	10
24Aug86♦ Deauville(Fr)	sf	*6fⓉStr	1:142	Prix Morny-G1 Stk95400	31	Head F	120 b	7.20		Sakura Reiko1201Shy Princess120noMiesque1203	Close up,led 150y to 170y out,lost 2nd on line	8
9Aug86♦ Deauville(Fr)	gd	*6fⓉStr	1:143	Prix de Lisieux Mdn (FT)20700	12	Head F	123 b	4.00		Miesque1232Proflare1231Lumen Dei1231	Tracked leader,led 1f out,ridden out	6

Mom's Command

ch. f. 1982, by Top Command (Bold Ruler)–Star Mommy, by Pia Star — **Lifetime record: 16 11 2 1 $902,972**

Own.– P. Fuller
Br.– Peter Fuller (Ky)
Tr.– Edward T. Allard

10Aug85- 8Sar	fst 1¼	:464 1:104 1:363 2:031	ⓕAlabama-G1	2 1 12½ 14 14½ 14	Fuller A	121	*.60	84-16	Mm'sCmmnd1214Fran'sValntn121¾FoxyDn12114 Ridden out 5
1Aug85- 8Sar	gd 7f	:221 :444 1:09 1:213	ⓕTest-G2	2 5 1hd 2hd 31½ 22	Fuller A	124	*.50	92-13	Lady's Secret1212Mom's Command124nkMajestic Folly118½ 10
	Gained place								
6Jly85- 8Bel	fst 1½	:461 1:103 2:031 2:32	ⓕC C A Oaks-G1	8 1 12 15 17 12½	Fuller A	121	*.50	60-20	Mom'sCmmnd1212½Bssrbn1214FoxyDn121½ Drifted out,clear 9
15Jun85- 8Bel	fst 1⅛	:45 1:092 1:493	ⓕMother Goose-G1	1 1 12 11½ 14½ 15½	Fuller A	121	*1.40	79-18	Mm'sCmmnd1215½LL'Argnt121nkWllowyMood1215¼ Ridden out 11
25May85- 8Bel	fst 1	:22 :441 1:09 1:354	ⓕAcorn-G1	8 1 17 16 14 13	Fuller A	121	*.70	86-11	Mm'sCmmnd1213LeL'Argent1219½Diplomette1211¼ Handily 8
11May85- 8Bel	fst 7f	:22 :443 1:091 1:221	ⓕComely-G3	9 1 11½ 11 12 14½	Fuller A	121	2.30	91-12	Mom'sCommnd1214½Majestic Folly113¾Clocks Secret1214¾ 9
	Ridden out								
19Apr85- 8GS	fst 1 1/16	:23 :462 1:102 1:413	ⓕCherry Blossom H 117k	8 1 12½ 11½ 13 14	Fuller A	121	*1.10	--	Mm'sCmmnd1214GoldenSilenc1136WllowyMood118¾ Handily 10
11Apr85- 8GS	fst 6f	:212 :433 1:082	ⓕGoldfinch H 66k	1 5 2½ 22½ 25 22½	Fuller A	123	*.50	--	ClocksScrt1142½Mm'sCmmnd123nkWllowyMood1205 Drifted out 6
23Mar85- 9Pim	sly 6f	:23 :46 :582 1:104	ⓕFlirtation 32k	5 1 13½ 16 18 119	Fuller A	119	*.40	92-21	Mm'sCommnd11919AppealingGirl1192¼ClassyCut1142 Easily 5
2Dec84- 8Hol	fst 1 1/16	:222 :454 1:104 1:44	ⓕHol Starlet-G1	16 3 3nk 1½ 1hd 57	Fuller A	120	16.20	--	Outstndngly1202¾Fran'sValntn1202½WsngUp120nk Weakened 16
27Oct84- 8Lrl	fst 1 1/16	:224 :454 1:104 1:433	ⓕSelima-G1	4 1 12½ 15 16 12½	McCarron G	119	17.10	90-13	Mom'sCommand1192½Diplomette119½Soliciting1192 Driving 7
14Oct84- 8Bel	fst 1	:222 :452 1:114 1:39	ⓕFrizette-G1	2 1 13 2½ 3½ 35¾	Fuller A	119	5.40	64-28	Charleston Rag1195¾Tiltalating119noMom's Command1191¼ 6
	Off poorly,weakened								
12Sep84- 8Bel	fst 6½f	:221 :452 1:11 1:174	ⓕAstarita-G2	2 10 11 2hd 12 11¼	Fuller A	116	19.10	87-14	Mom's Command1161¼Self Image1125¾Winter's Love112no 10
	Poor start,clear								
27Aug84- 8Sar	fst 6f	:221 :452 1:11	ⓕSpinaway-G1	2 6 31½ 35½ 45 46¼	Fuller A	119	15.30	79-16	Tiltalating1191¼Socible Duck1193½Contredance1191½ 7
	Steadied at start								
4Aug84-10Suf	fst 6f	:221 :453 :581 1:113	ⓕPriscilla 25k	5 2 2hd 2hd 1hd 1¾	Fuller A	116	3.40	83-21	Mm'sCmmnd116¾SheerIce1168½MyFriendFran1161½ Driving 8
17Jly84- 8Rkm	fst 5f	:221 :464 1:00	ⓕⓇFaneuil Miss 10k	5 11 85 66¼ 44 1hd	Carrasco B	113	44.70	84-21	Mm'sCmmnd113hdCircleFoot113nkMyFriendFrn113½ Driving 11

North Sider

dkbbr. f. 1982, by Topsider (Northern Dancer)–Back Ack, by Ack Ack — **Lifetime record: 36 15 7 5 $1,126,400**

Own.– Mrs Audrey Reed
Br.– Cisley Stable–Robert P. Levy (Ky)
Tr.– D. Wayne Lukas

21Nov87- 3Hol	fst 1¼	:471 1:113 1:364 2:024 3↑	ⓕBC Distaff-G1	2 4 54½ 67½ 614 625½	McCarron CJ	123	7.70	52-12	Sacahuista1192¼Clabber Girl1234Oueee Bebe119hd Weakened 6
	Previously owned by Paternostro & Lukas								
31Oct87- 8Kee	fst 1⅛	:462 1:101 1:354 1:483 3↑	ⓕSpinster-G1	3 7 62¼ 53½ 87¾ 911½	Perret C	123	*1.40e	82-14	Sacahuista1193Ms. Margi1192½Tall Poppy123no Tired 13
27Sep87- 8Bel	fst 1⅛	:462 1:092 1:35 1:483 3↑	ⓕRuffian H-G1	7 6 64½ 63¼ 78 106¼	Pincay L Jr	122	*.40e	78-19	ⒹSacahuista114hdCoupdeFusil1171¾ClabberGirl112½ Tired 12
12Sep87- 8Bel	fst 1	:223 :444 1:092 1:35 3↑	ⓕMaskette-G1	6 3 32 2hd 2hd 1nk	Cordero A Jr	123	1.20e	90-19	NorthSider123nkWisla1163½Funistrad116nk Strong handling 7
14Aug87- 8Sar	fst 7f	:213 :44 1:092 1:223 3↑	ⓕBallerina-G2	4 3 34½ 33½ 3nk 44	Romero RP	122	*.80e	85-21	I'mSweets119¾StormandSunshine1163PineTrLn122nk Weakened 5
19Jly87- 8Hol	fst 1¼	:453 1:091 1:344 2:003 3↑	ⓕVanity Inv'l H-G1	7 1 11 12 2½ 26½	Pincay L Jr	121	2.90	82-07	Infinidad1136½North Sider1212¾Clabber Girl1151¾ Tired 7
28Jun87- 8Bel	fst 7f	:222 :454 1:104 1:241 3↑	ⓕVagrancy H-G3	1 2 31½ 31 11 12	Cordero A Jr	121	2.30	81-19	NorthSidr1212StormandSunshine1172¾Funstrd1145½ Driving 6
20Jun87- 9Mth	fst 1 70	:233 :464 1:101 1:393 3↑	ⓕBud Breeders' H 155k	3 1 11 12½ 13 12½	Perret C	120	*.90	98-13	NorthSidr1202½BarbicueSauce112nkCoupdeFusl1133 Handily 7
5Jun87- 8Bel	gd 1⅛	:481 1:121 1:37 1:50 3↑	ⓕHempstead H-G1	2 1 12 13 1½ 54	Cordero A Jr	120	*.90	73-19	Catatonic116hdMs. Eloise1181Steal a Kiss1111½ Weakened 7
16May87- 8Bel	fst 1 1/16	:224 :453 1:102 1:414 3↑	ⓕShuvee H-G1	10 2 22½ 2hd 11½ 2no	Day P	120	*1.90	93-18	Ms.Eloise117noNorthSidr1207½Clmnn'sRos1141¾ Just failed 10
1May87- 7CD	fst 1 1/16	:24 :48 1:113 1:424 3↑	ⓕBud BC H 154k	2 3 42½ 2½ 22½ 46	Cordero A Jr	123	*.40e	88-12	QueenAlxandra117¾Infndd1162½I'mSwts1162¾ Flattened out 6
15Apr87- 9OP	fst 1 1/16	:232 :463 1:101 1:411 4↑	ⓕApple Blossom H-G1	1 2 1hd 11 13 14	Cordero A Jr	122	*.30e	95-18	NorthSidr1224FamilyStyle1202QuenAlxndr1192½ Ridden out 7
3Apr87- 9OP	fst 1 1/16	:224 :461 1:111 1:421 3↑	ⓕBud BC H 133k	1 3 33 2hd 12½ 14	Cordero A Jr	121	*1.30	90-17	NorthSider1214QueenAlexandra1221¾Ann'sBid1232¼ Easily 8
17Mar87- 8SA	fm 1⅛Ⓣ	:481 1:114 1:36 1:48 4↑	ⓕS Ana H-G1	5 5 52½ 43 34½ 35½	Cordero A Jr	120	5.80	81-17	Reloy1162Northern Aspen1193½North Sider120½ Evenly 7
1Mar87- 8SA	fst 1⅛	:454 1:103 1:36 1:484 4↑	ⓕS Margarita Inv'l H-G1	5 5 54½ 41 11½ 1hd	Cordero A Jr	117	2.40e	85-15	NorthSider117hdWinterTreasure1151¼FrauAltv117nk Driving 12
	Previously owned by Lettuce Farm & Paternostro								
7Feb87- 8SA	fst 1 1/16	:224 :461 1:103 1:423 4↑	ⓕS Maria H-G2	6 2 23 2½ 1½ 2¾	Delahoussaye E	118	11.70	87-14	Fran's Valentine121¾North Sider1182Infinidad1131 Gamely 8
28Jan87- 7SA	fst 1 1/16	:232 :47 1:113 1:441 4↑	ⓕAlw 45000	3 2 21½ 1hd 12½ 12	Pincay L Jr	118	*1.90	80-21	North Sider1182Ambra Ridge1141¼Sign Off1151¾ Drew out 8
2Nov86- 8BM	fst 1 1/16	:233 :47 1:111 1:431 3↑	ⓕⓇWatch Wndy H 50k	6 2 1hd 11 11½ 13	Baze RA	123	*.90	76-21	NorthSider1233Hertlftr1167GoldnTk1151 Dueled,ridden out 6
	Restricted to horses stabled at Bay Meadows								
12Oct86- 8BM	fst 1 1/16	:241 :473 1:122 1:433 3↑	ⓕTizna H 49k	2 3 31½ 31½ 2hd 2¾	Baze RA	123	*.70	73-19	Good Zar114¾North Sider123nkPetillante1154 Bid,failed 4
4Oct86- 6BM	fst 1	:231 :47 1:112 1:362 3↑	ⓕⓇBerry Bush H 25k	2 2 2½ 1½ 1hd 1no	Baze RA	121	*.60	86-16	North Sider121noWine Taster114nkBarbie Karen1145 Gamely 8
23Aug86- 9Aks	fst 1⅛	:494 1:15 1:403 1:55 3↑	ⓕQueen's H-G3	8 5 32 31 1hd 34	Baze RA	115	2.40	58-36	Oriental117Beauty Cream111North Sider115 Bumped start 9
26Jly86- 7Aks	fst 1 1/16	:24 :471 1:114 1:44 3↑	ⓕBud BC 123k	8 2 1hd 13 12 22½	Baze RA	115	2.00	80-23	Oriental1152½North Sider1153½Crystal Pleat1182 No match 9
4Jly86- 5Hol	fm 6fⓉ	:22 :444 1:083 3↑	ⓕHandicap 35000	5 3 1½ 11 2½ 54½	Delahoussaye E	118	7.40	94-00	Aberuschka1222Loucoum1152½Bold n Special110hd Weakened 7
20Jun86- 8Hol	fst 6f	:221 :452 :57 1:092 3↑	ⓕAlw 35000	2 5 41¾ 42½ 67 612¼	McCarron CJ	122	2.10	85-11	BoldNSpcl109½FolkArt1174Conn'sTj117hd Bumped hard start 6
7Jun86- 5Hol	fm 6fⓉ	:223 :452 :564 1:084 3↑	ⓕHandicap 35000	2 6 41¼ 42 42½ 43	Valenzuela PA	121	3.40	95-02	Lichi115noLoucoum1152½Regal Ties113½ Steadied break 6
9Feb86- 8SA	fst 1⅛	:464 1:11 1:363 1:494	ⓕLa Canada-G1	2 4 42½ 43½ 33½ 35¼	Delahoussaye E	118	6.80	75-16	Lady'sSecret1261¼Shywing1194NrthSidr1181¾ Bobbled start 6
1Feb86- 8SA	my 1 1/16	:221 :453 1:12 1:443 4↑	ⓕS Maria H-G2	3 5 611 42½ 34 35¾	Baze RA	118	5.20	72-24	LoveSmittn1202¼Johnc1213½NorthSdr1186 Wide into stretch 9
15Jan86- 8SA	fst 7f	:221 :44 1:084 1:213 4↑	ⓕS Monica H-G3	4 2 32½ 45 33 21¼	Pincay L Jr	119	12.80	91-14	HerRoyalty1201¼NrthSidr1192TkMyPctur117½ Saved ground 8
	Previously owned by Lettuce Farm								
28Dec85- 8BM	fst 1 1/16	:232 :47 1:104 1:414	ⓕBM Deb 51k	1 3 32 31 2½ 12½	Baze RA	125	*.40	83-14	NorthSider1252½CementCreek1143½BubbleBite118hd Handily 8
15Dec85- 8BM	fst 6f	:222 :451 :573 1:092	ⓕFoster City 48k	7 1 21 13 14 14	Baze RA	122	*.40	92-20	NorthSider1224ImpressiveAnnie1171BubbleBite1222 Easily 7
23Nov85- 8BM	fst 1 1/16	:233 :472 1:104 1:413	ⓕSan Jose H 51k	2 5 3nk 1½ 15 15	Baze RA	114	*1.50	84-15	NorthSider1145BubbleBite113nkRascalLass1202 Ridden out 7
18Nov85- 8BM	fst 1	:232 :473 1:12 1:362 3↑	ⓕAlw 18000	4 3 31 41½ 14 15	Baze RA	114	*.70	86-20	North Sider1145Normira1097Renee's Lark1161 Much best 8
24Oct85- 8BM	fst 6f	:224 :461 :581 1:104 3↑	ⓕAlw 17000	6 8 76½ 44½ 42¼ 23	Baze RA	117	*.60	82-23	Abstract Energy1173North Sider117noPirate Annie117hd 8
	Fractious in gate,broke in a tangle,very wide into stretch								
14Oct85- 4BM	fst 6f	:222 :453 :57 1:092	ⓕAlw 13000	6 4 23 2hd 16 17	Baze RA	120	*.90	92-18	NorthSidr1207Hylnd'sHHop1131½Prsuson1091 Not threatened 7
20Sep85- 1BM	fst 6f	:223 :453 :574 1:101 3↑	ⓕMd Sp Wt	1 2 1hd 1½ 14 16	Baze RA	116	*.90	88-17	NrthSidr1166SharpBrd116½MnhttnMgc116no Not threatened 6
13Sep85- 6Bmf	fst 6f	:224 :453 :581 1:11 3↑	ⓕMd Sp Wt	6 4 1hd 2hd 21½ 33¼	Baze RA	117	*.70	81-24	PeggyDee1173NobHillNative117nkNorthSidr117no Weakened 10

Open Mind

ch. f. 1986, by Deputy Minister (Vice Regent)–Stage Luck, by Stage Door Johnny **Lifetime record: 19 12 2 2 $1,844,372**

Own.– K. Makamura
Br.– Due Process Stables (NJ)
Tr.– D. Wayne Lukas

2Sep90- 8Bel	fst 1	:23 :452 1:094 1:353 3↑	ⒻMaskette H-G1	2 6 611 611 613	610½	Krone JA	123	2.80e	80-13	Go for Wand118²½Feel the Beat123noMistaurian116⁴	Outrun 6
10Aug90- 8Sar	fst 7f	:221 :45 1:091 1:22 3↑	ⒻBallerina-G1	3 8 713 812 511	511¼	Stevens GL	119	2.80e	84-13	FeeltheBeat119²FantasticFind116⁴ProperEvidence119²	Wide 8
Previously owned by E.V. Klein											
4Nov89- 6GP	fst 1⅛	:462 1:111 1:353 1:472 3↑	ⒻBC Distaff-G1	9 8 813 87½ 37	33¾	Cordero A Jr	119	5.20e	103-01	Bayakoa1231½Gorgeous1192¼Open Mind119⁵	Mild rally 10
15Oct89- 8Bel	fst 1¼	:491 1:131 1:383 2:051 3↑	ⒻBeldame-G1	6 5 511 66¾ 57½	57	Cordero A Jr	118	*.80	59-38	Tactile118nkColonialWaters1234½Ros'sCntn1232¼	No factor 6
24Sep89- 8Bel	fst 1⅛	:47 1:112 1:36 1:482 3↑	ⒻRuffian H-G1	5 5 56½ 43½ 21½	33¾	Cordero A Jr	120	2.00	81-24	Bayakoa1253½ColonlWaters118nkOpnMnd120⁹	Bid,weakened 6
12Aug89- 8Sar	my 1¼	:493 1:15 1:394 2:041	ⒻAlabama-G1	4 7 715 55 33½	1nk	Cordero A Jr	121	*.20e	79-23	OpnMind121nkDearlyLoved1211¾DreamDl121⁵	Up final yards 7
3Jly89- 8Bel	fst 1½	:483 1:124 2:042 2:322	ⒻC C A Oaks-G1	4 3 22 2hd 22	2no	Cordero A Jr	121	*.30	58-21	ⒹNiteofFun121noOpnMind121²⁰RoseDiamond1211½	Impeded 6
Placed first through disqualification											
11Jun89- 8Bel	fst 1⅛	:463 1:102 1:344 1:472	ⒻMother Goose-G1	4 5 52 2½ 1hd	1hd	Cordero A Jr	121	*.30	90-19	Open Mind121hdGorgeous121¹⁸Nite of Fun1212½	Driving 5
27May89- 8Bel	sly 1	:221 :45 1:101 1:352	ⒻAcorn-G1	8 11 98½ 2hd 11	14½	Cordero A Jr	121	*.40e	88-18	Open Mind1214½Hot Novel121⁴Triple Strike121²	Drew clear 11
5May89- 9CD	sly 1⅛	:48 1:121 1:373 1:503	ⒻKy Oaks-G1	2 4 33½ 24 21	12¼	Cordero A Jr	121	*.30e	89-19	OpnMnd1212¼ImaginaryLady121⁸Blondeinmotl1216½	Driving 5
1Apr89-11Lrl	fst 1¹⁄₁₆	:234 :464 1:111 1:43	ⒻPim Oaks 200k	1 7 78 42¾ 31	12	Cordero A Jr	122	*.40	94-19	OpenMind122²Dreamy Mimi122nkSeraglio114½	Brushed,clear 7
5Mar89-10GP	fst 1¹⁄₁₆	:242 :482 1:123 1:434	ⒻBonnie Miss-G2	2 4 44 42½ 1½	13	Cordero A Jr	121	*.40	82-20	Open Mind121³Seattle Meteor121¹Surging1145¾	Drew clear 6
1Feb89- 9GP	fst 7f	:22 :45 1:104 1:241	ⒻForward Gal-G3	5 8 813 79½ 23	12	Cordero A Jr	121	*2.30	83-24	OpnMnd121²Surgng114nkGorgsDoctor1189½	Steadied,handily 9
19Nov88- 7Aqu	fst 1⅛	:49 1:131 1:383 1:52	ⒻDemoiselle-G1	7 5 65½ 67 42½	1nk	Cordero A Jr	121	*.40e	75-20	Open Mind121nkDarby's Daughter1191¾Gild121hd	Driving 10
5Nov88- 5CD	my 1¹⁄₁₆	:232 :47 1:123 1:463	ⒻBC Juv Fillies-G1	8 11 1016 108¾ 42	11¾	Cordero A Jr	119	*.70e	75-20	OpnMind1191¾DarbyShuffle119nkLeaLucnd119¾	Driving,best 12
15Oct88- 7Bel	fst 1	:223 :452 1:103 1:364	ⒻFrizette-G1	6 4 46 35½ 23	2no	Cordero A Jr	119	*.30e	81-17	SomeRomnce119noOpnMind1196½Ms.GoldPole1191½	Mate won 7
18Sep88- 3Lrl	fst 7f	:224 :46 1:111 1:24	ⒻUSFG Lassie 95k	2 4 67¼ 68½ 45	24½	McCarron CJ	119	6.10	86-10	Ms.GoldPole1194½OpnMind119½SafelyKpt1191½	Wide,rallied 9
30Aug88- 7Mth	fst 6f	:223 :461 1:11	ⓈNJ Breeders 32k	3 5 52¼ 2hd 2½	1nk	Castaneda M	113	6.80	85-18	Open Mind113nkMs. Gold Pole116¹⁰Doc David115³	Driving 7
15Aug88-11Mth	fst 6f	:23 :464 1:124	ⓈMd Sp Wt	11 1 42 2½ 11	15	Castaneda M	115	10.90	76-18	OpnMnd115⁵OperationJonathon1182½RoyalNDr118nk	Driving 11

Outstandingly

b. f. 1982, by Exclusive Native (Raise a Native)–La Mesa, by Round Table **Lifetime record: 28 10 4 3 $1,412,206**

Own.– Harbow View Farm
Br.– Harbor View Farm (Ky)
Tr.–Lazaro S. Barrera

19Jan87- 8SA	fm 1⅛Ⓣ	:482 1:124 1:38 1:501 4↑	ⒻSan Gorgonio H-G2	6 2 21 41½ 31	53½	Stevens GL	120	*1.50	72-29	Frau Altiva117¹Auspiciante1221¼Solva1191¼	Tired 7
2Jan87- 8SA	fm 1⅛Ⓣ	:462 1:111 1:362 1:49 4↑	ⒻAlw 48000	3 3 35 42½ 11	11¼	Stevens GL	121	*.90	82-18	Outstandingly1211¼Frau Altiva117³New Bruce1142¼	Driving 8
23Nov86- 8Hol	fm 1⅛Ⓣ	:473 1:113 1:354 1:48 3↑	ⒻMatriarch Inv'l-G1	7 3 43 43 84¾	76½	Stevens GL	123	*2.00	81-13	Auspiciante1231½Aberuschka123¹Reloy120¾	Tired 12
1Nov86- 5SA	fst 1¼	:461 1:10 1:344 2:011 3↑	ⒻBC Distaff-G1	2 4 35 24 24	34½	Stevens GL	123	7.60	78-13	Lady'sSecrt1232½Frn'sVlntn123²Outstndngly123¾	Weakened 8
19Oct86- 8SA	fm 1⅛Ⓣ	:46 1:104 1:351 1:473 3↑	ⒻLas Palmas H-G2	4 2 32½ 32 1½	11½	Stevens GL	118	4.40	89-11	Outstandingly1181½Shywing118noJusticara1181¼	Driving 6
8Oct86- 5SA	fm *6½fⓉ	:222 :45 1:081 1:143 3↑	ⒻAtmn Dys H (Div 1) 50k	2 5 2½ 31½ 31½	31¼	Stevens GL	120	2.20	85-14	Lichi115noTax Dodge1191¼Outstandingly1201¼	Evenly 7
Run in divisions											
13Jly86- 9Hol	fst 1¼	:481 1:12 1:364 2:02 3↑	ⒻVanity Inv'l H-G1	4 2 21 31½ 34½	36¾	Stevens GL	118	6.10	75-15	MagnificntLindy116⁵DntstopThemusic1241¾Outstndingly1183½	5
Tired											
28Jun86- 8Hol	fst 1⅛	:462 1:11 1:354 1:484 3↑	ⒻMilady H-G2	2 4 54½ 63¼ 46½	46¼	Stevens GL	120	1.60e	87-12	DontstopThmusc1222¼MgnfcntLndy117hdTruffls110⁴	No rally 7
25May86- 8Hol	fm 1¹⁄₁₆Ⓣ	:25 :484 1:121 1:413 3↑	ⒻWilshire H-G2	3 1 1½ 1hd 1hd	1hd	Stevens GL	117	2.40	96-03	Outstandingly117hdLa Koumia118hdEstrapade1243½	Driving 5
10May86- 8Hol	fst 7f	:22 :444 1:091 1:214 3↑	ⒻA Gleam H-G3	2 1 53½ 53¾ 2hd	11¼	Stevens GL	120	2.80	95-12	Outstandingly1201¼Eloquack110½Shywing1205½	Driving 5
12Apr86- 8SA	fst 1¹⁄₁₆	:223 :46 1:104 1:432 4↑	ⒻⓇS Lucia H 88k	4 5 55½ 33 1½	14	Pincay L Jr	120	*1.30	84-19	Outstndingly120⁴LaMimosa116hdPalmReadr1181½	Ridden out 9
30Mar86- 8SA	fm 1¼Ⓣ	:481 1:124 1:363 2:01 4↑	ⒻS Barbara H-G1	6 5 66½ 78 77½	67½	Stevens GL	116	6.80	74-16	MountainBear119½Estrapade1243½RoylRegatta1162¼	Outrun 8
21Mar86- 8SA	fm 1⅛Ⓣ	:47 1:12 1:363 1:493 4↑	ⒻAlw 45000	4 6 69 64¾ 53¼	1½	Stevens GL	114	*1.30e	79-21	Outstandingly114½Water Crystals1153½Connie's Taj1141¼	6
Driving											
2Mar86- 1SA	fst 6½f	:211 :431 1:081 1:15 4↑	ⒻAmerigo Lady H 48k	2 6 710 713 411	24	Stevens GL	116	5.40	91-13	TakeMyPctur119⁴Outstndngly116hdHrRoylty123¾	Full of run 7
8Feb86- 1SA	fst 6f	:213 :444 :571 1:10 4↑	ⒻAlw 45000	7 2 77½ 64 53	21¾	Stevens GL	116	*2.10	86-19	GotYouRunnn1161¾Outstndngly116½CoulBy119²	Sluggish early 7
7Jly85- 8Hol	fst 1⅛	:464 1:104 1:351 1:472	ⒻHol Oaks-G1	2 6 611 610 413	417½	Shoemaker W	121	9.10	94-05	Fran's Valentine121hdMagnificent Lindy121⁹Deal Price1218½	6
Passed tired horses;Previously trained by Frank Martin											
15Jun85- 8Bel	fst 1⅛	:45 1:092 1:493	ⒻMother Goose-G1	10 11 109 1115 719	718¾	Guerra WA	121	12.00e	60-18	Mom'sCmmnd1215½LeL'Argent121nkWillowyMood1215¼	Outrun 11
25May85- 8Bel	fst 1	:22 :441 1:09 1:354	ⒻAcorn-G1	3 8 816 616 512	413¾	Velasquez J	121	8.20	72-11	Mom'sCommand121³LeL'Argent1219½Diplomett1211¼	No factor 8
11May85- 8Bel	fst 7f	:22 :443 1:091 1:221	ⒻComely-G3	2 9 98¾ 912 610	511¾	Velasquez J	121	4.50	79-12	Mom'sCommand1214½Majestic Folly1131¾Clocks Secret1214¾	9
Off slowly											
13Apr85- 9OP	fst 1¹⁄₁₆	:23 :463 1:104 1:431	ⒻFantasy-G1	9 8 97¾ 97¼ 68½	712½	Velasquez J	121	*1.80	72-17	Rascal Lass1181½Denver Express1133½Little Biddy Comet114²	11
Bumped second turn											
4Mar85- 9GP	fst 1¹⁄₁₆	:232 :482 1:124 1:444	ⒻBonnie Miss-G3	3 6 64 86¼ 74½	22	Bailey JD	121	*.40	75-19	LucyManette121²Outstandingly121nkMickBrckn121hd	Rallied 9
21Feb85- 9GP	fst 7f	:23 :463 1:114 1:243	ⒻAlw 30000	4 6 55 42½ 41	11¼	Bailey JD	121	*.30	81-24	Outstandngly1211¼MickBrckn121½Burk'sExprss114¾	Driving 6
16Dec84- 8Hol	gd 1¹⁄₁₆	:222 :453 1:103 1:432	Hol Futurity-G1	2 10 119 74 79	810¾	Guerra WA	118	9.60	- -	Stephan'sOdyssey121¹FirstNormn1211¼RghtCon121hd	Outrun 13
2Dec84- 8Hol	fst 1¹⁄₁₆	:222 :454 1:104 1:44	ⒻHol Starlet-G1	13 11 1211 65¼ 3nk	12¾	Guerra WA	120	6.00	- -	Outstandingly1202¾Frn'sVlntn1202½WsngUp120nk	Drew clear 16
10Nov84- 2Hol	fst 1	:223 :46 1:112 1:374	ⒻBC Juv Fillies-G1	8 9 98¾ 73¾ 41¼	2½	Guerra WA	119	22.80	- -	ⒹFran'sValntn119½Outstndngly1192¼DustyHrt119nk	Rallied 11
Placed first through disqualification											
28Oct84- 3Aqu	gd 7f	:221 :452 1:093 1:223	Alw 20000	3 3 69½ 57 410	410¾	Guerra WA	114	*.90	77-14	YoungMonrch1223½SunnyCabn117³SntorBrdy1174½	No factor 7
16Aug84- 8Sar	fst 6f	:221 :45 1:102	ⒻAdirondack-G2	7 6 65¾ 44 22½	2¾	Cordero A Jr	114	*1.40	87-21	Contredanc114¾Outstndngly1142¼Orntl1144¾	Wide,ducked in 7
29Jly84- 6Bel	fst 5½f	:223 :454 :574 1:041	ⒻMd Sp Wt	4 4 11½ 11½ 15	112	Cordero A Jr	117	2.50	94-15	Outstandingly117¹²Appealing Sam1175½Alice B. Tobin117no	7
Ridden out											

Pebbles (GB)

ch. f. 1981, by Sharpen Up (Atan)–La Dolce, by Connaught
Own.– Sheikh Mohammed al Maktoum
Br.– Warren Hill Stud–Mimika Financiera (GB)
Tr.– Clive E. Brittain

Lifetime record: 15 8 4 0 $1,457,271

Date	Track	Cond/Dist	Time		Race		Pos	Jockey	Wt	Odds	Speed	Finish	Field
2Nov85-6Aqu		fm 1⅜①	:48 1:12²2:02²2:27	3↑	B C Turf-G1	13 12 13¹³ 42½ 1¹	1nk	Eddery P	123	*2.20	106-00	Pebbles123nkStrawberry Road II126¹¼Mourjane126¹	All out 14
19Oct85◆ Newmarket(GB)	gd 1¼①Str	2:04³	3↑	Champion Stakes-G1 Stk205000		1³	Eddery Pat	126	4.50		Pebbles126³Slip Anchor122hdPalace Music129¹½	10
											Rated in7th,rallied to lead over 1f out,quickly clear	
6Jly85◆ Sandown(GB)	gd 1¼①RH	2:07¹	3↑	Eclipse Stakes-G1 Stk260000		1²	Cauthen S	130	3.50		Pebbles130²Rainbow Quest133¹½Bob Back133²	4
											Rated in last,sharp run to lead 3f out,comfortably	
18Jun85◆ Ascot(GB)	gd 1¼①RH	2:05⁴	4↑	Prince of Wales's Stakes-G2 Stk72000		2¹½	Cauthen S	130	1.25		Bob Back133¹½Pebbles130noCommanche Run133¹²	4
											Tracked leader,dueled 1f out,soon headed,won duel for 2nd	
26Apr85◆ Sandown(GB)	gd 1①RH	1:42²	4↑	Trusthouse Forte Mile-G2 Stk63400		1¹½	Cauthen S	130	*1.35		Pebbles130¹Vacarme126½Sarab126²½	7
											Tracked leaders,led 3f out,held well	
20Oct84◆ Newmarket(GB)	fm 1¼①Str	2:01	3↑	Champion Stakes-G1 Stk206000		2nk	Robinson P	119	7.50		Palace Music122nkPebbles119¹½Raft122nk	15
											Rank toward rear,sharp late run,gaining late.Tolomeo 9th	
20Jun84◆ Ascot(GB)	gd 1①RH	1:40³		⑤Coronation Stakes-G1 Stk64400		2¹½	Piggott L	130	*2.75		Katies130¹½Pebbles130⁵So FIne126¾	10
											Tracked leaders,dueled over 2f out,headed 100y out	
3May84◆ Newmarket(GB)	gd 1①Str	1:38		⑤1000 Guineas Stakes-G1 Stk197000		1³	Robinson P	126	8.00		Pebbles126³Meis El-Reem126½Desirable126¾	15
											Midpack,lacked room 2f out,led 1f out,drew clear	
19Apr84◆ Newmarket(GB)	gd 7f①Str	1:24³		⑤Nell Gwyn Stakes-G3 Stk28300		1¹	Robinson P	119	7.00		Pebbles119¹Leipzig119¹½Meis El-Reem119¹	9
											Led 3f out,met challenge 1f out,held gamely	
28Sep83◆ Newmarket(GB)	gd 6f①Str	1:14⁴		⑤Cheveley Park Stakes-G1 Stk93700		2nk	Robinson P	123	33.00		Desirable123nkPebbles123noPrickle123¾	12
											Toward rear,bid 2f out,2nd 1f out,dueled late,gamely	
26Aug83◆ Goodwood(GB)	fm 7f①RH	1:28³		⑤Waterford Candelabra Stakes-G3 Stk34700		5⁵¾	Mercer J	121	3.50		Shoot Clear121¹Satinette121³Tapaculo118¹½	8
											Rank in midpack,beaten 2f out	
17Aug83◆ York(GB)	gd 6f①Str	1:12¹		⑤Lowther Stakes-G2 Stk34800		44¼	Robinson P	123	5.50		Prickle123²½Desirable123nkChapel Cottage128¹½	9
											Close up,hard ridden over 1f out,faded late	
25Jun83◆ Newmarket(GB)	gd 6f①Str	1:14¹		⑤Childwick Stud Stakes Alw9100		1³	Robinson P	125	3.30		Pebbles125³Sajeda120¾Follow Me Follow125⁵	13
											Tracked leaders,led 1f out,ridden clear	
9Jun83◆ Newbury(GB)	gd 6f①Str	1:16²		⑤Kingsclere Stakes Alw10100		1⁴	Robinson P	117	12.00		Pebbles117⁴Refill117¹Valkyrie120³	7
											Rallied to lead over 1f out,drew clear in hand	
30May83◆ Sandown(GB)	yl 5f①Str	1:05		⑤Ann Boleyn Maiden Stakes Mdn5800		14	Robinson P	123	33.00		Sperrin Mist123¹Miss Mint123²Cutlers Corner123²	17
											Never a factor	

Perrault (GB)

ch. c. 1977, by Djakao (Tanerko)–Innocent Air, by Court Martial
Own.– Baron T. van Zuylen & Fradkoff
Br.– Sasse & Sheed (GB)
Tr.– Charles Whittingham

Lifetime record: 25 9 5 5 $1,489,942

Date	Track	Cond/Dist	Time		Race		Pos	Jockey	Wt		Odds	Speed	Finish	Field
18Sep82-8Bel		fst 1¼	:47³1:11³1:36 2:01	3↑	Marlboro Cup H-G1	3 2 2¹ 8²⁴ -	-	Pincay L Jr	128	b	3.70	--	Lemhi Gold115⁸³Silver Supreme117¾Pair of Deuces116⁹	8
	Pulled up,returned lame													
29Aug82-8AP	fm 1⅜①	:46²1:10¹1:35 1:58⁴	3↑	Bud Million 1000k	7 5 5⁴ 3¹½ 1¹	1²½	Pincay L Jr	126	b	*1.30e	125-00	Perrault126²½Be My Native118nkMotavato126²¾	Drew out 14
15Aug82-8Dmr	fm 1⅛①	:48⁴1:12¹1:36²1:48²	3↑	Eddie Read H-G2	6 3 2½ 1¹ 3¹	3¹	Pincay L Jr	129	b	*.70	95-06	Wickerr119¹SpenceBay122½Perrault129¹½	Sluggish,bore out 7
13Jun82-8Hol	fst 1¼	:45²1:09¹1:33⁴1:59¹	3↑	Hol Gold Cup H-G1	4 4 4³ 2hd 1¹½	1¹	Pincay L Jr	127	b	*.70	95-15	Perrault127¹Erins Isle118¹½It's the One125²	Driving 7
18Apr82-8SA	fm *1⅜①	:46 1:58⁴ 2:45³	4↑	S Juan Capistrano H-G1	9 2 25 2hd 22½	38¾	Pincay L Jr	129	b	*.40e	90-06	Lemhi Gold121⁷Exploded118¹³Perrault129²½	Weakened 9
28Mar82-8SA	fm 1⅛①	:46²1:10²2:00 2:24	4↑	San Luis Rey-G1	5 1 1½ 11½ 1¹	13¼	Pincay L Jr	126	b	1.70e	95-05	Perrault126³Exploded126¹½John Henry126no	Ridden out 5
7Mar82-8SA	fm 1¼①	:45 1:09 1:34²1:59	4↑	S Anita H-G1	4 5 5⁷ 4¹¼ 1½	1no	Pincay L Jr	126	b	4.20e	94-07	ⒹPerrault126noJohnHenry130³½It'stheOne120nk	Drifted out 11
	Disqualified and placed second													
10Feb82-8SA	yl 1¼①	:47³ 1:38¹2:04³	4↑	Arcadia H-G3	7 4 44½ 1½ 11½	15	Pincay L Jr	124	b	*1.60	64-36	Perrault124⁵Silveyville117¹¹Le Duc de Bar111⁵	Handily 7
	Previously trained by Pierre Pelat													
8Nov81-8SA	fm 1⅛①	:47²1:10²1:59³2:23²	3↑	Oak Tree Inv'l-G1	5 5 42½ 55½ 7¹¹	7¹⁵	St Martin Y	126		7.70e	83-02	John Henry126nkSpence Bay126⁴½The Bart126no	Tired 7
4Oct81◆ Longchamp(Fr)	yl *1½①RH	2:35¹	3↑	Prix de l'Arc de Triomphe-G1 Stk591000		42¾	Samani H	130	b	27.00		Gold River127¾Bikala123noApril Run120²	24
												Tracked in 5th,finished well without threatening	
30Aug81◆ Deauville(Fr)	fm *1⅛①RH	2:58³	3↑	Grand Prix de Deauville-G2 Stk112000		1hd	St Martin Y	131	b	*1.20		Perrault131hdCastle Keep126¾Glenorum131¹½	11
												Rated in 6th,rallied to lead near line	
14Jly81◆ Saint-Cloud(Fr)	gd *1⅛①LH	2:38²	3↑	Prix Maurice de Nieuil-G2 Stk112000		12½	St Martin Y	130	b	*1.30		Perrault130²½Roi Guillaume113nkDom Menotti128²	10
												Unhurried in 5th,led 1f out,going away	
23May81◆ Evry(Fr)	sf *1½①LH	2:43³	4↑	Grand Prix d'Evry-G2 Stk60000		2hd	St Martin Y	124	b	6.50		Lancastrian124hdPerrault124²¾Kelbomec124²½	12
												Rated in 6th,rallied to lead 1f out,caught final strides	
10May81◆ Longchamp(Fr)	hy *1½①RH	2:49²	4↑	La Coupe-G3 Stk35300		1hd	St Martin Y	123	b	*2.60		Perrault123hdSon of Love123hdMonsieur Dagobert123¹	10
												Tracked in 3rd,sharp late run to lead near line	
20Apr81◆ Longchamp(Fr)	fm *1½①RH	2:33²	4↑	Prix d'Hedouville (Listed) Stk26500		31¼	St Martin Y	121	b	2.80		Lancastrian123¾En Calcat126½Perrault121¹½	10
												Rated behind leaders,bid 1f out,twice hit by rival's whip	
21Mar81◆ Saint-Cloud(Fr)	sf *1¼①LH	2:19¹	4↑	Prix Exbury-G3 Stk35500		2¹½	Lequeux A	126	b	4.50		Armistice Day128¹½Perrault126²Sabzawar123¹	9
												Rated behind slow pace,rallied to lead 1f out,headed 100y out	
19Oct80◆ Longchamp(Fr)	sf *1½①RH	2:41¹	3↑	Prix du Conseil de Paris-G2 Stk76500		53¼	Badel A	122	b	7.10		En Calcat126¹½Lancastrian124²Satilla117no	14
												Rated in 6th,led over 1f out to 170y out,faded	
31Aug80◆ Deauville(Fr)	gd *1⅝①RH	2:56	3↑	Grand Prix de Deauville-G2 Stk63700		2³	Badel A	118	b	10.10		Glenorum119³Perrault118nkVincent126²	13
												Tracked leader,led 2f to 1f out,one-paced to line	
4Aug80◆ Vichy(Fr)	gd *1½①RH	2:36	3↑	Grand Prix de Vichy-G3 Stk51000		2nk	Badel A	114		*3.00		Perouges132nkPerrault114¹½Brousoy117¹	10
												Tracked in 4th,2nd over 1f out,one paced,just saved 3rd	
14Jly80◆ Saint-Cloud(Fr)	sf *1⅝①LH	2:47	3↑	Prix Maurice de Nieuil-G2 Stk51000		33¾	Badel A	114		12.30		Buckpoint128³Proustille113³Perrault114hd	13
												Tracked in 4th,dueled briefly 1f out,led 100y out	
14Jun80◆ Saint-Cloud(Fr)	gd *1½①LH	2:46		Prix Sica Boy Alw20100		1½	Badel A	121		2.60		Perrault121½Maiymad126¹½Koreillo120hd	6
												Rated in 6th,brief bid 2f out,one-paced final furlong	
15May80◆ Longchamp(Fr)	fm *1⅝①RH	2:16¹		Prix de Nanterre Mdn12500		1½	Badel A	126		21.90		Perrault126½Tajtal126¾Dom Menotti126nk	9
												Tracked in 4th,dueled 1f out,led 100y out	
5Nov79◆ Maisns-Lfftte(Fr)	sf *1⅛①Str	2:04⁴		Prix Bagheera Mdn12200		42½	Lequeux A	123				Vezzani118²Al Ward123½Talk It Over123hd	11
												Rated in 6th,brief bid 2f out,one-paced final furlong	
5Oct79◆ Saint-Cloud(Fr)	gd *1①LH	1:47²		Prix Mieuxce Mdn12200		31¼	Lequeux A	123				Pedrillo123¾Shakapour123½Perrault123²	11
												Rated in 7th,bid 1½ furlong out,held by first two	
20Sep79◆ Maisns-Lfftte(Fr)	gd 7f①Str	1:28¹		Prix de l'Yser Mdn (FT) 12200		43½	Lequeux A	123				Arch121½Tarrago123¹Shakapour123²	13
												Chased in 6th,mild late gain	

Personal Ensign

b. f. 1984, by Private Account (Damascus)–Grecian Banner, by Hoist the Flag — Lifetime record: 13 13 0 0 $1,679,880

Own.– Ogden Phipps
Br.– Ogden Phipps (Ky)
Tr.– Claude McGaughey III

5Nov88- 6CD	my	1⅛	:474 1:12 1:381 1:52	3↑ ⒻBC Distaff-G1	6 6 58½ 58 34 1no	Romero RP	123	*.50	82-20	Personal Ensign123noWinning Colors119½Goodbye Halo1195	9
	Tight early,just up										
16Oct88- 8Bel	fst	1¼	:481 1:12 1:362 2:011	3↑ ⒻBeldame-G1	1 3 22 2hd 12 15½	Romero RP	123	*.10	92-16	PersonlEnsign1235½ClassicCrown118½ShmSy1187 Ridden out	5
10Sep88- 8Bel	fst	1	:224 :451 1:09 1:341	3↑ ⒻMaskette-G1	2 3 36 22 2hd 1¾	Romero RP	123	*.30	94-14	PersonalEnsgn123¾WinningColrs1185¼ShmSy11511¼ Driving	4
6Aug88- 8Sar	sly	1⅛	:472 1:113 1:353 1:474	3↑ Whitney H-G1	3 3 33 21 1hd 11½	Romero RP	117	*.80	96-12	PersonalEnsign1171½Gulch12417King'sSwan123 Brisk urging	3
4Jly88-10Mth	fst	1 1/16	:24 :472 1:104 1:414	3↑ ⒻMolly Pitcher H-G2	5 3 23 2½ 12½ 18	Romero RP	125	*.40	96-14	Personal Ensign1258Grecian Flight1197Le L'Argent1171	5
	Bumped,forced wide										
11Jun88- 7Bel	fst	1⅛	:471 1:112 1:353 1:473	3↑ ⒻHempstead H-G1	5 3 31½ 31 14 17	Romero RP	123	*.40	89-13	PersonlEnsgn1237HomtwnQun1092ClbbrGrl118nk Ridden out	5
15May88- 8Bel	fst	1 1/16	:23 :453 1:10 1:413	3↑ ⒻShuvee H-G1	5 3 33 2hd 1½ 11¾	Romero RP	121	*.70	94-15	Personal Ensign1211¾Clabber Girl1183½Bishop's Delight1112¾	6
	Driving										
18Oct87- 8Bel	fst	1¼	:493 1:134 1:382 2:042	3↑ ⒻBeldame-G1	8 2 2½ 13 14 12¼	Romero RP	118	1.30	76-23	PersnlEnsgn1182¼CoupdFusl1232½SlntTurn1183¾ Drew clear	10
10Oct87- 5Bel	fst	1	:223 :454 1:102 1:363	ⒻRare Perfume-G2	2 3 11 15 15 14¾	Romero RP	115	*.80	82-22	PrsnlEnsign1154¾OneFromHevn1183¾KyBd1181½ Ridden out	9
24Sep87- 5Bel	fst	1	:233 :464 1:113 1:361	3↑ ⒻAlw 33000	5 2 12½ 13 15 17¾	Romero RP	113	*.20	84-20	PersonalEnsign1137¾WithaTwist117nkRosaMay1176 Handily	5
6Sep87- 5Bel	fst	7f	:232 :462 1:103 1:231	3↑ ⒻAlw 31000	3 5 43 1hd 11½ 13¾	Bailey JD	113	*.70	86-19	PersonalEnsign1133¾ChicShirine1131¼WithTwst117½ Handily	6
13Oct86- 8Bel	fst	1	:232 :46 1:101 1:362	ⒻFrizette-G1	2 2 2½ 2hd 1hd 1hd	Romero RP	119	*.30	83-16	PersonalEnsign119hdCollins1195½FlyingKatuna119 Driving	3
28Sep86- 6Bel	my	7f	:231 :463 1:103 1:224	ⒻMd Sp Wt	5 7 22½ 11½ 17 112¾	Romero RP	117	*.90	88-15	Personal Ensign11712¾Graceful Darby1172¾Nastique1171½	7
	Hesitated start,clear										

Pleasant Colony

dkbbr. c. 1978, by His Majesty (Ribot)–Sun Colony, by Sunrise Flight — Lifetime record: 14 6 3 1 $965,383

Own.– Buckland Farm
Br.– T.M. Evans (Va)
Tr.– John P. Campo

19Sep81- 8Bel	my	1¼	:481 1:114 1:354 2:003	3↑ Marlboro Cup H-G1	5 5 79 66 45 46½	Velasquez J	123	*1.10	90-13	Noble Nashua1163¾Amber Pass1201½Temperence Hill1271¼	8
	Lacked response										
5Sep81- 8Bel	fst	1⅛	:461 1:094 1:343 1:471	3↑ Woodward-G1	7 5 66½ 55¾ 21½ 11¾	Cordero A Jr	123	*1.90	91-14	PleasantClny1231¾AmberPass1261½HerbWtr1162 Ridden out	9
15Aug81- 8Sar	sly	1¼	:463 1:112 1:372 2:034	Travers-G1	8 5 57½ 2hd 2½ 2hd	Cordero A Jr	126	*1.60e	81-20	WillowHour126hdPleasntColny1261¾LordAvie1264¼ Bore out	10
6Jun81- 8Bel	fst	1½	:482 1:141 2:04 2:29	Belmont-G1	11 11 119½ 34½ 34 31¾	Velasquez J	126	*.80	73-14	Summng126nkHghlndBld1261½PlsntColny12611 Finished well	11
16May81- 9Pim	fst	1 3/16	:473 1:113 1:362 1:543	Preakness-G1	12 8 77¼ 62¾ 2½ 11	Velasquez J	126	*1.50	97-14	Pleasant Colony1261Bold Ego1262Paristo1265 Driving	13
2May81- 8CD	fst	1¼	:451 1:101 1:36 2:02	Ky Derby-G1	7 17 1618 43 11½ 1¾	Velasquez J	126	3.50	87-12	PleasntColny126¾Woodchopper1263Partez1262¼ Ridden out	21
18Apr81- 9Aqu	fst	1⅛	:454 1:102 1:362 1:493	Wood Memorial-G1	5 3 413 37 13 13	Fell J	126	12.70	87-23	Pleasant Colony1263Highland Blade1265Cure the Blues1266	6
	Handily;Previously trained by Lee P. O'Donnell										
6Mar81- 9GP	fst	1⅛	:47 1:111 1:374 1:502	Florida Derby-G1	6 11 1118 911 57 513	Bracciale V Jr	122	3.90	67-17	Lord Avie1224½Akureyri122¾Linnleur1186 No factor	11
16Feb81- 9GP	fst	1 1/16	:241 :48 1:121 1:442	Fountain of Youth-G3	8 9 813 86 3nk 2no	Bracciale V Jr	122	16.70	79-23	Akureyri119noPleasant Colony122hdLord Avie1221½ Brushed	9
9Nov80- 8Aqu	fst	1⅛	:474 1:123 1:373 1:501	Remsen-G1	5 6 710 64¾ 32 2½	Bracciale V Jr	116	5.20	83-21	ⒹAkreyri117½PleasntColny1162FoolshTanner1133½ Impeded	8
	Placed first through disqualification										
27Oct80- 8Aqu	sf	1⅛Ⓣ	:484 1:144 1:411 1:544	Pilgrim 58k	12 12 1314 1213 57½ 2¾	Bracciale V Jr	115	42.90	69-30	Akureyri115¾Pleasant Colony1152Jetzier1222¼ Wide	14
13Oct80- 8Bow	fst	7f	:224 :453 1:11 1:25	©Mar Nursery (Div 1) 35k	10 4 75 75¼ 74 52¼	Brumfield D	113	6.50	78-23	John'sRoll116nkPantdShld114noMtchngGft119½ Lacked a bid	11
22Sep80- 2Med	fst	1 70	:224 :471 1:132 1:443	Md Sp Wt	8 7 711 49 13 19½	Asmussen CB	118	4.60	78-18	PleasntClny1189½Community Interest1185½Solid Credit1182½	8
	Drew clear										
1Sep80- 4Bel	fst	7f	:223 :461 1:112 1:243	Md Sp Wt	7 3 3½ 42 613 616	Brumfield D	118	27.90	63-21	Summing1185Academy H.1187Bay Ridge118nk Tired	7

Plugged Nickle

b. c. 1977, by Key to the Mint (Graustark)–Toll Booth, by Buckpasser — Lifetime record: 21 11 3 1 $647,206

Own.– J.M. Schiff
Br.– J.M. Schiff (Ky)
Tr.– Thomas J. Kelly

2May81- 8Aqu	gd	7f	:222 :451 1:094 1:23	3↑ Carter H-G2	2 5 45½ 54 34 53½	Vasquez J	123		*1.60	82-19	AmbrPass114½GuiltyConscienc1111Dunhm'sGft1161 Weakened	7
24Jan81- 9GP	sly	7f	:221 :444 1:093 1:223	3↑ Sprint Champ H 58k	2 4 31 34 34½ 45¼	Asmussen CB	124		1.90	86-20	King's Fashion1222½Jaklin Klugman1241½Joanie's Chief1081¼	7
	Weakened											
4Jan81- 8SA	fst	7f	:213 :433 1:073 1:202	Malibu (Div 1)-G2	4 5 75¼ 79½ 912 915	Asmussen CB	126		*1.10	83-07	Doonesbury1171¾Roper114hdUnalakleet1146 Dull try	9
1Nov80- 8Aqu	fst	1⅛	:483 1:131 1:372 1:501	3↑ Stuyvesant H-G3	7 1 11 11½ 17 16	Asmussen CB	122	b	*1.60	84-25	PluggdNickle1226Dr.Ptchs1152¾RngofLght116hd Ridden out	10
18Oct80- 8Aqu	fst	7f	:223 :443 1:084 1:212	3↑ Vosburgh-G1	5 2 31 32 21 1½	Asmussen CB	123		5.10	94-12	PluggdNickle123½JaklinKlugman1231Dav'sFrnd126¾ Driving	9
30Aug80- 8Bel	fst	1	:222 :444 1:091 1:341	Jerome H-G2	3 2 2hd 2hd 33 37	Fell J	124		2.30	90-17	JaklinKlugmn122nkFappiano1146¾PlggdNckl1244 Bore out	6
16Aug80- 8Sar	fst	1¼	:454 1:101 1:361 2:024	Travers-G1	5 4 53¼ 43½ 42¼ 48¼	Fell J	126		*1.80	78-13	TemprnceHill1261½FirstAlbrt126noAmbrPss1266¾ Weakened	9
3Aug80- 8Sar	fst	1⅛	:462 1:103 1:361 1:492	Jim Dandy-G3	3 5 45½ 3½ 1½ 1nk	Fell J	128		*.50	88-12	PluggdNckle128nkCurrntLegnd1211¼HerbWatr114½ Driving	8
20Jly80- 8Bel	fst	7f	:23 :453 1:092 1:221	3↑ Tom Fool-G3	6 2 21½ 2hd 12 13	Fell J	121		2.60	91-16	PluggedNickle1213Dr.Patches1191½Isella1191¼ Ridden out	6
3May80- 8CD	fst	1¼	:48 1:124 1:373 2:02	Ky Derby-G1	11 1 31½ 32 68½ 78¼	Thornburg B	126		2.60	79-11	GenuineRisk1211Rumbo1261JaklinKlugman1264 Weakened	13
19Apr80- 8Aqu	fst	1⅛	:472 1:113 1:37 1:504	Wood Memorial-G1	10 1 11 11 11½ 11½	Thornburg B	126		*.50	81-17	PluggdNickle1261½ColonlMoran126hdGnunRsk1213¾ Driving	11
29Mar80- 9GP	fst	1⅛	:473 1:112 1:363 1:501	Florida Derby-G1	8 2 11 12 15 16	Thornburg B	122		*.40	81-19	PluggedNickle1226NakedSky1221½LordGallant1181½ Easily	8
10Mar80- 9GP	fst	7f	:223 :452 1:10 1:223	Hutcheson 29k	2 5 63½ 31½ 12 17	Thornburg B	122		*.80	91-27	PlggdNckle1227Executon'sRson122½OneSon114½ Ridden out	6
26Feb80- 9Hia	fst	6f	:22 :452 1:094	Alw 14000	2 4 34½ 31½ 32 24	Thornburg B	122		2.30	90-22	GoldStage1224PluggdNickle122¾SonofaDodo1154 No match	7
11Nov79- 8Aqu	my	1⅛	:48 1:122 1:372 1:502	Remsen-G2	6 1 11½ 13 15 14¾	Thornburg B	122		*.80	83-24	Plugged Nickle1224¾Googolplex117½Proctor1134¾ Handily	8
27Oct79- 9Pim	fst	1 1/16	:24 :47 1:112 1:434	Lrl Futurity-G1	4 5 65½ 11 13½ 11¾	Thornburg B	122		4.60	86-14	PluggedNickle1221¾GoldStage1222NewRegent1223½ Driving	8
17Oct79- 3Aqu	fst	1	:234 :461 1:103 1:353	Alw 15000	2 3 31½ 1½ 15 19¼	Vasquez J	115		*1.00	88-17	Plugged Nickle1159¼Buck's Turn1172Self Pressured1153¾	7
	Ridden out											
6Oct79- 5Bel	fst	6f	:223 :453 1:104	Alw 16000	3 3 22 22 24 21½	Rocco J5	110	b	3.00	86-21	Speed City1151½Plugged Nickle1102Imaromeo1151½ Bumped	7
15Sep79- 8Bel	fst	7f	:222 :451 1:092 1:22	Futurity-G1	5 3 11½ 12 37 713	Cordero A Jr	122	b	7.30	79-11	Rockhill Native1224Sportful1224¼Gold Stage1221½ Tired	8
29Aug79- 7Bel	sly	6½f	:223 :46 1:104 1:17	Alw 17000	2 4 1hd 1hd 11½ 21½	Vasquez J	118		*.90	89-15	SonofaDodo1181½PluggedNickle1183½ITakeAll115nk 2nd best	4
4Aug79- 6Sar	fst	6f	:22 :452 1:104	Md Sp Wt	11 6 2hd 1½ 11 11½	Vasquez J	118		8.80	86-12	Plugged Nickle1181½Buck Island1182¾Now and Then1181	12
	Ridden out											

Precisionist

ch. c. 1981, by Crozier (My Babu)–Excellently, by Forli **Lifetime record: 46 20 10 4 $3,485,398**

Own.– F.W. Hooper
Br.– F.W. Hooper (Fla)
Tr.– L. William Donovan

24Dec88-10Crc	fst 7f	:222 :45 1:104 1:243 3↑	Sunny Isle H 87k	5 7 3nk 32½ 1215 1212½	Perret C	123	*.70	79-15	PositionLeader1171¼ThRdRolls114noAbovNorml114¾	Faltered	12
Previously trained by John W. Russell											
10Dec88-8Hol	fst 1⅛	:46 1:102 1:354 1:483 3↑	Native Diver H-G3	7 2 11 11½ 2hd 2hd	McCarron CJ	123	1.90	94-15	CutlassReality124hdPrecisonst1232¾Pynt1162	Sharp effort	7
20Nov88-8Hol	fm 1⅛Ⓣ	:463 1:101 1:342 1:463 3↑	Citation H-G2	10 1 11½ 11 12½ 2nk	McCarron CJ	121	*2.30	95-10	Forlitano118nkPrcsonst1213½SkpOutFront1171¾	Held gamely	11
5Nov88-4CD	sly 6f	:21 :441 :562 1:102 3↑	BC Sprint-G1	6 6 42¼ 43½ 53¼ 52¼	McCarron CJ	126	7.40	89-20	Gulch126¾PlaytheKing1261Aflet126½	Wide lt.,lacked rally	13
22Oct88-8Aqu	fst 1	:223 :451 1:09 1:34 3↑	NYRA Mile H 567k	4 1 1½ 1½ 21 31½	Vega A	124	3.20	94-18	Forty Niner121nkMawsuff1151½Precisionist124nk	Weakened	6
10Sep88-8Dmr	fst 1	:223 :453 1:092 1:343 3↑	Bud BC H 148k	3 1 1½ 1hd 11½ 1¾	McCarron CJ	125	*.30	95-12	Precisionist125¾Lively One1142He's a Saros1161¾	Driving	4
28Aug88-8Dmr	fst 1⅛	:453 1:093 1:343 1:471 3↑	Cabrillo H-G3	4 1 11½ 11 15 13½	McCarron CJ	122	*.20	94-12	Precisionst1223½ConqurngHro1136CrcusPrnc115½	Ridden out	4
1Aug88-8Dmr	fst 1	:222 :453 1:091 1:331 3↑	Alw 48000	5 1 12½ 11½ 13½ 14	McCarron CJ	114	*.80	102-12	Precisionist1144Candi'sGold1162½RdAttck1155½	Ridden out	5
16Jly88-8Bel	fst 7f	:23 :461 1:101 1:222 3↑	Tom Fool-G2	4 3 1½ 1hd 45½ 48¾	McCarron CJ	119	2.40	81-22	King's Swan128¾Gulch1286Abject1192	Set pace,tired	4
29Jun88-8Hol	fst 1	:224 :45 1:094 1:343 4↑	Alw 55000	6 - - - - -	McCarron CJ	115	*.90	- -	Epidaurus1151RedAttack117nkMidwestKing1161¼	Lost rider	7
Previously trained by L.R. Fenstermaker											
1Nov86-7SA	fst 1¼	:46 1:101 1:343 2:002 3↑	BC Classic-G1	2 2 21 22 23½ 32½	Stevens GL	126	1.70	84-13	Skywalker1261½Turkoman1261½Precisionist1261¾	Bumped 7/8	11
13Oct86-8SA	fst 1⅛	:463 1:102 1:354 1:482 3↑	Yankee Valor H 94k	2 1 1hd 1½ 13½ 14½	Stevens GL	127	*.60	87-19	Precisionist1274½Garthorn1242Tasso1171½	Ridden out	5
13Sep86-8Bel	fst 1¼	:473 1:11 1:354 2:00 3↑	Marlboro Cup H-G1	1 1 11½ 13 2hd 21½	Velasquez J	127	*1.20	96-11	Turkoman1231½Precisionist1278¾RooArt119½	Best of others	5
30Aug86-8Bel	fst 1⅛	:453 1:092 1:334 1:46 3↑	Woodward-G1	5 2 21½ 22½ 1hd 14¾	McCarron CJ	126	*1.20	97-14	Precisionst1264¾Ldy'sScrt1215½PrsonlFlg1105¾	Drew clear	5
16Aug86-9Mth	sly 1⅛	:464 1:103 1:353 1:484 3↑	Iselin H-G1	2 2 21½ 2hd 2hd 22¼	McCarron CJ	125	1.70	88-16	RooArt1172¼Precisionist1251¼Lady'sSecret1206	Held place	5
20Jly86-9Hol	fst 1¼	:454 1:091 1:343 2:002 3↑	Hol Gold Cup H-G1	1 2 2½ 1hd 2hd 32	McCarron CJ	127	*.90	88-06	SuperDiamond1181½Alphabatim120½Prcisionst1276	Weakened	6
1Jun86-8Hol	fst 1	:222 :441 1:082 1:333 3↑	Californian-G1	1 2 21½ 11 11½ 1½	McCarron CJ	126	*.50	95-14	Precisionist126½SuperDiamond1173½Skywalker1212½	Driving	7
13Apr86-8SA	fst 1⅛	:451 1:093 1:35 1:473 4↑	S Bernardino H-G2	1 2 1½ 12½ 1½ 1nk	McCarron CJ	126	*.80	91-15	Precisionist126nkGreinton1268Encolure11614½	Driving	4
2Mar86-8SA	fst 1¼	:451 1:091 1:34 2:00 4↑	S Anita H-G1	4 2 21 22½ 32½ 63¼	McCarron CJ	126	*1.20	86-13	Greinton122¾Herat1122Hatim118nk	Tired	13
25Jan86-8SA	fst 1 1/16	:232 :461 1:094 1:411 4↑	S Pasqual H-G2	5 2 1hd 1½ 13½ 14½	McCarron CJ	126	*.30	95-11	Precisionist1264½BareMinimum113¾MyHabitony1163½	Easily	6
30Nov85-8Hol	my 6f	:214 :443 :562 1:084 3↑	Nat'l Sprint Champ-G3	5 3 31½ 21 31 42¾	McCarron CJ	124	*.40	97-09	Pancho Villa1221Charging Falls1221½Temerity Prince122nk		6
Wide stretch											
2Nov85-3Aqu	fst 6f	:22 :444 1:082 3↑	BC Sprint-G1	2 4 31½ 32 3½ 1¾	McCarron CJ	126	3.40	99-10	Precisionist126¾Smile124¾Mt. Livermore1261¼	Driving	14
23Jun85-8Hol	fst 1¼	:461 1:093 1:342 1:582 3↑	Hol Gold Cup H-G1	6 1 12½ 12 1hd 21¾	McCarron CJ	125	*1.00	118-00	Greinton1201¾Precisionist1251¼Kings Island1125	Weakened	6
9Jun85-10Hol	fst 1	:23 :45 1:083 1:323 3↑	Californian-G1	2 2 2½ 2½ 21½ 22¾	McCarron CJ	126	*.60	107-02	Greinton1192¾Precisionist1263½LordatWar1261¼	No excuse	4
19May85-8Hol	fst 1	:221 :444 1:083 1:324 3↑	Mervyn LeRoy H-G2	5 1 1hd 12½ 14 14	McCarron CJ	126	*.60	109-08	Precisionist1264Greinton1211My Habitony1151¾	Easily	5
13Apr85-8SA	fst 1⅛	:45 1:09 1:342 1:47 4↑	San Bernardino H-G2	3 2 21½ 2½ 1½ 2nk	McCarron CJ	127	1.40	94-13	Greinton120nkPrecisionist127hdAl Mamoon11510	Gamely	6
9Mar85-8SA	fst 6½f	:213 :44 1:084 1:152 4↑	Potrero Grande H 76k	6 5 3½ 21½ 41¾ 63¾	McCarron CJ	128	*.90	89-14	FiftySixinaRow117hdHulaBlaze1201½Coyotero114nk	Drifted	6
3Feb85-8SA	fst 1¼	:453 1:094 1:343 2:001	C H Strub-G1	5 1 12½ 1½ 1hd 1no	McCarron CJ	125	*1.10	88-12	Precisionist125noGrenton117½GtDncr12616	Strong handling	5
19Jan85-8SA	fst 1⅛	:47 1:103 1:35 1:472	San Fernando-G1	5 1 12½ 11½ 12½ 14	McCarron CJ	126	*1.70	92-16	Precisionist1264Greinton120nkGate Dancer1268½	Handily	7
26Dec84-8SA	fst 7f	:222 :441 1:083 1:212	Malibu-G2	5 4 31 1hd 11 12¾	McCarron CJ	126	*1.00	93-15	Precisionist1262¾Bunker1173½Milord1154	Ridden out	6
10Nov84-7Hol	fst 1¼	:453 1:103 1:37 2:032 3↑	BC Classic-G1	7 1 3½ 613 721 727¾	McCarron CJ	122	7.70	- -	Wild Again126hd[D]Gate Dancer122½Slew o' Gold1265	Tired	8
22Sep84-10LaD	fst 1¼	:462 1:102 1:35 2:001	Super Derby-G1	1 2 11½ 13½ 13 2hd	Shoemaker W	126	1.70	107-04	GateDancer126hdPrecisionist12611BgPstol1267	Game effort	8
3Sep84-8Dmr	fst *1¼	:451 1:09 1:34 1:564 3↑	Del Mar H-G2	10 1 16 13 12½ 11¾	McCarron CJ	116	*1.20	93-18	Precisionist1161¾Pair of Deuces1163Super Diamond1172¾		10
Never headed											
19Aug84-8Dmr	fm 1⅛Ⓣ	:471 1:112 1:36 1:48	Dmr Derby H-G2	7 2 11½ 1½ 32½ 76½	McCarron CJ	124	*2.70	91-05	TsunamiSlew1193PrinceTrue119noMajesticShore115¾	Tired	12
22Jly84-8Hol	fst 1¼	:453 1:101 1:35 1:594	Swaps-G1	6 1 11½ 12 17 110	McCarron CJ	123	3.70	92-15	Precisionist12310PrincTru120hdMjstcShor1141½	Ridden out	7
30Jun84-8Hol	fst 1⅛	:46 1:103 1:354 1:483	Silver Screen H-G2	1 1 11½ 11 3nk 31½	McCarron CJ	121	*1.30	84-20	Tights119noM. Double M.1161½Precisionist1211¼	Weakened	6
5May84-8Hol	fm 1Ⓣ	:23 :454 1:10 1:341	Spotlight H 67k	1 1 11½ 11½ 34 69¾	Guerra WA	123	*1.10	87-12	Tights1193½Loft1151Prince True1182½	Bumped,bore out	10
8Apr84-8SA	fst 1⅛	:452 1:10 1:36 1:49	S A Derby-G1	4 1 13 12 13 21¼	McCarron CJ	120	*1.10	83-16	MightyAdversry1201¼Precsonst120nkPrncTru1202½	Game try	8
3Mar84-8SA	fst 1	:22 :444 1:091 1:35	San Rafael-G2	2 1 12 12½ 12½ 15	McCarron CJ	120	3.00	93-14	Precisionist1205Fali Time1221¼Commemorte118¾	Driving	6
11Feb84-8SA	fst 7f	:222 :442 1:092 1:224	San Vicente-G3	5 2 2½ 2hd 1½ 2nk	McCarron CJ	122	*.60	86-18	Fortunate Prospect119nkPrecisionist122½Tights1172	Sharp	5
25Jan84-8SA	fst 6f	:212 :441 :562 1:09	San Miguel 64k	2 3 2hd 1½ 12½ 12	McCarron CJ	122	1.30	93-19	Precisionist1222FortuntProspct1203Commmort1201½	Driving	5
18Dec83-8Hol	fst 1 1/16	:222 :454 1:101 1:413	Hol Futurity-G1	5 1 1½ 2hd 77¾ 1011½	McCarron CJ	121	*1.90	75-14	FaliTime121½BoldT.Jay1213½Lif'sMgc1183	Checked,weakened	12
25Nov83-8Hol	gd 1Ⓣ	:233 :473 1:122 1:373	Hoist the Flag (Div 2) 83k	4 1 12 12½ 11 1½	McCarron CJ	116	*.80	80-22	Precisionist116½Fali Time1202½Tights1153	Driving	8
28Oct83-8SA	fst 6½f	:214 :442 1:094 1:161	Alw 22000	1 1 21½ 1½ 13 14½	McCarron CJ	113	*1.10	89-19	Precsnst1134½DonnrPrty1173½Fortun'sKngdm1173½	Handily	7
23Jly83-8Hol	fst 6f	:214 :441 :564 1:092	Juv Champ-G2	9 1 53¼ 46½ 510 514½	Lipham T	117	*.60	75-21	Althea11710Rejected Suitor1171Auto Commander1171½		9
Lacked a rally											
13Jly83-6Hol	fst 6f	:221 :45 :573 1:101	Md Sp Wt	1 3 13 16 16 17½	Lipham T	116	*1.00	86-19	Precisionist1167½TriumphantBanner116noFaliTm1165	Easily	8

Princess Rooney

gr. f. 1980, by Verbatim (Speak John)–Parrish Princess, by Drone **Lifetime record: 21 17 2 1 $1,343,339**

Own.– Paula Tucker
Br.– Ben & Tom Roach (Ky)
Tr.– Neil Drysdale

10Nov84-5Hol	fst 1¼	:471 1:113 1:37 2:022 3↑	ⒻBC Distaff-G1	4 2 2hd 1½ 13 17	Delahoussaye E	123	*.70	- -	Princess Rooney1237Life's Magic119¾Adored1232	Drew off	7
27Oct84-7Kee	fst 1⅛	:484 1:133 1:382 1:502 3↑	ⒻSpinster-G1	7 3 34 32 11½ 16	Delahoussaye E	123	*.80	85-25	PrncssRny1236LuckyLuckyLucky119½Hthrtn1232	Drew clear	9
9Oct84-7Kee	fst *7f	1:244 3↑	ⒻAlw 22340	4 3 3nk 1½ 12 14½	Delahoussaye E	123	*.20	99-13	PrncssRooney1234½QunofSong1232½RglVlly1232	Ridden out	6
26Aug84-8Dmr	fst 1 1/16	:23 :462 1:102 1:402 3↑	ⒻChula Vista H-G3	4 3 21 2½ 12½ 12½	Valenzuela PA	123	*1.00	98-13	PrincessRney1232½FlagdLun1152¼MomnttoBuy1162½	Driving	5
15Jly84-8Hol	fst 1⅛	:461 1:10 1:341 1:461 3↑	ⒻVanity Inv'l H-G1	1 3 32½ 21 2½ 1hd	Delahoussaye E	120	5.30	98-15	Princess Rooney120hdAdored12010Salt Spring1131½	Driving	7
16Jun84-8Hol	fst 1 1/16	:23 :46 1:091 1:41 3↑	ⒻMilady H-G2	3 5 65¾ 56½ 37½ 22½	Hawley S	122	4.10	87-16	Adored1192½Princess Rooney1221Lass Trump1173½	Gamely	7
13May84-0Hol	fst 1 1/16	:23 :462 1:102 1:414 3↑	ⒻHawthorne H-G2	3 4 3½ 2½ 22 34	Delahoussaye E	123	-	82-18	Adored117noHolidayDancr1164PrncssRoony12311	Weakened	4
Exhibition race - No wagering											
30Mar84-8SA	fst 1	:22 :452 1:101 1:354 4↑	ⒻⓇSusan's Girl 44k	2 2 21 2½ 2hd 1no	Delahoussaye E	122	*1.10	89-18	PrincssRooney122noBaraLss1178½Cpch1193	Brushed,driving	4
Previously trained by Joseph H. Pierce Jr											
14Jan84-8Hia	fm 1 1/16Ⓣ	1:414 4↑	ⒻBal Harbour 23k	4 2 2hd 1½ 31½ 43	Perret C	117	-	86-14	Aspen Rose1121Pat's Joy1191Jubilous1171	Drifted out	10
No wagering,tote malfunction											
19Dec83-8Med	fst 6f	:231 :463 1:103 3↑	ⒻAlw 20000	2 5 31½ 1hd 21½ 21	Vasquez J	120	*.30	89-11	PrimDeLaPrim1121PrincssRny1203½Myr'sBst114½	Lost whip	5
Awarded first purse money;Previously trained by Frank Gomez											
28May83-8Bel	fst 1	:23 :452 1:094 1:35	ⒻAcorn-G1	6 3 21½ 21½ 23 27½	Vasquez J	121	*1.10	82-18	Ski Goggle1217½Princess Rooney121nkThirty Flags1216		9
Altered course											
6May83-8CD	fst 1⅛	:47 1:12 1:373 1:504	ⒻKy Oaks-G1	1 1 11 11 11½ 11¼	Vasquez J	121	*.20	88-15	PrincssRooney1211¼BrightCrocus1212Bemissed121½	Driving	7
23Apr83-7Kee	sly 1 1/16	:231 :463 1:113 1:452	ⒻAshland-G2	4 2 1hd 1hd 12½ 19½	Vasquez J	121	*.20	79-24	PrincssRooney1219½Shamivor1149Dcson1167½	Drifted,clear	6
13Apr83-7Kee	fst *7f	1:272	ⒻAlw 27700	8 1 21 2hd 13 110	Vasquez J	123	*.30	86-21	PrincssRney12310FiestyBelle1143½SlvrdSlk1131	Handily	8
5Mar83-7GP	fst 7f	:221 :45 1:103 1:234	Alw 30000	2 8 31½ 3½ 1½ 1½	Vasquez J	114	*.20	85-19	PrncssRny114½Morgnmorgnmorgn1152¼Alchs1152¾	Driving	8
23Oct82-6Med	fst 1 1/16	:234 :471 1:11 1:43	ⒻGardenia-G2	6 1 1½ 12 17 111	Vasquez J	121	*.30	94-11	PrincessRooney12111For Once'nMyLife1183GoldSpruce11812		7
In hand											

10Oct82- 8Bel	fst 1	:223 :461 1:113 1:39	(F)Frizette-G1	2 1 1hd 11½ 16 18	Fell J	119	*1.30 70-29	PrincessRny119⁸WinnngTck1193½WkndSurprs119nk	Handily 13
11Sep82- 9Crc	fst 7f	:222 :454 1:102 1:234	(F)Melaleuca 27k	7 1 11 12½ 18 112	Pennisi FA	116	*.20 97-14	PrincssRooney116⁶Hiusoanso114⁴Rina'sMissy114⁶	Easily 8
1Sep82- 7Crc	fst 7f	:222 :46 1:111 1:251	(F)Alw 10000	1 2 1½ 11½ 110 118	Pennisi FA	116	*.90 90-18	PrncssRooney116¹⁸CourtUnon116nkFlwlssDmond116¹¼	Easily 5
7Jun82- 7Crc	fst 5f	:223 :463 :593	(F)Alw 9500	1 3 1½ 11½ 13 14	Pennisi FA	114	*1.20 94-15	PrincssRny114⁴Ishudhdtht107noRoylty Mss117⁶	Ridden out 6
22May82- 3Crc	fst 5f	:224 :47 1:002	(F)Md Sp Wt	9 8 3nk 1hd 12 13	Pennisi FA	115	*2.10 90-14	Princess Rooney115³Rilia115²Marie V.115¹	Driving 9

Relaxing

b. f. 1976, by Buckpasser (Tom Fool)–Marking Time, by To Market
Own.– O. Phipps
Br.– O. Phipps (Ky)
Tr.– Angel Penna

Lifetime record: 28 13 2 5 $590,030

10Oct81- 8Bel	fst 1½	:48 1:123 2:021 2:282 3↑	J C Gold Cup-G1	2 10 1011 43 21½ 3¾	Cordero A Jr	123	3.30 77-14	John Henry126hdPeat Moss126¾Relaxing123hd	Wide 11
27Sep81- 8Bel	fst 1⅛	:462 1:102 1:344 1:473 3↑	(F)Ruffian H-G1	2 4 45 3½ 1hd 1¾	Cordero A Jr	123	*.90 89-19	Relaxing123¾Love Sign1205¾Jameela122²	Driving 4
5Sep81- 8Bel	fst 1⅛	:461 1:094 1:343 1:471 3↑	(F)Woodward-G1	6 9 911 88¾ 7½ 45	Velasquez J	120	4.80 86-14	PleasntColny1231¾AmberPass1261½HerbWater116²	Checked 9
23Aug81- 7Del	fst 1¼	:462 1:102 1:352 2:01 3↑	(F)Delaware H-G1	3 9 815 42 11 12¾	Cordero A Jr	119	*.60 95-15	Relaxing1192¾Wistful1211Lady of Promise1111	Ridden out 10
11Apr81- 8Aqu	fst 1¼	:472 1:11 1:353 2:004 3↑	Excelsior H-G2	6 4 48½ 318 38 35¼	Cordero A Jr	125	*.40 87-22	Irish Tower1274¾Ring of Light113½Relaxing125¹	Late bid 6
14Mar81- 9Bow	fst 1¼	:48 1:122 1:373 2:043 3↑	JB Campbell H-G2	8 6 611 42½ 1½ 13	Cordero A Jr	123	2.80 97-25	Relaxing123³Irish Tower1282½Peat Moss112¹	Easily 9
10Jan81- 8Aqu	fst 1⅛●	:483 1:132 1:384 1:514 3↑	Assault H 55k	1 4 31 2hd 15 14	Cordero A Jr	122	*.20 87-24	Relaxing122⁴StiffSentence1103½LarkOscillaton109⁵	Easily 5
13Dec80- 8Aqu	fst 1⅝●	:484 1:402 2:051 2:422 3↑	Gallant Fox-G2	3 9 913 22 1½ 12	Encinas RI	120	*.50 106-10	Relaxing120²Fool's Prayer11413Dallasite1115½	Ridden out 10
6Dec80- 8Aqu	fst 1⅛●	:474 1:12 1:372 1:491 3↑	(F)Firenze H-G2	7 7 77 63½ 11½ 14½	Velasquez J	118	*.90 100-14	Relaxing1184½SugarandSpice115noPlankton121²	Ridden out 8
27Nov80- 7Aqu	fst 1⅛	:48 1:122 1:362 1:483 3↑	(F)Handicap 35000	4 6 31½ 12½ 19 112	Cordero A Jr	122	*.70 92-24	Relaxing12212Bien Fait110³General J.108¼	Handily 6
9Nov80- 7Aqu	gd 1⅛	:50 1:162 1:42 2:182 3↑	(F)Handicap 35000	4 6 77½ 2hd 15 16½	Cordero A Jr	118	*1.20 79-21	Relaxng1186½ExactlySo110nk[D]ProudBarbara114⁴	Ridden out 7
26Oct80- 8Aqu	sf 1⅜(T)	:514 1:18 2:10 2:351 3↑	(F)Long Island H-G3	4 3 2½ 21 25 29	Cordero A Jr	113	2.70 56-35	TheVeryOne119¹Relaxing113¼ProudBarbara11313	Drifted out 5
9Oct80- 6Med	gd 1⅜(T)	:50 1:15 1:393 2:161 3↑	(F)Queen Charlotte H-G3	5 4 41¼ 4¾ 53¼ 43½	Cordero A Jr	113	4.50 80-14	TheVeryOne1191¾HeyBu115nkRiddle'sReply11413	Weakened 10
1Sep80- 8Bel	fm 1¼(T)	:474 1:114 1:362 2:004 3↑	(F)Flower Bowl H-G2	3 8 814 85¼ 78 63½	Vasquez J	112	4.70 86-12	JustaGameII124²HeyBabe114noEuphrosyne112nk	No menace 11
17Aug80- 8Sar	fm 1⅛(T)	:48 1:124 1:363 1:49 3↑	(F)Diana H-G2	2 7 47½ 42 45¼ 3nk	Vasquez J	113	14.90 82-18	JustaGameII123nkTheVeryOne117hdRelaxing113¼	Rallied 9
21Jun80- 8Bel	fm 1¼(T)	:49 1:13 1:363 2:002 3↑	(F)New York H-G3	6 3 32 21½ 45½ 65¾	Encinas RI	115	2.90 86-11	JustaGmeII121¹Poppycock112hdPleasTryHrd1132¼	Bid, tired 6

Previously trained by Floreano Fernandez

5Apr80- 8SA	fst 1 1/16	:231 :462 1:10 1:403 4↑	(S)S Lucia H 55k	7 5 69 69½ 510 37½	Pincay L Jr	120	*2.30 90-10	ImageofReality1187FlamingLeaves121¾Relaxng120½	Mild bid 8
23Mar80- 8SA	fm 1⅛(T)	:472 1:12 1:36 2:004 4↑	(S)S Barbara H-G1	4 8 87¾ 43 32 31½	McHargue DG	118	6.20 84-14	Sisterhood1181Petron'sLove114nkRelxng1181½	Lacked room 10
13Mar80- 5SA	gd 1⅛(T)	:472 1:12 1:37 1:492 4↑	(F)Alw 22000	12 7 74¼ 51¾ 41¾ 1¼	Pincay L Jr	117	*1.70 80-20	Relaxing1171¼T.V. Caper115²Island Kitty114nk	Driving 12

Previously trained by John Dunlop

10Nov79◆ Doncaster(GB)	sf *1¼(T)LH 2:214	Armistice Stakes Alw8000	11½	Carson W	129	3.30	Relaxing129½Tahitian King135⁴Wrmington135³	4
							Rated at rear, rallied to lead 150y out, driving	
29Oct79◆ Chepstow(GB)	gd 1½(T)LH 2:451	Mademoiselle Stakes (Lady Amateurs) Alw2100	11½	Guest E	140	*.65	Relaxing140½Abielle135⁷Wingau147²	19
							Progress 4f out, led over 2f out, ridden out	
13Oct79◆ Ascot(GB)	gd 1½(T)RH 2:483 3↑	(F)Princess Royal Stakes-G3 Stk30000	41½	Starkey G	118	14.00	Alia115¹Crystal Queen115hdOdeon118¾	11
							Toward rear, progress 2f out, hung	
5Oct79◆ Lingfield(GB)	fm 1¼(T)LH 2:064	Hartfield Stakes Alw3900	17	Carson W	127	*2.00	Relaxing1277Tantot1172Persian Risk1202½	10
							5th stretch 2½ out, led over 1f out, easily clear	
22Sep79◆ Ayr(GB)	yl 1¼(T)LH 2:143	Brodick Alw4500	46½	Johnson E	128	*1.10	Pinaka134⁴Pendles Secret128¾Theydon Prince131½	10
							Trailed, 7th 2f out, mild late gain	
13Sep79◆ Salisbury(GB)	gd 1¼(T)RH 2:094	(F)Netheravon Maiden Stakes Mdn2900	18	Starkey G	123	*3.30	Relaxing1238Tantot123noRed Jay1231½	11
							Long drive to lead over 1f out, quickly clear	
31Aug79◆ Sandown(GB)	gd 1¼(T)RH 2:111	Autumn Maiden Stakes Mdn3500	76	Carson W	123	7.00	Wearmouth1261½Hay Reef1232Jakaroo126½	12
							Sweating, never a factor	
18May79◆ Newbury(GB)	gd 1⅜(T)LH -	Shaw Maiden Stakes Mdn5000	77¼	Muddle R	123	5.50	Tyrondero126¹Beau Reef126hdBalinger126³	19
							Toward rear, some late progress. Time not taken	
21Apr79◆ Newbury(GB)	gd 7f(T)Str 1:303	Bucklebury Maiden Stakes Mdn (FT)4400	24	Piggott L	123	*1.60	Sandfornia123⁴Relaxing123½Hay Reef123nk	14
							Midpack, bid over 1f out, no chance with winner	

Rhythm

b. c. 1987, by Mr. Prospector (Raise a Native)–Dance Number, by Northern Dancer
Own.– Ogden Mills Phipps
Br.– Ogden Mills Phipps (Ky)
Tr.– Claude McGaughey III

Lifetime record: 20 6 3 4 $1,592,532

8Jun91- 7Bel	fst 1⅛	:442 1:084 1:342 1:463 3↑	Nassau County H-G2	4 9 917 781½ 77 713¾	Cordero A Jr	115	6.60e 82-08	Festin1167Gervazy112nkFarma Way1232¼	Flattened out 10
17May91- 8Bel	fst 1	:234 :464 1:11 1:361 3↑	Handicap 47000	5 4 42 32 34 34¾	Cordero A Jr	122	*1.00 84-14	FarewllWv114noSoundofCnnons1164¾Rhythm122⁵	Lacked rally 6
23Mar91-11GP	fst 1¼	:472 1:11 1:351 2:01 3↑	Gulf Park H-G1	6 7 710 612 614 613½	Perret C	118	5.30 83-17	Jolie's Halo1193Primal117noChief Honcho1181¼	No rally 8
9Feb91- 9GP	fst 1⅛	:454 1:102 1:35 1:472 3↑	Donn H-G1	3 12 1213 1111 911 814¼	Perret C	121 b	*1.60 86-06	Jolie'sHalo1148SportsView116nkSecretHello116hd	No rally 12
26Jan91- 8GP	fst 1⅛	:242 :481 1:12 1:422 3↑	Creme Fraiche 75k	5 3 34½ 33 31½ 2nk	Perret C	121 b	*.60 101-10	NewYrkSwll111nkRhythm121½Mrcds Won112⁷	Drifted, missed 5
27Oct90- 9Bel	fst 1¼	:454 1:094 1:353 2:021 3↑	BC Classic-G1	7 11 1173 63¾ 811 813½	Perret C	121 b	*2.60 72-15	Unbridled1211IbnBey126¹ThirtySixRd121no	Bid, tired badly 14
15Sep90- 8Bel	fst 1⅛	:451 1:083 1:331 1:454 3↑	Woodward H-G1	3 7 612 66½ 64½ 32¾	Perret C	120 b	3.10 102-09	Dispersal123½QuietAmercn1171½Rhythm120no	Belated rally 7
18Aug90- 7Sar	fst 1¼	:472 1:112 1:362 2:023	Travers-G1	3 11 1311 79½ 32½ 13½	Perret C	126 b	6.50 91-09	Rhythm1263½ShtGnSctt126nkSrRchrdLws1263½	Wide, driving 13
28Jly90-10Mth	fst 1⅛	:471 1:111 1:363 1:491	Haskell Inv'l H-G1	5 5 42 3nk 41¾ 32½	Perret C	121 b	2.90 86-10	RstlssCon1182¼BarondVaux117nkRhythm121no	Lacked fin bid 7
30Jun90- 8Bel	fst 1⅛	:462 1:094 1:343 1:472	Dwyer-G2	3 3 32 21 1½ 12½	Perret C	123	1.30 95-03	Profit Key1231½Rhythm123½Graf114²	Bore out, gamely 4
9Jun90- 7Bel	gd 1⅛	:474 1:122 1:363 1:49	Colin-G3	5 5 65½ 62½ 2½ 121	Perret C	122	*.60 89-13	Rhythm1222¼Senator to Be1151½Paradise Found1152½	8
	Wide, good handling								
21May90- 7Bel	fst 7f	:224 :452 1:094 1:222 3↑	Alw 33000	1 5 65 53 21 11½	Perret C	113	*1.10 92-20	Rhythm113½SenatortoBe1122½FarewllWave119⁵	Going away 7
7Apr90- 8Aqu	gd 1	:22 :441 1:082 1:334	Gotham-G2	1 5 53¾ 65½ 68½ 57¾	Perret C	121	3.60 85-14	ThirtySixRed114½SenorPete123½BurntHlls1141¾	No factor 10
3Mar90-10GP	fst 1 1/16	:232 :473 1:122 1:443	Fountain of Youth-G2	6 3 41½ 54½ 1012 108¼	Perret C	122	2.90 80-14	Shot Gun Scott122½Smelly119noUnbridled117¾	Faltered 13
10Feb90-10GP	fst 7f	:214 :442 1:102 1:242	Hutcheson-G3	9 1 78 77¾ 47½ 78	Perret C	122	*.90 76-18	Housebuster1193Yonder1221Stalker114¾	Tired 11
4Nov89- 8Bel	fst 1 1/16	:232 :462 1:111 1:433	BC Juvenile-G1	3 5 52¾ 11 12 12	Perret C	122	2.60e 93-01	Rhythm122²Grand Canyon122½Slavic122¹	Driving 12
14Oct89- 8Bel	fst 1⅛	:231 :46 1:11 1:373	Champagne-G1	1 4 33½ 1hd 2½ 1½	Perret C	122	2.30e 77-26	Adjudicating114⁶Rhythm1223Senor Pete1222¼	Gamely 6
24Sep89- 6Bel	fst 7f	:23 :471 1:13 1:253	Alw 30000	4 6 52¾ 52½ 1½ 14	Cordero A Jr	122	*.50 74-21	Rhythm122⁴Hot Candy1173½Give a Buck117²	Ridden out 7
15Sep89- 9Bel	gd 7f	:223 :453 1:103 1:24	Md Sp Wt	3 4 42 2½ 11 13	Perret C	118	2.40 82-18	Rhythm118³ThirtySixRed1182¼JamesHarper1189¼	Ridden out 10
11Aug89- 6Sar	fst 5f	:223 :463 :59	Md Sp Wt	1 4 42½ 31½ 34½ 37¾	Perret C	118	*.80 83-19	Three Way Split1187Prone118¾Rhythm118nk	Weakened 8

Risen Star

dkbbr. c. 1985, by Secretariat (Bold Ruler)–Ribbon, by His Majesty — **Lifetime record: 11 8 2 1 $2,029,845**

Own.– L. Roussel III & Lamarque Stable
Br.– Arthur Hancock III & Leone J. Peters (Ky)
Tr.– Louie J. Roussel III

11Jun88-8Bel	fst	1½	:471 1:114 2:013 2:262	Belmont-G1	5	2	24	16	110	114¾	Delahoussaye E	126	*2.10	88-13	RisenStar12614¾Kingpost1262Brian'sTime12611¼ Ridden out	6
21May88-9Pim	gd	1 3/16	:47 1:111 1:363 1:561	Preakness-G1	3	4	31½	31	12	11¼	Delahoussaye E	126	6.80	86-11	RisenStar1261¼Brian'sTime1261¼WinnngColors1212½ Driving	9
7May88-8CD	fst	1¼	:464 1:112 1:36 2:021	Ky Derby-G1	1	13	1315	99¼	67½	33¼	Delahoussaye E	126	5.50	83-11	WinningColors121nkFortyNiner1263RisnStr126½ Very wide	17
16Apr88-8Kee	fst	1 1/16	:24 :48 1:122 1:424	Lexington-G2	5	5	53½	53½	2½	1hd	Vasquez J	118	3.20	92-18	Risen Star118hdForty Niner12112Stalwars1182 Driving	5
13Mar88-11FG	fst	1 1/16	:241 :473 1:12 1:431	La Derby-G3	1	6	67½	67	42½	11¾	Romero SP	120	2.60	96-14	Risen Star1201¾Word Pirate118¾Pastourelles1181¾ Driving	7
27Feb88-10FG	fst	1 40	:233 :461 1:122 1:40	Derby Trial 23k	11	9	914	55½	22	11	Romero SP	120	*1.10	93-20	Risen Star1201Pastourelles1153½Jim's Orbit1221 Driving	12
6Feb88-10FG	gd	1 1/16	:24 :473 1:124 1:463	Lecomte H 24k	7	5	55	21	21	21¼	Romero SP	122	*.30e	78-21	Pastourelles1131¼RisenStar1223RunPaulRun1141 Held place	7
2Jan88-8FG	gd	1 1/16	:24 :49 1:141 1:473	©Alw 9200	5	5	52½	11	14	110	Romero SP	119	*.30	74-26	Risen Star11910Mr. Buttercup1161Proper Duty1194½ Easily	7
6Dec87-9FG	fm	*7½fⓉ	:241 :481 1:144 1:341	©Alw 8400	10	12	914	65¼	13	14	Romero SP	120	*.40	78-18	Risen Star1204Quick Bob1174½Jacumlea1201 Easily	12
	Previously owned by L.J. Roussel III;previously trained by Rene Gebbia															
11Oct87-10LaD	fst	7f	:231 :462 1:102 1:223	Sport of Kings Fut 210k	5	3	31½	32	36	215	Snyder L	121	2.40	80-21	Success Express12115Risen Star1212¾Big Snoz12113 Tired	6
24Sep87-9LaD	fst	6½f	:222 :453 1:12 1:19	Minstrel 40k	3	9	53½	66¼	43½	11	Walker BJ Jr	112	*.90	80-27	RisnStr1121BoldChadr1151½SholSrchr115½ Soundly bumped	9

Roving Boy

b. c. 1980, by Olden Times (Relic)–Black Eyed Lucy, by Prince Royal II — **Lifetime record: 9 6 2 0 $843,675**

Own.– R.E. Hibbert
Br.– Robert E. Hibbert (Ky)
Tr.– Joseph Manzi

2Nov83-8SA	fst	1 1/16	:224 :46 1:104 1:433	Alibhai H-G3	6	4	33	43	21½	1no	Delahoussaye E	124	*.40	83-23	Roving Boy124noHula Blaze1102½Lagoon Lover115no	6
	Broke down past finish line															
14Oct83-8SA	fst	6½f	:213 :444 1:093 1:154 3↑	Alw 30000	2	5	44¼	34	11½	2hd	Delahoussaye E	115	*.50	91-19	CivicLeader117hdRovingBoy1153ShadyFox1106 Just missed	7
12Dec82-8Hol	fst	1 1/16	:222 :454 1:101 1:414	Hol Futurity 761k	1	6	41	2hd	1hd	1nk	Delahoussaye E	121	1.70	86-20	RovingBoy121nkDesertWine1212FifthDivision1214 Driving	9
30Oct82-8SA	fst	1 1/16	:223 :45 1:091 1:413	Norfolk-G2	1	5	34	3nk	11½	14½	Delahoussaye E	118	*1.50	93-10	Roving Boy1184½Desert Wine1183½Aguila1181¼ Easily	9
8Sep82-8Dmr	sl	1	:222 :461 1:123 1:384	Dmr Futurity-G2	8	5	35½	2½	2½	1½	Delahoussaye E	117	*1.60	74-30	Roving Boy117½Desert Wine12011Balboa Native1144 Driving	9
25Aug82-8Dmr	fst	1	:222 :454 1:094 1:352	Balboa 53k	2	5	43½	43	32	11½	Delahoussaye E	115	6.90	91-12	RvngBoy1151½Encourgr1152½FullChok1174½ Bobbled,driving	5
13Aug82-6Dmr	fst	1	:221 :46 1:121 1:372	©Md Sp Wt	7	1	12	12	13	16	Delahoussaye E	117	*2.00	81-17	RvingBoy1176Morry'sChamp1173½DebonairHerc1172 Driving	10
31Jly82-6Dmr	fst	6f	:22 :453 :584 1:113	©Md Sp Wt	8	5	4¾	2hd	2hd	2½	Delahoussaye E	118	19.90	79-15	Be a Scholar118½Roving Boy1184Jolly Be First1182½ Sharp	9
21Jly82-6Dmr	fst	5½f	:22 :453 1:04	©Md Sp Wt	2	10	1116	1121	1123	715	Pincay L Jr	118	7.70	76-17	EchoGrande1181½Mezzo1181¼InflationBeater1186 No threat	11

Royal Heroine (Ire)

dkbbr. f. 1980, by Lypheor (Lyphard)–My Sierra Leone, by Relko — **Lifetime record: 21 10 4 2 $1,217,397**

Own.– R.E. Sangster
Br.– B.L. Ryan (Ire)
Tr.– John H.M. Gosden

25Nov84-8Hol	yl	1⅛Ⓣ	:484 1:122 1:361 1:492 3↑	ⒻMatriarch-G1	1	2	2½	2½	2hd	11	Toro F	123	*.80	83-17	Royal Heroine1231Reine Mathilde1202Sabin1232¼ Driving	6
10Nov84-4Hol	fm	1Ⓣ	:223 :453 1:084 1:323 3↑	BC Mile-G1	10	5	63¾	53	3½	11½	Toro F	123	*1.70e	105-01	Royal Heroine1231½Star Choice126nkCozzene126nk Driving	10
9Sep84-8Dmr	fm	1⅛Ⓣ	:484 1:124 1:363 1:482 3↑	ⒻRamona H-G1	7	5	62¾	61¾	65¾	22½	Toro F	126	*.60	93-05	Flag de Lune1152½Royal Heroine126hdSalt Spring115¾ Wide	9
26Aug84-9AP	fm	1¼Ⓣ	:482 1:122 1:372 2:012 3↑	Bud Arl Million-G1	1	1	1½	1½	2hd	21¾	Toro F	122	14.70	85-15	JohnHenry1261¾RoyalHeroin1223GtodlSol126no Best of rest	12
11Aug84-8Dmr	fm	1Ⓣ	:23 :47 1:113 1:351 3↑	ⒻPalomar H-G3	8	4	33	32	21½	1nk	Toro F	125	*.60e	97-06	ⒹRoyal Heroine125nkMoment to Buy115¾L'Attrayante1203	8
	Drifted in,brushed;Disqualified and placed third															
1Jly84-8Hol	fm	1⅛Ⓣ	:464 1:104 1:343 1:471 3↑	ⒻBeverly Hills H-G2	8	7	76	63	1hd	11¾	Toro F	123	*.70	94-06	RylHeroine1231¾Adored121nkComedyAct118nk Bumped,clear	9
17Jun84-8Hol	fm	1 1/16Ⓣ	:23 :471 1:101 1:401 3↑	Inglewood H-G3	8	6	53¼	63¾	41	1½	Toro F	116	4.60	98-06	RoyalHeroine116½BelBolide120½VinStBenet118hd Driving	13
18Mar84-8SA	fm	1⅛Ⓣ	:46 1:104 1:351 1:482 4↑	ⒻSanta Ana H-G1	7	5	-	-	-	-	Toro F	122	2.90	- -	Avigaition1182¾Pride of Rosewood1161¾L'Attrayante122¾	9
	Fell over downed rival															
20Nov83-6Hol	fm	1⅛Ⓣ	:463 1:113 1:354 1:481	Hol Derby (Div 1)-G1	5	5	57	1hd	11	1¾	Toro F	119	3.70	89-13	RoyalHeroine119¾Interco1223½PacMani1223 Brushed,driving	11
	Previously trained by Michael R. Stoute															
6Nov83-8SA	fm	1¼Ⓣ	:474 1:134 1:374 2:021 3↑	ⒻYellow Ribbon-G1	9	9	75½	86¼	86¾	710	Swinburn WR	119	40.20	66-24	Sangue1231½L'Attrayante1192Infinite119½ Outrun	12
2Oct83♦ Longchamp(Fr)	fm	*1⅛ⓉRH	1:50 3↑	ⒻPrix de l'Opera-G2 Stk63700						11½	Swinburn WR	123	*2.40		Royal Heroine1231½Fly With Me121nkLittle Meadow121hd Rated in 6th,split horses to lead 1f out,ridden out	18
10Sep83♦ Doncaster(GB)	sf	1ⓉLH	1:424 3↑	ⒻSceptre Stakes (Listed) Stk25000						1nk	Swinburn WR	122	*1.10		Royal Heroine122nkFlamenco1181Gaygo Lady119¾ Always close up,led 3f out,held gamely	6
12Aug83♦ Newbury(GB)	gd	*7fⓉLH	1:282 3↑	ⒻHungerford Stakes-G3 Stk35900						22½	Swinburn WR	118	4.00		Salieri1232½Royal Heroine1181½Tecorno1212½ Tracked in 5th,bid over 1f out,always held by winner	10
6Jly83♦ Newmarket(GB)	gd	1ⓉStr	1:411 3↑	Child Stakes-G3 Stk13200						12	Swinburn WR	117	*2.00		Royal Heroine1172Flamenco1201½Lindas Fantasy1173 Tracked leader,led 3f out,ridden out.Annie Edge 5th	8
4Jun83♦ Epsom(GB)	sf	1½ⓉLH	2:404	ⒻEnglish Oaks-G1 Stk205000						718¼	Swinburn WR	126	4.50		Sun Princess12612Acclimatise1262½New Coins1261½ Lathered up,rated in 6th,never threatened	15
28Apr83♦ Newmarket(GB)	gd	1ⓉStr	1:413	Ⓕ1000 Guineas-G1 Stk140000						21½	Swinburn WR	126	10.00		Ma Biche1261½ⒹRoyal Heroine126hdFavoridge126½ Led 2f out,faded,back up for 2nd;Disqualified from 2nd place purse	18
14Apr83♦ Newmarket(GB)	gd	7fⓉStr	1:30	ⒻNell Gwyn Stakes-G3 Stk23700						31½	Swinburn WR	119	3.00		Favoridge1191½Annie Edge119hdRoyal Heroine1191 Tracked leaders,bid 1½f out,saved 3rd	9
18Aug82♦ York(GB)	gd	6fⓉStr	1:13	ⒻLowther Stakes-G2 Stk34200						21½	Starkey G	123	*1.75		Habibti1231½Royal Heroine1233Annie Edge123nk Tracked in 4th,rallied to lead 1f out,soon headed,2nd best; Previously trained by Mick Ryan	8
24Jly82♦ Ascot(GB)	gd	6fⓉStr	1:152	ⒻPrincess Margaret (Listed) Stk9800						12½	Robinson P	123	4.00		Royal Heroine1242½Henry's Secret127noBright Crocus1271½ Tracked leader,led 1f out,drew clear	6
7Jly82♦ Newmarket(GB)	gd	6fⓉStr	1:131	ⒻPrincess Maiden Stakes Mdn7300						13	Robinson P	123	12.00		Royal Heroine1233Montrevie1233The Babe123¾ Tracked leaders,led 1½f out,easily clear	20
26Jun82♦ Doncaster(GB)	yl	6fⓉStr	1:153	ⒻLonsdale Maiden Stakes Mdn1800						43½	Lowe J	123	33.00		Bright Cone123noSuper Entente1233Jumaireh123½ Prominent,bid 2f out,one-paced final furlong	15

Sacahuista

b. f. 1984, by Raja Baba (Bold Ruler)–Nalees Flying Flag, by Hoist the Flag
Own.– Beal & French Jr
Br.– G. Watts Humphrey Jr & William S. Farish (Ky)
Tr.– D. Wayne Lukas

Lifetime record: 21 6 7 2 $1,298,842

15Oct88- 3Bel	fst	6f	:221 :451 1:094	3↑ⒻAlw 41000	1 2 47½ 48 35 2¾	Romero RP	115	b	*.60	89-17	Starita115¾Sachust1154¾Poculton1156½	Wide,finished fast	4
25Sep88- 8Bel	fst	1⅛	:47 1:11 1:352 1:48	3↑ⒻRuffian H-G1	1 6 73½ 1115 1123 1023	Stevens GL	119	b	*1.50e	64-16	ShamSay113¾ClassicCrwn1156MakeChang114nk	Bobbled start	11
12Aug88- 8Sar	fst	7f	:221 :442 1:084 1:213	3↑ⒻBallerina-G1	6 2 41½ 53 57½ 57¾	Santos JA	119	b	3.00	86-08	Cadillacing116nkThirty Zip116hdReady Jet Go1115½	Tired	6
21Nov87- 3Hol	fst	1¼	:471 1:113 1:364 2:024	3↑ⒻBC Distaff-G1	5 1 12 12½ 12½ 12¼	Romero RP	119	b	2.90	78-12	Sacahuista1192¼Clabber Girl1234Oueee Bebe119hd	Driving	6
31Oct87- 8Kee	fst	1⅛	:462 1:101 1:354 1:483	3↑ⒻSpinster-G1	2 1 1½ 11 12½ 13	Romero RP	119	b	*1.40e	94-14	Sacahuista1193Ms. Margi1192½Tall Poppy123no	Ridden out	13
27Sep87- 8Bel	fst	1⅛	:462 1:092 1:35 1:483	3↑ⒻRuffian H-G1	12 1 1hd 11 12½ 1hd	Migliore R	114	b	*.40e	84-19	[D]Sacahuista114hdCoupdeFusil1171¾ClbbrGrl112½	Lugged in	12
	Disqualified and placed third												
12Sep87- 9Pha	fst	1 1/16	:233 :47 1:103 1:424	ⒻCotillion H-G3	4 1 1hd 1½ 1½ 1nk	Perret C	119	b	4.30	90-18	[D]Sacahuist119nkSlntTurn1187½SnglBld1175	Caused bumping	8
	Disqualified and placed second												
6Aug87- 8Sar	fst	7f	:213 :433 1:08 1:21	ⒻTest-G2	11 3 53½ 45½ 48½ 59¼	McCarron CJ	121	b	6.90e	88-14	VerySbtle1215¼UptheApalache1213½SlntTrn121hd	Weakened	14
19Jly87- 8Hol	fst	1¼	:453 1:091 1:344 2:003	3↑ⒻVanity Inv'l H-G1	1 4 46 55½ 55½ 511¼	Antley CW	109	b	8.30	78-07	Infinidad1136½NorthSidr1212¾ClbbrGrl1151¾	Wide into str	7
12Jly87- 8Hol	fst	1⅛	:461 1:101 1:354 1:483	ⒻHol Oaks-G1	3 2 1hd 2hd 1½ 2½	Stevens GL	121	b	*1.60	93-09	PerchancetoDream121½Sachst1215PnBlLdy1212	Outfinished	6
20Jun87- 8Hol	fst	1 1/16	:222 :453 1:101 1:43	ⒻPrincess-G2	1 4 41½ 31½ 22½ 2nk	Stevens GL	122	b	2.30	94-11	RansomedCaptive116nkSchst1221¼VrySbtl1222	Saved ground	6
6Jun87- 8Hol	fst	7f	:22 :443 1:093 1:223	ⒻRailbird-G3	3 2 2½ 32 33½ 36½	Stevens GL	122	b	1.90	84-17	VerySbtle1225½JoeytheTrp1171Schust122	No late response	4
30Nov86- 8Hol	fst	1	:224 :454 1:101 1:36	ⒻHol Starlet-G1	3 3 2½ 21½ 22½ 2½	Pincay L Jr	120	b	*1.20	82-16	Very Subtle120½Sacahuista12011Infringe1201¼		6
	Bobbled break,lugged out backside,through stretch												
1Nov86- 2SA	fst	1 1/16	:221 :453 1:101 1:431	ⒻBC Juv Fillies-G1	8 5 57 79 713 410¾	Pincay L Jr	119	b	*1.90	74-13	Brave Raj1195½Tappiano1193½Saros Brig1191¾	Rallied	12
5Oct86- 8SA	fst	1 1/16	:22 :453 1:102 1:443	ⒻOak Leaf-G1	5 3 21½ 2½ 1½ 12¼	McCarron CJ	115	b	1.90	78-15	Sacahuista1152¼Silk'sLady115nkDelicatVn115nk	Drew clear	7
10Sep86- 8Dmr	fst	1	:222 :452 1:101 1:353	Dmr Futurity-G1	1 1 1hd 2½ 1hd 2no	Day P	117	b	4.90	90-11	Qualify114noSacahuista117½Brevito1165	Sharp	9
	Previously owned by L.R. French Jr												
29Aug86- 6AP	fst	7f	:221 :45 1:101 1:232	ⒻArl-Wash Lassie-G1	6 2 2½ 2hd 2hd 21¼	McCarron CJ	122	b	3.20	84-19	DelicateVine1221¼Sacahuista122¾RulingAngl1221½	2nd best	6
14Aug86- 8Sar	fst	6f	:22 :452 1:11	ⒻAdirondack-G2	6 1 2½ 2hd 1hd 11	McCarron CJ	119	b	*.30	85-20	Sacahuista1191Collins1144½Release the Lyd1162	Driving	7
30Jly86- 8Sar	fst	6f	:22 :452 1:103	ⒻSchuylerville-G3	5 2 21 1hd 12½ 13½	McCarron CJ	115	b	*2.20	87-13	Sacahuist1143½OurLttlMrg1141¾Collns1144	Leaned in,clear	9
11Jly86- 6Hol	fst	5½f	:222 :454 :574 1:042	ⒻMd Sp Wt	10 1 11 1hd 14 19	McCarron CJ	118	b	9.20	92-14	Sacahuista1189Ninepaytheline113nkAlwysWomn1182½	Easily	11
5Jun86- 5Hol	fst	5f	:222 :462 :593	ⒻMd Sp Wt	3 4 88½ 810 67 56¼	Valenzuela PA	118		14.90	82-16	PrchncetoDream118hdRomnGem1184QuickMssngr1181	Outrun	9

Safely Kept

dkbbr. f. 1986, by Horatius (Proudest Roman)–Safely Home, by Winning Hit
Own.– Jayeff B Stable & Weisbord
Br.– Mr & Mrs David Hayden (Md)
Tr.– Alan E. Goldberg

Lifetime record: 31 24 2 3 $2,194,206

4Oct91- 9Med	fst	6f	:22 :442 1:084	3↑ⒻBud BC H-G3	4 2 21½ 2½ 1hd 12	Stevens GL	128	L	*.40	98-12	SafelyKpt1282BrghtCndls1141¾DvlshTouch1152¾	Ridden out	7
8Sep91- 3Pim	fst	6f	:23 :461 :582 1:11	3↑ⒻDistaff H 95k	5 4 1hd 1hd 1hd 1½	Stevens GL	130	L	*.30	90-12	Safely Kept130½In the Curl1181¾Wood So112nk	Driving	6
4Aug91- 9Mth	my	1 70	:23 :461 1:101 1:40	3↑ⒻBud BC H-G3	3 1 1½ 32 33 34¾	Wilson R	123	L	*.70	91-08	Toffeefee1154½Colonial Waters117nkSafely Kept1233¼		7
	Not good enough												
20Jly91- 9Lrl	fst	6f	:213 :434 :57 1:083	3↑F J DeFrancis 300k	5 6 67 32½ 32½ 36¼	Black CA	121	L	2.50	92-15	Housebuster1265Clever Trevor1231¼Safely Kept1213¼		6
	Dwelt,not driven late												
30Jun91- 8AP	fst	7f	:223 :453 1:101 1:23	3↑ⒻBud BC H 155k	1 4 11 11½ 13½ 17½	Perret C	126	L	*.30	88-17	SaflyKpt1267½NurseDopey1184½TokenDanc1142½	Ridden out	7
6Jun91- 8Bel	fst	6f	:223 :454 1:10	3↑ⒻGenuine Risk-G2	3 1 11½ 1½ 1½ 12	Perret C	122		*.20	90-12	Safely Kept1222Missy's Mirage1093Token Dance1173	Easily	5
11May91- 9GS	fst	6f	:214 :443 1:082	3↑ⒻBud BC H-G3	4 2 11 1½ 1½ 11¼	Black CA	128	L	*.30	101-09	SafelyKept1281¼AvieJane1178½TokenDance1159½	Ridden out	4
	Previously owned by Jayeff B. Stable & Weisbord												
27Oct90- 3Bel	fst	6f	:214 :442 1:093	3↑BC Sprint-G1	4 1 11 2hd 1hd 1nk	Perret C	123		12.20	91-11	Safely Kept123nkDayjur1234Black Tie Affair1262¼		14
	Saved ground,gamely												
14Oct90- 8Bel	fst	6f	:214 :441 1:08	3↑Boojum H-G3	4 1 21 21 42½ 42¾	Perret C	120		*1.60	96-09	Carson City1161Mr. Nickerson1211¼Once Wild118½	Weakened	6
22Sep90- 9Med	sly	6f	:213 :442 1:091	3↑ⒻBud BC-G3	1 5 1hd 2hd 1hd 1nk	Krone JA	127	L	*.50	96-12	Safely Kept127nkSexy Slew1151¾Diva's Debut1202½	Driving	7
9Sep90- 2Pim	fst	6f	:223 :454 :574 1:11	3↑ⒻDistaff H 95k	6 3 2hd 1½ 13½ 11¼	Krone JA	126	L	*.20	91-14	Safely Kept1261¼Amy Be Good1172¼Run Spot1133½	Easily	6
18Aug90- 8Pim	fst	6f	:22 :444 :564 1:09	3↑De Francis Dash 350k	5 1 2hd 42½ 56 46½	Antley CW	121	L	*.80	94-08	NorthernWolf1202½Glitterman1241½Sewickly1262½	Willingly	7
4Jly90-10FL	fst	6f	:213 :434 1:094	3↑Bud BC 183k	1 3 1½ 1hd 13 12¼	Perret C	117		*.30	97-15	Safely Kept1172¼Northern Crush1134For Really1092	Easily	7
7Jun90- 8Bel	fst	6f	:22 :451 1:101	3↑ⒻGenuine Risk-G2	3 3 1½ 12 13½ 13	Perret C	122		*.20	88-15	SafelyKept1223Div'sDbut11913Lvtton1178	As rider pleased	4
12May90- 8GS	fst	6f	:22 :45 1:092	3↑ⒻBud BC-G3	1 3 11 11 13 14	Perret C	125		*.05	96-13	SafelyKept1254MollyBolt1113½ProudEmilia112½	Good effort	6
18Apr90- 8Kee	fst	6f	:221 :452 1:102	3↑ⒻTbred Club of Am-G3	2 4 11 11½ 13½ 13½	Perret C	123		*.20	90-11	SafelyKpt1233½Volterra112noMdcnWomn1173	Sluggish start	5
1Mar90-10GP	fst	6f	:214 :451 1:11	3↑ⒻAlw 24000	3 2 2hd 1hd 14 15½	Perret C	122		*.20	90-19	SafelyKept1225½Cutlasee1152¼SpiritofFighter1191¾	Easily	6
4Nov89- 4GP	fst	6f	:214 :44 1:09	3↑BC Sprint-G1	13 1 11½ 1½ 12 2nk	Perret C	121		6.90	101-04	Dancing Spree126nkSafely Kept121nkDispersal1241	Gamely	13
	Previously owned by B. Weisbord												
8Oct89-10Pim	fst	6f	:23 :461 :582 1:111	ⒻColumbia 100k	5 2 11 11½ 13 14½	Perret C	122		*.10	90-18	SafelyKept1224½Cojinx119½KathleentheQueen1173	Drew off	5
10Sep89- 2Pim	fst	6f	:223 :45 :57 1:10	3↑Ⓕ[R]Distaff H 95k	2 1 1½ 11½ 13½ 14¾	Perret C	124		*.10	96-09	SafelyKept1244¾IntheCurl116¾RunSpot1101¼	Bumped,clear	6
3Aug89- 8Sar	fst	7f	:22 :442 1:081 1:212	ⒻTest-G1	3 5 11 11 14 11½	Perret C	121		2.80	95-14	SafelyKept1211½FntstcFnd1146Cojnx11616	Slow st.,driving	5
16Jly89- 8Bel	fst	6f	:213 :45 1:113	ⒻPrioress-G2	3 5 22½ 13 17 13¾	Cordero A Jr	118		*.30	81-22	SafelyKpt1183¾Cojinx1144TheWayIt'sBinn1144½	Ridden out	5
4Jly89- 3Mth	fst	6f	:204 :431 1:083	3↑ⒻRegret 33k	1 3 12½ 13 18 15½	Wilson R	116		*.30	97-13	SafelyKept1165½ReadyJetGo116noFeeltheBeat11610½	Easily	4
8Jun89- 8Bel	gd	6f	:214 :443 1:092	3↑ⒻGenuine Risk-G2	4 1 11½ 14 15 14	Cordero A Jr	114		*.70	92-14	Safely Kept1144Aptostar1224Cagey Exuberance1223	Driving	4
6May89- 9GS	fst	6f	:212 :44 1:083	3↑ⒻBud BC H-G3	3 2 15 15 14 12¾	Vigliotti MJ	108		*2.30	99-16	Safely Kept1082¾Social Pro1167Kerygma117hd	Driving	9
9Apr89-11Lrl	fst	6f	:221 :453 :582 1:113	Ⓕ[S]Politely 60k	7 5 2hd 1hd 14 14	Wilson R	118		*.40	85-22	SaflyKpt1184NoblestHeart1145SkatngLdy1151¾	Ridden out	11
	Previously trained by Carlos A. Garcia												
18Sep88- 3Lrl	fst	7f	:224 :46 1:111 1:24	ⒻUSFG Lassie 95k	5 6 2hd 11½ 1hd 35	Desormeaux KJ	119		*.40	86-10	Ms.GoldPole1194½OpenMind119½SafelyKept1191½	Weakened	9
14Aug88- 9Pim	fst	6f	:23 :462 :58 1:103	Ⓕ[S]Smart Angle 50k	1 3 12 13½ 15 19½	Desormeaux KJ	114		*.10	93-16	SaflyKpt1149½HardHeadedWoman1124HayRoll1106½	Handily	7
	Previously owned by Dark Hollow Farm												
24Jly88- 9Pim	fst	5½f	:222 :46 :582 1:05	ⒻPlaypen 54k	3 4 12 13 15 17½	Desormeaux KJ	110		*.30	96-21	SfelyKpt1107½TruxtonTwo110hdCrclthFloor1142	Ridden out	7
21Jun88- 4Pim	fst	5f	:221 :454 :583	ⒻMd Sp Wt	6 3 13 14 14 16½	Desormeaux KJ	119		*.40	92-19	SafelyKept1196½CirclethFloor1196¾PchIsl119hd	Going away	7
7Jun88- 4Pim	fst	5f	:22 :452 :583	ⒻMd Sp Wt	2 2 1hd 2hd 2½ 2½	Sarvis DA	119		*2.20	91-19	BeansBeans119½SafelyKpt1192¼CirclthFloor1195½	Game try	7

Slew o' Gold

b. c. 1980, by Seattle Slew (Bold Reasoning)–Alluvial, by Buckpasser — Lifetime record: 21 12 5 1 $3,533,534

Own.– Equusequity Stable
Br.– Claiborne Farm (Ky)
Tr.– John O. Hertler

10Nov84- 7Hol fst 1¼ :45³ 1:10³ 1:37 2:03² 3↑ BC Classic-G1 4 5 59½ 2½ 2hd 3½ Cordero A Jr 126 *.60e -- WildAgain126hd[D]GateDancer122½Slewo'Gold1265 Roughed 8
Placed second through disqualification
20Oct84- 8Bel fst 1½ :49³ 1:14¹ 2:03⁴ 2:28⁴ 3↑ J C Gold Cup-G1 5 2 22 12½ 14½ 19¾ Cordero A Jr 126 *.10 76-17 Slwo'Gld1269¾HalBoldKng1211BoundngBsqu1263 Ridden out 5
29Sep84- 8Bel fst 1¼ :47⁴ 1:11³ 1:36⁴ 2:02² 3↑ Marlboro Cup H-G1 6 4 3½ 11½ 11½ 11¾ Cordero A Jr 129 *.80 86-19 Slewo'Gold1291¾CarrdeNskra1192CanadnFctor1142½ Driving 9
15Sep84- 8Bel sly 1⅛ :45¹ 1:09² 1:34⁴ 1:47⁴ 3↑ Woodward-G1 6 2 3½ 21½ 21 1½ Cordero A Jr 126 *.70 88-18 Slew o' Gold126½Shifty Sheik1163Bet Big1163¾ Driving 6
4Aug84- 8Sar fst 1⅛ :46⁴ 1:10 1:35¹ 1:48³ 3↑ Whitney H-G1 1 1 2hd 2hd 1hd 11¾ Cordero A Jr 126 *.40 92-13 Slewo'Gold1261¾TrackBarron11711¼Thumbsucker115 Easily 3
2Jly84- 1Bel gd 1 :22³ :44⁴ 1:09² 1:34² 3↑ Alw 36000 1 2 24 1hd 13 17½ Cordero A Jr 115 *.40 93-15 Slewo'Gld1157½CannonShll1151¾NorthrnIc1083¼ Ridden out 5
Previously trained by Sidney Watters Jr
15Oct83- 8Bel fst 1½ :48 1:12³ 2:01 2:26¹ 3↑ J C Gold Cup-G1 3 5 63¼ 2½ 12 13 Cordero A Jr 121 3.00e 89-14 Slwo'Gld1213HighlandBlad126nkBoundngBsqu1211½ Driving 11
24Sep83- 8Bel fst 1¼ :47² 1:11¹ 1:36¹ 2:01³ 3↑ Marlboro Cup H-G1 2 2 1hd 13 1½ 2nk Cordero A Jr 119 4.80 92-17 HighlandBlade117nkSlewo'Gld119½BtsMotl1244 Wide,missed 9
3Sep83- 8Bel fst 1⅛ :45⁴ 1:09² 1:34 1:46³ 3↑ Woodward-G1 6 7 42 21 1hd 1no Cordero A Jr 118 4.00e 94-13 Slew o' Gold118noBates Motel1235Sing Sing1195 Driving 10
13Aug83- 8Sar gd 1¼ :46⁴ 1:10¹ 1:35² 2:01 Travers-G1 1 2 2½ 2hd 2hd 21¾ Cordero A Jr 126 *2.40 93-11 PlayFellow1261¾Slewo'Gold1262¼Hyperborean1262½ Gamely 7
30Jly83- 9Mth fst 1⅛ :46³ 1:10² 1:36 1:49¹ Haskell H-G1 5 8 87 44 51¾ 64 Cordero A Jr 124 *1.00 85-17 DeputdTstmony124nkBetBig1162Parftmnt116½ Lacked room 10
11Jun83- 8Bel fst 1½ :47² 1:11³ 1:59⁴ 2:27⁴ Belmont-G1 1 3 21½ 1½ 21 23½ Cordero A Jr 126 *2.50 77-14 Caveat1263½Slewo'Gld1261¾Barberstown126no Led,weakened 15
29May83- 8Bel fst 1⅛ :45³ 1:09¹ 1:33⁴ 1:46⁴ Peter Pan-G3 5 4 2½ 12½ 18 112 Cordero A Jr 126 *.80 93-11 Slew o' Gold12612I Enclose1233¾Foyt1176 Ridden out 5
7May83- 8CD fst 1¼ :47¹ 1:11⁴ 1:36⁴ 2:02¹ Ky Derby-G1 1 7 78 75½ 33 43¼ Cordero A Jr 126 10.10 83-10 Sunny'sHalo1262DesrtWine126nkCaveat1261 Bothered start 20
23Apr83- 8Aqu fst 1⅛ :48¹ 1:12¹ 1:37² 1:51 Wood Mem (Div 2)-G1 1 6 52 41¾ 1hd 1nk Maple E 126 *1.30 80-24 Slewo'Gold126nkParfaitement126½HighHonors1269¾ Driving 7
13Apr83- 1Aqu fst 1⅛ :48³ 1:12³ 1:37⁴ 1:50⁴ Alw 23000 4 2 1hd 11 16 17¾ Cordero A Jr 117 *1.00 81-19 Slewo'Gold1177¾LawTalk1171¼ElCubanaso117¾ Ridden out 6
19Mar83-10Tam fst 1$\frac{1}{16}$:24 :48 1:13 1:47¹ Tampa Derby 100k 2 5 42½ 43½ 23 2¾ Rivera H Jr 118 2.30 82-21 Morganmorganmorgan118¾Slew o' Gold118¾Quick Dip1186 14
Steadied,checked
5Mar83-10Tam fst 1$\frac{1}{16}$:23² :47⁴ 1:13² 1:47² Sam F Davis 12k 4 7 86¾ 43 32½ 33¾ Molina VH 118 *.40 78-23 Saverton1181¾TwoTurnsHome1202Slewo'Gold1181¼ Mild bid 8
13Nov82- 8Aqu gd 1⅛ :48² 1:12⁴ 1:37⁴ 1:50¹ Remsen-G1 11 4 52½ 53 610 612 Lovato F Jr 115 *1.80e 72-20 PaxinBello1131¾Chummng1158PrimitivePleasre113hd Tired 11
23Oct82- 9Aqu fst 1 :23³ :47 1:12¹ 1:37² Alw 20000 8 2 2½ 1hd 11½ 11¾ Lovato F Jr 117 3.70 79-21 Slew o'Gold1171¾LastTurn1172¾Chumming1222¾ Ridden out 9
15Oct82- 3Aqu fst 6½f :23² :47 1:12¹ 1:18⁴ Md Sp Wt 8 1 2½ 2½ 1½ 1nk Cordero A Jr 118 *.60 81-26 Slew o' Gold118nkCountertrade1186Majesty Cove1182½ 8
Lugged in,driving

Smile

dkbbr. c. 1982, by In Reality (Intentionally)–Sunny Smile, by Boldnesian — Lifetime record: 27 14 4 3 $1,664,027

Own.– Frances A. Genter Stable
Br.– F.A. Genter Stable Inc (Fla)
Tr.– Flint S. Schulhofer

7Mar87-10GP fst 1$\frac{1}{16}$⊗ :23⁴ :47³ 1:11⁴ 1:44³ 3↑ GP Bud BC H 133k 3 2 2½ 1hd 22½ 45½ Vasquez J 120 *.90 72-25 BolshoBoy1164ArctcHonymoon1141LttlBoldJohn115½ Gave way 5
24Jan87-10Hia fst 1⅛ :46⁴ 1:10⁴ 1:36 1:48⁴ 3↑ Seminole H-G2 1 1 2½ 1hd 1½ 65¼ Vasquez J 121 *1.40 82-17 LaunchaPegass1151½Arctic Honeymn116hdDarnThatAlarm118nk 8
Weakened
3Jan87- 7Crc fst 1$\frac{3}{16}$:48³ 1:13 1:39¹ 1:59³ 3↑ Bud BC H 143k 5 2 2½ 1hd 12½ 21½ Vasquez J 122 *.90 117-14 ArcticHoneymoon1141½Smle1229DrnThtAlrm120no Gave way 6
1Nov86- 3SA fst 6f :21¹ :43³ :55⁴ 1:08² 3↑ BC Sprint-G1 1 4 2½ 1hd 1hd 11¼ Vasquez J 126 11.00 96-13 Smile1261¼PineTreeLane1231¾BedsidePromise1261¼ Driving 9
27Sep86- 8Pha sly 7f :21² :44 1:09² 1:22¹ 3↑ Bud BC 148k 5 1 33 43¼ 44¼ 611¾ Cordero A Jr 122 *.90 84-17 LazerShow1128¼IAmtheGame115noPurplMountain114¾ Wide 7
30Aug86- 6AP fst 1 :22² :44³ 1:08¹ 1:34 3↑ Equipoise Mile H-G3 4 2 3½ 11 13 15 Vasquez J 121 *1.30 91-15 Smile1215Taylor's Special1242Red Attack1143½ Ridden out 7
26Jly86- 9Aks fst 1⅛ :48 1:11² 1:36³ 1:49² 3↑ Cornhusker H-G2 2 1 11 11 1hd 34 Vasquez J 120 *1.10 86-23 Gourami1162½Honor Medal1141½Smile1201 Tired 7
13Jly86- 9Cby gd 1⅛ :46⁴ 1:10¹ 1:35 1:48 3↑ Canterbury Cup H 165k 3 1 11 11 12 1½ Vasquez J 119 *.80e 103-09 Smile119½Dramatic Desire1131¼Forkintheroad1163½ Driving 9
5Jly86- 6Bel fst 1$\frac{1}{16}$:23² :46¹ 1:10² 1:42² 3↑ Alw 40000 6 2 11 13½ 15 14¼ Vasquez J 115 *.40 90-15 Smile1154¼ValiantLark1153½LittleMissouri1155 Ridden out 6
22Jun86- 8Bel fst 6f :22¹ :44³ 1:09 3↑ True North H-G2 2 2 21 2hd 2½ 44¼ Vasquez J 119 4.30 93-19 PhoneTrck127¾LoveThatMac1173½Cullendale111hd Weakened 5
26May86- 8Bel fst 1 :23² :45⁴ 1:09¹ 1:33³ 3↑ Metropolitan H-G1 6 2 31 3nk 53 77½ Vasquez J 121 6.70 89-11 Garthorn1241¼LoveThatMc117noLdy'sScrt120nk Stumbled st. 8
10May86- 7Bel fm 6f(T) :22 :44³ 1:09¹ 3↑ Alw 36000 12 2 1hd 1½ 11½ 12 Vasquez J 119 *1.90 94-19 Smile1192[DH]Fortunate Prospect119[DH]Roving Minstrel1191 12
Drew clear
16Nov85- 8Aqu sly 7f :21³ :44² 1:09 1:21⁴ 3↑ Vosburgh-G1 3 5 25 32 46½ 49¾ Vasquez J 124 *.50 82-22 AnothrReef1242¾PanchoVilla1244¾WhoopUp1262¼ Weakened 6
2Nov85- 3Aqu fst 6f :22 :44⁴ 1:08² 3↑ BC Sprint-G1 11 1 21 1hd 1hd 2¾ Vasquez J 124 6.40 98-10 Precisionist126¾Smile124¾Mt. Livermore1261¼ Gamely 14
13Oct85- 6Bel gd 1(T) :23¹ :46 1:10² 1:36² 3↑ Handicap 40000 1 1 1hd 1hd 2hd 35 Vasquez J 116 3.20 78-25 Chief's Crown1252½Intensify1142½Smile11612 Gave way 5
Previously trained by Carl Nafzger
18Aug85- 9Cby fst 1 70 :23¹ :46² 1:09⁴ 1:40¹ 3↑ Alw 20000 3 1 11 11 1hd 22½ Oldham J 120 *.40 104-11 Come Summer1122½Smile1202Ridan Clarion116½ Failed 6
21Jly85- 9FP fst 1⅛ :46⁴ 1:11¹ 1:36² 1:49 FP Derby-G3 3 2 11 12 12½ 14 Vasquez J 123 *.30 104-18 Smile1234Premier Partner1143Clever Allemont1235¾ Easily 7
Previously trained by Frank Gomez
6Jly85- 8AP fst 1¼ :47⁴ 1:11² 1:36 2:01³ American Derby-G1 5 1 11½ 11½ 11 31¾ Vasquez J 123 *.70 87-15 Creme Fraiche1231Red Attack114¾Smile1237 Tired 5
15Jun85- 8AP sly 1⅛ :48³ 1:13 1:38 1:51¹ Classic-G1 4 1 11½ 12 15 17½ Vasquez J 117 *.90 75-27 Smile1177½RedAttack1141¾CleverAllemont1231¼ Ridden out 6
1Jun85- 8AP fst 1 :22³ :44³ 1:08⁴ 1:34³ Sheridan-G2 1 2 26 23 21½ 2¾ Vasquez J 124 *.50 87-15 Banner Bob124¾Smile124noClever Allemont1243 Tired 5
18May85- 9Crc fst 7f :22 :44³ 1:10¹ 1:23⁴ Carry Back 68k 1 1 21 11½ 16 111½ Vasquez J 123 *.05 97-13 Smile12311½Paravon112nkHickoryHillFlyer114½ Ridden out 7
9May85- 0Crc fst 7f :22³ :45³ 1:10² 1:23³ Alw 4 2 12½ 13 19 110¾ Vasquez J 116 - 98-13 Smile11610¾SingleBidder1169¾NowICn1164 Speed in reserve 4
Exhibition race run between 6th and 7th races - No wagering or purse
20Oct84- 9Crc fst 1$\frac{1}{16}$:24¹ :48³ 1:13¹ 1:46³ [R]In Reality (FSS) 400k 10 1 11 1½ 11½ 12 St Leon G 120 *.20 86-16 Smle1202EmergencyCall12014½CovertOperaton1201¾ Driving 12
29Sep84- 9Crc sly 7f :22² :46 1:11¹ 1:24³ [R]Affirmed (FSS) 120k 4 4 22½ 1½ 15 17 St Leon G 118 *.40 93-18 Smile1187Kejinsky118¾Emergency Call1187 Ridden out 11
25Aug84- 9Crc fst 6f :22² :46² 1:13³ [R]Dr.Fgr(FSS)(Div2) 42k 8 2 11½ 12 16 14 St Leon G 116 *.40 83-19 Smile1164Water Gate1162[D]Hickory Hill Flyer116nk Easily 10
4Aug84- 9Crc fst 5½f :22³ :47 1:00¹ 1:07 Criterium (Div 2) 40k 1 7 13 12 12½ 12½ St Leon G 114 2.60 90-21 Smile1142½Spend a Buck116hdCherokee Fast1164½ Easily 7
Run in divisions
16Jun84- 2Crc sly 5f :22⁴ :46⁴ 1:00¹ Md Sp Wt 6 4 1hd 1hd 1½ 13 St Leon G 115 7.30 91-18 Smile1153Valid Likeness1157Cosmic Dust115hd Drew clear 10

Snow Chief

dkbbr. c. 1983, by Reflected Glory (Jester)–Miss Snowflake, by Snow Sporting — Lifetime record: 24 13 3 5 $3,383,210

Own.– Grinstead & Rochelle
Br.– Blue Diamond Ranch (Cal)
Tr.– Melvin F. Stute

7Jun87- 8Hol fst 1⅛ :46⁴ 1:10⁴ 1:35³ 1:48¹ 3↑ Californian-G1 2 2 21 2½ 21½ 31 Solis A 126 b 1.90 95-17 JudgeAnglucc1181IronEys115noSnwChf1262¾ Bobbled start 8
17Apr87- 9OP fst 1⅛ :46³ 1:10¹ 1:34³ 1:46³ 4↑ Oaklawn H-G2 7 2 1hd 1½ 11½ 1¾ Solis A 123 b *.80 101-11 Snow Chief123¾Red Attack112½Vilzak1081½ Driving 7
29Mar87-10GP fst 1¼ :49 1:13⁴ 1:38² 2:02⁴ 3↑ Gulf Park H-G1 1 1 12 2hd 2½ 34¾ Solis A 124 b *.70 76-24 SkipTrial1184½CremeFraich120nkSnwChf124nk Taken out st 4
8Mar87- 8SA fst 1¼ :45⁴ 1:10¹ 1:35 2:00³ 4↑ S Anita H-G1 3 2 2hd 2hd 32½ 57 Valenzuela PA 126 b 2.40 79-15 Broad Brush122noFerdinand1256½Hopeful Word117nk 9
Bumped into stretch
8Feb87- 8SA fst 1¼ :46⁴ 1:10² 1:34³ 2:00 C H Strub-G1 7 1 11 1½ 11½ 1no Valenzuela PA 126 b 2.40 89-14 SnowChf126noFrdnnd1264½BrodBrsh1267 Bumped hard late 8
18Jan87- 8SA fst 1⅛ :48² 1:12¹ 1:36³ 1:49 San Fernando-G1 5 1 1hd 1hd 2hd 33 Valenzuela PA 126 b *.90 81-19 VarietyRd123nkBrodBrsh1262¾SnwChf1263½ Stumbled start 8
26Dec86- 8SA fst 7f :22² :44⁴ 1:09 1:21³ Malibu-G2 4 5 31 3nk 11½ 21¼ Valenzuela PA 126 b *1.40 91-13 Ferdinand1231¼SnwChief1261½DonB.Blue1144 Bumped start 12
5Jly86- 8Hol fst 1 :22¹ :44³ 1:08 1:32⁴ Silver Screen H-G2 1 3 21½ 35 38½ 311 Solis A 127 b *.60 88-08 Melair1156½Southern Halo1134½Snow Chief127hd Tired 12

26May86- 9GS fst 1¼ :47 1:112 1:372 2:03 Jersey Derby-G2 5 1 12½ 1½ 12 12 Solis A 126 b *.60 89-20 Snow Chief1262Mogambo1261½Tasso1261¼ Kept to drive 10
17May86- 8Pim fst 1 3/16 :472 1:11 1:36 1:544 Preakness-G1 2 2 2½ 2hd 14 14 Solis A 126 b 2.60 93-18 SnowChief1264Frdnnd1266½BrodBrush126no Strong handling 7
3May86- 8CD fst 1¼ :451 1:101 1:37 2:024 Ky Derby-G1 12 4 43 41 911 1119½ Solis A 126 b *2.10 63-10 Ferdinand1262¼BoldArrangemnt126¾BrdBrush126nk Gave way 16
6Apr86- 5SA fst 1⅛ :471 1:11 1:36 1:483 S Anita Derby-G1 3 2 11½ 12 12½ 16 Solis A 122 b *.30 86-15 Snow Chief1226Icy Groom1221Ferdinand122¾ Ridden out 7
1Mar86- 9GP fst 1⅛ :464 1:12 1:38 1:514 Florida Derby-G1 12 1 11½ 1½ 12½ 1¾ Solis A 122 b *1.50 73-29 Snow Chief1221¾Badger Land1225Mogambo122nk Driving 16
2Feb86- 8BM sly 1 1/16 :223 :452 1:093 1:423 El Camino Real Derby-G3 2 2 21½ 2hd 1hd 12½ Solis A 120 b *.70 79-28 Snow Chief1202½Badger Land120½Darby Fair1207 In hand 6
12Jan86- 8SA fst 7f :221 :444 1:091 1:213 ⓢCal Br Champ 115k 7 2 52½ 61¾ 11 14 Solis A 126 b *.40 92-11 SnowChief1264VarietyRoad115nkAirPirate1174½ Ridden out 8
15Dec85- 8Hol fst 1 :22 :443 1:09 1:341 Hol Futurity-G1 9 5 2hd 13½ 15 16½ Solis A 121 b 2.90 92-09 SnowChief1216½ElectricBlue121noFerdinnd121nk Ridden out 10
29Nov85- 8Hol sly 1⊗ :221 :451 1:11 1:37 Hoist the Flag 191k 5 5 66½ 24 24 25 Solis A 120 *1.10 73-20 DarbyFair1205SnowChief1202¼AcksLikaRuler114¾ 2nd best 6
2Nov85-14SA fst 1 :232 :473 1:121 1:362 ⓢBJ Ridder 108k 4 6 53½ 32 32 1hd Solis A 122 *.40 86-13 SnwChief122hdVarietyRoad115½RaisedonStag11510½ Driving 7
13Oct85- 8SA fst 1 1/16 :221 :454 1:103 1:443 Norfolk-G1 2 6 55½ 56 32½ 13 Solis A 118 *1.50 78-17 Snow Chief1183Lord Allison1181¼Darby Fair1181½ Driving 9
2Oct85- 8SA fst 7f :221 :451 1:101 1:233 Sunny Slope 76k 5 6 76¾ 54¾ 44 2nk Solis A 119 *2.30 82-17 LouisianaSlew115nkSnowChief1194½DonB.Blue115¾ Rallied 8
11Sep85- 8Dmr fst 1 :231 :471 1:113 1:36 Dmr Futurity-G1 5 4 52¼ 41 34½ 32½ Solis A 117 7.80 85-15 Tasso117nkArewehavingfunyet1172½Snow Chief1173¼ Evenly 6
4Sep85- 8Dmr fst 6f :221 :451 :564 1:10 ⓡRancho Santa Fe 54k 7 1 52¾ 25 21½ 1¾ Meza RQ 117 7.20 88-17 SnwChief1171¾LittleRedCloud1172½QuickTwst1141¼ Driving 7
30Jun85- 5Hol fst 5½f :212 :433 :562 1:024 Desert Wine 51k 4 9 614 617 614 69½ Meza RQ 115 8.40 -- Hilco Scamper1174½Little Red Cloud1173½Sir Mahmoud116½ 9
In close st
19Jun85- 5Hol fst 5f :224 :452 :573 ⓢMd Sp Wt 4 6 2½ 1hd 1hd 12½ Meza RQ 118 2.20 -- SnwChf1182½GloryPath118noWindatHsBck1184½ Ridden out 10

Spend a Buck

b. c. 1982, by Buckaroo (Buckpasser)–Belle de Jour, by Speak John **Lifetime record: 15 10 3 2 $4,220,689**

Own.– Hunter Farm
Br.– Irish Hill Farm & R.W. Harper (Ky)
Tr.– Cam Gambolati

17Aug85- 9Mth fst 1⅛ :464 1:094 1:341 1:464 3↑ Monmouth H-G1 3 1 12 11½ 1½ 1no Pincay L Jr 118 *.50 101-10 SpendaBck118noCarrdeNaskra1209ⒹRumptious1121 Driving 6
27Jly85- 9Mth fst 1⅛ :47 1:104 1:354 1:483 Haskell Inv'l H-G1 7 1 1½ 1½ 1hd 23¾ Pincay L Jr 127 *.70 88-13 SkipTrial1163¾SpendaBuck1271CremeFraiche1264 Gave way 7
27May85- 9GS fst 1¼ :452 1:09 1:35 2:023 Jersey Derby-G3 5 1 1hd 1½ 1½ 1nk Pincay L Jr 126 *.05 -- SpendaBuck126nkCremeFraiche126hdElBasco1264¾ Driving 9
4May85- 8CD fst 1¼ :454 1:093 1:344 2:001 Ky Derby-G1 10 1 16 16 15 15¼ Cordero A Jr 126 4.10 96-08 SpndaBck1265¼Stphn'sOdyssy126½Chf'sCrown126nk Driving 13
20Apr85- 8GS fst 1⅛ :453 1:092 1:34 1:454 Garden State 304k 2 1 13½ 13 16 19½ Cordero A Jr 122 *.40 -- Spend a Buck1229½I Am the Game1175½Do It Again Dan115nk 9
Ridden out
6Apr85- 8GS fst 1 :223 :452 1:10 1:352 Cherry Hill Mile H 244k 7 1 12½ 12 16 110½ Cordero A Jr 122 1.70 -- SpndaBck12210½IAmtheGme115¾KingBabar1161¼ Ridden out 14
23Mar85- 8Aqu fst 7f :224 :453 1:093 1:221 Bay Shore-G2 1 6 31 41¼ 34½ 35½ Cordero A Jr 123 *1.40 84-23 Pancho Villa1143¾El Basco1141¾Spend a Buck1232 9
Weakened under impost
10Nov84- 1Hol fst 1 :222 :45 1:10 1:361 ©BC Juvenile-G1 3 1 1hd 12½ 11 31½ Cordero A Jr 122 6.40 -- Chief'sCrwn122¾Tank'sPrspct122¾SpndBck1226½ Weakened 10
18Oct84- 8Med fst 1 1/16 :23 :46 1:111 1:45 Young America-G1 4 1 11½ 11 1½ 2¾ Cordero A Jr 122 *1.00 83-22 ScriptOhio119¾SpendaBck122nkTank'sProspect1192 Gamely 11
22Sep84- 9AP fst 1 :222 :444 1:10 1:38 Arl Wash Futurity-G1 6 3 21 2hd 1½ 1½ Hussey C 122 2.90 71-24 SpendaBuck122½Dusty'sDarby1222½VivaMaxi1221¾ All out 7
2Sep84-11RD fst 1 1/16 :234 :473 1:12 1:451 Cradle H 125k 6 2 11 14 18 115 Hussey C 120 *1.20 80-18 SpendaBuck12015GrandNative1206Alex'sGame120nk Easily 13
16Aug84- 7Crc fst 6f :223 :461 1:124 Alw 15000 1 1 11½ 14 16 19½ Hussey C 112 *.50 87-23 SpendaBuck1129½SecretGoal1128½Mr.Introienne1143 Handily 5
4Aug84- 9Crc fst 5½f :223 :47 1:001 1:07 Criterium (Div 2) 40k 4 2 23 22 22½ 22½ Hussey C 116 *.60 87-21 Smile1142½SpendaBuck116hdCherokeeFast1164½ Held place 7
25Jly84- 8Crc fst 5½f :224 :463 :592 1:06 Alw 11000 3 1 1½ 11½ 13 14 Hussey C 113 2.40 95-20 Spend a Buck1134Mr. Introienne1161½Playing Politics1144½ 8
Ridden out;Previously raced in name of D.W. Diaz
14Jly84- 2Crc fst 5½f :23 :47 1:001 1:071 Md Sp Wt 6 3 11½ 1hd 12 1nk Hussey C 116 5.50 89-19 SpndaBck116nkHckoryHllFlyr1163SuprbAnswr1163½ Driving 12

Steinlen (GB)

b. c. 1983, by Habitat (Sir Gaylord)–Southern Seas, by Jim French **Lifetime record: 45 20 10 7 $3,300,100**

Own.– D. Wildenstein
Br.– Allez France Stables Ltd (GB)
Tr.– D. Wayne Lukas

27Oct90- 6Bel gd 1Ⓣ :223 :454 1:10 1:351 3↑ BC Mile-G1 11 4 42 63 53 41½ Santos JA 126 4.90 88-15 RoyalAcademy122nkItsallgreektom122¾Prolo122½ Mild rally 13
6Oct90- 8Bel fst 1¼ :473 1:112 1:352 2:003 3↑ J C Gold Cup-G1 2 3 31½ 67½ 615 625¾ Santos JA 126 14.30 68-11 Flying Continental126nkDe Roche122¾Izvestia1216¼ Tired 6
2Sep90- 8AP fm 1¼Ⓣ :483 1:13 1:364 1:593 3↑ Arl Million-G1 11 2 21½ 22 42½ 36½ Santos JA L 126 3.30 107-00 GoldenPhesnt1261¼WthApprovl1265¼StnIn126nk Lacked rally 11
12Aug90- 8Sar gd 1⅛Ⓣ :464 1:104 1:353 1:482 3↑ Bernard Baruch H-G2 5 2 2½ 2hd 12 22 Santos JA 126 *.30 86-11 Who'stoPay1102SteinIn1263RiverofSn1158 Not good enough 5
21Jly90- 8Atl fm 1 3/16Ⓣ :484 1:114 1:354 1:52 3↑ Caesars Int'l H-G2 7 1 11 1½ 11½ 13¾ Santos JA L 124 *1.60 103-10 Steinlen1243¾Capades1121¼Alwuhush1211 Driving 8
4Jly90- 8Hol fm 1⅛Ⓣ :464 1:102 1:351 1:474 3↑ American H-G2 5 2 21 2hd 1½ 2¾ Pincay L Jr L 125 *1.60 88-16 ClassicFame117¾Steinlen1251½PleasantVarty1162½ Held 2nd 7
28May90- 8Hol gd 1½Ⓣ :483 1:131 1:374 2:03 3↑ Hol Turf H-G1 3 2 25 21 21 1nk Pincay L Jr 124 3.80 78-22 Steinlen124nkHawkster1225½Santangelo110hd Driving 6
13May90- 8Hol fm 1⅛Ⓣ :484 1:121 1:352 1:47 3↑ John Henry H-G2 5 2 21 1hd 2hd 32 Santos JA 126 1.80 91-09 GoldenPheasnt1201¾ClassicFame117nkStnIn1261¾ Lost whip 5
8Apr90- 8SA fm 1Ⓣ :213 :45 1:09 1:332 4↑ El Rincon H-G2 5 4 42 32½ 21 1hd Santos JA 125 *1.00 96-05 Steinlen125hdBruho1175Wonder Dancer111¾ Driving 6
4Mar90- 5SA fm 1Ⓣ :214 :45 1:09 1:342 4↑ Arcadia H-G3 7 3 48 57¼ 54½ 74¾ Santos JA 126 *1.20 86-18 Prizd1241HappyToss115hdOntheMenu1122¾ Needed response 9
4Nov89- 7GP gd 1Ⓣ :232 :472 1:112 1:371 3↑ BC Mile-G1 2 4 52½ 63¼ 21 1¾ Santos JA 126 1.80 88-13 SteinIn126¾Sabona126½MostWIcom126nk Rough trip-driving 11
21Oct89- 8Kee yl 1⅛Ⓣ :483 1:132 1:39 1:522 3↑ Bud BC-G3 4 4 53½ 51¾ 1hd 1hd Santos JA 126 *.30 80-20 Steinlen126hdCrystal Moment1263Posen126nk Driving 10
3Sep89- 8AP fm 1¼Ⓣ :491 1:134 1:391 2:033 3↑ Arl Million-G1 4 2 22 32 3½ 1½ Santos JA 126 5.30 76-25 Steinlen126½LadyinSilver117½YankeeAffair126hd Driving 13
13Aug89- 8Sar sf 1⅛Ⓣ :501 1:14 1:381 1:51 3↑ Bernard Baruch H-G1 6 3 32½ 32½ 1½ 15 Santos JA 121 *1.90 72-28 Steinlen1215Soviet Lad111¾Brian's Time1122 Ridden out 8
2Aug89- 5Sar fm 1 1/16Ⓣ :24 :481 1:112 1:41 3↑ Daryl's Joy (Div 1)-G3 8 3 32 11 11½ 12½ Cordero A Jr 122 *.40 92-08 SteinIn1222½ExpensvDcson1172SprkIngWt1101 Stumbled st. 8
4Jly89- 8Hol fm 1⅛Ⓣ :481 1:112 1:344 1:471 3↑ American H-G1 4 2 21½ 2½ 1hd 2no Stevens GL 121 *.80 92-12 MisterWonderflII115noStenIn121hdPrnk1171½ Bumped start 8
18Jun89- 8Hol fm 1 1/16Ⓣ :233 :461 1:093 1:393 3↑ Inglewood H-G2 3 2 23½ 21 11½ 12¼ Stevens GL 120 *1.00 96-10 Steinlen1202¼Pasakos1152Mi Preferido117½ Bumped early 7
14May89- 8Hol fm 1⅛Ⓣ :462 1:094 1:334 1:461 3↑ John Henry H-G1 3 2 2½ 1hd 1hd 2¾ Stevens GL 121 *2.80 96-08 Peace116¾Steinlen121½Pay the Butler1161½ Held on well 8
30Apr89- 8Hol fm 1Ⓣ :231 :46 1:091 1:33 3↑ Premiere H-G3 5 2 2½ 2hd 2hd 21 Stevens GL 121 *1.70 98-06 Peace1151Steinlen121nkPolitical Ambition1222½ Gamely 8
9Apr89- 8SA fm 1Ⓣ :234 :473 1:113 1:353 4↑ El Rincon H 107k 3 3 41¾ 42 42 31½ Pincay L Jr 122 *1.50 91-15 Political Ambition121½Patchy Groundfog1181Steinlen122nk 5
Well up throughout
9Mar89- 8SA fm 1Ⓣ :23 :461 1:093 1:341 4↑ Alw 60000 6 1 11 11 11 1nk Pincay L Jr 118 *.70 100-00 SteinIn118nkPc1165ExclusvPrtnr116¾ Bumped st.,lunged in 6
5Nov88- 7CD gd 1Ⓣ :233 :472 1:123 1:383 3↑ BC Mile-G1 3 4 33 43 43 24 Pincay L Jr 126 37.40 92-04 Miesque1234Steinlen126hdSimplyMajestc1261¼ Gained place 12
23Oct88-10Lrl fm 6fⓉ :221 :452 :574 1:102 3↑ Lrl Dash 200k 8 4 711 713 64¾ 1no Pincay L Jr 124 7.60 90-15 StenIn124noMc'sFghtr117½Fourstrdv117½ Lugged in driving 11
8Oct88- 8Bel sf 1Ⓣ :24 :484 1:144 1:42 3↑ Kelso H-G3 5 3 3½ 32 57¾ 67¾ Stevens GL 121 *1.70 47-60 San'stheShadow116¾Posen117½Tinchen'sPrince1144¾ Tired 7
27Aug88- 7Sar gd 1 1/16Ⓣ :242 :473 1:114 1:432 3↑ Bud BC H-G3 5 1 1½ 1hd 1hd 1nk Day P 120 *.40 80-23 Steinlen120nkIron Courage113½Barood1103 Driving 6
14Aug88- 8Sar fm 1⅛Ⓣ :47 1:094 1:333 1:464 3↑ Bernard Baruch H-G1 7 1 1½ 1½ 1hd 2½ Day P 120 2.80 92-14 My Big Boy113½Steinlen120nkWanderkin115¾ Held well 9
4Jly88- 8Hol fm 1⅛Ⓣ :471 1:104 1:334 1:462 3↑ American H-G1 4 1 11 12 1hd 21 Stevens GL 121 *.70 95-06 SkipOutFront1151Steinlen121hdWorldCourt1131 Held place 4
19Jun88- 8Hol fm 1 1/16Ⓣ :24 :47 1:10 1:402 3↑ Inglewood H-G2 4 1 12½ 13½ 15 12½ Stevens GL 119 2.10 92-10 SteinIn1192½DeputyGovernor1201¾Galunpe115no Ridden out 9
15May88- 8Hol fm 1⅛Ⓣ :463 1:10 1:34 1:46 3↑ John Henry H-G1 7 1 12½ 11½ 11 22 Stevens GL 120 3.80 96-05 DeputyGovernr1182StenIn120½StopthFghtng115½ Rank early 8
1May88- 8Hol fm 1Ⓣ :23 :454 1:091 1:331 3↑ Premiere H-G3 6 4 31½ 11½ 11½ 1hd Stevens GL 119 *1.90 98-06 Steinlen119hdSiyah Kalem1151Neshad115hd Bumped start 8
10Apr88- 8SA fm 1Ⓣ :222 :454 1:101 1:344 4↑ El Rincon H 147k 1 1 11 1½ 12½ 11¾ Stevens GL 117 4.10 101-12 Steinlen1171¾Political Ambition120hdNeshad1173½ Driving 9
26Mar88- 5SA fm 1Ⓣ :23 :463 1:11 1:354 4↑ Alw 54000 3 3 2hd 1hd 13½ 15 Stevens GL 114 4.90 96-12 Steinlen1145Sanam1142¼Le Belvedere1141¾ Ridden out 7
12Mar88- 7SA fst 1 1/16 :224 :46 1:103 1:431 4↑ Alw 55000 5 6 63½ 51¾ 54½ 75 Stevens GL 114 14.20 80-19 No Marker114hdMasterful Advocate1174Forkintheroad114nk 8
Bid,faltered
21Jan88- 8SA fm 1⅛Ⓣ :473 1:12 1:372 1:503 4↑ Alw 55000 3 3 31 21½ 33½ 33½ Stevens GL 114 14.30 70-26 Temperate Sil1202¾Ivor's Image115¾Steinlen1141½ 12
Bumped start,lugged in stretch;Previously trained by Robert Frankel

30Oct87- 8SA gd 1⅛(T) :471 1:122 1:37 1:501 3↑ Alw 45000 2 9 1014 1011 78½ 76 Delahoussaye E 116 *3.00 70-24 ConquerngHero118hdWrldCourt1091¼GallntArchr1141¼ Wide 10
Previously trained by Patrick-Louis Biancone
26Aug87♦ Deauville(Fr) sf *1(T)Str 1:413 3↑ Prix Quincey-G3 Stk48200 51¾ Boeuf D 130 11.00 Tobin Lad1201½Pasticcio126noLibertine117nk 9
Pressed in 3rd,lacked rally,one-paced late
18Aug87♦ Deauville(Fr) sf *1(T)RH 1:443 3↑ Prix du Cercle Listed28400 31 Mosse G 131 10.00 Ephialtes128¾Dom Valory128nkSteinlen131½ 10
Tracked in 4th,bid 1½f out,lost 2nd near line
23Jly87♦ Saint-Cloud(Fr) sf *1(T)LH 1:431 4↑ Prix Sir Gallahad Listed34000 33¾ Cruz AS 130 1.50 Ephialtes123nkIstikal1303Steinlen130½ 4
Led to over 1f out,one-paced
30May87♦ Saint-Cloud(Fr) sf *1(T)LH 1:452 4↑ Prix Lovelace Listed34000 11½ Cruz AS 126 *.10 Steinlen1261½Al Joharah1181½Herald's Voice1192½ 4
Rated in last,dueled 1½f out,led 1f out,handily
20Apr87♦ Longchamp(Fr) fm*1⅛(T)RH 1:523 4↑ Prix de la Butte Mortemort Listed29000 13 Cruz AS 127 *2.30 Steinlen1273North Verdict127hdMachado130nk 9
Well placed in 3rd,led 1½f out,drew clear 1f out
9Apr87♦ Evry(Fr) sf *1⅛(T)LH 2:004 4↑ Prix de Savigny Alw17300 1¾ Cruz AS 128 7.20 Steinlen128¾Simsim1192½Herald's Voice119½ 15
Close up,ridden to lead final 16th,driving
27Mar87♦ Maisns-Lfftte(Fr) hy *1¼(T)RH 2:183 4↑ Prix Flechois Alw18700 11½ Cruz AS 119 13.50 Steinlen1191½Fabulous Pearl1281½Swedish Princess1212½ 14
Tracked in 4th,led 100y out,ridden out
15Jun86♦ Chantilly(Fr) fm*1(T)RH 1:363 Prix de Pontarme Listed28000 75 Lequeux A 120 13.00 Thrill Show1231½Majestic Voice123hdStar Maite130hd 14
Trailed to 1½f out,mild late gain
29May86♦ Longchamp(Fr) fm*1(T)RH 1:414 Prix du Pre-Catalan Alw22300 2¾ Legrix E 123 8.00 Green Mount123¾Steinlen1231½Shecky Red1182 8
Rated toward rear,finished well without threatening
26Apr86♦ Evry(Fr) hy *1(T)LH 1:494 Prix de la Beauce Mdn20500 39 Legrix E 123 2.20 Magical Wonder1235Forbidding1234Steinlen1234 6
Tracked in 3rd,never threatened,beaten 1½f out

Sunday Silence

dkbbr. c. 1986, by Halo (Hail to Reason)–Wishing Well, by Understanding
Lifetime record: 14 9 5 0 $4,968,554
Own.– Gaillard & Hancock III & Whittingham et al
Br.– Oak Cliff Thoroughbreds Ltd (Ky)
Tr.– Charles Whittingham

24Jun90- 8Hol fst 1¼ :464 1:101 1:343 1:594 3↑ Hol Gold Cup H-G1 4 4 31½ 2hd 2hd 2hd Valenzuela PA 126 *.50e 98-09 CriminalType121hdSndaySilnce1263½OpnngVrs1192¾ Gamely 7
3Jun90- 9Hol fst 1⅛ :471 1:104 1:351 1:48 3↑ Californian-G1 2 1 1½ 1½ 11½ 1¾ Valenzuela PA 126 *.10 94-14 Sunday Silence126¾Stylish Winner1153Charlatan III111 3
Awkward break;Previously owned by Gaillard & Hancock III & Whittingham
4Nov89-10GP fst 1¼ :461 1:102 1:35 2:001 3↑ BC Classic-G1 8 4 35 21½ 2hd 1nk McCarron CJ 122 2.00 107-01 SndaySlnc122nkEsyGr1221BlushngJohn1269¾ Good handling 8
24Sep89-10LaD fst 1¼ :471 1:121 1:374 2:031 Super Derby-G1 7 5 42½ 1hd 14 16 Valenzuela PA 126 *.40 85-15 SundaySilence1266BigEarl126hdAweInspiring126nk Drew out 8
23Jly89- 8Hol fst 1¼ :473 1:114 1:362 2:014 Swaps-G2 2 1 11½ 12½ 14 2¾ Valenzuela PA 126 *.20 82-18 Prized120¾Sunday Silence12610Endow1231¼ Lugged out late 5
10Jun89- 8Bel fst 1½ :47 1:111 2:004 2:26 Belmont-G1 6 3 21½ 21 24½ 28 Valenzuela PA 126 *.90 82-13 Easy Goer1268Sunday Silence1261Le Vygr12612 Second best 10
20May89-10Pim fst 1 3/16 :462 1:093 1:341 1:534 Preakness-G1 7 4 33 32 1hd 1no Valenzuela PA 126 2.10 98-10 Sunday Silence126noEasy Goer1265Rock Point1262 8
Bumped,steadied,brsh
6May89- 8CD my 1¼ :463 1:112 1:374 2:05 Ky Derby-G1 10 4 46½ 31 11½ 12½ Valenzuela PA 126 3.10 72-28 Sunday Silence1262½Easy Goer126hdAwe Inspiring126¾ 15
Steadied st,swerved
8Apr89- 5SA fst 1⅛ :453 1:093 1:344 1:473 S A Derby-G1 4 3 32 2½ 16 111 Valenzuela PA 122 2.40 91-12 Sunday Silence12211Flying Continental122¾Music Merci122½ 6
Jostled start
19Mar89- 8SA fst 1 1/16 :221 :451 1:091 1:423 San Felipe H-G2 5 4 24 24 12 11¾ Valenzuela PA 119 2.90 88-16 SundaySilnce1191¾Flying Continental1183½Music Merci1243½ 5
Broke awkwardly
2Mar89- 7SA sly 6½f :213 :443 1:084 1:152 Alw 32000 5 2 1hd 11 13½ 14½ Valenzuela PA 119 *.90 93-18 SndaySilnce1194½HeroicType119¾MightBRght1193½ Driving 7
3Dec88- 3Hol fst 6½f :22 :443 1:094 1:163 Alw 24000 1 5 31½ 1½ 11½ 2hd Gryder AT 120 1.80 92-12 Houston120hdSunday Silence1201¼Three Times Older1172 7
Lugged out lt
13Nov88- 2Hol fst 6f :22 :444 :564 1:092 Md Sp Wt 9 2 21½ 1½ 14 110 Valenzuela PA 118 *.70 95-13 SundaySilnce11810Moment of Time118¾Northern Drama1181¼ 10
Veered out st
30Oct88- 6SA fst 6½f :214 :451 1:102 1:17 Md Sp Wt 11 7 32 2hd 11 2nk Valenzuela PA 118 *1.50 85-13 CroLover118nkSndaySlnc1187½GrnStorm118hd Raced greenly 12

Sunshine Forever

b. c. 1985, by Roberto (Hail to Reason)–Outward Sunshine, by Graustark
Lifetime record: 23 8 6 3 $2,084,800
Own.– Darby Dan Farm
Br.– John W. Galbreath (Ky)
Tr.– John M. Veitch

4Nov89- 9GP gd 1½(T) :483 1:132 2:033 2:28 3↑ BC Turf-G1 6 8 1210 1314 1412 1414½ Cordero A Jr 126 18.20 70-13 Prized122hdSierra Roberta1191Star Lift126nk Outrun 14
22Oct89-11Lrl sf 1¼(T) :50 1:153 1:42 2:073 3↑ Bud Int'l-G1 7 2 21½ 78½ 79¾ 68 Cordero A Jr 126 b 7.00 51-38 Caltech1221¾YankeeAffair1262½MistrWondrfulII1261¼ Tired 11
14Oct89- 6Bel fm 1¼[T] :501 1:141 1:38 2:014 3↑ Handicap 50000 3 3 52 32 24 23 Cordero A Jr 122 *1.20 82-18 Coosaragga1153SnshnForvr1221¾CrystlMomnt1132¼ 2nd best 9
30Sep89- 1Bel gd 1 1/16(T) :232 :47 1:112 1:424 3↑ Alw 50000 6 4 54½ 65½ 610 57¾ Cordero A Jr 115 *.60 74-27 Maceo115nkPosen1152½Valid Fund1154½ Wide 6
7May89- 8Aqu sf 1 1/16(T) :261 :522 1:18 1:501 3↑ Fort Marcy H-G3 3 4 43½ 42½ 43 31½ Cordero A Jr 126 *.20 52-46 Arlene's Vlntn112¾Frstardave113¾SnshineFrvr1263¾ Rallied 5
11Feb89-10GP fm 1 1/16(T) :234 :47 1:101 1:41 3↑ Can Turf H-G2 3 5 55½ 53½ 33 23 Cordero A Jr 126 *1.30 92-12 Equalize1263SunshineForever1262¼MiSelecto1162 Steadied 7
5Nov88- 9CD gd 1½(T) :513 1:143 2:084 2:351 3↑ BC Turf-G1 2 2 21 3½ 2hd 2½ Cordero A Jr 122 2.10 - - GreatCommunicatr126½SnshineFrever122¾IndianSkimmr1239 10
Gamely
23Oct88- 7Lrl fm 1¼(T) :474 1:122 1:374 2:03 3↑ Bud Int'l-G1 4 3 21 1½ 2hd 1nk Cordero A Jr 122 *.80 82-15 SunshineForever122nkFranklyPerfct122½Squll1221¼ Driving 14
9Oct88- 8Bel sf 1½(T) :521 1:172 2:072 2:334 3↑ Turf Classic-G1 1 1 1½ 11½ 12½ 14¾ Cordero A Jr 121 *2.10 55-45 SnshineForvr1214¾MyBigBoy126¾MostWelcom126hd Driving 9
24Sep88- 8Bel fm 1⅜[T] :491 1:142 1:383 2:142 3↑ Man o' War-G1 9 5 42½ 1hd 11½ 1½ Cordero A Jr 120 *1.70 85-15 SnshineForevr120½PythButlr1261MyBgBoy1261½ Brushed,drv 9
20Aug88- 7WO fm 1¼(T) :472 1:122 1:362 2:00 3↑ Arl Million-G1 8 12 52½ 21½ 32½ 31¼ Velasquez J 118 3.95 106-07 MillNative126¾Equaliz126½SunshnForvr1181½ Finished well 14
30Jly88- 8Bel sf 1½(T) :503 1:154 2:07 2:321 3↑ Sword Dancer H-G1 2 4 42 43½ 33 21½ Cordero A Jr 114 *1.00 61-37 Anka Germania1171½Sunshine Forever1141¾Carotene1144¾ 7
Finished strong
10Jly88- 8Bel fm 1¼[T] :50 1:134 1:381 2:03 Lexington-G2 3 3 31½ 1½ 1½ 11¾ Cordero A Jr 123 *.60 79-18 SunshineForever1231¾HodgesBay114hdAskNot114nk Driving 8
24Jun88- 8Bel fm 1 1/16(T) :241 :464 1:11 1:411 Hill Prince-G3 5 4 31 1hd 12½ 16 Cordero A Jr 114 1.90 90-10 SunshineForever1146Posen1212¾KrisGreen1144 Ridden out 7
8Jun88- 5Bel fm 1 1/16(T) :24 :452 1:091 1:401 3↑ Alw 33000 1 4 410 36½ 11 13¼ Cordero A Jr 112 *.60 95-05 SnshineForevr1123¼Hertnc1171TurnngforHom1172¾ Driving 10
22May88- 8Bel yl 1(T) :23 :473 1:123 1:382 Saranac-G2 5 6 66¼ 53¼ 23½ 2¾ Cordero A Jr 114 4.70 72-27 Posen123¾Sunshine Forever1144½Blew by Em1171 Checked 8
9May88- 5Aqu gd 1⅛(T) :494 1:144 1:404 1:53 3↑ Alw 31000 12 5 52½ 41½ 21 11¾ Cordero A Jr 115 *.50 70-25 SnshineForever1151¾SultrySeason1163I'veDoneMyTime112no 12
Going away
25Apr88- 7Aqu fm 1 1/16(T) :232 :472 1:12 1:442 3↑ Md Sp Wt 7 6 59½ 46 23 13 Cordero A Jr 115 *1.00 83-18 SnshineForever1153ProfitbyEntry1152OnBorrowdTime1242½ 10
Drew clear
17Dec87- 5Hia fst 1⅛⊗ :491 1:134 1:384 1:512 Md Sp Wt 9 5 44½ 45½ 37½ 311½ Guerra WA 119 3.60 62-24 Fancy Hoofer1197Samurai Steel1194½Sunshine Forever1198 11
Lacked resp
16Oct87- 6Bel fm 1 1/16(T) :234 :474 1:123 1:452 Md Sp Wt 8 7 56 32 1hd 2hd Bailey JD 118 2.60 69-26 SmartLad118hdSnshineForevr1185¾RuntoDylght1185 Gamely 11
9Sep87- 6Bel fst 7f :224 :461 1:104 1:232 Md Sp Wt 6 5 87½ 710 711 511¾ Bailey JD 118 68.50 73-15 Firery Ensign1182½Cherokee Colony1185Foolish McDuff1183¾ 13
No threat
21Aug87- 4Sar fst 6f :222 :462 1:12 Md Sp Wt 5 11 1011 911 86¾ 79 Bailey JD 118 24.10 71-14 Digress1182Yurtu1181¾Gnome's Treasure1181 No factor 12
12Aug87- 3Sar gd 7f :223 :463 1:114 1:243 Md Sp Wt 1 11 54½ 75½ 912 815¾ Bailey JD 118 20.90 63-22 FortRily1186¾John'sConcord118nkForvrSlvr1183½ No factor 12

Swale

dkbbr. c. 1981, by Seattle Slew (Bold Reasoning)–Tuerta, by Forli **Lifetime record: 14 9 2 2 $1,583,660**

Own.– Claiborne Farm
Br.– Claiborne Farm (Ky)
Tr.– Woodford C. Stephens

9Jun84- 8Bel	fst 1½	:492 1:133 2:021 2:271	Belmont-G1	6 1 11 11½ 13 14	Pincay L Jr	126		*1.50	84-10	Swale1264Pine Circle1263Morning Bob126hd	Ridden out	11
19May84- 8Pim	fst 1 3/16	:451 1:091 1:342 1:533	Preakness-G1	5 2 22½ 31½ 55½ 76¾	Pincay L Jr	126		*.80	95-07	Gate Dancer1261½Play On1263½Fight Over126¾	Bothered	10
5May84- 8CD	fst 1¼	:472 1:114 1:363 2:022	Ky Derby-G1	15 3 31½ 12 15 13¼	Pincay L Jr	126		3.40	85-19	Swale1263¼CoaxMeChad1262AttheThreshold126nk	Drew off	20
17Apr84- 7Kee	sly 1 1/16	:233 :471 1:112 1:452	Lexington 53k	2 2 32½ 25½ 25 28	Pincay L Jr	123		*.10	71-23	He Is a Great Deal1118Swale1237½Timely Advocate1127½		5
	Best of others											
31Mar84-10GP	fst 1⅛	:463 1:101 1:344 1:473	Florida Derby-G1	7 2 2½ 2hd 1½ 1¾	Pincay L Jr	122		2.70	94-14	Swale122¾Dr. Carter1227Darn That Alarm1221	Driving	9
17Mar84- 9GP	fst 1 1/16	:234 :473 1:111 1:43	Fountain of Youth-G2	7 3 2½ 2hd 32 31½	Maple E	122		*.40	84-17	DarnThatAlrm112½CounterftMoney1121Swl122nk	Weakened	8
7Mar84- 9GP	fst 7f	:223 :452 1:093 1:221	Hutcheson-G3	10 3 3nk 2hd 1hd 18	Maple E	122		*1.00	93-21	Swale1228ForHalo1141DarnThatAlarm1122¼	Wide,ridden out	12
5Nov83- 8Med	fst 1 1/16	:224 :461 1:112 1:451	Young America-G1	7 5 47½ 33 22 1no	Maple E	122		2.30	83-20	Swale122noDisastrous Night1193Dr. Carter1196	Driving	16
8Oct83- 7Kee	fst 1 1/16	:232 :471 1:112 1:44	Breeders' Futurity-G2	3 3 2hd 1hd 1hd 1hd	Maple E	121		*1.10	86-14	Swle121hdSpender1212½BackBayBarrister121½	Wide,driving	8
10Sep83- 8Bel	fst 7f	:223 :452 1:103 1:24	Futurity-G1	4 2 1½ 1hd 2½ 1no	Maple E	122		*1.60	82-15	Swale122noShuttle Jet122¾Hail Bold King1225	Driving	5
21Aug83- 8Sar	fst 6½f	:214 :451 1:104 1:172	Hopeful-G1	3 7 32 21½ 1hd 33¼	Maple E	122		3.40	82-23	Capitol South1222¾Don Rickles122½Swale122hd	Weakened	13
1Aug83- 8Sar	my 6f	:221 :46 1:123	Sar Spl-G2	4 5 2hd 12 14 1¾	Maple E	117		2.60	77-24	Swale117¾Shuttle Jet1173¾Big Walt117½	Driving	7
21Jly83- 4Bel	fst 6f	:223 :454 1:112	Md Sp Wt	7 2 12 16 14 11¼	Maple E	118		*.60	85-20	Swale1181¼Capitol South1181¼Legatee1187¾	Driving	7
7Jly83- 4Bel	fst 5f	:223 :454 :58	Md Sp Wt	2 3 1½ 11½ 1½ 22½	Maple E	118		*.70	96-19	Shuttle Jet1182½Swale1186Rowdy Yates1181	Lugged in	8

Tasso

b. c. 1983, by Fappiano (Mr. Prospector)–Ecstacism, by What a Pleasure **Lifetime record: 23 9 4 4 $1,207,884**

Own.– Farish & Robins (Lessees)
Br.– G. Robins & T.H. Sams (Fla)
Tr.– Neil Drysdale

13Dec87- 8Hol	fm 1½Ⓣ	:483 1:13 2:022 2:27	3↑ Hol Turf Cup-G1	14 13 1312 108¾ 107¼ 94½	Toro F	126	b	13.90	81-16	Vilzak126nkForlitano1262¼Political Ambition122hd		14
	Lacked needed rally											
29Nov87- 8Hol	fm 1⅛Ⓣ	:474 1:11 1:35 1:472	3↑ Citation H-G2	9 7 62¼ 74 52¾ 53	Delahoussaye E	119	b	*2.00	88-11	Forlitano120¾Conquering Hero115nkIfrad115¾	Wide	12
16Nov87- 8SA	fm 1¼Ⓣ	:484 1:14 1:39 2:044	3↑ Ⓡ H P Russell H 84k	11 8 85½ 106¾ 75 3nk	Delahoussaye E	120	b	*1.90	63-34	GllntArchr115noWrldCourt117nkTsso1201½	Wide throughout	11
3Sep87- 8Dmr	fm 1⅛Ⓣ	:48 1:131 1:383 1:51	3↑ Alw 40000	2 4 410 54½ 41½ 1½	Delahoussaye E	116	b	2.30	78-22	Tsso116½HopefulWord117hdQuntllon1161¾	Boxed in stretch	6
8Aug87- 8Dmr	fst 1 1/16	:224 :454 1:10 1:404	3↑ San Diego H-G3	4 6 67 64¼ 54½ 56	Delahoussaye E	117	b	*1.50	90-10	Super Diamond123½Nostalgia's Star1161Good Command1142¾		7
	Wide ⅜ turn											
28Jun87- 8Hol	fst 1¼	:46 1:093 1:343 2:003	3↑ Hol Gold Cup H-G1	11 9 96 43 32 21¼↓	McCarron CJ	115	b	4.30	88-12	Ferdinnd1241¼[DH]JudgeAnglucc118[DH]Tsso1154	Wide into str	11
7Jun87- 8Hol	fst 1⅛	:464 1:104 1:353 1:481	3↑ Californian-G1	3 6 55 63½ 65½ 53¾	Pincay L Jr	117	b	5.30	92-17	JudgAngelucc1181IronEys115noSnwChf1262¾	Wide into str	8
14May87- 8Hol	fst 1	:232 :461 1:101 1:35	4↑ Alw 45000	2 6 53¾ 52¾ 42½ 1hd↓	Pincay L Jr	117	b	*1.30	88-13	[DH]Tsso117[DH]Metronomc117hdSouthrnHlo1172½	Wide into str	6
2May87- 8Hol	fst 7f	:213 :434 1:082 1:21	3↑ Triple Bend H 80k	3 5 511 511 56½ 56	Delahoussaye E	120	b	5.30	93-13	BedsidePromise1242Zabaleta1181¾BoldrThanBold1182	Wide	5
13Oct86- 8SA	fst 1⅛	:463 1:102 1:354 1:482	3↑ Yankee Valor H 94k	3 5 46 48 47½ 36½	Pincay L Jr	117	b	4.50	80-19	Precisionist1274½Garthorn1242Tasso1171½	Broke slowly	5
5Sep86- 8Dmr	fst 1 1/16	:222 :454 1:102 1:414	El Cajon 55k	5 6 75½ 31½ 1½ 13	Pincay L Jr	117	b	*1.00	91-16	Tsso1173SouthernHalo114½BrghtTom114½	Wide into stretch	9
26May86- 9GS	fst 1¼	:47 1:112 1:372 2:03	Jersey Derby-G2	3 8 813 66 35½ 33½	Pincay L Jr	126	b	3.40	85-20	Snow Chief1262Mogambo1261½Tasso1261¼	Stride late	10
7May86- 8Aqu	fst 1	:224 :46 1:101 1:353	Withers-G2	5 7 85¾ 85¼ 44½ 22¾	Pincay L Jr	126	b	*.70	85-15	ClearChoic1262¾Tsso1264¾LndngPlot1262¾	Best stride late	10
19Apr86- 8Aqu	fst 1⅛	:472 1:111 1:361 1:503	Wood Memorial-G1	4 3 53 65½ 46 42	Pincay L Jr	126	b	*.80	80-18	Broad Brush126½Mogambo126nkGroovy1261¼	Wide	7
5Apr86- 8Aqu	fst 1	:222 :444 1:083 1:343	Gotham-G2	6 7 811 811 56½ 32	Pincay L Jr	123		2.00	91-18	Mogambo121¾[D]Groovy1141¼Tasso1231	In close after start	9
	Placed second through disqualification											
15Mar86- 7Aqu	fst 7f	:231 :461 1:11 1:234	Manassa Mauler 55k	2 8 53½ 31 1hd 13	Maple E	122		*.60	82-23	Tasso1223Lil Tyler122noRiomundo115no	Driving	9
	Previously owned by Robins & Waldemar Inc											
2Nov85- 1Aqu	fst 1	:222 :452 1:104 1:361	©BC Juvenile-G1	7 7 85¾ 64½ 33 1no	Pincay L Jr	122	b	5.60	85-10	Tasso122noStorm Cat1221¾Scat Dancer122no	Just up	13
19Oct85- 7Kee	fst 1 1/16	:232 :474 1:121 1:46	Breeders' Futurity-G2	9 4 31 2hd 12½ 16	Pincay L Jr	121	b	*.90	76-24	Tsso1216ReglDreamer1213½ThunderngForc121hd	Ridden out	11
9Oct85- 7Kee	fst *7f	1:272	Alw 33040	1 4 43 65½ 2½ 2¾	Pincay L Jr	121		*.30	85-18	FarawayIsland112¾Tasso1218SonoftheDesert1211½	Rallied	7
11Sep85- 8Dmr	fst 1	:231 :471 1:113 1:36	Dmr Futurity-G1	6 5 31½ 2½ 22 1nk	Pincay L Jr	117		*1.00	88-15	Tasso117nkArewehavingfunyet1172¼Snow Chief1173¼	Driving	6
17Aug85- 7Dmr	fst 1	:222 :463 1:114 1:363	Alw 23000	1 4 42 22 2hd 14	Delahoussaye E	118		*.60	85-17	Tasso1184Speedy Shannon1187½Salerno Beach1184½	Easily	6
22Jly85- 3Hol	fst 6f	:222 :46 :582 1:103	Md Sp Wt	5 7 77½ 55¼ 32½ 11	Pincay L Jr	118		2.10	94-07	Tasso1181Bright Tom1187Darby Fair1181¼	Driving	7
31May85- 4Hol	fst 5f	:222 :454 :582	Md Sp Wt	4 8 77½ 69 38½ 36½	Pincay L Jr	118		3.40	--	MightyTrip1181DarbyFair1185½Tasso1184½	Rank post parade	10

Temperence Hill

b. c. 1977, by Stop the Music (Hail to Reason)–Sister Shannon, by Etonian **Lifetime record: 31 11 4 2 $1,567,650**

Own.– Loblolly Stable
Br.– Dr A.F. Polk Jr (Ky)
Tr.– Joseph B. Cantey

12Nov81- 6Med	fst 1¼	:471 1:113 1:363 2:022	3↑ Med Cup H-G2	9 10 64 32½ 34 43½	Maple E	124	b	5.90	86-14	Princelet110¾Niteange114¾Peat Moss1212	Lacked bid	14
10Oct81- 8Bel	fst 1½	:48 1:123 2:021 2:282	3↑ J C Gold Cup-G1	4 9 99¼ 96½ 83¾ 64	Maple E	126	b	6.60	74-14	John Henry126hdPeat Moss126¾Relaxing123hd	Wide	11
19Sep81- 8Bel	my 1¼	:481 1:114 1:354 2:003	3↑ Marlboro Cup H-G1	3 7 68½ 56 34½ 35¼	Maple E	127	b	4.10	92-13	Noble Nashua1163¾Amber Pass1201½Temperence Hill1271¼		8
	Lacked response											
5Sep81- 8Bel	fst 1⅛	:461 1:094 1:343 1:471	3↑ Woodward-G1	9 8 87½ 77¼ 56 55¾	Maple E	128	b	11.40	85-14	PleasntClny1231¾AmberPass1261¼HerbWtr1162	Raced wide	9
19Aug81- 1Sar	fm 1 3/16Ⓣ	:484 1:122 1:362 1:552	3↑ Alw 35000	6 5 54½ 53½ 66 55	Maple E	122	b	2.50	84-13	Manguin115noScythianGold1192¼TheLibrlMmbr1152	No factor	6
18Jly81- 8Bel	fst 1½	:492 1:134 2:013 2:26	3↑ Brooklyn H-G1	5 6 77 810 713 817	Maple E	128		2.30	73-15	Hechizado1164TheLiberlMembr113¾PeatMoss1113¼	No factor	10
4Jly81- 8Bel	sly 1¼	:473 1:114 1:36 2:02	3↑ Suburban-G1	1 4 49 45 33½ 1hd	MacBeth D	127		3.20	90-20	Temperence Hill127hdRing of Light115¾Highland Blade113nk		8
	Brushed,driving											
14Jun81- 8Hol	fst 1¼	:453 1:093 1:344 2:002	3↑ Hol Gold Cup H-G1	2 4 55¼ 75¾ 56¾ 56	Maple E	129		3.20	83-16	[D]Caterman120hdEleven Stitches1222½Super Moment117nk		10
	Lacked room											
25May81- 8Hol	fst 1⅛	:452 1:101 1:353 1:482	3↑ Californian-G1	3 4 411 52½ 32½ 2hd	Maple E	130		*1.60	87-15	ElevenStitches122hdTemprnceHill130nkKilijaro1233¾	Sharp	12
10Apr81- 9OP	fst 1 1/16	:232 :464 1:112 1:432	4↑ Oaklawn H-G2	4 5 43 1hd 1½ 12	Maple E	126		*.60	91-18	TemprnceHll1262SunCtchr1231¾Uncool1142½	Brushed,clear	5
28Mar81- 9OP	fst 1 1/16	:244 :49 1:13 1:441	4↑ Razorback H-G2	1 5 56½ 31 2hd 1nk	Maple E	124		*.40	87-21	TemprnceHill124nkBlueEnsign1133Belle'sRulr1124½	Driving	6
25Oct80- 8Aqu	sf 1½Ⓣ	:514 1:192 2:13 2:393	3↑ Turf Classic-G1	5 4 33 68 711 716	Maple E	121		2.40	27-57	Anifa1233Golden Act1265John Henry126nk	Tired	8
18Oct80-10LaD	gd 1¼	:491 1:143 1:393 2:063	Super Derby 500k	3 4 25 1½ 13 15½	Maple E	126		*.50	92-19	TemprnceHill1265½FirstAlbert126½CactusRoad126no	Driving	8
4Oct80- 8Bel	fst 1½	:494 1:15 2:051 2:301	3↑ J C Gold Cup-G1	1 3 43 1½ 13 15½	Maple E	121		2.30	69-19	TemprncHll1215½JohnHnry1262IvoryHuntr1263¼	Ridden out	7
6Sep80- 7Bel	fst 1⅛	:45 1:092 1:341 1:47	3↑ Marlboro Cup H-G1	6 8 811 74¼ 55 511¾	Maple E	119		6.20	80-15	Wintr'sTl1234½GlorousSng117nkJklnKlugmn1183½	No factor	8
16Aug80- 8Sar	fst 1¼	:454 1:101 1:361 2:024	Travers-G1	3 9 915 55 3nk 11½	Maple E	126		3.80	86-13	TemperenceHill1261½FirstAlbert126noAmbrPss1266¾	Driving	9
19Jly80- 8Bel	fst 1½	:513 1:163 2:05 2:283	3↑ Brooklyn H-G1	1 2 32 45½ 48 410½	Maple E	114	b	2.10	66-20	Winter'sTale1205StateDinner1213½RingofLight1142	Tired	5
5Jly80- 8Bel	fst 1⅛	:451 1:091 1:353 1:49	Dwyer-G2	7 6 611 57½ 46 21	Maple E	129	b	8.20	81-17	AmberPass1141TempernceHill129hdComptroller1193	Rallied	8
22Jun80- 8Bel	hd 1Ⓣ	:23 :452 1:093 1:334	Saranac-G2	2 10 1210 1211 911 77¾	Maple E	128	b	4.90	88-05	KeytoContent1143CurrentLegnd114½BenFab1233	No threat	13
7Jun80- 8Bel	my 1½	:501 1:151 2:04 2:294	Belmont-G1	3 7 85 3½ 2hd 12	Maple E	126	b	53.40	71-17	Temperence Hill1262Genuine Risk1211½Rockhill Native1262		10
	Brisk urging											

31May80- 7Bel fm 1 1/16Ⓣ :224 :454 1:10 1:423 3↑ Alw 35000 6 4 512 412 33 31¾ Maple E 113 b 8.10 81-19 FrenchColonial121nkPerceran1171½TemprncHll113no Gaining 6
26May80- 8Key fst 1⅛ :472 1:113 1:362 1:484 Pa Derby-G3 7 7 713 610 612 511¼ Haire D 122 b *.70 80-15 LivelyKing1224Mutineer122nkStutzBlackhawk1224 No rally 7
10May80- 8Aqu fst 1 :232 :454 1:091 1:342 Withers-G2 3 7 78¾ 69½ 28 25½ Haire D 126 b 3.30 88-13 ColonlMoran1265½TemperenceHill1264¼J.P.Brothr126½ Wide 7
12Apr80- 9OP fst 1⅛ :462 1:104 1:382 1:503 Ark Derby-G1 8 9 918 89¾ 41¾ 11¼ Haire D 123 b 4.60e 90-21 TemperencHll1231¼Bold'NRullng1173¾SunCtchr120nk Driving 10
29Mar80- 7OP sly 1 70 :234 :48 1:124 1:421 Alw 25000 1 3 31½ 33 23 24¾ Maple E 121 b 1.60 80-23 Loto Canada1214¾Temperence Hill1211¾Raise a Kid1122½ 7
2nd best
15Mar80- 9OP fst 1 70 :22 :452 1:112 1:424 Rebel H 64k 3 12 1117 814 44 12¼ Haire D 114 b 16.50 82-22 Temperence Hill1142¼Royal Sporn1112½Be a Prospect123hd 15
Drew out
4Mar80- 8OP fst 1 70 :234 :48 1:134 1:434 3↑ Alw 15000 4 3 44 43½ 32½ 1½ Maple S 114 b 3.00 77-24 TemprnceHll114½Tonimarow1142ElGatoGrande1144½ Driving 8
26Feb80- 4OP fst 6f :221 :47 1:132 3↑ Md Sp Wt 3 7 611 56½ 25 1¾ Maple S 114 b *.80 78-24 TemprnceHill114¾WrongSurf1156TailbackTodd1148 Driving 8
29Sep79- 4Bel fst 6½f :23 :463 1:103 1:164 Md Sp Wt 7 9 84¼ 96¾ 712 715 Maple S 118 b 16.40 77-12 Inland Voyager1188Preferred List118hdRaise a Crown1181¼ 12
Wide
4Aug79- 2Sar fst 6f :22 :451 1:102 Md Sp Wt 1 9 109¾ 89 78 68½ Maple E 118 5.30 79-12 Dressage1185¼Attengur1182½TrafficBreaker118no No factor 11
22Jly79- 4Bel fst 6f :221 :461 1:113 Md Sp Wt 9 6 1112 1114 912 410¾ Maple E 118 11.00 73-18 Fappiano1183½Buck Island1186¾Rectory118½ Late gain 11

Theatrical (Ire)

b. c. 1982, by Nureyev (Northern Dancer)–Tree of Knowledge, by Sassafras
Lifetime record: 22 10 4 2 $2,943,627
Own.– A.E. Paulson
Br.– Mr & Mrs B.R. Firestone (Ire)
Tr.– William I. Mott

21Nov87- 6Hol fm 1½Ⓣ :471 1:111 2:001 2:242 3↑ BC Turf-G1 12 4 48 11½ 1hd 1½ Day P 126 *1.80e 99-00 Theatrical126½Trempolino1223½VillgStrII126nk Long drive 14
Previously owned by Firestone & Paulson
24Oct87- 8Aqu fm 1⅜Ⓣ :501 1:142 1:382 2:152 3↑ Man o' War-G1 5 2 22 2hd 1hd 12½ Day P 126 *.30 94-07 Theatricl1262½LeGloriux121½MdnghtCousns1266 Ridden out 8
26Sep87- 8Bel sf 1½Ⓣ :491 1:133 2:044 2:291 3↑ Turf Classic-G1 5 2 27 1½ 12 13¾ Day P 126 *1.00 78-25 Theatrical1263¾RiverMemories1164¼Talkno1268¾ Ridden out 6
6Sep87- 8AP fm 1¼Ⓣ :482 1:133 1:383 2:022 3↑ Bud Arl Million-G1 4 3 2½ 11 23 34¾ Day P 126 2.30 77-27 Manila1261½Sharrood1263¼Theatrical1263¾ Tired 8
1Aug87- 8Bel fm 1½Ⓣ :491 1:132 2:024 2:26 3↑ Sword Dancer H-G1 2 1 1hd 21½ 23½ 23 Day P 124 *.40 91-10 ⒹDance of Life1223Theatrical1245½Akabir1144 Checked 4
Placed first through disqualification
13Jun87- 8Bel fm 1⅜Ⓣ :50 1:14 1:381 2:14 3↑ Bowling Green H-G1 1 3 33 33 2hd 11 Day P 123 *1.30 87-24 Theatrical1231Akabir116nkDance of Life121nk Ridden out 10
30May87- 8Bel fm 1¼Ⓣ :481 1:123 1:362 2:004 3↑ Red Smith H-G2 5 3 32 42¼ 31 11¾ Day P 122 2.80 90-24 Theatrical1221¾DanceofLife1221¼Equalize112hd Ridden out 11
21Feb87-10Hia fm 1½Ⓣ 2:283 3↑ Hia Turf Cup H-G1 6 1 1hd 11 1½ 1nk Day P 121 *1.30 87-14 Theatrical121nkLong Mick1151½Creme Fraiche1185 Lasted 8
31Jan87-10Hia fm 1 3/16Ⓣ 1:54 3↑ Bougainvillea H-G2 11 9 85 62¼ 33½ 22 Day P 122 *1.60 85-14 Akabir1132ⒹTheatrical122nkFlying Pidgeon1201 Bore in 14
Disqualified and placed 14th;Previously trained by Robert Frankel
7Dec86- 8Hol fm 1½Ⓣ :474 1:121 2:01 2:254 3↑ Hol Turf Cup Inv'l-G1 2 1 2hd 1½ 11 3nk Stevens GL 126 *1.20e 93-09 Alphabatm126hdDahar126nkTheatrcl126½ Rider dropped whip 8
1Nov86- 6SA fm 1½Ⓣ :472 1:111 2:003 2:252 3↑ BC Turf-G1 1 2 22½ 21 1hd 2nk Stevens GL 126 2.70e 88-07 Manila122nkTheatrical1263¾Estrapade1232¾ Gamely 9
12Oct86- 8SA fm 1½Ⓣ :464 1:111 2:003 2:26 3↑ Oak Tree Inv'l-G1 5 5 53½ 22 22 22¼ Stevens GL 126 *.40e 83-12 Estrapade1232¼Theatricl1265½UptownSwll126½ Best of rest 10
Previously trained by Dermot K. Weld
31Aug86- 8AP fm 1¼Ⓣ :471 1:113 1:371 2:004 3↑ Bud Arl Million-G1 14 11 108½ 107 99½ 1010¾ Cauthen S 126 *2.10e 79-11 Estrapade1225Divulge126hdPennine Walk126½ Pinched st. 14
Previously owned by B.R. Firestone
27Jly86♦ Dusseldorf(Ger) gd *1½ⓉLH 2:273 3↑ Grosser Preis von Berlin-G1 Stk80400 22 Kinane MJ 132 6.20 Acatenango1322Theatrical1323¼Orfano1171½ 8
Tracked leaders,bid 1½f out,chased winner home
20Jun86♦ Ascot(GB) fm 1½ⓉRH 2:291 4↑ Hardwicke Stakes-G2 Stk73300 712 Kinane MJ 124 *2.75 Dihistan121¾St. Hilarion1264Iroko1211 10
Progress 2½f out,drifted badly right,weakened
Previously owned by B.R. Firestone
2Nov85- 6Aqu fm 1½Ⓣ :48 1:122 2:022 2:27 3↑ BC Turf-G1 14 8 810 107¼ 117¼ 117 Piggott L 122 3.80e 99-00 Pebbles123nkStrawberryRoadII1261¼Mourjan1261 Raced wide 14
8Sep85♦ Phoenix Park(Ire) hy 1¼ⓉRH 2:091 3↑ Phoenix Champion Stakes-G1 Stk564000 77½ Kinane MJ 123 8.00 Commanche Run1323Bob Back132¾Damister123no 11
Brief progress 4f out,never threatened.Triptych 10th
29Jun85♦ The Curragh(Ire) gd 1½ⓉRH 2:294 Irish Derby-G1 Stk370000 2½ Kinane MJ 126 6.00 Law Society126½Theatrical1262½Damister126hd 13
Rallied to lead 2f out,headed 100y out.Triptych 5th
5Jun85♦ Epsom(GB) gd 1½ⓉLH 2:361 Epsom Derby-G1 Stk458000 725 Piggott L 126 10.00 Slip Anchor1267Law Society1266Damister126no 14
Tracked in 6th,weakened 3f out,drifted left
11May85♦ Leopardstwn(Ire) yl 1¼ⓉLH 2:134 Derrinstown Derby Trial-G2 Stk51600 14 Kinane MJ 123 *1.00 Theatrical1234Northern Plain1262Lord Duke1233 8
Tracked in 4th,led 2f out,soon clear,drifted slightly
27Apr85♦ The Curragh(Ire) gd 1⅜ⓉRH 2:252 Ballysax Stakes Stk11500 12 Piggott L 123 2.50 Theatrical1232Leading Counsel13112Snow Plant123nk 6
Steadied start,5th early,rail bid,angled out,led 1f out
15Oct84♦ Gowran Park(Ire) fm 1 1/16ⓉRH 1:372 Kilkenny EBF Maiden Mdn3200 11 Kinane MJ 126 *1.10 Theatrical1261Pala Chief1263Jazz Ballet126no 16
Tracked in 4th,dueled 1f out,led 100y out,handily

Tiffany Lass

dkbbr. f. 1983, by Bold Forbes (Irish Castle)–Sally Stark, by Graustark
Lifetime record: 10 8 1 1 $534,943
Own.– A.U. Jones
Br.– Aaron U. Jones (Ky)
Tr.– Lazaro S. Barrera

13Jun87- 8Hol fst 1⅛ :454 1:101 1:351 1:481 3↑ ⒻMilady H-G1 4 2 22½ 2½ 22½ 22¾ Stevens GL 120 2.20 93-11 SeldomSeenSue1172¾TiffanyLass1204½FrauAltv115½ 2nd best 7
9May87- 9Hol fst 1 :222 :444 1:084 1:333 3↑ ⒻHawthone H-G2 3 2 21 32½ 35½ 38 Stevens GL 123 *.60 87-10 Seldom Seen Sue1144Clabber Girl1164Tiffany Lass1236 5
Lacked response
29Apr87- 8Hol fst 6f :214 :444 :564 1:092 3↑ ⒻSilver Spoon 62k 4 2 2½ 2½ 1hd 1¾ Stevens GL 123 *1.10 96-13 Tiffany Lass123¾Luisant1182¼Seldom Seen Sue116½ Gamely 4
2May86- 9CD fst 1⅛ :463 1:11 1:371 1:503 ⒻKy Oaks-G1 1 2 32 22 2hd 1hd Stevens GL 121 *1.20 89-14 TiffanyLass121hdLifeattheTop121nkFamlyStyl121hd Driving 12
12Apr86- 9OP fst 1 1/16 :232 :471 1:113 1:42 ⒻFantasy-G1 1 1 1hd 1hd 1½ 12½ Stevens GL 121 3.40 91-16 Tiffany Lass1212½Lotka1162Turn and Dance112hd Drew out 8
22Mar86-10FG fst 1 1/16 :23 :462 1:114 1:45 ⒻFG Oaks-G3 5 3 34 21 2½ 1¾ Frazier RL 121 *1.00 87-17 TiffanyLass121¾PatriciaJ.K.1211½TurnandDnc1125½ Driving 6
2Mar86-10FG fst 1 1/16 :234 :48 1:14 1:46 ⒻDavona Dale 38k 9 4 53¾ 53 21½ 13 Frazier RL 122 *.30 82-25 TiffanyLass1223SuperSet1225PortofDeparture117½ Easily 10
15Feb86-10FG fst 6f :214 :462 :582 1:11 ⒻThelma 47k 1 4 1hd 2hd 13 19 Frazier RL 112 *.70 90-24 Tiffany Lass1129Best in Class122½My Mafalda1123½ Easily 9
9Jan86- 8FG sl 6f :222 :471 :593 1:124 ⒻAlw 9000 6 2 32½ 2hd 12 15 Frazier RL 119 *.50 81-32 TiffanyLass1195TwelveMileLimit1148PrttyPlum1191½ Easily 7
24Dec85- 6Hol fst 6f :22 :453 :573 1:10 ⒻMd Sp Wt 3 6 31 31 21½ 11 Stevens GL 118 *.80 94-12 TiffanyLass1181Barbarn1184½Bggr'sWllt1183½ Saved ground 11

Track Robbery

ch. f. 1976, by No Robbery (Swaps)–Left at Home, by Run for Nurse
Own.– Summa Stable
Br.– E. Kitchen (Ky)
Tr.– John W. Russell

Lifetime record: 59 22 12 7 $1,098,537

Date	Cond	Dist	Fractions	Race	PP	St	1c	2c	Str	Fin	Jockey	Wt	Eq	Odds	Spd	Top finishers	Comment	Fld
8Jan83-8SA	fm	1⅛Ⓣ	:45 1:091 1:333 1:462	4↑ ⒻSan Gorgonio H 84k	4	1	11½	1hd	1110	118	Valenzuela PA	122		6.00	87-05	Castilla1221StarPastures119hdCatGirl115½	Fin. after 6f	11
5Dec82-8Hol	fm	1⅛Ⓣ	:463 1:104 1:344 1:472	3↑ ⒻMatriarch (Div 2) 172k	2	1	14	13	3nk	42¼	Valenzuela PA	123		4.00	91-08	Castilla120hdSangue1231½Star Pastures123¾	Steadied	9
26Nov82-6Med	fst	1⅛	:464 1:12 1:383 1:52	3↑ ⒻLong Look H-G2	4	1	13	11½	35½	69½	Valenzuela PA	124		*.70	63-21	LadyDean1212¾Prismatical114nkCleverGuest1093½	Gave way	6
30Oct82-7Kee	sly	1⅛	:461 1:10 1:35 1:474	3↑ ⒻSpinster-G1	6	1	12	12	16	19	Valenzuela PA	123		4.00	98-08	TrackRbbry1239BlushWthPrd1191½OurDrlng1192¼	Ridden out	9
				Previously trained by Robert L. Wheeler														
18Aug82-8Dmr	fst	1 1/16	:223 :452 1:091 1:40	3↑ ⒻChula Vista H 77k	1	2	21½	31½	411	414	Delahoussaye E	123		*1.10	86-21	Matching1166Miss Huntington116noCat Girl1178	Faltered	4
11Jly82-8Hol	fst	1⅛	:462 1:101 1:352 1:48	3↑ ⒻVanity H-G1	1	1	1½	1½	2hd	21½	Delahoussaye E	123		2.30	87-16	Sangue1201½Track Robbery1231½Cat Girl1172	Game try	7
27Jun82-8Hol	fst	1 1/16	:231 :461 1:102 1:413	3↑ ⒻMilady H-G2	6	1	11½	11	2hd	22½	Delahoussaye E	124		*1.10	84-12	Cat Girl1142½Track Robbery124noAck's Secret1235	Gamely	6
23May82-8Hol	fm	1⅛Ⓣ	:461 1:102 1:341 1:464	3↑ ⒻGamely H-G2	8	1	11	1hd	21½	42	Delahoussaye E	125		*1.70	94-05	Ack'sSecrt1221MissHuntington117¾Vocalist114nk	Weakened	9
7Apr82-9OP	fst	1 1/16	:233 :472 1:123 1:451	4↑ ⒻApple Blossom H-G1	5	1	11	1½	2hd	1no	Delahoussaye E	124		*.90	82-30	Track Robbery124noAndover Way1205½Jameela1231	Driving	6
20Mar82-8SA	fst	1⅛	:454 1:094 1:344 1:471	4↑ ⒻS Ana H-G2	5	1	11	11½	12½	15¼	Delahoussaye E	123		2.30	93-12	TrackRobbery1235¼Manzanera1171¼Ack'sSecret1231¼	Driving	8
28Feb82-8SA	fst	1⅛	:453 1:092 1:35 1:473	4↑ ⒻS Margarita H-G1	1	2	2hd	1hd	2hd	22½	Delahoussaye E	123		6.80e	88-09	Ack'sSecrt1182½TrackRobbry1231PstForgttng1222½	Gamely	10
13Feb82-8SA	fst	1 1/16	:223 :46 1:101 1:42	4↑ ⒻS Maria H-G2	2	4	43½	42½	33	32½	Delahoussaye E	124		2.70e	88-16	Targa1142½Jameela124hdTrack Robbery124¾	Rallied	8
6Jan82-8SA	hy	1⅛	:474 1:123 1:393 1:523	4↑ ⒻSan Gorgonio H 79k	3	1	11½	11	1½	1½	Delahoussaye E	123		*.80	66-34	TrackRbbry123½RainbowConnection1177Targa11411	Driving	5
13Dec81-8Hol	fst	1⅛	:463 1:103 1:361 1:493	3↑ ⒻSilver Belles H 107k	3	1	11	1hd	1hd	2hd	Delahoussaye E	123		4.40	81-21	HappyGuess117hdTrackRobbery1232½Targa112hd	Just missed	6
5Dec81-8BM	yl	1⅛Ⓣ	:474 1:133 1:40 1:542	3↑ ⒻCal Jockey Club H 107k	3	2	22	21½	1hd	1nk	Mena F	124		*1.00	68-24	TrckRbbry124nkBrryBush1201½Tolt111½	Headed str,came back	7
21Nov81-8BM	sf	1 1/16Ⓣ	:232 :483 1:144 1:502	3↑ ⒻChildren's Hosp H 56k	5	1	11½	11½	1½	1½	Mena F	125		*.90	56-44	Track Robbery125½Tolita112½Noaah1181	Gamely	10
18Oct81-8SA	fm	1⅛Ⓣ	:451 1:094 1:341 1:47	3↑ ⒻLas Palmas H-G3	4	1	11	2hd	22½	44¾	Valenzuela PA	122		3.60e	87-12	Ack'sSecrt1191¾QntoConqur123nkBrryBush1182¾	No excuse	9
30Aug81-8Dmr	fm	1⅛Ⓣ	:464 1:104 1:361 1:484	3↑ ⒻRamona H-G2	5	2	2hd	1hd	3½	31½	Valenzuela PA	123		*2.90	92-10	QueentoConqr120½AmbrEver1121TrckRbbry1231½	Weakened	10
19Aug81-8Dmr	fst	1 1/16	:222 :45 1:093 1:413	3↑ ⒻChula Vista H 81k	6	1	17	13	31	36	Valenzuela PA	125		*1.50	86-17	Save Wild Life118½Princess Karenda1205½TrackRobbery1251¼	Used in pace	6
12Jly81-8Hol	fst	1⅛	:453 1:091 1:341 1:47	3↑ ⒻVanity Inv'l H-G1	7	1	17	14½	14½	13½	Valenzuela PA	120		3.70	94-14	TrackRbbry1203½Princess Karenda118nkSave Wild Life1173¼	Never threatened	7
13Jun81-8Hol	fm	1⅛Ⓣ	:46 1:101 1:341 1:464	3↑ ⒻBeverly Hills H-G3	2	1	15	13	12	11¼	Valenzuela PA	120		3.60	96-10	TrackRobbery1201¼PrincessKarenda1214½SaveWildLife1152½	Driving	5
31May81-8Hol	fm	1 1/16Ⓣ	:231 :463 1:111 1:404	3↑ ⒻWilshire H-G3	6	1	13	1½	12	1¾	Valenzuela PA	118		4.80	95-09	TrackRobbry118¾LuthMusic1151¾SaveWildLife1161½	Driving	6
6May81-8Hol	fm	1 1/16Ⓣ	:23 :461 1:101 1:41	3↑ ⒻⓇMatinee H(Div1) 43k	3	1	11½	2hd	2hd	33½	Valenzuela PA	122		3.80	90-09	Targa1103Ack's Secret122½Track Robbery1221½	Weakened	6
24Apr81-8Hol	fm	1⅛Ⓣ	:454 1:11 1:354 1:481	3↑ ⒻGamely H-G2	2	1	11½	11½	1hd	46	Valenzuela PA	118		24.10	83-12	Kilijaro1272½PrincessKrnd1212½WshngWll1221	Used in pace	6
11Apr81-8SA	fst	1 1/16	:221 :452 1:10 1:414	4↑ ⒻⓇS Lucia H 56k	6	2	21	53½	912	916	Lipham T	124		*2.20	76-15	Finance Charge1135½Si1151¾Swift Bird1182¾	Tired	10
7Mar81-8SA	fst	1⅛	:46 1:094 1:352 1:48	4↑ ⒻSanta Ana H-G3	2	2	2½	2½	11½	22	Delahoussaye E	119		4.30	87-11	QueentoConquer1212TrckRbbry1195Ack'sScrt1235	No match	7
20Feb81-8SA	fm	1⅛Ⓣ	:464 1:104 1:351 1:472	4↑ ⒻAlw 40000	1	1	12	12½	11	11½	Pincay L Jr	120		*1.80	90-10	TrackRobbery1201½GrafittiGal1151Hthr'sTurn1131¾	Driving	8
31Jan81-8SA	gd	1 1/16	:23 :462 1:104 1:431	4↑ ⒻS Maria H-G2	4	1	11½	1hd	22½	22	Pincay L Jr	117		4.10	83-23	GloriousSong1272TrckRbbry1175MssHuntngton11310	Gamely	4
22Jan81-8SA	fst	1 1/16	:224 :46 1:10 1:411	4↑ ⒻAlw 40000	1	1	11	11½	14	12	Pincay L Jr	117		2.60e	95-14	Track Robbery1172Princess Toby1186Miss Huntington1134	Not threatened	7
16Jan81-8SA	fst	1 1/16	:231 :463 1:11 1:42	4↑ ⒻAlw 40000	7	2	24	21	2½	31½	Pierce D	119		*1.30e	89-12	Kankm115noPrncssToby1171½TrckRbbry1191½	Bid,not enough	7
4Oct80-8BM	fm	1 1/16Ⓣ	:231 :47 1:114 1:434	3↑ ⒻTizna H 45k	11	1	15	12	1½	51½	Lipham T	115		8.40	87-09	Fresca121noNoaah114nkLusty Try112nk	Failed to last	11
9Aug80-8Dmr	fm	1Ⓣ	:231 :462 1:102 1:344	3↑ ⒻPalomar H-G3	1	1	1½	1hd	33	99	Lipham T	113		6.30e	91-05	A Thousand Stars115noWishing Well1212½Devon Ditty120nk	Done after 6f	9
31Jly80-8Dmr	fm	1 1/16Ⓣ	:24 :483 1:122 1:431	3↑ ⒻAlw 35000	4	1	12½	1½	1½	2¾	Lipham T	116		3.00	92-07	PrincessToby116¾TrackRobbery116¾More So1133	Hung late	6
11Jly80-8Hol	fm	1 1/16Ⓣ	:23 :463 1:101 1:401	4↑ ⒻAlw 50000	6	2	33	22	32½	44	Lipham T	117		14.70e	94-09	Love You Dear117¾Princess Toby122nkA Thousand Stars1173	Lacked rally	8
28Jun80-8Hol	fm	1⅛Ⓣ	:471 1:112 1:35 1:472	3↑ ⒻBeverly Hills H-G3	3	3	32½	41¼	32	62¾	Lipham T	113		9.60e	90-12	CountryQueen122noWishngWell122½TheVeryOne117nk	Hung	10
13Jun80-8Hol	fst	1 1/16	:222 :452 1:084 1:411	4↑ ⒻMarket Basket 50k	2	3	22	33	611	612	Lipham T	117		26.10	77-13	SplendidGrl1151½Picea1124½Canonzton1171¼	Done after 6f	7
1Jun80-5Hol	fm	1Ⓣ	:23 :461 1:10 1:354	4↑ ⒻAlw 40000	7	2	3½	2½	1hd	1no	Lipham T	114		25.90	90-10	TrackRobbery114noOutremer1143Conveniently1162½	Gamely	7
15May80-8Hol	fst	6f	:22 :442 :563 1:083	4↑ ⒻAlw 35000	4	4	1½	3nk	62¼	78½	Olivares F	115		34.20	85-13	Canonization117nkDouble Deceit1152Outremer1152½	Tired	7
3May80-8Hol	fst	6f	:213 :434 :552 1:073	4↑ ⒻAlw 35000	7	1	47	46½	510	69½	Olivares F	115		9.10e	89-13	SplendidGirl1152¾DoublDct1171½ShnHgh1142½	Flattened out	7
				Previously owned by Blue Sky Stable; previously trained by Phil Schvaneveldt														
16Dec79-10TuP	fst	6½f	:213 :434 1:09 1:154	ⒻMolly Butler H 14k	2	9	41½	42½	89	107½	Kato A	115	b	6.40	84-19	Maurita1122Megabuck112noGaelicGiggl110nk	Done after ½	11
2Dec79-10TuP	fst	6½f	:214 :45 1:094 1:161	Az Republic H 12k	10	2	11½	11½	75¼	1314	Powell JP	115	b	3.60	76-22	Ken'nBold117nkHourLong1151½FullFlm1204	Faltered stretch	14
11Nov79-8TuP	fst	6f	:214 :442 :562 1:094	Alw 4300	6	3	31	3½	23	2nk	Powell JP	115	b	*.50	88-17	VestdWys113nkTrckRbbry1153½LustyVkng1141	Strong finish	7
4Nov79-9TuP	fst	5f	:213 :444 :57	Black Canyon H 11k	6	4	44	43½	24	37½↓	Powell JP	117	b	2.90	84-20	Nervous John1233½Full of Flame119[DH]Track Robbery117	Between horses early	8
22Sep79-11Alb	fst	1	:233 :464 1:12 1:393	Alb Derby H 23k	2	1	12	12	21	21¼	Powell JP	118	b	*1.30	81-23	HappyIrishman1191¼TrackRobbery1183½TurquoisPrncss1112¼		12
18Aug79-9Cen	gd	1 1/16	:232 :471 1:122 1:474	ⒻLady & Dove 13k	2	2	13	16	16	12½	Powell JP	116	b	*.30	68-26	Track Robbery1162½Nalees Battle1161½Lady Go Marching1162	Wide,ridden out	8
5Aug79-9Cen	fst	1⅛	:471 1:122 1:38 1:512	Cen Derby 22k	3	2	2½	11½	21	2hd	Kato A	112	b	*.80	88-16	Keen'n Bold114hdTrack Robbery1122To Erin112hd	Gamely	8
19Jly79-7Aks	fst	1 70	:224 :461 1:104 1:423	ⒻPrincess 26k	5	3	3nk	31	2½	2hd	Kato A	120	b	2.40	85-19	MerryThought114hdTrackRbbery1204TurquoisePrincess118½	Dueled outside	8
5Jly79-7Aks	my	6f	:222 :451 1:112	ⒻGood Life 26k	10	5	3½	2hd	1hd	1nk	Kato A	116		3.90	80-25	Track Robbery116nkRappid Action1144Merry Thought114nk	Outside,driving	10
24Jun79-9Cen	fst	1	:23 :462 1:122 1:392	Turf Club Centre H 6.3k	6	3	3½	11½	12	1nk	Kato A	124	b	*.60	82-14	Track Robbery124nkAiles Sound114½To Erin115½	Lasted	13
10Jun79-9Cen	my	6f	:212 :44 :563 1:102	Turn of the Cntry H 5.6k	2	2	1½	13	14	16	Kato A	121	b	*.40	88-16	TrackRobbery1216Mr. Moon Babe115¾Tatty Walk1122	Easily	6
28May79-8Cen	fst	5½f	:22 :45 :572 1:04	Alw 2800	7	4	2hd	1½	13	14	Kato A	112	b	*.60	92-15	Track Robbery1124Gravitational1141Alliance Royal1162	Much the best	8
30Mar79-9TuP	fst	6f	:214 :443 :57 1:10	Alw 4500	7	1	2½	1½	15	16	Kato A	114	b	3.10	87-26	TrackRbbry1146VestedWays1132ShdyJck114½	Much the best	7
12Nov78-10LA	gd	6f	:213 :45 :584 1:114	ⒻSaddleback 22k	8	4	33	33½	65¾	68¾	Harris W	117	b	9.20	82-13	Sateen115hdScotts Princess1153½Go Zulu Sis1171¼	Tired	10
30Sep78-8Cen	fst	6f	:222 :451 :573 1:11	Alw 2800	3	6	41	2½	1½	11	Andrews EH	118	b	*.50	85-18	TrackRobbery1181TattyWalk1156Babu'sGlory116nk	Bit wide	6
16Sep78-6Cen	fst	5½f	:214 :443 :564 1:032	Alw 2600	4	6	42	31	12	15	Lintner K	113	b	*1.80	95-13	TrackRobbery1135TattyWalk1151CaptainNygeia1121½	Easily	8
3Sep78-9Cen	fst	6f	:212 :441 :563 1:093	Gold Rush Fut (Div 2) 59k	2	4	43½	32½	34½	35¼	Andrews EH	119	b	3.40	87-13	NativoRango122nkTorpedoAlley1195TrckRbbry1198	Evenly	9
29Jly78-8Cen	fst	6f	:221 :453 :581 1:111	Alw 2400	1	2	1½	12	14	16	Andrews EH	115	b	*1.40	84-18	Track Robbery1156To Erin1132½Rising Rullah1151	Easily	9
2Jly78-9Cen	fst	5½f	:22 :451 :572 1:041	ⒻM Brown (Div 2) 23k	9	6	2½	31	26	28	Andrews EH	119	b	14.20	83-19	Gazette1198TrackRobbery1193½CallMeDanny116hd	2nd best	12
10Jun78-5Cen	fst	5f	:222 :474 1:013	ⒻMd Sp Wt	1	10	42½	2½	12	1nk	Kato A	119	b	*1.50	74-25	Track Robbery119nkHoney Lamb1191Top Hop1092	Lasted	10

Turkoman

dkbbr. c. 1982, by Alydar (Raise a Native)–Taba, by Table Play

Lifetime record: 22 8 8 3 $2,146,924

Own.– Saron Stable
Br.– Corbin Robertson (Ky)
Tr.– Gary Jones

1Nov86- 7SA	fst	1¼	:46 1:101 1:343 2:002	3↑ BC Classic-G1	1	9	916	88½	36½	21¼	Day P	126		*1.60	86-13	Skywalker1261¼Turkomn1261¼Precisonst1261¾	Wide stretch 11
4Oct86- 8Bel	fst	1½	:504 1:16 2:041 2:28	3↑ J C Gold Cup-G1	1	3	42½	42¾	32	2hd	McCarron CJ	126		*.50	80-14	CremeFraiche126hdTurkmn1264¾DanzgConnctn1211¼	Gamely 6
13Sep86- 8Bel	fst	1¼	:473 1:11 1:354 2:00	3↑ Marlboro Cup H-G1	4	5	59	33	1hd	11½	Stevens GL	123		1.40	98-11	Turkoman1231½Precisionist1278¾Roo Art119½	Driving 5
17Aug86- 8Sar	my	7f	:214 :441 1:082 1:211	3↑ Forego H-G2	2	8	815	813	35½	2¾	McCarron CJ	124		*1.30	95-11	Groovy118¾Turkoman1244¾Innamorato110nk	Rallied 8
26May86- 8Bel	fst	1	:232 :454 1:091 1:333	3↑ Metropolitan H-G1	7	8	814	75¾	64½	41½	McCarron CJ	125		*1.20	95-11	Garthorn1241¼LoveThatMac117noLady'sSecrt120nk	Five wide 8
18Apr86- 9OP	fst	1⅛	:473 1:11 1:354 1:472	4↑ Oaklawn H-G2	2	3	35	21	2hd	11½	McCarron CJ	123		*.80	97-12	Turkoman1231½Gate Dancer123hdRed Attack11424	Driving 4
29Mar86-11Hia	fst	1¼	:471 1:101 1:334 1:583	3↑ Widener H-G1	1	6	613	44	33	1½	McCarron CJ	121		*1.20	105-06	Turkoman121½Darn That Alarm112noGate Dancer1249	Driving 6
7Mar86- 9Hia	fst	6f	:21 :433 1:081	3↑ Tallahassee H 39k	8	8	916	915	56½	12¾	McCarron CJ	120		*1.00	99-16	Turkoman1202¾Beveled1131½Cost Conscious1111	Driving 9
14Dec85- 8Hol	fst	1	:221 :444 1:091 1:341	Affirmed H-G3	6	9	911	76	33	11¼	McCarron CJ	121		*1.50	92-14	Turkomn1211¼BannerBob1215½FloatingReserve1171¼	Driving 10
17Nov85- 6Hol	fm	1⅛Ⓣ	:47 1:104 1:344 1:464	Hol Derby (Div 1)-G1	8	6	510	47½	78	79½	McCarron CJ	122		*1.10	- -	CharmingDuke1223½Herat1222¾LaKoumia119½	Lacked response 13
	Run in divisions																
2Nov85- 7Aqu	fst	1¼	:464 1:11 1:362 2:004	3↑ BC Classic-G1	3	7	78¾	63½	43	34	Vasquez J	122		7.70	88-10	ProudTruth122hdGtDncr1264Trkomn1225¾	Steadied far turn 8
16Oct85- 8Bel	fst	7f	:231 :464 1:11 1:222	3↑ Alw 27000	2	6	65¼	43½	13½	110	Vasquez J	114		*.50	90-22	Trkmn11410PurplMountn1141¾AccordngtoLuk1145	Ridden out 6
17Aug85- 8Sar	fst	1¼	:481 1:114 1:361 2:011	Travers-G1	2	1	2½	2½	2½	22¼	McHargue DG	126		7.60	92-08	Chief's Crown1262¼Turkoman1263Skip Trial126½	Weakened 7
21Jly85- 8Hol	fst	1¼	:47 1:104 1:36 2:012	Swaps-G1	3	8	76½	63¾	31	2no	McHargue DG	115		*1.90	105-04	Padua115noTurkomn1153½Don't Say Halo1202¾	Fast finish 8
29Jun85- 7Hol	fst	1	:222 :444 1:084 1:334	Silver Screen H-G2	2	9	910	89¾	56¼	43½	McHargue DG	118		*1.50	100-00	PanchoVilla118½ProudestDoon1182Nostalg'sStr1181	Crowded 9
16Jun85- 5Hol	fst	1	:23 :453 1:10 1:341	Alw 32000	3	6	66¼	33	12½	13½	McHargue DG	115		*.80	102-02	Turkoman1153½Ascension1164Sapient1142½	Ridden out 7
20Apr85- 8GG	fst	1⅛	:474 1:112 1:361 1:483	Cal Derby-G2	9	8	75½	32	33½	22½	McHargue DG	115		*1.70	87-13	Hajji'sTreasure1152½Trkomn115noNostlg'sStr1163½	Gamely 10
30Mar85- 8GG	fst	1 1/16	:222 :452 1:093 1:411	Gold Rush 56k	10	8	911	85¼	45	2hd	McHargue DG	115	b	*1.60	97-13	ProtctYourslf117hdTrkomn115nkFullHonr1151½	Just missed 10
3Mar85- 6SA	fst	1 1/16	:224 :461 1:102 1:432	©Alw 28000	9	5	42½	42¼	64	33	Hawley S	114	b	*1.40	81-14	BoldrThanBold118noAscenson1093Trkomn1141¼	Drifted out 9
30Jan85- 9SA	fst	1 1/16	:232 :473 1:114 1:433	Alw 25000	5	6	74½	64¼	33	31½	Hawley S	114	b	*.50	81-17	RoyalOlympia1151½RelaunchTun114hdTrkmn1141½	Lugged in 7
13Jan85- 4SA	fst	1 1/16	:224 :462 1:112 1:42	©Alw 24000	5	6	63	3½	2½	22½	Hawley S	114	b	3.60	88-13	Skywalkr1182½Turkoman1146Royal Olympia115½	Wide turn 7
19Dec84- 6Hol	sly	6f	:223 :463 :594 1:123	Md Sp Wt	8	9	99¾	66¼	22	1½	Hawley S	118	b	2.80	86-15	Turkoman118½Bloom's Beau1183½Time of the Fox118½	10
	Wide ⅜ turn,drifted in late																

Vanlandingham

b. c. 1981, by Cox's Ridge (Best Turn)–Populi, by Star Envoy

Lifetime record: 19 10 3 3 $1,409,476

Own.– Loblolly Stable
Br.– Loblolly Stable (Ky)
Tr.– Claude McGaughey III

5Apr86- 9OP	fst	1 1/16	:231 :454 1:10 1:42	4↑ Razorback H-G2	9	2	21½	21	11½	2½	Day P	125		*.50e	90-16	RedAttack111½Vanlandingham1251½InevitablLdr111hd	Bested 9
2Mar86- 8SA	fst	1¼	:451 1:091 1:34 2:00	4↑ S Anita H-G1	11	3	32½	58	811	812¼	MacBeth D	125		10.60	77-13	Greinton122¾Herat1122Hatim118nk	Tired 13
15Feb86-10GP	fm	1 1/16	:23 :463 1:093 1:40	3↑ Can Turf H (Div 2)-G2	7	2	21	2hd	11½	1½	MacBeth D	126		*.80	100-02	Vndlandinghm126½EndsWell1155Dr.Schwrtzmn1183¼	Driving 8
8Dec85- 8Hol	fm	1½Ⓣ	:492 1:15 2:042 2:282	3↑ Hol Cup Inv'l-G1	11	2	11	11½	1hd	32¾	MacBeth D	126		8.30	- -	Zoffany1262½Win126nkVanlandingham1262	Weakened 13
16Nov85- 9Lrl	sf	1½Ⓣ	:511 1:171 2:092 2:353	3↑ D C Int'l-G1	4	1	12	12	12	11	MacBeth D	126		7.10	41-55	Vanlandingham1261Yashgan126noJupiterIsland1261¼	Driving 10
2Nov85- 7Aqu	fst	1¼	:464 1:11 1:362 2:004	3↑ BC Classic-G1	2	2	2½	41	77	715	Day P	126		4.50	77-10	Proud Truth122hdGate Dancer1264Turkoman1225¾	8
	Steadied near stretch																
5Oct85- 8Bel	my	1½	:492 1:132 2:03 2:27	3↑ J C Gold Cup-G1	1	1	11	12	11½	12½	Day P	126		3.20	85-19	Vnlndinghm1262½GateDancr1267½CrmFrch1212¼	Ridden out 7
14Sep85- 8Bel	fst	1¼	:47 1:11 1:361 2:011	3↑ Marlboro Cup H-G1	7	1	11	1hd	3½	31	Day P	122		8.80	91-09	Chief'sCrown119nkGateDancr125¾Vnlndnghm122hd	Weakened 9
31Aug85- 8Bel	gd	1⅛	:461 1:10 1:341 1:463	3↑ Woodward-G1	2	3	31½	23	24½	24	Day P	123		2.40	90-10	Track Brn1234Vanldghm1231½Chf's Crown121½	Best rest 6
3Aug85- 8Sar	fst	1⅛	:474 1:112 1:351 1:473	3↑ Whitney H-G1	2	3	32	34½	35	34¾	Day P	124		*1.10	92-11	TrackBarrn124½CarrdNskr1204¼Vnlndnghm1241¾	Bobbled st. 5
4Jly85- 8Bel	fst	1¼	:463 1:10 1:342 2:01	3↑ Suburban H-G1	2	1	1½	1½	12	18¾	MacBeth D	115		8.60	93-17	Vanlandingham1158¾Carr de Naskra120nkDramatic Desire1091	9
	Brisk urging																
16Jun85- 9CD	fst	1⅛	:473 1:112 1:36 1:484	4↑ Stephen Foster H 56k	1	1	1½	1½	1½	1½	Day P	121		*.10	98-10	Vanlndinghm121½Manantil1121½SovrgnExchng1132½	Driving 7
31May85- 8CD	fst	7f	:221 :444 1:092 1:22	4↑ Alw 22490	5	3	12	13	14	16	Woods CR Jr	115		*.30	97-13	Vanlandingham1156Jetabid112¾Another Tom1124	Easily 5
5May84- 8CD	fst	1¼	:472 1:114 1:363 2:022	Ky Derby-G1	12	4	63½	1111	1518	1619	Day P	126		6.00e	66-19	Swale1263¼CoaxMeChd1262AtthThrshold126nk	Returned sore 20
31Mar84- 9OP	fst	1 1/16	:214 :444 1:094 1:41	Rebel H 117k	7	4	34	2½	1½	11¼	Day P	115		*1.20	103-05	Vnlndinghm1151¼WndFlyr1186½Lvsumdoubl1123	Drew clear 10
2Mar84- 8OP	fst	1	:222 :45 1:093 1:351	Alw 17500	4	2	1hd	11	15	110	Day P	121		*.70	- -	Vanlandinghm12110DirtyBirdie1212½SharprThn112½	Handily 7
26Jan84- 7Aqu	my	1 1/16⊡	:233 :48 1:123 1:441	Alw 22000	7	1	1½	1hd	11½	13	Lovato F Jr	117		3.00	91-10	Vnlndinghm1173Charmed Rook117nkLeroy S.1176	Drew out 9
7Jan84- 5Aqu	fst	1 1/16⊡	:24 :49 1:15 1:48	Alw 22000	3	3	31½	2½	22	26	Lovato F Jr	117		*1.10	66-24	Lt.Flag1176Vnlndnghm1177½Coopr'sHwk1172½	Best of others 7
26Nov83- 1CD	fst	1	:234 :473 1:132 1:382	Md Sp Wt	8	1	12	11	1½	11½	Day P	117		*.90	77-21	Vanlandingham1171½Pemcor1177Thunder Chick1142	Handily 11

Wayward Lass

dkbbr. f. 1978, by Hail the Pirates (Hail to Reason)–Young Mistress, by Third Martini

Lifetime record: 25 9 7 6 $435,237

Own.– Flying Zee Stable
Br.– H.A. Luro (Fla)
Tr.– Jose Martin

20Sep81- 1Bel	gd	1 1/16	:24 :48 1:131 1:454	3↑ ⒻHandicap 35000	4	2	21	12½	15	16	Asmussen CB	124		*.20	73-27	WaywrdLass1246Nora'sLass1137SweetMaid1196	Ridden out 4
10Sep81- 8Bel	fst	7f	:222 :451 1:10 1:23	3↑ ⒻAlw 32000	1	4	43	32	2½	11	Asmussen CB	115		4.90	87-16	Wayward Lass1151Highest Regard1156¾Cherokee Frolic1181½	5
	Driving																
27Jun81- 8Bel	fst	1½	:474 1:114 2:014 2:281	ⒻC C A Oaks-G1	2	3	31½	31½	21½	22¼	Asmussen CB	121		5.00	77-16	[D]RealPrize1212¼WaywrdLss1212¼BannerGala12113	Impeded 6
	Placed first through disqualification																
5Jun81- 8Bel	fst	1⅛	:47 1:11 1:354 1:484	ⒻMother Goose-G1	2	2	2½	2½	11	1nk	Asmussen CB	121		13.10	83-17	WywrdLss121nkHeavnlyCause1212¾BannerGala1211¾	Driving 8
15May81- 8Pim	sly	1 1/16	:231 :47 1:113 1:441	ⒻBlack-Eyed Susan-G2	2	2	2½	42¾	32½	23	Asmussen CB	121		3.00	81-18	Dame Mysterieuse1213Wayward Lass121¾Real Prize1211¾	7
	Finished strong																
1May81- 8CD	fst	1 1/16	:25 :484 1:13 1:434	ⒻKy Oaks-G1	1	3	3½	2½	32½	35	Asmussen CB	121		8.40	84-17	HeavnlyCause121noDeLaRose1215WaywrdLss1213	Weakened 6
18Apr81- 7Kee	fst	1 1/16	:23 :464 1:112 1:44	ⒻAshland-G2	3	4	43½	32	3½	2¾	Asmussen CB	121		5.00	85-20	TrulyBound121¾WywrdLss121¾DameMysterieus12110	Gamely 5
4Apr81- 9OP	fst	1 1/16	:233 :471 1:122 1:434	ⒻFantasy-G1	4	6	52¾	42½	34	35¼	Asmussen CB	121		2.20	84-19	Hvnly Cse121hdNl's Brqte1215¼WywrdLass1214½	Weakened 9
15Mar81- 8Aqu	fst	1 1/16⊡	:234 :473 1:112 1:433	ⒻLevel Best 56k	2	2	2hd	13	1½	31	Asmussen CB	121		*.20	95-10	RealPrize114hdInTrueForm1121WaywardLss1214¼	No excuse 7
15Feb81- 8Aqu	fst	1⅛⊡	:473 1:121 1:37 1:50	ⒻRuthless-G3	4	2	21½	14	18	111	Asmussen CB	121		*.20	96-11	WywrdLss12111RealPrize115½FbulousMusc1124	Ridden out 7
31Jan81- 8Aqu	fst	1 1/16⊡	:232 :473 1:122 1:433	ⒻSearching 54k	2	3	1hd	13	18	112	Asmussen CB	118		*.10e	96-11	WywrdLss11812RealPrize1131½FabulousMusic1125¾	Driving 6
17Jan81- 7Aqu	fst	1 1/16⊡	:24 :482 1:141 1:453	ⒻBusanda 56k	4	3	32½	21	14	17	Asmussen CB	116		3.00e	86-23	WywrdLss1167InTruForm1122ExplosvKngdom11210	Drew clear 10
1Jan81- 8Aqu	fst	6f⊡	:222 :454 1:112	ⒻRosetown 56k	2	6	2hd	43	44	33¾	Hernandez R	115		*1.00	83-21	Vandanya1122¾InTrueForm1131WywrdLss115nk	Well up,placed 7
7Dec80- 8Aqu	fst	6f⊡	:221 :451 1:101	ⒻTreetop 55k	4	2	21½	22½	23½	2¾	Cordero A Jr	122		4.90	92-08	DameMysterieuse122¾WywrdLss1221InTrueForm1157	Gamely 5
18Nov80- 7Med	fst	6f	:224 :47 1:121	ⒻAlw 14000	2	5	33	34	36	48½	Wilson R	120		3.20	73-23	Seed the Cld109½Dame Mystrse1208Drop a Gem120hd	Bled 6
1Nov80- 8Key	fst	6f	:222 :454 1:113	ⒻSchuykill 28k	3	3	23	24	23	1½	Wilson R	114		6.80	84-21	WaywardLss114½SurePrincess1132½Ruler'sDncr115¾	Driving 9
11Oct80- 4Bel	fst	6f	:223 :46 1:11	ⒻMd Sp Wt	1	1	2½	2hd	1½	11½	Lovato F Jr5	113		*1.40	87-17	Wayward Lass1131½Sight1182½Banner Gala1183¼	Ridden out 11
29Sep80- 4Bel	fst	6f	:222 :46 1:112	ⒻMd Sp Wt	1	1	24	43½	22	23¾	Lovato F Jr5	112	b	3.50	81-19	Dame Mystrse1173¾Waywd Lass1123¾Real Prize1176	2nd best 10
5Sep80- 2Bel	fm	1 1/16Ⓣ	:23 :472 1:124 1:471	ⒻMd Sp Wt	6	1	11½	1½	1½	54	Asmussen CB	117	b	*.90	56-34	Carduel117nkGdynia1171½Fabled Morn1171	Used up 12

29Aug80- 8Bel	fm 7fⓉ	:23 :46 1:094 1:232	ⒻEvening Out 56k	2	4	21½	64½	612	719	Asmussen CB	112	b	9.60	68-13	De La Rse114hdBrvo Ntive11210Prime Prspt1132¾	Brief foot 7
15Aug80- 2Sar	gd 1 1/16[T]	:241 :482 1:13 1:462	ⒻMd Sp Wt	6	1	11½	11	21½	24½	Cordero A Jr	117	b	*1.20	73-22	Seaholme1174½WywrdLss1172¼Zimbaba1171½	Best of others 10
4Aug80- 6Sar	fm 1[T]	:242 :483 1:133 1:38	ⒻMd Sp Wt	6	2	11½	13	2hd	21¾	Cordero A Jr	117		*1.70	87-12	BravoNative1171¾WaywardLass1172Seaholme1171½	2nd best 9
23Jly80- 4Bel	sly 7f	:232 :471 1:113 1:242	ⒻMd Sp Wt	3	4	2½	2½	24	29	Cordero A Jr	117		*1.50	71-22	Heavenly Cause1179WaywrdLass1176Zimbaba1174½	2nd best 8
2Jly80- 3Bel	fst 5½f	:222 :454 :583 1:051	ⒻMd Sp Wt	8	6	32½	45½	47½	35	Cordero A Jr	117		4.40	84-17	PrimeProspct1171¼QueenDesignate1123¾WywrdLss1171	Wide 9
23Jun80- 4Bel	fst 5½f	:224 :462 :584 1:052	ⒻMd Sp Wt	3	8	46	47	37½	36	Cordero A Jr	117		6.30	82-15	FamousPartner1172Shalomar1174WywardLass1171¼	Rallied 9

Winning Colors

ro. f. 1985, by Caro (Fortino II)–All Rainbows, by Bold Hour — **Lifetime record: 19 8 3 1 $1,526,837**

Own.– Eugene V. Klein
Br.– Echo Valley Horse Farm Inc (Ky)
Tr.– D. Wayne Lukas

4Nov89- 6GP	fst 1⅛	:462 1:111 1:353 1:472 3↑	ⒻBC Distaff-G1	8	5	55½	66½	921	924¼	Stevens GL	123		5.20e	83-01	Bayakoa1231½Gorgeous1192¼Open Mind1195	Tired badly 10
21Oct89- 7Aqu	fst 1⊗	:23 :451 1:091 1:334 3↑	ⒻBud BC H 156k	1	3	2½	31	43½	48¼	McCarron CJ	119		*.60	85-05	Wakonda1164Foresta1081½Toll Fee1112¾	Tired 5
30Sep89- 9TP	fst 1 1/16	:233 :471 1:373 1:444 3↑	ⒻBud BC 155k	7	1	1½	11	13	12	McCarron CJ	115		*.70	86-28	WinningColors1152GrecianFlight1232½LawyrTlk1234	Driving 7
9Sep89- 8Bel	fst 1	:233 :461 1:101 1:353 3↑	ⒻMaskette-G1	1	1	11½	1½	34½	48½	Perret C	123		*.50	78-15	MissBrio1161¼ProperEvidnc1165½Aptostr1231¾	Used in pace 5
26Aug89- 1Sar	fst 6f	:23 :454 1:101 3↑	ⒻAlw 41000	5	1	2hd	1hd	1½	14¼	Day P	115		*.40	89-16	Winning Colors1154¼Royal Rexson1151½Lake Valley1155¼	Stumbled,handily 5
13May89- 8Bel	fst 1 1/16	:224 :444 1:09 1:404 3↑	ⒻShuvee H-G1	2	1	1½	1hd	78	721¾	Stevens GL	121		1.30	76-16	Bankr'sLady1222¼Rose'sCantn1171¼GrcnFlght1171¼	Stopped 7
29Apr89- 8Hol	fst 7f	:214 :442 1:09 1:213 3↑	ⒻA Gleam H-G3	4	4	2hd	1½	2hd	44½	Stevens GL	123		*.40	91-10	Daloma1151¾Survive1162¾Behind the Scenes116hd	Weakened 7
5Nov88- 6CD	my 1⅛	:474 1:12 1:381 1:52 3↑	ⒻBC Distaff-G1	8	1	12½	12½	11½	2no	Stevens GL	119		4.00e	82-20	Personal Ensign123noWinning Colors119½Goodbye Halo1195	Just failed 9
15Oct88- 8Kee	fst 1⅛	:472 1:12 1:372 1:51 3↑	ⒻSpinster-G1	2	1	1hd	11½	32½	415	Stevens GL	119		*.30	64-24	HailaCab1233WillaontheMove1192Integra12310	Gave way 5
10Sep88- 8Bel	fst 1	:224 :451 1:09 1:341 3↑	ⒻMaskette-G1	4	1	15	12	1hd	2¾	Stevens GL	118		2.10	93-14	PersonlEnsign123¾WinningColrs1185¼ShamSy11511¼	Gamely 4
11Jun88- 8Bel	fst 1½	:471 1:114 2:013 2:262	Belmont-G1	3	1	2½	410	524	641¾	Stevens GL	121		2.20	46-13	Risen Star12614¾Kingpost1262Brian's Time12611¼	Stopped 6
21May88- 9Pim	gd 1 3/16	:47 1:111 1:363 1:561	Preakness-G1	5	2	2hd	2hd	22	32½	Stevens GL	121		*1.90	83-11	Risen Star1261¼Brian's Time1261¼Winning Colors1212½	Brushed,bckstr 9
7May88- 8CD	fst 1¼	:464 1:112 1:36 2:021	Ky Derby-G1	11	1	13½	13	13½	1nk	Stevens GL	121		3.40	86-11	WinningColrs121nkFortyNiner1263RsnStr126½	Strong drive 17
9Apr88- 5SA	fst 1⅛	:453 1:092 1:344 1:474	S A Derby-G1	5	1	11½	12½	17	17½	Stevens GL	117		*2.60	90-13	WinnngColors1177½LivelyOne1221¼MPrfrdo1222½	Ridden out 9
13Mar88- 8SA	fst 1 1/16	:222 :454 1:10 1:42	ⒻS A Oaks-G1	1	1	11	11	15	18	Stevens GL	117		2.10	91-15	WinningClrs1178JeannJons1171¼GoodbyHlo1179	Ridden out 4
20Feb88- 8SA	fst 1	:221 :461 1:11 1:364	ⒻLas Virgenes-G1	4	2	12½	11	1hd	2nk	Stevens GL	119		*.70	84-18	GoodbyeHalo123nkWnnngClrs1198SdB.Fst1157½	Just failed 5
20Jan88- 8SA	fst 1	:22 :454 1:11 1:363	Ⓕ[R]La Centinela 80k	2	1	11½	12½	14	16½	Stevens GL	114		*.70	85-22	WinningColrs1146½LittlePssword1143Forwrnng1161	Handily 7
27Dec87- 3SA	fst 6f	:214 :444 :57 1:094	ⒻAlw 32000	1	5	12½	12	13½	13½	Stevens GL	114		*1.30	89-17	Winning Colors1143½Floral Magic1182¾Constantly Right1161¼	Slow st.,veered in 6
13Aug87- 3Sar	fst 7f	:221 :453 1:11 1:241	ⒻMd Sp Wt	9	3	1½	11½	14	12½	Romero RP	117		*1.90	81-14	Winning Colors1172½Epitome1174Bippus1171½	Ridden out 11

Zaccio

ch. g. 1976, by Lorenzaccio (Klairon)–Delray Dancer, by Chateaugay — **Lifetime record: 42 22 7 3 $288,124**

Own.– Mrs L.C. Murdock
Br.– Blue Bear Stud (Ky)
Tr.– W. Burling Cocks

7Oct84- 6Mid	fm *1¼Ⓣ	2:172 3↑	Alw 500	6	9	51½	11½	11¼	14	Hendriks R	146		-	--	Zaccio1464Past Glory1425Night Fever1442	Ridden out 10
29Sep84- 6Fx	fm *1Ⓣ	1:464 3↑	Alw 1000	2	3	1½	2nk	21½	21¼	Hendriks R	146		-	--	Local Kid1461¼Zaccio1466Fiddler's Dam1411	5
15Sep84- 8Fai	yl *1 5/16Ⓣ	2:19 3↑	Alw 1000	4	5	56¾	31	69	611½	Hendriks R	140		*.80e	--	Yale Key133¾Locust Grove1521½Heart of the Desert1435½	7
21Nov82- 4Cam	fm *2¾ S'Chase	5:11 4↑	Colonial Cup 50k	9	7	49½	43¼	14	18	Hendriks R	162		-	--	Zaccio1628Sailor's Clue16210Double Wrapped1591¼	Easily 13
3Nov82- 8Lrl	yl 1 1/16Ⓣ	:23 :472 1:133 1:461 3↑	Alw 10000	8	3	49	715	817	823	Adams JK	116		3.40	49-33	SunandShine1152½GrayDude116nkDevoir1139	Fin. after ½ 8
8Oct82- 6Bel	fm 2⅝ S'Chase	4:523 4↑	Temple Gwathmey H 42k	4	3	32½	15	13	13¼	Hendriks R	163		*.60	--	Zaccio1633¼Shaban1421½Double Reefed1493¾	Ridden out 5
25Sep82- 6Fai	fm *1 5/16Ⓣ	2:142 3↑	Alw 1000	5	7	44½	41¼	1nk	12¾	Hendriks R	143		1.70e	--	Zaccio1432¾Abelard's Lust1551¼Oh So Choosy1491¼	Driving 13
26Aug82- 8Sar	gd 2⅜ S'Chase	4:19 4↑	NY Turf Writers H 43k	2	3	24	23	11	1nk	Hendriks R	161		*1.40	--	Zaccio161nkGive a Whirl1467¼Running Comment1456	Driving 7
16Aug82- 4Sar	fm 2 1/16 S'Chase	3:451 3↑	Handicap 25000	1	3	2½	16	110	116	Morris GL	159		*.80	--	Zaccio15916LeapngFrog1401½DoubleReefed1532¾	Easy score 6
6Aug82- 6Sar	fm 2 1/16 S'Chase	3:424 4↑	Lovely Night H 43k	2	5	48	25	1½	22	Morris GL	159		*1.60	--	Quiet Bay1512Zaccio1594¼Uncle Edwin1558	Gamely 7
29Jly82- 8Del	fm 1 1/16Ⓣ	:24 :48 1:122 1:44 3↑	Alw 8500	10	10	1114	1012	815	612	Smith GP	117		2.30	72-13	Big Curley1225½Going Aground1131Brown Gold1064½	Outrun 12
9Jly82- 6Bel	fm 1½Ⓣ	:483 1:134 2:03 2:272 3↑	Handicap 25000	7	5	55	44½	59	513	Maple E	117		4.30	74-13	Cookie120½Give a Whirl1092Double Reefed121¾	No factor 7
28Jun82- 8Del	fm 1 1/16Ⓣ	:241 :474 1:12 1:441 3↑	Alw 10000	2	4	410	48	45	24½	Smith GP	119		4.70	78-19	GildedAge1214½Zaccio119hdPhiladelphialwyr1192½	Game try 6
3Apr82- 4AtH	fm *2 S'Chase	3:50 4↑	Delta Cup H 24k	2	1	1½	11¼	2nk	31	Morris GL	159		-	--	Double Reefed146¾Daddy Dumpling146nkZaccio159	Tired 3
27Mar82- 5Cam	fm *2¼ S'Chase	4:104 4↑	Carolina Cup 15k	1	3	34	21½	1nk	21½	Morris GL	160		-	--	Quiet Bay1441½Zaccio1609Archange d'Or1442	Gave way 4
22Nov81- 4Cam	gd 2¾ S'Chase	5:143 4↑	Colonial Cup Int'l 50k	4	8	65¾	45½	11	111	Morris GL	160		-	--	Zaccio16011Al Arof1513Sailor's Clue160nk	Ridden out 9
7Nov81- 3Mtp	gd *2½ S'Chase	4:534 4↑	Noel Laing H 4.9k	2	4	44¼	110	112	115	Morris GL	158		-	--	Zaccio15815Cookie14818Yellow Boy141	4
31Oct81- 6FH	yl *2 5/16 S'Chase	5:16 4↑	S K Martin H 15k	1	1	1½	63¼	69¾	623	Morris GL	160		-	--	Uncle Edwin142½Al Arof14612Pestamystic1371½	6
17Oct81- 5Fx	hd *2⅝ S'Chase	4:584 4↑	Grand National H 16k	1	2	12	14	1½	1nk	Cushman J	159		-	--	Zaccio159nkSailor's Clue154	2
3Oct81- 8Med	fm 1 1/16Ⓣ	:222 :462 1:114 1:432 3↑	Alw 13000	4	9	911	810	89¼	814	Maple E	118		*2.80	71-15	The Missing Gift1131½Miroslav1142Hasty Tasty1131	Outrun 10
29Aug81- 3AP	sf *2⅜ S'Chase	4:44 4↑	Arl H 32k	3	4	56	519	546	556	McWade R	161		*.50	--	Double Reefed137nkUncle Edwin13534Snailwell138hd	Tired 5
21Aug81- 4Sar	fm 2 1/16 S'Chase	3:392 3↑	Handicap 25000	1	2	1½	11½	2½	24½	McWade R	164		*1.30e	--	Codicioso1464½Zaccio1646½Triple Try14414	Best of others 8
14Aug81- 7Sar	fm 1 1/16[T]	:234 :482 1:12 1:422 3↑	Alw 21000	1	11	1110	1111	95¾	96¼	Montoya D	117		11.20	92-10	RedWingPrince1143½Santo'sJoe117¾SpartnMystc112no	Outrun 11
10Oct80- 6Bel	fm 2⅝ S'Chase	4:544 4↑	Temple Gwathmey H 43k	2	4	46	-	-	-	Small D Jr	160		*.80	--	LeapingFrog1481½Marti'sAngr1581½BluNrco1331½	Lost rider 7
14Aug80- 6Sar	fm 2⅜ S'Chase	4:141 4↑	NY Turf Writers H 43k	1	2	21½	11	21½	11¼	McWade R	157		*1.10	--	Zccio1571¼RunningComment1422¼LeapingFrog1522¼	Driving 7
1Aug80- 6Sar	gd 2 1/16 S'Chase	3:451 4↑	Lovely Night H 43k	4	2	2½	2½	2½	11¾	McWade R	155		*1.30	--	Zccio1551¾Martie'sAnger1601¾LeapngFrog1531¼	Ridden out 8
17Jly80- 4Del	fm 2¼ S'Chase	4:224 4↑	Indian River 12k	3	1	12	12	12	14½	McWade R	152		*.60	--	Zaccio1524½Baronial1423¼Leaping Frog1549	Handily 4
18Jun80- 3Mth	fm *2¼ S'Chase	4:21 4↑	Mid Summer H 15k	4	2	31½	12½	14	13	McWade R	153		*.60e	--	Zaccio1533Town and Country1401¼Leaping Frog1582	Driving 6
24May80- 5Pro	gd *3 S'Chase	5:514 4↑	Hard Scuffle 20k	5	3	31¼	41¼	21	21¼	McWade R	140		-	--	Martie's Anger1511¼Zaccio1405Leaping Frog15616	5
27Apr80- 4Lex	yl *2½ S'Chase	5:121 4↑	Pillar 17k	1	2	11	1nk	1hd	1hd	McWade R	148		-e	--	Zaccio148hdDaddy Dumpling15018Schoeller15412	5
12Apr80- 3SoP	fm *2¼ S'Chase	4:211 4↑	Sandhills Cup H 15k	3	6	42½	31¾	2nk	31	McWade R	155		-e	--	Archanged'Or1431Martie'sAnger158noZaccio155¾	Held well 7
29Mar80- 4Cam	gd *2⅛ S'Chase	4:104 4↑	Handicap 12500	2	3	22¼	33¼	13	16	McWade R	152		-	--	Zaccio1526Popular Hero1441Tan Jay1581½	Ridden out 7
22Mar80- 4Aik	fm *1⅞ S'Chase	3:53 4↑	Handicap 7500	1	5	46	2nk	13	15	McWade R	149		-	--	Zaccio1495Alizar1324Empty Wallet1465	Handily 5
18Nov79- 1Cam	fm *2 S'Chase	3:424	Alw 7500	5	6	32½	14	18	121	Skiffington T Jr	154		-	--	Zccio15421ClassSymbl1442ChanceRomance1463½	Ridden out 7
11Oct79- 4Bel	sf 2 S'Chase	3:531 3↑	Alw 11000	2	5	43	15	11½	1¾	McWade R5	138		*1.70	--	Zccio138¾AcadmicFreedom13621BillyComLtly1482¼	Driving 7
24Aug79- 4Sar	fm 2 1/16 S'Chase	3:411 3↑	Alw 11000	8	2	23	11½	11½	2nk	Skiffington T Jr	139		*.70	--	Parson'sWaiting135nkZaccio13918PumpkinPie1404	Bobbled 8
10Aug79- 4Sar	fm 2 1/16 S'Chase	3:434 3↑	Alw 10000	1	11	106¼	43½	1hd	19¼	Skiffington T Jr	137		*1.50	--	Zccio1379¼RunningComment139hdBillyComeLtly1561½	Easily 11
12May79- 2Fai	fm *1⅞ S'Chase	3:422 3↑	Md Sp Wt	3	2	4¾	1hd	1½	12	McWade R7	135		1.80	--	Zaccio1352Odd Man1568Abbots Walk1566	In hand 6
28Apr79- 1Fx	gd *2 S'Chase	3:42 4↑	Md Sp Wt	3	3	21	11½	-	-	McWade R7	132			--	Ventarron15415Royal Greed1568Lochcruin15410	Lost rider 7
21Apr79- 3Clm	fm *1Ⓣ	1:43 3↑	Alw 1000	4	3	32½	31¼	1hd	11	McWade R5	139		-	--	Zaccio1391Cheviot1582½Ten Ducks131½	Driving 8
14Apr79- 2SoP	fm *7fⓉ	1:32 3↑	Md Sp Wt	6	3	31	2nk	1¾	12½	Skiffington T Jr	132		-	--	Zaccio1322½Sacred Melody1468Elsaik1454	Drew out 6
31Mar79- 2Cam	fm *7fⓉ	1:302 3↑	Md Sp Wt	7	7	1210	78	39	38	Skiffington T Jr	145		-	--	Cheviot1537Sky News1501Zaccio1453	Rallied 13

Going Global

THE 1990's

by Jay Privman

B ILL MOTT SAT IN THE FILM theater of Belmont Park, a small room hidden in the bowels of the racetrack, just around the corner from the jockeys' room. It was nearly dusk on October 28, 1995, and the trainer was flush with excitement and pride over having just watched his horse Cigar win the Breeders' Cup Classic. It was Cigar's 12th consecutive victory, completed a perfect 10-for-10 campaign that year, and secured for Cigar the titles of both Horse of the Year and champion older horse.

Cigar was 5, an age when many horses with his accomplishments are immediately whisked off to stud. But Allen Paulson, Cigar's owner, got into the sport because he likes to watch his horses run. Cigar in 1995 had raced in Florida, California, Arkansas, Maryland, and Massachusetts. And now Mott and Paulson were looking for new worlds to conquer.

"He'll race next year," Mott said, "but he'll have a different type of campaign."

The face of racing was changing demonstrably in the 1990's, and Cigar came along at the opportune time. Racing always had been an international sport. Horses from the United States often were sent by boat to Great Britain at the beginning of the

century. Midway through the century, the Washington, D.C., International laid the groundwork for the Breeders' Cup Turf, a late-season race designed to bring together the world's premier grass horses. The Breeders' Cup, launched in 1984, succeeded in bringing the best of Europe's runners to the United States for a championship event.

But the frequency and ease of international racing skyrocketed in the 1990's. The Japan Cup, in November, and races in Hong Kong in December became increasingly desirable targets. Horses could fly there in less time than it took to travel by van from Kentucky to Florida. Trainer Leo O'Brien sent a New York-bred, Fourstars Allstar, to The Curragh and won the Irish 2000 Guineas. Dr Devious was purchased in Europe for Sid and Jenny Craig by bloodstock agent Murray Friedlander, came to the United States for the Kentucky Derby, then returned to Great Britain and won the Epsom Derby.

In the Middle East, Sheikh Mohammed bin Rashid al-Maktoum audaciously decided to have his best runners winter in Dubai before heading back to Europe. Those horses would race with the stable name Godolphin, named for one of the three founding stallions of the modern Thoroughbred. In

Godolphin's first year of operation, Lammtarra, having spent the winter in Dubai, won the Epsom Derby, a grueling 1½-mile race, in his first start of the year. Godolphin later would send horses to Australia for the Melbourne Cup, and to the United States for the Kentucky Derby. Sheikh Mohammed also organized the Emirates World Championship Series, which linked some of the world's premier races, such as the Japan Cup, Melbourne Cup Breeders' Cup Turf, and Breeders' Cup Classic. Daylami, who raced for Godolphin, won the first Emirates World Series in 1999, when he completed his year with an overpowering victory in the Breeders' Cup Turf.

In 1995, Sheikh Mohammed startled the racing world by announcing his country would play host, beginning the following March, to the Dubai World Cup. The purse would be $4 million, $1 million more than the Breeders' Cup Classic, with a winner's share of $2.4 million, making it the richest race in the world. Having earned the title of Horse of the Year with Cigar, and looking for new challenges, Mott felt the Dubai World Cup was the ideal forum to establish Cigar's place in history.

Cigar was on the verge of proving himself one of the great horses of the century. He had blossomed under Mott's care, but the foundation had been laid years earlier. The Triple Crown, particularly the Kentucky Derby, increasingly became the focal point of owners and trainers during the 1990's. Trainers such as Bob Baffert, D. Wayne Lukas, and Nick Zito focused their entire operations around developing classic runners. And they were amazingly successful. Those three trainers won 7 of the

Two-time Horse of the Year Cigar ushered in a new era of international competition in 1996, when he traveled to the Middle East and won the inaugural running of the Dubai World Cup.

10 Kentucky Derbies run in the 1990's. Frequently, though, they went through a number of horses trying to find the right one. Some runners were pushed early and often to see if they were worthy of going to the Derby, and a number fell by the wayside and never were the same again.

Cigar, however, was not forced to try to make the classics. As a son of grass stakes winner Palace Music, Cigar had a pedigree that indicated he would do better on turf. He never raced at age 2, and did not win his first race – at six furlongs on dirt at Hollywood Park, in only his second start – until May 9, 1993, eight days after that year's Kentucky Derby was won by Sea Hero.

"He had a good-sized frame, but his muscles hadn't filled into that frame," said Alex Hassinger Jr., who trained Cigar for his first nine races. "He seemed like a route horse, and he seemed like a horse who would get better with time. I didn't know if that meant three months, six months, or a year or two, but I felt he'd get better. We also were having trouble with his knees. He wasn't the kind of horse who would hold up well under all those dirt races. That, along with his pedigree, is why we pointed him for the grass. So we raced him on turf. And by going slow, we had a horse for later on."

Cigar needed arthroscopic surgery to remove a chip in a knee at the end of his 3-year-old season. After he recuperated, Paulson decided to switch trainers. He sent Cigar to Mott in New York.

Cigar's first race for Mott was July 8, 1994. He finished fourth in an allowance race on the turf at Belmont Park. Three more losses, all in turf allowance races, followed. On October 28, Mott put Cigar back on the dirt, in a one-turn mile race at Aqueduct. Sent off at 7-2 in a six-horse field, Cigar romped by eight lengths. He was now 3 for 14. Yet that victory was the first step Cigar took on his path to greatness. He came back and won the NYRA Mile to close out 1994, then headed to Florida, where he took over as the best horse in America.

The baton was passed on February 11, 1995. Just as Cigar entered the backstretch and took the lead in the Donn Handicap at Gulfstream Park, the race favorite, Holy Bull, the 1994 Horse of the Year, was pulled up with a career-ending injury. Cigar won by 5 ½ lengths, but few noticed, the attention being focused on Holy Bull. Cigar, though, quickly made a name for himself. He traveled throughout the country and won everywhere he went.

His name, along with the winning streak, helped Cigar break through and capture the consciousness of America's sports fans. He was featured in magazines such as People, Sports Illustrated, Esquire, Newsweek, and Cigar Aficionado. Funny thing was, Cigar was not named for a tobacco product. Paulson, an accomplished pilot who made his fortune first by developing and patenting airplane parts, and then as head of Gulfstream Aerospace, named Cigar for an aviation checkpoint in the Gulf of Mexico, approximately 100 miles west of Tampa, Florida.

Paulson had once stopped in Dubai during a record around-the-world flight. But Cigar had never been out of the country until March 16, 1996, when he boarded a plane bound for Dubai, with a stopover at Shannon Airport in Ireland. "We got to Ireland on the 17th," recalled Tim Jones, Mott's assistant, who accompanied Cigar on the flight. "We couldn't get any gas for the plane. The stopover was supposed to take 45 minutes. But we sat on the tarmac for four hours. No one was around. It was St. Patrick's Day."

The trip alone was daunting. Dubai was 7,000 miles from Florida, where Cigar had spent that winter, and where he had won the Donn Handicap for the second straight year. But Cigar also was fighting a quarter crack and a bruise in his right front hoof. The injuries forced him to miss nearly two weeks of training and a start in the Santa Anita Handicap, and resulted in an accelerated workout schedule in order to prepare him for the World Cup. He also had to adjust to the time change – Dubai is nine hours ahead of Miami – and the desert climate, as well as an unfamiliar surface and racetrack.

Cigar's arrival thrilled Sheikh Mohammed, for Cigar's presence gave instant credibility to the inaugural World Cup. "I had a dream, and now they are all here," Sheikh Mohammed said. "If Cigar wins, he will be champion of the world."

There were 11 horses in the race, but Cigar was clearly the star. Though betting is prohibited in Dubai, he was the race favorite in Great Britain and the United States. His opposition included the top American runner Soul of the Matter, along with Godolphin's main challenger, Halling.

The race was run at night, under the lights of Nad al-Sheba racetrack. Around the world, attention was riveted on the World Cup. Bookmakers' shops in London were filled that afternoon. In Manhattan, the race was broadcast live on New York City's offtrack betting channel. In California, fans crawled out of bed early and headed to Santa Anita, where the race was shown at 7 a.m. local time.

Cigar, with Jerry Bailey riding, stalked the early pacesetters, moved for the lead with a half-mile to go, and took over with a quarter-mile remaining. But in midstretch, Soul of the Matter, ridden by Gary Stevens, came with a furious rush.

"He looked like he was beat," Mott recounted. "The first thing that flashed into my mind was the time we had missed training him. As a result, he had to work three times in eight days and then ship halfway around the world. We put a lot of pressure on him. It was an unusual training schedule. There was nothing nice and smooth and steady about it. When Soul of the Matter ran to him, I thought, 'There's the 13 days we missed.' It was the first time he'd been in a head-to-head battle since the streak started. In the other races, he'd leave everyone for dead with a half-mile to go. He'd run by the pacesetters, and the come-from-behind horses couldn't catch him. We didn't know what would happen when he was challenged."

He responded like a champion. Despite the trip, the missed training, and the sore foot, Cigar fought off Soul of the Matter and won by a half-length. From Dubai to London, to New York and Los Angeles, a collective roar went up. No one had known what to expect, and no one could have expected anything better. "It was pretty awesome," Mott said.

Cigar had now won 14 races in a row, and was closing fast on the record of 16 straight set by Citation nearly 50 years earlier. Cigar returned to the United States and won the Massachusetts Handicap for No. 15, then went to Arlington International Racecourse for a specially designed race, the Arlington Citation Challenge. Despite carrying 130 pounds, breaking from the outside post in a field of 10, and being forced to race wide the whole trip, Cigar won by 3½ lengths to tie Citation.

The attempt to break the record would come in the Pacific Classic at Del Mar on August 10. Cigar was training well, Mott said, but was starting to show some wear and tear, particularly on the inside of his right front foot. "He was developing foot problems," Mott said. "He had a quarter crack with a patch on it. We were dealing with issues we hadn't had the previous year."

Still, Mott was confident Cigar would win. "Every time I went over with him, I felt I had the best horse," he said. "Of course, you had to have racing luck, but you get to the point where you think he's going to repeat the previous 16."

Mott and Bailey feared one opponent, the speedy Siphon. He had won the Hollywood Gold Cup a few weeks earlier, beating Geri, a Mott-trained horse whom Bailey had ridden. "We didn't want Siphon to get an easy lead and steal the race. We wanted to keep him within range," Mott said. "I think the thing that we forgot is that we had Cigar, not Geri."

Cigar followed Siphon into the first turn of the 1¼-mile race, but when Dramatic Gold loomed up outside Cigar around the first turn, Bailey used Cigar to hold his position. Cigar, his competitive juices flowing, then got into a duel with Siphon. They sped through the second quarter in 22⅘ seconds, and the third quarter in 23⅖. They reached the six-furlong mark in 1:09⅕. By the time they hit the quarter pole, having run a mile in 1:33⅗, both Cigar and Siphon were spent.

Dare and Go, like Siphon, was trained by Richard Mandella. He took advantage of the wicked early pace and roared past both Cigar and Siphon, then drew off to a 3½-length victory. Cigar, in a remarkable effort, still finished second, some seven lengths in front of Siphon. He had won the battle, but lost the war. A Del Mar record crowd of 44,181, which had sent Cigar off at 1-10, was stunned into silence. The streak was over.

"It was something we had braced for," Mott said. "If you keeping taking them over, eventually they're going to get beat. But I was pretty grateful for what we had had."

Later that evening at the barn, Mott noticed something he would never forget. Cigar always liked people, and attention. He was attuned to the click of a camera shutter, and the telltale crinkling of a peppermint being unwrapped from cellophane.

"Bailey went over to give him a peppermint, but he wouldn't take it," Mott said. "I know horses don't think like humans, but he acted like he knew something was different, like he knew he got beat. I don't think he was proud. All the other times, he was a proud horse."

Cigar raced just three more times. He won once, and twice lost in photo finishes. He closed his career with a third-place finish in the 1996 Breeders' Cup Classic. But he had done enough earlier in the year, particularly in Dubai, to be rewarded with the Horse of the Year title for the second straight year. He was the only horse to receive that honor twice in the 1990's.

Mott and Bailey rode his coattails. Mott won Eclipse Awards as champion trainer in both 1995 and 1996, and in 1997, at age 45, became the youngest trainer inducted into the National Museum of Racing's Hall of Fame. Bailey won Eclipse Awards as champion jockey in 1995 and 1996, then added a third straight in 1997.

Mott, Paulson, and Paulson's wife, Madeleine, understood Cigar's place in history, and his importance to racing, and thus took him around the country so fans could see him. Cigar's sendoff was equally inspired. One week after his final race, Cigar was paraded before the National Horse Show at Madison Square Garden. Five blocks of Seventh Avenue were cordoned off to accommodate the horse van. Children rushed to the outside of the ring to pet Cigar, who was ridden by Bailey.

Cigar retired with record earnings of $9,999,815, but the streak is his enduring legacy, both for the number of races won and for the breadth and scope of where Cigar ran. He traveled across the country, and then halfway around the world, while winning 16 straight races. His campaign was unprecedented – nine tracks, six states, two continents, and four time zones. No horse had accomplished so much with such an ambitious racing and travel schedule, and that is why Cigar must rank as one of the all-time greats.

Cigar would be remembered only for his racing career, however. There would be no little Cigarettes trying to follow in his footsteps. Cigar was infertile, and eventually was retired to the Kentucky Horse Park. For Mott, it was an oddly perfect ending.

"I'm sure people will criticize me, but I'm satisfied that that's the way it turned out," Mott said. "As great a sire as Secretariat was, people always said he wasn't that good, because they tended to compare his offspring to him. That's not fair. If Cigar had turned out to be a mediocre stallion, I would have had to listen to that, people saying he wasn't that good a stallion because he didn't reproduce himself. So when I heard he was infertile, for me it was less traumatic than when he lost at Del Mar. I had no emotion. I just thought, 'It's over.'"

Cigar's success and popularity fueled a rebirth in interest in American racing. Ideas that had crashed and burned early in the decade were born anew. The American Championship Racing Series, a nationally televised group of races for older horses that ran from 1991-93, died because of infighting among the member tracks. When the series was disbanded, Barry Weisbord, the organizer, said, "I think the ACRS is a martyr, or let's say a wasted opportunity." An attempt to create a centralized national office failed miserably midway through the decade when Thoroughbred Racing Associations member tracks refused to remove the handcuffs from J. Brian McGrath, who was hired as the commissioner. But some of McGrath's core beliefs – organizing licensing and corporate sponsorships

A horse of uncommon gameness, Silver Charm won the Kentucky Derby and Preakness by tight margins, and came back as a 4-year-old to win the Dubai World Cup in another photo.

among the tracks – were cornerstones of the National Thoroughbred Racing Association, which was launched in 1998 and took over from the TRA as the sport's national office.

The NTRA, led by Commissioner Tim Smith, grew out of a concept first proposed by Fred Pope, a Kentucky advertising executive, who created the National Thoroughbred Association as a means for owners to control the financial destiny of the sport. One of the NTRA's first missions was to enhance racing's presence on television. A series of races for older horses trod the same ground as the ACRS pioneers, and an aggressive national advertising campaign was launched, featuring the waiflike actress Lori Petty screaming "Go Baby Go."

The combination of racing's increased television exposure, the emphasis on Triple Crown races, and the success of Cigar in Dubai came together gloriously for Silver Charm and his silver-haired trainer, Bob Baffert. Media savvy, quick with a quip, and possessed of horses who could flat-out run, Baffert

became the most recognizable figure in the sport in the late 1990's. He won both the Kentucky Derby and the Preakness Stakes in consecutive years, with Silver Charm and Real Quiet – both of whom won Eclipse Awards as champion 3-year-old – but Silver Charm was the stable's star.

Baffert, like D. Wayne Lukas and Nick Zito, made the Triple Crown, particularly the Derby, the focal point of his training operation. But Baffert's Derby winners had accomplished careers as older horses, too, in part because he gave them lengthy vacations following the classics. After nearly sweeping the Triple Crown in 1997, Silver Charm got a six-month break, then embarked on his 1998 campaign. The main goal was the Santa Anita Handicap. But when Silver Charm came up with a foot bruise on the eve of that race, an audible was called, and plans were made to send him to Dubai.

Had Cigar lost the inaugural Dubai World Cup, the course of history might have changed. But Americans took the first three spots in Dubai the year Cigar won, and then American-based runners finished 2-3 in the second Dubai World Cup. In just two runnings, it had become a premier target, the spring's counterpart to the Breeders' Cup Classic.

Silver Charm was flown to Dubai and, in one of the most courageous performances of the decade, re-rallied after being passed at midstretch – "Silver Charm is coming again. This is incredible," race-caller Derek Thompson exclaimed – to beat Swain in a photo finish.

Baffert had an amazing year. In addition to the Dubai World Cup, he almost won the Triple Crown with Real Quiet, who lost the Belmont Stakes by a nose to Victory Gallop. And Baffert sent out Silverbulletday to a victory in the Breeders' Cup Juvenile Fillies, which secured an Eclipse Award for her. Silverbulletday also was the champion 3-year-old filly of 1999, a year when Baffert received the Eclipse Award as champion trainer for the third straight year.

Baffert started his training career with Quarter Horses before switching to Thoroughbreds. He wore cowboy boots, jeans, and sunglasses, and concentrated on winning Triple Crown races. He was following a path first cleared by Lukas.

By the end of the century, Lukas had won 12 Triple Crown races, including four Kentucky Derbies, three of which were won in the 1990's, and 15 Breeders' Cup races. His horses had won more than $200 million in purses, and nearly two dozen Eclipse Awards. But for Lukas, the 1990's were a tumultuous decade, filled with the highest highs and the lowest lows.

Lukas guided Criminal Type to the Horse of the Year title in 1990, which included victories over Sunday Silence in the Hollywood Gold Cup and over Easy Goer in the Metropolitan Mile. But behind the scenes, Criminal Type's owner, Calumet Farm, was struggling to stay afloat in a financial whirlpool. A number of horses had to be sold, including a 2-year-

Serena's Song was an iron filly for trainer D. Wayne Lukas, setting an earnings record for a North American-based female and defeating males on two occasions.

old named Strike the Gold, who would go on to become the first of two Derby winners for Nick Zito. Calumet's prized stallion, Alydar, the sire of Strike the Gold, died under mysterious circumstances. Calumet was named champion breeder for 1990, and had the Horse of the Year. A year later, the farm, which was run by J. T. Lundy, declared bankruptcy. Creditors like Lukas lost millions.

Calumet's property was saved from developers by Henryk de Kwiatkowski, who purchased the historic farm. Calumet's priceless collection of trophies was kept from being parceled out by an auction house after sufficient funds were raised in an effort spearheaded by James E. Bassett III, chairman of the board of Keeneland Association.

In December 1993, Lukas's son and chief assistant, Jeff, was trampled by the colt Tabasco Cat and suffered severe head injuries. Jeff Lukas fell into a coma and nearly died, and though he survived and returned to work for his father, the injuries left him unable to handle as much responsibility as he had before the accident.

Yet Tabasco Cat got Lukas rolling again. Tabasco Cat won both the Preakness and the Belmont in 1994, the first two of six consecutive Triple Crown race victories for Lukas. In 1994, Lukas led the nation in purse earnings and won the Eclipse Award as champion trainer. He swept the Triple Crown events in 1995 with two different horses, Thunder Gulch (Derby, Belmont) and Timber Country (Preakness), then won the 1996 Derby with Grindstone. None of those horses, however, raced beyond age 3.

In 1999, Lukas was on the verge of wrapping up the Triple Crown. Charismatic, who twice was risked in claiming races, emerged as the best colt of his generation with upset victories in both the Derby and the Preakness. But he finished third in the Belmont, and suffered career-ending fractures to his left front leg. Once again, tragedy raced head-and-head with triumph in the Lukas barn. Lukas's year ended on an upswing, with upset victories in the Breeders' Cup by Cash Run in the Juvenile Fillies and Cat Thief in the Classic, and a Horse of the Year trophy for Charismatic.

Lukas's iron horse was a filly, Serena's Song, who won the Eclipse Award as champion 3-year-old filly in 1995. In three years of racing, she started 38 times, won 18 – including 11 Grade 1 races – and earned $3,283,388, a record for a North American-based female. She beat the boys twice at age 3, in the Haskell Invitational and the Jim Beam Stakes, and just missed at age 4 in the Whitney Handicap.

Serena's Song was owned by Bob and Beverly Lewis, who had a remarkable run of success. They owned Silver Charm and Charismatic, and twice in three years won the Derby and Preakness before suffering crushing losses in the Belmont. The exuberant couple, both in their 70's and married more than 50 years, charmed the sport with their enthusiasm, sportsmanship, and generosity. They were rewarded with the Eclipse Award of Merit in 1997.

Serena's Song was part of a golden era for fillies and mares in the 1990's. Bayakoa, an Argentine import who arrived in this country with a nervous disposition, thrived under the patient care of trainer Ron McAnally. She won 21 of 39 starts – including 12 Grade 1 races in the United States – and earned the second of her two championships in 1990. McAnally then mined the same vein and came up with another Argentine import, Paseana, who also was a two-time Eclipse Award winner. A hearty mare who won graded stakes at age 8, Paseana captured 10 Grade 1 races, including two runnings of Santa Anita's storied Santa Margarita Invitational Handicap. Both Bayakoa and Paseana won the Breeders' Cup Distaff.

Sky Beauty, who would bring tears to the eyes of her trainer, Allen Jerkens, when she won, took 15 of 21 starts, including 10 Grade 1 races. She swept the New York Racing Association's triple crown for 3-year-old fillies in 1993, and got an overdue Eclipse Award the following year. Trainer Charlie Whittingham, in the twilight of his career, brilliantly managed the turf mare Flawlessly, who won three consecutive runnings of both Del Mar's Ramona Handicap and Hollywood Park's Matriarch Stakes. A two-time champion, Flawlessly always needed plenty of rest after her late-season campaigns, and Whittingham always was accommodating.

Two other veteran trainers wrapped themselves in glory in the latter part of their careers: Jimmy Croll, with Housebuster, and Sonny Hine, with Guilty Conscience, had trained champion sprinters, but each of them ended up both training and owning a Horse of the Year in the 1990's. Holy Bull and Skip Away provided bookends around Cigar, and preceded Silver Charm, during an exciting run for 3-year-olds and up during the decade.

Croll acquired Holy Bull when a longtime client, Rachel Carpenter, left the colt to him in her will. Holy Bull won 7 of his first 8 starts, and entered the 1994 Kentucky Derby as the 2-1 favorite. But he

trained poorly at Churchill Downs, and ran to those works. He finished 12th. Croll then wisely took Holy Bull off the Triple Crown trail, and mapped out a schedule that resulted in him being named Horse of the Year.

Holy Bull whipped older horses in the Metropolitan Mile, but he earned his greatest respect in his last two starts of the year. In the Travers Stakes, run at the same 1¼-mile distance of the Derby, Holy Bull was forced into fractions of 46⅕ seconds for the first half-mile and 1:10⅖ for six furlongs. The stretch-running Concern seemed poised to take advantage of the crackling pace, and when he roared outside Holy Bull at the top of the stretch, Saratoga's racecaller, Tom Durkin, cleverly announced, "There is cause for Concern." Holy Bull, however, would not be denied. He bravely

Though he floundered as the 2-1 favorite in the Kentucky Derby, the steel-gray Holy Bull buzzed through the competition for the remainder of his 1994 campaign. After a dominating victory over the best older horses in the country in the Woodward, he was named Horse of the Year despite passing the Breeders' Cup.

fought off Concern and won by a neck. It was 17 lengths back to the third horse, Tabasco Cat, who had won the Preakness and Belmont that year.

Holy Bull then closed out his season with a five-length romp against older horses in the Woodward Stakes. He passed the Breeders' Cup Classic but secured Horse of the Year when Concern defeated older horses in the Classic. Holy Bull's 1995 campaign came to a sudden end in his second start of the year, when he suffered a career-ending injury in the Donn Handicap. Cigar won the Donn, and went on to be Horse of the Year. Cigar held the title as best older horse for two years, before relinquishing it to Skip Away.

Sonny Hine and his wife, Carolyn, purchased Skip Away as a 2-year-old in training. Hine trained Skip Away, and Carolyn was listed as the owner, but this was a partnership through and through. Skip, as Carolyn affectionately called him, became a member of the Hine family. They treated him as if he were a son, showering him with love and affection, and sticking up for him when he was not given credit the Hines believed he was due.

Just as Holy Bull passed the baton to Cigar in the 1995 Donn, so Cigar passed the baton to Skip Away in the 1996 Jockey Club Gold Cup. By that point, Skip Away already had won the Blue Grass Stakes and the Haskell Invitational, and had finished second in both the Preakness and the Belmont, but the Jockey Club Gold Cup announced his arrival. Skip Away was named champion 3-year-old and was ready to assert himself as the best older horse in the country.

In 1997, Skip Away won the Jockey Club Gold Cup for the second straight year and completed his season with a runaway six-length score in the Breeders' Cup Classic, a race to which he was supplemented for $480,000. He was the champion older horse, beating out such accomplished runners as Formal Gold, who defeated Skip Away three times that year and earned one of the highest Beyer Speed Figure of the decade, a 125. But Skip Away missed out on Horse of the Year, which went to the unbeaten 2-year-old Favorite Trick. The Hines were crushed, even though Carolyn was rewarded with the Eclipse Award as champion owner.

Determined to prove that Skip Away should have been Horse of the Year, the Hines designed an aggressive 1998 campaign to showcase Skip Away. He won his first seven starts of the year, racing in Florida, Maryland, Massachusetts, California, New Jersey, and New York, earning points like a politician campaigning in primaries. Although Skip Away lost his final two starts, including the Breeders' Cup Classic to Awesome Again, he was named Horse of the Year and, for the second straight year, champion older horse. Skip Away won 18 of 38 starts, including 10 Grade 1 races, and earned $9,616,360, second only to Cigar.

While Holy Bull, Cigar, and Skip Away were succeeding each other, Lonesome Glory was a constant in the steeplechase division. He was the champion at age 4 in 1992, again in 1993, 1995, 1997, and finally at age 11 in 1999, becoming the only five-time Eclipse Award-winning steeplechaser. Lonesome Glory won the Colonial Cup at Camden, South Carolina, three times. He was bred and owned by Kay Jeffords, was trained by Bruce Miller, and was ridden by Miller's daughter Blythe.

Favorite Trick, who beat out Skip Away for Horse of the Year in 1997, became only the second 2-year-old to earn that title, following Secretariat in 1972. Favorite Trick, who won all eight of his starts, was a precocious little fellow, but he proved versatile, too. He won dashing 4 ½ furlongs in April, and completed the year with a 5 ½-length romp going 1 1/16 miles in the Breeders' Cup Juvenile in November. His trainer, Patrick Byrne, also sent out that year's champion 2-year-old filly, Countess Diana.

Favorite Trick may have been a Horse of the Year, but the most talked-about 2-year-old of the nineties was Arazi. A Kentucky-bred who began his career in France, Arazi won 6 of his first 7 starts, all on turf, before arriving in Kentucky with trainer Francois Boutin for the 1991 Breeders' Cup Juvenile. In one of the most electrifying performances of the decade, Arazi darted through traffic down the backstretch and around the far turn to go

European star Arazi created a stir with his blowout victory in the 1991 Breeders' Cup Juvenile, but surgery on both knees following the race compromised his ability. He was never the same, and finished eighth as the favorite in the Kentucky Derby.

from 13th to second, then roared past Bertrando and drew off to win by 4¾ lengths while being geared down by his jockey, Pat Valenzuela. He was the champion 2-year-old colt, got support for Horse of the Year, and immediately became the future-book favorite for the 1992 Kentucky Derby.

Arazi needed arthroscopic surgery on both knees following the Breeders' Cup, and did not have the proper time to prepare for the Derby. He had one prep race in France before returning to Kentucky. He was rattled by the crowds that pressed against the rail during training hours in the days prior to the race. Despite the obstacles, he was sent off as the 9-10 favorite. Skeptics, though, abounded. The morning of the race, turf writer Dick Jerardi had had enough of the Arazi hype.

"I've decided what Arazi will be good for," Jerardi announced. "Years from now, when another overrated horse comes along, we'll be able to say, 'He's just another Arazi.'" Arazi proved Jerardi prophetic. Arazi made another powerful move on the turn in the Derby, but flattened out and finished eighth.

A.P. Indy, who was scratched with a quarter crack the morning of the 1992 Derby, went on to win the Belmont Stakes and the Breeders' Cup Classic to take that year's titles as Horse of the Year and champion 3-year-old colt. Arazi, six months after the Derby, returned from France and, remarkably, was sent off the 3-2 favorite in the Breeders' Cup Mile. He finished 11th and was retired, but his co-owners, Allen Paulson and Sheikh Mohammed al-Maktoum, had forged a partnership that would later pay off with Cigar's participation in the first Dubai World Cup.

There are disappointments, of which Arazi was surely one, and then there are heartbreaks. There is a difference. With a disappointment, you shrug your shoulders and move on. A heartbreak, though, makes you question and doubt, and curse the fates. And there was no greater heartbreak than the 1990 Breeders' Cup, the darkest day in American racing since Ruffian died as a result of injuries suffered in her 1975 match race against Foolish Pleasure.

It was the first Breeders' Cup run at Belmont Park, and the crisp fall air made it a perfect afternoon for racing. But disaster struck early. Mr. Nickerson and Shaker Knit suffered fatal injuries in the Breeders' Cup Sprint, setting the tone for the day.

That year's Distaff brought together two champions from 1989. Bayakoa and Go for Wand both had won Breeders' Cup races at Gulfstream Park, and they came into the 1990 Distaff atop their respective divisions. The first mile of the 1⅛-mile race was dazzling. Go for Wand, a 3-year-old, and the 6-year-old Bayakoa hooked up from the start, and drew away from their rivals. They were locked together, Go for Wand on the inside, Bayakoa on the outside, the crowd of 51,236 enthralled by the pure desire of both.

And then, without warning, Go for Wand fractured her right front ankle at the sixteenth pole. She nose-dived to the dirt, then her instincts compelled her to stand. The sight of her struggling was horrifying. Go for Wand was euthanized immediately, and was buried the next day at Saratoga. "It should be a victory, but it isn't," said Ron McAnally, Bayakoa's trainer. "They give their lives for our enjoyment."

As dusk began to gather over Belmont Park, Unbridled won the Classic, becoming the first horse to win that race and the Kentucky Derby in the same year. But that feat was overshadowed by the numbing events earlier in the day.

The sport lost others, both human and equine, during the decade. Trainers Laz Barrera, Francois Boutin, Henry Clark, W. Burling Cocks, Buddy Hirsch, Horatio Luro, Jack Price, Willard Proctor, Rodney Rash, Woody Stephens, Mesh Tenney, Harry Trotsek, Bob Wheeler, Charlie Whittingham, and Frank Wright; jockeys Eddie Arcaro and Eric Guerin; cinematographer Joe Burnham; photographer Kathryn Dudek; racetrack owners Edward J. DeBartolo and Robert Strub; racecaller Fred Capossela; steward Keene Daingerfield; sports impresario Sonny Werblin; auctioneer John Finney;

Heatbreak marred the running of the 1990 Breeders' Cup at Belmont Park. Three horses, including the brilliant champion Go for Wand, suffered fatal injuries.

celebrated grooms Clem Brooks and Eddie Sweat; owner-breeders Leslie Combs II, Rex Ellsworth, Thomas Mellon Evans, Daniel Galbreath, Frances Genter, Warner Jones, Howard Keck, Gene Klein, Paul Mellon, Stavros Niarchos, Alfred G. Vanderbilt, Frank Whitham, and Zenya Yoshida; and respected writers Pete Axthelm, Jim Bolus, Mary Jane Gallaher, Bob Harding, Kent Hollingsworth, Bill Leggett, Oscar Otis, and Whitney Tower all died.

Racehorses Great Communicator, Izvestia, Pleasant Stage, Prairie Bayou, and Three Ring were taken too soon. Death also claimed the retired horses Ack Ack, Bayakoa, Best Pal, Blushing Groom, Damascus, Easy Goer, Flying Paster, Forego, Grey Dawn II, and Sir Ivor, and three of this century's greatest stallions, Mr. Prospector, Nijinsky II, and Northern Dancer.

Bill Shoemaker retired as a jockey in 1990 with a record 8,833 victories, began training, and one year later was paralyzed in a car accident. Julie Krone, who became the first female jockey to win a classic when she captured the 1993 Belmont with Colonial Affair, retired in 1999. Hall of Fame trainer MacKenzie Miller, long associated with philanthropist Paul Mellon, retired two years after the two gentlemen of the turf won the Kentucky Derby with Sea Hero. Johnny Longden, the only man to both ride and train a Derby winner, stopped training. Trainer Gary Jones and jockeys Steve Cauthen and Sandy Hawley also retired, as did Lester Piggott, after a brief comeback that saw him win the 1990 Breeders' Cup Mile on Royal Academy.

Animal rights became an increasingly important issue. Organizations such as Re-Run, United Pegasus Foundation, and the Thoroughbred Retirement Fund

Michael Dickinson turned in one of the great training feats of all time when he sent out Da Hoss (RIGHT) to win the 1998 Breeders' Cup Mile off only a minor prep race following a two-year layoff.

helped to give retired racehorses a dignified way to live out their lives, but the sickening death of Exceller in a Swedish slaughterhouse in July 1997 was a reminder that more needed to be done.

The robust American economy was good for business. Sales prices at the top end of the market boomed. Total sales at the 1999 auctions were a record $1 billion. The average at the benchmark Keeneland July Yearling Sale in 1999 was up 21 percent from the previous year. The economic gains helped American breeders hold on to the best stallions, unlike the early 1990's, when horses such as Forty Niner and Sunday Silence were whisked off to Japan.

Tracks struggled with increased competition from casinos and state-run lotteries. "We have lost our exclusive franchise, and yet we are being regulated as if the old system still applied," said Ogden Mills Phipps, chairman of The Jockey Club. When Arlington International Racecourse could not get additional gambling approved for track grounds, owner Richard Duchossois elected not to race in 1998 or 1999. But some tracks, such as Delaware Park and Prairie Meadows, were able to put slot machines on track grounds, then watched their bottom lines and purses soar. The proliferation of simulcasting also kept purses and revenues high during the decade. But while handle was up, and big events, such as the Breeders' Cup and Triple Crown races, attracted record crowds, ontrack attendance on a daily basis was declining. Full-card simulcasting came to California, Florida, and Kentucky. New York became the last state to allow horses to race on antibleeding medications such as Lasix.

Racetracks became sought-after properties. Frank Stronach's Magna Entertainment purchased Santa Anita, Gulfstream Park, Golden Gate Fields, Remington Park, and Thistledown. Churchill Downs acquired Hollywood Park, Calder Race Course, and Ellis Park, and opened Hoosier Park in Indiana. Lone Star Park opened in Texas and became a raging success, while Sam Houston and Retama Park both rebounded from shaky starts. Fair Grounds was rebuilt after being destroyed by fire. Suffolk Downs reopened to great success. Emerald Downs opened in Washington State to replace longtime fan favorite Longacres. But nothing could save Ak-Sar-Ben or Detroit Race Course, and Atlantic City barely had a pulse.

Laffit Pincay Jr. put an exclamation point on his Hall of Fame career when on Dec. 10, 1999, he rode his 8,834th winner, passing Shoemaker's record for victories by a jockey. But Russell Baze, who won 400 races every year from 1992 through 1998, was on a pace to eventually catch Pincay. Michael Dickinson was trying to bring European-style training methods to the United States. He owned his own facility in Maryland, and used it as the launching pad for a startling comeback by Da Hoss, who won the 1996 Breeders' Cup Mile, was off for nearly two years, then had one prep before a repeat victory in the 1998 Mile.

Racing looked far different from how it did at the beginning of the century. Racetracks were changing hands, with the power being concentrated among a core group of businessmen. The impact of the Internet raised possibilities never before dreamed of for betting and flow of information. New home-wagering ventures were altering how and where fans placed their bets. Sports fans largely were tuning out the droning sameness of racing's weekday cards, but major events sparked record interest, and summertime meets at Del Mar and Saratoga were thriving. Stallions shuttled between Northern and Southern Hemispheres. And trainers and owners were increasingly emboldened to race their horses around the world. These were the trends racing was embracing as the sport dove headlong into the next millennium.

CHAMPIONS

PAST PERFORMANCES

THE 1990's

•1990•
•2-Year-Old Male *Fly So Free* •2-Year-Old Filly *Meadow Star* •3-Year-Old Male *Unbridled*
•3-Year-Old Filly *Go for Wand* •Handicap Horse *Criminal Type* •Handicap Mare *Bayakoa*
•Grass Horse *Itsallgreektome (M) Laugh and Be Merry (F)* •Sprinter *Housebuster* •Steeplechase *Morley Street*
•**HORSE OF THE YEAR** Criminal Type

•1991•
•2-Year-Old Male *Arazi* •2-Year-Old Filly *Pleasant Stage* •3-Year-Old Male *Hansel* •3-Year-Old Filly *Dance Smartly*
•Handicap Horse *Black Tie Affair* •Handicap Mare *Queena* •Grass Horse *Tight Spot (M) Miss Alleged (F)*
•Sprinter *Housebuster* •Steeplechase *Morley Street*
•**HORSE OF THE YEAR** Black Tie Affair

•1992•
•2-Year-Old Male *Gilded Time* •2-Year-Old Filly *Eliza* •3-Year-Old Male *A.P. Indy* •3-Year-Old Filly *Saratoga Dew*
•Handicap Horse *Pleasant Tap* •Handicap Mare *Paseana* •Grass Horse *Sky Classic (M) Flawlessly (F)* •Sprinter *Rubiano*
•Steeplechase *Lonesome Glory*
•**HORSE OF THE YEAR** A.P. Indy

•1993•
•2-Year-Old Male *Dehere* •2-Year-Old Filly *Phone Chatter* •3-Year-Old Male *Prairie Bayou*
•3-Year-Old Filly *Hollywood Wildcat* •Handicap Horse *Bertrando* •Handicap Mare *Paseana*
•Grass Horse *Kotashaan (M) Flawlessly (F)* •Sprinter *Cardmania* •Steeplechase *Lonesome Glory*
•**HORSE OF THE YEAR** Kotashaan

•1994•
•2-Year-Old Male *Timber Country* •2-Year-Old Filly *Flanders* •3-Year-Old Male *Holy Bull*
•3-Year-Old Filly *Heavenly Prize* •Handicap Horse *The Wicked North* •Handicap Mare *Sky Beauty*
•Grass Horse *Paradise Creek (M) Hatoof (F)* •Sprinter *Cherokee Run* •Steeplechase *Warm Spell*
•**HORSE OF THE YEAR** Holy Bull

•1995•
•2-Year-Old Male *Maria's Mon* •2-Year-Old Filly *Golden Attraction* •3-Year-Old Male *Thunder Gulch*
•3-Year-Old Filly *Serena's Song* •Handicap Horse *Cigar* •Handicap Mare *Inside Information*
•Grass Horse *Northern Spur (M) Possibly Perfect (F)* •Sprinter *Not Surprising* •Steeplechase *Lonesome Glory*
•**HORSE OF THE YEAR** Cigar

•1996•
•2-Year-Old Male *Boston Harbor* •2-Year-Old Filly *Storm Song* •3-Year-Old Male *Skip Away*
•3-Year-Old Filly *Yanks Music* •Handicap Horse *Cigar* •Handicap Mare *Jewel Princess*
•Grass Horse *Singspiel (M) Wandesta (F)* •Sprinter *Lit de Justice* •Steeplechase *Coreggio*
•**HORSE OF THE YEAR** Cigar

•1997•
•2-Year-Old Male *Favorite Trick* •2-Year-Old Filly *Countess Diana* •3-Year-Old Male *Silver Charm*
•3-Year-Old Filly *Ajina* •Handicap Horse *Skip Away* •Handicap Mare *Hidden Lake*
•Grass Horse *Chief Bearhart (M) Ryafan (F)* •Sprinter *Smoke Glacken* •Steeplechase *Lonesome Glory*
•**HORSE OF THE YEAR** Favorite Trick

•1998•
•2-Year-Old Male *Answer Lively* •2-Year-Old Filly *Silverbulletday* •3-Year-Old Male *Real Quiet*
•3-Year-Old Filly *Banshee Breeze* •Handicap Horse *Skip Away* •Handicap Mare *Escena*
•Grass Horse *Buck's Boy (M) Fiji (F)* •Sprinter *Reraise* •Steeplechase *Flat Top*
•**HORSE OF THE YEAR** Skip Away

•1999•
•2-Year-Old Male *Anees* •2-Year-Old Filly *Chilukki* •3-Year-Old Male *Charismatic* •3-Year-Old Filly *Silverbulletday*
•Handicap Horse *Victory Gallop* •Handicap Mare *Beautiful Pleasure* •Grass Horse *Daylami (M) Soaring Softly (F)*
•Sprinter *Artax* •Steeplechase *Lonesome Glory*
•**HORSE OF THE YEAR** Charismatic

A.P. Indy

dkbbr. c. 1989, by Seattle Slew (Bold Reasoning)–Weekend Surprise, by Secretariat — **Lifetime record: 11 8 0 1 $2,979,815**

Own.– Farish, Goodman, Kilroy & Tsurumaki
Br.– W.S. Farish III & W.S. Kilroy (Ky)
Tr.– Neil Drysdale

31Oct92-10GP	fst 1¼	:454 1:10 1:35 2:001	3↑ B C Classic-G1	4	6	84½	42½	2hd	12	Delahoussaye E		121		*2.10	100-03	A.P. Indy1212Pleasant Tap126½Jolypha1181½	Hand ride	14
10Oct92- 8Bel	gd 1¼	:461 1:10 1:35 1:584	3↑ J C Gold Cup-G1	5	7	715	62¾	54	36¾	Delahoussaye E		121		2.90	90-04	Pleasant Tap1264½Strike the Gold1262¼A.P. Indy121½		7
	Bobbled pnchd br																	
13Sep92- 8WO	fst 1⅛	:473 1:122 1:382 1:513	Molson Million-G2	2	3	32½	55½	63¾	52½	Delahoussaye E		126		*.70	85-18	Benburb119½Elated Guy117½Vying Victor119hd	Gave way	7
	Previously owned by Tomonori Tsurumaki																	
6Jun92- 8Bel	gd 1½	:47 1:114 2:011 2:26	Belmont-G1	1	4	42½	3½	2½	1¾	Delahoussaye E		126		*1.10	100-00	A.P.Indy126¾MyMemoirs126nkPnBluff12613¼	Strong handling	11
24May92- 8Bel	fst 1⅛	:453 1:10 1:351 1:472	Peter Pan-G2	6	5	53½	1½	12½	15½	Delahoussaye E		126		*.50	92-08	A.P.Indy1265½ColonyLight1144¾BerkleyFitz1142	Ridden out	7
4Apr92- 5SA	fst 1⅛	:461 1:102 1:361 1:491	S Anita Derby-G1	3	4	42½	43	31	11¾	Dlhoussaye E	B	122		*.90	84-11	A.P.Indy1221¾Bertrando122nkCasualLies1223½	Wide,driving	7
29Feb92- 8SA	fst 1	:223 :46 1:10 1:352	San Rafael-G2	5	3	31½	2½	22½	1¾	Dlhoussaye E	B	121		*.50	90-12	A.P. Indy121¾Treekster1169Prince Wild118½	Determinedly	6
22Dec91- 5Hol	fst 1 1/16	:23 :464 1:11 1:424	Hol Futurity-G1	11	9	95¾	63¼	1hd	1nk	Dlhoussaye E	B	121		3.20	87-17	A.P. Indy121nkDance Flr1215½Casl Lies1212	Wide ridden out	14
4Dec91- 8BM	fst 1	:23 :464 1:112 1:362	Alw 21000	1	1	1hd	1hd	11	13	Dlhoussaye E	B	117		*.20	88-19	A.P.Indy1173KalookanBoy1173½FabulousPol117no	Ridden out	8
27Oct91- 6SA	sl 6½f	:214 :453 1:113 1:181	Md Sp Wt	4	8	87¼	63½	31½	14	Dlhoussaye E	B	117		*1.30	79-24	A.P. Indy1174Dr Pain1173½Hickman Creek1172		9
	Lacked room ¼,swung out,handily																	
24Aug91- 4Dmr	fst 6f	:221 :451 :572 1:101	Md Sp Wt	2	5	54½	46½	47	45½	Dlhoussaye E	B	117		*2.30	82-11	Shrp Bandit1172½Anonymsly1172¾Rchd of Engld117nk	Gaining	7

Ajina

dkbbr. f. 1994, by Strawberry Road (Whiskey Road)–Winglet, by Alydar — **Lifetime record: 17 7 3 2 $1,327,915**

Own.– Allen E. Paulson
Br.– Allen E. Paulson (Ky)
Tr.– William I. Mott

26Jly98- 8Del	fst 1¼	:473 1:121 1:381 2:041	3↑ ⒻDelaware H-G3	1	2	11	1hd	3½	64¾	Smith ME		120		1.80	83-07	Amrllo110¾TuxdoJncton1152¼TmlyBrod110no	Dueled,gave way	9
20Jun98- 8Bel	fst 1 1/16	:222 :444 1:083 1:394	3↑ ⒻHempstead H-G1	4	3	42	43	55	413	Smith ME		122		*1.70	87-12	Mossflower11412Glitter Woman120noColonial Minstrel1181		6
	Lacked response																	
16May98- 4Pim	fst 1⅛	:462 1:102 1:354 1:483	3↑ ⒻPim Distaff H-G3	2	1	1½	1½	13½	13	Bailey JD		120		*.50	97-13	Ajina1203NskrColors112nkPocho'sDrmGrl1133½	Rail,driving	8
11Apr98- 6OP	fst 1 1/16	:231 :464 1:114 1:44	4↑ ⒻBayakoa 40k	7	3	21½	31½	88½	811½	Day P		112		*.40	76-10	Water Street113nkProper Banner1161Western Flick116nk		8
	Fractious loading,forward,nothing left																	
8Nov97- 4Hol	fst 1⅛	:454 1:091 1:342 1:471	3↑ ⒻBC Distaff-G1	1	4	31½	32	1hd	12	Smith ME	B	120		4.80e	90-06	Ajina1202Sharp Cat1203½Escena1231	Driving	8
19Oct97- 9Bel	fst 1⅛	:463 1:103 1:352 1:481	3↑ ⒻBeldame-G1	8	4	32	31½	22	22	Smith ME		119		2.90	87-12	Hidden Lake1232Ajina1192Jewel Princess1231¼	Held well	8
16Aug97- 8Sar	fst 1¼	:48 1:121 1:363 2:021	ⒻAlabama-G1	6	1	11½	1½	2hd	21¼	Smith ME		121		*.75	96-16	Runup the Clrs1211¼Ajina1213½Tomisue's Delt12112	gamely	6
	Yielded grudgingly																	
19Jly97- 9Bel	fst 1¼	:48 1:121 1:354 2:002	ⒻC C A Oaks-G1	3	1	11	13½	15	12¼	Smith ME		121		1.15	95-08	Ajina1212¼Tomisue'sDelight1218KeyHunter12115	Ridden out	5
21Jun97- 9Bel	fst 1⅛	:454 1:102 1:353 1:482	ⒻMother Goose-G1	2	2	21½	21½	1hd	11¼	Smith ME		121		18.00	13-13	Ajina1211¼Sharp Cat1211½Tomisue's Delight12111		6
	Stalked,strong urging																	
31May97- 9Bel	fst 1	:221 :443 1:084 1:342	ⒻAcorn-G1	3	5	53½	53½	35	37¼	Santos JA		121		23.00	85-14	Sharp Cat1212½Dixie Flag1214¾Ajina1211¼	Saved ground	7
1May97- 8CD	fst 7f	:222 :45 1:094 1:223	ⒻLa Troienne 113k	3	1	52¼	42¾	56½	411	Bailey JD		121		3.90	84-08	StarofGoshen11511PearlCity115noFlyingLurn116no	No rally	8
6Apr97- 9OP	fst 1 1/16	:231 :464 1:114 1:423	ⒻFantasy-G2	1	1	2hd	31½	37½	314	Bailey JD		121		1.90	81-16	Blushing K.D.1216Valid Bonnet1218Ajina1216		5
	Bore out 1st turn,rail,little left																	
9Mar97-10GP	fst 1 1/16	:231 :462 1:10 1:431	ⒻBonnie Miss-G2	2	3	34	35	39	413	Bailey JD		119		5.70	78-16	GlitterWoman1177¼SouthernPlaygirl119¾DixieFlg1145	Faded	5
30Nov96- 7Aqu	fst 1⅛	:493 1:142 1:402 1:533	ⒻDemoiselle-G2	9	3	2½	2½	1½	17	Day P		121		*1.05	72-21	Ajina1217Hidden Reserve1144½Biding Time114¾	Mild urging	9
10Nov96- 9Aqu	fst 1	:23 :46 1:111 1:362	ⒻTempted-G3	5	4	43½	3nk	2½	1½	Bailey JD		112		2.65	88-17	Ajina112½Glitter Woman1147Aldiza1141		7
	Checked,pinched break,wide,prevailed																	
13Oct96- 2Bel	fst 7f	:223 :461 1:104 1:232	ⒻMd Sp Wt	5	5	31½	3nk	13	13	Bailey JD		117		*1.70	84-11	Ajina1173Recoleta1175Runup the Colors1171½	Drew away	11
15Sep96- 2Bel	fst 6f	:222 :46 :581 1:103	ⒻMd Sp Wt	1	2	21	21	21½	22½	Bailey JD		116		3.75	86-08	URUnforgettabl1162½Ajn1169MssQun1161	No match,clear 2nd	10

Anees

b. c. 1997, by Unbridled (Fappiano)–Ivory Idol, by Alydar — **Lifetime record: 4 2 0 1 $609,200**

Own.– The Thoroughbred Corp
Br.– Farfellow Farms Ltd (Ky)
Tr.– Alex L. Hassinger Jr

6Nov99- 8GP	fst 1 1/16	:221 :46 1:101 1:421	©BC Juvenile-G1	9	14	148	87¾	41¾	12½	Stevens GL	L	122	b	30.30	96-00	Anees1222½ChiefSttl122¾HghYld1222¼	Bumped start,drifted	14
10Oct99- 7SA	fst 1	:221 :454 1:094 1:353	Norfolk-G2	2	6	68½	39½	35	35	Stevens GL	LB	118	b	9.50	88-15	DxUnon118½ForstCmp1184½Ans1189½	Inside move,bested rest	6
3Sep99- 3Dmr	fst 1	:224 :47 1:12 1:373	Md Sp Wt	5	4	44	41¾	1hd	12	Stevens GL	LB	118	b	4.90	84-09	Anees1182SilverAx1182½GltyMomnt1181½	4 wide bid,driving	8
21Aug99- 5Dmr	fst 5½f	:22 :452 :574 1:042	Md Sp Wt	9	6	918	919	814	613	Dsrmeaux KJ	LB	118		7.70	78-14	Tavasco1183½BraveSlew118nkVlntVson118¾	Lugged out start	9

Answer Lively

b. c. 1996, by Lively One (Halo)–Twosies Answer, by Two's a Plenty — **Lifetime record: 14 4 4 0 $938,296**

Own.– John A. Franks
Br.– John Franks (Ky)
Tr.– Bobby C. Barnett

2Oct99- 8LaD	fst 1¼	:463 1:10 1:353 2:002	Super Derby-G1	1	1	12	1hd	612	619	Gonzalez CV	L	126		4.10	83-09	EctonPark1262Menifee1262Pineaff1266	Pace,gave way drive	8
5Sep99- 8RP	fst 1⅛	:47 1:114 1:364 1:492	Rem Park Derby-G3	7	1	11	11	11½	21½	Gonzalez CV	LB	115		1.90	91-07	Temperence Time1191½Answer Lively1151Stellar Brush1244¾		8
	Could not last																	
1May99- 8CD	fst 1¼	:474 1:122 1:372 2:031	Ky Derby-G1	7	6	53	64	74¾	105¾	Perret C	L	126		37.00	83-14	Charismatic126nkMenifee126¾Cat Thief1261¼	In tight 1st turn	19
10Apr99-10OP	fst 1⅛	:46 1:101 1:36 1:491	Ark Derby-G2	7	3	32	32	46	59¾	Solis A	L	122		2.10	81-16	Valhol1184½Certain1222TorrdSnd1181	Stalked 4-wide,empty	7
	Awarded fourth purse money																	
14Mar99- 9FG	fst 1 1/16	:24 :48 1:124 1:432	La Derby-G2	7	3	32	3½	2½	2hd	Day P	L	122		1.80	94-20	Kimberlite Pipe122hdAnswer Lively122hdEcton Park1222¼		8
	3w turn,forced out																	
21Feb99- 9FG	fst 1 1/16	:232 :473 1:123 1:444	Risen Star 125k	1	4	52¾	64¼	32	2no	Day P	L	122		*.70	87-21	Ecton Park114noAnswer Lively122½Kimberlite Pipe1221½		12
	2w,outfinished																	
30Jan99- 9FG	fst 1	:223 :453 1:113 1:382	Lecomte H 100k	11	6	65¼	43	54	77¼	Albarado RJ	L	122		*.50	80-20	Some Actor114noDesert Demon1141½SilverChdr114¾		14
	Wide,6w,4w,no impact																	
7Nov98- 4CD	fst 1 1/16	:231 :463 1:113 1:44	BC Juvenile-G1	4	3	33½	3½	12	1hd	Bailey JD	L	122		*2.70	91-07	AnswerLively122hdAly'sAlley122¾CatThief1225½	Hard drive	13
18Oct98- 8Kee	fst 1 1/16	:223 :454 1:111 1:44	Breeders' Futurity-G2	1	1	2hd	12	11	2nk	Gonzalez CV	L	121		2.40	88-20	Cat Thief121nkAnswer Lively1213½Yes It's True1214½		8
	In bit tight 1st turn																	
3Oct98- 5LaD	fst 6½	:221 :444 1:10 1:163	Sport of Kings Fut 77k	10	1	2½	2½	14½	19	Gonzalez CV	L	120		*.50	91-15	AnswerLvly1209KodAct1203½BrssyWlls1205	Ridden out,sharp	10
20Sep98- 1LaD	fst 6f	:222 :46 :573 1:10	Alw 16000	6	2	31½	2hd	14	19	Gonzalez CV	L	113		*1.50	94-17	Answer Lively1139BlueAutumn119½TrickyMocha1194		7
	Rated,ridden out																	
19Jly98- 9LS	fst 6f	:211 :442 :573 1:111	Middleground 153k	11	1	12½	11½	41¼	56¼	Gonzalez CV	L	121	b	3.70	80-13	WingsofJones1211BrassyWlls1213¼Lou'sCnd1211½	Speed,tired	11
28Apr98- 3Kee	fst 4½f	:221 :461 :523	Md Sp Wt	4	1	1½		12	16½	Albarado RJ	L	118	b	3.30	93-08	Answer Lively1186½Hidden City1182½Fantastisch1182½		8
	Bore out,jolted foe start,pace,mild urging																	
9Apr98- 4Kee	my 4½f	:222 :453 :514	Md Sp Wt	9	7	32		34	413	Albarado RJ	L	118	b	2.80	84-15	TacticlCt1187ShortGo1185RokbysChrm1181	Stalked,weakened	10

Arazi

ch. c. 1989, by Blushing Groom (Red God)–Danseur Fabuleux, by Northern Dancer — Lifetime record: 14 9 1 1 $1,208,475
Own.– A.E. Paulson & Sheikh Mohammed Maktoum
Br.– Ralph Wilson Jr (Ky)
Tr.– Francois Boutin

31Oct92- 7GP fm 1Ⓣ :222 :454 1:09 1:324 3↑ B C Mile-G1 3 4 43 52¼ 1010 119 Valenzuela PA 122 *1.50 100-00 Lure1223ParadiseCrk122nkBrfTruc1221½ Saved ground,tired 14

4Oct92♦ Longchamp(Fr) sf *1ⓉRH 1:44 3↑ Prix du Rond Point-G2 Stk141000 14 Cauthen S 123 *1.20 Arazi1234Calling Collect123hdAlhijaz1301½ 11
Rated in 5th,sharp run to lead over 1f out,quickly clear

20Sep92♦ Longchamp(Fr) gd *1¼ⓉRH 2:072 3↑ Prix du Prince d'Orange-G3 Stk66900 36 Cauthen S 121 *.40 Arcangues1266Prince Polino121hdArazi1213 5
Unhurried in last,outside bid 2f out,lost 2nd near line

16Jun92♦ Ascot(GB) gd 1ⓉRH 1:392 St. James Palace-G1 Stk373000 52¼ Cauthen S 126 *.90 Brief Truce126noZaahi1261½Ezzoud126no 8
Rated in 6th,progress 2½f out,evenly late.Rodrigo de Triano 4th

2May92- 8CD fst 1¼ :464 1:111 1:363 2:03 Ky Derby-G1 17 17 1712 31½ 43 88¼ Valenzuela PA B 126 *.90 87-06 LilE.Tee1261CasualLis1263¼DncFloor1262 Bid 8 wide,tired 18
Originally teletimed in 2:04

7Apr92♦ Saint-Cloud(Fr) sf *1Ⓣ:H 1:48 Prix Omnium II (Listed)38200 15 Cauthen S 128 *.20 Arazi1285Supermec1282½River Majesty128½ 8
Unhurried in 5th,smooth rally to lead 2f out,drew clear in hand

2Nov91- 6CD fst 1 1/16 :231 :463 1:12 1:443 ©B C Juvenile-G1 14 13 85¼ 2hd 15 15 Valenzuela PA B 122 *2.10 92-09 Arazi1224¾Bertrando1223½Snappy Landing122hd 14
Drifted out in stretch,taken in hand last 70 yards;Previously owned by Allen E. Paulson

5Oct91♦ Longchamp(Fr) yl *1ⓉRH 1:442 Grand Criterium-G1 Stk356000 13 Mosse G 123 *.20 Arazi1243Rainbow Corner123hdSeattle Rhyme123¾ 6
Trailed to 3f out,sharp run between horses to lead 1f out,easily

8Sep91♦ Longchamp(Fr) gd *7fⓉRH 1:204 Prix Salamandre-G1 Stk147000 15 Mosse G 123 *.20 Arazi1235Made of Gold123nkSilver Kite123nk 8
Tracked in 3rd,sharp run to lead 2f out,quickly clear

18Aug91♦ Deauville(Fr) gd *6fⓉStr 1:131 Prix Morny-G1 Stk275000 13 Mosse G 123 *.50 Arazi1233Kenbu120¾Lion Cavern1232 4
Handily placed in 2nd,led 2f out,quickly clear

21Jly91♦ Maisns-Lfftte(Fr) gd *5½fⓉStr 1:052 Prix Robert Papin-G2 Stk99500 11½ Mosse G 123 *.80 Arazi1231½Showbrook1233Steinbeck1232 6
Tracked in 4th,rallied to lead 1f out,handily

3Jly91♦ Longchamp(Fr) yl *5fⓉStr :583 Prix du Bois-G3 Stk54800 1¾ Mosse G 124 1.40 Arazi124¾Steinbeck121½Woldwide1214 4
Pressed in 3rd,led 170y out,driving

12Jun91♦ Evry(Fr) gd *6fⓉStr 1:141 Prix La Fleche (Listed)34600 13 Head F 121 1.90 Arazi1213Tabac1262Valley Road121hd 7
Well placed in 3rd,led 1f out,drew clear

30May91♦ Chantilly(Fr) gd *5fⓉStr :59 Prix d'Orgemont Mdn (FT)28800 22½ Head F 123 *1.50 Steinbeck1232½Arazi123nkGramatique1183 6
Led to 1f out,saved 2nd

Artax

dkbbr. c. 1995, by Marquetry (Conquistador Cielo)–Raging Apalachee, by Apalachee — Lifetime record: 25 7 9 3 $1,685,840
Own.– Paraneck Stable
Br.– Vinery & Carondelet Farm (Ky)
Tr.– Louis Albertrani

6Nov99- 6GP fst 6f :22 :44 :554 1:074 3↑ BC Sprint-G1 5 7 2hd 11 11½ 1½ Chavez JF L 126 f 3.70 103-00 Artax126½KonaGold1262¾BgJg126½ Took over,lasted,driving 14

16Oct99- 9Bel fst 6f :221 :443 :554 1:073 3↑ Forest Hills H-G2 1 2 11 1hd 14½ 16½ Chavez JF L 120 f *1.85 103-11 Artax1206½Good and Tough1181½Intidab116nk 7
Sharp speed,ridden out

25Sep99- 9Bel fst 7f :221 :443 1:083 1:213 3↑ Vosburgh-G1 4 6 1hd 1hd 13 13½ Chavez JF L 126 f 4.30 94-09 Artax1263½Stormin Fever126hdMountain Top126½ 6
Speed outside,driving

6Sep99- 9Sar fst 7f :221 :441 1:081 1:211 3↑ Forego H-G2 1 9 73½ 75½ 44 55¼ Smith ME L 117 f 8.50 94-12 Crafty Friend119nkAffirmed Success1191¼Sir Bear1192¼ 9
Hustled,no rally

11Aug99- 9Sar fst 6f :224 :452 :57 1:09 3↑ A Phenomenon H-G2 2 4 1½ 1hd 2hd 21½ Smith ME L 117 f 7.00 94-12 Intdb1131½Artx1172¾YsIt'sTru117½ Set pace inside,gamely 7

31Jly99- 9Pha fst 6f :214 :44 :563 1:082 3↑ Pha BC H-G3 1 9 4¾ 3nk 43½ 21¼ Decarlo CP L 119 f *.70 100-09 Loaded Gun1141¼Artax119¾Power by Far115hd Off very slow 9

4Jly99- 8Bel fst 7f :223 :444 1:08 1:203 3↑ Tom Fool H-G2 3 4 31 3½ 33 35¾ Smith ME L 117 f 2.45 93-08 Crafty Friend116¾Affirmed Success1195Artax117hd 5
Speed 3 wide,faded

5Jun99- 8Bel fst 6f :212 :442 :564 1:093 3↑ True North H-G2 4 7 65 41¾ 3nk 2¾ Chavez JF L 119 f *1.00 92-10 Kashtry110¾Artx119¾ThTrdr'sEcho1111 Pinched back,gamely 9

15May99- 7Pim fst 6f :231 :453 :571 1:091 3↑ Md BC H-G3 5 8 52¼ 3nk 23 58½ Chavez JF L 116 f - 90-06 Yes It's True1134¾The Trader's Echo109½Purple Passion114¾ 8
Broke slowly,impeded by patron at ⅛,ran for purse money only

2May99- 8Aqu fst 7f :223 :444 1:08 1:20 3↑ Carter H-G1 9 3 2hd 2½ 1½ 13¼ Chavez JF L 114 f 5.10 102-11 Artax1143¼Affirmed Success1192½Western Borders1132½ 9
Speed outside,driving

10Apr99- 7Aqu fst 6f :213 :433 :551 1:072 3↑ Bold Ruler H-G3 5 2 2hd 2½ 21½ 22½ Chavez JF L 115 f 4.00 98-07 KllyKp1232½Artx1156¾BrushdOn115nk Speed outside,2nd best 5

21Mar99- 8Aqu fst 7f :223 :45 1:093 1:22 4↑ Alw 46000 3 8 1hd 1½ 2hd 2no Velasquez C L 115 f *.75 92-15 Iron Will119noArtax1152Well Noted1151¼ Set pace,gamely 8
Previously trained by Randy Bradshaw

3Mar99- 6SA fst 1 :223 :454 1:10 1:354 4↑ OClm 100000 5 2 31 43 44½ 56½ Antley CW LB 118 3.70 86-19 Klinsman120½Bold Words1184½River Keen1181¼ 5
Stalked pace,weakened

6Feb99- 8SA fst 1⅛ :452 1:092 1:343 1:473 Strub-G2 5 1 15 11½ 68¼ 721¼ Solis A LB 119 b 6.30 76-12 Event of the Year1192¾Dr Fong1214½Hanuman Highway1171¾ 7
Speed,inside,gave way

16Jan99- 7SA fst 1 1/16 :231 :47 1:104 1:41 San Fernando BC-G2 4 1 1hd 2hd 56 716 McCarron CJ LB 120 4.20 82-16 Dixie Dot Com1164½Event of the Year1224½Old Topper118½ 8
Dueled,weakened,steadied

26Dec98- 8SA fst 7f :23 :452 1:09 1:212 Malibu-G1 3 7 1hd 1½ 2½ 21½ McCarron CJ LB 119 4.00 96-08 RunManRun1151½Artax1192EventoftheYear121nk Inside duel 10

20Nov98- 4Hol fst 7½f :22 :45 1:09 1:273 3↑ OClm 100000 3 4 1hd 2hd 22 28½ McCarron CJ LB 115 *.80 84-15 SeaofSecrets1168½Artax1154½Emalt1178 Dueled,second best 5

2May98- 8CD fst 1¼ :453 1:103 1:353 2:021 Ky Derby-G1 12 10 1010 1211 1329 1339½ McCarron CJ L 126 11.50 55-02 Real Quiet126½Victory Gallop1262¼Indian Charlie126hd 15
Slow start,wide

4Apr98- 5SA fst 1⅛ :46 1:094 1:342 1:47 S Anita Derby-G1 6 4 33½ 32 33 39¼ McCarron CJ LB 120 2.60 92-03 Indian Charlie1202¼Real Quiet1207Artax1206 Bid,3rd best 7

14Mar98- 8SA fst 1 1/16 :224 :464 1:104 1:413 San Felipe-G2 1 1 1½ 1½ 11½ 1hd McCarron CJ LB 122 *1.20 95-10 Artax122hdRealQuiet1197ProsprousBd1166 Very game inside 5

1Feb98- 7SA fst 1 1/16 :224 :46 1:101 1:421 S Catalina-G3 1 1 1hd 1hd 11½ 15½ McCarron CJ LB 114 2.10 92-17 Artx1145½SouvnrCopy1203Alln'sOop1173½ Inside,clearly best 6

2Jan98- 6SA fst 1 1/16 :224 :464 1:11 1:424 Alw 46000 6 2 11 12 2hd 2½ Solis A LB 115 *.40 88-15 Futurstc115½Artx11510CrftyFlght115no Off bit slow,gamely 6

14Dec97- 7Hol fst 1 1/16 :223 :454 1:101 1:411 Hol Futurity-G1 7 5 51¾ 31½ 3½ 21 McCarron CJ LB 121 3.40 94-11 RealQuiet1211Artax1211¾Nationalor1211 Lugged in bit ⅛ 11

16Nov97- 9Hol gd 1 1/16⊗ :23 :47 1:123 1:451 Md Sp Wt 5 3 23½ 11 16 19 McCarron CJ LB 119 *1.30 75-29 Artax1199Availability1198Codeact1193 Ridden out 7

26Oct97- 6SA fst 7f :231 :46 1:104 1:23 Md Sp Wt 1 7 51¾ 51½ 41¾ 37½ McCarron CJ LB 120 4.00 81-14 Classic Cat1206Crypt de Chine1201½Artax120no 8
Off bit slow,steadied at gap and past ½

Banshee Breeze

b. f. 1995, by Unbridled (Fappiano)–Banshee Winds, by Known Fact — **Lifetime record: 18 10 5 2 $2,784,798**
Own.– James B. Tafel & Jayeff B Stables
Br.– James B. Tafel (Ky)
Tr.– Carl A. Nafzger

6Nov99- 3GP fst 1⅛ :462 1:094 1:343 1:472 3↑ ⒻBC Distaff-G1 3 6 53 44½ 21 2¾ Day P L 123 f 2.20 99-00 BeautiflPleasre123¾BansheeBreeze1231¼HeritageofGold1231¼ 8
Stdy bkstr,bid,hung
16Oct99- 6Kee fst 1⅛ :462 1:102 1:351 1:47 3↑ ⒻSpinster-G1 7 6 54½ 52¾ 41½ 22½ Day P L 123 f *.30 97-09 Keeper Hill1232½Banshee Breeze123noA Lady From Dixie1231 9
5 wide trip,bid,2nd best
27Aug99- 8Sar sly 1¼ :47 1:103 1:351 2:022 3↑ ⒻPersonal Ensign H-G1 6 4 47½ 25 23½ 22¼ Bailey JD L 124 f *.70 94-20 Beautiful Pleasure1132¼Banshee Breeze1241½Keeper Hill1182¼ 6
Game finish outside
7Aug99- 8Sar fst 1⅛ :48 1:112 1:363 1:494 3↑ ⒻGo for Wand H-G1 5 4 31½ 21 1hd 1½ Bailey JD L 124 f *.65 87-16 BansheeBreeze124½BeautifulPleasre1138¾HeritageofGold1172 5
Inside trip,driving
5Jun99-10CD fst 1⅛ :482 1:124 1:372 1:50 3↑ ⒻFleur de Lis H-G3 4 4 42 3½ 1½ 1½ Albarado RJ L 124 f *.30 93-12 Banshee Breeze124½Silent Eskimo1144½MdowVist109¾ 4
Bid 4w,drifted in ⅛
9Apr99- 9OP fst 1 1/16 :223 :452 1:094 1:413 4↑ ⒻApple Blossom H-G1 2 5 59 41½ 1hd 11¼ Bailey JD L 122 f *.70 96-11 Banshee Breeze1221¼Sister Act1149¾Silent Eskimo112nk 6
Bold move,all out
28Feb99-10GP fst 1 1/16 :25 :482 1:114 1:424 3↑ ⒻRampart H-G2 5 3 21½ 2½ 1½ 15½ Bailey JD L 122 f *.60 93-16 Banshee Breeze1225½Glitter Woman1194Timely Broad1143½ 5
Drew away,ridden out
7Nov98- 8CD fst 1⅛ :473 1:12 1:37 1:494 3↑ ⒻBC Distaff-G1 4 4 33½ 32 21½ 2no Bailey JD L 120 f *.80 95-07 Escena123noBansheeBrez1205KprHll120½ 4w 2nd turn,missed 8
Previously owned by James B. Tafel
17Oct98- 9Kee fst 1⅛ :461 1:103 1:35 1:47 3↑ ⒻSpinster-G1 5 5 53½ 31 15½ 112 Albarado RJ L 119 f *.80 101-05 Banshee Breeze11912Runup the Colors123½Aldiza1233½ 8
Bumped start,ridden out
22Aug98- 8Sar fst 1¼ :474 1:122 1:374 2:032 ⒻAlabama-G1 4 5 53½ 2hd 12 16 Bailey JD L 121 f 2.35 91-09 Banshee Breeze1216Lu Ravi121nkManistique1216½ 6
Quick 4w move,driving
25Jly98- 8Bel fst 1½ :491 1:142 2:044 2:312 ⒻCCA Oaks-G1 6 4 31½ 1½ 1½ 1nk Bailey JD L 121 f 1.90 87-20 Banshee Breeze121nkKeeper Hill12117Best Friend Stro12121 6
3 wide,driving
27Jun98- 8Bel fst 1⅛ :454 1:10 1:342 1:473 ⒻMother Goose-G1 9 7 85¼ 54 48 34 Davis RG L 121 5.10 88-16 Jersey Girl1211Keeper Hill1213Banshee Breeze1211 11
Bumped start,steadied
1May98- 9CD fst 1⅛ :484 1:133 1:384 1:52 ⒻKy Oaks-G1 6 7 62 41½ 11½ 2nk Bailey JD L 121 4.10 84-14 Keeper Hill121nkBanshee Breeze1213¾Really Polish121½ 13
6-wide,led,gamely
4Apr98- 8Kee fst 1 1/16 :232 :47 1:104 1:43 ⒻAshland-G1 5 5 41 32 42 34½ Romero RP L 120 2.60 88-12 WellChosen1151Let1153½BansheeBrez120no No late response 7
16Mar98-11GP fst 1 1/16 :24 :482 1:134 1:462 ⒻBonnie Miss-G2 4 5 54½ 63½ 21 11½ Romero RP 114 *1.90 75-33 Banshee Breeze1141½Santaria1142Cotton House Bay1142½ 8
Lugged in stretch,strong handling,clear
1Mar98- 5GP fst 7f :222 :453 1:11 1:242 ⒻAlw 31000 10 3 52½ 3½ 12½ 18 Romero RP 120 *2.00 78-21 Banshee Breeze1208Chandelle1204¾Appealing Pride1205 10
5-wide,driving
8Feb98- 4GP fst 7f :224 :462 1:121 1:251 ⒻMd Sp Wt 11 1 74¼ 41¾ 1½ 12¾ Romero RP 120 6.40 74-21 BansheeBreez1202¾CorlS120hdAdddGold1205½ 4-wide,driving 12
21Jun97- 1CD fst 5½f :22 :454 :582 1:051 ⒻMd Sp Wt 12 12 88½ 77½ 58 79½ Peck BD 119 11.80 84-08 Lolabell1197½Ghostpasser119noPuddlejump1191 12
Drifted out start,wide trip

Bayakoa (Arg)

b. f. 1984, by Consultant's Bid (Bold Bidder)–Arlucea, by Good Manners — **Lifetime record: 39 21 9 0 $2,817,524**
Own.– Mr & Mrs F.E. Whitham
Br.– Haras Principal (Arg)
Tr.– Ronald McAnally

19Apr91- 9OP fst 1 1/16 :222 :451 1:093 1:411 4↑ ⒻApple Blossom H-G2 4 5 56 54 69½ 614½ Pincay L Jr L 125 *.70 81-14 DegenerateGl1151¼Chron1212FttoScout1165 Four wide early 6
16Feb91- 8SA fst 1⅛ :462 1:101 1:351 1:482 4↑ ⒻS Margarita H-G1 2 1 11½ 1hd 22 22 Pincay L Jr LB 126 *.80 86-12 Little Brianne1192Bayakoa1261¾A Wild Ride1192¼ Held 2nd 7
2Feb91- 8SA fst 1 1/16 :224 :462 1:104 1:413 4↑ ⒻS Maria H-G1 3 1 1hd 2½ 45 411 Pincay L Jr LB 128 *.20 84-11 LittleBrianne1172LunElgnt1142½Somthngmrry1146½ Faltered 4
27Oct90- 5Bel fst 1⅛ :462 1:103 1:354 1:491 3↑ ⒻBC Distaff-G1 4 2 2½ 2hd 2½ 16¾ Pincay L Jr 123 1.10 88-15 Bayakoa1236¾ColonialWaters1232½VlyMd119nk Driving,clear 7
6Oct90- 8Kee fst 1⅛ :47 1:103 1:343 1:47 3↑ ⒻSpinster-G1 7 2 2hd 12 13 13 Pincay L Jr LB 123 *.80 99-11 Bayakoa1233Gorgeous1236Luthier's Launch123no Ridden out 8
1Sep90- 8Dmr fst 1 1/16 :23 :462 1:10 1:403 3↑ ⒻChula Vista H-G2 4 1 11 2hd 2hd 1no Pincay L Jr LB 127 *.40 98-02 Byakoa127noFantasticLook1134½FormdableLdy1121¾ Gamely 5
4Aug90- 8Dmr fst 1 1/16 :231 :463 1:10 1:402 3↑ San Diego H-G3 5 1 1½ 1½ 22½ 22¼ Pincay L Jr LB 122 *.50 97-05 QuietAmericn1152¼Byakoa1223½Bosphorus112½ Second best 6
16Jun90- 8Hol fst 1 1/16 :231 :462 1:10 1:411 3↑ ⒻMilady H-G1 2 2 21½ 21 2½ 12¼ Pincay L Jr 127 *.10 94-08 Bayakoa1272¼Fantastic Look1137½Kelly1108 Ridden out 4
19May90- 8Hol fst 1 :223 :442 1:083 1:34 3↑ ⒻHawthorne H-G2 5 4 3½ 3½ 11 14 Pincay L Jr 125 *.50 94-12 Bayakoa1254StormybutValid1193½FantasticLook1151¼ Wide 5
18Apr90- 9OP gd 1 1/16 :231 :463 1:103 1:402 4↑ ⒻApple Blossom H-G2 1 1 12 12 1½ 22¾ Pincay L Jr 126 *.10 97-21 Gorgeous1222¾Bayakoa12610½Affirmed Classic11210 Gamely 4
4Mar90- 8SA fst 1¼ :454 1:094 1:344 2:011 4↑ S Anita H-G1 3 3 55½ 912 916 1029 Pincay L Jr 122 *1.90 59-18 Ruhlmann1211¾CriminlType119hdFlyingContinentl121½ Wide 10
18Feb90- 8SA sly 1⅛ :463 1:104 1:36 1:482 4↑ ⒻS Margarita H-G1 4 2 1hd 12 13½ 16 McCarron CJ 127 *.50 94-18 Byakoa1276Gorgeous1255Luthier's Launch1135 Easy winner 4
4Feb90- 5SA gd 1 1/16 :233 :473 1:113 1:43 4↑ ⒻS Maria H-G1 2 1 1½ 11½ 14 13½ McCarron CJ 126 *.30 88-18 Bayakoa1263½Nikishka1172¼Carita Tostada1124½ Much best 4
4Nov89- 6GP fst 1⅛ :462 1:111 1:353 1:472 3↑ ⒻBC Distaff-G1 1 2 21 11½ 12 11½ Pincay L Jr 123 *.70 107-01 Bayakoa1231½Gorgeous1192¼Open Mind1195 Driving 10
14Oct89- 8Kee fst 1⅛ :47 1:104 1:35 1:474 3↑ ⒻSpinster-G1 4 1 13 16 17 111½ Pincay L Jr 123 *.40 95-21 Baykoa12311½GoodbyeHalo1231½SharpDance1193 Ridden out 6
24Sep89- 8Bel fst 1⅛ :47 1:112 1:36 1:482 3↑ ⒻRuffian H-G1 2 1 11½ 12 11½ 13½ Pincay L Jr 125 *1.30 85-24 Bayakoa1253½Colonial Waters118nkOpen Mind1209 Driving 6
2Sep89- 8Dmr fst 1 1/16 :221 :451 1:094 1:414 3↑ ⒻChula Vista H-G2 2 2 32 31 65¼ 615 Pincay L Jr 127 *.70 76-11 Goodbye Halo1201¾Flying Julia1124½Kool Arrival1152¾ 6
Gave way early
15Jly89- 8Hol fst 1⅛ :463 1:102 1:343 1:471 3↑ ⒻVanity H-G1 5 1 11½ 11½ 14 15 Pincay L Jr 125 *.70 101-11 Bayakoa1255FlyingJulia1123½GoodbyHlo122no Rated on lead 6
17Jun89- 9Hol fst 1 1/16 :231 :46 1:101 1:42 3↑ ⒻMilady H-G1 1 2 11½ 11½ 11½ 11 Pincay L Jr 124 *.20 90-15 Bayakoa1241FlyingJulia1134½CaritTostd115½ Finished well 5
20May89- 8Hol fst 1 :223 :443 1:081 1:324 3↑ ⒻHawthorne H-G2 5 1 1½ 12½ 13½ 14½ Pincay L Jr 122 *.60 99-07 Bayakoa1224½Goodbye Halo1233½Behind the Scenes114½ 5
Clear throughout
19Apr89- 9OP fst 1 1/16 :23 :47 1:111 1:413 4↑ ⒻApple Blossom H-G1 5 1 11½ 11½ 14 14 Pincay L Jr 120 1.10 93-22 Bayakoa1204Goodbye Halo1259Invited Guest1163 Wide 6
19Feb89- 8SA fst 1⅛ :461 1:102 1:351 1:482 4↑ ⒻS Margarita Inv'l H-G1 7 2 12 13 14 12 Pincay L Jr 118 3.50 87-21 Bykoa1182GoodbyeHalo1255½NoReviw117½ Veered out start 7
28Jan89- 8SA fst 1 1/16 :23 :461 1:101 1:41 4↑ ⒻS Maria H-G2 1 1 13½ 12½ 11½ 2¾ Pincay L Jr 118 4.00 95-14 MissBrio119¾Byko1181½Annoconnr1224½ Broke through gate 7
5Jan89- 8SA sly 1 :222 :453 1:101 1:362 4↑ ⒻAlw 55000 1 1 11¾ 15 110 112 Pincay L Jr 117 *.60 86-17 Bayakoa11712Small Virtue118¾Oueee Bebe116nk Easily 6
17Dec88- 7Hol gd 7f :213 :44 1:09 1:22 3↑ ⒻAlw 35000 1 5 11 11 12½ 22 Gryder AT 117 3.80 92-17 Miss Brio1162Bayakoa1172¾Valdemosa1173½ No match 7
30Oct88- 8SA fm 1Ⓣ :223 :46 1:093 1:344 3↑ ⒻMidwick H 112k 8 2 11 11½ 41½ 1013¼ Gryder AT 116 8.50 87-13 Balbonella1162¾Choritzo1182½Davie's Lamb1181 Faltered 10
6Oct88- 8SA fm 1Ⓣ :23 :461 1:101 1:343 3↑ ⒻAlw 60000 9 1 11½ 1½ 21 23 Gryder AT 121 *1.40 98-00 Daloma1093Byko1213½MssAlto1161¼ Lugged out backstretch 10
5Sep88- 5Dmr fst 1 :222 :453 1:094 1:34 3↑ ⒻⓇJune Darling 49k 5 1 11½ 12½ 16 110 Gryder AT 117 8.00 96-12 Bayakoa11710QueenForbes115½CaritaTostd119¾ In hand late 8
6Aug88- 8Dmr fm 1 1/16Ⓣ :232 :463 1:102 1:412 3↑ ⒻⓇOsnitas H (Div 2) 64k 2 1 11½ 1½ 2hd 53¼ Gryder AT 117 6.10 90-09 Choritzo115nkMy Virginia Reel1201¾Fiara1201¼ Rank early 6
29May88-10Cby fm 1Ⓣ :23 :461 1:10 1:343 3↑ ⒻLady Canterbry H 150k 11 1 13½ 13 12½ 66½ Velasquez J 115 b *2.30 90-04 Balbonella1152Nature'sWay1162½Dv'sLmb118½ Flattened out 12
11May88- 8Hol fm 1Ⓣ :231 :46 1:10 1:341 4↑ ⒻAlw 46000 1 1 11½ 11 12½ 12½ Pincay L Jr 117 3.20 93-07 Bayakoa1172½Quadrada116hdNew Bride1143½ Hand ride 9
Rank 7/8,vanned off due to heat prostration. Previously trained by Jorge Machado
1Nov87♦ Hipodromo(Arg) my*1LH 1:343 3↑ Gr Pr Palermo-G1 112 Lezcano M 111 *2.05 Bayakoa11112Laborioso118¾Speeding Light1186 11
Stk20200
Led throughout,clear 4f out,easily
10Oct87♦ San Isidro(Arg) fm*1ⓉLH 1:33 3↑ Gr Pr San Isidro-G1 21½ Lezcano M 110 4.70 Cautin1311½Bayakoa1105Gorbot1331½ 9
Stk15100
Tracked leader,led 3f out,headed 1f out

23Aug87♦ Hipodromo(Arg) fst*1LH 1:344 (F)Polla de Potrancas-G1 Stk22500 23 Riveiro R 123 34.10 Podeica1233Bayakoa1232Abloom123nk 17
Led to 2f out,second best;Previously trained by OL Finarelli

18Jly87♦ San Isidro(Arg) fm*1(T)LH 1:371 (F)Gr Pr 1000 Guineas-G1 Stk23800 910¼ Riveiro R 123 6.10 Pero Yo Se1232½Fiara1233Ecumenica123¾ 14
Tracked in 3rd,weakened 2f out

21Jun87♦ San Isidro(Arg) fm*7f(T)LH 1:232 (F)Pr Mas Valente Alw6000 14 Riveiro R 121 6.65 Bayakoa1214Pinuela1213Rumbilla121nk 11
Pressed pace,led 1½f out,drew clear

17May87♦ Hipodromo(Arg) fst*7½fLH 1:312 (F)Gr Pr Jorge de Atucha-G1 Stk22900 613¾ Riveiro R 121 6.05 Candila1216Fichada1211Matricule121¾ 10
Led to 2f out,weakened

10Apr87♦ Hipodromo(Arg) fst*5fStr :563 (F)Pr Mister Prieto Mdn4000 17 Riveiro R 121 *1.20 Bayakoa1217Cogotuda1212½Fulleria121nk 8
Wire to wire,drew clear in hand

15Feb87♦ Hipodromo(Arg) fst*5fStr :584 (F)Pr Villares Mdn4800 22 Riveiro R 121 3.35 Scherezade1212Bayakoa121¾Mi Cachorra1214 11
Led to 1f out,dueled briefly,outfinished

Beautiful Pleasure

b. f. 1995, by Maudlin (Foolish Pleasure)–Beautiful Bid, by Baldski **Lifetime record: 14 7 2 2 $1,916,578**

Own.– John C. Oxley
Br.– Farnsworth Farm (Fla)
Tr.– John T. Ward Jr

6Nov99- 3GP fst 1⅛ :462 1:094 1:343 1:472 3↑ (F)BC Distaff-G1 5 2 11½ 13 11 1¾ Chavez JF L 123 3.00 100-00 BeautiflPleasre123¾BansheeBreeze1231¼HeritageofGold1231¼ 8
Drifted late,driving

10Oct99- 5Bel sly 1⅛ :453 1:091 1:341 1:473 3↑ (F)Beldame-G1 1 1 15 13½ 12 14¾ Chavez JF L 123 2.40 93-23 Beautiful Pleasure1234¾Silverbulletday1196Catinca1237¾ 5
Strong pace off rail

27Aug99- 8Sar sly 1¼ :47 1:103 1:351 2:022 3↑ (F)Personal Ensign H-G1 4 1 15 15 13½ 12¼ Chavez JF L 113 4.70 96-20 Beautiful Pleasure1132¼Banshee Breeze1241½Keeper Hill1182¼ 6
Soon clear,driving

7Aug99- 8Sar fst 1⅛ :48 1:112 1:363 1:494 3↑ (F)Go for Wand H-G1 4 1 11½ 11 2hd 2½ Chavez JF L 113 3.45 86-16 BansheeBreeze124½BeautiflPleasre1138¾HeritageofGold1172 5
Speed off rail,gamely

19Jun99- 8Bel fst 1 1/16 :231 :461 1:094 1:403 3↑ (F)Hempstead H-G1 4 3 31 2hd 2½ 2½ Chavez JF L 112 4.20 93-06 Sister Act117½Beautiful Pleasure1129¼Catinca1224¾ 6
Drifted late,gamely

22May99- 8Bel fst 1 :223 :45 1:09 1:341 3↑ (F)Shuvee H-G2 3 2 21½ 2hd 41¾ 43¾ Chavez JF L 113 3.40 89-13 Catinca121½Sister Act1171½Tap to Music1151¾ 6
Speed in hand,weakened

23Apr99- 7Kee fst 7f :222 :442 1:083 1:211 4↑ (F)Alw 48054 1 4 1½ 1½ 12½ 15½ Chavez JF L 115 *.70 96-03 Beautiful Pleasure1155½My Wild Rose1182Quanah120hd 4
Ducked in,drifted

14Nov98- 8CD fst 1 :223 :452 1:093 1:342 3↑ (F)CD Distaff-G2 3 9 75 52¾ 31 33 Chavez JF L 110 3.70 98-11 Dream Scheme1131½Sister Act1111½Beautiful Pleasure1108¾ 9
Sluggish start,no gain

16Oct98- 5Kee fst *7f :223 :453 1:103 1:252 3↑ (F)Alw 39980 3 7 52½ 41¾ 1hd 16 Chavez JF L 110 *1.00 102-06 BeautifulPleasure1106CuantoEs115½Antoniette1132 Driving 11

9Apr98- 7Kee my 7f :222 :45 1:102 1:234 (F)Alw 46460 6 4 21 31½ 54 410 Day P L 119 *1.40 76-15 Flashstorm1192AuntAnne1194TrickyMove1194 Pressed,tired 6

8Nov97- 2Hol fst 1 1/16 :224 :46 1:102 1:42 (F)BC Juv Fillies-G1 13 11 64½ 43 711 1021 Bailey JD LB 119 7.60 69-06 Countess Diana1198½Career Collection1194Primaly1192 14
Bit awkward start,wide

11Oct97- 8Kee fst 1 1/16 :23 :454 1:092 1:451 (F)Alcibiades-G2 2 2 2½ 21 22½ 33 Bailey JD L 118 *.50 79-24 Countess Diana1182¾Lily O'gold118hdBeautiful Pleasure118¾ 6
Pressed,weakened

21Sep97- 7Bel fst 1 :224 :454 1:094 1:353 (F)Matron-G1 2 1 11 11 15 14½ Bailey JD L 119 *1.05 86-12 BeautifulPleasre1194½DiamondontheRun1191¾Carrielle11912 11
Broke slowly,clear early,ridden out

25Aug97- 4Sar fst 6½f :221 :454 1:103 1:172 (F)Md Sp Wt 8 2 3nk 11½ 14 15 Bailey JD L 118 *1.10 90-13 BeautifulPleasre1185TffyDvenport11810TilliOfStrfford1182¾ 8
Ridden out

Bertrando

dkbbr. c. 1989, by Skywalker (Relaunch)–Gentle Hands, by Buffalo Lark **Lifetime record: 24 9 6 2 $3,185,610**

Own.– 505 Farms & Nahem
Br.– Ed Nahem (Cal)
Tr.– John Shirreffs

14Jan95- 5SA gd 7f :221 :442 1:083 1:212 4↑ San Carlos H-G2 3 3 1½ 32 52¾ 65 Stevens GL LB 120 b 5.70 90-12 Softshoe Sure Shot114½Ferrara115½Subtle Trouble115nk 7
Rail,gave way

2Jan95- 8SA fm 1⅛(T) :47 1:12 1:364 1:491 4↑ San Gabriel H-G2 2 2 21½ 21½ 44½ 69¾ Romero RP LB 120 b 5.40 63-27 Romarin1191¼Inner City1161Ianomami1161 Stalked,gave way 6

26Nov94- 8Aqu fst 1 :223 :454 1:111 1:36 3↑ NYRA Mile-G1 3 1 2½ 95½ 1018 1024¾ Stevens GL 121 b 5.00 63-28 Cigar1117Devil His Due1242½Punch Line1121 Dueled,tired 12

5Nov94-10CD fst 1¼ :463 1:111 1:363 2:022 3↑ B C Classic-G1 12 1 12 3½ 53½ 67¼ Stevens GL L 126 b 8.80 93-07 Concern122nkTabascoCat1221½DramtcGold1221½ Tired,inside 14

15Oct94- 5SA fst 1⅛ :453 1:10 1:341 1:463 3↑ Goodwood H-G2 3 1 13½ 11½ 3nk 1nk Stevens GL LB 120 b 3.70 100-13 Bertrando120nkDramaticGold1151Tossofthecoin1157½ 6
Rail,brushed 1/16,came back

17Sep94- 8Bel fst 1⅛ :462 1:102 1:343 1:464 3↑ Woodward-G1 7 1 11 2½ 56¼ 512 Valenzuela PA 126 b 23.50 85-10 HolyBull1215DevilHisDue1261½ColonialAffair1263½ Used up 8

13Aug94- 4Dmr fst 1¼ :442 1:083 1:334 1:592 3↑ Pacific Classic-G1 3 1 1½ 77½ 817 834 Valnzuela PA LB 124 b *2.40 66-10 TinnersWy1241BstPl1244½DrmtcGold1175½ Rail,dueled,tired 9

28Jly94- 8Dmr fm 1(T) :23 :47 1:11 1:361 3↑ (R)Wickerr 66k 4 1 11½ 12 11½ 11¼ Valnzuela PA LB 121 b *1.50 89-11 Bertrando1211¼Bon Point116noDaros114½ Gamely 6
Previously trained by Robert Frankel

6Nov93- 8SA fst 1¼ :464 1:111 1:36 2:004 3↑ B C Classic-G1 7 1 11½ 11 11½ 22 Stevens GL LB 126 b *1.20e 89-10 Arcangues1262Bertrando1261¾Kissin Kris1221¼ Second best 13

18Sep93- 8Bel sly 1⅛ :453 1:094 1:342 1:47 3↑ Woodward-G1 4 1 15 12½ 17 113½ Stevens GL 126 b *.90e 94-15 Bertrando12613DevilHisDu1263VllyCrossng126hd Ridden out 6

21Aug93- 3Dmr fst 1¼ :46 1:094 1:341 1:592 3↑ Pacific Classic-G1 1 1 11½ 1½ 11½ 13 Stevens GL LB 124 b 3.10e 100-00 Bertrando1243MissionaryRidg124¾BstPl1242 Inside,driving 7

24Jly93-11Mth fst 1⅛ :462 1:103 1:354 1:491 3↑ Iselin H-G1 2 1 11½ 1½ 3½ 32½ Solis A L 119 b *.90 86-15 ValleyCrossing113hdDevilHisDue1232¼Bertrando1198 Tired 8

3Jly93- 3Hol fst 1¼ :462 1:101 1:35 2:00 3↑ Hol Gold Cup H-G1 2 1 11½ 11 2½ 22½ Solis A LB 118 b 3.50e 94-05 Best Pal1212½Bertrando1185½Major Impact114nk Good try 10

31May93- 9Bel fst 1 :221 :441 1:083 1:341 3↑ Metropolitan H-G1 7 1 1½ 1hd 1hd 21½ Stevens GL 121 b 4.00 95-03 Ibero1191½Bertrando121nkAlydeed1242½ Gamely 9

6Mar93- 5SA fst 1¼ :471 1:11 1:351 2:002 4↑ S Anita H-G1 4 1 11 1hd 31½ 99¾ McCarron CJ LB 120 b 2.40e 83-13 SirBufort119noStrRcrut117hdMjorImpct1141¾ Brushed start 11

7Feb93- 8SA fst 1¼ :472 1:114 1:354 2:003 C H Strub-G1 1 1 11½ 11 1½ 21¼ McCarron CJ LB 122 b *.30 91-11 SiberianSummr1181¼Brtrndo1222MjorImpct1183 Outfinished 8

16Jan93- 8SA sly 1⅛ :46 1:103 1:364 1:511 San Fernando-G2 3 1 11 11½ 16 19 McCarron CJ L 120 b *1.50e 77-30 Bertrndo1209StarRecruit120¾TheWckdNorth1164 Coasted in 8

26Dec92- 8SA fst 7f :222 :45 1:081 1:203 Malibu-G2 7 1 11 1hd 2hd 3¾ McCarron CJ LB 120 b *1.40e 98-09 StaroftheCrop118½TheWckdNrth116nkBrtrndo1205½ Game try 11
Previously owned by 505 Farms, Headley & Nahem;previously trained by Bruce Headley

4Apr92- 5SA fst 1⅛ :461 1:102 1:361 1:491 S Anita Derby-G1 1 1 11 11 1½ 21¾ Solis A B 122 b 1.10 82-11 A.P. Indy1221¾Bertrando122nkCasual Lies1223½ Held 2nd 7

15Mar92- 8SA fst 1 1/16 :222 :454 1:101 1:423 San Felipe-G2 4 1 1hd 1hd 12½ 1¾ Solis A B 122 b *.40 90-13 Bertrando122¾Arp1161¾Hickman Creek1161½ Hard drive 6

2Nov91- 6CD fst 1 1/16 :231 :463 1:12 1:443 (C)B C Juvenile-G1 5 1 11½ 1hd 25 25 Solis A B 122 b 2.50 87-09 Arazi1224¾Bertrando1223½Snappy Landing122hd 2nd best 14

13Oct91- 8SA fst 1 1/16 :221 :454 1:102 1:424 Norfolk-G1 3 1 11½ 11½ 14 19 Solis A B 118 b *1.50e 89-16 Bertrando1189Zurich118¾Bag118¾ Ridden out 9
Previously owned by G. Headley

11Sep91- 8Dmr fst 1 :214 :45 1:102 1:362 Dmr Futurity-G2 4 1 11 11 14 13½ Solis A B 114 b 8.70 84-18 Bertrando1143½Zurich1144½Star Recruit1152 All out 10

25Aug91- 9Dmr fst 6f :214 :444 :571 1:101 (S)Md Sp Wt 3 3 1½ 2hd 1½ 12 Solis A B 117 b 4.00 88-12 Bertrando1172Ebonair1171Simple King1124½ All out 11

Best Pal

b. g. 1988, by Habitony (Habitat)–Ubetshedid, by King Pellinore
Own.– Golden Eagle Farm
Br.– Mr & Mrs John C. Mabee (Cal)
Tr.– Richard Mandella

Lifetime record: 47 18 11 4 $5,668,245

15Jan96- 8SA	fst 1 1/16	:232 :472 1:11 1:413	4↑ San Pasqual H-G2	5 6 84½ 84½ 87½ 813½	McCarron CJ	LB 120	2.20	73-16	Alphabet Soup118¾Luthier Fever1152Cezind1144½	No rally	9
11Nov95- 8SA	fst 1⅛	:46 1:102 1:352 1:483	3↑ [S]Cal Cup Classic H 250k	5 6 75¾ 42¾ 22 21¼	McCarron CJ	L 124	*.80	89-17	LuthierFever118¼BestPl1242SemiMaar116nk	Closed gamely	10
18Oct95- 7SA	fst 1	:231 :462 1:10 1:351	3↑ Skywalker 65k	2 4 43 42¼ 41¾ 11	McCarron CJ	L 120	*1.10	93-16	BstPl1201GeengerMan114¾SlewofDmscus1203½	Determinedly	6
2Jly95- 6Hol	fst 1¼	:453 1:092 1:34 1:592	3↑ Hol Gold Cup H-G1	6 7 712 58 67¾ 57	McCarron CJ	L 120	8.30	96-04	Cigar1263½TinnersWay118hdTossofthecon118½	Mild late bid	8
11Jun95- 6Hol	fst 1⅛	:464 1:103 1:351 1:473	3↑ Californian-G1	3 6 66¼ 64¼ 42¼ 44¼	McCarron CJ	L 120	*1.50	91-08	Concern122¾Tossofthcon118½TnnrsWy1161	4 wide into lane	8
15Apr95- 9OP	fst 1⅛	:462 1:104 1:352 1:471	4↑ Oaklawn H-G1	1 5 57½ 53½ 43½ 47½	McCarron CJ	L 121	4.00	95-13	Cigar1202½Silver Goblin1194Concern1221	Middle move	7
11Mar95- 5SA	wf 1¼	:45 1:091 1:334 1:591	4↑ S Anita H-G1	10 9 915 66 42½ 2hd	McCarron CJ	L 122	*1.50e	99-12	UrgentRequest116hdBestPl1221DareandGo120hd	Strong rally	10
12Feb95- 8SA	fst 1⅛	:451 1:093 1:343 1:472	4↑ San Antonio H-G2	3 7 79 21 11 13	McCarron CJ	L 121	*1.80	96-12	Best Pal1213Slew of Damascus119½Tossofthecoin1171¾		10
	Big inside move										
22Jan95- 8SA	fst 1 1/16	:232 :471 1:103 1:411	4↑ San Pasqual H-G2	5 4 55 44 44 43¼	McCarron CJ	L 122	*.90	86-15	DelMarDennis1182Slew ofDamascus1201¼Tossofthecoin117no		6
	Wide trip										
4Dec94- 9Hol	fst 1⅛	:462 1:102 1:353 1:482	3↑ Native Diver H-G3	6 7 74¼ 73¼ 1½ 14	McCarron CJ	L 121	*1.50	92-10	BstPl1214Tossofthcon1173½RoylChrot1142½	5 wide 2nd turn	7
5Nov94- 10CD	fst 1¼	:463 1:111 1:363 2:022	3↑ BC Classic-G1	6 6 75 83¾ 65 53¼	McCarron CJ	L 126	5.80e	97-07	Concern122nkTabasco Cat1221½Dramatic Gold1221½		14
	7-wide stretch,no threat										
24Sep94- 9TP	my 1⅛	:492 1:133 1:374 1:501	3↑ Ky Cup Classic 376k	4 4 41¾ 31 46 33½	McCarron CJ	L 115	*1.30	78-20	Tabasco Cat1202Mighty Avanti1151½Best Pal1151½		6
	Checked ¼ pole,no late response										
13Aug94- 4Dmr	fst 1¼	:442 1:083 1:334 1:592	3↑ Pacific Classic-G1	7 7 810 4½ 2hd 21	McCarron CJ	L 124	3.90e	99-10	TinnersWay1241BestPl1244½DrmtcGold1175½	4 wide 2nd turn	9
22Jly94- 3Hol	fst 7f	:221 :444 1:09 1:211	3↑ [S]Answer Do 61k	2 4 510 59½ 53¼ 12¾	Desormx KJ	LB 117	*.40e	98-10	BstPl1172¾Marmoe117¾YearsofDrmng1215	Strong hand ride	5
	Previously trained by Gary Jones										
13Feb94- 8SA	fst 1⅛	:464 1:103 1:35 1:472	4↑ San Antonio H-G2	7 9 87¼ 72¾ 66½ 710¼	Black CA	LB 121	*1.80	86-14	TheWickedNorth1164½[D]HillPass116½Region1174½	Raced wide	9
22Jan94- 8SA	fst 1 1/16	:231 :47 1:11 1:41	4↑ San Pasqual H-G2	1 6 75 64 41¼ 21¾	Black CA	LB 122	2.40	88-12	HillPass1151¾BestPl122¾LottryWnnr116hd	5 wide into lane	7
6Nov93- 8SA	fst 1¼	:464 1:111 1:36 2:004	3↑ BC Classic-G1	4 4 43½ 63½ 98¼ 1010½	Black CA	LB 126	1.80	80-10	Arcangus1262Brtrndo1261¾KssnKrs1221¼	Drifted out,tiring	13
16Oct93- 8SA	fst 1⅛	:451 1:092 1:344 1:48	3↑ [S]Cal Cup Classic H 250k	1 5 512 55¼ 1½ 13½	Black CA	LB 126	*.30	93-10	Best Pal1263½Native Boundary1161¼Goldigger's Dream1071¼		7
	Wide,handily										
21Aug93- 3Dmr	fst 1¼	:46 1:094 1:341 1:592	3↑ Pacific Classic-G1	7 6 42 2½ 21½ 33¾	Black CA	LB 124	*.40	96-00	Bertrando1243MissionaryRidg124¾BstPl1242	Weakened a bit	7
3Jly93- 3Hol	fst 1¼	:462 1:101 1:35 2:00	3↑ Hol Gold Cup H-G1	5 5 54½ 21 1½ 12½	Black CA	LB 121	*1.10	97-05	Best Pal1212½Bertrando1185½Major Impact114nk	Driving	10
31May93- 8Hol	fm 1⅜Ⓣ	:474 1:112 1:343 1:573	3↑ Hol Turf H-G1	6 5 32½ 21 32½ 23½	Black CA	LB 122	7.40	102-00	Bien Bien1193½Best Pal122nkLeger Cat116hd	Game for 2nd	8
10Apr93- 8OP	fst 1⅛	:464 1:102 1:353 1:483	4↑ Oaklawn H-G1	2 7 812 710 65 32½	Desormx KJ	L 123	2.80	90-19	Jovial1171¼LilE.Tee1231¼BestPl1231¼	Lost footing,4 wide	10
6Mar93- 5SA	fst 1¼	:471 1:11 1:351 2:002	4↑ S Anita H-G1	1 8 76½ 73¾ 74¾ 55	Desormx KJ	LB 124	*1.40	88-13	Sir Beaufort119noStar Recruit117hdMajor Impact1141¾		11
	Wide,climbing,lost shoe										
24Jan93- 8SA	fst 1 1/16	:234 :47 1:11 1:414	4↑ San Pasqual H-G2	3 3 33½ 3½ 1hd 22¾	Desormx KJ	LB 124	*1.00	92-15	Jovl1152¾[D]BstPl124½Mrqutry118hd	Came out,impeded foe ⅝	7
	Disqualified and placed fifth										
9May92- 10Pim	fst 1 3/16	:473 1:112 1:354 1:544	4↑ Pim Spl H-G1	7 3 31½ 31 22 44¼	Desormx KJ	L 126	*.60	84-23	StriketheGold114¾FlySoFree1161¼TwlghtAgnd1222¼	Gave way	7
11Apr92- 8OP	fst 1⅛	:46 1:094 1:351 1:48	4↑ Oaklawn H-G1	6 5 55 53¼ 1½ 11½	Desormx KJ	L 125	*.70	96-20	BestPal1251½SeaCadet120½TwilightAgenda1234	4 wide⅜	7
7Mar92- 5SA	fst 1¼	:46 1:094 1:34 1:59	4↑ S Anita H-G1	4 5 53¼ 1½ 13 15½	Desormx KJ	LB 124	*1.70	99-10	Best Pal1245½Twilight Agenda1242¼Defensive Play1153		7
	Wide,ridden out										
9Feb92- 8SA	fst 1¼	:463 1:102 1:35 1:594	C H Strub-G1	5 3 31 1hd 11½ 11¼	Desormx KJ	LB 124	*1.20	95-11	Best Pal1241¼Dinard1208Reign Road118¾	Wide,ridden out	8
	Four wide backstretch,steadied near 3/8 pole										
18Jan92- 8SA	fst 1⅛	:47 1:111 1:353 1:481	San Fernando-G2	4 7 73¾ 4¾ 1½ 13½	Desormx KJ	LB 122	2.80	89-21	Best Pal1223½Olympio1225½Dinard120½	Wide,ridden out	9
30Nov91- 8Hol	fm 1⅛Ⓣ	:472 1:111 1:342 1:454	3↑ Citation H (Div 2)-G2	5 3 32 42 52¼ 21¾	Desormx KJ	LB 119	4.80	99-07	Fly Till Dawn1191¾Best Pal119nkWolf1191	Wide trip	8
9Nov91- 8SA	fst 1⅛	:471 1:103 1:354 1:49	3↑ [S]Cal Cup Classic H 250k	2 3 31 2hd 1hd 2hd	Valenzuela PA	L 124	*.40	85-18	Charmonnier112hdBstPl1247ElgntBrgn1172¾	Carried out ¼	10
22Sep91- 10LaD	fst 1¼	:462 1:11 1:36 2:004	Super Derby-G1	4 3 311 32½ 44 46½	Valenzuela PA	L 126	*.90	99-02	Free Spirit's Joy1262½Olympio1261Zeeruler1263	Bumped	7
10Aug91- 3Dmr	fst 1¼	:454 1:094 1:341 1:594	3↑ Pacific Classic 1000k	6 5 64 32 22½ 11	Valenzla PA	LB 116	4.90	--	BstPl1161TwlghtAgnd1242¾Unbrdld1241¼	Wide backstretch	8
7Jly91- 8Hol	fst 1¼	:462 1:103 1:353 2:003	Swaps-G2	4 3 21½ 21 2hd 14	Valenzla PA	LB 116	*1.40	94-05	BestPl1164CorportRport114¾ComplngSound1237	Ridden out	4
	Previously trained by Ian Jory										
16Jun91- 8Hol	fst 1⅛	:47 1:103 1:344 1:474	Silver Screen H-G3	1 2 21½ 2½ 11½ 2nk	Valenzla PA	LB 123	*.90	95-07	Compelling Sound118nkBest Pal1233½Caliche's Secret1175		5
	Edged for win										
18May91- 10Pim	fst 1 3/16	:461 1:101 1:35 1:54	Preakness-G1	5 6 54 32½ 35 511	Stevens GL	L 126	2.70	84-14	Hansl1267CorporateRport1262¾MnMnstr126½	Bid wide,tired	8
4May91- 8CD	fst 1¼	:462 1:111 1:372 2:03	Ky Derby-G1	15 10 87 72¾ 52½ 21¾	Stevens GL	LB 126	5.20	93-04	Strike the Gold1261¾Best Pal1261¾Mane Minister126hd		16
	Saved ground,2nd best										
6Apr91- 5SA	fst 1⅛	:462 1:101 1:351 1:48	S Anita Derby-G1	5 5 53¾ 41¾ 1½ 2½	Stevens GL	LB 122	*1.60	89-11	Dinard122½Best Pal1221¾Sea Cadet1222	Wide backstretch	9
3Mar91- 8SA	gd 1	:231 :47 1:104 1:354	San Rafael-G2	2 3 33½ 2hd 2hd 3½	Stevens GL	LB 121	2.30	87-13	Dinard118hdApollo118½Best Pal1218	Saved ground	5
9Dec90- 8Hol	fst 1	:22 :443 1:094 1:352	Hol Futurity-G1	7 8 73¾ 42 1½ 11	Santos JA	LB 121	*1.10e	87-20	BestPal1211GeneralMeeting121hdReignRoad1215	Wide trip	9
27Oct90- 7Bel	fst 1 1/16	:23 :46 1:103 1:432	ⒸBC Juvenile-G1	9 4 62½ 3½ 44½ 65¾	Valenzuela PA	122	1.80	79-15	FlySoFree1223TakMeOut1222LstMountn122hd	Bobbled start	11
7Oct90- 8SA	fst 1 1/16	:223 :461 1:102 1:424	Norfolk-G1	7 2 21 2½ 13 14½	Valnzuela PA	LB 118	*.50e	89-12	Best Pal1184½Pillaring1181½Formal Dinner1182	Much best	12
12Sep90- 8Dmr	fst 1	:223 :461 1:101 1:352	Dmr Futurity-G2	9 2 21 1½ 12 13½	Valnzuela PA	LB 120	*1.10e	89-14	Best Pal1203½Pillaring116hdGot to Fly1176	Came in early	11
22Aug90- 8Dmr	fst 7f	:22 :443 1:093 1:221	Balboa-G3	4 2 32½ 32½ 11 12	Valnzuela PA	LB 119	1.60	90-11	Best Pal1192Xray1172¾Sunshine Machine1174½	Driving	7
27Jly90- 8Dmr	fst 6f	:22 :451 :571 1:09	[S]I'm Smokin 50k	5 2 21 1hd 13 17	Valnzuela PA	L 118	*.50	95-11	BestPal1187JustasSwift118hdWarfarePrinc1131¼	Ridden out	5
23Jun90- 8GG	fst 5½f	:21 :44 :561 1:023	Ladbroke Futurity 100k	7 6 75¾ 76 35 22½	Hansen RD	117	4.90	97-09	Broadway'sTopGun1202½BestPal1172½Sunshine Machine1173		10
	Closed well										
18May90- 4Hol	fst 5f	:214 :45 :573	Md Sp Wt	5 4 32 31½ 21½ 1½	Valenzuela PA	117	4.80	94-07	Best Pal117½Barrage1177Just as Swift1172½	Driving	10

Black Tie Affair (Ire)

gr. c. 1986, by Miswaki (Mr. Prospector)–Hat Tab Girl, by Al Hattab
Own.– Jeffrey Sullivan
Br.– Stephen D. Peskoff (Ire)
Tr.– Ernie T. Poulos

Lifetime record: 45 18 9 6 $3,370,694

2Nov91- 8CD	fst 1¼	:482 1:123 1:38 2:024	3↑ BC Classic-G1	8 1 11½ 11 11 11¼	Bailey JD	LB 126 b	4.00	96-09	Black Tie Affair1261¼Twilight Agenda1262½Unbridled126nk		11
	Well rated										
14Sep91- 8AP	sly 1⅛	:463 1:104 1:362 1:492	3↑ Wash Park H-G2	3 1 11 12 13½ 17½	Sellers SJ	LB 120 b	1.50	87-31	BlackTieAffar1207½SummrSqull11918½ScrtHllo11425	Driving	4
1Sep91- 11Mth	fst 1⅛	:462 1:102 1:351 1:474	3↑ Iselin H-G1	7 1 1½ 1½ 1hd 1nk	Day P	LB 119 b	4.10	99-03	BlckTieAffr119nkFarmaWy122½ChfHoncho1153¼	Game score	8
11Aug91- 9Aks	fst 1⅛	:464 1:103 1:353 1:483	3↑ Cornhusker H-G3	1 1 1½ 11 12 13½	Day P	LB 124 b	*.30	102-10	Black Tie Affair1243½Bedeviled1174Whodam1135	Driving	5
13Jly91- 9Det	fst 1⅛	:474 1:12 1:372 1:494	3↑ Mich Mile H-G2	4 1 11 11 11½ 12½	Day P	LB 122 b	*.60	95-16	Black Tie Affair1222½Whiz Along1102Solo Matt113¾		11
	Confidently ridden										
22Jun91- 9CD	fst 1⅛	:474 1:114 1:362 1:494	3↑ Stephen Foster H-G3	5 1 11 11 12½ 12¾	Diaz JL	LB 119 b	*1.20	99-06	BlackTieAffar1192¾PrvtSchool111noGrydr1153	In hand late	5
27May91- 8Bel	fst 1	:22 :441 1:091 1:352	3↑ Metropolitan H-G1	9 2 42 66 99¾ 911	Diaz JL	122 b	14.70	82-16	In Excess1172¼Rubiano1111¾Gervazy1141½	Done early	14
4May91- 8Aqu	fst 7f	:224 :452 1:084 1:211	3↑ Carter H-G1	2 1 2½ 31½ 23 22¼	Diaz JL	123 b	7.10	94-17	Housebuster1222¼BlackTiAffr1232½Grvzy116no	Saved ground	8
12Apr91- 8Kee	fst 7f	:222 :452 1:09 1:214	3↑ Commonwealth BC-G3	6 2 21½ 21½ 2½ 11	Diaz JL	LB 124 b	7.10	101-12	BlackTieAffair1241Housebustr1244ExmplryLdr115hd	Driving	6

23Mar91- 9OP fst 1 1/16 :233 :472 1:112 1:422 4↑ Razorback H-G2 3 2 21 2hd 1hd 32¼ Diaz JL LB 118 8.80 88-11 Bedeviled1152Din'sDancer117nkBlackTieAffair118hd Gamely 7
24Nov90- 8Haw fst 1¼ :474 1:122 1:374 2:032 3↑ Bud Gold Cup H-G2 5 1 1½ 1½ 11½ 11½ Diaz JL LB 116 b 8.30 84-30 BlackTieAffair1161½MiSelecto115¾SilverTowr1126½ Driving 10
27Oct90- 3Bel fst 6f :214 :442 1:093 3↑ BC Sprint-G1 11 6 89½ 58 47½ 34¼ Pincay L Jr 126 b 53.20 87-11 SafelyKept123nkDayjur1234BlckTAffr1262¼ Wide,mild rally 14
21Sep90-10LaD fst 7f :222 :45 1:093 1:222 3↑ Island Whirl H 100k 3 4 21½ 32½ 32½ 21½ Velasquez J L 120 b *.80 96-14 Potentiality1131½Black Tie Affair1201Ankles1131 Gamely 8
25Aug90- 9AP fst 1 :221 :444 1:092 1:36 3↑ Equipoise Mile H-G3 3 2 21½ 1hd 11½ 13½ Velasquez J L 119 b *.30 91-16 Black Tie Affair1193½Bio1128New Plymouth1103 Driving 4
11Aug90- 7AP sly 1 :232 :462 1:111 1:354 3↑ Handicap 28000 4 2 1hd 1½ 13 17½ Velasquez J L 121 b *.70 92-18 Black Tie Affair1217½Bio113¾Old Stories112½ Ridden out 6
21Jly90-10LaD fst 6f :213 :441 1:10 3↑ Bud BC 139k 7 3 64½ 47 45 31¾ Guidry M L 120 b *1.00 95-08 Glitterman118½SilentReflex1161¼BlackTiAffr120nk Rallied 8
17Jun90- 8AP fst 7f :221 :442 1:083 1:211 3↑ Isaac Murphy H 48k 1 4 1hd 2hd 21½ 24¼ Guidry M 119 b 1.60 100-10 BeauGenius1214¼BlackTieAffr1193Trtmtr1132 Saved ground 5
28May90- 8Bel fst 1 :223 :45 1:091 1:342 3↑ Metropolitan H-G1 9 2 32½ 33 56 610½ Guidry M 117 b 132.90 86-18 Criminal Type120nkHousebuster1131½Easy Goer1273 Tired 9
5May90- 8Aqu my 7f :212 :434 1:091 1:22 3↑ Carter H-G1 2 3 49 66¾ 63 47¾ Guidry M 119 b 11.10 84-17 DancngSpree1232DncngPrtns115hdSwckly1195¾ Lacked rally 7
12Apr90- 8Kee fst 7f :231 :452 1:083 1:22 3↑ Commonwealth BC-G3 5 1 2hd 2hd 1hd 1hd Guidry M 121 b 32.10 99-09 BlackTieAffair121hdShakerKnit1152Momsfurrr118nk Driving 9
24Mar90- 8Spt fst 6f :232 :462 :582 1:111 4↑ J R Johnston Mem 53k 1 1 24 34½ 24 26 Guidry M 124 b 1.50 91-17 DeeLance1246BlackTieAffair124½Brett'sLick1242 2nd best 7
4Nov89- 4GP fst 6f :214 :44 1:09 3↑ BC Sprint-G1 7 9 1112 915 914 913¼ Razo E Jr 124 b 74.60 88-04 Dancing Spree126nkSafely Kept121nkDispersal1241 13
Bumped after start
16Sep89- 9AP fst 1 :232 :461 1:103 1:354 Sheridan-G3 6 1 1hd 1hd 1hd 1½ Razo E Jr 118 b 4.90 82-27 BlackTieAffair118½Bio1201¾AndovrMn1232¼ All out,driving 9
3Sep89- 7AP fst 6f :222 :453 1:094 3↑ Handicap 40000 2 6 1hd 1½ 12½ 2no Razo E Jr 115 b *1.50 91-15 Carborundum115noBlackTieAffr115hdThRdRolls1122¾ Gamely 9
12Aug89- 5AP fst 7f :223 :451 1:103 1:234 3↑ Handicap 35000 7 2 3½ 2½ 1½ 11¼ Razo E Jr 113 b 2.60 83-19 BlackTieAffr1131¼YukonJoey111¾ContactGam1122¾ Driving 7
29Jly89- 6AP fst 6f :223 :451 1:093 3↑ Alw 25000 2 5 1½ 1½ 1½ 1nk Razo E Jr 115 b 4.70 92-12 Black TieAffair115nkThe Red Rolls1222Highland Ruckus1174½ 6
Driving
20Jly89- 8AP sl 1 :233 :47 1:121 1:373 3↑ Alw 31000 1 1 1½ 1½ 11½ 2½ Razo E Jr 113 b 5.30 72-36 Joel115½Black Tie Affair1132¼All Nonesense1133¼ Gamely 7
1Jly89- 9AP fm 1 1/16(T) :23 :461 1:11 1:431 Arl Heights 56k 2 2 21 22½ 32½ 88¼ Razo E Jr 119 b 18.10 83-15 Ebros1152½Ruszhinka113¾Downtown Davey119hd Tired 8
18Jun89- 9Haw fm 7½f(T) :233 :462 1:104 1:293 Oil Capitol H 52k 7 7 63¼ 42 34 55¾ Razo E Jr 116 b *2.20 87-10 Tex's Zing1201½All Nonesense1182¼J.C.'s Darlin Boy116¾ 11
Bid,weakened
27May89- 7Spt fst 1⅛ :461 1:111 1:364 1:501 Ill Derby-G2 6 7 68 68¾ 511 611¾ Razo E Jr 117 b 55.60 82-18 [D]Notation119hdMusicMerci1242½Endow124½ Rallied briefly 7
13May89- 7Spt fst 1 1/16 :241 :481 1:132 1:464 T D Nash H 111k 1 3 3½ 2½ 33½ 45½ Razo E Jr 118 b 20.40 74-18 Endow1214Notation117nk[D]Nooo Problema1181¼ Weakened 10
Placed third through disqualification
30Apr89- 8Spt fst 6f :231 :463 :584 1:122 3↑ Bud BC H 87k 3 7 67½ 56¼ 54¼ 31¾ Razo E Jr 112 b 2.80 86-21 Daddy Rex116nkWolf Ticket1161½Black Tie Affair1121¼ 7
Drifted wide turn
23Apr89- 8Spt fst 1 :242 :481 1:13 1:392 Bold Favorite H 54k 9 2 2½ 2½ 1hd 1no Razo E Jr 118 b 3.10 83-24 Black Tie Affair118noNooo Problema1194All Nonesense1203½ 9
Brushed with rival;Previously owned by Hudson River Farm;previously trained by Walter C. Reese
24Feb89- 9GS fst 6f :223 :454 1:102 Bold Reasoning 21k 5 5 4¾ 31 34 44 Madrid A Jr 122 b 1.60 86-13 Dim Lights1223O.K. at Cards118noE.E. Express1181 Tired 6
12Feb89- 8Pha fst 1 :224 :453 1:11 1:374 [R]Cupid 21k 4 4 3nk 1hd 11 2hd Petersen JL 116 b 6.40 85-19 Keewatin116hdBlackTieAffr1166½RacingRascal116¾ Bumped 7
4Feb89- 9GS gd 6f :222 :452 1:10 Del Valley 32k 5 3 43¼ 44¼ 46¼ 46½ Madrid A Jr 115 b 2.50 85-17 Cheerfy1193DimLights1152½GreatestProspect1151 Even try 6
14Jan89- 8Pha gd 1 70 :23 :46 1:11 1:421 Philmont 30k 4 3 52¼ 64¾ 55 49¼ Madrid A Jr 119 b *1.60 75-16 A.M. Swinger1155Executive Edition1151¼Racing Rascal1153 11
Steadied turn
30Dec88- 6Med fst 6f :221 :451 1:102 Deputy Minister 40k 7 5 31½ 31½ 31½ 2nk Madrid A Jr 118 b 3.30 90-10 OedipusAppeal114nkBlckTAffr118noWrgod112no Just missed 7
24Dec88- 9Pha sly 6½f :221 :444 1:104 1:173 Allegheny 28k 3 6 53¼ 42½ 3½ 2hd Madrid A Jr 118 b 2.90 85-27 Dixieland Brass114hdBlack Tie Affair1182½Robin's Erik1146 7
Just missed
9Dec88- 7Med fst 1 :234 :471 1:121 1:382 Slewpy 40k 6 5 31½ 51¼ 66 69½ Verge ME 118 b 10.00 73-16 Doc's Leader1202¼Heliport115¾Seminole Slewpy116nk Faded 7
28Nov88- 8Med sly 6f :223 :454 1:101 Alw 25000 5 5 52¾ 34½ 48½ 39 Verge ME 119 b *1.50 82-19 Cheerfy1177½Fightin'Buck1171¼BlackTieAffair119no Even try 6
6Nov88- 8Pha fst 7f :222 :443 1:10 1:232 Malus 22k 7 2 3nk 32½ 3½ 11½ Verge ME 119 b 4.10 90-22 BlackTieAffr1191½Doc'sLdr1211¾Chrfy119½ Came in,driving 7
29Oct88- 9Pha fst 1 1/16 :224 :462 1:113 1:453 Heritage 69k 4 1 1hd 31½ 55 47¼ Verge ME 117 b *3.00 69-22 Doc'sLeadr1171¼Alydrome1143½SeminolSlwpy1172½ Gave way 11
5Oct88- 8Pha fst 6f :221 :463 1:124 Alw 11500 2 6 44½ 2hd 12½ 17 Verge ME 120 *1.10 77-23 BlackTieAffair1207EltonsAppl1141¾CuttrEx114¾ Drew clear 7
28Sep88- 5Pha fst 6f :222 :462 1:121 Md Sp Wt 6 6 31 1½ 2hd 11 Verge ME 118 4.30 80-21 BlackTieAffair1181Thunder God1185½First Grade Reader1181 10
Driving

Boston Harbor

b. c. 1994, by Capote (Seattle Slew)–Harbor Springs, by Vice Regent **Lifetime record: 8 6 1 0 $1,934,605**

Own.– Overbrook Farm
Br.– Overbrook Farm (Ky)
Tr.– D. Wayne Lukas

2Feb97- 5SA fst 1 1/16 :222 :451 1:092 1:423 Santa Catalina 105k 6 3 3½ 1hd 34½ 414¾ Bailey JD B 123 *.90 75-09 Hello1201¾Bagshot1168Carmen'sBby1205 Broke inward,tired 8
26Oct96- 8WO fst 1 1/16 :231 :464 1:11 1:432 B C Juv-G1 2 1 11½ 12½ 11 1nk Bailey JD 122 2.40 92-92 BostonHarbor122nkAcceptible1222½Ordway1222½ 10
Good handling,inside
11Oct96- 8Kee fst 1 1/16 :24 :474 1:121 1:451 Breeders' Futurity-G2 1 1 11½ 11 11 1½ Bailey JD 121 *.20 83-22 Boston Harbor121½Blazing Sword1212½Haint1214½ 5
Lost lead 1/16,came again,bobbled slightly late,driving
21Sep96- 7TP wf 1 1/16 :224 :461 1:101 1:424 Ky Cup Juv-G3 1 1 11½ 11½ 14 17 Barton DM 120 *.40 91-10 Boston Harbor1207Play Waki for Me1186Dr. Spine1125½ 8
Pace,attempted to lug in ⅛ briefly,in hand
1Sep96- 9EIP fst 7f :22 :45 1:094 1:223 EIP Juv 100k 4 1 1½ 11 15 16 Barton DM 121 *.30 100-11 Boston Harbor1216Near the Bank1132Mountain Lion1122 6
Mild hand ride,swerved in for stride, 1/16,much best
26Jly96- 7Sar my 6f :213 :45 :571 1:101 Sanford-G3 1 4 21½ 21 24 210½ Bailey JD 118 1.75 79-12 KellyKp11810BostonHrbor118nkSyFlordSndy1154½ Held place 8
29Jun96- 9CD fst 6f :213 :451 :572 1:094 Bashford Manor-G3 3 8 53 31½ 12 14 Luzzi MJ 115 *1.00e 94-12 Boston Harbor1154Prairie Junction1151½Nobel Talent115hd 8
Jostled,forced in start,exchanged brushes 3/16,driving,clear
25May96- 1CD fst 5f :231 :47 :59 Md Sp Wt 9 2 11 11½ 13½ 15 Barton DM 118 4.40 93-12 BostnHarbr1185BrndonJR1181½Rnwd118no Sharp,ridden out 9

Buck's Boy

b. g. 1993, by Bucksplasher (Buckpasser)–Molly's Colleen, by Verbatim **Lifetime record: 28 15 5 2 $2,600,830**

Own.– Quarter B Farm
Br.– Irish Acres Farm (Ill)
Tr.– P. Noel Hickey

6Nov99- 9GP gd 1½(T) :47 1:103 2:243 3↑ BC Turf-G1 5 1 11½ 11 1hd 34½ Gomez GK L 126 6.40 89-02 Daylami1262½Royal Anthem1262Buck'sBoy1261¼ 14
Off hedge,weakened;1/4 fraction unavailable
25Sep99- 8WO fm 1⅜(T) :481 1:12 1:36 2:13 3↑ Sky Classic H-G3 3 1 12 11 2hd 22½ Landry RC L 124 *.20 99-00 Dawson's Legacy1142½Buck's Boy1242¼Thornfield11612 5
Faltered upper stretch
10Sep99- 7WO gd 1⅛(T) :463 1:102 1:343 1:47 3↑ Alw 49761 4 1 13 13 16 110½ Landry RC L 122 *.35 95-11 Buck'sBoy12210Cracker'sFolly1226SunshnJourny1225 Easily 4
7Nov98- 9CD fm 1½(T) :491 1:134 2:033 2:283 3↑ BC Turf-G1 2 1 11 12½ 12 11¼ Sellers SJ L 126 3.60 92-09 Buck's Boy1261¼Yagli1261¾Dushyantor126no Steady urging 13
10Oct98- 8Bel sf 1½(T) :484 1:134 2:06 2:331 3↑ Turf Classic Inv-G1 2 1 12 11½ 13½ 13 Sellers SJ L 126 *1.45 70-30 Bck'sBoy1263Cetewyo1266LzyLod1263 Lost whip,ridden out 6
12Sep98- 9Bel fm 1⅜[T] :484 1:134 1:374 2:13 3↑ Man o' War-G1 5 2 21½ 21½ 1hd 21¼ Fires E L 126 4.20 93-10 Dylm1261¼Buck'sBoy1262¾IndyVdul126hd Speed,clear,gamely 9
26Jly98- 8WO fm 1⅜(T) :503 1:144 1:384 2:152 3↑ H K Jockey Club-G1C 3 1 11 11 13 12¼ Fires E L 121 *.85 90-17 Bck'sBoy1212¼CrownAttorny1191¾Trrmoto115nk Wire to wire 6
Previously trained by Hilary A. Pridham
4Jly98-10Lrl fm 1¼(T) :48 1:113 1:354 2:002 3↑ Fort McHenry H 100k 4 2 22 2½ 11 12 Fires E L 118 *.50 91-16 Buck's Boy1182Winsox1161¼Casey Tibbs1141¾ Driving 7
6Jun98- 8Bel fm 1¼[T] :464 1:104 1:342 1:581 3↑ Manhattan H-G1 3 2 22½ 12½ 11½ 32¼ Fires E L 117 4.70 99-05 ChiefBerhrt1221¾Dvonwood113½Bck'sBoy1171½ Bid,weakened 9

23May98-10Pim fm 1½Ⓣ :50 1:151 2:04 2:281 3↑ Riggs H 75k 3 1 11½ 1½ 11 11¼ Prado ES L 117 *.40 104-08 Buck'sBoy1171¼Cetewayo1121¼LordZad1128¾ Rail,ridden out 8
Previously trained by P. Noel Hickey
4Apr98-10OP fst 1⅛ :464 1:11 1:36 1:481 4↑ Oaklawn H-G1 4 1 12 11½ 42 77¼ Fires E L 115 7.20 88-15 Precocity1141¼Frisk Me Now1171½Phantom on Tour117¾ 7
Clear,gave way badly
7Mar98-10GP fm 1½Ⓣ :472 1:111 2:003 2:232 3↑ Pan American H-G2 3 1 11½ 12 11½ 1¾ Fires E L 115 5.00 111-00 Bck'sBoy115¾AfricanDncr115¾RoylStrnd1142½ Well handled 9
14Feb98-10GP fm 1⅜Ⓣ :474 1:123 1:362 2:122 3↑ GP BC H-G2 2 1 12 12 12 2¾ Fires E L 115 8.00 93-06 FlagDown120¾Buck'sBoy1152CopyEditor1161½ Sharp effort 12
8Nov97-7Hol fm 1½Ⓣ :471 1:11 1:593 2:234 3↑ BC Turf-G1 1 1 11 11 2½ 45¼ Guidry M LB 126 35.40 93-02 ChifBrhrt126¾Borg119½FlgDown1264 Lively pace,tired late 11
Previously trained by Hilary A. Pridham
11Oct97-9Haw fst 1¼ :47 1:112 1:361 2:002 3↑ Haw Gold Cup H-G3 7 1 16 13 11½ 11¼ Guidry M L 114 3.10 103-11 Buck'sBoy1141¼CairoExpress1154¾BeboppinBby115hd Driving 7
20Sep97-7AP yl 1 1/16Ⓣ :233 :461 1:111 1:433 3↑ [S]WH Bishop H 53k 5 1 12 11½ 13 12¼ Guidry M L 117 1.60 88-12 Buck'sBoy1172¼CanyonRun1224ChrysalisHouse1167 Driving 5
30Aug97-7AP fm *1 1/16Ⓣ :232 :46 1:092 1:402 3↑ [S]My Trip 31k 6 2 2hd 1½ 1hd 23¼ Guidry M L 117 *.90 100-00 CanyonRun1193¼Bck'sBoy1171¾LmonGrss113hd Couldn't last 7
6Aug97-7AP fst *1 1/16 1:454 3↑ Alw 32240 2 1 11 11 12 12 Guidry M L 119 *.80 110-17 Bck'sBy1192RuggedBuggr1196½RcoupthCsh1162½ Ridden out 5
28Jun97-5AP fm 1Ⓣ :243 :48 1:113 1:351 3↑ Alw 31000 6 2 2½ 1½ 11½ 12¾ Guidry M L 116 4.30 96-03 Buck's Boy1162¾Lord Comet116½Going Far1161½ Driving 7
8Jun97-8AP fst 1⊗ :233 :473 1:131 1:38 3↑ Alw 29040 5 2 2½ 11½ 17 113½ Guidry M L 116 *.50 86-17 Bck'sBoy11613PolarIceCaps116nkCherokeeSag119nk Handily 6
Previously trained by P. Noel Hickey
19Apr97-11Spt fst 1 1/16 :23 :474 1:124 1:441 3↑ [S]Milwaukee Ave H 65k 6 4 43 21½ 42 67¼ Nolan PM L 114 b 5.20 83-20 Polar Expedition1232½Beboppin Baby117¾Mr.Gorgff1131¼ 10
Bore out 1st turn;Previously trained by Doug Matthews
3Apr97-8OP fst 1 :224 :46 1:104 1:374 4↑ Alw 30000 5 6 65 31 31 4¾ Nolan PM L 116 11.30 89-19 [DH]Truckee116 [DH]O'steven116nkCapt. Tiff's Beau114½ 9
Bid,flattened out;Previously trained by P. Noel Hickey
30Sep96-8AP gd *1Ⓣ :234 :471 1:112 1:361 3↑ Alw 21402 7 3 32 22½ 43½ 66 Gomez GK 114 *1.40 87-08 GoingFar114¾CosaDivolo116noGlnSvoy1162½ Wide,tired,bled 10
14Sep96-7AP fm 1 1/16Ⓣ :233 :474 1:114 1:423 3↑ Alw 23042 1 6 65 65½ 31½ 2¾ Gomez GK 114 5.80 92-09 Jaunatxo114¾Buck's Boy1145Glen Savoye116¾ Four wide bid 9
18Aug96-3AP fst 6f :223 :453 :581 1:111 3↑ [S]Alw 18500 5 4 21 2hd 12½ 1nk Gomez GK 117 *.90 89-15 Buck's Boy117nkLimitless1142¾Slicker1173½ All out 8
Previously owned by Irish Acres Farm
27Jly96-7AP wf 1 :23 :46 1:112 1:382 3↑ [S]Alw 21000 8 2 2½ 2½ 12 11¼ Gomez GK 114 *1.70 77-23 Buck'sBoy1141¼SoftSho114noBll'sDusty1133 Stalked,driving 10
8Jly96-1AP fst 6f :224 :464 :591 1:12 3↑ [S]Md Sp Wt 3 1 2½ 11½ 15 113 Gomez GK 115 *.80 85-18 Buck'sBoy11513SilkenStar1158½PurpleLover1221½ In hand 6
17Jun96-9AP sly 1⅛⊗ :484 1:142 1:423 1:562 3↑ [S]Md Sp Wt 6 3 42½ 32½ 44 514¾ Gomez GK 114 *2.20 47-36 Aron'sJohnHenry1142¾RocknRobbi113nkBlueSksForbuck113nk 9
Wide,faded

Cardmania

dkbbr. g. 1986, by Cox's Ridge (Best Turn)–L'Orangerie, by J.O. Tobin

Lifetime record: 77 17 12 20 $1,522,783

Own.– Jean Couvercelle
Br.– Delta Thoroughbreds Inc (Ky)
Tr.– Derek Meredith

28Apr95-7Hol fst 6f :212 :433 :552 1:074 3↑ Los Angeles H-G3 8 3 99¾ 88½ 67 34 Nakatani CS LB 119 7.20 97-06 ForestGazelle1161LuckyForever1143Cardmani1191 Wide trip 10
14Apr95-8Kee fst 7f :224 :452 1:092 1:22 3↑ Commonwealth BC-G2 5 2 31 62½ 85 85½ Bailey JD L 113 7.90 86-10 GoldenGear118hdTurkomatic112nkLitdeJustice121nk Tired 8
11Mar95-8SA wf 6½f :213 :441 1:081 1:143 4↑ Potrero Grande H-G3 3 2 43 55 63½ 23½ Dlhoussaye E LB 119 2.70 95-07 LitdeJustice1153½Cardmn119hdPhonRobrto116½ Game for 2nd 6
12Feb95-8SA fst 1⅛ :451 1:093 1:343 1:472 4↑ San Antonio H-G2 1 5 68 74¾ 68 66½ Dlhoussaye E LB 117 12.40 89-12 BestPal1213SlwofDmscus119½Tossofthcon1171¾ Saved ground 10
28Jan95-8SA fst 6f :21 :433 :56 1:082 4↑ Palos Verdes H-G3 3 7 910 109 51½ 22 Dlhoussaye E LB 120 *1.80 93-11 D'hllvnt1172Crdmn1202¾SubtlTroubl115hd Best stride late 10
14Jan95-5SA gd 7f :221 :442 1:083 1:212 4↑ San Carlos H-G2 4 2 41½ 53¾ 42½ 41¼ Dlhoussaye E LB 120 2.10 94-12 Softshoe Sure Shot114½Ferrara115½Subtle Trouble115nk 7
Fell back,late bid
10Dec94-9Hol fst 6f :212 :434 :553 1:081 3↑ Underwood BC-G3 8 2 86½ 87¼ 74¾ 21½ Dlhoussaye E LB 120 3.10 97-07 WekivaSprings1181½Cardmania120noGundaghi120¾ Wide rally 9
5Nov94-4CD fst 6f :211 :443 :563 1:093 3↑ BC Sprint-G1 12 8 128 126½ 66 31½ Dlhoussaye E L 126 22.60 97-01 Cherokee Run126hdSoviet Problem1231½Cardmania126no 14
Wide stretch,finished well
15Oct94-4SA fst 6f :213 :442 :564 1:084 3↑ Ancient Title BC H-G3 1 6 88¼ 88¼ 87½ 46¾ Dlhoussaye E LB 121 4.20 86-08 Saratoga Gambler1133Uncaged Fury114nkConcept Win1173½ 8
Broke through gate
8Jan94-8SA fst 7f :22 :443 1:084 1:211 4↑ San Carlos H-G2 3 2 54½ 54 42½ 1¾ Dlhoussaye E LB 122 1.90 96-07 Cardmania122¾The Wicked North1172½Portoferraio1151 7
4 wide into lane
6Nov93-2SA ft 6f :21 :434 :56 1:083 3↑ BC Sprint-G1 5 5 96½ 66½ 54½ 1nk Dlhoussaye E LB 126 5.30 94-04 Cardmania126nkMeafr123½GlddTm1241¼ 5 wide,strong finish 14
17Oct93-5SA fst 6f :212 :434 :56 1:08 3↑ Ancient Title H-G3 3 4 41¾ 43½ 4½ 12½ Dlhoussaye E LB 116 6.00 97-09 Cardmania1162½Music Merci1172Bahatur114no 4 wide rally 8
18Sep93-4BM fst 6f :221 :442 :562 1:084 3↑ BM BC H 155k 7 8 87½ 87¾ 34 21½ Baze RA LB 116 3.30 90-14 LuckyForevr1141½Crdmn1162½Schrndo1152½ Rallied far wide 9
21Aug93-8Dmr fst 7f :221 :443 1:083 1:211 3↑ O'Brien H 87k 6 1 53½ 54 43 3¾ Stevens GL LB 116 6.00 93-09 Slerp117nkPortoferraio114½Cardmania116no Wide trip 7
3Jly93-8Hol fst 7f :213 :434 1:081 1:204 3↑ Triple Bend H-G3 6 7 78¾ 79 54 2¾ Dlhoussaye E LB 116 7.80 99-09 NowListen116¾Cardmania116½StaroftheCrop1203 Wide trip 10
11Jun93-7Hol fst 5½f :214 :441 :56 1:021 3↑ [R]Porterhouse 56k 6 6 68½ 610 66½ 35 Dlhoussaye E B 119 2.10 96-09 Knight Prospector1143½Anjiz1161½Cardmania1192 Wide trip 6
16May93-8Hol fst 6f :214 :441 :561 1:083 3↑ Los Angeles H-G3 6 7 77½ 77¼ 75½ 52½ Black CA B 117 21.10 95-08 StaroftheCrop119nkFabulous Champ116hdWild Harmony1161 7
Awkward start,wide
18Apr93♦ Sha Tin(HK) yl *7fⓉRH 1:221 3↑ Hong Kong Int'l Bowl (Listed) 45½ Cruz AS 126 8.60 Glen Kate123noHelene Star1261½Quicken Away1264 14
Stk388000
Tracked leaders in 3rd,lacked rally,faded 1f out
27Mar93-8SA fst 6½f :213 :442 1:083 1:144 4↑ Potrero Grande H-G3 1 8 73¼ 43 33 25 Dlhoussaye E B 117 8.00 93-09 GraySlewpy1185Crdmnia1172½StaroftheCrop1191 No match 8
21Feb93-10TuP fst 6f :211 :431 :544 1:064 3↑ Phoenix Gold Cup H-G3 6 2 32½ 22 32½ 33 Hansen RD 121 *1.90 97-09 HonortheHero1132½B.G.'sDrone112½Crdmani1211¼ Late gain 8
30Jan93-4SA fst 6f :213 :44 :561 1:084 4↑ Palos Verdes-G3 2 4 2hd 1hd 1½ 31¼ McCarron CJ B 117 11.70 92-11 MusicMerci114nkStaroftheCrop1191Crdmn1172¾ Good effort 7
9Jan93-8SA my 7f :221 :444 1:092 1:221 4↑ San Carlos H-G2 1 1 1hd 1hd 21½ 25 Black CA 117 4.80 87-15 Sir Beaufort1205Cardmania117½Excavate114½ Held 2nd 6
12Dec92-8Hol fst 6f :221 :451 :571 1:091 3↑ VO Underwood H-G3 4 2 2½ 31 33 31½ McCarron CJ 124 10.10 92-15 Gundaghia1161¼GraySlewpy124nkCrdmn1246½ Brushed start 5
27Nov92-8Hol fm 5½fⓉ :214 :442 :554 1:02 3↑ Hol Turf Express H 200k 4 6 63¼ 63¼ 64 83½ Black CA B 118 25.60 92-05 Answer Do121noRepriced118noGundaghia1171¼ Weakened 11
31Oct92-4GP fst 6f :213 :433 :553 1:081 3↑ BC Sprint-G1 6 8 74 118 1210 129 McCarron CJ 126 31.70f 93-00 Thirty Slews126nkMeafara1203Rubiano126no Through early 14
12Oct92-8SA fst 6f :21 :433 :553 1:082 3↑ Ancient Title BC H-G3 6 4 76¾ 55 54½ 42½ McCarron CJ B 119 18.50 91-14 GraySlewpy118nkTrickMe1141¼LightofMorn1171 Wide trip 9
9Aug92♦ Hoppegartn(Ger) gd 6½fⓉRH 1:143 3↑ Grosser Preis von Berlin-G3 11 Lequeux A 132 19.20 Mr Brooks132½Monde Bleu1321Dream Talk1323½ 12
Stk231000
Soon pushed along to keep pace,weakened over 2f out
4Jly92♦ Hamburg(Ger) gd *6fⓉStr 1:07 3↑ Holsten Trophy-G3 49¼ Badel A 132 4.80 Dream Talk1347Montepulciano1212¼Princess Nana119hd 4
Stk134000
Tracked in 3rd,weakened 1½f out
25May92♦ Sandown(GB) gd *5fⓉStr 1:001 3↑ Temple Stakes-G2 53½ Lequeux A 129 12.00 Snaadee1292Blyton Lad129nkMedaille d'Or129nk 9
Stk115000
In touch for a half,lost place entering final furlong
9May92-8Hol fst 6f :22 :443 :563 1:083 3↑ Los Angeles H-G3 4 4 43½ 43½ 32 11¾ Dlhoussaye E B 118 6.00 97-08 Cardmania1181¾GrySlwpy1193½RobynDncr1192 4 wide stretch 5
Previously trained by Myriam Bollack
12Apr92-8Kee fst 7f :222 :451 1:094 1:222 3↑ Commonwealth BC-G3 4 2 32 2½ 41¼ 43 Perret C B 121 2.90 94-12 Pleasant Tap1162½To Freedom115noRun on the Bank118½ 6
Carried out pole
22Mar92-8SA sly 6½f :22 :45 1:101 1:17 4↑ Potrero Grande H-G3 4 2 3½ 2½ 2hd 11 Dlhoussaye E B 117 3.20 85-16 Cardmania1171Frost Free1173½Answer Do1237 Brushed 3½ 4
7Mar92-6SA fst 6½f⊗ :221 :444 1:082 1:144 4↑ Zooron H 63k 5 6 64 53½ 43 1nk Dlhoussaye E B 116 3.80 96-06 Cardmania116nkFrostFr1181¼Doyouswhts1143 4 wide stretch 10
22Feb92-8SA fst 5½f :213 :441 :554 1:02 4↑ El Conejo H 106k 2 4 42½ 41¾ 32½ 32¾ McCarron CJ B 116 6.00 102-06 GraySlewpy1141¾FrstFree1191Crdmania1162¾ Always close 5
11Jan92-8SA fst 7f :221 :441 1:082 1:211 4↑ San Carlos H-G2 7 7 58½ 57½ 56½ 44 McCarron CJ B 116 4.20 93-11 Answr Do1201½Individlist115hdMdia Pln1162½Stumbled st,wide 7
14Dec91-8Hol fst 6f :212 :442 :563 1:084 3↑ V O Underwood-G3 3 6 54½ 53½ 52¾ 31 Badel A B 120 8.90 95-09 Individualist114hdThrtySlws1171Crdmn1203 4 wide stretch 8
29Nov91-8Hol fm 5½fⓉ :214 :44 :551 1:012 3↑ Turf Expr H (Div 2) 112k 5 6 42 32 3½ 31 Guignard G B 116 17.20 -- Answer Do120¾Apollo115nkCardmania116½ Good effort 8
20Oct91♦ San Siro(Ity) hy *5fⓉStr :584 Premio Omenoni-G3 1½ Badel A 119 5.30 Cardmania119½Magrana1193GoldFutures119nk 10
Stk99600
Tracked in 4th,led 170y out,held gamely

17Aug91♦	Deauville(Fr)	yl	*5f(T)Str	:593	3↑	Prix Piaget Hcp51000	1hd	Badel A	121	4.70	Cardmania121hdTamara's Twinkle1131Merry Hunter121¾	Pressed pace,dueled halfway,led near line,all out	16
3Aug91♦	Deauville(Fr)	yl	*6f(T)Str	1:122	3↑	Prix de la Municipalite et du District Hcp53900	2nk	Badel A	121	8.50	Merry Hunter118nkCardmania121nkRangoon121½	Pressed pace,dueled final furlong,outgamed	18
16Jly91♦	Maisns-Lffitte(Fr)	gd	*6f(T)Str	1:111	3↑	Prix de la Boe Hcp34300	11	Badel A	121	10.00	Cardmania1211Rechetnikov108hdGinger Candy1301	Tracked leader,led 1f out,driving	16
4Jly91♦	Evry(Fr)	gd	*6½f(T)Str	1:173	4↑	Prix de Marcoussis (Apprentices) Clm22600	1hd	Benoist O5	131	3.40	Cardmania1314Light Moon127¾Cervino111½	Chased clear leader,led 100y out,held gamely	9
25Jun91♦	Saint-Cloud(Fr)	gd	*1(T)LH	1:424	4↑	Prix des Heliotropes Clm26200	33½	Benoist O5	122	24.00	Jet Jeans1201½Radar Limit1212Cardmania1223	Midpack,progress into 4th 2½f out,one-paced final furlong	16
24Apr91♦	Evry(Fr)	sf	*6f(T)Str	1:132	4↑	Prix Teddy Hcp19200	105½	Badel A	122	5.00	Light Moon112nkMill Lady123hdSharpvite126nk	Tracked in 5th on rail,one paced	18
11Apr91♦	Longchamp(Fr)	gd	*7f(T)RH	1:203	4↑	Prix des Gravilliers Hcp55700	12	Badel A	118	7.00	Idefix127nkPlatinum Dancer119¾Positano117¾	Chased in 5th,bumped on rail over 1f out,unable to recover	18
30Mar91♦	Maisns-Lffitte(Fr)	sf	*6f(T)Str	1:142	3↑	Prix du Rey Hcp36900	31¾	Badel A	123	3.50	Platinum Dancer1201½Heart Noble130nkCardmania123nk	Dueled early,2nd halfway,lost 2nd near line	17
13Mar91♦	Maisns-Lffitte(Fr)	hy	*6f(T)Str	1:152	4↑	Prix Prince Chevalier Alw21300	2¾	Badel A	126	12.00	Nityo121¾Cardmania126hdReinstate121½	Tracked in 4th,2nd halfway,held by winner	13
2Nov90♦	Evry(Fr)	sf	*6f(T)Str	1:152	3↑	Prix du Lunain Hcp23700	11	Badel A	128	4.50	Ginger Candy1191½Sulmona1342Nao119no	Dueled to 1½f out,weakened	15
15Oct90♦	Maisns-Lffitte(Fr)	gd	*6f(T)Str	1:113	4↑	Prix de Menil-Vicomte Hcp23900	4¾	Badel A	128	8.50	Graphus126½King of Sun107nkSharpvite130hd	Rated in 6th,strong run over 1f out,gaining late	12
29Sep90♦	Evry(Fr)	gd	*1(T)LH	1:384	3↑	Prix d'Epernon Hcp40200	85¾	Badel A	127	13.00	Graveron133noJilgueno1241½Blue de Valois136½	Never a factor	17
16Sep90♦	Longchamp(Fr)	gd	*7f(T)RH	1:213	4↑	Prix du Pont de Flandre Hcp22800	97¾	Badel A	126	6.50	Despatch130hdBrenton1102½Elviss117½	Never a factor	16
8Sep90♦	Evry(Fr)	gd	*6f(T)Str	1:111	3↑	Prix Paris-Turf Hcp39600	3¾	Lawniczak D	121	9.50	Vitola117½Platinum Dancer119nkCardmania121¾	Tracked in 6th,finished well without threatening	18
29Aug90♦	Deauville(Fr)	gd	*6f(T)Str	1:143	3↑	Prix des Entraineurs Alw14200	12½	Bollack M	161	*1.60e	Cardmania1612½Pretty Liloy150nkWise Bird143½	Tracked leaders,led 150y out,going away Race in which all riders are trainers	12
18Aug90♦	Deauville(Fr)	yl	*1(T)RH	1:48	4↑	Prix de Barfleur Clm28500	21½	Badel A	128	*1.70	Prince Florent1181½Cardmania128nkZingaro1161	Chased clear leader,led 1½f out to 100y out,second best	9
12Jly90♦	Evry(Fr)	gd	*1(T)LH	1:361	4↑	Handicap de l'Essonne Hcp57300	63¾	de Smyter M	119	17.00	Forest Angel1311½Mephistopheles112nkDom Valory130hd	Well placed in 7th,evenly late	18
27Jun90♦	Longchamp(Fr)	hy	*7f(T)RH	1:273	4↑	Prix de la Chaussee Clm35800	3½	Badel A	128	*.80	Appolino124hdMorgause121½Cardmania1281½	Rated at rear,bid 2f out,finished well	10
18Jun90♦	Longchamp(Fr)	gd	*7f(T)RH	1:223	4↑	Prix de Fausses-Reposes Clm26600	12	Badel A	128	*1.90	Cardmania1282Elviss1201½Sumotori122½	Tracked in 3rd,led 1½f out,clear 1f out,handily	10
12Jun90♦	Chantilly(Fr)	yl	*1(T)RH	1:421	4↑	Prix du Bois Saint-Denis Clm26200	1½	Badel A	128	*1.50	Cardmania128½Morgause1232Millery122hd	Led to halfway,3rd 3f out,came again to lead near line	10
31May90♦	Chantilly(Fr)	gd	*1(T)RH	1:381	4↑	Prix de Chaumont Clm26200	32½	Badel A	127	2.50	Normandy Dancer119½Solido1272Cardmania1272	Tracked leader,effort over 1f out,one-paced late	6
22May90♦	Maisns-Lffitte(Fr)	gd	*1(T)Str	1:394	4↑	Prix de Chatou Clm22200	11	Badel A	130	5.40	Cardmania1301Moknine126¾Armero119½	Tracked leader,led before halfway,ridden out	15
7May90♦	Saint-Cloud(Fr)	gd	*1(T)LH	1:434	4↑	Prix de Grignon Clm18000	11½	Badel A	123	4.20	Cardmania1231½Riche Mare128hdMoknine123no	Dueled early,settled in 6th,rallied to lead 1f out,ridden out	20
16Apr90♦	Longchamp(Fr)	sf	*1(T)RH	1:431	4↑	Prix des Bouleaux Clm17700	14	Badel A	123	14.00	Solido128nkL'Ambitieux123nk[DH]Il Danieli128	Tracked in 6th,weakened 2f out	19
29Mar90♦	Saint-Cloud(Fr)	gd	*1(T)LH	1:42	4↑	Prix de Bernay Clm22700	2¾	Badel A	126	8.20	My Genelle122¾Cardmania1261½Rooty126½	Rated in 7th,4th 2f out,2nd 100y out,held by winner	15
15Mar90♦	Evry(Fr)	gd	*1(T)LH	1:404	4↑	Prix de Corbeil Hcp51800	12	Lawniczak D	117	72.00	Jilgueno103nkLe Scoot114½Arctic Swell108nk	Dueled for a half,4th 3f out,weakened over 1f out	17
2Mar90♦	Maisns-Lffitte(Fr)	hy	*1(T)Str	1:453	4↑	Prix de Conches Clm19000	14	Badel A	126	8.50	My Genelle124noBouche d'Aigre1142Carridge126no	Never a factor	18
24Nov89♦	Maisns-Lffitte(Fr)	sf	*7f(T)Str	1:304		Prix de Limours Clm16200	53¼	Badel A	130	13.00	Jame's Song121noIcy Calm121½Oh Lucky Day1191½	Toward rear,progress 1½f out,finished well	23
31Oct89♦	Maisns-Lffitte(Fr)	sf	*1⅛(T)Str	1:542		Prix de Chanteloup Clm16800	14	Badel A	128	6.50	Catabell1262½Trickiest1161Swift Legs Dancer119hd	Never a factor	25
23Oct89♦	Saint-Cloud(Fr)	fm	*1(T)LH	1:424		Prix Arreau Clm15900	32	Badel A	128	3.70	Catabell1261½Lyphard's Fire121½Cardmania1282½	Rated in midpack,rail bid 2f out,3rd 1f out;	15
						Previously trained by Christiane Head							
1Oct89♦	Saint-Cloud(Fr)	gd	*1(T)LH	1:431		Prix de Carville Clm14900	11½	Guignard G	126	*1.30	Cardmania1261½Off Stage117½Jame's Song113½	Toward rear,sharp run to lead 150y out.Claimed for $18,137	12
26Aug89♦	Deauville(Fr)	sf	*1(T)RH	1:473		Prix Caprice Clm18100	54	Guignard G	130	4.50	Margousier1271Le Scoot124nkVictory Queen1182	Rated toward rear,finished well without threatening	15
20Jly89♦	Saint-Cloud(Fr)	fm	*1(T)LH	1:41		Prix de Mantes Clm24700	34½	Head F	130	*2.50	My Genelle1223Swift Legs Dancer1301½Cardmania130¾	Rated at rear,10th 2f out,wide run to get up for 3rd	14
17Jun89♦	Saint-Cloud(Fr)	gd	*1(T)LH	1:441		Prix de Giberville Clm29800	12	Guignard G	122	*1.80	Cardmania1282Hercle1213[DH]Golden Mountains122	Rated in 9th,5th 2f out,led 1f out,ridden clear	13
5Jun89♦	Saint-Cloud(Fr)	sf	*1(T)LH	1:46		Prix Memorandum Mdn19000	31½	Guignard G	123	2.20	Susperregui123hdBoutonnement1181½Cardmania123hd	Tracked in 3rd,bid over 1f out,not good enough	11
26Apr89♦	Evry(Fr)	sf	*1(T)LH	1:452		Prix de la Beauce Mdn18700	2nk	Mosse G	123	*1.50	Prospector'sImage123nkCardmnia123¾SilverRiverman1231½	Tracked in 5th,led over 1f out,dueled 170y out,gamely	13
15Nov88♦	Saint-Cloud(Fr)	sf	*7f(T)LH	1:29		Prix Pitchoury Mdn21400	32½	Guignard G	123	*1.50	Idefix1192Creator123½Cardmania123¾	Tracked in 3rd,2nd 2f out,outfinished	12
31Oct88♦	Saint-Cloud(Fr)	sf	*7f(T)LH	1:292		Prix Samourai Mdn20900	31	Mosse G	123	8.70	Mistralien1231Aliocha123hdCardmania1232	Tracked in 5th,2nd 1f out,lost 2nd on line	17
10Oct88♦	Saint-Cloud(Fr)	gd	*1(T)LH	1:443		Prix du Vallon Mdn (FT)20100	44½	Moore GW	123	15.00	Forest Guard123½Nursery Slope1232½Strange Alliance1231½	Raced in midpack,mild late gain	13

Charismatic

ch. c. 1996, by Summer Squall (Storm Bird)–Bali Babe, by Drone — Lifetime record: 17 5 2 4 $2,038,064

Own.– Robert B. Lewis & Beverly J. Lewis
Br.– Parrish Hill Farm & W.S. Farish (Ky)
Tr.– D. Wayne Lukas

5Jun99- 9Bel	fst 1½	:473 1:12 2:014 2:274	Belmont-G1	4 2	2½	1hd	2½	31½	Antley CW	L 126		*1.60	103-06	Lemon Drop Kid126hdVision and Verse1261½Charismatic1264¾	Pressed pace,steadied midstr,game,broke down after finish	12
15May99-10Pim	fst 1 3/16	:451 1:101 1:351 1:551	Preakness-G1	6 10	107¾	83¾	13	11½	Antley CW	L 126		8.40	89-09	Charismatic1261½Menifee126hdBadge1262½	5 wide move,drifted 3/16,driving	13
1May99- 8CD	fst 1¼	:474 1:122 1:372 2:031	Ky Derby-G1	16 7	73½	31½	2½	1nk	Antley CW	L 126		31.30	89-14	Charismatic126nkMenif126¾CtThf1261¼	3 wide trip,driving	19
18Apr99- 8Kee	fst 1 1/16	:231 :464 1:103 1:41	Lexington-G2	5 6	42½	31½	2hd	12½	Bailey JD	L 115		12.10	103-07	Charismatic1152½Yankee Victor115¾Finder's Gold1152	3 wide 2nd turn,driving	12
3Apr99- 5SA	fst 1⅛	:471 1:112 1:361 1:484	S Anita Derby-G1	8 6	63¾	64	57	48¼	Pincay L Jr	LB 120		44.30	83-13	General Challenge1203½Prime Timber1203½Desert Hero1201¼	Improved position some	8
6Mar99- 7BM	fst 1 1/16	:224 :46 1:10 1:431	El Cam Real Derby-G3	2 6	67½	64¾	33½	2hd	Warren RJ Jr	LB 115		10.60	83-24	Cliquot115hdCharsmtc1153½NoClBrd117¾	Angled out,rallied	7
19Feb99- 6SA	fst 7f	:214 :434 1:081 1:212	Alw 50000	2 4	59½	59	36½	25	Pincay L Jr	LB 117		17.20	93-08	Apremont1195Charismtc1172Forstry1197	Finished willingly	5
11Feb99- 6SA	fst 6½f	:214 :442 1:102 1:171	Clm 62500	8 7	86¼	65	54	2nk	McCarron CJ	LB 117		2.70	82-17	[D]What Say You110nkCharismatic117nkVlleyDon1171	6w,bothered near ⅛;Placed first through disqualification	9
31Jan99- 8SA	gd 1 1/16	:234 :473 1:12 1:424	S Catalina-G2	2 5	54¼	55	57½	513½	Pincay L Jr	LB 117		30.10	75-15	General Challenge1173Buck Trout1201Brilliantly1153½	Bit tight ⅞,weakened	5
16Jan99- 5SA	fst 1 1/16	:233 :472 1:114 1:44	Alw 54000	8 7	75¾	73½	73½	54	Pincay L Jr	LB 117		17.90	79-16	Mr. Broad Blade116hdBrilliantly1161Outstanding Hero1162	Bit tight ¾	10
27Dec98- 1SA	fst 6½	:213 :441 1:09 1:152	Alw 50000	5 7	78¼	76¾	85¼	34½	Pincay L Jr	LB 117		23.10	87-06	Bright Vlour1164Outstanding Hero116½Charismatic117nk	Outside,late for 3rd	8
21Nov98- 1Hol	fst 6½f	:222 :453 1:104 1:171	Md 62500	3 5	42	41½	12	15	Pincay L Jr	LB 119		*1.30	80-20	Charismatic1195Wandering1192Pick Up Stixs1196	Rail trip,clearly best	6
17Oct98- 4SA	fm 1Ⓣ	:232 :472 1:13 1:381	Md Sp Wt	4 1	11	73¾	812	925¾	McCarron CJ	LB 120	b	3.40	42-28	LxingtonBch120noDancingMjsty1201¼CompnyApproval1203½	Speed,stopped	9
1Oct98- 1SA	fst 1	:221 :452 1:104 1:37	Md Sp Wt	2 1	13½	11	22	310¼	Pincay L Jr	LB 120	b	2.10	78-14	Crowning Storm12010NorthernAvn120nkCharismatic1204	Inside,edged for 2nd	7
23Aug98- 2Dmr	fst 5½f	:223 :46 :583 1:05	Md Sp Wt	2 3	3½	3nk	42½	45	McCarron CJ	LB 118	b	*.70	83-11	OutinFront1182RoundFour118hdKonCost1183	3-deep,weakened	4
25Jly98- 2Dmr	fst 6f	:222 :454 :582 1:112	Md Sp Wt	2 6	11	12	2½	31½	Nakatani CS	LB 118	b	*2.00	80-12	PrizedDemon118½Sybyby1181Chrsmtc1186	Inside,outfinished	8
20Jun98- 3Hol	fst 5f	:222 :453 :574	Md Sp Wt	3 4	44¾	35	68½	613¼	Flores DR	B 118		12.20	81-15	O'ryFntsm1182½Arstotl1182BuckTrout1183½	Inside,weakened	6

Cherokee Run

dkbbr. c. 1990, by Runaway Groom (Blushing Groom)–Cherokee Dame, by Silver Saber — Lifetime record: 28 13 5 5 $1,531,849

Own.– Jill E. Robinson
Br.– George Onett (Fla)
Tr.– Frank A. Alexander

17Apr95- 8Aqu	fst 6f	:214 :441 :561 1:084	3↑ Bold Ruler H-G3	5 2	55	43	31½	42½	Smith ME	125		*.65	95-08	Rizzi1121¼LitetheFuse1111EvilBr116nk	Rail,flattened out	6
10Mar95- 9GP	fst 7f	:224 :45 1:084 1:213	3↑ GP Sprint H 100k	3 4	2½	2hd	1½	12½	Smith ME	L 122		1.50	95-15	Cherokee Run1222½Waldoboro1131½Evil Bear116no	Driving	6
5Nov94- 4CD	fst 6f	:211 :443 :563 1:093	3↑ B C Sprint-G1	11 7	93	31½	21	1hd	Smith ME	L 126		*2.80	99-01	ChrokeRn126hdSovtProblm1231½Crdmn126no	Fully extended	14
17Sep94- 5Bel	fst 7f	:222 :443 1:09 1:214	3↑ Vosburgh-G1	7 2	22	22½	11	3¾	Perret C	126		2.40	93-08	Harln126½AmericnChance126nkCherokRn1261	Bid,weakened	10
7Aug94- 8Sar	fst 6f	:222 :451 :563 1:083	3↑ A Phenomenon H-G3	7 4	62½	4¾	2hd	2½	Perret C	120		*.70	97-03	Boundary117½CherokeeRn1202½ICan'tBelv1132	Rallied wide	7
16Jly94- 9Lrl	fst 6f	:214 :444 :563 1:084	3↑ De Francis Mem Dash-G2	1 6	54	31½	11	12¼	Perret C	114		*1.70	96-12	CherokeeRn1142¼BoomTownr119½FuManSlew107½	Driving	11
26Jun94- 7Bel	fst 7f	:233 :462 1:101 1:221	3↑ Tom Fool-G2	1 3	1½	11½	11	2hd	Perret C	121		*1.80	92-16	VirginiaRapids124hdChrokeeRn1211¾Boundry1192¾	Gamely	5
30May94- 8Bel	fst 1	:224 :45 1:092 1:334	3↑ Metropolitan H-G1	2 5	54	2½	22½	25½	Perret C	118		16.70	88-09	HolyBull1125½CherokeeRn118noDevilHisDue1222	Held place	10
7May94- 9Bel	fst 7f	:223 :451 1:091 1:212	3↑ Carter H-G1	9 4	31	3½	1hd	31½	Davis RG	119		*1.90	94-06	VirginiaRpds1181¼PunchLn114nkChrkRn1193¾	Bid,weakened	11
2Apr94- 8Aqu	fst 1	:233 :46 1:092 1:342	3↑ Westchester H-G3	7 3	32	21½	1hd	3¾	Perret C	119		*1.00	95-16	Virginia Rapids116½Colonial Affair121nkCherokee Run1192¼	Bid,weakened	7
16Mar94- 9GP	fst 7f	:223 :452 1:094 1:22	4↑ Alw 47600	1 5	2hd	11	11	12¼	Perret C	115		*.50	93-08	CherokeeRun1152¼Swedaus119noHold Old Blue1151½	Driving	6
10Oct93- 6Bel	fst 1	:231 :454 1:094 1:351	Jamaica H-G2	2 1	2hd	1½	1½	34½	McCauley WH	120		4.20	87-09	MiClo1162¾Prospctor'sFlg1131¾ChrokRun120¾	Dueled inside	8
21Aug93- 7Sar	fst 1¼	:47 1:113 1:37 2:014	Travers-G1	1 3	32½	72	63¾	710	Day P	126		7.70e	85-10	SeaHero1262KissinKris1261Miner'sMark126hd	Saved ground	11
1Aug93-11Mth	fst 1⅛	:461 1:102 1:361 1:492	Haskell H-G1	4 2	31	43	35	410½	Day P	123		*.80	77-21	KissinKris1182¼StormTower1198DryBean113hd	No late bid	7
3Jly93- 8Bel	my 1⅛	:454 1:093 1:344 1:473	Dwyer-G2	6 2	2½	1½	12	16	Day P	123		1.70	91-11	CherokeeRn1236Minr'sMrk1231¼SlvrofSlvr1232¾	Ridden out	6
5Jun93- 9Bel	gd 1½	:484 1:132 2:024 2:294	Belmont-G1	1 2	2hd	11½	68	613	Antley CW	126		4.20	68-15	ColonialAffair1262¼KissinKris126¾WldGl1262	Nothing left	13
15May93-10Pim	fst 1 3/16	:464 1:111 1:37 1:563	Preakness-G1	12 3	41¼	42	1hd	2½	Day P	126		9.40	78-18	PrairieBayou126½CherokeeRun1267ElBakan126nk	Stubbornly	12
24Apr93- 9CD	sly 1	:23 :462 1:113 1:372	Derby Trial-G3	2 2	1hd	11	13	13	Day P	L 122		*.70	92-27	Cherokee Run1223Darien Deacon1149Ground Force1172	Ridden out,much best	9
6Apr93- 8Kee	fst 7f	:222 :45 1:091 1:211	Lafayette-G3	5 1	2½	2½	1½	13½	Day P	L 118		*1.50	103-07	Cherokee Run1183½Poverty Slew1123Williamstown1211	Sharp,ridden out;Previously trained by Frank Gomez	8
20Mar93- 8GP	sly 7f	:223 :453 1:101 1:231	Swale-G3	7 4	42	41¼	21½	3½	Bailey JD	114		*.90	87-12	PrmrExplosn114hdDemalootDemashoot113nkCherokeeRn1142¼	Closed willingly	8
5Mar93- 7GP	fst 7f	:234 :473 1:112 1:231	Alw 37290	3 2	2½	1½	15	15	Vasquez J	117		*.90	87-16	Cherokee Run1175Wild Gale1176Ziao112	Ridden out	4
26Dec92-10Crc	fst 1 1/16	:241 :483 1:141 1:481	What a Pleasure-G3	6 4	51¼	21	2½	2½	Vasquez J	115		*.60	79-15	Virgil Cain115½Cherokee Run1152¼Kassec1122	Bumped near far turn,gamely	7
16Dec92- 9Crc	fst 1 70	:241 :483 1:13 1:451	Alw 21000	3 4	42	31½	11½	11½	Vasquez J	120		*.40	87-20	Cherokee Run1201½Ziao1121¼Game Red112nk	Driving	7
22Nov92- 9Crc	gd 7f	:223 :461 1:11 1:234	Alw 22500	2 4	35½	32½	11½	12¾	Vasquez J	114		*.40	96-10	Cherokee Run1142¾Virgil Cain1144Dr. Roses Hope1124	Strong handling	5
27Oct92- 7Crc	fst 6f	:22 :453 :58 1:11	Alw 17600	6 1	43	31½	13	15½	Vasquez J	116		*1.90	96-14	CherokeeRun1165½VirgilCain1162WakeMeatNoon1161	Driving	6
12Aug92- 8Crc	fst 6f	:22 :453 :583 1:121	Alw 15500	1 7	62¾	43	12	12½	Vasquez J	114		3.70	90-17	Cherokee Run1142½Pride of Burkaan1125Aspen Fortune112no	Driving,5-wide	7
16Jly92- 7Crc	fst 5½f	:221 :46 1:062	Alw 15500	3 2	31	21	31	58½	Vasquez J	116		*1.40	- -	Stacey's Bird1162It'sali'Iknownfact116noAspen Fortune1146½	Faltered	6
27Jun92- 3Crc	sly 5f	:222 :462 :591	Md Sp Wt	6 4	3½	2hd	12½	11	Vasquez J	116		9.40	107-07	CherokeeRn1161VanguardKnght1163MdnghtCook1112½	Driving	8

Chief Bearhart

ch. c. 1993, by Chief's Crown (Danzig)–Amelia Bearhart, by Bold Hour

Own.– Sam–Son Farms
Br.– Richard D. Maynard (Can)
Tr.– Mark Frostad

Lifetime record: 26 12 5 3 $3,462,014

29Nov98♦ Tokyo(Jpn)	fm*1½①LH 2:25⁴ 3 ↑ Japan Cup-G1 Stk3099000		45	Santos JA	126 b	6.60		El Condor Pasa121²½Air Groove121½Special Week126²	15
								Rated in 14th,progress over 2f out,finished well.Maxzene 5th	
7Nov98- 9CD	fm 1½① :49¹ 1:13⁴ 2:03³ 2:28³ 3 ↑ B C Turf-G1	8 13 12¹⁰ 9⁹½ 5⁸	4³	Santos JA	L 126 b	6.50 89-09		Buck'sBoy126¹½Yagl126¹³Dushyntor126no Circled five wide 13
18Oct98- 6WO	fm 1½① :52¹ 1:16¹ 2:04³ 2:29³ 3 ↑ Can Int'l-G1	3 6 5⁶ 4² 3¹	2²	Santos JA	L 126 b	*1.50e 82-17	RoylAnthm119²ChiefBehrt126½PrdGround119³ Second best 8
27Sep98- 8WO	yl 1⅜① :49¹ 1:13 1:37³ 2:15³ 3 ↑ Sky Classic H-G2C	3 6 6⁹½ 5⁴³ 1³	1³½	Santos JA	L 125 b	*.25e 89-11	ChiefBrhrt126³GreenMeansGo114½DesrtWvs112² Handily 6
5Sep98- 8WO	fm 1½① :51 1:15⁴ 2:05² 2:30 3 ↑ Niagara BC H-G1C	5 4 6³½ 4¹½ 1½	1²¾	Santos JA	L 123 b	*.30e 82-18	ChiefBrhrt123²¾GrnMnsGo113½CrownAttorny117½ Driving 6
15Aug98- 8Sar	fm 1½Ⓣ :52³ 1:18² 2:07² 2:29² 3 ↑ Sword Dancer H-G1	6 3 3¹½ 3¹ 5³¾	5³½	Santos JA	L 123 b	*1.20 66-17	Cetewyo115⅝VI'sPrnc113nkDushyntor119²½ 3 wide each turn 6
11Jly98- 8Bel	fm 1⅜① :50³ 1:14⁴ 1:38² 2:13² 3 ↑ Bowling Green H-G2	6 6 6⁵ 6⁷½ 6⁴¼	3⁴¼	Santos JA	L 124 b	*.30 84-12	Cetewayo112²Officious113²½Chief Bearhart124½ 6
	Hard ridden final turn							
6Jun98- 8Bel	fm 1½①Ⓣ :46⁴ 1:10⁴ 1:34² 1:58¹ 3 ↑ Manhattan H-G1	1 9 9¹³ 8⁷½ 3³	1½¾	Santos JA	L 122 b	*.65e 101-05	ChiefBrhrt122½¾Dvonwood113½Buck'sBoy117½ Strong finish 9
22Apr98- 8Kee	yl 1½① :52³ 1:18¹ 2:07⁴ 2:31³ 4 ↑ Elkwood-G3	5 4 5⁴ 5³ 5²½	2¾	Santos JA	L 122 b	*.70 81-19	African Dancer114¾Chief Bearhart122½Chorwon114nk 5
	Followed slow pace 5 or 6 wide,closed well,too late							
8Nov97- 7Hol	fm 1½① :47¹ 1:11 1:59³ 2:23⁴ 3 ↑ B C Turf-G1	5 8 8⁵½ 5²½ 3¹	1¾	Santos JA	LB 126 b	*1.90 98-02	ChfBrhrt126¾Borg119½FlgDown126⁴ 4-wide 2nd turn,in time 11
19Oct97- 8WO	fm 1½① :50⁴ 1:14⁴ 2:04³ 2:29 3 ↑ Can Int'l-G1	2 6 5³½ 1² 1²½	1²½	Santos JA	L 126 b	*.65e 83-11	ChiefBerhrt126²½DownthAsl126³½Romnov119⁸½ Last to first 6
28Sep97- 9WO	fm 1⅜① :49² 1:13² 1:37³ 2:13² 3 ↑ Sky Classic H-G2C	1 6 6⁴½ 2hd 1⁴	1⁶	Santos JA	L 123 b	*1.05 100-05	Chief Bearhart123⁶Honor Glide119⁵½Intheblinkofani118¹½ 6
	Much the best							
4Jly97- 6AP	fm 1½① :51 1:15⁴ 2:05³ 2:29² 3 ↑ S & Stripes B C H-G3	2 6 6⁴½ 5³ 3½	2hd	Santos JA	L 199 b	*1.40 99-11	LakeshoreRod113hdChfBrhrt119¹¾Awd119½ 3 wide ½,missed 9
14Jun97- 3WO	fm 1⅛① :45³ 1:09¹ 1:33³ 1:46¹ 3 ↑ King Edward B C H-G3	1 8 8¹⁰ 8⁵ 2½	1³½	Santos JA	L 119 b	*.85e 95-05	ChiefBrhrt119³½CrownAttorny119nkKrdsh124¹¾ Clearly best 8
25Apr97- 8Kee	fm 1½① :49¹ 1:14² 2:04¹ 2:28² 4 ↑ Elkhorn-G2	8 6 4⁵ 4³ 3²	1½	Santos JA	L 114 b	1.90 98-11	ChiefBearhrt114½SnkEys113³Lssgny122¹ 3 wide,stiff drive 8
11Apr97- 8Kee	fm 1① :23 :46² 1:10² 1:34² 4 ↑ Maker's Mark Mile-G3	5 9 9¹¹ 8¹⁰ 7⁶¾	2½	Santos JA	L 114 b	6.70 95-06	Influent116½Chief Bearhart114½Foolish Pole113¹½ 9
	Altered course inside ⅛,closed fast							
26Oct96- 9WO	gd 1½① :50 1:15² 2:05⁴ 2:30¹ 3 ↑ B C Turf-G1	14 6 7³½ 4²½ 11⁹½	11¹¹	Hawley S	L 121 b	20.10 66-18	Pilsudski126½Singspiel126½Swain126²½ 5 wide 2nd turn 14
29Sep96- 8WO	sf 1½① :51 1:16² 2:07¹ 2:33¹ 3 ↑ Can Int'l-G1	5 4 4²½ 2¹ 2³	2²	Hawley S	L 118 b	7.80 60-31	Singspiel126²Chief Bearhart118³Mecke126³½ Solid effort 7
25Aug96-11WO	fm 1½① :50² 1:15¹ 2:03⁴ 2:28³ Ⓡ Breeders'-G1C	3 7 4⁴ 1½ 1⁴	1⁹½	Walls MK	L 126 b	*1.35e 85-15	ChiefBearhrt126⁹½FirmDancer126½Selunch126¹½ Going away 9
25Jly96- 2WO	fm *1⅜① 2:16 3 ↑ Alw 27400	2 1 3¹ 3²½ 1²	1²½	Hawley S	L 109 b	*.50 --	Chief Bearhart109²½Set Ablaze113²Quest for Approval121⁵½ 5
	Clearly best							
7Jly96- 8WO	fst 1¼ :46 1:11¹¹ 1:37 2:03⁴ Ⓡ Queen's Plate-G1C	2 13 13¹⁴ 9⁸½ 5⁸	4³¾	Hawley S	L 126 b	*2.55 88-12	VctorCooly126½Stphnots126¾KrstyKrunch126½½ Rallied wide 13
23Jun96- 6WO	fst 1⅛ :45⁴ 1:09⁴ 1:36² 1:50 Ⓡ Plate Trial-G2C	4 8 9¹⁸ 8¹⁷ 5⁷	3²	Hawley S	126 b	1.70 94-12	Northface126¾FirmDancer126½½ChiefBerhrt126¹½ Wide rally 9
26May96- 5WO	fst 1¹⁄₁₆ :23² :47¹ 1:13² 1:45 Alw 25600	9 10 9¹³ 6³½ 1²½	1⁶½	Hawley S	115 b	3.85 84-19	Chief Bearhart115⁶½Bold Decision118¾Lorries ManeMan115⁹½ 10
	Bobbled,bold 5 wide bid,ridden out							
13Apr96- 4Kee	fm 1¹⁄₁₆① :22⁴ :46⁴ 1:11⁴ 1:42 Alw 41360	3 6 6⁴½ 5³¼ 4⁴	3⁶	Romero RP	114 b	8.70 91-10	Trail City112³Krigeorj's Gold115³Chief Bearhart114⁶ 10
	Angled 5 wide late,no response							
23Mar96- 6FG	fm *1½① :24² :49 1:13⁴ 1:39² Md Sp Wt	9 6 7⁷¼ 4¹½ 1¹½	1⁴	Romero RP	119 b	6.50 84-17	Chief Bearhart119⁴Mister Eye119¹½Chorwon119¹½ 12
	5w bid,incrsd margin							
25Jul95- 5WO	fst 5f :22³ :45³ :58 Md Sp Wt	2 5 6⁵½ 6⁹¼ 4¹²	4¹⁰	Ramsammy E	115 b	10.75 82-11	FrozenIce120⁴½RareAdmrl120³½IslndGldtor115² Belated bid 8

Chilukki

b. f. 1997, by Cherokee Run (Runaway Groom)–Song of Syria, by Damascus

Own.– Stonerside Stable
Br.– Mr & Mrs R.S. West & Mr & Mrs M. Miller (Ky)
Tr.– Bob Baffert

Lifetime record: 7 6 1 0 $762,723

6Nov99- 4GP	fst 1¹⁄₁₆ :22³ :45⁴ 1:10¹ 1:43¹ Ⓕ BC Juv Fillies-G1	3 3 3²½ 1hd 2hd	2¹½	Flores DR	L 119	*1.50 90-00	CshRun119¹½Chlukk119½Surfsd119½ Stalked,led,outfinished 9
9Oct99- 8SA	fst 1 :23 :46³ 1:10⁴ 1:36 Ⓕ Oak Leaf-G1	2 2 3¹ 2hd 1¹	1¹¼	Flores DR	LB 118	*.50 91-11	Chilukk118¹¼AbbyGrl118⁴¼Spn118½ Drifted in ⅛,driving 5
29Aug99- 7Dmr	fst 7f :22¹ :44³ 1:10 1:23² Ⓕ Dmr Debutante-G1	1 4 2½ 1¹ 1³	1¹	Flores DR	LB 121	*.20 86-12	Chlukk121¹Spn115⁴Sh'sClssy116⁵½ Dueled,clear,held driving 7
7Aug99- 8Dmr	fst 6½f :21⁴ :44³ 1:09⁴ 1:16² Ⓕ Sorrento-G2	1 4 1hd 1¹ 1⁴	1⁶	Flores DR	LB 121	*.20 89-11	Chilukki121⁶November Slew117³She's Classy117¹⁰ 6
	Inside,clear,easily							
26Jun99- 7CD	fst 5½f :22² :45³ :57² 1:03³ Ⓕ Debutante-G3	6 1 1¹¹ 1hd 1³	1⁵¼	Martinez W	L 121	*.30 100-09	Chilukki121⁵¼Miss Wineshine112¹¼Ccili's Crown115no 9
	Widened,ridden out							
31May99- 9CD	fst 5½f :21³ :44³ :57¹ 1:04 Ky BC-G3	1 1 1½ 1hd 1³	1⁴¾	Abarado RJ	L 112	*.40 98-09	Chilukki112⁴¾Barrier115¾SkyDweller115¹¾ Pace,hand urging 7
28Apr99- 1CD	gd 4½f :22 :44³ :51 Ⓕ Md Sp Wt	3 2 1hd 1³	1⁹¼	Flores DR	L 118	*1.10 105-15	Chilukki118⁹¼Shattered Heart118⁵Sweet Dixie118¹ 10
	Off inside,driving							

Cigar

b. c. 1990, by Palace Music (The Minstrel)–Solar Slew, by Seattle Slew

Own.– Allen E. Paulson
Br.– Allen E. Paulson (Md)
Tr.– William I. Mott

Lifetime record: 33 19 4 5 $9,999,815

26Oct96-10WO	fst 1¼ :46² 1:10⁴ 1:35² 2:01 3 ↑ B C Classic-G1	7 7 8⁵¾ 5³¾ 4¹	3nk	Bailey JD	L 126	*.65 106-02	AlphabetSoup126noLouisQuatorze121hdCigar126½ 5-wide bid 13
5Oct96-10Bel	fst 1¼ :47³ 1:11² 1:35⁴ 2:00³ 3 ↑ JC Gold Cup-G1	6 3 3⁴½ 3¹½ 3¹	2hd	Bailey JD	L 126	*.20 94-10	SkipAway121hdCigr126²LousQutorz121¹ Drifted,outfinished 6
14Sep96- 8Bel	fst 1⅛ :46¹ 1:10² 1:34³ 1:47 3 ↑ Woodward-G1	4 4 4²½ 3¹ 1¹½	1⁴	Bailey JD	L 126	*.35 95-10	Cigar126⁴L'Carriere126½Golden Larch126¾ Ridden out 5
10Aug96- 6Dmr	fst 1¼ :45⁴ 1:09¹ 1:33³ 1:59⁴ 3 ↑ Pacific Classic-G1	4 2 2¹ 1hd 2½	2³½	Bailey JD	LB 124	*.10 94-07	Dare and Go124³½Cigar124⁷Siphon124⁸ Led,outfinished 6
13Jly96-10AP	fst 1¼ :46¹ 1:10¹ 1:35³ 1:48¹ 3 ↑ Citation Challnge 1075k	10 7 6³ 3¹½ 1½	1³½	Bailey JD	L 130	*.30 103-16	Cigar130³½Dramatic Gold118nkEltish118² Ridden out,wide 10
1Jun96-10Suf	fst 1⅛ :45⁴ 1:10¹ 1:36¹ 1:49³ 3 ↑ Mass H 500k	3 4 3⁴ 1² 1⁴	1²½	Bailey JD	LB 130	*.10 95-08	Cigar130²PersonalMerit111¹⁰Prolanzr112nk 3 path,easily 6
27Mar96♦ NadAlSheba(Dub) fst*1¼LH 2:03⁴ 4 ↑ Dubai World Cup Stk4000000		1½	Bailey JD	124	-	Cigar124½Soul of the Matter124⁸¾L'Carriere124³½ 11
	5th after 1f,bid 4f out,led 2f out,dueled 1½f out,prevailed							
10Feb96-10GP	fst 1⅛ :46⁴ 1:10⁴ 1:35³ 1:49 3 ↑ Donn H-G1	1 3 3² 2hd 1³	1²	Bailey JD	L 128	*.20 92-12	Cigar128²Wekiva Springs117⁴Heavenly Prize115³ 8
	Six wide top str,easily best							
28Oct95- 8Bel	my 1¼ :48¹ 1:12¹ 1:35³ 1:59² 3 ↑ B C Classic-G1	10 3 3¹ 1¹½ 1²	1²½	Bailey JD	L 126	*.70 97-08	Cgr126²½L'Crrr126½UncountdFor126¾ Four wide bid,driving 11
7Oct95-10Bel	wf 1¼ :48 1:11²1:36 2:01¹ 3 ↑ JC Gold Cup-G1	6 3 3¹½ 2½ 1²	1¹	Bailey JD	L 126	*.35 88-14	Cigar126¹Unaccounted For126⁹¾Star Standard121² 7
	Carried 7 wide,gamely							
16Sep95- 9Bel	fst 1⅛ :45⁴ 1:09³ 1:34 1:47 3 ↑ Woodward-G1	5 3 3⁴ 2½ 1³½	1²¾	Bailey JD	L 126	*.10 97-09	Cigar126²¾Star Standard121³Golden Larch126¾ Under wraps 6
2Jly95- 6Hol	fst 1¼ :45³ 1:09²1:34 1:59² 3 ↑ Hol Gold Cup H-G1	1 4 4² 1¹ 1³	1³½	Bailey JD	LB 126	*.90 103-04	Cigar126³½Tinners Way118hdTossofthecoin118½ 8
	4 wide ½,strong handling							
3Jun95-10Suf	fst 1⅛ :47¹ 1:10² 1:35¹ 1:48³ 3 ↑ Mass H 750k	6 4 3³ 2½ 1³½	1⁴	Bailey JD	LB 124	*.20 110-05	Cigar124⁴Poor but Honest107⁵½Double Calvados113nk 6
	Rated 3w,mild urging							
13May95-10Pim	fst 1⅛ :48 1:11²1:35¹1:53³ 4 ↑ Pim Special H-G1	1 1 1¹½ 1¹½ 1⁵	1²½	Bailey JD	L 122	*.40 106-02	Cigar122²½Devil His Due121²¾Concern121⁴½ Ridden out 6
15Apr95- 9P	fst 1⅛ :46² 1:10⁴1:35²1:47¹ 4 ↑ Oaklawn H-G1	4 4 4⁵ 4¹½ 1hd	1²½	Bailey JD	L 120	*1.70 103-13	Cigar120²½Silver Goblin119⁴Concern122¹ 7
	Bumped,hit by opponent's whip,driving							

5Mar95- 9GP fst 1¼ :472 1:114 1:364 2:024 3↑ Gulf Park H-G1 9 4 45 1hd 15 17½ Bailey JD L 118 *.50 88-19 Cigar1187½Pride of Burkaan1141Mahogany Hall1132 11
Six wide bkstr,six wide top str,ridden out
11Feb95- 9GP fst 1⅛ :462 1:103 1:363 1:493 3↑ Donn H-G1 4 1 12 1hd 1½ 15½ Bailey JD L 115 4.00 89-13 Cigar1155½Primitive Hall1121½Bonus Money1123½ 9
Five wide top str,drifted out,driving
22Jan95-10GP fst 1 1/16 :231 :464 1:112 1:431 4↑ Alw 33000 5 1 1hd 11 11½ 12 Bailey JD L 122 *.50 92-13 Cigar1222Upping the Ante1198¾Chasin Gold1221 8
Crowded,bumped start,driving
26Nov94- 8Aqu fst 1 :223 :454 1:111 1:36 3↑ NYRA Mile-G1 6 4 42 11½ 17 17 Bailey JD 111 8.90 88-28 Cigar1117DevilHisDue1242½PunchLine1121 Wide,ridden out 12
28Oct94- 6Aqu fst 1 :222 :443 1:094 1:353 3↑ Alw 34000 6 2 12 13 16 18 Smith ME 117 3.50 90-23 Cigar1178Golden Plover1193½Gulliviegold1092 Handily 6
7Oct94- 8Bel fm 1 1/16[T] :232 :463 1:104 1:412 3↑ Alw 36000 2 4 35 2½ 34½ 38½ Krone JA 117 3.40 80-15 UnaccountdFor1142½SameOldWish1196Cgr117½ Flattened out 6
16Sep94- 7Bel fm 1Ⓣ :23 :452 1:083 1:33 3↑ Alw 34000 10 8 77¼ 45 66¾ 78½ Bailey JD 117 *1.90 89-13 Jido1082½BrmudaCedr1142LimtdWr1132 Wide,flattened out 11
8Aug94- 1Sar fm 1⅛[T] :472 1:12 1:363 1:483 3↑ Alw 34000 1 4 43½ 42 3½ 33 Smith ME 117 3.20 89-11 MyMogul1191½NextEndvr1191½Cgr117nk Lacked room stretch 8
8Jly94- 7Bel fm 1 1/16[T] :243 :482 1:123 1:43 3↑ Alw 34000 5 2 1hd 2hd 43 49 Smith ME 117 *1.70 72-16 DancingHuntr117½Compdr1173I'mVryIrsh1115½ Dueled,tired 5
Previously trained by Alex Hassinger Jr
20Nov93- 6Hol fm 1⅛Ⓣ :461 1:102 1:341 1:464 Hol Derby-G1 9 4 55 41¼ 64½ 1114½ Valnzuela PA LB 122 24.80 76-08 ExplsiveRed1221¼JeuneHomm122nkErlofBrkng122½ Wide trip 14
5Nov93- 8SA fm 1⅛Ⓣ :48 1:121 1:36 1:48 Volante H-G3 4 3 43 32½ 21½ 22 Valnzuela PA LB 118 7.70 77-21 EasternMemories1132Cigar118nkSnkEys120½ Bid,outfinished 9
25Sep93- 5BM fm 1 1/16Ⓣ :23 :453 1:10 1:413 Ascot H-G3 1 5 44 41¼ 12 3½ Valnzuela PA LB 117 4.10 102-03 Siebe115nkNonproductiveasset114hdCigar1172¼ Held well 11
3Sep93- 8Dmr fm 1Ⓣ :224 :47 1:11 1:35 3↑ Alw 40000 4 2 21½ 21 2hd 2½ McCarron CJ LB 115 3.30 95-04 Kingdom of Spain119½Cigar115½Saturnino1173 Sharp effort 6
18Aug93- 5Dmr fm 1 1/16Ⓣ :231 :472 1:111 1:414 3↑ Alw 36000 5 4 53½ 43½ 3nk 12¾ McCarron CJ LB 115 *1.90 97-04 Cigr1152¾OurMotionGrantd122hdTheBerklyMn1142¼ Driving 10
12Jun93-10Hol gd 1 1/16Ⓣ :231 :48 1:113 1:412 Alw 39000 10 7 73 42 31½ 31¾ Valnzuela PA LB 117 2.90 87-11 4 wide stretch 10
23May93- 9Hol fm 1 1/16Ⓣ :232 :471 1:103 1:411 Alw 39000 11 3 31 2½ 11½ 41¾ Valnzuela PA L 117 3.80 88-10 Pleasedontexplain117½Stately Warrior115½Fleet Wizard115¾ 12
Weakened a bit
9May93- 3Hol fst 6f :22 :443 :564 1:092 Md Sp Wt 3 6 21 1½ 13 12¼ Valenzuela PA 117 5.20 93-11 Cigr1172¼GoldnSlwpy1165½FmousFn115hd Off slowly,driving 6
21Feb93- 6SA gd 6f :214 :452 :58 1:104 Md Sp Wt 9 7 65½ 65¼ 68 713 Valenzuela PA 118 5.10 70-18 Demigod118nkCardiac1182[D]SirHutch1182½ Wide backstretch 9

Correggio (Ire)

b. g. 1991, by Sadler's Wells (Northern Dancer)–Rosa Mundi, by Secretariat **Lifetime record: 15 6 3 2 $274,725**
Own.– William C. Lickle
Br.– Ballydoyle Stud (Ire)
Tr.– Janet E. Elliot

12Jly98- 9Del fm *2¼ Hurdles 4:142 4↑ Midsummer Hurdle 50k 5 1 1hd 1hd 511 621 Kingsley A Jr 160 1.90 -- PrimeLegacy1429SerenityPrayer1521½Teb'sBnd1481 Faltered 8
9May98- 6PW yl *3 Hurdles 5:514 4↑ Iroquois-G1 6 1 12 12 1hd 33¼ Kingsley A Jr 156 - -- RowdyIrishmn156¾Confdnt1562½Crrggo15638 Weakened late 6
18Apr98- 3Mid fm *2½ Hurdles 5:422 4↑ Temple Gwathmey H-G2 5 1 13 12 2½ 29 Kingsley A Jr 162 - -- To Ridley1529Correggio1621¼Smart Jaune1464½ Gamely 5
11Apr98- 4AtH fm *2⅜ Hurdles 4:40 4↑ Atlanta Cup-G1 3 - - - - - Kingsley A Jr 158 - -- Soaringoverseattle1428½SerenityPryr1504PrmLgcy1424 Fell 5
10May97- 6PW fm *3 Hurdles 5:302 4↑ Iroquois-G1 2 1 12¼ 12½ 18 19¼ Kingsley A Jr 156 -- Correggio1569¼Lonesome Glory156½Confidente1563¼ Handily 6
17Nov96- 5Cam fm *2¾ Hurdles 5:092 4↑ Colonial Cup-G1 7 1 11 11½ 12 11 Teter J 160 -- Correggio1601Stop and Listen162¾Mr Yankee162¾ Driving 12
26Oct96- 5FH sf *2⅝ Hurdles 5:104 4↑ BC Grand Nat H-G1 3 1 11¼ 11 12 13 Kingsley A Jr 138 -- Correggio1383Mr Yankee1401½Rowdy Irishman1542½ Driving 10
29Sep96- 4Fx yl *2⅛ Hurdles 4:121 3↑ Alw 12500 9 1 11¼ 15 13 15 Teter J 146 -- Correggio1465Winterton15623Duraznillo152½ In hand 10
16Sep96- 8Pha sf 1⅛Ⓣ :503 1:174 1:444 1:59 3↑ Md Sp Wt 11 6 54½ 32 12 13½ Castillo RE 122 3.80 61-35 Correggio1223½Psychothrpy1221¼Pondrously116½ Drew clear 11
13Nov94- 2Cam fm *2¼ Hurdles 3:58 RG Woolfe Mem 25k 8 2 11¼ 1½ 23 28 Miller C 149 -- MacheteRoad1458Corrggio1492½UnitedCongress149½ Gamely 12
Previously trained by Charles O'Brien
19Sep94◆ Listowel(Ire) sf 2LH 4:193 Devon Inn 3YO Hurdle 34½ O'Dwyer C 158 5.00 Brief Reunion1543Nun's Island1541½Correggio1583½ 15
Alw8500 Led,clear at 3rd,headed 2 out,brushed 1 out,evenly late
15Sep94◆ Dundalk(Ire) yl 1½ⓉLH 2:403 3↑ Riverstown Maiden 515¾ Roche C 126 *1.25 Father Sky126¾Native Joy1233½Better Style1231½ 16
Mdn5000 Tracked leader,led halfway,headed over 2f out,weakened
22Aug94◆ Tralee(Ire) yl 2LH 3:512 Kellihers Electricl 3YO Hurdle 12 O'Dwyer C 145 7.00 Correggio1452Celibate1452½Dr Leunt14512 17
Alw8400 Led at 2nd,mistakes 4 and 3 out,won driving
2Jly94◆ Naas(Ire) gd 1¼ⓉLH 2:082 Virginia EBF Maiden 55 Roche C 121 *2.25 Bhavnagar1211½Muzrak121¾Bubbly Prospect1212½ 16
Mdn7100 Broke alertly,taken back to 4th,drifted and bumped 1½f out
1Jun94◆ The Curragh(Ire) gd 1¼ⓉStr 2:102 Curragh Bldstk Agency EBF Mdn 2hd Roche C 126 5.00 Better Choice126hdCorreggio1262½Ivory Reef126nk 12
Mdn5100 Led to halfway,tracked leader,led again 1f out,caught at line

Countess Diana

b. f. 1995, by Deerhound (Danzig)–T.V. Countess, by T.V. Commercial **Lifetime record: 14 7 2 0 $1,117,186**
Own.– Kaster & Kaster & Propson et al
Br.– Richard S. Kaster (Ky)
Tr.– Mary Jo Lohmeier

21Oct99- 9Kee fm 1 1/16Ⓣ :23 :47 1:113 1:414 3↑ ⒻAlw 51450 3 1 11 12 12 13 Perret C L 117 2.80 93-06 Countess Diana1173Tsso'sMgcRoo1174Aslwfwht117½ 9
Controlled pace,driving
25Sep99- 9TP fst 1 1/16 :234 :474 1:121 1:444 3↑ ⒻTP BC-G3 3 1 1hd 1hd 43½ 715 Prado ES L 114 f 3.60 64-24 RubySurpris1181Lt1183½FrnchBrds114nk Out in strip,faded 8
22Aug99- 8Sar fst 7f :22 :443 1:092 1:23 3↑ ⒻBallerina H-G1 5 3 2½ 22 96½ 917 Chavez JF L 116 f 4.40 73-16 Furlough114noBourbonBll171½[DH]Ctnc121 Tired after a half 10
8Aug99- 6Sar sly 6½f :213 :444 1:10 1:163 3↑ ⒻAlw 55000 5 1 11 11 15 15¾ Chavez JF L 117 f *1.00 91-18 Countess Diana1175¾MemoryCll1141½CottgeGrdn1144¼ 6
Strong pace,handily;Previously trained by William I. Mott
12Sep98- 8Bel fst 1⅛ :47 1:12 1:371 1:493 ⒻGazelle H-G1 4 2 1hd 1hd 5¾ 69½ Sellers SJ L 117 3.30 72-25 Tap to Music1121¼Keeper Hill1221French Braids1151 7
Between rivals,tired
27Jun98- 8Bel fst 1⅛ :454 1:10 1:342 1:473 ⒻMother Goose-G1 5 2 1½ 2½ 24 45 Sellers SJ L 121 6.80 87-16 Jersey Girl1211Keeper Hill1213Banshee Breeze1211 11
Stayed well inside
7Jun98- 8Bel fst 1 :223 :452 1:101 1:361 ⒻAcorn-G1 4 1 31½ 42 57½ 511½ Sellers SJ L 121 *1.00 71-22 Jersey Girl1212¾Santaria121noBrave Deed1211¾ Used up 10
13May98- 8Bel fst 7f :213 :443 1:091 1:223 ⒻNassau County-G3 4 1 45½ 44 23 22½ Sellers SJ L 118 *.75 86-12 Jersey Girl1212½Countess Diana1189Foil11418 4
Stumbled break,rallied inside, 2nd best;Previously trained by Patrick B. Byrne
8Nov97- 2Hol fst 1 1/16 :224 :46 1:102 1:42 ⒻBC Juv Fillies-G1 8 2 2½ 11 12½ 18½ Sellers SJ LB 119 *2.00 90-06 CountessDian1198½CrrCollcton1194Prmly1192 Clear,driving 14
11Oct97- 8Kee fst 1 1/16 :23 :454 1:092 1:451 ⒻAlcibiades-G2 6 1 1½ 11 12½ 12¾ Sellers SJ L 118 1.70 82-24 Countess Diana1182¾Lily O'gold118hdBeautiful Pleasure118¾ 6
Rated on pace,swerved,nearly misstepped 3/16,driving
29Aug97- 8Sar gd 7f :222 :454 1:102 1:24 ⒻSpinaway-G1 1 1 1½ 1½ 14 16½ Sellers SJ L 121 *.85 85-15 CountssDian1216½BrcDrftr121hdAuntAnn1212½ Kept to task 5
Previously owned by Nancy & Richard Kaster
23Jly97- 9Sar fst 6f :221 :453 :573 1:101 ⒻSchuylerville-G2 1 2 1½ 1½ 12 12 Sellers SJ L 116 2.30 90-13 CountssDiana1162LoveLock1195Sequence1162 Game effort 6
28Jun97- 7CD fst 5½f :221 :454 :573 1:034 ⒻDebutante-G3 1 1 1hd 2hd 11½ 2½ Sellers SJ L 115 *1.70 99-08 LoveLck115½CountssDiana1159QuckLp115nk Dueled,2nd best 13
Previously trained by Carlos A. Garcia
6Jun97- 3Pim fst 4½f :222 :452 :512 ⒻMd Sp Wt 5 1 22 21 1½ Johnston MT 119 6.20 106-11 CountessDiana119½BracDrifter11910Epistola119hd Driving 7

Criminal Type

ch. c. 1985, by Alydar (Raise a Native)–Klepto, by No Robbery — Lifetime record: 24 10 5 3 $2,351,817

Own.– Calumet Farm
Br.– Calumet Farm (Ky)
Tr.– D. Wayne Lukas

15Sep90- 8Bel fst 1⅛ :45¹ 1:08³ 1:33¹ 1:45⁴ 3↑ Woodward H-G1 1 4 32 21½ 43½ 64¾ Santos JA 127 *1.00 100-09 Dispersal123¼Quiet American117½Rhythm120nk Tired 8
4Aug90- 7Sar fst 1⅛ :48⁴ 1:12² 1:36² 1:48³ 3↑ Whitney H-G1 1 1 11½ 12 13 11½ Stevens GL 126 *.40 94-06 CriminalType1261½DancingSpree1212½MiSelcto1177¼ Driving 6
24Jun90- 8Hol fst 1¼ :46⁴ 1:10¹ 1:34³ 1:59⁴ 3↑ Hol Gold Cup H-G1 2 2 2½ 1hd 1hd 1hd Santos JA 121 2.40 99-09 CriminlType121hdSundaySilence1263½OpnngVrs1192¾ Gamely 7
28May90- 8Bel fst 1 :22³ :45 1:09¹ 1:34² 3↑ Metropolitan H-G1 6 3 21 21½ 21½ 1nk Santos JA 120 8.40e 97-18 CrimnlTyp120nkHousbustr1131½EsyGor1273 Drifted out late 9
12May90-10Pim fst 1 3/16 :46⁴ 1:10³ 1:34² 1:53 4↑ Pim Spl H-G1 8 2 21½ 22 21½ 1nk Santos JA 117 7.70 101-16 CriminlType117nkRuhlmann1241¼DeRoch1141½ Jostled break 10
14Apr90- 8OP fst 1⅛ :46² 1:10² 1:35² 1:47¹ 4↑ Oaklawn H-G1 6 4 32 21 45 47¾ Pincay L Jr 119 1.70 89-17 Opening Verse1182¼De Roche1142Silver Survivor1163½ 8
Wide first turn
1Apr90- 8SA fst 1⅛ :46 1:09³ 1:34² 1:47¹ 4↑ San Bernardino H-G2 1 3 32½ 34½ 23 22 Pincay L Jr 119 1.70 98-11 Rhlmnn1232CrmnlTyp1191½StylshWnnr113¾ Winner too tough 6
4Mar90- 8SA fst 1¼ :45⁴ 1:09⁴ 1:34⁴ 2:01¹ 4↑ S Anita H-G1 9 5 77 26 24 21¾ Solis A 119 5.80 86-18 Ruhlmann1211¾Criminal Type119hdFlying Continental121½ 10
Wide into lane
11Feb90- 8SA fst 1⅛ :45² 1:09⁴ 1:36 1:49 4↑ San Antonio H-G2 2 3 35 33 1½ 11 Solis A 117 4.70 91-14 CrimnlTyp1171StylshWnnr1136½Rhlmnn1224½ Strong effort 7
28Jan90- 8SA fst 1 1/16 :22⁴ :46 1:10³ 1:42² 4↑ San Pasqual H-G2 7 3 32½ 21½ 21 1½ McCarron CJ 114 7.60 91-19 CriminalType114½LivelyOne122½PresentValue1214½ Driving 8
12Jan90- 8SA fst 1 :22² :45⁴ 1:10² 1:36 4↑ Alw 47000 7 4 42½ 42 3½ 11¼ Pincay L Jr 122 1.40 87-22 Criminal Type1221¼Script1112Lowell1152 Wide final ⅜ 7
17Dec89- 7Hol fst 1 :23 :45⁴ 1:10 1:34³ 3↑ Alw 30000 3 1 2hd 2hd 12 15 Pincay L Jr 118 *1.30 91-14 CriminlType1185GoodDeliverance1163½Chrltn1161¾ Driving 8
18Nov89- 6Hol fst 1 :22³ :45¹ 1:09³ 1:34² 3↑ Alw 30000 3 2 31 41½ 42½ 33¼ Pincay L Jr 121 3.10 89-17 KingTaufan1181¼GoodDeliverance1162CrimnlType1211 Wide 7
2Nov89- 7SA fst 1 :23³ :47¹ 1:11⁴ 1:35³ 3↑ Alw 37000 4 1 1hd 2hd 3nk 2no Pincay L Jr 119 *1.20 91-16 Splurgr111noCrmnlTyp119¾Mr.DndyDncr1154½ Bumped start 6
22Oct89- 5SA gd 1⅛⊗ :46 1:10 1:35¹ 1:47⁴ 3↑ Alw 37000 4 1 11 11 2hd 2hd Delahoussaye E 119 3.80 96-09 Sepoy117hdCriminlType1197Charlatan117¾ Ducked in,bumped 8
8Oct89- 3SA fst 1 1/16 :23³ :47 1:11 1:42³ 3↑ Alw 34000 7 2 1hd 1hd 1hd 1½ McCarron CJ 118 4.70 88-17 Criminal Type118½Kaboi1143Stephen's Sooner1172¾ 7
Jostled early,driving
13May89- 7Hol fst 1 1/16 :23¹ :47¹ 1:11² 1:43³ 4↑ Alw 28000 2 5 31 1hd 2hd 31½ McCarron CJ 116 *1.40 80-11 Remar116nkPureExpense1191¼CrmnlTyp1162½ Lacked response 7
24Apr89- 9SA fm 1⅛Ⓣ :46³ 1:11² 1:36³ 1:49³ 3↑ Alw 36000 3 6 54 42¾ 54¼ 48¼ McCarron CJ 120 *1.90 71-19 NorthrnDrama112¾OrneryGuest1143ElitRgnt1224½ No mishap 9
12Apr89- 7SA fst 1 1/16 :23³ :47¹ 1:11 1:42² 4↑ Alw 36000 7 5 4¾ 1½ 2½ 33¼ Pincay L Jr 118 *2.30 86-14 Awesome Bud120¾Elite Regent1202½Criminal Type1181 8
Previously trained by Patrick-Louis Biancone
5Nov88♦ Saint-Cloud(Fr) sf *1½ⓉLH 2:36⁴ Prix Le Fabuleux (Listed) Stk33600 833 Kessas JL 121 33.00 Robore1233Valuable1204Plaza Gizon1261½ 8
Chased in 4th behind clear leader,weakened 2f out
28Sep88♦ Saint-Cloud(Fr) fm*1½ⓉLH 2:34³ Prix Sicambre (Listed) Stk31900 57 Legrix E 123 13.00 Hello Calder1232Andaroun1230Opposite Abstract1231 5
Tracked slow pace in 3rd,4th 2f out,weakened final furlong
27Sep87♦ Longchamp(Fr) yl *1ⓉRH 1:44² Prix des Chenes-G3 Stk56000 67 Boeuf D 121 5.00 Harmless Albatross1182½Baranof1212½Titus Groan121hd 9
In touch in 5th,never threatened
24Aug87♦ Deauville(Fr) sf *1ⓉRH 1:46⁴ Prix de Caen Mdn21100 1½ Boeuf D 123 5.20 Criminal Type123½Pintoriccio1231½Antiqua123nk 7
Tracked in 4th,taken wide into stretch 3f out,led 100y out
3Aug87♦ Clairefontaine(Fr) sf *1ⓉRH 1:41³ Prix des Tritons Alw13600 2no Boeuf D 119 10.00 Hymen119noCriminal Type119½Le Play1191½ 13
Tracked in 3rd,bid 1½f out,led 170y out,caught on line

Dance Smartly

dkbbr. f. 1988, by Danzig (Northern Dancer)–Classy 'n Smart, by Smarten — Lifetime record: 17 12 2 3 $3,263,836

Own.– Sam-Son Farms
Br.– Sam-Son Farms (Can)
Tr.– James E. Day

5Sep92- 9AP fm 1 3/16Ⓣ :48⁴ 1:12² 1:36¹ 1:54 3↑ ⒻBeverly D-G1 6 2 2½ 2½ 21½ 31¾ Day P L 123 *1.60e 94-08 Kostroma1231½RubyTiger123nkDanceSmartly1232 Mild rally 13
15Aug92- 9AP gd 1 1/16Ⓣ :23⁴ :47² 1:12 1:42² 3↑ ⒻArl Bud BC H 154k 4 2 21½ 21½ 1hd 32 Day P 123 *.20 92-13 Alcando1131¼Explosive Kate112¾Dance Smartly1233 Faded 6
19Jly92- 8WO sf 1⅜Ⓣ :51² 1:18³ 1:44² 2:12² ⓇMaturity-G1C 5 1 2hd 1½ 11½ 1½ Day P L 121 *.05e 39-61 DnceSmrtly121½SwordDance1262½ShinyKey126nk Ridden out 6
14Jun92- 7WO fm 1⅛Ⓣ :44⁴ 1:09 1:34 1:46 3↑ K Edward Gold Cup-G3 1 6 66½ 63¾ 2hd 2no Day P L 119 *.40e 97-06 ThundrRegnt113noDncSmrtly1191½TotofRum1193 Just missed 11
2Nov91- 4CD fst 1⅛ :47¹ 1:11⁴ 1:37⁴ 1:50⁴ 3↑ ⒻBC Distaff-G1 10 5 65½ 42½ 1hd 11½ Day P LB 120 *.50e 94-09 DnceSmrtly1201½Versailles Treaty1202¾BroughttoMind123½ 13
Driving clear
15Sep91- 9WO fst 1⅛ :48² 1:12¹ 1:36⁴ 1:49¹ Molson Million-G2 10 3 21 2½ 2hd 12 Day P 116 1.65 106-11 Dance Smartly1162Shudanz1176Majesterian1171 Hand ride 10
18Aug91- 8WO yl 1½Ⓣ :47 1:12 2:05⁴ 2:31² ⓇBreeders'-G1C 6 3 33½ 11½ 14½ 18 Day P 121 *.30e 83-17 Dance Smartly1218Shiny Key126hdJanuary Man1265 Handily 10
28Jly91- 8FE fst 1 3/16 :45⁴ 1:10 1:36³ 1:56³ ⓇPrince of Wales-G1C 5 3 32 32 11½ 12 Day P 121 *.10e 99-03 DnceSmrtly1212ProfssorRbbt1262¾Shudnz1264¾ Ridden out 6
7Jly91- 8WO fst 1¼ :47² 1:11⁴ 1:37¹ 2:03² ⓇQueens Plate-G1C 3 4 42 32 11½ 18 Day P 121 *.55e 91-15 DanceSmartly1218WildernessSong1213½Shudanz126½ Easily 9
16Jun91- 8WO fst 1⅛ :48 1:12³ 1:38³ 1:51¹ ⒻⓇCan Oaks-G1C 3 3 21½ 2½ 1hd 14½ Day P 121 *.05e 96-19 DanceSmrtly1214½Wilderness Song12110Platinum Paws1211½ 8
Hand ride
1Jun91- 9WO fst 1 1/16 :24 :48³ 1:12² 1:43³ ⒻSelene-G1C 6 3 32 32½ 2hd 13¼ Swatuk B 120 *.50e 96-10 DnceSmrtly1203¼ThroughFlight123nkAreydne113hd Handily 9
4May91- 9WO fst 6f :22² :45³ 1:10³ ⒻStar Shoot-G3C 2 6 42½ 31 1½ 12½ Swatuk B 120 *.35e 92-14 DanceSmrtly1202½DiamondSyl1164½Areydne1141¼ Hand ride 7
27Oct90- 4Bel fst 1 1/16 :22³ :45⁴ 1:11 1:44 ⒻBC Juv Fillies-G1 7 1 1hd 1hd 22 36 Hawley S 119 b 13.50e 76-15 MeadwStr1195PrivatTreasur1191DncSmrtly1194½ Weakened 13
15Sep90- 7WO yl 1Ⓣ :23² :46⁴ 1:11⁴ 1:39² ⒻNatalma (Div 1)-G2C 3 1 1½ 1hd 12 1½ Hawley S 116 b *1.10 77-18 DanceSmrtly116½ⒹLadyBeGreat1144½Malbay1141½ In hand 8
13Aug90- 8FE sly 6f :23 :47 1:13¹ ⒻⓇOnt Deb-G2C 7 1 41½ 33 21 22½ Hawley S 116 *.45 81-20 RegalPennant1152½DanceSmrtly1167¼UnrlAffr1161½ Mild bid 8
1Aug90- 8WO fst 5½f :22² :46¹ 1:05 ⒻAlw 23200 4 1 2hd 1hd 12½ 14¾ Hawley S 116 *.50 95-10 DanceSmartly1164¾SilentBattle1164Kaydann117nk Hand ride 8
7Jly90- 3WO fst 5½f :22⁴ :46¹ 1:06¹ ⒻMd Sp Wt 3 6 43 22 11 13½ Driedger I 114 *.50 89-11 Dance Smartly1143½Kaydanna119¾Chili Lee1192½ Authority 6

Daylami (Ire)

gr. c. 1994, by Doyoun (Mill Reef)–Daltawa, by Miswaki — Lifetime record: 21 11 3 4 $4,594,647

Own.– Godolphin Racing Inc
Br.– His Highness the Aga Khan's Studs S.C. (Ire)
Tr.– Saeed bin Suroor

6Nov99- 9GP gd 1½Ⓣ :47 1:10³ 2:24³ 3↑ BC Turf-G1 3 6 54½ 33 2hd 12½ Dettori L L 126 *1.60 94-02 Dylm1262½RoylAnthm1262Buck'sBoy1261¼ Drew clear,driving 14
3Oct99♦ Longchamp(Fr) hy *1½ⓉRH 2:38² 3↑ Prix de l'Arc de Triomphe-G1 Stk1432000 923½ Dettori L 131 4.00 Montjeu123½El Condor Pasa1316Croco Rouge1315 14
Unhurried in 8th,weakened 1½f out
11Sep99♦ Leopardstwn(Ire) sf 1¼ⓉLH 2:08² 3↑ Irish Champion Stakes-G1 Stk897000 19 Dettori L 130 1.50 Daylami1309Dazzling Park1202½Dream Well130½ 7
Tracked in 3rd,led over 1½f out,drew clear.Royal Anthem 5th
24Jly99♦ Ascot(GB) gd 1½ⓉRH 2:29² 3↑ King George VI & Queen Eliz St-G1 Stk954000 15 Dettori L 133 3.00 Daylami1335Nedawi133½Fruits of Love1332½ 8
Rated in 4th,5th 3f out,led 1½f out,drew clear.Oath 7th
4Jun99♦ Epsom(GB) yl 1½ⓉLH 2:40¹ 4↑ Coronation Cup-G1 Stk324000 1¾ Dettori L 126 4.50 Daylami126¾Royal Anthem1262Dream Well1261 7
Rated in 4th behind slow pace,long drive to lead 100y out
23May99♦ The Curragh(Ire) gd 1 5/16ⓉRH 2:10³ 4↑ Tattersalls Gold Cup-G1 Stk134000 22½ Dettori L 126 *1.00 Shiva1232½Daylami1261Make No Mistake1261½ 6
Tracked leader,led 2f out,headed 1f out,2nd best.Insatiable 4th
28Mar99♦ NadAlShba(UAE) fst*1¼LH 2:00³ 4↑ Dubai World Cup-G1 Stk5000000 54¼ Velazquez JR 126 - Almutawakel126¾Malek126¾Victory Gallop1261½ 8
Tracked leaders,bumped after 3f,trailed halfway,mild late gain
17Oct98♦ Newmarket(GB) gd *1¼ⓉStr 2:03³ 3↑ Champion Stakes-G1 Stk641000 32¼ Dettori L 128 *1.20 Alborada120nkInsatiable1282Daylami1281 10
Rated in 6th,outpaced 3f out,bid 2f out,briefly 2nd,faded late

12Sep98- 9Bel fm 1⅜T :484 1:134 1:374 2:13 3↑ Man o' War-G1 2 5 5½ 6¾ 44 1¼ Bailey JD L 126 *1.25 94-10 Dylm126¼Buck'sBoy126¾IndyVdul126hd Finished fast,clear 9
25Jly98♦ Ascot(GB) gd 1½ⓉRH 2:29 3↑ King George & Queen Eliz St-G1 Stk994000 43 Kinane MJ 133 6.00 Swain1331High-Rise1211½Royal Anthem121½ 8
Tracked in 4th,mild bid & drifted right 1½f out,one-paced late
4Jly98♦ Sandown(GB) gd 1¼ⓉRH 2:064 3↑ Eclipse Stakes-G1 Stk397000 1½ Dettori L 133 *1.50 Daylami133½Faithful Son1336Central Park122½ 7
Tracked in 4th,rallied to lead 2f out,ridden out
16Jun98♦ Ascot(GB) yl 1¼ⓉRH 2:081 3↑ Prince of Wales's Stakes-G2 Stk196000 3½ Dettori L 134 *2.00 Faithful Son129nkChester House117nkDaylami1343½ 8
Tracked in 3rd,bid & in tight 1½f out,angled out,gaining late
24May98♦ The Curragh(Ire) gd 1¼ⓉRH 2:061 4↑ Tattersalls Gold Cup-G2 Stk106000 11½ Dettori L 130 *1.25 Daylami1301½Stage Affair1243Quws1277 5
Tracked in 3rd,led over 1f out,driving.Dr Johnson 4th,Ebadiyla 5th;
Previously owned by H.H. Aga Khan;previously trained by Alain de Royer-Dupre
7Sep97♦ Longchamp(Fr) gd *1ⓉRH 1:37 3↑ Prix du Moulin de Longchamp-G1 Stk251000 33½ Mosse G 123 3.50 Spinning World1283Helissio128½Daylami123nk 9
Rated in 6th,finished well without threatening.Rebecca Sharp 7th
17Aug97♦ Deauville(Fr) gd *1ⓉStr 1:342 3↑ Prix Jacques le Marois-G1 Stk275000 22 Mosse G 123 2.50 Spinning World1302Daylami1236Neuilly1233 6
Behind,rallied to lead briefly 1½f out,2nd best.Starborough 4th
17Jun97♦ Ascot(GB) gd 1ⓉRH 1:381 St James's Palace Stakes-G1 Stk373000 35 Mosse G 126 3.50 Starborough1261Air Express1264Daylami126½ 8
Rated in 6th,angled out 2f out,one-paced late.Desert King 4th
11May97♦ Longchamp(Fr) sf *1ⓉRH 1:423 Poule d'Essai des Poulains-G1 Stk294000 12 Mosse G 128 1.60 Daylami1282Loup Sauvage1282½Visionary128¾ 6
Rated in last,sharp run to lead 100y out,driving.Yalaietanee 4th
20Apr97♦ Longchamp(Fr) gd *1ⓉRH 1:394 Prix de Fontainebleau-G3 Stk62800 12 Mosse G 128 2.00 Daylami1282Loup Sauvage128noFine Fellow1281 6
Tracked in 3rd,led 170y out,driving.Majorien 4th
2Nov96♦ Saint-Cloud(Fr) sf *1¼ⓉLH 2:154 Criterium de Saint-Cloud-G1 Stk133000 2¾ Mosse G 126 *.80e Shaka126¾Daylami1262Sendoro1262½ 10
Unhurried in 8th,rallied to lead 1f out,soon headed,second best
7Oct96♦ Evry(Fr) gd *1ⓉLH 1:442 Prix Herod (Listed) Stk46700 12 Mosse G 128 *.60 Daylami1282Bartex1282Herakles128nk 6
Tracked leader,led 1f out,easily clear
16Sep96♦ Longchamp(Fr) yl *1ⓉRH 1:482 Prix de Fontenoy-EBF Mdn (FT)34900 11½ Mosse G 128 *1.60 Daylami1281½Rate Cut128nkVisionary1282 9
Rated in 6th,led 1f out,not fully extended

Dehere

b. c. 1991, by Deputy Minister (Vice Regent)–Sister Dot, by Secretariat **Lifetime record: 9 6 2 0 $723,712**
Own.– Due Process Stable
Br.– Due Process Stable (Ky)
Tr.– Reynaldo H. Nobles

19Feb94- 9GP gd 1 1/16 :224 :453 1:102 1:443 Fountain of Youth-G2 6 5 58½ 53 1½ 1¾ Perret C L 119 2.40e 87-19 Dehere119¾Go for Gin1191¼Ride the Rails1173¾ 6
Five wide final turn,driving
5Feb94- 1GP fst 1 1/16 :241 :482 1:124 1:433 Alw 38610 1 1 1½ 1½ 1hd 2¾ Smith ME L 115 *.10 91-12 Ride the Rails115¾Dehere11512Senor Conquistador1153 4
Set pace,four wide backstr,gave way grudgingly
6Nov93- 6SA fst 1 1/16 :223 :462 1:104 1:424 B C Juvenile-G1 7 4 44½ 31 42½ 812½ McCarron CJ B 122 *.70 77-10 Brocco1225BluminAffair1221½TabascoCat1223 Bid,gave way 11
16Oct93- 7Bel fst 1 :231 :463 1:12 1:354 Champagne-G1 2 2 23 21 12 14 McCarron CJ 122 *.30 89-12 Dehere1224Crary122¾Amathos122½ Ridden out 6
18Sep93- 6Bel sly 7f :222 :453 1:101 1:231 Futurity-G1 4 5 41½ 34 32½ 2½ McCarron CJ 122 *.40 86-14 Holy Bull122½Dehere1225Prenup1228 Bumped break,wide 6
29Aug93- 8Sar fst 6½f :222 :453 1:092 1:154 Hopeful-G1 3 1 1hd 2hd 1½ 12½ McCarron CJ 122 *.40 96-09 Dehere1222½Slew Gin Fizz1222Whitney Tower1221¼ Handily 7
13Aug93- 8Sar fst 6f :221 :454 :581 1:102 Sanford-G3 2 5 52 51½ 1½ 15 McCarron CJ 122 *.40 90-07 Dehere1225Prenup1225½Distinct Reality1222¾ 6
Blocked,altered course,driving
29Jly93- 9Sar fst 6f :214 :45 :572 1:094 Saratoga Special-G2 1 9 31 41½ 52 1nk Maple E 117 *2.10 93-10 Dehere117nkSlew Gin Fizz1172Whitney Tower1175¾ 9
Broke slowly,steadied,alt course ⅛ pl,driving
30Jun93- 5Mth fst 5f :222 :463 :59 Md Sp Wt 1 12 63¼ 64¾ 32½ 14 Bravo J 118 *.90 86-19 Dehere1184Justinthefastlane1184¾Luckie Peri1184 12
Broke slow,5-wide,ridden out

Eliza

b. f. 1990, by Mt. Livermore (Blushing Groom)–Daring Bidder, by Bold Bidder **Lifetime record: 12 5 2 2 $1,095,316**
Own.– Allen E. Paulson
Br.– Allen E. Paulson (Ky)
Tr.– Alex L. Hassinger Jr

28Dec94- 3SA fst 6½f :22 :443 1:083 1:15 3↑ ⒻⓇMarket Basket 60k 8 5 53 31 33 44½ Stevens GL LB 115 3.30 92-10 KeyPhrase1141Pirat'sRvng1163½VlvtTulp122no Wide to turn 8
10Oct94- 8SA fst 1 1/16 :23 :47 1:103 1:403 3↑ ⒻLady's Secret H 106k 2 4 41½ 31 410 523¾ Antley CW L 119 4.50 68-17 Hollywood Wildcat1242½Exchange1213Dancing Mirage11314 5
Off step slow,pinched after start
3Sep94- 5Dmr fst 6½f :214 :44 1:082 1:144 3↑ ⒻⓇJune Darling 66k 7 3 1½ 13 12 33 Valnzuela PA LB 120 *1.40 94-06 Starolamo1162¾Nijivision114nkEliza120½ Speed,weakened 7
19Jun93- 8Hol fst 1 1/16 :223 :452 1:09 1:422 ⒻPrincess-G2 1 1 11½ 12 21 48¼ Valnzuela PA LB 119 *.30 81-11 FittoLead117hdSwazi'sMoment115hdPassingVic1198 Faltered 5
30Apr93- 9CD fst 1⅛ :47 1:122 1:383 1:522 ⒻKy Oaks-G1 8 5 54½ 31 2hd 21¼ Valnzuela PA L 121 *.60 81-17 Disput1211¼Elz121nkQunpool121nk Made lead,weakened late 11
3Apr93- 5SA fst 1⅛ :464 1:101 1:352 1:49 S A Derby-G1 4 2 2½ 1½ 2hd 31 Valnzuela PA LB 117 3.20 84-12 Personal Hope122¾Union City122nkEliza1171½ Game try 7
7Mar93- 8SA fst 1 1/16 :23 :471 1:11 1:424 ⒻS A Oaks-G1 7 2 2½ 12 15 12¼ Valnzuela PA LB 117 1.80 81-14 Eliza1172¼Stalcreek1171Dance for Vanny1171¾ Driving 9
31Oct92- 5GP fst 1 1/16 :231 :47 1:103 1:424 ⒻB C Juv Fillies-G1 9 3 3nk 11 11½ 11 Valnzuela PA L 119 *1.20 98-03 Eliza1191EducatedRsk119½Botts'nJck1195½ Strong handling 12
17Oct92- 8Kee fst 1 1/16 :223 :461 1:10 1:431 ⒻAlcibiades-G2 3 2 2 11½ 17 14 Valnzuela PA LB 118 *.80 88-23 Eliza1184Avie's Shadow1185True Affair1184 Easily 6
19Sep92-10AP fst 1 :233 :463 1:122 1:392 ⒻArl Lassie-G2 2 1 12 13 18 112 Valnzuela PA L 119 *.90 69-35 Eliza11912Banshee Winds1193Tourney1191½ Stumbled 6
19Aug92- 8Dmr fst 7f :214 :441 1:092 1:223 ⒻSorrento-G3 7 2 1½ 11½ 1hd 23½ Valnzuela PA B 117 *1.10 83-12 Zoonaqua1173½Eliza1171Medici Bells117nk Held 2nd 11
9Aug92- 6Dmr fst 5½f :211 :44 :562 1:03 ⒻMd Sp Wt 6 6 3½ 1hd 11 12¼ Stevens GL 117 1.90 96-05 Eliza1172¼Set Them Free1175Nijivision1172 Handily 10

Escena

b. f. 1993, by Strawberry Road (Whiskey Road)–Claxton's Slew, by Seattle Slew **Lifetime record: 29 11 9 3 $2,962,639**
Own.– Allen E. Paulson
Br.– Allen E. Paulson (Ky)
Tr.– William I. Mott

7Nov98- 8CD fst 1⅛ :473 1:12 1:37 1:494 3↑ ⒻBC Distaff-G1 7 1 12 12 11½ 1no Stevens GL L 123 3.00 95-07 Escena123noBansheBrz1205KprHll120½ Out in strip,driving 8
28Aug98- 8Sar fst 1¼ :474 1:123 1:374 2:04 3↑ ⒻPersonal Ensign H-G1 3 1 1½ 11 1hd 66 Bailey JD L 123 *.85 82-16 Tomisue's Delight1152Tuzia114nkOne Rich Lady1141½ 8
Set pace,gave way
2Aug98- 8Sar fst 1⅛ :472 1:112 1:361 1:494 3↑ ⒻGo for Wand H-G1 5 1 11 1hd 1hd 2no Bailey JD L 124 *.30 87-16 Aldiza114noEscn1243Tomsu'sDlght1162 Dug in determinedly 7
27Jun98- 7Hol fst 1⅛ :481 1:113 1:353 1:48 3↑ ⒻVanity Inv H-G1 6 2 2hd 1hd 1½ 12 Bailey JD LB 124 *.40 86-18 Escena1242HousDncr11510Dffrnt119¾ Dueled,led,clear late 7
6Jun98-10CD fst 1⅛ :482 1:123 1:372 1:50 3↑ ⒻFleur de Lis H-G3 3 1 1½ 11 13 16 Sellers SJ L 123 *.60 94-19 Escena1236One Rich Lady1131½Tomisue's Delight1186 5
Pace,steady drive
1May98- 7CD fst 1 1/16 :234 :473 1:121 1:444 3↑ ⒻLouisville BC H-G2 3 3 41½ 2hd 13½ 14 Bailey JD L 119 *.70 87-14 Escena1194One Rich Lady1133½Three Fanfares109hd 10
Drew clear stretch
10Apr98-10OP fst 1 1/16 :224 :461 1:101 1:404 4↑ ⒻApple Blossom H-G1 7 4 3½ 11 13 12½ Bailey JD L 117 3.10 104-13 Escena1172½Glitter Woman1195Toda Una Dama1157 7
Confident handling 3w
1Mar98-10GP fst 1 1/16 :241 :474 1:12 1:443 3↑ ⒻRampart H-G2 5 2 21 2½ 1hd 22 Bailey JD L 119 1.70 82-24 Dance for Thee1132Escena119½GlitterWoman1216¼ 6
Not good enough

1Feb98- 9GP fst 1 70 :24 :48 1:114 1:411 3↑ ⒻSabin H-G3 3 4 32 21 2½ 2hd Bailey JD L 119 *.70 90-14 Radiant Megan113hdEscena119¾Biding Time1131½ Sharp 7
8Nov97- 4Hol fst 1⅛ :454 1:091 1:342 1:471 3↑ ⒻB C Distaff-G1 7 5 41¾ 21½ 31 35½ Bailey JD LB 123 4.80e 84-06 Ajina1202Sharp Cat1203½Escena1231 Best of rest 8
13Oct97- 9Bel fm 1⅛T :472 1:104 1:344 1:47 3↑ ⒻAthenia H-G3 3 1 1½ 1hd 31½ 45 Bailey JD L 119 *.60 100-10 Rapid Selection1131¼Dynasty114nkPreachersnightmare1113½ 6
Dueled,tired
24Aug97- 7AP gd 1 3/16Ⓣ :473 1:114 1:363 1:541 3↑ ⒻBeverly D-G1 3 2 21½ 21 41½ 65¼ Day P L 123 5.40 94-15 MemriesofSilver123nkMaxzene1233¼DanceDesign123no Tired 6
2Aug97- 8Dmr fm 1⅛Ⓣ :50 1:14 1:38 1:494 3↑ ⒻRamona H-G1 7 2 2½ 2hd 11 1¾ Day P LB 115 6.60 86-16 Escena115¾RealConnection1151¼Dffrnt121½ Clear 1/16,held 7
28Jun97- 9Bel fst 1 1/16 :223 :452 1:094 1:404 3↑ ⒻHempstead H-G1 9 5 42 41½ 56 510 Bailey JD L 115 9.10 85-13 Hidden Lake1172Twice the Vice1212Jewel Princess1245¼ 9
Chased wide,tired
24May97- 9Bel fst 1 :222 :443 1:094 1:351 3↑ ⒻShuvee H-G2 8 2 31½ 2hd 33 35 Day P L 116 3.30 83-17 HiddenLake1154FltFltFt1201Escn116¾ Forced pace,weakened 9
2May97- 7CD fst 1 1/16 :242 :481 1:121 1:423 3↑ ⒻLouisville BC H-G2 4 4 42½ 53½ 22 23½ Day P L 116 3.20 94-05 Halo America1203½Escena1164Rare Blend116½ 7
Broke in tangle,angled 4 wide stretch,2nd best
11Apr97- 9OP sf 1 1/16 :231 :463 1:104 1:413 4↑ ⒻApple Blossom H-G1 4 4 43 32½ 23 45½ Day P L 116 5.80 94-12 Halo America1174Jewel Princess124hdDifferent1211½ 8
Flattened out drive
12Mar97-10GP fm *1 1/16Ⓣ :241 :483 1:121 1:42 4↑ ⒻAlw 39000 5 1 1½ 1hd 1½ 11¼ Day P L 116 *.80 91-07 Escna1161¼RebeccaMae116¾Chris'Diamond1161½ Ridden out 8
8Sep96- 9Bel sly 1⅛ :454 1:094 1:35 1:48 ⒻGazelle H-G1 1 5 44½ 32½ 21½ 21¼ Day P L 121 2.90 89-16 MyFlag1211¼Escna1211¼TopScrt1172 Saved ground,2nd best 6
17Aug96- 8Sar wf 1¼ :483 1:131 1:374 2:03 ⒻAlabama-G1 4 2 21½ 1hd 2½ 24 Day P L 121 3.75 90-14 Yanks Music1214Escena121½My Flag1213¼ Bid,held 2nd 7
27Jly96- 8Sar wf 7f :212 :431 1:074 1:21 ⒻTest-G1 1 7 32½ 21½ 46 511½ Bailey JD L 115 *1.45 89-08 CapoteBelle1152½FlatFletFt1153½JJ'sdrm1234 Chased,tired 8
22Jun96- 9Bel wf 1⅛ :441 1:081 1:341 1:474 ⒻMother Goose-G1 3 3 3½ 11½ 11½ 2nk Day P L 121 *1.20 91-12 YanksMusic121nkEscena1215½CarRfl1216 Yielded grudgingly 7
3May96- 9CD fst 1⅛ :47 1:112 1:37 1:494 ⒻKy Oaks-G1 1 1 11 11½ 11 2nk Day P L 121 3.00 97-06 PikePlaceDancer121nkEscena1215½CrRfl1212 Could not last 6
5Apr96- 9OP fst 1 1/16 :232 :471 1:121 1:434 ⒻFantasy-G2 7 3 31 11 13 17 Day P 117 2.60 88-19 Escn1177Antspnd121½SkTrl117hd Stalked 3-wide,ridden out 7
13Mar96-10GP fst 1 1/16 :241 :483 1:133 1:453 ⒻBonnie Miss-G2 4 4 42 32 1hd 21½ Day P 114 4.00 77-29 My Flag1171½Escena1147¼La Rosa1175¾ 5
Threw head up st,away slowly,tried to get out 1st turn,best of rest
24Feb96- 6GP fst 1 1/16 :233 :474 1:122 1:442 ⒻAlw 30000 6 4 41¾ 1hd 14 14½ Bailey JD 117 *1.10 86-11 Escena1174½Bright Time117¾Marfa's Finale1174 Ridden out 10
25Nov95- 6Aqu fst 1⅛ :47 1:123 1:383 1:504 ⒻDemoiselle-G2 5 6 54 42 24 38¼ Bailey JD 112 2.60 78-09 La Rosa1148Quiet Dance114nkEscena11217 No late bid 7
26Oct95- 7Bel fst 6f :222 :46 :582 1:112 ⒻAlw 32000 4 6 52¼ 4¾ 11 12½ Bailey JD 116 *.45 84-17 Escena1162½Echo Echo Echo116¾Hello Brian118no 7
Steadied,blocked early
1Oct95- 2Bel fst 6f :222 :463 :584 1:113 ⒻMd Sp Wt 6 6 76¾ 52½ 11½ 14½ Perez RB 117 22.30 83-19 Escn1174½Crly'sCrown1179Adordncr1174 Five wide,going away 10

Favorite Trick

dkbbr. c. 1995, by Phone Trick (Clever Trick)–Evil Elaine, by Medieval Man **Lifetime record: 16 12 0 1 $1,726,793**
Own.– LaCombe Stables
Br.– Mr & Mrs M.L. Wood (Ky)
Tr.– William I. Mott

7Nov98- 7CD fm 1Ⓣ :231 :462 1:104 1:351 3↑ B C Mile-G1 3 1 3½ 1hd 32 87½ Day P L 123 *2.60 85-09 DaHoss126hdHawkslyHill1264¼Labeeb1261½ Dueled,weakened 14
17Oct98- 8Kee fm 1Ⓣ :221 :461 1:104 1:35 3↑ Kee B C Mile-G2 5 1 1½ 1½ 11½ 13½ Day P : 123 3.00 93-08 FavoriteTrick1233½SovietLine126noWildEvent1262 Driving 5
29Aug98- 7Sar fst 7f :22 :442 1:091 1:223 Kings Bishop-G2 7 1 54½ 59 51¾ 52 Day P L 124 *1.25 90-12 SecretFrm121¾Mnt121¾Sctmndu116nk Traffic inside stretch 8
9Aug98- 8Sar fst 1⅛ :464 1:112 1:363 1:50 Jim Dandy-G2 3 3 32½ 42 41¾ 1no Day P L 119 *1.95 86-22 Favorite Trick119noDeputyDiamond114nkRaffie'sMajsty1141½ 7
Split rivals,got nod
19Jly98- 9Mth fst 1 1/16 :232 :47 1:11 1:43 Long Branch 100k 3 1 1hd 1hd 1hd 1hd Day P L 116 *.20 86-14 FavrtTrck116hdTomrrowsCt1133½ArctcSwp1142¼ Long drive 6
2May98- 8CD fst 1¼ :453 1:103 1:353 2:021 Ky Derby-G1 7 5 46 54 710 812½ Day P L 126 4.40 82-02 Real Quiet126½Victory Gallop1262¼Indian Charlie126hd 15
Bid inside,tired
11Apr98- 9OP fst 1⅛ :46 1:104 1:372 1:494 Ark Derby-G2 8 2 2hd 1hd 11 3nk Day P L 122 *.40 87-10 Victory Gallop122hdHanuman Highway118hdFavriteTrick1223 9
Dueled,clear,weakened
14Mar98- 5GP fst 7f :221 :444 1:094 1:224 Swale-G3 5 4 42½ 42 22 11¾ Day P L 122 *.30 86-18 Favorite Trick1221¾Good and Tough114nkDice Dancer1132½ 9
Previously trained by Patrick B. Byrne
8Nov97- 6Hol fst 1 1/16 :223 :452 1:092 1:412 B C Juvenile-G1 3 3 31½ 11 12½ 15½ Day P LB 122 *1.20 94-06 Favorite Trick1225½Dawson's Legacy122nkNationalore122¾ 8
Inside,ridden out
18Oct97- 8Kee fst 1 1/16 :232 :463 1:111 1:431 Breeders' Futurity-G2 1 3 33 32½ 31 13 Day P L 121 *.40 92-21 Favorite Trick1213Time Limit121nkLaydown121½ 5
5 wide stretch,steady drive
30Aug97- 8Sar fst 7f :214 :45 1:103 1:234 Hopeful-G1 4 4 43 44 2½ 11½ Day P L 122 *.45 86-12 Favorite Trick1221½K.O. Punch1225Jess M1227½ Ridden out 7
13Aug97- 9Sar my 6½f :213 :444 1:101 1:17 Sar Spl-G2 1 3 32 2½ 11½ 13½ Day P L 122 *.70 92-19 Favorite Trick1223½Case Dismissed114nkK.O. Punch1198 5
Rail trip,drew clear
28Jun97- 9CD fst 6f :21 :444 :571 1:094 Bashford Manor-G3 8 3 32 21½ 21 14½ Day P L 121 *.50 94-08 FvrtTrck1214½DoublHonor1151½CowboyDn1184 Driving clear 8
26May97- 9CD gd 5½f :223 :462 :583 1:044 Ky B C 106k 8 4 43½ 41½ 13 18½ Day P L 121 *1.40 95-05 FavoriteTrick1218½JessM115nkCutieLuttie1125 Ridden out 8
3May97- 3CD fst 5f :214 :454 :583 WHAS 117k 9 2 3½ 2hd 2hd 1nk Day P L 117 7.00 95-05 FavritTrck117nkCowboyDn1207SoldrFld117½ Dueled,driving 13
25Apr97- 2Kee fst 4½f :231 :471 :531 Md Sp Wt 2 1 1hd 11½ 11½ Day P 118 *1.20 90-16 Favorite Trick1181½Bright Nova1187Northern Impact1185 8
Dueled,driving

Fiji (GB)

b. f. 1994, by Rainbow Quest (Blushing Groom)–Island Jamboree, by Explodent **Lifetime record: 12 8 1 2 $894,480**
Own.– HRH Prince Fahd bin Salman
Br.– Newgate Stud Company (GB)
Tr.– Neil Drysdale

15Oct99- 8Kee fm 1 3/16Ⓣ :474 1:113 1:363 1:534 3↑ ⒻVinery First Lady 558k 8 8 77½ 33½ 32½ 34¼ Bailey JD L 117 *1.40 98-00 Happyanunoit1194Pleasant Temper119nkFiji1171½ 9
Bid,no late response
2Oct99- 9SA fm 1¼Ⓣ :47 1:104 1:35 1:592 3↑ ⒻYellow Ribbon-G1 1 4 44½ 41¾ 62¾ 63½ Bailey JD LB 123 *2.00 87-10 Spanish Fern1231¼Caffe Latte1181¼Shabby Chic118½ 7
Chased,no late bid
8Nov98- 8SA fm 1¼Ⓣ :491 1:142 1:391 2:051 3↑ ⒻYellow Ribbon-G1 6 7 74¼ 31 1hd 12 Dsrmeaux KJ LB 122 *.80 62-38 Fij1222DSeeYouSoon1221¾Sonja'sFth122nk 3 wide bid,driving 10
1Aug98- 8Dmr fm 1⅛Ⓣ :49 1:123 1:36 1:472 3↑ ⒻRamona H-G1 4 7 74½ 63¼ 43¾ 36 Dsrmeaux KJ LB 125 *.40 92-03 See You Soon114½Sonja's Faith1135½Fiji1251¼ 8
Off bit slow,crowded,between foes,4-wide into lane
7Jun98- 6Hol fm 1⅛Ⓣ :473 1:104 1:343 1:472 3↑ ⒻGamely BC H-G1 5 6 52¼ 31 1hd 13 Dsrmeaux KJ LB 123 *.60 86-16 Fiji1233KoolKatKatie119nkSquek1161¾ Off slow,4-wide ½ 6
18Apr98- 7SA fm 1¼Ⓣ :473 1:12 1:36 2:001 4↑ ⒻS Barbara H-G2 1 3 33½ 1½ 13 15½ Dsrmeaux KJ LB 119 *.40 87-18 Fiji1195½Pomona1154Ecoute1141½ Clear,much best 5
21Mar98- 8SA fm 1⅛Ⓣ :50 1:143 1:381 1:494 4↑ ⒻS Ana H-G2 6 2 2½ 2hd 1½ 14½ Dsrmeaux KJ LB 115 *1.90 80-21 Fij1154½ShkthYok1161GoldnArchs120nk Gamely kicked clear 6
19Feb98- 2SA fm 1⅛Ⓣ :491 1:131 1:381 1:51 4↑ ⒻAlw 57000 4 3 2hd 11½ 15 19 Dsrmeaux KJ LB 117 *.40 74-30 Fiji1179Alzora1155Miss Universal116nk 6
Squeezed bit start,ridden out
25Jan98- 8SA fm 1Ⓣ :244 :482 1:12 1:353 4↑ ⒻAlw 50000 4 4 32 32 21 1½ Dsrmeaux KJ LB 116 *.90 81-23 Fiji116½Griega1154Ava Knowsthecode1151 Gamely 8
27Dec97- 3SA fm 1⅛Ⓣ :491 1:124 1:363 1:483 3↑ ⒻAlw 50200 6 1 11 1hd 2hd 2no Dsrmeaux KJ LB 114 2.10 87-13 Sixy Saint115noFiji1147½Signoretta1161¼ 7
Broke slowly,stumbled slightly,game effort;Previously trained by Henry Cecil
25Jly97♦ Chepstow(GB) gd 1¼ⓉLH 2:082 3↑ ⒻDaffodil Stakes (Listed) 1no Fallon K 119 3.00 Fiji119noBint Baladee1171¼Dances With Dreams118½ 8
Stk30700
Tracked in 4th,rallied to lead 3f out,hard ridden to hold
17Sep96♦ Sandown(GB) gd 1ⓉRH 1:432 ⒻEBF Maiden Stakes 11¾ Eddery Pat 123 *.55 Fiji1231¾Alphabet1231½Listed Account123no 7
Mdn8400
Led virtually throughout,ridden out

Flanders

ch. f. 1992, by Seeking the Gold (Mr. Prospector)–Starlet Storm, by Storm Bird — Lifetime record: 5 4 0 0 $805,000

Own.– Overbrook Farm
Br.– Overbrook Farm (Ky)
Tr.– D. Wayne Lukas

5Nov94- 5CD fst 1 1/16 :23 :461 1:112 1:451 ⒻB C Juv Fillies-G1 2 1 2hd 2½ 1hd 1hd Day P 119 *.40e 88-07 Flanders119hdSerena's Song1194Stormy Blues119½ 13
Stiff drive,brushed stretch,vanned off lame

8Oct94- 6Bel fst 1 1/16 :231 :464 1:121 1:434 ⒻFrizette-G1 1 1 13 14 110 121 Day P 119 *.30 83-17 Flanders11921Change Fora Dollar119¾Pretty Discreet11910 4
Ridden out

17Sep94- 4Bel fst 1 :23 :462 1:11 1:35 ⒻMatron-G1 4 1 11½ 1½ 1½ 13¼ Day P 119 *.60 88-10 Flanders1193¼Stormy Blues1194½Pretty Discreet119½ 6
Disqualified from purse money

29Aug94- 8Sar fst 7f :214 :444 1:101 1:23 ⒻSpinaway-G1 2 5 11 11½ 12½ 14¾ Day P 119 4.10 90-13 Flanders1194¾SeaBreezer119½StormyBlues119nk Mild drive 6

10Aug94- 5Sar fst 5f :223 :46 :58 ⒻMd Sp Wt 5 4 41½ 1hd 11 17½ Day P 117 f *.60 93-09 Flanders1177½Jovial Joust1176½Share the Fun117¾ Handily 8

Flat Top

dkbbr. g. 1993, by Alleged (Hoist the Flag)–Lady of the Light, by The Minstrel — Lifetime record: 14 6 2 0 $244,450

Own.– Mrs Henry A. Gerry
Br.– Landon Knight (Ky)
Tr.– Janet E. Elliot

22Nov98- 5Cam fm *2¾ Hurdles 5:112 4↑ Colonial Cup 100k 4 2 22 2½ 2½ 15¾ Ryan CG L 156 - -- Flat Top1565¾Romantic156nkDictador1561¼ Drew clear 8

24Oct98- 5FH fm *2⅝ Hurdles 4:552 4↑ Grand Nat'l BC H-G1 5 1 11 1½ 1½ 11¼ Patterson B L 156 - -- Flat Top1561¼Romantic156¾Mario1563½ Driving 7

4Oct98- 8Cnl gd 2¼ Hurdles 4:014 4↑ Ferguson Mem H-G2 9 1 12 2hd 1hd 1½ Patterson B L 142 6.10 -- FlatTop142½ApproachingSquall1421Mro1501¼ Dueled,driving 9

7Sep98- 1Sar yl *2 1/16 Hurdles 3:461 4↑ Handicap 45000 4 3 21½ 1hd 21½ 25½ Patterson B L 142 3.55e -- Romntc1525½FltTop1422SmnolSprt1302½ Good run final turn 8

12Aug98- 1Sar sf *2 1/16 Hurdles 3:444 4↑ Alw 40000 5 1 13½ 11½ 2hd 53½ Kingsley A Jr L 148 *1.90e -- Grenade1482½It's a Giggle146noDalton River148¾ 7
Struggled after last

1Nov97- 3Pmt yl *2⅜ Hurdles 4:09 3↑ ⓇUS ChSupreme 75k 4 2 1½ 11 2¾ 22½ Clancy S L 149 - -- Teb's Blend1452½Flat Top1492Willstown14527 Gamely 6

11Oct97- 4Mor fm *2¼ Hurdles 4:19 3↑ ⓇArt McCashin 30k 4 1 11¼ 1¾ 11 1no Clancy S L 145 16.30 -- Flat Top145noDictador1502½Clearance Code150no Driving 9

1Jun97- 3Suf fm *2¼ Hurdles 4:243 4↑ Alw 14700 7 2 22½ 2½ 45½ 410¾ Delozier JW III L 146 2.40 -- Brigade of Guards1551¼Thelightfntistic1515Gliding1434½ 7
Chased,stopped

17May97- 3Mal hd *2¼ Hurdles 4:26 3↑ Alw 20000 6 2 45½ 55 44½ 410¾ Delozier JW III L 142 - -- SmartJaune1448StreetView1482½BrgdofGurds148nk No excuse 6

17Nov96- 3Cam fm *2 5/16 Hurdles 4:15 RG Woolfe Mem 25k 12 1 1¾ 1½ 1½ 12 Teter J L 149 - -- Flat Top1492Ratify1492Tomahawk Warrior1451 Driving 12
Previously owned by Timothy-N-Rye Stable;previously trained by Jeff Teter

5Oct96- 6Mid gd *2⅛ Hurdles 4:093 Md Sp Wt 3 3 520 23 2hd 11½ Teter J L 150 - -- FlatTop1501½Soaringoversettl1506Hrdhddrshmn1508 Driving 14
Previously owned by Kenneth L. & Sarah K. Ramsey;previously trained by Niall M. O'Callaghan

27May96- 7AP sly 1 :231 :472 1:151 1:44 3↑ Md 10000 8 4 813 828 845 848 Gryder AT 113 b 7.30 -- Skat Kat1221¾Go Big Red1084Longhaul Titus108½ 8
Gave way,eased

17May96- 4CD fst 1 1/16 :232 :471 1:121 1:451 3↑ Md 15000 11 9 1015 1116 1224 1226¾ Bourque CC L 114 6.30 58-11 StardustMiner1193LightHeart1152½Andrewsmyman1051¼ 12
Never close

23Mar96- 6FG fm *1Ⓣ :242 :49 1:134 1:392 Md Sp Wt 2 9 911 1011 911 812½ Emigh CA 119 12.60 72-17 ChiefBerhrt1194MstrEy1191½Chorwon1191½ Lugged out early 12

Flawlessly

b. f. 1988, by Affirmed (Exclusive Native)–La Confidence, by Nijinsky II — Lifetime record: 28 16 4 3 $2,572,536

Own.– Harbor View Farm
Br.– Harbor View Farm (Ky)
Tr.– Charles Whittingham

27Aug94- 6AP fm 1 3/16Ⓣ :473 1:113 1:364 1:552 3↑ ⒻBeverly D-G1 8 4 55 43½ 21½ 2½ McCarron CJ L 123 *2.00 89-09 Hatoof123½Flawlessly123½Potridee123½ Prominent late 8

6Aug94- 8Dmr fm 1⅛Ⓣ :473 1:113 1:361 1:481 3↑ ⒻRamona H-G1 1 4 46 41 1hd 1hd McCarron CJ LB 124 1.30 95-02 Flwlssly124hdHollywdWldct1241¼Skmbl1162 4 wide 2nd turn 5

3Jly94- 8Hol fm 1⅛Ⓣ :48 1:111 1:35 1:472 3↑ ⒻBeverly Hills H-G1 1 4 42½ 41¾ 51¾ 3nk McCarron CJ LB 124 1.60 87-14 Corrazona119nkHollywood Wildcat124noFlawlessly1241 7
Lacked room on rail ¼-⅛

12Jun94- 8Hol fm 1⅛Ⓣ :464 1:10 1:341 1:462 3↑ ⒻGamely H-G1 5 6 65½ 52¼ 32 35 McCarron CJ LB 124 *.70 87-10 Hollywood Wildcat1222¼Mz. Zill Bear1142¾Flawlessly124nk 6
Broke slightly in air,5 wide 2nd turn

28Nov93- 7Hol fm 1⅛Ⓣ :47 1:104 1:343 1:463 3↑ ⒻMatriarch-G1 2 5 63¾ 51¾ 1½ 1nk McCarron CJ LB 123 *.90 91-09 Flwlssly123nkToussud1232Skmbl123hd Awaited room 2nd turn 7

6Nov93- 5SA fm 1Ⓣ :223 :454 1:092 1:332 3↑ BC Mile-G1 4 5 74½ 77 99 910 McCarron CJ LB 123 3.10 88-04 Lure1262¼Ski Paradise1201¾Fourstars Allstar126hd 13
Tight quarters 1st turn

28Aug93- 9AP gd 1 3/16Ⓣ :492 1:133 1:38 1:553 3↑ ⒻBeverly D-G1 2 3 21½ 21 11 2no McCarron CJ L 123 *.50 88-11 ⒹLet'sElope123noFlawlssly123nkVBorghs123no Bumped late 7
Placed first through disqualification

7Aug93- 8Dmr fm 1⅛Ⓣ :47 1:104 1:354 1:481 3↑ ⒻRamona H-G1 2 2 26 33½ 21½ 11 McCarron CJ LB 125 *.90 95-03 Flawlessly1251Heart of Joy1141Let's Elope118½ 7
Floated out ¼,brushed 3/16,ridden out

27Jun93- 8Hol fm 1⅛Ⓣ :481 1:112 1:351 1:47 3↑ ⒻBeverly Hills H-G1 4 3 31½ 2½ 12½ 19 McCarron CJ LB 123 .90 89-11 Flwlssly1239Jolyph121noPrtyCtd1172 Drew off,kept to task 4

29Nov92- 7Hol fm 1⅛Ⓣ :471 1:104 1:34 1:46 3↑ ⒻMatriarch-G1 6 5 53½ 53 33½ 11 McCarron CJ LB 123 *1.40 94-07 Flawlessly1231Super Staff1232Kostroma123½ Strong finish 9

8Nov92- 8SA fm 1¼Ⓣ :471 1:112 1:35 1:591 3↑ ⒻYellow Ribbon Inv'l-G1 7 4 43 21½ 21 2no McCarron CJ LB 123 *.70 91-09 SuperStaff123noFlawlessly1233½Cmpgnrd123hd Resolute try 9

18Oct92- 8SA fm 1⅛Ⓣ :481 1:114 1:35 1:464 3↑ ⒻLas Palmas H-G2 4 3 33½ 32 21½ 2¾ McCarron CJ LB 124 *.50 84-22 Super Staff116¾Flawlessly1244Re Toss115½ Boxed in ⅜ 7

15Aug92- 8Dmr fm 1⅛Ⓣ :513 1:153 1:384 1:50 3↑ ⒻRamona H-G1 4 1 1½ 1½ 12 13 McCarron CJ LB 123 1.40 86-11 Flwlssly1233RToss115hdPolmc116½ Set slow pace,ridden out 7

28Jun92- 8Hol fm 1⅛Ⓣ :49 1:12 1:35 1:47 3↑ ⒻBeverly Hills H-G1 3 1 1hd 1½ 2hd 1hd McCarron CJ LB 122 1.90 89-12 Flawlessly122hdKostroma1241¾Alcando1131 Ultra game 5

1Dec91- 8Hol fm 1⅛Ⓣ :471 1:104 1:344 1:463 3↑ ⒻMatriarch-G1 3 7 84¾ 72¾ 1hd 11¾ McCarron CJ L 120 6.30 97-07 Flawlessly1201¾FirthGroom123½FrtLst123no 5-wide stretch 14

10Nov91- 8SA fm 1¼Ⓣ :492 1:142 1:374 2:01 3↑ ⒻYellow Ribbon-G1 6 3 32 31 42 22 McCarron CJ LB 119 5.00 81-17 Kostroma1232Flawlessly119½FiretheGroom123hd Good effort 13

5Oct91- 8SA fm 1Ⓣ :22 :454 1:102 1:332 ⒻH C Ramser H 112k 10 7 73¼ 2½ 2hd 1½ McCarron CJ LB 123 *.70 96-09 Flawlssly123½Gravieres1174½ZamaHummer1172 Game effort 10

25Aug91- 8Dmr fm 1⅛Ⓣ :482 1:131 1:373 1:492 ⒻDmr Oaks-G3 2 5 54 52 2hd 12 McCarron CJ L 120 *.70 91-09 Flawlessly1202SettlSymphony120½Fowd1201¼ Speed to spare 6

10Aug91- 8Dmr fm 1Ⓣ :231 :463 1:102 1:344 ⒻSan Clemente H 109k 8 6 54 4¾ 1½ 11¾ McCarron CJ L 120 *1.50 98-04 Flawlessly1201¾GoldFlc1142¼MssHghBld1172 4-wide stretch 9

5Jly91- 7Hol fm 1 1/16Ⓣ :24 :482 1:124 1:422 ⒻⓇStreet Dancer 61k 4 3 32½ 31 2hd 11¾ McCarron CJ L 118 *1.70 83-09 Flwlssly1181¾Jol'sPrncss114hdSprucory1143½ Strong effort 6
Previously trained by Richard E. Dutrow

19Jan91- 7Aqu fst 1 70⊡ :241 :472 1:111 1:414 ⒻBusanda 69k 7 3 44½ - - - Krone JA 121 *1.40 -- I'maThriller1124WinCraftyLady1165I'mTickldPnk112hd Bled 7

9Dec90- 8Aqu fst 1 1/16⊡ :241 :484 1:134 1:463 ⒻTempted-G3 4 6 51¾ 42 3nk 1hd Bailey JD 121 4.60 75-25 Flawlessly121hdDebutnt'sHlo1211½SlptThruIt1141¼ Driving 12

17Nov90- 8Aqu gd 1⅛ :50 1:153 1:41 1:534 ⒻDemoiselle-G2 6 1 1½ 1hd 2hd 44¼ Cordero A Jr 119 5.50 63-39 Debutant's Halo1162Private Treasure121nkSlept Thru It1122 7
Weakened

27Oct90- 4Bel fst 1 1/16 :223 :454 1:11 1:44 ⒻBC Juv Fillies-G1 5 12 1210 108½ 88½ 712¾ Pincay L Jr 119 46.20 69-15 Meadow Star1195Private Treasure1191Dance Smartly1194¼ 13
Improved position

6Oct90- 7Bel fst 1 :224 :461 1:11 1:352 ⒻFrizette-G1 1 3 2½ 21 26 314¼ Bailey JD 119 5.20 78-11 MeadwStr11914ChampagneGlow119nkFlwlssly1193¼ Weakened 5

27Sep90- 9Med fm 1 1/16Ⓣ :221 :461 1:111 1:433 ⒻGardenia-G3 15 7 63½ 42 2hd 14½ Bailey JD 112 7.50 79-21 Flawlessly1124½SweetSarita114noMadamSandie1121¾ Driving 15

14Sep90- 4Bel fst 6f :214 :451 1:11 ⒻMd Sp Wt 5 3 33½ 31 2hd 11¼ Bailey JD 117 8.90 84-16 Flawlessly1171¼I'm a Thriller117¾Boots1173 Driving 6

13Jun90- 4Bel fst 5f :221 :46 :584 ⒻMd Sp Wt 6 6 42½ 44 44½ 410 Cordero A Jr 117 8.50 84-20 MeadowStar1175¼WinCrafty Lady117¾My Fantazy1174 Tired 7

Fly So Free

ch. c. 1988, by Time for a Change (Damascus)–Free to Fly, by Stevward

Lifetime record: 33 12 5 3 $2,330,954

Own.– Thomas F. Valando
Br.– Bruce Hundley & Wayne Garrison (Ky)
Tr.– Flint S. Schulhofer

6Nov93- 2SA	ft 6f	:21 :434 :56 1:083 3↑	BC Sprint-G1	11 8 119 118¾ 910 910	Bailey JD	126	8.00	84-04	Cardmania126nkMeafara123½Gilded Time1241¼	5-wide	14
18Sep93- 4Bel	sly 6f	:222 :451 :57 1:092 3↑	Fall Highweight H-G2	8 7 33 31 2½ 1½	Bailey JD	135	4.10	93-14	FlySoFree135½DemalootDemashoot1261½TakeMOut1343	Driving	10
15Aug93- 9Sar	fst 7f	:221 :442 1:084 1:214 3↑	Forego H-G2	5 9 76½ 75¼ 44½ 46¼	Bailey JD	116	1.90	90-12	Birdonthewire1171½Harlan1102¼SnorSpdy1172½	Broke in air	9
10Jly93- 8Bel	fst 7f	:224 :45 1:083 1:204 3↑	Tom Fool-G2	2 2 31 43 22 21¾	Krone JA	119	*.90	97-08	Birdonthewire1191¾Fly So Free1192Take Me Out1194		5
	In tight ¼ pole										
31May93- 9Bel	fst 1	:221 :441 1:083 1:341 3↑	Metropolitan H-G1	6 7 73¾ 61¾ 41¾ 44¼	Krone JA	118	6.20	93-03	Ibero1191½Bertrando121nkAlydeed1242½	Wide trip	9
6May93- 8Bel	fst 7f	:224 :452 1:084 1:21 3↑	Alw 40000	5 1 2½ 21 11½ 13¼	Krone JA	117	*.30	98-08	Fly So Free1173¼Majesterian1171½Shining Bid1171	Driving	5
10Apr93- 8Aqu	fst 1	:232 :452 1:084 1:343 3↑	Westchester H-G3	10 1 31 32 1hd 2¾	Krone JA	118	*1.20	90-26	Bill of Rights110¾Fly So Free1181¼Loach1133½	Gamely	10
6Mar93- 8GP	fst 6½f	:214 :442 1:083 1:15 4↑	Alw 31000	4 6 66 44 23 24¾	Santos JA	114	2.40	97-09	Alydeed1224¾Fly So Free114noCold Digger1133	Gamely	7
3Oct92- 6Bel	fst 7f	:223 :452 1:10 1:224 3↑	Vosburgh H-G1	5 7 61¾ 73½ 66 57½	Day P	126	*1.60e	82-17	Rubiano126¾SheikhAlbadou1261¼SaltLk1234¼	No threat,wide	8
13Sep92- 8Bel	fst 6f	:221 :444 :562 1:09 3↑	Fall Highweight H-G2	1 4 53½ 43 44½ 43¼	Day P	134	2.70	92-12	SaltLake128½BurnFair126¾BelongtoMe122hd	Rallied wide	6
8Aug92- 8Mth	fst 1⅛	:453 1:09 1:341 1:464 3↑	Iselin H-G1	2 4 44½ 55½ 76 914½	Krone JA	117	2.90	90-00	Jolie's Halo116hdOut of Place1131Valley Crossing1111½		11
	Flattened out										
28Jun92- 7Bel	fst 1 1/16	:233 :463 1:101 1:412 3↑	Alw 47000	4 2 2hd 2hd 1½ 12	Krone JA	115	*.40	95-14	FlySoFree1152HonestEnsign115½SilverEnding1191¼	Driving	4
6Jun92- 7Bel	my 1⅛	:444 1:082 1:334 1:463 3↑	Nassau County H-G2	8 4 42½ 52¼ 62½ 79¾	Santos JA	116	*2.30	86-08	StriketheGold116nkPlsntTp1191½SltrySong1112¾	Wide,tired	9
9May92- 10Pim	fst 1⅜	:473 1:112 1:354 1:544 4↑	Pim Spl H-G1	5 1 1½ 2hd 12 2¾	Santos JA	116	7.40	87-23	StriketheGold114¾FlySoFree1161¼TwilightAgnd1222¼	Gamely	7
11Apr92- 8OP	fst 1⅛	:46 1:094 1:351 1:48 4↑	Oaklawn H-G1	1 4 42 43 44½ 56¼	Santos JA	118	6.00	90-20	Best Pal1251½Sea Cadet120½Twilight Agenda1234	Steadied	7
21Mar92- 10OP	fst 1 1/16	:23 :46 1:101 1:424 4↑	Razorback H-G2	8 6 68 49 49 45¼	Santos JA	121	*.70	82-15	Tokatee115½On the Edge112nkTotal Assets1104½	Four wide	9
2Nov91- 8CD	fst 1¼	:482 1:123 1:38 2:024 3↑	BC Classic-G1	5 4 54 42½ 34 44	Santos JA	B 122	27.70	92-09	BlackTieAffair1261¼TwlghtAgnd1262½Unbrdld126nk	Bid,hung	11
15Sep91- 9WO	fst 1⅛	:482 1:121 1:364 1:491	Molson Million-G2	4 2 32 32 59½ 49	Santos JA	126	*1.25	97-11	DanceSmartly1162Shudanz1176Majesterin1171	Couldn't stay	10
17Aug91- 8Sar	fst 1¼	:472 1:112 1:36 2:011	Travers-G1	3 3 32½ 31½ 32½ 32¾	Santos JA	126	4.10	95-06	CorporateReport126nkHansel1262½FlySoFree1263	Willingly	6
28Jly91- 8Sar	fst 1⅛	:462 1:103 1:354 1:484	Jim Dandy-G2	1 3 42 31½ 2hd 11¼	Santos JA	126	2.10e	93-08	Fly So Free1261¼Upon My Soul1143Strike the Gold1283		8
	Rank early,drv										
7Jly91- 8Bel	fst 1⅛	:454 1:10 1:354 1:491	Dwyer-G2	5 1 2hd 21 31½ 33½	Bailey JD	126	*.50	79-17	LostMountain1231SmoothPrformnc1142½FlySoFr1267	Weakened	7
8Jun91- 6Bel	fst 7f	:22 :45 1:10 1:23	Riva Ridge-G3	6 10 117¾ 84 3½ 12	Bailey JD	122	*.50	89-10	Fly So Free1222Formal Dinner1222½Dodge1221¼		11
	Bumped start,six wide,driving										
4May91- 8CD	fst 1¼	:462 1:111 1:372 2:03	Ky Derby-G1	1 4 42 3½ 42 54¼	Santos JA	B 126	3.30	91-04	Strike the Gold1261¾Best Pal1261¾Mane Minister126hd		16
	Came out st,bore in far turn										
13Apr91- 8Kee	gd 1⅛	:473 1:12 1:354 1:482	Blue Grass-G2	3 2 21 21½ 2½ 23	Santos JA	B 121	*.30	90-07	StriketheGold1213FlySoFr1213¼NoworkAllPly1214½	No excuse	6
16Mar91- 10GP	fst 1⅛	:464 1:113 1:371 1:502	Florida Derby-G1	3 4 43 21 12 11	Santos JA	122	*.40	85-13	FlySoFree1221StriketheGold1184Hansel1222¾	Hard drive	8
23Feb91- 10GP	fst 1 1/16	:223 :454 1:101 1:441	Fountain of Youth-G2	1 4 4¾ 1½ 12½ 16	Santos JA	122	*.50	92-12	Fly So Free1226Moment of True1171½Subordinated Debt1134		10
	Hard drive										
2Feb91- 10GP	fst 7f	:22 :442 1:094 1:231	Hutcheson-G2	8 8 52¾ 82¾ 41¾ 11	Santos JA	122	*1.10	90-08	FlySoFree1221ToFredm119noSunnyndPlsnt114nk	Strong race	10
27Oct90- 7Bel	fst 1 1/16	:23 :46 1:103 1:432	ⒻBC Juvenile-G1	3 3 3½ 1hd 1½ 13	Santos JA	122	*1.40	85-15	FlySoFree1223TakMeOut1222LostMountn122hd	Driving,clear	11
6Oct90- 6Bel	fst 1	:222 :451 1:101 1:353	Champagne-G1	9 6 74½ 67¼ 11½ 15¼	Santos JA	122	3.70	91-11	FlySoFree1225¼HappyJazzBand122nkSubordinated Debt1221¼		13
	Wide,driving										
21Jly90- 7Bel	fst 5½f	:221 :453 :583 1:042	Tremont BC-G3	4 7 57½ 47 47½ 45½	Bailey JD	117	*1.80	91-15	Hansel1153Vermont1152½Stately Wager115hd	Stumbled start	7
8Jly90- 6Bel	fst 5½f	:222 :454 :573 1:043	Alw 27000	2 5 42½ 42½ 41¾ 1¾	Bailey JD	117	1.60	96-10	FlySoFree117¾AlsknFrost1172¼SlfEvdnt1191¼	Strong finish	7
22Jun90- 5Mth	fst 5½f	:222 :453 :574 1:041	Alw 16500	4 4 42½ 31 33½ 34	Bruin JE	120	*.70	93-12	Fighting Affair1172¼Alaskan Frost1171¾Fly So Free12014		5
	Lacked response										
14May90- 4Bel	fst 5f	:222 :453 :574	Md Sp Wt	1 2 31½ 1hd 14 18¼	Santos JA	118	*1.70	99-11	FlySoFree1188¼StatlyWagr118nkMonongh11182¼	Ridden out	8

Gilded Time

ch. c. 1990, by Timeless Moment (Damascus)–Gilded Lilly, by What a Pleasure

Lifetime record: 6 4 0 1 $975,980

Own.– Milch & Silverman & Silverman
Br.– Harry T. Mangurian Jr (Fla)
Tr.– Darrell Vienna

26Dec93- 8SA	ft 7f	:22 :044 1:084 1:21	Malibu-G2	1 3 1hd 1hd 1hd 611¾	McCarron CJ	LB 116	*.80	86-09	Diazo120½Concept Win1162Mister Jolie116no	Dueled,tired	8
6Nov93- 2SA	ft 6f	:21 :44 :56 1:083 3↑	B C Sprint-G1	2 6 33 21½ 31½ 3¾	McCarron CJ	LB 124	5.40	93-04	Cardmania126nkMeafara123½Gilded Time1241¼	Sharp try	14
31Oct92- 8GP	ft 1 1/16	:223 :46 1:102 1:432	B C Juvenile-G1	3 5 41½ 3½ 2hd 1¾	McCarron CJ	L 122	*2.00	95-03	Gilded Time122¾It'sali'lknownfact122½River Special1225		13
	Rank,brushed										
26Sep92- 9AP	sly 1	:222 :452 1:103 1:374	Arl Wash Futurity-G2	3 2 21 2hd 15 15½	McCarron CJ	L 121	*1.10	77-29	Gilded Time1215½Boundlessly1214Rockamundo121¾	Handily	6
8Aug92- 10Mth	fst 6f	:212 :44 :554 1:074	Sapling-G2	5 6 41 3½ 2½ 1½	McCarron CJ	L 122	*1.10	102-05	GilddTime122½WildZon1227½GrtNvgtr1223¼	Wide str,driving	8
15Jly92- 4Hol	fst 6f	:221 :452 :573 1:101	Md Sp Wt	5 8 45 2½ 11 14	Stevens GL	B 117	*.70	89-12	Gilded Time1174Chayim1172¼Gulable1172		8
	Poor start,wide early,handily										

Go for Wand

b. f. 1987, by Deputy Minister (Vice Regent)–Obeah, by Cyane

Lifetime record: 13 10 2 0 $1,373,338

Own.– Christiana Stable
Br.– Christiana Stables (Pa)
Tr.– William Badgett Jr

27Oct90- 5Bel	fst 1⅛	:462 1:103 1:354 1:491 3↑	ⒻBC Distaff-G1	2 1 1½ 1hd 1½ -	Romero RP	119	*.70	--	Bayakoa1236¾Colonial Waters1232½Valay Maid119nk	Fell	7
7Oct90- 8Bel	fst 1⅛	:453 1:091 1:331 1:454 3↑	ⒻBeldame-G1	5 2 2½ 2½ 12 14¾	Romero RP	119	*.10	105-09	GofrWnd1194¾ColonialWtrs1238¾BuythFrm1232¼	Ridden out	5
2Sep90- 8Bel	fst 1	:23 :452 1:094 1:353 3↑	ⒻMaskette H-G1	1 2 21½ 2½ 11 12½	Romero RP	118	*.30	91-13	GofrWnd1182½FeeltheBeat123noMisturn1164	Good handling	6
11Aug90- 8Sar	gd 1¼	:481 1:112 1:36 2:004	ⒻAlabama-G1	3 1 11 12 12½ 17	Romero RP	121	*.50	100-09	Go for Wand1217Charon12148Pampered Star121	Ridden out	3
2Aug90- 8Sar	fst 7f	:221 :443 1:081 1:21	ⒻTest-G1	2 8 2½ 2hd 11½ 12	Romero RP	124	*1.20	100-05	GoforWnd1242ScreenProspct1182¼TokenDnce1182½	Driving	10
10Jun90- 8Bel	fst 1⅛	:46 1:102 1:353 1:484	ⒻMother Goose-G1	6 2 21 21½ 11½ 11¼	Romero RP	121	*.80	90-20	GoforWnd1211¼Charon1214¼StellaMadrid1212¾	Wide,driving	6
4May90- 9CD	my 1⅛	:481 1:13 1:39 1:524	ⒻKy Oaks-G1	1 4 42 31½ 22 23	Romero RP	121	*.30	81-20	Seaside Attraction1213Go for Wand1213Bright Candles1212½		10
	Flattened out										
21Apr90- 8Kee	my 1 1/16	:243 :482 1:122 1:433	ⒻAshland-G1	5 3 1½ 11½ 14 15	Romero RP	121	*.30	88-12	Go for Wand1215Charon1217½Piper Piper1128	Driving	5
10Apr90- 8Kee	my *7f	1:262	ⒻBeaumont-G3	6 2 32 3nk 14½ 18½	Romero RP	122	*.40	95-05	GoforWand1228½Trumpet's Blare119hdSeasideAttraction119½		6
	Ridden out										
4Nov89- 5GP	fst 1 1/16	:234 :472 1:12 1:441	ⒻBC Juv Fillies-G1	4 5 63½ 43½ 31 12¾	Romero RP	119	2.50	90-01	GofrWnd1192¾SweetRoberta119½StellaMdrd1192	Drew clear	12
14Oct89- 7Bel	fst 1	:23 :454 1:11 1:384	ⒻFrizette-G1	6 2 21 22 22½ 2½	Romero RP	119	*1.00	70-26	StellaMdrd119½GofrWnd1195¼DncColony1191¾	Finished well	7
2Oct89- 2Bel	sly 1	:231 :462 1:114 1:363	ⒻAlw 32000	9 1 11½ 13 16 118¼	Romero RP	116	*1.50	82-26	GoforWand11618¼InFullCry116½Jen'sWish1166	Ridden out	9
14Sep89- 2Bel	fst 6f	:221 :452 1:103	ⒻMd Sp Wt	6 3 33 11 12½ 14	Romero RP	117	2.40	86-15	Go for Wand1174Nina1171½Worth Avenue117nk	Drew clear	9

Golden Attraction

b. f. 1993, by Mr. Prospector (Raise a Native)–Seaside Attraction, by Seattle Slew

Lifetime record: 11 8 1 1 $911,507

Own.– Overbrook Farm
Br.– Overbrook Farm (Ky)
Tr.– D. Wayne Lukas

21Sep96- 9TP sly 1 1/16 :234 :464 1:11 1:422 3↑ Ⓕ TP Breeders' Cup-G2 4 1 12½ 11½ 12½ 11½ Stevens GL 114 1.30e 93-02 Golden Attraction1141½Bedroom Blues1173BttyVn1191½ 8
Well ridden,driving
18Aug96- 8Sar fst 7f :222 :444 1:09 1:214 3↑ Ⓕ Ballerina H-G1 3 2 11 2hd 43 615½ Bailey JD 116 6.00 81-09 ChaposaSprings120½CapoteBell1171BrodSml1144 Speed,tired 6
8Aug96- 7Sar fst 6f :214 :45 :571 1:103 3↑ Ⓕ Alw 50600 3 5 11½ 12 12½ 12¼ Bailey JD 115 *.45 88-11 Golden Attraction1152¼Little Buckles1224Wild Lightning1171 5
Handily
28Oct95- 2Bel my 1 1/16 :23 :462 1:11 1:422 Ⓕ B C Juv Fillies-G1 3 1 1½ 1½ 1hd 32 Stevens GL 119 *1.10 85-08 My Flag119½Cara Rafaela1191½Golden Attraction11917 8
Four wide,weakened
7Oct95- 5Bel wf 1 1/16 :23 :46 1:111 1:424 Ⓕ Frizette-G1 5 1 1hd 12½ 12 1¾ Stevens GL 119 *.80 85-14 Golden Attraction119¾My Flag1198½Flat Fleet Feet11912 5
Vigorous hand ride
16Sep95- 4Bel fst 1 :22 :443 1:094 1:361 Ⓕ Matron-G1 2 2 21½ 2½ 1½ 1nk Stevens GL 119 *.45 82-09 Golden Attraction119nkCara Rafaela1195½My Flag1192 8
Drift,strong handling
28Aug95- 8Sar fst 7f :22 :451 1:101 1:234 Ⓕ Spinaway-G1 3 3 1½ 11½ 2½ 1¾ Stevens GL 121 *2.30 87-18 GoldenAttractn121¾FlatFleetFeet1211WesternDreamer1213½ 8
Dueled,came again
6Aug95- 8Mth sly 6f :212 :45 :573 1:104 Ⓕ Sorority-G3 6 1 34 1hd 21 2¾ Barton DM 119 *.70 84-14 Crafty but Sweet119¾Golden Attractn1194½Carelss Heirss1192 6
Outfinished
21Jly95- 8Sar fst 6f :213 :443 :571 1:104 Ⓕ Schuylerville-G2 6 2 2hd 2hd 1hd 12½ Barton DM 121 3.15 87-10 GoldenAttractn1212½DaylightCome112hdWestrnDreamr1213½ 8
Dueled,game
2Jly95-10CD fst 5½f :22 :453 :573 1:04 Ⓕ Debutante 105k 2 5 1½ 1½ 12½ 1½ Barton DM 115 *1.20e 103-04 GoldenAttractn115½WesternDreamer1213½TipicallyIrish115¾ 9
Ridden out
4Jun95- 2Hol fst 5f :22 :46 :582 Ⓕ Md Sp Wt 7 4 21½ 21½ 11 14½ Stevens GL B 118 *.40 92-10 Gldn Attrctn1184½Fillycap118hdWdybvt1183½ Ridden out 7

Hansel

b. c. 1988, by Woodman (Mr. Prospector)–Count on Bonnie, by Dancing Count

Lifetime record: 14 7 2 3 $2,936,586

Own.– Lazy Lane Farms Inc
Br.– Marvin Little Jr (Va)
Tr.– Frank L. Brothers

17Aug91- 8Sar fst 1¼ :472 1:112 1:36 2:011 Travers-G1 2 2 21 2hd 2½ 2nk Bailey JD 126 1.90 98-06 Corporate Report126nkHansel1262½Fly So Free1263 6
Tore tendon of left foreleg in upper str
27Jly91-10Mth gd 1⅛ :46 1:101 1:351 1:48 Haskell H-G1 1 3 3½ 22 36½ 313 Bailey JD L 126 *.50 85-15 Lost Mountain118hdCorporate Report12013Hansel1262½ 5
Steadied entering 1st turn,rank briefly
8Jun91- 8Bel fst 1½ :463 1:113 2:02 2:28 Belmont-G1 5 3 1hd 11½ 12½ 1hd Bailey JD 126 4.10 90-08 Hansel126hdStrike the Gold1263Mane Minister1262½ 11
Drifted late,lasted
18May91-10Pim fst 1 3/16 :461 1:101 1:35 1:54 Preakness-G1 4 3 31½ 2hd 15 17 Bailey JD L 126 9.10 95-14 Hansel1267Corporate Report1262¾Mane Minister126½ 8
Drifted out-driving
4May91- 8CD fst 1¼ :462 1:111 1:372 2:03 Ky Derby-G1 6 5 63½ 52 74¾ 1010¾ Bailey JD LB 126 *2.50 84-04 Strike the Gold1261¾Best Pal1261¾Mane Minister126hd 16
Tiring,ducked in
21Apr91- 8Kee fst 1 1/16 :242 :474 1:111 1:423 Lexington-G2 3 2 21½ 1½ 15 19 Bailey JD LB 121 *.30 91-09 Hansel1219Shotgun Harry J.1152¾Speedy Cure1183 4
Jumped tracks late,much the best
30Mar91-10TP fst 1⅛ :453 1:093 1:341 1:463 Jim Beam-G2 3 3 41¼ 31½ 1½ 12½ Bailey JD LB 121 4.60 112-00 Hansl1212½Richman1216WilderThnEvr121½ Impressive score 11
16Mar91-10GP fst 1⅛ :464 1:113 1:371 1:502 Florida Derby-G1 7 5 54½ 32 43½ 35 Day P L 122 4.70 80-13 Fly So Free1221Strike the Gold1184Hansel1222¾ Bore out 8
23Feb91-10GP fst 1 1/16 :223 :454 1:101 1:441 Fountain of Youth-G2 2 5 84 68 610 511¼ Day P 119 6.10 81-12 FlySoFree1226MomntofTrue1171¼SbordntdDbt1134 No rally 10
22Sep90- 8AP gd 1 :23 :452 1:104 1:362 Arl-Wash Futurity-G2 1 3 31½ 51½ 31 1nk Day P 122 *1.40 89-17 Hansel122nkWalesa1221¼Discover1223¼ Blocked turn 7
25Aug90- 8Sar my 6½f :22 :443 1:093 1:161 Hopeful-G1 1 6 35½ 35½ 33½ 24½ Day P 122 6.50 95-04 Deposit Ticket1224½Hansel122¾Link122nk No match 6
11Aug90-10Mth my 6f :213 :444 1:11 Sapling-G2 1 8 52½ 34 35½ 35¼ Day P 122 *1.40 81-17 DepostTckt1223¾AlsknFrost1221½Hnsl122no Green,mild gain 9
21Jly90- 7Bel fst 5½f :221 :453 :583 1:042 Tremont BC-G3 5 5 32 2½ 2½ 13 Romero RP 115 3.40 97-15 Hansel1153Vermont1152½Stately Wager115hd Brisk urging 7
7Jun90- 4AP fst 5f :224 :464 :591 Md Sp Wt 4 6 31 1hd 13 13½ Romero RP 118 *1.10 93-14 Hansel1183½Bandito Barney1184Roman Envoy118½ Handily 10

Hatoof

ch. f. 1989, by Irish River (Riverman)–Cadeaux d'Amie, by Lyphard

Lifetime record: 21 9 4 1 $1,864,063

Own.– Sheikh Maktoum al Maktoum
Br.– Gainsborough Farm Inc (Ky)
Tr.– Christiane Head

5Nov94- 9CD fm 1½Ⓣ :464 1:103 2:00 2:262 3↑ B C Turf-G1 2 13 107¾ 76 41½ 21½ Swinburn WR 123 12.70 110-00 Tikkanen1221½Hatoof1231½Paradise Creek126½ 14
Lacked room early,gamely
15Oct94♦ Newmarket(GB) gd 1¼ⓉStr 2:053 3↑ Champion Stakes-G1 5¾ Swinburn WR 127 *1.50 Dernier Empereur130noGrand Lodge124nkMuhtarram130hd 8
Stk468000
Led for a half,tracked leader,outpaced 1½f out,gaining late
27Aug94- 6AP fm 1 3/16Ⓣ :473 1:113 1:364 1:552 3↑ Ⓕ Beverly D-G1 3 7 78 65 42 1½ Swinburn WR 123 2.90 90-09 Hatoof123½Flawlessly123½Potridee123½ Late wide rush 8
31Jly94♦ Deauville(Fr) yl *1ⓉStr 1:364 3↑ Ⓕ Prix d'Astarte-G2 1¾ Swinburn WR 126 *1.30 Hatoof126¾Ski Paradise130nkLunafairy1192 8
Stk94500
Held up in last,late rally to lead 50y out,driving
29May94♦ Longchamp(Fr) gd *1⅛ⓉRH 1:513 3↑ Prix d'Ispahan-G1 43¾ Swinburn WR 124 *2.70 Bigstone128nkMuhtarram1281½Marildo1282 7
Stk150000
Tracked in 4th,bid over 2f out,led 2f to 1½f out,faded
6Nov93- 7SA fm 1½Ⓣ :483 1:122 2:012 2:25 3↑ B C Turf-G1 8 7 85¾ 73¾ 52½ 53¾ Swinburn WR B 123 15.30 89-04 Kotshn126½BnBn1261¼Luzur126¾ Steadied far turn,weakened 14
16Oct93♦ Newmarket(GB) gd 1¼ⓉStr 2:064 3↑ Champion Stakes-G1 13 Swinburn WR 126 *2.50 Hatoof1263Ezzoud129noDernier Empereur1242 12
Stk534000
Toward rear,joined leaders 3f out,led 2f out,ridden clear
27Sep93♦ Maisns-Lfftte(Fr) hy *1¼ⓉStr 2:08 3↑ La Coupe de M-Laffitte-G3 14 Swinburn WR 129 2.50e Hatoof1294Baya124nkSawasdee1234 9
Stk60000
Unhurried in 5th,lacked room 3f out,led 2f out,easily clear
24Jun93♦ Longchamp(Fr) fm *1¼ⓉRH 2:073 4↑ La Coupe-G3 41¾ Swinburn WR 127 *.60 D'Arros1231Marildo130½Diese124nk 5
Stk59300
Trailed to 1f out,outside bid,never threatened
30May93♦ Longchamp(Fr) fm *1⅛ⓉRH 1:503 4↑ Prix d'Ispahan-G1 43½ Swinburn WR 124 *1.00e Arcangues1281½Misil128½Shanghai1281½ 7
Stk158000
Trailed for nearly a mile,wide rally 1½f out,hung
7May93♦ Saint-Cloud(Fr) yl *1ⓉLH 1:433 4↑ Prix du Muguet-G3 1¾ Swinburn WR 127 3.00 Hatoof127¾Shanghai1301½Northern Crystal126½ 5
Stk95600
Tracked leader in 2nd,led final furlong,held well
18Oct92- 4WO yl 1¼Ⓣ :492 1:16 1:421 2:074 3↑ Ⓕ E P Taylor-G2 5 6 65 53 43 11¼ Swinburn WR 118 *2.00 62-45 Hatoof1181¼Urban Sea1181¼Hero's Love123hd Ridden out 12
4Oct92♦ Longchamp(Fr) sf *1⅛ⓉRH 2:022 3↑ Ⓕ Prix de l'Opera-G2 1½ Swinburn WR 126 *1.80 Hatoof126½La Favorita1211Ruby Tiger128no 12
Stk142000
Behind,9th 2½f out,hard ridden,strong bid 1f out,led near line
6Sep92♦ Longchamp(Fr) sf *1ⓉRH 1:403 3↑ Prix du Moulin de Longchamp-G1 32½ Mosse G 120 6.20 All at Sea120nkBrief Truce1232½Hatoof1202 10
Stk320000
Held up in 6th,ridden 2f out,finished well
16Aug92♦ Deauville(Fr) sf *1ⓉStr 1:404 3↑ Prix Jacque le Marois-G1 53½ Swinburn WR 120 16.00 Exit to Nowhere1301Lahib130hdCardoun123nk 14
Stk342000
Never far back,effort over 1f out,one-paced.StarofCozzene 4th

17May92♦ Longchamp(Fr) gd *1ⓉRH	1:37	ⒻPoule d'Essai des Pouliches-G1 Stk317000	6¾	Swinburn WR	128	*1.70	Culture Vulture128½Hydro Calido128¾Guislaine128nk	Tracked in 2nd,outpaced 2f out,evenly late	9
30Apr92♦ Newmarket(GB) gd 1ⓉStr	1:392	Ⓕ1000 Guineas-G1 Stk335000	1hd	Swinburn WR	126	5.00	Hatoof126hdMarling126¾Kenbu126½	Well placed,dueled 2f out,drifted left,led 150y out,just held	14
10Apr92♦ Maisns-Lfftte(Fr) yl *7fⓉStr	1:274	ⒻPrix Imprudence (Listed) Stk37800	2nk	Swinburn WR	128	*.60e	Kenbu128nkHatoof128²½Plume Magique1281	5th early,tracked entrymate after 2f,led briefly,outfinished	6
6Oct91♦ Longchamp(Fr) yl *1ⓉRH	1:403	ⒻPrix Marcel Boussac-G1 Stk237000	2nk	Eddery Pat	123	7.50	Culture Vulture123hdHatoof1231Vereine123½	Reserved behind,hampered 3f out,strong late run,just missed	14
18Sep91♦ Longchamp(Fr) gd *1ⓉH	1:401	ⒻPrix d'Aumale-G3 Stk65300	2no	Guignard G	121	4.00	Guislaine121noHatoof1211Lady Normandy125½	Toward rear,wide bid 2f out,finished fast,just missed	12
3Sep91♦ Longchamp(Fr) sf *1ⓉRH	1:464	ⒻPrix de Toutevoie Mdn (FT)31700	11	Guignard	123	2.20	Hatoof1231Eastern Exodus123½Formidable Flight1232	Led to 1½f out,dueled,led again near line	6

Heavenly Prize

b. f. 1991, by Seeking the Gold (Mr. Prospector)–Oh What a Dance, by Nijinsky II

Lifetime record: 18 9 6 3 $1,825,820

Own.– Ogden Phipps
Br.– Ogden Phipps (Ky)
Tr.– Claude McGaughey III

10Feb96-10GP	fst 1⅛	:464 1:104 1:353 1:49	3↑ Donn H-G1	4 7 63¾ 56¼ 39	36	Day P	L 115	6.50	86-12	Cigar1282Wekiva Springs1174Heavenly Prize1153		8
	Eight wide top str,late rally											
28Oct95- 4Bel	my 1⅛	:454 1:092 1:332 1:46	3↑ ⒻB C Distaff-G1	8 9 912 814 512	213½	Day P	L 123	*.80e	88-08	Inside Information12313Heavenly Prize1232¼Lakeway1231		10
	Second best,inside											
7Oct95- 7Bel	wf 1⅛	:48 1:121 1:361 1:483	3↑ ⒻBeldame-G1	2 4 42½ 45 22½	2¾	Day P	L 123	*.65	88-14	Serena'sSong119¾HeavnlyPrz1236¾Lkwy1236¾	Finished well	5
20Aug95- 8Sar	fst 1¼	:48 1:124 1:382 2:04	3↑ ⒻJ A Morris H-G1	4 6 68 3½ 12½	18½	Day P	127	*.15	84-16	HeavnlyPrize1278½ForcngBd1082CnnmonSugr1142	Ridden out	8
23Jly95- 8Sar	fst 1⅛	:471 1:111 1:371 1:494	3↑ ⒻGo for Wand H-G1	3 4 46½ 45½ 12½	111	Day P	123	*.35	87-13	HeavenlyPrize12311ForcingBid1082LttlBuckls1113¾	Handily	5
18Jun95- 9Bel	fst 1 1/16	:23 :46 1:102 1:431	3↑ ⒻHempstead H-G1	4 3 34½ 34 2½	11¼	Day P	122	1.00	83-17	HeavnlyPrize1221¼LttlBuckls11110SkyButy1243	Going away	4
21Apr95- 9OP	fst 1 1/16	:224 :454 1:103 1:423	4↑ ⒻApple Blossom-G1	5 6 68½ 55½ 21	11	Day P	120	*1.00	94-15	HeavenlyPrize1201HaloAmrc1164Psn1225	3 wide ¼,driving	6
2Apr95- 9OP	fst 1 1/16	:232 :47 1:11 1:422	3↑ ⒻOP Bud BC 148k	6 3 33½ 34½ 25	23½	Day P	121	*.20	91-17	Halo America1153½Heavenly Prize1219Biolage111nk		6
	Washy in post parade											
5Nov94- 6CD	fst 1⅛	:474 1:121 1:373 1:503	3↑ ⒻB C Distaff-G1	3 6 21½ 32½ 21½	2nk	Day P	120	2.10	91-07	OneDreamer123nkHeavnlyPriz1201½MssDomnqu1231¼	Bid,hung	9
8Oct94-11Bel	fst 1⅛	:463 1:112 1:361 1:484	3↑ ⒻBeldame-G1	3 4 45½ 31½ 11	16	Day P	119	—	87-17	HeavnlyPrize1196EductdRsk12310ClssyMrg12311	Ridden out	4
	Exhibition race,no wagering											
4Sep94- 8Bel	fst 1⅛	:461 1:101 1:35 1:471	ⒻGazelle H-G1	3 5 54 41½ 2½	16½	Smith ME	123	*.70	95-05	HvnlyPrize1236½CnnmonSugr1181¾SovrgnKtty1181	Handily	5
13Aug94- 8Sar	fst 1¼	:48 1:12 1:372 2:031	ⒻAlabama-G1	2 4 42 1hd 11½	17	Smith ME	121	5.20	88-23	HeavnlyPrize1217Lakeway12111SovrgnKtty1211¼	Mild drive	7
23Jly94- 9Sar	sly 7f	:221 :442 1:09 1:22	ⒻTest-G1	2 8 76 78½ 34	33	Smith ME	121	*1.50	92-12	Twist Afleet1141Penny's Reshoot1182Heavenly Prize12110		8
	Brk slw,blcked ¼ pl											
18Jun94- 7Bel	fst 6f	:221 :452 :57 1:09	ⒻPrioress-G2	2 6 54½ 3½ 22	22¼	Smith ME	121	*.70	94-10	Penny's Reshoot1162¼Heavenly Prize1216Becky's Shirt1141½		6
	Broke slowly											
12Mar94- 7GP	fst 6f	:214 :45 :573 1:101	ⒻWhat a Summer 51k	6 11 97½ 75¼ 45	22½	Smith ME	118	*1.00	87-10	Swift and Classy1162½HeavenlyPrize118¾Shananie'sBeat116no		13
	Seven wide top str,rallied											
6Nov93- 3SA	fst 1 1/16	:232 :472 1:112 1:43	ⒻBC Juv Fillies-G1	4 4 42 32 31½	33	Smith ME	119	*1.90	77-10	PhoneChatter119hdSardula1193HeavenlyPriz119½	Inside bid	8
16Oct93- 4Bel	fst 1	:224 :451 1:10 1:352	ⒻFrizette-G1	5 6 62½ 2hd 12½	17	Smith ME	119	2.40	91-12	HeavnlyPrize1197FctsofLov1194¾Footng1192½	Wide,driving	7
15Sep93- 5Bel	fst 6f	:224 :462 :583 1:104	ⒻMd Sp Wt	4 4 52¾ 2hd 12½	19	Smith ME	117	*1.40	86-19	HeavnlyPriz1179AmyBeHappy1171¾Vibelle117nk	Ridden out	7

Hidden Lake

b. f. 1993, by Quiet American (Fappiano)–Friendly Circle, by Round Table

Lifetime record: 22 7 4 6 $947,489

Own.– Robert N. Clay & Tracy Farmer
Br.– Charles Nuckols Jr & Sons (Ky)
Tr.– John C. Kimmel

8Nov97- 4Hol	fst 1⅛	:454 1:091 1:342 1:471	3↑ ⒻBC Distaff-G1	8 6 64¼ 66½ 810	722	Migliore R	LB 123	1.70	68-06	Ajina1202Sharp Cat1203½Escena1231	Gave way	8
19Oct97- 9Bel	fst 1⅛	:463 1:103 1:352 1:481	3↑ ⒻBeldame-G1	1 2 21 1½ 12	12	Migliore R	L 123	*2.30	89-12	HiddenLake1232Ajin1192JwlPrncss1231¼	Stalked,drew clear	8
27Jly97- 8Sar	fst 1⅛	:473 1:114 1:361 1:493	3↑ ⒻGo for Wand-G1	6 1 11½ 1½ 2hd	1hd	Migliore R	L 123	*.70	88-17	Hidden Lake123hdFlat Fleet Feet1202Clear Mandate1133		7
	Hard drive,gamely											
28Jun97- 9Bel	fst 1 1/16	:223 :452 1:094 1:404	3↑ ⒻHempstead H-G1	7 3 21 2½ 12	12	Migliore R	L 117	4.90	95-13	Hidden Lake1172Twice the Vice1212Jewel Princs1245¼	game	9
24May97- 9Bel	fst 1	:222 :443 1:094 1:351	3↑ ⒻShuvee H-G2	4 5 55 4¾ 12½	14	Migliore R	L 115	8.80	88-17	HiddenLake1154FlatFleetFt1201Escn116¾	Well placed,clear	9
	Previously trained by Walter Greenman											
3May97- 6CD	fst 7f	:224 :452 1:094 1:221	4↑ ⒻHumana Distaff H-G3	4 8 54 53½ 21	2¾	Dsrmeaux KJ	L 115	5.40	96-05	Capote Belle118¾Hidden Lake115nkJ J'sdream1173½		8
	4 wide bid,2nd best;Previously owned by D.E. Weir											
11Apr97- 9OP	wf 1 1/16	:231 :463 1:104 1:413	4↑ ⒻApple Blossom H-G1	8 5 55 53½ 68	611	Dsrmeaux KJ	L 116	18.60	89-12	HaloAmerica1174JewelPrincess124hdDiffrnt1211½	Wide trip	8
	Previously owned by Estate of J.E. Weir & D.E. Weir											
9Mar97- 7SA	fst 1⅛	:48 1:121 1:364 1:491	4↑ ⒻS Margarita H-G1	6 3 3½ 31½ 21	3¾	McCarrn CJ	LB 114	10.40	86-12	Jewel Princess125½Top Rung116nkHidden Lake1143		6
	Game between foes late											
16Feb97- 8SA	fst 1 1/16	:231 :464 1:101 1:413	4↑ ⒻS Maria H-G1	5 6 54½ 42¾ 43	46½	McCarrn CJ	LB 116	10.80	88-12	JewelPrincess1235Cat'sCradle118½TopRung1171	Inside trip	7
29Dec96- 5SA	gd 7f	:222 :443 1:091 1:22	ⒻLa Brea-G2	6 6 55¼ 54 22	11	McCarrn CJ	LB 115	6.60	92-10	HddnLake1151Bll'sFlg1193TffnyDmond1154½	Closed gamely	7
	Previously owned by D.E. & J.E. Weir											
16Jun96- 9CD	fst 1 1/16	:231 :464 1:112 1:431	ⒻDogwood H 82k	6 4 33 31 42½	33	Valdivia J Jr	L 114	4.00	92-12	GinnyLynn121½Evrhop1212½HddnLk1141½	4 wide,no late gain	7
25May96- 9CD	fst 1	:23 :453 1:101 1:352	ⒻEdgewood 83k	7 2 32 32½ 23	23	Day P	L 114	*.90	93-09	Everhope1143HiddnLake1143Mariuka112no	Stalked,2nd best	7
5May96- 8Hol	fst 7f	:214 :444 1:093 1:222	ⒻRailbird-G2	4 5 69 63¼ 42	43¾	McCarrn CJ	LB 118	2.40	86-10	Supercilious1211¾TiffnyDmond1181¾RwGold121nk	Inside bid	6
10Mar96- 4SA	fst 1 1/16	:232 :473 1:112 1:43	ⒻS Anita Oaks-G1	2 5 43½ 33 33½	35¼	McCarrn CJ	LB 117	5.70	75-19	Antespend1172¼Cara Rafaela1173Hidden Lake1172½		5
	Rank,steadied early											
18Feb96- 8SA	fst 1	:222 :463 1:104 1:362	ⒻLas Virgenes-G1	2 5 56½ 54½ 43½	35	McCarron CJ	B 116	6.20	82-18	Antespend1202½Cara Rafaela1222½Hidden Lake1161¾		6
	Bobbled,lacked late bid											
28Jan96- 8SA	fst 7f	:222 :453 1:093 1:223	ⒻSanta Ynez-G3	6 6 54¼ 43 33½	31½	McCarron CJ	B 116	*1.20	87-15	Raw Gold1211Pareja121½Hidden Lake1167½	Slow late gain	6
6Jan96- 3SA	fst 6½f	:213 :443 1:091 1:154	ⒻAlw 42000	1 6 68¾ 63½ 32½	1nk	McCarron CJ	B 117	*1.50	91-11	Hidden Lake117nkDancing Prism1173½Babeinthewoods1177		6
	Closed gamely											
18Nov95- 6Hol	fst 7f	:222 :452 1:093 1:214	ⒻMaker's Mark 106k	3 5 56 44 24	24	McCarron CJ	B 114	4.10	89-10	Advcg Star1144Hidden Lake1143½Stga Flwr1212½	2nd best	6
18Oct95- 8SA	fst 6f	:214 :45 :571 1:093	ⒻAnoakia 78k	1 7 54 53¼ 41½	2½	McCarron CJ	B 115	9.30	88-12	Canta'sCrusade115½HiddnLake115nkThankyourlckystar1163½		8
	Bit awkward start,4 wide into lane											
27Aug95- 8Dmr	fst 7f	:214 :441 1:09 1:222	ⒻDmr Debutante-G2	9 12 1210 1210 78½	810½	Blanc B	B 115	26.40	79-10	Batroyale1194Proud Dixie1172General Idea1161	No rally	12
5Aug95- 4Dmr	fst 6f	:22 :452 :574 1:103	ⒻMd Sp Wt	4 7 78½ 77 63¾	11¼	Blanc B5	B 113	3.80	88-09	Hidden Lake1131¼Passion Flower118½Ticket to Houston118½		8
	Far wide rally											
16Jly95- 4Hol	fst 5f	:221 :453 :58	ⒻMd Sp Wt	3 8 77½ 59 54½	31	McCarron CJ	B 118	19.80	93-09	Blacktie Bid118½Totally Spellbound118½Hidden Lake118½		9
	Finished well											

Hollywood Wildcat

dkbbr. f. 1990, by Kris S. (Roberto)–Miss Wildcatter, by Mr. Prospector — Lifetime record: 21 12 3 3 $1,432,160
Own.– Marjorie & Irving Cowan
Br.– Irving & Marjorie Cowan (Fla)
Tr.– Neil Drysdale

10Feb95- 8SA fst 7f :224 :454 1:093 1:213 4↑ ⒻLittle Brianne 65k 4 4 31½ 31 12½ 14½ Dlhoussaye E LB 121 *.70 94-14 Hollywood Wildcat1214½Nijivision1152Flying in the Lane1131¼ 5
Impressively
5Nov94- 6CD fst 1⅛ :474 1:121 1:373 1:503 3↑ ⒻB C Distaff-G1 6 2 42 64¼ 68 68¼ Delahoussaye L 123 *1.80 83-07 One Dreamer123nkHeavenly Prize1201½Miss Dominique1231¼ 9
Pressed,tired
10Oct94- 8SA fst 1 1/16 :23 :47 1:103 1:403 3↑ ⒻLady's Secret H 106k 3 1 11 1hd 1½ 12¼ Dlhoussaye E LB 124 *.70 92-17 HollywdWildct1242¼Exchng1213DncngMrg11314 Mild urging 5
6Aug94- 8Dmr fm 1⅛Ⓣ :473 1:113 1:361 1:481 3↑ ⒻRamona H-G1 5 5 57 52½ 42 2hd Dlhoussaye E LB 124 *.80 95-02 Flawlessly124hdHollywood Wildcat1241¼Skimble1162 5
Awaited room 2nd turn
3Jly94- 8Hol fm 1⅛Ⓣ :48 1:111 1:35 1:472 3↑ ⒻBeverly Hills H-G1 4 7 74½ 63½ 61¾ 2nk Dlhoussaye E LB 124 *1.00 87-14 Corrzon119nkHollywdWldct124noFlwlssly1241 Closed gamely 7
12Jun94- 8Hol fm 1⅛Ⓣ :464 1:10 1:341 1:462 3↑ ⒻGamely H-G1 2 3 43 63½ 2½ 12¼ Dlhoussaye E LB 122 2.70 92-10 Hollywood Wildcat1222¼Mz. Zill Bear1142¾Flawlessly124nk 6
Strong rally
5Feb94- 8SA fst 1⅛ :472 1:112 1:361 1:484 ⒻLa Canada-G2 2 1 2hd 22½ 34 35¼ Dlhoussaye E LB 122 *.50 84-12 Stalcreek119¾Alyshn1154½HollywoodWldct122¾ Dueled,tired 4
6Nov93- 4SA fst 1⅛ :464 1:11 1:36 1:481 3↑ ⒻB C Distaff-G1 6 2 21½ 2hd 1hd 1no Dlhoussaye E LB 120 *1.30 89-10 Hollywood Wildcat120noPaseana1232½Re Toss1231 8
Lost whip 70 yards out,gamely
11Oct93- 8SA fst 1 1/16 :224 :461 1:101 1:41 3↑ ⒻLady's Secret 106k 1 3 32 2hd 11½ 12 Dlhoussaye E LB 117 *.70 90-07 HollywdWildct1172RToss1172WddngRng1134½ Clearly best 5
22Aug93- 8Dmr fm 1⅛Ⓣ :472 1:114 1:362 1:481 ⒻDel Mar Oaks-G2 3 4 44½ 52¼ 53 11 Dlhoussaye E LB 120 *.80 95-09 HollywoodWildcat1201PossiblyPerfect1201¾MiamiSnds120nk 10
Boxed in 3/8-3/16
1Aug93- 5Dmr fm 1Ⓣ :221 :46 1:102 1:344 ⒻSan Clemente H 83k 8 6 55 53 11½ 14½ Dlhoussaye E LB 120 *2.10 97-13 Hollywood Wildcat1204½MiamiSnds1161¼BealStreetBlues1171 10
7 wide stretch,handily
11Jly93- 8Hol fst 1⅛ :462 1:103 1:353 1:482 ⒻHol Oaks-G1 4 2 21 2½ 1hd 11¾ Dlhoussaye E LB 121 16.60 95-13 HollywoodWildcat1211¾FittoLead1216½Adorydr121no Driving 9
Previously trained by Emanuel Tortora
19Jun93- 9Crc fst 7f :222 :45 1:10 1:232 ⒻAzalea 100k 4 5 31 3½ 41 33¼ Coa EM L 117 f 5.30 95-01 Kimscountrydiamnd1151¾Nijivsion1131½HollywoodWldct117no 10
Lacked response
9Apr93- 9OP fst 1 1/16 :231 :474 1:124 1:441 ⒻFantasy-G2 1 6 52½ 31 65¼ 610 Arguello FA Jr L 121 f 11.60 70-19 Aztez Hill1215Adorydar1172Stalcreek117½ Inside 7
20Mar93- 10Tam fst 1 1/16 :233 :48 1:123 1:453 ⒻFlorida Oaks 100k 1 10 117½ 107¾ 46¼ 22 Lopez RD L 121 f *1.70 93-07 Star Jolie1112Hollywood Wildcat121nkJacody113¾ 11
Hung wide to stretch
7Mar93- 7GP fst 6f :221 :45 :572 1:102 ⒻReal Quillo 31k 3 1 41½ 31 22 31 Bailey JD L 117 1.30 88-13 Our Sweet Meg113noGatorCo Ed1081Hollywood Wildcat1173¾ 6
Weakened
12Sep92- 10Crc fst 7f :222 :46 1:113 1:25 ⒻⓇSusan's Girl 125k 1 6 53¾ 63¾ 611 614½ Arguello FA Jr L 118 *.50 75-14 Boots 'n Jackie1182Exercising1182½Sigrun1183 Faltered 8
1Aug92- 9Mth fst 6f :214 :451 :58 1:104 ⒻSorority-G3 3 3 55½ 44 21½ 14 Arguello FA Jr L 119 3.60 87-16 HollywoodWildcat1194FamilyEntrprize1193¾D'Accrdrss119nk 6
Drew out
12Jly92- 10Crc fst 5½f :221 :462 1:063 ⒻMelaleuca 50k 2 4 41½ 32 12½ 12½ Arguello FA Jr L 114 *1.20 - - HollywoodWldct1142½Debbie'sBliss118hdⒹBoots'nJackie1121 12
Driving
7Jun92- 9CD fst 5½f :224 :472 1:06 ⒻDebutante 59k 1 1 31½ 5¾ 1hd 13 Arglio FA Jr LB 116 7.80 92-13 HollywoodWildct1163CosmicSpeedQueen1181DixieBand1152 14
Driving;Previously owned by Irving Cowan
15Apr92- 3Crc fst 4½f :224 :472 :534 ⒻMd Sp Wt 3 1 2½ 1hd 15 Douglas RR 116 2.30 - - Hollywood Wildcat1165Marti Huizenga116¾Supah Gem116nk 6
Driving

Holy Bull

gr. c. 1991, by Great Above (Minnesota Mac)–Sharon Brown, by Al Hattab — Lifetime record: 16 13 0 0 $2,481,760
Own.– Warren A. Croll Jr
Br.– Pelican Stable (Fla)
Tr.– Warren A. Croll Jr

11Feb95- 9GP fst 1⅛ :462 1:103 1:363 1:493 3↑ Donn H-G1 9 2 22 — — — Smith ME 127 *.30 - - Cigar1155½Primitive Hall1121½Bonus Money1123½ 9
Pulled up 5½ furlong pole,lame left front
22Jan95- 9GP fst 7f :223 :451 1:093 1:22 3↑ Olympic H 100k 5 3 21 2hd 11½ 12½ Smith ME 126 *.40 93-15 Holy Bull1262½Birdonthewire1192¾Patton115¾ 6
Raced well out in the track early,six wide top str,ridden out
17Sep94- 8Bel fst 1⅛ :462 1:102 1:343 1:464 3↑ Woodward-G1 5 2 21 1½ 13 15 Smith ME 121 *.90 97-10 Holy Bull1215Devil His Due1261½Colonial Affair1263½ 8
Bump brk,ridden out
20Aug94- 7Sar wf 1¼ :461 1:102 1:354 2:02 Travers-G1 1 2 2hd 14 11½ 1nk Smith ME 126 *.80 94-06 Holy Bull126nkConcern12617Tabasco Cat1261 Hard drive 5
31Jly94- 10Mth fst 1⅛ :472 1:112 1:354 1:481 Haskell Inv H-G1 3 1 12 12½ 11½ 11¾ Smith ME 126 *.20 93-07 Holy Bull1261¾Meadow Flight1181¾Concern1181 Ridden out 6
3Jly94- 8Bel fst 1 1/16 :222 :451 1:092 1:41 Dwyer-G2 1 1 11 11½ 13 16¾ Smith ME 124 *.30 97-14 Holy Bull1246¾Twining1225Bay Street Star1199 Handily 4
30May94- 8Bel fst 1 :224 :45 1:092 1:334 3↑ Metropolitan H-G1 6 1 11 1½ 12½ 15½ Smith ME 112 *1.00 94-09 HolyBull1125½CherokeeRun118noDevilHisDue1222 Driving 10
7May94- 8CD sly 1¼ :471 1:114 1:373 2:033 Kentucky Derby-G1 4 6 53½ 99 1212 1218¼ Smith ME 126 *2.20 76-06 Go for Gin1262Strodes Creek1262½Blumin Affair126¾ 14
Off slow,in tight start,tired badly
16Apr94- 9Kee fst 1⅛ :474 1:123 1:374 1:50 Blue Grass-G2 1 1 13 12 11½ 13½ Smith ME 121 *.60 84-26 Holy Bull1213½Valiant Nature1215Mahogany Hall1212¼ 7
Sharp,ridden out
12Mar94- 10GP fst 1⅛ :46 1:10 1:344 1:472 Florida Derby-G1 6 1 12½ 12½ 15 15¾ Smith ME 122 2.70 100-06 HolyBull1225¾RidetheRails122noHalo'sImag1221 Ridden out 14
19Feb94- 9GP gd 1 1/16 :224 :453 1:102 1:443 Fountain of Youth-G2 4 1 1½ 21 68 624¼ Smith ME 119 *1.30 63-19 Dehere119¾GoforGin1191¼RidetheRails1173¾ Stopped badly 6
30Jan94- 9GP fst 7f :213 :44 1:081 1:211 Hutcheson-G2 1 4 11½ 11½ 2½ 1¾ Smith ME 122 *.50 97-11 Holy Bull122¾Patton1133You and I1193 5
Broke inward start,raced well off rail,ridden out
23Oct93- 11Crc fst 1 1/16 :23 :462 1:113 1:461 ⓇIn Reality 400k 9 1 11½ 12 14 17½ Smith ME 120 *.50 88-12 HolyBull1207½RusticLight1201ForwardtoLd1201½ Ridden out 12
18Sep93- 6Bel sly 7f :222 :453 1:101 1:231 Futurity-G1 2 1 11 11 12½ 1½ Smith ME 122 3.10 87-14 Holy Bull122½Dehere1225Prenup1228 All out 6
2Sep93- 7Bel fst 6½f :22 :441 1:094 1:17 Alw 28000 3 1 1½ 1hd 12½ 17 Smith ME 119 *.90 88-15 Holy Bull1197Goodbye Doeny1173End Sweep119½ Ridden out 6
Previously owned by Targan Stable
14Aug93- 7Mth fst 5½f :213 :444 :571 1:034 Md Sp Wt 1 3 11 11½ 11½ 12½ Rivera L Jr 118 *1.10 95-17 Holy Bull1182½Palance1187½Hold My Tongue1189 Driving 9

Housebuster

dkbbr. c. 1987, by Mt. Livermore (Blushing Groom)–Big Dreams, by Great Above — Lifetime record: 22 15 3 1 $1,229,696

Own.– Robert P. Levy
Br.– Murphy Stable & Blanche P. Levy (Ky)
Tr.– Warren A. Croll Jr

2Nov91- 2CD fst 6f :21 :442 1:091 3↑ BC Sprint-G1 2 6 22 21 2hd 99 Perret C B 126 *.40 92-02 Sheikh Albadou1243Pleasant Tap126½Robyn Dancer126nk 11
Bobbled start,bothered by rivals whip str,came back lame
28Sep91- 8Bel fst 7f :231 :454 1:094 1:214 3↑ Vosburgh-G1 1 5 31 31 1½ 15½ Perret C 126 *.40 95-14 Housebuster1265½Senator to Be126nkSunshine Jimmy1262½ 6
Stumbled start,driving
25Aug91- 8Sar fst 7f :214 :434 1:08 1:21 3↑ Forego H-G2 3 4 1hd 1½ 12 1no Perret C 126 *.60 100-12 Housebuster126noSenorSpeedy1121CleverTrvor1202½ Driving 6
20Jly91- 9Lrl fst 6f :213 :434 :57 1:083 3↑ F J DeFrancis 300k 2 2 32½ 42½ 21½ 15 Perret C 126 *2.40 98-15 Housebuster1265ClevrTrvor1231¼SflyKpt1213¼ Wide,driving 6
27May91- 8Bel fst 1 :22 :441 1:091 1:352 3↑ Metropolitan H-G1 4 1 11½ 1hd 44½ 810¼ Perret C 124 *.90 83-16 In Excess1172¼Rubiano1111¾Gervazy1141½ Speed,tired 14
4May91- 8Aqu fst 7f :224 :452 1:084 1:211 3↑ Carter H-G1 1 4 1½ 11 13 12¼ Perret C 122 *1.30 96-17 Housebuster1222¼BlackTieAffair1232½Gervazy116no Driving 8
12Apr91- 8Kee fst 7f :222 :452 1:09 1:214 3↑ Commonwealth BC-G3 4 3 11½ 11½ 1½ 21 Perret C B 124 *.30 100-12 BlackTieAffair1241Housbustr1244ExmplryLdr115hd 2nd best 6
16Mar91- 6GP fst 7f :22 :442 1:091 1:214 3↑ Deputy Minister H 50k 8 3 3½ 3nk 2hd 23 Perret C 122 *.40 94-07 Unbridled1193Housebuster122noShuttleman1145 Gamely 9
29Sep90- 8Bel fst 7f :213 :44 1:082 1:21 3↑ Vosburgh-G1 4 5 42 2½ 33½ 615 Perret C 122 *.30 84-11 Sewickley1264½SunshineJmmy122¾Glttrmn1261¾ 4-wide,tired 9
3Sep90- 8Bel fst 1 :223 :444 1:084 1:34 Jerome H-G1 5 2 21 1½ 16 113 Perret C 126 *.40 99-10 Housebuster12613Citidancer114¾D'Prrot1122 Good handling 5
18Aug90- 8Sar fst 7f :213 :441 1:084 1:214 King's Bishop-G3 8 1 33 2½ 15 13¼ Perret C 122 *.30 96-05 Housebstr1223¼Poppiano115nkSunshine Jimmy1155 Handily 9
23Jun90- 8AP fst 1 :23 :452 1:093 1:343 Sheridan-G3 3 1 11 12 13 14½ Perret C 123 *.05 98-13 Housebstr1234½Spanish Drummer11510½Copelan's Game1139½ 5
Under wraps
28May90- 8Bel fst 1 :223 :45 1:091 1:342 3↑ Metropolitan H-G1 3 1 11 11½ 11½ 2nk Perret C 113 2.40 97-18 CriminalType120nkHousebuster1131½EasyGoer1273 Good try 9
9May90- 8Bel fst 1 :223 :452 1:10 1:344 Withers-G2 6 1 11 1½ 11½ 12 Perret C 126 *.50 95-14 Housebustr1262ProfitKey1264SunnyServe1264½ Ridden out 6
28Apr90- 9CD fst 1 :222 :453 1:111 1:373 Derby Trial-G3 5 2 11 11½ 12 15¼ Perret C 122 *.20 89-26 Housebustr1225¼PrivatSchool119½FllngSky1173 Ridden out 6
11Apr90- 0Kee fst 7f :22 :45 1:084 1:224 Lafayette-G3 1 1 1hd 12½ 15 111 Perret C 121 - 95-09 Housebstr12111SacraHoxen11427CritclChoc113 Ridden out 3
17Mar90- 5GP fst 7f :223 :444 1:091 1:221 Swale-G3 2 2 1½ 1½ 12 11 Perret C 122 *.90 95-15 Housebstr1221SummerSquall1226ThirtySixRd1138¾ Handily 6
10Feb90-10GP fst 7f :214 :442 1:102 1:242 Hutcheson-G3 5 5 1hd 1hd 14 13 Romero RP 119 1.90 84-18 Housebuster1193Yonder1221Stalker114¾ Driving 11
16Jan90- 9GP fst 6f :22 :452 1:112 Spectacular Bid 50k 5 5 31 1½ 13½ 12¼ Perret C 114 *1.50 88-20 Housebuster1142¼FitContendr1132½Stalker1145 Ridden out 8
Previously trained by Ronald L. Benshof
24Nov89- 9Med fst 6f :213 :442 1:094 Morven BC 48k 3 2 1hd 11 16 17 Madrid A Jr 113 4.00 93-14 Housbstr1137Thoddsonchoc119noBoldHour'sLck1134¾ Easily 8
8Nov89- 4Med sly 6f :214 :45 1:111 Md Sp Wt 6 3 2hd 1hd 12 12¾ Krone JA 118 *.50 86-17 Housebuster1182¾Mr.MichaelJ.1181BigTedK.118hd Easily 11
17Oct89- 2Med sly 6f :212 :443 1:103 Md Sp Wt 8 3 41 1hd 2½ 32¼ Chavez JF 118 3.70 87-14 Stalker1182Canadian Roy118nkHousebuster1181 Weakened 8

Inside Information

b. f. 1991, by Private Account (Damascus)–Pure Profit, by Key to the Mint — Lifetime record: 17 14 1 2 $1,641,805

Own.– Ogden Mills Phipps
Br.– Ogden Mills Phipps (Ky)
Tr.– Claude McGaughey III

28Oct95- 4Bel my 1⅛ :454 1:092 1:332 1:46 3↑ ⒻB C Distaff-G1 1 4 1½ 11½ 16 113½ Smith ME 123 *.80e 102-08 Inside Information12313Heavenly Prize1232½Lakeway1231 10
Bobbled start,hand ride
8Oct95- 8Kee fst 1⅛ :48 1:121 1:371 1:50 3↑ ⒻSpinster-G1 4 3 31½ 21 1hd 1hd Smith ME 123 *.50 84-16 Inside Information123hdJade Flush1234Mariah's Storm1233 4
Fractious gate,broke in tangle,exchanged brushes stretch,driving
16Sep95- 6Bel fst 1 1/16 :231 :46 1:092 1:404 3↑ ⒻRuffian H-G1 5 2 1½ 14 110 111 Smith ME 125 *.10 95-09 InsideInformtn12511Unlawful Behavior110noIncinerate1121¼ 6
Easily
13Aug95- 8Sar gd 7f :224 :46 1:10 1:222 3↑ ⒻBallerina H-G1 3 6 52¼ 21½ 22 26 Smith ME 126 *.40 88-07 Classy Mirage1196InsideInformatn1264½Laura's Pist'ette1125 6
Stumbled badly break
4Jly95- 9Mth fst 1 1/16 :234 :464 1:101 1:434 3↑ ⒻMolly Pitcher H-G2 3 2 2hd 1hd 14 16¾ Smith ME 124 *.30 86-21 InsideInformation1246¾JadFlush1151¾HloAmrc1184¼ Handily 5
3Jun95-10Mth fst 1 70 :224 :462 1:111 1:414 3↑ ⒻMth Bud B C H-G3 2 3 3½ 1hd 11½ 12¼ Smith ME 123 *.30 93-20 Inside Information1232¼MorningMeadow1155Incinerate11610 5
Came in some upper stretch,driving
20May95- 8Bel wf 1 :224 :462 1:102 1:35 3↑ ⒻShuvee H-G1 1 2 2hd 11 13 15½ Santos JA 119 2.25e 88-24 Inside Information1195½Sky Beauty12616Restored Hope1152 4
Ridden out
26Apr95- 7Kee fst 7f :224 :453 1:093 1:213 4↑ ⒻAlw 45590 4 2 1½ 12½ 13 14 Smith ME 118 *.30 93-11 Inside Information1184Traverse City1184½Scoop th' Gold114½ 6
Ridden out,sharp
18Nov94- 6Aqu fst 6½f :224 :454 1:094 1:16 3↑ ⒻAlw 42000 4 5 2½ 11½ 15 18 Smith ME 120 *.15 101-14 InsideInfrmatn1208Little Buckles112hdReach for Clever11710 5
Handily
12Jun94- 8Bel fst 1⅛ :451 1:083 1:332 1:462 ⒻMother Goose-G1 2 2 1½ 2hd 33 310¼ Smith ME 121 *.70 89-14 Lakeway1214¼Cinnamon Sugar1216Inside Information121nk 6
Dueled,weakened
8May94- 8Bel my 1 :224 :452 1:093 1:341 ⒻAcorn-G1 3 1 11½ 12½ 16 111 Smith ME 121 *.50 92-17 InsideInformtn12111CinmnSugr1211½SvrgnKtty1213¾ Handily 5
23Apr94- 8Kee fst 1 1/16 :242 :491 1:14 1:464 ⒻAshland-G1 4 2 2½ 1½ 13 15½ Smith ME 121 *.80 75-41 InsideInformton1215½Buntng112nkPrvtSttus1182 Ridden out 6
5Mar94-10GP fst 1 1/16 :231 :462 1:103 1:424 ⒻBonnie Miss-G2 6 5 41½ 2hd 1hd 12¾ Smith ME 114 3.00 96-06 Inside Information1142¾Cinnamon Sugar113nkJade Flush1144 10
Fully extended
21Feb94- 1GP fst 1 1/16 :241 :481 1:122 1:431 ⒻAlw 29000 3 1 11½ 11 11½ 1nk Smith ME 118 *.60 94-09 InsideInformatn118nkCinnamonSugar12111True byTwo1185½ 5
Driving
6Feb94- 7GP fst 7f :224 :453 1:10 1:22 ⒻAlw 25000 7 3 2hd 1hd 11½ 17 Smith ME 118 *1.10 93-11 InsideInfrmatn1187BlushingBlond118nkMiss Prospectr1215½ 9
Six wide bkstr,angled inward leaving bkstr,ridden out
2Nov93- 6Aqu fst 1 :232 :464 1:121 1:382 ⒻAlw 30000 3 2 31 2hd 31½ 33 Smith ME 116 *.80 69-28 Sovereign Kitty116noBunting1163Inside Information1166¾ 7
Checked break,wide
15Sep93- 3Bel fst 6f :223 :462 :584 1:113 ⒻMd Sp Wt 4 5 43 2hd 13 17½ Smith ME 117 1.90 82-19 Inside Information1177½Jade Flush117½Miss Applause1172¾ 7
Wide,ridden out

Itsallgreektome

gr. g. 1987, by Sovereign Dancer (Northern Dancer)–Sans Supplement, by Grey Dawn II — Lifetime record: 29 8 10 2 $1,994,618

Own.– Jhayare Stables
Br.– Sugar Maple Farm (Fla)
Tr.– R.B. Hess Jr

26Feb94- 8SA fm 1¼Ⓣ :472 1:112 1:36 2:003 4↑ ⓇSan Marino H 82k 5 6 610 64½ 79 718 Desormx KJ LB 120 b 2.20 66-16 Semillon1162¼Memento Mori114noAlex the Great1141¾ 7
Very wide into lane
17Jan94- 3SA fm 1Ⓣ :223 :454 1:093 1:343 4↑ Alw 55000 4 6 611 610 56½ 22¼ Dlhoussaye E LB 116 b 2.30 90-08 RobberRamble1152¼Itsallgrktom116nkBonPont1151¼ Late bid 6
Previously trained by Wallace Dollase
15Nov92- 8CD yl 1⅛Ⓣ :483 1:122 1:364 1:491 3↑ River City H 112k 8 8 66 64½ 43½ 4½ Nakatani CS LB 122 b *2.10 89-10 Cozzene'sPrince117noLotusPool118½Stgcrft114no Hung late 8
7Mar92- 8SA gd 1Ⓣ :23 :462 1:094 1:343 4↑ Arcadia H-G3 5 8 87½ 74¾ 53¼ 2¾ Valenzla PA LB 123 *2.50 89-20 FlyTillDawn120¾Itsallgrktom123½Qthf1151¼ 5-wide stretch 11
5Jan92-10Hia fm 1½Ⓣ 2:281 3↑ Hia Turf Cup H 200k 1 2 2½ 1½ 1hd 2nk Velasquez J L 124 b *.40 86-14 CrystalMoment113nkItsallgreektome1241PassagereduSoir1152½ 13
Outfinished
15Dec91- 8Hol fm 1½Ⓣ :52 1:173 2:064 2:30 3↑ Hol Turf Cup-G1 1 3 41¾ 52 32 2hd Desormx KJ LB 126 b *1.40 73-21 Miss Alleged123hdItsallgreektome1261½Quest for Fame126¾ 7
Boxed in ¼ out,4-wide into stretch,game try

2Nov91- 7CD fm 1½Ⓣ :504 1:154 2:062 2:304 3↑ BC Turf-G1 8 2 2½ 2hd 1hd 2½ Velasquez J LB 126 b 4.70 95-06 MissAllegd123½Itsallgreektom1262QustforFm1262 Game try 13
12Oct91- 8Kee fm 1⅛Ⓣ :471 1:111 1:36 1:482 3↑ Keeneland BC-G3 6 4 3½ 1hd 11 12¼ Velasquez J LB 126 b 1.40 103-00 Itsallgrktome1262¼OpenngVrs1264SuprAbound1261½ Driving 6
1Sep91- 9AP fm 1¼Ⓣ :473 1:111 1:354 1:592 3↑ Arl Million-G1 5 5 67½ 88 88½ 76 Sellers SJ L 126 4.90 95-07 Tight Spot126hdAlgenib122nkKartajana123nk Evenly 10
10Aug91- 3Dmr fst 1¼ :454 1:094 1:341 1:594 3↑ Pacific Classic 1000k 1 6 53½ 45 55½ 65½ Nakatani CS LB 124 7.80 - - BestPal1161TwilightAgnda1242¾Unbrdld1241¼ Saved ground 8
29Jun91- 4Hol fst 1¼ :464 1:101 1:341 1:592 3↑ Hol Gold Cup-G1 9 6 54 33 34 32¾ Nakatani CS LB 119 8.30 97-00 Mrqutry110hdFrmWy122¾Itsllgrktom1193½ Wide to far turn 9
27May91- 8Hol fm 1¼Ⓣ :481 1:114 1:36 2:00 3↑ Hol Turf H-G1 4 5 58½ 34½ 1hd 2¾ Nakatani CS LB 123 *1.60 92-09 Exbourne119¾Itsallgreektome123½Prized1233½ No mishap 6
3May91- 8CD fm 1⅛Ⓣ :48 1:111 1:352 1:471 4↑ ET Turf Classic-G3 8 6 66 65¾ 4¾ 2no Nakatani CS LB 123 b *1.40 109-00 Opening Verse116noItsallgreektome1233Pedro the Cool112nk 11
Crowded early
14Apr91- 8Kee gd 1⅛Ⓣ :494 1:143 1:384 1:511 4↑ Elkhorn-G2 1 2 2hd 2½ 11½ 1¾ Baze RA LB 123 b *.60 89-13 Itsallgrktom123¾PrtArmy113¾SprkO'Dn113¾ Fully extended 7
23Mar91- 8GG yl 1Ⓣ :241 :483 1:124 1:384 3↑ S F Mile H-G3 1 6 68½ 65¾ 65 42 Nakatani CS LB 124 b *.90 82-16 Forty Niner Days113nkExbourne1161½Blaze o' Brien116nk 6
Rallied inside
16Dec90- 8Hol fm 1½Ⓣ :474 1:123 2:011 2:244 3↑ Hol Turf Cup-G1 1 6 86¾ 63¼ 11 11 Nakatani CS LB 122 b *2.50 97-04 Itsallgrktom1221Mshkour1262LvthDrm126hd 4-wide stretch 14
11Nov90- 8Hol fm 1⅛Ⓣ :464 1:101 1:342 1:463 Hol Derby-G1 6 10 107¾ 97¼ 43 1hd Nakatani CS LB 122 b 2.80 95-09 Itsallgreektome122hdSeptiemCl1222Anshn122¾ Bumped 1/16 12
27Oct90- 6Bel gd 1Ⓣ :223 :454 1:10 1:351 3↑ BC Mile-G1 6 6 53 21 2½ 2nk Natakani CS 122 b 36.90 90-15 RoylAcademy122nkItsallgreektome122¾Prolo122½ Sharp try 13
22Sep90- 8BM fm 1 1/16Ⓣ :234 :48 1:114 1:431 Ascot H-G3 5 6 63¾ 31½ 11 11 Nakatani CS LB 122 b *.70 89-14 Itsallgrektom1221NoblDr.112½ProforSur117hd Rallied wide 7
19Aug90- 8Dmr fm 1⅛Ⓣ :483 1:131 1:371 1:493 Dmr Derby-G2 4 8 89 76½ 44½ 23 Baze RA LB 122 b 4.00 87-08 ⒹTight Spot1223Itsallgreektome1221¾Predecessor122¾ 10
Troubled trip;Placed first by disqualification - ruling rescinded 9/26/90
5Aug90- 8Dmr fm 1 1/16Ⓣ :241 :48 1:112 1:414 La Jolla H-G3 4 4 46½ 45¼ 32½ 2no Garcia JA L 119 b *1.80 98-04 Tight Spot118noItsallgreektome1194Music Prospector1181 6
Just missed
10Jun90- 8Hol fm 1⅛Ⓣ :474 1:113 1:36 1:474 Cinema H-G2 10 9 96¾ 85½ 2½ 31 Nakatani CS 117 b 2.70 88-10 Jovial1151Mehmetori113noItsllgrktom1172½ Nipped for 2nd 10
26May90- 8Hol fm 1 1/16Ⓣ :23 :461 1:093 1:401 Will Rogers H-G3 2 6 77½ 76¼ 1½ 11¾ Nakatani CS 114 b 13.50 94-06 Itsallgreektome1141¾Warcrft120½BllCov116nk Broke slowly 9
5May90- 6Hol fm 1Ⓣ :23 :454 1:092 1:343 Spotlight BC H 109k 8 8 76 64½ 2hd 1no Nakatani CS 112 31.90 91-08 Itsallgreektome112noWarcraft120nkRobyn Dancer115½ Wide 9
4Mar90- 3SA fst 1 1/16 :24 :483 1:13 1:441 Alw 37000 6 5 41½ 51¾ 46½ 47¾ Davis RG 118 b 2.80 74-18 Warcraft1206Apprised120hdOh Wow1201¾ Broke awkwardly 8
9Feb90- 7SA fst 6f :213 :443 :57 1:101 Alw 34000 1 8 85½ 86¾ 59 49½ Davis RG 120 b 6.40 75-23 BurntHills120noOneMoreWork1203TalentedPirat1206½ Outrun 8
6Jan90- 5SA fst 6f :213 :434 :56 1:084 Alw 34000 2 7 52¼ 41¾ 42 41¼ Davis RG 120 b 9.40 91-09 PhantomX.120½BurntHills120¾DuetotheKing117no Evenly 10
21Sep89- 9LaD fst 7f :223 :461 1:122 1:26 Super Derby Juv 50k 7 7 66½ 55½ 713 720½ Davis RG 116 *1.40 57-25 CopperKenny1122¼RocketGibralter116½LeCounty1161¼ Dull 8
26Aug89- 6Dmr fst 6f :214 :45 :572 1:10 Md Sp Wt 6 9 64½ 44 33 1nk Davis RG 117 28.10 88-13 Itsallgreektome117nkDachi's Folly117hdJet West1172 11
Prevailed in hard drive

Jewel Princess

b. f. 1992, by Key to the Mint (Graustark)–Jewell Ridge, by Melyno

Lifetime record: 29 13 4 7 $1,904,060

Own.– Stephen & Stephen & The Thoroughbred Corp
Br.– Farnsworth Farms (Fla)
Tr.– Wallace Dollase

8Nov97- 4Hol fst 1⅛ :454 1:091 1:342 1:471 3↑ ⒻBC Distaff-G1 4 7 89¼ 89½ 56¼ — Nakatani CS LB 123 *1.00e - - Ajina1202Sharp Cat1203½Escena1231 Pulled up,walked off 8
19Oct97- 9Bel fst 1⅛ :463 1:103 1:352 1:481 3↑ ⒻBeldame-G1 2 7 66½ 55½ 34½ 34 Nakatani CS L 123 f 2.30 85-12 HiddenLak1232Ajn1192JwlPrncss1231¼ Broke slowly,rallied 8
20Jly97- 8Hol fst 1⅛ :463 1:101 1:341 1:462 3↑ ⒻVanity H-G1 1 3 34½ 43½ 33½ 34 Nakatani CS LB 123 *.90 90-04 Twice the Vice121hdReal Connection1144Jewel Princess1236½ 5
Inside to ⅛,weakened
28Jun97- 9Bel fst 1 1/16 :223 :452 1:094 1:404 3↑ ⒻHempstead H-G1 8 8 87 74½ 34½ 34 Nakatani CS L 124 *1.55 91-13 HiddnLake1172TwicetheVice1212JewlPrncss1245¼ Late gain 9
11Apr97- 9OP wf 1 1/16 :231 :463 1:104 1:413 4↑ ⒻApple Blossom H-G1 3 8 88¼ 75¾ 44 24 Nakatani CS L 124 *.90 96-12 Halo America1174Jewel Princess124hdDifferent1211½ 8
Angled out upper stretch,up for place
9Mar97- 7SA fst 1⅛ :48 1:121 1:364 1:491 4↑ ⒻS Margarita H-G1 2 4 51¾ 53¼ 32 1½ Nakatani CS LB 125 *.40 87-12 JewlPrincss125½TopRung116nkHiddenLak1143 Determinedly 6
16Feb97- 8SA fst 1 1/16 :231 :464 1:101 1:413 4↑ ⒻS Maria H-G1 4 5 65½ 53¾ 21½ 15 Nakatani CS LB 123 *1.00 95-12 JewelPrincess1235Cat'sCrdl118½TopRung1171 Clear,driving 7
26Oct96- 6WO fst 1⅛ :482 1:123 1:363 1:482 3↑ ⒻB C Distaff-G1 1 5 43½ 42½ 2½ 11½ Nakatani CS L 123 2.40 104-02 Jewel Princess1231½Serena's Song1231¾Different1235¼ 6
Driving inside
6Oct96- 5SA fst 1 1/16 :224 :454 1:094 1:414 3↑ ⒻLady's Secret BC H-G2 1 5 510 44½ 32½ 2½ Nakatani CS LB 122 *.60 85-16 TopRung116½JewlPrincess1221¾SleepEsy1165 Closed gamely 5
Previously owned by Martha J. & Richard J. Stephen
21Jly96- 9Hol fst 1⅛ :464 1:102 1:343 1:47 3↑ ⒻVanity H-G1 2 3 41½ 1hd 11 13 Nakatani CS LB 120 2.50 98-10 JewelPrincss1203Srn'sSong125¾TopRung116½ Clear,driving 6
23Jun96- 9Hol fst 1 1/16 :224 :461 1:094 1:404 3↑ ⒻMilady BC H-G1 5 5 56 54 41½ 2¾ Nakatani CS LB 120 1.80 96-09 TwicetheVice120¾JwlPrncss1201¼Urbn1171 5 wide into lane 5
25May96- 8Hol fst 1 1/16 :233 :464 1:102 1:411 3↑ ⒻHawthorne H-G2 1 6 58 57 32 2hd McCarrn CJ LB 120 *.90 95-08 Borodislew119hdJwlPrncss120½Urbn1186 Bobbled start,game 6
3May96- 7CD fst 1 1/16 :242 :474 1:12 1:422 3↑ ⒻLouisville BC H-G2 3 5 55½ 32½ 2½ 1nk McCarron CJ L 118 2.00 99-06 Jewel Princess118nkSerena's Song1237½Naskra Colors1133½ 6
Off bit slow,angled 6 wide stretch,leaned in brushed,1/8,driving
10Mar96- 7SA fst 1⅛ :48 1:122 1:364 1:492 4↑ ⒻS Margarita H-G1 6 8 63¼ 64 45 3¾ Solis A LB 119 2.00 85-19 Twice the Vice117nkSleep Easy115½Jewel Princess1192¾ 8
Bumped near ⅜,wide into lane
11Feb96- 6SA fst 1⅛ :472 1:112 1:364 1:492 ⒻLa Canada-G2 2 6 63¾ 52 2hd 12½ Solis A LB 119 *.90 86-19 Jewel Princess1192½Dixie Pearl1161¼Privity117¾ 6
Broke slow and slightly in air,shut off start,awaited room ¼
20Jan96- 8SA fst 1 1/16 :233 :472 1:113 1:414 ⒻEl Encino-G2 2 4 41½ 2hd 2hd 12½ Solis A LB 117 2.70 86-16 Jewel Princess1172½Sleep Easy1193½Urbane1191¾ Gamely 4
Previously owned by Richard J. Stephen
30Dec95- 8SA fst 7f :224 :452 1:084 1:212 ⒻLa Brea-G2 2 6 55 64½ 45½ 33¾ Nakatani CS LB 119 3.20 91-08 ExoticWood1192Evil'sPc1191¾JwlPrncss1191¼ Along for 3rd 6
4Nov95- 8SA fst 1 1/16 :224 :46 1:101 1:412 ⒻLinda Vista BC H-G3 1 4 46½ 21 13 19 McCarron CJ LB 118 2.80 88-17 JewelPrincess1189RaduCool1153½SkiDancr1185 Kept to task 5
14Oct95- 8SA fm 1Ⓣ :232 :47 1:112 1:363 ⒻH C Ramser Sr 107k 1 10 1013 87 55¼ 3¾ Pincay L Jr LB 117 *2.20 82-17 SkiDancer117nkRaduCool114½JewelPrncss1174 Finished well 10
20Aug95- 8Dmr fm 1⅛Ⓣ :474 1:123 1:372 1:493 ⒻDmr Oaks-G1 6 5 510 54¼ 53 52½ Solis A LB 120 7.40 85-11 BailOutBecky120noSleepEsy1201¼TopRuhl120¾ Mild late bid 9
29Jly95- 2Dmr fm 1Ⓣ :224 :462 1:111 1:36 ⒻSan Clemente H-G3 6 6 55 42 1½ 11¾ McCarron CJ LB 115 10.40 90-11 JewelPrncss1151¾Aurtt1192ScrtchPpr1192 4 wide into lane 6
20May95- 8Hol fm 1 1/16Ⓣ :24 :48 1:12 1:413 ⒻHoneymoon H-G3 5 5 63½ 62¾ 42¾ 55¾ Antley CW LB 116 15.00 82-12 Auriette117¾Artica1193Top Shape1181¾ 5 wide into lane 6
30Apr95- 8Hol fm 1Ⓣ :221 :451 1:10 1:343 ⒻSenorita BC-G3 3 7 68½ 54¼ 43½ 53½ Antley CW LB 118 3.50 86-12 Top Shape114nkArtica118nkAuriette1162¾ Mild bid 10
8Apr95- 8BM fm 1Ⓣ :234 :473 1:123 1:38 ⒻSan Jose BC 69k 5 5 43 41¾ 21 12 Chapman TM LB 115 2.40 83-16 Jewel Princess1152Slew Del Siglo1153½Whatninspirtion1133 6
Rallied wide
12Mar95- 8SA fst 1 1/16 :233 :473 1:12 1:423 ⒻS A Oaks-G1 2 5 41½ 53 59½ 525¼ McCarron CJ LB 117 11.40 57-23 Serena'sSong117hdUrban11714Mr'sShb117no Inside,gave way 5
22Feb95- 8SA fm 1Ⓣ :234 :484 1:141 1:39 ⒻAlw 50000 1 4 43½ 42½ 41½ 11 Nakatani CS LB 114 5.90 71-30 Jewel Princess1141Kuda114nkArtica117½ Up late stages 6
Previously owned by Michael H. Sherman;previously trained by Lee A. Sherman
4Dec94- 1Crc fst 1 1/16 :234 :481 1:142 1:503 ⒻAlw 17500 5 5 43½ 22 1½ 12½ Castillo H Jr 117 6.50 66-32 Jewel Princess1172½With a Princess1201StaceyLcey1173¼ 6
4-wide,driving
13Nov94- 3Crc sly 7f :233 :471 1:132 1:272 ⒻMd 30000 5 6 31½ 22 2hd 1¾ Castillo H Jr 117 7.40 75-22 Jewel Princess117¾Shocking Pleasre1199½Nualgorhythm117nk 6
Ducked in st,driving
27Oct94- 3Crc fst 5½f :222 :47 1:003 1:073 ⒻMd 20000 7 7 56¾ 510 510 38½ Ramos WS 118 6.50 76-17 LetsGotoIt1186Glitterchck1182½JwlPrncss118nk Late rally 7

Kotashaan (Fr)

dkbbr. c. 1988, by Darshaan (Shirley Heights)–Haute Autorite, by Elocutionist
Lifetime record: 22 10 5 2 $2,810,528
Own.– La Presle Farm
Br.– Wertheimer et Frere (Fr)
Tr.– Richard Mandella

28Nov93♦ Tokyo(Jpn) fm*1½ⓉLH 2:242 3↑ Japan Cup-G1 Stk3650000 2¹¼ Desormeaux KJ 126 *4.20 Legacy World126¼Kotashaan126hdWinning Ticket121nk 16
Toward rear,stumbled 1st turn,rallied 2f out,rider misjudged finish
6Nov93- 7SA fm 1½Ⓣ :483 1:122 2:012 2:25 3↑ BC Turf-G1 13 9 96¾ 31½ 2hd 1½ Dsrmeaux KJ LB 126 *1.50 93-04 Kotashaan126½Bien Bien1261¼Luazur126¾ 4-wide,driving 14
10Oct93- 8SA fm 1½Ⓣ :482 1:121 2:001 2:25 3↑ Oak Tree Inv'l-G1 4 2 2hd 11½ 12 14 Dsrmeaux KJ LB 124 *.50 93-07 Kotashaan1244Luazur1245½Let's Elope12121 Clear,driving 4
5Sep93- 8Dmr fm 1⅜Ⓣ :494 1:142 1:384 2:15 3↑ Dmr Inv'l H-G2 7 4 43½ 52½ 31½ 2no Dsrmeaux KJ LB 123 *.40 87-10 Luazur116noKotashaan1232¾Myrakalu1141 7
Off slowly,5 wide into drive
8Aug93- 8Dmr fm 1⅛Ⓣ :481 1:121 1:363 1:482 3↑ Eddie Read H-G1 2 6 64 62¾ 4¾ 13 Dsrmeaux KJ LB 122 *.90 94-06 Kotashaan1223Leger Cat116½Rainbow Corner114no 6
Carried out 8 wide ¼,strong rally,handily
18Apr93- 4SA fm *1¾Ⓣ :473 1:593 2:224 2:45 4↑ San Juan Cap H-G1 1 5 54 42½ 32½ 1no Dsrmeaux KJ LB 121 *.90 100-12 Kotashaan121noBnBn1191¼Frs12310 Off slowly,boxed in ¼ 5
21Mar93- 8SA fm 1½Ⓣ :473 1:113 2:00 2:234 4↑ San Luis Rey-G1 1 4 32 3nk 1½ 11¼ Dsrmeaux KJ LB 124 *.80 99-01 Kotashaan1241¼Bien Bien12413Fast Cure1247 Ridden out 4
15Feb93- 8SA yl *1½Ⓣ :494 1:15 2:052 2:273 4↑ San Luis Obispo-G2 1 7 76½ 53 11½ 17 Dsrmeaux KJ LB 114 1.80 - - Kotshn1147CarnvlBby113nkThNm'sJmmy1151¾ Wide,handily 8
23Jan93- 8SA gd 1¼Ⓣ :482 1:131 1:371 2:013 4↑ San Marcos H-G2 4 7 74¾ 41¾ 42 21 Dsrmeaux KJ LB 116 12.80 78-21 StarofCozzene1201Kotshaan1162CrnvlBby1121½ Good effort 7
1Jan93- 8SA gd 1⅛Ⓣ :474 1:114 1:361 1:481 4↑ San Gabriel H-G3 8 8 73½ 74¼ 64 46¾ Walls MK LB 114 20.10 71-10 Star of Cozzene1183Bistro Garden1143Leger Cat115¾ 9
Wide backstretch
19Nov92- 8Hol fm 1 1/16Ⓣ :231 :47 1:11 1:412 3↑ Alw 50000 1 6 63¾ 64 64½ 59 McCarron CJ B 115 2.10 89-22 Star of Cozzene1141¼Super May1144½Memo1143 6
Off slowly,rank early,wide
27Apr92- 8SA fm 1¼Ⓣ :472 1:114 1:353 1:594 4↑ [R]San Jacinto H 110k 2 4 32 32 65 44½ McCarron CJ B 119 *1.50 83-20 Missionary Ridge119¾Fanatic Boy1182Latin American1161¾ 8
Stumbled badly ⅜
4Apr92- 8SA fst 1⅛ :462 1:102 1:35 1:471 4↑ San Bernardino H-G2 3 7 65 64½ 54½ 55¼ McCarron CJ B 117 4.50 89-11 AnothrReview1143DefensivPly1151¼Loch116¾ No punch lane 11
12Mar92- 8SA fm 1Ⓣ :231 :463 1:094 1:333 4↑ Alw 44000 3 6 54 52¾ 31½ 11¼ McCarron CJ B 121 *1.60 95-05 Kotashn1211¼RegalGroom117hdMujzf121hd Off slowly,wide 9
Previously trained by Andre Fabre
19Sep91♦ Maisns-Lffitte(Fr) yl *1¼ⓉStr 2:03 3↑ La Coupe de Maisons-Laffitte-G3 Stk59000 21½ Guignard G 119 *1.20 Tel Quel1191½Kotashaan1191½April Night123½ 9
Tracked close up in 3rd,led 1f out,no answer to winner
15Aug91♦ Deauville(Fr) gd *1¼ⓉRH 2:064 Prix Guillaume d'Ornano-G2 Stk85500 3nk Guignard G 124 *1.00e Glity121nkArcangues127hdKotashaan1242 6
Well placed in 4th,strong rally over 1f out,gamely
23Jun91♦ Longchamp(Fr) yl *1¼ⓉRH 2:051 Grand Prix de Paris-G1 Stk421000 32¼ Guignard G 128 13.00 Subotica128nkSillery1282Kotashaan128nk 9
Tracked in 4th,bid 2f out,evenly late.Cudas 4th
19May91♦ Longchamp(Fr) gd *1¼ⓉRH 2:062 Prix la Force-G3 Stk57900 1nk Guignard G 123 *1.40 Kotashaan123nkFunny Baby1231½John Balliol1235 6
Track in 4th,in tight 1f out,sharp run to lead near line
30Apr91♦ Longchamp(Fr) sf *1 5/16ⓉRH 2:253 Prix de Courcelles (Listed)36300 1no Guignard G 123 4.30 Kotashaan123noRancher123½Malmsey1232 8
Settled in 5th,rallied to lead on line
7Apr91♦ Longchamp(Fr) sf *1⅜ⓉRH 2:19 Prix Noailles-G2 Stk88100 55½ Guignard G 128 17.00 Pistolet Bleu128¾Subotica1283Pigeon Voyageur128no 9
Tracked in 4th,mild bid 2f out,faded late
30Nov90♦ Maisns-Lffitte(Fr) hy *1⅛ⓉRH 2:064 Prix Manitou III Mdn33200 11½ Guignard G 121 *1.60 Kotashaan1211½Cudas121hdPactolo121hd 15
Tracked in 4th,rallied to lead 1f out,driving.Matrun 5th
16Nov90♦ Saint-Cloud(Fr) hy *1ⓉLH 1:554 Prix Gardefeu Mdn (FT)33800 2nk Doleuze O 118 13.00 Svetlana120hdKotashaan1182½La Carene1202½ 18
Well placed in 5th,finished well,gaining at line

Laugh and Be Merry

dbbr. f. 1985, by Erin's Isle (Busted)–Imaflash, by Reviewer
Lifetime record: 26 9 7 3 $482,937
Own.– Pin Oak Stable
Br.– Pin Oak Farm (Ky)
Tr.– Angel Penna Jr

29Sep90- 9Med fm 1⅜Ⓣ :49 1:134 1:381 2:154 3↑ ⒻQueen Charlotte H-G3 4 4 41½ 31½ 1hd 11¼ McCauley WH 118 *.30 92-15 LghandBeMrry1181¼MissUnnameable1131¾MemoriesofPam1134 8
Driving
9Sep90- 8Bel fm 1¼[T] :473 1:113 1:354 2:001 3↑ ⒻFlower Bowl H-G1 5 3 33 31 1½ 1½ McCauley WH 115 *1.10 99-01 LaughandBeMerry115½Foresta1153GailyGaily117nk Driving 13
28Jly90- 9WO fm *1⅛Ⓣ 1:444 3↑ ⒻBud BC H-G2C 3 6 63¾ 42½ 23 21½ McCauley WH 119 *.85 110-00 Fieldy1241½LaughandBeMrry119½SttlSngu1154½ Lacked rally 8
16Jun90- 8Bel fm 1¼[T] :471 1:104 1:341 1:582 3↑ ⒻNew York H-G2 5 4 43 32 21 2no McCauley WH 114 *1.60 108-03 Capades119noLaugh and Be Merry1146Key Flyer1091¼ 7
Gamely,just missed
2Jun90- 5Bel fm 1 1/16[T] :243 :472 1:11 1:404 3↑ ⒻHandicap 47000 5 2 24 21½ 11½ 13¼ McCauley WH 119 *1.80 101-04 LaughandBeMrry1193¼Highland Penny1202½Ann Alleged113nk 6
Hand ride
7Apr90- 9GP fm 1½Ⓣ :472 1:111 1:593 2:241 3↑ ⒻOrchid H-G2 7 3 2hd 2hd 11½ 2hd McCauley WH 113 2.50 104-01 Coolawin112hdLaughandBeMrry1134¼GlyGly1213½ Just failed 10
17Mar90- 7GP hd 1 1/16Ⓣ :231 :463 1:10 1:401 3↑ ⒻBuckram Oak H-G3 2 4 45 43 42½ 1no McCauley WH 112 4.10 100-04 LaughandBeMrry112noSummrSecrtary114noPrincessMora1131¼ 12
Driving
17Feb90- 6GP fm 1Ⓣ :234 :48 1:12 1:352 4↑ ⒻAlw 24000 5 6 64 32 2½ 1½ McCauley WH 119 *1.30 97-03 LghandBeMrry119½Contumelious1177MotlSwng1192 Driving 11
7Nov89- 5Aqu fst 1⅜⊗ :49 1:393 2:174 3↑ ⒻAlw 36000 1 3 46 21½ 15 18¾ McCauley WH 117 *.80 90-18 LaughandBeMerry1178¾Moment of Dare115noD'or Etoile1171 6
Ridden out
22Oct89- 8Aqu fst 1⅜ :483 1:133 1:383 2:142 3↑ ⒻLong Island H-G2 5 4 53 41¼ 55½ 511¾ Samyn JL 112 2.20 96-15 Warfie1111¼River Memories1136½Noble Links1112 Faltered 6
29Sep89- 9Med yl 1⅜Ⓣ :471 1:131 1:382 2:163 3↑ ⒻQueen Charlotte H-G3 12 3 34 2½ 22½ 22¾ Samyn JL 113 5.60 79-24 SpruceFir1172¾LghandBeMrry1134½Epmthus114nk 2nd best 12
16Sep89- 7Bel yl 1¼[T] :501 1:151 1:41 2:064 3↑ ⒻFlower Bowl H-G1 5 6 54 54 711 816¼ Samyn JL 113 8.30 44-40 RiverMemories1121¾Capades1162¼MissUnnameable1161¼ Tired 11
14Aug89- 8Sar gd 1⅛[T] :484 1:13 1:373 1:501 3↑ ⒻDiana H-G2 4 4 46½ 32½ 43 31¾ Antley CW 114 9.30 87-18 [D]Wooing111nkGlowing Honor1151½Laugh and Be Merry114nk 9
Finished well
2Jly89- 8Bel fm 1⅜[T] :482 1:124 1:36 2:123 3↑ ⒻSheepshead Bay H-G2 2 5 31½ 32½ 41½ 32¼ Santos JA 112 6.80 92-13 Love You byHeart1181Nastique1171¼LaughandBeMerry112no 10
Lacked room
17Jun89- 8Bel sf 1¼[T] :503 1:153 1:402 2:054 3↑ ⒻNew York H-G2 5 4 43½ 21½ 22 22½ Santos JA 112 10.80 62-35 MissUnnameable1082½[D]LghandBeMrry1121¼LoveYoubyHrt119½ 8
Bore in;Disqualified and placed fourth
31May89- 5Bel fm 1¼[T] :51 1:164 1:403 2:033 3↑ ⒻAlw 33000 8 6 42½ 32 24 22¼ Samyn JL 119 *1.30 74-17 Starofanera1122¼LaughandBeMrry1191¼Highland Penny119½ 9
Held place
1Apr89- 8Hia fm *1⅛Ⓣ 1:503 3↑ ⒻKey Largo 50k 6 6 65¾ 51¾ 32½ 51½ Samyn JL 115 4.70 76-22 Judy'sRedShoes1221FrauleinLieber112noFirstPrediction115½ 11
Weakened
19Feb89-10GP fm 1½Ⓣ :472 1:122 2:023 2:264 3↑ ⒻOrchid H-G2 13 3 56½ 11 2hd 3½ Samyn JL 110 38.20 89-09 GailyGaily110noAnkaGrmania120½LghndBMrry1101 Weakened 13
23Jan89- 8GP fm 1½Ⓣ :50 1:144 2:044 2:284 4↑ ⒻAlw 19000 3 6 64½ 2½ 1hd 11¼ Samyn JL 119 *1.80 80-14 LghandBeMrry1191¼LadyofMyArt1193½FntGlow1172 Driving 12
1Jan89-10Crc fm 1½Ⓣ :483 1:123 2:012 2:262 3↑ ⒻLa Prev Inv'l H-G2 4 8 87½ 117¼ 95¾ 74½ Samyn JL 110 28.50f 89-06 Judy'sRdShoes120½GailyGly111½BeutyCrm118nk No menace 14
11Dec88- 9Crc fm *1⅛Ⓣ 1:453 3↑ ⒻMy Chrmr H (Div 2) 48k 11 11 125½ 127½ 65¼ 46 Gonzalez MA 111 55.40 84-10 Judy'sRedShoes1173½Orange Motiff1131¼Chores at Dawn1131¼ 13
Late gain
6Nov88- 6Aqu fst 1⅛ :481 1:131 1:394 1:533 3↑ ⒻAlw 31000 2 3 35½ 32½ 14 15 Santos JA 115 2.50 67-26 LaughandBeMrry1155[D]BlackBeavr115nkFinez1151¾ Driving 6
14Oct88- 5Bel fm 1Ⓣ :232 :471 1:12 1:371 3↑ ⒻAlw 29000 10 6 44 42½ 32 27¼ Santos JA 114 17.30 72-22 TimelyBusiness1147¼LaughandBeMrry114hdCourtaflame114¾ 12
Gained place

19Jun88- 1Bel fst 1 1/16 :231 :46 1:103 1:424 ⒻAlw 29000 5 5 612 615 621 627¾ Santos JA 118 10.30 60-21 Maplejinsky1165½Near1184Bai Shun1163¼ Outrun 6
18May88- 6Bel sly 1 :23 :461 1:12 1:391 ⒻMd Sp Wt 9 4 2½ 2½ 11 1hd Santos JA 121 *2.00 69-19 LaughandBeMrry121hdEdistoLight1213JolScot1215¾ Driving 9
13Jan88- 5GP fst 1 1/16 :234 :483 1:143 1:48 ⒻMd Sp Wt 7 7 62¾ 41½ 22½ 22½ MacKinze HA 121 13.90 58-28 KeytotheStage1212½LaughandBeMrry1212½Words Hurt1211½ 12
2nd best

Lit de Justice

gr. c. 1990, by El Gran Senor (Northern Dancer)–Kanmary, by Kenmare **Lifetime record: 36 10 8 6 $1,398,677**

Own.– Evergreen Farm

Br.– Swettenham Stud & Mrs Julian G. Rogers (Ky)

Tr.– Jenine Sahadi

26Oct96- 5WO fst 6f :213 :44 :561 1:083 3↑ B C Sprint-G1 5 13 1311 106¾ 44 11¼ Nakatani C L 126 b *4.00 100-08 Lit de Justice1261¼Paying Dues126nkHonour and Glory1231¼ 13
Perfect trip,finished fast
17Aug96- 8Dmr fst 7f :214 :44 1:081 1:203 3↑ Pat O'Brien H-G3 8 8 713 57¾ 54½ 33½ Nakatani CS LB 123 b *.80 93-12 Alphabet Soup1183½Boundless Momnt116noLitdeJustice123no 8
4 wide turn
28Jly96- 8Dmr fst 6f :22 :443 1:08 3↑ Bing Crosby B C H-G3 6 3 68¼ 42½ 2½ 13½ Nakatani CS LB 121 b *1.10 99-07 LitdeJustice1213½ConcptWin116noGoldLnd1161¾ Ridden out 6
6Apr96- 8SA fst 6½f :221 :444 1:082 1:142 3↑ Potrero Grande BC H-G3 6 4 64¾ 43 45 47¾ Solis A LB 122 b 1.80 90-08 Abaginone1156Dramatic Gold117½Kingdom Found1181¼ 6
5 wide,no bid
2Mar96- 9SA fst 7f :224 :453 1:094 1:221 4↑ San Carlos H-G2 5 7 87¼ 75¾ 62½ 31½ Nakatani CS LB 123 b *.70 89-14 Kingdom Found1161¼Lakota Brave114nkLit de Justice123½ 8
6 wide into lane
4Feb96- 8SA fst 6f :212 :44 :561 1:084 4↑ Palos Verdes H-G3 8 8 79 76½ 44 11½ Dlhoussaye E LB 122 b *1.10 94-11 LitdeJustice1221½Siphon119½LakotaBrv115nk Strong finish 9
7Jan96- 8SA fst 5½f :212 :441 :553 1:014 4↑ El Conejo H 104k 3 4 68 66 11½ 15½ Nakatani CS LB 119 b 2.40 101-09 Lit de Justice1195½A.J. Jett1124Fu Man Slew116½ 6
4 wide¼,ridden out
17Dec95- 9Hol gd 1Ⓣ :24 :474 1:12 1:36 3↑ Alw 55000 3 9 99 84½ 72 2no Nakatani CS LB 115 b *1.60 83-17 Bon Point115noLit de Justice1151¼Polish Admiral1161¼ 9
Closed gamely
28Oct95- 3Bel my 6f :213 :442 :562 1:09 3↑ B C Sprint-G1 5 12 1312 119 66 32¼ Nakatani CS L 126 b 14.50f 94-08 Desert Stormer123nkMr. Greeley1232Lit de Justice126nk 13
8 wide¼,belatedly
16Sep95- 7Bel fst 7f :222 :444 1:092 1:222 3↑ Vosburgh-G1 3 13 1110 129¾ 1310 138½ Nakatani CS L 126 b 4.00 80-13 NotSrprsng126noYouandI126noOurEmblm1261 Broke slowly 13
19Aug95- 8Dmr fst 7f :214 :434 1:08 1:20 3↑ Pat O'Brien H-G3 7 7 711 78½ 1½ 16½ Nakatani CS LB 118 b 4.50 101-06 Lit de Justice1186½D'hallevant1172¼Pembroke1191¼ 7
Balked gate,handily
15Jly95- 9Hol fm 5½fⓉ :204 :423 :541 1:002 3↑ Hol Bud B C H 153k 1 4 411 411 44½ 23 Black CA LB 119 b 4.50 102-00 Pembroke1203Lit de Justice119hdCyrano Storm1182¾ 5
Finished well for 2nd
18Jun95-11Hol gd 1 1/16Ⓣ :24 :48 1:113 1:412 4↑ Alw 60000 6 6 63 32 21½ 21¾ Nakatani CS LB 114 b *1.70 87-13 Jahafil1141¾LtdJustc1142¾InnrCty1165 Bore out final ⅛ 7
20May95- 3Hol fst 6½f :214 :434 1:07 1:131 3↑ Rich Cream H 47k 3 3 416 416 413 413 Nakatani CS LB 121 b *1.10 90-04 Lucky Forever1185Blumin Affair1163D'hallevant1205 4
Balked gate,no speed
14Apr95- 8Kee fst 7f :224 :452 1:092 1:22 3↑ Commonwealth B C-G2 1 6 62¼ 42 1hd 3½ Nakatani CS L 121 b 2.80 91-10 Golden Gear118hdTurkomatic112nkLit de Justice121nk 8
Inside bid,good try
11Mar95- 8SA wf 6½f :213 :441 1:081 1:143 4↑ Potrero Grande H-G3 6 6 69¼ 67½ 11½ 13½ Nakatani CS LB 115 b *1.20 99-07 Lit de Justice1153½Cardmania119hdPhone Roberto116½ 6
5 wide ¼,handily
18Feb95- 8SA fst 5½f :212 :441 :56 1:021 4↑ El Conejo H 110k 5 7 77¼ 54¼ 5½ 22 Nakatani CS LB 115 b *1.10 97-08 Phone Roberto1142[D]Lit de Justice1151Lost Pan112¾ 8
Disqualified and placed sixth
18Jan95- 3SA fst 6½f :212 :441 1:09 1:154 4↑ Alw 53000 1 6 67½ 53¼ 12 12½ Nakatani CS LB 118 b *1.40 93-14 LitdeJustice1182½VirtuousRegent1172¾Marmoe1162 Handily 6
3Dec94- 7Hol fm 1Ⓣ :231 :463 1:103 1:351 3↑ Alw 42000 8 8 810 51¾ 21½ 1½ Nakatani CS LB 116 b *1.70 88-16 LitdeJustice116½Saltgrass1142Prclssly116¾ Circled field 9
16Oct94- 8SA fm 1Ⓣ :23 :46 1:091 1:334 3↑ Col Koester H-G2 1 4 41¾ 41¾ 42¼ 54¼ Desrmeaux KJ L 115 b 6.70 93-16 BonPoint116½Journlism1202JohannQuatz1171¼ Saved ground 5
27Aug94- 2Dmr fm 1 1/16Ⓣ :242 :492 1:133 1:433 3↑ Alw 44534 2 7 76 53½ 31½ 1nk Nakatani CS L 119 *.70 88-11 Lit de Justice119nkEastern Spirit1221¾Arinthod122½ 9
4 wide into lane
30Jly94- 7Dmr fm 1 1/16Ⓣ :233 :48 1:13 1:441 3↑ Alw 44534 4 7 78½ 75¼ 54¼ 2½ Nakatani CS LB 119 *1.30 84-12 Wesnorth119½Lit de Justice1193½Latin Book119hd 10
Previously trained by Alain de Royer-Dupre
12Jun94♦ Chantilly(Fr) gd *1ⓉRH 1:364 4↑ Prix du Chemin de Fer du Nord-G3 Stk60500 32¼ Mongil W 123 12.00 Zabar1272Jeune Homme129nkLit de Justice1232 6
Well placed in 3rd,2nd 2f out,lost 2nd near line
4Jun94♦ Maisns-Lfftte(Fr) sf *1ⓉRH 1:423 4↑ Prix Pegase (Prix Durbar) Alw20200 1¾ Mongil W 123 *2.30 Lit de Justice123¾Djanord127nkEnjoy Plan1272½ 12
Settled mid-pack,bid 2f out,dueled 1½f out,prevailed
29Apr94♦ Saint-Cloud(Fr) gd *1ⓉLH 1:432 4↑ Prix Prince Chevalier Alw20400 2hd Mongil W 124 4.00 Reference Lisa118hdLit de Justice124nkOcean Orbit1211 7
Unhurried in 5th,strong late run,just missed
27Nov93♦ Maisns-Lfftte(Fr) sf *1ⓉStr 1:434 3↑ Prix Tantieme (Listed) Stk35500 2nk Mongil W 123 6.50 What Katy Did120nkLit de Justice123¾IrishProspector1231½ 7
Held up toward rear,rallied 1f out,gaining at line
10Nov93♦ Evry(Fr) sf *6fⓉStr 1:20 3↑ Prix Contessina (Listed) Stk35600 21½ Mongil W 123 10.00 Huron Warrior1231½Lit de Justice123½Way West1232 11
Rated in 6th,bid 2f out.finished well
21Oct93♦ Maisns-Lfftte(Fr) hy *6fⓉStr 1:163 3↑ Prix d'Ecajeul Hcp53900 94½ Boeuf D 126 12.00 Raftsong114hdAttaris1132Palme121hd 17
Never a factor
10Oct93♦ Longchamp(Fr) sf *1 1/16ⓉRH 1:542 Prix de la Roseraie Alw30000 55 Boeuf D 128 6.50 Sacrement128¾Ilbiri128½Rustic Belle124¾ 10
Reserved in 8th,finished well without threatening
29Sep93♦ Evry(Fr) sf *6½fⓉStr 1:222 3↑ Prix Aly Khan (Amateur riders) Alw20500 88 Deasistrem C 145 *1.50 Zelda142¾Illuminator1452Mixmatch142¾ 9
Missed break,well behind throughout
2Apr93♦ Maisns-Lfftte(Fr) sf *7fⓉStr 1:302 Prix Bubbles Alw30800 41¾ Mongil W 128 3.50 Matelot128hdEgoiste1281Cyrano Storme128¾ 6
Dwelt,soon 4th.bid over 1f out,hung
18Nov92♦ Evry(Fr) sf *1ⓉLH 1:533 Prix des Chenes-G3 Stk63400 66¼ Mongil W 123 9.00 Dancienne1201Dernier Empereur123nkRanger1232½ 6
Behind in 5th,never threatened
19Sep92♦ Evry(Fr) gd *6½fⓉStr 1:162 Criterium d'Evry (Listed) Stk41300 2nk Boeuf D 121 5.70 Firm Friend118nkLit de Justice1211½Borodislew118nk 8
Rated in 6th,dueled 1f out,outgamed
1Sep92♦ Evry(Fr) sf *6fⓉStr 1:151 Prix d'Ommeel (EBF) Alw29500 33½ Mongil W 128 2.50 Firm Friend1241½Ski Paradise1202Lit de Justice128½ 9
Well placed in 3rd,never catching first two
22Aug92♦ Deauville(Fr) sf *7fⓉStr 1:273 Challenge d'Or Piaget (Lst-Rs) Stk616000 46¼ Mongil W 126 14.00 Master Peace1262½Top Salse126¾Marchand de Sable1263 18
Rated in 8th,mild late gain
1Aug92♦ Deauville(Fr) yl *6fⓉStr 1:133 Prix Yacowlef (Lst-1st timers) Stk42100 42¼ Boeuf D 126 5.00 Wixon122nkGold Splash122½Berdansk1261½ 5
Led to 1½f out,faded

Lonesome Glory

ch. g. 1988, by Transworld (Prince John)–Stronghold, by Green Dancer
Own.– Mrs Walter M. Jeffords Jr
Br.– Walter M. Jeffords Jr (Ky)
Tr.– F. Bruce Miller

Lifetime record: 44 24 5 6 $1,400,068

23Apr99- 9Kee fm *2½ Hurdles 4:36 4↑ E Royal Chase-G1 2 3 33 33 1hd 12 Miller B L 154 *.80 -- Lonesome Glory1542DltonRiver154nkMaster McGrath154hd 7
Stalked pace,driving
27Mar99- 5Cam fm *2¼ Hurdles 4:22⁴ 4↑ Carolina Cup-G1 5 6 54½ 32 1hd 16¾ Miller B L 154 - -- Lonesome Glory1546¾Assurance1541¼Romantic15415 Handily 6
22Nov98- 5Cam fm *2¾ Hurdles 5:11² 4↑ Colonial Cup 100k 7 6 67 76½ 51½ 59½ Miller C L 156 - -- Flat Top1565¾Romantic156nkDictador1561¼ No threat 8
27Aug98- 9Sar fm *2⅜ Hurdles 4:12 4↑ NY Turf Writers H-G1 4 7 77 76 613 617 Miller B L 162 *1.30 -- Hokan142nkRomantic1433Sundin142hd Lacked response 7
28Jun98-12CD fm *2½ Hurdles 4:28² 4↑ Hard Scuffle H-G1 3 3 44 31½ 1½ 11½ Miller B L 158 3.30 -- Lonesome Glory1581½Clearance Code150noNinepins1402½ 8
Inside trip,driving
16Nov97- 4Cam fm *2¾ Hurdles 5:11² 4↑ Colonial Cup-G1 4 9 93¼ 82¾ 3nk 1½ Miller B L 156 -- LonsmGlry156½RowdyIrshmn156noMstrMcgrth1567¾ Driving 10
21Aug97- 9Sar sf 2⅜ Hurdles 4:31 4↑ NY Turf Writers H-G1 6 5 58 44 34 34 Miller B L 156 *1.00 -- Bisbalense1422Confidnt1402LonsomGlry156½ Flattened out 6
31Jly97- 9Sar fm 2116 Hurdles 3:42¹ 4↑ AP Smthwck Mem H-G2 3 5 42 42 45 45½ Miller B 160 2.05 -- BrigadeofGuards1442WaterSkippr1402¾Mro156¾ No late bid 6
10May97- 6PW fm *3 Hurdles 5:30² 4↑ Iroquois-G1 1 5 55 58¼ 28 29¼ Miller C L 156 -- Correggio1569¼LonesomeGlory156½Confidente1563¼ Held on 6
12Apr97- 5Cam fm *2¼ Hurdles 4:27² 4↑ Carolina Cup-G1 3 4 63 22½ 2½ 11½ Miller B L 154 -- LonsmeGlry1541½HudsonBay1569¾PrimeLegcy1547¾ Driving 6
17Nov96- 5Cam fm *2¾ Hurdles 5:09² 4↑ Colonial Cup-G1 2 11 106½ 54 512 520 Miller B 162 -- Correggio1601Stop and Listen162¾Mr Yankee162¾ Mild bid 12
26Oct96- 5FH sf *2⅝ Hurdles 5:10⁴ 4↑ BC Grand Nat H-G1 6 3 21¼ 55 64¾ 68¼ Miller B 168 f -- Corrggio1383MrYankee1401½RowdyIrshmn1542½ Early speed 10
12Oct96- 2Mor gd *1½Ⓣ 2:54⁴ 3↑ Alw 2500 6 7 74¾ 55 2hd 2nk Miller C 165 *1.20 -- Rowdy Irishman165nkLonesome Glory1651½Bisblens165hd 12
Wide,just missed
20Jan96♦ Haydock(GB) sf 3LH 6:21⁴ 5↑ Peter Marsh Limited Hcp Chase-G2 Stk47100 413½ Miller B 164 2.25 ScottonBanks160½Smith'sBand14713GarrisonSavannah153hd 6
Tracked leader,mistake 6th,outpaced 5 out,brief bid,one paced late
1Dec95♦ Sandown(GB) gd 2916RH 5:08¹ 5↑ Crowngap Construction Hcp Chas Hcp16200 111 Miller B 140 2.75 LonesomeGlory14011EgyptMillPrince15115KingCredo14014 4
Rated in 4th,bid 3 out,led last,ridden clear.Remittance Man 4th
12Nov95- 4Cam gd *2¾ S'Chase 5:20¹ 4↑ Colonial Cup 100k 7 8 76½ 52¼ 1½ 11¼ Miller B 162 -- LonesmeGlry1621¼RowdyIrishman1621½Mistco1622¼ Driving 9
17Aug95- 9Sar fm 2⅜ Hurdles 4:12⁴ 4↑ NY Turf Writers H 107k 4 5 517 65½ 1½ 1nk Miller B 166 *1.25 -- Lonesome Glory166nkMistico1604½Rowdy Irishman1423 6
Reserved,closed late
27Jly95- 1Sar fm 2116 Hurdles 3:40² 4↑ AP Smithwick H 50k 4 5 710 52 2½ 11 Miller B 164 *1.10 -- LonsomGlry1641IrshApproch1461Mstco160½ Wide,drew clear 8
13May95- 8PW gd *3 Hurdles 5:32⁴ 4↑ Iroquois 93k 4 3 34 41½ 1hd 12¾ Miller B 156 -- LonesmeGlory1562¾Confdnt15612VctornHll1562¼ Ridden out 5
22Apr95- 3Mid fm *2½ Hurdles 4:37² 4↑ Temple Gwathmey H 50k 1 4 411 34½ 22 21 Miller B 164 -- MasterMcGrath1471LonesomeGlory16420IrishApproach14710 5
Lost whip
1Apr95- 6Cam fm *1⅜Ⓣ 2:19⁴ 3↑ Alw 2500 4 5 52 41 31 12 Miller B 150 96-14 LonesmeGlry1502HudsonBay1471TheFrugalKing1503 Handily 10
13Nov94- 4Cam fm 2¾ S'Chase 5:08¹ 4↑ Colonial Cup 100k 1 7 41 42¼ 2½ 1hd Miller B 162 -- LonesomeGlory162hdMistico16221VictorianHill162¾ Driving 8
22Oct94- 3FH fm *2⅝ Hurdles 4:58 4↑ BC Grand National 143k 2 4 43 53 3nk 34 Miller B 156 -- WarmSpell1562½MasterMcGarth1561½LonesomGlory1561¼ 6
Bid,hung
18Aug94- 9Sar sf 2⅜ Hurdles 4:30 4↑ NY Turf Writers H 109k 3 7 78 68¼ 46½ 37½ Miller B 168 1.90e -- Mistco1684CheerngNews1423½LonesomGlory168nk Late gain 8
14May94- 7PW gd *3 Hurdles 5:28³ 4↑ Iroquois 100k 1 6 715 - - - Miller B 168 -- Mistico16815Warm Spell16822Victorian Hill16835 Fell 7
23Apr94- 3Mid fm *2⅝ Hurdles 4:41³ 4↑ Temple Gwathmey H 50k 2 3 36 35 21½ 1nk Miller B 164 -- LonesmGlry164nkWarmSpell1629CheeringNews1448 Driving 5
2Apr94- 6Cam fm *1⅜Ⓣ 2:21 3↑ Alw 1000 6 3 33¾ 24 21 1nk Miller B 154 -- LonesmGlry154nkMessagePad1516GrenHghIndr1544 Driving 6
14Nov93- 4Cam fm *2¾ S'Chase 5:07⁴ 4↑ Colonial Cup 100k 4 9 95½ 95 52¼ 34½ Miller B 160 -- Declare Your Wish1622¾Simonov1511¾LonesomeGlory1602 11
Late rally
16Oct93-10Bel sf 2⅝ S'Chase 4:53² 3↑ BC Chase 250k 1 9 97½ 41½ 2½ 18½ Miller B 156 1.80 -- Lonesome Glory1568½Highland Bud1565Mistico1564 Driving 9
26Sep93- 2Fx gd *2Ⓣ 3:31 3↑ Alw 1000 5 2 35 3½ 18 18 Miller B 150 -- Lonesome Glory1508Cheering News150hdFlown1508 Easily 6
22May93- 3Pro gd *3 Hurdles 5:58⁴ 4↑ Handicap 25000 2 3 22 32¼ 21¾ 2no Miller B 159 -- Talkin Butter146noLonesome Glory15910Break Clean1435 4
1May93- 6GrM gd *3 Hurdles 5:19³ 4↑ Handicap 25000 1 4 327 321 22 1hd Miller B 153 -- Lonesome Glory153hdCircuit Bar1508Delessio1466 Up in time 8
12Dec92♦ Cheltenham(GB) sf 21116LH 5:41⁴ 4↑ Sport of Kings Challenge Stk23500 1hd Miller B 155 20.00 Lonesome Glory155hdAl Mutahm14725Beebob14210 4
Tracked in 3rd,shaken up approaching last,led near line
7Nov92- 3Pmt gd *2⅜ S'Chase 4:08 4↑ Delta Airline 50k 5 4 39 49½ 32½ 32½ Miller B 153 -- Green Highlander150noMistico1542½Lonesome Glory1534 6
Lacked response
24Oct92- 2FH fm *2½ S'Chase 4:46² 4↑ Supreme 50k 2 5 47½ 68½ 2½ 1½ Miller B 149 -- Lonesome Glory149½Hodges Bay1501½Bel Ange153nk Driving 9
9Oct92- 7Bel yl 2½ S'Chase 4:41¹ 4↑ Queen Mother Supr 50k 1 3 43½ 42½ 33 2¾ Lawrence J II 149 2.70 -- BelAnge149¾LonsomGlry1497GrnHghIndr1505¼ Finished well 7
27Sep92- 2Fx yl *2Ⓣ 3:28³ 3↑ Alw 1000 1 6 52 2hd 1½ 1nk Miller B 150 -- LonesomGlry150nkHero'sHour1476HodgesBay1472½ Driving 10
23May92- 3Pro fm *2½ S'Chase 4:04² 3↑ Alw 20000 2 3 3½ 2¾ 12 13½ Lawrence J II 142 -- LonesmGlry1423½Hopscotch147¾RunwyRomnc152 Ridden out 5
9May92- 7PW fm 1½Ⓣ 2:36¹ 3↑ Sp Wt 2000 6 4 415 49 31 1nk Daniels P 145 -- LonesomeGlory145nkFuller'sFolly1507Brdford15010 Driving 9
19Apr92- 4Mid gd *2⅛ S'Chase 3:55³ 4↑ OClm 15000 10 9 44½ 41½ 42½ 1nk Thornton C 141 -- LonesmeGlry141nkTrulyNolen1445SteadyMoney1445 Driving 10
12Oct91- 5Fai gd *2116 S'Chase 4:02³ 3↑ Md Sp Wt 4 7 96 41½ 1hd 12 Thornton C 140 6.60 -- LonesmeGlry1402ParadeMrch13712RuntoCourt1524½ Rallied 10
5Oct91- 3Mid hd *1¼Ⓣ 2:18¹ 3↑ Md Sp Wt 4 7 73¾ 78½ 410 414½ Miller B 145 -- Big Estero1506Rock Eagle1628Starting Game147½ Rallied 12
2Sep91- 8Fai hd *7fⓉ 1:28 3↑ Md Sp Wt 4 9 97½ 41½ 21 32½ Miller B 147 *2.60 -- Abacus1492¼Rangeless144nkLonesome Glory1472¾ 11
27May91- 1Fai fm *1⅜Ⓣ 2:12² 3↑ Md Sp Wt 8 8 96¾ 83½ 77 515½ Miller B 142 5.10 -- Steeple Chaser1521Dawn Attack1371½Phoenix Force1364 9

Lure

b. c. 1989, by Danzig (Northern Dancer)–Endear, by Alydar
Own.– Claiborne Farm & Nicole P. Gorman
Br.– Claiborne Farm & The Gamely Corp. (Ky)
Tr.– Claude McGaughey III

Lifetime record: 25 14 8 0 $2,514,809

5Nov94- 7CD fm 1Ⓣ :23¹ :46¹ 1:09⁴ 1:34² 3↑ B C Mile-G1 14 5 73¾ 64¼ 99 99¾ Smith ME 126 *.90 86-00 Barathea1263Johnn Quatz126hdUnfinished Symph1231½ 14
Wide,gave way
8Oct94- 5Bel fm 1Ⓣ :23 :45³ 1:09⁴ 1:34 3↑ Kelso H-G3 3 3 36 2½ 1½ 2no Smith ME 128 *.30 92-15 Nijinsky's Gold114noLure1282¼A in Sociology117nk Gamely 7
Previously owned by Claiborne Farm
12Aug94- 8Sar fm 1⅛Ⓣ :48¹ 1:11² 1:34³ 1:46 3↑ B Baruch H-G2 4 3 2½ 21 11 11 Smith ME 125 *1.00 97-10 Lure1251Paradise Creek1266Fourstardave1146 Driving 5
26Jun94- 7Atl fm 1316Ⓣ :47³ 1:10² 1:34¹ 1:52³ 3↑ Caesars Intl H-G1 1 1 11 2hd 21 1no Smith ME 123 *.60 98-06 Lure123noFourstars Allstar1171½Star of Cozzene1211½ 5
Jumped shadow backstretch,driving
20May94-11Pim fm 1⅛Ⓣ :48⁴ 1:13¹ 1:36⁴ 1:48² 3↑ ET Dixie H-G2 3 2 2hd 2hd 11 2¾ Smith ME 124 *.50 92-14 Paradise Creek124¾Lure1245½Astudillo115½ Gamely 5
6May94- 8CD gd 1⅛Ⓣ :47 1:11¹ 1:36¹ 1:48¹ 3↑ ET Classic H-G2 3 3 23½ 32 21 24 Smith ME 123 *.30 86-10 PrdsCrk1184Lur1232½YukonRobbry1162½ Bid inside,no match 7
15Apr94- 8Kee yl 1⅛ :49² 1:15¹ 1:40² 1:53³ 4↑ Elkhorn-G2 4 1 11 1½ 14 14 Smith ME 123 *.30 69-31 Lure1234Buckhar1202Pride of Summer1203 Easily,much best 5
6Nov93- 5SA fm 1Ⓣ :22³ :45⁴ 1:09² 1:33² 3↑ B C Mile-G1 12 2 11 11 11½ 12¼ Smith ME B 126 *1.30 98-04 Lure1262¼Ski Paradise1201¾Fourstars Allstar126hd 13
Forced out 1st turn,strong handling
16Oct93- 6Bel sf 1Ⓣ :22⁴ :45⁴ 1:10³ 1:35⁴ 3↑ Kelso H-G3 2 6 43 31 11½ 13¼ Smith ME 125 *.70 83-29 Lure1253¼Paradise Creek1205Daarik112½ Driving 10
30Jly93- 8Sar fm 1116Ⓣ :24 :47¹ 1:11 1:40³ 3↑ Daryl's Joy-G3 2 4 43½ 41½ 11 13 Smith ME 122 *.20 90-15 Lure1223Fourstardav1222ScottthGrt1151¼ Rated,ridden out 6
27Jun93- 5Atl fm 1316Ⓣ :47 1:10⁴ 1:35 1:53¹ 3↑ Caesars Intl H-G2 1 1 12 12 12 21 Smith ME 123 *.80 94-08 StarofCozzene1201Lure1239¼Finder'sChoic1142¼ Led,failed 7
6Jun93- 8Bel gd 1½Ⓣ :48¹ 1:12 1:35³ 1:58⁴ 3↑ ET Manhattan-G2 5 3 2hd 2hd 11 2¾ Smith ME 124 *.60 95-14 Star of Cozzene118¾Lure1247Solar Splendor1122¼ 8
Stumbled break,raced gamely

14May93-11Pim	fm 1⅛Ⓣ	:464 1:104 1:351 1:473	3↑ ET Dixie H-G3	8 3 2½ 1hd 13½ 11½	Smith ME	124	*.80	97-03	Lure1241½Star of Cozzene1192Binary Light1151¾	Driving	8
30Apr93-8CD	fm 1⅛Ⓣ	:47 1:104 1:342 1:461	3↑ ET Classic H-G3	4 1 1½ 11 11½ 1¾	Smith ME	123	*1.10	100-00	Lure123¾Star of Cozzene1182Cleone116no	Good handling	8
4Apr93-7Kee	fm 1Ⓣ	:23 :454 1:102 1:342	4↑ Alw 27360	7 2 1hd 1½ 12½ 14	Smith ME	123	*.50	98-08	Lure1234RocketFuel118nkKiri'sClown112½	Ridden out,sharp	7
31Oct92-7GP	fm 1Ⓣ	:222 :454 1:09 1:324	3↑ B C Mile-G1	1 1 12½ 11 13½ 13	Smith ME	122	5.40	109-00	Lure1223ParadiseCreek122nkBriefTruce1221½	Good handling	14
10Oct92-5Bel	sf 1Ⓣ	:222 :46 1:102 1:361	3↑ Kelso H-G3	4 2 32 21 22 22¾	Smith ME	111	2.70	78-19	Roman Envoy1172¾Lure1112Val des Bois1184	2nd best	9
14Sep92-7Bel	fm 1 1/16 [T]	:243 :47 1:104 1:41	3↑ Alw 33000	7 2 2½ 12 15 110¼	Smith ME	113	*1.00e	93-14	Lure11310Mucho Precious1173¼Scuffleburg115½	Ridden out	9
6Jun92-6Bel	my 7f	:213 :441 1:084 1:222	Riva Ridge-G3	5 4 44½ 45 77¾ 611	Smith ME	122	2.00	81-08	Superstrike1151¼ThreePeat1222½Windundermywings115nk	Gave way	7
21Apr92-8Kee	my 1 1/16	:232 :471 1:122 1:44	Lexington-G2	1 3 31½ 11 1hd 2nk	Smith ME	B 118	.40	86-16	MyLuckRunsNorth115nkLure1184Agincourt1158	Just failed	5
4Apr92-8Aqu	fst 1	:221 :434 1:081 1:353	Gotham-G2	2 4 1hd 1hd 2hd 14½	Smith ME	114	*.60	84-21	[DH]Lure114[DH]Devil His Due1144½Best Decorated114nk	Bobbled,brushed	8
15Mar92-7Aqu	fst 6f	:23 :47 :584 1:111	Alw 27000	7 2 2½ 2hd 13 18¾	Smith ME	117	*.40	85-25	Lure1178¾CourtingPleasre1171WinnngForc1172¼	Ridden out	9
12Oct91-8Bel	fst 1	:22 :45 1:102 1:363	Champagne-G1	6 8 83¾ 73¾ 811 613¾	Bailey JD	122	*1.50	73-16	TritoWatch1227½SnappyLandng1223½PnBluff122no	No threat	15
25Sep91-1Bel	sly 7f	:221 :451 1:094 1:232	Alw 27000	4 3 33 21½ 21½ 21¼	Bailey JD	117	*.40	86-14	DevilonIce1221¼Lure11714CraftyCoventry119hd	Good effort	5
13Jun91-4Bel	fst 5f	:212 :44 :561	Md Sp Wt	8 6 2½ 2½ 11 15	Bailey JD	118	*1.00	107-05	Lure1185In a Walk1182¾Money Run1183	Drifted,ridden out	8

Maria's Mon

gr/ro. c. 1993, by Wavering Monarch (Majestic Light)–Carlotta Maria, by Caro
Lifetime record: 7 4 1 1 $507,140
Own.– Pin Oak Stable & Mrs Morton Rosenthal
Br.– Morton Rosenthal (Ky)
Tr.– Richard Schosberg

4Aug96-8Sar	fst 1⅛	:472 1:111 1:35 1:471	Jim Dandy-G2	3 4 32½ 44½ 715 627¼	Davis RG	119 f	3.35	74-19	Louis Quatorze124nkWill's Way11415Secreto de Estado1143	Rated,tired	8
17Jly96-7Bel	fst 6½f	:223 :453 1:094 1:16	3↑ Alw 44000	5 6 43 41½ 41½ 23¼	Davis RG	115 f	*.60	91-08	May I Inquire1223¼Maria's Mon115hdThree Diamonds1141¾	Traffic 3/16 pl,mild rally;Previously owned by Mrs Morton Rosenthal	7
7Oct95-9Bel	wf 1 1/16	:223 :451 1:102 1:421	Champagne-G1	8 3 58 41½ 1½ 13¾	Davis RG	122	2.60	88-14	Maria's Mon1223¾Diligence122¾Devil's Honor122¾	Six wide,mild drive	8
16Sep95-5Bel	fst 1	:224 :453 1:093 1:35	Futurity-G1	6 4 41½ 1hd 1½ 12¾	Davis RG	122	3.65	88-09	Maria's Mon1222¾Louis Quatorze1221¼Honour and Glory1222	Wide,challenged,game	7
27Aug95-8Sar	fst 7f	:222 :453 1:102 1:232	Hopeful-G1	2 7 1½ 1hd 32 36½	Davis RG	122	3.10	82-12	Hennessy1223¼Louis Quatorze1223¼Maria's Mon1229	Dueled,weakened	7
21Jly95-7Sar	fst 6f	:213 :45 :573 1:104	Sanford-G3	3 5 2hd 1hd 12 12¼	Davis RG	115	*1.00	87-10	Maria'sMon1152¼Seekr'sRwrd1156FroznIc112hd	Dueled,clear	11
4Jly95-2Bel	fst 5½f	:23 :464 :583 1:043	Md Sp Wt	7 4 2½ 2hd 17 110½	Davis RG	116	*1.70	92-17	Maria's Mon11610[D]Louis Quatorze1163¾Shawklit Power1163½	Ridden out	7

Meadow Star

ch. f. 1988, by Meadowlake (Hold Your Peace)–Inreality Star, by In Reality
Lifetime record: 20 11 1 2 $1,445,740
Own.– Carl Icahn
Br.– Jaime S. Carrion (Fla)
Tr.– Leroy Jolley

31Oct92-6GP	fst 1⅛	:47 1:104 1:353 1:48	3↑ ⒻBC Distaff-G1	11 13 126½ 114½ 87¾ 77¾	Day P	L 123	37.00	89-03	Paseana1234VersaillesTreaty123½MagicIMaidn1191½	Outrun	14
11Oct92-8Kee	fst 1⅛	:48 1:123 1:371 1:494	3↑ ⒻSpinster-G1	10 7 74½ 74 46 38¼	Day P	LB 123	10.70	78-25	Fowda1232¼Paseana1236Meadow Star1232½	Duck,carried out	10
20Sep92-8Bel	fst 1 1/16	:231 :464 1:10 1:412	3↑ ⒻRuffian H-G1	6 4 52 31½ 54¼ 58¾	Bailey JD	112	4.60	86-15	VersaillesTreaty120½QuickMischief1163Nannerl1192¼	Tired	6
25May92-5Bel	fst 6½f	:224 :453 1:094 1:162	3↑ ⒻAlw 41000	1 4 31½ 2½ 33½ 32¾	Santos JA	117	*1.10	88-10	MakinFaces1172½PupptShw119½MdwStr1177¼	Altered course	5
14Apr92-8Kee	fst 6f	:22 :452 1:093	3↑ ⒻTbred Club of Am-G3	3 8 76 77 74 76¼	Santos JA	B 123	*.80	89-10	Ifyoucouldseemenow120hdHarbourClub1173MadamBear117no	Slow start	8
21Sep91-8Bel	fst 1 1/16	:233 :462 1:103 1:413	3↑ ⒻRuffian H-G1	5 4 43 52 64 67½	Bailey JD	117	2.90	86-14	Queen120½ShrpDnc1141¼LdyD'Accord113nk	Drifted badly str	7
1Sep91-8Bel	fst 1	:232 :462 1:101 1:344	3↑ ⒻMaskette-G1	1 6 67½ 65½ 55½ 47¾	Bailey JD	118	*.80	88-07	Queena123hdFit to Scout123nkScreen Prospect1167½	Broke outward,drifted out	6
6Jly91-8Bel	gd 1¼	:462 1:101 1:343 2:002	ⒻC C A Oaks-G1	1 2 23½ 2½ 22 27	Bailey JD	121	1.20	88-05	Lite Light1217Meadow Star1212Car Gal1218¼	2nd best	6
9Jun91-8Bel	fst 1⅛	:492 1:132 1:363 1:484	ⒻMother Goose-G1	2 1 12 1hd 1hd 1no	Bailey JD	121	.90	85-18	MeadowStr121noLiteLight12115NaleesPn121no	Wide,driving	4
25May91-8Bel	fst 1	:231 :462 1:113 1:372	ⒻAcorn-G1	3 4 41 1½ 12 16	Bailey JD	121	*.60	83-17	Meadow Star1216Versailles Treaty1212½Dazzle Me Jolie1212¾	Drifted,ridden out	6
20Apr91-8Aqu	fst 1⅛	:463 1:104 1:354 1:482	Wood Memorial-G1	6 4 45½ 31½ 44½ 410½	Antley CW	121	2.00	84-23	CahillRoad1263LostMountn1266HappyJazzBand1261¼	Tired	10
30Mar91-8Aqu	gd 1	:242 :49 1:14 1:38	ⒻComely-G2	5 2 2½ 2hd 2½ 11¾	Antley CW	121	*.30	72-28	MeadowStr1211¾DoItWithStyle1143I'maThrllr1181¾	Driving	5
16Mar91-6Aqu	fst 7f	:233 :472 1:111 1:23	ⒻQueen of the Stage 44k	5 1 2½ 1hd 12½ 14¾	Antley CW	121	*.10	87-22	MeadowStr1214¾Nany'sAppeal118½ChristnCzrn1144¼	Driving	5
27Oct90-4Bel	fst 1 1/16	:223 :454 1:11 1:44	ⒻBC Juv Fillies-G1	9 8 52½ 3½ 12 15	Santos JA	119	*.20	82-15	MeadwStar1195PrivatTrsur1191DncSmrtly1194¼	Drifted,drv	13
6Oct90-7Bel	fst 1	:224 :461 1:11 1:352	ⒻFrizette-G1	4 1 1½ 11 16 114	Santos JA	119	*.10	92-11	MeadwStr11914ChampagnGlow119nkFlwlssly1193¼	Drew off	5
16Sep90-8Bel	fst 7f	:222 :452 1:101 1:224	ⒻMatron-G1	2 3 33½ 32 12 16	Santos JA	119	*.20e	90-14	MeadowStr1196Verbasle1193ClarkCottage1192¼	Drew clear	6
27Aug90-8Sar	fst 6f	:214 :451 1:101	ⒻSpinaway-G1	8 3 43 43 21 12	Santos JA	119	*.70	93-12	MeadwStr1192GardenGal1191GoodPotntl1198½	Wide,driving	8
1Aug90-8Sar	fst 6f	:221 :46 1:111	ⒻSchuylerville-G2	2 3 43½ 42½ 2hd 13	Antley CW	119	*1.00	88-08	MeadwStr1193GardnGal1196PryrfulMss1143	Steadied,clear	7
18Jly90-8Bel	fst 5½f	:22 :454 1:041	ⒻAstoria BC-G3	4 4 36½ 33 31½ 11¼	Santos JA	113	*1.90	98-16	Meadow Star1131¼Sweet Sarita1146Pay'n and Play'n1122	Strong handling	6
13Jun90-4Bel	fst 5f	:221 :46 :584	ⒻMd Sp Wt	5 4 2½ 1½ 1½ 15¼	Santos JA	117	2.20	94-20	MeadwStr1175¼WinCraftyLdy117¾MyFntzy1174	Brisk urging	7

Miss Alleged

b. f. 1987, by Alleged (Hoist the Flag)–Miss Tusculum, by Boldnesian
Lifetime record: 15 5 4 3 $1,746,118
Own.– Fares Farms
Br.– Carl M. Freeman (Ky)
Tr.– Charles Whittingham

26Apr92-8SA	fm *1¾Ⓣ	:472 2:00 2:234 2:462	4↑ San Juan Cap H-G1	5 6 63¼ 54½ 46 27	McCarron CJ	LB 118	*1.20	94-12	Fly Till Dawn1217Miss Alleged118¾Wall Street Dancer1141¼	Steadied,boxed in backstretch,angled out 3/8,4 wide 1/8	9
5Apr92-8SA	fm 1¼Ⓣ	:48 1:12 1:36 1:593	4↑ ⒻS Barbara H-G1	1 6 54½ 53½ 32 21¼	McCarron CJ	LB 124	1.90	88-12	Kostroma1211¼MissAllegd1242½FreeatLst117½	Saved ground	6
17Feb92-8SA	gd 1½Ⓣ	:493 1:152 2:043 2:283	4↑ San Luis Obispo H-G3	1 6 52½ 53 53½ 33	McCarron CJ	LB 121	*1.30	68-29	Quest for Fame1211¾Cool Gold Mood1141¼Miss Alleged1213	4-wide into lane	9
15Dec91-8Hol	fm 1½Ⓣ	:52 1:173 2:064 2:30	3↑ Hol Turf Cup-G1	7 5 31½ 3½ 2½ 1hd	McCarron CJ	LB 123	2.90	73-21	Miss Alleged123hdItsallgreektome1261¼Quest for Fame126¾	Game effort;Previously trained by Pascal Bary	7
2Nov91-7CD	fm 1½Ⓣ	:504 1:154 2:062 2:304	3↑ BC Turf-G1	12 6 84¼ 52¼ 52¼ 1½	Legrix E	LB 123	42.10f	96-06	MissAlleged123½Itsallgreektome1262QustforFm1262	Driving	13
19Oct91-11Lrl	sf 1¼Ⓣ	:493 1:144 1:412 2:062	3↑ Bud Int'l-G1	10 4 54 62¾ 74½ 54¼	Legrix E	123	11.00	70-38	Leariva1231¾Sillery122½Goofalik1261¼	Needed rally	13
6Oct91◆ Longchamp(Fr)	sf *1½ⓉRH	2:312	3↑ Arc de Triomphe-G1 Stk1483000	1111½	Legrix E	127	43.00		Suave Dancer1232Magic Night1201Pistolet Bleu1233	Toward rear,in tight 2f out,never a factor.Generous 8th	14
22Sep91◆ Longchamp(Fr)	gd *1¼ⓉRH	2:102	3↑ Prix Prince d'Orange-G3 Stk59700	2nk	Legrix E	122	1.75		Passing Sale126nkMiss Alleged1221½Glity1261½	Rallied to lead over 1f out,caught near line.Cudas 5th	5

30Jun91♦ Saint-Cloud(Fr)	gd *1$\frac{1}{2}$ⓉLH	2:28	3↑ Grand Prix de Saint-Cloud-G1 Stk41200	4$^{4\frac{1}{2}}$	Legrix E	131	13.00	Epervier Bleu134^{3}Rock Hopper134$^{\frac{3}{4}}$Passing Sale134^{1} Unhurried in 6th,mild late gain	12
8Jun91♦ Evry(Fr)	sf *1$\frac{1}{2}$ⓉLH	2:35^{2}	4↑ Grand Prix d'Evry-G2 Stk99300	3$^{3\frac{1}{2}}$	Legrix E	122	5.00	Wajd120^{2}Epervier Bleu126$^{1\frac{1}{2}}$Miss Alleged122^{nk} Tracked leader,outfinished	7
20May91♦ Saint-Cloud(Fr)	gd *1$\frac{1}{2}$ⓉLH	2:37^{2}	4↑ Prix Jean de Chaudenay-G2 Stk86800	3^{4}	Legrix E	129	1.50	Dear Doctor128$^{1\frac{1}{2}}$Passing Sale132$^{2\frac{1}{2}}$Miss Alleged129^{nk} Tracked in 4th,bid 2f out,hung	6
16Sep90♦ Longchamp(Fr)	gd *1$\frac{1}{2}$ⓉRH	2:29^{3}	ⒻPrix Vermeille-G1 Stk228000	2^{nk}	Boeuf D	128	8.00	Salsabil128^{nk}Miss Alleged128$^{\frac{1}{2}}$In the Groove128$^{\frac{1}{2}}$ Never far away,led briefly 1f out,dueled,outgamed.Wajd 4th	9
24Jun90♦ Longchamp(Fr)	sf *1$\frac{1}{2}$ⓉRH	2:41^{3}	ⒻPrix de Malleret-G2 Stk90400	1^{2}	Legrix E	128	*1.00	Miss Alleged124^{2}Whitehaven121^{1}Ruby Tiger121^{8} Tracked in 4th,rallied to lead 150y out,handily	4
27May90♦ Longchamp(Fr)	gd *1$\frac{5}{16}$ⓉRH	2:13	ⒻPrix de Royaumont-G3 Stk54200	1^{1}	Boeuf D	123	*1.10	Miss Alleged123^{1}VueCvlir123^{hd}SvourusLdy123^{3} Tracked leader,led 1f out,handily	4
15May90♦ Longchamp(Fr)	gd *1$\frac{3}{8}$ⓉRH	2:26^{3}	ⒻPrix de Celles St Cloud Mdn (FT)30300	1^{2}	Legrix E	123	2.70	Miss Alleged123^{2}Passagere du Soir123$^{1\frac{1}{2}}$Eliush123^{1} Well placed in 3rd,led over 1f out,drew clear	7

Morley Street (Ire)

ch. g. 1984, by Deep Run (Pampered King II)–High Board, by High Line
Own.– Michael Jackson
Br.– M. Parkhill (Ire)
Tr.– Toby Balding

Lifetime record: 47 21 7 3 $888,696

16Dec95♦ Ascot(GB)	gd 3$\frac{3}{16}$RH	6:18	4↑ Long Walk Hurdle-G1 Stk67300	8	McCoy AP	161	11.00	Silver Wedge161^{4}Putty Road161^{5}Top Spin161^{nk} Always behind,lost touch 4 out,distanced	11
17Nov95♦ Ascot(GB)	gd 2$\frac{1}{2}$RH	4:58	4↑ Ascot Hurdle-G2 Stk36300	3$^{13\frac{1}{2}}$	Bradley G	154	25.00	Large Action154$^{1\frac{1}{2}}$Atours159^{12}Morley Street154 Rated in 4th,bid 3 out,weakened approaching last	5
11Sep94♦ Merano(Ity)	sf 2$\frac{1}{2}$RH		4↑ Corsa Siepi di Merano Stk103000	4$^{4\frac{3}{4}}$	Bradley G			Vaquero155$^{\frac{1}{2}}$Amazing Feat148$^{\frac{3}{4}}$Reckless William155^{3} Rated at rear,mild bid 4 out,evenly late.Time not taken	7
17Aug94♦ York(GB)	gd 1$\frac{3}{4}$ⓉLH	2:56^{2}	3↑ Ebor Handicap Hcp227000	19	Williams J	133	33.00	Hasten to Add129$^{\frac{1}{2}}$Admiral's Well120$^{1\frac{1}{2}}$Solartica111^{no} Always behind.Halkopous 16th	21
25Jun94♦ Newcastle(GB)	fm 2ⓉLH	3:24^{4}	3↑ Northumberland Plate Hcp Hcp170000	4$^{1\frac{1}{4}}$	Williams J	120	40.00	Quick Ransom120^{no}Hasten to Add114^{1}Tioman Island131^{nk} Behind,progress 4f out,gaining late.Further Flight(136) 16th	20
16Jun94♦ Ascot(GB)	gd 2$\frac{1}{2}$ⓉRH	4:27^{3}	4↑ Ascot Gold Cup-G1 Stk289000	8$^{25\frac{1}{2}}$	Williams J	128	40.00	Arcadian Heights128$^{\frac{3}{4}}$Vintage Crop128^{7}Sonus128$^{3\frac{1}{2}}$ Never a factor.Oh So Risky 6th	9
27Apr94♦ Ascot(GB)	yl *2ⓉRH	3:35^{4}	4↑ Sagaro Stakes-G3 Stk61300	11$^{31\frac{1}{4}}$	Williams J	124	20.00	SafetyinNumbrs120$^{\frac{3}{4}}$CairoPrince120$^{1\frac{1}{4}}$ArcdianHeights124^{nk} Always behind.Oh So Risky 7th,Flakey Dove 9th	13
15Mar94♦ Cheltenham(GB)	2$\frac{1}{16}$LH	4:02^{1}	4↑ Champion Hurdle-G1 Stk260000	-	Bradley G	168	16.00	Flakey Dove163$^{1\frac{1}{2}}$Oh So Risky168$^{\frac{3}{4}}$Large Action168$^{1\frac{1}{2}}$ Bumped at 1st,never recovered,tailed off,eased before 3 out	15
11Dec93♦ Cheltenham(GB)	2$\frac{5}{8}$LH	5:16^{1}	5↑ Tripleprint Gold Cup Hcp Chase-G3 Stk80800	7$^{55\frac{1}{2}}$	Frost J	164	14.00	FragrantDawn142^{3}YoungHustlr155$^{\frac{3}{4}}$FreelineFinishing144^{20} Mistake at 8th,always behind,distanced.Egypt Mill Prince 9th	11
13Nov93♦ Cheltenham(GB)	2$\frac{9}{16}$LH	5:18^{4}	5↑ Mackeson Gold Cup Hcp Chase-G3 Stk83100	9$^{54\frac{1}{2}}$	Guest R	167	20.00	BradburyStar162^{7}EgyptMillPrince143^{4}GenrlPershing165$^{2\frac{1}{2}}$ Rated at rear,well behind,brief progress at 11th	15
29Oct93♦ Newmarket(GB)	2ⓉRH	3:34	3↑ George Stubbs Rated Hcp (Listed) Stk24000	3$^{4\frac{3}{4}}$	Williams J	133	12.00	My Patriarch127^{4}Ritto113$^{\frac{3}{4}}$Morley Street133^{nk} Rated at rear,finished well without threatening	12
3Apr93♦ Aintree(GB)	2LH	3:46	4↑ Aintree Hurdle-G1 Stk76300	1$^{1\frac{1}{2}}$	Bradley G	161	6.00	Morley Street161$^{1\frac{1}{2}}$Granville Again161^{2}Flown161^{hd} Rated at rear,cruised up after 2nd last,steadied,led late	6
16Mar93♦ Cheltenham(GB)	2$\frac{1}{16}$LH	3:51^{2}	4↑ Champion Hurdle-G1 Stk213000	12$^{16\frac{1}{2}}$	Bradley G	168	20.00	Granville Again168^{1}Royal Derbi168$^{2\frac{1}{2}}$Halkopous168^{3} Chased leaders,weakened 2 out.Vintage Crop 6th,Flown 8th	18
6Feb93♦ Sandown(GB)	2$\frac{1}{16}$RH	4:06^{3}	5↑ AGFA Hurdle Alw22500	5	Dunwoody R	164	1.85	Mole Board149^{6}Valfinet154^{20}Ruling149^{15} Rated in 4th,2nd at 5th,weakened quickly over 2 out,distanced	5
12Dec92♦ Cheltenham(GB)	2$\frac{1}{8}$LH	4:23^{4}	4↑ Bula Hurdle-G2 Stk56100	3^{16}	Dunwoody R	162	1.85	Halkopous156^{10}Granville Again162^{6}Morley Street162^{nk} Tracked in 4th,always one-paced.Oh So Risky 4th,Kribensis 5th	6
20Nov92♦ Ascot(GB)	2$\frac{1}{2}$RH	4:54^{4}	4↑ Ascot Hurdle-G2 Stk36100	2^{hd}	Dunwoody R	164	2.50	Muse154^{hd}Morley Street164^{8}Tyrone Bridge154$^{2\frac{1}{2}}$ Rated at rear,sharp bid 3 out,led after last,caught near line	7
15Nov92♦ Cheltenham(GB)	2$\frac{1}{16}$LH	4:26^{3}	4↑ Elite Hurdle Alw58800	1^{1}	Dunwoody R	162	-	Morley Street162^{1}Granville Again156^{2}Oh So Risky159^{3} Rated in 3rd,bid over 1f out,led after last,held well	4
23Oct92♦ Doncaster(GB)	gd 2$\frac{1}{16}$ⓉLH	3:45^{2}	3↑ Doncaster Writers Stakes Alw8400	1$^{3\frac{1}{2}}$	Williams J	131	2.10	Morley Street131$^{3\frac{1}{2}}$Jungle Dancer131^{hd}Glaisdale116^{20} Rated in 4th,progress 3f out,led 1f out,drew clear	5
4Apr92♦ Aintree(GB)	gd 2$\frac{1}{2}$LH	4:46^{2}	4↑ Aintree Hurdle-G1 Stk78500	1$^{\frac{1}{2}}$	Dunwoody R	161	*.80	Morley Street161$^{\frac{1}{2}}$Minorettes Girl156^{10}Forest Sun161^{10} Unhurried,progress halfway,led after 2 out,idled,just held	6
10Mar92♦ Cheltenham(GB)	gd 2LH	3:57^{2}	4↑ Champion Hurdle-G1 Stk229000	6$^{7\frac{1}{2}}$	Frost J	168	*2.00	Royal Gait168$^{\frac{1}{2}}$Oh So Risky168^{no}Ruling168^{6} Settled behind leaders,mild bid 2 out,weakened.Chirkpar 7th	16
1Feb92♦ Leopardstwn(Ire)	yl 2LH	3:51^{3}	4↑ Irish Champion Hurdle (Listed) Stk78700	2no	Frost J	164	*.70	Chirkpar161^{no}Morley Street164$^{\frac{3}{4}}$Minorettes Girl159^{4} Rated toward rear,rallied to lead 1 out,caught on line	9
15Nov91♦ Ascot(GB)	gd 2$\frac{1}{2}$RH	4:52^{4}	4↑ Ascot Hurdle-G2 Stk46100	1^{nk}	Frost J	164	*.45	Morley Street164^{nk}King's Curate164^{7}Danny Harrold154^{7} Rated in 5th,mistake 3 out,led run-in,held gamely	6
12Oct91- 3Fai	gd *2$\frac{5}{8}$ S'Chase Ridden out	5:10^{3}	3↑ BC Chase 250k 7 6 4$^{7\frac{3}{4}}$ 4^{3} 1^{3}	1$^{9\frac{3}{4}}$	Martinez AV	156	*.60 - -	MrlyStreet156$^{9\frac{3}{4}}$Declare Your Wish156$^{15\frac{1}{2}}$Cheering News146^{hd}	12
12Sep91♦ Doncaster(GB)	gd 2$\frac{1}{4}$ⓉLH	3:56	3↑ Doncaster Cup-G3 Stk70800	2no	Williams J	126	33.00	Great Marquess129^{no}Morley Street126^{4}Haitham126^{hd} Rated in last,rallied 2$\frac{1}{2}$f out,just missed	8
20Aug91♦ York(GB)	gd *2ⓉLH	3:30	Lonsdale Stakes (Listed) Stk38000	4$^{35\frac{1}{2}}$	Williams J	126	9.00	Supreme Choice112$^{2\frac{1}{2}}$Retouch126^{3}Bondstone126^{30} Rated in 5th,progress halfway,weakened 3f out	7
6Apr91♦ Aintree(GB)	yl 2$\frac{1}{2}$LH	4:54^{2}	4↑ Aintree Hurdle-G1 Stk92000	1^{6}	Frost J	161	*1.35	Morley Street161^{6}Nomadic Way161^{5}Run for Free161^{no} Jumped well,led on bit after 2nd last,finished strongly	9
12Mar91♦ Cheltenham(GB)	yl 2LH	3:54^{4}	4↑ Champion Hurdle-G1 Stk253000	1$^{1\frac{1}{2}}$	Frost J	168	*4.00	Morley Street168$^{1\frac{1}{2}}$Nomadic Way168^{hd}Ruling168^{5} Progress halfway,dueled and hit 3rd last,led 2 out,drifted,all out	24
1Mar91♦ Newbury(GB)	yl 2$\frac{9}{16}$LH	5:07^{3}	4↑ Berkshire Hurdle-G2 Stk30800	1^{2}	Frost J	166	*.70	Morley Street166^{2}Danny Harrold159^{20}Vagador166 Progress 7th,led 2 out,hampered by loose horse over 1 out,driving	6
26Dec90♦ Kempton(GB)	gd 3RH	6:17^{2}	5↑ Feltham Novices Chase-G1 Stk73900	-	Frost J	161	*1.60	Sparkling Flame161^{15}Ardbrin161Man on the Line161 Jumped left,not fluent in 3rd,weakened and eased before 3 out	7
15Dec90♦ Ascot(GB)	gd 2$\frac{1}{2}$RH	4:54^{1}	5↑ Noel Novices Chase-G2 Stk31900	2^{8}	Frost J	164	*.50	RemittanceMan161^{8}MorlyStreet164^{10}BraveDefender157$^{3\frac{1}{2}}$ Mistake 3rd,jumped left,chased winner 4 out,second best	5
3Dec90♦ Worcestor(GB)	gd 2$\frac{1}{2}$LH	5:25^{4}	5↑ Fred Rimell Meml Novices Chase Alw11500	1^{2}	Frost J	162	*.15	Morley Street162^{2}Popeswood152$^{\frac{1}{2}}$Pamber Priory152^{20} Rated in 2nd,led at 5th,headed briefly at 7th,won under wraps	9

16Nov90♦ Ascot(GB) gd 2½RH 4:45 4↑ Ascot Hurdle-G2 Stk47000 1³ Frost J 164 *.80 Morley Street164³Sabin du Loir154¹⁵Brabazon154³ 5
Rated in last,2nd at 7th,led on bit 1 out,won under wraps
20Oct90- 2Bel sf 2⅝ S'Chase 4:53¹ 3↑ BC Chase 250k 11 5 5⁴ 4²½ 1⁴ 1¹¹ Martinez AV 156 *2.00 -- MrlyStrt156¹¹SummrColony156³Moonstruck156¹¾ Ridden out 12
6Oct90♦ Goodwood(GB) *2ⓉB 3:49⁴ 3↑ Gatwick South Terminal Stakes Alw12500 1hd Williams J 125 10.00 Morley Street125hdMichelozzo125¹⁰Indian Baba120¹½ 9
Rated at rear,long drive to lead near line
7Apr90♦ Aintree(GB) fm 2½LH 4:39² 4↑ Aintree Hurdle Stk62500 1¹⁵ Frost J 160 *.80 Morley Street160¹⁵Joyful Noise160³Ikdam160¹⁵ 6
Confidently ridden,led after 2nd last,quickly clear
13Mar90♦ Cheltenham(GB) gd 2LH 3:50³ 4↑ Champion Hurdle Stk128000 5¹²¼ Frost J 168 10.00 Kribensis168³Nomadic Way168¾Past Glories168½ 19
Rated in touch,lacked rally
23Dec89♦ Chepstow(GB) sf 2½LH 5:17 4↑ Sport of Kings Challenge Hurdle Alw37700 2¾ Frost J 160 *.60 Propero155¾Morley Street160¹⁰Calabrese155⁴ 8
Rated toward rear,progress halfway,left in lead 3 out,headed late
9Dec89♦ Cheltenham(GB) fm 2½LH 5:02² 4↑ Sport of Kings Challenge Hurdle Alw37700 1⁷ Frost J 160 *.55 Morley Street160⁷Deep Sensation155²½Ikdam155½ 8
Rated at rear,long drive to lead 1 out,drew clear
25Nov89♦ Newbury(GB) gd 2 1/16LH 3:48² 4↑ Gerry Feilden Hurdle Stk25300 2⁶ Frost J 157 3.50 Cruising Altitude157⁶Morley Street157⁴Nomadic Way154¹ 8
Progress at 5th,2nd over 2 out,second best.Royal Derbi 6th
8Apr89♦ Aintree(GB) hy 2½LH 5:08² 4↑ Mumm Prize Novices Hurdle Stk25400 1¹½ Frost J 159 3.50 Morley Street159¹½Trapper John155¾Undaunted155³⁰ 10
Tracked leaders,lost place 4 out,led last,drifted left,driving
15Mar89♦ Cheltenham(GB) sf 2½LH 5:17² 4↑ Sun Alliance Novices Hurdle Stk77400 4¹⁰½ Frost J 161 5.00 Safar's Lad161⁵Trapper John161⁵Knight Oil161½ 22
Smooth progress 4 out,bid over 1 out,weakened run-in
8Feb89♦ Ascot(GB) gd 2RH 3:55 4↑ AF Budge Novices Hurdle Stk16100 1³ Frost J 170 *.80 Morley Street170³Penny Forum164²Lalitpour170⁶ 7
Mistake 4th,led approaching last,ridden out
31Dec88♦ Newbury(GB) gd 2 9/16LH 5:04⁴ Ramsbury Hurdle Alw8500 1¹⁵ Frost J 157 *1.10 Morley Street157¹⁵Cash Is King152⁶Lapiaffe152¹⁰ 7
Rated at rear,sharp run to lead over 1 out,handily
2Dec88♦ Sandown(GB) gd 2RH 4:05¹ Nat'l Hunt Guide Novices Hurdle Alw7100 1² Frost J 154 2.50 Morley Street154²Pipers Copse158⁷The Artful Rascal154⁵ 17
Rallied approaching last,ridden to lead near line
5Nov88♦ Sandown(GB) gd 2ⓉRH 3:55⁴ EBF Marten Julian NH Flat Race Alw5200 1¹ Charlton A⁴ 158 *.70 Morley Street158¹Gaelic River156⁶Scampered143hd 22
Toward rear,progress 3f out,led over 1f out,comfortably
8Apr88♦ Aintree(GB) gd 2ⓉLH 4:05 4↑ Supreme Nat'l Hunt Flat Race Alw4000 2½ Charlton A 156 *1.60 Black Mocassin162½Morley Street156⁶Alekhine156⁷ 16
Progress 6f out,led 2f out,caught near line
12Mar88♦ Sandown(GB) gd 2ⓉRH 4:02 4↑ Flyers Nat'l Hunt Flat Race Alw3900 1¹² Charlton A⁷ 147 16.00 Morley Street147¹²Alekhine154¾Errant Knight154⁴ 22
Midpack,rallied to lead over 1f out,handily

Northern Spur (Ire)

b. c. 1991, by Sadler's Wells (Northern Dancer)–Fruition, by Rheingold
Lifetime record: 15 6 4 3 $1,616,792
Own.– Charles J. Cella
Br.– Swettenham Stud &Partners (Ire)
Tr.– Ronald McAnally

22Jun96- 4Atl fm 1 3/16Ⓣ :50¹ 1:14² 1:38 1:55³ 3↑ Caesars Int'l H-G1 6 1 1hd 2hd 3¹ 3³½ McCarron CJ L 122 1.80 81-18 Sandpit122¹¾DplomtcJt117¹¾NorthrnSpr122¾ Weakened late 8
27May96- 9Hol fm 1¼Ⓣ :48 1:11² 1:35³ 1:59² 3↑ Hol Turf H-G1 5 4 4¹² 4⁴½ 3³ 2³½ McCarron CJ L 123 *1.60 87-09 Sandpit120³½Northern Spur123¾Awad119¹¾ Second best 6
1May96- 8Hol fm 1 1/16Ⓣ :23³ :46⁴ 1:10² 1:39¹ 4↑ Alw 60000 2 2 2² 2½ 1hd 1¹ McCarron CJ L 122 *1.30 100-08 NrthrnSpr122¹WvyRun116nkUnusulHt117½ Confident handling 6
19Feb96- 8SA gd *1½Ⓣ :49 1:14³ 2:05 2:30¹ 4↑ San Luis Obispo H-G2 5 3 2½ 1½ 2¹ 4³½ McCarron CJ L 123 *1.00 83-13 Windsharp115¾Wandesta114²¾Virginia Carnival115hd 6
Reserved,bid,tired late
28Oct95- 7Bel sf 1½Ⓣ :52³ 1:19 2:13⁴ 2:42 3↑ B C Turf-G1 12 2 2½ 1¹ 1½ 1nk McCarron CJ L 126 3.95 -- NorthrnSpr126nkFreedomCry126²Crng126²½ Fully extended 13
8Oct95- 8SA fm 1¼Ⓣ :49 1:13⁴ 1:37⁴ 2:02¹ 3↑ Oak Tree Inv'l-G1 8 2 2¹ 2hd 1¹ 1¹½ McCarron CJ L 124 4.70 79-21 NorthernSpur124¹½Sandpit124³RoyalChrot124³ Clearly best 8
27Aug95- 8AP fm 1¼Ⓣ :46² 1:10³ 1:35¹ 1:58³ 3↑ Arl Million-G1 9 6 6⁷ 7²¾ 10⁷¾ 10¹⁴¾ McCarron CJ 126 5.60 90-01 Awad126²¼Sandpit126nkThe Vid126½ Wide throughout,bled 11
6Aug95- 8Dmr fm 1⅛Ⓣ :48¹ 1:12 1:36 1:48¹ 3↑ Eddie Read H-G1 2 8 8⁶¼ 8⁵½ 4³ 3²¾ McCarron CJ 118 5.50 92-16 Fastness115¹¼Romarin119¹½NorthernSpur118² Finished well 8
Previously trained by Andre Fabre
1Oct94♦ Longchamp(Fr) yl *1⅞ⓉRH 3:13 Prix de Lutece-G3 Stk70500 2½ Jarnet T 128 *.40 The Little Thief121½Northern Spur128²Sheshara118⁵ 6
Led,dueled final furlong,failed
11Sep94♦ Longchamp(Fr) sf *1½ⓉRH 2:34⁴ Prix Niel-G2 Stk128000 2¹½ Peslier O 128 11.00 Carnegie128¹½Northern Spur128¹½Sunshack128nk 10
Well placed in 3rd,led 1½f out,headed 150y out.Celtic Arms 4th
26Jun94♦ Longchamp(Fr) sf *1⅞ⓉRH 3:16² Prix Hubert de Chaudenay-G2 Stk93900 1² Jarnet T 123 *.20 Northern Spur123²Bayrika120⁴Party Season123⁶ 4
Led to halfway,tracked in 3rd,led again 1f out,driving
30May94♦ Saint-Cloud(Fr) gd *1¾ⓉLH 3:04¹ Prix du Lys-G3 Stk60200 1¹½ Jarnet T 123 1.40 Northern Spur123¹½Sans Ecocide123¾Cafe Milano123²½ 5
Wire to wire,met challenge 1f out,driving
12May94♦ Longchamp(Fr) gd *1½ⓉRH 2:32³ Prix de l'Avre (Listed) Stk36700 3¹ Mongil W 128 7.50e Bataillon128hdCafe Milano128¹Northern Spur128¾ 12
Tracked in 3rd,dueled 1-1/2f out,faded late.The Little Thief 6th
16Nov93♦ Saint-Cloud(Fr) hy *1¼ⓉLH 2:23⁴ Prix Saraca (Listed) Stk35500 2¾ Guillot S 123 *.90 Red Rubin120¾Northern Spur123²½Exit Line120nk 4
Led,repelled first challenge over 1f out,headed 100y out
17Oct93♦ Compiegne(Fr) sf *1⅛ⓉLH 1:57³ Prix du Tremble Mdn14600 1³ Guillot S 123 *1.30 Northern Spur123³Stylish Condor116²Kabriz128¹½ 12
Led throughout,drew clear over 1f out,handily

Not Surprising

ch. g. 1990, by Medieval Man (Noholme II)–Tenderly Calling, by Always Gallant
Lifetime record: 61 23 4 5 $1,112,302
Own.– Robert E. Van Worp
Br.– Raven Brook Farm Inc (Fla)
Tr.– Judson Van Worp

2May99- 9Tam fm 5fⓉ :21⁴ :44⁴ :56³ 3↑ Alw 14600 9 3 4³¾ 6⁴½ 7⁵ 5⁴¼ Garcia JJ L 114 f *2.10 -- FlshyLink114¹¼AdorbleRcr114¹WrittnApprovl115¹½ 10
Well placed,no rally
20Jun98-12Crc fst 6f :21³ :45¹ :58 1:11² 3↑ Miami Beach Spr H 300k 7 7 11⁷¾ 12¹⁷ 12²¹ 12²⁸½ Rivera JA II L 112 59.80 62-22 Heckofaralph115¹ThunderBreeze113³NicholasDs115² Outrun 13
25May98-11Crc fst 6f :21⁴ :45¹ :57⁴ 1:11¹ 3↑ Alw 25000 6 5 3¹½ 3¹½ 3⁶ 3⁷½ Rivera JA II L 115 6.30 83-19 Nicholas Ds117⁵½PerfectPrmir115²Not Surprising115¾ 8
Couldn't keep pace
2May98- 8Tam fst 7f :22⁴ :45⁴ 1:10⁴ 1:23³ 3↑ Alw 13000 4 4 3²½ 3¹½ 1¹½ 1⁴ Whitley K L 119 *.70 95-13 Not Surprising119⁴King Willow119¹¼Sailing Sain119¹ 10
Kept to pressure
21Apr98- 9Tam fst 6f :22¹ :45² :57³ 1:10³ 3↑ Alw 12200 3 3 5⁴¼ 3³½ 3⁴ 2¾ Henry WT L 119 *.70 98-14 Bubba Higgins119¾Not Surprising119²¾Flashy Link119no 9
Gaining outside
4Apr98- 8Hia fst 6f :21⁴ :45 :58¹ 1:09³ 3↑ Hia Sprint Champ 50k 6 6 6⁵ 6²¾ 5⁴¾ 5¹²½ Henry WT L 117 5.90 79-22 WstrnBordrs114³½NcholsDs116¹½Hckofrlph118⁶¼ No response 7
24Feb98- 9Tam fst 5½f :23¹ :46² 1:04¹ 4↑ Alw 11400 8 3 4²½ 2hd 1½ 1²¼ Henry WT L 116 *.90 100-15 Not Surprising116²¼Adorable Racer119⁴Threshold116¾ 8
Kept to pressure
6Apr97- 9Hia fst 7f :23 :45² 1:09⁴ 1:22⁴ 3↑ Hia Sprint Chp H 50k 7 3 2¹ 3¹ 6⁶½ 7⁹ Henry WT L 116 4.30 83-21 Stormy Do112³¼Derivative111¹½Thats Our Buck113¹½ Tired 11
7Mar97- 9GP sly 6f :21³ :44² :57¹ 1:11 4↑ Alw 50000 3 4 3⁶ 2⁵ 3⁴ 5² Davis RG 117 *1.70 83-22 SonicSignl117noStormyDo115½TuxdoLndng115no Faded 3 path 6
16Feb97-10GP fst 6f :22² :44⁴ :57² 1:09³ 3↑ Deputy Minister H 75k 5 1 5³½ 4¹½ 6⁵½ 5⁷¼ Henry WT 116 6.40 85-10 Templado113²¼SeaEmperor114noPunchLine119³½ No threat 6
5Oct96- 7Bel fm 1Ⓣ :23³ :46³ 1:10¹ 1:34² 3↑ Kelso H-G3 10 2 3¹ 5²¼ 9⁸¾ 9¹³¾ Castillo H Jr 113 30.50 76-15 SameOldWsh113hdDHoss120nkVolochn116hd Forced pace,tired 10

21Sep96- 9Bel	fst 7f	:23 :454 1:084 1:211 3↑	Vosburgh-G1	3	4	41½	62¾	64½	54½	Davis RG		126		12.60	90-15	Langfuhr1261¼Honour and Glory122¾Lite the Fuse1262½		8
	Saved ground,tired																	
2Sep96- 9Sar	fst 7f	:22 :442 1:091 1:214 3↑	Forego H-G2	7	6	56½	69	55	44½	Davis RG		118		4.50	92-11	Langfuhr110nkTopAccount1154LitetheFuse121nk	No late bid	7
8Aug96- 9Sar	fst 6f	:214 :441 :554 1:081 3↑	A Phenomenon-G2	2	2	43	43½	45½	49¼	Davis RG		120		6.50	91-11	Prospect Bay1131¾Honour and Glory1195Lite the Fuse1232½		7
	Saved ground,no rally																	
20Jly96-11Lrl	fst 6f	:213 :434 :562 1:084 3↑	De Francis Mem Dash-G2	2	6	67½	76¾	65	45½	Castillo H Jr		117		4.60	93-11	LitetheFuse117noMdowMonstr1191¾ProspctBy1143¾	Very wide	7
4Jly96- 8FL	gd 6f	:22 :451 :572 1:104 3↑	FL BC-G3	3	6	43	33	23	3½	Castillo H Jr		119		*1.10	89-25	Forest Wildcat119hdFriendly Lover115½Not Surprisingly1197¼		8
	Willingly																	
8Jun96- 7Bel	fst 6f	:213 :44 :561 1:09 3↑	True North H-G2	7	8	65¼	64½	33½	11	Davis RG		121		2.80	97-08	NotSrprisng1211ProspctBy1132¾ForstWldct114½	Going away	8
26May96- 8Bel	fst 6f	:223 :453 :57 1:091 4↑	Handicap 46000	6	3	42	3½	11½	13	Castillo H Jr		122		*2.25	96-16	Not Surprising1223Kings Fiction110hdDistinct Reality110hd		6
	Going away																	
5May96- 9Bel	my 7f	:222 :442 1:082 1:204 3↑	Carter H-G1	1	6	64	55	76½	914	Perret C		121		4.30	83-10	Lite the Fuse121hdFlying Chevron1153Placid Fund114½		10
	Lacked response																	
6Apr96- 9Hia	fst 7f	:232 :453 1:094 1:222 3↑	Hia Sprint Ch H 50k	7	2	72¾	31	11½	12¾	Perret C		118		*.80	94-17	Not Surprising1182¾Constant Escort1122Excelerate113½		8
	Outside turn,five wide top str,ridden out																	
24Mar96- 8Hia	fst 6f	:221 :443 :57 1:10 3↑	Dade County 28k	1	4	2hd	61¾	68	69½	Davis RG		119		*.70	81-08	CrftyChris113hdOur Exuberant Lad1131¾Constant Escort1132		6
	Inside,stopped																	
18Feb96-10GP	fst 6f	:213 :443 :571 1:103 3↑	Deputy Minister H 50k	4	5	47½	67½	66½	56¾	Davis RG		123		*.80	80-21	Jess C's Whirl1153Buffalo Dan117nkPatton1142½		6
	Wide top str,failed to menace																	
28Oct95- 3Bel	my 6f	:213 :442 :562 1:09 3↑	BC Sprint-G1	3	2	84¾	75	44	42½	Davis RG		126		*3.30	93-08	DesertStormer123nkMr.Greeley1232LtdJustc126nk	Mild gain	13
16Sep95- 7Bel	fst 7f	:222 :444 1:092 1:222 3↑	Vosburgh-G1	10	2	42½	42	2½	1no	Davis RG		126		*3.25	89-13	NotSrprisng126noYoundI126noOurEmblm1261	Fully extended	13
23Aug95- 9Sar	fst 7f	:223 :45 1:09 1:214 3↑	Forego H-G2	4	2	33½	32	11	14	Davis RG		121		4.70	97-15	NotSrprisng1214OurEmblem1135LitetheFus123nk	Drew away	4
6Aug95- 8Sar	wf 6f	:22 :451 :571 1:093 3↑	A Phenomenon H-G2	9	1	53½	42	21½	12	Davis RG		115		*3.15	93-17	Not Surprising1152Chimes Band1191Mining Burrah116no		10
	Four wide,drew clear																	
4Jly95- 7FL	fst 6f	:212 :442 :563 1:09 3↑	FL Bud BC-G3	2	6	42½	31	1½	11½	Davila JR Jr		113		4.50	99-13	NotSurprising1131½FriendlyLovr1193Schossbrg1159	Driving	9
	Previously owned by Robert Van Worp Jr																	
17Jun95- 9Bel	fst 1⅛	:462 1:104 1:354 1:49 3↑	Brooklyn H-G2	9	5	42	31	56	814	Davis RG		112		9.60	73-22	YouandI1151KeyContndr1121SlckHorn1137¼	Four wide,tired	9
29May95- 9Bel	gd 1	:221 :441 1:083 1:343 3↑	Metropolitan H-G1	3	7	65¼	43	33½	45	Davis RG		113		20.80	85-17	You and I1121Lite the Fuse1132½Our Emblem1141½		9
	Bid inside,flattened																	
29Apr95-11Hia	sly 1⅛	:464 1:104 1:35 1:481 3↑	Seminole H 50k	1	6	22½	1½	12	12½	Castillo H Jr	L	117		2.10	101-09	NotSurprsng1172½PrideofBurkan1171Byton1148	Ridden out	9
1Apr95- 8Hia	fst 7f	:233 :46 1:093 1:221 3↑	Hia Sprint Ch H 50k	2	6	41¼	31½	2hd	12	Davis RG	L	114		12.30	98-11	NotSurprising1142EvilBear118¾TurfStr1121	Driving,inside	10
11Mar95- 9GP	gd 1 1/16Ⓣ	:224 :464 1:104 1:41 3↑	Ft Lauderdale H-G3	5	5	73¾	96¾	63½	98½	Henry WT	L	114		28.00	83-18	TheVid1203FlyingAmericn113nkDJ's Rainbow1141¼	Gave way	12
18Feb95-11Tam	fst 1 1/16	:233 :464 1:111 1:442 3↑	Tam Bud BC 77k	4	3	32	3½	16	1hd	Henry WT	L	114		3.20	100-00	NotSurprising114hdMightyAvanti1135Bostrous1131½	All out	12
28Jan95-10Tam	fst 7f	:224 :452 1:101 1:231 3↑	BC Super 45k	8	8	74¼	21	3nk	32½	Henry WT	L	122		*.20	99-11	Boistrous1102½Mr.Tooth116noNotSurprising1227½	Bid,hung	9
7Jan95- 9Tam	gd 6f	:223 :461 :581 1:104 3↑	Pelican H 28k	9	2	56½	41¼	16	111½	Henry WT	L	113		*.90	98-16	Not Surprising11311Honor Colony116noReigning Glory122no		12
	Strong race																	
25Jly94- 8Crc	sly 1 1/16⊗	:243 :491 1:133 1:454 3↑	Handicap 22000	4	6	62½	53½	45	58¼	Ramos WS	L	117		*.60	82-10	SilentLk1121¼DprtngCloud1132¾Jck'sHop1124	Showed little	6
16Jly94-11Crc	fst 1⅛	:471 1:122 1:384 1:523 3↑	Spend a Buck H 100k	5	4	42	62½	35	54¼	Valles ES	L	115		12.30	86-14	Daniel'sBoy111¾It'sl'lknownfct1103AggrssvChf115nk	Faded	8
25Jun94-11Crc	fst 7f	:232 :462 1:103 1:232 3↑	Emerald Dunes H 100k	6	3	52¼	42½	53	52½	Henry WT	L	116		2.90	92-12	Swedaus111nk[DH]Score a Birdie113 [DH]Daniel's Boy111¾		7
	Seven wide top str,lacked response																	
4Jun94- 9Crc	yl 5fⓉ	:221 :46 :574 3↑	Largo Mar H 100k	1	8	93½	83½	32½	22	Henry WT	L	116		6.60	93-05	CoolAir1182NotSurprising1161½AbsentRussian112nk	Rallied	12
14May94- 6LaD	fst 1⅛	:482 1:121 1:364 1:492 3↑	Ark-La-Tex H-G3	9	4	43½	42	78	78½	Henry WT	L	115		5.30	93-17	Nelson1162¼Eequalsmcsquared1151DixiePokerAce1151	Tired	10
23Apr94-10Hia	sly 1⅛	:453 1:102 1:352 1:482 3↑	Seminole H 100k	7	5	54½	21½	1½	11¾	Henry WT	L	114		11.90	102-11	NotSrprisng1141¾[D]Dnl'sBoy111¾NorthrnTrnd1161¾	Driving	8
3Apr94- 9Hia	fst 7f	:223 :444 1:091 1:214 3↑	Sprint Ch H 50k	11	2	3½	2½	31½	33	Sellers SJ	L	113		24.10	97-09	[D]Jack Livingston110hdD.J. Cat1153Not Surprising1132		11
	Steadied midstretch,gamely;Placed second through disqualification																	
19Feb94-10Tam	fst 1 1/16	:233 :473 1:122 1:442 3↑	Tam Bud BC 78k	12	6	62½	2hd	12½	22	Henry WT	L	113		3.70	98-12	PrideofBurkaan1132NotSurprising1132Rplton1222½	2nd best	12
29Jan94-10Tam	gd 7f	:224 :454 1:11 1:243 3↑	BC Super 47k	4	7	43½	43	1½	12	Henry WT	L	122		*1.50	95-15	NotSrprisng1222PremirAngl122½JunkBondKng1132½	Driving	12
8Jan94-10Tam	fst 6f	:223 :453 :58 1:102 3↑	Pelican 28k	3	1	31	52½	12½	13	Henry WT	L	116		2.80	100-13	NotSurprsng1163OhSoStriking1153½BobtheHt1181½	Driving	12
	Previously trained by William P. White																	
8Dec93- 9Crc	fst 5f	:214 :453 :581	Handicap 22000	1	5	64¾	65¾	33	32¼	Ramos WS	L	118	f	3.60	103-12	GreyCountr116noProbablCll1162¼NotSurprsng1183	Good try	9
23Oct93- 8Crc	fst 7f	:22 :45 1:092 1:222 3↑	Miami Beach H 75k	7	7	104½	96½	915	915½	Lee MA	L	112	f	35.10	88-07	SongofAmbition1163½CoolinIt113nkDnl'sBoy1172½	No threat	12
26Sep93-11Crc	fst 6½f	:221 :443 1:10 1:164 3↑	Cooper Cty H 20k	7	1	41¼	42¾	34½	46¾	Lee MA	L	114	f	5.70	93-07	SongofAmbtn116nkD.J.Ct119½MyLuckRnsNrth1126	Weakened	7
1Sep93- 9Crc	fm *5fⓉ	:583	Handicap 22000	8	1	75¼	67	64¼	1¾	Lee MA	L	119	f	*1.30	- -	Not Surprising119¾My Boy Cary111½Sergio's Turn112no		10
	Eight wide top str,driving																	
30Jly93- 1Crc	fst 7f	:232 :461 1:102 1:224 3↑	Handicap 22000	3	4	22½	21½	45	46	Lee MA	L	112	f	4.90	95-04	MyLuckRunsNurth1111Humbugboo1162¼ColorfulCrw1132¾		5
	Weakened																	
11Jly93- 1Crc	sly 5f	:223 :461 :59	Alw 19900	4	4	32	31½	21½	11	Lee MA	L	118	f	1.70	101-07	NotSurprising1181AspenFortune1162½TradeBll114nk	Driving	5
19Jun93-10Crc	fst 7f	:221 :45 1:093 1:223	Carry Back H 100k	4	6	53½	53½	46½	57	Lee MA	L	117	f	2.50	95-01	Humbugaboo1122½Signoir Valery1124¼Kassec113hd		8
	Failed to menace																	
6Jun93-10Crc	fst 6f	:213 :444 :57 1:10	Needles H 22k	1	5	33½	32	21	11¼	Lee MA	L	117	f	3.80	98-07	Not Surprising1171¼Humbugaboo1141Ships in the Night1102¼		7
	Six wide top str,driving																	
17Oct92-11Crc	fst 1 1/16	:233 :473 1:123 1:473	[R]In Reality (FSS) 410k	13	11	108¼	1414	1414	710½	Lee MA		120		10.40	78-11	SilverofSilver1204Crafty120noFierySpcl1202½	Belated bid	15
19Sep92-10Crc	fst 7f	:214 :444 1:104 1:243	[R]Affirmed (FSS) 125k	10	10	85¼	75¼	57¾	56¾	De'Oliveira WG		118		2.90	85-11	Fiery Special1182Ships in the Night1183½Gentle Patrick118nk		10
	Lacked response																	
6Sep92-10Crc	fst 7f	:23 :461 1:114 1:25	Turnberry Isle 50k	3	4	41¼	2hd	2hd	1½	De'Oliveira WG		116		*.70	90-12	NotSurprising116½Ducd'Sligovil1123Dotsappel1124	Driving	5
22Aug92-11Crc	fst 6f	:212 :444 :58 1:114	[R]Dr Fager 75k	5	9	54¼	34	31	1hd	De'Oliveira WG		116		2.10	92-13	Not Surprising116hdGentle Patrick116¾Fiery Special1164½		9
	Driving,lugged in																	
9Aug92-11Crc	fst 6f	:213 :451 :581 1:113	Alw 22000	2	6	67	54	1½	12	De'Oliveira WG		114		9.80	93-11	Not Surprising1142Thats Our Buck1182½It's a Runaway116nk		6
	Drifted in,driving																	
19Jly92-10Crc	fst 5½f	:221 :454 1:053	Criterium 50k	8	4	21½	21	32½	66¾	De'Oliveira WG		116	b	15.60	- -	ThirtyTwoSlew1184SummerSet1121It'saRunaway1161	Stopped	8
5Jly92- 5Crc	fst 5½f	:222 :46 1:053	Alw 15500	2	9	75¼	64¾	44	35	Douglas RR		116		7.70	- -	Thirty Two Slew1163It's a Runaway1162Not Surprising1161		9
	Late rally 5 wide																	
2May92- 3Crc	fst 5f	:224 :472 1:003	Md Sp Wt	8	8	75	43¾	1hd	12¾	Lee MA		116		3.50	- -	NotSrprisng1162¾MyMax1161¼LeaderoftheLaw1161½	Driving	12

Paradise Creek

dkbbr. c. 1989, by Irish River (Riverman)–North of Eden, by Northfields **Lifetime record: 25 14 7 1 $3,386,925**

Own.– Masayuki Nishiyama
Br.– Mr & Mrs Bertram R. Firestone (Va)
Tr.– William I. Mott

27Nov94♦ Tokyo(Jpn) fm*1½ⓣLH 2:23³ 3↑ Japan Cup-G1 Stk3968000 2no Day P 126 4.00 MarvelousCrown126noParadiseCrk126¼RoyceandRyce126¼ 14
Rated in mid-pack,rallied 2f out,dueled final 16th,just missed
5Nov94- 9CD fm 1½ⓣ :46⁴ 1:10³ 2:00 2:26² 3↑ B C Turf-G1 13 4 1½ 1hd 1½ 3³ Day P L 126 *.80 109-00 Tikkann122½Htoof123½PrdsCrk126½ Drifted out,weakening 14
15Oct94-10Lrl fm 1¼ :46¹ 1:10² 1:35³ 1:59³ 3↑ D C Int'l-G1 6 7 6⁵ 2³ 1hd 1⁵½ Day P L 126 *.20 96-10 ParadiseCreek1265½Redcll126noBnfcl1263¾ Wide,ridden out 9
28Aug94-10AP fm 1¼ⓣ :48 1:11² 1:35² 1:59³ 3↑ Arl Million-G1 12 6 6⁵¼ 4³½ 2²½ 1¾ Day P L 126 *1.80 99-04 ParadiseCrk126¾Fanmore126½Muhtarram126½ Driving wide 14
12Aug94- 8Sar fm 1⅛ⓣ :48¹ 1:11² 1:34³ 1:46 3↑ B Baruch H-G2 1 4 3¹ 3² 2¹ 2¹ Day P 126 1.10 96-10 Lure1251Paradise Creek1266Fourstardave1146 Willingly 5
11Jun94- 7Bel fm 1⅜Ⓣ :46² 1:10 1:33⁴ 1:57³ 3↑ ET Manhattan-G1 2 2 1½ 1½ 1³ 1⁶¾ Day P 124 *.30 102-02 ParadiseCrek1246¾SolrSplndor112½RvrMjsty1137 Ridden out 7
20May94-11Pim fm 1⅛ⓣ :48⁴ 1:13¹ 1:36⁴ 1:48² 3↑ ET Dixie H-G2 4 3 4²¼ 4²¾ 2¹ 1¾ Day P L 124 1.30 93-14 Paradise Creek124¾Lure1245½Astudillo115½ Driving 5
6May94- 8CD gd 1⅛ⓣ :47 1:11¹ 1:36¹ 1:48¹ 3↑ ET Classic H-G2 6 4 4⁶ 4³ 1¹ 1⁴ Day P L 118 3.30 90-10 Paradise Creek1184Lure1232½Yukon Robebry1162½ 7
4-wide,ridden out
12Mar94-11GP fm 1 1/16ⓣ :23¹ :47 1:10² 1:39¹ 3↑ Fort Lauderdale H 100k 4 4 4³½ 4² 2hd 1¾ Smith ME L 125 *.70 100-02 Paradise Creek125¾Bidding Proud115¾Social Retiree1141¼ 9
Ridden out,inside;Previously owned by Bertram R. Firestone
29Jan94- 9GP fm 1⅛ⓣ :47² 1:11¹ 1:34³ 1:47³ 3↑ Canadian Turf H-G2 7 3 3¹½ 2¹ 1½ 1³¼ Smith ME L 123 *.40 93-11 Paradise Creek1233¼Glenfiddich Lad113¾Nijinsky's Gold113nk 8
Hand ride
8Jan94- 9GP fm 1 1/16ⓣ :24 :47³ 1:11¹ 1:40⁴ 3↑ Appleton H-G3 5 4 4³ 3½ 1¹½ 1³ Smith ME L 121 *1.20 92-14 ParadiseCrek1213FourstrsAllstr117nkEltJblr111no Handily 8
28Nov93- 5Hol fm 1⅛ⓣ :47 1:10² 1:33⁴ 1:45⁴ 3↑ Citation H-G2 3 1 1hd 1hd 1½ 2²¼ Day P LB 120 *2.10 93-09 Jeune Homme1142¼Paradise Creek120noJohannQuatz1202 8
Inside duel
6Nov93- 5SA fm 1ⓣ :22³ :45⁴ 1:09² 1:33² 3↑ B C Mile-G1 6 4 4²½ 5⁴½ 8⁷½ 8⁸ Day P LB 126 8.20 90-04 Lure1262¼Ski Paradise1201¾Fourstars Allstar126hd 13
Carried out 1st turn
16Oct93- 6Bel sf 1ⓣ :22⁴ :45⁴ 1:10³ 1:35⁴ 3↑ Kelso H-G3 10 2 3² 2½ 2¹½ 2³¼ Day P 120 3.00e 80-29 Lure1253¼Paradise Creek1205Daarik112½ Second best 10
30Apr93- 8CD fm 1⅛ⓣ :47 1:10⁴ 1:34² 1:46¹ 3↑ ET Classic H-G3 1 4 4² 4²½ 3³ 4²¾ Day P L 123 2.70 97-00 Lure123¾StarofCozzene1182Clon116no Lacked late response 8
31Mar93- 8GP fm 1 1/16ⓣ :23⁴ :47⁴ 1:11³ 1:41⁴ 4↑ Handicap 55000 4 2 3³ 3⁴ 2¹½ 1¹ Day P L 122 *.50 87-12 ParadiseCrk1221SylvaHond1131FlyngAmrcn1112 Ridden out 7
22Nov92- 8Hol fm 1⅛ⓣ :45³ 1:09³ 1:34¹ 1:47¹ Hol Derby-G1 5 3 2½ 1½ 1½ 1no Day P LB 122 *1.50 88-15 Paradise Creek122noBien Bien1221¼Kitwood122hd Gamely 12
31Oct92- 7GP fm 1ⓣ :22² :45⁴ 1:09 1:32⁴ 3↑ B C Mile-G1 11 6 6³¾ 6³¾ 4⁴ 2³ Day P 122 30.30f 106-00 Lure1223Paradise Creek122nkBrief Truce1221½ Good effort 14
3Oct92- 9Med fm 1 1/16ⓣ :23² :46³ 1:10¹ 1:40² Palisades B C H 77k 4 2 2¹½ 2¹ 2½ 2¹ Smith ME 119 *.40 95-01 Bidding Proud1161Paradise Creek119nkMaryland Moon1142½ 6
No match late
7Sep92- 9AP fm 1¼ⓣ :48² 1:13 1:37³ 2:01 Secretariat-G1 3 4 3² 4² 3²½ 2½ Smith ME 123 *2.40 91-05 Ghazi114½ParadiseCreek1231¾TangoCharl117hd Strong rally 10
6Aug92- 8Sar fm 1⅛ⓣ :47 1:10¹ 1:34 1:46³ Hall of Fame-G2 4 1 1½ 1¹½ 1² 1¹ Smith ME 115 *1.30 97-03 ParadiseCrk1151SmilingandDancin1191¾SpectaculrTide122hd 8
Driving
22Jly92- 7Bel fm 1 1/16ⓣ :23⁴ :46³ 1:10 1:40 3↑ Alw 31000 5 2 2¹½ 2¹ 1hd 1²¼ Smith ME 113 *.50 96-15 ParadiseCrk1132¼VictoryCross1176TimberCt111hd Driving 9
18Jun92- 7Bel fm 1 1/16ⓣ :23² :46¹ 1:10 1:40² 3↑ Alw 29000 10 2 2¹ 1¹ 1⁴ 1⁴ Perret C 112 b *1.00 94-11 Paradise Creek1124Scuffleburg1136Alfaares117½ Handily 11
24Aug91- 8Sar fst 6½f :21³ :44² 1:10³ 1:17³ Hopeful-G1 9 2 6⁶ 5⁸¾ 3⁶ 4⁹¼ Cordero A Jr 122 3.40 78-14 Salt Lake1229Slew's Ghost122hdCaller I.D.122hd 4-wide 9
19Jly91- 5Bel fm 7fⓣ :22⁴ :45⁴ 1:10³ 1:22³ Md Sp Wt 2 12 5²½ 4¹½ 1² 1¹¹ Smith ME 118 3.00 92-08 ParadiseCreek11811ForeverFighting118hdJayG1181¼ Handily 12

Paseana (Arg)

b. f. 1987, by Ahmad (Good Manners)–Pasiflin, by Flintham **Lifetime record: 36 19 10 2 $3,171,203**

Own.– Sidney H. Craig
Br.– Haras Vacacion (Arg)
Tr.– Ronald McAnally

23Jly95- 7Hol fst 1⅛ :46¹ 1:10³ 1:35³ 1:48¹ 3↑ ⒻVanity H-G1 4 4 4⁶½ 3²½ 4⁷ 5¹¹½ McCarron CJ LB 123 *1.30 80-09 Private Persuasion1143Top Rung1162¾Wandesta1194½ 7
Mild bid ⅜,weakened
25Jun95- 4Hol fst 1 1/16 :23² :46³ 1:10¹ 1:41² 3↑ ⒻMilady H-G1 3 5 5⁹¼ 5⁵ 3³½ 2³½ McCarron CJ LB 123 *.80 90-14 Pirate's Revenge1163½Paseana1234Private Persuasion1161¾ 5
Best of others
28May95- 9Hol fst 1 1/16 :22³ :45² 1:09⁴ 1:42² 3↑ ⒻHawthorne H-G2 4 6 6¹¹ 6³¾ 3½ 1² McCarron CJ LB 122 2.10 89-13 Paseana1222Pirate'sRvng117¾TopRung1178 4 wide into lane 7
21Apr95- 9OP fst 1 1/16 :22⁴ :45⁴ 1:10³ 1:42³ 4↑ ⒻApple Blossom-G1 1 3 3⁶ 3³½ 3²½ 3⁵ McCarron CJ L 122 2.00 89-15 HeavnlyPrize1201HaloAmeric1164Psn1225 Mild middle move 6
26Feb95- 8SA fst 1⅛ :47 1:11 1:36 1:48⁴ 4↑ ⒻS Margarita H-G1 2 3 4³ 3²½ 3² 2² McCarron CJ LB 123 1.30 87-16 QueensCourtQn1202Pasna123½KlassyKm1169 Game effort 5
5Feb95- 8SA fst 1 1/16 :22⁴ :46¹ 1:09² 1:41³ 4↑ ⒻS Maria H-G1 3 4 5²¼ 4⁵½ 3⁴½ 2⁴½ McCarron CJ LB 123 2.20 82-15 Queens Court Queen1184½Paseana123¾Key Phrase1173½ 5
Closed willingly
28Aug94- 8Dmr fst 1 1/16 :22⁴ :46¹ 1:10¹ 1:40² 3↑ ⒻChula Vista H-G2 2 3 3³½ 3²½ 3½ 1no McCarron CJ LB 123 *.30e 104-03 Paseana123noExchange120¾MagicIMaidn118nk Determinedly 4
6Mar94- 8SA fst 1⅛ :46⁴ 1:10⁴ 1:36 1:49 4↑ ⒻS Margarita H-G1 6 5 4¹½ 4¹¼ 1½ 1²¾ McCarron CJ LB 123 *1.10 88-18 Paseana1232¾KalitaMelody117hdStalcreek1192 Kept to task 9
12Feb94- 8SA fst 1 1/16 :23¹ :47¹ 1:11 1:41⁴ 4↑ ⒻS Maria H-G1 3 4 3½ 3½ 2¹½ 2no McCarron CJ LB 124 *.70 86-14 SupahGem116noPsn124noAlysbll1161½ Drifted out near wire 7
6Nov93- 4SA fst 1⅛ :46⁴ 1:11 1:36 1:48¹ 3↑ ⒻBC Distaff-G1 3 4 3²½ 3¹ 2hd 2no McCarron CJ LB 123 2.50 89-10 Hollywood Wildcat120noPaseana1232½Re Toss1231 Game try 8
17Oct93- 8Kee my 1⅛ :46³ 1:10³ 1:35³ 1:48² 3↑ ⒻSpinster-G1 3 4 3² 3¹ 2¹ 1¹ McCarron CJ L 123 *1.20 92-07 Pasean1231GryCshmr1234Jcody1191 Brushed 3/16,hard drive 9
19Sep93- 8Bel my 1 1/16 :23² :46⁴ 1:10³ 1:41³ 3↑ ⒻRuffian H-G1 1 3 4⁴½ 4² 5⁷ 5²⁰¾ McCarron CJ 125 *1.20 72-16 SharedInterest1142½Dsput1153TrnbckthAlrm1232¼ Gave way 5
18Jly93- 8Hol fst 1⅛ :47² 1:10² 1:35¹ 1:47³ 3↑ ⒻVanity H-G1 3 4 5¹¾ 1½ 1¹½ 2¹¼ McCarron CJ LB 126 *.70 97-10 Re Toss1151¼Paseana1262¼Guiza1143 Clear,overtaken 8
12Jun93- 8Hol fst 1 1/16 :23 :46 1:09⁴ 1:41³ 3↑ ⒻMilady H-G1 1 5 4² 3¹ 1hd 1½ McCarron CJ LB 125 *.40 93-13 Paseana125½Bold Windy114½Re Toss1165 Hard drive,gamely 7
16Apr93- 9OP fst 1 1/16 :23 :46¹ 1:10³ 1:41⁴ 4↑ ⒻApple Blossom H-G1 1 4 4³ 4¾ 1²½ 1³½ McCarron CJ L 124 *.40 92-13 Paseana1243½Looie Capote1154½Luv Me Luv Me Not114nk 9
4 wide,2nd turn
28Feb93- 8SA fst 1⅛ :48¹ 1:12¹ 1:36⁴ 1:49² 4↑ ⒻS Margarita H-G1 2 2 3½ 1½ 1hd 2hd McCarron CJ LB 125 *.40 83-17 Southern Truce115hdPaseana1251¾Guiza1143 9
Rider dropped rein briefly⅛
6Feb93- 8SA fst 1 1/16 :23² :47² 1:10⁴ 1:41¹ 4↑ ⒻS Maria H-G1 3 3 3¹½ 3² 2¹ 2²¼ McCarron CJ LB 126 *.70 96-12 Race the Wild Wind1172¼Paseana1261¼Southern Truce1164½ 6
Not enough late
31Oct92- 6GP fst 1⅛ :47 1:10⁴ 1:35³ 1:48 3↑ ⒻBC Distaff-G1 14 4 3½ 1hd 1³ 1⁴ McCarron CJ L 123 2.70e 97-03 Paseana1234Versailles Treaty123½Magical Maiden1191½ 14
Strong hand ride
11Oct92- 8Kee fst 1⅛ :48 1:12³ 1:37¹ 1:49³ 3↑ ⒻSpinster-G1 4 5 6³ 5² 2² 2²¼ McCarron CJ LB 123 *.50 84-25 Fowda1232¼Paseana1236MeadwStar1232½ Broke awkwardly 10
30Aug92- 4Dmr fst 1¼ :46¹ 1:10² 1:35 2:00⁴ 3↑ Pacific Classic 1000k 2 2 2½ 3½ 3¹½ 5⁶¼ McCarron CJ LB 119 *1.70 89-11 MissionaryRidge1243½DefnsivePlay124nkClrt1242 Weakened 7
19Jly92- 8Hol fst 1⅛ :47 1:10³ 1:35¹ 1:48 3↑ ⒻVanity H-G1 2 2 2hd 1hd 1¹½ 1² McCarron CJ LB 127 *.30 94-12 Paseana1272Fowda1181¼Re Toss1153 Driving 6
13Jun92- 8Hol fst 1 1/16 :22³ :45⁴ 1:10 1:41² 3↑ ⒻMilady H-G1 7 6 5³ 4¾ 1¹½ 1²¾ McCarron CJ LB 125 *.40 94-12 Paseana1252¾Re Toss115¾Fowda1191¾ Wide,handily 7
17Apr92- 9OP fst 1 1/16 :23³ :46⁴ 1:11 1:42 4↑ ⒻApple Blossom H-G1 1 4 3³ 2hd 1³ 1⁴½ McCarron CJ L 124 *.40 91-23 Paseana1244½FitforaQueen1213½SldoutFront1092 Ridden out 8
1Mar92- 8SA fst 1⅛ :46¹ 1:10¹ 1:34⁴ 1:47² 4↑ ⒻS Margarita Inv'l H-G1 1 2 2²½ 2¹½ 1hd 1²¼ McCarron CJ LB 122 *.40 93-15 Pseana1222¼LaramieMoon1166ColourChart1182½ Ridden out 5
8Feb92- 8SA fst 1 1/16 :22³ :46¹ 1:10⁴ 1:41⁴ 4↑ ⒻS Maria H-G1 1 2 1½ 1½ 1¹½ 1²½ McCarron CJ LB 120 *.80 94-16 Paseana1202½ColourChrt1181¾Campagnarde1171¼ Ridden out 5
5Jan92- 8SA sly 1⅛⊗ :47 1:12³ 1:39³ 1:53⁴ 4↑ ⒻS Gorgonio H-G2 1 2 2¹½ 1³ 1²½ 1²½ McCarron CJ LB 118 *.60 91-31 Paseana1182½Laura Ly11216Reluctant Guest11723 Handily 4
23Nov91- 8Hol fst 1 1/16 :23 :46⁴ 1:11¹ 1:42³ 3↑ ⒻSilver Belles H-G2 4 2 1hd 2hd 1½ 1⁵½ McCarron CJ 117 *1.70 88-18 Pseana1175½Damewood116nkLunaElegante117½ Clear,driving 6
14Oct91- 3SA fst 1 1/16 :23¹ :47¹ 1:11¹ 1:42² 3↑ ⒻManta H 61k 4 3 4²½ 4¹ 3² 2² McCarron CJ 117 2.20 89-16 LaCharlatna1172Pasen1171PmprdStr1131¾ Wide backstretch 6
13Apr91♦ San Isidro(Arg) fm*1⅛ⓣLH 1:46² 3↑ ⒻClasico Abril-G2 Stk16500 1²½ Sarati M 122 *.70 Paseana1222½Inimitable1322½Sereana1321½ 9
Tracked in 3rd,led 2f out,handily
30Mar91♦ San Isidro(Arg) fm*1⅜ⓣLH 2:14² 3↑ ⒻClasico Federico de Alvear-G2 Stk16400 4²½ Garcia M 120 2.05 Fail132hdBallesta1202½Teresine132no 9
Tracked in 3rd,bid 2f out,weakened final 16th
8Dec90♦ San Isidro(Arg) fm*1¼ⓣLH 2:01² 3↑ ⒻCopa de Plata-G1 Stk24400 7¹⁰ Sarati M 119 *1.10 Jewellery119hdFail132nkCampagnarde119nk 12
Never a factor

3Nov90♦ San Isidro(Arg) gd *1¼Ⓣ LH 1:592 ⒻGran Premio Enrique Acebal-G1 Stk34000 14 Sarati M 123 2.15 Paseana1234Pupy Hill123nkJewellery123½ 10
Tracked in 5th,sharp run to lead over 1f out,quickly clear
14Oct90♦ Hipodromo(Arg) fst *1¼ LH 2:022 ⒻGran Premio Seleccion-G1 Stk47600 38½ Sarati M 123 5.20 Campagnarde1231½Silver Beauty1237Paseana123¾ 16
Tracked in 4th,3rd 4f out,no further response
21Sep90♦ Hipodromo(Arg) fst *1⅛ LH 1:502 ⒻClasico Francisco J Beazley-G2 Stk15300 11½ Garcia M 123 3.95 Paseana1231½Silver Beauty1246Campagnarde1232½ 11
Rated in 6th,2nd 2f out,led over 1f out,driving
22Aug90♦ San Isidro(Arg) fm *7fⓉ LH 1:214 ⒻPremio Baluarte Alw3900 14 Sarati M 123 *.65e Paseana1234Caramel Toss1234KsteelMi1238 7
Tracked leader,led 2f out,drew clear
1Aug90♦ San Isidro(Arg) fm *7fⓉ LH 1:23 ⒻPremio Cerrito Mdn3000 11½ Sarati M 123 *1.75 Paseana1231½La Calada1234Mining Lark1232 14
Tracked in 3rd,4th halfway,rallied to lead 1f out,handily

Phone Chatter

ch. f. 1991, by Phone Trick (Clever Trick)–Passing My Way, by Pass the Glass **Lifetime record: 15 5 3 1 $838,741**
Own.– Herman Sarkowsky
Br.– Herman Sarkowsky (Ky)
Tr.– Richard Mandella

13Jan96- 8SA fst 6f :212 :44 :56 1:082 4↑ ⒻAlw 55000 4 5 512 58½ 58 46¾ Pincay L Jr LB 117 b 6.70 89-10 Igotrhythm1143Ballerina Gal122¾Angi Go1223 No threat 5
15Nov95- 8Hol fm 1Ⓣ :23 :462 1:10 1:341 3↑ ⒻⓇFlawlessly 61k 7 5 2½ 31 84 76¾ Dsrmeaux KJ L 116 b 4.70 85-10 Twice the Vice1201¼Norcliffe Dancr116nkReau Perralt117½ 8
Drifted out into lane
9Sep95- 8Dmr fm 1 1/16Ⓣ :24 :481 1:114 1:422 3↑ ⒻPalomar-G2 3 5 55½ 55 77¼ 56½ Pincay L Jr L 117 b 9.50 86-07 Morgana1181½Yearly Tour1181¼Lady Affirmed117hd 7
Drifted wide 2nd turn
19Jly95- 8Hol fm 1Ⓣ :242 :481 1:121 1:354 4↑ ⒻMelvn Durslag 75k 2 3 32 42½ 41¼ 2½ Pincay L Jr L 117 b 4.10 83-15 Morgana118½Phone Chatter117½Fondly Remembered118¾ 6
4 wide into lane
8Jun95- 8Hol fst 7f :222 :452 1:091 1:21 3↑ ⒻAlw 60000 3 5 55½ 54 56 37 Black CA LB 118 2.10 90-07 PrivatePersuson1164LunrSpook1173PhnChttr118½ Wide trip 5
28Dec94- 8SA fst 7f :221 :443 1:09 1:214 ⒻLa Brea-G2 7 6 710 76½ 65½ 43¾ Pincay L Jr 117 1.80 89-10 Top Rung115¾Klassy Kim1191Twice the Vice1192 7
Wide early,checked a bit 1/16
16Oct94- 8Kee fst 1⅛ :473 1:113 1:362 1:484 3↑ ⒻSpinster-G1 6 4 64 68½ 813 823¼ Nakatani CS 119 2.20 67-24 Dispute1231½LetsBeAlert1197MssDominique1232½ Gave way 8
12Sep94- 8Dmr fst 1 :221 :452 1:094 1:344 3↑ ⒻVieille Vigne H 66k 1 3 32 31 31½ 2¾ Pincay L Jr 119 *.40 95-03 Miss Dominique117¾Phone Chatter119½Pub Rivr11311 5
Floated out into lane
25Aug94- 8Dmr fst 6½f :214 :441 1:083 1:15 ⒻCERF 60k 6 3 64 33 32 11 Pincay L Jr 117 *.50 96-13 Phone Chatter1171Airistar120½Klassy Kim11510 Driving 6
6Nov93- 3SA fst 1 1/16 :232 :472 1:112 1:43 ⒻBC Juv Fillies-G1 6 6 53 42½ 2½ 1hd Pincay L Jr B 119 2.30 80-10 PhoneChatter119hdSardula1193HeavenlyPrz119½ 4-wide trip 8
9Oct93- 8SA fst 1 1/16 :222 :462 1:104 1:413 ⒻOak Leaf-G1 5 3 32 3½ 1hd 1½ Pincay L Jr B 117 5.00 96-10 PhoneChatter117½Sardul1167½TrckyCod1153 Drifted out ¼ 6
4Sep93- 8Dmr fst 7f :214 :443 1:091 1:213 ⒻDmr Debutante-G2 8 6 77¼ 55 46½ 27½ Pincay L Jr B 119 2.00 87-10 Sardula1167½Phone Chatter119nkBallerina Gal1142½ 8
Off a bit awkwardly,wide trip
14Aug93- 8Dmr fst 6½f :214 :443 1:094 1:161 ⒻSorrento-G3 5 5 56 55¼ 33 12¾ Pincay L Jr B 117 4.90 90-13 Phone Chatter1172¾Rhapsodic121½Noassemblyrequired1174½ 6
Rough start,bumped 3/16,driving
4Jly93- 4Hol fst 5½f :214 :454 :582 1:043 ⒻMd Sp Wt 3 6 65½ 44 33 11¾ Pincay L Jr B 117 2.80 89-11 PhoneChatter1171¾StrongColors1172CocoLuv1173½ Driving 8
20Jun93- 4Hol fst 5f :214 :443 :571 ⒻMd Sp Wt 5 7 88 77¼ 68 66½ Pincay L Jr B 117 *3.50 91-08 Dance With Grace1172Smilin' Irish Eyes1172¾MlibuLight1171 10
Took up 3/16

Pleasant Stage

b. f. 1989, by Pleasant Colony (His Majesty)–Meteor Stage, by Stage Door Johnny **Lifetime record: 10 2 3 2 $844,272**
Own.– Buckland Farm
Br.– Mrs Thomas M. Evans (Ky)
Tr.– Christopher Speckert

11Jly92- 8Bel fst 1¼ :50 1:133 1:38 2:032 ⒻC C A Oaks-G1 2 6 64 31 33 32½ Bailey JD 121 2.10 71-18 TurnbacktheAlrm1211¼EasyNw1211¼PleasntStg1211 Rallied 6
7Jun92- 8Bel fst 1⅛ :452 1:093 1:352 1:484 ⒻMother Goose-G1 2 7 710 79 79¾ 718¾ Delahoussaye E 121 b 1.80 66-22 TurnbacktheAlarm1212¼EasyNow1211¾QueenofTriumph121¾ 7
Dull try
23May92- 8Bel fst 1 :224 :453 1:10 1:35 ⒻAcorn-G1 6 12 118 83¼ 32 22 Delahoussaye E 121 b 4.30 93-07 ProspectorsDelite1212PlsntStge1211½TurnbacktheAlrm1215¾ 12
Broke slow
1May92- 9CD fst 1⅛ :481 1:122 1:38 1:512 ⒻKy Oaks-G1 4 6 65¼ 54¾ 43 2½ Delahoussaye E 121 b 3.40 86-13 LuvMeLuvMeNot121½PlsntStage121½ProspectorsDelite121nk 6
Lean in brushed
18Apr92- 8Kee fst 1 1/16 :23 :464 1:11 1:423 ⒻAshland-G1 9 10 99½ 89¼ 58 46½ Delahoussaye E 121 *2.00 84-15 ProspectrsDelite1212½SpinnngRound1211LuvMeLvMeNt1213 10
Appeared to shy while lugging inside at ⅛ pole,no threat
8Mar92- 8SA fst 1 1/16 :232 :464 1:11 1:431 ⒻS A Oaks-G1 3 8 76¾ 55 54¼ 41¾ Delahoussaye E 117 *1.90 85-13 GoldnTreat117noMagicalMaiden1171QueensCourt Queen117¾ 8
Broke slowly
2Nov91- 3CD fst 1 1/16 :234 :474 1:124 1:462 ⒻB C Juv Fillies-G1 14 12 95¼ 115 43 1hd Delahoussaye E 119 5.80 83-09 Pleasant Stage119hdLa Spia1192½Cadillac Women119nk 14
Sluggish start,altered course 3/16 pole,driving
14Oct91- 8SA fst 1 1/16 :231 :464 1:112 1:432 ⒻOak Leaf-G2 2 5 56 42 31½ 12 Dlhoussaye E B 116 6.50 86-16 Pleasant Stage1162Soviet Sojourn1163La Spia1155½ 5
Off slowly,lugged in lane
6Sep91- 6Dmr gd 1 :224 :463 1:113 1:37 ⒻMd Sp Wt 6 5 45 33½ 22½ 22 Dlhoussaye E B 116 *1.70 79-16 QueensCourtQueen1162PleasntStage1169IllustriousLady1163½ 7
Best of rest
18Aug91- 4Dmr fst 6f :22 :451 :574 1:103 ⒻMd Sp Wt 1 8 811 78 58½ 36 Ortega LE B 117 33.50 80-11 Captivant1175½Praslin117½Pleasant Stage1172 8
Broke awkwardly,lugged in1/4 while green,quickened strongly

Pleasant Tap

b. c. 1987, by Pleasant Colony (His Majesty)–Never Knock, by Stage Door Johnny **Lifetime record: 32 9 9 5 $2,721,169**
Own.– Buckland Farm
Br.– T.M. Evans (Va)
Tr.– Christopher Speckert

31Oct92-10GP fst 1¼ :454 1:10 1:35 2:001 3↑ BC Classic-G1 13 11 106½ 96¼ 31½ 22 Stevens GL 126 2.50 98-03 A.P. Indy1212Pleasant Tap126½Jolypha1181½ Finished well 14
10Oct92- 8Bel gd 1¼ :461 1:10 1:35 1:584 3↑ J C Gold Cup-G1 6 5 57½ 2hd 12½ 14½ Stevens GL 126 3.40 97-04 PleasantTap1264½StrikthGold1262¼A.P.Indy121½ Going away 7
19Sep92- 8Bel fst 1⅛ :463 1:102 1:344 1:47 3↑ Woodward-G1 6 4 54 64 42 21¾ Delahoussaye E 126 1.90 92-06 SultrySong1261¾PleasantTap126hdOutofPlc126no Up for 2nd 8
18Jly92- 8Bel fst 1¼ :46 1:102 1:352 2:001 3↑ Suburban H-G1 2 5 39 32 1hd 11½ Delahoussaye E 119 2.00 90-16 Pleasant Tap1191½Strike the Gold1191¼Defensive Play1155 7
Ducked out,driving
6Jun92- 7Bel my 1⅛ :444 1:082 1:334 1:463 3↑ Nassau County H-G2 7 8 814 75¼ 51½ 2nk Delahoussaye E 119 5.30 96-08 Strike the Gold116nkPleasant Tap1191½Sultry Song1112¾ 9
Sted,blocked turn
25May92- 8Bel fst 1 :222 :444 1:082 1:333 3↑ Metropolitan H-G1 10 11 117¼ 87 43 22¼ Delahoussaye E 119 6.70 100-05 DixieBrass1072¼PlesntTp1191¾InExcss121nk Rallied,inside 11
2May92- 7CD fst 7f :224 :452 1:094 1:221 4↑ Chl Downs H-G3 5 6 82½ 73½ 42 1no Delhoussaye E B 120 *.80 99-02 PleasntTap120noTakMOut1202CntrllRod113¾ Brsh wire drvg 9
12Apr92- 8Kee fst 7f :222 :451 1:094 1:222 3↑ Commonwealth BC-G3 3 6 66½ 64½ 2hd 12½ Delhoussaye E B 116 *.90 97-12 PleasntTap1162½ToFreedom115noRunontheBank118½ Driving 6
20Feb92- 8SA fst 6f :22 :443 :562 1:084 4↑ Alw 50000 3 4 54 55½ 54 21¼♦ Delhoussaye E B 121 *1.80 91-16 Rushmore1151¼[DH]ValiantPete117[DH]PleasntTap121½ Rallied 5
11Jan92- 8SA fst 7f :221 :441 1:082 1:211 4↑ San Carlos H-G2 1 6 711 710 69 66¼ Delhoussaye E B 119 b *1.90 91-11 AnswerDo1201½Individualist115hdMedPln1162½ Broke slowly 7
30Nov91- 8Hol fm 1⅛Ⓣ :472 1:111 1:342 1:454 3↑ Citation H (Div 2)-G2 3 6 76½ 73½ 74¼ 85¾ Flores DR 116 b 20.40 95-07 Fly Till Dawn1191¾Best Pal119nkWolf1191 No mishap 8
Run in divisions

2Nov91- 2CD fst 6f :21 :442 1:091 3↑ BC Sprint-G1 7 8 1113 1110 63¼ 23 Delhoussaye E B 126 b 8.80 98-02 Sheikh Albadou1243Pleasant Tap126½Robyn Dancer126nk 11
8-wide stretch,lugged in
12Oct91- 8SA fst 1⅛ :47 1:103 1:343 1:474 3↑ Goodwood H-G2 2 5 53 43½ 45 34½ Pincay L Jr B 117 b 3.70 86-15 The Prime Minister115noMarquetry1194½Pleasant Tap1173½ 6
5-wide stretch
7Sep91- 3Dmr fst 6½f :224 :452 1:10 1:161 3↑ Alw 50000 5 3 41¾ 42 21½ 11¾ Solis A B 121 b 2.80 87-15 PleasntTap1211¾[D]MediaPlan1171½AsktheMn115nk Wide trip 5
30Mar91- 8SA fst 1⅛ :461 1:10 1:342 1:47 4↑ San Bernardino H-G2 9 8 75¼ 62¾ 54½ 34 Solis A B 116 b 5.80 91-07 Anshan115noLouis Cyphre1124Pleasant Tap116no Wide trip 9
9Mar91- 5SA fst 1¼ :46 1:101 1:344 2:001 4↑ S Anita H-G1 6 9 98½ 43 23½ 33½ Solis A B 115 b 36.20 89-10 Farma Way1202¾Festin115¾Pleasant Tap1155½ 4-wide ⅞ 10
10Feb91- 8SA fst 1¼ :461 1:102 1:344 2:004 C H Strub-G1 1 7 77 77¾ 67¾ 56¼ Delhoussaye E B 116 b 5.30 84-10 DefnsvPly122hdMyBoyAdm1171¼InExcss1214½ Ducked in early 7
19Jan91- 8SA fst 1⅛ :462 1:101 1:341 1:463 San Fernando-G2 7 9 88 83¾ 67 510 Solis A B 120 b 3.10 87-09 In Excess1264Warcraft1202¾Go and Go1231¼ Wide trip 9
26Dec90- 8SA fst 7f :22 :441 1:083 1:213 Malibu-G2 7 9 1012 99¼ 54½ 11¼ Solis A B 117 b 3.70 95-10 PleasntTap1171¼Bedevld1201½DutothKng1171¼ Broke slowly 10
1Dec90- 8Hol fst 1⅛ :464 1:103 1:351 1:472 3↑ Native Diver H-G3 3 6 66½ 55½ 32½ 2no Solis A B 115 b 6.30 97-09 Warcraft117noPleasntTap115nkGoandGo1151¼ Bumped start 7
27Oct90- 8Bel gd 1½Ⓣ :494 1:153 2:041 2:293 3↑ BC Turf-G1 1 5 74½ 96½ 911 815¾ Bailey JD 121 b 10.40 66-15 IntheWings126½WithApprovl1261½ElSnor1262½ Saved ground 11
4Oct90- 8Bel fst 1¹⁄₁₆ :232 :462 1:104 1:421 3↑ Alw 50000 8 4 31½ 1½ 11½ 13¼ Cordero A Jr 113 b 2.60 91-18 PleasantTap1133¼OutofPlace1122IndianToss1154 Drew clear 8
21Sep90- 9Med fst 1⅛ :462 1:093 1:343 1:471 Pegasus H-G1 6 2 21½ 32½ 64½ 710½ Desormeaux KJ 115 b 7.70 88-01 SilverEnding1192MusicProspectr116½RunwyStrm1131½ Tired 12
5May90- 8CD gd 1¼ :46 1:11 1:373 2:02 Ky Derby-G1 9 12 1113 44 36 39½ Desormeaux KJ 126 b 40.70 91-00 Unbridled1263½SummerSquall1266PlesntTp1263 In close st. 15
24Apr90- 8Kee fst 1¹⁄₁₆ :231 :464 1:111 1:432 Lexington-G2 9 7 63 51¼ 31½ 22 Desormeaux KJ 115 b 11.40 87-11 Home at Last1182Pleasant Tap1155Thirty Slews1162½ 9
Lacked room ⁵⁄₁₆ pole
18Mar90- 8SA fst 1¹⁄₁₆ :224 :463 1:11 1:42 San Felipe H-G2 11 10 96¼ 107¼ 99¼ 614¾ Delahoussaye E 119 b *2.70 78-16 RealCash1135½Warcrft117¾MuscProspctr1173 Never menaced 12
4Feb90- 9SA gd 1 :223 :463 1:113 1:38 Alw 37000 4 8 43 33 3½ 11¼ Delahoussaye E 118 b *1.00 77-18 PleasantTap1181¼T.V.Rebel118¾VideoRanger116no Driving 10
25Nov89- 8Hol fm 1Ⓣ :232 :473 1:112 1:353 Hoist the Flag-G2 10 6 2½ 2hd 1hd 2no Delahoussaye E 118 b 4.50 86-13 Single Dawn114noPleasant Tap1182¾Doyouseewhatisee121nk 12
Rough start
4Nov89- 8GP fst 1¹⁄₁₆ :232 :464 1:111 1:433 BC Juvenile-G1 1 12 1211 127¼ 88¼ 66½ Delahoussaye E 122 11.30 86-01 Rhythm1222Grand Canyon1221¾Slavic1221 Without speed 12
4Oct89- 8SA fst 7f :221 :444 1:10 1:222 Sunny Slope 80k 6 6 711 710 31 1¾ Delahoussaye E 116 12.40 88-15 PleasntTp116¾GrandCanyon1154Doyouseewhats1196 Driving 7
9Sep89- 6Dmr fst 6f :22 :452 :572 1:091 Md Sp Wt 9 6 65½ 63¼ 44 34¼ Baze RA 117 19.70 88-11 GrandCanyn1172½JetWest1171¾PleasntTp1174 Troubled trip 9
19Aug89- 4Dmr fst 6f :221 :451 :571 1:093 Md Sp Wt 2 7 715 715 714 69¾ Delahoussaye E 117 22.00 80-14 Social Jokes117½Profit Key1173Silver Ending117no Outrun 7

Possibly Perfect

b. f. 1990, by Northern Baby (Northern Dancer)–Avasand, by Avatar **Lifetime record: 18 11 2 4 $1,377,273**

Own.– Blue Vista Inc
Br.– Mr & Mrs Robert Witt (Ky)
Tr.– Robert Frankel

26Aug95- 6AP fm 1³⁄₁₆Ⓣ :484 1:13 1:372 1:544 3↑ ⒻBeverly D-G1 7 3 2½ 2½ 11 1¾ Nakatani CS 123 *.70 96-06 Possibly Perfect123¾Alice Springs123noAlpride123hd 7
Rated early,driving
5Aug95- 8Dmr fm 1⅛Ⓣ :491 1:132 1:373 1:494 3↑ ⒻRamona H-G1 6 2 31 21 21 11¼ Nakatani CS B 123 *1.20 87-12 Possibly Perfect1231¼Morgana115hdYearly Tour116hd 7
In tight leaving first turn,gamely
2Jly95- 9Hol fm 1⅛Ⓣ :471 1:101 1:342 1:463 3↑ ⒻBeverly Hills H-G1 5 4 32½ 42½ 2½ 21¾ Desrmeaux KJ B 124 *.70 90-10 Alpride1151¾PossblyPrfct1241Wndst1196½ 4 wide into lane 6
4Jun95- 9Hol fm 1⅛Ⓣ :472 1:112 1:344 1:464 3↑ ⒻGamely H-G1 5 1 11½ 11 12 11¾ Desrmeaux KJ B 123 *.50 91-12 PossiblyPrfct1231¾LadyAffirmed1141Don'tReadMyLips1151¾ 6
Ridden out
14May95- 9Hol fm 1¹⁄₁₆Ⓣ :234 :473 1:103 1:401 3↑ ⒻWilshire H-G2 5 1 1hd 2hd 1hd 11¾ Desrmeaux KJ B 121 *.50 95-09 PossiblyPrfect1211¾Morgana116½AubIndnn1193½ Ridden out 5
2Apr95- 7SA fm 1Ⓣ :232 :481 1:12 1:36 4↑ ⒻAlw 60000 3 2 31 2hd 13 1½ Nakatani CS B 114 *.90 86-19 PossiblyPrfct114½FantasticKim1171¾Wnd115½ Hand ridden 7
10Apr94- 8SA fm 1¼Ⓣ :472 1:114 1:36 2:002 4↑ ⒻS Barbara H-G1 5 2 21½ 1½ 11½ 1½ Desrmeaux KJ B 121 *.70 85-15 Possibly Perfect121½Pracer1152¾Waitryst114½ Gamely 5
19Mar94- 8SA yl 1⅛Ⓣ :501 1:142 1:382 1:51 4↑ ⒻSanta Ana H-G1 7 1 11½ 11 11 11¾ Desrmeaux KJ B 119 2.30 64-36 Psbly Prfct1191¾Hero's Lve1201½[D]Waitryst115hd Held game 7
27Feb94- 8SA fm 1Ⓣ :231 :47 1:102 1:344 4↑ ⒻBuena Vista H-G3 3 3 21 3½ 3½ 42 Desrmeaux KJ B 120 *1.30 89-11 LadyBlessington119noSkimbl1181½Hro'sLov121½ Outfinished 9
Awarded third purse money
14Nov93- 8SA fm 1¼Ⓣ :50 1:144 1:382 2:024 3↑ ⒻYellow Ribbon Inv'l-G1 11 1 11 1hd 11 11¼ Nakatani CS B 118 16.60 73-27 PossiblyPerfct1181¼Trbulton118hdMtuschk122no Well rated 13
30Oct93- 8Kee yl 1⅛Ⓣ :484 1:134 1:403 1:533 ⒻQueen Elizabeth C-G1 5 3 21 41¾ 2hd 32½ Day P 121 2.40 66-31 Tribulation1212MmSnds121½PsblyPrfct1213 Weakened late 9
2Oct93- 11LaD fm 1¹⁄₁₆Ⓣ :231 :484 1:14 1:444 ⒻDe Bartolo H 100k 4 6 64½ 52¼ 1hd 13½ Desormeaux KJ 119 *.70 83-10 Possibly Perfect1193½Lady Tasso116½She's a Little Shy114½ 11
Lost footing,ridden out
22Aug93- 8Dmr fm 1⅛Ⓣ :472 1:114 1:362 1:481 ⒻDel Mar Oaks-G2 2 1 1½ 1½ 1½ 21 Desrmeaux KJ B 120 7.20 94-09 Hllywd Wildct1201PsblyPrfct1201¾MiamiSands120nk Sharp 10
25Jly93- 8Hol fm 1¹⁄₁₆Ⓣ :232 :461 1:103 1:413 Alw 39000 1 2 25 22 11 11¼ Desrmeaux KJ B 117 2.30 88-11 Possibly Perfect1171¼Capel1172Minjinsky1172¾ 7
Drifted in ⅛,ridden out
23Jun93- 5Hol fm 1⅛Ⓣ :471 1:111 1:354 1:483 3↑ ⒻMd Sp Wt 1 3 31 1hd 12½ 13½ Desrmeaux KJ B 116 3.40 81-11 Possibly Perfect1163½Starlet Minister115noIndio Rose1151¼ 10
Previously trained by Antonio Spanu
8Oct92♦ Evry(Fr) sf *1ⓉLH 1:454 ⒻPrix de Saint-Eutrope Alw33300 51½ Asmussen CB 128 9.00 Hawk Beauty128hdNakama124¾Kiruna128½ 12
Led for 7 furlongs,met challenge gamely,faded near line
21Sep92♦ Maisns-Lfftte(Fr)sf *1ⓉRH 1:423 ⒻPrix Sauge Pourpree Alw33100 31¼ Jarnet T 128 11.00 Dancienne128½Mariemma128¾Possibly Perfect1281½ 13
Close up in 4th,bid for lead 1½f out,no late foot
3Jly92♦ Maisns-Lfftte(Fr)sf *6fⓉStr 1:13 ⒻPrix de la Marne Mdn (FT)32900 32¼ Asmussen CB 128 23.00 Myza1281½Quelle Affaire128¾Possibly Perfect128½ 11
Raced in 7th,4th on rail 1f out,no further response

Prairie Bayou

ch. g. 1990, by Little Missouri (Cox's Ridge)–Whiffling, by Wavering Monarch **Lifetime record: 12 7 3 0 $1,450,621**

Own.– Loblolly Stable
Br.– Loblolly Stable (Ky)
Tr.– Thomas Bohannan

5Jun93- 9Bel gd 1½ :484 1:132 2:024 2:294 Belmont-G1 5 11 - - - - Smith ME 126 *2.70 - - ColonialAffair1262¼KissinKris126¾WildGal1262 Broke down 13
15May93- 10Pim fst 1³⁄₁₆ :464 1:111 1:37 1:563 Preakness-G1 3 10 97¼ 85½ 2hd 1½ Smith ME 126 *2.20 79-18 Prairie Bayou126½Cherokee Run1267El Bakan126nk 12
Steadied backstretch
1May93- 8CD fst 1¼ :463 1:111 1:364 2:022 Ky Derby-G1 5 16 1613 94¾ 63½ 22½ Smith ME 126 *4.40 97-07 SeaHero1262½PrairieByou126hdWildGal126nk 6-wide,gamely 19
10Apr93- 8Kee fst 1⅛ :481 1:121 1:37 1:493 Blue Grass-G2 8 8 87½ 83¼ 1hd 12 Smith ME 121 3.70 87-16 Prairie Bayou1212Wallenda121noDixieland Heat121¾ 9
5-wide,ridden out
27Mar93- 11TP fst 1⅛ :472 1:113 1:372 1:504 Jim Beam-G2 1 8 87¾ 74¾ 11½ 1¾ McCarron CJ 121 *1.20 79-18 Prairie Bayou121¾Proudest Romeo1212Miner's Mark1215 9
5-wide,driving
20Feb93- 8Aqu fst 1¹⁄₁₆[•] :24 :483 1:131 1:451 Whirlaway B C 110k 4 5 2½ 2½ 1hd 13 Smith ME 117 *.40 79-24 Prairie Bayou1173Rohwer1143Slews Gold1147 Driving 5
24Jan93- 8Aqu fst 1 70[•] :243 :48 1:122 1:424 Count Fleet 68k 1 5 45½ 31½ 1½ 13 Smith ME 117 *.90 88-24 Prairie Bayou1173Slews Gold1175½Rohwer1175 Driving 6
13Jan93- 8Aqu sly 1 70[•] :24 :493 1:142 1:433 Pappa Riccio 52k 2 4 45 44 21½ 21¼ Smith ME 117 *1.30 83-20 Bert's Bubbleator1171¼Prairie Bayou1171Classi Envoy11716 4
Mild rally
20Dec92- 10Lrl my 1⅛ :484 1:134 1:393 1:524 Inner Harbor 50k 6 8 89¾ 65½ 2hd 2no Velazquez JR 122 *1.50e 76-32 Jorge of Mexico113noPrarie Bayou1223½Ozan113¾ 9
Wide,bumped,hung;Previously trained by Anthony Reinstedler
18Nov92- 7CD fst 1¹⁄₁₆ :24 :474 1:132 1:45 Alw 28700 9 9 1010 96¾ 1½ 13 Bartram BE B 121 *2.40 89-15 Prairie Bayou1213Enchanting Future1184Colonial Miner1234 11
Ridden out
10Nov92- 4CD fst 1¹⁄₁₆ :241 :482 1:143 1:461 Md Sp Wt 6 11 911 63½ 11½ 11½ Bartram BE B 119 6.60 83-22 PrairieBayou1191½UnionCity1193Waxahach1197 Wide,driving 11
14Oct92- 5Kee fst 7f :222 :46 1:112 1:234 Md Sp Wt 9 11 64¼ 85 89¾ 710 Miller DA Jr B 119 8.10 80-14 TurnofftheLits1194CountryEldr119¾ChrmdHlo119no No rally 12

Queena

b. f. 1986, by Mr. Prospector (Raise a Native)–Too Chic, by Blushing Groom — **Lifetime record: 17 10 2 1 $565,024**

Own.– Emory A. Hamiton
Br.– Emory Alexander (Ky)
Tr.– Claude McGaughey III

2Nov91- 4CD fst 1⅛ :471 1:114 1:374 1:504 3↑ ⒻBC Distaff-G1 13 11 1214 118¼ 85¾ 55 Smith ME 123 5.70 89-09 DanceSmrtly1201½VersaillesTreaty1202¾Brought toMind123½ 13
Broke slowly,7-wide into stretch
21Sep91- 8Bel fst 1 1/16 :233 :462 1:103 1:413 3↑ ⒻRuffian H-G1 6 5 53½ 31 2½ 1½ Cordero A Jr 120 2.10 94-14 Qna120½SharpDance1141¼LadyD'Accord113nk Wide,driving 7
1Sep91- 8Bel fst 1 :232 :462 1:101 1:344 3↑ ⒻMaskette-G1 6 3 31½ 31½ 21 1hd Cordero A Jr 123 3.70 96-07 Queena123hdFittoScout123nkScreenProspect1167½ Wide drv 6
4Aug91- 8Sar fst 7f :214 :441 1:084 1:22 3↑ ⒻBallerina-G1 3 6 53 43½ 42½ 1hd Smith ME 119 3.00 95-08 Queena119hdMssy'sMrge1112DremTouch1103½ Blocked turn 9
23Jun91- 8Bel fst 7f :221 :45 1:091 1:22 3↑ ⒻVagrancy H-G3 7 3 41 2½ 1½ 1no Smith ME 115 *.90 94-07 Queena115noMissy'sMirage1091½Gottagetitdone1112 Driving 10
20May91- 8Bel fst 7f :224 :46 1:11 1:241 3↑ ⒻAlw 41000 2 3 1½ 22 1hd 13 Smith ME 119 1.80 83-16 Queena1193Dreamy Mimi1192Token Dance119nk Going away 5
12Feb91- 9GP fst 6f :221 :453 1:101 4↑ ⒻAlw 21000 9 4 37 42½ 32½ 32¼ Bailey JD 120 1.90 92-12 Avie Jane1152Ivory Princess115nkQueena1203½ Hung 9
Previously raced under name of Emory Alexander
17Jan91- 9GP gd 6f :22 :454 1:113 3↑ ⒻFirst Lady H 50k 8 2 53½ 54 54½ 52½ Bailey JD 115 3.70 84-22 Spirit of Fighter1182Mistaurian115hdLove's Exchange128hd 9
Bumped,gaining
22Nov90- 9Lrl fst 7f :232 :463 1:104 1:231 3↑ ⒻStraight Deal H 100k 4 10 21½ 21½ 21½ 2½ Smith ME 116 *.90 90-14 Iceycindy113½Queena1163½Thirty Eight Go Go114hd Hung 10
21Oct90- 9Bel fst 7f :222 :444 1:091 1:222 3↑ ⒻFirst Flight H-G2 1 5 3½ 42¾ 3½ 12½ Bailey JD 113 5.90 92-18 Queena1132½QuckMischief115¾APennyIsaPnny1222½ Driving 5
22Sep90- 9Med sly 6f :213 :442 1:091 3↑ ⒻBud BC-G3 4 6 57¼ 44½ 54¼ 54½ Smith ME 113 9.10 91-12 SafelyKpt127nkSxySlw1151¾Dv'sDbut1202½ Lacked response 7
23Aug90- 7Sar fst 7f :231 :463 1:102 1:224 3↑ ⒻAlw 30000 3 4 1hd 1½ 1½ 1nk Smith ME 119 2.30 91-16 Queena119nkAishah1142¾Moon Drone1124 Long drive 6
4Aug90- 6Sar fst 6f :223 :46 1:101 3↑ ⒻAlw 28000 6 2 32 3½ 2hd 1½ Smith ME 114 *1.20 93-04 Queena114½Rumgumption1124LovlyHrss114¾ Strong handling 10
9Jly90- 1Bel fst 7f :23 :47 1:114 1:244 3↑ ⒻAlw 27000 1 3 1½ 11 11½ 12 Smith ME 122 2.60 80-20 Queena1222Mime113½Unite and Conquer1176 Hand ride 6
21Jun90- 7Bel fst 6f :224 :464 1:121 3↑ ⒻMd Sp Wt 5 3 2hd 1½ 13 16 Smith ME 122 *.90e 78-22 Queena1226Timetocheckin1144By Descent1141¼ Brisk urging 9
30Apr90- 4Aqu my 7f :23 :471 1:13 1:263 3↑ ⒻMd Sp Wt 2 6 53½ 42½ 44½ 43½ Smith ME 124 *.90 65-26 DancinBaba115noIncaLegacy1151½GabrlP.1152 Lacked rally 7
31Mar90- 1Aqu sly 6f :214 :452 1:112 4↑ ⒻMd Sp Wt 1 6 45 45½ 33 22¼ Smith ME 122 4.00 81-18 JustBeLucky1222¼Queena1222FullTill1153 Steadied,green 8

Real Quiet

b. c. 1995, by Quiet American (Fappiano)–Really Blue, by Believe It — **Lifetime record: 20 6 5 6 $3,271,803**

Own.– Michael E. Pegram
Br.– Little Hill Farm (Ky)
Tr.– Bob Baffert

27Jun99- 5Hol fst 1¼ :47 1:102 1:342 1:593 3↑ Hol Gold Cup-G1 2 3 42 41½ 31½ 1½ Bailey JD **LB** 124 b *.90 97-03 RealQuiet124½Budroyal124nkMlk1247 Trapped rail 2nd turn 4
29May99-13Suf fst 1⅛ :472 1:11 1:36 1:49 3↑ Mass H-G2 2 2 21 3½ 32 33¼ Stevens GL **LB** 121 b *.80 88-16 Behrns118½RunnngStg1132¾RlQut1214½ 3p,bid 2nd,weakened 6
8May99- 6Pim fst 1 3/16 :47 1:111 1:36 1:541 3↑ Pim Special H-G1 5 3 32½ 33 2hd 1nk Stevens GL **L** 120 b 1.90 94-19 Real Quiet120nkFree House1245Fred Bear Claw1132 5
Aim 3w,dueled,long drive
18Apr99- 7LS fst 1 :24 :471 1:111 1:353 3↑ Texas Mile-G3 5 4 34½ 1½ 2½ 2nk Stevens GL **L** 116 b *.50 94-15 Littlebitlivly116nkRlQut1161¾Alln'sOop1134¾ Outfinished 8
7Mar99- 8FG fst 1⅛ :483 1:124 1:364 1:49 4↑ New Orleans H-G3 6 3 21½ 21 2½ 2½ Desormeaux KJ **L** 122 b *.50 94-13 Precocity118½RlQut122nkAlln'sOop108¾ 3w,4w,bid,no match 6
6Jun98- 9Bel fst 1½ :483 1:132 2:024 2:29 Belmont-G1 7 6 31 1½ 14 2no Desormeaux KJ **L** 126 b *.80 99-09 Victory Gallop126noReal Quiet1266Thomas Jo1261¼ 11
Wide move turn,drifted out,bumped rival late,gamely
16May98-10Pim fst 1 3/16 :462 1:11 1:354 1:543 Preakness-G1 10 8 69 51¾ 1½ 12¼ Desormeaux KJ **L** 126 b 2.50 92-13 Real Quiet1262¼Victory Gallop126¾Classic Cat1263¾ 10
Very wide entering stretch,lugged in 1/16,driving
2May98- 8CD fst 1¼ :453 1:103 1:353 2:021 Ky Derby-G1 3 8 68 11 11½ 1½ Desormeaux KJ **L** 126 b 8.40 94-02 Real Quiet126½Victory Gallop1262¼Indian Charlie126hd 15
Broke to inside,bid far turn,clear,lasted
4Apr98- 5SA fst 1⅛ :46 1:094 1:342 1:47 S Anita Derby-G1 7 6 56½ 54½ 22½ 22¼ Dsrmeaux KJ **LB** 120 b 3.00 99-03 Indian Charlie1202¼Real Quiet1207Artax1206 7
Lost rein briefly 2nd turn,split foes ⅛,2nd best
14Mar98- 8SA fst 1 1/16 :224 :464 1:104 1:413 San Felipe-G2 5 3 32½ 3½ 21½ 2hd Dsrmeaux KJ **LB** 119 b 4.10 95-10 Artax122hdReal Quiet1197Prosperous Bid1166 Came back on 5
18Jan98- 7GG sly 1 1/16 :222 :461 1:104 1:431 Golden Gate Derby 200k 7 7 66¼ 66½ 814 822½ Dsrmeaux KJ **LB** 120 b *1.10 63-19 Clover Hunter1206½Mantles Star1201½Allen's Oop1204 8
Wide,dull effort
14Dec97- 7Hol fst 1 1/16 :223 :454 1:101 1:411 Hol Futurity-G1 2 4 41½ 21 1hd 11 Dsrmeaux KJ **LB** 121 b *1.50e 95-11 Real Quiet1211Artax1211¾Nationalore1211 Gamely 11
29Nov97-11CD fst 1 1/16 :232 :47 1:12 1:434 Ky Jockey Club-G3 6 10 75½ 42½ 53½ 31¾ Flores DR **L** 116 b 12.40 90-09 Cape Town113½Time Limit1191¼Real Quiet1161½ 11
Bumped from both sides start,bobbled,up rail,good try
18Oct97- 3SA fst 1 1/16 :232 :472 1:122 1:441 Md Sp Wt 7 6 52 42 2hd 13 Dsrmeaux KJ **LB** 120 b 1.60 82-19 RealQuiet1203Opine1207SydnyHrbor1205 4w,clearly best 7
5Sep97- 6Dmr fst 1 :221 :454 1:104 1:363 Md Sp Wt 7 6 78 54½ 34½ 48 Stevens SA **LB** 118 f 2.20e 79-13 OldTrst1182½Johnbll1185½JustRulr118no Just missed third 9
24Aug97- 8SFe fst 7f :221 :444 1:10 1:234 Indian Nations Fut 571k 2 8 95½ 66½ 56½ 32¾ Stevens SA **L** 120 f 4.60 86-12 Grady120nkGeneralGem1202½RealQuit1202½ 4 wide,willingly 12
8Aug97- 8SFe fst 7f :22 :442 1:10 1:234 Fut Trial 10k 1 7 2hd 2hd 25 37½ Stevens SA **L** 120 f 2.10 81-15 GeneralGem1207Thtsknf120½RlQut1205 Dueled rail,weakened 10
19Jly97- 7Hol fst 5½f :221 :443 :562 1:023 Md Sp Wt 4 2 41¼ 32½ 33½ 36½ Flores DR **LB** 118 2.30 93-08 MeadowPrayer1184½KonaWind1132RelQt11813 Best of others 6
29Jun97- 1CD gd 6f :212 :451 :572 1:10 Md Sp Wt 1 5 34 44½ 36 38½ Steiner JJ **L** 118 f 10.70 84-07 Polished Brass1181½Tropic Lightning1187Real Quiet1185 10
Held position
15Jun97- 1CD fst 5f :22 :451 :574 Md Sp Wt 1 2 46 45½ 58½ 710 Steiner JJ **L** 119 f 5.00 89-12 DiceDancer1191PolishedBrass1195DaDevl1192½ Inside,tired 11

Reraise

b. g. 1995, by Danzatore (Northern Dancer)–Get Us to Paris, by Policeman — **Lifetime record: 8 7 1 0 $891,630**

Own.– Class Racing Stable & Fey & Opas & Sinatra
Br.– Willard Sergent (Ky)
Tr.– Craig Dollase

2May99- 3GG gd 6f :222 :444 :562 1:083 3↑ Oakland H 98k 1 3 11 12½ 12½ 12½ Nakatani CS **LB** 125 *.10 97-12 Reraise1252½Early Pioneer113hdSaylo115½ Won as pleased 4
8Apr99- 9OP fst 6f :21 :434 :554 1:082 4↑ Count Fleet Sprint H-G3 1 4 1hd 1hd 13½ 12¾ Nakatani CS **L** 122 *.30 102-12 Rrs1222¾RunJohnny1141¾EJHrly1151¼ Quick pace,ridden out 6
Previously owned by Fey & Dollase & Han & Sinatra
7Nov98- 6CD fst 6f :21 :441 :561 1:09 3↑ BC Sprint-G1 3 3 1½ 11 12½ 12 Nakatani CS **L** 124 3.80 98-03 Reraise1242GrandSlam124hdKonGold1261 Drew clear,driving 14
Previously owned by Fey & Han & Sinatra
26Sep98- 8TP fst 6f :212 :441 :561 1:082 Ky Cup Sprint-G2 1 7 1½ 11½ 18 112 Nakatani CS **L** 116 *.70 99-13 Rerais11612CoplnToo114nkMrBrt1144 Off inside,ridden out 7
20Aug98- 6Dmr fst 7f :22 :441 1:092 1:221 3↑ OClm 80000 4 4 11½ 11½ 11 24½ Delhoussye E **LB** 116 b *.70 84-14 YoungatHeart1174½Reraise1162Zede117½ Speed,outfinished 5
4Jly98- 3Hol fst 6f :22 :441 :56 1:082 Playa del Rey 68k 6 1 1½ 1hd 1½ 16 Delhoussye E **LB** 116 b *1.00 95-14 Reraise1166Souvenir Copy122½Full Moon Madness1173½ 6
Kicked clear,driving
27May98- 7Hol fst 6f :221 :45 :571 1:092 3↑ Alw 42000 2 4 11 1hd 1hd 13 Delhoussye E **LB** 116 b *1.30 90-18 Reraise1163ShotMd1145Wyn'sChoc1163½ Inside,kicked clear 5
Previously owned by Matlow & Opas & Sinatra;previously trained by Richard P. Matlow
29Oct97- 2SA fst 6f :214 :45 :573 1:10 Md 62500 6 8 64¾ 64¼ 41¾ 12 Delhoussye E **LB** 120 6.20 88-16 Reraise1202LuckySandman1203TruelyYours1206 Wide to lane 9

Rubiano

ro. c. 1987, by Fappiano (Mr. Prospector)–Ruby Slippers, by Nijinsky II

Own.– Centennial Farm
Br.– Third Kirsmith Racing Associates (Va)
Tr.– Flint S. Schulhofer

Lifetime record: 28 13 6 1 $1,273,457

Date	Track	Cond	Dist	Fractions	Final	Race	Pos	Calls	Jockey	Wt	Odds	Speed	Finish	Comment	Field
31Oct92- 4GP	fst 6f	:21³:43³ :55³	1:08¹	3↑ BC Sprint-G1	10 1	11⁶½ 8⁵¾ 56	33¾	Krone JA	126	*2.10	99-00	Thirty Slews126ⁿᵏMeafara120³Rubiano126ⁿᵒ	Fin. well 14
3Oct92- 6Bel	fst 7f	:22³:45²	1:10 1:22⁴	3↑ Vosburgh-G1	4 4	71¾ 31½ 31½	1³	Krone JA	126	*1.60e	90-17	Rubiano126¾Sheikh Albadou126¹¼Salt Lake1234½	8
		Blocked,altered course											
16Aug92- 8Sar	my 7f	:22¹:45¹	1:10 1:22²	3↑ Forego H-G2	6 1	74½ 52½ 2hd	13¼	Krone JA	124	*1.00	93-14	Rubiano124³½Drummond Lane115¹½Diablo114⁴	Wide,driving 8
18Jly92- 7Bel	fst 7f	:22⁴:45³	1:09² 1:21³	3↑ Tom Fool-G2	2 2	54 43 1½	11	Krone JA	126	*1.70	96-12	Rubiano126¹Take Me Out119¹½Arrowtown119¹	Driving 8
25May92- 8Bel	fst 1	:22²:44⁴	1:08² 1:33³	3↑ Metropolitan H-G1	7 8	107 107¼78	81¹⅓	Santos JA	120	4.10	91-05	Dixie Brass107²¼Pleasant Tap119¹³In Excess121ⁿᵏ	Tired 11
2May92- 8Aqu	fst 7f	:22 :44¹	1:08¹ 1:21²	3↑ Carter H-G1	7 3	76 74½ 42½	1hd	Santos JA	118	2.90	98-07	Rubiano118ʰᵈKid Russell112¹½In Excess122¹¾	Wide driving 9
22Mar92- 8Aqu	fst 1	:24 :47	1:10³ 1:34⁴	3↑ Westchester H-G3	4 2	2½ 2½ 11	1ⁿᵒ	Santos JA	117	*1.20	88-25	Rubiano117ⁿᵒOut of Place115²Wild Away111²	All out 6
26Oct91- 8Aqu	fst 1	:22³:44⁴	1:08³ 1:33³	3↑ NYRA Mile H-G1	9 9	104½104 83½	1hd	Santos JA	116	5.00	94-08	Rubiano116ʰᵈSultry Song111¹Diablo112ⁿᵏ	Driving 15
20Oct91- 8Bel	fst 1	:24 :47²	1:11 1:35²³	3↑ Handicap 47000	2 4	31 1hd 11½	1ⁿᵒ	Santos JA	121	1.80	93-07	Rubiano121ⁿᵒCrackedbell118⁵Shots Are Ringing108¼	5
		Saved ground,driving											
19Sep91- 8Bel	fst 1	:23³:46²	1:10¹ 1:34⁴	3↑ Alw 47000	2 4	52½ 2½ 11	1hd	Santos JA	115	*.90	96-07	Rubino115ʰᵈCrckdbll122ⁿᵏFftysvnvtt115¹½	Lugged in drive 6
25Aug91- 8Sar	fst 7f	:21⁴:43⁴	1:08 1:21	3↑ Forego H-G2	5 2	55 64 53½	43½	Smith ME	116	6.60	96-12	Housebustr126ⁿᵒSenorSpeedy112¹ClvrTrvor120²½	Four wide 6
13Jly91- 8Bel	sly 7f	:22¹:44²	1:08³ 1:21⁴	3↑ Metropolitan H-G1	2 4	43½ 44 23	22½	Bailey JD	121	*.80	93-08	Mr. Nasty119²½Rubiano121½Senor Speedy119¹⁴	2nd best 4
27May91- 8Bel	fst 1	:22 :44¹	1:09¹ 1:35²	3↑ Metropolitan H-G1	13 9	64½ 3½ 21½	22½	Bailey JD	111	24.30	91-16	In Excess117²¼Rubiano111¹¾Gervazy114¹½	Rallied wide 14
4May91- 8Aqu	fst 7f	:22⁴:45²	1:08⁴ 1:21¹	3↑ Carter H-G1	4 5	53 42½ 46	44¾	Smith ME	113	12.50	91-17	Housebuster122²¼BlackTiAffr123²¼Grvzy116ⁿᵒ	Saved ground 8
29Mar91- 8Aqu	gd 1	:23¹:46	1:09³ 1:34⁴	3↑ Westchester H-G3	2 3	22½ 32 21	11¾	Bailey JD	111	7.50	88-17	Rubiano111¹¾Senor Speedy113³Killer Diller115⁸½	Driving 9
2Mar91-10GP	fst 1⅛	:48 1:11² 1:35⁴	1:48	3↑ Broward H 75k	5 7	72¾ 54 69	61²⅜	Castillo H Jr	110	10.90	84-17	ChiefHoncho116¼½NoMarkr112¹½Barkada114²	Bid,stopped 7
9Feb91- 9GP	fst 1⅛	:45⁴1:10²1:35	1:47²³	3↑ Donn H-G1	12 9	98¾ 85¼ 811	611¼	Santos JA	113	29.50	89-06	Jolie'sHalo114⁸SportsView116ⁿᵏSecretHllo116ʰᵈ	No threat 12
14Jan91- 9GP	fst 1¹⁄₁₆	:24 :48¹	1:12 1:43²⁴	4↑ Alw 25000	6 4	44 41 11	11	Bailey JD	112	2.00	96-05	Rubiano112¹Allied Flag114¹⁰Out of Place114ⁿᵏ	Stiff drive 7
3Nov90- 8Aqu	fst 1	:22³:45³	1:08³ 1:32⁴	3↑ NYRA Mile-G1	8 7	62½ 12¹⁶12¹⁵	12¹⁹¼	Santos JA	111	2.70e	79-14	QuietAmricn116⁴¾DancingSpre119ⁿᵒSwckly124²	Done early 12
20Oct90- 8Bel	fst 1	:22⁴:45	1:09² 1:35³	3↑ Jamaica H-G2	4 3	31½ 11 11½	2ⁿᵏ	Cordero A Jr	114	4.10	91-17	ConfidntialTalk111ⁿᵏRbiano112½SunshinJimmy114²½	Gamely 7
26Sep90- 8Bel	fst 7f	:23 :45⁴	1:09² 1:21⁴	3↑ Alw 41000	2 6	42 41½ 41	2ⁿᵏ	Santos JA	113	*1.90	95-12	Six Speed113ⁿᵏRubiano113¾Two Eagles115¹¾	Rallied 8
29Aug90- 6Bel	fst 6½f	:22²:45²	1:10¹ 1:16³	3↑ Alw 28000	6 1	56 44¼ 1½	13	Santos JA	113	*2.10	94-14	Rubiano113³Senor Speedy113ʰᵈDancinwiththedevil112²¼	8
		Saved ground,clear; previously trained by H. Allen Jerkens											
30Jly90- 6Bel	fm 1 ⊤	:23 :45⁴	1:10¹ 1:34¹	3↑ Alw 31000	6 6	66½ 63½ 811	71³¼	Bailey JD	111 b	*1.90	81-06	GoDtch112³CommissionBrt111½DfnsPolcy117¾	Nothing left 9
20Jly90- 6Bel	fst 1	:22¹:45	1:10² 1:23	3↑ Alw 28000	3 4	32 23 27	25	Bailey JD	111 b	2.70	84-19	Carson City112⁵Rubiano111⁸½Any Minute Man117½	2nd best 6
3Apr90- 3GP	fst 7f	:22¹:45³	1:11²1:25	Alw 19000	2 5	2hd 2½ 11½	14	Vasquez J	122 b	*.60	81-26	Rubiano122⁴Joe's Lad117ⁿᵏBudd Believes110²½	Drew clear 7
25Mar90- 3GP	fst 6f	:21³:44⁴	1:11²	Alw 23000	1 6	2¹ 22 22½	2½	Smith A Jr	122 b	3.60	87-17	Dr. Jimmy122¹Rubiano122¾Joe's Lad117⁹¼	Rallied 6
2Mar90- 8GP	fst 7f	:22¹:45	1:10³ 1:24	Alw 19000	8 2	3ⁿᵏ 52½ 811	81²¼	Migliore R	122	1.90	73-17	Gervazy122½HomeatLast122ʰᵈThirtySixRed122²¾	Gave way 10
30Jan90- 7GP	fst 6f	:22¹:46¹	1:12	Md Sp Wt	2 11	21½ 2½ 14	14	Migliore R	122	*1.70	85-19	Rubiano122⁴FallingSky122⁵Thewhlsofjustc122ⁿᵏ	Drew clear 12

Ryafan

b. f. 1994, by Lear Fan (Roberto)–Carya, by Northern Dancer

Own.– Juddmonte Farms
Br.– Juddmonte Farms (Ky)
Tr.– Robert Frankel

Lifetime record: 10 7 1 0 $1,346,353

Date	Track	Cond	Dist	Fractions	Final	Race	Pos	Calls	Jockey	Wt	Odds	Speed	Finish	Comment	Field
30Nov97- 6Hol	yl 1¼⊤	:51²1:16²1:40³	2:05⁴	3↑ (F)Matriarch-G1	7 2	21 2½ 12	1hd	Solis A	B 120	*2.00	63-29	Ryafan120ʰᵈMaxzene123²¾Yokama123ⁿᵒ	Gamely 8
		Previously trained by John H.M. Gosden											
2Nov97- 7SA	fm 1¼⊤	:50¹1:15 1:39³	2:03³	3↑ (F)Yellow Ribbon-G1	7 3	32½ 2½ 11	11¼	Solis A	B 118	2.60	70-29	Ryafan118¹¼Fnjc122¹½MmorsofSlvr122¹	Gamely kicked clear 8
4Oct97- 8Kee	fm 1⅛⊤	:46⁴1:11 1:35	1:46³	3↑ (F)QE II Cup-G1	3 3	31½ 41 31	11½	Solis A	121	2.80	96-07	Ryafan121¹¾Auntie Mame121ⁿᵏGolden Arches121ⁿᵏ	8
		Checked nearing 1st turn,rail trip,driving											
2Aug97 ◆	Goodwood(GB)	gd 1¼⊤RH	2:05³	3↑ (F)Nassau Stakes-G2 Stk139000		12½		Hills M	121	*2.25		Ryafan121²½Entice118²Papering127³	7
		Tracked in 3rd,2nd 3f out,led 2f out,ridden out.Last Second 5th											
9Jly97 ◆	Newmarket(GB)	gd 1⊤Str	1:38²	3↑ (F)Falmouth Stakes-G2 Stk97800		1¾		Eddery Pat	118	4.00		Ryafan118¾Ocean Ridge118⁶Theano127²	7
		Tracked in 3rd,led 150y out,driving.Rebecca Sharp 6th											
8Jun97 ◆	Chantilly(Fr)	sf *1⁵⁄₁₆⊤RH	2:08¹	(F)Prix de Diane (French Oaks)-G1 Stk425000		44		Dettori L	126	12.00		Vereva126¹½Mousse Glacee126²Brilliance126¹½	12
		Led to over 1f out,weakened late.Always Loyal 6th											
24May97 ◆	TheCurragh(Ire)	yl 1⊤Str	1:42¹	(F)Irish 1000 Guineas-G1 Stk227000		43½		Dettori L	126	*3.00		Classic Park126¹Strawberry Roan126²¼Caiseal Ros126ⁿᵒ	10
		Tracked in 4th,3rd 1½f out,no rally.Oh Nellie 5th,Seebe 6th											
6Oct96 ◆	Longchamp(Fr)	yl *1⊤RH	1:39⁴	(F)Prix Marcel Boussac-G1 Stk263000		1hd		Dettori L	123	*2.00e		Ryafan123ʰᵈYashmak123²¼Family Tradition123¹½	13
		Well placed in 4th,dueled entrymate 1f out,gamely prevailed											
8Sep96 ◆	TheCurragh(Ire)	gd 7f⊤Str	1:26¹	(F)Moyglare Stud Stakes-G1 Stk242000		2½		Eddery Pat	123	4.50		Bianca Nera123½Ryafan123ⁿᵏAzra123ʰᵈ	10
		Tracked in 3rd,led 3f out to 1½f out,faded,back up for 2nd											
29Jun96 ◆	Doncaster(GB)	gd 7f⊤Str	1:30⁴	(F)EBF Lonsdale Maiden Stakes Mdn8400		11¼		Eddery Pat	123	*1.25		Ryafan123¹½Ajayib123¹½Elrayahin123³½	7
		Led throughout setting modest pace,held well											

Saratoga Dew

b. f. 1989, by Cormorant (His Majesty)–Super Luna, by In Reality

Own.– Charles F. Engel
Br.– Mrs Helen B. Chenery (NY)
Tr.– Gary Sciacca

Lifetime record: 11 8 1 0 $541,580

Date	Track	Cond	Dist	Fractions	Final	Race	Pos	Calls	Jockey	Wt	Odds	Speed	Finish	Comment	Field
31Oct92- 6GP	fst 1⅛	:47 1:10⁴1:35³	1:48	3↑ (F)B C Distaff-G1	4 1	1½ 3½ 12¹³	12¹³¼	McCauley WH	119	*2.00	83-03	Paseana123⁴VrsaillesTrety123³MgclMdn119¹½	Used on pace 14
10Oct92- 6Bel	gd 1⅛	:45³1:09³1:34¹	1:46⁴	3↑ (F)Beldame-G1	1 1	11 1½ 16	16	McCauley WH	119	2.00	95-04	SaratogaDew119⁶VersaillsTrty123⁶Coxwold123⁶½	Mild drive 5
2Sep92- 8Bel	fst 1⅛	:46 1:10¹1:34⁴	1:47³	(F)Gazelle H-G1	2 2	23½ 22 1hd	11½	McCauley WH	120	*1.00	91-10	Saratoga Dew120¹½Vivano114⁴¼Tiney Toast113⅜	Mild drive 6
15Aug92- 8Sar	my 1¼	:47¹1:11²1:36²	2:02³	(F)Alabama-G1	5 1	11 11½ 11	2ⁿᵒ	McCauley WH	121	6.70	91-09	November Snow121ⁿᵒSaratoga Dew121¹¾Pacific Squall121ⁿᵒ	7
		Gamely											
25Jly92-10FL	gd 1⅛	:23³:47³	1:12¹1:45	(F)(S)N Y Oaks 100k	5 2	2½ 1½ 12	16½	McCauley WH	112	*.40	92-20	SratogaDw112⁶½Noble'sHoney109²⁷She'saQun112ⁿᵒ	Handily 6
27Jun92-10Mth	fst 1 70	:22¹:45⁴	1:10²1:41³	(F)Post-Deb-G2	7 11	9¹⁰ 69¼ 68½	69¼	McCauley WH	119	2.70	79-16	Diamond Duo113ⁿᵏC.C.'s Return115⁶Miss Legality121ʰᵈ	12
		No solid rally											
3Jun92- 8Bel	fst 7f	:22⁴:45⁴	1:10²1:23²	3↑ (F)(S)Hyde Park H 86k	5 6	1½ 2½ 1hd	1ⁿᵏ	McCauley WH	114	2.40	87-12	SrtogaDw114ⁿᵏMissIronSmoke114³Bn'sMomnt114²½	Driving 7
28Mar92- 8Aqu	fst 1	:23 :46²	1:11²1:37¹	(F)Comely-G2	7 2	21 21 2hd	11	McCauley WH	114	*.80	76-31	Saratoga Dew114¹City Dance112½Looking for Win114¹⁰	7
		Hard drive											
16Mar92- 8Aqu	fst 7f	:22⁴:46²	1:11³1:24³	(F)Over All 54k	8 4	2½ 2½ 13	14¾	McCauley WH	116	*1.60	82-25	SaratogaDw116⁴¾MissCoverGirl116ʰᵈGiveNotc118¹¼	Driving 9
8Feb92- 6Aqu	fst 6f	:23 :46⁴	1:11⁴	(F)(S)Alw 27000	4 2	1½ 1hd 16	111½	McCauley WH	121	*.70	84-22	SaratogaDew121¹¹½BeSpcial116¹½Aint'ShNc116⅜	Ridden out 6
19Jan92- 6Aqu	fst 6f	:23³:48²	1:14	(F)(S)Md Sp Wt	11 9	5³ 1½ 14	15¾	McCauley WH	121	8.90	73-27	SaratgaDew121⁵¾MontanaGal121²Kyle'sKreem121⁵	Handily 11

Serena's Song

b. f. 1992, by Rahy (Blushing Groom)–Imagining, by Northfields
Own.– Robert B. & Beverly J. Lewis
Br.– Dr Howard Baker (Ky)
Tr.– D. Wayne Lukas

Lifetime record: 38 18 11 3 $3,283,388

9Nov96- 8CD fst 1 :22 :442 1:092 1:361 3↑ ⒻCD Distaff-G2 6 3 32½ 1½ 11½ 2¾ Barton DM 125 *.50 91-23 Fast Catch109¾Serena's Song125noBedroom Blues1126 9
Lunged out start,stalked,bid,led,game try
26Oct96- 6WO fst 1⅛ :482 1:123 1:363 1:482 3↑ ⒻB C Distaff-G1 3 2 21½ 21 1½ 21½ Stevens GL 123 2.70 102-02 Jewel Princess1231½Serena's Song1231¾Different1235¼ 6
3 path,good try
6Oct96- 9Bel fst 1⅛ :464 1:102 1:342 1:47 3↑ ⒻBeldame-G1 4 1 1½ 11 11 2¾ Stevens GL 123 *.95 94-12 Yanks Music119¾Serena's Song1233Clear Mandate1231 6
Pressured,held well
14Sep96- 9Bel fst 1116 :233 :471 1:111 1:414 3↑ ⒻRuffian H-G1 4 2 1½ 11 11 2nk Stevens GL 126 *.75 90-10 Yanks Music116nkSerena's Song1269Head East108nk 6
Yielded grudgingly
25Aug96- 9Mth fst 1116 :232 :464 1:103 1:412 3↑ P H Iselin H-G1 6 2 2hd 1hd 1hd 33¼ Barton DM 115 *1.60 106-05 Smart Strike1152¼Eltish1161Serena's Song115½ Weakened 7
3Aug96- 8Sar fst 1⅛ :47 1:102 1:352 1:483 3↑ Whitney H-G1 9 1 11 12½ 12½ 2nk Bailey JD 116 3.55 94-06 Mahogany Hall113nkSerena's Song1161Peaks and Valleys121½ 9
Sharp,yielded late
21Jly96- 9Hol fst 1⅛ :464 1:102 1:343 1:47 3↑ ⒻVanity H-G1 6 4 31 41¼ 32 23 Bailey JD B 125 *1.60 95-10 JewelPrincess1203Seren'sSong125¾TopRung116½ 4 wide trip 6
29Jun96- 9Bel fst 1116 :234 :462 1:10 1:413 3↑ ⒻHempstead H-G1 5 4 2½ 2½ 11½ 13¾ Bailey JD 125 *.40 91-13 Serena'sSong1253¾Shoop115hdRestoredHope114¾ Mild drive 8
1Jun96-10CD fst 1⅛ :463 1:11 1:363 1:501 3↑ ⒻFleur de Lis H-G3 8 3 21 1hd 1½ 1½ Stevens GL 124 *.60 95-15 Serena's Song124½Halo America1171¼Alcovy1176 9
Brushed gate start,leaned in bumped,hand urging
18May96- 4Pim my 1⅛ :47 1:104 1:361 1:493 3↑ ⒻPim Distaff H-G3 2 1 11 11 12½ 11½ Stevens GL 123 *.30 90-18 Serena's Song1231½Shoop1166¼Churchbell Chimes1145½ 4
Ridden out
3May96- 7CD fst 1116 :242 :474 1:12 1:422 3↑ ⒻLouisville BC H-G2 4 1 1½ 11 1½ 2nk Stevens GL 123 *.60 99-06 Jewel Princess118nkSerena's Song1237½Naskra Colors1133½ 6
Pace,4 wide,brushed ⅛ pole,could not last
12Apr96- 9OP sly 1116 :23 :46 1:102 1:413 4↑ ⒻApple Blossom H-G1 2 2 21½ 21 21½ 33 Stevens GL 124 *.60 96-11 Twice the Vice1171½Halo America1151½Serena's Song1242½ 7
Stalked,bid ¼,flattened out
2Mar96- 7SA fst 1¼ :462 1:102 1:354 2:02 4↑ S Anita H-G1 11 4 52 2hd 43 712½ Stevens GL B 114 6.00 74-16 MrPurple1162LuthierFever1145JustJava1143 Led into lane 11
17Feb96- 6SA fst 1116 :234 :473 1:103 1:421 4↑ ⒻSanta Maria H-G1 5 2 31 1hd 11½ 11¼ Stevens GL B 124 *.30 84-21 Serena's Song1241¼Twice the Vice1183Real Connection1141¼ 5
Ridden out
27Jan96- 8SA fst 7f :222 :444 1:084 1:212 4↑ ⒻS Monica H-G1 1 1 2½ 2hd 1hd 1½ Stevens GL B 123 *1.10 95-12 Serna'sSng123½ExoticWood1184½KlssyKm116nk Game inside 6
28Oct95- 4Bel my 1⅛ :454 1:092 1:332 1:46 3↑ ⒻB C Distaff-G1 6 3 32 33½ 38½ 518¾ Stevens GL 119 2.50 83-08 InsideInformation12313HvnlyPrz1232¼Lkwy1231 Tired badly 10
7Oct95- 7Bel wf 1⅛ :48 1:121 1:361 1:483 3↑ ⒻBeldame-G1 4 1 12 14 12½ 1¾ Stevens GL 119 2.05 89-14 Serena's Song119¾Heavenly Prize1236¾Lakeway1236¾ 5
Uncontested lead,game
23Sep95- 9TP fst 1116 :231 :463 1:103 1:413 3↑ ⒻTP Bud BC-G2 1 3 32½ 2½ 21 25½ Stevens GL 119 *.20 94-15 Mrh'sStorm1175½Srn'sSong1194½Alcovy1177 Bid,second best 5
3Sep95- 8Bel fst 1⅛ :464 1:101 1:342 1:471 ⒻGazelle H-G1 2 2 2½ 1½ 15 17 Stevens GL 124 *.35 96-09 Serena's Song1247Miss Golden Circle113nkGolden Bri1214¼ 6
Ridden out
30Jly95-11Mth fst 1⅛ :46 1:102 1:353 1:484 Haskell Inv H-G1 8 3 2hd 11½ 13½ 1¾ Stevens GL 118 *1.50 90-09 Serena's Song118¾Pyramid Peak1203½Citadeed1182 Driving 11
8Jly95- 9Bel fst 1¼ :474 1:12 1:372 2:034 ⒻC C A Oaks-G1 4 3 31½ 11½ 1½ 21½ Stevens GL 121 *.20 76-21 Golden Bri1211½Serena's Song1218Change Fora Dollar1212 6
Took lead 316,weakened
9Jun95- 8Bel fst 1⅛ :463 1:111 1:363 1:501 ⒻMother Goose-G1 6 1 2hd 1½ 13 13 Stevens GL 121 *.05 81-24 Serena's Song1213Golden Bri1216Forested12112 Ridden out 6
19May95-10Pim fst 1⅛ :47 1:112 1:36 1:482 ⒻBlack Eyed Susan-G2 6 2 21½ 2½ 12 19 Stevens GL 122 *.40 96-14 Serena's Song1229Conquistadoress1151¼RareOpportnity1157 7
Ridden out
6May95- 8CD fst 1¼ :454 1:101 1:353 2:011 Kentucky Derby-G1 13 1 11½ 1hd 42½ 1611½ Nakatani CS 121 *3.40e 95-00 Thunder Gulch1262¼Tejano Run126hdTimber Country126¾ 19
Hard pressed,tired
1Apr95-11TP fst 1⅛ :463 1:111 1:362 1:493 Jim Beam-G2 3 1 1hd 11 14 13½ Nakatani CS 116 *.90 95-20 Serena'sSng1163½TejanoRn1215Meck1214 Sharp,ridden out 8
12Mar95- 8SA fst 1116 :233 :473 1:12 1:423 ⒻS A Oaks-G1 4 2 2½ 2½ 12½ 1hd Nakatani CS B 117 *.70 82-23 Serena'sSong117hdUrbn11714Mr'sShb117no Gamely,just held 5
19Feb95- 8SA fst 1 :224 :46 1:10 1:352 ⒻLas Virgenes-G1 1 1 1hd 2hd 1hd 11¼ Nakatani CS B 122 *.50 92-17 Serena'sSong1221¼Ct'sCrdl118nkUrbn1162 Very game effort 7
29Jan95- 8SA fst 7f :223 :444 1:083 1:212 ⒻSanta Ynez BC-G3 5 1 1hd 2hd 11½ 12 Nakatani CS B 123 1.50 95-09 Serena'sSong1232Cat'sCradl1212CllNow1214½ Much the best 5
17Dec94- 9Hol fst 1116 :233 :464 1:104 1:414 ⒻHol Starlet-G1 5 1 1hd 1hd 11½ 1no Nakatani CS B 120 *.40 92-13 Serena'sSong120noUrbane1203½SkiDancer1204 Game on rail 5
5Nov94- 5CD fst 1116 :23 :461 1:112 1:451 ⒻB C Juv Fillies-G1 12 3 1hd 1½ 2hd 2hd Nakatani CS 119 7.00 88-07 Flanders119hdSerena's Song1194Stormy Blues119½ 13
Brushed stretch,stubbornly
8Oct94- 8SA fst 1116 :222 :454 1:094 1:414 ⒻOak Leaf-G1 1 1 1½ 1½ 11½ 12¾ Nakatani CS B 115 3.70 86-11 Serena's Song1152¾Call Now1154½Mama Mucci11511 5
Strong hand ride
3Sep94- 8Dmr fst 7f :214 :434 1:081 1:212 ⒻDmr Deb-G2 3 5 62½ 63½ 33½ 49¾ Stevens GL B 119 2.90 86-06 Call Now1154½How So Oiseau1191¾Ski Dancer1163½ 9
Broke out,bumped,no late bid,returned bleeding from mouth
12Aug94- 8Dmr fst 6½f :213 :443 1:091 1:154 ⒻSorrento-G2 6 1 42¼ 4½ 21 32 Stevens GL B 121 *.60 90-13 HowSoOiseau1172SkiDancr117noSern'sSong1218 4 wide turn 8
25Jly94- 8Hol fst 6f :22 :451 :572 1:10 Hol Juv Chm-G2 4 2 52¼ 52½ 43½ 2½ Stevens GL B 117 1.50 89-12 Mr Purple117½Serena's Song1171½Cyrano1171½ 7
Awaited room ¼,5 wide into lane
9Jly94- 4Hol fst 6f :213 :443 :57 1:10 ⒻLandaluce-G2 9 1 31½ 21 1½ 14½ Stevens GL B 116 *1.20 90-11 Serena'sSong1164½Embroidred1162Cat'sCradl1162¾ Handily 10
25Jun94- 3Hol fst 5f :22 :45 :572 ⒻMd Sp Wt 8 1 1½ 12½ 18 110 Stevens GL B 118 1.80 97-10 Serena'sSong11810ValidAttraction118hdGuise1183¾ Easily 8
12Jun94- 9CD fst 5½f :22 :453 :581 1:051 ⒻDebutante 92k 1 8 1hd 2hd 41½ 45½ Barton DM 112 6.50 91-09 Chargedupsycamore1211Phone Bird1161½Our Gem1163 9
Dueled,weakened,brushed,checked 116
28May94- 1CD fst 5f :223 :46 :59 ⒻMd Sp Wt 11 11 87 78½ 58½ 56½ Sellers SJ 119 3.20 91-11 Phone Bird1193MeMy119nkB J Shiny Gold1192 Wide stretch 12

Silver Charm

gr/ro. c. 1994, by Silver Buck (Buckpasser)–Bonnie's Poker, by Poker
Own.– Robert B. & Beverly J. Lewis
Br.– Mary Lou Wootton (Fla)
Tr.– Bob Baffert

Lifetime record: 24 12 7 2 $6,944,369

12Jun99- 9CD fst 1⅛ :464 1:11 1:352 1:471 3↑ S Foster H-G2 3 4 44½ 42½ 44 48½ Antley CW L 123 1.40 98-03 Victory Gallop1205Nite Dreamer110¾Littlebitlively1152¾ 7
Hopped start,weakened
28Mar99♦ NadAlShba(UAE) fst*1¼LH 2:003 4↑ Dubai World Cup-G1 614¼ Stevens GL 126 - Almutawakel126¾Malek126¾Victory Gallop1261½ 8
Stk5000000
Tracked in 5th,weakened over 2f out.Daylami 5th,RunningStag 7th
6Mar99- 5SA fst 1¼ :472 1:112 1:352 2:003 4↑ Santa Anita H-G1 1 3 31½ 42¼ 41½ 31 Stevens GL LB 124 *1.00 97-11 Free House123½Event of the Year119½Silver Charm1243 6
Came back on outside
30Jan99-10GP fst 1⅛ :463 1:102 1:353 1:481 3↑ Donn H-G1 12 9 99¼ 76¾ 63½ 35¼ Stevens GL L 126 *.80 91-14 PuertoMadro1202¾Bhrns1132¼SlvrChrm126nk Mild wide rally 12
10Jan99- 8SA fst 1116 :242 :472 1:104 1:413 4↑ San Pasqual H-G2 3 3 38½ 36 31 11¼ Stevens GL LB 125 *.30 95-10 Silver Charm1251¼Malek1193½Crafty Friend1182 5
Rallied,good handling
27Nov98-11CD fst 1⅛ :472 1:112 1:361 1:49 3↑ Clark H-G2 2 1 1hd 2hd 2½ 1hd Stevens GL L 124 *.30 99-14 Silver Charm124hdLittlebitlively1131Wild Rush117½ 8
Dueled,headed,gamely
7Nov98-10CD fst 1¼ :473 1:12 1:371 2:02 3↑ BC Classic-G1 8 4 52¼ 2½ 1hd 2¾ Stevens GL L 126 2.50 94-07 AwesomeAgain126¾SilvrChrm126nkSwn126no Led,drifted late 10
17Oct98- 8SA fst 1⅛ :464 1:101 1:343 1:471 3↑ Goodwood BC H-G2 5 3 31½ 3½ 1hd 12½ Stevens GL LB 124 *.50 100-07 SilverCharm1242½Free House1242½ScoreQuick1156 Driving 6
26Sep98-10TP fst 1⅛ :462 1:10 1:343 1:472 3↑ Ky Cup Classic H-G3 1 3 31 2hd 2hd 11↓ Stevens GL L 123 *.50 100-16 DH Silver Charm123 DH Wild Rush11717Acceptible1175 5
Long drive,brushed

(Silver Charm — continued)

Date	Track/Cond	Dist	Times				Race	Pos						Jockey	Wt	Odds	Sp	Finish order	Fld
25Jly98- 8Dmr	fst 1 1/16	:23 :464 1:102 1:41				3↑	San Diego H-G3	4 2	21	31	510	527		Stevens GL	LB 125	*.30	72-09	MudRoute1176Hal'sPal11351/2Benchmrk11751/2 Stalked,gave way	5
13Jun98- 9CD	fst 11/8	:464 1:11 1:36 1:483				3↑	Stephen Foster H-G2	1 3	44	31	11/2	21		Stevens GL	L 127	*.40	100-07	Awesome Again1131Silver Charm12751/2Semoran11521/4	7
	Drifted in final 1/16,brushed,outfinished																		
28Mar98◆	NadAlShba(UAE) fst*11/4LH	2:041				4↑	Dubai World Cup-G1 Stk4000000					1no		Stevens GL	126	-		Silver Charm126noSwain12621/2Loup Sauvage126no	9
	Tracked in3rd,led over 2f out,repelled challenges,all out																		
7Feb98- 8SA	wf 11/8	:472 1:11 1:344 1:471					Strub-G2	3 2	311/2	31/2	12	14		Stevens GL	LB 123	*.30	100-06	SilverChrm1234MudRoute1172Bagshot1177 Strong handling	6
17Jan98- 8SA	fst 11/16	:241 :482 1:121 1:414					San Fernando BC-G2	1 2	211/2	21/2	1hd	11		Stevens GL	LB 122	*.20	94-12	Silver Charm1221Mud Route11631Lord Grillo12010 Gamely	4
26Dec97- 8SA	fst 7f	:222 :45 1:092 1:212					Malibu-G1	6 5	511/4	42	31	21/2		Stevens GL	LB 123	*.30e	96-13	Lord Grillo1191/2Silver Charm1233Swiss Yodeler1152	9
	Lacked room 7/16 to past 1/8																		
7Jun97- 9Bel	fst 11/2	:491 1:134 2:04 2:284					Belmont-G1	2 3	21/2	1hd	11/2	23/4		Stevens GL	L 126	*1.05	89-14	Touch Gold1263/4Silver Charm1261Free House12614	7
	Game effort,wide,drifted late																		
17May97-10Pim	fst 13/16	:464 1:102 1:352 1:544					Preakness-G1	7 4	311/2	211/2	21	1hd		Stevens GL	L 126	3.10	93-15	Silver Charm126hdFree House126hdCaptain Bodgit12611/4	10
	3 wide turns,floated out late,up																		
3May97- 8CD	fst 11/4	:472 1:121 1:371 2:022					Ky Derby-G1	5 6	42	31/2	1hd	1hd		Stevens GL	L 126	4.00	93-05	Silver Charm126hdCaptain Bodgit12631/2Free House1263	13
	4-wide bid,all out																		
5Apr97- 6SA	fst 11/8	:45 1:09 1:342 1:473					S Anita Derby-G1	3 2	2hd	2hd	11/2	2hd		Stevens GL	LB 120	2.10	95-10	Free House120hdSilver Charm1202Hello120no Game effort	10
16Mar97- 7SA	fst 11/16	:223 :46 1:101 1:422					San Felipe-G2	6 5	54	54	321/2	23/4		McCarron CJ	LB 122	*1.10e	90-12	FreeHouse1193SilvrChrm1221KngCrmson1163/4 Slowly gaining	9
8Feb97- 6SA	fst 7f	:222 :444 1:084 1:21					San Vicente-G3	5 7	311/2	421/2	1hd	113/4		McCarron CJ	LB 120	2.60e	100-13	Silver Charm12013/4Free House1202Funontherun1141/2	9
	Broke thru gate,perfect inside trip																		
11Sep96- 8Dmr	fst 7f	:223 :451 1:093 1:224					Dmr Futurity-G2	7 3	21	31	21	1hd		Flores DR	LB 116	1.60e	86-15	SilvrCharm116hdGoldTribute11531/2SwissYodelr12121/4 Gamely	7
24Aug96- 6Dmr	fst 51/2f	:214 :444 :57 1:031					Md Sp Wt	2 2	1hd	11/2	111/2	111/4		Flores DR	LB 118	*.40e	97-09	Silver Charm11811/4Gold Tribute1188So Easy1185	8
	Inside duel,jumped shadow late																		
10Aug96- 3Dmr	fst 6f	:214 :444 :572 1:10					Md Sp Wt	2 3	1hd	1hd	11/2	24		Flores DR	B 118 b	2.80e	85-08	Deeds Not Words1184Silver Charm1181Constant Demand11833/4	8
	Inside duel																		

Silverbulletday

b. f. 1996, by Silver Deputy (Deputy Minister)–Rokeby Rose, by Tom Rolfe
Own.– Michael E. Pegram
Br.– Highclere Inc & Clear Creek (Ky)
Tr.– Bob Baffert

Lifetime record: 18 14 1 0 $2,821,750

Date	Track/Cond	Dist	Times	Race	Pos					Jockey	Wt	Odds	Sp	Finish order	Fld
6Nov99- 3GP	fst 11/8	:462 1:094 1:343 1:472	3↑ (F)BC Distaff-G1	6 5	421/2	23	43	6111/4		Bailey JD	L 120	*1.60	89-00	BeautiflPleasre12333/4BansheeBreeze12311/4HeritageofGold12311/4	8
	Close up,faded														
100ct99- 5Bel	sly 11/8	:453 1:091 1:341 1:473	3↑ (F)Beldame-G1	3 2	25	231/2	22	243/4		Bailey JD	L 119	*.45	88-23	Beautiful Pleasure12343/4Silverbulletday1196Catinca12373/4	5
	Rail,lost whip 1/8 pole														
11Sep99- 8Bel	fst 11/8	:453 1:093 1:342 1:473	(F)Gazelle-G1	1 5	41	3nk	131/2	113/4		Bailey JD	L 124	*.20	93-15	Silverbulletday12413/4Queens' Word1132Awful Smart1153/4	6
	3 wide,clear,driving														
21Aug99- 8Sar	fst 11/4	:492 1:134 1:383 2:023	(F)Alabama-G1	6 5	54	2hd	12	19		Bailey JD	L 121	*.40	95-13	Silverbulletday1219Strolling Belle1213Gandria12161/2	7
	When asked,ridden out														
10Jly99- 9Mth	fst 11/16	:234 :471 1:111 1:43	(F)Mth BC Oaks-G2	4 3	211/2	21/2	11	15		Bailey JD	L 121	*.05	86-14	Silverbulletday1215Boom Town Girl1211Bag Lady Jane11612	4
	Drew off,handily														
5Jun99- 9Bel	fst 11/2	:473 1:12 2:014 2:274	Belmont-G1	3 1	11/2	3nk	531/2	71011/4		Bailey JD	L 121	5.10	95-06	Lemon Drop Kid126hdVision and Verse12611/2Charismatic12643/4	12
	Set pace,gave way														
14May99-11Pim	fst 11/8	:47 1:104 1:351 1:474	(F)Black Eyed Susan-G2	1 1	11/2	151/2	141/2	12		Stevens GL	L 122	*.10	104-12	Silverbulletday1222Dreams Gallore11716VeVStr11531/4	7
	Pace inside,ridden out														
30Apr99- 9CD	fst 11/8	:473 1:121 1:371 1:494	(F)Ky Oaks-G1	5 6	621/2	2hd	121/2	12		Stevens GL	L 121	*.10	94-13	Silverbulletday1212Dreams Gallore12143/4Sweeping Story1216	7
	Hand urged,clearly best														
3Apr99- 8Kee	my 11/16	:223 :46 1:104 1:413	(F)Ashland-G1	6 4	371/2	311/2	111/2	17		Bailey JD	L 123	*.30	100-15	Silverbulletday1237MarleyVale11541/2Gold From theWest11541/2	6
	3wd,widened in hand														
13Mar99- 9FG	sly 11/16	:24 :484 1:133 1:444	(F)FG Oaks-G3	7 6	421/2	311/2	11/2	13		Stevens GL	L 121	*.30	87-27	Silverbulletday1213Runwy Vnus112noBrushed Halory11411/4	7
	4wd,3w bid,clear late														
20Feb99- 9FG	fst 11/16	:242 :482 1:13 1:441	(F)Davona Dale-G3	1 5	45	211/2	111/2	121/4		Stevens GL	L 122	*.10	90-21	Silverbulletday12221/4Brushed Halory114nkOn a Soapbox11963/4	8
	Bobbled,inside,driving														
28Nov98- 9CD	fst 11/16	:24 :473 1:121 1:434	(F)Golden Rod-G3	4 4	321/2	11	16	110		Stevens GL	L 122	*.10	92-05	Silverbulletday12210Here I Go1133Lefty's Dollbaby11361/2	6
	3 wide,drew off														
7Nov98- 5CD	fst 11/16	:232 :471 1:12 1:433	(F)BC Juv Fillies-G1	5 5	54	31	12	11/2		Stevens GL	L 119	*.80	92-07	Silverbulletday1191/2Excellent Meeting11921/2Three Ring119nk	10
	6w 2nd turn,driving														
11Oct98- 8Kee	fst 11/16	:224 :454 1:104 1:421	(F)Alcibiades-G2	2 5	56	1hd	11	121/2		Stevens GL	L 118	*1.00	97-00	Silverbulletday11821/2Extended Applause1187Grand Deed1181	11
	4 wide,hand urging														
29Aug98- 8Dmr	fst 7f	:214 :441 1:092 1:221	(F)Dmr Debutante-G2	1 3	2hd	11	211/2	471/2		Delhoussye E	LB 121	*1.60	81-13	Excellent Meeting11551/2Antahkarana1152Colorado Song115hd	9
	Dueled,weakened														
8Aug98- 8Dmr	fst 61/2f	:214 :443 1:103 1:172	(F)Sorrento-G2	4 3	421/2	2hd	12	12		Stevens GL	LB 121	*.70	84-15	Silverbulletday1212Excellent Meeting1171/2Colorado Song1175	7
	3 deep turn,driving														
27Jun98- 7CD	fst 51/2f	:214 :451 :574 1:043	(F)Debutante-G3	4 4	31/2	2hd	111/2	113/4		Martinez W	L 115	*.30	96-10	Silverbulletday11511/2The Happy Hopper11531/4Mncr'sRos11533/4	9
	Stalked,steady drive														
13Jun98- 3CD	fst 51/2f	:22 :453 :58 1:043	(F)Md Sp Wt	9 4	311/2	21/2	16	111		Sellers SJ	L 118	*1.00	96-11	Silverbulletday11811ForvrMisi11811DrivThruBlus1181	12
	Much best,ridden out														

Singspiel (Ire)

b. c. 1992, by In the Wings (Sadler's Wells)–Glorious Song, by Halo — **Lifetime record: 20 9 8 0 $5,950,217**
Own.– Sheikh Mohammed al Maktoum
Br.– Mohammed al Maktoum (Ire)
Tr.– Michael R. Stoute

19Aug97♦ York(GB) gd *1 5/16 ⓉLH 2:12 3↑ Juddmonte International Stakes-G1 Stk533000 — 1 1½ Dettori L 131 4.00 — Singspiel131 1½Desert King123 1½Benny the Dip123 1¼ 4 — Tracked leader,led over 2f out,handily.Bosra Sham 4th
26Jly97♦ Ascot(GB) sf 1½ⓉRH 2:36² 3↑ King George VI & Queen Eliz-G1 Stk816000 — 4 4¾ Dettori L 133 4.00 — Swain133 1Pilsudski133 1¼Helissio133 2½ 8 — Rated in 5th,4th 3f out,bid 2f out,briefly 3rd,weakened late
6Jun97♦ Epsom(GB) gd 1½ⓉLH 2:37⁴ 4↑ Coronation Cup-G1 Stk312000 — 1 5 Dettori L 126 *1.25 — Singspiel126 5Dushyantor126½Le Destin126 4 5 — Led for 5f,tracked leader,led 3½f out,clear 2f out,handily
3Apr97♦ NadAlSheba(Dub) fst *1¼LH 2:02 4↑ Dubai World Cup (Listed) Stk4000000 — 1 1¼ Bailey JD 126 — Singspiel126 1¼Siphon126 1½Sandpit126 2½ 12 — 3rd early,rated in 5th,rail bid to lead 2f out,driving.No betting
24Nov96♦ Tokyo(Jpn) fm *1½ⓉLH 2:23⁴ 3↑ Japan Cup-G1 Stk3229000 — 1 no Dettori L 126 6.60 — Singspiel126 noFabulous la Fouine117 1¼[DH]Helissio121 15 — Rated in 6th,dueled 2f out,all out,very game.Awad 5th,Pentire 8th
26Oct96- 9WO gd 1½Ⓣ :50 1:15² 2:05⁴ 2:30¹ 3↑ B C Turf-G1 — 10 4 2hd 1hd 1hd 2 1¼ Stevens GL L 126 *1.10e 76-18 — Pilsudski126 1¼Singspiel126 1¼Swain126 2½ Clear,good effort 14
29Sep96- 8WO sf 1½Ⓣ :51 1:16² 2:07¹ 2:33¹ 3↑ Canadian Int'l-G1 — 7 3 2 1½ 1 1 1 3 1 2 Stevens GL L 126 *1.90 62-30 — Singspiel126 2Chief Bearhart118 3½Mecke126 3½ Mild drive 7
14Sep96♦ Goodwood(GB) gd 1¼ⓉRH 2:07² 3↑ Select Stakes-G3 Stk62100 — 1 1 Asmussen CB 129 *1.10 — Singspiel129 1Wall Street119 8Farasan119 2½ 4 — Led throughout,ridden out
9Jly96♦ Newmarket(GB) gd 1½ⓉRH 2:29 3↑ Princess of Wales's Stakes-G2 Stk98800 — 2 1¼ Kinane MJ 128 1.75 — Posidonas133 1¼Singspiel128 2½Annus Mirabilis128 2½ 8 — Rated in 6th,progress 3½f out,bid 2f out,held by winner
8Jun96♦ Epsom(GB) gd 1½ⓉLH 2:40² 4↑ Coronation Cup-G1 Stk277000 — 2 nk Kinane MJ 126 2.25 — Swain126 nkSingspiel126 5De Quest126 no 4 — Tracked leader,bid 2f out,always held by winner
27Apr96♦ Sandown(GB) gd 1¼ⓉRH 2:06³ 4↑ Gordon Richards Stakes-G3 Stk49900 — 1 3 Dettori L 122 *1.10 — Singspiel122 3Pilsudski122½Naked Welcome122½ 11 — Tracked in 5th,led 3f out,drew clear.Prince of Andros 6th
8Sep95♦ Doncaster(GB) yl 1½ⓉLH 2:45⁴ Troy Stakes (Listed) Stk35300 — 1 2½ Kinane MJ 123 *.30 — Singspiel123 2½Jumairah Sun118 4Tenorio123 3 — Tracked leader,led 3f out,met challenge 2f out,won ridden out
15Aug95♦ York(GB) gd *1½ⓉLH 2:29⁴ Great Voltigeur Stakes-G2 Stk126000 — 2 no Kinane MJ 121 2.50 — Pentire124 noSingspiel121 3½Luso126 4 4 — Tracked leader,led 2½f out,dueled final furlong,gamely
8Jly95♦ Sandown(GB) gd 1¼ⓉRH 2:05² 3↑ Eclipse Stakes-G1 Stk416000 — 2 nk Kinane MJ 122 4.50 — Halling133 nkSingspiel122 3Red Bishop133 4 8 — Tracked pacesetting winner,bid 1f out,not good enough.Eltish 5th
25Jun95♦ Longchamp(Fr) gd *1¼ⓉRH 2:02¹ Grand Prix de Paris-G1 Stk418000 — 2 nk Kinane MJ 128 4.00e — Valanour128 nkSingspiel128¾Diamond Mix128 1½ 10 — Wide in 8th,7th 2½f out,rallied 1½f out,gaining late
9May95♦ Chester(GB) gd *1½ⓉLH 2:38² Chester Vase-G3 Stk78500 — 4 4¾ Swinburn WR 122 *1.00 — Luso122 hdCourt of Honour126¾Maralinga122 4 7 — Rated toward rear,wide bid over 2f out,one-paced late
29Apr95♦ Sandown(GB) gd 1¼ⓉRH 2:07² Thresher Classic Trial-G3 Stk116000 — 2 nk Swinburn WR 122 8.00 — Pentire122 nkSingspiel122 1½Balliol Boy122 3 8 — Rated in 5th,dueled final 16th,gamely. Luso 4th,Torrential 5th
8Oct94♦ Ascot(GB) gd 7fⓉStr 1:27¹ Hyperion Conditions Stakes Alw26500 — 2 8 Swinburn WR 123 2.25 — Celtic Swing123 8Singspiel123 10Winners Choice125 nk 6 — Rated in last,progress 2½f out,chased winner home
21Sep94♦ Chester(GB) yl 7fⓉLH 1:35 Marford Maiden Stakes Mdn8800 — 1 2½ Dettori L 126 *.65 — Singspiel126 2½Embryonic126 2Maybe Today116 1½ 8 — Chased leading group,pushed along halfway,led over 1f out
6Sep94♦ Leicester(GB) gd *7fⓉStr 1:23 David Millns Mdn Stakes (Div1) Mdn9600 — 5 2¾ Reid J 126 5.00 — Mandarina121 noShahid126 2½Oakbury126 hd 16 — Sluggish start,late progress through last quarter

Skip Away

gr/ro. c. 1993, by Skip Trial (Bailjumper)–Ingot Way, by Diplomat Way — **Lifetime record: 38 18 10 6 $9,616,360**
Own.– Carolyn H. Hine
Br.– Anna Marie Barnhart (Fla)
Tr.– Hubert Hine

7Nov98-10CD fst 1¼ :47³ 1:12 1:37¹ 2:02 3↑ B C Classic-G1 — 6 3 2 1 4¾ 6 3¼ 6 4 Bailey JD L 126 b *1.90 91-07 — AwesomeAgn126¾SlvrChrm126 nkSwain126 no Pressed,empty 10
10Oct98-10Bel sly 1¼ :46² 1:09³ 1:34¹ 2:00³ 3↑ JC Gold Cup-G1 — 4 1 2hd 2 2 3 4 3 10¼ Bailey JD L 126 b *.35 81-14 — Wagon Limit126 5½Gentlemen126 4¾Skip Away126 4 6 — Dueled outside,faded
19Sep98-10Bel fst 1⅛ :45² 1:09 1:34¹ 1:47⁴ 3↑ Woodward-G1 — 2 2 1½ 1 1 1 2 1 1¾ Bailey JD L 126 b *1.10 91-18 — Skip Away126 1¾Gentlemen126 6RunningStag126 9 5 — About his business
30Aug98-11Mth fst 1⅛ :46³ 1:10 1:34⁴ 1:47¹ 3↑ P H Iselin H-G2 — 4 3 2hd 1 1 1hd 1 no Bailey JD L 131 b *.05 102-09 — Skip Away131 noStormin Fever113 9Testafly114 2¾ Driving 7
28Jun98- 7Hol fst 1¼ :46² 1:09³ 1:34 2:00 3↑ Hol Gold Cup-G1 — 2 1 1 1 1hd 1 1 1 1¾ Bailey JD LB 124 b *.40 95-05 — Skip Away124 1¾Puerto Madero124 1Gentlemen124 3 8 — Gamely kicked clear
30May98- 9Suf fst 1⅛ :46² 1:10¹ 1:34⁴ 1:47¹ 3↑ Mass H-G3 — 1 1 1 2½ 1 2 1 3½ 1 4¼ Bailey JD L 130 b *.30 103-07 — Skip Away130 4¼Puerto Madero116 4¾K.J.'s Appeal113 4 5 — 2 path,ridden out
9May98- 7Pim gd 1 3/16 :47 1:11² 1:35⁴ 1:54¹ 3↑ Pim Special H-G1 — 4 1 1 3 1 2½ 1 3 1 3¼ Bailey JD L 128 b *.20 94-16 — Skip Away128 3¼Precocity115 nkHot Brush113¾ Driving 5
28Feb98-10GP fst 1¼ :46³ 1:10¹ 1:35¹ 2:03¹ 3↑ Gulf Park H-G1 — 2 2 2 1 1 2½ 1 3 1 2¼ Bailey JD L 127 b *.10 95-16 — Skip Away127 2¼Unruled112 1¾Behrens114 1¼ Driving,clear 6
7Feb98-10GP fst 1⅛ :46³ 1:10⁴ 1:36² 1:50 3↑ Donn H-G1 — 3 2 3 1½ 1hd 1 3 1 2¾ Bailey JD L 126 b *.40 87-24 — SkipAway126 2¾Unruled112½SirBr113 nk 3-wide bid,hand ride 10
8Nov97- 8Hol fst 1¼ :46¹ 1:09³ 1:33⁴ 1:59 3↑ B C Classic-G1 — 1 3 3 1 1 4 1 5 1 6 Smith ME L 126 b *1.80 102-06 — Skip Away126 6DeputyCommnder123¾[D]Whiskey Wisdom126 3 9 — Much best,driving
18Oct97- 9Bel wf 1¼ :47 1:10 1:33⁴ 1:58⁴ 3↑ J C Gold Cup-G1 — 1 2 2½ 1 1 1 6 1 6½ Bailey JD L 126 b 1.45 103-04 — Skip Away126 6½Instant Friendship126 10Wagon Limit121¾ 7 — Contested pace,gamely
20Sep97- 9Bel fst 1⅛ :47¹ 1:11¹ 1:35 1:47² 3↑ Woodward-G1 — 2 1 2hd 3 2½ 3 3½ 2 5½ Sellers SJ L 126 b 1.35 87-15 — FormalGold126 5½SkpAwy126 nkWll'sWy126 40 Game,2nd best 5
23Aug97- 9Mth fst 1 1/16 :22⁴ :45² 1:09 1:40¹ 3↑ PH Iselin H-G2 — 1 4 4 4 3 2½ 2 5 2 5¼ Sellers SJ L 124 b *.90 101-07 — Formal Gold121 5¼Skip Away124 2½Distorted Humor115 6 4 — 3-wide bid,2nd best
2Aug97- 8Sar fst 1⅛ :47 1:10⁴ 1:35² 1:48¹ 3↑ Whitney H-G1 — 2 3 3 2½ 3 1½ 3 3 3 6½ Sellers SJ L 125 b *1.10 88-25 — Will's Way117 noFormal Gold120 6½Skip Away125 9½ 6 — Lacked response
4Jly97- 9Bel fst 1¼ :47² 1:12 1:37¹ 2:02¹ 3↑ Suburban H-G2 — 1 2 3½ 3 1½ 3½ 1 1½ Sellers SJ L 122 b *1.00 86-23 — Skip Away122 1½Will's Way116¾Formal Gold120 15 6 — Shuffled back ½ pl,awaited room turn,determinedly
31May97-11Suf fst 1⅛ :47¹ 1:10⁴ 1:35¹ 1:47⁴ 3↑ Mass H-G3 — 3 2 2½ 1hd 1hd 1hd Sellers SJ L 119 b *.70 104-01 — SkpAwy119 hdFormlGold114 3½Wll'sWy114 2¼ 2 wide,long drive 6
10May97- 9Pim fst 1 3/16 :46³ 1:10 1:34³ 1:53 3↑ Pim Spl H-G1 — 8 4 4 2½ 3 2 2 1½ 2½ Sellers SJ L 119 b 3.30 101-17 — Gentlemen122½Skip Away119 6½Tejano Run114 8 8 — Three wide both turns,gamely
20Apr97- 7LS fst 1 :23² :46¹ 1:09³ 1:34² 3↑ Texas Mile 250k — 5 6 5 2½ 4 3½ 3 4 3 7½ Sellers SJ L 11 b *.60 - - — Isitingood123 3Spiritbound116 4½Skip Away116 2½ 7 — 5 wide first turn,empty drive
1Mar97-10GP fst 1¼ :46 1:10⁴ 1:35⁴ 2:02¹ 3↑ Gulf Park H-G1 — 2 2 2 1 2hd 2hd 2 2¼ Sellers SJ L 122 b *.40 89-19 — Mt. Sassafras113 2¼Skip Away122 nkTejano Run114 2 Gamely 6
8Feb97-10GP fst 1⅛ :47 1:10⁴ 1:35 1:47² 3↑ Donn H-G1 — 7 2 2 1 2 1½ 2 2 2 1¼ Sellers SJ L 123 b *.70 99-04 — Formal Gold113 1¼Skip Away123 6Mecke120 hd Rallied 3 path 10
5Oct96-10Bel fst 1¼ :47³ 1:11² 1:35⁴ 2:00³ 3↑ J C Gold Cup-G1 — 4 2 2½ 2½ 1 1 1hd Sellers SJ L 121 b 5.80 94-10 — Skip Away121 hdCigar126 2Louis Quatorze121 1 Hard drive 6
15Sep96- 9WO fst 1⅛ :46⁴ 1:10³ 1:36 1:49 WO Million-G1 — 1 5 5 5 5 3¼ 1hd 1 4 Sellers SJ L 126 b *1.15 101-09 — SkipAwy126 4VictorCooley119 noStephanotis119 3½ Drew away 7
24Aug96- 7Sar fst 1¼ :46¹ 1:10³ 1:36¹ 2:02² Travers-G1 — 3 4 3 2 3 1 3 1½ 3 1¾ Santos JA L 126 b *1.45 95-03 — Will's Way126¾Louis Quatorze126 1Skip Away126 3½ 7 — In tight ¾ pl,wide turn

4Aug96-10Mth fst 1⅛ :461 1:094 1:342 1:473 Haskell Inv'l H-G1 2 4 43 3½ 3½ 11 Santos JA L 124 b *.60 103-01 Skip Away1241Dr. Caton1151Victory Speech1214½ Driving 7
23Jun96-14Tdn fst 1⅛ :461 1:104 1:353 1:474 Ohio Derby-G2 10 5 52 1½ 13 13½ Santos JA LB 122 b *.70 103-08 Skip Away1223½Victory Speech1189¼Clash by Night118nk 10
Widened,brisk hand ride
8Jun96- 9Bel fst 1½ :464 1:104 2:02 2:284 Belmont-G1 13 6 2hd 11½ 1½ 21 Santos JA L 126 b 8.00 89-13 Editor'sNote1261SkipAwy1264MyFlg1216 Long drive,gamely 14
18May96-10Pim fst 1 3/16 :461 1:094 1:342 1:532 Preakness-G1 11 2 22 21½ 21½ 23¼ Sellers SJ L 126 b 3.30 98-10 Louis Quatorze1263¼Skip Away1263Editor's Note1262½ 12
Bid far turn,2nd best
4May96- 8CD fst 1¼ :46 1:103 1:35 2:01 Ky Derby-G1 16 5 64½ 108¾ 1319 1216¾ Sellers SJ L 126 b 7.70 84-04 Grindstone126noCavonnr1263½PrncofThvs126nk 5 wide tired 19
13Apr96- 9Kee wf 1⅛ :462 1:101 1:344 1:471 Blue Grass-G2 5 2 1hd 1½ 14½ 16 Sellers SJ L 121 b 4.60 98-10 Skip Away1216Louis Quatorze1211½Editor's Note1213 7
Dueled,driving clear impressivey
16Mar96-10GP fst 1⅛ :462 1:094 1:343 1:474 Florida Derby-G1 3 5 46½ 46½ 24 36¼ Sellers SJ L 122 b 7.90 92-07 Unbridled's Song1225¾Editor's Note122½Skip Away1222¼ 9
Seven wide top stretch,weakened
10Feb96- 8GP fst 1 1/16 :233 :474 1:114 1:441 Alw 26000 4 5 31½ 11 17 112 Sellers SJ L 117 b *1.10 87-12 Skip Away11712Hedge120noNatural Selection1201½ 12
Crowded,bumped turn,five wide final turn,driving
10Jan96- 1GP fst 1 1/16 :23 :463 1:114 1:454 Alw 26000 1 4 54 58 528 - Bailey JD 117 *.40 - - Blushing Jim1171½HedMinistr1171¼Night Runner1177¾ 5
Eased str in distress
25Nov95- 7Bel fst 1⅛ :471 1:114 1:373 1:501 Remsen-G2 1 5 42½ 32 1hd 2nk Bailey JD 112 2.30 89-09 Tropcool112nkSkpAwy1122CrftyFrnd1133 Yielded grudgingly 11
29Oct95- 7Bel fst 1 :223 :461 1:113 1:37 Cowdin-G2 7 3 31 2½ 2hd 2no Wilson R 122 5.30 78-19 Gator Dancer122noSkip Away1223In Contention1224¾ 8
Lost bob,gamely
6Oct95- 9Med fst 1⊗ :23 :463 1:104 1:371 World Appeal 40k 10 6 62½ 34½ 36 33¼ Wilson R 115 1.80 87-10 SpicyFact1153½PlayItAgnStn117noSkpAwy1159 Even finish 10
16Aug95- 5Mth fst 1 :24 :474 1:13 1:39 Md Sp Wt 2 3 23 11½ 19 112¼ Wilson R 118 *.80 83-17 SkpAwy11812ClashbyNight1187½DarnThatErc1134½ Drew off 8
9Jly95- 9Mth fm 5f(T) :22 :451 :572 Gilded Time 33k 4 7 77½ 66½ 45 21½ Marquez CH Jr 112 5.00 85-13 ColdSnap1181½SkipAway1121Cobb'sCreek1211¾ Closed well 7
16Jun95- 5Mth fst 5f :22 :462 :584 Md Sp Wt 2 10 87½ 79½ 59 48¾ Marquez CH Jr 118 *.80e 81-18 ColdSnap1134¼Foolspruce1182BeauCoup1182½ Broke slowly 10

Sky Beauty

b. f. 1990, by Blushing Groom (Red God)–Maplejinsky, by Nijinsky II **Lifetime record: 21 15 2 2 $1,336,000**
Own.– Georgia E. Hofmann
Br.– Sugar Maple Farm (Ky)
Tr.– H. Allen Jerkens

18Jun95- 9Bel fst 1 1/16 :23 :46 1:102 1:431 3↑ (F)Hempstead H-G1 1 2 23½ 24 37½ 311¾ Smith ME 124 *.75 71-17 Heavenly Prize1221¼Little Buckles11110Sky Beauty1243 4
Drifted,tired
20May95- 8Bel wf 1 :224 :462 1:102 1:35 3↑ (F)Shuvee H-G1 4 3 31 21 23 25½ Krone JA 126 *.35 82-24 Inside Information1195½Sky Beauty12616Restored Hope1152 4
Wide,no match
3May95- 7Bel wf 7f :222 :454 1:091 1:212 3↑ (F)Vagrancy H-G3 1 4 31½ 41½ 11½ 14 Smith ME 125 *.35 94-06 Sky Beauty1254Aly's Conquest1148Through the Door11019 4
Rated on rail,4 wide far turn,handily
5Nov94- 6CD fst 1⅛ :474 1:121 1:373 1:503 3↑ (F)B C Distaff-G1 8 7 84¾ 54 912 912¼ Smith ME 123 1.90 79-07 One Dreamer123nkHeavenly Prize1201½Miss Dominique1231¼ 9
Tired,not abused late
17Sep94- 6Bel fst 1 1/16 :232 :46 1:101 1:413 3↑ (F)Ruffian H-G1 3 2 21 2hd 11 11¼ Smith ME 130 *.40 94-10 Sky Beauty1301¼Dispute1172¼Educated Risk114nk Driving 5
24Jly94- 8Sar fst 1⅛ :47 1:11 1:363 1:492 3↑ (F)Go for Wand-G1 1 1 1½ 11½ 12½ 110½ Smith ME 123 *.10 89-19 Sky Beauty12310Link River123noLife is Delicious1237½ 5
Drifted,ridden out
19Jun94- 8Bel fst 1⅛ :474 1:113 1:351 1:472 3↑ (F)Hempstead H-G1 4 1 1½ 1hd 1hd 1nk Smith ME 128 *.30 94-16 SkyBeauty128nkYou'dBeSurprisd11812SchwayBabyS'way1097 5
Headed,driving
21May94- 8Bel fst 1 1/16 :231 :454 1:093 1:403 3↑ (F)Shuvee H-G1 2 2 2hd 1hd 14 19½ Smith ME 125 *.30 99-12 SkyBeauty1259½ForAllSeasns1133LooiCpot112no Ridden out 4
4May94- 8Bel fst 7f :222 :451 1:09 1:213 3↑ (F)Vagrancy H-G3 6 4 53¼ 31 11 13 Smith ME 122 *.40 95-11 Sky Beauty1223For All Seasons1147¾Pamzig107¾ Ridden out 6
6Nov93- 4SA fst 1⅛ :464 1:11 1:36 1:481 3↑ (F)B C Distaff-G1 1 5 65½ 52¼ 32 54¼ Smith ME 120 4.30 85-10 HollywoodWildcat120noPasn1232½RToss1231 4 wide 2nd turn 8
10Oct93- 7Bel fst 1 :231 :461 1:103 1:353 (F)Rare Perfume-G2 4 2 21 2½ 1hd 11¾ Smith ME 124 *.30 85-09 Sky Beauty1241¾Fadetta112nkFor All Seasons114nk Driving 6
14Aug93- 9Sar fst 1¼ :464 1:112 1:371 2:032 (F)Alabama-G1 3 3 35 2hd 2hd 11½ Smith ME 121 *.70 87-20 SkyBeauty1211½FuturePretns1211¾SlkyFthr1211½ Hard drive 8
11Jly93- 8Bel fst 1¼ :47 1:103 1:353 2:012 (F)C C A Oaks-G1 5 2 2½ 1hd 11½ 1½ Smith ME 121 *.10 84-16 SkyBeauty121½FuturePretense1212SilkyFeather1213 Driving 5
6Jun93- 9Bel fst 1⅛ :464 1:11 1:361 1:493 (F)Mother Goose-G1 4 2 21 2½ 12 15 Smith ME 121 *.50 83-21 Sky Beauty1215Dispute1213½Silky Feather1215 Handily 4
8May93- 8Bel fst 1 :224 :453 1:10 1:352 (F)Acorn-G1 6 3 2½ 1hd 12 15¼ Smith ME 121 *.40 91-17 SkyBeauty1215¼EducatedRisk1212½InHerGlory1215¾ Handily 6
13Mar93-10GP fst 1 1/16 :24 :491 1:14 1:433 (F)Bonnie Miss-G2 1 2 21½ 21 2½ 2¾ Maple E 114 *1.30 91-15 Dispute114¾Sky Beauty1143Lunar Spook1174¾ Best of rest 6
19Sep92- 5Bel fst 7f :222 :46 1:103 1:231 (F)Matron-G1 2 8 41¾ 3½ 1½ 12¾ Maple E 119 *.40 88-11 SkyBeauty1192¾EducatdRisk1192¼FmlyEntrprz1192¼ Driving 9
31Aug92- 8Sar fst 6f :22 :45 :571 1:094 (F)Spinaway-G1 1 4 33 31 2½ 11¾ Maple E 119 *.30 95-11 (D)Sky Beauty1191¾Family Enterprize11910(D)TryintheSky1192½ 5
Disqualified and placed third
13Aug92- 8Sar fst 6f :214 :451 :572 1:10 (F)Adirondack-G2 7 2 47 33 2hd 13½ Maple E 116 1.70 94-13 Sky Beauty1163½Missed the Storm1147Distinct Habit1213 7
Ridden out
15Jly92- 6Bel fst 5½f :222 :454 1:041 (F)Alw 27000 3 2 2½ 1hd 11½ 12½ Maple E 121 *1.10 94-14 SkyBeauty1212½TenaciousTiffany1187Clrwthflr116½ Driving 7
3Jly92- 3Bel fst 5f :22 :453 :58 (F)Md Sp Wt 3 3 41½ 41 1½ 12 Maple E 117 5.30 91-11 Sky Beauty1172Port of Silver117¾Quinpool1174¾ Driving 8

Sky Classic

ch. c. 1987, by Nijinsky II (Northern Dancer)–No Class, by Nodouble **Lifetime record: 29 15 6 1 $3,240,398**
Own.– Sam-Son Farm
Br.– Sam-Son Farms (Can)
Tr.– James E. Day

31Oct92- 9GP fm 1½(T) :474 1:112 2:00 2:24 3↑ BC Turf-G1 3 5 31½ 31½ 1hd 2no Day P L 126 *.90 101-00 Fraise126noSky Classic1262Quest for Fame1261 Game try 10
3Oct92- 7Bel fm 1½(T) :481 1:114 1:594 2:242 3↑ Turf Classic Inv-G1 6 3 42 42 1hd 11¾ Day P 126 *1.00 103-06 SkyClassic1261¾Fraise1262½SolarSplendor126nk Mild drive 6
6Sep92-10AP fm 1¼(T) :482 1:114 1:352 1:594 3↑ Arl Million-G1 6 4 55½ 53½ 1½ 2hd Day P L 126 *1.20 98-03 DearDoctr126hdSkyClssc126nkGoldnPhsnt1262¼ Game 2nd 12
16Aug92- 9AP fm 1¼(T) :491 1:13 1:371 2:003 3↑ Arlington H-G2 3 5 44 53¼ 31 11¼ Day P L 125 *.30 94-09 SkyClassic1251¼(D)PlateDancer115¾Duckaroo112hd Driving 9
28Jun92- 5Atl fm 1 3/16(T) :462 1:092 1:334 1:521 3↑ Caesars Int'l H-G2 2 8 87½ 63¾ 33 11¼ Day P L 123 *.70 99-08 SkyClassic1231¼CheninBlanc1151LotusPool114½ Ridden out 9
7Jun92- 7Bel yl 1¼[T] :48 1:121 1:371 2:022 3↑ ET Manhattan H-G2 8 5 55 31 2½ 13 Day P 123 *1.20 78-22 SkyClssc1233RomnEnvoy1111¼LgrCt1161¼ Blocked ¼,driving 11
15May92-10Pim fm 1⅛(T) :483 1:122 1:36 1:474 3↑ E T Dixie H-G3 8 6 67¼ 66 32 1½ Day P L 122 *1.00 96-11 SkyClassic122½FourstarsAllstar1162SocilRtr1121¾ Driving 10
1May92- 8CD fm 1⅛(T) :471 1:102 1:342 1:462 3↑ E T Turf Classic-G3 4 5 41¼ 31½ 2hd 2½ Day P LB 123 *1.60 103-00 Cudas117½SkyClassic1231½FourstarsAllstar118no 2nd best 12
22Apr92- 8Kee fm 1(T) :233 :464 1:112 1:362 4↑ Fort Harrod-G3 3 5 52¼ 61¼ 64 41½ Day P B 122 *1.10 95-05 Shudanz114nkTo Freedom113nkCudas1171 No late rally 9
2Nov91- 7CD fm 1½(T) :504 1:154 2:062 2:304 3↑ BC Turf-G1 1 1 1½ 1hd 2hd 44½ Day P B 126 3.30 91-06 Miss Alleged123½Itsallgreektome1262Quest for Fame1262 13
Pace,weakened
20Oct91- 8WO fm 1½(T) :482 1:123 2:03 2:274 3↑ Rothmans Int'l-G1 6 3 31½ 1½ 1hd 11 Day P 126 *.75e 101-05 Sky Classic1261Panoramic1261Tot of Rum126hd Driving 11
22Sep91- 8WO fm 1¼(T) :454 1:102 1:352 2:003 3↑ (R)Seagram Cup H-G3C 3 6 66 42¼ 3½ 11¾ Day P 122 *.90 97-06 Sky Classic1221¾(D)Izvestia1252½Karmani1191¼ Hand ride 7
21Jly91-10WO fm 1¼(T) :474 1:122 1:36 2:011 (R)Can Maturity-G1C 4 4 44¼ 3½ 11½ 11½ Walls MK 126 *.05e 94-12 SkyClassic1261½Secret'nClassy1262BrrBush1262½ Ridden out 5
16Jun91- 9WO fm 1⅛(T) :451 1:083 1:333 1:461 3↑ K Edward Gold Cup H-G3 7 6 65½ 43½ 1½ 14½ Day P 119 *.45e 93-07 SkyClassic1194½SlewofAngels1111¼Jalaajel116½ Hand ride 7
2Jun91- 8WO fm 1 1/16[T] :23 :46 1:093 1:411 4↑ (R)Connaught Cup-G3C 4 5 56 24½ 11½ 12½ Day P 115 *.65 98-07 SkyClassic1152½StormyGladitor1191½Grncus1172½ Hand ride 6
1May91- 8CD fm 1⅛(T) :481 1:122 1:372 1:491 3↑ Alw 27870 3 5 53¾ 63 2hd 13 Day P B 116 *1.20 99-01 Sky Classic1163Alaqua118hdSpark O'Dan1182¼ 9
Jostled 3/16,ridden out
14Apr91- 8Kee gd 1⅛(T) :494 1:143 1:384 1:511 4↑ Elkhorn-G2 6 1 1hd 1½ 21½ 63 Day P B 113 b 4.50 86-13 Itsallgreektome123¾Pirate Army113¾Spark O'Dan113¾ 7
Shied,misstep 3/16

16Mar91- 7GP fst 1 1/16 :232 :473 1:114 1:44 4↑ Alw 30500 8 8 84¼ 85¾ 87½ 87¾ Day P 112 5.70 85-13 Gun Deck113¾Rowdy Regl1121½Lucky Tent114½ Wide stretch 8
23Nov90- 8CD gd 1⅛ :474 1:12 1:373 1:503 3↑ Clark-G3 7 4 45 44½ 54 57½ Swatuk B LB 113 26.70 87-14 SecretHello1152Din'sDncr1194DRoch1211½ Never threatened 7
27Oct90- 8Bel gd 1½(T) :494 1:153 2:041 2:293 3↑ BC Turf-G1 3 3 2½ 109¼ 1116 1126¼ Hawley S 121 38.20 56-15 In the Wings126½With Approval1261½El Senor1262½ Used up 11
14Oct90- 7WO sf 1½(T) :50 1:151 2:082 2:344 3↑ Rothmans Int'l-G1 5 2 21½ 11 2½ 21¼ Hawley S 118 21.95 65-37 FrenchGlory1261¼SkyClassic1183Cozzene'sPrinc1181 Gamely 10
30Sep90- 9WO sf 1¼(T) :481 1:13 1:383 2:051 3↑ Niagara H-G3 9 3 3nk 1hd 1hd 65¼ Hawley S 115 b 3.45 69-26 Hodges Bay117noShellac116noSteady Power1152½ Tired 13
15Sep90- 9WO yl 1[T] :232 :47 1:112 1:373 Alw 28500 4 6 54½ 33 32½ 31½ Hawley S 119 *.45 84-18 Noble Concorde1141½Viking King115noSky Classic1197½ 6
Closed willingly
8Oct89- 7WO fst 1 1/16 :231 :47 1:122 1:46 Grey-G3 5 5 25 1½ 12½ 13½ Hawley S 122 *.35 79-21 Sky Classic1223½La Dolce Vita117¾Halo's Honey1133 7
Ducked in,handily
24Sep89- 8WO fm 1 1/16(T) :223 :45 1:101 1:422 [R]Cup & Saucer-G1C 11 8 64¼ 2hd 16 110 Hawley S 122 *.25 92-15 SkyClassic12210TruthSquad122hdFrenchKing1222½ Handily 11
10Sep89- 5WO fm 1[T] :23 :471 1:114 1:36 Summer-G3 2 9 84¾ 4¾ 11½ 15½ Hawley S 122 *1.20 97-09 SkyClassic1225½D'Parrot1224DestinationMoon122¾ Handily 11
23Aug89- 8WO fm *7f[T] :234 :473 1:14 1:261 Md Sp Wt 6 3 53¼ 52¾ 12 15 Hawley S 115 *.35 85-00 SkyClssc1155DestinationMoon120½VikingKng1201¼ Handily 10
22Jly89-10WO fst 6f :222 :45 1:101 [R]Vandal-G3C 3 6 42 21 21 2hd Hawley S 115 *.55 92-14 EverSteady122hdSkyClassic1155¾Halo'sHoney115¾ Game try 7
24Jun89- 9WO fst 5½f :224 :463 :59 1:06 [R]Clarendon-G3C 4 7 42 42 32 21¼ Hawley S 115 *.60 86-19 Ever Steady1171¼Sky Classic1152Briar Bush1178 Steadied 7

Smoke Glacken

gr/ro. c. 1994, by Two Punch (Mr. Prospector)–Majesty's Crown, by Magesterial **Lifetime record: 14 10 2 1 $759,560**
Own.– Karkenny & Levy & Roberts
Br.– Perry M. Rosebrock (Md)
Tr.– Henry L. Carroll

19Jly97-10Lrl fst 6f :223 :444 :57 1:092 3↑ De Francis Mem-G2 2 1 11 13½ 11½ 11½ Perret C L 113 *.40 97-15 SmokeGlackn1131½WiseDusty112hdCapoteBelle110¾ Driving 7
28Jun97- 3Mth fst 6f :213 :441 :554 1:082 Jersey Shore BC-G3 1 3 11 12 12½ 12½ Perret C L 122 *.10 100-12 SmkeGlckn1222½Prtnr'sHro1158¼KngBuck1157¾ Ridden out 4
7Jun97- 7Bel fst 7f :224 :453 1:083 1:204 Riva Ridge-G3 6 2 11 11½ 12 13¼ Perret C L 123 *.70 97-05 SmokeGlckn1223¼Trafalgr1231WldWondr120nk Kept to task 6
20Apr97- 8Kee fst 1 1/16 :23 :47 1:11 1:431 Lexington-G2 2 1 1½ 2½ 22 28½ Perret C L 118 *.70 83-08 Touch Gold1158½Smoke Glacken1183Deeds Not Words112¾ 5
Reared start,appeared rank,drifted out,1st turn,pace,2nd best
16Mar97- 9FG fst 1 1/16 :224 :453 1:101 1:423 La Derby-G3 8 1 13 12 12 3½ Perret C L 122 *.70 96-17 Crypto Star118hdStop Watch118½Smoke Glacken1223½ 9
Rank on lead,settled,clear drive,grudgingly
1Mar97- 9OP sly 1 :224 :47 1:123 1:383 Southwest-G3 6 1 12 12½ 14 18 Perret C L 117 *.60 86-27 Smoke Glackn1178PhantomonTour1223½AlwaysMyPlace1132½ 8
Slow to settle,ridden out
8Feb97- 9OP my 6f :224 :461 :591 1:114 Mountain Valley 53k 3 2 1½ 12 12 13½ Perret C L 119 *.10 82-24 Smoke Glacken1193½Prosong1161½Near the Bank1191¼ 5
Dueled,shook free
12Jan97- 9FG fst 6f :214 :45 :564 1:092 Black Gold H 41k 1 3 22½ 1½ 11 15½ Perret C L 122 *.50 97-10 Smoke Glacken1225¼TrufstSlew11414Auto Be a Hero111 3
Restrained,easily
15Sep96- 8Bel fst 1 :222 :45 1:101 1:351 Futurity-G1 7 3 3nk 1½ 34 514 Perret C 122 *.90 73-13 Traitor1225½NightinReno1226HarleyTune122½ Dueled wide 9
31Aug96- 8Sar fst 7f :213 :441 1:093 1:233 Hopeful-G1 6 1 2hd 11 15 19 Perret C 122 7.00 88-12 Smoke Glacken1229Ordway1222Gun Fight122¾ Kept to drive 8
17Aug96-11Mth fst 6f :211 :44 :563 1:101 Sapling-G2 4 7 2hd 1hd 11½ 11¾ Perret C 122 2.50 92-08 SmkeGlckn1221¾HarleyTun1224¾CountryRnbow122¾ Driving 10
28Jly96- 9Mth fst 5½f :22 :451 :574 1:043 Tyro 40k 1 4 2hd 2hd 2hd 11 Perret C 116 *.70 96-08 Smoke Glacken1161Johnny Legit1162¼Partner's Hero1163½ 9
Brushed stretch,driving
12Jly96- 8Mth fst 5½f :221 :452 :574 1:043 Md Sp Wt 3 1 11 12½ 19 18½ Mojica R Jr 118 *.80 96-15 SmokeGlackn1188½Mary'sSocialite1184½Fromsilvertogld1181¾ 7
Handily;Previously owned by William Roberts
30Jun96- 2Mth sly 5½f :214 :451 :582 1:052 Md Sp Wt 7 1 1hd 1½ 2hd 2½ Mojica R Jr 118 9.80 91-12 Confide118½SmokeGlackn1184¼CapturetheGold1185 Gamely 7

Soaring Softly

ch. f. 1995, by Kris S. (Roberto)–Wings of Grace, by Key to the Mint **Lifetime record: 16 9 1 3 $1,270,433**
Own.– Phillips Racing Partnership
Br.– Galbreath & Phillips Racing Partnership (Ky)
Tr.– James J. Toner

6Nov99- 7GP gd 1⅜(T) :491 1:14 1:383 2:134 3↑ (F)BC F&M Turf-G1 12 8 96 83¾ 31½ 1¾ Bailey JD L 123 *3.60 87-02 SorngSoftly123¾Cortt123hdZomrdh123hd 4 wide rally,up late 14
3Oct99- 6Bel fm 1¼[T] :504 1:15 1:383 2:012 3↑ (F)Flower Bowl H-G1 6 7 62 4½ 3nk 11 Bailey JD L 118 3.05 84-16 SorngSoftly1181Cortt118¾Mossflowr115½ 4w move,driving 7
5Sep99- 9Sar fm 1⅛(T) :473 1:112 1:342 1:454 3↑ (F)Diana H-G2 6 7 75 53 52¾ 53¾ Smith ME L 118 *2.10 97-07 Heritage of Gold1151Khumba Mela114nkMossflower114½ 9
3 wide move 2nd turn
17Jly99- 8Bel fm 1¼[T] :503 1:151 1:391 2:021 3↑ (F)New York H-G2 4 5 43 2½ 1hd 1no Smith ME L 117 *1.20 80-13 SorngSoftly117noTmpco116¾Angull119hd 3w turns,got nod 6
31May99- 9Bel fm 1⅜(T) :522 1:16 1:391 2:15 3↑ (F)Sheepshead Bay H-G2 4 2 41 44 14½ 15½ Smith ME L 114 2.90 80-19 Soaring Softly1145½Starry Dreamer114¾Pinafore Park1133¼ 6
Quick inside move
8May99- 8GS fm *1⅛(T) :473 1:123 1:371 1:49 3↑ (F)Vineland H 50k 3 3 38 33½ 2½ 13 Smith ME L 115 *1.00 100-13 Soaring Softly1153AbsolutelyQun1182HousVrgn1122 6
Control 3w drew off
17Apr99- 7Kee fm 1⅛(T) :472 1:111 1:353 1:482 4↑ (F)Alw 58500 4 8 87¼ 810 63½ 1½ Sellers SJ L 115 3.50 87-18 Soaring Softly115½Mocha Mocha1151Riotous Miss1151 9
Rail,hand urging
1Mar99- 8GP fm *1⅛(T) :503 1:144 1:393 1:511 4↑ (F)Alw 34000 8 8 73½ 75 2hd 11¼ Smith ME L 116 4.10 80-05 SorngSoftly1161¼MomntsOfMgc1161¾GurrEtPx118½ 9
4 wide,edged away
5Dec98- 6Aqu fst 1 1/16[•] :233 :482 1:124 1:453 3↑ (F)Alw 43000 4 4 51¾ 33½ 23½ 2¾ Gryder AT L 114 2.70 80-21 Light Bail116¾Soaring Softly1141½Global Star1161¼ 6
Finished strongly
20Nov98- 7Aqu fst 1 :233 :47 1:113 1:37 3↑ (F)Alw 43000 6 4 43½ 21½ 26 39¼ Gryder AT L 114 3.05 75-24 Santaria1148One Run Baby1141¼Soaring Softly1144½ 6
Wide move,weakened
1Nov98- 6Aqu fst 1 :243 :481 1:124 1:374 3↑ (F)Alw 43000 4 4 44 31½ 43 35 Gryder AT L 114 5.00 75-33 Christmas List1143Santaria1142Soaring Softly1141 5
Wide trip,no rally
27Jun98- 8Bel fst 1⅛ :454 1:10 1:342 1:473 (F)Mother Goose-G1 3 9 75 84½ 716 619½ Gryder AT L 121 28.00 72-16 Jersey Girl1211Keeper Hill1213Banshee Breeze1211 11
Between rivals,no rally
7Jun98- 8Bel fst 1 :223 :452 1:101 1:361 (F)Acorn-G1 9 7 85 75½ 45½ 44½ Davis RG L 121 38.50 78-22 JerseyGirl1212¾Santaria121noBraveDed1211¾ Belated rally 10
24Apr98- 5Kee fst *7f :214 :443 1:10 1:263 (F)Alw 43495 3 7 75¼ 64 2hd 12½ Sellers SJ L 119 *1.90 96-08 SorngSftly1192½JudthLynn119nkCuntoEs1221½ 4-wide,driving 9
11Nov97- 5Aqu wf 1 :223 :451 1:11 1:374 (F)Md Sp Wt 5 4 68½ 35 11 14 Smith ME 119 *2.10 81-20 SoaringSftly1194NewDircton1144GrtRspct1198½ Going away 9
18Oct97- 1Bel wf 7f :223 :453 1:093 1:22 (F)Md Sp Wt 4 5 65 53½ 34 310 Bravo J 119 5.20e 81-09 Azarba11910PrettyBlue119noSorngSoftly1192½ Rallied wide 7

Storm Song

b. f. 1994, by Summer Squall (Storm Bird)–Hum Along, by Fappiano **Lifetime record: 12 4 1 2 $1,020,050**

Own.– Dogwood Stable
Br.– W.S. Farish & O.M. Phipps (Ky)
Tr.– Nicholas P. Zito

31May97- 9Bel	fst 1	:221 :443 1:084 1:342	ⒻAcorn-G1	1 3 32 32½ 47 711¼	Bravo J	L 121	5.90	81-14	SharpCat1212½DixieFlag1214¾Ajn1211¼	Broke slowly,rushed	7
2May97- 9CD	fst 1⅛	:474 1:114 1:37 1:501	ⒻKy Oaks-G1	7 8 84¾ 65½ 57 49¾	Perret C	L 121	18.00	83-05	Blushing K.D.1212½Tomisue's Delight121¾[D] Sharp Cat1216½	5-wide bid,flattened out.Placed third after disqualification	9
5Apr97- 8Kee	fst 1 1/16	:232 :464 1:112 1:434	ⒻAshland-G1	5 4 36½ 36 38 38½	Perret C	L 121	4.80	80-22	GlttrWmn1216½Anklt1212StrmSng1216	No threat,best of rest	6
9Mar97- 10GP	fst 1 1/16	:231 :462 1:10 1:431	ⒻBonnie Miss-G2	1 4 44 411 515 522	Perret C	L 122	3.60	69-16	GlittrWoman1177¼SouthernPlaygirl119¾DixFlg1145	Stopped	5
9Feb97- 10GP	fst 1 70	:234 :47 1:101 1:391	ⒻDavona Dale-G3	4 4 47 44½ 49 514	Perret C	L 121	1.30	85-08	Glitter Woman1149City Band1214Southern Playgirl121¾	Lacked response	6
26Oct96- 4WO	fst 1 1/16	:223 :46 1:104 1:433	ⒻB C Juv Fillies-G1	4 7 65 53½ 1½ 14½	Perret C	L 119	*1.60	91-02	StormSng1194½LoveThtJzz1193¼CrtclFctor1194½	Ridden out	12
6Oct96- 8Bel	fst 1 1/16	:222 :451 1:093 1:422	ⒻFrizette-G1	6 3 33½ 31 11½ 14	Perret C	L 119	2.85	87-12	StormSong1194SharpCat1196Aldiza1196½	Well placed,clear	7
15Sep96- 7Bel	fst 1	:224 :452 1:10 1:36	ⒻMatron-G1	4 4 36 32 32 21	Perret C	119	6.50	82-13	SharpCat1191StormSng1192½FabulouslyFst1192	Steady gain	6
30Aug96- 8Sar	fst 7f	:221 :443 1:10 1:233	ⒻSpinaway-G1	6 5 52½ 54½ 77½ 610½	Day P	121	4.50	78-12	Oath121¾Pearl City121noFabulously Fast1219	No rally	9
12Aug96- 8Sar	fst 6½f	:214 :452 1:104 1:173	ⒻAdirondack-G2	9 2 53 51¾ 1hd 16	Day P	113	6.80	87-10	Storm Song1136Last Two States1131[DH] Larkwhistle116	Wide,going away	9
1Aug96- 4Sar	sly 6f	:22 :454 :582 1:114	ⒻAlw 38147	5 6 31½ 42½ 54 45¾	Day P	117	*.45e	76-13	LastTwoStts115¾Pntls1174Crodl1171	Bumped break,no rally	6
19Apr96- 3Kee	fst 4½f	:222 :453 :513	ⒻMd Sp Wt	6 5 41¼ 1hd 14	Day P	117	5.90	103-08	StormSong1174Dblo'sStory1172NaughtynHaughty1171¼	Ridden out,sharp	10

The Wicked North

ch. c. 1989, by Far North (Northern Dancer)–Wicked Witchcraft, by Good Behaving **Lifetime record: 17 8 4 1 $1,180,750**

Own.– Philip & Sophie Hersh Trust
Br.– Edward Zurek (Ky)
Tr.– David Bernstein

2Jly94- 3Hol	fst 1¼	:47 1:102 1:35 2:003	3↑ Hol Gold Cup H-G1	2 3 31½ 31½ 44½ 48¾	Dsrmeaux KJ	LB 122	*.60	85-08	Slew of Damascus117¾Fanmore116½Del Mar Dennis1167½	Drifted wide,gave way	5
5Jun94- 8Hol	fst 1⅛	:46 1:094 1:334 1:463	3↑ Californian-G1	1 2 21 32 31½ 1nk	Dsrmeaux KJ	LB 120	*.80	101-05	TheWickedNorth120nkKingdomFnd1161¾Slew ofDamscs1163½	Up final strides	7
16Apr94- 10OP	fst 1⅛	:463 1:101 1:352 1:474	4↑ Oaklawn H-G1	5 2 31 22 1hd 11½	Dsrmeaux KJ	L 119	*.90	99-16	TheWckdNrth1191½DevlHsDu120hdBrothrBrown116½	Driving	12
5Mar94- 5SA	fst 1¼	:472 1:112 1:352 2:00	4↑ S Anita H-G1	3 1 2½ 1hd 11½ 11½	Dsrmeaux KJ	LB 118	*1.80	95-07	[D]TheWickedNorth1181½Stuka1151¼BienBn120no	Came in 3/16. Disqualified and placed fourth;Previously owned by Philip Hersh	8
13Feb94- 8SA	fst 1⅛	:464 1:103 1:35 1:472	4↑ San Antonio H-G2	8 2 2hd 1½ 13 14½	Dsrmeaux KJ	LB 116	6.40	96-14	TheWickedNorth1164½[D]HillPass116½Region1174½	Big effort	9
8Jan94- 8SA	fst 7f	:22 :443 1:084 1:211	4↑ San Carlos H-G2	6 4 32 42 31½ 2¾	Solis A	LB 117	*1.10	95-07	Cardmania122¾ThWckdNrth1172½Portofrro1151	Outfinished	7
6Nov93- 9SA	fst 7f	:214 :441 1:082 1:204	3↑ Smile H 100k	7 4 22 31½ 21½ 23½	Smith ME	LB 117	*2.90	95-04	Memo1183½The Wicked North117hdIbero1201	No match late	12
23Oct93- 9Lrl	yl 1Ⓣ	:24 :48 1:124 1:38	3↑ D C Int'l-G1	3 1 1½ 2hd 41½ 79	Black CA	L 126	3.50	71-32	Buckhar1261½[D]Cleone126noMaryland Moon1262	Checked,in tight ⅛	8
6Sep93- 5BM	fm 1 1/16Ⓣ	:223 :46 1:101 1:414	3↑ San Fran H-G3	7 2 22 21 11½ 12½	Solis A	LB 114	3.20	101-01	TheWickedNrth1142½TheTenderTrack1172SlewofDamscs115¾	Held gamely	7
1Aug93- 8Dmr	fst 6f	:22 :444 :562 1:082	3↑ Bing Crosby H-G3	5 1 2hd 2hd 2hd 1hd	Black CA	LB 116	7.80	97-05	The Wicked North116hdThirty Slews1211Black Jack Road115½	Jumped track marks near 1/16,gamely	6
16Jan93- 8SA	sly 1⅛	:46 1:103 1:364 1:511	San Fernando-G2	5 2 21 21½ 26 39¾	Nakatani CS	LB 116	2.90	67-30	Bertrndo1209StarRecruit120¾TheWickdNrth1164	Weakened	8
26Dec92- 8SA	fst 7f	:222 :45 1:081 1:203	Malibu-G2	2 2 21 42 32½ 2½	Nakatani CS	LB 116	4.30	98-09	Star of the Crop118½The Wicked North116nkBertrando1205½	Late surge	11
21Nov92- 8Hol	fst 1 1/16	:23 :46 1:101 1:41	Laz Barrera H-G3	2 1 1hd 1hd 1hd 2nk	Dsrmeaux KJ	LB 116	*1.20	96-09	Star Recruit117nkThe Wicked North116½Lottery Winner115no	Game try	7
8Nov92- 7SA	fst 1	:23 :461 1:102 1:354	3↑ Alw 36000	5 1 2hd 1hd 11½ 13	Dsrmeaux KJ	LB 115	*1.10	88-17	The Wicked North1153Double O'Slew1153½Desert Sun1164	Driving	8
9Oct92- 7SA	fst 1	:23 :462 1:101 1:352	Alw 32000	2 1 1½ 12½ 12½ 12½	Dsrmeaux KJ	LB 117	2.20	90-18	The Wicked North1172½So EverClever117½Turbulent Kris1201	Ridden out	9
7Sep92- 6Dmr	fst 6½f	:214 :443 1:09 1:152	3↑ Md Sp Wt	3 4 1hd 1½ 14 15	Dsrmeaux KJ	LB 118	3.30	96-09	TheWickdNrth1185Penningtn1185Compeii118nk	Ridden out	12
22Dec91- 9Hol	fst 6½f	:213 :443 1:10 1:164	Md Sp Wt	2 9 812 812 67¼ 65¾	Pincay L Jr	118 b	15.00	82-09	Saron Lake1181¼Play Ten1181Treekster118nk	Broke slowly	9

Thunder Gulch

ch. c. 1992, by Gulch (Mr. Prospector)–Line of Thunder, by Storm Bird **Lifetime record: 16 9 2 2 $2,915,086**

Own.– Michael Tabor
Br.– Peter M. Brant (Ky)
Tr.– D. Wayne Lukas

7Oct95- 10Bel	wf 1¼	:48 1:112 1:36 2:011	3↑ JC Gold Cup-G1	4 2 21 45 49½ 514	Stevens GL	121 b	3.05	74-14	Cigar1261UnaccountedFor1269¾StrStndrd1212	Stalked,tired	7
23Sep95- 10TP	fst 1⅛	:473 1:114 1:364 1:492	3↑ Ky Cup Classic 396k	5 5 43 4½ 2hd 11	Stevens GL	121 b	*.20	96-15	Thunder Gulch1211Judge T C1121½Bound by Honor1138	Leaned in,bumped start,brushed ⅝,hard drive	6
19Aug95- 8Sar	fst 1¼	:471 1:112 1:371 2:033	Travers-G1	5 4 42 1hd 1½ 14½	Stevens GL	126 b	*.75	86-22	Thunder Gulch1264½Pyramid Peak1262Malthus1262½	Broke in air,wide,going away	7
23Jly95- 8Hol	fst 1⅛	:462 1:101 1:353 1:49	Swaps-G2	4 2 2½ 21 1hd 12	Stevens GL	B 126 b	*.90	88-09	Thunder Gulch1262Da Hoss118¾Petionville120¾	Gamely	7
10Jun95- 9Bel	fst 1½	:501 1:151 2:052 2:32	Belmont-G1	10 3 2½ 2½ 1hd 12	Stevens GL	126 b	*1.50	70-25	Thunder Gulch1262Star Standard1263½Citadeed1261½	3 or 4 wide,driving,clear	11
20May95- 10Pim	fst 1 3/16	:471 1:104 1:352 1:542	Preakness-G1	11 5 53½ 54 4¾ 3¾	Stevens GL	126 b	3.80	101-08	Timber Country126½Oliver's Twist126nkThunder Gulch1264	Wide bid,good try	11
6May95- 8CD	fst 1¼	:454 1:101 1:353 2:011	Kentucky Derby-G1	16 6 54 3nk 11½ 12¼	Stevens GL	126 b	24.50	106-00	Thunder Gulch1262¼Tejano Run126hdTimber Country126¾	4-wide,stiff drive	19
15Apr95- 7Kee	fst 1⅛	:49 1:131 1:372 1:491	Blue Grass-G2	4 3 31 3½ 42 44½	Day P	121 b	*1.30	83-13	Wild Syn1212½Suave Prospect121hdTejano Run1212	Leaned in,bumped 1st turn,came up empty	6
11Mar95- 10GP	fst 1⅛	:471 1:113 1:362 1:493	Florida Derby-G1	7 3 31½ 2hd 21½ 1no	Smith ME	122 b	2.00	89-11	Thunder Gulch122noSuave Prospect1225Mecke1222	Forced outward deep str,fully extended	10
18Feb95- 9GP	fst 1 1/16	:231 :464 1:11 1:431	Fountain of Youth-G2	9 7 51¾ 3nk 1hd 1nk	Smith ME	119 b	4.70	92-16	Thunder Gulch119nkSuave Prospect1174Jambalaya Jazz1193½	Wide backstr,seven wide top str,fully extended	12
18Dec94- 8Hol	fst 1 1/16	:224 :46 1:093 1:403	Hollywood Futurity-G1	1 4 47 47 35 26½	Nakatani CS	B 121 b	3.80	91-04	Afternoon Deelites1216½Thunder Gulch12110A.J. Jett121½	Second best	5
26Nov94- 7Aqu	fst 1⅛	:481 1:14 1:402 1:534	Remsen-G2	9 7 74½ 41¾ 21 1nk	Stevens GL	115	5.60	67-28	Thunder Gulch115nkWestern Echo1193Mighty Magee114¾	Previously owned by K.E. Ellenberg & Mutual Shar Stable;previously trained by John C. Kimmel	10
11Nov94- 8Aqu	fst 1	:23 :461 1:111 1:372	Nashua-G3	6 5 43 42 43½ 44¾	Bailey JD	112	*1.35	76-21	Devious Course1142Mighty Magee1122¾Old Tascosa122no	Saved ground	7

23Oct94- 8Aqu	my 7f	:22² :45⁴ 1:11¹ 1:24³	Cowdin-G2	4 5 66½ 65 33½ 22½	Velazquez J R	122	4.40	78-19	Old Tascosa122²½Thunder Gulch122¹½AdamsTrail122²¼		8

Up for place

| 4Oct94- 3Bel | fst 6f | :22⁴ :46³ :58³ 1:11 | Md Sp Wt | 4 3 73¾ 31 31 1no | Velazquez J R | 118 | *1.00 | 86-14 | ThundrGulch118noPorphyry118½LstEffort118¹½ | Wide,driving | 9 |

Previously owned by Mutual Shar Stable

| 16Sep94- 3Bel | fst 6f | :22⁴ :46³ :58⁴ 1:11¹ | Md Sp Wt | 2 2 42½ 41½ 31 3nk | Velazquez J R | 118 | 6.50 | 85-10 | Crusader's Story118noPorphyry118nkThunder Gulch118¹½ | | 8 |

Took up,hit rail ⅛ pl

Tight Spot

b. c. 1987, by His Majesty (Ribot)–Premium Win, by Lyphard

Own.–Anderson & VHW Stable & Whitham

Br.– Verne H. Winchell (Ky)

Tr.– Ronald McAnally

Lifetime record: 21 12 3 1 $1,566,100

16Aug92- 8Dmr	fm 1⅛Ⓣ	:47⁴ 1:11¹ 1:35² 1:47¹ 3↑	Eddie Read H-G1	2 2 1hd 2hd 31 44	Pincay L Jr	LB 125	*1.50	96-02	Marquetry118noLuthirEnchntur116hdLgrCt115⁴	Saved ground	7
21Mar92- 8GG	fm 1⅛Ⓣ	:23⁴ :47¹ 1:10⁴ 1:35² 3↑	S F Mile H-G3	1 1 11½ 1½ 1hd 1nk	Pincay L Jr	LB 125	*.80	101-03	Tight Spot125nkNotorious Pleasure116½Forty Niner Days116¹		9
28Feb92- 8SA	fm 1Ⓣ	:23 :45³ 1:09² 1:33² 4↑	Alw 55000	5 1 11 13 13 11½	Pincay L Jr	LB 121	*.60	96-04	Tight Spot121¹½Laxey Bay116noEton Lad114¾	Ridden out	6
2Nov91- 5CD	fm 1Ⓣ	:24 :48 1:12² 1:37² 3↑	BC Mile-G1	12 7 31 2hd 51¼ 96↓	Pincay L Jr	LB 126	2.80	91-06	Opening Verse126¹½Val des Bois126noStar of Cozzene123²¼		14

Dueled,tired

1Sep91- 9AP	fm 1¼Ⓣ	:47³ 1:11¹ 1:35⁴ 1:59² 3↑	Arl Million-G1	7 3 21½ 21 2½ 1hd	Pincay L Jr	L 126	*1.80	101-07	Tight Spot126hdAlgenib122nkKartajana123nk	All out	10
11Aug91- 8Dmr	fm 1⅛Ⓣ	:47² 1:11² 1:35¹ 1:47¹ 3↑	Eddie Read H-G1	7 1 13½ 11½ 12½ 13½	Pincay L Jr	LB 125	*1.10	102-02	TightSpot125³½ValdesBois115nkMadjarist116nk	Ridden out	7
4Jly91- 8Hol	fm 1⅛Ⓣ	:47² 1:10² 1:34¹ 1:46 3↑	American H-G2	1 1 11½ 11½ 11½ 11	Pincay L Jr	LB 123	*1.70	100-08	Tight Spot123¹Exbourne122½Super May118½	Ridden out	8
8Jun91- 8Hol	fm 1¹⁄₁₆Ⓣ	:24¹ :47³ 1:11 1:40¹ 3↑	Inglewood H-G2	3 1 12½ 13 14 14½	Pincay L Jr	LB 121	*.80	94-07	TightSpot121⁴½Somethingdifferent116hdRzn114no	Ridden out	8
8May91- 8Hol	fm 1Ⓣ	:47 1:10¹ 1:33² 1:44⁴ 4↑	Alw 50000	2 1 11½ 11½ 11 11	Pincay L Jr	LB 117	*1.40	106-01	Tight Spot117noHigh Rank115⁵Tarsho114¹½	Held gamely	5
19Aug90- 8Dmr	fm 1⅛Ⓣ	:48³ 1:13¹ 1:37¹ 1:49³	Dmr Derby-G2	9 1 11½ 11½ 12½ 13	Pincay L Jr	LB 122	*1.10e	90-08	Ⓓ TightSpot122³Itsallgrektom122¹²½Prdcssor122²½	Came over	10

Disqualified and placed 10th - ruling rescinded 9/26/90

5Aug90- 8Dmr	fm 1¹⁄₁₆Ⓣ	:24¹ :48 1:11² 1:41⁴	La Jolla H-G3	6 2 2½ 2hd 12 1no	Delhoussaye E	L 118	2.30	98-04	Tight Spot118noItsallgrktom119⁴MuscProspctor118¹	Driving	6
22Jun90- 7Hol	fm 1Ⓣ	:23⁴ :47² 1:11² 1:41³	Ⓡ Star Dust 79k	5 1 1½ 1½ 11½ 12	Delahoussaye E	117	2.60	87-15	TightSpot117²Predecessor114hdKeptHisCool112no	Driving	7
21Apr90- 8GG	fst 1⅛	:44⁴ 1:08³ 1:34 1:46⁴	Cal Derby-G3	9 4 42 43½ 49½ 413¾	Black C A	115	2.70	77-14	StalwartCharger115²⁴MusicPrspctr117³⁴Tsu'sDawning117³½		12

Evenly

31Mar90- 10TP	my 1⅛	:46³ 1:11² 1:37² 1:49²	Jim Beam-G2	10 3 2hd 2½ 48 518	Black C A	121	4.50	80-20	Summer Squall121²½Bright Again121⁸Yonder121⁶	Gave way	10
3Mar90- 8SA	fst 1	:23 :46⁴ 1:11¹ 1:36³	San Rafael-G2	7 2 21½ 21 22½ 22½	Black C A	115	13.70	81-22	MisterFrisky115²½TightSpot115²LandRsh115⁶½	Good effort	7
28Jan90- 8GG	fst 1	:22² :45³ 1:09⁴ 1:34	El Cerrito H 53k	1 2 3½ 2hd 11 12½	Hansen R D	115	4.70	95-14	TightSpot115²½MuchDivorced116½DragRace119⁷	Hard ridden	6
17Dec89- 3Hol	fst 1¹⁄₁₆	:23¹ :47² 1:12 1:43²	Md Sp Wt	6 1 11 1½ 12½ 17	Delahoussaye E	117	*.70	83-14	TightSpot117⁷Carrie'sGlory117¾HawaiianPass117¹	Easily	7
26Nov89- 2Hol	gd 1¹⁄₁₆	:23³ :47¹ 1:11⁴ 1:43⁴	Md Sp Wt	4 1 1½ 1hd 1hd 24	Delahoussaye E	117	3.80	77-21	AssyrianPirate117⁴TightSpot117hdRiflemaker117⁴	Weakened	8
12Nov89- 4SA	fst 1	:23¹ :47 1:12¹ 1:42²	Md Sp Wt	4 1 1½ 2hd 22½ 22½	Baze R A	118	3.30	82-14	LandRush118⁴Riflemaker118⁵½TightSpot118¹	Weakened	8
14Oct89- 4SA	fst 6½f	:22 :45¹ 1:10³ 1:17	Md Sp Wt	2 1 2hd 1hd 2½ 2²	Baze R A	117	*1.70	83-15	ElToreo117²TightSpot117⁴GoodFieldNoHit117⁵	Held place	6
9Sep89- 6Dmr	fst 6f	:22 :45² :57² 1:09¹	Md Sp Wt	8 4 21 3½ 66 712½	Solis A	117	10.00	79-11	Grand Canyon117²½Jet West117¹¾Pleasant Tap117⁴	Wide	9

Timber Country

ch. c. 1992, by Woodman (Mr. Prospector)–Fall Aspen, by Pretense

Own.– Gainesway Stable & Overbrook Farm & Lewis

Br.– Lowquest Ltd (Ky)

Tr.– D. Wayne Lukas

Lifetime record: 12 5 1 4 $1,560,400

| 20May95- 10Pim | fst 1³⁄₁₆ | :47¹ 1:10⁴ 1:35² 1:54² | Preakness-G1 | 7 6 64¾ 66 3½ 1½ | Day P | 126 | *1.90 | 102-08 | Timber Country126½Oliver's Twist126nkThunder Gulch126⁴ | | 11 |

Wide bid,driving

| 6May95- 8CD | fst 1¼ | :45⁴ 1:10¹ 1:35³ 2:01¹ | Kentucky Derby-G1 | 15 14 13¹² 11 15½ 10⁵¾ 32½ | Day P | 126 | *3.40e | 104-00 | Thunder Gulch126²½Tejano Run126hdTimber Country126¾ | | 19 |

Angled in between horses,gamely

| 8Apr95- 5SA | fst 1⅛ | :46² 1:10 1:34⁴ 1:47⁴ | Santa Anita Derby-G1 | 8 6 64 66¼ 35½ 41½ | Day P | B 122 | 1.80 | 93-07 | Larry the Legend122hdAfternoon Deelites122nkJumron122¹ | | 8 |

Steady late gain

| 19Mar95- 5SA | fst 1¹⁄₁₆ | :23 :46³ 1:10¹ 1:42 | San Felipe-G2 | 3 4 42 42 22 21 | Day P | B 122 | 2.20 | 84-17 | Afternoon Deelites119¹Timber Country122²Lake George116¹⁴ | | 4 |

Slow late gain

| 4Mar95- 5SA | gd 1 | :24 :48⁴ 1:13¹ 1:37³ | San Rafael-G2 | 2 5 52¾ 53¼ 32 32 | Day P | B 121 | *.70 | 79-27 | Larry theLegend118¹FandarelDancr118¹TimberCountry121³½ | | 5 |

Good effort

| 5Nov94- 8CD | fst 1¹⁄₁₆ | :23¹ :47 1:12³ 1:44² | B C Juvenile-G1 | 7 9 73½ 41¼ 1½ 12 | Day P | 122 | *2.40 | 92-07 | Timber Country122²Eltish122³Tejano Run122¹¼ | | 13 |

Checked 1st turn,steadied ⅝,ridden out

| 8Oct94- 8Bel | fst 1¹⁄₁₆ | :23² :46¹ 1:11¹ 1:44 | Champagne-G1 | 10 1 3nk 1hd 1hd 1½ | Day P | 122 | 3.70 | 82-17 | Timber Country122½Sierra Diablo126²½On Target122nk | | 11 |

Stumbled break,wide drive

14Sep94- 8Dmr	fst 7f	:21³ :44 1:09³ 1:22¹	Del Mar Futurity-G2	5 7 8¹¹ 7¹⁰ 32½ 31	Nakatani C S	B 119	6.00	91-10	On Target115½Supremo115½TimberCountry119¹⁰	Good effort	9
24Aug94- 8Dmr	fst 6½f	:22¹ :45 1:10 1:16³	Balboa-G3	7 4 52½ 53¾ 31½ 1nk	Solis A	B 117	8.40	88-12	TmbrCountry117nkDsrtMrg115nkSuprmo117⁴	5 wide into lane	7
6Aug94- 6Dmr	fst 6½f	:22 :45¹ 1:10¹ 1:16³	Md Sp Wt	5 5 42½ 31½ 3½ 1½	Solis A	B 117	*1.00e	88-08	Tmbr Cntry117½Dgrs Scnrio117³Tac Sqd117²½	Inside rally	9
2Jly94- 10CD	fst 6f	:21¹ :45¹ :57² 1:10¹	Bashford Manor-G3	13 10 8⁴½ 54¼ 68 6⁹	Pincay L Jr	117	*1.60e	86-09	Hyroglyphic116⁶Boone'sMll116¹Hobgobln116nk	Lacked rally	13
2Jun94- 5Hol	fst 5f	:22 :45¹ :57³	Md Sp Wt	4 6 7⁶ 76½ 65 36¼	McCarron C J	B 117	9.90	90-03	Aponus All117¹½Seattle Saint117⁵Timber Country117nk	Wide	8

Unbridled

b. c. 1987, by Fappiano (Mr. Prospector)–Gana Facil, by Le Fabuleux

Own.– Frances A. Genter Stable Inc

Br.– Tartan Farms Corp (Fla)

Tr.– Carl A. Nafzger

Lifetime record: 24 8 6 6 $4,489,475

| 2Nov91- 8CD | fst 1¼ | :48² 1:12³ 1:38 2:02⁴ 3↑ | BC Classic-G1 | 7 11 10¹⁶ 85¾ 45½ 33¾ | Perret C | LB 126 | 4.30 | 92-09 | Black Tie Affair126¹¼Twilight Agenda126²½Unbridled126nk | | 11 |

Mild rally

6Oct91- 8Kee	fst 1⅛	:47² 1:11² 1:36 1:48⁴ 3↑	Fayette H-G2	1 5 56½ 43½ 31½ 23	Perret C	LB 122	1.90	88-17	SummrSquall122³Unbridled122²½SecrtHllo115¹¾	Veered out	5
10Aug91- 3Dmr	fst 1¼	:45⁴ 1:09⁴ 1:34¹ 1:59⁴ 3↑	Pacific Classic 1000k	8 7 79 56 44½ 33¾	Perret C	LB 124	6.20	--	Best Pal116¹Twilight Agenda124²½Unbridled124¹½	Came on	9
3Aug91- 5AP	fst 7f	:22³ :44⁴ 1:08⁴ 1:21 3↑	Alw 25500	2 6 610 610 25 16½	Day P	L 122	*.40e	98-12	Unbridled122⁶½SpnshDrummr119¹½Prfcton117³	Strong finish	7
11May91- 9Pim	fst 1¼	:46⁴ 1:10 1:34¹ 1:52² 4↑	Pim Spl H-G1	4 5 510 57½ 610 610	Perret C	L 122	2.40	93-13	FarmaWay119³SmmrSqll120²½Jol'sHlo119nk	Weakened,bled	7
13Apr91- 8OP	sly 1⅛	:46³ 1:10⁴ 1:35⁴ 1:48 4↑	Oaklawn H-G1	5 8 8¹⁵ 8¹⁵ 75³ 56	Day P	L 124	2.00	89-03	Festin115¾Primal115³½Jolie's Halo120¹	Belated rally	8
16Mar91- 8OP	fst 7f	:22 :44² 1:09¹ 1:21⁴ 4↑	Deputy Minister H 50k	4 9 814 814 34 1½	Day P	L 119	3.10	97-07	Unbridled119³Housebuster122noShuttleman114⁵	Ridden out	9
27Oct90- 9Bel	fst 1¼	:45⁴ 1:09⁴ 1:35³ 2:02¹ 3↑	BC Classic-G1	14 13 13¹¹ 96¾ 32½ 11	Day P	121	6.60e	86-15	Unbridled121¹IbnBey126¹ThirtySixRed121no	Strong drive	14
23Sep90- 10LaD	fst 1¼	:46² 1:11¹ 1:36¹ 2:02	Super Derby-G1	9 9 94¾ 32 43½ 23½	Velez J A Jr	L 126	*.90	102-00	HomeatLast126²½Unbridled126nkCee'sTzzy126¹	Six wide ⅜	9
3Sep90- 8AP	fm 1¼Ⓣ	:49¹ 1:13¹ 1:37² 2:01³	Secretariat-G1	4 7 75¾ 63½ 3nk 2¾	Fires E	L 126	*.50e	103-03	SuperAbound114¾Unbridld126¹½SuperFan117¾	Brushed start	8
18Aug90- 4AP	fst 1	:22⁴ :45¹ 1:09² 1:34² 3↑	Alw 23500	1 4 42 21 13 11¹½	Fires E	L 112	*.30	99-12	Unbridled112¹¹Lampkin Cache116½Remington's Pride119⁴	Much the best	8
9Jun90- 8Bel	gd 1½	:48 1:12¹ 2:01⁴ 2:27¹	Belmont-G1	5 6 42½ 44½ 46 412¾	Perret C	126	*1.10	81-13	GoandGo126⁸¹ThirtySixRd126²BrondVux126²½	Bid wide,tired	9
19May90- 1Pim	fst 1³⁄₁₆	:47 1:10⁴ 1:35³ 1:53³	Preakness-G1	6 9 87½ 54 2hd 22½	Perret C	126	*1.70	96-12	SmmrSquall126²Unbrdld126⁹MstrFrsky126¾	Best of others	9
5May90- 8CD	gd 1¼	:46 1:11 1:37³ 2:02	Ky Derby-G1	8 11 12¹⁴ 2½ 11 13½	Perret C	126	10.80	101-00	Unbrdld126³½SummrSquall126⁴PlsntTp126³	Tight st.,driving	15

14Apr90- 8Kee my 1⅛ :474 1:121 1:351 1:483 Blue Grass-G2 4 5 52 41¾ 31½ 33¾ Perret C 121 4.10 87-10 SmmerSquall1211¾LandRush1212Unbridld1213 Flattened out 5

17Mar90-10GP fst 1⅛ :482 1:123 1:39 1:52 Florida Derby-G1 4 5 42 41¾ 31 14 Day P 122 2.50 77-22 Unbridled1224Slavic122nkRunTurn1221 Brushed str,driving 9

3Mar90-10GP fst 1 1/16 :232 :473 1:122 1:443 Fountain of Youth-G2 5 10 127 99¼ 51¾ 3½ Day P 117 7.60e 87-24 Shot Gun Scott122½Smelly119noUnbridled117¾ Lacked room 13

14Jan90-10Crc fst 1⅛ :483 1:131 1:384 1:522 Trop Park Derby-G3 4 3 32 32½ 43½ 55¾ Perret C 119 *1.30 91-11 Run Turn1174¼Country Day112hdShot Gun Scott119½ Tired 8

24Dec89-10Crc fst 1 1/16 :233 :481 1:131 1:451 What a Pleasure 56k 9 8 85½ 74¼ 2hd 15 Velez JA Jr 112 *1.50 96-11 Unbridled1125Fiery Best1172½Alwys Rng115nkBumped,drew clear 10

22Oct89-10Crc fst 1 1/16 :25 :494 1:143 1:473 ⓇIn Reality (FSS) 450k 4 10 85¼ 54¼ 32 22¾ Velez JA Jr 120 5.20 81-19 Shot Gun Scott1202¾Unbridled120¾Swedaus1203½ Rallied 14

24Sep89- 9Cby fst 1 :231 :461 1:11 1:371 Cby Juvenile 150k 1 4 74½ 42½ 2½ 2½ Smith ME 120 5.20e 89-15 Appealing Breeze120½Unbridled1204½Table Limit1203½ Hung 7

13Sep89- 8AP sly 7f :223 :461 1:112 1:24 Arch Ward 37k 1 5 54½ 54 312 319¾ Smith ME 115 3.30 62-31 Karen'sTom1122¾SecretHello12217Unbridld1157½ No threat 5

23Aug89- 8AP fst 6½f :221 :45 1:104 1:171 Waukegan BC 55k 7 7 79½ 613 38½ 37 Smith ME 116 *1.10 82-21 SecretHello1165Karen'sTom1132Unbridld1161¼ Broke inside 8

2Aug89- 4AP fst 6f :223 :461 1:113 Md Sp Wt 10 11 64¾ 11½ 17 110½ Smith ME 122 *3.10 82-20 Unbrdld12210½SoundofCannons122½HomeatLast122nk Easily 12

Victory Gallop

b. c. 1995, by Cryptoclearance (Fappiano)–Victorious Lil, by Vice Regent **Lifetime record: 17 9 5 1 $3,505,895**

Own.– Prestonwood Farm Inc

Br.– Tall Oaks Farm (Ont)

Tr.– W. Elliott Walden

1Aug99- 9Sar fst 1⅛ :47 1:104 1:36 1:483 3↑ Whitney H-G1 2 7 810 65¾ 2hd 1no Bailey JD L 123 *.90e 93-07 VictoryGllop123noBhrns12312Ctnus1133 Quick outside move 8

12Jun99- 9CD fst 1⅛ :464 1:11 1:352 1:471 3↑ S Foster H-G2 1 7 711 76¼ 11½ 15 Bailey JD L 120 *1.30e 107-03 Victory Gallop1205Nite Dreamer110¾Littlebitlively1152¾ 7
Hand urging,sharp

28Mar99♦ NadAlShba(UAE) fst*1¼LH 2:003 4↑ Dubai World Cup-G1 Stk5000000 31½ Bailey JD 126 - Almutawakel126¾Malek126¾Victory Gallop1261½ 8
Tracked in 4th,wide bid 1½f out,hung.Silver Charm 6th

3Mar99- 3GP fst 1 1/16 :25 :483 1:123 1:434 4↑ Alw 44000 1 5 42½ 41¼ 11 12¾ Bailey JD L 119 *.30 88-28 Victory Gallop1192¾Delay of Game119¾Dancing Guy1155¾ 5
Steady hand ride

7Nov98-10CD fst 1¼ :473 1:12 1:371 2:02 3↑ BC Classic-G1 1 10 1013 85¼ 51¾ 41 Solis A L 122 7.50 94-07 Awesome Again126¾Silver Charm126nkSwain126no 10
Strong rally between

29Aug98- 9Sar fst 1¼ :484 1:13 1:372 2:032 Travers-G1 7 5 52½ 32 31½ 2no Solis A L 126 *1.20 91-09 Coronado'sQuest126noVictoryGallp126noRaffie'sMajesty1265 7
Wide,finished fast

9Aug98-11Mth fst 1⅛ :47 1:104 1:353 1:483 Haskell Inv H-G1 5 5 58½ 45 33 21¼ Stevens GL L 125 1.20 94-13 Coronado's Quest1241¼Victory Gallop125½Grand Slam1188¼ 6
Rallied inside turn,checked behind winner late

6Jun98- 9Bel fst 1½ :483 1:132 2:024 2:29 Belmont-G1 9 10 97 57½ 24 1no Stevens GL L 126 4.50 99-09 VctoryGllp126noRlQut1266ThomsJo1261¼ Hard drive,gamely 11

16May98-10Pim fst 1 3/16 :462 1:11 1:354 1:543 Preakness-G1 9 7 89¼ 4¾ 2½ 22¼ Stevens GL L 126 *2.00 90-13 Real Quiet1262¼Victory Gallop126¾Classic Cat1263¾ 10
Wide far turn,gamely

2May98- 8CD fst 1¼ :453 1:103 1:353 2:021 Ky Derby-G1 13 14 1516 75½ 33½ 2½ Solis A L 126 14.60 93-02 Real Quiet126½Victory Gallop1262¼Indian Charlie126hd 15
6 wide,strong finish

11Apr98- 9OP fst 1⅛ :46 1:104 1:372 1:494 Ark Derby-G2 5 7 88¾ 85¼ 21 1hd Solis A L 122 7.80 87-10 VictoryGallop122hdHanumanHighway118hdFavoriteTrick1223 9
Waited ¼,angled out,brushed foe 3/16,willingly three wide

21Mar98- 9OP fst 1 1/16 :231 :473 1:131 1:443 Rebel-G3 7 4 53 31 1hd 1hd Coa EM L 119 4.10 85-24 Victory Gallop119hdRobinwould1146Whataflashyactor114¾ 10
3w bid,lost whip 3/16,came in,bumped foe ⅛,brushed late,game;Previously owned by Speriamo Stable;previously trained by Mary E. Eppler

1Nov97-10Lrl sly 1⅛ :49 1:141 1:40 1:533 Laurel Futurity-G3 3 4 45 44½ 33½ 21¾ Johnston MT L 122 *1.40 68-35 Fight for M'Lady1221¾Victory Gallop122½Essential1229½ 6
Circled,rallied

11Oct97- 9Cnl fst 1 :22 :444 1:101 1:364 Chenery 100k 5 6 66¼ 43½ 31½ 1¾ Johnston MT L 119 1.80 93-00 Victory Gallop119¾Fight for M'Lady1153½PersonalFv1193¼ 8
Swung wide ¼,driving

1Sep97- 9Cnl fst 7f :222 :451 1:093 1:223 New Kent 54k 3 4 52½ 55 21 12 Johnston MT L 114 8.90 - - Victory Gallop1142Unreal Madness1205Luisita's Choice1142½ 6
Bumped start,4-wide bid,strong handling

2Aug97- 1Lrl fst 7f :232 :481 1:141 1:264 Md Sp Wt 8 4 1hd 1hd 15 18¾ Prado ES L 120 1.90 75-17 VictoryGallop1208¾Essential1205¼DoIEver120nk Ridden out 8

20Jly97- 1Del fst 5f :23 :472 :593 Md Sp Wt 8 5 84½ 76¼ 78 59¾ McCarthy MJ 118 5.20 76-20 Carreras1184¾He's a Charm1184½Duck Grayson118nk Outrun 8

Wandesta (GB)

ch. f. 1991, by Nashwan (Blushing Groom)–De Stael, by Nijinsky II **Lifetime record: 21 7 3 5 $1,255,283**

Own.– Juddmonte Farms Inc

Br.– Juddmonte Farms Inc (GB)

Tr.– Robert Frankel

1Dec96- 7Hol fm 1¼Ⓣ :49 1:131 1:364 2:00 3↑ ⒻMatriarch-G1 12 8 85½ 73½ 42½ 1½ Nakatani CS LB 123 5.70 88-10 Wandsta123½Windsharp1231¾MemoriesofSlvr120¾ Wide rally 12

3Nov96- 5SA fm 1¼Ⓣ :491 1:133 1:364 2:003 3↑ ⒻYellow Ribbon-G1 1 8 88 63¾ 62¾ 52 Nakatani CS LB 122 *.90 93-07 Donna Viola122½Real Connection122hdDixie Pearl122nk 8
Blocked on rail ¼ to past 1/16

13Oct96- 5SA fm 1⅛Ⓣ :48 1:12 1:353 1:463 3↑ ⒻLas Palmas H-G2 1 4 44 32 12½ 12 Nakatani CS LB 120 *1.00 97-03 Wndst1202RlConncton1131¾Alprd1204½ Rail trip,ridden out 5

20Apr96- 5SA fm 1¼Ⓣ :49 1:14 1:374 2:02 4↑ ⒻSanta Barbara H-G2 4 4 32½ 32½ 32 35½ Nakatani CS LB 121 *.80 82-12 Auriette1163½Angel in My Heart1192Wandesta1217½ 5
Forced out,squeezed after start,bumped hard,forced out past ⅜

24Mar96- 5SA fm 1½Ⓣ :481 1:121 2:023 2:274 4↑ San Luis Rey-G1 2 6 74½ 53¾ 2½ 2nk Nakatani CS LB 117 *2.10 80-20 Windsharp117nkWandesta1172¼Silver Wizard1224 7
Bumped,blocked,came through tight quarters ⅛,led 1 1/16,gamely

19Feb96- 8SA gd *1½Ⓣ :49 1:143 2:05 2:301 4↑ San Luis Obispo H-G2 4 5 31 2½ 11 2¾ Nakatani CS LB 114 4.20 86-13 Windsharp115¾Wandesta1142¾Virginia Carnival115hd 6
Tracked leaders,bid,led,outfinished

14Jan96- 8SA fm 1⅛Ⓣ :484 1:122 1:363 1:49 4↑ ⒻSan Gorgonio H-G2 4 5 44 43 1½ 13 Nakatani CS L 119 2.60 85-15 Wandesta1193Matiara1182½YearlyTour1171½ Strong handling 6

26Nov95- 6Hol fm 1¼Ⓣ :493 1:132 1:363 2:001 3↑ ⒻMatriarch-G1 10 6 84¼ 105 104¼ 31¼ Nakatani CS L 123 6.50e 86-10 Duda1231Angel in My Heart120nkWandesta123no Wide rally 14

12Nov95- 8SA fm 1¼Ⓣ :471 1:122 1:372 2:013 3↑ ⒻYellow Ribbon Inv-G1 9 7 75¼ 94½ 54 64½ Nakatani CS LB 122 *2.80e 78-18 Alpride122½Angel in My Heart118hdBold Ruritana1221¼ 12
Rail trip,awaited room 2nd turn

23Jly95- 7Hol fst 1⅛ :461 1:103 1:353 1:481 3↑ ⒻVanity H-G1 1 6 710 54½ 35½ 35¾ Nakatani CS LB 119 2.00 86-09 PrivatePersuson1143TopRung1162¾Wndst1194½ Mild late bid 7

2Jly95- 9Hol fm 1⅛Ⓣ :471 1:101 1:342 1:463 3↑ ⒻBeverly Hills H-G1 1 5 56¾ 55 41½ 32¾ Nakatani CS LB 119 3.30 89-10 Alpride1151¾Possibly Perfect1241Wandesta1196½ 6
Boxed in upper stretch

29May95- 9Hol fm 1¼Ⓣ :481 1:12 1:354 1:593 3↑ Hol Turf H-G1 6 8 104½ 85¾ 86 89½ Day P LB 114 6.90 80-10 EarlofBarking1152¼Sandpit122hdSavno117¾ 6 wide 2nd turn 10

9Apr95- 8SA fm 1¼Ⓣ :50 1:133 1:374 2:013 4↑ ⒻSanta Barbara H-G1 7 4 42½ 31½ 2½ 12 Nakatani CS LB 118 *1.10 82-18 Wandsta1182YearlyTour116noMorgana1164 Strong handling 7

18Mar95- 8SA fm 1⅛Ⓣ :491 1:133 1:38 1:50 4↑ ⒻSanta Ana H-G1 5 5 56½ 41¼ 41¼ 12 Nakatani CS LB 115 1.90 79-21 Wandesta1152Yearly Tour116¾Aube Indienne120nk 7
Awaited room 2nd turn,split rivals past ⅛

19Feb95- 4SA fm 1⅛Ⓣ :474 1:13 1:382 1:503 4↑ ⒻAlw 46000 3 3 44 31½ 31½ 1nk Nakatani CS LB 120 *.50 76-24 Wandest120nkRubyCro1203½MllNuts117½ Rode rail,best late 10

27Nov94- 7Hol gd 1⅛Ⓣ :484 1:131 1:371 1:492 3↑ ⒻMatriarch-G1 3 7 83¾ 83¾ 51¾ 3½ Nakatani CS LB 120 10.60 76-17 Exchange123hdAubeIndienne123½Wndsta1201¼ 5w into lane 8
Previously trained by Roger Charlton

6Nov94- 8SA fm 1¼Ⓣ :47 1:112 1:362 2:021 3↑ ⒻYellow Ribbon Inv-G1 1 1 12½ 1½ 55 918 Day P LB 118 *2.20e 58-24 AubeIndnne122½FondlyRmmbrd122nkZoonqu1221 Speed,tired 11

17Aug94♦ York(GB) gd *1½ⓉLH 2:28 3↑ ⒻYorkshire Oaks-G1 Stk215000 622½ Carson W 123 6.00 Only Royale1336Dancing Bloom133½State Crystal1233 7
Well placed in 3rd,weakened over 2½f out

7Aug94♦ Deauville(Fr) gd *1 11/16ⓉRH 2:574 3↑ ⒻPrix de Pomone-G2 Stk94000 22½ Eddery Pat 119 3.00 Bright Moon1322½Wandesta1193Molesnes132no 7
Tracked in 3rd,led 3f out,headed 1f out,no further response

16Jly94♦ Newmarket(GB) gd 1½ⓉRH 2:31 3↑ ⒻAphrodite Stakes (Listed) Stk25700 11¾ Dettori L 116 4.50 Wandesta1161¾Darrery1282Moon Carnival128no 11
Prominent in 5th,led over 1f out,driving

22Oct93♦ Doncaster(GB) gd 7fⓉStr 1:284 EBF Flaxton Maiden Stakes Mdn10900 614 Eddery P 121 4.00 Golden Nashwan1263½Moving Arrow1263Faal Mario1262½ 15
Tracked in 4th,drifted left 1f out,one-paced

Warm Spell

ch. g. 1988, by Northern Baby (Northern Dancer)–Smilin' Sera, by Explodent **Lifetime record: 19 12 3 1 $457,964**

Own.– John K. Griggs
Br.– Robert G. Kluener (Ky)
Tr.– John K. Griggs

13Nov94- 4Cam	fm 2¾	S'Chase	5:08^{1}	4↑ Colonial Cup 100k	3	6	7^{3½}	-	-	-	Lawrence J II	162		--	Lonesome Glory162^{hd}Mistico162^{21}Victorian Hill162¾	Fell	8
22Oct94- 3FH	fm *2⅝	Hurdles	4:58	4↑ B C Grand Nationl 143k	4	3	3^{2¼}	2^{1}	1^{hd}	1^{2½}	Lawrence J II	156		--	WrmSpll156^{2½}MasterMcGrth156^{1½}LonsmeGlry156^{1¼}	Driving	6
18Aug94- 9Sar	sf 2⅜	Hurdles	4:30	4↑ NY Turf Writers H 109k	7	8	8^{11}	7^{8¾}	5^{8½}	5^{8}	Lawrence J II	168	*1.20	--	Mistico168^{4}Cheering News142^{3½}Lonesome Glory168^{nk}		8
	Wide,lacked rally																
28Jly94- 1Sar	sf 2 1/16	Hurdles	3:47^{4}	4↑ Handicap 50000	1	7	7^{12}	4^{2¼}	2^{hd}	1^{2½}	Lawrence J II	164	2.50	--	Warm Spell164^{2½}Mistico168^{1¾}Cheering News146^{nk}	Driving	7
14May94- 7PW	gd *3	Hurdles	5:28^{3}	4↑ Iroquois 100k	6	4	4^{13}	2½	2^{8}	2^{15}	Lawrence J II	168		--	Mistico168^{15}Warm Spell168^{22}Victorian Hill168^{35}		7
	Bid,outrun by winner																
23Apr94- 3Mid	fm *2⅝	Hurdles	4:41^{3}	4↑ Temple Gwathmy H 50k	1	2	2^{4}	2^{3}	1^{1½}	2^{nk}	Lawrence J II	162		--	LonesomeGlory164^{nk}WarmSpll162^{9}ChrngNws144^{8}	2nd best	5
9Apr94- 3AtH	fm *2⅛	Hurdles	3:55^{4}	4↑ Rob HumphryCH 100k	4	5	6^{4¾}	3^{3}	4^{1}	1½	Lawrence J II	164		--	Warm Spell164½Rolling Cart142^{2}Castleworth144^{6}	Driving	7
19Aug93- 9Sar	gd 2⅜	Hurdles	4:15^{2}	4↑ NY Turf Writers 118k	4	3	6^{8}	2^{1½}	1^{1½}	1^{5}	Lawrence J II	161	1.80	--	Warm Spell161^{5}Castleworth142^{2}Darby Sky145^{4}	Driving	9
29Jly93- 1Sar	fm 2 1/16	Hurdles	3:42^{4}	4↑ Handicap 46000	7	8	5^{9½}	3^{1}	1^{hd}	1¾	Lawrence J II	158	*1.70	--	Warm Spell158¾Castleworth140^{12}Rolling Cart145^{1½}	Gamely	10
8May93- 7PW	gd 3	Hurdles	5:43	4↑ Iroquois 100k	6	1	2^{nk}	2^{1}	3^{1½}	2^{2½}	Lawrence J II	163	-	--	Mistico168^{2½}Warm Spell163^{3}Darby Sky168^{5}	Strong bid	7
18Apr93- 3Mid	gd *2⅝	Hurdles	5:08	4↑ Temple Gwathmy H 50k	1	1	1^{2}	2^{hd}	1^{3}	1^{5}	Lawrence J II	156		--	Warm Spell156^{5}Ninepins154^{2½}Woodlast142^{1¼}	Ridden out	7
3Apr93- 4AtH	fm *2⅛	Hurdles	4:00^{3}	4↑ Ath Cup H 100k	4	6	5^{3}	-	-	-	Griggs K	156		--	Ninepins150^{1½}Circuit Bar149^{hd}Lexington Ball138^{5}	Fell	8
4Jun92- 4Bel	fm 2	S'Chase	3:36^{3}	4↑ Handicap 45000	1	2	2^{2½}	2^{hd}	1^{6}	1^{7½}	Griggs K	148	*.80	--	WarmSpell148^{7½}NordicSurpris142^{nk}Woodlst144^{nk}	Mild drive	7
9May92- 9PW	fm 3	S'Chase	5:31^{4}	4↑ Iroquois 100k	8	2	2^{1}	2^{1½}	2¾	3^{2}	Griggs K	158		--	VictorianHill168^{1¾}Mistico168^{nk}WarmSpll158^{6½}	No response	8
26Apr92- 4Lex	fm *2½	S'Chase		4↑ Coca Cola H 25k	3	2	3^{3}	2¾	1^{7}	1^{7}	Lawrence J II	148		--	Warm Spell148^{7}Mistico142^{3}Three Bells for Me139^{6}	Handily	4
	Fractional times unavailable																
4Apr92- 5AtH	fm *2⅛	S'Chase	4:04	4↑ Alw 30000	7	2	2^{nk}	1^{5}	1^{1½}	1^{2½}	Lawrence J II	145		--	WarmSpell145^{2½}TalkinButter149^{5}[D]Rainlough141^{hd}	Driving	7
16Nov91- 5Cam	fm *2	S'Chase	3:36^{1}	Alw 15000	6	1	1^{1}	1^{1½}	1½	1^{2¼}	Griggs K	151		--	Warm Spell151^{2¼}Plusser148^{1}Hero's Hour148^{15}	Driving	13
19Oct91- 4GrM	fm *2¼	S'Chase	4:32	Alw 15000	9	7	2^{2½}	1^{2}	1^{6}	1^{15}	Griggs K	150		--	WrmSpll150^{15}WiseOne145^{12}BlackSeaDancr138^{5}	Ridden out	10
21Jly91- 3Sar	fm 2 1/16	S'Chase	4:01^{2}	3↑ Md Sp Wt	9	7	6^{14}	1^{1}	1^{4}	1^{10}	Cooney P	138		--	WamSpell138^{10}Tuniche155^{6}LdsCstl155^{6}	Brilliant first out	9

Yanks Music

b. f. 1993, by Air Forbes Won (Bold Forbes)–Traipsing, by Darby Creek Road **Lifetime record: 9 7 2 0 $787,600**

Own.– Audrey H. Cooper & Michael Fennessy
Br.– Irish American Bloodhorse Agency Ltd (Ky)
Tr.– Leo O'Brien

6Oct96- 9Bel	fst 1⅛	:46^{4} 1:10^{2} 1:34^{2} 1:47	3↑ Ⓕ Beldame-G1	6	3	3^{1½}	2^{1}	2^{1}	1¾	Velazquez JR	119	2.30	95-12	Yanks Music119¾Serena's Song123^{3}Clear Mandate123^{1}		6	
	Well placed,determined																
14Sep96- 9Bel	fst 1 1/16	:23^{3} :47^{1} 1:11^{1} 1:41^{4}	3↑ Ⓕ Ruffian H-G1	2	4	4^{2}	2^{1}	2^{1}	1^{nk}	Velazquez JR	116	2.10	90-10	YanksMsic116^{nk}Serena'sSong126^{9}HedEst108^{nk}	Determinedly	6	
17Aug96- 8Sar	wf 1¼	:48^{3} 1:13^{1} 1:37^{4} 2:03	Ⓕ Alabama-G1	3	4	3^{5}	2^{hd}	1½	1^{4}	Velazquez JR	121	6.30	94-14	Yanks Music121^{4}Escena121½My Flag121^{3¼}	Well placed,clear	7	
6Jly96- 8Mth	fst 1 1/16	:23^{4} :47 1:10^{3} 1:42^{1}	Ⓕ Mth BC Oaks-G2	4	3	4^{1¾}	4^{2}	3^{4½}	2^{3}	Velazquez JR	121	*.30	102-00	TopSecrt114^{3}YnksMsic121^{1}MesabiMadn121^{4¾}	Earned place	5	
22Jun96- 9Bel	wf 1⅛	:44^{1} 1:08^{1} 1:34^{1} 1:47^{4}	Ⓕ Mother Goose-G1	5	5	5^{4½}	4^{2½}	2^{1½}	1^{nk}	Velazquez JR	121	2.10	91-12	YanksMusic121^{nk}Escena121^{5½}CrRfl121^{6}	5w,determinedly	7	
18May96- 9Bel	wf 1	:21^{4} :44^{2} 1:09^{1} 1:34^{3}	Ⓕ Acorn-G1	3	7	7^{3½}	7^{2}	4^{3}	2½	Velazquez JR	121	*.80	89-14	Star de Lady Ann121½Yanks Music121^{1½}Stop Traffic121^{2}		12	
	Bumped early,steadied,blocked turn																
18Apr96- 7Aqu	fst 7f	:22^{4} :45^{3} 1:10^{1} 1:22^{1}	Ⓕ Alw 35000	3	6	6^{4}	6^{2½}	1^{1}	1^{5½}	Velazquez JR	114	2.15	97-09	Yanks Music114^{5½}Stop Traffic116^{1½}Zee Lady114^{3}		8	
	Five wide,going away																
23Nov95- 6Aqu	fst 1	:23^{1} :46^{1} 1:11^{3} 1:37^{3}	Ⓕ Alw 33000	4	3	3^{4½}	2½	1^{3}	1^{3¾}	Migliore R	116	2.00	81-20	YanksMussc116^{3¾}Break Through113^{2}Flume118^{7}		6	
	Lugged in,ridden out																
5Nov95- 2Aqu	fst 6f	:22^{2} :46^{2} :58^{3} 1:11	Ⓕ Md Sp Wt	9	6	6^{7}	3^{2}	1^{3}	1^{9¾}	Velazquez JR	118	2.75	87-11	YnksMsc118^{9¾}CelestialGlanc118^{2½}SwtEmmLou118½	Handily	9	

CHAMPIONS

APPENDICES

EXPLANATION OF PAST PERFORMANCES

Color, sex, year of birth, sire, sire's sire, dam, dam's sire

Name of horse, Country of origin (if foreign)

Owner, Breeder, state where bred

Speed rating and track variant

Starts, 1st, 2nd, 3rd, earnings

Secretariat

ch. c. 1970, by Bold Ruler (Nasrullah)–Somethingroyal, by Princequillo

Own.– Meadow Stable
Br.– Meadow Stud Inc (Va)
Tr.– L. Laurin

Lifetime record: 21 16 3 1 $1,316,808

Fractional times

28Oct73- 8WO	fm 1⅝ⓣ	:47² 1:37³	2:41⁴ 3 ↑ Can Int'l-G2	12	2 21½	15	112	16½	Maple E	117	b	*.20	96-04	Secretariat1176½BigSpruce126½GoldenDon117¾	Ridden out 12
8Oct73- 7Bel	fm 1½ⓣ	:47 1:11³ 2:00 2:24³	3 ↑ Man o' War-G1	3	1 1³	11½	1³	1⁵	Turcotte R	121	b	*.50	103-01	Secretariat121⁵Tentam126⁷½Big Spruce126½	Ridden out 7
29Sep73- 7Bel	sly 1½	:50 1:13² 2:01⁴ 2:25⁴	3 ↑ Woodward-G1	5	2 2½	1hd	21½	24½	Turcotte R	119	b	*.30	86-15	ProveOut126⁴½Secretariat119¹¹CougarII126½	Best of rest 5
15Sep73- 7Bel	fst 1⅛	:45³ 1:09¹ 1:33 1:45²	3 ↑ Marl Cup Inv'l H 250k	7	5 51¼	3½	12	13½	Turcotte R	124	b	*.40e	104-07	Secretariat124³½Riva Ridge127²Cougar II126⁶½	Ridden out 7
4Aug73- 7Sar	fst 1⅛	:47⁴ 1:11 1:36 1:49¹	3 ↑ Whitney H-G2	3	4 3¹	2½	2hd	2¹	Turcotte R	119	b	*.10	94-15	Onion119¹Secretariat119½Rule by Reason119²	Weakened 5
30Jun73- 8AP	fst 1⅛	:48 1:11¹ 1:35 1:47	Invitational 125k	4	1 1³	12½	16	19	Turcotte R	126	b	*.05	99-17	Secretariat126⁹My Gallant120ⁿᵏOur Native120¹⁷	Easily 4
9Jun73- 8Bel	fst 1½	:46¹ 1:09⁴ 1:59 2:24	Belmont-G1	1	1 1hd	120	128	131	Turcotte R	126	b	*.10	113-05	Secretariat126³¹TwiceaPrince126½MyGllnt126¹³	Ridden out 5
19May73- 8Pim	fst 1³⁄₁₆	:48¹ 1:11² 1:35³ 1:54²	Preakness-G1	3	4 1½	12½	12½	12½	Turcotte R	126	b	*.30	98-13	Secretariat126²½Sham126⁸Our Native126¹	Handily 6
	Daily Racing Form time 1:53 2/5														
5May73- 9CD	fst 1¼	:47² 1:11⁴ 1:36¹ 1:59²	Ky Derby-G1	10	11 69½	2½	1½	12½	Turcotte R	126	b	*1.50	103-10	Secretariat126²½Sham126⁸Our Native126½	Handily 13
21Apr73- 7Aqu	fst 1⅛	:48¹ 1:12¹ 1:36³ 1:49⁴	Wood Memorial-G1	6	7 66	55½	45½	3⁴	Turcotte R	126	b	*.30e	83-17	Angle Light126ʰᵈSham126⁴Secretariat126½	Wide,hung 8
7Apr73- 7Aqu	fst 1	:23¹ :45¹ 1:08³ 1:33²	Gotham-G2	3	3 1hd	12	1½	1³	Turcotte R	126	b	*.10	100-08	Secretariat126³ChampagneCharl117¹⁰Flush117²½	Ridden out 6
17Mar73- 7Aqu	sly 7f	:22¹ :44⁴ 1:10 1:23¹	Bay Shore-G3	4	5 56	53	1hd	14½	Turcotte R	126	b	*.20	85-17	Secretariat126⁴½ChmpgnChrl118²½Impcunous126ⁿᵒ	Mild drive 6
18Nov72- 8GS	fst 1¹⁄₁₆	:24¹ :47² 1:12 1:44²	Garden State 298k	6	6 46¼	3³	11½	13½	Turcotte R	122	b	*.10e	83-23	Secretariat122³½Angle Light122½Step Nicely122¾	Handily 6
28Oct72- 7Lrl	sly 1¹⁄₁₆	:22⁴ :45⁴ 1:11² 1:42⁴	Lrl Futurity 133k	5	6 5¹⁰	5³	1⁵	1⁸	Turcotte R	122	b	*.10e	99-14	Secretariat122⁸Stop the Music122⁸Angle Light122¹	Easily 6
14Oct72- 7Bel	fst 1	:22⁴ :45¹ 1:09⁴ 1:35	Champagne 146k	4	11 98½	53½	1½	12	Turcotte R	122	b	*.70e	97-12	ⒹSecretariat122²StopheMusic122²StepNicely122¹½	Bore in 12
	Disqualified and placed second														
16Sep72- 7Bel	fst 6½f	:22³ :45³ 1:10 1:16²	Futurity 144k	4	5 65½	53½	12	11¾	Turcotte R	122	b	*.20	98-09	Secretariat122¹¾StoptheMusic122⁵SwiftCourr122²½	Handily 7
26Aug72- 7Sar	fst 6½f	:22⁴ :46³ 1:09⁴ 1:16¹	Hopeful 86k	8	8 96½	1hd	14	1⁵	Turcotte R	121	b	*.30	97-12	Secretariat121⁵FlighttoGlory121ⁿᵏStopthMusc121²	Handily 9
16Aug72- 7Sar	fst 6f	:22⁴ :46¹ 1:10	Sanford 27k	2	5 5⁴	41	1½	1³	Turcotte R	121	b	1.50	96-14	Secretariat121³Lnd'sChf121⁶NorthstrDncr121³½	Ridden out 5
31Jly72- 7Sar	fst 6f	:23¹ :46² 1:10⁴	Alw 9000	4	7 73¾	3½	1hd	11½	Turcotte R	118	b	*.40	92-13	Secretariat1181½Russ Miron118⁷Joe Iz118²½	Ridden out 7
15Jly72- 4Aqu	fst 6f	:22¹ :45² 1:10³	ⒸMd Sp Wt	8	11 66½	43	1½	16	Feliciano P⁵	113	b	*1.30	90-14	Secretariat113⁶Master Achiever118¾Be on It118⁴	Handily 11
4Jly72- 2Aqu	fst 5½f	:22² :46¹ :58⁴ 1:05	ⒸMd Sp Wt	2	11 107	108¾ 75½	41¼		Feliciano P⁵	113	b	*3.10	87-11	Herbull118ⁿᵏMaster Achiever1181Fleet 'n Royal118ⁿᵒ	12
	Impeded,rallied														

Age, sex restrictions, class of race, purse

Odds to $1 (* indicates favorite)

Date, race, track abbreviation, track condition, distance, surface

Post position, fractional calls with margins, finish with margins

Jockey, weight carried, equipment

First three finishers with weight carried and margins, comment line number of starters

416 CHAMPIONS

ABBREVIATIONS FOR TYPES OF RACES

Alw 15000	Allowence race, $15,000
Alw 15000s	Starter allowance (number indicates minimum claiming price horse must have started for to be eligible)
Clm 10000	Claiming race (entered to be claimed for $10,000)
Hcp 10000s	Starter handicap race. Number indicates minimum claiming price horse must have started for to be eligible
Md Sp Wt	Maiden Special Weight race (for non-winners)
MCl 32000	Maiden Claiming race (entered to be claimed for $32,000)
Handicap 40k	Overnight handicap race (purse of $40,000)
Ky Derby-G1	Graded Stakes race, with name of race (North American races are graded in order of status, with G1 being the best)
PrincetonH 40k	Ungraded, but named Stakes race (H indicates handicap) Purse value is $40,000

SYMBOLS

▣	=	Inner dirt track	Ⓢ	=	Race for state-breds only
Ⓓ	=	Disqualified (symbol located next to odds and in company line)	Ⓡ	=	Restricted race for horses who meet certain conditions
DH	=	Dead-Heat (symbol located in company line if horses are among first three finishers)	©	=	restricted to colts and geldings
			Ⓕ	=	Race for fillies, or fillies and mares
			Ⓣ	=	Main turf course
♦	=	Dead-Heat (symbol used next to finish position)	Ⓣ	=	Inner turf course
			⊗	=	Race taken off turf
3↑	=	Race for 3-year-olds and up	*	=	About distance
♦	=	Foreign race (outside of North America)	+	=	Start from turf chute
			wc	=	Widener Course

FRACTIONAL TIMES

Distance		Fractional Times		
3½ f	—	1/4	3/8	finish
4 f	—	1/4	3/8	finish
4½ f	—	1/4	1/2	finish
5 f	—	1/4	1/2	finish
5½ f	1/4	1/2	5/8	finish
6 f	1/4	1/2	5/8	finish
6½ f	1/4	1/2	3/4	finish
7 f	1/4	1/2	3/4	finish
7½ f	1/4	1/2	3/4	finish
1 mile	1/4	1/2	3/4	finish
1 m 70 yds	1/4	1/2	3/4	finish
1 1/16	1/2	3/4	mile	finish
1 3/16	1/2	3/4	mile	finish
1 1/4	1/2	3/4	mile	finish
1 3/8	1/2	3/4	mile	finish
1 1/2	1/2	3/4	1 1/4	finish
1 5/8	1/2	mile	1 1/4	finish
1 3/4	1/2	1 1/4	1 1/2	finish
1 7/8	1/2	1 1/4	1 3/4	finish
2 miles	1/2	1 1/2	1 3/4	finish
2 1/8	1/2	1 1/2	1 3/4	finish

TRACK CONDITIONS

DIRT TRACKS

fst	=	Fast
wf	=	Wet-Fast
gd	=	Good
sly	=	Sloppy
my	=	Muddy
sl	=	Slow
hy	=	Heavy
fr	=	Frozen
cpy	=	Cuppy

TURF & STEEPLECHASE

hd	=	Hard
fm	=	Firm
gd	=	Good
yl	=	Yielding
sf	=	Soft
hy	=	Heavy

EQUIPMENT & MEDICATION

b	=	Blinkers
f	=	Front bandages
r	=	Bar shoe
w	=	whip
s	=	spurs
B	=	Butazolidin
L	=	Lasix (furosemide)

TRACK ABBREVIATIONS

ABBREV	TRACK NAME	STATE	ABBREV	TRACK NAME	STATE
AC	Agua Caliente	MX	Due	Dueling Grounds	KY
Agm	Agawam	MA	EIP	Ellis Park	KY
Aik	Aiken	SC	Emp	Empire City	NY
Aks	Aksarben	NE	Esx	Essex Park	AR
Alb	Albuquerque	NM	EvD	Evangeline Downs	LA
AP	Arlington Park	IL	Fai	Fair Hill	MD
Aqu	Aqueduct	NY	Fax	Fairfax	VA
AtH	Atlanta Hunt	GA	FE	Fort Erie	ON
Atl	Atlantic City	NJ	FG	Fair Grounds	LA
BB	Blue Bonnets	QU	FH	Far Hills	NJ
Bel	Belmont Park	NY	FL	Finger Lakes	NY
Ben	Bennings	DC	Fon	Fonner Park	NE
BM	Bay Meadows	CA	FP	Fairmount Park	IL
Bmf	Bay Meadows Fair	CA	Fx	Foxfield	VA
Bow	Bowie	MD	GG	Golden Gate	CA
BPT	Belmont Park Terminal	NY	GP	Gulfstream Park	FL
Bri	Brighton Beach	NY	Gra	Gravesend	NY
Bue	Butte	MT	Grd	Greenwood	ON
Cam	Camden	SC	GrM	Great Meadows	VA
Cby	Canterbury	MN	GS	Garden State Park	NJ
CD	Churchill Downs	KY	Ham	Hamilton	ON
CDA	Coeur d'Alene	ID	Haw	Hawthorne	IL
Cen	Centennial	CO	HdG	Havre de Grace	MD
CI	Coney Island	OH	Hel	Helena	MT
Clm	Clemmons	NC	Hia	Hialeah Park	FL
Con	Connaught Park	ON	Hol	Hollywood Park	CA
Crc	Calder Race Course	FL	HP	Hazel Park	MI
Dad	Dade Park	KY	Hrm	Harlem	IL
Dal	Dallas	TX	Jam	Jamaica	NY
Dar	Darby Downs	OH	JnD	Jefferson Downs	LA
Del	Delaware Park	DE	Jua	Juarez	MX
Det	Detroit	MI	Kee	Keeneland	KY
Dev	Devonshire Park	ON	Key	Keystone	PA
Dmr	Del Mar	CA	Knw	Kenilworth	ON
DoP	Douglas Park	KY	LA	Los Alamitos	CA
Dor	Dorval Park	QU	LaD	Louisiana Downs	LA
DRn	Deep Run	VA	Lag	Lagoon	UT

ABBREV	TRACK NAME	STATE	ABBREV	TRACK NAME	STATE
Lak	Lakeside	IN	PR	El Commandante	PR
Lat	Latonia	KY	Pro	Prospect	KY
LD	Lincoln Downs	RI	Pur	Purchase Hunts	NY
Lex	Lexington	KY	PW	Percy Warner	TN
LF	Lincoln Fields	IL	Ran	Randall Park	OH
Lga	Longacres	WA	RB	Red Bank	NJ
Lib	Liberty Bell Park	PA	RD	River Downs	OH
Lig	Ligonier	PA	Rkm	Rockingham Park	NH
Lrl	Laurel	MD	SA	Santa Anita Park	CA
LS	Lone Star	TX	Sac	Sacramento	CA
Lxt	Lexington	KY	SAP	Old Santa Anita Park	CA
Mal	Malvern	PA	Sar	Saratoga	NY
MBr	Meadow Brook	NY	SH	Strawberry Hill	VA
Med	Meadowlands	NJ	She	Sheepshead Bay	NY
Mgo	Marengo	VA	Sol	Solano	CA
Mid	Middleburg	VA	SoP	Southern Pines	NC
Mor	Morven Park	VA	Spt	Sportsman's Park	IL
MP	Morris Park	NY	SR	Santa Rosa	CA
Mth	Monmouth Park	NJ	StL	St. Louis	MO
Mtp	Montpelier	VA	Suf	Suffolk Downs	MA
Nar	Narragansett	RI	Syr	Syracuse	NY
Nvl	Nashville	TN	Tam	Tampa Bay Downs	FL
Nwp	Newport	KY	Tan	Tanforan	CA
Oak	Oakland	CA	Tdn	Thistledown	OH
Oky	Oakley	OH	Tij	Tijuana	MX
OMP	Old Monmouth Park	NJ	Tim	Timonium	MD
OP	Oaklawn Park	AR	TP	Turfway Park	KY
OWP	Old Washington Park	IL	TrP	Tropical Park	FL
Pal	Palmetto	SC	Try	Tryon	NC
Pen	Penn National	PA	TuP	Turf Paradise	AZ
Pha	Philadelphia Park	PA	UH	United Hunts	NY
Pim	Pimlico	MD	Uni	Unionville	PA
PiR	Piping Rock	NY	War	Warrenton	VA
Pln	Pleasanton	CA	Was	Washington Park	IL
PM	Portland Meadows	OR	Wnr	Windsor	ON
Pmt	Pine Mountain	GA	WO	Woodbine	ON

ABOUT THE AUTHORS

GLENYE CAIN has been the bloodstock correspondent for *Daily Racing Form* since May of 1999. Previously Cain was news editor and features editor of The Thoroughbred Times; was the editor of Equine Athlete; and worked for the Thoroughbred Owners and Breeders Association and National Thoroughbred Racing Association. Cain received the 1995 Story of the Year Award for the Chronicle of the Horse and was the 1999 winner of the Kent Hollingsworth Award for reporting excellence.

STEVEN CRIST was named CEO, Editor and Publisher of *Daily Racing Form* in August, 1998. Crist covered horse racing as a New York Times reporter and columnist from 1981 to 1990; was founding editor-in-chief of The Racing Times in 1991-92; served on Governor Mario Cuomo's Commission on Racing in the 21st Century from 1993 to 1995; and was a vice president of the New York Racing Association from 1995 to 1997. He is the author of two books, Offtrack and The Horse Traders.

DAVID GRENING has covered Thoroughbred racing since 1991. He worked the Delaware Valley circuit for the Trentonian (N.J.) and was also the correspondent in that area for the Blood-Horse from 1991-94. In May 1994, he joined the New York Post where he covered New York racing and the national scene for four years before joining *Daily Racing Form* as its New York correspondent in Sept. 1998. He also worked as the New York correspondent for Thoroughbred Times during his four-year tenure at the Post.

JOE HIRSCH, an internationally recognized racing figure for most of the last 50 years, is considered the dean of America's turf writers. *Daily Racing Form's* executive columnist, who has worked for the paper since 1948, has covered more major American races than any other journalist. Hirsch's work has been honored with virtually every major award in his profession. He is the only turf writer in win the Eclipse Award and the Lord Derby Award from the Horse Race Writers of England. Among his many other accolades include The Jockey Club Medal, the Walter Haight Award, the William H. May Award from the Association of Racing Commissioners International, and an entire day in his name from the state of Kentucky. Hirsch most recently wrote "The First Century," a history of Thoroughbred racing from 1894-1994, and collaborated with Jim

Bolus on "Kentucky Derby: The Chance of a Lifetime."

JAY PRIVMAN has been the national correspondent for *Daily Racing Form* since October 1998. He is the lead writer on events such as the Triple Crown and Breeders' Cup. Prior to that, he was a West Coast correspondent for The New York Times for six years, and a staff writer with the Los Angeles Daily News for nine years. Privman served as the West Coast Editor for The Racing Times, and was also a West Coast correspondent for Thoroughbred Times from 1985 to 1998. Privman does extensive television work, most notably as an analyst for FOX on the "NTRA Champions on FOX" series. Privman is a five-time winner of the Red Smith Kentucky Derby Writing Contest, and three times has received honorable mentions in the Eclipse Awards for his writing

DAVE LITFIN was a call-taker with *Daily Racing Form* from 1982 until the fall of 1984, when he joined the New York Racing Association's publicity department just as Slew o' Gold was setting out to sweep the Woodward, Marlboro Cup and Jockey Club Gold Cup. Four years later, he left the NYRA to serve brief stints at Racing Action and the New York Daily News, but came back to the Form in 1990 and has been the lead New York handicapper since the spring of 1991. In addition to a twice-weekly column entitled "Handicapper's Corner," Litfin has authored two well-received handicapping books: "Dave Litfin's Expert Handicapping," and "Real-Life Handicapping."

JAY HOVDEY, executive columnist for *Daily Racing Form*, is a two-time Eclipse Award winner for magazine writing whose work also has appeared in Reader's Digest, the New York Times, the Los Angeles Times, and such Thoroughbred racing publications as The Blood-Horse, Thoroughbred Times, The Racing Times, Horsemen's Journal, Spur Magazine, Pacemaker International, and Keiba Book of Japan. He is the author of three books on horse racing, including "Whittingham: A Thoroughbred Racing Legend" and "Cigar: America's Horse." Hovdey is a two-time winner of the David F. Woods Award for coverage of the Preakness Stakes, a two-time winner of the Joe Hirsch Award for coverage of the Breeders' Cup, winner of Canada's Sovereign Award for feature writing, and winner of the Charles Englehard Award for turf writing. In 1995 he was honored by his peers with the Walter Haight Award for career excellence in racing journalism.

PAULA WELCH was the Special Projects Editor for *Daily Racing Form* from 1996 to 2000. In addition to researching and collecting the data for the past performances in Champions, Welch also coordinated the material for the Graded Stakes Yearbook from 1995 through 1998. A 1992 graduate of the Racetrack Industry Program at the University of Arizona, Welch currently is the technical support manager for Essential Data Control Systems.